Manual of Woody Landscape Plants:

Their Identification, Ornamental Characteristics, Culture, Propagation and Uses

Fourth Edition

MICHAEL A. DIRR
Department of Horticulture
University of Georgia
Athens, Georgia

ILLUSTRATIONS BY
MARGARET STEPHAN,
ASTA SADAUSKAS,
NANCY SNYDER,
and
BONNIE DIRR

Copyright © 1975, Revised 1977, Revised 1983, Revised 1990
MICHAEL A. DIRR

ISBN 0-87563-344-7

Published by
STIPES PUBLISHING COMPANY
10 – 12 Chester Street
Champaign, Ilinois 61820

Dedication

To

The Dirr Family

PREFACE TO THE FOURTH EDITION

The forty-sixth year of a satisfying life . . . each day exciting, rich and active, greets (coincides with) this, the fourth edition. My children have literally grown up with the *Manual,* now 15 years young. Katie, our oldest ventures forth to college, Matt becomes a high school junior and Susy reaches the 8th grade ladder. Doubtfully, will they become horticulturists but they have an inherent appreciation for the environment and a sense of responsibility for its integrity. My wife, Bonnie, has penned approximately 300 pen and ink drawings for the new edition and is as much a part of the *Manual* as I am.

The new edition is substantive with approximately 200 new species and over 500 cultivars. As current as the *Manual* purports to be, it is already marginally out-of-date since new cultivars are introduced daily. New woody plant introductions come from myriad sources and their introduction and description never flow through a single clearinghouse. In recent years, the nursery industry has become enthused about introducing and promoting new plants. Universities, Botanical Gardens and Arboreta have instituted plant introduction schemes to earn recognition and, hopefully, a few dollars to foster continued research. Plants are patented and trademarked with alarming frequency, even though most will fall by the wayside. The great challenge for this author is to stay current and provide the reader with accurate information concerning the new cultivars.

I decided to publish and offer a PLANT INTRODUCTION NEWSLETTER for those with the passion and need to stay current relative to old and new introductions. Instead of waiting 5 to 10 years for a new edition of the *Manual,* each subscriber will receive two issues (depending on volume of information, possibly more) per year with the latest plant introductions, their characteristics, availability, and other pertinent information. Also, as new information surfaces relative to plants already included in the *Manual,* it will be transmitted through the NEWSLETTER. A good example might be the latest thinking on the dogwood anthracnose (*Discula*) which the popular press has blown out of proportion relative to its garden severity. For a subscription to the newsletter send $10.00 to

PLANT INTRODUCTION NEWSLETTER
C/O DR. MICHAEL A. DIRR.
1270 HOLLOW CREEK LANE
WATKINSVILLE, GA 30677

The Newsletter will be sent in early July and early January.

Upon reflection, the past nine years develop rather sharp edges . . . students who passed through my classes are now active in the profession. My hope is that they received a measure of inspiration and education. My association with Dr. Allan Armitage, friend and colleague, as we studied, photographed and enjoyed plants in many gardens but most vividly in the rain and cold at Edinburgh Botanical Garden . . . the only two souls in the unrivaled three and one-half acre rock garden. . . . Gardeners are not defined by economics, social status, or education. Their willingness to seek and share dissolves the barriers to forming friendships. The plant becomes the common bond . . . all other nuances and quirks seem trivial.

I have watched our Georgia garden evolve over the past eleven years . . . metamorphasizing, maturing, expressing itself . . . with memories tied to each plant, yet the quiet anticipation of those to come. Perhaps the philosophy of all garden makers is best reflected in the Chinese proverb . . . "A garden, where one may enter in and forget the whole world, cannot be made in a week, nor a month, nor a year; it must be planned for, waited for and loved into being."

As always, I welcome comments from readers and over the years have made numerous garden pen pals. I discovered that the plant world is imbued with amusing individuals. Perhaps we should not all be released at the same time.

Michael A. Dirr
Athens, Georgia
March, 1990

Acknowledgements

A book is a collection of loose ends that until gathered and collated serve no significantly useful purpose. Many people assisted with the synthesis of the fourth edition and their efforts are greatly appreciated. To Ms. Alice Richards, Ms. Vickie Waters, Mrs. Dorothy J. Callaway, Ms. Andrea Simao, Mrs. Betty Johnson, Ms. Karin Helfman . . . sincere thanks. To my wife Bonnie, who penned 300 new drawings, often from material that was less than whole . . . your artistry, patience and endurance are laudable.

The front cover photograph is *Aesculus parviflora*

INTRODUCTION TO THE USE OF THE MANUAL

Each plant type (taxon) is discussed in a defined sequence and usually accompanied by a line drawing and identification characteristics related to leaf, bud, and stem. Certain plants are discussed under the heading "Related Species". This approach was taken to avoid repetition and at the same time allow for a significantly greater number of plant discussions.

The plant's scientific, common, and family names are the first items treated under each description. After the family name has been listed for a particular genus it is usually omitted for the other species within the genus. The latin names are as accurate and current as is feasible. *The International Code of Botanical Nomenclature* (1972); and *International Code for Nomenclature of Cultivated Plants* (1980) were followed for scientific names while *Standardized Plant Names* (1942) was used, where feasible and logical, for common names. *Hortus III* (1976) was consulted and followed (where feasible) for a complete update on scientific names. If a scientific name was recently changed both the old and new names are listed.

Common names are a constant source of confusion and embarrassment. I have attempted, in most cases, to use the common name which is widely spoken. Certain plants might have 3 to 5 common names and they are usually included after the "accepted" common name. Common names should be written in lower case unless part of the name is proper and then the first letter of only the proper term is capitalized. For example, sugar maple would be written with lower case letters while Japanese maple would be written with the capital J. This is the accepted method for writing common names in scientific circles and should be familiar to the student. In this text and many others common names are written with capital first letters. This was done to set the name off from the rest of the sentence and make it more evident to the reader.

The family name was included so that the reader could begin to see the common floral or fruit bonds which exist among genera which are dissimilar to each other in vegetative (leaf, bud, stem, habit) characters. For example, Kentucky Coffeetree does not appear similar or related to Redbud but the similarity of fruits should imply a familial relationship.

The use of SIZE delineations is a moot question and almost any description can be challenged due to the great variation which is to be found in a native population compared to a landscape population. I have attempted to estimate sizes which might be attained under "normal" landscape situations and, in many instances, have listed maximum heights so that the reader might get a feel for the differences. Plants can be maintained at various heights and widths by proper pruning. If a plant is listed as 25 feet in height and one only has space for a 20 foot specimen this is no reason to avoid using the tree. There are simply too many variables which affect the size of a tree or shrub. Plants which appear gnarled and dwarfed on high mountain tops where the soil is dry, rocky, and the exposure windy and cold, may grow to be gentle giants in the moist, fertile, well-drained soils of the valley below. Do not attempt to evaluate the size of a tree in one individual's yard with that in another's even though both may be of the same age. The conditions under which they are growing may be very different.

HARDINESS ratings are risky business since many factors other than low temperatures affect plant survival in a specific area. The hardiness zones mentioned in this book follow those compiled by the Arnold Arboretum. A picture of the map is presented on page 3.

The U. S. Department of Agriculture also publishes a hardiness map which is slightly different from the Arnold Arboretum map (See page 4). Each zone includes 10°F increments and is split into an *a* and *b* zone with the lower temperature occurring in the *a* zone. Since the maps do not coincide it is difficult to compare hardiness ratings but the following cross comparisons of USDA zones versus Arnold zones may serve as a guide.

USDA Hardiness Zones	Arnold Hardiness Zones
Zone 1 — below 50°F	Zone 1 — -50°F and below
Zone 2 — -50 to -40°F	Zone 2 — -50 to -35°F
Zone 3 — -40 to -30°F	Zone 3 — -35 to -20°F
Zone 4 — -30 to -20°F	Zone 4 — -20 to -10°F
Zone 5 — -20 to -10°F	Zone 5 — -10 to -5°F
Zone 6 — -10 to 0°F	Zone 6 — -5 to 5°F
Zone 7 — 0 to 10°F	Zone 7 — 5 to 10°F
Zone 8 — 10 to 20°F	Zone 8 — 10 to 20°F

Hardiness ratings are meant only as a guide and should not be looked upon as a limiting factor in plant use. Large bodies of water, well-drained soil, wind protection, and adequate moisture will help to increase hardiness. I used *Ilex cornuta* 'Burfordii', a Zone 7 plant, in a protected part of my Illinois garden. Temperatures in the winter of 1975-76 dropped as low as -8°F yet the plant was not injured. Many plants such as forsythia are limitedly flower bud hardy but quite shoot hardy. Plants, such as *Abelia* × *grandiflora*, are best considered weakly shoot hardy and are often killed to the ground in central Illinois but, as with herbaceous perennials, develop new shoots and will make an attractive show during the growing season since it flowers on new wood.

Hardiness is a dual-edged sword for heat, like cold, can limit successful growth of certain plants. Unfortunately, heat tolerance has not been studied to any degree. *Acer platanoides,* Norway Maple, languishes in the heat of Zone 8. The same is true for most firs, spruces, and white-barked birches. The reasons for their lack of adaptability are unknown but rest assured heat stress, high night temperatures, and/or perhaps lack of sufficient chilling to satisfy bud rest, contribute to plant decline. There is no guarantee that a species which performs well in Boston or Cincinnati will do likewise in Atlanta or Orlando. The hardiness zone ratings have been expanded to include the most suitable range for the culture of a specific plant.

In many instances, I have offered a ballpark estimate of flower bud or plant low temperature tolerance. These predictions are based on extensive observations and laboratory cold hardiness determinations that Dr. Orville M. Lindstrom and I have conducted on many taxa. Use these as a guide and not absolute values. One should never allow hardiness ratings to solely determine whether he/she will use a specific plant. Since plants have not been known to read what is written about them in terms of hardiness, they often surprise one and grow outside of their listed range of adaptability.

HABIT as used in this book should supply the reader with a mental picture of the ultimate form or outline of the plant and should prove useful to landscape architecture and design students.

RATE of growth refers to the vertical increase in growth unless specified differently. Rate, as is true for size, is influenced by numerous variables such as soil, drainage, water, fertility, light, exposure, ad infinitum. The designation *slow* means the plant grows 12″ or less per year; *medium* refers to 13 to 24″ of growth per year; and *fast* to 25″ or greater.

TEXTURE refers to the appearance of the plant in foliage and without foliage. A plant that is fine in leaf may be extremely coarse without foliage. Best landscape effects are achieved when similar textures are blended. For example, a planting of catalpa next to a weeping willow is a definite contrast of textures.

The BARK COLOR and texture were included so that the reader could develop an appreciation for these ornamental characters. Too often they are overlooked and omitted as integral parts of the plant's aesthetic qualities. Considering that most deciduous trees and shrubs are devoid of foliage for six months in the northern states, it behooves us to use trees and shrubs with good bark character. To my way of thinking trees like *Acer griseum, Stewartia* spp., and *Ulmus parvifolia* are more beautiful without foliage.

LEAF COLOR refers to the shade of trees in summer as well as the colors attained in fall. Again, nutritional and soils factors can partially influence the degree of greenness and to a lesser extent the quality of fall color for fall color is very strongly genetically controlled.

HARDINESS ZONES of the UNITED STATES and CANADA

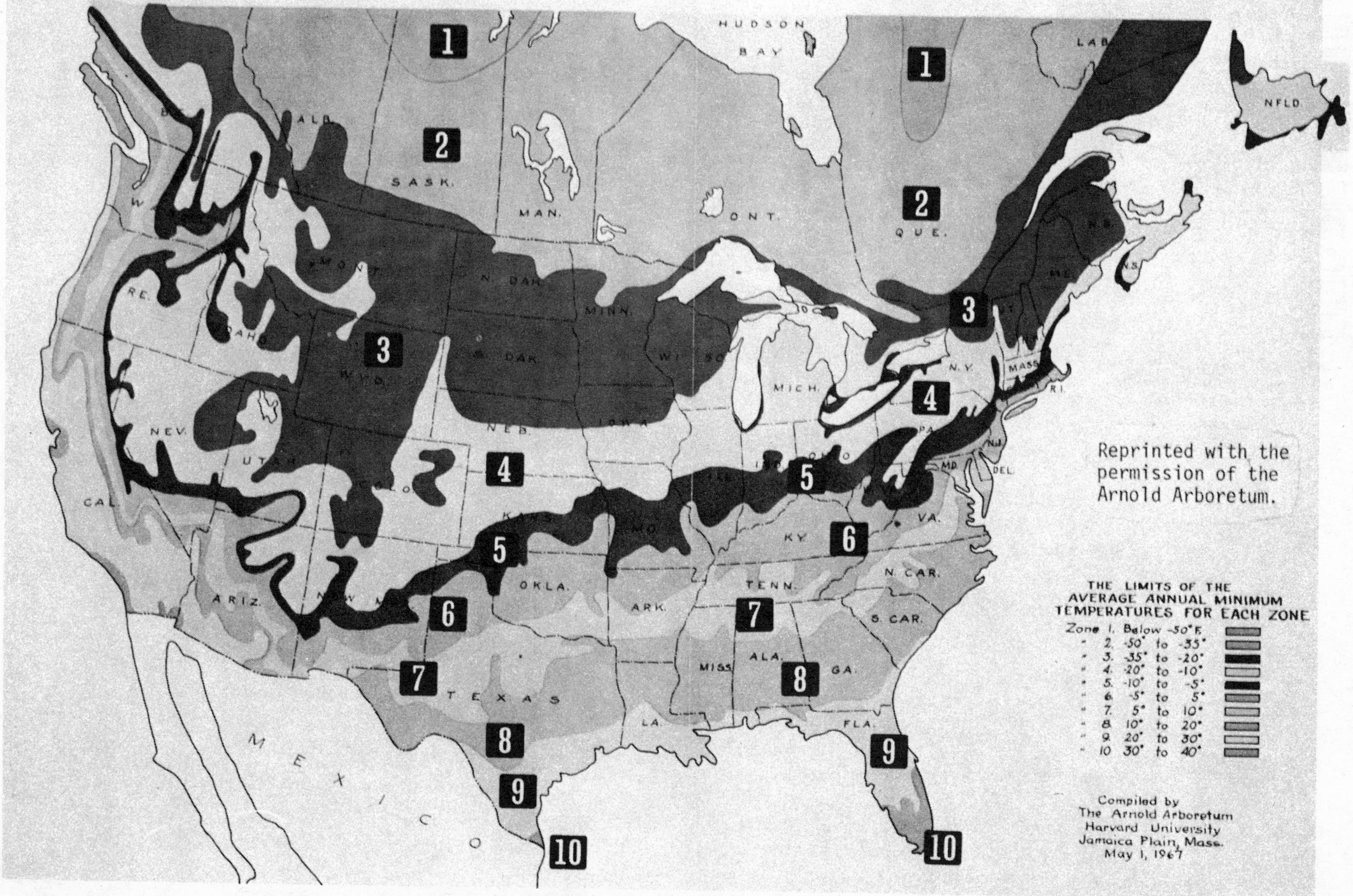
HUDSON BAY
ALB.
SASK.
MAN.
ONT.
QUE.
LAB.
NFLD.
N.B.
N.S.
ME.
MASS.
R.I.
N.Y.
PA.
N.J.
MD.
DEL.
VA.
N. CAR.
S. CAR.
GA.
FLA.
ALA.
MISS.
TENN.
KY.
OHIO
MICH.
ILL.
WIS.
MINN.
IOWA
MO.
ARK.
LA.
OKLA.
KAS.
NEB.
N. DAK.
S. DAK.
MONT.
WYO.
COLO.
UTAH
NEV.
IDAHO
ORE.
WASH.
CAL.
ARIZ.
N. MEX.
TEXAS
MEXICO
1
2
3
4
5
6
7
8
9
10
Reprinted with the permission of the Arnold Arboretum.
THE LIMITS OF THE AVERAGE ANNUAL MINIMUM TEMPERATURES FOR EACH ZONE
Zone 1. Below -50° F.
" 2. -50° to -35°
" 3. -35° to -20°
" 4. -20° to -10°
" 5. -10° to -5°
" 6. -5° to 5°
" 7. 5° to 10°
" 8. 10° to 20°
" 9. 20° to 30°
" 10 30° to 40°
Compiled by
The Arnold Arboretum
Harvard University
Jamaica Plain, Mass.
May 1, 1967

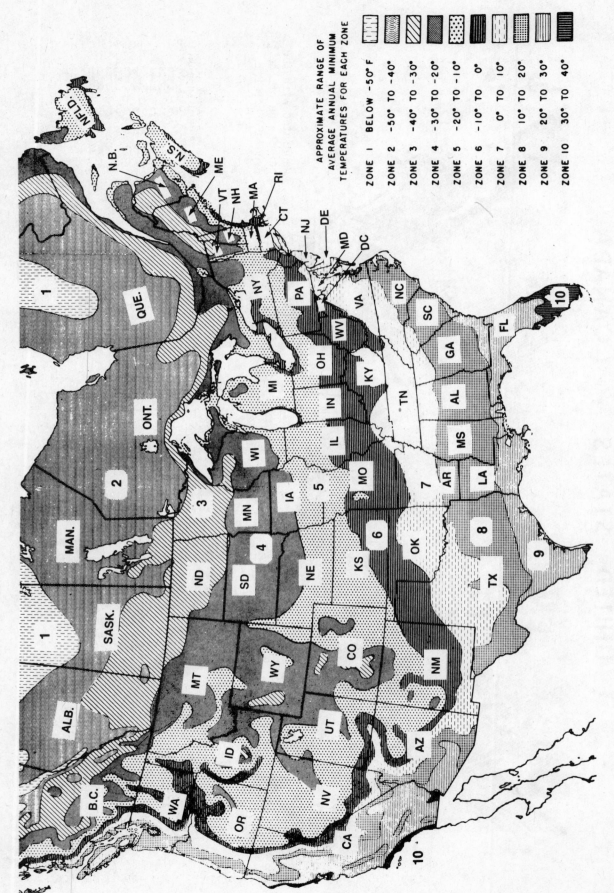

Zones of plant hardiness.

FLOWERS are discussed in terms of color, size, fragrance, period of effectiveness (based on my observations in central Illinois, Boston and Athens-Atlanta, GA) and the type of inflorescence. Some plants bear monoecious flower (both sexes on same plant) while others are dioecious (sexes separate). This has profound implications if one is interested in fruit production. It does no good to buy 5 female American Hollies unless a male plant accompanies them. The male is necessary for pollination and subsequent fruit set. A good rule of thumb to apply to flowering as treated in this book is to add 4 to 5 weeks to Georgia dates to equate them with central Illinois-Boston and reverse the procedure for Illinois-Boston dates to bring them into harmony with Athens-Atlanta. Unless dates are specified as Georgian, they refer to central Illinois–Boston.

FRUIT discussion covers the type of fruit for each particular plant (i.e., whether it is a drupe, pome, berry); the size and color; period of effectiveness; persistence; and ornamental value.

The CULTURE section discusses the ease of transplanting, soil, light, pruning, pollution tolerance, and other factors which govern the successful growth of a particular plant type.

DISEASES AND INSECTS is a listing of problems encountered with various plant types. If a particular insect or disease is a significant problem it is usually discussed in some detail. Surprisingly most plants require limited maintenance. Ask yourself how often you have sprayed for insects or diseases on your ornamental plants.

LANDSCAPE VALUE is an arbitrary judgement on my part as to the best location or use for a particular plant in the landscape. Plants can be tailored to specific locations by pruning and other manipulations. The "pigeon holing" of plants is by far the worst crime one can commit. Certain plants are used for celebrated locations in the landscape and have become stereotyped. Blue Colorado Spruce or a White Birch are common occurrences in the front yard. Purpleleaf Plum is used on the corners of foundation plantings. Yews and many junipers are often reserved for foundation plantings. The effective use of a particular plant requires a thorough knowledge of all the factors discussed under that plant. It does no good to use a plant that has lovely flower and fruit qualities in wet soils if it is not adapted to this condition.

CULTIVARS are important components of the modern landscape and have been selected for growth habit, flower, fruit, pollution tolerance and myriad other factors. I have attempted to list the more common and recent introductions which are worthy of landscape consideration. Almost every juniper which is now sold is a cultivar which has been selected for good foliage and/or growth habit. The same could be said for many plants and you will note that many cultivar names are probably more familiar to you than the species.

PROPAGATION section lists the most effective methods of seed and vegetative reproduction. One of my research interests is in the area of propagation and much of the information in this section is based on actual experience. This section has been significantly expanded in this edition and often includes references for the individual requiring additional information.

RELATED SPECIES section discusses plant types which are similar to the species in many characters but differ in a few areas such as size, flower, or fruit color. Also included are those plants which are of negligible importance in the landscape but are worth considering if native to a particular area. Other plants discussed include plants which are limitedly known and available but seem to have excellent landscape potential.

ADDITIONAL NOTES is a potpourri of facts, trivia, or minutia related to the use of plant parts for food, fiber and man's enjoyment.

NATIVE HABITAT discusses the natural distribution or range of a particular plant type. The introduction or cultivation date is the earliest record of the plants.

PLANT MORPHOLOGY

In order to successfully identify woody plants it is necessary for an individual to have a keen awareness (working knowledge) of taxonomic terminology and concise mental pictures of leaf, bud, stem, flower and fruit morphology. The glossary in the back of the text capably defines the terminology. This section is devoted to line drawings of woody plant morphological characters which will aid in the identification of various plant types. Definitions and examples are also included.

LEAF MORPHOLOGY

ANGIOSPERM LEAF TYPES

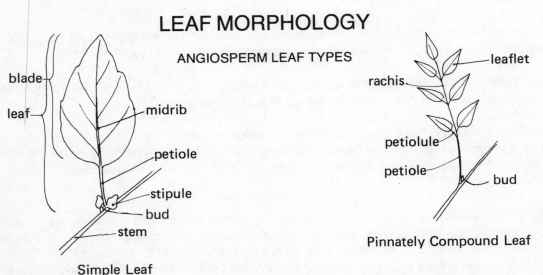

Simple Leaf

Pinnately Compound Leaf

The position of the bud determines whether the leaf is simple or compound. In this case the bud is located in the axil of a single leaf and the stem, therefore, the leaf is classified as simple.

In this case the bud is located in the axil of a structure with more than one leaf, therefore, the leaf is termed compound. Compound leaves are composed of anywhere from three (*Acer griseum*) to 400 to 1500 leaf-like structures in the case of *Albizia julibrissin.*

OTHER TYPES OF COMPOUND LEAVES

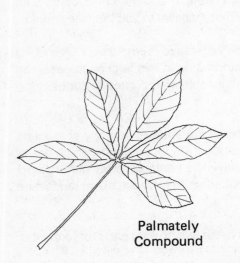

Palmately Compound

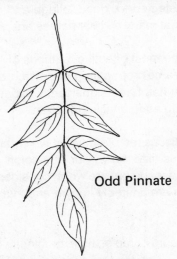

Odd Pinnate

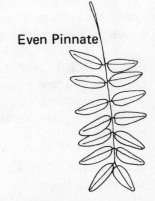

Even Pinnate

In this situation each leaflet is attached to a common point. Ex: *Aesculus, Acanthopanax, Parthenocissus quinquefolia.*

A compound pinnate type of leaf with an odd number of leaflets. Ex: *Acer negundo* has 3 to 5 leaflets. *Fraxinus americana* has 5 to 9 leaflets.

A compound pinnate type of leaf with an even number of leaflets. Ex: *Gleditsia, Caragana.*

Bipinnately Compound

Bipinnately compound leaves are twice divided. What was considered the leaflet of the pinnately compound leaf is now another leaf-bearing axis to which additional leaflets are attached. The new leaf bearing axes are referred to as pinnae. Each pinna has a certain number of leaflets. Ex: *Gymnocladus, Albizia, Gleditsia* (in certain instances).

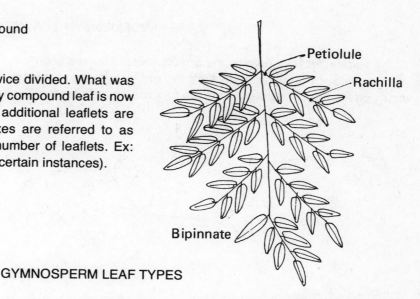

Petiolule

Rachilla

Bipinnate

GYMNOSPERM LEAF TYPES

Cone-bearing or naked seeded plants often display different leaf types than those associated with angiosperm plants. Not all conifers (or cone-bearers) have evergreen foliage (exceptions include *Taxodium, Metasequoia, Larix,* and *Pseudolarix.*)

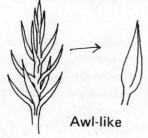

Awl-like

The needles (leaves) are shaped like an awl. They are usually very sharp to the touch. Many *Juniperus* (Junipers) exhibit awl-shaped foliage. This character is manifested in juvenile forms of juniper, however, there are many species and cultivars (*Juniperus communis, J. procumbens, J. chinensis* 'Pyramidalis' to name a few) which possess the awl-like or needle foliage in youth and old age.

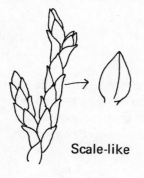

Scale-like

Scale-like foliage overlaps like the shingles on a roof or the scales on a fish. This type of foliage is relatively soft to the touch. *Thuja, Chamaecyparis, Cupressus, Calocedrus* and many *Juniperus* species exhibit this type of foliage.

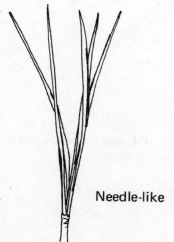

Needle-like

Needle-like foliage is typical of several evergreen genera and species. The drawing depicts the foliage of a 5-needled pine. In the genus *Pinus* the leaves (needles) are usually contained in fascicles of 2, 3, 2 and 3, or 5. Other species such as *Abies, Picea, Cedrus, Pseudotsuga,* and *Taxus* have the needles borne singly or in clusters along the stem. The needles may be relatively flat (2-sided) or angular (often quadrangular) in cross-section. See the respective genera for a detailed discussion of their leaf morphology.

ARRANGEMENT OF LEAVES

Many vegetative keys employ the arrangement of leaves and buds as a basis for separation. The use of the four categories by the student allows him/her to categorize plants into groups and assists in eliminating many plants from consideration in the process of positive identification.

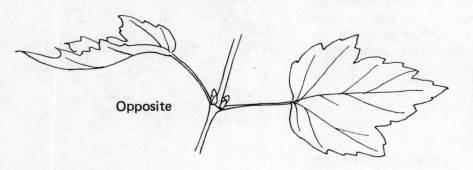

Opposite

Leaves and buds directly across from each other on the stem. Ex: *Acer, Lonicera, Deutzia, Viburnum.*

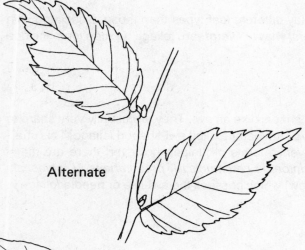

Alternate

Leaves and buds are spaced in alternating fashion along the axis of the stem and seldom, if ever, are seated directly across from each other. Ex: *Betula, Fagus, Quercus, Celtis, Ulmus, Carya, Juglans.*

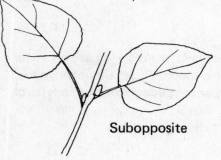

Subopposite

Subopposite refers to a condition where the leaves and buds are not spaced sufficiently far apart to be considered alternate nor are they perfectly opposite, hence, the term subopposite. Ex: *Rhamnus cathartica, Cercidiphyllum japonicum, Chionanthus virginicus.*

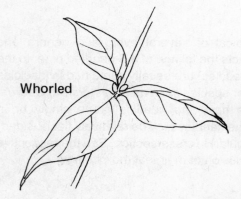

Whorled

Whorled refers to a condition when three buds and leaves (or more) are present at a node. Ex: *Catalpa, Hydrangea paniculata* 'Grandiflora', *Cephalanthus occidentalis.*

TYPES OF VENATION

**Elm
Pinnate**

Pinnate. The leaf has a prominent central vein (often termed the midrib) which extends from the base, where the petiole attaches to the blade, to the apex of the leaf. If the interveinal areas were removed the overall effect would be that of a fishbone. Pinnate venation occurs in the leaves of many plant types. The elm (*Ulmus*) and oak (*Quercus*) are classic examples.

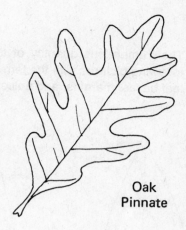

**Oak
Pinnate**

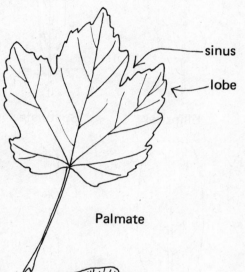

—— sinus

—— lobe

Palmate

Palmate. There are several main veins all of approximately equal size which extend from the base of the leaf to the apex of the lobe or margin of leaf. Ex: *Acer, Platanus, Cercis.*

Dichotomous

Dichotomous. A very limited type of venation, the most familiar representative of which is *Ginkgo biloba*. The basal veins extend for a distance and then branch forming a "Y" type pattern.

Parallel

Parallel. Typical of many monocotyledonous plants. The veins run essentially parallel to each other along the long axis of the leaf. Ex: *Zea* (corn), *Ruscus, Danae.*

LEAF SHAPES

The tremendous quantity of terminology related to leaf shapes can be confusing. Association of the following pictures with the terms will help to alleviate the burden of strict terminology. This also applies to leaf bases, margins, and apices.

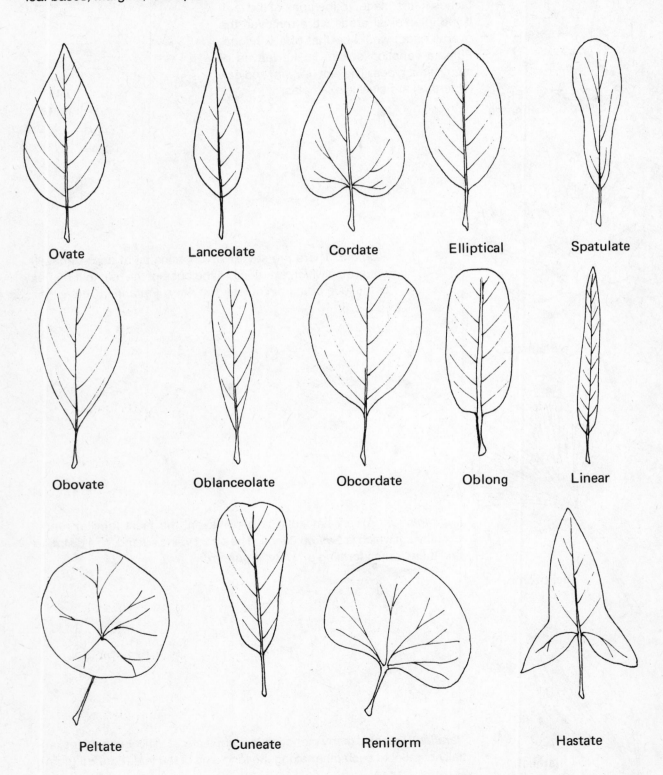

Ovate   Lanceolate   Cordate   Elliptical   Spatulate

Obovate   Oblanceolate   Obcordate   Oblong   Linear

Peltate   Cuneate   Reniform   Hastate

LEAF BASES, MARGINS, APICES

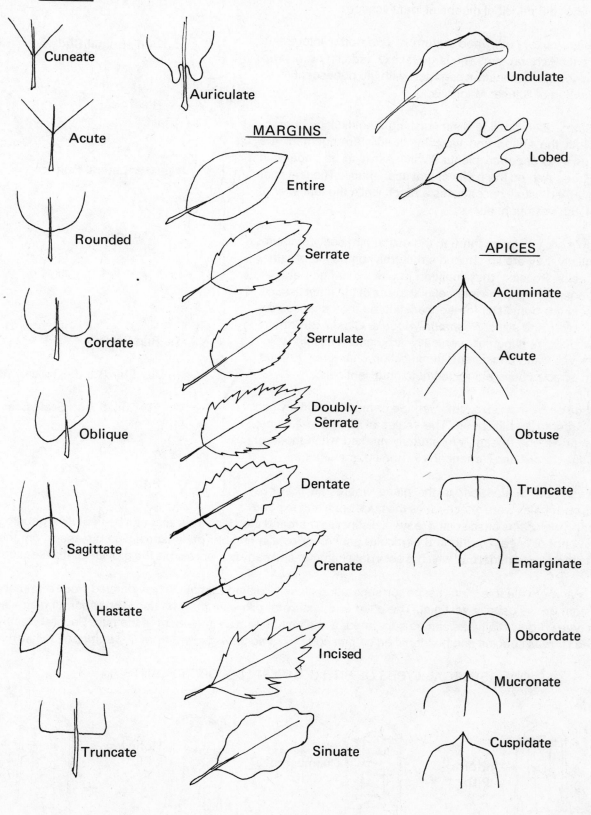

BASES

Cuneate

Acute

Rounded

Cordate

Oblique

Sagittate

Hastate

Truncate

Auriculate

MARGINS

Entire

Serrate

Serrulate

Doubly-Serrate

Dentate

Crenate

Incised

Sinuate

Undulate

Lobed

APICES

Acuminate

Acute

Obtuse

Truncate

Emarginate

Obcordate

Mucronate

Cuspidate

STEM AND BUD MORPHOLOGY

Deciduous woody plant identification in winter must be based on stem, bud and bark characters. Buds and stems offer the principal means of identification.

The shape, size, color, and texture of *buds* offer interesting identification characters. The large, sticky, reddish brown bud of Common Horsechestnut contrasts with the pubescent, soft-textured bud of Saucer Magnolia.

Leaf Scars often provide distinguishing identification characters. Both the shape and vascular bundle arrangement are often used to separate plants. White Ash can be separated from Green Ash on the basis of leaf scar shape. The leaf scar of White Ash usually possesses a notch while the leaf scar of Green Ash is straight across.

Lenticels are produced through the action of a cork cambium. Essentially they are lip-shaped structures composed of rather corky cells. Possibly they function in gas exchange between the atmosphere and the intercellular areas of the plant tissues. Lenticels are beneficial for identification as they possess different colors and sizes. *Rhamnus frangula,* Glossy Buckthorn, has whitish, rectangular, vertically arranged lenticels which offer a valid and consistent identification character. *Prunus,* cherry, species have elongated horizontal lenticels.

Bud Scales by their size, color, shape or markings offer good characters for identification. The scales of *Ostrya virginiana,* American Hophornbeam, are striately marked while those of *Carpinus caroliniana,* American Hornbeam, are smooth.

Terminal Bud Scale Scar is the place where the previous year's bud scales were attached. As the buds open and expand in Spring the scales abscise and leave a distinct scar around the stem. This scar can be useful for gauging the amount of linear growth in a particular season or over a number of seasons. The distance from the scar to the new terminal bud which is set in late summer and early fall represents the growth for that season.

Pith is a very valuable plant tissue for separating closely related plants. Pith is derived from a primary meristem and is usually vestigial. The color and texture of pith can often be used for separating similar plant types. Forsythia types can be separated by the texture and arrangement of the pith. Several closely related *Cornus* species can be identified by pith color [*C. amomum* (brown) from *C. sanguinea* (white)].

- Terminal Bud
- Leaf Scar
- Lateral Bud
- Lenticel
- Bud Scale
- Vascular Bundle Trace
- Terminal Bud Scale Scar
- Pith

SEVERAL TYPES OF PITH COMMON TO WOODY PLANTS

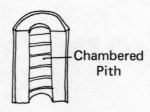
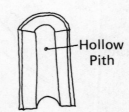

Uniform Pith Chambered Pith Hollow Pith Excavated Pith

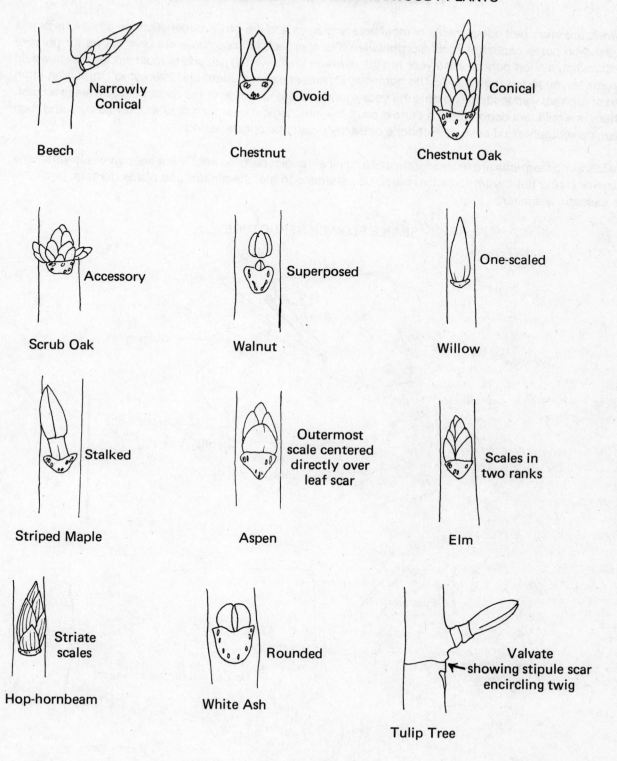

BUD TYPES FREQUENTLY FOUND IN WOODY PLANTS

Narrowly Conical

Beech

Ovoid

Chestnut

Conical

Chestnut Oak

Accessory

Scrub Oak

Superposed

Walnut

One-scaled

Willow

Stalked

Striped Maple

Outermost scale centered directly over leaf scar

Aspen

Scales in two ranks

Elm

Striate scales

Hop-hornbeam

Rounded

White Ash

Valvate showing stipule scar encircling twig

Tulip Tree

FLORAL MORPHOLOGY

Flowers are important components of most botanical keys and the positive identification of various plants is based on some aspect of floral morphology. This approach is acceptable but only allows for positive identification a short period of the year (on the average the flowering periods of most woody plants would average seven to fourteen days). The homeowner, nurseryman, student and interested plantsman often wish or are required to identify plants the year-round and the use of features other than flowers is a must. If there is significant doubt about a certain plant the most logical approach is to wait for flowers and then consult a reputable text such as Rehder's or Bailey's great taxonomic works.

The following diagrams are representative of a "typical" angiosperm flower. There are numerous variations in flower shape but the reproductive parts, i.e., stamens (male, staminate) and pistils (female, pistillate) are essentially similar.

SIMPLE FLOWER STRUCTURE

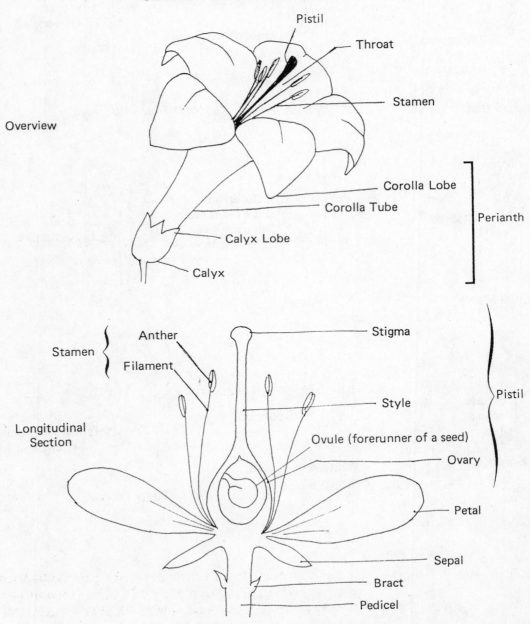

Flowers which have all the parts (sepals, petals, stamens, and a pistil or pistils) are termed *complete*. *Incomplete* flowers lack one or more whorls of floral parts such as the petals. *Imperfect* flowers lack either stamens or pistils. *Perfect* flowers have both stamens and pistils. *Monoecious* means that staminate and pistillate flowers are present on the same plant but in different structures (*Betula, Carpinus, Ostrya, Carya, Quercus, Fagus*). *Dioecious* means the staminate and pistillate flowers are borne on different plants (Examples include *Gymnocladus dioicus, Ilex, Lindera,* and *Cercidiphyllum*). *Polygamo-monoecious* refers to a condition where perfect, pistillate and staminate flowers occur on the same tree. *Polygamo-dioecious* implies perfect and pistillate flowers on the same plant or perfect and staminate flowers. Several woody plants which show polygamous characters include *Gleditsia, Fraxinus, Chionanthus, Osmanthus,* and *Morus*.

INFLORESCENCES

Flowers are borne on structures which are referred to as inflorescences. An inflorescence is a collection of individual flowers arranged in some specific fashion. The following are some of the representative types found in both woody and herbaceous plants.

Spike. Individual flowers are sessile on the elongated axis (peduncle). The male flower of *Betula, Carpinus, Alnus, Populus, Quercus, Salix* and *Carya* are spikes with a special name termed catkin or ament (Indeterminate).

Spike

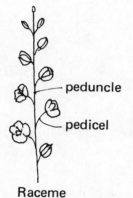

peduncle

pedicel

Raceme

Raceme. In the simplest terms it is a modification of a spike with the individual flowers stalked (on a pedicel). *Cladrastis, Laburnum, Wisteria* possess racemose flowers (Indeterminate).

Corymb. An indeterminate (can continue to elongate) inflorescence in which the individual flowers are attached at different points along the peduncle. The outer flowers open first. *Malus, Prunus,* and *Iberis* show corymb inflorescences.

Corymb

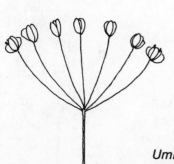

Umbel

Umbel. An indeterminate inflorescence in which the pedicels of the individual flowers radiate from about the same place at the top of the peduncle. Flowers open from outside in. *Hedera helix, Aralia, Daucus* (carrot) are examples.

16

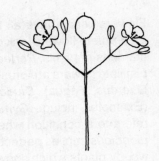

Cyme. A determinate, flat or convex inflorescence, the central or inner flowers opening first. *Cornus, Viburnum, Geranium* are examples.

Cyme

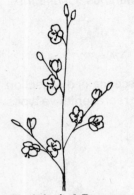

Panicle. An indeterminate inflorescence with repeated branching. Panicles can be made up of many racemes, spikes, corymbs, cymes, or umbels. Racemose-panicles are found in *Pieris, Koelreuteria;* spikose-panicles in corn; corymbose-panicles in *Pyracantha;* umbellose-panicles in *Aralia.*

Panicle (of Racemes)

Solitary. Indicates a single flower with a pedicel attached to the stem. *Magnolia, Calycanthus, Kerria* and many other woody plant flowers fall into this category.

Solitary

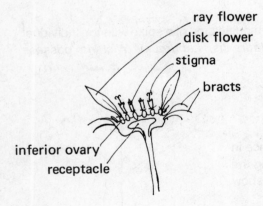

ray flower
disk flower
stigma
bracts
inferior ovary
receptacle

Head. The typical inflorescence of the family Asteraceae (Compositae). Made up of ray (sterile) and disk (fertile) flowers which are arranged on a flattened receptacle. *Chrysanthemum, Rudbeckia* are examples.

Head

A *spadix* is a specialized type of inflorescence typical of many tropical plants. The showy part is the bract or spathe while the spike-like structure which is partially surrounded by the spathe bears the fertile flowers. Examples include *Anthurium, Spathiphyllum, Caladium, Calla* and *Philodendron.*

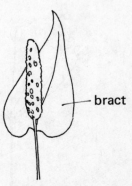

bract

Spadix

FRUIT MORPHOLOGY

The longitudinal section of the "typical" flower offers a representative view of the ovary. The ovary is the forerunner of the fruit and is defined as an unripened fruit. The ovary is composed of carpel(s) which are highly modified leaf-like structures which inclose ovules (forerunner of seeds). An ovary may be composed of one carpel (simple fruit) or two or more carpels (compound fruit). Fruits are very important considerations in woody landscape plants for they offer good ornamental assets (color, texture) and positive identification features through late summer, into fall, and often persist until spring of the year following maturation. The fruits of *Ilex* (Holly) are often colorful for a long period of time while fruits of *Prunus* (Cherry), some *Malus* (Flowering Crabapples), and several *Crataegus* (Hawthorns) persist briefly after ripening (2 to 4 weeks).

The following classification scheme for fruits along with their definitions and line drawings should afford an idea of the diversity of fruit types which are manifested by woody or herbaceous plants.

I. SIMPLE FRUITS

  A. Dry Fruits

    1. *Indehiscent fruits* (not splitting open at maturity)

      a. *Achene* — one-seeded fruit with seed attached at only one place to the pericarp. Pericarp is very close-fitting and does not split open, at least along regular established lines. Examples: Buckwheat, Sunflower, Calendula.

      b. *Caryopsis* — similar to an achene but the pericarp is adherent to the seed, the two often being indistinguishable (seed coat is inseparable from the pericarp). Examples: Corn, Wheat.

      c. *Samara* — usually one-seeded (not always) with a membranous wing which develops from the pericarp. Examples: Maple, Ash, Elm.

      d. *Nut* — a bony, hard, one-seeded fruit. The pericarp is bony throughout. Examples: Oak, Chestnut and Filbert.

      e. *Utricle* — similar to an achene but the ovary wall is relatively thin and inflated so it fits only loosely around the seed. Examples: Goosefoot, Pigweed.

      f. *Nutlet* — diminutive of nut. Examples: Hornbeam, Birch, Hophornbeam.

    2. *Dehiscent fruits* (splitting open when mature)

      a. *Legume* (Pod) — composed of one carpel and opens along two sutures; characteristic of most members of the Fabaceae (Leguminosae); contains several to many seeds. Examples: Redbud, Honey-locust, Coffeetree, Black Locust.

      b. *Follicle* — composed of one carpel but splits open at maturity along one suture exposing several to many seeds. Examples: Larkspur, Columbine, Peony, Milkweed, Spirea, individual fruits of Magnolia.

      c. *Capsule* — many-seeded fruits formed from more than one carpel. The carpels are united. *Loculicidal Capsule* opens along midrib; *Septicidal Capsule* divides through the partitions. Examples: Rhododendron, Mockorange, Deutzia, Forsythia, and Lilac.

d. *Silique* — composed of two carpels which separate at maturity, leaving a thin partition between. Example: Mustard family.

e. *Silicle* — a short, broad silique. Examples: Shepherd's Purse, Peppergrass.

f. *Pyxis* — type of capsule which opens around a horizontal ring, the top of fruit falling away like a lid. Example: Purslane.

B. Fleshy Fruits

1. *Berry* — the entire pericarp (exo, endo, meso-carp) is fleshy. Examples: Tomato, Date, Banana, Blueberry, Cranberry, Honeysuckle.

   a. *Hesperidium* — a berry with a leathery rind. Examples: Orange, Lemon, Grapefruit.

   b. *Pepo* — a berry with a hard rind and fleshy inner matrix. Examples: Watermelon, Squash, Pumpkin.

2. *Drupe* — the pericarp is clearly differentiated into three layers; exocarp is the epidermis; middle layer, the mesocarp, is fleshy; and the inner layer, the endocarp, is stony. Examples: Cherry, Peach, Plum, Sassafras, Viburnum, Holly and numerous other woody ornamental plants.

3. *Pome* — the pericarp is surrounded by the floral tube (hypanthium) which becomes fleshy and tasty. Examples: Apple, Pear, Quince.

II. AGGREGATE FRUITS

Develop from a single flower which contains many pistils. Several to many fruitlets are massed on one receptacle. Examples: Raspberry—aggregate of drupes; Strawberry—aggregate of achenes; Tuliptree—aggregate of samaras; Magnolia—aggregate of follicles; Osageorange—aggregate of drupes.

III. MULTIPLE FRUITS

Consists of several flowers which are more or less united into one mass. Examples: Fig, Pineapple, Mulberry.

FRUIT TYPES

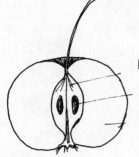

Endocarp

Seed

Receptacle

POME
*(Malus, Pyrus,
Chaenomeles)*

Seed

Endocarp

Mesocarp

DRUPE
*(Prunus, Viburnum,
Celtis, Sassafras)*

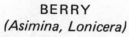

Pericarp

(Fleshy Matrix)

Seed

BERRY
(Asimina, Lonicera)

SAMARA
(Ulmus)

SCHIZOCARP
(Acer)

SAMARA
(Fraxinus)

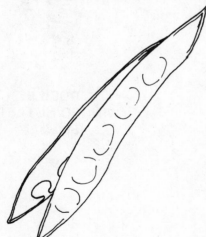

LEGUME (POD)
*(Robinia, Cercis,
Gleditsia)*

CAPSULES
*(Kalmia, Forsythia,
Rhododendron)*

ACORN
(Quercus)

20

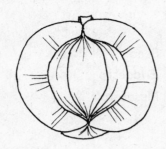

NUT WITH DEHISCENT HUSK
(Carya)

NUTLET
(Carpinus)

CONE
(Tsuga, Pinus, Abies)

AGGREGATE OF SAMARAS
(Liriodendron)

MULTIPLE FRUIT OF SMALL DRUPES
(Morus)

STROBILE: WINGED NUTLET
(Betula)

AGGREGATE OF FOLLICLES
(Magnolia)

THE USE OF KEYS FOR IDENTIFYING WOODY PLANTS

A key is, in esssence, an artificial contrivance which outlines specific morphological features in an organized manner that allows the identifier (user) to eventually arrive at a specific plant or at least reach a point where he/she can consult other references for further separatory information. The information in many keys is geared to flower and fruit morphology; however, keys have been constructed from leaf, stem, bud, root, plant habit, anatomical traits and about any other feature be it macro- or micro-scopic.

A key is an aide to plant identification but far from the sole answer as many individuals would lead one to believe. Plants are variable entities! They may be in flower an average of only 7 to 14 days. The leaves of deciduous trees and shrubs, in the northern climes, are present, at most, 5 to 7 months. Bud and stem colors change drastically from fall through winter and into spring. A key that includes all season features is the utopian necessity but does not exist. Keys are often based on one or two morphological traits which suffice for a single time period. Gardening enthusiasts and those who work in horticultural related businesses must be able to identify plants throughout the seasons. I have seen more mixed up landscape plantings of birch, witchhazel, and honeysuckle simply because the buyer and seller could not distinguish between and among the various species. The Illinois campus is a monument to this problem for pink and white flowering honeysuckles were mixed unintentionally in hedges; Japanese and Mentor Barberries confused in the same planting; and Gray and European White Birch in total chaos. These examples are not isolated for I have seen foul-ups like this in many landscape situations. The moral is that plants must be learned by the characteristics which will permit separation in any season.

A key is a supplement and should not be used as the sole mode for teaching and/or learning plants. Innumerable times I have heard people say they can always "key" the plant out. Yet when I asked them to define several of the simple terms used in keys they were boggled. The successful use of a key demands a specific level of horticultural and botanical expertise. Considerable practice, patience, taxonomic vocabulary, and a more knowledgeable plant person (who can tell you if the answer is correct) are the necessary prerequisites. If one makes the wrong choice in the dichotomy of the key, he/she is hopelessly lost.

Too often keys attempt to simplify and reduce morphological characters to a paradigm. Maples are often construed as having the "typical" five-lobed leaves when; in fact, the genus *Acer* possesses species with trifoliate, compound pinnate, simple pinnate, and simple palmate leaves. The same is true for oaks where one gets the impression that White and Bur Oak leaves are characteristic of the genus. If one looks at enough oaks he/she quickly finds this more the exception than the rule.

A typical woody plant key for several *Cornus*, dogwood, species might be constructed like the following.

A. Leaves alternate. *C. alternifolia*

A. Leaves opposite.

    B. Flowers and fruits in open cymes or panicles, pith white, buff or brown.

        C. Fruits cream colored, inflorescence paniculate, pith buff. *C. racemosa*

        C. Fruits cream or bluish, inflorescence cymose, pith white or brown.

            D. Fruits and pith white. *C. sericea*

            D. Fruits porcelain-blue or bluish white, pith brown. *C. amomum*

    B. Flowers sessile in compact umbels, true flowers surrounded by 4 conspicuous, white, petal-like bracts.

        C. Bracts emarginate (indented). *C. florida*

        C. Bracts acuminate (long pointed). *C. kousa*

A key starts with a general categorization (alternate versus opposite) and gradually works to the smallest component. The above example is geared to 6 dogwood species and shows the pathway of least resistance for "keying out a plant". One would note that the leaves are opposite or alternate. If alternate, the plant in question is *C. alternifolia*. The opposite branch offers 5 possibilities which can be separated without great difficulty assuming floral and fruit structures can be examined.

The following books offer valuable "keys" for distinguishing among plants. See bibliography for complete citation.

Apgar, Austin C. *Ornamental Shrubs of the United States* and *Trees of the Northern United States.*

Bailey, L.H. *Manual of Cultivated Plants.*

Blackburn, Benjamin. *Trees and Shrubs in Eastern North America.*

Core, Earl L., and Nelle P. Ammons. *Woody Plants in Winter.*

Curtis, Ralph W., et al. *Vegetative Keys to Common Ornamental Woody Plants.*

Gray, Asa. *Gray's Manual of Botany* (revised by M.C. Fernald).

Harlow, William M. *Fruit Key and Twig Key.*

Rehder, Alfred. *Manual of Cultivated Trees and Shrubs.*

Sargent, Charles S. *Manual of the Trees of North America.* Vol. I and II.

Trelease, William. *Winter Botany.*

Vietel, Arthur T. *Trees, Shrubs and Vines.*

PLANT NOMENCLATURE

Any discussion of plants should be prefaced by an explanation of how and why plants are named as well as a general understanding of the concepts of genus, species, variety, cultivar, and forma, all of which are used in this text. The following article (written by this author) was published in the *American Horticulturist* 54:32-34 (1975) and is reprinted here with only minor changes.

Recently I read a column by a noted garden authority (writer) who attempted to define the makeup of a plant's scientific name. His ideas and those of the taxonomic world were miles asunder. A name is a handle by which we get to know certain people, places and plants. We learn to recognize specific characters, for example, an individual's facial expressions, voice, or walk, which make him or her different from another. Plants are not unlike people in this respect for they possess characteristics which set them apart. Sugar Maple, Acer *saccharum* Marsh., possesses opposite, simple, 5-lobed, medium to dark green leaves, sharp-pointed, imbricate, scaly, gray-brown to brown winter buds, upright-oval growth habit and brilliant yellow to burnt orange to red fall color. These features bring to this species an identity of its own which permit identification and separation from other types.

But what is this thing called a species? What do the latinized terms signify? How did the present system for naming plants evolve? Actually a historical sojourn would uncover several interesting facts concerning plant nomenclature. Before the Linnean system (binomial system) was accepted as a standard for naming plants, nomenclature was literally a disaster. Plants were named *Descriptively!* Latinized adjectives were added until sufficient verbiage was present to allow differentiation among plants. These latinized terms usually described morphological features of the plant. For example, the common carnation which is now *Dianthus caryophyllus* L. was, before 1753, "Dianthus floribus solitariis, squamis calycinis subovatis brevissimus, corollis crenatis." The Japanese Maple, *Acer palmatum* Thunb., was "Acer orientalis, hederae folio" which, figuratively translated, means oriental ivy-leaved maple. Obviously, students of plant materials were at a distinct disadvantage in the embryonic stages of nomenclature. If this latinization approach seems cumbersome or confusing consider for a moment the *Common Name* syndrome. The common name of a specific plant in one part of the state, country or world often is not the same in another. *Carpinus caroliniana* Walt., American hornbeam, has been called the water beech, blue beech, ironwood and musclewood. *Nymphaea alba* L., the European white waterlily has 15 English common names, 44 French, 105 German, and 81 Dutch for a total of 245 common names. The term Mayflower means different things to different people. In the Middle West it refers to *Podophyllum* (mayapple), in New England to *Epigaea repens* (trailing arbutus), in England to *Caltha palustris* (marsh marigold), and in the West Indies to a member of the pea family.

The question which arises is how was this chaos made orderly? It is credited to Carl von Linne more commonly known by his pen name of Linnaeus. His book, *Species Plantarum* (1753), signaled the beginning of the binomial system of nomenclature. Essentially it means that plants acquire two latinized names, one representing the *genus* and the other termed the *specific epithet,* which in combination with the generic name constitute the *species* by means of which all plants or animals are known by all people in all countries who speak or write of them with precision. Take, for example, the European white waterlily. It is known to everyone as *Nymphaea alba,* however, it becomes a different entity when spoken of in common name terminology.

Those who work with and read about plants are continually exposed to the concepts of genus, species, variety, cultivar, and forma. These terms appear in every nursery catalog, gardening article or publication concerning plants. However, what do they signify? Is there any practical significance to them and will understanding their meaning enhance one's appreciation of plants?

The *genus* is weakly defined as a more or less closely related and definable group of plants comprising one or more species. The genus is a category whose components (i.e. species) have more characters in common with each other than they do with components of other genera within the same family. Similarity of flowers and fruits is the most widely used feature although roots, stems, buds, and leaves are used. There may be a single species comprising a genus such as in the case of *Ginkgo* where the species *Ginkgo biloba* L. is the only member. *Cercidiphyllum* possesses only one species, *Cercidiphyllum japonicum* Sieb. and Zucc. (Katsura-tree), a beautiful tree of Japanese and Chinese origin. At the other end of the spectrum the genus *Rosa* (rose) contains between 100 and 200 species. The generic name is written with a capital letter and underlined [*Quercus* (oak)]. The plural of genus is genera and not the often used genuses.

Possibly the most important unit of classification is the *species,* however, the term is more a concept than an absolute entity. Lawrence noted that botanists of every generation have attempted to define the term species for which there may be no single definition. L.H. Bailey defined a species as a kind of plant or animal distinct from other kinds in marked or essential features that has good characters of identification, and may be assumed to represent a continuing succession of individuals from generation to generation. He then went on to say that the term is incapable of exact definition for nature is not laid out in formal lines. Actually, the species term is a concept, the product of each individual's judgment. My concept of a species can be depicted by a bell-shaped curve. In any population of trees, shrubs or people there are those which fit under the common characteristic in the peak portion of the curve. These individuals adhere to the marked or essential identification features. Certain individuals do not fit the stereotype and appear to belong at the fringes of the bell curve. Intergrading between the normal types and the extremely divergent types are those of moderate adherence to the essential features but exhibiting some variance perhaps in degree of pubescence (hairiness) or some other salient features. A casual stroll through the woods, meadow or any area where native stands of trees, shrubs, wild flowers and grasses co-exist will illucidate the great variation that exists within a species. All sugar maples within a given geographic area are not similar. They are members of the species, *Acer saccharum* Marsh., but exhibit discernible differences. A species name is composed of the following components and written as follows.

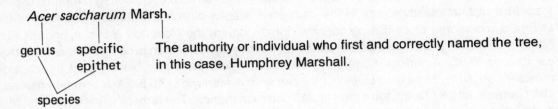

Acer saccharum Marsh.

genus   specific   The authority or individual who first and correctly named the tree,
epithet   in this case, Humphrey Marshall.

species

Note that the species name is always underlined or italicized and the specific epithet is lower case. The plural of species is species and the authority name does not have to be included in normal writing. Species is often abbreviated sp. (singular) or spp. (plural).

The term *variety* as used in the botanical sense constitutes a group or class of plants subordinate to a species and is usually applied to individuals displaying rather marked differences in nature. The crux is that these differences are inheritable and should show in succeeding generations. The difference between the thornless common honeylocust (*Gleditsia triacanthos* L. var. *inermis* Willd.), a true variety, and the species, common honeylocust (*Gleditsia triacanthos*), is the absence of thorns on the former. Seed collected from the variety will yield predominantly thornless seedlings, although a small percentage of the population will exhibit the thorny character. The redleaf Japanese barberry (*Berberis thunbergii* DC var. *atropurpurea* Chenault.), a true variety, yields 90 percent or greater redleaf progeny when grown from seed. Unfortunately, variety is often confused, and used interchangeably, with the term *cultivar* (a term coined by L.H. Bailey). The variety term is always written with the species, in lower case, and with the abbreviation var. placed before the variety term and the term underlined. The plural of variety is varieties. For example, the pink flowering variety of the white flowering dogwood (*Cornus florida* L.) may be written as follows.

Cornus florida var. *rubra*

A relatively new term and one which has important implications in horticultural circles is that of *cultivar*. A cultivar is an assemblage of cultivated plants which is clearly distinguished by any characters (morphological, physiological, cytological or chemical) and which when reproduced (sexually or asexually) retains its distinguishing characteristics. The difference between Norway maple (*Acer platanoides* L.) and the cultivar Crimson King (*Acer platanoides* 'Crimson King') is the purplish maroon foliage color of the cultivar. This cultivar cannot be reproduced from seed (hence does not fit the definition of variety) and must be reproduced vegetatively (grafting) to maintain the foliage characteristic. Essentially all other characters of identification between this species and the cultivar are similar. *Cedrus deodara* Loud. 'Kashmir', Kashmir Deodar cedar, is similar to the species in leaf, stem, bud and other morphological characters except it is much hardier. Kashmir was the only plant of 200 set in nursery rows in Concordville, Pennsylvania which survived a rapid temperature drop to 25°F below zero. Obviously this difference is not apparent to the eye, as in the previous example, but the selection of this cultivar permits the use of this beautiful specimen much further north than could be accomplished with the species. This difference between the cultivar and species is of a cytological nature possibly related to protoplasmic resistance to low temperature stresses. Sexually reproduced cultivars include those plants (annuals such as petunias, marigolds, and asters) which are propagated from seed derived from the repetitive crossing of two or more parental breeding stocks maintained either as lines or clones. A few woody plant cultivars are seed-produced, but these are the exception rather than the rule. The seed-produced cultivars may be uniform for fall color or fruit but other characteristics, like growth habit, may vary considerably among seedlings. A *line* consists of a group of plants that are largely homozygous (similar in genetic makeup). *Clone* is a group of plants which originated from a single individual and, therefore, is genetically homogenous.

Cultivar names are written with single quotes and the first letter of each word comprising the term is capitalized or the insertion of cv. before the term and the deletion of the single quotes.

Example: *Acer platanoides* 'Crimson King'

or

Acer platanoides cv. Crimson King

It is possible to have a cultivar of a variety. *Cornus florida* var. *rubra* is the pink flowering form of the flowering dogwood. A cultivar of this variety is Cherokee Chief which possesses deeper red flowers. The term would read *Cornus florida* var. *rubra* 'Cherokee Chief'.

The basics of plant nomenclature are relatively simple to comprehend. A fuller, deeper appreciation of the great diversity which nature offers can be developed through an understanding of the previous discussion. A knowledge of the systematic naming of plants also has practical implications. Consider the great variation in the red maple, *Acer rubrum* L. The purchase of a seedling-grown tree does not guarantee red flowers in spring nor brilliant red fall color, for trees may range from yellow to red in flower and fall color. The purchase of *Acer rubrum* 'October Glory', 'Autumn Flame' or 'Red Sunset' cultivars guarantees a tree with outstanding red to scarlet fall color for these trees were selected for their consistent ability to color.

The least important unit of classification is the *forma* (plural *formae*). In everyday horticultural parlance it is seldom used. A forma is a trivial variation that occurs in nature on a sporadic or random basis. Flower and fruit color variations are most often given forma status. For example, an orange-fruited form of the typical red-fruited *Ilex verticillata* is known. Correctly it is designated as *I. verticillata* f. *aurantiaca*. The red-flowered form of the yellow-flowered spicebush becomes correctly *Lindera benzoin* f. *rubra*. A forma generally does not come true-to-type from seed and to maintain the particular characteristic, vegetative propagation is necessary. The forma designation precedes the term and is designated with an f. or forma. The term is always lower case and underlined.

Abelia × grandiflora — Glossy Abelia
(a-bē′ li-a gran-di-flō′ra)

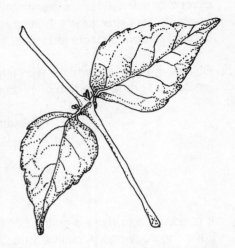

FAMILY: Caprifoliaceae

LEAVES: Opposite, simple, ovate, 1/2 to 1 1/2″ long, half as wide, acute, rounded or cuneate at base, dentate, lustrous dark green above, turning bronze-red in winter, paler beneath and glabrous, except bearded near base of midrib; petiole 1/8″ long.

BUDS: Small, ovoid, with about 2 pairs of rather loose scales.

STEM: Young-pubescent, reddish brown, fine textured appearance; older stem-exfoliating and split to expose light inner bark, leaf scars connected by a stipular line.

SIZE: 3 to 6′ by 3 to 6′; usually at the low end of the range in northern areas; have seen 8′ high plants in the south.

HARDINESS: Zone 5 but best in Zone 6 to 9,–5 to –10°F appears to coincide with stem kill; flowers still present in November in Zone 8, indicating tissue has not hardened.

HABIT: Often a spreading, dense, rounded, multistemmed shrub with arching branches; in the north is often killed back to ground or snow line and quickly grows back into a rather dense small shrub; at times somewhat loose in outline.

RATE: Medium to fast.

TEXTURE: Medium-fine in all seasons.

LEAF COLOR: Lustrous dark green in summer, bronze-green to bronze-red to bronze-purple in late fall and into winter; shows semi-evergreen tendency and leaves hold late into fall or early winter; in the south leaves persist through winter.

FLOWERS: White-flushed pink, funnel-shaped, 3/4″ long and wide, throat 5-lobed, slightly fragrant, 2 to 5 together in leafy panicles at end of lateral branches, 3/4″ long sepals (2 to 5 per flower) develop a purplish tinge and persist for months; May-June through frost; flowers on new growth of season; usually profuse, prolific flowering plant but does not produce an overwhelming display like forsythia.

FRUIT: One-seeded, leathery achene with no ornamental value; have never seen a stray seedling and suspect the plant may be essentially sterile.

CULTURE: Easily grown, transplant balled and burlapped or from containers; prefers well-drained, moist, acid soil; full sun up to 1/2 shade; often damaged in severe winters and proper siting is necessary; will require pruning of dead wood in north.

DISEASES AND INSECTS: None serious but leaf spots, mildew and root rots have been reported.

LANDSCAPE VALUE: Excellent for textural effects, handsome in flower, often used as a bank cover, mass or facing plant; used as a hedge in southern areas; combines well with broadleaf evergreens; safest when used in Zone 6 and south.

CULTIVARS:

    ‘Francis Mason’—A rather difficult to digest yellow color on new leaves, some completely golden, most bordered in rich yellow with a yellow-green middle; less vigorous than the species; I admit to growing this form among variegated *Vinca minor,* golden-edged yucca, *Sedum* ‘Autumn Joy’, and *Spiraea × bumalda* ‘Goldflame’ with a few blue Siberian iris seedlings thrown in for good measure. Every year I promise to readjust the composition but to date it remains intact.

    ‘Prostrata’—Low-growing, more compact form with smaller leaves, purple-green color in winter.

    ‘Sherwood’—More dense and compact in habit, leaves smaller and more refined than those of species, 3 to 3 1/2′ high and 4 to 4 1/2′ wide, occasional reversions to the species should be removed; ‘Nana’ may be synonymous; plants on the Georgia campus are quite lovely, do not become as ragged as A. × grandiflora; in winter the small leaves turn purple-green; good plant for massing in sun or partial shade.

    ‘Variegata’—A variegated form has been reported but to my knowledge is not in cultivation in this country.

PROPAGATION: Softwood cuttings root readily; I have rooted this plant with 100% success any time foliage was present using 1000 ppm IBA; cuttings collected in November rooted well; seeds should be sown when ripe.

MAINTENANCE CONSIDERATIONS: Trouble-free, easy to maintain plant requiring occasional pruning to keep it well coiffured; hard pruning in late winter is recommended to rejuvenate old plants; plants will flower the same year after pruning.

ADDITIONAL NOTES: The hardiest and most free-flowering of the abelias; best reserved for eastern and southern gardens. Result of a cross between *A. chinensis* × *A. uniflora.*

RELATED SPECIES:

Abelia chinensis, (ăbē'li-a chī-nen'sis), Chinese Abelia, is a 5 to 7' high upright spreading shrub. The young branches are covered with reddish tomentum; the leaves are dark green, lighter green beneath with serrate margins; flowers are white, fragrant, two or more per cluster, appearing July to September. One of the parents of *A.* × *grandiflora.* I have rooted the plant from cuttings collected in fall at the Brooklyn Botanic Garden with the same procedure as described under *A.* × *grandiflora.* China. Introduced 1844. Zone (6)7 to 9.

Abelia 'Edward Goucher' is a hybrid between *A.* × *grandiflora* and *A. schumannii* and tends to be intermediate in habit between the parents. The leaves tend toward *A.* × *grandiflora* while the darker-colored purple-pink flowers reflect the influence of *A. schumannii*; leaves are often borne in whorls; average 5' by 5' at maturity; flowers from May-June until frost; resulted from a cross made at the Glenn Dale Plant Introduction Center by Edward Goucher in 1911; best reserved for Zone 6 to 9; showier in flower than *A.* x *grandiflora* but unfortunately less hardy, probably 5 to 10°F less so.

Abeliophyllum distichum — Korean Abelialeaf or White Forsythia
(a-bē-li-o-fĭl'um dis'tĭ-kum)

FAMILY: Oleaceae

LEAVES: Opposite, simple, entire, 2 to 3 1/2" long, spreading in two ranks, ovate to elliptic-ovate, acuminate, broad-cuneate or rounded at base, appressed pilose on both sides, medium green to dark green; petiole 1/12 to 1/5" long.

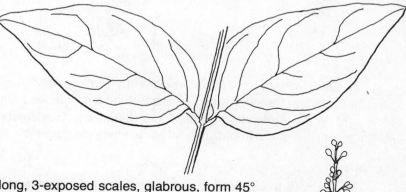

BUDS: Imbricate, brown, small, 1/10" long, 3-exposed scales, glabrous, form 45° angle with stem; flower buds exposed, purplish, small, evident through winter months.

STEM: Slender, light brown to tan, glabrous, 4-sided, with prominent ridges on vigorous stems; second year stems develop a shreddy, stringy condition; pith-white, finely chambered through nodes and internodes.

SIZE: 3 to 5' by 3 to 4' (perhaps wider).

HARDINESS: Zone 5 to 8, can grow in Zone 4; reports from the University of Minnesota Landscape Arboretum (−25 to −30°F) indicated the flower buds may be injured in a severe winter but are more dependable than *Forsythia* × *intermedia* types.

HABIT: Multistemmed (often straggly) small shrub of rounded outline developing arching branches; at times rather ragged looking and disheveled.

RATE: Depending on situation will range from slow to fast; has the ability to produce long trailing branches in a single season.

TEXTURE: Medium in leaf, perhaps medium-coarse in winter.

LEAF COLOR: Medium to dark green in summer; no significant change in fall.

FLOWERS: Perfect, white or faintly tinged pink, 4-petaled, 3/8 to 5/8″ across, fragrant, borne in 1/2 to 1 1/2″ long axillary racemes in March-April before the leaves.

FRUIT: Two-celled compressed rounded capsule which is winged all around; similar to an elm fruit; not ornamental.

CULTURE: Easily transplanted; adapted to many soils, preferably those that are well-drained; proper siting is important; acid or alkaline conditions; full sun or very light shade; renew frequently by heavy pruning immediately after flowering.

DISEASES AND INSECTS: None serious.

LANDSCAPE VALUE: Provides early spring color to an otherwise dull landscape; since the flowers are borne along the leafless stems they make quite a show; makes a nice companion shrub to forsythia; best if set off by a dark green background; more suitable than forsythia for plains states but not as showy.

CULTIVARS: A pink form exists but, to my knowledge, is unnamed; I have seen it growing next to the typical species and it is a uniform pink.

PROPAGATION: Easily rooted from softwood cuttings; in England it it is propagated by cuttings of half-ripened wood taken in July, and treated with IBA or IAA; bottom heat may be helpful; seeds should be sown when ripe.

MAINTENANCE CONSIDERATIONS: Have observed old, overgrown plants that looked like a tangle of vines and brush; needs to be renewal pruned every 3 to 4 years; prune to 6 to 12″ from ground in late winter.

ADDITIONAL NOTES: Certainly not the best of the deciduous shrubs but early flowering enough that it avoids competition from better plants; often ragged and straggly in habit and needs to be rejuvenated; have observed it in full flower at Bernheim Arboretum, Clermont, Kentucky, after exposure to approximately −18°F.

NATIVE HABITAT: Central Korea. Introduce 1924.

Abies — Fir
Pinaceae

Firs are limitedly used in midwestern and southern landscapes but often appear in the northeastern and northwestern United States. There are about forty species found in Europe, Northern Africa, temperate Asia and on the American continent from Canada to Guatemala. In youth they are mostly conical and extremely symmetrical in outline, and some types may grow over 200′.

MORPHOLOGICAL CHARACTERISTICS

Monoecious trees, evergreen, habit symmetrically pyramidal, or narrow-conical while young, or with age becoming large forest trees; trunk simple, rarely forked; bark usually smooth, thin on young trees, often thick and furrowed at the base on old trees; branchlets smooth, or grooved in a few species; winter-buds usually resinous; leaves spirally inserted, often spreading in 2 ranks (pectinate), linear or linear-lanceolate, entire, sessile, contracted above the base, leaving on falling a circular scar, usually flattened and grooved above, in most species with 2 white or pale stomatic bands and keeled beneath, rarely with stomata above, rarely 4-sided and with stomata on all 4 sides, rounded and variously notched or pointed at the apex; male flowers in cones composed of numerous scales, each with two ovules adaxially at the base and subtended by a narrow exserted or included bract; scales falling at maturity from the persistent axis; seeds ovoid or oblong; wing large and thick; cotyledons 4 to 10.

GROWTH CHARACTERISTICS

The firs would be considered slow-growing landscape plants especially when planted outside of their native habitats. It is safe to generalize that the majority of species are conical to pyramidal, almost spirelike, in outline. From this aspect they are somewhat difficult to work into the small, residential landscape. There are many cultivars among the various species including prostrate, compact, pendulous, contorted, fastigiate, yellow-foliaged, and blue-foliaged types. These cultivars fall in the novelty category and are difficult to find in the landscape trade; however, they do add different textures, colors and shapes not available from the fir species.

CULTURE

Firs require moist, well-drained, acid soil and high atmospheric moisture coupled with cooler temperatures. The hot, dry summers which occur in the midwest and south tend to limit their landscape usefulness. Firs are not suited for city plantings and do not tolerate air pollution. Transplanting is best accomplished in the spring using balled and burlapped specimens. Pruning should be kept to a minimum for when older branches are removed new growth seldom develops and, consequently, the trees become ragged and unkempt. They are most appropriately sited in full sun but light shade is also acceptable.

DISEASES AND INSECTS

Firs do not seem to be extensively troubled with disease and insect pests. At least this was true for firs which I have seen in landscape plantings. Needle and twig blight, leaf cast, rusts, cankers, shoestring root rot, wood decay, balsam twig aphid, bagworm, caterpillars, spruce spider mite, scale, balsam woolly aphid, spruce budworm and dwarf mistletoe (plant parasite) have been listed as problems.

PROPAGATION

Seed is the principal means of propagation. Dormancy of fir seed appears to be both physical and physiological in nature. There is considerable variation between seed lots in degree of dormancy. Part of this variability in dormancy is attributable to time of collection, methods of processing, seed cleaning, and storage. Seed is typically stratified under cool, moist conditions at 34° to 41°F for 14 to 28 days.

Cuttings have been rooted but the percentages were low and this approach is not practical on a commercial basis. The cultivars are usually grafted and some type of a side graft is most appropriate.

LANDSCAPE USE

Abies balsamea and *Abies fraseri,* which are grown for Christmas trees, only do well in colder climates. Their stiff, rigid habit and specific cultural requirements place a restriction on extensive use. They are best employed in groupings, near large buildings, as specimens and screens.

SELECTED SPECIES

Based on observations I have made at various arboreta and in landscape plantings around the midwest and east the following firs would be my first choice.

Abies cilicica	Cilician Fir
Abies concolor	White Fir
Abies homolepis	Nikko Fir
Abies procera	Noble Fir

Other firs which are worthwhile include:

Abies alba	Silver Fir
Abies balsamea	Balsam Fir
Abies cephalonica	Greek Fir
Abies firma	Momi Fir
Abies fraseri	Fraser Fir
Abies holophylla	Manchurian Fir
Abies koreana	Korean Fir
Abies mariesii	Maries Fir
Abies nordmanniana	Nordmann Fir
Abies veitchii	Veitch Fir

Abies balsamea — Balsam Fir
(ā′-bēz bâl-sā′mē-a)

LEAVES: Variable, 5/8 to 1″ long, 1/20 to 1/16″ wide, horizontally arranged in 2 lateral sets with a V-shaped parting between, apex slightly notched, upper surface shining dark green with interrupted lines of stomata towards the tip, lower surface with 2 gray bands of stomata, typical balsam odor.

BUDS: Small, ovoid or globular, resinous and seemingly varnished, brownish.

STEM: Smooth, covered with fine, soft grayish hairs.

SIZE: 45 to 75′ in height by 20 to 25′ in spread.

HARDINESS: Zone 3 to 5(6), suitable in higher elevations of the southeast.

HABIT: Stiff in habit, symmetrically pyramidal or narrow-conical when young before losing its pyramidal habit with age.

RATE: Slow.

TEXTURE: Medium.

BARK: Dull green, later with grayish areas, smooth except for numerous raised resin blisters; eventually breaking up into small reddish brown, irregular scaly plates, 1/2″ thick.

LEAF COLOR: Lustrous dark green with white stomatic bands below.

FLOWERS: Male-catkin-like, yellow, developing from the underside of the leaf axil.

FRUIT: Cone, dark violet when young, 2 to 4″ long, turning gray-brown and resinous at maturity; soon after the ripening of the seeds the scales fall off leaving only the central axis.

CULTURE: Shallow rooted, readily transplanted balled and burlapped; adaptable to cold climates and there makes its best growth; prefers well-drained, acid, moist soil, however, in the wild it often forms pure stands in swamps but does best in association with spruce on ground which is better drained; it also grows on higher ground and is found in dwarfed, matted, pure stands, or entangled with Black Spruce, *Picea mariana,* near the windswept summits of mountains where great extremes in temperature occur. More shade tolerant than other firs but will not withstand polluted areas.

DISEASES AND INSECTS: Troubled by spruce budworm, woolly aphid and several canker diseases; see general *Abies* discussion.

LANDSCAPE VALUE: Used mainly as a specimen tree and popular as a Christmas tree. Does not hold its needles very long in a dry house and for this reason is not as desirable as the pines. In youth it looks good but under the hot, dry conditions soon loses the older needles and becomes open and unkempt.

CULTIVARS: Many named selections, few of which are available in commerce.

    f. *hudsonia*—I see this form always listed as 'Hudsonia', a rather cute, compact, 1 to 2′ high broad mound with numerous short branches; needles radially arranged, dark green above, silvery beneath, about 1/2″ long, never bears cones, found in White Mountains of New Hampshire.

    'Nana'—Possibly the same thing as f. *hudsonia,* dwarf globose with dark green needles, whitish stomatic lines on underside.

PROPAGATION: A brief stratification period of 15 to 30 days in moist medium at 34 to 41°F is recommended.

ADDITIONAL NOTES: I have seen this species growing in the barren rock on tops of Cadillac Mountain in Maine; the resin from this tree was used to mount thin specimens under slides but has now been supplanted by other materials.

NATIVE HABITAT: Native over a wide part of North America, especially in the higher altitudes from Labrador to Alberta to Pennsylvania. Cultivated 1696.

Abies cilicica — Cilician Fir
(ā′-bēz si-li′-see-ka)

LEAVES: Spreading upward and forward, 3/4 to 1 1/4″ long, 1/10 to 1/12″ wide, on weaker branches outward and upward forming a V-shaped depression, rounded or acute and slightly 2-notched at apex, shining bright green above, with narrow whitish bands beneath.

Abies cilicica, Cilician Fir, has thrived for many years in Spring Grove, Cincinnati, OH where the largest plants approach 60 to 70′ high. They are distinctly columnar-spirelike, varying very little from base to apex in width. The foliage from a distance is more gray-green than the normal dark green of most firs. The species has survived in the heavy clay soils and −25°F temperatures and deserves consideration at least in the midwestern states. Cones 6 to 10″ long, 2 to 2 1/2″ wide, cylindric and reddish brown. Asia Minor, Syria. In the wild often grows in association with Cedar-of-Lebanon on calcareous, limestone-based rocky soils with hot dry summers and mild rainy winters. Introduced 1855. Zone 5 to 6.

Abies concolor — White (Concolor) Fir
(ā′-bēz kon′-kul-er)

LEAVES: Curving outwards and upwards or almost vertically arranged on the stems, 1 1/2 to 2 1/2″ long and 1/12 to 1/10″ wide, flattened, glaucous on both surfaces, apex short-pointed or rounded, upper surface slightly convex, not grooved, with faint lines of stomata, lower surface with 2 faint bands of stomata separated by a green band, both sides more or less bluish green.
BUDS: Large, broadly conical, blunt, covered with resin which conceals the scales, light brown.
STEM: First year, glabrous or minutely downy, yellowish green; second year, grayish or silvery.

SIZE: 30 to 50′ in height by 15 to 30′ in spread; can grow to 100′ or more.
HARDINESS: Zone 3 to 7.
HABIT: Conical and branched to the base, the branches on the upper half of the tree tend to point upward, the lower horizontal or deflected downward, creating a rather rigid, stiff appearance in the landscape.
RATE: Slow to medium; one authority reported that this species will grow 50 to 60′ in 30 to 60 years.
TEXTURE: Medium.
BARK: Smooth on young stems except for resin blisters; 4 to 7″ thick on old trunks, ashy gray and divided by deep irregular furrows into thick, horny, flattened ridges.
LEAF COLOR: Bluish or grayish green with pale bluish bands beneath; new growth a light rich green or bluish green; on some forms a silvery-blue.
FLOWERS: Inconspicuous, monoecious; staminate-red or red-violet.
FRUIT: Cones are stalked, cylindrical, 3 to 6″ long, 1 1/2 to 1 3/4″ wide, pale green before maturity often with a purplish bloom, finally brown.
CULTURE: The best fir for the midwest and east; transplant balled and burlapped; while withstanding heat, drought and cold equally well, it prefers and makes best growth on deep, rich, moist, well-drained gravelly or sandy-loam soils; dislikes heavy clay. This species requires less moisture than other western firs and can exist on dry, thin layers of partially decomposed granite or nearly barren rocks. Although full sun is preferable, it will tolerate light shade. Root system, according to some authorities, is shallow and wide spreading while others indicated there is a tap root; seems to hold its needles better than any other fir; a 30-year-old specimen at my former residence attested to this; a degree more tolerant of city conditions than other fir species.
DISEASES AND INSECTS: None serious.
LANDSCAPE VALUE: Because of its growth habit and softer effect it could well replace the spruces in the landscape; beautiful foliage, especially those trees with bluish needles.
CULTIVARS: There are at least 20 cultivars that I have run across in the literature and possibly more.

‘Candicans’—Large bright silver-blue needles on a narrow upright tree.

‘Compacta’—Irregularly dwarf compact shrub with bright blue 1 to 1 1/2″ long needles.

‘Violacea’ (f. *violacea*)—Offers silver blue needles of great beauty; from a distance might be mistaken for one of the silvery-blue forms of *Picea pungens* var. *glauca;* I can still see (12 years later) a handsome specimen in the meadow by Bussey Brook at the Arnold Arboretum; although this form is usually grafted, apparently similar forms occur in nature and seed-beds.

PROPAGATION: Seed shows variability in its chilling requirements; a period of 30 days in moist medium at 41°F is recommended; cuttings taken in early December failed to root without treatment but rooted 50% after treatment with 100 ppm IBA/24 hour soak; in another study, cuttings taken in early December rooted 73% with the above treatment but did not root at all without treatment; in another study, cuttings taken in late January rooted 76% in eight months without treatment, and 100% after treatment with 8000 ppm IBA talc; in other work, cuttings rooted best when taken in March and treated with 100 ppm IBA for 24 hours.

NATIVE HABIT: Colorado to southern California, northern Mexico and New Mexico. Introduced 1872.

Abies firma — Momi Fir
(ā′-bēz fir′-ma)

LEAVES: Arranged in a comb-like pectinate fashion, to 1 1/2″ long, broadest at about the middle, sharply two-pointed at apex on young plants, becoming obtuse or emarginate on older plants, dark green above and furrowed with a few stomatal lines near the apex, lighter green beneath with 2 gray-green bands; of the firs described here this one is quickly noticeable by the sharp prickly apex.

Abies firma, Momi Fir, has been praised for heat tolerance among firs and indeed is growing in the Mobile, AL, Athens, GA, and Raleigh, NC areas. The plants I have observed were significantly short of spectacular. Sargent considered it the most beautiful of Japanese firs, in which country it can grow 120 to 150′. Most widely distributed fir in Japan and is found in dry and moist sites. Under cultivation, 40 to 50′ is more realistic, but I have seen nothing approaching this size. Might be worth trying by the conifer collector. Cones 3 1/2 to 5″ long by 1 1/2 to 2″ wide, brown. Introduced 1861. Zone 6 to 9.

Abies fraseri — Fraser Fir, Southern Balsam Fir, Southern Fir
(ā′-bēz frā′zer-ī)

LEAVES: Crowded, directed forward, pectinate below, 1/2 to 1″ long, 1/24″ broad, entire or emarginate at apex, flat, grooved, shining dark green above, with stomates above near apex, with 2 broad bands of 8 to 12 stomatic lines beneath.

STEMS: Gray or pale yellowish brown, in the first winter reddish brown, very resinous.

SIZE: 30 to 40′ in height by 20 to 25′ in spread; occasionally to 70′ high.

HARDINESS: Zone 4 to 7, suitable in higher elevations of southeast (2000′).

HABIT: Pyramidal, with horizontal, stiff branches, opening up with age.

RATE: Slow.

TEXTURE: Medium.

LEAF COLOR: Shining dark green with stomata above near the apex and two broad bands of 8 to 12 stomatic lines beneath.

FLOWERS: Monoecious.

FRUIT: Cones ovoid or cylindrical, 1 1/2 to 2 1/2″ long and 1 to 1 1/4″ broad, purple when young becoming tan-brown; bracts much protruded and bent downwards so as to hide the scales.

CULTURE: Transplants well when root pruned, does better in dry situations than *Abies balsamea* but prefers a moist, well-drained loam and sun or partial shade.

LANDSCAPE VALUE: Excellent evergreen in the right climate; like Balsam suffers in hot, dry weather; Fraser has become a favored Christmas tree in the southern highlands and North Carolina State University has an active research program with the species; truly a beautiful Christmas and ornamental tree.

CULTIVARS:

'Prostrata'—Slow-growing, spreading, mounded, can grow 4 to 5' high by 12 to 14' wide, needles like the species, originated in East Boxford, MA, 1916.

PROPAGATION: Seed, again actual recommendations vary somewhat but a cold period of 15 to 30 days would probably be somewhat beneficial. See Dirr and Heuser (1987) for an overview of cutting propagation.

NATIVE HABITAT: Native to the mountains of West Virginia, North Carolina, and Tennessee at altitudes of 3000 to 6000'. Introduced 1811.

Abies homolepis — Nikko Fir
(ā'-bēz hō-mō-lep'us)

LEAVES: Needles form almost a solid cushion without the distinct pectinate arrangement, glossy dark green above, 2 white bands below, 1/3 to 1 1/8" long, slight notch at rather flat apex; the lowest leaves are the largest and spread horizontally, each succeeding rank is smaller and more erect producing a narrow or scarcely perceptible V-shaped opening at the top.

Abies homolepis, Nikko Fir, is a tree of great formal beauty that has prospered in Bernheim Arboretum, Clermont, KY. The tree is densely clothed with branches to the base and forms a rather fat pyramidal spire, not as narrow and lose as some firs. Probably will grow 30 to 50' under cultivation but grows 100 to 130' in its native Japan. Cones cylindrical, 4 to 5" long, green in youth and pale brown when mature. For midwestern and eastern states, it is worth trying. Introduced 1861. Zone 4 to 6(7).

Abies koreana — Korean Fir
(ā'-bēz kôr-ē-ā'na)

LEAVES: Thickly set on stem, 1/2 to 3/4" long, 1/16 to 1/12" wide, notched or rounded at apex which is the broadest point of needle, dark green above, two whitish bands below divided by a thin green midrib.

Abies koreana, Korean Fir, is a slow growing, rather small-statured 15 to 30' high, compact tree. Most notable characteristic is the rich violet-purple, some would argue blue, 2 to 3" long, 1" wide cone that occurs on 3 to 5' high plants. Appears slightly more heat tolerant than many firs but still best in cold climates. 'Horstmann's Silberlocke' is a handsome, irregular branching form with the needles curling up and revealing the bright silver lower surface. 'Prostrata' is a reasonably common, rich green, low growing type. Korea. Introduced 1908. Zone 5 to 6(7).

Abies lasiocarpa — Rocky Mountain Fir
(ā'bēz lā-si-ō-kär'pa)

LEAVES: Much crowded and directed forward and upward, 1 to 1 1/2" long, acute or rounded at apex, rarely emarginate, pale bluish green, stomatiferous above and slightly grooved, with silvery-gray stomatal bands below.

Abies lasiocarpa, Rocky Mountain Fir, is a large, 100 to 160' high tree with grayish or chalk-white bark. Cones are oblong-cylindric, 2 to 4" long and dark purple. 'Glauca' is a rich silver-blue needle form, habit is pyramidal. 'Glauca Compacta' is a dwarf pyramid with silver-blue congested foliage. In general it is not well suited to culture in the east and midwest but I have seen variety *arizonica* which is a smaller rich blue green pyramid and has a thick corky creamy white bark. The needles of the variety are distinctly emarginate, whiter beneath and distinctly pectinate. Forms a narrow pyramid. Found at high altitudes in north Arizona and northern New Mexico. Introduced 1901. Zone 5 to 6(7). The species from Alaska to Oregon, Utah and northern New Mexico. Introduced 1863.

Abies nordmanniana — Nordmann Fir
(ā′-bēz nôrd-man-ē-ā′na)

LEAVES: Directed forward and densely covering the branches, 3/4 to 1 1/2″ long, 1/16 to 1/12″ wide, apex rounded and notched, lustrous dark green above, midrib sunken, 2 white bands below.

Abies nordmanniana, Nordmann Fir, is perhaps the handsomest of the firs. Stately, elegant with almost black green needles it may grow 40 to 60′ under cultivation but in the wild grows to 200′. Many old +100′ specimens exist in England. Cones are 5 to 6″ long, 1 3/4 to 2″ wide, cylindrical or tapered to apex, reddish brown. 'Pendula' has weeping branches and is a rather curious but not aesthetic sight. 'Prostrata' is a slow growing form with a trailing habit. Caucasus, Asia Minor. Introduced 1848. Zone 4 to 6.

Abies procera — Noble Fir
(ā′bēz prō′ser-a)

LEAVES: Crowded above, the lower ranks spreading outward, those of the middle rank much shorter, appressed to the branchlet, curving upwards near the base, pectinate below and curved, 1 to 1 1/8″ long, 1/16″ wide, scarcely broadened, rounded or slightly notched at apex, grooved, bluish green, stomatiferous above, with narrow pale bands below.
BUDS: Roundish, resinous, surrounded at base by a collar of long pointed scales free at the tips.
STEM: In youth covered with a reddish brown minute pubescence.

SIZE: 50 to 100′ under landscape conditions, 180 to 270′ in height in native stands.
HARDINESS: Zone 5 to 6(7).
HABIT: Symmetrically pyramidal or narrow; conical in youth; mature trees develop a long, clear, columnar trunk, with an essentially domelike crown.
RATE: Slow to medium, will reach 75′+ in 30 to 60 years; trees 100 to 120 years of age are commonly 90 to 120′ in height.
TEXTURE: Medium.
BARK: Gray and smooth for many years, with prominent resin blisters; eventually dark gray, often tinged with purple and broken up into thin, nearly rectangular plates separated by deep fissures on old trunks; bark about 1 to 2″ thick; this is thin in comparison to other trees and specimens are often ruined by fire.
LEAF COLOR: Bluish green, stomatiferous above with narrow pale bands below.
FLOWERS: Inconspicuous, monoecious.
FRUIT: A large, cylindrical cone, 6 to 10″ long by approximately 3″ broad, green before maturity, finally turning purplish brown.
CULTURE: Readily transplanted balled and burlapped if properly root pruned, prefers a moist, deep, cool, well-drained soil, sun or partial shade and dislikes high pH soils as well as windy conditions; good growth is also made on thin rocky soils if provided with an abundance of moisture.
DISEASES AND INSECTS: Damaged by the spruce budworm, woolly aphid and several canker diseases.
LANDSCAPE VALUE: Can be used as a specimen tree however best adapted in its native habitat.
CULTIVARS:
  'Glauca'—Extremely glaucous foliage and a liberal cone bearer.

PROPAGATION: Stratified and non-stratified seeds gave good germination percentages.
NATIVE HABITAT: Native to the Cascade Mountains of Washington, Oregon and the Siskiyou Mountains of California. Western United States. Introduced 1830.

Abies veitchii — Veitch Fir
(ā′bēz vētch′ē-ī)

LEAVES: One half to (+)1″ long and about 1/16″ wide, flattened, gradually tapering to the base, apex truncate, notched; upper surface dark green, shining, grooved; lower surfaces with 2 conspicuously broad white bands of stomata.
BUDS: Small, nearly globular, resinous, grayish brown.
STEM: Green, reddish brown to brown, more or less clothed with short pubescence.

SIZE: 50 to 75′ high by 25 to 35′ in spread.
HARDINESS: Zone 3 to 6.
HABIT: A broadly pyramidal tree with horizontal, spreading branches.
RATE: Slow to medium; one authority reported 20 to 50′ in height after 20 to 30 years.
TEXTURE: Medium.
LEAF COLOR: Lustrous dark green above with prominent, chalky-white bands below.
FLOWERS: Inconspicuous, monoecious.
FRUIT: Cones are sessile, cylindrical, 2 to 3″ long, 1 1/4″ broad and bluish purple when young, becoming brown.
CULTURE: Transplants well balled and burlapped if properly root pruned; prefers moist, well-drained soils; sun or partial shade; dislikes high pH soils; supposedly performs acceptably in semi-urban conditions.
DISEASES AND INSECTS: As is the case with most firs it is troubled by the spruce budworm, woolly aphid and several canker diseases.
LANDSCAPE VALUE: Because of its extremely hardy nature and handsome foliage it should be considered more often for a specimen tree.
PROPAGATION: There appears to be a significant increase in germination percentage with stratified versus non-stratified seeds; stratify in a moist medium for 15 to 30 days at 41°F; cuttings taken in late December rooted 60% with 8000 ppm IBA-talc; not at all without treatment; rooting of winter cuttings has also been improved by IBA, 40 ppm soak for 24 hours.
NATIVE HABITAT: Central and southern Japan. Introduced 1865.

Acanthopanax sieboldianus — Fiveleaf Aralia
(a-kan-thō-pā′naks sē-bōl-dē-ā′-nus)

FAMILY: Araliaceae
LEAVES: Alternate, palmately compound, partly fascicled on short spurs; leaflets 5 to 7, subsessile, obovate to oblong-obovate, 1 to 2 1/2″ long, 1/3 to 1″ wide, acute, cuneate, crenate-serrate, rich bright green, glabrous; petiole—1 to 3″ long.
BUDS: Solitary, sessile, conical-ovoid with about 3 exposed scales.
STEM: Light brown, warty, with 1 or 2 slender arching prickles beneath each narrow leaf-scar; pith-solid, ample, white; leaf scars narrowly crescent shaped or U-shaped, somewhat raised.

SIZE: 8 to 10′ by 8 to 10′
HARDINESS: Zone 4 to 8.
HABIT: Erect, upright-growing deciduous shrub with arching stems which gradually flop over to form a rounded outline; can be maintained in a more upright fashion with proper pruning.
RATE: Medium to fast in good soil; grows remarkably fast under less-than-ideal conditions.
TEXTURE: Medium in all seasons.

LEAF COLOR: Rich bright green, leafing out by late March—early April in Athens and holding late into fall; I have observed a full complement of leaves as late as mid-November; fall color is non-existent.

FLOWERS: Unisexual, usually dioecious, small, greenish white, borne in a spherical umbel, 3/4 to 1″ diameter, which terminates a 2 to 4″ long slender stalk, arises from cluster of leaves on one-year-old wood, May–June.

FRUIT: Sparingly produced in cultivation, 1/4″ wide, 2 to 5-seeded black berry; Bailey noted only the pistillate form was in cultivation and produced no fruit for lack of a suitable pollinator; perhaps other members of the genus can act as pollinators.

CULTURE: Readily transplanted and cultured; adapts to unfavorable conditions; prefers well-drained soil, acid or alkaline, sand to clay, full sun to heavy shade, withstands heavy pruning, seems to tolerate polluted conditions.

DISEASES AND INSECTS: Nothing serious although a leaf spot has been reported.

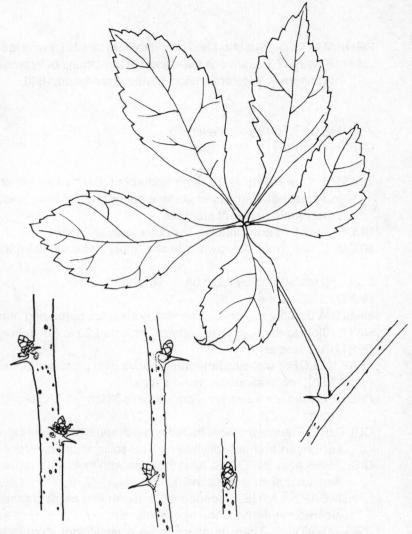

LANDSCAPE VALUE: Tremendous plant for cities; have seen this plant performing magnificently under the worst conditions; quite tolerant of dry soils; makes a good screen or barrier; tends to sucker and may need to be restrained; will withstand considerable shade or full sun.

CULTIVARS:

'Variegatus'—A handsome form, the leaves bordered creamy-white; will grow 6 to 8″ high and wide; Bean considered it one of the daintiest of variegated shrubs; I first saw this plant at the Oxford Botanic Garden, England, and was quite taken with its handsome variegation pattern; this plant would make an excellent focal point in a shady shrub border.

PROPAGATION: Seed requires a warm:cold treatment and 6 months warm:3 months cold should suffice; easily rooted from softwood cuttings; root cuttings and division also work; August-collected cuttings rooted 93% when treated with 8000 ppm IBA + Thiram and placed under mist.

NATIVE HABITAT: Japan, Cultivated 1859.

RELATED SPECIES:

Acanthopanax henryi, (a-kan-thō-pā′naks hen′rē-ī), Henry's Aralia, is a sturdy, upright, strongly multistemmed shrub growing 8 to 10′; the dull dark green, rough-surfaced leaves hold late into fall; greenish flowers give way to inky-black, 3/8″ long fruits in 1 1/2 to 2″ diameter umbels, fruits persist for a time and are rather attractive. This species fruits commonly in cultivation. 'Nana' grows about 1/2 to 2/3 the size of the species and forms a solid, impenetrable thicket of upright, multispined, grayish stems. China. 1901. Zone 5 to 7.

ADDITIONAL NOTES: None of these plants will supersede the viburnums for ornamental qualities but where pollution tolerant, low-maintenance plants are needed they may have a place; they make superb barrier plants because of nodal spines.

Acer buergeranum — Trident Maple
(ā′ser ber-jār-ā′num)

FAMILY: Aceraceae

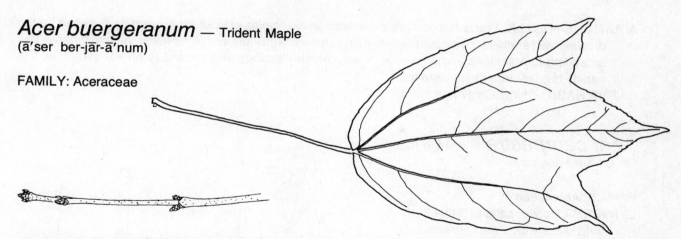

LEAVES: Opposite, simple, 3 lobed, 1 1/2 to 3 1/2″ across, 3 nerved at base and rounded or broad-cuneate, lobes triangular, acute and pointing forward, entire or slightly and irregularly serrate, pubescent while young, soon glabrous, very lustrous green; petiole about as long as blade.

BUDS: Imbricate, terminal—1/8″ long, rich brown, 4-angled, pyramid-shaped, pubescent on edge of scales, scales sharply acute; laterals—smaller, somewhat appressed, otherwise similar.

STEM: Slender, pubescent, gray-brown, small lenticels, pith-solid, greenish white; second-year stems becoming darker brown and lose pubescence.

SIZE: 20 to 25′ perhaps to 30 to 35′; spread approaches height.

HARDINESS: Based on performance during the difficult winters of 1976 and 77 to 78 when temperatures in the midwest ranged from −15 to −25°F, I would rate this plant Zone 5 to Zone 8 to 9.

HABIT: Distinctly oval-rounded to rounded outline; very lovely small tree; tendency toward multiple and low branching unless trained to a single stem.

RATE: Slow to medium, over time would be considered a slow grower.

BARK: On 2 to 3″ diameter trunks becomes gray-brown-orange and develops an exfoliating, platy, scaly character.

LEAF COLOR: New growth often rich bronze to purple maturing to glossy dark green in summer, changing to yellow, orange and red in fall; colors later than many maples (late October—early November); can be very good but is often variable; trees in Mt. Auburn Cemetery, Cambridge, Mass turned a lovely combination of yellow to red; a 30′ tree on the Georgia campus colors a rich rose to red.

FLOWERS: Greenish yellow, borne in downy umbel-like corymbs with the leaves in April–May; scarcely noticeable.

FRUIT: Samara, 3/4 to 1″ long, the wings 1/4″ wide, parallel or connivent, mature in October–November.

CULTURE: Transplants readily but best moved balled and burlapped in spring; well drained, acid soil; displays good drought resistance; full sun; has received plaudits from many plantsmen; may suffer breakage in severe ice and snow storms; have moved it in full leaf successfully.

DISEASES AND INSECTS: None serious, see *A. saccharinum* for listing of maple problems.

LANDSCAPE VALUE: Vary handsome small patio, lawn, or street tree; might work well in planter boxes; definitely should be used more extensively; makes a good bonsai specimen; in Japan it is widely planted as a street tree; reports on quality of fall coloration are somewhat contradictory; significant variation does occur; trees which I have seen in Massachusetts were outstanding and the late Professor Clancy Lewis, Michigan State, described a tree on campus which turned a good red with some purple; reports from Morton Arboretum, Chicago, IL, note that it can be used in that area with proper siting.

CULTIVARS: Dwarf and variegated forms exist; anyone interested in specifics should read J.D. Vertrees, *Japanese Maples,* Timber Press.

PROPAGATION: Seed, 3 months at 41°F works well; cuttings from mature trees are difficult to root but cuttings taken from 2-year-old seedlings rooted 75 to 95% depending on treatment (nothing, 10000 ppm NAA, 3000 or 8000 ppm IBA talc); cuttings collected in late June rooted 60% when treated with 20000 ppm IBA talc, fine sand, intermittent mist.

ADDITIONAL NOTES: I have noticed great variation in the leaves with some accurately depicted by the drawing while others show a rounded-lobing pattern with deeper-cut sinuses; variety *trinerve* has spreading lateral lobes; margins of all lobes coarsely toothed and underside of leaf glaucous; this variety is considered a juvenile form.

NATIVE HABIT: China. Cultivated 1890.

Acer campestre — Hedge Maple
(ā'ser kam-pes'trē)

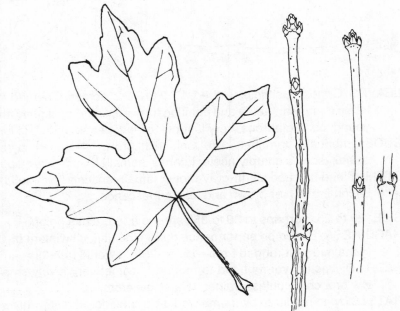

FAMILY: Aceraceae

LEAVES: Opposite, simple, 2 to 4″ long and wide, dark green above, pubescent beneath, 3 to 5 rounded, entire lobes, deep dark green; petiole 4″ long, when detached yields a milky sap.

BUDS: Terminal—imbricate, 1/8″ long, grayish brown to brownish black, tips of scales often pubescent and chaffy; laterals—appressed, smaller.

STEM: Slender, glabrous, light brown, somewhat lustrous, lenticelled; second year stems gray-brown, more prominently lenticelled; stems often develop corky fissures; pith-solid, white.

SIZE: 25 to 35′ (45′), occasionally 70 to 75′; spread would be comparable to height, especially on specimens 30 to 35′ high.

HARDINESS: Zone (4)5 to 8.

HABIT: Usually rounded and dense, often branched to the ground making grass culture difficult; some trees display a pyramidal-oval outline; can be easily limbed up.

RATE: Slow, 10 to 14′ over a 10 to 15 year period; can be pushed in the nursery and may average 2′ per year in youth.

TEXTURE: Medium in all seasons.

BARK: Gray-black, lightly ridged-and-furrowed, resembles bark of Norway Maple.

LEAF COLOR: Handsome dark green in summer changing to yellow-green or yellow in fall; does not color consistently in midwest or south but trees in the Arnold Arboretum colored a lovely yellow; one of the latest trees to color developing along with Norway Maple in late October—early November and remaining effective for a long period; a tree on the Georgia Campus has colored bright yellow on several occasions.

FLOWERS: Few, green, initially in erect corymbs, May, ineffective.

FRUIT: Samara, 1 1/4 to 1 3/4″ long, 1/3 to 1/2″ wide, nutlet often pubescent, wings horizontally spreading, forming a 180° angle from wing to wing.

CULTURE: Readily transplanted; extremely adaptable; prefers rich, well-drained soil but performs admirably in high pH soils; also does well in acid situations (pH 5.5 and above); tolerant of dry soils and compaction; air pollution tolerant; full sun or light shade; withstands severe pruning.

DISEASES AND INSECTS: None serious.

LANDSCAPE VALUE: Excellent small lawn specimen, street tree in residential areas and perhaps cities, good under utility lines because of low height; can be pruned into hedges and is often used for this in Europe; probably the best maple for dry, alkaline soils; have observed trees in the Salt Lake City, Utah area which were 30 to 40′ high and wide with a full complement of healthy foliage in October.

CULTIVARS:

'Compactum'—A dwarf, multistemmed shrub of very close, compact growth, 2 to 4′ (6′) high and usually broader than high; very effective and handsome dwarf shrub; have noticed some tip dieback as a result of low temperatures; apparently not as hardy as the species; develops a good yellow fall color under proper environmental conditions; have attempted to root softwood cuttings but with no success; Arnold Arboretum experienced 68% rooting on August cuttings treated with 8000 ppm IBA-talc; found in 1874.

'Eastleigh Weeping'—Pendulous habit; raised in Eastleigh nursery of Hilliers & Sons.

'Fastigiatum'—Upright form with corky branches, leaves 5-lobed, hairy beneath, found in the wild about 1930; to my knowledge not present in commerce.

'Postelense'—Leaves golden yellow when young gradually changing to green, interesting in spring but losing the yellow color with the advent of warm weather.

'Queen Elizabeth'—Small to medium sized tree, rounded with a flat top, more vigorous than the species, branches at 45° angle, leaves darker green and larger than the species, fall color yellowish; introduced by J. Frank Schmidt and Sons, Boring, OR. Queen Elizabeth is the trademark name, 'Evelyn' the cultivar name.

'Schwerinii'—Leaves purple when unfolding, finally turning green.

PROPAGATION: Seed requires a warm/cold period for germination, 68 to 86°F for 30 days followed by 36 to 40°F for 90 to 180 days; I have raised many seedlings following this procedure; soaking seeds in warm water followed by 3 months at 41°F has a positive effect; softwood cuttings collected on June 4, treated with 8000 ppm IBA-talc, placed under mist with bottom heat rooted 79%; timing appeared to be critical.

MAINTENANCE CONSIDERATIONS: Surprisingly durable small maple that is not common in American gardens; essentially pest and disease free; will take considerable pruning and is a familiar inhabitant of the hedge rows encountered along English roads.

ADDITIONAL NOTES: A variable species and at least 4 varieties are recognized: *austriacum, hebecarpum, leiocarpum,* and *tauricum;* appears to be significant variation in degree of leaf lobing and pubescence; used as a hedge in Europe and some of the famous hedges at Schönbrunn, near Vienna, form perpendicular walls 35′ high.

NATIVE HABIT: Europe, Near East and Africa. Introduced in colonial times into the United States.

Acer carpinifolium — Hornbeam Maple
(ā′ser car-pīn′-ĭ-fō-lē-um)

LEAVES: Opposite, simple, ovate-oblong, 3 to 5″ long, long acuminate, subcordate to truncate, doubly serrate, glabrous or nearly so at maturity, dark green; petiole—1/2″ long.

BUD: Terminal—imbricate, 1/8 to 3/16″ long, ovoid, 4-sided, lustrous blood red, edge of scales light brown, pubescent at collar where petiole abscised; laterals 1/2 size of terminal.

STEM: Slender, lustrous gray-green-brown, slightly lenticelled, glabrous, angular.

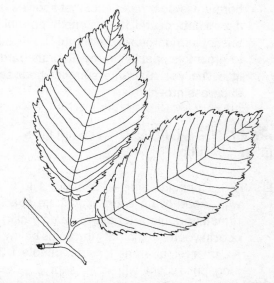

Acer carpinifolium, Hornbeam Maple, may have the most appropriate common name of any maple. The leaves are atypical for maple, resembling in shape and character those of *Carpinus caroliniana.* The dark green leaves change to rich gold and brown in autumn. Habit is often vase shaped, multistemmed and round headed. Landscape size would range from 20 to 25′ although most that I have seen were smaller than this. In Japan, it is described as growing to 50′. Bark is smooth and gray. The greenish flowers (May) are borne in short glabrous racemes and the 3/4″ long samaras diverge at a right or obtuse angle. Prefers a moist, well drained soil and some shade. I would surmise that in the wild this tree exists as an understory plant. Can be rooted from August cuttings using 8000 ppm IBA talc. Japan. Introduced 1881. Zone (4)5 to 7.

Acer cissifolium — Ivy-leaved Maple
(ā′ser sis-ĭ-fō′lē-um)

LEAVES: Opposite, trifoliate, each leaflet 1 1/2 to 3″ long, ovate or obovate to elliptic, long acuminate, cuneate, medium green above, glabrous, whitish tufts in axils of veins below, prominent mucronate, *Zelkova*-like serrations, terminal leaflet stalked, petiolule about 1″ long, laterals 1/2″ long; petiole—3 to 4″ long, reddish purple.
BUDS: Terminal—reddish purple, 3/16″ long, valvate, pubescent, lower part of bud glabrous, lustrous; laterals similar, 1/2 as long, appressed.
STEM: First year—slender, reddish purple, prominently pubescent; second year—gray-brown with an onion skin effect.

Acer cissifolium is extremely rare in cultivation but certainly worthy of consideration. Young trees are upright-oval in outline but with age may become distinctly mushroom-like and broad spreading at least with open-grown specimens. Ultimate height and spread range from 20 to 30′. The medium green foliage changes to yellow and red in fall although I have not seen good color on the trees I've observed. Flowers are born in 2 to 4″ long slender racemes; the samaras are 1″ long and diverge at an angle of 60° or less. Fruit set may be abundant but the percentage of solid seed is low. Cuttings of this species can be readily rooted. Cuttings collected in mid-August, treated with 8000 ppm IBA talc rooted 100%; those that were wounded had heavier root systems. The branches are intricate and low slung, often growing parallel with the ground but still twisting and turning in elegant fashion. The smooth, slightly dimpled gray bark is an added feature. Prefers well-drained, moist, acid soil and a partially shaded location although plants I have seen in full sun were performing well. The species is supposedly allied to *Acer negundo* but this is like allying a Rolls Royce with a Pinto; the only similarity being trifoliate leaves in the case of the trees, with 4 wheels in the case of the cars. A close relation that I have seen at the Morris Arboretum is *Acer henryi* but that species is larger. Japan. Introduced 1875. Zone 5, possible 4 to 8, but not as vigorous in the south. I have attempted to grow this species in my Georgia garden with little success. Extreme summer heat seems to suppress growth.

Acer diabolicum — Devil Maple
(ā′-ser dī-à-bol′-ī-kum)

LEAVES: Opposite, simple, 5-lobed, 4 to 6″ across, with broad-ovate short-acuminate coarsely and remotely dentate lobes, extremely silky-pubescent in youth, at maturity the veins below densely so, interveinal areas less so; petiole 1 3/4 to 2″ long, pubescent, with milky sap.
STEM: Young-whitish and pubescent, finally glabrous and red-brown.

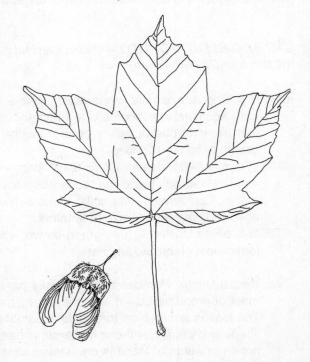

Acer diabolicum, Devil Maple, is not well known in American gardens and is seldom seen in European gardens but is certainly a handsome tree, possibly best reserved for the collector. The habit is rounded with ultimate landscape size approximately 20 to 30'. A tree has prospered in the Arnold Arboretum for years. In my mind, the most recognizable trait is the thick bristly nutlet of the samara. The wings are upright or spreading, 1 1/4 to 1 3/4" long; fruits occur on a 1/2 to 2" long stalk; dioecious: yellow flowers before the leaves, male fascicled on pendulous, pilose pedicels, sepals connate; female flowers in several-flowered racemes, with sepals and petals distinct and of equal length. Species appears adaptable but has not been tested extensively. 'Purpurascens' offers emerging purple-red leaves, flowers and fruits; the color is lost with maturity. Harris *The Plantsman* 83(5):35 to 58. stated that it is simply the male tree with attractive red flowers. Mountains of Japan. Cultivated 1850. Zone 5 to 7.

Acer ginnala — Amur Maple
(ā'ser jin-nā'-la)

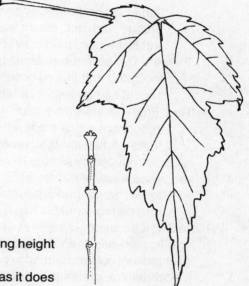

LEAVES: Opposite, simple, 1 1/2 to 3" long, 3 lobed, middle lobe is much longer than the 2 lateral lobes, doubly serrate, dark green and lustrous above, light green beneath; petiole 1/2 to 1 3/4" long.

BUDS: Small, 1/8" long, imbricate, reddish brown or lighter, glabrous.

STEM: Glabrous, slender, gray-brown; rougher and striped on older branches.

FRUIT: Samaras hang on late into fall; wings virtually parallel; persistent into spring.

SIZE: 15 to 18', possibly to 25' in height, spread equal to or exceeding height especially multi-stemmed specimens.

HARDINESS: Zone 2 to 8; does not perform as well in Zone 7 and 8 as it does further north.

HABIT: Multi-stemmed large shrub or small tree often of rounded outline; shape is variable and can be successfully tailored to specific landscape requirements by pruning.

RATE: Over a period of 10 to 20 years the growth in height would average 12 to 20'; however, in extreme youth can be induced into rapid growth by optimum fertilizer and moisture.

TEXTURE: Medium-fine in leaf; medium in winter.

BARK: Grayish brown on older branches; smooth with darker striations like serviceberry.

LEAF COLOR: Handsome dark glossy green in summer changing to shades of yellow and red in fall; does not fall color consistently; best coloration is seen in full sun situations; extreme variation in fall coloration and selections should be made for this trait; one of the first trees to leaf out, often in full leaf by late March in Athens, Georgia.

FLOWERS: Yellowish white, fragrant as the leaves unfurl in April to May, borne in small (1 to 1 1/2" diameter) panicles; one of the few maples with fragrant flowers.

FRUIT: Samara, 3/4 to 1" long, wings nearly parallel, red to brown, variable in coloration but there are several good red fruiting types available; red color most vibrant in June–July; fruits ripen September–October.

CULTURE: Very easy to transplant; quite adaptable to wide range of soils and pH ranges; performs best in moist, well-drained soil; withstands heavy pruning; can be successfully grown as a container plant; full sun or light shade.

DISEASES AND INSECTS: Relatively free of problems although can be affected by several of the pests listed under Silver Maple; *Verticillium* has been a problem on 'Compactum' and 'Flame'.

LANDSCAPE VALUE: Small specimen, patio tree, screen, grouping, massing, corners or blank walls of large buildings; very popular maple in east and midwest; certainly one of the hardiest; seems to do better in shade than many maples; tends toward multistemmed character and this would limit street tree use; one of the better maples for above-ground container use.

CULTIVARS:

'Compactum'—Supposedly more dense and compact than 'Durand Dwarf' but based on limited observations this does not appear true; shows vigorous growth and may reach 5 to 6′ and larger; leaves are lustrous dark green, about the size of the species, and color a good red-purple in fall; leaves 1/4 developed by early March in my garden; full flower by mid April; wonderfully fragrant and certainly a worthy garden plant. Plants in my garden made over 2′ of growth in a single season and had to be cut back to maintain compactness; in 10 years in the Dirr garden the plant is now 12′ high and 20′ wide, densely branched and serves as an effective barrier. Introduced by J.V. Bailey Nursery, Newport, Minnesota.

'Durand Dwarf'—Dwarf, shrubby type, branches more dense than 'Compactum'; will grow 3 to 5′ high with a similar or greater spread; leaves are about 1/2 the size of the species; summer leaf color lighter green than 'Compactum'; fall color is often poor but can range from yellow to bronze, orange and red; colors early (early October); easily rooted from cutting; originated from a witches broom before 1955 in Durand Eastman Park, Rochester, New York.

'Flame'—Dense shrub or small tree with red fruits and fiery red fall color; several nurserymen have indicated that this selection is superior to seedlings of the species; 'Flame' is seed grown and should be somewhat variable in fall and fruit color.

'Red Fruit'—A collective term for types whose fruit color a brilliant red; Minnesota Landscape Arboretum has a clone whose fruits turn a good red; based on observations in 1976 the tree fruits so heavily that vegetative growth is somewhat reduced. 'Red Wing' is included here (Introduced by McKay Nursery in Wisconsin).

var. *semenowii*—An interesting shrubby type (10 to 15′) with smaller, more graceful, deeper cut lobes; would make an effective screen or barrier; leaves are lustrous dark green in summer turning red-purple in fall; it is a geographical form found farther to the west, in Turkestan.

PROPAGATION: Seed—stratify at 68 to 86°F for 30 to 60 days followed by 41°F for 150+ days, or light scarification and then stratification for 90 days at 41°F; 3 to 4 months at 41°F also induces good germination; softwood cuttings collected in June rooted 90% in peat:perlite under mist with 1000 ppm IBA treatment; one of the easiest maples to root from cuttings; success can be variable and timing is critical—generally the earlier the better for maximum rooting.

ADDITIONAL NOTES: This species is closely allied to *A. tataricum* but differs principally in the shape of the leaf.

NATIVE HABITAT: Central and northern China, Manchuria and Japan. Introduced 1860.

Acer griseum — Paperbark Maple
(ā′ser gris′ē-um)

LEAVES: Opposite, trifoliate, 3 to 6″ long, elliptic to ovate-oblong, each leaflet 2 to 2 1/2″ long, half as wide, apex acute, base cuneate, middle leaflet short-stalked, coarsely toothed; lateral leaflets almost sessile, not as toothed, lower surface distinctly pubescent especially on the veins, bluish green above, pale green to glaucous beneath; petiole distinctly pubescent, 2 to 3″ long.

BUDS: Imbricate, brownish black, 1/16 to 1/8″ long, sharply pointed, reminiscent of Sugar Maple buds except for size and color; distinctly pubescent at base of bud, almost a collar of hairs surrounds the terminals and laterals.

STEM: Fine branches, pubescent at first, rich brown; stems develop exfoliating character during their second and third year which becomes more pronounced with age; bark color varies but is usually a cinnamon brown; leaf scars are surrounded by tufts of hairs; pith-white, solid, becoming brown on older stems.

SIZE: 20 to 30′ in height; spread one-half or equal to height; can reach 40 to 50′ but usually smaller under cultivation.

HARDINESS: Zone 4 to Zone 8; not as happy in the south but performs reasonably well; in the past listed as Zone 5.

HABIT: Upright-oval, oval or rounded; usually favoring the latter two descriptions; the splendid specimens on the University of Illinois campus are extremely variable but tend toward the oval-rounded habit; the specimens at the Arnold Arboretum offer age and, with age, *Acer griseum* assumes a dignity unmatched by other trees; a trip to view the Arnold's magnificent specimens is justified in any season; the oldest specimen in the United States exists in the Arnold Arboretum (83 years as of this publication date).

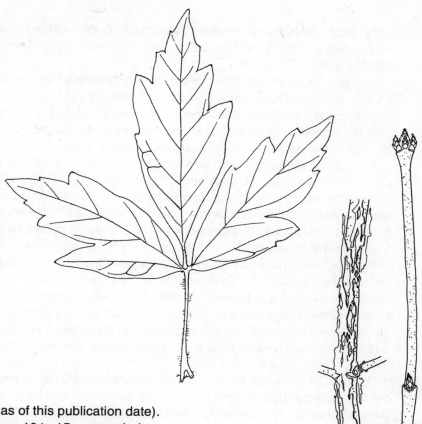

RATE: Slow, 6 to 12″ per year over a 10 to 15 year period.

TEXTURE: Medium-fine in leaf and winter habit.

BARK: Young stems rich brown to reddish brown; older wood (1/2″ diameter or greater) a beautiful cinnamon or red-brown as the bark exfoliates to expose these colors; second year wood usually starts to exfoliate, thus the exquisite bark character develops at a very young age; old trunks lose some of the exfoliating character but retain the rich brown colors; significant variation in degree of flakiness, and if a young tree does not exhibit a striking exfoliating character, this will carry into maturity; verbal descriptions cannot do justice to this ornamental asset and only after one has been privileged to view the bark first hand can he or she fully appreciate the character; snow acts as a perfect foil for the bark and accentuates its qualities.

LEAF COLOR: Flat dark to bluish green in summer changing to bronze, russet-red or red in fall; fall color can be spectacular but in seven years at Illinois I never once witnessed anything but muted green-red-brown colors; however, while on sabbatical leave at the Arnold Arboretum I was fortunate enough to have seen spectacular red coloration; in Georgia fall color is a muted red; *Acer griseum* is the last of the trifoliate maples *(A. mandshuricum, A. nikoense, A. triflorum)* to color and may hold some leaves into early November as far north as Boston.

FLOWERS: Few or solitary, greenish, on pendulous, 1″ long, pubescent peduncles.

FRUIT: Samara, 1 to 1 1/2″ long, pubescent, woody nutlet, wings diverge at a 60 to 90° angle.

CULTURE: Transplant balled and burlapped or as a container-grown plant in spring; adaptable to varied soils; prefers well-drained and moist but performs well in clay soils; pH adaptable; full sun.

DISEASES AND INSECTS: None serious.

PROPAGATION: Difficult, the biggest problem is poor seed quality; seeds are often void as is true for the other trifoliate maples; fruits we collected had 1% and 8% viable seeds; seeds will germinate after 90 days stratification at 41°F in moist peat; however, the fruit wall is so tough the root radical cannot penetrate and will spiral around within the structure; after stratification, I have removed the embryos and the majority continued to grow; commercial production of this species involves fall planting and waiting for two years for germination to begin; see Stimart, *HortScience* 16:341–343 (1981) "Factors regulating germination of trifoliate maple seeds;" I have conducted many experiments with cuttings and of two or three thousand mature woody cuttings have had one root; Brotzman (*PIPPS.* 30:342–

345, 1980) showed strong clonal differences in rooting among trees of *Acer griseum;* with 6 clones, rooting ranged from 17 to 80% using June collected cuttings from semi- to mature trees, wounding, treating with 2% IBA, mist.

It is well documented that cuttings taken from seedlings will root with relative ease (*PIPPS.* 34:570–573, 1984) and some nurserymen produce them this way; by continually cutting the young seedlings back juvenility is maintained; even when rooted the cuttings should not be disturbed until they have gone through a dormant period. The basic recipe: Seedling stockblock, pruned in March (Rhode Island) to induce long shoots, 3rd week in June (timing is critical; wood can't be too hard or soft), sand, 8″ long cutting, tip removed with only 1 pair of leaves remaining, 8000 ppm IBA-talc, 3″ deep in medium, mist, Benlate and Captan applied regularly, rooting takes place in 8 to 10 weeks, lifted with a spading fork, average 60% rooting. Rooted cuttings are potted in 2 1/2″ clay pots in soil:peat:sand and placed pot to pot in the greenhouse to reroot. Plants syringed and given bottom heat until mid October. Pots moved to deep pit house, covered with 1/2″ peat moss and watered in. Maintained at minimum 28°F during winter. When shoots emerge in spring (June) plants are planted in outdoor beds under 50% shade. After 3 years they are sold for lining out material or transplanted to field. We have budded *Acer griseum* on *Acer saccharum* in August with about 40% success: the budded-stock was dug, brought into the greenhouse and grew 18 to 30″ the first three months; I know of one commercial grower who produces *Acer griseum* by grafting on *Acer saccharum;* I am a degree skittish about long term prospects because of possible incompatabilities. See also *PIPPS* 19:346–349 (1969) and Dirr and Heuser, *The Reference Manual of Woody Plant Propagation,* for more details.

ADDITIONAL NOTES: *Acer griseum* is becoming more evident in commerce; not inexpensive but worth the expenditure; I grew some seedlings of *A. griseum* and one showed intermediate characteristics between the maternal parent and Sugar Maple; it is definitely a hybrid and shows tremendous vigor, slightly fissured bark, trifoliate and simple leaves and beautiful red fall color. There are known hybrids between *A. nikoense* and *A. griseum.* Might be reasonable to assume that all trifoliate maples will hybridize with each other.

NATIVE HABITAT: Central China. Introduced by Veitch in 1901.

RELATED SPECIES:

Three closely allied species, all with magnificent ornamental attributes, are presented here for the purposes of comparison and appreciation.

Acer mandshuricum—Manchurian Maple
(ā′ser mand-shör′i-kum)

LEAVES: Opposite, trifoliate, terminal leaflet 3 to 5″ long, 1 to 1 1/4″ wide, lanceolate, pointed, saw-toothed, glabrous except on midrib and larger veins; lateral leaflets shorter with a 1/4″ long petiolule, terminal petiolule 1/2 to 1″ long, medium to dark green above, glaucous beneath; petiole glabrous, reddish, 2 to 6″ long.

BUDS: Imbricate, brownish black, glabrous; terminal—3/8″ long, angled; laterals smaller, 1/4″ long, appressed, angled; slight spiral hook to the buds.

STEM: Slender, 1st year somewhat lustrous brown, glabrous, covered with numerous, elongated vertical lenticels; 2nd year becoming gray-brown with slight vertical fissuring.

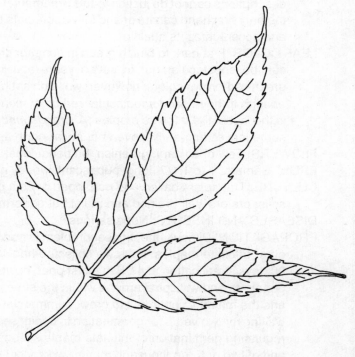

BARK: Smooth, gray, somewhat beech-like, and maintaining this character into old age.

Acer mandshuricum, Manchurian Maple, is a fantastic small tree that develops an upright-spreading crown. Height approaches 30 to 40' and spread slightly less. The insect and disease-free foliage turns a magnificent rose-red to red in early October. It is one of the earliest of all maples to develop fall color. Norway Maple is totally green while Manchurian is in full spectacle. Fruits glabrous; wings spreading at a right or obtuse angle, the nutlets thick and reticulate, samara averaging 1 to 11/2″ in length. A beautiful, small specimen tree that is worth the effort to procure. The most magnificent specimens I have observed are at the Arnold Arboretum and Smith College Botanic Garden. During my sabbatical at the Arnold, I watched the fall color peak by October 5 to 7 and the leaves completely abscise by October 10 to 12. Native to Manchuria, Korea. Cultivated 1904. Zone 4 to 7 (?).

Acer nikoense—Nikko Maple
(ā′ser nik-ō-en′sē)

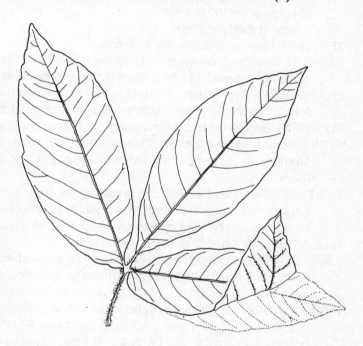

LEAVES: Opposite, trifoliate, leaflets ovate to elliptic-oblong, 2 to 5″ long, middle-short stalked, lateral ones subsessile, acute, obtusely dentate or nearly entire, medium green above, villous-pubescent beneath; petiole 1 to 1 1/2″ long, densely pilose.
BUDS: Imbricate, pyramid-shaped.
STEM: Slender, angled, brownish, prominently lenticelled, with pilose pubescence near end of stem; glabrous the 2nd year.

Acer nikoense, Nikko Maple, is a lovely, slow-growing, vase-shaped, round-headed, 20 to 30′ high tree. Although slow growing, it is interesting throughout the seasons and would make a fine specimen for the small property. The leaves are bronzy when emerging, changing to medium green in summer and finally glorious yellow, red and purple in fall. The fall color is not as brilliant as the other three trifoliates at least as I observed them at the Arnold. The fall color peaks in mid-October in Boston. Some trees develop a muted, subdued red. Bark is, like *A. mandshuricum,* a handsome smooth gray to grayish brown. Flowers are yellow, 1/2″ diameter, produced usually 3 together on drooping pedicels, 3/4″ long, May. Fruit is a thick, densely pubescent samara, 1 to 2″ long; the upright wings curved inward or spreading at a right angle. This species seems to prefer a well-drained, loamy, moist, slightly acid soil. Seven year old trees were 8 to 12′ high and 5″ in diameter at Wooster, Ohio. I have seen it performing well in the vicinity of Louisville, KY and Cincinnati, OH. Truly a beautiful tree but, like *Acer griseum,* the fruits are often devoid of solid seed and germination is a two-year process. Native to Japan, central China, now quite rare in its native haunts. Introduced 1881. Zone (4)5 to Zone 7.

Acer triflorum—Three-flower Maple
(ā′ser trī flō′rum)

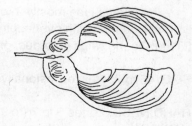

LEAVES: Opposite, trifoliate, leaflets ovate-lanceolate, dark green, 2 to 3″ long, 1″ wide, irregularly serrate, acuminate, leaf bases uneven, some cuneate or rounded, scattered pubescence above, veins pubescent beneath, especially mid-vein with long hispid hairs, margins of leaves with prominent hairs; basal leaflets short-stalked, terminal leaflet with a 1/4 to 1/2" stalk; petiole 2 to 3" long, pubescent.

BUDS: Imbricate, brownish black, scales tipped with short, whitish pubescence, 1/16 to 1/8" long, resemble *Acer griseum* buds; distinct pilose pubescence at nodes around base of buds.

STEM: Slender, brown, angled, abundant small lenticels, pilose pubescent at apex; 2nd and 3rd year stems brownish, exfoliating.

SIZE: 20 to 30' in height, comparable spread; may grow to 45' in the wild.

HARDINESS: Zone 5 to 7; there is a small specimen at the Minnesota Landscape Arboretum which might indicate Zone 4 hardiness.

HABIT: Small, upright-spreading tree of rather delicate proportions; the few open grown trees I have observed were full, dense and round-headed while those in more confined areas developed an upright-spreading outline.

RATE: Slow in the landscape.

TEXTURE: Medium through the seasons.

BARK: Outstanding; on young stems weakly exfoliating, while mature bark is ash-brown, loose, and vertically fissured; the exfoliation is not as pronounced as with *Acer griseum.*

LEAF COLOR: Dark green changing to rich yellow and reds in fall; overall effect is orange and based on Arnold Arboretum observations is truly beautiful; also rose-red to red; third of trifoliates to color.

FLOWERS: In clusters of 3, terminating short, 2-leaved shoots; hence, common name Threeflower Maple

FRUIT: Samara, wings 1 to 1 1/4" long, 3/8 to 5/8" wide, spreading at an angle of 120°; nutlets are thick, prominently pubescent; fruit-stalk hairy, about 5/8" long; fruits reminiscent of *Acer griseum* but are more hairy.

CULTURE: Transplant balled and burlapped or from a container; prefers acid, moist, well-drained soil; English reference indicated that a plant growing in chalk (limestone) collapsed and died; in early stages should be kept moist and adequately fertilized.

DISEASES AND INSECTS: None serious.

LANDSCAPE VALUE: Simply an outstanding small specimen maple, lovely foliage, exquisite bark and small habit contribute to the overall landscape effectiveness; would make a fine lawn specimen, focal tree in border planting, or perhaps small street tree; uses for good trees are endless.

PROPAGATION: Seed—same difficulty as with *A. griseum;* requires warm-cold; takes two years in nature; can be grafted on other trifoliates; Brotzman [*PIPPS* 30 (1980)] achieved 58% rooting with June collected cuttings treated with 2% IBA talc, silica sand, poly house.

ADDITIONAL NOTES: One of my favorites; the bark and fall color cannot be adequately described in words; not easy to propagate and obtain, but a real treasure for the discriminating gardener; the Arnold Arboretum has some fine specimens and all seem to color a bit differently which is related to seedling variation; Gary Koller has an excellent article on the species in *Horticulture* 57(10):32–35. 1979.

NATIVE HABIT: Manchuria and Korea. Introduced 1923.

Acer macrophyllum — Oregon Maple, Bigleaf Maple
(ā'ser mak-rō-fil'um)

FAMILY: Aceraceae

LEAVES: Opposite, simple, 8 to 12" across, glossy dark green above, pale beneath, 3 to 5 toothed lobes, the middle lobe mostly 3-lobed; petiole yields a milky sap when detached, 10 to 12" long.

BUDS: Rounded with overlapping scales.

STEM: Young twigs glabrous, green to reddish brown.

SIZE: 45 to 75' tall, occasionally reaching 100', usually smaller under cultivation; trunk diameter reaching 3 to 4'.

HARDINESS: Zones 5 to 7 (to 9 in West)

HABIT: Young trees with erect branches, becoming more rounded at maturity.

RATE: Slow to medium.
TEXTURE: Coarse in summer and winter.
BARK: Gray to reddish brown, furrowed with small flattened platelets.
LEAF COLOR: Dark glossy green changing to yellow-orange in fall.
FLOWERS: Yellow, fragrant, produced in 4 to 8″ long nodding racemes appearing with the leaves in April–May; each flower is approximately 1/3″ across.
FRUIT: Samara, approximately 1 1/2″ long, nutlet covered with brown pubescence, wings nearly glabrous, forming a 60° angle from wing to wing.
CULTURE: Prefers cool moist environment such as that in its native Pacific Northwest.
LANDSCAPE VALUE: Too many superior maples in the midwest and east but perhaps worthy of consideration in the west; have seen at Morris Arboretum in Pennsylvania and the tree appeared prosperous; perhaps too coarse because of large leaves for the average landscape.
ADDITIONAL NOTES: Have seen in the Portland, Oregon area where the tree is quite common. Seems to pop up in fence rows and waste areas not unlike Norway maple in the northern states.
NATIVE HABITAT: Alaska to Southern California. Introduced 1812.

Acer miyabei — Miyabe Maple
(ā′ser mi-ya′bē-ī)

LEAVES: Opposite, simple, 4 to 6″ wide, 3 to 5″ high, mostly 5-lobed, each lobe with prominent indentations, long acuminate, cordate, flat to semi-lustrous dark green above, lower surface olive-green, pubescent, prominently so on veins, tufts of hairs in axils; petiole 4 to 7″ long, pubescent, with milky sap.
BUDS: Terminal imbricate, 1/8 to 3/16″ long, brownish, bud scales edged with fine pubescence; laterals similar but smaller and hidden by petiole bases.

STEM: Lustrous brown, angled, glabrous.
BARK: Grayish, scaly but in long strips.

Acer miyabei, Miyabe Maple, is an upright-oval to rounded small tree growing 30 to 40′, either open or densely branched. The habit is quite lovely and may remind one of the outlines of Acer campestre or Acer buergeranum. The leaves stay green into October and then turn rapidly to pale yellow and fall soon thereafter. The flowers are greenish yellow, borne in slender-stalked, 10- to 15-flowered pyramidal corymbs in May. The wings of the fruits horizontally spreading, the nutlet silky-hairy, averaging 1 3/4 to 2″ in length. Culturally the species prefers moist, well-drained soils probably on the acid side. Several specimens are doing quite well in the Morton Arboretum where the soil could best be described as a clay loam. Propagation has been a problem as vegetative and seed attempts have met with limited success. Fall planting or 3 months cold stratification will overcome dormancy. Percent sound seed is usually low. Seed should be collected as early as possibly to prevent seed coat drying and a subsequent deeper dormancy. The species is very close to A. campestre and may have similar dormancy problems. Cuttings from 55-year old tree rooted 20, 37, and 23% with 0.5, 1.0 and 1.5% IBA-5 second dip; cuttings from 7-year-old hedge plants rooted 57, 70, 40, and 43% with 0.1, 0.5, 1.0, and 1.5% IBA-5 second dip, respectively. The Morton Arboretum has indicated that grafting onto volunteer seedlings has proved successful as well as onto seedlings of Acer campestre. The species is hardy to Zone 4 and I have seen a specimen doing quite well at the Minnesota

Landscape Arboretum where winter temperatures may drop to –30°F. Would make a nice specimen tree for the small residential area. The discovery of this rare tree took place quite by accident when Prof. C.S. Sargent of the Arnold Arboretum was waiting for a train at Iwanigawa, a railroad junction in Yezo, Japan. He had some time before the train arrived and, as any good plantsman, strolled out of the town to a small grove of trees. In this grove, occupying a piece of low ground on the borders of a small stream was *A. miyabei* covered with fruit. Japan. Introduced 1892.

Acer negundo — Boxelder, Ash-leaved Maple
(ā'ser nĕ goon'dō)

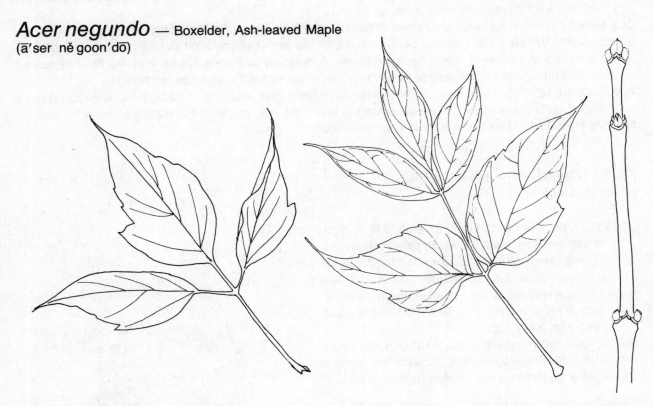

LEAVES: Opposite, pinnately compound, 3 to 5 (7 to 9) leaflets, ovate or lance-oblong, 2 to 4″ long, coarsely serrate or terminal one lobed, bright green above, glabrous, lighter green beneath and slightly pubescent or eventually glabrous; petiole 2 to 3″ long.

BUDS: 1/4″ long, greenish or reddish scales covered with silky hairs, two scales often split exposing inner, more pubescent scales.

STEM: Green to reddish brown, often covered with a waxy whitish bloom that can be rubbed off, glabrous; leaf scars encircle twig and meet at a sharp angle; malodorous when bruised; pith-large, white, solid.

SIZE: 30 to 50′ in height, can reach 70′, but this is the exception; spread variable but usually equal to or greater than height.

HARDINESS: Zone 2 to 9.

HABIT: Usually rounded to broad-rounded in outline, branches develop irregularly to support the uneven crown; often a small "alley cat" tree with multi-stemmed character and ragged appearance.

RATE: Fast, extremely so when young, the wood is weak and will break up in ice and wind, can grow 15 to 20′ in a 4 to 6 year period.

TEXTURE: Owing to ragged habit, the tree is coarse in all seasons; perhaps a degree unfair and the best forms grade to medium.

BARK COLOR: Gray-brown, slightly ridged and furrowed.

LEAF COLOR: Light green on the upper surface and grayish green below in summer, foliage turns yellow-green to brown in fall; usually of no ornamental consequence; along with *Acer mandshuricum* one of the earliest maples to develop fall color.

FLOWERS: Dioecious, yellowish green, March to April, male flowers born in corymbs; female in slender pendulous racemes and usually in great quantity; not ornamentally effective but worth avoiding the female forms if the tree has to be used.

FRUIT: Samara, maturing in September or October, usually profusely borne, persisting into winter, the pair forming an angle of 60° or less.

CULTURE: Easy to transplant, actually native to stream banks, lakes, borders of swamps but performs well out of its native habitat in poor, wet or dry soils and cold climates; pH adaptable; full sun; a necessary tree under difficult conditions where few other species will survive; usually a short-lived tree.

DISEASES AND INSECTS: Described under Silver Maple; boxelder bugs make nice pets.

LANDSCAPE VALUE: Extensive use is limited due to lack of ornamental assets; however, has been used in Great Plains and Southwest; falls in same category as *Ulmus pumila, Ailanthus altissima* and *Morus alba;* the cultivars have some landscape merit.

CULTIVARS: When traveling through Europe, the variegated forms of Boxelder are everywhere in evidence. They can be particularly striking and for that reason are treated here in detail.

'Auratum'—The leaflets entirely yellow; in proper climate will retain this color into fall; Bean considered it one of the best golden colored trees; have seen in Europe where the plant may be cut back in winter to force long shoots that provide vivid yellow leaf color; used as a filler in shrub borders to provide color.

'Aureo-marginatum' ('Aureo-variegatum')—Dr. J.C. Raulston, North Carolina State Univ., led a group of Southeasterners, including the author, through Germany, and to my delight we chanced upon an experiment station that had a handsome tree with yellow-bordered leaves. Up close and personal the leaves were rather striking, but better used at a theme park. The tree was 15 to 20′ tall.

'Baron'—Selection from Morden Arboretum, Canada, male, free of seed, grows 35 to 50′. Hardy in Zone 2.

'Elegans'—Have seen small plants at Bressingham Gardens and the leaves are edged with a handsome irregular yellow margin; the plant does not appear as vigorous as 'Aureo-marginatum'.

'Flamingo'—A rather curious form with brilliant pink new shoots that age to green with a white border. The color is best in cool weather and plants should be cut back in late winter to encourage vigorous new extension growth. I have seen the plant used in English gardens and it is most effective from May–June. Late in the season the pink color occurs in the new growth and is not as vibrant. Older leaves are quite similar to 'Variegatum' and this form could be a branch sport of same; originated in Holland.

'Sensation'—More controlled, slower growth and improved branch structure than species, medium green summer foliage, brilliant red in fall, rounded habit, 30′ by 25′, Zone 2 to 7, a 1989 Schmidt introduction.

'Variegatum'—A common form with irregular white margined leaves; I consider it one of the most effective of variegated small trees; a female clone and the fruits are variegated like the leaves; will revert to green or produce albino leaves; must be carefully pruned; originated as a branch sport in the nursery of M. Fromant at Toulouse, France in 1845; one of the most beautiful specimens of this cultivar resides at Smith College Botanic Garden; best in Zone 5 to 8.

Several geographical varieties exist including var. *californicum* with pubescent leaves and stems and var. *violaceum* with purplish or violet branches covered with a glaucous bloom.

PROPAGATION: In general a 2 to 3 month treatment at 40°F is necessary; however, pretreatment of seeds for 2 weeks by soaking in cold water or mechanical rupture of pericarp are recommended before stratification; cuttings will root readily and for the cultivars this may be the preferred route; softwood material treated with 8000 ppm IBA in talc rooted readily when taken as late as mid-September.

MAINTENANCE CONSIDERATIONS: Not the neatest tree and certainly should not be used if better trees are available. Female trees are actually ugly because fruits hang like dirty brown socks through fall and early winter. The various colored foliage types can be rather cheerful but in the south (Zones 7 and 8) require special siting under pines or some form of partial shade. At the University's Botanical Garden a small tree of 'Variegatum' always developed leaf burn in summer.

ADDITIONAL NOTES: Not my favorite tree but kind of pleasant when exposing its yellow-green flowers in early spring before most trees have even awakened; found along streams and rivers; will withstand periodic flooding; probably the most aggressive of the maples in maintaining itself in unfavorable sites; can become a noxious weed.

NATIVE HABITAT: Virtually the entire United States and southern Canada. Cultivated 1688.

Acer palmatum — Japanese Maple
(ā′ser pal-mā′tum)

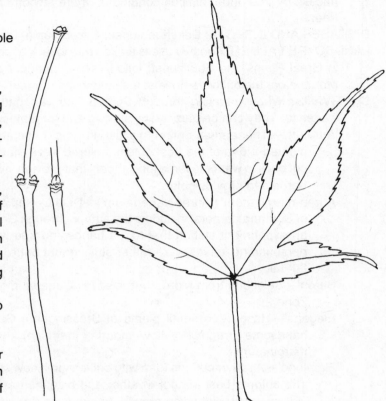

LEAVES: Opposite, simple, 2 to 5″ long, deeply 5 to 7 to 9 lobed, lobes being lance-ovate to lance-oblong in shape, acuminate, subcordate doubly serrate; color varies depending on cultivar.

BUDS: Tend toward valvate character, small, green or red, hidden by base of petiole, frequently double terminal buds; margin of leaf scar much elevated forming flaring collar around bud; remind one of Easter eggs sitting in grass.

STEM: Glabrous, slender, usually green to red, often with a glaucous bloom.

SIZE: 15 to 25′ in height, spread equal to or greater than height; great variation in this species due to large number of cultivars which are common in commerce; many of the *dissectum* types only reach 6 to 8′ and become quite mound-like in shape; the species can reach 40 to 50′ in the wild state; magnificent specimens along the east coast from Boston to Washington that approach 40 to 50′.

HARDINESS: Depending on cultivar, Zones 5 and 6 to 8; does quite well in Zone 8 and provides excellent fall color in November.

HABIT: Species tends towards a rounded to broad-rounded character, often the branches assume a layered effect similar to Flowering Dogwood; the plant can be grown as a single-stemmed small tree or large multi-stemmed shrub; perhaps the greatest ornamental attributes are exposed in the latter situation.

RATE: Over many years a slow grower but in youth will tend toward the medium rate; about 10 to 15′ over a 10 year period.

TEXTURE: Fine to medium-fine in leaf depending on the cultivar; of similar texture during winter.

BARK: Young stems vary from green to polished or bloomy reddish purple and red; older branches assume a gray cast; handsome for bark character but often not considered for this feature due to over-shadowing by excellent foliage.

LEAF COLOR: The species is green in summer, becoming yellow, bronze, purple or red in the fall; many of the var. *atropurpureum* types turn a magnificent red in fall; leaves hold late and are often present into November.

FLOWERS: Small, red to purple, May–June, borne in stalked umbels (possibly corymbs), quite attractive on close inspection.

FRUIT: Samara, 1/2 to 3/4" long, wings 1/4 to 3/8" wide, much incurved, the pair forming a broad arch; wings often turning a good red especially those of the var. *atropurpureum* series; ripen in September–October.

CULTURE: Transplant balled and burlapped or as a container plant into moist, high organic matter, well drained soil; protect from sweeping winds and late spring frosts for the young foliage is sensitive to cold; tends to leaf out early and many nurserymen and gardeners have lost a year's growth or the entire plant to frost; ideally provide dappled shade; if too much the plants grow slowly and the purple types become more green (still lovely though); too little they may literally cook in the summer sun; provide supplemental moisture and mulch.

I have been amazed at Japanese maple performance in Zone 8. Certainly some specimens fry in the heat and during the summer of 1988, one of our worst drought periods, young plants that were not provided supplemental water turned up their toes (roots) and died. Minimal attention will reward the gardener manyfold.

DISEASES AND INSECTS: Actually surprisingly few; have had a real problem with rooted cuttings in plastic houses that leafed out early. The high humidity promoted *Botrytis* infection which literally killed 80 fine specimens in about three days.

LANDSCAPE VALUE: Probably one of the most flexible maple species as far as landscape uses; magnificent specimen, accent plant, shrub border, grouping, bonsai; definitely lends an artistic and aristocratic touch; considering the tremendous heat in the south I am amazed at the number of choice specimens; even in full sun the plant does reasonably well; the purple-leaf forms appear to lose the pronounced color earlier in the growing season; there are a number of Japanese Maples, including *'Dissectum Atropurpureum'*, in the Athens area and most have prospered.

CULTIVARS: In the previous edition many cultivars were included; here I have included a selected few and recommend that anyone serious about cultivars consult the 2nd Edition of J.D. Vertrees magnificent reference, *Japanese Maples,* Timber Press, Portland, Oregon; most of those presented are available in commerce.

NON-DISSECTED TYPES:

var. *atropurpureum* ('Atropurpureum')—Leaves reddish purple, 5 to 7(9) lobed, color usually fades with maturity and summer heat, excellent in spring and fall for red coloration; seedlings produced from seeds of the type are variable in leaf coloration; the better red-leaved seedlings generally command a superior price; several plants in the Botanical Garden are somewhat disappointing since the purplish red spring leaf color only persists into June before turning green; if one wants superior foliage color then choose a good cultivar.

'Bloodgood'—Based on my observations over the years perhaps the best for deep reddish purple leaf color retention; have seen good color in summer in the Boston area, a slow-growing, small round-headed tree probably maturing in the 15 to 20' range; excellent red fall color; the leaves ranging from 4" long to 5" wide; also has beautiful red fruits; commonly propagated from cuttings and one of the easier to root and overwinter cultivars; possibly originated at Bloodgood Nursery, Long Island, NY.

'Burgundy Lace'—Growing next door to 'Bloodgood' at the Arnold Arboretum but does not hold the reddish purple color as well; turns purple-bronze-green in summer, the sinuses are cut almost to the point of attachment of the blade to the petiole and each lobe is finely serrated and cut along the margins; leaves average 4" long by 3 1/2" wide; usually a small tree about 10 to 12' high and 12 to 15' wide; another good form for American gardens.

'Moonfire'—A relatively new introduction from the Red Maple Nursery, Media, PA, an excellent purple-red leaf form that holds color during the summer and will not bronze like many var. *atropurpureum* forms; 7(5) lobed leaves turn crimson in fall, leaf size ranges from 3 to 5" in length and about 4 1/2" wide; habit is upright in youth gradually broadening with maturity, will grow about 15' high.

'Oshio beni'—The new growth emerges a vibrant orange-red to red but unfortunately loses the color in late spring–early summer, becoming bronze to greenish red; fall color is rich scarlet; the

7-lobed leaves average 3″ long and 3 to 4″ wide, margins are finely serrate like the species; will grow 15 to 20′ and develops a spreading habit.

'Ozakazuki'—An old cultivar with 7 evenly serrated lobes, bright green leaves that turn a rich crimson in the fall, considered one of the best for autumnal coloration; becomes a round-topped 15 to 20′ high tree at maturity.

'Sango Kaku' ('Senkaki')—A common cultivar and often praised for the brilliant coral fall and winter color of the young stems; the color is striking but as the branches mature the color is lost and only the first and second year growth show rich coloration; 5 to 7 lobed leaves with doubly serrate margins, leaves about 2″ long by 2 1/2″ wide, new leaves are reddish tinged, become light green in summer and finally yellow gold with light red overtones in fall; habit is upright with numerous smaller "twiggy" stems; will grow 20 to 25′ high by 18 to 22′ wide.

'Scolopendrifolium'—Quite a handsome green, 5-lobed leaf form with the lobes cut to the point of attachment, each lobe only 1/4 to 1/2″ wide with irregularly toothed margins; entire leaf about 3″ long by 4″ wide; yellow fall color; leaf effect is quite digitate or finger-like; strong growing form to 15′ developing a rounded canopy at maturity.

'Scolopendrifolium Rubrum'—As above but not as vigorous, more bushy growing 6 to 8′ high; reddish purple new leaves turn bronzy red-green in summer and reddish in fall; handsome form and appears adapted to Zone 8.

DISSECTUM GROUP ('Dissectum', var. *dissectum*)

Perhaps the most refined of all maples, the 7, 9, or 11 lobes are cut to the point of attachment with each lobe in turn finely cut and each division toothed. The cultivars vary in the fineness of the cutting as well as color.

var.*dissectum atropurpureum* ('Dissectum Atropurpureum')—Leaves deep red, a compact, slow-growing shrub of mounded, pendulous outline; usually growing 6 to 8′ but I have seen plants in the 10 to 12′ category; the entire plant appearing as a mound of rich, purple-red, ferny foliage; the color fading to purple-green or green with time and in fall turning glorious burnt orange that implies the plant is on fire; perhaps the most magnificent aspect of the plant is the twisted, contorted branching pattern; it is an architectural masterpiece that only a higher being could create; these forms set fruit and the resultant seedlings will yield plants of different colors and degrees of ferniness.

'Crimson Queen'—New growth bright crimson-red which Vertrees states persists throughout the entire growing season; plants I have seen in the south lose the color and become more bronze-green to red; fall color is in the scarlet range; this is a strong growing 7 to 9 to 11 lobed form that is popular in commerce; will eventually grow 8 to 10′ by 12′; develops handsome cascading branches.

'Ever Red'—Interesting 7-lobed form of var. *dissectum atropurpureum* with the newly emerging leaves covered with fine silky pubescence, pubescence soon fades and the deep purple red color becomes prominent; does not hold the color as prominently as 'Crimson Queen' and fades to bronze-green in the heat of the summer; fall color is bright red; vigorous form with cascading, pendulous growth habit and old specimens 15′ are known; apparently many plants sold as 'Ever Red' are in fact something else.

'Filigree'—A handsome yellow-green 7-lobed var. *dissectum* type that is overlain with minute dots and flecks of pale cream and gold; leaves turn a rich golden in fall; this cultivar is romantically delicate and provides a bright element in shady locations; forms a rounded cascading 6 by 9′ mound.

'Garnet'—I grew this var. *dissectum atropurpureum* form in my Illinois garden where the rich gemstone garnet color faded to a purple green; when grown in shade the leaf maintains a greenish cast but develops the garnet color in sun; a vigorous form that will grow 10′ high; leaves are slightly more coarse than most var. *dissectum atropurpureum* types; fall color is a good red; common in commerce and one of the more available types.

'Ornatum'—An old var. *dissectum atropurpureum* cultivar that I have kind of grown up with; the new leaves are more bronze-red than 'Garnet' and 'Ever Red' and during summer turn largely green;

fall color is often an excellent crimson-red; 7-lobed leaves are finely dissected and delicate; grows 6 by 9′ or more; has lost popularity due to better colored foliaged types but still reasonably common.

'Red Filigree Lace'—A relatively new form of var. *dissectum atropurpureum* with deep purple-red or maroon leaf color that is retained into summer and then turns rich crimson in fall; 7-lobed leaves that are more finely dissected than other cultivars presented here, leaves are 2 to 3″ long and 3 to 3 1/4″ wide; typical habit of the Dissectum group, but not as fast as 'Crimson Queen' and 'Garnet'.

'Tamukeyama'—Mr. Don Shadow, Winchester, TN considers this the best of the purple dissected group; the 7 to 9 lobed leaves are not as finely dissected as 'Crimson Queen', 'Red Filigree Lace', or 'Ever Red'; leaves average 3 to 3 3/4″ long and 4 to 4 1/2″ wide; the young foliage is deep crimson-red and matures to purple-red and holds quite well; an old cultivar that according to Vertrees was listed as early as 1710; 50 to 100 year-old plants are 13′ high.

'Viridis'—This is probably a catch-all term for all green-leave dissected types; 'Viride' is occasionally listed in nursery catalogs; the leaves vary from 7 to 9 lobed with the usual dissections; fall color is yellow-gold to red; in my travels I have observed beautiful green leaf dissected forms; they have a place in almost any garden.

'Waterfall'—Considered the best green leaf dissected form with 7 to 9 multi-dissected lobes; leaves are larger than typical 'Viridis' types ranging from 3 to 5″ long, 3 to 5″ wide; the rich green foliage holds up well in Zone 8 heat; fall color is golden with reddish suffusions; I have a small plant and it is truly a beautiful form; will grow 10′ high and 12 to 14′ wide.

Many variegated foliage cultivars are described but are limitedly available to the general gardening public and must be sought from speciality producers. Vertrees' wonderful book is a must for anyone interested in Japanese Maples. One's eyes are opened to an entirely new adventure in gardening.

PROPAGATION: Based on the literature I have reviewed, a book could be written on *Acer palmatum* propagation. See Dirr and Heuser, 1987, and also James Wells, "How to propagate Japanese Maples" *American Nurseryman* 151(9):14. In general, seed should be collected when green or red before it dries on the tree; it can be planted directly and should germinate the following spring; dried seed should be soaked in water at 110°F for 2 days followed by stratification; dried seed from Japan when pretreated in a "normal" manner germinated over a 5 year period; seed that is collected green/red, cleaned, dusted with Captan, stratified in moist peat for 90 to 150 days at 40°F and sown should germinate. Many cultivars are grafted but choice of understock is important. Softwood cuttings are rooted by taking 6 to 8″ lengths (smaller on less vigorous cultivars), wounding, applying high IBA (20000 ppm); placing in peat:perlite under mist; when rooted they should be left undisturbed until they have gone through a dormant period or transferred to supplemental light and induced into growth; I have rooted softwood cuttings that were collected in July, wounded, treated with 10000 ppm IBA quick dip, placed in peat:perlite under mist; roots developed only from wounded area; rooting took 2 months. Anyone serious about Japanese Maple propagation should consult *The Reference Manual of Woody Plant Propagation* for detailed information.

NATIVE HABITAT: *Acer palmatum* is native to Japan, China, Korea. Introduced to England in 1820. Long cultivated by the Japanese.

RELATED SPECIES:

Acer circinatum—Oregon Vine Maple
(ā′ser sir-sin-ā′tum)

LEAVES: Opposite, simple, (5)7 to 9(11) lobed, 3 to 5″ long and wide, almost circular in general outline, but heart shaped at the base, lobes unequal or doubly toothed, glabrous, dark green above, petiole 1 to 1 1/2″ long.

Acer circinatum, Oregon Vine Maple, grows commonly as a large multi-stemmed tree in the 10 to 20′ range. I have seen numerous specimens in the Vancouver, British Columbia area and they are predominantly shrubby and start to develop a tinge of fall color in August–early September. Fall color is variable, ranging from yellow-orange to red, the new spring growth is reddish tinged. The reddish purple sepals subtend small dull white petals and make a handsome display against the conspicuous crimson bud scales. Red fruits about 1 1/2″ long with the wings spreading horizontally, develop in late spring. Found in moist woods, along streambanks from British Columbia south to northern California. It appears to perform reasonably well in drier situations but will develop earlier fall coloration. 'Monroe' has deeply cut leaves like *A. japonicum* 'Vitifolium'. 'Little Gem' is a compact roundish shrub with smaller leaves than the species. Zone 5 to 6 on east coast. I tried to grow a plant in my Illinois garden but was unsuccessful. Introduced 1826.

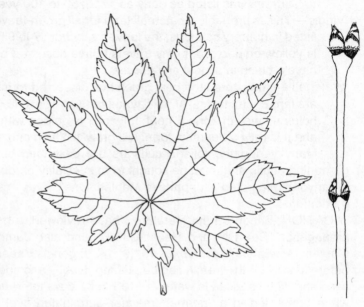

Acer japonicum—Fullmoon Maple
(ā′ser ja-pon′-i-kum)

LEAVES: Opposite, simple, roundish, 3 to 6″ across, 7 to 11-lobed, lobes ovate to lanceolate, long pointed, sharply and irregularly toothed, cordate, rich green, tuft of whitish pubescence at end of downy leaf stalk on upper side, underside with whitish hairs on veins and in their axils; petiole 1 to 1 1/2″ long, pubescent when young.

BUDS: Similar to *A. palmatum* in every way, bud is valvate, lustrous red; collars flare and produce "nest" effect, collars are fringed with hairs.

STEM: 1st year: slender, glabrous, reddish green, angled, slightly bloomy, smooth, nodes flattened (similar to *Cercidiphyllum*); pith-white, solid; 2nd year: marked color change—becoming brown, lightly fissured; sharp demarcation between current and last season's growth; pith—whitish to tan.

Acer japonicum, Fullmoon Maple grows 20 to 30′ in height with a comparable or larger spread (can reach 40 to 50′ in the wild). Leaves are an extremely handsome soft green changing to rich yellow and crimson in fall. Purplish red 1/2″ diameter flowers are produced in April before the leaves on long stalked nodding corymbs. Fruit is 1″ long and wings range from nearly horizontal to forming an obtuse angle. Culture is similar to *Acer palmatum.* Japan. Zone 5 to 7. The following cultivars are probably more common than the species in gardens and include:

'Aconitifolium'—Lobes extend to 1/2 or 1/4″ of the end of petiole, each lobe (9 to 11) being again divided and sharply toothed; magnificent crimson fall color; rounded bushy habit to 8 to 10′ in height; one of the most beautiful of all fall coloring shrubs.

'Aureum'—Leaves golden yellow and effective during the summer; reaching 10 to 20′ in height with a comparable spread; literally lights up a garden; have seen listed as a selection of *Acer shirasawanum* which is probably where it belongs.

'Itayo'—Leaves larger than the species with good yellow fall color.

'Junshitoe'—Leaves smaller than the species, 2 to 3″ across.

'Vitifolium'—Excellent type because of the rich purple, crimson, and orange fall colors, leaves are large, up to 6″ long and wide and of grape-like shape; beautiful plant at Longwood Gardens, that, in fall color, is a garden, to 20′; have seen this labeled as 'Aconitifolium' but the leaves are not as deeply cut and do not develop the vibrant red color of 'Aconitifolium'.

Acer oliverianum
(ā′ser ol-i-vĕr-ē-ā′num)

LEAVES: Opposite, simple, 2 to 4″ long and wide, 5-lobed, truncate or subcordate, lobes ovate, caudate-acuminate, finely serrate, middle lobe with 5 to 8 pairs of lateral veins, finely reticulate, medium green above, lustrous and glabrous beneath; petiole 2 to 3″ long.
BUDS: Essentially valvate, ovoid, almost triangular in outline, glabrous, glossy reddish purple, about 1/8″ long and wide, presents a squat appearance when nestled against the stem.
STEM: Medium, terete, glabrous, lustrous purple to green, often covered with a waxy bloom.

'Vitifolium'

Acer oliverianum is a relatively unknown small (15 to 25′) maple with characteristics similar to *A. palmatum*. The fall colors are rich shades of orange and red. I was first introduced to the tree at the old USDA Bamboo Station in Savannah, GA where the plant has prospered for many years. The habit is upright-spreading with the more or less horizontal branching of *A. palmatum*. The most impressive aspect is the tremendous heat tolerance since Savannah is in Zone 9 (+20 to +30°F). The tree grows in sandy soil and is perhaps more drought tolerant than *A. palmatum*. The 1 to 1 1/4″ long fruits have nearly horizontal wings while those of *A. palmatum* are more incurved. A few Georgia nurserymen have started to grow the species and the tree may prove a valuable addition to Zone 9. Zone 7 to 9. Central China. Introduced 1901.

Acer pseudosieboldianum—Purplebloom Maple
(ā′ser sū-do-sē-bōl-dē-a′-num)

LEAVES: Similar to *Acer japonicum;* 9 to 11-lobed, doubly-serrate lobes.
BUDS: Similar *A. japonicum;* silky, rusty brown hairs are evident at point where bud attaches to stem.
STEM: Red to reddish-purple, glabrous.

Acer pseudosieboldianum is a lovely small tree similar to *A. japonicum* and *A. palmatum* and rather difficult to differentiate from unless detailed characteristics are applied. E.H. Wilson noted that in its native Manchuria and Korea it assumes wonderful tints of orange, scarlet and crimson. As I viewed it in the Arnold Arboretum during the fall of 1978 the colors approximated a green-brown haze. A freeze effectively eliminated the possibility of good fall color. Cultivated 1903. Zone 5.

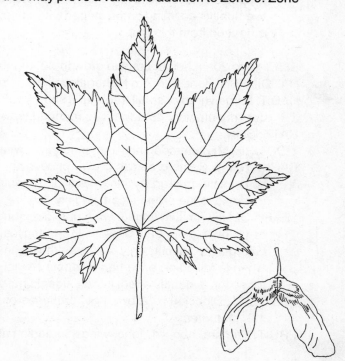

Acer sieboldianum—Siebold Maple
(ā′ser sē-bōl-dē-a′num)

Acer sieboldianum is similar to the previous but differs in the yellow flowers (purple on *A. pseudosiebol-dianum*) and pubescence of the stems. The pubescence appeared to be a constant character. Fall color is yellow orange and had started to develop by Oct. 16, 1978 at the Arnold. A report from the Morton Arboretum, Lisle, Illinois, listed the fall color as intense red. Unfortunately the same freeze (Oct. 23) that eliminated the fall color of *A. pseudosieboldianum* also eliminated this species. Japan. Cultivated 1880. Zone 5.

ADDITIONAL NOTES: These maples are outstanding landscape plants; almost a guaranteed success in any landscape if sited and cultured properly; the cultivars of *A. palmatum* have become a passion for some gardeners.

Acer pensylvanicum — Striped Maple, also called Moosewood, Whistlewood
(ā′ser pen-sĭl-van′-ĭ-kum)

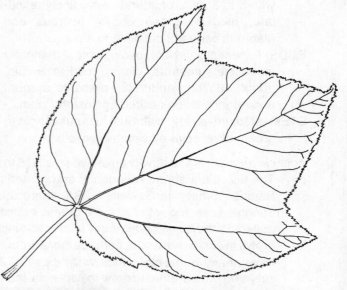

LEAVES: Opposite, simple, roundish obovate, 3-lobed at apex, 5 to 7″ long and as wide, sub-cordate, the lobes pointing forward, acuminate, serrulate, ferrugineous-pubescent beneath when young, finally glabrous; petiole 1 to 3″ long, rufous pubescent when young, finally glabrous or nearly so.

BUDS: Glabrous, 1/3 to 1/2″ long, blunt, 2 scales, valvate; terminal—almost 1/2″ long, much longer than the lateral buds, covered by 2 thick, bright red, spatulate, boat-shaped prominently keeled scales, inner scales green; stalk about 1/25″ long, red, glossy.

STEM: Smooth, stout, green changing to red or reddish brown; lenticels few; leaf scars "U" shaped, almost encircling twigs, older stems eventually becoming green striped with white; very handsome for this characteristic; snake bark term is derived from this trait.

SIZE: 15 to 20′ in height but can grow to 30′ or more in the wild, spread is less than or equal to height.

HARDINESS: Zone 3 to 7 in higher elevations of southern Appalachians.

HABIT: Large shrub or small tree with a short trunk and ascending and arching branches that form a broad but very uneven, flat-topped to rounded crown.

RATE: Slow.

TEXTURE: Medium-coarse in leaf, medium in winter.

BARK: Young stems greenish brown or reddish; young branches (1/2″ or greater) are green and conspicuously marked by long, vertical, greenish white stripes, hence, the name Striped Maple; old trunks lose the pronounced striping.

LEAF COLOR: Pinkish tinged when unfolding, bright green at maturity; apparently a great concentration of yellow pigments is present in the leaves; leaves change to vibrant yellow in autumn; in North Georgia the species only occurs on the highest peaks and is unbelievably spectacular in mid-October when in fall color; have had students collect leaves during this time and bring them back to Athens for positive identification; if the students notice, then the pigmentation must be sensational.

FLOWERS: Dioecious, yellow, May, produced on pendulous, slender 4 to 6″ long racemes, each flower 1/3″ diameter.

FRUIT: Samara, about 1″ long, wings spreading at a wide angle, born on a 1″ long pedicel.

CULTURE: Does not proliferate under cultivation, prefers partially shaded woods; well-drained, cool, moist, slightly acidic soils; in native range exists as an understory plant which provides an index of its shade tolerance; have seen on rocky mountainsides in Massachusetts growing in the most inhospitable of situations; not amenable to culture where heat and drought are common denominators.

DISEASES AND INSECTS: See Silver Maple discussion.

LANDSCAPE VALUE: Very inadequate lawn specimen but for naturalizing purposes has possibilities; bark is lovely and for that reason worth considering if conditions can be supplied.

CULTIVARS:

'Erythrocladum'—Young stems turn a bright coral-red after leaf fall; had only read about this form until viewing it first hand in Boston and England; spectacular coral-pink-red stems with white striations that literally glow in winter; introduced by Späth's nursery in 1904.

PROPAGATION: Seed, 41°F for 90 to 120 days; I have tried cuttings with no success; *Acer capillipes* and *A. tegmentosum* have been rooted with good success (see *PIPPS* 30:342); seed of the above and following species that I have collected was void of embryos; this could relate to the lack of a suitable male for pollination.

MAINTENANCE CONSIDERATIONS: Although lovely trees because of bark and fall color, they offer little in the way of urban toughness; bark is thin and subject to mower and weed-eater damage; plants appear canker susceptible under stress; I can never remember seeing a prospering snakebark maple under adverse conditions; reserve for cooler climates, moist, well-drained soil and perhaps partial shade.

NATIVE HABITAT: Quebec to Wisconsin, south to northern Georgia. Introduced 1755.

RELATED SPECIES:

There are several asiatic maples with similar floral and bark characteristics. They are discussed here in encapsulated form. None is widely available in commerce. I have observed all species in my travels and have attempted here to highlight the differences.

Acer capillipes
(ā'ser ka-pil'i-pēz)

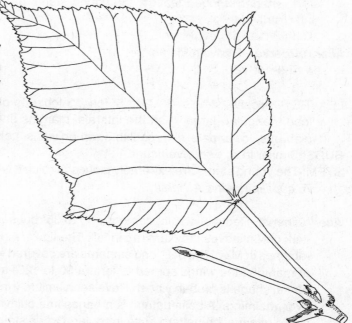

LEAVES: Opposite, simple, 4 to 7″ long, 3 to 5″ wide, 3-lobed, the lateral lobes much shorter, acuminate, cordate, prominently serrate from apex to base, glabrous above and below; gummy substances in axils of veins; petiole—1 1/2 to 2 1/2″ long, glabrous, channeled above, reddish.

BUDS: Similar to *A. pensylvanicum*.

STEM: Greenish purple to reddish purple, with white striations, terete, glabrous.

Acer capillipes is a small (30 to 35′ high) round-headed tree that often branches close to the ground. The young leaves are reddish and upon maturity turn dark green. Fall color may be yellow to red but trees I have observed were injured by a freeze before turning. Young branches are greenish to reddish brown with whitish stripes; the bark eventually becomes grayish brown and ridged and furrowed. Very handsome small tree and the most beautiful specimen in this country is located at the Arnold Arboretum. The greenish white 1/3″ diameter flowers occur in slender 2 1/2 to 4″ long pendulous racemes. The samara is 3/4″ long and the wings form a 120° to 180° angle. Japan. Introduced 1892. Zone 5 to 7. This is probably the most heat tolerant of the Snakebark maples.

Acer davidii—David Maple
(ā'ser dā-vid'ē-ī)

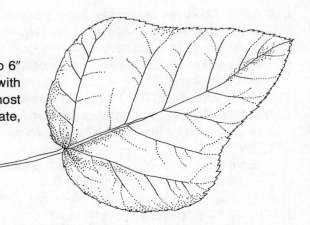

LEAVES: Opposite, simple, ovate to ovate-oblong, 3 to 6″ long, acuminate, subcordate or rounded at base, with a central midrib and no prominent lobes like most snakebark species; unequally crenate-serrulate, green beneath and rufous-villous on veins when young, finally glabrous or nearly so, lustrous dark green; petiole 3/4 to 2″ long.

BUDS AND STEM: Similar to *A. capillipes,* younger branches green or purplish red becoming striped with white.

Acer davidii, David Maple, is seldom seen in cultivation outside botanical gardens and arboreta. I have observed only small trees although the species can grow 30 to 50′. The leaves, being unlobed, are easily distinguished from most other species. The yellowish flowers (May) are borne in slender, pendulous, 2 to 3″ long racemes; the female on longer inflorescences than the males. The 1 1/4″ long glabrous fruits spread horizontally. Apparently there are different forms of the species in cultivation. Common in English gardens and certainly a stellar performer there. Is not as well adjusted to U.S. conditions except in the Pacific Northwest. Central China. Introduced 1879 and 1902. Zone 5 to 7 in cool mountain regions.

‘Ernest Wilson’ is a small compact tree with lustrous dark green, triangular-shaped, essentially unlobed leaves; bark is green with white stripes.

‘George Forrest’ is a medium sized, more open growing form with attractive dark green, triangular shaped 3-lobed leaves; the young stems are rhubarb red and later become red with white stripes.

Acer rufinerve—Redvein Maple
(ā'ser rū-fi-ner'vē)

LEAVES: Opposite, simple, 2 1/2 to 5″ long, 3-lobed to obscurely 5-lobed, truncate or cordate, terminal lobe triangular, larger than the laterals, margins finely and irregularly toothed, dark green above, glabrous, lower pale with reddish down on veins; petiole 1 to 2″ long, pubescent in youth.

BUDS: Similar to *A. pensylvanicum.*

STEM: The young stems are extremely glaucous (bluish white) which separates it from *A. pensylvanicum,* *A. capillipes,* and *A. hersii.*

Acer rufinerve, Redvein Maple, can grow 30 to 35′ but seldom attains that size in the United States. The dark green leaves may turn red in fall. The flowers are borne in 3″ long erect rusty-brown pubescent racemes in May. The 3/4″ long samaras are covered with reddish brown pubescence which falls away at maturity; the wings spread to form a 90 to 120° angle. This species can be grown in full sun but partial shade is probably best. Have seen limitedly in cultivation in the U.S. and the trees were never overwhelming. ‘Albolimbatum’ is a handsome cultivar with white splashed and marbled leaves, the entire variegation pattern quite irregular. Green stems show good white striation pattern. Have only seen the plant at Edinburgh Botanic Garden and on every visit always make the journey to view this most handsome foliaged maple. ‘Winter Gold’ offers bright, golden yellow winter bark which changes to yellow-green in spring and summer; smaller in habit but otherwise similar to the species; 4-year-old tree is 6.5′ high, 2′ wide, hardy to Zone 5, selected from open pollinated seedlings by Peter Douwsma in Olinda, Victoria, Australia. Japan. Introduced 1879. Zone 5 to 7.

Acer tegmentosum—Manchustriped Maple
(ā′ser teg-men-tō′sum)

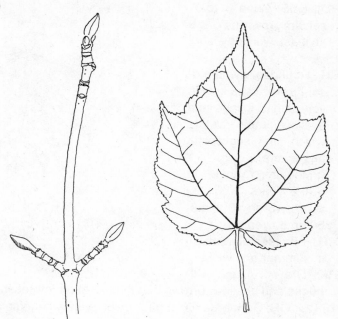

LEAVES: Opposite, simple, 3 to 5-lobed, margin finely and uniformly serrate, 4 to 6″ high and wide, pale green above, paler (glaucous) beneath, glabrous, acuminate, cordate; petiole 2 1/2 to 3 1/2″ long, glabrous, with a groove at the point of attachment.

BUD: Similar to *A. capillipes.*

STEM: Rich green to greenish purple, glabrous, bloomy; 2nd year develop a vertical white fissured pattern, becomes more prominent with time.

Acer tegmentosum, Manchustriped Maple, is a small oval to rounded tree reaching 20 to 30′ in height. Most of the trees I have observed in cultivation had 5-lobed leaves although the literature states unlobed to 3 and 5-lobed. The lateral lobes are much smaller than the terminal lobes. The pale green leaves may turn golden yellow in fall. Yellowish green flowers occur in 3 to 4″ long pendulous racemes. The samaras are 1 1/4″ long and form a wide angle or are nearly horizontal. Fine specimens are located at the Rowe and Arnold Arboreta. Based on rather incomplete information about the "Snakebarks" I would opt for this species for general garden purposes, although *Acer capillipes* seems well adapted. Manchuria, Korea. Introduced 1892. Zone 4 to 7.

ADDITIONAL NOTES: The striped maples are not easy to distinguish especially in winter dress. Even leaves do not provide totally reliable features. They will never become commonplace in American gardens. It is certainly invigorating to stumble upon a specimen for the unusual bark is both beautiful and a dead giveaway as to relative identification. Many snakebark species are known and quite similar in general characteristics. In my travels through European gardens, it became evident that my knowledge of the striped bark maples was, at best, superficial. The following are listed for the collector to pursue: *A. crataegifolum, A. micranthum, A. grosseri, A. hersii, A. laxiflorum* and *A. morrisonense.* All of the snakebarks have stalked valvate buds which allows the snakeophile to choose a good key and proceed with caution.

Acer platanoides — Norway Maple
(ā′ser plat-an-oy′-dēz)

LEAVES: Opposite, simple, 4 to 7″ across, 5-lobed, lobes sharp pointed (acuminate), remotely dentate, lustrous dark green above, lustrous beneath often with hairs in axils of veins; milky sap is visible when petiole is removed from stem, petiole 3 to 4″ long.

BUDS: Terminal—imbricate, 1/4 to 3/8″ long, rounded, scales plump, fleshy, lustrous, greenish maroon to maroon, essentially glabrous except for pubescence at edge of scales, 6 to 8 scaled, two accessory buds 1/3 to 1/2 size, usually with 2 evident scales; terminal when cut in cross section will exude milky sap if slight pressure is applied; lateral buds 1/8″ long, often appressed, 2 to 3 scaled, greenish to maroon.

STEM: Stout, smooth, glabrous, lustrous olive brown, lenticelled, leaf scars meet to form a sharp angle; pith solid, white; 2nd year stems lose luster, become more gray-brown.

SIZE: 40 to 50′ in height occasionally over 90′, usually spread is 2/3's or equal to height.

HARDINESS: Zone 3 to 7, seldom grown in Zone 8 at least with any success.

HABIT: Rounded, symmetrical crown, usually with very dense foliage and shallow root system which limit successful turf culture.

RATE: Medium, 10 to 12' in 5 to 8 years, 30' in 20 years, 45' in 40 years, 60' in 60 years.

TEXTURE: Medium-coarse in summer and winter.

BARK: Grayish black with ridges and shallow furrows that form a rather interesting textural effect.

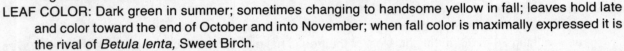

LEAF COLOR: Dark green in summer; sometimes changing to handsome yellow in fall; leaves hold late and color toward the end of October and into November; when fall color is maximally expressed it is the rival of *Betula lenta,* Sweet Birch.

FLOWERS: Perfect, yellow or greenish yellow, each flower 1/3" diameter, April before the leaves, produced in erect, many flowered corymbs; quite effective in the early spring landscape; one of the most floriferous maples; the entire tree a thing of great beauty.

FRUIT: Samara, maturing in September–October; samaras wide spreading, each 1 1/2 to 2" long, glabrous, with virtually horizontally spreading wings.

CULTURE: Easy to transplant; well adapted to extremes in soils, will withstand sand, clay, acid to calcareous soils, seems to withstand hot, dry conditions better than Sugar Maple; tolerates polluted atmosphere, especially those containing ozone and sulfur dioxide; intolerant of 2,4-D; in the south (Zone 8 and higher) the warm summer nights retard growth, trees simply are not as vigorous as in northern latitudes; 'Crimson King' has been planted numerous times and usually disappears over time; the species grew 8.3" per year over a 10-year period; more resistant to leaf scorch than *A. rubrum* and its cultivars but very poor fall color.

DISEASES AND INSECTS: *Verticillium* wilt, anthracnose, some leaf scorch; some cities are skittish about the long-term prospects for this tree.

LANDSCAPE VALUE: Over-used and probably over-rated tree; the species and several of the cultivars, especially 'Crimson King', are overplanted; has been used as lawn, street and park tree; should be given considerable room for it does cover large areas; often creates many problems along streets; the cultivars offer the greatest hope for the landscape.

CULTIVARS:

'Alberta Park' (Moeller)—Straight, vigorous grower that forms a beautiful proportional head with width 25% less than the height; not narrow like 'Emerald Queen'; no frost cracking in certain locations where all other varieties have; excellent tough green foliage.

'Almira'—Small (20 to 25') globe shaped, round-headed and twiggy.

'Aureo-marginatum'—Leaves with three deep, long-pointed lobes, margined with yellow.

'Cavalier'—Very compact with rounded habit, almost a large globe; 30 to 35' tall.

'Charles F. Irish'—More rounded in outline.

'Cleveland'—Upright oval to oval-rounded, not as wide spreading as species, dense dark green foliage, excellent golden yellow fall color, coarsely branched, 6.4' high and 2.7' wide after 4 years; considered one of the best Norway cultivars for urban plantings, 40 to 50' high by 30 to 40' wide.

'Columnare'—In my mind no one has ever adequately described the differences between this and 'Erectum'; I offer the following based on a great deal of observation; 'Columnare' is an old cultivar having been raised in the nursery of Simon-Louis at Plantieres in 1855; the leaves are smaller and shallower lobed than the species; the habit is that of a fat column with branches that spread at a 60 to 90° angle from a central trunk; height approximates 60'; spread 15 to 20'.

'Crimson King'—Rich maroon leaf color throughout the growing season; probably the most vigorous of all persistent red leaved forms; could be called a horticultural exclamation point in the landscape; grew 19' by 16' in 10 years; originated as a seedling of 'Schwedleri' in Orleans, France and put into commerce in 1946; the flowers are maroon-yellow; slower growing than 'Schwedleri'; 40 to 50' by 35 to 45'; grew 5.2" per year over a 10-year period in Wichita tests; slow growing and poorly adapted especially in the southeast.

'Crimson Sentry'— A dense, columnar form, dark purple foliage in spring and summer; a bud sport of 'Crimson King'; slower growing than 'Crimson King', 25' by 15'.

'Deborah'— Introduction from Holmlund Nursery, Gresham, Oregon; brilliant red new growth, wrinkled margins, eventually changing to dark green; seedling of 'Schwedleri'; rounded to broad rounded outline; like 'Schwedleri' but with a straight leader, 50' by 45'.

'Dissectum'—One of the many cut-leaf forms, leaves finely cut, margins crinkled, small bushy tree; put into commerce about 1845; other cultivars with unusual leaf lobing patterns include 'Cucullatum' (absolutely abominable) and 'Palmatifidum'; others exist.

'Drummondi'—Light green leaves edged with white, supposedly the best of its class, 23' high and 13.9' wide after 10 years; reverts and must be pruned; common in Europe, develops a rounded outline, probably 30 to 40' and as wide.

'Emerald Lustre' (Bailey) ('Pond' is cultivar name) —Vigorous, prolific branching as a young tree, good branching structure; new leaves with a reddish tinge, glossy deep green foliage with wavy margin; better branching than 'Emerald Queen'.

'Emerald Queen'—Ascending branches, oval-rounded outline, rapid grower, dark green leaves, similar to 'Summershade'; fall color is bright yellow; 26' high and 20.7' wide after twenty years; one of the best Norway cultivars for urban plantings, 50' by 40' at landscape maturity.

'Erectum'—Columnar with short lateral branches; the Lombardy poplar of Norway maples.

'Faasens Black'—Lustrous purplish brown leaves, folded upwards at the margins, young leaves not wrinkled, red fall color under the proper environmental conditions, put into commerce about 1936; I asked a nurseryman how to tell this cultivar from 'Crimson King' and he said that after a rain 'Faasens Black' would hold the water in the rim formed by the upfolded margins; 'Crimson King' did not; there was never any mention of color differences. I have compared 'Faasens Black' to 'Crimson King' and, indeed, the leaf differences are as manifest as described.

'Faasens Redleaf'—Red leaf form, 14' high and 17.5' wide after 10 years; severe leaf scorch and died soon after planting.

'Fairview'—A seedling of 'Crimson King'; dark red foliage becomes dark green.

'Globosum'—Dense, formal globe habit only growing to a height of 15 to 18'; usually grafted or budded at 6 to 7' height; similar to 'Almira'; 5' high and 5' wide after 4 years; provides a lovely lollipop effect in the landscape.

'Goldsworth Purple'—Light reddish brown when young becoming deep, dull, blackish purple and remaining so until autumn; young leaves wrinkled; put into commerce about 1949.

'Greenlace'—Interesting form with a deeply cut, lacelike leaf; upright branching habit (50'), fast growing.

'Jade Glen'—Similar to species, supposedly rapid growing and extremely sturdy, produces a more open rounded canopy, 40 to 50' by 40 to 50'.

'Laciniatum'—Smaller and more twiggy tree than the type, of more erect, narrow habit; leaves tapering and wedge-shaped at base, the lobes ending in long, often curved clawlike appendages, the oldest of named varieties (1792).

'Lamis'—Vigorous straight trunk; better branching than 'Emerald Luster' with a lighter colored leaf tip; selected by Bailey Nursery and sold under the trademark name 'Crystal'.

'Lorbergii'—Leaves palmately divided to base of leaf but tips ascending from plane of leaf; a dense, rounded, very slow growing tree with a central leader; 60 to 70', 1881.

'Olmsted'—Upright, similar to 'Columnare', grows 35' high and 15' wide.

'Oregon Pride' (TM) (= 'Cutleaf')—Cutleaf form with gold-bronze fall color, fast growing with a heavy crown.

'Parkway'—Broader form of 'Columnare' (probably 'Erectum'), maintaining a strong central leader, essentially oval in outline with dark green summer foliage, 40' by 25'; cultivar name is 'Columnarbroad'.

'Royal Red'—Similar to 'Crimson King' but slower growing, supposedly better maroon color; supposedly hardier than 'Crimson King' but there is an underlying suspicion that the two are in fact the same tree...only the names are different; averaged 2.6" per year over a 10-year period in Wichita tests; severe leaf scorch and borers.

'Schwedleri'—Common older form with purplish red spring foliage changing to dark green in early summer, wider spreading than most selections, slightly hardier than 'Crimson King'; 17.5' high and 21' wide after 10 years; parent of 'Crimson King' and 'Deborah'; cultivated since at least 1869. Averaged 5.3" per year over a 10-year period and developed severe leaf scorch.

'Stand Fast'—Very dwarf, sparingly branched, leaves small, dark green, ruffled and clustered at the ends of branches; 47 year old tree only 30" high; have seen at Longwood Gardens, a curiosity at best.

'Summershade'—Rapid growing, heat resistant and upright-rounded in habit, maintains a single leader; the foliage is more leathery than the other varieties and retained later in the fall; 12' high and 10.6' wide after 4 years; at maturity almost rounded in outline; ranked extremely high in the Shade Tree Evaluation Trials conducted at Wooster, Ohio. Averaged 10.4" of growth per year over a 10-year period; proved the most vigorous of Norway maples in Dr. Pair's tests, produced less scorch than either Sugar or Red Maple, but did not develop appreciable fall color.

'Superform'—Rapid growing with straight trunk and heavy dark green foliage; 22.6' high and 21' wide after 10 years; 50' by 45' at maturity.

'Waldeesii'—White interveinal areas; have seen at Edinburgh Botanic Garden and the tree literally grabs the passerby; would "cook" in heat of summer in US.

PROPAGATION: Seed, 41°F for 90 to 120 days in moist peat or other media; the cultivars are budded on seedling understocks; recent work indicated that the species can be rooted from softwood cuttings collected in mid-June, treated with 8000ppm IBA talc, placed under intermittent mist with bottom heat (*PIPPS* 29: 345–347, 1979).

ADDITIONAL NOTES: A very popular maple and probably will continue to be in demand; often the bark splits on the species and cultivars on the south or southwest side of the trunk where the sun warms the bark and then sudden low temperatures cause contraction and splitting occurs; often termed "frost cracks".

NATIVE HABITAT: Continental Europe, where it is widely spread in a wild state from Norway southwards; also has escaped from cultivation in United States.

Acer pseudoplatanus — Planetree Maple; also called Sycamore Maple
(ā'ser soo-dō-plat'an-us)

LEAVES: Opposite, simple, 3 to 6" across, 5 lobed, cordate, lobes ovate, coarsely crenate serrate, veins impressed, dark green and glabrous above, greenish white beneath, sometimes pubescent on veins, leaf is leathery; petiole 2 to 3 1/2" long.

BUDS: Terminal large, greenish, slightly pointed, imbricate, glabrous, 1/4 to 1/3" long, only single buds above leaf scar; buds similar to Norway, but remain green through winter; lateral buds smaller than terminal.

STEM: Glabrous, gray-brown, dull, lenticelled, slightly 4-sided, leaf scars do not meet as is the case in Norway Maple.

SIZE: 40 to 60' in height under most landscape conditions but specimens of over 100' are known, spread two-third's of, or equal to height; impressive tree in England where it thrives in the cooler climate.

HARDINESS: Zone 4 to 7, not suited to the south.

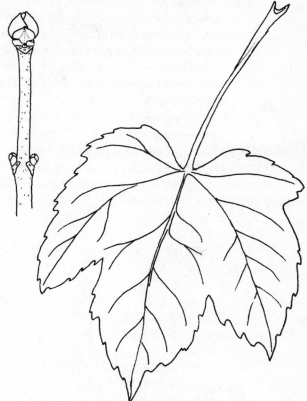

HABIT: Tree with upright, spreading branches forming an oval to rounded outline; can become a
massive tree with maturity.

RATE: Medium, 10 to 12′ in 5 to 8 years.

TEXTURE: Medium in leaf and winter.

BARK: Grayish, reddish brown to orangish; flaking
into small, rectangular scales, exposing orangish brown inner bark.

LEAF COLOR: Dark green in summer; fall color a
dingy brown or possibly with a tinge of yellow.

FLOWERS: Perfect, yellowish green, May, born in
pendulous panicles, 2 to 4″ long.

FRUIT: Samara, maturing in September–October,
each samara 1 1/4 to 2″ long, forming angle of
about 60°.

CULTURE: Transplant balled and burlapped in
spring; very adaptable to soil types, preferably
well-drained; tolerates high lime to acid conditions and exposed sites; will withstand the full
force of salt-laden winds in exposed places
near the sea; often listed as a salt tolerant
species and has been used extensively in the
Netherlands; full sun or light shade; abundant
throughout Europe, almost weedlike.

DISEASES AND INSECTS: Cankers, subject to
considerable dead wood and requires ample maintenance for that reason.

LANDSCAPE VALUE: Probably too many better maples for this species to ever assume any popular status
in American gardens; where conditions warrant (exposed, saline environment) it might be used to
good advantage; in evidence everywhere in Europe; actually makes a magnificent tree; have seen
80 to 100′ high specimens in England.

CULTIVARS: Too numerous to expound upon but a few of the more "outstanding" that have crossed my
path are included here.

'Atropurpureum' ('Spaethii', 'Purpureum').—Leaves dark green above, rich purple beneath, a rather
pretty form and reasonably common in the United States, especially handsome when the leaves
are backlighted; will come partially true-to-type from seed, aphids love it, produces large
quantities of fruit, vigorous, has grown 26′ high and 25′ wide after 10 years in Oregon tests;
introduced in 1883 through Späth's nurseries; grew 11.3″ per year over a 9-year period in
Kansas tests, developed severe leaf scorch, sunscald and high borer infestations.

'Brilliantissimum'—A real show stopper as the new leaves unfold shrimp pink and later to pale
cream to yellow-green and finally off-green; slow growing round-headed tree; I was in
Hidcote Garden, England, on a miserable rainy May day and this plant was the first thing
that caught my eye; widely used in European gardens, would have to be sited in some shade
in the United States.

'Erectum'—An upright form, rather wide, compared to many erect types, not particularly outstanding.

'Erythrocarpum'—Form with red samara wings, rather effective, reportedly wild in the Alps of Bavaria,
have seen this form or something similar at Stourhead in England, the bright red wings are
effective in June.

'Leopoldii'—A form with yellowish pink and purple stained leaves; originated about 1860; there seems
to be some confusion about this cultivar for plants that I have seen did not color pink or purple
but were distinctly white and green, the variegation pattern almost resembling that of a marble
cake; other forms of the same character are 'Simon Louis Frères' and 'Tricolor'. I have chased
the 'Marble Cake' variegated forms around botanical gardens and books with little success. The
labels only confuse me.

'Prinz Handjery'—I first saw this at the Arnold Arboretum and identified it as 'Brilliantissimum'. The label indicated I was incorrect. The new foliage is a rich shrimp pink; the literature says yellow above, purple beneath. It is a slow growing bushy tree but more open than 'Brilliantissimum'.

f. *variegatum*—Bean applies this term to any form with yellowish or yellowish white blotched and/or striped leaves. These variegated forms are often derived from seed and thus would show some variation in degree of variegation. The trees appear amazingly vigorous and specimens 80 to 90' are known.

'Worleei'—Leaves soft yellow-green at first then yellow and finally green with reddish petioles; raised in Germany.

PROPAGATION: Seed, 41°F for 90 plus days in moist peat; cultivars are budded onto seedlings.

ADDITIONAL NOTES: Old world tree, cannot compete with American or Asiatic species for fall color; considerable number along the New England coast especially Cape Cod and coastal Rhode Island.

NATIVE HABITAT: Europe, western Asia. Cultivated for centuries.

Acer rubrum — Red Maple, Scarlet Maple, Swamp Maple
(ā'ser rū'brum)

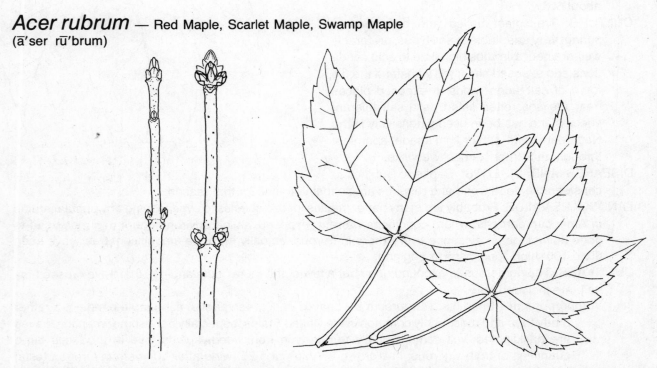

LEAVES: Opposite, simple, 2 to 4(5)″ long and wide, 3 although often 5 lobed, triangular ovate lobes and sinuses are irregularly toothed (in Silver Maple the sinuses are entire), medium to dark green above, grayish beneath with hairy veins, new growth and petioles often red; petiole 2 to 4″ long.

BUDS: Imbricate, red to green, blunt and several scaled, 1/16 to 1/8″ long with rounded bud scales (Silver Maple scales are slightly pointed); flower buds in clusters often encircling nodes, flower buds spherical, edge of scales finely pubescent.

STEM: Glabrous, lenticelled, green-red-brown; when crushed does not have rank odor; usually green becoming red as winter progresses.

FLOWER: Flowers are borne with petals; Silver Maple flowers without them.

BARK: Young—smooth, light gray; old—dark gray and rough, scaly and/or ridged and furrowed.

SIZE: 40 to 60' in height, but occasionally reaches 100 to 120' in the wild; spread less than or equal to height.

HARDINESS: Zone 3 to 9, best to select Red Maples for a specific area that have been grown from seed collected there; ample evidence to suggest provenance is important for hardiness. See Dirr and Lindstrom *Amer. Nurseryman* 169(1):47–55(1989).

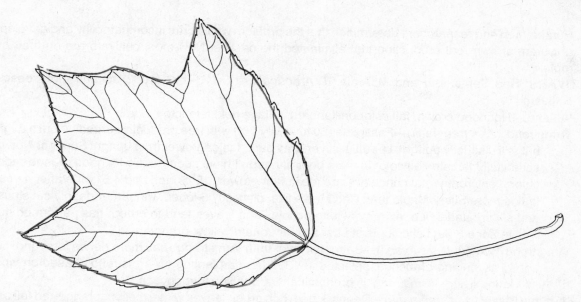

HABIT: In youth often pyramidal or elliptical, developing ascending branches which result in an irregular, ovoid or rounded crown.

RATE: Medium to fast; 10 to 12′ in 5 to 7 years.

TEXTURE: Medium-fine to medium in leaf; medium in winter.

BARK: Soft gray or gray-brown; see above.

LEAF COLOR: Emerging leaves are reddish tinged gradually changing medium to dark green above with a distinct gray cast beneath; fall color varies from greenish yellow to yellow to brilliant red; Red Maple does not always have brilliant red fall color and unscrupulous plantsmen who offer seedling trees and guarantee red fall color are frauding the public.

FLOWERS: Red, rarely yellowish; mid to late March into April, in dense clusters before the leaves, each flower on a reddish pedicel at first quite short but lengthening as the flower and fruit develop; the stigmas and styles as well as the small petals are the showy part of the flower; I have seen trees which are predominantly pistillate, largely staminate or monoecious; all are showy; the male does not have the intense red color compared to the female. On the Georgia campus some trees are in flower in January, others February, and others early March; great spread of flowering times.

FRUIT: Samara, often but not always reddish maturing to brown; on slender drooping pedicels 2 to 3″ long, wings 3/4″ long, 1/4″ wide, spreading at a narrow to about a 60° angle.

CULTURE: Transplants readily as a small specimen bare root, or balled and burlapped in larger sizes, move in spring; very tolerant of soils, however, prefers slightly acid, moist conditions; tolerant of ozone and intermediately tolerant of sulfur dioxide; occurs naturally in low, wet areas and is often one of the first trees to color in the fall; shows chlorosis in high pH soils, in the past this was thought to be due to iron deficiency, however, recent research has shown that manganese is the causal agent; not particularly urban tolerant, although planted in ever-increasing numbers in cities; averaged 11″ per year in Wichita tests over a 9-year period; tremendous variation in growth rates from seedling material, considerable leaf scorch.

DISEASES AND INSECTS: Leaf hoppers will cause considerable damage, also borer that attacks young terminals.

LANDSCAPE VALUE: Excellent specimen tree for lawn, park or street; does not tolerate heavily polluted areas; does not grow as fast as *Acer saccharinum*, Silver Maple, however, is much preferable because of cleaner foliage, stronger wood and better fall color; Red Maple is the light that brightens the fall color sky throughout the northern midwestern and northeastern states; the fall color can be so dazzling and combined with a backdrop of *Pinus strobus* paints a picture that no master could duplicate; the only thing consistent about Red Maple fall coloration is the inconsistency from tree to tree; some remain almost green or at best yellow-green, others bright yellow, others flaming orange or red. In the 1970's many budded trees of *A. rubrum* began to decline for no apparent reason.

Nurserymen and researchers determined that the problem was a graft incompatability and developed a system of own-root production that eliminated the decline. Now most cultivars are on their own roots.

CULTIVARS: See Santamour and McArdle, *J. Arboriculture* 8:110–112 (1982) for the more obscure cultivars.

'Ablaze'—Rounded crown, fall color brilliant red, foliage held late into the fall.

'Armstrong' (*A.* × *freemanii*)—Fastigiate (50 to 70' by 15') with tree gradually spreading out a degree but still distinctly upright, beautiful silver-gray bark, faster grower than upright Sugar or Norway; essentially female; fall color is often poor although I have seen trees with good orange-red fall color if environmental conditions are ideal; fast grower, 15.4' high and 4.5' wide after 4 years; leaf is more Silver Maple than Red Maple like, distinctly 5-lobed with rather deeply cut sinuses and silvery underside, extremely long petioles and leaves tend to droop; has performed quite well in Zone 8 but fall color is at best an inadequate yellow-orange.

'Armstrong Two' (*A.* × *freemanii*)—Better fall color than 'Armstrong', has more dense form and more tightly ascending branches, selected in 1960 from a planting of 'Armstrong'; based on what I see in the trade, 'Armstrong' is predominant, a Scanlon introduction.

'Autumn Blaze' (*A.* × *freemanii*)—Deeply lobed, rich green leaves with excellent orange-red fall color that persists later than many cultivars, dense oval-rounded head with ascending branch structure and central leader, rapid growth and Zone 4 hardiness, may be more drought tolerant than true *Acer rubrum* cultivars, early reports indicate fall color is excellent; selected by Glenn Jeffers, Fostoria, OH in late 1960's, 50' by 40'.

'Autumn Fantasy' (*A.* × *freemanii*)—Upright-oval form, with 5-lobed leaves more closely resembling Silver than Red Maple, attractive crimson fall color, original tree from central Illinois, introduced by Bill Wandell.

'Autumn Flame'—Good looking selection, eventually forming a rounded outline (to 60'), excellent and early red fall color, smaller leaves that color earlier than the species; grew 21' high and 24' wide after 10 years; severely injured during the horrendous winter of 1976 to 77 in the Chicago area, trees as large as 5" diameter were killed, 80 to 90% loss of fall planted stock was reported, has slipped somewhat in popularity especially with all the new introductions. Grew 1'1" per year in Wichita tests over a 10-year period; colored early and developed considerable leaf scorch.

'Autumn Glory'—Upright tree with oval spreading crown, selected for exceptional red fall color, doubtfully being produced in commerce.

'Autumn Radiance'—Dense oval form, green summer foliage turning brilliant orange-red in fall. Zone 4.

'Bowhall'—Upright form with a symmetrical, narrow pyramidal head, wider than 'Armstrong', good yellowish-red fall color; I have equated this cultivar with 'Columnare', but erroneously so; although literature says good red fall color, I have seen yellow-orange with some red in midveins; 50' by 15'.

'Celebration' (*A.* × *freemanii*)—Upright habit, uniform growth and strong crotch angles; dense foliage starts to color in September with a cast of red turning to gold in October; a male, introduced by Lake County Nursery Exchange; mature tree 45' high and 20 to 25' wide, leaves similar to Silver Maple, fall color is yellowish green in Madison, WI.

'Columnare'—A very handsome, narrow columnar-pyramidal form that is a degree slower growing and more compact than 'Armstrong' but to me preferable because of darker green foliage and excellent orange to deep red fall color; grew 12.5' high and 3.6' wide after 4 years; predominantly male; leaves are 3-lobed with rounded leaf bases and shallow lobes toward the apex; pictured in Garden and Forest, 1894, at which time it was 80' high.

'Doric'—Upright form, not to the degree of 'Armstrong', female, selected by Ed Scanlon, branches at 30° angle, ascend to two thirds the height of the tree, leathery glossy leaves turn red in fall, doubtfully in commerce.

'Embers'—A tree with narrow habit in youth maturing to a rounded outline, lustrous green summer foliage turns consistent bright red in fall, vigorous and hardy.

'Excelsior'—Teardrop shape, upsweeping branches can be observed early in life, fall color orange-red, 35 to 40', Zone 3.

'Gerling'—Small broad pyramidal form, eventually becoming rounded, densely branched, yellow to red fall color. 25′ high by 35′ wide.

'Globosum'—Compact, dwarf form with scarlet flowers.

'Karpick'—Dense narrow form, 40 to 50′ tall, by 20′ wide, distinct red twigs and green foliage turning yellow or red in fall, Schichtel introduction, named after Frank E. Karpick, former city forester of Buffalo, NY.

'Landsburg'—Medium sized tree with brilliant red fall color; oval habit, growing to 50′ tall; selected from a tree in northern Minnesota. Zone 3. Bailey introduction.

'Lee's Red' (*A.* × *freemanii*)—Brilliant red fall color, foliage not as deeply divided as that of Silver Maple.

'Marmo' (*A.* × *freemanii*)—A selection from the Morton Arboretum, habit is distinctly broad-columnar, the leaves start to color in mid September (Lisle, IL) with red dominating and green patches interspersed, color lasts for 2 to 4 weeks and is outstanding, the leaves are intermediate between the parents, the wood is considered moderately tough, 60-year-old specimen is 70′ by 35 to 40′, leaves 5-lobed with sinuses toothed 2/3 the depth of the sinuses, and more closely resembles Silver than Red Maple, flowers staminate. Zone 4.

'Morgan' (*A.* × *freemanii*)—One of the fastest growing red maples, habit open, brilliant orange-red to red fall color, colors well in mild climates, supposedly brightest of all red maples, vigorous cultivar growing 60 to 70′, pistillate flowers, 'Indian Summer' is US name; hardier than the typical cultivars, valid as Zone 4, selected at Morgan Arboretum, MacDonald College, Quebec.

'Northwood'—Rounded-oval crown with branches ascending at a 45° angle, dark green summer foliage; good orange-red fall color and adaptability to the rigors of the Minnesota climate. Selected from a native seedling population near Floodwood, MN by Leon Snyder, and introduced by University of Minnesota. In Spring Grove, Cincinnati, OH, turns yellow-orange-red; definitely not as effective for fall color in the southern states. Some indication that growth habit is rather irregular and unruly.

'October Brilliance'—Excellent red fall color, well shaped tight crown, delayed leaf emergence in spring, reduces chance of frost injury, 40′ by 30′, Zone 5 to 7.

'October Glory'—Good oval-rounded (40 to 50′) form but tends to hold its lustrous dark green leaves late and the intensity of the brilliant orange to red fall color may be impaired by early freezes; can be spectacular when right; grew 11′ high and 6.4′ wide after 4 years; suffered in extreme winter of 1976–77. Superb for fall coloration in the south and has been better than 'Red Sunset' in Zone 8. Both are excellent but with 'October Glory' the red color is more intense and has lasted into mid November in my garden. I watched closely the development of fall color in 1988 and witnessed red to orange-red to a dying ember red. The colors changed with time and weather conditions. This form and 'Red Sunset' are the dominant selections in the market place. This is a female form and wings of the fruits are reddish tinged. The patent has expired but the name is trademarked. Introduced by Princeton Nursery. Possibly the most impressive aspect of 'October Glory' is the ability to develop excellent red fall color in latitudes were environmental conditions are not 'perfect' for expressions of maximum color. Averaged 1′1″ per year in Wichita tests over a 10-year period; developed good fall color late in the season that persisted for 3 to 4 weeks.

'Phipps Farm'—A selection by Weston Nurseries, Hopkinton, MA, for intense red fall coloration and adaptability to the rigors of the New England climate; this form may have been dropped since it did not appear in the 1988 catalog.

'Red Skin' (Schichtel)—A rounded form characterized by large thick foliage and early reddish maroon fall color, 40′ by 40′, Zone 3.

'Red Sunset'—One of the best Red Maple cultivars, excellent orange to red fall color, colors before 'October Glory', lovely pyramidal to rounded outline; 13.6′ high and 7.8′ wide after 4 years; one of the highest rated trees in Ohio Shade Tree Evaluation tests; came through the 1976–77 (−20 to −25°F) winter as the only unscathed patented Red Maple now superseded in cold hardiness by 'Northwood' and others; considered the best by many nurserymen and landscape designers; 'Franksred' is the cultivar name, Red Sunset the trademark name; ultimately 45 to 50′ by 35 to

40′; a female. Grew 1′1″ in Wichita tests in 9 years; develops good branch angles, bright red fall color, but still showed some leaf scorch.

'Scanlon'—Forms a compact conical crown of dense branches and colors rich orange-red in fall; Scanlon introduction, no longer common in cultivation.

'Scarlet Sentinel' (*A.* × *freemanii*)—(Schichtel Nursery, NY). According to the literature, columnar, fast-growing, good rich green leaves, yellow-orange to orange-red fall color, leaves 5-lobed, closely resembling Silver Maple, flowers pistillate, probably the fastest-growing upright maple, bark smooth and shiny; my observations indicate that this form is anything but upright, more toward oval-rounded, have seen at Spring Grove in Cincinnati; 'Scarsen' is cultivar name, Scarlet Sentinel the trademark; 45′ by 25′.

'Schlesingeri'—Introduced for superior rich red to reddish purple fall color, forms a large (60′ to 70′) upright spreading rounded crown at maturity; the earliest Red Maple and for that matter shade tree to color; by September 15, 1978 at the Arnold Arboretum it had developed full coloration, color holds for a long time (20 to 30 days); female; 12.6′ high and 6.9′ wide after 4 years; largely fallen out of favor since the introduction of the "better" fall coloring, smaller types; still a magnificent tree; discovered by C.S. Sargent of the Arnold Arboretum on the grounds of a Mr. Schlesinger; an old cultivar dating back to the 1880's.

'Shade King'—Upright oval head, well branched in first year; leaves dark green, slightly serrated, 50′, Zone 4.

'Silhouette'—A Bill Wandell introduction about which I can find no information; may be an *A.* × *freemanii* type.

'Tilford'—Globe headed, uniform in shape, vigorous, red to yellow fall color, 35′ by 35′; averaged 9″ per year over a 7-year period; developed leaf scorch and high borer infestations.

'W.J. Drake'—Selected for the pattern of fall coloration with the outside of the leaf coloring a deep red and this color progressing toward the green middle.

'Variegatum'—Leaves variegated; have seen one specimen of a marbled white variegated leaf type that was a rather weak grower; the new growth was reddish pink owing to the normal red pigment coupled with the white areas.

PROPAGATION: Seeds mature in early summer and will germinate without pretreatment although stratification for 60 to 75 days at 41°F or a cold water soak for 2 to 5 days will hasten and unify germination; softwood cuttings can be rooted readily and considerable work has been undertaken with the various cultivars; the idea being to put these maples on their own roots and avoid the incompatibility problems; over the years my students and I have propagated many red maples from cuttings. A few hints follow: use healthy stock plants, preferably firm wooded, mature leaved cuttings, single or multiple node, 5000 ppm IBA in 50% alcohol or similar concentration of KIBA, peat:perlite, mist that is applied evenly and without fail, and cuttings should root in 3 to 5 weeks. For detailed information see Dirr and Heuser, *The Reference Manual of Woody Plant Propagation*.

ADDITIONAL NOTES: The cultivars should be used in preference to seedling stock if consistent, good red fall color is desired; Red Maple is definitely a candidate for regional selection; a good fall coloring selection from a mature population is needed in the southern states; Red Maple has been called a cosmopolitan species because of its adaptability to swamps, bottomlands, mixed forest situations, and rocky uplands; the early spring flowers are attractive and forewarn that spring is just "around the corner".

NATIVE HABITAT: Newfoundland to Florida west to Minnesota, Oklahoma and Texas. Introduced 1860.

Acer saccharinum — Silver Maple, also called Soft, White, River Maple
(ā′ser sak-kär-ī′-num)

LEAVES: Opposite, simple, 3 to 6″ across, 5-lobed, with deeply and doubly acuminate lobes, the middle often 3-lobed, bright green above, silvery white beneath and pubescent when young; petiole 3 to 5″ long.

BUDS: Vegetative-imbricate, flattened, ovoid, 2 outer scales form a "V" shaped notch, appressed, 1/8 to 3/16" long, lustrous red or reddish brown on outside of scales, edges fringed with short pubescence; flower-imbricate, globose, accessory, often in dense, compact, umbel-like clusters, 1/8 to 3/16" high, margins of scales prominently fringed.

STEM: Similar to Red Maple except with rank odor when bruised, moderate, terete, lustrous red to brown, glabrous, slender vertical lenticels; pith-solid, white; 2nd year stem becoming gray.

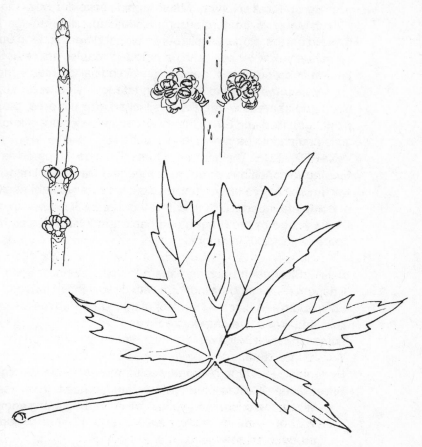

SIZE: 50 to 70' in height and can grow 100 to 120'; spread is usually about 2/3's the height.

HARDINESS: Zone 3 to 9.

HABIT: Upright with strong spreading branches forming an oval to rounded crown with pendulous branchlets which turn up at the ends.

RATE: Fast, 10 to 12' in 4 to 5 years from a small newly planted tree is not unreasonable, unfortunately with fast growth comes a weak-wooded tree, often will break up in wind, ice, and snow storms; fastest growing American maple species.

TEXTURE: Medium in leaf, but coarse in winter; may appear somewhat dissheveled in winter.

BARK: On young branches (1" or more) color is an interesting gray or gray-brown and can be mistaken for the bark of *Acer rubrum;* however, the color is usually darker (or with a tinge of red) compared to that of *Acer rubrum*.

LEAF COLOR: Medium green above, gray or silver beneath in summer; fall color is usually a green-yellow-brown combination; a tinge of red is evident with certain trees during the fall but this is the exception rather than the rule, some of the red fall color may be attributable to hybridization with *A. rubrum.*

FLOWERS: Perfect, predominantly staminate or pistillate, or essentially monoecious; greenish yellow to red, without petals, opening before *Acer rubrum,* usually in early to mid-March; borne in dense clusters similar to Red Maple, some trees are as showy as Red Maple, female shower than male.

FRUIT: Samara, not ornamentally important, wings spreading at an 80 to 90° angle, 1 1/3 to 2 1/3" long, matures in late May–June, one of the largest fruited maples.

CULTURE: Of the easiest culture, transplants well bare root or balled and burlapped; tolerant of wide variety of soils but achieves maximum size in moist soils along stream banks and in deep, moist soiled woods; prefers slightly acid soil; will cause sidewalks to buckle and drain tiles to clog because of vigorous, gross feeding root systems; one of the best trees for poor soils where few other species will survive and for these areas should be considered.

DISEASES AND INSECTS: Anthracnose (in rainy seasons may be serious on Sugar, Silver Maples and Boxelder), leaf spot (purple eye), tar spot, bacterial leaf spot, leaf blister, powdery mildow, *Verticillium* wilt (Silver, Norway, Red and Sugar are most affected), bleeding canker, basal canker, *Nectria* canker, *Ganoderma* rot, sapstreak, trunk decay, forest tent caterpillar, green striped maple worm, maple leaf cutter, Japanese leafhopper, leaf hopper, leaf stalk borer, petiole borers, bladder-gall mite, ocellate leaf gall, Norway Maple aphid, boxelder bug, maple phenacoccus, cottony maple scale (Silver Maple is tremendously susceptible), other scales (terrapin, gloomy, and Japanese), flat-headed borers, Sugar Maple borer, pidgeon tremex, leopard moth borer, metallic borer, twig pruner, carpenter worm, whitefly and nematodes; maples are obviously susceptible to a wide range of insect and disease problems; several physiological problems include scorch where the margins of the leaves become necrotic and brown due to limited water supply; this often occurs on newly planted trees and in areas where there is limited growing area (planter boxes, narrow tree lawns, sidewalk plantings); Red and Silver Maple also show extensive manganese chlorosis in calcareous or high pH soils and should be grown in acid soils.

LANDSCAPE VALUE: The use of this tree should be tempered as it becomes a liability with age; possibility for rugged conditions or where someone desires fast shade; there are far too many superior trees to warrant extensive use of this species; in its native habitat along streams it withstands several weeks of complete inundation but cultivated trees will do well in dry soils; the English consider the Silver Maple a tree of great beauty in habit and foliage; I saw magnificent specimens in Europe, some approaching 100′ in height.

CULTIVARS:
  'Blair'—Stronger branching pattern than the species; 50 to 70′ high, Zone 4.
  'Crispum'—Dense growing form with deeply lobed leaves and crinkled margins.
  'Laciniatum'—A catch-all term for plants whose leaves are more deeply divided than the type; 'Beebe' and 'Wieri' are categorized here.
  'Lutescens'—New leaves orangish yellow in color turning yellowish green at maturity. Introduced before 1883.
  'Pyramidale'—A type of broadly columnar habit, maintaining central leader, 70′ high, 40′ wide.
  'Silver Queen'—More upright oval-rounded habit, fruitless, and leaves are bright green above with silvery lower surface, yellow fall color, becoming common in commerce. 50′ by 40′. Averaged 2′7″ per year in Wichita tests over a 10-year period; although listed as seedless, trees did produce some fruits.
  'Skinner'—A cut-leaf form with bright green foliage and a pyramidal outline; lateral branches more slender and horizontal.
  'Wieri'—Branches pendulous, leaf lobes narrow and sharply toothed; discovered in 1873 by D.B. Wier.

PROPAGATION: Seed has no dormancy and germinates immediately after maturing; seedlings grow in every idle piece of ground and gradually overtake an area; cuttings have been taken in November and rooted with 84% efficiency; softwood cuttings root readily; treat like Red Maple.

ADDITIONAL NOTES: This species has been and will continue to be overplanted; it is one of the nurseryman's biggest moneymakers because of fast growth and ease of culture; responds well to heavy fertilization and watering; with selection a better class of Silver Maples will enter the marketplace; like Red Maple, seed source selection is important to insure cold hardiness.

NATIVE HABITAT: Quebec to Florida, to Minnesota, Nebraska, Kansas, Oklahoma, and Louisiana. Introduced 1725.

Acer saccharum — Sugar Maple; often called Rock Maple or Hard Maple
(ā′ser săk-kär′um)

LEAVES: Opposite, simple, 3 to 6″ long and across, 3 to 5 lobed, cordate, acuminate, slightly coarsely toothed with narrow and deep sinuses; lighter green than Black Maple and not as pubescent.

BUDS: Terminal-imbricate, long and sharp pointed, cone-shaped, 3/16 to 1/4″ long, gray-brown, glabrous or hairy at apex; axillary buds 1/2 as long as terminal, hairs are found at upper edge of leaf scar and are brown in color.

STEM: Brown, often lustrous, glabrous, angled, lenticels are small and not as conspicuous as those of Black Maple.

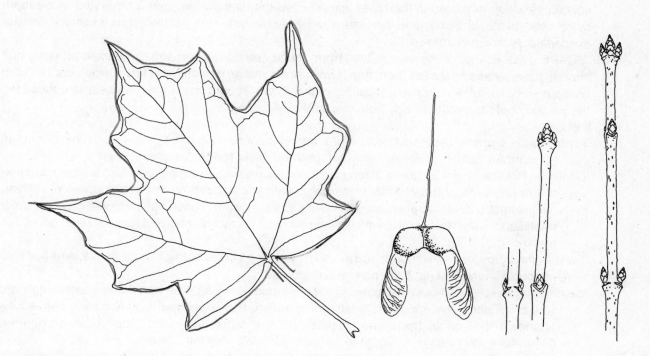

SIZE: A landscape size of 60 to 75′ is often attained; potential to 100 to 120′ in height; the spread is variable but usually about 2/3's the height although some specimens show a rounded character.

HARDINESS: Zone 4 to 8.

HABIT: Upright-oval to rounded; usually quite dense in foliage.

RATE: Slow, possibly medium in youth; the size of one recorded specimen was 23′ in 28 years and 62′ in 128 years; obviously this indicates that Sugar Maple is of slow growth; however, has grown 23′ high and 23′ wide in ten years in Oregon tests.

TEXTURE: Medium in leaf and winter; I have seen delicately branched specimens of a distinct upright-oval character which appeared fine in winter character.

BARK: Young trees develop a smooth, gray-brown bark; with age the bark becomes deeply furrowed, with long irregular thick plates or ridges, sometimes quite scaly; bark is tremendously variable on this species; some trees from a distance remind one of a Shagbark Hickory.

LEAF COLOR: Usually a medium to dark green in summer (not as dark as Norway or Black Maple); changing to brilliant yellow, burnt orange and limited red tones in autumn; there is great variation in fall color among members of this species; the New England types seems to show more orange and red then the southern Indiana, Ohio, and Illinois group which develops a beautiful golden yellow; cultivated trees in Georgia develop good fall coloration.

FLOWERS: Perfect, staminate or pistillate apetalous, campanulate, 1/5 to 1/4″ long, greenish yellow, borne on 1 to 3″ long pendulous hairy pedicels in subsessile corymbs; stamens exserted in the staminate flower, before the leaves in April; attractive in a subtle way.

FRUIT: Samara, glabrous, 1 to 1 3/4″ long, somewhat horseshoe-shaped with nearly parallel or slightly divergent wings, maturing September–October.

CULTURE: Transplant balled and burlapped; prefers well-drained, moderately moist, fertile soil; pH-no preference although a slightly acid soil seems to result in greater growth; does not perform well in tight, compacted situations such as planter boxes, small tree lawns or other restricted growing areas; not extremely air pollution tolerant; tolerates shade and is often seen on the forest floor under a canopy of leaves gradually developing and assuming its place in the climax forest; susceptible to salt.

DISEASES AND INSECTS: Leaf scorch (a physiological disorder) can be a serious problem caused by excessive drought; *Verticillium* wilt; in the early sixties many New England Sugar Maples were declining or dying and the cause was unknown; this "Maple Decline" was attributed to drought conditions which persisted in the fifties and affected the overall vigor of the trees and made them more susceptible to insect and disease attacks; apparently, the problem has subsided for the noticeable decline has ceased.

LANDSCAPE VALUE: One of the best of the larger shade and lawn trees; excellent for lawn, park, golf course, possibly as street tree where tree lawns are extensive; definitely not for crowded and polluted conditions; beautiful fall color and pleasing growth habit, suffers from extended heat and if used in the South should be located away from stressful sites.

CULTIVARS:

'Arrowhead'—Upright, pyramidal head with a strong leader and dense branching, yellow to orange fall color 60′ tall by 30′ wide; Schichtel, Orchard Park, NY, introduction.

'Bonfire'—Polished medium green 5″ long by 5″ wide leaves which supposedly turn brilliant carmine-red in fall, canopy broad oval, vigorous grower and appears to be fastest growing cultivar, exhibits good heat tolerance and resistance to leaf hopper; I have not observed good fall color on this form, the best to date was yellow-orange; fall color iin midwest has not been good; 50′ by 40′.

'Cary'—Slow-growing form, shorter and more compact than the species; foliage dense, one-half size of species, long-lasting; habit narrow bell-shaped.

'Commemoration'—Vigorous, fast-growing oval-rounded 50′ by 38′ tree with dense canopy, calipers well at an early age, moderately spreading crown; heavy textured glossy dark green leaves abundant throughout the crown, resistant to leaf tatter, fall color deep yellow-orange-red occurring 10 to 14 days earlier than species, a Bill Wandell introduction.

var. *conicum*—Dense, conical habit; have seen numerous forms in the wild that approximate this description.

'Endowment'—Columnar, compact cylindrical head, rapid growth, scorch free summer foliage, orange-red fall color, a Siebenthaler introduction.

'Fairview'—Sturdy broad-oval tree growing 50′ by 40′, leaves emerald green, changing to orange in fall, supposedly calipers faster than other cultivars.

'Flax Mill Majesty' (= 'Majesty')—Flax Mill Nursery Inc., Cambridge, NY. Fast-growing, symmetrically ovoid, large thick dark green leaves turning red-orange in fall, free from frost crack and sun scald, thick branching structure, perhaps 2 to 3 times the branch number of the species.

'Globosum'—Round headed form, 20 year-old plant being 10′ by 10′, good yellow fall color; not common.

'Goldspire'—Densely columnar, leathery dark green foliage, highly resistant to scorch, rich bright yellow-orange fall color, a Princeton introduction.

'Greencolumn'—Form of *A. nigrum* selected by Bill Heard of Des Moines, Iowa. Found growing in a stand in the central part of the state; selected for upright, columnar shape, maintains a central leader, 65′ high, 25′ wide; leaves yellow-orange in fall; hardy in Zone 4, worthwhile trying in Zone 3; displays visible characteristics and functional qualities that indicate successful performance in the midwest.

'Green Mountain'—Dark green leathery foliage with good scorch resistance; supposedly orange to scarlet in fall but reports from midwest indicate yellow and from Pacific Northwest yellow-red; upright oval crown; supposed hybrid of *Acer saccharum* and *Acer nigrum;* quite heat tolerant and performs better than species in dry restricted growing areas; 7.2′ and 5′ wide after 4 years. 70′ high by 45′ wide; Princeton Introduction. Averaged 1′1″ growth per year over a 10-year period in Wichita tests; developed severe leaf scorch.

'Lanco Columnar'—Broad columnar form, resists summer scorch and frost crack, excellent fall color.

'Legacy'—Crown heavier with better distribution of leaves throughout; glossy dark green leaves thicker with heavy wax; approximately 1.5 times thicker than species, no leaf tatter, good red or sometimes yellow-orange fall color; has proven superior in South, appears to be the best of the newer, drought resistant cultivars.

'Moraine'—Fast-growing form, conical habit, fall color gold-orange-scarlet; no summer leaf scorch or frost cracking, a Siebanthaler Nursery introduction.

'Newton Sentry' ('Columnare')—Found by the entrance to Newton Cemetery, Newton, MA and introduced by F.L. Temple, a Cambridge, MA nurseryman around 1885–86; Temple described the original tree as 30′ high and only 2.5′ in diameter at the top; the leaves leathery, thick and dark green; in 1983 the original tree was 50′ high, 14′ wide, with a 16″ caliper; it is the most upright of all maples and presents a rather harsh winter silhouette; generally it does not maintain a single central leader above 6′ from the ground, the major and minor branches are laden with short stubby branchlets, fall color is yellow-orange like the species.

'Seneca Chief'—Narrow tree with oval crown; dense branching; fall color orange to yellow, a Schichtel introduction.

'Skybound'—Upright, tight almost oval crown, excellent yellow-orange fall color, introduced by Synnesvedt Nursery, Illinois.

'Slavin's Upright'—Upright form with strongly ascending branches.

'Summer Proof'—Vigorous spreading form; heat tolerant and does not suffer from windburn.

'Sweet Shadow'—Leaves deeply cut, each lobe also cut, medium green, orange fall color, most trees I have seen were rounded, although literature says vase-shaped; have seen this cultivar at a number of locations throughout the midwest and east, appears to be adaptable; growth quite vigorously.

'Temple's Upright' ('Monumentale')—Often confused with 'Newton Sentry' but maintaining a central leader well into the crown, the major branches ascending and absence of short stubby lateral branchlets; the outline is distinctively elliptical and the branches ascend and gently curve upwards; a 98-year-old tree in the Arnold Arboretum was 60′ high, 17′ wide with a 16″ diameter.

'Wright Brothers'—Broad cone-shaped head, brilliant fall color of mottled gold, pink, orange and scarlet; rapid growth rate, calipers at approximately twice the rate per year as seedling *A. saccharum,* non frost cracking, resistant to scorch, hardy to −25°F.

PROPAGATION: Seed should be stratified in moist medium for 60 to 90 days at 41°F; cuttings collected in early June and treated with 1000 ppm IBA-talc rooted 57%; not considered easy to root from cuttings; all cultivars are budded on seedling understocks.

ADDITIONAL NOTES: *Acer saccharum* is an outstanding native tree, unexcelled for fall color; sap is boiled down to make maple syrup; a trip to a sugar camp in February or March is a unique experience; takes about 40 gallons of sap to make a gallon of syrup; trees are being selected with the highest possible sugar content.

NATIVE HABITAT: Eastern Canada to Georgia, Alabama, Mississippi and Texas. Introduced 1753.

RELATED SPECIES:

Acer barbatum *(floridanum),* (ā′ser bar-bā′tum), Florida Maple, Southern Sugar Maple, is mentioned here because of its possible use as a Sugar Maple substitute in the south. It is essentially smaller in all parts compared to *A. saccharum* and occurs as a small spreading, 20 to 25′ high understory tree from Virginia to Florida, Louisiana, southern Arkansas and eastern Oklahoma and Texas. It is usually found along streams and swamps in both the Piedmont and Coastal Plain. If planted in the same area as *A. saccharum,* it normally flowers about two weeks earlier and colors two weeks later. The 3/4 to 1 1/4″ long fruits have an angle of 60 to 70°. The autumnal fall coloration is usually yellow and not as vibrant as the northern form. Some botanists list this as a subspecies or variety of *Acer saccharum.* Zone 7 to 9.

Acer leucoderme, (ā′ser lū-kō-dēr′mē), Chalkbark or Whitebark Maple, is another southern variation of Sugar Maple. It is quite similar to *A. barbatum* but is supposedly more pubescent on the underside of the leaf. I have studied herbarium specimens and would say that the two are quite difficult to separate. The wings of the fruits spread at a wider angle than those of *A. barbatum. Acer leucoderme* is found in drier, upland woods in the Piedmont from North Carolina to Georgia, Louisiana, eastern Oklahoma and Texas. It occurs as an understory species and matures at about 25 to 30′. In the UGA Botanical Garden, numerous specimens occur and in fall put on a dazzling show that rivals *Acer saccharum.* Trees vary from yellow-orange to deep red. Several nurserymen are growing this species and hopefully it will be "accepted" by the landscape designers and public. It is smaller in all parts compared to Sugar Maple and displays good dry soil tolerance. Zone 5 to 9.

Acer nigrum—Black Maple
(ā'ser nī'grum)

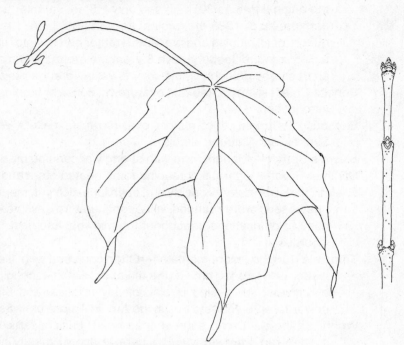

LEAVES: Opposite, simple, 3 to 6″ wide, 3 to 5 lobed, deeply cordate with closed sinus, lobes acute, sides of blade drooping, dull green above, yellow green beneath, pubescent; petioles usually pubescent, often enlarged at base, stipules present, 3 to 5″ long.

BUDS: Imbricate, pubescent, much more so than Sugar Maple, tend to be plumper than Sugar Maple buds and gray-dust-brown in color; 2 axillary buds at terminal, 1/2 to 3/4 as long as terminal.

STEM: Straw colored with prominent lenticels; much more so than Sugar Maple.

Acer nigrum, Black Maple, is extremely similar to *A. saccharum* and is often difficult to differentiate. The principal differences are the drooping lateral leaf lobes, the stipules that are present at the base of the petiole, the more pubescent underside of the leaf and the yellow fall color. Growth habit and size are similar to *A. saccharum.* Perhaps the most important difference is the supposed greater heat and drought tolerance of Black compared to Sugar Maple. At times I have trouble accepting this because in the midwest, plants of both grow side by side and appear equally satisfied. Black Maple is found further west in Minnesota, Iowa, Kansas and Arkansas and selections from these populations might exhibit greater drought tolerance. Grew 4″ per year over a 9-year period in Wichita tests; large bare-root trees did not establish well and developed some leaf scorch. 'Greencolumn', listed under *A. saccharum,* is a Black Maple selection from Iowa. Black Maple should never be slighted for it is equal to Sugar Maple in ornamental characteristics and perhaps superior in tolerance to hostile growing conditions. The yellow fall color needs no apologies. Quebec and New England to New York, West Virginia, and Kentucky, west to South Dakota, Iowa, Kansas and Arkansas. Introduced 1812. Zone 4 to 8.

Acer spicatum — Mountain Maple
(ā'ser spī-kā'tum)

LEAVES: Opposite, simple, 3-lobed or sometimes slightly 5-lobed, 2 to 5″ long, cordate, lobes ovate, acuminate, coarsely and irregularly serrate, dark yellowish green and smooth above, paler beneath and covered with a short grayish down.

BUDS: Usually less than 1/4″ long, stalked, pointed, red but dull with minute, appressed, grayish hairs, 2 visible scales (valvate).

STEM: Young stems grayish pubescent, developing purplish red, or often greenish on one side, minutely pubescent with short, appressed, grayish hairs, particularly about the nodes and toward the apex. Leaf scars are narrowly crescent shaped.

SIZE: Variable, but 10 to 30′ in height over its native range.

HARDINESS: Zone 2 to 7 at high elevations.
HABIT: Shrub or small, short trunked tree of bushy appearance.
RATE: Slow to medium.
TEXTURE: Medium.
BARK: Thin, brownish or grayish brown, smooth, eventually becoming slightly furrowed or warty.
LEAF COLOR: Dark yellowish green in summer, changing to yellow, orange and red in fall.
FLOWERS: Small, perfect, greenish yellow, borne in erect, 3 to 6″ long racemes in June, each flower on a slender stalk about 1/2″ long.
CULTURE: Transplant balled and burlapped; actually not well adapted to civilization and prefers cool, shady, acid, moist situations similar to where it is found in the wild.
DISEASES AND INSECTS: None serious.
LANDSCAPE VALUE: Limited; however, if native worth leaving; have observed it on the highest mountain in Georgia peeking its little head out of a mixed understory; leaves among native maples are unmistakable.
PROPAGATION: Seed requires 90 to 120 days at 41°F.
NATIVE HABITAT: Labrador to Saskatchewan, south to northern Georgia and Iowa. Introduced 1750.

Acer tataricum — Tatarian Maple
(ā′ser ta-tär′ī-kum)

LEAVES: Opposite, simple, 2 to 4″ long, usually unlobed, irregularly double serrate; bright green above, often pubescent when young on veins beneath; on adult trees leaves are essentially unlobed, on young trees or vigorous shoots leaves may be 3 to 5 lobed and resemble *Acer ginnala;* often very difficult to separate these two maples; petiole 3/4 to 2″ long.
BUDS: Imbricate, small, 1/8 to 1/4″ long, reddish brown to brownish black, glabrous to slightly hairy.
STEM: Slender, glabrous, reddish brown to brown, angular, dotted with numerous lenticels.

SIZE: 15 to 20′ in height with a comparable spread; can grow to 30′ in height.
HARDINESS: Zone 3 to 8, seldom seen in Zone 7 to 8 and like *Acer ginnala,* best reserved for cooler climates.
HABIT: A large multi-stemmed shrub of bushy habit or a small, rounded to widespreading tree; have seen handsome tree specimens.
RATE: Slow to medium.
TEXTURE: Medium in foliage and in winter habit.
LEAF COLOR: Medium to dark green in summer; yellow, red and reddish brown in fall; very variable; leaves fall earlier than those of *Acer ginnala.*

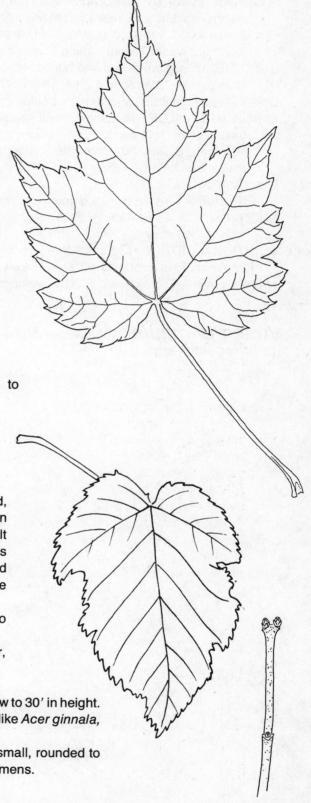

FLOWERS: Greenish white, April–May, borne in upright 2 to 3″ long panicles; not overwhelmingly ornamental but a definite asset in the landscape.

FRUIT: Samara, 3/4 to 1″ long, wings almost parallel, red, variable in intensity of color, August, effective 3 or more weeks before turning brown, fruit on some trees is green to brown.

CULTURE: Transplant balled and burlapped, tolerant of adverse conditions including drought; similar to *Acer ginnala*. Averaged 10″ per year in Wichita tests over a 9-year period.

DISEASES AND INSECTS: None particularly serious.

LANDSCAPE VALUE: Handsome small specimen tree for the limited residential landscape, street tree use, perhaps planter boxes, groupings; could be used more than is currently being practiced; Michigan State and Ohio State campuses and Missouri Botanical Garden have handsome specimens.

CULTIVARS:

'Rubrum'—Leaves color a blood red in the fall.

PROPAGATION: Seed, 41°F for 90 to 180 days; cuttings collected in mid August rooted 77% when treated with 10,000 ppm IBA talc.

ADDITIONAL NOTES: Nice small tree with landscape attributes similar to *Acer ginnala;* not common in commerce and probably never will be owing to pronounced similarity to *A. ginnala*.

NATIVE HABITAT: Southeast Europe, western Asia. Introduced 1759.

Acer truncatum — Purpleblow Maple, Shantung Maple
(ā′ser trun-kā′-tum)

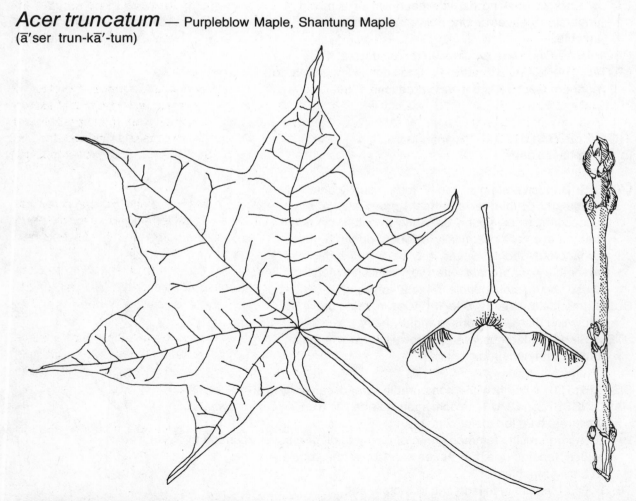

LEAVES: Opposite, simple, 3 to 5″ wide, not as high, 5-lobed, each lobe triangular in shape, two basal lobes drawn out, often truncate at base, lobes acuminate, dark green above, paler beneath, glabrous except at point of attachment to petiole where axillary tufts of pubescence occur; petiole 2 to 4″ long, glabrous, contains milky sap.

BUDS: Terminal-imbricate, plump, reddish brown, 4-sided, 1/4″ high, essentially glabrous, tips of upper scales with pubescence, resembles Norway Maple bud; laterals much smaller.

STEM: Moderate, lustrous reddish brown, glabrous, slightly lenticelled, leaf scars meet at a point like Norway.

SIZE: 20 to 25′ in height with a spread slightly less than or equal to height.

HARDINESS: Zone 4 to 8, will withstand −20 to −25°F (Zone 4), successful at Morton Arboretum and Minnesota Landscape Arboretum.

HABIT: Small, rounded-headed tree of neat outline with a regular branching pattern; often densely branched and foliaged.

RATE: Slow.

TEXTURE: Medium in all seasons.

BARK: Often tinged with purple when young; older branches assuming a gray-brown color.

LEAF COLOR: Reddish purple when emerging (very beautiful) gradually changing to dark glossy green in summer; fall color, as observed at the National and Arnold Arboreta, was an excellent combination of yellow-orange-red; some trees glistening yellow-orange.

FLOWERS: Greenish yellow, 1/3 to 1/2″ diameter, each on a slender stalk 1/2″ long, borne in erect branching, 3″ diameter corymbs in May.

FRUIT: Samara, 1 1/4 to 1 1/2″ long, forming an angle of about 90°, wings may spread obtusely.

CULTURE: Apparently a relatively hardy tree which thrives under conditions similar to those required for *Acer griseum;* I have seen several specimens and they appeared vigorous and healthy in midwest, east, and the Middle Atlantic States. Averaged 1′4″ per year over a 9-year period and developed purplish fall color and purplish fruits.

DISEASES AND INSECTS: None particularly serious, tar spot has been reported.

LANDSCAPE VALUE: A very lovely small maple with potential for street or residential areas; do not know why the tree is not better known; appears to have potential for urban areas; resistant to leaf scorch and may prove a valuable addition to the list of urban trees; I have a small plant in my garden and am encouraged by performance in Zone 8. Dr. John Pair, Kansas State, has championed this fine tree because of heat and drought tolerance; his article in *PIPPS* 36:403–408 (1988) presents a fine ornamental and propagational overview.

CULTIVARS:

'Norwegian Sunset' ('Keithsform')—An upright oval outline with good branch structure and uniform canopy structure, glossy dark green foliage turns orange-red to red in fall, should exhibit more heat and drought tolerance than typical Norway, 35 by 25′, hardy to −25°F, hybrid between *Acer truncatum* and *A. platanoides,* a 1989 Schmidt introduction.

'Pacific Sunset' ('Warrenred')—An upright spreading, rounded crown form with finer branch structure than 'Norwegian Sunset', very glossy dark green summer foliage colors, bright red in fall, colors a little earlier than 'Norwegian Sunset', *Acer truncatum* × *A. platanoides* hybrid, hardy to −25°F, a 1989 Schmidt introduction.

PROPAGATION: 30 to 60 days cold moist stratification produced 85% or higher germination; June cuttings from a 10-year-old tree rooted 71 and 79% after treatment with 1000 and 5000 ppm IBA solution, respectively. *Acer truncatum* and *A. T.* subsp. *mayrii* are monoecious but male and female flowers do not open at the same time; hence, most seeds are void of embryos.

NATIVE HABITAT: Northern China. Introduced 1881.

RELATED SPECIES: *Hortus III* includes *A. mono* as a subsp. of *A. truncatum.* I do not agree with this assessment but include them here for the sake of brevity.

Acer truncatum subsp. **mono**—Painted Maple

LEAVES: Opposite, simple, 5-lobed (7), 3 to 6″ across, each lobe tapering to a long, narrow acuminate apex, entire, truncate or cordate, dark green above, lighter beneath, pubescent on veins; petiole 2 to 4″ long, pubescent, milky sap at base.

BUDS: Terminal; imbricate, ovoid, 4 to 6 scaled, 3/16 to 1/4″ long, weakly 4-sided, deep purplish red with a luster, edges of scale finely pubescent, apex of bud silky pubescent.

STEM: Slender, glabrous, reddish brown to purple, no prominent lenticels.

Acer truncatum subsp. *mono,* Painted Maple, is a lovely small to medium sized landscape tree. The habit is somewhat vase-shaped with the branches forming a dome-like crown at maturity (30 to 40′). The dark green leaves may turn yellow orange in fall but on trees that I observed the leaves died off green because of early freezes. The greenish yellow flowers appear in 2 to 3″ long corymbose racemes in April–May. The samaras are 3/4 to 1 1/4″ long and spread almost horizontally. The bark is Japanese Maple-like, smooth, gray,

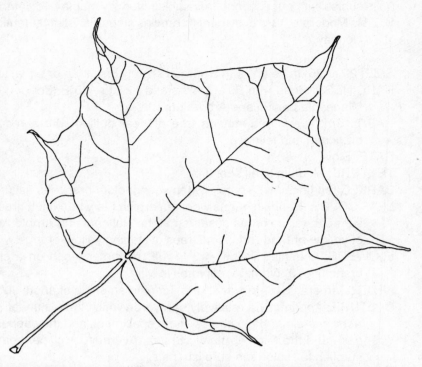

broken only by irregular, shallow, longitudinal fissures. This is one of the most beautiful trees in the Arnold Arboretum and as one walks along the Meadow Road this beautiful mushroom-headed tree looms on the horizon directly in front of the Japanese maples. Although similar to *A. truncatum* it differs in the larger leaves, more uniform habit and smoother bark. Other closely related taxa include *Acer cappadocicum* and *A. truncatum* subsp. *mayrii,* both of which have milky sap. The unfolding leaves of subsp. *mayrii* are a rich bronze and extremely attractive. The yellowish flowers remind of Norway Maple. China, Manchuria and Korea. Introduced 1880. Zone 5 to 8.

Acer cappadocicum—Coliseum Maple
(ā′ser kap-a-do′-sē-kum)

LEAVES: Opposite, simple 5 to 7 lobed, 3 to 6″ across, cordate at base, lobes triangular-ovate, long acuminate, entire, rich green and finely reticulate beneath with axillary tufts of hairs; petiole 4 to 8″ long, milky sap at base of petiole.
STEM: Remains green the second year.

Acer cappadocicum, Coliseum Maple, is virtually unknown in commercial horticulture and in many respects could be confused with *Acer truncatum* and subspecies *mono* and *mayrii.* A principal difference is that in subsp. *mono* the second year stems become gray-brown and wrinkled or fissured. The habit is rounded and landscape size approximates 25 to 30′. The yellow flowers occur with the leaves in 2″ long glabrous coymbs. The samara ranges from 1 1/4 to 1 3/4″ long and the wings spread at a wide angle. Tree appears quite adaptable and might be considered for more culturally difficult sites. 'Aureum' is a rather handsome yellow leaf form that emerges yellow, changes to green in summer and finally yellow in autumn. 'Rubrum' offers blackish red unfolding leaves that gradually change to green although the young tips of branches still maintain a reddish coloration. In England, this form has grown over 70′ high. In addition, several varieties are known which differ in leaf characteristics, primarily size and lobing. Caucasus and western Asia to Himalayas. Introduced 1838. Zone 5 to 7.
ADDITIONAL NOTES: I am not sure anyone has this particular group accurately straightened out; various references are somewhat contradictory. This group of trees deserves greatest landscape consideration. The future offers a place for these trees because of environmental and pest resistances.

Actinidia arguta — Bower Actinidia, Tara Vine
(ak-ti-nid'-ē-a âr-gū'ta)

FAMILY: Actinidiaceae

LEAVES: Alternate, simple, broad-ovate to elliptic, 3 to 5″ long, abruptly acuminate, rounded to subcordate at base, rarely cuneate, setosely and sharply serrate, lustrous dark green above, green beneath and usually setose on midrib; petiole 1 1/2 to 3″ long, sometimes setose, sometimes reddish purple.

BUDS: Small, concealed in the thickened cortex above the leaf scar, the end bud lacking.

STEM: Stout, brownish, heavily lenticelled (vertical), glabrous; pith-brown, lamellate; leaf scars raised with single bundle trace (looks like an eyeball).

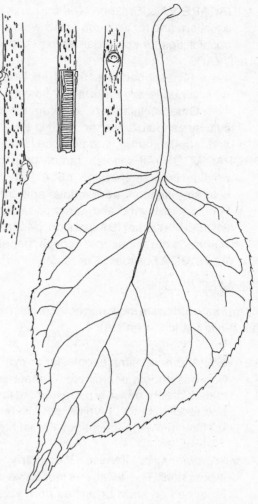

SIZE: 25 to 30′ in height but seems to be limited only by the structure to which it is attached.

HARDINESS: Zone 3 to 8, often described as the hardy kiwi.

HABIT: Vigorous, high climbing, twining vine which requires support.

RATE: Fast, can grow 20′ in 2 to 3 years time.

TEXTURE: Medium in leaf; medium-coarse in winter; actually the tangled, jumbled thicket of winter stems would be considered coarse by most observers.

LEAF COLOR: Lustrous dark green in summer, petioles often with slight reddish tinge; fall coloration is yellowish green, leaves hold late and seldom show any change; beautiful, disease-free foliage.

FLOWERS: Polygamo-dioecious, delicately fragrant, whitish or greenish white, 3 or more together in axils of leaves, each about 4/5″ across, and 1/2 to 3/4″ long; sepals green, ovate-oblong, blunt; waxy petals orbicular, white tinged with green, very concave and incurving giving the flowers a globular shape; numerous dark purple anthers; ovary with a short, stout style, at the top of which about 20 stigmas radiate like the spokes of a wheel; May–June, essentially hidden by the foliage, bee pollinated and one male can pollinate up to 8 females.

FRUIT: A greenish yellow, 1 to 1 1/4″ long by 3/4″ wide ellipsoidal berry with lime-green flesh, chocolate-colored seeds; fruits have been described as possessing flavors ranging from insipid (unripe) to pleasant (?) to that of strawberries, melons, gooseberries and bananas; I sampled a ripe fruit at Fred and Mary Ann McGourty's in mid-October, 1984 and was, what's the term, pleasantly surprised by the mild mixed flavor; the species is effectively dioecious and a male must accompany the female for best fruit set; has received considerable attention in recent years as an edible landscape plant and a partial substitute for *Actinidia deliciosa (A. chinensis)*, True Kiwi, in cold climates; advantages of *A. arguta* fruits include the hairless nature, no peeling, high vitamin C (10 times higher than oranges), as much potassium as a 6″ long banana, high in fiber, low in calories and sodium free; two mature vines (male and female) may produce up to 10 gallons of fruit per year; fruits can be stored up to 16 weeks in the refrigerator.

CULTURE: Like most rampant vines easy to transplant; this is probably the most vigorous of the *Actinidia* species; will tolerate any type soil but best sited in infertile soil to reduce rapid growth; full sun or partial shade; needs considerable pruning and this can be accomplished about any time of year; probably one of the most adaptable vines, for best fruit production, each winter the stems should be cut back to 8 to 10 buds.

DISEASES AND INSECTS: None serious.

LANDSCAPE VALUE: Good vine for quick cover but can rapidly overgrow its boundaries; the foliage is excellent and for problem areas where few other vines will grow *Actinidia arguta* could be used; has possibilities for home garden use especially in cold climates.

CULTIVARS:

'Issai' is described in a 1988 Stark Nursery catalog as hermaphrodite (perfect flowered) and no male is necessary for fruit set, flowers and fruits as a young plant.

Other cultivars are appearing in commerce and their net worth is unknown. Ideally, the better cultivars should flower and fruit at a young age, possess bisexual or perfect flowers (no need for male and female plants), and produce large, 1 to 1 1/2″ long fruits that ripen early in fall.

PROPAGATION: All species can be propagated by seed; stratification for 3 months at 41°F in a moist medium is recommended, but *A. kolomitka* has shown a double dormancy and requires a warm plus cold stratification; tremendous amount of cutting research especially on *A. chinensis* (see Dirr and Heuser); softwood and hardwood cuttings have been successful; June–July cuttings, slightly firm, 3000 to 5000 ppm IBA-solution, peat:perlite and mist would be a good starting point; there are literally hundreds of recipes for success; generally rooting percentages will fall in the 50 to 80% category.

NATIVE HABITAT: Japan, Korea, Manchuria. Cultivated 1874.

RELATED SPECIES:

Actinidia chinensis (now correctly *A. deliciosa*)—Chinese Gooseberry or Kiwi Fruit
(ak-ti-nid′ē-a chī-nen′sis)

LEAVES: Alternate, simple, obicular or oval, 3 to 5″ (7″) long, cordate at base, rounded, emarginate or on vigorous shoots acuminate, crenate-serrulate; newly emerging leaves purplish gradually changing to dark green, densely pubescent at first, finally slightly hairy above and densely tomentose beneath with reddish hairs on veins; petiole densely covered with reddish hairs; 1 1/2 to 3″ long.

STEM: Thick, brown, with shaggy brown hairs; pith whitish to yellowish and solid.

Actinidia chinensis, Chinese Gooseberry, has received considerable attention in recent years for fruit production. The foliage is attractive and the 1 1/2″ diameter, creamy-white fragrant flowers are produced on short branches from year-old wood. The plant is functionally dioecious and male and female plants are necessary for good fruit set. The fruit is an elongated, 1 to 2″ long, hairy, edible brownish green berry. The fruit in the produce section of the grocery store that you have no earthly idea of its identity is probably Kiwi. Requires well drained, moderately moist soil; full sun or partial shade; no significant pest problems. Makes a good cover for a fence, trellis, arbor or pergola. Rapid growth rate and coarse-textured, luxuriant foliage are principle landscape assets. It is used in Europe as a wall and arbor cover. Many cultivars, probably the most famous in the United States is 'Hayward' (female) and 'Chico Male'. Has been promoted as a potential fruit crop in the southeast with marginal success. Sixty-eight percent of the Kiwi crop is produced in New Zealand with the U.S. producing 12%. Interestingly, the New Zealanders consume 5% of the production, while the U.S. consumes 12%. New Zealand has accomplished miracles with this plant and is responsible for the common name Kiwi and popularizing the plant worldwide. National Geographic (May 1987) presented a fine article with numerous trivial pursuit questions. For example, an average 100-acre New Zealand dairy farm earns $30,000 U.S. yearly; the same acreage in Kiwis can bring in $1,000,000 U.S.; plants may grow as much as 8″ in 24 hours; and a fine white wine, often mistaken for a Riesling is made; the crop is now worth $40,000,000 annually in the U.S. China. Introduced 1900. Zone 8 to 9.

Actinidia kolomikta—Kolomikta Actinidia
(ak-ti-nid′ē-a kō-lō-mik′ta)

LEAVES: Alternate, simple, broad-ovate, 3 to 6″ long, 3 to 4″ wide, cordate, acuminate, sharply and uniformly serrate, 6 to 8 vein pairs, glabrous, slightly pubescent on veins beneath; petiole 1 to 1 1/2″ long, essentially glabrous.

BUDS: Perhaps superposed with one imbedded in leaf scar and the other small and globose.
STEM: Rich brown, glabrous, prominently lenticelled, nodes appear swollen; pith rich brown, finely chambered.

Actinidia kolomikta, Kolomikta Actinidia, is a deciduous twining vine growing 15 to 20′ and more. The foliage is purplish when young, developing particularly on the pale plant a white to pink blotch at the apex which may extend to the middle and beyond. I can't confirm the statement about males being more showy than females from observations, but have read it in literature on several occasions. The leaves are about 5″ long and the variegated foliage is therefore quite showy. Supposedly this variegation is more colorful when the plant is grown on calcareous soils. Certain plants one only reads about and for a long time I could only imagine the leaf coloration. Having watched this vine through the growing season at the Arnold Arboretum and observing other specimens including a magnificent plant on the administration building at Wisley Gardens, I believe this species is worth more than a second glance. On a garden tour that I led to England there was more interest in this plant than any other. The vividness of the variegation is often reduced by hot weather. The white, fragrant, 1/2″ diameter flowers are produced 1 to 3 from the leaf axils in May–June. The stamens are yellow. Fruit is a sweet, edible, greenish yellow, oblong-ovoid, 1″ long berry that ripens in September–October. Not as vigorous as *A. arguta* but appears well adapted to any reasonably well drained soil. Excessive fertilizer and shade will reduce leaf coloration. Mature plants tend to show pronounced leaf coloration. Cuttings collected in June, treated with 8000 ppm IBA rooted 40%. Does not seem to be as easy to root as other *Actinidia* species. See general propagation recommendation under *A. arguta.* Northeastern Asia to Japan, central and western China. Introduced about 1855. Zone 4 to 8 (?). Actually, this species is listed as hardy to −45°F.

Actinidia polygama—Silver-vine
LEAF: Alternate, simple, broad-ovate to ovate, oblong, 3 to 6″ long, acuminate, rounded or subcordate at base, appressed serrate, usually setose on the veins beneath, on male plants the upper half or almost the whole leaf silver white or yellowish; petioles bristly.

Actinidia polygama, (ak-ti-nid′ē-a pō-lig′a-ma), Silver-vine, is probably the weakest grower of the *Actinidia* group. It may grow 15′ but is definitely not as vigorous as *A. arguta.* The 3 to 5″ long leaves of staminate plants are marked with a silver-white to yellowish color. Cats apparently are attracted to this plant and will maul the foliage. The leaves of female plants are a duller green than *A. arguta.* The flowers are white, 1/2 to 3/4″ across, 1 to 3 together, fragrant, June–July; the fruit is an edible 1″ long, greenish yellow berry of little ornamental significance. Differs from previous species in the solid, white pith. Roots readily from softwood cuttings. Native to Manchuria, Japan and central China. Introduced 1861. Zone 4 to 7.
ADDITIONAL NOTES: An interesting group of vines but seldom used in modern landscaping; their adaptability to difficult situations should make them more popular; the difference in foliage colors between male and female plants is a rarity among dioecious plants. Do not be disappointed if young plants of *A. kolomikta* and *A. polygama* do not develop the pronounced leaf coloration; the juvenile nature and high nutrition appear to suppress color formation; an excellent article on the *Actinidia* species appeared in *The Plantsman* 6(3):167–180 (1984) by Philip McMillan Browse.

Adina rubella
(a-dī′na rö-bel′la)

FAMILY: Rubiaceae
LEAVES: Opposite, simple, elliptic-ovate, to 2″ long, entire, acute, rounded, lustrous dark green above, paler and pubescent on veins beneath.
STEM: Slender, reddish brown, pubescent.

Adina rubella is a handsome lustrous dark green foliaged small shrub that is essentially unknown in American gardens. One lone plant on the Georgia campus has served as a favorite test plant that almost all visitors have been asked to identify. The reader can guess the results. The habit is upright spreading, about 8 to 10′ at maturity. I have seen the species in Bernheim Arboretum, Clermont, KY, where it was prospering. In northern latitudes it is a dieback shrub. White, slightly fragrant flowers occur in 1/2 to 3/4″ diameter rounded heads in June–July to October in Athens. Although not 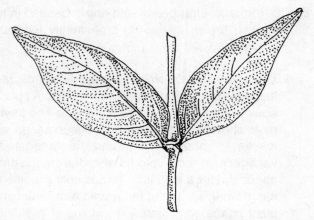 overwhelming, they are curiously interesting and remind of the more common buttonbush, *Cephalanthus occidentalis.* Requires nothing more than well drained soil and partial shade appears to serve it best. Southern China. Zone 7 to 9.

Aesculus californica — California Buckeye
(es′-kū-lus kal-i-fôr′-ni-ka)

LEAVES: Opposite, compound palmate, 5 (4 to 7) leaflets, each 3 to 6″ long, elliptic-oblong to lance-oblong, acuminate, narrowed or rounded at the base, sharply serrate, glabrous, lustrous dark green above; petioles 3 to 4″ long, petiolules 1/2 to 1″ long.

BUDS: Imbricate, lance-shaped, pointed at tip, dark brown, quite sticky, probably more so than *A. hippocastanum.*

STEM: Stout, gray-brown to reddish when young, glabrous, with age becoming lighter.

BARK: Essentially smooth and light to pale silver, reminding of American Beech bark; have seen native trees in California and the silvery-gray bark color really stands out.

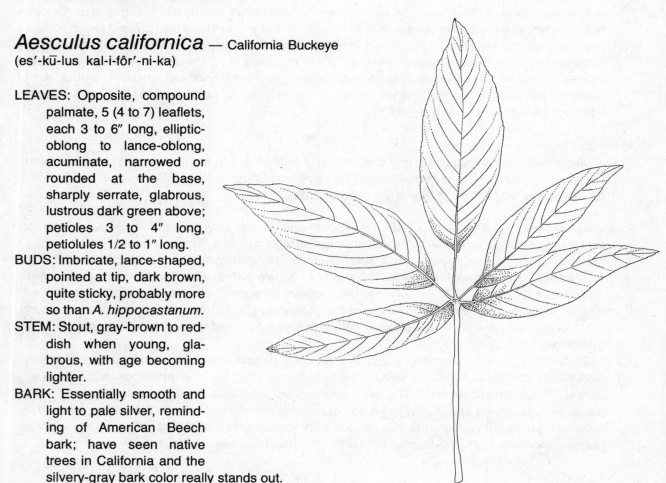

Aesculus californica, California Buckeye, to my knowledge is not grown on the east coast but in California and European gardens, it prospers. My first introduction to the tree occurred in June at the Strybing Arboretum in San Francisco. The plant was at the tail-end of the flowering season but still spectacular. The habit is broad globose to rounded with a regular, symmetrical branching structure (15 to 20′ tall). The lustrous dark green foliage is striking. It occurs naturally on dry soils in canyons and gullies and drops its leaves in July–August but if given ample moisture will hold them into fall. Interestingly, the tree does well in England with the cooler climate and moist atmospheric conditions.

I circled a buckeye for 20 minutes at the Bath Botanic Garden before admitting I did not know its identity. The label said *A. californica*! Flowers are primarily white but may be pink, fragrant, and occur in 4 to 8″ long, 2 to 3″ wide panicles. The stamens extend beyond the petals and provide a feathery texture. The 2 to 3″ long pear shaped, smooth capsule contains 1 to 2, 1 1/2 to 2″ wide pale orange-brown seeds. Probably a marginal tree for eastern conditions but I now have a small plant that is growing reasonably well. The high night temperatures and humidity may wreak havoc. Seed will germinate without pretreatment and, like all *Aesculus* seeds, dries and shrivels rapidly. Plant after collection in beds or deep containers. Generally buckeyes develop a long taproot as a seedling. Good plants for the collector. See McMillan Browse and Leiser, *The Plantsman* 4:54–57 (1982) for a detailed analysis of the species. California. Introduced 1855. Zone 7 to 8(?).

Aesculus glabra — Ohio Buckeye, also called Fetid Buckeye
(es′-kū-lus glā′bra)

FAMILY: Hippocastanaceae

LEAVES: Opposite, palmately compound, 5 leaflets, rarely 7, elliptic to obovate, 3 to 6″ long, acuminate, cuneate, finely serrate, pubescent beneath when young, nearly glabrous at maturity, medium to dark green; petiole approximately 3 to 6″ long.

BUDS: Imbricate, ovoid, sessile, terminal–2/3″ long, brown, with prominently keeled scales, hairy on margins, lateral buds smaller.

STEM: Stout, pubescent at first becoming glabrous and red-brown to ash-gray with disagreeable odor when bruised.

BARK: Ashy gray, thick, deeply fissured and plated.

SIZE: Usually in the range of 20 to 40′ in height with a similar spread although can grown to 80′; the largest specimen I have seen is located on the campus of Wabash College, Crawfordsville, Indiana, however the tree is in poor condition.

HARDINESS: Zone 3 to 7.

HABIT: Rounded to broad-rounded in outline, usually low branched with the branches bending down toward the ground and then arching back up at the ends; actually quite handsome in foliage; very dense and therefore difficult to grow grass under.

RATE: Medium, 7 to 10′ over a 6 to 8 year period.

TEXTURE: Medium-coarse in leaf; coarse in winter.

BARK: Ashy-gray, rather corky-warty, and on the older trunks much furrowed and scaly.

LEAF COLOR: Bright green when unfolding (very handsome) changing to dark green in summer; one of the first trees to leaf out (often late March–early April) and also one of the first to defoliate in fall; fall color is often yellow but at times develops a brilliant orange-red to reddish brown, best termed a pumpkin orange.

FLOWERS: Perfect, greenish yellow, 1″ long, 4 petaled, borne in early to mid-May in 4 to 7″ long by 2 to 3″ wide terminal panicles; not overwhelming but handsome when viewed close-up, flowers occur with foliage and tend to get lost in the shuffle.

FRUIT: Capsule, light brown, dehiscent, 1 to 2″ long, broadly obovoid, with a prickly (echinate) cover similar to Common Horsechestnut but not as pronounced; the seeds (buckeyes) are usually borne solitary;

no childhood is complete without a pocketful of buckeyes!; the seeds are poisonous but nonetheless often eaten by hungry squirrels; only American buckeye with a prickly fruit, although the closely related *A. arguta* is often spiny.

CULTURE: Transplant balled and burlapped into moist, deep, well-drained, slightly acid soil; tends to develop leaf scorch and prematurely drop leaves in hot, droughty situations; found native in bottom-lands along banks of rivers and creeks; full sun or partial shade; prune in early spring.

DISEASES AND INSECTS: Leaf blotch is very serious on this species and *A. hippocastanum;* the leaves develop discolored spots which gradually change to brown; powdery mildew is also a problem and some trees appear gray in color; other problems include leaf spot, wood rot, anthracnose, canker, walnut scale, comstock mealybug, white-marked tussock moth, Japanese beetle, bagworm, flat-headed borer; if a problem occurs, and it is likely to be on the two species mentioned above, consult your extension agent for proper diagnosis and control measures; another significant problem is leaf scorch which is physiological in nature; the margins of leaves become brown and curled; trees located in tight planting areas are especially susceptible although it has been noted as occurring on selected trees even in moist years.

LANDSCAPE VALUE: I value this species as a good native tree best left in the wild or natural setting; a good tree for parks and large areas; definitely not recommended for streets or the small residential landscape; when selecting a tree many factors should be considered and I believe the messiness and lack of ornamental attributes limit extensive use; I have seen trees planted in narrow (3′ wide) tree lawns completely defoliated by late August; I still remember my Dad pointing out the tree on our squirrel hunting trips in southern Ohio. My main interest was collecting pocketfuls of shiny brown seeds. The squirrels probably wondered who was more squirrelly.

CULTIVARS:

var. *nana*—Woodlanders, Aiken, SC has a dwarf shrubby form that flowers at a young age and comes true to type from seed, makes a rather handsome small rounded bush.

PROPAGATION: Seed should be stratified in a moist medium for 120 days at 41°F; *Aesculus* seed should be collected as soon as capsules show a tendency toward dehiscence; it is often a race with the hungry squirrels to see who wins; much of stored material is fats and lipids and the seeds degenerate rapidly; best to sow in fall and cover to a depth equal to the seed's height; cultivars are usually grafted onto *A. hippocastanum, A. glabra* or *A. octandra.*

NATIVE HABITAT: Pennsylvania to Nebraska, Kansas and Alabama. Cultivated 1809.

RELATED SPECIES:

Aesculus arguta—Texas Buckeye

LEAVES: Opposite, compound palmate, 7 to 9 leaflets, each leaflet 2 to 5″ long, lanceolate to obovate-lanceolate, deeply and doubly serrate with obtuse teeth, glabrous at maturity, medium green; petiole as long as leaflet.

Aesculus arguta, (es′-kū-lus âr-gū′ta), Texas Buckeye, is a small tree (15 to 20′) or more commonly a low shrub of rather ungainly proportions. In general, it is similar to the above but smaller in all parts. Has been listed as a variety by some botanists. Leaflets are narrower than Ohio Buckeye and usually 7 to 9 per leaf. Although native to east Texas the species can be grown as far north as Boston and I know of an established specimen at Mt. Airy Arboretum, Cincinnati that withstood -25°F. The Mt. Airy tree is 20′ high and has set many fruits. East Texas. 1909. Zone 4 to 8.

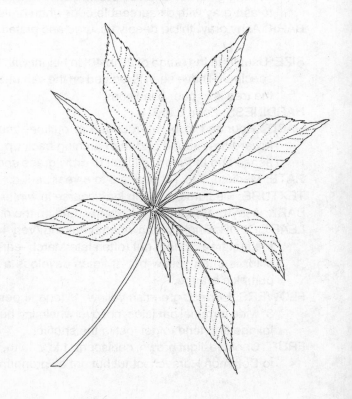

Aesculus flava *(Aesculus octandra)*—Yellow Buckeye
LEAVES: Opposite, compound palmate, generally 5 leaflets, each 4 to 6″ long, oblong-obovate or narrow
elliptic, acuminate, cuneate, finely serrate, dark green above, yellow green and pubescent beneath
when young, essentially glabrous at maturity; petiole 3 to 4″ long.

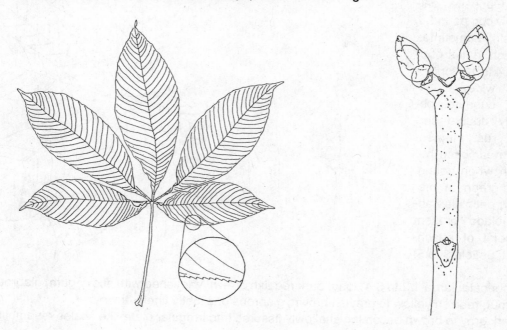

Aesculus flava (*A. octandra*), (es′-kū-lus flā′va), Yellow Buckeye, is, to me, the most beautiful of the large
growing *Aesculus*. The upright-oval to slightly spreading crown often reaches 60 to 75′ in height. The
dark green leaves (5-leaflets) may turn a pumpkin color in fall and do not appear to be as troubled
by foliar diseases as *A. glabra*. The bark is a rather curious combination of gray and brown with large,
flat, smooth plates and scales comprising old trunks. The yellow (tinge of green) flowers are borne
in erect 6 to 7″ long by 2 to 3″ wide panicles in May. The fruit is smooth, pear-shaped, 2 to 2 1/2″ long
capsule usually containing 2 seeds. There are magnificent trees in Sosebee Cove, North Georgia
that ascend fully 90′. The most beautiful trees in cultivation that I have seen are housed at Spring
Grove, Cincinnati, Ohio. Many of these trees range from 60 to 80′ in size. Prefers a deep, moist, well
drained root run. A very handsome buckeye and preferable to the Ohio Buckeye for landscape
situations. Pennsylvania to Tennessee and northern Georgia, west to Ohio and Illinois. Introduced
1764. Zone 3 to 8.

Aesculus × hybrida represents a group of hybrids between *A. flava* and *A. pavia*. The flowers are
yellow-red to reddish; the red trait being inherited from *A. pavia*. These hybrids also have glands as
well as hairs on the margins of the petals which is indicative of *A. pavia*. I have seen many trees with
yellowish red flowers, sometimes labeled as *A. flava*; others as *A. × hybrida*. Fortunately or
unfortunately, there are a significant number of *Aesculus* hybrids many with *A. pavia* as one parent.
The range of flower color is extreme and it is very difficult to accurately categorize them. The
Minnesota Landscape Arboretum has given one of these hybrids a cultivar name *A × arnoldiana*
'Autumn Splendor'. This cultivar is the result of a cross between *A. glabra × A. × hybrida* and
maintains dark green summer leaf color while changing to brilliant red in fall. See *HortScience*
24:180–181 (1989) for complete description of 'Autumn Splendor'.
ADDITIONAL NOTES: Buckeyes are beautiful trees when properly grown. I delight in an early spring
walk in the woods when the leaves of buckeyes are unfurling their rich green to deep purple-green
leaves.

Aesculus hippocastanum — Common Horsechestnut, European Horsechestnut
(es'-kū-lus hip-ō-kas-tā'num)

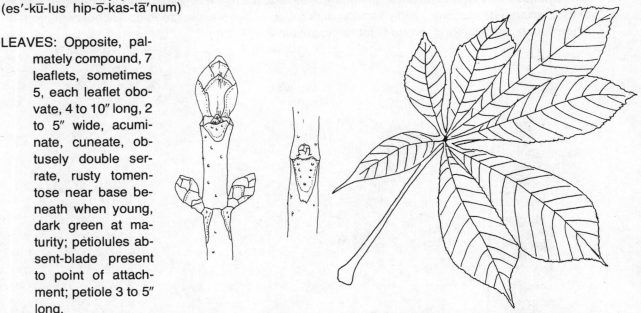

LEAVES: Opposite, palmately compound, 7 leaflets, sometimes 5, each leaflet obovate, 4 to 10″ long, 2 to 5″ wide, acuminate, cuneate, obtusely double serrate, rusty tomentose near base beneath when young, dark green at maturity; petiolules absent-blade present to point of attachment; petiole 3 to 5″ long.

BUDS: Imbricate, large 1/2 to 3/4″ long, dark reddish brown, varnished with sticky gum, glabrous.

STEM: Stout, reddish yellow to grayish brown, glabrous or slightly finely-downy.

BARK: Dark gray to brown becoming shallowly fissured into irregular plate-like scales resembling bark of apple trees.

SIZE: 50 to 75′ in height, will usually develop a 40 to 70′ spread, can grow to 100′ or larger.

HARDINESS: Zone 3 to 7 and possibly 8 although does not perform well in Athens, Georgia.

HABIT: Upright-oval to rounded in outline, making a very striking specimen especially as the new leaves emerge.

RATE: Medium, 12 to 14′ over a 6 to 8 year period.

TEXTURE: Medium to coarse in leaf; definitely coarse in winter.

BARK: Dark gray to brown, on old trunks becoming platy, exfoliating, and exposing orangish brown inner bark.

LEAF COLOR: Light yellow green when unfolding, changing to dark green at maturity; fall color is often a poor yellow and often the leaves develop a brown color; have seen trees in Europe with reasonably good yellow fall color; one of the earliest trees to leaf out but still later than *A. glabra*.

FLOWERS: Perfect, each flower with 4 or 5 petals, white with a blotch of color at the base which starts yellow and ends reddish; flowers borne in 5 to 12″ long and 2 to 5″ wide terminal panicles in early to mid May; very showy and, at one time, much over-planted in the eastern states for that reason.

FRUIT: Light brown, spiny, dehiscent, 2 to 2 1/4″ diameter capsule containing one, sometimes two seeds; matures in September–October.

CULTURE: Transplant balled and burlapped into moist, well-drained soil; full sun or light shade; pH adaptable; prune in early spring; avoid extremely dry situations.

DISEASES AND INSECTS: See under Ohio Buckeye.

LANDSCAPE VALUE: Park, arboretum, campus, commercial grounds, golf courses and other large areas—not for small residential properties; abundant through the eastern states, virtually every campus has a horsechestnut; the blotch and mildew limit extensive use; widely used in Europe; gardens such as Versailles, Schwetzingen and many English parks are well endowed with this species.

CULTIVARS:
   'Baumannii'—Double white flowers, no fruits, flowers last longer than the type, the best of the garden forms handsome and impressive in flower; discovered by A.N. Baumann near Geneva; occurred as a branch sport on a tree in the garden of Mons. Duval around 1820.

There are other cultivars with white and yellow variegation as well as cutleaf, compact, fastigiate, and weeping types. Most are to be avoided except for the fanatical collector. I have observed many of the variegated leaf types in European gardens and some are rather handsome. Doubtfully would they prosper in the United States.

PROPAGATION: Cultivars are grafted on the species; seeds require 3 to 4 months at 41°F.

ADDITIONAL NOTES: A cherished plant in European countries but not so much in the United States; my wife and I sat on a bench in Hyde Park, London, and watched boys collect the nuts as if they were nuggets; boys play a game of "conkers"; in addition they make great ammunition, and provide food for squirrels and deer.

NATIVE HABITAT: Greece and Albania in the mountainous, uninhabited wilds; introduced 1576; once thought to be native to India.

RELATED SPECIES:

Aesculus × carnea, (es'-kū-lus × kär'nē-a), Red Horsechestnut, resulted from a cross between *A. pavia* and *A. hippocastanum.* Little is known of the origin of the hybrid except that it probably occurred in Germany. It is one of the most popular trees in England and in May the rose-red flowers are spectacular. The flowers are borne on a 6 to 8″ high and 3 to 4″ wide panicle. The globose, 1 1/2″ diameter capsules are slightly prickly. The species comes true-to-type from seed which is unusual for most hybrids. The theory behind this quirk is unraveled here. The original *A. × carnea* was probably a diploid with 40 chromosomes, as in the parents. At some stage, spontaneous doubling took place thus resulting in an 80 chromosome complement. There are reports that *A. × carnea* does and does not breed true. This could be explained if, assuming the doubling took place on the original tree, scions or seeds were collected and distributed. Some would be of the 40 chromosome complement; others the 80. It is illogical to assume this spontaneous doubling took place in every bud and consequently the above rationale. *Aesculus × carnea* makes a splendid rounded to broad-rounded 30 to 40′ tree in our country. In Europe, the species is listed as growing 60 to 80′ although I saw no trees of that magnitude and Red Horsechestnut was everywhere in evidence. The lustrous dark green leaves are composed of 5, occasionally 7, leaflets. The leaflets are smaller than those of *A. hippocastanum.* The buds are not quite as large or as sticky as *A. hippocastanum.* 'Briotii' has deeper red colored and larger (to 10″ long) panicles. There are several yellow-variegated forms as well as a pendulous type but these are uncommon. 'Briotii' originated in 1858 from seed grown at Trianon in France. Madison, Wisconsin indicated that young trees were severely injured or killed during the severe 1976 to 77 winter. Minnesota Landscape Arboretum mentioned that a tree north of St. Paul has flowered for a number of years. *A. × carnea* is not as susceptible to blotch and mildew as *A. hippocastanum.* In October, I was walking along a street in Salt Lake City, Utah and noticed *A. × carnea* interplanted in a tree lawn with *A. hippocastanum.* The foliage of the latter was paper-bag brown while *A. × carnea* was lush lustrous dark green. A pronounced difference in growth habit was evident with *A. × carnea* rounded and *A. hippocastanum* upright-oval. 'O'Neill' was included in the last edition with a note about the double-flowered nature. I found out through correspondence that it was not double-flowered as advertised. I have since observed the plant in flower at the Strybing Arboretum in San Francisco and the flowers are a fine red, better than 'Briotii', and occur in 10 to 12″ long panicles. To my knowledge, Weston Nurseries, Hopkinton, MA is the only eastern source for the plant.

Aesculus × plantierensis, (es'-kū-lus plan-ti-er-en'sis), is the result of a backcross of *A × carnea × A. hippocastanum.* Flowers are a soft pink or red with a yellow throat, panicles to 12″ long. The tree does not set fruit and the fact that it is a triploid explains this sterility. Raised in the nursery of Simon-Louis Frères, at Plantières, near Metz, France.

Aesculus indica — Indian Horsechestnut
(es'-kū-lus in'-di-ka)

LEAVES: Opposite, compound palmate, 7 (5 to 9) leaflets, short stalked, obovate-lanceolate, 6 to 10″ (12″) long, finely serrate, glabrous, lustrous dark green above and with a distinct undulating margin.
BUDS: Imbricate, gray-brown.
STEM: Stout, gray-green to green-brown.

Aesculus indica, Indian Horsechestnut, is perhaps the finest of the genus for foliage and flower effect. In the U.S., maximum cultural success would be realized in the Pacific Northwest. My fondest recollections are derived from yearly June visits to Kew Gardens, where several spectacular 40 to 50′ high specimens line the entrance walk. The habit is best described as oval-rounded but there is a classic, undefinable dignity inherent in this species that sets it apart from the more pedestrian *A. hippocastanum.* The summer foliage is a lustrous dark green and in fall may develop salmon to orange-red colors. The flowers occur in 12 to 16″ long, 4 to 5″ wide erect cylindrical panicles and are as close to awe-inspiring as an *Aesculus* can get. Each 4-petaled flower is about 1″ long, white, with the upper two petals blotched yellow and red at base, the lower shorter pair pale rose. The stamens protrude about 3/4″ beyond the petals. The overall flower effect is pink to pinkish rose. Fruit is a 2 to 3″ rounded roughened (not spiny) capsule. Prefers moist soil, full sun and an even cool climate. Tremendous park and large estate, or commercial grounds tree. 'Sydney Pearce' has deeper pink flowers in tighter panicles that are freely borne. I have seen the tree at Kew and only wish I could grow it. Northwestern Himalayas. Introduced 1851. Zone 7?

Aesculus parviflora — Bottlebrush Buckeye
(es'-kū-lus pâr-vĭ-flō'-ra)

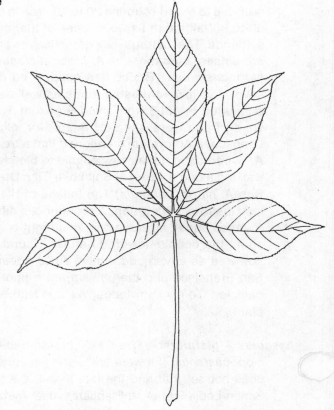

LEAVES: Opposite, palmately compound, 5 to 7 leaflets, nearly sessile, elliptic to oblong-obovate, 3 to 8″ long,1 1/4 to 4″ wide, acuminate, crenate-serrulate, medium to dark green above, grayish and pubescent beneath.
BUDS: Weakly imbricate, usually with 4 exposed scales, terminals— 1/5 to 1/4″ long, laterals smaller, scales minutely pubescent and glaucous, gray-brown in color.

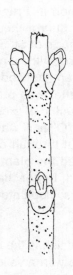

STEM: Stout, gray-brown, with raised light brown lenticels; leaf scar half encircling bud, vascular bundle traces forming a face-like image, usually 3 to 6 in number.

SIZE: 8 to 12′ in height, spreading to 8 to 15′; I have seen a large specimen at the Arnold Arboretum that ranges between 15 and 20′ high.
HARDINESS: Zone 4 to 8 (9).

HABIT: Wide-spreading, suckering, multi-stemmed shrub with many upright, slender branches; often with an irregular, spreading almost stratified appearance; excellent form and texture in the branching structure.

RATE: Slow on old wood but shoots which develop from the base will grow 2 to 4′ in a single season.

TEXTURE: Medium-coarse in summer and winter.

LEAF COLOR: Medium to dark green in summer, changing to yellow-green in fall; foliage is little troubled by diseases which afflict *A. glabra* and *A. hippocastanum*; have observed excellent bright yellow color on plants; expression of good fall color appears to be strongly dependent on ideal environmental conditions.

FLOWERS: White with 4 petals, 1/2″ long, stamens thread-like and pinkish white, standing out an inch from the petals, anthers red; produced June–July on cylindrical 8 to 12″ long and 2 to 4″ wide panicles; outstanding in flower; there are few summer flowering plants which can rival this species; many flowers in the same inflorescence are male, others perfect; I wait with anxious anticipation for the plant to flower in my garden which it normally does from early to mid June. In 1985, the flowers were effective from June 7 through 23. In my mind, it is one of the handsomest of all native southeastern flowering shrubs.

FRUIT: Dehiscent, 1 to 3″ long, pear-shaped, light brown smooth capsule; have not noticed abundant fruit set in northern states possibly because of shortness of growing season; in more southerly areas significant fruit set often occurs, ripen in late September to early October, Athens.

CULTURE: Transplant balled and burlapped or from a container in early spring into a moist, well-drained soil that has been adequately prepared with organic matter; prefers acid soil but is adaptable; full sun or partial shade; in fact, seems to proliferate in shade; pruning is seldom necessary; can be rejuvenated by pruning to ground.

DISEASES AND INSECTS: None serious compared to Ohio Buckeye and Common Horsechestnut.

LANDSCAPE VALUE: Excellent plant for massing, clumping or placing in shrub borders; actually a handsome specimen plant; very effective when used under shade trees and in other shady areas; W.J. Bean noted, "no better plant could be recommended as a lawn shrub"; even if it never flowered it would be a superb shrub for foliage effect; a full grown, broad spreading specimen appears to be flowing across the landscape; perhaps the greatest planting anywhere in the world is located at Bernheim Arboretum, Clermont, Kentucky; will proliferate in the shade of Green Ash and flower superbly.

CULTIVARS:

var. *serotina*—Flowers 2 to 3 weeks later than the species; leaflets supposedly less pubescent than species; Alabama, introduced 1919.

'Rogers'—Selection made by J.C. McDaniel of the University of Illinois from seedlings he grew from seed of var. *serotina* collected at Missouri Botanical Garden; it is named for Dr. Rogers in whose yard it grows in Urbana, Illinois; flowers later than the species and variety; inflorescences fully 18 to 30″ long, very striking; in the early editions it was stated that this selection did not sucker as profusely as the species; this is not true for in recent years I noticed considerable basal suckering.

PROPAGATION: Seed should be planted as soon as it is collected and should never be allowed to dry out; root cuttings, 2 1/2 to 3″ long, buried in sand in a cool place in December and then set in the field in spring produced plants; May collected softwood cuttings from shoots which had developed from roots were treated with 0, 1000, 10000, and 20000 ppm IBA/50 percent alcohol; the cuttings were placed in peat:perlite under mist; the respective rooting percentages were 70, 80, 20 and 10 for various treatments; the 10000 and 20000 treatments resulted in premature defoliation and death; for more details see Burd and Dirr, 1977, Bottlebrush Buckeye: Ornamental Characteristics and Propagation, *The Plant Propagator* 23(4):6–8.

NATIVE HABITAT: *A. parviflora* ranges from South Carolina to Alabama and Florida. Introduced 1785.

RELATED SPECIES:

Aesculus pavia—Red Buckeye
(es'-kū-lus pā'vē-a)

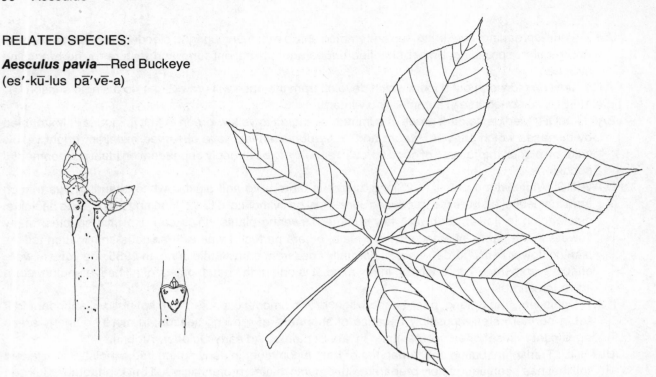

LEAVES: Opposite, palmately compound, 5(7) leaflets, short stalked, oblong-obovate or narrow elliptic, 3 to 6″ long, acuminate, irregularly and often double serrate, glabrous or slightly pubescent beneath, often lustrous dark green.

BUDS: Terminal-imbricate, large, 1/3 to 1/2″ long, brownish, glabrous, laterals—much smaller than terminal.

STEM: Stout, olive-brown in color with raised light brown lenticels; leaf scars triangular to shield-shape with "V" arrangement of leaf traces.

Aesculus pavia, Red Buckeye, is a small clump-forming, round-topped shrub or small tree reaching 10 to 20′ in height under cultivation and spreading that much or more; can grow 30 to 36′ in the wild; handsome lustrous dark green foliage with no appreciable fall color; flowers in 4 to 8″ long, 1 1/2 to 3″ wide panicles, each flower 1 1/2″ long, with the 4 to 5 petals glandular at the margins, stamens about length of petals, April–May; fruit a flat, rounded, smooth, dehiscent capsule with 1 or 2 lustrous brown seeds, ripening in October; handsome small tree in flower; flowers well in rather dense shade but becomes open; best in full sun; is not prone to severe mildew of *A. hippocastanum* but may contract blotch; best to provide a moist, well-drained soil; loses its leaves early, often by late September; 'Atrosanquinea' has deeper red flowers and 'Humilis' is a low or even prostrate shrub with red flowers in small panicles. Native from Virginia to Florida and Louisiana. Introduced 1711. Zone 4 to 8. There are a number of other red or yellow-red flowered species that are similar to *Aesculus pavia* in certain features.

It is fair to say that the variation in the species is tremendous as it extends from coastal North Carolina to the Edwards Plateau of Texas. I have seen seedling beds of *A. pavia* with both yellow and red flowers. Interestingly 2 to 3-year old plants will flower. Wyatt and Harden, *Brittonia* 9:147–171, 173–195 (1957) mentioned that populations of *A. pavia* from the Edwards Plateau of Texas are uniformly yellow-flowered but otherwise similar to typical red flowered plants. Wyatt and Lodwick, *Brittonia* 33:39–51 (1981) indicate sufficient differences that the yellow flowered population is *A. p.* var. *flavescens;* the red types *A. p.* var. *pavia*. Plants of typical *A. pavia* have red, tubular flowers with exserted stamens and are effectively pollinated by ruby-throated hummingbirds. Plants of var. *flavescens* have yellow, campanulate flowers with included stamens that can be pollinated effectively by large bees.

Aesculus splendens is listed by Rehder as a distinct species and several horticulturists feel strongly about its authenticity. Perhaps the most striking difference is the dense pubescence on the underside of the leaflets that persists until leaf fall. The few plants I have observed had scarlet flowers compared to the red of *A. pavia.* Exists as a 10 to 15′ high shrub or small tree. Hardin includes it with *A. pavia.* Alabama to Mississippi and Louisiana. Introduced 1911. Zone 6 to 9.

 I checked herbarium specimens of *A. discolor* var. *mollis, A. pavia,* and *A. sylvatica.* I could see no consistent difference in leaf characteristics except that *A. sylvatica* is more glabrous and generally has yellow-green flowers. *A. sylvatica* was listed as growing as tall as 30′. *Aesculus pavia* varies from pubescent on the midvein on the underside of the leaf to soft velvety pubescent. I did not find a completely glabrous specimen of *A. pavia.* Size notations on *A. pavia* ranged from 5 to 10′ to 25′. *A. discolor* var. *mollis* has a dense velvety pubescence on the underside of the leaflets, but is otherwise similar to *A. pavia.* It would be difficult for the amateur (me) to distinguish between the pubescent forms of *A. pavia* and *A. d.* var. *mollis.*

Aesculus sylvatica (A. georgiana) — Painted Buckeye
(es′kū-lus sil-vat′i-ka)

LEAVES: Opposite, compound palmate, 5 leaflets, each 4 to 6″ long, 1 1/2 to 2 1/2″ wide, ovate to obovate, tapering at apex and base, finely and often doubly serrate, pubescent in youth finally glabrous or hairy on margins below petiole.

BUDS: Similar to *A. pavia;* imbricate, reddish brown, 3/8 to 1/2″ long, glabrous, tips of scales mucronate.

STEM: Stout, terete, smooth, light gray-brown, glabrous; leaf scars shield shaped, large in relation to stem diameter. Similar to *A. pavia;* it is quite difficult to separate *A. sylvatica* and *A. pavia* by bud and stem characteristics.

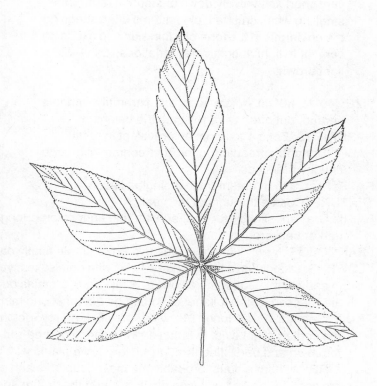

Aesculus sylvatica, Painted Buckeye, has become a cherished horticulural friend since my arrival in Georgia. The plant is abundant in moist woods in the piedmont of Georgia, existing as a (6 to 15′ tall) shrub or small tree in the understory. The leaves emerge in late March–early April in the Athens area and vary from green to a reddish purple. The flowers (bisexual and male) occur together in a 4 to 8″ long panicle during April–May. The panicle is often broader than that of *A. pavia.* Flower color is tremendously variable and ranges from yellow-green, yellow, pink to red, often pink, touches of red and yellow green in the same inflorescence. Fruit set has been minimal on plants in the University Botanical Garden. The leathery, 3-valved, smooth, 1 to 2″ thick capsule contains 1 to 3 shiny dark brown seeds. Prefers a moist, humusy soil in partial shade and makes an excellent naturalizing plant. Found mixed with beech, maple, oak and hickory in the Botanical Garden often on gentle slopes. Virginia to Georgia, west to Tennessee and Alabama. Introduced 1905. Zone 6 to 9.

Ailanthus altissima — Tree of Heaven
(ā-lan′thus al-tis′-ĭ-ma)

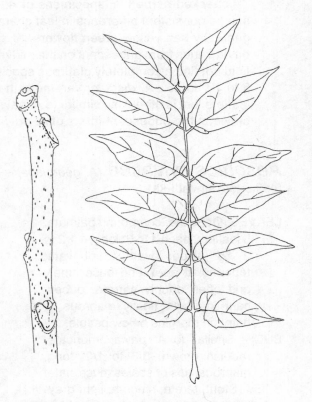

FAMILY: Simaroubaceae

LEAVES: Alternate, pinnately compound, 18 to 24″ long, leaflets—13 to 25, stalked, lance-ovate, 3 to 5″ long, usually truncate at base, finely ciliate, with 2 to 4 coarse teeth near base, glabrous and glaucescent beneath; petiolules—1/4 to 3/4″ long.

BUDS: Terminal-absent, lateral buds relatively small, 1/6″ or less long, half spherical, reddish brown, downy, scales-thick, the 2 opposite lateral scales generally alone showing.

STEM: Stout, yellowish to reddish brown, covered with very short fine velvety down or smooth; rather rank-smelling when crushed; older stems often shedding the epidermis in the form of a thin skin and exposing very fine light longitudinal striations; pith—wide, light brown.

SIZE: 40 to 60′ in height with an extremely variable spread, but often 2/3's to equal the height.

HARDINESS: Zone 4 to 8; not as prevalent in south.

HABIT: Upright, spreading, open and coarse with large chubby branches.

RATE: Fast, 3 to 5′ and more in a single season.

TEXTURE: Coarse throughout the year.

BARK: Grayish, slightly roughened with fine light colored longitudinal streaks in striking contrast to the darker background.

LEAF COLOR: Newly emerging leaves bronze-purple finally dark green in summer, no fall color.

FLOWERS: Dioecious, although some trees with both sexes; yellow-green, borne in 8 to 16″ long panicles in early to mid-June; male flowers of vile odor; females odorless; effect is often lost because flowers are masked by the foliage; of course no one of sound mind will use the plant for flower effect.

FRUIT: Samara, 1 1/2″ long, 1/2″ wide, thin, flat, narrow-oblong, tapering at both ends with one seed in the center; slight twist to fruit; yellow-green to orange-red, effective in late summer, finally changing to brown and persisting through winter; some plants with good red fruit.

CULTURE: Without a doubt probably the most adaptable and pollution tolerant tree available; withstands the soot, grime and pollution of cities better than other species.

DISEASES AND INSECTS: *Verticillium* wilt, shoestring root rot, leaf spots, twig blight and cankers have been reported; verticillium is the most destructive of these pests; none are particularly serious.

LANDSCAPE VALUE: For most landscape conditions it has *no* value as there are too many trees of superior quality; for impossible conditions this tree has a place; selections could be made for good habit, strong wood, better foliage which would make the tree more satisfactory; I once talked with a highway landscape architect who tried to buy *Ailanthus* for use along polluted highways but could not find an adequate supply; I always knew a specialist growing *Ailanthus* could make money! An update on the money potential of *Ailanthus* is in order; in January, 1982 I received a letter from a gentleman who grew *Ailanthus,* advertised in a local paper and did not sell one; he should have grown *Acer griseum.*

CULTIVARS:

'Erythrocarpa'—Pistillate type, with dark green leaves and red fruit.

'Metro'—Handsome confined crown, a male, Wandell introduction.

'Pendulifolia'—Branches erect as in the type but the longer leaves hang downward, rather than being horizontally disposed as in species; have attempted to locate this form to date without success.

PROPAGATION: Seed which I have worked with required no pre-treatment although 60 days in moist medium at 41°F is a recommendation; root pieces will work.

ADDITIONAL NOTES: Since the last edition (1983), abundant *Ailanthus* literature has appeared almost like *Ailanthus* sprouts. There is considerable interest in what makes *Ailanthus* tick. Perhaps the most vocal opponent of the tree was Peter Feret, *J. Arboriculture* 11:361–368 (1985). He stated "...In all the ailanthus seedlings I handled during the course of seed source trials, I never found one without leaf glands, and never saw growth forms or phenological mutants of redeeming horticultural utility. I do not recommend ailanthus as an urban tree, as a species for short rotation biomass production or as a substitute for pines or junipers on droughty sites. When it comes to pollution, I would prefer to search for new plant varieties for those sites than to encumber them with a tree species having as many disadvantageous traits as has ailanthus". Another author posed the question "Arboreal riffraff or ultimate tree?"

NATIVE HABITAT: China, naturalized over much of the United States. Introduced 1784.

RELATED SPECIES:

Picrasma quassioides—India Quassiawood
FAMILY: Simaroubaceae
LEAVES: Alternate, compound pinnate, 10 to 14" long, 9 to 15 leaflets, each 1 3/4 to 4" long, subsessile, ovate to oblong-ovate, acuminate, broad cuneate or nearly rounded at the oblique base, crenate serrate, lustrous dark green above, lighter beneath and glabrous except on midrib when young.

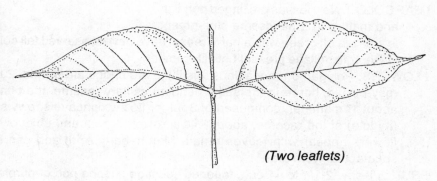

(Two leaflets)

BUDS: Terminal-naked, rich brown, pubescent.
STEM: Coarse, reddish brown, marked by conspicuous lenticels.

Picrasma quassioides, (pi-kraz'mă kwă-zē-oi'dēz), India Quassiawood, is virtually unknown in American gardens and exists in perhaps only a handful of arboreta. The tree develops a rounded outline, eventually growing 20 to 40' high. The rich green summer foliage may turn orange and red in fall. The 1/3" diameter green perfect flowers occur in 6 to 8" long, loose corymbs. The red, pea-sized obovoid berry ripens with the calyx still attached. There is a tree in the Arnold Arboretum which indicates a Zone 6 hardiness rating. The most unique identification feature is the terminal naked bud with two fuzzy brown pubescent primordia slightly clasped like hands in prayer. The tree might hold a future for urban conditions but has never been adequately tested. Distributed in the wild over a wide area from Japan, Korea, through China to the Himalayas. Introduced 1890.

Akebia quinata — Fiveleaf Akebia
(a-kē'bē-ă kwi-nā'ta)

FAMILY: Lardizabalaceae
LEAVES: Alternate, palmately compound, 5 leaflets (sometimes 3 or 4), obovate or elliptic to oblong-obovate, 1 1/2 to 3" long, emarginate, rounded or broad cuneate at base, bluish green above, glaucous beneath; petiolules 1/2" long.
BUDS: Imbricate, glabrous, small, sessile, ovate, with 10 to 12 mucronate scales.

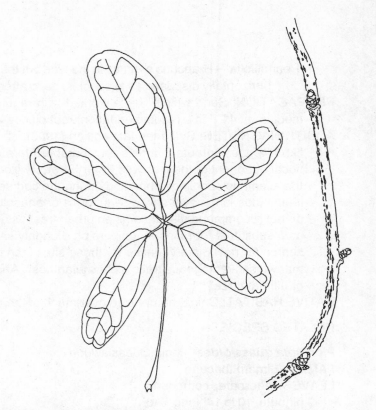

STEM: Slender, rounded, green becoming brown, glabrous, heavily lenticelled, leaf scars with 6 or more traces in a broken ellipse, half elliptic, much raised.

SIZE: 20 to 40′, essentially restricted by the structure upon which it grows.

HARDINESS: Zone 4 to 8, deciduous in northern climates, more evergreen in warm; at Illinois I noticed the plants kept some basal foliage in winter; at Georgia is completely deciduous; literature seems to indicate one thing, the plant does another.

HABIT: Twining vine or a rampant ground cover.

RATE: Fast.

TEXTURE: Medium-fine, a little rougher in winter.

LEAF COLOR: New leaves are tinged purplish and mature to a handsome blue-green; leaves die off green with a hard freeze; have never observed fall color; leafs out by early–mid March in Georgia, foliage present until December.

FLOWERS: Polygamo-monoecious, pistillate are chocolate-purple, 2 to 5 together, staminate, lighter rosy-purple, borne in the same pendent axillary raceme, the pistillate at the ends (outside) and about 1″ diameter, composed of 3 rather fleshy concave showy sepals, the staminate at the end (middle) of the raceme, about 1/4″ across, fragrant and uniquely attractive on close inspection; flowers appear with leaves in late March–early April and can be lost among the foliage; not spectacular from afar.

FRUIT: Fleshy, 2 1/4 to 4″ long, fattened sausage shaped pod of purple-violet color and covered with a waxy bloom, inside is a central pulpy whitish core with numerous imbedded blackish seeds; ripens in September–October; for best fruit set hand pollination has been suggested but I have observed fruit set at the Arnold Arboretum without any man-made influences; it could be that the plant is self-sterile or male flowers do not open at the same time the gummy stigmatic surface is receptive; Dr. J.C. Raulston has assembled a tremendous collection of species and cultivars of *Akebia* at the North Carolina State Arboretum which are displayed on a pergola at the entrance to the garden; in late October I observed abundant fruit set, more so than on any other plants, that might suggest cross fertility or vines that open over a staggered period; fruits are supposedly edible.

CULTURE: Transplant from container, extremely fast to establish; adaptable to drought and moisture, sun or shade, displays excellent landscape toughness, major problem is vigor for it can consume a piece of landscape real estate in short order.

DISEASES AND INSECTS: None serious.

LANDSCAPE VALUE: Excellent fast cover but seldom seen in typical landscape situations; good choice for trellises, arbors, pergolas, fences and other structures, will require pruning to keep it in bounds.

CULTIVARS:

'Alba'—Quite a departure from the species, this form offers white flowers and white fruits.

'Rosea'—More lavender or light purple than pink; much lighter colored compared to species.

PROPAGATION: Softwood cuttings will root readily, use 1000 to 3000 ppm IBA-solution; division is also a possibility; seed requires a cold moist stratification for one month although 30% germination occurred with freshly sown seed.

NATIVE HABITAT: Central China to Korea and Japan. Introduced 1845.

RELATED SPECIES

Akebia × pentaphylla (a-kē′bē-â̂ pen-ta-fil′á) is a hybrid between *A. quinata* and *A. trifoliate* with 3 to 5 leafleats intermediate in characteristics between the two parents.

Akebia trifoliata—Three-leaflet Akebia
(a-kē′bē-ă trī-fō-li-ā′ta)

LEAVES: Alternate, compound palmate, 3-leaflets, each 1 1/2 to 4″ long, broad ovate to ovate, emarginate, rounded or truncate at base, undulate or irregularly and shallowly lobed, sometimes entire, bluish green above, glaucescent or greenish beneath, the leaflets stalked with the terminal leaflet stalk three times those of the laterals.

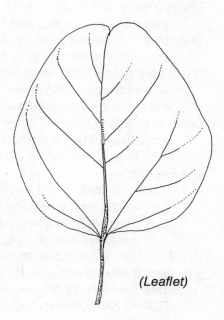

Akebia trifoliata, Three-leaflet Akebia, is seldom seen in American gardens but is a worthy twining climber, possibly less cold-hardy than *A. quinata.* The flowers are similar to *A. quinata* with the 3/4 to 1″ diameter pistillate maroon-red flowers and the pale purple, smaller numerous stamens on short 1 1/2″ long pedicels, March–April. The sausage-shaped, 3 to 5″ long, 1 1/2 to 2 1/2″ diameter pale violet pod ripens in fall and splits from the base to reveal rows of black seeds embedded in the white pulp. Same general landscape uses as *A. quinata.* Not quite as vigorous or high climbing. Central China to Japan. Introduced before 1890. Zone 5 to 8.

(Leaflet)

Albizia julibrissin — Albizia, also called Silk-tree and Mimosa
(al-biz′i-a jū-li-bri′sin)

FAMILY: Fabaceae
LEAVES: Alternate, bipinnately compound, to 20″ long, with 10 to 25 pinnae, each with 40 to 60 leaflets, leaflets falcate, oblong, very oblique, 1/4 to 1/2″ long, ciliate and sometimes pubescent on midribs below, often does not leaf out until late May or early June.
BUDS: Terminal absent, laterals with 2 to 3 scales, small, rounded, brownish.
STEM: Slender, greenish, heavily lenticelled, glabrous, angled.

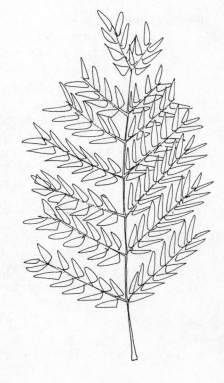

SIZE: 20 to 35′ in height; spread similar or greater.
HARDINESS: Zone 6 to 9, based on considerable observation and laboratory hardiness testing, temperatures below −5°F for any period of time will result in injury.
HABIT: Vase-shaped, often multiple stemmed, broad-spreading, forming a flat-topped crown.
RATE: Fast.
TEXTURE: Fine in leaf; medium in winter.

BARK: On larger branches and trunks relatively smooth, gray-brown.

LEAF COLOR: late to leaf out, dark green at maturity, no fall color as leaves die off green when killed by frost.

FLOWERS: Light to deep pink, the numerous thread-like, 1″ or more long pink stamens create a brush-like effect; flowers borne in slender-peduncled heads in May, June, July and August.

FRUIT: Pod, 5 to 7″ long, 1″ wide, light gray-brown, thin, September–October, and persisting into winter and often until the following spring, usually becoming uglier with age.

CULTURE: Transplants readily, extremely adaptable, will withstand drought, high pH and soil salinity; withstands excessive wind; flowers best in full sun.

DISEASES AND INSECTS: Unfortunately very susceptible to a vascular wilt disease; this disease seems to be widespread and numerous plants in the south show evidence of infection; often killed to ground and develops shoots from roots creating a mass of suckers; webworm can be highly destructive.

LANDSCAPE VALUE: Not a quality plant because of insect and disease problems; sets prodigious quantities of fruits and effectively seeds itself in waste and road-side situations; foliage and flowers provide a tropical effect; unless a wilt-immune clone is found I would avoid using the species.

CULTIVARS:

'Charlotte' and 'Tryon'—Wilt resistant clones, but undocumented reports indicate these are not without problems; doubtfully available in commerce.

'E.H. Wilson' ('Rosea')—Whether or not these two are synonyms is a moot question but they (it) show increased hardiness to perhaps –15°F.

PROPAGATION: Seed dormancy is due to a hard seed coat and acid scarification for 30 minutes permits germination to ensue; root cuttings collected in spring will produce shoots which can be easily rooted [See Fordham, *PIPPS* 16:190–193 (1966)].

ADDITIONAL NOTES: Very popular throughout the southern states; its day of reckoning has come due to the wilt disease; as one drives along Interstate 75 through Tennessee and Georgia, *A. julibrissin* is everywhere in evidence; many plants survive only as root sprouts, because the main portion of the tree has been killed by the disease.

NATIVE HABITAT: Iran to central China. Introduced 1745.

Alnus glutinosa — Common Alder, also called Black or European Alder
(al′nus glū-tĭ-nō′sa)

FAMILY: Betulaceae

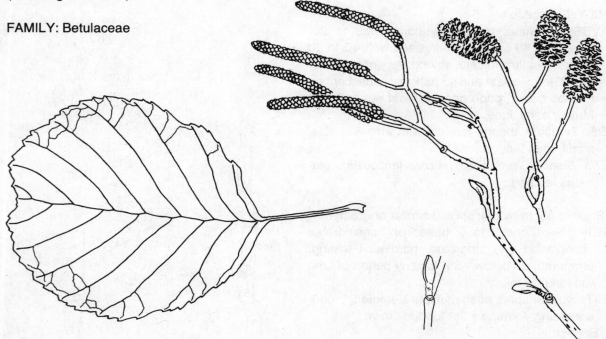

LEAVES: Alternate, simple, 2 to 4″ long, 3 to 4″ wide, oval or orbicular to suborbicular, usually broad cuneate, very gummy when young, rounded or emarginate at apex, coarsely and doubly serrate, dark green, glabrous above, axillary tufts beneath, 6 to 8 vein pairs; petiole 1/2 to 1″ long.

BUDS: Stalked, 1/4 to 1/2″ long, reddish or reddish purple, valvate.

STEM: Glabrous, green-brown, finally brown, pith-small, three sided, continuous.

FRUIT: Nutlet, borne in persistent 1/3 to 1/2″ long oval strobiles, on 1/2 to 1″ long peduncles; the long peduncle permits separation from *A. incana.*

SIZE: 40 to 60′ in height with a spread of 20 to 40′, can grow to 90 to 100′, often shrubby in inhospitable situations.

HARDINESS: Zone 3 to 7.

HABIT: Often weak pyramidal outline and at other times developing an ovoid or oblong head of irregular proportions; small trees show a pyramidal habit; often grown multistemmed and, in fact, has more ornamental appeal when cultured in this fashion.

RATE: Fast in youth, tends to slow down when abundant flowering and fruiting occur, although will average 24 to 30″ per year over a 20 year period; the wood is not as weak and brittle as *Acer saccharinum,* Silver Maple.

TEXTURE: Medium in leaf and in winter.

BARK: Young bark is often a lustrous gray-green or greenish brown and changes to polished brown with age.

LEAF COLOR: Dark glossy green in summer, fall color does not occur as the leaves abscise green or brown; I have read British literature which reported that fall color may be a good yellow; the foliage is extremely handsome and little troubled by insects or diseases.

FLOWERS: Monoecious, reddish brown male flowers in 2 to 4″ long catkins, 3 to 5 together; rather handsome but seldom noticed by most individuals; purplish females borne in a distinct egg-shaped strobile, March.

FRUIT: A small winged nutlet borne in a persistent 1/3 to 2/3″ long egg-shaped woody strobile; maturing in October–November and persisting through winter; brown through late fall and winter.

CULTURE: Transplants readily; prefers moist or wet soil but performs well in dry soils; full sun or partial shade; seems to be tolerant of acid or slightly alkaline soils; prune in winter or early spring; if used along waterways will seed in along the banks and eventually cover large areas; I have seen the species growing submerged in the water; for extremely wet areas the tree has distinct possibilities; a nitrogen fixing species; does not perform well in the heat of the south.

DISEASES AND INSECTS: Powdery mildew attacks the female strobili but this is rarely serious, cankers can be a problem, leaf rust—rarely serious, woolly alder aphid, alder flea beetle, alder lace bug, leaf miner, and tent caterpillar; have seen a few serious tent caterpillar infestations.

LANDSCAPE VALUE: Perhaps for difficult, wet sites such as those encountered along highways, in parks and other large areas; does well in infertile areas and has the ability to fix atmospheric nitrogen; widely used throughout Europe; have seen its roots submerged yet plants appear to thrive; to my mind a better plant than many willows and poplars but not as popular (no pun intended); as a biomass source the alders would make good choices; of 35 species, 33 have been reported to fix nitrogen.

CULTIVARS:

'Aurea'—Leaves golden yellow, fading to green with time, quite handsome in May–June especially as seen in the English landscape; would probably succeed in more northern locations in the U.S.; not a vigorous grower; introduced around 1860.

'Charles Howlett'—Variously shaped and variegated leaves, yellow to orange streaked bark, slightly less vigorous than the species; discovered in Chandler's Ford, Hampshire, England in 1982.

'Imperialis'—A form with deeply and finely cut light green leaves; much more prominently incised than 'Laciniata', the sinuses cut more than halfway to the midrib; it is fair to say that in youth the tree is ungainly but I have observed several handsome specimens in England that inspire me to try one in my garden; behind the Spread Eagle Hotel in Midhurst, England are several beautiful specimens.

'Laciniata'—Leaves cut and lobed but not to the degree of 'Imperialis'; lobes not prominently serrated and almost triangular in outline; a vigorous form growing 50 to 70′ high; in existence probably before 1819.

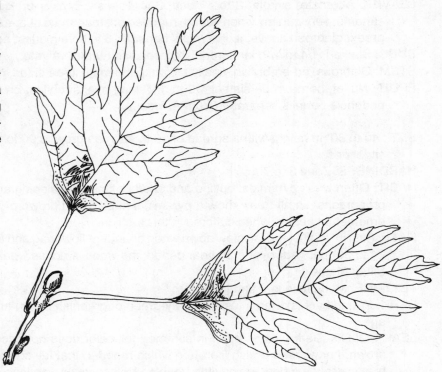

'Pyramidalis' ('Fastigiata')—Good looking form of upright columnar habit, 40 to 50′, resembling Lombardy Popular; definitely should be used more extensively; occasionally seen in midwestern arboreta but not common in commerce; might make a suitable substitute for *Populus nigra* 'Italica'.

PROPAGATION: The following applies to all the alders discussed herein. Seed requires a cold period and 3 months at 41°F for fall sowing should suffice; seeds are similar to birch and have a low survival rate; strobiles should be collected as they begin to change from green to brown; there is some indication that fresh seed will germinate without a cold treatment; once the seeds are dried then moist-cold becomes necessary; information on cutting propagation is scant but June and July collected cuttings treated with 8000 ppm IBA have been rooted at a 20 to 40% rate; cultivars are usually grafted onto the species.

NATIVE HABITAT: *Alnus glutinosa* is indigenous to Europe (including Britain), western Asia and northern Africa; long cultivated; escaped from cultivation in the United States and is frequently observed forming pure stands along waterways.

RELATED SPECIES:

Alnus cordata—Italian Alder
(al′nus kor-dā′tă)

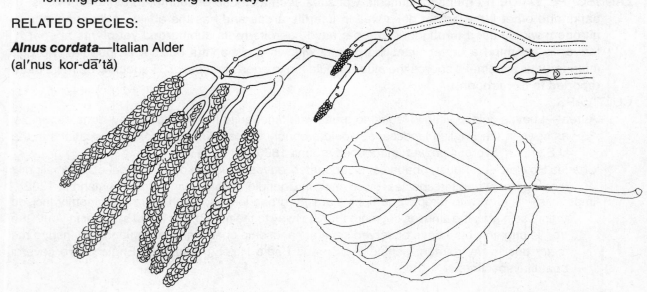

LEAVES: Alternate, simple, 2 to 4″ long, 3/4 to as much in width, broad-ovate to roundish, abruptly acuminate, cordate at base, finely serrate, glabrous above, lustrous dark green, lighter beneath with brownish tufts in axils of veins; petiole 1/2 to 1 1/2″ long, slender, glabrous.

FRUIT: Large, egg-shaped, 1 to 1 1/4″ long, 5/8 to 3/4″ wide, erect, woody strobile, often occurring in 3's; persistent and offering a consistent identification feature; the largest fruit of the cultivated alders.

Alnus cordata, Italian Alder, forms a 30 to 50′(70′) high pyramidal to pyramidal rounded tree. Resembles to a degree Littleleaf Linden in outline. In many respects, from a distance, it resembles the Common Pear in appearance. Bark is a glistening brown in youth. Thrives in infertile, dry, high pH soils but is most at home near water. Perhaps the most beautiful of the alders for landscape use but little known and grown. Have seen it thriving in midwest. Corsica and southern Italy. 1820. Zone 5 to 7.

Alnus incana—White or Gray Alder
(al′nus in-kān′-a)

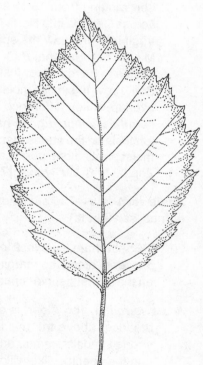

LEAVES: Alternate, simple, 2 to 4″ long, 1 1/4 to 2 1/4″ wide, ovate, oval or obovate, apex acute, base rounded or cuneate, double serrate and usually slightly lobulate, dull green above, impressed veins, grayish beneath, 9 to 12 vein pairs; petiole 1/2 to 1″ long, pubescent.

BUDS: Distinctly stalked, 1/4 to 1/2″ long, reddish, more or less whitened with fine down, slightly sticky within.

STEM: Slender, finely downy or glabrous, grayish brown, hairy towards tips especially of fruiting twigs.

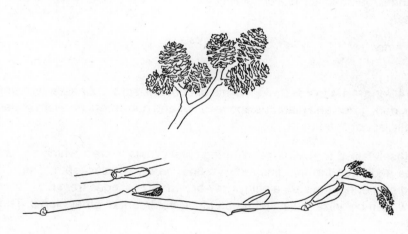

Alnus incana, White or Gray Alder, is a large pyramidal-oval tree 40 to 60′ in height with dull dark green foliage. Next to *Alnus glutinosa* the commonest of the alders and is useful for planting in cold (Zone 2), wet places. It is closely allied to *Alnus rugosa* and, at one time, the Speckled Alder was listed as *Alnus incana* var. *americana.* There are several cultivars of *Alnus incana* which are more common in the landscape than the species:

'Aurea'—Leaves are yellow, young stems are reddish yellow and remain so throughout the winter, young catkins orangish; have seen in England during September and the yellow leaf color is essentially past but the orange male catkins are quite distinct.

'Laciniata'—The handsomest of the many cut-leaved types with the blade divided into 6 or 8 pairs of lobes reaching 2/3's or more of the way to the midrib, leaves light green; apparently there are many cut-leaf forms of the species all varying in degrees of fineness.

'Pendula'—A fine form with pendulous branches and gray-green leaves; leaves are actually dark green above, gray-breen below; the branches decidedly pendulous and the entire tree quite attractive; large specimen in the Palmengarten, Frankfurt, West Germany, that makes the trip justifiable.

This species can be distinguished from *A. glutinosa* by the shape and color of the leaves. Europe and the Caucasus; long cultivated in Europe; not common in America. Zone 2 to 6.

Alnus rugosa—Speckled Alder
(al'nus rū-gō'sa)

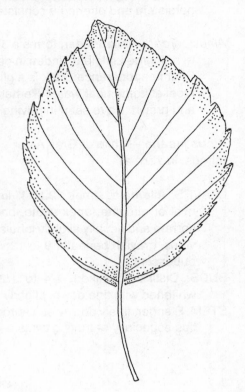

LEAVES: Alternate, simple, 2 to 4 1/2″ long, ovate, acute or obtuse, cuneate, with a row of 2 distinctly different-sized teeth along the margin, dull dark green, glabrous, and somewhat wrinkled on the upper surface, paler and covered with rusty-red hairs below; petiole short, stout, smooth, white dotted.

Alnus rugosa, Speckled Alder, is usually a coarse shrub or small tree ranging from 15 to 25′ tall. It occurs in a broad band across Canada into North Dakota south to West Virginia and Virginia. I first saw the species along the Concord River in Minuteman National Park in Concord, MA...or did I? There seems to be much confusion between this and *A. serrulata.* Both grow in similar moist habitats and their native ranges overlap. A key difference is the more even serrations of *A. serrulata. Alnus rugosa* has distinct 1/6 to 1/3″ long whitish lenticels on the stems; hence, the name Speckled Alder. For moist areas along ponds and streambanks it is a possibility. Zone 3 to 6. Cultivated 1769.

Alnus serrulata—Tag or Hazel Alder
(al'nus ser-ū-lā'ta)

LEAVES: Alternate, simple, 2 to 4″ long, 1 1/4 to 2 1/2″ wide, ovate or obovate, acute, cuneate, with uniform fine teeth along the margin, dark green and glabrous above, paler and pubescent beneath especially on the veins; petiole-smooth, about 1″ long.

Alnus serrulata, Tag Alder, is closely allied to *A. rugosa,* differing chiefly in its leaves, which are usually broadest above the middle and have the margins set with fine, nearly regular teeth. The habit is strongly multistemmed and suckering, the bark a shiny gray-brown. Size ranges from 6 to 10′ to 20′ and the species, like willow, can colonize moist soil areas to the detriment of other plants. The 1/2″ long, 1/4″ wide oval cone-shaped fruit persists through the winter months. The fruits are smaller than those of *A. rugosa.* Neither this nor *A. rugosa* will take the nursery industry by storm. In fact, I do not know of a nurseryman that grows either. Abundant in southern states along streams and lakes. In my mind there is little difference between this and the above species. Very beautiful in February–March when the yellow-

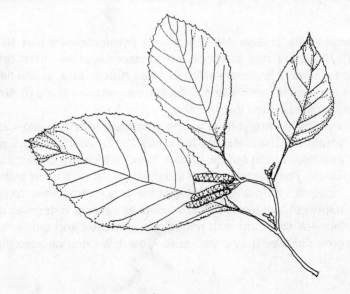

brown catkins are waving in the early spring breezes. Zone (4)5 to 9. Maine south to Florida and Louisiana.

ADDITIONAL NOTES: None of the alder species mentioned here are widely cultivated in the United States. They make excellent plants for use along stream banks and in poor soil areas. There is considerable interest in their potential for biomass and subsequent energy production. Interestingly, *Alnus* has been tissue culture propagated by researchers at the University of Minnesota. In early spring, as their elongating yellow-brown catkins sway with the warm breezes, they provide interesting color to an otherwise drab landscape. *Alnus rubra,* Red Alder, a west coast species, makes a large and quite beautiful tree. I have seen large trees in Muir Woods, California that were magnificent. The West is endowed with a number of other species including *A. sinuata,* Sitka Alder, *A. rhombifolia,* White Alder, *A. oblongifolia,* Arizona Alder, and *A. tenuifolia,* Mountain Alder. They are beyond the scope of this book and Elias, *Trees of North America,* provides excellent coverage. Three species, *Alnus Maritima, A. nepalensis, A. nitida* flower in autumn; the others before or with the leaves in spring.

Amelanchier arborea — Downy Serviceberry also called Juneberry, Shadbush, Servicetree or Sarvis-tree

(am-el-ang′-kē-er ar-bor′-ē-a)

FAMILY: Rosaceae

LEAVES: Alternate, simple, generally obovate, less often ovate, elliptic or oblong, 1 to 3″ long, acute or acuminate, usually cordate at base, sharply serrate nearly or quite at base, when young densely tomentose beneath, less so above, tomentum usually partly persistent, when unfolding grayish pubescent; petiole 3/8 to 1 1/4″ (1 1/2″).

BUDS: Terminal-present, 5 to 7 scaled, laterals of similar size, 1/3 to 1/2″ long, imbricate, narrowly ovate to conical, sharp pointed, greenish yellow, more or less tinged with reddish purple, glabrous or with white silky hairs at apex and edges of scales, mostly appressed; tend to show a slight spiraling; color is higly variable; variable from green to maroon.

STEM: Slender, olive-green to red-brown often covered with a gray skin, generally smooth, glabrous, with slight taste of bitter almonds; pith green, small.

SIZE: 15 to 25′ in height with a variable spread; can grown to 40′ but this is rare under cultivation.

HARDINESS: Zone 4 to 9.

HABIT: Multistemmed large shrub or small tree with a rounded crown of many small branches; often dissipates in old age to a rounded form; beautiful in winter dress with an understated elegance.

RATE: Medium, 9 to 10′ in 5 to 8 year period.

TEXTURE: Medium-fine in leaf; medium in winter.

BARK: Grayish, smooth but streaked with longitudinal fissures, often with a reddish cast, very ornamental; in extreme age becoming ridged and furrowed and scaly.

LEAF COLOR: Grayish tomentose when emerging and gradually changing to a medium to dark green in summer; fall color can vary from yellow to apricot-orange to dull, deep dusty red; one of our finest small trees for fall coloration; may color and drop early in the fall.

FLOWERS: Perfect, white, borne in pendulous racemes, 2 to 4″ long, mid to late March in Athens, GA, mid to late April in Boston, MA, about the time the leaves are emerging and about 1/2 normal size; effective for 4 to 7 days depending on weather; very ornamental but briefly persistent; weakly malodorous.

FRUIT: Berry-like pome, orange-shaped, 1/4 to 1/3″ diameter, changing from green to red and finally to purplish black, bloomy, slightly sweetish, and birds love them; ripens in June; actually matures over a 3 to 4 week period and must be picked before birds clean the plant; ripe fruits are *better* than highbush blueberries; I have had serviceberry pie and it ranks in the first order of desserts.

CULTURE: Transplant balled and burlapped into moist, well drained, acid soil; will tolerate full sun or partial shade; in the wild commonly found along borders of woodlands, streambanks and fence rows in open country, although also occurs on hillsides and mountain slopes where conditions are drier; from my own observation I would expect the Amelanchiers to perform well in many types of soils; not particularly pollution tolerant; rarely require pruning.

DISEASES AND INSECTS: Rust (cedar serviceberry rust, comparable to cedar apple and hawthorn rusts), witches' broom caused by a fungus, leaf blight, fire blight, powdery mildews, fruit rot, leaf miner, borers, pear leaf blister mite, pear slug sawfly and willow scurfy scale. Have observed reasonable amount of leaf spot which disfigures leaves and causes early defoliation; many of the newer cultivars are free of any serious insects and diseases; over the years I have been advised that fireblight was a problem; interestingly in 1988, the Athens–Atlanta area suffered the worst fireblight on pears, apples and other rosaceous plants in my 10 years in the area; serviceberries on campus and at the Botanical Garden were essentially free of infestation; a local nurseryman had fireblight on 'Cumulus' but this could have been related to the high nutritional status of the plants.

LANDSCAPE VALUE: Very pleasing in a naturalistic planting and probably used to best advantage there; blends in well on the edges of woodlands near ponds and streambanks; blends into shrub borders especially with evergreen background; serviceberries are now used in all facets of landscaping but their most effective use is as described above.

CULTIVARS: In the previous edition no selections were listed except under *A. alnifolia* and *A. laevis* and these were of no significance in the midwest, east and south. In the past seven years the entire scene has changed with at least eight new introductions and a few older ones that are being offered in commerce. They are presented here in alphabetical order with the suspected parentage. Unfortunately, *Amelanchier* taxonomy is not clear and I have pieced the information together and will be pleased to entertain other observations and ideas.

'Autumn Brilliance'—An *A.* × *grandiflora* selection. Bill Wandell, Urbana, IL has introduced a number of excellent shade tree selections as well as the amelanchier with the poetic name 'Autumn Brilliance'. It will reach 20 to 25' at maturity. White flowers, edible fruits, clean summer foliage, persistent leaves and brilliant red fall color are notable attributes. Light gray bark, attractive in winter; grows faster and will produce 6 to 8' high heavily branched plant from an 18 to 24" liner in 3 years. Hardy to –35°F.

'Autumn Sunset'—A particularly fine form of *A. arborea,* or perhaps *A.* × *grandiflora.* I selected it in 1986 from seedling plants on the University of Georgia campus, Athens. The habit is rounded with a strong single trunk. The plant's flowers and summer foliage are typical of *A. arborea,* and the principal attributes are superior leaf retention and rich, pumpkin-orange fall color. Fall color in the Athens area develops from late October to mid-November and its consistent from year to year. 'Autumn Sunset' displays excellent heat and drought tolerance and did not drop a leaf in the worst drought of the century (1986). The plant was probably grown from a southern seed provenance. Hardiness tests indicate it will tolerate –24°F or lower. If adequately cold hardy, it could be one of the best amelanchiers. I suspect its ultimate size will average 20 to 25'.

'Ballerina'—A selection of *A.* × *grandiflora* made by the Experiment Station at Boskoop, Netherlands, from plants sent as *A. ovalis* by Hillier and Sons, Winchester, England. It is an upright shrub or small tree with spreading branches. The young leaves are broad elliptic, finely saw-toothed, 2 to 3" long and 1 1/4 to 1 1/2" wide, bronze-colored, essentially without pubescence. They turn glossy dark green in summer and finally purple-bronze in fall. The pure white flowers average 1 to 1 1/8" in diameter and occur 6 to 8 together in a 3 to 5" long fleecy raceme that is more or less pendent. The 3/8 to 1/2" diameter fruit is bright red, turning purplish black when ripe. It is tender and sweet. This selection will grow 15 to 20' high and is hardy in Zone 4. One source indicated this is a hybrid with *A. laevis* and the other parent unknown. Named in 1980. Several American nurseries are growing this selection; a southeastern nurseryman reported the fall color as brick red; essentially free of fire blight.

'Cole'—A designation I will use for lack of a better name. Dr. Ed Hasselkus, University of Wisconsin, mentioned that this selection of *A.* × *grandiflora* has exceptional red fall color. The Cole Nursery

Co., Circleville, OH grew, but did not name it. At least one nursery in the U.S. (Briggs Nursery, Olympia, WA) has the plant and will be producing it through tissue culture.

'Cumulus'—An introduction from Princeton Nurseries, Princeton, NJ. According to Dr. Hasselkus, this is a selection of *A. laevis*. It grows 20 to 30' high, 15 to 20' wide, and is hardy in Zone 4. It has fleecy white flowers in spring and bright yellowish to orange-scarlet fall color. Plants I have observed displayed a distinct upright-oval outline in youth, which would make this form useful for street tree plantings or where lateral branch spread must be restricted. Unfortunately, 'Cumulus' has been grafted or budded in the past, and several plants I have observed had suckers developing from the rootstock. Supposedly less prone to suckers than other forms. Fire blight was devastating during the 1988 growing season in the southeastern U.S.

'Forest Prince'—A × *grandiflora* selection with clean, healthy summer foliage and good orange-red fall color; pure white flowers offer a billowy appearance, opening over the length of the the stems instead of at the tip; a Klehm Nursery introduction.

'Princess Diana'—A selection of *A.* × *grandiflora* from the garden of Tom Watson's parents in Milwaukee, WI. Abundant white flowers, clean foliage, 3/8" diameter edible fruits and outstanding red fall color (appearing in early October in Cambridge, WI), provide superlative ornamental traits. The habit can be multi- or single-stemmed; plants from tissue culture develop the multistemmed habit. Watson estimates 25' by 15 to 20' for the mature landscape size. Plants will flower in their third year out of tissue culture. I have seen photographs of fall color and found a triple take necessary to assure myself that the color was as good as the print. This form is hardy to at least −35°F. Report from Galen Gates, Chicago Botanic Garden, indicates this form has not fall colored as well as the original plant.

'Prince Charles'—An *A. laevis* form that flowers ahead of the leaves, thus offering a prominent display. The bronzy red new foliage matures to a pleasant green and develops orange-red fall color. Again, the 3/8" diameter fruits are edible. This is an upright form (probably maturing about 25' by 15'), selected from a number of *A. laevis* that Mr. Watson and Dr. Ed Hasselkus, were evaluating. The final selection was a plant growing in the University of Wisconsin Arboretum.

'Prince William'—Probably a hybrid, with *A. canadensis* as one parent. The habit is shrubby, like that of a typical *A. canadensis,* with landscape size approximating 8' or possibly taller by 6' wide. The emerging leaves are reddish tinged (suggesting *A. laevis* parentage) developing a rich glossy green and finally an orange-red in fall. The edible fruit averages about 1/2" in diameter. Plants may flower the second year out of tissue culture. This form was selected in the Madison, WI area and is hardy to −25 to −30°F.

'Robin Hill'—Grows 20 to 30' high by 12 to 15' wide, and is hardy in Zone 4. It is another *A.* × *grandiflora* form, but the pink color resides in the buds and fades as the flowers unfurl. The color is intense in cool weather but fades rapidly if the weather is hot and dry at flowering time, yellow to red fall color, good tree form.

'Rubescens'—Grows 20 to 25' tall and is hardy in Zone 4. It is another *A.* × *grandiflora* form, which arose as a seedling in Seneca Park, Rochester, NY. It has been in cultivation since 1920. The flowers are purplish pink in bud and open to a light pink. In my forays through the Arnold Arboretum, I chanced upon this most handsome form. With the renewed interest in amelanchiers, enterprising nurserymen should resurrect this clone. In England, this form is described as developing excellent autumn color.

'Springtime'—A compact, 12' tall selection of *A. canadensis;* provides a graceful column of white flowers; supposedly has brilliant fall color but no mention was made of what color; introduced by Lake County Nursery Exchange, Perry, Ohio.

'Strata'—A form of *A.* × *grandiflora* selected by Dr. Hasselkus because of its strong horizontal branching. It is in the University of Wisconsin Arboretum and was originally bought as a seedling from Tures and Sons Nursery in Kingston, IL. The fall color is said to have "tinges of orange".

'Tradition'—A strong tree form with a central leader and excellent branching habit, showy white flowers, heavy fruiting, fall color a blaze of orange and red; grows to 25' tall; listed as *A. canadensis,* but is probably a selection of one of the other species, Lake County introduction.

PROPAGATION: Cold stratification for most species is recommended; 90 to 120 days at 41°F in moist medium would suffice; tissue culture has opened the floodgates for new introductions and Knight Hollow Nursery (Dr. Deborah McCown), Madison, WI and Briggs Nursery (Mr. Bruce Briggs), Olympia, WA, have been successful. For specific tissue culture recipes see Dirr and Heuser, 1987. In the past I have had miserable success with cuttings, but have listened to many people and have developed a reasonably safe procedure. Timing is important and cuttings should be taken when the growth extension has ceased, the end leaf is maturing and the stem tissue is firming. Over the past three years, 3000 to 10000 ppm KIBA-quick dip has produced good results, May 12, 1988 cuttings of 'Autumn Sunset', 10000 ppm KIBA quick dip, peat:perlite, mist resulted in 72% rooting; results have been as high as 96%; leave cuttings in the bed or rooting cells, take through an overwintering period and sell preferably as 2-year-old liners; overwintering losses can be a problem especially if cuttings are transplanted immediately after rooting.

NATIVE HABITAT: Main to Iowa, south to northern Florida and Louisiana. Introduced about 1746.

RELATED SPECIES:

Amelanchier alnifolia—Saskatoon Serviceberry

LEAVES: Alternate, simple, 1 to 2 1/2″ long, 1 to 1 1/2″ wide, broad-oval to suborbicular, rounded to slightly indented at apex, rounded to heart-shaped at base, sharply and coarsely toothed especially on the upper one-half of the margins, pale to dark green above, paler beneath, glabrous; petiole—1/2″ to 1″ long, pubescent or glabrous.

Amelanchier alnifolia, (am-el-ang′-kē-er al-ni-fō′lē-a), Saskatoon Serviceberry, deserves mention because of its development for commercial fruit production. It is closely allied to *A. florida* and much confused with that species. It is distinguished by the smaller flowers (3/4″ diameter) and the thicker, rounder leaves. It is also smaller in habit but according to the literature ranges from 3 to 18′ in height. The 1/3 to 1/2″ diameter berries are bluish purple when ripe (July), juicy and edible. Prairie Indians mixed it with buffalo meat and fat to make pemmican, their principal winter food. It tolerates harsh climates and alkaline soil. 'Regent' is a compact shrub with excellent foliage; 'Success' produces an abundance of fruit. Native to Great Plains from Manitoba and Saskatchewan to Nebraska. Cultivated 1918. Zone 4 to 5.

Amelanchier asiatica—Asian Serviceberry

LEAVES: Alternate, simple, 1 1/2 to 3″ long, ovate to elliptic-oblong, acute, rounded to subcordate at the base, finely serrate along the margin, densely woolly when young.

Amelanchier asiatica, (am-el-ang′-kē-er ā-shi-at′i-ka), Asian Serviceberry, is a tree of very graceful form growing from 15 to 25′ (40′) high; flowers are white, fragrant, and borne about 2 to 3 weeks after *A arborea* when the leaves are about full size; fruit is purple-black, edible, about 1/3″ diameter. Native to China, Korea, and Japan. Zone 5. Winter buds are a very deep red and quite different in that respect from most of our native types.

Amelanchier canadensis—Shadblow Serviceberry, Thicket Serviceberry
(am-el-ang′kē-er kan-a-den′sis)

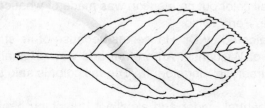
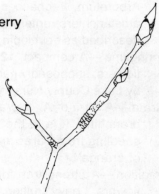

LEAVES: Alternate, simple, elliptic to oblong, 1 1/2 to 2 1/2″ long, 1/2 to 1 1/4″ wide, rounded, rarely cordate, finely and uniformly toothed, sometimes entire near base, woolly when young ultimately becoming glabrous.

BUDS: Imbricate, slender, conical, 1/4 to 3/8″ long, 5 to 7-scaled, greenish to reddish purple, some pubescence often evident under edges of scales, outside of scales glabrous.

STEM: Slender, brown with gray onion-skin effect, glabrous, small lenticels; pith-solid, green, small.

HABIT: Upright, suckering, tightly multistemmed shrub; distinctly different in habit from *A. arborea* and *A. laevis* with which it is often confused.

Amelanchier canadensis, Shadblow Serviceberry, is often confused with *A. arborea* and, in fact, the two are used interchangeably in the nursery trade. *A. canadensis* as now understood is a shrub with erect stems, spreading by means of sucker growths from the base, 6 to 20′ tall, occurring in bogs and swamps from Maine to South Carolina along the coast; the white flowers are borne in erect, compact, 2 to 3″ long racemes in late March on the Georgia Campus and the petals are more distinctly and uniformly obovate than in *A. arborea* or *A. laevis* and somewhat shorter, 3/5″ long; fruit is black, juicy and sweet. This species flowers about one week after *A. arborea.* The fall color is often yellow and gold but I have seen specimens with sprinklings of orange and red. Zone 3 to 7 (8).

Amelanchier florida—Pacific Serviceberry
(am-el-ang′-kē-er flor′-i-da)

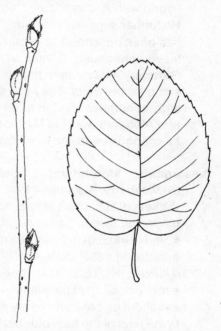

LEAVES: Alternate, simple, broad-oval to ovate, 3/4 to 1 1/2″ long, truncate or subcordate at base, coarsely and sharply toothed above the middle, rarely below, quite glabrous or slightly floccose-tomentose at first.

BUDS: Ovoid to ellipsoidal, acute or acuminate, dark chestnut-brown, glabrous or puberulous, 1/4 to 3/4″ long, scales of the inner ranks ovate, acute, brightly colored, coated with pale silky hairs.

STEM: Slender, pubescent when they first appear, bright red-brown and usually glabrous during their first season, darker second year, ultimately dark gray-brown.

BARK: Light brown, slightly tinged with red, smooth or slightly fissured.

Amelanchier florida, Pacific Serviceberry, is a shrub of erect stems to 10′ or more high or a small tree; flowers are white, about 3/4 to 1 1/4″ across, borne 5 to 15 together in erect racemes; fruit purplish black, juicy and edible although the birds do not seem to bother it like the fruit of other species. There was a specimen on the Illinois campus and the flowers never compared with *A. arborea, A.* × *grandiflora* or *A. laevis.* In fact they paled by comparison. Also, the fruits often dried on the plant like raisins. Fresh fruits were not tasty. Have seen *A. florida* listed as a synonym of *A. alnifolia.* Southern Alaska to Idaho and Northern California introduced 1826. Zone 2.

Amelanchier × *grandiflora,* (am-el-ang′-kē-er × gran-di-flō′ra), Apple Serviceberry, is a hybrid between *A. arborea* × *A. laevis* with young leaves purplish and pubescent. The flowers are larger, on longer more slender racemes, tinged pink in bud. Cultivated since 1870. Zone 4 to 9.

Amelanchier laevis—Allegheny Serviceberry
(am-el-ang′-kē-er lē′vis)

LEAVES: Alternate, simple, elliptic-ovate to ovate-oblong, 1 1/4 to 3″ long, short acuminate, subcordate or rounded at base, quite glabrous and purplish when young.

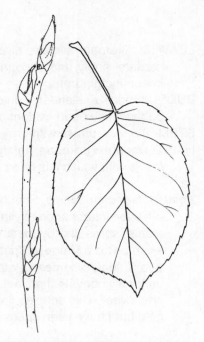

BUDS: Imbricate, similar to *A. arborea,* usually 1/2″ long, green tinged with red, the inner scales lanceolate, bright red above the middle, ciliate with silky white hairs.

STEM: Slender, glabrous, reddish brown 1st year, dull grayish brown in their second season.

Amelanchier laevis, Allegheny Serviceberry, is closely allied to *A. arborea* but differs by reason of the bronzy color of the unfolding leaves and their lack of pubescence as well as the almost glabrous pedicels and peduncle of the inflorescence. The fruit is black and sweet. The fruits were preferred by the American Indians. Many birds and animals are also extremely fond of them. Have observed in North Georgia mountains in full flower in mid April on rocky soils. The leaves are a distinct purple bronze and the flowers occur in nodding, fleecy, to 4″ long panicles. In Europe, a closely related species, if not the same, is described as *A. lamarckii.* Bean suggests it is possibly a hybrid with *A. canadensis,* along with *A. laevis,* as the parents. He further suggests that it might be a microspecies and is, therefore, effectively apomictic. Apomixis has been described as occurring in *A. laevis.* See Campbell et al. 1985. "Apomixis in *Amelanchier laevis,* shadbush." *Amer. J. Bot.* 1397–1403. It has naturalized in England, Netherlands, and Germany. I have seen the plant in relative abundance in the Netherlands and Germany and have sampled the fruits. They are sweet, edible, 3/8″ across and rich purple-black at maturity. I noticed a great number used in large containers in German cities. Native from Newfoundland to Georgia and Alabama, west to Michigan and Kansas. In Georgia has been free of fireblight and produced an orange-red to brick red fall color. Cultivated 1870. Zone 4 to 8(9).

Amelanchier stolonifera, (am-el-ang′kē-er stō-lon-if′ĕr-a), Running Serviceberry, is a small 4 to 6′ stoloniferous shrub which forms small thickets of stiff, erect stems; flowers are white; fruit is purplish black, glaucous, sweet, juicy and of good flavor, ripening in July. Native from Newfoundland and Maine to Virginia in non-calcareous soils. Introduced 1883. Zone 4.

ADDITIONAL NOTES: The *Amelanchier* species as a group make excellent landscape plants. They offer four season interest and excellent edible fruit. To my mind and stomach, a serviceberry pie is the rival of the best blueberry pie. The serviceberries are difficult to separate and are confused in the nursery profession. Unless flowers and developing leaves are present it is difficult to accurately separate *A. arborea, A. canadensis, A. laevis* and *A.* × *grandiflora. A. arborea* is native to the Piedmont woods of Georgia and is one of the first shrubs/trees to flower. Considering the wide-spread range of adaptability of the *Amelanchier* species, it is surprising they are not more commonly used.

For a more detailed account of *Amelanchier* species, see Dirr, 1987. *American Nurseryman* 166(5):66–83. *Amelanchier* taxonomy is fraught with difficulty and certainly not clear-cut. It is reasonably fair to state that what one orders and receives is not necessarily the same in the world of serviceberries. Although many nursery catalogs list *A. canadensis,* in fact, what is sold is *A. arborea, A.* x *grandiflora* and *A. laevis.* In recent works (Elias), I noticed *A. laevis* was listed as a synonym of *A. arborea.* I doubt if many people would agree with this. Two worthwhile readings are Jones. 1946. "American species of *Amelanchier*". *Illinois Biological Monograph* 20:1–126 and Robertson. 1974. "Genera of Rosaceae–*Amelanchier*". *J. Arnold Arboretum* 55:633–640.

Amorpha fruticosa — Indigobush Amorpha, also called Bastard Indigo
(am-ôr′fa frū-ti-kō′-sa)

FAMILY: Fabaceae

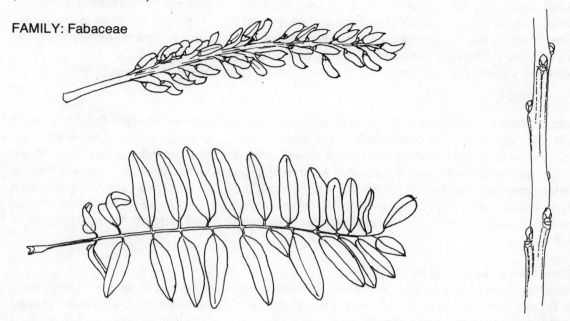

LEAVES: Alternate, pinnately compound, 13 to 33 leaflets, oval or elliptic, 1/2 to 1 1/2″ long, rounded at ends, mucronate, finely pubescent or glabrate; short thread-like stipule at base of each leaflet and transparent dots on the blade.

BUDS: Imbricate, often superposed, essentially glabrous, appressed, brownish gray.

STEM: Gray to brown, slender, often looks dead.

SIZE: Variable 6 to 20′ tall with a 5 to 15′ spread; a planting on the Illinois campus was about 12′ tall and 8 to 10′ wide.

HARDINESS: Zone 4 to 9.

HABIT: Ungainly deciduous shrub developing a leggy character with the bulk of the foliage on the upper 1/3 of the plant.

RATE: Medium in youth.

TEXTURE: Medium in foliage, coarse in winter.

LEAF COLOR: Light bright green in summer, slightly yellowish in fall; late leafing shrub, hard freeze turns foliage brown.

FLOWERS: Perfect, purplish blue with orange anthers, each flower 1/3″ long, June, borne in 3 to 6″ long upright spikes; flowers are not extremely showy but the colors are unusual.

FRUIT: Small, 1/3″ long, warty, kidney-shaped pod; persistent into winter and offers a good identification feature.

CULTURE: Transplants readily; does extremely well in poor, dry, sandy soils; pH adaptable; full sun; prune in late winter or early spring to keep the plant looking somewhat neat.

DISEASES AND INSECTS: Plants may be completely defoliated by the uredinal stage of the rust *Uropyxis amorphae;* other problems include leaf spots, powdery mildew and twig canker; I have also observed a gall forming insect which causes a swelling of the spent inflorescences; inside the gall is a small larva similar to those found in galls of oaks.

LANDSCAPE VALUE: Not a great deal of worth attached to this plant; perhaps for poor soil areas where few plants will survive; spreads easily by seeds and can become a noxious weed; interestingly many horticultural forms are listed but I have never seen one in gardens or nurseries.

CULTIVARS:

‘Dark Lance’—Rich green globular plant with purple flowers (petals) that subtend golden brown filaments, grew 14′ by 6 1/2′ in 6 years, selection from the wild by Mr. Benny J. Simpson, hardy Zone 5 to 9.

PROPAGATION: Seed has an impermeable coat and dormant embryo; light acid scarification for 5 to 8 minutes in sulfuric acid followed by cold stratification is recommended; cold stratification may not be necessary based on some research results I have read; softwood cuttings can be rooted; untreated softwoods from 1, 2 and 5-year-old plants rooted 89, 88 and 89%, respectively; division, especially of *A. brachycarpa, A. canescens* and *A. nana,* is effective; one researcher reported that July cuttings treated with 480 ppm Ethrel and placed in peat:perlite rooted well.

NATIVE HABITAT: Connecticut to Minnesota, south to Louisiana and Florida. Introduced 1724.

RELATED SPECIES:

Amorpha brachycarpa, (am-ôr′fa brak-i-kâr′pa), is a small dense, rather fine-textured shrub growing about 3′ high and wide. The purple flowers are borne in 1 to 2″ long cylindrical, terminal panicles during July. Not common in cultivation but a lovely addition to the summer garden. The Arnold Arboretum has probably the best collection of *Amorpha* species in North America. I consider this the best of the species for garden use. Missouri. Introduced 1920. Zone 5. *Amorpha nana,* Fragrant False Indigo, is similar but differs in having 13 to 19 leaflets compared to 21 to 45 for the above. It also occurs over a wider range from Manitoba and Saskatchewan to Iowa and New Mexico. Introduced 1811. Zone 2.

Amorpha canescens—Leadplant Amorpha
LEAVES: Alternate, compound pinnate, with 15 to 45 leaflets, entire leaf curved and 2 to 5″ long, each leaflet 1/3 to 1″ long, elliptic to oblong-lanceolate, acute or obtuse, rounded at base, densely grayish pubescent on upper and lower surfaces.

Amorpha canescens, (am-ôr′fa ka-nes′enz), Leadplant Amorpha, grows 2 to 4′ high and spreads 4 to 5′. The habit is broad, rounded and flat-topped. The foliage is an interesting gray-green in summer and can be used for contrast. Flowers are similar to the above species. Should be used as a herbaceous perennial, accent plant, or useful in rock gardens. Can be propagated by cuttings; seed should be treated similar to *A. fruticosa.* Native from Michigan and Saskatchewan to Indiana, Texas and northern Mexico. Introduced 1812. Zone 2.

Ampelopsis brevipedunculata — Porcelain Ampelopsis
(am-pel-op′sis brev-i-ped-unk-ū-lā′ta)

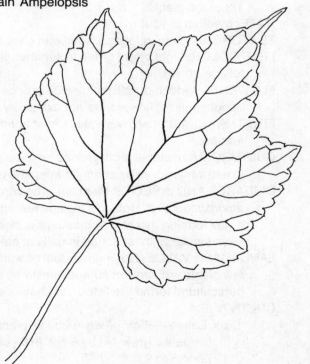

FAMILY: Vitaceae
LEAVES: Alternate, simple, 2 1/2 to 5″ long, broad-ovate, acuminate, cordate, 3 rarely 5-lobed, the lateral lobes broadly triangular-ovate, spreading, coarsely serrate, pilose beneath, dark green above with short pubescence, bristly hairy beneath; hairy petioles as long as blade or slightly shorter.
BUDS: Subglobose, solitary though collaterally branched in development, sessile, with 2 or 3 scales, brownish.
STEM: Hairy when young, angled or nearly terete, brownish; pith-continuous, white.

SIZE: 10 to 15 to 25′ and more.
HARDINESS: Zone 4 to 8.
HABIT: Vigorous vine clinging by tendrils; not as dense as some vines, but certainly vigorous.
RATE: Fast, can grow 15 to 20′ in a single season; however, this is the exception.

TEXTURE: Medium-coarse in leaf and winter.

LEAF COLOR: Dark green in summer, not much different in fall; no appreciable fall coloration.

FLOWERS: Perfect, greenish, unimportant; borne in long stalked cymes in July and August; flowers on new growth of season so can be cut to ground in late winter to maintain control and will still produce flowers and fruits the same season.

FRUIT: Berry, 1/4 to 1/3″ diameter, yellow to pale lilac and finally to bright blue; often all colors are present in the same infructescence; effective in September and October.

CULTURE: Easily transplanted, adaptable to many soils except those that are permanently wet; best fruiting occurs in full sun; requires adequate support for climbing; plants should be sited where the root growth can be restricted, for under this condition, fruiting is optimized.

DISEASES AND INSECTS: Some of the problems which are common to *Parthenocissus* could prove troublesome on *Ampelopsis* species; Japanese beetles can be a genuine problem.

LANDSCAPE VALUE: Another vine which is rarely visible in the landscape; the fruit is extremely handsome and is probably unrivaled by any other woody plant in vitality of color; could be effectively integrated into a landscape by growing on a fence or over a rock pile; rapid cover for unsightly objects and valuable for that reason; unfortunately, Japanese beetles love the foliage and can render a green vine a missing object in short order; one authority calls the fruits an amethyst blue color.

CULTIVARS:

'Elegans'—A rather interesting type with slightly smaller leaves, variegated with white; greenish white and tinged pinkish when young; not as vigorous as species and would be a good choice for locations where the species is too aggressive; handsome; supposedly comes true-to-type from seed; introduced before 1847.

var. *maximowiczii*—Leaves more deeply lobed, 3 to 5 lobes, interesting for textural difference compared to species; I planted this variety on a drain spout at my Illinois home and in a single growing season it started to grow in the window; vigorous to a fault.

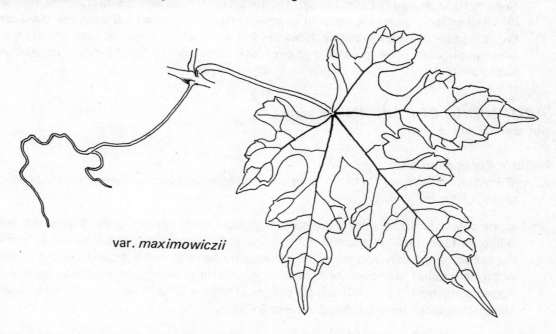

var. *maximowiczii*

PROPAGATION: All species are easily rooted from leafy cuttings of firm growth taken in June, July and August; *A. brevipedunculata* cuttings taken in early summer, untreated, and planted in sand rooted 90 percent in 30 days under mist; doubtful if a hormone treatment is needed to improve rooting; seed when cleaned and sown will germinate in rather irrational percentages; a 30-day or longer cold period may improve germination; and, in our studies, seeds proved easy to germinate when removed from flesh and cold stratified for 3 months.

NATIVE HABITAT : China, Korea, Japan and the Russian Far East. Cultivated 1870.

RELATED SPECIES:

Ampelopsis aconitifolia, (am-pel-op′sis ak-on-ĭt-i-fō′li-a), Monks Hood Vine, is a slender luxuriant vine with delicate, deep glossy green, 3- to 5-foliate leaves. The vine grows 15 to 25′ and can develop as much as 12 to 15′ of linear growth in a single season. The flowers are perfect, greenish, August, borne in cymes. The fruits are dull orange or yellow, sometimes bluish before maturity, 1/4″ diameter, effective in September and October. Valued for delicate foliage; offers variation in texture; can be used on fences, rock piles, walls and other structures. Native to northern China. Zone 4 to 7.

Ampelopsis arborea, (am-pel-op′sis är-bō′rē-a), Pepper Vine, is a common occurrence in the southern United States and is considered by many to be a pernicious pest. The bipinnately compound, 4 to 8″ long leaves are composed of numerous 1/2 to 1 1/4″ long, broad-ovate or rhombic-ovate to obovate leaflets, apex acute to acuminate, broad-cuneate to rounded at base, terminal leaflet stalked, lateral ones short-stalked to subsessile, coarsely toothed, dark green. The young slender somewhat angular stems are purplish and glabrous or nearly so. The 1/3″ diameter berries are dark purple at maturity but go through the same color transitions as *A. brevipedunculata.* The species is particularly rampant and is seldom cultivated. My first introduction came at the Atlanta Botanical Garden where it smothered a chain-link fence. Quite beautiful in fruit. Virginia to Missouri, Florida, Texas, and Mexico. Introduced 1700. Zone 7 to 9.

Ampelopsis humulifolia, (am-pel-op′sis hū-mū-li-fō′li-a), Hops Ampelopsis, is a climbing, shrubby vine with lustrous bright green 3 to 5-lobed foliage with rounded sinuses resembling that of *Vitis* (true grape) in shape and texture. This species has been confused with *A. brevipedunculata,* but differs in the thicker, firmer leaves which are whitish beneath. The fruit is not borne profusely. The color ranges from pale yellow, changing partly or wholly to pale blue. Native to northern China. Introduced 1868. Zone 5.

ADDITIONAL NOTES: I remember learning *A. brevipedunculata* in my plant materials courses at Ohio State in 1963 and did not see it again until the fall of 1975 when several students, who were involved in a fruit collecting project, brought in several clusters. Having not seen the plant for 12 years, I hesitated to immediately identify it, but the fruit color struck a mental note which I translated to *A. brevipedunculata.* The moral is that once one sees the fruit he/she never forgets which plant to associate it.

Andrachne colchica — Andrachne
(an-drac′nē kol′chi-ka)

FAMILY: Euphorbiaceae
LEAVES: Alternate, simple, 1/4 to 3/4″ long, one half as wide, ovate, obtuse, rounded at base, entire, rich green, glabrous.

Andrachne colchica, Andrachne, is a wispy 2 to 3′ high shrub with rich green foliage that would serve as a filler or facer plant in a shrub border. The plant is most interesting as a hardy member of the Euphorbiaceae family and my initial introduction came during sabbatical at the Arnold Arboretum where this rather unknown shrub labored in relative obscurity. Flowers and fruits are not showy. Appears to almost thrive with neglect but would require full sun. August cuttings can be rooted. Asia Minor. Introduced before 1990. Zone 5 to 8 (?).

Andromeda polifolia — Bog-rosemary
(an-drom′e-da pol-i-fō′li-a)

FAMILY: Ericaceae
LEAVES: Alternate, simple, evergreen, linear-oblong, 1 to 1 1/2″ long, 1/8 to 1/3″ wide but appearing narrower because of the recurved margins, blue green to dark green above, glaucous or slightly tomentose beneath.

Andromeda polifolia, Bog-rosemary, is an extremely interesting, slow growing (1 to 2′ high by 2 to 3′ wide) evergreen shrub with creeping rootstocks and upright limitedly branched stems. The foliage is stiff, leathery textured and deep dark green. The flowers are perfect, white tinged pink, 1/4″ long, urn-shaped; borne in May at the end of the shoots in umbels. The fruit is a capsule. The species requires a peaty or sandy soil which is constantly moist and cool; full sun or light shade; best to move it as a container grown plant; in the wild it is most commonly found in peat or sphagnum bogs. A very lovely and interesting plant for edging or naturalized conditions but very exacting as to culture. Not very common in the trade but I have seen it offered in several garden centers as well as through mail order firms. I attempted to grow a compact form of the species in Illinois but with meager success. I planted it in pure peat and provided sufficient water. No doubt, the high summer heat and humidity were not to its liking. Found in colder parts of northern hemisphere and significant variation must occur over such diverse terrain. Various epithets such as 'Nana,' 'Compacta,' 'Compacta Alba,' 'Grandiflora Compacta,' and 'Congesta' have been applied to compact forms. *Andromeda glaucophylla* is similar with linear leaves and short erect pubescence on the lower surface. Flowers are borne on shorter pedicels than *A. polifolia.* Newfoundland and Laborador to Manitoba, south to New Jersey, Indiana and Minesota. Cultivated 1829. Zone 2 to 6. *Andromeda polifolia* is native to north and central Europe, northern Asia, North America south to New York and Idaho. Cultivated 1786. Zone 2 to 6 (higher elevations in the south).

Aralia spinosa — Devils-walkingstick or Hercules-club
(a-rā′li-a spī-nō′sa)

FAMILY: Araliaceae

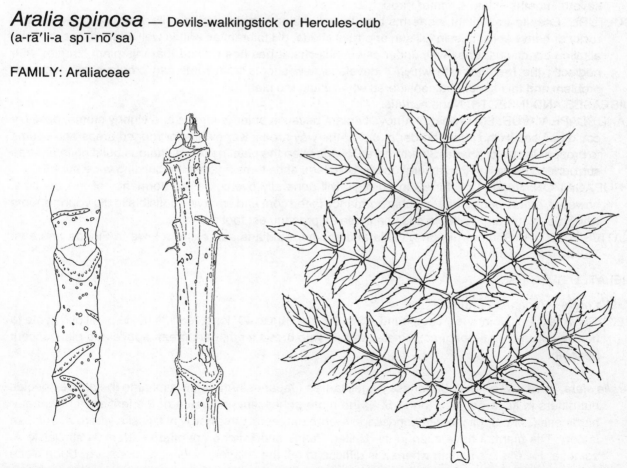

LEAVES: Alternate, bi- to tri-pinnately compound, 32 to 64″ long, rachis with scattered prickles, leaflets ovate, 2 to 4″ long, acuminate, serrate, glaucous and nearly glabrous beneath; petiole to 10″ long; entire leaf presents a tropical effect.

BUDS: Ovoid-conical, solitary, with few scales.

STEM: Stout, gray-straw colored, glabrous, with prickles; leaf scars fully half encircling stem, bundle traces 15 in a single series; pith-large, pale.

SIZE: 10 to 20' in height although can grow to 30 to 40'.

HARDINESS: Zone 4 to 9.

HABIT: Large, few-stemmed shrub or small tree with stout, coarse branches forming an obovate outline; often renews itself by developing shoots from the base and forms a dense thicket of impenetrable branches; I have seen a large planting like this in Mt. Airy Arboretum, Cincinnati, Ohio, and the overall effect is quite handsome (soft-textured) in summer with the compound foliage; however, in winter the planting is extremely coarse.

RATE: Slow to medium on old wood, but fast on shoots which develop from roots.

TEXTURE: Medium, possibly medium-fine in leaf; appearing coarse in winter.

LEAF COLOR: Medium to dark green, sometimes lustrous, changing to subdued yellow-green and yellow; an occasional leaf turns purple; have seen in recent years reasonable yellow to purple fall coloration on selected plants, never consistent across the species.

FLOWERS: Perfect, small, whitish, produced from July to August in large 12 to 18" diameter pubescent umbellose-panicles at the end of the branches; interestingly handsome in flower; akin to a lacy veil over the top of the plant; flowers last for a long time but the July to early September flowering period refers to the periods of time in which individuals in a given geographic area will flower; during my sabbatical I monitored flowers from late July to early September at the Arnold Arboretum.

FRUIT: Drupe, purple-black, 1/4" long, late August into October, produced in great quantity and are either eaten by birds or fall soon after ripening; the infructescence turns a pinkish red and is attractive for several months in late summer through early fall.

CULTURE: Easy to transplant, performs best in well-drained, moist, fertile soils, but also grows in dry, rocky or heavy soils; best in full sun or partial shade; pH tolerant as will do well under acid or slightly alkaline conditions; does well under city conditions; it has been noted that this plant "thrives with neglect"; the freedom with which it develops new shoots from roots can create a maintenance problem and this should be considered when siting the plant.

DISEASES AND INSECTS: None serious.

LANDSCAPE VALUE: Somewhat of a novelty plant because of large leaves and clubby stems; possibly could be used in the shrub border or out-of-the-way areas; worthwhile for rugged areas and seems to prosper in sun or shade; Swarthmore College used the plant next to a campus building in an area surrounded by walks; the textural quality of foliage and stems against the building were superb.

PROPAGATION: Seed, 41°F for 60 to 90 days will generally overcome the dormancy of this species; however, other species have double dormancy (seed coat and embryo); possible to dig young shoots which develop from the roots and use these as propagules; root cuttings.

NATIVE HABITAT: Southern Pennsylvania and southern Indiana and eastern Iowa to Florida and east Texas. Introduced 1688.

RELATED SPECIES:

Aralia elata—Japanese Angelica-tree

LEAVES: Alternate, bipinnately compound, 16 to 32" long, up to 40" long, leaflets ovate or elliptic ovate to narrow ovate, 2 to 5" long, acuminate, serrate with broad teeth, dark green above and glaucescent beneath.

Aralia elata, (a-rā'li-a ē-lā-ta), Japanese Angelica-tree (Japanese Aralia), is similar to the above species but differs in its larger size (30 to 50'); the more pubescent underside of the leaflets; and greater hardiness (Zone 3, Minnesota Landscape Arboretum reports this hardy at Chaska where *A. spinosa* is not). The plants I have seen in the United States and Europe appeared extremely similar to *A. spinosa.* Here is a situation where it is difficult to tell the "player" without a scorecard. Upon close examination the pubescence differences seem to hold up and the veins run to the end of the serrations on *A. elata* and anastomose in *A. spinosa;* the stems are not as spiny as *A. spinosa;* 'Aureo-variegata' has leaflets edged with an irregular border of golden-yellow, a most beautiful form but a weak grower; 'Pyramidalis' is an upright form with smaller leaflets than the species; 'Variegata' offers an irregular creamy white border along the margin of the leaflet. 'Silver Umbrella'—Noted this in Dr. Raulston's North Carolina State University Arboretum newsletter; no description of the leaf but is probably a silver to creamy edged variegated form; listed as growing 10′ by 6′. I saw several cultivars at Treasures of Tenbury in England and Mr. John Treasure, the owner, bemoaned the fact that they were so slow growing and provided limited amounts of bud wood. He purchased his plants from Holland and noted they commanded a premium price. Most of the variegated forms are produced in Dutch nurseries. Japan, Korea, Manchuria, and Russian Far East. Introduced 1830.

Araucaria araucana — Monkey Puzzle, Chilean Pine
(ar-â-kā′ri-ä ar-â-kā′na)

FAMILY: Araucariaceae

LEAVES: Evergreen, spirally arranged, radially spreading, essentially 2-ranked, ovate-lanceolate, spiny pointed stiff leaves, 1 to 2″ long, 1/2 to 1″ wide, slightly concave above, lustrous dark green on both sides, persisting alive for 10 to 15 years and then indefinitely when dead; needles densely packed about 24 to an inch of stem.

HABIT: Unique and easily identifiable because of stiff, gaunt, rather scary growth habit; belongs in a horror movie; branches are produced in tiers (whorls of 5 to 7), are minimally branched and protrude horizontally for a distance from the center of the trunk and then ascend in a gentle arch skyward.

Araucaria araucana, Monkey Puzzle, was essentially unknown to this author until introduction in European gardens. Surprisingly hardy (Zone 7) and a report indicated the plant had been grown in Knoxville, TN. Probably better adapted to the west coast but for novelty purposes worth a try in the coastal southeastern region. A large tree, 50 to 80′ with a pyramidal-oval outline at maturity; the lower limbs are often lost creating a slender bole and a crown restricted the the upper 1/2 to 1/3 of the tree. Essentially dioecious and the male flowers occur in 3 to 5″ long cylindrical catkins; female in 5 to 8″ thick pineapple-shaped cones that take two years to mature. I saw a cone in California and decided that there were no rakes strong enough to compete. The conical seeds are 1 1/2″ long by 3/4″ wide. Certainly an imposing specimen, especially in English gardens. Quite difficult to utilize in garden-making and should be used as a single specimen or perhaps in widely spaced groupings. Soil should be cool and moist. Seems to prosper in cooler, continental climates. *Araucaria heterophylla,* Norfolk Island Pine, is suitable for Zone 10 conditions and is quite common in Hawaii. It has received wide favor as a houseplant. Makes a rather attractive plant were adapted. Chile, Argentina. Introduced 1795.

Arbutus unedo — Strawberry Tree
(är-bū′tus ū′-ne-dō)

FAMILY: Ericaceae

LEAVES: Alternate, evergreen, narrowly oval to obovate, 2 to 4″ long, 1/2 to 3/4″ wide, acute, cuneate, serrate, lustrous dark green above, glabrous; petiole 1/4″ long, glandular, red.

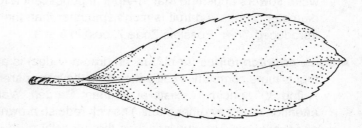

SIZE: 15 to 30′ with a similar habit.

HARDINESS: Zone 7 to 9.

HABIT: A small shrub in the southeast United States but in Europe a large shrub or round-headed small tree.

RATE: Slow.

TEXTURE: Medium fine throughout the season.

BARK: Handsome beyond description with rich reddish brown coloration and shredding fibrous texture; becomes twisted (spiraled) and gnarled with age, certainly one of the most beautiful features of this species.

LEAF COLOR: Lustrous dark green.

FLOWERS: Perfect, urn-shaped like blueberry, about 1/4″ long, white to pinkish, in 2″ long and wide panicles from October–November; not spectacular in flower but certainly alluring; have seen in flower in early December in Aiken, SC.

FRUIT: A 3/4″ diameter, sub-globose, orange-red, berry-like, granular surfaced drupe with mealy flesh; ripens the year following flowering; have seen flowers and ripe fruits present at the same time; the fruit is striking.

CULTURE: Have finally procured a plant for my garden and look forward to moving it around until the ideal situation is realized; observations indicate the plant is easy to grow and in California it grows well in dry (once established) and moist, well drained garden soils; apparently also quite salt-tolerant, sun or shade.

DISEASES AND INSECTS: None serious

LANDSCAPE VALUE: Handsome out of season plant for the discriminating gardener, certainly an eye catcher in a shrub border where the off-season flowers and normal-season fruits dominate.

CULTIVARS:

'Compacta'—Slower growing, deep green form that does not flower as heavily as the species; contorted branching structure, picturesque and probably no bigger than 5′ after 8 to 10 years; have seen reports in literature that note this form flowers and fruits continuously.

'Elfin King'—A common compact form that bears abundant flowers and fruits; am most impressed with this small bushy form that will probably mature between 5 and 10′.

'Quercifolia'—Appears in European literature but I have not come across the plant in gardens; dark green dissected leaves with reddish veins; flowers and fruits like the species.

'Rubra'—Rich dark pink flowers, slightly less vigorous and hardy than species; Bean describes it as virtually lost to cultivation.

NATIVE HABITAT: Southwestern Ireland where it attains greatest proportions to the Mediterranean region. Cultivated for centuries.

RELATED SPECIES:

Arbutus andrachne—Madrone
(är-bū′tus an-drac′nē)

LEAVES: Alternate, simple, evergreen, 2 to 4″ long, 1 to 2″ wide, lustrous dark green above, paler and glabrous below, toothed on young and vigorous shoots, but entire when mature; petiole 1/2 to 1″ long.

STEM: Glabrous which separates it from the glandular-hairy nature of *A. unedo*.

Arbutus andrachne, Madrone, is a 10 to 20′ evergreen shrub with the ornamental traits of *A. unedo*. The white flowers appear in March–April in pubescent 2 to 4″ long and wide panicles. The globose 1/2″ diameter orange-red fruit is much smoother than that of *A. unedo*. Native of southeastern Europe. Introduced 1724. Possible Zone 7, best in 8 to 9.

Arbutus andrachnoides (är-bū′tus an-drac-noy′dēz) is a hybrid between *A. unedo* and *A. andrachne* that is more common in cultivation than the latter parent; it is strongly intermediate in characteristics. A fine 30′ specimen exists at Bodnant Garden, Wales and on every garden tour receives more attention than any other plant. The rich reddish brown branches literally grab even the most passive of passers-by. The sun enriches the intensity of the bark color. A most handsome tree probably reserved for more even, cool climates than the United States. Found wild in Greece and was hybridized in England around 1800.

Arctostaphylos uva-ursi — Bearberry, also called Kinnikinick, Mealberry, Hog Cranberry, Sandberry, Mountain Box, Bear's Grape

(ark-tō-staf′i-los oo′-va er′si)

FAMILY: Ericaceae

LEAVES: Alternate, simple, obovate or obovate-oblong, 1/4 to 1 1/4″ long, 1/4 to 1/2″ wide, cuneate, revolute, glabrous, lustrous dark green above, lighter beneath; petiole 1/4″ long.

BUDS: Solitary, sessile, ovoid with about 3 exposed scales.

STEM: Minutely tomentulose-viscid, becoming glabrate; leaf scars small, crescent-shaped, bundle trace one; older branches covered with papery, reddish to ashy exfoliating bark.

SIZE: 6 to 12″ in height by 2 to 4′ in width, spreading to infinity.

HARDINESS: Zone 2 to 5 or 6; have seen in Zone 8.

HABIT: Low growing, glossy leaved evergreen ground cover forming broad, thick mats; single plant may cover an area 15′ in diameter.

RATE: Slow.

TEXTURE: Fine.

LEAF COLOR: Glossy bright green to dark green in summer, bronze to reddish in fall and winter; the foliage effect is unique and quite different from most ground covers.

FLOWERS: Perfect, white tinged pink, small (1/6 to 1/4″ long), urn-shaped, April to May, borne in nodding racemes; dainty and beautiful.

FRUIT: Fleshy drupe, lustrous bright red, 1/4 to 1/3″ diameter, late July through August and persisting; beautiful on close inspection.

CULTURE: One of the more interesting species as far as cultural requirements; difficult to transplant and container-grown plants or large mats of plants should be used; although found in diverse soils and habitats it does best in poor, sandy, infertile soils; full sun or partial shade; pH 4.5 to 5.5 is preferable; exhibits good salt tolerance (I have seen the plant growing right next to beach grass on the beaches of Cape Cod); set plants 12 to 24″ apart; pruning is seldom necessary; never fertilize.

DISEASES AND INSECTS: Black mildew, leaf galls and rust have been reported; in recent years have noticed a leaf type gall that disfigures the plant; use resistant cultivars.

LANDSCAPE VALUE: Outstanding ground cover for that different effect; has been called "the prettiest, sturdiest, and most reliable ground cover"; good bed preparation for this one plant alone is worth the effort.

CULTIVARS:

'Alaska'—Compact flat growing form with small, round, dark green leaves.

'Big Bear'—Large, shiny dark green leaves and large red fruits, reddish winter leaf color.

'Massachusetts'—Small, dark green leaved, flat growing form with good resistance to leaf spot and leaf gall, abundant pinkish white flowers followed by red fruits, originated from Massachusetts seed grown in Oregon by Bob Tichner.

'Point Reyes'—Dark green leaves closely spaced on the stems, reasonable heat and drought tolerance.

'Radiant'—Leaves lighter green and more widely spaced than 'Point Reyes'; bears abundant bright red fruit that persists into winter.

'Rax'—A prostrate form with leaves smaller than the type; original clone was discovered in eastern Australia.

'Tilden Park'—Dark green closely set oval foliage on a 2 to 3″ high by 2 to 3′ wide plant.

'Vancouver Jade'—Introduction from University of British Columbia Botanical Garden, lustrous dark green summer foliage, good deep red winter color, resistance to leaf spot, flowers white with pink tinge, red fruits like those of species.

'Wood's Red'—Large, bright red fruits on a compact form, small dark green leaves turn reddish in winter; an American clone that received the Award of Merit from the Royal Horticultural Society.

PROPAGATION: Seeds have impermeable seed coats and dormant embryos; acid scarification for 3 to 6 hours followed by 2 to 3 months of warm and 2 to 3 months of cold stratification resulted in 30 to 60% germination; nursery practice involves 2 to 5 hours in acid followed by summer planting with germination taking place the following spring; at one time, based on the literature, I reported that cuttings were somewhat difficult to root; based on my work and the new work of others I would say this is not true; cuttings collected July 28 and treated with IBA rooted 80% in sand:peat under mist;

October and December cuttings treated essentially as above rooted 70% to 80% in about 6 weeks; see Dirr and Heuser 1987 for specifics.

ADDITIONAL NOTES: Although considered to be a strong acidophile by gardeners, it is equally at home on limestone and siliceous rock and is a vigorous colonizer of exposed, sandy soils; there are magnificent colonies on Cape Cod that thrive in the most infertile sand; the "emerald carpet" of ground covers; have seen in Aiken, SC where the plant was prospering; certainly would not recommend for wholesale use in the southeast, but for small areas may be worth a try.

NATIVE HABITAT: Circumboreal covering Europe, Asia, North America, south to Virginia, northern California. Cultivated 1800.

Ardisia japonica — Japanese Ardisia, Marlberry
(är-diz′i-a ja-pon′i-ka)

FAMILY: Myrsinaceae

LEAVES: Alternate, simple, evergreen, crowded at end of stems and appearing whorled, elliptic-oval, 1 1/2 to 3 1/2″ long, 3/4 to 1 1/2″ wide, tapered at both ends, sharply serrate, glabrous except on midrib, lustrous dark green; petiole—1/4″ long, puberulous.

Ardisia japonica, Japanese Ardisia, is a magnificent, bold-textured 8 to 12″ high evergreen ground cover that to a degree resembles *Helleborus orientalis* in leaf texture but is not as coarse. The dark green leaves are leathery. The white, 1/2 diameter, star-shaped, 5 narrow, ovate-petaled flowers are borne in 2 to 6, rarely many-flowered racemes (forming a panicle) in July-August. The rounded 1/4″ diameter, red drupes mature in September–October and persist. Culturally, an acid, organic, moist, well-drained soil is best. It spreads rapidly and forms a solid ground cover. Prefers partial to full shade and is an ideal choice for woodsy, shaded situations. Callaway Gardens, Pine Mountain, Georgia, has beautiful plantings and this is where I first came to appreciate this species' potential for ground cover use in the south. Propagation is easiest by division. Have rooted stem cuttings that were collected in late February, in fact, have found the various cultivars easy to root. Apparently variable in degree of hardiness; probably best in Zone 8 and 9 although it is mentioned as being hardy in Zone 5 and 6. Hardiness has never been well defined and until Dr. Raulston provided me with several plants, my observational experience was limited. During the difficult winter (–3°F) of 1983–84 in Athens plants were killed to the ground but came back from the roots. The variegated forms were less cold hardy than the green leaf types. Raulston noted that the variegated forms die back to the ground at about 15°F but will regrow from the roots. Plants are protected on the north side of my home and were injured in the relatively mild winter of 1986–87. The foliage may not harden quickly in the fall and an early freeze induces injury. Many forms exist including those with varying degrees of variegation. They are beautiful plants probably best reserved for shady protected areas in moist, loose soil. Japan, China. Introduced about 1830.

CULTIVARS:

'Beniyuki'—Leaves irregularly shaped and notched—wide bands (more than 1/2″ wide) of white on edges.

'Chiyoda'—Leaves irregularly shaped and notched—thin bands (less than 1/4″ wide) of white on edges.

'Hakuokan'—One of the largest and most vigorous cultivars—heavily variegated white on edges.

'Hinode'—A large and vigorous plant with broad band of yellow variegation in the center of leaves.

'Hinotsukasa'—Irregular rounded "teeth" on margins of leaf. Main blade green but "teeth" often (not always) white. From distance has a "dotted" look.

'Ito-Fukurin'—An elegant, subtle cultivar—light silvery-gray leaves with a very thin margin of white outlining each leaf.

Aristolochia durior — Dutchman's Pipe
(a-ris-tō-lō′ki-a dū′ri-ôr)

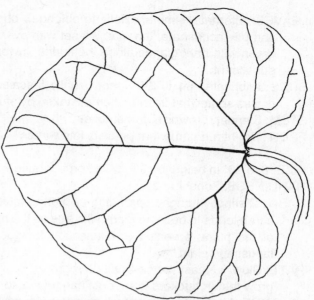

FAMILY: Aristolochiaceae

LEAVES: Alternate, simple, 4 to 10″ (12″) long, almost as wide, heart- or kidney-shaped, pointed or obtuse, dark green and glabrous above, pale green and pubescent beneath, finally glabrous; petiole—1 to 3″ long.

BUDS: Superposed, 3, one above the other, appear to be enclosed in stem tissue, upper largest, greenish, glabrous.

STEM: Green, glabrous, nodes swollen, leaf scars form a horse-shoe crescent around buds; pith-white, greater than 1/2 the diameter of the stem.

Aristolochia durior, Dutchman's Pipe, will never make the best seller list but in bygone days was a staple for screening front porches. I have seen many sunscreens fashioned from a trellis covered with Dutchman's Pipe. It is a vigorous, climbing, twining vine that can grow 20 to 30′. Given the appropriate arbor, trellis, pergola or pillar, it will cover the structure in a single season. The large leaves form a solid screen and are certainly more attractive than bamboo curtains and related tack. The unusual flowers by virtue of their shape give rise to the common name. They occur 1 or 2 together from the axils of the leaves in May or June. They are yellow-green and glabrous on the outside; at the mouth the perianth tube (1 to 1 1/2″ long) contracts to a small orifice, spreading into 3-lobed, smooth, brownish purple limb 3/4″ across. The fruit is a 6-ribbed, 2 to 3″ long capsule. Appears to thrive in about any soil as long as it is moist and well drained. Leaves may wilt under droughty conditions. Will withstand full sun or partial shade. Propagate by division or July cuttings. A rooting compound should be used. For best germination, seeds should be stratified for 3 months at 40°F or sown in fall. Also listed as *A. macrophylla* and some botanists have placed the species in the genus *Isotrema.* Pennsylvania to Georgia, west to Minnesota and Kansas. Introduced 1783 by John Bartram. Zone 4 to 8.

Aronia arbutifolia — Red Chokeberry
(a-rō′ni-a âr-bū-ti-fō′li-a)

FAMILY: Rosaceae

LEAVES: Alternate, simple, elliptic to oblong or obovate, 1 1/2 to 3 1/2" long, 1/2 to 3/4" wide, acute or abruptly acuminate, the margins set with even, black-tipped teeth, the upper surface lustrous dark green with dark glands along the midrib, lower with permanent gray tomentum; petiole—1/3" long, pubescent.

BUDS: Imbricate, 1/4 to 3/8" long, usually 5-scaled, green tinged red, often completely red, glabrous, scales somewhat fleshy, often mistaken by students for an *Amelanchier.*

STEM: Slender, brownish, tomentose.

FRUIT: Bright red pome that persists into winter.

SIZE: 6 to 10' in height by 3 to 5' in spread; quite variable, tends to sucker and forms a colony.

HARDINESS: Zone 4 to 9.

HABIT: Distinctly upright, spreading-suckering multistemmed shrub, somewhat open and round topped; shrub tends to become leggy with age as the majority of the foliage is present on the upper 1/2 to 1/3 of the plant; breeding and selection for good habit, foliage and fruit could result in a superior landscape plant.

RATE: Slow, at least the case with the growth of plants I have recorded in the midwest; in good soil will grow faster; suckers from roots can grow 2 to 3' in a season.

TEXTURE: Medium in leaf; medium-coarse in winter although good fruit quality tends to minimize the ragged habit.

LEAF COLOR: Lustrous deep green above, grayish tomentose beneath in summer, changing to red, rich crimson or reddish purple in fall.

FLOWERS: White or slightly reddish (anthers), about 1/3" diameter; flowers early to mid April in Athens, May in most Zone 5 areas; borne in 9 to 20-flowered, 1 to 1 1/2" diameter corymbs, not overwhelming.

FRUIT: Pome, 1/4" diameter, bright red; September through November and later; fruits are firm and glossy into January in midwest, borne in great abundance along the stems; called Chokeberry because of the astringent taste, even the birds do not like it.

CULTURE: Finely fibrous root system, transplants well, prefers soil with adequate drainage but seems well adapted to many soil types, even poor soils; seems to tolerate both wet and dry soils; full sun or half shade, however, best fruit production occurs in full sun; tends to sucker.

DISEASES AND INSECTS: Leaf spots, twig and fruit blight results in gray, powdery mold over affected plant parts, round-headed apple borer; none serious.

LANDSCAPE VALUE: Border, massing, groups; very effective fruit character in the fall; the most useful way to compensate for the leggy character is to mass this species; extremely effective when used in this manner; almost a sea of red in fall and winter; might be a good choice for highway use because of adapatability and brilliant fruit display; a large mass on the Georgia campus which is now reaching fruiting maturity has been spectacular.

CULTIVARS:

'Brilliantissima'—In the last edition, my description of this cultivar was abruptly terse; having observed this form in greater numbers I am giving it a first class rating. It is superior to the species because of the almost waxy, lustrous dark green leaves that turn brilliant scarlet in fall, the more abundant flowers and the glossier, larger, more abundant red fruit. In fall color it is equal and perhaps superior to *Euonymus alatus.* I have had excellent success (80%) rooting it from softwood (June) cuttings using 4000 ppm IBA quick dip, peat:perlite, mist; plants continued to grow after rooting. This cultivar grows 6 to 8' (10') and forms a suckering colony not unlike that of the species; can be propagated by division.

'Erecta'—An upright form that as I studied it at the Arnold appeared to show hybrid characteristics between *A. arbutifolia* and *A. elata;* upright in habit and not as beautiful as the two species or the above cultivar; fruit not as colorful as the species.

PROPAGATION: Seeds, stratify in moist peat for 90 days at 33 to 41°F; cuttings, softwood root readily; untreated cuttings taken in early summer rooted 92% in six weeks in sand medium; best results obtained when the basal cut was made 1/2" below a node; division is also a practical way to increase the plant in small numbers; nothing more than a sharp spade and steel-toed boots work wonders.

NATIVE HABITAT: Massachusetts to Florida, west to Minnesota, Ohio, Arkansas and Texas. Introduced 1700.

RELATED SPECIES:

Aronia melanocarpa—Black Chokeberry

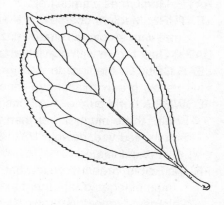

LEAVES: Alternate, simple, 1 to 3″ long, 3/4 to 2″ wide, obovate, abruptly acuminate, or obtusish, finely and regularly serrate, lustrous dark green above with dark glands on the midrib, lower surface light green and entire leaf glabrous; petiole—1/4″ or less.

Aronia melanocarpa, (a-rō′ni-a mel-an-ō-kâr′pa), Black Chokeberry, is similar to *A. arbutifolia* except the leaves and stems are glabrous and the fruit is blackish purple. This species grows 3 to 5′ (10′) and tends to sucker profusely thus forming large colonies. Again, a very adaptable species for I have seen it growing in low wet areas in the Chicago area and on dry, sandy hillsides in Wisconsin. Fall color can be a good wine red and the purplish black, 1/3 to 1/2″ diameter fruits are also handsome. Propagation is as described under *A. arbutifolia*. Variety *elata* is considered superior for landscape use and I would agree with this assessment. I have seen plants of var. *elata* 10 to 12′ high although it is usually smaller. It has larger leaves, flowers and fruits. It was listed in "The Top Ten-Plus-One-Shrubs for Minnesota", *Minnesota Horticulturist* 106(6):152–154. June–July. 1978. Nova Scotia to Florida, west to Michigan, introduced about 1700. Zone 3 to 8(9). Very diverse over its range and also forming natural hybrids with *A. arbutifolia*.

Aronia prunifolia, (a-rō′ni-a prū-ni-fō′li-a), Purple-fruited Chokeberry, is similar to *A. melanocarpa* except it is larger (12′). The fall color is good wine-red or purplish red. The flowers are white, about 1/2″ across borne in terminal corymbs in late April through early May. The fruit is a lustrous, 1/3″ diameter, purplish black drupe that may abcise after the first frost. According to Rehder, this species is intermediate between *A. arbutifolia* and *A. melanocarpa,* but is not a hybrid. Current thinking, with which I concur, has it that *A. prunifolia* is a hybrid species. Native from Nova Scotia to Florida, west to Indiana. Cultivated 1800. Zone 4 to 7(8).

Asimina triloba — Common Pawpaw
(à-sim′i-nà trī-lō′ba)

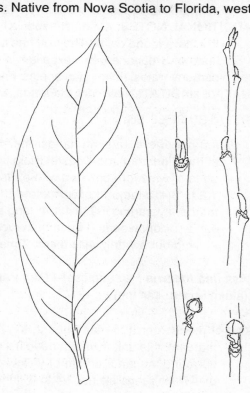

FAMILY: Annonaceae

LEAVES: Alternate, simple, entire, 6 to 12″ long, obovate-oblong, apex short acuminate, base uniformly tapering, medium green, usually glabrous at maturity; petiole—1/3″ long.

BUDS: Terminal bud naked, larger than laterals, pubescent, dark brown; lateral buds naked, obliquely superposed; flower buds—pubescent, globose to rounded, 2 to 3 scaled.

STEM: Essentially glabrous at maturity, brown, with fetid odor when broken; pith-continuous, white, with firmer greenish diaphragms at intervals in second year's growth.

SIZE: 15 to 20′ high and wide; will grow 30 to 40′ in height in favorable locations.

HARDINESS: Zone 5 to 8.

HABIT: Multistemmed shrub or small tree with short trunk and spreading branches forming a dense pyramidal or round-topped head; tends to sucker and forms rather loose colonies in the wild; presents a semi-tropical appearance.

RATE: Medium as a small tree.

TEXTURE: Medium-coarse in leaf and in winter habit; the summer foliage tends to droop and presents the tree with an overall sleepy (lazy) appearance; easily recognizable by this feature.

BARK: Dark brown with grayish areas when young; becoming rough and slightly scaly with maturity.

LEAF COLOR: Medium to dark green above, paler green beneath in summer changing to yellow or yellow-green in fall; have observed brilliant yellow fall color on selected trees.

FLOWERS: Lurid purple, 1 to 2″ across; early to mid May in Zone 5; borne singly; there are six petals, the outer three much larger than the inner three; flowers before or as leaves are developing on thick, often recurved, downy, 1/2 to 3/4″ long pedicels; not particularly showy but interesting; seldom seen by the uninitiated.

FRUIT: Edible, greenish yellow berry finally turning brownish black, 2 to 5″ long, of many shapes—sometimes elongated, at other times rounded, has a taste similar to a banana, usually containing 2 to 3 almost 1″ long dark brown flattish seeds.

CULTURE: Somewhat difficult to transplant and should be moved as a small (3 to 6′) balled and burlapped or container grown plant; prefers moist, fertile, deep, slightly acid soils; does well in full sun; have seen extensive groves of Pawpaw along Sugar Creek (Turkey Run State Park, Indiana) growing in very dense shade; however, the trees were of open, straggly habit.

DISEASES AND INSECTS: None serious.

LANDSCAPE VALUE: Interesting native tree which could be used for naturalizing in moist, deep soils along streams; the fruits have a sweet, banana-like flavor and are eaten by man and animal; interesting species but its landscape uses are limited; have seen at the edges of woodlands where it provided a rather striking pose; will never replace Bradford Pear but has a place in specific situations.

CULTIVARS: Not readily available but three of the best include 'Davis', 'Overleese' and 'Sunflower'; these forms bear 3 to 6″ long fruits that average between 5 and 12 ounces each; 'Overleese' may produce fruits that weigh one pound or more.

PROPAGATION: Seeds possess a dormant embryo and possibly an impermeable seed coat and should be stratified in a moist medium for 60 days at 41°F; germination may be erratic.

ADDITIONAL NOTES: Animals (especially racoons) seem to relish the fruits; the epithet *triloba* refers to the three-lobed calyx. The fruit has a fragrant aroma and a custard-like texture of a banana and the taste of a banana pear; excellent source of Vitamins A and C; high in unsaturated fats, proteins, carbohydrates, richer than apples, peaches or grapes in K,P,Mg,S; also good balance of amino acids.

NATIVE HABITAT: New York to Florida, west to Nebraska and Texas. Introduced 1736.

RELATED SPECIES:

Asimina parviflora, (à-sim′i-nà pär-vi-flō′ra), Dwarf Pawpaw, is a reasonably common 6 to 8′ high shrub of the Piedmont and Coastal Plain from Virginia to Mississippi. The dark green 4 to 7″ long leaves, up to 4″ wide, are covered with a rusty pubescence beneath. The brownish purple flowers average 1/2 to 3/4″ wide and occur before the leaves in April in Georgia. The fruit is small compared to *A. triloba,* averaging 1/2 to 1 1/4″ long and about 1/2″ wide, seeds are about 1/2″ wide. Often found in sandy or dry woods. I have observed the plant on several occasions in the Athens area. Not very striking but a worthwhile plant. Zone 7 to 9.

Asimina incarna (A. speciosa)—Flag Pawpaw
(à-sim′i-nà in-kär′-na)

Out of respect for a former student, Mr. Mark Callahan, who consistently baffled me with unusual quiz material, this unknown but beautiful species is included. The 1 1/2 to 2″ diameter white outer petals surround the inner cream or yellow ones and appear in March to June depending on location. The oval fruits range from 1 3/4 to 3″ long and contain 1/2″ long seeds. The habit is typically shrubby, 4 to 5′ high with dark gray bark. Found in the sandhills from southeastern Georgia to northeastern Florida. Probably Zone 8 to 9.

Aspidistra elatior — Cast-iron Plant, Bar-room Plant
(as-pi-dis′tra ē-lā′ti-ôr)

FAMILY: Liliaceae

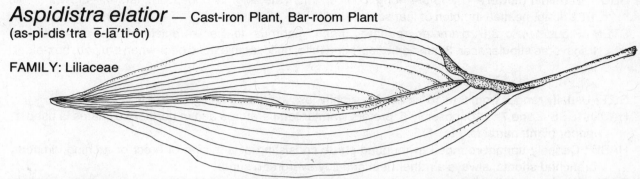

LEAVES: Evergreen, long ovate, parallel venation, blade 12 to 18″ long, dark green, entire, glabrous, acute apex; petiole 8 to 12″ long.

SIZE: 1 1/2 to 2′ high, 2 to 3′ wide.
HARDINESS: Zone 7 to 9, injured at 0°F, portion of the leaves turned brown, literally killed to the ground at –3°F in Athens; Zone 7 is probably over-optimistic unless the plant is protected.
HABIT: Upright clumps of evergreen foliage that develop from rhizomes.
RATE: Slow.
TEXTURE: Coarse.
LEAF COLOR: Lustrous dark green; wonderful contrast with lighter foliage colors; old brown leaves need to be removed in spring or entire plant cut to ground.
FLOWER: Purple, insignificant; occur underground and are only appreciated by moles.
CULTURE: Easily grown, provided a few simple rules are followed; prefers *full to partial* shade; deep, rich, well drained soil; should be sheltered from winter winds; displays excellent drought tolerance.
DISEASES AND INSECTS: None serious; scale has been mentioned.
LANDSCAPE VALUE: Excellent for low light areas; good plant for textural contrast; at the Georgia Botanical Garden it is planted under a ramp and receives limited light yet is a tremendous performer; can be used in containers, as an edging along walks, in masses or for accent; also makes a good indoor plant.
CULTIVARS:
  'Akebono'—White variegation on margin, much better than the striped form.
  'Variegata'—Leaves have alternate stripes of green and white in varied widths; will lose pronounced variegation if grown in high fertility soil; quite attractive and does add interesting color; less hardy than the species. Other selections include 'Milky Way' with white spots on leaf surface; 'Variegata Asher'—leaf centers flushed white with age; and 'Variegata Exotica' with parchment whitish variegations.
PROPAGATION: Division of established clumps.
ADDITIONAL NOTES: Does well in Coastal, Piedmont and lower south; called Bar-room Plant because of its ability to thrive under spittoonish conditions.
NATIVE HABITAT: Himalayas, China, Japan.

Aucuba japonica — Japanese Aucuba
(â-kū′ba ja-pon′ik-a)

FAMILY: Cornaceae
LEAVES: Opposite, simple, leathery, elliptic-ovate to el-

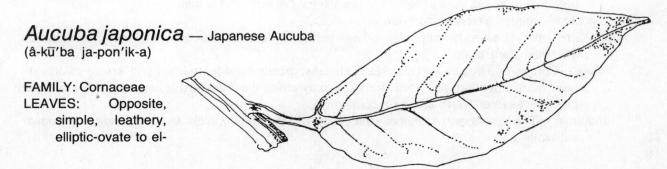

liptic-lanceolate, 3 to 8″ long, 1 1/2 to 3″ wide, acute to acuminate, broad cuneate at base, entire to remotely coarsely dentate toward the apex, glabrous, lustrous dark green above, lighter beneath; petiole—1/2 to 2″ long.

BUDS: Terminal (flower)—1/2 to 3/4″ long, conical, imbricate, slightly pubescent; lateral—brown, small, 1/32″ long, nestled in notch of leaf scar.

STEM: Stout, 1/4 to 3/8″ diameter, rounded, green, glabrous, leaf scars shield shape, connected by transverse stipular scar, 3 bundle traces; pith-white, solid, ample; fetid odor when bruised, box-elder-like.

SIZE: Usually ranges from 6 to 10′ in height, slightly less in spread; can grow to 15′.

HARDINESS: Zone 7 to 10, possibly 6, prefers warmer temperatures and in northern climates is used as indoor plant; hardy to 0 to −5°F.

HABIT: Densely upright-rounded to rounded shrub consisting of a thicket of erect or arching, limitedly branched shoots; always a rather neat and tidy evergreen shrub.

RATE: Slow, can easily be forced into more rapid growth with water and fertilizer.

TEXTURE: Medium, although medium-coarse could be easily argued.

LEAF COLOR: Dark lustrous green throughout the seasons; needs to be sited in shade, at least in south, for younger leaves when exposed to hot sun will blacken.

FLOWERS: Dioecious, purple, male flowers borne in upright, terminal, 2 to 4 1/2″ long panicles, individual flowers 1/3″ wide, with 4, occasionally 5 petals; female in shorter inflorescences from the axils of the leaves; March–April; in Athens flowers in mid to late March.

FRUIT: An ellipsoidal, 1/2″ long, scarlet, one-seeded, berry-like drupe; matures in October and November and persists through the following spring; quite handsome but often hidden by the foliage; anywhere from 1 to 5 present in leaf axil.

CULTURE: Easily transplanted, most plants are container-grown and present no transplanting problem; prefers well-drained, moist, high organic matter soils; must be sited in shade; has been known to grow under beeches, lindens and horsechestnuts were grass will not grow; tolerates polluted conditions extremely well; winter shade is also required for the leaves may become sickly green.

DISEASES AND INSECTS: In the last edition I reported no serious problems but in recent years have witnessed considerable stem dieback, at times just an occasional branch, others half the plant; *Sclerotium raulsoni* may be the causal agent for it girdles the stems.

LANDSCAPE VALUE: Used extensively in the south under the canopy of large trees and in ground cover plantings to break up the monotony of the sea of green; used in foundation plantings especially on the north and east side of homes; the variegated types add a touch of brightness to dark corners; also nice in groupings; remains quite dense even in heavy shade.

CULTIVARS: Many cultivars have been selected over the centuries and their nomenclature is somewhat confused. The following represent some of the more common types.

'Crassifolia'—A male form with large, leathery, dark green leaves; 'Macrophylla' is similar but female.

'Crotonifolia'—Large leaves are finely speckled with yellow; separate authorities list the sex as male and female.

'Fructo Albo'—Leaves white variegated, the fruits pinkish cream, female.

'Golden King'—Broadly golden variegated, male.

'Longifolia' (var. *longifolia*)—A catch-all name for narrow leaved forms; many have been introduced into cultivation; some male, others female; true 'Longifolia' is female; leaves may be 5″ long, only 1/4″ wide and faintly toothed; 'Augustifolia' ('Angustata') is male.

'Maculata'—leaves blotched yellowish white, male.

'Mr. Goldstrike'—Leaves heavily splashed with bold gold markings, much more intense than common gold dust plant, male.

'Nana'—Compact form, one-half the size of species, growth habit more erect and female selections bear more abundant fruit; also better display since the fruits are borne above the foliage; probably several 'Nana' clones in commerce.

'Picturata'—The leaves with a distinct solid yellow blotch in their middle and surrounded by smaller yellow flecks.

'Rozannie'—Flowers perfect, producing fruits in the absence of a male, forms a spreading compact shrub about 3′ high, leaves green, broad elliptic with a few coarse teeth near the apex.

'Salicifolia'—A green-leaved form with narrow, serrated leaves, a female.

'Serratifolia'—A rather handsome clone with large teeth along the margin; may also be listed as 'Dentata'.

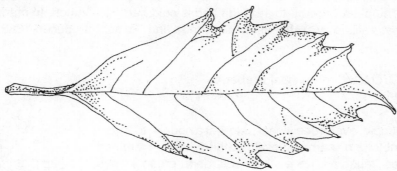

'Sulphur'—Wide, golden yellow edges with dark green centers, leaves serrated, female, the same as 'Sulphurea Marginata', an old cultivar dating from 1800's.

'Variegata'—The true Gold Dust Plant, introduced ahead of the species in 1783 from Japan by John Graeffer; this is the yellow-flecked form and is female; there are numerous variegated types— some are stable and others revert back to the green condition of the species.

PROPAGATION: Interestingly, I can find no information on seed propagation and on several occasions have attempted to germinate seeds without success. Cuttings root easily, about any time of the year; I have had 100% success by treating cuttings with 3000 ppm IBA—quick dip; cuttings should be firm.

ADDITIONAL NOTES: Certainly a popular landscape plant from Zone 7 south; an attempt could be made to straighten out some of the cultivar confusion. In recent years, popularity in the south has declined most probably related to the devastating freeze of 1983–84 when the leaves were knocked from many plants. Generally, stem tissue was not killed and regrowth was slow. In 1989, I see more 'Variegata' still alive and it appears slightly hardier than the species or other cultivars.

NATIVE HABITAT: Japan. Variegated form was introduced in 1783; the green form in 1861.

Baccharis halimifolia — Groundsel-bush
FAMILY: Asteraceae

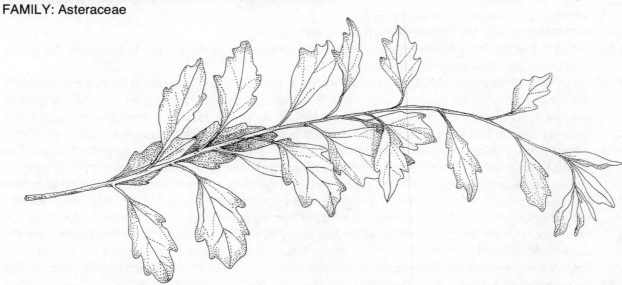

LEAVES: Alternate, simple, obovate to oblong, 1 to 3″ long, 1/4 to 1 1/2″ wide, acute, cuneate, coarsely toothed, upper leaves may be entire, both surfaces resinous dotted, gray-green; petiole 1/8 to 1/4″ long.

Baccharis halimifolia, (bak′ȧ-ris ha-li-mi-fō′li-ȧ) Groundsel-bush, is a handsome, unusual native multi-stemmed deciduous shrub with soft gray green to rich green leaves. The habit is distinctly oval to rounded. Makes a good mass or filler plant in difficult soil areas. Common along the coast of Georgia (quite salt tolerant) where in late summer and fall the white fruits appear as a froth over the top of the plants. The actual white color is the silky hairs on the pappus of the pistillate flowers much like the dandelion. The plant grows 5 to 12′ high and is cold hardy to Boston. In many inland areas in Georgia it has naturalized. Massachusetts to Florida and Texas. Introduced 1683. Zone 5 to 9.

Berberis candidula — Paleleaf Barberry
(bēr′ber-is kan-did′ū-la)

LEAVES: Alternate, simple, evergreen, linear, 3 to 9 at a node, 1 to 2″ long and 1/2″ wide, oblong or narrowly oval, leathery, spiny margined, edges of leaves recurved under, lustrous dark green above, glaucous white beneath, glabrous, cuneate, acute with spine like apex; petiole—1/16″ or smaller.

BUDS: Loosely aggregated scales arise in center of leaves, nondescript.

STEM: Light brown, glabrous, angled, zig-zag, 3-pronounced spines, each about 1/2″ long at node; pith-white, solid.

SIZE: 2 to 4′ in height, spreading to 5′.

HARDINESS: Zone 5 to 8 (9); −10°F or below will take the leaves off.

HABIT: Low growing, dense, evergreen shrub of hemispherical habit with branches rigidly arching and covered with three-prong spines.

RATE: Slow.

TEXTURE: Medium-fine in all seasons.

LEAF COLOR: Dark glossy green above, whitish below in summer; leaves often turn bronze to wine-red in fall and winter.

FLOWERS: Perfect, bright yellow, 5/8″ diameter, borne singly on a 1/2″ long pedicel in May–June; very dainty and appealing; unfortunately lost among the foliage.

FRUIT: True berry, purplish, bloomy, 1/2″ long, August–September.

CULTURE: Transplants readily; prefers moist, well-drained, slightly acid soils; full sun or light shade; withstands pruning well; fertilize in spring.

DISEASES AND INSECTS: Nothing exceptionally serious.

LANDSCAPE VALUE: Very handsome and beautiful plant for rock gardens; used in Europe in groupings or masses; could be used as a ground cover.

PROPAGATION: This discussion applies to barberries in general: I have rooted cuttings using 1000 ppm IBA/50% alcohol (KIBA might be better than the acid), peat:perlite, under mist with 90% or greater efficiency; barberries, in general, can be rooted from softwood cuttings; excessive moisture in the rooting bench is problematic and as soon as cuttings are rooted misting should be curtailed; I have rooted many different barberry species and cultivars utilizing the technique described above; the literature is full of "how to's" related to rooting barberry; I think it is probably more important how the cuttings are handled at the end of the cycle than the beginning; the deciduous types should be rooted from June through August while the evergreen types can be done at this time but also are amenable to September–October collection and sticking with rooting occurring 6 to 8 weeks later. Seeds should be removed from the pulp and sown in the fall with normal winter temperatures satisfying the cold-stratification period or placed in a moist medium and provided 3 months at 41°F and sown in flats in the greenhouse; damping off of seedlings can be a problem and fungicidal treatments may be appropriate; barberries have a high percentage (90 to 99%) of sound seed.

NATIVE HABITAT: *B. candidula* is native to central China. Introduced 1894.

RELATED SPECIES:

Berberis × **chenaultii,** (bĕr′ber-is sha-nōw′ē-ī), Chenault Barberry, is a hybrid that is probably the equal of *B. julianae* for cold hardiness. The plant grows 3 to 4′ high and slightly greater in spread. The lustrous dark green leaves turn a rich bronze-red with the onset of cold weather. Flowers and fruits are sparse compared to *B. julianae*. *Berberis* × *chenaultii* resulted from crosses between *B. gagnepainii* and *B. verruculosa,* and several selections were named. It is questionable whether one is buying the species or the named selections. The original crosses were made by Chenault of Orleans, France, around 1933. Zone 5 to 8.

Berberis × **frikartii,** (bĕr′ber-is frik-är′tē-ī), Frikart's Barberry, is a hybrid between *B. candidula* and *B. verruculosa*. The type as first raised by Frikart of Stäfa, Switzerland around 1928. Mr. H. van de Laar in 1972 applied the grex name to these hybrids. The current 8 clones show hybrid vigor and differ from their parents in supposed lighter green leaves. I have seen 'Amstelveen' and 'Telstar' in England and am hard pressed to tell them from the parental species. 'Telstar' formed a 4′ high, flat-topped clump in 5 years at Kew. 'Amstelveen' is slightly less vigorous.

Berberis gagnepainii, (bĕr′ber-is gag-ne-pān′ē-ī), Black Barberry, serves as a parent for several of the hybrids but is doubtfully available commercially in this country. The plant ranges between 3 1/2 and 5″ in height and is usually higher than wide at maturity. The glossy, dark green, 1 1/4 to 4″ long leaves are the largest of the evergreen species mentioned here. *B. gagnepainii* has not proven hardy where winter temperatures range from −5° to −15°F.

Berberis × **gladwynensis** (bĕr′-ber-is glad-win-en′sis) 'William Penn' was introduced by the Henry Foundation of Gladwyne, PA. Its habit is dense and mounded, and plants mature at about four feet. The foliage is a lustrous dark green and turns a beautiful bronze in winter. Bright yellow flowers in April–May. The foliage may be the handsomest of any evergreen barberry. Unfortunately, the plant is not well known. It is represented in only a limited number of arboreta. Since the last edition this selection has picked up steam and is now being produced by major container growers. The parents are *B. verruculosa* and *B. gagnepainii*. Hardiness is suspect, and temperatures below −10° will probably eliminate it from the landscape. I saw a planting killed to the ground in Mt. Airy Arboretum after exposure to −17°F. One reference reported that this plant was hardy to −25 to −30°F but I don't believe it and neither does the plant. Continuous snow cover may permit survival at lower temperatures.

Berberis julianae — Wintergreen Barberry
(bĕr′-ber-is jū-lē-ā′na)

LEAVES: Alternate, simple, evergreen, narrow-elliptic to lanceolate or oblanceolate, 2 to 3″ long, 1/3 to 1/2″ wide, spiny-serrate, lustrous dark green above, much paler and indistinctly veined beneath, rigidly coriaceous, often 5 leaves at a node;petiole-1/3 to 5/8″ long.
STEM: Slightly angled, yellowish when young, light yellowish gray or yel-

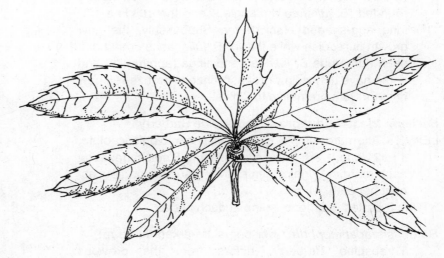

lowish brown the second year, spines rigid, 3-parted, 1/2 to 1 1/4" long; the inner bark and wood is yellow.

Berberis julianae, Wintergreen Barberry, is probably the hardiest of the evergreen barberries, although I have observed considerable leaf burning and abscission after exposure to temperatures of –6°F. Desiccating winds play a role in the browning and leaf drop observed on this species in northern states. On the University of Georgia campus in Athens, the leaves are retained through winter but may bronze or turn a good wine-red. The species forms a 6 to 8' (10') mound of dense branches and foliage when properly maintained. Bean mentioned a 10' high by 12' wide 'luxuriant rounded mass of foliage'. It is almost inpenetrable to students, children and dogs; for that reason, it makes a good barrier or hedge. The lustrous, dark green foliage is handsome throughout the growing season. Abundant yellow flowers (mid to late March-Athens) are followed by bluish black, 1/3" long oval fruits that may persist into fall. 'Nana' appears to be a good cultivar but is seldom available commercially. It grows about half the size of the species and forms a solid mound. Several southern nurseries have started to grow the plant for it makes an effective mass planting on commercial properties. 'Spring Glory' is a selection with brilliant coloration to the new shoot growth; leaves and stems are tinted red to bronze-red. Mr. Don Shadow, Winchester, TN, first pointed out the plant to me. Based on initial observations it is superior to the species and will prove a worthy landscape plant with time. Pruning tends to ruin the plant and throughout the southeast, especially on campuses, it is reduced to a 30 to 42" high hedge. The lower branches lose their foliage with time and plants become open and ratty. Ideally, let the plant go and develop the naturally dense rounded habit or cut to within 6 to 12" of the ground and allow for complete rejuvenation. Central China. Introduced 1900. Zone 5 to 8.

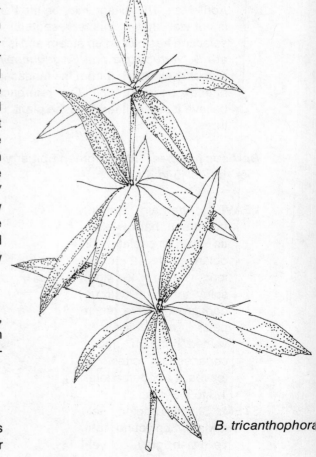

Berberis sanguinea, (bẽr'ber-is san-gwin'ē-a), Red-pedicel Barberry, and *B sargentiana,* (bẽr'ber-is särjent-ē-āna), Sargent Barberry, deserve mention because of their fine evergreen foliage, yellow flowers, and red maturing to black fruit. Both are dense in habit growing 6 to 9' high and 6' wide. I have seen them used in Zones 6 to 8 and feel they are worthy of consideration. *Berberis sargentiana* continues to fascinate me for I never see it in commerce only in botanical gardens and arboreta yet, according to Bean, it was described as the only evergreen barberry known to be hardy at the Arnold Arboretum. I did not locate it during sabbatical. In most respects, it is like *B. julianae,* except the leaves are larger, 1 1/2 to 5" long, 1/2 to 1 1/4" wide, dark green (without prominent luster of *B. julianae*), the stems are rounded (*B. julianae* are angled), and the fruit is a 1/3" long egg-shaped black berry. Supposedly, the new growth is reddish while that of *B. julianae* is not. I have seen numerous *B. julianae* seedlings (apparently) and some have rich yellow green, bronze to bronze-red new growth. Both are native to China.

Berberis triacanthophora — Threespine Barberry
LEAVES: Alternate, simple, evergreen, linear to oblanceolate, 1 to 2" long, 1/8" (1/2") wide, with 1 to 5 setose teeth on each margin, bright green above, glaucous or glaucescent beneath.
STEM: 3-parted, 5/8" long, spine at each node.

Berberis triacanthophora, (bẽr'ber-is trī-a-kan-thof'o-rà), Threespine Barberry, differs from the previous evergreen species in that the flowers are pale yellow or

B. tricanthophora

whitish, tinged red outside, producing a pink effect overall. Fruit is bluish black, slightly bloomy, 1/3″ diameter. The plant matures at three to five feet and tends to be more open than other evergreen species. The foliage is bright green above, somewhat glaucous on the underside and some leaves turn reddish purple in winter. Spines are 3-parted and vicious. I had one plant in my garden and was never impressed by its performance. Central China. Introduced 1907. Zone 5 to 8.

Berberis verruculosa — Warty Barberry

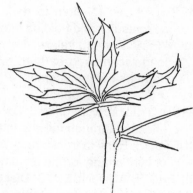

LEAVES: Alternate, simple, evergreen, 1/2 to 1 1/2″ long, elliptic or ovate to ovate-lanceolate, tapering at both ends, leathery, margins recurved and remotely spiny-toothed, glabrous, lustrous dark green above, glaucous beneath, leaves arranged in clusters along the stems.

STEM: Rounded, light brown, covered with tiny dark brown excrescences which give the bark a rough surface; spines are slender, 3-parted, 1/2 to 3/4″ long.

Berberis verruculosa, (bĕr′ber-is ver-uk-ū-lō′sa), Warty Barberry, grows to 3 to 6′ and forms a dense evergreen shrub. Leaves are small and lustrous dark green above, whitish beneath and remain green, become purplish green or turn rich mahogany in winter. The flowers are golden yellow, 5/8 to 3/4″ diameter. Fruit is violet-black, bloomy, 1/3″ long. Closely related to *B. candidula.* Western China. Introduced 1904. Zone 5. Although listed as hardy in Zone 5 it was severely injured above the snowline during the winter of 1975–76 in Illinois and lowest recorded temperature was −8°F. *Berberis candidula* growing next to it was not affected. It is similar to and often confused with *B. candidula.* Based on my experience with the two species, the following differences seem relatively constant. The leaves of warty barberry are not as white on their underside, although this characteristics appears less than absolute, and the stems are covered with tiny, wart-like excrescences. Height may approach 3 to 6′ compared to 3′ for *B. candidula.* 'Compacta' has been listed, but I have not seen the plant in cultivation.

ADDITIONAL NOTES: I could ramble for pages over the various species of evergreen barberries. They can be among the handsomest of landscape plants when properly groomed. The reciprocal is also true. In traveling through European gardens I noticed an abundance of evergreen barberries of great foliage and floral beauty. On the west coast especially in the San Francisco area I observed a number of the same species. Some of the best include *B. darwinii,* Darwin Barberry; *B. empetrifolia,* Crow Barberry; *B. linearifolia,* Jasperbells Barberry, and *B. × stenophylla,* Rosemary Barbery. New hybrids will continue to appear in the years ahead.

Berberis koreana — Korean Barberry
(bĕr′ber-is kō-re-ā′na)

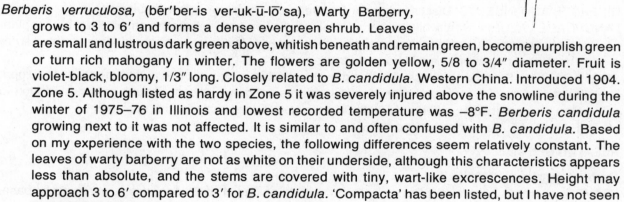

LEAVES: Alternate, simple, obovate or elliptic, 1 to 3″ long, rounded at apex, cuneate at base, rather densely spinulose-serrulate, reticulate beneath, medium to dark green above, strongly veined beneath; petiole-1/4 to 1/2″ long.

STEM: Moderate, reddish to purple-brown, bloomy, grooved, glabrous, with 1 to 5 spines, usually 3, each spine flattened and nearly 1/4″ wide.

SIZE: Rather dense shrub growing 4 to 6′ (8′) high and usually slightly less in spread.
HARDINESS: Zone 3 to 7.

HABIT: Multistemmed oval to haystack-shaped plant of rather dense constitution; however, it does sucker from the roots and at times becomes quite unruly in its growth habit; will form large, clump-type colonies.

RATE: Medium.

TEXTURE: Medium in all seasons; this species has larger foliage than most barberries.

STEM COLOR: Young shoots are reddish and bloomy.

LEAF COLOR: Medium to dark green in summer changing to deep reddish purple in the fall; often spectacular and holding late (November).

FLOWERS: Perfect, yellow, 1/4″ diameter, each flower on a 1/2″ long pedicel, borne in drooping, 3 to 4″ long racemes in early to mid May-Boston; borne after foliage has matured but still quite showy, perhaps the handsomest of the deciduous barberries for flower although I know plantsmen who will argue this contention.

FRUIT: True berry, bright red, covered to varying degrees with a waxy bloom, egg-shaped, 1/4 to 3/8″ long, effective through fall and into winter.

CULTURE: Easy to transplant; will tolerate about any soil except those that are permanently wet; full sun or light shade; prune anytime; extremely cold hardy.

DISEASES AND INSECTS: Discussed under *B. thunbergii;* usually very few problems.

LANDSCAPE VALUE: A worthwhile barberry for foliage, flower, and fruit: makes an excellent barrier plant and I have seen it used in mass plantings with a degree of success; presents an inpenetrable barrier to unwanted neighbors; best in northern gardens.

PROPAGATION: Softwood cuttings of young growth collected in May or June and treated with 1000 ppm IBA rooted readily; most barberry species have internal dormancy and require cold stratification to stimulate germination; a period fo 60 to 90 days at 41°F is suitable for this species.

NATIVE HABITAT: Korea. Introduced 1905.

RELATED SPECIES:

Berberis gilgiana—Wildfire Barberry

LEAVES: Alternate, simple, elliptic or elliptic-obovate to oblong, 1 to 2″ long, acute, attenuate at base, remotely serrate, dull green above, either glabrous or slightly pubescent, gray-green below.

STEM: Grooved, 1/4 to 1″ long, usually 3 parted spines.

Berberis gilgiana, (bĕr′ber-is gil-jē-a′na), Wildfire Barberry, has excellent garden potential, but very few people know the plant. A mature specimen may be 6 to 8′ high and densely branched to form a rounded outline. The rich green foliage is attractive throughout the growing season and changes to beautiful shades of yellow, orange and red in fall. The bright yellow flowers are borne in spike-like, pendulous, 2 to 3″ long racemes in May. They are followed by reddish fruits that persist into fall. This is an extremely attractive barberry at least worthy of trial by nurserymen. The species is hardy to −15°F and possibly lower. North, central China. Introduced 1910. Zone 5 to 7.

Berberis vulgaris—Common Barberry

LEAVES: Alternate, simple, oval or obovate, 1 to 2″ long, obtuse, rarely acutish, finely toothed, thin, dull green.

Berberis vulgaris, (bĕr′ber-is vul-gār′is), Common Barberry, grows 6 to 10′ high producing a mass of stems; erect at the base, branching and spreading outwards at the top into a graceful, arching or pendulous form. The foliage is dull green, about 1 to 2″ long. Flowers are yellow and borne in 2 to 3″ long pendulous racemes in May. Fruit is a bright red or purple, 1/3 to 1/2″ long, egg-shaped berry which becomes effective in fall and persists. W.J. Bean is manifest in his praise of this shrub but in America it is a significant problem for it has escaped from cultivation and serves as the alternate host for the wheat rust, *Puccinia graminis.* In some states the laws require the destruction of Common Barberry on this account. Native to Europe, North Africa and temperate Asia. Long cultivated. Zone 3 to ?.

Berberis × mentorensis — Mentor Barberry; result of cross between *B. julianae* and *B. thunbergii*.

(bĕr'ber-is men-tor-en'sis)

FAMILY: Berberidacae

LEAVES: Alternate, simple, elliptic-ovate, 1 to 2″ long, subcoriaceous, sparingly spinulose toothed toward apex, very dark green, pale beneath; tends to be semi-evergreen or hold leaves late in fall.

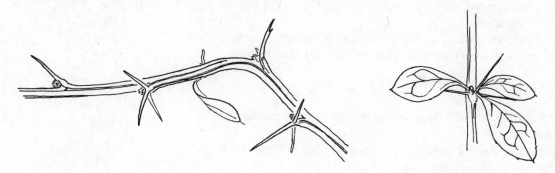

BUDS: Small and scaly, usually 6 pointed scales borne on spurs which is true for most barberries.

STEM: Glabrous, usually three-spined, grooved, inner bark and wood yellow as is true for all barberries; 3-spined on older branches, young stems often have only a single spine.

SIZE: 5′ in height by 5′ to 7′ in spread; have seen specimens 5 to 7′ high and 10 to 12′ wide.

HARDINESS: Zone 5 to 8; does not seem as prosperous in the south (Zone 8) yet both parents are adapted.

HABIT: Upright, stiff, with many slender stems, becoming bushy with age, very regular and rounded in outline.

RATE: Medium to fast, good rapid growing hedge plant.

TEXTURE: Medium in foliage, medium in winter.

LEAF COLOR: Dark green, leathery in nature; often developing yellow-orange-red late in fall; have observed leaves as late as December 5 in Boston, Massachusetts. A California reference noted it is evergreen to −5°F but in my 10 years in Athens it has always become deciduous; the lowest temperature was −3°F and one winter temperatures did not drop below 18°F.

FLOWERS: Yellow, usually April-May, not as showy as other species but still attractive; flowers in mid to late March in Athens, GA.

FRUIT: I have never observed fruit on this hybrid and assume it is sterile; possibly a triploid?; one parent is bright red-fruited; the other bluish black.

CULTURE: Easily transplanted, very adaptable; full sun to 1/2 shade situations; well drained soil is preferable.

DISEASES AND INSECTS: None serious, although *Verticillium* wilt has been reported; see under *B. thunbergii*.

LANDSCAPE VALUE: Excellent hedge plant because of uniform growth rate; makes an excellent barrier plant because of thorny nature of stems; can be used for massing, shrub border and foundation plant; possibly the best of the barberries for hedging in the midwest and east; makes a beautiful dense, mounded shrub if left to its own genetic code and not that of the pruning shears.

PROPAGATION: Roots readily and one report mentioned that cuttings collected in early August and treated with 8000 ppm IBA rooted 100% by late September.

ADDITIONAL NOTES: Result of breeding work of M. Horvath, Mentor, Ohio. Introduced 1942. Although considered quite hardy, severe top damage occurred during the winters of 1976–77, 77–78 when temperatures dropped to −25°F in the midwestern states.

Berberis thunbergii — Japanese Barberry
(bĕr′ber-is　thun-bĕr′jē-a)

LEAVES: Alternate, simple, very unequal, obovate to spatu-
late-oblong, 1/2 to 1 1/4″ long, obtuse, rarely acute, sometimes spine-tipped, narrowed at base into a petiole 1/12
to 1/2″ long, quite entire, bright green above, glaucescent
beneath, leaves borne in clusters along the branches.

BUDS: Small, ovoid, solitary, sessile, about 6 pointed scales
born on spurs.

STEM: Reddish brown, angled or grooved, glabrous, single
spine, 1/2″ long (usually), does not always hold true.

SIZE: 3 to 6′ by 4 to 7′; Bean mentions plants 8′ high and 15′
wide.

HARDINESS: Zone 4 to 8; not as robust in heat of Zone 8 but
performs reasonably well.

HABIT: Much branched, very dense rounded shrub usually broader than tall at maturity.

RATE: Medium.

TEXTURE: Medium fine to medium in leaf, medium to coarse in winter; tends to attract leaves, papers,
cans and bottles due to dense, multi-stemmed habit; I have personally looked upon this shrub as a
winter garbage can because of this ability; truly requires a spring cleaning.

LEAF COLOR: Bright green in summer changing to orange, scarlet, and reddish purple in the fall; usually
quite variable in fall color; one of first shrubs to leaf out in spring; this is true for most of the deciduous
barberries.

FLOWERS: Perfect, yellow, 1/3 to 1/2″ across, borne on a 1/2″ long pedicel, April–May, solitary or 2
to 4 in umbellate clusters, actually not showy for individual flowers are small and borne under the
foliage.

FRUIT: Bright red, 1/3″ long, ellipsoidal berry, October and persisting into winter; excellent winter effect
and should be considered more often for its fruits.

CULTURE: Easily transplanted as a container plant; extremely adaptable, withstands dry conditions; will
not withstand extremely moist conditions; best in full sun; tolerates urban conditions better than many
shrubs.

DISEASES AND INSECTS: Bacterial leaf spot, anthracnose, root rots, rusts (Japanese Barberry is not
susceptible), wilt, mosaic, barberry aphid, barberry webworm, scale, and northern root-knot
nematode; usually barberries are little troubled under ordinary landscape conditions.

LANDSCAPE VALUE: Hedge, barrier, groupings; the cultivars offer different foliage colors and forms and
therefore other landscape possibilities.

CULTIVARS: In the last edition I mentioned that more new cultivars were on the way. Well, they have
arrived. Probably another 10 to 15 have been introduced or actively promoted since the 1983
edition. I have left the old and embellished them with new observations and added many of the
new cultivars.

var. atropurpurea—The foliage assumes reddish or purplish shades. There is extreme variation
among seed-grown progeny, and selections have been made for superior red-purple coloration.
The history of this plant is interesting—the original plant arose in the nursery of Renault in
Orleans, France, about 1913, but it was not distributed until 1926. At first, the plant was
propagated vegetatively, but it was later discovered that it would come relatively true to type
from seed. Many nurserymen still grow it from seed and rogue the off-color seedlings. The
red-purple foliage becomes more greenish if the plants are sited in shade. This is true of the
various named selections of var. atropurpurea. The yellow flowers are tinged with purple, but

the fruits are the same bright red as those of the species. Generally grows about the same size as the species.

var. *atropurpurea* 'Baggatelle'—A compact form like 'Crimson Pygmy' except the leaves are slightly glossier, considered slower growing, more compact (16″ high) and with smaller leaves (1″ long); a most beautiful selection with vivid red-purple leaves, originated at Van Klaverin, Boskoop and introduced in 1971, supposedly a hybrid between 'Kobold' and 'Atropurpurea Nana'.

var. *atropurpurea* 'Crimson Pygmy'—This is the most popular Japanese Barberry selection. This low, dense plant grows 1 1/2 to 2′ tall and 2 1/2 to 3′ wide. The foliage color is best when the plant is grown in full sun. The plant was raised by Van Eyck in Boskoop, Holland, in 1942. Unfortunately, it has been sold under the names 'Little Gem', 'Little Beauty', 'Little Favorite' and 'Atropurpurea Nana'. It is an excellent landscape plant from Chicago, IL, to Atlanta, GA, and can be used for a multitude of purposes. A 12-year-old plant may be 2′ high and 5′ wide.

var. *atropurpurea* 'Crimson Velvet'—A form described as possessing fuchsia new foliage that deepens to smokey maroon, the color holding throughout the growing season, vigorous grower, fall color is a good red, probably similar to var. *atropurpurea* in size and habit; introduced by Lake County Nursery Exchange, Perry, Ohio.

var. *atropurpurea* 'Dart's Red Lady'—Large, dark purple-black leaves, good autumn color, semi-spreading habit; have seen in Mr. Adrian Bloom's great garden and was impressed by intensity of foliage color; have seen in September at Sissinghurst and although the purple was distinct it was not as vibrant as in the spring.

var. *atropurpurea* 'Erecta'—It is similar to var. *atropurpurea,* except that its habit is more upright. It was found at Marshall Nurseries, Arlington, Nebraska in a block of two-year seedlings.

var. *atropurpurea* 'Golden Ring' ('Golden Rim' in Europe may be the same thing?)— This is a reddish purple-leaved form similar to the variety in growth habit but with a green or yellow-green border around the margin of each leaf. The effect is not noticeable except on close inspection.

var. *atropurpurea* 'Harlequin'—New foliage a mottle of pink, cream and purple; forms a tight, rather compact shrub about 4′ high, a Dutch introduction.

var. *atropurpurea* 'Helmond Pillar'—Distinct upright form reminiscent of 'Erecta' but narrower and with reddish purple leaves, good red autumn color, reasonably common in English gardens, probably grows 4 to 5′ by 2′ wide; narrower at base than top.

var. *atropurpurea* 'Intermedia'—This cultivar was selected from a group of seedling 'Crimson Pygmy' plants at Zelenka Evergreen Nursery Inc., Grand Haven, MI. It grows much faster than 'Crimson Pygmy', with good reddish purple foliage. Its mature size averages about three feet; good looking plant.

var. *atropurpurea* 'Pink Queen'—Young foliage nearly red like 'Rose Glow', later leaves more brown with pink-red, gray and white specks and stripes, turns good red in fall, probably 4′ by 4 to 6′ wide, has also been listed as 'Atropurpurea Rosea'.

var. *atropurpurea* 'Red Bird'—This is a selection made by Willis Nursery Co., Inc., Ottawa, KS, prior to 1959. It has better color and larger leaves and is more compact than *atropurpurea*.

var. *atropurpurea* 'Red Chief'—Vivid reddish purple new foliage that becomes green-purple-brown with maturity, leaves 1 1/2″ long by 1/2″ wide, stems also bright reddish purple, orange-red to orange-purple fall color, grows 6′ by 8′.

var. *atropurpurea* 'Red Pillar'—Red to reddish purple leaves, good orange-red fall color, dense upright column at maturity, 4 to 5′ by 1 1/2 to 2′.

var. *atropurpurea* 'Rose Glow'—Spaargen & Sons of Holland raised this selection about 1957. The new foliage is rose-pink, mottled with deeper red-purple splotches. The colors gradually mature to a deep reddish purple. The ultimate size is about 5 to 6′. I have grown 'Rose Glow' in Urbana, IL, and Athens, GA, with excellent success. First leaves are purple, the new shoots that follow produce the characteristic mottled color. Has become extremely popular in the south. A good form.

var. *atropurpurea* 'Sheridan's Red'—A single observation at the Royal Botanic Garden, Hamilton, Ont., Canada, is sufficient reason for including this selection. The leaves are larger and more leathery than those of *atropurpurea,* and were a vivid red-purple in mid-August.

'Aurea'—This plant is a definite knockout if one is looking for contrast. The leaves are a vivid yellow and hold this color except in shade, where they become yellow-green. Surprisingly, the yellow foliage does not seem to burn or scorch, even in southern landscapes. 'Aurea' is a dense, relatively slow-growing shrub, eventually reaching a height of 3 to 4'. Apparently it does not flower or fruit heavily. 'Bonanza Gold' grows 1 1/2 to 2' by 2 to 2 1/2', bright gold leaves, red fruit.

'Erecta'—A fine selection seldom available commercially, it was introduced by Horvath after five generations of selections for upright habit. This cultivar grows 4 to 5' high and 8 to 10' wide, but only after a great many years. Each branch is distinctly upright, and very few laterals are produced. The fall color varies from yellow or orange to red and can be truly spectacular. 'Erecta' was patented by Cole Nursery Co., Painesville, OH, in 1936. Another name applied to this clone is Truehedge Columnberry.

'Globe'—This patented selection has also been listed as 'Nana' and 'Compacta'. The habit is that of a globe. Its mature height ranges from 2 and 3', with a spread about twice that. The foliage is a uniform dark green and may be reddish in fall.

'Green Carpet'—Light green, oval to rounded leaves turn good yellow-orange-red in fall, develops a spreading growth habit, 3' by 5', a Dutch introduction.

'Green Ornament'—Good dark green, 1/2 to 1 1/4", rounded-elliptic foliage on an upright ascending shrub that will average 5' by 3' at landscape maturity, a free-fruiting form with glossy red fruits, fall color brownish yellow.

'Kelleriis'—A compact 4 to 5' by 4 to 5' form with medium green foliage that is speckled and splashed with white variegation on the new shoots, variegation persists into fall, a Dutch introduction.

'Kobold'— Introduced by Van Klavern of Boskoop, Holland, around 1960. Its habit is similar to that of a compact Japanese Holly or boxwood, and in summer offers a visual substitute. The new foliage is rich green, becoming lustrous dark green with maturity. In fall, it is off-yellow, with perhaps a tinge of red. Flowers and fruits are sparsely produced. This selection grows 2 to 2 1/2' at maturity and forms a perfect mound without pruning. It is tremendous addition to the list of landscape barberries.

'Minor'—It was grown from seed collected at the Arnold Arboretum in 1892. The leaves, flowers and fruits are smaller than those of the species. The habit is dense, rounded and compact, reaching a height of 3 1/2 to 5'.

'Silver Beauty'—A sprawly grower with variegated green and white foliage; it is not uniform in variegation patterns. It does not appear to possess the vigor of the species. It is also listed as 'Argenteo-marginata'.

'Sparkle'—The plants, even when young, have arching horizontal branches and maintain a dense constitution into old age. The plant grows 3 to 4' high and slightly wider at maturity. The glossy, rich, dark green, almost leathery foliage turns a fluorescent reddish orange in fall. Abundant yellow flowers are followed by persistent bright red fruits. Did not do particularly well in my Georgia garden but have seen handsome specimens in the Cincinnati area. Introduced by Synnesvedt Nursery, IL.

'Thornless'—Because most barberries carry thorns, this one is somewhat of a novelty. The habit is globe-like, with a mature size of about 4 by 6'.

'Variegata'—There are several variegated froms mentioned in the literature, and it is questionable how different they are. This cultivar originated as a chance seedling among 20,000 plants in the nurseries of Alex Toth, Madison, OH. The leaves are predominantly green with spots, splotches, or dots of white, light gray and yellow. Have seen an 'Aureo-marginata' described that has green, yellow, pink new leaves and pink stems; grew 3' by 4' in 6 years.

'Vermillion'—Dense, compact form, 3 to 3 1/2' high, green summer foliage turning vermillion-red in fall.

NATIVE HABITAT: Japan. Introduced about 1864.

Betula lenta — Sweet Birch, also called Black or Cherry Birch
(bet'ū-la lĕn'ta)

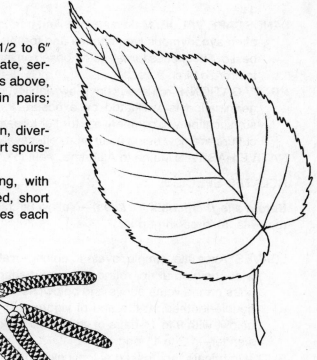

FAMILY: Betulaceae

LEAVES: Alternate, simple, ovate or ovate-oblong, 2 1/2 to 6″ long, 1 1/2 to 3 1/2″ wide, acuminate, mostly cordate, serrated, often doubly, glossy dark green and glabrous above, paler beneath and hairy on veins, 10 to 13 vein pairs; petiole—1/2 to 1″ long, pubescent.

BUDS: Imbricate, conical, sharp pointed, reddish brown, divergent, terminal-absent on long shoots; buds on short spurs-terminal.

STEM: Slender, light reddish brown, glabrous, shining, with strong wintergreen flavor when chewed or smelled, short spur-like lateral shoots abundant, bearing 2 leaves each season.

SIZE: Possiby 40 to 55′ in height in a landscape situation with a spread of 35 to 45′; in the wild may reach 70 to 80′ in height.

HARDINESS: Zone 3 to cool mountain areas of Georgia and Alabama.

HABIT: Pyramidal and dense in youth forming an irregular, rounded, sometimes wide spreading crown at maturity.

RATE: Medium, 20 feet over a 20 year period.

TEXTURE: Medium in leaf and winter.

BARK COLOR: Glistening reddish brown to almost black on young trees, reminds of wild black cherry, *Prunus serotina* bark, with prominent horizontal lenticels; on mature trees brownish black and breaking up into large, thin, irregular, scaly plates.

LEAF COLOR: Lustrous dark green in summer changing to golden yellow; exhibits the best fall color of the commonly cultivated birches especially in midwest (among *B. nigra, B. papyrifera, B. pendula,* and *B. populifolia*).

FLOWERS: Monoecious, staminate catkins, 2 to 3″ long; the male flowers on birches are apparent on the tree during the winter as they are formed during summer and fall of the year prior to flowering; the pistillate flowers are enclosed in the bud and are borne upright while the male catkins are pendulous; the birches flower in April before the leaves; they possess a hidden beauty which is lost to most people because they have never examined or considered the birches as flowering species, on *B. lenta* male 3 to 4″ long; female 1/2 to 1″ long.

FRUIT: Small winged nutlet, occurring in a 3/4 to 1 1/3″ long, 3/5″ wide strobile.

CULTURE: Reaches its best development in deep, rich, most, slightly acid, well-drained soils; however, is often found on rocky, drier sites; has performed reasonably well on the heavy soils of the midwest.

DISEASES AND INSECTS: Birches are subject to many problems and the following list is applicable to this and the species which follow unless otherwise noted; leaf spots, leaf blisters, leaf rust, canker (black, paper, sweet and yellow birches are particularly affected), dieback, wood-decay, and mildew are the most commonly noted pathogens; insects include aphids, witch-hazel leaf gall aphid, birch skeletonizer, leaf miner (gray, paper, white are very susceptible), bronze birch borer and seed mite gall.

LANDSCAPE VALUE: Makes an excellent tree for parks, naturalized areas, does not have the white bark often synonymous with birches and for this reason is often shunned; Dr. Wyman mentions it is the best of the birches for fall color; based on midwest and eastern observations, I would agree; resistant to bronze birch borer.

PROPAGATION: Birch seeds have low viability, but produce numerous nutlets (1/2 to 1 million) per pound; germination is facilitated by exposure to light, never plant seeds too deeply; one month cold stratification will compensate for light treatment. Many cultivars are grafted but cuttings and tissue culture are now being used more effectively. See Dirr and Heuser, 1987.

NATIVE HABITAT: Maine to Alabama, west to Ohio. Introduced 1759.

RELATED SPECIES:

Betula alleghaniensis *(B. lutea)*—Yellow Birch
(bet′ū-la al-lĕ-gā′-nē-en′sis)

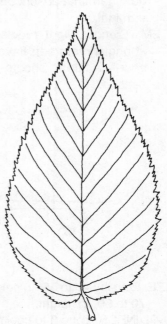

LEAVES: Alternate, simple, ovate to oblong-ovate, 3 to 5″ long, 1/2 as wide, pointed at tip, rounded or heart-shaped at base with pale hairs on the veins above and below, nearly glabrous at maturity, double-toothed, at the end of vigorous shoots often pubescent below, with 9 to 11 pairs of veins, dull dark green above; petiole slender—1/2 to 1″ long.

BUDS: Imbricate, appressed at least along the lower part of the stem, often hairy.

STEM: Slender, dull-light yellowish brown, exhibiting the faint odor and taste of wintergreen, bark has a bitter taste.

CATKINS: Fruiting catkins 1 to 1 1/2″ long, 3/4″ thick, erect; short-stalked or subsessile, fatter than those of *B. lenta;* back of scales are pubescent, those of *B. lenta* are not or sparingly so.

Betula alleghaniensis, Yellow Birch, is similar to *B. lenta* but grows 60 to 75′ and occasionally 100′ in height. The leaves are dull dark green above, pale yellow-green beneath in summer changing to yellow in fall. Bark on young stems and branches is yellowish or bronze and produces thin papery shreds, gradually changing to reddish brown and breaking into large, ragged edged plates. It prefers moist, cool soils and cool summer temperatures as it does not perform well in hot, dry climates. An important lumber tree as the wood is used extensively for cabinets, furniture, flooring and doors. Native to Newfoundland to Manitoba, south to high peaks of Georgia and Tennessee. Cultivate 1800. Zone 3 to 7, only in higher elevations in south.

ADDITIONAL NOTES: Rather difficult to separate these two species; often found together especially in the Appalachian range to North Georgia. They are beautiful in fall color and valuable for lumber but their lack of white bark precludes their ever becoming popular landscape species. Oil of wintergreen can be distilled from the stem and bark of these species.

Betula nigra — River Birch, also termed Red Birch
(bet′ū-la nī′gra)

LEAVES: Alternate, simple, 1 1/2 to 3 1/2″ long, 3/4 to 2 1/2″ wide, rhombic-ovate, sharp pointed, doubly serrate, or shallowly lobed, base wedge shape, lustrous medium to dark green above, glaucous beneath with 7 to 9 pairs of impressed veins; petiole—1/4 to 1/2″ long, downy.

BUDS: Imbricate, small, less than 1/5″ long, light chestnut brown, sometimes pubescent, more or less appressed.

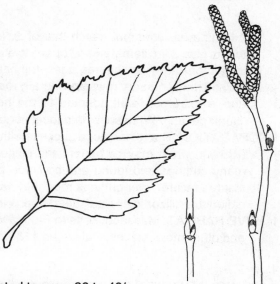

STEM: Pubescent at first, later essentially glabrous, reddish brown, with warty excrescences.

BARK: Young trunks and branches thin, shining, light reddish brown to cinnamon brown, peeling freely; older trunks, dark reddish brown, deeply furrowed, broken into irregular plate-like scales.

SIZE: 40 to 70′ and may reach 90′ in height; spread 40 to 60′.

HARDINESS: Zone 4 to 9.

HABIT: Pyramidal to oval-headed in youth, often rounded in outline at maturity; the trunk is usually divided into several large arching branches close to the ground; the tree is more handsome when grown as a multi-stemmed specimen.

RATE: Medium to fast, over a 20 year period can be expected to grow 30 to 40′.

BARK: On branches 2″ or greater diameter, exfoliating into papery plates and exposing the inner bark which is colored gray-brown to cinnamon-brown to reddish brown; various authors list the color as salmon-pink but this is stretching the fact; there is tremendous variability in bark color among trees, native populations exhibit extreme variability in bark color; most River Birch are seedling grown so differences in bark and other characteristics are the rule and not the exception; the biological world is composed of shades of gray and not black and white; there simply are no stereotypes in the species category; one cannot unequivocally say that all River Birch (or any other species) will have the same leaf, bark, or fall color; it is folly to think like this in relation to biological systems; old bark of River Birch becomes brown and develops a ridged and furrowed character.

LEAF COLOR: Lustrous medium to dark green in summer changing to yellow in fall and soon dropping; the fall color on River Birch is seldom effective.

FLOWERS: Male in 2 to 3″ long, slender dark brown catkins.

FRUIT: Small nutlet, born in a 1 to 1 1/2″ long, 1/2″ thick cylindric, pendulous catkin, ripens and sheds seed in spring.

CULTURE: Transplants well; best adapted to moist soils and is usually found in the wild along stream banks and in swampy bottomlands which are periodically flooded; will survive in drier soils although reaches its maximum development in moist, fertile areas; prefers an acid soil (6.5 or below) for chlorosis will develop in high pH situations. In early March I was putting a rope swing over our creek and had to cut a branch from this species; the end of the branch actually produced a steady stream of sap. Moral: don't prune this birch and other birches until summer. They are "bleeders" and should not be cut when the sap is flowing.

DISEASES AND INSECTS: Probably the most trouble free birch but in moist years, I have noticed significant leaf spot that may cause premature defoliation of older (interior) leaves.

LANDSCAPE VALUE: Very handsome specimen tree for estates, parks, golf courses, campuses and other large areas; particularly well suited to areas which are wet a portion of the year yet may be quite dry in the summer and fall; handsome for bark character and should receive wider landscape use as it becomes better known; the iron chlorosis on high pH soils has been extremely common in the midwest, for this reason I would test the soil and make sure it read pH 6.5 or below before planting River Birch; River Birch is being planted more widely in the south; on the University of Georgia campus it is used effectively in a multiplicity of situations; the most widely distributed birch in the United States and definitely the best choice for hot climates.

CULTIVARS: 'Heritage'—A patented selection introduced by Mr. Earl Cully, Jacksonville, IL; over the 8 years since the last edition this introduction has earned a place in the birch hall of fame; it is commonly grown and superior to the run-of-the-mill seedlings, generally produced through tissue culture and rooted cuttings; tremendous vigor and side by side comparisons in a southern nursery show 'Heritage' outgrowing the seedlings by 50%, leaves are larger, glossier dark green and less prone to leaf spot; fall color, like the species, is variable but in October of 1987 and 1988 was an excellent yellow in the

Athens area; does not match that of *B. lenta* but what does; the bark starts to exfoliate on young trunks (1 to 2″ in diameter) and opens to a white to salmon-white on young stems eventually darkening to salmon-brown as the tree ages, the bark is in every way superior to row run seedlings and I have walked many nursery rows and literally marvelled at the fine coloration; is cold hardy to at least −40°F and is extremely well adapted to the heat of Zone 8; interestingly side-by-side comparisons of 'Heritage' and 'Whitespire' in a local nursery indicate 'Heritage' is superior in every characteristic.

PROPAGATION: I have had good success with softwood cuttings treated with 1000 ppm IBA/50% alcohol (KIBA in water may be better) and placed in peat:perlite under mist; over the years I have rooted many cuttings and found one common denominator: any period of dryness on the leave surface insures failure; after cuttings root, they will produce a flush of growth especially if a light application of liquid fertilizer is applied; seed ripens in the spring and should be direct sown.

NATIVE HABITAT: Massachusetts to Florida west to Minnesota and Kansas; restricted to stream banks and other moist places. Cultivated 1736.

Betula papyrifera — Paper Birch, also called Canoe or White Birch
(bet′ū-la păp-ĭ-rif′ĕr-ă)

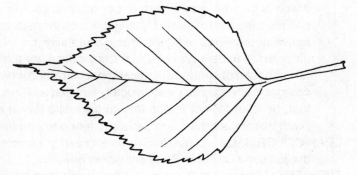

LEAVES: Alternate, simple, ovate to narrow ovate, 2 to 4″ (5 1/2″) long, 2/3 as wide, acuminate, rounded or sometimes wedge shaped, coarsely and doubly serrate, glabrous and dark green above, pubescent on veins beneath, 3 to 7 pairs of lateral veins; petiole-about 1″ long, pubescent.

BUDS: Imbricate, 1/4 to 1/2″ long, ovate, pointed, divergent, brown-black, lustrous, scales downy on margin.

STEM: Smooth or somewhat hairy, reddish brown, young stem-lightly glandular.

BARK: Trunk and older branches chalky-white, peeling or easily separated into thin paper-like layers.

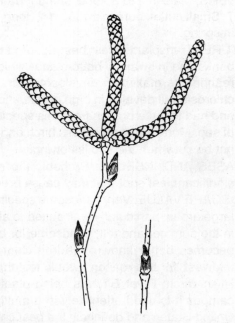

SIZE: 50 to 70′ in height with a spread equal to one-half to two-thirds the height; Rehder noted it may reach 90 to 120′ in height.

HARDINESS: Zone 2 to 6(7).

HABIT: Loosely pyramidal in youth developing an irregular, oval to rounded crown at maturity; usually maintaining its branches close to the ground unless limbed up; handsome as a single or multi-stemmed specimen.

RATE: Medium to fast, over a 10 to 20 year period averaging 1 1/2 to 2′ of growth per year.

TEXTURE: Medium in leaf and in winter habit.

BARK: Thin, smooth, reddish brown on young branches, becoming creamy-white in the third to fourth year, perhaps the whitest of all birches; peels freely to expose a reddish orange inner bark; old trunks become marked with black; in general the bark stays whiter longer than that of *B. pendula*.

LEAF COLOR: Usually dull dark green in summer changing to yellow in fall; I rate this second to *Betula lenta* for excellence of fall color; this is one of the trees that contribute to the magnificent fall color spectacle in our northern forests.

FLOWERS: Staminate, brown, 2 to 4″ long, usually born in 2's or 3's; female in erect 1 to 1 1/4″ long greenish catkins.

FRUIT: Small nutlet, borne on a 1 to 1 1/2″ long, pendulous catkin.

CULTURE: Transplants readily as balled and burlapped specimen; best adapted to colder climates; adapted to a wide variety of soils; does best on well-drained, acid, moist, sandy or silty loams; full sun; not a particularly tough tree and should not be used in difficult, polluted areas; based on midwest observations much more tolerant to high pH soils than *B. nigra*.

DISEASES AND INSECTS: Much more resistant to bronze birch borer than *B. pendula*.

LANDSCAPE VALUE: Handsome for bark and fall color attributes; good in parks, estates and large area plantings; splendid in winter when framed against evergreens.

PROPAGATION: Seed requires no cold period but when exposed to 9 plus hours of light per 24 hour period germinated 30%; 2 to 3 months of cold at 41°F will compensate for light; nursery practice involves fall sowing with germination occurring in spring; this applies to all birch species presented here except *B. nigra;* there is considerable interest in accelerated growth of birches especially *B. papyrifera* and *B. pendula;* Krizek, *PIPPS.* 22:390–395, reported that *B. papyrifera* would produce white bark in 2 rather than 3 years; it is more responsive to light than *B. pendula;* optimum seedling growth requires 77°F day/65°F night; long days (16 hr); good air movement and adequate moisture and nutrition. Cuttings can be rooted with significant attention to detail; an English report (*PIPPS.* 18:67–68) indicated that 6 to 8″ long cuttings collected on August 18 and September 1, treated with 2000 ppm IBA-quick dip rooted well; also 8000 ppm IBA-talc gave 100% rooting; best not to disturb rooted cuttings but allow them to go through natural dormancy cycle and pot them during their spring flush; I have had poor success rooting this species.

NATIVE HABITAT: Labrador to British Columbia and Washington south to Pennsylvania, Michigan, Nebraska, and Montana. It is the most widely east-west distributed of all North American birches. Introduced 1750.

RELATED SPECIES:

There are many varieties described but their separation is fraught with difficulty. These geographical variants are probably only of significant interest to the botanist and forester. I am afraid nurserymen have paid little attention to seed source.

ADDITIONAL NOTES: The bark has been used for utensils, canoes, and wigwam covers. After fire, Paper Birch often seeds large areas where mineral soil was exposed; and especially on moist sites it forms nearly pure stands. There is evidence that this species at least in the midwest is a much better landscape species than *B. pendula*. Although susceptible to the borer, especially stressed trees, it seems to perform better than the European White Birch.

Betula pendula — European White Birch (formerly listed as *B. alba* and *B.verrucosa*)
(bet′u-la pen′du-la)

LEAVES: Alternate, simple, broadly ovate, sometimes rhomboidal to diamond-shaped, 1 to 3″ long, 3/4 to 1 1/2″ wide, slenderly tapered at apex, broadly wedge-shaped or truncate at base; doubly serrate, glabrous, lustrous dark green, dotted with glands on both surfaces; petiole—1/2 to 3/4″ long.

BUDS: Imbricate, curved, pointed, brownish black.

STEM: Glabrous, resinous-glandular (results in warty appearance), brown, smoother than paper or gray.

BARK: Whitish, does not peel (exfoliate) to degree of Paper Birch; with age trunk becomes black with relatively small amount of white bark showing.

SIZE: 40 to 50′ in height with a spread one-half to two-third's the height, may reach 80 to 100′ or more in the wild.

HARDINESS: Zone 2 to 6 (7).

HABIT: Gracefully pyramidal in youth, developing an oval pyramidal to oval outline with time while maintaining the graceful pendulous branching habit; sometimes rounded in outline.

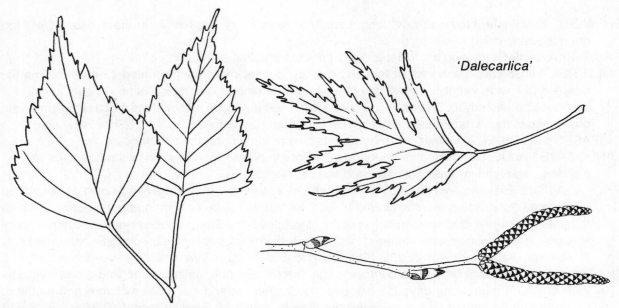

'Dalecarlica'

RATE: Medium to fast, growing 30 to 40′ over a 20 year period.

TEXTURE: Medium-fine in leaf; medium in winter habit.

BARK: Brownish in youth (1 to 1 1/2″ diameter) changing to white on larger branches and with time developing black fissured areas.

LEAF COLOR: Dark glossy green in summer often changing to a poor yellow or yellow green; leafs out early in spring; seems to hold the green leaves later into fall than the other species; have seen excellent fall color in Michigan and New England.

FLOWERS: Staminate, 1 1/2 to 3 1/2″ long, usually in 2's, sometimes singly or in 3's.

FRUIT: Small nutlet, produced in 3/4 to 1 1/4″ long by 1/3″ wide cylindrical catkins, shed in fall.

CULTURE: Transplants readily; should be moved in spring; does best in moist, well drained, sandy or loamy soil but will tolerate wet or dry soils; more pH tolerant than *B. nigra;* should be pruned in summer or fall as pruning in late winter or early spring causes the tree to "bleed" excessively.

DISEASES AND INSECTS: See under *B. lenta;* leaf miner and bronze birch borer are serious pests; I do not recommend European White Birch because of the borer; it can be controlled but most people wait until considerable injury has occurred and then it is too late to save the tree; the top is infected first; if one has specimen trees a regular spray program is a worthwhile investment.

LANDSCAPE VALUE: Very popular tree gracing the front or back yard of one out of three homes in parts of midwest; still widely sold by many nurserymen and, unfortunately, purchased by the uninitiated; tree has been extensively used for lawns, parks, and cemeteries; if a suitable white-barked alternative can be found it should be planted.

CULTIVARS:

'Birkalensis' (Also spelled 'Bircalensis')—Each leaf has 3 or 4 acute lobes on each margin that reach one half way to the middle, tree is columnar in habit.

var. *crispa* (f. *crispa*)—Has been confused with 'Dalecarlica' but the leaves are more regularly and less deeply cut; often listed as 'Laciniata'; found wild in several localities in Scandinavia.

'Dalecarlica'—A very distinct tree, branches and leaves pendulous; the whole tree very elegant; the leaves are lobed to within 1/8 to 1/4″ of the midrib, the lobes lanceolate, coarsely toothed with long slender points, ends of basal lobes curving backward; the most common form in cultivation. Bean in the 1988 supplement stated that the plant in commerce described as 'Dalecarlica' is actually 'Laciniata', the leaves of 'Laciniata' are supposedly 2″ long and those of 'Dalecarlica' about 3″, in the United States the plant I know as 'Dalecarlica' fits the 3″ leaf characteristic.

'Elegans'—Branches hanging almost perpendicularly, leader erect; a mop.

'Fastigiata'—Branches erect, of columnar habit, resembling a Lombardy Poplar; there is a recorded specimen in England which measures 95′; holds foliage later than other cultivars; actually this is a rather ugly upright cultivar and the bark appears to turn darker faster than the species; the habit is never very uniform for in winter the upright branches look like bundles of sticks tied together, branches are curved, leaves normal.

'Golden Cloud'—Introduced by Bressingham Gardens in England for 'the gleaming' bark of the Silver (White) Birch and in late spring reddish shoots emerge, unfolding as bright golden leaves. The leaves become deeper gold in the summer in sun, less intense in partial shade; fall color is yellow, growth rate is similar to the species and white bark should develop in 2 to 3 years; have seen in Mr. Adrian Bloom's garden and the leaves are a distinct golden yellow; would probably burn in heat of midwestern and eastern United States; I suspect it will perform best in a cool continental climate, leaves normal.

'Gracilis'—A small tree without a central leader (15 to 20'), with finely cut leaves and drooping branches; stems are produced in clusters like elongated witches brooms, almost ponytail-like, leaves finer and more deeply lobed than 'Dalecarlica'.

'Obelisk'—Found in northern France in 1956 and put into commerce by P.L.M. van der Ban, upright like 'Fastigiata' with a narrower crown and whiter bark; strong straight ascending branches, leaves normal.

'Purple Rain'—New foliage displays lustrous vivid purple color that is retained through the season, a lovely contrast of purple foliage and white bark, leaves normal, tissue culture is being used to produce the plants, a Monrovia introduction.

'Purpurea'—Leaves deep reddish purple gradually losing the strong color with the coming of summer. I have never been pleased with the landscape performance of this cultivar, lacks vigor and the purple leaf color fades in the heat of the summer, sounds wonderful in catalog descriptions but acts as a borer magnet and is not worth spending money for, named clones include 'Purple Splendor' and 'Scarlet Glory', leaves normal.

'Rocky Mountain Splendor'—A broadly pyramidal to oval tree with medium green summer foliage that turns yellow in fall, has white bark, cold hardy in Rocky Mountain states, 45' by 30', considered a hybrid between *B. pendula* and *B. occidentalis (B. fontinalis),*–30 to –40°F hardiness, a 1989 Schmidt introduction.

'Tristis'—A clone similar to 'Elegans' developing a central leader, the side branches extending and arching, forming a tall ovate crown, leaves normal.

'Trost Dwarf'(Often listed as 'Trost's Dwarf')—Too many people have gotten excited about a rather inferior witches broom-like compact shrubby form of the species; actually there has been a great deal of promotion behind the plant that could have been better spent behind a good form of *Fothergilla gardenii;* the habit is best described as "bushy", probably 3 to 4' high and wide after 8 to 10 years, the rich green leaves are almost threadlike, perhaps a good collectors item but doubtfully for mainstream American gardens.

'Youngii'—Branches are slender and perfectly pendulous, without a leading stem; best to graft on a standard; have seen this cultivar at several gardens and it always reminded me of a fat mop head; however, a plant at Bodnant Gardens, Wales, had been trained so the branches grew horizontally for a distance and were then allowed to weep; this specimen was truly spectacular; have also seen it staked until a 10 to 12' high leader developed and then allowed to weep; leaves normal.

PROPAGATION: Seed will germinate with proper light treatment or 2 to 3 months of stratification at 41°F will compensate; cuttings treated with 50 ppm IBA for 32 hours rooted 25%; cultivars are grafted on seedling understock.

NATIVE HABITAT: Europe (including Britain), especially high altitutdes and parts of northern Asia. Long cultivated.

RELATED SPECIES:

The descriptions of *B. platyphylla* var. *japonica* and var. *szechuanica* are presented as they appear in the third edition with the following additions since new facts concerning their bronze borer resistance have come to light. Both varieties have been reported to contract the borer. The University of Wisconsin seed source of var. *japonica* shows good resistance. See Dirr, *Weeds, Trees, and Turf* 20(2):51, 54, 1981 for more details. The key differences between the two varieties are: var. *japonica* has thinner leaves that abscise earlier; finer and less warty stems; less tolerance to wet soils; and better leaf miner resistance.

Betula platyphylla, (bet′ū-la plat-i-fil′-la), Asian White Birch, is probably represented in cultivation by the varieties *japonica* and *szechuanica.* Dr. Ed. Hasselkus, University of Wisconsin, mentioned that while other birches, especially *B. pendula,* were dying out in the U. of W. Landscape Arboretum this birch continued to thrive. The original planting of three still exists which would indicate bronze birch borer resistance. Variety *japonica* would be the preferred tree under landscape conditions for it is rather large (85′), with thin spreading branches and pure white bark on the trunk. Under landscape conditions the tree would grow 40 to 50′. The Wisconsin trees are 25 to 30′ with a relaxed, pyramidal habit and have maintained a dominant central leader. The leaves are about 1 1/2 to 3″ long, glossy dark green and shaped somewhat like those of *B. pendula* but differ by virtue of being broader with axillary tufts beneath, more numerous veins and usually single toothing. Bean noted that in England it thrives well in cultivation. Native to Japan and the Okhotsk peninsula. Cultivated since 1887. Zone 4. To date, I like what I have seen of the tree and based on observations of an old tree in the Arnold Arboretum the bark character (whiteness over time) may be better than *B. pendula.* The variety *szechuanica* is more open and wide spreading than the above but according to Bean a rather graceless tree, with a silvery-white bark. The leaves are thick, blue-green, and remain on the tree longer than other birches. *Betula platyphylla* var. *szechuanica* 'Purpurea'—I had never heard of this selection until paging through a Studebaker (1988–89) nursery catalog; the new leaves are described as deep purple and contrast with the white bark, leaves mature to purple-green. Is it, in fact, a purple leaf *B. pendula* type? Distinguished from var. *japonica* by the leaves which are dotted with glands beneath. Native to western China. Introduced 1872. Zone 5.

Without becoming excessively repetitive let me warn the gardener and nurseryman that both *B. platyphylla* var. *japonica* and *B.p.* var. *szechuanica* are susceptible to borer. Only 'Whitespire' from the original selection by Dr. Hasselkus, University of Wisconsin is borer-free. In a 1989 telephone conversation, he reiterated the original introduction was borer free. Unfortunately, many trees have been sold as 'Whitespire' that were actually grown from seed from the original tree. Be sure that the trees you buy were produced by tissue culture or cuttings from the original. The tree is not totally resistant to leaf miner but is less susceptible than *B. papyrifera.* Hasselkus feels that the tree's resistance to borer can be related to the tree's heat tolerance which means it is under less stress in hot climates and thus better able to resist infestation. 'Whitespire' has survived –30°F at Madison and after 27 years was 33′ high and 14′ wide with a distinctive spire-like form. It is fine textured in stem and foliage and the glossy dark green leaves turn yellow in fall. The chalky white non-exfoliating bark is marked with black triangles at the base of lateral branches. The original seed was collected by John L. Creech of the U.S. Plant Introduction Station in 1951 from a single tree in an open field above Shibuyu Onsen at 5000′ in the Yatsugatake Mountains. Dr. Hasselkus planted 5 trees from these seeds and selected to the one with the best developed white bark and habit. Tom Pinney in an October 15, 1986 'Whitespire' birch update reported that seedling trees of 'Whitespire' under stress did contract the borer. He emphasized that plants in good vigor were more resistant. 'Whitespire' seedlings in a local (Zone 8) nursery have not looked as inspiring as Heritage River Birch. Time will tell, but to date I have not been as impressed with 'Whitespire' in the south as some literature leads one to believe.

ADDITIONAL NOTES: Other birches are more suitable for the midwest and should be used in preference to *B. pendula;* when purchasing a "white" birch make sure of the scientific name, for any birch with white bark is a "white" birch. Santamour, *American Nurseryman* 156(11):61 (1982) presented interesting data relative to which white-barked birches are least susceptible to borer. The trees were surveyed in their tenth year in the Washington, DC area. The borer attacks started in the fifth growing season with borer populations remaining extremely high until the survey. *Betula papyrifera* grew slowly but 84% of the trees survived; *B. pendula* showed variable borer susceptibility depending on seed source. Survival varied from 15% to 75%. *Betula platyphylla* var. *japonica* from five seed sources showed 1 out of 127 trees alive and the lone survivor was also infested. Interestingly, this variety was the most adaptable and fastest growing *but* the most susceptible. Santamour suggests that the concept of plants under stress being more susceptible to borer might be re-examined. *Betula populifolia* survived 75% and shows some borer resistance.

Betula populifolia — Gray Birch, also called Old Field Birch, White Birch, Poverty Birch, and Poplar Birch

(bet'ū-la pop-ū-li-fō'lē-a)

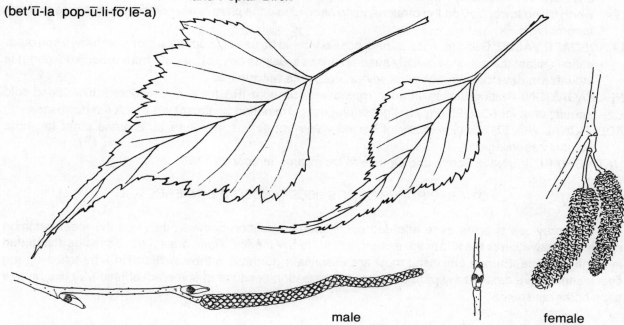

male   female

LEAVES: Alternate, simple, 2 to 3 1/2″ long, 1 1/2 1/4″ wide, triangular-ovate or deltoid, long acuminate, truncate at base, coarsely or doubly serrate, glutinous when young, 6 to 9 vein pairs, lustrous dark green above, glabrous, 6 to 9 vein pairs; petiole—3/4 to 1″ long, dotted black glands.

BUDS: Imbricate, 1/4″ or less in length, brownish, smooth, somewhat resinous, ovate, pointed, divergent; scales finely downy on margin.

STEM: Slender, bright reddish brown or grayish, roughened by warty resinous exudations, glabrous.

BARK: Dull chalky-white (older branches), close, not peeling, with distinct dark triangular patches below insertion of branches.

MALE CATKIN: Borne singly at end of branches, 2 to 3 1/2″ long; most effective way to separate this species from other cultivated birches.

SIZE: 20 to 40′ in height with 30′ representing an average size; spread is about 10 to 20′.

HARDINESS: Zone 3 to 6 (7).

HABIT: Narrow, irregularly open, conical crown with slender branches ending in fine stems that are often pendulous; usually a multiple stemmed tree in the wild but can be grown single-stemmed; has a tendency to develop shoots from the roots and often forms thickets; one of the smallest of the birches and usually short-lived (15 to 25 years).

RATE: Medium to fast, averaging 2′ per year over a 10 to 15 year period; often forms pure stands in cut-over or burned forest lands in a very short time.

TEXTURE: Medium-fine in leaf; medium in winter habit.

BARK: Thin, smooth, reddish brown on young trunks becoming chalky white with prominent, triangular black patches below the bases of the branches; loses color quickly, becoming dirty gray, does not peel readily.

LEAF COLOR: Dark glossy green in summer changing to yellow in fall; leafs out early and provides a nice touch of "spring green".

FLOWERS: Staminate, 2 to 3 1/2″ long, catkin borne singly at the end of the branches, rarely in 2's.

FRUIT: Small nutlet, borne in 3/4 to 1 1/4″ long by 1/4″ diameter cylindrical catkin.

CULTURE: Transplant balled and burlapped in spring; relishes in the poorest of sterile soils; will grow on sandy, rocky, gravelly sites and also heavier soils; tolerates wet and dry conditions; full sun, intolerant of competition and this should be considered if it is used in the landscape; will develop chlorosis in extremely high pH soils.

DISEASES AND INSECTS: Leaf miner, cankers, probably more resistant to bronze birch borer; leaf miner as I have seen it in New England, can literally turn a green tree into a Kraft (brown) bag; certainly not worth trying to control, on the other hand no need to use the plant in the contrived landscape and ask for problems.

LANDSCAPE VALUE: Good for naturalizing, possibly could be used in poor soils along highways and other difficult sites; the ability to quickly seed an area as well as develop shoots from roots (suckering) is valuable in developing rough sites where few plants will survive.

PROPAGATION: Cuttings taken in July treated with 50 ppm IBA for 6 hours rooted 30%; seed-cold stratification for 60 to 90 days or light during the germination treatment will break the dormancy.

ADDITIONAL NOTES: Commercially of limited value but serves in nature as a nurse plant for more valuable seedlings.

NATIVE HABITAT: Nova Scotia and Ontario to Delaware. Introduced 1780.

OTHER BIRCHES OF POSSIBLE LANDSCAPE INTEREST

The previous species were afforded considerable attention because they are the most common species in cultivation or the wild in the eastern half of North America. There are about 40 species distributed in North America, Europe and Asia; most are essentially northern in their distribution. The following are species that have crossed my path or created a sensation because of some advertised trait like bronze birch borer resistance.

Betula albo-sinensis — Chinese Paper Birch

LEAVES: Alternate, simple, ovate to ovate-oblong, 2 to 3″ long, 1 to 1 1/2″ wide, acuminate, rounded or sometimes subcordate, doubly serrate and often slightly lobulate, dark green above, light green and glandular below, with 10 to 14 vein pairs that may be silky hairy or glabrous; petiole—1/4 to 3/4″ long, 1/3″ wide, sparingly silky or glabrous.

Betula albo-sinensis, (bet′ū-la al′-bō-sī-nen′sis), Chinese Paper Birch, is a little known and grown species with an exquisite bark character rivaled by few trees. E.H. Wilson in his *Aristocrats of the Trees* noted that "the bark is singularly lovely, being a rich orange-red or orange-brown and peels off in sheets, each no thicker than fine tissue paper, and each successive layer is clothed with a white glaucous bloom". Foliage is dark yellow-green in winter changing to yellow in fall. The habit is rounded and size in a landscape situation would range from 40 to 60′ although it can grow 80 to 90′. The variety *septentrionalis* is similar but differs in the oblong-ovate rather than ovate leaves, distinctly glandular young shoots, silky hairs on veins beneath and prominent axillary tufts of hair. I have seen the species at Vineland Station, Ontario, Canada. The tree was about 25′ tall and the bark had a distinct orangish cast but the exfoliating character was not evident. It was my privilege to view a mature, 40 to 45′ high and 40 to 50′ wide specimen on the Isle of Mainau in the Lake of Constance, Germany. The trunk and major branches of this impressive specimen were covered with lichens but the younger branches showed the "orange-brown, orange to yellowish orange and orange-gray." Common in European gardens, seldom seen in American. Western China. Zone 5. Introduced 1908. The species was introduced in 1910. Zone 5. Central and western China.

Betula davurica —Dahurian Birch

LEAVES: Alternate, simple, 2 to 4″ long, 1 1/2 to 3″ wide, rhombic-ovate, acute or acuminate, cuneate, unequally dentate-serrate, dark green and glabrous above, gland-dotted beneath, 6 to 8 vein pairs, pubescent on veins below; petiole—1/4 to 1/2″ long.

Betula davurica, (bet'-ū-la dav-ūr'i-ka), Dahurian Birch, is apparently used on the east coast to a small degree. The species grows 40 to 50' in height and has rather wide and spreading branches. A 72 year old tree at the Arnold is 35' by 40'. The summer foliage is dark green changing to yellow in fall. The bark is not unlike that of *B.nigra,* River Birch, exfoliating in curly flakes of warm brown to reddish brown. An adequate description of the bark is difficult for the flakes appear to puff out from the trunk rather than curl off in papery flakes and sheets like *B. nigra.* Most trees I have observed were small and appeared to lack significant vigor, lacks graceful arching branches and twigginess of *B. nigra.* Tolerates dry, infertile soils better than *B. nigra.* Three months cold stratification produced the best germination. Native to Manchuria, northern China, and Korea. Introduced 1883. Zone 4 to 5.

Betula ermanii — Erman Birch
LEAVES: Alternate, simple, 2 to 4" long, 1 1/2 to 2 1/2" wide, triangular-ovate, acuminate, truncate or subcordate, unequally coarsely serrate, usually glandular beneath or pubescent on veins, 7 to 11 vein pairs; petiole-1/4 to 1 1/2" long, warty.

Betula ermanii, (bet'ū-la er-man'ē-ī), Erman Birch, is a pyramidal-oval tree in youth said to grow to 100'. The few trees I have seen possessed a creamy or pinkish white, peeling bark that was the rival of any birch species. The bark comes off in large papery sheets. Mr. Don Shadow reported that it did not perform well in his nursery (Zone 7). Three months cold stratification produced good germination. Northeast Asia, Japan. Cultivated 1880. Zone 5.

Betula grossa — Japanese Cherry Birch
LEAVES: Alternate, simple, 2 to 4" long, one-half as wide, ovate to oblong-ovate, acuminate, , subcordate at base, coarsely double toothed, glandular beneath, with 10 to 15 vein pairs with silky pubescence, lustrous dark green; petiole—1/2 to 1" long, silky.

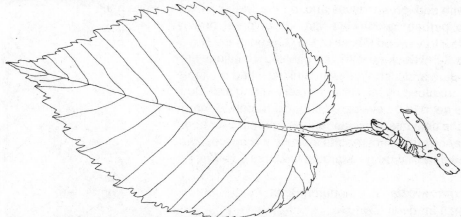

Betula grossa, (bet'ū-la grō'sa), Japanese Cherry Birch, reminds of *B. lenta* and *B. alleghaniensis* with its aromatic wintergreen stems. The lustrous dark green leaves turn a good yellow in fall. The beautiful, rich, polished, reddish brown cherry-like bark is especially handsome. The Arnold Arboretum has a lovely specimen of pyramidal outline about 25' high. Japan. Introduced 1896. Zone 4.

Betula jacquemontii — Whitebarked Himalayan Birch
LEAVES: Alternate, simple, ovate, 2 to 3" long, rounded or slightly cuneate at base, double-serrate, dark green above, glandular below, pubescent on veins, with 7 to 9 vein pairs; petiole—1/2 to 1" long.

Betula jacquemontii, Whitebarked Himalayan Birch, is an enigma in the world of white-barked birches. In its finest form, the bark is a beautiful cream-white and probably the most striking of all the white-barked birches. I attended a nursery conference at Pershore Horticultural College, England, in 1989 and listened to the speakers question the authenticity of what is being offered in the trade as this species. The literature is equally fun to wade through since Krüssmann, Bean, Rehder, et al. have slightly different views. Bean remarks that the bark is not always white and may be pale-colored, ochre-cream, ochre-brown or light pinkish brown. The whitest barked trees I have seen in European gardens were *B. jacquemontii* or *B. utilis*. *B. utilis* is highly variable like *B. jacquemontii* and may house *B. jacquemontii* as a variety. Ashburner and Shilling, 1985, "*Betula utilis* and its varieties." (*The Plantsman* 7(2):124) give *jacquemontii* variety status. They state that *B. jacquemontii* occurs in the western Himalayas, has whiter bark and fewer veins. *Betula utilis* var. *utilis* has browner bark and more vein pairs (10 to 14). I was wandering through Edinburgh Botanic Garden, Scotland and chanced upon a young planting (10 to 15′ high) of what I thought was *B. jacquemontii*. Bark was beautiful white on some seedlings and polished brown on others. All were labeled as *B. utilis*. Next time I will count vein pairs.

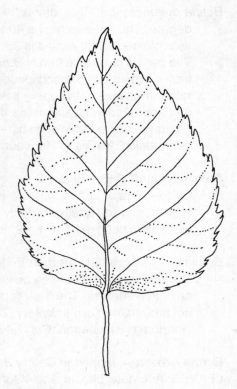

Betula jacquemontii is being grown by several west coast growers and shipped into the midwest and east. Dr. Raulston at North Carolina State thinks it might survive better if grafted on *B. nigra*. Raulston builds a strong case for the southeastern nursery industry to at least test this birch. In the North Carolina State Arboretum, he reported no borer infestation on vigorous plants, the oldest of which grew 25′ high with a 7″ diameter trunk in 6 years. The white bark appeared in the second year on plants set out from a quart liner. Cuttings have been rooted successfully (90%) in July, 1000 to 3000 ppm IBA-talc, mist. He has also grafted the species on *B. nigra* and plants grew 3 to 4′ in one year. The tree is pyramidal oval with dark green leaves and, on the best form, milky white bark.

Two perhaps worthwhile hybrids of great beauty include 'Grayswood Ghost' at the Garden of the Royal Horticultural Society at Wisley with superb foliage and white bark and 'Jermyns' with striking white bark that was introduced by the Hillier Nursery in England. Both clones need to be evaluated under U.S. conditions.

At one time this "species" showed promise for borer resistance but recent reports indicate it is susceptible. The adaptability range is probably Zones 5 to 7?

Betula maximowicziana — Monarch Birch
(bet′ū-la max-im-ō-wix-ē-ā′-na)

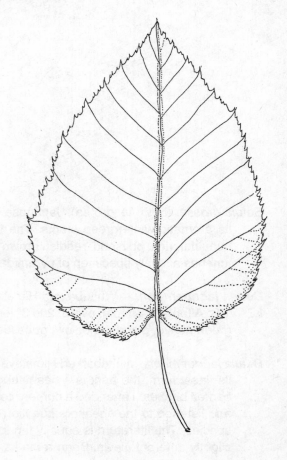

LEAVES: Alternate, simple, broad-ovate, 3 to 6″ long, 3/4 as wide, acuminate, deeply cordate at base, doubly serrate, pubescent on young trees, nearly glabrous on old trees, with 10 to 12 pairs of veins, dark green; petiole— 1 to 1 1/2″ long.

Betula maximowicziana, Monarch Birch, has attained heights of 100′ or more in its native habitat of Japan, however, experimental plantings in arboretums in the United States have indicated that it will generally be closer to 45 to 50′. The habit is roundish and of a mop-like nature. Leaves on seedlings and young trees are densely pubescent and purple veined on the lower surface. The foliage is dark green in summer changing to yellow in fall. The leaves and catkins (male 4 to 5″ long; fruiting 2 to 2 1/2″ long by 1/3″ wide, 2 to 4 together) are the largest of all known hardy birches. The young branches are reddish brown eventually becoming gray or whitish and the bark splits into long, broad thin sheets which cling to the tree in shaggy masses. I have seen trees labeled as *B. maximowicziana* at the Holden Arboretum, Mentor, Ohio and they were truly beautiful; however, the older bark was a uniform white, the leaves were small (about the size of *B. papyrifera*) and the leaf bases were not cordate as is supposedly typical for *B. m.* Significant advantages of this birch are the complete resistance to bronze birch borer and, unlike other birches, the tolerance to urban environments. According to Cole Nursery Co., Circleville, Ohio, this species grows about 33 percent faster than *B. pendula* or *B. papyrifera*. The very confusing aspect of the Monarch Birch is the fact that what we (horticulturists) are calling *B. m.* does not fit the taxonomic description. Drs. P.C. Kozel and R.C. Smith have an interesting article in *Horticulture.* 54(1):36, 1975, "The Monarch Birch", from which much of the above information was abstracted. Since the last edition it has been documented that the Holden and Cole trees were not Monarch. See Santamour and Meyer. *American Nurseryman* 145(12):7. Since the last edition I have seen several trees of the "real thing" and they bore no resemblance to what is in the trade as Monarch. A few comments follow: I chased the tree all over Winkworth Arboretum in England and was disappointed with what I discovered. The habit was pyramidal-oval and the bark rather unglamorous dirty gray brown. In fact, I saw no evidence of white even on the younger branches. The bark did not exfoliate in shaggy masses and was rather smooth in appearance. This shagginess could be a variable trait. The leaves and male catkins were the largest I have seen on a birch. At the Arnold Arboretum, several recently planted *B. maximowicziana* specimens have a distinct pyramidal habit and reasonably good white bark. Also the leaves turned a good yellow in October. I believe these were from wild collected seed when Drs. Spongberg and Weaver were in Japan. If they prove leaf miner and bronze birch borer resistant perhaps someone should consider vegetative propagation. Probably good only in cooler climates and Don Shadow reported poor growth at his nursery in Winchester, TN. From discussions with nurserymen, the true Monarch is not very cold hardy. It perished at −20°F in Illinois field tests. Native to northern Japan. Introduced 1888. Zone 5 to 6.

Betula nana — Dwarf Birch
LEAVES: Alternate, simple, rounded or occasionally broader than long, 1/4 to 1/2″ diameter, round toothed, lustrous dark green above, net veined below, glabrous, 2 to 4 vein pairs; petiole 1/12″ or less with a fringed stipule on each side.

Betula nana, (bet′ū-la nā′na), Dwarf Birch, is a neatly rounded, 2 to 4′ high and wide shrub with lustrous dark green, orbicular, 1/4 to 1/2″ wide, conspicuously round-toothed leaves. This is a very dainty shrub that is both beautiful and provides a challenge for one's plant material friends. It is found in the northern latitudes of Europe and North America in moist habitats. Among the shrubby birches it is distinguished by its round-toothed, orbicular leaves and the absence of warts or glands on the stems. Cultivated 1789. Zone 2. Other shrubby species that may be of interest but are decidedly larger than *B. nana* include *B. glandulifera, B. glandulosa, B. humulis* and *B. pumila.*

Betula occidentalis — Water Birch
LEAVES: Alternate, simple, 1 to 2″ long, 3/4 to 1 1/2″ wide, glandular, broad-ovate, rounded or slightly heart shaped, pointed, double-serrate, dull dark green and slightly hairy above, paler and glabrous below, 3 to 5 vein pairs; petiole—1/4 to 1/2″ long, at first hairy, finally glabrous.

Betula occidentalis (formerly *B. fontinalis*), (bet′ū-la ok-si-den-tā′lis), Water Birch, is a handsome, small (20 to 30′) shrubby tree with close reddish brown bark. I first made its acquaintance on a trip to Salt Lake City. It is a rather graceful tree with slender spreading and pendulous branches. I do not know of plants east of the Mississippi. Native from Alaska to Oregon and through Rocky Mountains to Colorado. Introduced 1874. Zone 4.

Betula schmidtii — Schmidt Birch
LEAVES: Alternate, simple, 1 1/2 to 3″ long, 1 to 1 3/4″ wide, ovate, slender pointed, rounded or wide
   cuneate at base, finely and irregularly serrate, 9 to 11 vein pairs, dark green above, hairy on veins
   below; petiole—1/6 to 1/8″ long, hairy.

Betula schmidtii, (bet′ū-la schmid′tē-ī), Schmidt Birch, is a rather unusual species noted for its wood
   which is too heavy to float in water. The tree makes a fine ornamental with excellent summer foliage
   followed by golden yellow fall color. The brownish black bark falls off in small, irregular-shaped plates.
   There is a fine specimen at the Arnold Arboretum. In cultivation it forms a neat rounded outline and
   will grow 20 to 40′ high although in the wild it is reported growing 60 to 100′. Japan, Korea and
   Manchuria. Introduced 1896. Zone 5.

There is abundant literature on the birches and to sift through it all is akin to sieving the sand on the
beaches of the world. There is considerable confusion regarding the various white-barked birches. If you
have a desire to confuse a botanist hand him or her a handful of birch leaves and run. See Richard
Weaver's, The Ornamental Birches, *Arnoldia* 38(4):117–131 (1978) and Santamour and McArdle, Checklists of Cultivars in *Betula* (Birch). *J. Arbor.* 15(7):170–176 (1989).

Bignonia capreolata *(Anisostichus capreolata)*— Crossvine
(big-nō′ni-a kap-rē-ō-lā′ta)

FAMILY: Bignoniaceae
LEAVES: Opposite,   semi-
   evergreen to evegreen, trifoliate, leaflets 2, stalked,
   the rachis ending in a
   branched tendril clinging
   by small disks, leaflets
   oblong-ovate to oblong-lanceolate, 2 to 6″ long, 1/2
   to 2″ wide, obtusely acuminate, cordate, entire,
   glabrous, lustrous dark green in summer changing
   to reddish purple in winter; petiole—about 1/2″ long;
   petiolules-curved, 1/2 to 3/4″ long.

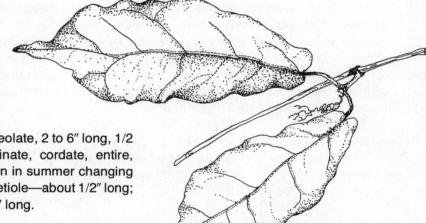

SIZE: Depending on structure, will climb 30 to 50′; usually
   less.
HARDINESS: Zone 6 to 9, possibly 5.
HABIT: Semi-evergreen to evergreen self-clinging vine climbing by tendrils; will cover trees or often snakes
   along the ground.
RATE: Fast.
TEXTURE: Medium.
LEAF COLOR: Dark green in summer, developing reddish purple cast in cold weather; foliage is not dense
   and does not make a solid cover like many vines unless provided with sufficient sun.
FLOWERS: Perfect, brown to brownish orange or brownish red to orange and orange-red on the outside;
   the typical wild form that I commonly see is reddish with yellow to orangish inside, each flower shaped
   like a trumpet to broad funnel form-campanulate, 1 1/2 to 2″ long, 3/4 to 1 1/2″ wide at the end of the
   corolla, borne 2 to 5—together in short-stalked cymes, interesting mocha fragrance on the wild type,
   flowers open in mid-April in Athens with an effective 3 to 4 week period; curiously attractive, yet
   effective because of the large numbers of flowers.
FRUIT: Slender, compressed, 4 to 7″ long capsule, green initially, finally brown.

CULTURE: Easily grown, prefers moist well-drained soils, will grow in heavy shade but best flowering is achieved in full sun; have observed plants that were covered with water for 2 to 4 weeks in March/April and still flourished; inherently tough plant; needs to be pruned and trained under cultivation.

DISEASES AND INSECTS: None serious.

LANDSCAPE VALUE: Handsome foliage and flowers are principal ornamental features; in the wild is often thin and sparse flowering; excellent for covering a fence or trellis; should be more widely used.

CULTIVARS:

'Atrosanguinea'—Flowers dark red-purple; leaves narrower and longer than species; the plant I have grown as 'Atrosanguinea' is more orange-red than purple-red and the flowers are more narrow-trumpet shaped than the species. Interestingly, the color inside is similar to the outside.

PROPAGATION: Seed requires no pretreatment; cuttings root readily when taken in June and July; I have lifted plants that were trailing on the ground and noticed an abundance of roots all along the vine; this is a good indication that the plant is easily rooted.

ADDITIONAL NOTES: The vine climbs by tendrils but the tendrils are subtended by small disks that allow the plant to cement itself to wood and masonry structures; will readily climb a tree or porous concrete and brick; on trail walks that I have led at the UGA Botanical Garden people frequently ask about the identity of the *Bignonia;* apparently very few people are familiar with it; common name, Crossvine, is derived from appearance of the stem in cross section.

NATIVE HABITAT: Virginia and southern Illinois to Florida and Louisiana. Cultivated 1653.

Broussonetia papyrifera — Paper Mulberry, Tapa-cloth Tree
(broo-so-nesh'ē-a pap-i-rif'er-a)

FAMILY: Moraceae

LEAVES: Alternate, occasionally opposite, simple, ovate, 3 1/2 to 8″ long, acuminate, cordate at base, coarsely dentate, on young plants often deeply lobed, dull green and scabrous above, soft-pubescent beneath; petioles—1 1/4 to 4″ long, sap milky.

BUDS: Moderate, conical, solitary, sessile, outer scale longitudinally striped, grayish brown, appear similar to "dunce" caps.

STEM: Stout, coarse, gray-green, finally gray-brown, thickly downy, almost to the point of being hispid, covered with prominent orange-brown lenticels; pith—large, white, with a green diaphragm at each node.

SIZE: 40 to 50′ in height with a comparable or greater spread; usually smaller under cultivation.

HARDINESS: Zone 6 to 10.

HABIT: Tree with wide-spreading branches forming a broad-rounded crown; usually low branched; often shrubby and forming colonies in waste areas, tends to sucker profusely and can assume weed-like proportions if not controlled.

RATE: Fast, 20 to 30′ over a 6 to 8 year period; a genuine weed.

TEXTURE: Medium-coarse in all seasons.

BARK: Gray-brown, shallowly ridged-and-furrowed on large trunks; often assuming the appearance of kneaded bread; there are magnificent old specimens at Colonial Williamsburg with well-developed trunks and interesting bark.

LEAF COLOR: A rather innocuous dull green changing to yellow-green in fall; fall color is not great but trees can be readily spotted because of the mottle of yellow-green that is produced; seems as if one leaf turns all yellow, another stays green and the pattern is repeated over the entire tree; leaves of vigorous shoots are often highly lobed while those on mature specimens show little lobing.

FLOWERS: Dioecious, male borne in cylindrical, often curly, woolly, 1 1/2 to 3″ long and 1/4″ wide, yellowish catkins; female flowers in a ball-like, 1/2″ diameter head; May in north, early April in Athens.

FRUIT: Red, 3/4″ diameter, aggregate of drupes; September, have seen fruits on a tree at Brooklyn Botanic Garden in late September; most plants in Athens are apparently male for I have never seen a single fruit.

CULTURE: Easy to grow; thrives in any soil; does well in dirt and grime of cities; tolerates heat and drouth; highly alkaline soils; full sun.

DISEASES AND INSECTS: Canker, root rot, dieback, leaf spot, root knot nematode.

LANDSCAPE VALUE: Often planted for ornament; sometimes used as a street tree, casts heavy shade and will send up shoots from the roots; W.J. Bean mentions that this tree can make a nice street specimen; have seen at Colonial Williamsburg where it is used rather effectively; a weed in the south.

CULTIVARS:

'Aurea'—Don Shadow found this rather curious form with rich yellow leaves, the color most pronounced in spring and fading with the heat of the summer; the plant is growing in Don's Dad's garden in Winchester, TN.

'Cucullata'—A male tree with curious leaves whose margins are curled upwards, so as to give the leave the shape of a boat.

'Laciniata'—A dwarfish clone with the leaf reduced to a stalk and the three main veins, ends of which have a small, narrow, variously shaped blade.

PROPAGATION: Softwood cuttings collected in July and August of short shoots with a heel attached will root readily; root cuttings would also work quite well; seed requires no pretreatment; three months cold produced good germination but no control was included to determine whether the cold enhanced germination.

ADDITIONAL NOTES: Interesting tree which is closely allied to the mulberries *(Morus)* but is less woody. The common name is derived from the use of the bark for paper, and in the Polynesian islands for the fiber, which is made into a cloth.

NATIVE HABITAT: China, Japan. Cultivated 1750. Occasionally naturalized from New York to Florida and Missouri.

Buddleia davidii — Butterfly-bush, Summer Lilac
(bud'lē-a dā-vid'ē-ī)

FAMILY: Loganiaceae

LEAVES: Opposite, simple, ovate-lanceolate to lanceolate, 4 to 10″ long, 1 to 3″ wide, acuminate, cuneate, closely serrate or serrulate, gray-green to dark green above and glabrous, white-tomentose beneath, leaf color among cultivars varies significantly and this should be considered when reading the above description; petiole—very short.

BUDS: Naked, 2-scaled, pubescent, grayish green.

STEM: Stout, prominently angled, 4 to 6 to 8 sided, in youth covered with pubescence, finally glabrous.

SIZE: Large shrub 10 to 15′ high but usually ranging from 5 to 10′; quite tender and frequently killed back to the ground in northern areas.

HARDINESS: In Chicago, Illinois a herbaceous perennial; in Atlanta, Georgia a large rather unkempt woody shrub; can be grown in Zones 5 through 9.

HABIT: Rather succulent caned, large, arching shrub; in many respects better pruned to the ground in spring since it flowers on new growth of the season.

RATE: Fast, when cut to ground in spring will easily reach 5 to 8′ high by fall.

TEXTURE: Medium throughout the seasons.

LEAF COLOR: Overall effect is a gray-green to blue-green, rather subdued but serves as a handsome accompaniment to other more obtrusive foliaged shrubs; leaves appear late in spring and hold late in fall, in Athens during mild winters (+15°F or above) some foliage persists; no fall color.

FLOWERS: Perfect, usually lilac, orange at the mouth, delightfully fragrant, borne in 4 to 10″ long upright or nodding panicles; June (Athens) through frost on new growth, cut off old inflorescences and plant will bloom all summer.

FRUIT: Two-valved, septicidal, 1/4 to 1/3″ long capsule; not ornamentally important; the entire dried infructescence might be used in arrangements; best to remove the spent flowers before they go to fruit.

CULTURE: Easily transplanted, almost weedlike in its ability to survive; prefers well drained, fertile soils; full sun; prune before growth ensues in spring, the more vigorous the growth the larger the flower panicles; in Europe the plant has become an "urban dweller" and grows from loose mortar joints and sidewalk cracks, amazingly durable plant.

DISEASES AND INSECTS: None serious, nematodes in south.

LANDSCAPE VALUE: Valued for summer flowering; makes a fine addition to the shrub or perennial border; have seen it used in mass with good success; definitely not a single specimen shrub; fine for cut-flower use but flowers do not last long; inflorescences vary from 6 to 30″ in length; attracts butterflies in profusion. Since arriving in Georgia this plant has become a mainstay in my garden and deserves consideration by all gardeners. Attracts an amazing array of butterflies and bees. Numerous new or resurrected older cultivars have become available. The Nanho series which was presumably derived from the var. *nanhoensis,* which is more compact than the type and usually about 3 to 5′ high, are excellent for the smaller garden. In early October, 'Nanho Purple' was still flowering prolifically in Ithaca, NY. The planting was most effective since a large mass had been allowed to drift through the Cornell Plantations.

CULTIVARS: Numerous, the following are some of the best.

'African Queen'—Dark violet, panicles 7 to 9″ long.

'Black Knight'—Very dark purple, vigorous grower, may be slightly hardier than other clones.

'Border Beauty'—Deep lilac-purple flowers, heavy flowering, strongly branched, a lower growing form, about 2/3's the size of the species.

'Charming'—Pink flowers in 1 to 2′ long panicles, each flower with an orange throat, upright and strong growing.

'Darkness'—Wide spreading arching habit and deep blue to purple-blue flowers.

'Dubonnet'—Dark purple flowers, each flower with a light orange throat, strong upright grower, panicles to 14″ long.

'Empire Blue'—Rich violet-blue flowers with orange eye, panicles 6″ to 1′ long, somewhat upright habit, silvery green foliage, strong grower, well branched, 6 to 7′ high.

'Fascination' ('Fascinating')—Broad panicles of vivid lilac-pink, 14 to 18″ long, one report noted up to 32″ long, 2 to 3″ wide, very strong grower.

'Fortune'—Long cylindrical racemes of soft lilac flowers each with a yellow eye, prolific flowering.

'Harlequin'—A rather handome form with cream variegated leaves, the new leaves yellow, aging white, flowers reddish purple, not as vigorous and smaller than 'Royal Red' of which it is a sport.

'Ile de France'—Dark violet flowers with a yellow throat, abundant flowers in panicles to 28″ long, light green leaves on a well branched shrub.

'Lochinch' (a hybrid between *fallowiana* ö *davidii*)—I could not resist the temptation to include this more vigorous, large growing form with sweetly scented lavender-blue flowers, each with a large orange eye that occur in 12″ long panicles. I first spied the plant at Wakehurst Place in West Sussex, England. Will grow 12 to 15′ high and as wide. Cut to ground to rejuvenate and will flower on new growth of the season. Leaves are 8 to 10″ long, gray-green above and silvery-gray below; should be adaptable to Zones 6 to 8.

'Nanho Alba'—Compact form with spreading habit, slender leaves and white flowers.

'Nanho Blue'—Mauve-blue flowers, small gray-green leaves, compact grower.

'Nanho Purple'—Purple flowers, spreading dwarf habit about 5′ high, silver green foliage, hybrid between *B. d.* var. *nanhoensis* and *B. d.* 'Royal Red'.

'Opera'—Strong growing form with deep purple-red flowers.

'Orchid Beauty'—Less vigorous than the species with mauve flowers.

'Peace'—Arching habit, 2/3's the size of species, white flowers with orange throat.

'Petite Indigo' (var. *nanhoensis* type)—Monrovia nursery introduction with lilac-blue flowers, small gray-green leaves on a compact, much branched shrub.

'Petite Plum' (var. *nanhoensis* type)—Reddish purple flowers with an orange eye, foliage more dark green than above and longer persistent, Monrovia introduction.

'Pink Delight'—A recent Dutch introduction with true deep pink fragrant flowers, panicles 12 to 15″ long, gray-green leaves, compact growth habit, have seen in England and the flower color is excellent.

'Royal Red'—Rich purple-red flowers on up to 20″ long panicles, considered the best "red" form.

'Snow Bank'—Pure white flowers.

'White Bouquet'—White flowers with an orange throat in 8 to 12″ long panicles.

'White Profusion'—White flowers in small 6 to 8″ long panicles.

PROPAGATION: Seed requires no pre-treatment; cuttings collected from June through August root readily; I have used 3000 ppm IBA quick dip; once rooted remove cuttings from the bench or turn off mist; they deteriorate rapidly with excess moisture.

NATIVE HABITAT: China. Cultivated 1890.

RELATED SPECIES:

Buddleia alternifolia — Alternate-leaf Butterfly-bush

(bud′lē-a al-ter-ni-fō′-li-a)

LEAVES: Alternate, simple, lanceolate, 1 1/2 to 4″ long, 1/4 to 1/2″ wide, narrowed toward the acute or obtusish apex, cuneate, entire, dull dark green above, with grayish white scurfy tomentum beneath; petiole—about 1/8″ long.

Buddleia alternifolia, Alternate-leaf Butterfly-bush, is a large shrub or small tree that grows 10 to 20′ in height. The habit is lax and long pendulous shoots flay their supple arms in the slightest breeze. The dull dark green leaves take on a grey cast from a distance and provide interesting foliage color. The bright lilac-purple flowers appear in dense clusters in June from the axils of the previous season's wood. The flowers are fragrant but not to the degree of many *B. davidii* cultivars. Prefers loose loamy soil and a sunny position. Has been likened to a gracious, small-leaved, weeping willow when not in flower and a sheer waterfall of soft purple when it is. I have had more difficulty rooting this from softwood cuttings than the *B. davidii* cultivars. 'Argentea' has appressed silky hairs which give the leaves a silvery sheen. This is a most handsome form and preferable to the species. This is the hardiest of the butterfly bushes, and the first to flower. Zone 5. Native to northwestern China. Introduced 1914.

Buddleia globosa — Orange Butterfly-bush

LEAVES: Alternate, simple, elliptic-ovate to lanceolate, 3 to 8″ long, about 1/4 as wide, acuminate, cuneate, crenate, dark green, rugose and glabrous above, covered with light brown pubescence below; petiole—1/4″ long.

Buddleia globosa, (bud′lē-a glō-bō′sả), Orange Butterfly-bush, is a robust 10 to 15′ high and wide semi-evergreen to deciduous shrub of rather open gaunt habit. The bright yellow, fragrant, 3/4″ diameter rounded flowers occur 8 to 10 together in a terminal 6 to 8″ long panicle in opposite pairs, each flower on a 1 to 1 1/2″ long pedicel. Flowers in June in England and probably early to mid May in the Athens area. Flowers on previous season's wood and should not be pruned until after flowering. Actually a striking shrub in flower and certainly worthy of consideration by Zone 8 and 9 gardeners. Prefers a loamy, well drained, moist soil and ample sunlight. 'Lemon Ball' is later flowering than the species with lemon-yellow flowers. Chile, Peru. Introduced 1774. Zone 7 to 9.

Buddleia × weyeriana, (bud'lē-a wāy-ēr-i-ā'-na) is a hybrid between *B. globosa* × *B. davidii* var. *magnifica.* This is probably superior to *B. globosa* and is now being offered in the United States, especially the form 'Sun Gold' ('Sungold') with 3/4″ diameter yellow-orange, fragrant flowers, a sport of 'Golden Glow'. Due to the nature of the parents, the flower colors in the seedlings can be quite variable. 'Golden Glow' is a strong growing form with pale yellowish orange flowers with a trace of lilac (from *B. davidii*). 'Moonlight' has cream-yellow flowers with a trace of lilac-pink and a dark orange throat. Hybrid originated about 1915. Probably slightly hardier than *B. globosa.*

ADDITIONAL NOTES: Many botanical varieties of *B. davidii* are spread over central and western China; most of the garden varieties descended from seed Wilson collected in Hypeh and Szechuan during the years 1900–1908; there are many other *Buddleia* species but none, to my mind, are as effective as the types described above for American gardens. See Maunder, *The Plantsman* 9(2):64–60 (1987) for a discussion of the tender *Buddleia* species.

Buxus microphylla — Littleleaf Box or Boxwood
(buk′sus mī-krō-fil′a)

FAMILY: Buxaceae

LEAVES: Opposite, simple, obovate to lance-obovate, 1/3 to 1″ long, 1/6 to 1/3″ wide rounded or emarginate, cuneate, entire, usually medium green often turning yellowish brown in winter.

BUDS: Small, solitary, sessile, ovoid with 1 to 2 pairs of visible, scarcely specialized scales.

STEM: Slender, green, flat, grooved between each pair of leaves, stems appear sharply quadrangular, glabrous.

SIZE: 3 to 4′ in height by 3 to 4′ in spread.

HARDINESS: Zone 6, although some cultivars of the variety *koreana* will grow in Zone 4, to Zone 9.

HABIT: Evergreen, much branched, compact, dense, rounded or broad-rounded shrub.

RATE: Slow.

TEXTURE: Medium-fine in all seasons.

LEAF COLOR: Medium green in summer changing to repulsive yellow-green-brown in winter.

FLOWERS: Apetalous, in axillary or terminal clusters consisting of a terminal pistillate flower and several staminate flowers, March-April; not showy but fragrant; bees become quite active when this species is in flower.

FRUIT: Three-celled capsule, each valve 2-horned, seeds shining black.

CULTURE: Transplant balled and burlapped or from a container into well-drained soil; responds well to mulching with peat or leaf mold for roots require cool moist conditions; full sun or light shade; protect from drying winds and severe low temperatures; often necessary to shade newly transplanted plants from summer sun; boxwood should not be cultivated around since it is a surface rooter; in the south partial shade is preferable, although plants, especially of the variety *japonica,* appear to prosper in full sun.

DISEASES AND INSECTS: Canker, blight, leaf spots, root rot, winter injury and sun scald (physiological injury), mealybugs, scales, boxwood psyllid, boxwood leaf miner, giant hornet, boxwood webworm, nematodes and boxwood mite; most of these problems are more prevalent on *Buxus sempervirens;* root rot (*Phytophthora*) is a problem in inadequately drained soils and is usually manifested by an off-color to the foliage.

LANDSCAPE VALUE: Excellent as hedge plant, for foundations, edging situations, formal gardens; too often pruned into a green meatball and allowed to haunt a foundation planting; if used properly boxwood can be a superb plant.

CULTIVARS:

'Compacta'—Small, dense, slow growing form with excellent dark green foliage; 47-year-old plant is 1' by 4'.

'Curly Locks'—Have seen this rather unusual twisted branched form in Georgia on occasion, can be espaliered on walls, fences, etc., makes a dense mound of yellow green foliage, 3 by 4' high.

'Green Beauty' (var. *japonica* form)—Compact habit and glossy dark green foliage color, less hardy than 'Winter Gem', considered hardy to –10°F; holds color in cold weather and is greener than var. *japonica* in the heat of the summer.

'Green Pillow'—Similar to 'Compacta' except the leaves are twice as large, deep dull green.

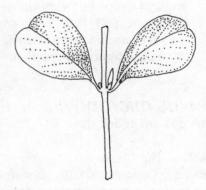

var. *japonica*—Sometimes listed as a species but doubtfully so; have seen plants labeled as *japonica* but could not be sure if they were correct; 3 to 6' high loose shrub, stems glabrous, winged, leaves 1/3 to 1" long, and often as broad, rounded or notched at apex, cuneate at base, flowers (occur at terminals) more freely than the species. Japan. Introduced 1860. Zone 6 to 9. Better adapted to southeast; apparently heat and nematode resistant.

'Kingsville Dwarf' (var. *japonica* form)—compact and slow growing form selected by Mr. Henry Hohman, Kingsville, MD.

var. *koreana*—Extremely hardy geographical variety of the species; the foliage turns yellowish brown in the winter; leaves 3/5" long, obovate to elliptic-oblong, margins inrolled, venation scarcely visible in upper surface, young stems and petioles hairy; somewhat loose and open in habit and twice as wide as high at maturity; the best choice for northern areas; has survived some miserable winters (–20 to –25°F); grows 2 to 2 1/2' high, Zone 4.

'Morris Midget' (var. *japonica* form)—Low mounded slow growing, 1 by 1 1/2' after many years, yellow-green notched leaves.

'Pincushion' (var. *koreana* form)—Low mounded 1 1/2 by 2' with light green foliage that turns bronze in winter, hardy form.

'Richardii' (var. *japonica* form)—Darker green, larger leaves notched at apex, more vigorous to 6' and hardy to 0°F.

'Sunnyside' ('Sunnyside Largeleaf') (considered a form of var. *japonica*)—A large leaf form with good winter hardiness, remains green with a slight bronze cast during the winter, had a plant in my Georgia garden and was not impressed by performance; developed bronze-yellow-green winter color even in Zone 8; will grow 6' by 6'.

var. *sinica*—Although not exactly sure of the status of this variety, I present it for the reader since var. *koreana* and var. *japonica* are common in commerce; the former in the north, the latter in the south; the Chinese Box grows 3 to 18' in its native habitat; the 1 1/4" long, ovate to obovate lustrous green leaves have visible venation on the upper surface (unlike var. *koreana*), emarginate at apex with petiole and basal midrib puberulous. Introduced about 1900. Zone 6 to 9.

'Tall Boy' (var. *koreana* form)—Loose upright to rounded form, 4 by 5', medium green foliage, becoming bronze-brown in winter.

'Tide Hill'—Cultivar of the var. *koreana* with green foliage all winter; 20-year-old plant is 15" by 5'.

'Winter Beauty'—Good mounded form with dark green foliage; have seen in a windswept nursery situation in northern Illinois and the foliage was a coppery green, no broadleaf evergreen maintains "normal" leaf color under those conditions, a seedling selection of *B. microphylla* var. *koreana.*

'Winter Gem' (var. *koreana* form)—Apparently quite comparable to 'Wintergreen' with all the traits of that cultivar although described in another catalog as having rich deep velvety green foliage, grows 2' high; might be a rename, listed in 1989 Monrovia catalog.

'Wintergreen'—The original introduction constituted more than one clone and multiple plants were released by Scarff Nursery Co., New Carlisle, OH; today the plant I see labeled as 'Wintergreen' is quite uniform and suspect the best form has been selected and propagated over the years; this is a handsome light green, small leaved form that performs superbly in colder climates; at the Chicago Botanic Garden, Glencoe, IL, considerable use has been made of this fine selection for low hedges and the like; in warmer climates where other forms can be grown it is probably not preferable.

var. *koreana* × *B. sempervirens* hybrids—A handsome and valuable group of boxwoods with the hardiness and compactness of var. *koreana* and the good leaf color of *B. sempervirens.* Introduced by Sheridan Nursery Co., Oakville, Ontario, Canada, the plants have found application in northern landscapes and are now widely grown. Have observed all selections at Royal Botanic Garden, Hamilton, Ontario, in December and was impressed by retention of dark green color. The following are selections from this cross:

'Green Gem'—A green mound, actually described by introducer as a perfect round ball, hardier than var. *koreana* 'Winter Beauty', slow growing, requires little pruning, deep green foliage through winter, 2 by 2', roots easily and makes a salable plant faster than *B. m.* var. *koreana,* also sets very little fruit compared to var. *koreana.*

'Green Mountain'—Forms a perfect wide pyramidal oval, is the most upright of this group of hybrids, small dark green leaves, excellent for hedging, 5' by 3'.

'Green Mound'—Forms an attractive mound of dark green foliage, grows 3' by 3'.

'Green Velvet'—Rounded, full bodied, slow growing with small dark green leaves similar to 'Green Gem', 3' by 3'.

PROPAGATION: Seed apparently requires a cold period of 1 to 3 months to facilitate good germination although seed will germinate without pretreatment. Cuttings root readily anytime of year; have had good success with 1000 ppm IBA, quick dip, peat:perlite, mist or poly-tent; abundant literature on boxwood cutting propagation; see Dirr and Heuser, 1987.

NATIVE HABITAT: Japan, Introduced 1860.

RELATED SPECIES:

Buxus harlandii — Harland Boxwood

Buxus harlandii, (buk′sus har-lan′dē-ī), Harland Boxwood, is occasionally seen in southern landscapes (Zone 8 to 9) and is something of a mystery as to exact identity. The form in cultivation is probably a clone from *B. microphylla* var. *sinica.* The lustrous leathery dark green leaves are 1 1/2″ long, distinctly obovate, emarginate at apex on a 2 to 3′ high and wide mounded shrub. I have grown a plant for three years and it has performed admirably but during the −3°F (1985) winter in Athens, the leaves were killed. Interestingly, Bean says the leaves are only 1/4″ wide but a ruler indicated the leaves on the Harland Clone in my garden were greater than 1/2″ wide at the widest point. Krüssmann mentioned that *B. harlandii* cultivated in German nurseries is probably a form of *B. microphylla* var. *japonica.* Perhaps it is a hybrid.

Buxus sempervirens — Common Box or Boxwood
(buk′sus sem-per-vī′renz)

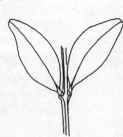

LEAVES: Opposite, simple, elliptic or ovate to oblong, 1/2 to 1″ long, about 1/2 as wide, obtuse or emarginate at apex, dark green above, light or yellowish green beneath, and usually lustrous on both sides; midvein on lower side wide and cream to yellowish; petiole short and minutely hairy.

STEM: Somewhat angled (squarish) but not like *Buxus microphylla,* minutely hairy.

SIZE: 15 to 20′ in height with an equal or greater spread; can grow to 30′ but this size is rarely attained; actually makes a handsome small tree.

HARDINESS: Zone 5 to 6 depending on cultivar, to 8.

HABIT: Dense, multibranched evergreen of rounded or broad-rounded outline that holds its foliage to the ground; old, over-grown specimens in Spring Grove Cemetery, Cincinnati, Ohio, with 4 to 6″ diameter trunks were cut back to 1 to 2′ from the ground and have developed new shoots and are filling in nicely; the new growth however is extremely sensitive to winter injury. Have seen tremendous winter damage that occurred when box was pruned too late in season (August). Apparently tissue never hardened properly and was literally blitzed by low temperatures.

RATE: Slow, but faster than *B. microphylla.*

TEXTURE: Medium-fine in all seasons.

LEAF COLOR: Lustrous dark green above, light or yellowish green below in all seasons; will brown in severe winters in the face of desiccating winds.

FLOWERS: Creamy, in clusters developing from leaf axils, without petals, the female flower often terminal in the cluster, the male subterminal, the male with 4 sepals and 4 stamens that are longer than the sepals; female with 6 sepals and a 3-loculed ovary, flowers occur in April–May and are fragrant.

FRUIT: A 1/3″ long, 3-horned dehiscent capsule, each valve containing 2 lustrous seeds.

CULTURE: Similar to *B. microphylla* except does best from Boston to north Georgia, this species has prospered in climates that do not have extremes of summer heat or winter cold; appears quite adaptable.

DISEASES AND INSECTS: See under *B. microphylla.*

LANDSCAPE VALUE: Excellent specimen and is used extensively in east and south; good for hedges, massing, topiary work, formal gardens, might be called the 'aristocrat' of the hedging plants.

CULTIVARS: There are numerous cultivars and anyone contemplating boxwood gardening should visit the National or Arnold Arboreta which have rather extensive collections. In my mind most cultivars are almost indistinguishable and once they are put to the shears no one can reliably separate them. There is an American Boxwood Society that "Boxophiles" should consider joining if all other societies are full.

'Angustifolia'—Treelike in habit with leaves 1 to 1 1/4″ long, 'Longifolia' may belong here.

'Argenteo-variegata'—Leaves variegated with white.

'Aureo-variegata'—Leaves variegated with yellow.

'Bass'—Medium-sized, densely branched form with slightly larger foliage than 'Inglis' and the dark green color is retained through winter.

'Bullata' (also known as 'Latifolia Bullata')—Low growing form with short blunt leaves that are decidedly dark green, 8′ by 10′.

'Elegantissima'—A rather pretty creamy margined form that I have seen used with good taste at Callaway Gardens. In dappled pine shade it presented a rather peaceful repose nestled among the bright vivid Kurume azaleas. I don't know how it would do in full sun in the south. Not as vigorous as the species but certainly not docile either, probably 5 to 8′ by 5 to 8′ in 15 years. May revert and green branches should be removed.

'Graham Blandy'—Striking, narrow upright outline; introduced from Blandy Experimental Farm in Virginia.

'Handsworthiensis'—Wide, strong growing, upright form with dark green foliage; makes a good hedging plant.

'Inglis'—Hardy form, densely pyramidal in habit with good dark green foliage in winter; supposedly hardy to −20°F.

'Myrtifolia'—Low growing form, 4 to 5′ tall; leaves 1/3 to 3/4″ long and 1/3″ wide.

'Newport Blue'—Foliage is bluish green, habit is densely rounded; 14-year-old plant is 18″ by 3′, grows 3 to 5″ per year, selected in 1940's by Boulevard Nurseries, RI.

'Northern Beauty'—A form that survived the terrible winters of 1976–77, 77–78 with no foliage burn.

'Northern Find'—Hardy form selected from a group of plants at Cookville, Ontario, Canada, where it withstood temperatures of –30°F; doubtfully hardy to this temperature.

'Northland'—Hardy form from central New York state; 14-year-old plant is 4′ by 5′ with dark green foliage all winter.

'Pendula'—Form with pendulous branchlets that grows into a small tree.

'Pullman'—Selected by W.A.P. Pullman, Chicago, Illinois, for incredible vigor and hardiness (–20°F), starts growth in mid May and is not injured by late freezes; rounded, dense habit and will probably grow to about 6′ in height.

'Rosmarinifolia'—Low shrub with leaves 1/6 to 1/4″ wide, about the smallest of any cultivar.

'Suffruticosa'—Dense, compact, slow growing form ideal for edging; leaves quite fragrant and considered the least susceptible to box leaf miner; susceptible to nematodes; 150-year-old plants are about 3′ high; this is a centuries old boxwood that is considered the standard or "True Edging" Boxwood; it can be kept a few inches high or will grow 4 to 5′ after many years; if left alone it reminds of clouds fused together, leaves obovate-rounded, 1/3 to 3/4″ long.

'Vardar Valley'—In the previous edition I commented on the beauty of this low-growing flat-topped mounded form, 2 to 3′ by 4 to 5′, excellent dark blue-green foliage; unfortunately over the years it has been brow-beaten by the cold weather and even in Cincinnati was severely injured at –25°F while *B. microphylla* var. *koreana* was not injured. Based on more recent observations, about –15°F (Zone 5) coincides with some injury. We have used a few plants in the horticultural garden and they lacked vigor possibly because of nematodes; all developed bronze leaf condition and were removed.

'Welleri'—Dense, broad form, 13-year-old plant is 3′ by 5′ and green throughout the winter; this is a good form and does well in the midwest.

'Zehrung'—Robust dark green foliage form with a columnar growth habit; listed in 1988–89 Studebaker Nursery Catalog.

PROPAGATION: Cuttings root readily; I use 1000 ppm IBA/50% alcohol and achieve excellent results; seeds need no pretreatment although a slight chilling will unify germination.

ADDITIONAL NOTES: Wood is of a hard, bony consistency and good for carving. The foliage has a distinctly malodorous fragrance. Boxwood through the years has been associated with formal gardens. Boxwood parterres and hedges can be seen in many of the great gardens of Europe and America. W.J. Bean put it so straightforwardly when he noted that boxwood was among the most useful of garden plants but not the most beautiful. An excellent practical article on boxwood was penned by Flint, *Horticulture* 65(3):50–59 (1987).

Common Box is truly a beautiful plant and is a staple of many southeastern formal gardens. Colonial Williamsburg, especially around the Governor's Mansion, offers wonderful examples of formal boxwood use. Unfortunately, culture is not without some difficulty and in the lower south, nematodes and root rot, especially in heavy clay soils contribute to decline over time. On the Georgia campus in a rather handsome formal boxwood garden, plants were declining badly. The entire planting was removed, soil sterilized, and new plants installed. After 4 years most plants are still vigorous although a few are developing the characteristic discoloration. The old plants had developed the bronze-yellow to orange color, started to thin out and drop leaves and lacked vigor. These are tell-tale signs that something needs to be adjusted. The root knot nematode's tell-tale symptoms are manifested by stunted roots with a bunchy dark appearance.

NATIVE HABITAT: Southern Europe, northern Africa, western Asia. Long cultivated and steeped in legend and lore.

Callicarpa japonica — Japanese Beautyberry
(kal-i-kär′-pa ja-pon′-i-ka)

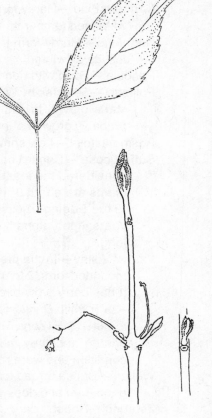

FAMILY: Verbenaceae

LEAVES: Opposite, simple, elliptic to ovate-lanceolate, 2 to 5″ long, 1 1/2 to 2″ wide, long acuminate, cuneate, serrulate, medium green with yellowish glands beneath, nearly glabrous, petiole—1/6 to 1/3″ long.

BUDS: Small, superposed, often distinctly stalked or the uppermost developing the first season, round or fusiform oblong, naked, or the smaller appearing to have 2 nearly valvate scales.

STEM: Round, slender, gray-buff, pubescent, with a purplish tinge when young, glabrous at maturity.

SIZE: 4 to 6′ in height by 4 to 6′ in spread; have seen plants 10′ high.

HARDINESS: Zone 5 to 8; −5 to −10°F will usually result in stem dieback.

HABIT: Bushy, rounded shrub with arching branches, probably best cut to ground in late winter.

RATE: Fast.

TEXTURE: Medium in all seasons.

LEAF COLOR: Medium green in summer becoming faintly yellowish to purplish in fall; sometimes almost pinkish lavender fall color.

FLOWERS: Perfect, pink or white; July (Boston); many flowered cymes, 1 to 1 1/2″ across, not showy, occur on new growth of the season from June (Athens) to August in Athens.

FRUIT: Berry-like drupes, 1/6″ across, violet to metallic-purple; borne in rather loose 1 to 1 1/2″ diameter cymes; effective in October and more so for about 2 weeks after the leaves fall off; doubtfully as showy or as abundant as *C. americana, C. dichotoma,* or *C. bodinieri;* some will argue this and I have observed excellent fruit on *C. japonica* in arboreta where other seedlings or species were present; I grew this species in Georgia and it never fruited like *C. dichotoma* (which see); also *C. dichotoma* fruits consistently from year to year without other seedlings or species for possible cross-pollination.

CULTURE: Readily transplanted; well drained soil; full sun or light shade; prune to within 4 to 6″ of the ground every spring as the flowers are produced on new growth; avoid excess fertility.

DISEASES AND INSECTS: Leaf spots, black mold, and various stem diseases, none of these are serious.

LANDSCAPE VALUE: Most effective when planted in groups in the shrub border; the fruit is very attractive and unusual in color among woody plants; best to treat as a herbaceous perennial in northern areas.

CULTIVARS:

'Leucocarpa'—White fruits, good looking plant, not readily available in commerce, certainly less offensive in color than the species; leaves of this form are lighter green than the species.

PROPAGATION: Softwood cuttings root readily in sand under mist, in fact, all *Callicarpa* root readily from softwood cuttings, roots will form in 7 to 14 days; seeds require cold, moist stratification.

NATIVE HABITAT: Japan. Introduced 1845.

RELATED SPECIES:

Callicarpa americana — American Beautyberry

LEAVES: Opposite, simple, elliptic-ovate to ovate-oblong, 3 1/2 to 6″ long, 1/2 as wide, acuminate, cuneate, crenate serrate, medium green and pubescent above, tomentose and glandular below; petiole—1/2 to 1″ long.

Callicarpa americana, (kal-i-kär′pa a-mer-i-kā′na), American Beautyberry or French Mulberry, is a rather coarse, 3 to 8′ high, loose, open shrub that is found throughout the southeast. The 3 1/2 to 6″ long, extremely pubescent, anemic medium green leaves are the largest and coarsest of the species discussed here. The light lavender-pink flowers are borne in axillary cymes on new growth from June into August. The 1/4″ diameter, violet to magenta fruits are produced in profusion. The nodes of the stems are literally encircled by the fruit clusters. Fruit ripening proceeds over a long time period. Makes a good shrub for naturalizing or massing. Have seen it used under pine trees with excellent effect. Denser and more fruitful in sun. Does better with ample root moisture; when overgrown cut back as described under *C. japonica.* Variety *lactea* is white-fruited. Southwest Maryland to North Carolina, Arkansas, south to Mexico and the West Indies. Zone 7 to 10.

C. americana

Callicarpa bodinieri — Bodinier Beautyberry

LEAVES: Opposite, simple, narrow oval or lanceolate, 2 to 5″ long, 1 to 2 1/4″ wide, acuminate, cuneate, denticulate or dentate, dull dark green above and slightly pubescent, distinctly so beneath, particularly on veins; petiole—1/5 to 1/2″ long.

Callicarpa bodinieri, (kal-i-kär′pa bō-din-i-er′ī), Bodinier Beautyberry, is rarely cultivated in American gardens, but the British consider it the finest species for their gardens. The shrub reaches 6 to 10′ at maturity and has erect branches much more distinct than *C. americana* or *C. dichotoma* in this character. Flowers are lilac, but flowers of seedling plants vary from lavender to rich purple. The 1/8 to 1/6″ diameter fruit is a glossy bluish lilac and a white-fruited form also exists. The fruits of this species are borne in a fashion similar to *C. japonica* and in my opinion do not make the best show. The infructescences of both species are loose and the fruits do not seem to persist as well as *C. americana* or *C. dichotoma. C. japonica* can be distinguished from *C. bodinieri* by its narrower glabrous leaves and glabrous inflorescences. Variety *giraldii* is glabrous above and less pubescent beneath. 'Profusion' (a Dutch selection) is a more fruitful form with 1/6″ wide violet fruits that occur 30 to 40 together per infructescence. Abundant fruits even on young plants. Leaves may turn a pinkish purple in fall. Szechuan, Hupeh, Shensi provinces of China. Introduced 1887. Zone 6 to 8.

Callicarpa dichotoma — Purple Beautyberry

LEAVES: Opposite, simple, elliptic to obovate, 1 to 3″ long, 1/2 as wide, acuminate, cuneate, coarsely serrate except at apex and base, glabrous above, glandular and sparingly pubescent beneath; petiole—1/8″ long.

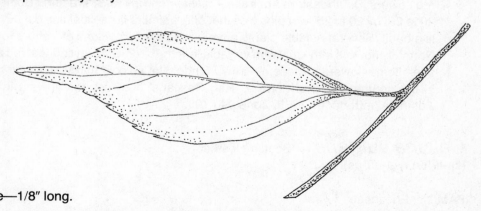

Callicarpa dichotoma, (kal-i-kär′pa dī-kot′ō-ma), Purple Beautyberry, is the most graceful and refined of the species. The species grows 3 to 4′ high with a slightly greater spread. The long slender branches arch and touch the ground at their tips. The medium green leaves are borne in one plane along the stem rather than radiating, as is true for the other species. The small pinkish lavender, 3/4″ diameter cymes are borne on stalks above the foliage from June to August. The 1/8″ diameter, lilac-violet fruits are perfectly displayed, with the foliage acting as a foil. A white-fruit form, var. *albifructus,* is also quite attractive. I have one plant of *C. dichotoma* by my driveway that was raised at Illinois from seed which I received in a seed exchange with Smith College Botanic Garden. Three plants resulted and the one I brought south proved to be a bountiful fruiter without the presence of other plants for cross-pollination. In fruit, it draws much comment with the ultimate being, "What is it?" I took several rooted cuttings to a regional American Rhododendron Society meeting and after presenting a slide lecture on this and other plants the Society auctioned off the rooted cuttings for $7.00 each. I have grown or observed all the species listed herein and consider *C. dichotoma* the best garden form. Eastern and central China. Japan. Introduced 1857. Zone 5 to 8.

ADDITIONAL NOTES: There are few fruiting shrubs that can compete with the beautyberries in October when they are at their fruiting best. When used in mass the effect is spectacular. Should be treated as herbaceous perennials in most gardens.

Callistemon citrinus (C. lanceolatus)—Lemon Bottlebrush
(kal-i-sté′mon si-trī′nus)

FAMILY: Myrtaceae

LEAVES: Alternate, simple, evergreen, lanceolate, 1 to 3″ long, 1/4″ wide, acute, reddish when young, finally bright green, midrib and axillary veins elevated.

Callistemon citrinus, Lemon Bottlebrush, is one of the plants that every traveler to Florida wants to carry back to the frozen north. The spectacular red bottlebrush-like flowers are sufficient reason to become excited. The red stamens occur in 2 to 4 1/2″ long by 2″ wide spikes at the end of the branches sporadically throughout the year. Have seen flowers in December, March and summer at various Zone 9 locations. Habit is a large, upright shrub that will grow 10 to 15′. The plant is often trained into a standard and makes a rather attractive small tree. *Citrinus* is derived from the lemon scent of the bruised foliage. The capsule like fruits are compressed and look like small buttons along the stem. They persist for several years. This species is the most tolerant of heat, cold and adverse soils. Will grow in dry soils but best growth is achieved in moist, well-drained situations in full sun. Have seen it used as a tub or container plant in northern areas. Must be protected in a cool house during winter. Used in reasonable numbers along Georgia's coast where it occasionally is injured. Temperatures dropped to 11°F along the Georgia coast in 1983–84 and so did the *Callistemon.* Probably reserved for Zone 9. Cultivars include 'Splendens' with glossy carmine-red stamens that are twice as long as the norm and a propensity to flower heavily on young plants; 'Compacta' grows 4′ by 4′ with smaller red flowers. Southeastern Australia. *Callistemon viminalis,* Weeping Bottlebrush, is a round-headed, 20 to 25′ by 20 to 25′ weeping tree that offers similar floral qualities but more graceful weeping willow like habit. Several notable plants have been seen by millions of visitors to Disney's Magic Kingdom. Normally flowers May-July with variable length, 1 1/2″ wide, cylindrical red spikes. Have seen some flowers in December in Orlando. Not as cold hardy as *C. citrinus* and best in the southern part of Zone 9. 'Red Cascade' has rosy-red flowers in abundance. Australia. Introduced 1788. Zone 9 to 10.

Calluna vulgaris — Scotch Heather
(ka-lū′na vul-gā′ris)

FAMILY: Ericaceae

LEAVES: Opposite, simple, evergreen, scale-like, 4-ranked, giving a squarish shape to the shoot, sessile, keeled, oblong-ovate, 1/25 to 1/8″ long, sagittate at base, puberulous or nearly glabrous, closely packed, appearing almost scale-like.

BUDS: Small, solitary, sessile, angularly globose, with about 3 scales.

STEM: Very slender, terete; pith—very small, roundish, continuous.

SIZE: 4 to 24″ in height; spread 2′ or more.

HARDINESS: Zone 4 to Zone 6 (7).

HABIT: Upright branching, small evergreen ground cover with dense, leafy ascending branches forming thick mats; old plants become unkempt and need an occasional pruning to keep them respectable.

RATE: Slow.

TEXTURE: Fine in all seasons.

LEAF COLOR: Medium green in summer; winter color varies from green to bronze. Cultivars may be silver, yellow to red.

FLOWERS: Perfect, rosy to purplish pink, urn-shaped sepals showy part of 1/4″ long flower, 4-lobed corolla; borne in 1 to 12″ long racemes in July-September; exquisite, dainty, refined plants especially when in flower; bees are especially fond of the flowers and the honey they give is regarded as special quality.

FRUIT: Four-valved 1/10″ long capsule, October, not ornamental.

CULTURE: Move as a container-grown plant in spring; prefer acid (pH 6 or less), sandy, organic, moist, perfectly drained soils; avoid sweeping winds as plants are very susceptible to drying; full sun or partial shade, however, plants do not flower as profusely in shade; prefer low fertility soils, otherwise become ratty looking; do not over fertilize, prune in early spring before new growth starts; do not cultivate soil around plants; mulch and water during dry periods. Raulston reported a 20 to 25% loss per year in the Raleigh, NC area.

DISEASES AND INSECTS: Japanese beetle, two-spotted mite and oyster shell scale.

LANDSCAPE VALUE: Good ground cover plant, edging, rock garden; excellent flowers and foliage put this plant at the top of my groundcover list; fastidious as to soil requirements and attention to cultural details is necessary.

CULTIVARS: There are so many cultivars that it would be impossible to do justice to them; recently I read a report that stated there are 663 heather cultivars and 338 are in private gardens. This is actually amazing because *Calluna vulgaris* is a monotypic species and all variants have arisen within the genetic limits of one species. In September, 1981 I visited the private garden of Mr. and Mrs. R. Cameron, Great Compton, Kent, England, and was over-whelmed with the diversity of form, color and texture of *Calluna* cultivars. The Camerons had assembled 200 different heathers and displayed them in a most pleasing fashion. At one time I thought growing *Calluna* in the midwest was nigh to impossible, but I raised seedlings and outplanted them in my garden. They performed magnificently and, by rooting cuttings, I distributed them to my gardening friends. A few cultivars I might recommend based on observation in the United States include:

var. *alba*—white flowers. There are several named 'Alba' forms with double and larger flowers.

'County Wicklow'—One of the best double pink forms with 3 to 6″ long inflorescences, prostrate to 9″, dark green foliage, July to September.

'H.E. Beale'—A vigorous, durable, silvery double pink form, strong branching, to 18″, flower in August-October.

'Robert Chapman'—Most interesting form with greenish yellow summer foliage changing to orange-red and reddish in winter, 8 to 10″ long rose-purple flowers in August-September, colorful to the point of being gauche.

PROPAGATION: Seed should be sown on peat moss; there is no dormancy and germination takes place in 2 to 3 weeks; I have raised many *Calluna* plants this way; softwood cuttings treated with 1000 ppm IBA quick dip, rooted in 2 to 3 weeks in a peat:perlite medium under mist.

RELATED SPECIES: The genus *Erica* is closely related but differs in the innumerable species (200 plus); the linear, spreading leaves (rather than closely packed as in *Calluna*) arranged in whorls of 3 or 4, sometimes 5 or 6; and the globular to cylindrical corolla with the 4-small teeth at the contracted opening (calyx showy part of *Calluna* flower) corolla only one-half as long. The *Erica* species flower in winter or spring; *Calluna* in summer or fall although some heaths, *E. ciliaris, E. cinerea* and others flower in summer and fall. A few that I have seen and would recommend include *E. carnea,* Spring

Heath, with rosy-red flowers and two cultivars 'Springwood White' and 'Springwood Pink' which I have seen at local garden centers; all flower in January through March. *E. cinerea*, Bell Heath, Twisted Heath, with purple flowers from June to September and its numerous cultivars. *E. tetralix*, Crossleaf Heath, with rose-colored flowers from June to September/October. *E. vagans*, Cornish Heath, with pinkish purple flowers from July to October. *Erica* requires essentially the same care as *Calluna*. They are not as cold hardy and do not appear to be as happy in American gardens as *Calluna*. I have seen numerous *Erica* types in European gardens and they are truly beautiful especially when used in mass.

ADDITIONAL NOTES: The moors of northern England and Scotland are covered by the heathers and heaths (*E. cinerea*) and become beautiful in late summer and autumn. On a recent trip we crossed through the English mountains into Wales and the heather was about the only plant in evidence and provided the kind of setting one associates with English horror movies.

Many excellent books are available on heathers and heaths and should be consulted. Several of the best include:

Chapple, F.J. 1952. *The Heather Garden*, W.H. and L. Collingridge LTD. London. Covers *Calluna*, *Daboecia* and *Erica* with numerous cultivar descriptions.

Underhill, T.L. 1971. *Heaths and Heathers*, David and Charles, Newton Abbot, England. Newer and more detailed concerning cultivar descriptions. Thirty-three pages of *Calluna vulgaris* cultivars presented. I counted 27 cultivars with the 'alba' prefix; many were synonyms but it affords some idea of possible similar selections. Appears to be the most complete.

Proundley, B. and V. Proundley. 1983. *Heathers in Color*. Blandford Press, Dorset England. Significant color of good quality which adds to the book's pleasure. Includes *Calluna, Daboecia* and *Erica* with descriptions of cultivars.

Over the years of visiting European gardens, I have returned to the United States with a much greater appreciation for this species and its garden uses. Perhaps the finest display occurs in Mr. Adrian Bloom's garden, Foggy Bottom, at Bressingham. He has skillfully integrated heathers, heaths, conifers, deciduous shrubs and small trees to produce unbelievable summer and even more striking winter combinations. Certainly a garden worth visiting. Several notable collections of heathers and heaths include Wisley and Edinburgh Botanic Garden.

I found a heather in a Georgia garden, propagated and grew it for several years but it has not flowered. It is in a peat:sand soil and is vegetatively happy. Does high heat restrict flower development?

NATIVE HABITAT: *Calluna vulgaris* is found in Europe, Asia Minor, and has naturalized in northeastern North America. Cultivated for centuries.

Calocedrus decurrens (*Libocedrus decurrens*)—California Incensecedar
(kal-o-sed′rus de-ker′enz)

FAMILY: Cupressaceae

LEAVES: In 4's closely pressed, equal in size, oblong-obovate, apex finely pointed and free, narrowing to base, dark green; on ultimate branches about 1/4″ long; on main shoots about 1/2″ long, lateral pair boat-shaped, almost wholly ensheathing the facial pairs; glandular, emitting an aromatic odor when crushed, lustrous dark green.

STEM: Branchlets flattened, terminating in dense, fan-like sprays in which the ultimate branches point forward at an acute angle.

SIZE: 30 to 50′ high by 8 to 10′ wide; can grow to 125 to 150′ high in the wild.

HARDINESS: Zone 5 to 8.

HABIT: Stiff or narrowly columnar in youth, very regular in outline, with a distinct formal character even in old age; a beautiful conifer that is often confused with arborvitae.

RATE: Slow-medium, in proper soil and atmosphere may grow 50 to 70′ after 30 to 50 years.

TEXTURE: Medium.

BARK: Thin, smooth, and grayish green or scaly and tinged with red on young stems; on old trunks—thick (3 to 8"), yellowish brown to cinnamon-red, fibrous, deeply and irregularly furrowed.

LEAF COLOR: Shiny dark green, borne in vertical sprays; holds color well in winter months.

FLOWERS: Monoecious, male-oblong with 12 to 16 decussate stamens.

FRUIT: Cones cylindric, 3/4" long, 1/4 to 1/3" wide at base, tapered, reddish brown or yellowish brown when ripe in early autumn, remaining on the tree until spring, lowest pair of cone-scales half as long as the others, seeds 1/3" long, awl-shaped, with a large wing on one side, a small one on the other.

CULTURE: Prefers moist, well-drained, fertile soil; full sun or light shade, not tolerant of smoggy or wind-swept conditions, shows good adaptability to different soil types, may be somewhat difficult to transplant.

DISEASES AND INSECTS: A heart rot caused by *Polyporus amarus* is this tree's most destructive single enemy; other conspicuous, but seldom damaging, diseases are a brooming *Gymnosporangium* rust and a leafy mistletoe.

LANDSCAPE VALUE: Handsome specimen for large areas and formal plantings; not used enough; the plant that your neighbor will wonder about; the plant does quite well in the south and one 70' high specimen in Athens attests to its tolerance of heat and drought; very formal and should probably be restricted to that style of landscaping; Longwood Gardens has a fine grove all of which are distinctly columnar; also performing well on Oklahoma State Campus, Stillwater, OK.

CULTIVARS:

'Aureo-variegata'—A rather interesting yellow-variegated form; the size of the yellow variegation varying from a small spot to an entire spray; first saw this at the Parc Floral, Orleans, France and was genuinely dazzled (also blinded).

PROPAGATION: Propagated by seed, which requires a stratification period of about 8 weeks at 32° to 40°F for good germination; I have had poor success trying to grow this species; cuttings are difficult and I have been unable to root a single cutting; can be grafted on *Thuja occidentalis.* Nicholson, *The Plant Propagator* 30(1):5–6 (1984) used mid-November cuttings, 75°F bottom heat, poly tent, 50 to 60°F air temperature, obtained 92, 66, 58 and 8% rooting with 2500 ppm NAA dip, 2500 ppm NAA + 2500 ppm IBA dip, 200 ppm IBA-24 hour soak, and control (0), respectively.

ADDITIONAL NOTES: Habit is broadly conical in the wild with spreading branches; in cultivated trees the branches are usually short and the outline is columnar. Most trees in cultivation appear to be the cultivar 'Columnaris' which is narrow, columnar. Have seen the plant in abundance in Portland, OR area, appears better adapted and more vibrant. Interestingly, it has performed quite well in the heat of Zone 8. Might be worth additional testing in midwest and south.

NATIVE HABITAT: Western United States from Oregon to Nevada and lower California. Introduced 1853.

Calycanthus floridus — Common Sweetshrub, also called Carolina Allspice or Strawberry-shrub
(kal-i-kan'-thus flôr'-i-dus)

FAMILY: Calycanthaceae

LEAVES: Opposite, simple, entire, ovate or elliptic to narrow-elliptic, 2 to 5" long, acute or acuminate, rarely obtuse, cuneate or rounded at base, dark green and slightly rough to the touch above, grayish green and densely pubescent beneath; petiole—1/3" long.

BUDS: Superposed in a single bud-like aggregate, sessile, round or oblong, brown hairy, without evident scales, the end bud lacking; buds concealed by base of petiole.

STEM: Aromatic when bruised, stout, glabrous, gray-brown, compressed at the nodes appearing angled; pith—relatively large, somewhat 6-sided, white, continuous; leaf scars—U or horseshoe-shaped, raised, 3 bundle traces.

SIZE: 6 to 9' in height by 6 to 12' in spread.

HARDINESS: Zone 4 to 9; have seen it injured in Zone 4; −15° to −20°F is the break point.

HABIT: Dense, bushy, rounded or broad rounded shrub of regular outline; is often straggly and unkempt in the wild.

RATE: Slow to medium.

TEXTURE: Medium in leaf and in winter.

LEAF COLOR: Dark green in summer, yellowish in fall, but usually not effective; leaves persist late (November); have observed quite excellent fall color, definitely varies from year to year.

FLOWERS: Perfect, dark reddish brown, 2″ across, very fruity fragrance, May and flowering sporadically into June and July, borne singly from the leaf axil; flowers on current season's growth and wood of previous season; sepals and petals numerous and similar; in my garden it may be in flower by early April.

FRUIT: Urn-shaped receptacle, somewhat capsule-like at maturity and enclosing many one-seeded rich brown achenes, September-October and persisting through winter.

CULTURE: Easily transplanted; adaptable to many soils, preferably a deep, moist, loam; shade or sun, but does not grow as tall in sun as in shaded places; prune after flowering; appears to adapt to acid and alkaline soils.

DISEASES AND INSECTS: Very resistant shrub.

LANDSCAPE VALUE: Worthwhile plant for every garden, especially welcome in the shrub border or around an outdoor living area where the sweet strawberry-banana-pineapple scent can permeate the entire area; great variation in flower odor and it is best to smell before buying; this is a trouble-free plant that can be meshed into any garden setting.

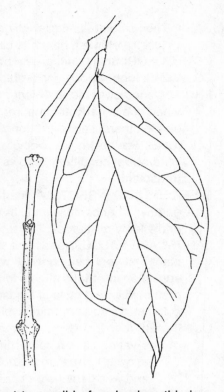

CULTIVARS: A yellow-flowered form exists but is not well known; supposedly Henry Hohman, Kingsville, MD, had the plant; Callaway Gardens, Gene Cline, Canton, GA and Jane Symmes, Madison, GA have the plant but its origin is lost to antiquity; I have a plant provided by Mrs. Symmes and it has tremendous fragrance—as good as I have ever experienced on *any* sweetshrub; the foliage is lustrous dark green and the habit dense and mounded; in the last edition I mentioned naming the shrub after my oldest daughter, Katherine; someone decided this was not kosher and named it 'Athens' so the plant with these two names is actually one and the same; the plant has brought great delight to our garden and home and virtually every garden could make use of such a plant; cut branches (from April to May) are frequently brought into the house and provide a heady fragrance; in the last edition, I mentioned only 50% success with rooting, since that time better techniques have evolved that insure 80% or greater success; they include: firm wooded cuttings (as late as August), peat:perlite, mist, 10000 ppm KIBA (water soluble) and 10,000 ppm IBA-alcohol produced 93 and 82% rooting, respectively; in the past with soft cuttings, alcohol has injured the stem tissue; in this study the wood was quite firm and more resistant to alcohol. In 1988 trials, 3000 and 5000 ppm KIBA from early June and early July cuttings produced 77 and 87% rooting, respectively. I was told that this cultivar reproduced partially true-to-type from seed but have found this not true with populations I grew. Seeds were collected from an isolated plant in my garden, hence, no cross-pollination, and in 3 years flowered the typical reddish-maroon-brown color of the species. Most were fragrant but even some seedlings exhibited no delightful fragrance.

'Edith Wilder'—A form that I have only seen at Mrs. Gertrude Wister's garden in Swarthmore, PA. It has the typical deep brown-maroon-red flower of the species and excellent fragrance; needs to be propagated by an enterprising nurseryman.

'Purpureus'—A form with purplish leaves. I have not seen this clone.

'Urbana'—A selection by the late great plantsman Professor J.C. McDaniel, University of Illinois, for sweet fragrance and the typical species flower color.

PROPAGATION: I have collected seeds in December and sown them immediately with good results; they could have naturally stratified outside; 3 months at 41°F is recommended. I collected seeds just as the urn-shaped receptacle was changing from green to brown (August); the seed coats could be easily broken with the fingernail, these seeds (achenes) germinated 90% 3 weeks after planting; in follow-up work I collected the receptacles when they were brown and withered, extracted the seed which at this time had bullet-hard seed coats; out of 75 seeds planted, one germinated; my guess is that the dormancy of *Calycanthus* is probably due to the seed coat and not strict internal embryo dormancy. July-collected cuttings rooted 90% in sand in 60 days when treated with 8000 ppm IBA talc; however, I have seen reports of only 30% success at this same time. I have rooted softwood cuttings with poor success using 1000 or 3000 ppm IBA-quick dip; the alcohol seems to cause the leaves to defoliate ahead of cuttings treated with talc; see report under cultivars for best cutting procedure.

ADDITIONAL NOTES: All parts and particularly the wood when dry exude a camphor-like fragrance. Supposedly the bark was used as a substitute for cinnamon.

NATIVE HABITAT: Virginia to Florida. Introduced 1726.

RELATED SPECIES:

Based on my studies I am not sure there are related species at least among the eastern types. They should all be included under the above species. *Calycanthus fertilis,* Pale Sweet-shrub, supposedly has less pubescent leaves and flowers with no scent. Great quantities of fruit are set. *Calycanthus mohrii,* Mohr Sweetshrub, is similar to *C. fertilis* with more ovate leaves and rounded or heart shape leaf bases. I have looked at a lot of *C. floridus* native populations in the southeast and can find the characteristics of all three species in any one population. *C. occidentalis,* California Sweetshrub, is similar to the above but has larger parts and exposed leaf buds. The California Sweetshrub, *C. occidentalis,* is more common in English gardens. It appears more vigorous and I have seen 12 to 15′ high plants. The flower color is lighter and the fragrance is minmal and, based on actual nose tests, not at all pleasant. Where the fragrant type eastern species can be grown this should not be considered. Considered hardy in Zone 6.

Camellia japonica — Japanese Camellia
(ka-mēl′i-a ja-pon′i-ka)

FAMILY: Theaceae

LEAVES: Alternate, simple, evergreen, ovate to elliptic, 2 to 4″ long, abruptly acuminate, cuneate, serrate, each serration tipped with a black gland, lustrous dark green above, glabrous, firm, leathery, almost plastic texture, underside with black gland-like dots; petiole—1/4″ long.

BUDS: Flower—imbricate, green, pubescent on upper portion, rounded-conical, 3/4″ long, 1/2″ wide; vegetative—imbricate, green, glabrous, angular-conical, 1/4 to 3/8″ long, both buds may be present at same node.

STEM: Moderate, rich brown, covered with blackish lenticels, glabrous; pith—white, spongy; leaf scars crescent shaped to nearly elliptical; one bundle trace.

SIZE: 10 to 15′ (20 to 25′), 6 to 10′ wide.

HARDINESS: 7 to 9; in Athens-Atlanta area numerous plants killed at −3°F during 1985 winter.

HABIT: Usually dense pyramid of lustrous dark green foliage; some forms more open than others and a bit more graceful; have also seen forms that are columnar-pyramidal; in general rather stiff, stodgy and formal.

RATE: Slow.

TEXTURE: Medium to medium-coarse.

LEAF COLOR: Lustrous dark green through the seasons; if sited in full sun some discoloration may occur in winter; this is not, however, absolute.

FLOWERS: Perfect, non-fragrant except for a few cultivars, axillary, solitary, rarely 2 to 3 together, 5 to 7 petals in the species to numerous petals in the doubles, 3 to 5″ across; white, pink, rose, red, about every conceivable combination; some flowers are variegated; may open from November through April in the Athens, GA area; cold is their biggest enemy and turns the flowers to brown mush; beautiful when unadulterated by the weather.

FRUIT: Rather unusual loculicidal woody capsule that houses 1 to 3 seeds; seeds are brown, subglobose or angular and about 1″ long, ripen in fall.

CULTURE: Easily transplanted from containers; prefer moist, acid, well-drained, high organic matter soils; plants in high pH soils do not prosper; best to mulch since root system is not particularly deep; should be sited in partial shade; too much shade or sun results in depressed flowering; have balled plants in a nursery and most of the root system was in confined area around the trunk; prune anytime but most logically after flowering; cold is a limiting factor in Zones 7 and 8; plants are often grown in conservatories in the northern states.

DISEASES AND INSECTS: Spot disease on leaves, black mold on leaves and stems, leaf gall, leaf spot, flower blight, stem cankers, root rot, leaf blight, virus induced flower and leaf variegation, tea scale (serious pest in south), Florida red scale, numerous other scales, mealy bugs, weevils, Fuller rose beetle, thrips, spotted cut worm, numerous other insects, root-nema; physiological disorders include bud drop, chlorosis, oedema, sunburn, salt injury.

LANDSCAPE VALUE: A cherished plant in southern gardens but the devastating freeze of 1983–84 and 1985 killed old venerable specimens with 12 to 16″ trunk diameters. On the Georgia campus a few survived, many were killed to the ground and resprouted, and others perished. The flowers are beautiful and a shrub in full regalia is an object of great beauty. Unfortunately, with flowers opening from December to April in the Athens area, many times the petals are turned brown from the cold. I suspect anything below 32°F for a time will cause some petal deterioration. I *had* seen entire collections of nothing but *Camellia japonica* without much feeling for placement and design considerations. The plant is coming back and being used in borders, mixed plantings and as an accent or focal point in protected courtyards or against walls. Careful siting in Zone 8 is a must. Also choose the cultivars based on cold hardiness since this dictates whether the plant will survive.

CULTIVARS: Numerous, in fact, confused to the point of hopelessness; professional and amateurs have bred, selected, and introduced new cultivars, any attempt at a list would be superfluous so I will recommend that interested parties join the American Camellia Society. Mr. Gerald Smith, former Extension Specialist, University of Georgia, and gardener, provided a list of some of the hardier types. (See Univ. of Georgia Cooperative Extension Bulletin #813, *Camellia Culture for Home Gardeners*.) They include:

'Bernice Boddy'—Flowers semi-double, shaded light pink, very cold hardy flower buds.

'Debutante'—Light pink, early flowering, peony type, complete double.

'Flame'—Late-flowering red form, very cold hardy flower buds, semi double.

'Governor Mouton'—Red and white variegated flowers, cold hardy buds.

'Kumasaka'—Dark pink, late, cold hardy, incomplete double.

'Lady Clare'—Flowers large, semi-double, dark pink, above average cold hardiness.

'Lady Vansittart'—Variable colors on same plant from semi-double white, pink to red, very shiny dark green pointed leaves, above average cold hardiness.

Magnoliaeflora'—Light pink, cold hardy, semi-double, compact plant.

'Pink Perfection'—Formal double, pink.

'Rev. John G. Drayton'—Flowers semi-double, carmine-rose, late-blooming.

'White Empress'—White, early, above average hardiness, incomplete double.

PROPAGATION: Seed requires no pretreatment if taken from the capsules and planted immediately; if seeds dry out they should be covered with hot water (190°F) and allowed to imbibe for about 24 hours; after this time they can be placed in seed flats. Cuttings are best collected from May to September and in the fall, about November; cuttings should be taken from the current season's growth just below the fifth node; 3000 to 8000 ppm IBA is effective; sand and peat or peat and perlite, mist or poly-tent are the other important ingredients. West Coast and southern propagators have reported good success from July-August cuttings from clean, container-grown stock plants. Camellias are also grafted and air-layered.

NATIVE HABITAT: China, Japan. Cultivated 1742.

RELATED SPECIES:

Camellia oleifera — Tea-oil Camellia

LEAVES: Alternate, simple, evergreen, 1 to 3″(5″) long, 3/4 to 1 1/4″ wide, broad elliptic or oblanceolate to obovate, acuminate, serrate, leathery, lustrous dark green, glabrous; petiole-short, hairy.

Camellia oleifera, (kȧ-mēl′i-a ō-lē-if′ĕr-ȧ), Tea-oil Camellia, is not well known in cultivation but may be one of the hardiest camellias. In most respects it is similar to *C. sasanqua* and has been hybridized with that species. The 2 to 2 1/2″ wide, white flowers appear in the leaf axils from October to January. At North Carolina State Arboretum, I have seen the species (hybrids) in flower in October. Interestingly, these plants had survived –9°F, were 12 to 15′ high and vigorous. Flower color was variable white to pink, possibly because of the hybrid parentage. The leaves of *C. sasanqua* are thinner (not as leathery), smaller, and blunter-pointed. China. Zone 7(?) to 9.

Camellia sasanqua — Sasanqua Camellia
(ka-mēl′i-a sa-san′kwa)

LEAVES: Similar to *C. japonica* but smaller, obovate or narrowly oval 1 1/2 to 3″ long, 1/3 to 1/2 as wide, lustrous dark green, hairy on midrib above and below, rounded teeth on the margin; petiole—pubescent.

BUDS: Similar, one-half size of *C. japonica,* pubescent.

STEM: Slender, compared to *C. japonica,* brown, and covered with prominent pubescence.

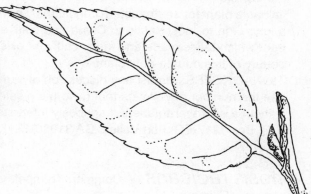

Camellia sasanqua, Sasanqua Camellia, tends to be smaller, 6 to 10′ high (15′), and more refined than *C. japonica.* It, too, forms a broad densely branched evergreen pyramid. The leaves are a lustrous dark green and considerably smaller than those of *C. japonica.* The flowers are usually smaller (2 to 3″ diameter) and more open than *C. japonica* but no less diverse in color, or degree of doubleness. They open ahead of *C. japonica* and range from September into December in the Athens area. This species has the same basic cultural requirements as *C. japonica* but is considered less hardy. I have observed specimens in full sun that were quite healthy. After the two devastating winters of 1976–77 and 1977–78 almost all the *C. sasanqua* were eliminated from the camellia collection at the National Arboretum (Zone 7) whereas many *C. japonica* survived. Based on 1983–84 freeze damage, this species survived better than *C. japonica.* Large flowering specimens in 1987 and 1988 were of this species which indicated better freeze survival or subsequent regrowth than *C. japonica.* The plant is more refined and more lax and open than *C. japonica* and is more attractive from a landscape point of view. A very easy way to tell *C. japonica* from *C. sasanqua* is by the pubescent stems of the latter. China, Japan. Introduced 1811. Zone 7 to 9. Cultivars include:

'Bonanza'—Deep red, semi-peony form, large flower.

'Daydream'—White edged deep rose, single large flowers.

'Jean May'—Shell pink, semi-double to double, large.

'Mine-No-Yuki'—White, double, large, sets buds heavily.

'Pink Snow'—Light pink, semi-double, large, more vigorous than 'Mine-No-Yuki', does not bud as quickly.

'Setsugekka'—White, semi-double, large ruffled petals.

'Sparkling Burgandy'—Ruby rose overlaid with lavender sheen, peony-form.

'Yuletide'—Red, with yellow stamens, single.

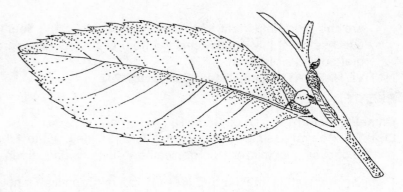

Camellia sinensis — Tea
LEAVES: Alternate,   simple, evergreen, elliptic, 2 to 4 1/2″ long, 1/3 as wide, serrate, lustrous dark green above; petiole—short.

Camellia sinensis, (ka-mēl′i-a sī-nen′sis), Tea, is one of the great, unsung treasures of the *Camellia* world for use in Zone 7 to 9 gardens. It is distinguishably hardier than the above species and makes a fine 4 to 6′ high and wide evergreen shrub especially adapted to shady environments. The 1 to 1 1/2″ diameter, fragrant, white-petalled, yellow-stamened flowers open in September-October (Athens) and continue into November, usually 1 to 3 produced from the leaf axils on 1/2″ long pedicels; unfortunately flowers are hidden by the leaves and do not jump out like those of the brethren above. The fruit is a 3/4″ long shiny capsule with 1 or 2 seeds. The plant is not particular about soil or exposure and will perform quite well in full sun. It also displays high heat and drought tolerance and could prove a valuable plant for southeastern conditions. I have propagated July-August cuttings but they do take a long time to root. Native to China and cultivated for centuries by the Chinese. This is the plant from which tea is made and many cultivars exist. Next time you read the tea leaves, reflect on the beauty of this double-duty plant.

ADDITIONAL NOTES: Almost any discussion of camellias is superfluous. It staggers the imagination to see the number of cultivars that have been selected. It would be difficult to separate the "players" without a scorecard (label). If seriously interested consider joining the American Camellia Society, P.O. Box 1217-FG, Fort Valley, GA 31030-1217.

Campsis radicans — Common Trumpetcreeper, Trumpet Vine
(kamp′sis rad′-i-kanz)

FAMILY: Bignoniaceae
LEAVES: Opposite, pinnately compound, 6 to 15″ long, 7, 9 to 11 leaflets, short-stalked, elliptic to ovate-oblong, each leaflet 3/4 to 4″ long, 1/4 to 2″ wide, coarsely and angularly toothed, with a long acuminate apex, lustrous dark green above, glabrous, pubescent beneath especially on veins.
BUDS: Small, mostly solitary, sessile, triangular, compressed, with 2 or 3 pairs of exposed scales.
STEM: Light brown, glabrous, aerial rootlets develop between nodes; pith-solid, pale brown; leaf scar-crater-like like depression with one bundle trace, bud sits on top of leaf scar, leaf scars connected by hairy ridge.

SIZE: 30 to 40′ high, actually will scramble and climb over everything in its path.
HARDINESS: Zone 4 to 9.
HABIT: Rampant, deciduous, clinging (rootlike holdfasts), strangling vine; at its best on fenceposts for when it

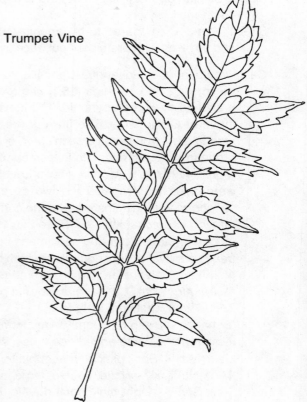

reaches the top of the post it forms an immense whorl of stems; makes the post appear as if it is about to fly; needs frequent pruning.

RATE: Fast; keep your legs moving when in the vicinity of this plant.

TEXTURE: Medium in summer, coarse in winter.

LEAF COLOR: Lustrous dark green changing to yellow-green in fall and not effective; late leafing, as late as early May in Athens.

FLOWERS: Perfect, corolla rich orange and scarlet, trumpet-shaped, 2 1/2 to 3″ long, 1 1/2″ wide at mouth with triangular teeth, borne 4 to 12 together in terminal cymes from June (Athens) to September; flowers on new growth of the season; tremendous variation in flower color from orange to red in southeast; the corolla sometimes spotted on the outside.

FRUIT: A 3 to 5″ long, 3/4″ wide capsule; each loaded with numerous flattened seeds with 2 large transparent wings.

CULTURE: If you can not grow this, give up gardening; grows in any soil and also prospers in sidewalk cracks; extremely rampant in rich soil; best to prune back to a few buds in spring; I suspect if the developing fruits are removed the plant will flower even more heavily into late summer.

DISEASES AND INSECTS: Blight, leaf spots, powdery mildew, plant hoppers, scale and whitefly occur but are not serious enough to warrant controls.

LANDSCAPE VALUE: Good for screening, covering rock piles, have seen it used tastefully over trellises and lath structures; good pruning is a necessity to keep it in bounds.

CULTIVARS:

'Crimson Trumpet'—A strong growing form with pure glowing red flowers without any trace of orange.

'Flava' (var. *flava*)—Handsome form with yellow, perhaps orange-yellow flowers, cultivated 1842, this is a particularly handsome form and in my mind preferable to the species; one of the most beautiful specimens I have seen is found in Mr. Airy Arboretum, Cincinnati, Ohio; easily rooted from cuttings.

'Praecox'—Flowers red, appearing in June; I have seen many forms in the south that approach red to scarlet; the midwestern type appears to have more orange.

PROPAGATION: Seeds germinate more uniformily when given 2 months at 41°F or fall sown; softwood cuttings (June-July) root readily and root cuttings work well; in fact it is hard to get rid of this plant because of its propensity to sucker from root pieces.

NATIVE HABITAT: Pennsylvania to Missouri, Florida and Texas. Introduced 1640.

RELATED SPECIES:

Campsis grandiflora, (kamp′sis gran-di-flō′-ra), Chinese Trumpetcreeper, grows 20 to 30′ and is similar to *C. radicans* in most respects. The deep orange and red corolla is widely trumpet-shaped, 2 to 3″ long and wide with 5-broad, rounded lobes. Flowers on new growth with 6 to 12 flowers per pendulous panicle. The leaflets (7 or 9) are glabrous, 1 1/2 to 3″ long, 1/2 as wide, long-pointed, and coarsely toothed. The inflorescence paniculate and the flowers are longer than *C. radicans.* Native to Japan. Introduced 1800. Zone 7 to 9.

Campsis × tagliabuana, (kamp′sis × tag-lē-a-bwa′na), is a hybrid between *C. g.* × *C. radicans* and is intermediate in characteristics. The first plant to be identified as a hybrid arose in the nursery of the Tagliabue brothers near Milan. Many forms were distributed by French nurseries; the finest and most common being 'Mme. Galen' which was put into commerce in 1889. It makes a spectacular show in flower and is superior and hardier than *C. grandiflora.* Have seen in coastal Georgia where it prospers in the summer heat; an indefatigable flowerer. Zone 5, probably best in 6 to 9.

ADDITIONAL NOTES: The common name is appropriately derived. A genetic engineer should transfer the genes from this species to some of the more tempermental ornamental plants.

Caragana arborescens — Siberian Peashrub
(kăr-a-gā′na   ar-bō-res′-enz)

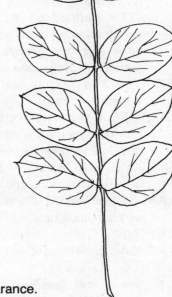

FAMILY: Fabaceae

LEAVES: Alternate, evenly pinnately compound, 1 1/2 to 3″ long, 8 to 12 leaflets, each leaflet obovate to elliptic-oblong, 1/2 to 1″ long, rounded at apex and acuminate, pubescent when young, later glabrescent, bright green, stipules linear, spine tipped, developing into a pair of stiff 1/4″ spines at each node, this is more prevalent on wild rather than cultivated specimens.

BUDS: Weakly imbricate, light brown in color, scales-chaffy in nature.

STEM: Green in color, remaining so for several years, angled from the nodes, with pale, horizontal lenticels, usually of scurfy appearance.

SIZE: 15 to 20′ in height with a spread of 12 to 18′.

HARDINESS: Zone 2 to 7.

HABIT: Erect, oval shrub, often taller than broad with moderate, sparse branches; can also be grown as a tree; branches may be so erect as to create a fastigiate appearance.

RATE: Medium to fast.

TEXTURE: Medium in summer, coarse in winter.

LEAF COLOR: Light bright green in summer; briefly yellow-green in fall.

FLOWERS: Perfect, bright yellow, 1/2 to 1″ long, early to mid May on previous year's wood when the leaves are 2/3's to fully developed; borne singly or up to 4 in fascicles.

FRUIT: A pod, 1 1/2 to 2″ long, yellow-green changing to brown, with 3 to 5 seeds, matures July/August, makes popping sound as pod opens.

CULTURE: Very easy to grow; extremely cold hardy and able to tolerate poor soils, drought, alkalinity, salt as well as sweeping winds; an extremely adaptable but limitedly ornamental plant; nitrogen fixing.

DISEASES AND INSECTS: Nothing too serious although leaf-hoppers can disfigure young growth.

LANDSCAPE VALUE: Good for hedge, screen, windbreak where growing conditions are difficult; I would not recommend it for wholesale use.

CULTIVARS:

'Lorbergii'—Leaflets reduced to linear proportions, each 1/4 to 3/4″ long, 1/25 to 1/12″ wide; flowers are also narrower; has an overall ferny appearance; not bad for textural quality; saw it at one nursery identified as *Robinia pseudoacacia* 'Lorbergii'—close, but no cigar; found in Lorberg's Nursery, Germany and introduced around 1906.

'Nana'—A dwarf, rather stunted form with stiff contorted branches; similar in leaf and flower to the species upon which it is grafted; Arnold Arboretum has a nice specimen; 17-year-old plant may be 6′ high and 3′ wide.

'Pendula'—Stiffly weeping form that when grafted on a standard makes a rather pleasant ornamental; several plants at Niagara Falls, Canadian side are beautiful; leaves and flowers as in the species.

'Sutherland'—An upright form that would be effective for screening; have seen it at Minnesota Landscape Arboretum and was quite impressed.

'Walker'—Much like 'Lorbergii' in leaf character but strongly weeping; arose from a cross between 'Lorbergii' and 'Pendula' at Morden Research Station, Canada.

PROPAGATION: Apparently seed dormancy is shallow and/or caused by an impermeable seed coat; stratification for 15 days at 41°F or longer is recommended; cold water and preferably hot water (180°F) soaks have induced 80% plus germination; a light acid scarification (5 minutes) would probably be effective or simply plant in fall and let nature take its course. 'Nana', 'Lorbergii', 'Pendula' and the species have been rooted at 80% levels when collected in May, June, July and treated with 3000 to 8000 ppm IBA-talc; the weeping type is usually grafted on a standard to produce a rather handsome small tree.

NATIVE HABITAT: *Caragana arborescens* is found in Siberia, Mongolia. Introduced 1752.

RELATED SPECIES:

There are many *Caragana* species but it is doubtful that any will ever become extremely popular. The two best collections I have seen are at the Arnold and Minnesota Landscape Arboreta. Minnesota has a particularly large collection. Most of the following remarks are based on evaluations of those collections.

Caragana aurantiaca, (kãr-a-gā'na â-ran-ti-ā'ka), Dwarf Peashrub, is a small (4' high), graceful shrub that is armed with triple-spines. The dark green leaves and orange-yellow flowers which hang from the underside of the stem is a long row, 3 to 4 to the inch, make it particularly attractive. Siberia to Afghanistan and Turkestan. Cultivated 1850, lost and reintroduced 1887. Zone 4.

Caragana frutex, (kãr-a-gā'na frū'teks), Russian Peashrub, is an upright, unarmed, suckering shrub growing 6 to 9' high. There are 4, stalked, closely spaced, 1/4 to 1" long, dark green leaflets per leaf which distinguishes this from *C. pygmaea* and the other species treated here. The bright yellow, 1" long flowers appear in May-June. 'Globosa' is a diminutive form of globe-shape growing 2' high and wide. Southern Russia to Turkestan and Siberia. Introduced 1752. Zone 2.

Caragana maximowicziana, (kãr-a-gā'na maks-im-ō-wiks-i-ā'na), Maximowicz Peashrub, is a low, spreading, spiny form with 4 to 6, grass- to blue-green leaflets. Size ranges from 3 to 6' high and 1 1/2 to 2 times as wide. It has bright yellow flowers and is a rather pretty alternative to barberries for barrier planting. Western Szechuan and Kansu, China and eastern Tibet. Zone 2. Introduced by E.H. Wilson in 1910.

Caragana microphylla, (kãr-a-gā'na mī-krō-fil'la), Littleleaf Caragana, grows 6 to 10' high with a greater spread and has 12 to 18, 1/8 to 1/3" long, dull grayish green, oval to obovate leaflets. The light yellow, 3/4" long flowers are produced during May and June. Minnesota Landscape Arboretum lists cultivar 'Tidy' that description-wise sounds very much like the species. Siberia, northern China. Introduced 1789. Zone 2.

Caragana pygmaea, (kãr-a-gā'na pig-mē'-a), Pygmy Peashrub, is similar to *C. aurantiaca* and along with that species is considered the prettiest of the peashrubs. My field notes say only interesting, wispy form. Apparently it is very tolerant of dry, alkaline soils. There are 4-dark green leaflets per leaf. The 1" long yellow flowers are produced in May-June. Northwest China, Siberia. Introduced 1751. Zone 3.

Caragana sinica, (kãr-a-gā'na sin'-i-ka), Chinese Peashrub, is a spiny 5' by 8' shrub of rather pretty nature. There are 4 large, 1 1/2 by 3/4" on young plants, 1/4 to 3/4" long on mature growth, glossy dark green leaflets per leaf. The 1 1/4" long reddish yellow flowers were the first to open among all the peashrubs in the Arnold Arboretum collection, starting to show color on May 1. The bruised bark smells like anise. Northern China. Introduced 1773. Zone 5.

ADDITIONAL NOTES: As a group the *Caragana* species are little-used or known in American gardens. Their bright green foliage and pretty yellow flowers are certainly attractive. As a group, they display good dry soil tolerance and would be excellent choices for containers, dry banks, cuts and fills along highways. Some sucker which would make them ideal candidates for holding soil. Most species develop some sort of spines in the wild but under cultivation these are reduced or absent from certain species, particularly *C. arborescens* and *C. frutex,* upon which I have not seen spines.

Carpinus betulus — European Hornbeam
(kär-pī′nus bet′ū-lus)

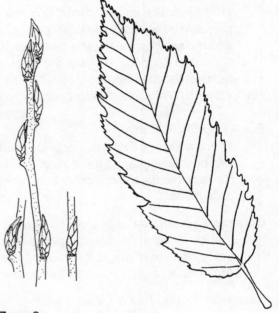

FAMILY: Betulaceae

LEAVES: Alternate, simple, ovate to ovate-oblong, sharply and doubly serrate, 2 1/2 to 5″ long, 1 to 2″ wide, cordate or rounded at base, short pointed at apex, similar to *Carpinus caroliniana* except leaf of thicker texture, 10 to 14 vein pairs, veins more impressed above; petiole 1/4 to 1/2″ long.

BUDS: Imbricate, angular-conical, usually appressed, brownish to reddish, curl around stem, scales with soft pubescence, 1/4 to 1/3″ long.

STEM: Glabrous, olive-brown, prominently lenticelled.

BARK: Smooth, steel gray, fluted, presenting muscle character of *C. caroliniana.*

SIZE: 40 to 60′ in height by 30 to 40′ in spread; can grow as wide as high; potentially can reach 70 to 80′ in height.

HARDINESS: Zone 4 to 7, have seen respectable plants in Zone 8.

HABIT: Pyramidal in youth, oval-rounded to rounded at maturity.

RATE: Slow to medium, about 10′ over a 10 year period, perhaps slightly faster; Ford, Secrest Arboretum Notes, Spring, 1984, mentioned rates of 16 to 20″ per year over a 7-year period in Wooster, OH.

TEXTURE: Medium-fine in leaf and winter habit; exquisitely tailored in winter with the slender branches dapperly arranged around the main leader.

BARK: Usually on old wood a handsome gray and the wood is beautifully fluted; akin to muscle-wood.

LEAF COLOR: Dark green in summer changing to yellow or yellowish green in fall; the summer foliage is usually very clean, i.e., no evidence of insect or disease damage.

FLOWERS: Monoecious, male not preformed as in *Betula,* nor ornamentally important, the male catkins, 1 1/2″ long, the female 1 1/2 to 3″ long, furnished with large conspicuous 3-lobed bracts, the middle lobe 1 to 1 1/2″ long, often toothed, borne in April, bracts produced in pairs and face each other.

FRUIT: Nut, ribbed, 1/4″ long, borne at the base of the above described bract, maturing September-October.

CULTURE: Transplant as a small (8 to 10′) tree balled and burlapped in spring; tolerant of wide range of soil conditions—light to heavy, acid to alkaline, but prefers well drained situations; performs best in full sun but will tolerate light shade; pruning is seldom required although this species withstands heavy pruning; partially tolerant of difficult conditions.

DISEASES AND INSECTS: None serious, in fact, unusually free of problems which lead to extensive maintenance; have noticed some leaf miner and dieback in Spring Grove, Cincinnati, Ohio.

LANDSCAPE VALUE: One of the very finest small landscape trees; excellent for screens, hedges, groupings, around large buildings, in malls, planter boxes, withstands pruning as well as or better than European Beech; a choice specimen with an air of aloofness unmatched by any plant; the many excellent cultivars are probably preferable to the species for landscape situations; widely used in England for hedges.

CULTIVARS: There are several cultivars that offer excellent color, texture and form. Unfortunately, several of the upright types are often confused in the trade.

    'Asplenifolia'—Leaves deeply and regularly double-toothed, the primary teeth large enough to be called lobes.

    'Columnaris'—A densely branched and foliaged, spirelike, slow-growing tree, usually maintaining a central leader; Bean noted that this cultivar developed an egg-shaped outline with time; however, the few trees I have seen were distinctly columnar; Wyman noted that 'Columnaris' has been confused in American gardens with 'Fastigiata', it is possible that 'Globosa' is confused with this form.

'Fastigiata'—The most common cultivar in cultivation; however, somewhat of a misnomer, because the plant develops an oval-vase shape, with distinct fan-ribbed branches, and may grow 30 to 40' (50') tall and 20 to 30' wide; it does not develop a central leader, and the foliage is more uniformly distributed along the branches than on 'Columnaris' and 'Globosa', where the foliage is concentrated at the perimeter of the branches; trees with a habit similar to 'Fastigiata' occur in the wild in France and Germany. Based on the tremendous variation in fastigiate types, it is obvious that there is confusion among upright-growing cultivars or that more than one fastigiate clone is in the trade. This cultivar grew 25' high and 14' wide after 10 years in Oregon tests; very highly rated (7th) in the Ohio Shade Tree Evaluation Tests; serves as an effective screen in winter because of the dense, compact, close-knit nature of the ascending branches; introduced before 1883.

'Globosa'—Rounded and globose in outline with no central trunk; the foliage is borne toward the perimeter of the branches; distinct when compared to the previous two cultivars and could, like them, serve as a screen even in winter because of the close-knit branches; slow-growing and at maturity may reach 15 to 20' in height.

var. horizontalis or 'Horizontalis'—A flat-topped form supposedly similar to *Crataegus crusgalli* (Cockspur Hawthorn) in outline.

'Incisa'—Similar to 'Asplenifolia' but differs by virtue of smaller and shorter leaves, which are coarsly and irregularly toothed with only about six pairs of veins.

'Pendula'—As I have seen the clone, a shrubby grower with weakly pendant branches; there is a clone listed by Bean as 'Pendula Dervaesii' which is more elegant than 'Pendula'; before 1873; in 1988 I saw a 30 to 40' high, 60' wide specimen probably of the latter at Sezincote Gardens in England. I believe the plant would be a welcome addition to American gardens; striking and singularly dominating; see Dirr, *American Nurseryman* 170(8):146 (1989).

'Purpurea'—The new foliage is purplish but rapidly fades to the dark green of the species; I have seen the cultivar in mid May, and the only purple evident was on the immature shoots.

var. *quercifolia* or 'Quercifolia'—The leaves are somewhat oaklike in shape; before 1783.

'Variegata'—Krüssmann lists both a white ('Albo-variegata') and this form—an irregular yellow patched and marked form; before 1770.

PROPAGATION: The best prescriptions for handling seed vary so several are presented here. Dormancy may be caused by conditions in the embryo and endosperm and stratification for 28 days at 68°F followed by 87 to 98 days at 41°F is recommended; seed should be collected green and sown if germination is expected the first spring; seed should be collected as wings are turning yellow and are still pliable; drying allows hard seed coat to develop and if this happens a warm followed by cold period is needed; seed that has not become hard-walled can be germinated if stratified for 3 to 4 months at 41°F. The best information on cuttings is derived from Cesarini, *PIPPS* 21:380–382.

1. Select healthy, vigorous stock plants. Cuttings should be six to eight inches long and wounded.
2. Cuttings should be taken about the time the last leaf reaches mature size and the last bud has not fully developed. This would probably coincide with the month of July.
3. Many rooting mediums were tested; however, the best was a mixture of perlite and peat moss.
4. Hormone concentrations must be high. 3000 ppm and 8000 ppm are not sufficiently high and a concentration of two percent IBA (20,000 parts per million) was required to successfully root *Carpinus betulus* 'Fastigiata'.
5. After rooting, the cuttings require a dormancy period. Placing them at a temperature of 32°F during the winter months satisfied the dormancy requirements, and, when budbreak ensued in March or April, the rooted cuttings were transplanted to containers.

Other work I have read corroborates Cesarini's findings. Cultivars are usually grafted onto seedlings of the species. Recently etiolation has increased the rooting potential of the species. See *PIPPS* 34:543–550 (1984) for specifics.

ADDITIONAL NOTES: Minumum seed bearing age is between 10 and 30 years. To date I have had poor success with seed propagation. The wood is extremely hard, heavy, and tough. Cogs, axils, and spokes were made of hornbeam. It is used extensively in English and continental Europe for hedges and allees. There are many fine specimens of this species and the cultivars in Cave Hill Cemetery, Louisville, Kentucky, and Spring Grove Cemetery, Cincinnati, Ohio. Perhaps the most spectacular specimens of the species are located in Lexington Cemetery, Lexington, Kentucky, although the Arnold Arboretum has several magnificent specimens, one a 50', oval-rounded, central leadered tree; another a superlative low-branched, wide-spreading form of broad-rounded proportions. Has performed well in Athens and Griffin, GA but is not available in commerce in the south. Beavers appear to love the tree and, in test plots at Griffin, chewed this species while ignoring *Zelkova, Prunus, Ilex,* and × *Cupressocyparis.* Tremendous influx of papers on *Carpinus* and the closely related *Ostrya* appeared in *The Plantsman.* The reader is referred to 7(3):173–191 (1985), 7(4):205–212 (1986), 7(4):212–216 (1986), and 8(2):112–117 (1986). More information than this book can present but excellent discussions of species and cultivars.

NATIVE HABITAT: Europe, Asia Minor, southeast of England. Long cultivated.

Carpinus caroliniana — American Hornbeam, also called Blue Beech, Ironwood, Musclewood, and Water Beech.

(kär-pī′nus ka-rō-lin-i-ā′-na)

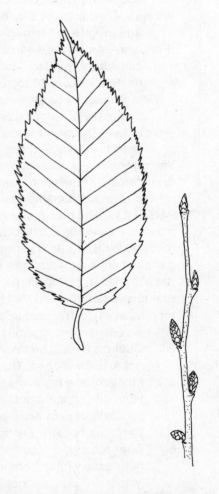

LEAVES: Alternate, simple, 2 1/2 to 5″ long, 1 to 2″ wide, ovate-oblong, acuminate, rounded or heart-shaped, sharply and doubly serrate, glabrous, dark green, pilose on veins beneath and with axillary tufts of hair, veins seldom forking at ends; petiole 1/4 to 1/2″ long, pubescent.

BUDS: Imbricate, small, 1/6 to 1/4″ long, 12, 4-ranked scales, narrowly ovate to oblong, pointed, reddish-brown-black, more or less hairy, especially buds containing staminate catkins, terminal bud absent, scales—often downy on edges, frequently with woolly patch of down on tip.

STEM: Slender, dark red-brown, shining, smooth or often somewhat hairy; pith—pale, continuous.

BARK: Smooth, thin, dark bluish gray, close fitting, sinewy, fluted with smooth, rounded, longitudinal ridges; wood-heavy and hard.

FRUIT: Small, ribbed, seed-like nutlet enclosed by a veiny, generally 3-lobed bract about 1″ long.

SIZE: 20 to 30' in height and as wide, often smaller but with the potential to reach 40 to 50'; 65' high by 66' wide tree reported from Milton, NY; 68' high by 42' wide in Spring Grove, Cincinnati, OH.

HARDINESS: Zone 3 to 9.

HABIT: Small, multistemmed, bushy shrub or single-stemmed tree with a wide-spreading, flat or round-topped (often irregular) crown; some plants are quite uniform.

RATE: Slow, averaging 8 to 10' over a 10 year period; will grow faster with uniform moisture and fertility.

TEXTURE: Medium in leaf and winter.

BARK COLOR: On older branches develops a slate gray, smooth, irregularly fluted appearance; the overall appearance is comparable to the flexed bicep and forearm muscles and, hence, the name Musclewood.

LEAF COLOR: Dark green in summer changing to yellow, orange and scarlet in the fall; have seen trees of good yellow and others orange-red; considerable fall color variation exists; drops its leaves ahead of *Carpinus betulus.*

FLOWERS: Monoecious, male, 1 to 1 1/2″ long; female, 2 to 3″ long; the bracts 3-lobed, 1 to 1 1/2″ long, the middle lobe the widest (1″ diameter), toothed.

FRUIT: A nut(let), borne at base of 1 to 1 1/2″ long, 3-lobed bract; the middle largest and almost 1″ wide; entire infructescence 2 to 4″ long.

CULTURE: Somewhat difficult to transplant and should be moved balled and burlapped or from a container in spring; performs best in deep, rich, moist, slightly acid soils although will grow in drier sites; does well in heavy shade and is often found as an understory plant in forests; probably if used in the landscape should be sited in partial shade; does not take pruning as well as *C. betulus* and is probably an inferior tree except for fall color; I have observed this species in many landscape situations and believe it is much more adaptable than ever given credit; has prospered in calcareous soils of Illinois without evidence of chlorosis; has been used in shopping mall island plantings in Georgia and performed reasonably well.

DISEASES AND INSECTS: Leaf spots, cankers, twig blight, maple phenococcus scale, none of which are significantly serious although of late I have seen considerable dieback which appeared to be caused by canker.

LANDSCAPE VALUE: Best in naturalized situation; interesting native tree often seen in the woods and inappropriately called "beech" by the uninitiated; does well in wet soils and will tolerate periodic flooding; might be worth a longer look in man-made landscapes.

CULTIVARS:

'Pyramidalis'—The tree is supposedly V-shaped with a rounded top; a tree in the Arnold Arboretum at 43 years of age was 40′ tall and 33′ in spread; as I viewed it not too different from the species.

PROPAGATION: Seed, moist stratification at 68 to 86°F for 60 days followed by 41°F for 60 days; see *HortScience* 14(5):621–622 (1979) for good information on seed germination; in short authors found that green seeds collected in early September germinated 24% the following spring; those collected in late September germinated less than 1%; stratification for 15 and 18 weeks increased germination to 43 and 58%, respectively.

NATIVE HABITAT: Nova Scotia to Minnesota, south to Florida and Texas. Introduced 1812.

ADDITIONAL NOTES: Quite a nice native tree, usually found as an understory plant along rivers and streams throughout its native range where it withstands periodic flooding. This tree has a lot to offer our landscapes in subtle beauty. See Dirr, The hornbeams—Choice plants for American gardens. *American Nurseryman* 148(10):10–11, 46, 48, 50, 52 (1978) for more detailed information.

RELATED SPECIES:

There are a number of other species that one only sees in arboreta, botanical gardens and private plant collections. The following remarks are based on my observations.

Carpinus cordata, (kär-pī′nus kor-dā′ta), Heartleaf Hornbeam, is a rather large-leaved (2 1/2 to 5 1/2″ long, 1 1/2 to 1 3/4″ wide) species; the leaf bases of which are deeply heart-shaped and give rise to

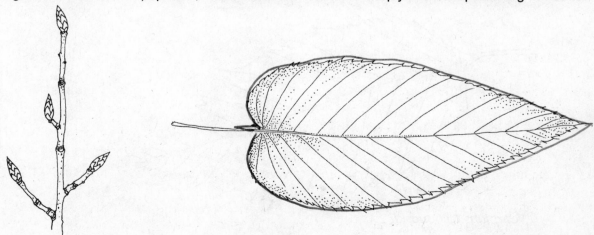

the specific epithet. The dark green leaves show no propensity to develop fall color. The habit is rounded and landscape size ranges from 20 to 30′ although the species can grow 40 to 50′ in the wild. The bark is totally different from the above species being slightly furrowed and scaly. The ovoid, rich brown winter buds are about 5/8″ long. The fruits are borne in cigar-shaped, 3 to 5″ long, 1 1/2″ wide catkins; the bracts closely overlapping, each bract folded and partially covering the nut; the entire infructescence reminding of *Ostrya virginiana*. *Carpinus japonica* has a similar fruiting structure. Japan. Introduced 1879. Zone 5.

Carpinus japonica, (kär-pī′nus ja-pon′i-ka), Japanese Hornbeam, is a small tree seldom growing more than 20 to 30′ in this country. The wide-spreading branches radiate like the ribs on a fan and the species can be identified by this feature. The ovate to oblong, 2 to 4 1/2″ long, 3/4 to 1 3/4″ wide, acuminate, weakly cordate to rounded, (a feature that separates it from *C. cordata*), doubly toothed, 20 to 24 vein-paired, deeply impressed dark green leaves do not color appreciably in the fall although the literature mentions red. The fruits are similar to those of *C. cordata* but shorter (2 to 2 1/2″ long). The bark is shallowly furrowed and scaly. The foliage is handsome and for this reason alone it is worth planting. Japan. Introduced 1879. Zone 4.

Carpinus orientalis, (kär-pī′nus ôr-i-en-tā′lis), Oriental Hornbeam, exists as a large shrub or small tree (20 to 25′) with an overall "U-shaped" branching pattern. The small glossy dark green leaves are 1 to 2″ long and 1/2 to 1″ wide. Again they do not color well in the fall although the literature says red. The bracts of this species are unlobed which separates it from *C. betulus* and *C. caroliniana*. The bark is similar, on a micro-scale, to *C. betulus* and *C. caroliniana*. The main branches and stems are twisted, presenting an interesting winter branch structure. In Wooster, OH, trees averaged 14 to 20″ in height per year over a 7-year period. Southeast Europe, Asia Minor. Introduced 1739. Zone 5.

Other species that the intrepid hornbeam lover might want to track down include *C. laxiflora*, Loose-flower Hornbeam (appropriately named); *C. tschonoskii*, Yeddo Hornbeam, and *C. turczaninovii*.

Carpinus japonica

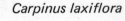

Carpinus laxiflora

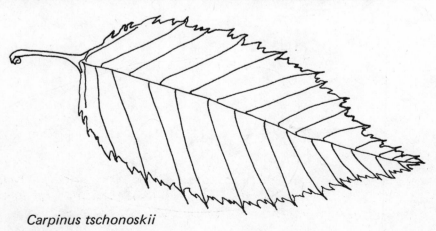

Carpinus tschonoskii

Carya — Hickory, Pecan, Bitternut
(kā'ri-a)

FAMILY: Juglandaceae

The hickories are treated as a group rather than individual entities because of their limited use in normal landscape situations. Although extremely beautiful and aesthetic native trees, they develop large taproots and are difficult to transplant. Most are large trees reaching 60′ or more and may drop leaves, stems, or fruits. Their size and limited ornamental assets, as well as the difficulty in transplanting, limit extensive landscape use. The nuts of several species are edible and utilized extensively by man and animal. The production of pecan, *Carya illinoensis,* is a large commercial business and research and breeding continues on this most important crop.

The flowers are monoecious with the male borne in drooping 3-branched catkins; the female in few flowered terminal spikes, developing with the leaves in April into early May. The fruits are bony, hard-shelled nuts encased in a 4-valved "husk" (involucre?) often splitting away but in some species persisting. They usually ripen in October and drop from the trees. The seeds are either bitter or sweet. In the wild, seed dissemination is largely through squirrels who bury them in the forest floor as a food reserve. The hickories are typically American trees and the following are some of the more common.

ADDITIONAL NOTES: *Carya* exhibit embryo dormancy and should be stratified in a moist medium at 33° to 40°F for 30 to 150 days. Prior to the cold treatment nuts should be soaked in water at room temperature for 2 to 4 days with 1 or 2 water changes per day. Cultivars are budded or grafted on seedling understocks. Pecan grafting is an art and science and for detailed information see Dirr and Heuser, 1987.

Carya cordiformis — Bitternut Hickory
(kā'ri-a kor-di-for'mis)

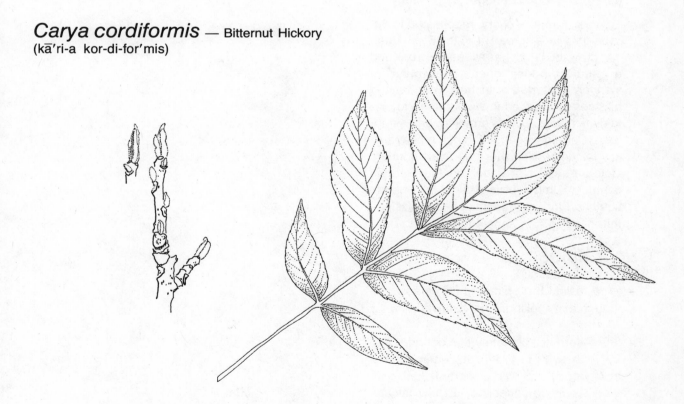

LEAVES: Alternate, pinnately compound, 6 to 10″ (15″) long, composed of 7, sometimes 5 or 9, leaflets, each 3 to 6″ long, 3/4 to 2 1/2″ wide, ovate to lanceolate, acuminate, sharply serrate, light green and glabrous above, pubescent below on midrib and veins; petiole and rachis-pubescent.

BUDS: Valvate scales, strikingly sulfur-yellow, terminal bud—2/5 to 3/5″ long, flattened, obliquely blunt pointed, scurfy-pubescent; lateral buds—more or less 4-angled, much smaller than the terminal.

STEM: Stout, buff, gray or reddish, smooth or slightly downy toward apex; pith—brown, solid.

Carya cordiformis, Bitternut Hickory, can grow to 50 to 75′ in height and larger. Professor McDaniel first introduced me to this species and pointed out the striking sulphur-yellow buds that permit distinction from other *Carya* species. It is usually a slender tree with rather irregular, cylindrical crown of stiff ascending branches, often widest at the top. Supposedly the fastest growing of the hickories. Seeds are bitter and squirrels tend to ignore them. Native from Quebec to Minnesota, south to Florida and Louisiana. Introduced 1689. Zone 4 to 9.

Carya glabra — Pignut Hickory
(kā′ri-a glā′bra)

LEAVES: Alternate, pinnately compound, 5 to 7 leaflets, usually 5, entire leaf 8 to 12″ long, each leaflet 3 to 6 1/2″ long, 1 to 2″ wide, the terminal leaflets largest, the lowest pair about 1/3 the size; terminal obovate, basal ovate-lanceolate, sharply toothed, dark yellowish green, glabrous above, except on midrib and veins beneath.

BARK: On young trees smooth, eventually developing rounded ridges, not shaggy.

Carya glabra, Pignut Hickory, reaches 50 to 60′ in height with a spread of 25 to 35′ although can grow to 100′. It has a tapering trunk and a regular, rather open, oval head of slender, contorted branches. Found along hillsides and ridges in well-drained to dry, fairly rich soils. Seeds are bitter and astringent. Certainly beautiful in rich golden yellow fall color. No other tree rivals it in late October-early November on the Georgia campus. Native from Maine to Ontario, south to Florida, Alabama and Mississippi. Introduced 1750. Zone 4 to 9.

Carya illinoensis — Pecan
(kā′ri-a il-in-oy-en′sis)
(*Hortus III* insists the epithet is *illinoinensis* although this spelling is not followed.)

LEAVES: Alternate, pinnately compound, 12 to 20″ long, 9, 11 to 17 leaflets, each leaflet 4 to 7″ long, 1 to 3″ wide, short-stalked, dark green, oblong-lanceolate, usually falcate, serrate or doubly serrate, glandular and tomentose when young, becoming glabrous; petiole—glabrous or pubescent.

BUDS: Valvate, 1/4 to 1/3″ long, dark brown, pubescent, ovoid, apex pointed, looks like a small roasted almond.

STEM: Stout, olive-brown, pubescent, leaf scar indented and partially surrounding bud.

Carya illinoensis, Pecan, will grow 70 to 100′ in height with a spread of 40 to 75′ and can reach 150′. Largest of the hickories, tall and straight with a uniform, symmetrical, broadly oval crown. Extremely difficult to transplant as it develops a long taproot. On a 6′ tree the taproot may extend 4′ or more. Prefers deep, moist, well-drained soil. The best hickory for fruits and many cultivars have been selected for outstanding fruiting characters. Native from Iowa to Indiana to Alabama, Texas and Mexico. Follows the river basins very closely. Introduced 1760. Zone 5 to 9. Makes an interesting ornamental in the midwest but does not bear liberal quantities of fruit. Abundant in south and trees are often low-branched and wide-spreading. This seems to be especially true of trees in orchard and cultivated situations. Pecans are a major hor-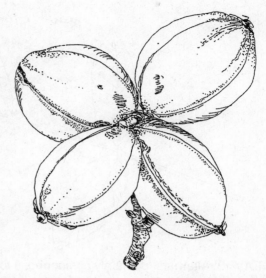ticultural crop in the southeast and southwest. For landscape purposes it is not a good tree because of insect and disease problems. Also the tree produces a high level of litter, especially in late summer and fall when infected leaves and maturing nuts start to abscise. Georgia has an excellent pecan research program that has served as the foundation for the industry. Many excellent publications on pecan culture are available from the Georgia Cooperative Extension Service. "Insect Pests and Diseases of the Pecan" USDA ARM-S-5 (1979) describes the biology of 40 insects and diseases that affect pecan.

Carya laciniosa — Shellbark Hickory
(kā′ri-a la-sin-i-ō′sa)

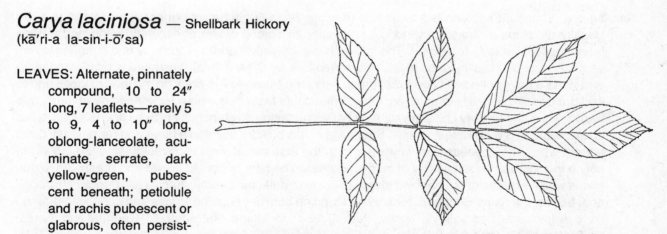

LEAVES: Alternate, pinnately compound, 10 to 24″ long, 7 leaflets—rarely 5 to 9, 4 to 10″ long, oblong-lanceolate, acuminate, serrate, dark yellow-green, pubescent beneath; petiolule and rachis pubescent or glabrous, often persistent during winter. Similar to *C. ovata* in bud, stem and bark characteristics; leaflets do not have hairs at tip of teeth like those of *C. ovata*; stem is often orange-brown in color; fruit is somewhat larger and nut is 4 to 6 ribbed versus 4 ribbed nut of *C. ovata.*

Carya laciniosa, Shellbark Hickory, Big Shellbark Hickory, King Nut Hickory, reaches 60 to 80′ in height or greater and forms a high branching tree with a straight slender trunk and narrow oblong crown of small spreading branches, the lower drooping, the upper ascending. The seed is sweet and edible. In many respects similar to *C. ovata* except it does not grow as large and tends to inhabit wet bottomlands, even those which are covered with water for a time. Possesses the interesting "shaggy" bark similar to *C. ovata.* Native from New York to Iowa, south to Tennessee and Oklahoma on deep, moist, fertile soils of floodplains and bottomlands. Introduced 1800. Zone 5 to 8.

Carya ovata — Shagbark Hickory
(kā′ri-a ō-vā′ta)

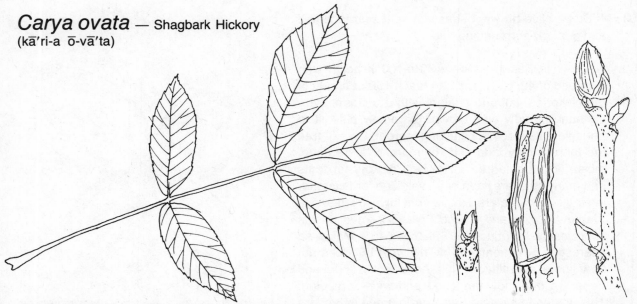

LEAVES: Alternate, pinnately compound, 8 to 14″ long, 5 leaflets, rarely 7, 4 to 6″ long, 1/2 to 2 1/2″ wide, elliptic to oblong-lanceolate, acuminate, serrate and densely ciliate, pubescent and glandular below when young, finally glabrous, deep yellow-green.

BUDS: Imbricate, terminal—1/2 to 1″ long, broadly ovate, rather blunt-pointed, brown, with 2 to 4 visible, overlapping, pubescent, loose fitting scales.

STEM: Stout, somewhat downy or smooth and shining, reddish brown to light gray; lenticels—numerous, pale, conspicuous, longitudinally elongated.

BARK: On old trunks shagging characteristically into long flat plates which are free at the base or both ends; usually more pronounced than Shellbark with plates more recurved.

Carya ovata, Shagbark Hickory, is a large tree reaching 60 to 80′ in height but can grow to 100 to 120′. Usually develops a straight, cylindrical trunk with an oblong crown of ascending and descending branches (similar to *C. laciniosa*). The foliage is a deep yellow green in summer and changes to rich yellow and golden brown tones in fall (this is also true for *C. laciniosa*). The seed is edible and quite sweet. As a boy I collected bags full of these nuts. The trees always grew on the lower slopes and in well drained alluvial soils of southern Ohio. What could taste better than Hickory smoked hams and bacon. Try some hickory chips in your next barbecue outing. Prefers rich and well drained loams, but is adaptable to a wide range of soils. Seedlings of this hickory develop a large and remarkably deep taproot which may penetrate downward 2 to 3′ the first season with a corresponding top growth of only a few inches. This is typical of many hickories. The bark is gray to brown and breaks up in thin plates which are free at the end and attached at the middle; the overall effect is a "shaggy" character and, hence, the name Shagbark Hickory. Is found on both drier upland slopes and deep well-drained soils in lowlands and valleys. Native from Quebec to Minnesota, south to Georgia and Texas. Cultivated 1629. Zone 4 to 8.

Carya tomentosa — Mockernut Hickory, White Hickory
(kar′i-a tō-men-tō′sȧ)

LEAVES: Alternate, compound pinnate, 6 to 12″ long, 5 to 7 leaflets, the upper pair 5 to 9″ long, 3 to 5″ wide; the lower pair 2/3 that size, oblong to oblong-lanceolate, acuminate, serrate, densely pubescent and glandular below, fragrant when bruised; petiole and rachis tomentose.

Carya tomentosa, Mockernut Hickory or White Hickory, although widespread in the eastern United States, is seldom encountered compared to *C. glabra* and *C. ovata*. The crown is narrow to broadly rounded and trees may average 50 to 60′ in height, although trees over 100′ are known. Bark, unlike *C.*

laciniosa and *C. ovata,* is dark gray, thin, with shallow furrows and narrow flat ridges forming a net-like pattern. The tree is found on ridges, dry hills and slopes but grows best in moist well-drained soil. Although considered the commonest species in the south, I have not seen a single plant in the Athens area while *C. glabra* is everywhere. If native, like other hickories, do not destroy. To find one in commerce would be difficult. Massachusetts to Ontario and Nebraska, south to Florida and Texas. Introduced 1766. Zone 4 to 9.

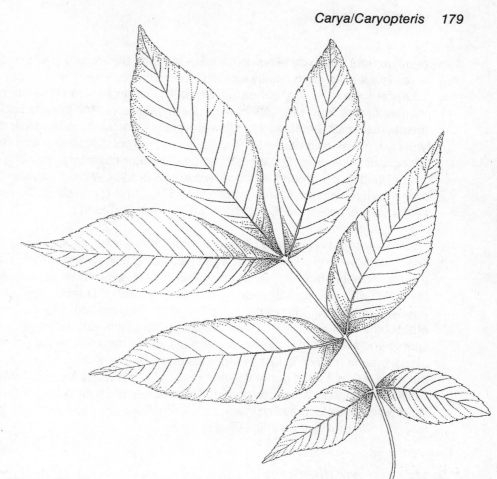

Caryopteris × clandonensis — Bluebeard, Blue-spirea, Blue-mist Shrub
(kar-i-op′tĕr-is klan-dō-nen′sis)

FAMILY: Verbenaceae
LEAVES: Opposite, simple, ovate, 1 to 2″ long, 1/2 to 1 1/4″ wide, acute, rounded, entire or with full teeth, dull green above, silvery tomentose beneath; petiole about 1/4″ long, pubescent.
STEM: Slender, 4-sided, pubescent, grayish green, nodes flattened.

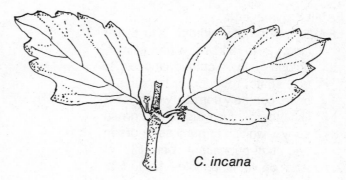

C. incana

Caryopteris × clandonensis, Blue-spirea, is a low (2′), mounded, almost herbaceous shrub that graces the late summer garden with lovely bright blue flowers. This species is the result of a cross between *C. incana* × *C. mongolica* and is the most common form in cultivation. The flowers are borne in small cymes from the axils of the uppermost leaves. It prefers a loose, loamy soil and full sun. Excessive fertility results in rampant growth. It should be treated as a herbaceous perennial and cut back in late winter. Flowers are borne on new growth of the season. Softwood cuttings root readily and should be removed from mist as soon as rooting is sufficient. The hybrid was raised in the garden of Arthur Simmonds at West Clandon, Surrey, England. The typical and original clone is named 'Arthur Simmonds'. Other clones include: 'Azure' with bright blue flowers; 'Blue Mist' with powder blue flowers; 'Dark Knight' with deep blue purple flowers; 'Ferndown' with dark green leaves and deeper blue flowers than 'Arthur Simmonds'; 'Heavenly Blue' with a compact habit and deeper blue flowers than 'Arthur Simmonds'; and 'Kew Blue', a dark blue flowered seedling from 'Arthur Simmonds' raised at Kew about 1945. 'Longwood Blue'—A mounded, gray-green foliage shrub reaching 4′ by 4′, flowers bluish violet, filaments are darker and the anthers blue-black, dies back to ground in winter but flowers on new growth. Zone 6 to 9.

Caryopteris incana, (kar-i-op′tēr-is in-kā′na), Common Bluebeard, grows 3 to 5′ and is rather loose and open. The leaves are coarsely toothed, almost lobed, 1 to 3″ long, 1/2 to 1 1/2″ wide, dull green and pubescent above, silvery pubescent beneath. The bright violet-blue fragrant flowers occur in hemispherical cymes from the axils of the uppermost leaves and literally encircle the stem. Has proven spectacular in Dr. Armitage's cut flower tests at Georgia. Much showier than the *C.* × *clandonensis* types but not as cold hardy. 'Blue Billows' is a low compact trailer with dense lavender-blue flowers throughout September-October. Longwood Gardens has a large planting of this cultivar and reported it was killed to the ground in the severe winter of 1976–77 but grew and flowered the next season. Japan to northwestern China. Introduced 1844. Zone 7; can be grown further north when treated as a herbaceous perennial. 'Candida' is a white-flowered form.

The *Caryopteris* make lovely garden shrubs. Their leaves, stems and flowers are pleasantly scented. Their late flowering period makes them valuable garden plants. Given a well-drained, loose soil and a sunny position they will prosper for years. I have grown *C.* × *clandonensis* for years and treat the plant with minimal maintenance, yet it responds with numerous light blue flowers from July to late August. I always cut the plant back in late winter and provide a handful of granular 10-10-10 fertilizer at the base. On occasion I have literally pulled plants out of the ground for relocation. Roots are sparse and stringy but I have never lost a plant after transplanting. Since flowers occur on new growth of the season nothing is lost by vigorous pruning early in the season. My observations indicate that the plant will fruit itself out of flowering much like *Hibiscus syriacus.* When the flower production is slowing in August, a feather pruning to induce new shoot growth will increase flower production. Worthwhile plant for massing in dry, sunny situations or for a filler in a low border where the gray-green foliage color provides an interesting diversion.

Castanea mollissima — Chinese Chestnut
(kas-tā′nē-a mol-lis′-i-ma)

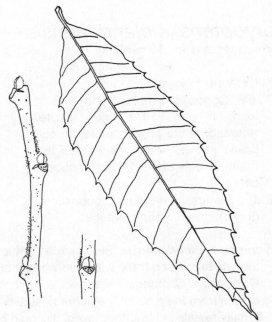

FAMILY: Fagaceae

LEAVES: Alternate, simple, 3 to 6 (8″) long, 2 to 3 1/2″ wide, ellipticoblong to oblong-lanceolate, acuminate, rounded or truncate at base, coarsely serrate, with bristle-like teeth, lustrous dark green above, whitish tomentose or green and soft-pubescent beneath at least on veins; petiole—1/4 to 1/2″ long, usually hairy.

BUDS: Two to 3 scales weakly overlapping, gray-brown, pubescent, 1/8 to 1/4″ long, ovoid.

STEM: Pubescent with long spreading hairs, olive-brown, prominent lenticels; pith—star-shaped, 4 to 5 sided; bark on second and third year stems is cherry-like in appearance.

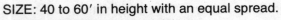

SIZE: 40 to 60′ in height with an equal spread.

HARDINESS: Zone 4 to 8 (9).

HABIT: Rounded in youth, developing a rounded to broad-rounded outline at maturity, usually low-branched.

RATE: Slow to medium, 4 to 7′ over a 3 to 4 year period.

TEXTURE: Medium throughout the seasons.

BARK: Gray-brown to brown and strongly ridged and furrowed.

LEAF COLOR: Reddish upon unfolding changing to a lustrous dark green in summer culminating with shades of yellow and bronze in fall; can be handsome and often long persistent.

FLOWERS: Pale yellow or creamy, of heavy, unpleasant odor, monoecious, staminate in erect cylindrical catkins, pistillate on the lower part of the upper staminate catkins, usually 3 female in a prickly symmetrical involucre, borne in a 4 to 5″ long and wide panicle in June (late May, Athens).

FRUIT: Nut, 2 to 3 enclosed in a prickly involucre which splits at maturity into 2 to 4 valves, fruits are edible and relished by man and animals; seed-grown trees often produce fruit after 4 to 5 years.

CULTURE: Easily transplanted when young (5 to 6′); prefer acid (pH to 5.5 to 6.5), well-drained, loamy soil; full sun; does well in hot, dry climates; responds well to fertilization; actually a very tough and seemingly durable tree that I have observed under a host of differing environmental conditions; actually might fall in the ornamental tree category of requiring minimal attention although nut production is not without problems.

DISEASES AND INSECTS: Blight (discussed under *C. dentata*), twig canker of asiatic chestnuts, weevils which damage the roots; this species is *not* immune to chestnut blight but resistant.

LANDSCAPE VALUE: Best as a replacement for the American Chestnut; valued for fruits; in the last edition I mentioned the possibility of street tree use but have seen too many instances of prickly burrs littering the ground, the fruits' prickly covers are a real nuisance and fall over an extended period of time making quick cleanup a somewhat dubious process.

PROPAGATION: Seed should be stratified under cool moist conditions for 60 to 90 days or fall planted; seeds deteriorate rapidly and should not be allowed to dry out; cuttings taken from young trees have been rooted.

ADDITIONAL NOTES: Interesting story relative to one man's love for the chestnut that may prove of interest to the reader. The Dunstan Hybrid chestnuts have been under development since 1950's. Dr. Robert Dunstan of North Carolina grafted an apparent blight free American strain onto Japanese Chestnut. When it flowered he crossed it with Chinese Chestnut. Using progeny from this cross he backcrossed it to the American parent. The resulting F_2 generation was moved to Alachua, FL where there are now 50 mature trees, none with blight despite attempts to induce fungal cankers by inoculation. Several superior trees have been grafted. They produce straight trunks, with heavy crops of sweet nuts, supposedly superior to Chinese Chestnut. Trees bear in 3 to 5 years.

NATIVE HABITAT: Northern China, Korea.
Introduced 1853 and 1903.

RELATED SPECIES:

Castanea dentata — American Chestnut
(kas-tā′nē-a den-tā′ta)

LEAVES: Alternate, simple, oblong lance shaped in outline, with cuneate base and long-pointed tips, numerous coarse, sharp pointed serrations, lustrous dark green above, glabrous at maturity on both surfaces, 5 to 8″ (11″) long, 1 3/4 to 2″ (3″) wide; petiole about 1/2″ long.

BUDS AND STEM: Glabrous, chestnut brown.

Castanea dentata, American Chestnut, was once native from southern Maine to Michigan, south to Alabama and Mississippi. Cultivated 1800. This tree was the queen of eastern

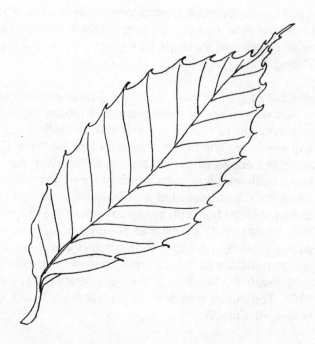

American forest trees but now is reduced to a memory. About 1906 a blight, *Endothia parasitica,* was introduced along the east coast and spread like wildfire through the forests. All that remains are isolated stump and root sprouts which developed after the parent tree was killed. The tree reached heights of 100′ and developed massive, wide-spreading branches, and a deep broad-rounded crown. The flowers are similar to those of *C. mollissima* however the fruits are reported as being much sweeter and more flavorful than the asiatic species although I know people who do not agree.

Castanea pumila — Allegheny Chinkapin

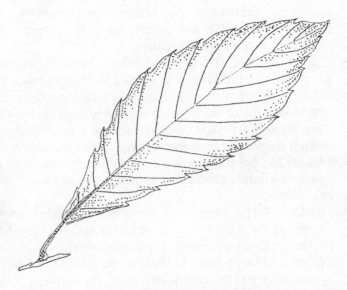

LEAVES: Alternate, simple, elliptic-oblong or oblong-obovate, 3 to 5″ long, 1 1/2 to 2″ wide, acute, rounded or broadly cuneate at the base, coarsely serrate, the teeth reduced to bristles, dark green above, whitish and hairy below; petiole 1/4 to 1/2″ long.

Castanea pumila, (kas-tā′nē-a pū′mila), Allegheny Chinkapin, has entered my plant life since moving south and makes, as I have seen it, a small shrub that could be used for naturalizing and providing food for wildlife. It can grow 20 to 25′ high but most often forms a 6 to 10′ high shrub. The fruit is about 1 1/2″ wide with normally a single (occasionally 2), 3/4 to 1″ long, dark brown sweet edible nut. The involucre is quite prickly. The species occurs in drier woodlands from Pennsylvania to Florida and west to Oklahoma and Texas. Introduced 1699. Zone 5 to 9.

Castanea sativa — Sweet, Spanish or European Chestnut

LEAVES: Alternate, simple, oblong-lanceolate, 4 1/2 to 9″ long, 2 to 3 1/2″ wide, acute or short acuminate, broad cuneate, rounded or subcordate at base, coarsely serrate, covered with a soft pubescence when developing, lustrous dark green above, glabrous on both surfaces at maturity; petiole—1/2 to 1″ long.

Castanea sativa, (kas-tā′nē-a sa-tī′va), Sweet, Spanish or European Chestnut, is not used in this country to any degree but is widespread in Europe, especially England. It is a magnificent, impressive, enormous (80 to 100′) tree that is found in parks and gardens. The rich brown bark is deeply furrowed and the ridges and furrows spiral around the trunk. On my first visit to England, this tree seemed to stand out above all others. It is an excellent choice for dry, rather sandy soils of acid persuasion. Many cultivars have been selected for fruiting characteristics and variegated, purple and cut-leaf forms have been selected for ornament. Although I have not seen the plant in the eastern United States, it might be worth trying, especially the garden forms. The variegated forms 'Albo-marginata' with creamy white margins and 'Aureo-marginata' with yellowish margins are quite striking. They grow slower than the species. Perhaps the species is restricted in the U.S. and, upon checking plant import restrictions, this was the case. At Petworth House in West Sussex, there existed several magnificent old specimens that were devastated by the terrible hurricane force winds of October 16, 1987. The trunks were fully 12′ in diameter. Southern Europe, western Asia, northern Africa. Long cultivated. Zone 5.

Catalpa speciosa — Northern Catalpa, also called Western Catalpa or Hardy Catalpa.
(ka-tal'pa spē-si-oo'sa)

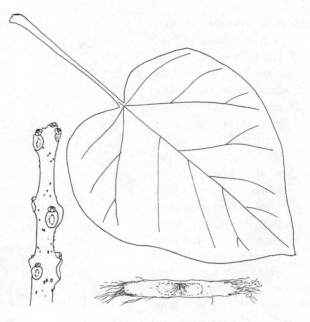

FAMILY: Bignoniaceae

LEAVES: Whorled or opposite, simple, ovate to ovate-oblong, 6 to 12″ long, 3 to 8″ wide, long acuminate, truncate to cordate, entire, medium green and glabrous above, densely pubescent beneath, scentless; petiole 4 to 6″ long.

BUDS: Terminal-absent, lateral buds small, hemispherical, 1/12″ high, scales-brown, loosely overlapping.

STEM: Stout, smooth or slightly short-downy, reddish to yellowish brown; lenticels large, numerous; leaf scars-round to elliptical with depressed center; bundle scars—conspicuous, raised, forming a closed ring; pith is solid, white.

FRUIT: Capsule, 8 to 20″ long, 1/2 to 3/5″ wide, wall thick, seeds fringed, persisting into late fall and winter.

SIZE: 40 to 60′ in height with a spread of 20 to 40′ but sometimes reaching 100′ or more in the wild.

HARDINESS: Zone 4 to 8 (9).

HABIT: Tree with a narrow, open, irregular, oval crown; can be quite striking in winter with bold rugged outline.

RATE: Medium to fast, 15′ over 7 to 8 year period.

BARK: Grayish brown on old trunks usually exhibiting a ridged and furrowed character although some trees exhibit a thick, scaly bark.

LEAF COLOR: Medium green although there is some variation in leaf color, some leaves are a bright green in summer, fall color a poor yellow-green to brownish, often falling before turning.

FLOWERS: Perfect, corolla white, 2″ long and wide, the tube bell-shaped, the lobes spreading and frilled at the margin, the lower one with yellow spots and ridges as in *C. bignonioides,* but less freely spotted with purple, borne in May-June, in large upright terminal panicles, 4 to 8″ long.

FRUIT: Capsule, green changing to brown, pendulous, 8 to 20″ long, about 1/2″ wide, persisting through winter, contains numerous fringed seeds.

CULTURE: Transplant balled and burlapped as a small tree; very tolerant of different soil conditions but prefers deep, moist, fertile soil; withstands wet or dry and alkaline conditions; sun or partial shade, seems to withstand extremely hot, dry environments.

DISEASES AND INSECTS: Leaf spots, powdery mildew, *Verticillium* wilt, twig blight, root rot, comstock mealybug, catalpa midge and catalpa sphinx.

LANDSCAPE VALUE: Limited value in the residential landscape because of coarseness; has a place in difficult areas but the use of this and the following species should be tempered.

PROPAGATION: Seeds germinate readily without pretreatment; cuttings—root pieces taken in December can be used for most species.

ADDITIONAL NOTES: Catalpa wood is usually quite brittle and frequently small branches are broken off in wind and ice storms. The wood in contact with the ground is extremely resistant to rot and has been used for railroad ties.

NATIVE HABITAT: Southern Illinois and Indiana to western Tennessee and northern Arkansas. Cultivated 1754.

RELATED SPECIES:

Catalpa bignonioides — Southern Catalpa, also called Common Catalpa and Indian Bean. (ka-tal′pa big-nō-ni-oy′dēz)

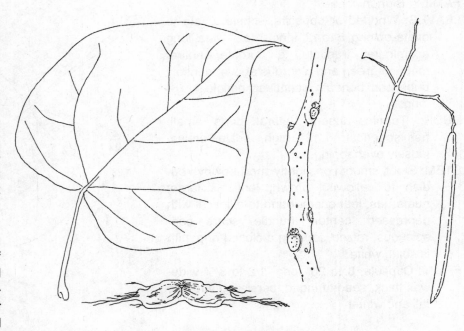

LEAVES: Whorled or opposite, simple, 4 to 8″ (10″) long, 3 to 8″ wide, apex—abruptly acuminate, base truncate to subcordate, light green and nearly glabrous above, slightly pubescent beneath, especially on veins, of unpleasant odor when crushed; petiole—4 to 6″ long. Similar to *C. speciosa* except on veins, of smaller size and rounded habit. Flowers 2 weeks later than *C. speciosa* and has a thinner walled fruit. End of seeds are tufted versus fringed of *C. speciosa*.

Catalpa bignonioides, Southern Catalpa, is smaller than *C. speciosa* reaching heights of 30 to 40′ with an equal or greater spread. It is broadly rounded in outline with an irregular crown composed of short, crooked branches. Flowers are white with 2 ridges and 2 rows of yellow spots and numerous purple spots on the tube and lower lobe, borne in broad, pyramidal panicles, 8 to 10″ long and wide, mid to late May, Athens, GA, mid to late June in Boston, about two weeks after *C. speciosa*. Fruit is a 6 to 15″ long capsule. 'Aurea' has leaves of a rich yellow which, in England, does not become dull or green during the summer; 'Nana' is an old (1850), dwarf, bushy form of French origin that is grafted on a standard to produce a mushroom or globe; this form rarely if ever flowers. Georgia, Florida, Alabama and Louisiana. Introduced 1726. Zone 5 to 9.

Catalpa bungei, (ka-tal′pa bun′gē-ī), is a small, bushy pyramidal to round-headed, 20 to 30′ high tree that has been confused with *C. b.* 'Nana'. Its leaves vary from 2 to 7″ long and 1 1/2 to 4 1/2″ wide.

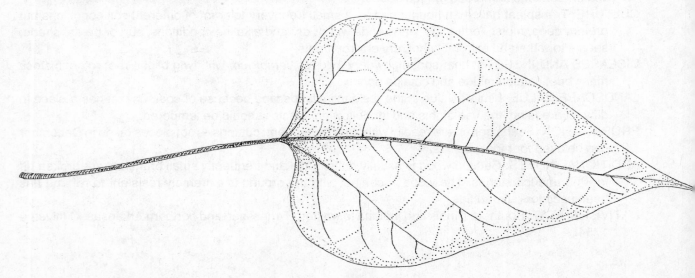

They are ovate, sometimes entire, but often scalloped with 1 to 6 large teeth on each side, mostly on the lower one-half of the leaf, glabrous at maturity. This species is rare in cultivation but there is one at the Arnold Arboretum which adheres closely to the above leaf description. Northern China. Cultivated 1877. Zone 5 to 8(?).

Catalpa × *erubescens,* (ka-tal′pa × ē-rū-bes′enz), represents a group of hybrids between *C. big-nonioides* and *C. ovata.* The hybrid has occurred at different times and places around the world resulting in several named clones. The best known form was raised by J.C. Teas at Bayville, Indiana around 1874 from seed of *C. ovata.* The unfolding leaves are purplish, broad-ovate or slightly 3-lobed, cordate, up to 10 to 12″ long, and pubescent beneath. The white flowers are smaller than *C. bignonioides* but more numerous and stained with yellow and minutely spotted with purple. In 'Purpurea' the emerging shoots are black-purple and gradually change to dark green, the petiole retaining the purple coloration. It is speculated that this clone was raised in the Meehan nurseries, Germantown, PA before 1886. Zone 5 to 8?

Catalpa fargesii, (ka-tal′pa far-jēs′ē-ī), Farges Catalpa, is mentioned here because of the unusual 1 1/2″ wide, rosy-pink to purple, purple-brown dotted flowers (June), produced 7 to 15 together in corymbs. I have seen this plant at the Arnold Arboretum and in flower it is lovely. Capsules are slender and range from 12 to 18″ long. The tree is open and not particularly attractive. It would be a good candidate for hybridization work. Western China. Cultivated 1900. Zone 5 to 8.

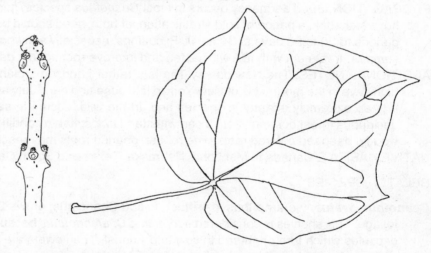

Catalpa ovata, (ka-tal′pa ō-vā′ta), Chinese Catalpa, is similar to other species except fruit is often longer, 8 to 12″, and thinner, less than 1/3″. Leaves are glabrous, almost completely so. Seeds are smaller than *C. speciosa* and *C. big-nonioides* and exhibit the fringed character of *C. speciosa. Catalpa ovata* is only mentioned here because of long, thing (1/3″ diameter) fruits. Flowers are yellowish white in 4 to 10″ high narrow pyramidal panicles and not as effective as *C. speciosa* or *C. bignonioides.* In the last edition I mentioned seedlings that I had grown of this species. In a single growing season some flowered and by the second all produced flowers. China. Introduced 1849. Zone 4 to 8.

Ceanothus americanus — New Jersey Tea, also called Redroot, Wild Snowball, Mountain Sweet

(sē-a-nō′thus a-mer-i-kān′us)

FAMILY: Rhamnaceae

LEAVES: Alternate, simple, ovate to obovate, 2 to 3″ long, 3/4 to 2″ wide, acute or acuminate, irregularly serrulate, dark green at maturity, with 3 conspicuous veins, pubescent or nearly glabrous beneath; petiole 1/4 to 1/2″ long.

BUDS: Sessile, ovoid, with several glabrate, stipular scales of which the lowest only are distinct.

STEM: Rounded, rather slender, more or less puberulent, green or brownish; pith relatively large, white, continuous; leaf scars small, half-round, somewhat raised; 1 transverse bundle-trace, more or less evidently compound, sometimes distinctly 3; stipules small, persistent or leaving narrow scars.

SIZE: 3 to 4' high by 3 to 5' in width.

HARDINESS: Zone 4 to 8, probably the hardiest of the *Ceanothus.*

HABIT: Low, broad, compact shrub with rounded top and slender upright branches; plants I have seen were quite low and dense.

RATE: Slow to medium.

TEXTURE: Medium in all seasons.

LEAF COLOR: Dark green in summer, perhaps yellow to tan in fall.

FLOWERS: Perfect, white, odorless, less than 1/8″ diameter, borne in 1 to 2″ long corymbose panicles at the ends of the stems in June and July.

FRUIT: Similar to a capsule, dry, triangular, 1/5″ wide, separating into 3 compartments at maturity, not showy.

CULTURE: Supposedly somewhat difficult to transplant; prefers light, well drained soil; tolerates dryness; full sun or shade; found on dry banks along highways throughout east; fixes atmospheric nitrogen; growing on dry hillside in Georgia Botanical Garden.

DISEASES AND INSECTS: Leaf spots and powdery mildew are two minor problems.

LANDSCAPE VALUE: This species is a parent of many of the hybrids which are used extensively in Europe and the west coast; may have a place in difficult areas.

PROPAGATION: Seed dormancy occurs in most *Ceanothus* species; germination has been induced by a hot water soak, a period of cold stratification, or both; seed should be stratified in a moist medium for periods fo 30 to 90 days at 34° to 41°F; cuttings, especially softwood, root readily when collected in summer; treatment with IBA will hasten and improve rooting to a degree.

ADDITIONAL NOTES: The New Jersey Tea is a rather handsome plant. I have seen it in flower along highways in the mountains of New York in late June and early July and it makes a rather pretty show. It is an extremely adaptable species and, in the wild, occurs in sandy woods, dry prairies, mixed deciduous forest communities. It can withstand inhospitable conditions due to presence of massive, woody, deep red colored roots. The robust, gnarled roots may reach diameters of 6 to 8″.

NATIVE HABITAT: Canada to Manitoba, Nebraska, Texas and South Carolina. Introduced 1713.

RELATED SPECIES:

Ceanothus ovatus, (sē-a-nō′thus ō-vā′tus), Inland Ceanothus, grows 2 to 3′ high and is quite dense in foliage. This species is considered superior to *C. americanus* because of its growth habit and the dry capsules which turn bright red in July and August. The flowers are white and minimally showy. The summer foliage is a shiny green while fall coloration is of no consequence. Best reserved for out of the way areas and naturalizing. Native from New England to Nebraska, Colorado and Texas. Cultivated 1830. Zone 4.

There are many species and hybrids of *Ceanothus,* most too tender or ill-adapted for the midwest, east and surprisingly south. I brought one of the blue-flowered hybrids from California to Georgia. The leaves abscised for no apparent reason and then grew back. The high humidity may be its downfall. I have seen many of the west coast species on the side of a mountain growing in sandy, rocky soil under dry atmospheric conditions. On the other hand, many of the *Ceanothus* hybrids appear to prosper in England. One particular hybrid group, *C. × delilianus,* a cross between the tender blue-flowered *C. coeruleus* of Mexico and *C. americanus* has given rise to beautiful blue and pink to rose flowered forms. One of the most beautiful blue forms is 'Gloire de Versailles' which I saw in several English gardens. This and the blue poppy, *Meconopsis* sp., are real show stoppers.

The Arnold Arboretum has a rather dainty light pink flowered *Ceanothus × pallidus* 'Roseus' that I find attractive. The plant forms a 2 to 3′ mound; the branches being terminated by soft pink flowers. Although injured by −6°F, it grew back and flowered in one growing season.

Ceanothus species are evergreen or deciduous, the flowers usually white or blue (rose), the leaves opposite or alternate, and the latter group having different vein patterns.

Cedrela sinensis — Chinese Cedrela or Chinese Toon
(se-drē'la sī-nen'sis)

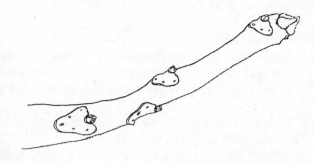

FAMILY: Meliaceae

LEAVES: Alternate, pinnately compound, 10 to 20″ long, leaflets 10 to 22, short-stalked, oblong to lance-oblong, 3 to 6″ long, acuminate, base unequal on each side of midrib, remotely and slightly serrate or nearly entire, pubescent beneath on veins or finally glabrous; young leaves smell like onions when crushed; reddish bronze in color on newly emerging leaves, eventually medium green; long petioled.

BUDS: Solitary, sessile, short-ovoid, with about 4 short-pointed, exposed scales; terminal much larger.

STEM: Coarse, terete, puberulent; pith large, homogenous, roundish, white becoming colored; leaf scars cordately elliptical-shield-shaped, slightly raised, large; 5 bundle-traces; no stipular scars; could be mistaken for *Ailanthus* on first inspection.

SIZE: 30 to 40′ tall under landscape conditions; can grow 60 to 70′ in the wild, often suckering and forming colonies.

HARDINESS: Zone 5 (6) to 8; has survived −25°F.

HABIT: Upright-oval, single-stemmed and from a distance resembles *Carya ovata;* variable, may also be multistemmed or suckering.

RATE: Medium to fast.

TEXTURE: Medium-coarse in summer; coarse in winter.

BARK: Brown, peeling off in long strips similar to that of *Carya ovata* in appearance but on a reduced scale.

LEAF COLOR: Reddish purple when unfolding, gradually changing to medium green in summer; fall color is of no consequence.

FLOWERS: Small, perfect, white, malodorous, campanulate, about 1/5″ long, borne in pendulous 12″ long panicles in June.

FRUIT: Woody capsule, about 1″ long, with winged seeds.

CULTURE: Quite adaptable to different soils; grows under extreme stess; possibly should be given a longer look.

DISEASES AND INSECTS: None serious.

LANDSCAPE VALUE: Has been used as a street tree in Philadelphia, PA, Santa Barbara, CA, and Paris, France.

CULTIVARS:

'Flamingo'—An interesting form with pink to cream colored new foliage that eventually changes to green; originated in Australia around 1930 and the name was first published in 1981.

PROPAGATION: Seed apparently requires no pretreatment although reported success varies; a one-month cold stratification is suggested; root cuttings will produce shoots; collect in October and later.

ADDITIONAL NOTES: Resembles *Ailanthus altissima* in morphological features except it does not bear the glandular teeth near the base of the leaflet and the leaves have an oniony smell. The young shoots are boiled and eaten as a vegetable by the Chinese. The tree was known to botanists since 1743, but was not introduced to Europe until 1862. By some strange happenstance this species was included in a planting on the Georgia campus. At first I thought it was *Ailanthus* but the onion-smell gave it away. Probably the most recent complete landscape treatment of the species is offered by Koller. *Arnoldia* 38:158–161 (1978).

NATIVE HABITAT: Northern and eastern China. Introduced 1862.

Cedrus atlantica — Atlas Cedar
(sē'drus ăt-lăn'tĭ-kă)

FAMILY: Pinaceae

IDENTIFICATION FEATURES: Closely related to *C. libani*, distinguished by the taller crown, less densely arranged branchlets, the bluish or dark green leaves which are mostly as thick as broad, the smaller cones (2 to 3" long) and the smaller seeds (1/2" long).

SIZE: 40 to 60' high by 30 to 40' wide but can grow to 120' in height by 90 to 100' spread; trees over 100' are relatively common in England.

HARDINESS: Zone 6 to 9; this and Deodar are the least cold hardy of the cedars.

HABIT: In youth and early maturity the form is stiff with an erect leader and the overall shape is pyramidal; unfortunately open and gaunt in youth and not as preferable to the customer on first inspection compared to *C. deodara* but a superior plant over time; in age it assumes a flat-topped habit with horizontally spreading branches; extremely picturesque and interesting tree, its beauty perhaps unmatched by any other conifer.

RATE: Slow (fast when young).

TEXTURE: Medium.

LEAF COLOR: Bluish green, varying in color from light green to silvery blue.

FLOWERS: Monoecious, male cones very densely set, erect, finger-shaped, 2 to 3" long, 1/2 to 5/8" wide, shedding clouds of yellow pollen in fall; usually more numerous on the lower portion of the tree (the above description applies to the other cedars); female borne in stout, erect cones, purplish initially, usually in the upper parts of the tree.

FRUIT: Cones rather short, long persistent, upright on upperside of branches, 3" long and 2" in diameter, requiring two years to mature; glaucous green while developing, finally brown.

CULTURE: Difficult to transplant and should be moved as a container plant; prefers a well-drained, moist, deep loamy soil but will tolerate sandy, clay soils if there is no stagnant moisture; sun or partial shade; needs shelter from strong, sweeping winds; preferably acid soil although withstands alkaline soils; does well in the heat of the south.

DISEASES AND INSECTS: Tip blight, root rots, black scale and Deodar weevil.

LANDSCAPE VALUE: A handsome specimen tree, particularly striking when fully mature; the cedars should never be considered for anything but specimen use; when they are surrounded by ample turf and allowed to develop naturally they have no garden rivals; not used enough in the south were *C. deodara* dominates because of its fuller, denser habit and faster growth in youth; unfortunately *C. deodara* will often die back starting at the top of the plant; to be sure, magnificent specimens of *C. deodara* can be found throughout the south and far west.

CULTIVARS:

'Argentea'—Perhaps the rest of the bluish needle forms, the whole tree is a beautiful pale silver-gray-blue color.

'Aurea'—A rather stiff form with yellowish needles, not as robust as the species.

'Fastigiata'—An upright form with good blue-green needles; have seen at Morris Arboretum, Pennsylvania; good looking plant; unfortunately, something is lost in translation with this cultivar since it will never develop the grandiose outline of the species.

'Glauca' (f. *glauca* by Bean)—Might well be listed as a true variety comparable to *Picea pungens* var. *glauca* as bluish forms can be selected from seedling populations; usually the foliage colors range from very blue to green in a given population; beautiful plant; there is a +80 year-old plant on the Georgia campus that evokes considerable comment.

'Glauca Pendula'—Weeping form with bluish foliage; the branches cascade like water over rocks; must be staked to develop a strong leader; truly a beautiful clone; have seen in many gardens and each is slightly different due to training, pruning and staking in the early years.

PROPAGATION: Seeds of *Cedrus* exhibit little or no dormancy; however, prechilling or cold stratification at 37° to 41°F for 14 days has been recommended.

ADDITIONAL NOTES: Closely related to *C. libani* from which it differs in the shoots always being downy and the cones do not taper above the middle so much. Bean noted that *C. atlantica* was thriving splendidly in various parts of the British Isles. At Kew Gardens, on dry, hot soil it grows more quickly and withstands London smoke better than *C. libani* or *C. deodara*.

NATIVE HABITAT: Algeria and Morocco on the Atlas Mountains. Introduced before 1840.

Cedrus deodara — Deodar Cedar
(se̅'drus de̅-o̅-där'-a)

LEAVES: One to 1 1/2″ long (occasionally 2″), needle-like, on current season's growth extension singly and spirally, 15 to 20 per whorl, dark green, glaucous or silvery, sharply pointed, on long shoots borne singly and spirally around the stem.

BUDS: Minute, ovoid, with brown scales which remain on the shoots after the appearance of young leaves.

STEM: Long stems bearing scattered leaves and short, spur-like stems with whorled leaves; stems usually clothed with a grayish down; silvery, glaucous appearance.

SIZE: 40 to 70′ after 30 to 40 years; supposedly can grow 150 to 200′ high with a spread of 150′.

HARDINESS: Zone 7 to 8 (9); references state hardy to −12°F, but this is generally not true, less cold hardy than *C. libani* and *C. atlantica*.

HABIT: Broadly pyramidal when young with gracefully pendulous branches; becoming wide spreading and flat-topped in old age; the most graceful cedar especially in youth.

RATE: Medium, grows about 2′ in a year when young.

TEXTURE: Fine, especially in youth.

LEAF COLOR: Light blue or grayish green, sometimes silvery in color.

FLOWERS: As described under *C. atlantica*.

FRUIT: Cones solitary to two together on short branchlets, ovoid or oblong ovoid, 3 to 4″ long by approximately 3″ broad; apex rounded, bluish, bloomy when young turning reddish brown at maturity.

CULTURE: If root pruned, transplants easily, prefers a well-drained and somewhat dry, sunny location and protection from sweeping winds; often container-grown to avoid transplanting difficulties.

DISEASES AND INSECTS: Tops die back because of canker (?), weevil, and/or cold.

LANDSCAPE VALUE: Excellent specimen evergreen because of extremely graceful and pendulous habit; in the last edition I mentioned planting 3 in my garden; 2 are dead because of cold and poor root systems (produced from cuttings); for a shorter term investment than the other cedars, it is acceptable.

CULTIVARS: I was somewhat remiss in the last edition not listing more cultivars and considered expanding the lists of the three *Cedrus* species treated herein. However, upon reflection, common sense took command and said...practice restraint. Many excellent conifer books including van Hoey Smith and van Gelderen, Bean, Boom, den Ouden and Boom, Welch, and Krüssmann have noteworthy lists. I counted 33 named forms of *C. deodara* alone in Krüssmann. Also many specialist evergreen nurseries have quite extensive lists. Iseli Nursery, Boring, OR, a wholesale producer of quality evergreens (plants in general) lists (1989 catalog) 19 forms of *C. deodara,* 13 of which are not listed in Krüssmann.

'Kashmir'—Hardy form, silvery blue-green foliage, survived rapid temperature drop of 25°F below zero; repeated trials in Illinois have met with failure; one of my University of Illinois colleagues and I were determined to grow this form and tried it in every imaginable microclimate except the greenhouse and all attempts met with winter kill and the lowest temperature experienced was −20°F; doubtfully much better than −5°F cold tolerance.

'Kingsville'—Similar to above, possibly hardier than 'Kashmir' but again met with the same fate as above.

'Shalimar'—An introduction by the Arnold Arboretum that displays good blue-green needle color and excellent hardiness in vicinity of Boston, MA; this, to date, is the hardiest cultivar. Grown from seed collected in a garden by that name in Srinigar in the Kashmir region of India in 1964; reports indicated growth of 9 to 15′ in 10 years from a cutting; has shown needle damage in severe winters but vastly superior to 'Kingsville' and 'Kashmir'; Don Shadow indicated it had survived at least −15°F in his Winchester, TN nursery; Nicholson, *The Plant Propagator* 30(1):5–6(1984) took 'Shalimar' cuttings in mid November (Boston), sand:perlite, 75°F bottom heat, poly tent in 50 to 60°F greenhouse, evaluated cuttings in April with 67% rooting from 5000 ppm IBA 5-second dip and 50% from 10,000 ppm dip.

PROPAGATION: Seed as described for *C. atlantica;* it should be noted that seed is oily and deteriorates quickly on drying; see Fordham, *Arnoldia* 37:46–47, 1977 for more details. Cuttings can be rooted and should be collected in October and later, treated with at least 8000 ppm IBA, given bottom heat and placed in a poly tent; rooting with various cultivars and the species ranged from 64 to 90%; cultivars of various species are often grafted on *C. deodara* because it has the most fibrous and compact root system.

NATIVE HABITAT: Himalaya from East Afghanistan to Garwhal. Introduced 1831.

Cedrus libani — Cedar of Lebanon
(sē′drus lib′an-ī)

LEAVES 30 to 40 per spur, 3/4 to 1 1/2″ long, needle-like, stiff, quadrilaterally compressed, broader than high, pointed at apex, dark or bright green.

STEM: Branchlets very numerous, densely arranged, spreading in a horizontal plane, short, glabrous or irregularly pubescent.

SIZE: 40 to 60′ after 40 to 70 years but can grow 75 to 120′ in height by 80 to 100′ spread.

HARDINESS: Zone 5 to 7.

HABIT: A stately tree with a thick, massive trunk and very wide-spreading branches, the lower ones sweeping the ground; pyramidal when young; superb in mature outline with horizontally disposed branches and a flat-topped crown.

RATE: Slow.

TEXTURE: Medium.

BARK: Gray-brown to brown forming a pebbled like appearance on old trunks; this applies to all the cedars.

LEAF COLOR: Dark or bright green.

FLOWERS: As previously described, yellow-brown, erect male catkins; pistillate purplish.

FRUIT: Cones stalked, solitary, upright, barrel-shaped, 3 to 5″ long by 2 to 2 1/2″ across, impressed at the apex, sometimes resinous, requiring two years to mature, purple-brown in color.

CULTURE: Somewhat difficult to transplant; a good, deep, well-drained loam; open, sunny, spacious location; intolerant of shade; needs a pollution-free, dry atmosphere; at the species level the hardiest type; has withstood −15 to −25°F temperatures in the Cincinnati area, but did suffer same dieback and needle burn.

DISEASES AND INSECTS: None serious.

LANDSCAPE VALUE: A specimen tree of unrivaled distinction, uniting the grand with the picturesque; the dark green foliage, stiff habit, and rigidly upright cones give this tree a popular interest; somewhat stiff in youth becoming more picturesque with age.

CULTIVARS:

'Argentea'—Could be listed as a true variety; leaves of a very glaucous (silvery-blue) hue; supposedly is found wild in the Cilician stands.

var. *brevifolia,* Cyprus Cedar, is generally smaller in all its parts compared to *C. libani;* the needles range from 1/4 to 1/2″ long, the cones are smaller and ultimate size (height) averages about 40′.

'Pendula'—Handsome form with gracefully pendulous branches; often grafted high to produce a small weeping tree.

'Sargentii'—A dwarf 3 to 5′ high mound with numerous horizontal branches and long dark green needles.

var. *stenocoma*—Extremely hardy form and more stiff and rigid than the species; a specimen on the Purdue campus, West Lafayette, IN and several handsome plants at the Arnold Arboretum attest to this; apparently raised from seeds collected in Cilician Taurus; preferred choice for cold climates.

PROPAGATION: Seed, see under *C. atlantica;* cuttings taken in November rooted 30% in sand:peat without treatment; the most difficult cedar to root from cuttings.

ADDITIONAL NOTES: All the *Cedrus* are exquisite, lovely trees but *C. libani* has received the most notoriety, and justifiably so. There are disagreements as to the exact taxonomic status of the various cedars. Some botanists regard them all as geographical forms of one species. One botanist divided them into four subspecies. No matter how they are allied taxonomically they offer incomparable beauty among the large conifers. The National Arboretum, Washington, D.C. has a notable collection of *Cedrus* as does Longwood Gardens.

NATIVE HABITAT: Asia Minor, best known for its historic stands in Lebanon, but attaining maximum size in the Cilician Taurus, Turkey. Further west it occurs in scattered locales as far as the Aegean. Introduced in colonial times.

Celastrus scandens — American Bittersweet
(sē-las′trus skan′denz)

FAMILY: Celastraceae

LEAVES Alternate, simple, ovate to oblong-ovate, 2 to 4″ long, acuminate, broad cuneate at base, serrulate, glabrous, lustrous dark green; petiole—1/4 to 1″ long.

BUDS: Brownish, small, sessile, solitary, sub-globose, with about 6, hard, mucronate scales, glabrous.

STEM: Brown to tan, lenticels scarcely noticeable; pith—solid, white; one bundle trace.

SIZE: Often listed as 20′ but seems to continue growing as long as there is something to climb upon.

HARDINESS: Zone 3 to 8.

HABIT: Vigorous, deciduous, twining vine or vine-like shrub which engulfs every fence in sight.

RATE: Fast; Wyman noted it can kill shrubs or small trees as it girdles the stems.

TEXTURE: Medium in leaf; medium-coarse in winter.

LEAF COLOR: Deep glossy green in summer; greenish yellow in fall.

FLOWERS: Polygamo-dioecious, primarily dioecious, yellowish white, not showy; borne in 2 to 4″ long terminal panicles, May–June.

FRUIT: Three-lobed capsule, 1/3″ across, yellow orange on the inside, with crimson seeds; ripens in October and is extensively collected and sold for dried flower arrangements.

CULTURE: Most nurserymen sell it as a small container plant; the problem occurs because the sexes are never labeled; in this respect, it is like holly for without the male, fruit set will be nonexistent; quite easy to grow as it withstands about any soil condition including those that are dry; pH adaptable; full sun for best fruiting; probably best to locate in a poor soil site as it will quickly overgrow its bounds when placed in good soil.

DISEASES AND INSECTS: Leaf spots, powdery mildews, crown gall, stem canker, *Euonymus* scale, aphids, and two-marked treehopper.

LANDSCAPE VALUE: Little, except in rough areas; could be allowed to scramble over rock piles, fences, old trees and the like; the fruit is handsome and is always welcome in arrangements.

PROPAGATION: Seeds have a dormant embryo and require after-ripening for germination; there is some evidence that the seed coat may have an inhibiting effect upon germination; seeds or dried fruits should be stratified in moist sand or peat for 2 to 6 months at 41°F; softwood cuttings root readily in sand without treatment, but rooting may be hastened or improved by treatment; cuttings collected in early August, treated with 8000 ppm IBA-talc rooted 83%; softwood cuttings of all species when collected in July and treated with IBA root readily.

RELATED SPECIES:

Celastrus loeseneri, (sē-las′trus lō-sen′ēr-ī), Loesener Bittersweet, is similar to *C. orbiculatus* but differs in its thinner, rounder leaves and the pith being lamellate. I have seen this plant at several gardens and was not sure of how it differed from the Oriental Bittersweet. It can grow to 20′. The greenish white flowers are produced in axillary cymes. The 1/3″ diameter fruits open to expose a yellow inner capsule and the red seed. Central China. Introduced 1907. Zone 4 to 8 (?).

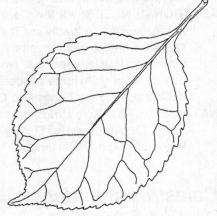

Celastrus orbiculatus — Chinese Bittersweet
LEAVES: Alternate, simple, obovate to orbicular, 2 to 5″ long, almost as wide, acute or acuminate, cuneate, crenate-serrate, lustrous rich green, glabrous; petiole—1/3 to 1″ long.
STEM: Rounded, pith solid, white.

Celastrus orbiculatus, (sē-las′trus ô-bi-kū-lā′tus), Chinese Bittersweet, is similar to the above but tends to be more rampant. The fruits are in axillary cymes which permits separation from *C. scandens.* Handsome in fruit but has become a rather noxious weed in the Northeastern United States. It has escaped from cultivation and is particularly abundant along roadsides in some parts of New England. Japan, China. Introduced 1870. Zone 4, possibly best in 5. Often developing a good yellow fall color.

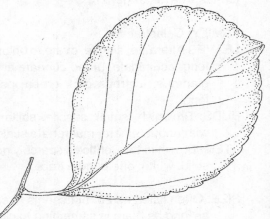

Celtis occidentalis — Common Hackberry
(sel′tis ok-si-den-tā′lis)

FAMILY: Ulmaceae
LEAVES: Alternate, simple, ovate to oblong-ovate, 2 to 5″ long, acute to acuminate, oblique and rounded or broad-cuneate at base, serrate except at base, bright green and usually smooth, lustrous or dull green above, paler below and glabrous or slightly hairy on veins; petioles 1/2 to 3/4″ long.
BUDS: Small, imbricate, 1/4″ long or less, downy, chestnut brown, ovate, sharp pointed, flattened, appressed, terminal—absent.
STEM: Slender, somewhat zigzag, light olive-brown, prominently lenticelled, more or less shining, more or less downy; wood of stem light greenish yellow when moistened; pith—white, finely chambered.
BARK: Trunk and older limbs with narrow corky projecting ridges which are sometimes reduced to wart-like projections.

SIZE: 40 to 60′ in height with a nearly equal spread can grow to 100′.
HARDINESS: Zone 2 to 9.
HABIT: In youth weakly pyramidal; in old age the crown is a broad top of ascending arching branches, often with drooping branchlets; not unlike the American Elm in outline; however, by no means as aesthetic.

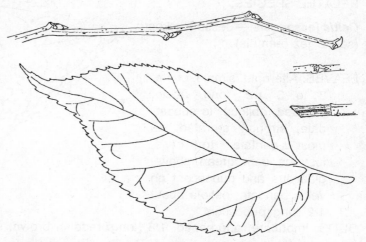

RATE: Medium to fast, 20 to 30′ over a 10 to 15 year period.

TEXTURE: Medium-coarse in leaf and in winter.

BARK: Grayish with characteristic corky warts or ridges, later somewhat scaly.

LEAF COLOR: Dull light to medium green in summer; yellow or yellow-green fall color.

FLOWERS: Polygamo-monoecious, staminate ones in fascicles toward base; the perfect and pistillate flowers above; solitary in the axils of the leaves; April–May with the emerging leaves.

FRUIT: Fleshy, orange-red to dark purple rounded drupe, 1/3″ diameter, borne on 1/2″ long peduncle, ripening in September and October, often persistent for several weeks; flavored like dates and relished by birds and wildlife; one hard seed which if bitten into will shatter teeth.

CULTURE: Easily transplanted bare root as a small tree or balled and burlapped in larger sizes; prefers rich, moist soils, but grows in dry, heavy or sandy, rocky soils; withstands acid or alkaline conditions; moderately wet or very dry areas; tolerates wind; full sun; withstands dirt and grime of cities.

DISEASES AND INSECTS: Leaf spots, witches' broom, powdery mildew, *Gonoderma* rot, hackberry nipple-gall, mourning-cloak butterfly and several scales are troublesome; personally I find the witches' broom often caused by an *Eriophyes* mite and the powdery mildew fungus, *Sphaerotheca phytophylla,* particularly offensive for trees are often totally disfigured by broom-like clusters of abnormal branch growth; some trees show resistance and might be propagated vegetatively to avoid this problem; the nipple gall is another serious problem as the leaves are often disfigured by these bullet-like appendages.

LANDSCAPE VALUE: Good tree for plains and prairie states because it performs admirably under adverse conditions; good for park and large area use; has the innate ability to grow in dry soils and under windy conditions; have observed some beautiful hackberries that need to be vegetatively propagated.

CULTIVARS:

'Chicagoland'—Develops a single upright leader, a 15-year-old tree was 26′ high and 14′ wide, a chance seedling selected by Roy Klehm, South Barrington, IL.

'Prairie Pride'—Selected by Bill Wandell; the foliage is thick, leathery, lustrous dark green and as a small tree develops a nice uniform, compact oval crown; does not develop witches broom and has lighter than usual fruit crops; young trees under cultivation show rapid upright growth and few spur branches; tree was initially somewhat difficult to propagate but is now being produced in commercial quantities.

'Windy City'—Another Klehm selection with upright spreading habit, attractive foliage and healthy growth rate.

PROPAGATION: Seed should be stratified for 60 to 90 days at 41°F in moist medium; this is a general recommendation for all species; cuttings have been rooted but the percentages were low.

ADDITIONAL NOTES: *C. occidentalis* is immune to Dutch elm disease. Best growth occurs in rich bottom lands of the Ohio River where trees in the original forest grew to be 5′ in diameter and 100′ high, living 150 to 200 years. The name Hackberry is a corruption of the Scottish Hagberry which in Britain was the Bird Cherry *(Prunus avium).*

NATIVE HABITAT: I have seen the Common Hackberry in about every imaginable situation—in flood plains, open fields, along roadsides and in fence rows. Quebec to Manitoba, south to North Carolina, Alabama, Georgia and Oklahoma. Cultivated 1636.

RELATED SPECIES:

Celtis jessoensis — Jesso Hackberry
(sel'tis jez-ō-en'sis)

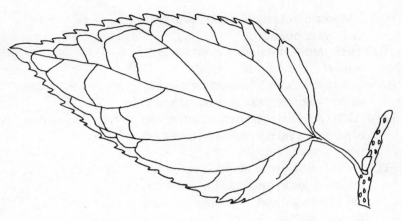

LEAVES: Alternate, simple, ovate,
2 to 3 1/2″ long, acute,
rounded, oblique, to subcordate, strongly serrated, almost dentate to base,
lustrous dark green above,
glaucous and pubescent on
veins beneath; petiole about
1/2″ long, pubescent.
BUDS: Imbricate, appressed, 1/8″ long, reddish brown, scales vari-colored, perhaps pubescent at
edges.
STEM: Slender, brown, zig-zag, pubescent, dotted with gray-brown lenticels; second year gray-green; end
of stem terminates in woody petiole base like *Eucommia;* pith did not show chambers.

Celtis jessoensis, Jesso Hackberry, will not ring anyone's plant material bell simply because it is so
uncommon. My good friend Gary Koller of the Arnold Arboretum introduced this species to me during
my sabbatical and after one-year of almost everyday evaluation I think it has a genuine place in the
landscape. The Arnold has several plants that are upright-spreading, 50 to 60′ (70′) high. The leaves
are the best dark green of any hackberry I have observed and completely free of nipple gall. Also no
"witches" broom was present. The Jesso Hackberries are planted next to the other hackberries, and
the elms and zelkovas are within throwing distance; so if serious insect or disease maladies were
associated with the species they should have been present. The bark is a smooth gray not unlike that
of *Cladrastis lutea* or beech. Korea, Japan. Introduced 1892 into the Arnold Arboretum and the trees
mentioned were derived from this accession. Zone 5.

Celtis laevigata — Sugar hackberry, Sugarberry
(sel'tis lev-i-gā'ta or lē-vi-gā'ta)

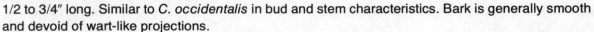

LEAVES: Alternate,
simple,   oblong-
lanceolate, some-
times ovate, 2 to
4″ long, 1 1/4″
wide, long-acumi-
nate and usually falcate, broad-
cuneate or rounded at base, entire
or sometimes with a few teeth, dark
green above, slightly paler
beneath, glabrous, thin; petioles
1/2 to 3/4″ long. Similar to *C. occidentalis* in bud and stem characteristics. Bark is generally smooth
and devoid of wart-like projections.

Celtis laevigata, Sugar Hackberry, is also known as the Sugarberry, Southern Hackberry or Mississippi
Hackberry. The tree can grow from 60 to 80′ in height and similar spread. The habit is rounded to
broad rounded with spreading, often pendulous branches. This tree is used extensively in the south
on streets, parks and large areas; have seen a great number used as street trees in Savannah, GA;
resistant to witches' broom; the fruit is orange-red to blue-black, very sweet and juicy, and relished
by birds. The common name is derived from the sweet taste of the fruits. Many of our best urban or
compact soil tolerant trees inhabit flood plain environments. Sugar Hackberry occurs in low wet areas

such as floodplains, bottomlands and sloughs, generally in clay soils. In Urbana, IL there were a number used around a downtown shopping mall that showed tremendous variation in foliage and habit. I believe Bill Wandell's 'All Seasons' Sugarberry was selected from one of these. 'All Seasons' has an excellent well balanced crown, full and fine-textured, small lustrous green leaves that turn good yellow in fall, heavy interior leaf population, smooth American Beech-like bark, excellent growth under adverse city conditions and cold hardiness to −25°F. Another selection is a purported cross between *C. laevigata* × *C. occidentalis* called 'Magnifica' and introduced by Princeton Nursery. It does not develop witches' broom. I have been unable to track other characteristics. Southern horticulturists need to work with this tree since many have been planted as street trees in the south and ample opportunity exists for superior introductions. Native from southern Indiana, Illinois to Texas and Florida. Cultivated 1811. Zone 5 to 9.

Cephalanthus occidentalis — Buttonbush
(sef-a-lan'thus ok-si-den-tā'lis)

FAMILY: Rubiaceae

LEAVES: Opposite, or whorled, simple, ovate to elliptic-lanceolate, 2 to 6″ long, about half as wide, acuminate, cuneate, entire, lustrous bright green above, lighter and glabrous or somewhat pubescent beneath; petiole 1/4 to 3/4″ long.

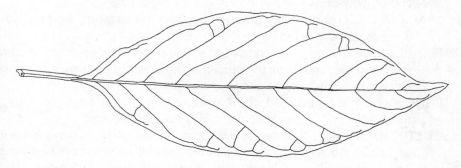

BUDS: Terminal-absent, laterals-solitary, sessile, conical, in depressed areas above the leaf scars, often superposed.

STEM: Moderate to stout, coarse, slightly pubescent or glabrous, weakly 4-sided, dirty gray brown to shining olive, prominent vertical lenticels; 2 to 3-year-old stems take on a reddish brown color and develop prominent fissures at the lenticels; ellipsoidal leaf scar with C-shaped bundle traces; scars connected by a line as in *Campsis radicans;* pith light brown, solid.

FRUIT: Rounded mass of nutlets persisting through winter.

Cephalanthus occidentalis, Buttonbush, is a rounded 3 to 6′ high, occasionally 10 to 15′ shrub (southern part of range), of rather loose, gangling proportions. The winter texture is quite coarse; however, the glossy summer foliage lends a medium texture. Leaves emerge late in spring and the plant looks dead until mid-May. The flowers are creamy-white, crowded in globular heads, without the projecting styles, 1 to 1 1/4″ across, on peduncles 1 to 2 1/2″ long in August. The fruit is a nutlet and the compound structure is present throughout winter. Culturally, Buttonbush is best adapted to moist situations, and in cultivation is averse to dryness. Probably best reserved for wet areas in a naturalized situation. The glossy foliage is quite attractive and the late flower is interesting. Easily propagated by softwood and hardwood cuttings. Softwood cuttings taken in late July and early August rooted 100 percent in sand:peat in one month without treatment. Seeds will germinate promptly without pretreatment. Native from New Brunswick to Florida, west to southern Minnesota, Nebraska, Oklahoma, southern New Mexico, Arizona and central California; also occurring in Cuba, Mexico and eastern Asia; have seen it growing in water; seems to prosper in such habitats. Introduced 1735. Zone 5 to 10.

Cephalotaxus harringtonia — Japanese Plum Yew
(sef-à-lō-tak′sus hăr-ing-tōn-i-a)

FAMILY: Cephalotaxaceae

LEAVES: Linear, evergreen, spirally arranged in 2 planes, forming a distinct V-shaped trough, 3/4 to 1 3/4″ long, abruptly pointed, lustrous dark green above, with 2 grayish bands beneath, each with about 15 rows of stomata.

SIZE: Variable, from a spreading 5 to 10′ evergreen shrub to a 20 to 30′ high small tree; the former predominant in the eastern United States.

HARDINESS: 5(6) to 9, amazing heat tolerance and should be the *Taxus* substitute for the south.

HABIT: Spreading evergreen shrub under normal landscape conditions; usually wider than high at maturity.

RATE: Slow.

TEXTURE: Medium-fine throughout the seasons.

BARK: Rich gray-brown on old trunks, exfoliating in strips.

LEAF COLOR: Lustrous dark green throughout the seasons, holds good color in winter unless sited in wind-swept, sunny locations.

FLOWERS: Dioecious, male composed of 4 to 6 stamens, enclosed in a bract and arranged in clusters of small rounded heads on the growth of the previous season, April–May; female composed of pairs of carpels in a mass of scales at base of stems.

FRUIT: Actually a naked seed, obovoid in shape, 1 to 1 1/4″ long, 3/4″ wide, on a 1/4 to 1/2″ long peduncle, turns a brown (olive to reddish brown) color at maturity.

CULTURE: Easily transplanted as a container grown plant, root system is white and rather fleshy like that of *Taxus;* requires moist well drained soil but once established will tolerate excess drought, have seen plants in full sun in virtual pure sand in Savannah, GA and was amazed at their quality; locate in shade but will tolerate full sun; one of the best needle evergreens for use in shade and heat in the south.

DISEASES AND INSECTS: None serious, although have seen some mite damage.

LANDSCAPE VALUE: Potential has not even been tapped for southeastern gardens; a superb and shade tolerant aristocratic evergreen for groupings, masses and accents; slow growing which frightens those who design with a juniper mentality, but the rewards over time are abundant.

CULTIVARS:

var. *drupacea*—Often listed as a species but current thinking places it in the varietal category; needles are generally shorter and plants I have seen were more bushy and spreading; native to Japan and Korea.

‘Duke Gardens’—A handsome 2 to 3′ tall and 3 to 4′ wide form that originated as a branch sport of ‘Fastigiata’ at Duke Gardens in Durham, NC; has all the desirable characteristics of a gracefully spreading yew.

‘Fastigiata’—A rotund columnar form that will grow 10′ tall and 6 to 8′ wide; the up to 2″ long leaves are black-green and spirally arranged on the stem but instead of appearing two ranked like the species are arranged in a bottlebrush fashion and present a rather unusual textural quality; Raulston mentioned that this is an old Japanese clone (more probably Korean) that was introduced into Europe about 1861; 20 to 25 year old plant at North Carolina State was 7′ high and wide; cuttings take 4 to 6 months to root and should be collected in December–March, 8000 ppm IBA-talc and mist.

‘Nana’—Occasionally seen but doubtfully is the same shrub that Rehder mentioned as 6′ high, spreading by suckers with upright, ascending stems. Creech, *Amer. Nurseryman* Jan. 15 (1986) reports that var. *nana* grows along the Sea of Japan on the coast of Honshu and is found in the dense conifer forests of Hokkaido.

‘Prostrata’—At best a topophytic form propagated from a lateral, horizontal shoot; 2 to 3′ high, 2 to 3′ in width, have seen the plant in Dutch gardens.

PROPAGATION: I could find no reliable references and suspect it shold be handled like *Taxus;* cuttings are rooted commercially and usually taken in winter months, treated with a rooting compound and left alone for 3 to 4 months; one report said rooting compound did not help; patience is the key factor; I have rooted a few cuttings but have found that it is one plant that will not hurry; after transplanting, plants do not grow off fast; probably takes 2 years from a rooted cutting to produce a one-gallon salable plant.

ADDITIONAL NOTES: Not the easiest genus to separate into identifiable species and at times the reader will come across *C. fortunei, C. harringtonia, C. drupacea,* et al. From a landscape perspective there is little difference. *Cephalotaxus fortunei* has longer, more slender needles to 3 1/2″ long. The plant grows into a large +10′ shrub under cultivation. I did once attempt to develop reliable methods of separation in Cambridge Botanic Garden's collection but decided that life was too short for such frustration.

NATIVE HABITAT: Japan, where it is distributed in the mountains from Kyushu to northern Honshu in moist, semi-shaded environments. Introduced 1830.

Cercidiphyllum japonicum — Katsuratree
(sĕr-si-di-fīl′-um ja-pon′-i-kum)

FAMILY: Cercidiphyllaceae

LEAVES: Opposite or subopposite, simple, 2 to 4″ long and as wide, suborbicular to broad ovate, obtusish, cordate at base, crenate-serrate, dark bluish green above, glaucescent beneath; leaf resembles redbud, purplish when unfolding.

BUDS: Two scales, not overlapping, terminal bud lacking, reddish, 1/16 to 1/8″ long, appressed, glabrous, angular.

STEM: Slender, swollen at nodes, brownish, glabrous; second year at each node 2 short "spur-type" growths develop that bear the male or female flower and a single leaf.

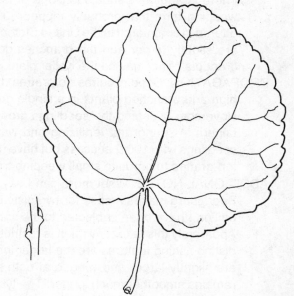

SIZE: 40 to 60′ in height and can reach 100′ in the wild; I have seen 40 to 50′ high trees with a 20 to 30′ spread and other trees of the same size with a spread equal to and in some cases greater than the height.

HARDINESS: Zone 4 to 8; several beautiful trees on the Georgia campus.

HABIT: Pyramidal in youth, full and dense even as a young tree; greatly variable with maturity, some trees maintaining pyramidal habit; others wide spreading; literature has ascribed a more upright habit to male trees, more spreading to female but I find this inconsistent with actual observations.

RATE: Medium to fast; once established about 14′ over a 5 to 7 year period and about 40′ over 20 years.

TEXTURE: Medium-fine in leaf; medium in winter habit.

BARK: Brown, slightly shaggy on old trunks with the ends loose; limitedly reminiscent of Shagbark Hickory bark; very handsome and quite refined compared to Hickory.

LEAF COLOR: New leaves emerge a beautiful reddish purple and gradually change to bluish green in summer; fall color varies from yellow to apricot with the emphasis on the yellow in the midwest; often a soft apricot-orange fall color develops; leaf is shaped like a *Cercis* (Redbud) leaf, hence, the generic name *Cercidiphyllum;* have seen magnificent apricot fall color on trees in New England but never red or scarlet that some literature ascribes to this tree; tends to be early leafing and should be in full fall color by mid October; the senescing (fall coloring) leaves give off a delightful spicy (cinnamon)/ brown sugar odor.

FLOWERS: Dioecious, male consists of a minute calyx and an indefinite number of stamens; pistillate of four green, fringed sepals, and four to six carpels, open from the late March to early April before the leaves; not showy.

FRUIT: Small, 1/2 to 3/4″ long dehiscent pods; borne 2 to 4 together on a short stalk; pods should be collected in October before they split; seeds are paper thin and winged.

CULTURE: Somewhat difficult to transplant; move as a balled and burlapped or container grown plant in early spring; soil should be rich, moist and well-drained; pH adaptable although seems to fall color better on acid soils; full sun; an effort should be made to provide supplemental watering during hot, dry periods during the initial time of establishment.

DISEASES AND INSECTS: None serious; sun scald and bark splitting may occur.

LANDSCAPE VALUE: Possibly a street tree but requires ample moisture in early years of establishment; excellent for residential properties, parks, golf courses, commercial areas; one of my favorite trees, overwhelming in overall attractiveness; if I could use only one tree this would be my first tree; I do not mind admitting to a few biases and for that reason have included a list of places where I have seen choice to magnificent specimens; they include Morton Arboretum, Arnold Arboretum, Spring Grove Cemetery, Morris Arboretum (what a specimen!), Hunnewell Estate, Callaway Gardens, Michigan State, University of Illinois, Purdue, Depauw, Smith College, University of Massachusetts, University of Georgia, University of Maine, off the town square in Amherst, MA (another wow specimen, now 100 years old), and Regis College, Weston, MA. The planting at Regis consists of numerous seedling trees lining either side of a long semicircular drive and in the fall it is absolutely unbelievable; worth first class airfare to see the spectacle.

CULTIVARS: 'Pendula' forms a mound of gracefully weeping branches which looked like blue-green water cascading over rocks; Spring Grove, Cave Hill Cemetery, Bernheim and Holden Arboreta have sizable specimens; it appears this cultivar will grow 15 to perhaps 25′; it is a fast growing form; I have tried unsuccessfully to root cuttings and now realize it must be grafted onto seedling understock. There is another pendulous clone of larger size; Gary Koller showed me a photograph of a large weeping form that probably topped 50′; it, too, was beautiful; *C. magnificum* 'Pendulum' is now offered in commerce in the United States. I suspect it is larger growing than *C. j.* 'Pendula'. The leaves are slightly larger and the branches do not appear to weep as strongly at an early age as *C. j.* 'Pendula'. This may be the Koller plant.

PROPAGATION: Seed requires no pretreatment and can be sown when mature; have produced 3 to 5′ high and branched plants in a single growing season by sowing seed in flats in the greenhouse in November. Keeping the seedlings growing under lights through winter, transplanting them to containers in spring and fertilizing and watering them regularly; have rooted softwood cuttings from seedlings with 100% success but have not been able to root cuttings from mature trees; cultivars are top-grafted to produce small weeping trees.

ADDITIONAL NOTES: What more can I say...See Spongberg. *J. Arnold Arboretum* 60:367–376. 1979. Spongberg makes a case for two distinct species, *C. magnificum* and *C. japonicum*. Since the last edition I have been subjected to the var. *magnificum* or, by some authorities, species *magnificum*. Apparently this taxonomic unit is restricted to Japan and does not grow as large as *C. japonica*. The distinguishing features are the larger leaf, more rounded shape and more cordate base. The seeds are slightly larger and winged at both ends (compared to one end of *C. japonica*). Also the bark remains smoother much longer. The typical form is actually var. *sinense* which occurs in China and tends to be more tree-like. Wilson described trees of *sinense* up to 130′ high and exceeding in height and girth all other deciduous, non-coniferous trees from China.

NATIVE HABITAT: China, Japan. Introduced 1865.

Cercis canadensis — Eastern Redbud
(ser'sis kan-a-den'sis)

FAMILY: Fabaceae

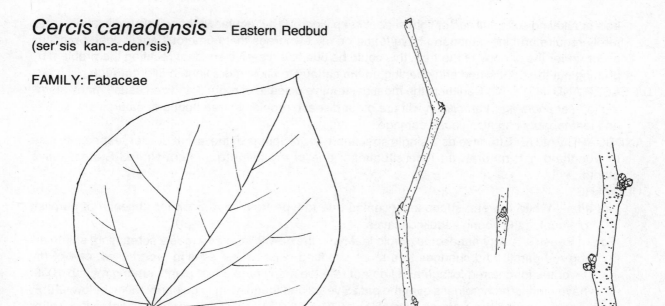

LEAVES: Alternate, simple, broad-ovate to suborbicular, (broadly heart-shaped), 3 to 5″ across, often wider than long, cordate, lustrous dark green, base with 5 to 9 prominent, radiating veins, petiole with conspicuous swelling just below blade, pubescent to glabrous beneath; petiole—1 1/2 to 2 1/2″ long.

BUDS: Terminal-absent, laterals—small, 1/8″ or less long, blunt, blackish red, somewhat flattened and appressed, one or more superposed buds often present, the uppermost the largest, bud scales—overlap, somewhat hairy on edges, about 2 visible to a leaf bud, several to a flower bud; flower buds more rounded than leaf buds and often clustered at each node.

STEM: Slender, glabrous, dark reddish brown to black, zigzag; pith—especially of older growth generally with reddish longitudinal streaks.

SIZE: 20 to 30′ in height by 25 to 35′ in spread.

HARDINESS: Zone 4 to 9, can be grown in Minnesota (Zone 3).

HABIT: Usually a small tree with the trunk divided close to the ground forming a spreading, flat-topped to rounded crown; very handsome with its gracefully ascending branches; "a native tree with a touch of class".

RATE: Medium, 7 to 10′ in 5 to 6 years.

TEXTURE: Medium-coarse in leaf; medium in winter.

BARK: Older bark black or brownish black usually with orangish inner bark peaking through; not often considered as a tree with interesting bark but it does possess ornamental value.

LEAF COLOR: New growth when emerging is a reddish purple and gradually changes to a dark, often somewhat lustrous green in summer; fall color is usually a poor yellow-green but can be an excellent yellow.

FLOWERS: Perfect, reddish purple in bud, opening to a rosy-pink with a purplish tinge, 1/2″ long; on a 1/2″ long pedicel; open in March–April and are effective for 2 to 3 weeks; borne 4 to 8 together, fascicled or racemose; often flowers are produced on old trunks 4 to 8″ in diameter; flowers at a young age, 4 to 6 years.

FRUIT: True pod (legume), brown, 2 to 3″ long, 1/2″ wide, October; reddish to green before maturity; may look a tad untidy with heavy fruit set.

CULTURE: Transplant balled and burlapped as a young tree in spring or fall into moist, well drained, deep soils; however, does exceedingly well in many soil types except permanently wet ones; adaptable to acid or alkaline soils; full sun or light shade; keep vigorous by regular watering and fertilization; trees rarely require pruning although I have found on my own trees that numerous small dead branches occur under the canopy of the tree; this could be due to excessive shade; I rectified the problem by pruning out the dead wood and opening up the canopy to allow more light to filter through.

DISEASES AND INSECTS: Canker is the most destructive disease of redbud and can cause many stems to die, leaf spots and *Verticillium* wilt are other disease problems; tree hoppers, caterpillars, scales and leafhoppers can also cause damage.

LANDSCAPE VALUE: Effective as a single specimen, in groupings in the shrub border, especially nice in woodland and naturalized type situations; one of my favorite eastern United States native plants.

CULTIVARS:

var. *alba*—White flowers; supposedly comes true to type from seed; look for absence of purplish pigment in the young seedling leaves.

'Forest Pansy'—A very handsome purple leaf type, the new foliage emerges a screaming, shimmering red-purple and changes to a more subdued color as the season progresses; one of my favorites for colored foliage and I do not rate too many purple leaf plants among my top 1000; have monitored hardiness over the past 5 years and found it not to be hardy much below −10°F; plants survived the extreme lows of the 1976–77 (−20 to −25°F) winter but did not leaf out after the winter of 1977–78 when the low was only −10°F but the average minimum for December through February was 10° lower than the normal; established plants were wiped out in Mt. Airy and Spring Grove, Cincinnati, Ohio; it is growing successfully in the UGA Botanical Garden but loses the intense color by late May–June when it becomes almost dark green; flowers are more rose-purple than the species and open a little later.

'Flame'—A rather interesting double-pink form that I believe is rather attractive yet nobody seems to be growing it; may be called 'Plena'; seldom sets fruit.

'Pinkbud'—A pure, bright true pink flower, discovered wild on an estate near Kansas City.

'Royal White'—A selection made by Professor J.C. McDaniel of the University of Illinois, Department of Horticulture for outstanding and abundant white flowers; the parent tree is located in Bluffs, Illinois; probably the most cold-hardy form; flowers larger than var. *alba* and open slightly earlier.

'Rubye Atkinson'—Flowers pure pink, may be a *Cercis reniformis* type.

'Silver Cloud'—A variegated form the leaves splotched, blotched and speckled with creamy-white; best grown in some shade; leaves show tremendous variegation pattern; less floriferous.

'Wither's Pink Charm'—Flowers soft pink without the purplish tint of the species.

PROPAGATION: Seeds have hard, impermeable seedcoats and internal dormancy; scarification in concentrated sulfuric acid for 30 minutes followed by 5 to 8 weeks of cold (41°F), moist stratification is recommended; see Frett and Dirr. *The Plant Propagator* 25(2):4–6, 1979 for more details on seed propagation; cultivars are budded on seedling understock.

ADDITIONAL NOTES: Redbud, like Flowering Dogwood, occurs over an extended range and plants grown from southern seed sources (Florida, Georgia) are not cold hardy in northern areas. Seed should be collected from local or regional sources. Interestingly, the Minnesota Landscape Arboretum is growing seedlings from one tree that has prospered at the University's Horticultural Research Center with the offspring showing the hardiness of the parent. The redbud is a breath of fresh air after a long winter. In my opinion one of our most beautiful native trees.

NATIVE HABITAT: New Jersey to northern Florida, west to Missouri and Texas and northern Mexico. Cultivated 1641.

RELATED SPECIES: No one has worked harder to promote redbuds than Dr. J.C. Raulston, North Carolina State University Arboretum, and his superlative treatise was published in the July 1986 No. 14 Arboretum Newsletter. Nine pages of single spaced type provide as great a synopsis as one could hope to locate. Additionally Raulston has brought to the Arboretum a virtual complete collection of species and is ardently working on the cultivars. See also *Amer. Nurseryman* 171(5): 39–51 (1990).

Cercis chinensis — Chinese Redbud
LEAVES: Alternate, simple, heart-shaped, 3 to 5″
long and wide, deeply cordate, lustrous
dark green above, glabrous, leathery, very
difficult to separate this species from *C.
canadensis.*

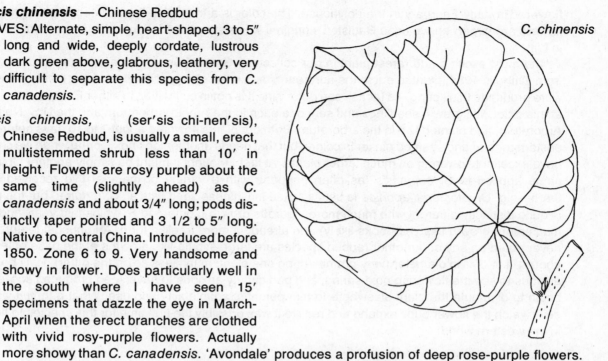

C. chinensis

Cercis chinensis, (ser′sis chi-nen′sis),
Chinese Redbud, is usually a small, erect,
multistemmed shrub less than 10′ in
height. Flowers are rosy purple about the
same time (slightly ahead) as *C.
canadensis* and about 3/4″ long; pods distinctly taper pointed and 3 1/2 to 5″ long.
Native to central China. Introduced before
1850. Zone 6 to 9. Very handsome and
showy in flower. Does particularly well in
the south where I have seen 15′
specimens that dazzle the eye in March-April when the erect branches are clothed
with vivid rosy-purple flowers. Actually
more showy than *C. canadensis.* 'Avondale' produces a profusion of deep rose-purple flowers.

Other species of merit in other parts of the U.S. and world include *C. occidentalis,* Western
Redbud, a shrub or small tree 10 to 12′ high which is native to California (Zone 7). *C. reniformis* is
closely related to *C. occidentalis* but ranges from Texas to New Mexico. Introduced 1901. Zone
7 to 9. I have seen the species or a selection called 'Oklahoma' that has the most lustrous waxy
rich green leaves of any redbud. 'Oklahoma' was discovered in the spring of 1964 in the Arbuckle
Mountains of Oklahoma, named and released by Warren and Son Nursery. Oklahoma City, OK
in 1965. The flowers are rich wine-red; the leaves rounded, thick textured, glossy, closely spaced;
budded trees flower after one year; T-bud in late July—early August. 'Texas White' offers similar
foliage and pure white flowers. Trees of both will grow 12 to 18′ tall. Whether this is normal for
the species I do not know. Tennessee Botanical Garden, Nashville, has a handsome specimen
of 'Oklahoma' (?) and Professor
McDaniel, Illinois, had a similar
form of *C. reniformis* at his Urbana home until *Verticillium* or
cold eliminated it. *C. siliquastrum,* Judas-tree, is the redbud of England and continental
Europe. It, as I have observed,
could easily be mistaken for our
native *C. canadensis.* In size it
ranges from 15 to 25′ but
specimens as large as 40′ are
known. Southern Europe,
western Asia. Cultivated since
ancient times. Zone 6. See
Robertson, *Arnoldia* 36: *Cercis*—The Redbuds (1976) for in
depth information.

Raulston provided me with a
plant of *C. chingii* and it

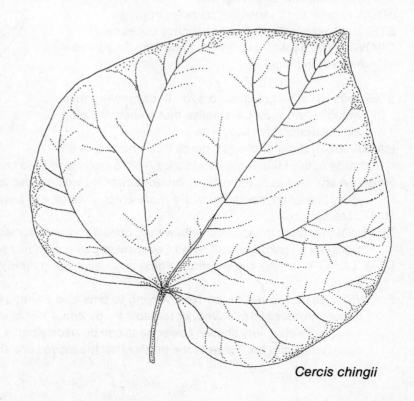

Cercis chingii

flowered in early February in the polyhouse. The color is a truer pink than *C. canadensis,* and the flowers are larger. I have used Raulston's original Newsletter description which is reproduced here in full:

"the most exciting and rarest plant in our collection. Grown from an accession of seed received from China in 1984, planted out to the arboretum bed in the spring of 1985, and our first few flowers were produced this spring. As far as I can determine it is not in cultivation in either Europe or the U.S. at this point. We grew 4 seedlings and sent one each to the Arnold Arboretum and the U.S. National Arboretum, and planted two in the arboretum. Both our plants flowered about 7 to 10 days before the eastern redbud and seemed pinker in color—but that needs another look next spring when we should have excellent flowering on much larger plants. At first I thought it might be simply another Chinese name applied to *C. chinensis* (as often happens with a variety of material I've received from there—e.g. *Cryptomeria japonica* is usually cited in Chinese seed lists as *C. fortunei*) but the plant is quite distinctly different with much more vigorous growth (some 4 to 5' whips last year, and that much more growth this year looks likely) and already a more treelike form. An unusual feature I've never noted on any of our other redbud species are large stipule-like growths at the base of leaves about 1/4 to 3/4" in diameter (*very* prominent on one plant, much less so on the other). I will be very anxious to see the flowering next spring, and particularly anxious to have seed produced so we can begin to distribute the plant elsewhere to test potential adaptability and use. What a thrill it was to daily watch the flower buds expand and realize it was possibly the first time for this species to flower in the western world!"

Chaenomeles speciosa — Common Floweringquince
(kē-nom'-e-lēz spē-si-ō'sa)

FAMILY: Rosaceae

LEAVES: Alternate, simple, ovate to oblong, 1 1/2 to 3 1/2" long, acute, sharply serrate, lustrous dark green above, glabrous, stipules large and conspicuous on current season's growth, up to 1 1/2" diameter, rounded, toothed.

BUDS: Similar to *C. japonica,* usually larger.

STEM: Slender, brownish, often slightly pubescent.

GROWTH HABIT: More upright in habit than *C. japonica;* 6 to 10' in height.

SIZE: 6 to 10' in height, spread 6 to 10' or greater; quite variable and may be smaller due to hybridization with *Chaenomeles japonica.*

HARDINESS: Zone 4 to 8 (9), no cultivars have proven hardy at the Minnesota Landscape Arboretum where lows can reach −25 to −30°F.

HABIT: A shrub of rounded outline, broad-spreading with tangled and dense twiggy mass of more or less spiny branches; some forms are more erect while others are quite rambling, variable in habit.

RATE: Medium.

TEXTURE: Medium in leaf; coarse in winter; collects leaves, bottles and trash in the twiggy network; rates highly as a "garbage can" shrub; over-rated plant, primarily because of flowers.

LEAF COLOR: Bronzy-red when unfolding gradually changing to dark, glossy green; fall color is nonexistent.

FLOWER: Scarlet to red in the type varying to pink and white; January-February-March in south; April further north; before leaves, borne solitary or 2 to 4 per cluster on old wood, each flower 1 1/2 to 1 3/4" diameter, very showy, flower buds can be killed when a freeze eliminates the expanding flower buds, usually in full flower in the north when the leaves are about one-half mature.

FRUIT: Pome, 2 to 2 1/2″ long and wide, yellowish green often with a reddish blush, fragrant, speckled with small dots (glands), ripening in October; fruits are quite bitter when eaten raw but when cooked are used for preserves and jellies.

CULTURE: Transplant balled and burlapped or from a container; adaptable to a wide range of soil conditions, performs well in dry situations; full sun or partial shade with best flowering in sun; develops chlorosis on high pH soils; renewal pruning either by eliminating the older branches or simply cutting the whole plant to within 6″ of the ground will result in more spectacular flower.

DISEASES AND INSECTS: Leaf spots result in premature defoliation, abundant rainfall in the spring and early summer can cause 50 to 75% defoliation by July; there are other problems (scale, mite) but none of an epidemic nature; aphids are prevalent on young stems and foliage.

LANDSCAPE VALUE: Excellent for flower effect when fully realized; range of flower colors is tremendous going from orange, reddish orange, scarlet, carmine, turkey red and white; there was a planting on the Illinois campus which in full flower was beautiful, however, during the rest of the year (50 to 51 weeks) the planting was intolerable; often used for hedge (makes a good barrier), shrub border, massing, grouping; I evaluate this species and its many cultivars as a single season plant (flower) and have discovered too many superior (multi-season) plants to justify using this extensively in the landscape; unfortunately it will continue to be widely sold because many people are only interested in flowers when in essence, this feature is the most short-lived of all ornamental attributes.

CULTIVARS: Abundant; Wyman noted that the Arnold Arboretum was growing 150 forms; most appropriate to check with the local nurseryman and note the color he has available; white, pink and scarlet tend to be the most commonly available colors; during sabbatical I evaluated the *Chaenomeles* collection at the Arnold and was left with the feeling that the differences between and among many of the cultivars were so minute as to be meaningless. I have included a few here that the nurseryman or homeowner might consider.

'Cameo'—One of the best double forms with fluffy, peachy-pink (apricot pink) flowers borne in profusion.

'Jet Trail'—A white-flowered sport of 'Texas Scarlet' with the qualities of the parent.

'Minerva'—Cherry-red flowers on a compact, low-growing shrub.

'Nivalis'—Upright form of vigorous constitution with pure white flowers.

'Spitfire'—A vivid red flowered form of upright habit.

'Texas Scarlet'—Many consider this the best tomato-red flowered form because of its spreading habit and profuse flowers that are borne on a rather compact spreading plant.

'Toyo-Nishiki'—Upright grower with pink, white, red and combination colored flowers on the same branch, very pretty, has shown greater susceptibility to fireblight than others.

PROPAGATION: Cuttings collected in August, dipped in 1000 ppm IBA solution rooted 100% in peat:perlite medium under mist; seed requires 2 to 3 months at 41°F.

ADDITIONAL NOTES: Often flowers sporadically late into spring and, again in fall, will show some color; interesting but not overwhelming as are the flowers which develop in late winter and early spring.

NATIVE HABITAT: China, cultivated in Japan. Introduced before 1800.

RELATED SPECIES:

Chaenomeles japonica — Japanese Floweringquince
(kē-nom′-e-lēz ja-pon′i-ka)

LEAVES: Alternate, simple, broad-ovate to obovate, 1 to 2″ long, obtuse or acutish, coarsely crenate-serrate, glabrous; stipules large on young shoots, ovate or broadly heart-shaped, 1/4 to 3/4″ wide.

BUDS: Imbricate, solitary, sessile, round-ovoid, with few exposed scales, brown.

STEM: Slender, dark gray to brown, glabrous, sometimes spiny.

GROWTH HABIT: Low growing, densely branched shrub to 3′.

Chaenomeles japonica, Japanese Floweringquince, forms an interlacing network of thorny stems in a wide-spreading usually 2 to 3′ high framework; flowers orange-red, scarlet or blood-red on year-old wood; each flower about 1 1/2″ across, early to mid April (before *C. speciosa*); fruit is a greenish yellow, fragrant, 1 1/2″ diameter pome, late September to October. A ratty shrub whose use should be tempered by astute judgment; not as ornamental as *C. speciosa;* native of Japan. Cultivated 1874. *Chaenomeles × superba* represents a hybrid species between *C. japonica × C. speciosa.* Usually they are low spreading shrubs, 4 to 5′ in height; most characters are intermediate between the parents; flower colors range from white, pink, crimson to shades of orange and orange-scarlet. Quite difficult to distinguish among various *C. × superba* forms and *C. speciosa* forms.

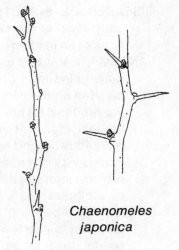

Chaenomeles japonica

Chamaecyparis — Falsecypress
Cupressaceae

At one time I would have said that the falsecypress might as well be omitted from midwestern and southern landscapes but the more I travel the more convinced I become that many of the cultivars are suitable for these regions. *Chamaecyparis* is generally considered the least important of the smaller evergreens used in contemporary landscaping. They appear frequently on the east and west coast in cooler, more humid regions. All, except *C. thyoides* of eastern North America, are native of the lands bordering the Pacific Ocean, two in western north America and the other three in Formosa and Japan. With the exception of *C. formosensis* all the species are hardy. Cultivars of *C. obtusa* and *C. pisifera* are most common in the U.S. trade although *C. lawsoniana* has yielded many cultivars that are used extensively in European gardens. The leaves of seedling and juvenile plants are very distinct from those of adult trees, being needle-like or awl-shaped, up to 1/3″ long and spreading. Formerly plants with these features were placed in the genus *Retinospora,* but this genus is no longer recognized. It is interesting to note that some juvenile forms of more recent origin, having produced neither cones nor reversion shoots, still cannot be placed with certainty, either as to species or even to genus. It is easy to confuse *Thuja* with *Chamaecyparis,* however, the cones differ and the lateral leaves nearly cover the facial in the former, whereas in the latter, the facial leaves are more exposed.

MORPHOLOGICAL CHARACTERISTICS
Monoecious trees, pyramidal, leading shoots nodding; branchlets mostly frond-like, usually flattened; leaves opposite, scale-like (awl-shaped only in the juvenile state), ovate to rhombic, pointed or obtuse; flowers borne terminally on lateral branchlets; male flowers ovoid or oblong, yellow, rarely red, often conspicuous by their large number, stamens with 2 to 4 anther-cells; female flowers small, globular, less conspicuous; cones globose, short-stalked, solitary, ripening the first season (except *C. nootkatensis,* cones of which ripen in the second year); scales 6 to 8 (seldom 4, or 10 to 12), peltate, pointed or bossed in the middle; seeds (1)–2, rarely up to 5 per scale, slightly compressed; wings broad, thin, cotyledons 2.

GROWTH CHARACTERISTICS
The *Chamaecyparis* species are large pyramidal, almost columnar trees with pendulous branches at the tips. All but *C. thyoides* can regularly grow to over 100 feet in native stands; however, they are generally (about 50%) smaller under landscape conditions and can be maintained at suitable heights by proper pruning. The species are seldom in evidence in landscape plantings but many of the cultivars are excellent and offer diversity of form, color and texture.

CULTURE
Falsecypress does best in full sun in rich, moist, well-drained soil. They thrive in a cool, moist atmosphere where they are protected from drying winds. *C. thyoides* is found in fresh-water swamps and bogs, wet depressions and along stream banks and would obviously withstand less than perfect drainage. *C. obtusa* and *C. pisifera* types seem best adapted to the midwest and south. Fall or spring transplanting with a ball

of soil or as a container plant are satisfactory. Pruning is best accomplished in spring although branches can be removed about anytime.

DISEASES AND INSECTS
Falsecypress is relatively free of serious problems although blight *(Phomopsis juniperovora)*, witches broom, spindle burl gall, root rot and other minor insect pests have been noted.

PROPAGATION
Seed germination is usually low, due in part to poor seed quality, and also to various factors of embryo dormancy. In general, 2 to 3 months at 41°F is advisable. See specific recommendations under each species. Softwood or hardwood cuttings are the principal means of propagation although a few difficult to root types may be grafted.

LANDSCAPE USE
Falsecypress can be used for about any landscape situation if the proper cultivar is chosen. They make good hedges, screens, foundations, and border plants. Some of the cultivars make strong accent or specimen plants and their use should be tempered so as not to detract from the total landscape. If not properly cared for the species will become ratty, open, and sorrowful looking. As a genus, this is relatively unimportant when compared to *Thuja, Juniperus,* and *Taxus;* for few plants are used in contemporary midwestern and southern landscapes.

SELECTED CULTIVARS
The following cultivars are recommended for general use. Most of these are available in the trade.
- *C. nootkatensis* 'Pendula'
- *C. obtusa* 'Filicoides'
- *C. obtusa* 'Nana'
- *C. obtusa* 'Nana Gracilis'
- *C. obtusa* 'Tetragona Aurea'
- *C. pisifera* 'Boulevard'
- *C. pisifera* 'Filifera'
- *C. pisifera* 'Filifera Aurea'
- *C. pisifera* 'Plumosa' and types
- *C. pisifera* 'Squarrosa' and types

Chamaecyparis lawsoniana — Lawson Falsecypress or Port Orford Cedar
(kam-e-sip′ä-ris lâ-sō-ni-ā′na)

LEAVES: Closely pressed, arranged in opposite pairs marked with indistinct white streaks on the under-surface; the lateral pair keel-shaped, 1/16 to 1/12″ long, slightly overlapping on the facial pair, which are rhomboidal and much smaller, about 1/20″ long, often glandular pitted, those on the main axis oblong, unequal; the lateral pair 1/4″, the facial pair 1/5″ long, with short or long spreading points.
STEM: Flattened, frond-like, arranged in a horizontal plane; entire spray deep green to glaucous green and not developing the prominent whitish markings on the underside.

SIZE: Almost impossible to estimate landscape size but 40 to 60′ high under landscape conditions is reasonable; can grow 140 to 180′ high and greater in the wild.
HARDINESS: Zone 5 to 7, possibly 8; does not thrive in excessive heat.
HABIT: A pyramidal to conical tree with massive, buttressed trunk and short ascending branches, drooping at the tips and ending in flat sprays.
RATE: Medium.
TEXTURE: Medium.
BARK: Silvery brown to reddish brown, fibrous, divided into thick, rounded ridges separated by deep irregular furrows 6 to 10″ thick on old trees.

LEAF COLOR: Glaucous green to deep green above.

FLOWERS: Monoecious, staminate-crimson, pistillate steely-blue.

FRUIT: Cones numerous, globose, 1/3" across, at first bluish green, afterwards reddish brown, bloomy; scales 8, with thin, pointed, reflexed bosses, each with 2 to 4 seeds; seeds oblong, appressed, glossy brown, broadly winged.

CULTURE: Transplanted balled and burlapped if root pruned; prefers well-drained, moist soil; full sun or partial shade; shelter from winds, supposedly does not like chalky soils; in south inadequate drainage and high night temperatures spell doom.

DISEASES AND INSECTS: Until recently it was thought this tree to be insect and disease free, but there is a fungus, *Phytophthora lateralis,* which is devastating the species; it does its main damage by rotting the root system, which in turn kills the tree.

LANDSCAPE VALUE: A very handsome specimen with beautiful foliage and graceful habit for gardens and plantations where it can be grown; has numerous variations for form and color.

CULTIVARS: The number of selections staggers even the most ardent plantsman. For some unknown reason, I have never gotten excited with the species and the cultivars. In recent years, I have mellowed and now appreciate how truly stately and elegant the larger forms can be especially as viewed in European gardens. Many dwarf forms exist and are available from specialist nurseries. I have not seen outstanding, in most cases even mediocre, specimens in the eastern United States. Practicality points toward *C. obtusa* and *C. pisifera* for the eastern United States. Interestingly some of the large west coast producers like Monrovia and Iseli do not list *C. lawsoniana* or its cultivars. Krüssmann in *Manual of Cultivated Conifers* lists 238 cultivars of *C. lawsoniana.*

PROPAGATION: Germination of Falsecypress seed is characteristically low, due in part to poor seed quality, and also to various degrees of embryo dormancy. Sound, unstratified seeds of *C. lawsoniana* have germinated completely on moist paper in less than 28 days at diurnally alternating temperatures of 86°F for 8 hours and 68°F for 16 hours with light during the warm periods. However, in Britain, presowing stratification has yielded the most consistent results. Stratification for 60 to 90 days at 41°F is recommended. This species is easily propagated by cuttings taken in fall. Cuttings taken in October and placed untreated in sand:peat rooted 90% or more. Untreated cuttings taken in January rooted equally well but more slowly. IBA treatments will hasten rooting.

ADDITIONAL NOTES: This species performs best where there is an abundance of soil and atmostpheric moisture although it is less exacting in this respect than Redwood, *Sequoia sempervirens,* and frequently occurs on rather high, dry, sandy ridges which are often 30 to 40 miles inland.

NATIVE HABITAT: Southwestern Oregon and isolated parts of northwestern California. Introduced 1854.

Chamaecyparis obtusa — Hinoki Falsecypress
(kam-e-sip′ä-ris ob-tū-sa)

LEAVES: Closely pressed, of 2 sizes, the lateral pair much the larger, boat-shaped, 1/12" long, blunt at the apex or with a minute point; the smaller pairs about 1/24" long, triangular, with a thickened apex, all prominently lined beneath with white X-shaped markings produced by a coating of wax along the margin, dark green above.

STEM: Flattened, slightly drooping at the tips.

SIZE: 50 to 75′ in height with a 10 to 20′ spread.

HARDINESS: Zone 4 to 8; some cultivars are being grown in Athens, GA.

HABIT: A tall, slender pyramid with spreading branches and drooping, frondlike branchlets.

RATE: Medium (25′ in 20 years).

TEXTURE: Medium.

BARK: Reddish brown, shed in long narrow strips.

LEAF COLOR: Shining dark green above, whitish markings beneath.

FLOWERS: Monoecious, staminate yellow, pistillate solitary.

FRUIT: Cones short-stalked, solitary, globose, 1/3″ across, orange-brown; scales 8, rarely 10, depressed on the back and with a small mucro; seed-2 to 5 on each scale, convex or nearly triangular on both margins, often with 2 glands, wings narrow, membranous.

CULTURE: Supposedly somewhat difficult to transplant but most of the cultivars are container-grown and move without great difficulty as is true with most *Chamaecyparis;* this species prefers a moist, well-drained soil and moderately humid atmosphere in a sunny, protected (from wind) area; according to an English reference the species and its cultivars thrive in moist, neutral soils and in those that have decided acid tendencies; from my own observations I would have to rank the cultivars of this species about the best suited for landscape use.

LANDSCAPE VALUE: Useful as a specimen; dwarf forms valuable for rock gardens and that different landscape touch; dark green foliage is particularly handsome.

CULTIVARS:

'Crippsii'—Broad pyramid, branches spreading, branchlets broadly frond-like, tops decurving, rich golden yellow, changing to green within plant, yellowish at ends of sprays.

'Filicoides'—A bush or small tree of open, irregular habit, branches long and straggly, clothed with dense pendulous clusters of fern-spray, green foliage.

'Nana'—Very slow growing type to about 3′ in height and slightly broader, a 90 year-old specimen was 20″ high and 25″ wide; often confused with the following cultivar.

'Nana Gracilis'—Has thick dark green foliage; grows slowly to a height of about 6′ and has a spread of 3 to 4′; makes a pyramidal bush; fine form.

It is hopeless to list all the cultivars of this species. Many are so close in morphological features that as small plants it is impossible to distinguish among them. I have seen the fine dwarf conifer collection at the Arnold Arboretum and was thoroughly impressed by the many types of falsecypress. Mr. Al Fordham, the propagator at the Arnold, showed me some seedlings of Hinoki Falsecypress which had been grown from seed collected from a dwarf clone. The variation was endless and the possibilities for introducing more dwarf forms existed. I also saw a large seedling population which was grown from a yellow foliaged form of *C. pisifera.* Again, there were many different types for some had yellow foliage, some blue or bluish green, others had juvenile needles while some showed adult foliage. The bottom line translates to production of new and different cultivars of falsecypress is about as simple as sowing seed.

PROPAGATION: Considerable variation in cutting rootability among different cultivars of this species; cuttings of the species and the cultivars 'Nana', 'Compacta', 'Lycopodioides', 'Filicoides', 'Gracilis' and 'Magnifica' were taken eleven times between late September and late January; the average percentage of rooting of untreated cuttings was 41%. Rooting of cuttings treated with 50 to 100 ppm IBA/18 to 24 hours soak, or 8000 ppm IBA-talc was 96%. Cutting wood was collected from current season's growth although 2 and 3-year-old wood also rooted; untreated cuttings rooted equally well when taken from September through January.

NATIVE HABITAT: Japan and Formosa. Introduced 1861.

RELATED SPECIES:

Chamaecyparis nootkatensis, (kam-e-sip'ä-ris noot-ka-ten'sis), Nootka Falsecypress, Alaska-cedar, Yellow-cypress, is a medium-sized tree reaching 60 to 90′ in the wild but one-half of that under cultivation. The crown is conical and composed of numerous drooping branches with long, pendulous, flattened sprays. The leaves are a dark bluish green or grayish green, 1/8 to 1/4″ long, pointed, scale-like, with the tips often diverging, occasionally glandular on the back; turning brown during the second season but persistent until the third. The leaves do not possess white markings on the underside and are rank-smelling when bruised or rubbed. Branchlets are often quadrangular. Cones 1/3 to 1/2″ across, globose, glaucous, with 4(6) scales furnished with a triangular pointed boss, ripens in 2nd year. This species does best where both soil and atmospheric moisture are abundant. Not seen in cultivation too extensively compared to *C. obtusa* and *C. pisifera* and their clones. There is a rather attractive pendulous form ('Pendula') that has become increasingly common in the eastern United States. Beautiful, graceful, elegantly arranged pendulous branches and rich green foliage. Native from Coastal Alaska to Washington; the Cascades to Oregon. Zone 4 to 7 (8). Introduced 1853.

Chamaecyparis pisifera — Sawara or Japanese Falsecypress
(kam-e-sip′ä-ris pī-sif′ēr-a)

LEAVES: Appressed, long pointed, ovate-lanceolate, with slightly spreading tips, obscurely glandular, dark green above, with whitish lines beneath; branchlets flattened, 2-ranked and arranged in horizontal planes.

SIZE: 50 to 70′ in height by 10 to 20′ in width.
HARDINESS: Zone 4 to 8.
HABIT: A pyramidal tree with a loose open habit and numerous branchlets thickly covered with slender feathery sprays.
RATE: Medium.
TEXTURE: Medium.
BARK: Rather smooth, reddish brown, peeling off in thin strips, extremely handsome.
LEAF COLOR: Dark green above with whitish lines beneath.
FLOWERS: Monoecious, small, inconspicuous.
FRUIT: Cones crowded, short-stalked, globose, 1/4″ across, yellowish brown; scales 10 to 12, soft-woody, upper side wrinkled, the middle depressed, with a small mucro at the depression; seeds 1 to 2, ovoid, bulbous on both sides, glandular; wing broad, membranous, notched above and below.
CULTURE: Moist, loamy, well-drained; humid climate; sunny, open conditions; prefers lime-free soils.
LANDSCAPE VALUE: Handsome when small but may lose its beauty with old age as the lower branches die; the chief advantage lies in the many cultivars which have a place in various parts of the landscape, especially in rock gardens or as accent plants.
CULTIVARS:
　‘Boulevard’ (‘Squarrosa Cyano-viridis’)—Foliage is similar to above but silvery blue-green in summer and grayish blue in winter; up to 10′ high and rather narrow-pyramidal, reasonably heat-tolerant.
　‘Filifera’—Has drooping stringy branches and forms a dense mound, usually no higher than 6 to 8′ after 10 to 15 years although can become quite large; very fine textured, a lovely and different accent plant.
　‘Filifera Aurea’—Similar to above with yellow foliage; quite striking, rather obtrusive especially in winter; 15 to 20′.
　‘Plumosa’—Foliage is very soft textured, almost feathery in constitution; large plant 30 to 50′, tree-like.
　‘Plumosa Aurea’—Soft, feathery golden yellow foliage; retains considerable color throughout the summer and ranks among the best in this respect; slower than above but easily 20 to 30′ high.
　‘Squarrosa’—Foliage is almost needle-like, very feathery, definitely not flat and frond-like; soft gray-green foliage; large plant, 30 to 40′.
PROPAGATION: Cuttings should be taken in October, November and December, treated with 1000 ppm IBA and placed in sand:peat; there are other manipulations which can be performed to increase rootability but the above should work for most clones.
ADDITIONAL NOTES: Four more or less distinct foliage classes are distinguishable, each harboring a number of cultivars. Logically, one should attempt to assess the foliage category for an unknown cultivar and then proceed with the detective work. The categories include:
　1.　*Normal:* Foliage is similar to the species and cultivars vary in color and/or habit.
　2.　*Filifera* (Threadleaf Falsecypress): The main branchlets become stringy and cord-like without the typical flattened sprays of the normal group. The silver markings on the underside of the foliage are not detectable. The most common form in cultivation is ‘Filifera Aurea’, a rather ghastly form that can grow 15 to 20′ high. In my worst dreams, the large specimen by the waterfall at Longwood Gardens always surfaces. ‘Filifera’, the green form, can grow 40 to 50′. ‘Filifera Nana’ is a handsome dwarf green form that is preferable to its large relative. Occasionally a ‘Filifera Aurea Nana’ is listed but the ultimate size is unknown to this author. Plants I have seen appear more compact and rounded than ‘Filifera Aurea’. ‘Golden Mop’ is a true compact yellow-foliaged form that is sold in the United States.

3. *Plumosa* (Plume Falsecypress): In most respects like the species but more airy and ferny in texture because the opposite awl-shaped leaves stand out at a 45° angle to the stem. Even though the leaves are awl shaped they are soft to the touch unlike many junipers with a common form. Grows into a good size, 20 to 30′ high tree under cultivation. The silver markings are distinguishable on the underside of the sprays. On the Illinois and Georgia campuses, 'Plumosa' has survived (notice I did not say prosper) for many years. 'Plumosa Aurea', as mentioned under cultivars, is common in the trade. Plants over 60′ high have been recorded.

4. *Squarrosa* (Moss Falsecypress): Has the feel of a soft fluffy stuffed animal and serves as a substitute pacifier for adult gardeners who are embarrassed to carry their furry bears. Foliage shows a more juvenile condition than plumosa types. Foliage is dense, silvery glaucous blue and borne on rather billowy branches; the entire plant becoming irregularly fluffy. Needles are about 1/4″ long, narrow, flat, glaucous on both surfaces and stand out 45 to 90° from the stem. 'Boulevard' as described above, is one of the most common. 'Squarrosa Pygmaea' is a cuddly, soft blue foliaged globe that provides sparkle to a rock garden. This clone is quite common and tends to produce reversion shoots which should be removed. 'Squarrosa' is a large plant and many fine specimens occur in New England, especially Cape Cod where 30 to 40′ is the norm.

    Perhaps southern gardeners have missed the landscape boat by not experimenting with the cultivars of *C. obtusa* and *C. pisifera*. I suspect that the high summer night temperatures (+ 65°F) may contribute to their slower growth in the south. A neighbor has a number of *C. p.* 'Boulevard' that were 3′ high in 1979 and are 8′ in 1989. A campus plant in full sun and compacted soil grew even less. This same plant appeared to develop more brown dead needles toward the interior. Interestingly, I always query the students about the correct identification of 'Boulevard'. Most have no idea where to start with identification because keys were not written for juvenile foliage forms.

NATIVE HABITAT: Japan. Introduced 1861.

Chamaecyparis thyoides — Whitecedar Falsecypress or Atlantic Whitecedar
(kam-e-sip′ä-ris thī-oy′dēz)

LEAVES: Bluish green to glaucous-green with white margins, 1/10 to 1/12″ long, lateral pairs boat-shaped with sharp-pointed, spreading tips, facial pairs closely pressed, ovate-triangular, short-pointed, flat or keeled; most of the green to bluish leaves are marked on the back with a resinous gland; leaves turn brown the second year but persist for several years.

STEM: Branchlets slender, rather irregularly arranged (not flattened), spreading, not decurving, very thin.

SIZE: 40 to 50′ high, 10 to 20′ spread; can grow 75′ and larger.

HARDINESS: Zone 3 to 8.

HABIT: A slender column in youth, forming a narrow spirelike crown at maturity devoid of branches for 3/4's of its length.

RATE: Medium (25′ in 20 years).

TEXTURE: Medium.

BARK: Thin, on old trunks 3/4″ to 1″ thick, ashy gray to reddish brown.

LEAF COLOR: Green to bluish green turning brown the second year, but persistent for several years.

FLOWERS: Monoecious, small, staminate red or yellow and abundant; pistillate green, few.

FRUIT: Cones on small branchlets, globose, small, 1/4″ across, a bluish purple, bloomy; scales 4 to 5, rarely 6, acute often with a reflexed base; seeds 1 or 2 on each scale, oblong; wing narrow, as broad as the seed.

CULTURE: In the wild, characteristic of fresh-water swamps and bogs, wet depressions, or stream banks, and is rarely found except on such sites; extensive pure stands are the rule, occurring on shallow-peat covered soils underlain with sand; under cultivation it is best to provide a moist, sandy soil; prefers full sun and cannot compete with hardwood species.

DISEASES AND INSECTS: None serious.

LANDSCAPE VALUE: Useful on low lands and boggy sites where it is native; performs well in garden situations.

CULTIVARS: Over the past few years I have bumped into a few of the compact cultivars. Probably will never replace juniper but worth the effort for the true gardener.

'Andelyensis'—Compact, slow growing, broad pyramidal form to 10', always with several main branches at the top, i.e., never a clear central leader; bright blue-green in summer turning purplish green in winter, aromatic when bruised, produces abundant cones.

'Hopkinton'—Selected by Weston Nursery for narrow habit, rapid growth and aromatic blue-gray needles, produces numerous cones; might be worth using in moist areas where other Falsecypress, Leyland Cypress, upright junipers and yews would suffer.

PROPAGATION: Supposedly somewhat difficult to root from cuttings but cuttings taken in mid-November and treated with 125 ppm IBA/24 hour soak rooted 96% in sand:peat in 6 months; cuttings taken in mid-December and placed in sand:peat rooted 14% without treatment and 70% with 8000ppm IBA-talc.

ADDITIONAL NOTES: Quite an interesting species because of its adaptability to wet, boggy sites; not a good competitor in the wild and it avoids competition by growing in these wet habitats. I have seen considerable stands in Maine and Massachusetts. Perhaps one of the most beautiful is the White Cedar Swamp in the Cape Cod National Seashore where an interpretive trail walk leads one through a native stand.

NATIVE HABITAT: Eastern United States in swamps, along the Atlantic coast from Maine to Florida. Introduced 1727.

Chimonanthus praecox — Fragrant Wintersweet
(kī′mo-nan′thus prā′koks)

FAMILY: Calycanthaceae

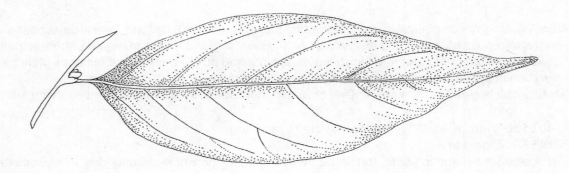

LEAVES: Opposite, simple, elliptic-ovate to ovate-lanceolate, 2 1/2 to 6″ long, acuminate, rounded or cuneate at base, entire, glabrous, lustrous dark green, rough to the touch above, almost like sandpaper; petiole—1/4 to 1/2″ long.

BUDS: Flower—imbricate, greenish brown, glabrous, appearing as stalked globes, 1/4 to 3/8″ long and wide, opening in December–January; vegetative—small, 1/8″ long, imbricate, green-brown, borne at 45° angle to stem, glabrous.

STEM: Somewhat squarish, stout, glabrous, shiny gray-brown, prominently covered with orangish brown lenticels, compressed at nodes, when bruised does not have the strong odor of *Calycanthus,* actually rather stinky; pith—white, solid, ample.

SIZE: 10 to 15′ high and 8 to 12′ wide in south, less in north to Philadelphia where the winters may regulate size.

HARDINESS: Zone 6 or 7 to 9.

HABIT: Large multistemmed shrub usually with fountain-like outline; with age becomes quite leggy and ragged; can be pruned to within 6 to 12″ of the ground in late winter and will rejuvenate.

RATE: Considered slow.

TEXTURE: Medium to coarse.

LEAF COLOR: Lustrous dark green changing to yellow-green in fall; does not overwhelm one in fall but the combination of yellow and green leaves is rather handsome, i.e., does not have to apologize for its fall performance; have observed foliage in early January in Athens, GA.

FLOWERS: Perfect, fragrant, transparent yellow on outside grading to purple in the middle, each flower 3/4 to 1″ across, borne singly on leafless branches in the axils of the previous summer's wood, opening over a long period of time depending on the mildness of the winter, often from December to January–February in the Athens–Atlanta, Georgia areas; may be injured by cold in more northern gardens; wonderfully fragrant when all goes right.

FRUIT: One to 2″ long urn-shaped receptacle, 5 to 8 shining brown fruits (achenes) are held within this structure; not ornamental; fruit set apparent by April, can be collected, harvested and sown by late May.

CULTURE: Easily transplanted; adaptable to varied soils, needs good drainage; prune out old canes after flowering; full sun or partial shade.

DISEASES AND INSECTS: None serious.

LANDSCAPE VALUE: In the southern states, it makes a prized winter flowering shrub; it appears that some protection (a courtyard, wall) prevents excessive flower bud damage; can be used in a shrub border but is best employed along walks and entrances to buildings; the fragrance is the principal ornamental characteristic; cut branches may be brought inside and used in floral arrangements; flowers were fully open in January, 1982 when 0°F temperatures and 4″ of snow graced the Athens area, surprisingly the flowers held up reasonably well although some injury occurred; my flower dates over the past 8 years indicate that mid-January is peak flowering period; flowers are never overwhelming but when backlighted by the sun almost sparkle.

CULTIVARS: To my knowledge the following cultivars are not common in this country; however, they are worth listing. There is need for a compact form of the species.

'Grandiflorus'—Flowers purer yellow and more showy than the species; may reach 1 3/4″ diameter but are not as fragrant; the leaves may be larger and the overall habit larger.

'Luteus' ('Mangetsu')—In the previous edition, I mentioned a pure golden yellow form without any trace of purple. The bright yellow petals are not transparent. I have one small plant that put out one flower in 6 years. In fact, my note says late January, 1984, pure golden yellow. Outstanding though it was, I wait for a second. The plant has been shuffled throughout my garden but appears less than satisfied. Seedlings I grew from campus plants at the same age are 6 to 8′ tall.

PROPAGATION: Seeds will germinate readily if collected in late May or June when the receptacles are changing from green to brown; at this stage the seed coat (actually pericarp wall) is quite soft and can be broken with a fingernail; if seeds are allowed to dry out and the seed coat becomes hard, germination is reduced to less than 5% compared to 90 plus percent for the soft seeds. Cuttings are described as difficult to root but my experiences at Georgia have led me to believe this is not the case. Cuttings were collected in late July from a mature, 15′ high shrub; they were given a 3000 ppm IBA quick dip and placed in peat:perlite under mist; the wood was quite hard and growth had stopped by the time the cuttings were taken; 70 percent of the cuttings developed strong root systems and 3 made it through winter. I suspect that cuttings taken from rejuvenated shrubs would root in higher percentages than old wood cuttings.

ADDITIONAL NOTES: See Dirr, *American Nurseryman* 154(8):9, 40, 42, (1981) for detailed information. Raulston gave me *Chimonanthus nitens,* which appears to be rank growing like its cousin but not as tall. The leaves are lustrous dark green, glabrous and 3 to 4″ long, 1 1/2″ wide, flowers are white, 3/4″ diameter, borne in the axils of the leaves, weakly fragrant. The plant will not replace *C. praecox* but offers interest for the collector. China.

NATIVE HABITAT: China. Introduced 1766.

Chionanthus virginicus — White Fringetree, Grancy Gray-beard, Old-man's-beard
(kī-ō-nan'thus ver-jin'i-kus)

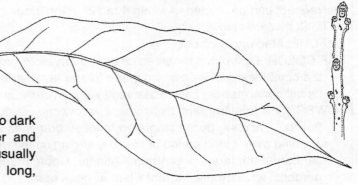

LEAVES: Opposite or subopposite, simple, narrow-elliptic to oblong or obovate-oblong, 3 to 8″ long, 1/2 as wide, acute or acuminate, cuneate, entire, medium to dark green and often lustrous above, paler and pubescent at least on veins beneath, usually becoming glabrate; petiole 1/2 to 1″ long, downy.

BUDS: Terminal-present, ovoid with keeled scales, acute, 1/8″ long, green to brown, 3 pairs of sharp-pointed keeled scales, angled appearance when looked upon from apical end.

STEM: Rather stout, green to buff to brown, glabrous or pubescent when young, slightly squarish, epidermis peeling to give onion-skin effect; have looked at many *C. virginicus* and some have quite hairy almost tomentose stems, others glabrous; have also noticed stem color is a rich dark purple-brown on certain plants and the color persists into late summer–fall.

SIZE: In the wild may reach 25 to 30′ with an equal spread but under landscape conditions is often a shrub or small tree 12 to 20′ with an equal spread.

HARDINESS: Zone 3 to 9.

HABIT: Large shrub or small tree with a spreading, rather open habit; often wider than high; the range of shapes is as variable as the stem characteristics, some open and straggly; others bushy, robust; others treelike.

RATE: Slow, under ideal conditions possibly 8 to 10′ in 10 years but plants I have observed in the midwest averaged only about 4 to 6″/year over a five year period; a 7-year old plant in my garden is 10′ high.

TEXTURE: Medium-coarse in leaf, fine in flower, medium in winter.

BARK: Gray, smooth on young branches; finally slightly ridged and furrowed.

LEAF COLOR: Medium to dark green, sometimes lustrous, in summer; fall coloring is usually yellowish-green-brown but can range from a bright to golden yellow; have observed good yellow on selected specimens.

FLOWER: Dioecious or polygamo-dioecious, white, slightly fragrant, males more effective than females because of longer petals, each petal 3/4 to 1 1/4″ long, 1/16 to 1/12″ wide, borne in 6 to 8″ long, fine, fleecy, soft textured panicles in May (early to mid in Athens) to early June just as leaves are expanding to point of complete development, on previous season's wood; one of our more handsome native plants in flower; each flower stalk of the panicle bears 3 flowers and emerges from the axil of a 1 to 1 1/2″ long leaf-like bract; bracts persist until fruits ripen.

FRUIT: Dark blue, bloomy, fleshy egg-shaped drupe, 1/2 to 2/3″ long, effective in August–September; interesting but often overlooked because the fruits are partially hidden by the foliage, birds relish them; invariably ripen by mid August in Athens.

CULTURE: Transplant balled and burlapped in spring; supposedly difficult to move although several nurserymen I have talked with indicated they have had no problems; prefers deep, moist, fertile, acid soils but is extremely adaptable; full sun; pruning is rarely required; in the wild is most commonly found along streambanks or the borders of swamps.

DISEASES AND INSECTS: None serious, occasionally scale, borer, perhaps ash, has been reported, leaf spots, powdery mildew and canker.

LANDSCAPE VALUE: Very beautiful specimen shrub, excellent in groups, borders, near large buildings; outstanding in flower; will do well in cities as it is quite air pollution tolerant; I would like to make a case for this as the national shrub for even dogwood does not carry itself with such refinement, dignity and class when in flower; possibly not considered sufficiently hardy but is prospering in Orono, ME,

Manchester, NH and Chicago, IL. In fact, the Manchester specimen by the Art Museum will perpetually linger in my memory as one of the largest specimens I have observed. On a chilly October day, Peter Kidd, Phil Caldwell and I perused every Manchesterian nook and cranny for unusual plants. I look forward to returning. Becoming more available in commerce and several mailorder firms like Wayside Gardens, Hodges, SC and Woodlanders, Aiken, SC offer the plant.

CULTIVARS: Although the plant is difficult to propagate vegetatively the Dutch have grafted selected forms onto *Fraxinus ornus* and *F. excelsior.* Doubtfully, will the plants be long lived. I saw Dutch grafted stock in a Georgia nursery and was impressed by the large leathery dark green leves but also noticed the suckering ash understock.

'Floyd'—The only American named clone that I know; named by Professor J.C. McDaniel, *PIPPS* 19(1969) for upright growth habit, neater large flower panicles, predominately male, but with some perfect flowers since a light smattering of fruit is produced; doubtfully in commerce.

The possibilities for selections are endless and a particularly fine lustrous dark green narrow-leaf seedling in my garden resists every propagation attempt. A correlation appears to exist between leaf width and petal diameter: the wider the leaf the wider the petal and conversely. Two to three-year-old plants may flower and I purchased two such plants for my garden. This is an indication that juvenility is lost at an early age which may correspond to miserable rooting results even with young seedlings.

PROPAGATION: Seed possesses a double dormancy and requires a warm period of 3 to 5 months, during which a root unit is made while the shoot remains dormant; then cold temperature at 41°F for one or more months overcomes the shoot dormancy; if sown in fall outside, seed germinates the second spring; first year seedlings do not put on much shoot extension; Dr. John Frett, one of my former graduate students, has extracted embryos from August collected seed and incubated them on a gibberellic acid:nutrient solution; these embryos greened up and produced both shoots and roots; based on John's work the dormancy is fairly complex and appears to involve a hard, bony endocarp that must be broken down, inhibitors in the endosperm and then a dormancy in the shoot portion of the embryo. Until 1987 I had never rooted cuttings and have taken wood from 3-year-old seedlings which should still be juvenile. Alcohol quick dips result in rapid deterioration of cuttings and talc preparations appear to be necessary. I suspect that cuttings taken from rejuvenated shrubs would root in higher percentages than old wood cuttings. Peter Del Tridici and I set up an elaborate rooting experiment at the Arnold with different rooting compounds and concentrations. Nothing worked on *C. virginicus* but some rooting did occur on *C. retusus*. *C. retusus* has essentially the same seed requirements (perhaps shorter) as *C. virginicus* but it can be rooted from cuttings. I know of one Tennessee nurseryman who is rooting *C. retusus* in commercial quantities. A Tennessee report noted that cuttings of *C. retusus* should be taken as they harden, wound, 8000 ppm IBA talc with early July and mid-July cuttings rooting 85 and 95%, respectively. In the past few years, I have used 10000 ppm KIBA on early June *C. retusus* cuttings, peat:perlite, mist, 8 to 10 week period, with 40 to 50% success. Have rooted *C. virginicus* in low percentages at the same time from a six-year-old plant using same procedure with perlite medium. Rooting took 12 to 14 weeks and several cuttings were successfully overwintered.

ADDITIONAL NOTES: I could ramble for pages but suggest the insatiable "Chionanthus-phile" read Fagan and Dirr, *American Nurseryman* 152(7):14–15, 114–117 (1980). Considered by the British to be one of the finest American plants introduced into their gardens. Although native to southeast, it is perfectly hardy in Maine and Minnesota. In the wild is found in a variety of habitats. A pink flowered form has been described but is nowhere to be found.

NATIVE HABITAT: Southern New Jersey to Florida and Texas. Introduced 1736.

RELATED SPECIES:

Chionanthus pygmaeus, (kī-ō-nan'thus pig-mē'us), Dwarf Fringetree, is a dwarf form from the sandy soils of Florida that flowers with the same intensity and character as *C. virginicus* yet on a smaller framework. I have seen plants in Aiken, SC about 3 to 4′ high literally dripping with large fleecy, white panicles in mid to late April.

Chionanthus retusus—Chinese Fringetree

LEAVES: Opposite, subopposite, narrow-elliptic to oblong or obovate-oblong and on some forms almost rounded, 3 to 8″ long, acute or acuminate, cuneate, lustrous dark green, either thick and leathery or rather thin, usually glabrous at maturity; petiole—1/2 to 1″ long.

Chionanthus retusus, (kī-ō-nan'thus rē-tū'-sus), Chinese Fringetree, is a large multistemmed shrub in cultivation but can be grown as a small tree. Usually reaches 15 to 25′ in height but may grow 30 to 40′ in the wild. The outline is spreading, rounded. The gray bark may be peeling or tightly ridged and furrowed. The leaves are leathery, often smaller than those of *C. virginicus,* and lustrous. The flowers are snow-white, (late April–early May in Athens) May–June, produced in erect, 2 to 3″ high and 2 to 4″ wide, cymose panicles, terminating young shoots of the year. It tends to be alternate in flowering abundance, although I have not noticed this tendency on plants in the Athens area. Fruit is an ellipsoidal, 1/2″ long, dark blue drupe which ripens in September through October. The flowers, fruits and foliage are highly ornamental but the fruit will only occur on female plants. Another asset is the handsome gray-brown bark which offers another season of interest. Quite variable in leaf characteristics and two distinct forms are commonly seen in cultivation in the United States. One is a tree with a distinct trunk and large, dark, rather dull green leaves; the other a shrubby form (15′) with rounded to oval-rounded, lustrous thickish dark green leaves that persist into early December in Athens. The latter is a wide spreading rounded shrub with long shoot extensions. The bark is a polished light brown and may exfoliate in papery curls. In the literature occasionally I see reference to var. *serrulatus* which appears to be nothing more than the seedling (juvenile) version with serrate leaves, a trait that is lost with maturity. I have grown seedlings and, indeed, they often have a serrate leaf margin. *Chionanthus retusus* is perhaps even more effective in flower than *C. virginicus* since the flowers occur at the ends of the new shoot extension. Prospers in the heat of the south and when finished flowering maintains a handsome dark green posture. One traveler in China compared it in flower to a dome of soft, fleecy snow. Pair reported excellent growth and heat tolerance in Wichita, KS tests. China, Korea, Japan. Introduced 1845. Zone 5 to 8. The finest tree in the country, perhaps the world, is located at the Arnold Arboretum.

Choisya ternata — Mexican-orange
(choiz'ē-a tēr-nā'ta)

FAMILY: Rosaceae
LEAVES: Opposite, generally trifoliate, evergreen, 3 to 6″ long, each sessile leaflet obovate, 1 1/2 to 3″ long, about as wide, rounded, cuneate, lustrous rich green, glabrous, when crushed emitting a pungent odor; petiole (rachis)—1 to 2″ long.

Choisya ternata, Mexican-orange, is a superb, densely rounded evergreen shrub that ranges from 6 to 8′ high and wide. For the adventuresome gardener where winter temperatures seldom drop below 5 to 10°F it is worthy of trial. The fragrant white flowers, each 1 to 1 1/4″ wide, occur in 3 to 6-flowered corymbs at the end of the shoots. I have seen the plant in flower in May and June in England but it will flower sporadically into winter. Requires a well-drained, acid, moist soil in full sun. No doubt high night temperatures especially in the south will prove problematic. Used as a specimen evergreen shrub and is one of the handsomest. 'Sundance' was introduced by Bressingham Gardens, England for its golden foliage that is richest on the young growth but persists throughout the seasons; also produces the fragrant white flowers. Introduced 1866. Zone 7 to 9.

Cinnamomum camphora — Camphor Tree
(sin-a-mō'mum cam-for'a)

FAMILY: Lauraceae

LEAVES: Alternate, simple, evergreen, oval or obovate, 3 to 6″ long, 1 1/2 to 3″ wide, acuminate, cuneate, entire, lustrous dark green and glabrous, fragrant when bruised, coriaceous, 3 to 4 vein pairs, the lower prominent and creating a palmate-like impression; petiole—3/4 to 1 1/4″ long.

SIZE: 40 to 60′ by 40 to 60′.

HARDINESS: Zone 9 to 10, 11°F killed 42″ diameter trees at Sea Island, Georgia.

HABIT: In youth a uniformly branched round headed evergreen tree of great beauty; at maturity similar but with wide spreading branches, very elegant in general architecture.

RATE: Fast.

TEXTURE: Medium throughout the seasons.

BARK: Gray-brown, ridged and furrowed, rather clean and attractive.

LEAF COLOR: New growth bronze-red and quite attractive, maturing to lustrous dark green, will discolor (yellow-green) in exposed windy locations during cold weather; drops old leaves in late winter/early spring.

FLOWERS: Perfect, fragrant, greenish white, 1/6″ wide, and produced in axillary, stalked, 2 to 3″ long panicles in May.

FRUIT: A blackish 1/3″ diameter drupe that is often borne in great abundance and becomes a nuisance especially in trafficked areas; not really showy since it blends with foliage.

CULTURE: Move as a young container or balled and burlapped tree; will make up quickly into a handsome specimen; acid, sandy or clay loam soil; will tolerate dry conditions once established.

DISEASES AND INSECTS: Root rot, *Verticillium* wilt; have not noticed any problems in the southeast.

LANDSCAPE VALUE: Handsome tree that is fast growing and suitable for warm (+20°F and above) climates; lovely shade tree but messy because of fruits; is a surface rooter and will compete with other plants; have seen a small stump sprout in Atlanta that dies back virtually every winter; best in coastal Georgia and south.

CULTIVARS:

'Majestic Beauty'—To this author's knowledge the first clone to be named, more uniform habit, larger richer green foliage than the species. A Monrovia introduction.

PROPAGATION: Collect fruits in fall, remove pulpy outer coating, sow outside and germination occurs in spring.

NATIVE HABITAT: Japan, China, Formosa. Introduced 1727.

Cistus laurifolius — Laurel Rock Rose
(sis'tus lâr-i-fō'lē-us)

FAMILY: Cistaceae

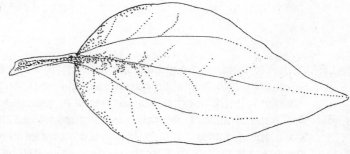

LEAVES: Opposite, simple, evergreen, oval-oblong, 1 1/2 to 3″ long, 3/4 to 1 1/2″ wide, long taper pointed, rounded, dark green and glabrous above, gray tomentose below, sticky on both surfaces; petiole—hairy, 1/2 to 3/4″ long, the bases of each leaf meeting and clasping the stem.

Cistus laurifolius, Laurel Rock Rose, was a plant I wrestled with to see whether it would find a place in this *Manual*. Obviously the plant won. I have never seen a *Cistus* in the east or south but have fallen in love (can a man do this?) with the various species from my European visits. The following description is somewhat general to purposely provide an overview. They are evergreen shrubs with opposite entire leaves that are usually fragrant when crushed. Most grow 1 to 3' to 6' high and form irregular mounds. Their real beauty resides in the 5-petaled, 2 to 3"(4") wide flowers of white, pink, and reddish shades, often with a deeper colored spot at the base of the petal. Flowers occur in great profusion in June and July (August). I can say I never met a Rock Rose that was not attractive. Ideally, full sun in a well-drained, reasonably dry situation is ideal. Transplant as container grown plants since they do not move readily bare root. Plants are native to the Mediterranean region and will, no doubt, suffer in the humidity of the southeast. The hardiest and most available species include: *C.* × *corbariensis,* a 1 1/2' high form with 1 1/2" diameter white flowers with a yellow spot at the base of the petal and with *C. laurifolius* the most hardy; *C. ladaniferus,* Gum Rock Rose, a 4 to 5' high shrub with sticky stems and leaves and 3 to 4" diameter white, red-brown spotted flowers; *C. laurifolius* is a 3 to 6' high shrub with sticky stems and leaves and 2 to 3" diameter white, yellow spotted, fragrant flowers, later than the above species from June to August; this is probably the hardiest species and small seedlings in my garden were fine at 23°F; will probably take 0 to 10°F with little damage; *C.* × *purpureus,* Orchidspot Rock Rose, is common in European gardens as a 1 1/2 to 3' mounded shrub with 2 to 3" wide reddish purple to lavender-pink flowers with a dark red basal spot. These species are best adapted along the west coast and areas with a Mediterranean climate. It never hurts to roll the dice when gardening and these plants are deserving. Seeds of *C. laurifolius* received in a seed exchange from Wisley Garden germinated immediately after sowing. Cuttings supposedly root without difficulty but I suspect with their Mediterranean heritage, the moisture should be minimized.

Cladrastis kentukea (lutea) — American Yellowwood, Virgilia
(klá-dras'tis ken-tuk'ē-a)

FAMILY: Fabaceae

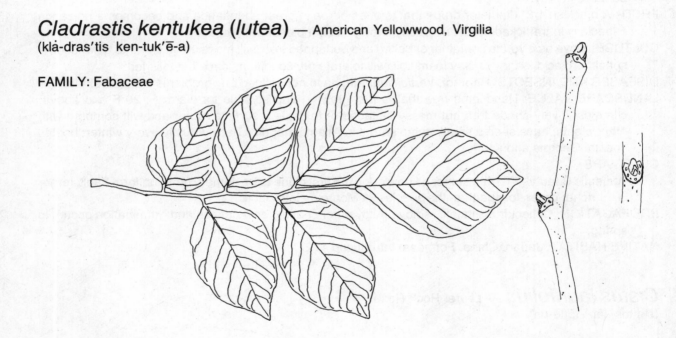

LEAVES: Alternate, odd-pinnately compound, (5) 7 to 9 (11) leaflets, entire leaf 8 to 12" long, each leaflet elliptic to ovate, acute, broad cuneate, glabrous, bright green, terminal the largest (4" by 2 1/2"), basal smaller to 1 1/2" long; petiole enlarged at base, enclosing bud.

BUDS: Terminal-absent, laterals-naked, superposed, the uppermost the largest and generally alone developing, flattened, closely packed together to form a pointed, bud-like, hairy brownish "cone", generally less than 1/4" long, nearly surrounded by the leaf scar.

STEM: Slender, more or less zigzag, smooth, bright reddish brown, often bloomy, odor and taste resembling that of a raw pea or bean.

BARK: Thin, gray to light brown, resembling dark of beech, beautiful and remaining so into old age.

SIZE: 30 to 50' in height with a spread of 40 to 55'.
HARDINESS: Zone 4 to 8; has proven hardy in Minnesota Landscape Arboretum and University of Maine.

HABIT: Usually a low branching tree with a broad, rounded crown of delicate branches.

RATE: Medium, 9 to 12′ over an 8 to 10 year period.

TEXTURE: Medium in foliage and winter; very handsome in foliage because of the bright green color of the leaves.

BARK: On older branches and trunks very smooth, gray and beech-like in overall appearance and texture; called Yellowwood because the heartwood is yellowish.

LEAF COLOR: Opening bright yellowish green gradually changing to bright green in summer; very prominent in a landscape when compared to the dark green of maples, oaks, or ashes; fall color may be a yellow to golden yellow.

FLOWERS: Perfect, white, fragrant, 1 to 1 1/4″ long; borne in 8 to 14″ long, 4 to 6″ wide at base, pendulous terminal panicles in (early May in Athens) May to early June; tends to produce the greatest abundance of flowers in alternate years or every third year; flowers when 12 to 18′ tall; bees really frequent the flower for nectar; in full flower the tree apears to be dripping with white rain; I grew a tree from seed that is now eight years old and has not flowered.

FRUIT: Pod, brown, October, 2 1/2 to 4″ long, 1/2″ wide, containing 4 to 6 flat brown hard coated seeds.

CULTURE: Transplant balled and burlapped as a small tree into well drained soil; tolerates high pH soils as well as acid situations, native on limestone cliffs and ridges; full sun; prune only in summer as the tree bleeds profusely if pruned in winter or spring; often develops bad crotches which can split or crack in storms; supposedly can fix atmospheric nitrogen.

DISEASES AND INSECTS: Very few problems are associated with this tree; *Verticillium* wilt has been reported; have never observed anything serious.

LANDSCAPE VALUE: Excellent tree for flowers and foliage; the medium size and spreading habit make it a choice shade tree for smaller properties; can be used as a single specimen or in groupings; there are beautiful specimens located on the University of Illinois campus, Spring Grove Cemetery, and the Arnold Arboretum; does not appear quite as prosperous in Zone 8 but a 30′ high specimen on the Georgia campus has flowered heavily over the years.

CULTIVARS:

'Rosea'—A beautiful pink flowered form that has been distributed by the Arnold Arboretum to several nurseries; original plant was located on grounds of Perkins School for the Blind, Watertown, MA; its origin is unclear.

PROPAGATION: Seed dormancy is supposedly caused by an impermeable seed coat and to a lesser degree by conditions in the embryo; scarify with sulfuric acid for 30 to 60 minutes plus mild stratification in moist sand or peat for 90 days at 41°F; root cuttings taken in December are an alternative method of propagation; see Frett and Dirr, *The Plant Propagator* 25(2):4–6 (1979) for a thorough insight into seed propagation of *Cladrastis;* based on that work embryo dormancy is not the limiting factor for seeds provided 0, 30, 60 and 120 minutes acid treatment germinated, 5, 41, 92 and 96%, respectively; simply a hard seed coat that must be rendered permeable.

ADDITIONAL NOTES: Common name is derived from the appearance of the freshly cut heartwood which is yellow; hence, yellowwood. Interestingly it is quite hardy and has flowered in the Minneapolis-St. Paul, MN area and at the University of Maine, Orono, where winter temperatures may range from –25 to –30°F. One report noted that new leaves may be injured by late spring frosts. An excellent article on yellowwood is by Robertson, *Arnoldia* 36(3): 137–150, 1977.

NATIVE HABITAT: North Carolina to Kentucky and Tennessee, nowhere very common; reference books show it scattered in Indiana, Illinois, Alabama, Mississippi, Arkansas, Missouri, Oklahoma. Generally occurs in rich well drained limestone soils in river valleys, slopes and ridges along streams. Introduced 1812.

RELATED SPECIES:

Cladrastis platycarpa — Japanese Yellowwood

LEAVES: Alternate, compound pinnate, 8 to 10″ long, 11 to 15 leaflets, each obliquely ovate, acuminate, cuneate to rounded, 1 1/2 to 4″ long, 1 to 1 1/2″ wide, dark green above, glabrous except on midrib and petiole; a small stipule is at the base of the petiolule of each leaflet.

C. platycarpa, (klȧ-dras'tis pla-ti-kȧr'pa), Japanese Yellowwood, is a rather handsome, small (20 to 40'), rounded tree with white, pea-like flowers produced in 4 to 6" high and 2 1/2 to 4" wide panicles. The 2" long by 1/2" wide pod is tapered at both ends and winged all around. There is a nice specimen in the Arnold Arboretum that flowers after *C. lutea*. Japan. Introduced 1919. Zone 5.

Cladrastis sinensis, (klȧ-dras'tis sī-nen'sis), Chinese Yellowwood, grows 30 to 50' high and wide. The compound pinnate leaves are composed of 9 to 13 (17) leaflets, each 3 to 5" long and 1 to 1 1/2" wide, obtuse or acute, rounded at base, bright green and glabrous above, rusty pubescent on midrib and petiole below. The blush white to pinkish flowers occur in July in 12" by 9", erect, terminal, pyramidal panicles. The calyx of each flower is covered with rusty pubescence. Pod is 2 to 3" long, 1/2" wide, flattened and smooth. Western and Central China. Introduced 1901. Zone 5 to 7 (8)?

Clematis × *jackmanii* — Jackman Clematis
(klem'a-tis jak'man-ī or jak'man-ē-ī)

FAMILY: Ranunculaceae
LEAVES: Opposite, pinnate, the upper ones often simple, leaflets ovate, entire, rather large, usually slightly pubescent beneath.
BUDS: Rather small, ovoid or flattened, sessile, solitary, with 1 to 3 pairs of exposed somewhat hairy scales.
STEM: Slender, light brown, ridged, with the 6 primary ridges prominent; pith-angular or star-shaped, white, continuous with thin firmer diaphragms at the nodes.

SIZE: 5 to 6' to 18' on the appropriate structure.
HARDINESS: Zone 3 to 8 (9).
HABIT: A vine whose stems twine around objects while the leaves clasp or fold over any object.
RATE: Fast, 5 to 10' in a single season.
TEXTURE: Medium in summer.
LEAF COLOR: Bright green to blue-green in summer, no fall color of any consequence.
FLOWERS: Perfect, violet-purple, 4 to 7" diameter, June (May in Athens) through until frost; usually borne solitary or in 3-flowered cymes, sepals are the showy portion.
FRUIT: Achene, with 1 to 2" long persistent style which is clothed with long silky hairs.
CULTURE: Attention to detail is important, the adage a warm top and cool bottom apply; transplant as a container plant in spring into light, loamy, moderately moist, well-drained soil (cool root environment); soil should be mulched; avoid extemely hot, sunny area; place the plant so it receives some shade during the day; higher pH soils 6 to 7.5 are often recommended as being optimum but personally I do not think it makes much difference if the pH is 4.5; avoid extremely wet conditions; I have seen clematis growing on mailboxes, posts and other structures where they are often trampled and abused; tougher than given credit!
DISEASES AND INSECTS: Leaf spot and stem rot can be a serious problem, black blister beetle, clematis borer, mites, whiteflies, scales and root-knot nematodes.
LANDSCAPE VALUE: Does not fit the absolute requirements of a woody plant but to omit these beautiful vines would be somewhat of an injustice to the reader; excellent for trellises, fences, rock walls, any

structure around which the stems and petioles twine is a good support; very beautiful in flower and many of the large flowered hybrids are worth experimenting with. The small flowered species and large flowered cultivars are all deserving of a place in the garden; every garden can house a clematis; on an English garden tour I visited a nursery, Treasures of Tenbury, a large clematis grower, and the owner, Mr. John Treasure, had a display garden that was open to the public; he demonstrated many different ways that clematis could be used and had them scrambling over shrubs, evergreens, up trees, on walls, ad infinitum. I have copied his approach with some success and allowed a plant to clamber over an *Itea japonica*. The effect is striking and the *Itea* has problems with its identity.

CULTIVARS: Here I have attempted to bring some order to what in the last edition was a rather chaotic treatment of cultivars; they are divided by groups.

Jackman Group—Probably the most popular group of hybrids in American gardens; this group includes *C.* × *jackmanii* raised in 1858 at Jackman and Sons of Woking, Surrey, England and varieties raised later using it as one of the parents; this group flowers on new growth in July and August with some varieties flowering until frost. Stems can be cut back hard as buds swell; their stems may also be cut back within 4 to 6″ of origin, thus allowing a larger framework to develop.

'Comtesse de Bouchard'—Medium size flowers of soft satiny pink with a slight overlap of lavender; yellow stamens, vigorous and free flowering, June–August.

'Crimson Star'—Vigorous, floriferous red form.

'Gipsy Queen'—Rich violet-purple, large star-shaped flowers.

'Hagley Hybrid'—Shell pink flowers with chocolate-brown anthers, free flowering.

jackmanii 'Alba'—Large 4 to 5″ diameter single white flowers with a bluish tinge around the margin of each sepal.

jackmanii 'Rubra'—Flowers are deep red; sometimes double on old wood.

jackmanii 'Superba'—Improved form of *jackmanii* with rich violet-purple, 5″ diameter flowers.

'Madame Baron Veillard'—Lilac-rose, 4 1/2 to 6″ across, vigorous grower.

'Madame Edouard Andre'—Rich crimson with yellow stamens and pointed sepals, very free flowering.

'Mrs. Cholmondeley'—Sparse flowering with pale blue 6″ diameter flowers.

'Perle d'Azur'—Sky blue flowers, vigorous.

'Star of India'—Reddish plum with a red bar.

'Victoria'—4 to 5″ diameter light blue flowers, vigorous and free flowering.

Lanuginosa Group—Many lovely hybrids are included here that have *C. lanuginosa* as one parent. Many of the cultivars will flower in June if a proportion of the previous year's growth is left. If cut back to within 2 to 4′ of the ground each spring, new shoots will grow quickly and more abundant bloom can be expected later. Some within the group produce double flowers on old and single on new wood.

'Beauty of Worcester'—Deep blue with white stamens, double on old, single on young wood.

'Candida'—Off-white with white centers, large flowers.

'Crimson King'—Double crimson flowers from old wood, single from new, free flowering, large flowered, less vigorous in growth than many.

'Elsa Spath'—Profuse intense blue flowers, darker towards the center.

'Fairy Queen'—Flesh pink, with bright central bars, large flowers.

'Henryi'—Magnificent large, 4 to 5″ diameter, white flowers with dark stamens, free flowering; flowers on old wood in June and again in late summer on new.

'King Edward VII'—Large orchid flowers with deep mauve bar in center.

'King George V'—Flesh pink, each sepal with a dark central bar.

'Lady Northcliffe'—Deep lavender blue with white stamens, 5 to 6″ diameter.

'Lord Neville'—Rich deep blue with wavy-margined sepals; flowers on old wood in June and later on new growth.

'Maureen'—Velvety royal purple.

'Nelly Moser'—Large pale mauve-pink flowers with a deep pink bar in the center of each sepal, very free flowering, one of the most popular.

'Prins Hendrik'—Azure-blue, pointed sepals.

'Ramona'—Large lavender-blue flowers with dark anthers, excellent for June flower on old wood.

'Violet Charm'—Rich violet.

'W.E. Gladstone'—Large, silky lavender, purple anthers, vigorous and free flowering.

'William Kennett'—Lavender-blue with dark stamens; margins of sepals crinkled.

Patens Group—Derived from *C. patens;* flower typically on previous year's wood; some varieties produce sparse smaller flowers in late summer. Prune dead and broken growth in spring. After flowering, a portion of old shoots should be cut back severely to encourage them to break, thus producing flowering wood for the following spring.

'Barbara Dibley'—Large rich rosy-violet flowers with deeper bars.

'Barbara Jackman'—Deep violet, striped deep carmine, May–June, again in September.

'Bees Jubilee'—Mauve pink with carmine bars and pink stamens.

'Daniel Deronda'—Large, violet-blue, paler at center with creamy stamens, often double.

'Gillian Blades'—Pure white.

'Kathleen Wheeler'—Plummy-mauve.

'Lasurstern'—Deep lavender blue, with conspicuous white stamens and broad, tapering, wavy margined sepals.

'Lincoln Star'—Bright red with pale edges to sepals and maroon stamens.

'Marcel Moser'—Mauve with a deep carmine bar, sepals tapered.

'Marie Boisselot'—Large, pure white with cream stamens and broad, rounded overlapping sepals, vigorous and free flowering.

'Miss Bateman'—Medium-size white flowers with a cushion of chocolate stamens.

'Mrs. N. Thompson'—Deep violet with a scarlet bar, pointed sepals.

'Percy Picton'—Very large flowers of rosy purple.

'The President'—Large (6″) deep violet flowers with pointed sepals.

'Vyvyan Pennell'—Deep violet blue suffused purple and carmine in the center, fully double, May through June, single flowers in autumn.

Viticella Group—Derived from *C. viticella;* this is essentially a summer flowering group and can be pruned back hard in spring. If greater height is desired it is possible to retain a lower woody framework and reduce the previous season's growth to within 6″ of their origins on the more permanent woody framework. In essence, this group may be treated similar to the Jackman Group.

'Ascotiensis'—A bright blue with long pointed sepals, very floriferous.

'Duchess of Sutherland'—Petunia red with a darker bar on each tapered sepal, often double.

'Ernest Markham'—Glowing red-violet flowers with a velvety sheen, sepals rounded, 3 to 4″ diameter flowers.

'Huldine'—Pearly-white, the pointed sepals with a mauve bar on the reverse, vigorous and free flowering, 3 to 4″ diameter.

'Lady Betty Balfour'—Large rich blue-violet flowers with yellow stamens, vigorous late flowering form.

'Madame Julia Correvon'—Deep wine-red.

'Margot Koster'—Small, rosy pink flowers in abundance.

'Mrs. Spencer Castle'—Large, pale heliotrope, sometimes double, May and June and again in fall.

'Venosa Violacea'—Violet blue.

'Ville de Lyon'—Bright carmine-red, deeper crimson on edges of sepals, golden stamens, 4″ diameter.

Florida Group—Origin married to *C. florida;* most of the hybrids have semi-double to double flowers. They flower in late spring on previous year's wood and are not pruned until after flowering is complete.

'Bell of Woking'—Pale mauve, double.

'Duchess of Edinburgh'—Large double, rosette-like, white with green shading, scented.

'Kathleen Dunford'—Semi-double rosy-purple flowers.

PROPAGATION: Seeds have dormant embryos and stratification for 60 to 90 days at 33° to 40°F is recommended. I have a feeling that embryos may not be fully developed or possible inhibitors exist in the fruit coat that slow germination. Seeds of *C. maximowicziana* were collected in November, sown directly in flats in a warm greenhouse and germinated 3 1/2 months later. The warm temperatures facilitate the development of the embryo to a point where it will germinate. *Clematis orientalis* and *C. tangutica* received in the Wisley Seed Exchange germinated 3 weeks after planting. Over the years, I have germinated many species and have not observed an absolute cold requirement for any. Cuttings, summer, single internode with cuts between the nodes have given good results with large flowered types; see Evison, *PIPPS* 27:436–440 (1977), "Propagation of *Clematis*" for an excellent discussion of the subject.

ADDITIONAL NOTES: Two excellent reference books on *Clematis* are suggested: Markham, Ernest, 1935. *Clematis.* Charles Scribner, NY. Excellent treatment of species. Lloyd Christopher. 1977. *Clematis.* William Collins Sons and Co. Ltd. London. Probably the best reference with color plates showing hybrid and species characteristics. Also excellent descriptions. Possibly being revised as I write this. Actually the more I read the book the more tempted I am to remove the section on *Clematis* in the *Manual.*

Other *Clematis* Species and Cultivars

Clematis armandii —Armand Clematis
(klem'a-tis är-man'dē-ī)

LEAVES: Opposite, compound pinnate, 3 leaflets, evergreen, each leaflet 3 to 6″ long, 1 to 1 1/2″ wide, lustrous dark green, prominently 3-veined, oblong-lanceolate to ovate, rounded or slightly heart-shaped at base, pointed, glabrous.

Clematis armandii, Armand Clematis, would be a beautiful plant if it did not flower. A fast growing vine that quickly covers a fence, trellis or similar structure. The large, glossy green, leathery leaves provide a handsome foil for the white, fragrant flowers that appear in March–May. Have monitored its flowering sequence in the Athens, GA area. It often starts in mid-March and is finished by mid-April. Individual flowers are 2 to 2 1/2″ in diameter with 4 to 7 sepals and occur in panicles on the previous season's growth. Can be grown from Zone 7 south. Have seen it used tastefully at Callaway Gardens, Pine Mountain, Georgia. 'Apple Blossom' has broad sepals of white shaded pink, especially on the reverse side; the unfolding leaves are a bronzy-green. 'Farquhariana' has pink flowers. 'Snowdrift' has pure white flowers. Introduced 1900 by E.H. Wilson. Central and western China. In 1981, –5°F killed the plant to the ground in exposed locations.

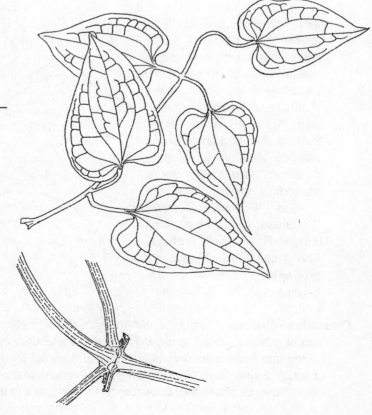

Clematis maximowicziana (C. paniculata) — Sweetautumn Clematis
(klem'a-tis max-im-ō-wix-ē-ā'-na)

LEAVES: Opposite, pinnately compound, 3 to 5 leaflets, 1 to 4″ long, acute, subcordate or rounded at base, entire or sometimes lobed, glabrous, dark blue-green.
BUDS: Small, with 1 to 3 pairs of rather hairy scales.
STEM: Straw colored, 12 to 18 ridged; ridges are actually vascular bundles; pith—white.

Clematis maximowicziana, Sweetautumn Clematis, is a rampant, rampaging vine which engulfs every structure in sight. The flowers are white, 1 1/4″ across, fragrant, 6 to 8 sepals, August into September and October, borne in many flowered axillary and terminal panicles; quite literally make the whole plant look like a new fallen snow; probably the easiest *Clematis* to grow as it seems to thrive with neglect. Flowers in late August–early September in my Georgia garden; extremely vigorous to the point of viciousness. Soft fragrance is delightful and I allow the plant to scramble over crape myrtles, sedums and baptisias. Japan. 1864. Zone 5 to 8(9).

Clematis montana, (klem'a-tis mon-tan'a), Anemone Clematis, is a vigorous, almost rampant, white flowering species. The 2 to 2 1/2″ diameter, 4-sepaled flowers occur singly on a glabrous 2 to 5″ long peduncle in May–June. Makes a great plant for covering walls, rock piles, and arbours. 'Alexander' has creamy-white, sweetly scented flowers; 'Elizabeth' has large, slightly fragrant soft pink flowers in May and June; 'Grandiflora' is a strong growing Chinese form that produces an abundance of 2 1/2 to 3″ diameter white flowers; var. *rubens* is a rosy-red flowered, vigorous, hardy form that was introduced by Wilson in 1900, the flowers appear later than those of the species, easy to root from cuttings; 'Superba' offers deep pink flowers. 'Tetrarose' is a vigorous tetraploid with purplish pink 3″ diameter flowers; the foliage has a bronzish cast; var. *wilsonii* has larger white flowers (3″) and flowers in July and August. Himalayas, central and western China. 1831. Zone 5.

Clematis orientalis, (klem'a-tis ôr-i-en-tā'lis), Oriental Clematis, is a more restrained, perhaps 10 to 20′ high clematis that offers delightful, slightly fragrant, 1 1/2 to 2″ diameter yellow flowers in August and September. The flowers occur singly on 2 to 4″ long pedicels and produce a 3″ diameter tuft of glistening, feathery achenes. Fruits are in various stages of development while flowers continue to open. Similar to *C. tangutica* but more delicate. *Clematis tangutica* is larger flowered and has pubescent stems and flower stalks. See *The Plantsman* 7(4):192–204 (1986) for an excellent discussion of these and related species. Iran to Himalayas. Introduced 1731. Zone (5)6 to 9.

Clematis tangutica, (klem'a-tis tan-gū'ti-ka), Golden Clematis, has bright yellow, 3 to 4″ diameter flowers, June–July, solitary, listed as handsomest of yellow flowered *Clematis;* silky seed heads. Mongolia to northwestern China. 1890. Zone 5.

Clematis texensis, (klem'a-tis teks-en'sis), Scarlet Clematis, has carmine or bright scarlet flowers, urn-shaped, narrowed at the mouth, about 1″ long and 3/4″ wide; June–July through until frost; solitary and nodding. 'Duchess of Albany' is a pink flowered form with more spreading sepals than the species. 'Gravetye Beauty', 'Countess of Onslow', and 'Etiole Rose' belong here. The species does not propagate readily from cuttings. Texas. 1878. Zone 4.

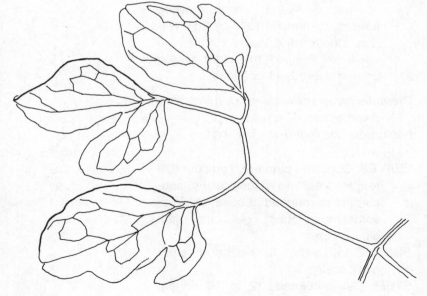

Clematis virginiana, (klem'a-tis vĕr-jin-ē-ā'na), Virginsbower, is a handsome vine growing 12 to 20′ with bright green summer foliage. The flowers are whitish (supposedly this is a dioecious species with staminate flowers showy white, pistillate more dull); borne in 3 to 6″ long axillary leafy panicles in July through September. Good vine for native situations; other types are more effective in flower. Native from Nova Scotia to Manitoba, south to Georgia and Kansas. Introduced 1720. Zone 4 to 8.

Clematis vitalba, (klem'a-tis vī-tàl'ba), Traveler's Joy or Old Man's Beard, has white, 1″ diameter, almond scented flowers in July through September which are borne in axillary and terminal 3 to 5″ panicles. Common name comes from the fact the flowers are slightly fragrant and odor proves refreshing to the traveler on a hot summer's day. Europe, northern Africa. 1820. Zone 4.

Clematis viticella, (klem'a-tis vī-ti-sel'la), Italian Clematis, has purple, rosy-purple or violet, 1 to 2″ diameter, 4-sepaled flowers which are born in June through August singly or in 2's or 3's. The flowers are extremely dainty and hang bell-like from slender stalks. Cultivars include:
'Abundance'—Delicately veined flowers of soft purple.
'Alba Luxurians'—White flowers, tinted mauve, dark purple anthers.
'Kermesina'—Deep purple wine-red flowers.
'Nana'—Dwarf form about 3′ high.
'Plena'—Double purple flowers, an old clone.
'Royal Velours'—Velvety purple flowers.
'Rubra'—An old red-flowered form.
Southern Europe to western Asia. 1578. Zone 4.

Clerodendron trichotomum — Harlequin Glorybower
(kle-rō-den'dron trī-kō-tō'mum)

FAMILY: Verbenaceae
LEAVES: Opposite, simple, ovate to elliptic, 4 to 9″ long, 2 to 5″ wide, acuminate, broad cuneate to truncate, entire (usually) or sparsely toothed, dark green above, pubescent beneath, malodorous when bruised; petiole—1 to 4″ long, pubescent.
STEM: Coarse, green, finally brown, pubescent, soft, with pith like a *Sambucus,* nodes flattened.

Clerodendron trichotomum, Harlequin Glorybower, has missed the last three editions of the *Manual* but finally was brought on board. Over the years, my feelings toward this plant have ebbed and flowed like the tide. In flower and fruit it is delightful but at its worst has the appearance of an overturned Dempster Dumpster. The habit, even in Zone 8, is that of a dieback shrub probably seldom growing more than 10′. It can form a small 15′ tree but needs some assistance since suckers will develop. I have seen it as far north as the Brooklyn Botanic Garden but there it was a herbaceous perennial. The dark green leaves die off green. Flowers occur late, often July and continue into fall while the fruits are developing. It is not uncommon to find flowers and developed fruits at the same time. Individual flowers are white, 1 to 1 1/2″ wide, tubular at the base and spreading into 5 narrow oblong lobes at the mouth. Flowers occur in long stalked cymes from the upper leaves, the inflorescence averaging 6 to 9″ across. The reddish, leathery, 1/2″ long, 5 angled and 5-lobed calyx subtends a pea-size (1/4″ diameter) bright blue drupe and is actually spectacular on close inspection. Prefers moist, well-drained soil in full sun but I have seen plants in partial shade, albeit open in habit, with decent flower and fruit. I grew the plant for 4 years and never saw a flower or fruit and chucked it. Should be used in a shrub border or other area where it can blend with the woodwork until it does something. Eastern China, Japan. Cultivated 1880. Zone 6(7) to 9.

Clethra alnifolia — Summersweet Clethra
(kle'thra al-ni-fō'li-a)

FAMILY: Clethraceae
LEAVES: Alternate, simple, obovate-oblong, 1 1/2 to 4″ long, 3/4 to 2″ wide, acute to short acuminate, cuneate, sharply serrate, glabrous or nearly so on both sides, with 6 to 10 pairs of veins, lustrous dark green above; petiole—1/8 to 3/4″ long, pubescent.
BUDS: Small, loosely scaled, solitary, sessile, ovoid.
STEM: Brown, pubescent, rounded or obscurely 3-sided; pith—light brown, continuous.

SIZE: 3 to 8′ high and 4 to 6′ wide, apt to be variable because of soil effects, larger in moist soil.

HARDINESS: Zone 3 to 9.

HABIT: Oval, round-topped, erect, dense leafy shrub, often suckering to form broad colonies.

RATE: Slow to medium.

TEXTURE: Medium in all seasons.

LEAF COLOR: Late to leaf out in spring; lustrous deep green in summer; pale yellow to rich golden brown in fall; fall color develops about mid October and can persist for 3 to 4 weeks.

FLOWERS: Perfect, white, delightfully fragrant, 1/3″ across, July into August, effective 4 to 6 weeks, borne on current season's growth in 2 to 6″ long and 3/4″ wide upright racemes or panicles; lovely to look at but even lovelier to smell; the bees constantly hover about; produced on new growth of season.

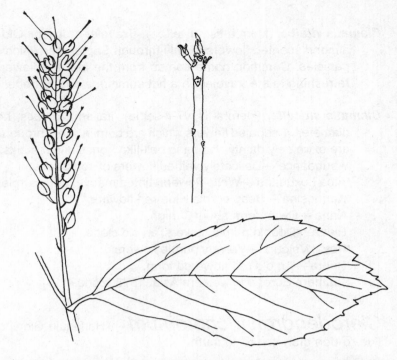

FRUIT: Dry, dehiscent capsule, persisting through winter and offering a good identification characteristic.

CULTURE: Transplant balled and burlapped or as a container plant into moist, acid soil which has been supplemented with organic matter; supposedly difficult to establish; grows naturally in wet places; withstands acid soil; shade or full sun; salty conditions of seashore; prune in early spring; I have found this plant easy to grow.

DISEASES AND INSECTS: Tremendously pest free although mite damage might occur in dry seasons.

LANDSCAPE VALUE: Excellent for summer flower, shrub border, good plant for heavy shade and wet areas; I would like to see this plant used a lot more than it is; the foliage is very handsome and the overall winter habit is clean; does not have the dirty habits of *Weigela* and *Lonicera;* the fragrance is tremendous; fall color is a worthwhile attribute.

CULTIVARS

‘Paniculata’—Large terminal panicles, vigorous grower, and is superior to the type, introduced 1770.

‘Pink Spires’—Buds pink to rose, open to soft pink and do not fade to white.

‘Rosea’—Flowers buds pink; flowers at first pinkish fading to pinkish white, glossy dark green leaves, beautiful form, introduced 1906. I have grown this for 10 years in Georgia, the flower color does not fade any worse in the south than the north; good plant for partial shade.

PROPAGATION: Cuttings taken in summer root readily in sand and peat without treatment but treatments may hasten rooting; have rooted the species and ‘Rosea’ by taking July cuttings, 1000 ppm IBA, sand or peat:perlite, under mist; the cuttings will root in 2 weeks at 90 to 100%; seed can be sown when ripe and requires no stratification.

ADDITIONAL NOTES: The late flowering is an asset to the summer garden; the preferred species is *C. alnifolia* because of its availability and adaptability. All seem to prefer moist, acid, organic soils.

NATIVE HABITAT: Maine to Florida. Introduced 1731.

RELATED SPECIES:

Clethra acuminata — Cinnamon Clethra

LEAVES: Alternate, simple, 3 to 8″ long, ovate-elliptic or elliptic to elliptic-oblong, acuminate, broad cuneate or rounded, serrulate, lustrous dark green above, pubescent below; petiole—1/4 to 1 1/4″ long.

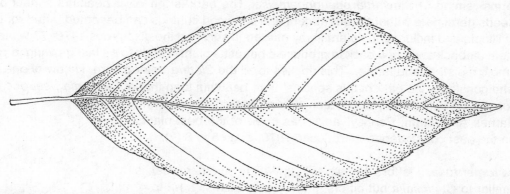

Clethra acuminata, (kle'thra a-kū-min-ā'-ta), Cinnamon Clethra, is a medium-sized, often suckering shrub or a small tree of rather gaunt proportions. Its landscape size would approximate 8 to 12' but in the wild it can reach 15 to 20'. The dark green, 3 to 6" (8") leaves are toothed toward the apex. The white, fragrant flowers are borne in 3 to 8" long, solitary, cylindrical terminal racemes in July. The bark can be a beautiful polished cinnamon-brown color but I have seen every imaginable combination of brown, with some trunks showing an exfoliating character. In the wild, it grows on rather dry, rocky, gravelly mountain sides. Seeds germinate without pretreatment and softwood cuttings root as above. Common on Brasstown Bald in North Georgia where it grows on rocky soils. The plants on Brasstown have cinnamon-brown exfoliating scaly bark. Selections could be made for superior characteristics. Found in the mountains from Virginia to West Virginia to Georgia and Alabama. Introduce 1806. Zone 5 to 8.

Clethra barbinervis — Japanese Clethra

LEAVES: Alternate, simple, oval or obovate, 2 to 5" long, 1 to 2 1/4" wide, acuminate, cuneate, sharply serrate, lustrous dark green and glabrous above, at maturity pubescent on veins below; petiole—1/4 to 3/4" long.

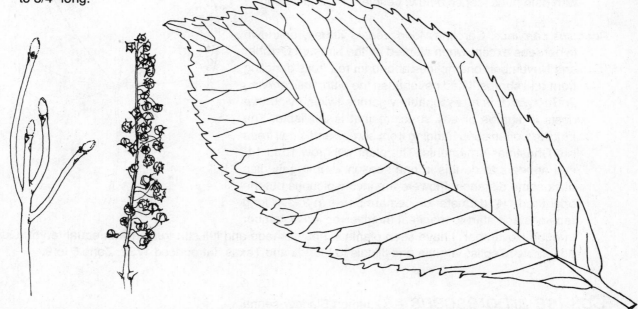

Clethra barbinervis, (kle'thra bàr-bin-er'vis), Japanese Clethra, is a beautiful large shrub or small tree (10 to 20' high) that is seldom seen in cultivation in the United States. One specimen at the Arnold Arboretum is about 18' high. The leaves are dark green and tend to be clustered at the end of the branch, presenting a whorled appearance. The fragrant, white, 1/3" diameter flowers are borne in 4 to 6" long terminal racemose panicles from July to August. The bark is a beautiful, smooth, polished, gray to rich brown and may display an exfoliating character. In many respects the best forms remind of *Stewartia pseudocamellia*. The bark is the most beautiful aspect of this plant. Seeds germinate without pretreatment and softwood cuttings can be rooted. I had rooted a cutting at Illinois and included the plant in my garden. It survived the disastrous 1976–77 winter with slight stem dieback and grew back to produce a beautiful plant. Tends to be fast growing in youth if given ample moisture and fertility. This applies to all the *Clethra* treated here. I know of one nurseryman who considers the bark of this species more beautiful than that of *Stewartia pseudocamellia* or *S. koreana*. There is great variation among individuals and the Barnes Arboretum, Pennsylvania, has three of the best plants on the east coast. Japan. Introduced 1870. Zone 5 to 8 (?).

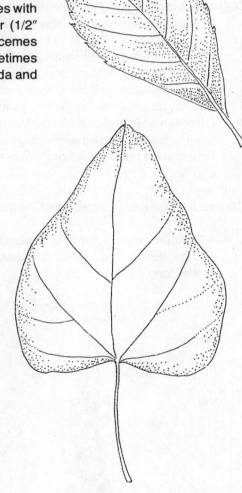

Clethra tomentosa, (kle′thra tō-men-tō′sa), Woolly Summersweet, is similar to *C. alnifolia* but differs in the downy stems, 1 1/2 to 4″ long, 1/2 to 2″ wide, obovate, serrated on terminal half leaves with their thick, pale tomentum, 7 to 10 vein pairs, and larger (1/2″ diameter), white, fragrant flowers borne in 6″ long woolly racemes in August–September. Usually grows 6 to 8′. Sometimes regarded as a variety of *C. alnifolia*. North Carolina to Florida and Alabama. Introduced 1731. Zone 5 to 9.

Cocculus carolinus — Carolina Moonseed
(kok′ū-lus ka-ro-lī′-nus)

FAMILY: Menispermaceae
LEAVES: Alternate, simple, orbicular to triangular-ovate, 2 to 4″ long, 3 to 7 veined, rounded and mucronate at apex, rounded to subcordate at base, entire or often obscurely lobed, lustrous deep green and glabrous above, covered with pale pubescence below; petiole—1 1/2 to 4″ long.

Cocculus carolinus, Carolina Moonseed, is virtually unknown in gardens except when planted by the birds. In October and November, one notices abundant red fruits dangling from odd shrubs. I had never seen the plant until arriving in Georgia. It is a reasonably vigorous twining vine that nests in shrubs or any structure that is available. The fruits are often seen hanging from shrubs and small trees like Christmas ornaments. The plant will grow 10 to 14′ and appears to do this in one season as it largely dies back some distance. Flowers are inconspicuous but the bright red 1/4″ diameter drupes are borne in 2 to 4″ long racemes and start to manifest themselves in September through November. I have seen plants in heavy shade and full sun fruiting with equal fervor. Quite adaptable to soils. Virginia and Illinois to Florida and Texas. Introduced 1732. Zone 5 to 9.

Colutea arborescens — Common Bladder-senna
(ko-lū′-tē-a âr-bor-es′enz)

FAMILY: Fabaceae
LEAVES: Compound, odd-pinnate, 9 to 13 leaflets, 3 to 6″ long, each leaflet 1/2 to 1″ long, elliptic to obovate, usually emarginate to mucronate, bright green, membranous with fairly distinct venation.

BUDS: Small, usually superposed and the upper promptly developing into slender branches, with 2 to 4 visible scales or leaves, appressed-pubescent.

STEM: Moderate, terete except for shortly decurrent lines from the nodes; pith moderate, rounded, continuous; leaf scars alternate, broadly crescent shaped, much elevated; bundle-traces 1 or 3 or the middle one divided; stipules persistent on the sides of the leaf cushion.

SIZE: 6 to 8' high and about as wide at maturity; may grow larger (12').

HARDINESS: Zone 5 to 7.

HABIT: Strong growing shrub of bushy habit; becomes leggy at base.

RATE: Medium to fast.

TEXTURE: Medium in leaf; possibly medium-coarse in winter.

LEAF COLOR: Bright green in summer; fall color is not effective.

FLOWERS: Yellow, 3/4" long, pea-shaped, the standard with red markings; (May) June through July; borne in 6 to 8-flowered, 1 1/2 to 4" long racemes; produced on current season's growth; very pretty flowers.

FRUIT: Inflated and bladder-like pod, 3" long and 1 to 1 1/2" wide; greenish to slightly reddish near the base; maturing July through September; rather interesting but drying soon after maturing and assuming the dirty brown socks posture.

CULTURE: Root system is sparingly branched and plants should be grown in and transplanted from containers; easily grown in almost any soil except waterlogged; prefers full sun; prune back to old wood in winter; tends to show some dieback and may not always be the tidiest shrub.

DISEASES AND INSECTS: None serious.

LANDSCAPE VALUE: Most authorities consider this species too coarse and weedy for the home landscape; because of its adaptability, it could be successfully used in poor soil areas where more ornamental shrubs would not grow; I have seen the species and the cultivar 'Bullata' in July at the Arnold Arboretum; at this time their foliage was in immaculate condition and they were the match of any other shrub for summer foliage effect.

CULTIVARS:

'Bullata'—A dwarf form of dense habit whose 5 to 7 leaflets are small, rounded and somewhat bullate; probably about 1/3 to 1/2 the size of the species at maturity; not the handsomest plant.

'Crispa'—A low growing form with leaves wavy on the margins.

PROPAGATION: Seeds have a hard seed coat and should be scarified in concentrated sulfuric acid for 30 to 60 minutes; steeping seeds in hot water (190°F) for 24 hours also works; half-ripened cuttings collected in early November (England) rooted 29 percent without treatment, failed to respond to NAA but rooted 73 percent after treatment with 100 ppm IBA/18 hr.

ADDITIONAL NOTES: Only *Koelreuteria* and *Staphylea* among hardy woody plants have similar fruits. The fruits explode when squeezed. W.J. Bean noted that "its accommodating nature had made it, perhaps, despised in gardens." *Colutea* will never supersede forsythia in gardens.

NATIVE HABITAT: Mediterranean region and southeastern Europe. Introduced 1570.

RELATED SPECIES:

Colutea* × *media is a hybrid between *C. arborescens* and *C. orientalis* with bluish green foliage. Each leaf is composed of 11 to 13, obovate, 3/4 to 1" long leaflets. Flowers show evidence of *C. orientalis* for they are brownish red to a coppery hue and quite attractive. The 3" long inflated pod often turns solid lime-green, pink or bronze, reddish or reddish purple. There is a nice specimen at the Arnold Arboretum. Originated before 1790, given the name *C.* × *media* in 1809, where it was cultivated in the Botanic Garden of Berlin. Zone 5. Koller [*PIPPS* 32:598 (1982)] described several interesting facets of the plant's behavior; matures into a 6 to 10' high rounded shrub that is hardy to +10°F. Peak flowering occurs in mid May (Boston) with scattered blossoms throughout summer. Colors range from the typical yellow to those with blends or tints of copper, pink or reddish brown.

Comptonia peregrina — Sweetfern
(komp-tō′ni-a per-i-grī′na)

FAMILY: Myricaceae

LEAVES: Alternate, simple, linear-oblong, deeply pin-
natifid with roundish-ovate, oblique, often mucronulate lobes, 2 to 4 1/2″ long and 1/3 to 5/8″ wide, pubescent, fragrant; looks somewhat like a fern frond; hence, the name Sweetfern; pale green when emerging, eventually dark green often lustrous; petiole 1/8 to 1/4″ long.

BUDS: Globular, minute, solitary, sessile, with 2 or about 4 exposed scales, hairy; pistillate catkins crowded at the ends of the stems, 1/4″ long, cylindrical, pale brown, hairy.

STEM: Young stems green or yellowish or reddish brown and covered with resin dots, older stems yellowish brown with shining surface, somewhat hairy, oldest are reddish purple or coppery brown.

SIZE: 2 to 4′ high and can spread 4 to 8′, actually indefinite for it suckers profusely.

HARDINESS: Zone 2 to 5 or 6.

HABIT: Deciduous shrub with slender, often erect branches developing a broad, flat-topped to rounded outline as it spreads and colonizes.

RATE: Slow to medium.

TEXTURE: Medium-fine in leaf and no worse than medium in winter; the interesting fern-like foliage gives the plant a gentle, woodsie, graceful appearance.

LEAF COLOR: Dark green, almost lustrous, in summer; falls green or greenish brown in autumn.

FLOWERS: Monoecious (usually), staminate with 3 to 4, usually 4, stamens, borne in cylindric catkins; female-ovary surrounded with 8 persistent bracts at the base, borne in globose-ovoid catkins, April or early May, not showy, of yellow-green color.

FRUIT: Nutlet, 1/5″ long, olive-brown, borne in a distinct burr-like cluster of bracts.

CULTURE: Not the easiest plant to move; people have suggested digging large pieces of sod and, hopefully, getting sufficient roots to effect establishment. Recent work has sown that Sweetfern can be container-grown and successfully transplanted from containers. See *PIPPS* 24:364–366, 1974. Sweetfern does best in peaty, sandy, sterile, acid soils. Some authorities indicated moist soils are beneficial, however, I have seen this plant in New England growing all over cuts and fills along highways. Sweetfern has the ability to fix its own nitrogen and this partially explains the adaptability to poor, infertile soils; full sun or partial shade.

DISEASES AND INSECTS: Nothing serious.

LANDSCAPE VALUE: Interesting plant with aromatic foliage and stems; can be used for highways and other waste areas where the soil is sandy, infertile and somewhat dry; might be used in naturalistic landscaping where typical "ornamentals" tend to languish; a nice novelty plant for the collector.

PROPAGATION: Cuttings taken from mature wood rooted poorly. Cuttings taken from juvenile growth rooted readily when treated with 3000 ppm IBA and placed under mist. Best to collect juvenile stems 3″ or less in length. The principal means of propagation is by root pieces which are dug in late winter or early spring before growth starts. The root pieces should be 4″ long if 1/16″ in diameter and 2″ long if 3/8 to 1/2″ in diameter. The medium should be fine sand and Sphagnum peat. The cuttings should be placed horizontally at a 1/2″ depth and will develop shoots and additional roots. As the new juvenile shoots develop they can be collected for cutting wood. Seed propagation has met with limited success but Del Tredici and Torrey, *Botanical Gazette* 137(3):262–268. 1976, showed that seeds treated with 500 ppm gibberillic acid (GA_3) germinated 20%, those scarified and then treated with GA_3 germinated 80%; their paper is interesting and should be obtained by anyone who is serious about seed propagation of this species.

ADDITIONAL NOTES: Similar to *Myrica* but differs in the monoecious flowers and fern-frond type leaves. I had the plant in my Illinois garden and it was performing fantastically. I planted it in a peat:soil mixture. For best growth an acid soil appears mandatory. It is a nitrogen-fixing species and forms nodules in association with an Actinomycete fungus which is quite different from the *Rhizobium*-induced nodules on many leguminous plants.

NATIVE HABITAT: Nova Scotia to Manitoba, south to North Carolina. Introduced 1714; found primarily on sandy, gravelly, infertile soils; abundant along roadsides in New England, New York, Pennsylvania.

Cornus alba — Tatarian Dogwood
(kôr′nus al′ba)

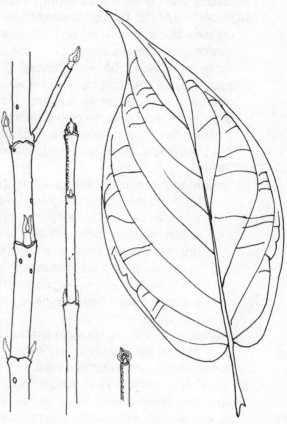

FAMILY: Cornaceae

LEAVES: Opposite, simple, ovate to elliptic, 2 to 4 1/2″ long, 1/2 as wide, acute to acuminate, usually rounded at base, entire, rugose, and often somewhat bullate above and dark green, glaucous beneath, with 5 to 6 pairs of veins; petiole 1/3 to 1″ long.

BUDS: Appressed, valvate, pubescent, deep red-brown-black in color.

STEM: Slender, hairy to glabrous, lenticels prominent, long oval, vertical, beautiful deep-red in winter; pith—white, solid, ample.

FRUIT: Drupe, white or slightly bluish, stone higher than broad, flattened at each end.

SIZE: 8 to 10′ in height, spread is variable ranging from 5 to 10′.

HARDINESS: Zone 2 to 7(8) but performing poorly in south, possibly because of canker susceptibility; have not seen a planting persist in Zone 8.

HABIT: Usually distinctly erect in youth, arching somewhat with age, the long branches sparsely branched creating an open, loose appearance; the lack of lateral bud development along the shoots is interesting; the branching (when it occurs) appears at the tops of the shoots.

RATE: Fast.

TEXTURE: Medium in leaf, medium in winter although the rich red winter stems reduce the bold harshness of the erect ascending stems.

STEM COLOR: In winter the stems change to a blood-red color; the summer color is strongly greenish with a tinge of red; the color transformation can be correlated with the short, cool days of fall and the abscission of foliage which coincides quite well with the initiation of red coloration; the oldest canes should be removed as the young stems develop the most vivid reds.

LEAF COLOR: Soft yellow-green in early spring gradually changing to lustrous dark green; fall color is often a good reddish purple, however, some plants exhibit very limited coloration.

FLOWERS: Perfect, yellowish white, May–June, after the leaves have matured, in 1 1/2 to 2″ diameter flat-topped cymes, effective 7 to 10 days; the flowers are not overwhelmingly effective; sporadic flowering may occur into the summer months.

FRUIT: Drupe, whitish or slightly blue tinted, about 3/8″ across, June to July, interesting but not long persistent; the stone (endocarp and seed) higher than wide, flattened at each end; the fruit has ornamental appeal but is little recognized by most gardeners; in fact, a question to the most knowledgeable of gardeners concerning the fuit colors of the "red-stemmed" dogwoods (C. alba, C. baileyi, C. sericea) would probably yield an I do not know response.

CULTURE: Fibrous rooted, relatively easy to transplant; adapted to varied soil conditions but prefers a moist, well-drained situation; sun or partial shade; quite vigorous and is apt to overgrow neighboring shrubs; prune 1/3 of old wood every year or cut to ground (6 to 12″ actually) in late winter; new growth of the season has the most brilliant winter stem color.

DISEASES AND INSECTS: Crown canker, flower and leaf blight, leaf spots, powdery mildews, twig blights, root rots, borers (at least seven kinds), dogwood club-gall, leaf miner, scales, and other lesser insects; the borers can be serious especially on stressed, weak growing trees.

LANDSCAPE VALUE: Difficult to use as a single specimen plant, best in shrub border, especially in large masses along roadsides, ponds and other large display areas; definitely adds color to the winter landscape; probably does not spread as rapdily as *C. sericea* and, hence, more desirable for the home landscape; the red-stemmed dogwoods are difficult to separate by winter characteristics especially as small plants and one is never absolute as to which species he is purchasing; use with discretion for this species is a strong focal point in the landscape and may actually detract from the other plant materials; tremendous interest in winter gardening in Europe and the trend is slowly crossing the Atlantic; have seen wonderful examples at Mr. Adrian Bloom's garden at Bressingham; this plant, more specifically the cultivars, make a tremendous show.

CULTIVARS:

'Argenteo-marginata' ('Elegantissima')—Leaves with an irregular creamy-white margin, the center a subdued grayish green; winter stems red; there is considerable confusion related to this cultivar and nurserymen often list it as *C. elegantissima* thus relegating it to species status which is incorrect; this is a rather pretty form and if used correctly adds a nice color touch to gardens, especially in shady areas; 'Variegata' (which may not be the correct name) is a distinctly different form with creamy white margins and dark green centers, and it is also more vigorous than 'Argenteo-marginata'; side by side there is a distinct difference in leaf coloration but I do not believe anyone in the United States has bothered to separate the two cultivars in commerce.

'Aurea'—The leaves are suffused with soft yellow; have seen in England where it looked fine; in the heat of our country I do not know how it would hold up; fall color is a striking birch yellow.

'Gouchaultii'—The leaf margin is yellow and rose, the center of the leaf green and rose; becoming partly white on the margin. *Hillier's Manual* suggested that there is no difference between this cultivar and 'Spaethii', at least among the plants in cultivation; 'Gouchaultii' is more vigorous with more silvery variegation compared to 'Spaethii', stems dark blood-red in winter.

'Kesselringii'—The stems turn dark brownish purple in winter; grows 6 to 9'; not overwhelming.

'Sibirica'—The stems are bright coral-red and the fruit is a bluish color; this cultivar is often offered in the trade but what is being sold is anyone's guess; 'Sibirica' differs from the species in the two characteristics mentioned above as well as having more rounded leaves with a short apex and a less vigorous nature; the bright stem color is best on stems of the current season's growth and this should be kept in mind during pruning; I saw several plants at the Arnold Arboretum, labeled 'Sibirica', and each was different from the other; there was a rather weak growing shrub by the pond at the foot of the lilac collection that adhered to the "true" description of 'Sibirica'; a clone called 'Westonbirt' is listed but according to W.J. Bean does not differ from "true" 'Sibirica'.

'Spaethii'—The foliage is strongly bordered with yellow; less vigorous than 'Gouchaultii'. I have seen this used in the hedge collection at the Royal Botanic Gardens, Hamilton, Ontario, in August, and would rate it the brightest yellow of any hardy, yellow-leaved type; this clone maintains the bright yellow color throughout the summer and does not show any signs of scorch; the story goes that the cultivar originated on a stem of the species, on which was grafted a white-variegated scion; the scion died and just beneath the point of union a yellow-variegated shoot developed; it could be that some callus formation had taken place before the scion died and the resultant yellow-foliaged form was, in fact, a graft-chimera. There is some indication in the literature that 'Aurea' and 'Spaethii' are the same plant but the plants I have seen labeled as each differ by the characteristics described.

PROPAGATION: Seed should be treated like *C. sericea;* most nursery production is by cuttage; I have seen nursery operations where the long stems are cut into 8 to 10" cuttings in fall or winter and directly stuck into the field; softwood and hardwood cuttings root readily and time of year; use 1000 ppm IBA-dip on June–July cuttings; one of the easiest dogwoods to root.

ADDITIONAL NOTES: Good choice for winter color especially in the northern states where shades of brown dominate; for a rather humorous look at "red-stemmed" dogwoods see Dirr. *American Horticulturist* 56(2):18–21. 1977. "In search of the elusive red-stemmed dogwood."

NATIVE HABITAT: Siberia to Manchuria and northern Korea. Introduced 1741.

Cornus alternifolia — Pagoda Dogwood
(kôr′nus al-ter-ni-fō′li-a)

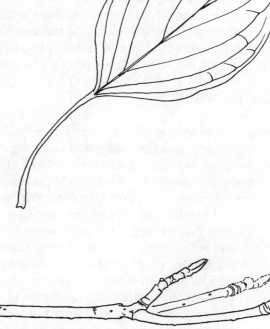

LEAVES: Alternate—but crowded near ends of twigs, appearing as if whorled, simple, elliptic-ovate, 2 to 5″ long, 1 to 2 1/2″ wide, acuminate, cuneate, entire, nearly glabrous above, medium to dark green, glaucescent beneath and appressed pubescent, with 5 to 6 pairs of veins; petiole—1 to 2″ long.

BUDS: Flower—1/4″ long, purplish, essentially glabrous at base, pubescent toward tip, valvate, terminally born; vegetative—minute, valvate, minutely hairy.

STEM: Slender, usually greenish to reddish or purplish to dark purplish brown, shiny, somewhat bloomy and glabrous; pith—white.

SIZE: 15 to 25′ in height, possibly 1 1/2 times that in spread.

HARDINESS: Zone 3 to 7.

HABIT: Spreading, horizontal, low-branched tree or large shrub with broadly horizontal branches forming horizontal tiers; interesting branching habit.

RATE: Slow initially, medium when established.

TEXTURE: Medium in leaf and winter habit; excellent textural effects because of the strong horizontal branches which are almost parallel with the ground; the sympodial or "Y"-type branching pattern creates an unusual effect.

STEM COLOR: Variable but first and second year stems are often lustrous brown to purple; quite handsome on close inspection; older bark gray and slightly ridged- and-furrowed.

LEAF COLOR: Medium to dark green, fall color can develop reddish purple; usually not developing outstanding fall color.

FLOWERS: Yellowish white, sickeningly fragrant, effective 7 to 10 days, May to early June; borne in 1 1/2 to 2 1/2″ diameter flat-topped upright cymes; the flowers are not eye catching but are sufficiently showy to be of ornamental value in the late spring landscape.

FRUIT: Drupe, bluish black, bloomy, 1/4 to 1/3″ across; July–August; not long persisting; the fruit stalk turning a pinkish red; fruit changing from green to red to blue-black at maturity; quite handsome.

CULTURE: Fibrous, spreading root system, transplants best as young plant; requires moist, acid, well-drained soil; seems to do best in a partially shaded situation although I have observed plants in full sun which appeared quite prosperous; does best in colder climates; keeping the root zone moist, acid, and cool is the key to success.

DISEASES AND INSECTS: Leaf spot, twig blight or canker are problems, see under *C. alba*.

LANDSCAPE VALUE: Possibly for naturalizing, where horizontal characteristics are needed, shrub border, where sharp vertical architectural lines are present; interesting dogwood, little used for it has rough competition from *Cornus florida*.

CULTIVARS:

'Argentea'—Leaves variegated with white, tends toward shrubby habit; a very pretty variegated form with leaves smaller than the species; although introduced before 1900 in the United States it is not common in American gardens; I have observed it in many European gardens; really stands out in a crowd; does not grow as large as *C. controversa* 'Variegata', perhaps 15'.

PROPAGATION: Seed requires a variable period of warm (2 to 5 months) followed by 2 to 3 months of cold; at Illinois I had some success with softwood cuttings but the percentage was low; during sabbatical I had 100% success; cuttings should be rooted and allowed to overwinter and break bud before potting; this is true for many dogwoods, especially tree types.

NATIVE HABITAT: New Brunswick to Minnesota south to Georgia and Alabama. Introduced 1760.

RELATED SPECIES:

Cornus controversa, (kôr'nus kon-trō-ver'sa), Giant Dogwood, is a strikingly picturesque, horizontally branched, wide spreading tree reaching 30 to 45' under cultivation but up to 60' in the wild. The creamy white flowers are borne in 3 to 7" diameter flat-topped cymes in May–June. The 1/4" diameter fruit progresses from a reddish to purple or blue-black color in August–September. The dark green leaves range from 3 to 6" long and 2 to 3" wide with a 1 to 2" long petiole. They have 6 to 8, sometimes 9, vein pairs. In fall, the leaves may turn purple but I have not noticed good fall coloration on this species. Seeds require 5 months warm followed by 3 months cold; softwood cuttings root readily and should not be disturbed after rooting; I collected cuttings on August 24, treated them with 8000 ppm IBA-quick dip, sand:perlite and in 8 weeks had 100% rooting with unbelievably profuse root systems. 'Variegata' has an irregular, creamy white border, the leave being long, narrow and lanceolate, usually less than 1 1/2" wide, and often unequally sided and somewhat deformed; again this cultivar is evident in many English gardens. It is more vigorous than *C. alternifolia* 'Variegata' and makes a more stunning sight. Certainly one of the handsomest trees in cultivation resides in the Bath Botanic Garden, England. Two of the most notable American specimens of the species are located at the Arnold (30 to 35' high) and Secrest (45' by 48') Arboreta. Raulston reported it was the fastest (3 to 5' per year) of all dogwoods at Raleigh, NC. Perhaps more urban tolerant than other dogwoods. Has been used as a street tree in Swarthmore, PA. Japan, China. Introduced 1880. Zone 5 to 8, possibly hardy in 4.

Cornus amomum — Silky Dogwood
(kôr'nus ȧ-mō'mum)

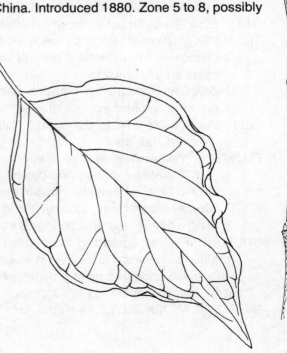

LEAVES: Opposite, simple, elliptic-ovate or elliptic, 2 to 4" long, 1 to 2 1/4" wide, short acuminate, usually rounded at base, medium to dark green and nearly glabrous above, glaucous beneath and with grayish white or brownish hairs on the veins, 4 to 7 vein pairs. petiole—1/3 to 2/3" long, pubescent.

BUDS: Flower-terminally borne, hairy, valvate, nearly sessile, relatively small; vegetative-valvate, appressed, pubescent, small.

STEM: slender, purplish, rarely greenish, appressed pubescence especially on younger branches, second year wood showing distinct fissuring pattern; pith-brown, solid.

SIZE: 6 to 10' in height by 6 to 10' in spread.

HARDINESS: Zone 5 to 8.

HABIT: Rounded, multistemmed shrub usually twiggy and round-topped in youth, becoming open with age; often straggly, unkempt and without ornamental appeal.

RATE: Medium (possibly fast).

TEXTURE: Medium in foliage; medium-coarse in winter.

STEM COLOR: Young branches reddish purple, sometimes greenish; older wood is brownish purple and develops brown fissured areas.

LEAF COLOR: Medium to dark green in summer; fall color is often green to brown although various authors mention reddish purple as a possibility; have seen purple fall coloration but it was not spectacular.

FLOWERS: Yellowish white, not fragrant, June, 7 to 10 days, borne in upright, 1 1/2 to 2 1/2" diameter, flat-topped, slightly villous cymes.

FRUIT: Drupe, 1/4" across, bluish often with white blotches, almost porcelain blue, rather attractive; unfortunately persisting only a brief time in August, for the birds and other forces of nature quickly ravage the fruits.

CULTURE: Native in low woods, along streams and borders of swamps over much of the eastern United States; fibrous rooted, easily transplanted; quite adaptable but prefers moist, partially shaded situations although it performs well in full sun and with less than optimum moisture.

DISEASES AND INSECTS: Scale may present a problem, see under *C. alba*.

LANDSCAPE VALUE: Possibly massing, shrub borders, naturalizing, in moist and wet soils where many shrubs do not grow well; probably too coarse and with limited ornamental assets to ever become a common landscape shrub but, like all plants, in the proper setting it has a place; in full sun in the Georgia Botanical Garden a plant has gown 10' by 15'.

PROPAGATION: Seed, 90 to 120 days at 41°F will break the dormancy; cuttings, softwood, taken in July rooted well without hormonal treatment; rooting can be enhanced with IBA treatment, probably 1000 to 3000 ppm IBA best.

NATIVE HABITAT: Massachusetts to Georgia, west to New York and Tennessee. Introduced 1658.

RELATED SPECIES: There are a number of related taxa that do not show a dime's worth of difference but have been listed as species and varieties by various authorities. They are included here so the reader can practice splitting taxonomic hairs.

Cornus asperifolia, (kôr′nus as-per-i-fō′li-à), Roughleaf Dogwood, and the variety *drummondii* are more or less pubescent cousins of *C. amomum*. I have seen *C. asperifolia* in Kansas and identified it as *C. amomum*. It can grow to 15' in height and sometimes makes a small tree to 40 to 45'. Flowers and fruits are similar to *C. amomum* although fruit is usually white. Pith is brown like *C. amomum*. The leaves of var. *drummondii* are hairy above with thicker softer pubescence below and about 5 vein pairs. Ontario to Florida, west to Iowa, Kansas and Texas. Cultivated 1836. Zone 4 to 8 (9).

Cornus obliqua (*C. purpusii*), (kôr′nus ō-blē′kwà), Pale Dogwood, is similar to *C. amomum* but is usually more loosely branched and the stems are purple to yellowish red. It grows in wet soils. Quebec, Minnesota, and Kansas, southern Pennsylvania, Illinois and Missouri. Cultivated 1888. Zone 3.

Cornus canadensis — Bunchberry
(kôr′nus kan-a-den′sis)

LEAVES: Alternate, appearing whorled at top of stem, oval to obovate, 1 to 3" long, acute, glabrous or slightly appressed-pubescent, glossy dark green, 2 to 3 vein pairs.

SIZE: 3 to 9″ high, wide spreading but in a slow fashion.
HARDINESS: Zone 2 to 6, best in cold climates.
HABIT: Beautiful deciduous ground cover, in favorable areas form-
    ing a carpet-like mat.
RATE: Slow.
TEXTURE: Medium-fine in all seasons.
LEAF COLOR: Shiny dark green in summer changing to red and
    vinous-red in fall.
FLOWERS: Fertile flowers greenish white, not showy; bracts are
    borne in four's, white, appearing from May through July, very
    striking in flower.
FRUIT: Scarlet, berry-like drupe, 1/4″ diameter, ripening in August
    and later; persisting quite late or until eaten by the birds; again very lovely.
CULTURE: Sod cut from established plantings is probably the best mode of transplanting; requires moist,
    acid soil rich in organic matter; prefers a cool atmosphere; partial or full shade; needs frequent
    watering until well-established; mulching with acid material such as peat moss or pine needles is
    recommended.
DISEASES AND INSECTS: None serious.
LANDSCAPE VALUE: Probably one of our most beautiful native ground covers; fastidious as to culture
    but worth the effort; excellent under pines, broadleaf evergreens and other acid-requiring plants.
PROPAGATION: Moving pieces of sod is the most practical way; seeds require a warm plus cold
    stratification period; one report noted 60 minutes of acid followed by 60 to 90 days of cold resulted
    in high germination.
NATIVE HABITAT: Southern Greenland to Alaska, south to Maryland, west to South Dakota, New Mexico,
    and California; found at high altitudes in cool, moist woods, and on hummocks in bogs.

Cornus florida — Flowering Dogwood
(kôr′nus flôr′-i-da)

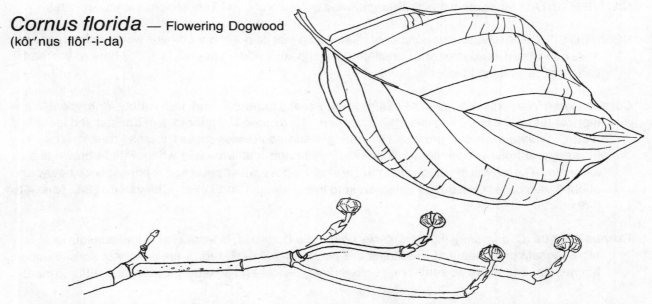

LEAVES: Opposite, simple, oval or ovate, 3 to 6″ long, 1 1/2 to 3″ wide, abruptly acuminate, broad cuneate
    to rounded at base, nearly glabrous and dark green above, glaucous beneath and usually only
    pubescent on the veins, with 6 to 7 vein pairs; petiole 1/4 to 3/4″ long.
BUDS: Flower—usually at end of stem, globose, biscuit shape, flattened, valvate, covered by 2 large silky
    appressed pubescent scales; vegetative—small, valvate, slender, almost hidden by raised leaf scar;
    leaf scars usually completely encircling stem.
STEM: Slender, green to purple, sometimes bloomy, pubescent when young, finally glabrous.
BARK: Broken into small squarish and rectangular blocks, the entire effect reminiscent of an alligator's
    back.

SIZE: Variable with location, in some areas 20' in height represents a magnificent specimen, however, the tree can reach 30 to 40' in height with a spread equal to or considerably greater than the height.

HARDINESS: Zone 5; this is a misnomer for seedling material from southern sources is not adequately hardy under Zone 5 conditions; plants which are sold in Zone 5 should be grown from seed collected from trees indigenous to those areas; I have observed far too many Flowering Dogwoods in the midwest with minimal flower production principally caused by lack of flower bud hardiness; if possible, always ask the nurserymen where the trees are grown and this, in turn, will save considerable disappointment when in 3 to 5 years time the trees show limited flowering; grows into Zone 9.

HABIT: Shrub (seldom) or small, low-branched tree with spreading horizontal lines, layered effect, usually with a flat-topped crown and often wider than high at maturity; excellent plant for winter habit, very unique.

RATE: Slow upon transplanting, gradually assuming a medium rate.

TEXTURE: Medium in foliage; medium or fine in winter; the soft gray to purple young stems silhouetted against snowy or evergreen backgrounds are as handsome as the flowers (almost).

STEM COLOR: Young stems are often purplish, gradually turning grayish; older wood (3 to 4" diameter) becomes scaly (grayish brown) and develops an "alligator" hide appearance.

LEAF COLOR: A handsome bronze-green to yellow-green when unfolding, usually a good dark green in summer, fall color is a consistent red to reddish purple; one of the most consistent trees for excellent fall color; tremendous variation from seedling grown material in all characteristics (habit, fall color, flower).

FLOWERS: True flowers are greenish yellow and unimportant, each 1/4" across, in a crowded 1/2" wide head, showy parts of inflorescences are the 4 white bracts which are obovate or emarginate, about 2" long, the entire involucre (bracts) 3 to 4" across, occur in April to May, effective for 10 to 14 days depending on the weather; true flowers are borne in short stalked cymes (umbels?) and are subtended by the handsome bracts; normally in full regalia in mid April (Athens, GA).

FRUIT: Drupe, glossy red, 1/3" long, ovoid, 3 to 4 or more in a "cluster", ripening in September to October and can persist until mid December; birds seem to devour them or they often simply abscise after ripening; tremendous variation in fruit retention; have seen fruits as late as early February in Athens.

CULTURE: Even as a small tree (3 to 4') move balled and burlapped; provide an acid, well drained soil with sufficient organic matter; mulch to maintain a cool, moist, soil; place in partial shade although full sun is acceptable; this particular species grows wild over the eastern United States and if you have ever witnessed a woodland dotted in flower, the reason for its popularity becomes evident; trees planted in poorly drained soils and open areas where summer water is limited invariably decline and die; not pollution tolerant.

DISEASES AND INSECTS: It seems that everytime I pick up a trade publication there is an article on Flowering Dogwood insects or diseases; there is no question that this species is susceptible to a number of troublesome pests including borer and various petal and leaf spots; a recent scientific paper concluded that the more stressed the tree the more likely it is to become infested with borer; an article on Dogwood diseases by Lambe and Justis. *Ornamentals Northwest.* June–July, 1978 lists many *C. florida* diseases; this is worth obtaining; the old axiom in the north was never plant a dogwood in a hot, dry site but in the south I have seen trees in full sun, in acid, clay soil doing splendidly; the summers of 1980, 81, 87 and 88 were exceptionally dry and although newly planted dogwoods declined, established trees fared reasonably well. Since the last edition a prominent leaf and stem anthracnose, *Discula* has weakened and/or killed many dogwoods in the Middle Atlantic and New England states. Was also discovered in North Georgia on native dogwoods but has not been found to any degree in the Athens-Atlanta area. Several state and federal agencies are working on the disease. The symptoms include small, purple-rimmed leaf spots or large tan blotches that may enlarge and kill the entire leaf; infected leaves may cling to stems after normal leaf fall; twigs may die back several inches and all the way to the main stem; epicormic (water sprouts) often form up and down the main stem and on major branches; these also become infected and die; bracts may also be infected if rainy conditions prevail during flowering: trees are often killed 2 to 3 years after the first attack; disease discovered in late 1970's; by 1986 discovered in nine northeastern states and as far south as West Virginia, in 1987 found in northern Georgia; several fungicides are reasonably effective for controlling the disease.

LANDSCAPE VALUE: The aristocrat of native flowering trees, often overplanted but never becomes obnoxious as is the case with forsythia, deutzia and spirea; a plant with four-season character (excellent flower, summer and fall foliage, fruit, and winter habit); excellent as specimen, near a patio, corners of houses and larger buildings, parks, groupings; especially effective against a red brick background where the flowers are accentuated, as is the branching habit in winter; Dr. Wyman considers it the best ornamental of all the natives growing in northern United States; has the quality of flowering before the leaves and consequently vegetative competition is minimized.

CULTIVARS:

The selections are numerous and to select the best may be like rolling the dice...one takes his/her chances. To minimize chance, I talked with John Pair (and read his publications), Wichita, KS, and used my eyes. Many new cultivars have been introduced since the last edition and Santamour and McArdle *J. Arbor.* 11(1):29–36 (1985) offer a cultivar checklist of the large-bracted dogwoods.

'Abundance'—Probably same as 'Cloud 9'.

'American Beauty Red'—Attractive foliage and pretty deep red flowers.

'Apple Blossom'—Light pink flowers—shading to white in the center.

'Barton'—A large, white-flowered form with overlapping bracts that flowers heavily as a young plant and is well suited for culture in Zone 6 through 8; this cultivar has performed extremely well at the Georgia Botanical Garden.

'Belmont Pink'—Flowers (bracts) blushed pink, apparently no longer in cultivation.

'Big Girl'—Large white flowers.

'Bonnie'—A selection from Louisiana State University with 6″ diameter white flowers and showy red fruits.

'Cherokee Chief'—Flowers rich ruby-red and new growth reddish; bracts may develop a spotting, has been serious in Athens area; one of the most popular red-bracted forms.

'Cherokee Daybreak'—Leaves green and white and hold color without scorching in hot weather, turn pink to deep red in fall, vigorous, upright in habit, white bracts, Commercial Nursery introduction.

'Cherokee Princess'—White with large bracts, early flowering, heavy flowering every year.

'Cherokee Sunset'—Pinkish red tipped new growth, matures to green with a broad irregular margin of yellow that will not burn in the heat of summer, fall color ranges from pink through red to purple, the bracts are a good red, excellent vigor and resistance to anthracnose, have seen in a nursery field in Tennessee and believe it will prove a great success, Commercial Nursery introduction, Decherd, TN.

'Cloud 9'—Slow growing with showy white overlapping bracts, profusely flowering when young, spreading habit, considered one of the best and Pair rated it one of the most flower bud hardy.

'Compacta'—Dwarf plant reaching 4′ tall in 8 to 10 years.

'Dekalb Red'—Semi-dwarf habit, bracts wine-red.

'Fastigiata'—Maintains upright habit only while young; have seen a large specimen at Bernheim Arboretum and the branches were fairly erect although some of the outer branches were starting to spread, white bracts.

'First Lady'—Variegated yellow and green foliage, a bit difficult to work into the common landscape, more vigorous than 'Welchii' and does not tend to "burn", but loses most of its variegation in Zone 8.

'Fragrant Cloud'—White flowers, profuse, similar to 'Cloud 9', slightly fragrant.

'Gigantea'—Large flowered form, flower bracts 6″ from tip to tip.

'Green Glow'—Listed as fastest growing of all dogwoods, upright, tight and compact, single white, heavy flowering, leaves with interesting light green blotches surrounded by darker green margin.

'Golden Nugget'—Bronzy gold margined leaves more vigorous than 'Welchii'.

'Hillenmeyer'—Outstanding early blooming white-bracted form.

'Hohman's Gold'—Variegated golden yellow and green foliage that turns deep red in fall; fall color is spectacular, yellowish areas lighter red than green areas.

'Imperial White'—Large white bracts, "flower" diameter to 6".

'Junior Miss'—A rather attractive, large flowered form, the outer portion of the bracts a deep pink grading to whitish in the center; grew next to 'Cherokee Chief' in the Georgia Botanical Garden and made the latter pale by comparison; it also contracted no bract spotting (anthracnose) while 'Cherokee Chief' was heavily infected.

'Magnifica'—Flower bracts white, about 4" from tip to tip.

'Mary Ellen'—Flowers double, white.

'Moon'—Form with unusually large bracts; very floriferous.

'Multibracteata'—Double form.

'Mystery'—Bracts white with reddish spots; compact habit, resists drought.

'New Hampshire'—Hardy, white flower producing clone from Atkinson, New Hampshire; gave a talk in New Hampshire several years back and we had a lively discussion on whether this tree still existed; consensus was no!

'October Glory'—A selected strain of own-rooted pink dogwood with brilliant red fall color, a Princeton introduction.

'Pendula'—Weeping form with stiffly pendulous branches and white flowers; may come true to type from seed; original clone was raised in Meehan's nursery, Philadelphia before 1880; not a particularly attractive weeping form; in my estimation there are several weeping forms in the trade.

'Pink Flame'—Bracts pink, leaves with yellow variegation, wrinkled; selected from a sport of *C. florida* var. *rubra.*

'Pink Sachet'—Similar to 'Cherokee Chief' but with pronounced fragrance to flowers resembling gardenia, honeysuckle and sweetshrub.

'Plena'—Double white form, catch-all term for double types.

f. *pluribracteata* ('Pluribracteata')—A "double" form with 7 to 8 large bracts and many aborted smaller ones.

'Poinsett'—Compact, vigorous-growing form; yellow berries in center of red fall leaves gives this cultivar its name.

'President Ford'—A fast growing, multicolored yellow and green form; the foliage of which remains effective until after 3 or 4 killing frosts.

'Prosser Red'—Bracts dark red.

'Purple Glory'—A purple-leaf form that holds this color through the growing season; in October the leaf color is a dark, almost black purple; dark red flowers.

var. *pygmaea* or 'Pygmaea'—Considerable confusion exists within this taxon; there are several (many?) dwarf clones in cultivation; essentially they are rounded to globose and have excellent dark green foliage; some flower, others do not; degree of dwarfness varies for one plant at Longwood Gardens is a good 6 to 8' high; not a bad plant for effect; white bracts.

'Rainbow'—Variegated deep yellow and green; turns carmine-red in fall, white bracts in spring.

'Red Cloud'—Bracts pink; leaves with crinkled margins.

'Red Giant'—Bracts red with white tips.

'Reddy'—Flowers and leaves red.

'Redleaf'—Bracts red; leaves remain reddish year-round.

'Rich-red'—Red flowered form.

'Roberts Pink'—A vigorous growing pink dogwood for the deep south.

'Royal Red'—New foliage opens blood-red, turns red in fall; flowers are deep red and very large.

var. *rubra*—Pink to pinkish red flowers, considerable variation in color; the history of this variety is not clear but it was apparently first discovered in Virginia; it is a beautiful plant when properly grown; the flowers are not as cold hardy as the white form (at least those from northern sources);

during the winter of 1976–77 and 77–78 when the outer bracts of many of the white trees were injured, the entire flower (4-bracts) was killed on the pink form; tends to open a few days later than the typical white form.

'Salicifolia' ('Boyd's Willowleaf')—Whether these two names are synonymous is a moot question; 'Salicifolia' is a small, mounded tree, the leaves being very narrow and willow-shaped, it has a rather fine texture and to my knowledge does not flower.

'September Dog'—Flowers in September, rather than spring, flower buds begin to develop in August but instead of entering dormancy, continue to mature and flower, no fruits are formed.

'Spring Song'—Deep rose-red flowers.

'Springtime'—Selection from Spring Grove, Cincinnati, large white overlapping bracts, 5″ across tip to tip.

'Steele's Fastigiate'—Upright branching form with darker green foliage and larger flowers than typical.

'Stokes Pink'—Pink bracts, on a medium size upright tree, good in warm climates.

'Sweetwater Red'—Deep red flowers and reddish foliage, good red-purple fall color.

'Tricolor'—White bracts, leaves with white irregular margin, flushed rose-pink, turning purple in fall with rose-red margins.

'Weaver's White'—Large white bracts, unique foliage, does well in deep south.

'Welchii'—Leaves are a combination of green, creamy white and pink; stands out in a crowd; definite clashing of color; best in partial shade; spectacular rose red to red purple fall color; white bracts.

'Welch's Bay Beauty'—Particularly handsome white double form with flowers like *Gardenia*; 7 sets of whorled bracts, 4.5 to 5.5″ diameter, performs better in south, holds leaves longer and develops good autumn color, 20′; probably not as hardy as 'Pluribracteata'.

'White Bouquet'—Heavy and consistent display of large pure white bracts on a compact plant.

'White Cloud'—Numerous creamy white flowers especially when plant is very young.

'White Giant'—Large white bracts.

'Williams Red'—A deep rose-red flowering form for the deep south.

'Willsii'—Leaves gray-green with white margins; leaves somewhat puckered.

'World's Fair'—Bracts white, produced at an early age, stocky trunk, large diameter limbs, drought resistant, hardy to −7°F.

f. *xanthocarpa* ('Xanthocarpa')—Yellow-fruited form; again several clones in cultivation; the stems show no trace of red-pigment and I suspect the fall color would be yellowish.

PROPAGATION: Seed, dormant embryo, 100 to 130 days at 41°F. Cuttings, softwood, collected immediately after the flowering period ended, rooted readily in three weeks; softwood cuttings collected in June rooted 56 percent in sand under mist, when treated with 10000 ppm IBA, quick dip, after 8 weeks; this same clone rooted 93 percent in peat:perlite under mist in 10 weeks with the same hormonal treatment; apparently, the acidity of the medium influenced the degree of rooting since other factors were constant. Also see Savella *PIPPS* 30:405–406. 1980. "Propagating pink dogwoods from rooted cuttings"; one of the most important aspects is to allow the rooted cuttings to go through a dormant period and when growth ensues then pot them.

ADDITIONAL NOTES: A most important ornamental tree in commercial nursery production. Millions of seedlings and budded trees are produced every year. For the gardener, the heavy budded large bracted cultivars are worth considering. For producers a paper by Badenhop and Glosgow, *J. Environmental Horticulture* 3(2):49–52 (1985) discusses a production system and costs for propagating dogwoods from softwood cuttings. They estimated a cost of $0.34 per rooted cutting and reported growers in the future will be producing part of their dogwood crop by cuttings.

An excellent new (1988) Extension publication, *A Guide to the Commercial Propagation of Dogwoods* by Coartney, Lukham and Smeal, Virginia Tech, Blacksburg, VA is available. Covers all facets of seed, cutting, budding production.

NATIVE HABITAT: Massachusetts to Florida, west to Ontario, Texas and Mexico. Cultivated 1731.

RELATED SPECIES:

Cornus nuttallii — Pacific Dogwood
(kôr′nus nū-tal′ē-ī)

LEAVES: Alternate, simple, elliptic-ovate to obovate, 3 to 5″ long, 1 1/2 to 3″ wide, short acuminate, broad cuneate, appressed pilose when young, at maturity only beneath or glabrous, 5 to 6 vein pairs; petiole—1/4 to 1/2″ long.

Cornus nuttallii, Pacific Dogwood, is the West Coast edition of *C. florida* and is a beautiful tree in its own right. The principal difference resides in the flower; the true flowers purple and green, crowded into a dense 3/4″ diameter head; these are surrounded by 4 to 8, usually 6, showy bracts; each bract is oval to obovate, pointed and ranges from 1 1/2 to 3″ long and 1 to 2″ wide; creamy white then white or flushed with pink; the true flowers are not enclosed by the bracts as in *C. florida* and are subject to the vagaries of weather. Fruit is an orange to red ellipsoidal 1/3″ long drupe. This is a beautiful dogwood in flower but it does not appear suited to the eastern United States. 'Corigo Giant' is larger growing and flowered than the species; bracts up to 8″ across, overlapping, with large, heavy textured green leaves and wonderful fall color; 'Goldspot' has leaves that are splashed, spotted and mottled with creamy-yellow markings and the white bracts are larger than the species. 'Eddie's White Wonder' is the result of a cross between *C. florida* and *C. nuttallii;* it is supposedly better adapted to east coast conditions than *C. nuttallii* but has not proven that suitable; a large east coast mailorder nursery firm who specializes in unusual woody plants has dropped this cultivar from its list; the flowers resemble *C. nuttallii* in that the overwintering flowers are not enclosed by the bracts.

I have observed 'Eddie's White Wonder' at the Arnold Arboretum where it was marginally subsistent owing to cold and the uncovered flower buds which appear much more cold susceptible. There is a fine plant at N.C. State Arboretum that could get one excited, with distinct upright habit without the layered appearance of *C. florida.* I am skittish about cold hardiness and Dr. Elwin Orton, Rutgers University, reported that *C. nuttallii* flowers "blasted" in Zone 6 (USDA) (−10 to 0°F) and plants were not vegetatively hardy. He also mentioned that the flower buds of 'Eddie's White Wonder' were subject to desiccation and/or winterkill in central New Jersey, and floral display was poor. Hybrids between *C. nuttallii* and *C. florida* have resembled *C. nuttallii* and were only marginally winter hardy. Also, as trees increase in caliper, bark split is common on the south and/or southwest side. Hybrids of *C. nuttallii* and *C. kousa* are typically upright in habit with naked flower buds and the usual "blasting" in winter. Vegetatively plants are more cold hardy than *C. nuttallii* and *C. florida* hybrids but still exhibit bark split. See *PIPPS* 35:655–661 (1985) for more details.

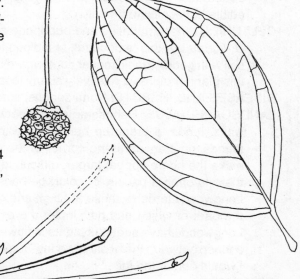

Cornus kousa — Kousa Dogwood
(kôr′nus koo′sa)

LEAVES: Opposite, simple, elliptic-ovate, 2 to 4″ long, 3/4 to 1 3/4″ wide, acuminate, cuneate, dark green above, glaucous and appressed—pilose beneath and with large axillary fulvous tufts of hairs; petiole—1/4 to 1/2″ long.

BUDS: Flower—Formed at end of stem, fattened and globose at base with 2 valvate silky appressed pubescent bud scales forming a sharp apex; vegetative—valvate, appressed, brownish black, usually longer than those of *C. florida*.

STEM: Slender, light tan with tinges of purple and green, essentially glabrous.

BARK: Exfoliating with age and forming a mottled mosaic of gray, tan and rich brown.

SIZE: About 20 to 30′ in height with an equal spread; can be smaller or larger depending on the area of the country.

HARDINESS: Zone 5 to 8; at one time no one thought this plant could be grown in the south; Callaway Gardens disproved that; flower buds are definitely more cold hardy than those of *C. florida;* should be given a Zone 4 designation.

HABIT: In youth, vase-shaped in habit, with age, forming a rounded appearance with distinct stratified branching pattern; very strong horizontal lines are evident in old age.

RATE: Slow, possibly medium in early stages of growth.

TEXTURE: Medium in leaf and winter character; very handsome in the winter because of horizontal branching character.

BARK COLOR: Older wood often develops multicolored gray-tan-rich brown areas due to exfoliating nature of the bark.

LEAF COLOR: Dark green in summer foliage changing to reddish purple or scarlet in fall, persisting for 3 to 5 weeks, significant variation in intensity of fall color.

FLOWERS: The true flowers are small and inconspicuous and are produced in a 5/8″ diameter rounded umbel on an upright 2″ long peduncle that originates from short lateral spurs at the end of a small 2 to 4-leaved twig; the creamy white bracts are the showy part of the inflorescence and are borne in June (mid-May, Athens), approximately 2 to 3 weeks after those of *Cornus florida;* the 4 bracts are taper-pointed, 1 to 2″ long, 1/4 to 3/4″ wide; the flowers, being stalked, are raised above the foliage creating a milky way effect along the horizontal branches; the bracts persist for up to 6 weeks and longer; in the aging process they often become pinkish. Tremendous interest in a pure pink or rose bracted form but most start white and age to pink; in late June of 1988 at Bodnant Gardens, Wales, I saw a deep rose-pink bracted *C. kousa;* I suspect that the cooler temperatures contribute to more intense pink/rose; have seen more trees in Europe with good pinkish bract color than in U.S.

FRUIT: Drupe, pinkish red to red, borne in 1/2 to 1″ diameter, globose syncarp (resemble a raspberry in appearance); borne on a 2 to 2 1/2″ long pendulous stalk; late August through October, very effective, edible but somewhat mealy.

CULTURE: Transplant balled and burlapped as young specimen, considered more difficult to grow than *C. florida* but this is doubtful, fastidious for acid, well drained soil, seems to perform best in sandy soil with good organic matter content; well worth the extra cultural efforts needed to successfully grow this plant; requires a relatively sunny location; more drought resistant than *C. florida*.

DISEASES AND INSECTS: None serious, some borer damage reported.

LANDSCAPE VALUE: Handsome small specimen tree or shrub, excellent near large buildings or blank walls, tends to break up harshness with horizontal structure, works well in shrub border or in a foundation planting at the corner of the house; the horizontal lines break up the vertical lines and make the home appear larger; difficult to overuse this plant; the flowers appear in May–June when there is often a paucity of color; perhaps the finest specimens in the United States are located at Longwood Gardens; these 30′ high and 40′ wide trees are low branched with rather massive trunks, the bark of which has developed the exfoliating characteristics to the maximum; in my travels to Longwood I have seen the plants in flower, fruit, fall color and winter bark and can say that if I had to choose between the best Flowering Dogwood for my garden or one of Longwood's Kousa Dogwoods, I would opt for the latter.

CULTIVARS:

'Big Apple'—A large spreading tree with heavy textured dark green leaves and very large fruit; hardy to −5°F; a Polly Hill introduction.

var. *chinensis*—According to Wyman and Bean there is not much botanical difference between this form and the species, however, under cultivation the variety grows more freely and the flowers are larger than those of any form; introduced by E.H. Wilson from Hupeh, China in 1907; it can grow to 30'; the bracts range from 1 1/2 to 2 1/2" long, 3/4 to 1" wide; the fruits as described by E.H. Wilson are sweet and edible; I have sampled the fruits of this variety and the species and can honestly say I prefer Snicker's Bars; the bracts start off a soft green and gradually change to white; certainly one of the most beautiful of all flowering trees.

'Dwarf Pink'—Bracts light pink, growth habit low spreading, reaching 6 to 9' tall; found wild in Gumma Prefecture of Japan.

'Elizabeth Lustgarten'—Distinct weeping tendency to upper branches, forms graceful rounded crown, leading branches weep 2' from highest point of curve, 7' high and 4 to 5' wide after 12 years, selected from seedlings grown by Baier Lustgarten, at Lustgarten Nurseries, Long Island.

'Fanfare'—Plant with fastigiate upright growth habit; hardy to −20°F.

'Gay Head'—Tree of medium size, bracts of different sizes and curved or ruffled; hardy to −5°F; a Polly Hill introduction.

'Gold Star'—Foliage splashed with broad central band of gold through spring and summer, will revert to green as is true for many plants with the center variegation, supposedly reddish stems that set off the foliage, introduced by Dutch nurserymen who got it from Japan. I have seen the plant on several occasions and it is quite handsome but appears quite slow growing; bracts are white.

'Lustgarten Weeping'—Another weeping form; Jim Cross, Environmentals, Long Island, told me that this was a beautiful specimen because the flowers are positioned along the weeping stems so that they are directly in view, 12 year old plant was 10' wide and 2 to 3' high; all branches arch over 12 to 15" above ground; needs to be grafted on a standard to produce a small weeping tree.

'Madame Butterfly'—An extremely floriferous plant with flowers borne on long pedicels and bracts turning vertical about the midpoint of their length, giving the appearance of butterflies on the branches.

'Milky Way'—Cultivar of var. *chinensis* with very floriferous habit; I have witnessed this specimen at Mill Creek Valley Park, Youngstown, Ohio, and was amazed at the flower and fruit production compared to the species this was a very broad, bushy form suitable for the small landscape; this may be a commercially manufactured name for the variety; nevertheless it appears more floriferous than the species and for that reason deserves to be mentioned.

'Moonbeam'—Flowers 7 to 8" in diameter, on long peduncles inclined so blooms are visible at eye level; plant hardy to −20°F.

'National'—Large creamy white bracts on a vigorous vase-shaped tree, fruits are larger than normal; U.S. National Arboretum introduction.

'Nell Monk'—Large broad bracts overlap at their edges, extremely floriferous, grown from seed collected at Nymans, England in 1968 and registered in 1987.

'Prolific'—White flowered bracts in June, slightly hardier than *C. florida*.

'Rochester'—More vigorous than the species.

'Rosabella'—A fine rose pink bract form that is offered through Wayside Gardens.

'Silverstar'—Plant has upright arching, vase-shaped growth habit; smooth exfoliating bark, hardy to −20°F.

'Snowboy'—The gray-green leaf has a creamy white narrow margin with occasional splashes of yellow throughout the leaf; again, not a particularly stable form and not particularly vigorous.

'Speciosa'—Dark green leaves curling slightly at margins impart an interesting bicolor effect, large white bracts (Vermeulen).

'Square Dance'—Upright growth habit with flowers most visible from above; hardy to −5°F; a Polly Hill introduction.

'Summer Stars'—A Bill Flemer introduction from Princeton Nursery; bracts hang on up to 6 weeks after the initiation of flowering; the fruits supposedly develop with the bracts still present; dark green foliage changes to reddish purple in fall.

'Triple Crown'—Small plant with dainty growth habit that flowers heavily with blooms mostly in triple clusters; hardy to −20°F.

'Twinkle'—Habit upright, compact; flowers with 6 to 9 bracts; wine-red fall color.

'Variegata'—There is probably more than one variegated form in cultivation; the one plant I have seen at the Arnold Arboretum is rather unstable and the white marked leaves may revert to green.

'Weaver's Weeping'—Exceptionally heavy flower display on weeping branches.

'Wilton'—Flowers more persistent than typical.

'Xanthocarpa'—Yellow-fruited form.

It is worth noting that *C. kousa* is variable from seed and I have seen selected seedling populations with immense bracts (3″ long) and fruits (1 to 2″ across); some of these may find their way into the trade in the future.

PROPAGATION: Cuttings, somewhat more difficult to root than *C. florida* but various investigators have been able to achieve 50% success from softwood cuttings treated with IBA; from my own experience, softwood cuttings collected in June rooted 50 percent with 10000 ppm IBA-quick dip when placed in peat:perlite under mist after 12 weeks; all cuttings had callused and possibly would have rooted with increasing time; best not to disturb cuttings after rooting; seed is easily germinated and requires 3 months at 41°F.

ADDITIONAL NOTES: Dr. Elwin Orton, Rutgers University, has conducted outstanding work in woody ornamental plant breeding with *Ilex* and *Cornus*. I present information relative to crosses between *C. florida, C. kousa,* and *C. nuttallii*. For full article see *PIPPS* 35:655–661 (1985). Dr. Orton's goals were increased vigor, borer resistance, pink bracts perhaps on *C. kousa*. The best of his crosses produced five clones of *C. kousa* × *C. florida*. Four are intermediate in floral display and anthesis (flower opening) with the upright habit (in youth) of *C. kousa*. Three have white bracts; one soft pink bracts. The fifth clone resembles *C. florida* with a low, spreading habit of growth and floral display sufficiently early to overlap plants of *C. florida*. The bracts of all are intermediate in shape to those of the parents. Interestingly, the floral bracts do not enclose the true flowers as tightly as either parent. Many are more vigorous than the parents, i.e., display hybrid vigor and are highly resistant to dogwood borer. Vegetatively they have been winter hardy at New Brunswick, NJ although some floral bract injury has occurred following a severe winter.

Orton also mentions that the *C. kousa* genetic base from the original introductions was so narrow that plants show inbreeding depression, i.e., reduced vigor, rounded compact habit of growth, spindly branches and small leaves. Seed should be collected from open pollinated seedlings rather than a single isolated clone.

NATIVE HABITAT: Japan, Korea, China. Introduced 1875.

Cornus macrophylla — Bigleaf Dogwood
(kôr′nus mak-rō-fil′à)

LEAVES: Opposite, simple, ovate to elliptic-ovate, 4 to 7″ long, 2 to 3 1/2″ wide, acuminate, rounded at base, dark green above and slightly rough, grayish green beneath with appressed pubescence, 6 to 8 vein pairs; petiole—1/4 to 1 1/2″ long.

Cornus macrophylla, Bigleaf Dogwood, is virtually unknown in the United States but might be worth a close inspection. It is a small tree of essentially rounded outline that will grow 25 to 35′ high. Based on observations at the Arnold Arboretum, this tree might have possibilities in dry soils and could perhaps be adapted to street tree or large outdoor container use. The large, 4 to 6″ diameter, cymose-like panicles of yellowish white flowers occur in July and August at a time when precious few other trees show any color. The 1/4″ diameter, globose fruits color reddish purple and at maturity are blackish purple. In most respects the fruits are similar to *C. alternifolia*. The bark is a relatively smooth gray. Interestingly it roots readily from softwood cuttings; July 28 cuttings produced tremendous root systems (100% rooting) when treated with 4000 ppm IBA-quick dip and placed in sand:perlite under mist. Gary Koller, Arnold Arboretum, believes this tree could be a valuable addition to the list of urban trees. Himalaya, China, Japan. Introduced 1827. Zone 5 to 7(?).

Cornus mas — Corneliancherry Dogwood
(kôr′nus mas)

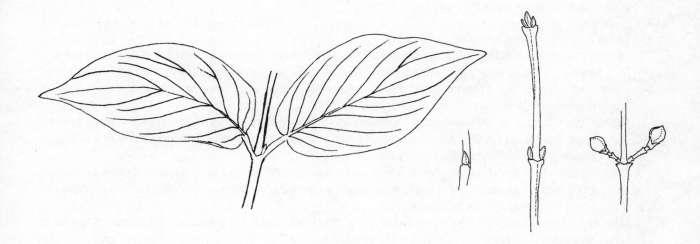

LEAVES: Opposite, simple, ovate to elliptic, 2 to 4″ long, 3/4 to 1 1/2″ wide, acute to acuminate, broad-cuneate at base, appressed-pilose on both sides, dark green above, with 3 to 5 pairs of veins; petiole about 1/4″ long.
BUDS: Flower—borne in axillary position, appear stalked, valvate, globose, without sharp apex, yellow green-brown in color, appressed pubescence; vegetative—valvate, more divergent than other dogwood vegetative buds, greenish with silky appressed pubescence.
STEM: Slender, angled on young stems, usually red above—green below, branches minutely appressed-pilose; pith white, solid.

SIZE: 20 to 25′ in height by 15 to 20′ in width.
HARDINESS: Zone 4 to 8 but not as robust in the south and flowers do not appear as large or vivid.
HABIT: Large multistemmed shrub or small tree of oval-rounded outline, usually branching to the ground making successful grass culture impossible; it is possible to remove the lower branches and the result is a small tree of rounded habit; excellent way to use this plant; may sucker profusely.
RATE: Medium.
TEXTURE: Medium in foliage and in winter habit.
BARK: Exfoliating, flaky, often gray brown to rich brown, rather attractive, not as showy as that of *C. officinalis.*
LEAF COLOR: Dark green often somewhat glossy, attractive summer foliage; fall color can be purplish red, usually very poor fall color, often the leaves fall off green.
FLOWERS: Yellow, (opens mid February in Athens) March, effective for three weeks, borne in short stalked umbels before the leaves from the axils of the previous season's wood; each flower about 1/6″ diameter; each umbel about 3/4″ diameter, enclosed before opening in four downy boat-shaped bracts; very effective in the early spring landscape for it receives little competition from other flowering shrubs.
FRUIT: Oblong drupe, 5/8″ long and about 1/2″ wide, bright cherry-red, July, often partially hidden by the foliage; the fruits are used for syrup and preserves; I have observed specimens with fruit more abundantly borne than that often found on sour cherry trees; selections should be made for both flower and fruit production; although edible one must be hungry.

CULTURE: Transplants well when young, move balled and burlapped; adaptable as far as soil types and pH are concerned, but prefers rich, well drained soil; sun or partial shade; I would rate this the most durable of the larger dogwood types for midwestern conditions.

DISEASES AND INSECTS: None serious, actually a very pest-free plant.

LANDSCAPE VALUE: Shrub border, hedge, screen, foundation planting, around large buildings, optimum effect is achieved if the plant has a dark green or red background so the early yellow flowers are accentuated; this species is not used enough in the modern landscape; makes an excellent small tree and should be used this way more often.

CULTIVARS:

'Alba'—White-fruited form.

'Aurea'—A rather striking golden foliaged form that is relatively common in English botanical gardens, striking in June when it literally glows, I suspect the color diminishes with the heat of summer.

'Aureo-elegantissima' ('Elegantissima')—Leaves yellow or with an unequal border of yellow, others tinged with pink; introduced before 1872.

'Flava' (var. *flava*)—A yellow-fruited form; the fruits bigger than those of the species and sweeter, have had good (100%) success rooting this clone from August 8 (Boston) collected cuttings, treating with 3000 ppm IBA-quick dip.

'Golden Glory'—An upright, abundant flowered form introduced by the Synnesvedt Nursery Company of Illinois it has been a good plant for Chicago and the northern midwest where the choice of early flowering shrubs is limited.

'Nana'—There is a low growing, small-leaved form that might be useful in landscape situations; apparently at least two forms are in cultivation.

'Variegata'—The margins of the leaves are irregularly colored creamy white; this, like *C. alternifolia* 'Argentea', is a rather striking variegated plant.

PROPAGATION: Seed should be stratified in moist medium for 120 days at 68 to 86°F followed by 30 to 120 days at 34 to 56°F; cuttings, softwood, treated with IBA root in high percentages; my successes have not been great but I have rooted the species using June–July cutting wood.

NATIVE HABITAT: Central and southern Europe and western Asia. Cultivated since ancient times.

RELATED SPECIES:

Cornus chinensis, (kôr′nus chī-nen′sis), is similar to *C. officinalis* but differs in the whitish pubescence on the underside of the leaves and from both *C. officinalis* and *C. mas* by the long tapered sepals and black fruits. The flowers are sulfur-yellow and more numerous than *C. mas* and the trunk is smooth and palm-like. The leaves can become quite large and can grow one foot. Central and south China. Introduced 1950 by Frank Kingdon Ward. Not too hardy. Zone 9.

Cornus officinalis, (kôr′nus o-fis-i-nā′lis), Japanese Cornel Dogwood, is similar to *C. mas* except, according to the literature, in the dense, rusty-colored patches of down in the axils of the veins on the lower surface and the more open habit. It may have more vein pairs (5 to 7). Although not common in arboreta or gardens the Secrest Arboretum has grown a number of plants since 1929. One 46-year-old tree was 22′ high and 35′ wide. Plants there survived temperatures of −20°F. The following comparisons between the two species are based on close scrutinization over the past 10 years. Axlillary tufts of brown down do occur on leaves of *C. officinalis* but this is not con-

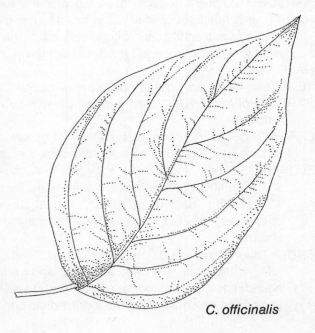

C. officinalis

sistent from tree to tree. The bark of *C. officinalis* is much more showy with rich gray, brown and orange colors on the same trunk. *C. officinalis* flowers about one week ahead of *C. mas* but the fruits ripen considerably later usually in September. Fruits of *C. officinalis* are more insipid. Winter buds of *C officinalis* are covered with rusty-brown pubescent. The overall flower effect is superior to *C. mas* and a tree in full flower on a March–April day is a thing of great beauty. I have had poor success rooting this species from softwood cuttings (20 percent). Japan, Korea. Cultivated 1877. Zone 5 to 8.

ADDITIONAL NOTES: *C. mas* was one of the first shrubs (way ahead of *Forsythia*) to flower in the midwest and northeast; it would have a difficult time competing with the late April and May flowering trees and shrubs but flowering when it does, it is a star; the classic case of being in the right place at the right time.

Cornus racemosa — Gray Dogwood
(kôr′nus ra-se-mō′sa)

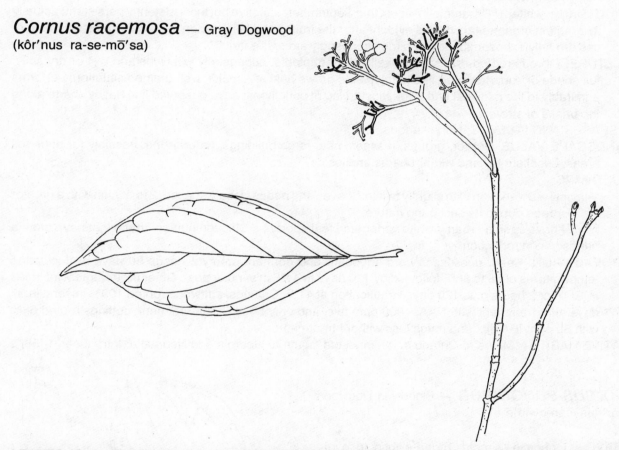

LEAVES: Opposite, simple, narrow-elliptic to ovate-lanceolate, 2 to 4″ long, one half as wide, long acuminate, cuneate, 3 to 4 vein pairs, dark almost gray green, appressed-pubescent or nearly smooth, glaucous beneath; petiole—1/2 to 3/4″ long.

BUDS: Flower—terminally borne, more plump than vegetative buds, slightly appressed hairy; vegetative-valvate, very small in relation to flower buds, almost hidden by leaf scar.

STEM: Slender, young stems—somewhat angled, tan to reddish brown, essentially glabrous; older stems—decidedly gray; pith—small, white to brown, usually light brown.

FRUIT: Pedicels remain red into late fall and early winter.

SIZE: 10 to 15′ in height by 10 to 15′ in width; actually it is difficult to define the spread of this shrub for it suckers profusely from the roots and forms a large colony of plants extending in all directions from the original plant; this should be considered when employing this plant in the home landscape for it often oversteps its boundaries.

HARDINESS: Zone 4 to 8.

HABIT: Strongly multistemmed, erect growing, suckering shrub with short spreading branches towards apex of stems; forms a colony because of suckering nature.

RATE: Slow from old wood, however, shoots which develop from roots grow very fast (3 to 5' in a season).

TEXTURE: Medium-fine in leaf, medium in winter, probably more interesting and valuable in winter than in the foliage periods.

STEM COLOR: Three-year-old wood or greater is a distinct gray and quite attractive; the first and second year stems are a light reddish brown and form an interesting contrast; the inflorescences are reddish pink and are effective into December; the total winter character is valuable in the landscape.

LEAF COLOR: Dull gray-green to dark green in summer foliage, assuming purplish red tones in fall; fall color is usually not spectacular; could be some worthwhile selections made for fall coloration.

FLOWER: Whitish, late May to early June, borne in 2″ diameter cymose panicles which terminate almost every stem, effective for 7 to 10 days.

FRUIT: Drupe, white, 1/4″ diameter; August into September; effective but inconsistently persistent; actually its greatest ornamental effect is evident after the fruits have fallen when the reddish pink inflorescences are fully exposed; over 100 birds supposedly savor the fruits.

CULTURE: Fibrous rooted, transplants well; very adaptable, supposedly will withstand wet or dry soils; full shade or sun; however, like many plants grows best in a moist, well-drained situation; performs admirably in the midwest under the most trying of conditions; have observed it in heavy shade along the banks of streams.

DISEASES AND INSECTS: None serious.

LANDSCAPE VALUE: Border, groups, masses, near large buildings, naturalizing, possibly for poor soil areas, excellent fall and winter characteristics.

CULTIVARS:

'Slavinii'—Dwarf form with slightly twisted leaves, the nodes closely spaced, 2 to 3' high with a greater spread due to its suckering nature.

I have seen a creamy white variegated leaf sport at a Chicago nursery that might have been a handsome introduction.

PROPAGATION: Seed, possesses hard endocarp and dormant embryo, needs 60 days at fluctuating temperatures of 68 to 86°F followed by 120 days at 41°F in sand or peat. Other pretreatment includes H_2SO_4 for 2 hours plus 120 days stratification at 41°F. Cuttings, softwood rooted 100% in sand in 37 days after treatment with NAA, 1000 ppm talc, and only 8% without treatment; cuttings rooted 66% with 80 ppm IBA dip, and much less without treatment.

NATIVE HABITAT: Maine to Ontario and Minnesota, south to Georgia and Nebraska. Introduced 1758.

Cornus sanguinea — Bloodtwig Dogwood
(kôr′nus san-gwin′ē-a)

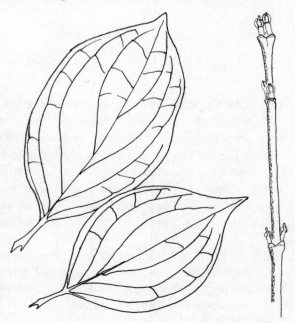

LEAVES: Opposite, simple, broad-elliptic to ovate, 1 1/2 to 3″ long, 3/4 to 1 3/4″ wide, acuminate, rounded or broad-cuneate at base, dark green above, villous on both sides, more densely so and lighter green beneath, with 3 to 5 pairs of veins; petiole—1/8 to 3/4″ long.

BUDS: Flower—terminally borne, pubescent with grayish silky hairs, fatter than vegetative buds which are valvate, appressed, coated with gray silky appressed pubescence.

STEM: Slender, appressed hairy, usually purple or dark blood-red, often greenish on lower side; older branches greenish gray in color; pith— white.

SIZE: 6 to 15′ in height, with spread ranging from 6 to 15′, variable.

HARDINESS: Zone 4 to 7.

HABIT: A large, unkempt, sloppily dressed, spreading, round-topped, multi-stemmed shrub of a dense, twiggy nature; suckers freely from the roots and forms a colony much like *C. racemosa*.

RATE: Slow to medium on old wood, fast on shoots which develop from roots.

TEXTURE: My opinion is somewhat biased, but I would rate it coarse in all seasons; very difficult to blend into the landscape; a proverbial "sore thumb" plant.

STEM COLOR: I have never understood the name bloodtwig for the stems are usually more green than blood-red; often the stem portion exposed to the sun is red and the rest is green; Bean noted that the name is derived from its fall color and not the young bark; there is considerable variation in habit and stem color.

LEAF COLOR: Dull, dark green in summer changing to blood-red autumnal color according to many authorities; this shrub has never shown good fall color as I have observed it and is usually a sickly greenish purple.

FLOWERS: Dull white, of fetid odor, profusely produced in late May to early June in 1 1/2 to 2″ diameter flat-topped pubescent cymes, effective 7 to 10 days, the total effect of the flowers is somewhat reduced by the abundant foliage.

FRUIT: Drupe, 1/4″ across, shining purplish black, August–September, almost unnoticeable for they blend in with the dark green foliage.

CULTURE: Fibrous rooted, easily transplanted, very adaptable, supposedly tolerates lime better than other dogwoods; sun or partial shade; needs frequent pruning to keep it clean (presentable).

DISEASES AND INSECTS: None serious.

LANDSCAPE VALUE: Possibly shrub border, massing, screening; definitely not for specimen use or the small residential landscape; too large and clumsy, tends to look out of place with age.

CULTIVARS:

'Atrosanguinea'—Branches of a deep red color.

'Variegata'—Leaves mottled with yellowish white; apparently a number of variegated forms have been in cultivation at various times but are not spectacular.

'Viridissima'—A rather attractive form with yellowish green winter stems; best color occurs on current year's growth; Arnold Arboretum has several attractive plants.

PROPAGATION: Cuttings taken in late June rooted 44% without treatment, and 68% in three weeks after treatment with 30 ppm IBA, 12 hour soak; seeds require warm (3 to 5 months) followed by cold (3 months) periods.

NATIVE HABITAT: Europe. Long cultivated.

Cornus sericea (Formerly *C. stolonifera*)—Redosier Dogwood
(kôr′nus ser-ē′sē-a)

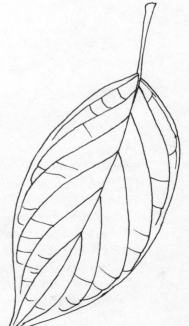

LEAVES: Oppostie, simple, ovate to oblong-lanceolate, 2 to 5″ long, 1 to 2 1/2″ wide, acuminate, rounded at base, medium to dark green above, glaucous beneath, with about five pairs of veins; petiole—1/2 to 1″ long.

BUDS: Flower—terminally borne, valvate, hairy, silky-appressed pubescence; vegetative—valvate, appressed, elongated, essentially no difference between this species and *C. alba*.

STEM: Slender, upright, bright red to dark blood red, appressed pubescence on younger stems; lenticels similar to *C. alba* except per internode; pith—white, large.

FRUIT: Drupe, white, globose; stone as broad as high or slightly broader, rounded at base.

SIZE: 7 to 9′ in height spreading to 10′ or more.

HARDINESS: Zone 2 to 8, although not performing well in Zone 8.

HABIT: Loose, broad-spreading, rounded, multistemmed shrub with horizontal branches at base; freely stoloniferous as it spreads by underground stems.

RATE: Fast, quite vigorous.

TEXTURE: Medium in leaf and in winter.

STEM COLOR: Red, various authorities list the stem color as dark blood-red, dark purplish red, brilliant red; very handsome and eye appealing in a winter setting especially with a sprinkling of snow to set off the stem color.

LEAF COLOR: Medium to dark green in summer; purplish to reddish in the fall, fall color is variable but can be an excellent reddish purple.

FLOWERS: Dull white, borne in 1 1/2 to 2 1/2″ diameter flat-topped cymes in late May to early June, flowers are adequate but not overwhelming; flowering sporadically through summer.

FRUIT: Drupe, 1/3″ diameter, white, borne in August-September, briefly effective; have observed several extremely fruitful specimens with large infructescences of milky white fruit.

CULTURE: Fibrous rooted, easily moved bare root or balled and burlapped; extremely adaptable to wide range of soil and climatic conditions; does best in moist soil and is often observed in the wild in wet, swampy situations.

DISEASES AND INSECTS: There is a twig blight (canker) which can wreak havoc on this species and the cultivars; scale can be a problem and I have noticed a wealth of bagworms.

LANDSCAPE VALUE: Excellent for massing in large areas, along highways, parks, golf courses; interesting stem color makes it suitable for shrub border use in residential landscapes; can be an effective bank cover for it holds soil quite well; beautiful when framed by snow.

CULTIVARS:

'Cardinal'—A good bright red (cherry red) stemmed form released by Minnesota Landscape Arboretum. Dr. Pellett brought many wild collected provenances to Minnesota for various research activities and selected one of the best red stemmed forms.

var. *coloradensis*—This variety has smaller leaves, brownish stems and bluish white fruits; it ranges from the Yukon and Manitoba to New mexico and California.

var. *coloradensis* 'Cheyenne'—Good selection for blood-red stem color; shows growth habit of the species but does not grow as tall.

'Flaviramea'—Form with yellow stems, often inflicted with canker, nonetheless widely sold and planted; should be used with taste for a small planting goes a long way on any residential landscape; first offered by Spath Nursery, Germany, 1899/1900, who received it from the Arnold Arboretum; also listed as Golden-twig Dogwood and 'Lutea'.

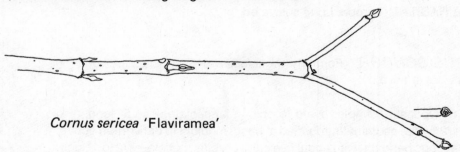

Cornus sericea 'Flaviramea'

'Isanti'—Compact form with bright red stem color, shorter internodes which make for a denser plant; does contract considerable leaf spot in wet weather; Minnesota introduction.

'Kelseyi'—Low-growing, neat, compact form, 24 to 30″ in height, nice facing plant in the shrub border to hide the "leggy" shrubs in the background; stems less colorful than the species; quite susceptible to leaf spot; fall color not as good as species.

'Nitida'—Stems are green, leaves glossy green, habit more vigorous and upright than 'Flaviramea', the winter stems a pea green color.

'Silver and Gold'—A new 1987 introduction from Mt. Cuba Center, Delaware that occurred as a branch sport from *C. s.* 'Flaviramea'; the leaves have a creamy irregular border around the margin and the variegation pattern is stable; the stem color is yellow which sets it apart from all the other variegated leaf forms which have red stem coloration.

'Sunshine' (*C. s.* var. *occidentalis*)—A large 10 to 12' high shrub with a general pale yellow or chartreuse foliar glow. Leaves are variable in variegation and may be all of one hue (yellow) or have yellow margins and an irregular green center, more rarely they are creamy white margined with a central green blotch; leaves on young shoots average 4 to 6" long and 2 to 2 1/2" wide, stem coloration is red; introduced by University of Washington Arboretum and described in the Bulletin 47(2):24. 1986. Arboretum received the cuttings from Mr. G.W. Nadermann, Oakville, WA in 1941. Apparently occurred as a branch sport in the wild.

PROPAGATION: Seed should be stratified for 60 to 90 days at 41°F. I have rooted cuttings with 90% success any time leaves were present by treating the cuttings with 1000 ppm IBA-quick dip. Hardwood cuttings placed in the field in late winter also give 90 to 100% success without treatment.

NATIVE HABITAT: Newfoundland to Manitoba, south to Virginia, Kentucky and Nebraska. Cultivated 1656.

RELATED SPECIES:

Cornus alba, (kôr′nus al′bȧ), is closely allied to *C. sericea* and some authors consider *C. sericea* a subspecies of *C. alba;* the vegetative differences are nonexistent.

Cornus baileyi, (kôr′nus bā′lē-ī), is similar and much confused with *C. sericea* from which it differs in the shoots and lower surface of the leaves being distinctly woolly and in not being stoloniferous; the stem color also is duller and browner red; usually found native on sandy soils and is recommended for this situation in the landscape. Native to Ontario and Minnesota to Pennsylvania and Indiana with a Zone 4 hardiness designation; *Hortus III* reduces it to a form of *C. sericea* and *Seeds of Woody Plants in the United States* treats it as a synonym of *C. sericea;* they are almost impossible to distinguish and I doubt if one could locate a taxonomist who would be willing to risk his reputation by identifying the red-stemmed dogwoods.

ADDITIONAL NOTES: Nurserymen tend to sell all three species, *C. alba, C. baileyi,* and *C. sericea* as red-stemmed dogwoods. The homeowner is at the mercy of the garden center operator or nurseryman and the differences in growth habit and stem color in old age are different enough to warrant correct labeling by the seller.

Cornus walteri — Walter Dogwood
(kôr′nus wâl′ter-ī)

LEAVES: Opposite, simple, oval, 2 to 4 1/2" long, 1 1/4 to 2" wide, tapered at both ends, slender pointed, dark green above with fine appressed hairs, more abundant on lower surface, 3 to 5 vein pairs; petiole to 1" long.

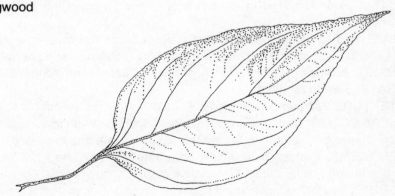

Cornus walteri, Walter Dogwood, is a rather unusual dogwood with true alligator-hide bark and a tree-type stature. I have seen the species at two gardens in the United States and came away with the feeling that it is a meritorious plant deserving of wider use. It can grow 30 to 40' high and wide. The 3/8" diameter, white flowers are produced in 2 to 3" diameter corymbose-cymes in June. The 1/4" diameter, globose black fruit matures in August–September. Cuttings do not root as readily as those of *C. macrophylla.* Seed requires a warm/cold period possibly as much as 4 months of each phase. A related species, *C. coreana,* Korean Dogwood, is a larger tree (50 to 60') with similar flower and fruit characteristics. The bark is perhaps more blocky. The Arnold had a large specimen and the Sercrest Arboretum lays claim to the biggest plant that I know of in this country. Korea. Introduced 1918. Zone 5. *C. walteri* is native to central China. Introduced 1907. Zone 5.

Corylopsis glabrescens (C. gotoana) — Fragrant Winterhazel
(kôr-i-lop'sis glā-bres'enz)

FAMILY: Hamamelidaceae

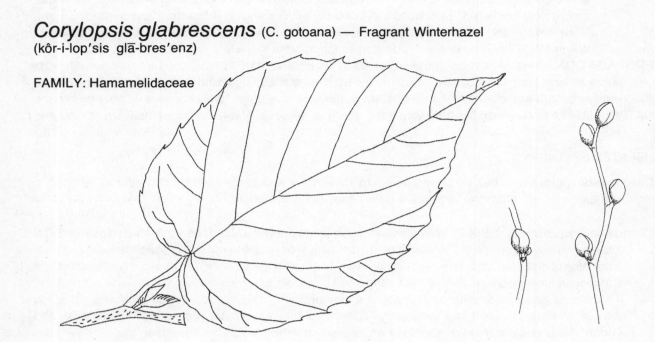

LEAVES: Alternate, simple, ovate, acuminate, cordate to subcordate, 2 to 4″ long, 1 1/4 to 3″ wide, sinuate-dentate with bristle-like teeth, dark green, glaucescent beneath and sparingly silky on the veins or sometimes slightly pubescent when young, thin, 7 to 11 vein pairs; petioles slender, 1/2 to 1″ long.
BUDS: Rather large, sessile, solitary or finally short-stalked and collaterally branched, directly in the axil, fusiform or ovoid, with about 3 glabrous scales, greenish brown to brown.
STEM: Rounded, zig-zag, moderate or slender, mostly glabresent; pith small, angular, continuous.

SIZE: 8 to 15' in height with a similar spread; can be grown as a small tree.
HARDINESS: Zone 5 to 8, the hardiest of the *Corylopsis* and possibly the best choice for northern gardens.
HABIT: A wide-spreading, dense, somewhat flat-topped, rounded, multi-stemmed shrub.
RATE: Slow to medium.
TEXTURE: Medium in leaf; possibly medium to medium-coarse in winter.
LEAF COLOR: Dark green above, glaucescent beneath in summer; fall color varies from yellow-green to clear gold, often the leaves remain green late and are killed by a freeze.
FLOWERS: Perfect, pale yellow, fragrant, borne in 1 to 1 1/2″ long pendulous racemes; bracts boat-shaped, silky inside, flower stalk glabrous, flowering in April before the leaves develop.
FRUIT: Two-valved, dehiscent capsule, about 1/4″ across, not ornamental, seeds black.
CULTURE: Transplant balled and burlapped into moist, acid, preferably well-drained soil which has been amended with peat moss or leaf mold; full sun or light shade; should be sheltered as they flower early and are susceptible to late spring frosts; this is especially true in the midwest and south where invariably there is a warm period in March and the buds of many plants swell and often open only to succumb to the early April freeze, pruning should be accomplished after the flowers pass; plants flower in early March in Athens, GA.
DISEASES AND INSECTS: As is true with many members of the Hamamelidaceae, this genus is free of significant problems.

LANDSCAPE VALUE: Good plant for early spring flower color and fragrance; could be successfully integrated into the shrub border; worthwhile considering if a protected area is available in the garden; over the years I have grown very fond of the *Corylopsis* species; in full flower they are as beautiful as any plant that could grace a garden; probably best used against an evergreen background; the Swarthmore College campus, Arnold Arboretum and Longwood Gardens probably have the best collections on the Eastern Seaboard; have seen plants injured at Morton and Dawes Arboreta after the 1976–77 winter when temperatures dropped –20 to –25°F; this included flower buds and stem tissue; *Corylopsis* does reasonably well in the south; the North Carolina State Arboretum, Raleigh and Callaway Gardens have specimens.

PROPAGATION: Seeds are difficult and require an extended 5 month/3 month: warm/cold period; softwood cuttings root readily and I have collected cuttings throughout June, July and August, provided a 1000 ppm IBA-quick dip and achieved 90 to 100% success; the root systems are profuse but the cuttings, in my experience, resist moving and should be allowed to go through a dormancy cycle; when new growth ensues they can be transplanted; this approach appears to be true for many of the Hamamelidaceae; see Verstage, *PIPPS* 29:204–205, 1979. "Propagation of *Corylopsis*".

NATIVE HABITAT: Japan. Introduced 1905.

RELATED SPECIES: There is a certain commonality about the Winterhazels and if one can identify a particular species then he can identify the others at least to the generic level; apparently their taxonomy is somewhat confused and I recommend the following article for additional reading: Li. *Morris Arboretum Bulletin.* 13(4):63–68. 1963. "The cultivated *Corylopsis*".

Corylopsis pauciflora — Buttercup Winterhazel

LEAVES: Alternate, simple, ovate to broad-ovate, 1 1/2 to 3″ long, 1 to 2″ wide, acute, obliquely cordate to subcordate, with a few bristle-like teeth, glabrous and bright green above, silky on veins below; petiole—1/3 to 3/4″ long, slender.

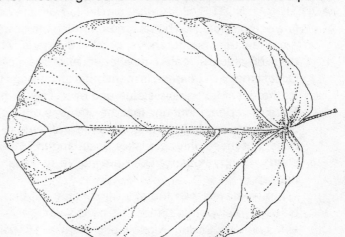

Corylopsis pauciflora, (kôr-i-lop′sis paw-si-flō′rà), Buttercup Winterhazel, is a small (4 to 6′) shrub of spreading habit with fragrant primrose-yellow flowers, about 3/4″ diameter, produced 2, sometimes 5 on short inflorescences. I have seen this species at the National Arboretum, Washington, D.C. and Arnold Arboretum and was quite impressed with the floral display as well as the overall daintiness of the entire shrub compared to *C. glabrescens, C. spicata* and *C. willmottiae.* This would be a good choice for modern gardens. Flowers about mid to late April in vicinity of Boston, MA. Needs to be protected from incessant wind, full sun and high pH soils. Best suited to a woodland setting. Japan and Taiwan. Introduced 1862. Zone 6 to 8.

Corylopsis platypetala

LEAVES: Alternate, simple, ovate or broadovate to elliptic, 2 to 4″ long, short acuminate, cordate or subcordate, sinuate-dentate with bristle-like teeth, glabrous and dark green above, glaucous beneath; petiole-slightly glandular.

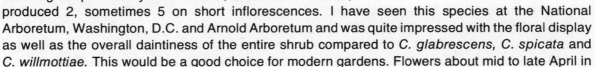

Corylopsis platypetala, (kôr-i-lop′sis plat-i-pet′ȧl-ȧ), grows 8 to 10′ and larger under cultivation with specimens as large as 20′ high and 10′ wide being reported. Its leaves develop a glaucous waxy bloom when grown in full sun. The fragrant, pale yellow flowers are borne in 8 to 20-flowered, 1 to 2″ long racemes. It was introduced by E.H. Wilson in 1907 with Hupeh, China where it is a common shrub growing in thickets and along margins of woods. This is a very ornamental species and is allied to *C. willmottiae* from which it differs by some minute floral characteristic. Zone 6 to 8.

Corylopsis spicata — Spike Winterhazel

LEAVES: Alternate, simple, orbicular-ovate or orbicular-obovate, 2 to 4″ long, 2 to 3″ wide, abruptly short acuminate, obliquely cordate to rounded, sinuate-denticulate with bristle-like teeth, new growth purplish, later dull dark to blue green, glaucous and downy beneath; petiole—1/2 to 1″ long, woolly.

Corylopsis spicata, (kôr-i-lop′sis spi-kā′tȧ), Spike Winterhazel, is a wide-spreading, 4 to 6′ (10′) high shrub that forms a rather attractive mass of crooked, flexible branches at maturity. I have seen specimens twice as wide as high and in flower they were spectacular. The yellow, fragrant flowers occur 6 to 12 together on a 1 to 2″ long pendulous raceme in April (mid March, Athens). The emerging leaves are a rich vinous purple and eventually change to bluish green. This is one of the most beautiful of the *Corylopsis* and ranks at the top of my list as an early flowering shrub. It is native to the mountains of Japan. Two 50-year-old plants in the Morris Arboretum were 8′ high and 12′ wide. A floriferous hybrid between *C. spicata* and *C. pauciflora* is in cultivation. Introduced 1863. Zone 5 to 8.

Corylopsis willmottiae — Willmott Winterhazel

LEAVES: Alternate, simple, oval or obovate, 2 to 4″ long, short acuminate, subcordate or truncate, sinuate-dentate with mucronate teeth, bright green and glabrous above; rather glaucous and downy below, especially on the veins, 7 to 10 vein pairs; petiole—1/4 to 3/4″ long, glabrous or slightly pubescent.

Corylopsis willmottiae, (kôr-i-lop′sis wil-mot′i-ē), Willmott Winterhazel, is seldom seen in cultivation in the United States. It is a rather large, 6 to 12′ high shrub with glabrous brown stems that are dotted with numerous lenticels. The winter buds are pale shining green and stalked. The fragrant flowers are soft greenish yellow and borne in 2 to 3″ long pendulous racemes. This species was discovered and introduced by E.H. Wilson in 1908 from western China in Sikang province. Zone 6. A cultivar 'Spring Purple' has plum-purple young shoots that eventually change to green.

ADDITIONAL NOTES: Somewhat similar to *Hamamelis* and *Parrotia,* its hardy allies, but differing in the flower morphology. The raceme on which the flowers are borne is really a short branch. At the base are a few thin, membranous, bract-like organs, which are not accompanied by flower, but from the axils of which a leaf is developed after the flowers farther along the raceme have developed. Occasionally *C. gotoana* is mentioned as perhaps the best garden species. The literature is not clear as the exact taxonomic status and often lists *C. gotoana* as a synonym for *C. glabrescens.* Ohwi, *Flora of Japan,* mentions that the stamens of *C. gotoana* are nearly as long as the petals; those of *C. glabrescens* half as long. Also the leaf teeth of *C. gotoana* are shorter than those of *C. glabrescens,* but these characteristics according to Morley and Chao are not sufficient to warrant species status. Happy hunting! Both are native to Japan and based on Ohwi's account occur in similar habitats.

I have stayed with the older taxonomy but Morley and Chao, *J. Arnold Arb.* 58:372–415 (1977) place *C. platypetala* under *C. sinensis* var. *calvescens, C. willmottiae* is included with *C. sinensis* var. *sinensis.* 'Spring Purple' becomes a cultivar of *C. sinensis.* The authors reduced the 33 species that have been described to 7. Wow!

Corylus americana — American Filbert
(kôr′-i-lus å-mer-i-kā′nå)

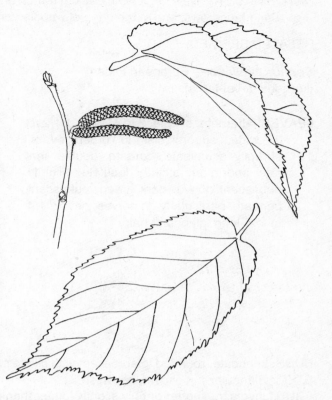

FAMILY: Betulaceae

LEAVES: Alternate, simple, 2 1/2 to 6″ long, 1 1/2 to 2 1/2″ wide, broad-ovate to broad-elliptic, apex short-acuminate, heart-shaped or rounded at base, sparingly pubescent and dark green above, soft pubescent beneath; petiole about 1/2″ long, glandular hairy.

BUDS: Imbricate, globose, gray-pubescent, 1/6 to 1/4″ long, greenish brown to purplish.

STEM: Young branches glandular-pubescent, brown; pith—continuous, 3-sided, pale or brown.

FRUIT: Involucre downy, deeply cut and toothed, about twice as long as the 1/2″ long, slightly flattened nut, usually tightly enclosing it, deeply and irregularly lobed.

SIZE: Listed as 8 to 10′ by many authorities but usually grows larger, 15 to 18′, spread approximately 2/3's the height.

HARDINESS: Zone 4 to 9.

HABIT: Strongly multistemmed shrub forming a rounded top with a leggy or open base, often with widespreading rather straight stems branched toward their extremities.

RATE: Medium to fast.

TEXTURE: Medium-coarse in summer and winter, this is also true for the types treated under the related species category.

LEAF COLOR: Dark green in summer, muddy yellow-green in fall, sometimes with a reddish tint, usually of negligible importance.

FLOWERS: Monoecious, male in catkins, 1 1/2 to 3″ long, yellowish brown, quite showy in early spring, March; female flowers inconspicuous, the stigma and style barely protruding out of the bud, color is a rich red; male catkins have opened as early as February 1 in Athens.

FRUIT: Nut, 1/2″ long, set in an involucre nearly twice its length, involucre is downy and deeply notched, maturing in September–October.

CULTURE: Transplant balled and burlapped or as a container plant into well drained, loamy soil; pH adaptable; full sun or light shade; prune anytime; tends to sucker from the roots and must often be thinned out to maintain a respectable appearance.

DISEASES AND INSECTS: Blight, crown gall, black knot, leaf spots, Japanese leafhopper, caterpillar, scales; I have not noticed extensive problems with *Corylus* although nurserymen have indicated that *Corylus avellana* 'Contorta' is affected by a blight which injures leaves and branches.

LANDSCAPE VALUE: The American Hazel is best reserved for naturalizing and other nonformal areas; the European Filbert and especially the cultivars might lend themselves to selected landscape situations; the species are too large for contemporary landscapes.

PROPAGATION: Three months cold stratification or fall plant; softwood cuttings of *C. avellana* and *C. maxima* var. *purpurea* have been rooted but percentages were low; I have never had any success with *C. maxima* var. *purpurea;* have tried *C. avellana* 'Cortorta' with no success; logically if this form were put on its own roots the suckering experienced with grafted forms would not be a problem. See Dirr and Heuser 1987 for a good overview of *Corylus* propagation.

ADDITIONAL NOTES: All shrubby filberts should be used with restraint in the landscape; probably not good choices for small properties; squirrels love the nuts.

NATIVE HABITAT: New England to Sasketchewan and south to Florida, often found in moist and dry areas, along fencerows, and at the edge of woodlands. Introduced 1798.

RELATED SPECIES:

Corylus avellana — European Filbert
(kôr′i-lus a-vel-lā′nå)

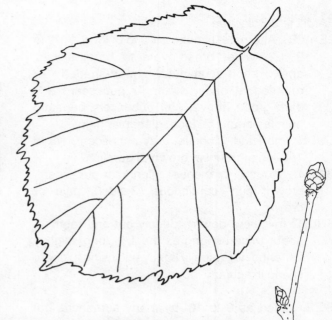

LEAVES: Alternate, simple, 2 to 4″ long, 1 1/2 to 3″ wide, suborbicular to broad ovate, abruptly acuminate, cordate, double serrate and often slightly lobulate, slightly pubescent above, dark green, pubescent beneath, particularly on nerves; petiole 1/4 to 1/2″ long, glandular hairy.

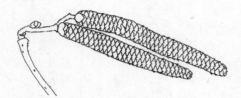

BUDS: Imbricate, rounded, glabrescent with ciliate scales, small, 1/6 to 1/3″ long, greenish.
STEM: Glandular-pubescent, brownish.
FRUIT: Involucre shorter or only slightly longer than nut.

Corylus avellana, European Filbert, grows from 12 to 20′ in height, can be a small tree, but usually forms a dense thicket of erect stems and develops extensive shoots from the roots. Nut is 3/4″ long, set in an involucre about as long as the nut, the margins are cut into shallow, often toothed lobes; native to Europe, western Asia, and northern Africa; prized for its nuts in European countries; this is one of the species that is grown for nut production. Zone 4 to 8.

CULTIVARS:
‘Aurea’—A yellow leaf type, a rather weak-growing form; have seen at Wisley, color does not persist.
‘Contorta’—8 to 10′, stems curled and twisted, quite an attraction when properly grown, often called Harry Lauder's Walkingstick; discovered about 1863 at Frocester, Gloucestershire, England in a hedgerow; leaves also twisted, best for winter effect; male catkins open later than those of species; have never seen fruits on this form; almost always grafted on the species and the understock suckers result in maintenance nightmares.

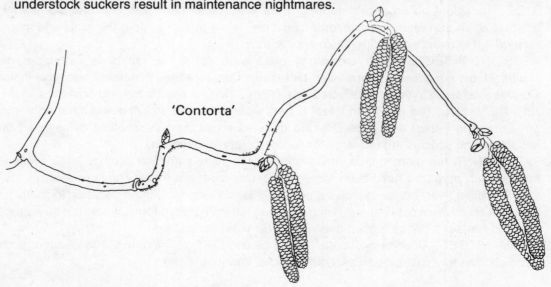

‘Contorta’

'Fusco-rubra'—A purple leaf form; the purple not as dark as that of *C. maxima* var. *purpurea;* have seen at Holden Arboretum and, from a distance, am hard pressed to separate from *C. m.* var. *purpurea.*

'Heterophylla'—A form with smaller leaves than the species, the leaves being lobed about one-third of the distance to the midrib, each lobe triangular and sharply toothed; also listed as 'Laciniata'; finally tracked the plant in Munich Botanic Garden, not sensational.

'Pendula'—Rather interesting form with distinctly weeping branches; if grafted on a standed it forms a broad inverted soup-bowl head; there is a shrubby form at the Arnold Arboretum approximately 8′ high and 16′ wide.

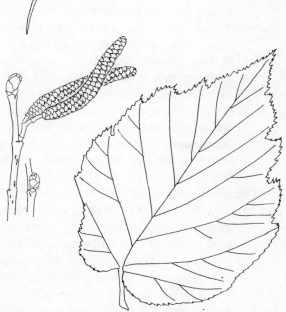

Corylus cornuta, (kôr′i-lus kôr-nū′tȧ), Beaked Filbert, is included here because of its interesting beaked fruits. It is a smaller (4 to 8′ high and wide), more refined shrub than the others. The leaves range from 1 1/2 to 4 1/2″ long and 1 to 3″ wide. The unopened male catkin is 1/2 to 1″ long and the nut only about 1/2″ long. The involucre (husk) that covers the nut is extended, forms a slender beak 1 to 1 1/2″ beyond the nut. Quebec to Sasketchewan south to Missouri and Georgia. Introduced 1745. Zone 4 to 8.

Corylus maxima var. ***purpurea*** — Purple Giant Filbert
(kôr′-i-lus maks′-i-ma pēr-pū′rē-ȧ)

Similar to *Corylus avellana* except with dark purple leaves (2 to 5″ long, 1 1/2 to 4″ wide, petiole—1/4 to 1/2″ long, glandular) in spring fading to green in summer; buds and catkins retain purplish cast; involucre and young fruits are also purplish.

Purple Giant Filbert is a large shrub reaching 15 to 20′ in height, with leaves of a dark purple gradually fading to dark green during the summer months; can be grown from Zone 4 to 8 but in the south the leaves quickly change to green, usually by early June; often in full leaf by mid April in Athens. This variety flowers later than *C. americana* or *C. avellana.* The species is native to southern Europe and is a parent of the filberts that are grown in English orchards; the involucre encloses and protrudes beyond the nut distinguishing it from *C. avellana.* Species is native to southeastern Europe, Western Asia. Long cultivated. Has been rooted using 4000 ppm IBA talc, 3 peat: 1 sand medium with 64% rooting after 6 months.

Corylus colurna — Turkish Filbert or Hazel
(kôr′-i-lus ko-lur′na)

LEAVES: Alternate, simple, broadly ovate to obovate, 2 1/2 to 6″ long, acuminate, cordate, doubly serrate or crenate-serrate, sometimes lobulate, nearly glabrous above, pubescent on veins beneath; petiole—1/2 to 1″ long.

BUDS: Large—1/3″, softly pubescent, green-tinged brown.

STEM: Glandular-pubescent, gray-grown, coarse, with fissures up and down the stem, becoming more pronounced in second year.

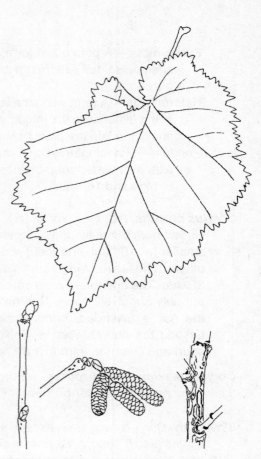

SIZE: 40 to 50′ in height with a spread of 1/3 to 2/3's the height, can grow to 70 to 80′.

HARDINESS: Zone 4 to 7.

HABIT: Broad pyramidal, very stately and handsome in form, usually with a short trunk and the bottom branches touching the ground.

RATE: Medium, 35′ over a 20 year period; 50′ in 50 years.

TEXTURE: Medium in leaf and winter.

BARK: Pale brown, older bark develops a flaky character and as scales fall off a brown or orange-brown bark is exposed.

LEAF COLOR: Dark green in summer, potentially yellow to purple in autumn but seldom handsome, drops yellow-green; have seen considerable variation in degree of greenness and texture of leaf with some extremely leathery; the summer foliage is very handsome and seems to be free of insect and disease problems.

FLOWERS: Male catkins, 2 to 3″ long; female, inconspicuous as only the two free styles protrude from the bud scale; tree with flowers of little ornamental appeal but the catkins in early spring (March) can be rather handsome.

FRUIT: Nut, 1/2 to 5/8″ diamter, the involucre about 1 1/2 to 2″ long, nuts are closely grouped 3 or more together; involucre deeply incised, fimbriated, twice the length of the nut, covered with a fine pubescence mixed with gland-tipped bristles, September–October.

CULTURE: Thrives in hot summers and cold winters; tolerant of adverse conditions, a well drained, loamy soil is preferable; pH adaptable; full sun; actually a very excellent tree but little known and grown; supposedly somewhat difficult to propagate; somewhat difficult to transplant and needs supplemental watering the first few summers until it re-establishes; once established, the tree is quite drought tolerant.

DISEASES AND INSECTS: None serious.

LANDSCAPE VALUE: Excellent formal character, possibly for lawns, street tree use, also city conditions, where maples exhibit scorch this tree is still green and vigorous; little used and under-appreciated tree in the United States; occasionally found in arboreta and campus settings; always distinct because of unique outline, heavy textured leaves, fruit and bark; difficult to locate in commerce but worth the hunt, has not performed well in Wichita, KS tests.

PROPAGATION: Most of the shrubby *Corylus* require 2 to 6 months of cold temperature before the germination will occur; also warm alternated with cold stratifications are recommended; cuttings of the shrubby species can be rooted but are difficult; I have never had good luck; in general cuttings should be taken in June, July or August and treated with a high IBA level (10,000 ppm); *C. maxima* var. *purpurea* has been rooted 100% from late July cuttings using 10,000 ppm IBA; 'Contorta' has also been rooted 60% using similar procedures; 'Contorta' and var. *purpurea* are grafted on seedling understocks and the suckers from the understock often overgrow the scion.

NATIVE HABITAT: Southeast Europe, western Asia. Introduced 1582.

Cotinus coggygria — Common Smoketree or Smokebush
(kō-tī′nus ko-gīg′ri-a)

FAMILY: Anacardiaceae

LEAVES: Alternate, simple, oval to obovate, 1 1/2 to 3 1/2″ long, rounded or slightly emarginate at apex, entire, glabrous, well marked with parallel veins, bluish green; petiole 1/2 to 1 1/2″ long.

BUDS: Small, 1/16″ long, solitary, sessile, with several imbricate dark red-brown scales, acute.

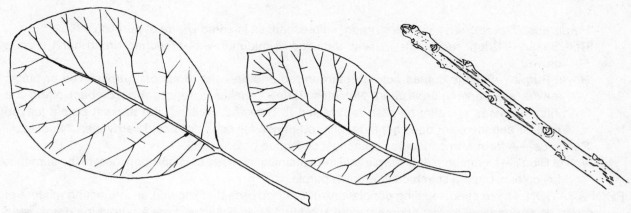

STEM: Stout, brown or purplish, bloomy, with numerous small lenticels, glabrous; pith—orange-brown, solid, when crushed emitting strong odor; leaf scars not lobed, deep bloomy purple color around the leaf scars.

SIZE: 10 to 15′ in height by 10 to 15′ spread.

HARDINESS: Zone 4, preferably 5 to 8, perhaps 9.

HABIT: Upright, spreading, loose and open, often wider than high, multi-stemmed shrub; when pruned develops very long slender shoots creating a straggly, unkempt appearance.

RATE: Medium.

TEXTURE: Medium in leaf; coarse in winter.

LEAF COLOR: Late leafing, late April–early May in Athens; medium blue-green in summer and yellow-red-purple in fall; fall color is often poorly developed but at times is spectacular especially on cultivars.

FLOWERS: The flower is rather ineffective for each 5-petaled yellowish flower is about 1/8″ in diameter and sparsely borne, (May, Athens) June, the real show occurs as a result of the hairs (pubescence) on the pedicels and peduncle of the large 6 to 8″ long and wide panicle; the hairs often pass through several color changes but at their best are a smoky pink; they are effective from June into August–September; the purple-leaf types have purplish hairs.

FRUIT: A rather small 1/4″ wide, kidney-shaped, dry reticulate drupe.

CULTURE: Fibrous rooted, readily transplanted; adaptable to widely divergent soils and pH ranges; dry and rocky soils; prefers well drained loam and sunny exposure.

DISEASES AND INSECTS: None of serious magnitude; however, rusts, leafspot, leaf rollers and San Jose scale can attack this species; *Verticillium* can be a problem.

LANDSCAPE VALUE: Good in shrub border, possibly in masses or groupings, not for single specimen use but usually employed in that fashion, the plant is employed for accent or a striking focal point, have seen it used in many European gardens in such a fashion, often the purple-leaf types are cut to the ground in late winter to force vigorous shoot growth which is more colorful than the normal shoot extensions.

CULTIVARS: Several interesting purple leaf and flower forms; of special note is 'Velvet Cloak'.

'Daydream'—Floriferous form with dense, ovoid, heavily produced, fluffy inflorescences that mature a rich brownish pink, green leaves, this is one of the handsomest of the cultivars and its habit is rather dense.

'Flame'—Selected for its brilliant orange-red fall coloration; inflorescences pink.

'Foliis Purpureis'—Leaves purplish when young, later purplish green to green, inflorescence usually pinkish, one of many clones with similar characteristics; name may not be taxonomically correct.

'Nordine'—A selection made at the Morton Arboretum, Lisle, IL and supposedly resembling 'Royal Purple' in leaf color, leaves hold purplish red color well into summer, fall foliage yellow to orange-yellow, hardiest of purple-leaf smoke bushes.

'Notcutt's Variety'—As I saw it at the Oxford Botanic Garden a dark maroon-purple leaved form; the color strikingly rich and almost impossible to properly photograph (at least for me); the inflorescence purplish pink; this has also been listed as 'Foliis Purpureis Notcutt's Variety' and 'Rubrifolius'.

'Purpureus' (f. *purpureus*)—Leaves green, inflorescences in some shade of purplish pink.

'Red Beauty'—Bright red purple initially, dark red at maturity, well branched broad habit, strong grower.

'Royal Purple'—Foliage comes out rich maroon-red and darkens to almost purplish red or black; leaves are darker purple than 'Notcutt's Variety'; makes a reasonably compact plant; the inflorescences are also purplish red; raised at Boskoop, Holland; the darkest purple leaved cultivar and the color does not fade; rich red-purple fall color, less cold hardy than 'Nordine'.

'Pendulus'—A form with pendulous branches; cultivated before 1885.

'Velvet Cloak'—Handsome dark purple-leaf form maintaining good color through most of the summer; fall color is often a spectacular reddish purple.

PROPAGATION: I have seen seedling populations of *C. coggygria* that showed an interesting mixture of green and purple leaf forms; apparently the seed had been collected from a purple-leaf form; seed requires 30 to 60 minutes of acid followed by 3 months at 41°F; nursery practice involves fall sowing with germination occurring in spring; cuttings are not the easiest thing to root but June, July cuttings root 80 or greater percent when treated with 10000 to 20000 ppm IBA; cuttings should be over-wintered in flats or beds and not disturbed until growth ensues in spring; Kelly and Foret, *PIPPS* 27:445–448 (1977) showed that cuttings of *C. coggygria* rooted best in early June (86%) compared to 33% when collected on July 24; a 1425 ppm IBA + 1425 ppm NAA + 50 ppm boron quick dip improved rooting percentage and quality; I have had 80 to 100% success with softwood (June) cuttings treated with 1000 ppm IBA-quick dip, peat: perlite, mist.

NATIVE HABITAT: Southern Europe to central China and Himalaya. Cultivated 1656.

RELATED SPECIES:

Cotinus obovatus — American Smoketree
(kō-tī′nus ob-ō-vā′tus)

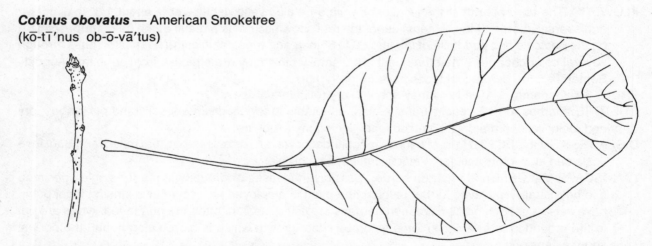

LEAVES: Alternate, simple, entire, obovate to elliptic-obovate, 2 to 5″ long, 1/2 as wide, rounded at apex, cuneate at base, bluish to dark green, silky pubescent beneath when young; petiole—1/2 to 1 1/2″ long.

Similar to *C. coggygria* except leaf-scars lobed, stems orangish and usually an upright tree or shrub to 30 feet; the leaf scar lobing is a variable and unreliable characteristic in spite of what the keys say.

Cotinus obovatus, American Smoketree, Chittamwood, is a large upright shrub or small, round-headed tree growing 20 to 30′ high. The bluish to dark green leaves turn a magnificent yellow, orange, red and reddish purple in the fall. In fact, it may be the best of all American shrub trees for intensity of color. In observing this tree through the midwest, east and south, I am amazed at the beauty and consistency of the excellent fall color. It was my good fortune to spend several days in October, 1981, with Mr. Don Shadow, Shadow Nurseries, Winchester, TN. Don took me to the mountains near Winchester where I saw *C. obovatus* in its fall splendour. There were shrub and tree forms, but all were various shades of the colors mentioned previously. The bark is also a beautiful gray to gray-brown and mature trunks become scaly reminding of the scales of a fish. Don is rooting the plant from softwood cuttings and apparently timing is quite important if success is to be experienced. One of the first things I mentioned to Don is that someone should be making selection for fall colors. Don had a twinkle in his eye so the question had already been answered. In Snyder's *Trees and Shrubs for Northern Gardens,* cultivar 'Red Leaf' is described as having especially good fall color. Interestingly the flowers are dioecious with the male being showier than the female. Panicles range from 6 to 10″ long and three-quarter's as wide. Fruit production is sparse. Will grow in the same situations as *C. coggygria* and is particularly well adapted to limestone soils for this is where it occurs in the wild. During the Civil War, it was almost lost because of its use for a yellow to orange dye. Found in restricted localities in Tennessee, Alabama, and the Edwards Plateau of Texas where it reaches its greatest numbers. Introduced 1882. Zone (3) 4 to 8.

ADDITIONAL NOTES: Two excellent articles that cover a multitude of *C. obovatus* virtues include Koller and Shadow, *American Nuerseryman* 159(9):155–161 (1984) and *Arnoldia* 44(2):17–22. Propagation as reported in the latter article consists of taking cuttings just before new season's growth hardens, pinching off soft tips, using 8000 ppm IBA talc or quick dip, suitable medium, 47% shade cloth, 15 second mist every 15 minutes, making sure cuttings are not overwatered for they deteriorate quickly; reduce mist as soon as cuttings root which may be as fast as 16 days to 4 to 6 weeks.

A recent introduction is *Cotinus* 'Grace', from a cross made in summer of 1978 by Peter Dummler of Hillier Nurseries; interestingly seeds were acid scarified for 3 hours and planted with germination occurring in 12 days. No cold stratification was given. The hybrids will be known as the Dummler Hybrids. 'Grace' was named after Mr. Dummler's wife and has a massive pink flower panicle, 14″ high by 11″ wide, leaves are 4 to 6″ long, 3″ wide, light red when young, darkening with age, petiole—red and 2″ long, in fall turns red, orange and yellow; will probably mature about 20′, received an award of merit from the Royal Horticultural Society in 1983.

Cotoneaster apiculatus — Cranberry Cotoneaster
(kō-tō-nē-as′ter ā-pik-ū-la′tus)

FAMILY: Rosaceae

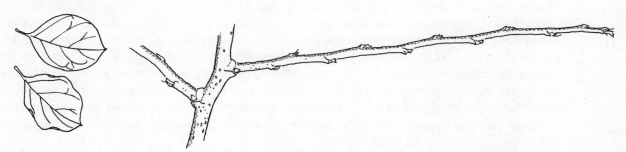

LEAVES: Alternate, simple, suborbicular to orbicular-ovate, 1/4 to 3/4″ long and wide, apiculate, occasionally rounded or even notched, glabrous at maturity or only slightly ciliate, lustrous dark green above, glabrous, lower slightly pubescent, undulating margin; petiole—1/4″ long.

BUDS: Similar to *C. lucida* except smaller.

STEM: Reddish purple with appressed pubescence; older stems gray-brown and ragged in appearance; when bruised or broken, stems emit a distinct maraschino cherry odor; this smell is more distinct on the low growing types.

SIZE: 3′ in height by 3 to 6′ in spread.

HARDINESS: Zone 4 to 7; best in colder climates.

HABIT: Low, wide spreading shrub with stiff, cold branching pattern, young shoots growing herringbone fashion from the older ones; tends to mound upon itself forming dense, impenetrable tangles where leaves, bottles, and paper penetrate but rakes cannot enter; somewhat of a "garbage can" shrub but useful because of good foliage and fruit.

RATE: Slow, growth can be accelerated in youth with optimum watering and fertilization, will cover an area fairly fast.

TEXTURE: Fine in leaf, but often coarse in winter because of its "pack-rat" ability to store many unwanted articles.

LEAF COLOR: Dark glossy green, extremely handsome for its summer foliage effect; changing to good bronzy-red or purplish tones in fall and holding its fall color often into late November.

FLOWERS: Perfect, pinkish, late May to early June, solitary, small, not ornamentally overwhelming but attractive.

FRUIT: Pome, 1/4 to 1/3" diameter, cranberry-red, August through September (October–November), borne singly, quite attractive for this feature alone, often heavy fruiting.

CULTURE: Transplant from a container; almost all low-growing cotoneasters are container grown; prefers moist, well-drained soil but will grow in about any situation except those that are permanently wet; light sandy soil and heavy clays are acceptable; acid or alkaline, in fact does extremely well in high pH soils; withstands considerable drought once established; displays medium to high soil salt tolerance.

DISEASES AND INSECTS: Mites, in dry situations, can render this species brown; fireblight occasionally presents a problem.

LANDSCAPE VALUE: Effective as bank cover, foundation plant, near wall where branches can hang over, facer plant in shrub border, ground or large area cover, used around campuses a great deal; have seen it used with *Myrica pensylvanica* and the combination is beautiful in summer foliage; probably overused by landscape architects and nurserymen especially in midwest but, nonetheless, a valuable landscape plant which offers good foliage and fruit; can present a maintenance problem for it is difficult to clean leaves and trash out of the interior of the plant; was surprised to see this species performing so well in the Salt Lake City-Provo, Utah areas; on Brigham Young's campus the plants were much more heavily fruited than I had ever noticed in the midwest and east; observed significant winter kill after exposure to −20°F during winter of 1976–77; does not perform well in heat of Zone 8; rated the most popular *Cotoneaster* in a 1989 *American Nurseryman* survey.

CULTIVARS:

'Blackburn'—A more refined and compact form; has appeared in a few midwest nurseries.

PROPAGATION: Seeds should be scarified in acid for 60 minutes and then provided 60 plus days at 41°F; seeds have a hard endocarp; the degree of hardness varies among species and consequently the time of acid treatment should vary; see *Contrib. Boyce Thompson Inst.* 6:323–338 (1934) for detailed information on seed germination; in general softwood cuttings of all cotoneasters root readily if treated with 1000 to 3000 ppm IBA-quick dip and placed in peat:perlite or sand under mist; from my experiences it is doubtful if there is a species or cultivar that cannot be rooted with some measure of success; many of the groundcover types like the above, *C. dammeri* and cultivars frequently root where the prostrate stems touch moist soil.

NATIVE HABITAT: Western China. Introduced 1910.

RELATED SPECIES:

Cotoneaster adpressus — Creeping Cotoneaster
(kō-tō-nē-as′ter ad-pres′us)

LEAVES: Alternate, simple, broadly ovate or obovate, 1/4 to 5/8" long, acute or obtusish, mucronate, lustrous dark green and glabrous on both surfaces except with a few scattered hairs beneath, wavy margined, somewhat scoop shaped; petiole—1/2" long; leaf much like *C. apidulatus* perhaps more undulating; plants I have seen have lustrous dark green leaves but some literature says dull green.

Cotoneaster adpressus, Creeping Cotoneaster, is a very dwarf, close growing, compact, rigidly branched, 1 to 1 1/2′ high shrub, spreading 4 to 6′ and rooting where branches touch the soil. The leaves are dark glossy green; flowers are solitary or in pairs, white tipped rose; fruit-pome, 1/4″ diameter, dark red. Regarded by some authorities as a variety of *C. horizontalis*. According to Rehder hardy in Zone 4. This is a beautiful cotoneaster rivaling or surpassing *C. apiculatus* for fruit effect, more common in east than midwest; var. *praecox* is a more vigorous form growing to 3′ high and 6′ wide; the leaves (1/2 to 1″ long) and red fruits (1/3 to 1/2″ long) are larger; even with the above described differences I find it difficult to separate the variety and species and both of these from *C. apiculatus;* the leaves of *C. adpressus* and the variety have a rather undulating surface that is quite distinct; western China. Introduced 1896; the variety cultivated 1905; a cultivar that masquerades under the name 'Little Gem' or 'Tom Thumb' is known; it forms a dense, closely branched, broad-spreading mound of lustrous dark green leaves; it is a beautiful plant but its exact affinity is unknown; in the last edition of this work it was listed with *C. horizontalis* but is probably more properly placed here; another cultivar called 'Boer' out of Holland looks promising because of the large red fruits that color early and remain on the plant into winter.

Cotoneaster dammeri — Bearberry Cotoneaster
(kō-tō-nē-as′ter dam′er-ī)

LEAVES: Alternate, simple, evergreen, elliptic to elliptic-oblong, acutish or obtusish, mucronulate, rarely emarginate, cuneate, 3/4 to 1 1/4″ long, 1/4 to 5/8″ wide, glabrous and lustrous dark green above, glaucescent and slightly reticulate beneath, strigose pubescent at first, soon glabrous,4 to 6 vein pairs, petiole—1/4″ long; semi-evergreen to evergreen in protected areas; usually deciduous in exposed locations; leaves assuming a purplish tinge in late fall and winter.
BUDS: Like all cotoneaster—similar; see under *C. lucidus.*
STEM: Relatively fine, quite pubescent when young, changing to reddish brown at maturity.

SIZE: 1 to 1 1/2′ in height, spread 6′ and more due to ability to root freely where branches contact soil.
HARDINESS: Zone 5 to 8.
HABIT: Very low, prostrate, evergreen to semi-evergreen shrub, with slender-creeping stems keeping close to the ground, will cover a large area in a short period of time; branches root readily when in contact with the soil.
RATE: Fast.
TEXTURE: Fine in all seasons.
LEAF COLOR: Lustrous dark gren in summer and fall, assuming a dull dark green to reddish purple color in winter.
FLOWERS: White, 1/3 to 1/2″ diameter, solitary or in pairs, borne in (late April, Athens) late May, not overwhelming.
FRUIT: Pome, 1/4″ wide, globose or top shaped, usually with 5 nutlets, bright red, late summer, good for color, however, usually sparsely produced.
CULTURE: Transplants well from containers, adaptable but prefers well drained soil; occurs wild on heaths (peaty areas) and rocky ground; one of the easiest cotoneasters to grow.
DISEASES AND INSECTS: Subject to usual problems; I have noticed great quantities of aphids on this plant; in the south has not been as fireblight susceptible as some species.
LANDSCAPE VALUE: The species and cultivars are among the best evergreen ground covers; excellent on banks, gentle slopes, masses, shrub border, low facing shrub, foundation and as a possible espaliered effect; the solid carpet of glossy green is difficult to duplicate with other ground covers; extremely fast growing and can cover an area faster than *C. apiculatus* or *C. adpressus;* has picked up steam in the southeast nursery and landscape trades and is really the only cotoneaster of commercial consequence; can be directly rooted in the container and will become a 12 to 18″ well

branched salable plant in a single growing season; used extensively on banks and for large area cover; unfortunately, does not hold up over time and can become ratty in 3 to 5 years.

CULTIVARS:

'Coral Beauty' ('Royal Beauty', 'Pink Beauty')—Excellent free fruiting form with coral-red fruits, rich glossy evergreen foliage, 1' by 3 to 6'; certainly does not rival *C. apiculatus* or *C. adpressus* for fruit effect but is slightly superior to 'Skogholm'; I have seen many patches of this since the last edition and it grows taller than 1'; often 2 to 2 1/2'; a good quick fix and possibly more handsome than 'Skogholm'; more commonly listed as 'Royal Beauty' in commerce; 'Royal Carpet' is also similar.

'Eichholz'—Perhaps a hybrid between *C. dammeri* and *C. microphyllus* var. *colcheatus;* grows 10 to 12" high, small (1/2 to 3/4" long) bright green leaves assume yellow to orange red color in autumn, carmine-red fruits.

'Lowfast'—Supposedly extremely hardy with good dark glossy green foliage; abundant glossy red fruits, 12" high.

'Major'—A more vigorous selection with leaves 1 to 1 1/2" long, some leaves turning yellow-orange with the onset of cold weather, more winter hardy than species.

'Moon Creeper'—A low-growing, mat-forming selection with lustrous dark green foliage, becoming more common in the southeast.

var. *radicans*—Virtually unknown in the Unitd States but a particularly good low-growing form and, as I have seen it, will doubtfully grow 4 to 6" high, leaves about 1/2" long and more founded than 'Coral Beauty' and 'Skogholm', petiole 1/5 to 3/5" long; 'Major' is apparently confused with this type; var. *radicans* is quite common in English gardens where it makes a fine lustrous dark green carpet.

'Skogholm'—An extremely vigorous form with prostrate or serpentine branches; will grow 1 1/2 to 3' high; a two year old plant may be 3' across and can spread several feet each year; it is not a free fruiting form; used this cultivar extensively in my Illinois garden; really covers an area fast; tends to send up vertical shoots which should be cut off to maintain ground cover effect; 'Skogholm' was raised in Sweden and put into commerce about 1950.

'Streibs Findling'—First saw in 1987 in the Bundesgartenschau in Dusseldorf, Germany, later to discover that the flat growing, 4 to 6" long, dark blue-green leaf form was first raised in Germany, foliage is not quite as lustrous as other cultivars and is probably no longer than 1/2", produces white flowers and red fruits but their relative abundance is unknown.

PROPAGATION: Cuttings, anytime during the growing season, treat with 1000 ppm IBA, quick dip, peat:perlite, mist, 100% rooting; perhaps the easiest *Cotoneaster* to root.

NATIVE HABITAT: Central China. Introduced 1900.

RELATED SPECIES:

There are two sections of cotoneasters, those with pinkish, upright petals called Cotoneaster and those with white, spreading, more or less orbicular petals called Chaenopetalum. *C. adpressus, apiculatus, divaricatus, horizontalis* and *lucidus* belong to Cotoneaster; the others treated herein are of the section Chaenopetalum.

Cotoneaster congestus — Pyrenees Cotoneaster

LEAVES: Alternate, simple, evergreen, oval or obovate, about 1/3" long, 1/3" wide, obtuse, cuneate, dull dark green above, whitish beneath at first, becoming glabrous; petiole—1/12" long, slender, nearly glabrous.

STEM: Pubescent when young, glabrous at maturity.

Cotoneaster congestus, (kō-tō-nē-as'ter kon-jes'tus), Pyrenees Cotoneaster, is not well known but appears to warrant consideration. It is an evergreen shrub of low, compact, dense outline, 1 1/2 to 2 1/2' high and wide. The branches, instead of spreading, are decurved and the whole shrub forms a compact, rounded mass resembling a small haystack. The leaves are dull green (effect is blue-green) above and do not assume the glossiness of the previous species. The 1/4" diameter flowers are pinkish white. The bright red, rounded, 1/4″ diameter fruits are attractive. It makes a handsome small evergreen for the rock garden, or for small borders where it will not be overrun by more aggressive shrubs. Himalayas. Introduced 1868. Zone 6 to 8.

Cotoneaster conspicuus — Wintergreen Cotoneaster

LEAVES: Alternate, simple, evergreen, ovate, oval and oblanceolate to linear-obovate, 1/6 to 1/4″ long, 1/12 to 1/4″ wide, obtuse and often mucronulate at apex, shining black-green and glabrous above, gray and pubescent below.
STEM: Pubescent at maturity.

Cotoneaster conspicuus, (kō-tō-nē-as′ter   kon-spik′-u-us), Wintergreen Cotoneaster, is an evergreen shrub of variable habit, usually prostrate or spreading, 3 to 4′ high but in some forms growing to 8′ tall or more. At Wisley, saw an 8′ by 10′ dense shrub with abundant fruits. The glossy dark green leaves are extremely small, and the underside of the leaf is gray and woolly. The white flowers range from 3/8 to 1/2″ diameter. The bright, shining, dark red purple globose to obovoid fruit averages 3/8″ in diameter. It is considered one of the better fruiting shrubs because the fruits are not attractive to birds and usually persist throughout the winter. Variety *decorus* ('Decorus'), Necklace Cotoneaster, is listed as a relatively prostrate form (12 to 15″) with short rigid branches, silvery foliage and abundant fruits. At Wisley, the plant labeled as *decorus* was 5′ high and more green than silver. Western China. Introduced 1925. Zone 6 (7) to 8.

Cotoneaster microphyllus — Little-leaf Cotoneaster

LEAVES: Alternate, simple, evergreen, obovate to obovate-oblong, 1/4 to 1/2″ long, half or less wide, obtuse, rarely acutish or emarginate, cuneate, lustrous dark green above, densely woolly below.
STEM: Pubescent when young.

Cotoneaster microphyllus, (kō-tō-nē-as′ter   mī-krō-fil′us), Little-leaf Cotoneaster, is an evergreen shrub of low-spreading or even prostrate habit, rarely more than 2 to 3′ high. The 1/4 to 1/2″ long, deep glossy green leaves create a light airy texture; the leaves are grayish and woolly beneath. The 1/3″ diameter white flowers are followed by 1/4″ diameter, rounded, scarlet-red fruits. This species is closely allied to *C. congestus* and *C. conspicuus.* Himalayas. Introduced 1824. Zone 5 to 8. Several varieties and cultivars have been selected:
    var. *colcheatus*—This form is more prostrate and compact in habit with broader, brighter geen leaves.
    'Emerald Spray'—This selection displays a distinctive spreading, arching dense growth habit. The leaves are glossy emerald green. Flowers are white and the red fruit is about 1/3″ in diameter. In areas of high humidity this cultivar is quite susceptible to fireblight.
    var. *thymifolius* ('Thymifolius')—A dwarf or prostrate shrub, with numerous rigid branches; the shining deep green leaves are narrower than in the species and are made to appear more so by the curling under of the margins.
ADDITIONAL NOTES: The above three cotoneasters are probably more susceptible to fireblight and their use should be tempered in the south. Generally, the three species flower about mid April in Athens, mid May Boston.

Cotoneaster divaricatus — Spreading Cotoneaster
(kō-tō-nē-as′ter di-vār-i-kā′tus)

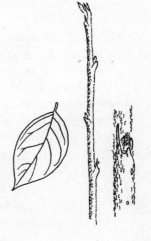

LEAVES: Alternate, simple, elliptic or broad-elliptic, acute at ends or rounded at apex, 1/3 to 1″ long, 1/4 to 5/8″ wide, lustrous dark green above, lighter and slightly pubescent or glabrous beneath, 3 to 4 vein pairs; petiole about 1/12″ long.
BUDS: Similar to other cotoneasters.

STEM: Slender, purple, appressed pubescent, older stems becoming dark brown.

SIZE: 5 to 6′ in height with a comparable or larger spread (6 to 8′).

HARDINESS: Zone 4 to 7 (8).

HABIT: Spreading, multistemmed shrub of rounded outline, outer branches are long, slender, and tend to droop creating a fine appearance.

RATE: Medium to fast.

TEXTURE: Fine in leaf; medium-fine in winter; tremendous textural asset in the shrub border.

LEAF COLOR: Dark glossy green, unexcelled for summer leaf color; fall color can be outstanding with the leaves changing to fluorescent yellow-red-purple combinations which persist for 4 to 6 weeks.

FLOWERS: Rose, solitary or in threes, late May to early June, not spectacular, somewhat masked by the foliage.

FRUIT: Pome, 1/3″ long and 1/4″ wide, egg-shaped, red to dark red, early September through November, one of the handsomest in fruit of the Chinese cotoneasters but not overwhelming from long distances.

CULTURE: Same as described for *C. lucidus.*

DISEASES AND INSECTS: One of the most desirable, ornamental, and trouble-free of the cotoneasters although susceptible to the typical problems which beset cotoneasters.

LANDSCAPE VALUE: Multi-faceted shrub, can be successfully used in foundation plantings, hedges, groups, borders, masses; blends well with other plants; foliage is unrivaled in summer and fall; integrates well with broadleaf evergreens.

PROPAGATION: Seed, as described for *C. apiculatus;* cuttings, softwood collected in early June, dipped in 1000 ppm IBA solution, rooted 90% in three months in sand under mist (personal experience); another worker reported 100% rooting in six weeks with untreated cuttings collected in early July.

ADDITIONAL NOTES: Always one of my favorite medium sized cotoneasters in the midwest and east; have one plant on the Georgia campus that has plugged along for years; apparently not well adapted to the heat; appears less prone to mites and fireblight than many cotoneasters.

NATIVE HABITAT: Central and western China. Introduced 1907.

Cotoneaster horizontalis — Rockspray or Rock Cotoneaster
(kō-tō-nē-as′ter hôr-i-zon-tā′lis)

LEAVES: Alternate, simple, suborbicular to broad-elliptic, acute at ends and mucronate at the apex, 1/5 to 1/2″ long, about three-fourths as wide, lustrous dark green, glabrous above, sparingly strigose-pubescent beneath; petioles 1/12″ long, strigose-pubescent; leaf blade lies flat and does not have the undulating character of *C. apiculatus* or *C. adpressus.*

STEM: The interesting fishbone pattern in which the branches are borne provides a distinct identification feature (see drawing).

SIZE: 2 to 3′ in height, spreading 5 to 8′.

HARDINESS: Zone 4, this might be somewhat open to question; some damage after 20°F during winter of 1976–77, best no further than Zone 7, had a rather large planting on campus that succumbed to mites and lace bug; definitely not as adaptable as *C. dammeri* and cultivars.

HABIT: Usually a low, flat, dense shrub with branches spreading horizontally; the branches almost form tiers and create a very unusual layered effect; often used against walls in England where the plant grows easily 6 to 10′ high.

RATE: Slow to medium.

TEXTURE: Fine in leaf, possibly medium when defoliated although the branch detail does contribute to a rather fine winter character.

LEAF COLOR: Excellent glossy dark green in summer changing to reddish purple combinations in fall; leaves hold late often into late November.

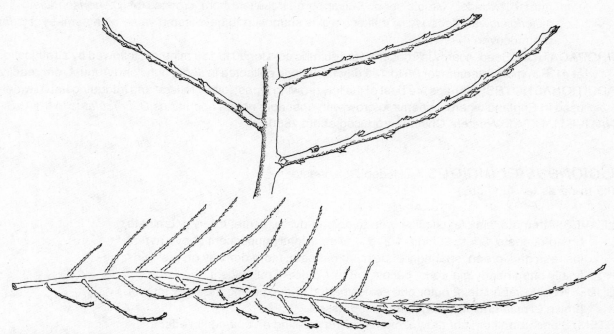

FLOWERS: Perfect, pink, rather small (1/4″ diameter), borne in mid to late May and into early June; single or 2 together, subsessile; flowers are very small but when present in great quantity make a nice show; the bees seem to like the flowers as I was almost stung collecting cuttings from a particularly handsome plant at the Holden Arboretum, Mentor, Ohio.

FRUIT: Small pome, bright red, 1/5 to 1/4″ diameter; effective in late August through October; not as showy as *C. apiculatus* and *C. adpressus,* but borne in sufficient numbers to be considered showy.

CULTURE: Same as described for *C. lucidus;* this species is deciduous or semi-evergreen to almost evergreen depending on location; in northern locations it would tend toward the former, in southern towards the latter; I have seen the plant in March at Bernheim Arboretum, Clermont, KY, completely evergreen; in Georgia the plant is tardily deciduous.

DISEASES AND INSECTS: Same as discussed under *C. lucidus.*

LANDSCAPE VALUE: Nice ground cover plant; I have seen it used by gradually descending steps and it fit in very well; would work as bank cover, in masses or groupings; used for espalier, especially on walls.

CULTIVARS:

'Hessei'—Considered a hybrid between *C. horizontalis* and *C. adpressus* var. *praecox,* deciduous irregularly branched shrub with decurving branches, small 1/4 to 3/5″ long, round or broad elliptic, lustrous dark green leaves, pinkish red flowers in May–June, globose 1/4″ wide red fruits with 2 to 3 nutlets, originated by H.A. Hesse, Weener, West Germany before 1933; has been in the midwest for a time and is being pushed by a plant evaluation program in the Chicago, IL area.

'Perpusilla'—A very prostrate form with leaves about 1/4″ long; a handsome clone. I grew this form in my Illinois garden; it is definitely more prostrate than the species and the lustrous dark green leaves are handsome; unfortunately it is one of the most susceptible to fireblight (see Davis and Peterson, *J. Arboriculture* May, 1976, Susceptibility of Cotoneasters to Fireblight); may be considered a variety.

'Robusta'—A clone I observed at the Morton Arboretum; considerably more upright (3′ high) and vigorous than the species; a free-fruiting form.

'Saxatilis'—More compact than the species with distinct "fish bone" branching pattern; quite prostrate with smaller leaves; sparse fruiting; introduced by Hesse of Germany in 1950.

'Variegatus'—Leaves are edged with white; considered one of the daintiest of variegated shrubs; from my experience, it is certainly one of the slowest growing, turns rose-red in autumn.

'Wilsonii'—The one plant I saw appeared similar to 'Robusta'.

Two named hybrids, 'Gracia' and 'Valkenburg', resulted from crosses of *C. horizontalis* × *C. salicifolius* var. *floccosus*. 'Valkenburg' is supposed to have some value as a semi-evergreen groundcover.

PROPAGATION: Seed, scarify in concentrated sulfuric acid for 90 to 180 minutes, followed by stratification at 41°F in moist medium for 90 to 120 days. Cuttings collected in June, July, and August root readily.

ADDITIONAL NOTES: Perhaps the best of the low growing types; lovely foliage and intriguing habit; widely used in England where it seems to grow with abandon; not as popular as *C. apiculatus* in the U.S.

NATIVE HABITAT: Western China. Introduced about 1880.

Cotoneaster lucidus — Hedge Cotoneaster
(kō-tō-nē-as'ter lū'si-dus)

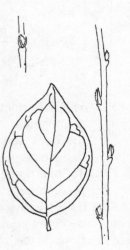

LEAVES: Alternate, simple, elliptic-ovate to oblong-ovate, acute, rarely acuminate, broad-cuneate, 3/4 to 2″ long, 1/2 to 1″ wide, slightly pubescent above at first, lustrous dark green, sparingly pubescent beneath, more densely on the veins, finally often nearly glabrous; petiole 1/8 to 1/5″ long, pubescent.

BUDS: Weakly imbricate, 2 outer bud scales parted and exposing the hairy interior, brown to pale gray in color, usually appressed.

STEM: Slender, buff or light brown, often peeling creating an onion-skin effect.

SIZE: 6 to 10′ high and as wide.

HARDINESS: Zone 3 to 7.

HABIT: Erect, round topped shrub with slender spreading branches, usually taller than broad.

RATE: Medium.

TEXTURE: Medium in leaf; depending on whether the plant is left unpruned or made into a hedge; medium to coarse, respectively, in winter.

LEAF COLOR: Lustrous dark green in summer; yellow to red combinations in fall; actually very effective but little praised for its fall coloration.

FLOWERS: Pinkish white, rather small and ineffective, mid to late May; borne in 2 to 5-flowered cymes.

FRUIT: Berry-like pome, black, globose, 2/5″ diameter, with 3 or 4 nutlets, September and persisting.

CULTURE: In general cotoneasters have sparse root systems and should be moved balled and burlapped or preferably as a container plant; they prefer well drained, loose, fertile soil with adequate moisture but do quite well in dry, poor soils tolerant of wind; pH adaptable; somewhat tolerant of seaside conditions; prune almost anytime; once established they are very vigorous, strong growing landscape plants; full sun or light shade.

DISEASES AND INSECTS: Leaf spots, canker, fire blight, hawthorn lace bug, scales, spider mites, cotoneaster webworm, sinuate pear tree borer, and pear leaf blister mite.

LANDSCAPE VALUE: Primarily used as a hedge because of upright branching habit; excellent for screens or groupings because of handsome foliage; tends to be overused as a hedge; often plants are stereotyped as to landscape use and this plant has been relegated to the status of hedge plant.

PROPAGATION: Seed should be scarified in concentrated sulfuric acid for 5 to 20 minutes followed by cold stratification in moist peat at 40°F for 30 to 90 days. Cuttings rooted well when taken in early July; reports that this species can be difficult to root from cuttings.

NATIVE HABITAT: Siberia and other parts of northern Asia. Cultivated 1840.

RELATED SPECIES:

Cotoneaster acutifolius, (kō-tō-nē-as'ter a-kū-tī-fō'li-us), Peking Cotoneaster, is confused with *C. lucidus* in the trade. The principal difference is in the foliage which is dull green, not shining and more hairy. Native to Mongolia, northern and western China and the eastern Himalaya. Zone 4. Introduced 1883. Bean considers this an inferior cotoneaster and possibly a poor form of *C. lucidus*.

Cotoneaster multiflorus — Many-flowered Cotoneaster
(kō-tō-nē-as′ter mul-ti-flō′rus)

LEAVES: Alternate, simple, broad-ovate to ovate, acute to obtuse, rounded or broad cuneate at base, 3/4 to 2 1/2″ long, 1/2 to 1 1/2″ wide, bluish green above, at first tomentose beneath, soon glabrous; petioles—1/4 to 1/2″ long.

BUDS: Similar to other cotoneasters.

STEM: Purple when young, to reddish green and finally gray; slightly pubescent to glabrous.

SIZE: 8 to 12′ and greater in height (17′ specimens on Illinois campus) and 12 to 15′ in spread.

HARDINESS: Zone 3 to 7.

HABIT: Upright, spreading, weeping or mounded at maturity with long arching branches forming a fountain much like Vanhoutte Spirea, *S. ö vanhouttei.*

RATE: Medium; once well established develops very rapidly.

TEXTURE: Medium-fine in foliage; medium-coarse in winter; looks a bit naked in the winter landscape and is difficult to conceal due to large size.

LEAF COLOR: Soft gray-green when unfolding, changing to gray or blue-green in mature leaf; fall color not much different or with a hint of yellow; summer foliage is different which adds unusual contrasting color to the normal green complement of most shrubs.

FLOWERS: White, each flower about 1/2″ diameter, early to mid-May, abundantly produced in 3 to 12 or more flowered corymbs, unpleasantly scented; very spectacular in flower as the flowers are borne upright along the stem on slender peduncles and effectively use the gray-green foliage as a background for accentuation of their beauty; could be mistaken for *Spiraea ö vanhouttei* but is most definitely a superior plant.

FRUIT: Berry-like pome, 1/3″ diameter, red, late August holding into early October, borne in great quantities, appears with the foliage and falls before leaf abscission, so the total ornamental effect is somewhat masked; very beautiful in full fruit; I rate this the best flowering and fruiting shrub of the large deciduous cotoneaster group.

CULTURE: Supposedly somewhat difficult to transplant, should be root pruned to develop good, fibrous root system, probably well adapted to container production at least in small sizes; strongly prefers well drained soil, sunny, airy location and no standing water.

DISEASES AND INSECTS: Comparing the cotoneasters on the Illinois campus, this species was the most trouble-free and exhibited abundant growth every year; I have not observed the fireblight or mite problem which have occurred frequently on *C. apiculatus,* although fireblight has been reported as troublesome.

LANDSCAPE VALUE: Requires room to spread, shrub border, massing, parks, golf courses, almost any public area because of low maintenance aspect; there are several large (16 to 18′) specimens on the Illinois campus which are bountiful in flower and fruit, unfortunately, I was never able to successfully propagate them from cuttings.

CULTIVARS:

var. *calocarpus*—Leaves longer and narrower than the type; fruits larger and more numerous; W.J. Bean termed this variety "a singularly beautiful fruit bearing shrub".

PROPAGATION: Cuttings, collected in June by this author, treated with 1000 ppm IBA solution, placed in sand under mist yielded 1% root cuttings; according to an Illinois nurseryman, *C. multiflorus* roots readily from June-collected softwood cuttings. Seed should be treated as described under *C. apiculatus.*

NATIVE HABITAT: Western China. Introduced 1900.

RELATED SPECIES:

Cotoneaster racemiflorus var. ***soongoricus,*** (kō-tō-nē-as′ter rā-sem-i-flō′rus soon-gôr′i-kus), Sungari Redbead Cotoneaster, is similar in form, but slightly hardier (Zone 3) with bluer foliage and great abundance of pink (rose) fruits; in cultivation it has proven to be a graceful and exceptionally free fruiting shrub, thriving in dry, sandy soil; native of central Asia, introduced by E.H. Wilson, the great plant explorer. Western China. Introduced 1910.

ADDITIONAL NOTES: These species are little known and used, but definitely should be brought to the gardener's eye; asset in any garden while the liability shrubs (forsythia, deutzia, mock-orange) continue to be overplanted.

Cotoneaster salicifolius — Willowleaf Cotoneaster
(kō-tō-nē-as'ter sal-is-i-fō'li-us)

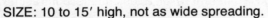

LEAVES: Alternate, simple, evergreen, oval-oblong to ovate-lanceolate, 1 1/2 to 3 1/2″ long, 1/3 to 3/4″ wide, dark green, rugose and glabrous above, pubescent and glaucous below, 5 to 12 prominent impressed vein pairs; leaves of species and most cultivars assume a purplish tinge in winter.

SIZE: 10 to 15′ high, not as wide spreading.
HARDINESS: Zone 6 to 8.
HABIT: Large evergreen shrub of spreading, arching habit, will become leggy at base unless pruned.
RATE: Medium.
TEXTURE: Medium through the seasons.
LEAF COLOR: Lustrous dark green during the growing season, may develop a suffusion of plum-purple during the winter months; appears to be pigment in the leaves of the low growing types which may, in fact, be hybrids with *C. dammeri.*
FLOWERS: Individual flowers small, white, borne in woolly 2″ diameter flat-topped corymbs, May-June; floral effect is not really potent due to leaf competition, flowers generally stinky.
FRUIT: Bright red, 1/5 to 1/4″ wide, subglobose, with 2 or 3 nutlets, often persisting through winter.
CULTURE: Move as a container plant; best in moist well-drained acid soil or approaching neutral pH soil, sun or partial shade, may be tougher than given credit and should be tested, especially in the southern states, for relative worth.
DISEASES AND INSECTS: As described under *C. lucidus;* I keep looking for significant fireblight infestations but, to date, have not observed same.
LANDSCAPE VALUE: Large evergreen shrub valued for fruits especially in European gardens; perhaps more important as a parent in some of the larger fruited or lower growing ground cover types.
CULTIVARS:
'Autumn Fire' ('Herbstfeuer')—A good, rather lax growing evergreen groundcover; it grows 2 to 3′ high; the 1 1/2 to 2 1/4″ long leaves are extremely glossy and leathery; scarlet fruits contrast nicely with the foliage and persist into winter; the leaves assume a reddish purple tinge in the winter months; at one time this was considered of hybrid origin but is now placed under *C. salicifolius.*
'Emerald Carpet'—More compact, tighter habit and smaller foliage than the species, white flowers, red fruits, a Monrovia introduction.
var. *floccosus*—Probably more common in cultivation and is semi-evergreen in the north. The lustrous dark green leaves are smaller (3/4 to 2 1/2″ long); the flowers in smaller corymbs (to 1″ diameter); the fruits wider (1/4″ diameter) than *C. salicifolius.* It is a very graceful variety. *C. salicifolius* is a variable species and has given rise to seedlings of diverse growth habit.
'Gnom' ('Gnome')—Low-growing, 8 to 12″ high evergreen ground cover, leaves 1″ long, lance-shaped, lustrous dark green above, floccose-tomentose beneath; have watched this form at Wisley over the years and am really impressed by low-growing nature.

'Parkteppich'—A good looking evergreen ground cover usually taller than 'Autumn Fire'; unfortunately like that cultivar never proved hardy in my Illinois garden; leaves—1″ long, 1/3″ wide.

'Repens' ('Repandens')—Some references say this cultivar does not exist but I have seen it enough to be positive it does; this is a good low-growing, evergreen to semi-evergreen form with lustrous dark green foliage (1 to 1 1/4″ long), and small red fruits; I have observed it being used in the Cincinnati, Ohio area with considerable success; depending on the degree of snow cover and severity of temperatures it ranges from evergreen to semi-evergreen; I do not doubt that this is the situation with most of these groundcover types; it also goes under the names 'Avondrood' and 'Dortmund'; foliage becomes reddish purple in winter.

'Saldam'—Similar to 'Autumn Fire' but leaves remain green through winter.

'Scarlet Leader'—Excellent, low growing, ground hugging, dark glossy green ground cover; this cultivar was planted on a steep bank at the Georgia Botanical Garden and in one complete growing season formed a solid mat; have seen no mites or fireblight; have used it in my garden where it grew 2 to 3′ high and 6 to 8′ wide, develops a red-purple winter leaf color; definitely grows larger than the literature ascribes.

ADDITIONAL NOTES: A good reivew article on the ground cover cotoneasters appeared in *Dendroflora* 1966. No. 3:20–27; much of the information included here was extraced from the article. I was sent a branch of this species by a lady who wanted to know which viburnum she had in her garden.

NATIVE HABITAT: Western China. Introduced 1908.

RELATED SPECIES:

Cotoneaster lacteus (*C. parneyi*) — Parney Cotoneaster
(kō-tō-nē-as′ter lak′tē-us)

LEAVES: Alternate, simple, evergreen, 1 1/4 to 2 1/4″ long, 3/4 to 1 1/4″ wide, obovate or broadly oval, obtuse and mucronate, rounded or broad cuneate, dark green above, whitish tomentose beneath, 6 to 9 prominent vein pairs.

Cotoneaster lacteus, Parney Cotoneaster, is a 6 to 10′ high evergreen shrub that has prospered on the Georgia campus despite record cold and drought and a tremendous fireblight epidemic. For those reasons it is worthy of inclusion. The white flowers (off-scented) occur in 2 to 3″ wide corymbs in mid May in Athens. Again, like *C. salicifolius,* the effect is not overwhelming. The 3/10″ long, 1/8″ wide red fruits (with 2 nutlets) are handsome and persist through winter. Will never take the place of evergreen holly in the southeast but offers different texture and form. Zone 6 to 8. Western China. Introduced 1930.

Crataegus crusgalli — Cockspur Hawthorn
(krȧ-tē′gus krus-gā′li)

FAMILY: Rosaceae

LEAVES: Alternate, simple, obovate to oblong-obovate, usually rounded at apex, cuneate, 1 to 4″ long, 1/3 to 1 1/2″ wide, sharply serrate above the entire base, quite glabrous, subcoriaceous, dark glossy green; petiole 1/4 to 1/2″ long.

BUDS: Applies to the genus: solitary or collaterally branched in spine formation, sessile, round or oblong-ovoid, with about 6 exposed fleshy and bright red to reddish brown scales.

STEM: Moderate or slender, terete, usually armed with slender, numerous, 1 1/2 to 3″ long thorns.

SIZE: 20 to 30′ in height with a spread of 20 to 35′.

HARDINESS: Zone 3 to 7.

HABIT: Broad-rounded, low branched tree with wide spreading, horizontal thorny branches which are densely set and make it difficult to grow grass under.

RATE: Slow to medium, 10 to 14' over 6 to 10 years.

TEXTURE: Medium-fine in leaf; medium in winter.

LEAF COLOR: Lustrous dark green in summer; bronze-red to purplish red in fall.

FLOWERS: Perfect, 1/2 to 2/3" diameter, white, of disagreeable odor, May, effective for 7 to 10 days, borne in 2 to 3" diameter flat corymbs, flowers with 10 stamens, pink anthers, usually 2 styles.

FRUIT: Pome-like drupe, deep red, 3/8 to 1/2" diameter; ripening in late September, October and persisting into late fall.

CULTURE: Transplant balled and burlapped in early spring as a small tree; tolerant of many soils but they should be well drained; pH adaptable, however, I have noticed a few trees with chlorosis; full sun; tolerates soot and grime of cities; prune in winter or early spring.

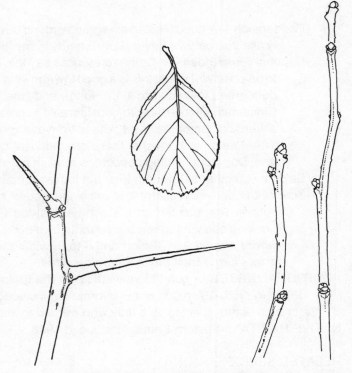

DISEASES AND INSECTS: Fireblight, leaf blight, rusts (at least 9 species attack hawthorns), leaf spots, powdery mildews, scab, aphids, borers, western tent caterpillar, apple leaf blotch miner, lace bugs, apple and thorn skeletonizer, plant hopper, scales and two spotted mite. Hawthorns, though lovely ornamentals, are severely affected by pests, the cedar hawthorn rust has been extremely bad as has the leaf blotch miner especially on *C. crusgalli*; the rust can affect the leaves, stems and fruits; I have seen it on all species treated here except *C.* × *lavallei*.

LANDSCAPE VALUE: Single specimen, groupings, screens, barrier plant, hedges; on the Illinois campus this species was effectively used around large buildings and softened the strong vertical lines; extensive use around residences must be tempered with the knowledge that the 2" long thorns can seriously injure small children; in fact, I would not use this hawthorn in the landscape where small children are apt to play.

CULTIVARS:

var. *inermis*—Thornless type with the good features of the species; I had three under evaluation and found them to be vigorous and attractive trees; flowers and fruits similar to the species; have seen 'Crusader' listed which is nothing more than a rename for var. *inermis*.

'Hooks'—A densely foliaged round headed form, 15 to 20' high and wide, with disease resistant dark green foliage, white flowers, 3/8 to 1/2" diameter red fruits, fewer thorns than species.

PROPAGATION: Seed should be immersed in acid for 2 to 3 hours (seed should be dry) then warm stratified at 70 to 77°F for 120 days followed by 135 days at 41°F; other species do not have the bony endocarp and require only the warm-cold treatment; selected clones are budded on seedling understock.

NATIVE HABITAT: Quebec to North Carolina and Kansas. Introduced 1656.

RELATED SPECIES:

Crataegus punctata, (kra̍-tē'gus punk-tā'ta̍), Thicket Hawthorn, grows 20 to 35' high and is usually wider than tall at maturity. The leaves are dull grayish green in summer. Flowers are white, fruit is dull red, 3/4" diameter, ripening in October and falling soon after. Listed as quite susceptible to rust. Quebec to Ontario, Illinois to Georgia. Introduced 1716. Zone 4 to 7.

'Aurea' (f. *aurea*)—Yellow fruits and could be considered a variety or forma as it has been found in the wild.

var. *inermis* ('Ohio Pioneer')—An essentially thornless type selected from a tree at the Secrest Arboretum, Wooster, Ohio, with good vigor, growth, and fruiting characteristics; I have seen the parent tree in flower and it is quite spectacular. This tree was found growing in the Secrest Arboretum nursery in 1962. At 10 years of age it had developed only three small thorns. The abundant white flowers are followed by dark red fruits in September or October. It is commercially available.

ADDITIONAL NOTE: Only a few birds like the fruits of *Crataegus* and, consequently, they remain effective for a long time.

Crataegus laevigata (*C. oxyacantha*) — English Hawthorn
(krȧ-tē′gus lē-vi-gā′tȧ)

LEAVES: Alternate, simple, broad-ovate or obovate, cuneate, lobes rounded or pointed, 1/2 to 2 1/2″ long, 2/3's as wide, with 3 to 5 broad serrulate, obtuse or acutish lobes, glabrous, dark green; petiole—slender, 1/4 to 3/4″ long.

Crataegus laevigata, English Hawthorn, is a shrubby, low branching, round topped tree with a close, dense head of stiff zig-zag ascending thorny (to 1″ long) branches reaching 15 to 20′ in height and 12 to 20′ in spread. The foliage is a deep dark green in summer, and does not color appreciably in fall. Flowers are white, with 20 stamens, anthers red, 2 or 3 styles, 5/8″ diameter, mid May, borne in 5 to 12-flowered corymbs. Fruit is scarlet, 1/4 to 1/2″ long, ripening in September and October. The cultivars offer the greatest diversity in the landscape and include:

var. *aurea*—Fruit bright yellow.

'Autumn Glory'—Good growth habit, glossy green foliage, single white flowers and giant red fruit; however, probably a Zone 5 plant; very susceptible to fireblight.

'Crimson Cloud'—A selection by Princeton Nurseries with good red single flowers and resistance to the leaf blight which is so troublesome to *C. l.* 'Paul's Scarlet'; each flower has a white star-shaped area in the center; glossy red fruits; supposedly does well under city conditions; I was unduly harsh on this tree having seen only young plants that were not impressive in flower; since 1983. I have observed a number of good sized specimens with excellent flower.

'Paul's Scarlet' ('Paulii')—Flowers double, red, with a tinge of rose, the most showy of all the hawthorns, arose as a branch sport about 1858 on a tree of the double pink var. *rosea-plena;* it was propagated by Mr. Paul who showed it at the International Horticultural Exhibition in 1866 under the name 'Paul's New Double Scarlet Hawthorn'; unfortunately, tremendously susceptible to hawthorn leaf spot or blight, *Entomosporium maculatum,* which in wet seasons may cause the tree to defoliate by July; in full flower a beautiful sight.

var. *plena* ('Plena')—Flowers double, white, with few fruits; Purdue University has several trees and they are attractive in flower.

var. *rosea* ('Rosea')—Flowers light rose, single, occurring frequently in the wild.

var. *rosea-plena* ('Rosea Flore Plena')—Flowers light rose, double.

var. *rubra*—A good fruiting form with 3/8″ diameter bright red fruits; flowers single, white.

A hybrid, *C.* × *mordenensis,* resulted from crosses between *C. laevigata* 'Paul's Scarlet' and *C. succulenta* at Morden Experimental Station, Manitoba, Canada. 'Toba' is a selection with double white fragrant flowers that age to pink. The dark green leaves are larger than *C. laevigata* with 2 to 4 lobes. The few plants I saw in Ohio were not very healthy and appeared to suffer from the same problem as 'Paul's Scarlet'. This form and others were selected for their high degree of resistance to rust. There is also a graft incompatability problem that may explain the reason for the decline. 'Snowbird' is a double white form that originated as an open pollinated seedling of 'Toba'; considered to be hardier than 'Toba'. 'Toba' is relatively common in the trade but doubtfully superior to *C. crusgalli* or *C. phaenopyrum*. Grows 20′ by 20′ with an upright rounded outline; fruit is red, 3/8″ long.

NATIVE HABITAT: *C. laevigata* is native to Europe, northern Africa. Long cultivated. Zone 4 to 7.

Crataegus × *lavallei* — Lavalle Hawthorn
(krȧ-tē'gus la-vāl'ē-ī)

LEAVES: Alternate, simple, elliptic to oblong-obovate, acute, cuneate, 2 to 4″ long, 1 to 2 1/2″ wide, unequally serrate from below the middle, slightly pubescent above when young, finally glabrous and lustrous dark green, pubescent beneath, especially on veins; petiole 1/4 to 3/4″ long.

STEM: Greenish, glabrous, glaucous, usually without the numerous prominent thorns of *C. crusgalli* or *C. phaenopyrum*.

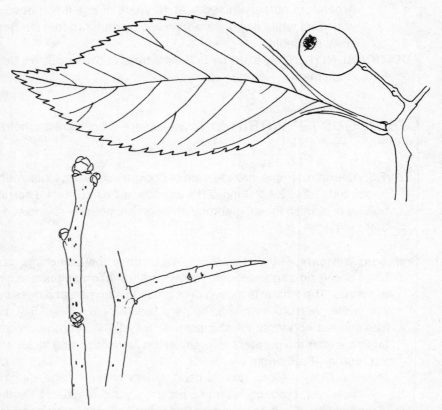

Crataegus × *lavallei*, Lavalle Hawthorn, is a hybrid between *C. stipulacea* (*C. mexicana*) and *C. crusgalli*. It is a small, dense, oval-headed tree growing 15 to 30′ tall, about 2/3's as wide. The foliage is a lustrous dark green in summer followed by bronzy or coppery-red colors in fall. Flowers are white, 3/4″ diameter, 20 stamens, 1 to 3 styles, late May; borne in 3″ diameter, erect corymbs. Fruit is brick red to orange-red speckled with brown, 5/8 to 3/4″ diameter pome-like drupe which ripens in November and persists into winter. I have seen many specimens and most exhibited a one-sided habit. They are not the most uniform growing trees; is used a great deal in European countries. This hybrid species arose at several gardens and was first described in 1880. Three years later Carriere published an account of a similar hawthorn, *C. carrierei,* and his clone is often designated 'Carrierei' but incorrectly so. Listed as *C.* × *carrierei* in some gardens. 'Lavalle' is quite free of rust and appears as adaptable as any hawthorn. Zone 4 to 7.

Crataegus mollis — Downy Hawthorn
(krȧ-tē'gus mol'lis)

LEAVES: Alternate, simple, broad ovate, 2 to 4″ long and almost as broad, sharply and doubly serrate and with 4 to 5 pairs of short and acute lobes, medium green, densely pubescent beneath at first, later chiefly on the veins; petiole 1 to 2″ long.

STEM: Moderate, thorns to 2″ long, curved, stout or absent; older branches turn a grayish cast.

Crataegus mollis, Downy Hawthorn, is a rounded to wide-spreading tree with varying degrees of thorniness reaching 20 to 30′ in height. The branches take on a gray cast and are quite different from most hawthorns. The young leaves are very downy when unfolding and gradually change to a flat medium green in summer and can turn yellow to bronze to bronze-red in fall. Flowers are white, 1″ diameter, 20 stamens, pale yellow anthers, 4 to 5 styles, malodorous, early May (one of the earliest flowering hawthorns), borne in 3 to 4″ diameter corymbs. Fruit is red, 1/2 to 1″ diameter, subglobose, ripening

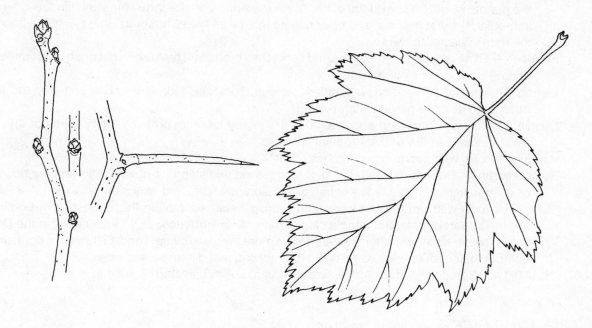

in late August and September and falling soon after. Good native trees but extremely variable; not for the modern landscape as there are too many superior species and cultivars. Leaves are often so badly infected by rust that the entire plant appears to be suffering from the measles. Southern Ontario to Virginia, west to South Dakota and Kansas. Cultivated 1683. Zone 3 to 6.

Crataegus nitida — Glossy Hawthorn
(krȧ-tē′gus nit′i-da)

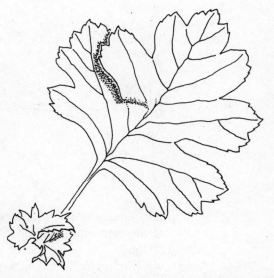

LEAVES: Similar to *C. laevigata* but more deeply 3 to 7-lobed, lobes more narrow and acute with only a few teeth at the apex, usually larger and of a rich polished green color.

FLOWERS AND FRUITS: The name Singleseed is derived from the fact that the fruit has a single stone; the flower a single style; *C. laevigata* has 2 to 3 styles and 2 nutlets (stones).

THORNS: *C. monogyna* is more formidably armed than *C. laevigata*. The species is abundant throughout the English countryside and the fabled hedges that line virtually every roadway are composed principally of *C. monogyna* but also *C. laevigata*.

Crataegus monogyna, Singleseed Hawthorn, is a round headed, densely branched tree with slightly pendulous branches and moderate thorny character which grows to 20 to 30′ high. The summer foliage is a rich, polished green; flowers are white, Bean calls the odor the sweetest of open-air perfumes, 5/8″ diameter, mid to late May, borne in corymbs. Fruit is red, 3/8″ diameter, one-seeded (hence the name Singleseed), effective in September and October. The species is seldom seen in American gardens with the exception of 'Stricta', an upright form. Unfortunately the species and cultivars are susceptible to leaf diseases and I have noticed an abundance of mites on 'Stricta'. Cultivars include:

'Biflora' (Glastonbury Thorn)—Flowers in mild seasons in mid-winter, producing the rest of the flowers in May; this cultivar has much tradition; Joseph of Arimathea, after the crucifixion of Christ, went to England to found Christianity; at Glastonbury he prayed a miracle might be performed so that the people would be convinced of his divine mission; when he thrust his staff into the ground, it immediately burst into leaf and flower, although it was then Christmas day; this is the basis for the name Glastonbury Thorn.

'Flexuosa'—Slow-growing form with twisted corkscrew branches; have seen but doubt its commercial appeal because of slow growth.

'Inermis Compacta' ('Pygmaea')—A rather curious, compact, thornless mushroom-headed form; have seen at a few gardens; interesting.

'Laciniata'—Leaves deeply cut and the lobes irregularly toothed; probaby many forms of this type since it occurs in the wild at irregular intervals.

'Pendula'—Form with pendulous branches.

'Semperflorens'—Form with small, 1/2 to 1″ long leaves and slender branches; flowers continuously or at intervals from May until August; dwarf, shrubby habit and very slow growing.

'Stricta'—A form with upright branches and narrow habit resembling in the best form Lombardy Poplar; apparently several upright clones have been introduced at various times; in the United States I have observed what appeared to be more than one clone; some distinctly upright; others fatter in their middle; very susceptible to fireblight, leaf diseases and mites.

NATIVE HABITAT: Europe, northern Africa, western Asia. Long cultivated. Zone 4 to 7.

Crataegus nitida — Glossy Hawthorn
(krȧ-tē′gus n̩it′i-da)

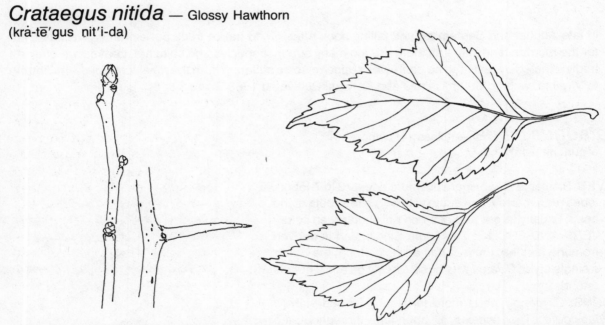

LEAVES: Alternate, simple, elliptic to oblong-obovate, acuminate, cuneate, 1 to 3″ long, one half as wide, coarsely serrate and often slightly lobed, dark green and lustrous above, paler below, glabrous; petiole—1/2″ long.

STEM: Slender with thorns to 2″ long, straight, often thorns minimal or absent.

Crataegus nitida, Glossy Hawthorn, grows to 30′ and forms a dense, rounded outline. The foliage is lustrous dark green (extremely shiny) in summer and turns orangish to red in the fall. Flowers are white, small, mid to late May, borne in 1 to 2″ diameter corymbs. Fruits is dull red, 3/8 to 5/8″ diameter, ripening in October–November and persisting into spring. This species is similar to *C. viridis,* Green Hawthorn. Illinois to Missouri and Arkansas. Introduced 1883. Zone 4 to 6. In my opinion a very handsome hawthorn.

Crataegus phaenopyrum — Washington Hawthorn
(krȧ-tē′gus fē-nō-pī′rum)

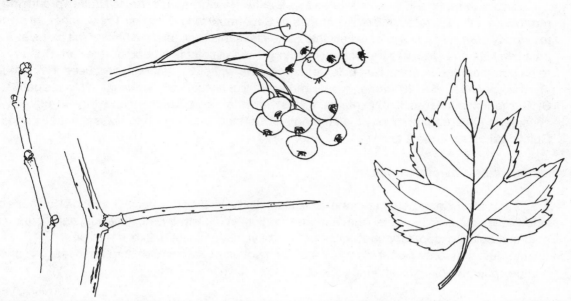

LEAVES: Alternate, simple, broad to triangular-ovate, acute, truncate or subcordate, 1 to 3″ long, 3/4 to 2 1/4″ wide, sharply serrate and 3 to 5 lobed, dark green and lustrous above, paler beneath; petiole about 1″ long.

STEM: Brown, slender, with very slender 1 to 3″ long thorns.

Crataegus phaenopyrum, Washington Hawthorn, grows to 25 to 30′ high with a 20 to 25′ spread. The overall effect is a broadly oval to rounded, dense, thorny tree. The foliage is a reddish purple when unfolding gradually changing to lustrous dark green at maturity; fall color varies from orange to scarlet through purplish; flowers are white, 20 stamens, pink anthers, 2 to 5 styles, 1/2″ diameter, not badly scented compared to *C. mollis* and *C. crusgalli,* early June, effective for 7 to 10 days (the last of the cultivated hawthorns to flower); borne in many flowered terminal and axillary corymbs. Fruit is bright glossy red, 1/4″ diameter, coloring in September and October and persisting all winter. Excellent single specimen plant, screen, near buildings, streets, borders, hedges. This species is often grown as a tree or shrub form and is designated as such in nursery catalogs. In the south, hawthorns are not widely planted in the landscape but on the University of Georgia campus this species has been outstanding for fruit display. Many people remark about the attractive fruit and want to know the plant's identity. The thorns present a problem and the tree should not be used in high traffic areas. Cultivars include:

'Clark'—Heavy fruiting clone.

'Fastigiata'—Columnar type with flowers and fruits smaller than the species.

'Vaughn' *(c. crusgalli × c. phaenopyrum)*—Excellent for the abundance of glossy fruit it produces; have observed tremendous rust on leaves, stems and fruits, probably 15 to 20′ by 15 to 20′.

NATIVE HABITAT: Virginia to Alabama and Missouri. Introduced 1738. Zone 3 to 8; not as vigorous in the south.

OTHER HAWTHORNS

Crataegus succulenta — Fleshy Hawthorn

LEAVES: Alternate, simple, broad elliptic to obovate, 2 to 3″ long, 1 1/4 to 2 1/2″ wide, acute or short acuminate, cuneate, coarsely and doubly serrate, lustrous dark green above, glabrous below at maturity, veins parallel in 4 to 7 pairs.

STEM: Purplish brown with 1 1/2 to 2″ long thorns, prominently borne.

Crataegus succulenta, (krȧ-tē′gus suk-ū-len′tȧ), Fleshy Hawthorn, is a heavy fruiter producing bright
red, 3/8 to 1/2″ diameter pome-like drupes in September and October. I remember this tree from
my woody plant materials courses at Ohio State and can still picture the heavy fruit crops as I walked
past this tree on my way to the botany building. The fall color is a good purple-red. Does not seem
to be common and in many respects (foliage, flower white, 3/4″ across, produced in rounded 3″ or
greater corymbs, 15 to 20 stamens, pink anthers, 2 to 3 styles, fruit) is similar to *C. crusgalli.* Charles
S. Sargent considered it one of the 6 best hawthorns in America and that is quite a tribute
considering the great number which are native. Quebec and Ontario to Massachusetts and Illinois.
Cultivated 1830. Zone 3 to 6.

Crataegus viridis — Green Hawthorn

LEAVES: Alternate, simple, oblong-ovate to elliptic, 1 1/2 to 3 1/2″ long, 3/4 to 2 1/2″ wide, acute or
acuminate, cuneate, serrate, the terminal portion shallowly lobed, lustrous dark green above,
glabrous below except for pubescence in axils of veins; petiole—1/2 to 1 1/2″ long.
STEM: Glabrous, gray-brown, thorns up to 1 1/2″ long but often absent; older stems silver-gray and finally
a large caliper trunk exfoliating to expose orange brown inner bark.

Crataegus viridis, (krȧ-tē′gus vir′i-dis), Green Hawthorn, is a rounded, sharply thorny, spreading, dense
tree growing 20 to 35′ high and wide. The foliage is a lustrous medium green in summer and can
change to purple and scarlet in the fall. Flowers are white, 20 stamens, pale yellow anthers, 2 to 5
styles, 3/4″ diameter, mid May, borne in 2″ diameter corymbs. The fruits are bright red, 1/4 to 1/3″
diameter, coloring in September–October and persisting.
  'Winter King'—Selection with lovely rounded habit, almost vase-shaped branching structure and
distinct gray-green bloomy stems. The fruits are larger than the species and a good red,
one-half inch diameter; fruits persist into winter and are among the handsomest of all
hawthorns. Introduced by the Simpson Orchard Co. of Vincennes, IN in 1955. Could be a
hybrid as it does not match the characteristics of the species; less susceptible to rust than
other thorns but I have seen the fruits badly infected when the leaves showed very little
infection. This and *C. phaenopyrum* are the two most outstanding hawthorns for landscape
use.

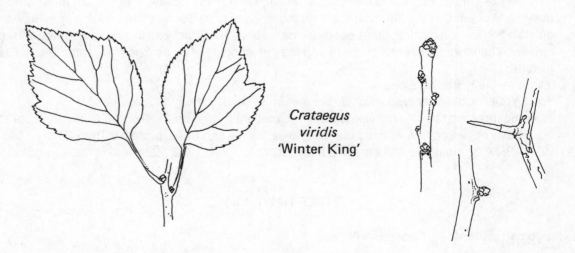

*Crataegus
viridis*
'Winter King'

NATIVE HABITAT: Maryland and Virginia to Illinois, Iowa, Texas and Florida. Cultivated 1827. Zone 4 to 7.

Cryptomeria japonica — Japanese Cryptomeria, Japanese Cedar
(krip-tō-mē′ri-a ja-pon′-i-ka)

FAMILY: Taxodiaceae

LEAVES: Evergreen, spirally arranged, persisting 4 to 5 years, awl-shaped, 4-angled, 1/4 to 3/4″ long, the first leaves of the year shorter than the later ones, curving inwards, sometimes slightly twisted, pointed forwards, keeled on both surfaces, margins entire, apex tapering to a blunt point, base spreading and clasping the shoot, stomata on each surface.

STEM: Green, glabrous; the branchlets spreading or drooping, eventually deciduous.

SIZE: 50 to 60′ high by 20 to 30′ wide; can grow to 100′.

HARDINESS: Zone 5 to 6, hardy to Boston, Massachusetts and south to Zones 8 and 9.

HABIT: A pyramidal or conical tree with a stout trunk and erect, wide-spreading branches with numerous branchlets; relatively graceful in habit.

RATE: Medium, can grow 50 to 60′ after 30 to 40 years; in the lower midwest (Cincinnati) trees are much slower growing.

TEXTURE: Medium.

BARK: Reddish brown peeling off in long strips; beautiful bark.

LEAF COLOR: Bright green to bluish green in summer; during the winter the needles take on a bronzy hue (brown if in windy locations), becoming green again in spring.

FLOWERS: Monoecious, inconspicuous.

FRUIT: Cones are terminal, globular, 1/2 to 1″ broad and dark brown, composed of 20 to 30 scales, each with 3 to 5 seeds.

CULTURE: Easy to grow; prefers a rich and deep, light, permeable, acid soil with abundant moisture; open, sunny location, shelter from high winds.

DISEASES AND INSECTS: Leaf blight and leaf spot, have noticed a branch dieback, particularly in southeast.

LANDSCAPE VALUE: An accommodating tree, graceful, stately and handsome; useful as a specimen or for avenues; a fine evergreen, when properly grown as pretty as any conifer.

CULTIVARS: Many cultivars (over 50) are known and some, because of their smaller size, are more appropriate for residential landscaping.

    'Compacta'—Compact, conical tree to 45′ high, needles short, stiff and bluish green, 'Lobbii Compacta' is sometimes applied to this form.

    'Elegans'—Juvenile form of tall bushy habit, 9 to 15′ (30′), the soft feathery 1/2 to 1″ long green summer foliage turns brownish red in winter, fluffy looking juvenile foliage, less hardy than species.

    'Elegans Nana' ('Elegans Compacta' is probably correct)—As above but flattened, globose, compact and slow growing; 3′ high; needles bluish green becoming purplish tinged in winter.

    'Globosa'—This neat, dense, dome-shaped form grows 2 to 3′ high and 2 1/2 to 3 1/2′ wide in 10 to 15 years; the bluish green adult needles assume a rusty-red color in winter.

    'Lobbii'—Considerable confusion in my mind relative to correct identity; plants I have seen labeled as 'Lobbii' were probably 'Yoshino'; true 'Lobbii' is an upright pyramidal-columnar form with denser and less pendulous branching than species, needles are longer and deeper green, and may bronze in cold weather, 20 to 40′.

    'Lycopodioides'—A rather curious, loose growing evergreen shrub, the branches long, slender and snake-like; a novelty item.

    'Vilmoriniana'—Compact, 1 to 2′ high mound of dense foliage; good collector's item or rock garden plant.

    'Yoshino'—Handsome form like the species with rich bright blue-green summer foliage that becomes slightly bronze-green in cold weather, grows fast and develops a handsome form without extensive pruning, 30 to 40′, is now being grown by southern nurserymen.

PROPAGATION: Seed germination is usually quite poor; the seed should be soaked in cold water (32°F) for about 12 hours, then put moist into plastic bags and stored at 34°F for 60 to 90 days before sowing;

bags should be left open for adequate aeration; 3 months warm followed by 3 months cold supposedly results in good germination; cuttings taken in summer and fall will root, although slowly; the older literature reports effective treatments of 40 to 80 ppm IBA soak for 24 hours; based on some work I did at Illinois it is probably best to collect cuttings in November (have also done it in August); treat with 10,000 ppm IBA-quick dip, place in peat:perlite, under a poly tent; rooting took place 2 or 3 months later but was generally good with large numbers of thick white roots.

ADDITIONAL NOTES: A lovely conifer where it can be grown; not used enough in the southern states where it thrives; with proper cultivar selection the plant could be used in almost any landscape.

NATIVE HABITAT: China and Japan, and was originally discovered in the former country in 1701 by James Cunningham, and by Kaempfer in Japan in 1692. Introduced into America 1861.

Cunninghamia lanceolata — Common Chinafir
(kun-ing-ham′i-à lan-sē-ō-lā′ta)

FAMILY: Taxodiaceae

LEAVES: Evergreen, spirally arranged, those on the main axis standing out from all around the stem, those on the underside of the branches turning upwards by a basal twist so that all appear to spring from the sides and surface of the shoot; persisting 5 or more years and remaining dry and dead on the branches for several years more; lanceolate, curving backwards, 1 to 2 3/4″ long, 1/16 to 1/8″ wide at the base, green or glaucous green, margins finely toothed, apex a long slender point; stomata in a broad band on each side of the midrib on the under-surface.

SIZE: 30 to 75′ in height, 10 to 30′ wide; 150′ in native haunts.

HARDINESS: Zone (6) 7 to 9; is growing at the Secrest Arboretum, Wooster, Ohio, where temperatures drop to −20°F; tips of branches are killed every winter.

HABIT: Pyramidal with slightly pendulous branches, giving the appearance of an exotic-looking tree; often rather ragged.

RATE: Slow to medium; supposedly can grow 20 to 30′ after 15 years.

TEXTURE: Medium-fine.

BARK: Brown, scaling off in long irregular strips, exposing the reddish inner bark.

LEAF COLOR: Bright medium green or glaucous to bluish green; often discoloring in cold weather, more or less bronze-green.

FLOWERS: Monoecious; male flowers in terminal clusters; female flowers terminal.

FRUIT: Cones usually several together, rarely solitary, globose, ovoid, 1 1/2″ broad.

CULTURE: Prefers moist, acid, well-drained soils; not very hardy; grows best in open spaces shaded by trees and protected from windswept sites.

DISEASES AND INSECTS: None serious.

LANDSCAPE VALUE: Only of value in the warmer parts of the country; possibly used as a specimen or mass planting; in youth reasonably attractive but becoming "seedy" with age as the old dead needles cling to the branches; common in the south and I have seen 60′ high trees; in most landscapes seems out of place.

CULTIVARS:

'Glauca'—Leaves with a conspicuous glaucous bloom, attractive when young, perhaps more cold hardy than the species.

PROPAGATION: Cuttings can be rooted and November appears to be the best time; high hormone treatments, 8000 ppm IBA and above are recommended; a poly-tent and bottom heat are advisable; the cuttings may retain the growth characteristics of the branch from which they were collected; if from a lateral shoot they grow laterally; if from a vertical they grow upright; in propagation circles this is called topophysis.

ADDITIONAL NOTES: Highly prized tree in China and, next to bamboo, is the most useful for all around work. The wood is light, soft, fragrant, pale yellow or almost white, easily worked, durable, and used for housebuilding, indoor carpentry, masts, planking, box-making, and largely for coffins. The wood is very rot resistant in contact with the soil. In the wild, under forest conditions, it develops a long, straight, mast-like trunk, 80 to 150′ high, clear of branches for half its height. It has the ability when cut to produce sprouts from roots and revegetate an area. Watched a 30′ specimen being cut to the ground and 3 years later it had resprouted to 10′.

NATIVE HABITAT: Central and southern China. Introduced 1804.

× *Cupressocyparis leylandii* — Leyland Cypress
(kū-pres-ō-si′pa-ris lā-lan′dē-ī)

FAMILY: Cupressaceae (Intergeneric hybrid between *Cupressus macrocarpa* and *Chamaecyparis nootkatensis*).

LEAVES: Very similar to those of *C. nootkatensis* but less odorous when bruised, branchlets flattened or somewhat quadrangular.

SIZE: 60 to 70′ under landscape conditions; can grow over 100′, spread 1/5 to 1/8 the height or less.

HARDINESS: Zone 6 to 10, possibly 5.

HABIT: Magnificent, noble, needled evergreen forming a columnar to pyramidal outline.

RATE: Fast, easily 3′ a year in youth, 100′ in 60 years.

TEXTURE: Fine, feathery foliage contributes to the gracefulness of the species.

BARK: Reddish brown, scaly.

LEAF COLOR: Bluish green on the type, upper and lower side of sprays of the same color.

FRUIT: Cone 1/2 to 3/4″ diameter, 8 scales, with about 5 seeds per scale.

CULTURE: Transplants readily from a container, should not be field-grown as roots are somewhat stringy and plants are difficult to ball and burlap, many southern nurserymen are successfully digging the tree with mechanical tree diggers; adaptable to extremes of soil; acid or calcareous; withstands salt spray; even on "poor" sites plants from cuttings have grown 48′ in 16 years; requires full sun, definitely thins out in shady environments.

DISEASES AND INSECTS: None serious; canker has appeared that causes branch dieback to main trunk, can be controlled with fungicide; I have not seen it but some Christmas tree growers mentioned the problem.

LANDSCAPE VALUE: In the last edition I looked into the crystal ball and predicted the tree would become popular in the southeast; in a sense its acceptance has snowballed not simply as an ornamental evergreen but also as a Christmas tree; production is now in the hundreds of thousands; from the gardeners' perspective the plant should be purchased in a 1, 3, or 7 gallon container, plants in containers are not as dense as field (soil) grown material but will fill in quickly without pruning once installed in the landscape; my neighbor and I planted one gallon plants 4′ apart and in 2 years had 6 to 7′ plants that were touching at the base; the plant's growth rate is truly amazing; no matter what the literature states the plant grows faster in reasonably fertile, moist, well-drained soil compared to the extremes on either side; the plant can be pruned almost indefinitely to maintain a certain shape (plasticity); excellent for quick screens, groupings, hedges; possibly not a long term landscape investment (10 to 20 years) but it gets where it is going in a hurry and provides functional service; interestingly the Christmas tree growers sell this for much more than Virginia Pine yet it makes a salable tree in a shorter period of time; many cultivars have been introduced and here I attempt to present a clear picture of their characteristics based on observation and the literature.

CULTIVARS:

‘Castlewellan Gold’ (‘Castlewellan’)—Rather handsome golden yellow foliage form that is not quite as bright as *Thuja orientalis* ‘Aurea Nana’; in cool European climates the color persists through the summer but in Georgia is best in fall, winter and early spring, becoming light green, but handsomely so, in summer; I collected a branch February 18, 1989 to check intensity of color and was not impressed by the gold color but prior to this temperatures were in the 70's which may account for minimal coloration. I have grown a plant for three years and the vigor is exceptional, unfortunately, the color is not as potent in hot weather; origin is interesting since a coning branch broke off *Cupressus macrocarpa* 'Lutea', Forest Park, Castlewellan, County Down, Ireland; a tree of the golden needle form of *Chamaecyparis nootkatensis* grew nearby, the seeds were sown with the hope that hybridization might have occurred and one seedling proved such and was propagated; the clone was put into commerce around 1970; foliage is arranged as on 'Haggerston Gray'.

'Goldconda'—A new introduction that I know very little about; golden needles and a compact pyramidal outline; considered an improvement on 'Castlewellan Gold' for the intensity of yellow-gold pigmentation, one small plant has held excellent golden yellow foliage color during the winter of 1989, cursory evaluations indicate much brighter and persistent than 'Castlewellan Gold'.

'Green Spire'—Narrow columnar, very dense, with rich green foliage, branchlets spaced irregularly and at varying angles to stem, directed forward on an even plane, central leader often poorly developed, raised in 1888 (clone 1) at Haggerston Castle.

'Haggerston Grey'—More open than 'Leighton Green'; the green foliage with a slight pale gray cast, branchlets arising and lying in 2 planes at right angle, frequently in opposite and decussate pairs, the smallest branchlets often in tufts; raised in 1888 (clone 2); differs from 'Leighton Green' in the decidedly irregular lateral branches.

'Harlequin'—A silvery variegated form that arose from a branch sport of 'Haggerston Grey'; it develops multiple leaders and is not so pretty in variegation pattern as 'Silver Dust'; described about 1975.

'Hillspire'— Described as a large narrow pyramidal tree with bright green foliage; I have never seen this form listed except in 1989 Iseli Nursery Catalog; could it be another name for 'Green Spire'?

'Hyde Hall'—Dwarf, slow-growing form that arose as a witches' broom on a plant in Essex, England; rather flame shaped in outline with dark green, soft semi-juvenile foliage like a miniature *Chamaecyparis lawsoniana* 'Erecta'.

'Leighton Green'—Tall, columnar form with central leader and rich green foliage, branchlets and their divisions in one plane recalling those of the pollen parent, *Chamaecyparis nootkatensis*; consistent cone bearer; raised in 1911 (clone 11); in actuality there is little difference in foliage color between this and 'Haggerston Grey'.

'Naylor's Blue'—The most glaucous foliaged of the cultivars; the bluish green foliage most noticeably glaucous in winter; more loosely branched and open; raised in 1911 (clone 10), available in U.S.; I have grown this in my garden and find it the most distinctive of the green or blue-green foliage forms; needles are distinctly blue-green, branching is more loose and irregular and the plant is not as upright and narrow as 'Haggerston Grey' or 'Leighton Green'; it is being produced in southern nurseries; appears a little slower growing than the other types.

'Robinson's Gold'—Foliage arranged like 'Leighton Green' perhaps brighter yellow when young; bronze-yellow in spring, gradually turning lemon-green and gold-yellow; fast growing but more compact and densely branched and conical than 'Leighton Green'; original plant 25' by 10' in 20 years; found in 1962 by George Robinson in Belvoir Park, Belfast, Northern Ireland was a self-sown seedling; always fascinating how plants "find" their way into cultivation.

'Silver Dust'—Although described as a branch sport of 'Leighton Green' I have genuine difficulty making the habit and needle characteristics fit; the green foliage is splotched, streaked and splashed with creamy white; from a distance, it is difficult to separate it from the typical forms; appears to grow slightly slower than 'Haggerston Grey' or 'Leighton Green' but based on plant performance in the Dirr garden will grow 2' per year; in rooting studies this rooted faster and in higher percentages than other cultivars; 'Leighton Green' is more difficult to root than other cultivars; taxonomically I am not sure of exact status but is a rather handsome subdued variegated conifer for Zone 6 to 9; have observed prosperous plants in Savannah, GA area, made an effort to compare 'Silver Dust' branches to the literature and what I know as 'Haggerston Grey' and 'Leighton Green'; 'Silver Dust' coincides more closely with 'Haggerston Grey'.

'Stapehill Hybrid' (*Cupressus macrocarpa* × *Chamaecyparis lawsoniana*)—Similar to 'Leighton Green' in appearance with darker blue-green heavily textured foliage, the undersides of the sprays blue-gray-green; developed in the Barthelemy Nursery, Stapehill, Winborne, Dorset, England in 1940; not common in the U.S.

PROPAGATION: The last edition went overboard on propagation information; in recent years numerous studies have been published and tell of success in summer, fall and winter; from our experience, February–March cuttings with brown wood, 5000 to 8000 ppm IBA-50% alcohol quick dip, 2 perlite:1 peat, mist with bottom heat or (what we use) a wire frame that is covered with plastic and 2 layers of 50% shade cloth, cuttings are syringed twice a day, rooting will occur in 6 to 10 weeks and should approach 80%; a local nurseryman sticks cuttings in summer, about 10,000 ppm IBA and has excellent success; Whalley *PIPPS* 29:190–197 (1979) presented strong evidence for taking cuttings in February; 'Haggerston Grey'; 'Leighton Green', and 'Stapehill' rooted 87, 70, 99%, respectively, when treated with 3000 ppm IBA-talc, peat and sand, mist, 68°F medium temperature; cuttings collected in May, August, September *always* rooted in lower percentages sometimes 50% less. See Dirr and Frett, *HortScience* 18(2):204–205 (1983) and Dirr and Heuser, 1987.

ADDITIONAL NOTES: The cross first originated at the estate of Mr. Naylor, Leighton Hall, Welshpool, Wales in 1888 (6 seedlings) and again in 1911 (2 seedlings planted at Leighton Hall); also in a garden at Ferndown, Dorset in 1940 (2 seedlings). The six seedlings were taken by Naylor's brother-in-law, C.J. Leyland, and planted on his property, Haggerston Castle, Northumberland, in 1892–93. Five of the original plants still existed in 1970 and are the parents by asexual propagation of × *C. leylandii,* Clones 1 to 5. The derivation of the clonal names is evident from the brief history presented here.

Two other × *Cupressocyparis* species, × *C. notabilis* and × *C. ovensii* have been described. × *C. notabilis* was grown from seed collected in 1956 from a specimen of *Cupressus glabra* growing at Leighton Hall, Montgomeryshire. In 23 years, the original seedlings had grown about 40′ high. The foliage is dark grayish green. The other parent is *C. nootkatensis.* × *C. ovensii* is a hybrid between *Cupressus lusitanica* and *Chamaecyparis nootkatensis* raised from seed collected in 1961 from a specimen of *C. lusitanica.* The hybrid exhibits a strong influence of the Nootka parent and produces large flattened sprays of drooping, dark glaucous green foliage. In approximately 20 years the plant grew 35′ high. For an excellent account of the origin of Leyland Cypress see A.F. Mitchell. 1972. *Conifers in the British Isles.* HSMO. London.

Cupressus arizonica — Arizona Cypress
(ku-pres'us ar-i-zon'ic-a)

FAMILY: Cupressaceae

LEAVES: Evergreen scales closely overlapping, scale-like, flattened to branchlet, and superposed in 4 rows, about 1/16″ long, acutely pointed, pale green to gray-green, occasionally blue-green; the overall effect is like a braided bullwhip and since the scales are pressed against the stem the foliage is soft-textured.

BRANCHLETS: Irregularly arranged, not planar as in most *Chamaecyparis* species, the final divisions 1/20″ wide and quadrangular in cross section.

BARK: Handsome red, smooth, peeling in flakes, on mature trees dark brown, ridged and furrowed and fibrous.

SIZE: 30 to 40′ high by 15 to 20′ wide.
HARDINESS: Zone 7 to 9.
HABIT: Rather handsome graceful pyramid with fine textured foliage.
RATE: Medium.
TEXTURE: Fine.
BARK: Interesting especially on middle-aged trees, shiny, red to brown bark exfoliates in scales.
LEAF COLOR: Green, gray-green to blue-green.
FLOWERS: Monoecious, with male in small oblong cones, yellowish in color; female in a subglobose cone.

FRUIT: Globose cone with 6 to 8 flat or slightly depressed scales, each contracted into a short mucro (point), 1 to 1 1/4″ wide, scales are peltate which separates them from arborvitae; their size separates them from *Chamaecyparis.*

CULTURE: All species prefer hot, dry conditions, well drained soil, full sun (thin out significantly with competition), transplant as a container grown specimen.

DISEASES AND INSECTS: In the proper environment generally trouble-free, in the southeast subject to canker (possibly *Coryneum* sp.) and are not long lived.

LANDSCAPE VALUE: Excellent specimen, windbreak, tall screen, interestingly at one time widely grown in southeast and odd trees may be seen, have seen seedlings in great abundance on dry, abandoned slopes around Athens; suspect the species is best reserved for the southwest and west; will never compete with ö *Cupressocyparis leylandii* in the southeast.

CULTIVARS:

'Gareei'—Silver-blue foliage.

'Pyramidalis' (var. *conica* or *pyramidalis*)—Narrowly conical with glaucous blue leaves.

PROPAGATION: Seeds require cold moist stratification for one month; cuttings have not been easy to root for this author and excessive moisture induced rapid decline; I suspect the ventilated polytent method (warm bottom, cool top) would work best; November to December may be the best months to collect cuttings, use 2000 to 5000 ppm IBA.

NATIVE HABITAT: Central and southern Arizona. Introduced 1887.

RELATED SPECIES: It is fair to state that the *Cupressus* are difficult to identify. The species that is often listed as *C. glabra,* which is a dense, bushy tree with a spreading crown and has gray to blue leaves, is often sold as *C. arizonica* and for 10 years I have been trying to determine the identity of a 35 to 40′ specimen on the Georgia campus that, unfortunately, has never coned. Some authorities consider *C. glabra* a variety of *C. arizonica.*

Cupressus macrocarpa,(ku-pres′us ma-kro-câr′pa), Monterey Cypress, is an artistic, horizontally branched, often flat-topped tree in its native environs of the Monterey peninsula in California. The trees are genuinely beautiful. Habit is narrow and pyramidal in youth becoming picturesque with age. Plants grow 30 to 40′ (50′). The needles are a rich dark green and as handsome as any in the genus. The 8 to 14 scaled cones are 1 to 1 1/3″ wide, grouped 1 to 2 together on short thick stalks. Unfortunately, the species is tremendously susceptible to a canker (*Coryneum* sp.) that has killed many trees especially those planted away from the coast. In San Francisco's Golden Gate Park, I witnessed numerous trees dying and being removed. The species displays excellent salt tolerance. It is one of the parents of × *Cupressocyparis leylandii* and I wonder when the same disease will manifest itself on the intergeneric hybrid. Numerous cultivars of *C. macrocarpa* have been selected over the years. The golden needled forms are more prevalent in Europe and are best reserved for cool climates. 'Donard Gold' and 'Golden Cone' are two that have crossed my path. 'Contorta' is sold in the United States and becomes broad upright in habit with bright green twisted new foliage. Introduced 1838. Zone 7 to 9. Not for high humidity areas of the southeastern states.

Cupressus sempervirens, (ku-pres′us sem-per-vī′renz), Italian Cypress, has always been an enigma to me. The plant in its familiar cultivated form is a narrow column, which has crossed my path numerous times. The species has dark green foliage and horizontal branches. Apparently three selections dominate the cultivated market and include 'Roylei' with bright green needles and stiff upright habit, 'Stricta' a narrow-columnar form with green foliage, and 'Glauca' ('Stricta Glauca') with genuine rich blue-green foliage and columnar habit. All look like exclamation points and their use needs to be restrained. 'Swane's Golden', also spelled 'Swain's Gold', is a slow growing narrow columnar form with green golden foliage throughout the year; grows like 'Skyrocket' juniper. The selections can grow 20 to 30′ and higher. I have seen 'Stricta' used in Charleston, SC where it was relatively prosperous. Southern Europe and western Asia. Zone 7 to 9.

Cyrilla racemiflora — Swamp Cyrilla, Leatherwood
(sī-ril′a̍ rā-sem-i-flō′-ra̍)

FAMILY: Cyrillaceae

LEAVES: Alternate, simple, evergreen, semievergreen or deciduous, oblong or oblanceolate, 1 1/2 to 4″ long, 1/2 to 1 1/4″ wide, obtuse, cuneate, lustrous dark green above, bright green and reticulate beneath, glabrous; petiole 1/4″ long.

BUDS: Small, 1/16 to 1/12″ long, deltoid, sitting directly above and flat across the leaf scar.

STEM: Moderate, gray-brown, glabrous, raised ridges from center of base of leaf scar giving stem angled appearance; shield shaped leaf scar with what appears to be a single bud scar.

SIZE: Usually 10 to 15′ high and wide, but can grow 25 to 35′.

HARDINESS: Zone 5 to 10, have seen at Louisville, KY, Mentor, OH, and Boston, MA; is distinctly deciduous in cold climates and may be killed back in extremely cold winters.

HABIT: Large shrub or small tree; usually a rather sprawling-spreading rounded shrub of great beauty; develops a stout eccentric trunk from which numerous wide-spreading branches arise; branches contorted and twisted.

RATE: Medium.

TEXTURE: Medium.

LEAF COLOR: Lustrous rich green holding late in fall and eventually turning orange and scarlet; the beautiful foliage is sufficient reason to use this shrub; in deep south may hold leaves into the following season; has been evergreen in mild seasons in my garden.

FLOWERS: Perfect, white, fragrant, 5-petaled, 1/5″ across, in slender 3 to 6″ long and 1/2 to 3/4″ wide racemes that appear in a horizontal whorl at the base of the current season's growth; flowers quite showy and rather light and airy in texture; June–July; flowers late June–early July in my garden.

FRUIT: A 1/2″ long, roundish, 2 celled, loculicidally dehiscent capsule, mature in August–September, persist into winter; rather interesting.

CULTURE: Not well documented but prefers a high organic matter, moist, acid, well-drained soil; full sun to partial shade; in the wild found in swamps; actually once established appears difficult to kill.

DISEASES AND INSECTS: None serious.

LANDSCAPE VALUE: Simply a beautiful shrub for foliage and flowers; can be successfully grown from Zone 6 south; have seen it used by the edge of a lake with great success; seems to belong in a naturalistic setting; a good shrub border plant in the home landscape; does not compete well with other species; used in a large bed in front of the house and many people ask me why it is there; there is no good reason except I like it, have pruned the lower branches and suckers to expose rather handsome smooth brown bark; the contorted, twisted spiraled stems are beautiful; needs room to expand.

PROPAGATION: Seeds can be directly sown; root cuttings will work; August cuttings treated with 10,000 ppm IBA rooted 100%; over the years I have rooted the plant many times, firm wooded cuttings from June into September can be easily rooted.

NATIVE HABITAT: In its broadest sense a single species ranging from Virginia to Florida, also West Indies and eastern South America. Introduced 1767.

RELATED SPECIES:

Cliftonia monophylla, (klif-tōn′e-a̍ mon-ō-fil′a̍), Buckwheat-tree or Titi, is similar to the above and is found in the same locations in the wild. It forms a medium-sized (6 to 12′ (18′) high) evergreen shrub. The lustrous dark green evergreen leaves are 1 to 2″ long. The white

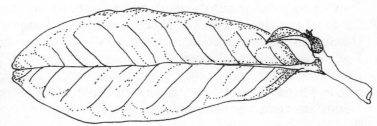

or rose fragrant flowers are borne in 1 1/2 to 2 1/2" long and 5/8" wide racemes in March–April. The ovoid, indehiscent, 3 to 4-winged fruit looks like a buckwheat fruit; hence the common name. Has the same cultural requirements as *Cyrilla*. The foliage is beautiful and the fragrant flowers a fine asset. In the Coastal plain, this and *Cyrilla* make great bee-pasture and are a source of "Titi" honey. Have seen it in Canton, Georgia where temperatures as low as –16°F have occurred. Georgia to Florida and Louisiana. I took 5 cuttings from a plant in my garden in July; treated them with 3000 ppm IBA; had 80% rooting by October; no wound; rooting takes 2 to 3 months. Introduced 1806. Zone 7 to 9, perhaps 6.

Cyrilla parviflora, (sī-ril′à par-vi-flō′rà), Small Cyrilla, is a Florida native with smaller leaves, 3/4 to 1 1/2" long, 1/4 to 1/2" wide, and 1 to 3" long floral racemes. Although not common in commerce, Woodlanders, Aiken, SC has offered the plant. Might be a better choice for the small garden but foliage, as I have observed it, is sparse and not as handsome as big sister's.

ADDITIONAL NOTES: These species are highly unusual but worthy landscape plants, especially in native situations. Their foliage effect alone is sufficient reason for using them. Flowers are more spectacular on *Cyrilla*.

Cyrtomium falcatum — Japanese Holly-fern
(sĕr-tō′mi-um fal-kā′tum)

FAMILY: Polypodiaceae
LEAVES: Evergreen, 1 to 2′ long, leaflets holly-like with prominent serrations, lustrous dark green above, 1 to 2" long, one-half as wide, leathery, underside of leaf developing numerous sori (spore clusters) in summer–fall.

Reserved strictly for the southern United States, the Japanese Holly-fern is one of those plants that northerners drool over the first time they see it. At the first meeting, it takes awhile for the fact to sink in that one is looking at a true fern. The lustrous dark green leaves form a lovely 1 to 2′ high and wide mound. As the young fiddle heads unroll (early to mid April) the entire frond assumes an attractive yellow-green color before maturing to dark green. The plant tolerates partial to heavy shade and is ideal for the moist site on the north side of a structure. Prefers moist, well-drained, high organic matter soils. There are no serious insect or disease problems. 'Compactum' has shorter leaves than the species and 'Rochfordianum' has more incised leaflets that produce a finer texture than the species. Restricted to Zone 8 (+10 to +20°F) and warmer conditions. Grew this for a number of years but lost foliage in late April to a freak freeze as the young fronds were developing; also lost all plants at –3°F during the 1983–84 winter.

Cytisus scoparius — Scotch or Common Broom
(sī′ti′-sus skō-pā′ri-us)

FAMILY: Fabaceae
LEAVES: Alternate, 3-foliate, obovate or lanceolate, 1/4 to 5/8" long, sparingly appressed pubescent, the upper leaves reduced to 1 leaflet, bright to medium green.
BUDS: Small, solitary, sessile, round-ovoid, with about 4 often indistinct scales.
STEM: Slender, finely granular, green, almost winged on the ridges; bright green in summer and winter; pith—small, roundish, continuous.

SIZE: 5 to 6′ when open grown and twice that when used in shrub borders and tight situations; spread is equal to or considerably greater than height.
HARDINESS: Zone 5 to 8.

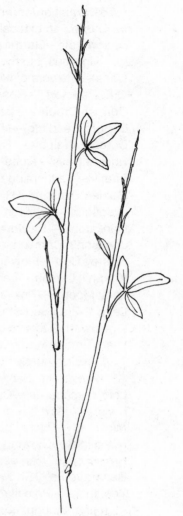

HABIT: A broad, rounded-mounded, deciduous shrub with very erect, slender grass green stems and twigs; can become ratty in appearance.

TEXTURE: Medium-fine if kept in bounds during summer; similar texture in winter.

STEM COLOR: Distinctly angled stems of grass green color, very sttractive in winter; young stems maintain green color, older stems become gray-brown.

LEAF COLOR: Light to medium green in summer; fall color of no consequence.

FLOWERS: Perfect, glowing yellow, 1″ long and 4/5″ across, May–June, profusely borne along the stems on old wood either singly or in two's.

FRUIT: 1 1/2 to 2″ long pod, hairy along the margins, not ornamental.

CULTURE: Supposedly does not transplant well but I have had good success with container-grown material; prefers sandy, infertile soils which are somewhat on the dry side; full sun; pH adaptable; prune after flowering; relatively easy to grow; tends to seed itself in; old plants may die out but new ones always seem to be coming along, cut back old overgrown plants.

DISEASES AND INSECTS: Leaf spot and blight can kill the plants; small irregular spots first appear on the leaf blades, enlarge rapidly, and cause a blotch or blight.

LANDSCAPE VALUE: Very good plant for poor soils; has been used for stabilizing sandy right-of-ways along eastern highways; I have seen it used in Massachusetts along highways and it made an effective cover; yields a fantastic splash of color when in flower; a midwest nurseryman told me the plant rarely lasts more than 5 years; I witnessed tremendous injury after winter of 1977–78 when the low temperatures reached −8°F but the mean low temperature for December, January, February was 10° below normal; in general *Cytisus* will seed and can establish fairly large colonies; does quite well in south, where it often seeds in waste areas. On our yearly garden tours the first plants our guests ask about are broom and gorse (*Ulex*); everyone is in the twilight zone from the flight but after boarding the bus outside Gatwick and seeing the repeated dashes of bright yellow along the M23 (motorway) the inevitable question surfaces . . . what is that plant? My colleague and I proceed to tell them and explain how the plant is often used in English gardens for May–June color; in many gardens a single plant is spotted among ground covers or heathers and literally erupts in a floral volcano; there is a tendency in the United States to use the plant in masses especially for color splashes along highways; several years past a Georgia Department of Transportation official called me and wanted to know where to locate 700 yellow brooms for a highway interchange; I had no answer but the GDOT official persisted for the plants were installed and are certainly attractive in flower.

My general belief is that brooms should be viewed as temporary but beautiful garden plants. If one dies replace it for the floral display is worth the effort. Quite sandy soil and salt tolerant as many seedlings exist on Cape Cod, MA.

CULTIVARS: The brooms are not popular landscape plants in the United States but in Europe they appear everywhere. The color range is rather fantastic moving from white to yellow to red with all combinations and permutations in the flower. The Dutch are breeding brooms and have introduced a number of fine forms. Several years past at the International Garden Festival in Liverpool, England, I visited the Dutch exhibit where they had displayed several of their new broom hybrids. 'Boskoop Ruby' with rich garnet flowers was one of the best, yet I have not seen it in English or American gardens or literature. Maybe too many selections are available; certainly many too similar to warrant naming (actually end up being named), that fall by the commercial and gardening wayside.

A few mail order firms in the United States offer 4 or 5 broom selections but to my knowledge no one carries an extensive list and what is listed below is nothing more than a futuristic shopping list:

'Burkwoodii'—Garnet red (standard red-carmine, wings red-brown with a narrow gold border) flowers; vigorous, bushy.

'Carla'—Flowers pink and crimson lined with white.

'C.E. Pearson,'—Rose, yellow, red flowers; reasonably common in commerce.

'Cornish Cream'—Cream and yellow, bushy, open habit.

'Donard Seedling'—Mauve-pink and flame-red, loose habit.

'Dorothy Walpole'—Rose-pink with velvety crimson wings.

'Enchantress'—Rose-pink and carmine, spreading bushy outline.

'Firefly'—Yellow and rich mahogany-crimson, bushy.

'Golden Sunlight'—Rich golden yellow, very free-flowering, vigorous arching habit.

'Goldfinch'—Crimson and yellow, pink and yellow wings.

'Hookstone'—Flowers lilac and orange.

'Johnson's Crimson'—Clear crimson, free flowering, graceful arching habit.

'Killiney Red'—Flowers bright red, dwarf, compact habit.

'Knaphill Lemon'—Lemon-yellow flowers.

'Lady Moore'—Pinkish yellow and orange-flame, loose branching.

'Lena'—Ruby-red standards and wings, pale yellow keels, freely borne, compact, comparatively dwarf, 3 to 4' high.

'Lilac Time'—Many conflicting descriptions; the plant in the trade is a compact grower with deep reddish purple flowers; certain literature ascribes a lilac color to the standard with lighter colored wings; the plant was obviously mislabeled in nursery circles.

'Lord Lambourne'—Creamy yellow and maroon-crimson, branching and spreading.

'Luna'—Yellow flowers.

'Minstead'—Fuchia purple and white, slender arching habit.

'Moonlight'—Glowing moonlight yellow (actually cream-white) flowers, nodding growth habit.

'Nova Scotia'—An extra hardy form offered by Wayside Gardens with intense yellow flowers.

'Red Favorite'—Showy red flowers on an upright stemmed, compact mounding shrub.

'Zeelandia'—Pale lilac-pink and red, long arching sprays.

A final thought concerning performance in the south crossed my mind. Mr. Will Corley, Horticulturist, Griffin, GA, evaluated a tremendous number of *Cytisus* for adaptability. He was interested in persistence, flower quality, growth habit, hardiness, etc. The bottom line . . . he did not find a single taxon that was well adapted.

PROPAGATION: Seeds should be soaked in hot water or acid soaked to break seed coat dormancy; for germination, diurnally alternating temperatures of 68°F (night) and 86°F (day) for 28 days are recommended; it may require 30 minutes or more in acid, apparently there is no embryo dormancy; seeds are usually produced in abundance. Two to 3″ long cuttings with a heel taken in August and September, placed in sand in cold frames, will develop roots by spring; various species and cultivars have been rooted anytime from June to December by treating the cuttings with a relatively high IBA level (8000 ppm); a loose medium is recommended since root systems are somewhat brittle.

NATIVE HABITAT: Central and southern Europe. Long cultivated.

RELATED SPECIES: It is beyond the scope of this book to treat extensively all the *Cytisus* species and related genera. I have included several that deserve a closer look.

Cytisus decumbens, (sī′ti′-sus dē-kum′benz), Prostrate Broom, smothers the ground in May–June with a sea of bright yellow. The species grows about 6″ high. The leaves are simple, sessile, 1/4 to 3/4″ long, 1/8 to 1/6″ wide, oblong or obovate, pubescent, especially beneath. The 1/2 to 5/8″ long flowers occur singly, in two's or three's from the axils of previous season's wood. Pod is 3/4 to 1″ long, pubescent, 3 to 4 seeded. The five angled stems are sparsely pubescent. This species is confused with *C. procumbens* but is more pubescent. A fine choice as a low-ground cover in full sun or in the rock garden. Southern Europe. Introduced 1775. Zone 5.

Cytisus hirsutus, (sī-ti′sus hĕr-sūt′us), Hairy Broom, is a dwarf, 2 to 3′ high and wide shrub with rounded, slender, pubescent (not appressed) stems. The trifoliate leaves are composed of 3/8″ long, half as wide, oval to broadly obovate leaflets; their undersurface hairy. The 1″ long yellow flowers occur 2 to 4 together in axillary clusters; the standard stained brown in the center. Pod 1 to 1 1/2″ long, flattened shaggily hairy. This species is not as showy as *C. scoparius* or *C. ö praecox* but is considered the hardiest of the brooms. It is being successfully grown in Minnesota where some stem dieback occurs but flowering occurs heavily on the basal portion of the plant. This species can be distinguished from the other species treated here by its rounded stems. Southeastern Europe. Cultivated 1739. Zone (4) 5. Variety *hirsutissimus* is a sturdier, more erect form with more pubescent parts.

Cytisus × praecox, (sī-ti′sus × prē′koks), Warminster Broom, is a hybrid complex resulting from crosses between *C. purgans* (yellow) and *C. multiflorus* (white). The typical and original clone should be known as *C. ö pracox* 'Warminster'. It is a large shrub (10′) like *C. multiflorus,* but with denser and heavier masses of young branches. Leaves mostly simple about 1/2″ long, silky-pubescent like the long shoots. The sulfur-yellow flowers are produced in abundance during May but are of a rather unpleasant odor. It first appeared among seedlings of *C. purgans* in the nursery of Messrs. Wheeler of Warminster about 1867. It sets fertile seed but the resultant plants revert more or less to one or the other parents. Selections have been made and include 'Albus'—white; 'Allgold'—deep yellow flowers; and 'Gold Spear' (also known as 'Canary Bird') with profuse, bright yellow flowers; 'Hollandia'—flowers salmon-pink to rosy pink on a robust 4′ shrub, flowers profusely borne, common in U.S.

ADDITIONAL NOTES: The brooms literally light up a landscape. They are effective in mass and, like forsythia, can be blinding when used in this manner. *Ulex europaeus,* Gorse, is a close relative but with extremely spiny branches; the gold-yellow flowers are equally attractive and I have seen it in abundance along English highways where it flowers at the same time as the broom. Gorse more or less flowers all season long in England and is found on sandy infertile soils and disturbed sites. Appears to be somewhat of a colonizer. Raulston has grown the golden-foliaged form in Raleigh. The species could be likened to a green porcupine. Zone (7) 8. Flint, *Horticulture* 65(6):46–52 (1987) presented an excellent overview of *Cytisus* and *Genista.*

Danae racemosa — Alexandrian-laurel
(da′nȧ-ē̄ rā-se-mō′sȧ)

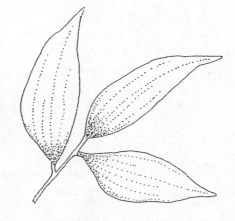

FAMILY: Liliaceae
LEAVES: In this case, the "leaves" are modified stems (phyl-loclades) but serve the same function; alternate, oblong-lanceolate, 1 1/2 to 4″ long, 1/4 to 1 1/2″ wide, rich green on both surfaces, taper pointed, abruptly narrowed at base and scarcely stalked.

Danae racemosa, Alexandrian-laurel, is an elegant, refined evergreen shrub that grows 2 to 4′ high and wide. The habit is gracefully arching. The lustrous rich green leaves are handsome throughout the year. The greenish yellow flowers are rather inconspicuous but the fleshy orange-red, 1/4 to 3/8″ diameter berry is quite attractive. Prefers a moist, well-drained soil in shade. "Foliage" discolors in sun and open exposed situations. The "foliage" is excellent for use inside as the cut branches remain fresh a long time. Not common in the south but certainly worthy of cultivation. Has no serious insect or disease problems but have noticed some leaf spot on plants at Callaway Garden. Division of the parent plant will work. Native to northern Iran and Asia Minor. Introduced 1713. Zone 8 to 9.

Daphne cneorum — Rose Daphne
(daf'nē nē-ō'rum)

FAMILY: Thymelaeaceae

LEAVES: Alternate, simple, evergreen, 3/4 to 1″ long, 1/8 to 1/5″ wide, crowded, oblanceolate, usually obtuse and mucronulate, cuneate, lustrous dark green above, glaucescent and glaucous beneath.

BUDS: Sessile, usually solitary but sometimes superimposed or collaterally branched, ovoid, with 4 to 6 exposed scales.

STEM: Moderate, rounded or somewhat 4-sided; pith small, roundish, continuous; leaf-scars crescent-shaped, small, exceptionally elevated; 1 bundle-trace.

SIZE: 6 to 12″ in height by 2′ or more in spread.

HARDINESS: Zone 4 to 7.

HABIT: A low spreading evergreen shrub with long, trailing and ascending branches forming low, loose masses.

RATE: Slow.

TEXTURE: Medium-fine in all seasons although may look ragged in winter.

LEAF COLOR: Dark green throughout the year.

FLOWERS: Bright rosy-pink, 1/2″ across, delightfully fragrant; April and May and often flowering again in late summer; borne in 6 to 8-flowered umbels; often reminds one of the flower of Candytuft; literally smother the foliage and produce an ocean of rose-pink; sepals are showy part of flower.

FRUIT: Yellowish brown drupe.

CULTURE: Transplant as a container plant; does not move readily; should be done in early spring or early fall; there is considerble incongruity in soil recommendations but the following composite was gleaned from several sources; prefer well-drained, moist, near neutal (pH 6 to 7) soil; light shade, possibly full sun in coastal areas; snow-cover is beneficial; protect with pine boughs where winter sun and wind present a problem; mulch to maintain moist root zone; prune annually after the plants have become established, preferably after flowering and before mid-July; the plant resents disturbance and once located should be left there permanently; have grown many daphnes, some as many as three times, they die for no explicable reason; to date have lost *Daphne odora* and several cultivars, *Daphne* × *burkwoodii* and 'Carol Mackie', *Daphne caucasica;* interestingly when they decide to go it is usually with haste...one day green...the next day crinkled, dry looking leaves; still in the first order of landscape plants and as I write this my *D. odora* 'Aureomarginata' and 'Alba' are at the end of the flowering sequence but their sweet fragrance is still hovering about; one or two branches in a vase will perfume a room.

DISEASES AND INSECTS: Leaf spots result in brown spots on both sides of the leaves, crown rot occurs more commonly on plants in shady areas; twig blight, canker, viruses, aphids, mealy-bud and scales present problems; virus may be the culprit when plants die for no logical reason; have seen virus-induced distortion of leaves of *D. odora.*

LANDSCAPE VALUE: Good small evergreen ground cover; works well in a rock garden or slightly shady spots; very fastidious as to culture and perhaps *Iberis sempervirens* is a decent substitute especially for midwestern states; over the past 5 years I have come across many Daphnes and can honestly say have not met one I do not like; this particular species is a real gem and my first significant exposure came when I visited the garden of Mr. Larry Newcomb, Sharon, MA., author of *Newcomb's Wildflower Guide;* Larry was showing me through his extensive wildflower garden and at the end of the tour as we were about to enter his house, by the stoop, was a tremendous bed of *D. cneorum* in full flower; he said that it received no special care and yet thrived; have seen time and again in rock gardens throughout Europe, absolutely stunning in flower; can never seem to get enough of this wonderful plant.

CULTIVARS:

'Alba'—White flowers and rather dwarfish habit.

'Eximia'—Larger leaves and flowers, the buds crimson opening rose-pink; have seen many times at Edinburgh Botanic Garden.

'Pygmaea' (var. *pygmaea*)—A rose-pink, free flowering form with prostrate branches.

'Ruby Glow'—Dark pink flowers on a 6 to 12″ high framework of dark green foliage; Lake County Nursery Introduction, Perry, OH.

'Variegata'—A very beautiful, dainty, cream-edged leaf form of vigorous constitution; flowers like the species, I first saw this cultivar in Wisley Gardens, England and wanted to collect cuttings; a plant of delicate, quiet beauty; a model for other variegated plants to emulate.

var. *verlotii*—Leaves up to an inch long and about 1/8″ wide, rose-pink flowers, the perianth tube 5/8″ long, resulting in larger flowers than the species; quite handsome.

PROPAGATION: Seed of most species requires a cold treatment of 2 to 3 months. Cuttings (December) of *D. cneorum* failed to root without treatment but rooted 56% after treatment with 100 ppm IAA/16 hour soak; July cuttings rooted 74% without treatment, and 93% with 1000 ppm IBA-talc; I have rooted *Daphne odora* with 100% efficiency in two separate tests; July cuttings from the Georgia campus and November cuttings from Longwood Gardens were treated with 3000 ppm IBA-quick dip, peat:perlite, mist, root systems were profuse; rooting takes about 8 weeks; cuttings of *D.* × *burkwoodii* and *D. cneorum* that I collected on August 24, treated with 8000 ppm IBA-quick dip failed to root.

At one time I thought *Daphne odora* propagation was as easy as cutting warm butter but have had up and down success since the last edition of the book; timing appears important and possibly best to take cuttings after growth flush hardens in June and July; I have watched cuttings "sit" in the rooting bench for months and never do anything; excess moisture is not conducive to good rooting and a covered frame using polyethylene and shade cloth might be beneficial; make sure the stock is clean, i.e., virus free before collecting cuttings; virus infection may be the largest hindrance to good rooting.

Lamb and Nutty, *The Plantsman* 8(2):109–111 (1986) present interesting observations on propagation of daphnes. A summary follows. In Ireland (Kinsealy), June, July, August cuttings gave the most consistent results. Depending on species, percentages ranged from 28 to 96% with 50 to 70% being average. Treatment consisted of 8000 ppm IBA-talc, Captan, 2 peat moss:1 sand medium, mist; rooting time ranged from 7 to 11 weeks. Seeds should be collected before they change color, cleaned and sown; some, but not complete, germination will occur the first year; plants can also be grafted or layered.

NATIVE HABITAT: Europe, from Spain to Southwest Russia. Introduced 1752.

RELATED SPECIES:

Daphne × **burkwoodii**, (daf′nē × berk-wood′e-ī), Burkwood Daphne, is a cross between *D. cneorum* × *D. caucasica*. The flowers are creamy white to pinkish tinged, fragrant, and borne in dense, terminal, 2″ diameter umbels in May. Individual flowers are about 1/2″ wide while the red drupes are about 1/3″ wide. This species is performing quite well at the Morton Arboretum in Lisle, Illinois. The species will grow 3 to 4′ high. Zone 4 to 8. There are two clones, one termed 'Arthur Burkwood' the other 'Somerset' which have received considerable attention. Apparently, when the original cross was made only three seeds resulted but all germinated. Of the three plants, one died and the other two are the clones listed. Both forms make vigorous bushes to at least 3′, but of the two, 'Somerset' is larger and can grow to 4′ high and more in diameter. The foliage is semi-evergreen on both and, in this respect, intermediate between the parents. Wyman noted that a 20-year-old specimen was 4′ high and 6′ wide, very rounded and dense. This group is supposedly easily propagated by cuttings taken in summer and treated with IBA. Plants of *D.* × *burkwoodii* that I have seen maintain their foliage into late November–early December but finally lose all their leaves. They make superb garden plants and the dense, broad mounded form is particularly well suited to the small garden. A most beautiful and unusual clone is 'Carol Mackie' with delicate cream-edged leaf margins and fragrant light pink flowers; it grows to about 3′ high and slightly wider; I have observed this clone in the University of Maine's display garden; it has withstood temperatures as low as −30°F without injury; in my mind this is a most lovely variegated cultivar. There are several forms with variegated foliage. All are fine garden plants. See *Amer. Nurseryman* 170(11):7–9 (1989) for a discussion of the variegated clones.

For gardeners this is the preferred species because of quality attributes, slightly tougher garden constitution and commercial availability.

Daphne caucasica—Caucasian Daphne

LEAVES: Alternate, simple, oblanceolate, 1 to 1 3/4″ long, 1/3 to 1/2″ wide, obtuse, rarely acuminate, pale green above, glaucous beneath, glabrous.

Daphne caucasica, (daf′nē kâ-kas′i-ka), Caucasian Daphne, is a deciduous 4 to 5′ high and wide shrub that produces fragrant white flowers in groups of 4 to 20 in May and June and sporadically thereafter. The Scott Arboretum, Swarthmore College, is particularly high on this species and introduced me to the plant for the first time. The delightful fragrance and the long season of flower are desirable traits. A plant found its way to Georgia, was happily growing in a 3-gallon container, awaiting a new home in my garden. Unfortunately, the plant curled up the root apices, performed a Daphne Death, and withered away into oblivion. Early reports from the Philadelphia area noted the ease of culture. I have read some literature that states it is tempermental. One of the parents of *D.* × *burkwoodii.* Zone 6 to 8. Caucasus. Cultivated 1893.

Daphne genkwa—Lilac Daphne

LEAVES: Mostly opposite, occasionally alternate, 1 to 2″ long, 1/2 to 5/8″ wide, acute, pubescent on veins beneath.

Daphne genkwa, (daf′nē genk′wȧ), Lilac Daphne, grows 3 to 4′ high, is deciduous and composed of erect, slender, sparsely branched stems. Flowers are lilac-colored, produced during May at the nodes of naked wood of the previous year in stalked clusters. Native to China. Introduced 1843. Zone 5. Easily propagated by cuttings taken when the new growth is very soft. Very beautiful in flower but rather temperamental in the garden. It is unique among *Daphne* species because of the opposite leaves. Barnes Foundation, Merion, PA, has a specimen that I was fortunate to see in flower...beautiful but lacking fragrance.

Daphne giraldii—Giraldi Daphne

LEAVES: Alternate, simple, crowded at end of branches in a whorled fashion, oblanceolate, 1 1/2 to 3″ long, 1/4 to 5/8″ wide, blunt or pointed and mucronate, cuneate, glaucescent below, glabrous.

Daphne giraldii, (daf′nē ji-ral′dē-ī), Giraldi Daphne, is a deciduous 2 to 3′ high shrub of bushy habit. The flowers are fragrant, golden yellow, produced during May in umbels terminating the young shoots, 4 to 8 per inflorescence. The fruit is an egg-shaped, 1/4″ diameter, red drupe which matures in July–August. It is quite hardy (Zone 3) but difficult to culture successfully. Native of northwestern China. Introduced 1910.

Daphne mezereum—February Daphne

LEAVES: Alternate, simple, oblanceolate, 1 1/2 to 3 1/2″ long, 1/4 to 3/4″ wide, obtuse to acute, cuneate, dull blue-green above and gray-green below, glabrous.

Daphne mezereum, (daf′nē me-zē′rē-um), February Daphne, is a semi-evergreen to deciduous, erect branched shrub growing 3 to 5′ high and as wide, usually becoming leggy at the base. The flowers are lilac to rosy-purple, very fragrant, produced from the buds of the leafless stems in late March to early April, grouped in 2's and 3's, each flower 1/2″ across. The fruit is a red, 1/3″ diameter drupe which matures in June. Species must be self-fertile since I have observed heavy fruit set on an isolated plant at the Biltmore Gardens. Several authorities have noted that the shrub will do well for years and then suddenly die. No one has a good explanation for the whims of *Daphne,* however, there is a lethal virus which affects *D. mezereum* and this could explain its sudden failings. The variety *alba* has dull white flowers and yellowish fruits; comes true to type from seed and is found in the wild. Selections called 'Paul's White' and 'Bowles White' have pure white flowers. 'Autumnalis' flowers in the fall and the flowers are larger than the species and equally fragrant and colored. It does not usually bear fruit. *D. mezereum* and the clones can be propagated, although not very easily, by cuttings taken and planted in a mixture of peat moss, loam and sand. Native of Europe and Siberia; found wild, although limitedly so in England; occasionally naturalized in northeastern states. Introduced in colonial times. This is a most enchanting *Daphne* because of the deliciously fragrant flowers. It flowers before most shrubs and, cut branches, when brought into a house provide a delightful spring perfume. Leaves may start to emerge from end of stem while flowers remain on previous season's growth. Have seen considerable scale injury on this species.

Daphne odora—Fragrant or Winter Daphne
(daf'nē ō-dō'rȧ)

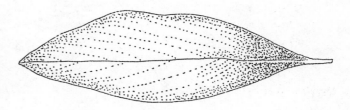

LEAVES: Alternate, simple, evergreen, elliptic-oblong, 1 1/2 to 3 1/2" long, 1/2 to 1" wide, dark green, glabrous, entire, pointed and tapered equally at both ends.

Daphne odora, Winter Daphne, is a densely branched, mounded evergreen shrub that reaches 4 feet in height and width. In the south I have never seen plants larger than 3 feet. The fragrant, rosy-purple flowers are borne in one-inch diameter terminal heads during February-March. The flowers last a long time and I have seen them showing color in January and persisting into March. The fragrance is wonderful. This species performs well in shade and does not appear as fastidious about soil types as some *Daphne* species. The plant is usually offered in containers and presents no transplanting problems. What a wonderful plant! Temperamental, trying, but worth all the attention. I have charted flower times since the last edition to indicate how flowering responses vary from year to year, I offer the following: full flower—February 28, 1983, March 9, 1984, March 1, 1986, February 14, 1989. Choice plant where people can sense its presence...i.e., by a walk, entrance. I know a great gardener, Mrs. Robert T. Segrest, in Athens, who puts it in a container by the entrance to her home so she can enjoy the fragrance. Native to China. Zone 7 to 9.

'Alba'—White flowers (actually off-white)

'Aureo-marginata'—A handsome clone that is hardier than the species, the leaves are faintly margined with yellow and the flowers are reddish purple on the outside and lighter (nearly white) within; survived –3°F with some leaf injury while the leaves of the species and 'Alba' were killed completely; also a form with similar leaf variegation and white flowers is known.

'Mazelii'—Flowers are borne in terminal clusters and also out of the axils of the leaves subtending the cluster, the flowers are pinkish outside, whitish within.

'Variegata'—The yellow-margins are more pronounced than those of 'Aureo-marginata' and the flowers pale-pink.

ADDITIONAL NOTES: A choice group of plants for the garden but unfortunately fastidious as to cultural requirements. One can travel to private and public gardens without ever seeing a wealth of *Daphne.* English authorities speculated that most *Daphne* species do best in limestone soils; however, in the Arnold Arboretum several species are growing in a soil of pH 5 to 5.5 and in the Athens, GA area many plants of *D. odora* are growing well in soils of pH 4.5 to 5. Anyone interested in *Daphne* should read Brickell and Mathew. *Daphne: The genus in the wild and cultivation.* The Alpine Garden Society, 1976. Numerous other species beyond the scope of the *Manual* and the following are worth considering: *D. laureola, D. collina, D. pontica, D. retusa,* and *D. tangutica* have crossed my path in European gardens but their relative garden worthiness in the United States is unknown. Excellent down-to-earth *Daphne* article appeared in *Horticulture* 66(4):16–22. 1988.

Davidia involucrata — Dove-tree, sometimes called Handkerchief Tree
(dā-vid′-i-a   in-vol-ū-krā′tà)

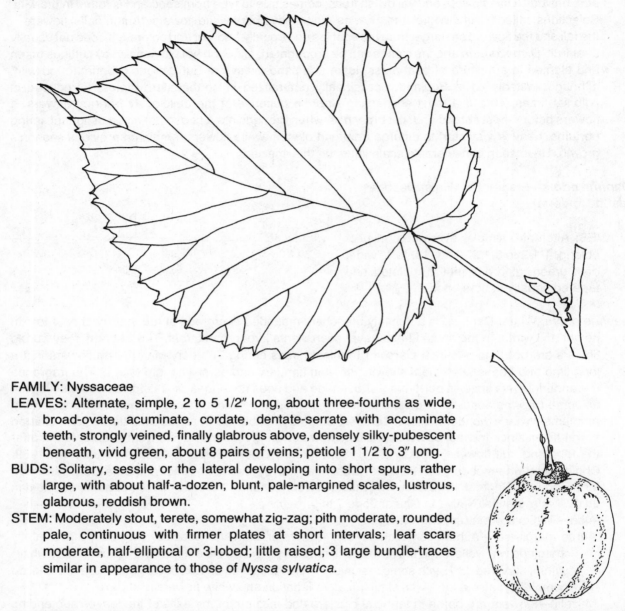

FAMILY: Nyssaceae

LEAVES: Alternate, simple, 2 to 5 1/2″ long, about three-fourths as wide, broad-ovate, acuminate, cordate, dentate-serrate with accuminate teeth, strongly veined, finally glabrous above, densely silky-pubescent beneath, vivid green, about 8 pairs of veins; petiole 1 1/2 to 3″ long.

BUDS: Solitary, sessile or the lateral developing into short spurs, rather large, with about half-a-dozen, blunt, pale-margined scales, lustrous, glabrous, reddish brown.

STEM: Moderately stout, terete, somewhat zig-zag; pith moderate, rounded, pale, continuous with firmer plates at short intervals; leaf scars moderate, half-elliptical or 3-lobed; little raised; 3 large bundle-traces similar in appearance to those of *Nyssa sylvatica*.

SIZE: Under cultivation 20 to 40′ high and as wide; supposedly in the wild can roam from 40 to 65′ in height.

HARDINESS: Zone 6 to 8, probably not fully hardy as a young tree, once established performs well.

HABIT: Broad pyramidal tree, resembling a linden, especially in youth; loosening with age but still distinctly pyramidal in outline.

TEXTURE: Medium in leaf; would also be medium in winter.

BARK: Orange, brown, scaly, handsome, adds winter interest to the plant.

LEAF COLOR: Bright green in summer, leaves supposedly strong scented when unfolding, I have not noticed an objectionable odor; fall color of no consequence and dies off green or brown; leaves hold late and are often killed by a hard freeze with the majority of the leaves falling at the same time.

FLOWERS: Andro-monoecious, crowded in a 3/4″ diameter rounded head at the end of a 3″ long pendulous peduncle; staminate flowers composed of numerous long stamens with white filaments and red anthers, forming a brush-like mass; pistillate reduced to an egg-shaped ovary, with a short 6-rayed style and a ring of abortive stamens at the top; the real beauty of the *Davidia* lies in two large bracts which subtend each flower, they are white or creamy white, of unequal size, the lower being the larger (7″ long by 4″ wide); the upper bract being 3 to 4″ long and 2″ wide; they are effective for 10 to 14 days in May; often the tree does not flower until about 10-years-of-age and even then some trees do not flower every year; tends to show alternate year patterns like many crabapples.

FRUIT: Solitary, ovoid, 1 1/2″ long drupe, green with a purplish bloom; becoming russet-colored and speckled with red when ripe; contains a single, hard, ridged nut (endocarp) with 3 to 5 seeds; matures in fall.

CULTURE: Transplant balled and burlapped; prefers a well-drained, moist soil that has been amended with peat moss and the like; prefers light shade but will tolerate sun if the soil is kept moist; water during drought periods; prune in winter.

DISEASES AND INSECTS: None serious.

LANDSCAPE VALUE: Acclaimed by many gardening enthusiasts as the most handsome of flowering trees; that is quite an accolade when one thinks of all the beautiful flowering trees we have at our disposal; the obvious use is that of a specimen; any tree so grand should not be hidden in the shrubbery; Wyman noted that, for all its good features, it has the bad habits of being slow to flower, does not consistently flower every year and, even though stem and vegetative bud hardy, may not set flower buds in colder climates; during sabbatical at the Arnold Arboretum I was fortunate enough to witness the tree in full flowering spectacle; when observed in flower there is an insatiable urge to secure a plant for one's garden; it should be mentioned that the tree will grow in the south; there are beautiful trees at Hills and Dales, LaGrange, GA and there was once a lovely specimen on the Georgia campus; the finest specimens I have seen are at the Arnold Arboretum, Swarthmore College and Hills and Dales.

CULTIVARS: Variety *vilmoriniana* differs from the species in that the underside of the leaves are yellowish green or somewhat glaucous, slightly downy on the veins at first but otherwise glabrous; the variety is more common in cultivation than the species and is hardy in Zone 5.

PROPAGATION: According to Bean it is easily propagated by cuttings or by seed; one research report stated that hardwood cuttings taken in mid-January rooted 20 percent without treatment and there was no response to IBA; leaf-bud cuttings taken in September treated with 3000 ppm IBA-talc, placed in sand, shaded, and frequently syringed, rooted 85 percent in five weeks; I was able to root several cuttings from an old tree at the Arnold but was unable to keep the cuttings alive. A relatively recent cutting propagation account appeared in *The Plantsman*. Seeds are doubly-dormant and require a warm-cold treatment; they should be placed in moist medium and kept at 68 to 86°F until the radicle emerges, than transferred to cold for 3 months; after this they can be planted; nursery practice involves fall planting with germination taking place two springs later; often multiple seedlings result from a single fruit since each fruit may contain 3 to 5 seeds.

NATIVE HABITAT: Native to China in West Szechuan and parts of West Hupeh. Introduced 1904.

Deutzia gracilis — Slender Deutzia
(dūt′si-a gras′i-lis)

FAMILY: Saxifragaceae

LEAVES: Opposite, simple, oblong-lanceolate, 1 to 3″ long, 3/8 to 5/8″ wide, long acuminate, broad-cuneate or rounded at the base, unequally serrate, with scattered stellate hairs above, flat deep green, nearly glabrous beneath.

BUDS: Ovoid, nearly sessile, with several pairs of outer scales, glabrate, brownish; this bud description is applicable to the following species.

STEM: Yellowish-gray-brown, glabrous; leaf scars—linear; pith—white, hollow after a time.

SIZE: 2 to 4′ high by 3 to 4′ in width; can grow to 6′ high.

HARDINESS: Zone 4 to 8.

HABIT: A low, broad mound, graceful and free flowering, with slender ascending branches.

RATE: Slow to medium.

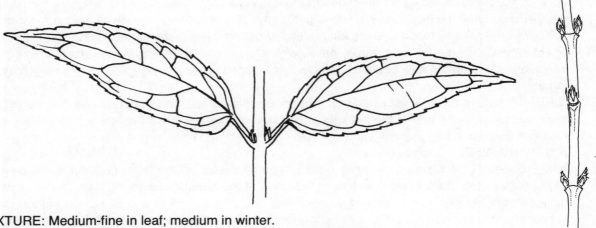

TEXTURE: Medium-fine in leaf; medium in winter.

LEAF COLOR: Flat deep green in summer, does not color effectively in fall.

FLOWERS: Perfect, pure white, 1/2 to 3/4″ across; mid to late May (Mid to late April, Athens); borne in erect racemes or panicles, 1 1/2 to 3″ long; the plants are literally covered with flowers and are quite attractive at this time of year; effective for 10 to 14 days.

FRUIT: Dehiscent brown capsule, not effective.

CULTURE: Transplant readily, best moved in spring; any good garden soil is acceptable; pH adaptable; full sun or very light shade; prune after flowering.

DISEASES AND INSECTS: Leafspots, aphids, and leaf miner; basically problem free plants.

LANDSCAPE VALUE: This is probably the best of the deutzias and makes a good hedge, mass, facer or shrub border plant; deutzias have lost favor over the years and, in my opinion, rightfully so; they offer only good flowers and the rest of the year are often bedraggled; I noticed that there was not one plant in the Arnold Arboretum's extensive collection that did not need considerable pruning after the winter of 1978–79 when the low temperature was –6°F; plants on the Illinois campus were less than well dressed and usually possessed an allotment of dead branches; possibly the best way to handle the plant when it looks bedraggled is a rather complete pruning to within 6″ of the ground; this will induce new shoot growth; some of the pink or rose-red flowered forms are beautiful but these are less hardy than *D. gracilis* or *D.* × *lemoinei.*

CULTIVARS: *D. gracilis* was used as a parent of several hybrid deutzias including *D.* × *rosea (D. g.* × *D. purpurascens)* with pink petals on the outside and paler within; the cultivar 'Carminea' is a selection from the *D.* × *rosea* group with pale rosy pink petals within, darker pink outside and in bud, about 3/4″ across, in large panicles; it is a rather spreading plant, with arching branches, to about 3′ high; W.J. Bean calls it one of the most delightful of dwarf deciduous shrubs.

'Nikko'—A compact, perhaps 2′ high by 5′ wide small leaved, graceful, almost groundcover shrub that offers good white flowers, rich green foliage and deep burgundy fall color. This plant has been kicked around in a taxonomic sense and may be listed as *Deutzia gracilis* var. *nakaiana,* 'Nana', or perhaps as a species; I have seen small plants and believe it has a place in a sunny rock or hillside garden; possibly a zone less hardy than *D. gracilis.*

PROPAGATION: All deutzias can be easily rooted from softwood cuttings collected any time in the growing season; ideally collect slightly firm softwoods, use 1000 ppm KIBA dip, peat:perlite, mist and root systems should be profuse in 3 to 4 weeks; seeds can be sown when collected.

ADDITIONAL NOTES: Deutzias, although usually dependable for flower display, rarely overwhelm one at any time of the year. In northern areas they require annual pruning to remove the dead wood and to keep them looking acceptable. The summer foliage is a blasé green while fall color and fruits are not interesting. The crux of the matter is that if one has limited garden space he/she should look elsewhere for ornament; but in large landscapes, especially shrub borders, the excellent flower display provided by the deutzias is warranted.

About 50 species are known worldwide and many hybrids have been produced over the years. The United States nurseries offer a small number of species compared to European establishments. In

English gardens, deutzias are often woven into the fabric of the shrub border and after flowering blend in with the green woodwork. In the United States they are upstaged by viburnums that offer multi-season attributes.

A few miscellaneous types that are encountered every so often in the United States include *Deutzia × kalmiifolia (D. parviflora × D. purpurascens)* growing 4 to 5′ high with light green foliage that may turn plum-purple in fall, and good pink flowers, 5 to 12 in an umbellate panicle. Also, occasionally 'Mont Rose' with fuschia purple flowers, crimped at the margin and 2 to 3 1/2″ long sharply toothed leaves; 'Contraste' has larger flowers similar to 'Mont Rose' but with a darker stripe on the back of the petals, habit is gracefully arching; 'Magician' is similar to 'Contraste' but the petals are edged with white; 'Perle Rose' has pale pink, freely borne flowers, slightly smaller than the others described here; and 'Pink Pompon' with deep carmine buds opening to strong pink outside and borne in dense, hemispherical corymbs. All of the above cultivars originated from unknown but suspected parentage of *D. longifolia, D. discolor, D. purpurascens* and/or *D. × elegantissima*.
NATIVE HABITAT: Japan. Introduced 1880.

Deutzia × elegantissima — Elegant Deutzia
(dūt′si-a × el-e-gan-tis′i-mȧ)

Elegant Deutzia is another Lemoine creation probably combining *D. purpurascens* and *D. sieboldiana*. The typical form grows 4 to 6′ high with an upright branching habit. The oval-oblong leaves are 2 to 3″ long, short acuminate, irregularly serrate, rugose and dull green with stellate pubescence beneath. The individual pinkish (outside) white flowers average 3/4″ diameter and are carried in many flowered loose, erect cymes in June. 'Rosealind' has been popularized in the United States and, indeed, is a beautiful 4 to 5′ high form with deep carmine-pink flowers.

Deutzia × lemoinei — Lemoine Deutzia
(dūt′si-a le-moi′nē-ī)

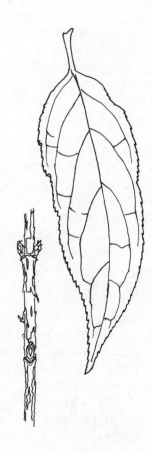

LEAVES: Opposite, simple, elliptic-lanceolate to lanceolate, 1 1/2 to 2 1/2″ long, on shoots to 4″ long, 1/2 to 1 1/4″ wide, long acuminate, cuneate at base, sharply serrulate, green on both surfaces, with scattered 5 to 8 rayed hairs beneath.
STEM: Glabrous or nearly so, older with brown exfoliating bark; pith—white.

Deutzia × lemoinei, Lemoine Deutzia, grows 5 to 7′ tall with a similar spread. It is a very twiggy, dense, round, erect branched shrub. The flowers are pure white, 5/8″ across, after *D. gracilis* usually about late May; borne in 1 to 3″ long erect pyramidal corymbs. Some authorities say this species is more beautiful and effective than *D. gracilis*. It is considered one of the hardiest and is being successfully grown in Madison, WI and Chaska, MN (−30°F). Was never as impressed with the hybrid species compared to *D. gracilis*. The parentage is *D. gracilis* by *D. parviflora* and was raised by Lemoine of Nancy in 1891. Several cultivars of importance include 'Avalanche' and 'Compacta'. 'Avalanche'—Bears white flowers in small clusters on arching branches, very dense and compact, about 4′ high; should be possibly placed under *D. × maliflora*. 'Compacta'—Dwarf and compact in habit, pure white, large flowers in dense clusters, could be the same as 'Boule de Neige'.

Deutzia × *magnifica* — Showy Deutzia
(dūt′si-a × mag-nif′i-ka)

Showy Deutzia, is the result of a cross between *D. scabra* × *D. vilmoriniae;* raised by Lemoine of Nancy and put into commerce from 1909. This hybrid species is often listed as growing 6′ high but I have seen 8 to 10′ specimens. The plant is strongly multistemmed, usually leggy at the base, and clothed with foliage over the upper one-half. The flowers are the best I have seen among the deutzias. They are white, double, borne in dense 1 1/2 to 3″ long panicles in late May or early June (early to mid May, Athens) and are extremely eye-catching. Originated before 1910. Zone 5. Several clones include:

'Eburnea'—Single white flowers in loose panicles, each flower bell-shaped.

'Erecta'—Single white flowers in large erect panicles.

'Latiflora'—Single white flowers 1″ or more across with wide spreading petals borne profusely in erect panicles.

'Longipetala'—Single white flowers with long, narrow petals.

'Staphyleoides'—Single white flowers with reflexed petals.

Deutzia scabra — Fuzzy Deutzia
(dūt′si-a skā′bra)

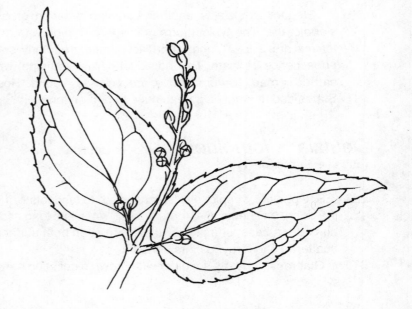

LEAVES: Opposite, simple, ovate to oblong-lanceolate, 1 to 4″ long, up to 2″ wide, acute or obtusely acuminate, usually rounded at the base, crenate-denticulate, dull green, stellate-pubescent on both sides with 10 to 15-rayed hairs; sandpaper texture.

STEM: Brown, rarely gray-brown, tardily exfoliating bark; stellate pubescent when young; pith—brown, excavated, finally hollow.

Deutzia scabra, Fuzzy Deutzia, grows 6 to 10′ tall with a spread of 4 to 8′. It is an oval or obovate, round topped shrub, taller than broad, with spreading, somewhat arching branches with brown peeling bark; often straggly in appearance. Flowers pure white or tinged pink outside, 1/2 to 3/4″ long and wide, borne in upright, 3 to 6″ long cylindrical panicles; flowers 10 to 14 days after *D. gracilis,* usually in early June in the midwest and vicinity of Boston. Cultivars include:

'Candidissima'—Double, pure white.

'Flore-pleno'—Double, white, tinged with rosy-purple on outside of corolla.

'Godsall Pink'—Double, clear pink flowers.

'Pride of Rochester'—Similar to the above but the rosy tinge is paler; put into commerce by Ellwanger and Barry; often seen in older midwest and New England landscapes.

'Punctata'—Single, pure white flowers, with leaves strikingly marbled with white and 2 or 3 shades of green; will revert to the typical green state.

'Watereri'—Flowers 1″ across, single, petals rosy outside.

I remember a specimen on the Illinois campus that resided next to the old faculty club which, alas, is now a parking lot. This was the coarsest of the three species I taught (*D. gracilis, D.* × *lemoinei*) but generally the most reliable for consistent year-to-year flower. Unfortunately, it is a coarse shrub and now outmoded by some of the newer green meatballs. Japan, China. Introduced 1822. Zone 5 to 7(8).

Diervilla sessilifolia — Southern Bush-honeysuckle
(dī-ẽr-vil′a̍ ses-sil-i-fō′li-a̍)

FAMILY: Caprifoliaceae

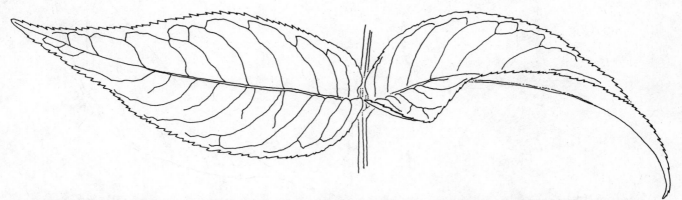

LEAVES: Opposite, ovate-lanceolate, 2 to 6″ long, half as wide, acuminate, cordate or rounded at base, sharply serrate, subsessile, glabrous except on the midrib above; new foliage with a bronze-purple cast changing to dark green.
BUDS: Often superposed, sessile, oblong, appressd, with about 5 pairs of exposed scales.
STEM: Rounded, brownish, with 4 crisp-puberulent ridges decurrent from the nodes; pith—moderate, pale, continuous.

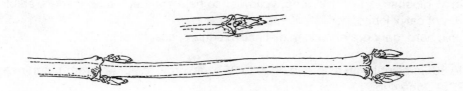

Diervilla sessilifolia, Southern Bush-honeysuckle, is a low growing, suckering, 3 to 5′ high and 3 to 5′ wide or greater spreading, deciduous shrub; the foliage is glossy dark green and seldom colors in fall although European literature indicates good red-purple fall coloration; the flowers are sulfur yellow, 1/2″ long, June-July into August; borne in 2 to 3″ diameter, 3 to 7-flowered cymes on current season's growth; very adaptable and should be pruned back in early spring; makes a good filler, possibly facer plant; roots readily from cuttings; a tremendously tough plant; this plant prospered in the evaluation tests at Illinois where it was exposed to −20°F and incessant winds; would be a good choice for rough cuts and fills, banks, perhaps even planters or containers in outside areas; foliage is not troubled by insects or diseases; have seen this species in north Georgia and the Smokey Mountains where it forms a solid thicket on the side of mountains and stream banks; will withstand shade but is best in full sun; a closely related species, *D. lonicera,* Dwarf Bush-honeysuckle, is found from Newfoundland to Sasketchawan, south to Michigan and North Carolina but has not proven as vigorous as *D. sessilifolia* in Minnesota Landscape Arboretum tests; it differs in having short (1/8″ long) petioled leaves; *D. rivularis,* Georgia Bush-honeysuckle, occurs over a range similar to *D. sessilifolia* but the leaves are pubescent on both sides. *D.* × *splendens,* a hybrid between *D. sessifolia* and *D. lonicera* is known and listed in European literature and garden catalogs. Supposedly, it develops good purple-red autumn color.

Diospyros virginiana — Common Persimmon
(dī-os′pir-os vĕr-jin-i-ā′nȧ)

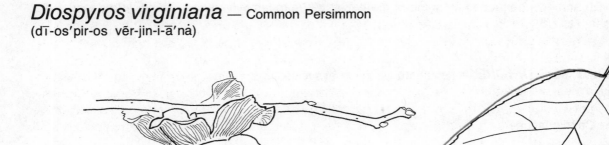

FAMILY: Ebenaceae

LEAVES: Alternate, simple, 2 1/4 to 5 1/2″ long, 3/4 to 2″ wide, ovate to elliptic, rounded at base, lustrous dark green above, paler beneath, glabrous at maturity or with minimal pubescence on the midrib; petiole 1/3 to 1″ long, pubescent.

BUDS: Solitary, sessile, with 2 greatly overlapping scales, 1/4″ long, ovoid, acute, reddish black, glabrous, terminal bud lacking.

STEM: Slender, gray-red-brown, pubescent or glabrous.

FRUIT: Berry, globose, 1 to 1 1/2″ long, yellowish to pale orange, 1 to 8 seeded, edible, subtended by 4 persistent calyx lobes, persistent into winter.

BARK: Thick, hard, dark gray-black, in distinctive square, scaly blocks.

SIZE: 35 to 60′ in height with a spread of 20 to 35′; can grow to 90′ or larger but this rarely occurs.

HARDINESS: Zone 4 to 9.

HABIT: Tree with slender oval-rounded crown, often very symmetrical in outline.

RATE: Slow to medium; one authority reported 15′ over a 20 year period in England.

TEXTURE: Medium in leaf and winter.

BARK: On old trunks the bark is thick, dark gray or brownish to almost black and is prominently broken into scaly, squarish blocks; handsome and easily recognizable.

LEAF COLOR: Dark green and often lustrous above, paler beneath in summer changing to yellow-green, yellow, or reddish purple in fall; yellow-green is the usual fall color in central Illinois although the late Professor J.C. McDaniel, Department of Horticulture, University of Illinois, selected a clone that consistently colored a beautiful reddish purple; in the south the trees turn a consistent yellow to reddish purple every fall; the fall color is more pronounced and consistent than what I observed on trees in the north.

FLOWERS: Dioecious, although sometimes both sexes present on same tree; white or whitish to greenish white, shaped like a blueberry, flowers constricted at their mouth, often tinged green on the end of the 4 corolla lobes, staminate usually in threes about 1/3″ long, with 16 stamens; pistillate short-stalked, solitary, 3/5″ long, borne in May-June; the peduncles of the male flower persistent and woody, delightfully fragrant.

FRUIT: An edible berry, yellowish to pale orange, 1 to 1 1/2″ across, subtended by 4 persistent calyx lobes; ripens after frost in late September through October, although cultivars are available which produce edible fruit without frost treatment.

CULTURE: Somewhat difficult to transplant and should be moved balled and burlapped as a small tree in early spring; prefers moist, well-drained, sandy soils but will do well on low fertility, dry soils; in southern Illinois the tree grows on coal stripped lands and often forms thickets on dry, eroding slopes; pH adaptable; full sun; prune in winter; does well in cities.

   I have pedaled my bike many miles along local backroads and everywhere in evidence is persimmon. Apparently animals of all makes move the fruits around and act as "Johnny Persimmon Seeds". The plant is found in pastures, fence rows, roadside ditches and a hundred other less than hospitable sites. It also suckers rudely and can form thickets or naturalized type stands. Worthwhile leaving if in a naturalized situation.

DISEASES AND INSECTS: In years past, I would have said totally free but have noticed, maybe I was not looking previously, a distinct blackish leaf spot that affects the leaves and presents a measley appearance. Plants can look pretty sick in the summer and fall months. Lots of variability in susceptibility.

LANDSCAPE VALUE: Interesting native tree, possibly for naturalizing, golf courses, parks; could be integrated into the home landscape but there are too many superior trees to justify extensive use.

CULTIVARS: I did not know how many cultivars existed but found an excellent article by Goodell, *Arnoldia* 42(4):102–133 that provides an excellent perspective of *D. virginiana* and *Actinidia arguta.* 'Early Golden' is the standard for early ripening. 'Garretson', 'Killen', 'John Rick', 'Florence', 'George', 'Mike', 'Wabash', 'Morris Burton', 'Juhl', 'Hick', 'Richards', 'Evelyn', 'Utter', 'Pieper', and 'William' are also mentioned in the article. Anyone interested in this or other native fruit and nut trees should consider joining North American Fruit Explorers, c/o Ray Walker, Box 711, St. Louis, MO 63188 and Northern Nut Growers Association, c/o John English, RR #3, Bloomington, IN 61701.

PROPAGATION: Seed, stratify in sand or peat for 60 to 90 days at 41°F; cultivars are grafted on seedling understock; root cuttings will work.

ADDITIONAL NOTES: The wood of *D. virginiana* is heavy, hard, strong and close grained and is used for golf club heads, billiard cues, flooring and veneer; the fruits are palatable and frequented by wildlife such as racoon, opossum, skunk, foxes, white-tailed deer and other species.

NATIVE HABITAT: Connecticut to Florida west to Kansas and Texas. Introduced 1629. Frequently encountered in abandoned fields, in fence rows and along highways.

RELATED SPECIES:

***Diospyros kaki*—**Japanese Persimmon
(dī-os′pir-os ka′kī)

LEAVES: Alternate, simple, elliptic-ovate to oblong-ovate or obovate, 2 1/2 to 7″ long, 1 1/2 to 3 1/2″ wide, broad cuneate to weakly cordate, glabrous, lustrous dark green above, lighter and pubescent beneath, leathery and strongly veined; petiole—1/2 to 1″ long, pubescent; easily distinguished from the above by larger leaves, buds and fruits.

Diospyros kaki, Japanese Persimmon, first came to my attention at the grocery store and most recently on a drive through south Georgia where I saw a most unusual mop-headed, small tree dripping with large egg-shaped to rounded, 3 to 4″ diameter yellow-orange fruits. In subsequent travels, I have seen trees distinctly upright. In fact in Tulsa, OK I saw a Japanese Persimmon that had the upright habit of *Pyrus communis,* Common Pear. The fruit ripens after the leaves fall and considerable variation exists among cultivars as far as size, shape and quality. The lustrous dark green leaves turn a handsome yellow-orange-red in the fall. The species is dioecious with the male flowers in threes' about 2/5″ long, with 16 to 24 stamens; the female 1/2 to 3/4″ long; both whitish. Flowers appear on current season's growth in May-June; the fruits ripen in October and later. The tree can grow 20 to 30′ high and wide but is usually smaller. The habit is low-branched and wide-spreading with semi-pendulous outer branches. Requires moist, well-drained soil and full sun. Could be used as a container or tub plant; integrated into the border. Many cultivars have been selected over the centuries. Native to China, long cultivated in China and Japan for its fruit; introduced into Europe 1796, but little known before 1870. Zone 7 although best in 8 and 9.

CULTIVARS of *D. kaki* include:

'Chocolate'—Brown sweet flesh, actually a group of selections with cocoa-brown flesh that when ripe is moist and tasty.

'Eureka'—Bright orange-red tomato shaped fruits, must be fully ripe.

'Fuyu'—Golden orange skinned fruit with firm apple-like flesh, about the size of a handball but shaped like a tomato, non-astringent even before completely ripe, a most popular variety and ordinarily seedless.

'Fuyu Giant'—Similar but produces larger fruits, perhaps as much as 40% larger, non astringent.

'Hachiya'—Handsome tree form with large conical (3 1/2 to 5″ long, 2 1/2″ broad), essentially seedless fruits, needs to be soft before eaten, outside orange-red, flesh orange-yellow.

'Tamopan'—Large acorn-shaped fruit, often 5″ across, astringent unless fully ripe.

'Tanenashi'—Brilliant orange cone-shaped fruits, heavy production, essentially seedless, must be fully ripe, otherwise astringent taste.

Dirca palustris — Leatherwood
(dir′ka pa-lus′tris)

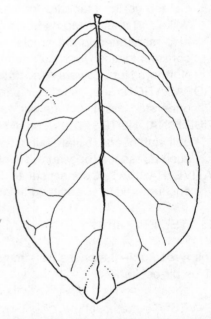

FAMILY: Thymelaeaceae

LEAVES: Alternate, simple, elliptic to obovate, 1 to 3″ long, about one-half as wide, obtuse, cuneate, entire, light green above, glaucescent beneath and pubescent when young; short petioled, about 1/8″ long.

BUDS: Small, solitary, short conical, with about 4 indistinct dark silky scales; end-bud lacking.

STEM: Slender, light brown becoming olive or darker, with conspicuous small white lenticels; gradually enlarged upwards through the season's growth; called leatherwood because the bark is very leathery and it is quite difficult to remove a piece of broken stem.

SIZE: Variable over its native range; 3 to 6′ in height with a similar spread.

HARDINESS: Zone 4 to 9.

HABIT: Much branched, rather dense, oval to rounded shrub in cultivation when sited in full sun; irregular, open and spreading in the wild.

RATE: Slow.

TEXTURE: Medium.

LEAF COLOR: Light green, by some authorities yellow-green; one of the first shrubs to leaf out in spring; may turn clear yellow in fall, can be very effective in fall color.

FLOWERS: Perfect, pale yellow, 3 to 4 in an inflorescence; not overwhelming but interesting by virtue of their March to April flowering date; has been in full flower in early March at the Georgia Botanical Garden.

FRUIT: Oval drupe, 1/3″ long, pale green or reddish; containing one large shining, brown seed; June–July; seldom seen as it is hidden among the leaves and falls soon after maturity.

CULTURE: Thrives in moist to wet, shady areas; prefers a deep soil supplied with organic matter; in Turkey Run State Park, Indiana, the plant appears to follow the water courses through the ravines and occurs in the alluvial soils.

DISEASES AND INSECTS: None serious, although I have observed scale infestations on selected plants.

LANDSCAPE VALUE: Interesting native shrub well-adapted to moist shady areas; if natural in an area it is worth leaving; the flowers are borne on leafless stems and are interesting; I have become very fond of this plant over the years; the rich green foliage is very distinct and the fall color can be an excellent yellow; in hot sun it does not have the handsome leaf color that occurs in a semi-shaded situation.

PROPAGATION: Seed can be sown as soon as ripe; seed requires a cold period of about 3 months to facilitate germination; the only definitive published information reported that cleaned fruits (pulp removed) sown immediately outside (Boston) germinated 54% in the spring; at the Georgia Botanical Garden, two side-by-side seedlings set prodigious quantities of fruits and numerous seedlings have germinated around the bases of these plants. Cuttings have proven difficult to root and I have had no success; layering offers a method of vegetative reproduction.

ADDITIONAL NOTES: The Indians used the bark for bow strings and fish lines and in the manufacture of baskets.

NATIVE HABITAT: New Brunswick and Ontario to Florida and Missouri. Introduced 1750.

Disanthus cercidifolius
(diz-an'thus ser-sid-i-fō'li-us)

FAMILY: Hamamelidaceae

LEAVES: Alternate, simple, thickish, broad-ovate to rounded, blunt and rounded at apex, cordate or truncate, 2 to 4 1/2″ long, about as wide, entire, bluish green, glabrous; petiole 1 to 2″ long.

A magnificent, but rare, plant that is worthy of the discriminating gardener's attention. One of the purposes of this book is to introduce readers to unusual plants that are not common in the nursery trade. This is one such attempt. *Disanthus cercidifolius* becomes a broad spreading shrub of slender branches. The ultimate height ranges between 6 and 10′ (15′). The bluish green leaves turn combinations of claret-red and purple, often suffused with orange. It is one of the most beautiful shrubs for fall color. The leaves resemble those of *Cercis* in shape and, hence, the specific epithet, *cercidifolius.* the perfect, dark purple, 1/2″ diameter, 5-petaled flowers are borne in axillary pairs in October. The fruit is an obovoid, dehiscent capsule containing several glossy black seeds in each cell. The fruit ripens in October of the year following flowering. It is not the easiest plant to grow and requires a deep, moist, high organic matter soil in light shade and protection from strong wind. The Morris and Taylor Arboreta have fine specimens which I had the privilege of viewing. It is a knockout and certainly worth securing for one's garden. Someone, actually Roger Gossler, Gossler Farms Nursery, 1200 Weaver Road, Springfield, OR 97478-9663, heard my prayers and sent a plant that has prospered for the last 5 years on the north side of our home in shade and a relatively moist soil. Incidentally, for those looking for rare plants at reasonable prices, Gossler offers the créme de le créme. In the ensuing years, cuttings have been rooted 100% using firm June cuttings, 10,000 ppm IBA, perlite:peat, mist; after rooting they are potted, lightly fertilized and continue to grow. Much easier to root than the literature indicates. A monotypic genus occurring in Japan. Introduced 1892. Hardy to at least −20°F. Zone 5 to 8.

Elaeagnus angustifolia — Russian-olive
(ē-lē-ag'nus an-gus-ti-fō'li-a̍)

FAMILY: Elaeagnaceae

LEAVES: Alternate, simple, oblong-lanceolate to linear-lanceolate, 1 to 3″ long, 3/8 to 5/8″ wide, dull green and scaly above, silvery-scaly beneath, acute to obtuse, usually broad-cuneate at base; petiole—1/5 to 1/3″ long.

BUDS: Small, solitary, gray-brown, sessile, round, conical or oblong, with about 4 exposed silvery scales.

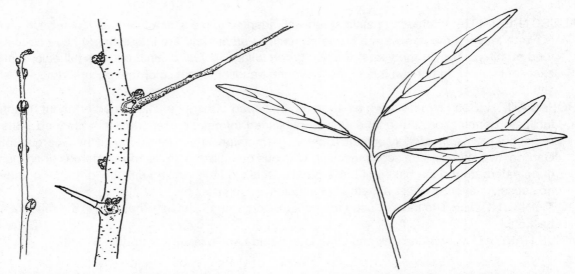

STEM: Young branches silvery, sometimes thorny, covered with scales; older branches assuming a glistening brown color; pith—brown.

SIZE: 12 to 15′(20′) tall and as wide, occasionally will grow 30 to 40′.
HARDINESS: Zone 2 to 7.
HABIT: Large shrub or small tree of rounded outline, often quite open and of light texture.
RATE: Medium to fast.
TEXTURE: Medium-fine in leaf; medium in winter.
LEAF COLOR: Silver-green to gray-green in summer and one of the most effective plants for gray foliage.
FLOWERS: Perfect, apetalous, calyx tube campanulate, with 4 spreading lobes as long as the tube, silvery or whitish outside, yellow inside, 3/8″ long, fragrant, May, one to three together in each leaf axil.
FRUIT: Drupe-like, most correctly considered an achene covered by a fleshy perianth, 1/2″ long, yellow and coated with silvery scales, August through September, the flesh is sweet and mealy and in the Orient a sherbet is made from it.
CULTURE: Transplants readily, can be grown in any soil, but does best in light, sandy loams; withstands seacoast, highway conditions, drought and alkali soils; prefers sunny open exposure; can be pruned into a tight structure; the secret to keeping this plant looking good is to keep it vigorous; have seen in Colorado where it appeared more vigorous than in midwest and east; displays high degree of salt tolerance, especially to soil salts; fixes atmosphere nitrogen making it amenable to poor soils, does not perform well in heat of the south.
DISEASES AND INSECTS: Leaf spots, cankers, rusts, *Verticillium* wilt, crown gall, oleaster-thistle aphid, and scales; *Verticillium* can wreak havoc on this species and for this reason it has lost favor as a highway plant in many parts of the midwest.
LANDSCAPE VALUE: For grayish foliage effect it is difficult to beat; can be used for hedges, highways, seacoasts, about anywhere salt is a problem; possibly an accent plant in the shrub border; better in dry climates than moist.
CULTIVARS:
    'Red King'—Rich rust-red fruits.
PROPAGATION: Seed should be stratified for 60 to 90 days at 41°F; cuttings collected in mid-October rooted after treatment with 40 ppm IBA for two hours but the percentage was poor; seed is the preferred method of propagation.
NATIVE HABITAT: Southern Europe to western and central Asia, Altai and Himalayas. Long cultivated in Europe.

RELATED SPECIES:

Elaeagnus commutata—Silverberry

LEAVES: Alternate, simple, ovate to oblong or ovate-lanceolate, 1 1/2 to 3 1/2″ long, 3/4 to 1 1/4″ wide, acute or obtuse, cuneate, both sides covered with glistening silvery white scales; petiole—1/8″ long.
STEM: Silvery white like the leaves.

Elaeagnus commutata, (ē-lē-ag′nus kom-mū-tā′ta), Silverberry, is a 6 to 12′ high and wide shrub of erect habit with rather slender branches. It suckers profusely and forms colonies. The 1 1/2 to 3 1/2″ long, 3/4 to 1 1/2″ wide, oval to narrowly ovate leaves are covered on both surfaces with silvery white scales. The leaves are the showiest of the *Elaeagnus* species treated here. The fragrant, silvery-yellow, tubular, 1/2″ long flowers are produced in great numbers in the leaf axils during May. The fruit is a silvery, 1/3″ long, egg-shaped drupe that ripens in September-October. At Illinois, in our test plots, this species contracted scale and performed poorly. At the University of Maine, in their test area, it appeared more vigorous. It makes a rather striking shrub because of the silvery foliage but is rather untidy in growth habit. Have not seen in the southeast and doubt whether it would survive in the humidity and heat. Eastern Canada to Northwest Territory, south to Minnesota, South Dakota and Utah. Introduced 1813. Zone 2 to 5 or 6. The only species native in North America.

Elaeagnus multiflora—Cherry Elaeagnus

LEAVES: Alternate, simple, elliptic or ovate to obovate-oblong, 1 1/2 to 2 1/2″ long, 3/4 to 1 1/2″ wide, short acuminate to obtusish, broad cuneate, green above with scattered tufted hairs, silvery-brown beneath with a mix of tiny silver scales and larger brown ones; petiole—1/4″ long.

Elaeagnus multiflora, (ē-lē-ag′nus mul-ti-flō′ra), Cherry Elaeagnus, is a wide spreading almost flat-topped shrub with rather stiff branches (grows 6 to 10′ high and as wide). Foliage is a silvery green (green above, silvery-brown below); fruits are red scaly, 1/2″ long on a 1″ pedicel, oblong, of pleasant acid flavor, June–July; birds seem to like the fruits; as adaptable or more so than *E. angustifolia.* The 5/8″ long, 3/5″ wide flowers are fragrant and of the same color as the underside of the leaf. They occur in April and May from the axils of the leaves. This is a rather handsome species and the scaly-red fruits that hang from the underside of the branches are beautiful. The leaves are more green than the other species treated here. A specimen at the Arnold Arboretum was 8 to 10′ high, 10 to 12′ wide, dense, mounded and beautiful in fruit during late June into July. China, Japan. 1862. Zone 5 to 7. Has not proven hardy at Minnesota Landscape Arboretum.

Elaeagnus umbellata—Autumn Elaeagnus, Autumn-olive
(ē-lē-ag′nus um-bel-lā′-ta)

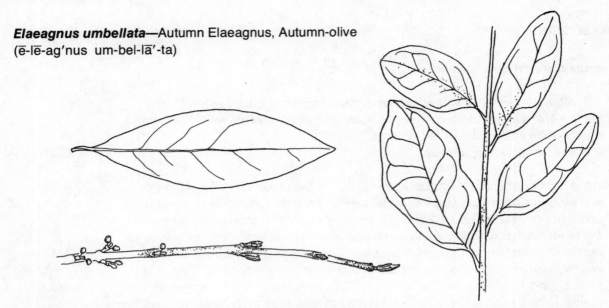

LEAVES: Alternate, simple, elliptic to ovate-oblong, 2 to 4″ long, 3/4 to 1 1/2″ wide, obtuse to short-acuminate, rounded to broad cuneate at the base, often with crisped margin, usually with silvery scales above when young, sometimes glabrous, bright green above at maturity, silvery beneath and usually mixed with brown scales; petiole—1/3″ long.

STEM: Silver brown with many brownish scales which give a speckled appearance, spines may be present; pith—rich brown.

Elaeagnus umbellata, Autumn Elaeagnus or Autumn-olive, is a large (12 to 18′ tall by 12 to 18′ wide, sometimes 20 to 30′ across), spreading, often spiny branched shrub. The foliage is bright green above, silver green beneath; the 1/2″ long funnel-shaped, silvery-white, fragrant flowers occur in May–June (early-mid May, Athens); globose fruits are silvery mixed with brown scales finally turning red, 1/4 to 1/3″ long, ripening in September to October; fruits are borne in great numbers on short 1/4″ long stalks and appear to almost encircle the stem; becomes a noxious weed with time for birds spread the seeds everywhere; 'Cardinal' is a Soil Conservation Service introduction that grows to 12′, fruits heavily and thrives in low-fertility, acid, loamy and sandy soils and displays excellent drought tolerance; sold for conservation purposes; not a plant for the home landscape. In the south, this species has escaped and can be found in abundance in almost any untended location; appears to adapt quite well to light shady pine woods; the sweet fragrance is inescapable in early May, in fact, I can ride home from work (8 miles) and notice almost a continuum of fragrance. 'Titan' is a new upright introduction that grows 12′ high and only 6′ wide with the other attributes of the species. Lake County Introduction. China, Korea, Japan. 1830. Zone 3 to 8.

ADDITIONAL NOTES: The *Elaeagnus* species offer good foliage color, fragrant flowers and silvery to red fruits; unfortunately, several species are pestiferous and become weeds with time. I have seen numerous bird-planted *E. umbellata* in Georgia. At Illinois I conducted salt tolerance research with *E. angustifolia* and found that it was almost impossible to kill with soil applications. Apparently Russian-olive does not accumulate the Na or Cl ions and is able to survive in saline environments. Anyone interested in salt tolerant trees and shrubs should see Dirr, *J. Arboriculture,* 2:209–216 (1976) "Selection of trees for tolerance to salt."

Elaeagnus pungens — Thorny Elaeagnus
(ē-lē-ag′nus pun′jenz)

LEAVES: Alternate, simple, evergreen, margins as if ruffled (crisped), 2 to 4″ long, 1/4 to 1 3/4″ wide, linear-ovate, acute, cuneate, glabrous and lustrous dark green above, prominently covered with

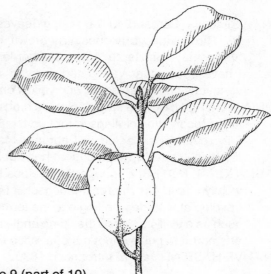

punctate scales below, giving silver sheen to entire lower surface, major veins appearing brown; petiole—1/4 to 1/2" long, brown, covered with brown scales.

BUDS: Loosely aggregated brownish scales (4) give appearance of fingers glued together, 1/8 to 1/4" long; apparently some buds are leaf buds, others develop into spines; both present at same node; spine continues to grow and produces leaves.

STEM: Moderate, terete, brown, densely covered with scales, will develop rather nasty 2 to 3" long thorns that are covered with brown scales, pith—greenish white, solid.

SIZE: 10 to 15' high, similar spread.

HARDINESS: Zone 6, succeeds in the Philadelphia area, to 9 (part of 10).

HABIT: In its natural form a genuine horror; long shoots wander in disarray from all areas of the plant; best described as a rather unkempt, dense, spreading more or less thorny shrub; needs a good tailor.

RATE: Fast, does not adequately describe the speed with which it grows.

TEXTURE: Coarse, but some of the better cultivars fall in the medium category.

LEAF COLOR: Glossy dark green above; silvery with a hint of brown beneath, some leaves brown on underside.

FLOWERS: Perfect, silvery white, fragrant (similar to that of *Gardenia*), 1/2" long, tubular but flaring above the ovary, usually in three's from the leaf axis, October–November, often lost among the leaves but the fine fragrance stimulates the olfactory senses.

FRUIT: Seldom seen, a 1/2 to 3/4" long, scaly brown at first, finally red drupe; fruits develop in April and May and attract birds; very similar to those of *E. multiflora*.

CULTURE: Easily grown, actually a weed in the south, adaptable to varied soils and withstands considerable drought; sun or shade, tends to become thin in shade but still makes an acceptable plant; tolerates salt spray and apparently air pollutants; requires frequent pruning and regrowth of shoots following pruning is problematic.

DISEASES AND INSECTS: None serious, but spider mites do occur in dry weather.

LANDSCAPE VALUE: Not for the small property; has been used extensively for highway landscaping in the south; rest areas along interstates seem to abound with this plant; good for banks, hedges, screens, natural barriers; tends to sucker which makes it good for stabilizing soils; leaves were injured at –3°F in 1983–84 but did grow back as stems and buds were not hurt.

CULTIVARS: Many, names appear to be confused.

'Aurea'—Leaves bordered with bright yellow ('Aureo-picta').

'Dicksonii'—Leaves bordered with a broad gold margin, with some leaves completely gold toward the apex.

'Frederici'—Small, narrow 1 to 1 3/4" long leaves, the cream-colored or pale yellow center bordered with a thin margin of green, have seen in England, not particularly striking and appears as if sick.

'Fruitlandii'—Supposedly symmetrical in outline; leaves slightly larger and more rounded than the species, wavy, silvery beneath.

'Golden Rim'—Apparently a branch sport of 'Maculata', leaves green in center with gold margins, originated in Holland, have not seen in the United States.

'Maculata' ('Aureo-variegata')—Large leaves are marked with a deep yellow blotch of variable size in their center; often, between the yellow and green areas is an intermediate yellowish shade; this cultivar will revert back to the type and these branches must be cut out; I have seen plants that showed virtually complete reversion; common in the south but almost gauche, reversions to both yellow and green shoots occur.

'Marginata'—Leaves with silvery white margins.

'Simonii'—Larger (2 to 4 1/4″ long) leaves than the type with bright green upper surface, very silvery undersides, branches gray-brown, not thorny; similar to 'Fruitlandii'?

'Variegata'—Similar to 'Aurea' but border color yellowish white, very irregular and narrow.

I have seen other variegated cultivars but do now know how different they are. Only so many variations can be selected with yellow on the inside or yellow on the outside.

PROPAGATION: Not the easiest plant to root; use firm wood cuttings and some cold (October–November) may precondition cuttings to root better; 8000 ppm to 20,000 ppm IBA-talc have been used successfully; cuttings collected in February–March, 6″ long from previous season's growth, 8000 ppm IBA-talc, 2 peat: 1 sand, bottom heat, poly tent or mist rooted 90 to 100% in 8 weeks.

ADDITIONAL NOTES: *E. pungens* develops long shoots almost devoid of leaves that give it a wild and woolly effect. The interesting aspect of these shoots is the spine development. The spines normally develop at a 45 degree angle to the terminal end of the shoot; however, if in contact with a structure such as a trellis or fence the spine angle is reversed and the spines act almost like hooks. If you ever attempted to pull a shoot out of a fence this effect is obvious.

NATIVE HABITAT: Japan. Introduced 1830.

RELATED SPECIES:

Elaeagnus × ebbingii, (ē-lē-ag′nus × eb-bing′ē-ī), is a suspected hybrid between *E. macrophylla* and *E. pungens*. A batch of six seedlings was raised by S.G.A. Doorenboos in 1929; all six were propagated and two clones are still in commerce; supposedly more vigorous than the species. Based on observations, *E. × ebbingei* is not as wild and woolly as *E. pungens*; may show semi-evergreen tendencies but is evergreen in mild climates. From the original seedlings, two were named: 'Albert Doorenbos' with large 3 to 5″ long, 2 to 2 1/4″ wide leaves that more closely resemble *E. macrophylla* and 'The Hague' with narrower leaves, 3 to 4″ long, 2″ wide and resembles *E. pungens*. More recently a particularly handsome form, 'Gilt Edge' with soft yellow-gold prominent margins and a light green center has entered the marketplace; this is a particularly fine form that I have seen in many English gardens and has found its way into American commerce (Monrovia Nurseries). I have also seen a form called 'Clemson' which is somewhat similar but with lighter margins. It is probably not in the trade. 'Limelight' has leaf splashed pale gold to gold and is particularly striking in summer months, losing some of its intensity in cold weather. Probably Zone 6 to 9.

Elliottia racemosa— Georgia Plume, Elliottia
(el-i-ot′ti- a rā-se-mō′sá)

FAMILY: Ericaceae

LEAVES: Alternate, simple, narrowly oval or obovate, 2 to 5″ long, 3/4 to 1 3/4″ wide, tapering at both ends, dull dark green or blue green and glabrous above, paler and slightly pubescent beneath; petiole 1/4 to 1/2″ long, pubescent.

BUDS: Terminal 1/4″ long, 2 distinct scales form cone-like structure, glabrous, light brown; laterals 1/16″ long, ovoid, indistinctly scaled (2), rather stiff, almost mucronate, leaf scars elliptical with one bundle trace.

STEM: Moderate, lustrous brown, glabrous, somewhat angled; in second year developing vertical fissures.

Elliottia racemosa, Georgia Plume, is a beautiful large shrub or small tree found in isolated localities in Georgia and South Carolina. It tends to sucker from the roots and form colonies 8 to 12′ high although larger trees are known. The real show occurs from mid June to early July (in Georgia) when the pure white, slightly fragrant, 4 petaled flowers occur in 4 to 10″ long terminal racemes or panicles. The fruit is a flattened-globose, 3/8″ diameter capsule that houses the small winged seeds. The plant is magnificent in flower and would tantalize anyone's gardening palette. After flower it fades into relative obscurity and is quite difficult to identify unless one knows exactly what to look for. It has a historic past and many articles have been written of which I recommend Miller. *American Forest* 84(2):

"Wildfire's child." 1978. It has not found its way into gardens owing to the supposed difficulty of propagation but Al Fordham of the Arnold Arboretum worked out an excellent method from root cuttings. See *PIPPS* 29:284–287 (1979) for specifics. Interestingly, it is growing as far north as Boston, MA in the Arnold Arboretum where I have photographed it in full flower. South Carolina and Georgia. Cultivated 1813. Zone 5 (once established) to 8 (9).

Elsholtzia stauntonii — Staunton Elsholtzia
(el-shōlt'si-à stawn-tō'nē-ī)

LEAVES: Opposite, simple, lanceolate, slenderly tapered at both ends, acuminate, coarse triangular teeth except at ends, 2 to 6" long, 1/2 to 1 1/2" wide, bright green above, pale and covered with minute dots beneath, glabrous on both surfaces, minutely downy on margins; when crushed emitting a mint-like odor.

Elsholtzia stauntonii, Staunton Elsholtzia, is a semi-woody, 3 to 5' high and wide shrub that has no great merit other than the purplish pink flowers that occur in spikose panicles at the end of the stems in September and October. Each spike is normally 4 to 8" long and about 1" wide. It prefers a well-drained soil and a sunny site. It is probably best to prune the plant before new growth starts. Since it flowers on new wood of the season the flower effect is not impaired. Watched the plant at the Arnold Arboretum during sabbatical and never envisioned it as a major force in the garden. Should be treated almost like a herbaceous perennial in the north since it flowers on new growth of the season. Seed has no apparent dormancy and softwood cuttings can be rooted. Northern China. 1905. Zone 4 to 8.

Enkianthus campanulatus — Redvein Enkianthus
(en-ki-an'thus kam-pan-ū-lā'tus)

FAMILY: Ericaceae
LEAVES: Alternate, simple, mostly crowded at the end of branches, elliptic to rhombic-elliptic, 1 to 3" long, 1/2 to 1 1/4" wide, acute or acuminate, appressed-serrulate with aristate teeth, dull dark green, with scattered bristly hairs above and on the veins beneath; petiole 1/3 to 5/8" long.

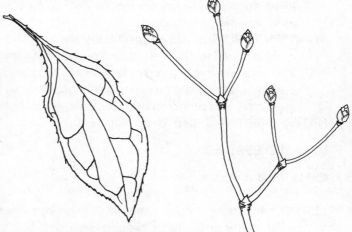

BUDS: Minute, sunken and in the notch of the leaf scar, solitary, sessile, indistinctly scaly, the flower buds large, ovoid, imbricate, about 1/3" long.
STEM: Slender, 3-sided or rounded, often reddish in youth, becoming brown, glabrous.

SIZE: 6 to 8' in cold climates but can grow from 15 to 30'; have seen 12 to 15' high specimens in the east, immense specimens in England fully 20' high and spectacular.
HARDINESS: Zone 4 to 7.
HABIT: Narrow, upright shrub or small tree with layered branches and tufted foliage.
RATE: Slow.
TEXTURE: Medium in all seasons.
LEAF COLOR: Bright to medium green (almost blue-green) in summer; brilliant yellow to orange and red in fall, often variable in quality of coloration.

FLOWERS: Perfect, creamy yellow or light orange, veined with red, 1/3 to 1/2″ long; May-June, about the time the leaves are developing, in pendulous umbel-like racemes, from terminal bud of previous year's growth; very dainty and delicate; corolla bell-shaped with 5 rounded lobes.

FRUIT: Dehiscent capsule, 5 valved, egg-shaped, 3/4″ long, borne upright on a recurved pedicel.

CULTURE: Similar to rhododendrons, definitely acid soil requiring; full sun or partial shade.

DISEASES AND INSECTS: None serious, scale has been reported.

LANDSCAPE VALUE: Excellent for flower and fall color, nice specimen, combines well with rhododendrons, lovely around a patio.

CULTIVARS:

'Albiflorus'—White flowers with no veins, actually somewhat off-white (cream); fall color may approach orange-red.

var. *palibinii*—Red flowers, each flower 1/3″ long, borne in a distinct raceme.

'Red Bells'—Flowers redder toward tip than normal, basal 1/3 of corolla creamy yellow and lightly veined with red.

'Renoir'—Named by Rob Nicholson, Arnold Arboretum, this form offers subdued yellow flowers with pink lobes.

'Showy Lantern'—Selected by the late Mr. Ed Mezitt, Weston Nurseries, for large solid pink flowers; dark green foliage turns rich scarlet, wide and upright with dense branching from the ground.

'Sikokianus' (var. *sikokianus*)—Considered by Nicholson, *Amer. Nurseryman* 166(6):83 (1987), the darkest flowered *Enkianthus;* unopened flowers are maroon with violet undertones; when open the color is dark brick red with shrimp pink streaks.

'Weston Pink Strain'—One of the pioneer nurseries of New England, Weston at Hopkinton, MA, has selected forms for good pink corolla coloration; their 1988 catalog has a wrap-around color photo of the deep, almost rose-pink form; by growing seedlings from these superior types they have increased the opportunity for better pink coloration.

PROPAGATION: Seed, see under *Calluna,* very easy to grow from seed, almost like beans; cuttings collected in late May rooted 80% without treatment; have rooted the species from July softwoods using 1000 ppm IBA-quick dip; overwinter survival after rooting may be a problem; tissue culture is commercially practiced.

ADDITIONAL NOTES: Not all *Enkianthus* are created equal. Their floral beauty is really evident only upon close inspection. The interesting growth habit and fall color make them valuable landscape plants. The consistent red fall color forms should be propagated vegetatively. I have observed leaves of *E. campanulatus* dying off green and those of other plants a brilliant red; excellent practical article on the genus was authored by Nicholson, *Amer. Nurseryman* 166(6):83 (1987).

NATIVE HABITAT: Japan. Cultivated 1870.

RELATED SPECIES:

Enkianthus cernuus

LEAVES: Alternate, simple, elliptic to rhombic-obovate or obovate-oblong, 3/4 to 1 1/2″ long, 1/2 to 2/3 as wide, acute or obtusish, crenate-serrulate, bright green above, glabrous, or slightly pubescent on midrib below.

Enkianthus cernuus, (en-ki-an'thus sĕr'nū-us), is a rather pretty 5 to 10′ high white flowering shrub. Each flower is bell-shaped, 1/4″ long and borne in a nodding 10 to 12-flowered raceme in May. Variety *rubens* is a beautiful rich deep red flowered form. Have seen in full flower at Biltmore Gardens in mid May and was most impressed by the deep color. Not as large in habit, leaf or flower as the species. Japan. Cultivated 1900. Zone 5. The red-flowered form is a plant of great beauty.

Enkianthus deflexus—Bent Enkianthus

LEAVES: Alternate, simple, oval, obovate or lanceolate, produced in a pseudo-whorled cluster at the end of the branch, 1 to 3″ long, 1/2 to 1 1/3″ wide, acute at apex, cuneate at base, serrulate, strigose on midrib beneath and sparingly hairy above and below.

Enkianthus deflexus, (en-ki-an'thus dē-fleks'us), Bent Enkianthus, is a narrow, upright shrub with layered branches reaching 10 to 20′ in height. Foliage is dark green in summer, scarlet in fall; flowers are yellowish red with darker veins, 1/2″ diameter, May, borne in umbel-like racemes; flowers are larger and showier than Redvein, however, not as hardy. Himalayas, western China. 1878. Zone 5 to 6.

Enkianthus perulatus—White Enkianthus

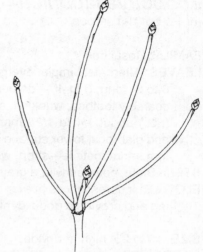

LEAVES: Alternate, simple, narrow oval to obovate, clustered, 1 to 2″ long, 1/2 as wide, acute, sharply appressed-serrulate, glabrous and bright green above, pubescent on veins below; petiole—about 1/2″ long.

Enkianthus perulatus, (en-ki-an'thus per-ū-lā'tus), White Enkianthus, grows to 6′ high and about as wide. The foliage is bright green in summer, scarlet in fall; flowers are white, urn-shaped, 1/3″ long, early May before the leaves in 3 to 10-flowered nodding umbel-like racemes. This is a neater shrub than the other species but hard to find in the trade; Koller (*Green Scene,* Sept. 1975) described a 60 to 70-year-old plant at the Morris Arboretum that was 9′ tall and 15′ wide. The branching pattern is somewhat tiered resulting in an oriental look. 'Compacta' is a dwarf cultivar only 18″ high and 25″ wide after 30 years; it only started to flower within the last few years. Japan. Introduced 1870. Zone 5 to 7?

Epigaea repens — Trailing Arbutus
(ep-i-jē′à rē′penz)

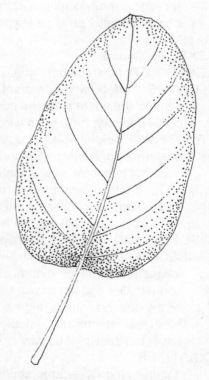

LEAVES: Alternate, simple, evergreen, ovate or suborbicular to oblong-ovate, 1 to 3″ long, 3/4 to 2″ wide, rounded and mucronulate, rarely acute at apex, subcordate or rounded at base, ciliate, glossy dark green above, rough and covered with persistent stiff hairs on both surfaces; petiole 1/4 to 3/4″ long, pubescent.

Epigaea repens, Trailing Arbutus (Ericaceae), is, like *Andromeda polifolia,* one of the untamed members of Ericaceae. It resists cultivation but is deserving of every attempt that die-hard plantsmen make. The habit is one of a flat (4 to 6″ high by 2′ spread) evergreen mat which forms dense cover; in favorable locations it will carpet large areas but, alas, intrusion and disturbance by man puts it to rot. The foliage is leathery, of a rather dark glossy green, slightly bronzed by rusty hairs. The flowers are perfect, white through pink, 5/8″ long by 1/2″ wide, exceedingly fragrant, April, 4 to 6 together in a dense terminal raceme. Fruit is a whitish, berry-like 1/2″ diameter capsule. Extremely difficult to transplant and perpetuate; requires an acid, sandy or gravelly soil which has been mulched with decayed oak leaves or pine needles; best to move as a container-grown plant for the delicate roots are easily injured; shade or partial shade is advisable but freedom from man and his activities are even more necessary. This plant could be one where a mycorrhizal association plays a significant role in its survival. It could be transplanted specimens do not develop the fungal relationship that is necessary for their survival. A very dainty, delicate evergreen ground cover that presents a challenge to every individual who considers him- or herself a true plant-person. There is a cultivar termed 'Plena' which is a double-flowered type. Usually propagated from cuttings although large pieces of "sod" may be utilized. Native from Massachusetts to Florida west to Ohio and Tennessee. Introduced 1736. Zone 2 to 9. The state flower of Massachusetts.

Eriobotrya japonica — Loquat
(er-i-ō-bot′ri-à ja-pon′i-kà)

FAMILY: Rosaceae

LEAVES: Alternate, simple, evergreen, variable in size, usually 6 to 9″ long, 3 to 4″ wide but up to 12″ long, and 5″ wide, coarsely toothed, wrinkled, strongly set with parallel veins (ribs) about 1/4 to 1/2″ apart, lustrous dark green above and glabrous, lower surface covered with a grayish brown tomentum; petiole—short, woolly.

STEM: Stout, covered with a grayish woolly pubescence.

FLOWER: Inflorescences are formed in summer prior to flowering and provide a good identification feature.

SIZE: 15 to 25′ high and wide.

HARDINESS: Zone 8 to 10, leaves were severely injured in exposed locations after exposure to 0°F; killed at −3°F in Athens.

HABIT: Small evergreen tree or more often a large, broad spreading shrub forming a rounded outline; have observed it as an espalier on large expanses of brick.

RATE: Medium.

TEXTURE: Coarse.

LEAF COLOR: Lustrous dark green above; lower surface covered with a brownish tomentum.

FLOWERS: Perfect, white, fragrant, 1/2 to 3/4″ across, 5-petaled, borne in a 3 to 6″ long, stiff, terminal panicle, the entire structure covered with a dense brown pubescence; flowers anytime from November to January; have seen it in flower during September in Savannah, GA.

FRUIT: Edible, pear-shaped, or oblong, 1 to 1 3/4″ long, yellow pome that ripens in April through June; in eastern Asia, southern Europe and the southern United States the plant is grown for its edible fruit; does not fruit in Athens–Atlanta area; farther south will set large quantities of fruit.

CULTURE: Easily grown, prefers moist, well-drained, loamy soil but will withstand coarse alkaline soils and a measure of drought; do not over fertilize as fireblight can be troublesome; withstands pruning quite well; site in full sun but will tolerate partial shade; probably should be grown in Zone 9.

DISEASES AND INSECTS: Fireblight.

LANDSCAPE VALUE: A beautiful evergreen shrub especially valued because of the lustrous dark green foliage; excellent for textural effects; has been utilized for street tree plantings in the south; makes a fine espalier against a wall; used as a lawn tree in Florida; displays good drought tolerance based on my observations during the summers of 1980 and 1981 in Athens, Georgia where one-inch of rain fell in four months and temperatures approached 90 to 100°F every day; have not seen fruit in middle south but does fruit heavily in lower south.

CULTIVARS:

'Golden Nugget'—Large abundant pear-shaped, flavorful yellow-orange fruit; this selection is commercially available; 'Champagne', 'MacBeth', and 'Thales' are also listed.

'Variegata'—Leaves variegated with white, rather attractive.

PROPAGATION: Seed requires no cold treatment; June-July cuttings have been rooted.

NATIVE HABITAT: China, Japan. Introduced 1784.

Eucommia ulmoides — Hardy Rubber Tree
(ū-kom′-i-a ul-moy′dēz)

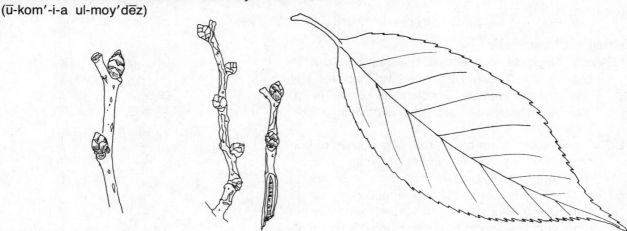

FAMILY: Eucommiaceae

LEAVES: Alternate, simple, 3 to 6″ long, about 1/2 as wide, elliptic or ovate to oblong-ovate, acuminate, broad-cuneate or rounded, serrate, lustrous dark green and glabrous above and slightly rugose at maturity; leaf when torn exhibits rubbery substance.

BUDS: Imbricate, sessile, ovoid, chestnut brown, 3/16″ long, terminal lacking, ending in a leaf.

STEM: Stout, bloomy, olive-brown; pith—chambered; bark when stripped exhibiting elastic (rubbery) strings.

SIZE: 40 to 60′ in height with an equal or greater spread.

HARDINESS: Zone 4 to 7; has survived −20°F at the Secrest Arboretum.

HABIT: Rounded to broad-spreading tree of dapper outline at maturity; in youth somewhat pyramidal in outline.

RATE: Medium, 30′ over a 20 year period.

TEXTURE: Medium in all seasons.

BARK: On old trees, ridged-and-furrowed, of a gray-brown color and reasonably attractive; in China the bark is valued as a tonic and for its medicinal properties.

LEAF COLOR: Lustrous dark green in summer (very handsome); fall color is non-existent as the leaves fall green or a poor yellowish green.

FLOWERS: Dioecious, inconspicuous and ornamentally unimportant, staminate clusters of brown stamens, female—consisting of a single pistil.

FRUIT: Capsule-like with compressed wings, 1 1/2″ long, oval-oblong, notched at apex, one seeded, like a large, waxy, fleshy elm fruit.

CULTURE: Transplants readily; very soil tolerant; resists drought; pH adaptable; full sun.

DISEASES AND INSECTS: None serious.

LANDSCAPE VALUE: Excellent shade tree for many areas; outstanding summer foliage that is completely free of pests; excellent for midwest; never has become popular and is doubtfully as urban tolerant as given credit.

PROPAGATION: Seeds require 2 to 3 months cold moist stratification; the only published report indicates that chloromone (1-naphthyl-acetamine) induced 57% rooting from a 50-year-old tree and 85% from an unspecified plant; cuttings should be taken just as the new growth is forming.

ADDITIONAL NOTES: Only rubber producing tree for the central and northern parts of the country; rubber content is about 3% on a dry weight basis, however, the extraction is difficult; *ulmoides* refers to the leaf shape which is similar to that of elm, *Ulmus*. Barker, *J. Arboriculture* 10(8):233–235 (1984), built an impressive case for the species in urban areas and reported that 34 trees planted in 6′ wide tree lawns in Cleveland, OH in 1952 were 25 to 30′ high with an average 14″ trunk diameter in 32 years. His data indicate that the tree will suffer some tip dieback at −20°F. Also tree is adaptable to soils ranging above pH 7 but intolerant to poor drainage.

NATIVE HABITAT: Central China. Introduced 1896.

Euonymus alatus — Winged Euonymus
(ū-on'i-mus a̍-lā'tus)

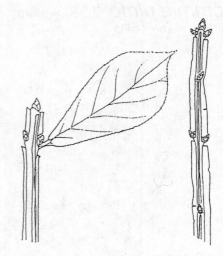

FAMILY: Celastraceae

LEAVES: Opposite to subopposite, simple, elliptic to obovate, 1 to 3″ long, 1/2 to 1 1/4″ wide, acute, finely and sharply serrate, medium to dark green, glabrous or somewhat downy beneath; petiole 1/12″ long.

BUDS: Imbricate, green-brown-red, 6 to 8 pairs of bud scales, conical, ovoid, acute, glabrous, strongly divergent, actually breaking the continuous wing.

STEM: Green to brown with 2 to 4-armed corky wings (prominent), wings 1/4 to 1/2″ broad, generally the more vigorous shoots have the biggest wings, glabrous.

SIZE: 15 to 20′ in height, similar in spread; here is a classic example of how the size descriptions given in the literature do not adequately estimate the actual landscape size; usually listed at 9 to 10′, this shrub defies description and develops into a 15 to 20′ well-preserved specimen.

HARDINESS: Zone 4 to 8(9).

HABIT: Mounded to horizontal, spreading, flat-topped shrub, usually broader than high; extremely effective and well-preserved in the winter landscape; does not develop the "garbage can" look of many shrubs, always an aristocrat even under the most demanding of conditions; makes a rather handsome small tree if pruned properly.

RATE: Slow.

TEXTURE: Medium in leaf; medium in winter, the distinctive corky-winged branches are very effective in the winter landscape and their beauty is renewed with each new fallen snow.

LEAF COLOR: Flat medium to dark green, very clean looking foliage, fall color is usually a brilliant red; one of the most consistent fall coloring shrubs, seldom disappointing; colors as well in the midwest and south as it does in the eastern states; over the years I have seen a million(?) plants in fall color; interestingly, although clonal (or is it), variation in degree of red coloration is evident; a few nurserymen have selected for superior fall color and growth habit.

FLOWERS: Ornamentally unimportant, perfect, yellow-green, 3-flowered cyme, May to early June, early April in Athens.

FRUIT: A 1/4 to 1/3″ long capsule, red, September through late fall, not particularly showy for fruits are borne under the foliage; seed is actually the ornamental part of fruit as it possesses an orange-red seed coat (aril) which is exposed when the capsule dehisces; by the time the leaves have fallen many of the fruits have also abscised thus minimizing the ornamental quality; effect may vary from year to year.

CULTURE: Easily transplanted balled and burlapped; very adaptable plant tolerating widely divergent soils; seems to do well in heavy shade and still develop good fall color; not tolerant of water logged soils, best growth is achieved in well-drained soils; pH adaptable; withstands heavy pruning; shows stress in droughty soils; root system is quite fibrous and develops a mass of roots at the soil surface; ideally should be watered and/or mulched in hot, dry situations.

DISEASES AND INSECTS: None serious; does not contract scale; have seen a leaf anthracnose in the south especially on container-grown plants that were overhead watered.

LANDSCAPE VALUE: Unlimited and, therefore, overused; excellent for hedging, in groups, as a specimen plant, borders, screening, massing; plants used near water are very effective in the fall where the brilliant red foliage color is reflected off the water; makes an excellent foundation plant because of horizontal lines, clean foliage, and interesting stem characters; still one of the finest landscape plants for American gardens and new selections add some diversity to the typical form; in early November I chanced upon a spectacular hedge in flaming fall color at Hershey Gardens, Hershey, PA; the air was cool, the sunlight rich, the bluegrass green, the sky blue and the hedge rich almost fluorescent red...a sight to behold.

CULTIVARS:

'Angelica'—Almost twice as dense and compact as the species with vibrant red fall color.

'Compactus'—Corky wings not as pronounced, sometimes almost absent, appears to be a variable trait; branches more slender and more densely borne, overall rounded outline, 10', definitely not a small diminutive form; makes an excellent hedge or screen without pruning; not as hardy as the species, will be injured in severe (–25°F) winters.

'Nordine Strain'—Named after Mr. Roy Nordine, former propagator, Morton Arboretum; selected from seedlings of the Korean strain; more compact than species and branches close to the ground; also more fruitful; considerably hardier than 'Compactus'.

'October Glory'—A bushy, compact, 6 to 8' high form of *E. alatus* with brilliant red fall color. A Princeton introduction.

'Rudy Haag'—A more compact form than 'Compactus' with pinkish red fall color; 15 year-old plants being 4 to 5' high and wide; Bernheim Arboretum has a fine planting of this selection; no doubt will become extremely popular with exposure. In the last edition I commented about the potential for this plant and several nurserymen are starting to produce large numbers; Mr. Don Shadow, who is usually ahead of the pack with "new" plants has significant production of this form; my opinion has not changed about this cultivar, it will become a dominant plant in the market place.

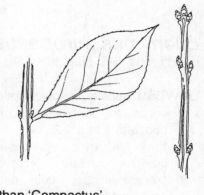

PROPAGATION: Seeds should be cleaned and provided 1 to 3 months cold moist stratification; cuttings, anytime in leaf, 1000 ppm to 3000 ppm IBA-quick dip; I have had 100% success every time with 'Compactus' and 'Rudy Haag'; the plant develops a deep bud rest and cannot practically be induced to grow by anything but cold treatment; I have found 90 to 120 days at 40°F sufficient to induce bud break of terminal and lateral buds; any time period less than this has resulted in only terminal bud growth or no growth; would be a good plant to experiment with for inducing continuous growth as it grows slowly and in short flushes; interestingly, hardwood cuttings did not root, in fact, no callus was evident.

NATIVE HABITAT: Northeastern Asia to central China. Introduced about 1860.

Euonymus americanus — American Euonymus, Strawberry-bush
(ū-on'i-mus a̍-mer-i-kā'nus)

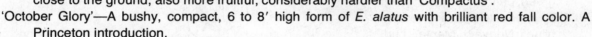

LEAVES: Opposite, simple, lance-ovate to lanceolate, 1 1/2 to 3 1/2" long, 1/3 to 1 1/4" wide, acuminate, cuneate, glabrous, crenate-serrate, flat medium green, turning yellow-green in fall; petiole—1/12" long.

Euonymus americanus, Strawberry-bush, will never take the place of its aristocratic brother, *E. alatus,* but in fruit elicits tremendous interest and for that reason is given ink in this book. It is a most obscure plant until September–October when the warty, scarlet capsules open to display scarlet seeds. One of its common names, "Hearts-a-Burstin", is derived from this character. Strawberry-bush is a loose, suckering, 4 to 6' high, green-stemmed shrub that resides in the shadows of the forest giants. The 1/3" diameter, greenish purple, 5-petaled (unusual for *Euonymus,* usually 4-petaled) flowers appear singly or in threes in summer. The 1/2 to 3/4" diameter fruits follow. Nice plant for naturalazing. A plant in heavy fruit is beautiful. I am amazed that a native plant tucked away in the recesses of a remote forest can be infected by *Euonymus* scale. This species is particularly susceptible and garden worthiness may be questionable. Native from New York south to Florida and west to Texas. Introduced 1697. Zone 5(6) to 9.

Euonymus europaeus — European Euonymus
(ū-on'i-mus ū-rō-pē'us)

LEAVES: Opposite, simple, elliptic-ovate to lance-oblong to obovate, 1 to 3 1/2″ long, 1/3 to 1 1/4″ wide, acuminate, crenate, cuneate, glabrous, crenate-serrate, dull dark green; petiole 1/4 to 1/2″ long.

BUDS: Imbricate, plump, resembling Norway Maple bud, greenish often tinged with red.

STEM: Slender, green-red, glabrous the first year, usually becoming light gray-brown the second.

FRUIT: Capsule, 4 lobed, 1/2 to 3/4″ wide, pink to red, seed white, aril orange.

SIZE: 12 to 30′ high and 10 to 25′ wide.
HARDINESS: Zone 3 to 7, doubtfully suited for the south.
HABIT: Narrow upright shrub or tree when young, broadening with age, taller than broad at maturity, usually rounded in outline at maturity.
RATE: Medium to fast.
TEXTURE: Medium in leaf and winter.
LEAF COLOR: Dull dark green in summer; fall color varies from yellow-green to yellow to a good reddish purple; one of the first plants to leaf out in spring, early April in Urbana, IL.
FLOWERS: Perfect, 4-petaled, yellowish green, 1/2″ across, May, 3 to 5 flowered, 1 to 1 1/2″ long cyme, not showy.
FRUIT: Dehiscent capsule, 1/2 to 3/4″ across, of pink to red color, 4-lobed, opening to expose orange seeds; September into November; quite attractive in fruit.
CULTURE: Transplant balled and burlapped; tolerant of moist soils as long as they are well-drained; pH adaptable; full sun or partial shade; very tough and tolerant.
DISEASES AND INSECTS: See under *E. fortunei;* the most significant problem is scale and all the tree species on the Illinois campus were affected; timing of spray application is very important in the control of scale; should be applied when the young crawlers are moving about; based on a great number of observations I do not believe there is a tree *Euonymus* that is not susceptible to scale; I have seen entire collections in arboreta and botanical gardens that were laden with the insects; the whitish scales infest the leaves, stems and older trunks and even the fruits; if not controlled they can devastate a planting; I hesitate to recommend these susceptible types because of the scale problem.
LANDSCAPE VALUE: All of the tree *Euonymus* can be used in groupings, screens and massings; they do not make good specimens simply because of lack of ornamental characters; their flowers are not showy and the principle landscape value resides in the fruits.
CULTIVARS:
'Albus' or var. *albus*—Fruit white; does not produce the rich effect of the species but is very striking in contrast with it.
'Aldenhamensis'—Brilliant, large pink capsule borne on longer, more pendulous stalks than the species; more fruitful than the species; appeared sometime before 1922.
var. *intermedius*—A heavy fruiter with bright red capsules; supposedly enormous crops of fruits.

'Nana'—Compact form, 2 1/2 by 2' after 8 years from a rooted cutting, more tender than the species, flowers and fruit have not been observed.

'Red Cascade'—A free-fruiting form, there is a cultivar called 'Red Caps' which, according to several individuals in the midwest, has proven the best of the tree *Euonymus;* rosy red capsules with orange seeds occur in abundance, whether 'Red Caps' and 'Red Cascade' are synonyms for the same plant is not known by this author; Wyman noted that the color of the fruit may vary slightly, but when viewed from a distance there is little to choose among them, unless one is very particular about the exact shade of red or pink color in the fruits.

PROPAGATION: Seed should be stratified at 68 to 77°F for 60 to 90 days followed by 32 to 50°F for 60 to 120 days; cuttings should be taken in June and July and treated with IBA.

NATIVE HABITAT: Europe to western Asia. Escaped from cultivation in the United States.

RELATED SPECIES:

Euonymus atropurpureus—Eastern Wahoo
(ū-on'i-mus at-rō-pêr-pū'rē-us)

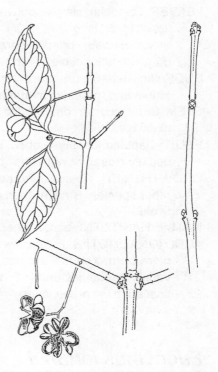

LEAVES: Opposite, simple, elliptic to ovate-elliptic, 1 1/2 to 5″ long, 3/4 to 2 1/4″ wide, acuminate, serrulate, dark green, pubescent beneath; petiole 1/3 to 2/3″ long.

BUDS: Small, green tinged red, appressed, with 5 to 6 scales.

STEM: Slender, greenish, glabrous, usually more or less (mostly less) 4-angled, often with slight corky lines.

FLOWERS: Dark purple, 4-petaled, 1/3″ diameter, June–July, in 7 to 15-flowered in 2 to 3 times branched cymes.

FRUIT: Smooth capsule, deeply 4-lobed, crimson, glabrous, seed brown with scarlet aril; attractive in fruit.

GROWTH HABIT: Large shrub or small tree with wide, flat-topped, irregular crown, 12 to 24′ high; seldom seen in gardens.

NATIVE HABITAT: New York to Florida, west to Minnesota, Nebraska, Oklahoma and Texas. Introduced 1756. Zone 4 to 9.

Euonymus bungeanus—Winterberry Euonymus
(ū-on'i-mus bun-jē-ā'nus)

LEAVES: Opposite to subopposite, simple, elliptic-ovate to elliptic-lanceolate, 2 to 4″ long, 3/4 to 1 3/4″ wide, long acuminate, broad-cuneate at base, serrulate, glabrous, light to medium green; petiole 1/3 to 1″ long.

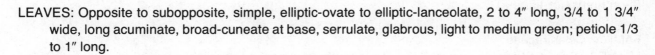

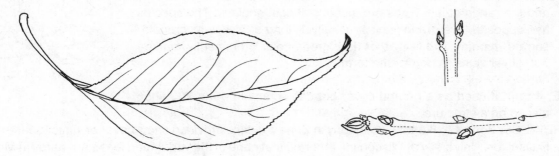

BUDS: Terminal (unique), outer bud scales upright creating a stockade-like appearance around meristem; lateral-imbricate, appressed, green-red-brown.

STEM: Slender, often weeping, greenish, glabrous, almost round, often with slight corky lines.

FLOWERS: Yellowish (green), 1/4″ diameter, anthers purple, produced in 1 to 2″ long cymes, 4-petaled, May, not showy.

FRUIT: Smooth capsule, deeply 4-lobed, yellowish to pinkish white, seeds white, seeds white or pinkish with orange aril, usually open at apex; is beautiful in fruit but unfortunately very susceptible to scale.

GROWTH HABIT: Rounded small shrub or tree with pendulous branches to 18 to 24′ in height. During my Illinois years, I watched a particularly fine specimen slowly deteriorate due to scale infestation. In rich pink fruit the tree was handsome.

NATIVE HABITAT: Northern China and Manchuria. Introduced 1883. Zone 4. Variety *semipersistens* has leaves and fruits which remain late in fall; var. *pendulus* has weeping branchlets.

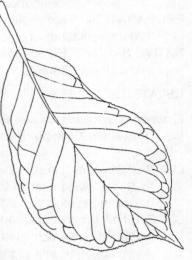

Euonymus hamiltonianus var. *sieboldianus*—Yeddo Euonymus
(ū-on′i-mus ham-il-tō-nē-a′nus sē-bol-dē-a′nus)
(Euonymus yedoensis)

LEAVES: Opposite, simple, obovate to obovate-oblong, sometimes elliptic, 2 to 5″ long and 1 3/4 to 2 1/2″ broad, abruptly acuminate, broad-cuneate, crenate-serrulate, dark green in summer, reddish purple in fall; petiole 1/4 to 1/2″ long.

BUDS: Similar to *E. europaeus;* terminal bud looks something like Norway Maple bud, greenish in summer, purplish in winter.

STEM: Stout, coarse compared to other shrub-tree species, greenish red, glabrous.

FRUIT: Capsule, deeply 4-lobed, pinkish purple, aril orange, seed white, usually closed or with small opening.

GROWTH HABIT: Coarse textured small tree or shrub, much coarser than other species. Smaller than other shrub-tree species, 10 to 15′ high. Tremendously susceptible to scale.

NATIVE HABITAT: Japan, Korea. Introduced 1865. Zone 4.

ADDITIONAL NOTES: *E. hamiltonianus* is confused and the available literature does not make things any more clear. Yeddo Euonymus appears as described above, as its own species, *E. yedoensis,* or the variety *yedoensis* under *E. hamiltonianus*. It can be rather attractive especially in fall but the scale susceptibility prevents any recommendation for garden use unless one is willing to spray at regular intervals.

Euonymus fortunei — Wintercreeper Euonymus
(ū-on′i-mus fôr-tū′nē-ī)

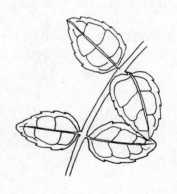

FAMILY: Celastraceae

LEAVES: This is a variable species because it sports (mutates) so readily and the range of leaf types produced is almost endless. The species has opposite, evergreen leaves, usually 1″ long or less, with crenate-serrate margins and leaves of dark green color prominently marked with silver veins. A nonfruiting form.

SIZE: 4 to 6″ if used as a ground cover but can scramble 40 to 70′ when placed on a structure.

HARDINESS: Zone 4 to 8 and 9; not happy in Zone 4 unless provided snow cover or winter shade; Dr. Ed Hasselkus, University of Wisconsin, reported that none of the variegated forms are hardy in Madison, WI.

HABIT: Evergreen ground cover or high climbing, true clinging vine; many of the adult types make 1 1/2 to 3′ mounding woody evergreen shrubs.

RATE: Fast.

TEXTURE: Medium-fine to medium depending on cultivar.

LEAF COLOR: Depends on cultivar but the species as I interpret it has small leaves less than 1″ long, the leaves are dark green almost bluish green with silver-nerved veins; the morphology changes considerably from the juvenile to the adult forms.

FLOWERS: Only on adult types; perfect, greenish white, 4-parted, June–July, axillary cymes; not particularly showy.

FRUIT: Dehiscent capsule 1/3″ diameter usually with a pinkish to reddish color which opens to expose the seeds which have an orange aril (fleshy seed coat), October–November and often persisting.

CULTURE: Extremely easy to culture, transplants readily; tolerant of most soils except swampy, extremely wet conditions; tolerates full sun and heavy shade; pH adaptable.

DISEASES AND INSECTS: Anthracnose, crown gall (bacterial disease of considerable importance), leaf spots, powdery mildews, aphids, thrips, and scales (these have proved lethal on many plantings especially those containing 'Vegetus', 'Coloratus', and the tree species such as *E. europaeus*, *E. bungeanus* and *E. hamiltonianus* var. *sieboldianus*); many plantings have been ruined by scale.

LANDSCAPE VALUE: Multitudinous depending on cultivar; ground cover, vine, wall cover, low hedge, massing and groupings; tremendous variation occurs as a result of vegetative mutations; I have remained silent through three editions and cannot restrain myself in this, the fourth; the number of variegated cultivars has exceeded the wildest imaginations of a rock star; yellow margins are thick, thin, yellow blotches occur on the inside and entire leaves are yellow; from 17′ away they all look the same; whenever I think of yellow *E. fortunei* my mind drifts to a particularly oppressive and depressing mass planting at Western Electric off I-85 heading to Atlanta; a yellow piece of plastic on the bank would have been as effective; an occasional plant for spot color in a border or rock garden is acceptable; some Atlanta landscapers are having second thoughts about wholesale use because of decline in heavy wet soils.

CULTIVARS:

'Acutus'—A rapidly growing dark green foliaged form that is relatively prostrate; may be more than one clone of this in the trade.

'Andy'—Described as a var. *carrieri* selection; slow growing shrub with large green leaves with white margins that turn rosy pink in cold weather, a Weston Nursery introduction.

'Azusa'—Ground cover type with prostrate branches, small dark green leaves with lighter colored veins; underside of foliage turns intense maroon in winter.

'Berryhillii'—Upright form with leaves 1 1/2 to 2″ long; 5-year-old plants are 2 1/2′ tall, definitely upright, and the leaves are evergreen, plant at Arnold was 7 to 8′ high and 6′ wide, looks like it might have some *E. kiautschovicus* blood based on leaf shape and growth habit.

'Canadale Gold'—Large light green leaves are bordered with golden yellow, the color is deeper on new growth; forms a sturdy compact plant; variegation is substantial.

'Canadian Variegated'—Forms an 18″ by 3′ compact shrub with small waxy green leaves strikingly edged in white; this is probably the same as 'Harlequin'.

'Carrierei'—Semi-shrub form or climbing if supported, leaves glossy deep green about 2″ long; fruiting freely; adult state of var. *radicans,* may grow 6 to 8′; also listed as var. *carrierei,* flowers 4-parted, 5 or more at end of a slender stalk (cyme), fruit 1/3″ across, green with red tinge, seed with a yellow-orange aril.

var. *coloratus* (often listed as 'Coloratus')— Vigorous ground cover form, foliage is a deep glossy green and turns plum-purple in the winter; there seem to be several clones in the nursery trade; some clones do not develop the good plum-purple color on both leaf surfaces, while others show excellent color over the entire plant; have observed more scale on this, especially in south, in recent years.

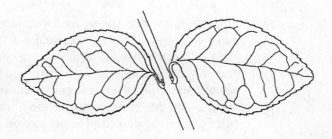

Leaves: Without the prominent venation, usually lustrous dark green, 1 to 2″ long, changing to purple during the winter; this variety is variable for often the underside of the leaf is purple and the upper portion green; usually nonfruiting; supposedly introduced to the U.S. from Japan in 1914.

'Dart's Blanket'—A relative newcomer in America, found in Holland; thick, waxy, 1 to 2″ long dark green leaves; supposedly displays excellent salt tolerance; use as a ground cover near the ocean or where deicing salts present a problem; tends to be wide spreading and grows to 16″ in height; the leaves become bronzed in autumn and purplish red beneath; a juvenile form first distributed in 1969, considered an improvement on 'Coloratus'; also 'Dart's Carpet,' 'Dart's Dab,' and 'Dart's Ideal' have been described.

'Emerald Beauty'—Grows 6′, spreads 8 to 10′ and bears abundant pink capsules with orange seeds.

'Emerald Charm'—Shrub of erect habit to 3′; leaves broad elliptic, glossy green on both surfaces; fruits yellowish white with orange seed coats; adult form introduced by Corliss Brothers, Ipswich, MA.

'Emerald Cushion'—Dwarf mounded form, dense branching habit, holds rich green foliage, 12″ by 18″.

'Emerald Delight'—Possesses the largest leaves of any of the Emerald series, and some of the richest foliage color on any broadleaf evergreen; leaves emerge light green edged with yellow; later becoming intense green with creamy borders; a vigorous spreading plant, distributed by Conard-Pyle.

'Emerald Gaiety'—Small, erect form of dense branching habit, distinguished by the pronounced irregular white margin on the deep green, 3/4 to 1 3/4″ diameter, rounded leaves, margin becomes pink tinged in winter, 4 to 5′; will climb if planted next to a structure.

'Emerald 'n Gold'—Low growing, tight branching habit, 1 1/2 to 2′ high (have seen larger); foliage dark glossy green with yellow margins, 1 to 1 1/2″ long, leaves turn pink-red in cold weather.

'Emerald Leader'—Similar to 'Emerald Beauty' in fruitfulness but grows to 5′ with a 30″ spread.

'Emerald Pride'—Small, erect form with lustrous dark green foliage and a close branching habit, 4 to 5′, spreading 42″.

'Emerald Surprise'—An unusual foliage mixture of green, gold and creamy white on an upright branched shrub, introduced by Conard Pyle.

'Erecta'—Often a catchall term for upright woody forms of the species.

'Gold Spot'—Dark green foliage with bright gold centers; upright and stronger growing than most forms; could this be the same as 'Sun Spot', simply a rename?

'Gold Tip'—Leaves edged with gold, aging to creamy white; may also appear under the name 'Gold Prince'.

'Gold Prince'—Vigorous, mounded form with new foliage tipped a bright gold; older leaves turn solid green; considered hardiest of all variegated *Euonymus fortunei* types; grows to 2′ and more; handsome foliage.

'Gracilis'—Used to designate a group of variable and inconstant forms which possess variegated white or yellow or pink foliage.

'Green Lane'—A better green foliage form and not as upright growing as 'Sarcoxie', will mature about 4′ by 4 to 6′; thick lustrous dark green leaves do not (supposedly) windburn and remain vibrant year-round, it develops pinkish fruits with orange seeds, considered superior to 'Sarcoxie' and 'Vegetus'.

'Ivory Jade'—Large rich green leaf with ivory margin; white portion develops pink color in cold weather; grows 2′ high and develops a low spreading habit.

'Kewensis'—Dainty prostrate form with leaves about 1/4″ to 5/8″ long, 1/8 to 1/4″ in width; forms low mat only several inches high; if allowed to climb a tree it develops the *radicans* character and flowers and fruits; the basal portion however retains the 'Kewensis' characteristics.

'Longwood'—Another good, small leaved form collected on Mt. Tsukuba, Japan; survived −25°F and 106°F; more vigorous and larger leaved than 'Kewensis' or 'Minimus'.

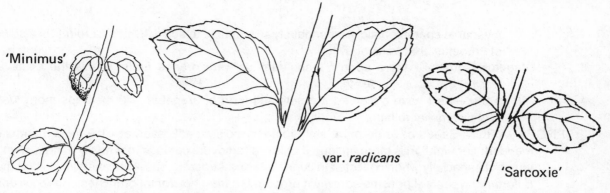

'Minimus'

var. *radicans*

'Sarcoxie'

'Minimus'—Low growing form with leaves 1/4 to 1/2″ long; a plant in my Georgia garden is performing well; shows excellent vigor and good heat tolerance; in overall effect a large-leaved form of 'Kewensis'; distributed by Simon-Louis Fréres in 1912.

var. *radicans*—Intermediate form trailing or climbing, fruiting, leaves ovate or broad-elliptic to elliptic, 1 1/2 to 2″ long, acute or obtusish, distinctly serrate, of thicker texture, veins obsolete; this variety represents an intermediate stage between the species and the 'Vegetus' type; trailing or climbing in habit forming woody stems and exhibiting sporadic flowering and fruiting; leaves are shiny medium to dark green and wavy in appearance; very unstable and numerous variegated branch sports can be found on a large plant.

'Sarcoxie'—Upright form to 4′(6′) with glossy 1″ long leaves; polished dark green leaves are partially whitish veined; genuinely confused in the nursery trade; I have seen many clones that were named 'Sarcoxie' but each differed in various characteristics; I have seen heavy fruit crops on this form (white tinged pink); raised by Sarcoxie Nursery, Missouri in 1950.

'Sheridan Gold'—Deep green foliage has sunshine yellow coloring in a full sun situation, color supposedly richer than most golden forms, leaves variable being greenish yellow, spotted yellow or completely yellow; forms a densely branched, mounded, 20″ high shrub.

'Silver Gem'—Leaves like 'Silver Queen' but smaller with a white border and reddish speckles, strong climbing shrub to 6′.

'Silver Queen'—An old name attached to a low, shrubby type with metallic dark green leaves with creamy yellow margins on new growth, finally cream-white margins; again have seen several descriptions; probably a sport var. *radicans* or *carrierei;* may fruit.

'Sparkle 'n Gold'—Branch sport with large leaves with a dark green center and broad borders of brilliant gold, it is a mounded form growing 12 to 18″ (36″) tall and twice as wide, advertised as having the brightest gold of any *E. fortunei* type; somebody has to be fibbing because the hype that accompanies every new gold leaved introduction says the same thing.

'Sun Spot'—Rounded, compact, shapely form (3′ by 6′) with good winter hardiness; thick green leaves with pronounced yellow centers; the leaves inside the plant being of the same variegated pattern as the leaves at the stem tips; margin is a dark green.

'Sunshine'—The leaves are bordered with bold gold margins, the center is gray-green; reasonably fast grower.

'Variegatus'—Perhaps another catchall term for variegated types of var. *radicans;* I have observed so many variegated sports on the adult form of *E. fortunei* that the reasons for the multitude of named color sports becomes immediately evident; I have collected variegated shoots from a plant in Spring Grove and rooted them; I also had the good sense not to name them; this form as well as some of the others are unstable and will revert to any number of color combinations (albino to green); is about the same taxonomic status as 'Gracilis'.

'Vegetus'—Somewhat similar to var. *radicans;* however, a heavy fruiting form; the leaves are medium green without the venation and of a more rounded, thick nature; actually the super-adult form; an upright shrub to 4 to 5′ or a true clinging vine if trained; leaves are broad-elliptic to nearly suborbicular, 1 to 2″ long, acute or obtusish, crenate-serrate, dull green to medium-green; fruiting freely, however, this is

a variable characteristic, tremendously susceptible to scale; 'Dart's Cardinal' is a selected form of 'Vegetus' that fruits heavily.

'Vegetus Cardinal'—More upright than 'Vegetus' with orange fruits; is this the same as 'Dart's Cardinal'?

'Woodland'—As I have observed it a selected form of 'Vegetus' with perhaps more lustrous and slightly smaller foliage.

PROPAGATION: Seeds have dormant embryos and moist stratification at 41°F for 3 months is recommended; germination is more uniform if arils are removed; cuttings root easily almost any time of the year but especially when collected in June, July and August. It should be mentioned that many of the *E. fortunei* types will become sprawly if propagated from horizontal branches and more upright from vertical leaders.

ADDITIONAL NOTES: *Euonymus fortunei* behaves similar to *Hedera helix*; the juvenile form is non-flowering and of different leaf morphology; the adult form flowers and fruits and shows great variation in leaf morphology; in Spring Grove, I have noticed plants on trees that have every imaginable shape and some branches produce variegated sports; I have rooted cuttings of these variegated plants; someone needs to stop introducing new cultivars and straighten out the confusion that now exists; I recommend selecting the 5 or 6 best and leaving it go at those.

NATIVE HABITAT: China. Introduced 1907.

Euonymus japonicus — Japanese Euonymus
(ū-on'i-mus ja-pon'i-kus)

LEAVES: Opposite, simple, evergreen, obovate to narrowly oval, 1 to 3″ long, 3/4 to 1 3/4″ wide, lustrous dark green, leathery, glabrous, tapered at base, blunt or rounded at apex, serrated except at base; petiole 1/4 to 1/2″ long.

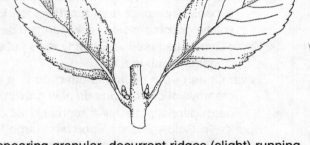

BUDS: Typically *Euonymus;* imbricate, conical, 6 to 8-scaled, green with edges of scales tinged red in winter, glabrous, 1/4″ long; terminal—similar but larger.

STEM: Stout, somewhat squarish, green, glabrous, appearing granular, decurrent ridges (slight) running from sides of leaf scar to next node, small brownish-black glandular dot on either side of petiole at point of attachment to stem, nodes somewhat flattened; emit boxelder-like odor when bruised; pith—green.

SIZE: 10 to 15′ high, about 1/2 that in width, supposedly can grow to 25′ but I have seen nothing approaching that in the U.S., 5 to 10′ is more common under landscape conditions; saw a particularly nice tree form in CA.

HARDINESS: Zone 7 to 9; severely injured at –3°F in Athens area; leaves killed but buds produced new leaves in spring; variegated types are more tender than the species.

HABIT: Very dense oval shrub when growing in full sun; more open in shade.

RATE: Medium to fast.

TEXTURE: Medium.

LEAF COLOR: Lustrous waxy dark green.

FLOWERS: Perfect, greenish white, 4-petaled, 1/3″ diameter, borne in 5 to 12 flowered, stalked cymes, June.

FRUIT: Four-valved, 1/3″ diameter, pinkish capsule, orange aril, late summer, early fall, not usually effective.

CULTURE: Easily transplanted, adaptable to varied soils; appear to do well in Piedmont clays of Georgia; withstands salt spray; full sun to heavy shade; withstands heavy pruning; more widely used in Europe especially in coastal areas; over the years I have walked the cities of Hastings, Eastbourne, and

Brighton in England and have observed the plant fully exposed to maritime conditions; appears about as salt tolerant as any broadleaf evergreen.

DISEASES AND INSECTS: Crown gall, anthracnose, mildew, leaf spots, aphids, euonymus scale.

LANDSCAPE VALUE: Has lost favor in the south where it is most at home; excessively stiff in habit and prone to significant diseases; have not observed its use in many modern day landscapes; often a symbol of a hamburger establishment and used in great numbers in such locations; used as a houseplant.

CULTIVARS: Many, the variegated types will revert; excessive fertility tends to promote reversion.

'Albo-marginatus'—Leaves bordered with a slight margin of white.

'Aureus'—The bright yellow center bordered with green; often reverts to the type; stems are yellow, common in south but not worthy of use, have seen plants being stocked at a local chain store with 1/3 of the branches already green; may also be listed as 'Aureo-variegata' and 'Aureo-pictus'.

'Aureus'

'Grandifolia'—Large shiny green leaves and a compact tightly branched habit.

'Latifolius Albo-marginatus'—Broad oval leaves with a wide margin of white; more vigorous and probably better than 'Albo-marginatus'; center of leaf gray-green.

'Macrophyllus'—Larger leaves (green) than the type.

'Microphyllus'—A dwarf, small-leaved form with distinctly erect branches; leaves dark green, oval-lanceolate, 1/2 to 1″ long, 1/8 to 1/3″ wide, not as hardy as the type, grows 1 to 3′ high, has been used on the Georgia campus with success; is often a scale's best friend.

'Microphyllus Pulchellus'—Small leaves suffused with yellow.

'Microphyllus Variegatus'—like 'Microphyllus' except the waxy petite deep green leaves have white margins, not a plant for every landscape; from a distance it is difficult to discern whether the plant is sick or variegated.

'Ovatus Aureus'—Leaves oval or ovate with a broad irregular margin of rich yellow that suffuses into the green center.

'Silver King'—Large pale green leaves with creamy white margins; may be an American name for an older clone; upright grower.

Other cultivars are known but are doubtfully available in commerce.

PROPAGATION: Cuttings root easily.

NATIVE HABITAT: Japan, Introduced 1804.

Euonymus kiautschovicus — Spreading Euonymus
(ū-on′i-mus kī-atch-ov′i-cus)
(formerly *E. patens*)

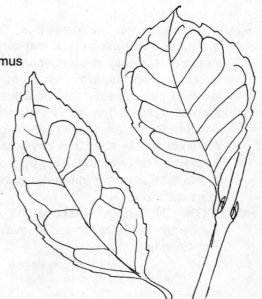

LEAVES: Opposite, simple, evergreen, semi-evergreen or deciduous, broad-elliptic or obovate to oblong-obovate or elliptic-oblong, 2 to 3″ long, 3/4 to 1 3/4″ wide, acute or obtuish, cuneate, crenate-serrulate, lustrous dark green, subcoriaceous with obsolete veins beneath; petiole 1/6 to 1/3″ long.

BUDS: Imbricate, conical, sharp pointed, greenish and often tinged with red in winter, perhaps becoming straw brown in winter.

STEM: Slender, green, rounded, not developing the straw-brown color until the second or third year.

Euonymus kiautschovicus, Spreading Euonymus, is a semi-evergreen (also evergreen or deciduous) shrub of rounded habit reaching 8 to 10′ in height; the foliage is a good dark green in summer but usually burns in winter and looks quite unkempt. Flowers are greenish white, 4-parted, 1/3″ diameter, and borne in loose, erect 1 1/2 to 4″ wide cymes in July–August; the flies and bees hover about this shrub when in flower and it is not a good plant for patio areas and like; fruit capsule is pink, seed coat is orange-red, matures in October–November; decent plant for informal hedges, screens, and massing; not as susceptible to scale as *E. fortunei* and tree types, but on the Georgia campus have seen heavy infestations on plants; the cultivars:

'Dupont'—Hybrid form with large leaves (2 1/2″) and vigorous growth habit; 4-year-old plants are 4′ tall, quite hardy; a somewhat confusing clone.

'Hobbs'—Good looking dense, mounded form with lustrous dark green leaves; have seen at Bernheim Arboretum.

'Manhattan'—Hybrid, excellent dark green glossy foliage form with leaves 2 1/2″ long and 1 1/4″ wide; has not proven particularly hardy and was killed to snowline in Illinois during rugged winters of 1976–77 and 77–78; will grow back rapidly; forms a rounded 4 to 6′ high evergreen shrub; easily rooted from cuttings; has a rather strange history and supposedly came out of Manhattan, KS from where the cultivar name is derived; have seen plants 8′ high and 12′ wide.

'Newport'—A form similar to 'Manhattan' but not as vigorous, flowers at same time as *E. kiautschovicus*; probably a hybrid.

'Paulii'—A glossy dark green leaved form, more upright than 'Manhattan' with greater hardiness; 5′ by 5′ at maturity; leaves leathery, broad-ovate to rounded; flowers ahead of *E. kiautschovicus*.

'Sieboldiana'—Supposedly with good foliage and not as suceptible to scale as other types, do not know origin but have seen it listed in a nursery catalog.

The cultivars are superior to the species. Native to eastern and central China. Introduced 1860. Zone 5 to 8.

Euonymus nanus var. *turkestanicus* — Dwarf Euonymus
(ū-on′i-mus nā′nus ter-ke-stan′i-kus)

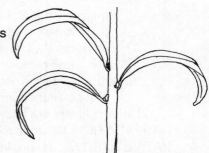

LEAVES: Alternate, whorled or occasionally opposite, simple, evergreen, semi-evergreen to deciduous, narrow-to-linear-oblong, 1 1/2 to 3″ long, 1/4 to 1/2″ broad, not revolute, bluish green.

Euonymus nanus var. *turkestanicus,* Dwarf Euonymus, is a small (3′) shrub with erect slender branches and leaves which may be alternate, opposite, or subopposite. The foliage is of a bluish green consistency in summer and changes to brilliant red tones in fall. The 4-petaled flowers are about 1/6″ across, brownish purple, and borne 1 to 3 on a slender stalk in May. The fruit is a 4-lobed, pink capsule; the seeds are brown and not wholly covered by the orange aril. The variety *turkestanicus* is the type in cultivation. The species is native from Caucasian Mountains to western China. Introduced 1830. Zone 2 to 6. This plant performed well in central Illinois and the fall color was brilliant. It is easily rooted from softwood cuttings treated with a quick-dip of 1000 ppm IBA. I have changed my opinion on this plant and doubt seriously whether anyone will take it into their hearts or gardens. Generally too straggly and unkempt to be given serious garden consideration.

ADDITIONAL NOTES: A good paper that anyone serious about *Euonymus* should read is "An account of *Euonymus* in cultivation and its availability in commerce." *The Plantsman* 3(3): 133–166, 1981, by Roy Lancaster.

Evodia daniellii — Korean Evodia
(ē-vō'di-a   dan-i-el'ē-i)

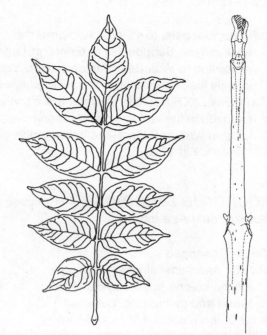

FAMILY: Rutaceae

LEAVES: Opposite, pinnately compound, 9 to 15″ long, leaflets (5)7 to 11, ovate to oblong-ovate, 2 to 5″ long, acuminate with obtusish point, rounded at base, sometimes broad-cuneate or subcordate, finely crenulate, lustrous dark green above and glabrous, pubescent below on the midrib and in the axils of the veins; petiole 1 1/2 to 2 1/2″ long.

BUDS: Solitary, sessile, ovoid, 1 pair of rather indistinct scales, terminal-puberulent, gray-brown; exposed and visible; differing from *Phellodendron* where the buds are hidden by the petiole base.

STEM: Round or somewhat 4-angled or wrinkled; pith— moderate, somewhat angular, firm, continuous; leaf scars broadly crescent-shaped, low; 3 bundle-traces.

SIZE: Will probably grow 25 to 30′ high under landscape conditions but can reach 50′; the spread is equal to or greater than the height.

HARDINESS: Zone 4 to 8; I have seen excellent specimens at the Morton Arboretum, Lisle, Illinois, which showed good vigor and abundant fruit; also a reasonably thrifty plant on the Georgia campus.

RATE: Medium to fast, especially in youth; seedlings which I grew in containers reached 5 to 6′ in a single growing season.

TEXTURE: Medium in leaf and in winter.

BARK: Older stems and branches develop a smooth gray appearance which is interrupted at irregular intervals by raised lenticels; reminds of beech bark.

LEAF COLOR: Dark lustrous green in summer; the foliage is quite free of pests and diseases and looks as good in August as it did when first maturing in May; fall color is of no consequence as the leaves usually drop green or yellowish green.

FLOWERS: Small, white, borne in 4 to 6″ broad, flattish corymbs on current season's growth in June, July–August; the flowers are borne in great quantities and provide quite a show when few other plants are in flower; bees love them.

FRUIT: Capsule, composed of 4 to 5 carpels which split from the top; red to black in color and effective in late August through November; the fruits are very effective from an ornamental standpoint; seeds are lustrous brownish black, about the size of buckshot.

CULTURE: I have found this species easy to transplant; seems to prefer a well drained, moist, fertile soil; pH adabtable; full sun; may be a bit tender when young and should be well sited and mulched; one authority noted that any soil is acceptable for culturing this plant.

DISEASES AND INSECTS: None of any consequence.

LANDSCAPE VALUE: A very interesting tree, but unfortunately little known and used; a lovely small tree which can be used in the small landscape; excellent summer foliage, flower, and fruit characters make this tree worthy of additional use; Wyman noted that the wood is comparatively weak and splits easily and the tree is short-lived (15 to 40 years); I have observed numerous Evodias through the midwest, east and south and have not noticed any serious problems; this tree might warrant a close look especially for urban areas.

PROPAGATION: Seeds which were sent from the Morris Arboretum, Philadelphia, were direct sowed and germinated almost 100 percent.

NATIVE HABITAT: Northern China, Korea. Introduced by E.H. Wilson in 1905.

RELATED SPECIES:

Evodia hupehensis, (ē-vō′di-a hoo-pe-en′sis), Hupeh Evodia, is closely allied to *E. daniellii* and may be an ecotype. Supposedly it differs in larger stalked leaflets and the longer beak of the fruit, but according to W.J. Bean the characters are not reliable. *E. hupehensis* can grow to 60′ and may be slightly less hardy than *E. daniellii*. Native to central China. Introduced 1907. Zone 5 to 8.

ADDITIONAL NOTES: The Evodias are closely allied to *Phellodendron* but differ in the buds which are exposed in the leaf axils rather than covered by the base of the petiole as in *Phellodendron*. *Evodia* is often written *Euodia* and this was the original spelling as rendered by the Forsters who founded the genus in 1776.

Exochorda racemosa — Common Pearlbush
(ek-sō-kôr′da ra-se-mō′sa)

FAMILY: Rosaceae

LEAVES: Alternate, simple, elliptic to elliptic-oblong or oblong-obovate, acute and mucronate, cuneate, 1 to 3″ long, about 1/2 as wide, entire or on vigorous shoots serrate above the middle, whitish beneath, glabrous.

BUDS: Moderate, solitary, sessile, ovoid, with about 10 more or less pointed and fringed scales.

STEM: Round, slender, brown, glabrous, roughened by lenticels and longitudinal fissures; pith—small, continuous, pale.

SIZE: 9 to 15′ by 10 to 15′.

HARDINESS: Zone 4 to 8; does extremely well in Zone 8.

HABIT: An upright, slender branched, loose, irregular shrub becoming floppy and often unkempt with age; often somewhat fountain-like in outline.

RATE: Medium.

TEXTURE: One of the earliest leafing shrubs and plants usually are in full leaf by early April (Athens, GA); medium in leaf, coarse in winter.

BARK: Old branches, 1 to 2″ diameter, develop a scaly bark of gray, brown and orange-brown combinations, rather attractive.

LEAF COLOR: Medium green in summer; no fall color of any consequence.

FLOWERS: Perfect, white, 5-petaled, 1 1/2″ across, odorless; (March, Athens) April–May (7 to 14 days); borne in 6 to 10 flowered, 3 to 5″ long racemes at ends of short lateral stems from branches of previous year, each expanding bud reminds of a pearl, excellent for floral effect as the entire end of a branch appears in flower.

FRUIT: Broad turbinate, 5-valved, dehiscent, 1/3″ wide capsule ripening in October and persisting, green to yellow-brown and finally rich brown.

CULTURE: Transplant balled and burlapped or as a container plant in early spring; prefers well-drained, acid, loamy soil; full sun or partial shade; prune after flowering; pH adaptable.

DISEASES AND INSECTS: None serious.

LANDSCAPE VALUE: Good for flower effect, probably should be reserved for the shrub border; can be spectacular in flower but soon fades into oblivion; does quite well in Athens-Atlanta areas and is in flower by late March to early April; the plant thrives with neglect and is amazingly tough considering the heat and drought that it takes in stride in the southeast.

PROPAGATION: Seeds will germinate sporadically when sown directly; a short stratification (30 to 60 days) improves germination; cuttings should be collected in June, July and August and treated with 3000 to 8000 ppm IBA talc or quick dip for best results; in general these recommendations apply to the species treated here.

NATIVE HABITAT: Eastern China. Introduced 1849.

RELATED SPECIES:

Exochorda giraldii, (ek-sō-kôr′da jir-al′dē-ī), Redbud Pearlbush, is closely allied and very similar to the above but less available. The young shoots are pinkish and the petioles and veins of mature leaves maintain this color through summer. The variety *wilsonii* has flowers 2″ across, and is more upright and floriferous. 'Irish Pearl' is a hybrid between *E. racemosa* × *E. g.* var. *wilsonii* with greater vigor; almost 2″ diameter pure white flowers, borne 8 to 10 on racemes; the entire flowering shoot 20 to 36″ long. Northwestern China. Introduced 1897. Zone 5.

Exochorda korolkowii—Turkestan Pearlbush

LEAVES: Alternate, simple, obovate, 1 1/2 to 3 1/2″ long, 3/4 to 1 1/2″ wide, acute or obtusish, mucronulate, toothed toward apex on vigorous shoots, dark green, glabrous; petiole—1/4 to 1/2″ long.

Exochorda korolkowii, (ek-sō-kôr′da kôr-ōl-kōw′-ē-ī), Turkestan Pearlbush, is a vigorous shrub (10 to 12′ high) much in the mold of *E. racemosa.* The pure white, 1 1/2″ diamter flowers occur in 3 to 4″ long erect racemes in April–May about the same time as the other Pearlbushes. In fact, I was evaluating the Pearlbush collection at the Arnold Arboretum on May 8, 1979 and could find few differences among the true species listed here. The only species that appeared inferior to the others was *E. serratifolia* which had poor flower quality. Turkestan. Introduced 1878. Zone 5.

Exochorda × macrantha (ek-sō-kôr′da mȧ-kran′tha) is a hybrid between *E. racemosa* and *E. korolkowii* and a shrub of great beauty producing a raceme of flowers from every bud of the previous year's growth. 'The Bride' grows only 3 to 4′ tall and is quite bushy. I have seen the plant in several gardens, and it is indeed compact and refined compared to the two species which grow 12 to 15′. It was raised by Messrs. Lemoine of Nancy about 1900. It produces a 3 to 4″ long, 6 to 10-flowered raceme, each flower 1 1/4″ diameter, from every bud of the previous year's growth.

ADDITIONAL NOTES: Pearlbushes will never take over the horticultural world but they are rather pretty, trouble free shrubs. The finest specimen I have observed is located at Mt. Auburn Cemetery, Cambridge, MA. It is about 18′ high and 22 to 25′ wide. The larger Pearlbushes might be trained as a small tree. In Illinois after a particularly devasting ice storm I noticed several large broken branches.

Fagus grandifolia — American Beech
(fā′gus gran-di-fō′li-ȧ)

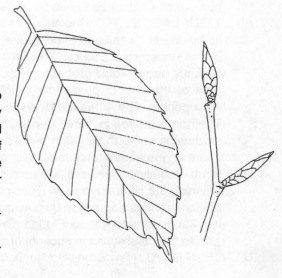

FAMILY: Fagaceae

LEAVES: Alternate, simple, ovate-oblong, 2 to 5″ long, 3/4 to 2 1/2″ wide, acuminate, broad-cuneate at base, coarsely serrate, glossy dark green above and light green and usually glabrous below or with tufts of hairs in the axils of the veins and along the midrib, silky when unfolding; more veins than *F. sylvatica* (11 to 15 pairs); petiole 1/4″ or longer.

BUDS: Imbricate, slender, 3/4 to 1″ long, brown, apex sharp-pointed.

STEM: Slender, somewhat zigzag, smooth, shining, silver-gray especially on older stems.

SIZE: 50 to 70′ in height with a maximum of 100 to 120′; spread is usually less than or equal to the height, although many specimens especially those in forest stands assume an upright-oval shape.

HARDINESS: Zone 3 to 9.

HABIT: A sturdy, imposing tree often with a short trunk and wide spreading crown, a picture of character in a native situation.

RATE: Slow, possibly medium in youth, averaging 9 to 12′ over a 10 year period.

TEXTURE: Medium throughout the season.

BARK: Thin, smooth, light bluish gray almost silvery on young stems; similar on mature trees but darker.

LEAF COLOR: Silvery green when opening, gradually changing to dark green in summer; fall color is a beautiful golden bronze and the leaves (especially on the lower portion of the tree) often persist into winter.

FLOWERS: Monoecious; male and female separate on the same tree; male in globose heads; pistillate in 2- to 4-flowered spikes, however, sometimes at base of staminate inflorescence; usually flowers in April to early May.

FRUIT: Three-winged nut, solitary or 2 to 3, partly or wholly enclosed by a prickly involucre about 3/4″ long, the prickles recurved; nut is edible.

CULTURE: Transplant balled and burlapped in spring; moist, well-drained, acid (pH 5.0 to 6.5) soil is preferable; will not withstand wet or compacted soils; soils with oxygen concentrations of less than 10 to 15% are not suitable; root system is shallow and it is difficult to grow grass under this tree; does best in full sun although withstands shade; prune in summer or early fall.

DISEASES AND INSECTS: The following problems have been reported but are not particularly serious; leaf spots, powdery mildew, bleeding canker, leaf mottle, beech bark disease, cankers, aphids, brown wood borer, beech scale, two-lined chestnut borer and caterpillars.

LANDSCAPE VALUE: Beautiful native tree; restricted to large area use; beautiful in parks, golf courses, and other large areas; a beech forest is worth viewing especially in early spring and again in fall; the boat has been missed as far as the use of this tree in the landscape; young trees can be moved successfully and will establish and prosper; I have seen examples in the southeast of American Beech and European Beech, planted at the same time, the American Beech outgrows and out-performs the European species; American Beech is more amenable to culture in Zones 7 through 9 than the European; unfortunately, no named selections of American Beech exist while the European has numerous; in a sense, a beech is planted for posterity and my children and yours will enjoy its grandeur.

PROPAGATION: Seed, 41°F for 90 days in moist sand; I have opened numerous prickly involucres only to be disappointed by shriveled and hollow seeds; according to several references large crops of seed may occur at 2- to 3-year or longer intervals; their germination rate is high, usually approaching 95 percent; American Beech shows a propensity to sucker from the roots and small trees often occur in the vicinity of mature specimens; beech would obviously seed naturally but the predominant number of small trees I have observed, especially in native stands, appear to be root sprouts.

ADDITIONAL NOTES: F.B. Robinson has termed the beech "The Beau Brummel of trees but clannish and fastidious as to soil and atmosphere, magnificent specimen casting a dense shade which does not permit undergrowth." J.U. Crockett noted, "If the word noble had to be applied to only one kind of tree, the honor would probably go the beech." The nuts were once fed to swine and were a favorite food of the extinct passenger pigeon, squirrels, blue jays, titmice, grosbeaks, nuthatches and woodpecker. The American Beech is a variable species and there are at least three different races. The northern type is "Gray Beech" found from Nova Scotia to the Great Lakes, and on the higher mountains of North Carolina and Tennessee, mainly on neutral to alkaline soils. "White Beech" is found on the southern coastal plain and northward on poorly drained acid sites. Between these two forms, mainly on well-drained acid sites and mixing with them is "Red Beech." These races are anything but clear-cut and all types of intermediate forms occur. I like to think of American Beech as one contiguous population displaying the "typical" species characteristics that allow one to identify it in Minnesota as well as Florida. On the other hand, there are differences of a trivial nature much akin to the differences in accents of people from Boston and Atlanta.

NATIVE HABITAT: New Brunswick to Ontario, south to Florida and Texas. Introduced 1800.

Fagus sylvatica — European Beech
(fā′gus sil-vat′i-ka)

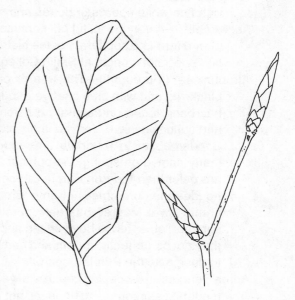

LEAVES: Alternate, simple, 2 to 4″ long, 1 1/2 to 2 1/2″ wide, may be 5″ by 3″, ovate or elliptic, acute, broad-cuneate or rounded at base, undulate, entire or obscurely toothed, lustrous dark green above, light green beneath, glabrous at maturity, silky and ciliate when young; 5 to 9 vein pairs; petiole 1/4 to 1/2″ long, downy.

BUDS: Similar to *F. grandifolia.*

STEM: Similar, except olive-brown in color.

GROWTH HABIT: Tends to branch close to ground; dense, upright, oval character when young.

SIZE: 50 to 60′ in height with a spread of 35 to 45′; can reach 100′ in height.

HARDINESS: Zone 4 to 7; does not do well in extreme heat.

HABIT: Densely pyramidal to oval or rounded, branching to the ground; very formal (stately) in outline.

RATE: Slow to medium, 9 to 12′ over a 10 year period; an English reference noted 35′ in 20 years, much slower growing in the south.

TEXTURE: Actually fine when first leafing out, otherwise of medium texture in full foliage and winter.

BARK: Smooth, gray, usually darker than the American Beech; developing an elephant hide appearance on old trunks; a beauty unmatched by the bark of other trees.

LEAF COLOR: When unfolding a tender shimmering green unmatched by any other tree gradually changing to lustrous dark green in summer followed by rich russet and golden bronze colors in fall; the leaves are slow to emerge and do not fully develop until sometime in May.

FLOWERS: Essentially as described for American Beech.

FRUITS: Nuts triangular, 5/8″ long, usually 2 enclosed in 3/4 to 1″ long, hard, woody, four lobed husk covered with bristles, borne singly on an erect pubescent pedicel.

CULTURE: More tolerant of soils than American Beech but otherwise requirements are comparable.

DISEASES AND INSECTS: Some bark disease problems.

LANDSCAPE VALUE: There is no finer specimen tree; so beautiful that it overwhelms one at first glance, excellent for public areas, also makes an excellent hedge for it withstands heavy pruning; the cultivars are especially beautiful and at least one will blend into every landscape; my favorites are 'Asplenifolia', 'Fastigiata', 'Pendula', and 'Riversii'.

CULTIVARS: There are a great number of cultivars which have developed in the wild and under cultivation. The European Beech is one of my great plant loves and in this edition I have expanded the list of cultivars based on the literature and my observations. Many of these are not available in this country and perhaps have even been lost to cultivation. It is interesting that no named cultivars have arisen from the American Beech considering the tremendous number that have occurred within the concept of the species, *Fagus sylvatica.* Had an opportunity to tromp around Germany with Dr. J.C. Raulston and made an attempt to look at every beech that crossed my path. Also at Trompenburg Arboretum in Rotterdam have seen a tremendous collection of unusual cultivars. This revised listing reflects my most recent observations.

'Albo-variegata'—Leaves smaller than the type, margin coarser and irregularly undulate, streaked irregularly with yellowish white; the term f. *albo-variegata* is used to represent leaves blotched and striped with white; saw several different forms of this, some apparently more stable than others; only for the collector.

'Ansorgei'—Leaves narrow lanceolate, only 1/2 to 1″ wide, of a dark brownish red; slow growing, loose and open in outline, unusual and delicate.

'Argenteo-marmorata'—Leaves of the first spring flush are green, those in the second irregular dotted with fine white specks or dotted and marbled.

'Asplenifolia'—A very beautiful but confused cultivar (with 'Laciniata') with gracefully cut leaves that offer a fern-like appearance; the lustrous dark green leaves turn excellent golden brown in fall; fine specimens occur at Smith College, Niagara Falls and Spring Grove.

'Atropunicea' ('Purpurea')—The true or original purple leaf beech; the young leaves are a deep black-red and with time change to purple-green and often almost green; the purple leaf beech has been found on several occasions in the wild; the only authenticated source from which horticulturists have derived their stock occurred before 1772 in the Hanleiter Forest near Sonderhausen in Thuringia; it reproduces somewhat true-to-type from seed and has produced many named off-spring; the popular 'Cuprea', Copper Beech, designates trees whose leaves are paler than the true Purple Beech; I have seen so many trees labeled 'Cuprea' that I have no idea the correctness of any; 'Brocklesby' has deep purple leaves that are larger than the norm; 'Swat Magret' has dark purple leaves that supposedly retain their coloring until late summer; other forms have arisen and are discussed below; apparently the name 'Atropunicea' may not be perfectly correct and names like 'Purpurea' and 'Purpurea Latifolia' are being used to designate the Purple Beech.

'Aurea Pendula'—A weeping beech with yellow leaves which become somewhat green in the summer months; handsome and unusual, not common in gardens or commerce; originated as a branch sport in 1900; introduced 1904.

'Aurea-Variegata'—Leaves margined with yellow.

'Bornyensis'—The trunk is upright and straight from which the branches hang down to form a green fountain or cone; found in Borny, France about 1870.

'Colcheata'—A dwarf, slow-growing, cone-shaped form; leaves about 1 1/2″ long, concave beneath, obovate and tapering to an acute base; margins toward apex with deep dentations (mini-lobes).

'Cockleshell'—A slow growing, somewhat columnar form with lustrous leaves that are smaller than those of 'Rotundifolia'; discovered about 1960 in Hillier's Nursery; have seen this only once at the Holden Arboretum and identified it as 'Rotundifolia'; it is a rather handsome plant.

'Comptoniifolia'—Similar to 'Asplenifolia' except the linear-lanceolate leaves are more abundant; it is a weaker grower; cultivated before 1864 in Germany.

'Crarae'—Asymmetrically ovate and recurved leaves with oblique-cuneate and slightly auriculate bases, deeply lobed along the margins, sinuses are cut one-fourth to one-third the distance to the midrib; parent tree in Crarae Gardens, Inverary, Argyll, Scotland.

'Crispa'—Growth normal but upright; leaves narrowly elliptical with the edges deeply cut and a little frizzy (hairy).

'Cristata'—Leaves bunched at end of shoots, very short petioled, coarsely triangular toothed, the apex decurved, crumpled resembling a cockscomb flower.

'Dawyck' ('Dawyckii', 'Fastigiata')—There is considerable confusion about the upright beeches; 'Fastigiata' has been introduced but technically is different from 'Dawyckii' which is rigidly columnar to narrowly cone-shaped and maintains this condition without pruning; it can grow 80′ and more high while spreading only about 10′; it was found wild near the Scottish country estate Dawyck, Peeblesshire in 1864 and cultivated there; about 1907 the Hesse Nursery of Weener, Hanover, Germany, obtained scions and introduced it commercially in 1913; among the handsomest of all upright-columnar trees.

'Dawyck Gold'—Introduced by J.R.P. van Hoey Smith in 1973; originated in 1968 as the result of a cross between 'Dawyck' and 'Zlatia'; it is narrow columnar in habit with golden yellow leaves in spring that color similarly in the fall; see *The Garden* 105(7), 1980 for complete details on this and the next cultivar.

'Dawyck Purple'—As above but leaves of a deep purple color; the tops of the shoots turned slightly inward; narrower, more open growth habit than 'Dawyck Gold'.

'Foliis Variegatus'—The leaves variegated with white and yellow, with red and purple stains interspersed.

'Grandidentata'—Leaves broadly elliptical, margin coarse and evenly dentate, the teeth angular, cuneate at base; not as handsome as 'Asplenifolia'; possibly a branch sport, found in Germany around 1810.

'Interrupta'—Leaves irregular and deformed, often part of the blade is only connected by the venation.

'Laciniata'—A rather confusing group of serrated-leaf beeches; leaves ovate-lanceolate, with 7 to 9 deep and regular serrations on each side, the sinuses extending about one-third of the way to the midrib, known since 1792 and considerable variation in degree of serration occurs on any one tree.

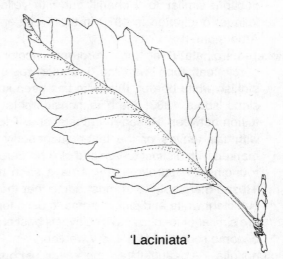

'Laciniata'

'Latifolia' (f. *latifolia*)—A form with larger, sturdier leaves than the type, often up to 6 and 7″ long, 5 1/2″ wide, on young trees.

'Luteo-variegata'—Leaves marked with yellow blotches, margins yellow; stronger growing than 'Albo-variegata'.

'Miltonensis'—A weeping form of great beauty; apparently quite confused; Bean has an excellent account of this cultivar.

'Pagnyensis'—A weeping form with a wide umbrella-shaped crown; has to be grafted on a standard or otherwise does not grow upright like typical 'Pendula'.

'Parkanaur'—Unique parasol appearance, extremely contorted older branches, 160-year-old parent tree is 10′ by 17′.

'Pendula' (f. *pendula*)—I have never seen one I didn't love and no two are exactly alike; a most beautiful weeping form, sometimes the branches are horizontal for a distance and then turn down forming a large tent-like mass; other trees have a central leader from which the branches hang down at various angles from 60 to 45° to almost "arms at one's side"; I can cite numerous examples of splendid Weeping Beeches but the finest is located at the Hunnewell Estate, Wellesley, MA; the center of the tree died out and the outer branches layered forming a copse; the entire tree (multiple trees) covers an area the size of a basketball court; a magnificent feeling to walk into this biologically domed coliseum.

'Purple Fountain'—This interesting form resulted as a seedling of 'Purpurea Pendula'; it differs in the narrow upright growth and the central stem from which the branches hang down in loose cascading fashion; the purple foliage is not as dark as the parent's; like the parent's it fades in the summer heat; a plant was 12′ high and 3′ wide at the base; introduced by Grootendorst in 1975.

'Purpurea Nana'—Compact, 10′ high, 6′ wide, oval form with small purple-brown leaves.

'Purpurea Pendula'—A broad mushroom shaped weeping purple-leaf form that never becomes too large; the largest specimens I have seen were about 10′; the leaves fade to purple-green in summer; a slow grower; it does not develop a central leader and the branches develop in a broad arch; originated in Germany about 1865.

'Purpurea Tricolor'—Purplish leaves are edged and striped with rose and pinkish white, leaves narrower than usual; this may be the same as 'Roseo-marginata'.

'Quercifolia'—Similar to 'Laciniata' types?; intermediate between 'Laciniata' and 'Grandidentata'.

'Remillyensis'—An umbrella-shaped form with tortuous branches.

'Riversii'—A deep purple form that supposedly holds this color into summer; trees I have seen turn purple-green like many of the Purple Beech cultivars; it was raised and distributed originally by Messrs. Rivers of Sawbridgeworth, England; the new spring leaves are perhaps the darkest (blackest) purple of any form and from my experience difficult to properly photograph.

'Rohanii'—A vigorous grower with brownish purple leaves, the margins of the leaves somewhat undulating, edged with rounded shallow teeth, and almost crisped; the color fades with time;

supposedly originated from a cross between a purple beech ('Brocklesby') and 'Quercifolia' in 1894.

'Rohan Gold'—Another J.R.P. van Hoey Smith introduction; similar to 'Rohanii' but with yellowish foliage; originated in 1970 in the Trompenburg Arboretum.

'Roseo-marginata' ('Tricolor', 'Purpurea Tricolor')—A purple-leaf form with an irregular rose and pinkish white border, this form has been known since about 1883; there is considerable confusion between 'Roseo-marginata' and 'Tricolor' with the leaves of the latter supposedly well marked with distinct cream and pink borders surrounding the purple center; I have seen many 'Roseo-marginata' and must admit that there is sufficient white and pink in some to pass for the 'Tricolor' version; Bean suggests that the two are similar or identical; this cultivar is best provided some shade for the creamy-pink areas often become scorched in hot, dry weather.

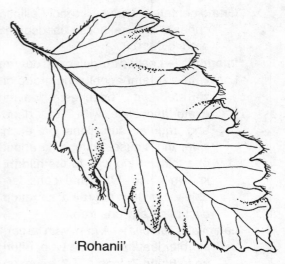

'Rohanii'

'Rotundifolia'—A beautiful tree, the leaves lustrous deep dark green, rounded, and 1/2 to 1 1/2″ in diameter, very closely set on the branches, usually with 4 vein pairs; it leafs out about two weeks later than the species; the habit is dense, pyramidal-oval to pyramidal-rounded; one of the most handsome forms of the European Beech; there is a splendid 40 to 50′ high specimen at the Arnold Arboretum.

'Rotundifolia'

'Spaethiana'—One of the most beautiful deep purple leaf beeches, the veins of which are usually lighter than the intervenal areas; it holds the color well, probably better than any other purple form; leafs out about one week later than most other beeches; introduced by Späth Nursery about 1920.

'Tortuosa' (f. *tortuosa*)—A variable form with uniquely twisted trunk and branches; usually wide-spreading and mounded forming a dome of foliage and sometimes referred to as the Parasol Beech; occurs in the wild in several European countries; the foliage is normal; this is a beautiful form especially in winter when the branches are highlighted by snow; supposedly comes about 60 percent true to type from seed; seldom grows more than 10 to 15′ high; there are several magnificent specimens in the Arnold Arboretum; found for the first time about 1845 in France.

'Viridi-variegata'—The dark green leaves are marked with light green blotches; put into commerce about 1935.

'Zlatia'—Normal habit but slow growing; new leaves yellow and fading to green in summer; discovered in 1890 near Vranje, Serbia; this form may belong to *F. moesiaca* since it was found in its range of distribution.

PROPAGATION: Seed should be stratified for 3 to 5 months at 41°F or fall sown; I have attempted to root soft and hardwood cuttings on several occasions but to no avail; cultivars are pot grafted usually in the winter months; tissue culture might prove extremely useful here; some interesting work by Dr. Bassuk and coworkers from Cornell on etiolation and banding relative to rooting cuttings; see *PIPPS* 34:543–550 (1984) for specifics.

ADDITIONAL NOTES: I have many "favorite" trees and this certainly ranks near the top; unfortunately it does not do well in the heat of the southern states (Zone 8) and was severely injured, especially on exposed sites in the midwest during the difficult winter of 1976–77 (–20 to –25°F). It appears to reach its maximum size from Boston south to Washington, D.C. Some of the most beautiful forms of European Beech can be found at Longwood Gardens, Swarthmore College, Arnold Arboretum and Mt. Auburn Cemetery.

NATIVE HABITAT: Europe, Long cultivated.

Fatsia japonica — Japanese Fatsia
(fat′si-à ja-pon′i-kà)

FAMILY: Araliaceae

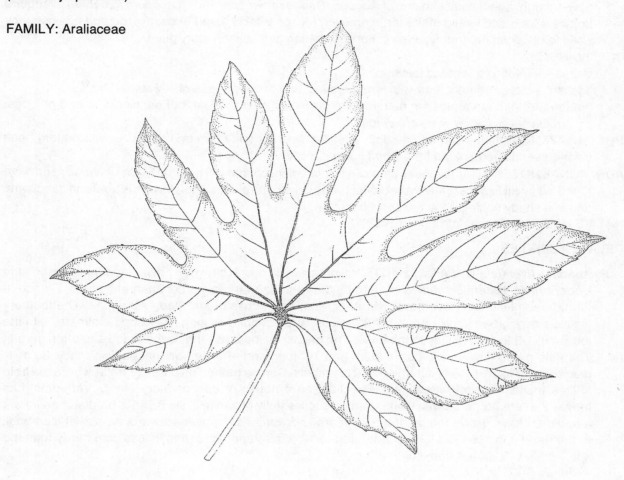

LEAVES: Alternate, simple, evergreen, deeply palmately 7 to 9 lobed, leathery, usually broader than high, 6 to 14″ (16″) across, cordate, divided beyond the middle into oblong-ovate, acuminate, serrate lobes with rounded sinuses, lustrous dark green above, paler beneath, glabrous; petiole—4 to 12″ long, round, smooth.

STEM: Stout, coarse, usually unbranched, green, marked with large leaf scars.

SIZE: 6 to 10′ high by 6 to 10′ wide; can grow to 15′ but this is rare.

HARDINESS: Zone 8 to 10; Athens-Atlanta, Georgia areas are the upper limit; if not sited in a shady courtyard or against a wall it is doomed to failure in these areas; tolerant to about +10°F, literally blitzed at −3°F.

HABIT: Rather rounded and open but I have seen plants that were quite full and dense.

RATE: Moderate.

TEXTURE: Coarse, tropical in effect, but exciting for the unique boldness it brings to a garden.

LEAF COLOR: Lustrous dark green through the seasons; will brown if sited in full sun and windy exposure.

FLOWERS: White, in 1 1/2″ diameter umbels which form a large terminal unbellose-panicle; October to November; flower stalks white like flowers; has flowered outdoors at Callaway Gardens, Pine Mountain and at Mrs. Robert Segrest's garden, Athens, GA.

FRUIT: Subglobose, fleshy, black, 1/3″ diameter drupe.

CULTURE: Transplants readily from containers; prefers moist, acid, high organic matter soils but tolerant of light-sandy to heavy-clay soils with less than adequate drainage; responds to fertility; full shade is preferable; excessive wind and winter sun may cause injury.

DISEASES AND INSECTS: None serious.

LANDSCAPE VALUE: Excellent for bold textured effect but not exactly easy to blend with other plants; I have thought about combinations of *Aucuba, Danae racemosa,* and *Cyrtomium falcatum;* all require or love shade and would make for interesting foliage effects; used in courtyards and against brick walls to break up monotony; used in north as house and conservatory plant.

CULTIVARS:
'Aurea'—Golden variegated leaves.
'Moseri'—More compact form with larger leaves; one of the parents of × *Fatshedera lizei.*
'Variegata'—White variegation patterns are dispersed over the leaf, but principally at end of lobes; have seen at Kew, very pretty form.

PROPAGATION: Cuttings should be taken after the wood is fairly firm and provided with bottom heat; cleaned seeds germinated 58% when sown directly.

ADDITIONAL NOTES: I learned these plants in a houseplant course at The Ohio State University and have found it difficult to accept them as outdoor hardy landscape plants. Their foliage is bold and handsome and in a shady setting, they have much to offer.

NATIVE HABITAT: Japan. Introduced 1838.

RELATED SPECIES:

× *Fatshedera lizei* (fatz-hed'ĕr-à liz-ē'ī) is an intergeneric hybrid between *Fatsia japonica* 'Moseri' and *Hedera helix* 'Hibernica' raised in 1910 by Messrs. Lizè Fréres, nurserymen of Nantes, France. It forms a semi-climbing evergreen shrub or vine, and is useful for shady situations. The leathery lustrous dark green leaves are 4 to 10″ across, and not quite as long, five-lobed, palmate, with the lobes cut 1/3 to 1/2 the way to the base. The petiole is about as long as the blade and often purple. The pale green flowers are borne in an 8 to 10″ long and 4″ wide terminal panicle made up of 1″ diameter, 12 to 36-flowered hemispherical umbels. Can be trained on a wall or trellis where the bold foliage makes a strong statement. Excellent as a house or conservatory plant. 'Variegata' has leaves that are bordered with white. Can be successfully grown in Zone 8 and is hardier than *Fatsia japonica.* I have grown the plant for six years and watched it grow backward. At –3°F it died back to the ground in 1984 but has regenerated to 12″. The variegated form is less cold hardy than the species. Easily rooted from cuttings.

Feijoa sellowiana — Guava, Pineapple Guava
(fē-jō'à sel-lōw-i-ā'nà)

FAMILY: Myrtaceae

LEAVES: Opposite, simple, evergreen, oval or ovate, entire, blunt at apex, tapered or rounded at the base, 1 to 3″ long, 3/4 to 1 1/2″ wide, dark almost bluish green and glabrous above except when young, whitish, felted and conspicuously veined beneath; petiole—1/4″ or less, pubescent.

SIZE: 10 to 15′, spread to 10′; at one time 8 to 10′ specimens at Callaway Gardens.

HARDINESS: Zone 8, considered hardy to 10°F; killed to ground at –3°F in Athens.

HABIT: Evergreen shrub or small tree of bushy habit; plants I have seen were quite dense; apparently will spread if not pruned and can become rather loose and open.

RATE: Fast.

TEXTURE: Medium.

LEAF COLOR: Dark green above, grayish beneath; gray-green effect due to whitish pubescence on underside of leaf.

FLOWER: Perfect, solitary, produced in leaf-axils of current year's shoots, 1 1/4 to 1 3/4″ wide and borne on a pubescent, pendulous, 1 to 1 1/2″ long pedicel, 4 sepals are reflexed, 4 petals red in center, whitish at margin, stamens numerous, erect, 3/4 to 1″ long, rich crimson, May-June.

FRUIT: Green tinged red, maturing to yellow, 1 to 3″ egg-shaped berry, edible, with a rich aromatic flavor; ripen in late summer and early fall into January depending on climate; taste likened to pineapple with overtones of spearmint.

CULTURE: Prefers well drained, light loamy soil; full sun, tolerant of partial shade if fruit is not a factor; tolerant of salt spary; prune after flowering.

DISEASES AND INSECTS: None serious.

LANDSCAPE VALUE: Excellent for foliage effect and flowers; suitable for screens and hedges; has been used at Callaway Gardens with good success; in colder areas of the south the tips of the shoots are killed and this has the effect of pruning; supposedly can grow 15 to 25′ but this is probably only realized under south Florida and west coast conditions in the United States.

CULTIVARS:

'Coolidge'—Self-fruiting selection, small fruit with mild flavor.

'Nazemeta'—Large, excellent fruit, self-fruitful.

'Pineapple Gem'—Self-fruiting selection.

'Superba'—Self-sterile, round fruits, plant with 'Coolidge' to insure abundant fruiting.

'Trask'—Large fruit with deep green skin, skin is thicker and grittier than parent but pulp quality is good, productive and ripens early, self-fruitful.

'Variegata'—Leaves with white variegation.

PROPAGATION: Seeds can be sown when removed from the pulp; cuttings are the preferred method but published success is variable; I have not been able to root the plant; the parent plant influences rooting success, 15 clones that averaged 10 years of age rooted 4 to 76% when evaluated 7 months later; 3 to 4″ long 2 leaf cuttings, August, rooted 75%, a rooting chemical has proven beneficial, possibly in the 3000 to 8000 ppm range.

ADDITIONAL NOTES: Beautiful shrub; flowers are delicate and spectacular; may require cross pollination to set fruit; plant on Georgia campus is now 6′ high after being killed to ground at –3°F in 1983–84 winter.

NATIVE HABITAT: Southern Brazil and Uruguay; discovered by Friedrich Sellow in 1819.

Ficus carica — Common Fig
(fī′kus kar′i-kȧ)

FAMILY: Moraceae

LEAVES: Alternate, simple, 3 to 5-lobed, 4 to 8″ long, and on occasion even larger in length and width, cordate, depth of sinuses variable, lobes usually scalloped into broad rounded teeth, dark green, both surfaces scabrous with short stiff hairs; petiole 1 to 4″ long.

Ficus carica, Common Fig, forms a rather coarse, broad rounded shrub. Size varies from 10 to 15′. The

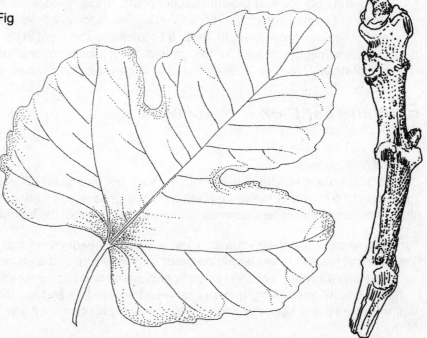

dark green leaves provide an interesting textural effect in the landscape. The flowers are produced on the inside of a concave receptacle which when mature is enlarged and fleshy and contains the true fruits (achenes). The Common Fig is often seen around older homes in the south and at one time was widely planted. It prefers a moist, well-drained soil but appears to be adaptable to less-than-ideal conditions. Unfortunately, excessive cold will cause injury and it is best grown in Zone 8 through 10. I have grown rather fond of this plant over the past 10 years, especially because of the large, rugged leaves. Unfortunately, −3°F killed most shrubs one-half-way to the ground. Most returned to a normal state. Several good cultivars include 'Brown Turkey' with purple-brown fruit and 'Comadria' a choice white fig blushed violet, thin skinned with sweet white to red flesh. Western Asia and eastern Mediterranean region. Cultivated since early times.

Ficus pumila — Climbing Fig
(fī'kus pū'mil-à)

Juvenile leaf

Adult leaf

FAMILY: Moraceae
LEAVES: *Juvenile* (more common), alternate, simple, evergreen, obliquely heart shaped, pointed, 3/4 to 1 1/4″ long, 2/3's as wide, medium green, usually glabrous above, pubescent below; petiole—very short; *Adult* (fruit-bearing state), more leathery, ovate, cordate, pointed, 2 to 4″ long, 1/2 as wide, rich dark green above, pale beneath, net-veined; petiole—pubescent, 1/2″ long.

Ficus pumila, Climbing Fig, seems out of place in outdoor gardens since it usually covers the inside of conservatory walls in northern gardens. However in the south it is a regular feature on masonry structures. The small medium green juvenile leaves form an interesting mosaic and become dense and matted with time. Both juvenile (about 1″ long) and mature leaves (2 to 4″ long) develop. The vine climbs by aerial rootlets and can literally cement itself to porous materials. Prefers a moist, well drained soil and high humidity; can be sited in full sun or partial shade; may need considerable pruning in deep south but cold controls growth in upper south. In many respects, the juvenile/mature stages parallel those of *Euonymus fortunei.* 'Minima' is a juvenile form with very small leaves; 'Variegata' has white and green mottled leaves. In 1982, 0°F defoliated the plant in the Athens area. In 1984, −3°F killed the same plant half way to the ground but it has recovered and now (1990) blankets the wall completely. Zone 8 to 10. Native of China, Formosa, and Japan. Introduced into cultivation in 1759.

Firmiana simplex — Chinese Parasol Tree
(fir-mē-ā'nà sim'pleks)

FAMILY: Sterculiaceae
LEAVES: Alternate, simple, 6 to 8″ long and wide but often over 12″ especially on vigorous young plants, usually 3-lobed, but often 5-lobed, with the general appearance of a maple leaf, cordate at base, glabrous or pubescent beneath; petiole—2/3's to about the length of the blade.

Firmiana simplex, Chinese Parasol Tree, is a round-headed tree that will grow 30 to 45′ high. Its chief interest resides in the large rich green leaves which lend an almost tropical appearance. The stem and bark on young trees are smooth, gray-green and add winter interest. The yellowish-green flowers occur in 10 to 20″ long terminal panicles in June-July and are followed by pea-sized fruits that are attached to the edges of leaflike carpels that split open soon after flowering. The first time I saw the fruit I was intrigued by the pattern of seed development. Classically, angiosperms are hidden-seeded plants and the carpel walls usually enclose the seeds from view. I collected seeds that had dried and sowed them directly. Germination was sporadic but good. Seeds that were stratified for about 2 months did not germinate any better. A tree on the Georgia campus often develops reasonable yellow fall color. I doubt seriously whether the plant has a place in commerce. China, Japan. Introduced 1757. Zone 7 to 9.

Fontanesia fortunei
— Fortune Fontanesia
(fon-tā-nē′zi-a for-tū′nē-ī)

FAMILY: Oleaceae
LEAVES: Opposite, simple, lanceolate or ovate-lanceolate, 1 to 4 1/2″ long, 1/3 to 1″ wide, acuminate, cuneate, entire, lustrous bright green, glabrous; petiole—1/2″ long.

Fontanesia fortunei, Fortune Fontanesia, is only included because one of my mentors, Dr. Ken Reisch, brought the plant to my attention many (now 27) years ago during my plant material courses at Ohio State. The plant has succumbed to progress, i.e., new construction but I can picture this graceful 12′ high, multistemmed, almost bamboo-like, unperturbable shrub. The foliage is what makes the plant run for the greenish white flowers, each 1/6″ long, occur in 1 to 2″ long panicles and do not overwhelm. The fruit is a 3/8″ long, flat, oblong samara with winged margins and a notched apex. For difficult sites and rough areas it would prove servicable. In many respects, it has privet-like characteristics and is tougher to propagate so pales by commercial comparison. 'Titan' was selected by Cole Nursery Co., Circleville, OH (now out of business) for more upright habit and better foliage; 3″ high cuttings grew 76″ tall and 65″ wide in 3 growing seasons; this plant needs to be used in tough highway and urban sites. China. Introduced 1845. Zone 4 to 8?

Forsythia × intermedia — Border Forsythia
(fôr-sith′i-à in-tēr-mē′di-a)

FAMILY: Oleaceae
LEAVES: Opposite, simple, toothed usually on the upper one-half, ovate-oblong to oblong lanceolate, 3 to 5″ long, medium to dark green above, lighter below, glabrous; petiole—1/2″ long.

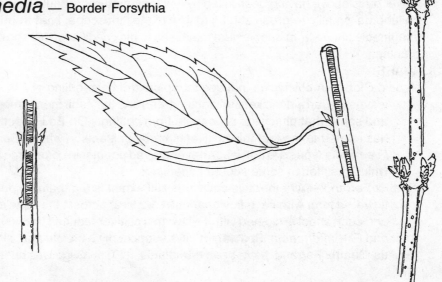

BUDS: Imbricate, conical, light yellow-brown with a tinge of green, about 1/4″ long, borne several together in the axils, usually rather loosely scaled.

STEM: Often somewhat squarish or 4-sided, yellowish brown and strongly lenticellate; pith—chambered in the internodes, solid at the nodes.

SIZE: 8 to 10′ high by 10 to 12′ wide.

HARDINESS: Vegetatively hardy in zone 4, however, flower buds are often killed in Zone 5, acceptable in 6 to 8 (9).

HABIT: Upright, rank growing deciduous shrub, differentially developing upright and arching canes which give it the appearance the roots were stuck in an electric socket; always needs grooming, one of the most overrated and over-used shrubs!

RATE: Fast.

TEXTURE: Medium in leaf; wild in winter.

LEAF COLOR: Medium to dark green in summer; green or yellow green in fall, sometimes with a tinge of purple; have seen respectable fall color on certain plants in the Athens area, leaves hold late (November) and may turn a deep burgundy.

FLOWERS: Perfect, 1 1/4 to 1 1/2″ long, pale to deep yellow, 4-lobed corollas, scentless although I have detected a slight privet odor on occasion, usually March-April for 2 to 3 weeks; borne 1 to 6 together or often in 2's and 3's on old wood; the justifiable reason for using forsythia is the wonderful flower effect in early spring; in the midwest one was easily frustrated waiting for a swaggering golden yellow shrub to appear in the spring landscape only to find that a significant portion of the flower buds were killed by cold; in Athens I have charted the flowering times with occasional flowering as early as late January but the peak normally early to mid March.

FRUIT: Two-celled dehiscent brown capsule, 1/3″ long, often housing many winged seeds, not ornamental; have collected and germinated seeds of *F. × intermedia* but never kept the seedlings until flowering.

CULTURE: Fibrous, transplants readily bare root or balled and burlapped; prefers a good, loose soil but will do well in about any soil; full sun to maximize flower; pH adaptable; withstands city conditions; prune after flowering either by cutting plant to ground or removing the oldest stems.

DISEASES AND INSECTS: Crown gall, leaf spots, dieback, four-lined plant bug, Japanese weevil, northern root-knot nematode and spider mites; none of which are extremely troublesome.

LANDSCAPE VALUE: Chief value is in the early spring flower; forsythias do not belong in foundation plantings but are often used there; shrub border, massing, groupings, bank plantings are the most appropriate places; the early spring color is a strong selling point and when forsythia is in flower it is one of the hottest selling items at a garden center; often injured by late freezes and flower quality is reduced; I have seen forsythia flowers a beautiful golden yellow one day and with a hard freeze over night they are transformed to brown mush; temperatures about −10 to −15°F appear to coincide with flower bud kill; it is common in the north to see forsythia flowering only below the snowline; those flower buds above having been killed by low temperatures; should be planted with other spring bulbs, hellebores, small evergreen shrubs to tie it to the landscape; I have seen the plant pruned into every imaginable shape from bubble gum machines to pink cadillacs; this shrub was not made for extensive pruning.

CULTIVARS:

'Arnold Giant'—A colchicine induced tetraploid from a seedling of *F. × intermedia* 'Spectabilis'; the leaves are larger, thicker and darker green and the habit more erect; it is sparse in flower number and somewhat difficult to propagate from cuttings; Dr. Ed Hasselkus, University of Wisconsin, has related to me that this cultivar is hardy in Madison where 'Beatrix Farrand' and other *F. × intermedia* types are not; it has never proved popular in commerce but has been used in crosses which resulted in some superior seedlings.

'Beatrix Farrand'—Whether this cultivar is still extant is a debatable point but there is a vivid-yellow flowered form with each flower about 1 1/2 to 2″ across; the flowers are borne in great numbers and each shoot is clothed with yellow; this cultivar resulted from crosses between 'Arnold Giant' and *F. × intermedia* 'Spectabilis'; it is supposedly a triploid and all subsequent clones identified as 'Beatrix Farrand' have been tetraploids; it (?) is a vigorous bush easily growing 8 to 10′ high and wide; I chuckle somewhat at the thought of all the nutritional, propagation and hardiness experiments that have been conducted over the years with this cultivar(?); another plant with this name is vigorous, erect, with dull bluish green, coarsely serrated teeth; flowers are 3/4 to 1″ long, 3/8″ wide and soft yellow, more or less nodding, fruits are borne in abundance; foliage is considered ugly and habit is gaunt.

'Densiflora'—Introduced by Späth Nurseries, Berlin, Germany in 1888; the result of seedling selection from *F. × intermedia;* the flowers are light yellow, the corolla lobes about 1 1/4″ long, spreading, not markedly revolute; borne singly, crowded along stem, its habit is spreading with pendulous branches like *F. suspensa.*

'Goldzauber'—Flowers dark yellow resembling those of 'Lynwood', medium sized, thin branched shrub, result of a cross between 'Lynwood' and 'Beatrix Farrand'.

'Karl Sax'—Of bushier habit and not as tall as 'Beatrix Farrand'; the deep yellow flowers are a shade darker than 'Beatrix Farrand'; the flowers may be 1 3/4″ across and are more or less horizontally disposed so their deep yellow throats provide a golden glow to the entire shrub; it is a tetraploid and shows better flower bud hardiness than 'Beatrix Farrand'; this clone resulted from 'Arnold Giant' × *F. × intermedia* 'Spectabilis' and was named for Dr. Karl Sax, Director of the Arnold Arboretum, who with his students worked on improving the genus *Forsythia;* originated about 1944 as did 'Beatrix Farrand'.

'Lynwood' ('Lynwood Gold')—A branch sport of 'Spectabilis' which originated in the garden (Lynwood) of Miss Adair in Northern Ireland; the owner noticed a branch that had flowers which were more open and better distributed along the stem than those on the rest of the plant; the Slieve Donard Nursery of Newcastle introduced it in 1935; the brilliant yellow flowers are slightly lighter than 'Spectabilis'; the habit of growth is upright; nurserymen in this country call it 'Lynwood Gold' which is incorrect.

'Minigold'—Described as growing one-half the size of the species with typical yellow flowers.

'Nana'—Low, dwarf form, a 20-year-old plant being 5′ high and 8′ wide; leaves may be simple, lobed and sometimes compound, pith is solid at nodes, chambered in internodes; very slow to flower and may take 7 years from a cutting before the greenish yellow flowers appear; originated in the midwest.

'Parkdekur'—Deep yellow flowers up to 2″ wide, abundant, on a semipendulous branched shrub, result of a cross between 'Beatrix Farrand' and 'Spectabilis'.

'Primulina'—A chance seedling discovered by Alfred Rehder of the Arnold Arboretum in 1912; the flowers are pale yellow and the growth habit similar to 'Spectabilis'; it has been largely superseded by 'Spring Glory'.

'Spectabilis'—Has been the standard by which all others are judged; called Showy Border Forsythia; a vigorous shrub that will grow 10′ high and wide; the leaves being ovate-lanceolate and 3 to 4 1/2″ long; the rich bright yellow flowers may be as much as 1 1/2″ across and contain the usual 4 corolla lobes as well as 5 and 6; the flowers occur profusely from the axils of the stems; this cultivar is also more flower bud hardy than 'Beatrix Farrand'; introduced by Späth Nurseries in 1906.

'Spring Glory'—A branch sport of 'Primulina' discovered in 1930 by M. Horvath of Mentor, Ohio; the 1 1/2″ wide, sulfur-yellow flowers are densely produced along the stems; it grows to about 6′ in height; introduced into the trade by Wayside Gardens, in 1942.

'Tremonia'—A rather curious form with deeply cut leaves; the plants I have seen were not particularly vigorous; they were upright-spreading; introduced into the Arnold Arboretum in 1966 from the Dortmund Botanic Garden, Dortmund, West Germany.

'Variegata'—Have seen probably more than one form with creamy variegated leaves; unfortunately, unstable and will revert to green, also weak growing.

'Vitellina'—The deep yellow flowers are about the smallest (1 1/4 to 1 1/2″ diameter) of the *F. × intermedia* types; the habit is rather erect; put into commerce by Späth in 1899.

A corollary to the above is necessary to fully understand the background of these cultivars. In 1878 Hermann Zabel, Director of the Municipal Garden in Munden, found seedling forsythias in the Botanic Garden of Gottingen which were the result of crosses between *F. viridissima* and *F. suspensa* var.

fortunei. In 1885 he described this as *F.* × *intermedia* which has been the source of the garden forms we utilize today. It is interesting to note that the introduction of these garden forms took place largely at the Späth Nurseries around 1900 and the Arnold Arboretum in the 1940's. It might be worth someone's time to produce new forms with better habit and greater bud hardiness. See *Arnoldia* 31:41–63 (1971), The story of forsythia.

PROPAGATION: Seeds will germinate without a pretreatment but one to two months at 41°F appears to improve and unify germination; seeds that were cold stratified for 3 months produced radicles in the bag; softwood cuttings are easy to root; I always give them 1000 ppm IBA quick dip and in 3 to 4 weeks the mass of white roots is so great it is difficult to remove them from the media; hardwood cuttings can also be rooted.

RELATED SPECIES:

Forsythia 'Arnold Dwarf' resulted from a cross between *F.* × *intermedia* and *F. japonica* var. *saxatilis*. It flowers (greenish yellow) sparsely and plants may not produce any flowers until they are 5 to 6-years-old. Produces 1 to 2″ long, strongly serrated, bright green leaves. Principal landscape value is the comparatively low habit. Six-year-old plants may be 3′ tall and 7′ across. It makes an excellent bank or large area cover for wherever the branches touch the soil, roots invariably develop. Longwood Gardens has effectively used the plant on a 30 to 40% bank next to the Idea Garden. I have watched the plants form a solid mass of foliage and the entire planting is a bright green, somewhat irregular mass of semi-arching and prostrate shoots. Does not produce the carpet effect of *Vinca*, *Pachysandra* and *Hedera*. Developed at the Arnold Arboretum in 1941 by Dr. Sax. Zone 5 to 8.

Forsythia europaea—Albanian Forsythia
(for-sith′i-à u-rō′pē-a)

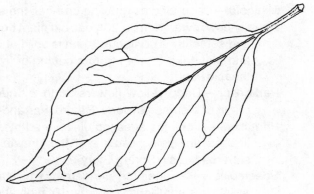

LEAVES: Alternate, simple, ovate to ovate-lanceolate, 2 to 3″ long, 3/4 to 1 1/2″ wide, acute,
   rounded or broad cuneate, usually entire or
   with a few teeth on leaves of vigorous shoots,
   thick texture, glabrous, dark green; petiole—
   1/6 to 1/3″ long.
STEM: Green, more rounded than *F.* × *intermedia*,
   glabrous, dotted with lenticels, pith—chambered.

Forsythia europaea, Albanian Forsythia, is an upright shrub growing to about 6′ in height. The pale yellow flowers are about 3/4 to 1″ long and occur singly or 2 to 3 together. Considered the least snowy of the forsythias when in flower. It was discovered about 1897 in northern Albania. It is allied to *F. viridissima* but differs in the ovate leaves and lanky habit. Zone 5. About at hardy as *F. suspensa*. Report said hardy to −20°F.

Forsythia mandschurica, (fôr-sith′i-à mand-shoor′i-ka), 'Vermont Sun', is an almost unknown entity in the United States but represents probably the most flower-bud hardy type for northern gardens. The species itself is essentially unknown for it does not appear in Rehder, *Hortus III*, Krüssmann or Bean. I will offer the history of this cultivar. In 1940 Montreal Botanical Gardens obtained cuttings of *F. mandschurica* from Mr. L. Ptitsin of Harbin, Manchuria. The University of Vermont obtained cuttings from MBG in 1968. After extensive evaluation Drs. Pellett and Evert registered the name 'Vermont Sun' in August, 1978. Through field and laboratory testing, its flower bud hardiness is estimated between −25°F and −30°F. It flowers about one week earlier with larger, darker yellow flower buds than *F. ovata*. It is an upright, erect shrub that will grow 6 to 8′ high and slightly less in width. I have seen the plant in flower at the Vermont Horticultural Research Center and can recommend it for those climates that suffer harsh winters. It does not hold a candle to the

F. × *intermedia* types so do not think of it in those terms. Softwood cuttings collected in June treated with 3000 ppm IBA-talc placed in vermiculite under mist rooted 85% in 3 months. See *HortScience* 19:313–314 (1984).

Forsythia ovata—Early Forsythia
(for-sith′i-a ō-vā′ta)

LEAVES: Alternate, simple, ovate or broad-ovate, 1 1/2 to 3 1/2″ long, 1 1/4 to 2 1/2″ wide, abruptly acuminate, truncate, or sometimes subcordate or broad cuneate, nearly entire to coarsely toothed, dark green, glabrous; petiole—1/4 to 1/2″ long.
STEM: Rounded (terete), gray-brown, glabrous, covered with small darkish lenticels; pith—chambered.

Forsythia ovata, Early Forsythia, is a rather stiff, spreading shrub that will grow 4 to 6′ high and wide. A fine specimen at the Arnold is 6′ high and 8 to 10′ wide. The bright yellow (tinge of green), 1/2 to 3/4″ wide flowers are among the earliest of all forsythia to open usually appearing in March-April. The flowers are usually solitary. This species is interesting because of its flower bud hardiness. It has survived −20°F temperatures and flowered satisfactorily in Vermont tests (see *HortScience* 14:623–624. 1979. Forsythia flower bud hardiness). Hybrids have been produced between *F. suspensa* and *F. ovata* and a colchicine-induced tetraploid called 'Tetragold' was raised in Holland and distributed about 1963. It is a low growing (3′), bushy shrub with large (1 1/4″ wide) deep yellow flowers. 'Ottawa' came out of Canada and is more flower bud hardy, more vigorous with heavy floral production, and flowers 7 to 10 days earlier than other cultivars. 'French's Florence' is a 4 to 5′ high shrub with smaller and lighter yellow flowers than the species but with greater flower bud hardiness. Korea. Introduced 1917. Zone 4 to 7. Hardy to −25°F.

Forsythia suspensa var. *sieboldii*—Weeping Forsythia
(fôr-sith′i-a sus-pen′sa sē-bōl′ dē-ī)

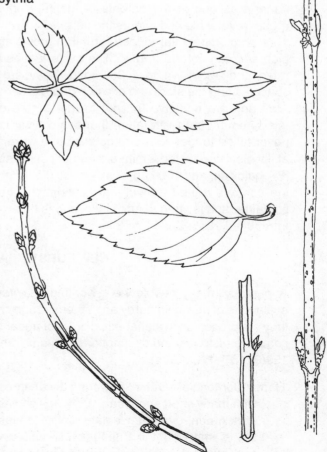

LEAVES: Opposite, simple, sometimes 3-parted or 3-foliate, ovate to oblong-ovate, 2 to 4″ long, 1 to 2″ wide, acute, broad cuneate or rounded at base, coarsely toothed, medium to dark green; petiole 1/2″ long.
STEM: Pith—hollow in internodes and solid at the nodes, yellowish brown stem color; also stem appears more rounded than *F.* × *intermedia.*

Forsythia suspensa var. *sieboldii,* Weeping Forsythia, grows 8 to 10′ tall and 10 to 15′ wide. The habit is upright, arching, almost fountain-like with slender, long, trailing, pendulous branches. The flowers are golden yellow, 1 to 1 1/4″ across, April, usually 1 to 3 together. This plant does not flower as heavily as *F.* × *intermedia.* Considerable confusion abounds as to the true name for 'Weeping Forsythia'. Variety *sieboldii* is the form with the long trailing branches. I have seen the branches hanging over walls where they resemble brown ropes in winter. The branches can be trained on a wall or suitable structure and can grow 20 to 30′

high. In addition, if planted near a low-branched tree it will grow into and over the host plant. It is a most graceful shrub but lacks the strong floral display of *F. × intermedia* types. Variety *fortunei* is the upright version of *F. suspensa* with stiffer, erect or arching shoots. In variety *atrocaulis* the young shoots and unfolding leaves are dark purple, the older stems a rich brown; 'Nyman's Variety' is a selection from var. *atrocaulis* with soft yellow (ivory yellow) flowers about 1 3/4″ across; it is of erect habit and one of the last forsythias to flower. Other cultivars include 'Decipiens' with single flowers and 'Pallida' with washed out yellow flowers; both raised by Späth around 1905–06 and now scarce. China. Zone 5 to 8.

Forsythia viridissima—Greenstem Forsythia
(fôr-sith'i-a vir-i-dis'si-ma)

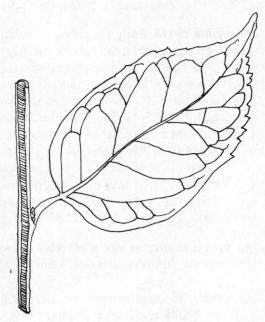

LEAVES: Opposite, simple, elliptic-oblong to lanceolate, 3 to 6″ long, 3/4 to 1 1/2″ wide, rarely obovate-oblong, broadest about or above the middle, tapering at both ends, dark green, serrated toward the apex or sometimes entire; petiole—1/4 to 1/2″ long.

STEM: Often greenish, pith chambered through nodes and internodes on young branches, or finally all excavated on old wood.

Forsythia viridissima, Greenstem Forsythia, grows 6 to 10′ high with a similar spread. The habit is stiff and upright, more or less flat-topped. Flowers are bright yellow with a slight greenish tinge, 1″ long, April, 1 to 3 together. This species is rather pretty in flower and usually flowers one or two weeks later than *F. suspensa*. Its chief claim to fame is as one of the parents of the *F. × intermedia* group. A valuable and interesting cultivar is 'Bronxensis'. This is a compact flat-topped form that grows about 12″ high and can spread 2 to 3′. The ovate leaves are serrated and about 3/4 to 1 3/4″ long. They are closely spaced along the stem and of a rich bright green. The primrose yellow flowers occur in late March to April and are effective but not to the degree of the *F. × intermedia* types. There is a myth or misstatement in the literature that this cultivar is difficult to root. This is absolutely false for I have never failed to root softwood cuttings that were treated with 1000 ppm IBA-quick dip. In fact, when at Illinois, I conducted a mini-experiment using softwood cuttings and 0, 1000, 5000 and 10,000 ppm IBA-quick dip and 1000 ppm NAA quick dip. After 4 weeks the cuttings were evaluated and we found the controls rooted as well as the hormone treatments. This cultivar grows extremely well in a container and is often seen in landscapes throughout the midwest. *F. viridissima* is native to China. Introduced 1845. Zone 5 to 8.

NEW FORSYTHIA SELECTIONS

Apparently, many people were working on forsythia over the past eight years for a literal yellow avalanche of new cold hardy and other strange characteristic forsythias have been introduced. Here, they are presented in alphabetical order or under the individual who introduced the plant(s). For rather complete histories and descriptions of the cold-hardy cultivars of *Forsythia,* see *Amer. Nurseryman* 159(9):167–173 (1984).

'Happy Centennial'—A free flowering dwarf spreading shrub growing 2 to 2 1/2′ high and 3 to 5′ wide with many short secondary branches and abundance of 1 3/4 to 2″ long, 1/2 to 1″ wide, leathery dark green, ovate-lanceolate, entire leaves; the fragrant golden yellow flowers are 1 1/4 to 1 3/4″ diameter, 3/4 to 1″ long usually with several flowers per node; supposedly quite cold hardy and suspect −20°F flower bud hardiness; derived from (*F. ovata* 'Ottawa' × *F. europaea*) crossed with an unknown seedling found in the ornamental gardens at Central Experimental Farm, Ottawa, Canada; see *HortScience* 22(1):165 (1987) for more details.

'Meadowlark'—Introduction from North and South Dakota State Universities and the Arnold Arboretum; bright yellow flowers in profusion on a 6 to 9′ high rather unkempt semi-arching shrub, leaves are dark green and pest free, flowers bud hardy to −35°F; found by Dr. Harrison Flint at the Arnold Arboretum in heavy flower while a mass planting of 'Spectabilis' surrounding the plant was nearly devoid of flowers from the 1966–67 cold winter; a cross between *F. ovata* and *F. europaea* and originated from the breeding work of Dr. Karl Sax and Haig Derman at the Arnold; is being grown commercially in the midwest.

'New Hampshire Gold'—Drooping, single, cold hardy yellow flowers on a 5′ high mounded shrub, developed by Paul Joly, Windsor Road Nursery, Cornish, NH; result of a cross between 'Lynwood' and *F. ovata* 'Ottawa' and *F. europaea.*

'Northern Sun'—Has never failed to flower over a 12-year period at Minnesota Landscape Arboretum where −30°F is common, 8 to 10′ high shrub, possibly a hybrid between *F. ovata* and *F. europaea.*

'Sunrise'—Bright yellow flowers, 2 to 3 per node, medium green leaves, squarish stems, full dense habit, 5′ by 5′, flower bud hardy to −20°F, offspring of *F. ovata* and a selected plant purchased as *F. ovata;* an Iowa State University introduction.

Van der Werken Irradiated 'Lynwood' Cultivars: A rather interesting story of irradiation-induced mutant forsythias is presented in *Amer. Nurseryman* 167(1):127–132 (1988) that resulted in the ultimate release of 5 (too many) cultivars. Abbreviated descriptions follow. All plants were released by Hendrick van der Werken, University of Tennessee, Knoxville, TN. Actual flower bud hardiness is unknown but suspect a Zone 6 to 8 distinction is safe.

'Fairy-Land'—A small, fine-textured shrub, 3 to 4′ high, 5 to 6′ wide, 2 to 4 flowers per node, each flower with 4 to 8 lobes, leaves 3″ long, 1/2″ wide.

'Lemon-Screen'—An upright fan-like habit, with lemon-yellow, 1 1/2 to 1 3/4″ long flowers, 4 per node, and chartreuse foliage in spring; foliage turns green in summer and exhibits a golden glow where exposed to full sun; plant may grow 8 to 10′ in 5 years.

'Minikin'—Small linear leaves, 1 1/2″ long, 1/4″ wide, on a 1/2″ long petiole; 1/2″ wide, yellow flowers with recurved petals, 2 per node, internodes short, only 1/4 to 3/4″ long; 2 to 2 1/2′ by 3 to 4′ in 5 years.

'Pygmy-Red'—The name reflects the high anthocyanin (red pigment) in the young shoots, also the leaves develop maroon fall color on their upper side; 3 1/2 to 4′ high and 5′ wide in 5 years; flowers 1 1/4 to 1 1/2″ wide with 4(5) lobes, 2 flowers per node; internodes 1/2 to 1 1/2″ long.

'Tinklebell'—A rigid, upright, semi-dwarf growing 4 to 5′ high, flowers young, 2 to 4 flowers per node, with 4 (5 to 6) petal lobes, internodes short, leaves 2 to 3″ long, 1/2″ wide, also listed as 'Tinkle-Bells.'

Fothergilla gardenii — Dwarf Fothergilla
(foth-ér-gil′a gar-dē′nē-ī)

FAMILY: Hamamelidaceae

LEAVES: Alternate, simple, obovate to oblong, rounded or broad cuneate, 1 to 2 1/2″ long, 3/4 to 1 3/4″ wide, dentate above the middle, dark green above, pale or glaucous and tomentose beneath; petioles—1/4 to 1/3″ long, pubescent; leaves resemble those of *Hamamelis vernalis.*

BUDS: Stalked, oblique, obovate or oblong, with 2 caducous scales, often collaterally branched, the end bud largest.

STEM: Rounded, light brown, zig-zag, slender, dingy stellate-tomentose; pith—small, somewhat angular, continuous, for a time greenish.

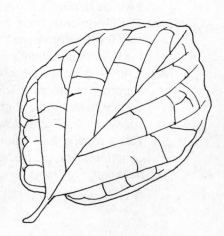

SIZE: 2 to 3' in height, similar or greater in spread; many stories about the size of this plant; in the U.S. I have seen 5 to 6' tall plants; Raulston reported 10' tall plants in Europe.

HARDINESS: Zone (4)5 to 8(9).

HABIT: Small shrub with slender, crooked, often spreading branches, rounded in outline; forms a rather dense mound at maturity; suckers, some plants more so than others, and forms colonies.

RATE: Slow.

TEXTURE: Medium in foliage, medium in winter.

LEAF COLOR: Dark green, to a degree almost blue-green, summer foliage, quite attractive, somewhat leathery in texture; fall color is a brilliant yellow to orange to scarlet, often a combination of colors in same leaf; coloration develops late, often mid November in Athens.

FLOWER: White, fragrant, actually apetalous; showy parts are the stamens (white filament, yellow anthers), borne in terminal, 1 to 2" long by 1" diameter spikes, April to early May, flowers appear before leaves, actually look like small bottle-brushes, honey-scented, lasting for 10 to 14 days; in some years the flowers and emerging leaves may appear together.

FRUIT: Capsule, not showy, 2-valved with 2 shining black seeds.

CULTURE: Move balled and burlapped or as a container-grown plant; requires acid, peaty, sandy loam; does well in partial shade, flowers and colors best in full sun; requires good drainage; have read the exhortations of one author who noted that *Fothergilla* species in general will tolerate clay soils and pH of 6.8 to 7.5. Admittedly, horticultural literature is not infallible but there are too many reports, especially out of England, where soils are often chalky (high pH) that list the plant as totally unsuitable for limey soils. My own experience, and I have grown countless fothergillas, is to maintain a moist, well drained acid soil and the plant will prosper.

DISEASES AND INSECTS: Trouble free, making it worthy of wider landscape use.

LANDSCAPE VALUE: Foundation plantings, borders, masses, excellent for interesting flowers, good summer foliage and outstanding fall color; good in combination with rhododendrons and azaleas, and other ericaceous plants.

CULTIVARS: Reasonable variation in summer foliage and fall colors as well as growth habit to warrant selection. Since the last edition several clones have been named.

‘Blue Mist’—A handsome glaucous blue foliage form with a rather wispy delicate mounded growth habit, the leaves hold late and do not fall color as spectacularly as some other forms, also may not be quite as cold hardy as the species, introduced by the Morris Arboretum. I like the plant and find the summer foliage color an interesting diversion from the typical green, roots easily from softwood cuttings, in fact, cuttings collected on September 13, 1988 from a container grown plant, treated with 3000 ppm KIBA-quick dip, rooted 100% in six weeks; in 1989, the worst year for fall coloration in my 11 years in Georgia, ‘Blue Mist’ developed sickly yellow-green coloration while ‘Mt. Airy’ leaves were spectacular orange-red.

‘Eastern Form’—Listed by Gossler Farms Nursery as the typical form with small oval foliage, dark green leaves that turn yellow-orange-red, and the normal white flowers.

‘F$_2$ Hybrid’—Dr. Darrel Apps, Chadds Ford, PA showed me a particularly fine form that was growing with 2 or 3 other seedlings from the same population. It was intermediate in size with perhaps the best red to purple, almost fluorescent color I have witnessed on any shrub. There is a chance it will be named and introduced. It is an improvement over both species.

‘Jane Platt’—Selected from the Portland Garden of John and Jane Platt; the habit is more cascading than the ‘Eastern Form’, the leaves narrow rather than oval, and the fall color brilliant yellow-red, the flowers are slightly longer than ‘Eastern Form’, grows 3' high, a Gossler introduction.

‘Mount Airy’—A clone I selected from Mt. Airy Arboretum, Cincinnati, OH for good dark green foliage, superb, consistent yellow-orange-red fall color, abundant flowers, vigorous constitution, more upright habit (3 to 5'), also shows a suckering tendency that is stronger than many plants; has survived −25°F and flowered; collected 189 cuttings on July 24, 1988, 3000 ppm KIBA with 100% rooting in 7 weeks and 100% overwinter survival; this form appears easy to grow in containers and even under high nutrition has developed spectacular fall color; possibly a hybrid between *F. gardenii* and *F. major*.

PROPAGATION: The best seed information comes from Mr. Alfred Fordham, Propagator, at the Arnold Arboretum [See *Arnoldia* 31:256–259 (1971)]; seeds are somewhat difficult to germinate for they exhibit a double dormancy and pretreatment must be accomplished in two stages, seeds require warm fluctuating temperatures followed by a period of cold. *Fothergilla major* seeds have required exceptionally long warm periods with 12 months being optimum; after warm treatment they should be placed at 40°F for 3 months. *Fothergilla gardenii* has germinated well after 6 months of warm pretreatment followed by 3 months at 40°F. Cuttings, wood taken from suckers or root cuttings yielded good results, best with bottom heat; *F. major*—untreated cuttings taken when shrubs were in flower rooted 67% in sandy soil in 60 days; June cuttings set in sand:peat rooted 67% without treatment, and 100% in 42 days after treatment with 200 ppm IAA/24 hours; for some reason the two species treated here have been listed as difficult to root; I have a "love affair" with these shrubs and would like to describe some of my propagation adventures (see Dirr. *Horticulture* 40(12):38–39. 1977. Fothergillas: A garden aristocrat.); softwood cuttings can be readily rooted when collected in June, July and as late as August; they should be treated with IBA-quick dip and placed in peat:perlite under mist; one experiment (see *The Plant Propagator* 24(1):8–9, 1978) we conducted with *F. major* involved 0, 1000, 2500, 5000 and 10,000 ppm IBA-quick dip treatments and 1000 ppm NAA-quick dip; *all* cuttings, even the controls, rooted 80 to 100%; the greatest numbers of roots were produced with the highest IBA levels but surprisingly the NAA treatment resulted in the greatest number of roots; *F. gardenii* is also easily rooted; I have found that if the cuttings are still growing when rooted they can be transplanted, if not the following handling practice should apply; often after rooted cuttings are transplanted they enter a dormancy from which they never recover; the problem can be avoided if the cuttings, when rooted, are left in the flats and hardened off; the flats of dormant cuttings are transferred to cold storage, which is maintained at 34°F; in February or March the flats are returned to a warm greenhouse and when growth appears the cuttings are potted; over the years I have propagated thousands of both species and firmly believe I have made, along with my colleagues, a propagation mountain out of a molehill; standard procedure now includes 3000 ppm KIBA quick dip, 2 perlite: 1 peat, in 3 by 3 by 3 1/2″ deep cells, mist, root in 4 to 7 weeks, remove from mist and leave be or apply 100 ppm nitrogen solution; rooted cuttings will often put out a flush of growth after the application; +90% of the cuttings overwinter regardless of the growth flush.

ADDITIONAL NOTES: Anyone interested in furthering their *Fothergilla* education should consult Dr. Richard Weaver's excellent article in *Arnoldia* 31:89–97 (1971), and Flint, *Horticulture* 43(9):12–16 (1984).

NATIVE HABITAT: Introduced 1765. All species are localized in the southeastern United States; *F. gardenii* is a Coastal Plain species and is often found around the edges of ponds or boggy type depressions called pocasins, from North Carolina to southern Alabama and the Florida panhandle.

Fothergilla major — Large Fothergilla
(foth-ēr-gil′a mā′jor)

LEAVES: Alternate, simple, suborbicular to oval or obovate, cordate or truncate, 2 to 4″ long, from 2/3's to as wide, coarsely crenate-dentate or sometimes denticulate above the middle, glabrous and dark green above, glaucous and stellate-pubescent beneath at least on the veins, leathery; petioles 1/3″ long, tomentose.

BUDS: Moderate or small, stalked, oblique, obovate or oblong, with 2-caducous scales, often collaterally branched; terminal largest.

STEM: Rounded, zig-zag, slender, dingy stellate-tomentose or more or less glabrescent, pith rather small, somewhat angular, continuous, for a time greenish; leaf-scars 2 ranked, half-rounded or deltoid, small, slightly raised; stipule-scars unequal, one short the other elongated; 3 bundle-traces, more or less compound or confluent.

SIZE: 6 to 10′ in height; slightly less to a similar spread.
HARDINESS: Zone 4 to 8.

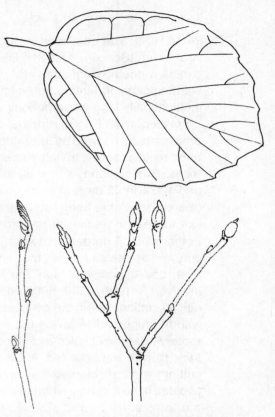

HABIT: A rounded, multistemmed shrub with mostly erect stems; very dense due to the leaves which are closely borne along the stems; have seen rounded and upright-oval versions.

RATE: Slow, actually medium in youth with ample water and fertilizer.

TEXTURE: Medium in leaf and winter.

LEAF COLOR: Dark green in summer; fall color ranges from yellow to orange and scarlet often with all colors present in the same leaf; one of our more handsome native fall coloring shrubs.

FLOWERS: Whitish, apetalous, the showy portion of the flower being the stamens, borne in 1 to 2″ bottlebrush-like spikes in April to early May; the flowers are fragrant and remind one of the smell of honey.

FRUIT: Two-valved, dehiscent capsule, 1/2″ long, splitting at the top, usually containing two shiny black seeds.

CULTURE: The need for acid soil conditions is of paramount importance; most authorities indicated that *Fothergilla* species are not suitable for limy soils; have observed a light green (yellow-green) margin around the leaf on stressed plants, see *F. gardenii* for further discussion.

DISEASES AND INSECTS: See under *F. gardenii*.

LANDSCAPE VALUE: Excellent shrub for the residential landscape; adds considerable color from April to October by virtue of flower and fall color; the summer foliage is a leathery dark green and is not affected by diseases or insects; probably best used in the shrub border but could be employed in groupings, masses and foundation plantings.

CULTIVARS:

'Huntsman'—A form with good red fall color that was introduced to the U.S. from England.

PROPAGATION: See under *F. gardenii*.

ADDITIONAL NOTES: This species and *F. monticola,* Alabama Fothergilla, are quite similar and are now treated as one species, *F. major;* in the past, plants with more glabrous vegetative parts were listed as *F. monticola;* also *F. monticola* was supposedly smaller in size (6′) but these differences are not absolute; the current thinking is the lumping of the two species into the *F. major* category. This brief discussion has been left in the fourth edition in case people wonder what happened to *F. monticola.*

I have had many opportunities to propagate, grow and evaluate the two species treated here. I can say without equivocation that they are among the most beautiful shrubs for autumn coloration. No two are exactly alike which adds to their interest. In fact, often every leaf is colored differently. I do believe there is an opportunity for selection of superior flowering and fall coloring types by observant plantsmen. I have planted both species in my Georgia garden in full sun which appears to be a mistake because they are not thriving as they did at my Illinois garden. Some shade and soil moisture in hot climates may be a necessity.

The Arnold Arboretum has identified a hybrid between the two species which offers intermediate size and other characteristics. This could be a most valuable shrub for modern landscapes.

NATIVE HABITAT: Indigenous to the Allegheny Mountains from northern North Carolina and Tennessee to northern Alabama. Introduced late 1800's.

Franklinia alatamaha — Franklinia, Franklin Tree
(frank-lin′i-a ȧ-la-ta-ma′ha)

FAMILY: Theaceae

LEAVES: Alternate, simple, 5 to 6″ long, up to 3″ across, obovate-oblong, acute, gradually narrowed into a short petiole, remotely serrate, shiny dark green above, pubescent below.

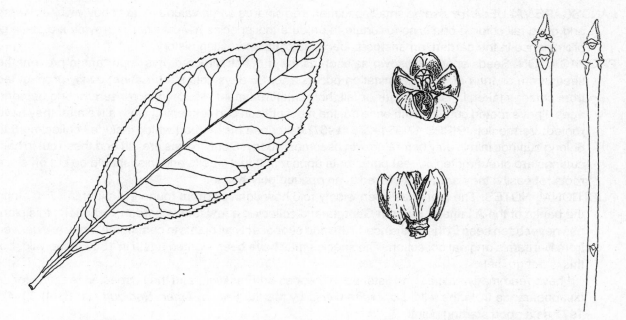

BUDS: Terminal—elongated, silky, pubescent, grayish brown, scales weakly overlap, 1/4 to 1/2″ long; laterals—conical-ovoid, brownish pubescent, 1/16″ long, sit above leaf scar, appearing partially imbedded.

STEM: Moderate, terete, young stems silky-pubescent, green to brown, dotted with numerous small lenticels; pith rather large, coffee-colored, continuous; leaf-scars half-round, or shield-shaped, scarcely raised; 1 bundle-trace, transverse or V-shaped, compound; strange odor to bruised stems.

SIZE: 10 to 20′ (30′) in height by 6 to 15′ wide.

HARDINESS: Zone 5 to 8(9).

HABIT: Small tree or shrub with upright, spreading branches, often leafless in their lower reaches, giving the plant an open, airy appearance; not unlike *Magnolia virginiana* in habit.

RATE: Medium, proper water and fertilizer induces excellent growth.

TEXTURE: Medium in all seasons.

BARK: Smooth, gray, broken by irregular vertical fissures; trunks assume a slight fluted condition; very attractive feature.

LEAF COLOR: Lustrous dark green in summer changing to orange and red in fall; very handsome foliage, leaves hold late, have recorded them present in early to mid November, Boston.

FLOWERS: Perfect, white, 5-petaled, yellow center of stamens, very striking, 3″ across, fragrant, solitary, slightly cup-shaped; late July into August and weakly into September.

FRUIT: Woody, 5-valved capsule, 1/2 to 3/4″ in diameter, splitting into 10 segments; a rather curious fruit on close inspection and one which is not easily forgotten, several flattened-angular seeds in each cell.

CULTURE: Somewhat hard to transplant because of sparsely fibrous root system; best to move as a small container or balled and burlapped specimen; requires moist, acid, well-drained soil which has been supplied with ample organic matter; full sun or light shade but best flowering and fall coloration occur in full sun.

DISEASES AND INSECTS: Wilt caused by *Phytophthora cinnamoni* species is serious in propagating beds and container-grown plants [see *J. Arboriculture* 6(4):89–92. 1980 for details]; interestingly in the south this species does not perform as well as it does in the north; there is speculation that a disease associated with cotton infects *Franklinia;* since the organism is soil-borne and cotton once covered most of the Piedmont there is no "safe" place to culture the tree; some of the best specimens are located at the Arnold Arboretum and Longwood Gardens.

LANDSCAPE VALUE: A handsome small specimen tree or large shrub valued for the showy white flowers and good fall color; if one is so fortunate to procure this species he/she should provide it a place of prominence in the garden; an aristocrat because of its interesting history.

PROPAGATION: Seeds should be sown as soon as the fruit has matured, it is important to prevent the seeds from drying out; best germination occurs after 30 days cold stratification; easily propagated from cuttings taken in late summer or fall; hormonal treatment results in increased rooting percentages. I have rooted cuttings with ease but the most difficult part is keeping them alive after they have rooted; Vermeulen. PIPPS 17:254–255 (1967) described his method which includes collecting 5 to 6″ long cuttings in mid July before growth becomes woody, 5 or 6 leaves are left and these cut in half; cuttings are direct rooted in peat pots, roots appear in 3 to 4 weeks and mist should be cut off since roots rot easily; they are overwintered in an opaque poly-house.

ADDITIONAL NOTES: The story has been widely told how John Bartram found this plant in 1770 along the banks of the Altamaha River in Georgia and collected a few for his garden; strangely, this plant has never been seen in the wild since 1790, and supposedly all plants in commerce today are derived from Bartram's original collection. The species may have been sighted again in 1803 in the wild, but this is not gospel.

I have read many articles and listened to theories on *Franklinia* and the suspected reasons for its disappearance from the wild. I offer *Franklinia* by Martha Prince, *Amer. Horticulturist* 56(4):39–41. 1977 as a good starting point.

NATIVE HABITAT: Once, the wilds of Georgia.

RELATED SPECIES:

Gordonia lasianthus—Loblolly-bay
LEAVES: Alternate, simple, evergreen, obovate-lanceolate, 4 to 6″ long, acute, cuneate, lightly serrate, glossy dark green above, lighter green below.

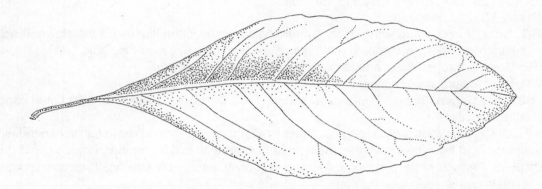

Gordonia lasianthus, (gôr-dō′ni-à lā-zi-an′thus), Loblolly-bay, is sometimes confused with *Franklinia* and at one time *Franklinia* was referred to as "The Lost Gordonia". Loblolly-bay is a wet soil species found throughout the Coastal Plain from Virginia to Florida to Louisiana. It has evergreen leaves, 2 1/2″ diameter white flowers with yellow stamens (similar to *F. alatamaha*) which appear in May and continue to October on the Georgia campus. It is a slender, narrow-conical, open tree that grows about 30 to 40′ under cultivation. This species suffers under cultivation and I have seen too many young plants die from a wilt type symptom. Perfectly drained soils are necessary under cultivation although the plant grows submerged, at least for a time, in the wild. Possibly the conditions in swamps result in such low pH that the causal organism does not grow. Also, young trees are usually open and rather unappealing. Zone 8 to 9. Dr. Orton produced hybrids between this and *Franklinia* in an attempt to trace the origin of the latter. His interesting work appeared in *Amer. Assoc. Bot. Gard. Arb. Bull.* 11(4):81–84. 1977.

Fraxinus americana — White Ash
(frak′si-nus a-mer-i-kā′na)

FAMILY: Oleaceae

LEAVES: Opposite, pinnately compound, 8 to 15″ long, 5 to 9 leaflets, usually 7, stalked, 2 to 6″ long, 1 to 3″ wide, ovate to ovate-lanceolate, acute to acuminate at apex, rounded or tapered at base, usually entire, or edged near the apex or the entire margin with remote serrations, dark green and glabrous above, glaucous beneath and usually glabrous; petiolules of lateral leaflets 1/3″ long, terminal 1/2 to 1″ long; petiole—yellowish, glabrous, round, with a slight groove above.

BUDS: Terminal present, 2 to 3 pairs of scales, semi-spherical to broadly ovate, scurfy, and more or less slightly downy, rusty to dark brown to sometimes almost black; terminal about 1/4″ long, usually broader than long; buds inset in the leaf scar.

STEM: Stout, rounded, smooth and shining, grayish or greenish brown often with a slight bloom, brittle, flattened at nodes at right angles to leaf scars; leaf scars "U" shaped with deep to shallow notch; vascular bundles forming open "C" shape.

SIZE: 50 to 80′ in height with a spread of similar proportions, can grow to 120′.

HARDINESS: Zone 3 to 9.

HABIT: In youth weakly pyramidal to upright oval, and in old age developing an open and rather round topped crown; unique in maintaining a central leader in youth with an even distribution of branches.

RATE: Medium, 1 to 2′ per year over a 10 to 15 year period.

TEXTURE: Medium in leaf; medium-coarse in winter.

BARK: Ashy-gray to gray-brown, furrowed into close diamond-shaped areas separated by narrow interlacing ridges; on very old trees slightly scaly along the ridges.

LEAF COLOR: Dark green above and paler beneath in summer changing to yellow to deep purple and maroon colors in fall; I have seen trees with yellow fall color as well as individuals of dark, intense, maroon color; colors early, often by late September, and most leaves abscised by mid to late October.

FLOWER: Dioecious (possibly polygamo-dioecious), usually unisexual, apetalous, both sexes appearing in panicles before the leaves, not ornamentally important, calyx minute, campanulate, corolla absent, green to purple, April.

FRUIT: Samara, 1 to 2″ long, 1/4″ wide, of no ornamental quality, body rounded in cross-section; wing extending about 1/3 of the way down the body.

CULTURE: Easily transplanted, makes its best growth on deep, moist, well drained soils but also withstands soils which are not excessively dry and rocky; seems to be pH adaptable; full sun; prune in fall; not as adaptable as the Green Ash but much superior to it as an ornamental.

DISEASES AND INSECTS: Ashes are susceptible to many problems and the following list is applicable to the plant types which follow as well as White Ash. Leaf rust, leaf spots (many), cankers (many), dieback has been associated with White Ash (probably mycoplasms), ash borer (can be very destructive), lilac leaf miner, lilac borer, carpenter worm, brown-headed ash sawfly, fall webworm, ash flower gall (flowers develop abnormally and galls are evident on white ash male flowers throughout the winter, caused by a mite), oyster shell scale, and scurfy scale.

LANDSCAPE VALUE: One would wonder if the ashes have any value after reading that impressive list of insects and diseases; vigorous growing trees do not develop that many problems but homeowners should always be on the lookout and when something seems awry should call a tree specialist or seek help through their county extension office; the White Ash is a handsome native tree for parks and other large areas; I hesitate to recommend it for extensive homeowner use because of size and potential pest problems.

CULTIVARS: These selected clones are much preferable to seedling grown trees and should be sought out if a White Ash is desired.

'Autumn Applause'—Densely branched oval form with close-knit branches, produces reliable maroon fall color, narrower leaflet than typical White Ash, somewhat drooping appearance to the leaf, 40' by 25', male, Wandell introduction.

'Autumn Blaze'—First adapted White Ash for the prairie region of Dakotas and Canada, oval form with purple fall color, female but described as having light fruit set, Morden introduction.

'Autumn Purple'—A fine selection of pyramidal-rounded outline with deep green leaves and handsome reddish purple fall color, a male tree; I have seen the tree in fall color in the midwest and east and the color was a more subdued reddish purple in the midwest compared to a rich deep red on Maine's campus; fall color may hold 2 to 4 weeks, the leaflets are glossy which also contributes to the beauty, 45' by 60'.

'Champaign County'—Tight dense crown and lustrous leaves that show no appreciable fall color (yellow); the heavy trunk is so stout that whips supposedly do not need staking; strong central leader, 45' by 30'.

'Chicago Regal'—Vigorous, upright growth habit, 18-year-old tree was 30' by 15', deep green foliage turns regal purple with earth tones, bark is resistant to frost cracking, a Klehm introduction.

'Elk Grove'—Vigorous upright growth habit, lustrous dark green foliage that turns rich royal purple, bark resistant to frost cracking, a Klehm introduction.

'Greenspire'—A narrow upright form with dark green leaves that turn dark orange in autumn, a Princeton introduction.

'Manitoo' ('Manitou')—Noteworthy because of its narrow, upright growth habit; a Canadian introduction.

'Rosehill'—Dark green summer foliage, bronze-red fall color, tolerant of poor, alkaline soils; may not be as hardy as 'Autumn Purple', seedless, 50' by 30', have seen in Raleigh, NC where fall color was yellow-bronze-red and not very effective.

'Royal Purple'—Royal purple autumn foliage, shapely upright growth habit, 30' by 25' in 24 years, resistant to frost cracking, a Klehm introduction.

'Skyline'—Oval form with central leader, symmetrical branching and good crotch angles, glossy medium green leaves turn orange-red, 50' by 40', seedless.

PROPAGATION: Seeds germinate best with warm stratification at 68 to 86°F for 30 days followed by cold at 41°F for 60 days; cultivars are budded onto seedling understocks in summer.

ADDITIONAL NOTES: Truly a beautiful tree in fall color; in my travels through central and southern Indiana I have seen magnificent specimens 70 to 80' high and wide. Unfortunately White Ash does not like harsh conditions. Much noise has been made about ash decline which results in dieback for no apparent reason. Appears to be a combination of factors impinging on the health of the tree plus mycoplasm like organisms.

NATIVE HABITAT: Nova Scotia to Minnesota, south to Florida and Texas. Introduced 1724.

Fraxinus pennsylvanica — Green Ash. Formerly listed as *F. p. var. lanceolata* while Red Ash was listed as *F. pennsylvanica*. Both Red and Green are now included in the same species.
(frak'si-nus pen-sil-van'i-ka)

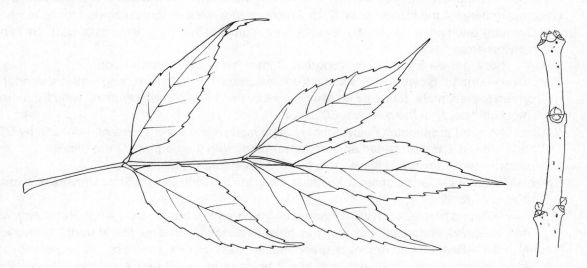

LEAVES: Opposite, pinnately compound, up to 12″ long, 5 to 9 leaflets, 2 to 5″ long, 1 to 2″ wide, ovate to oblong-lanceolate, acuminate, broad-cuneate, crenate serrate or entire, lustrous medium to dark green and essentially glabrous above, pubescent beneath.

BUDS: Dark rusty brown, smaller and narrower than those of the White Ash, woolly, set above leaf scar, leaf scars nearly straight across at the top.

STEM: Rounded, rather stout, densely velvety downy or glabrous, leaf scar not notched, vascular bundles forming closed "C" shape.

SIZE: 50 to 60′ in height by about 1/2 that in spread, although can grow to over 80′.

HARDINESS: Zone 3 to 9.

HABIT: Softly pyramidal when young, developing an upright, spreading habit at maturity with 3 to 5 main branches and many coarse, twiggy branchlets which bend down and then up at the ends; the crown is extremely irregular and the overall habit somewhat difficult to describe; sometimes rather unsightly.

RATE: Fast, 2 to 3′ per year in the landscape over a 10 year period; budded trees may grow 8 to 12′ in a single season.

TEXTURE: Medium in leaf; quite coarse in winter.

BARK: Similar to White Ash.

LEAF COLOR: Variable, but often a shiny medium to dark green in summer changing to yellow in the fall; fall coloration is inconsistent and seed-grown trees provide only disappointment; can be spectacular when right.

FLOWER: See description for White Ash; produced on old wood just below new shoot, green to reddish purple, April.

FRUIT: Samara, 1 to 2″ long, 1/4″ or less wide, wing extending half-way or more down the cylindrical body.

CULTURE: Transplants readily and grows about anywhere; hence, its tremendous popularity; actually this is strange for it is found native in moist bottomlands or along stream banks; however, once established it tolerates high pH, salt, drought, and sterile soils; requires full sun; prune in fall. Interestingly, 'Marshall's Seedless' and 'Summit' averaged 1′7″ and 1′4″ per year, respectively, in Wichita, KS tests but both were attacked by borers.

DISEASES AND INSECTS: See White Ash; borers and scale are significant problems.

LANDSCAPE VALUE: In a way, this tree has been overplanted because of its adaptability; it has been used for streets, lawns, commercial areas, parks, golf coarses and about any other area one can think of; best for plains' states where few trees proliferate but somehow has become the favorite of many plnt people; one of the real problems is the use of seedling grown trees for they often fruit and in so doing become a significant nuisance; have observed a number of Green Ash in the south, some are performing reasonably well, others less so.

CULTIVARS: Since the last edition, a number of selections have been introduced. In fact, I doubt if anyone could accurately list the top three cultivars. I have seen several of the variegated forms in England and Germany and find them virtually unredeeming. 'Aucubaefolia' and 'Variegata' continue to haunt me in my dreams.

'Aerial'—Tight, narrow crown; branch sport of 'Summit'; a Wandell introduction.

'Bergeson'—Upright growth habit, straight trunk, vigorous, fast to caliper, long lustrous slender dark green leaves, male, found by Melvin Bergeson, Fertile, MN; possibly along with 'Patmore' the most cold hardy of the cultivars, 50' by 35'.

'Cardan'—A seed propagated cultivar that is supposedly quite borer resistant, released by USDA-SCS and SEA for farmstead and windbreak planting in the northern Great Plains.

'Cimmaron'—Rich dark green leaves turn brick-red in autumn, male, 60' by 30'.

'Dakota Centennial'—Globe shaped, seedless selection by North Dakota State University, extremely hardy, 40 to 50'.

'Emerald'—Round headed form with glossy dark green leaves, bark like Common Hackberry, 45' by 40', seedless, perhaps not as hardy as other selections, introduced by Marshall Nursery.

'Honeyshade'—Beautiful, glossy dark green leaflets, fast grower, seedless, unfortunately seldom seen in commerce, does not look like it belongs to the Green Ash tribe, Klehm Nursery introduction.

'Jewell'—Shiny dark green leaves, well branched form, fruitful.

'Kindred'—Maintains a central leader, fast growing, good foliage, seedless, good hardiness, selected by Ben Gilbertson, Kindred, ND.

'King Richard'—Glossy deep green foliage, uniform upright growth habit, male, a Klehm introduction.

'Marshall's Seedless'—Male form with glossy dark green foliage; more vigorous and has less insect problems than the species; lustrous dark green foliage, yellow fall color; may be more than one clone originally introduced, 50' by 40'.

'Newport' (Bailey, Bailey's Select Green Ash)—Straight trunk, good branching, foliage similar to 'Marshall's Seedless', male, a Bailey Nursery introduction.

'Patmore'—Upright branching, oval head, more uniform and symmetrical than 'Marshall's Seedless', growth rate in nursery slower than 'Marshall's Seedless', equal to 'Summit', 5 to 7 glossy dark green, neatly serrated leaflets, male, hardier than 'Marshall's Seedless', discovered by Richard Patmore, Brandon, MN, as a native seedling in Vegreville, Alberta, near Edmonton, probably hardy to −50°F, 45' by 35'.

'Prairie Spire'—Compact grower with an upright oval form, seedless, hardy, North Dakota State University introduction.

'Robinhood'—Lustrous, vibrant green foliage and vigorous, upright growth habit, male, a Klehm introduction.

'Sherwood Glen'—Uniform upright tree with thick deep green foliage, a Klehm introduction.

'Skyward'—Narrow constricted crown, good leaf texture, heavy rough bark, purple fall color, a Wandell introduction.

'Summit'—Upright, pyramidal, glossy foliage selection out of Minnesota tends to drop its leaves two weeks earlier in the fall than 'Marshall's Seedless'; straight central leader; foliage not as lustrous or dark green as 'Marshall's Seedless' but more refined; excellent golden yellow fall color; considerable confusion whether male or female although older trees I have seen did not fruit; 45' by 25'.

'Urbanite'—Broad, pyramidal form with thick, leathery, lustrous dark green leaves and a deep bronze fall color, bark appears resistant to sun scald, seedless, 50' by 40', Wandell introduction.

PROPAGATION: Seed requires warm (68°F), moist stratification for 60 days, followed by 120 days at 32 to 41°F; cultivars are budded onto seedling understocks.

NATIVE HABITAT: Nova Scotia to Manitoba, south to northern Florida and Texas. Introduced 1824.

OTHER *FRAXINUS:* Other *Fraxinus* of landscape importance but of significantly less concern than the previous species include:

Fraxinus angustifolia—Narrowleaf Ash

LEAVES: Opposite, compound pinnate, 6 to 10″ long, 7 to 13 leaflets, each 1 to 3″ long, 1/3 to 3/4″ wide, oblong-lanceolate to narrow-lanceolate, acuminate, cuneate, sharply and remotely serrate, dark green above, lighter beneath, glabrous.
BUDS: Brown, which separates it from the closely allied *F. excelsior.*

Fraxinus angustifolia, (frak′si-nus an-gus-ti-fō′li-à), Narrowleaf Ash, is a tree reaching 60 to 80′ in height. The specimens I have seen were upright-oval in habit with lustrous dark green leaflets of more refined nature than the two American species discussed above. At Kew Gardens, London, I saw a 60 to 70′ specimen of the species. It makes a good looking tree where it can be properly grown. Native of the western Mediterranean and northern Africa. Cultivated 1800. Zone 5.

Fraxinus excelsior—Common or European Ash
(frak′si-nus ek-sel′si-or)

LEAVES: Opposite, compound pinnate, 10 to 12″ long, leaflets 7 to 11, essentially sessile, ovate-oblong to ovate-lanceolate, 2 to 3 1/2″ long, 1 to 1 1/3″ wide, acuminate, cuneate, serrate, dark green above, lighter green beneath, glabrous except villous along the midrib beneath; rachis—usually pubescent.
BUDS: Black, pubescent, sessile, with 2 to 3 pairs of opposite scales.
STEM: Usually rounded, somewhat flattened at nodes, glabrous at maturity, grayish or grayish brown.

Fraxinus excelsior, Common or European Ash, grows 70 to 80′ with a 60 to 90′ spread, reaching on favored sites from 100 to 140′ in height. Forms a round-headed, broad spreading outline, the lower branches upcurving. Foliage is dark green in summer and drops off green or develops a casual yellow. Prefers a deep, moist, loamy soil and thrives on limestone (calcareous) soils; one of the largest of European deciduous trees and much planted there. Has not had overwhelming acceptance in America because of borer susceptibility and the fact that our native ashes make better landscape plants. Many cultivars are available and the following are a few or the more popular.

'Aurea'—Young shoots yellow; older bark yellowish, quite noticeable in winter; fall color deep yellow; slow growing.
'Aurea Pendula'—Branches weeping and forming a flat, umbrella-like head, young shoots yellow.
'Globosa'—A dense rounded head, 30′ in height with a 20′ spread; leaves smaller than the type.
'Gold Cloud'—Yellow leaves and stems, leaves turn yellow in fall; rapid growing, seedless.
'Hessei'—Leaves are simple and prominently toothed, lustrous dark green; very vigorous; upright oval to rounded; seedless; has shown good pest resistance compared to the species and other ashes; I had three in the Illinois evaluation plots and found them to be extremely hardy and vigorous; little fall color as the leaves stay green late into fall; trees form a stright sturdy trunk,

well filled with branches, and almost flat topped at maturity, 60′, Zone 4. One of the highest rated trees in the Ohio Shade Tree Evaluation Tests. Unfortunately, this cultivar has proven almost as susceptible to borers as the species; shows great vigor and averaged 1′ 6.3″ per year over a 9 year period in Wichita, KS tests; Dr. John Pair noted that despite the excellent vigor there was much borer damage.

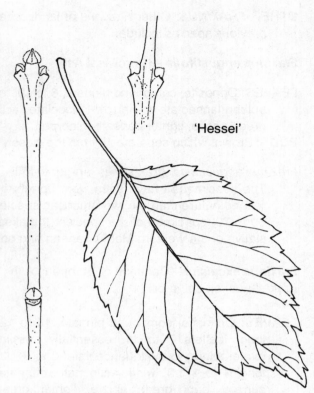

'Hessei'

'Jaspidea', 'Jaspidea Pendula'—Sometimes seen in botanic gardens; the former has yellow leaves when young with good yellow fall color; grows more vigorously, taller and open than 'Aurea'; the latter is a weeping form with similar leaf traits.

'Kimberly' ('Kimberly Blue')—Santamour and McArdle, *J. Arboriculture* 9(10):271–279 (1983) and 10(1):21–32 (1984) published checklists of North American and European Ash cultivars. They straighten the confusion concerning this selection. It was selected by Kimberly Nursery, Kimberly, Idaho about 1936. Characteristics include attractive compact symmetrical form, sturdy rapid growth, seedless. The authors noted that the tree has lost favor in recent years because of a "virus" or "decline"; not proven hardy at the Minnesota Landscape Arboretum and was also injured in the Chicago area during the harsh (–20° to –25°F) winter of 1976–77.

'Pendula'—Branches all weeping, forming a spreading umbrella-like head; this appears the most popular weeping tree in England and I have seen magnificent specimens throughout the cities and countryside; it does make a rather interesting tree and I will always remember a large, imposing specimen that reminded of a mop in Canterbury and a grizzled old specimen in Oxford Botanic Garden; the tree descends from the middle 1700's, female.

'Rancho'—Small (30′) round headed type, with dark green leaves and yellow fall color.

There are numerous other cultivars of Common Ash but their use is negligible or nonexistent in this country. Native of Europe and Asia Minor. Cultivated for centuries. Based on evaluations at arboreta in the midwest I would estimate a Zone 5 to 7 adaptability range.

Fraxinus holotricha

LEAVES: Opposite, often whorled, compound pinnate, (5)9 to 13 leaflets, mostly 11, each leaflet elliptic or oblong-elliptic to lanceolate or broad elliptic, 1 1/2 to 2 3/4″ long, 1/2 to 3/4″ wide, acuminate, cuneate, serrate, most stalked on 1/3″ long petiolules, can be sessile, lustrous green, essentially glabrous above, with pubescence below.

BUDS: Often whorled, especially on young vigorous shoots, pubescent, brown black.

Fraxinus holotricha, (frak′si-nus hol-ō-tri′ka), 'Moraine', Moraine Ash, is a round headed tree 30 to 40′ in height with a similar spread; very susceptible to borer injury; has a finer texture than many ashes; watched trees in Urbana, IL literally succumb to borer. Actually the tree was uniformly rounded, light foliage texture and rather handsome. Simply could not handle adversity.

Fraxinus nigra—Black Ash

LEAVES: Opposite, compound pinnate, 7 to 11 leaflets, oblong or oblong-lance shaped, 3 to 5″ long, 1 to 2″ wide, long acuminate, obliquely cuneate or rounded, serrate with small incurved teeth, dark green

and glabrous above, lighter and hairy at base
and on midrib below; all leaflets except terminal one are sessile.
BUDS: Black.

Fraxinus nigra, (frak′si-nus nī′gra), Black Ash, is a
small to medium-sized tree reaching 40 to 50′
in height and developing a rather narrow, open
crown. The bark is scaly and flaky rather than
ridged-and-furrowed. In the wild it occurs in
wet places: low wet woods, cold swamps, and
periodically inundated river bottoms. Does not
have much to recommend it for ornamental
use. 'Fallgold' is a seedless, clean, disease-
free foliage form with long persisting golden
fall coloration and upright growth habit. Native
from Newfoundland to Manitoba, south to
Delaware, Virgina and Iowa. Introduced 1800.
Zone 2 to 5. (Extremely hardy).

Fraxinus ornus—Flowering Ash

LEAVES: Opposite, compound pinnate,
5 to 8″ long, 5 to 9, usually 7
leaflets, each 2 to 4″ long, 3/4 to 1
3/4″ wide, oblong to ovate, terminal
one obovate, abruptly pointed,
broad cuneate, irregularly serrate,
dull dark green and glabrous
above, pubescent on base of midrib
below.
BUDS: Pubescent, grayish brown.

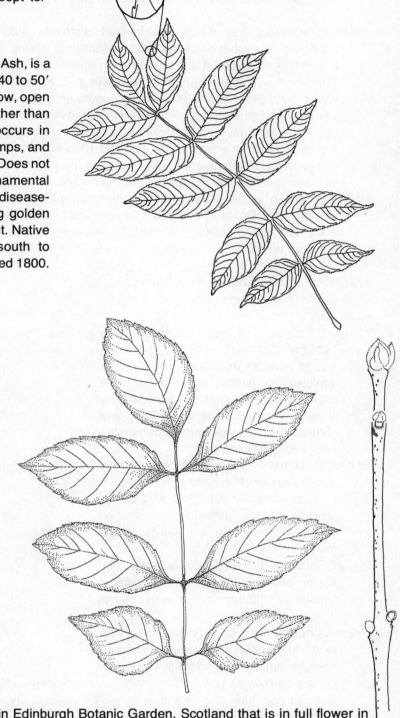

Fraxinus ornus, (frak′si-nus ôr′nus),
Flowering Ash, reaches 40 to 50′ in
height and develops a rounded,
spreading head; hardy to −10°F
(Zone 5 to 6). The flowers are
showy, fragrant, and borne in 5″
long panicles in May. This is one of
the few ashes which has a corolla
and calyx. This species has long
been popular in European gardens
and has been cultivated there for
over 300 years. Beautiful specimen in Edinburgh Botanic Garden, Scotland that is in full flower in
June. It makes a superb show and tempts one to at least try the tree. The bark is smooth and gray,
not unlike that of European Beech. Native to southeastern Europe and western Asia. Introduced
1700. Zone 5 to 6.

Fraxinus oxycarpa

LEAVES: Very closely allied to *F. angustifolia* and often treated as a subspecies, often whorled, 3 to 7
leaflets, 1 1/2 to 2 1/2″ long, half this in width, lanceolate to narrow-elliptic, acute or acuminate,

cuneate or long-cuneate, sessile, finely to coarsely serrate; the principal difference between this and *F. angustifolia* is a band of hairs on each side of the midrib at its base.

Fraxinus oxycarpa, (frak′si-nus ok-si-kär′pȧ), is closely allied to *F. angustifolia* and by some authorities is treated as a subspecies. Its chief distinction is a band of hairs on either side of midrib at the base. It also is less vigorous and smaller with a smoother bark. I only know this tree through its cultivar 'Raywood' which was raised in Australia. It is a handsome tree somewhat narrow in habit when young but opening up with age. The compound pinnate leaves are composed of 7 to 9, sharply serrated, lustrous dark green leaflets. The leaves are usually whorled or present in 4's immediately under the terminal bud. The leaves turn a rich plum purple in fall if sited in full sun and a somewhat dryish situation. It will probably average 40 to 50′ in height under cultivation but a 47-year-old tree has grown to 80′ in height. I have seen it at the Arnold Arboretum and in California. It might deserve a closer look from the nursery trade. 'Flame' has a symmetrical rounded outline and narrow, lustrous dark green leaflets that turn rich deep burgundy and then, to a flame color, 30′, a Scanlon introduction; 'Golden Desert' is a small round headed tree (20′) with green foliage that turns to gold about July, a Scanlon introduction. Native to southeastern Europe, lower Danube, Asia Minor and the Caucasus. Zone 5 to 8(9).

Fraxinus quadrangulata—Blue Ash
(frak′si-nus kwa-drang-ū-lā′ta)

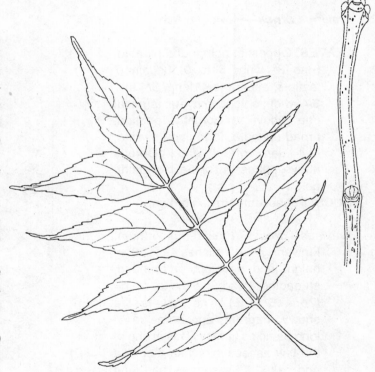

LEAVES: Opposite, pinnately compound, 7 to 14″ long, (5)7 to 11 leaflets, 2 to 5″ long, 1 to 2″ wide, short stalked, ovate to lanceolate, acuminate, broad-cuneate or rounded and unequal at base, sharply serrate, lustrous dark green, and glabrous above, pubescent along midrib near base beneath.

BUDS: Dark gray to reddish brown, slightly puberulous or often hairy-tomentose.

STEM: Stout, usually 4-angled and corky-winged, brown, glabrous at maturity; vascular bundles in a lunate arrangement.

BARK: Rather thin, gray, divided into plate-like scales, often shaggy; inner bark contains substance which turns blue on exposure.

Fraxinus quadrangulata, Blue Ash, grows 50 to 70′ in height and develops a slender, straight, slightly tapered trunk which supports a narrow, rounded, often irregular crown of spreading branches. The leaves are dark green in summer changing to pale yellow in fall. It frequents dry, limestone, upland soils. Does not seem to be a fast grower and is somewhat difficult to propagate. Bark is different from other ashes for on old trunks it is broken into scaly plates. The inner bark contains a mucilaginous substance which turns blue on exposure. 'True Blue'—an excellent fairly fast growing square-twigged blue ash classified as a calciphyte capable of tolerating 'sweet' soils. Keeps green color throughout the growing season—does not "yellow out" like the species. Small narrow leaves: full crown as it matures, 80′ by 40′. Minnesota Arboretum reports good success with the species. Grew 8.5″ per year over 9 years in KS. Showed good drought tolerance, did contract borer. Native from Michigan to Arkansas and Tennessee. Introduced 1823. Zone 4 to 7.

Fraxinus tomentosa—Pumpkin Ash

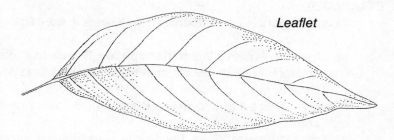

Leaflet

LEAVES: Opposite, compound pinnate, 10 to 18″ long, 7 to 9 leaflets, oblong-lanceolate or ovate, 3 to 9″ long, 1 1/2 to 3 1/2″ wide, slender pointed, rounded or broad cuneate, entire or slightly toothed, dark green and glabrous above, soft pubescent below especially on midrib and veins, petiolules of lower leaflets 1/4″ long, rachis round not grooved or winged.

Fraxinus tomentosa, (frak′si-nus tō-men-tō′sa), Pumpkin Ash, is strictly a tree of deep swamps and inundated river bottoms which may grow 80 to 100′ or more. The crown is open and narrow, with small spreading branches; the leaflets are quite large reaching 10″ in length. Native from western New York to southern Illinois, Louisiana, and northwestern Florida. Introduced 1913. Zone 5 to 9.

Gardenia jasminoides — Cape Jasmine
(gär-dē′nia jas-min-oy′dēz)

FAMILY: Rubiaceae

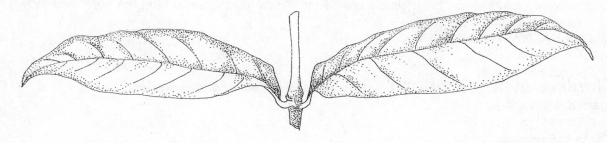

LEAVES: Opposite or whorled, simple, evergreen, lanceolate to obovate, 2 to 4″ long, one-half as wide, short-acuminate, cuneate, entire, thickish, lustrous dark green, leathery.
STEM: Green, moderate, glabrous.

SIZE: 4 to 6′ by 4 to 6′.
HARDINESS: Zone 8 to 10, marginal in Zone 8 but has survived –3°F; killed to ground but regenerated.
HABIT: Dense, rounded evergreen shrub with a sort of "blend into the woodwork constitution" after flowering.
RATE: Medium.
TEXTURE: Medium.
LEAF COLOR: Very beautiful, lustrous dark green, quite leathery in texture.
FLOWERS: Perfect, waxy white, solitary, exceedingly fragrant, 2 to 3″ diameter, May, June, July.
FRUIT: Orange, fleshy, ovate, 1 1/2″ long berry.
CULTURE: Easily transplanted from containers; requires acid, moist, well-drained, high organic matter soils; protect from winter winds and cold; full sun to partial shade; injured severely at 0°F.
DISEASES AND INSECTS: Powdery mildew, canker (*Phomopsis gardeniae*), aphids, scale, mealybugs, white flies, thrips, mites, nematodes; requires a degree of attention to keep it looking thrifty; white flies are particularly troublesome.
LANDSCAPE VALUE: Excellent for fragrant flowers and handsome foliage; should be sited near patio or where people will notice the fragrance; flowers open over a long period of time; requires considerable maintenance.

CULTIVARS:
'August Beauty'—Large double white flowers, heavy flowering, May-October, 4 to 6′ high vigorous shrub.

'Fortuneiana'—Leaves larger than species; flowers to 4″ diameter, double and carnation like.

'Golden Magic'—Fairly double pure white flowers age to deep golden yellow, plants grow 3′ by 2′ in 3 years.

'Mystery'—Large 4 to 5″ diameter double white flowers on a large 4 to 6′ (8′) rather upright growing shrub.

'Radicans' ('Prostrata')—A handsome, small-leaved almost creeping version of the species; the small, lustrous leaves are especially handsome and coupled with the 1″ diameter fragrant flowers make this a better choice for many more landscapes than the species; grows 2 to 3′ high and spreads 4′, forms a graceful flowing evergreen shrub; good mass or facing plant; not particularly hardy; severely injured in exposed locations in Athens when low temperature was +12°F.

'Radicans Variegata'—Like the above but with a creamy white leaf margin, same floral characteristics as 'Radicans'; may produce branch reversions which need to be removed.

'Variegata'—A handsome creamy-variegated leaf form that is doubtfully as hardy as the species; have seen at North Carolina State Arboretum and was impressed.

'Veitchii'—Grows 2 to 4′ high and produces 1 to 1 1/2″ diameter white flowers, flowers profusely.

'Veitchii Improved'—Grows taller than 'Veitchii' to 5′ and produces slightly larger flowers in greater numbers.

PROPAGATION: Softwood cuttings root easily in June, July, August; have germinated seeds from wild collected material in China; simply sowed the seeds after removal from the berry and they germinated.

NATIVE HABITAT: China.

Gaultheria procumbens — Checkerberry or Creeping Wintergreen
(gawl-thēr′i-à prō-kum′benz)

FAMILY: Ericaceae

LEAVES: Alternate, simple, evergreen, oval to obovate, rarely suborbicular, 3/4 to 1 1/2″ long, 1/2 to 7/8″ wide, obtuse and apiculate, crenate-serrate often with bristly teeth, lustrous dark green above, turn reddish with the onset of cold weather, strong aroma of wintergreen when bruised, glabrous; petiole—1/6″ long.

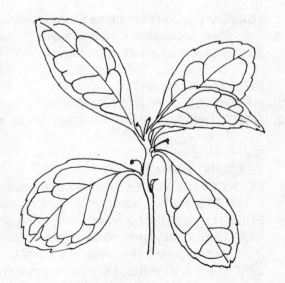

Gaultheria procumbens, Checkerberry or Creeping Wintergreen, is a low growing (6″), creeping, evergreen ground cover. The leaves turn reddish with the advent of cold weather. When crushed they emit a wintergreen odor and have been a source of this oil in the past. Flowers are perfect, pinkish white, 1/4″ long, nodding, solitary, borne May through September. The fleshy, 3/8″ long scarlet capsule is present in July through April of the following year. The oil is also extracted from the fruits. Culturally, acid, moist, high organic matter soils prove optimum. Using pieces of sod in spring or early fall are the easiest ways of transplanting. 'Macrocarpa' is a compact free-flowering form that produces a great quantity of fruits. Native from Newfoundland to Manitoba, south to Georgia and Michigan. Introduced 1762. Zone 3. Makes a fine ground cover where it can be successfully grown.

Gaylussacia brachycera — Box Huckleberry
(gā-lu-sā′shi-ȧ bra-kis′e-rȧ)

FAMILY: Ericaceae

LEAVES: Alternate, simple, evergreen, 1/3 to 1″ long, about 1/2 as wide, elliptic, slightly revolute, glabrous, glossy dark green above, paler beneath; very short petioled.

BUDS: Solitary, sessile, ovoid, small, with 2 or some 4 or 5 exposed scales; terminal lacking.

STEM: Slender, roundish; pith small, 3-sided or rounded, continuous; leaf-scars low, crescent-shaped or 3-sided; 1 bundle-trace.

SIZE: 6 to 18″ high, spreading indefinitely.

HARDINESS: Zone 5.

HABIT: Dwarf evergreen shrub spreading by underground rootstocks and forming a solid mat.

RATE: Slow.

TEXTURE: Medium-fine in all seasons.

LEAF COLOR: Glossy dark green, although when grown in full sun often has reddish cast; becoming deep bronze to reddish purple in winter.

FLOWERS: Perfect, self-sterile but cross-fertile, white or pinkish, 1/4″ long, urn-shaped, May through early June; borne in short, axillary, few-flowered racemes near the end of the shoot.

FRUIT: Berry-like drupe, bluish, ripening in July-August.

CULTURE: Another ericaceous plant which requires considerable cultural manipulation if success is to be had; requires an *acid,* loose, well drained soil supplied with organic matter; preferably partial shade.

DISEASES AND INSECTS: None particularly serious.

LANDSCAPE VALUE: A very lovely, intriguing evergreen ground cover well suited to areas underneath pine trees and rhododendrons where the soil is acid and well drained.

PROPAGATION: Untreated seeds are slow to germinate; warm followed by cold stratification is recommended; fluctuating warm temperatures of 68 to 86°F for 30 days followed by 50°F for 27 days and 47 days resulted in 80 percent and 96 percent germination of sound seeds; cuttings are variable based on my work; August cuttings treated with 8000 ppm IBA quick dip rooted only 20% while 'Amity Hall North' rooted 80% with the same treatment; other work reports excellent success with fall cuttings and 8000 ppm IBA talc.

ADDITIONAL NOTES: Rare American plant, lost to American gardens for a time but was reintroduced through the efforts of the Arnold Arboretum. It has been theorized that one particular stand (colony) in the Amity-Hall area of central Pennsylvania covering an area of 300 acres and a mile long originated from one plant and is over 12,000 years old; whether this is totally true is somewhat suspect but it does make for interesting reading.

NATIVE HABITAT: In the mountains and hills from Pennsylvania to Virginia, Kentucky and Tennessee. Introduced 1796.

Gelsemium sempervirens — Carolina Yellow Jessamine
(jel-sē′mi-um sem-pẽr-vī′renz)

FAMILY: Loganiaceae

LEAVES: Opposite, simple, evergreen, lanceolate or oblong-lanceolate, rarely ovate, 1 to 3 3/4″ long, 1/3 as wide, acute or acuminate, rounded, lustrous dark green and glabrous above, entire; short petioled.

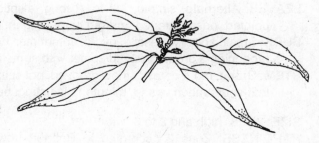

BUDS: Several pairs of scales rather loosely aggregated together.

STEM: Thin, wiry, greenish to brown, glabrous.

SIZE: 10 to 20', will climb trees or scramble over fences, rock piles and other structures; can develop a 3 to 4' mound of tangled stems if left to its own devices.

HARDINESS: Zone 6 to 9.

HABIT: Twining evergreen vine with thin, wiry stems; becomes more dense when sited in full sun.

RATE: Medium to fast; like most vines the better the soil the faster the growth.

TEXTURE: Fine.

LEAF COLOR: Lustrous dark green developing a slight yellow-green or purple-green cast in winter.

FLOWERS: Perfect, yellow, fragrant, solitary or in cymes, 1 1/2" long, funnelform with 5 short imbricate lobes; February into April; often flowers again in fall but sporadically; usually peaks in late march in the Athens area.

FRUIT: Compressed, 1 1/2" long capsule, summer.

CULTURE: Prefers moist, well-drained, organic matter laden soils but is quite adaptable; acid or slightly alkaline; best flowering in full sun but will grow and flower in shade; often found in shady situations in the wild; has a tenacious constitution.

DISEASES AND INSECTS: None serious.

LANDSCAPE VALUE: Used in a multitude of ways in southern gardens; on fences, mailboxes, downspouts, trellises, structures, as a ground cover, in planters where it spills gracefully over the sides; quite beautiful in the wild where it scrambles into the crown of small trees (especially redbud and dogwood in the Georgia Botanical Garden) and lights them with bright yellow; especially noticeable along the highway when in flower; after flowering the vines become almost nondescript.

CULTIVARS:

'Pride of Augusta' ('Plena')—Double flowering form, from a distance scarcely discernible from the species, handsome on close inspection.

PROPAGATION: Seeds, semi-hardwood or hardwood cuttings; cuttings collected in August rooted 100% when treated with 3000ppm IBA and placed in peat:perlite under mist.

ADDITIONAL NOTES: All parts of the plant are poisonous.

NATIVE HABITAT: Virginia to Florida and Texas to Central America. Introduced 1640.

RELATED SPECIES:

Gelsemium rankinii, (jel-sē′mi-um ran-ki′nē-ī), Swamp Jessamine, has been popularized by Dr. Raulston at North Carolina State and is certainly deserving of consideration by Zone 7 to 9 gardeners. In most characteristics it is like *B. sempervirens* except it flowers spectacularly in October and November and waits for warm weather during the winter months to put forth an occasional yellow flower. Also flowers prolifically in March-April. I have a single plant and have been delighted with its performance. This is certainly a plant for the future. The flowers are not fragrant and usually occur in 2 to 3-flowered cymes. the fruit is also smaller (1/2" long) than that of *G. sempervirens*. Found in swamps in North Carolina to Florida where it is rare in the wild. Zone 7 to 9.

Genista tinctoria — Common Woadwaxen or Dyer's Greenwood
(je-nis′ta tink-tō′ri-à)

FAMILY: Fabaceae

LEAVES: Alternate, simple, 1/2 to 1" long, elliptic-oblong to oblong-lanceolate, nearly glabrous, apex pointed, base rounded, margin hairy-fringed, rich green.

BUDS: Small, solitary, sessile, ovoid, sometimes developing the first season or collaterally branched and producing a green grooved spine, with some half-dozen scales.

STEM: Green, more or less stripe-grooved, not spiny; stipules persistent; pith small, rounded, continuous; leaf-scars much raised, minute; 1 indistinct bundle-trace.

SIZE: 2 to 3' high and 2 to 3' wide.

HARDINESS: Zone 2 according to Rehder; however, plants are killed back severely at Minnesota Arboretum, probably best in Zone 4 to 7.

HABIT: Low shrub with almost vertical, slender, green, limitedly branched stems; spiky and twiggy in effect.

RATE: Slow, possibly medium.

TEXTURE: Fine to medium-fine in all seasons when well maintained.

STEM COLOR: Green.

LEAF COLOR: Bright green in summer; no fall color.

FLOWERS: Yellow, 1/2 to 3/4″ long, produced on erect racemes, 1 to 3″ long, occurring on new growth from June to September although peak period is June and limited flowering may occur after that.

FRUIT: Pod, 1/2 to 3/4″ long, glabrous, 8 to 12-seeded.

CULTURE: Somewhat difficult to transplant and once located should not be moved; prefers hot, sunny location in relatively infertile soils which are dry and loamy or sandy; succeeds in acid or neutral soils and thrives on limestone; can be pruned back after flowering and will flower sporadically again.

DISEASES AND INSECTS: None serious.

LANDSCAPE VALUE: Good low growing plant for poor, dry soil areas; will add an element of color to the landscape; the few that I have seen were quite handsome and would make a nice addition to the landscape; might be used in midwest.

CULTIVARS:

‘Plena’—A dwarf, semi-prostrate shrub, with more numerous petals of a more brilliant yellow color.

‘Royal Gold’—Stems erect, up to 2′ high; flowers golden yellow in terminal and axillary racemes, forming a narrow panicle.

There are numerous geographical varieties which differ in habit, leaf morphology and flower characteristics; Bean noted that *G. tinctoria* in its modern acceptation may be taken to cover a group of allied forms put under one variable species.

PROPAGATION: Seeds should be the preferred method of propagation; they germinate best when given a 30 minute acid scarification followed by a water soak; many hard seeded legumes can be handled this way; it is difficult to estimate the time of acid scarification and this needs to be worked out for each species and often each seed lot; late July, August and September appear to be ideal times for cuttings; they can be placed in sand in an outdoor frame and should be rooted by the following spring; good results can be obtained with 8000ppm IBA and a sand:peat medium.

NATIVE HABITAT: Europe, western Asia. Cultivated 1789.

RELATED SPECIES:

Genista lydia (je-nis′ta lē′di-a) has received attention in recent years because of the abundant, bright yellow, 3/8″ long flowers produced on a 2′ high, lax, loose, arching shrub composed of slender 4 to 5 angled, glabrous green stems. Leaves are linear, 3/8″ long, 1/16″ wide, and spaced 1/2″ apart along the stem. Flowers explode in May-June and are extremely handsome. Requires well drained soil and a full sun location. The common type in cultivation is procumbent. Balkans, western Asia. Introduced 1927. Zone (6)7 to 9.

Genista pilosa, (je-nis′ta pī-lō′sa), Silkyleaf Woadwaxen, is a low growing (1 to 1 1/2′) procumbent shrub in youth, finally forming a low, tangled mass of slender, twiggy shoots. The 1/4 to 1/2″ long, narrow-obovate, margins folded upward, silvery haired leaves and stems are a grayish green and provide a nice contrast. The flowers are bright yellow, produced singly or in pairs from the leaf-axils, forming a crowded 2 to 6″ long raceme. ‘Goldilocks’ produces abundant gold flowers. ‘Vancouver Gold’ grows 1′ high by 3′ wide and is covered with bright golden flowers in spring. Promoted by University of British Columbia Botanical Garden in Vancouver, looks like a yellow blanket in flower. Demands sandy, gravelly, dry soils for best growth. Native to much of Europe. Cultivated 1789. Zone 5 to 8?

ADDITIONAL NOTES: The woadwaxens (there are numerous species) are not well known in American gardens. They are popular in Europe where most are found wild. The Morton Arboretum has a small collection which I first saw in the summer of 1975; most were low growing, spreading shrubs with handsome foliage colors. In Europe, *Genista* is everywhere in evidence. One particularly outstanding golden-yellow, spiny branched species was *Genista hispanica,* Spanish Woadwaxen. Anyone interested in the *Genista* species needs to move beyond the scope of this book.

Ginkgo biloba — Ginkgo, often called Maidenhair Tree
(gingk′gō bī-lō′ba)

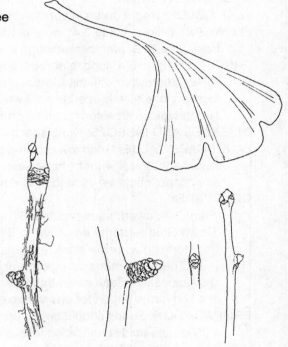

FAMILY: Ginkgoaceae

LEAVES: Alternate, simple, in clusters of 3 to 5 on spurs or alternate on long shoots, fan shaped, dichotomously veined, more or less incised or divided at the broad summit, 2 to 3″ long, 2 to 3″ wide, bright green, glabrous; petiole 1 1/2 to 3 1/2″ long.

BUDS: Imbricate, mounded, often acute, brownish.

STEM: Stout, light brown 1st year, becoming gray with stringy peeling bark; prominent blackish spurs evident on older stems.

SIZE: 50 to 80′ in height with a tremendously variable spread ranging from 30 to 40′ to ultimately wider than high at maturity; the species can grow to 100′ or more.

HARDINESS: Zone 3 to 8 (9); performing well in Minnesota and Georgia; also have seen fine trees in the coastal southeast and a particularly fine specimen in St. Augustine, FL.

HABIT: Usually pyramidal in outline when young; in old age often becoming wide spreading with large, massive, picturesque branches; it is quite difficult to adequately describe the habit of this tree due to the tremendous variation in plants grown from seed; the male tree is supposedly more upright than the pistillate form; however, I have seen either side of the fence with male and female plants.

RATE: Slow to medium, probably 10 to 15′ over a 10 to 12 year period although with adequate water and fertilizer this tree will grow very fast; interesting Kansas study with 'Autumn Gold'—4.5″ growth per year over a 9-year period; a famous old tree at Kew Gardens (one of the best I've seen) planted in 1762 was 56′ high 128 years later, tends to indicate that over time the species is slow growing.

TEXTURE: Medium in leaf and coarse in winter but not objectionable.

BARK: Usually gray-brown ridges with darker furrows, actually quite handsome in the overall effect.

LEAF COLOR: Bright green on both surfaces in summer changing to an excellent yellow in fall; I would like to say that the yellow fall color is consistent from year to year but this is not the case; a freeze will cause the leaves to drop almost overnight whether they have colored or not; has colored spectacularly in the Athens area; I have been impressed with the performance of Ginkgo in the south.

FLOWERS: Dioecious, male flowers (green) are borne on the short shoots in cylindrical, 1″ long catkins during March-April; the female on a 1 1/2 to 2″ long pedicel bearing 1 or 2 greenish ovules.

FRUIT: Actually not a true fruit but simply a naked seed; tan to orangish in color, plum-like in shape, 1 to 1 1/2″ long; the fleshy covering on the seed (female gametophyte) is extremely messy and malodorous and, for this reason, only male trees should be planted; the sperm which fertilze the egg are motile (swimming) and depend on water for accomplishing their mission; the seed is eaten by the Japanese and is reported to be well flavored; may take 20 years or more before a seedling *Ginkgo* flowers.

CULTURE: Transplants easily and establishes without difficulty; prefers sandy, deep, moderately moist soil but grows in almost any situation; full sun; very pH adaptable; prune in spring; air pollutant tolerant; a durable tree for difficult landscape situations; displays good soil salt tolerance; quite heat tolerant, does well in Zones 8 and 9 of the southeast.

DISEASES AND INSECTS: Extremely free of pests although several leaf spots of negligible importance have been reported.

LANDSCAPE VALUE: Excellent city tree, public areas, perhaps too large for street use but is used extensively for this purpose; a well developed Ginkgo is an impressive sight; often looks out of place in the small residential landscape because of unique foliage and winter habit; tends to be somewhat gaunt and open in youth but with time becomes one of the most spectacular of all trees; fall color alone is sufficient reason to plant the tree.

CULTIVARS:

'Autumn Gold'—A handsome symmetrical broad conical form, very regular in shape, 50′ by 30′, perhaps broader later, excellent golden yellow fall color, considered one of the best of the *Ginkgo* cultivars for this character, male, introduced by Saratoga Horticultural Foundation, CA, about 1955.

'Fairmount'—Narrow upright pyramidal form, male, selected from a tree in Fairmount Park, Philadelphia, tree still exists.

'Fastigiata'—(f. *fastigiata*)—Arguably there is more than one clone of the upright columnar type and several have been given cultivar names; ideally the selection should be male, in Vine Street Cemetery in Cincinnati, OH there is a large avenue planting of a distinct columnar form, apparently male, that predates the newer named selections.

'Lakeview'—Compact conical form, male, a Scanlon introduction.

'Mayfield'—Narrow columnar habit like Lombardy Poplar, male, selected around 1948 in Ohio.

'Magyar'—Uniform upright branching habit, male, apparently a Princeton Nursery introduction; have never seen this tree and do not know the details of its origin.

'Palo Alto'—Nicely formed specimen, representative of the species, Scanlon.

'Princeton Sentry'—Probably the best of the upright types, not perfectly columnar, i.e., like a fat telephone pole, but slightly tapered to the apex and slightly fatter at the base, yellow fall color, male, a Princeton introduction.

'Pendula' (f. *pendula*)—Actually, like f. *fastigiata,* a gathering place for plants with various degrees of pendulosity; the few plants of 'Pendula' I have seen were anything but...for the branches are horizontal for a distance but show no distinct weeping character like a weeping European Beech; I suspect that *Ginkgo* exhibits topophytic growth and if budwood is taken from a lateral branch the resulting plants show the arm-extended growth character.

'Santa Cruz'—Male, gold fall coloring form, umbrella form, low and spreading, Scanlon introduction.

'Saratoga'—Similar to 'Autumn Glory' in habit with distinct central leader, rich yellow fall color, male, introduced by Saratoga Horticultural Foundation.

'Shangri-la'—Uniform compact crown with good dense branching habit, excellent yellow fall color, fast growing, 40′ by 30′, a Wandell introduction.

Other cultivars: 'Aurea', 'Epiphylla', 'Laciniata', 'Tit', 'Tremonia', 'Variegata' have been listed. Of these, I have only seen 'Variegata' which is irregularly streaked with yellow but unstable and reverts to the green form unless carefully pruned.

PROPAGATION: Collect in mid-fall, remove pulp, place seeds in moist sand for 10 weeks at 60 to 70°F to permit embryos to finish developing; then seeds are stratified for 60 to 90 days at 41°F; reports have also indicated that freshly cleaned seed will germinate if directly sown; apparently some cold (1 to 2 months) improves germination; nursery practice involves fall planting; I have had good success rooting June cuttings from mature trees with 8000 ppm IBA quick dip, mist; cuttings root in 7 to 8 weeks; it appears 8000 to 10,000 ppm IBA is about ideal for stimulating good rooting; the cultivars are budded on seedling understock.

ADDITIONAL NOTES: W.J. Bean considers the Ginkgo "undoubtedly one of the most distinct and beautiful of all deciduous trees." It is a true gymnosperm and differs significantly from the angiosperms in the reproduction process. Anyone interested in botanical sidelights will find the history of the Ginkgo fascinating reading. One of the oldest trees, growing on earth for 150 million years and was native in North America at one time. The problem in determining the sex of Ginkgo is that they do not "fruit" until they are quite old (20 to 50 years). Always be leary when buying unnamed clones for this reason alone.

NATIVE HABITAT: Eastern China. Introduced 1784.

Gleditsia triacanthos var. *inermis* — Thornless Common Honeylocust
(gle-dit′si-à trī-a-kan′thōs in-ēr′mis)

FAMILY: Fabaceae

LEAVES: Alternate, pinnately or bipinnately compound, 6 to 8″ long, rachis pubescent all around, grooved, pinnate leaves with 20 to 30 oblong-lanceolate leaflets, 1/3 to 1 1/2″ long, 3/16 to 5/8″ wide, remotely crenate-serrulate, pubescent on midribs beneath; bipinnate leaves with 8 to 14 pinnae, the leaflets 1/3 to 1″ long, glossy bright green; base of petiole swollen and enclosing bud.

BUDS: Terminal-absent, laterals small, about 5 more or less distinct at a node, some scaly, others naked.

STEM: Shining, smooth, reddish to greenish brown, often mottled or streaked, zigzag with enlarged nodes.

SIZE: Tremendously variable in the cultivated types but usually in the range of 30 to 70′ in height with a comparable spread; in the wild often grows to over 100′.

HARDINESS: Zone 3 to 9; most cultivars do not perform well in heat, humidity and heavy soils of the southeast.

HABIT: Usually a tree with a short trunk and a rather open spreading crown; light-shaded and consequently grass will grow up to the trunk; a very delicate and sophisticated silhouette which, unfortunately, has led to abuse by landscape planners.

RATE: Fast, as a young tree will grow 2′ or more per year over a 10 year period.

TEXTURE: Medium-fine in leaf (almost fine); medium in winter.

BARK: On old trees grayish brown, broken up into long, narrow, longitudinal and superficially scaly ridges which are separated by deep furrows.

LEAF COLOR: Bright green in summer; clear yellow to yellow green in fall; leaves fall early.

FLOWERS: Polygamo-dioecious, perfect and imperfect flowers on same tree, greenish yellow, May-June, fragrant and nectar laden, not showy, male in clustered, downy, 2″ long racemes; females in few flowered racemes.

FRUIT: Pod, reddish brown to brownish, strap-shaped, 7 to 8″ long up to 18″, about 1″ wide; seeds oval, shining dark brown and hard as a bullet; entire pod often irregularly twisted.

CULTURE: Readily transplanted; withstands a wide range of conditions although reaches maximum development on rich, moist bottomlands or on soils of a limestone origin; tolerant of drought conditions; high pH; salt tolerant (in fact has proven to be the most salt-tolerant tree growing along Chicago freeways); full sun; prune in fall; one of our most adaptable native trees but overused.

DISEASES AND INSECTS: Leaf spot, cankers, witches' broom, powdery mildew, rust, honeylocust borer, midge pod gall, webworm and spider mites; webworm can literally defoliate the tree; after the decline of the American Elm, honeylocust and the many cultivars were extensively used as a substitute; unfortunately the insects and diseases have caught up with this tree in the urban landscapes and let us hope its fate is not similar to that of the predecessor; monogamous planting can lead to problems and for that reason I would strongly recommend using a diversity of trees and shrubs. In 1980 I returned to the Illinois campus to visit friends and as we walked the campus it became evident that the hundreds (thousands) of honeylocusts planted on the campus in the 1950's and 1960's were in trouble. Large trees were being removed from the Quadrangle for fear they might fall over and hurt students (perhaps faculty also), since one had already fallen over. The threat of liability will do wonders for campus beautification. The trees over the years had been subjected to every scourge mentioned above and apparently tremendous root rot had put the trees in a precarious way. Interestingly, the entire population was gradually removed and planted with four different species (no honeylocust).

    The tree is beautiful but is not without problems. An aggressive canker, *Thyronectria austro-americana* causes wilt, cankers or both. In Colorado, the most diseased trees were between 12 and 20 years old, 20 to 30′ high and 6 to 12″ diameter. 'Sunburst' is the most susceptible cultivar. See *Amer. Nurseryman* 156(8):52–53 (1982) for details.

LANDSCAPE VALUE: At one time I would have said an excellent lawn tree for filtered shade but no more; it is overused by everyone and consequently the novelty has worn off; we might be looking for a replacement for this tree if serious insect and disease problems continue.

CULTIVARS: Haserodt and Sydnor, *J. Arbor.* 9(7):186–189 (1983) reported on the growth characteristics of 5 cultivars after 15 years in the Ohio Shade Tree Evaluation Tests at Wooster, OH. Height/width of 'Imperial' was 25′/24′; 'Moraine'—32′/28′; 'Shademaster'—32′/25′; 'Skyline'—35′/26′; 'Sunburst' — 32′/24′.

'Bujotii' ('Pendula')—A very elegant, pendulous tree; branches and branchlets very slender; leaflets narrower than the species, often mottled with white.

'Continental'—Vigorous narrow crown of stout branches, large leaves, fine leaflets, dark blue-green color, virtually seedless, 60 to 70′, a Princeton introduction.

'Elegantissima'—Dense, shrubby habit, with elegant foliage; original plant grew 13′ in 25 years; should be grafted on *G. t.* var. *inermis* understock; might be suitable under low wires and other structures.

'Fairview'—Strong, sturdy growth habit, habit is similar to 'Moraine', produces one grade larger than most cultivars; a McGill introduction.

'Green Glory'—(50 to 75′) Vigorous grower with strong central leader, pyramidal when young; retains foliage later than other types; shows some resistance to webworm damage; essentially fruitless.

'Halka'—Strong growing, 40′ by 40′, large oval-rounded to round headed with greater fullness and less pendulous branching than typical form, essentially fruitless.

'Imperial'—(30 to 35′) Graceful, spreading branches at right angles to main trunk, rounded outline; produces a few pods; Minnesota reports some dieback in severe winters; 1′7.9″ per year over a 10-year period in Wichita, KS tests.

'Majestic'—(60 to 65′) Spreading but more upright branched than above; excellent dark green foliage; one of the more popular clones; 1′10.8″ per year over a 10-year period in Wichita, KS tests.

'Marando'—New form with semi-weeping habit, dark green leaves, dark brown bark, seedless.

'Maxwell'—Somewhat irregular grower, horizontally spreading branches; reputed hardy to low temperature.

'Moraine'—The first of the thornless honeylocusts to be patented (1949); broad, graceful in outline; 40 to 50′; fruitless; good dark green changing to golden yellow in fall; shows greater resistance to webworm than some of the new introductions; possibly should be considered the standard by which the others are judged.

'Perfection'—An excellent well scaffolded tree developing an early crown, slightly broader than 'Skyline' but not as spreading as 'Imperial,' dark green foliage, 50′ by 35′.

'Pin Cushion'—Interesting novelty form; foliage is borne in bunches along the stem; I have seen three planted together and the shade produced was not dense enought to protect an ant.

'Ruby Lace'—Ruby red when first unfolding, purplish bronze later and finally green, a poor specimen, ungainly, as bad as a cultivar can be; webworms love it.

'Shademaster'—Ascending branches, dark green leaves, strong growing, essentially podless; several horticulturists consider this the best, 45′ by 35′, 1′10.7″ per year over a 10 year period in Wichita, KS tests.

'Skyline'—(45′ by 35′) Pyramidal form with ascending branches (60 to 90° angle), compact, dark green leaves, bright golden yellow fall color; another good form; Cole introduction; more upright than most forms; 1′9″ per year over 10 years in Wichita, KS tests.

'Summergold'—Open, elegant lazy appearance, bright golden new growth turning to yellow-green, 40 to 50′.

'Summer Lace'—Strong growing, graceful appearance, light green foliage turns dark green, dark shiny bark, 60 to 70′.

'Sunburst'—(30 to 35′) Broad pyramidal head, golden leaves on new growth changing eventually to bright green, somewhat hard to digest.

'True Shade'—(40′ by 35′)—Broad oval form, fine textured medium green foliage turns yellow in fall, fast growing; branch angles approximate 45°.

PROPAGATION: Seeds should be scarified in concentrated sulfuric acid for 1 to 2 hours; they will then germinate readily; cultivars are budded on seedling understock.

ADDITIONAL NOTES: The pods contain a sweetish, gummy substance from which the name honeylocust is derived. The species, *Gleditsia triacanthos,* is laden with multibranched thorns and should not be considered for landscape situations. It should be mentioned that very few of the clones are completely fruitless. The polygamous nature of the flowers usually allows for some perfect flowers and, hence, fruit will occur.

NATIVE HABITAT: Pennsylvania to Nebraska and south to Texas and Mississippi. Introduced 1700.

Gymnocladus dioicus — Kentucky Coffeetree
(jim-nok′là-dus dī-ō-ē′kus)

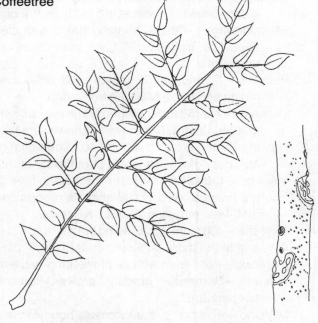

FAMILY: Fabaceae

LEAVES: Alternate, bipinnately compound, to 36″ long and 24″ wide, with 3 to 7 pairs of pinnae, the lower usually reduced to simple leaflets, the upper with 6 to 14 leaflets; leaflets ovate or elliptic-ovate, entire, 1 1/2 to 3″ long, acute, rounded or cuneate at base, dark green, almost bluish green, pubescent beneath when young; short petioled, swollen at base.

BUDS: Terminal—absent, laterals—small, bronze, pubescent, partially sunken, scarcely projecting beyond surface of twig, surrounded by an incurved downy rim of bark, axillary bud in depression at top of leaf scar, one or sometimes 2 superposed buds present; sometimes 2 lateral scales visible.

STEM: Very stout, more or less contorted, brown or slightly greenish, glabrous or often velvety downy; pith—wide, salmon-pink to brown.

BARK: Dark brown, characteristically roughened with tortuous, recurved, scale-like ridges which are distinct even upon comparatively young branches.

SIZE: 60 to 75′ in height by 40 to 50′ in spread although can grow to 90′.

HARDINESS: Zone 3 to 8.

HABIT: Usually develops vertically ascending branches which form a narrow, obovate crown; picturesque; bare limbed and somewhat clumsy looking in winter; the finest specimen I know exists on the Illinois campus.

RATE: Slow to medium, growing 12 to 14' over a 10 year period.

TEXTURE: Medium in leaf; coarse, but not offensively so, in winter.

BARK: Rough, with hard, thin, firm and scaly ridges curling outward (recurving) along their edges; very unique and interesting bark pattern which develops on 1 to 2" diameter branches; grayish brown to dark brown.

LEAF COLOR: One of the latest trees to leaf out in spring, usually emerging about May 5 to May 20 in midwest; new leaves are pinkish to purplish tinged gradually changing to dark green, almost dark bluish green in summer; fall color is often ineffective (some yellow) but on some trees is excellent.

FLOWERS: Dioecious or polygamo-dioecious, greenish white, late May to early June, each flower 3/4 to 1" long, pubescent, borne in large 8 to 12" long, 3 to 4" wide pyramidal panicles (female); on the male tree the panicle is about 1/3 the length of the female; interesting on close inspection; female fragrant like the best rose; males may be also but have never noticed.

FRUIT: Reddish brown to brownish black, leathery pod, 5 to 10" long, 1 1/2 to 2" wide, containing a few, large, blackish brown, hard-shelled, rounded seeds imbedded in a sweet, sticky pulp; ripens in October, but hang on tree through winter; good crops produced alternately or on three year cycles.

CULTURE: Transplant balled and burlapped into deep, rich, moist soil for best growth; however, adaptable to a wide range of conditions such as chalk (limestone), drought, and city conditions; full sun; prune in winter or early spring; wood may be somewhat brittle.

DISEASES AND INSECTS: None serious.

LANDSCAPE VALUE: A choice tree for parks, golf courses and other large areas; at times somewhat dirty for the pods, leaflets and rachises are falling at different times; the tree has interesting characters especially the bold winter habit and handsome bark; essentially unknown in south but a young 5 to 6' high tree grew 20' high in 5 years on the Georgia campus. The tree is absolutely beautiful and results in a number of "What is it?" questions. The yellowish rachises have persisted until February.

CULTIVARS: 'Variegata' is virtually unknown and I saw for the first time a small tree in Kew Gardens, the gray-green foliage was irregularly peppered and streaked with creamy white variegation; from a distance the variegation pattern was not pronounced but on close inspection is lovely; the combination of pinkish to purplish new growth and variegation is quite handsome, not as strong growing as the species.

PROPAGATION: Seed should be scarified in concentrated sulfuric acid for 4 to 6 hours; I have left seeds in the acid for 24 hours and still got 90% germination; Frett and Dirr. *The Plant Propagator* 25(2):4–6, 1979 reported that 0, 2, 4, 8, 16, 32 hours of acid scarification resulted in 7, 93, 100, 95, 83, and 87 percent germination, respectively; root cuttings, 3/8" diameter, 1 1/2" long, December, can be used to vegetatively propagate the tree. Tom Tracz, former student, when he was with Synnesvedt Nursery, propagated three clones from root cuttings; interestingly one grew 50 to 100% faster than the other two clones, there is room for a good male tree and Tom's work indicated root cuttings will work. Deb McCown, Knight Hollow Nursery, Madison, WI has successfully propagated a male form in tissue culture.

ADDITIONAL NOTES: The seeds are great fun to throw and hit with a baseball bat. The seeds were used by the early settlers to Kentucky as a coffee substitute; hence, the tree's common name. Selections should be made for good male forms and these, in turn, propagated vegetatively. This tree has been slighted in the landscape industry and, considering its cultural tolerances, would make a valuable addition to the list of "tough" trees. Ford (*Secrest Arboretum Notes.* Autumn, 1975) reported that the leaves and seeds are poisonous to man and the seed and fruit contain the alkaloid cytisine. Cattle have been poisoned by drinking from pools of water into which seed pods have fallen. He speculated that roasting the seed may destroy its toxic principal(s). I mention this because in my youth I ate the sweetish gummy substance that lined the inside of the pod. Maybe that's what is wrong with me today.

NATIVE HABITAT: New York and Pennsylvania to Minnesota, Nebraska, Oklahoma and Tennesee where it occurs in deep, rich soils in bottomlands, deep ravines and moist slopes. Introduced before 1748.

Halesia carolina — Carolina Silverbell
(ha-lē′zhi-ȧ kȧ-rō-lī′na)

FAMILY: Styracaceae

LEAVES: Alternate, simple, ovate or elliptic to ovate-oblong, 2 to 5″ long, about 1/3 to 1/2″ as wide, acuminate, cuneate or rounded at base, serrulate, tomentose at first, dark green and soon glabrous above, pubescent beneath; petiole 1/4 to 1/2″ long.

BUDS: Terminal—absent laterals ellipsoid to ovoid, superposed, 1/8 to 1/4″ long, with thick, broad-ovate dark brown to red-black acute puberulous scales, rounded on the back, slightly stalked.

STEM: Slender, glabrous or densely pubescent becoming slightly pubescent or remaining glabrous, brown; pith—white, chambered, 1 bundle trace; stem becoming stringy on 2nd year wood.

SIZE: 30 to 40′ in height with a spread of 20 to 35′; may grow up to 80′.

HARDINESS: Zone 4 to 8.

HABIT: Low branched tree with a comparatively narrow head and ascending branches or often with several spreading branches forming a broad, rounded crown.

RATE: Medium, 9 to 12′ over a 6 to 8 year period.

TEXTURE: Medium in all seasons.

BARK: Gray to brown to black combination, ridged and furrowed with flat somewhat lustrous ridges which develop into scaly plates; intermediate branches are gray and streaked with darker vertical fissures.

LEAF COLOR: Dark yellowish green in summer; changing to yellow or yellow green in fall; usually dropping very early in fall.

FLOWERS: White, rarely pale rose, bell-shaped, 1/2 to 3/4″ long, shallowly 4-lobed, flowering on year-old wood; borne on pendulous 1/2 to 1″ long stalks in axillary (cymose) 2 to 5-flowered clusters in April to early May; flowers early to mid April in Athens and effective for 10 to 14 days, flowers emerge before or with the leaves; a subtle beauty not appreciated by most people.

FRUIT: Oblong or obovoid, 4-winged dry drupe, 1 1/2″ long, green changing to light brown, effective in September into late fall, containing 2 to 3 seeds.

CULTURE: Transplants readily balled and burlapped; prefers rich, well-drained, moist, acid (pH 5 to 6), high organic matter soils; sun or semi-shade; in the wild often occurs as an understory tree on the slopes of mountains, particularly along the streams; will become chlorotic in high pH soils.

DISEASES AND INSECTS: Exceptionally pest resistant.

LANDSCAPE VALUE: One of my favorite small native trees; often neglected in this country but definitely with a place in shrub and woodland borders; handsome lawn tree; set off best with an evergreen background; rhododendrons grow well beneath silverbells.

CULTIVARS:

'Meehanii'—This interesting form was found in Meehan's nursery at Germantown, PA, as a solitary plant in a bed of seedling-grown *Halesia carolina;* it forms a rounded shrub to 12′; the flowers are smaller than those of the species and apparently borne in great quantities; leaves coarser and more coarsely wrinkled.

'Rosea' (var. *rosea*)—I read a great deal about different plants but like to confirm the literature by actually seeing the plant; I have read that 'Rosea' is a pink form whose color is dependent on climate and soil; I have seen at least two pink forms, one with rich pink color and rather delicate flowers; the other pink blushed and large flowered; the first is worthy of distribution for it is a tree of great beauty; I have rooted both the clones mentioned above from August cuttings using 3000 ppm IBA quick dip, peat:perlite, mist; the pink corolla color is expressed regardless of climate but hot weather may reduce intensity of coloration.

PROPAGATION: Seed must be moist stratified at 56° to 86°F for 60 to 120 days, followed by 60 to 90 days at 33 to 41°F; I have germinated seed but it was no easy task; I provided warm and cold as mentioned above and sowed the seeds in the greenhouse with no resultant germination; back into the cooler for another 60 days of cold and finally the seedlings came up; nursery production involves fall planting and two years of patience; student at Tennessee excised embryos from green or brown fruits and found they grew normally, embryo from stratified fruits germinated in 4 days; this work indicates that the dormancy may be related solely to physical factors, i.e., thick fruit wall; see Gersbach and Barton, *Contributions Boyce Thompson Inst.* 4:27–37. 1932. "Germination of seeds of the silverbell, *Halesia carolina*." I have collected softwood cuttings from a tree on the Illinois campus, treated with 1000 ppm IBA/50% alcohol, placed in peat:perlite under mist and received 80 to 90% rooting; after this initial success one of my graduate students, Ms. Sue Burd, undertook a detailed study; she sampled *Halesia* in May, June, July and August; cuttings rooted 80 to 100 percent when treated with IBA in the range of 2500 to 10,000 ppm; cuttings are easy to overwinter.

NATIVE HABITAT: West Virginia to Florida and eastern Oklahoma, on wooded slopes and along stream-banks. Introduced 1756.

RELATED SPECIES:

Halesia diptera—Two-winged Silverbell

LEAVES: Alternate, simple, elliptic or obovate, 3 to 5 1/2″ long, 1 1/2 to 3″ wide, abruptly long acuminate, cuneate or rounded, remotely sinuate-serrulate with minute callous teeth, dark green and glabrous above, pubescent at least on veins below; petiole—1/2 to 3/4″ long.

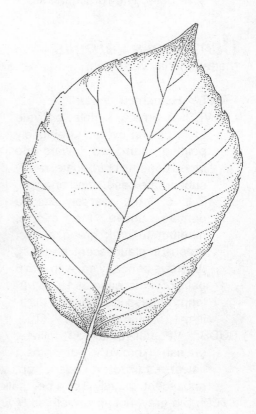

Halesia diptera, (ha-lē′zhi-à dip′tēr-a), Two-winged Silverbell, is a beautiful, small, rounded tree (20 to 30′), usually multiple stemmed or low-branched. It is, unfortunately, not well known in gardens. The 4-lobed, white, 3/4″ long, bell-shaped flowers occur on 1/2 to 3/4″ long pendulous slender pedicels in May. The corolla is deeply cut and the flowers are more refined than those of *H. carolina*. The flowers arrive 7 to 14 days later than *H. carolina*. The 1 1/2 to 2″ long, 3/4″ wide dry drupes have two longitudinal, 1/4 to 3/8″ wide wings. The common name is derived from the shape of the fruit. I have changed my mind on this species and recommend it highly. It makes a rather pretty small tree with leaves and bark not unlike that of *H. carolina*. Found in moist sites from South Carolina and Tennessee to Florida and Texas. Introduced 1758. It has withstood -25°F in Cincinnati and flowered profusely. Have not been able to root this from cuttings.

Halesia monticola, (ha-lē′zhi-ȧ mon-ti-kō′la), Mountain Silverbell, is similar to *H. carolina* but differs in having larger flowers, larger fruits and larger habit often reaching 60 to 80′ with well developed single or double leaders and a conical habit; some trees develop bushy crowns. Cultivar termed 'Rosea' has pale pink flowers. There is a variety *vestita* with more pubescent leaves that are often rounded at the base. It is a large tree that appears to maintain a central leader. Native from North Carolina to Tennessee and Georgia in the mountains at altitudes not less than 3,000′. Introduced 1897. Zone 5 to 8.

Halesia parviflora—Little Silverbell

LEAVES: Alternate, simple, ovate, 2 to 4″ long, 1 to 2″ wide, irregularly wavy along margin, fine toothed, dark green.

Halesia parviflora, (ha-lē′zhi-ȧ pär-vi-flō′ra), Little Silverbell, is a large shrub or small tree that supposedly grows 25 to 30′ high. The only plant I have seen was about 8 to 12′ and somewhat shrubby. The white flowers are the smallest of the group being only 1/4 to 1/2″ long, while the fruits range from 1 to 1 1/2″ long, with 4 narrow, essentially equal wings. Native in the woods and hillsides of the Coastal Plain of northern Florida and Mississippi. Zone 6 to 9.

ADDITIONAL NOTES: The largest specimens of *H. carolina* and *H. monticola* I have seen are located on the campus of Purdue University, West Lafayette, Indiana. *H. carolina* is about 40 to 50′ in height while *H. monticola* is probably 50 to 60′. *H. monticola* is now included with *H. carolina* by some authorities and this thinking is probably justified since it is extremely difficult to distinguish between the two species. If anyone is interested in the logic behind the merger of *H. monticola* with *H. carolina,* I recommend Spongberg *J. Arnold Arboretum* 57(1):54–73. "Styracaceae hardy in temperate North America." Little did I know that the piece of property upon which my home rests is inundated by silverbells. They grace the slope above the creek and some extend their branches over the water.

Hamamelis vernalis — Vernal Witchhazel
(ham-ȧ-mē′lis vêr-nā′lis)

FAMILY: Hamamelidaceae

LEAVES: Alternate, simple, obovate to oblong-ovate, obtusely pointed, narrowed toward the broad cuneate or truncate, rarely subcordate base, often unequal, 2 to 5″ long, coarsely sinuate dentate above the middle, medium to dark green above, green or glaucescent beneath, glabrous or nearly so, with 4 to 6 pairs of veins; petioles 1/4 to 1/2″ long, pubescent; leaves—thickish.

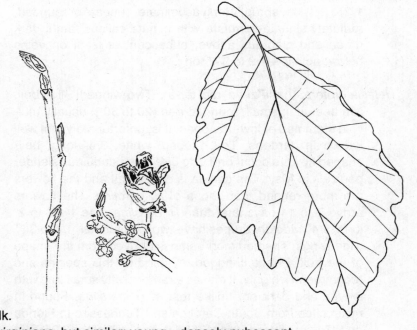

BUDS: Vegetative-naked, foliose, grayish brown, tomentose; flower—stalked, rounded, tan, pubescent, usually 3 or 4 per stalk.

STEM: Old-gray, not as smooth as *H virginiana,* but similar; young—densely pubescent.

SIZE: 6 to 10′ high and greater in spread; have seen 10 to 15′ high specimens; one of the largest is located at Longwood Gardens.

HARDINESS: Zone 4 to 8; second hardiest witchhazel after *H. virginiana*.

HABIT: Multistemmed, dense, rounded shrub, quite neat in appearance but variable in form; branches are often low and serpentine bending up at their extremities to form a broad-rounded outline, will sucker and form large colonies.

RATE: Medium.

TEXTURE: Medium in leaf and in winter.

STEM COLOR: Older stems, 3-year or greater, assume a gray to grayish brown color; quite attractive.

LEAF COLOR: Medium to dark green in summer, changing to golden yellow in fall, fall color persists for 2 to 3 weeks and is often outstanding, fall color develops late.

FLOWERS: Yellow to red, variable, 1/2 to 3/4″ across, 4-petaled, each about 1/2″ long, usually the inner surface of the calyx lobe is red and the petals are yellow, some plants exhibit solid yellow, orange, or red; pungently fragrant, January through February–March and effective for 3 to 4 weeks, borne in few flowered (3 to 4) cymes; petals roll up on very cold days and in a protective sense, avoid freeze damage; this "adaptive" mechanism extends the flowering period.

FRUITS: Capsule, dehiscent, 2-valved, splitting in September–October, expelling the black seeds; green-yellow to brown and interestingly attractive in a quiet manner.

CULTURE: Supposedly somewhat difficult to transplant; my experience indicated no problem if handled as a container or balled and burlapped specimen; root pruning has been advocated for increasing root development; native on gravelly, often inundated banks of streams, performs best in moist situations; has grown admirably in poorly drained, clay soils; does well in full sun or 3/4's shade; pH adaptable; much more tolerant of high pH than *H. virginiana*.

DISEASES AND INSECTS: None serious, gall on leaves caused by a wasp can become rather ugly, at its worst reminds of Hackberry nipple gall.

LANDSCAPE VALUE: Durable plant for east and midwest; used effectively on University of Illinois campus in groupings near large buildings, also in planter boxes, would make a good screen, unpruned hedge; unusual because of the early flower date; selections should be made for good floriferous character, dense habit and excellent fall color; will often hold old leaves and they compete with flowers.

CULTIVARS:

'Carnea'—Petals red at base grading to orange at tip, calyx red, 1/2″ long, 1/12″ wide, kinked, slightly twisted; deep flower color and worth growing for that reason alone.

'Christmas Cheer'—Professor McDaniel showed me this selection 18 years ago and its presence in commerce by Gossler Farms Nursery provides impetus to mention the characteristics, selected from the garden of Dr. James Gerdemann for flowering around Christmas in Urbana, IL.

'Lombarts Weeping'—Petals orange-red at base, orange toward the end, 1/3″ long, kinked, calyx red-pink; is not weeping just low growing, tends to hold its old leaves; a form called 'Pendula' has crossed my path at Van Dusen Botanical Garden, Vancouver, BC; the plant was about the same as an octopus, high in the middle and a million leaders radiating in all directions, this may in fact be 'Lombarts Weeping.'

'Red Imp'—Hillier selection with claret-red petals at base, grading to copper at tips, calyx claret-red.

'Sandra'—When I first read about this in *The Garden* I wrote to England asking how to procure plants and was told that a large mail order firm would be selling them in the U.S.; unfolding leaves are suffused with plum-purple, changing to green and lightly flushed with purple on the underside, in fall turning orange and red; the flowers are cadmium yellow; although my prayers were answered by Gossler the plant has not lived up to its billing; at the Arnold Arboretum the fall color was at best suffused with orange, the same in my garden and not as vibrant as some seedlings, also the new growth is a far cry from plum-purple, at best bronze-green; flowers are not outstanding.

'Squib'—Petals cadmium yellow with a green calyx.

PROPAGATION: Seed, difficult due to double dormancy but results have been obtained by stratifying seed for 60 days at 68°F plus 90 days at 41°F. Seeds germinate more readily than *H. virginiana*. Cuttings, collected in early June, wounded, 10 sec. 1000 ppm IBA/50% alcohol dip, placed in sand under mist rooted 70 to 80% in 3 months; this species is generally easy to root. Although described as easy, cuttings of this and the other witchhazels have peculiar quirks. Rooting is easy but their overwinter survival difficult. Ideally, to insure survival, induce a flush of growth *after* rooting. For complete details on the witchhazel rooting story see Dirr and Heuser, 1987. Another good reference is Lamb and Nutty, *The Plantsman* 6(1):45–48 (1984).

NATIVE HABITAT: Missouri to Louisiana and Oklahoma. Found on gravelly, often inundated banks of streams. Introduced 1908.

Hamamelis virginiana — Common Witchhazel
(ham-à-mē′lis vẽr-gin-i-ā′na)

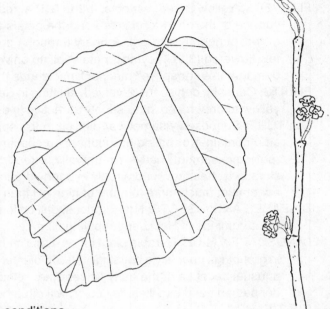

LEAVES: Alternate, simple, obovate or elliptic, obtusely short-acuminate or obtusish, narrowed toward the base and subcordate, rarely broad-cuneate, 3 to 6″ long, 2 to 3-1/2″ wide, coarsely crenate-dentate, medium to dark green, nearly glabrous or pubescent on the veins beneath, with 5 to 7 pairs of veins; petioles 1/4 to 1/2″ long, pubescent; leaves—thinnish.

BUDS: Naked, brownish, tomentose, flower buds—stalked, globose, opening in the fall, usually 3 or 4 on a bent stalk.

STEM: Slender, older stems—glabrous, smooth, gray; young stems—brownish, pubescent; pith—small, green, continuous.

SIZE: 20 to 30′ in height by 20 to 25′ in spread; 15 to 20′ is more appropriate under landscape conditions.

HARDINESS: Zone 3 to 8(9).

HABIT: Small tree or large shrub with several large, crooked, spreading branches forming an irregular, rounded, open crown; architecturally the branches are beautiful.

RATE: Medium.

TEXTURE: Probably would be considered medium-coarse in leaf as well as winter habit, tends toward openness and gangliness but still makes an attractive shrub.

BARK: Smooth gray to grayish brown on 2-year-old stems to 80-year-old trunks.

LEAF COLOR: Medium green in summer yielding to good yellow in the fall, can be spectacular.

FLOWERS: Yellow, fragrant, four strap-like crumpled petals, each 1/2 to 2/3″ long, calyx lobes are yellowish to reddish brown inside, November; I have observed specimens in full flower in mid October and others as late as early December; flowers are borne in 2 to 4 flowered cymes, effective for about 2 to 4 weeks depending on weather; often in full fall color at the time of flower thus reducing the quality and effectiveness of the flowers.

FRUIT: Capsule, 1/2″ long, dehiscing at the distal end; do not discharge the seeds until 12 months after flowering.

CULTURE: Similar to *H. vernalis;* full sun or shade; somewhat tolerant of city conditions; prefers a moist soil; avoid extremely dry situations.

DISEASES AND INSECTS: None serious, although when planted near birch trees a peculiar insect makes small galls on the underside of the foliage, like hackberry nipple gall.

LANDSCAPE VALUE: Native shrub covering much of eastern United States and therefore valuable in a naturalized situation, best reserved for the shrub border, near large buildings in shaded areas; probably too large for the small residential landscape; considerable selections could be made for quality and abundance of flower and the absence of foliage during the flowering period; when open grown this makes a wonderful shrub especially in fall as the leaves turn a gorgeous yellow and the fragrance of the flowers permeates the cool autumn air; Kalmthout Arboretum, Belgium, has selected forms that drop their leaves ahead of flowering.

PROPAGATION: Seed, same as described for *H. vernalis;* cuttings, I have had little success rooting this species; cuttings taken and handled as described for *H. vernalis* yielded 2 to 5% rooting; an Illinois nurseryman told me this was easy to root; softwood cuttings from young plants (3 to 5 years old) have been rooted using 10,000 ppm IBA; have read published reports of 80% and higher rooting but cuttings must be collected early; mature cuttings from old plants do not root as easily.

ADDITIONAL NOTES: The extract witchhazel is distilled from the bark of young stems and roots. It is found in moist, shady areas along streambanks throughout its range. Plants in the wild are often rather ragged but if placed in full sun make a large rounded shrub of great stability.

NATIVE HABITAT: Canada to Georgia, west to Nebraska and Arkansas. Introduced 1736.

RELATED SPECIES:

Hamamelis macrophylla, (ham-à-mē′lis mak-rō-fil′a), Southern Witchhazel, is closely related and for the previous editions I chose to ignore it until actually seeing the plant in flower with leaves present in early December at Aiken, SC. The epithet *macrophylla* is certainly unjustified for the leaves are small, one half to two third's the size of *H. virginiana*. Also the undersides are distinctly pubescent. It is smaller in all characteristics and flowers on the plant I saw were small and disappointing. For the collector. South Carolina to Florida, Arkansas and Texas. Introduced 1928. Zone 6 to 9.

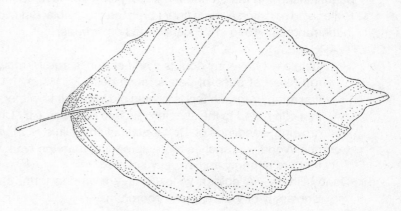

Hamamelis mollis — Chinese Witchhazel
(ham-à-mē′lis mol′lis)

LEAVES: Alternate, simple, obicular-obovate to obovate (appearing roundish), 3 to 6″ long, 3/4's as wide, short acuminate, obliquely cordate to sub-cordate at base, sinuately denticulate, dull green and pubescent above, grayish tomentose beneath; petioles about 1/4″ long, stout and densely pubescent.

BUDS: Vegetative—1/2″ long, stalked, scales (2 to 3) tightly fitted together, densely pubescent, grayish brown; laterals smaller; one smaller outer scale appears to partially envelop the darker brown part; flower—on a crooked stalk, 2 to 4 together, egg-shaped, gray-brown, densely pubescent.

STEM: Slender, terete, grayish pubescence on first year stem, partially remaining on second, becoming gray and glabrous.

SIZE: 10 to 15′ high and wide, potential to 20′ and greater.
HARDINESS: Zone 5 to 8.

HABIT: Large shrub or small tree of oval to rounded outline, branches often spreading; usually more compact than *H. × intermedia* and *H. virginiana.*

RATE: Slow.

TEXTURE: Medium.

BARK: Smooth, gray on older branches.

LEAF COLOR: Medium green in summer, somewhat dull, can be a spectacular yellow to yellow-orange in fall.

FLOWER: Perfect, yellow with rich red-brown calyx cups, fragrant, 4-petaled, each petal strap-shaped, 5/8″ long, not wavy as in *H. japonica,* February to March, lasting for a long time.

FRUIT: Two-valved, dehiscent capsule splitting at maturity ejecting two jet black seeds.

CULTURE: Transplant balled and burlapped; prefers moist, acid, well-drained, organic soils; full sun or partial shade; the least hardy of the species treated here.

DISEASES AND INSECTS: None serious, although Japanese Beetles have been described as eating foliage of *H. × intermedia.*

LANDSCAPE VALUE: This is a fine species and is probably the most fragrant of the group; makes a beautiful show in March and the finest planting I have seen in this country is located at Swarthmore College; to my mind a much finer shrub than forsythia; unfortunately the least hardy and temperatures in the range of -10 to -15°F can injure flower buds.

CULTIVARS:

'Brevipetala'—I have my doubts whether this is true *H. mollis* or a hybrid; flowers deep yellow, with red blush at base of petals, each petal 3/5″ long, 1/12″ wide, kinked, slightly twisted, heavy flowering, fragrant, tends to hold old leaves into winter, the pubescence on the lower surface is thin compared to the species; put into commerce by Chenault's nurseries around 1935, upright growing; seedlings of 'Brevipetala' display little *H. mollis* affinity.

'Coombe Wood'—Branches more spreading than the type with slightly larger golden yellow flowers that are strongly and sweetly scented.

'Donny Brook'—A golden yellow heavy flowering form, apparently introduced by Brian Mulligan, University of Washington Arboretum.

'Early Bright'—Brighter yellow flowers that open 3 to 4 weeks ahead of the species, flowers in mid January at Swarthmore, PA; original 37-year-old plant is 15′ by 15′.

'Goldcrest'—Large flowers of a rich golden yellow suffused claret at base; strong and sweet scent, often later than other *H. mollis* cultivars.

'Pallida'—Soft sulfur-yellow flowers, each petal about 3/4″ long, reddish purple calyx cup, flowers profusely borne, sweetly fragrant, raised in the garden of the Royal Horticultural Society; leaves do not resemble those of *H. mollis* as they are somewhat lustrous above with sparse stellate hairs beneath; may be *H. × intermedia* type, one of the best.

PROPAGATION: Seed—3 months warm followed by 3 months cold has resulted in good germination; June cuttings treated with high IBA (1%) rooted well. See cuttings under *H. vernalis.*

NATIVE HABITAT: Central China. Introduced 1879.

RELATED SPECIES: Out of sequence here in order to introduce the two parents of *H. × intermedia* (*H. japonica × H. mollis*).

Hamamelis japonica—Japanese Witchhazel
(ham-á-mē′lis ja-pon′i-ka)

LEAVES: Alternate, simple, suborbicular to broad-ovate, or elliptic, 2 to 4″ long, 1 1/4 to 2 1/2″ wide, acute or rounded at apex, rounded or subcordate, rarely broad-cuneate at base, margins wavy, 5 to 8 vein pairs that run forward at an acute angle from the midrib, lower surface densely pubescent when young, essentially glabrous by late summer, medium to dark green; petiole—1/4 to 3/4″ long, downy.

BUDS: Terminal, 2 to 3 scales clumped together, naked, 1/4″ long, dusty pubescent; flower—1 to 3, ovoid, 1/4″ long, deep dusty brown, pubescent, borne on a crooked stalk.

STEM: Slender, gray-brown, scattered orangish brown lenticels, glabrous except near tip where slight pubescence remains.

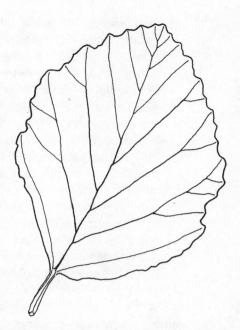

Hamamelis japonica, Japanese Witchhazel, is a spreading, at times almost flat-topped, sparsely branched shrub or small tree growing 10 to 15′ high. Most of the plants I have seen in cultivation were wide-spreading shrubs. The leaves often have a sheen and in fall turn rich combinations of yellow, red, and purple. The yellow, 2/3″ long, very narrow, strap-shaped, wrinkled and crinkled (akin to crepe paper), 4-petaled flowers occur 2 to 3 together on the leafless branches in February–March. The calyx lobes vary from green to reddish brown to red on the inside. The fragrance is not as strong as *H. mollis.* Several varieties and cultivars of note include:

var. *arborea*—A tall growing form with horizontally disposed branches, flowers yellow, small, faint, sweet scent, produced in abundance, fall color yellow, a beautiful plant, introduced 1862.

var. *flavopurpurascens*—Petals suffused with red, overall effect is not staggering; calyx cup dark purple, reddish yellow fall color, a rather wide-spreading shrub. Japan. Introduced 1919.

'Sulphurea'—Petals yellow, 3/8″ long, crimped, calyx cup red on inside, faint sweet odor, large shrub with spreading, ascending branches.

'Zuccariniana'—Petals good butter yellow with no tinge of red, greenish inside the calyx, 3/5″ long, 1/12″ wide, kinked and twisted, flowering late February into March, erect in youth, spreading with age, to 15′ high, yellow fall color.

Although not common in this country it is a handsome shrub especially in its loose wide-spreading branching pattern. Japan. Introduced 1862. Zone 5 to 8.

Hamamelis × intermedia (ham-à-mē′lis × in-ter-mē′di-a) represents a group of hybrids between *H. japonica × H. mollis* with intermediate characteristics. Originally described by Alfred Rehder in 1945 from plants growing in the Arnold Arboretum. Plants display hybrid vigor and may grow 15 to 20′ high. They are usually upright-spreading and rather loosely branched if not pruned. They flower from late January into mid March (north) depending on the cultivar. Their flower colors range from yellow to red. The red flowered types may show more red fall coloration than the yellow-flowered types but this is not absolute. Cultivars have been raised in several countries but the greatest concentration has come from Kalmthout Arboretum. Mr. de Belder, owner of the Arboretum, provides an account of some of the Kalmthout introductions in *J. Royal Hort. Soc.* 94:85, 1969. Lancaster also provides a valuable account of the *Hamamelis* species and cultivars in *Gardeners Chronicle* 167, 1970. Also, I offered a reasonably complete account in *Amer. Nurseryman,* 157(5): 53–62 (1983).

CULTIVARS: The number is now staggering and without a scorecard it is difficult to separate the best. I have included a reasonably complete list and would be pleased to hear of cultivars not appearing here. Personal favorites include 'Arnold Promise', 'Jelena', and 'Pallida' (see under *H. mollis*).

'Allgold'—Deep yellow flowers with a reddish calyx cup abundantly borne on ascending branches; yellow fall color.

'Arnold Promise'—Raised and introduced by the Arnold Arboretum, clear yellow flowers with a reddish calyx cup, each petal almost an inch long, fragrant, large shrub, the original plant about 20′ high and wide; during by sabbatical I monitored the flowering progression of the original plant; it showed significant color in late February 1979 and still had a measure of color in mid March; this cultivar is being grown by American nurserymen. I am afraid that this cultivar has become my favorite among the yellow types, flowers are definitely later than the others and my

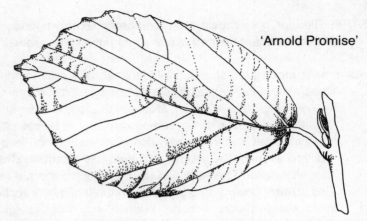

'Arnold Promise'

field notes indicate that flowers were still present on April 12, 1986; in 1984, flowers were just opening on February 4 and losing their effect on March 9; in 1989 full flower occurred on March 24; time of optimum effectiveness truly varies from year to year; based on our propagation and cultural research this is an easy form to root using 5000 to 10,000 ppm KIBA quick dip; in 1988, cuttings collected on April 27, May 26, June 1, June 10, and July 19 and treated with 5000 ppm KIBA rooted 100, 78, 61, 77 and 83%, respectively; rooted cuttings will set a greater number of flower buds their second year; this form appears to produce heavy crops of flowers every year.

'Carmine Red'—Red-orange flower effect, each petal about 4/5″ long, kinked, twisted and rolled; strong grower of spreading habit; yellow fall color.

'Diane'—Kalmthout introduction, one of the best red-flowering forms, better than 'Ruby Glow' but still more copper-red than red; rich yellow-orange-red fall color; each petal 3/5 to 4/5″ long, 1/15″ wide, calyx purple-red, faintly fragrant, petals bronze colored red, shiny, lighter at ends, turning bronze with age; have seen in flower on several occasions and was not as impressed as I hoped to be; flowers *are not* red, also old leaves persist more so on this form than some and must be removed to maximize flower effect.

'Feuerzauber' ('Magic Fire', 'Fire Charm')—Excellent orange-red flowers, each petal about 3/4″ long, kinked, twisted, fragrant.

'Golden'—Good clear yellow with deep pink blush at base of petal, 5/8″ long, extremely kinked, slightly twisted.

'Hiltingbury'—Pale copper flowers of medium size, large shrub of spreading habit with large leaves that turn orange, scarlet and red in fall; seedling of *H. japonica* var. *flavopurpurascens.*

'Improved Winter Beauty'—A second generation seedling from 'Winter Beauty' and more floriferous than the parent.

'James Wells'—Abundant golden yellow flowers; have one plant that has flowered so profusely that the branches are almost hidden by the flowers.

'Jelena' ('Copper Beauty')—A Kalmthout introduction; excellent in flower and from a distance glows like copper; each 1″ long petal is red toward base, orange in middle and yellow at the tip, kinked, twisted, rich orange-red fall color, beautiful shrub.

'Luna'—Each petal burgundy at base, light yellow to the tip, 4/5″ long, kinked, twisted.

'Moonlight'—Pale sulfur-yellow, claret-red at base, medium-size, strong, sweet fragrance, kinked and twisted petals, large shrub with ascending branches, yellow fall color.

'New Red'—Starts deep red, eventually turning orange-brown.

'Nina'—Deep yellow flowers, each petal 1″ long, heavily produced, apparently not common in cultivation.

'Orange Beauty'—Deep yellow flowers verging on orange-yellow, abundant, fragrant.

'Primavera'—Primrose-yellow, each petal 3/5″ long, 1/16″ wide, sweet scent, exceedingly floriferous, vigorous, a late flowering form; a Kalmthout introduction.

'Rubra'—Good red until anthesis, afterward orange, 4/5″ long petals, kinked and twisted.

'Ruby Glow'—Coppery red flowers maturing to reddish brown, 3/5″ long petals, kinked and twisted, somewhat erect in habit, fall color combinations of orange and red; original plant over 20′ high and 20′ wide.

'Sunburst'—Listed under *H. mollis* but more properly belongs in the hybrid category; its lemon yellow, scentless flowers are produced in abundance during January and February; the petals may be almost 1″ long by 1/12″ wide; may hold some of its leaves through winter, obscuring the flowers.

'Vesna'—Dark yellow petals stained red at the base; 4/5 to 1″ long, 1/16 to 1/12″ wide and more twisted and crumpled than other *H.* × *intermedia* forms, with a strong, sweet scent; the calyx is claret red, which imparts an overall orange effect intermediate between 'Winter Beauty' and 'Jelena'.

'Westerstede'—Probably a *H.* × *intermedia* form, although it is often listed as a cultivar of *H. mollis;* primrose-yellow petals average 3/5″ long and are straight; flowers appear in late February and last into March.

'Winter Beauty'—Flowers similar to 'Orange Beauty' but petals are slightly longer (3/5 to 4/5″) and more twisted with more red staining on the basal third; little or no fragrance; raised by Hokaneya Nurseries, Yokohama, Japan and is said to be a cross between *H. mollis* and *H. japonica* 'Zuccariniana'.

There are additional cultivars but information is scant on their specifics. In early March at Longwood Gardens I saw 'Jelena', 'Ruby Glow' and *H. mollis* 'Brevipetala' in full flower and they were spectacular. November 2, 1981, I witnessed them in gorgeous fall color. Why these plants are not in greater use is beyond me. They are lovely, maintenance-free plants. The *H.* × *intermedia* types set good seed and no doubt many new seedlings will be selected and introduced over the years. Hopefully, evaluation and screening will be rigorous for a glut of rather indistinguishable cultivars is not needed. Compactness would be a good trait to select for. Seed requires about 3 months warm followed by 3 months cold. A key to good rooting success is taking cuttings as early as obtainable. Our work (Athens) indicates late April to end of May is the best time.

Hedera helix — English Ivy
(hed′ĕr-a hē′liks)

FAMILY: Araliaceae

LEAVES: Alternate, simple, evergreen, of juvenile shoots—3 to 5 lobed, 1 1/2 to 4″ long, about as wide, dark green and lustrous above, often with whitish veins, pale or yellowish green beneath; on mature (flowering branches)—ovate to rhombic and often lighter green in color, entire, rounded to cuneate at base.

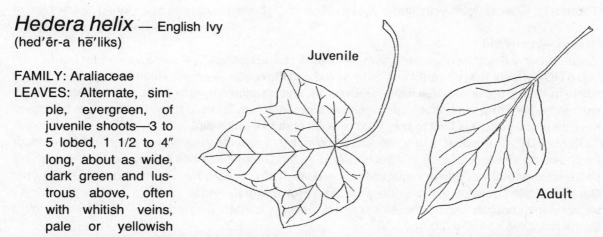

Juvenile

Adult

SIZE: 6 to 8″ high when used as a ground cover; can climb to 90′ as a vine.

HARDINESS: Zone 4 to 9, largely depends on cultivar selection.

HABIT: Low evergreen ground cover, rooting at the nodes, or a high climbing, true-clinging vine attaching itself to structures with root-like holdfasts.

RATE: Fast.

TEXTURE: Medium in all seasons.

LEAF COLOR: Dark green and often lustrous above, often with whitish veins on juvenile leaves; on mature plants foliage is a bright, lustrous green without the prominent whitish veins.

FLOWERS: Perfect, only occuring on the "Adult" form, greenish white, borne in globose umbels, September–October.

FRUIT: Berry-like, black drupe, 1/4″ across, containing 2 to 5 seeds, April or May following flowering, apparently the fruits are poisonous.

CULTURE: Transplants readily; growth is maximized in rich, fairly moist, organic, well-drained soil; full sun or heavy shade; not a bad idea to protect from winter sun and wind as the leaves develop necrotic areas; may require considerable pruning to keep it in bounds; tolerates acid and alkaline soil; shows a fair degree of salt tolerance.

DISEASES AND INSECTS: Bacterial leaf spot and canker, leaf spots, powdery mildews, aphids, caterpillars, mealybugs, scales, and two-spotted mite; mites and leaf spots can be serious.

LANDSCAPE VALUE: Ground cover with many uses; good in heavy shade, can look especially nice when given proper cultural conditions; has a nice effect when grown on trees or buildings; the adult form develops high up in trees or on buildings; the leaf morphology of the adult form is different from the vigorous normal type and the plant becomes quite woody.

CULTIVARS: A staggering number of ivy cultivars exist. There is an ivy society and an ivy handbook for those who are so inclined. I have included only a handful of the hardy forms. As one moves further south the number of selections that can be successfully grown increases. Ivy identification is fraught with difficulty.

'Baltica'—A hardy form with smaller leaves; introduced by Missouri Botanical Garden; unfortunately, not as hardy as advertised and 'Bulgaria' and 'Hebron' have proven hardier.

'Bulgaria'—One of the hardiest forms based on Wisconsin tests; a Missouri Botanical Garden introduction.

'Hebron'—Hardy form.

'Hibernica'—Large shiny leaf form, supposedly quite popular in cultivation. I cannot tell it from the others.

'Rochester'—Hardy form.

'Rumania'—Similar to 'Bulgaria'.

'Thorndale'—Hardy form with larger leaves than the species; proved itself during the winter of 1976–77.

'Wilson'—Hardy form.

'238th Street'—Supposedly a hardy form with adult characteristics, not subject to winter burn.

PROPAGATION: Seed, the pericarp must be removed and the seeds stratified; I tried an experiment using whole fruits and those with fruit walls removed; the germination only took place with the seeds which were extracted from the fruit; all seedlings were similar to the juvenile form. Cuttings can be rooted anytime of the year; it is best to use 1000 to 3000 ppm IBA-quick dip.

ADDITIONAL NOTES: I believe every individual knows ivy. It is used as a house plant and for outdoor purposes. Its shade tolerance is legendary and on the Georgia campus superb beds of English Ivy proliferate under the shade of water and willow oaks. It effectively covers trees and other structures. Old plants often develop a 4 to 6″ diameter light brown slightly ridged-and-furrowed trunks. For ivy afficienados consider joining the American Ivy Society, c/o Mr. Bill Redding, P.O. Box 520, West Carrollton, Ohio 45449-0520.

NATIVE HABITAT: Caucasian Mountains. Cultivated since ancient times.

RELATED SPECIES:

Hedera canariensis—Algerian Ivy
(hed'ĕr-à kà-nâri-en'-sis)

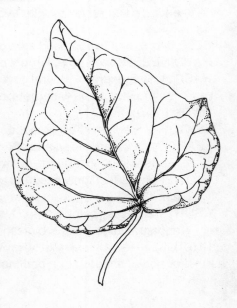

LEAVES: Alternate, simple, evergreen, 2 to 6″ (8″) long, shallowly 3 to 7 lobed in the juvenile state, heart shaped at base, leathery, glossy dark green; petiole and stems burgundy-red.

Hedera canariensis, Algerian Ivy, is not common in southern gardens but can be successfully grown in Zones 9 and 10. The large leaves and rampant growth provide solid cover. Used at Sea Island, GA, and during 1983–84 at 11°F was essentially eliminated. Grows well in coastal areas and is obviously quite salt tolerant. Best above 20°F. Native of the Canary Islands, Madeira, the Azores, Portugal and northwestern Africa as far east as Algeria.

Hedera colchica—Colchis Ivy
(hed'ēr-á kol'chi-ká)

LEAVES: Alternate, simple, evergreen, ovate or heart shaped, leathery, dull dark green, 3 to 7″ (10″) across, entire or slightly lobed with a few sharp teeth, fragrant when crushed.

Hedera colchica, Colchis Ivy, compares to English Ivy in most respects except it is larger leaved and presents a slightly coarser texture. Have seen it in test planting at the Griffin, Georgia Experiment Station in full sun and dry soil performing magnificently. Very fast growing. 'Dentata Variegata' offers a creamy-white border and has proven adaptable in my Georgia garden. Native to the region south of the Caspian and westward through the Caucasus to the Pontic ranges of Asiatic Turkey. Zone 6 to 9.

Hibiscus syriacus — Shrub Althea, also called Rose-of-Sharon
(hī-bis'kus si-ri-ā'kus)

FAMILY: Malvaceae

LEAVES: Alternate, simple, palmately veined and 3-lobed, ovate or rhombic-ovate, 2 to 4″ long, often coarsely toothed with rounded or acutish teeth, broad-cuneate or rounded at base, medium green, often lustrous, glabrous except a few hairs on the veins beneath; petiole 1/4 to 1″ long.

BUDS: Not evident, their position usually occupied by the scars of fallen inflorescences or branch-vestiges.

STEM: Rounded, fluted near the dilated tip, glabrescent, gray; pith—small, white, continuous with green border; leaf-scars crowded at tip, half round or transversely elliptical, raised, shortly decurrent in more or less evident ridges.

FRUIT: A dehiscent, 5-valved, upright, brown capsule which persists through winter and offers a valid identification character.

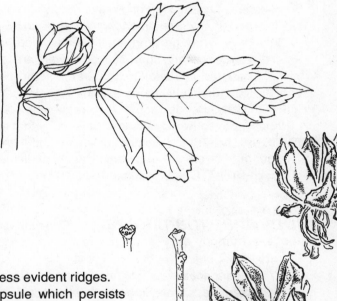

SIZE: 8 to 12′ in height by 6 to 10′ wide.

HARDINESS: Zone 5 to 8 (9); have observed severe injury at -20°F.

HABIT: Shrub or small tree, very erect but occasionally spreading, with numerous upright branches.

RATE: Medium.

TEXTURE: Medium in leaf; medium to medium-coarse in winter.

LEAF COLOR: Medium green in summer, holding late or changing to a poor yellow in fall; late leafing out in spring.

FLOWERS: Perfect, 5-petaled, white to red or purple or violet, or combinations, single and double, short stalked, broad campanulate, 2 to 4″ across; July, August through September, solitary on new year's growth; have seen plants in flower by mid to late April in Athens, GA.

FRUIT: Dehiscent capsule, 5-valved and persisting through winter.

CULTURE: Move as a small plant (5′ or less); transplants well; grows in about any soil except those which are extremely wet or dry; does best in moist, well-drained soils which have been supplemented with peat moss, leaf mold or compost; pH adaptable; full sun or partial shade; prefers hot weather; prune back heavily in early spring, or prune back to 2 or 3 buds in spring to get large flowers.

DISEASES AND INSECTS: Leaf spots, bacterial leaf spot, blights, canker, rust, aphids, Japanese beetle, mining scale, foliar nematodes and white-fly.

LANDSCAPE VALUE: Valuable for the late season flowers, groupings, masses, shrub borders but does not deserve specimen use; has and can be used for screening and hedges; not one of my favorite plants but has certainly been accepted by the gardening public.

CULTIVARS: Too many to discuss; see Wyman's list in *Shrubs and Vines for American Gardens;* several new cultivars have been introduced by the National Arboretum in recent years; they include:

'Aphrodite'—Erect growing, multiple-stemmed, low branched shrub, 9 1/2' high and 8' wide in 14 years. Solitary, short-stalked flowers are dark pink with a prominent dark red eye spot, 4 1/2 to 5″ in diameter, blooming from June to September. Heavy-textured foliage, reliably hardy to Zone 5, triploid.

'Diana'—A triploid with large pure white flowers that remain open at night, the foliage is a waxy dark green; it sets very little fruit and flowers over a long period in summer; Dr. Egolf bred this cultivar; see *Baileya* 17:75–78 (1970) for specifics.

'Helene'—Essentially white with a reddish purple blush at the base; a triploid and does not set much fruit, if any; see *American Nurseryman* 154(6):11, 66–67. 1981.

'Minerva'—Erect growing, multiple-stemmed, low branched shrub, 8 1/2' high and 7' wide in 14 years. Solitary, short-stalked flowers are lavender with traces of pink overcast and a prominent dark red eye spot, 4 to 5″ in diameter, profuse blooming from June to September. Lustrous foliage, reliably hardy to Zone 5, triploid.

PROPAGATION: Seeds require no pretreatment and self-sown seedlings can be a nuisance in the landscape; softwood cuttings, June–July, root readily when treated with 1000 ppm IBA.

ADDITIONAL NOTES: Have grown 'Diana' and 'Helene' without becoming attached, do not show great vigor but flowers are excellent; 'Diana', particularly, is weak, humpy, rather wimpy form.

NATIVE HABITAT: China, India. Introduced before 1600.

Hippophae rhamnoides — Common Seabuckthorn
(hi-pof′ā-ē ram-noy′dēz)

FAMILY: Elaeagnaceae

LEAVES: Alternate, simple, linear to linear-lanceolate, 1 to 3″ long, 1/8 to 1/4″ wide, acutish, upper surface dark gray-green and not as scaly as the silvery gray undersurface.

BUDS: Shrivelled and ragged with 2 thin, very loose scales, end bud lacking; on male plants flower buds are conical and conspicuous; on female-smaller and rounded.

STEM: Commonly with terminal and axillary twig-spines, stellately pubescent and with silvery or brownish small peltate scales, slender, subterete; pith—small, brown, round, continuous.

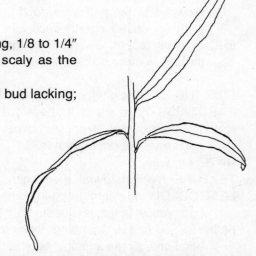

SIZE: 8 to 12 to 30' tall with a spread of 10 to 40'.

HARDINESS: Zone 3 to 7.

HABIT: Large shrub or small tree, spreading and irregularly rounded, loose and open; staminate trees are more erect than the spreading pistillate trees; tends to sucker and form large colonies.

RATE: Medium.

TEXTURE: Medium-fine in leaf; medium-coarse in winter.

LEAF COLOR: Silver-green in summer, grayish green in fall.

FLOWERS: Essentially dioecious, yellowish before leaves in March or April, borne in axillary racemes on previous season's branches.

FRUIT: Bright orange, drupe-like, globose to egg-shaped , short-stalked, 1/4 to 1/3″ long, September, persisting through April of the following year, apparently very acid and birds to not bother it.

CULTURE: A bit difficult to get established; seems to do better in sandy, relatively infertile soil than in rich soil; prefers sand with a moist subsoil; sunny open area; withstands salt spray; supposedly a ratio of 6 females to 1 male is sufficient for pollination, pollen is carried by the wind; nitrogen fixing.

DISEASES AND INSECTS: None serious.

LANDSCAPE VALUE: One of the best plants available for winter fruit color; good for color contrast because of summer foliage and fruit; works well in masses, borders, and along the seashore for stabilizing sand; could be an effective plant for highway use where salt-spray is a problem; seldom available in commerce and since there is no way to determine the sex of seedling grown plants, there is a chance that one will end up with non-fruiting plants.

PROPAGATION: I have grown many seedlings but have had a tough time growing them on; seeds should be stratified for 90 days at 41°F and they will then germinate like beans; in the rich Illinois prairie soils the plant languished; cuttings are apparently difficult but root cuttings will work, also layering and division of the suckers that occur around the parent plant.

ADDITIONAL NOTES: Abundant in Europe; widely planted in the Netherlands and parts of Germany and France as a roadside cover; the fruit is handsome as is the soft grayish green foliage.

NATIVE HABITAT: Europe to Altai Mountains, western and northern China and north and western Himalayas.

Hovenia dulcis — Japanese Raisintree
(hō-vē′ni-a dul′sis)

FAMILY: Rhamnaceae

LEAVES: Alternate, simple, broad-ovate to elliptic, 4 to 6″ long, 3 to 5″ wide, acuminate, subcordate or rounded and usually unequal at base, coarsely serrate, glabrous or pubescent on veins beneath, prominently 3-veined, lustrous dark green; petiole 1 1/4 to 2″ long.

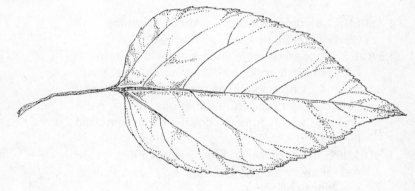

BUDS: Dark brown, hairy, rather small, superposed, sessile, ovoid, with 1 or 2 exposed scales; no terminal.

STEM: Villous to glabrous, terete, slender, zig-zag, rich brown, small dot-like lenticels; pith relatively large, pale, continuous, pale or white, round; leaf-scars round-heart-shaped, somewhat elevated; buds sit in notch formed by leaf scar.

SIZE: Usually reaching 30′ under cultivation; the spread would be about 2/3's to equal the height; can grow 40 to 45′.

HARDINESS: Zone 5, probably safest in the southern areas of Zone 5 to 7(8).

HABIT: Small, handsome tree of upright-oval to rounded outline with clean, ascending main branches and a paucity of lateral branches.

RATE: Medium.

TEXTURE: Medium in all seasons.

BARK: Flat gray to gray-brown, rather wide ridges with shallow, darker furrows, very nice effect, especially pleasing bark, very soft gray and recognizable from a distance.

LEAF: Handsome lustrous dark green in summer, no appreciable fall color, perhaps yellow under ideal conditions.

FLOWERS: Perfect, greenish white, 1/3″ diameter, borne on many-flowered, 2 to 3″ diameter cymes; June and July.

FRUIT: Fleshy drupe, 1/3″ diameter, light grayish or brown; the fleshy branches of the inflorescence are reddish; the fleshy branches are sweet and are chewed by the Japanese and Chinese; mature in September–October; actually not bad tasting.

CULTURE: Not too difficult to culture; limited information is available on this species but I have seen the plant performing admirably in a planter on the Southern Illinois Campus at Edwardsville, at the Missouri Botanic Garden, St. Louis, National Arboretum, Washington, D.C., Swarthmore College, and at the Arnold Arboretum; in all cases the soils, exposures, and maintenance levels were different yet the trees were vigorous and healthy; supposedly thrives in sandy loams.

DISEASES AND INSECTS: Nothing serious.

LANDSCAPE VALUE: A small lawn or street tree; hardiness may be a problem; could be used in planters.

PROPAGATION: Seed requires a considerable acid scarification period and somewhere between 1 and 2 hours is sufficient; recently published paper by Frett, *HortScience* 24(1):52 (1989) indicates best germination 93.8% with 45 minutes acid followed by 90 days cold stratification, 45 minutes acid produced 36% germination; apparently there is a type of embryo dormancy.

ADDITIONAL NOTES: The Dawes Arboretum, Newark, Ohio, had a rather sizable tree that was killed during the 1976–77 winter when temperatures dipped to -22°F in that area.

NATIVE HABITAT: China; cultivated in Japan and India. Cultivated 1820.

Hydrangea anomala subsp. *petiolaris* (formerly *H. petiolaris*) — Climbing Hydrangea
(hī-dran′jē-à à-nom′a-là pet-i-ō-lā′ris)

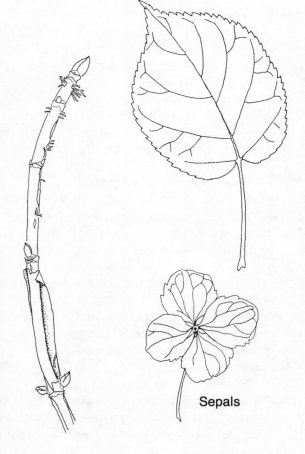

FAMILY: Hydrangeaceae (Also included in Saxifragaceae by some authorities)

LEAVES: Opposite, simple, broad-ovate to ovate-oval, acute or acuminate, cordate or rounded at base, 2 to 4″ long, nearly as wide, serrate, nearly glabrous, dark green and lustrous above, paler and often with tufts of down in the vein-axils beneath; petioles ranging from 1/2 to 4″ long.

BUDS: Imbricate, greenish brown, sometimes tinged red, shiny, 2 loosely overlapping scales visible, essentially glabrous.

STEM: Brown, with peeling, exfoliating shaggy bark (handsome), developing root-like holdfasts along the internodes.

SIZE: Almost unlimited in ability to climb tall trees, perhaps 60 to 80′ in height; obviously can be maintained at lower heights but the inherent ability to cover large structures is present; has been used as a bush in the open, will cover rock piles, walls and other structures.

HARDINESS: Zone 4 to 7(8), not as vigorous in south.

HABIT: True clinging vine and climbing by rootlike holdfasts; interesting in that it develops in more than one plane and gives depth to the structure it is covering; the branches protrude out from the structure to which the vine is attached creating interesting shadows unlike that obtainable with *Parthenocissus* and juvenile *Hedera helix*.

RATE: Slow in the establishment process, but quite vigorous after roots are established.

TEXTURE: Medium-fine in leaf; medium in winter habit.

Sepals

STEM COLOR: Older stems (3 years or more) develop an exfoliating character much like *Acer griseum* (Paperbark Maple); the bark color is a rich cinnamon-brown and unparalleled by any other hardy vine.

LEAF COLOR: Glossy dark green in summer foliage, exquisitely handsome, a rare jewel in the crown of vines; the leaves stay green late into fall and essentially abscise green.

FLOWERS: White, late June to early July, effective for 2 weeks or longer, borne in 6 to 10″ diameter flat-topped corymbs with the outer flowers (sepals) sterile and showy (1 to 1 3/4″ across) and the inner flowers fertile, dull white, and weakly attractive, sweet fragrance; overall flower effect is magnificent; inflorescence borne on 1 to 1 1/2″ long stalk.

FRUIT: Capsule, not ornamentally important.

CULTURE: Somewhat show to develop after transplanting, requires rich, well-drained, moist soil; full sun or shade; best used on east or north exposure in adverse climates; should be grown and handled as a container plant to avoid excessive abuse in transplanting.

DISEASES AND INSECTS: None serious compared to those listed for *H. arborescens.*

LANDSCAPE VALUE: The best vine! As Wyman so succinctly stated, ''There is no better clinging vine''; excellent for massive effect on brick or stone walls, arbors, trees and any free structure; becomes quite woody, so needs ample support; the extra cultural care required in establishment is rewarded many times over in ornamental assets for the excellent foliage, flowers and winter bark effect make this species a four-season plant.

PROPAGATION: Somewhat difficult to root, I have collected cuttings in July, treated with 1000 ppm IBA and received 5% rooting; supposedly the optimum time to secure cutting wood is late spring or early summer before the stems turn brown; July cuttings have been rooted using 8000 to 10,000 ppm IBA; see Dirr and Heuser, 1987, for detailed procedures; seed needs no pretreatment and can be directly sown; cold period of 1 to 2 months will hasten and unify germination.

NATIVE HABITAT: Japan, China. Introduced 1865.

RELATED SPECIES: Unfortunately an enterprising taxonomist reduced the above to subspecies classification. *Hydrangea petiolaris* has been around for a long time and is still not well known. With the name change it will take another 50 years before the garden public catches up with the new name. My good friend, the late Professor Emeritus Clarence E. Lewis, once noted that *H. petiolaris* has been listed as such for 100 plus years so why change the name when it has been universally accepted. McClintock, *A Monograph of the Genus Hydrangea,* is the basis for this change. The real kicker in this change is that not all taxonomists agree. Bean, for example, treats *H. petiolaris* as a species. Alas, if I had nothing better to do with my time than split taxonomic hairs I would have myself bound and shelved in the archives.

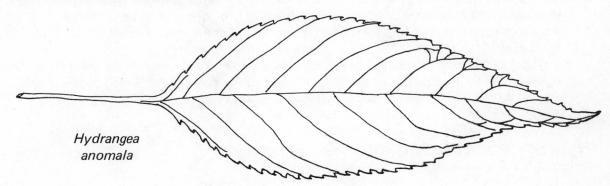

Hydrangea anomala

Hydrangea anomala (hī-dran′jē-a̅ a̅-nom′a̅-la̅) differs from the above in the elliptic-ovate, 3 to 6″ long, 1 to 3″ wide, pointed, rounded, triangular or round toothed, lustrous dark green leaves. Corymbs are smaller (6 to 8″ across), with fewer sterile sepals (2/3 to 1 1/2″ diameter) and 9 to 15 stamens instead of 15 to 22 as in *H. anomala* subsp. *petiolaris.* The inflorescence tends to be more lax and floppy than subsp. *petiolaris.* The Arnold Arboretum has both vines on the north wall of the Administration Building and in June-July they are magnificent. The elliptic-ovate leaves of *H.*

anomala permit easy separation from the more rounded leaves of the subspecies. Probably not as hardy as the subspecies. Himalaya, China. Introduced 1839. Zone 5 to 7(8).

Schizophragma hydrangeoides — Japanese Hydrangea-vine

LEAVES: Opposite, simple, suborbicular or broad-ovate, 2 to 4″ long, short acuminate, rounded to cordate at base, coarsely dentate, lustrous dark green, essentially glabrous; petiole—1 to 3″ long, reddish.

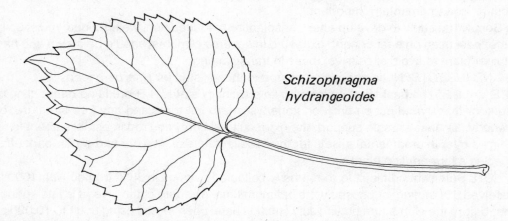

Schizophragma hydrangeoides

Schizophragma hydrangeoides, (skiz-ō-frag′má̇ hī-dran-jē-oy′dēz), Japanese Hydrangea-vine, is an allied but quite distinct climber. The vine stays flat and does not develop the protruding woody framework of *H. a.* subsp. *petiolaris* The leaves are much more coarsely toothed and the sterile flowers are composed of a single ovate entire sepal compared to the 3 to 5-parted sepals of *H. a.* subsp. *petiolaris*. The inflorescences are flat-topped and 8 to 10″ wide, showing a slight drooping tendency compared to the rather rigid inflorescence of *H. a.* subsp. *petiolaris*. It is in full flower just after *petiolaris*. Requires about the same cultural mainpulations as subsp. *petiolaris*. Found in woods and forests in the mountains of Japan where it often grows in association with *H. a.* subsp. *petiolaris*. This is a true clinging vine and cements itself by rootlike holdfasts. 'Roseum' is a lovely form with rose-flushed bracts. It is in this country and hopefully will find its way into cultivation. Cultivated 1880. Zone 5 to 7(8). I have rooted late July cuttings with 3000 ppm IBA.

Schizophragma integrifolium, (skiz-ō-frag′má̇ in-teg-ri-fō′li-um), Chinese Hydrangea-vine, differs from the above in its entire or sparingly denticulate, 4 to 6″ long leaves, the immense 10 to 12″ wide inflorescences, and the 2 to 3″ long single ovate sepal. Central and western China. Introduced 1901 by Wilson. Zone 7(?).

ADDITIONAL NOTES: All of the above are lovely vines and make excellent choices on brick and stone buildings. As I write this, I recall beautiful plants of subsp. *petiolaris* at Spring Grove, Smith College and the Arnold Arboretum that would make believers of every gardener.

Hydrangea arborescens — Smooth Hydrangea
(hī-dran′jē-á̇ âr-bō-res′enz)

LEAVES: Opposite, simple, ovate to elliptic, 2 to 8″ long, 2 to 6″ wide, acuminate, rounded or cordate at base, serrate, dark green, glabrous or sometimes puberulous beneath; petioles 1 to 3″ long.
BUDS: Imbricate, 4 to 6 scaled, greenish brown, divergent, 1/8″ long, glabrous, much longer than *H. paniculata* buds.
STEM: Stout, gray-tan-brown, young branches essentially glabrous, smooth, without gray streaks; older stems-exfoliating; pith-relatively large, roundish, continuous, whitish.

SIZE: 3 to 5′ in height by 3 to 5′ and larger in spread; suckers freely from roots and will cover large areas if not maintained.

HARDINESS: Zone 3 to 9.

HABIT: Usually low growing, clumpy rounded shrub with many weak, shreddy barked non-branched canes; often broader than high at maturity.

RATE: Fast, almost weedy.

TEXTURE: Coarse in leaf, flower and winter habit.

LEAF COLOR: Dark green in summer, fall color is green to brown, although leaves may die off a pleasing lemon-yellow in certain years, generally nondescript.

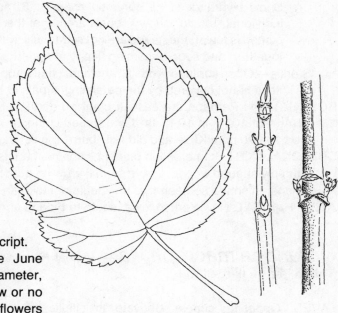

FLOWERS: Fertile flowers, dull white, late June through September, borne in 4 to 6″ diameter, much branched, flattish corymbs with few or no large white sterile flowers; actually the flowers pass from apple green to white to brown; probably best to cut off flowers at the early brown stage as they are ornamentally valueless after this time; flowers open one month or more before those of *H. paniculata,* open early to mid June, Athens.

FRUIT: Capsule, 8 to 10 ribbed, of no ornamental consequence.

CULTURE: Fibrous rooted, transplants well; very adaptable; however, proliferates in rich, well-drained, moist soil; pH adaptable; prefers partial shade, however, does well in full sun if soil moisture is sufficient; often requires supplemental watering in hot dry summers; probably should mow it off with a lawnmower in late fall or early spring; flowers on new wood; leaves appear "dog-earred" under drought conditions.

DISEASES AND INSECTS: Bacterial wilt, bud blight, leaf spot, powdery mildew, rust, aphids, leaf tier, rose chafer, oystershell scale, two-spotted mite, and nematodes have been reported on this and other species. I have grown 'Annabelle' for 8 years and have never had a single problem. First have the problem diagnosed by a county agent or university specialist and accept their current control recommendations.

LANDSCAPE VALUE: Consider this species as a herbaceous perennial in colder climates; some flowers are so heavy as to weight the stem to the ground thus creating a very unkempt and unruly specimen; perhaps in the shrub border or massing in some shady, out-of-the-way area; in the last edition I beat the plants into verbal submission but after growing and loving 'Annabelle', I have tempered my earlier remarks; if cut to the ground in late winter and lightly fertilized, by June or July the regrowth will produce stunning flowers that are effective for a month in the south, two months in Zone 5; as flowers fade cut them at the base, strip the leaves, tie by their bases and hang to dry; we have done this for years and the sepals do not shatter and make excellent dried bouquets; in fact they could be dyed or painted for more colorful effects; I usually get two flushes of flower, the first in June, and after pruning, the second in August-September.

CULTIVARS:

'Annabelle'—Selected by J.C. McDaniel of the University of Illinois for its extremely large corymbs (up to 1′ across) and the fact it flowers 10 to 14 days later than 'Grandiflora'; heads are more erect on the stem with a more nearly symmetrical radius, and are usually larger in total diameter than those of 'Grandiflora' grown under the same conditions; have seen it growing from Orono, ME to Clermont, KY to Athens, GA; has become one of the most popular hydrangeas and is widely available from nurserymen; this is definitely a superior plant and was introduced by a true plantsman and gentleman; the history of this selection is presented in *PIPPS* 12:110 (1962).

'Grandiflora'—This is the type commonly available from nurseries, often referred to as the Hills of Snow Hydrangea; the corymbs are 6 to 8″ across with primarily sterile white flowers; the individual "sterile" showy sepals are larger than 'Annabelle', but the total number of flowers in a head is fewer; the heads are not so radially symmetrical, looking like four parts loosely pushed together, and soon becoming floppy in appearance.

'Sterilis'—Often confused with 'Grandiflora', flatter topped head, showing some areas of small perfect flowers not covered by the persisting sepals of the showy flowers.

PROPAGATION: Perhaps the easiest plant on earth to root, softwood cuttings, May–June, 1000 ppm KIBA, root 100% in 10 to 14 days; rooted cuttings continue to grow after removal from mist; have used 10,000 ppm KIBA and did not "burn" the cuttings.

ADDITIONAL NOTES: Interesting plant in its native haunts, and often found growing out of rock crevices in deeply shaded woods. I have seen it growing out of the sandstone cliffs in Turkey Run State Park, Indiana, in shade so deep that one could not take an effective photograph.

NATIVE HABITAT: New York to Iowa, south to Florida and Louisiana. Introduced 1736.

Hydrangea macrophylla — Bigleaf Hydrangea
(hī-dran′jē-à mak-rō-fil′a)

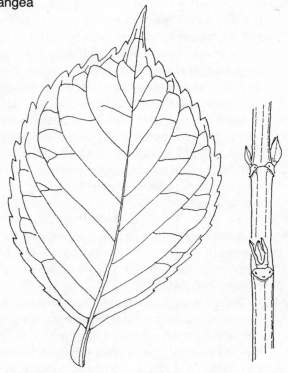

LEAVES: Opposite, simple, obovate to elliptic or broad-ovate, 4 to 8″ long, two-third's as wide, short-acuminate, broad cuneate at base, coarsely serrate with triangular obtusish teeth, lustrous medium green above, rather fleshy texture and greasy to the touch, glabrous or slightly puberulous beneath; petioles stout, 1/2 to 1 1/4″ long, leaving large scars, the opposite one contiguous.

STEM: Light brown, scarcely branched, often dying back in winter; pith—large, white.

SIZE: 3 to 6′ in height but can grow to 10′; spread would be equal to or greater than the height.

HARDINESS: Zone 6 to 9, does not do well in Zone 5 unless extremely well sited, as one goes south and east this becomes a very common plant; however, in the northern states it is rare to see it in full flower; qualification is necessary for I have seen the plant in Urbana, IL withstand -20°F; it never flowered, but did come back from the crown to produce a respectable mound of foliage; since flowers are set (largely) on last year's growth, if the shoots are killed then flowering is history; I have seen the most magnificent flowering specimens on Cape Cod; in Zone 8, Athens, where the plant should prosper, 2 flowering years out of 3 might be considered good; the plant is soft and succulent and does not harden and the tops of the plant are killed.

HABIT: Rounded, suckering shrub of many erect, usually unbranched, thick stems.

RATE: Fast.

TEXTURE: Medium-coarse in leaf although coarse is a definite possibility; coarse in winter, in fact, irreparably so.

STEM COLOR: Of a light, shiny, gray- or straw-brown color.

LEAF COLOR: Leaves are quite large (4 to 8″ long) and are a lustrous medium green in summer; the leaves are quite fleshy (succulent) with a greasy consistency.

FLOWERS: Very difficult to adequately describe the typical species flower because of the numerous selections; the sterile, outer flowers are pink or bluish, entire or toothed, up to 2″ or more in diameter, the fertile flowers are usually blue or pink; both are borne in large, broad, flat-topped, much branched, cymose corymbs; July through August; June-July in Athens; have seen in flower in early June in Athens.

FRUIT: Capsule, 1/4 to 5/16″ long, not showy.

CULTURE: Transplant as a container plant into moist, well-drained soil which has been amended with peat moss, leaf mold and the like; will withstand seashore conditions and actually flourish near the shore; full sun or partial shade; pruning is an art with the *Hydrangea* species and one must know the requirements of each type; this species flowers from buds formed on previous season's growth and any pruning should be done right after flowering; often winter killed in north and no flowering occurs. The flower color on some cultivars is strongly affected by the pH of the soil in which they are growing. The ray flowers are often the most affected. The color changes depend on the concentration of aluminum ions in the soil. This depends in turn on the acidity of the soil, being highest on very acid soils and lowest where the soil is alkaline. The color range depends on the cultivar, but the bluest shades are always produced on the most acid soils. A pH range of 5.0 to 5.5 is listed as satisfactory for inducing blue coloration while pH 6.0 to 6.5 and probably slightly higher is best for pink coloration.

DISEASES AND INSECTS: See under *H. arborescens,* although none particularly serious.

LANDSCAPE VALUE: Probably a good plant for the shrub border in southern areas; not adequately winter hardy in the northern states and is often killed back to the ground, the only benefit then is the foliage; this plant and the numerous cultivars are widely planted in the east and south; makes a good flower display, good choice for coastal areas.

CULTIVARS: Unbelievably large number of cultivars many of which are not hardy. W.J. Bean's *Trees and Shrubs Hardy in the British Isles,* Vol. II; Hillier's *Manual of Trees and Shrubs;* and Haworth-Booth's, *The Hydrangeas,* offer a wealth of cultivars and the technical information concerning them. Wyman has a list in his book based on his observations. Quite an interesting species with many lovely garden forms. The cultivars are divided into two groups: the *hortensias* which have essentially sterile flowers that are borne in large globose corymbs. These usually form solid masses of white, pink, red and/or blue which are often so heavy they cause the stem to bend. The *lacecaps* have a center of fertile, relatively non-showy flowers and an outer ring of showy, sterile flowers which together afford a pinwheel effect.

Hortensias

'All Summer Beauty'—Small plant with rich blue flowers in acid soil, prolific flowering, will be different shade of pink/blue in near neutral soil, 3 to 4′, will supposedly flower on the new growth of the season.

'Blue Prince' ('Blauer Prinz')—Pink or purplish, medium blue in acid soil, dense corymbs, moderate height, one of the hardiest.

'Compacta'—Supposedly more compact than 'Nikko Blue' with darker green leaves, blue in acid soil.

'Domotoi'—Individual flowers large and doubled, pale pink or blue, in an attractive regular shaped head; literature is confusing as it reports the form as being both vigorous and weak growing, may become fasciated and distorted if too well fed, about 3′ high.

'Forever Pink'—Good compact, 3′ high form with 4″ diameter pink flower heads that become rose-red in cool weather, flowers earlier than other types often in June, keeps good foliage color until frost.

'Nikko Blue'—An old form that is quite vigorous, 6′, with large rounded deep blue inflorescences in acid soil.

'Otaksa'—Pink or blue flowers, red leaf stalks, rather weak stems which bend down under the weight of wet flower heads, 3′ high, an old Chinese variety.

'Westfalen'—Pure vivid-crimson or deep purple-blue, free and perpetual flowering, richest colored of all, 2 1/2′ high.

Lacecaps

'Blue Wave'—Ray flowers with 4 wavy-edged sepals, rich blue in acid soils, otherwise pink or lilac, a vigorous shrub 6' high and as wide with bold foliage, grows best in light shade, a seedling of 'Mariesii'.

'Coerulea'—Perfect flowers a deep blue, ray flowers blue or white, one of the hardier forms, Zone 6, cultivated 1846.

'Lanarth White'—Fertile flowers blue or pink, ray florets pure white, starting in July and lasting into August, a hardy form, 3' high and wide, very good old form.

'Mariesii'—A few sterile flowers are scattered among the fertile ones and are similar in shape to the normal ray flowers that edge the inflorescence, flowers are nearly always pink or mauve-pink (pale blue on very acid soils), grows 4 to 5' high.

'Quadricolor'—Supposedly the best of the variegated leaf types with shades of white, cream, lime and green in each leaf, more variegation than 'Variegata'.

'Variegata'—Leaves edged with creamy-white, very attractive, flowers blue in acid soil; 3' high, nice accent plant, not particularly strong grower.

PROPAGATION: Best to propagate from softwood cuttings of late May, June, July growth; also semi-hardwood and hardwood cuttings will root; rooting is hastened with IBA treatment although the rooting percentage will approach 100 without any treatment.

NATIVE HABITAT: Japan.

RELATED SPECIES:

Hydrangea serrata

LEAVES: Opposite, simple, lanceolate, ovate-elliptic, 2 to 6″ long, 1 to 2 1/2″ wide, acuminate, cuneate, finely or coarsely serrate, dark green and usually glabrous above, veins beneath often with short appressed or curled hairs.

Hydrangea serrata (hī-dran'jē-a ser-rā'ta) is allied to the above but is not as robust, has slender stems, relatively narrow leaves and smaller flowers and seed capsules. It is found in mountain woodlands and is considerably hardier than *H. macrophylla.* Several beautiful cultivars include 'Bluebird' with pale pink or blue ray flowers, early flowering, and a vigorous (5'), drought-resistant constitution; 'Preziosa' has a hortensia type inflorescence that is rather small (3 to 4″) but the flowers start pink with a deeper shade at the edge and later change to crimson with deeper shades of the same color. This is a hardy and free flowering form that does well in sun or half shade, 4' high. I saw this in England and was genuinely impressed by the rich flower color. Japan, Korea. Cultivated 1870. Zone 5(6) to 7.

Hydrangea paniculata — Panicle Hydrangea
(hī-dran'jē-a pan-ik-ū-lā'ta)

LEAVES: Opposite, sometimes whorled, especially on flowering stems, simple, elliptic or ovate, acuminate, rounded or cuneate at base, 3 to 6″ long, 1 1/2 to 3″ wide, serrate, dark green and sparingly pubescent or nearly glabrous above, setose pubescent beneath, particularly on the veins; petiole 1/2 to 1″ long.

BUDS: Imbricate, rounded, globose, 4 to 6 scaled, glabrous, brownish in color, sometimes with whorled character.

STEM: Stout, reddish brown, bark showing gray vertically streaked areas; older bark often peeling and more gray in color.

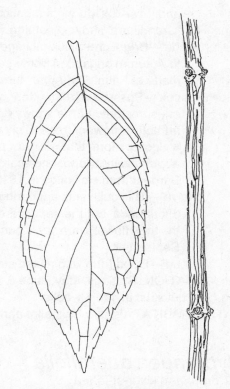

SIZE: 15 to 25′ in height by 10 to 20′ in spread; quite variable in size, often 10′ or less.

HARDINESS: Zone 3 to 8, probably the most cold-hardy hydrangea species.

HABIT: Upright, coarsely spreading, low-branched tree or large shrub, the branches assuming a semi-arching condition under the weight of the flowers; often rather straggly and unkempt with age.

RATE: Fast.

TEXTURE: Coarse the year round but peaking when denuded of leaves yet possessed with browned remains of the inflorescence; actually spent flowers should be removed in September or earlier.

STEM COLOR: Older wood, 1 to 2″ or greater, assumes a gray-brown, ridged and furrowed look; often quite handsome especially when lower branches are removed and the sun shadows are allowed to develop; especially handsome is the bark on cultivar 'Praecox' when treated in this fashion.

LEAF COLOR: Dark green, possibly a tinge of luster to the summer foliage, fall color is green with a hint of yellow, sometimes a tinge of reddish purple appears, never spectacular.

FLOWERS: White changing to purplish pink, mid July on, borne in pyramidal panicles approximately 6 to 8″ long, two-thirds as wide at base, the bulk of the flowers are fertile, yellowish white, not showy; a few flowers are sterile and showy; flowers last for long periods while going through the color transformation.

FRUIT: Capsule, ornamentally without appeal.

CULTURE: Similar to *H. arborescens,* prefers good loamy, moist, well-drained soil; sun or partial shade; remove inflorescences in September as they are then turning brown; flowers on new wood as does *H. arborescens* and can be pruned in winter or early spring; very hardy plant; the most adaptable and most urban tolerant, difficult to kill.

DISEASES AND INSECTS: Same as previously described for *H. arborescens.*

LANDSCAPE VALUE: Several astute plantsmen have termed this species a "Monstrosity in the Landscape"; difficult to blend into the modern landscape because of extreme coarseness; totally disgusting in late fall and winter with inflorescences still evident; overplanted in the past but little used in modern landscapes; grows very fast and will provide a large splash of white at a time when few plants are in flower; possibly should be reserved for the shrub border or the neighbor's yard; I have observed this plant through the seasons and always came to the same conclusion—a "loner" in the landscape; making somewhat of a comeback in recent years; good pruning can do a great deal to make this a better plant.

CULTIVARS:

'Floribunda'—Sterile flowers more numerous but not sufficiently so to conceal the fertile flowers; sepals about 5/8 to 3/4″ long, 4 to 5 in number, overlapping, flowers late July into September.

'Grandiflora'—Almost all flowers are sterile and large; forming a tight panicle of white then purplish pink and finally brown; the inflorescences (normally 6 to 8″ long) can reach sizes of 12 to 18″ in length and 6 to 12″ wide at the base; this is the most common form and still widely available from nurseries. To produce the large panicles mentioned it is necessary to thin the plant to 5 or 10 primary shoots; these, if properly fertilized and watered, will produce immense heads that literally weight the branches down; I have seen plants handled like this at Bernheim Arboretum and it is a welcome change from the normal shrub-tree type; this form was introduced from Japan in 1862; goes under the name PeeGee Hydrangea; I monitored flowering times of this and 'Praecox' during sabbatical at the Arnold; on July 10, 1978, 'Praecox' was in flower while 'Grandiflora' showed nothing.

'Kyushu'—Bright green, lush foliage, numerous white panicles of sterile and fertile flowers, from July to Autumn; originated from seeds collected by Collingwood Ingram in Japan; selection actually made at Kalmthout Arboretum, Belgium, listed in 1989 Bressingham catalog.

'Praecox'—Possesses a smattering of sterile, showy flowers integrated with the fertile, non-showy ones, majority of the showy flowers are located at the base of the inflorescence; interestingly attractive; flowers three to six weeks earlier than 'Grandiflora' about late June in Zone 8;this is a vigorous form that will grow between 10 and 15′ in height; the sepals are grouped 4-together, about one inch long, and scarcely overlap; raised at Arnold Arboretum from seeds collected by Sargent from Hokkaido in 1893; hardier than 'Grandiflora'.

'Tardiva'—This cultivar is appearing in more and more American nurseries; it is somewhat similar to 'Floribunda' but the sepals are mostly in 4's compared to 5's; the inflorescence about 6″ long, the ray flowers are less numerous and smaller (1/2 to 3/4″ long); it flowers quite late in September.

'Unique'—Good form with mixed sterile and fertile florets, from 1989 Bressingham catalog.

PROPAGATION: Cuttings, May, June & July, softwood, root readily in sand:peat medium, with 1000 ppm IBA quickdip in 4 to 5 weeks.

NATIVE HABITAT: Japan, Sakhalin, and eastern and southern China. Introduced 1861.

Hydrangea quercifolia — Oakleaf Hydrangea
(hī-dran′jē-a kwĕr-si-fō′li-a)

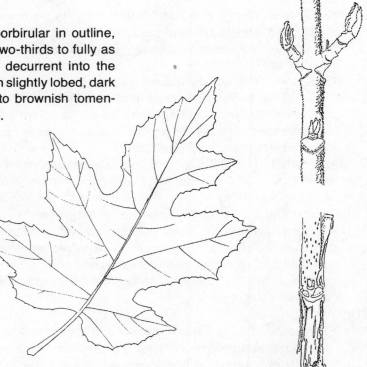

LEAVES: Opposite, simple, ovate to suborbirular in outline, sinuately 3 to 7 lobed, 3 to 8″ long, two-thirds to fully as wide, usually truncate at base and decurrent into the petiole, lobes broad, serrate and often slightly lobed, dark green and glabrous above, whitish to brownish tomentose beneath; petiole 1 to 2 1/2″ long.

BUDS: Imbricate, 4 to 6 scaled, divergent, brownish, tomentose; terminal—much larger than laterals.

STEM: Stout, pubescent on young growth, brownish, older stems with prominent lenticels, exfoliating cinnamon-brown bark; large leaf scars—prominent, inverted—triangular in shape with prominent vascular bundle scars; pith—light brown.

SIZE: 4 to 6′ (8′) in height; spread as wide and wider as it suckers from roots.

HARDINESS: Zone 5 to 9.

HABIT: Upright, little branched, irregular, stoloniferous shrub forming mounded colonies.

RATE: Slow to medium.

TEXTURE: Pleasantly coarse in leaf; coarse in winter, but handsome by virtue of exfoliating bark.

STEM COLOR: Young stems intensely brownish tomentose, older stems (3 year and more) exfoliating to expose a rich brown inner bark; quite attractive but often overlooked.

LEAF COLOR: Deep green, sometimes glossy in summer, changing to shades of red, orangish brown and purple in fall; quite spectacular in fall color; seems to be great variability in the fall color among progeny of this species; selections should be made for this feature alone; new growth grayish green, leaves emerge folded in prayer and open to their 180° angle position from surface to surface, handsome in early spring; leaves hold late, often into late November–early December and in winter of 1988–89 when lowest temperature was 21°F until February 22, many fall (winter?) colored leaves were still on the plants.

FLOWERS: White, changing to purplish pink and finally brown, outer flowers sterile, 1 to 1 1/2″ diameter; fertile flowers numerous, lacking character or good color; late June through July and persisting, in Athens, flowers invariably at their best in late May–early June; borne in 4 to 12″ long erect panicles; the cultivars are considerably more showy in flower than the straight species.

FRUIT: Capsule, not showy.

CULTURE: Somewhat tender as a young plant and should be protected in Zone 5; stems and buds may be injured when winter temperatures go much below -10°F; requires moist, fertile, well-drained soil; sun or partial (1/2) shade; wise to mulch to maintain a cool, moist root environment; if terminal buds are lost during winter, no flowers will be produced; in the north it is possibly best to consider this plant for its excellent foliage and if flowering occurs accept it as an added bonus; prune after flowering; excellent plant for southern gardens.

DISEASES AND INSECTS: Observations have led me to believe this species is quite trouble-free; leaf blight has been listed as a problem.

LANDSCAPE VALUE: Somewhat difficult to use in the residential landscape because of coarseness; the shrub border, massing or shady situations offer possibilities; excellent foliage makes it worthy of consideration; in common use at the Georgia Botanical Garden and those plants which have a moist root run and a modicum of shade do better than plants in exposed, dry, full sun situations; plants may show premature fall coloring as early as August if stressed; saw a wonderful combination planting with *Oxydendrum arboreum* surrounded by a planting of *H. quercifolia;* in late October both were in fall color and the effect was striking.

CULTIVARS:

'Harmony'—Mostly sterile, large paniculate inflorescences, 12″ long, white, will weigh down the branches, interesting and unusual but not as elegant as 'Snowflake' and 'Snow Queen'.

'PeeWee'—Compact form, probably 2 to 3′ by 2 to 3′ with leaves and flowers more refined, has received rave notices from Atlanta gardeners who have observed it.

'Roanoke'—Loose and more open inflorescence than 'Harmony', will weigh down the branches.

'Snowflake'—Multiple bracts or sepals emerge on tops of older ones creating a double-flowered appearance; 12 to 15″ long panicles, actually the most beautiful of the sterile flowered forms; as is true with 'Harmony' and 'Roanoke', the heads are heavy and the branches may be weighed down, but never to the degree of those two, prefers moist soil and partial shade.

'Snow Queen'—An improvement of the species with larger and more numerous sterile florets that provide a more dense solid appearance, the inflorescences are held upright and do not "flag" like many seedling plants, leaves are dark green and seem to hold up in the sun better than seedlings, leaves turn deep red-bronze in fall, flowers turn a good pink as they mature, nurserymen have been impressed with this plant, a Princeton Nursery introduction.

LOUISIANA NURSERY CULTIVARS: Louisiana Nursery, Opelousas, LA has introduced several cultivars; a brief description of each per their catalog is provided.

'Cloud Nine'—Showy, large handsome white flowers.

'Gloster Form'—Vigorous, with 5 petals (probably means sepals on each flower), does exceptionally well in the south.

'Joe McDaniel'—Vigorous with large showy white flowers, collected in the south by Professor McDaniel.

'John Wayne'—Selected from Florida, large white showy flowers, does well all over the south.

'Late Hand'—Choice late flowering clone with large "hand-like" lobed leaves and pretty white flowers; extends flowering season about one month.

'Luverne Pink'—An attractive bushy medium-sized clone with pretty white flowers aging to a deep pink.

'Picnic Hill'—A vigorous bushy form with short internodes and handsome flowers.

'Sikes Dwarf'—A dwarf clone, 2 to 2 1/2' high, up to 4' across, pretty white flowers and attractive leaves.

'Tennessee Clone'—Attractive leaves and bold white flowers.

To heighten the confusion I have selected two strong growing, 8 to 10' high clones with elegant dark green summer foliage and burgundy red fall color; the flowers occur in 12" long upright to semi-arching panicles, one is named 'Alice', the other 'Alison'; both are easy to propagate, in fact, cuttings were collected September 13, 1988, 5000 ppm KIBA dip, 2 perlite: 1 peat, mist, rooted 100% in 4 weeks; similar success with 'Snowflake'.

PROPAGATION: Seed can be sown at once and will germinate; should be relatively fresh; layers and division of the parent plant provide a means of vegetative propagation; over the years I have had real problems with rooting; currently successes are 90% plus; too much moisture is a problem; our standard procedure is firm wood cuttings in May, June, and into September, 5000 ppm KIBA dip, well drained medium, either all perlite or 2 perlite: 1 peat, intermittent mist, 4 to 6 weeks rooting time.

ADDITIONAL NOTES: Spring Grove, Cincinnati, OH has mass planted the species throughout the grounds and in June and July it makes a spectacular show. In my mind, should always be afforded some shade even in northern areas.

NATIVE HABITAT: Georgia, Florida and Mississippi. Introduced 1803.

Hydrangea sargentiana — Sargent Hydrangea
(hī-dran′jē-a sar-jen-tē-ā′na)

LEAVES: Opposite, simple, ovate, 4 to 5" long, 2 to 3" wide on flowering shoots, 6 to 10" by 4 to 7" on non-flowering shoots, short-acuminate, rounded or subcordate, crenate-serrate, dull dark green and hairy above, reticulate and densely hairy beneath; petiole—1 to 3" long, bristly.

STEM: Stout, ribbed, clothed with stiff bristles and small erect hairs.

Hygrangea sargentiana, Sargent's Hydrangea, is not well known in the United States, except in gardens in the Pacific Northwest. It is probably inferior to the species mentioned above for the midwest, east and south. However, after observing the mixture of pinkish white sterile florets and deep rose-lilac fertile flowers it is difficult to at least not mention the plant. If it never flowered, there would be interest from the large hairy leaves and bristly-hairy stems. Flowers occur during July and August in a 6 to 9" wide flat corymb with the 1 1/4" diameter sterile flowers on the outside. The entire inflorescence is bristly. Develops into a large 6 to 10' high mounded shrub; would require moisture and shade along the eastern corridor. Have seen in shade and moist soils in English gardens, most notably at Hidcote. In Europe, I see this species often listed as a subspecies of *H. aspera* which has somewhat similar characteristics. *Hydrangea sargentiana* is native to central China. Introduced 1907. Zone 7 to 9.

Hypericum prolificum — Shrubby St. Johnswort
(hī-per′i-kum prō-lif′i-kum)

FAMILY: Guttiferae, Hypericaceae

LEAVES: Opposite, simple, narrow-oblong to oblanceolate, 1 to 3" long, 1/4 to 1/2" wide, obtuse, dark lustrous green or bluish green above and pellucid-punctate; short petioled.

STEM: Two-angled, light brown, glabrous; older stems with exfoliating bark.

SIZE: 1 to 4' high by 1 to 4' spread (up to 5' high).

HARDINESS: Zone 3 to 8.

HABIT: A small, dense little shrub with stout, stiff, erect stems, rounded, variable in size.

RATE: Slow.

TEXTURE: Medium-fine in leaf; medium in winter.

BARK: On older stems light brown and exfoliating.

LEAF COLOR: Dark lustrous green in summer, perhaps could be considered bluish green; no fall color of consequence.

FLOWERS: Perfect, 3/4 to 1″ diameter, bright yellow, late June through July and August, borne in axillary and terminal few-flowered cymes, quite lovely in flower.

FRUIT: A dry, dehiscent, 3-valved capsule; persists all winter and could be used for dried arrangements, offers a good identification feature.

CULTURE: Best transplanted from a container; does extremely well in dry, rocky soils; full sun or partial shade; pH adaptable, does extremely well in calcareous soils; observations lead me to believe this is an excellent plant for dry, heavy soil areas; prune in early spring.

DISEASES AND INSECTS: In the last edition I mentioned that the genus was little troubled by insects and diseases. I have changed my mind. Over the years I have grown 'Hidcote', *H. androsaemum, H. olympicum* and a host of other species that were obtained in a seed exchange with The Royal Horticultural Society. Seeds germinated without any treatment and produced handsome plants. Once in the garden they developed a wilt or melting out that obliterated all. The only species that has handled the heat, humidity, and poorly drained soils, is *H. calycinum* and its performance has been less than satisfactory. I would estimate 2 to 3 years of landscape usefulness in the south, and this may be generous. As a final note, I had 'Hidcote' all over the garden and lost every one.

LANDSCAPE VALUE: Nice plant for summer colors because of excellent yellow (buttercup-colored) flowers; would work well in the shrub border; possibly in groupings or in mass; I do not believe the Hypericums have been adequately explored and developed as landscape plants in the United States.

PROPAGATION: Cuttings root readily, softwood collected in Juny—July treated with 1000 ppm IBA and placed in sand under mist gave good rooting; seeds of almost all species will germinate without any pretreatment.

NATIVE HABITAT: New Jersey and Iowa to Georgia. Introduced about 1750.

RELATED SPECIES:

Hypericum androsaemum—Tutsan

LEAVES: Opposite, simple, ovate, up to 3 1/2″ to 4″ long, 2 to 2 1/4″ wide, blunt, cordate, dark blue green, sessile, slightly aromatic when bruised, about the largest leaved of the hardy hypericums.

STEM: Brown, 2-angled.

Hypericum androsaemum, (hī-per′i-kum an-drō-sē′mum), Tutsan, is doubtfully in cultivation to any degree in the U.S. but in Europe is found in abundance. This makes a vigorous, spreading, bushy shrub 2 to 3′ high. The leaves are among the largest of the hardy hypericums. The light yellow, 3/4″ diameter flowers occur 3 to 9 together in cymose clusters at the terminus of the stem and lateral branches. The fruit is a totally different berry-like capsule that transgresses from red to purple to almost black at maturity and is filled with a wine-colored juice. I saw it in fruit during September in Amsterdam and could not properly identify the species. In fruit, at least, it presents a genuine curve ball for a plantsman who is use to the American species. Appears to tolerate shady situations and is somewhat of a weed in European gardens. Western Europe, northern Africa, northwest Yugoslavia. Cultivated before 1600. Zone 6 to 8.

Hypericum buckleyi—Blueridge St. Johnswort

LEAVES: Opposite, simple, obovate to elliptic, 1/4 to 1″ long, rounded at apex, cuneate, rich green.
STEM: Brown, slender, 4-angled.

Hypericum buckleyi, (hī-per′i-kum buk′lē-ī), Blueridge St. Johnswort, is a low growing (1′), spreading, decumbent, yellow-flowering shrub. North Carolina to Georgia. Introduced 1889. Zone 5 to 8.

Hypericum calycinum—Aaronsbeard St. Johnswort

LEAVES: Opposite, simple, ovate-oblong to ovate, 2 to 4″ long, obtuse, slightly odorous, dark green above, glaucous beneath, subcoriaceous, sessile.
STEM: Brown, obscurely 4-angled.

Hypericum calycinum, (hī-per′i-kum kal-ē-sī′num), Aaronsbeard St. Johnswort, is a stoloniferous semi-evergreen shrub with procumbent or ascending stems growing 12 to 18″ high and spreading 18 to 24″. The tops of the plant often winter-kill in severe cold but since it flowers on new wood little damage is done. The leaves are dark green above and glaucous beneath. The flowers are a screaming bright yellow, 3″ across, borne singly or rarely 2 to 3 together on new wood in June through September. Easily transplanted in spring; does well in poor sandy soil; full sun or partial shade; best mowed to the ground to induce new growth each spring. Makes a rather handsome groundcover plant as it grows fast and effectively covers an area in a short time. Over the past 8 years this has become common in the southeast but seldom flowers like I have seen it in the Pacific Northwest and Europe. Apparently flowers are not set prolifically on new growth of the season since regrowth after winter injury has produced minimal flowers, at least in the south. Roots easily from softwood cuttings (84% when taken in early summer and set in sand without hormone treatment in 42 days). Native to southeastern Europe, Asia Minor. Introduced 1676. Zone 5 to 8.

Hypericum densiflorum—Dense Hypericum

LEAVES: Opposite, simple, linear-oblong to linear, 1 to 2″ long, 1/4″ wide, revolute, rich blue-green.
STEM: Brown, 2-edged.

Hypericum densiflorum, (hī-per′i-kum den-si-flō′rum), Dense Hypericum, grows to 4 to 6′ in height with a 3 to 4′ spread. The habit is upright oval, taller than broad and densely twiggy and leafy. The foliage is deep green in summer; flowers are golden yellow, 1/2″ across, July through September, borne in many flowered corymbs. It is an ally of *H. prolificum* but has smaller flowers and leaves. New Jersey to Florida, Missouri and Texas. Introduced 1889. Zone 5 to 8.

Hypericum frondosum—Golden St. Johnswort
(hī-per′i-kum fron-dō′sum)

LEAVES: Opposite, simple, entire, ovate-oblong to oblong, 1 to 2 1/4″ long, mucronate, pellucid-dotted, rich bluish green.
STEM: With thin exfoliating reddish bark on older branches, branches 2-edged.

Hypericum frondosum, Golden St. Johnswort, grows to 3 to 4′ high with a similar spread. Often an upright shrub with rather stout branches; bark is reddish brown and exfoliating; foliage is a very handsome, distinct bluish green; flowers are bright yellow, 1 to 2″ diameter, with the stamens forming a dense brush 3/4″ across, June–July, solitary. Fruit is a 1/2″ high, broad-based, 3-celled reddish brown capsule. 'Sunburst' is lower growing than the species (3′ by 4′) and makes a lovely mass plant; this cultivar has proven superior in midwest tests. The British consider it the handsomest of the American species in cultivation in their country. South Carolina and Tennessee to Georgia and Texas. 1747. Zone 5 to 8.

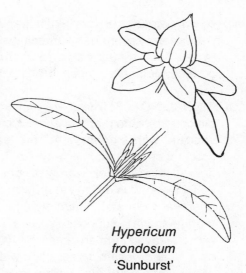

Hypericum
frondosum
'Sunburst'

Hypericum 'Hidcote'

For the past three editions and now this I have attempted to find the correct place for this lovely cultivar. Current thinking (?) has it a hybrid of *H.* × *cyanthiflorum* 'Gold Cup' and *H. calycinum,* where previously it was placed with *H. patulum.* No doubt, it grows taller than I gave it credit, although in the United States I never saw it above 3′ high; invariably the shoots would be killed in winter but the vigorous regrowth and splendid, profusely borne 2 1/2 to 3″ wide waxy golden yellow flowers overcame the dieback deficiency. Peak flowering in my garden was late May to late June with sporadic flowers into fall. The old flowers became brown and looked messy. Unfortunately, I watched the complete decline of all Hidcotes in my garden and have largely given up on this and other species. Mention is made in European literature of a virus or virus-like disease which causes the flowers to become malformed. Where it can be grown, the shrub is first rate. The dark green lanceolate, 2″ long leaves are a fine backdrop to the flowers. Grows 3 (5′) high and wide. Zone (5)6 to 9.

Hypericum kalmianum—Kalm St. Johnswort

LEAVES: Opposite, simple, linear-oblong to oblanceolate, 1 to 2″ long, 1/8 to 1/3″ wide, bluish green above, glaucous beneath, and dotted with transparent glands.
STEM: Brown, 4-angled.

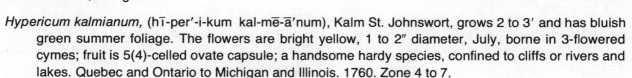

Hypericum kalmianum, (hī-per′-i-kum kal-mē-ā′num), Kalm St. Johnswort, grows 2 to 3′ and has bluish green summer foliage. The flowers are bright yellow, 1 to 2″ diameter, July, borne in 3-flowered cymes; fruit is 5(4)-celled ovate capsule; a handsome hardy species, confined to cliffs or rivers and lakes. Quebec and Ontario to Michigan and Illinois. 1760. Zone 4 to 7.

Hypericum × *moseranum,* (hī-per′i-kum × mō-sēr-ā′num), Moser's St. Johnswort, is a hybrid between *H. patulum* and *H. calycinum* that was raised in Moser's nursery at Versailles in 1887. It is a compact plant of tufted habit and sends up reddish tinted, arching, 1 to 1 1/2′ long shoots each season. The blue-green leaves are intermediate, about 2″ long. Flowers occur from July to October, 1 to 5 at the end of the shoot with only one flower opening at a time. Each flower is 2 to 2 1/2″ across with broad overlapping golden-yellow petals and stamens whose anthers are pinkish purple. It should be treated like a herbaceous perennial and cut back to the ground in winter. It is considered more hardy than *H. patulum,* which died back in my Athens, GA garden. The cultivar 'Tricolor' will always stick in my mind for as I walked through Wisley Gardens I came upon this handsome white and rose variegated plant that looked like a hypericum. I found the label which confirmed my suspicions. This is not as hardy as the species and is not as vigorous. Zone 7(?).

Hypericum patulum—Goldencup St. Johnswort

LEAVES: Opposite, simple, semi-evergreen to evergreen, 1 to 2 1/2″ long, ovate, ovate-oblong to lanceolate-oblong, obtuse and usually mucronulate, dark green above, glaucous beneath.

Hypericum patulum, (hī-per'i-kum pat'ū-lum), Goldencup St. Johnswort, grows to 3' and is a semi-evergreen to evergreen spreading shrub. Flowers are golden yellow, 2" diameter, July, solitary or in cymes. Variety *henryi* is more vigorous than the species, flowers are larger (2 1/2" across); probably correctly *H. beanii.* Japan. 1862. Zone 6 to 7.

ADDITIONAL NOTES: There are numerous *Hypericum* species and to me they are all attractive. It is difficult to locate many in commerce. *Hypericum galioides,* Bedstraw St. Johnswort, an evergreen species, with extremely narrow leaves; and *Hypericum olympicum,* Olympic St. Johnswort, a procumbent, handsome gray-green leaved species, with large 1 1/2 to 2" diameter bright yellow flowers, are definitely worthy of consideration. I turn around and find a species or cultivar that should be included. It is difficult to draw the *Hypericum* line. *H. × inodorum* 'Elstead', a hybrid between *H. androsaemum* and *H. hircinum,* looks more like the former but is more compact and the fruits are orange-scarlet. Supposedly quite susceptible to a disease which weakens the plant. There is a golden-leaved form and suspect that 'Ysella' is this plant. 'Gold Pansy' is also listed and appears to be a *H. androsaemum* selection with golden yellow flowers and red to black fruits, often all present at the same time. Also visible is *H. kouytchense,* a 2 to 4' high semi-evergreen shrub with 2 1/2" diameter golden yellow flowers. An old cultivar that I have seen at the Arnold Arboretum and other places is 'Sungold' which appears mired in synonymy with this species. In many respects, it reminded of 'Hidcote', except not as large or deep yellow flowered.

Iberis sempervirens — Candytuft
(ī-bē'ris sem-pĕr-vī'renz)

FAMILY: Brassicaceae
LEAVES: Alternate, simple, evergreen, linear-oblong, 1/2 to 2" long, 1/8 to 3/16" wide, obtuse, entire, dark green.

SIZE: 6 to 12" high, spreading with time and forming handsome evergreen mats.
HARDINESS: Zone 4 to 8 (9).
HABIT: Dwarf evergreen ground cover of sprawling habit.
RATE: Slow to medium; under good cultural conditions will fill an area reasonably fast.
TEXTURE: Fine in summer; possibly medium in winter as it looks a bit rough.
LEAF COLOR: Dark green and handsome.
FLOWERS: Perfect, white, borne in terminal 1 to 1 1/2" diameter racemes which engulf the plant and give the appearance of a drift of snow; April-May and lasting for several weeks; spent flowers should be removed; flowers in late March in Athens, GA.
FRUIT: A silique, orbicular-elliptic, 1/4" long, not showy.
CULTURE: Easy to transplant; I have moved seedlings and container plants with great success; prefer loose, loamy, average fertility soil; if fertility levels are excessive the plants become loose, leggy and open; full sun or partial shade; pH adaptable, prune heavily after flowering.
DISEASES AND INSECTS: Club root, damping off, downy and powdery mildews, and white rust.
LANDSCAPE VALUE: Excellent plant for early color; contrasts well with tulips and other bulbs; I have used it as drifts interplanted with woody shrubs; even after flowering it can look quite good if it is maintained as described under culture.
CULTIVARS:
'Christmas Snow' ('Snowflake')—Flowers twice, early in season and again in fall, may grow 1' high and 2' wide, leaves dark green; flowers in 2" diameter trusses.
'Little Gem'—More dwarf than the type, only 6" tall and quite hardy; leaves are smaller and finer in texture.

'Purity'—Similar to 'Little Gem' in habit with large inflorescences.
PROPAGATION: Seed represents an easy method, sow as soon as mature; softwood cuttings root easily
    and I have used this method to reproduce seed grown plants which were especially floriferous.
NATIVE HABITAT: Southern Europe, western Asia. Introduced 1731.

Idesia polycarpa
(i-dē′zē-a pol-i-kar′pa)

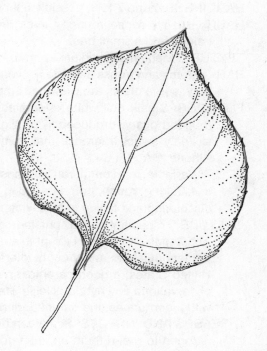

FAMILY: Flacourtiaceae
LEAVES: Alternate, simple, ovate to oblong-ovate, 5 to 10″
    long, 2/3's as wide, acuminate, cordate or subcordate,
    remotely crenate-serrate, deep green above, glaucous
    below, glabrous except in leaf axils; petiole—2 1/2 to 6″
    long, with 1 to 3 obvious concave glands toward the
    middle.

SIZE: 40 to 60′ and as wide.
HARDINESS: Zone 6 to 9.
HABIT: In youth pyramidal, with age becoming rounded.
RATE: Fast.
TEXTURE: Coarse
BARK: Relatively smooth, grayish.
LEAF COLOR: Dark green, no appreciable fall color.
FLOWERS: Dioecious, yellow-green, apetalous, fragrant, in
    terminal panicles in June; male 5 to 6″ long, each flower
    1/3″ wide, sepals covered with brownish pubescence;
    female individual smaller but in a large panicle.
FRUIT: Multiple seeded, pea sized red berry, borne in 4 to 8″ long pendulous panicles and swaying with
    the fall breezes; beautiful in fruit, unfortunately it takes a male and female to guarantee fruit set and
    very few gardeners can afford the space necessary for the trees.
CULTURE: Transplant as a young container grown specimen or balled and burlapped material, prefers
    loose, moist, well drained soil and with proper fertility grows like a weed, full sun and frost protection
    as a young tree.
DISEASES AND INSECTS: None serious.
LANDSCAPE VALUE: Only for large areas where multiple trees can be grouped for success, beautiful in
    fruit and the tree provides a Catalpa-like texture, i.e., coarse; interesting about hardiness for in Boston
    (Arnold Arboretum) it is a stump sprout, in Brooklyn Botanic Garden a 60′ tree and in Washington,
    DC (National Arboretum) a rather handsome grove of fruiting 25 to 30′ high trees; have not seen in
    Zone 8.
PROPAGATION: On many occasions, I have raised seedlings by simply cleaning fruits and sowing
    cleaned seed; within 2 weeks germination was rampant; have also sown entire fruits and been
    successful.
NATIVE HABITAT: Southern Japan, central and western China. Introduced 1864.

Ilex cornuta — Chinese Holly
(ī′leks kôr-nū′ta)

FAMILY: Aquifoliaceae
LEAVES: Alternate, simple, evergreen, short-stalked, oblong-rectangular, 1 1/2 to 4″ long, 1 to 3″ wide
    with 3 strong almost equal spines at the broad apex and 1 or 2 spines on each side at the base, spines
    can vary from 5 to 9, or on older plants rounded at the base, lustrous dark green above, yellow-green

below, leaves of old specimens show fewer spines, almost plastic in texture, extremely lethal to work around; petiole—1/6″ long.

SIZE: 8 to 10′ (15′) and perhaps to 25′, often wider than high at maturity.

HARDINESS: Zone 7 to 9, possibly 6 if protected.

HABIT: Bushy, dense rounded evergreen shrub, can be trained into a small tree.

TEXTURE: Medium to medium-coarse.

BARK: Stems and trunks become a lovely relatively smooth gray; some plants are grown as small trees and are limbed up to show off the bark.

FLOWERS: Small, dull white, 4-petaled, 1/4 to 1/3″ wide, male with 4 stamens, female—large green rounded ovary, produced in prodigious quantities in the axils of the leaves; male flowers have a sickenly sweet fragrance that is much more potent than the female's, late March—early April in Athens, GA.

FRUIT: Variable, from bright red to almost blood-red at least on some campus plants I have observed, 1/4 to 1/3″ long, round, borne on 1/3 to 5/8″ long stalk, abundant, persisting through winter, handsome, discoloring and falling in cold winters about February.

CULTURE: Transplant from a container; almost all *Ilex cornuta* types are container-grown; very adaptable, withstands drought; pH adaptable, extremely heat tolerant; an amazingly durable holly that displays tremendous heat and drought tolerance, has survived the worst droughts on record in southeastern United States; a good parental species for introducing heat tolerance into the progeny; based on observations any hybrid ('Nellie Stevens', 'China Boy', 'China Girl', 'John T. Morris', 'Lydia Morris') with *I. cornuta* as one parent performs reasonably well in the heat.

DISEASES AND INSECTS: Scale can be a problem, many heavily fruited hollies need an application of nitrogen to green them up, numerous diseases, many related to nursery production of hollies and Lambe *PIPPS* 29:536–544 (1979) presents an excellent overview; beyond the scope of this book to summarize but leaf spots, cankers, die-back, root rots and nematodes; these problems vary in severity with species and cultivars; my own ranking of resistant species and cultivars in the south (Zone 7 to 9) would start with *I. vomitoria, I. cornuta, I. × attenuata, I. opaca, I. × koehneana, I. latifolia, I. cassine, I. × meserveae* and *I. crenata;* lots of room to maneuver and add species but for the evergreen species this is a good attempt.

LANDSCAPE VALUE: The species is seldom used in contemporary landscaping but the cultivars are abused to the point of boredom; the uses are numerous depending on the cultivar.

CULTIVARS:

'Anicet Delcambre'—Long, narrow, slightly twisted lustrous dark green leaves and a single terminal spine, female, have seen abundant fruit on this clone.

'Avery Island'—Large yellow fruits and lustrous dark green foliage.

'Berries Jubilee'—Medium-sized, 6 to 10′ high form with large leaves and large fruit clusters inside the foliage canopy.

'Burfordii'—Considered a dense rounded shrub about 10′ in height but when left unchecked it makes a large, rather dense tree or shrub 20 to 25′ high; the lustrous dark green leaves usually have a single terminal spine but on occasion two lateral spines may develop; the fruit set is heavy and will occur without pollination (parthenocarpically); plants at Callaway Gardens are fully 20′ high and, in fruit, are beautiful; it is not a bad idea to prune away the lower branches thus making a small tree; have seen it killed to the ground at Bernheim Arboretum when temperatures reached −18°F; easily

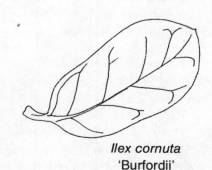

Ilex cornuta
'Burfordii'

rooted; one of the most popular *I cornuta* forms; discovered about 1900 in Westview Cemetery, Atlanta.

'Cajun Gold'—A large shrub on the order of 'Burford' with golden margined leaves, red fruits.

'Carissa'—LEAVES: Alternate, simple, evergreen, ovate, 2 to 3″ long, 1 to 1 1/2″ wide, cuneate or slightly rounded, entire, leathery to the point of plasticity, transparent rim around margin, glabrous, lustrous, waxy dark green above, flat olive green beneath; petiole — 1/4″ long; some leaves develop a bullate condition. Dense, dwarf form 3 to 4′ high and 4 to 6′ wide at maturity, leaves have a single terminal spine and may show a bullate or puckered condition; it is a branch sport of 'Rotunda' and will revert to the 'Rotunda' form on occasion; older plants are more prone to this than young ones. I have not seen it fruit, definitely less cold hardy than 'Dwarf Burford'.

'Dazzler'—Upright, somewhat irregular selection that grows to 10′ and more; heavy fruiting, 5-spined leaf; Dr. John Pair, Wichita Field Station, noted it was the most fruitful of *I. cornuta* types in his tests.

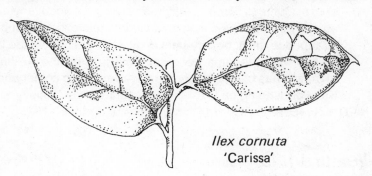

Ilex cornuta
'Carissa'

'D' Or'—A yellow-fruited form that is quite similar to 'Burfordii', leaves lustrous dark green and with only a terminal spine; as I understand the origin it was found as a branch sport on the normal Burfordii in Columbus, GA; quite a handsome plant; Callaway Gardens has some nice specimens.

'Dwarf Burford' ('Burfordii Nana')—Compact form [5 to 6′ (8′)] with smaller and usually single-spined leaves, does not fruit as heavily as Burford, fruits smaller and darker red, leaves show a blistered or bullate condition; 10′ plants on Georgia campus, much faster growing than given credit.

'E.A. McIlhenny'—Shield shaped leaves and scarlet fruits.

'Grandview'—Dense compact bushy form with smaller leaves than the species, a male.

'James Foret'—Mostly 5-spined, red fruits.

'Jungle Gardens'—Excellent nearly flat dark green leaves with variable spines from 1 to 7, scarlet fruits.

'Lottie Moon'—Compact form intermediate between 'Burfordii' and 'Rotunda'.

'Needlepoint'—Similar to 'Anicet Delcambre' but with larger leaves, plants I have seen look suspiciously alike; this is a good fruiter with a more delicate leaf than 'Burford' types.

'O'Spring'—Irregular, upright form with cream colored leaves, new foliage with a purple tinge, does best in partial shade.

'Rotunda'—A compact, dense, mounded form with 5(7)-spined leaves that make an impenetrable thicket; it grows 3 to 4′ high and 6 to 8′ across; widely used in south; a female clone and I have observed occasional fruit set; very tough, durable plant.

'Rotunda'

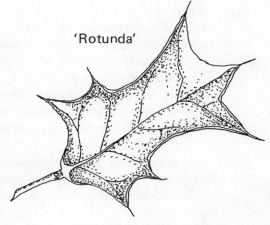

'Shangri-La'—Fast growing female clone with vermillion red fruit that matures in June and remains until the following March.

'Tall Stallion'—Male tree type for pollination.

'Willowleaf'—Large shrub (15′) with long, narrow, slightly twisted leaves; blood red fruits.

PROPAGATION: In general there are a lot of different stories about holly seed germination. Take the following for its net worth and then heed what Mr. Gene Eisenbeiss has to say about germinating seeds. In general, *Ilex* seeds exhibit a deep dormancy that is caused partly by the endocarp surrounding the seed coat and partly to conditions in the embryo. According to J. Bon Hartline, an Illinois holly grower, the best way to handle holly seed is as follows. The fruits should

be collected in fall, the pulp crushed and washed away. Seeds which float should be discarded, since they are usually not viable. Seeds of *I. crenata, I. vomitoria, I. glabra,* and of some *I. opaca* of southern origin will germinate in a very short time after being properly handled. *Ilex aquifolium, I. cornuta, I. verticillata, I. serrata, I. decidua,* and most *I. opaca* seeds require a longer period—up to 18 months before all seeds germinate. Patience is probably the necessary ingredient in holly seed propagation for it is the length of time rather than the cold treatment which aids germination. I visited Gene Eisenbeiss at the National Arboretum and asked him about the secrets of success. He showed me his operation and basically it consists of patience. The nutlets (pyrenes) are removed from the mealy part of the fruit and sown in a suitable medium, placed in a plastic bag; as I remember in a room where temperature is about 70 to 75°F. When the seeds start to germinate they are moved to the greenhouse. Cuttings of most evergreen types root about anytime of year. There are, no doubt, differences among species and cultivars but I have had excellent success with 1000 to 3000 ppm IBA-quick dip, peat:perlite, mist; bottom heat is often helpful. Since the last edition, thousands of hollies have been rooted in our research work. For most species and cultivars, we take the cuttings when the first flush of growth has hardened and treat with a rooting compound like IBA. We have used 1000 to 5000 ppm KIBA depending on taxon. Rooting of the deciduous types is discussed under *Ilex verticillata.*
NATIVE HABITAT: Eastern China, Korea. Introduced 1846.

Ilex crenata — Japanese Holly
(ī'leks kre-nā'ta)

LEAVES: Alternate, simple, evergreen, crowded, short-stalked, elliptic or
   obovate to oblong-lanceolate, 1/2 to 1 1/4" long, 1/4 to 5/8" wide,
   acute, cuneate or broad-cuneate, crenate-serrulate or serrulate,
   lustrous dark green above, glabrous, of hard texture, dotted beneath
   with blackish pellucid glands.
STEM: Normally green on current season's growth turning gray-green to
   gray-brown in 2nd or 3rd year.
GROWTH HABIT: Except for the species, usually a much branched shrub of dense, rigid, compact habit.

SIZE: Very difficult to ascertain from the literature the actual size of the species, listed as reaching 20' by
   various authorities; in actuality a shrub 5 to 10' high with a similar or greater spread.
HARDINESS: Zone 5 to 6 depending on cultivar to 8, does not do as well in the south as in Zone 5 to 7.
HABIT: Usually a dense, multi-branched evergreen shrub of rounded or broad rounded outline; apparently
   quite variable in the wild.
RATE: Slow.
TEXTURE: Medium-fine in all seasons.
LEAF COLOR: Lustrous dark green in summer and winter.
FLOWERS: Dioecious, unisexual, dull greenish white, staminate in 3 to 7 flowered cymes; pistillate solitary
   in leaf-axils of current season's growth, May-June, not at all showy but if one is interested in
   determining the sex of any particular holly, inspection of the flowers is the only logical way.
FRUIT: Berry-like black drupe, globose, 1/4" diameter, September-October, and persistent into spring in
   Zone 8, borne under the foliage and, therefore, somewhat inconspicuous, only female plants have
   fruits.
CULTURE: Transplants readily balled and burlapped or from a container; most plants are container grown;
   prefers light, moist, well-drained, slightly acid soils; sun or shade adaptable; seems to do well in city
   gardens; prune after new growth hardens off; will withstand severe pruning; have seen chlorosis in
   high pH soils.
DISEASES AND INSECTS: Spider mites can be serious, nematodes in south and black knot (*Thielaviopsis
   basicola*) disease; *I. crenata* is quite susceptible to *Thielaviopsis.*
LANDSCAPE VALUE: Excellent for textural differences in foundation plantings, hedges, and masses;
   hedges in Japan have been maintained for so long that they can be walked on; very handsome and

worthwhile landscape plant; often overused and abused; used in masses, along walks and on gradual slopes on virtually every college campus; often massacred with a pruning shears to produce "handsome" pieces of geometric sculpture; actually nicer if left to their own genetic control, perhaps remove and odd branch here or there for shaping but otherwise stand back and enjoy.

CULTIVARS: The Japanese Holly is prone to cultivarism and over the centuries numerous forms have been selected. Mr. Gene Eisenbeiss, National Arboretum, estimates that there are as many as 380 names in the literature with about 100 of these synonyms. There are at least 60 cultivars being offered by the trade. Their identification is fraught with difficulty and a reasonable list is presented here.

'Allen Seay'—Upright form with lustrous dark green leaves similar in shape to 'Microphylla', holds good color during the winter; withstood −23°F with minimal damage.

'Angelica'—Low spreading form with long narrow leaves, quite hardy.

'Beehive'—Dense, compact mounded form, slightly wider than high, excellent lustrous dark green foliage, 1/2″ long, 1/4″ wide, good hardiness, selected by Dr. Elwin Orton, Rutgers from 21,000 seedlings, originated as a cross of 'Convexa' × 'Stokes'.

'Bennett'—Semi-upright with dark green foliage.

'Black Beauty'—Selected by Girard Nursery, Geneva, Ohio for lustrous dark green foliage, compact habit, and extreme hardiness, Zone 5.

'Border Gem'—Dense, low growing type with lustrous dark green foliage and good hardiness, Zone 5; has survived winters of −8°F and looked fantastic; 'Hetzii', on the other hand, was winter killed at this temperature.

'Buxifolia'—A compact pyramidal form that grows to 15′ in height; the leaves are oblong-lanceolate; a 10 year-old plant may be 6 to 8′.

'Compacta'—Compact, globose outline to 6′; leaves lustrous dark green, obovate, flat, 3/4″ long; young stems are purple; little pruning is required to produce a compact, heavy plant; over the years I have seen a number of 'Compacta' forms and they are not all the same; probably a catch-all term.

'Convexa'—One of the hardiest forms, 40-year-old plant somewhat vase-shaped in habit but extremely dense is 9′ tall and 24′ wide, takes pruning for hedging; leaves 1/2″ long, convex above, concave beneath, somewhat bullate; of Japanese origin, Zone 5; a female clone that is often heavy with black fruits; severely injured at −20°F; susceptible to iron and nitrogen deficiency and spider mites.

'Dwarf Pagoda'—Selected by Dr. Orton from his holly breeding program at Rutgers University in 1972; female with tiny leaves 5/16 to 7/16″ long by 1/4″ wide, short internodes, branching irregular; result is an extremely heavy foliage effect and artistic form; grows 2″/year, hardy to 0°, from seedling population of 'Mariesii' × 'John Nasal'.

'Fastigiata'—A narrow fastigiate form with thick slightly convex dark green leaves, good choice as an accent plant, E.L. Bennett introduction, Greenbrier Farms, VA.

'Foster No. 1'—A cold hardy form that survived −23°F with minimal injury.

'Glass'—(Zone 5) Male clone of *Ilex crenata* 'Microphylla' with compact upright habit and slightly smaller leaves (1/2″ long); frozen to ground after exposure to −20°F.

'Glory'—Small compact globe form with 1/4 to 4/5″ long, 1/8 to 3/8″ wide flat lustrous dark green leaves, after 12 growing seasons at Bernheim Arboretum, Clermont, KY, the plant was over 5′ high and about 8′ wide; the most impressive trait is cold hardiness, Flint and Hubbuch, *Amer. Nurseryman* 169(3):154 (1989) reported 'Glory' survived −23°F with minimal injury.

'Golden Gem'—Leaves golden, habit low and spreading, the color is best developed in sunny location.

'Green Dragon'—Male clone, otherwise similar to 'Dwarf Pagoda'.

'Green Island'—(Zone 5) Loose and open shrub form, usually growing twice as broad as tall; 11-year-old plant is 3′ by 6′, matures less than 5′, lustrous medium green foliage.

'Green Luster' ('Green Lustre')—Similar to above with leaves darker and more lustrous; injured by −20°F; good looking foliage; grows about twice as wide as tall, somewhat flat-topped.

'Green Splendor'—Broad pyramidal form with lustrous leaves that are slightly larger than 'Microphylla'; survived winters of 1977–78 and 83–84 with limited leaf damage.

'Helleri'—Dwarf, mounded, compact form; 26-year-old plant is 4' by 5' with leaves about 1/2" long, Zone 5; leaves less lustrous than most; good form, does well in Zone 8.

'Hetzii' (Zone 5)—Larger form of 'Convexa' with bigger (1/2 to 1" long) convex leaves of lustrous dark green, grows 6 to 8' and several plants on the Georgia campus are easily 8', appears quite adaptable to Zone 8 conditions, not as cold hardy as 'Convexa', a female and the fruits are larger than those of 'Convexa'.

'Highlander'—Tall, pyramidal, rather loose form that grows to 6' and greater; interestingly this cultivar has shown good cold tolerance; has performed well at Bernheim Arboretum and at Wichita, Kansas.

'Highlight'—Branch sport from 'Microphylla' with 1" by 3/8" wide leaves, 15-year-old plant 13' by 11', discovered by W.F. Kosar around 1956, extremely lustrous dark green leaves, more difficult to propagate than the other forms.

'Howard'—Spreading form maturing at about 6' high, the obovate-oblong leaves are slightly convex.

'Ivory Tower'—Spreading form with yellowish white fruits.

'Jersey Pinnacle'—Dense self-compacting, upright in habit, glossy dark green leaves, might serve as a standard upright type like 'Helleri' does for spreading, Orton introduction.

'Kingsville Green Cushion'—Dense, low growing form, 10-year-old plant is 8" by 32".

'Major'—Similar to 'Rotundifolia', flat dark green leaves, grows thicker without extensive pruning.

'Mariesii'—Stiffly erect female clone with one or several upright stems and small, 5/8" long, 1/4" wide, rounded leaves.

'Maxwellii'—Mounded habit and small leaves reminiscent of 'Microphylla', supposedly more gray-green than dark green.

'Microphylla'—(Zone 5) Leaves smaller than the species; upright shrub or small tree in habit.

'Midas Touch'—Variegated form with yellow green foliage, a branch sport of a seedling from a cross of a yellow-fruited clone × *I. crenata* (male); most leaves exhibit yellow sectors and light green areas in addition to normal pigmentation, occasional green shoots develop that must be pruned out; Orton introduction.

'Noble Upright'—Somewhat pyramidal form with excellent cold hardiness, survived –23°F with minimal injury.

'Northern Beauty'—Similar to 'Hetzii' but more compact and hardy, good lustrous foliage.

'Petite Point'—Upright growth habit, somewhat pyramidal, good in south, difficult to propagate.

'Pin Cushion'—A compact globe with small leaves.

'Recurvifolia'—Spreading growth habit, elongated flat leaf and light green foliage.

'Repandens'—Spreading form of compact habit with narrow lustrous dark green leaves; quite handsome, usually 2 to 3' high and 4 to 6' wide.

'Rotundifolia'—A somewhat confusing cultivar, but the ones I have seen have large, 1/2 to 1" long leaves, and tend to grow upright-rounded to about 8 to 12', called Bigleaf Japanese Holly; completely defoliated after exposure to –18°F; a male form.

'Sentinel'—Tall upright form with glossy, convex foliage; male, have seen it listed as heavy fruiting, good cold hardiness.

'Steeds'—Lustrous dark green flat leaves, upright pyramidal habit, might be a good choice for hedging.

'Stokes'—Similar to 'Helleri' but not as hardy or compact in habit; low, dense rounded habit, glossier leaves; no injury after exposure to –18°F, male.

'Tiny Tim'—A low, spreading form to 3', similar to 'Helleri' but supposedly more hardy.

'Variegata'—Leaves spotted or blotched with yellow.

'Wayne'—Low-growing, spreading form similar to 'Helleri'; 3' by 6' and more.

'William Jackson'—Horizontal branched form similar to 'Repandens'.

'Yellow Fruited Clone'—Raulston described it as a pale lime-green, not yellow, fruited type; small leaves, will form a rounded outline, 5 to 8' diameter.

NATIVE HABITAT: Japan, Korea. Introduced 1864.

Ilex glabra — Inkberry
(Ī′leks glā′bra)

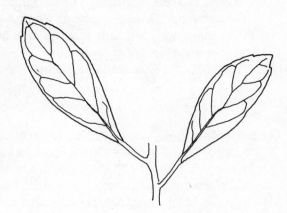

LEAVES: Alternate, simple, evergreen, obovate to oblanceolate, 3/4 to 2″ long, 1/3 to 5/8″ wide, acute or
obtusish, cuneate, with few obtuse teeth near apex
or entire, dark green and lustrous above, glabrous,
leaves are very thin compared to *I. crenata* forms
with which it is often confused; petiole 1/8 to 1/4″
long.

STEM: Slender, green, pubescent at first, finally
glabrous; normally hold green color longer than *I.
crenata* types.

SIZE: 6 to 8′ in height by 8 to 10′ in spread; however, variable depending on growing conditions.

HARDINESS: Zone 4 to 9; more hardy than *I. crenata* but leaves will burn in severe winters (−15 to −20°F).

HABIT: Upright, much branched, erect-rounded evergreen shrub, somewhat open with age and often
losing the lower leaves; tends to sucker and form colonies.

RATE: Slow, fast from sucker shoots.

TEXTURE: Medium in all seasons.

LEAF COLOR: Dark green and often lustrous in summer, sometimes becoming light yellow-green in
summer, have observed severe foliage burn after −20°F temperatures.

FLOWERS: Similar to *I. crenata;* male borne 3 or more together on a slender stalk, female solitary, each
with 6(8) creamy petals, flowers open late, usually late May in Athens.

FRUIT: Berry-like, black drupe, 1/4″ diameter, September through until May of the following year, often
hidden by the foliage but usually more showy than *I. crenata* fruits.

CULTURE: Somewhat similar to *I. crenata* except prefers moist, acid soils and in the wild is common in
swamps where it forms large clumps; withstands heavy pruning quite well and renewal of old plants
is suggested; avoid extremely high pH soils, quite shade tolerant, best in full sun with ample root
moisture.

DISEASES AND INSECTS: Seems to be quite free of problems, have observed leaf spot.

LANDSCAPE VALUE: Excellent (especially the cultivars) for foundation, hedges, masses, accent plant.

CULTIVARS:

'Compacta'—A dwarf, female clone with tighter branching and foliage than the species; introduced
by Princeton Nursery; found in a group of seedlings; grows 4 to 6′ high, will become leggy at
base.

'Georgia Wine'—Mr. Bill Craven, Twisted Oaks Nursery, Waynesboro, GA has discovered a form that
turns lovely burgundy during the winter, will release it in the next few years.

'Ivory Queen' and 'Leucocarpa'—Rather unusual white fruited forms growing 6 to 8′ high; easily
rooted from cuttings; fruit color is off-white. 'Leucocarpa' was discovered in January 1955 in
Jackson County, FL by Frank W. Woods; displays good cold tolerance; a plant at Griffin, GA is
now 8′ by 12′ with lustrous green foliage.

'Nigra'—Purplish foliage in winter.

'Nordic'—Compact rounded form with lustrous deep green leaves, grows 3 to 4′ by 3 to 4′, has proven
quite cold hardy, described as a male and I have not checked the plants in my garden to
determine sex, as yet no fruit production; unfortunately, like 'Compacta' will drop lower leaves
and probably needs to be pruned back to make it dense.

'Shamrock'—Handsome compact form with lustrous dark green leaves, is slower growing than
'Compacta' and 'Nordic', plants in the Georgia Botanical Garden have performed well, leaves
smaller, flat.

'Steed' ('Stead')—Another compact form that I have not seen.

'Squat'—Like 'Steed', a compact form but I do not know the origin.

PROPAGATION: Same as for *I. crenata;* 1000 ppm IBA quick dip, 100% rooting in 4 to 6 weeks.

ADDITIONAL NOTES: Spreads by underground stems (stolons or rhizomes) and is the only holly to sucker in this manner. Grew the cultivar 'Compacta' in my Illinois garden. In spite of what the literature says it becomes leggy with time. Leaves were burned at –20°F but no stem tissue was injured. It is a good holly for moist to wet areas.

NATIVE HABITAT: Nova Scotia to Florida, west to Mississippi. Introduced 1759.

RELATED SPECIES:

Ilex coriacea, (ī'leks cor-ē-ā'sē-á), Large or Sweet Gallberry, is a large version of *I. glabra* that is not as handsome. Leaves average 1 1/2 to 2 1/2″ long, and 1/2 to 1 1/2″ wide. Serrations are generally more numerous than *I. glabra.* The lustrous black fruits are globose and average about 1/3″ wide. Grows 10 to 15′ high and is found in pocosins and wet areas throughout Coastal Plain. Zone 7 to 9.

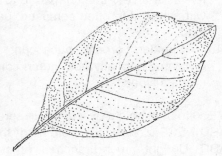

Ilex opaca — American Holly
(ī'leks ō-pā'ka)

LEAVES: Alternate, simple, evergreen, elliptic to elliptic-lanceolate, 1 1/2 to 3 1/2″ long, half as wide, with large remote spiny teeth, teeth may be minimal on older plants, especially toward the tips of the plant, rarely nearly entire, dull to dark green above, yellowish green beneath; petiole 1/4 to 1/2″ long, grooved, minutely downy.

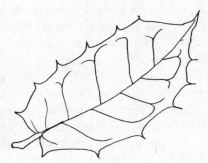

SIZE: 40 to 50′ in height with a spread of 18 to 40′; usually smaller, 15 to 30′ in height is more reasonable under normal landscape conditions, takes a long time to get where it is going.

HARDINESS: Zone 5 to 9.

HABIT: Densely pyramidal in youth with branches to the ground, becoming in age open, irregular, and picturesque, high branching, the branches at a wide angle and contorted.

RATE: Slow.

TEXTURE: Medium in all seasons.

LEAF COLOR: Dull to dark yellow green; great variation among trees but, in general, not a particularly handsome leaf; use superior lustrous dark green leaved cultivars.

FLOWERS: Similar to *I. crenata;* staminate in 3 to 9-flowered cymes; pistillate solitary, dull white; about the latest evergreen holly to flower, May in Athens.

FRUIT: Berry-like, dull red rounded drupe, 2/5″ diameter, borne singly on 1/4″ long stalk, maturing in October and persisting into winter; fruit display can be spectacular on good selections.

CULTURE: Transplant balled and burlapped or from a container in spring into good, moist, loose, acid, well-drained soil; partial shade or full sun; avoid extremely dry, windy, unprotected places; does not tolerate poor drainage under cultivation; use 1 male for every 2 to 3 females; prune in winter; air pollution tolerant; have seen chlorosis in high pH soils. American Holly is more cold hardy than given credit but is not wind tolerant; if protected from winter sun and desiccating winds, cold hardy selections should withstand –20 to –25°F; in Illinois I have seen winters where virtually all the leaves were removed from plants *yet* the stem and bud tissue survived and a new flush of growth covered the scars of winter; Ford, Secrest Arboretum Notes, Spring 1983, reported that 48 cultivars of *I. opaca* were outplanted at Wooster, OH; there were striking differences among cultivars with 'Kildare' averaging 15″ per year, 9 averaged 11″ per year, average growth is 6″ per year; 'Christmas Carol' which averaged 15″ per year over a 6 year period in the protected test garden was moved to an exposed site and averaged 2″ per year in 8 growing seasons; the moral is that microclimate can make a big difference in plant performance.

DISEASES AND INSECTS: This species is affected by many problems including holly leaf miner, bud moth, scales, beetles, whitefly, berry midge, southern red mite, tar spot, leaf spots, cankers, bacterial blight, twig die back, spot anthracnose, leaf rot, leaf drop, powdery mildews, spine spot (nonparasitic) and leaf scorch (physiological); leaf miner and scale are particularly troublesome.

LANDSCAPE VALUE: Specimen plant, grouping; requires male and female for fruit set; I feel there are too many superior hollies to justify extensive use of this species but the list of cultivars is endless; on the east coast and south this is a favored plant; again, do not use seedlings; use one of many superior cultivars.

CULTIVARS: There are more than 1000 cultivar names and if one is extremely interested *The International Checklist of Cultivated Ilex,* put out by the U.S. National Arboretum, is a must; desirable characteristics in holly cultivars should include annual bearing, large and bright colored fruits, good foliage, and dense habit; American Holly appears to be regionally adapted and it is best to check with a local nurseryman for the best varieties in a given area.

'Amy'—Large, spiny lustrous leaves and abundant large red fruit.

'Angelica'—Fast growing large form with large leaves and fruit.

'Cardinal'—Compact, slow-growing form with small dark green leaves and abundant small, light red fruit.

'Canary'—Yellow-fruited form, heavy producer, leaves light green with small spines.

'Carolina #2'—Good dark green form with heavy bright red fruit production, fairly common in southeast; looks a little open in youth, becoming fuller with maturity.

'Croonenburg'—Compact, pyramidal, columnar tree with deep green leaves that are less spiny than the species; fruits heavily every year, the plant is monoecious bearing flowers in the ratio of 10 female: 1 male; good fruiter.

'Farage'—An excellent form with large dark green, deeply spined leaves and lustrous persistent red fruits.

'Goldie'—Heavy yellow-fruiting form with dull green leaves.

'Greenleaf'—Becoming more popular in southeast, strong growing pyramidal form with glossy medium green, spiny foliage, margin is somewhat undulating, bright red fruits at an early age, in cold hardiness tests leaves and stems were hardy to −22°F.

'Howard'—Dark green leaves, almost spineless, abundant bright red, medium-sized berries, good looking clone that fruits heavily every year on the Georgia campus.

'Jersey Knight'—A male with lustrous dark green leaves, a handsome form, Orton introduction.

'Jersey Princess'—Female version of above, good foliage, abundant red fruits, Orton introduction.

'Manig'—Large dark green closely spaced leaves with large spines, large, glossy dark orange-red fruits.

'Merry Christmas'—Lustrous dark green small to medium-sized short spined leaves on a fast growing densely foliaged and branched tree, lustrous ellipsoidal bright red fruits.

'Miss Helen'—Thick dark green leaves, glossy red fruits ripen early, dense conical tree.

'Old Heavy Berry'—Vigorous, large dark green leaved selection that produces heavy crops of large red fruits.

'Stewart's Silver Crown'—The leaf margins are edged in cream, it is a female; the parent tree is 25′ high and wide.

'Wyetta'—Fast growing conical to pyramidal form with dense branching habit, glossy dark green foliage and large showy fruits.

PROPAGATION: Although I have rooted *I. opaca* many times from cuttings my experiences with 'Jersey Knight' and 'Jersey Princess' might prove valuable to other propagators. Dr. Orton sent cuttings in late December which I wounded, treated with 3000 ppm IBA-quick dip, placed in peat: perlite under mist and provided bottom heat (75°F). In 6 weeks a number of cuttings had rooted and the bulk of the roots originated from the wounded area. The cuttings were wounded (1″) on only one side and this is where the root systems were formed with the unwounded side showing essentially no root development.

NATIVE HABITAT: Massachusetts to Florida, west to Missouri and Texas. Introduced 1744. *Ilex opaca* is frequently encountered in shady woods throughout the southeast. Apparently birds disseminate the seeds. In these situations the plants are rather thin and open. They become much denser in full sun.

Ilex pedunculosa — Longstalk Holly
(ī'leks pe-dunk-ū-lō'sa)

LEAVES: Alternate, simple, evergreen, ovate or elliptic, 1 to 3″ long, 3/4 to 1 1/4″ wide, acuminate, rounded or broad-cuneate at base, entire, persistent for 3 years, glabrous, lustrous dark green; petiole 1/2 to 3/4″ long.
STEM: Slender, somewhat flattened, brownish green.

SIZE: 20 to 30′ in height but usually smaller under cultivation, perhaps 15′.
HARDINESS: Zone 5, has survived in Illinois field plots under the most adverse conditions: heavy soils, dry, sweeping winds, and intense summer heat.
HABIT: Large shrub or small tree of dense habit and handsome foliage.
RATE: Slow to medium.
TEXTURE: Medium in all seasons.
LEAF COLOR: Very beautiful lustrous dark green in summer; in exposed areas develops a yellow-green cast during winter; remind of *Kalmia latifolia* leaves.
FLOWERS: Male in clusters; female usually solitary, borne on current season's growth.
FRUIT: Berry-like, bright red drupe, 1/4″ diameter, borne singly on 1 to 1 1/2″ long pedicels, October and persisting into November.
CULTURE: Similar to *I. opaca;* from my observations perhaps not as fastidious as to soils.
DISEASES AND INSECTS: None serious, at least I have not seen any serious problems.
LANDSCAPE VALUE: One of the hardiest evergreen red fruiting hollies; should be used more than it is; apparently not well known; to me this is the most handsome of the evergreen hollies that can be grown in northern gardens; at its best, the habit is dense but still loose enough to show some grace; the beautiful fruits hang down on long pedicels and seem to be relished by birds; the Arnold Arboretum has several specimens by the corner of the Administration Building that rival any holly in cultivation; have seen it after the 1976 to 77 winter at Bernheim where temperatures dropped to −18°F and *no* injury was evident when all around other hollies dropped like flies. Have not seen in Zone 8, suspect like other holly species may not be very heat tolerant. Fred Galle, formerly of Callaway Gardens, Pine Mountain, GA, said the plant never performed well there.
PROPAGATION: I have had good success with cuttings, in fact, cuttings taken in February rooted 80% with 1000 ppm IBA/50% alcohol; have also rooted them in July and August with equal success.
NATIVE HABITAT: Japan, China. 1892.

Ilex verticillata — Common Winterberry, Black Alder, Coralberry, Michigan Holly
(ī'leks ver-ti-si-lā'ta)

LEAVES: Alternate, simple, 1 1/2 to 3″ long, 1/2 to 1″ wide, elliptic or obovate to oblanceolate or oblong-lanceolate, acute or acuminate, cuneate, serrate or double serrate, dark green above, usually pubescent beneath, at least on the veins; petiole 1/4 to 1/2″ long.
BUDS: Imbricate, small, 1/16″ long, globose, brownish, buds smaller then leaf scar.
STEM: Slender, angled, olive-brown to purplish brown, glabrous or finely pubescent, lenticelled; second year stem developing an onion-skin effect; leaf scar half-elliptical, somewhat raised, with two small blackish projections at either side; pith—white, excavated, appearing chambered.

SIZE: 6 to 10′ in height with a similar spread, can grow to 20′ but this is rare under landscape conditons.
HARDINESS: Zone 3 to 9.

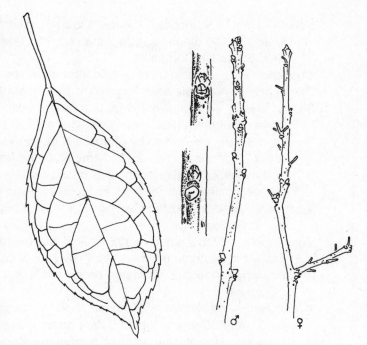

HABIT: Oval-rounded, deciduous shrub with dense complement of fine twiggy branches; tends to sucker and form large multistemmed clumps.

RATE: Slow, in youth can be induced into medium growth with adequate fertilizer and water.

TEXTURE: Medium in summer and winter.

BARK: Dark gray on old stems, interesting architectural twist to the branches.

LEAF COLOR: Deep rich green in summer; no significant fall color; although occasionally yellow to purple-tinged.

FLOWERS: Male in clusters of 6 or more in the leaf axils; female flowers fewer, usually singly or in three's on short peduncles.

FRUIT: Berry-like rounded drupe, bright red, 1/4″ across and often in pairs, ripening in late August-September and persisting into January depending on bird populations, make a magnificent show, often spectacular and without rival in the winter landscape.

CULTURE: Transplant balled and burlapped or as a container plant; adaptable to wet conditions (native to swampy areas) and does well in light and heavy soils; prefers moist, acid (pH 4.5 to 6.5), high organic matter soils; full sun or partial shade; will develop chlorosis in high pH soils.

DISEASES AND INSECTS: Tar spots, leaf spots, and powdery mildew, nothing serious.

LANDSCAPE VALUE: Excellent for mass effect, shrub borders, water side and wet soils; requires male and female for fruit set; I have seen several mass plantings which were outstanding; superior when the red fruits are framed by snow.

CULTIVARS: Introducers' names in parentheses.

'Afterglow'—Seedling selection by Simpson Nursery in 1960, introduced in 1976, 30-year-old plant is multistemmed, slow-growing, compact globe shaped, 10′ high and wide, glossy green leaves are smaller than average, fruits are globose or subglobose, 5/16″ long and 11/32″ diameter, borne singly or in 3's, on short pedicels, orange to orange-red, hardy to Zone 4.

'Aurantiaca' (Gulf Stream Nursery) (*I.v.* f. *aurantiaca* is botanically correct)—Abundant orange fruits about 1/4 to 1/3″ in diameter. Fruits do not persist as well as several of the red forms. They may start orange-red and fade to orange-yellow. Early flowering. Birds do not seem to bother the fruits.

'Bright Horizon' (Hill)—Bright red, 1/2″ diameter fruits. Small plants show a bushy habit.

'Cacapon' (Neal)—Compact type similar to 'Afterglow' but more upright. Abundant true red fruits. Glossy, dark green red crinkled leaves. Intermediate in height (6 to 8′).

'Chrysocarpa' (*I. v.* f. *chrysocarpa* is botanically correct)—A yellow-fruited form that does not fruit as heavily as many of the red selections. Fruits are handsome, especially before harsh weather. Birds do not bother it as much as red forms. Found several times in the wild in Massachusetts. This form exhibits early leaf drop compared to the red-fruited types.

'Christmas Gem' (Jenkins)—Red fruited. Has not performed well in Wichita, KS. Not much known about this clone.

'Earlibright' (Hill)—An orange-red fruited form from Martha's Vineyard.

'Fairfax' (Neal)—Heavy red fruit on a fairly compact plant. Fruit still present in late February at Swarthmore College, Swarthmore, PA. Will grow 8 to 10′ high.

'Hopperton' (Simpson)—Not a valid name yet. Has red 1/2″ diameter fruits and light gray bark.

'Jackson' (Neal)—A male form to accompany 'Cacapon', 'Fairfax', and 'Shaver'.

'Maryland Beauty' (Jenkins)—An introduction from Maryland.

'Mill Creek'—I first observed this cultivar at Swarthmore College, Swarthmore, PA.

'Nana' (Hampton Nurseries)—Grows 3 to 5' high; compact, rounded. Persistent, bright red fruit, 3/8 to almost 1/2" diameter, larger than *I. verticillata*. Lustrous dark green leaves. Popularly called 'Red Sprite' or 'Compacta'.

'Quansoo' (Hill)—A male plant named after a swimming beach on Martha's Vinyard.

'Quitsa' (Hill)—A female selection (red fruit) from Martha's Vinyard.

'Shaver' (Neal)—An excellent large orange-red fruiting form. Upright compact growth habit. Glossy leaves. Southern type, slow growing. Perhaps largest fruits of all selections.

'Sunset'—Seedling selection by Simpson Nursery in 1960, named in 1983, 30-year-old original plant is 8' by 9'; fruits are red, 7/16" diameter, borne singly on 1/8" long pedicels or in 3 short branched peduncles; original selection was based on dark olive-brown stem color, vigor, spreading habit, longer fruit than 'Winter Red' and heavy fruiting characteristic.

'Tiasquam'—Red-fruited female from Martha's Vineyard. Have seen plants in late February with abundant red fruits.

'Winter Gold'—Branch sport of 'Winter Red' discovered in 1984 at Simpson Nursery, Vincennes, IN; habit is multistemmed, rounded, 7' by 7'; leaf color is lighter green than 'Winter Red'; fruits are pinkish orange, 3/8" diameter, borne singly on a 1/16" pedicel or 3 together, considered hardy in Zone 4.

'Winter Red'—Introduced by Simpson Nursery, multistemmed, erect, deciduous rounded shrub, 9' by 8' after 30 years, lustrous dark green leaves, bright red, 3/8" diameter fruits are borne in tremendous profusion, intense color is maintained throughout the winter, have seen in a local nursery in early February with bright red fruit still persisting in good condition, truly one of the best introductions and now widely available.

(*Ilex verticillata* × *Ilex serrata*):

'Apollo' (National Arboretum)—Male form to accompany 'Sparkleberry'. Upright, ascending branches, 10 to 12' high and wide. New growth distinctly reddish maturing to dark green.

'Autumn Glow' (Orton)—Bushy form, slightly more erect than 'Harvest Red'. Landscape size approximates 6 to 8' high and slightly wider. Orton mentioned that a 20-year-old plant was 10' by 12'. Red fruits are retained until Christmas but bleach out earlier. Originally described as developing fiery orange fall color with bright flashes of yellow, but this has not held up for mature plants; generally yellow-green at best.

'Bonfire' (Simpson)—Originally listed as an *I. serrata* selection but probably belongs here. Masses of small red fruits ripen early in the fall while leaves are still green. Slender branches droop from the weight of the fruit. Small plants fruit heavily. Grows 8 to 10' high. See under *I. serrata*.

'Christmas Cheer' (Gulf Stream Nursery)—Small red fruits. At one time considered an *I. serrata* form but probably a hybrid.

'Harvest Red' (Orton)—Slightly deeper and larger red fruits than 'Autumn Glow'. Lustrous, dark green summer foliage that supposedly turns deep red-purple in fall, but plants I have observed were yellow-green. Fruits are not as large as the best *I. verticillata* forms. An 18-year-old plant is 9' by 16'.

'Raritan Chief' (Orton)—A male to accompany 'Autumn Glow' and 'Harvest Red'. Resulted from crossing a hybrid of *I. serrata* × *I. verticillata* with an unrelated female *I. verticillata*. Low, dense, spreading habit with handsome, lustrous, dark green foliage. Branches are rather brittle, so care should be exercised in handling. Grew 6 1/2' by 12' in 15 years.

'Sparkleberry' (National Arboretum)—The 3/8" diameter brilliant red fruits persist into winter, often into March. Distinctly upright, becoming somewhat leggy with age. Original plant was 12' high after 16 years. Hill noted that if she were restricted to a single pair of deciduous hollies, 'Sparkleberry' and 'Apollo' would be her first choices. 'Sparkleberry' received the prestigious Styer Award from the Pennsylvania Horticultural Society in 1987.

PROPAGATION: Cuttings, softwood, root readily. June or July cuttings treated with 1000 to 3000 ppm IBA-quick dip, peat:perlite, mist will root 90 to 100% in 6 to 8 weeks. On one occasion, I stratified fruits for 3 months at 41°F and had about 70 germinate out of 300; I tried the same thing again and did not have a single one germinate; see propagation under *I. cornuta*.

ADDITIONAL NOTES: *I. verticillata* is an amazing plant. I have seen it growing in fresh water ponds on Cape Cod, the entire root system completely submerged. Some stems on these plants were 4″ in diameter. The fruit will often stay showy into January. It makes a choice plant along lakes and ponds especially in fall when the fruit-laden branches are reflected off the water.

NATIVE HABITAT: Native in swamps from Nova Scotia to western Ontario, west to Wisconsin, south to Florida and west to Missouri; the most northerly distributed of the hollies native in America. Introduced 1736.

RELATED SPECIES:

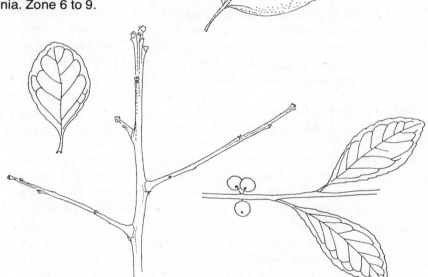

Ilex amelanchier, (ī′leks am-el-ang′kē-er), Serviceberry or Swamp Holly, has beautiful velvet-red to cerise-red, almost fluorescent, 1/4 to 1/3″ diameter persistent fruits. The only plant I have seen was at the Henry Foundation, Gladwyne, PA. Unfortunately, fruit was sparse. The leaf margins are entire or serrated, with an elongated bristle tip to each serration. The species occurs in sandy swamps and wet woods on the coastal plain from southeastern Virginia. Zone 6 to 9.

Ilex decidua—Possumnaw
(ī′leks dē-sid′ū-a)

LEAVES: Alternate, simple, obovate to obovate-oblong, 1 1/2 to 3″ long, 1/3 to 3/4″ long, usually obtusish, cuneate, obtusely serrate, dark green and lustrous above and with impressed veins, pale and pubescent on the midrib beneath, thickish; petiole—1/6 to 1/3″ long, pubescent.

BUDS: Small, imbricate, reddish brown, globular, glabrous, 1/16″ long.

STEM: Grayish, variable, on some plants a very soft gray, on others a grayish brown; the lateral branches are produced in great quantities and result in a very bushy main stem; short laterals sometimes appearing spur-like.

Ilex decidua, Possumhaw, will grow to 20 to 30′ in the wild but 7 to 15′ in height with 3/4's to equal that in spread is more reasonable under cultivation. Habit is that of a shrub or small tree, much branched with horizontal and ascending branches. Often suckers develop at the base of the plant and produce lateral thickets. Foliage is glossy dark green in summer, yellow in fall; fruits are orange to scarlet, singly to 3 together, supposedly 1/4 to 1/3″ diameter and ripen in September, often persisting until the following April; better adapted to alkaline soils than *I. verticillata;* the stems are usually very light gray and stand out against an evergreen background. Native from Virginia to Florida, west to Texas. Cultivated 1760. Zone (4)5 to 9.

Ilex decidua cultivars:

'Byers Golden' (Byers)—Excellent yellow-fruited form. I have seen fruits in good condition in February. Large plant. Has been difficult to propagate and is not readily available.

'Council Fire' (Hartline)—Bushy, upright, oval in outline. Fruit remains orange after others turn dark. Plants grown in a North Alabama nursery and a Tennessee nursery still had abundant, colorful fruits in mid-March. Fruits are borne in dense clusters along the stem. Grew 6 1/2′ by 5 1/2′ in nine years at Wichita, KS.

'Pocahontas' (Hartline)—Larger growing and more upright than 'Council Fire' and 'Sundance'. Red fruits, not as persistent as those of 'Council Fire'.

'Red Cascade'—Simpson Nursery introduction selected in 1965 and named in 1987; 30-year-old plant is 20′ by 20′ with a rounded habit with horizontal undulating branches which produce a weeping appearance, stems are an intense gray color, leaves glossy dark green, fruits are 5/16″ diameter, borne singly on 3/16″ long dark purplish pedicels; fruiting spurs with up to 7 closely spaced fruits, Zone 6 hardiness.

'Red Escort'—Simpson Nursery introduction named and introduced in 1987; 30-year-old parent is 25′ by 20′ with a globe-shaped crown, leaves are glossy dark green, considered one of the best males for habit and foliage, possibly the first named male clone, Zone 6 hardiness.

'Reed'—An older, red-fruited form that is probably not in commercial production. I have seen it at Simpson Nursery and was impressed by the bright red fruit.

'Sentry'—A Simpson Nursery introduction in 1987, 25-year-old plant is 20′ by 10′ with a columnar habit; leaves are less glossy green than typical *I. decidua*, leaves abscise early; fruits are 1/4″ long and 5/16″ diameter, subglobose, borne singly on dark purplish 1/4″ long pedicels, fruits also occur 6 to 7 on each spur, fruit is more firm than typical *I. decidua*, Zone 6 hardiness.

'Sundance'—Broad, spreading bushy habit, very vigorous, abundant orange-red fruits that color early and persist late into winter, grew 7′ by 6′ in nine years at Wichita.

'Warren Red'—Originated as a branch sport by Otis Warren and Son Nursery, Oklahoma City, OK, purchased before 1955 by Simpson Nursery and named by Robert Simpson, original plant is 25′ by 20′, more upright branching, lustrous dark green leaves, bright glossy red 5/16″ diameter, globose fruits occur singly or 2 to 6 per fruiting spur, fruiting is heavy and fruits are long persistent, a particularly handsome form and probably a zone hardier than the typical species.

Ilex laevigata, (ī′leks lē-vi-gā′ta), Smooth Winterberry, is closely allied to *I. verticillata* except the fruits are borne singly, are slightly larger, and the leaf petioles are shorter. The plant grows to about 10′, usually with upright branches. The leaves are somewhat glossy, elliptic, oval, or sometimes lanceolate, 1 to 3 1/2″ long, the margins finely serrulate. The fruits are orange-red, 1/3″ diameter, and supposedly can be set without pollination. There is a yellow-fruited cultivar called 'Hervey Robinson'. Native in swamps and low woods from Maine to New Hampshire, south to northern Georgia. Introduced 1812. Zone 4. The leaves turn yellow in the fall.

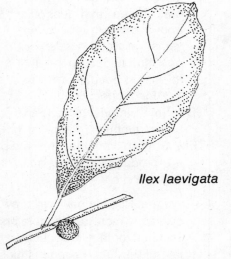

Ilex laevigata

Ilex longipes, (ī′leks lon′ji-pēz), Georgia Holly, is another deciduous holly nurserymen might want to consider. It is akin to *I. decidua.* The shiny, bright red, persistent fruits of *I. longipes* measure 1/4 to 1/2″ in diameter and occur on 1 to 1 1/2″ long stalks. The shiny light green leaves are oblanceolate (widest above the middle) and serrate toward the apex. To date, *I. longipes* has no known cultivars. It is native to Florida, west to Louisiana. I suspect temperatures between −10°F and −15°F will result in some stem injury, although the species is growing in the Arnold Arboretum. This species, like *I. decidua,* develops fruit on side spurs up and down its stems.

Ilex montana, (ī′leks mon-ta′na) (*I. monticola*), Mountain Holly, can actually achieve tree status, reaching as high as 40′, with a trunk that measures 10 to 12″ in diameter, but usually it is more shrubby, growing to about a third to half this size. I first chanced upon the species in North Georgia at 4,700′ above sea level on Brasstown Bald. The 2/5″ diameter rich red fruits do not persist like those of the other species and cultivars discussed. The species is usually found on well-drained, wooded slopes from New York to Tennessee, Georgia and eastern Alabama. The 2 1/2 to 6″ long leaves are the largest of the species treated here. In the tests at Wichita, KS, this species grew slowly (3' in 9 years), developed severe leaf scorch and produced few tiny red fruits. Zone 5 to 7.

Ilex serrata — Finetooth Holly
(ī′leks ser-rā′tá)

LEAVES: Alternate, simple, elliptic or ovate, 1 to 3″ long, 1/3 to 1″ wide, acute or acuminate, serrulate, dull green above, pubescent beneath; petiole 1/3″ long or less, downy.

Ilex serrata, Finetooth Holly, is similar to *I. verticillata* except the fruits are smaller (about 1/4″ diameter) and not as bright, and the leaves are more finely toothed. The species may grow 12 to 15′ high with spreading branches; however, under landscape conditions 4 to 8′ is more logical. The red fruits are abundantly borne and extremely showy after the leaves fall. The fruits ripen early, often in late August and persist for a long period and cut branches make excellent indoor decorations. Native to Japan and China. Introduced 1866. Zone 5 to 7(8).

'Bonfire'—Originated from a group of 150 seedlings at Simpson Nursery in 1957, introduced in 1983 as 'Bonfire', 30-year old plant is 12′ high with a spreding habit and mound-shaped crown, fruits are globose to ovoid, red, 5/16″ diameter, either singly or 2 to 4 on branched peduncles, selection was based on vigorous growth, spreading habit, fruiting at a young age, and persistence, hardy at least to the Chicago area, Zone 5 to 8.

'Koshobai'—A dwarf from Japan with abundant tiny 1/18″ wide, red, persistent fruits. Habit is twisted and twiggy, new growth rich purple. Japanese name means "plum of youth." Very slow growing and probably not a good garden plant but suitable for bonsai.

'Leucocarpa'—A white-fruited form that is quite striking. The National Arboretum has a handsome specimen that was heavily laden with fruit in early December.

'Xanthocarpa'—A yellow-fruited form.

OTHER HOLLIES OF LANDSCAPE IMPORTANCE

Ilex × ***altaclarensis*** (*I. aquifolum* × *I. perado*), (ī′leks × al-tá-klār-en′sis), Altaclara Holly, has evolved over the years to include a group of hollies that have larger, evergreen leaves, flowers, fruits, and greater vigor then the parents. The ones I have seen look more like *I. aquifolium.* Several notable cultivars include:

'Camelliifolia' — A fine form with lustrous dark green leaves up to 5″ long and 2″ wide; the leaves are essentially entire but some leaves develop 1 to 8 spines; the long stems, petioles, and base of

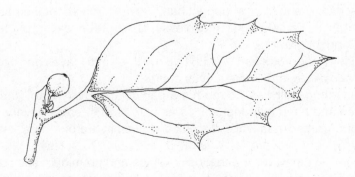

midrib are purplish; it is a female with rather large, dark red berries. 'Camelliifolia Variegata' is a branch sport with gray-green center and yellow-green margin.

'James G. Esson' — A beautiful, undulating, spiny-leaved form, the leaves being dark green; it makes a splendid specimen especially when the lustrous red fruits are present; the name does not fit the plant's sex; Longwood Gardens has a fine plant; leaves smaller than 'Camelliifolia' and habit is more open.

'J.C. Van Tol' — Fast growing form with regular crops of red fruits.

'Wilsonii' — Leaves broad-elliptic or obovate, spiny, up to 5″ long, 3″ wide, glossy green, red fruits, grows 30′ high or more, a vigorous form; best grown in Zone 7 and south.

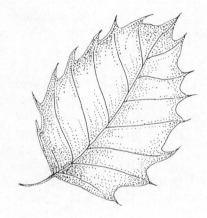

Ilex aquifolium, (ī′leks a-kwi-fō′li-um), English Holly, has a lustrous dark green, undulating, spiny-margined leaf that is quite distinct from other hollies. The leaves vary considerably in size ranging from 1 to 3″ long and 3/4 to 2 1/2″ wide. Seed-grown trees tend to have extremely spiny leaves but as the trees mature the spines decrease progressively with age and entire-margined leaves may be found in the tops of old plants. The dull white fragrant flowers occur during May from the leaf axils and give rise to 1/4″ diameter, round, red drupes. There are numerous cultivars of this species and published estimates approach 200. In a survey of hollies grown by U.S. nurseries, Klingaman (*American Nurseryman* 154(12):10–11, 106–119, 1981) reported only 24 types. English Holly makes a dense, 30 to 50′ high (to 80′) evergreen tree that is well clothed with branches even in old age. It is especially attractive in fruit. In addition, many of finest holly hybrids (*I.* × *meserveae,* 'Nellie Stevens') have the species as one parent. Supposedly for best fruit set a male English Holly needs to serve as pollinator. The following list is derived from Klingaman's Survey.

'Argenteo-marginata' — Dark green leaves marked with whitish margins, female.

'Aureo-marginata' — A designation for yellow margined types of which many have been named; in the common form the leaf is spiny margined and with a bright yellow border.

'Balkans' — Noted for cold hardiness, both male and female forms are offered, survived Kansas tests, glossy dark green leaves, upright habit, considered about the hardiest English Holly.

'Boulder Creek' — Female with large, glossy, black-green leaves; did reasonably well in Wichita, KS tests, upright growing.

'Ciliata Major' — Vigorous female with flat, ovate-elliptic leaves on which the spines point forward in the plane of the leaf, some leaves entire.

'Ferox' (Hedgehog Holly) — To me not a particularly lovely plant, the leaves are smaller than the species and have marginal spines as well as stiff, erect, silvery spines on the surface, male; 'Ferox Argentea' has white-margined leaves; in 'Ferox Aurea' the margin is green, the center yellow.

'San Gabriel' — Female form with glossy foliage and prominent spines.

'Sparkler' — Fast-growing, upright, free-fruiting form that sets heavy crops earlier than most cultivars.

'Zero' or 'Teufel's Weeping' — Erect form with long, thin, graceful branches, female, reasonably hardy, survived Kansas tests. Best grown in lower part of Zone 6 to 9. Europe, northern Africa and western Asia.

***Ilex* × *aquipernyi*,** (ī′leks × ȧ-kwi-pēr′nē-ī), is the result of crosses between *I. aquifolium* × *I. pernyi*. The habit is densely pyramidal while the evergreen foliage is lustrous dark green. 'Aquipern' is a male clone and 'San Jose' a female. 'San Jose' is hardy but best success is achieved under Zone 6 conditions. Proved extremely hardy in Kansas tests. The fruits are bright red and of good size. I have rooted cuttings of 'San Jose' with 100 percent success. Supposedly this hybrid species can grow 20 to 30′ high. 'San Jose' is popular on the west coast. 'Brilliant' is cone shaped, 10 to 20′ high, dense foliaged, twice as large as *I. pernyi* with a few pronounced teeth, sets abundant red fruits supposedly without pollination.

Ilex* × *attenuata 'Fosteri' — Foster's Hybrid Hollies
(ī′leks × ȧ-ten-ū-ā′tȧ)

LEAVES: Evergreen, alternate, simple, elliptic to oblong-ovate, 1 1/2 to 3″ long, about 1/2 as wide, spiny pointed and with 1 to 4 spreading spiny teeth on each side, glossy dark green.

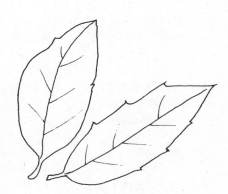

Ilex × *attenuata* 'Fosteri' represents a group of interspecific hybrids between *Ilex cassine* × *I. opaca*. There are selected clones known as Foster #1 through #5 made by E.E. Foster of Bessemer, Alabama. Foster #2 and #3, the most popular of this group in the south and the ones most often sold as Foster Holly, are used in general landscape work as foundation plants, hedges, and specimen plants. Both #2 and 3 are typically small-leaved, glossy green, with a spiny margin and have a compact, pyramidal growth habit. They are heavily fruited as is *I. cassine*. Foster #4 is a male plant while #1 and 5 are more like inferior forms of *I. opaca* and have been discarded. They make dense, narrow-conical 20 to 30′ trees of great beauty. The red fruits persist through winter. Zone 6 to 9. Easily rooted from cuttings. Foster #2 is the most popular form and is offered widely in the nursery trade. It makes a splendid 25′ high slender conical tree with rich deep red fruit. Several other selections, either from the wild or controlled crosses, have been made. They are correctly *Ilex* × *attenuata* selections.

'Alagold' — A yellow fruited form, apparently a seedling of 'Foster's #2'.

'Eagleston'—Upright almost shrubby form without the defined terminal leader of 'Foster's #2', foliage medium to dark green, entire or with some spines toward the apex, red fruits, vigorous grower, southern nurserymen are starting to grow this form.

'East Palatka' — Discovered in the wild near East Palatka, FL in 1927, it produces 1/4″ diameter bright red fruits in abundance, the dark green leaves may be entire or only toothed near the apex, this is looser and more airy than 'Foster's #2'; in the Georgia Botanical Garden, plants of this, 'Foster's #2' and 'Savannah' are planted in the Entrance Court Garden, all are quite different in habit, foliage and fruiting characteristics; in hardiness tests 'East Palatka' is less cold hardy than 'Foster's #2' and 'Savannah'.

'Hoosier Waif' — Originated as a "wild" seedling in Monroe County, IN, introduced by Dr. R.B. Rypma, Ohio University, 14-year-old plant is a dwarf spreading evergreen shrub, 2 1/2′ by 6′ with drooping branches, fruit is deep red, globose, 1/4″ diameter, borne singly on 3/16″ long pedicels or 2 to 3 per branched peduncle, supposedly hardy to −20°F.

'Hume #2' — A tall 30 to 35′ high loosely conical tree with lighter green leaves than 'East Palatka' and 'Foster's #2', the fruits are almost fluorescent red, small and reflect the *I. cassine* parentage, the leaves are somewhat rounded like 'East Palatka' but essentially spineless except at apex.

'Hume #4' — Supposedly has more spines than 'Hume #2'; I have rooted cuttings of 'Hume #4' and the leaves and fruits are larger.

'Nasa' — Resembles a compact 'Foster's #2', probably grows 8 to 10′ high, 4 to 6′ wide, dark green leaves, about 1 1/2″ long, 1/3″ wide.

'Oriole' (*I. myrtifolia* × *I. opaca*) — A slow growing, compact form with large exposed red fruit; after 25 years the original plant was 6' high and 6' wide; I have not been impressed with this form or 'Tanager' of the same parentage and compact, slow growing; was 6' by 7' after 25 years.

'Savannah' — A tremendously popular form in the southeast because of large fluorescent red fruits that are borne in great abundance; the habit is loosely pyramidal and the foliage light green, in summer and fall when the fruits are ripening, a tremendous movement of nitrogen (I assume) from the leaves to the maturing fruits results in chlorotic foliage subtending the fruits, the leaves remind of *I. opaca* and are generally spiny from the middle to the apex and larger than those of 'Foster's #2', 'East Palatka' and 'Hume #2'; will grow 25 to 30' high.

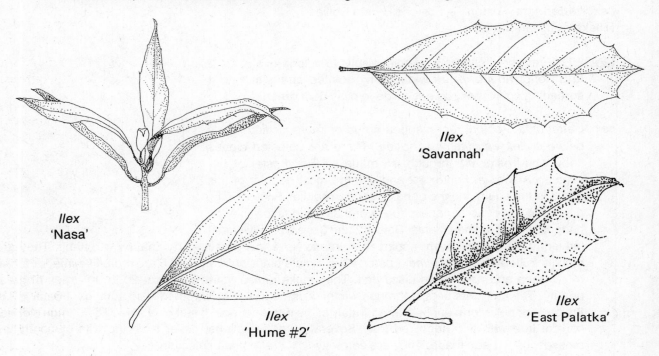

Ilex
'Nasa'

Ilex
'Savannah'

Ilex
'Hume #2'

Ilex
'East Palatka'

Ilex cassine — Dahoon
(ī′leks kȧ-sī′nē)

LEAVES: Alternate, simple, evergreen, 2 to 4″ long, oblong or oblanceolate, acute or rounded, cuneate, glossy medium green, entire or with a few sharp mucronate teeth near apex, essentially glabrous at maturity; petiole 1/4″ long.

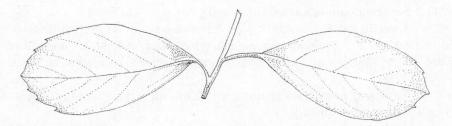

Ilex cassine, Dahoon, is seldom seen in American gardens but deserves mention because of the garden hybrids between it and *Ilex opaca.* Typically it forms a small evergreen tree 20 to 30′ high and 8 to 15′ wide in the wild. Zone 7 to 9. The 1/4″ diameter fruits range from red to almost yellow. The variety *myrtifolia* (*I. myrtifolia*) is closely allied but differs in smaller leaves, 3/8 to 1″ long by 3/8 to 3/4″ wide, with the midrib very prominent beneath and by the smaller fruits. 'Lowei' is yellow fruited with dark green leaves. Several nurserymen have made selections for improved fruiting characteristics. Although the fruits are smaller than *I. opaca* and *I.cornuta* they are borne in great quantities. In addition, the color is much brighter. The fruits occur 1 to 3 at a node on 3/4″ long pedicels. The species is native in moist woods of the Coastal Plain region south and west to Texas. Introduced by Mark Catesby in 1726. The variety has a more coastal distribution than the species. Hybrids between the species and *I. opaca* occur naturally in the wild. Selections have also been made, the most notable of which include *I.* × *attenuata* 'East Palatka', 'Hume #2', 'Savannah' and the Fosteri hybrids.

Ilex × 'Clusterberry' ('Nellie Stevens' × *I. leucoclada) is* a spreading shrub that grows 6 to 10′ high. The large, leathery, dull green evergreen leaves and large clusters of brick red fruits are the principal assets. Hardy to Zone 7. Released in 1978.

Ilex × 'Dr. Kassab' (*I. cornuta* × *I. pernyi*) is a beautiful dark green leaved, broad pyramidal evergreen form that grows 15 to 20′ high. It is a female and offers excellent red fruits. I had the good fortune of meeting Dr. Kassab who showed me around his Philadelphia area garden. He has a deep love of plants and his fine garden was a testimony to his enthusiasm. Like so many visits, there is never enough time to ask all the questions and sort out the pertinent details. There is no better fraternity than that bound by the love of plants.

Ilex × 'Ebony Magic' is an upright pyramidal form with excellent leathery lustrous dark green spiny leaves and brilliant large orange-red fruits. Fruits persist through spring. The parentage appears *I. rugosa* and *I. aquifolium* but I have not been able to document this. Conflicting reports on hardiness are given with Zone 4 and Zone 6 designations. One nurseryman reported it was hardier than the Blue Hybrids. A male, 'Ebony Male' can be used to pollinate 'Ebony Magic'. Name is derived from the dark color of the stem and leaves; originated as a natural (?) hybrid found wild in Germany; will form a strong pyramidal upright tree 20′ by 10′ with heavy crop of deep orange-red fruits that persist into spring.

Ilex × 'Emily Brunner' (*I. cornuta* × *I. latifolia*) is a fine broad, dense pyramidal female form that grows to 20′ high. The large evergreen leaves are a good dark green. Zone 7 to 9. It was introduced by Mr.

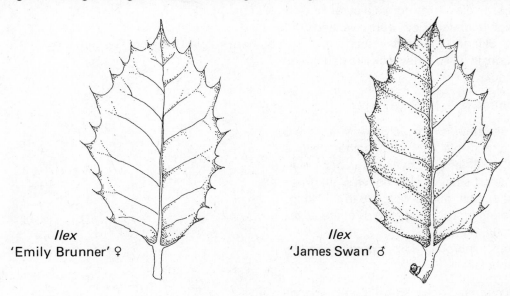

Ilex
'Emily Brunner' ♀

Ilex
'James Swan' ♂

Don Shadow, Winchester, TN. Don tells the story how a lady brought a plant into the greenhouse when he was an undergraduate at Tennessee. Don knew this plant was special and acquired the plant. It is a good choice for southern gardens. 'James Swan' is the male pollinator for 'Emily'. Several plants of 'Emily' have fruited abundantly on the Georgia campus. The large red fruits essentially encircle the stems. Temperatures around −3°F injured many leaves but did not kill stem tissue.

Ilex 'Hopewell Myte' [(*I. serrata* × *I. verticillata*) 'Sparkleberry' × *I. serrata*] — Originated as a controlled cross made in 1980 by Dr. R.B. Rypma at Ohio University Botanical Garden, Athens, Ohio; original plant is a low spreading dwarf shrub, 2' by 4', fruits are small, 1/4" diameter, red, borne singly or in fascicles of 2 to 3, hardiness to −15 to −20°F.

Ilex integra, (ī'leks in-te'gra), Nepal Holly, is a large 30' high evergreen tree with lustrous, almost black-green leaves and abundant subglobose, 1/3 to 1/2" diameter red fruits on 1/4" long stalks. The leaves average 2 to 4" long, 3/4 to 1 1/4" wide, and are essentially entire. This is more vigorous than *I. rotunda,* at least plants I have seen, and produces handsome fruit crops. Japan. Introduced 1864. Zone 9, perhaps 8. Has performed well in Savannah, GA area for many years. Reported hardy in Memphis, TN.

Ilex × 'John Morris' and 'Lydia Morris' represent male and female hybrid hollies selected from seedlings which resulted from crosses between *I. cornuta* 'Burfordii' × *I. pernyi.* They exhibit a dense pyramidal shrub-type habit and possess lustrous dark green, almost black-green evergreen foliage. The leaves are tightly borne along the stems and are extremely spiny. Very handsome in foliage and the female form produces cardinal red fruits. The plants were named after the individuals who donated land for the establishment of the Morris Arboretum, Philadelphia, Pennsylvania. Hardy in Zone 6, shakily so in Zone 5. These plants were killed after exposure to −20°F during 1976–77 winter. After 30 years, the original 'John T. Morris' was 15' high and 12' across. 'Lydia Morris' forms a pyramidal shrub to 12' high and wide. Both were released in 1961 by Henry Skinner. Plants have performed well at the Georgia Botanical Garden and are 15' high and 10' wide; in outline they look like dark green haystacks.

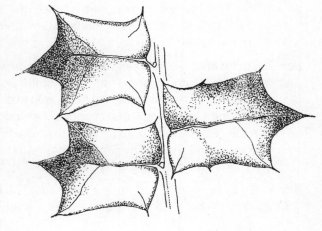

Ilex × **koehneana** — Koehne Holly

LEAVES: Alternate, simple, elliptic-ovate, 2 to 3 1/2" long, 1 to 1 1/2" wide, leathery, with 8 to 12, 1/16" long, spiny teeth on each margin, lustrous dark green above, light green beneath, glabrous; petiole 1/8 to 1/2" long.

BUDS: Imbricate, 1/8" long, ovoid, acute at tip, glabrous, purple.

STEM: Stout, glabrous, glossy, purplish above, green below.

Ilex × **koehneana,** (ī'leks kō-nē-ā'na),) Koehne Holly, is the grex name for hybrids between *I. aquifolium* and *I. latifolia.* 'Ruby' and 'Jade' are two rather non-descript hybrids, the former languishing as a shrub at the

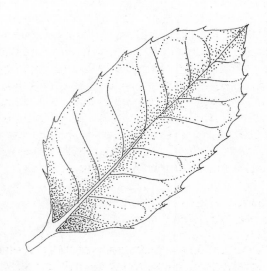

National Arboretum. The only clone I see with regularity is 'Wirt L. Winn', a beautiful glossy moderately spiny margined dark green leaf form that bears handsome large red fruits in abundance. The habit is distinctly pyramidal and landscape size approximates 20 to 25' in height. Interestingly this plant has withstood the heat and drought of the southeast and prospered while its *I. aquifolium* parent languished. At –3°F leaves were slightly injured. Cuttings of 'Wirt L. Winn' collected June 29 and August 17, 10,000 ppm KIBA, peat:perlite, mist, rooted 100%. This hybrid is much easier to root than *I. latifolia*. Zone 7 to 9.

Ilex latifolia — Lusterleaf Holly
(ī'leks lat-i-fō'li-à)

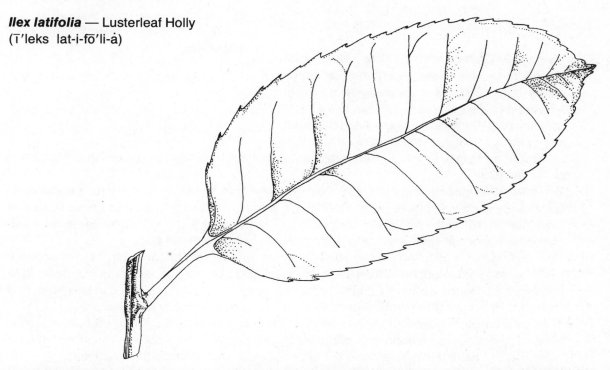

LEAVES: Alternate, simple, evergreen, leathery, oblong, 4 to 8″ long, 1 1/2 to 3″ wide, tapered equally at both ends, marginal teeth coarse and not spiny, lustrous dark green above, lower surface yellow green, glabrous; petiole — 1/2 to 1″ long.

Ilex latifolia, Lusterleaf Holly, is a large, pyramidal evergreen tree. Although not common in the south, it certainly ranks among the best of the broadleaf evergreens. Specimens on the University of Georgia campus growing in one-half shade are quite dense. Landscape size approximates 20 to 25'. The large lustrous dark green leaves hold their color throughout the year. The deep dull red, 1/3″ diameter fruits are borne in dense axillary clusters and almost completely encircle the stems. Fruits hold into February-March but lose color and become dull, washed out red. Given a well drained soil it appears to thrive. Holds up under drought conditions at least based on my Georgia observations. Offers the texture of *Magnolia grandiflora* yet without the inherent messiness. Japan. Introduced 1840. Zone 7 to 9. A relatively new hybrid, 'Mary Nell' named after the wife of former University of Illinois professor J.C. McDaniel, is starting to make waves in the southeast. The habit is pyramidal and the leaves spiny, lustrous dark green. It sets great quantities of bright red fruits. The parentage is (*I. cornuta* × *I. pernyi*) × *I. latifolia*. Hardiness should approximate Zone 7 to 9. A selection called 'Mary Nell Sibling' with 3 1/2″ long, glossy deep green spiny leaves and bright red fruits was selected from the same cross. The form I have seen in cultivation is the first mentioned.

Ilex × meserveae — Meserve Hybrid Hollies
(ī'leks me-sērv'ī-ē)

In the last edition I lumped everything together in a continuous never-ending paragraph that defied logic. This edition I chose to list the cultivars in alphabetical order. Mrs. F. Leighton Meserve (hence, ×

meserveae) of St. James, NY made crosses between the cold hardy *I. rugosa,* Prostrate Holly, and *I. aquifolium,* English Holly, that resulted in this magnificent series of introductions. Subsequent introductions were not always of the same parentage as above. Mrs. Meserve was honored for her work and received the American Horticultural Society's Citation for Outstanding Contributions to Amateur Horticulture. Conard Pyle purchased rights to introduce, grow, and market the plants and has been highly successful with these plants.

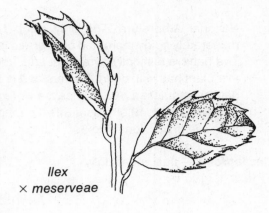

Ilex
× *meserveae*

'Blue Angel' — Offers crinkled, glossy dark green foliage, large shiny deep red drupes, and a full dense habit, 8′ by 8′, slowest growing of the females and also the least cold hardy. At –17°F (Cincinnati OH) every leaf was killed (browned); interestingly I have seen the plant since and it has recovered so stems and buds were not injured; definitely the "dumpiest" of the group, introduced in 1973.

'Blue Boy' — A 1964 introduction that was considered inferior to 'Blue Prince' and later introductions but actually is an acceptable plant. The habit is shrubby, 10 to 15′ high, and I have observed older plants (15′ high) with a full compliment of lustrous dark green foliage; the patent has expired and this cultivar is starting to appear more commonly in the trade.

'Blue Girl' — A 1964 introduction like the above except a female with bright red fruits; this appears faster growing and more open than 'Blue Princess' but I have no absolute data to substantiate the statement, forms a shrubby upright, pyramidal outline, 8 to 10′ (15′) by 6 to 8′, patent has expired on this cultivar; in Kansas tests this was the most cold hardy female form.

'Blue Maid'— Considered one of the hardiest of the group, fast growing, forms a broad 15′ high pyramid and produces a good crop of red fruits similar to 'Blue Princess' in size. Conard Pyle promoted this as one of the hardiest, but 'Blue Princess' and 'Blue Girl' are hardier.

'Blue Prince'— A dense lustrous, leathery dark green male form that produces abundant pollen, habit is dense and somewhat broad pyramidal but again tends toward a shrubby nature, can easily be pruned into any shape, will grow 8 to 12′ high; essentially no discoloration of foliage at –17°F, one of the hardiest, along with 'Blue Princess' introduced 1972.

'Blue Princess'— An improved 'Blue Girl' (some will argue this) with more abundant darker red fruit, lustrous darker bluish green foliage, the habit is broad and shrubby and size approximates 15′ high by 10′ wide, considered by many who have grown and evaluated this plant as the best fruit producer.

'Blue Stallion' — A male form with purplish stems and lustrous dark green "snag-free" foliage (i.e., not spiny margined), grows faster than 'Blue Prince', a good pollinator for 'Blue Princess' and the other female forms for it supposedly flowers over a long time frame in spring.

Other Meserve Hybrids

'China Boy'— A compact mounded form that is stated to mature at 10′ by 8′; plants I have seen were rounded, compact with glossy green foliage, this cultivar is a pollinator for 'China Girl'; excellent cold hardiness, probably in the range of –20°F, based on observations this is more cold hardy than the Blue series, shows increased heat tolerance compared to Blue series, result of a cross between *I. cornuta* and *I. rugosa,* introduced 1979.

'China Girl'— A handsome female form with abundant large 1/3″ diameter red fruits, foliage is a lustrous green but not as dark as the Blue series, also the leaves tend to cup, i.e., the margins turn down and in, a trait that easily separates it from the Blue series, habit is rounded, 10′ by 10′ at maturity, but all plants I have seen to date were 3 to 5′ by 3 to 5′, my first introduction came at Longwood Gardens, in the Idea Garden, where a number had been planted in a hedge arrangement, interspersed with several 'China Boy' for pollination, the foliage and fruiting effects were fabulous considering the December time frame, same parentage as 'China Boy', excellent heat tolerance. Pair showed unequivocally that 'China Girl' was more heat tolerant than the true Blue hybrids and reported that 'China Girl' survived record high temperatures in 1983 that killed the Blue hybrids growing next to them.

'Dragon Lady'— (*I. aquifolium* × *I. pernyi*) is more correctly listed as an *I. aquipernyi* (which see) form; habit is distinctly pyramidal-columnar with lustrous dark green, spiny margined leaves and large red fruits, have seen it used as a backdrop for the perennial border at Longwood, makes an excellent barrier plant, definitely less cold hardy than the Blue or China series, probably mature at 15 to 20' by 4 to 6'. I suspect −5 to −10°F will cause some leaf damage. 'Blue Stallion' can serve as an effective pollinator.

'Golden Girl'—Broad pyramidal habit, dense satiny foliage, brilliant yellow fruits, the first yellow fruited introduction, 1989.

A few final thoughts relative to the Meserve Hybrids: In a sense, they have been warmly embraced by northern gardeners. In the south, the true Blue (*I. aquifolium* and *I. rugosa*) do not perform well in the heat of Zone 8 and 9. If shade is provided the plants are acceptable but still do not measure up to plants I have seen in Boston MA, Hershey PA, Columbus OH and Philadelphia PA. I tried to grow *I. rugosa* in Georgia but the heat reduced it to rubble. Also *I. aquifolium* is not well adapted to the southeast, possibly because of the high summer night temperatures and poorly drained soils. They are worth a try but use should be tempered. The new 'China Boy' and 'China Girl' series look exceptionally promising north and south. *I. cornuta* contributes heat tolerance to these hybrids. Their only drawback is, perhaps, less handsome foliage.

All the Meserve Hybrids can suffer from winter desiccation and in the Burlington, VT area, I witnessed extensive leaf kill above the snowline with stems, for the most part, still alive; the low temperature was about −20°F; the bottom line for any broadleaf evergreen in northern latitudes if the ground is frozen, the wind blowing, the sun bright, some water loss from the leaves is inevitable. No replacement water is available since the ground is frozen and eventually, especially over time, some or all exposed leaves may die.

Drs. John Pair and Steve Still conducted outstanding practical research showing the effect of exposure on the blue hollies. They built a structure that offered various sun/shade exposures during winter and planted 'Blue Angel', 'Blue Maid', 'Blue Prince' and 'Blue Princess'. Air temperatures on south and southwest sides were as high as 109°F and 118°F, respectively; low temperature was −10°F. All cultivars survived with 'Blue Angel' most seriously injured. 'Blue Princess' was the hardiest and most fruitful, shoot growth was greatest on 'Blue Prince' and 'Blue Maid'. Plants grew best on north, northeast, and northwest exposures where summer temperatures were relatively cool and foliage temperature fluctuations in summer were reduced. See *HortScience* 17(5):823–825 (1982); *HortScience* 22(2):268–270 (1987) and *Amer. Nurseryman* 159(9):51–52 (1984).

Ilex × 'Nellie R. Stevens' is a putative hybrid between *I. aquifolium* × *I. cornuta*. The habit is that of a large evergreen shrub or small broad pyramidal tree 15 to 25' high. The leaves are lustrous dark green, slightly bullate, with 2 or 3 teeth on each side. The fruit is red, rounded, 1/4 to 1/3" wide, and the female flowers can be effectively pollinated by male *I. cornuta* which flower at a similar time. Heavily fruitful and fruit develops parthenocarpically. Hardy in Zone 6 to 9. Very vigorous plant and relatively fast growing. One of the best hollies for the southern states. It was released by G.A. Van-Lennep, Jr., St. Michael, MD. in 1954. It is

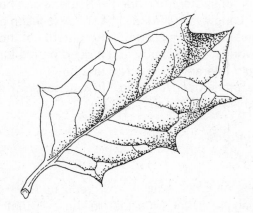

named for the owner, Nellie R. Stevens, Oxford, MD. 'Edward J. Stevens' is a large male clone that is useful for pollinating 'Nellie.'

Ilex pernyi — Perny Holly
(ī'leks pĕr'nē-ī)

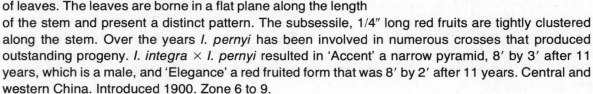

LEAVES: Alternate, simple, evergreen, 5/8 to 2″ long, 3/8 to 1″ wide, rhombic or quandrangular-ovate, 1 to 3 spines on each side, the upper pair the longest, but shorter than the terminal spine, glabrous, dark green above, leaves crowded together in more or less one plane; petiole — 1/12″ long, puberulous.

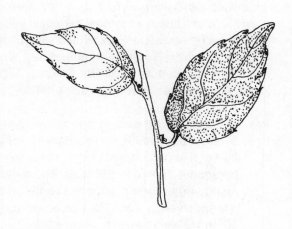

Ilex pernyi, Perny Holly, is not common in American gardens but has been used for breeding purposes. Easily distinguished by its upright habit (9 to 12′ high by 4 to 6′ wide) and rather open outline. Flower buds are purplish and tightly clustered in axils of leaves. The leaves are borne in a flat plane along the length of the stem and present a distinct pattern. The subsessile, 1/4″ long red fruits are tightly clustered along the stem. Over the years *I. pernyi* has been involved in numerous crosses that produced outstanding progeny. *I. integra* × *I. pernyi* resulted in 'Accent' a narrow pyramid, 8′ by 3′ after 11 years, which is a male, and 'Elegance' a red fruited form that was 8′ by 2′ after 11 years. Central and western China. Introduced 1900. Zone 6 to 9.

Ilex rotunda, (ī'leks rō-tun'dȧ), Lord's Holly, is occasionally found in Zone 9 where it makes a small evergreen tree. The dark green ovate or elliptic, obtuse or acute, rounded or cuneate, entire leaves average 1 1/2 to 4″ long with 1/2 to 1″ long petioles. The 1/4″ diameter bright red fruits are borne in umbels on 1/4″ pedicels and look like a red shower in fall and winter. Fruits hold into winter in the Savannah, GA area. Difficult to propagate from cuttings and mid January cuttings did not root at all under our typical procedure. Japan and Korea. Introduced about 1850. Zone 8(9). Injury coincides with 5°F, killed outright at −9°F.

Ilex rugosa, (ī'leks rū-gō'sȧ), Prostrate Holly, has ovate, 1 to 1 1/2″ long, 5/8 to 3/4″ wide, obtuse, rounded to cuneate, serrate, glabrous, wrinkled, leathery dark green leaves. It is a low-growing (1 to 1 1/2′ high), almost prostrate evergreen shrub that, although paling to a degree with the larger types, makes a rather handsome shrub. The solitary, roundish, red, 1/4″ diameter fruits ripen in September. I have seen it at Longwood Gardens in a shady location performing quite well. It is a one of the parents of the Meserve hybrids. Quite hardy and a good parent for breeding cold tolerant hollies. Not at all heat tolerant and not recommended for Zone 7 to 8. Japan, Sakhalin. Introduced 1895. Zone 3 to 6 (7).

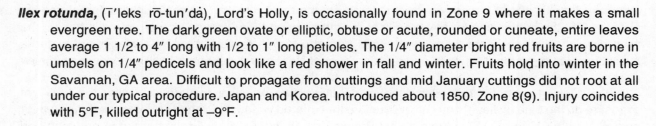

Ilex vomitoria — Yaupon
(ī'leks vom-i-tō'ri-ȧ)

LEAVES: Alternate, simple, evergreen, narrowly oval to ovate, tapered at base, blunt at apex, 1/2 to 1 1/2″ long, 1/4 to 3/4″ wide, margin shallowly toothed usually to the base which separates it from *I. crenata,* glabrous, lustrous dark green; no blackish glands evident on underside; petiole 1/8″ long.
STEM: Young stems quite downy, purplish initially, finally whitish gray and glabrous.

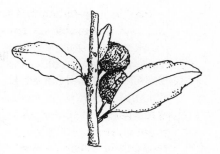

SIZE: 15 to 20′ in height, usually less in spread; can grow larger.

HARDINESS: 7 to 10.

HABIT: Very picturesque, upright, irregularly branched shrub or small tree.

RATE: Medium to fast, responds well to high fertility; 2 to 3′ of new growth occurred in a single season on plants at the Georgia Botanical Garden.

TEXTURE: Medium-fine.

BARK: White to gray, quite striking; good idea to limb up older specimens to expose and highlight the handsome bark.

LEAF COLOR: New growth with a purplish tinge but soon lost and turning a lustrous dark green.

FLOWERS: Dioecious, greenish white produced in axillary clusters on year-old wood, males numerous on 1/8″ long peduncles, females solitary or in pairs mid-April, later than *I. cornuta* types.

FRUIT: Translucent, 1/4″ diameter scarlet drupe, usually borne in prodigious quantities and persisting into spring; fruit is truly beautiful.

CULTURE: Easily transplanted, adaptable to varied soils from quite dry to extremely wet; found native in wet swampy areas; tolerant of salt spray; perhaps the most adaptable small leaved evergreen holly for southern gardens.

DISEASES AND INSECTS: None serious although a leaf miner has been listed; shows much greater propensity to succeed under southern conditions compared to *Ilex crenata* and cultivars.

LANDSCAPE VALUE: Multitudinous uses incuding informal screens, hedges, specimens, barriers, espaliers; takes pruning well; the cultivars are widely used for mass and foundation plantings; also maks a good topiary plant.

CULTIVARS: Difficult to track all the cultivars; other forms exist.

'Folsom's Weeping' — A selection similar to 'Pendula', female, narrow in habit.

'Grey's Little Leaf' — A cute diminutive small leaf form, foliage about 1/3 as wide as the species, new growth reddish purple, have seen only once and wondered why the plant is not more common, nice delicate, fine textured plant.

'Jewel' — Female form selected for its heavy fruit production, rounded compact outline.

'Nana' — Dwarf, compact form with smaller leaves than the species, new growth rich yellow-green without the purplish tinge associated with 'Shillings'/'Stokes', grows 3 to 5′ high and slightly wider after many years, a female based on my observations but fruit is usually hidden by the close-knit branches, branches are quite brittle and I have noticed a few branches dying at random on shrubs in the Georgia Botanical Garden and on campus; close examination indicated the branches had been broken; very fine cultivar but over used; a 25-year-old plant may be 5′ high and 8 to 10′ wide; makes a gigantic mounded cushion if not pruned.

'Pendula' (f. *pendula*) — I have decided this is a convenient holding area for any weeping form of the species; on the Georgia Campus there are male and female forms, one particular grouping of male plants was 20 to 25′ high; interestingly they had to be relocated due to construction, the plants were cut back, dug, and transplanted successfully, the basal trunk diameter was about 10″.

'Poole's Best' — A heavily fruited, strong growing, compact selection.

'Pride of Houston' — Medium-sized shrub with heavy fruit set.

'Shadow's Female' — An excellent large dark green, almost rounded leaf female form, with bright red translucent fruits, makes a large shrub or small tree and have seen it pruned into topiary form, probably several degrees hardier than the typical forms in cultivation, suspect about −10°F.

'Shillings/Stokes Dwarf' — One and the same, a more compact form than 'Nana' with smaller leaves, purplish new shoot extension, I have difficulty separating 'Nana' from this clone when plants are isolated; together the differences are more evident, 3 to 4′ by 3 to 4′, male.

'Straughn's' — A relative newcomer that appeared most promising as a boxwood substitute because of its billowy, rounded habit, supposedly less susceptible to breakage than 'Nana' but plants will often open up in the center almost like they have been pulled apart, will grow as large as

'Nana' perhaps more so, when I first saw the plant, I had great hopes; hopes are now tempered with the problem mentioned.

'Yawkey' — A yellow-fruited selection.

'Yellow Berry' — Yellow fruits that persist.

PROPAGATION: I had not worked with this species until moving to Georgia and learned quickly that it is difficult to root. My successes (?) range from 0 to about 50%. Nurserymen have reported similar percentages to 100%. Early March cuttings of 'Nana', 'Pendula', 'Shillings' and a heavily pruned plant of the species rooted 30, 20, 30, and 100%, respectively, in 9 weeks after 8000 ppm IBA quick-dip, peat:perlite, mist. An Alabama report mentioned 100% success with October cuttings of 'Pendula' rooted in poly houses. Possibly the use of KIBA would be beneficial.

ADDITIONAL NOTES: Easily separated from *Ilex crenata* by virtue of red fruits compared to black fruits, gray stems compared to green stems, red-purple veined new leaves compared to all green leaves and lack of dots or glands on the lower surface. The epithet *vomitoria* refers to the use the leaves were put by the Indians. They made an infusion of the leaves and drank freely until vomiting was induced. This cleansed them of any impurities of body and soul. A book titled *Black Drink, A Native American Tea,* University of Georgia Press, tells the fascinating story of *Ilex vomitoria.*

NATIVE HABITAT: New York, Long Island to central Florida and west to Texas. Introduced 1700.

Illicium floridanum — Florida Anise-tree
(il-iss'i-um flôr-i-dā'num)

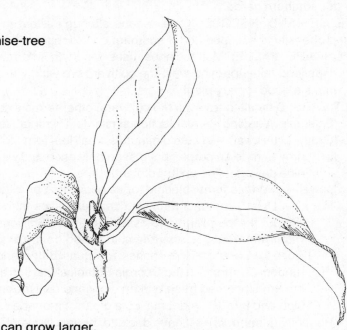

FAMILY: Illiciaceae

LEAVES: Alternate, simple, evergreen, elliptic to elliptic-lanceolate, 2 to 6″ long, half as wide, acute, cuneate, entire, glabrous, lustrous dark green above, pale beneath; petiole — 1/2″ long; reddish purple which separates it from *I. parviflorum;* highly aromatic when bruised or crushed.

SIZE: 6 to 10′ high, slightly less in spread, can grow larger.

HARDINESS: Zone 7 to 9, survived –9°F, in laboratory hardiness tests survived –15°F.

HABIT: Much branched, upright shrub usually compact in outline; require pruning in early years to keep in shape.

RATE: Medium.

TEXTURE: Medium.

LEAF COLOR: Dark green; leaves with age droop like a large-leaved rhododendron.

FLOWERS: Perfect, 1 to 2″ diameter, borne singly on a 1/2 to 2″ long pedicel, maroon-purple, odor is rather strange, composed of 20 to 30 strap-shaped petals, April-May; rather interesting but not overwhelming, has started to flower in late March in Athens and continued until late April.

FRUIT: One-seeded, dehiscent follicles 11 to 15, arranged in a whorl, one-inch diameter, at first green then yellow and finally brown, maturing in August-September, have a star-like configuration, distinct, seeds BB-like, brown, shiny.

CULTURE: Best tranplanted from containers, prefers moist, well-drained, high organic matter soils; partial to heavy shade; have actually waded into swamp-like areas to photograph the plant; appears to thrive under moist to almost wet conditions, in full sun leaves are lighter green and not as handsome as those on shade-grown plants.

DISEASES AND INSECTS: None serious.

LANDSCAPE VALUE: The entire shrub has a strong pungent odor and is simply wonderful to have in the garden; the flowers are beautiful but malodorous (April in the Piedmont area of Georgia); could be utilized in shrub borders, in shady, moist corners; Callaway Gardens has a planting in their wildflower garden area and the plant blends quite nicely into a naturalistic type setting.

CULTIVARS: A white flowered form ('Alba') is available; I have seen it at Woodlanders, Aiken, S.C., it is a superb addition to the list of broadleaf evergreens with white flowers.

    'Hally's Comet' — Has more red on the petals and they are slightly reflexed.

      Godfrey (1988) reported that white and pink flowered forms were intermixed with the red flowered type in the wild. I have also seen a variegated leaf form.

PROPAGATION: Seeds germinate readily and according to Fred Galle, Callaway Gardens have self-sown there to the point of weediness. I collected cuttings in late August, treated them with 3000 ppm IBA and had 100 percent rooting in 4 to 6 weeks; firm wooded cuttings of all species described here root easily.

NATIVE HABITAT: Florida to Louisiana. Found in moist wooded ravines, along or even in the small streams or seepage areas. Discovered by Bartram in western Florida in 1766. Introduced into cultivation in 1771.

RELATED SPECIES:

Illicium anisatum — Japanese Anise-tree

LEAVES: Alternate, simple, evergreen, 2 to 4″ long, 3/4 to 1″ wide, lustrous medium to dark green, narrowly oval, blunt at apex, cuneate at base, glabrous, tapering to a short petiole; confused in the southeast with hardier *I. parviflorum* (which see), the leaves of *I. anisatum* are borne more perpendicular to the stem and are often slightly dog-eared compared to upright leaves on upper stems (at 45° angle) of *I. parviflorum*.

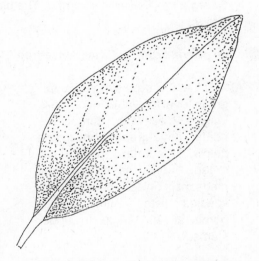

Illicium anisatum, (il-iss′i-um an-iss-ā′tum), Japanese Anise-tree, makes a rather dense medium to broad, pyramidal broadleaf evergreen shrub or small tree 6 to 10′ (15′) high. The habit is more formal than *I. parviflorum* and the few plants I have seen do not sucker and form large colonies like *I. parviflorum*. The creamy (pale greenish yellow) up to 30 petaled, 1″ diameter nonfragrant flowers normally occur in March-April, however, at Callaway Gardens flowers have opened in late February. Flowers develop on 1″ long pedicels from the leaf axils. Fruit is a 1″ diameter, star-shaped, aggregate of follicles. At one time considered hardier than *I. floridanum* and *I. parviflorum* but the freeze of 1983–84 (−3°F) eliminated this species while the others were not affected. Requires moist, well-drained, reasonably rich soil and partial shade for best performance. Native to China and Japan. Introduced 1790. Zone 8 to 9.

Illicium henryi, (il-iss′i-um hen′rē-ī), Henry Anise-tree, is a 6 to 8′ (to 15′) high, densely pyramidal broadleaf evergreen shrub with leathery, glossy dark green, 4 to 6″ long, 1 to 2″ wide (1/2 to 3/4″ long petiole) leaves. The 1 to 1 1/2″ diameter up to 20-petaled flowers vary from pink to deep crimson. The flowers develop from the leaf axils on 1 to 1 1/2″

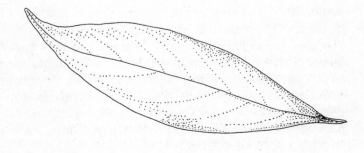

long arching pedicels. This is a virtual unknown in American gardens but might prove a genuine gem with greater exposure. I have seen plants at Strybing Arboretum, San Francisco, and Woodlanders, Aiken, SC. The flowers open in April-May and are more colorful and aesthetic than those of *I. floridanum*, *I. anisatum* and *I. parviflorum*. Will make a good shade tolerant plant and could be effectively mixed with winter flowering plants like *Camellia*. Hardiness is unknown, but Zone 7 to 9 is possible. Western China.

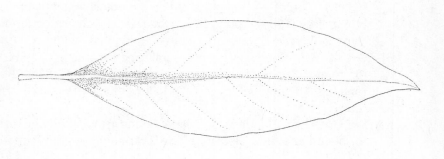

Illicium mexicanum, (il-iss′i-um mek-si-kā′num), Mexican Anise-tree, is another unknown broad-leaf evergreen that will grow in stature with exposure. Leaves are lustrous dark green. The habit is pyramidal. Flowers are reddish and 1 1/2 to 2″ across. Raulston mentioned that flowers appeared in autumn in Raleigh, NC, however a small plant at Georgia has flowered in spring. The plant has proved hardy in Raleigh, NC and should grow in Zone 7 to 9.

Illicium parviflorum — Small Anise-tree

LEAVES: Alternate, simple, ever-green, oval to oval-elliptic, 2 to 4″ long, 1/2 as wide, abrupt, cu-neate, olive-green above and below, glabrous, petiole — green; leaves have the most pleasant "anise" odor of the species listed here; leaves borne at 45° angle to upper stems.

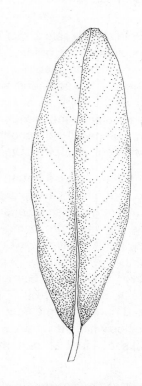

Illicium parviflorum, (il-iss′i-um par-vi-flō′rum), Small Anise or Anise-tree, has surfaced as the most rugged landscape per-former among the *Illicium* species. Although thoroughly confused with *I. floridanum* and *I. anisatum* the differences are manifest. Habit is upright pyramidal to prominently suckering unless restrained. I have seen plants in Savannah and Pine Mountain, GA about 15 to 20′ tall. On our campus, 8 to 10′ masses have drifted along for many years. The olive-green foliage is handsome and provides a slightly different color than the lustrous dark green of many broadleaf evergreens. Will tolerate extremely moist soils and does well in dry situations. The best *Illicium* for sun and shade. Flowers are small, no bigger than 1/2″ wide, 6 to 12 petaled and yellow-green in color. Flowers appear in May-June, sporadically into fall and go virtually unnoticed. There is no noticeable odor. Easily rooted from cuttings. A most vigorous and worthwhile plant for southern gardens. Excellent large foliage mass or screen. Found in wet areas in southern Georgia and Florida. Zone 7 to 9.

Indigofera kirilowii — Kirilow Indigo
(in-di-gof'ēr-à kir-il-ōw'eī)

LEAVES: Alternate, compound pinnate, 7 to 11 leaflets, entire leaf — 4 to 6″ long, each leaflet — sub-orbicular to obovate or elliptic, 1/2 to 1 1/4″ long, mucronate, broad cuneate or rounded at base, rounded at apex, bright green above, sparingly appressed-pubescent on both sides.

Indigofera kirilowii, Kirilow Indigo, is a low, dense suckering shrub with erect stems that grows 3′ in height. The foliage is bright green in summer. The flowers are rose-colored, 3/4″ long, borne in June and July in dense 4 to 5″ long erect racemes on current season's growth. Extremely adaptable species which does well in calcareous soils; branches may be killed to the ground in severe winters but new shoots quickly develop from the roots. Might be used as a ground cover for difficult areas. The flowers are somewhat masked by the foliage. Probably should be treated as a herbaceous perennial in northern areas. *Indigofera gerardiana* (*I. heterantha*), Himalayan Indigo, has succeeded at the Arnold Arboretum. It grows about 2 to 4′ high and has 13 to 21 leaflets. The rosy purple, 1/2″ long flowers occur in a 3 to 5″ long raceme. The racemes are produced from the leaf-axils in succession from the base upwards, on the terminal portion of the shoot. Has flowered from second week in July to second week in September, in Boston. *Indigofera incarnata*, Chinese Indigo, is encountered now and again in American gardens. The leaves are composed of 7 to 13, 1 to 2 1/2″ long, dark green leaflets. The 3/4″ long pink flowers occur in 4 to 8″ long slender racemes in July and August. Variety *alba* has white flowers and is considerably hardier. The leaves appear somewhat bleached green. The species and variety form a 1 to 1 1/2′ high tangled meshwork of stems. Have seen the variety used effectively as a ground cover. *I. kirilowii* is native of northern China, Korea and southern Japan. Introduced 1899. Zone 4 to 7 (8).

Itea virginica — Virginia Sweetspire
(ī-tē'à vēr-jin'-i-ka)

FAMILY: Saxifragaceae, Iteaceae or Escalloniaceae depending on the authority.

LEAVES: Alternate, simple, deciduous, semi-evergreen or evergreen, elliptic or obovate to oblong, acute or short acuminate, usually cuneate at the base, 1 1/2 to 4″ long, 3/4 to 1 1/4″ wide, serrulate, glabrous and lustrous dark green above, often sparingly pubescent beneath; petiole 1/8 to 1/4″ long, pubescent, grooved on upper side.

SIZE: 3 to 5′ in height, possibly to 10′, spread variable but normally wider than high.

HARDINESS: Zone 5 to 9.

HABIT: Shrub with erect, clustered branches, branched only near the top; have seen plants in full sun that were densely branched and wider than high; will form rather large colonies if left unchecked; much fuller in sun exposures, becomes rounded, arching in habit.

RATE: Medium, fast with adequate nutrition and moisture.

TEXTURE: Medium.

LEAF COLOR: Dark green in summer changing to reddish purple, scarlet and crimson with the advent of fall; often persisting quite long in fall; fall color can be a spectacular fluorescent red, at −3°F leaves were essentially removed from the plant, at 15 to 20°F virtually an evergreen to semi-evergreen shrub.

FLOWERS: Perfect, white, lightly fragrant, 1/3 to 1/2″ diameter, borne in upright, dense, pubescent, 2 to 6″ long and 5/8″ wide racemes, terminating short, leafy twigs; June-July; sufficiently abundant to make the shrub very attractive; flowers in May in the Piedmont of Georgia.

FRUIT: Five-valved capsule, 1/4 to 1/3″ long, narrow, pubescent, persistent.

CULTURE: Easily transplanted from a container; however, pieces of the plant can be divided and successfully transplanted; prefers moist, fertile soils and in the wild exists in wet places; full sun or shade; amazingly adaptable and has displayed drought tolerance; appears pH adaptable.

DISEASES AND INSECTS: None serious.

LANDSCAPE VALUE: An interesting native shrub valued for fragrant flowers at a time when few plants are in flower; best situated in moist or wet areas in the garden; on some specimens the fall color is fantastic; not utilized enough in American gardens; it would make a good choice for naturalizing in moist areas of the garden; not given sufficient credit for drought tolerance which is considerable. I have collected it in the Piedmont area of Georgia along streams where it literally grows at the water's edge in moist, cool soil; it is rather straggly, thin, and open in the wild but becomes more dense under cultivation; holds its leaves into December in the Athens area and some leaves, in a mild winter, will persist until spring.

CULTIVARS:

'Henry's Garnet' — A superb selection from the Swarthmore College campus with brilliant reddish purple fall color and up to 6″ long flowers. Both fall color and flowers are superior to the species. Grows 3 to 4′ high and 1 1/2 times as wide; has proven cold hardy to −20°F and thrives in the heat of Zone 8; easily rooted from softwood cuttings; I have grown this for a number of years and believe it has a great future in American gardens; received prestigious Styer award; laboratory hardiness tests indicate tolerance to −20°F.

PROPAGATION: Seed requires no pretreatment; softwood cuttings root easily in four weeks with or without IBA treatment; I have collected cuttings from wild plants in late August, treated them with 3000 ppm IBA quick-dip and they have rooted 100 percent; this success applies to the related species.

NATIVE HABITAT: Pine barrens of New Jersey to Florida, west to Missouri and Louisiana. Introduced 1744.

RELATED SPECIES:

Itea ilicifolia, (ī-tē′à̇ i-lis-i-fō′li-a), Holly Sweetspire, is a true evergreen, 6 to 12′ high shrub with lustrous dark green, spiny-jagged margined, 2 to 4″ long, 1 1/2 to 2 3/4″ wide leaves. The greenish white flowers occur in 6 to 12″ long, 1/2″ wide racemes in July. Prefers moist, well drained soil, partial shade and protection from desiccating winds. Used in English gardens and is a most elegant shrub. Should prove hardy in Zone 8 to 9 and Raulston has successfully grown it in Raleigh. Easily rooted from softwood cuttings.

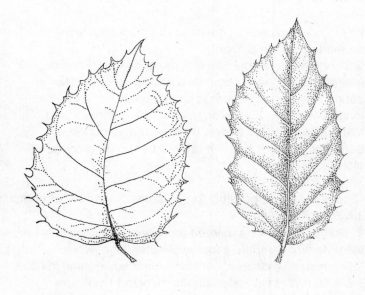

Itea japonica, (ī-te′ à̇ ja-pon′i-kà̇), 'Beppu' ('Nana'), was introduced by the National Arboretum. It makes a rather handsome, 2 to 2 1/2′ high, spreading mound of rich green summer foliage that turns reddish purple in fall and persists into winter. The flowers are smaller than those of *I. virginica* but similar in color and fragrance. It is very fast growing and because of its suckering nature would make a good ground cover. Easily rooted from softwood cuttings. Eleven years ago I brought a rooted cutting to Athens and planted it in the Botanical Garden. The plant, with numerous cuttings removed, is 4 to 5′ high and considerably wider due to its suckering nature. The 'Nana' epithet is actually a misnomer since the plant grows taller than *I. virginica*. Fall color, on occasion, has been a bright red and other times red-purple. Leaves will persist into winter at 15 to 20°F. The plant is not as hardy as *I. virginica* and some stem injury is possible at 0 to −10°F.

Jasminum nudiflorum — Winter Jasmine
(jas′mi-num nū-di-flō′rum)

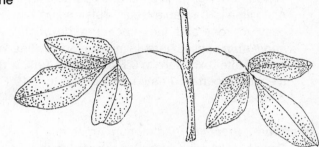

FAMILY: Oleaceae

LEAVES: Opposite, pinnately compound, 3 leaflets, each leaflet ovate to oblong-ovate, 1/2 to 1 1/4″ long, one third to half as wide, narrowed at ends, mucronulate, entire, ciliolate, deep lustrous green; petiole—1/3″ long.

STEM: Slender, trailing, green, glabrous, angled, almost 4-sided.

SIZE: 3 to 4′ high, 4 to 7′ wide; can grow 12 to 15′ if trained on a wall or trellis.

HARDINESS: Zone 6 to 10, perhaps hardy in Zone 5, at least woody hardy.

HABIT: A broad spreading mounded mass of trailing branches arising from a central crown; can consume large areas with time for the trailing branches root in contact with moist soil and form new plants.

RATE: Fast.

TEXTURE: Fine.

BARK: Stems are fairly effective in the winter landscape; the green stands out in contrast to the grays and browns.

LEAF COLOR: Deep lustrous green in summer; no fall color of any consequence.

FLOWERS: Perfect, solitary and axillary along the previous season's growth, salver-shaped, with slender corolla tube, about 1 1/2 to 2″ long and 3/4 to 1″ across, usually 6 wavy lobes, bright yellow, waxy red in bud, non-fragrant, opening from January to March but peaking in February; never as potent as forsythia because the flowers open over a long period; responds to the slightest degree of warm weather; -3°F killed all flower buds.

FRUIT: Two-lobed, black berry; seldom seen in cultivation; I have never seen the fruit on cultivated plants.

CULTURE: Transplants readily; almost approaches weed status because of its widespread adaptability; prefers well drained soil but does well in poor soils and is moderately drought resistant; full sun or shade (flowering is reduced); probably should be rejuvenated every 3 to 5 years by cutting plant to within 6″ of ground; roots where branches touch soil and tends to colonize an area; actually difficult to remove once it is established.

DISEASES AND INSECTS: None serious.

LANDSCAPE VALUE: A good plant for banks and poor soil areas where a cover is desired; often used for massing and works well along walls where the trailing branches flow over the side; often used to face down leggy shrubs; flower is lovely but foliage and tenacity may be the best assets.

CULTIVARS: 'Aureum'—Leaves blotched with yellow.

PROPAGATION: Cuttings root readily; I have had good success in July with 3000 ppm IBA quick dip, peat:perlite and mist; root systems were fantastic; probably could root the plant anytime of year and without a rooting hormone.

NATIVE HABITAT: China. Introduced 1844.

RELATED SPECIES:

Jasminum floridum, (jas'mi-num flôr'i-dum), Showy Jasmine, is a half-evergreen to evergreen, 3 to 5′ high shrub
that produces a mass of slender, arching, quadrangular,
glabrous, green stems. This species is easily separated
from the previous because the leaves are alternate. The
dark green leaves are composed of 3 to 5 leaflets, each
leaflet 1/2 to 1 1/2″ long and 1/4 to 5/8″ wide. The yellow,
1/2 to 3/4″ long, 5-lobed flowers open over a long time
period from April into June and sporadically into the fall.
At no time is the display really outstanding. It is extremely
easy to root and the procedure described under *J.*
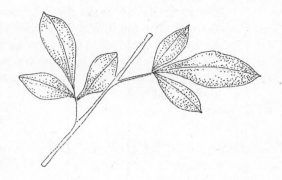
nudiflorum applies here. In my opinion, the fine foliage is more valuable than the flowers. Plants were
injured after exposure to 0°F during the 1982 winter. All leaves had abscised and considerable stem
dieback occurred. I estimate that +5 to +10°F is about the break point. China. Introduced 1850.
Zone 8 to 10.

Jasminum mesnyi, (jas'mi-num mes'nē-ī),
Primrose Jasmine, is better adapted to the
lower south. The species will grow 5 to 6′
(9′) high and evelops the mounded habit
and long trailing branches common to *J.*
nudiflorum. The oppositely arranged, pinnately compound, lustrous dark green
leaves are composed of 3 leaflets, each
from 1 to 3″ long and 1/3 to 3/4″ wide. The
bright yellow, 1 1/2 to 1 3/4″ diameter
flowers are produced singly on 1/2 to 1 1/2″
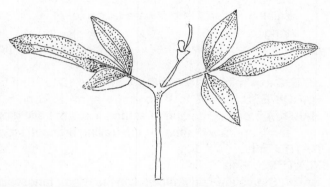
long pedicels in early spring through midsummer (sporadically). The corolla is often semi-double,
composed of 6 to 10 divisions, each 1/3 to 1/2″ wide and rounded at the end. Closely allied to *J.*
nudiflorum but is larger in all its parts and flowers later, usually about late March into April in the
Athens area. China. Introduced 1900. Zone 8 to 9.

Jasminum officinale, (jas'mi-num ō-fis-i-nā'lē), Common White Jasmine, is a deciduous or semi-
evergreen climbing or spreading shrub growing 10 to 15′ and if trained on a wall 30 to 40′. The
oppositely arranged, pinnately compound rich green leaves have 5 to 9 leaflets, each 1/2 to 2 1/2″
long and 1/6 to 1″ wide. The 3/4 to 1″ long and wide, 4 to 5-lobed corolla is white and appears in June
through October; the flowers are deliciously fragrant. One of the cherished plants in English gardens
and there has been cultivated since time immemorial. 'Affine' has flowers tinged pink on the outside
and broader calyx lobes. In 'Aureo-variegatum' ('Aureum') the leaves are blotched yellow and
'Grandiflorum' has larger, more showy flowers, up to 1 1/3″ across. Native the Caucasus, northern
Iran, Afghanistan, the Himalaya and China. Cultivated since ancient times. Zone 8 to 10, doubtfully
hardy in Zone 8 of the southeast.

Juglans—Walnut
FAMILY: Juglandaceae

The walnuts are treated in this text as a group similar to the format under *Carya*. The flowers are
imperfect (monoecious); male catkins preformed, appearing as small, scaly, conelike buds, unbranched;
female in 2 to 8 flowered spikes. Fruit is a nut with the outer ovary wall (exocarp and mesocarp) semifleshy;
the endocarp is hard and thick-walled, while the seeds are sweet and quite oily. The flowers are wind

pollinated. Walnuts are important timber trees and the Black Walnut, *Juglans nigra,* is a prime timber tree. The following are the more important species. An excellent paper, *Walnuts for the Northeast* appeared in *Arnoldia* 44:1–19 (1984) by Edward Goodell. He traces history, commercial production, biology, culture, cultivars and myriad additional facts. What is abundantly evident is the volume of information available on nut culture. Goodell mentions that over 500 *J. nigra* cultivars have been selected and named. 'Thomas' is the only one I see with any regularity in nursery catalogs.

ADDITIONAL NOTES: Seed of most *Juglans* species have a dormant embryo and the native species also have a hard outer wall. Dormancy can be broken by stratification at 41°F. The cultivars are grafted on seedling understocks.

Juglans cinerea — Butternut
(jū′glanz sin-ēr′ē-à)

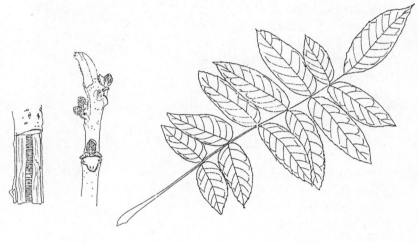

LEAVES: Alternate, pinnately compound, 10 to 20″ long, (7) 11 to 19 leaflets, each leaflet 2 to 5″ long, 3/4 to 2 1/4″ wide, oblong-lanceolate, acuminate, obliquely rounded, appressed-serrate, dark green and finely pubescent above, pubescent and glandular beneath, petiole and rachis covered with gland-type sticky hairs.

BUDS: Densely pale downy, terminal bud large-1/2 to 1″ long, flattened, oblong to conical, obliquely blunt-pointed; lateral buds smaller, ovate, rounded at apex, 1 to 3 superposed buds generally present above axillary bud.

STEM: Stout, reddish buff to greenish gray, pubescent or smooth, bitter to taste, coloring saliva yellow when chewed; pith — chocolate brown, chambered; leaf scar—large, conspicuous, 3-lobed, inversely triangular, upper margin generally convex, seldom slightly notched, surmounted by a raised, downy pad.

BARK: Ridged and furrowed, ridges whitish, furrows grayish black, inner bark becoming yellow on exposure to air, bitter.

Juglans cinerea, Butternut, reaches 40 to 60′ in height with a spread of 30 to 50′ although it can grow to 100′. The tree is usually round topped with a short, usually forked or crooked trunk and somewhat open, wide-spreading crown of large horizontal branches and stout, stiff branches; relatively slow growing as is true for most walnuts and hickories (excluding *J. nigra*); prefers moist, rich, deep soils of bottom lands although it grows quite well in drier, rocky soils, especially of limestone origin; the 1 1/2 to 2 1/2″ long tapered-oblong fruit is covered with gland tipped sticky hairs, the actual endocarp (hard portion) is 1 to 1 1/2″ long with a sharp point, the seeds are sweet, edible and very oily; the inner bark has mild cathartic properties and was used in older times as an orange or yellow dye. Native from New Brunswick to Georgia, and west to the Dakotas and Arkansas. Cultivated 1633. Zone 3 to 7. Ranges much further north and occurs at higher elevations than *J. nigra.*

Juglans nigra — Black Walnut
(jū′glanz nī′gra)

LEAVES: Alternate, pinnately compound, 12 to 24″ long, (11) 15 to 23 leaflets, the terminal one often missing, each leaflet 2 to 5″ long, 3/4 to 2″ wide, ovate-oblong to ovate-lanceolate, acuminate, rounded at base, irregularly serrate, at first minutely pubescent above, finally nearly glabrous and somewhat lustrous, dark green, pubescent and glandular beneath, leaves fragrant when crushed, petiole and rachis minutely downy.

BUDS: Pale silky-downy; terminal buds ovate, 1/3″ long, scarcely longer than broad; lateral buds smaller, often superposed, grayish.

STEM: Stout, densely gray-downy to smooth and reddish buff, bitter to taste and coloring saliva yellow when chewed; pith—buff, paler than that of Butternut, chambered; leaf scar-upper margin distinctly notched, no downy pad above leaf scar.

BARK: Dark brown to grayish black, divided by deep, narrow furrows into thin ridges, forming a roughly diamond shaped pattern.

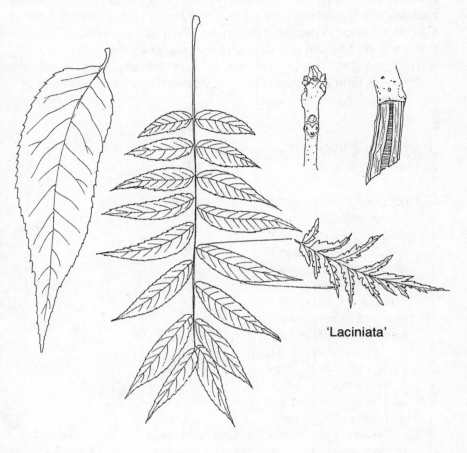

'Laciniata'

Juglans nigra, Black Walnut, is a large tree to 50 to 75′ in height and often a similar spread when open grown. The species may reach a maximum height of 125 to 150′. Usually develops a full, well formed trunk which is devoid of branches a considerable (1/2 to 2/3′s) distance from the ground; the crown is oval to rounded and somewhat open; prefers deep, rich, moist soils and here maximum growth occurs; tolerates drier soils but grows much more slowly under these conditions; develops an extensive taproot and is difficult to transplant; the globose glabrous light green nuts average 1 1/2 to 2″ thick, grainy surfaced, the sculptured wall (endocarp) is blackish and 1 to 1 1/2″ across; the wood is highly prized and has been used for cabinets, gunstocks and many furniture pieces. The wood is so valuable that "Walnut Rustlers" have developed sophisticated techniques to remove trees such as midnight operations and the use of helicopters. Tremendous call for walnut veneer and; hence, the high value placed on the tree. 'Laciniata' has leaflets that are finely dissected; makes a rather pretty tree. Native from Massachusetts to Florida and west to Minnesota and Texas. Cultivated 1686. Zone 4 to 9.

Juglans regia — Persian, Common, English Walnut
(jū′glanz rē′ji-à)

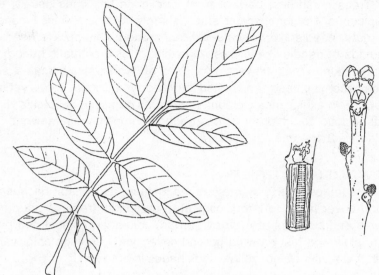

LEAVES: Alternate, pinnately compound, 5 to 9 leaflets, rarely to 13, 2 to 5″ long, elliptic to obovate, to oblong-ovate, acute or acuminate, entire, rarely and chiefly on young plants obscurely serrate, medium to dark green, glabrous except small axillary tufts of hairs beneath.

BUDS: Terminal—2 to 3-fold larger than lateral, 1/4 to 1/3″ long, valvate with scales barely overlapping, pubescent, brownish.

STEM: Stout, olive-brown when young, grayish on old branches; pith — uniformly chambered, brownish in color.

Juglans regia, Persian, Common, or English Walnut, is a tree which develops a rounded, often spreading and open crown ultimately reaching 40 to 60′ in height with a comparable or greater spread. Prefers a deep, dry, light loamy soil; does not do well in wet or poor subsoil areas; like most walnuts should be pruned in summer or fall; 1 1/2 to 2″ diameter nuts are edible, thin shelled and widely available in stores; actual seeds (with hard covering) abscise or are released from fleshy outer covering unlike the other walnuts mentioned here; they do not have the wild, nutty taste of *J. nigra* but are much easier to shell; there are many cultivars of this tree but two which are well adapted to cold conditions are 'Carpathian' which was brought to Canada from the mountains of Poland and supposedly bears heavy crops even when winter temperatures drop to -40°F, and; 'Hansen', an annual bearer, shells are very thick, easily shelled and the nut meats (seeds) are classed as excellent with the highest percent of kernel reported; the tree is located at Clay Center, Ohio, southeast of Toledo. This particular tree might make a nice ornamental because of quality characters where it can be grown. In addition several lobed or cut-leaf forms ('Heterophylla' and 'Laciniata') as well as a pendulous form ('Pendula'), are in cultivation. Native to southeastern Europe to Himalayas and China. Long cultivated.

Juniperus—Juniper
Cupressaceae

Junipers would have to rank as the toughest of evergreen landscape plants for they will grow and are used in all parts of the United States and, for that matter, the world. They include 50 to 70 species widely distributed throughout the temperate and subtropical regions of the Northern Hemisphere and south of the equator in Africa. Thirteen species are native to the United States. The majority of types used in landscape plantings are found in the species *J. chinensis, J. communis, J. horizontalis, J. sabina, J. scopulorum* and *J. virginiana,* with a few important cultivars found in *J. conferta, J. davurica, J. procumbens,* and *J. squamata.* For some strange reason the common name of *J. virginiana* is Eastern Redcedar with all other species known as junipers. The wood of the tree species is used for furniture (cedar chests), paneling, novelties, posts, poles, fuel, and pencils. The fleshy cones ("fruits") are used in medicine, varnish and for flavoring an alcoholic beverage known as gin.

MORPHOLOGICAL CHARACTERISTICS

Trees or shrubs; bark of trunk and main branches usually thin, shredding, rarely scaling; buds conspicuous, 1/8″ long, scales small, sharply pointed or buds inconspicuous and naked; leaves opposite or ternate, needle-like or scale-like, on young plants always needle-like, older plants have both forms, upperside of needle-like leaves with white or blue stomatic bands; male flowers united into an ovoid or oblong catkin, female flowers composed of 3 to 8 valvate scales, some or all bearing 1 to 2 ovules; the scales becoming fleshy and united into a berry-like cone; cones variously shaped, brown when young and covered with a thick mealy bloom, afterwards dark blue or blackish blue, ripening the second or third year; seeds elliptic to oblong, obtuse-ended, sometimes somewhat 3-angled in section, glossy brown; cotyledons 2 or 4 to 6.

GROWTH CHARACTERISTICS

It is impossible to stereotype the junipers as to habit because the species vary from low-growing, ground cover types to larger conical to pyramidal trees (*J. scopulorum* and *J. virginiana*). Among the species and cultivars are narrow, broad, columnar, conical and pyramidal; small and large spreading; globe, slow and fast growing ground cover types. Foliage color varies from lustrous dark green to light green, blue, silver-blue, yellow and shades in between.

CULTURE

Junipers are most successfully moved balled and burlapped or as container plants. In fact, most junipers are now grown in containers, especially the ground cover and shrubby types. They prefer open, sunny locations and light, sandy, low or high pH, moderately moist soils but will grow will in about any situation. They are very tolerant of dry, clay soils and some types will grow in sand. They exhibit good air pollution tolerance and will withstand the dirt and grime of cities as well as any conifer. They have been used as windbreaks with good success. Some types (*J. c.* var. *sargentii, J. conferta* and cultivars) show good salt tolerance. When junipers are located in heavy shade they become open, thin and ratty. Junipers withstand heavy pruning and for this reason make good hedges. A good rule of thumb is "if you cannot grow junipers, then do not bother planting anything else."

DISEASES AND INSECTS

Twig blight (*Phomopsis juniperovora*), cedar-apple rust, wilt, rocky mountain juniper aphid, bagworm, juniper midge, scale, webworm, redcedar bark beetle, and mites. Junipers have a number of very serious problems including blight (usually manifested in a tip dieback and sometimes whole plants are killed) and bagworm (so bad that plants are often completely stripped of foliage). *J. horizontalis* and cultivars (especially 'Plumosa'), *J. procumbens,* and *J. chinensis* 'San Jose' are especially susceptible to blight.

PROPAGATION

Seed and cutting propagation are adequately discussed under *J. chinensis.* Some cultivars are grafted on understocks of *J. virginiana, J. chinensis,* or *J. chinensis* 'Hetzii'. They are pot grafted using a side graft in February or March in the greenhouse.

LANDSCAPE VALUE

There is no limit to the use of junipers in landscape situations. They make excellent screens, hedges, windbreaks, ground covers, foundation plants, rock garden plants, groupings, and specimens. Because of their ease of culture and ubiquitous landscape value they are often overused almost to the point of monotony. Whole foundation plantings are often composed of nothing but junipers. Another problem is that consideration is seldom given to ultimate landscape size and in a few years plants have overgrown their boundaries. Many of the newer, smaller, better-foliaged types should be used in place of the cumbersome *J.c.* 'Pfitzeriana' and 'Hetzii'. Also it is important to consider the degree of shade in which the junipers will be grown. They can become "ratty" looking in a short time period if sited in heavy shade.

ADDITIONAL NOTES

A strong diuretic, oil of juniper, is extracted from juniper berries and these are also used in flavoring gin. The utilization of juniper berries in the making of gin dates back many centuries. British gin is prepared by distilling a fermenting mixture of maize, rye and malt. Then the resulting liquid is redistilled after juniper and sometimes coriander have been added.

Juniperus chinensis — Chinese Juniper
(jū-nip'ĕr-us chī-nen'sis)

LEAVES: Of 2 kinds, adult branches with the ultimate divisions about 1/25″ in diameter, clothed with 4 ranks of leaves in opposite pairs which are closely pressed, overlapping and rhombic in outline, 1/16″ long, blunt or bluntly pointed, the outer surface convex, green with a paler margin marked with a glandular depression on the back; juvenile leaves awl-shaped, 1/3″ long, spreading, in whorls of 3, or in opposite pairs, with a green midrib and 2 glaucous bands above, convex beneath, ending in a spiny point.

CONES: Dioecious, male is yellowish or brownish, numerous, usually borne on adult branchlets, occasionally on branchlets bearing juvenile foliage; female, ripening the second year, at first whitish blue, bloomy, when ripe brown, sub-globose or top-shaped, 1/3″ to on some forms 1/2″ in diameter, composed of 4 to 8 scales, seeds 2 to 5.

SIZE: Tree to 50 or 60′ in height, averages 15 to 20′ in spread, rarely represented in this country.

HARDINESS: Zone 3 to 9 depending on cultivar.

HABIT: Tree or shrub; most typically an erect, narrow, conical tree; sometimes very slender, sometimes bushy.

RATES: Slow to medium.

TEXTURE: Medium.

BARK: Gray-brown lightly ridged and furrowed, coming off in thin strips.

LEAF COLOR: Green to blue-green to grayish green.

FLOWERS: Dioecious, staminate flowers yellow-brown to orange-yellow, start to show color and shed pollen in March (Athens, GA), pistillate greenish, trees with flowers of both sexes occasionally occur.

FRUIT: Cones globose or oblong irregularly globose, 1/3″ across, at first whitish blue bloomy, when ripe dark brown, seeds oblong-obtuse or nearly 3-angled, glossy brown.

CULTURE: Trnasplant balled and burlapped or from a container; prefers moist, well drained conditions; full sun; pH adaptable, quite tolerant of calcareous soils.

DISEASES AND INSECTS: *Phomopsis* blight (kills young shoots, prevalent in early spring and wet weather); relatively trouble-free juniper.

LANDSCAPE VALUE: Depending on cultivar they can be used as a ground cover, foundation plant, hedge, screen, specimen, and mass planting.

CULTIVARS:

'Ames'—Initially grows as dwarf spreading shrub; with time develops a broad pyramidal shape 8 to 10′ high, steel blue foliage initially, turning green when mature, leaves needle-like; raised and introduced by T.J. Maney, Iowa State, Ames, Iowa, in 1948; other forms introduced by Professor Maney include 'Iowa', 'Maney' and 'Story'; a 14-year old plant was 9′ high and 4′ wide at the base; this is a female and I have seen a few cones, does not appear to cone heavily; originated from seed of *J. chinensis* var. *sargentii*.

'Angelica Blue'—Finer, brighter blue foliage than Blue Pfitzer, easier to propagate, introduced by Angelica Nurseries.

'Aquarius'—A branch sport of 'Hetzii' with blue-green foliage, compact habit, fills out more readily than 'Pfitzeriana Compacta', 4′ by 6′ after 19 years, a Lake County Nursery introduction.

'Arctic'—Bluish green needles cover this wide spreading form that grows 18 to 20″ high and 5 to 6′ across, considered to be hardier than most of the Pfitzeriana types.

'Armstrong'—Dwarf form to 3 to 4' high with an equal or greater spread, branches horizontally spreading, leaves are primarily scale-like and soft to the touch except at the base; bright green, hold color in cold weather; a branch sport of Pfitzer introduced by Armstrong Nurseries in 1932.

'Aurea'—Upright type with golden foliage, has a mixture of needle and scale-type foliage.

'Blaauw'—Foliage is a rich blue-green, dense growing, upright form, reminds me of a number of wide "V's" stacked upon each other, 4 to 6' high and wide (?); introduced from Japan by J. Blaauw and Company of Holland about 1924.

'Blue and Gold'—A strong upright-vase shaped form with blue and cream foliage intermixed, resembling 'Hetzii' in outline; probably 8 to 10' high and slightly less in spread, Raulston reports growth at 1 1/2' per year.

'Blue Cloud'— Large spreading ground cover type with dense blue-gray foliage.

'Blue Point'—Pyramidal form with a tear drop outline, extremely dense branching, blue-green, needle and scale-like foliage; listed as 7 to 8' tall but will grow larger.

'Blue Vase'—Vase-shaped form with good summer and winter foliage; supposedly intermediate between upright and spreading type; dense steel blue primarily scale-like foliage; moderate growth rate, 4 to 5' high, 3 to 4' wide; have seen 10 to 15' high plants in Georgia.

'Columnaris Glauca'—narrowly columnar, 24', loose in branching habit, needles awl-shaped, silvery-gray; 'Columnaris' is similar but has deep green foliage.

'Dropmore'—An extremely slow-growing form with a dense habit with extremely small (1/8" long) leaves, collected by F.L. Skinner, Dropmore, Manitoba.

'Fairview'—Narrow-pyramidal, vigorous growing, leaves mostly subulate, on some branches scale-like, bright green, silver berry-like structures (cones) during late summer and fall; rather handsome upright form.

'Fruitlandii'—Spreading form of vigorous growth, compact, dense with bright green foliage; actually an improved form of 'Pfitzeriana Compacta'; 3' by 6'.

'Globosa'—Apparently rare in cultivation; three forms, gray, green and gold, were imported from a Japanese nursery; true 'Globosa' is dense, rounded, symmetrical, light green, male, a 24-year-old plant was 6' by 7'.

'Globosa Cinerea'—Similar to 'Blaauw' but broader and less ragged; foliage in winter is gray-green rather than the blue-gray of 'Blaauw'.

'Gold Coast'— Graceful, compact, spreading form with golden yellow new growth that persists and deepens in cold weather, could be considered a refined, compact version of 'Pfitzeriana Aurea'; introduced by Monrovia Nursery, supposedly holds color better in winter than 'Old Gold'.

'Gold Sovereign'—A branch sport of 'Old Gold' with bright yellow foliage color year round, more compact and slow growing than 'Old Gold' (rate estimated as one-half), 16 to 20" by 24", a Bressingham Nursery introduction.

'Gold Star'—Compact form with light blue-green foliage accented by golden yellow branches, resistant to root problems, 4' by 6', Conard-Pyle introduction.

'Hetzii'—Large, rapid-growing, upright-spreading form, branches in all directions, 15' by 15' but usually less, leaves scale-like, glaucous, a few leaves awl-shaped; bears liberal quantities of small glaucous cones; typical landscape size approximates 5 to 10' high, found in a batch of seedlings from the West Coast before 1948; considered a hybrid between *J. virginiana* 'Glauca' and *J. chinensis* 'Pfitzeriana'; introduced by Hetz Nursery, Fairview, PA; roots easily from cuttings, transplants readily and is often used as an understock for grafting upright junipers.

'Hetzii Columnaris'—Upright pyramidal form, similar to 'Keteleeri' with scale and awl-shaped leaves; needles are bright green, 10 to 15' high, female with heavy cone production; has performed well in southeast.

'Hetzii Glauca'—Semi-erect form with light blue foliage; intermediate between the previous two, grows 5 to 7' high.

'Hills Blue'—Similar to 'Pfitzeriana Glauca' but making a lower, flatter plant.

'Iowa'—Forms a rather loose pyramid of blue-green foliage, it is more spreading and less compact than 'Ames' and more green in color; some fruiting; leaves awl-shaped and scale-like; 13 year old plant was 10' by 4'.

'Kaizuka' ('Torulosa')—Hollywood Juniper; this form is appropriately named for it belongs in California and I have seen it used in abundance in that state; leaves scale-like, vivid green, female, branches slightly twisted resulting in a Japanese effect; can be grown as a shrub or tree; will grow 20 to 30' high; excellent heat and salt tolerance, used widely in the southeast; a blue-green foliage form and a variegated form with rather bold creamy white markings are available in commerce.

'Kallays Compacta'—Another compact form of Pfitzer; deep green leaves and a preponderance of juvenile foliage; a rather flat-topped form growing 2 to 3' high and up to 6' wide; originated at Kallay Nursery, Painesville, Ohio.

'Keteleeri'—Broadly pyramidal tree with a stiff trunk and loose, light to medium green foliage, leaves scale-like, very pointed, cones with a recurved stalk, globose, 1/2 to 3/5" across, initially grayish green, finally glossy light green; has been a popular form over the years and is common in midwestern landscapes, 15 to 20'.

'Kohankies Compact'—A dense, globose sport of Pfitzer that originated at the old Kohankie Nursery, Painesville, Ohio; not common in cultivation.

'Kuriwao Gold'—Upright reasonably thick branched, bright green needles with golden midrib, foliage effect from a distance is gold-green, forms an upright fat teardrop shape, airy texture, 4 to 5' high and 3' wide.

'Kuriwao Mist'—Open pyramidal form with creamy silver to golden gray-green foliage.

'Kuriwao Sunburst'—Open pyramidal shape, soft green foliage, tipped bright green to yellow.

'Maney'—Bushy, semi-erect form, as broad as high, leaves acicular, bluish, bloomy, reports from Minnesota indicate it grows about 6' high and wide, one of the best for cold climates, female, 7' high by 12' wide after 13 years.

'Mathot'—Similar to 'Kallays Compacta' in habit, but dense, juvenile leaves in pairs about 1/3" long with bluish green band above, green below, the upper surface is turned out giving a general glaucous appearance; originated at Mathot Nursery, Holland 1940.

'Milky Way'—Fast growing, low-spreading form, 3 to 4' high, dark green foliage with stippled markings of cream.

'Mint Julep'—Compact grower with arching branches creating a low fountain-like form, foliage is a brilliant mint green; actually looks like a very green, compact Pfitzer; introduced by Monrovia around 1971, 4 to 6' high, greater spread.

'Mordigan'—Dark green foliage, taller and more blocky than Pfitzer, 7' by 5'; a golden foliage form, 'Mordigan Aurea', is known.

'Mountbatten'—Dense, pyramidal, narrow form to 12', similar to *J. communis* 'Hibernica'; foliage grayish green, most acicular.

'Nick's Compact'—A relatively flat-topped, wide spreading form with green, slight blue overcast foliage, more needle than scale-like foliage, grew 2 1/2' by 6' in eight years, a male, same as 'Pfitzeriana Compacta'?

'Obelisk'—Forms a narrow pyramid about 8 to 10' high, leaves juvenile with sharp apices, glaucous gray foliage; introduced by F.J. Grootendorst and Sons.

'Old Gold'—Similar to Pfitzer only more compact, foliage bronze-gold, permeating the plant; color is retained through winter; a branch sport of 'Armstrong'? a Grootendorst introduction, 3' by 4'.

'Pfitzeriana ('Pfitzerana' in *Hortus III*)—The granddaddy of juniper cultivars; probably the most widely planted juniper, wide spreading, variable form, usually listed as growing about 5' high and 10' wide, actually can grow larger than these values; foliage scale-like and awl-shaped, bright green, original plant was a male; main branches emerge at a 45° angle and the young shoots show a slight pendulous tendency; much more handsome in youth, often becoming ragged with age; interestingly this cultivar does well in the north (-25°F) and in the mid to deep south; named by Späth for his friend W. Pfitzer. As I travel through Europe, specimens of Pfitzer approaching 10' high and 20 to 25' wide appear, the Morton Arboretum listed a 26-year-old plant that was 5' by 20'; Nordine, *PIPPS* 12:122 (1962) listed 12 clones (branch sports) of 'Pfitzeriana'.

'Pfitzeriana Aurea'—Similar to Pfitzer in growth but flatter and not as large, branchlets and leaves tinged golden yellow in summer, becoming yellowish green in winter; only the young shoots are gold tinged, the body of the plant is green; I find this a rather attractive form that is not as obtrusive as some of the flagrantly yellow forms; branches emerge at a 30° angle compared to the 45° angle of Pfitzer.

'Pfitzeriana Compacta'—Bushy, compact, with greater proportion of awl-shaped leaves, grows 12 to 18″ high and up to 6′ across, the white upper surface of the needles gives an overall gray-green cast to the plant; grew 4′ by 4′ in 12 years, introduced by Bobbink and Atkins Nursery, Rutherford, N.J.

'Pfitzeriana Glauca' ('Blue Pfitzer')—Possibly more dense than Pfitzer with mixed leaves, markedly blue in older plants, becoming slightly purplish blue in winter; more prickly than 'Hetzii'; a male, handsome bluish foliage through the seasons in warmer climates, similar to Pfitzer in general growth characteristics.

'Pfitzeriana Moraine'—Green with blue cast, sharp needled form, 1 1/2′ by 5 to 6′ in 8 years; male.

'Pfitzeriana Nelson's Compact'—Dusty blue-green foliage, grew 3′ by 5′ in 5 years.

'Pfitzeriana Owens'—Compact low growing, 3 to 4′ high, mixture of juvenile and adult foliage, similar to 'Ozark Compact' but slightly hardier.

'Pfitzeriana Plumosa'—Spreading type with bluish green needles, 4′ by 8′ in 4 years, male.

'Plumosa'—Leaves mainly scale-like, deep green, male, however 'Hasselkus' noted it was female, 3 to 4′ high, broad spreading with short dense drooping branches; 'Plumosa Albovariegata' is peppered with creamy-white markings; 'Plumosa Aurea' has yellow-green growth that becomes more pronounced through the season and culminates in golden bronze during winter, more upright and stiff in outline; 'Plumosa Aureovariegata' is marked with deep yellow among the deep green foliage, another report indicated a mixture of scale and needle-like foliage that turns from light green to yellow to bronze-green in winter, habit is open and irregular with some branches completely needle-like; plant tends to have a one-sided development.

'Pyramidalis'—Male, dense columnar form with ascending branches, leaves acicular, bluish green, very pungent, often sold as *J. excelsa* 'Stricta'; not particularly handsome; there appear to be several clones with this designation.

'Ramlosa'—Spreading vase shape, similar to Pfitzer with feathery dark green foliage.

'Robusta Green'—Upright form with tufted brilliant green foliage; actually a rather handsome, somewhat irregular form; have seen plants about 15′ high, female, sets abundant cones.

'San Jose'—Creeping form, 12 to 18″ (24″) high and 6 to 8′ wide, spreads irregularly; foliage sage green, young plants tend to be acicular but with maturity there is a mixture of scale and needle-like foliages, quite susceptible to juniper blight but in the Georgia Botanical Garden it has thrived on a dry bank; introduced by W.B. Clarke, San Jose, California in 1935; sometimes confused with *J. davurica* 'Parsoni' but that form has more scale-like foliage.

'Sarcoxie'—Dense compact, low spreading form of Pfitzer, listed as Ozark Compact Pfitzer Juniper by Greenleaf Nursery.

var. *sargentii*—One of the best and by some treated as a species. I am in no position to argue and will stay with the format of the previous edition; low growing (18″ to 2′ high), wide spreading (7.5 to 9′ wide), branchlets 4-angled, leaves mostly scale-like in 3's, small, slightly grooved on back, blue-green, bloomy; cones blue, scarcely bloomy; seeds 3; resistant to juniper blight; branches have a whip-like appearance; discovered by C.S. Sargent on the coast of the North Island of Japan (Hokkaido) in 1892; found on seashores throughout Japan and on rocky cliffs in the mountains.

var. *sargentii* 'Compacta'—More compact than above with scale-like leaves light green, acicular leaves dark green, with very glaucous green top, margins bounded by a dark green edge.

var. *sargentii* 'Glauca'—Dwarf, much better in growth than 'Compacta'; branchlets thin, feathery, leaves blue-green, 1 1/2′ by 6′.

var. *sargentii* 'Viridis'—Similar to var. *sargentii* but leaves light green year round.

'Saybrook Gold'—Considered the brightest gold foliaged *J. chinensis* type, primarily needle-like foliage, foliage bright yellow in summer, more bronze-yellow in winter, horizontal spreading type probably 2 to 3′ high by 6′ wide, Girard Nursery introduction.

'Sea Green'—Compact spreader with fountain-like, arching branches, dark green (mint green) foliage; 4 to 6' high, 6 to 8' wide; good looking form, more upright than 'Pfitzeriana', foliage darkens in cold weather.

'Sea Spray'—According to Hines Nursery who introduced the shrub it is a better ground cover than 'Blue Rug', 'Bar Harbor' or var. *tamariscifolia;* grows 12 to 15" high and 6' wide, blue-green relatively soft-textured foliage; center branches stay full and dense; resistant to water molds, root rot and juniper blight; hardy to –20°F; a sport of 'Pfitzeriana Glauca', introduced in 1972; I like what I have seen to date.

'Shoosmith'—A dwarf, compact, globose or pyramidal form.

'Spartan'—A fast, dense grower of tall, pyramidal or columnar habit, of rich green color and very handsome appearance, a Monrovia introduction, may grow to 20' high.

'Spearmint'—Dense columnar-pyramidal habit to 15', 3 to 4' wide, bright green foliage color, soft, predominantly scale-like foliage.

'Story'—Upright and slender symmetrical small tree with horizontal branching and dark green foliage; a Maney introduction, 12' by 3' after 13 years; male.

'Stricta'—In youth somewhat flattened and conical with all juvenile blue-gray foliage, distinctly prickly; has the untidy habit of holding onto its foliage for several years, not a good plant.

'Sulphur Spray'—Semi-prostrate habit, soft light green foliage with white tips giving silvery appearance overall.

'Variegata'—Conical form, slow growing, juvenile and adult blue green leaves, irregularly splashed with creamy white.

'Viridis'—Pyramidal, teardrop shape in outline, dense branching, gray green foliage.

'Wintergreen'—Pyramidal, dense, rich green foliage.

PROPAGATION: Invaluable needle evergreens displaying cosmopolitan personalities that allow them to survive where other landscape plants succumb. Most are dioecious or occasionally monoecious trees, shrubs, or ground covers that "flower" in spring with the berry-like cones ripening the first or second (occasionally third) season. Each cone contains 1 to 4, to 12 seeds. Collect ripened fruits in late fall or winter, clean by maceration, dry seeds and store in sealed containers under refrigeration.

An expanded discussion of juniper propagation is necessary because of their importance to the nursery industry and the tremendous volume of literature. Simply stated, there is no ubiquitous recipe for all junipers. Some root easily; others with difficulty. Many upright types must be grafted. Cutting propagation is broken down by category.

CONDITION OF STOCK PLANT: A vigorous, healthy plant is superior to an overgrown plant that has been setting for 10 years unattended in a corner of the nursery. Major growers stress that cuttings taken from their container grown plants are superior. They root in higher percentages and have better root systems.

TIMING: Generally, cuttings should be taken after several hard frosts or freezes. Major container juniper growers take cuttings in December to March. References point to any time from July through April. The data presented for summer rooting indicated that percentages were not as high as for late fall-winter rooting. It is truly a mixed bag as far as timing is concerned. November through February is considered optimum. Cuttings of *J. horizontalis* 'Plumosa' rooted 65% in August, 52% in September, 91% in October, 100% in December, 96% in February, 33% in April and 2% in June. A large grower noted that the best time to take cuttings from a physiological standpoint was when they had stopped growing. In one study, junipers were rooted year-round but best rooting occurred between November and December with 4000 ppm IBA-dip. *J. chinensis, J. communis, J. horizontalis, J. sabina* and *J. squamata* were easier to root than *J. scopulorum* and *J. virginiana.*

HORMONE: The standard recommendation throughout the literature is 3000 ppm IBA-solution or talc for easy-to-root types, 8000 IBA-solution or no hormone to 4.5% IBA-talc. Based on published data, a hormone definitely serves to improve rooting. The following hormones and concentrations are used by the largest and most successful juniper growers in the world; 600 to 5000 ppm IBA-solution; 3000, 8000, 3.0%, 4.5% IBA talc or 2000 ppm IBA + 1000 ppm NAA-solution; 5000 ppm IBA-solution; 1870 ppm to 1.0% IBA-solution; 1.6% IBA-talc; 3000 to 8000 ppm

IBA-talc; 3.0 to 4.5% IBA-talc. About all this indicates is that everyone does it differently. Virtually all nuerserymen/researchers agree that a hormone is beneficial. The reason for the disparity of rates is that easy-to-root types like *J. horizontalis* would be treated with a low hormone concentration, difficult-to-root types like 'Maneyi,' 'Blaauw', *J. virginiana* cultivars, etc., with higher levels. There are several reports that indicate greener cuttings (July–August) require greater hormone concentrations than those taken later.

Senior author has observed alcohol burn on juniper cuttings, especially those taken in summer or early fall, although damage (basal burn) has occurred on *J. conferta* (one of the most susceptible) in January through March. A study [*The Plant Propagator* 29(2):8–10 (1983)] with *J. chinensis* 'Hetzii' confirmed and quantified this observation, 5000 ppm to 2.0% IBA in 50% ethanol or prolonged exposure to 50% ethanol (2 minutes) caused basal end necrosis (burning) and reduced rooting. KIBA (water soluble formulation) at similar IBA concentrations and exposure times did not damage cuttings and resulted in slight increases in percent and number of roots. Rooting ranged from a low of 18% (1250 ppm IBA in 50% ethanol-2 minute dip) to 86% (5000 ppm KIBA-water-2 minute dip).

CUTTINGS: SIZE/CONDITION/WOUNDING/BOTTOM HEAT/ROOTING TIME: Four to 6″ long cuttings with a tinge of brown (mature) wood seem to be preferred. If actively growing July–August cuttings are taken this type of wood is not possible. Cuttings are stripped one-third to one-half. This, in effect, provides a wound which appears to assist in juniper rooting. In general, stockier, larger cuttings root better than small spindly ones. Bottom heat (66 to 68°F) is used by some growers and not by others. It should be advantageous if cuttings are rooted outside in cold frames or poly houses in ground beds where the air temperature is rather cool. Rooting time varies from 6 to 8 weeks to 12 weeks and possibly longer. I have noticed that *J. conferta* (January, February, March) rooted quickly and appeared to require less heat than other conifers. In a controlled study using outdoor ground beds with and without bottom heat with two media (bark or peat: perlite), *J. conferta* rooted under all conditions (better and faster with bottom heat) while Leyland Cypress in the non-heated frames did nothing (not even callus). It may be that junipers have a lower heat requirement for the root initiation process to proceed.

I worked for a nurseryman during college who took all his juniper cuttings in the late summer, provided IBA-talc treatment, sand, on a shaded greenhouse bench, syringed when needed and waited patiently for 3 to 5 months for rooting. He had good success with a wide range of junipers.

MEDIUM: The choice of media is about like the hormone rate . . . variable. Sand, sand: peat, bark, sandy soil, peat: perlite, vermiculite, etc., have been used successfully. In a comparative study, vermiculite, sand: peat, soil: peat: perlite proved better than sand or German peat.

WATER/SANITATION: Mist in summer months with hand syringing or controlled mist in fall-winter months. Observations indicate junipers do not require a great amount of water during the rooting process. Keep medium moist, but not wet. Do not leave a continual film of moisture on cuttings. Water tends to bead in axils of the needles and the opportunity for fungal invasion (*Phomopsis*) is excellent. Some growers dip all the cuttings in a Benlate-Captan solution before preparing them for rooting. Again, it is a mixed bag as far as those that do and don't. The large growers practice preventative medicine.

AFTERCARE: Cuttings can be rooted in place and allowed to go through the winter and transplanted into containers in spring. The better the root system, the more successful the transplanting. Junipers present no special problems as far as aftercare. Proper cultivation and fertility practices yield a high quality juniper.

GRAFTING: Many upright forms of *J. chinensis, J. virginiana* and *J. scopulorum* are grafted because they do not root easily. Choice of understock has been argued for 40 years in the Plant Propagator's Proceedings with *Juniperus chinensis* 'Hetzii' the clear leader followed by seedling *J. virginiana,* the cultivar 'Skyrocket' and a strange juniper called *J. pseudocupressus.* A large nursery noted 'Sky Rocket' was an excellent understock because it is straighter and more graftable and resists fungal diseases better than 'Hetzii' and *J. virginiana.* 'Hetzii' or 'Hetz Columnaris', however, are the most popular. Understocks should be 1/4 to 1/3″ diameter, cleaned 3 to 4″ from soil of needles, etc., tops evened up. Process can run from December–

February. The potted understock is brought inside and evidence of root growth is a signal to start. Understocks are sprayed with a fungicide prior to grafting. Scionwood is collected (like cutting wood) from vigorous stock plants, is 5 to 6″ long with 1 to 2″ brown wood at base, lower 2″ are cleaned, soft growth at top is removed, scions dipped in fungicidal solution, side-grafted, wrapped and allowed to heal in greenhouse bench, 25% of grafts are healed in 2 weeks, most are healed after 5 to 6 weeks. Watch for new growth on scion as an index to successful healing, Grafts can be placed under shade or moved to containers for growing on.

ADDITIONAL NOTES: The species is almost an unknown entity under cultivation but is adequately represented by the numerous cultivars which vary in size from prostrate, spreading types to upright tree forms. P.J. Van Melle, an American nurseryman, has an interesting hypothesis concerning the numerous cultivars of *J. chinensis.* He says that the original species *J. chinensis* L. was inadequately defined by Linnaeus and that certain true varieties within *J. chinensis* should have been listed as species. He also noted that numerous natural and garden hybrids have occurred between *J. c.* and *J. sabina* all of which are listed under *J. c.* Mr. Van Melle stated that the name *J. chinensis* has come to include "everything but the kitchen stove—a loose aggregate, incapable of definition in terms of a species". He proposed to limit the use of *J. chinensis,* to resuscitate *J. sphaerica* and to raise *J. sheppardii* to specific status. He also proposed a new hybrid species, *J.* × *media,* to contain all the more or less bush-like forms in which *J. sabina* was discernible by the characteristic savin odor of the bruised foliage. He relegated *J. chinensis* var. *sargentii* to species level, *J. sargentii.* Van Melle did a considerable amount of study but his work has not been fully accepted by the botanical world. One taxonomist said that "Van Melle is probably right, but a lot more work will have to be done on these junipers before we can accept all he says—it will mean scrapping so much in all the books."

Anyone who has taken a close look and smell of the *J. c.* cultivars will see some truth in Van Melle's hypothesis. In recent years, more literature is including many of the spreading cultivars in the *J.* × *media* category.

NATIVE HABITAT: China, Mongolia and Japan. Introduced 1767.

Juniperus communis — Common Juniper
(jū -nip′ĕr-us kom-mū′nis)

LEAVES: Awl-shaped, persisting for 3 years, tapering from the base to a spiny point, sessile, spreading at a wide angle from stem, about 3/5″ long, concave above with a broad white band, sometimes divided by a green midrib at the base, bluntly keeled below, needles consistently ternate.

BRANCHLETS: Triangular with projecting ridges, the leaves in whorls of 3.

CONES: Usually dioecious, male solitary, cylindrical, 1/3″ long, yellow stamens in 5 to 6 whorls. Female, solitary, 1/2″ long, ripening the second or third year, green when young, bluish or black when ripe, covered with a waxy bloom; globose or slightly longer than broad, 1/3 to 1/2″ diameter with 3 minute points at the top, the 3 scales of which the fruit is composed usually gaping and exposing the seeds; seeds, 2 to 3, elongated, ovoid, 3-cornered, with depressions between.

SIZE: 5 to 10′ (rarely to 15′, known to 40′) by 8 to 12′ spread.

HARDINESS: Zone 2 to 6 (7); does not do well in deep south.

HABIT: A medium-sized tree with ascending and spreading branches or more often a much-branched, sprawling shrub; prostrate in some forms.

RATE: Slow.

TEXTURE: Medium.

BARK: Reddish brown, scaling off in papery sheets.

LEAF COLOR: Green-gray to blue-green in summer; often assuming a yellow or brownish green in winter, often discolors worse than *J. chinensis* forms.

FLOWERS: Dioecious; staminate yellow.

FRUIT: Cones sessile or short-stalked, globose or broadly ovoid, 1/3 to 1/2″ across, bluish black or black, glaucous bloomy, ripening the second or third season; seeds usually 3, elongated ovoid, tri-cornered with depressions between; fruits used as diuretic, flavoring of gin.

CULTURE: Transplants readily; grows on the worst possible land, common on dry, sterile soils, rock outcroppings and waste lands; withstands wind; tolerant of calcareous soils, will tolerate neutral or acid soils; extremely hardy; full sun; amazing in its adaptability to diverse soil and climatic conditions. Not as heat tolerant as *J. chinensis, J. conferta, J. davurica, J. horizontalis* and *J. virginiana.*

DISEASES AND INSECTS: Susceptible to juniper blight and other problems mentioned on the culture sheet.

LANDSCAPE VALUE: Can be handsome ground cover for sandy soils and waste places, useful for undergrowth and naturalized plantings; best represented in the landscape by the cultivars; used in European gardens to some degree and the northern United States, is adaptable to heat and possibly heavy clay and poorly drained soils; also the competition from the major landscape species is intense and under aesthetic scrutinization, *J. communis* often does not measure up.

CULTIVARS:
'Compressa'—Dwarf, cone-shaped form, dense, very slow growing, 2 to 3′ tall, leaves awl-shaped, thin, with a conspicuous silvery band above, margin narrow, green, dark green beneath.

'Depressa'—Dwarf, broad, low, vase-shaped, essentially prostrate shrub, rarely above 4′ high, glaucous band on upper surface with green margin; although listed as a cultivar in many collections it should properly be variety *depressa;* as such it represents the eastern North American segment of *J. communis;* it occurs in the most inhospitable soils including dry, sandy, stony or gravelly; extremely vigorous and hardy; tends to discolor (brown) in winter months.

'Depressa Aurea'—Yellow foliaged form, new shoots strongly colored, fading with time, otherwise similar to above, rather depressing especially in winter.

'Effusa'—A wide spreading low ground cover with rich green color on the lower needle surface, silvery band above, holds color during winter, 9 to 12″ (18″) by 4 to 6′, similar to 'Repanda' but winter color is inferior and habit is more open.

'Gold Beach'—Excellent dwarf form with green foliage, 5 year-old plants are 5″ tall and 2′ across; in early spring, new growth is yellow, later turning green.

'Gold Cone'—Narrow form of slow growth with golden yellow foliage color.

'Golden Shower'—Upright bushy pyramidal form with bright golden yellow new shoots; foliage becomes bronze-yellow during cold weather.

'Green Carpet'—Ground cover form with bright green new growth that matures to dark green, 4 to 6″ high by 2 1/2 to 3′ wide.

'Hibernica'—Dense, upright in habit, can grow 10 to 15′ high, foliage bluish white to near the apex above, margin narrow, green, bluish green beneath; a poor plant in American gardens; called Irish Juniper.

'Hornibrookii'—Low growing (12 to 20″) ground cover with short (1/4″ long) sharp needles, silver white broad band above, green and keeled below, appears rich silver-green in summer, losing its luster in winter and becoming brownish; branches lie flat on ground in youth, discovered in 1923 by Murray Hornibrook in County Galway, West Ireland.

'Repanda'—A low growing form that maintains the best foliage color of the low growing types; medium green foliage turning yellowish green in winter, grows to 15″ high, the soft, coarse-textured foliage is densely set on slightly ascending branches, nodding at the tips, plants form nearly uniform circles.

'Sentinel'—A narrow columnar form with rich green foliage that will mature between 5 and 10′.

'Suecica'—Similar to 'Hibernica' except the tops of the branchlets droop; leaves bluish green, about as lousy as above; listed as Swedish Juniper.

PROPAGATION: Refer to *J. chinensis.*

ADDITIONAL NOTES: The oil distilled from the fleshy cones ("berries") is used for medicinal and flavoring purposes (gin). There are numerous varieties and cultivars of this species none of which compete effectively with the *J. chinensis, J. horizontalis* and *J. virginiana* types. For those who want in depth information see Den Ouden and Boom, Jackson and Dallimore and Welch (1979). I was wandering around on a 6600′ high mountain a short distance from Lucerne, Switzerland when what do I see but patches of *Juniperus communis*. Two things in life are inescapable: taxes and *J. communis*. Variety *montana* (var. *nana,* var. *saxatilis*) is the prostrate, often mat forming type from which numerous selections have been made.

NATIVE HABITAT: *J. communis* has a wider distribution than any other tree or shrub; common in north and central Europe and also occurs in the mountains of the countries bordering on the Mediterranean. it is also found in Asia Minor, the Caucasus, Iran, Afghanistan, the western Himalaya, the United States and Canada. In the United States it occurs from New England to Pennsylvania and North Carolina. I have seen old farmland in Massachusetts completely overgrown with this species and the range of forms seemed infinite. One could select cultivars until the cows came home. The whole point is that with junipers we have reached a cultivar glut and the addition of more only compounds and confuses the issue.

Juniperus conferta — Shore Juniper
(jū-nip′ĕr-us kon-fĕr′tà)

LEAVES: Crowded, overlapping, awl-shaped, 1/4 to 5/8″ long, 1/16″ wide, ternate, glaucous green, tapering to a prickly point, deeply grooved above with one band of stomata, convex below and green.

CONES: Produced in abundance, globose, 1/3 to 1/2″ diameter, dark blue or bluish black, bloomy at maturity and appearing silvery; seeds, 3, 3-angled, ovate, with longitudinal grooves on back, acuminate.

SIZE: 1 to 1 1/2′ (2′) in height by 6 to 9′ spread.

HARDINESS: Zone (5)6 to 9, widely planted in southern states; temperature below -10°F may result in injury; Schneider and Hasselkus, *Amer. Nurseryman* 158(2):38–59 (1983) reported severe burn and dieback at the University of Minnesota Landscape Arboretum.

HABIT: Dense, bushy, procumbent evergreen shrub.

RATE: Slow.

TEXTURE: Medium.

LEAF COLOR: Bright bluish green in summer, often bronze-green or somewhat yellow-green in winter.

FLOWERS: Dioecious, inconspicuous.

FRUIT: Cones subglobose, flat at base, 1/3 to 1/2″ across, dark blue or bluish black, bloomy at maturity; seeds, 3, 3-angled, ovate, with longitudinal grooves on back, acuminate.

CULTURE: Tolerant of poor soils, especially adapted to plantings in sandy soils of the seashore; full sun; does not tolerate excess soil moisture, will develop dieback in exceedingly moist situations.

DISEASES AND INSECTS: I have noticed a fair amount of dieback in large scale plantings in the south; there are numerous ground cover plantings on the Georgia campus and some have had to be removed because of the persistent dieback; plants in extremely heavy, water-logged soils seem to languish.

LANDSCAPE VALUE: A low ground cover, especially adapted for planting on sand dunes in the seashore area; actually one of the handsomest of the ground cover type junipers; good in mass, on banks, in planter boxes, around tall shrubs or trees; lovely draped over a wall; my years in the southern states have brought me a greater appreciation of the species and particularly the cultivars; on Jekyll Island, GA plants grow on a barrier sand mound exposed to the Atlantic Ocean yet have increased in size and actually prospered over the 11 years I have observed them; the species and cultivars grow quite well in clay soils *as long as* drainage is adequate but thrive in well drained situations; a landscape architect mentioned to me that the species and 'Blue Pacific' are more shade tolerant than the other junipers.

CULTIVARS:

'Blue Pacific'—Low trailing habit and ocean blue-green foliage color; distinctly different than the species and making a better ground cover; probably never grows more than 1′ high; appears to be hardier than the species; literature describes it as growing 2′ high but I have never seen plants this tall; needles shorter and more densely borne (spaced) along the stem than with the species or 'Emerald Sea'; the foliage color is superior to species or any other cultivar that I know; does not discolor as badly as the species in cold weather but loses some of the bluish sheen, considered hardier than the species but less hardy than 'Emerald Sea'.

'Blue Tosho'—A silver-green foliage form growing 1 1/2' by 4'.

'Boulevard'—Glaucous green foliage, a prostrate grower with all the main branches growing horizontally.

'Compacta'—Young plants prostrate, needles and branches closely spaced, needle color light green; stomatal band not so apparent on older growth because of needle color and horizontal growth pattern.

'Emerald Sea'—A National Arboretum introduction with good salt tolerance and a dense, low prostrate habit; abundant confusion about this plant but with a plant in my garden for the past two years the differences are evident; the foliage is akin to the species and not as blue as 'Blue Pacific', habit is larger and ultimate size will exceed 1', reports indicate 1 to 2' by 8 to 10' is possible; foliage color dulls slightly in winter but not to the degree of the species, needles are more loosely borne than 'Blue Pacific', considered hardier than the species or 'Blue Pacific' and without snow cover at least to -10°F or lower; will grow faster than 'Blue Pacific'.

'Silver Mist'—Raulston has promoted this handsome silver blue-green foliaged form that is more compact and dense than the species, summer foliage color is outstanding with needles developing a slight purplish cast in winter, could be the next major ground cover juniper cultivar in the southeast if adaptable.

PROPAGATION: Refer to *J. chinensis*.

ADDITIONAL NOTES: A fine juniper but like many good plants over-used and abused, especially in the southern states; has been widely used on the Georgia campus to the point of monotony.

NATIVE HABITAT: Found on the sea costs of Japan, especially on the sand dunes of Hakodate Bay in Hokkaido. Introduced 1915.

Juniperus horizontalis — Creeping Juniper
(jū-nip'ĕr-us hôr-i-zon-tā'lis)

LEAVES: Conspicuously glaucous, soft textured, almost feathery, of 2 kinds, mostly scale-like, about 1/6" long, closely appressed, in 4 ranks, ovate to oblong, shortly pointed, each with a glandular depression on the back, the awl-shaped leaves in opposite pairs; foliage usually turning a plum-purple color in winter, foliage has a plume-like texture.

CONES: On recurved stalks, bluish or greenish black, 1/4 to 3/4" long, seeds, 2 to 3.

SIZE: 1 to 2' high by 4 to 8' spread, variable but definitely low growing, spreading type.

HARDINESS: Zone 3 to 9.

HABIT: Low growing, procumbent shrub with long, trailing branches forming large mats.

RATE: Slow to medium may grow to a diameter of 10' over a 10 year period.

TEXTURE: Medium-fine.

LEAF COLOR: Green, glaucous, bluish green or steel-blue turning plum-purple in winter.

FLOWERS: Dioecious, inconspicuous.

FRUITS: Cones on recurved stalks, about 1/3" across, blue, slightly glaucous; seeds 2 to 3; seldom produced on cultivated plants.

CULTURE: Adaptable, withstands hot dry situations and slightly alkaline soils, seems to transplant readily, tolerant of heavy soils, native to sandy and rocky soils and exposed situations; found on sea cliffs, gravelly slopes and in swamps.

DISEASES AND INSECTS: *Phomopsis* blight (Juniper blight) can be extremely serious, spider mites.

LANDSCAPE VALUE: A low ground cover valued for its adaptability in sandy and rocky soils as well as tolerating hot, dry, sunny locations; used for slope plantings and facer evergreens, ground covers, masses, foundations and in containers; probably the most popular ground cover type.

CULTIVARS:

'Admirabilis'—A bluish green needle form that grows about 8″ to 1′ high and 8 to 10′ wide, the main branches are prostrate with the secondary branches and branchlets borne at a steep angle, primarily juvenile foliage but some scalelike, male, introduced by Plumfield Nurseries in 1953, turns darker green with purplish tips in winter.

'Adpressa'—Another Plumfield introduction, very dense and prostrate, seldom growing more than 10″ high, foliage green with tips glaucous green.

'Alberta'—Looks like 'Prince of Wales', 6″ high, medium green foliage turns bronzy green in summer, prostrate and dense habit.

'Alpina'—Dwarf creeping form, 2′ by 5′, leaves exclusively awl-shaped, bluish or gray-blue, changing to dull purple in autumn; highly susceptible to twig blight.

'Argenteus'—Blue foliage with whip-cord branches, 18″ high.

'Banff'—Bright silver-blue-green foliage, grows 6″ by 2 to 3′, not as vigorous as some types.

'Bar Harbor'—Low growing, spreading form, 1′ by 6 to 8′, leaves chiefly awl-shaped, loosely appressed, bluish green, turning more purple in the winter; probably a number of clones have been introduced under this name; comes from Mt. Desert Island, Maine, where it grows in crevices on the rocky coast and is frequently found within reach of the salt spray; in the best form(s), it makes a fine ground cover usually less than 12″ high; sometimes confused with 'Blue Rug' but 'Blue Rug' is female with more scale-like foliage, typical 'Bar Harbor' is male and turns more reddish purple than 'Blue Rug'; apparently more than one clone in cultivation since male and female forms are known.

'Blue Acres'—New foliage blue, blue-green with age, prostrate spreader, Sheridan Nursery introduction, 4″, female.

'Blue Chip'—Selected by Hill Nursery Co. for low prostrate habit and excellent blue foliage color in summer, tipped purplish in winter, 8 to 10″ high and 8 to 10′ wide with vertical branchlets arranged in rows; Welch mentions that it was raised from seed by the Jensen Nursery, Denmark in 1940; whether Hill's received it from Jensen is unknown; it is a tremendously handsome blue-foliaged form; I have seen it as late as August in Kentucky and the foliage was still a good blue. I rooted cuttings and brought a plant to Georgia where, unfortunately, it is not performing as well as in more northerly areas, not as prosperous in Zone 8 and 9 as further north.

'Blue Horizon'—Similar to 'Wiltonii' except it remains low and open, never mounding up in the center, male, blue-green turning bronze-green in winter.

'Blue Mat'—Dense, slow growing, 6″ high, prostrate type, with blue-green foliage, turns dark purplish green in winter.

'Coast of Maine'—Scaly blue-green foliage turns light purple in winter, male, vigorous, plant appears to open in center.

'Douglasii' ('Waukegan')—Trailing form, 1 to 1 1/2′ by 6 to 9′, steel blue foliage turning grayish purple through the winter; rapid growing form, introduced by Douglas Nursery, Waukegan, IL about 1855; good choice for sandy soils.

'Dunvegan Blue'—Low spreading form with a bright bluish green color that turns light purple in winter; also described as having silvery-blue color; introduced by Beaver Lodge Nursery, Alberta, Canada; texture and habit like 'Plumosa'.

'Emerald Isle'—Slow growing, compact form of low habit, rich green foliage, branchlets fern-like.

'Emerald Spreader'—Exceedingly low (7″), ground hugging spreader is heavily set with emerald green branchlets giving it a full, feathery appearance; lacks density, mounds in center, grading off toward the perimeter; a Monrovia introduction in 1967.

'Emerson'—Low growing form, 1′ by 9 to 15′, leaves acicular and scale-like, blue-green foliage turns dark purplish green in winter, slow growing, drought resistant, female, found in Black Hills of South Dakota and originally distributed as Black Hills Creeper.

'Fountain' ('Plumosa Fountain')—Gray-green foliage turns bright purple in winter, 15″ high, male, plant was selected for compact growth habit, similar habit and color to 'Plumosa'; selection from 'Plumosa' by D. Hill Nursery Co.

'Filicina'—Blue-green foliage turns pleasing bronze in winter, 4″ high, stays dense and low but has a few long scaly branches that overtop others, female and sparse fruiter; Schneider and Hasselkus consider it similar but superior to 'Admirabilis' and 'Prince of Wales' because of finer texture and greater density; 'Livida' is similar to 'Filicina' but superior because it is denser and lacks the long overtopping branches.

'Glenmore'—Light green needle foliage turns dark brown in winter, low growing extremely dense, flat branches overtop the plants, sparse cone producer, ugly in winter.

'Glomerata'—Extremely dwarf, 6″ high, leaves scale-like, green assuming dull plum purple color in winter, male, short nearly vertical branchlets with needles arranged like *Chamaecyparis*.

'Green Acres'—A dark green form that is similar to 'Blue Acres' in other features.

'Grey Carpet'—Creeping form with long, trailing branches forming low cushions, foliage more green than that of 'Bar Harbor', female, turns bronzy in winter.

'Grey Pearl'—Bright blue feathery foliage, branches more erect, compact form, 8″ by 16″ or more.

'Hermit'—Rather interesting shrubby type with blue-green foliage, somewhat similar to Pfitzer in habit; selected by Dr. R.B. Livingston, University of Massachusetts on Hermit Island, Maine; at one time thought to be a hybrid between *J. virginiana* and *J. horizontalis.*

'Hughes'—Low growing, 1′ by 9′, foliage silvery blue, distinct radial branching habit, good ground cover, holds blue-green color in winter with only a tinge of purple.

'Huntington Blue'—Wide spreading, dense branching habit, covered by intense blue-gray foliage, becomes slightly plum colored in winter, first saw at Cottage Hill Nursery in Alabama and misidentified it as 'Blue Chip', similar in growth habit.

'Jade River'—Silver-blue foliage, 8″ high ground cover form, mixture of scale and needle foliage, turns light purple in winter, male.

'Jade Spreader'—Very low, wide spreading form with dense jade green foliage which creates a heavy mat-like appearance, turns dark brownish purple in winter, male.

'Lime Glow'—A branch sport with lime green foliage, found by Larry Hatch, NC State University.

'Livida'—Juvenile foliage, deep grass green with a grayish bloom giving the plant an overall blue-green appearance, turns bronzy purple in winter, dense mat forming type, forms a 6″ high ground hugging circle.

'Livingston'—Procumbent type, generally 12 to 15″ high, steel blue summer foliage, bluish green in winter, mostly scale like foliage, female, from Hermit Island, ME; introduced by University of Vermont, 1972.

'Marcella'—Ground hugging type seldom more than 6″ high, bluish green juvenile foliage, female, open and lacks foliage density.

'Mother Lode'—Gold variegated form introduced by Iseli Nursery, OR.

'Petraea'—An early selection of ground cover inclination that grows 8 to 10″ high, bluish green juvenile foliage turning dull mauve in winter, female.

'Plenifolia'—Silvery blue needled foliage turns slight bronze-green during winter, grows 18″ high with branches borne at a 45° angle to ground, habit is open, highly susceptible to blight, introduced by Plumfield Nurseries around 1940.

'Plumosa'—Wide spreading, dense, compact form, 2′ by 10′, leaves awl-shaped and scale-like, blue-green to gray-green, purplish in winter, branches arise at a 45° angle to ground, introduced by Andorra Nurseries of Philadelphia in 1907; over the years this has proven to be one of the most popular junipers; can be seriously afflicted with blight; male.

'Plumosa Aunt Jemima'—Low, spreading, blue-green form growing about 8″ high and 4 to 5′ wide, supposedly reminds of a pancake; introduced by Hill's in 1957, male.

'Plumosa Compacta'—Compact form of 'Plumosa', dense branching, flat (18″ high) spreading; bronze-purple in winter, stays full in center, gray-green summer foliage, light purple in winter.

'P. C. Youngstown'—Similar to above but stays green all winter according to literature; this is not true for the plant will assume a purplish to bronze tinge in cold weather; however, this and the above are probably the same plant, male.

'Plumosa Fountain'—Flat growing form, 16" by 6', rapid growing, similar to 'Aunt Jemima'.

'Prince of Wales'—Very procumbent, 4 to 6" high, bright green with a bluish tinge caused by a waxy bloom, tinged purplish in winter months; acicular and scale-like foliage; introduced by Morden Experiment Station in 1967; collected in southern Alberta, Canada, considered cold hardy to −40°F, plant opens up in center with age.

'Procumbens'—Spreading, prostrate form, 6" by 12 to 15', leaves awl-shaped, soft, glaucous green, becoming bluish green with age; name may be incorrect but plants are encountered with this name.

'Prostrata'—Dark silvery green foliage, grows 6" high but lacks density with many long branches overtopping the plant, female.

'Pulchella'—A very slow-growing, dense, compact type, forming a symmetrical, 4 to 6" high mat that may spread to 3' and more, greenish gray, bronzy in winter, acicular leaves, male.

'Sun Spot'—Similar to 'Waukegan' but spotted yellow throughout the branches.

'Turquoise Spreader'—12" high, wide spreading form, densely covered with soft and feathery branchlets of turquoise green foliage, turns bronzy green with lavender tips in winter; vigorous grower, remains quite flat; juvenile foliage; a Monrovia introduction.

'Variegata'—Vigorous, 15" high form with creamy-white variegation, turns dark purple in winter, branches at 45° angle to ground, lacks density, female.

'Venusta'—Darker blue-green than species, grows less than 12".

'Webberi'—Extremely low, mat-like, spreading form of fine texture, bluish green foliage, 6" to 1' by 6 to 8', male, bronze-green in winter.

'Wilms'—Silvery green foliage in summer, turns brownish purple in winter, lower and more compact than 'Plumosa', considered a new and improved 'Plumosa', grows 12" high.

'Wiltoni' ('Wiltonii', 'Blue Rug')—Very flat growing form with trailing branches, 4 to 6" by 6 to 8', foliage-intense silver-blue, assumes light purplish tinge in winter, fairly fast growing; a female with 1/4" diameter silvery blue cones; found on Vinalhaven, an island off the coast of Maine in 1914; introduced by South Wilton Nurseries, Wilton, Connecticut; has become one of the most popular ground cover junipers in the U.S. and Europe; does quite well in the heat of the south; there are many beautiful established plants in the Athens area that are growing in soil with the consistency of blacktop.

'Winter Blue'—Similar to 'Plumosa' in habit with a pleasing light green summer foliage that becomes rich blue in winter.

'Wisconsin'—Selected in 1964 by Ed Hasselkus, University of Wisconsin near Brocks, Wisconsin, mixture of scale and needle blue-green foliage, turns dark purplish green in fall and winter, 8" high, mounds slightly with good radial habit, fast growing, no twig blight, male.

'Yukon Belle'—Bright silvery blue foliage, turns dark purplish green in winter, foliage is dense and fine-textured; winter foliage color like 'Wisconsin', ground hugging, broadly spreading, Zone 2.

PROPAGATION: Refer to *J. chinensis*.

NATIVE HABITAT: North America where it inhabits sea cliffs, gravelly slopes, even swamps (Nova Scotia to British Columbia, south to Massachusetts, New York, Minnesota, and Montana). Introduced 1836.

Juniperus procumbens — Japgarden Juniper (Listed as a variety of *J. chinensis* by *Hortus III*).
(jū-nip'ĕr-us prō-kum'benz)

LEAVES: Is three's, linear-lanceolate, spiny-pointed, about 1/3" long, concave above and glaucous with a green midrib toward the apex, lower surface convex, bluish with 2 white spots near the base below, from which 2 glaucous lines run down the edges of the pulvini.

SIZE: 8 to 12″ to 24″ high by 10 to 15′ spread; plants 3′ high and over 22′ wide are known.
HARDINESS: Zone 4 to 9.
HABIT: A dwarf, procumbent plant with long, wide-spreading, stiff branches; a beautiful ground cover in its finest form, tips of branches ascend often at a 20 to 30° angle to ground.
RATE: Slow, may cover 10′ diameter area in 10 years.
TEXTURE: Medium.
LEAF COLOR: Bluish green or gray-green.
FLOWERS: Dioecious, staminate yellow, pistillate greenish.
FRUIT: Cones subglobose, 1/3″ across; seeds 3, ovoid; cones not seen on cultivated plants.
CULTURE: Needs full sun; tolerant of many soils, thrives under adverse conditions, needs open situations, thrives will on calcareous soils.
DISEASES AND INSECTS: *Phomopsis* can be a problem.
LANDSCAPE VALUE: A handsome ground cover for beds, low borders, terraces, hillsides; can be pruned to retain size; in the previous edition I really beat on the species relative to *Phomopsis* susceptibility but since moving south have seen minimal problem on a great number of plants; foliage is beautiful and when properly grown both the species and 'Nana' make superb ground covers for full sun.
CULTIVARS:
'Greenmound'—Attractive light green foliage that does not brown out, grows with slight mounding habit, 8″ high and 6′ wide, a Hines introduction.
'Nana'—Dwarf, similar to species, forms a compact mat with branches one on top of the other, branchlets vary in length, spreading out as a compact mass of sprays, foliage bluish green, slightly purplish in winter, male; one of the best!; can become quite wide-spreading with time; have seen a 10 to 12′ wide plant at Longwood Gardens; may mound upon itself and become 2 to 2 1/2′ high after many years.
'Nana Californica'—Similar to 'Nana' but finer textured and with more pronounced blue-green color; slow-growing, ground-hugging, cushion-like form, 8″ high and spreading to 4′ or more; probably the same as 'Greenmound'.
'Variegata'—The bluish green foliage is streaked with creamy-white coloring; variegated forms by some authorities have been relegated to *J. davurica,* but the foliage is always needle-like on *J. procumbens* and predominantly scale-like with some needle on *J. davurica.*
PROPAGATION: Refer to *J. chinensis.*
NATIVE HABITAT: Mountains of Japan. Introduced 1843.

RELATED SPECIES:

Juniperus davurica, (jū-nip′ĕr-us dā-vūr′i-kȧ), Dahurian Juniper, is another confusing species that is apparently not common in cultivation. An 11-year-old plant was 2′ high and 8 to 9′ wide. 'Expansa' ('Parsoni'), which does well in the southern states and may have several names, develops stout, rigid, horizontally-spreading primary branches which do not lay on the ground but extend themselves slightly above. It builds upon itself and forms a dome-shaped mound about 2 to 3′ high and 9′ across. It carries a mixture of adult and juvenile dark green foliage. An attractive feature is the long, slender, filiform adult branches arranged in dense, rich looking sprays. 'Expansa Variegata' is boldly splashed with creamy-white over the plant on both adult and juvenile foliage. 'Expansa Aureospicata' is less vigorous than the above with primarily juvenile foliage and butter yellow variegation. The species is widely distributed in eastern Asia. 'Parsoni' is one of the best junipers in the southeast and displays excellent heat and some shade tolerance. It is vigorous and adaptable.

Juniperus sabina — Savin Juniper
(jū-nip′ĕr-us sȧ-bī′nȧ)

LEAVES: Scale-like, 4-ranked, in opposite pairs which are over-lapping, ovate, shortly pointed or blunt at the apex, about 1/20″ long, rounded on back, which usually bears a resin gland, leaves on young plants and older branchlets awl-shaped, spreading, straight, 1/6″ long, apex sharply pointed; green or bluish green and with a conspicuous midrib above; foliage when crushed emits a disagreeable odor and has a bitter taste; quite distinct among the junipers.

CONES: Dioecious usually; may have both sexes on one plant; female cones ripening in the autumn of the first year or the following spring, on recurved stalks, globose to ovoid, about 1/5″ diameter, brownish or bluish black, bloomy, composed of 4 to 6 scales, seeds 2 to 3, ovoid, furrowed.

SIZE: 4 to 6′ high by 5 to 10′ spread; supposedly can grow to 15′.

HARDINESS: Zone 3 to 7.

HABIT: A spreading shrub, upright in habit, stiff, somewhat vase-shaped; distinctly stiff branches borne at a 45° angle to the ground; extremely variable from groundcover to distinctly upright.

RATE: Slow.

TEXTURE: Medium.

LEAF COLOR: Dark green in summer, often a dingy green in winter showing a tinge of yellow, no purplish color in winter which allows easy separation, especially from the cultivars of *J. horizontalis*.

FLOWERS: Monoecious or dioecious.

FRUIT: Cones on recurved stalks, ripening in the first season or in the spring of the second season; seeds 1 to 3, ovoid, furrowed.

CULTURE: Does well on limestone soil, well drained and dry soils, and open, sunny exposures; withstands city conditions, best suited to colder climates.

DISEASES AND INSECTS: Juniper blight, see culture sheet.

LANDSCAPE VALUE: The species does not have a great deal to offer because of poor foliage and ragged nature; the cultivars are quite handsome especially the low growing types; they make excellent groundcovers, mass plants or foundation plants; I noticed that in many reports the var. *tamariscifolia* is listed as moderately to severely susceptible to juniper blight; I saw several handsome specimens of var. *tamariscifolia* at Purdue University's Horticultural Park, West Lafayette, Indiana, that showed no signs of blight while *J. procumbens*, *J. procumbens* 'Nana', and *J. horizontalis* and cultivars were heavily infested; apparently there are different clones in the trade with varying degrees of resistance; an excellent paper evaluating juniper susceptibility to *Phomopsis* appeared in the *J. Amer. Soc. Hort. Sci.* 94: 609–611 (1969).

CULTIVARS:

'Arcadia'—Growth habit dense and layered, 1 to 1 1/2′ by 4′, leaves predominantly scale-like, grass green; resistant to juniper blight; hardy in Zone 3, darker green than 'Skandia', less compact.

'Blue Danube'—Semi-upright yet more horizontal than the species, foliage bluish green, scale-like, awl-shaped inside the plant, Zone 4.

'Blue Forest'—Blue foliage, spreading growth habit with upturned sprays, 18″ high and wide spreading, blight free, hardy to -20°F.

'Broadmoor'—A dwarf, low-spreading, staminate form which looks like a neat form of var. *tamariscifolia* when young, but the plant tends to build up at the center with age, the main branches are strong and horizontally spreading; the branchlets short and reaching upwards; the sprays very short and occurring mainly on the upper side of the branches; the foliage is a soft grayish green and is resistant to juniper blight, this clone as well as 'Arcadia' and 'Skandia' were selected from many thousands of seedlings raised by D. Hill Nursery Co., Dundee, Illinois from seed imported near Petersburgh, Russia in 1933; all have proved resistant to juniper blight; Zone 4, will grow 2 to 3' high and 10' wide or more; I have been really impressed with this selection.

'Buffalo'—Similar to var. *tamariscifolia* with feathery branches and bright green foliage, 12″ high by 8′ wide in 10 years, female, retains good color in winter, Zone 2 to 3.

'Calgary Carpet'—A selection from 'Arcadia' with lower and more spreading growth habit, soft green foliage.

'Moor Dense'—A form with foliage color similar to 'Broadmoor,' but flatter growing, more tiered branching habit; a Monrovia introduction.

'Pepin'—Upright form with blue-green foliage, supposedly with greater blight resistance than typical *J. sabina*.

'Skandia'—Similar to 'Arcadia' with foliage mostly acicular and pale grayish green, 1 to 1 1/2′ by 10′ and more, Zone 3, female, blight resistant.

var. *tamariscifolia*—Low spreading, mounded form, branches horizontal, branchlets crowded, leaves awl-shaped, very short, nearly appressed, bluish green; grows 18″ tall and 10 to 15′ across in 15 to 20 years; susceptible to blight; often listed as 'Tamariscifolia'; found in the wild on the mountains of southern Europe and, hence, may deserve botanical categorization, i.e., variety or forma; apparently more than one clone in the nursery trade; a blue-green form is described, and listed as 'Tamariscifolia New Blue'.

'Variegata'—Dwarf form, 2 to 3′ by 3 to 4 1/2′, leaves scale-like, sprays streaked white.

'Von Ehren' ('Von Ehron')—Vase-shaped grower, 5′ by 5′, leaves awl-shaped, light to dark green, resistant to juniper blight; may grow 6 to 8′ high and 18 to 20′ wide.

PROPAGATION: Refer to *J. chinensis*.

ADDITIONAL NOTES: A very variable, spreading or procumbent shrub and one in which the numerous named selections are superior to the species types. Some of the cultivars are quite beautiful but do not seem to have the popular appeal of the *J. horizontalis* types.

NATIVE HABITAT: Mountains of central and southern Europe, western Asia, Siberia and Caucasus. Cultivated before 1580.

Juniperus scopulorum — Rocky Mountain Juniper, Colorado Redcedar
(jū-nip′ĕr-us skop-ū-lō′rum)

LEAVES: Scale-like, tightly appressed, rhombic-ovate, apex acute or acuminate, entire, back varying in color, dark or light bluish green, glaucous or light green and obscurely glandular.

CONES: Ripening the second year, globose, 1/4 to 1/3″ diameter, dark blue, glaucous bloomy; pulp sweetish; seeds 2, reddish brown, triangular, prominently angled and grooved.

SIZE: 30 to 40′ high by 3 to 15′ wide.

HARDINESS: Zone 3 to 7.

HABIT: A narrow, pyramidal tree often with several main stems.

RATE: Slow, most of the cultivars will average 6 to 12″ per year.

TEXTURE: Medium.

BARK: Reddish brown or gray, shredding but persistent.

LEAF COLOR: Varying in color from dark green or bluish green, glaucous or light green.

FLOWERS: Monoecious or dioecious; male has 6 stamens compared to 10 or 12 of *J. virginiana*.

FRUIT: Cones nearly globular, to 1/3″ across, dark blue, glaucous bloomy, ripening in the second year, pulp sweetish; seeds 2, triangular, reddish brown, prominently angled, grooved.

CULTURE: Withstands droughty conditions very well; same requirements as other *Juniperus*, not well adapted to humidity and high night temperatures of the southeast.

DISEASES AND INSECTS: *Phomopsis* blight, also serves as an alternate host for cedar apple rust.

LANDSCAPE VALUE: Valued for its use as screens, hedges, backgrounds and foundation plants, very nice blue cast to the foliage, more popular in upper midwest, plains and Rocky Mountain states.

CULTIVARS:

'Blue Creeper'—Low spreading habit, 2′ by 6 to 8′, bright blue foliage color that becomes more intense in cold weather, a Monrovia introduction.

'Blue Heaven' ('Blue Haven')—Neat pyramidal form, foliage strikingly blue in all seasons, heavy cone bearer, 20′ in 15 to 20 years.

'Chandler's Silver'—A broadly pyramidal form with bluish green foliage; may require pruning to keep it attractive.

'Cologreen'—Green (forest green) foliaged form that is susceptible to rust, forms a compact upright cone-like outline, 15 to 20′.

'Cupressifolia Erecta'—Dense, pyramidal, rich green, with undertones of silvery blue, needle-like foliage, to 20′.

'Dewdrop'—A broad pyramidal form with bluish green foliage.

'Erecta Glauca'—Upright bluish needled form, supposedly a good grower.

'Fairview'—Blue-green foliage and supposedly resistant to cedar apple rust.

'Gray Gleam'—Pyramidal, slow growing, male, foliage distinct silvery gray, becoming more brilliant in the winter, grows 15 to 20′ in 30 to 40 years.

'Green Ice'—Broad pyramidal tight-branched form, new growth is ice-green, mature foliage gray-green, color is best in colder climates, a Monrovia introduction.

'Hillborne Silver Globe'—A medium sized more or less globe-shaped form with bluish green foliage, susceptible to rust.

'Lakewood Globe'—Compact form with excellent blue-green foliage, 4 to 6′ in 10 years; several leaders may develop.

'March Frost'—Vigorous upright selection with good blue-green foliage.

'Medora'—Slender, columnar-pyramidal compact form with good blue-green foliage, slow-growing, selection from Badlands of North Dakota, male, named in 1954.

'Moffettii'—Pyramidal and dense, foliage heavy, silvery green, abundant cones.

'Montana Green'—Pyramidal, dense, compact, green foliage color.

'Moonglow'—A dense broad pyramidal selection, intense silver-blue foliage, 20′.

'North Star'—An upright green form that may suffer slight windburn.

'Pathfinder'—Narrow, pyramidal tree, regular in outline, leaves in flat sprays, distinctly bluish gray, 20′ high in 15 to 20 years.

'Silver King'—Essentially ground cover type that grows 24″ high with a wide-spreading, loose layered habit, scaly silvery green foliage holds color well in winter, although listed as male, some plants have male and female cones which is not unusual for *J. scopulorum* types.

'Skyrocket'—Probably the most narrow columnar juniper available, bluish green mostly acicular needles, has done well in midwest, reminds of a blue rocket sitting on the launching pad, actually this might be the best place for it in the landscape; if you want your landscape to have that third dimensional, outer space feeling, plant a couple hundred Skyrockets; formerly listed as a *J. virginiana* selection, 15′ plant may be only 2′ wide at base, roots readily from cuttings.

'Sterling Silver'—Compact pyramidal habit, with interesting twisting tight silver-blue foliage.

'Sutherland'—Strong growing, silver-green foliaged form, broad pyramidal to 20′.

'Table Top'—Flat-topped form with silvery blue foliage, grows 5 to 6′ high and 8′ across in 10 years, female, formerly listed as 'Table Top Blue', semi-upright in habit.

'Tolleson's Weeping Juniper'—Silver-blue foliage hangs string-like from arching branches; supposedly cold hardy anywhere in the country, interesting form; has been grown in south with some success, have seen as far south as Orlando, FL; there is also a form with soft green foliage ('Tolleson's Green Weeping').

'Welchii'—Narrow, columnar, compact growth habit, to 8′ tall, silvery new growth, changing to bluish green, handsome foliage.

'Wichita Blue'—Brilliant bright blue foliaged pyramidal form, 18′ or greater.

'Winter Blue'—Semi-prostrate spreading form, brilliant silver-blue foliage retains blue color in winter, found by Clayton Berg, Valley Nursery, Helena, MT.

PROPAGATION: See under *J. chinensis*.

NATIVE HABITAT: Found wild on dry, rocky ridges, usually above 5,000′, on the eastern foothills of the Rocky Mountains from Alberta to Texas, westward to the coast of British Columbia and Washington, and to eastern Oregon, Nevada, and northern Arizona. Introduced 1836.

Juniperus squamata — Singleseed Juniper
(jū-nip′ĕr-us skwȧ-mā′tȧ)

LEAVES: Awl-shaped, over-lapping, in whorls of 3, pressed together or slightly spreading, the upper part free and 1/8 to 1/6″ long, curved, tapering to a sharp point, grayish green with 2 grayish white bands, green beneath, convex, furrowed; old leaves persisting on the shoots and branchlets as dry brown scales.

CONES: Ellipsoidal, 1/4 to 1/3″ long, reddish brown becoming black when ripe in the second year; scales 3 to 6, pointed; seeds solitary, ovoid, ridged, with 3 to 4 depressions below the middle.

SIZE: Extremely variable and is difficult to ascertain the exact nature of the species; the cultivars are used in landscaping but the species is not cultivated.

HARDINESS: Zone 4 to 7 (8); heat and humidity of southeast have not been kind to the cultivars.

HABIT: Dwarf, decumbent, ascending or erect shrub; very variable over its wide geographical range; usually low to prostrate shrub, but in some forms capable of being trained as a small tree.

RATE: Slow.

TEXTURE: Medium.

LEAF COLOR: Grayish green to bright steely blue-green with two gray white bands.

FLOWERS: Monoecious; staminate yellow, pistillate green.

FRUIT: Cones elliptic, 1/4 to 1/3″ across, reddish brown, changing to purplish black; scales with a triangular mucro; seeds solitary, ovoid, keeled.

CULTURE: Adaptable, tolerates dry soils, not well suited to the heat and humidity of the southeast.

DISEASES AND INSECTS: Susceptible to bagworms.

LANDSCAPE VALUE: Cultivars are handsome, especially blue foliaged forms.

CULTIVARS: Many forms have been selected in Europe and are common in gardens. They appear to prosper in the cooler European climate and would be suitable for the northern states. Many are not commercially available but are now being produced in U.S. nurseries for eventual release. Ten years past 'Blue Star' was essentially unknown and now is reasonably common. Some of the new ground cover types are particularly attractive. Many of the descriptions have been extracted from European nursery catalogs and horticultural literature as well as synthesized from face to plant confrontations.

'Blue Alps'—Upright branching with arching slightly nodding branch tips, bright silver-blue needles, 5 to 6′ high by 2 to 2 1/2′ wide.

'Blue Carpet'—Handsome ground cover form with rich blue-gray-green foliage, 8 to 12″ by 4 to 5′ wide after 19 years, a mutation of 'Meyeri'.

'Blue Star'—A branch sport of 'Meyeri' found in about 1950; it is a slow-growing, low, rounded, squat plant, about as broad as high; the juvenile foliage is the same rich blue of 'Meyeri' but is more crowded on the branches; the plant does not develop the strong leaders of 'Meyeri' so it remains dense; it has remained stable under cultivation; I first saw the plant at Amstel Park, Amsterdam and it truly shone like a silver-blue star; rich foliage color is attractive, may decline under high humidity and high night temperatures, 3′ by 3 to 4′.

'Blue Swede'—Particularly attractive, almost Pfitzer growth habit, with rich blue-green foliage in summer turning metallic bluish gray in winter, 4′ by 4 to 5′.

'Chinese Silver'—Branches develop at a 45° angle to ground and the tips develop a semi-pendulous character, handsome, blue-silver-green foliage in summer, 4 to 5′ high, 5 to 6′ wide.

'Holger'—Semi-spreading form with yellowish new growth that becomes gray-green in summer and later, foliage does not resemble typical *J. squamata*, considered a possible hybrid between *J. squamata* and *J. chinensis* 'Pfitzeriana Aurea'; eventually grows 2 to 3′ high, 3 to 4′ wide, plants I saw were small but some literature indicates 6′ by 6′ at maturity.

'Loderi'—Columnar form, branches dense, upright, tips nodding, rich blue-green foliage, grows 3 to 5′ high.

'Meyeri'—Bushy, dense form, 5′ by 4′, foliage striking blue-white above, needle-like, quite exotic when young but the old dead needles persist and after a time the plant becomes a liability, often called the Fishtail Juniper; reported to grow as much as 6 to 8' high and 2 to 3' wide in 15 years; known to 20' high; female, introduced in 1910 (have seen 1914 also) by F.N. Meyer; many branch sports have arisen from 'Meyeri' resulting in cultivars 'Blue Star' and 'Blue Carpet'.

'Prostrata'—Prostrate, slow growing form, branchlets erect, short, green, leaves awl-shaped with bluish white bands above, margin broad, green; green and slightly keeled beneath, tips of leading shoots nod, 12", mounding in center, trailing off at edges, differs from 'Nana' in that the branch tips nod instead of turning up.

'Variegata'—Prostrate, spreading form, 10" by 4 to 5', new growth is cream colored.

PROPAGATION: Refer to *J. chinensis.*

ADDITIONAL NOTES: Often difficult to distinguish this species and the cultivars from *Juniperus procumbens* and its kin. 'Prostrata' is a particularly confusing form that is apparently quite confused in gardens and the nursery trade.

NATIVE HABITAT: Afghanistan, Himalayas, western China. Introduced 1836.

Juniperus virginiana — Eastern Redcedar
(jū-nip′ĕr-us vĕr-jin-i-ā′nȧ)

LEAVES: Scale-like leaves arranged in 4 ranks closely pressed and overlapping, about 1/16" long, short or long pointed, free at the apex, often with a small, oval, glandular depression on the back, shorter than the distance from the gland to the leaf-tip; leaves on older branchlets broader, about 1/12" long becoming brown and withered, juvenile leaves often present on adult trees, spreading, in pairs 1/5 to 1/4" long, ending in a spiny point, concave and glaucous above, green and convex beneath; bruised needles smell like a cedar chest or closet.

CONES: Dioecious, female cones ripening in one year, sub-globose, ovoid, up to 1/4" long, often glaucous; seeds 1 to 2, ovoid, furrowed, shining brown, cones can be quite handsome and some appear almost blue, and with the waxy bloom appear frosted.

SIZE: 40 to 50' high by 8 to 20' spread; extremely variable over its extensive native range.

HARDINESS: Zone 2 to 9.

HABIT: Densely pyramidal when young and slightly pendulous in old age; variable in the wild from almost columnar to broadly pyramidal.

RATE: Medium.

TEXTURE: Medium.

BARK: A handsome grayish to reddish brown, exfoliating in long strips.

LEAF COLOR: Medium green in summer becoming dirty green in winter, variable from tree to tree.

FLOWERS: Usually dioecious; staminate yellow, pistillate green; interesting in late winter, February into March, when the staminate yellow-brown cones are swelling and starting to release pollen; male trees take on a rather ugly yellow-brown color and are easily distinguished from female trees at this time of year, in actuality the male cones are noticeable in fall and beyond; female trees are lovely with the various colored cones, some greenish blue to frosted blue, often the female cones are so abundant that the tree literally glows; to my knowledge no one has ever selected for this trait.

FRUIT: Cones globular or ovoid, about 1/5" across, brownish violet, glaucous bloomy, ripening in the first season; seeds 1 to 2, ovoid, small, apex blunt-angular, deeply pitted, shining brown.

CULTURE: Easily transplanted balled and burlapped if root pruned; tolerant of adverse conditions, poor gravelly soils; acid and high pH soils; prefers a sunny, airy location, and a deep moist loam on well drained subsoil; will tolerate shade only in extreme youth.

DISEASES AND INSECTS: Cedar apple rust and bagworms.

LANDSCAPE VALUE: An excellent specimen and mass if used with care as to color combinations; useful for windbreaks, shelter belts, hedges, and topiary work; the cultivars are the truly ornamental plants of this species; the var. *crebra* is the northern form of the species and tends toward a narrow, conical habit; most of the selected clones have come from the northern form; the principal value of the species is the wood which is used for cedar chests, closet linings, pencils, carving and small ornamental work.

CULTIVARS:

'Blue Cloud'—Supposedly a hybrid between *J. v.* 'Glauca' and *J. chinensis* 'Pfitzeriana' that forms a large shrub with a glaucous gray-green foliage, long feathery young shoots emerge from all over the plant providing a rather aesthetic, but unkempt appearance, 4' by 6'.

'Burkii'—Narrow to broad pyramidal, 10 to 25' high, leaves acicular and scale-like, dull blue band above, narrow green margin, green beneath, steel blue with a slight purplish cast in winter, male, grew up with this cultivar in Cincinnati, OH.

'Canaertii'—Compact pyramidal form, leaves on young branchlets scale-like, on old ones awl-shaped, dark green; foliage tufted at ends of branches; cones small, grape-like, whitish blue bloomy, usually profusely produced, 20' tall in 15 years, very susceptible to rust, known to 35'; opens up with age becoming picturesque.

'Cupressifolia'—Pyramidal, loose, leaves cypress-like, soft yellow-green, female form, actually nomenclature is confused on this cultivar, probably should be called 'Hillspire'.

'Emerald Sentinel'—Pyramidal columnar form with dark green foliage, female, 15 to 20' by 3 to 5', Conard Pyle introduction.

'Glauca'—Narrow, columnar form to 25', leaves scale-like, appressed, some awl-shaped leaves inside the plant; silver-blue foliage is best in spring as it turns silver-green in summer, more than one clone is grown under this name.

'Globosa'—Dense, compact form; branchlets crowded, thin, green mostly adult foliage; bronze-brown in winter, 50-year-old plant is about 15' tall.

'Grey Owl'—Similar to Pfitzer in habit with small, appressed, soft silvery gray foliage; originated in 1938 in a batch of 'Glauca' seedlings; lower growing and wider spreading than 'Blue Cloud'; handsome spreading relatively compact, 3' by 6' form, female, sets abundant cones, possibly hybrid between *J. virginiana* 'Glauca' and 'Pfitzeriana'.

'Hillii'—Dense, columnar, slow-growing form, 6 to 16' high, leaves awl-shaped with a rather broad, bluish white band above, greenish blue beneath, conspicuously purple during winter, 8 to 12' in about 10 years.

'Hillspire'—Symmetrical conical-pyramidal habit with bright green foliage that is essentially maintained in winter, male, named 'Cupressifolia' in 1964 but that name was taken, renamed 'Hillspire' about 1963, introduced by D. Hill Nursery Co., Dundee, IL.

'Idyllwild'—Broad based pyramidal form, informal rugged upright branching, handsome dark green foliage.

'Kosteri'—Bushy form, 3 to 4' by 25 to 30', leaves loosely appressed, grayish blue, assuming a purplish cast, often confused with Pfitzer, but lower and wider spreading.

'Manhattan Blue'—Compact, pyramidal form, differing from 'Glauca' by the bluish green foliage;; male.

'Nova'—Narrow, upright, symmetrical form, extremely hardy, 10 to 12'.

'O'Connor'—Developed from a witches broom on *J. virginiana* 'Glauca' in former Donaldson Nursery, Sparta, KY, globe shape with steel-blue foliage.

'Pendula'—Form with spreading branches and pendulous branchlets; leaves mostly acicular, light green, 36 to 45' tall, female with bloomy blue-white cones.

'Princeton Sentry'—A compact, narrow form with soft textured dark green foliage that turns attractive purple-green in winter, a Princeton Nursery introduction.

'Pseudocupressus'—Narrow, columnar form with gray-green mostly scale-like foliage, 38' high plants are known; this name appears in propagation literature as an understock, first described about 1932.

'Pyramidalis'—Unfortunately a collective name for pyramidal growing forms; Hill Nursery Co. has a form named 'Dundee' which falls into the 'Pyramidalis' group; it has soft foliage which turns a purple-green in winter.

'Silver Spreader'—Wide spreading, low growing, branches rise at 30° angle to ground, silver-gray foliaged form introduced by Monrovia about 1955; somewhat similar to 'Grey Owl' but foliage is more silvery, a male, will probably grow (1 1/2') 2 to 3' by 4 to 6'.

'Stover'—A narrow symmetrical upright form with intense blue-gray foliage.

'Tripartita'—Dwarf, dense form, 4′ by 7.5′, branches stout, spreading, irregular, branchlets short; leaves acicular, fine, pale green or slightly glaucous, similar in habit to Pfitzer but does not grow as large and is a bit stiffer; assumes a slight purplish winter color.

PROPAGATION: Refer to *J. chinensis.*

ADDITIONAL NOTES: Closely related to *J. scopulorum* but differing in floral characteristics and in its habit of ripening seeds the first year. It can be distinguished from *J. chinensis* by its juvenile leaves being in pairs (rarely 3's) and by the adult leaves which are pointed and from *J. sabina* by the absence of true savin odor or bitter taste. Apparently this species can hybridize with *J. horizontalis.*

NATIVE HABITAT: East and central North America, east of the Rocky Mountains. Introduced before 1664.

OTHER SPECIES:

Juniperus deppeana 'McFetters' (*J. pachyphloea*) (jū-nip′ĕr-us dep-pē-ā′na), McFetters Alligator Juniper, was mentioned by Raulston as a genuine surprise because of rich blue foliage color, ease of propagation and 1 1/2′ growth per year. He received the plant from Mr. Tom Dilatush. The color is better than any *J. scopulorum* or *Cupressus* taxa in the North Carolina State University Arboretum. 'McFetters' was found in the mountains of Arizona. If like the parent, it should form a broad pyramidal or round-topped tree; the characteristic brown bark is broken into small, closely appressed "alligator hide" scales. Foliage is primarily scale-like. Arizona, New Mexico, southwest Texas and Mexico. Cultivated 1873. Zone 7 to 8.

Juniperus rigida—Needle Juniper

LEAVES: Always needle-like, spreading, linear-subulate, 1/3 to 3/4″ long, tapering from the middle into a spiny, extremely sharp point, triangular in cross-section, in whorls of 3 (ternate), upper surface grooved with a glaucous stomatic band, rest of needle bright green and keeled below.

CONES: Globose, 1/4 to 1/3″ wide, brownish black, bloomy, ripening the second year, seeds 1 to 3 in each scale.

Juniperus rigida, (jū-nip′ĕr-us rij′i-dȧ), Needle Juniper, has crossed the author's horticultural path on sufficient occasions that it deserves inclusion. In fact, several nurseries are starting to grow it. My most lasting impression came from a 20′ tall specimen at the Arnold Arboretum with a central leader, horizontal secondary branches and weeping tertiary branchlets. The habit is most elegant and lends itself to specimen or accent use in the garden. Is successfully growing in Raleigh, NC. Raulston notes that 'Pendula' which is probably the same as the species grew about 3′ per year at the NCSU Arboretum. The plant is female with attractive bluish black fruits. December–January cuttings with reddish coloration at the base, 8000 ppm IBA-talc, mist, rooted 90 to 95%. This could become a popular plant in the future. The habit is somewhat open and plants do not make good screens. Introduced by Veitch in 1861. Native to Japan, Korea, North China and apparently quite variable in the wild. Raulston has described 'Akebono' with sparkling white tipped shoots that will grow 15 to 20′ high.

Juniperus silicicola, (jū-nip′ĕr-us si-lis-i-kō′la), Southern Redcedar, is considered a separate species by some, but in most recognizable characteristics is simply *J. virginiana* with a southern coastal/Florida distribution. The trees are abundant on the Georgia coast and literally grow on the sand dunes, coastal marsh edges, and sandy soils. Handsome tree where native and often with a more open and wide spreading habit than typical *J. virginiana.* Possibly slightly larger male and female cones.

Kalmia latifolia—Mountain-laurel Kalmia or Mountain-laurel
(kal′mē-a̍ lat-i-fō′lē-a̍)

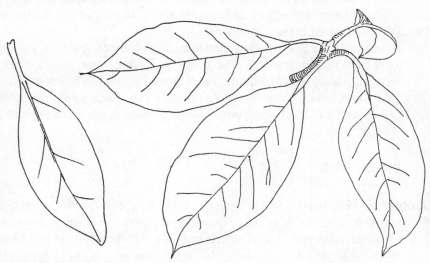

FAMILY: Ericaceae

LEAVES: Alternate, simple, evergreen, appearing irregularly whorled, elliptic to elliptic-lanceolate, 2 to 5″ long, 3/4 to 1 1/2″ wide, leathery, entire, acute or short acuminate, cuneate, dark green above, yellowish green beneath; petiole 1/4 to 1″ long.

SIZE: Variable, 7 to 15′ in height with a similar spread, supposedly can grow to 30 to 36′.

HARDINESS: Zone 4 to 9.

HABIT: Large, robust shrub which, if not crowded, is symmetrical and dense in youth; in old age becomes, open, straggly, loose, with picturesque gnarly trunks and limbs.

RATE: Slow, 4 to 8′ over a 10 year period.

TEXTURE: Medium in all seasons.

LEAF COLOR: New growth a light yellow green to bronze changing to glossy dark green at maturity; winter foliage color is usually a good dark green but in sun will become a yellowish green.

FLOWERS: Individually the most beautiful flower I know of especially as the buds are opening; variable from white to pink-rose to deep rose with purple markings within, 3/4 to 1″ across, broad-campanulate, May to June, borne in 4 to 6″ diameter terminal corymbs, each flower has 10 stamens which on first expanding are held in little cavities in the corolla; the "knee" (bend) formed by the filament is sensitive, and when the pollen is ripe, if touched, the anther is released; obviously insect pollination is facilitated in this manner.

FRUIT: Brown, 5-valved, dehiscent capsule, 1/4″ across, persistent through winter.

CULTURE: Easy to transplant because of fibrous root system; requires acid, cool, moist, well drained soil; full sun or deep shade but flowers best in sunnier locations; remove flowers immediately after fading; mulch to keep soil moist and to reduce cultivation; my observations indicate that many of the new cultivars introduced from Connecticut will not compete favorably in Zone 8 and 9 for soils are often heavy and inadequately drained; like *Rhododendron catawbiense* and cultivars, plants would best be served by planting on top of the ground and covering with pine bark.

DISEASES AND INSECTS: Leaf spot, blight, flower blight, whitefly, scale, lace bug, azalea stem borer and rhododendron borer.

LANDSCAPE VALUE: Excellent broadleaf evergreen for shady borders; exquisite in mass; magnificent in flower; one of our best and best loved native shrubs; excellent plant for naturalizing; again requires attention to cultural details; I tried, unsuccessfully, to grow the plant in my Illinois garden for it simply languished and died.

CULTIVARS: Information presented below was distilled from many references; the best checklist is Jaynes, *Bull. Amer. Assoc. Bot. Gard. Arbor.* 17(4): 99-106 (1983); also the revised edition of Dr. Jaynes, *Kalmia-The Laurel Book II,* Timber Press (1988) lists 46 cultivars and several formae. Most are included here.

‘Alba’—Pure white flowers, Eichelser introduction.

‘Alpine Pink’—Rich pink in bud opening to a medium pink with a white throat, good growth habit and foliage.

‘Bettina’—Reduced corolla, deep purplish pink when grown in full sun, faint in shade.

'Bravo'—Flower buds and open flowers dark pink, leaves are large and glossy dark green, new shoots have red stems, 3rd or 4th generation seedling from the late Ed Mezitt, Weston Nursery.

'Bridesmaid'—Rich deep pink in bud and heavily banded pink with a white center when open, low spreading habit.

'Bullseye'—Deep purplish cinnamon colored buds open to a creamy blossom with a broad purple band around the inside with a white throat and edge, new growth reddish bronze.

'Candy'—Buds and flowers deep pink, broad thick wavy leaves, petioles and young stems purplish red, a Weston Nursery introduction.

'Carol'—Bright red buds open to almost pure white, broad thick lustrous dark green leaves, wavy and twisted.

'Carousel'—Intricate pattern (starburst) of bright purplish cinnamon pigmentation inside the corolla, good grower, relatively easy to root.

'Clementine Churchill'—Tyrian rose outside, inside rose-red, good foliage and habit.

'Den Window'—Large flowers open light pink becoming deeper pink as they age, foliage is bluish green, purplish red new stems, robust grower.

'Elf'—Compact dwarf form with light pink buds, flowers white, habit 1/3 to 1/2 normal size, but flowers only slightly smaller than species.

'Emerald Sheen'—Medium pink buds open nearly white and mature to medium pink; outstanding feature is the thick textured, glossy rounded, convex dark green foliage borne on a compact plant.

'Freckles'—Buds light pink, opening to a creamy white flower with purple spots just above the 10 anther pouches.

'Fresca'—Flowers white banded with burgundy, selection of f. *fuscata*.

f. *fuscata*—Flowers with a broad brownish, purple or cinnamon band inside the corolla, called Banded Laurel.

'Goodrich'—Buds deep red, flowers with continuous cinnamon purple band when open, one of the darkest cultivars, difficult to propagate by cuttings, foliage susceptible to leaf spot.

'Heart of Fire'—Buds red, flowers deep pink, selected from 'Ostbo Red' seedling population for better foliage and habit; introduced by Melrose Nursery, Olympia, WA.

'Hearts Desire'—Buds dark red, flowers burgundy (cinnamon-red) with narrow white lip; better habit than 'Kaleidoscope'.

'Kaleidoscope'—Similar to 'Hearts Desire' but with larger white lip and brighter color to the bloom, giving more of a bicolor effect.

'Minuet'—Miniature form similar to 'Elf' but with broad maroon band inside corolla, buds light pink, leaves glossy dark green and narrow.

f. *myrtifolia*—Compact growing type less than 6′ tall, one half to one-third normal size, common name is Miniature Laurel, also listed as f. *minor* and f. *nana*.

'Nancy'—Buds pinkish red, opening to clear bright pink.

'Nathan Hale'—Red in bud open pink, symmetrical compact habit, thick shiny dark green foliage, petioles and stems of new growth purplish red.

'Nipmuck'—Intense red buds open creamy white to light pink, back of opened corolla is dark pink, rooted 91% over 9 year test period, light yellow-green foliage, upper foliage turns unattractive purplish color in fall.

f. *obtusata*—Dwarf, dense form with thick, leathery almost rounded leaves.

'Olympic Fire'—Large deep red buds open to pink flowers, seedling of 'Ostbo Red', good habit and foliage color, easier to root than 'Ostbo Red'.

'Olympic Wedding'—Flower buds pink, opening to pink flowers with a broken cinnamon colored band, broad flat dark green leaves.

'Ostbo Red'—Buds bright red, flowers soft deep pink, introduced by Melrose Nursery, Olympia, WA; first red budded selection named.

'Pink Charm'—Deep red-pink buds open to uniform rich pink, more deeply pigmented than 'Pink Surprise', a narrow and deeply red pigmented ring occurs on the inside and near the base of the corolla, October cuttings rooted 82 percent in a poly tent, peat:perlite, bottom heat with no auxin; annual bloomer.

'Pink Frost'—Large pink buds open to silvery pink flowers, then deeper pink, excellent wide lustrous foliage; cuttings root better than the species.

'Pink Star'—Flowers deep pink, star shaped, a seedling of 'Ostbo Red'.

'Pink Surprise'—Deep pink buds open to pink flowers, corolla has a crisp inner ring and 10 pigment flecks where the anthers are held, cuttings surprisingly easy to root, hence, the common name.

'Pinwheel'—Flowers maroon and edged in white, cinnamon flower with white center, scalloped edge.

f. *polypetala* ('Polypetala')—corolla cut to form five strap-like feathery petals, selection often lacks vigor.

'Quinnipiac'—Intense red buds open to soft light pink, rich dark green foliage, somewhat similar to 'Nipmuck' but a more compact plant with darker green foliage, prone to purple leaf spot especially if container grown, sister seedling of 'Nipmuck', rooted 77% over 9 year period.

'Raspberry Glow'—Deep burgundy buds open to deep raspberry pink flowers, foliage dark green.

'Richard Jaynes'—Red to raspberry red buds open to pink with silvery white sheen on the inside, heavy annual flowering, good glossy foliage, named after the famous *Kalmia* hybridizer.

'Sarah'—Vivid red buds open to bright pink-red, flowers for a long time, foliage and habit excellent.

'Sharon Rose'—Deep red buds, fading to pink, much like 'Ostbo Red', good habit, thick broad flat leaves, cuttings are relatively easy to root.

'Shooting Star'—White flowers with five distinct lobes that reflex, selected from the wild in North Carolina, flowers one week later than species and less hardy.

'Silver Dollar'—Pale pink buds, large (1 1/2″ diameter) white flowers twice the size of the species, leaves large, leathery dark green; selected in 1952 by Weston Nurseries.

'Snowdrift'—Compact mound-shaped plant with pure white flowers, broad dark green leaves.

'Splendens'—Flowers deeper pink than the type, described in 1896 in England and is the oldest named cultivar.

'Star Cluster'—Similar to 'Fresca', flowers with white edge and center maroon slightly interrupted band, may tolerate heavy soils better than most mountainlaurels.

'Stillwood'—Flower buds and flowers clear white when growing in full sun, essentially lacking pink pigment, selected from wild population in New Hampshire.

'Sunset'—Bright red buds and near red open, leaves narrow and twisted with thick blades, purplish red new petioles and stems, low spreading growth habit.

'Tiddlywinks'—A selection from forma *myrtifolia* much like 'Elf' in growth rate and form but with a broader, multiple-branching habit and deeper-colored flowers, medium to rich pink in bud and a soft or light pink when open; 10-year-old plant was 20″ by 30″.

'Tightwad'—Buds are pink if grown in full sun and remain in good condition for a month beyond the normal flowering period but never open.

'Tinkerbell'—Is a miniature laurel that is quite similar to 'Tiddlywinks,' flower color is generally a deeper pink, the stems of new growth are green compared to red of 'Tiddlywinks'; 10-year-old plant was 30″ by 40″.

'Twenty'—Dark pink in bud opening to medium pink, glossy dark green leaves, low compact habit twice as wide as high.

'Wedding Band'—Pink buds open to reveal a 1/4″ diameter solid maroon band, broad flat dark green leaves, good habit.

Weston Pink and Red-budded Selections—Long before the "Kalmia Kraze" this nursery envisioned a future for the species and over the years selected outstanding color forms. Seeds from the superior types are used to produce even better types and the evolution continues. A visit in late May-June will make a convert out of any non-believer.

'Willowcrest'—Willow-leaved foliage, light pink flowers.

'Yankee Doodle'—Red buds open to irregular maroon banded blossom with large white throat, yellow green foliage, a f. *fuscata* selection.

PROPAGATION: Seed should be directly sown on peat with lights to stimulate growth after germination; the seedlings are extremely small and hard to work with so it is necessary to get some size to them;

cuttings are extremely difficult to root but there are differences in rootability of various clones. Days could be spent discussing *Kalmia latifolia* cutting propagation. Some investigators have said a hormone treatment is a must while others say it does not make any difference. The mountain-laurel is inherently difficult to root from cuttings. I refer the reader to Fordham, *PIPPS* 27:479-483, 1977. "Propagation of *Kalmia latifolia* by cuttings". Taking vegetative propagation a step further, the interested reader should see Lloyd and McCown, *PIPPS* 30:421-427, 1980. "Commercially-feasible micropropagation of mountain-laurel, *Kalmia latifolia*, by use of shoot-tip culture". Kalmia is now being produced commercially through tissue culture which has literally opened the floodgate for the many new cultivars.

ADDITIONAL NOTES: Alfred Rehder called it "one of the most beautiful native American shrubs." Interestingly, *Kalmia latifolia* is found south to Florida. I think most gardeners consider this a cool climate plant. In the south it follows the water courses and is found scattered and in large thickets on the slopes above streams and rivers. By February, in the Athens, GA. area, the buds are already starting to elongate. There have been some interesting crosses between *K. hirsuta* and *K. latifolia*.

NATIVE HABITAT: Quebec and New Brunswick to Florida, west to Ohio and Tennessee. Introduced 1734.

RELATED SPECIES:

Kalmia angustifolia, (kal′mē-à an-gus-ti-fō′lē-à), Lambkill Kalmia, is a low growing (1 to 3′), blue-green foliaged, evergreen shrub of rounded spreading habit with 2 forms; one a compact, tufted grower; the other thin and open. Flowers are usually rose-pink to purplish crimson, 1/2″ across, in corymbs, June to July; two varieties include var. *rubra* with dark purple flowers and var. *candida* with white flowers; 'Hammonasset' is a compact, stoloniferous form with rich blue-rose flowers; discovered in 1961 in a population of 300 plants within a few hundred feet of the Hammonasset River, CT; Foliage may be poisonous if eaten in large amounts. The species is found on a variety of sites including rocky barrens, old pastures, wet sterile soils, often in semi-shade. Native from Newfoundland and Hudson Bay to Michigan and Georgia. Introduced 1736. Zone 1 to 6(7).

Kalopanax pictus—Castor-aralia
(kal-ō-pan′aks pik′tus)

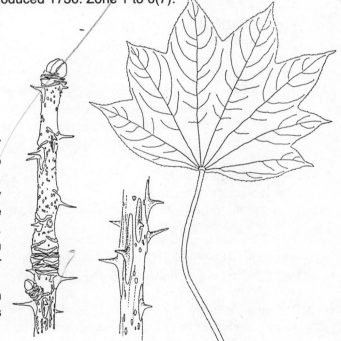

FAMILY: Araliaceae

LEAVES: Alternate, simple, palmately 5 to 7 lobed, 10 to 14″ wide on young trees, 7 to 10″ wide on mature trees, lobes shallow, triangular-ovate, long pointed, uniformly toothed, reaching 1/3 or less toward the center, lustrous dark green above, glabrous, paler beneath except with hairs in the axils of the veins; petiole often longer than the blade.

STEM: Coarse, stout, almost club-like, yellowish brown, glabrous, armed with numerous prominent broad based prickles.

SIZE: 80 to 90′ in height in the wild with a spread comparable to height; under cultivation sizes of 40 to 60′ are more in line.

HARDINESS: Zone 4 to 7, possibly 8 with cultural coddling.

HABIT: In youth—upright oval, coarse, gaunt and not particularly attractive; rather impressive at maturity, with massive oval-rounded outline.

TEXTURE: Coarse in leaf and in winter.

BARK: Armed with stout, broad-based, yellowish prickles on young stems; mature trunks blackish, deeply ridged and furrowed.

LEAF COLOR: Dark glossy green above, lighter green beneath, somewhat similar in shape to Sweetgum, *Liquidambar styraciflua;* changing to yellow or red in the fall, usually not good; have only observed yellow fall color.

FLOWERS: Perfect, white, July to early August, produced in numerous, small, 1″ diameter umbels, forming a large, flattish terminal umbellose-panicle, 12 to 24″ across, each individual flower is small, however they are borne in great quantity at the end of the shoots of the season, bees appear to love them.

FRUIT: Small, 1/6″ wide, globose drupe, black, late September-October, relished and soon devoured by birds.

CULTURE: Transplant balled and burlapped as a young specimen into deep, rich, moist soil; full sun exposure; prune during spring; supposedly tolerant of alkaline conditions; long lived and trouble free.

DISEASES AND INSECTS: None serious.

LANDSCAPE VALUE: Excellent large shade tree yielding a tropical effect because of the large leaves; nowhere common in commerce; in youth it is extremely coarse but given time makes an impressive tree; has proven hardy at the University of Wisconsin Arboretum; survived −22°F during the rugged 1976-77 winter; will never surpass Sugar Maple in popularity; in the Arnold Arboretum small seedlings can be found in abundance.

VARIETY: There is a variety termed *maximowiczii* with deeply lobed leaves reaching 2/3 the way to the center.

PROPAGATION: Dormancy of the seed is related to embryo condition (probably immature) and an impermeable seed coat; warm plus cold (41°F) stratification for 60 to 90 days may give reasonably prompt germination; soaking the seeds in sulfuric acid for 30 minutes will substitute for the warm period.

NATIVE HABITAT: Japan, Sakhalin, the Russian Far East, Korea and China. Introduced 1865.

Kerria japonica—Japanese Kerria
(ker′ē-á ja-pon′i-ká)

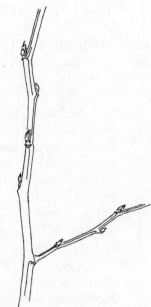

FAMILY: Rosaceae

LEAVES: Alternate, simple, ovate-lanceolate, 1 1/2 to 4″ long, about 1/2 as wide, acuminate, cuneate, double serrate, bright green and glabrous above, paler and slightly pubescent below on veins; petioles 1/4 to 1/2″ long.

BUDS: Imbricate, greenish brown, vari-colored, usually 5 exposed scales, glabrous.

STEM: Slender, green throughout winter, zig-zag, glabrous, glossy, supple.

SIZE: 3 to 6′ in height; spreading, with time, to 6 to 9′.

HARDINESS: Zone 4 to 9, flowered only above snow-line after −20°F.

HABIT: Stems distinctly upright arching forming a low, broad-rounded, dense twiggy mass becoming loose with age; stems are slender and refined in overall textural quality.

RATE: Somewhat slow in establishment, fast with time.

TEXTURE: Fine in foliage and winter.

STEM COLOR: Distinct yellowish green to bright green in winter, very noticeable and actually not objectionable, adds color to the winter landscape especially when used in mass.

LEAF COLOR: Leafs out early with young shoots emerging in March (Athens), bright green in summer usually exhibiting little change in fall and holding late, often late November (Athens), some yellow; leaves of flowering shoots smaller than those on barren shoots of the season.

FLOWERS: Bright yellow, 5-petaled, 1 1/4 to 1 3/4″ across, April to early May (very effective) for 2 to 3 weeks, borne solitary at the terminal of short leafy stems originating from previous year's growth; sporadically flowers through the season; prune after flowering, starts in late March to early April in Athens; in full sun, flowers tend to bleach out and look sickly, ideally site plant in partial shade or at least out of the afternoon sun.

FRUIT: Achene, seldom seen, not showy.

CULTURE: Transplant balled and burlapped or from a container; requires loamy, well-drained soil of moderate fertility; does well in full shade; actually best removed from full sun (flowers fade rapidly) in exposed locations; requires considerable pruning for dead branches are constantly evident; avoid winter damage by planting in a well-drained situation; if fertility levels are too high, the plant becomes weed-like and grows excessively with a resultant reduction in flowers; in spite of the cultural precautions, I find it an easy plant to grow.

DISEASES AND INSECTS: Leaf and twig blight, twig blight, canker, leaf spot, and root rot; the above are possibilities but I have not noticed serious problems.

LANDSCAPE VALUE: Interesting free-flowering shrub; could be used more extensively; borders, masses, facer plant to hide leggy specimens, possibly on highways or other large public areas where extensive masses of foliage and flowers are welcome and needed; tough plant, seems to withstand considerable abuse; does extremely well in south and flowers in late March in Athens, GA, and sporadically into early summer.

CULTIVARS:

'Aureo-variegata'—Leaves edged with yellow, 2″ long.

'Aureo-vittata'—Branches striped green and yellow, will revert, tried to track a plant in the Arnold Arboretum but by the time I found it, green stems predominated.

'Golden Guinea'—Flowers larger than the species and freely borne over a long period, rich green foliage, graceful delicate shrub.

'Picta'—Leaves edged white, handsome, not obnoxious like many variegated plants; good choice for massing; probably needs some shade in hot climates; single yellow flowers; a superb foliage shrub that with adequate moisture does not cook in the heat of the summer even in Zone 8, the central leaf color is a soft gray-green, flowers are profuse, will occasionally produce green shoots which must be removed, easy to propagate and grows sufficiently fast to have impact.

'Pleniflora'—Flowers double, almost golden yellow, nearly ball shaped, 1 to 2″ in diameter; flowers are more effective than those of species and longer lasting; it is quite different in habit from the species being more erect, gaunt and rather lanky; I have seen plants 6 to 8′ high and plants to 12′ have been reported; this form is quite common in southern gardens but is not as dainty as the species, opens in late March and still effective in late April, suckers freely.

'Shannon'—Vigorous form with larger flowers than typical species type, Cedar Lane Farms, Madison, GA has offered this form a number of years.

'Splendens'—Large buttercup yellow flowers.

PROPAGATION: Easily rooted using untreated cuttings collected in summer and fall; I have never had a problem rooting the species or the cultivars.

NATIVE HABITAT: Central and western China. Introduced 1834.

Koelreuteria paniculata—Panicled Goldenraintree, Varnish Tree
(kōl-rū-tē′ri-a pan-ik-ū-lā′ta)

FAMILY: Sapindaceae

LEAVES: Alternate, pinnate or bipinnately compound, 6 to 18″ long, 7 to 15 leaflets, each leaflet ovate to ovate-oblong, 1 to 4″ long, coarsely and irregularly crenate-serrate, at base often incisely lobed, rich green and glabrous above, pubescent on the veins beneath or nearly glabrous.

BUDS: Terminal-absent, laterals half-ellipsoid, sessile, with 2 exposed scales, brownish, 1/8 to 3/16″ long.

STEM: Stout, olive-buff to light brown, glabrous; glabrescent leaf scars—raised, rather large, shield-shaped; lenticels—prominent, orange-brown, raised; pith-solid, white.

SIZE: 30 to 40′ in height with an equal or greater spread.

HARDINESS: Zone 5, possibly lower part of 4, to 9, has not been reliably hardy in Madison, Wisconsin; young plants much more susceptible to winter damage; suspect -20 to -25°F will result in some stem injury.

HABIT: Beautiful dense tree of regular rounded outline, sparingly branched, the branches spreading and ascending.

RATE: Medium to fast, 10 to 12′ over a 5 to 7 year period.

TEXTURE: Medium in foliage, medium-coarse in winter.

BARK: Light gray-brown, ridged and furrowed on older trunks.

LEAF COLOR: Purplish red when unfolding, bright green at maturity changing to yellow and golden almost orange-yellow in fall but not coloring consistently; have had good yellow fall color on a tree in my garden, new leaves may be injured by late spring frosts.

FLOWERS: Perfect, yellow, each about 1/2″ wide, borne in a 12 to 15″ long and wide loose panicle in July, very showy; flowers in early June at Athens and early July at Urbana, IL.

FRUIT: Deshicent, papery, 3-valved capsule, 1 1/2 to 2″ long (changing from green to yellow and finally brown); seeds are black, hard, about the size of peas, August to October for complete color transformation.

CULTURE: Transplants well but best moved balled and burlapped as a small tree; adaptable to a wide range of soils; withstands drouth, heat, wind and alkaline soils; tolerates air pollutants; prefers full sun; prune during winter; averaged 1′5″ per year over a 9-year period in Wichita, KS tests.

DISEASES AND INSECTS: None particularly serious, although coral-spot fungus, leaf spot, canker, wilt and root rot have been reported.

LANDSCAPE VALUE: Excellent and unrivaled for late yellow flowers; one of the very few yellow flowering trees; excellent as a small lawn tree, for shading a patio; suggested as a street tree although supposedly somewhat weak-wooded; very lovely to look upon and lay under on a hot July day; choice specimen tree where space is limited; shows tremendous adaptability to extremes of soil.

CULTIVARS:

‘Fastigiata’—I have seen this clone at several gardens and found it to be extremely upright; 25′ high tree with 4 to 6′ spread; raised at Kew Gardens, England, from seeds received in 1888 from Shanghai; it flowers sparsely; I received seeds of this clone from Dr. S.M. Still when he was at Kansas State; unfortunately they were never planted so their ability to produce fastigiate types will never be known at least by this author; averaged 1′4″ per year over a 10-year period in KS test but was killed to ground in 78-79 winter, not as cold hardy as the species.

‘September’—Selection by J.C. McDaniel from a group of three trees on the Bloomington campus of the University of Indiana, two of which were in full flower on August 25, 1958; flowers first two weeks in September at the Arnold Arboretum, seedlings raised from the mother plant also exhibit the late flowering habit; is not as hardy as the species; probably does not harden off early enough in fall to avoid early freezes, possibly a hybrid between *K. paniculata* and *K. bipinnata*.

PROPAGATION: Seed has an impermeable seed coat and internal dormancy; scarification for 60 minutes in concentrated sulfuric acid followed by moist stratification at 41°F for 90 days is recommended; root cuttings collected in December represent a vegetative means of propagation; very easy to grow from seed, I have raised many seedlings.

ADDITIONAL NOTES: Although several authors mention the tree is weak-wooded I have never observed anything in the field that supports this. I have witnessed horrendous ice storms in Illinois and Georgia but absolutely no damage to *K. paniculata*. There are numerous plants in the Athens area from 8' to 35 to 40'. Damage to Siberian Elm, Water Oak, and Loblollybay from ice has been tremendous but I have not noticed a single broken limb on Goldenrain.

NATIVE HABITAT: China, Japan, Korea. Introduced 1763.

RELATED SPECIES:

Koelreuteria elegans, (*K. formosana*) (kōl-rū-tē′ri-a el′e-ganz), Flamegold, appears in Florida landscapes and forms a small 20 to 30' high rounded tree with the yellow flowers and rose fruits of *K. bipinnata*. The drive to Disney World has groupings of this species. It is distinctly less cold hardy and is reserved for Zone 9 to 10. Flowers in late summer-fall and the fruits are evident into December. Formosa, Fiji.

Koelreuteria bipinnata—*Bougainvillea Goldenraintree*

LEAVES: Alternate, bipinnately compound, 20″ long or longer and as wide, 8 to 11 pinnae, leaflets 2 to 3″ long, oval-oblong and entire to finely serrate, lustrous dark green.

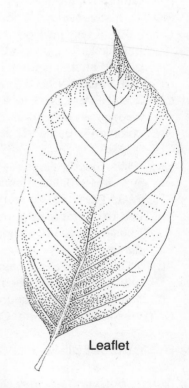

Leaflet

Koelreuteria bipinnata, (kōl-rū-tē′ri-a bī-pin-nā′ta), Bougainvillea Goldenraintree, was not given its just due in the last edition but has emerged in the past five years as a worthwhile, handsome, late summer flowering tree. Habit is distinctly upright-spreading with large, coarse thick stems that must be pruned in youth to induce a full dense crown. Height will approximate 20 to 30 (40′) and 2/3's this in width. The flowers occur in 12 to 24″ high, 8 to 18″ wide, upright panicles in late August-mid September in Athens. The effect is outstanding and since competition is nil the plant shines like a yellow star. The three-valved, 1 to 2″ long, pink to rose capsules develop shortly after flowering and hold color for 3 to 5 weeks. If the fruits are collected in the pink stage and dried the color will persist. A fine bouquet in our home is still colorful six years after collecting. Like *K. paniculata,* any well drained soil is suitable. Will withstand acid or alkaline conditions but requires full sun. Nurserymen indicate root systems may be sparse and trees should be root pruned or moved as a young container-grown plant. Two-year-old seedlings will flower. Interestingly, of all the plants in my garden, this produces the most stray seedlings. Even if some cold injury occurs on the tips of the branches, flowering will still occur since buds are set on the new growth of the season. Possibly 0 to -5° (-10°F) will induce some tip injury. Seeds sown in fall germinate the following spring. China. Introduced 1888. *Koelreuteria integrifolia* is occasionally listed but is nothing more than an old name for *K. bipinnata.*

Kolkwitzia amabilis—Beautybush
(kōlk-wit′zē-a à-mab′à-lis)

FAMILY: Caprifoliaceae

LEAVES: Opposite, simple, broad-ovate, 1 to 3″ long, 3/4 to 2″ wide, acuminate, rounded at base, remotely and shallowly toothed or nearly entire, ciliate, dull dark green above and sparingly hairy, pilose on the netted veins beneath; petiole-pilose, about 1/8″ long.

BUDS: Solitary, sessile, ovoid, with 3 to 4 pairs of scales.

STEM: Slender, round, villous at first, later glabrous and developing an exfoliating, brownish bark.

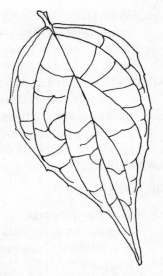

SIZE: 6 to 10′ in height and usually slightly smaller in spread, can grow to 15′.

HARDINESS: Zone 4 to 8.

HABIT: Upright arching, vase-shaped shrub, somewhat fountain-like in over-all effect; becomes leggy with age and most of the foliage is in upper one-half of the plant.

RATE: Fast.

TEXTURE: Medium in leaf; coarse in winter.

BARK: Light grayish brown and often exfoliating on older stems.

LEAF COLOR: Dull dark green in summer; slightly yellowish to reddish in fall.

FLOWERS: Perfect, pink, yellow in throat, flaring bell-shaped, two-together, 1/2″ long, about as wide at the mouth, May-early June, borne in 2 to 3″ diameter corymbs; the principal attribute of this plant is the flower, full flower mid April on the Georgia campus.

FRUIT: Bristly, ovoid, 1/4″ long dehiscent capsule, often long persistent, good identification feature.

CULTURE: Easily transplanted balled and burlapped; prefers well drained soil, pH adaptable; full sun for best flowering; older stems should be pruned out every year or to renew plant simply cut it to the ground after flowering; flowers on old wood.

DISEASES AND INSECTS: None serious.

LANDSCAPE VALUE: Probably belongs where it can develop alone, but hardly falls into the category of a specimen plant; rather pretty in flower but too coarse and cumbersome for many landscapes; rather common in England but seldom encountered in modern day U.S. landscapes.

CULTIVARS:

'Pink Cloud'; 'Rosea'—Clear strong pink flowers of good size and very floriferous, raised at Wisley in 1946; the second with more reddish flowers, introduced from Holland.

PROPAGATION: Seeds can be sown as soon as ripe or stored in air tight containers in a cool place for up to a year; plants grown from seeds will often show inferior, washed out, pink flower color; it is best to use softwood cuttings, as they root readily, and select wood from floriferous, good pink-colored plants.

ADDITIONAL NOTES: I have a difficult time acclimating myself to this shrub. In flower it is singularly effective; however, the rest of the year it gives one a headache. E.H. Wilson considered it one of the finest plants he introduced to cultivation.

NATIVE HABITAT: Central China. 1901.

RELATED SPECIES:

Dipelta floribunda—Rosy Dipelta
(dī-pel′tả flôr-i-bun′dả)

LEAVES: Opposite, simple, ovate to oval-lanceolate, 2 to 4″ long, 5/8 to 1 1/2″ wide, acuminate, rounded or cuneate, entire, or on vigorous shoots slightly denticulate, glabrous, dark green; petiole—1/4″ long.

Dipelta floribunda, Rosy Dipelta, is a large, oval-rounded, 10 to 15′ high shrub. The fragrant flowers are 1 to 1 1/4″ long, 1″ wide with 5 rounded, funnel-shaped, spreading lobes, pale pink and yellow in the throat. It is a rather pretty shrub and essentially unknown outside of arboreta. There is a fine specimen at the Arnold Arboretum. The fruit is unusual and resembles an elm samara being about 1/2 to 3/4″ long. Quite tolerant of acid or alkaline soil and requiring full sun. Central and western China. Introduced 1902. Zone 5 to 7?

Laburnum × *watereri* — Waterer Laburnum, Goldenchain Tree
(lȧ-bēr′num × wa-ter′-erī)

(Hybrid between *L. alpinum* and *L. anagyroides*)

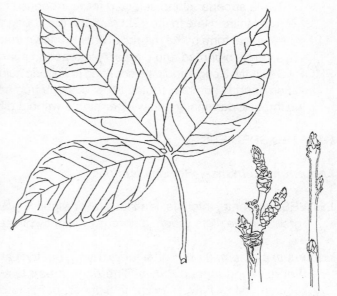

FAMILY: Fabaceae

LEAVES: Alternate, trifoliate, each leaflet elliptic to elliptic-oblong or elliptic-obovate, 1 1/4 to 3″ long, usually obtuse and mucronulate, broad cuneate, glabrous at maturity, bright green.

BUDS: Ovoid, small, 1/16 to 1/8″ long, with 2 to 4, exposed silvery-haired scales.

STEM: Slender to stout, olive, without prominent lenticels, green stem color is maintained into old wood, glabrous.

SIZE: 12 TO 15′ in height with a spread of 9 to 12′.

HARDINESS: Zone 5 to 7; not a plant for deep south conditions.

HABIT: Distinctly upright oval to round-headed small tree or shrub which usually loses the lower branches and is in need of a facer plant after a period of years.

RATE: Medium, 12 to 18″ per year over a 5 to 8 year period.

TEXTURE: Medium-fine in leaf; somewhat coarse in winter condition.

BARK: Olive green in color on young and old branches; eventually developing fissured areas.

LEAF COLOR: Bright green in summer with a bluish tinge; fall color is non-descript.

FLOWERS: Perfect, yellow, 3/4″ long, borne on 6 to 10″ long, pendulous racemes in May, extremely beautiful in flower.

FRUIT: Pod, slightly pubescent, October, not ornamentally effective.

CULTURE: Transplant balled and burlapped in spring as a small tree into moist, well drained soil; the plant is adaptable to many situations but prefers light shade in the hot part of the day; will not withstand standing water; also cold injury can be a problem; withstands high pH conditions; prune after flowering; should be looked upon as a short-lived tree in the midwest and probably east; not at all heat tolerant, possibly excessively high night temperatures, and therefore not suitable for the south, although a tree in Spartanburg, SC persists.

DISEASES AND INSECTS: Leaf spot, twig blight, laburnum vein mosaic, aphids and grape mealy-bug can affect this plant; the twig blight is often a serious problem.

LANDSCAPE VALUE: Good in the shrub border, near buildings, corners of houses; plant in a protected spot; very effective when grouped in threes and fives; makes a tremendous show in flower; truly a beautiful plant in flower and the German popular name, Goldregen (Golden Rain), is most appropriate; widely planted in Europe but not so common in the United States; at Bodnant Gardens, Wales, there is the famous "Laburnum Arch" with the plants trained across a structure about 50 to 75 yards long; the flowers cascade and the visitors can walk through this feature; my visit coincided with full flower and the effect was just overwhelming.

CULTIVARS:

'Alford's Weeping'—Pendulous in habit, discovered at Hillier's Nursery, England.

'Aureum' (*L. anagyroides*)—Leaves golden yellow; Bean considered it one of the prettiest of yellow-leaved trees, in commerce at least since 1874, have not yet seen.

'Pendulum' (*L. anagyroides* and *L. alpinum*)—Branches slender and weeping, considered a very graceful form; during my graduate student days at the University of Massachusetts I found a small weeping form on campus; it displayed distinctly weeping branches and was rather pretty in all of its parts; I assume the weeping forms flower but have not seen them.

'Vossii'—Often used as the specific epithet for *L. × watereri,* i.e., *L. × vossii,* when actually 'Vossii' is a superior clone selected for more dense habit and racemes which are up to 2′ long; raised in Holland late in the 19th century; the young stems are appressed hairy, not glabrous as in the typical form of the hybrid; a virus is known that causes a rosetting of foliage; in Wichita KS tests rarely bloomed and over a 7-year period averaged 4″ per year, finally dying.

PROPAGATION: Seed should be scarified in sulfuric acid for 15 to 30 minutes; cuttings — leaf bud cuttings taken in early summer rooted 80%; cuttings from root sprouts rooted 100%; apparently seeds have no internal dormancy and will germinate without difficulty when properly scarified.

RELATED SPECIES:

Laburnum alpinum — Scotch Laburnum

LEAVES: Alternate, trifoliate, leaflets oval or slightly obovate, 1 1/2 to 3″ long, acute, rounded, ciliate, deep green above, light green, glabrous or slightly pilose below; petiole—1 to 2″ long.

Laburnum alpinum, (là-bĕr′num al-pī′num), Scotch Laburnum, is a 20′ tree with a short sturdy trunk and flat to round-topped crown. The deep green leaflets are not as hairy as in *L. anagyroides.* The golden yellow flowers occur in slender, pendulous, 10 to 15″ long racemes in May; pod is 2 to 3″ long, flat, glabrous, upper suture winged and forming a knife-like edge. This is considered the superior garden species. Southern Alps, also occurring wild in the northern Apennines, northwest Yugoslavia and southern Czechoslovakia. Found in moister situations than *L. anagyroides.* Cultivated 1596. Zone 4 to 7.

Laburnum anagyroides — Common Laburnum

LEAVES: Alternate, trifoliate, leaflets elliptic to elliptic-oblong or elliptic-obovate, 1 to 3″ long, obtuse and mucronate, broad cuneate, rich green above, grayish green and silky pubescent below; petiole—2 to 3″ long.

Laburnum anagyroides, (là-bĕr′num ăn-ă-jī-roy′dēz), Common Laburnum, tends to be a low branched, bushy, wide spreading, 20 to 30′ high tree. The golden yellow flowers occur in cylindrical, pendulous, 6 to 10″ long downy racemes. Pods 2 to 3″ long, upper suture thickened and not winged as in *L. alpinum.* Central and southern Europe. Cultivated 1650. Zone 5 to 7.

+ **Laburnocytisus adamii,** (là-bĕr-nō-sī-tis′-us a-dam′ē-ī), is a curious anomaly of great interest with considerable garden value. It is a graft hybrid between *Cytisus purpureus* and *L. anagyroides* that appeared in the nursery of Jean Louis Adam near Paris in 1825. On the grafted plant a branch appeared with purplish yellow flowers intermediate between the parents. Further, when outplanted it was found to revert back and produce yellow, pinkish purple and the combination colored flowers. The vegetative portions of the plant show pure as well as intermediate characteristics of the two parents. I have seen this plant at Kew Gardens in flower and it is genuinely fascinating. They have a high quality educational exhibit showing the parents and the resultant + *L. adamii.* It makes a small 20 to 25′ high tree. The Arnold Arboretum has a plant. Zone 5 to 7.

ADDITIONAL NOTES: Seeds contain an alkaloid called cytisine, which can be fatal to children and adults. This compound is contained in all parts of the plant. Supposedly, one small seed can prove toxic to a small child. Extreme care should be exercised when using this plant in a public area.

Lagerstroemia indica — Common Crapemyrtle
(lā-gĕr-strē′mē-à in′di-kà)

FAMILY: Lythraceae

LEAVES: Opposite or the upper alternate or in whorls of three, very much privet-like, simple, 1 to 2 3/4″ long, 3/4 to 1 1/2″ wide, entire, subsessile, elliptic or obovate to oblong, acute or obtuse, broad-cuneate or rounded at base, dark green and often lustrous, glabrous or pilose along the midrib beneath, very small conical and deciduous stipules; very short petioled.

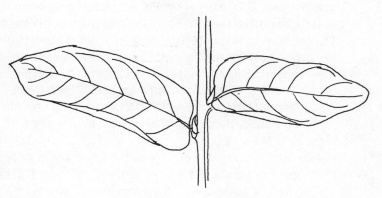

BUDS: Small, solitary, sessile, oblong, somewhat elbowed above base, closely appressed, with 2 acute ciliate scales.

STEM: Rather slender, angled often almost squarish with rather prominent wings, glabrous, greenish, red, or combinations, maturing to brown; older stems becoming smooth.

SIZE: Variable but based on observtions of plants from Washington, D.C.; Raleigh, N.C.; and Athens, GA., a range of 15 to 25′ in height seems reasonable; saw a 40 to 45′ plant in Savannah; the range of sizes is astronomical from 18″ up.

HARDINESS: Zone 7 to 9, -5 to -10°F is about the break point between a woody plant and herbaceous perennial.

HABIT: Small to medium size shrub or small tree of variable habit; often seen in multi-stemmed form with a cloud of foliage reserved for the upper 1/2 of the plant while the basal portion is leafless and only the handsome bark is evident.

RATE: Fast.

TEXTURE: Medium, possibly medium-fine in all seasons.

BARK COLOR: Smooth, gray, exfoliating and exposing vari-colored underbark which ranges from many handsome shades of brown to gray; the beautiful bark is a real landscape asset.

LEAF COLOR: New emerging leaves are yellowish green, bronze to reddish purple in color yielding to lustrous medium to dark green at maturity; fall coloration ranges from yellow, orange and red with all colors interspersed on the same tree; white flowered types often have yellow fall color; pink and red types show yellow, orange and red fall color.

FLOWERS: Perfect, 6-petaled, each flower 1 to 1 1/2″ wide, color varying from white, pink, purple to deep red on different plants; produced in 6 to 8″ long and 3 to 5″ wide panicles which terminate the current year's growth; July through September; petals crinkled.

FRUIT: A broad-ellipsoidal 6-valved dehiscent capsule, about 1/2″ wide and persisting through winter, seeds 3/8″ long and winged.

CULTURE: Transplant as a balled and burlapped or container-grown plant into moist, well-drained soil; prefers full sun; prune by removal of the deadwood or by cutting the plants almost to the ground in spring; this latter approach can be effectively used to produce large flowers and to keep the larger growing types in bounds; the species prefers hot, sunny climates and, obviously, is best suited for southern gardens.

DISEASES AND INSECTS: Powdery mildew, black spot, sooty mold, tip blight, leaf spot, root rot, aphid, and Florida wax scale are problems.

LANDSCAPE VALUE: Handsome and very beautiful specimen shrub or tree; often used in groups and underplanted with a ground cover; the dark green ground cover acts as a foil for the handsome bark; some of the smaller types are used as hedges, screens, masses; many of the new introductions from the National Arboretum are superior to the run-of-the-mill cultivars; crape myrtles are often given credit only for flower but many have superb fall color and excellent bark.

CULTIVARS: Flower colors range from white, pink, orchid to dark red. The National Arboretum, Washington, D.C. has an extensive breeding program with *Lagerstroemia*. The number of cultivars is staggering and I recommend *The Lagerstroemia Handbook/Checklist* by Egolf and Andrick, 1978. Descriptions of National Arboretum and other important cultivars are presented.

'Acoma'—Low spreading, semi-pendulous, semi-dwarf, multi-stemmed grow habit, 10′ high and 11′ wide in 15 years. Panicles are pure white with pronounced golden anthers, 6 to 7 1/2″ long and 3 1/2 to 5″ wide, blooming from late June to September. Young leaves are dark bronze-tinged, becoming dark green, turning to dark purple-red in fall. Mildew resistant. Young branches are red-purple, becoming gray brown, at maturity light gray that is exposed by exfoliating bark of older branches and trunk.

'Apalachee'—Upright, multi-stemmed large shrub or small tree, 12 1/2′ high by 8 1/2′ wide in 12 years. Panicles are light lavender, 5 1/2 by 9 1/2″ long and 5 1/2 to 7″ wide, blooming from mid July to September. Young leaves are glossy, glabrous and bronze-tinged, later dark green, becoming dull orange to russet in autumn. Mildew resistant. New shoots are glabrous, dull red, becoming gray-brown as the branches mature, later sinuous, mottled exfoliating branches and trunk reveal cinnamon to chestnut brown bark coloration.

'Biloxi'—Upright, multiple-stemmed, arched-crown, small tree, 20′ high and 12′ wide in 12 years. Panicles are pale pink, 5 1/2 to 7 1/2″ long, 4 1/2 to 7 1/2″ wide, blooming from July to late September. Young leaves are glabrous, light bronze becoming lighter tinged, glossy, slightly leatherly, becoming dark green, turning dark yellow-orange to orange-red to dark red in autumn. Mildew resistant. Young branches are glabrous, light brown becoming gray-brown, later sinuous, mottled, exfoliating bark of older branches and trunk reveals dark brown bark coloration.

'Byers Standard Red'—Upright tall growing form reaching 25′ in height, flowers soft red in mid July, fall color orange, good mildew resistance.

'Byers Wonderful White'—Upright form reaching 20′ in height, flowers clear white blooming in July, fall color yellow, good mildew resistance.

'Carolina Beauty'—Upright form reaching 20′ in height, flowers dark brick red blooming in mid July and later; fall color orange, poor mildew resistance.

'Catawba'—Globose medium habit, glossy dark green foliage, abundant compact inflorescences of dark purple florets, mildew resistant, flowers late July to September, 10 1/2′ by 11′ in 11 years, has been outstanding in my garden with reddish fall color.

'Centennial'—Dwarf compact globular shrub reaching approximately 3′ in height, flowers bright lavender, blooming mid June and later; fall color orange, sister to 'Victor', with similar habit and good mildew resistance.

'Centennial Spirit'—Upright shrub or small tree with generally 3 to 5 major stems with few secondary branches or suckers from base. Panicles are dark wine-red, with very little discoloration before falling, 8 to 12″ long and 4 to 8″ wide, blooming from late June through early October. Leaves are smaller and thicker than the species average, dark green turning red-orange in autumn. Mildew resistant. Strong stems keep inflorescences from drooping after summer rains. Has withstood -4°F without damage but was killed to soil line at -22°F, regrowing and flowering by July.

'Cherokee'—Compact, medium growth habit, 8′ by 7 1/2′ in 11 years, glossy heavy dark green foliage, numerous pyramidal inflorescences of brilliant red florets, mildew resistant, late July with good recurrent flowering through September, this cultivar has been confused since the introduction and plants I have grown were light red and infested with mildew. However, I have seen slides of the original introduction and the flowers were indeed brilliant red.

'Comanche'—Upright, multi-stemmed, broad spreading crown, large shrub or small tree, 11 1/2′ high and 12 1/2′ wide in 15 years. Panicles are coral-pink, 5 1/2 to 9 1/2″ long and 5 1/2 to 7″ wide, blooming from late July to mid-September. Young leaves are glossy, glabrous, light bronze, maturing to dark green and turning dark orange-red to dark purple-red in autumn. Young branches are brown-maroon becoming medium gray-brown; later sinuous, mottled, sandalwood as bark exfoliates on older branches and trunk.

'Conestoga'—Open growth habit, flowers open, medium lavender, change to pale lavender, early flowers starting in mid July and opening over a period of a month, slightly susceptible to mildew, 10' by 14' in 11 years, not impressive in my garden because of washed out lavender-pink color, flowers occur at the ends of long shoots and cause the stems to arch.

'Dallas Red'—Of interest because of excellent hardiness and Raulston noted it was the best of the *L. indica* cultivars at NC State Arboretum; he mentioned that the winters of 1984 and 1985 killed or severely injured 20' tall mature plants without touching 'Dallas Red'; grows fast and produces large deep "red" panicles; mildew resistance is not known by this author.

'Hardy Lavender'—Upright form reaching 20' in height, flowers medium lavender, blooming late July; fall color red, good mildew resistance.

'Hope'—Open growing dwarf form reaching 4' in height, flowers white, blooming mid June; fall color yellow, good mildew resistance.

'Hopi'—Spreading, semi-dwarf, multiple-stemmed, 7 1/2' high and 10' wide in 12 years. Panicles are medium pink, 4 to 5 1/2" long and 2 1/2 to 7" wide, blooming from late June to late September. Young leaves are glabrous, slightly pink overcast, becoming dark green, turning bright orange-red to dark red in autumn. Mildew resistant. Young branches are dark red-purple becoming gray-brown prior to light gray-brown at maturity. Most hardy of the semi-dwarf cultivars from the National Arboretum, withstood -24°F without injury.

'Lipan'—Upright, multiple-stemmed, large shrub or small tree, 13' high and 13' wide in 12 years. Panicles are medium lavender, 5 1/2 to 7" long and 6 to 8 1/2" wide, blooming from mid-July to mid-September. Young leaves are glabrous, slightly leathery, slightly bronze-tinged, becoming dark green, turning light orange to dull red in autumn. Mildew resistant. Young branches are red-purple, becoming medium gray-green, later sinuous, mottled near white to beige as the bark exfoliates from the older branches and trunk.

'Miami'—Upright, multiple-stemmed small tree, 16' high and 8 1/2' wide in 12 years. Panicles are dark pink, 5 1/2 to 9 1/2" long and 4 to 9 1/2" wide, blooming from early July to September. Young leaves are burgundy, becoming dark green, turning orange to dull russet in autumn. Mildew resistant. Young maroon shoots become gray-brown, later sinuous, mottled, dark chestnut brown as older branches exfoliate.

'Muskogee'—Large shrub or small tree, 21' high and 15' wide after 14 years, medium brown bark, glossy green leaves turn good red in autumn, prolific light lavender-pink flowers, each inflorescence 4 to 10" long, 4 to 5" wide, July to September, mildew resistant, produces landscape plant in 3 years, hybrid between *L. indica* × *L. fauriei,* have a 15' plant in my garden and am quite impressed by vigor and flower production, unfortunately, aphids are much more fond of this than 'Natchez' and sooty mold can really disfigure the plant; bark is a shiny light gray to tan and rather attractive but again does not measure up to 'Natchez'.

'Natchez'—Large shrub or small tree, 21' high and 21' wide after 14 years, dark cinnamon-brown, sinuous, mottled, exfoliating trunk bark that remains spectacular throughout the year, glossy dark green leaves that turn orange and red in fall, pure white flowers, 6 to 12" long, 4 to 7 1/2" wide panicle, late June, July into September, bark develops after about 5 years, *L. indica* × *L. fauriei,* widely planted in the southeast and is probably the dominant white flowering large tree type cultivar, cinnamon-brown bark is outstanding, good aphid resistance compared to 'Muskogee', fall color some years is nil since an early freeze will kill the leaves, others a pretty bronze-orange but never red at least in the south.

'Near East'—Open spreading form reaching 18' in height, flowers light pink, blooming mid July and later; fall color yellow-orange, moderately mildew resistant.

'Ocmulgee'—Small 3' by 3', dark green foliage form with glistening red-maroon buds that open to "red" flowers and literally smother the foliage in July-August, have grown this for a number of years along with 'Victor' and can tell very little difference; at times I think they are one and the same.

'Osage'—Semi-pendulous, arched crown, open-branched, multiple-stemmed, large shrub or small tree, 12′ high and 10′ wide in 12 years. Panicles are clear light pink, 6 to 8″ long and 4 to 6″ wide. Young leaves are glossy, glabrous, bronze-tinged, becoming dark green, slightly leathery, turning red to dark red in autumn. Mildew resistant. Young shoots are red-purple, becoming gray-brown, later sinuous, mottled, exfoliating bark of older branches and trunk reveal chestnut brown bark coloration.

'Pecos'—Globose, semi-dwarf, multiple-stemmed shrub, 8′ high and 6′ wide in 12 years. Panicles are medium pink, 6 to 8″ long and 5 to 7 1/2″ wide, blooming from early July to September. Young leaves are glossy, glabrous, heavily tinged bronze, becoming dark green, turning maroon to dark purple-red in autumn. Mildew resistant. Young branches are red-purple becoming gray prior to dark brown at maturity.

'Pink'—Upright form to 18′ tall, flowers bubblegum pink, blooming mid July, fall color yellow orange, moderate mildew resistance.

'Potomac'—Upright growth habit, 10′ by 7 1/2′, dense dark green foliage, large terminal inflorescences of clear medium pink, mid-July to October, grew this for a number of years but it suffered significant dieback and was removed, flower color is as close to bright pink as any, mildew susceptible.

'Powhatan'—Compact, medium growth habit, 10 1/2′ by 10 1/2′ in 11 years, glossy heavy foliage, abundant compact inflorescences of medium purple open in late July until late September, mildew resistant, I have trouble separating this from 'Catawba'.

'Prairie Lace'—Compact, upright semi-dwarf shrub, 4 to 6′ in height in 6 years, panicle 4 1/2 to 10″ long, 3 to 8″ wide, individual petals medium pink banded with pure white on the outer margin, blooming mid June through late September; leaves are smaller and thicker than the species. New leaves emerge wine-red, gradually turning very dark green, fall color red to red-orange, supposedly resistant to mildew but a small plant in our lath area contracted significant mildew.

'Purple'—Upright form to 20′ tall, flowers light purple, blooming mid July; fall color orange, moderate resistance to mildew.

'Regal Red'—Broad upright form reaching 16′ in height, flowers red, blooming mid July; fall color red-orange, mildew resistance good.

'Seminole'—Compact medium growth habit, 7 to 8′ high and 6 to 7′ wide, glossy medium green heavy foliage, numerous large globose inflorescences of clear medium pink from mid-July to September, florets open over a 6 to 8 week period with recurrent bloom, high mildew resistance; in my mind one of the best for intensity of vivid pink and quality of flower, as soon as first flowers fade I cut them off and a second heavy bloom occurs about 3 to 4 weeks later, aphids can be heavy.

'Sioux'—Upright multiple-stemmed, large shrub or small tree, 14′ high and 12′ wide after 10 years, panicles dark pink, 5 to 9″ long, 4 1/2 to 6 1/2″ wide, maintains intense flower color, blooming late July to mid September; young foliage glabrous, early bronze, leaves become glossy, slightly leathery, dark green turning light maroon to bright red in autumn, mildew resistant; young branches glabrous, dull red, maturing to gray brown, later sinuous, mottled, exfoliating bark of older branches and trunk reveals light medium gray-brown coloration.

'Tuscarora'—Large shrub or small tree, 15′ high and wide after 12 years, red-tinged immature leaves turn dark green and then orange-red in fall, the dark coral-pink flowers appear in 5 to 12″ long and 4 to 8″ wide panicles from early July with recurrent bloom until late September, the mottled, light brown bark is spectacular, mildew resistant; have not been as impressed with this because of lack of hardiness at least in the Athens area.

'Tuskegee'—Multiple-stemmed small tree with distinct horizontal branching, 14′ high by 18′ wide in 17 years, long tapered panicles dark pink to near red, 6 to 8 1/2″ long and 4 1/2 to 7″ wide, blooming early July to September; young foliage red tinged becoming glossy, subcoriaceous, dark green, turning orange-red in autumn, mildew resistant; young branches bright red glabrous, becoming gray-tan, then sinuous, exfoliating, mottled light gray-tan.

'Victor'—Dwarf compact form reaching 3′ in height, flowers dark red, blooming July-August; fall color reddish yellow, good mildew resistance.

'Wichita'—Upright multiple-stemmed small tree, 16′ high and 9′ wide in 12 years, long tapered panicles light magenta to lavender, 4 1/2 to 14″ long, 3 1/2 to 19″ wide, blooming early July to October; young foliage glossy, glabrous, bronze-tinged, becoming slightly leathery, dark green and turning russet to mahogany in autumn, mildew resistant; young branches glabrous, red-purple, becoming light gray, later sinuous, mottled, dark russet brown to dark mahogany and exfoliating, has proven difficult to root.

'William Toovey'—Vase shaped form, 15′ tall, flowers pink-red, blooming July-August; fall color red-orange, good mildew resistance.

'Yuma'—Upright multiple-stemmed large shrub or small tree, 13′ high and 12′ wide in 12 years; long-tapered panicles, medium lavender bicolored, 6 1/2 to 14″ long, 5 to 8 1/2″ wide, blooming in late July to late September; young foliage glabrous, dull bronze-tinged, later dark green, turning dull yellow-orange to russet to lighter mahogany in autumn, mildew resistant; young branches glabrous, red-purple becoming gray, later sinuous, mottled, light gray as the bark exfoliates on older branches and trunk.

'Zuni'—Globose, semi-dwarf multistemmed shrub, 9′ high by 8′ wide in 12 years, panicles medium lavender, 3 to 5 1/2″ long, 3 to 5″ wide, blooming mid-July to late September; young foliage glossy, glabrous, leathery, red-tinged with heavier pigmentation on leaf margins, becoming dark green and turning orange-red to dark red in autumn, mildew resistant, young branches glabrous, heavily pigmented red, becoming gray prior to light brown and gray on older branches and trunk.

PROPAGATION: Interestingly, seeds supposedly germinate best if given a 30 to 45 day cold treatment before sowing; however, I have collected seeds in January and sown them immediately with excellent germination taking place in 2 to 3 weeks. Softwood cuttings of young growth taken in late May, June, July or semihardwood cuttings will root; I have had great success with 1000 ppm IBA-quick dip on softwood cuttings in July-August; rooting takes place in about 3 to 4 weeks; if rooted early in season will continue to grow.

ADDITIONAL NOTES: Another plant I dreamed about growing when living in the deep freeze zone. Rooted cuttings in 4″ pots planted in May grew 3′ the first season and flowered. Plants respond to good fertility and moisture. There are so many wonderful cultivars available that I doubt if there is anyone who knows or grows the best of the lot. We need to refine the list to the best 10 in order to keep from confusing the gardening public. Some of the new National Arboretum introductions are worth considering since they have been bred for disease resistance, good flowering, and highly ornamental bark.

NATIVE HABITAT: China and Korea. Introduced 1747.

RELATED SPECIES:

Lagerstroemia fauriei, (lā-gĕr-strē′mē- à fȧr′ē-ī) was unknown in the United States until Dr. John Creech, U.S. National Arboretum, brought it back from Japan in the 1950's. Has been the basis of mildew resistance in many of Dr. Egolf's National Arboretum hybrids. Also, the rusty brown bark character has proven aesthetically exceptional. Some of the original seedlings found their way to North Carolina State and what is now Dr. Raulston's Arboretum. In October, 1987, I witnessed these most magnificent 20 to 25′ high, multistemmed, dark red-brown barked specimens. Flowers are white and not exceptional. Ohwi lists them as occurring in 2 to 4″ long panicles. Supposedly more difficult to root than *L. indica* with softwoods yielding 70% in 6 to 8 weeks. Plants grow 2 to 4′ per year and the excellent bark develops after three years from a cutting. This is hardier than *L. indica* and probably should be considered Zone 6 since plants have survived -10°F in Raleigh. 'Fantasy' will be released by North Carolina State University Arboretum. It has outstanding bark and will make a handsome small tree.

Larix decidua — European or Common Larch
(lār′iks dē-sid′ū-à)

FAMILY: Pinaceae

LEAVES: Of long shoots up to 1 1/4″ long, narrow, pointed or blunt, those of short shoots (spurs) 30 to 40 together, 1/2 to 1 1/2″ long, narrower and blunter than those of the long shoots, both kinds keeled below, bright green when young, eventually soft deep green, turning yellow in autumn.

BUDS: Terminal of long shoots globose, short-pointed, with many brown pointed scales; lateral buds shorter, blunter, buds of short shoots small, rounded.

STEM: Young gray or yellowish, furrowed, without pubescence; those of the second year roughened by cushion-like leaf bases of the previous year; short shoots dark brown or almost black, marked with as many rings as they are years old, the younger rings downy.

CONES: Ovoid, 1 to 1 1/2″ long, 3/4 to 1″ wide, scales rounded and entire above, striated, margin sometimes wavy.

SIZE: 70 to 75′ in height by 25 to 30′ in width; can grow 100 to 140′ high.

HARDINESS: Zone 2 to 6, struggle in Zone 7(8).

HABIT: Pyramidal, with horizontal branches and drooping branchlets, slender and supple in youth but irregular and lacking in dignity with age; this is a deciduous conifer, i.e., the needles abscise in the fall.

RATE: Medium to fast, 2 1/2′ a year in youth, slowing with time.

TEXTURE: Medium-fine in leaf; medium-coarse in winter.

BARK: On young trees thin, scaly; on old trees, thick, deeply fissured at the base exposing a reddish brown inner bark which contrasts with the grayish brown outer bark.

LEAF COLOR: Bright green in spring becoming a deeper green in summer and finally turning an ochre yellow in the fall; fall color can be spectacular.

FLOWERS: Monoecious, in early spring the attractive red, pink, yellow or green, 1/2″ long, egg-shaped female strobili and the smaller yellow male strobili cover the branchlets.

FRUIT: Cone, scales pubescent on the backside, 1 to 1 1/2″ long, changing from red to yellow-brown to brown at maturity, scales overlapping and *not* reflexed.

CULTURE: Readily transplanted when dormant; should have sufficient moisture, well-drained and sunny conditions although *L. laricina* often grows in wet or even boggy conditions in the wild; intolerant of shade, dry, shallow, chalky soils and polluted areas; prune in mid-summer.

DISEASES AND INSECTS: The larch case-bearer is a serious pest; this small insect appears in early May and eventually eats its way into the needles, causing them to turn brown for the remainder of the season; early and timely spring spraying will control them; also cankers, leaf cast, needle rusts, wood decay, larch sawfly, woolly larch aphid, gypsy moth, tussock moth and Japanese beetle can be serious problems; canker has been a problem in European forest plantings.

LANDSCAPE VALUE: Very effective for park and large area use as a screen or specimen plant; fall colors can be excellent, new growth is as elegant as that of any tree.

CULTIVARS:

‘Fastigiata’—Columnar, similar to Lombardy Poplar with short ascending branches.

f. *pendula* (‘Pendula’)—Represents those trees with branches of a distinct pendulous nature; no doubt, more than one form is in cultivation; the common form is usually grafted on a standard and allowed to cascade; some plants are as "elegant" as mop heads; others rather graceful and attractive.

PROPAGATION: Seeds of most species germinate fairly well without pre-treatment; there seems to be a mild dormancy, however, that varies somewhat among species and lots within species; it can be overcome by cold stratification in a moist medium for 30 to 60 days at 30° to 41°F; cuttings are difficult to root although low percentages can be achieved with proper timing; the cultivars are grafted.

NATIVE HABITAT: Northern and central Europe. Introduced in colonial times. The main home of this species lies in the mountains of central Europe from southeastern France through the main chain of the Alps eastward to the neighborhood of Vienna. Here it forms beautiful forests, often in association with *Pinus cembra*.

Larix kaempferi (formerly *L. leptolepis*) — Japanese Larch
(lār′iks kem′fĕr-ī)

LEAVES: 1 to 1 1/4″ long and 1/25″ wide; on short spurs 40 or more together, 1 1/2″ or longer; upper side of both kinds flat, glaucous, underside keeled and with 2 white bands, deep green.

BUDS: Small, oblong or conical, pointed, resinous with bright brown fringed scales.

STEM: Glaucous, covered in varying density with soft brownish hairs or sometimes without hairs, furrowed; short spurs stout, dark brown.

CONES: 1 to 1 1/2″ long and slightly narrower in width; scales about 1/2″ long and wide, rounded, with the upper edge rolled back giving the extended cones a rosette-like appearance.

SIZE: 70 to 90′ in height by 25 to 40′ in spread.

HARDINESS: Zone 4 to 7.

HABIT: Very open and pyramidal in habit with beautiful slender pendulous branchlets.

RATE: Medium to fast.

TEXTURE: Fine in foliage, coarse in winter.

BARK: Similar to *L. decidua*.

LEAF COLOR: Green, underside keeled with two white glaucous bands, turning yellowish gold in autumn.

FLOWERS: See *Larix decidua*.

FRUIT: Cones stalked, 1 to 1 1/2″ long and almost as wide, scales keeled forming a rosette appearance.

CULTURE: Readily transplanted when dormant; should have sufficient moisture, well-drained, sunny situations; susceptible to drought but tolerant of shallow, acid soils; intolerant of shade, chalk soils and polluted areas.

DISEASES AND INSECTS: Similar to other larches but more resistant to canker than *L. decidua*.

LANDSCAPE VALUE: Best ornamental among the larches but reserved for large areas such as a park, golf course, campus.

CULTIVARS:

'Blue Rabbit'—A narrow, pyramidal form with conspicuously glaucous foliage, not common.

'Dervaes'—Branches horizontal, branchlets drooping, leaves fresh green, handsome but uncommon.

'Pendula'—A weeping form with glaucous needles; I see various specimens labeled as either *L. decidua* 'Pendula' or this form and am really not sure how to differentiate between them; I have seen distinct, mop-headed forms with long trailing branches that look alike but are labeled differently; without cones it is difficult to tell; although the mature stems of *L. kaempferi* are reddish brown this does not seem to hold for the weeping form unless some are *L. decidua* forms labeled incorrectly.

PROPAGATION: As previously described.

ADDITIONAL NOTES: *Larix kaempferi* is difficult to distinguish from *Larix decidua* except shoots of the former are rich reddish brown, leaves blue-green to glaucous and wider, and broader cones with reflexed scales.

NATIVE HABITAT: Japan. Introduced 1861.

Larix laricina — Eastern or American larch (Tamarack)
(lār′iks lār-i-sī′na)

LEAVES: Light bluish green, 3/4 to 1 1/4″ long, 1/50″ wide, 3-sided, strongly keeled beneath, on short spurs 12 to 30 in a bundle.
BUDS: Rounded, glossy dark red, slightly resinous.
STEM: Thin, at first glabrous, bloomy, later dull yellowish brown or reddish brown.
CONES: Egg-shaped, small, 1/3 to 2/3″ long, 1/4 to 1/2″ wide, with 15 to 20 scales.

SIZE: 40 to 80′ high by 15 to 30′ spread, usually smaller in cultivation.
HARDINESS: Zone 1 to 4 or 5; hates the heat.
HABIT: Open and pyramidal with a slender trunk, horizontal branches and drooping branchlets.
RATE: Slow-medium.
TEXTURE: Medium-fine in foliage; coarse in winter.
BARK: Thin and smooth on young stems, later becoming 1/2 to 3/4″ thick, gray to reddish brown, scaly.
LEAF COLOR: Bright blue-green foliage turning yellowish in the fall; often showy in fall color.
FLOWERS: Monoecious, sessile; staminate yellow, pistillate rosy colored.
FRUIT: Cones are small, oval, 1/3 to 2/3″ long, 1/4 to 1/2″ broad, pendulous, glabrous, green or violet becoming brown when mature.
CULTURE: Moist soils, less tolerant of cultivation then *Larix decidua;* intolerant of shade and pollution; makes best growth in moist, well-drained, acid soils.
DISEASES AND INSECTS: Subject to Larch case-bearer, Larch sawfly, wood rot and several rust fungi.
LANDSCAPE VALUE: Excellent in groves and in moist soil; less tolerant of cultivation than *L. decidua,* best left in its native confines; have seen in Maine and Michigan in boggy areas.
CULTIVARS: None important.
PROPAGATION: See previous entry.
NATIVE HABITAT: Northern North America, from the Arctic Circle in Alaska and Canada southwards to northern Pennsylvania, Minnesota and Illinois. Introduced 1737.

Lavandula angustifolia — Common or English Lavender
(lȧ-van′dū-lȧ an-gus-ti-fō′li-ȧ)

FAMILY: Lamiaceae
LEAVES: Opposite, entire, evergreen, linear to lanceolate, 1 to 1 3/4″ long, up to 3/16″ wide, obtuse, revolute, green to gray-green above, white tomentose below.

SIZE: 1 to 2′ high, wider at maturity; plants as tall as 3 to 5′ have been reported.
HARDINESS: Zone 5 to 8(9).
HABIT: Evergreen subshrub with a well-developed woody base forming a broad cushion-like mound, refined and aristocratic.
RATE: Slow, although I have grown it from seed and in 2 years had bushy 10 to 12″ diameter plants.
TEXTURE: Fine.
LEAF COLOR: Grayish to bluish green throughout seasons, develops an off-color during winter; at its best in spring and summer when the new foliage is present, foliage is fragrant.
FLOWERS: Lavender-purple in the typical form but numerous selections have been made that vary from white and pink, through blue, violet to lilac and beyond; flowers borne in 1 1/2 to 2 1/2″ long spikes on extended, 2 to 6″ long peduncles; abundant flowers appear in June, July or August; dried flowers can be used for sachets.
FRUIT: Nutlet, not ornamental.

CULTURE: Readily transplanted from containers; prefers well-drained soil on the dry side; neutral to alkaline soil reaction is best; stalks should be removed after flowers fade; excessive moisture will literally do the plant in.

DISEASES AND INSECTS: None serious.

LANDSCAPE VALUE: An essential ingredient in herb gardens, can be used as a border or pruned to form a low hedge; often used in mass where both foliage and flowers produce a striking effect; a fine plant with many uses in the home landscape; the textural quality and foliage color can be used to great advantage to soften the effect of excessive broadleaf evergreens; the leaves, flowers, and dried seed heads are very fragrant; this is the English Lavender that has been cultivated in England since the early 16th century; it is the source of the true oil of lavender.

CULTIVARS: Many, probably hybrids of the above and *L. latifolia,* Spike Lavender; most are distinguished by flower and foliage color as well as time of flower and growth habit.

'Alba'—Pinkish white flowers, spikes 2 to 3″ long, stems about 20″ long.

'Hidcote'—Considered a cultivar of *L. angustifolia,* rich purple flowers born on 10 to 15″ long stalks, foliage is silvery, habit more compact; truly a handsome selection that was selected at Hidcote Garden before 1950.

'Munstead'—Associated with Gertrude Jekyll and Munstead House and Garden, flowering plants grow 16 to 18″ high, foliage 10 to 12″, greenish gray 1 to 1 1/2″ long, 1/24″ wide leaves, flowering spikes blue-lilac, 1 3/4 to 2 1/2″ long, 6 to 10 flowers per whorl, June-July; synonymous with 'Munstead Dwarf', 'Munstead Variety', 'Munstead Blue', and 'Nana Compacta'.

PROPAGATION: Seeds can be directly sown; a fine 10 to 12″ diameter plant can be expected in two growing seasons from seed. Cuttings can also be rooted and should be collected in August or September and placed in a cold frame or suitable structure; I have attempted to root the species but with minimal success primarily because of excessive moisture in the rooting beds (mist).

ADDITIONAL NOTES: I have always loved this plant and believe it is worthy of cultivation in every garden. The wonderful flowers and fragrant plant parts are sufficient reason for using it.

NATIVE HABITAT: Southern Europe, northern Africa; cultivated since ancient times.

Ledum groenlandicum — Labrador Tea
(lē′dum green-land′i-kum)

FAMILY: Ericaceae

LEAVES: Alternate, simple, evergreen, 3/4 to 2″ long, 1/4 to 1/2″ wide, elliptic or ovate to oblong, obtuse, margins recurved, glaucous and resinous, dark green above, covered with dark brown rust beneath, fragrant when crushed; petiole—1/6 to 1/4″ long.

BUDS: Solitary, sessile, somewhat compressed, small with about 3 exposed scales; the terminal flower buds large, round or ovoid, with some 10 broad mucronate, glandular-dotted scales.

STEM: Slender, rounded, young shoots densely covered with rusty tomentum; older branches reddish brown or copper-colored; pith small, somewhat 3-sided, spongy, brownish; leaf-scars mostly low, half-elliptical or bluntly cordate, the lowest transversely linear; 1 bundle-trace.

SIZE: 2 to 4′ in height by 2 to 4′ in spread.

HARDINESS: Zone 2 to 5.

HABIT: Dwarf evergreen shrub with erect branches forming a rounded mass, sometimes procumbent.

RATE: Slow.

TEXTURE: Medium-fine in all seasons.

LEAF COLOR: Deep dark green above, undersides covered with whitish or rusty brown hairs.

FLOWERS: Pefect, white, each flower 1/2 to 3/4″ across, borne in 2″ diameter corymbs from May through June.

FRUIT: Capsule, about 1/5″ long, not showy, 5-valved, opening from base to apex.

CULTURE: Transplants readily, fibrous rooted; prefers moist, sandy, peaty soils; found in swampy moors of northern latitudes; full sun or partial shade.

DISEASES AND INSECTS: Anthracnose, leaf galls caused by fungi, rusts and leaf spots.

LANDSCAPE VALUE: Another interesting and little known ericaceous plant which is good for cool, moist, swampy areas; the plants I have seen were attractive in flower.

CULTIVARS:

'Compactum'—Dense, neat shrub to 1' in height with short branches, very woolly stems, short broad leaves, and small flower clusters.

PROPAGATION: Seeds can be grown as described for *Calluna;* layers and cuttings can also be used; cuttings collected in October rooted 66 to 100% when treated with 8000 ppm IBA-talc.

NATIVE HABITAT: Greenland to Alberta and Washington, south to Pennsylvania and Wisconsin. Introduced 1763.

Leiophyllum buxifolium — Box Sandmyrtle
(lī-ō-fil'um buks-i-fō'li-um)

FAMILY: Ericaceae

LEAVES: Usually alternate (may also be opposite), simple, 1/8 to 1/2" long, 1/16 to 3/16" wide, oblong or obovate-oblong, to almost orbicular, lustrous dark green above, paler beneath, entire, short-petioled.

BUDS: Sessile, solitary, ovoid, appressed, with about 2 exposed scales.

STEM: Very slender, subterete, pith minute, continuous; leaf-scars more or less broken and then 4-ranked, minute, crescent-shaped or 3 sided, raised; 1 bundle-trace.

SIZE: 1 1/2 to 3' high and spreading 4 to 5'.

HARDINESS: Zone 5 to high elevations of the southeast.

HABIT: Small evergreen shrub of great variability in the wild; erect, prostrate or decumbent according to location and altitude; in cultivation usually a dense bush up to 1 1/2' high.

RATE: Slow.

TEXTURE: Fine in all seasons.

LEAF COLOR: Lustrous dark green in summer becoming bronzy with cold weather.

FLOWERS: Perfect, rosy in bud opening to white tipped with pink, each flower about 1/4" diameter; May through June; borne in terminal 3/4 to 1" diameter corymbs.

CULTURE: Transplant balled and burlapped or container-grown plants; prefer moist, sandy, acid soil supplied with peat and leaf mold; full sun or partial shade; will not tolerate drought, not an easy plant to establish but like *Ledum* and *Epigaea* is well worth the effort.

DISEASES AND INSECTS: None serious.

LANDSCAPE VALUE: Dainty and unusual plant for the rock garden; blends will with other broadleaf evergreens; in flower makes a solid froth of white; handsome garden plant.

CULTIVARS:

'Pinecake'—Low, dense, creeping plant, described as flowing over the ground "glacier-like", 5" high and 27" wide, discovered in the wild by Dr. Richard Lighty, near Chatham, Morris Co., NJ, will be a good ground cover for acid, sunny sites, Zone 5 to ?

PROPAGATION: Seed as described for *Calluna;* root cuttings, layering and stem cuttings also work; one authority noted the best method is by cuttings made of shoots 1 to 1 1/2" long in July or August, placed in peat:sand and provided bottom heat; October cuttings, 3000 ppm IBA-talc, rooted 100% in 8 weeks.

ADDITIONAL NOTES: The only species within the genus; resembles *Ledum* but can be distinguished by the small, quite glabrous, short-stalked to almost sessile leaves; the species is usually divided into three varieties.

NATIVE HABITAT: New Jersey southward, westward into the mountains of the Carolinas, Tennessee, and eastern Kentucky. Introduced 1736.

Leitneria floridana — Florida Corkwood
(light-neer′i-a flōr-i-dā′na)

FAMILY: Leitneriaceae

LEAVES: Alternate, simple, elliptic-lanceolate to lanceolate, 3 to 6″ long, half as wide, acuminate, cuneate, entire, bright green above, paler, reticulate and silky pubescent below; petiole— 1 to 2″ long, tomentose.

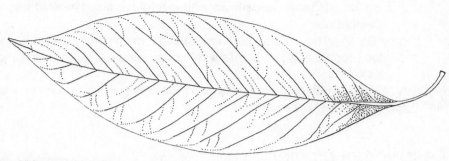

Leitneria floridana, Florida Corkwood, is a suckering 6 to 12′ high shrubby mass but in the wild can grow to 20′. Although ornamentally not particularly attractive it is rather interesting planted in moist soil along a brook or moist depression where it forms a large thicket of grove-like proportions. Flowers are dioecious and plants I have seen in cultivation are male and the flowers occur in 1 to 1 3/4″ long catkins before the leaves in March-April. The flowers are more curious than attractive. Fruit is an oblong 1/2 to 3/4″ long, 1/4″ wide light olive-brown drupe. The wood is extremely light, with a specific gravity less than cork. In the wild has been reported growing under water. A tough durable plant that is cold hardy well north of its range probably withstanding -20°F. Southern Missouri to Texas and Florida. Introduced 1894. Zone 5 to 9. Apparently not common in the wild.

Leptospermum scoparium — Broom Teatree
(lep-tō-spēr′mum skō-pā′ri-um)

FAMILY: Myrtaceae

LEAVES: Alternate, simple, evergreen, linear-oblong, 1/3 to 1/2″ long, 1/12 to 1/6″ wide, sharply acuminate, dark green, fragrant when bruised, dotted with transparent oil glands.

SIZE: 6 to 10(15′) high and slightly less in spread.

HARDINESS: Zone 9 to 10.

HABIT: Reasonably compact-rounded evergreen shrub with dense branching structure, quite refined because of small leaves.

RATE: Medium.

TEXTURE: Fine through the seasons.

LEAF COLOR: Medium green often with a purplish tinge.

FLOWERS: Perfect, white, 1/2″ diameter produced singly from the leaf axils in June-July, spectacular on the best cultivars.

FRUIT: Pea sized and shaped, many seeded woody capsule.

CULTURE: Transplant container-grown material; moist, fertile, acid, well drained soil; full sun to light shade, protect from sweeping winds, root rot may be a problem in poorly drained soils; shows good salt tolerance, necessary to site in a micro-climate for optimum growth, have seen used as a container plant in southeast which means it must be overwintered in a cool greenhouse or room.

DISEASES AND INSECTS: None serious.

LANDSCAPE VALUE: In San Francisco, CA, a handsome plant; in Athens, GA of dubious value because of humidity and possibly high night temperatures; superb in the shrub border or in a container for excellent flower effect.

CULTIVARS: Many have been named but few are grown in the United States.

‘Helen Strybling’—Offers gray-green foliage and large dark pink flowers.

'Nanum Tui'—A compact, 2′ high form with dark green foliage and white to pale pink flowers, darker at center.

'Red Damask'—Fully double, over 1/2″ diameter deep cherry-red flowers, exceptionally free flowering, dense habit, grows to about 6 to 8′ high, raised in 1940's by W.E. Lamments, University of California.

'Ruby Glow'—The old standard and the plant most common in cultivation, the flowers are deep red, fully double and 1/2″ across with bronzy foliage and red stems and a reasonably compact habit, 6 to 8′.

PROPAGATION: Cuttings of firm wood will root, collect in early to mid summer.

NATIVE HABITAT: New Zealand.

Lespedeza bicolor — Shrub Bushclover
(les-pe-dē′zà bī′kul-ēr)

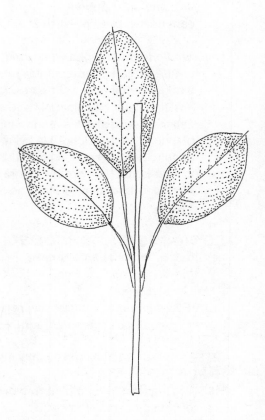

FAMILY: Fabaceae

LEAVES: Alternate, trifoliate, each leaflet 3/4 to 2″ long and two thirds to as much in width, broadly oval or obovate, midrib terminating in a small bristle, middle leaflet larger and longer petioluled than others, dark green above, pale below, glabrous or sparsely covered with appressed pubescence on both sides.

SIZE: 6 to 9′ (12′) high and wide.

HARDINESS: Zone 4 to 7 or 8; may die back in cold climates and is best treated as a herbaceous perennial.

HABIT: Upright, open, loosely branched shrub that can become wonderfully unkempt and disorderly if not properly pruned.

RATE: Medium to fast.

TEXTURE: Medium.

LEAF COLOR: Dark green usually with no appreciable fall color; leaves may turn yellow.

FLOWERS: Perfect, rosy-purple, 1/2″ long, produced in 2 to 5″ long racemes on current season's growth and are borne from the leaf axils of the uppermost 2′ of the shoot; July-August; not really overwhelming.

FRUIT: Downy, ovate, 1/3″ long, one-seeded pod.

CULTURE: Of the easiest culture given a well drained soil; excess fertility should be avoided; pH adaptable; full sun; prune in winter or before new growth ensues in spring.

DISEASES AND INSECTS: None serious.

LANDSCAPE VALUE: Best utilized in the border; could serve as a herbaceous perennial in the north; a specimen in the Arnold Arboretum was about 10 to 12′ but had no great beauty being rather open and mediocre in flower.

CULTIVARS:

'Summer Beauty'—Flowers occur over an extended period from July through September on a 5′ high spreading shrub; cut back to 6 to 12″ from the ground in late winter.

'Yakushima'—Grows about 12″ and forms a tight mound of foliage with smaller flowers and leaves than the species.

PROPAGATION: Seeds can be directly sown; when dry they might benefit from a slight acid treatment or hot water soak; softwood cuttings root easily.

NATIVE HABITAT: North China to Manchuria and Japan. Introduced 1856.

RELATED SPECIES:

Lespedeza thunbergii, (les-pe-dē'zȧ thun-bēr'jē-ī), Thunberg Lespedeza, is really the beauty among the beasts of this genus. It exists as a semi-woody plant that is usually killed back in cold weather. In terms of height, it can grow 3 to 6' in a single season. The flowering stems are so heavy they arch over producing a rather handsome fountain-like effect. The trifoliate leaves are bluish green. The real beauty of the plant lies in the rosy-purple, 1/2 to 5/8" long, pea-shaped flower. They are produced in up to 6" long racemes from the upper portion of the shoot, the whole constituting a 2 to 2 1/2' long, loose panicle. The flowers peak in late August through September. I saw a beautiful plant at the Parc Floral, Orleans, France sited by water that provided a reflective surface and acted to enhance the floral beauty. This same body of water was traversed by a small arching bridge which from the opposite side provided the perfect frame for photographing the plant. This plant will stick in my mind forever. After my initial introduction, I knew the plant must find a home in the Dirr garden. A friend in Swarthmore PA provided a clump which has been multiplied a thousand-fold and given to those who ask and those who do not. The plant has the curious habit of flowering in June in Zone 8 and again more heavily in late August-September. Growth is a large arching gracefully mounded shrub by the middle of summer. I used the plant with *Sedum* 'Autumn Joy', *Miscanthus* 'Gracillimus', *Buddleia davidii* (white flowered form) and the effect has been outstanding. Does extremely well under hot dry conditions. A white flowered form, 'Alba', possibly more correctly 'Albiflora', is rather handsome but more upright in habit and not as graceful as the species. In 1988, a pinkish white branch sport developed that might prove valuable. Also a white-variegated leaf form is in cultivation. The variegated pattern is rather subdued but handsome on close inspection. China, Japan. Introduced 1837. Zone 5 to 8.

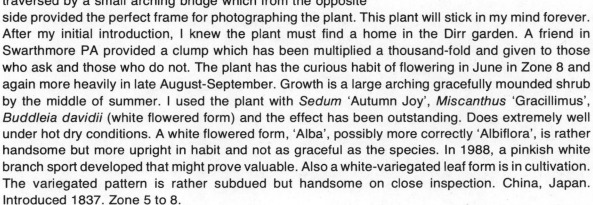

Leucophyllum frutescens — Texas Sage or Silverleaf

FAMILY: Scrophulariaceae
LEAVES: Opposite, simple, evergreen, elliptic to obovate, 1" long, silvery pubescent on both surfaces.

Leucophyllum frutescens, (lū-kō-fil'um frū-tes'enz), Texas Sage or Silverleaf, has become popular in recent years and is moving into southeastern markets. I have seen plants performing quite well; others dying. The species is typically a compact shrub probably 5 to 8' high and 4 to 6' wide but most of the new introductions will probably not grow as large. The evergreen, silvery pubescent on both surfaces, 1/2 to 1" long leaves provide a handsome contrast to dark green shrubs. The 1" wide rose-purple bell-shaped flowers appear in summer. Prefers low humidity environments and perfectly drained, acid or higher pH soil. Again like other southwest native plants, the humidity and high night temperatures of the eastern seaboard and southeastern states often prove lethal. Plant should be used in shrub border or possibly filler in herbaceous perennial borders. The cultivars include 'Alba' with white flowers, 'Compactum' of smaller habit with orchid-pink flowers; 'Green Cloud' is a compact form with dark green foliage and violet-purple flowers. 'Rain Cloud' (*L. minus* × *L. frutescens)*—Violet-blue flowers, large and inflated, 5' by 3' in 5 years; does well in calcareous soil where rainfall is less than 35", Zone 8. 'Thundercloud' (*L. candidum*)—Abundant dark purple flowers and dense globular habit, more floriferous than typical and has pleasing gray foliage; 30" by 20" in 3 years, superior to 'Silver Cloud', drought tolerant, Zone 8. Native to Texas and Mexico. Zone 8 to 9(?).

Leucothoe fontanesiana (L. catesbaei) — Drooping Leucothoe or Fetterbush
(lū-koth'ō-ē fon-tȧ-nē-zē-ā'na) (kāts'bē-ī)

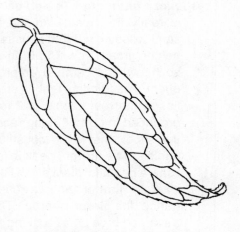

FAMILY: Ericaceae

LEAVES: Alternate, simple, evergreen, ovate-lanceolate to lanceolate, 2 to 5″ long, 1 to 1 1/2″ wide, long-acuminate, rounded or
broad-cuneate at base, appressed ciliate-serrulate on margins, lustrous dark green above, lighter beneath, glabrous or
with scattered hairs; petiole-1/3 to 2/3″ long.

STEM: Long, slender, with little or no lateral branch development,
greenish, reddish, to purplish in color, glabrous, shiny, solid
pith.

SIZE: 3 to 6′ by 3 to 6′.

HARDINESS: Zone (4)5 to 8, only in the coolest, shadiest locations
in the southern landscape.

HABIT: Very graceful evergreen shrub with long, spreading, arching branches clothed with long pointed
leaves and weighted down by the flowers; almost fountain-like in habit.

RATE: Slow to medium, 3 to 5′ in 4 to 5 years.

TEXTURE: Medium in all seasons.

LEAF COLOR: New growth of bright green or bronzy color eventually changing to lustrous dark green at
maturity develops a bronze to purplish coloration in winter.

FLOWERS: Perfect, white, fragrant, slenderly pitcher shaped, 1/4″ long, May, borne in 2 to 3″ long axillary
racemes from the leaf axils and hanging down; somewhat masked by the foliage.

FRUIT: Capsule, dehiscent, 1/6″ diameter, not showy.

CULTURE: Transplants readily, best moved as a container plant in spring; prefers acid, moist, well drained,
organic soil; will not withstand drought or sweeping, drying winds; prefers partial to full shade but will
grow in full sun if not too dry; rejuvenate by pruning to ground after flowering.

DISEASES AND INSECTS: Leaf spots can be troublesome as at least 8 species of fungi infect Leucothoe;
in recent years I have seen tremendous leaf spot; based on numerous observations over the years,
this plant should only be used in ideal situations because any stress appears to predispose the plant
to leaf spot which produces ugly lesions that often coalesce and consume the entire leaf, resulting
in abscission of leaves and death of plants; the literature ascribes greater resistance to L. axillaris
but it, too, is susceptible; also the hybrids like 'Scarletta' are quite susceptible; root rot problems can
also be serious; have seen tremendous thickets in North Georgia mountains but always along
streams in shade.

LANDSCAPE VALUE: Good facer plant, hides leggy plants, nice cover for a shady bank, massing,
grouping or shrub borders; contrasts nicely with dull rhododendron foliage, good as undergrowth
plant; leaf spot can render a plant unfit for any landscape.

CULTIVARS:

'Girard's Rainbow'—Selected by Girard Nursery, Ohio for its striking new growth which may emerge
white, pinkish, coppery and other combinations; with time the effect is reduced but it is a showy
evergreen shrub when the new leaves are emerging; cuttings collected on March 11, treated
with 3000 ppm IBA-quick dip, peat:perlite, mist, had rooted by April 12.

'Lovita'—Mounded compact habit and dense deep bronze foliage in winter, probably 2′ by 4′, a hybrid
between L. f. 'Nana' and L. f.?

'Nana'—Lustrous dark green foliage compliments a dense 2′ high, 6′ wide plant; this is a fine
selection but is not widely available in the trade; I noticed a fine old plant in the Arnold Arboretum
that was compact and handsome, there was no leaf spot but the plant was in a shady
environment; unfortunately, leaf spot does occur on 'Nana'.

'Rollisoni'—Rather obscure form with smaller leaves, 2 to 4″ long by about 1/2 to 3/4″ wide, relatively compact habit, 3′ by 6′, foliage lustrous dark green; several nurseries grow this form and consider it hardier than the species.

'Scarletta'—The first time I saw the plant I was impressed, several years later during a visit, the plants were gone...victims of leaf spot; my reason for excitement was the rich glossy scarlet (hint of purple) new growth that matures to dark green, foliage develops burgundy tones in fall and winter, will be more compact than the species, probably in the same range as 'Lovita'; I believe this is from the same parentage as 'Lovita'.

'Trivar'—Considered stronger growing than 'Girard's Rainbow' but not common in cultivation, red young leaves with cream-yellow-green variegation, developed around 1947 in New Jersey.

ADDITIONAL NOTES: *L. fontanesiana* makes a magnificent evergreen shrub in the cool, moist, shady environment along streams in north Georgia. It forms large thickets that are almost impenetrable. It is usually not as beautiful under cultivation especially in stressed situations.

NATIVE HABITAT: Virginia to Georgia and Tennessee in the mountains. Introduced 1793.

PROPAGATION: Direct sow the seed as described for *Calluna;* firm cuttings root readily when treated with 1000 ppm IBA/50% alcohol in peat:perlite under mist; actually cuttings collected in winter root readily when treated with 3000 to 8000 ppm IBA-talc or liquid.

RELATED SPECIES:

Leucothoe axillaris, (lū-koth′ō-ē ak-sil-lā′ris), Coast Leucothoe, is receiving wide favor in the nursery trade as a potential replacement or substitute for *L. fontanesiana.* Grows 2 to 4′ high (6′) and 1 1/2 times that in width, with spreading branches, zig-zagged towards the end. The leaves are leathery, dark glossy green. Flowers develop in axillary racemes, 1 to 2 1/2″ long, white, in April and May. This species is not particularly common in cultivation and in many respects resembles *L. fontanesiana.* It differs in comparatively shorter and broader, abruptly pointed leaves and fewer flowers (8 to 30) per inflorescence. Native from Virginia to Florida and Mississippi in lowland areas. Introduced 1765. Supposedly hardy in Zone 6, but based on observation of plants at 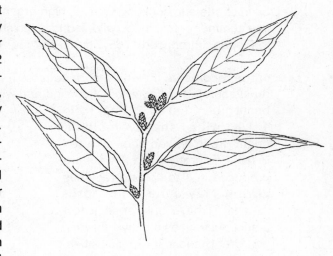 Millcreek Valley Park, Youngstown, Ohio and in Lake County, Ohio, nursery area, I would place it in Zone 5. This species will also contract the leaf spot disease and I have seen plants that were not in the best of condition. This species is similar to *L. fontanesiana* and much confused with it. From my observations I would say the differences, except for native range, are meager at best. Like *L. fontanesiana* it should be provided ideal cultural conditions.

Leucothoe keiskei, (lū-koth′ō-ē kēsk′ē-ī), Keisks Leucothoe, is a dwarf, rather compact, graceful evergreen shrub with 1 1/2 to 3 1/2″ long, 1/2 to 1 1/2″ wide, inconspicuously toothed dark green leaves. The young shoots are a shining red and the leaves become deep red in fall. The real beauty lies in the pure white, cylindrical, 1/2 to 5/8″ long, 1/4″ wide, nodding flowers that occur in short racemes during July. The flowers are the largest of the cultivated leucothoe. I was told that it is a rather temperamental garden plant. Japan. Introduced 1915. Zone 5.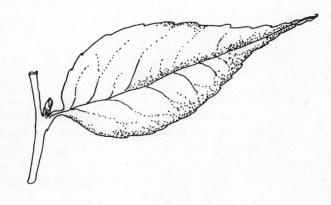

Leucothoe populifolia (now correctly *Agarista populifolia*)
(lū-koth′ō-ē pop-ū-li-fō′li-à)

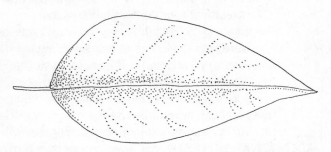

LEAVES: Alternate, simple, evergreen, ovate-lanceolate, glabrous, 1 1/2 to 4″ long, one half as
wide, acuminate, irregularly serrate or entire,
glossy rich green, new growth is tinged red or
purplish, stays green in winter.
STEM: Fine, green, shiny, glabrous, lamellate pith.

Leucothoe populifolia, Florida Leucothoe, is sel-
dom seen in cultivation but is probably superior to *L. axillaris* and *L. fontanesiana* at least for southern
gardens. The habit is lax, arching, and multistemmed. The plant tends to sucker and can be used to
great advantage along moist stream banks in shady situations. The glossy rich green foliage is not
as susceptible to leaf spot as *L. fontanesiana.* In fact, I have seen no signs of infestation on cultivated
plants. Cream-colored fragrant flowers are born in axillary racemes in profusion during May-June. It
makes a great companion with large-leaved rhododendrons, mountain-laurel and similar shrubs. It
grows 8 to 12′ high but can be maintained at any height with proper pruning. Given the correct
landscape setting, it blends in beautifully. Wonderful textural addition to a shade garden. One of the
most handsome choices for understory plantings or creating a naturalistic effect along streams. Must
be in shade and cool, moist, acid, high organic matter soils. Easily rooted from cuttings collected in
late summer or fall. In the wild, found in moist to wet hummocks and wet woodlands. South Carolina
to Florida. Introduced 1765. Zone 6 or 7 to 9.

Leucothoe racemosa, (lū-koth′ō-ē ra-se-mō′sà), Sweetbells Leucothoe, is a rather handsome deciduous shrub growing 4 to 6 1/2′ high and wide. It tends to sucker, producing a thicket effect. The
bright green, 1 to 2 1/2″ long, 1/2 to
1 1/4″ wide, shallow-toothed,
bright green leaves often turn red
in fall. The pretty white flowers are
produced in 1 to 4″ long racemes
during May-June (mid April-
Athens). I have only seen a few
plants but feel, as a native shrub, it
has great landscape possibilities.
Massachusetts to Florida and
Louisiana. Introduced 1736. Zone
5 to 9.

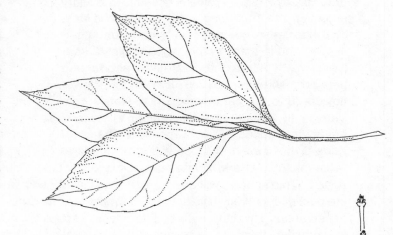

Ligustrum amurense — Amur Privet
(lī-gus′trum a-moor-en′sē)

FAMILY: Oleaceae
LEAVES: Opposite, simple, entire, elliptic to oblong, 1 to 2″
long, obtuse to acute, rounded or broad cuneate at base, ciliolate, glabrous except on midrib
beneath, dull green.
BUDS: Sessile, ovoid, small, with 2 or 3 pairs of exposed scales, brownish; typical for most privets.
STEM: New growth purplish, pubescent, older stems gray with some pubescence.

SIZE: 12 to 15′ high and 2/3's that in width or with a spread equal to the height.

HARDINESS: Zone 3 to 7, I have not seen the plant in Zone 8.

HABIT: Dense, upright, multi-stemmed shrub with a weak pyramidal outline.

RATE: Fast, all privets are fast growing shrubs.

TEXTURE: Medium-fine in leaf and in winter condition.

LEAF COLOR: Dull medium to dark green in summer; no fall coloration of any consequence.

FLOWERS: Perfect, creamy white, unpleasantly fragrant, May-June, 2 to 3 weeks, borne in axillary 1 to 2″ long panicles; flower effect is often lost because of use in hedges and flowers are cut off.

FRUIT: Berry-like rounded drupe, black, slightly gray-dusty with bloom, 1/4 to 1/3″ long, September-October, not particularly showy, persistent.

CULTURE: Transplant readily bare root, adaptable to any soil except those which are extremely wet; pH adaptable; full sun up to 1/2 shade; tolerant of smoke and grime of cities; does well in dry soils; prune after flowering.

DISEASES AND INSECTS: Anthracnose, twig-blight (affects *L. vulgare* more so than this species), leaf spots, galls, powdery mildew, root rots, privet aphid, leaf miners, scales, privet thrips, mealybugs, Japanese weevil, mites, whitefly and nematodes; in spite of this impressive array of problems, privets, in general, do well and rarely require spraying; the key is selecting the most reliable and hardy species.

LANDSCAPE VALUE: Hedging purposes, withstands pruning about as well as any plant; tends to be overused; there are many better hedging plants.

PROPAGATION: As a graduate student at the University of Massachusetts I was always attempting to propagate plants which were growing on campus. In winter I collected a quantity of *L. amurense* fruits and directly sowed one lot white removing the pericarp and cleaning the seed before sowing the second lot. The first batch did not germinate while batch two came up like beans. Apparently there is a chemical or physical barrier to germination which resides in the fruit wall. The usual recommendation for seed is 3 months at 41°F in a moist medium. Softwood cuttings root readily, in fact, I do not know why people would bother to propagate this group of plants any other way unless they are into breeding.

NATIVE HABITAT: Northern China. Introduced 1860.

RELATED SPECIES:

Ligustrum × ibolium, (lī-gus′trum ī-bō′li-um), Ibolium Privet, is a cross between *L. ovalifolium* and *L. obtusifolium*. It is more handsome than *L. amurense* for the foliage is a glossy dark green. Foliage is semievergreen to deciduous and ultimate landscape size ranges between 8 to 12′. Similar to *L. ovalifolium* but with pubescent stems and leaf undersides. Actually a rather handsome privet seldom available in commerce. Zone 4 to 7(8). Originated in Connecticut about 1910.

Ligustrum obtusifolium—Border Privet
(lī-gus′trum ob-too-si-fō′li-um)

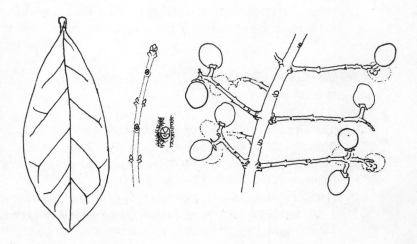

LEAVES: Opposite, simple, entire, elliptic to oblong or oblong-obovate, 1 to 2″ long, 1/3 to 1″ wide, acute or obtuse, cuneate or broad-cuneate, medium to dark green and glabrous above, pubescent beneath or only on midrib.

STEM: Green when young, possibly with a slight purplish tinge, pubescent; older stems gray, somewhat pubescent.

Ligustrum obtusifolium, Border Privet, grows 10 to 12′ tall with a spread of

12 to 15'. Usually a multistemmed shrub of broad horizontal outline, broadest at the top, much branched and twiggy with wide spreading branches. The foliage is medium to dark green in summer, sometimes turning russet to purplish in fall. Flowers are white, unpleasantly fragrant, early to mid June and later, borne in 3/4 to 1 1/2" long nodding panicles, usually numerous on short axillary branches. Fruit is a black to blue-black, slightly bloomy, 1/4" long, berry-like drupe which ripens in September and persists. Probably the best growth habit of the *Ligustrum* species and makes a good screen, background or hedge plant. The variety *regelianum* is low (4 to 5') with horizontal spreading branches and leaves regularly spaced in a flat plane (distichously) to give this plant a unique appearance. Extensively used for highway plantings, works well in mass, especially on banks and other large areas. Its leaves and stems are more pilose than the species. The species and variety are my favorite privets for northern climates. They rarely appear in southern gardens. 'Constitution' is a compact, dense form, 6 to 8' high and 8 to 10' wide in 10 years, leaves slightly twisted and smaller than normal, 1 to 1 1/4" long by 1/3" wide, hardy to –20°F, occurred as a chance seedling at the University of Tennessee, Knoxville. Japan. Introduced 1860. Zone 3 to 7.

Ligustrum ovalifolium—California Privet
(lī-gus'trum ō-val-i-fō'li-um)

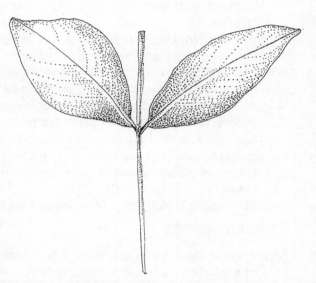

LEAVES: Opposite, simple, entire, evergreen, semi-evergreen to deciduous, 1 to 2 1/2" long, elliptic-ovate to elliptic-oblong, acute, broad-cuneate, lustrous dark green above, yellowish green below, glabrous; petiole—1/6" long.
STEM: Glabrous.

Ligustrum ovalifolium, California Privet, is a large, vigorous shrub forming a dense thicket of erect stems 10 to 15' high. It varies from deciduous to semi-evergreen (evergreen) depending on the severity of the climate. In Zone 8, the plant was evergreen to semi-evergreen (evergreen) every year except when temperatures dropped to –3°F. This was over a 10-year period. The dull white, heavy scented flowers are produced in 2 to 4" long and wide, crowded, stiff, erect, terminal panicles during June-July. The fruits are globose, shining black. Actually, this is a handsome privet and in moderate climates makes a fine screen or hedge. It is hardy at the Arnold Arboretum and deserves at least a Zone 5 designation. Like all privets, it thrives with neglect. 'Argenteum' has leaves that are bordered with creamy-white. 'Aureum' has only a green spot in the center, being bordered with golden yellow. It will revert to the type and several plants I have seen in collections were more green than yellow. Used extensively in English cities and it is common to see gold, green and mixed combinations in large hedge plantings. Extremely tough, durable plant. Japan. Cultivate 1847.

Ligustrum japonicum — Japanese Privet
(lī-gus'trum ja-pon'i-kum)

LEAVES: Opposite, simple, evergreen, entire, lustrous dark green, almost black-green, leathery, glabrous, broad-ovate to ovate-oblong, 1 1/2 to 4" long, 3/4 to 2" wide, obtusely short acuminate or acute to obtusish, usually rounded at base, 4 to 5 pairs of indistinct veins raised below, margin and midrib often reddish; petiole—1/4" long.
BUDS: Imbricate, more or less 4-sided, 1/8" long or less, brownish, glabrous.
STEM: Moderate, squarish, glabrous, green near apex finally gray-brown, profusely dotted with large, raised, light gray lenticels, nodes distinctly flattened; pith-green, solid.

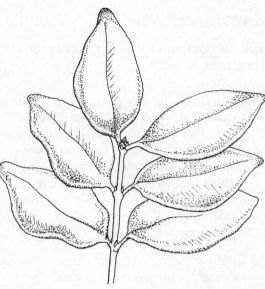

SIZE: 6 to 12′ high, 6 to 8′ wide; may grow 15 to 18′ high.

HARDINESS: Zone 7 to 10.

HABIT: Dense evergreen shrub of upright habit; can be grown as a small tree; frequently disfigured by pruning shears and assumes the geometric shape of a green meatball.

RATE: Fast.

TEXTURE: Medium.

BARK: Relatively smooth, gray, covered with large lenticels.

LEAF COLOR: Lustrous dark green.

FLOWERS: Perfect, creamy-white, fragrant, borne in 2 to 6″ high and wide, relatively tightly branched, terminal, pyramidal panicles in mid to late May (Athens); odor is typically privet and is offensive to many people; flowers are effective for a long time.

FRUIT: Lustrous black, 1/4″ diameter oval-rounded drupe, maturing in September-October and often persisting through winter; rather effective in the winter landscape; birds show no propensity to attack the fruits.

CULTURE: Easily transplanted; adaptable to varied soils; quite salt tolerant; sun or shade; withstands heavy pruning and is often fashioned into topiary subjects; probably the only soils this species will not grow in are those that are permanently wet.

DISEASES AND INSECTS: None serious, actually thrives with neglect.

LANDSCAPE VALUE: A favorite landscape plant in the south; has been used for everything imaginable: single specimen, foundations, screens, hedges, topiary, containers; very handsome when limbed up; almost has a sculptural quality about it.

CULTIVARS:

'Howard' ('Frazieri')—New leaves yellow turning green with maturity, usually some color present even late in the growing season that gives it away, plant is somewhat two-toned since emerging leaves are yellow, previous season's leaves green, not for the faint-of-heart.

'Korea Dwarf'—Collected by U.S. National Arboretum expedition in South Korea in 1985; team discovered a population of genetically dwarf plants on Taehuksen Island off the south coast; foliage and growth rate are 1/3 to 1/2 the species; Raulston believes it may have possiblilites in the green meatball market.

'Nobilis'—More cold hardy form, upright habit with large lustrous dark green foliage.

'Recurvifolium'—A slightly smaller leaved form with wavy leaf margin, leaves twisted at tip, perhaps more open than the species in growth habit, hardier than the typical species but the exact taxonomic status is unknown.

'Rotundifolium' ('Coriaceum')—Distinctly upright in habit, exceedingly stiff, 4 to 6′ high (usually less), leaves crowded (appear whorled), 1 to 2 1/2″ long, almost as wide, broadly oval or rounded, blunt or notched at apex, lustrous dark green, thick and leathery, flowers are white in 2 to 3″ long pyramidal panicles; fruits black, globose, 1/4″ wide; introduced by Fortune from Japanese gardens in 1860; some references have described it as a piece of living sculpture; I cannot print my impression; defoliated at -3°F, less hardy than species.

'Silver Star'—Deep green center with gray-green mottling and creamy-silver edges, slow growing, compact, erect habit, probably 6 to 8′.

'Suwanee River'—Leathery, somewhat twisted dark green leaves, compact habit, relatively slow growing to 3 to 5′; may be a hybrid between *L. j.* 'Rotundifolium' and *L. lucidum*.

'Variegatum'—Leaves margined and blotched with creamy white.

PROPAGATION: Cuttings roots readily; seeds can be planted in fall and will germinate the following spring.

NATIVE HABITAT: Japan, Korea. Introduced 1845.

RELATED SPECIES:

Ligustrum lucidum—Waxleaf, Glossy, or Chinese Privet
(lī-gus′trum lū′si-dum)

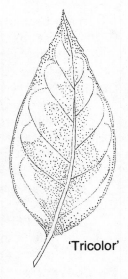

LEAVES: Opposite, simple, evergreen,
ovate to ovate-lanceolate, 3 to 6″ long,
1 to 2 1/2″ wide, acuminate or acute,
broad-cuneate, entire, glossy dark
green, with 6 to 8 pairs of veins usually
distinct above and below, veinlets
often impressed below; petiole—1/2
to 3/4″ long.
STEM: Glabrous.

'Tricolor'

Ligustrum lucidum, Waxleaf Privet, is
thoroughly confused with *L. japonicum* but need not be. In short, *L. lucidum* is
larger (20 to 25′) and more loose in outline; the leaves are larger, not as lustrous
dark green and have an opaque rim around the margin; leaves have 6 to 8 pairs
of veins often sunken on the underside whereas the 4 to 6 pairs of veins of *L.
japonicum* are raised; the flower and fruit panicles are larger (5 to 8″ long and
wide) and the 1/3 to 1/2″ long fruit is a dull blue-black. In addition, it flowers
about 2 to 3 weeks later than Japanese Privet. Both species are common
characters in southern landscapes. *Ligustrum lucidum* grows as tall as 40 to
50′ feet and becomes quite open in the process. 'Davison Hardy' is a cold hardy
(-10°F) form found on the Davison College campus, no tip injury or foliage burn
while all other plants of the same species were killed to the ground; parent plant
is 15″ in diameter (trunk) with handsome foliage, could be a valuable addition
to list of cold hardy broadleaf evergreens for quick screens, hedges, borders
and masses. 'Excelsum Superbum' is a fine creamy yellow margined form that
is a strong grower; have seen at Kew Gardens and was reasonably impressed.
'Tricolor' ('Variegatus') has young leaves with an irregular broad border turning
white with maturity, supposedly a handsome form, a tree 35′ high has been reported. *Ligustrum lucidum*
is as tolerant to soil conditions as *L. japonicum* and both can be expected to do well under a variety of
conditions. Native to China, Korea, Japan. Introduced 1794. Zone 8 to 10. Temperatures dropped to
−3°F in Athens during the 1983-84 winter and *L. lucidum* was severely injured or killed while *L.
japonicum* survived.

Ligustrum sinense — Chinese Privet
(lī-gus′trum sī-nen′sē)

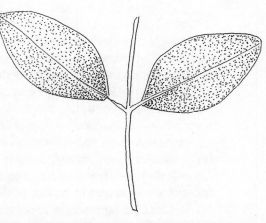

LEAVES: Opposite, simple, evergreen to semi-evergreen
(deciduous in cold climates), elliptic to elliptic-oblong, 1
to 3″ long, 1/2 to 1″ broad, acute to obtuse, broad cuneate,
entire, dull dark green above, pubescent on midrib below;
petiole—1/8″ long.
STEM: Pubescent with gray-yellow coloration.

Ligustrum sinense, Chinese Privet, is considered by the great
British plantsman, W.J. Bean, the best and most ornamental of deciduous privets. I challenge that conten-
tion and would rank it as a noxious weed, especially in the southern states. In addition, the flowers
are not better than those of *L. amurense, L. obtusifolium* and others. In the southern states, it has
escaped and is found about everywhere that birds fly. It has a tenacious constitution that allows it to

thrive in concrete crevices in back alleys and flood plains along rivers. It thrives in heavy shade and full sun and forms impenetrable thickets. The species grows 10 to 15' high and like most privets can be fashioned into innumerable forms. The species is not available in commerce but 'Variegatum' is offered. This cultivar has leaves that are bordered gray to creamy white. In cold weather the leaves loose the pronounced variegation pattern and turn more or less uniform sickly yellowish to grayish green. May revert to the species and odd branches need to be removed. The cultivar grows about 4 to 6' high and wide under typical landscape conditions, however have seen 15' high plants of virtual tree stature. It is reasonably manageable but does flower and fruit. The seeds when they germinate give rise to the green form (species). There are apparently two variegated forms: one creamy-yellowish green; the other with a true white variegation pattern. The variegated form is used extensively throughout the south. China. Introduced 1852. Zone 7 south.

Ligustrum × vicaryi — Golden Vicary Privet or Golden Privet
(lī-gus′trum vi-kâr′ē-ī)

Ligustrum × vicaryi, Golden Vicary Privet or Golden Privet, goes under many names in the trade. Result of a cross between *L. ovalifolium* 'Aureum' and *L. vulgare.* The habit is somewhat vase-shaped (oval-rounded) and the leaves are golden yellow the entire growing season especially if the plant is used in a sunny location. I do not find this shrub palatable but nurserymen claim they cannot grow enough of it. To each his own! If one must have golden foliage this plant is probably as good as any. Can grow 10 to 12' high so should be afforded adequate garden space. If grown in the shade the foliage turns a sickly yellow-green (more green than yellow) and the only medicine which cures this malady is full sun. In the heat of Zone 8, even in full sun, some color is lost especially on leaves in the interior of the canopy. Reports from the Minnesota Landscape Arboretum indicate that Vicary is not hardy with them, however, they have a form called the 'Storzinger Strain' which looks similar but does not winter kill as bad. I would guess this strain has significant *L. vulgare* blood based on leaf characteristics. Also from Minnesota is 'Hillside' which is a quite cold hardy yellow foliage strain. Interestingly, seedlings of Vicaryi show the yellow foliage condition. This could open the way for better selections. Vicaryi is rated Zone 5 to 8 and 'Storzinger Strain' Zone 4 to 9. Golden Vicary originated in the garden of Vicary Gibbs, Middlesex, England, before 1920.

Ligustrum vulgare — European Privet
(lī-gus′trum vul-gā′rē)

LEAVES: Opposite, simple, entire, oblong-obovate to lanceolate, 1 to 2 1/2″ long, 1/4 to 5/8″ wide, obtuse to acute, glabrous, dark green; petiole—1/8 to 2/3″ long.
STEM: Young branches green and minutely pubescent, finally glabrous, gray.

Ligustrum vulgare, European or Common Privet, is a stout, much branched shrub with irregularly spreading branches growing 12 to 15' high with a similar spread. The foliage is a distinct dark green in summer; flowers are white, of heavy, objectionable odor, mid-June, borne in dense, terminal, 1 to 3″ long panicles; the fruit is lustrous black, 1/3″ long, berry-like drupe which ripens in September and persists through March and later of the following year. This used to be the favored privet species but has lost some of its appeal and perhaps should be entirely omitted because of the better species. The anthracnose twig blight (*Glomerella cingulata*) which causes drying out of the leaves, blighting of stems and development of cankers is serious on this species. Cultivars include:
'Cheyenne'—A hardy form but still not capable of sustaining itself at the Minnesota Landscape Arboretum; grown from seed collected in Yugoslavia by E. Anderson; introduced by Cheyenne Field Station, U.S.D.A.; holds leaves late, often into December.
'Densiflorum'—Upright form with dense habit; maintaining this, if unpruned, for at least 20 years.
var. *italicum*—Holds the leaves longer than any variety, found in the southern range of the species.

'Lodense'—Low, dense, compact form; 22-year-old plant was only 4 1/2' tall; susceptible to a blight
for which there is no cure, holds leaves late, existed on Illinois campus for a number of years.
'Pyramidale'—Excellent hedge plant, somewhat pyramidal in habit.

Other cultivars with green, white and yellow fruits as well as variegated foliage are known,
probably 20 or more cultivars. Native to Europe, northern Africa, naturalized in eastern North
America. Zone 4 to 7.

Lindera benzoin — Spicebush
(lin-der'à ben'zō-in)

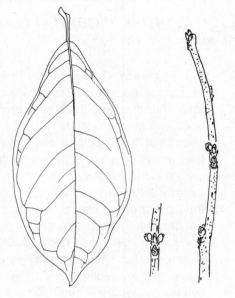

FAMILY: Lauraceae

LEAVES: Alternate, simple, oblong-obovate, 3 to 5″ long, 1 to
2 1/2″ wide, acute or short acuminate, cuneate at base,
entire, light green above, pale beneath, margins ciliate;
petiole—1/4 to 1/2″ long.

BUDS: Small, superposed, upper collaterally arranged producing
green, ovoid, stalked flower buds, vegetative buds with 3
scales, end bud lacking.

STEM: Rounded, slender, green or olive-brown with pale lenticels; pith — large, round, white, continuous; all parts of the
plant are aromatic when broken.

SIZE: 6 to 12' high with a similar spread.

HARDINESS: Zone 4 to 9.

HABIT: Usually rounded shrub in outline, somewhat loose and
open in the wild; dense, full, and broad-rounded in full sun.

RATE: Slow to medium.

TEXTURE: Medium in all seasons.

LEAF COLOR: Light green in summer changing to yellow in fall, often excellent yellow to golden yellow.

FLOWERS: Dioecious, greenish yellow, early to mid-April before the leaves, in axillary clusters, not
overwhelming but attractive; will open about mid-March in Athens, GA.

FRUIT: Oval drupe, 1/3 to 1/2″ long, bright scarlet, September, seldom seen since it is showy only after
the leaves fall and is borne only on pistillate plants, nevertheless, very ornamental.

CULTURE: Difficult to transplant because of coarsely fibrous root system and somewhat slow to reestablish; does best in moist, well-drained soils; full sun or 1/2 shade; does adequately in dry soils.

DISEASES AND INSECTS: None serious.

LANDSCAPE VALUE: Good shrub for the border or naturalizing; I have seen it growing in deep woods
where it is often rather thin and open; excellent for moist soil areas and semi-shady spots; in full sun
it makes a splendid plant in flower and fall color; a harbinger of spring.

CULTIVARS:

'Rubra' (f. *rubra*)—A brick-red, male-flowered selection from Hopkinton, R.I.; the winter buds are a
darker, red-brown color.

'Xanthocarpa' (f. *xanthocarpa*)—An orange-yellow fruited form that was discovered as a spontaneous plant at the Arnold Arboretum in 1967 by Alfred Fordham, the former propagator.

PROPAGATION: Seed should be stratified for 30 days at 77°F, followed by 90 days in peat at 34° to 41°
or 105 days in sand at 41°F. Have had good success with 90 days cold moist stratification. Cuttings
of half-ripe (greenwood) shoots will root but percentages are usually not high. I have had poor
success and have had only an occasional cutting root.

ADDITIONAL NOTES: The fruits are lovely and remind one of the fruits of *Cornus mas.* They are a brilliant
scarlet and singularly eye-catching in the autumn landscape on close inspection.

NATIVE HABITAT: Maine to Ontario and Kansas, south to Florida and Texas. Introduced 1863.

RELATED SPECIES:

Lindera obtusiloba—Japanese Spicebush
(lin-der′à ob-tū-si-lō′bà)

LEAVES: Alternate, simple, variable in shape (see below), but distinctly 3-veined, 2 1/2 to 5″ long, 1 1/4 to 4″ wide, lustrous dark green and glabrous above, pale and pubescent on the veins below; petiole 1/2 to 1″ long, pubescent.

Lindera obtusiloba, Japanese Spicebush, is a beautiful, large, multistemmed shrub or small tree that ranges from 10 to 20′ in height. Fourteen-year-old plants average 8 to 10′ in height and slightly less in width. The rather leathery, lustrous dark green leaves are variable in shape ranging from 3 lobed, left-hand mitten, right hand mitten, to no lobes. In October the leaves turn brilliant golden yellow,

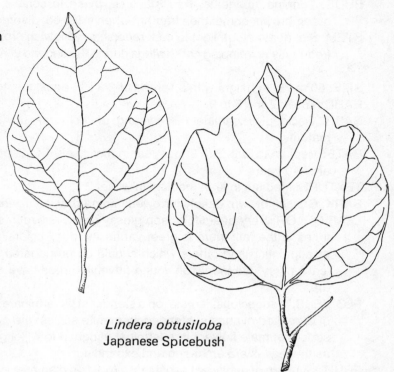

Lindera obtusiloba
Japanese Spicebush

color uniformly and remain effective for two weeks or longer. Surprisingly, it colors well in partial shade. I know of no other woody shrub that rivals it for intensity of yellow coloration. The flowers are similar to those of *L. benzoin* and appear 1 to 2 weeks earlier. The fruits are globose, 1/4″ wide, changing from red to shining black. The buds are plump, angular-ovoid and reddish in color, with one per node. Seeds will germinate after a 3 month cold period. July cuttings rooted 55 percent when treated with 8000 ppm IBA and placed under mist. This is a fine plant and is worthy of wider use. Hardy in Zone 6 although laboratory hardiness tests indicate it being hardy to -17°F. Japan, Korea, China. Introduced 1880.

Liquidambar styraciflua — American Sweetgum
(lik-wid-am′bär stī-ra-se-floo′a)

FAMILY: Hamamelidaceae

LEAVES: Alternate, simple, 4 to 7 1/2″ wide and about as long, 5 to 7 lobed with oblong-triangular, acuminate, star-shaped, finely serrate lobes, cordate at base, dark green and lustrous above, paler beneath except axillary tufts in axils of principal veins; petiole 2 1/2 to 4″ long.

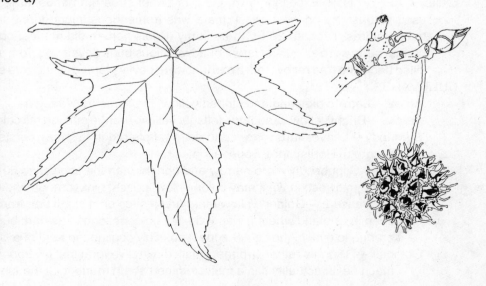

BUDS: Terminal imbricate, 6 to 8 scaled, ovate to conical, 1/4 to 1/2" long, laterals smaller, reddish green-brown, sometimes fragrant when crushed, divergent.

STEM: Slender to stout, light to dark reddish or yellowish brown, aromatic, rounded or somewhat angled, frequently developing corky wings during the second year; pith-star-shaped, solid, white or brownish.

SIZE: 60 to 75' in height with a spread of 2/3's to equal the height; can reach 80 to 120' in the wild.

HARDINESS: Zone 5 to 9.

HABIT: Decidedly pyramidal when young, of very neat outline; often with an oblong to rounded crown at maturity.

RATE: Medium to fast, 2 to 3' per year in moist soil; 1 to 2' per year in dry soil; 20.3' high and 14.5' wide after 10 years.

TEXTURE: Medium in leaf; medium in winter.

BARK: Grayish brown, deeply furrowed into narrow, somewhat rounded ridges.

LEAF COLOR: Very beautiful, deep glossy green above in summer, changing to rich yellow-purple-red tones in the fall; there is great variability in fall colors; I have seen sweetgums which were totally disappointing and others which should be propagated vegetatively for their fall color alone; holds leaves very late in fall; on young (juvenile) trees have seen leaves persist into February in Athens area.

FLOWERS: Monoecious, female, on a slender stalk terminated by a 1/2" diameter globose head consisting of 2-beaked ovaries subtended by minute scales; the ovaries coalescing at maturity to form a solid structure; male flowers in a terminal upright 3 to 4" long raceme; neither are showy, late April, May as the leaves are emerging and expanding.

FRUIT: Syncarp of dehiscent capsules, 1 to 1 1/2" diameter, persisting into winter, the seeds are brownish and winged; the fruit can be quite messy; good identification feature, fruits fall over an extended period from December to April and beyond, definitely a maintenance liability as a street or general lawn tree.

CULTURE: Transplant balled and burlapped in spring into deep, moist, slightly acid soil; full sun; the root system is fleshy and consequently is not greatly fibrous and takes a while to reestablish; have seen newly transplanted trees, even small trees, literally sit still for a year or so until root systems developed, leaves may be somewhat smaller the first growing season after winter or early spring transplanting; in the wild the tree occurs as a bottomland species on rich, moist, alluvial soils but is found on a great variety of sites; prune during the winter; not a good plant for city plantings and small areas where roots are limited in their development; avoid polluted areas; averaged 1'10" per year over a 10-year period in KS tests, most vigorous on moist sites.

DISEASES AND INSECTS: Bleeding necrosis, leaf spots, sweetgum webworm, caterpillars, cottony-cushion scale, sweetgum scale, walnut scale; iron chlorosis can be a problem on high pH soils.

LANDSCAPE VALUE: Excellent lawn, park, or street stree but needs large area for root development; used extensively on west coast; there was tremendous injury during the winter of 1976-77 when temperatures reached -20°F; a tree in my Illinois garden did not leaf out until June; apparently the normal buds were killed and latent or adventitious buds developed from stems and that had not been killed back; the tree recovered; trees that were newly planted in fall were essentially killed by the cold.

CULTIVARS:

'Aurea'—Leaves blotched and striped yellow, the same as 'Variegata'.

'Aurora'—Bright yellow variegated foliage, yellow, orange and red fall color on a small pyramidal tree.

'Burgundy'—Leaves turn wine-red to deep purple red in fall, may persist into winter, a selection by Saratoga Horticultural Foundation.

'Festival'—Supposedly more narrow and upright than the species to 60'; fall color has been yellow in the midwest; in west may color yellow, peach, pink, orange and red, Saratoga introduction.

'Golden Treasure'—Golden yellow margined leaves on a small tree framework, slow growing, have seen in England where it was vivid; fall color described as dark burgundy in the deeper areas, orange to pink in the lighter zones; possibly cook in the heat of a U.S. summer.

'Gumball'—I like this rather strange, small, diminutive form that is supposedly shaped like a gumball machine; in actuality it is a multistemmed shrub rounded at the top and gradually tapering to a rather wide base, leaves are normal size and I have not observed flowers or fruits; fall color is not particularly good; in Cincinnati and Boston I have seen it severely frozen back by temperatures of -6°F; it did recover from the injury; I estimate that anything below 0°F will result in some injury; I have rooted it from softwood cuttings collected in late August, 8000 ppm IBA-quick dip, mist, at a 100 percent rate; introduced by Hiram Stubblefield, McMinnville, TN.

'Kia'—Orange-red turning deep purplish in fall, pyramidal habit; supposedly narrow, spire-like outline.

'Lane Roberts'—An English introduction with rich black crimson-red fall color; have not seen it in the United States.

'Levis'—Branches show no corky bark and leaves color brilliantly in autumn.

'Moonbeam'—Green and cream in summer, turning pink and magenta in autumn, Duncan and Davies, New Zealand.

'Moraine'—More uniform and faster growing than the species; upright-oval habit with a medium branch texture and brilliant red fall color; I have seen this cultivar at the Ohio Agricultural Research and Development Shade Tree Evaluation Plots, Wooster, Ohio, and was impressed by the excellent glossy dark green foliage, as well as the good habit; has proven to be the most cold hardy cultivar surviving temperatures in the range of -20° to -25°F.

'Oconee'—A plant has grown on the Georgia campus for years, the habit is akin to 'Gumball' but more rounded and perhaps not as large at maturity; I estimate 8 to 10' (15') and 6 to 8' wide, makes a multistemmed tight shrub, fall color is superior to 'Gumball' and turns deep reddish purple in fall and holds for 3 to 4 weeks, hardiness is unknown but suspect more cold hardy than 'Gumball'.

'Palo Alto'—A more uniform growth habit than the species and the leaves turn orange-red in fall, Saratoga introduction.

'Rotundiloba'—In the last edition I had listed this form as 'Obtusiloba' which is incorrect; my knowledge about this tree was scanty in the 1983 edition but have seen enough to believe it could have an impact on tree planting in Zone 6 to 9; a large tree on NC State campus is more narrow pyramidal than the typical species type, leaves are lustrous dark green and turn, at least based on observations in 1987 and 1988, rich reddish purple fall color; on a previous visit to NC State, I remembered yellow fall color; Raulston reported color varies from year to year with a range of yellow to dark burgundy; the plant sets no fruit which is sufficient reason to grow it, probably hardy to -10°F, I have seen a branch reversion to the typical leaf shape and this should be kept in mind when growing the tree, was discovered in the wild in North Carolina in 1930.

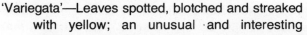

'Variegata'—Leaves spotted, blotched and streaked with yellow; an unusual and interesting variegated type that displays reasonable hardiness; the same as 'Aureum'?

'Worplesdon'—Unique narrow lobed leaves and apricot-orange fall color.

PROPAGATION: Seeds exhibit only a shallow dormancy, but germination rate is considerably increased by cold, moist stratification at 41°F for 15 to 90 days; leafy cuttings taken with a heel can be rooted under mist in summer; have tried to root a variegated seedling clone but without success; cultivars are normally budded or grafted.

NATIVE HABITAT: Connecticut, south to New York to Florida, southern Ohio, Indiana, Illinois, Missouri to Texas and Mexico. Introduced 1681.

RELATED SPECIES:

Liquidambar formosana—Formosan Sweetgum
(lik-wid-am'bär fôr-mō-sā'nȧ)

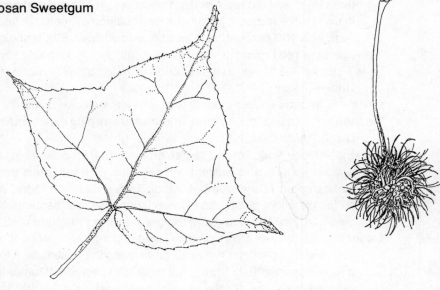

LEAVES: Alternate, simple, 3 lobed, middle triangular, laterals spreading, 2 to 4" high, 3 to 6" wide, apex long acuminate, base truncate to cordate, sharply serrate from apex to base, glabrous and lustrous dark green above, medium green and pubescent on veins below; petiole—2 to 3" long, glabrous.

BUDS: Imbricate, dark brown, 3/8 to 5/8" long, scales covered with silky brown pubescence; flower buds larger than vegetative, elongated conical and tapering at base.

STEM: Stout, terete, dark gray-brown, prominently lenticelled, glabrous; stem when bruised emits a slight sweet-spicy odor; pith-greenish, solid.

Liquidambar formosana, Formosan Sweetgum, will always place second to our native *L. styraciflua* in landscape use. It is a handsome species with distinct 3-lobed, lustrous dark green leaves that turn an excellent yellow in fall. The tree becomes quite large with time and one stately specimen on the University of Georgia campus is fully 50' tall and wide. A report from Mississippi State indicated that superior types were being selected for brilliant red fall coloration. A variety *monticola* is described as having plum purple new foliage, finally dull green, and changing to crimson in the autumn; whether this is a true variety has been questioned. The species flowers 2 to 3 weeks ahead of *L. styraciflua* and the beaks of the capsules are not as stiff and rigid. Interestingly, the species (perhaps all sweetgums) is self-sterile and the lone tree on the Georgia campus has never produced a stray seedling. Apparently its earlier flowering date prevents any potential cross-polination with *L. styraciflua.* The fruits do form and fall like the native species but are not as objectionable because of their less woody nature. 'Afterglow' appears in the California literature and is described as having lavender-purple new growth and rose-red fall color, the habit is broad asymmetrical. Native to Formosa, southern and central China from the coast to Szechuan and Hupeh, south to Kwantung province, and also occurs in Indochina. Introduced 1884. Zone 7 to 9. Wilson introduced the variety *monticola* from W. Hupeh in 1907. Zone 6 to 9(?).

ADDITIONAL NOTES: Wood is used for plywood, furniture, cabinet making, and other uses. The name Sweetgum is derived from the sap which has a sweet taste and gummy consistency. Sweetgum, in the south, is a primary invader of abandoned fields as well as flood plain areas. It makes its best growth on the rich, moist, alluvial clay and loam soils of river bottoms. The species has tremendous potential for landscape use and selections from the southern states need to be made for superior habit and fall color. The variation in fall color is truly astounding and on the Georgia campus there are trees that remain green into November and seldom color well while others literally appear to be on fire. A good fruitless form would be welcome; perhaps 'Rotundiloba' is the answer to the problem.

Liriodendron tulipifera—Tuliptree, also called Tulip Magnolia, Tulip Poplar, Yellow Poplar, and Whitewood.

(lir-i-ō-den′dron tū-li-pif′ēr-ȧ)

FAMILY: Magnoliaceae

LEAVES: Alternate, simple, 3 to 8″ across and as long, broad truncate apex, with a short acuminate lobe on each side and usually 3 to 4, acute or short-acuminate lobes on each side near the rounded or truncate base, bright green above, paler beneath; petiole 2 to 4″ long.

BUDS: Valvate, terminal—1/2″ long, greenish to reddish brown, covered with a bloom, white dotted, entire bud resembling a duck's bill; laterals similar but considerably smaller.

STEM: Slender to stout, lustrous greenish to red-brown, sometimes bloomy, aromatic when broken but with intensely bitter taste, distinct stipular scars surrounding stem; pith—chambered.

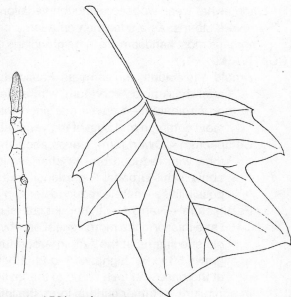

SIZE: 70 to 90′ in height with a spread of 35 to 50′; can grow to 150′ and greater.

HARDINESS: Zone 4 to 9, is being grown in Minnesota Landscape Arboretum but will never attain the size there that it does further south; it has withstood temperatures as low as -25°F without injury.

HABIT: In open-grown situations somewhat pyramidal in youth maturing to oval-rounded with several large sinuous branches constituting the framework; in the wild often free of branches for 70 to 80 percent of its height with only a narrow ovoid canopy at the upper reaches.

RATE: Fast, 15 to 20′ over a 6 to 8 year period; rapid growing especially when provided ample fertilizer and moisture.

TEXTURE: Medium in leaf and winter.

BARK: Grayish brown, furrowed into close, interlacing, rounded ridges which are separated by grayish crevices.

LEAF COLOR: Leaves emerge folded in flag-like outline, mature to bright green in summer, changing to golden yellow or yellow in fall, often superb during October and into early November; I have never given the species sufficient credit for fall coloration; truly an aristocratic tree.

FLOWERS: Perfect, with 6 greenish yellow petals in 2 rows, 3 reflexed sepals, interior of the corolla an orangish color; May to early June (often flowers by late April in Athens and continues for an extended period); solitary; may be slow to flower from seed although 6 to 10-year-old trees have flowered in the Athens area; flowers are often borne high in the tree and are missed by the uninitiated; a beautiful flower.

FRUIT: Cone-like aggregate of samaras, 2 to 3″ long, eventually turning brown in October and persisting through winter, good identification feature.

CULTURE: Transplant balled and burlapped in spring into deep, moist, well-drained loam; the root system is fleshy and often poorly branched; full sun; pH adaptable although prefers a slightly acid soil; prune in winter; has been used for street tree plantings in narrow tree lawns and usually develops leaf scorch or simply dies after a time; one tree grew 1′8″ per year over a 10-year period in KS tests, but 2 of 3 trees died because of drought and sunscald.

DISEASES AND INSECTS: Cankers, leaf spots, powdery mildews, root and stem rot, *Verticillium* wilt, leaf yellowing (physiological disorder), aphid, scale, and tuliptree spot gall; aphids are a real problem; the insect secrets liberal quantities of "honeydew" and the leaves of the plants are often coated with this substance which is then overrun with the sooty mold fungus, which causes a blackening and unsightliness of the leaves; the leaf yellowing problem can be a headache with newly planted as well as established trees which do not receive adequate water; the leaves abscise prematurely and create a mess that requires constant attention.

LANDSCAPE VALUE: Not a tree for the small residential property or streets; should be restricted to large areas and this type of situation only; a very large and magnificent plant when fully grown and developed; somewhat weak-wooded, although variation occurs among individuals, and may break up in ice and severe storms; as a specimen on a large property it has great beauty and in fall can be spectacular; perhaps most handsome in large groupings or groves where trees develop a spire-like habit.

CULTIVARS:

'Arnold'—Is actually the same as 'Fastigiatum', put into commerce by Monrovia Nursery and named after the Arnold Arboretum, where the scion wood was obtained.

'Aureo-marginatum'—Leaves margined with yellow or greenish yellow; quite handsome and is the most common and best of the variegated types; 'Majestic Beauty' by Monrovia is included here.

'Compactum'—Dwarf form, leaves about 1/2 the size of the species; the term possibly includes any form with reduced growth characteristics, Professor J.C. McDaniel had the plant described above in his Urbana, IL garden; it was a rather cute diminutive form that could have commercial possibilities where a reduced version of the species is required.

'Fastigiatum'—Narrow, with upright lateral branches that almost parallel the center leader; the more I see this form the more I question why it is not being grown commercially; there are magnificent old specimens at the Arnold Arboretum and I have seen it used in several European gardens; grows 50 to 60' high by 15 to 20(25)' wide, a handsome useful form; larger plants become fat at the base and lose some of the fastigiate character.

'Integrifolium'—Rather curious form, the lateral or lower lobes missing resulting in an almost rectangular leaf, have seen on occasion in gardens, not common.

'Medio-pictum' ('Aureo-pictum')—Leaves with yellow blotch in middle, the margin typical bright green, rather handsome but have only seen in botanical gardens; the exact name is unknown and the two listed have been used in the literature and on botanical garden labels to describe what appears to be the same plant.

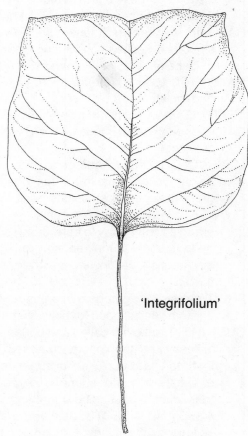

'Integrifolium'

'Tortuosum'—Supposedly with contorted stems but as I have seen it the leaves are distinctly tortuous, undulated and, rather innocuous; there is a form called 'Contortum' which resembles the 'Tortuosum' I have seen; 'Crispum' might be synonymous with both (?). Santamour and Mc-Ardle, *J. Arbor.* 10(11):309–312 (1984) report that 'Contortum' is the correct name for this form.

PROPAGATION: Seeds should be stratified in bags of peat moss or sand for 60 to 90 days at 41°F; percentage of sound seed is usually quite low. Cuttings, July collected, made with basal cut 1/2″ below node, rooted 52%; have rooted cuttings from stump sprouts with success. Cultivars must be grafted.

ADDITIONAL NOTES: Wood is used for furniture and other products; one of our tallest native eastern American deciduous species and can grow to 190'. The showy flowers depend on honeybees for cross-pollination and the honey is supposedly of excellent quality. I was amazed at the percentage of great specimens in Europe. In fact, they appear to be more suited to culture there than in their homeland.

NATIVE HABITAT: Massachusetts to Wisconsin, south to Florida and Mississippi. Cultivated 1663.

Lithocarpus henryi—Henry Tanbark Oak
(lith-ō-kär′pus hen′ri-ī)

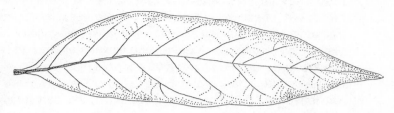

FAMILY: Fagaceae
LEAVES: Alternate, simple, evergreen, narrow-oblong, 4 to 8″(10″) long, 1 1/2 to 2″ wide, acute, cuneate, entire, leathery, lustrous medium green; petiole—1″ long.

Lithocarpus henryi, Henry Tanbark Oak, is an oval to rounded evergreen tree with good heat and drought tolerance. Plants have been growing in the southeast for years and appear adaptable. In winter, leaves turn yellow-green and appear to need fertilization. Fruits (acorns) are closely set on a 4 to 8″ long spike that occurs at the end of the shoot. Each acorn is globose, flattened at the top, 3/4″ wide and covered with a 1/8″ deep, shallow cap (involucre). A few Georgia nurserymen have offered this but acceptance has been slow. In youth the tree is somewhat open and no one is quite sure where to use it. In general the *Lithocarpus* differ from *Quercus* by erect spike flowers borne at the end of the shoots and spikes often with male and female flowers on the same structure.

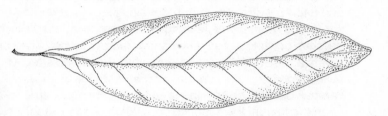

Lithocarpus edulis, (litho-ō-kär′pus ed′ū-lis), Japanese Tanbark Oak, tends toward a shrubby nature although I have seen small 20 to 25′ trees in Savannah, Ga. Leaves are 3 1/2 to 6″ long, 1 to 2 1/4″ wide, entire, blunt at apex, hard leathery texture, lustrous and darker green than above with a slight silvery sheen below, 9 to 11 vein pairs, petiole—1/3 to 1″ long. Leaves are darker green and do not discolor to the degree of *L. henryi*. Japan. *L. henryi* occurs in western Hupeh and eastern Szechuan, China. Zone 8 and 9 although *L. edulis* survived -3°F. Have grown *L. densiflorus* in my Georgia garden. Makes a handsome dense lustrous dark evergreen shrub/tree. Flowered in late October on Georgia campus. Leaves are toothed.

Lonicera—Honeysuckle
FAMILY: Caprifoliaceae

GENERAL NOTE: The number of honeysuckle species and cultivars is enormous. There are about 180 species and here I have presented an encapsulated treatment. In general they are of easy culture, propagate readily from seeds and cuttings, and are generally free of serious insects and diseases. I had the opportunity to evaluate the Arnold Arboretum's tremendous collection during sabbatical and have included a few species here that will be new to most readers.

Lonicera alpigena—Alps Honeysuckle
(lon-iss′ēr-à al-pi-jē′na)

LEAVES: Opposite, simple, ellilptic to oblong-ovate or oblong, 2 to 4″ long, 1 to 2″ wide, acuminate, rounded to cuneate, entire, dark green and glabrous above, lighter beneath and glabrous at maturity; petiole—1/2″ long.

Lonicera alpigena, Alps Honeysuckle, grows 4 to 8′ high, developing an erect, much branched habit. Like many honeysuckles, the winter habit is less than appealing and the only appropriate way to alleviate the situation is to hide the plant in the shrub border. Leaves are dark green and somewhat lustrous in summer; fall color is of no consequence. Flowers are yellow or greenish yellow, tinged dull red or brown-red; effective in May (north); borne in axillary peduncled pairs; each flower about 1/2″ long. The fruits are red, up to 1/2″ long, cherry-like, often united for a portion of their length. This is a rather distinct species because of the long flower stalks, large leaves and large fruits. The cultivar 'Nana' is a low, slow-growing form; a 63-year-old plant being only 3′ high. This makes a rather handsome broad-mounded dark green foliaged form. The leaves are large (up to 4″ long) and slightly crinkled. The leaves are pubescent on the lower surface, particularly the veins. The gray-brown bark shows a slight exfoliating characteristic. Native to the mountains of central and southern Europe. Introduced 1600. Zone 5 to 7.

Lonicera × *bella*—Belle Honeysuckle
(lon-iss′ēr-à × bel′la)

Lonicera × *bella,* Belle Honeysuckle, is the result of crosses between *L. morrowi* and *L. tatarica.* The hybrids were first raised in the Münden Botanic Garden from seeds received from the St. Petersburg (Russia) Botanic Garden before 1889. The plants will grow 8 to 10′ high and 8 to 12′ wide. The shrub develops a dense, rounded habit with spreading, somewhat arching branches. The foliage is bluish green in summer. Flowers vary in degrees of white to pink and usually fade to yellow. They are evident in early to mid-May (north). The fruit is a red, 1/4″ diameter berry which becomes effective in late June and July often persisting into fall but does not rival *L. tatarica* for abundance or showiness. A large mass was present on the Illinois campus but offered little in the way of aesthetics. Large foliage mass at best. Several selections have been made from the seedling populations and the best include 'Albida'—flowers initially white, fading to creamy yellow; 'Atrorosea'—dark rose with a lighter edge; 'Candida'—pure white flowers; 'Dropmore'—white flowers; and 'Rosea'—flowers deep pink. Zone 4 to 7.

Lonicera × *brownii*—Brown's Honeysuckle
(lon-iss′ēr-à brow′nē-ī)

A group of hybrids between *L. sempervirens* and *L. hirsuta* with the habit and general foliage characteristics of the former but somewhat hardier and with the corolla more or less two-lipped and glandular-pubescent on the outside. The typical form of the cross arose before 1853. Unfortunately, it shows the first parent's susceptibility to aphids. 'Dropmore Scarlet' was raised by F.L. Skinner, Dropmore, Manitoba. The red flowers appear in June and continue into October–November. This is considered to be the hardiest vine honeysuckle in the north. 'Fuchsioides' is used occasionally in European gardens but is less vigorous than 'Dropmore Scarlet' or *L. sempervirens.* The flowers are orangish red and not as large as the two mentioned above.

Lonicera caerulea—Bearberry Honeysuckle
(lon-iss′ēr-à se-rū′lē-à)

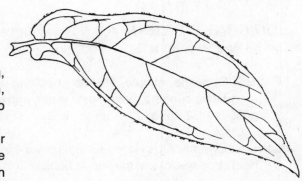

LEAVES: Opposite, simple, ovate, obovate or oblong, 1 1/2 to 3″ long, 1/4 to 1″ wide, acute to obtuish, rounded, entire, bright green, pubescent on midrib and veins below; petiole—1/8″ long, pubescent.

Lonicera caerulea, Bearberry Honeysuckle, is a rather dense, sturdy shrub that grows 4 to 5′ high. The yellowish white flowers give rise to bloomy bluish fruits. This is a highly variable species and occurs in the higher altitudes and latitudes of three northern continents. I grew it in the Illinois test plots and it never really proved superior to *L. tatarica, L. morrowi,* and *L. × bella,* which, in essence, provides reason for a strong inferiority complex. The blue fruits are interesting and var. *edulis* has sweetish edible fruits. Zone 2 to 5.

Lonicera fragrantissima — Winter Honeysuckle
(lon-iss′ĕr-à frā-gran-tis′i-mà)

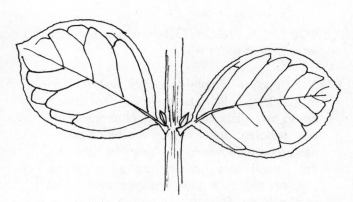

LEAVES: Opposite, simple, elliptic to broad-ovate, 1 to 3″ long, two-thirds to almost as wide, acute , broad cuneate at base, setose-ciliate, dull blue-green to dark green and glabrous above, setose on the midrib; petiole 1/3″ long.

BUDS: Imbricate, sessile, with numerous 4-ranked scales, slightly pubescent.

STEM: Slender, glabrous, light, often lustrous brown; pith—white, solid or slightly excavated.

SIZE: 6 to 10′ high (15′) by 6 to 10′ in spread.

HARDINESS: Zone 4 to 8 (9).

HABIT: Wide-spreading, irregularly rounded, deciduous shrub with tangled mass of slender recurving branches; holds foliage very late in fall and in southern states into winter.

RATE: Fast.

TEXTURE: Medium in leaf, medium-coarse in winter; this is true for most of the larger honeysuckles.

LEAF COLOR: Dull dark bluish or grayish green in summer; foliage holds late and falls green or brown; leafs out early in spring.

FLOWERS: Creamy white, lemon-scented and extremely fragrant, relatively small, March-early April (Urbana, IL) for a 3 to 4 week period; opens in January, peaks in February, still flowering in mid-March (Athens), borne in axillary peduncled pairs before the leaves; not very showy but certainly among the most fragrant of woody flowering shrubs, the sweet lemon fragrance is about the first of all woody shrubs, tremendous plant for pulling one out of the winter doldrums.

FRUIT: Berry, two-ovaries fuse, 1/4″ diameter, dark red, late May-early June, seldom seen for it is borne under foliage.

CULTURE: The following discussion applies to the honeysuckles; transplant readily, adapted to many soils and pH levels; prefer good loamy, moist, well-drained soil; abhor extremely wet situations; full sun to partial shade; pruning should be accomplished after flowering and, in fact, when honeysuckles become overgrown the best treatment is to cut them back to the ground as they readily develop new shoots.

DISEASES AND INSECTS: Leaf blight, leaf spots, powdery mildews, aphids, Russian aphid (causes brooming), woolly honeysuckle sawfly, four-lined plant bug, planthopper, green house whitefly, flea beetle, looper caterpillar, long-tailed mealybug, fall webworm, a few scale species.

LANDSCAPE VALUE: Makes a good hedge or screen plant; nice for fragrance, could be integrated into the shrub border; worthwhile to force branches inside in winter.

PROPAGATION: Most species show some embryo dormancy and stratification in moist media for 30 to 60 days at 41°F is recommended; some species have hard seed coats and warm followed by cold stratification is recommended. Cuttings of most species (softwood collected in June) root with ease under mist. Have rooted this species many times and discovered that one has to work to get less than 100%.

NATIVE HABITAT: Eastern China. Introduced 1845.

RELATED SPECIES:

Lonicera standishii, (lon-iss′ēr-a stan-dish′ē-ī), Standish Honeysuckle, is quite similar but not as good an ornamental. *Lonicera fragrantissima* differs by the absence of bristles on the young shoots, flower-stalks, and corolla; the leaf is shorter and the apex is not drawn out. Leaves of *L. standishii* are 2 to 4 1/2″ long, 3/4 to 2″ wide, oblong-lanceolate, acuminate, rounded with distinct pubescence below. Have seen a 9 to 10′ high plant in the Coastal Plain. China. Introduced about 1845. A hybrid, *L.* × *purpusii*, between the two species, has the fine fragrance of the parents. Zone 5 to 8(9) for both.

Lonicera × *heckrottii*—Goldflame Honeysuckle
(lon-iss′ēr-à × hek-rot′e-ī)

LEAVES: Opposite, simple, oblong or oval, 1 1/2 to 2 1/2″ long, glabrous, lustrous dark bluish green, firm, glaucous beneath, glabrous; scarcely petioled; upper leaves are fused at the base (connate) and form a disk that subtends the flower; new growth has a handsome purplish red tinge that becomes blue-green with maturity. The stems are purplish red and glabrous.

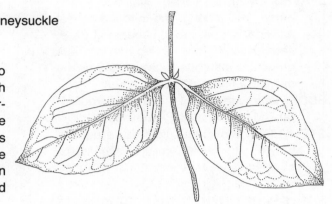

Lonicera × *heckrottii,* often called the Everblooming or Goldflame Honeysuckle, is a vine of unknown origin although the parentage is purported to be *L. sempervirens* × *L.* × *americana*. I would consider it the most handsome of the climbing honeysuckles. The flower buds are carmine and, as they open, the yellow inside the corolla is exposed. The outside gradually changes to a pink color and the total flower effect is strikingly handsome. The slightly fragrant flowers are borne in elongated peduncled spikes, with several remote whorls; in my garden flowers are evident in March-April into summer with sporadic recurrent bloom in fall. Foliage is essentially evergreen to 15 to 20°F. Fruit is described as red but I have never observed a single berry; 10 to 20′ high. Zone 4 but best in Zone 5 and south (9). Introduced before 1895. As long as new growth occurs flowers continue to develop.

Lonicera japonica—Japanese Honeysuckle
(lon-iss′ēr-à ja-pon′i-kà)

LEAVES: Opposite, simple, evergreen, semievergreen to deciduous, ovate to oblong-ovate, 1 1/4 to 3 1/4″ long, acute to short-acuminate, rounded to subcordate at base, pubescent on both sides when young, later glabrate above; petiole— 1/4″ long.
BUDS: Small, solitary, covered with 2 pubescent scales, superposed, sessile.

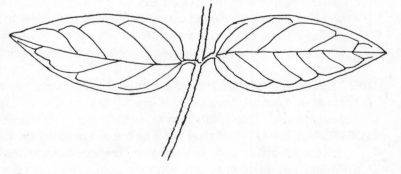

STEM: Reddish brown to light brown, covered with soft pubescence, twining; pith—excavated.

Lonicera japonica, Japanese Honeysuckle, is a weedy, twining vine growing from 15 to 30′. The dark green foliage is evergreen to semi-evergreen to deciduous depending on the severity of cold. Flowers are white (may be tinged pink or purple) turning yellow, fragrant; (early May in Athens) June through November, borne in peduncled pairs; usually a solid mass of white and yellow in full flower; fruit is a black, 1/4″ diameter berry ripening in August through October; a good, quick, ground, bank, or support cover but has escaped from cultivation and has become a noxious weed in many areas of the country. 'Aureo-reticulata' is an interesting cultivar with yellow netted markings throughout the leaf, the overall effect is that of reverse chlorosis, best grown in full sun, an interesting novelty plant; variety *purpurea* is a vigorous grower with rich purple tinted dark green foliage, purple-red flowers on outside, white inside, and coral red fruit; 'Halliana' has pure white flowers which change to yellow, very fragrant, vigorous grower. I am never sure whether to praise or curse this species for it has ruined many acres of native woodland understory by essentially out-competing and shading the native woodland flowers. It is vigorous to a fault and scarcely a fencerow in Georgia is free of the plant. The fragrance is quite appealing and can be sensed from the car at 65 miles per hour. A handsome and little-known taxon is var. *chinensis* (var. *repens*) that I have seen intermixed with the species. It is slightly less vigorous, flatter growing with glabrous leaves. The flowers are more colorful being reddish purple on the outside. Stems and leaves also show the purplish red coloration. Might be a better garden plant. Japan, China, Korea. Introduced 1806. Zone 4 to 9.

Lonicera korolkowii—Blueleaf Honeysuckle
(lon-iss′ēr-à kôr-ōl-kōw′ē-ī)

LEAVES: Opposite, simple, ovate to elliptic, 3/4 to 1 1/4″ long, 1/2 to 1″ wide, acute, cuneate to rounded, entire, pale bluish green, pubescent on both surfaces, petiole—about 1/4″ long; true *L. korolkowii* is distinct because of small leaves and glaucous blue foliage.

Lonicera korolkowii, Blueleaf Honeysuckle, is a loose, open, irregular shrub with slender, spreading and arching branches growing 6 to 10′ high and as wide although one authority listed mature size between 12 and 15′ high with an equal spread. The largest true example I have seen was 6′ high and wide. The downy shoots and pale, sea green, pubescent leaves give the shrub a striking gray-blue hue and hence the name Blueleaf Honeysuckle. The flowers are rose-colored (pinkish), each flower about 2/3″ long (corolla), borne in peduncled pairs from the leaf axils of short lateral branchlets in May. The fruit is a bright red berry which matures in July and August. Culturally this species is more difficult to establish than other honeysuckles and should be transplanted balled and burlapped. This is one reason why Blueleaf Honeysuckle is seldom seem in the trade. The cultivars include 'Aurora' with moderate purplish pink flowers and a profuse flowering nature, and 'Floribunda' which supposedly is more floriferous than the species. There is a variety *zabelii* which has deeper rose-pink flowers and glabrous leaves broader than the species. This variety is often confused with the cultivar 'Zabelii' which is purported to belong to *L. tatarica*. The University of Minnesota has introduced 'Freedom' which resembles *L. korolkowii* with blue-green foliage, white flowers, red fruits and freedom from the Russian aphid. Native to Soviet Central Asia, bordering parts of Afghanistan and Pakistan. Introduced 1880. Zone 4 to 7.

Lonicera maackii—Amur Honeysuckle
(lon-iss′ēr-à mak′ē-ī)

LEAVES: Opposite, simple, ovate-elliptic to ovate-lanceolate, 2 to 3″ long, 1/2 to 1 1/2″ wide, acuminate, broad-cuneate, rarely rounded at base, entire, dark green above, lighter beneath, usually pubescent only on the veins on both sides; petiole—1/8 to 1/5″ long, glandular-pubescent.
BUDS: Gray, pubescent, oblong or acute.
STEM: Grayish brown, short pubescence on current year's growth, finally glabrous; pith—brown, excavated in internodes, solid at nodes.

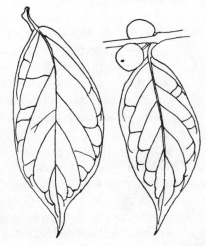

Lonicera maackii, Amur Honeysuckle, is a large, upright, spreading, leggy, deciduous shrub reaching 12 to 15′ in height with a similar spread. The foliage is medium to dark green in summer and the fall color is ineffective. The flowers are white changing to yellow, 1″ long, May creeping into early June, borne in axillary peduncled pairs. The fruit is a red, 1/4″ diameter berry which ripens in October and is eaten by the birds. Variety *podocarpa* flowers in early June, Zone 4 hardiness, and is a better flowerer. 'Rem Red' is a Soil Conservation Service, U.S.D.A. introduction that grows 8 to 12′ tall, produces abundant white maturing to yellow flowers and red fruits. It is a seed-produced cultivar. In my mind, I am doubtful about how different this is from the species. In the southern states, the species has escaped and the red fruits will be present into February and March. It appears that if other food is present, birds will pass over Amur Honeysuckle. The birds deposit the seeds in old shrub borders, hedges, wasteland and before one knows it, Amur Honeysuckle has taken over. Starts to leaf out in late February-early March with flowers by mid to late April in Athens. Shows amazing shade tolerance and exists as an understory plant in some woodlands. Truly a noxious weed. Manchuria and Korea. Introduced 1855–1860. Zone 2 to 8.

Lonicera maximowiczii var. *sachalinensis*—Sakhalin Honeysuckle
(lon-iss′ẽr-à mak-si-mō-wik′zē-ī sak-à-lī-nen′sis)

Lonicera maximowiczii var. *sachalinensis*, Sakhalin Honeysuckle, as my field notes say "was the most beautiful honeysuckle" in the Arnold's collection. It makes a dense, rounded to mounded, 6 to 8′ high shrub. The dark green, ovate, 1 1/2 to 3″ long, 3/4 to 1 1/2″ wide leaves may turn a golden yellow in fall. The 1 1/2″ long flowers are deep red, produced on a 1″ peduncle and the fruit is red. This is a handsome honeysuckle which is not well known. Northern Japan, Sakhalin, Korea and the Ussuri region. Probably too many honeysuckles are already in commerce to allow this a toe-hold, however, for foliage effect it is superior to the run-of-the-mill offerings. Introduced 1917. Zone 4 to 6(7)?

Lonicera morrowii—Morrow Honeysuckle
(lon-iss′ẽr-à môr-ōw′ē-ī)

LEAVES: Opposite, simple, elliptic to ovate-oblong or obovate-oblong, 1 to 2 1/2″ long, 1/2 as wide, acute or obtusish and mucronulate, rounded at base, sparingly pubescent above at least when young, gray to blue-green, soft-pubescent beneath; petiole 1/12 to 1/8″ long.
BUDS: Small, somewhat puberulent, blunt.
STEM: Grayish to light brown, pubescent when young, older stems a distinct gray, hollow.

Lonicera morrowii, Morrow Honeysuckle, grows 6 to 8′ high and 6 to 10′ wide forming a broad, rounded, dense, tangled mound with branches and foliage to the ground. Foliage is a grayish to bluish green in summer. Flowers are creamy-white changing to yellow, 3/4″ long, mid to late May, in peduncled pairs. Fruit is a blood-red, 1/4″ diameter berry ripening in July and August. Better than most honeysuckles as the foliage hugs the ground. Seldom seen in cultivation. Japan. 1975. Zone (3)4 to 6. 'Xanthocarpa' has white flowers and yellow fruits.

Lonicera nitida—Boxleaf Honeysuckle
(lon-iss′ẽr-à nit′i-dà)

LEAVES: Opposite, simple, evergreen, ovate to roundish, 1/4 to 5/8″ long, blunt, subcordate to broad-cuneate, entire, glossy dark green, glabrous; petiole—1/20″ long, minutely bristly.

Lonicera nitida, Boxleaf Honeysuckle, is totally confused with *L. pileata.* Boxleaf Honeysuckle is a dense, leafy shrub that grows to 5′ and higher. Have seen 6 to 8′ high plants in Europe. It is valued chiefly for the foliage. The creamy white, fragrant, 1/4″ long flowers are produced in axillary, short-stalked pairs. Based on actual smelling tests I can sense essentially no odor. The globular, bluish purple, translucent, 1/4″ diameter fruits appear in late summer. Have seen fruits on plants in Europe but never in America. Used extensively in Europe for hedges and masses; appears to tolerate more shade than many honesuckles. It is quite difficult to ascertain the exact nature of *L. nitida* for the plants in cultivation in the United States do not adhere to the species description. A key difference between this and *L. pileata* is the more rounded, smaller leaf. Several cultivars have been introduced and may, in fact, represent the species in cultivation.

'Baggesen's Gold'—A form with golden leaves and mounded almost haystack habit, color fades but not completely, with time; have seen 4 to 6′ high plants in England, better color under cool conditions.

'Elegant'—This form grows to about 3′ with horizontal or rather attractive slightly pendulous branches, leaves mat green, ovate to roundish ovate, 1/2″ long.

'Ernest Wilson'—Lateral branches drooping; leaves glossy bright green, mostly lanceolate-ovate or triangular ovate, less than 1/2″ long; have not noticed it in flower or fruit; probably offered as *L. nitida* in trade.

'Fertilis'—Branches arching or erect; leaves dark green and slightly more than 1/2″ long; flowers and fruits well.

'Graziosa'—A dense spreading shrub with small leaves.

'Yunnan'—Similar to 'Ernest Wilson' but differs by virtue of more erect lateral branches and slightly larger leaves not arranged in two ranks; also flowers more freely; has been distributed as *L. pileata* var. *yunnanensis;* have seen *L. yunnanensis* in the south which is apparently this clone or 'Ernest Wilson'.

ADDITIONAL NOTES: I first came in contact with the shrub on The Ohio State University campus. I collected cuttings, rooted them easily, and attempted to grow the plant in Urbana, Illinois. The -20°F winter effectively removed it from my landscape. Plants may display semi-evergreen tendencies in Zone 8. Native of western Szechuan and Yunnan, China. Introduced by Wilson in 1908. Zone 7 to 9.

Lonicera pileata—Privet Honeysuckle
(lon-iss′ĕr-a̤ pī-lē-ā′ta̤)

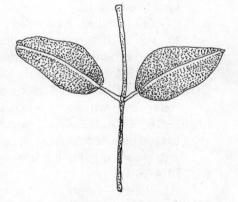

LEAVES: Opposite, simple, evergreen or semi-evergreen, ovate to oblong-lanceolate, 1/2 to 1 1/4″ long, 1/6 to 1/2″ wide, obtusish, cuneate, entire, lustrous dark green above, pale green and sparingly pubescent on midrib beneath or glabrous, sparingly ciliate; petioles—short.

Lonicera pileata, Privet Honeysuckle, is closely allied to *L. nitida* but differs in the larger, more elongated, lustrous dark green leaves. Yellowish white, 1/2″ long flowers occur in pairs during May and are not very effective. The translucent, rounded, amethyst fruit is about 1/5 to 1/4″ wide and handsome, but, again, has not been produced on U.S. plants. The habit is different being more spreading with horizontal branches that tend to build up on each other forming a rather graceful elegant 2 to 3′ high groundcover shrub. In Europe the plant is outstanding and appears to reach its aesthetic potential. In the eastern and southern United States, it struggles for identity. The habit is never as full or graceful and the leaves, especially in the heat of the south do not have the lustrous dark green character. Ideally, locate in well drained soil in shade or partial shade. At -3°F in Athens, plants were defoliated but developed new growth. *Lonicera pileata* is about 5 to 10°F more cold hardy than *L. nitida.* China. Introduced 1900. Zone 6 to 8.

Lonicera sempervirens — Trumpet Honeysuckle
(lon-iss'ēr-à sem-pēr-vī'renz)

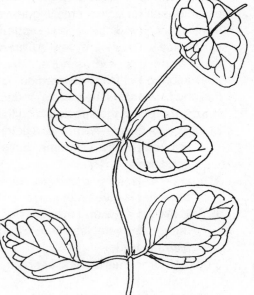

LEAVES: Opposite, simple, elliptic or ovate to oblong, 1 to 3″ long, 3/4 to 2″ wide, obtuse or acutish, usually cuneate, dark bluish green above, glaucous beneath and sometimes pubescent, 1 or 2 pairs below the inflorescence connate into an oblong disk, rounded or mucronate at ends; petiole—1/4″ long.

STEM: Twining, straw colored, glabrous; pith—excavated.

SIZE: 10 to 20′ and higher depending on structure.

HARDINESS: Twining vine, essentially deciduous but in Zone 8 to 9 will show semi-evergreen tendency in mild winters.

HABIT: Twining vine.

RATE: Fast.

TEXTURE: Medium, looks ragged during the summer months in the southeast but for 3 months from April to June is exceptionally handsome.

LEAF COLOR: New growth reddish purple or tinged some shade thereof turning bluish green at maturity; one of the earliest woody vines (plants) to leaf out, starting in late February-early March in Athens.

FLOWERS: Perfect, non-fragrant, variable in color from orange-red to red on the outside of the tubular corolla, generally yellow to yellow-orange inside, 1 1/2 to 2″ long, produced in a 3- to 4- whorled spike, each whorl with 4 to 6 flowers, borne at the end of the shoot, never axillary as in *L. japonica,* the corolla mouth with 4 upper lobes of equal proportions, not two-lipped as in the majority of honeysuckles; flowers on shoots produced from last year's wood but also sporadically on new growth of the season; exceptional full flower effect in April in Athens, especially when grown in full sun on a structure.

FRUIT: Red, 1/4″ diameter rounded berry, September-November, that at times is produced in abundance, other times sparingly or not at all; have seen heavy fruit set on isolated specimens so assume plant is not self-sterile.

CULTURE: Transplant as a small container-grown plant into moist well-drained, acid or near neutral soil, full sun but also tolerates dense shade, however, does not flower as profusely in the latter, provide support otherwise plant forms tangles on the ground, prune after flowering to shape and control, if pruned in late winter most of the flowers will be removed.

DISEASES AND INSECTS: None serious although a leaf spot has occurred on occasion; in recent years have observed heavy defoliation particularly on 'Sulphurea'.

LANDSCAPE VALUE: Great twining vine for the imaginative gardener, flowers and foliage are superb, should be placed on a trellis, picket fence, old shrub framework; I planted it next to a fence and trained it to grow along the top where it has formed a billowy cloud of foliage and flowers.

CULTIVARS:

'Magnifica'—Bright red, 2″ long flowers, interior yellowish; based on my observations of southeastern native populations 'Magnifica' could be f. *magnifica* since large bright red flowered forms are reasonably common.

'Manifich'—Lighter orange on the outside with a clear yellow inside, see Cresson, *Horticulture* 65(8):12–17 (1987).

'Sulphurea' ('Flava')—Beautiful pure yellow flowered form with the wonderful attributes of the species, new leaves emerge without reddish purple coloration of the species; a literal shower of yellow flowers and bright green foliage in April, a must for every garden, each year I become more antsy waiting for the first flower, in recent years has defoliated to various degrees by mid to late summer.

'Superba'—Have seen it listed as orange-scarlet to bright scarlet, leaves are supposedly more broad-oval; I suspect the comments made under 'Magnifica' apply here.

PROPAGATION: Clean seed from the pulp and provide 3 months cold moist stratification; cuttings when firm root easily, use 1000 ppm KIBA quick dip; after rooting, cuttings will produce new growth and make a salable plant in a single growing season; cuttings can be taken as early as April.

NATIVE HABITAT: Connecticut to Florida, west to Nebraska and Texas.

RELATED SPECIES: In the past I have resisted the temptation to include many of the vining species which are so common in European gardens but in this edition have opened the floodgates. Many are beautiful and serve the same landscape functions as *L. sempervirens*. An excellent article on Climbing Honeysuckles appeared in *The Plantsman* 4(4):236–252 (1983).

Lonicera caprifolium—Italian Honeysuckle
(lon-iss'ēr-a̓ cap-ri-fō'li-um)

LEAVES: Opposite, simple, obovate or oval, 2 to 4″ long, half as wide, rounded, cuneate, entire, dark green above and glaucous blue-green beneath; upper 2 to 3 pairs of leaves connate into acute disks subtending the flower.

STEM: Glabrous.

Lonicera caprifolium, Italian Honeysuckle, is a twining vine with fragrant, 1 3/4 to 2″ long, tubular (borne in whorls) yellowish white often tinged purplish on outside of the corolla flower. Flowers open in May-June and by this author have been confused with *L. periclymenum* which does not have the connately fused, disk-type leaves subtending the flower. Fruits are orange-red. 'Pauciflora' has flowers tinted rose on the outside of the corolla. Europe and western Asia. Cultivated for centuries. Zone 5 to 8?

Lonicera flava—Yellow Honeysuckle
(lon-iss'ēr-a̓ flā'va)

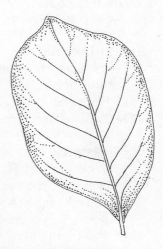

Lonicera flava, Yellow Honeysuckle, was introduced to me many years ago by Mr. Gene Cline of Canton, GA. He pointed out the difference between this and *L. sempervirens* 'Sulphurea'. The habit is weakly twining and not as robust as *L. sempervirens*. Leaves are bright green above, bluish green beneath, 1 3/4 to 3 1/4″ long, broad elliptic to elliptic, obtuse or acutish, the upper pairs connate at the base into a suborbicular or oval disk and usually mucronulate at tips. The orange-yellow 1 1/4″ long distinctly two-lipped flower occurs in whorls of 1 to 3 at the end of the shoot. Authors have ascribed a slight fragrance to no fragrance. I cannot sense any distinct fragrance. Fruits are orange and apparently not produced in great numbers. Flowers sometimes occur on a 1/2″ long peduncle. Quite difficult to locate in cultivation but a handsome vine well suited to semi-shady conditions and probably equally at home in sun if the soil is moist. North Carolina to Missouri, Arkansas and Oklahoma. Cultivated 1810. Zone 5 to 8.

Lonicera periclymenum—Woodbine Honeysuckle
(lon-iss'ēr-a̓ per-i-klī'men-num)

LEAVES: Opposite, simple, ovate or elliptic to ovate-oblong, 1 1/2 to 2 1/2″ long, 1 to 1 1/2″ wide, acute to obtuse, dark green above, bluish green below, essentially glabrous at maturity; petiole present on lower leaves, upper almost sessile but *never fused at the base* like *L. caprifolium*.

Lonicera periclymenum, Woodbine Honeysuckle, is akin to *L. caprifolium* and *L. sempervirens* and serves a similar landscape function. Will grow 10 to 20′ and twine around structures and itself. Flowers are fragrant, 1 1/2 to 2″ long, two tipped (unlike *L. sempervirens*), occurring in a peduncled spike in 3 to 5 whorls at the end of the shoots. Flower color is typically yellowish white with a purplish tinge but many of the cultivated forms have deeper purple outer corolla color. Fruits are red. 'Belgica' (Dutch) is a handsome form with purplish red outer color, yellowish within; the stems and leaves are purplish tinged; tends to be more bushy although plants I have seen were distinctly viny. 'Serotina' (Late Dutch) has dark purple flowers (outside), yellowish inside, becoming paler with maturity; flowers open over a long period and occur later than the species. Apparently true 'Serotina' has been usurped by an imposter clone and is not common in cultivation; the plant is evident in English gardens and at least in flower color fits the above description. A new cultivar, 'Berries Jubilee' is listed by Monrovia under this species but described as having lovely yellow flowers in summer and fall followed by attractive red fruits; foliage is blue-green above and glaucous gray beneath. The general characters do not fit true *L. periclymenum*. Europe, North Africa, Asia Minor, long cultivated. Zone 4 to 8(?).

Lonicera × tellmanniana, (lon-iss′ĕr-a tel-man-i-ā′na), Tellman Honeysuckle, is a hybrid between *L. tragophylla* and *L. sempervirens* 'Superba' that was raised around 1920 in Budapest, Hungary. The elliptical-ovate leaves are 2 to 3 1/2″ long, much larger than the previous mentioned species, bright green and densely borne. The growth is vigorous and it appears to have acquired the best characteristics of both parents. Flowers, in my opinion, are the showiest of the vining honeysuckles presented here. Slender tubed to about 2″ long with a diameter of 1″ across the two lips at the mouth of the corolla; the yellow-almost fluorescent, perhaps yellow-orange flowers are flushed in the bud stage at their tips with a red cast. About 6 to 12 flowers are borne at the end of the shoots. Zone 5 to 7(?).

Lonicera tatarica—Tatarian Honeysuckle
(lon-iss′ĕr-a ta-tār′i-ka)

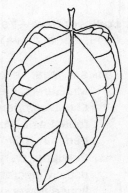

LEAVES: Opposite, simple, ovate to ovate-lanceolate, 1 1/2 to 2 1/2″ long, 1 to 1 1/2″ wide, acute to acuminate, rarely obtusish, rounded or subcordate at base, entire, bluish green, glabrous and glaucous beneath; petiole 1/12 to 1/4″ long.
BUDS: Flattened, closely appressed, elongated, with valvate lower scales, glabrous.
STEM: Green at first, finally brownish, glabrous; pith—brown, excavated.

Lonicera tatarica, Tatarian Honeysuckle, grows 10 to 12′ in height with a 10′ spread. The general habit is upright, strongly multi-stemmed with the upper branches arching and the overall effect one of a dense, twiggy mass. Foliage is bluish green in summer; flowers are pink to white (profusely borne), 3/4 to 1″ long, May, soon after the leaves develop, borne in peduncled pairs on a 1/2 to 1″ long stalk in the axils of the leaves. Fruit is a red, 1/4″ diameter berry which colors in late June into July and August. Has become a weed in many areas. Leafs out very early in spring. Often considered the "best" of the honeysuckles because of the many cultivars which include:
'Alba'—Flowers pure white.
'Arnold Red'—Darkest red flowers of any honeysuckle, supposedly resistant to Russian aphid.
'Grandiflora'—Large white flowers; sometimes called 'Bride'.
'Hack's Red'—Flowers deep purplish red.
'LeRoyana'—Dwarf variety, 3′ tall, poor flowerer, valued solely for dwarf character.
'Lutea'—Pink flowers, yellow fruit.
'Morden Orange'—Pale pink flowers and good orange fruits.
'Nana'—Flowers pink, dwarf habit, 3′ high at 9 years; apparently several different clones with this name.
'Parvifolia'—One of the best for white flowers.

'Rosea'—Flowers rosy pink outside, light pink inside.

'Sibirica'—Flowers deep rose.

'Valencia'—Upright, more compact, orange-fruited.

'Virginalis'—Buds and flowers are rose-pink; largest flowers of any *L. tatarica* form.

'Zabelii'—Dark red flowers similar to 'Arnold Red'; supposedly very susceptible to Russian aphid which causes "witches brooming".

Central Asia to southern Russia. Introduced 1752. Zone 3 to 8. In modern landscapes this is essentially an outmoded plant. Akin to the Edsel of deciduous shrubs. The Russian aphid has essentially rendered the plant a liability in the midwest and east. With wonderful viburnums to fill almost every nook and cranny of a garden this plant is headed for the recycling factory.

Lonicera xylosteum—European Fly Honeysuckle
(lon-iss′ēr-a zi-los′tē-um)

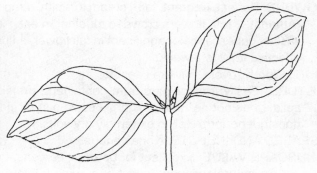

LEAVES: Opposite, simple, broad-ovate or ellip-tic-ovate to obovate, 1 to 2 1/2″ long, half or more than half as wide, acute, broad-cuneate to rounded at base, margins entire and sometimes fringed with pubescence, dark or grayish green and sparingly pubes-cent or glabrous above, paler and pubes-cent, rarely glabrate beneath; petiole—1/8 to 1/3″ long; pubescent.

BUDS: Brownish, woolly pubescent.

STEM: Pubescent, gray; pith—brown, excavated.

Lonicera xylosteum, European Fly Honeysuckle, develops into a rounded mound with spreading arching branches; grows 8 to 10′ with a spread of 10 to 12′. Foliage is a grayish green (has somewhat of a blue effect). The flowers are white or yellowish white, 5/8″ long, often tinged reddish; May; borne in peduncled pairs. Fruit is a dark red berry ripening in July and August. 'Claveyi' is a 3 to 6′ dwarf form recommended for hedges; however, I have seen plants that were 8 to 10′ high. 'Hedge King' is another selection by Clavey Nurseries and is a distinct narrow, upright grower which would be suitable for hedges. 'Emerald Mound' or 'Nana' is one of the very finest low growing, mounded honeysuckles. The foliage is a rich, bluish green and about the handsomest of any honeysuckle. I have seen this cultivar used in mass at the Minnesota Landscape Arboretum and must admit was handsomely impressed. Roots easily from cuttings and should become more popular with exposure. Ultimate landscape size should run 3′ with a 4 1/2 to 6′ spread; does not move well in leaf, yellowish white flowers and dark red berries. 'Miniglobe' is a 1981 introduction from Morden Research Station that resembles 'Emerald Mound' but is hardier and more compact with dense green foliage. Flowers and fruits are not conspicuous. Grows 3 to 4′ high and wide. Zone 3. Considered a *L.* × *xylosteoides* selection. Europe to Altai. Long cultivated. Zone 4 to 6.

Loropetalum chinense
(lō-rō-pet′a̍-lum chī-nen′sē)

FAMILY: Hamamelidaceae

LEAVES: Alternate, simple, evergreen, ovate-rounded, 1 to 2 1/2″ long, 3/4 to 1 1/4″ wide, apex pointed, oblique leaf base, finely toothed to essentially entire, dark green and rough above, paler beneath, pubescent; petiole—1/8″ long, pubescent.

BUDS: Imbricate, small, brown.

STEM: Slender, brown, densely pubescent; pith—solid, small, greenish.

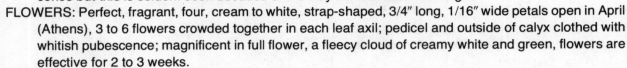

SIZE: 6 to 10′ high with a similar spread; have seen plants 15′ high and wide; Creech reported 30′ high trees in the Ise Grand Shrine Forest, Japan.

HARDINESS: Zone 8 to 9.

HABIT: Irregularly rounded evergreen shrub often developing whip-like branches; leaves are borne in a single plane along the stem.

RATE: Fast.

TEXTURE: Medium-fine.

BARK: On old stems exfoliates in large strips, very rich brown; actually handsome but seldom seen.

LEAF COLOR: Lustrous dark green throughout the seasons; underside of leaf is grayish green due to the dense pubescence but this is seldom seen because of the way the leaves are arranged.

FLOWERS: Perfect, fragrant, four, cream to white, strap-shaped, 3/4″ long, 1/16″ wide petals open in April (Athens), 3 to 6 flowers crowded together in each leaf axil; pedicel and outside of calyx clothed with whitish pubescence; magnificent in full flower, a fleecy cloud of creamy white and green, flowers are effective for 2 to 3 weeks.

FRUIT: Woody, ovoid, nut-like capsule.

CULTURE: Easily transplanted from containers; prefers acid, moist, well-drained, high organic matter soils; does not do well in high pH soils: sun or medium shade; withstands any amount of pruning; does not perform well in extremely dry soils.

DISEASES AND INSECTS: None serious.

LANDSCAPE VALUE: Excellent for borders, screens, foundations; loses something when pruned; has a certain naturalness that is lost by turning it into a green meatball; one of the first plants I used for landscaping my Georgia home; can be effective as a single specimen or in groupings; have seen it thriving in heavy shade; could be easily espaliered; -3°F seriously damaged or killed many plants in the Athens area, the plant in my garden was killed to about 6 to 12″ from ground but produced new shoots; leaves will probably show injury at 5°F; Creech mentions a plant as far north as Merion, PA.

CULTIVARS:

‘Roseum’—A rose flowered form that I have only seen in photographs; will be a tremendous addition to the southern garden; Arnold Arboretum has imported a plant and is working on increasing numbers; also in Dr. Raulston's NC State Arboretum.

PROPAGATION: Cuttings collected on July 28, treated with 3000 ppm IBA, alcohol quick dip, placed in peat:perlite under mist rooted about 80%. Based on my observations, the rooting medium should not hold too much moisture or the cuttings will rot; plants grown in containers were almost prostrate for a season and developed height later.

ADDITIONAL NOTES: Frequently misidentified; looks a bit like some of the honeysuckles and cotoneasters; looks nothing like a member of the witch-hazel family; definitely deserves to be more widely planted in southern gardens.

NATIVE HABITAT: China, one locality in Japan. Introduced 1880.

Lyonia lucida — Fetterbush Lyonia
(li-ō′ni-a lū′si-da)

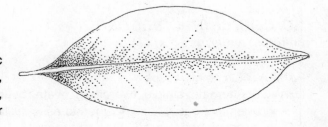

LEAVES: Alternate, simple, evergreen, broad elliptic to obovate to oblong, 1 to 3″ long, half as wide, abruptly acuminate, cuneate, entire, revolute, leathery, lustrous dark green above, lighter beneath, glabrous.

STEM: Glabrous, 3-angled.

Lyonia lucida, Fetterbush Lyonia, is a 3 to 5′ high suckering, open, arching evergreen shrub that I have never seen in good condition under cultivation. I grew it for a number of years in my Georgia garden and gave up because of weak growth and susceptibility to leaf spot. The pinkish white, up to 1/3″ long flowers occur in racemes from the axils of the leaves and are rather pretty. Prefers a moist, well drained soil and at least partial shade under cultivation. Probably best only in a naturalized situation. The foliage is quite handsome but does not hold up under even mild stress. Virginia to Florida and Louisiana. Introduced 1765. Zone 7 to 9.

Lyonia mariana — Stagger-bush
(li-ō′ni-a mar-i-a′nȧ)

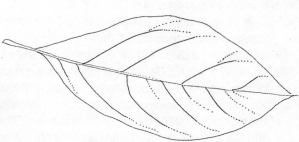

LEAVES: Alternate, simple, oblong, elliptic or narrowly obovate, 3/4 to 3″ long, acute or obtuse, cuneate, entire, medium to dark green, glabrous except for the pubescence on veins beneath.

Lyonia mariana, Staggerbush Lyonia, is a rather handsome deciduous cousin of *L. lucida.* The white or pinkish, 3/8 to 1/2″ long ovoid to tubular flower occurs in May–June on leafless racemes. The flowers are almost as handsome unopened because the calyx is tinged red. The foliage colors a good red in autumn. A worthy shrub for a moist well drained soil in a shrub border. Rhode Island to Florida, west to Tennessee and Arkansas. Introduced 1736. Zone 5 to 9.

Maackia amurensis — Amur Maackia
(mak′ē-ȧ ā-moor-en′sis)

FAMILY: Fabaceae

LEAVES: Alternate, compound, odd-pinnate, 8 to 12″ long, leaflets opposite or nearly so, short stalked, 7 to 11, elliptic to oblong-ovate, 1 1/2 to 3 1/2″ long, abrupt at apex, rounded at base, glabrous, grayish green when unfolding finally turning a dark almost olive-green, paler and glabrous below.

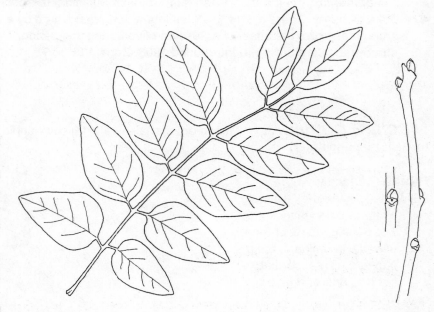

BUDS: Two exposed pale-margined scales, dark brown, somewhat ovoid, plumpish, similar in shape to the buds of *Koelreuteria.*

STEM: Dark grayish brown to black, usually glabrous, somewhat dingy in color and texture in winter; lenticels on older stems distinctly diamond-shape.

SIZE: Probably 20 to 30′ under cultivation but can grow to 45′ in the wild, usually as wide or wider than tall.

HARDINESS: Zone 3 to 7 (8), have found a tree in Zone 8, however, not as vigorous as further north.

HABIT: Small, round headed tree; quite dapper in outline when properly grown.

RATE: Slow, 12′ over a 20-year-period according to an English source, faster under U.S. conditions.

TEXTURE: Medium in all seasons.

BARK: Peeling with maturity, rich shining amber to brown, developing a curly consistency.

LEAF COLOR: Initially somewhat grayish green finally dark green; fall color is nonexistent.

FLOWERS: Perfect, dull white, closely set on stiff erect racemes, 4 to 6″ long, sometimes branched at the base, June–July, smell like new mown grass.

FRUIT: Pod, 2 to 3″ long, 1/3″ wide, flat.

CULTURE: Performs best in good, loose, well-drained, acid or alkaline soil; preferably sunny exposures; appears to be quite adaptable.

DISEASES AND INSECTS: Nothing particularly serious.

LANDSCAPE VALUE: Of interest for the late summer flowers; the specimens I have seen had very clean foliage and appeared quite vigorous; the more I see of this tree the more impressed I am by its durability and general adaptation; has survived at Minnesota Landscape Arboretum and performed spectacularly at Bernheim Arboretum and Swarthmore College; the foliage has a certain richness and the bronze-colored bark is quite attractive; I believe it would be a good candidate for street tree and container planting.

PROPAGATION: Seeds may be soaked in hot water overnight, then sown; 60 minutes acid will alleviate the seed coat dormancy and seeds will germinate readily.

ADDITIONAL NOTES: A little-known genus which is closely related to *Cladrastis* and may have by some authorities been put in that genus. It differs from *Cladrastis* in that the leaf-buds are solitary and not hidden by the base of the petiole; the leaflets are opposite and the flowers are densely packed in more or less erect racemes; genus commemorates a Russian naturalist, Richard Maack.

NATIVE HABITAT: Manchuria. Introduced 1864.

RELATED SPECIES:

Maackia chinensis, (mak′ē-ȧ chī-nen′sis), Chinese Maackia, is closely related to the above but is not quite as hardy. There are 11 to 13 leaflets which are covered by a silvery gray pubescence as they emerge and give the effect of a Russian-olive during this period. Tends to be a small, 20 to 30′ high shrub-tree. Central China. Introduced 1908. Zone 4 (5) to 7?

Maclura pomifera — Osage-orange, also called Hedge-apple and "bois d'arc".
(mȧ-klū′rȧ pō-mif′ēr-ȧ)

FAMILY: Moraceae

LEAVES: Alternate, simple, ovate to oblong-lanceolate, 2 to 5″ long, about one-half as wide, acuminate, broad-cuneate to subcordate at base, entire, glabrous, lustrous bright to dark green and glabrous above, lighter and pubescent on veins beneath; petiole 1/2 to 1 1/2″ long.

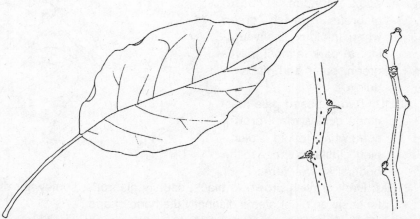

BUDS: Terminal-absent, laterals-small, globular, brown, depressed and partially imbedded in the bark, 5-scaled.

STEM: Stout, buff or orange-brown, glabrous, armed with straight, stout axillary spines, 1/2" long, exudes milky juice when cut.

SIZE: 20 to 40' in height with a comparable spread, can grow to 60'.

HARDINESS: Zone 4 to 9.

HABIT: Usually develops a short trunk and low, rounded, irregular crown composed of stiff, spiny, interlacing branches; some of the branches show a pendulous tendency.

RATE: Fast, 9 to 12' over a 3 to 5 year period.

TEXTURE: Medium in leaf; coarse in fruit and winter.

BARK: On old trunks, the bark develops ashy-brown or dark orange-brown with irregular longitudinal fissures and scaly ridges; the wood itself is of a characteristic orange color.

LEAF COLOR: Bright, shiny medium to dark green in summer; fall color varies from yellow-green to a good yellow and on occasion approaches fantastic.

FLOWERS: Dioecious, inconspicuous; female borne in June in dense globose heads on short peduncles; male in subglobose or sometimes elongated racemes.

FRUIT: A large (3) 4 to 6" wide globose syncarp of drupes covered with a mamillate rind, yellow-green in color, becoming effective in September and lethal in October if one is sitting under the tree; usually fall after ripening, a real mess.

CULTURE: One of our very tough and durable native trees; transplants readily; the poorer the site the better; withstands wetness, dryness, wind, extreme heat, acid and high pH conditions once established; full sun; male thornless selections could be made for inner city areas and other impossible sites where few plants will grow; 'Park' grew 1'7" per year over a 5-year period in KS tests.

DISEASES AND INSECTS: None serious—although a few leaf spots have been reported.

LANDSCAPE VALUE: Has been used for hedgerows in the plains states; not worth recommending for the residential landscape; has potential for rugged, polluted areas; wood is valuable for making bows and is amazingly rot resistant; I have seen patios made out of osage-orange logs which were quite handsome; the wood contains about 1% 2, 3, 4, 5-tetrahydroxystilbene, which is toxic to a number of fungi which may explain the decay resistance.

CULTIVARS:

var. *inermis*—A thornless type; also many people (nurserymen) are interested in selecting superior clones and, no doubt, the future will yield several cultivars; a true thornless form has proved elusive and to date there is no cultivar that is completely thorn-free; it seems that budwood or cuttings taken from thornless branches are not stable and will produce thorns at some period in the growth cycle.

Dr. John Pair, Kansas State University, has assembled a number of "thornless" clones and evaluated them for degree of thornlessness. The thorny habit is primarily a juvenile character and disappears with maturity. When thornless branches are propagated, the new growth develops a number of spiny branches. The following 3-year-old male budded trees (all about 10' high) carried the following number of thorns per node: 'Altamont'–0.39; 'Bois D'Arc Supreme'–0.25; 'Fan D'Arc'–0.36; 'Park'–0.47; 'Pawhuska': softwood–0.40/plant; hardwood–2.22/plant; 'Wichita': softwood–0; hardwood–0.05; budded on seedling–3.75. Based on his work, 'Wichita' appears the most thornless of the group. 'Double O' is a male form with pleasing upright crown, thornless except on juvenile stems, a Wandell introduction.

PROPAGATION: Seeds exhibit a slight dormancy which can be overcome by stratification for 30 days at 41° or by soaking in water for 48 hours. Softwood cuttings taken in July rooted 32% without treatment and 100% in 42 days after treatment with IAA; Dr. Pair has found that softwood cuttings from 3-year-old stock plants root readily with 5000 to 10000 ppm IBA; hardwood cuttings collected in January, given bottom heat, rooted in 6 weeks; these hardwood cuttings produced about 30" of growth in a single season which is about twice as much as a 2-year-old rooted softwood. For complete details see *The Plant Propagator* 30(1): 6 (1984). Has also been tissue cultured. See *HortScience* 23: 613–615 (1988).

ADDITIONAL NOTES: Select male trees; the large fruits are a nuisance and a problem around public areas as people will invariably use them for ammunition. The wood is used for fence posts, bow-wood, and rustic furniture. A bright yellow dye can be extracted from the wood. Squirrels often eat the seeds during the winter months and it is not unusual to see a small pile of pulp under the trees. An intergeneric hybrid between *Cudrania* and *Maclura*, × *Macludrania hybrida,* exists. An excellent reference on Osage-orange, its history and economic uses appeared in *Economic Botany* 35(1): 24–41, 1981, and should be consulted by anyone who seeks additional information.

NATIVE HABITAT: Arkansas to Oklahoma and Texas but grown far out of its native range. Introduced 1818.

Magnolia acuminata — Cucumbertree Magnolia
(mag-nō′li-a a-kū-mi-nā′ta)

FAMILY: Magnoliaceae

LEAVES: Alternate, simple, elliptic or ovate to oblong-ovate, or sometimes oblong-ovate, 4 to 10″ long, about half as wide, short acuminate, cordate, rounded or acute at base, entire, dark green above, soft pubescent and light green beneath; petiole—1 to 1 1/2″ long.

BUDS: Greenish to whitish, pubescent, covered (as is true for all magnolias) with a single keeled scale which on abscising leaves a distinct scar which appears as a fine line encircling the stem.

STEM: Moderate, brownish or reddish brown, glabrous; the leaf scars U-shaped; emits a spicy odor when bruised.

SIZE: 50 to 80′ in height with a comparable spread at maturity; in youth a distinctly pyramidal tree and the spread is always considerably less than the height.

HARDINESS: Zone 3 to 8.

HABIT: Pyramidal when young (20 to 30 years of age), in old age developing a rounded to broad-rounded outline with massive wide-spreading branches; an open grown Cucumbertree Magnolia is a beautiful tree.

RATE: Medium to fast, 10 to 15′ over a 4 to 6 year period.

TEXTURE: Medium-coarse in leaf, coarse in winter.

BARK: Relatively smooth gray-brown in youth becoming ridged and furrowed with flat gray ridges and relatively narrow vertical fissures, some scaling occurs on the flat gray ridges.

LEAF COLOR: Dark green in summer, abscising green or brown in fall; some trees develop a soft ashy-brown fall color which is actually quite attractive.

FLOWERS: Perfect, often self-sterile, however, some trees are self-fertile, greenish yellow petals, 2 1/2 to 3″ long, in two sets of 3, sepals 1 to 1 1/2″ long, slightly fragrant, May to early June, borne solitarily, not particularly showy for the flowers are borne high in the tree and often are masked by foliage; seedling grown trees may not flower until 20′ or more in height.

FRUIT: Aggregate of follicles, pinkish red, October, briefly persisting, 2 to 3″ long, looks (more or less) like a small cucumber; hence, the name Cucumbertree.

CULTURE: Transplant balled and burlapped in early spring into loamy, deep, moist, well drained, slightly acid soil; performs well in calcareous soils of midwest; does not tolerate extreme drought or wetness; full sun or partial shade; does not withstand polluted conditions; do not plant too deep; prune after flowering; another of the fleshy rooted type trees which have a minimum of lateral roots and practically no root hairs; trees which fall into this category are often difficult to transplant and care should be taken in the planting process.

DISEASES AND INSECTS: Basically free from problems; scale can occur now and then.

LANDSCAPE VALUE: Excellent tree for the large property; parks, estates, golf courses, naturalized areas; the trees appear pyramidal and compact in youth but this is misleading for with maturity 60 to 70' specimens with a spread of 70 to 85' and large, massive, spreading branches often develop.

CULTIVARS:

'Elizabeth'—Result of a cross between *M. acuminata* and *M. denudata.* The habit is neat and pyramidal but the genuine beauty resides in the finely tapering buds that open to display flowers of the clearest primrose-yellow; have not seen the plant but all reports indicate transparent yellow; at the Brooklyn Botanic Garden it opens from late April to mid-May; patented in 1977.

'Evamaria' *(M. acuminata × M. liliiflora)*—Unopened flower buds are purple, suffused with yellow shadings; open flower consists of 6 broadly rounded petals in two whorls of 3, the distinctive and unusual flower color is due to the contrasting shade of magenta-rose, suffused with a pale orange and yellow; patented in 1968, a Brooklyn Botanic Garden introduction.

'Golden Glow'—Flowers yellow, supposedly selected from a tree in the wild.

'Variegata'—Leaves blotched in a rather attractive manner with golden yellow.

'Woodsman'—J.C. McDaniel selected a cross between this species and *M. liliiflora* 'O'Neill'; the flowers are light purple-tinged and larger than the normal Cucumbertree type; technically, the cross is listed as *M. × brooklynensis* 'Woodsman'; registered in 1974.

'Yellow Bird'—Well-shaped pure yellow flowers that open earlier than *M. acuminata;* parentage described as 'Evamaria' backcrossed to *M. acuminata.*

PROPAGATION: Seeds exhibit embryo dormancy which can be overcome by 3 to 6 months of stratification in moist peat at 32° to 41°F; I have had excellent success with this species by removing the fleshy seed coat, stratifying for 90 days at 41°F and directly planting; magnolia seeds are quite oily and deteriorate rapidly if not properly handled; it is best to collect the fruits, extract the seed, remove their fleshy seed coats and either direct sow or provide a cold period as mentioned above.

Mr. Don Shadow relates an interesting story relative to cutting propagation of this species. He collected from young trees and stuck something approaching 6000 cuttings. Not a single one rooted which indicated rapid loss of juvenility even though the species does not flower until much older.

NATIVE HABITAT: New York to Georgia, west to Illinois and Arkansas. Introduced 1736.

RELATED SPECIES:

Magnolia acuminata var. **subcordata,** (sub-kor-dā'ta), Yellow Cucumbertree, is a large shrub or small bushy tree, 20 to 30' high, allied to *M. acuminata.* The leaves are smaller and comparatively broader being 4 to 6" long, 2 1/2 to 3 1/2" wide. They are more lustrous dark green and are covered with matted pubescence below. The flowers vary in size and color and resemble those of *M. acuminata* differing in their smaller size and yellow color. I have seen enough true *M. a.* var. *subcordata* to present a reasonably intelligent discussion. The tree is usually small, upright and at times shrubby. Flowers are more tulip-shaped, fuller, and closer to yellow. One exception is a giant +90' high tree at Longwood Gardens which is labeled as this taxon. Every piece of literature and eye to tree observation says otherwise. It flowers with the emerging leaves and can never compete with the early types, but is still a handsome plant. 'Miss Honeybee' is a good hardy yellow selection. Compact yellow flowered forms as well as a variegated ('Ellen') form are known. North Carolina and Georgia. Introduced 1801. Zone 5 to 8(9). Has withstood −25°F in Cincinnati, OH.

ADDITIONAL NOTES: The magnolias are a difficult group to treat. There are numerous species but the great confusion arises in the almost overwhelming plethora of cultivars. I have attempted to include the more important landscape species and cultivars. I recommend an outstanding book, *Magnolias,* by Neil G. Treseder, Faber and Faber, Boston, 1978 for anyone interested in advancing their knowledge of magnolias. The Magnolia Society Inc. publishes a newsletter that offers new information. Spongberg has an outstanding presentation of "Magnoliaceae Hardy in Temperate North America." *J. Arnold Arboretum* 57: 250–312. 1976.

Magnolia denudata (formerly *M. heptapeta*) — Yulan Magnolia
(mag-nō'li-a de-nū-dā'ta)

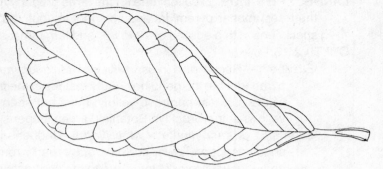

LEAVES: Alternate, simple, obovate to obovate-oblong, 4 to 6″ long, 2 to 3 1/2″ wide, short acuminate, tapering at base, entire, dark green and sparingly pubescent above, light green beneath and minutely pubescent chiefly on the nerves and slightly reticulate.

Magnolia denudata, Yulan Magnolia, is a small tree growing 30 to 40′ high with a similar spread. The flowers (9 petals) are white, fragrant, 5 to 6″ across and open before *M.* × *soulangiana* and are borne singly. Unfortunately this species responds to early warm spells and the flowers are often injured by late freezes. Very beautiful when unadulterated by the weather. Has been difficult to root from cuttings and is often grafted on *M.* × *soulangiana.* The var. *purpurascens* has rose-red flowers outside, pink inside. Several other commercially available cultivars include 'Purple Eye' with white flowers and a purple blush at the base of the tepals, habit is broader than typical species form; 'Swada' has perfectly formed creamy white flowers on a smaller plant and 'Wada' has smaller white flowers and is later flowering. I still consider this one of the most beautiful of all the early flowering magnolias. Young plants are distinctly upright and only with maturity does the plant become more open. Central China. 1789. Zone 5 to 8.

Magnolia grandiflora — Southern Magnolia, also called Evergreen Magnolia or Bull Bay.
(mag-nō'li-a gran-di-flō'ra)

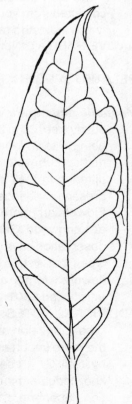

LEAVES: Alternate, simple, evergreen, obovate-oblong or elliptic, 5 to 10″ long, less than half as wide, obtusely short-acuminate or obtusish, cuneate at base, entire, dark green and lustrous above, often ferrugineous-pubescent beneath, firmly coriaceous; petioles stout, about 1 to 2″ long.
STEM: Coarse, green, glabrous or pubescent.

SIZE: 60 to 80′ in height with a spread of 30 to 50′.
HARDINESS: Zone (6)7 to 9, supposedly the brown back type is hardier than the green form but no quantitative evidence supports this.
HABIT: Densely pyramidal, low-branching, stately evergreen tree; generally distinctly columnar-pyramidal but some trees become as wide as tall.
RATE: Slow to medium; with water and fertilizer a fast grower.
TEXTURE: Even though the leaves are extremely large, the overall textural effect is medium-coarse.
BARK: Smooth gray on young and older trees although older trees may develop large scaly plates.
LEAF COLOR: Lustrous dark green above, lighter green below and often ferrugineous (rusty) pubescent beneath; leaves are messy and never seem to decompose, drop in spring and fall.
FLOWERS: Perfect, creamy white, beautifully fragrant (better than the best perfume), 8 to 12″ in diameter, solitary, in May–June, sporadically thereafter, usually with 6 petals, each petal thick, concave, broadly obovate and 4 to 6″ long; may take as long as 15 to 20 years for trees to flower which have been grown from seed; the literature is so full of burbles that one does not often know who or what to believe; over the years I have read statements about the slowness to flower from seed; a one-gallon container plant (1-year-old) flowered 3 years later in my

garden; after 9 growing seasons the plant is 20′ high and usually has a few open flowers by early May; there is a great deal of difference among seedlings and cultivars in earliness to, and degree of, flower; buy seedling-grown plants in flower if possible or select a reliable cultivar.

FRUIT: Rose-red, aggregate of follicles, 3 to 5″ long, splitting open to expose the red seeds; usually ripen in September–October–November; fruit heavily in the south; old "cone-like" structure falls in November–December and makes a mess.

CULTURE: Transplant balled and burlapped or from a container in winter or early spring; soil should be rich, porous, acidulous and well drained; full sun or partial shade; some authorities indicate it does best in partial shade, supposedly will tolerate as little as 3 hours of sunlight per day; must be protected from winter winds and sun in northern area; tolerates high soil moisture levels; often shocks, i.e., drops many interior leaves when transplanted, try to move young plants or those that have been root pruned.

DISEASES AND INSECTS: Essentially problem free; a paper in *J. Arboriculture* 11(9) (1985) presents information on the decline and death of Southern Magnolia that might be linked to a mycoplasm or bacterium; I have not noticed any serious problems.

LANDSCAPE VALUE: Specimen, widely used and planted in the southern states; needs room to develop; a very worthwhile and handsome tree; have seen it used as a screen, grouping and hedge; an almost indispensible part of the southern garden heritage; Yankees would kill to be able to grow this tree; never been successful with the species at the Arnold Arboretum although the Freeman hybrids *(M. grandiflora* × *M. virginiana)* have survived but certainly not thrived, have seen 'Edith Bogue' in Philadelphia that was handsome; the newer cultivars offer greater hope for the landscape and, to my way of thinking, seedling material is now outmoded.

CULTIVARS: I did a literature search for a talk on this species and found something approaching 125 cultivars that did not include the past 10 years. For many years, the biggest hindrance to growing the cultivars was propagation. Most had to be grafted which is a lost art in the United States. Most cultivars assembled here are historically noteworthy, and/or available in commerce. Louisiana Nursery, Route 7, Box 43, Opelousas, LA 70570 lists about 28 cultivars. Wow!

'Bracken's Brown Beauty'—Certainly one of the best selections, relatively compact and dense even in youth, forms multiple breaks from each shoot and thus makes a fuller specimen, leaves small, about 6″ long, leathery lustrous dark green above, rusty brown below with an undulating surface; flowers about 5 to 6″ diameter with 2 to 3″ long fruits, transplants better than many and does not drop as many leaves; ultimate size is unknown but will possibly mature around 30′, introduced by Ray Bracken, Easley, SC.

'Claudia Wannamaker'—A fine form with dark green foliage and medium rusty brown undersides, flowers at an early age, medium-broad pyramid, vigorous and more open than 'Bracken's', propagators report it relatively easy to root, widely planted in the southeast, Brailsford introduction, Orangeburg, SC.

'D.D. Blancher'—An upright selection with lustrous dark green leaves and rich orangish brown undersides, relatively easy to root, exceptionally handsome form, selected by Robbins Nursery, Willard, NC.

'Edith Bogue'—Excellent tight pyramidal form with lustrous dark green and narrow leaves, light tomentum on underside, possibly the most cold hardy clone; a large tree in the Morris Arboretum, Philadelphia, has withstood the test of cold, ice, and snow; Roger Gossler reports the branches less susceptible to breakage in heavy wet snows, 30′ by 15′, originated from Florida as a tree sent to Miss E.A. Bogue, Montclair, NJ.

'Glen St. Mary'—Lustrous dark green leaves, the underside of the leaf is bronzed by the felty pubescence; flowers at a younger age than most *M. grandiflora* forms, same as 'St. Mary'; compact bushy pyramidal form, 20′ by 20′, flowers in 2 to 3 years from a cutting.

'Gloriosa'—Flowers of great size and substance, very broad leaves, considered one of the finest.

'Goliath'—Superior flowering form with large flowers up to 12″ across, the leaves are broad, rounded and blunt at the end and glossy green, up to 8″ long, with a trace of pubescence on midrib below; reasonably compact habit.

'Hasse'—Rather unusual form with more upright growth habit, leaves smaller than species, extremely lustrous dark green, light rusty pubescence below, Brailsford introduction.

'Lanceolata' ('Exoniensis,' 'Exmouth')—Narrow pyramidal form, leaves narrower than species, rusty tomentose beneath; flowers particularly handsome often with another set of tepals in the center of the flower; one of the first selections, has existed for over 200 years.

'Little Gem'—Definitely the smallest of the forms presented here; wants to grow as a large dense shrub rather than with a single leader, leaves are small (4"), lustrous dark green and covered with a bronzy brown pubescence below, flowers smaller (3 to 4" diameter) but borne at a young age and continually, production slackens in summer heat, through October–November in Zone 8. Rooted cuttings have produced flowers in their first year in a one-gallon container; actually would make a good medium size screen or hedge plant, one of the best for smaller properties, possibly 20' high, 10' wide in 20 years. Monrovia introduction, selected by Warren Steed Nursery, Candor, NC.

'Main Street'—More columnar or fastigiate growth habit with oval, brown-backed leaves, Cedar Lane Farm, Madison, GA selection.

'Majestic Beauty'—Extravagantly large lustrous dark green leaves, profuse flowering and pyramidal outline; young plants are open; foliage is immense and somewhat coarse, veins appear as ribs, 35 to 50' by 20'.

'Margaret Davis'—Dark green brown back foliage, broad flame shape, tight branching structure, a Brailsford introduction.

'Ruff'—Large dark green leaves with red-brown indumentum.

'Russet'—Tight dense columnar-pyramidal form with small narrow dark green leaves covered with orangish brown indumentum below, appears to be more cold hardy. I have had a difficult time rooting this clone, Saratoga Horticultural Foundation introduction.

'Samuel Sommer'—Form of rapid growth, strong ascending habit and large (10 to 14" diameter) creamy white flowers, lustrous dark green foliage with heavy rusty pubescence below, becomes a handsome tree, 30 to 40' by 30'.

'Symmes Select'—Full and branched to the ground, lustrous dark green leaves with dark brown backs, large white flowers occur on young trees, Cedar Lane Farm introduction.

'Victoria'—Considered among the hardiest of all *M. grandiflora* introductions; was selected in Vancouver, B.C. for its lustrous foliage with brown pubescent undersides, used extensively in Pacific Northwest, seldom seen in southeast, 20' by 15'.

PROPAGATION: Seeds exhibit embryo dormancy and should be stratified for 3 to 6 months at 32 to 41°F; after working with this plant over the past five years I have created and found enough information to fill several pages; suggest the reader see Dirr and Heuser, 1987, or Dirr and Brinson, *Amer. Nurseryman* 162(9): 38–51 (1985); our recipe for cutting success involves firm wooded cuttings July–early September, 5000 to 10,000 ppm NAA-50% alcohol, IBA will also work, perlite, mist, with rooting taking place in 6 to 10 weeks; if by fourth week no swelling of the stem has taken place the cuttings will probably not root. Many other successful recipes depending on propagator. Use the most juvenile material possible for stock plants.

ADDITIONAL NOTES: Truly an aristocratic broadleaf evergreen and many old southern homes are graced with this tree. During the rugged winter of 1976–77 (-20°F) almost every tree in Champaign-Urbana was killed outright or at least to the ground. Similar response on trees in Spring Grove, Cincinnati, OH. Several survived and may represent the most cold-hardy clones available. Currently, propagating and conducting laboratory cold hardiness tests on these clones. Often found in the wild in moist areas and in alluvial soils under the shade of large trees.

NATIVE HABITAT: North Carolina to Florida and Texas. Cultivated 1734.

Magnolia kobus — Kobus Magnolia
(mag-nō′li-á kō′bus)

LEAVES: Alternate, simple, broad-obovate to obovate, 3 to 6" long, abruptly pointed, tapering to the cuneate base, dark green above, light green beneath and pubescent on the veins, finally glabrous or nearly so; petioles—1/2 to 3/4" long.

Magnolia kobus, Kobus Magnolia, in youth develops a pyramidal crown and eventually becomes round-headed. The tree grows 30 to 40′ high and often develops a multiple-stem character. The foliage is medium to dark green in summer and does not develop good fall color, although on occasion leaves die off golden brown. The flowers are white, slightly fragrant, 4″ across or less, 6 (9) petals, with a faint purple line at the base outside, petals soon falling, March-April. Does not flower well when young and may take as long as 30 years to reach full flowering potential although there is variation in this respect among progeny. Easily propagated from cuttings; I have seen several old specimens (35′) in flower at Cave Hill Cemetery, Louisville, Kentucky; they were like a white cloud. This, *M. salicifolia* and *M. stellata* are among the earliest magnolias to flower. Variety *borealis* represents a more vigorous, robust, larger (70 to 80′ high), pyramidal tree than the species. The leaves are 6 to 7″ long and the flowers average up to 5″ across. A seedling of variety *borealis* grown by C.S. Sargent of the Arnold Arboretum was still sparse flowering when almost 30-years-old, but 15 years later was making a fine display and bore more flowers in succeeding years. 'Wada's Memory' has 6″ diameter fragrant white flowers before the leaves, fast large growing, bronze foliage in spring, dark green in summer, butter yellow in fall; hybrid between *M. kobus* and *M. salicifolia.* Native to Japan. Introduced 1865. The species is hardy in Zone 4, the variety in Zone 3, grows well in Zone 8. Supposedly excellent for all types of soil, including limestone.

Magnolia liliiflora (formerly *M. quinquepeta*) — Lily Magnolia
(mag-nō′li-a li-lē-ī-flô′ra)

LEAVES: Alternate, simple, entire, obovate or elliptic-ovate, short-acuminate, tapering at base, 4 to 7″ long, 2 to 5″ wide, dark green and sparingly pubescent above, light green beneath and finely pubescent on the nerves.
BUDS: End bud enlarged, hairy.
STEM: Glabrous except near the tip.

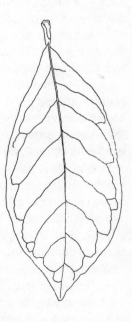

Magnolia liliiflora, Lily Magnolia, is a rounded, shrubby plant reaching 8 to 12′ in height with a similar spread. Often looks ragged in early fall when the leaves appear tattered, torn and mildewed. The 3 to 4″ wide flowers are vinous-purple outside and usually white inside, 6 petals, late April to early May, just before or as leaves are developing, borne singly. I have always admired this species for handsome flower but it does become somewhat ratty in habit and the foliage can look tired and worn by late summer. Has served as a good parent in several hybrids. Considered to be a native of China. Zone 5 to 8.
CULTIVARS:
'Gracilis'—More narrow, fastigiate habit, with narrower, deeper purple petals; leaves narrower, paler green.
'Nigra'—Larger flowers, 5″ across, petals 5″ long, dark purple outside and light purple inside, makes a less straggly bush than the species, flowers later than species.
'O'Neill'—Clone was selected by Professor J.C. McDaniel for good vigorous compact habit and very dark purple flowers, flowers heavily as a young plant, possibly the best clone.
'The Little Girl Hybrids'—For lack of a better name I will advance this. This is a group of hybrids that resulted from crosses between *M. liliiflora* 'Nigra' and *M. stellata* 'Rosea' or the reciprocal. The original crosses were made in 1955 and 1956 at the U.S. National Arboretum. The idea was to produce a group with good floral characteristics that would flower later than the star magnolia and thus avoid frost damage. They are all rather erect, shrubby growers and will probably

mature between 10 to 15′(20′). The flowers open before the leaves and make a magnificent display. Again in summer, sporadic flowers occur but are lighter colored owing to the heat. They root easily from softwood cuttings and have been successully flowered at the Minnesota Landscape Arboretum (Zone 3) and Athens, GA (Zone 8). Flower normally peaks around mid-March in Athens. The girls' names are 'Ann', 'Betty', 'Jane', 'Judy', 'Pinkie', 'Randy', 'Ricki', and 'Susan'. 'Ann' is my favorite. See *Horticulture* 58(5): 66, 1980 for additional details.

'Ann'—8 to 10′ high, 10′ wide, more open than 'Betty', deep purple-red, 7 to 9 petaled, slightly earlier than 'Betty', mid to late March in the Dirr garden, good grower.

'Betty'—10′, very upright, deep purple-red outside to white inside, 12 to 15 tepals.

'Jane'—Reddish purple outside and white inside.

'Judy'—Deep red-purple outside, whiter inside, erect growth habit.

'Pinkie'—Pale red-purple fading to pink on the outside to almost white at the apex, lightest of all hybrids, white on inside, 9 to 12 tepals, 5 to 7″ diameter.

'Randy'—Purple outside, white inside, nothing exceptional, narrow habit.

'Ricki'—Deep purple flower, white to purple shaded inside, nicer shrub than 'Randy'.

'Susan'—Red-purple long slender buds, essentially same color inside as out, 6 tepals opening to 5″ wide flowers, the tepals slightly twisted, relatively compact habit.

Magnolia × loebneri — Loebner Magnolia
(mag-nō′li-a lēb′nĕr-ī)

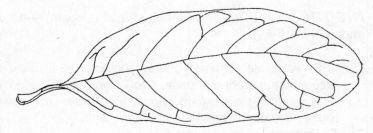

Magnolia × loebneri is the result of a cross between *M. kobus* and *M. stellata* made by Max Löbner of Pillnitz, Germany, shortly before World War I. In 41 years one of the original plants was 25′ high and 28′ wide. In general, the hybrid can be expected to mature between 20 and 30′ with a slightly greater spread. The habit is rounded to broad-rounded. The flowers typically have 12 petals, are fragrant and open in early to mid March in Athens, mid to late April in Boston. The hybrids are among the most beautiful of all magnolias and as I pen this (March 19, 1989) the 'Leonard Messel' in the garden is in full flower. The hybrids are quite vigorous and flower well in the second or third year from a cutting. In Athens, 'Leonard Messel' has always flowered later than *M. × soulangiana* and *M. stellata,* but in Zone 5 to 6 has opened 7 to 10 days earlier than *M. × soulangiana.* Cuttings are easy to root and grow off rapidly. I have not observed every deciduous Magnolia known to man but have watched with great satisfaction the superb flowering sequence of 'Ballerina', 'Leonard Messel', 'Merrill' and 'Spring Snow'. I have added a few cultivars in this edition that might be worthy of use. Several cultivars include:

'Ballerina'—A J.C. McDaniel introduction with up to 30 petals, fragrant, more so than 'Merrill' or 'Leonard Messel', pinkish in center, pure white over most of the flower, tends to escape late spring frosts; an F_2 seedling from 'Spring Snow' raised in 1963; have had good success (88%) rooting this clone from June softwoods treated with 10000 ppm IBA-quick dip, sand, mist in 8 weeks. Slightly smaller than 'Merrill' and 'Spring Snow', 15 to 20′.

'Donna'—Flat fragrant pure white 8″ diameter flowers.

'Leonard Messel'—A chance hybrid between *M. kobus* and *M. stellata* 'Rosea' raised in Colonel Messel's garden at Nymans, Sussex, England; the 12 petals are flushed with a purple-pink line along their center; fuschia pink on the back of the strap-shaped, undulating, crinkled tepals, white on the inside; this is a beautiful hybrid that peaked between April 22–30, 1979 at the Arnold Arboretum; in the Dirr garden typically early to mid March; 15–20′; it roots easily from softwood cuttings.

'Merrill'—A free flowering form raised from seed sown in 1939 at the Arnold Arboretum; there are 15 white petals, each flower about 3 to 3 1/2″ across, grows about twice as fast as *M. stellata* and the parent plant is 25 to 30′ high and slightly wider; it peaks in late April and is magnificent in flower resembling a white cloud; roots readily from cuttings; has performed well at the Minnesota Landscape Arboretum (Zone 3).

'Spring Joy'—White flowers flushed pink, 5 to 6″ across.

'Spring Snow'—A J.C. McDaniel introduction; the parent tree is in the President's garden on the University of Illinois campus; the pure white petals (15) hold their color well; it forms a 25 to 30′ high tree with a rounded outline; flowers a degree later and may escape late spring frosts, fragrant, many magnolia experts consider this the best of the white *M.* × *loebneri* types.

'Star Bright'—Fragrant pure white flowers.

Magnolia macrophylla — Bigleaf Magnolia
(mag-nō′li-a mak-rō-fil′à)

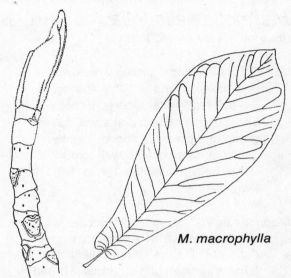

LEAVES: Alternate, simple, entire, oblong-obovate, 12 to 32″ long, 7 to 12″ wide, obtuse, subcordate-auriculate at base, bright green and glabrous above, silvery gray and downy below; petiole 2 to 4″ long.

BUDS: Large, tomentose, 1/2 to 1″ long.

STEM: Stout, pubescent at first, finally glabrous, coarse-textured.

M. macrophylla

Magnolia macrophylla, Bigleaf Magnolia, is a round-headed, cumbersome giant reaching 30 to 40′ in height. The flowers are creamy-white, 8 to 10″ and sometimes 14″ across, 6 petals, fragrant, solitary, June. The roundish, egg-shaped, rose-colored fruits are about 3″ long. The leaves are extremely large (12 to 32″ long) and give an overall coarse appearance which makes it difficult to use the tree in the landscape. It is an interesting sight when the leaves have fallen for the ground appears to be littered with large pieces of green and gray paper. This tree is not meant for the residential landscape and, along with the species treated herein, is reserved for parks, campuses and more fittingly the insatiable magnolia collector. The tree is particularly imposing and stately as an open-grown tree in a broad expanse of lawn. *Magnolia ashei,* Ashe Magnolia, is very similar with smaller leaves and a distinctly shrubby habit at least as I have seen plants in cultivation. Flowers (6″ across) as a young plant and have seen 4 to 6′ high plants with flowers and fruits. Most accurately in the 10 to 20′ height range, less in spread, at least cultivated specimens. Florida, Texas. It is also less cold hardy (Zone 6 to 9). Introduced 1933. There is a fine plant at Biltmore House, Asheville, N.C. Another closely allied species is *M. fraseri,* Fraser Magnolia. The general shape of the leaves is similar but they are smaller, with green undersides, being about 8 to 15″ long with a 2 to 4″ long petiole. The buds are glabrous and purple-green which distinguishes this species from the pubescent, silky buds of the above two species. Flowers are

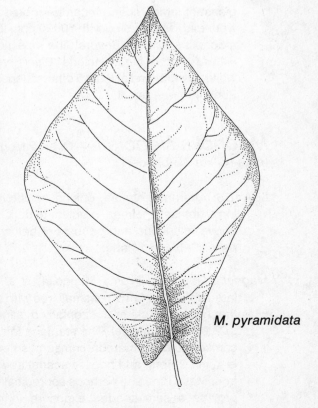

M. pyramidata

white, fragrant, 6 to 9 petaled, and 8 to 10″ across. Virginia to Georgia and Alabama. Introduced 1787. Zone 5 to 8(9). *Magnolia pyramidata,* Pyramid Magnolia, although uncommon in cultivation completes the true "bigleaf clan". Plants are generally small, 10 to 20′ high, with glabrous greenish buds and stems, leaves 6 to 9″ long with a distinct auriculate base. Leaves are green on the underside. Flowers are 3 to 5″ across, white and with a strong "turpentine" scent. Found in Georgia, Florida, and Alabama. Cultivated 1825. Zone 6 to 9. *Magnolia macrophylla* is an interesting native tree which occurs limitedly from Ohio to Florida west to Arkansas and Louisiana. 1800. Zone 5 to 8. All species are botanically interesting and horticulturally worthy. They will simply never become mainstream plants.

Magnolia salicifolia — Anise Magnolia
(mag-nō′li-à sal-is-i-fō′li-à)

LEAVES: Alternate, simple, narrowly oval to lanceolate, 1 1/2 to 4″ long, 5/8 to 1 1/2″ wide, tapered at both ends, blunt or pointed at apex, dull green and glabrous above, slightly glaucous and covered with minute down below; petiole—1/4 to 5/8″ long, slender.

Magnolia salicifolia, Anise Magnolia, is not well known in American gardens but is a handsome plant. It forms a slender, rather narrow to broad pyramid about 20 to 30′ high. The pure white, fragrant, 3 to 4″ diameter flowers are composed of six petals which open in April before the leaves. Fruits 2 to 3″ long, rose-pink with scarlet seeds. The stems when bruised emit a pleasant lemon scent. It can be rooted from June–July cuttings by wounding and treating with 10000 ppm IBA. One of the more difficult magnolias to root. Several fine selections, some possibly with *M. kobus* blood include 'Else Frye' with 6″ diameter white flowers, and at least 8 others. Japan. Introduced 1892. Zone 4 to perhaps 8.

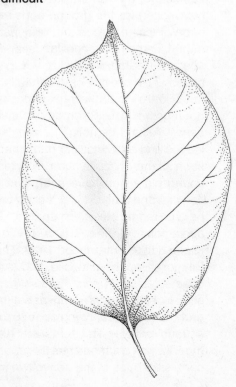

Magnolia sieboldii — Oyama Magnolia
(mag-nō′li-à sē-bōl′dē-ī)

LEAVES: Alternate, simple, oblong or obovate-oblong, 3 to 6″ long, obtusely pointed, medium to dark green and glabrous above, glaucous and pubescent below, 7 to 9 vein pairs; petiole—3/4 to 1″ long.

Magnolia sieboldii, Oyama Magnolia, is a superb, handsome large shrub (10 to 15′) or small tree with cup-shaped flowers that are borne either horizontally or slightly nodding on a 1 to 2 1/2″ long pedicel. The stamens form a pinkish to rose-crimson to deep maroon-crimson center. The carmine fruit is about 2″ long and houses scarlet seeds. Flowers appear from May–June and perhaps sporadically thereafter. Ideally provide a semi-shaded exposure in moist, fertile, well-drained soil. Have seen very few specimens in the eastern corridor, but enough to know the plant will grow. Two related species, *M. sinensis,* Chinese Magnolia, and *M. wilsonii,* Wilson Magnolia, as I have observed them are large (20′), more tree-like, with 3 to 4″ diameter, slightly cup-shaped pendulous flowers with crimson-purple stamens. To view the flowers at their best, one must walk under the tree and literally look up at the flowers. Flowers occur with the leaves and are usually at their best in May–June. Gossler mentioned that *M. sinensis* is more shrub-like than *M. sieboldii.* In fact, I have seen *M. sinensis* listed as a subspecies of *M. sieboldii.* The taxonomy is not totally clear-cut among the 3 species. All are first rate garden plants where adaptable. Best used in a mixed shady border with hostas, ferns, and wildflowers planted underfoot. *Magnolia sieboldii* is native to Japan and Korea. Introduced about 1865. Zone 6 to 8. *Magnolia sinensis*— western China. Introduced 1908. Zone 7 to 8? *Magnolia wilsonii*—western China. Introduced 1908. Zone 6 to 8.

Magnolia × *soulangiana* — Saucer Magnolia
(mag-nō′li-à) sū-lan-gē-ā′na)

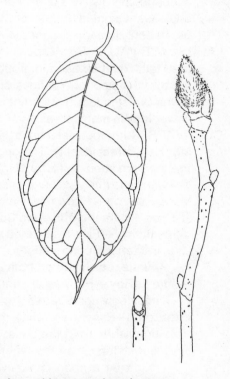

LEAVES: Alternate, simple, 3 to 6″ long, half as wide, obovate to broad-oblong, apex narrow and more or less abruptly short-pointed, base taper-pointed, dark green above, pubescent below.

BUDS: Terminal pubescent, silky to the touch, 1/2 to 3/4″ long, laterals smaller.

STEM: Brown, glabrous, with grayish lenticels, fragrant when crushed, with prominent stipular scars.

SIZE: 20 to 30′ in height with a variable spread, often about the same as height.

HARDINESS: Zone 4 to 9.

HABIT: Distinctly upright in youth and often grown as a multiple-stemmed shrub under nursery production; usually a large spreading shrub or small, low-branched tree with wide-spreading branches forming a pyramidal to rounded outline at maturity.

RATE: Medium, 10 to 15′ over a 10 year period.

TEXTURE: Medium-coarse in leaf; perhaps medium to medium-coarse in winter.

BARK COLOR: A handsome gray on older trunks, usually smooth, often with sapsucker damage.

LEAF COLOR: Medium to deep flat green in summer; sometimes (but not usually) an attractive yellow-brown in fall.

FLOWERS: Perfect, white to pink to purplish (variable when seed grown), often with 9 petals, usually the outside of the petals are flushed pinkish purple while the inside is whitish, 5 to 10″ diameter, campanulate, before the leaves in March–April, solitary; over the years I have possibly recorded the flowering dates of this tree more often than any other; in Athens flowers show color by late February and usually peak from March 1 to 15, in Savannah GA plants have been in full flower on February 19, so a 200 mile trip slightly southeast from Athens makes a two-week difference in full flower expression; flowers will persist and leaves follow quickly in some years so both are present; also the plant has the curious habit of flowering sporadically on new growth of the season but the flowers are never as brightly pigmented because of the heat and are often slightly twisted and mis-shaped; from rooted cuttings, 2 to 3-year-old plants will set flower buds which makes it a choice plant for nursery and garden center sales; a fine old 20 to 25′ high by 25 to 30′ wide specimen consumes a corner property on two heavily trafficked streets in Athens; when in perfect full flower, garden centers can't stock enough, when blitzed by the cold weather which happens

1 (2) out of 3 to 4 years, demand is lower; amazingly the tree can look stunning one bright late winter or early spring afternoon and with an overnight temperature drop to 25 to 28°F, become a mass of limp brown petals the next day.

FRUIT: Aggregate of follicles, August–September, seldom produced in significant numbers; in fact, I rarely see fruit.

CULTURE: The following discussion applies to the other magnolias in this section with one notable exception; magnolias have a fleshy root system with minimal lateral roots and root hairs and should be transplanted balled and burlapped or from a container; soil should be moist, deep, preferably acid (pH 5.0 to 6.5), and supplemented with leaf mold or peat moss; prefer full sun but will withstand light shade; do not plant too deep; prune after flowering; *M. denudata* and *M.* × *soulangiana* display good pollution tolerance; if pruning is necessary perform the task after flowering, ideally in early summer before all the flower buds are set for next year.

DISEASES AND INSECTS: Black mildews, leaf blight, leaf spots (at least 15 different ones), dieback, *Nectria* canker, leaf scab, wood decay, algal spot, magnolia scale, Tuliptree scale, and other scales; although this list is quite impressive I have not witnessed many problems. Perhaps the most unpleasant sight is the numerous circles of sapsucker holes that often ring the trees; apparently no permanent damage is done.

LANDSCAPE VALUE: Small specimen tree, often over-used but with ample justification; flowers when 2 to 4′ tall; could be used in groupings, near large buildings or in large tree lawns; roots need ample room to develop; one serious problem is that late spring frosts and freezes often nip the emerging flower buds; in fact, 1(2) out of every 3 or 4 years would be a conservative estimate for almost total flower loss in many areas.

CULTIVARS: Numerous selections have been made over the years and there is much confusion concerning their correct identity. The original hybrid was raised in the garden of Soulange-Bodin at Fromont, France from seed borne by *M. denudata* fertilized by pollen of *M. liliiflora*. The plant first flowered in 1826 and the cultivars have become the most popular of all magnolias in American gardens.

'Alba Superba'—Flowers white, outside of petals colored very light purplish, fragrant (Syn: 'Superba' or 'Alba'); the true 'Alba Superba' is of dense, erect habit.

'Alexandrina'—Flowers flushed rose-purple outside, inside of petals pure white, one of the larger and earlier flowering varieties, probably more than one clone, some lighter, others darker rose-purple, easily rooted from June cuttings, widely grown in the nursery trades.

'Andre LeRoy'—Flowers are dark pink to purplish on the outside, petals are white inside and flowers decidedly cup-shaped.

'Brozzonii'—Essentially white, flowers 10″ across when fully open; outside of petals tinged a pale purplish rose at the base; beautiful floriferous form that is about the last to flower perhaps 2 weeks later than the others, supposedly not as fragrant; makes a large plant 25 to 30′ high; might be a good choice where late spring frosts are a common occurrence; easily rooted, originated in France about 1873.

'Burgundy'—Flowers are a deep purple color of burgundy wine, flowers earlier than most varieties; easily rooted.

'Grace McDade'—Flowers are white with pink at the base of the petals; growth habit like 'Lennei'.

'Lennei'—Dark purplish magenta petals (6), white inside, each petal often 4″ long and wide, broad-obovate, concave; flowers later than the type and usually sporadically into summer; leaves are dark green and larger (8″ by 5″); the habit is that of a stiff broad shrub; many plants I have seen were more or less flat across the top; it arose in Italy and was introduced to Germany about 1854.

'Lennei Alba'—A pure white form of the above with goblet-shaped flowers (9 tepals) that appear about the same time or slightly later; seedling of 'Lennei', introduced by Kerssen, Aalsmer, Holland in 1931.

'Lilliputian'—Smaller light pink flowers and habit than species, slow grower.

'Lombardy Rose'—Lower surface of the petals is dark rose, upper surface white, flowers for several weeks, seedling of 'Rustica Rubra', free flowering and more upright in habit.

'Rustica Rubra'—Rose-red flowers, 5 1/2" diameter, inside of petals is white, this is purported to be a seedling of 'Lennei' but the flowers have more rose and it makes a larger, looser growing shrub; it is beautiful in flower.

'San Jose'—Large flowers, rosy-purple (rose-pink with milky white interior), fragrant, and a vigorous grower.

'Speciosa'—A late flowered white form, the petals flushed purple at the base; the outer whorl of petals reflexed at their midpoint; makes a rather dense tree.

'Verbanica'—Late flowering form opening about the same time as 'Brozzonii'; the petals rose on the outside but fading to white at the apex, the inner and medium petals are strap-shaped and usually tinted rose on the outside.

PROPAGATION: Seed should be stratified for 3 to 6 months in moist media at 32 to 41°F to overcome embryo dormancy. In general it is best to collect cuttings when the terminal (flower bud) is formed, cuttings should be wounded and dipped in 10,000 to perhaps 20,000 ppm IBA, peat:perlite, mist; rooting generally occurs in high percentages; this approach is much preferable to grafting. *M.* × *soulangiana* is more difficult to root than *M. stellata* or *M.* × *loebneri* but easier than *M. denudata;* for a thorough discussion of *Magnolia* propagation see Dirr and Heuser, 1987.

Magnolia stellata — Star Magnolia
(mag-nō'li-a ste-lā'ta)

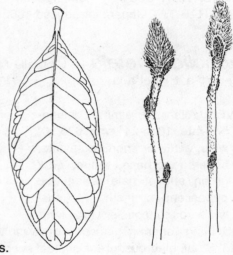

LEAVES: Alternate, simple, entire, obovate or narrow elliptic to oblong-obovate, 2 to 4" long, half as wide, obtusely pointed or obtusish, gradually tapering at base, glabrous and dark green above, light green and reticulate beneath and glabrous or appressed-pubescent on the nerves; petiole—1/4 to 1/3" long.

BUDS: Densely pubescent, flower buds 1/3 to 1/2" long; vegetative-smaller.

STEM: Slender, brown, glabrous, more densely borne than in *M.* × *soulangiana.*

SIZE: 15 to 20' in height with a spread of 10 to 15'.

HARDINESS: Zone 4 to 8(9).

HABIT: Dense oval to rounded shrub or small tree usually of thick constitution from the close-set leaves and stems.

RATE: Slow, 3 to 6' over a 5 to 6 year period.

TEXTURE: Medium in all seasons; possibly medium-fine.

LEAF COLOR: Dark green in summer, often yellow to bronze in fall.

FLOWERS: White, fragrant, 3 to 4" in diameter, 12 to 18 petals, each petal 1 1/2 to 2" long, narrowly oblong or strap-shaped, often wavy, at first spreading, finally reflexed, late February–early March in Athens and usually ahead of *M.* × *soulangiana* but at times in full flower at the same time, interestingly in the north seems to flower 10 to 20 days ahead of *M.* × *soulangiana,* flowers solitary opening before leaves, often flowering when less than one foot tall; flowers are delicate and since they open early are often at the mercy of the weather; late freezes and wind can severely damage the petals (tepals).

FRUIT: Aggregate of follicles, 2" long, twisted, and usually with only a few fertile carpels.

CULTURE: As discussed under *M.* × *soulangiana* this species should be protected as much as possible; try to avoid southern exposures since the buds will tend to open fastest in this location; prefers a peaty, organic-based soil; does quite well in heat of south.

DISEASES AND INSECTS: Basically trouble-free.

LANDSCAPE VALUE: Nice single specimen or accent plant; I have seen it used against red brick walls and the effect is outstanding; very popular plant and with justifiable reason, could be, and often is, integrated into foundation plantings; many excellent cultivars that are preferable to the species.

CULTIVARS: Many cultivars have been introduced although nothing resembling the *M.* × *soulangiana* complex. Request the better cultivars.

'Centennial'—Originated at Arnold Arboretum, 28 to 32 tepals (1 1/2 to 2″ long), more open flower (5 1/2″ across), and tepals are blushed with slight pink tinge on the outside, commemorates the 100 year anniversary of the Arnold Arboretum (1872–1972).

'Dawn'—White flower with pink stripe that runs length of tepal, pink color persists, 25 tepals.

'King Rose'—Buds develop pink, blush pink on the outside when open, 22 tepals, forms a large spreading shrub of dense twiggy growth.

'Rosea'—Flower buds pink, fading white at maturity; more than one clone with this name.

'Royal Star'—Possibly the best and quite common in commerce; pink buds open to 25 to 30 nearly pure white tepals, 3 to 4″ diameter, fragrant, slightly later than typical *M. stellata,* clean dark green foliage, upright densely branched shrub in youth, more rounded with age.

'Rubra'—Flowers are purplish rose, fading to pink, 16 tepals, compact shrub with yellow-green foliage.

'Waterlily'—Buds pink, eventually white, 14 tepals (have counted 24), slightly narrower than those of the species, highly fragrant; upright, bushy grower, late flowering, more than one clone under this name.

PROPAGATION: See *M.* × *soulangiana.*

NATIVE HABITAT: Japan. Introduced 1862.

Magnolia tripetala — Umbrella Magnolia
(mag-nō′li-a trī-pet′a-la)

LEAVES: Alternate, simple, oblong-obovate, 10 to 24″ long, 6 to 10″ wide, acute or short acuminate, cuneate at base, entire, dark green above, pale green and pubescent beneath, at least while young; petiole 1 to 2″ long.

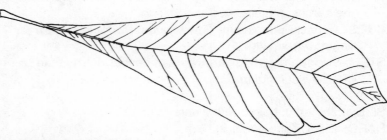

BUDS: Long, tapering, glaucous, greenish to purplish, glabrous.

STEM: Stout, glabrous, greenish, leaf scar-large, oval, very coarse textured stems.

Magnolia tripetala, Umbrella Magnolia, reaches 15 to 30′ but can grow to 40′. It is similar to *M. macrophylla* in many respects but the 6 to 9-tepaled flowers are 6 to 10″ across, creamy-white, and unpleasantly fragrant, May to early June (before *M. macrophylla*), solitary. The elongated, cone-shaped, 4″ long, rosy-red fruits mature in September-October. The leaves reach 10 to 24″ in length and are clustered near the ends of the branches and thus create an umbrella effect. Very difficult to utilize in the home landscape because of cumbersome characteristics. Ranges from southern Pennsylvania to northern Georgia and Alabama and west to central Kentucky and southwestern Arkansas. Introduced 1752. Zone (4)5 to 8. A hybrid between this and *M. virginiana* is called *M.* × *thompsoniana.* Professor J.C. McDaniel selected a clone and named it 'Urbana'. The leaves are a lustrous green, the flowers creamy white, about 3 to 5″ across, fragrant, and open over a long period from late May through June. This hybrid was first noticed around 1808 when Mr. Thompson found a distinct plant among seedlings of *M. virginiana.* It is, unfortunately, a shrub-tree of vigorous, unkempt habit and makes great long shoots in a single season. It will never replace *M.* × *soulangiana* or *M. stellata* in residential landscapes.

Magnolia virginiana — Sweetbay Magnolia, also called Laurel or Swamp Magnolia
(mag-nō'li-à vĕr-jin-ē-ā'na)

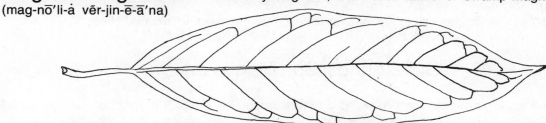

LEAVES: Alternate, simple, entire, evergreen, semi-evergreen to deciduous, elliptic to oblong-lanceolate, 3 to 5″ long, about one-half as wide, acute or obtuse, broad cuneate at base, rarely rounded, dark lustrous green above and glaucous beneath.

BUDS: Sparsely pubescent, somewhat silky.

STEM: Green, slender, glaucous, with prominent diaphragms.

SIZE: In the north 10 to 20′ by 10 to 20′; in the southern part of its range can grow to 60′ or more.

HARDINESS: Zone 5 to 9.

HABIT: Small, multi-stemmed, deciduous shrub of loose, open, upright spreading habit in the north; deciduous, semi-evergreen to evergreen in the south and forming a large pyramidal tree.

RATE: Medium to fast.

TEXTURE: Medium in all seasons.

LEAF COLOR: Dark green and often lustrous above, distinctly glaucous (silvery) beneath in summer.

FLOWERS: Creamy white, lemon-scented, 2 to 3″ diameter, 9 to 12 petals, May–June, solitary; usually not produced in great abundance, often continuously on leafy shoots from May–June to September; may be slow to flower in youth.

FRUIT: Aggregate of follicles, 2″ long, dark red, very handsome where the bright red seeds are exposed.

CULTURE: Different than most magnolias in that it does well in wet and even swampy soils; also tolerates shade; seems to grow best in warm climates; requires acid soil.

DISEASES AND INSECTS: None serious, chlorosis is the worst malady I have seen.

LANDSCAPE VALUE: I have always considered this a lovely, graceful, small patio or specimen tree; the foliage is handsome especially as the wind buffets the leaves exposing the silvery underside; winter damage is a distinct possibility in the northern part of Zone 5; excellent for the sweet fragrance of its flowers, never overwhelming in flower.

CULTIVARS:

var. *australis*—More pubescent branches and petioles; the southern representative and often larger, more tree-like and evergreen; rejected by one authority as a true variety but accepted by others; see Treseder's *Magnolias* for an interesting discussion.

'Henry Hicks'—A tree that was given to the Arthur Hoyt Scott Horticultural Foundation at Swarthmore College and has remained evergreen even at temperatures as low as -17°F; I have seen the parent tree and it is not particularly outstanding but does offer evergreen foliage.

There is great interest in hardy evergreen forms and selections have been made by various collectors and nurserymen. Perhaps in the succeeding years these plants will become available to gardeners.

PROPAGATION: Seed requires 3 to 5 months at 41°F for best results although the literature is not absolutely clear on the best time period; cuttings can be rooted and I have taken softwood material from 2 to 3 year old plants, treated with 1000 ppm IBA-quick dip, placed in sand under mist with 100% rooting; mature wood should be collected in June–July and treated with about 10,000 ppm IBA for best results; have had a difficult time rooting cuttings from mature trees.

ADDITIONAL NOTES: Really a beautiful plant, especially when the sweet-scented flowers are opening. As one drives through coastal and southern Georgia and Florida, the species is quite evident along streams and moist areas. It makes a large tree and is seen growing in a mixed association with sweetgum and other wet soil plants. I have seen tremendous chlorosis in the calcareous soils of the midwest.

NATIVE HABITAT: Massachusetts to Florida and Texas, near the coast. Introduced 1688.

Other Landscape Magnolias

In putting together this edition I reflected on the astronomical number of hybrids that have been introduced. The numbers exceed even the fondest dreams of the obsessed plantsperson. Often only the degree of shading on the outside of the tepals was justification for a new cultivar. Unfortunately, mainstream gardening America cannot absorb the many new magnolias. The days should be past when nurserymen offer only *M.* × *soulangiana* or *M. stellata*. The gardeners deserve the better cultivars.

'Galaxy'—Pyramidal, single trunk tree probably 20 to 30′ high; 12 tepals, 6″ across, red-purple to pink and open late enough to avoid spring frost damage, as late as 2 to 3 weeks after the frost sensitive magnolias, considered hardy in Zone 5 to 9, hybrid from a 1963 cross between *M. liliiflora* × *M. sprengeri* 'Diva', introduced by U.S. National Arboretum; may grow 30′ high by 10′ wide in 10 years.

'Gresham Hybrids'—Parentage mixed—*M. campbellii, M. veitchii, M.* × *soulangiana* cultivars; Zones 7 to 9.

'Darrell Dean'—Wine-red flowers, 12″ across, 9 to 12 broad tepals, rounded vigorous tree.

'Elisa Odenwald'—Cream and white, medium to large, fragrant, upright flaring growth habit.

'Frank Gladney'—Deep pink cup and saucer type flower, 10 to 12″ across, 12 tepals, creamy white inside, vigorous upright plants with broad green leaves.

'Joe McDaniel'—Dark red-violet, opening to well formed bowls, darkest colored of all, large upright habit.

'Mary Nell'—10″ diameter cup shaped flowers, 9 tepals tinged purple-red at the base, inside pure white, vigorous bushy grower.

'Peter Smithers'—Deep pink, 10″ diameter, white inner surface, fast vigorous upright grower.

'Royal Crown'—Vigorous tree with 12 tepaled red-purple flowers that open before the leaves with occasional flowering later, hardy to -10°F.

'Sweet Sixteen'—White candle-like 5″ long buds open into fragrant tulip shaped flowers, oval-rounded habit.

'Tina Durio'—White 10 to 12″ diameter flowers, profuse, flower late, fast grower.

'Todd Gresham'—Violet-rose and white flowers, 10 to 12″ across, 9 tepals, fast growing and vigorous, also produces abundant red fruits.

'Nimbus'—Vigorous small tree to 30′ with partially evergreen foliage, 6″ diameter, 8-tepaled ivory white fragrant flowers, smooth gray bark, considered hardy to -10°F; hybrid between *M. hypoleuca* and *M. virginiana,* product of the U.S. National Arboretum.

'Spectrum'—A sister seedling of 'Galaxy' with wider habit, flowers are larger and deeper colored and not as profuse, probably inferior to 'Galaxy'.

'Sundance'—Yellow flowers, Dr. August Kehr introduction.

'Yellow Fever'—Offers 6 to 8″ yellow fragrant flowers that are tinged light pink at the base of the tepals, flowers open before leaves appear and supposedly open late enough to avoid spring frosts.

Magnolia hypoleuca (*M. obovata*), (mag-nō′li-a hī-pō-loo′kȧ), White Bark Magnolia, always greeted my eye as I rounded the corner on the Arborway in Jamaica Plain heading for the Arnold Arboretum. I only studied the 30 to 40′ specimen on one occasion and then to simply admire the handsome gray bark. Leaves (8 to 18″ long) remind of *M. tripetala* except with a glaucous underside. The creamy-white, 8″ diameter strong scented flowers open in May–June with a conspicuous central mass of purplish red stamens in the center. The red fruit is cone-shaped, 5 to 8″ long, 2 1/2″ wide aggregate of follicles. Habit is open and gaunt and with leaves in a pseudo-whorl at the tips of the branches; the appearance resembles *M. tripetala.* Japan. Introduced 1865. Zone 5 to 7(8).

Magnolia × **wieseneri** (*M.* × *watsonii*) (mag-nō′li-a wīz′nĕr-ī) has only crossed my path once. The flowers are quite fragrant and some say overpowering. The ivory colored tepals with red stamens average 6 to 8″ across. The habit is somewhat ungainly. Possibly hardy to 10°F. A hybrid between *M. hypoleuca* and *M. sieboldii*. Probably 15 to 25′ high. Leaves are 4 to 8″ long and taper to a 1/4 to 1″ long petiole. The plant at Wakehurst Place, England, was rather coarse.

×*Mahoberberis*
Berberidaceae

× *Mahoberberis* is the result of intergeneric crosses between *Mahonia* and *Berberis.* The foliage varies from evergreen to semi-evergreen and from simple to compound on the same plant. Flowers and fruits are sparse or nonexistent. Having seen the following hybrids I would have to rate them poor quality ornamentals. They do have some interest for the plant collector and are chiefly found in arboreta although, to my surprise, I discovered several plants in Cave Hill Cemetery, Louisville, Kentucky.

× *M. aquicandidula,* (ma-hō-ber′ber-is a-kwi-kan-did′ū-la), resulted from a cross between *M. aquifolium* and *B. candidula.* The leaves are a leathery, glossy dark green, 1 to 1 1/2″ long, with 3 to 5 sharp spines on each margin of the leaf. The foliage turns brilliant scarlet, claret and other red-purple combinations in the winter. The habit is somewhat open and stiff and not attractive. Will probably grow 3 to 6′ at maturity. Zone 6, possibly 5. Lost most of its leaves after exposure to -6°F.

× *M. aquisargentiae,* (ma-hō-ber′ber-is a-qwi-sâr-jen′ti-ē), is a hybrid between *M. aquifolium* × *B. sargentiana.* In general it is more vigorous than the previous species (6′). The glossy evergreen to semi-evergreen foliage may be simple or compound pinnate on the same plant. Leaves will turn bronze to reddish purple in winter especially if sited in full sun. First introduced from Sweden in 1948. Zone 6. Foliage injured at -6°F.

× *M. neubertii,* (ma-hō-ber′ber-is new-ber′tē-ī), is the first *Mahoberberis* I had ever witnessed. It was growing in the shrub collection at the Arnold Arboretum and probably represents the worst of the lot. It is leggy, open, and the leaves are of a dull, semi-evergreen nature. Result of crosses between *Mahonia aquifolium* and *Berberis vulgaris.* Grows 4 to 6′ high. Zone 6. Dropped *all* leaves after exposure to -6°F. Originated in France in 1854.

Mahonia aquifolium — Oregongrapeholly or Oregon Grapeholly or Oregon Hollygrape
depending on who or what is writing the common name.
(ma-hō′ni-a a-kwi-fō′li-um)

FAMILY: Berberidaceae
LEAVES: Alternate, compound pinnate, evergreen, 6 to 12″ long, 5 to 9 leaflets, ovate to oblong-ovate, 1 1/2 to 3 1/2″ long, spine-tipped, rounded or truncate at base, sinuately spiny-dentate, lustrous dark green above, rarely dull, extremely stiff and leathery, usually turning purplish in winter.
BUDS: Rather small, except for the terminal which is ovoid with half-a-dozen exposed scales.
STEM: Roundish, stout, becoming gray-brown at maturity; pith—large, pale, continuous; leaf scars—narrow, low, half encircling the stem.

SIZE: 3 to 6′, will grow to 9′ in height; spread of 3 to 5′.
HARDINESS: Zone 4 to 5 to 8.
HABIT: Limited branching evergreen shrub with upright, heavy stems, often stoloniferous in habit, actually there seem to be two forms, one low and broad, dense and rounded; the other taller with upright branches, irregular and open, with lustrous foliage.

RATE: Slow, 2 to 3′ over a 3 to 4 year period.

TEXTURE: Medium in summer, medium-coarse in winter.

LEAF COLOR: Reddish bronze when unfolding, changing to light, glossy yellow-green and finally lustrous dark green in summer; purplish bronze in fall.

FLOWERS: Perfect, bright yellow, borne in fascicled, erect, 2 to 3″ long and wide terminal racemes (early to mid March, Athens) April, very handsome in flower; has slightly fragrant flowers but not to the degree of *Mahonia bealei.*

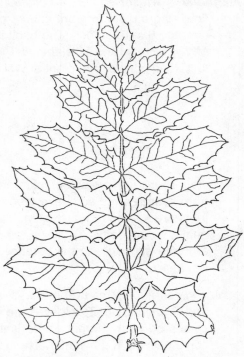

FRUIT: True berry, blue-black, bloomy, 1/3″ diameter, August–September, about a month earlier in Zone 8, look like grapes and, therefore, the common name grapeholly, may persist into December.

CULTURE: Transplant balled and burlapped into moist, well-drained, acid soil; avoid hot, dry soils and desiccating winds; preferably shade (will tolerate sun); tends to brown up very badly unless sited in a protected location; will develop chlorosis in high pH soils.

DISEASES AND INSECTS: Leaf rusts, leaf spots, leaf scorch (physiological problem caused by desiccating wind and winter sun), barberry aphid, scale, and whitefly.

LANDSCAPE VALUE: Foundation plant, shrub border, specimen, shady area; not the best of the broadleaves but certainly not the worst; has a place in the landscape but should be used with discretion; severely injured at -20°F.

CULTIVARS: Reasonable confusion about the exact taxonomic status of many of the cultivars since they might represent hybrids or intergrades of *M. aquifolium* and *M. repens.* I see significant variation in foliage color and density. Recently found a plant with *M. aquifolium* characteristics yet flowers at every node that resulted in a golden wand.

'Apollo'—Low growing variety with conspicuous golden orange flowers in dense heads, makes a good ground cover.

'Atropurpureum'—Leaves dark reddish purple in winter.

'Compactum'—Dwarf form with very glossy leaves and a bronze winter color; grows about 24 to 36″ in height, hardy to -10°F, a handsome form.

'Golden Abundance'—Heavy yellow flowers are born against bright green foliage; plants are vigorous, erect and dense, and covered with blue berries (Zone 5).

'King's Ransom'—A rather upright, dark green, closer to blue green leaf form that is being utilized in greater numbers every year, turns bronze-red-purple in winter, probably a hybrid.

'Mayhan Strain'—A dwarf form with glossy foliage and fewer leaflets per leaf and the leaflets arranged more closely on the rachis. The Mayhan Nursery who introduced this cultivar claims it is the result of 25 years of selection and the form can be maintained by seed propagation. Plant should grow between 30 to 42″ high.

'Moseri'—Bronze-red or orange new leaves, in spring the young growth is rich apricot; leaves turn to apple green and finally dark green.

'Orange Flame'—Blazing bronze-orange new foliage, contrasts with wine-red or deep green older leaves, erect grower, stout stems, needs full sun.

'Smaragd' ('Emerald')—Handsome glossy emerald-green leaves, assumes bronzy purple hue with advent of cold weather, deep yellow flowers occur in terminal and axillary racemes/panicles, habit is intermediate between 'Compacta' and larger growing types.

PROPAGATION: Seed should be stratified for 90 days as 41°F and should not be allowed to dry out after it is collected; best time to take cuttings is in November or after some exposure to cold, treat with 8000 to 10000 ppm IBA. If only a few plants are needed, simple division of the parent plant works well.

NATIVE HABITAT: British Columbia to Oregon. Introduced 1823.

RELATED SPECIES:

Mahonia 'Arthur Menzies' is a seedling that was selected in 1961 at Washington Park Arboretum, Seattle; yellow flowers occur in 5 to 10″ long, 8 to 10″ wide inflorescences in December–January; withstood +11°F, however, at Callaway Gardens was defoliated with stem damage at 0 to -5°F, tends toward a leggy upright cumbersome shrub but has the larger leaf of the *M.* × *media* hybrids. Zone (7)8 to 9. A *M. bealei* × *M. lomariifolia* hybrid.

Mahonia bealei—Leatherleaf Mahonia
(ma-hō′ni-a bēl′ē-ī)

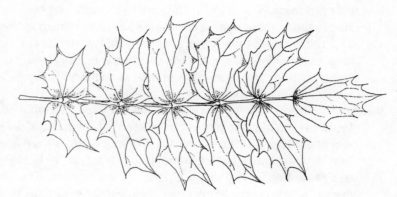

LEAVES: Alternate, compound pinnate, evergreen, 9 to 13 leaflets,
each leaflet 1 to 4″ long, 1 to 2″
wide, 3- to 5-nerved, endowed
with 5 to 7 prominent spines,
glabrous, sessile on rachis,
leathery, dull dark to blue green
above, pale green below; petiole
1 to 1 1/2″ long.

Mahonia bealei, Leatherleaf Mahonia, is a clumsy, upright, coarse evergreen shrub growing 6 to 10′ (12′) high. The foliage is dull dark to blue-green and very coriaceous; texture is coarse; flowers are lemon yellow and extremely fragrant, March–April, has flowered as early as mid-January in Athens and is normally in full flower by late February; 3 to 6″ long and 6 to 12″ wide inflorescence; fruit is a bluish berry maturing in July–August. Native to China. Introduced 1845. Zone (6) 7 to 9. On the Georgia campus the fruits mature in May–June. The fruits assume a bloomy, almost "robin's egg" blue color as they pass toward maturation. Seeds will germinate without cold stratification and can be sown as extracted from the fruits. Used in great numbers in the southeast and is particularly attractive in a shady corner of the garden where the fragrant flowers are particularly welcome. The fruits are especially attractive and occur in great numbers. Apparently the birds love the fruits since they are often removed shortly after ripening. Also, numerous seedlings develop in out-of-the-way places where only birds could disseminate the seeds. Flowers open from the base to the apex and are not as vivid in color or as showy from a distance as *M. aquifolium*. Hardiness has never been adequately documented but plants in Cincinnati were killed to the ground at -17°F. In 1983–84, at -3°F, Athens, there was leaf browning but nothing particularly severe. Possibly hardy in the -5 to -10°F range.

Mahonia fortunei — Chinese Mahonia
(ma-hō′ni-a fôr-tū′nē-ī)

LEAVES: Alternate, evergreen, pinnately compound, 6 to
10″ long, 5 to 9 leaflets, lanceolate to linear-lanceolate,
cuneate, 2 to 5″ long, 1/2 to 3/4″ wide, 5 to 15 forward
pointing spiny teeth on each margin, apex spine-
tipped, sessile, flat dark green above, paler beneath,
glabrous and marked with prominent netted veins;
petiole 1 to 2″ long.
STEM: Stout, generally 1/4″ or more in diameter, brown,
rough, typically yellow when cut.

Mahonia fortunei, Chinese Mahonia, is perhaps the most
beautiful mahonia because of its rather ferny foliage
and, when properly grown, compact, dense stature. It

grows 5 to 6′ high but in Zone 8 seldom reaches more than 3′ unless well protected. The yellow flowers occur in 2 to 3″ long, erect, cylindrical racemes in late March–April (Georgia). The purple-black fruits are seldom developed. It is a rather graceful shrub and not as lethal to the touch as *M. bealei.* Temperatures of 0 to 5°F will take the leaves off and -3°F killed the plant to the ground. It resprouted but is only 18″ tall after 4 growing seasons. In Savannah, GA (Zone 9), this species is tucked away in a shady nook in a park by the Savannah River and makes a stunning filler. Plants are vigorous and quite full. For warmer regions, this might be the *Mahonia* of choice. China. Introduced 1846.

Mahonia japonica, (ma-hō′ni-a jā-pon′i-ka), Japanese Mahonia, is quite similar to *M. bealei* and for landscape purposes serves the same function. Principal difference resides in the lax, loose spreading inflorescence with the flowers more distantly spaced and individual flowers subtended by bracts as long as the flower stalks. Based on the few plants I have seen, the differences are not manifest and, in fact, hybrids are probably common in cultivation. Japan. Zone 6 to 8.

Mahonia × media (*M. japonica × M. lomariifolia*), (ma-hō′ni-a × mē′di-a). The progeny of this cross resemble, at least the plants I have seen, *M. lomariifolia,* a rather tender species with a 10 to 24″ long leaf composed of 19 to 37 leaflets. Plants of *M. × media* are upright branched becoming rounded with time and grow larger than typical *M. japonica,* between 8 and 15′. Leaflets number 17 to 21, each averaging 2 1/2 to 4 1/2″ long, 1 to 1 1/2″ wide, handsome, somewhat glossy green. Flowers (lemon-yellow) occur at the ends of the branches in 10 to 14″ long, erect or spreading racemes. Plants are striking in flower. I have seen plants in flower ('Charity') in early January in England. They make great winter flowering shrubs where hardy which is at best in Zone 8 and 9 in the southeastern states. Cultivars include:
'Buckland'—Inflorescence up to 27″ across, composed of 13 to 14 primary racemes, slightly fragrant.
'Charity'—Soft yellow flowers, excellent shrub.
'Faith'—Closer to *M. lomariifolia* in habit and foliage but with soft-colored yellow flowers.
'Hope'—Soft bright yellow flowers, densely set.
'Lionel Fortunescue'—Fragrant yellow flowers occur in racemes that may reach 16″ long.
'Winter Sun'—More erect racemes than 'Charity'.

Mahonia nervosa, (ma-hō′ni-a nẽr-vō′sa), Cascades Mahonia, is a low, suckering evergreen (6 to 20, thick, up to 3″ long leaflets) shrub rarely reaching more than 12 to 18″. Flowers are yellow and borne in 8″ racemes; fruit purplish blue, 1/4″ diameter. British Columbia to California. Introduced 1822. Zone 5.

Mahonia repens, (ma-hō′ni-a rē′penz), Creeping Mahonia, is a low (10″), stoloniferous evergreen ground cover plant of stiff habit. Pinnately compound leaves (3 to 7 leaflets, 1 to 2 1/2″ long, spine toothed) are dull blue-green in summer; rich purple in winter. Flowers are deep yellow, April, borne in small racemes, 1 to 3″ long; fruit is black, grape-like, covered with a blue bloom, 1/4″ diameter, August-September. British Columbia to northern Mexico and California. Introduced 1822. Zone 5.

Malus — Flowering Crabapple
(Rosaceae)

I doubt if any treatment of flowering crabapples will ever be complete for as I write this someone is ready to introduce a new clone into the trade. The actual number of crabapple types is open to debate but across the country one could probably find 400 to 600 types. Crabapples tend to be cross fertile and freely hybridize. If one checked the parentage of many clones he or she would find that it was an open pollinated seedling, meaning that any number of trees within proximity of the fruiting tree could be the parent(s). There is a nice collection of crabapples on the University of Illinois campus and I collected fruits from many types and enjoyed watching the potpourri of seedlings which resulted. The diversity of foliage colors (light green, dark green, various tints of purple); leaf morphology (serrate, lobed, incised); and vigor (some seedlings grow 3 to 4 times faster than others) can be attributed to the heterogeneous genetic pool contributed by the many different parents. I was told a particular mass planting on campus was *M. hupehensis,* Tea Crabapple, a triploid which comes true-to-type from seed. The plants did not have the typical vase-shaped habit of the species and I found out why when the first group of seedlings developed. The leaves were different colors, shapes and sizes indicating anything but a species which breeds true from seed. I have attempted to assemble a fairly representative list of crabapples which are often grown and available from nurseries. The salient characteristics of flower, fruit, size and diseases are included. Many crabapples are almost worthless because of extreme susceptibility to apple scab, rust, fire blight, leaf spot and powdery mildew. Unfortunately, the most susceptible types seem to be the most popular (i.e., 'Almey', 'Hopa', 'Eleyi', 'Bechtels', 'Red Silver'). Considering the tremendous number of crabapples available only a handful or so meet the stringent requirements of excellent flower, fruit, habit and disease resistance. Many types are slightly susceptible to certain disease(s) and are perfectly acceptable provided their limitations are understood. I have used the late Dr. Lester Nichols, Pennsylvania State University, Dr. Ed Hasselkus, University of Wisconsin, Dr. Elton Smith of The Ohio State University and Dr. Malcolm Shurtliff, Univ. of Illinois, disease ratings based on their many years of collecting data regarding disease susceptibility. In certain instances no data were available and no evaluation is given. I have cross-checked many references in regard to the flower and fruit characters and strongly recommend the following references for further reading: TREES FOR AMERICAN GARDENS by Donald Wyman; TREES AND SHRUBS HARDY IN THE BRITISH ISLES, VOL. II by W.J. Bean; CRABAPPLES OF DOCUMENTED AUTHENTIC ORIGIN, National Arboretum Contribution No. 2 by Roland Jefferson; and FLOWERING CRABAPPLES by Arie den Boer. To my knowledge there is no current crabapple reference that is up to date. Since the last edition, about 80 *new* cultivars have been introduced; most are included here.

The following crabapples are my favorites (note the selection is not necessarily based on disease resistance as was strongly suggested in the above discussion).

M. × *atrosanguinea*—Carmine Crabapple   *M. hupehensis*—Tea Crabapple
M. 'Callaway'   *M. sargentii*—Sargent Crabapple
M. 'Donald Wyman'   *M.* 'Snowdrift'
M. floribunda—Japanese Crabapple   *M.* 'White Angel'
M. halliana var. *parkmanii*

There are few other trees or shrubs which approach the beauty of a crabapple tree in full flower. Ornamental crabapples are an outstanding group of small flowering trees for landscape planting. They are valued for foliage, flowers, fruit, and variations in habit or size. By using different species and cultivars, the flowering period can be extended from late April to late May and early June (late March to late April in Zone 8) with colors ranging from white through purplish red.

The small fruits, borne in the fall, are also effective, with colors of red, yellow, and green. Other features of this group are the small size (rounded, horizontal, pendulous, fastigiate, and vase-shaped). Crabapples are suited for home grounds, schools, parks, commercial and public buildings, and highway plantings.

CHARACTERISTICS

Deciduous trees and shrubs, rarely half evergreen; most are between 15 and 25' in height at maturity; often tremendous winter architecture because of unique branching.

Shape: Range from low mound-like plants to narrow upright or pendulous types.

Branches: Alternate, upright, horizontal, or drooping, rarely with spinescent branches.

Buds: Ovoid, with several imbricate scales, usually reddish brown with hairs protruding from the underside of the bud scales.

Bark: On old trunks, shiny gray-brown, scaly.

Flowers: White to pink or carmine to red to rose. Single flowers have 5 petals. Flowers occur in umbel or corymb-like racemes. Petals are small, suborbicular to obovate. Stamens 15 to 20, usually with yellow anthers. Ovary is inferior, 3 to 5 celled, styles present vary from 2 to 5, connate at base, perfect.

Fruit: A pome with persistent or deciduous calyx; colors range from red to yellow to green. If fruit is 2″ in diameter or less, it is a crabapple. If the fruit is larger than 2″, then it is classified as an apple.

HABITAT:

Twenty to 30 species of crabapples are scattered in the temperate regions of North America, Europe, and Asia. Currently, at least 100 to 200 types of crabapples are grown in North American nurseries, with at least 300 to 400 additional types in arboretums and botanical gardens. Dr. Nichols crabapple printout listed approximately 700 types.

GENERAL CULTURE:

Crabapples are quite adaptable to varying soil conditions, but have been observed to do best in a heavy loam. The soil, regardless of type, should be well drained, moist and acid (pH 5.0 to 6.5). Most crabapples are hardy and should be planted in full sun for best development of flowers and fruits. The Asiatic forms are much more resistant to insects and diseases than are the forms native to North America. In the southern states, crabapples are not as widely planted but, in general, types like *M.* 'Callaway', *M. floribunda, M. sargentii* and *M. sieboldii* var. *zumi* do well. Fireblight and woolly aphids are more prevalent in the southern states.

Generally crabapples require little pruning, but if any is done, it should be completed before early June. Most crabapples initiate flower buds for the next season in mid-June to early July and pruning at this time or later would result in decreased flower production the following year. Pruning may be done, however, to remove sucker growth, open up the center of the plant to light and air, to cut off out-of-place branches, and shape the tree.

PROPAGATION:

Practically all flowering crabs are self-sterile and are propagated by budding, grafting, or from softwood cuttings. Two crabapples are, however, commonly propagated from seed and come true to type; *M. hupehensis* and *M. toringoides.* The Sargent Crabapple is also frequently propagated from seed, but considerable variabtion in size occurs. Although the literature is conflicting on seed treatment I have found that a 2 to 3 month cold period will induce good germination.

Crabapples are often grafted, using a whip graft, or are budded in summer. Understocks, include the common apple; *M. robusta* and *M. sieboldii* seedlings have proven acceptable as has *M. baccata* where hardiness is a factor. The Malling rootstocks are now used routinely to reduce suckering and provide a better root system. In addition to grafting and budding, a few crabapples such as Arnold, Carmine, Sargent, or Japanese Flowering are propagated from softwood cuttings taken from mid-June through July. Anyone interested in cutting propagation should see Brown and Dirr. *The Plant Propagator* 22(4): 4–5, 1976. "Cutting propagation of selected flowering crabapple types" and Burd and Dirr. *PIPPS.* 27: 427–232, 1977. See Dirr and Heuser, 1987, for a more in depth discussion.

DISEASES AND INSECTS:

Fireblight. The diseased plants have the appearance of being scorched by fire. The first visible signs of infection are often a drying up of the tips of young shoots and bud-clusters. The disease is caused by bacteria which are spread by aphids, leaf hoppers, and bees. Carelessness in handling diseased leaves and branches, and failure to adequately disinfect pruning equipment contribute to the spread of the disease. Control of this disease is difficult. Cultural control practices such as pruning out diseased branches and avoiding excessive nitrogen fertilization should be employed. Use resistant cultivars when possible.

Cedar Apple Rust (Asiatic varieties are resistant). The disease appears on apple leaves in May as yellow (orange) leaf spots which subsequently enlarge, resulting in heavy leaf drop. The disease has as an alternative host *(Juniperus virginiana, J. horizontalis,* and *J. scopulorum).* Galls appear on junipers in early April and spores produced by these galls later infect apple trees.

Cultural control is possible by keeping a minimum distance of 500′ between apple and juniper plants. The disease can be prevented from spreading to apples by spraying the galls when they form in early April with a suitable fungicide. Crabapples can be sprayed with a fungicide when the galls appear on junipers (about mid-April to mid-May). Make 4 to 5 applications at 7 to 10 day intervals.

Apple Scab. The native North American species, Asiatic species, and hybrids and the fruiting apple (*Malus pumila*) are quite susceptible to this disease. Fruits show darkened, leathery spots with many small cracks. The leaves also have darkened spots which may look black or velvety. For control of scab use a suitable fungicide in late March before flowers show any color, and repeat the application at weekly or ten day intervals until petals have dropped and the fruits have set.

Canker. Several species of fungi cause canker on the trunks of crabapples. They often gain entrance through wounds made by lawn mowers and other maintenance equipment.

Scale. Three main types: San Jose, Oyster Shell, or Putman. Adequate control can be obtained by either using a dormant oil as a spray before bud break or with a suitable insecticide when the scales are in the crawling stage.

Borers (may be a serious problem). For cultural control, keep the plants growing well with adequate fertilization and watering practices.

Aphids. A serious problem generally only on native species. Adequate control can be obtained by spraying the trees with an insecticide.

Malus 'Adams'
FLOWERS: Single, 1 1/2″ diameter, carmine in bud, flowers fading to dull pink, annual.
FRUIT: Red, 5/8″ diameter, persistent.
HABIT: Rounded and dense, 24′.
DISEASES: Very resistant, proving to be a superior crabapple although slight fireblight, scab and mildew have been reported.

Malus 'Adirondack', a *Malus halliana* form, introduced by U.S. National Arboretum, bred by Dr. Egolf.
FLOWERS: Red buds, flowers large waxy white with red tinge.
FRUIT: Red to orange-red, 1/2″ diameter.
HABIT: Columnar, obovate, 10′ by 6′.
DISEASES: Resistant to scab, fireblight, rust and mildew, see *HortScience* 22:269–270 (1987).

Malus 'Albright'
FLOWERS: Single, deep pink.
FRUIT: Purplish red, 3/4″ diameter.
HABIT: Upright spreading.
DISEASES: Slight susceptibility to fireblight, frogeye leaf spot.

Malus 'Aldenham' ('Aldenhamensis'), *M.* × *purpurea* type
FLOWERS: Single and semidouble, expanding buds maroon-red, open purplish red fading to deep purplish pink, 1 3/4 to 2″ across.
FRUIT: Dark maroon-red to maroon-purple, shaded side green to bronze, 3/4 to 1″ diameter.
HABIT: Resembles 'Eleyi', 25′.

Malus 'Almey'
FLOWERS: Single, expanding buds deep maroon or purple-red, open purple-red with claw and base of petals and center vein pale lavender to nearly white, 1 4/5″ diameter.
FRUIT: Maroon, approximately 1″ across.
HABIT: Upright spreading tree to 24′.
DISEASES: Very susceptible to diseases, especially scab.

Malus 'Amberina'
FLOWERS: Deep red buds open to creamy white flowers.
FRUIT: Abundant, brilliant orange-red, persistent.
HABIT: Strongly upright, semi-dwarf reaching 10′, clean green summer foliage.

Malus 'American Beauty'
FLOWERS: Deep red, double, exceptionally large.
FRUIT: Apparently does not set fruit.
HABIT: 20 to 25′ tall, foliage with bronze cast.
DISEASES: Extremely scab susceptible.

Malus 'American Spirit'
FLOWERS: Deep rose.
FRUIT: Red, 1/2″ diameter.
HABIT: Rounded, 15 to 18′.

Malus 'Ames White'
FLOWERS: Single, pink to white.
FRUIT: Yellow.
DISEASES: Highly resistant.

Malus 'Angel Choir'
FLOWERS: Buds pale pink, opening to double white flowers.
FRUIT: Red, reaching 3/8″ diameter.
HABIT: Small upright tree reaching about 12′ in height.
DISEASES: Highly disease resistant.

Malus angustifolia — Southern Crabapple
(mā′lus an-gus-ti-fō′li-à)
FLOWERS: Single, pink to deep pink in bud, opening white, extremely fragrant, 1 to 1 1/4″ diameter.
FRUIT: Yellowish green, 3/4″ diameter.
HABIT: Rounded small tree to 20′, usually deciduous but may remain semi-evergreen in mild winters.
DISEASES: Rust susceptible like most native crabapples.
NOTES: Quite an attractive crabapple in native setting; have seen it flowering as early as late February at
    Tifton, Georgia, normally mid April in Athens.

Malus × *arnoldiana (floribunda* × *baccata);* originated at the Arnold Arboretum.
(mā′lus × är-nōl-di-ā′nà)
FLOWERS: Single, buds
    rose-red, flower phlox
    pink outside fading to
    white inside, 1 1/4 to 2″
    diameter, fragrant, an-
    nual or alternate.
FRUIT: Yellow and red, 5/8″ diameter.
HABIT: Mounded, dense branching, 25′ by
    25′.
DISEASES: Susceptible to scab and fireblight;
    a handsome tree in flower but highly sus-
    ceptible to scab.

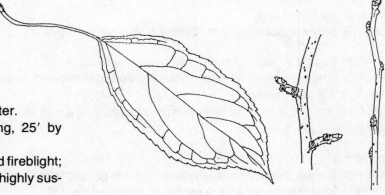

Malus × *atrosanguinea (halliana* × *sieboldii)*—Carmine Crabapple
(mā′lus × a-trō-san-gwin′ē-a̤)

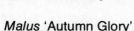

FLOWERS: Bud crimson, single, flower rose madder (pink) and 1 1/4″ diameter, annual; 'Shakespeare' is listed as a form that retains pink color without fading.

FRUIT: Dark red, 3/8″ diameter, not ornamental.

HABIT: Mounded, almost shrub-like, dense branching, 15 to 20′, very lovely small crabapple, good lustrous dark green foliage, usually partially lobed.

DISEASES: Very resistant to scab, have seen it listed as very susceptible to scab, variable to fireblight.

Malus 'Autumn Glory'

FLOWERS: Buds deep bright red, opening to blush white and full white; flowers heavily on spurs.

FRUIT: Glossy bright orange-red, oval, 1/4″ diameter, colors in August and remains firm into December-January.

HABIT: Upright to 12′, deep green, heavily textured leaves.

DISEASES: Highly resistant.

Malus 'Autumn Treasure'

FLOWERS: Single, buds red opening to white.

FRUIT: Gold, 1/4″ diameter, showy, colors early, persistent.

HABIT: Small weeper, refined form, 10′ high and wide; leaves medium to dark green.

DISEASES: Resistant.

Malus baccata — Siberian Crabapple
(mā′lus ba-kā′ta̤)

FLOWERS: Single, pink in bud, opening white, 1 1/2″ diameter, very fragrant, annual.

FRUIT: Bright red or yellow, 3/8″ thick.

HABIT: Tree, 20 to 50′ high, forming a rounded, wide-spreading head of branches.

DISEASES: Susceptible to scab; variable to fireblight.

M. b. 'Columnaris'

FLOWERS: Single, buds creamy-white, open pure white, 1 1/2″ across.

FRUIT: Yellow with a red cheek, approximately 1/2″ diameter.

HABIT: Distinctly upright columnar tree probably 4 to 5 times as tall as wide; does not seem to flower and fruit well, at least this was true for few trees I have observed, 30′ by 8′.

DISEASES: Supposedly very susceptible to fireblight.

M. b. var. *gracilis*

White flowers, 1 3/8″ diameter, more dense than the species with tips of the branches slightly pendulous and smaller leaves.

M. b. var. *himalaica*

FLOWERS: Buds pink opening to white.

FRUIT: Yellow.

DISEASES: Slightly susceptible to scab.

M. b. 'Jackii'
FLOWERS: Single, expanding buds white with touch of pink, open pure white, approximately 1 3/5″ diameter.
FRUIT: Purplish or maroon-red, tan on shaded side, 1/2″ diameter.
HABIT: An upright type with leaves of a remarkably deep green for a crabapple; probably grow 30 to 40′.
DISEASES: Slightly susceptible to fireblight and powdery mildew.

M. b. var. *mandschurica*
Flowers white, 1 1/2″ diameter, one of the first crabapples to flower, moderately to very susceptible to scab and powdery mildew, fruit bright red, 1/2″ diameter.

Malus 'Ballerina'
FLOWERS: Single, white buds open to large, very cupped, showy white flowers.
FRUIT: Bright yellow, about 1/2″ diameter, persistent.
HABIT: Upright to fan shaped, to 15′ high; dark green leaves.
DISEASES: Resistant.

Malus 'Barbara Ann' (A seedling of 'Dorothea').
FLOWERS: Double, deep purplish pink, fading to a light purplish pink, approximately 1 7/8″ diameter.
FRUIT: Purplish red, 1/2″ diameter.
HABIT: Rounded, 20′.
DISEASES: Severely susceptible to scab and slightly susceptible to frogeye leafspot.

Malus 'Baskatong'
FLOWERS: Single, expanding buds dark purplish red, open light purplish red with white claw, 1 3/4″ diameter.
FRUIT: Dark purplish red with many russet marks, 1″ diameter.
HABIT: Tree broad globose, 25 to 30′ by 25 to 30′.
DISEASES: Very resistant.

Malus 'Beauty'
FLOWERS: Single, expanding buds pink to rose-pink, open white and pinkish white, 2″ diameter, alternate.
FRUIT: Dark red, 1 3/5″ diameter, edible.
HABIT: Fastigiate, moderately columnar, 24′.
DISEASES: Very resistant.

Malus 'Beverly' — Originated at Morton Arboretum in 1940, one parent is *M. floribunda.*
FLOWERS: Single, buds red, opening to white, annual.
FRUIT: Excellent, bright red, 1/2 to 3/4″ across.
HABIT: Rounded, dense, 15 to 25′.
DISEASES: Fireblight can be severe under proper environmental conditions; Shurtleff listed it as highly resistant.

Malus 'Blanche Ames'
FLOWERS: Semidouble, 1 1/2″ diameter, pink and white, annual.
FRUIT: Yellow, 1/4″ diameter.
HABIT: Rounded and dense (24′).
DISEASES: Resistant to scab.

Malus 'Bob White'
FLOWERS: Buds cherry colored, flowers fade to white, 1″ diameter, fragrant, alternate.
FRUIT: Yellow to brownish yellow, 5/8″ diameter, persistent.
HABIT: Rounded, dense branching, 20′ by 20′.
DISEASES: Very susceptible to scab and fireblight.

Malus 'Bonfire'
FLOWERS: Single, red buds open to white.
FRUIT: Brilliant orange-red, abundant, 1/4″ diameter, colors early and persists until eaten by birds.
HABIT: Small, upright-rounded, 13 to 14′ high; medium to dark green leaves.

Malus 'Brandywine' (hybrid between 'Lemoinei' and 'Klehm's').
FLOWERS: Double, fragrant, deep rose pink.
FRUIT: Yellow green, 1″ diameter.
HABIT: Vigorous, symmetrical; leaves large, dark green with an overcase of wine-red, 15 to 20′ high and wide.
DISEASES: Moderate scab, severe rust.

Malus 'Bridal Crown'
FLOWERS: Pure white buds open to white, double flowers.
FRUIT: Reddish, 1/2″ diameter.
HABIT: Upright tree reaching 12′ in height.

Malus 'Burgundy' (Simpson introduction).
FLOWERS: Abundant, dark red, fragrant.
FRUIT: Maroon.
HABIT: Vase-shaped, slender.

Malus 'Burton'
FLOWERS: Single, buds pink opening to white
FRUIT: Yellow, 1 7/8″ diameter.
DISEASES: Highly resistant.

Malus 'Butterfly'
FLOWERS: Bright pink buds open to light pink flowers.
FRUIT: Bright red, 3/8″ diameter.
HABIT: Small tree reaching 10′ high.

Malus 'Callaway'
Perhaps one of the best white-flowered crabapples for southern gardens because of excellent disease resistance as well as an apparently minimal flower bud chilling requirement. Mr. Fred Galle of Callaway Gardens made this selection from a number of *M. prunifolia* crabapples that he had ordered from a northern nursery. He noted that one was distinctly different from the others and thanks to his keen horticultural eye an excellent crabapple has become available and is in wholesale production.
FLOWERS: Single, expanding buds pink, open white, 1 to 1 1/2″ across, early April in the Piedmont area of Georgia; flowers later than rosy-bloom types, about 7 to 10 days later.
FRUIT: Large, reddish maroon, 3/4 to 1 1/4″ diameter fruits that may persist for an extended time.
HABIT: 15 to 25′ round-headed tree with graceful constitution.
DISEASES: Possibly the best crabapple for southern gardens; I have observed no scab on 'Callaway' in years when 'Almey' and 'Hopa' were almost leafless; Nichols 1980 survey lists it as slightly suscep-tible to mildew and fireblight, moderate to rust.

Malus 'Candied Apple' (also 'Weeping Candied Apple').
FLOWERS: Red buds opening to pink, single.
FRUIT: Bright cherry red, 5/8″ diameter, persistent.
HABIT: Branches pendulous; rather heavy textured leaves with an overcast of red, 10 to 15′ high.
DISEASES: Slight to moderate scab susceptibility; was selected from a batch of 'Hopa' seedlings so its scab susceptibility is not surprising.

Malus 'Cardinal's Robes'
FLOWERS: Single, bright orange-red buds open to bright red.
FRUIT: Bright red, about 1/2″ diameter.
HABIT: Medium sized rounded tree to 15′; leaves dark green; bark like a cherry tree.
DISEASES: Resistant.

Malus 'Carnival'
FLOWERS: Single, pinkish red buds open to white.
FRUIT: Gold-orange-red, to 1/3″ diameter, distinctive and showy, remains firm and persistent until heavy
    freeze.
HABIT: Small rounded tree, 10′; heavy textured dark green leaves.

Malus 'Centennial'
FLOWERS: Single, white.
FRUIT: Red-yellow, 1 7/8″ diameter.
DISEASES: Highly resistant.

Malus 'Centurion' (A Bob Simpson introduction, var. *zumi* × 'Almey').
FLOWERS: Red buds open to rose-red, flowers when young.
FRUIT: Glossy cherry red, 5/8″ across, attractive for several months.
HABIT: Upright branching, becoming more oval-rounded with maturity, 25′ by 15 to 20′.
DISEASES: Highly resistant.

Malus 'Christmas Holly'
FLOWERS: Buds bright red, opening to white, single, 1 1/2 to 1 5/8″ diameter.
FRUIT: Very bright red, 3/8″ across, stays hard and bright until after Christmas.
HABIT: Small spreading tree 10 to 15′ high.
DISEASES: Slight scab susceptibility.

Malus 'Color Parade'
FLOWERS: Single, bright red buds open to white.
FRUIT: Coral with red cheek, 1/2″ diameter, colors early and remains firm.
HABIT: Refined semi-weeper, 10 to 12′ high and wide; dark green leaves.
DISEASES: Very resistant.

Malus 'Copper King'
FLOWERS: Single, white buds open to large, spice fragrance flowers.
FRUIT: Reddish copper, 1/2″ diameter.
HABIT: Small rounded tree, to 12′; leaves dark green, leathery, turning yellow to orange in fall.
DISEASES: Resistant.

Malus 'Coralburst'—Developed at Gardenview Horticultural Park, Strongsville, Ohio.
FLOWERS: Coral-pink buds open to double rose-pink flowers.
FRUIT: Few, 1/2″ diameter, bronze, reddish orange.
HABIT: Dainty, dwarf type forming a rounded bushy head, grows 8 to 10′, grown both as a shrub and
    grafted on a standard; small dark green foliage.
DISEASES: Slight scab susceptibility.

Malus 'Coral Cascade'
FLOWERS: Buds coral-red opening to blush white, annual.
FRUIT: Pink-coral-orange, 3/8″ diameter, oval, colors in September becoming deeper coral with frost and
    persisting into January.
HABIT: To 15′, medium weeper, leaves deep green.
DISEASES: Highly resistant.

Malus 'Coralene'
FLOWERS: Single, red pink buds open to white.
FRUIT: Coral pink and copper, firm, persistent, colors early.
HABIT: Small, refined semi-weeper, 12′ high; medium green leaves.
DISEASES: Resistant.

Malus coronaria — Wild Sweet Crabapple
(mā′lus kôr-o-nār-i-à)
FLOWERS: Single, white tinged with rose, fragrant like violets, 1 1/2 to 2″ diameter, pink in bud, essentially the last crabapple to flower along with *M. angustifolia* and *M. ioensis.*
FRUIT: Yellowish green, 1 to 1 1/2″ diameter, orange-shaped, very harsh and acid.
HABIT: A tree 20 to 30′ high with a short trunk and a wide-spreading head of gray branches.
DISEASES: Very susceptible to rust.

M. c. 'Charlottae'
FLOWERS: Double (12 to 18 petals), fragrant, expanding buds flesh pink, open pale pink, 1 1/2 to 2″ diameter, annual.
FRUIT: Dark green, 1 1/5″ diameter.
FOLIAGE: Leaves apparently may turn excellent color in fall.
DISEASES: Susceptible to diseases.

M. c. 'Nieuwlandiana'
FLOWERS: Double, expanding buds rose-red, open pink, 2 1/5″ diameter, annual, fragrant.
FRUIT: Yellowish green, 1 3/5″ diameter.

Malus 'Cotton Candy'
FLOWERS: Annual, deep pink buds opening up semi-double to fully double, 3-tiered blossoms of deep pink.
FRUIT: Deep yellow, 1/2″ across, browns and falls soon after ripening.
HABIT: Slow-growing, upright-rounded tree to 10′ with heavy textured deep green leaves.
DISEASES: Slight scab susceptibility.

Malus 'David' — Named by Arie den Boer in 1957 after his grandson.
FLOWERS: Pink in bud, opening white, single, 1 1/2″ diameter.
FRUIT: Scarlet, 1/2″ diameter.
HABIT: Nice rounded habit, reminds of *M. floribunda;* foliage tends to conceal flowers and fruit.
DISEASES: Slight fireblight susceptibility.

Malus 'Dolgo' — Introduced in 1917 by South Dakota Agr. Expt. Station.
FLOWERS: Pink in bud, opening white, 1 3/4″ diameter, fragrant, flowering well in alternate years.
FRUIT: Bright red, purple, almost fluorescent, 1 1/4″ diameter, ripening in July and falling by late August, can be used for jelly.
HABIT: Open, but vigorous, wide-spreading, 30 to 40′.
DISEASES: Resistant but with slight scab, fireblight, and frogeye leaf spot susceptibility.

Malus 'Donald Wyman'
FLOWERS: Single, expanding buds red to pink, opening to white, 1 3/4″ across, tends toward alternate year pattern, but even in "off" years, is still showy.
FRUIT: Glossy bright red, approximately 3/8″ diameter, abundant, persistent into winter.
HABIT: Large spreading form, 20′ high and 25′ wide; lustrous dark green foliage.
DISEASES: Slightly susceptible to powdery mildew.

Malus 'Dorothea'
FLOWERS: Semidouble, 10 to 16 petals, expanding buds carmine, open-rose pink not fading to white, approximately 1 4/5″ diameter.
FRUIT: Yellow, approximately 1 4/5″ diameter.
HABIT: Rounded, dense branching, branches somewhat horizontal, 25′.
DISEASES: Severely susceptible to scab and fireblight, slightly susceptible to powdery mildew.

Malus 'Doubloons'
FLOWERS: Bright red buds, double white flowers.
FRUIT: Yellow-gold, 1/3″ diameter.
HABIT: Dense, rounded tree, 10 to 12′ high.
DISEASES: Good resistance.

Malus 'Egret'
FLOWERS: Deep pink buds open to semi-double or double pinkish white flowers.
FRUIT: Round, red, 3/8″ diameter.
HABIT: Weeping, 6′ high.

Malus 'Eleyi'
FLOWERS: Deep red in bud, opening reddish purple, 1 1/4″ across.
FRUIT: Reddish purple, conical.
HABIT: Broad headed, rounded, 20 to 25′ high and wide, leaves reddish purple, later purple green.
DISEASES: Very susceptible to scab.

Malus 'Ellen Gerhart'
FLOWERS: Semi-double, pale pink.
FRUIT: Red, small, persistent, relished by birds.
DISEASES: Very susceptible to scab.

Malus 'Ellwangeriana'
FLOWERS: Single, pink and white, alternate.
FRUIT: Bright red, 5/8″ diameter.
DISEASES: Moderate fireblight susceptibility, slight rust and mildew.

Malus 'Evelyn'
FLOWERS: Single, expanding buds deep rose-red, open rose-red to deep rose red, 1 2/5″ diameter, alternate.
FRUIT: Greenish yellow and red, 1 2/5″ diameter.
HABIT: Erect, 20′, foliage purplish initially, bronze-green at maturity; fall color listed as red-orange, purple.
DISEASES: Very resistant.

Malus 'Fiesta'
FLOWERS: Single, red in bud, open white.
FRUIT: Bright burnt coral to orange-gold, 1/3″ diameter, firm, persistent.
HABIT: Semi-weeper with slender, refined branches, 15′; dark green leaves.
DISEASES: Resistant.

Malus 'Firebelle'
FLOWERS: Single, red in bud, white at maturity, borne in heavy clusters.
FRUIT: Bright red, 1/3″ diameter, round, firm, persistent.
HABIT: Rounded tree, 12′; dark green foliage.
DISEASES: Resistant.

Malus 'Firebrand'
FLOWERS: Single, red in bud, open white.
FRUIT: Brilliant orange-red, 1/4″ diameter, abundant, extremely showy.
HABIT: Round headed tree, 14′; deep green leaves.
DISEASES: Resistant.

Malus 'Fireburst'
FLOWERS: Single, bright cherry-red buds, white flowers.
FRUIT: Bright red, 1/4″ diameter, showy, persisting until hard freeze.
HABIT: Upright or slightly spreading, 15′; dark green leaves.
DISEASES: Resistant.

Malus 'Firedance'
FLOWERS: Red buds open to white flowers.
FRUIT: Abundant, red.
HABIT: Weeping, 5′ high.

Malus 'Flame'—University of Minnesota introduction.
FLOWERS: Single, expanding buds pink, open white, 1 1/2″ diameter, annual.
FRUIT: Bright red, 4/5″ across, persistent.
HABIT: Tree, 25′.
DISEASES: Extremely susceptible to diseases; one writer says highly resistant; I opt for the former.

Malus floribunda — Japanese Flowering Crabapple. Introduced from Japan in 1862.
(mā′lus flō-ri-bun′dá)

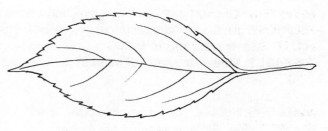

FLOWERS: Buds deep pink to red, flowers gradual-
    ly fading white, 1 to 1 1/2″ diameter, fragrant,
    annual.
FRUIT: Yellow and red, 3/8″ diameter, usually not
    persistent.
HABIT: Broad-rounded and densely branched, 15
    to 25′, one of the best crabapples, one that all
    others are compared to.
DISEASES: Slightly susceptible to scab and powdery mildew; moderately to fireblight.

Malus 'Garnet'
FLOWERS: Deep red buds open to blush white flowers.
FRUIT: Deep red, persistent.
HABIT: Small tree to about 8′ tall.
DISEASES: Resistant.

Malus 'Gibbs Golden Gage' — Originated in England in early 1920's.
FLOWERS: Single, buds pink, open white.
FRUIT: Yellow, 1″ diameter, waxy almost translucent.
HABIT: Small, rounded, 20′.
DISEASES: Highly resistant.

Malus 'Golden Dream'
FLOWERS: Single, red buds open white.
FRUIT: Bright yellow-gold, 1/4 to 1/3″ diameter, round, firm, persistent.
HABIT: Rounded tree, 12′; bright green foliage.
DISEASES: Resistant.

Malus 'Golden Galaxy'
FLOWERS: Single, pale pink buds, open white.
FRUIT: Bright gold, 1/2″ diameter, firm, persistent.
HABIT: Upright, fan-shaped, 16′; medium green leaves.
DISEASES: Resistant.

Malus 'Golden Gem'
FLOWERS: Single, white, 1 1/5″ diameter, pink buds.
FRUIT: Yellow, 1″ diameter, very freely borne and remaining long on the tree.
HABIT: Upright tree to 25′, spreads out with age.
DISEASES: Severely susceptible to fireblight; Shurtleff reports high resistance.

Malus 'Golden Hornet'
FLOWERS: Single, white, 1 1/5″ diameter, pink buds.
FRUIT: Yellow, 1″ diameter, very freely borne and remaining long on the tree.
HABIT: Upright tree to 25′, spreads out with age.
DISEASES: Severely susceptible to fireblight and scab.

Malus 'Goldilocks'
FLOWERS: Single, red buds open to white.
FRUIT: Golden copper, 1/4 to 1/3″ diameter, abundant, showy.
HABIT: Refined, semi-weeper, 15′; medium green leaves.

Malus 'Gorgeous'
FLOWERS: Single, 1 1/4″ diameter, pink buds followed by white flowers, annual.
FRUIT: Yellow, 1″ diameter, abundantly produced; have seen red listed for fruit color.
HABIT: Dense, rounded, 25 to 30′.
DISEASES: Moderate scab, slight fireblight and rust, severe mildew susceptibility.

Malus 'Guiding Star'
FLOWERS: Double, buds rose-pink, open white, 2 1/4″ diameter.
FRUIT: Yellow, 5/8″ diameter.
DISEASES: Slightly susceptible to scab, moderate to powdery mildew, very to fireblight.

Malus 'Gwendolyn'
FLOWERS: Single, pink flowers.
FRUIT: Red.
DISEASES: Resistant.

Malus 'Gypsy Dancer'
FLOWERS: Single, bright red buds, open white.
FRUIT: Red-orange-yellow-coral, 1/2″ diameter, brilliant, persistent.
HABIT: Very graceful, somewhat spreading tree, 14′; dark green leaves.
DISEASES: Resistant.

Malus halliana var. *parkmanii*
(mā′lus hâl-li-ā′ná pärk-man′ē-ī)
FLOWERS: Double (15 petals), neyron rose in bud, finally shell pink, 1 1/4″ diameter, annual, late flowering.
FRUIT: Dull red, 1/4″ diameter, obovoid.
HABIT: Upright, almost vase-shaped, dense branching, 15 to 18′; foliage leathery lustrous dark green.
DISEASES: Moderate rust and fireblight susceptibility.

Malus 'Harvest Gold'
FLOWERS: Single, pink in bud, white, flowers one week later than other crabs.
FRUIT: Gold, 3/5″ diameter, remaining colorful into December, and persisting until spring.
HABIT: Vigorous, moderately columnar, 30′ by 15′.
DISEASES: Highly resistant.

Malus 'Henningi' — Originated in Wrightsville, PA.
FLOWERS: Single, white.
FRUIT: Small, orange-red, 5/8″ diameter.
HABIT: Tree, upright-spreading, 25′ by 25′.
DISEASES: Highly resistant.

Malus 'Henry F. Dupont'
FLOWERS: Single and semidouble (5 to 10 petals), expanding buds purplish red to deep rose-red, open
    light purplish pink, fading to pale magenta, 1 1/2″ diameter, annual.
FRUIT: Brownish red, 1/3″ diameter.
HABIT: Rather open, low spreading, 20 to 30′; new foliage is maroon-red.
DISEASES: Severely susceptible to scab and fireblight, slightly susceptible to powdery mildew.

Malus 'Henry Kohankie'
FLOWERS: Buds pink, opening pinkish white to white, single, 1 1/4 to 1 1/2″ diameter.
FRUIT: Glossy red, ellipsoidal, 1″ diameter, persistent.
HABIT: Rounded, 18′ tall, similar spread.
DISEASES: Slight scab susceptibility.

Malus 'Hopa'
FLOWERS: Single, expanding buds dark red to purplish red, open rose-pink with almost white star in the center, approximately 1 1/2 to 2″ diameter.
FRUIT: Bright red to crimson, usually yellowish on shaded side, approximately 3/4 to 1″ diameter, ripen in August, drop by September.
HABIT: Spreading tree to 30′ high and wide.
DISEASES: This along with the old standards 'Almey' and 'Eleyi' should be on the discard list because of extreme disease susceptibility — especially to apple scab; in low rainfall areas probably acceptable.

Malus hupehensis (triploid, comes true to type from seed) — Tea Crabapple
(mā′lus hū-pe-en′sis)
FLOWERS: Deep pink buds, gradually fading white, 1 1/2″ diameter, fragrant, alternate; also a 'Rosea' form with pinker flowers.
FRUIT: Greenish yellow to red, 3/8″ diameter.
HABIT: Vase-shaped, decidedly picturesque, 20 to 25′ and larger.

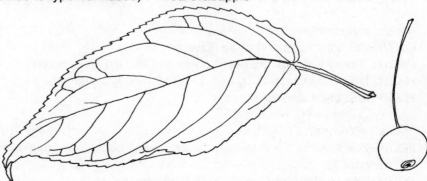

DISEASES: Severely susceptible to fireblight, never noticed any problems with trees on the Illinois campus; have also seen susceptibility listed as slight.

Malus hupehensis 'Cornell'
FLOWERS: Single, light pink in bud, open to pinkish white
FRUIT: Yellowish, turning red, 1/3″ diameter, persisting into winter.
HABIT: Vase-shaped.
DISEASES: Resistant to scab, cedar apple rust and leaf spot.

Malus 'Indian Magic' — A Bob Simpson introduction.
FLOWERS: Single, red buds open to deep pink, 1 1/2″ diameter.
FRUIT: Small glossy red, changing to orange, less than 1/2″ diameter, persisting.
HABIT: Rounded, 15 to 20′ by 15 to 20′.
DISEASES: Moderately susceptible to scab although Nichols in his 1980 survey reported severely
    susceptible to scab and slightly to rust; Shurtleff — moderately susceptible to scab.

Malus 'Indian Summer'
FLOWERS: Rose-red.
FRUIT: Bright red, 5/8 to 3/4″ diameter.
HABIT: Broad globe shape, 18′ by 19′; good fall color.
DISEASES: Resistant.

Malus ioensis — Prairie Crabapple
(mā′lus ī-ō-en′sis)
FLOWERS: Single, deep pink in bud, pink to white when open, fragrant, with the leaves, 1 1/2 to 2″
    diameter.
FRUIT: Dull yellowish green, 1 1/4 to 1 1/2″ diameter.
HABIT: Small, rounded tree, 20 to 30′ high and quite similar to *M. coronaria* in appearance differing in the
    more pubescent branches and undersides of the leaves.
DISEASES: Rust susceptible.

Malus ioensis 'Klehm's'
FLOWERS: Double, pink, fragrant, 2″ diameter.
FRUIT: Sparse, green, 1″ diameter.
HABIT: Rounded, 20 to 25′ tall, strong grower.
DISEASES: Resistant, but have seen reports of susceptibility to cedar apple rust.

Malus ioensis 'Plena' — Bechtel Crabapple
FLOWERS: Double (33 petals), buds and flowers pink, 2″ diameter, fragrant.
FRUIT: Green, 1 1/8″ diameter, few produced.
HABIT: Rounded, open, 30′; supposedly a 'Dwarf Bechtel' that grows about 8′ and has high fragrant double
    pink flowers is known.
DISEASES: Extremely susceptible to diseases, especially rust which induces foliage abscission.

Malus 'Jewelberry'
FLOWERS: Pink buds and white flowers.
FRUIT: Glossy red, 1/2″ diameter, persistent into fall, fruits heavily as a young tree.
HABIT: Dwarf, dense shrubby tree, 8′ by 12′, will grow larger.
DISEASES: Light scab and fireblight.

Malus 'Katherine'
FLOWERS: Double (15 to 24 petals), expanding buds deep pink, open pink fading to white, 2″ diameter,
    annual.
FRUIT: Yellow with a red cheek, 1/4″ diameter.
HABIT: Loose and open, 20′.
DISEASES: Resistant to scab and fireblight; also reportedly susceptible to scab.

Malus 'Kelsey'
FLOWERS: Semi-double, 10 to 16 petals, purplish red with a white marking at base of each petal.
FRUIT: 4/5″ diameter, shiny dark red-purple, persistent.
HABIT: Upright tree 18′ by 18′.

Malus 'Kibele'
FLOWERS: Dark red buds open rose-pink, single.
FRUIT: Dark burgundy red, 1/2″ diameter.
HABIT: Small, compact, spreading, maturing at 8′ and represents one of the smallest pink-flowered forms.
DISEASES: Slight scab, moderate fireblight.

Malus 'Kirk'
FLOWERS: Red buds open to white flowers.
FRUIT: Rich red, abundant, 7/8″ diameter.
HABIT: Upright rounded, 15′ in height.

Malus 'Koi'
FLOWERS: Single, red-pink buds, open white.
FRUIT: Bright orange-red, 1/2″ diameter, firm and persistent into February.
HABIT: Upright, fan-shaped tree, 14′; medium green leaves.
DISEASES: Resistant.

Malus 'Lady Northcliffe'
FLOWERS: Single, expanding buds rose-red, open pale pink fading to white, 1″ diameter.
FRUIT: Yellow and red, 3/5″ diameter.
DISEASES: Resistant to scab.

Malus 'Leprechaun'
FLOWERS: Red buds open to white flowers.
FRUIT: Very heavy, round, 1/8 to 1/4″ diameter, persistent.
HABIT: Small tree to about 8′.

Malus 'Limelight'
FLOWERS: Single, light pinkish buds, open white.
FRUIT: Lime-chartreuse, 1/2″ wide by 3/4″ long, firm and persistent until frozen.
HABIT: Rounded tree, 16′; heavy textured, leathery dark green leaves.
DISEASES: Resistant.

Malus 'Liset' — Originated in the Netherlands.
FLOWERS: Single, expanding buds dark crimson, open rose-red to light crimson, approximately 1 1/2″ diameter.
FRUIT: Dark crimson to maroon-red, glossy, approximately 1/2″ diameter, persistent.
HABIT: Rounded, dense, 15 to 20′; deep purplish green leaves.
DISEASES: Moderately susceptible to powdery mildew, slightly susceptible to fireblight.

Malus 'Little Troll'
FLOWERS: single, brilliant red buds, open white; numerous flowers form cascades along the branches.
FRUIT: Orange-red, 1/3″ wide, firm, persistent.
HABIT: Very refined, graceful weeper, 16′; dark green leaves.
DISEASES: Resistant.

Malus 'Louisa'
FLOWERS: Pink.
FRUIT: Yellow, 3/8" diameter, persistent.
HABIT: Broad weeping, 15' by 15', glossy dark green foliage.
DISEASES: Susceptible to scab.

Malus 'Lullaby'
FLOWERS: Red buds open to large ruffled coral, rose and white-tinted candy-striped semi double flowers.
FRUIT: Golden orange.
HABIT: Low, weeping form, about 6' in height; large deep green foliage.
DISEASES: Highly resistant.

Malus 'Luwick'
FLOWERS: Deep pink buds open to pale pink ruffled flowers.
FRUIT: Red, sparse.
HABIT: Weeping, reaching about 5' with narrow leaves.

Malus 'Madonna'
FLOWERS: Double, buds pink opening to white, blooms early and holds a long time.
FRUIT: Golden with red blush, 1/2" diameter.
HABIT: Compact upright, 20' tall by 10' wide; new growth bronze, mature dark green.
DISEASES: Tolerant.

Malus 'Makamik' — Developed about 1921 in Canada.
FLOWERS: Single, expanding buds dark red, open purplish red fading to a lighter tint, 2" diameter.
FRUIT: Purplish red, 3/4" diameter, good fruiter with fruits holding late.
HABIT: Rounded, 40', bronze foliage.
DISEASES: Severely susceptible to mildew, slightly susceptible to fireblight.

Malus 'Manbeck Weeper'
FLOWERS: Abundant pink and white blossoms.
FRUIT: Bright red.
HABIT: Strong central leader.
DISEASES: Resistant.

Malus 'Mandarin Magic'
FLOWERS: Single, buds reddish pink, open white.
FRUIT: Green cheeked with red, turning orange-cheeked, bright red and yellow, 1/2" wide by 3/4" long, firm and persistent, colors late.
HABIT: Spreading, 17'; dark green leaves.
DISEASES: Resistant.

Malus 'Maria'
FLOWERS: Rose-red buds open to fragrant reddish pink flowers which fade with age.
FRUIT: Shiny deep red, abundant, 1/2" diameter.
HABIT: Moderately weeping, 12' high; bronze new growth.
DISEASES: Resistant.

Malus 'Marshall Oyama'
FLOWERS: Single pink buds followed by white flowers, 1 5/8" diameter, annual.
FRUIT: Yellow and red, 1" diameter.
HABIT: Narrowly upright, 25' high.
DISEASES: Resistant to scab and fireblight.

Malus 'Mary Potter' — Introduced by Arnold Arboretum in 1947; supposedly a triploid and will come true from seed.
FLOWERS: Single, expanding buds pink, open white, 1″ diameter.
FRUIT: Red, 1/2″ diameter.
HABIT: Cross between *M.* × *atrosanguinea* × *M. sargentii* var. *rosea,* 10 to 15′ high, 15 to 20′ wide, dense, mounded, spreading, low-branched, a fine plant; lustrous dark green foliage.
DISEASES: Moderately susceptible to scab, powdery mildew, fireblight, and frogeye leaf spot; have not seen any serious problems.

Malus 'Matador'
FLOWERS: Single, bright red buds, open white.
FRUIT: Brilliant red, 1/3″ diameter, firm and persistent.
HABIT: Wide spreading tree, 14′; dark green leaves.
DISEASES: Resistant.

Malus 'Maysong'
FLOWERS: Single, pinkish white buds, open white.
FRUIT: Medium red, about 1/2″ diameter.
HABIT: Upright, narrow tree, 20′, becoming more spreading to vase shape with age; deep green, heavily textured leaves.
DISEASES: Resistant.

Malus × *micromalus* 'Midget' — Midget Crabapple *(M. baccata* × *M. spectabilis).*
(mā′lus mi-krō-mā′lus)
FLOWERS: Single, deep red in bud, opening to pale pink at edge, deeper pink in center.
FRUIT: Red, 1/2″ diameter.
HABIT: Small, erect branched tree.
DISEASES: Very susceptible to diseases.

Malus 'Mollie Ann'
FLOWERS: Deep red buds open to white flowers.
FRUIT: Buff-gold, 1/2″ diameter.
HABIT: Semi-weeping, growing to 8′.
DISEASES: Resistant.

Malus 'Molten Lava' — Lake County Nursery introduction.
FLOWERS: Deep red in bud, opening to single white, 1 1/2″ diameter flowers, annual.
FRUIT: Red-orange, 3/8″ across, remaining firm into early December.
HABIT: Wide-spreading weeper, 15′ by 12′, with attractive yellow bark in winter.
DISEASES: Highly resistant.

Malus 'Moonglow'
FLOWERS: Single, bright red buds, open white.
FRUIT: Lime-chartreuse with a rose cheek turning to pale lemon with a rose-coral cheek, 1/3″ diameter, firm and persistent.
HABIT: Rounded tree, 12′; dark green leaves.
DISEASES: Resistant.

Malus 'Mount Arbor Special'
FLOWERS: Carmine buds and flowers fade to dull pink.
FRUIT: Red, 3/4″ diameter, russet dotted, not persistent.
HABIT: Irregular.
DISEASES: Highly resistant.

Malus 'Narragansett' (National Arboretum introduction).
FLOWERS: Red buds open to white with pink tinge.
FRUIT: Cherry red with light orange underside, 1/2″ diameter.
HABIT: Broad-crowned small tree.
DISEASES: Resistant to scab, fireblight, rust and mildew.

Malus 'Oekonomierat Echtermeyer'
FLOWERS: Single, expanding buds deep purplish red, open purplish pink, 1 3/5″ diameter.
FRUIT: Purplish red before ripening, later turning a dark reddish brown to greenish brown, 1″ diameter.
HABIT: Semi-weeping, 15′ by 15 to 18′, purplish foliage when young, maturing purplish green.
DISEASES: Extremely susceptible to diseases, especially scab.

Malus 'Ormiston Roy'
FLOWERS: Single, expanding buds rose-red turning pale rose-pink, open white, 1 3/5″ diameter, annual.
FRUIT: Orange-yellow with reddish blush, 3/8″ diameter, persistent.
HABIT: Upright in youth, assuming the shape of *M. floribunda* with age but not as dense, 20′ by 25′.
DISEASES: Slight scab and rust, moderate fireblight.

Malus 'Pagoda'
FLOWERS: Single, bright carmine buds, open white.
FRUIT: Brilliant orange-red, 1/3″ diameter, firm and persistent.
HABIT: Small, rounded weeper, 12′; dark green leaves.
DISEASES: Resistant.

Malus 'Park Center'
FLOWERS: Light pink.
FRUIT: Golden, small.
HABIT: 25′, vigorous.
DISEASES: High resistance.

Malus 'Peter Pan'
FLOWERS: Single, bright red buds, open white.
FRUIT: Bright red, 1/4″ diameter, firm, persistent, turning copper red with heavy frosts.
HABIT: Rounded tree, 14′; medium green leaves.
DISEASES: High resistance.

Malus 'Pink Perfection' (Seedling from 'Katherine' × 'Almey').
FLOWERS: Red in bud, opening to large clear pink double flowers.
FRUIT: Sparse, yellow, 1/2″ diameter.
HABIT: 20′ by 20′.
DISEASES: Extremely scab susceptible.

Malus 'Pink Princess'
FLOWERS: Rose-pink, single.
FRUIT: Deep red, 1/4″ diameter, persistent.
HABIT: Low spreading, 15′ by 12′; reddish spring foliage turns reddish green.
DISEASES: Slightly susceptible to scale.

Malus 'Pink Spires'
FLOWERS: Full dark lavender buds open to lavender and fade to pale lavender, early.
FRUIT: Purplish red, persistent.
HABIT: Upright grower with copper-colored fall foliage, foliage reddish in spring, 25′.
DISEASES: Moderately susceptible to scab, slightly to fireblight and leaf spot.

Malus 'Prairifire'
FLOWERS: Buds red opening to dark pinkish red flowers.
FRUIT: Dark red-purple, small, persistent.
HABIT: Upright when young, later rounded, 20′ high and wide, new growth reddish maroon maturing to
    dark green.
DISEASES: Very resistant.

Malus 'Prince Georges'
FLOWERS: Double (50 to 61 petals), expanding buds deep rose-pink, open light rose-pink, 2″ diameter,
    annual, exceedingly fragrant, smells like a good rose.
FRUIT: Not known to produce fruit.
HABIT: Upright, dense, eventually rounded, 15 to 20′ by 15 to 20′.
DISEASES: Resistant although its parentage *(M. angustifolia* × *M. ioensis* 'Plena') suggests it should be
    rust susceptible.

Malus 'Professor Sprenger'
FLOWERS: Single, expanding buds pink, open white.
FRUIT: Orange-red, 1/2 to 5/8″ diameter, persistent into November-December.
HABIT: Densely upright spreading.
DISEASES: Highly resistant.

Malus 'Profusion'
FLOWERS: Single, expanding buds deep red, open purplish red fading to purplish pink, 1 3/5″ across.
FRUIT: Oxblood red, 1/2″ diameter, persistent.
HABIT: Small tree of excellent constitution, new foliage purple fading to bronze.
DISEASES: Moderately susceptible to powdery mildew, slightly susceptible to scab and fireblight.

Malus prunifolia — Plumleaf Crabapple
(mā′lus prū-ni-fō′li-a)
FLOWERS: Single, pink to red in bud, opening white, fragrant, 1 1/2″ diameter.
FRUIT: Round or ovoid, yellowish or red, 1″ diameter.
HABIT: Small tree.
DISEASES: Scab susceptible.

Malus p. var. *rinkii:* Differs in being more downy and having pink flowers (usually); highly scab susceptible.

Malus pumila 'Niedzwetzkyana' *(M. niedzwetzkyana* of some authors).
(mā′lus pū′mil-a̲)
Young leaves, flowers, fruit including the flesh, bark and wood of branches purplish red. This form is a
parent of many crabapples. Resistant to fireblight and variable resistance to scab. Often listed as highly
susceptible to scab and from my observations this is the case. One of the parents of the rosy bloom
group ('Almey', 'Chilko', 'Simcoe', 'Hopa', etc.)

Malus 'Purple Prince'
FLOWERS: Single, carmine-red buds, open to bright red.
FRUIT: Bluish purple with a fine blue cast, about 1/2″ diameter.
HABIT: Rounded, 17′; deep purple-green leaves; bark like a cherry.
DISEASES: Resistant.

Malus × *purpurea* 'Lemoine' *(M. niedzwetzkyana* × *M.* × *atrosanguinea)*
(mā′lus pēr-pū′rē-a̲ le-moyn)
FLOWERS: Single and semidouble, expanding buds dark red, open purple-red to crimson fading to lighter
    shades, 1 1/2″ diameter, annual.

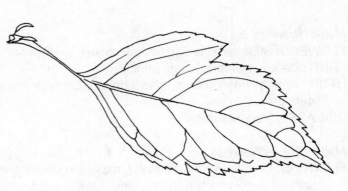

FRUIT: Purplish red, 5/8″ diameter.
HABIT: Dense wide spreading outline, 25′, leaves purplish when unfolding and becoming deep green later.
DISEASES: Highly susceptible to scab and fireblight.

Malus 'Radiant' — A University of Minnesota introduction.
FLOWERS: Single, expanding buds deep red, open deep pink, annual.
FRUIT: Bright red, approximately 1/2″ diameter, persistent.
HABIT: Compact, round-headed, 25 to 30′; young leaves reddish changing to green.
DISEASES: Very susceptible to scab.

Malus 'Red Baron' — Simpson Introduction, selected from Arnold Arboretum.
FLOWERS: Single, very deep red buds open to reddish to pink flowers.
FRUIT: Glossy dark red, 1/2″ across.
HABIT: Moderately columnar, 20′ by 12′; as broad as tall at maturity.
DISEASES: Severely susceptible to scab, slightly susceptible to fireblight and rust.

Malus 'Red Bird'
FLOWERS: Single, white.
FRUIT: Bright red, persistent.
HABIT: Rounded, 12 to 15′ high and wide.

Malus 'Red Jade' — Introduced by Brooklyn Botanic Garden.
FLOWERS: Single, expanding buds deep pink, open white, 1 3/5″ diameter, alternate.
FRUIT: Glossy red, 1/2″ diameter, birds like the fruits.
HABIT: Weeping, 15′ of a graceful pendulous nature; graft incompatibilities are a problem.
DISEASES: Moderately susceptible to scab and powdery mildew, have been reports of fireblight susceptibility.

Malus 'Red Jewel'
FLOWERS: White, single, abundant.
FRUIT: Bright cherry red, less than 1/2″ diameter, persisting with color until mid-December, color becomes darker in cold weather.
HABIT: Medium-sized, horizontally branched, rounded, 15′ by 12′.
DISEASES: Moderately susceptible to scab, fireblight, slightly to mildew.

Malus 'Red Peacock'
FLOWERS: Large, soft pink, ruffled.
FRUIT: Shiny red, 1/2″ diameter, persistent.
FOLIAGE: Clean dark green.

Malus 'Red Silver' — A South Dakota State University introduction.
FLOWERS: China-rose color, 1 1/2″ diameter, single, alternate.
FRUIT: Purplish red, 3/4″ diameter.
HABIT: Dense, 30′, with purplish red leaves turning reddish green.
DISEASES: Extremely susceptible to scab, the leaves fall off before your eyes in June or July.

Malus 'Red Snow'
FLOWERS: Orange-red buds open to creamy, slightly pinkish, 1 1/2″ diameter flowers.
FRUIT: Bright red, oblong, 5/16″ wide, persistent into December and January.
HABIT: Small tree 8 to 10′ high with long, graceful, arching branches and fine stems; leaves fine and narrow with a leathery texture, turn attractive gold in fall.
DISEASES: Highly resistant.

Malus 'Red Splendor'
FLOWERS: Single, expanding buds rose-red, open pink to rose-pink, 1 4/5″ diameter, alternate according to Dr. John Pair, Kansas State.
FRUIT: Red, 3/5″ diameter, persistent.
HABIT: Upright, more or less open tree 20 to 30′; dark reddish green foliage turning reddish purple in fall.
DISEASES: Slightly susceptible to scab, moderate to fireblight, in 1980 survey Nichols found severe scab.

Malus 'Red Swan'
FLOWERS: Light pink, bell-shaped flowers turn white.
FRUIT: Bright red, elliptical, 1/4 to 1/2″ diameter.
HABIT: Weeping, graceful, finely branched, to 10′.

Malus 'Robinson' — Introduced by C.M. Hobbs, Indianapolis.
FLOWERS: Single, crimson buds opening to deep pink flowers.
FRUIT: Dark red, 3/8″ diameter.
HABIT: Upright-spreading, dense branching, 25′.
DISEASES: Highly resistant.

Malus × *robusta* (Hybrids between *M. baccata* and *M. prunifolia*).
(mā′lus × rō-bus′tà)
FLOWERS: Single and semidouble, expanding buds white with trace of pink, open pure white.
FRUIT: Yellow and red to dark crimson, 1″ diameter.
HABIT: Oval-shaped, dense branching, 40′.
DISEASES: Resistant to scab, variable to fireblight.

M. × *r.* 'Erecta'
   Upright to moderate vase shaped habit when young, with maturity opens up as side branches are often weighted down with fruits, 40′, same flowers as above.

M. × *r.* 'Persicifolia'
   Single, white flowers; excellent red ornamental fruits, sometimes with a yellowish or brownish cheek, 3/4″ diameter; hang on late in season; slightly susceptible to scab and fireblight; leaves narrow, resembling a peach; 40′.

Malus 'Rockii'
FLOWERS: Single, pink buds opening to white flowers.
FRUIT: Bright red, approximately 1/2″ diameter.
DISEASES: Moderately susceptible to powdery mildew, slightly to scab.

Malus 'Rosseau'
FLOWERS: Single, expanding buds maroon-red, open purplish to rose-red with white claw, 1 3/5″ diameter, annual.
FRUIT: Carmine to light jasper red, 1″ diameter.
HABIT: Rounded, dense, 40′.
DISEASES: Resistant to scab and fireblight.

Malus 'Royal Ruby'
FLOWERS: Double, red-pink, 1 to 2″ across, annual flowers at an early age.
FRUIT: Red, 1/2″ across, limitedly produced.
HABIT: Vigorous, upright tree to 10 to 15′ with glossy dark green foliage.
DISEASES: Severely susceptible to scab.

Malus 'Royal Splendor'
FLOWERS: Single, red-pink buds, open white, produced in heavy cascades along the branches.
FRUIT: Brilliant red, about 1/2″ diameter, firm and persistent into midwinter.
HABIT: Spreading weeper, 10′ by 11 to 12′; green leaves.
DISEASES: Resistant.

Malus 'Royalty'
FLOWERS: Single, crimson, almost purple, annual, sparsely produced.
FRUIT: Dark red-purple, 5/8″ diameter, sparse.
HABIT: 15′ to 20′, upright, one of the best purple foliaged forms, leaves are glossy purple in spring, purple-green in mid-summer, and brilliant purple in fall.
DISEASES: Severely susceptible to scab and fireblight.

Malus sargentii — Sargent Crabapple
(mā′lus sär-jen′tē-ī)
FLOWERS: Single, red in bud opening white, 3/4 to 1″ diameter, fragrant, annual or alternate; this seems to be variable.
FRUIT: Bright red, 1/4″ diameter, birds like them.
HABIT: Mounded, dense branching, wide spreading, 6 to 8′(10′) high, one and one-half to twice that in spread.
DISEASES: Slightly susceptible to scab, fireblight and leaf spot.

M. s. 'Rosea'
Similar to species except flower buds darker pink in bud, 1 1/2″ across, taller growing and more susceptible to fireblight and scab, 8′ by 10′.

M. s. 'Roseglow'
A SCS, USDA, Rose Lake Plant Materials Center Release; 8′ high by 10′ wide, densely branched, white fragrant flowers, dark red, 1/4″ diameter fruit; seed produced cultivar.

Malus 'Satin Cloud'
FLOWERS: Buds pale white, open to pure white fragrant flowers.
FRUIT: Amber yellow, 3/8″ diameter.
HABIT: Dwarf with dense rounded crown; red fall color.

Malus × *scheideckeri* (Hybrid between *M. floribunda* and *M. prunifolia*).
(mā′lus shī-dek′ēr-i)
FLOWERS: Double (10 petals), pale pink, 1 1/2″ diameter, annual.
FRUIT: Yellow to orange, 5/8″ diameter.
HABIT: Upright, dense, vase-shaped, 20 to 30′.
DISEASES: Extremely susceptible to diseases and not a good landscape plant.

Malus 'Sea Foam'
FLOWERS: Deep red buds open to pure white flowers.
FRUIT: Bright red, 3/8 to 1/2″ diameter.
HABIT: Low, strongly weeping, 5′ or less ultimate height.
DISEASES: Highly resistant.

Malus 'Selkirk' — A Morden introduction in 1962.
FLOWERS: Rose-red, 1 1/2″ diameter, single to semi-double, annual or alternate, inconsistent.
FRUIT: Glossy purplish red, 4/5″ diameter; about the glossiest fruits of any crabapple.
HABIT: Open, upright, somewhat vase-shaped, 25′ by 25′.
DISEASES: Moderately susceptible to scab, fireblight and powdery mildew.

Malus 'Sensation'
FLOWERS: Single, carmine red in bud, open white.
FRUIT: Bright orange with red cheeks, 1/2″ wide, firm, persistent.
HABIT: Graceful, semi-weeper, 12′; dark green leaves.
DISEASES: Resistant.

Malus 'Sentinel' — A Bob Simpson introduction.
FLOWERS: Single, pale pink.
FRUIT: Small, red, 1/2″ diameter, persistent.
HABIT: Moderately columnar.
DISEASES: Slight scab and fireblight susceptibility.

Malus 'Serenade'
FLOWERS: Deep pink buds open to pale blush white flowers.
FRUIT: Pale yellow with orange-gold tinge, becoming burnt orange when mature.
HABIT: Graceful, semi-weeping, 12′ high.

Malus 'Shaker's Gold'
FLOWERS: Soft pink in bud, opening to white, 1 5/8″ across, single.
FRUIT: Light yellow then with frost to deeper yellow with orange cheeks touched with reddish, persistent
    and firm into January.
HABIT: Upright, spreading, to 16′.
DISEASES: Severely susceptible to fireblight.

Malus sieboldii
(mā′lus sē-bōl′dē-ī)
FLOWERS: Pink buds, fading white, fragrant, 3/4″ diameter; may also range from pale pink to rose.
FRUIT: Yellow to red, 3/8″ diameter, bearing annually, long persistent.
HABIT: Mounded, dense branching, rarely more than 10 to 15′ high but known to 30′ in the wild.

Malus sieboldii 'Fuji'
FLOWERS: Double, 13 to 15 petals, expanding buds purplish red, open greenish white with occasional
    traces of purplish red, approximately 1 1/2″ diameter.
FRUIT: Orange, approximately 1/2″ diameter, abundant.
HABIT: Large tree at maturity, original tree is 28′ high and 46′ wide; has ascending, declining and irregular
    branching.
DISEASES: Moderately susceptible to powdery mildew and scab.

Malus sieboldii var. *zumi*
FLOWERS: Single, pink in bud becoming white after opening, 1 to 1 1/4″ diameter, alternate.
FRUIT: Red, 3/8″ diameter, globose.
HABIT: Small tree of pyramidal habit, 20′; may become rounded, have seen considerable variation.
DISEASES: Moderately susceptible to scab.

Malus sieboldii var. *zumi* 'Calocarpa'
FLOWERS: Single, expanding buds deep red, open white to pinkish white, 1 2/5″ diameter, fragrant,
    annual, acts as a biennial bearer at times.

FRUIT: Bright red, 1/2″ diameter, abundant, persistent into December.

HABIT: Dense, rounded, rich lustrous dark green foliage, 25′ by 25′.

DISEASES: Slightly susceptible to scab, powdery mildew and severely susceptible to fireblight.

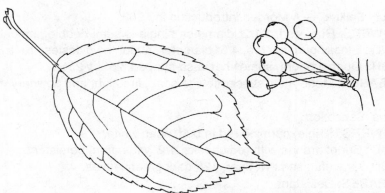

Malus sieboldii var. *zumi* 'Calocarpa'

Malus sikkimensis — Sikkim Crabapple
(mā′lus sik-ki-men′sis)
FLOWERS: Single, rose in bud, opening white, 1″ across, annual.
FRUIT: Pear-shaped, dark red with pale dots, 5/8″ long and wide.
HABIT: Small tree of low, bushy habit; distinct among crabapples because of the excessive development of stout, rigid branching spurs on the trunk.
DISEASES: Resistant to scab, susceptible to fireblight.

Malus 'Silver Moon' — A Bob Simpson introduction.
FLOWERS: Pink in bud, opening to white, 1 1/2″ diameter, flowers at terminals after tree is in full leaf, alternate.
FRUIT: Tiny, purple-red, persistent.
HABIT: Compact, narrow-upright, eventually moderately ovate, 20′ by 12′.
DISEASES: Moderate scab and frogeye leafspot, severe fireblight.

Malus 'Sinai Fire'
FLOWERS: Single, brilliant red buds, open white.
FRUIT: Brilliant orange-red with a waxy sheen, 1/4 to 1/3″ diameter, firm, persistent.
HABIT: Upright weeper with very downward weeping branches, 12′ high and wide; rich dark green leaves.
DISEASES: Very resistant.

Malus 'Sissipuk'
FLOWERS: Single, expanding buds deep carmine, open rose-pink fading to pale pink, 1 1/8″ diameter, annual.
FRUIT: Dark maroon-purple to oxblood red, 1″ diameter.
HABIT: Rounded, 40′.
DISEASES: Resistant to scab and fireblight.

Malus 'Snowcloud'
FLOWERS: Pink buds open to large double white flowers.
FRUIT: Yellow, 1/2″ diameter, not abundant.
HABIT: Upright, 22′ by 15′.
DISEASES: High susceptibility.

Malus 'Snowdrift' — Introduced by Cole Nursery.
FLOWERS: Single, expanding buds pink, open white, 1 1/4″ diameter, annual, abundant.
FRUIT: Orange-red, 3/8″ diameter.
HABIT: Rounded, dense, good vigorous grower, 15 to 20′ by 15 to 20′, heavy textured, lustrous dark green foliage.
DISEASES: Slightly susceptible to scab, 1980 evaluation lists it as severely susceptible to fireblight, have seen moderate listing.

Malus 'Snow Magic'
FLOWERS: Pink buds open to white flowers.
FRUIT: Deep red.
HABIT: Compact pyramidal.
DISEASES: Good resistance.

Malus 'Sparkler' — University of Minnesota introduction.
FLOWERS: Bright rose-red, abundant.
FRUIT: 1/3″ diameter, dark red.
HABIT: A flat-topped, wide-spreading tree, 15′ high and 24′ wide; new foliage emerges reddish, matures
     to dark green.
DISEASES: Scab susceptible.

Malus spectabilis — Chinese Crabapple
(mā′lus spek-tab′i-lis)
FLOWERS: Often double, deep rosy-red in bud, paling to blush-tint when fully open, 2″ diameter.
FRUIT: Yellow, 3/4 to 1″ diameter, poor fruiter.
HABIT: A tree to 30′ forming a rounded head of branches as wide as high.
DISEASES: Highly resistant to fireblight, variable to scab.

Malus spectabilis 'Riversii'
FLOWERS: Pink, double (up to 20 petals), 2″ diameter, alternate bearer.
FRUIT: Green, 1 1/4″ diameter, not effective.
HABIT: Open, 25′.
DISEASES: Highly resistant to fireblight, variable to scab.

Malus 'Spring Snow'
FLOWERS: White, considered sterile equivalent of 'Dolgo'.
FRUIT: Few to none.
HABIT: Dense upright oval tree, 20 to 25′ tall.
DISEASES: Severely susceptible to scab; slightly susceptible to cedar apple rust and fireblight.

Malus 'Spring Song'
FLOWERS: Deep rose buds open to light pink fading to white, flowers about 2″ across.
FRUIT: Bright red, 1/2″ diameter.
HABIT: Small upright compact rounded tree, 10′ high.
DISEASES: Resistant.

Malus 'Strathmore'
FLOWERS: Dark red.
FRUIT: Red-purple.
HABIT: Narrow vase-shaped, 20′ by 5 to 8′, reddish new foliage.
DISEASES: Highly susceptible.

Malus 'Strawberry Parfait'
FLOWERS: Red buds open to large, pink flowers with red margins; heavy bloomer.
FRUIT: Yellow with red blush, 1/2″ diameter.
HABIT: Open, vase shaped, 20′ by 25′; purple tinged new leaves become leathery dark green.
DISEASES: Very resistant.

Malus 'Sugar Tyme'
FLOWERS: Pale pink buds open to sugar white fragrant flowers.
FRUIT: Red, 1/2″ diameter, abundant, persistent.
HABIT: Upright oval, vigorous, 18′ by 15′.
DISEASES: Very resistant.

Malus 'Sunset'
FLOWERS: Orange-red buds open to bright red to mauve flowers.
FRUIT: Deep red.
HABIT: Small upright tree; leaves purple-red.

Malus 'Tanner'
FLOWERS: Single, white, 1 1/2″ diameter, alternate.
FRUIT: Red, 5/8″ diameter.
HABIT: Low, 20′.
DISEASES: Highly susceptible.

Malus 'Tea Time'
FLOWERS: Single, pale pink buds, open white.
FRUIT: Lime-chartreuse with a red cheek, 1/3″ diameter, firm and persistent.
HABIT: Upright, vase-shaped tree, 25′; dark green leaves.
DISEASES: Resistant.

Malus 'Thunderchild'
FLOWERS: Single, delicate pink to rose.
FRUIT: Dark red, purple, 1/2″ diameter.
HABIT: Compact upright spreading, broad oval to rounded.
DISEASES: Resistant.

Malus 'Tina'
FLOWERS: White, yellow centers, single, pink to red buds.
FRUIT: Red, small.
HABIT: Supposedly a dwarf Sargent type with low spreading form, 12 to 18″ high plant was 3 to 3 1/2′
        wide; will grow to 5′ in height.
DISEASES: Highly resistant.

Malus toringoides var. *macrocarpa*
(mā′lus tôr-in-goy′dēz mak-rō-kär′på)
FLOWERS: White, 3/4″ diameter, fragrant, alternate, expanding buds pink or pinkish white.
FRUIT: Pear shaped, 1″ diameter, yellow on shaded side, red on sunny side.
HABIT: Upright-pyramidal, dense branching, 25′.
DISEASES: Resistant to scab and rust.

Malus tschonoskii — Tschonoski Crabapple
(mā′lus shō-nos′kē ī)
FLOWERS: Slight pink finally white, not showy, 1 to 1 1/4″ diameter.
FRUIT: Yellow-green, somewhat russet-dotted, 1 to 1 1/4″ wide.
FOLIAGE: New leaves silver gray, changing to dark green and excellent apricot-red in fall, one of the best
        crabapples for fall color.
HABIT: Large tree, 30 to 40′ high.
DISEASES: Slight scab, severe fireblight.

Malus 'Van Eseltine' (a suspected hybrid between *M. spectabilis* × *M.* × *arnoldiana*).
FLOWERS: Double (13 to 19 petals), expanding buds deep rose to rose-pink, often pink fading to pale
        pink, 2″ diameter, alternate bearer.
FRUIT: Yellow, with brown or light carmine cheek, 3/4″ diameter.
HABIT: Narrowly upright, 20′ by 10′, vase-shaped crown.
DISEASES: Severely susceptible to scab and fireblight.

Malus 'Vanguard'
FLOWERS: Single, rose-red, 2″ diameter, annual.
FRUIT: Red, 5/8 to 3/4″ diameter, persistent.
HABIT: Dense, somewhat vase-shaped, 18′ by 10′.
DISEASES: Highly susceptible to scab.

Malus 'Velvet Pillar'
FLOWERS: Single, pink, sparse.
FRUIT: Red, 1/2″ diameter.
HABIT: Upright columnar, 20′ by 14′; dull purple foliage.
DISEASES: Scab susceptible.

Malus 'Volcano'
FLOWERS: Red buds open to white flowers.
FRUIT: Orange-red, 3/8 to 1/2″ diameter, abundant.
HABIT: Small upright tree, 10′ in height.
DISEASES: Highly resistant to scab.

Malus 'White Angel' (also termed 'Inglis')
FLOWERS: Single, 1″ diameter, pure white, heavy flowerer, expanding buds pink.
FRUIT: Glossy red, 1/2 to 3/4″ diameter, heavy fruiter, almost overbears.
HABIT: Tends toward a rounded tree but often irregular because of heavy fruit loads, 20′ by 20′; lustrous dark green foliage.
DISEASES: Slight scab and rust, slight to moderate fireblight.

Malus 'White Candle' — Introduced by Inter-State Nurseries, 1970.
FLOWERS: Semi-double, white, one reference said pale pink, 1 1/2″ diameter, borne in great quantity.
FRUIT: Red, 5/8″ diameter, limitedly produced.
HABIT: 12 to 15′ by 2 to 3′ wide, good upright type.
DISEASES: Slightly susceptible to scab and fireblight.

Malus 'White Cascade'
FLOWERS: Single buds deep pink, white flowers uniformly from top to bottom, gives the appearance of a cascading waterfall.
FRUIT: Yellow, small, pea-size.
HABIT: 10 to 15′, gracefully pendulous.
DISEASES: Resistant, based on current data; has not been extensively tested.

Malus 'Wies'
FLOWERS: Single, pink.
FRUIT: Very dark red to purple, 1/2 to 5/8″ diameter.
HABIT: Upright, leaves purplish.
DISEASES: Highly resistant.

Malus 'Wildfire'
FLOWERS: Single, bright red buds, open pink.
FRUIT: Brilliant red, 1/4 to 1/2″ diameter, firm, persistent.
HABIT: Semi-weeper with attractive form, 16′; dark reddish green leaves.
DISEASES: Resistant.

Malus 'Winter Gold'
FLOWERS: Single, expanding buds deep carmine, open white, 1 1/5″ diameter, alternate.
FRUIT: Yellow, occasionally with orange to pink blush, 1/2″ diameter, abundant, persistent.
HABIT: Broadly pyramidal, 20′ by 20′.
DISEASES: Slightly susceptible to powdery mildew and scab, moderately susceptible to fireblight.

Malus 'Woven Gold'
FLOWERS: Single, carmine red buds, open white.
FRUIT: Yellow-gold, 1/3″ wide in spur clusters, firm, persistent.
HABIT: Semi-weeping tree, 12′; dark green leaves.
DISEASES: Resistant.

Malus yunnanensis
(mā′lus yū-na-nen′sis)
FLOWERS: Single, white or with a faint pink tinge, 5/8″ diameter.
FRUIT: Red sprinkled with whitish dots, 1/2″ wide.
HABIT: Tree, 20 to 40′, leaves may turn orange and scarlet in fall; var. *veitchii* is the common form in
    cultivation and is narrowly ovate in habit, 20′ by 10′, white flowers, heavy textured foliage.
DISEASES: var. *veitchii*—slight scab, moderate powdery mildew and fireblight.

Malus 'Zumirang'
FLOWERS: White.
FRUIT: Red, 3/8″ diameter.
HABIT: Upright, broadly pyramidal to rounded.
DISEASES: Good resistance.

Malus 'Zumi Wooster'
FLOWERS: Salmon coral buds open to fragrant white flowers.
FRUIT: Abundant dark red fruits, 1/2″ diameter.
HABIT: Broadly ovate.
BARK: Tannish coral.
DISEASES: Unknown

Melia azedarach — Chinaberry, Pride of India
(mē′li-a ȧ-zēd′ȧ-rak)

FAMILY: Meliaceae
LEAVES: Alternate, bipinnately compound, 12 to 24″ long, half as wide, leaflets ovate
    to oval, slender pointed, unequally serrate at base, toothed or lobed, 1 1/2 to
    2″ long, 1/3 to 3/4″ wide, glabrous or slightly pubescent on midrib and petiolules
    when young, lustrous rich green.
BUDS: Small, 1/16″ high and wide, rounded, covered with brown pubescence, sits
    in a notch above leaf scar.
STEM: Stout, coarse, angled, olive-brown to brown, covered with light brown len-
    ticels; leaf scar large, shield shaped; malodorous when broken.

Leaflet

SIZE: 30 to 40′ high with a similar spread.
HARDINESS: Zone 7 to 10; severely injured or killed at -3°F; 'Umbraculiformis' was
    more seriously injured than the species.
HABIT: Round-headed tree composed of stiff coarse branches; not very appealing in the winter months.
RATE: Fast.
TEXTURE: Medium in summer; coarse in winter.
BARK: Gray-brown, ridged and furrowed.
LEAF COLOR: Lustrous rich green in summer, yellow-green in fall; colors about mid October into early
    November in Athens.
FLOWERS: Lavender-lilac, 3/4″ across, perfect, fragrant, borne in large, loose, 8 to 16″ long panicles in
    May; foliage is present when flowers open and much of the effect is lost, rather pretty on close
    inspection.

FRUIT: Sub-globose, 3/8 to 1/2″ diameter yellow drupe with a hard bony seed that ripens in September-October and persists into the following spring; every flower must result in a fruit, actually somewhat attractive.

CULTURE: A genuine weed tree; adaptable to about any situation; frequently seen along highways, fence rows and other waste areas; a rapid grower and very weak-wooded; interestingly trees that were killed to the ground in 1984 have resprouted and by 1988 were producing abundant fruit crops, apparently will flower as a small tree when seed grown.

DISEASES AND INSECTS: None of any consequence.

LANDSCAPE USE: None, in my estimation much worse that Tree of Heaven or Silver Maple; a genuine nuisance; apparently birds and animals disseminate the fruits to waste areas; it is rare to see a fence row in the south without a Chinaberry.

CULTIVARS:

'Umbraculiformis'—Like the species a true biological vagrant; called the Texas Umbrellatree because of its multistemmed habit and dome or umbrella-like outline; it reproduces true to type from seed and can be seen in the waste areas as well as in the yards of older residences; at one time this form must have been fashionable because 2 and 3 trees are often seen in a single landscape; said to have appeared originally on the battlefield of San Jacinto, Texas; grows 20 to 25′ high, not as cold hardy as the species.

PROPAGATION: Seed is the logical and preferred method; root cuttings will work.

ADDITIONAL NOTES: Not too much good that can be said about the tree except that it does not grow north of Zone 7; cultivated or naturalized in almost every warm temperate or subtropical country.

NATIVE HABITAT: Northern India, central and western China. Cultivated since the 16th century.

Menispermum canadense — Common Moonseed
(men-i-sper′mum kan-a-den′sē)

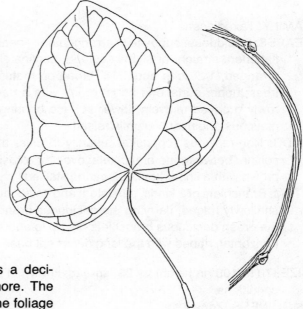

FAMILY: Menispermaceae

LEAVES: Alternate, simple, orbicular-ovate, 4 to 10″ long, 4 to 7″ wide, acute or obtuse, rounded or truncate at base, entire or shallowly angulate-lobed, dark green above, slightly pubescent beneath or nearly glabrous at maturity; petioles 2 to 6″ long, attached to the blade near, but not at base (peltate).

BUDS: Small, hairy, superposed, with the uppermost developing the inflorescence and the lower covered by the leaf scar, about 3-scaled.

STEM: Round, fluted, green becoming buff to shiny brown, glabrescent, leaf scars raised, crater-like; pith—white, solid; sieve tubes prominent, visible to the naked eye.

Menispermum canadense, Common Moonseed, is a deciduous, twining vine growing 10 to 15′ and more. The stems are very slender and require support. The foliage is dark green in summer and the leaves are quite large (4 to 10″) which makes for effective screening; very adaptable; grows back quickly (6 to 10′ in a single season); flowers dioecious, greenish yellow, borne on a long stalked raceme, fruit black; seed resembles a half-moon, hence, the common name; easily propagated by division. Quebec and Manitoba to Georgia and Arkansas. 1646. Zone 4 to 8. Almost a weed.

Mespilus germanica — Showy Mespilus
(mes'pi-lus jĕr-man'i-ka)

FAMILY: Rosaceae

LEAVES: Alternate, simple, oblong to oblong-lanceolate, 2 to 5" long, short acuminate, minutely toothed, dull green and pubescent above, more so beneath, essentially sessile, may turn yellowish to red-brown in fall.

STEM: Pubescent and armed with 1/2 to 1" long firm straight spines although cultivated trees I have seen in England were essentially thornless.

Mespilus germanica, Showy Mespilus, is a small (20'), rounded to broad-rounded tree composed of tightly woven branches producing a rather picturesque habit. On past garden tours to Europe, I have always quizzed people about its identity which looks like nothing in the normal realm of the Rose family. The white to lightly blushed pink, 1 to 1 1/2" diameter, 5-petaled flowers occur at the end of short leafy branches in May–June. The sepals provide a good identification feature for they are triangular at the base and extended into a long narrow point that reaches beyond the petals. Sepals are also woolly pubescent. Fruit is a brown, hard apple to slightly pear-shaped (more top shaped than anything), 1" wide pome with the sepals still present. Selections have been made for larger fruit size up to 2" diameter. Fruits ripen late, require frost or cold weather or need to be stored cold until the fruit softens. Jelly can be made from the fruits and I purchased my first vessel of same on a 1989 trip. The taste is perhaps similar to mayhaw *(Crataegus opaca)* jelly which is sold in the southeast. Ideally any well drained soil and a sunny location suit it best. Native to southeastern Europe to Iran. Long cultivated. Zone 5 to 8.

Metasequoia glyptostroboides — Dawn Redwood
(met-a-sē-kwoy'à glip-tō-strō-boy'dēz)

FAMILY: Taxodiaceae

LEAVES: Deciduous, opposite in arrangement, linear, flattened, straight or slightly curved, pectinately arranged, 1/2" long and 1/16" broad on mature trees; upper surface is bright green with a narrowly grooved midvein, lower surface bearing obscure lines of stomata, lighter green or slightly glaucous, the midrib slightly raised.

BUDS: Non-resinous (opposite), usually in pairs at the base of deciduous branchlets but sometimes solitary between the branchlets; ovoid or ellipsoid, about 1/4" long, scales light reddish or yellowish brown with a linear keel, appearing stalked.

STEM: Branchlets of 2 kinds, persistent and deciduous; the persistent—bright reddish brown when young, shallowly ridged, carrying the deciduous branchlets, numerous vegetative buds and a few leaves; the green deciduous branchlets are up to about 3" long, usually arranged distichously, more or less horizontal, ribbed with the long decurrent bases of up to 50 to 60 or more leaves.

SIZE: 70 to 100' in height by 25' spread, known to 120' high; 40 to 50' in 20 years under good growing conditions.

HARDINESS: Zone 4 to 8.

HABIT: Pyramidal, conical, with a single straight trunk in youth; supposedly developing a broad-rounded crown with age; the Missouri Botanic Garden has a beautiful complement of trees which were grown from seed distributed to them by the Arnold Arboretum; have seen many large trees over the years and all maintain the feathery-pyramidal growth habit.

RATE: Fast (50' in 15 to 20 years); 30-year-old-tree on William and Mary College campus is supposedly over 120' high.

TEXTURE: Fine in leaf, less so when defoliated.

BARK: Reddish brown when young, becoming darker, fissured and exfoliating in long narrow strips: base buttressing and developing an irregular fluted character.

LEAF COLOR: Bright green above changing to brown in fall; can be an excellent orange-brown to red-brown.

FLOWERS: Monoecious; male flowers in racemes or panicles; female solitary.

FRUIT: Cones pendulous, on long stalks, globose or cylindrical, female solitary, 3/4 to 1″ long and wide, dark brown, mature the first year, seeds small like those of arborvitae.

CULTURE: Easy to transplant; performs best in moist, deep, well-drained, slightly acid soils; is not well adapted to chalky soils; full sun; may grow late into summer and early fall and is damaged by an early freeze; should be well sited such as on a hill rather than a low area; seldom requires pruning due to neat, uniform, conical habit.

DISEASES AND INSECTS: The National Arboretum has lost some trees through canker infestations; prior to this there was no known serious problem; usually if a tree is around long enough and has been planted in sufficient numbers some insect or disease catches up with it; Japanese beetles will feed on the foliage.

LANDSCAPE VALUE: I have changed my opinion of this tree since I first learned it in my plant materials courses at Ohio State in 1963; at that time the tree was...well...just another tree but through closer association I find it a very lovely ornamental well suited to parks, golf courses and other large areas; would make a very effective screen, grouping or for use in lining long drives or streets; where it can be grown without problem of freeze damage it should be given adequate consideration; excellent in groves, along streams or lakes; Morris Arboretum has a beautiful grove along a stream.

CULTIVARS:

'National'—Habit conspicuously narrow-pyramidal, selection made in 1958 at National Arboretum, tree was 58′ high, 24′ wide and 23 years old; see *PIPPS* 31: 464 (1971).

'Sheridan Spire'—More upright than typical for the species.

PROPAGATION: Seeds, if viable, will germinate to a degree but one month cold stratification improves and unifies germination; abundant literature on cutting production, in general use firm wooded softwoods, June–August, 8000 ppm IBA talc or solution, mist and rooting should approach 80% or greater. Monrovia Nursery uses 4″ long hardwood cuttings, soak in chlorine water and fungicide, place in plastic bags for 30 days at 45°F, 3000 ppm IBA dip, place in outdoor rooting beds with bottom heat, 90% rooting in 4 months.

ADDITIONAL NOTES: The genus was described by Miki in 1941 from fossils discovered in Japan in Lower Pliocene strata. Extant specimens were found growing wild in China in the same year. The Arnold Arboretum sponsored an expedition to the area in 1944 and collected seeds, which were shared with other arboreta and botanical gardens around the world. This species has been growing and reproducing itself for 50 million years. It is amazingly fast growing and has infatuated many good horticulturists and botanists. I have seen it as far north as the University of Maine, Orono, but there the top is often killed back. One hot summer day, I bicycled all over the campus of William and Mary looking for the 100′ plus high trees that Mitchell described in *J. Royal Hort. Soc.* See *Arnoldia* 28: 113–123 for a full account of history, introduction and cultivation.

NATIVE HABITAT: Native of eastern Szechuan and western Hupeh, China. Introduced 1947–1948.

Michelia figo — Banana Shrub
(mī-kē′li-à fī′gō)

FAMILY: Magnoliaceae

LEAVES: Alternate, simple, evergreen, narrowly oval or slightly obovate, 1 1/2 to 4″ long, 1/2 to 2″ wide, initially covered with brownish pubescence, at maturity nearly glabrous, entire, lustrous and rich dark green; petiole 1/2″ long, brown pubescent.

STEM: Green, but covered with brown pubescence (down).

Michelia figo, Banana Shrub, is one of those plants that excites the plant lover but frustrates that individual when he/she attempts to locate it in commerce. It forms a dense, upright oval to rounded outline, 6 to 10′ (15′) high and wide. The lustrous dark green foliage is truly magnificent. During winter, the leaves, at least in the Piedmont, become yellow-green, especially on plants sited in full sun. The extremely fragrant, 1 1/2″ diameter, 6 to 9 tepaled, yellowish green, tinged purple flowers are borne on a 1/2″ long brown, downy peduncle in April through June. The flowers are initially covered with brown, downy bracts. Prefers well-drained, fertile, acid, sandy loam with high organic matter content and full sun to partial shade. It has no significant pest problems and is well-adapted to conditions in the Coastal Plain. The fragrance could be termed fruity—reminds of ripening cantaloupes and bananas. Has been used for foundations, single specimens, and groupings. A beautiful plant that was once widely planted in southeast, and should be brought back into commercial production. Unfortunately the flowers are not explosive and do not "fit" the modern concept of a quality landscape plant. "Stubbs Purple' has flowers that are more purple than the typical species form. Several hybrids between *M. doltsopa* (a tender, Zone 9 to 10, 3 to 7″ long, 1 1/4 to 3″ wide, lustrous dark green leaved form with soft creamy white, 3 to 4″ diameter, fragrant, 12 to 16 petaled flowers from the axils of the leaves in spring) and *M. figo* are known, technically listed as *Michelia* × *foggii* selections; 'Allspice' has exceedingly fragrant white flowers and handsome lustrous dark green foliage on a vigorous plant and 'Jack Fogg' with white flowers with a pinkish purple edging to the petals, glossy dark green leaves, upright habit. Other cultivars exist but probably represent overkill based on their descriptions. Hybrids are probably best in Zone 9. *Michelia doltsopa* as I have seen it is a distinctly upright pyramidal tree and I suspect most hybrids will be quite upright in outline. *Michelia figo* is native to China. Introduced 1789. Zone 7 to 10; best in Zone 8 and warmer.

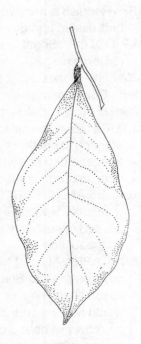

Microbiota decussata — Russian Arborvitae
(mī-krō-bi-ō′ta dē-ku-sā′ta)

FAMILY: Cupressaceae
LEAVES: Branchlets arranged in flattened sprays like *Thuja,* needles mostly scale-like and appressed, soft textured; spreading and needle-like on young and seedling plants or those grown in shade, bright green in summer, bronzy purple to brown in winter.

Microbiota decussata, Russian Arborvitae, has stirred considerable interest among gardeners since entering the marketplace. Abundant accolades have appeared in the literature and, indeed, when well grown the plant has few rivals among ground cover needle evergreens. In Europe, the plant appears more vigorous than in the hotter summers of the eastern/southern states. Plants grow about 12″ high and spread almost indefinitely. The tips of the shoots nod gracefully. One report mentioned a 14-year-old plant that was 12″ high and 15′ in diameter. Ideally, well drained moist soil is best but some shade is acceptable. I have grown a plant under an oak tree for the past four years and it looks miserable. The summer foliage is bright green and turns *Juniperus horizontalis* 'Plumosa' brownish purple in winter. Several clones are described with the Vancouver form supposedly better. Apparently monoecious species with female consisting of a single, naked, oval seed, surrounded at based by spreading scales. Discovered in 1921 near Vladivostock, Russia, growing above the tree line in the mountains. Considered hardy to -40°F and possibly lower. Zone 3 to 8?

Mitchella repens — Patridgeberry, also called Twinberry and Squawberry
(mi-chel′à   rē′penz)

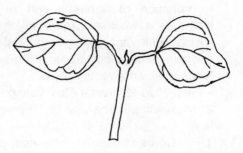

FAMILY: Rubiaceae
LEAVES: Opposite, simple, evergreen, 1/4 to 1″ long, of similar width, orbicular-ovate, obtuse, subcordate or rounded, lustrous above, often variegated with whitish lines; petiole about 1/8 to 1/4″ long.

SIZE: 2″, usually a biological pancake.
HARDINESS: Zone 3 to 9.
HABIT: Low growing, ground-hugging evergreen cover scarcely reaching above the ground.
RATE: Slow.
TEXTURE: Fine.
LEAF COLOR: Dark green and lustrous above, often with variegated whitish lines.
FLOWERS: White or pinkish, possibly tinged with purple, 4-lobed at mouth, narrow trumpet-shaped, 1/2″ long, extremely fragrant; borne over an extended period in late spring and early summer in erect short peduncled pairs; have seen in flower late May–early June in North Georgia mountains.
FRUIT: Berry-like globose drupe, red, 1/4″ diameter, fall into winter; somewhat irregular in shape due to fusion of two ovaries; in the wild it is not uncommon to see flowers and fruits appearing at the same time.
CULTURE: Best moved in sods being careful to maintain as much soil as possible; requires acid, moist, well-drained soil which has been abundantly supplied with acid leafmold or peat; requires shade; is sensitive to the encroachment of man.
DISEASES AND INSECTS: Several leaf diseases have been reported but none are serious.
LANDSCAPE VALUE: A worthwhile groundcover for the lover of plants; requires special attention and without it should not even be considered; the plants are collected from the wild and sold at Christmas time; there is one firm in Vermont which sells the Patridge-berry bowl, which consists of Rattlesnake plantain, moss and the above; good rock garden plant; I delight in finding small patches of this in the woods; it has a delicate beauty and is usually found in combination with mosses and lichens under the shade of the forest canopy where it forms a most beautiful natural garden.
CULTIVARS:
　f. *leucocarpa*—Listed as having white fruits; have never seen this but would like one for my garden.
PROPAGATION: Seed requires a 2 to 3 month cold period; cuttings can be rooted in November and through the winter months by using a poly tent and IBA treatment.
NATIVE HABITAT: Nova Scotia to Ontario and Minnesota, south to Florida, Arkansas and Texas. Introduced 1761.

Morus alba — White or Common Mulberry
(mō′rus ăl′bà)

FAMILY: Moraceae
LEAVES: Alternate, simple, undivided or lobed, dimorphic, serrate or dentate, ovate to broad-ovate, 2 to 7″ long, up to 6″ wide, acute or short acuminate, rounded or cordate at base, dark green and usually smooth above, pubescent on veins beneath or nearly glabrous; petiole 1/2 to 1″ long.
BUDS: Imbricate, terminal-absent, laterals-small, 1/8″ to 1/4″ long, ovoid, 3 to 6 scales, appressed, sharp or blunt pointed, light brown to reddish brown, often set oblique to leaf scar, margins of bud scales somewhat finely hairy.
STEM: Slender, yellowish green to brownish gray, smooth, more or less shining, slightly sweetish if chewed, bark exuding a white juice if cut on warm days.

SIZE: 30 to 50′ in height with a comparable spread, usually smaller.

HARDINESS: Zone 4 to 8(9).

HABIT: Usually an extremely dense, round topped tree with a profusion of tight-knit slender branches; often develops a witches' broom which gives the tree a messy, unkempt appearance; definitely one of the original garbage-can trees; often seen as a shrub in fence rows and waste areas.

RATE: Fast, 10 to 12′ over a 4 to 6 year period; Pair reported 2′ of growth per year over a 10-year-period in Wichita tests.

TEXTURE: Coarse throughout the year; perhaps somewhat unfair assessment-medium in summer in the best forms.

BARK: On younger branches (1 to 4″) an ashy-orange or light orangish brown, on larger trunks a brown color.

LEAF COLOR: Variable, dull yellow green to lustrous dark green in summer; fall color ranges from green to yellow-green to yellow in the best forms.

FLOWERS: Polygamo-dioecious (monoecious or dioecious according to Rehder), yellowish green, March–April, both sexes in stalked, axillary pendulous catkins, not showy, female 1/3 to 1/2″ long, male longer.

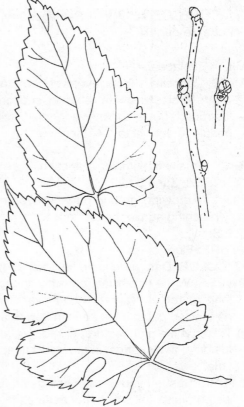

FRUIT: Multiple fruit of small fleshy drupes, white, pinkish or purplish violet, sweet, but insipid, 1/2 to 1″ long, June to July somewhat similar in size and shape to blackberry; birds love them and create fantastic messes because of cathartic properties.

CULTURE: Transplants readily, adaptable, withstands drought, urban and seaside (quite salt tolerant) conditions; full sun to light shade; prune in winter; similar to *Maclura* in cultural adaptability, grows best in moist, well-drained, fertile soils.

DISEASES AND INSECTS: Bacterial blight on leaves and shoots, leaf spots, cankers, powdery mildews, scales, two-spotted mites and other pests; in the southern states this species may be infested with many more problems.

LANDSCAPE VALUE: None; according to a landscape architect whose name will remain anonymous this tree has excellent color, texture, and form; possibly she and I are thinking of different trees; about the only beneficiaries are the birds and the silkworms; the tree was originally imported from China for the silkworm industry and unfortunately escaped and is now naturalized in Asia, Europe and America; several of the weeping forms and the fruitless types offer the greatest hope for the landscape.

CULTIVARS:

'Bellaire'—A mature male selection, multiple trunk and distinctive form.

'Chaparral'—Non-fruiting, bright green leaved weeping type, usually grafted on a standard.

'Fegyvernekiana'—Have seen this bush-like non-fruiting form that probably will never exceed 3 to 4′; makes a cute dense mound and every gardener needs at least one plant with such a name.

'Hampton'—Fruitless form selected from a 100-year-old specimen, wide spreading, picturesque habit, Pair introduction, Kansas State.

'Lingan'—A type with leathery, lustrous foliage, fruitless, fast growing, drought resistant and apparently somewhat salt resistant as it is often used for seashore plantings.

'Laciniata'—Leaves are deeply lobed, the lobes narrow, pointed and deeply serrated.

'Mapleleaf'—Dr. Pair calls this a standard in the trade but I am not sure where it belongs taxonomically; many years past I saw a plant like this in the Ohio Shade Tree Evaluation tests at Wooster with a large, lustrous dark green, lobed "maple-like" leaf, a male form.

'Pendula'—A form with slender pendulous branches and gnarled twisted growth habit; often in evidence in older landscapes; interesting but grotesque (also called Teas Weeping Mulberry), a fruiting clone, will grow 15 to 20′ high and wide.

'Pyramidalis'—Upright clone of conical habit, have not seen this.

'Stribling'—Another fruitless, fast growing clone; have seen excellent yellow fall color on this clone, appears quite cold hardy, survived -25°F at Spring Grove, Cincinnati, OH.

var. *tatarica*—Called the Russian Mulberry, hardiest of all the mulberries.

'Urbana'—Weeping, fruitless clone named by J.C. McDaniel, otherwise like 'Pendula'.

PROPAGATION: Seed, stratify for 60 days at 41°F to improve germination. Cuttings collected in late October rooted 30% without treatment and 87% in 13 weeks with IBA; have rooted August cuttings of 'Pendula' with 3000 ppm IBA-quick dip, peat:perlite, mist; over the years have rooted the various forms of *Morus alba* with excellent success; suspect that hardwood cuttings would root.

NATIVE HABITAT: China. Introduced into Jamestown, Virginia with the early settlers, cultivated since time immemorial in many European countries.

RELATED SPECIES:

Morus australis *(M. bombycis)*, (mō′rus aw-strā′liz) 'Unryu' ('Tortuosa') has been popularized by Dr. Raulston, NC State Arboretum and indeed his shrub or small tree has much to offer. I received a rooted cutting about 5 years past which is now 12′ tall, 8 to 10′ wide with a 6″ diameter trunk at the base. One year it was killed almost to the ground by an April freeze, but returned to the size listed above. Raulston reports 6 to 10′ growth per year. Ultimate landscape size is probably 20 to 30′. Leaves are large, 6 to 7″ long, lustrous dark

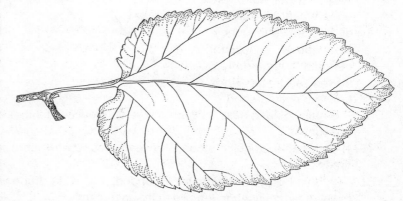

green and may turn a good bright yellow but have been killed off green on most occasions in my garden. The most interesting (curious) part of the plant's anatomy is the twisted corkscrew con-figurated branches which serve as a poor man's *Corylus avellana* 'Contorta'. Branches are not quite as twisted as 'Contorta' but are sufficiently pronounced to make an effective accent. Easily rooted from softwood and hardwood cuttings. Native to China. Zone 6 to 9. It tends to leaf out early and may be injured by late freezes. Apparently a female.

Morus rubra—Red Mulberry
(mō′rus rū′brȧ)

LEAVES: Alternate, simple, broad-ovate to oblong-ovate, 3 to 5″ (8″) long, abruptly long acuminate, truncate or subcordate at base, closely and sharply serrate, scabrous or sometimes smooth above, dark green, soft-pubescent below; petiole—1″ long.

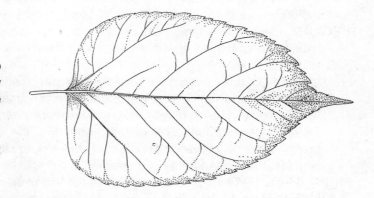

Morus rubra, Red Mulberry, reaches 40 to 70′ in height with a 40 to 50′ spread and is taller, more open, and irregular than *M. alba.* the large dark green leaves are quite noticeable and tend to attract the eye of even casual biologists. Fall color is subdued yellow. Fruits are red turning dark purple, juicy, edible and relished by birds. Native from Massachusetts to Florida, west to Michigan, Nebraska, Kansas and Texas. Introduced 1629. Zone 5 to 9. A better tree than *M. alba* and more fastidious as to soil requirements, preferring a rich, moist situation.

Myrica pensylvanica — Northern Bayberry
(mi-rī'kȧ pen-sil-van'i-ka)

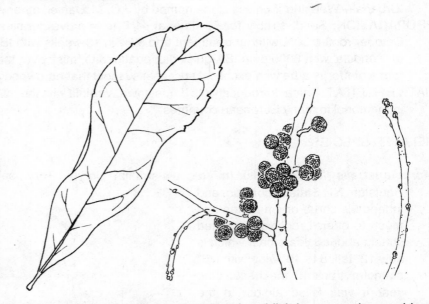

FAMILY: Myricaceae

LEAVES: Alternate, simple, deciduous to semi-evergreen, almost always deciduous in the north, obovate to oblong-obovate or oblong, 1 1/2 to 4″ long, 1/2 to 1 1/2″ wide, obtuse or acutish, shallowly toothed toward apex or entire, lustrous dark green and pubescent above, pubescent beneath, resin-dotted, leaves aromatic when bruised; petiole-short.

BUDS: Small, solitary, sessile, subglobose or ovoid, with 2 to 4 exposed, reddish brown scales, end-bud absent.

STEM: Rounded or angular, stoutish, resin-dotted when young; pith small, somewhat angled, continuous, green.

FRUIT: A small gray, waxy coated, rounded, 1/5″ wide drupe which persists throughout the winter; an excellent identification feature on female plants.

SIZE: 9′ is a good average for height, however, quite variable ranging from 5 to 12′ in height and could equal that in spread; tends to sucker and therefore forms large colonies.

HARDINESS: Zone (2)3 to 6, suspect into Zone 8 since I am growing a few plants successfully.

HABIT: Deciduous to semi-evergreen, upright-rounded, and fairly dense shrub; actually difficult to describe the habit of this plant; must be seen to be fully appreciated; suckers and forms large colonies, near the ocean a low windswept shrub, further away a large irregular colonizing mass.

RATE: Medium from old wood, probably fast from shoots which develop from roots.

TEXTURE: Medium in foliage, possibly could be considered medium-fine; medium in winter habit; a very handsome specimen in winter because of interesting branch pattern and the gray, waxy fruits on female plants.

LEAF COLOR: Deep lustrous green, dotted with resin glands beneath, leaves have a leathery texture, very aromatic when crushed as are all parts of the plant; fall color is nonexistent.

FLOWERS: Monoecious or dioecious, tends toward the dioecious character; male and female plants are required for good fuit development, not showy, the flowers borne in catkins with male (yellowish green) consisting of varying number of stamens; the female of a one-celled ovary with two stalkless stigmas; sepals and petals are absent; flowering in late March to April before the leaves.

FRUIT: Drupe, 1/6 to 1/5″ across, grayish white, endocarp covered with resinous, waxy coating, effective from September through April and later of the following year, borne in great quantities and usually covering the stems of female plants.

CULTURE: Transplant balled and burlapped or as a container plant; thrives in poor, sterile, sandy soil; has performed well in heavy clay soils; appears to be extremely adaptable; full sun to 1/2 shade;

withstands salt spray; chlorosis is a problem on high pH soils but can be corrected with soil treatments or iron sprays; displays excellent salt tolerance as evidenced by its natural proximity to the sea; tends to be low-growing along the coast where it is sculptured by the ocean spray and becomes larger inland; fixes atmospheric nitrogen; provenance may be extremely important for hardiness, although listed as Zone 2 to 3 hardy, plants have suffered damage at -20 to -25°F in midwest; if plants are going to be used in northern areas make sure plants were grown from northern seed sources.

DISEASES AND INSECTS: None serious.

LANDSCAPE VALUE: Excellent plant for massing, border, combines well with broadleaf evergreens, could be integrated into the foundation plantings, possibly for highway plantings and other areas where salts present a cultural problem; could be used in many poor soil sites.

PROPAGATION: Seeds, collect in October, remove the wax, stratify in moist peat for 90 days and the germination approaches 100%; I have had excellent success with this procedure. Cuttings, I conducted an experiment using 0, 1000, 2500, 5000, and 10,000 ppm IBA treatments; the cutting wood was collected June 14, after 8 weeks rooting was evaluated; no roots were produced at 0 or 1000 ppm IBA; rooting was 36, 53, 46% for 2500, 5000, and 10,000 ppm IBA treatments, respectively; see Dirr and Heuser (1987) for additional information.

ADDITIONAL NOTES: The wax is used for making the finely aromatic bayberry candles.

NATIVE HABITAT: Newfoundland to western New York, Maryland, and North Carolina. Primarily along the seashore. Introduced 1725.

RELATED SPECIES:

Myrica cerifera, (mi-rī′kȧ sēr-if′ĕr-ȧ), Southern Waxmyrtle, is best described as the southern evergreen extension of *Myrica pensylvanica*. However, it is distinctly different in leaf, fruit and growth habit. The leaves are narrowly 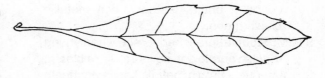 obovate or oblanceolate and extremely variable in size ranging from 4 1/2″ long to 2″ wide, but more typically 1 1/2 to 3″ long, and 1/3 to 3/4″ wide. They are usually serrate at the apex, glossy olive green and glabrous above, dotted with yellowish resin-glands beneath. The petiole is about 1/8 to 1/4″ long. In recent years, a leaf anthracnose that causes spotting and browning of the leaves has become evident. Also a "mosaic type" leaf distortion was reported in Florida. Leaves developed pale green blistered areas interspersed with dark green normal tissues. Actual culprit was a new species of eriophyid mole. See *Hortscience* 22:258–260 (1987). The gray, globose fruits are about 1/8″ wide and are sessilely massed in clusters of 2 to 6 on the previous season's growth. This is a beautiful, rather wispy broadleaf evergeen that will grow 10 to 15′ (20′) high and wide. It makes an excellent pruned screen and may be limbed up to form an attractive small tree. At Sea Island, GA, it is limbed up to expose the handome gray almost white bark. At the Georgia Botanical Garden, it has been used effectively to soften the vertical lines of the administration building and as a specimen plant. It tolerates infertile soils but responds trememdously to good watering and nutritional practices. I planted a small container-grown plant by one side of the entrance to our house and in a single growing season it grew 5′ high and wide. In the spring when the new growth develops, the rich 'bayberry candle' odor is evident. Its only limitation appears to be the sensitivity to cold for at 0°F plants were defoliated or the leaves severely browned. The stem tissue was not injuured. Also ice and snow loads effectively split several plants in the Athens area. It is tolerant of salt spray and will tolerate full sun or half shade. It has been reported as being used at Williamsburg in 1699. The species is receiving more attention in southeastern landscapes and several new introductions are on the way. Variety *pumila* is a small, 3 to 4′ high colonizing evergreen that occurs in low woods and sandy pinelands of the Coastal Plain. Variety *pumila* remained evergeen at 0°F. 'Fairfax' is a compact 4 to 5′ high speading colonizing form that was found by Mr. Bill Craven outside of Fairfax, SC. The leaves are about the same size as the species but lighter green. Deer do not bother the plant at all. I have grown the selection in my garden and have been impressed with its performance. Is hardy to at least 0°F and probably lower. 'Georgia Gem' is a small leaf, compact mounded form for ground cover and massing introduced by Bill Craven, Waynesboro, GA. 'Georgia

Gem' will grow 12 to 18″ high, 30 to 36″ wide with yellow-green to dark olive green leaves that are smaller than the species. Recently I heard of a large irregularly scalloped leaf seedling selection of *M. cerifera* from Selma, AL that shows good vigor and rich dark green foliage. Best cutting propagation results occurred in May–August with or without a rooting hormone. Zone (7)8 to 9. Found in Coastal Plain from Maryland to Texas.

Myrica gale, (mi-rī′kȧ gāl), Sweetgale, is a low growing, 2 to 4′ high, deciduous, bushy shrub with glossy, dark green foliage. In gardens the Sweetgale is grown for its pleasing foliage fragrance. Native to the higher latitudes of all the northern hemisphere. Cultivated 1750. Zone 1. In England the branches were used to flavor a home-made beer known as "gale-beer".

Nandina domestica — Nandina, Heavenly Bamboo
(nan-dē′na dō-mes′ti-kȧ)

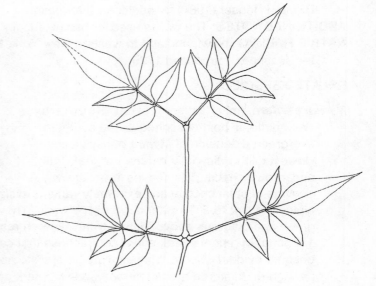

FAMILY: Berberidaceae

LEAVES: Alternate, tri-pinnately compound, evergreen, 12 to 20″ long and wide, each leaflet subsessile, elliptic-lanceolate, 1 1/2 to 4″ long, half as wide, acuminate, cuneate, entire, leathery, rich metallic bluish green.

STEM: Stout, unbranched, erect, when young reddish purple and covered with a bloom; later ugly brown; petiole bases ensheath stem; when cut shows yellow coloration typical of members of Berberidaceae.

SIZE: 6 to 8′ high, less in spread, can grow to 10′, tends to sucker and colonies wider than high are often evident in the landscape.

HARDINESS: Zone 6 to 9; at -3°F during 1983–84 winter plants showed variable response with some completely defoliated, others not affected; in general stem tissue was not hurt.

HABIT: Distinctly upright in outline, unless properly pruned becomes leggy at base with a flat-topped, spreading crown of foliage, spreads by rhizomes.

RATE: Medium.

TEXTURE: Medium, almost fine if not allowed to become leggy.

LEAF COLOR: New leaves coppery to purplish red becoming blue-green with age; tends to assume a reddish tint in winter especially when sited in full sun; this winter coloration trait is quite variable and there is no consistent rule of thumb; coloration depends on seedling, some redder than others.

FLOWERS: Perfect, pinkish in bud finally white with yellow anthers, each flower 1/4 to 1/2″ across, borne in erect, terminal, 8 to 15″ long panicles, May–June, will flower in heavy shade, usually in full flower in Athens about late May.

FRUITS: Spectacular, globular, 1/3″ diameter, two-seeded, bright red berry; ripening in September–October and persisting into and through winter; the large panicles are so heavy that the branches may bend; actually more showy than most hollies because the fruit is not hidden by the foliage.

CULTURE: Easily transplanted from containers; I doubt if anyone is growing *Nandina* in the field; adaptable to extremes of soil and exposure; prefers moist, fertile soil and here makes its best growth; full sun or shade; will grow in beds of ivy under the shade of large oaks and make a great showing; the canes do not branch and careful pruning must be practiced; best to thin out old stems every year or head back old canes at varying lengths to produce a dense plant.

DISEASES AND INSECTS: None serious; actually an amazingly trouble-free plant.

LANDSCAPE VALUE: The species has fallen out of favor because of the competition from the compact-growing cultivars; nice in groups or drifts; softens the effect of coarse-textured shrubs; has been used for every imaginable purpose; possibly not given sufficient plaudits for the tremendous environmental toughness; large plants exist by old homes throughout the south *in situ* for 100 or more years; the species could be used effectively to hide (camouflage) unwanted structures.

CULTIVARS: The nursery industry has realized the great potential for this plant and, in recent years, selected and introduced a number of fine cultivars. Dr. Raulston assembled a fine collection at the N.C. State Arboretum and published an excellent review in Newsletter 11, December, 1984 which has been abstracted here. Raulston lists many small, unusual forms that are not discussed here but may have interest for the collector.

'Alba'—White berried form; the fruits are really off-white and not particularly attractive; apparently comes true to type from seed; some almost yellowish white, foliage lighter green than red-fruited forms, new growth without red pigment, 4 to 6' high.

'Atropurpurea Nana' ('Nana Purpurea')—A rather upright, stiff, compact form that grows about 2' high; does not develop the graceful character of 'Harbour Dwarf'; usually yellow-green tinged with reddish purple throughout the growing season becoming uniformly red with the advent of cold weather; leaves do not have the gracefulness of the species of 'Harbour Dwarf', and are somewhat inrolled or cupped, probably from a virus infection; have never seen this form flower or fruit.

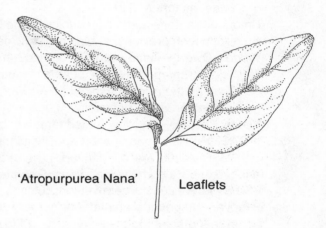

'Atropurpurea Nana'   Leaflets

'Fire Power'—Perhaps a virus-free 'Atropurpurea Nana', i.e., without the foliage distortion; I have had a plant for 4 years and the winter color is a fluorescent glowing red, the habit dense and compact and the foliage apparently virus free, at maturity 1 to 2' by 2'; originated in New Zealand.

'Gulf Stream' ('Compacta Nana')—Another good red winter foliage form that next to 'Moon Bay' in the Georgia Botanical Garden showed more intense red foliage color and more vigorous growth; leaves are flatter and larger than 'Moon Bay', will mature around 2 1/2 to 3 1/2' judging by early performance, good metallic blue-green summer foliage, forms a large compact mound, originated as branch sport of 'Compacta Nana' at Hines Nursery, Houston, TX.

'Harbour Dwarf'—Probably the finest compact form of *Nandina*; branches from the ground and forms a dense mound 2 to 3' high and slightly wider; with time will become one of the most widely used broadleaf evergreens in southern gardens; assumes reddish purple tinge of species in winter, extremely graceful form, flowers and fruits with age, inflorescence smaller than the species.

'Moon Bay'—After observing this for one year in the University's Botanical Garden I think it may have a great future; winter color was bright red, leaves are smaller than the species with a slight cupping tendency; summer leaf color is lighter green than the species; will probably mature around 1 1/2 to 2 1/2' and form a broad mound; originated as a chance seedling in a population of the species at Hines Wholesale Nursery, Houston, TX.

'Moyers Red'—May be a real winner for southern gardens as it is a tall growing form with good cold weather red pigment formation in the leaves; a local Georgia nursery has been growing this and the winter foliage color is a glossy reddish with a tinge of purple; Raulston reports flowers and fruits are pinker and redder, respectively, than other forms and fruits color 1 to 2 months ahead of the other, 2' high and 1 1/2' wide after 3 years, will grow 6' high.

'Nana' ('Pygmaea', 'Compacta')—Probably several clones have been selected under this umbrella; 'Nana' grows about 2 to 4' and forms a dense, stiff, leafy mound, again not as graceful as

'Harbour Dwarf', also minimal berry production; 'Compacta' may be synonymous with 'Harbour Dwarf', also minimal berry production, it may represent a form that is a scaled down version of the species growing 3 to 4′ high.

'Okame'—Like 'Atropurpurea Nana' with virus-free foliage, excellent uniform bright red foliage color early in season, will be mounded and compact like 'Atropurpurea Nana'.

'Pygmaea' ('Minima')—A reasonably tight mounded foliage mass with smaller species-like foliage, supposedly will grow 3′ high and produces bright red cold weather foliage.

'Royal Princess'—Individual leaflets narrower and reduced in size compared to species producing a finer textured effect; Raulston mentioned it may grow to sizes approximating the species.

'San Gabriel'—A fine textured form with blades extremely narrow creating a fine ferny appearance; I had a plant in the garden and was impressed by the textural qualities; unfortunately -3°F eliminated it, will be a compact possibly mounded form, 1 to 2′ high at landscape maturity.

'Umpqua Chief'—Medium sized, typical foliage, 3′ high by 2′ wide after 3 years, mature 5 to 6′.

'Umpqua Princess'—Smallest of the Umpqua series, typical foliage, after 3 years 2 1/2′ high and 2′ wide, mature at 3 to 4′.

'Umpqua Warrior'—Largest in habit with the biggest flowers and fruits, foliage and fruit panicle more open than previous, 4′ high and 3′ wide in 3 years, will grow 6 to 8′.

'Wood's Dwarf'—Have seen this on enough occasions to provide a reasonable assessment, much like 'Atropurpurea Nana' but the foliage appears virus free and develops good red winter color, may be the most compact of the dwarf forms, developed by Ed Wood when he was a student at Oregon State University, supposedly a compact seedling from a normal population.

'Yellow Fruited'—A yellow-fruited form has been described.

PROPAGATION: Seed germination specifications are variable, generally conceded that two years are required if seeds are fall planted; have read information that noted direct sowing of clean seed resulted in 65% germination, also a Georgia horticulturist collected seeds in January, cleaned and sowed with successful germination; cuttings are rooted after the growth has hardened using a variety of rooting compounds, an Alabama nursery uses 2500 ppm IBA + 1500 ppm NAA with good success; the largest breakthroughs have occurred in tissue culture and, commercially, numerous plants are being produced by this means; see Dirr and Heuser, 1987, for details.

NATIVE HABITAT: China. Introduced 1804.

Neillia sinensis — Chinese Neillia
(nēl′i-a̍ sī-nen′sis)

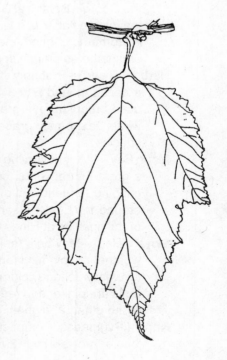

FAMILY: Rosaceae

LEAVES: Alternate, simple, ovate, 2 to 4″ long, 1 1/4 to 2 1/2″ wide, acuminate, coarsely toothed, or with small lobes that are again sharply toothed, essentially glabrous at maturity, rich green.

Neillia sinensis, Chinese Neillia, is rare outside of botanical gardens and arboreta. It is small, rounded in stature (5 to 6′ high), with refined foliage and delicate pink flowers making it worthy of wider use. The flowers are produced in a slender, nodding, 1 to 2 1/2″ long terminal raceme in May. There are 12 to 20 flowers per raceme. The foliage is a rich green and is not troubled by any insect or disease problems. It prefers a well drained, moist soil but appears to be adapted to less than ideal conditions. The glabrous brown stems develop a peeling characteristic with age. The plant could be used for massing and perhaps bank plantings or as a filler in the shrub border. Have grown the plant in my Georgia garden for a number of years and am less than excited about performance. High heat may reduce growth. Have seen excellent specimens in the north. Realistically, the plant will never become a force in the marketplace. Central China. Introduced 1901. Zone 5 to 7. A closely related species is *N. thibetica,* Tibet Neillia, which ranges from 3 to 6′ in height and has 2 to 6″ long slender terminal racemes bearing up to 60 rosy-pink flowers in May-June. Western China. Introduced 1910. Zone 5 to 7(8).

Nerium oleander — Oleander
(nē′ri-um ō-lē-an′dēr)

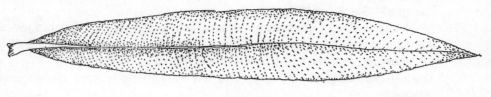

FAMILY: Apocynaceae

LEAVES: Opposite or in whorls of 3 to 4, evergreen, simple, linear-lanceolate, 3 to 5″ long, 1/2 to 3/4″ wide, apex acute, entire, leathery, dark green, with thick midrib and short petiole.

STEM: Stout, green, glabrous, shining.

SIZE: 6 to 12′ high with a similar spread; often smaller in mid-south because of occasional freeze injury; to 20′ high in deep south; have seen 20′ specimens along coast of Georgia.

HARDINESS: Zone 8 to 10, actually best in lower portion of Zone 8, below +15°F some foliar or stem damage is virtually guaranteed.

HABIT: Upright rounded bushy evergreen shrub; can be fashioned as a small tree in lower south.

RATE: Medium to fast; actually quite weed-like in its growth pattern.

TEXTURE: Medium-fine.

LEAF COLOR: Dark green throughout seasons.

FLOWERS: Perfect, 5-petaled, each flower 1 to 1 1/2″ across, borne in terminal cymes on new growth of the season from June–August and into mid-fall, fragrant, single or double, white, pink to red color range, quite handsome in flower; have seen the plant in flower literally year-round, although summer is peak time, flowers on new growth of the season and after the 1983–84 winter numerous plants were killed to the ground along the Georgia coast yet came back and flowered the same year.

FRUIT: A 5 to 7″ long, slender pod (may be a follicle) that is present in various states of maturity through summer and into fall; not ornamental and probably should be removed; small fringed seeds remind of *Catalpa* seeds.

CULTURE: Easily transplanted, well-adapted to coastal areas; displays high salt and wind tolerance, prefers well-drained soil, withstands dry conditions, responds to fertility, used in Florida in sandy highway medium plantings which is an indication of its adaptability; needs protection in upper parts of Zone 8; sun or partial shade; tolerates polluted conditions; supposedly withstands marshy soils; killed to ground after exposure to 0°F.

DISEASES AND INSECTS: Scale, aphids, mealybug, oleander caterpillar, bacterial gall.

LANDSCAPE VALUE: Excellent container or tub plant, foundations, borders, screens, groupings in coastal areas where wind and salt spray are problematic; displays good heat tolerance and could be used where there is a significant amount of reflected light; several years past I was traveling from San Francisco to Davis, CA and the highways were absolutely crammed with Oleander; it makes a great visual barrier and requires minimal maintenance.

CULTIVARS: Numerous; the following are representative of the color range available.

'Algiers'—Single dark red, intermediate between Petite types and species.

'Calypso'—Showy, single cherry red flowers, a hardy form.

'Cardinal'—Single red flowers.

'Casablanca'—Single, white, similar to 'Algiers' in habit.

'Cherry Ripe'—Single, brilliant rose-red flowers.

'Compte Barthelemy'—Double red flowers.

'Hardy Pink'—Single salmon-pink flowers; this is probably the cultivar that was planted on the University of Georgia campus; also a 'Hardy Red'.

'Hawaii'—Single salmon-pink flowers with yellow throats.

'Isle of Capri'—Single light yellow flowers.

'Mrs. Roeding'—Double salmon-pink flowers, grows 6' high, finer textured than species.

'Petite Pink'—Single, shell pink, dwarf, possibly 3 to 4' high.

'Petite Salmon'—Single, bright salmon-pink, dwarf, 3 to 4' high, both Petites Zone 9.

'Ruby Lace'—Ruby red flowers, wavy edged petals with a fringed lip, individual flowers large, up to 3", intermediate in growth habit.

'Sister Agnes'—Single pure white flowers, vigorous, 15 to 20' at maturity.

'Tangier'—Single, soft medium pink flower.

PROPAGATION: Seeds germinate without any pretreatment, the fringed seeds remind of catalpa; softwood cuttings root easily; cuttings collected in late July, given a 3000 ppm IBA dip, placed in peat:perlite under mist rooted well; plants can also be divided.

ADDITIONAL NOTES: Caution! All parts of the plant are poisonous. Green and dry wood contain the toxic principal.

NATIVE HABITAT: Southern Asia, Mediterranean region.

Neviusia alabamensis — Snow-wreath, Alabama Snow-wreath

(nev-i-ū'si-á al-a-bam-en'sis)

FAMILY: Rosaceae

LEAVES: Alternate, simple, 1 1/2 to 3 1/2" long, ovate to ovate-oblong, acute or acuminate, doubly serrate, those of shoots slightly lobed, nearly glabrous, medium green, pubescent on veins below; petiole—1/3" long, downy.

BUDS: Glabrate, rather small, solitary, sessile, ovoid, ascending, with about 6, somewhat keeled or striated scales.

STEM: Golden-brown, puberulent, slender, long, somewhat zig-zag, decurrently ridged from the nodes; pith relatively large, rounded, white, continuous.

SIZE: 3 to 6' high with an equal spread.

HARDINESS: Zone 4 to 8, growing at Morton Arboretum, Chicago, Illinois and Athens, GA.

HABIT: Upright deciduous shrub of somewhat straggly, open appearance with arching branches, eventually becoming rounded.

RATE: Slow to medium.

TEXTURE: Medium-fine in leaf; medium in winter.

FLOWERS: Perfect, apetalous, white, born in 3 to 8-flowered cymes in early to mid-May (early April, Athens); the stamens are the showy part of the flower and give a very feathery appearance to the plant, each flower borne on a 3/4" long pedicel with a bunch of 1/4 to 1/3" long stamens.

FRUIT: Achene, of no ornamental consequence.

CULTURE: Easily cultured; well drained soil, ample moisture; full sun or partial shade; prune after flowering.

DISEASES AND INSECTS: None serious.

LANDSCAPE VALUE: A novelty item for the plantsman who wants something different; the flowers are quite showy and interesting; reminds of a petal-less spirea; I had this plant in my Illinois garden under the shade of a gross-feeding *Prunus serotina* and it performed reasonably well; it will show moisture stress if sited in an excessively dry location; otherwise it is a trouble-free shrub that could be used in the shrub border; it is a great plant with which to stump your plant material friends.

PROPAGATION: Roots easily from softwood cuttings; division of the plant works quite well; I have received dormant divisions from the Morton Arboretum and had good success by potting them and growing them on in the greenhouse.

ADDITIONAL NOTES: Anyone interested in additional information should refer to R.A. Howard, *Arnoldia* 36(2): 57–65. 1976.

NATIVE HABITAT: One species in Alabama. Found near Tuscaloosa, AL by the Rev. R.D. Nevius in 1958.

Nyssa sylvatica — Black Tupelo, also known as Black Gum, Sour Gum, and Pepperidge.
(nis'à sil-vat'i-kà)

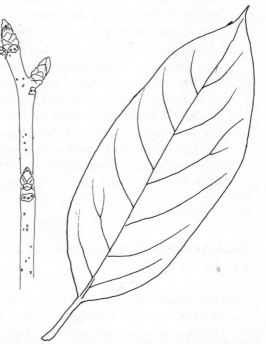

FAMILY: Nyssaceae

LEAVES: Alternate, simple, obovate or elliptic, 3 to 6″ long, 1 1/2 to 3″ wide, entire or remotely toothed, acute or obtusish, cuneate or sometimes rounded at base, lustrous dark green above, glaucescent beneath, pubescent on veins or glabrous at maturity; petiole 1/2 to 1″ long, often reddish.

BUDS: Imbricate, 1/8 to 1/4″ long, ovoid, vari-colored, yellow-brown to red-brown, smooth or slightly downy at tip, usually brownish on tip of scales.

STEM: Slender, glabrous or nearly so, grayish to light reddish brown, producing numerous short slow growing spurs; bundle traces 3, distinct, forming cavern-like entrance to stem; pith chambered.

SIZE: 30 to 50′ in height with a spread of 20 to 30′ can grow to 100′ or more but this size is rare.

HARDINESS: Zone 3 to 9.

HABIT: One of our most beautiful native trees; somewhat pyramidal when young with densely set branches, some of which are pendulous; in old age the numerous spreading and often horizontal branches form an irregularly rounded or flat-topped crown; I have seen 60′ specimens in Spring Grove, Cincinnati, OH which were distinctly upright-oval in outline; there is great variation in mature habit; the young trees take on the appearance of *Q. palustris*.

RATE: Slow to medium, 12 to 15′ over a 10 to 15 year period.

TEXTURE: Medium in leaf; medium in winter.

BARK: Dark gray, at times almost black, broken into thick, irregular ridges which are checked across into short segments, giving it a block-like or alligator hide appearance; this trait is variable and some trees have an almost scaly bark.

LEAF COLOR: Lustrous dark green in summer changing to fluorescent yellow to orange to scarlet to purple colors in the fall; one of our best, most consistent, and most beautiful trees in fall.

FLOWERS: Polygamo dioecious, appearing with the leaves, small, greenish white, borne in (female) 2 to 4 flowered axillary peduncled clusters; the male in many-flowered peduncled clusters, not ornamentally effective; the literature is not consistent on sexual characteristics and I have seen trees wholly male and wholly female; others with sporadic fruit set; polygamo-dioecious implies primarily dioecious but with the possibility of perfect (bisexual) flowers on the tree; this might explain limited fruit set sometimes observed on primarily male trees.

FRUIT: Oblong drupe, 3/8 to 1/2″ long, bluish black ripening late September through early October and eaten by many species of birds and mammals, on occasion fruits are present into November in the south.

CULTURE: Difficult to transplant because of taproot; move balled and burlapped in early spring; prefers moist, well drained, acid (pH 5.5 to 6.5), deep soils; however, in the wild it is found on dry mountain ridges, burned over forest land, or abandoned fields, and in cold mountain swamps; does not tolerate high pH soils; full sun or semi-shade and sheltered locations from winds are preferred; prune in fall; Pair reported 4 to 6″ of growth per year over an 8-year period in Wichita, KS tests.

DISEASES AND INSECTS: Cankers, leaf spots, rust, tupelo leaf miner and scale; none are particularly serious.

LANDSCAPE VALUE: Excellent specimen tree, acceptable street tree in residential areas, not for heavily polluted areas; outstanding summer and fall foliage and habit, lovely in a naturalized area; certainly one of the *best* and *most consistent* native trees for fall color.

PROPAGATION: Seeds exhibit moderate embryo dormancy and moist stratification for 60 to 90 days at 41°F is beneficial; I have raised numerous seedlings following this procedure. Generally not rooted from cuttings but a report in *The Plant Propagator* 14(4): 11–12 described a successful method. Shoots are forced in the greenhouse, 1 1/2″ long, 8000 ppm IBA talc, sand, 70°F bottom heat, mist, with rooting taking place in 2 to 3 weeks; cuttings are transplanted after 6 weeks and grow normally, rooting success of 95 to 100% was not unusual. Personally, I have had no success with the species from cuttings. Tissue culture has been successful.

ADDITIONAL NOTES: I have a great love for *N. sylvatica* and do not adhere to the difficult transplanting philosophy. If container-grown and moved in small sizes it will re-establish quite well. It responds well to water and fertilizer. I have seen it on rolling hills of southern Indiana, growing around fresh water ponds on Cape Cod and in a mixed forest association in the Piedmont of Georgia. In all situations, the glory of its fall coloration always stands out above its other features. Have made a selection for outstanding scarlet fall color.

NATIVE HABITAT: Maine, Ontario, Michigan to Florida and Texas. Introduced before 1750.

RELATED SPECIES:

Nyssa aquatica — Water Tupelo
(nis′à a-kwat′i-kà)

LEAVES: Alternate, simple, oblong-ovate or elliptic, 4 to 7″ long, 2 to 4″ wide, acute or acuminate, entire or often serrated, dark green above, paler beneath and either glabrous or slightly pubescent; petiole—to 2″ long.

BUDS: Small and roundish.

Nyssa aquatica,, Water Tupelo, is one of the most characteristic of southern swamp trees and is found on sites which are periodically under water. The distinguishing differences from *Nyssa sylvatica* include larger leaves to about 7″ long and larger fruit (about 1″ long) of reddish purple color with thin flesh and a deep, sharp ridged nutlet (endocarp). The trunk bulges conspicuously at the base but tapers rapidly to a long, clear trunk; the crown is rather narrow and open. The wood is commercially important as is that of *Nyssa sylvatica*. Native from Virginia to southern Illinois, Florida and Texas. Introduced before 1735. Chiefly found in the Atlantic and Gulf Coastal Plains and Mississippi River Valley. Zone 6 to 9.

Nyssa ogeche — Ogeechee Tupelo
(nis′à ō-gē′chē)

LEAVES: Alternate, simple, elliptic to obovate-oblong, 4 to 6″ long, acute to obtuse, entire, lustrous dark green and slightly pubescent above, pubescent or glabrous below.

Nyssa ogeche, Ogeechee Tupelo, is known for the 1/2 to 3/4″ diameter red fruits that are pleasantly flavored and have been used as a substitute for limes. Introduced 1806. South Carolina, Georgia, Florida. Zone 7 to 9.

Nyssa sinensis — Chinese Tupelo
(nis'a̅ sī-nen'sis)

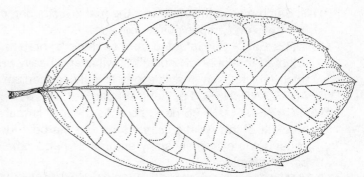

LEAVES: Alternate, simple, elliptic, 3 to 6″
long, tapering at both ends, dull dark
green above, paler green and lustrous
beneath; petiole—1/4″ long, hairy.

Nyssa sinensis, Chinese Tupelo, is a virtual
recluse and, to my knowledge, is hidden
in a select few gardens in the United
States. A young plant at the NC State Arboretum was gracefully pyramidal with a uniform branching
habit. Foliage in late October was developing yellow and red hues; the species may grow 30 to 50′
high. My knowledge is limited but initial observations indicate it may have potential. Central China.
Introduced 1902. Zone 7 to 9.

Osmanthus heterophyllus (formerly *O. ilicifolius*) — Holly Tea Olive, Holly Osmanthus,
False-holly

(oz-man'thus het-ē̄r-o-fil'us)

FAMILY: Oleaceae

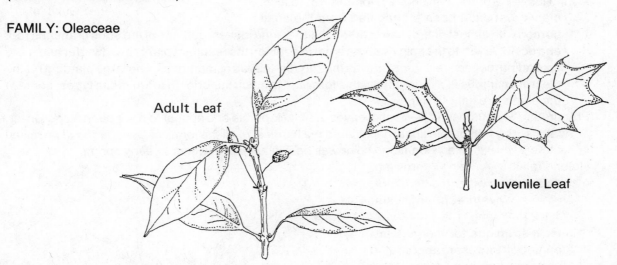

Adult Leaf

Juvenile Leaf

LEAVES: Opposite, simple, evergreen, elliptic or ovate to elliptic-oblong, 1 to 2 1/2″ long, 1 to 1 1/2″ wide,
spiny pointed, cuneate or broad-cuneate, with 1 to 4 pairs of prominent spiny teeth, rarely entire,
leathery, lustrous dark green above, yellowish green and veined beneath, glabrous; petiole—1/2″
long or less.
NOTE: In the adult stage the leaves at the top of the plant become oval or ovate and essentially entire;
have noticed that mature specimens are largely entire.

SIZE: 8 to 10′ (up to 20′) in height, spread slightly less; old plants on the Georgia campus are 12 to 15′
high and slightly wider; in youth the habit is distinctly upright.
HARDINESS: Zone 7 to 9.
HABIT: Dense, upright-oval to rounded evergreen shrub of impenetrable constitution.
RATE: Slow to medium.
TEXTURE: Medium throughout the seasons.
LEAF COLOR: Lustrous dark green above, yellow green beneath.
FLOWERS: In general, *Osmanthus* species may be perfect, polygamous, or dioecious; the flowers of this
species are white, 4-petaled, 1/4″ across with the petals reflexed, exceedingly fragrant, borne 4 to 5
together in axillary cymes during late September-October into early November. The flowers are
largely hidden by the foliage but the fragrance is overpowering; suspect this species is dioecious.

FRUIT: Seldom seen in cultivation; the fruit is a slender, ovoid, 3/8″ long, bluish black drupe; have seen a few fruits on campus plants, not showy.

CULTURE: Easily transplanted from containers; prefers fertile, moist, well-drained, acid soil but seems adapted to higher pH soils; will withstand heavy pruning; seems to display a fair degree of urban tolerance, full sun (may discolor slightly) to medium shade; more shade tolerant than given credit.

DISEASES AND INSECTS: None serious.

LANDSCAPE VALUE: Borders, screens, hedge, formal specimen, by walks and entrances; this is the hardiest of the Asiatic *Osmanthus* and the best for the upper south and northern areas along the coast but is extremely spiny and not as handsome as *O.* × *fortunei;* makes an excellent screen or barrier planting.

CULTIVARS: In most cases, the variegated forms are less hardy than the species.

'Aureomarginatus' ('Aureus')—Leaves margined with yellow.

'Gulftide'—A compact, upright form of the species with extremely glossy green foliage and prominent spiny margins and a slight twist; introduced by Gulfsteam Nursery; have seen plants 10 to 15′ high; leaves become progressively less spiny with maturity of the plant; more cold hardy than the species.

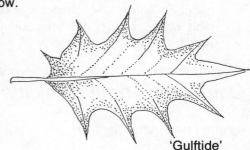

'Gulftide'

'Latifolius Variegatus'—Leaves broader than 'Variegatus'.

'Myrtifolius'—Perhaps a misnomer for this represents plants that have been propagated from the adult portion with almost entire, narrowly-oval, 1 to 2″ long leaves; cuttings of the adult branches root and do not revert to the spiny-leaved type; in addition the resultant plants are dwarfer and more spreading; collectively referred to as the "myrtle-leaved osmanthus," one large planting on the Georgia campus is almost wholly this form and is much superior to the juvenile types; some of the plants are fully 18′ high.

'Purpureus' ('Purpurascens')—Young leaves are black-purple and appear to have been dipped in tar; later green with purple tinge; considered the hardiest of all the forms of *O. heterophyllus;* raised at Kew in 1880; Raulston noted color was best in full sun in winter to early spring.

'Rotundifolius'—A slow growing, dwarf shrub with rigid, leathery, simple, evergreen, obovate, 1 1/2 to 2″ long, 1 to 1 1/4″ wide leaves, unique for margins are angled off to present a geometric pattern, lustrous dark green above, pale beneath, petiole 1/4″ long; grows 4 to 5′ high, have not seen it flower, although described as having fragrant

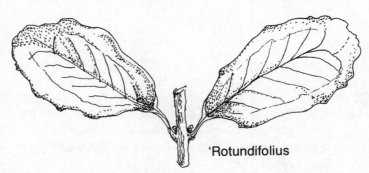

'Rotundifolius

flowers; slightly less cold hardy than the species for leaves were browned on a protected plant while the species was not injured.

'Variegatus'—Quite handsome shrub for color contrast; the leaves margined with creamy white; slower growing than the species and perhaps more upright in habit but equally dense; have had no success rooting this clone, 8 to 10′ only after many years, have seen it in full sun where it showed no burning; interestingly, the leaves were completely killed at -8°F but the stem and buds were not injured.

PROPAGATION: Cuttings apparently root readily but I have had no success; it could be related to timing; a nurseryman told me that cuttings should be collected just as new growth hardens in late spring or early summer. Rooting times are generally quite long with 3 to 4 months the norm. A Georgia nursery roots *O.* × *fortunei* and *O. fragrans* in July–August, 8000 ppm IBA talc, bark-sand, mist with good success. Cuttings are taken from young container-grown plants. Blazich and Acedo, *J. Envirn. Hort.* 7:133–135 (1989) rooted untreated *O. heterophyllus* 'Ilicifolius' in September and February at 92 and 81%, respectively.

NATIVE HABITAT: Japan, introduced 1856 by Thomas Lobb. Sargent describes *O. heterophyllus* as attaining the dimensions of a tree approaching 30′ in height and one foot or more in diameter.

RELATED SPECIES:

Osmanthus americanus — Devilwood
(oz-man′thus ȧ-mer-i-kā′nus)

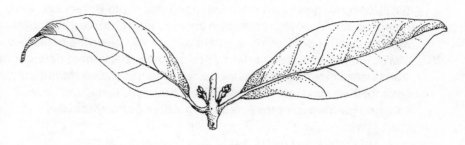

LEAVES: Opposite, simple, evergreen, lanceolate-ovate, 2 to 4 1/2″ long, 3/4 to 1 1/2″ wide, abruptly acute, cuneate, entire, leathery, lustrous dark olive green above, pale green beneath, prominent protruding midvein, laterals obscure, glabrous; petiole—1/4 to 3/4″ long.
BUDS: Imbricate, 1/4″ long, greenish brown, in upper leaf axils flower buds are preformed and elongated.
STEM: Stout, squarish, glabrous, green finally gray-brown, dotted with numerous pale lenticels; pith—white, diaphragmed, ample.

Osmanthus americanus, Devilwood, is by no means a common landscape shrub but deserves consideration in southern and perhaps northern gardens. Most people would not recognize it as an *Osmanthus* because the leaves are entire. The habit is open and loose (15 to 25′ high), an attribute that separates it from other species. The dark olive green leaves are handsome throughout the seasons. In the axils of the upper leaves, paniculate inflorescences are present from fall until late March–April (Athens) when the white, fragrant flowers open. The ovoid, 1/2″ long, dark blue drupe matures in September and may persist into spring of the next year. Cultural requirements are similar to *O. heterophyllus.* Can be used in naturalized situations. North Carolina to Florida and Mississippi. Found along swamp margins, hammocks and borders of streams. Cultivated 1758. Listed as Zone 6 but have seen it as far north as Cincinnati, Ohio. The most cold hardy *Osmanthus* species and should tolerate -20 to -25°F.

Osmanthus × fortunei — Fortune's Osmanthus
(oz-man′thus × fôr-tū′nē-ī)

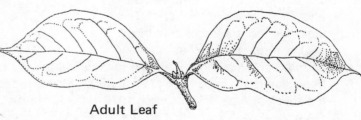

Adult Leaf

LEAVES: Opposite, simple, evergreen, 2 1/2 to 4″ long, 1 1/2 to 3″ wide, oval or slightly ovate, taper-pointed and spine-tipped, wedge shape, margins with up to 10 or 12 triangular, 1/6″ long, spine-tipped teeth on each side, leathery, lustrous dark green; some leaves especially those in the upper reaches of the plant display an adult condition and have no marginal spines (teeth).
BUDS: Imbricate, small, 1/8″ long, greenish brown, superposed, glabrous, emerge at 45° angle to stem.
STEM: Moderate, gray, glabrous, dotted with dark lenticels, compressed at nodes; pith—solid, green.

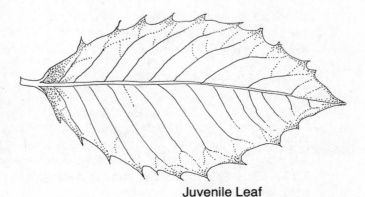

Juvenile Leaf

Osmanthus × *fortunei,* Fortune's Osmanthus, is a hybrid between *O. heterophyllus* and *O. fragrans.* It tends to be intermediate between the two parents in most characteristics. It is a large, dense, oval-rounded shrub that matures between 15 to 20'. It can be easily restrained at about any height. Two massive specimens on the Georgia campus are 20 to 25' high and wide and look like dark green haystacks. The 1/3" diameter, exceedingly fragrant white flowers are produced in axillary cymes in October–November; mid to late October has been the normal flowering period in Athens. Quite hardy compared to *O. fragrans* and preferable to that species in the upper south. Introduced from Japan in 1856. According to Bean the early introduction into Britain was a male. Whether this is true for the American introduction is not known but I have not observed fruit on this species. Apparently this hybrid was reconstituted in California where a clone was given the name 'San Jose'. Over the past few years I have looked at sufficient 'San Jose' to know the form is different from typical *O.* × *fortunei.* The leaves are longer, slightly more narrow and the spines more abundant and longer. 'Variegatus' is described as having broad white marginal serrations. *Osmanthus* × *fortunei* is quite common in southern gardens. Displays greater vigor than *O. heterophyllus* and, in my mind, is a better landscape plant.

Osmanthus fragrans — Fragrant Tea Olive
(oz-man'thus frā'granz)

LEAVES: Opposite, simple, evergreen, oblong-lanceolate to elliptic, 2 to 4" (5") long, long acuminate, cuneate, finely dentate or entire, leathery, lustrous dark green above, lighter, glabrous and distinctly veined below.

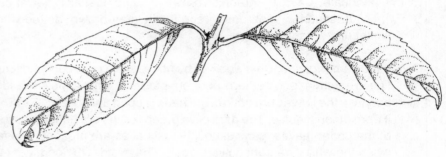

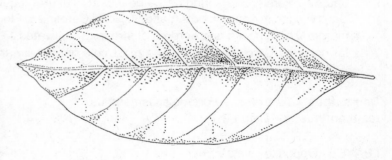

Osmanthus fragrans, Fragrant Tea Olive, is the least cold hardy of the species presented. In coastal areas it makes a large shrub or small tree, 20 to 30' high; further inland it may be damaged by low temperatures and thus reduced in size. The leaves which are larger than those of *O.* × *fortunei* are not as coarsely serrated and may be entire. The small white flowers are the most fragrant of the group and it has been stated that one or two of them will fill a fair-sized room with sweet perfume. My first contact with the species came in September, 1979 at the American Camellia Society Headquarters in Fort Valley, GA where it was in flower. I have also observed flowers in the spring, around early to mid-April in the Athens area. Probably grows too large for the average landscape but is certainly worth considering where hardy and space permits. Would make a fine container plant for use on the patio or near entrances. Forma *aurantiacus* has pale orange-colored flowers, and is a beautiful form. Species was severely injured in Athens area after exposure to 0°F. Plants were generally defoliated and young stems injured.

ADDITIONAL NOTES: *Osmanthus delavayi,* with 1/2 to 1" long, lustrous dark green, ovate to oval, prominently toothed leaves on a 6 to 8' and larger spreading framework is occasionally encountered. I have seen the plant only in European gardens and it is rather handsome. The white fragrant flowers are borne in terminal and axillary 4 to 8 flowered cymes. Each flower about 1/2" long and 1/2" wide with 4 reflexed lobes. Fruits are egg-shaped, 1/2" long, blue-black drupes. China. Introduced 1890. Zone 9 to 10, possibly 8.

   Also encountered in Europe was *O. decorus,* with 2 to 5″ long, 1/2 to 1 3/4″ wide, glossy dark green, leathery, firm textured, oval, generally entire leaves. White, fragrant, 1/3″ diameter flowers are borne in dense axillary clusters in April. Plants grow 5 to 10′ high and wider at maturity. Foliage reminds of an evergreen privet. Listed as *Phillyrea decora* in *Hortus III,* but most botanical gardens label it *O. decorus.* Native around the Black Sea. Zone 8 to 9?

Ostrya virginiana — American Hophornbeam, also known as Ironwood.
(os′tre̅-a̅ ve̅r-jin-e̅-a̅′na)

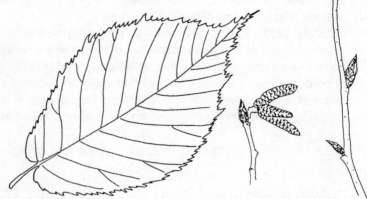

FAMILY: Betulaceae

LEAVES: Alternate, simple, 2 to 5″ long, half as wide, oval-lanceolate, acuminate, rounded or heart shaped, dark green and hairy on midrib and between veins above, paler and more pubescent beneath, sharply and doubly serrate, veins forking at ends; petiole—1/4″ long, pubescent.

BUDS: Imbricate, small, 1/8 to 1/4″ long, narrowly ovate, pointed, glabrous or finely downy, green to brown, slightly gummy especially within, strongly divergent, terminal absent; scales longitudinally striate.

STEM: Slender, dark reddish brown, often zigzag, for the most part smooth and shining.

FRUIT: Nutlet, enclosed in hop-like sac; staminate catkins, abundantly present, usually in 3's, good winter identification characteristics.

SIZE: A small tree averaging 25 to 40′ in height and 2/3's to equal that in spread; can reach 60′ but this is seldom attained.

HARDINESS: Zone 3 to 9.

HABIT: Very graceful small tree with many horizontal or drooping branches usually forming a rounded outline, somewhat pyramidal in youth.

RATE: Slow, probably 10 to 15′ over a 15 year period.

TEXTURE: Medium-fine in leaf, medium in winter.

BARK: Grayish brown, often broken into narrow, longitudinal strips which are free at each end.

LEAF COLOR: Dark green in summer changing to yellow in the fall, seldom effective and falling early.

FLOWERS: Monoecious, male catkins usually grouped in 3's and visible throughout winter, each about 1″ long; female visible in April.

FRUIT: A 1/3″ long nut(let), enclosed in an inflated, membranous, ovate, 3/4 to 1″ long involucre and resembling the fruit of hops, hence, the name Hophornbeam; entire infructescence 1 1/2 to 2 1/2″ long, 2/3 to 1 1/2″ wide

CULTURE: Transplant balled and burlapped or from a container in early spring into a cool, moist, well drained, slightly acid soil; often found in the wild growing in rather dry, gravelly or rocky soil; full sun or partial shade; prune in winter or early spring; somewhat slow to re-establish after transplanting.

DISEASES AND INSECTS: None serious, "witches' broom" occurs on occasion and results in broomy masses of small, bunchy, twiggy growths.

LANDSCAPE VALUE: Handsome medium sized tree for lawns, parks, golf courses, naturalized areas, and possibly streets; the species has performed well in city plantings and very narrow tree lawns; once established it makes excellent growth.

PROPAGATION: Seeds have an internal type of dormancy which is difficult to overcome; warm followed by cold seems to be the best treatment; one study reported that seeds collected fresh and sown immediately did not germinate, those given 3 months cold stratification germinated 2%, 3 months warm stratification followed by 3, 4, or 5 months cold produced 81, 92 and 92% germination, respectively.

RELATED SPECIES: I would be hard pressed to separate *O. carpinifolia,* (os-trē′ȧ kär-pi-ni-fō′li-ȧ), European Hornbeam, and *O. japonica,* (os-trē′ȧ ja-pon′i-kȧ), Japanese Hornbeam, from the above species without close scrutiny. During sabbatical, I admired one particularly handsome specimen of *O. virginiana* only to find out that upon checking the label it was *O. japonica.* The first species differs from *O. v.* by virtue of never having any glands on the hairs of the stems. *O. japonica* has fewer veins (9 to 12) compared to 12 to 15 of *O. virginiana* and more uniformly pubescent, velvety leaf surfaces. Good luck!

ADDITIONAL NOTES: *Ostrya virginiana* is an attractive, small to medium-sized tree that the American nursery industry has never pursued. In the wild, it grows on the drier slopes of woodlands where it exists as an understory species. Interestingly, in the Georgia Botanical Garden it is abundant on the slopes above the Oconee River flood plain and is totally absent in the areas that are periodically flooded. At this sharp juncture, *Carpinus caroliniana,* American Hornbeam, becomes the dominant understory plant and even grows on the river banks where its roots literally dangle their apices in the cool water.

NATIVE HABITAT: Cape Breton, Ontario to Minnesota, south to Florida and Texas. Introduced 1690.

Oxydendrum arboreum — Sourwood, also called Sorrel Tree or Lily of the Valley Tree
(ok-si-den′drum âr-bō′rē-um)

FAMILY: Ericaceae

LEAVES: Alternate, simple, elliptic-oblong to oblong-lan- ceolate, 3 to 8″ long, 1 1/2 to 3 1/2″ wide, acuminate, broad-cuneate, serrulate or entire, lustrous dark green and glabrous above, lighter green and spar- ingly pubescent on veins beneath; petiole—1/2 to 1″ long.

BUDS: Small, 1/16″ long, conical-globose, solitary, ses- sile, with about 6 scales; terminal lacking.

STEM: Glabrous or sparingly pubescent, olive or bright red, slender.

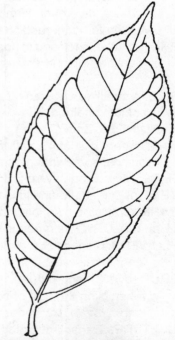

SIZE: 25 to 30′ in height and approximately 20′ in spread; can grow 50 to 75′.

HARDINESS: Zone 5, possibly 4, to 9.

HABIT: Pyramidal tree, with rounded top and drooping branches; very lovely outline.

RATE: Slow, 14 to 15′ over a 12 to 15 year period.

TEXTURE: Medium in all seasons.

BARK: Grayish brown to black, thick, deeply furrowed, and has rather scaly ridges that are often cut horizontally; resembling in its finest form the blocky bark of persimmon.

LEAF COLOR: Rich irridescent green in spring becoming lustrous dark green with maturity and turning yellow, red and purple in fall; often all colors on the same tree; I had a small tree in my Illinois garden that turned a brilliant red in fall; in the south this is one of the earliest and certainly best trees for fall coloration.

FLOWERS: White, urn-shaped, 1/4″ long, fragrant, June to early July in 4 to 10″ long and wide, drooping, racemose-panicles, excellent flowering tree, literally smother the foliage, remind of a lacy veil.

FRUIT: Dehiscent, 5-valved, 1/3″ long capsule, persistent, at first yellowish, finally brown, erect, good identification feature in winter months; pendulous in youth, upright at maturity.

CULTURE: Transplant as a young tree balled and burlapped or container grown into acid, peaty, most, well-drained soil; full sun or partial shade although flowering and fall color are maximized in sun; the pH should run 5.5 to 6.5 if possible; does reasonably well in dry soils; not for polluted or urban areas.

DISEASES AND INSECTS: Leaf spots and twig blight, neither of which are serious.

LANDSCAPE VALUE: Truly an all season ornamental; excellent specimen plant; it has so many attributes that it should only be considered for specimen use; many gardeners feel, among native trees, this is second only to Flowering Dogwood; certainly one of my favorite trees and in Bernheim Arboretum, Clermont, KY, is a grouping, actually a grove, that is contrasted with a forest background; it is one of the handsomest uses imaginable; also in New England have seen the species in combination with *Hydrangea quercifolia* and in fall color at the same time, the pinkish-red of the Sourwood and deep burgundy of Oakleaf Hydrangea were memorable.

PROPAGATION: I have attempted to root July cuttings using up to 10,000 ppm IBA-quick dip, peat:perlite, mist but have had no success; Dr. John Frett collected seeds from the wilds of Georgia and raised numerous seedlings by placing the seeds on a peat medium and placing the flats under mist until they germinated; he then moved the seedlings under fluorescent light where they proceeded to grow like weeds. Plants have been successfully produced through tissue culture.

NATIVE HABITAT: Found on well-drained, gravelly soils on ridges rising above the banks of streams from the coast of Virginia to North Carolina and in southwestern Pennsylvania, southern Ohio, Indiana, western Kentucky, Tennessee; Appalachians to western Florida and the coasts of Mississippi and Louisiana. Introduced 1747.

Pachysandra procumbens — Alleghany Pachysandra
(pak-i-san′drȧ prō-kum′benz)

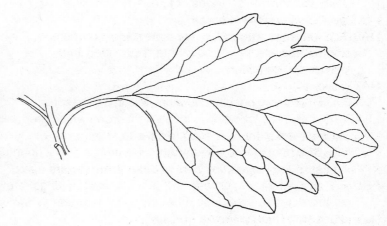

FAMILY: Buxaceae

LEAVES: Alternate, simple, evergreen, semi-evergreen to deciduous, 2 to 4″ long, 2 to 3″ wide, elliptic to obovate, much wider than those of *P. terminalis,* prominently toothed especially above middle, gray to blue-green, often with a gray mottle above, slightly pubescent below; petiole 1/2 to 1 1/2″ long.

SIZE: 6 to 10″ (12″) high.

HARDINESS: Zone 4 to 9.

HABIT: Deciduous to semi-evergreen to evergreen ground cover spreading by rhizomes.

RATE: Slow, perhaps medium if soil is loose, moist and acid.

TEXTURE: Medium.

LEAF COLOR: Flat green to bluish green, often mottled, does not possess the luster of *P. terminalis,* very handsome foliage; some plants have a snake-skin like mosaic on the upper surface of the leaves.

FLOWERS: White or pinkish, fragrant, borne on 2 to 4″ long spikes in March-April, spikes arise from buds at the base of the stem, all seem to emerge from the center of a plant and make a rather attractive show.

FRUIT: Dehiscent, 3-pointed capsule, seeds lustrous blackish brown.

CULTURE: Appears adaptable, prefers moist, acid, organic, well-drained soil; partial to full shade; in cold climates some protection is necessary if plants are to maintain a smattering of evergreen leaves; a plant sited in an exposed location in my Illinois garden died to the ground and did not flower while in a protected area in a neighbor's garden it maintained green foliage and flowered profusely.

DISEASES AND INSECTS: Apparently this species is not troubled by dieback problems, scale, or leaf spot which sometimes ruin plantings of *P. terminalis;* the Cornell Plantations, Ithaca, N.Y., has maintained beds for 12 years and had no serious disease or dieback.

LANDSCAPE VALUE: Excellent and different ground cover for shade, forms a soft carpet of gray-green leaves; have seen superior plantings at the Morton Arboretum, Arnold Arboretum and Atlanta Historical Society.

PROPAGATION: Cuttings of vigorous growth in June will root readily; Jack Alexander, propagator, Arnold Arboretum, and I found that 4000 and 8000 ppm IBA yielded excellent results. For a detailed discussion see Alexander and Dirr. *The Plant Propagator* 25(2):9–10, 1979.

ADDITIONAL NOTES: Plant is not widely available in commerce but is worth seeking out. I have observed enough excellent plantings to believe the plant should be more widely promoted and planted.

NATIVE HABITAT: Eastern Kentucky, West Virginia to Florida and Louisiana. Introduced 1800.

Pachysandra terminalis — Japanese Pachysandra or Spurge
(pak-i-san'drå tēr-mi-na'lis)

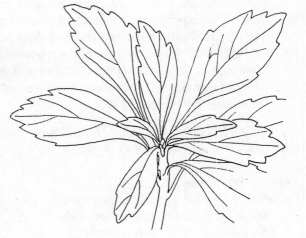

FAMILY: Buxaceae

LEAVES: Alternate, simple, evergreen, obovate to ovate, 2 to 4″ long, 1/2 to 1 1/2″ wide, dentate, 3-nerved at base, lustrous dark green above, glabrous; petiole—1/2 to 1″ long; leaves appear whorled at top of stem.

STEM: Upright, greenish, glabrous.

SIZE: 6 to 12″ high.

HARDINESS: Zone 4 to 8, does not perform as well in south as in northern areas.

HABIT: Evergreen ground cover spreading by rhizomes and forming a solid mat if provided the proper soil conditions.

RATE: Slow.

TEXTURE: Medium, possibly medium-fine in all seasons.

LEAF COLOR: New growth is a lovely light green which gradually changes to lustrous dark green; foliage will yellow if plants are sited in full sun or exposed windy situations.

FLOWERS: White, March to early April, borne in a 1 to 2″ long upright spike at the end of the shoot in the center of the leaves, females at base, male toward apex.

FRUIT: Berry-like drupe, whitish, 1/2″ long, some plantings rarely produce fruits; this is probably because all the plants are of one clone; the plant is probably self-sterile and several clones are necessary along with bees to insure fruit set.

CULTURE: Easily transplanted; prefers moist, well drained, acid soil abundantly supplied with organic matter (pH 5.5 to 6.5 is ideal); prefers shade and actually yellows in full sun, does extremely well under heavily shaded and shallow rooted trees; I have seen established plantings under the European Beech which provides one of the heaviest shades.

DISEASES AND INSECTS: Leaf blight, *Volutella pachysandrae* causes both leaf blight and also stem cankers, *Pachysandra* leaf tier, scale, mites and northern root-knot nematode.

LANDSCAPE VALUE: Probably the best ground cover for deep shade; singularly beautiful when the new growth emerges; one of my favorites; siting is important and in exposed locations of sun and wind extensive foliar discoloration and damage occur; have observed plantings that qualify as perfect; unfortunately in east and parts of midwest the use has reached monoculture proportions; *Volutella* can be serious and can ruin a planting unless fungicides are employed.

CULTIVARS:

'Green Carpet'—A superior cultivar because the foliage is not trailing in habit but grows close to the ground, forming a low, neat ground cover; foliage is smaller and deeper more waxy green than the species, many ground cover producers are growing this form.

'Green Sheen'—High, mirror-like gloss to the leaves which is retained for at least 3 years in sun or shade, selected by Dale Chapman of the University of Connecticut.

'Variegata' ('Silver Edge')—Leaves prominently mottled with white, is not as vigorous as the species and does not develop as fast; attractive in the right location.

PROPAGATION: Cuttings root readily with 1000 ppm IBA, peat:perlite, under mist; the best time to take cuttings (my experience) is after the spring flush of growth has hardened and leaves are fully mature; for my Illinois garden I rooted about 10 flats from campus cuttings; good rooting should take place in 6 to 8 weeks; freshly harvested seed germinated 20% in 30 days, scarified seeds germinated 90% in 34 days.

NATIVE HABITAT: Japan. Introduced 1882.

Parrotia persica — Persian Parrotia
(par-rō′ti-à pēr′si-kà)

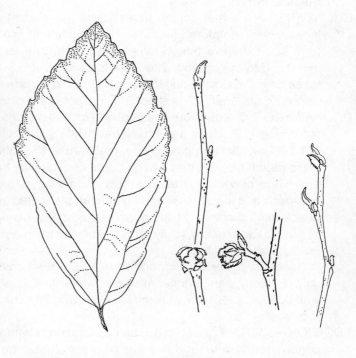

FAMILY: Hamamelidaceae

LEAVES: Alternate, simple, 2 1/2 to 5″ long, 1 to 2 1/2″ wide, oval to obovate-oblong, with large lanceolate caducous stipules, obtuse, rounded to sub-cordate at base, coarsely crenate-dentate above the middle or almost glabrous above, with sparse pubescence below, undulate, lustrous medium to dark green, similar in shape to *Hamamelis* and *Fothergilla* leaves; petiole 1/12 to 1/4″ long.

BUDS: Vegetative-stalked, with 2 outer scales, tomentulous, brownish; flower buds—globose, about 1/3″ diameter, quite pubescent, brownish black.

STEM: Slender, brownish, pubescent when young, finally becoming grayish brown and glabrous with maturity.

BARK: Exfoliating on old branches to expose gray, green, white, brown mosaic.

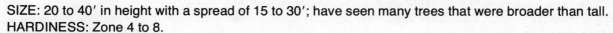

SIZE: 20 to 40′ in height with a spread of 15 to 30′; have seen many trees that were broader than tall.

HARDINESS: Zone 4 to 8.

HABIT: Small single-stemmed tree or large multistemmed shrub with an oval-rounded head of upright, ascending branches; also a form with wide-spreading branches.

RATE: Medium, 10′ over a 6 to 8 year period.

TEXTURE: Medium in leaf; medium-fine in winter.

BARK: Older branches and trunks develop an exfoliating gray, green, white, brown color reminiscent of *Pinus bungeana*, Lacebark Pine; the bark is a welcome asset in the winter landscape; takes considerable time before exfoliating bark occurs.

LEAF COLOR: Reddish purple when unfolding changing to lustrous medium to dark green during summer and developing brilliant yellow to orange to scarlet fall color; one of the most beautiful trees for foliage effect.

FLOWERS: Perfect, apetalous, before the leaves in March-April (early to mid February, Athens), the showy parts of the flower are the crimson stamens; most people miss the flowers which are, at best, curiously effective.

FRUIT: A capsule, ornamentally ineffective, 2-valved, seeds 3/8″ long, bright brown.

CULTURE: Transplant balled and burlapped in early spring; prefers well drained, loamy, slightly acid (pH 6.0 to 6.5) soils; will tolerate chalky soils; full sun, but will do well in light shade; prune in spring; appears to be extremely tolerant once established.

DISEASES AND INSECTS: Very pest-free tree, noticed significant Japanese beetle damage in the south.

LANDSCAPE VALUE: One of the best small specimen trees that I know; the foliage, bark and pest resistance make it a tree worth considering; excellent small lawn or street tree, could be integrated into foundation plantings around large residences; is definitely a topic of conversation; a fine accent plant; since this is one of my favorite plants I am claiming eminent domain and reciting the following litany of institutions that have fine specimens, a pilgrimage would be worth the reader's time; Barnes Arboretum*, Bernheim, Brooklyn Botanic Garden, Rowe*, Arnold*, Morton, Dawes Arboreta; Cave Hill and Spring Grove Cemeteries; Biltmore* and Cantigny Gardens; Michigan State and Swarthmore* campuses; those marked with an asterisk have exceptional specimens; perhaps the most beautiful and definitely the largest (50 to 60′) specimen I have seen occurs at the Jardin des Plantes, Paris.

CULTIVARS: In the last edition I mentioned the weeping form that had eluded my every attempt to locate....well, no more...for at Kew Gardens there is an 8 to 10′ high, 12 to 15′ wide, stiffly weeping form of superlative beauty, the habit is akin to a large umbrella with a long handle with the ribs extending to the ground. The trunk is 14 to 18″ in diameter and exfoliates like the species. One of these days I will locate one for my garden; I did receive a plant that was listed as 'Pendula' but appears nothing more than a side shoot, i.e., plagiotrophic growth, with a more or less horizontal nature.

PROPAGATION: Seeds should be stratified for five months at warm, fluctuating temperatures and then 3 months at 41°F. Cuttings—I have had 100% success with June-July cuttings treated with 1000 ppm IBA/50% alcohol and placed under mist. After the cuttings have rooted it is important to leave them in the medium where they can go dormant; after they have received an artificial or natural cold period and when new growth ensues they should be potted. I have had tremendous success with this approach and in cases where the cutting has rooted and the shoot is still growing have potted them directly with success. If cuttings are rooted in late May-June (Athens), they invariably produce a flush of growth especially if lightly fertilized after rooting. *Parrotia*, like *Fothergilla*, is not difficult to root or manage after rooting.

Report in *The Plant Propagator* 30(4):9 (1984) describes the following success: 6-year-old tree, July (Boston), sand:perlite, mist, overwinter in flats and analyzed in March of 1984—100% rooting with 8000 ppm IBA talc plus thiram, 95% with 24 hour soak 400 ppm KIBA, 65% untreated with poor root quality.

ADDITIONAL NOTES: In my mind, an outstanding ornamental tree that has few rivals. I have observed only limited fruit set and this was on a less-than-robust plant at William and Mary College. I had a nice small specimen in my Illinois garden which always evoked a "What is it?" from visitors. In Europe, I noticed the plants often tend to be more widespreading than plants in the United States.

NATIVE HABITAT: Iran, cultivated 1840, one species named after F.W. Parrot, German naturalist and traveler.

Parrotiopsis jacquemontiana
(par-rō-ti-op′sis jak-mon-ti-ā′na)

FAMILY: Hamamelidaceae

LEAVES: Alternate, simple, roundish or very broadly ovate, 2 to 3 1/2″ long and about as wide, margins with broad serrations, dark green and pubescent above to almost glabrous, dense pubesence on veins beneath; petiole 1/4 to 1/2″ long.

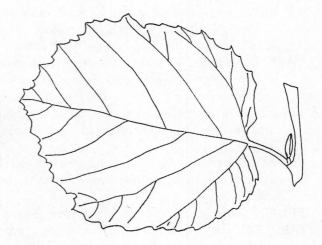

SIZE: 8 to 12′ high, usually not as wide, can grow 15 to 20′.

HARDINESS: Zone 5 to 7.

HABIT: Usually an upright shrub in this country although can become a small tree.

RATE: Slow.

TEXTURE: Medium.

BARK: Smooth gray on older branches.

LEAF COLOR: Dark green, no fall color of consequence; leaves hold late and may turn yellow.

FLOWERS: Perfect, apetalous, white, 1/2 to 1" wide produced in a short-stalked cluster and open from April to May and intermittently through summer, yellow stamens are showy, beneath the head of flowers are 4 to 6 petal-like bracts, white, 1/2 to 1" long, that constitute the showy part of the inflorescence.

FRUIT: Capsule containing shining brown, 1/6" long, oblong seeds.

CULTURE: Similar to *Parrotia*.

DISEASES AND INSECTS: None serious.

LANDSCAPE VALUE: Interesting and unusual shrub; rather pretty in flower; not well known and certainly not common.

PROPAGATION: Apparently seed has a long warm-cold requirement; cuttings collected in August rooted 100% when treated with 8000 ppm IBA-talc; cuttings should probably be allowed to pass through a dormant period before being transplanted.

NATIVE HABITAT: Himalayas. Introduced 1879.

Parthenocissus quinquefolia — Virginia Creeper, also called Woodbine.
(pär-thē-nō-sis′us kwin-ke-fō′li-à)

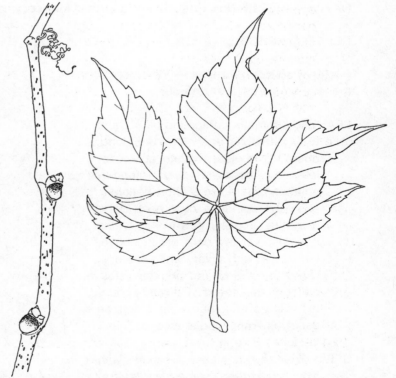

LEAVES: Alternate, compound palmate, (3) 5 leaflets, each stalked (1/3" long), elliptic to obovate-oblong, 1 1/2 to 4" long, 1/2 to 2 1/2" wide, acuminate, usually cuneate, coarsely and often crenately serrate, lustrous dark green above, glaucescent beneath, young growth bright waxy bronze to red; petiole—1 to 4" long.

BUDS: Often collateral, brownish, sessile, round-conical, with 2 to 3 exposed scales, end-bud absent.

STEM: Round, light brown, prominently lenticelled, glabrous leaf scars distinctly concave; pith—white, tendrils with 5 to 8 branches ending in adhesive tips, longer than those of *P. tricuspidata*.

SIZE: 30 to 50′ and more; the structure upon which it climbs is the limiting factor.

HARDINESS: Zone 3 to 9.

HABIT: Deciduous vine with tendrils which have 5 to 8 branches, each ending in adhesive like tips; has the ability to literally cement itself to the wall and therefore needs no support; good on trees, will also crawl along the ground.

RATE: Fast, 6 to 10′ and beyond in a single season.

TEXTURE: Medium in leaf, somewhat coarse in winter.

LEAF COLOR: New growth bronzish to reddish, rich lustrous deep green in summer; usually a purple-red to crimson-red in fall; first of all woody plants to color effectively; often noticeable in the tops of tall trees.

FLOWERS: Greenish white (yellowish green), June-July, in cymes which usually form terminal panicles; totally ineffective as they are borne under the foliage.

FRUIT: Berry, 1/4″ diameter, bluish black, bloomy, September-October, and only effective (actually noticeable) after the leaves have fallen.

CULTURE: Supposedly coarsely fibrous and slow to reestablish but I have never had any problem rooting or growing it; best grown in containers and moved from them to the final growing area: tolerates just about any kind of soil; full sun or full shade; exposed, windy conditions; polluted situations, city conditions; actually difficult to kill; have seen it growing in the most inhospitable situations, even in pure sand on Cape Cod; quite salt tolerant.

DISEASES AND INSECTS: Canker, downy mildew, leaf spots, powdery mildew, wilt, beetles, eight-spotted forester, leaf hoppers, scales and several other insects.

LANDSCAPE VALUE: Excellent, tough, low-maintenance cover for walls, trellises, rock piles; can be an asset if used properly; the ivy covered walls of most universities are not ivy covered but "creeper" covered; have seen the species growing on sand dunes in the company of *Rosa rugosa, Ammophila breviligulata, Myrica pensylvanica* and other salt tolerant species; if other vines fail this is a good choice; cements itself to structures and does not need support; may leave a residue on buildings that is difficult to remove; can became a weed as birds "plant" the seeds with reckless abandon.

CULTIVARS: Two varieties of some note include *engelmannii* with smaller leaflets than the species and *saint-paulii* with smaller leaflets but better clinging qualities.

PROPAGATION: Seed has a dormant embryo and stratification in cool moist sand or peat for 30 to 60 days at 41°F is recommended; softwood cuttings collected in August rooted 90% in 20 days without treatment; very easy to root from June, July or August cuttings, use 1000 ppm KIBA quick dip, peat:perlite, mist.

NATIVE HABITAT: New England to Florida and Mexico, west Ohio, Illinois and Missouri. Introduced 1622.

RELATED SPECIES:

Parthenocissus henryana — Silvervein Creeper
(pär-thē-nō-sis′us hen-rē-ā′nȧ)

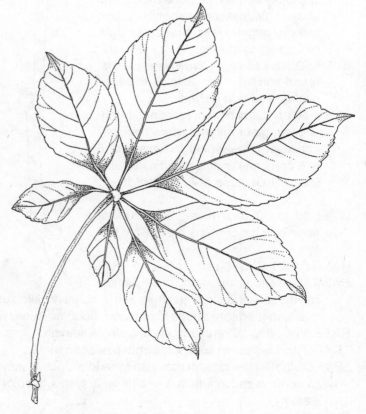

LEAVES: Alternate, compound palmate, 3 to 5 (7) leaflets, each 1 1/2 to 5″ long, about 1/2 as wide, obovate, oblanceolate, or narrowly oval, slender-pointed, tapered to a short petiolule, coursely toothed except near base, glabrous above, downy on veins beneath, velvety dark green above, variegated with silvery white and pink along the midrib and primary veins, although this does not always appear to hold true; deep purple on underside especially on young leaves; petiole 1 1/2 to 4 1/2″ long.

STEM: Four angled, glabrous, tendrils with 5 to 7 branches, cementing itself to structures by disk-like cups.

Parthenocissus henryana, Silvervein Creeper, is noteworthy for its distinct bluish green leaves which are veined with white in youth, and purple on their underside throughout the growing season. Fall color is also a good red to reddish purple. From a foliage standpoint this is the handsomest of the species treated here but the least hardy. Does reasonable in the south. Definitely more vigorous and handsome in colder climates. The leaf coloration does not hold in the heat. Have also noted more leaf spot on this than the other two treated here. Zone 7 to 8. Central China. Introduced about 1895.

Parthenocissus tricuspidata — Japanese Creeper, Boston Ivy
(pär-thē-nō-sis′us trī-kus-pi-dā′tȧ)

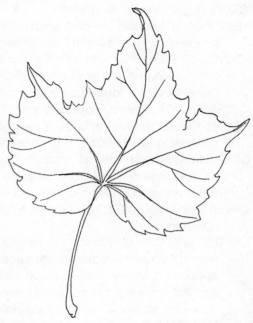

LEAVES: Alternate, simple, slender-stalked, broad-ovate, 4 to 8″ wide, 3-lobed with acuminate coarsely serrate lobes; or chiefly on the young plants and basal shoots, smaller and partly 3-foliate with stalked leaflets, glossy dark green, glabrous above, finely pubescent on veins beneath.
BUDS: Brownish-similar to previous species.
STEM: Squarish, tendrils 5 to 12, shorter than those of *P. quinquefolia,* prominent, vertically arranged lenticels, usually glabrous.

Parthenocissus tricuspidata, Japanese Creeper, is similar to *P. quinquefolia* in all respects except the foliage is usually more lustrous, the leaf is simple and 3-lobed and it is possibly not as hardy. It is excellent and can be used in the same situations as Virginia Creeper. 'Beverly Brooks' ('Beverley Brook' of Jackman in England)—has large leaves that turn brilliant shades of red and scarlet in fall. 'Green Showers' ('Green Spring'?) has essentially fresh green foliage that is larger than typical, up to 10″ wide, fall color is rich burgundy. 'Lowii' has small, 3 to 7-lobed leaves when young. 'Purpurea' has reddish purple leaves throughout the summer. 'Robusta' offers thick, waxy, glossy green leaves and excellent orange to red fall color, vigorous grower and leaves are often trifoliate (3 leaflets) and 4 to 8″ wide. Japan, Central China. 1862. Zone 4 to 8.

Paulownia tomentosa — Royal Paulownia, also called Empress Tree or Princess Tree.
(paw-lō′ni-a tō-men-tō′sa)

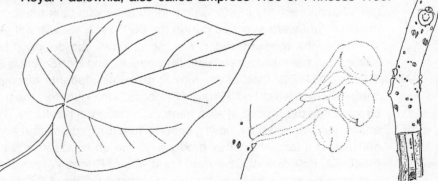

FAMILY: Scrophulariaceae, sometimes placed in Bignoniaceae.
LEAVES: Opposite, simple, broad-ovate to ovate, 5 to 10″ long and wide, acuminate, cordate, entire or sometimes shallowly 3-lobed, dark green and sparsely pubescent above, tomentose beneath; petiole about as long as blade; leaves on sucker growth may reach 2 to 2 1/2′ in diameter.
BUDS: Similar to *C. speciosa.*
STEM: Stout, pubescent when young, heavily lenticelled, with lip-like shape, olive-brown color.
PITH: Chambered, *Catalpa* pith is continuous.
FLOWERS: Panicle, formed in summer; individual flower buds appear as light brown, pubescent spheres through winter, excellent identification feature.

SIZE: 30 to 40' in height with an equal spread, may grow 50 to 60' but this is rare; trees over 80' high are known.

HARDINESS: Zone 5 to 9.

HABIT: Rounded, dense crown; resembles *C. bignonioides* in habit.

RATE: Fast, 14 to 17' in 4 to 5 years and can grow as much as 8 to 10' in a single year; the wood tends to be somewhat brittle.

TEXTURE: Coarse in all seasons.

LEAF COLOR: Medium to dark green in summer, fall color of no consequence as the leaves usually fall off green; watched leaves turn brown by a fall freeze when the temperature dropped to 24°F.

FLOWERS: Pale violet with darker spots and yellow stripes inside, reminds of a foxglove flower, 2" long, vanilla-scented, borne in April (May in north) before the leaves in 8 to 12" long pyramidal panicles; flower buds are formed during the summer prior to flowering and are a brown color and very evident during the winter; unfortunately the flower buds are often killed during the winter.

FRUIT: Ovoid, beaked dehiscent capsule, 1 to 2" long, not ornamentally overwhelming, persisting, containing up to 2000 small winged seeds.

CULTURE: Transplant balled and burlapped in early spring into moist, deep, well drained soil; will tolerate a wide range of soils but does best in the type mentioned; full sun or partial shade and sheltered from wind; withstands air pollutants and does well along coastal areas; prune in winter.

DISEASES AND INSECTS: Seldom troubled although leaf spots, mildew and twig canker have been reported.

LANDSCAPE VALUE: Falls in the same category as *Catalpa* except probably less desirable because of messiness and in northern climates the uncertainty of flowers; possibly for parks and other large areas; very dense shaded and therefore difficult to grow grass under; over the years have watched a grand avenue at Longwood Gardens and am always reluctant to criticize the tree after seeing them in flower, however, noticed especially in fall numerous leaves cascading at irregular intervals over the handsome lawn, there is always some "pick-up" necessary; old fruit capsules will persist and the tree can really look unkempt if they are not removed, I suspect Longwood Gardens spends considerable maintenance dollars.

CULTIVARS:

'Somaclonal Snowstorm'—I would like to say good things about this creamy variegated leaf form, the variegation streaked, flecked and blotched throughout the leaf; unfortunately, the plant in the Georgia Botanical Garden has reverted to green, considerable vigilence is necessary to keep it variegated, resulted from hypocotyl explants in tissue culture and introduced by Dr. Marcotrigiano of the University of Massachusetts, see *HortScience* 23: 226–227 (1988) for details.

PROPAGATION: The seeds exhibit no dormancy but light is necessary for germination; fresh seed has a germination capacity of 90 percent in 19 days with alternating temperatures of 68° and 86°F; eight hours of light were supplied during the 86°F cycle. Seeds will germinate like grass if placed on the surface of the medium under mist, never cover too deeply; I have grown many seedlings; tissue culture has been successful with the species, see *HortScience* 20: 760 (1985).

ADDITIONAL NOTES: One of my former graduate students discovered a white form on the Georgia campus which we called 'Georgia Princess'. Unfortunately the tree has never been propagated. The species has been used in strip mine reclamation in Kentucky. The wood is prized by the Japanese and is used for rice pots, bowls, spoons, furniture, coffins and air crates. There are 85,000 seeds per ounce and a large tree may produce 20 million seeds in a year. The tree was named after Anna Pavlovna, daughter of Czar Paul I and wife of Prince Willem of the Netherlands. It is tremendously fast growing and a 22-year-old tree reached a height of 62' and averaged 3 growth rings per inch. This is the wonder that appears in Sunday supplements. It does amazing things like "soar to 23' in two seasons; flower continuously from spring to summer; withstand -25°F and produce leaves 2 1/2' across". The actual fact is that it does none of the above. Cold is its biggest enemy and flower buds are often seriously injured or killed between 0 and -5°F. Escaped from cultivation in Georgia and has found a home along highway cuts and fills. It is intolerant of competition and will give way to other species with time.

NATIVE HABITAT: China. Introduced 1834. Escaped from cultivation from southern New York to Georgia.

Paxistima canbyi — Canby Paxistima (formerly spelled *Pachistima*), also called Rat-stripper.
(paks-iss′ti-ma kan′-bē-ī)

FAMILY: Celastraceae

LEAVES: Opposite, simple, evergreen, linear-oblong or narrow-oblong, 1/4 to 1″ long, 3/16″ or less wide, revolute and usually serrulate above the middle, lustrous dark green, glabrous; short petioled.

BUDS: Solitary, sessile, ovoid, appressed, very small, with about 2 pairs of exposed scales; the terminal somewhat larger with more visible scales.

STEM: Very slender, somewhat 4-sided, the bark becoming corky-thickened and transversely checked; pith minute, rounded, brownish, and spongy; leaf-scars minute, crescent-shaped, somewhat raised; 1 indistinct bundle-trace.

SIZE: One foot in height by 3 to 5′ in spread at maturity.

HARDINESS: Zone 3 to 7, shows good cold hardiness.

HABIT: Low growing evergreen shrub with decumbent branches which often root when in contact with the soil; relatively neat and compact.

RATE: Slow, can grow 12″ high by 2 to 3′ wide in 3 to 4 years.

TEXTURE: Fine in all seasons.

LEAF COLOR: Lustrous dark green in summer becoming somewhat bronzish in cold weather.

FLOWERS: Perfect, greenish or reddish, 1/5″ across, early May, borne in few-flowered 1/2″ cymes, not particularly showy.

FRUIT: Leathery capsule, white, 1/6″ long, of no ornamental consequence.

CULTURE: Easily transplanted, but best moved as a container-grown plant; prefers moist, well drained soil which has been well supplied with organic matter; in the wild it is found on calcareous, rocky soils; full sun or partial shade although is denser and more compact in full sun; rarely requires fertilizer or pruning; will tolerate high pH soils.

DISEASES AND INSECTS: Leaf spot and scale have been reported.

LANDSCAPE VALUE: Good evergreen ground cover which once established requires little or no attention; excellent when used in combination with broadleaf evergreens; makes a good facer plant or low hedge; does not appear too often in midwestern or southern gardens but is used on the east coast.

PROPAGATION: Plants can be divided; cuttings can be rooted easily; I have taken cuttings in late July, treated them with 1000 ppm IBA, placed them under mist and had good success. Another investigator collected softwood cuttings in summer, treated them with 3000 ppm IBA-talc and had 100% rooting in 6 weeks.

NATIVE HABITAT: Mountains of Virginia and West Virginia, found chiefly on calcareous soils. Cultivated 1880.

Perovskia atriplicifolia — Russian-sage
(pe-rof′ski-à a-tri-pli-si-fō′li-à)

FAMILY: Lamiaceae

LEAVES: Opposite, simple, rhomboidal or slightly obovate, 1 to 2″ long, 1/3 to 1″ wide, tapered at both ends, coarsely serrate, gray-green and slightly downy; petiole—1/12 to 1/3″ long.

Perovskia atriplicifolia, Russian-sage, is a beautiful plant when properly grown. It is semi-woody to herbaceous and reaches 3 to 5′. The foliage is a handsome gray-green. In August and September, violet-blue flowers occur in terminal 9 to 12″ long panicles. A mass planting, which is the only way to effectively utilize the plant, is without equal. The entire inflorescence, like the stems, is covered

P. Abrotanoides

with a fine whitish down which accentuates the color of the flowers. Locate in full sun in well-drained soil that is not excessively rich. It should be pruned back in spring to live wood as it generally winter kills in cold climates. I have propagated it from softwood cuttings but they should be removed from the mist bench soon after rooting for excess water is harmful. 'Blue Spire' has deeply lobed leaves, is of upright habit to 3' and bears the flowers in large panicles. One of the finest plantings in this country is located at Bernheim Arboretum. *Perovskia abrotanoides* is closely allied to *P. atriplicifolia* but differs in more deeply incised leaves, often almost to midrib; these segments are often again dissected. Afghanistan to western Himalayas and Tibet. Cultivated 1904. Zone 5 to 8.

Persea borbonia — Redbay
(pēr′se-á bôr-bōn′ē-á)

FAMILY: Lauraceae
LEAVES: Alternate, simple, evergreen, oblong to lance-oblong, 2 to 4″ long, obtuse, cuneate, lustrous medium green above, glaucescent below, glabrous; petiole 1/3″ long, pubescent.
BUDS: Naked.
STEM: Stout, green, ridged, usually glabrous, aromatic when bruised.

SIZE: 20 to 30′ (40′) high, two-thirds to equal this in spread.
HARDINESS: Zone (7)8 to 9, defoliated or killed to ground at -3°F.
HABIT: Oval to rounded large shrub or reasonably robust tree; have seen 40′ high single-trunked, round headed trees along coastal Georgia and North Carolina.
RATE: Medium.
TEXTURE: Medium to coarse.
BARK: Gray-brown, shallowly ridged and furrowed on old trunks, the ridges becoming scaly.
LEAF COLOR: Lustrous medium green, in winter often yellowish green, especially noticeable on plants in the Athens area.
FLOWERS: Perfect, creamy, in peduncled several flowered cymes, not showy, June; did a double take with a plant on the Outer Banks of North Carolina; I thought I was looking at *Nyssa* flowers.
FRUIT: Subglobose, 1/2″ long, dark blue to black drupe borne on a red peduncle; interestingly have had heavy fruit set on campus plants, ripen in October.
CULTURE: Doubtfully available in commerce except from specialty growers, should be moved as a container-grown plant, prefers moist, acid, well drained soil but in the wild occurs in swamps; I have seen plants growing submerged in North Carolina; interestingly appears to prosper under drier conditions as evidenced by performance on the Georgia campus; full sun or moderate shade.
DISEASES AND INSECTS: In the wild, the leaves are usually infected with a gall and appear swollen and watery, also rather ugly; on campus plants I have not noticed the problem.
LANDSCAPE VALUE: Coastal, native plant situations, appears quite salt-tolerant, best for naturalizing.
PROPAGATION: Seeds are the usual method and should be fall sown.
NATIVE HABITAT: Southern Delaware to Florida, in swamps. Introduced 1739.

Phellodendron amurense — Amur Corktree
(fel-ō-den′dron ă-moor-en′sē)

FAMILY: Rutaceae
LEAVES: Opposite, pinnately compound, 10 to 15″ long, 5 to 11(13) leaflets, ovate to lance-ovate, 2 1/2 to 4 1/2″ long, half as wide, entire, long-acuminate, rounded or narrowed at base, lustrous dark green above, glabrous beneath or with a few hairs along the base of the midrib.

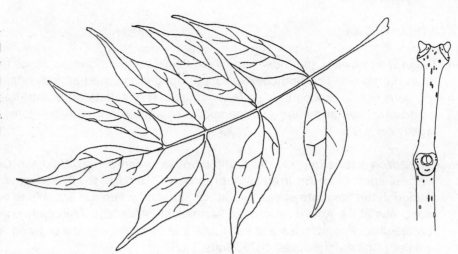

BUDS: Solitary, half-ellipsoid, compressed from the sides, silky with red or bronzed hairs so as to mask the overlapping of the two scales, enclosed by the base of petiole.

STEM: Stout, orange-yellow or yellowish gray, changing to brown, lenticels prominent, glabrous, leaf scars horseshoe-shaped, raised, rather large with bud setting in the "U" formed by the leaf scar; inner bark of young stems usually a bright yellowish green.

SIZE: 30 to 45' in height with an equal or greater spread.

HARDINESS: Zone 3 to 7, will grow in Zone 8 but is slow.

HABIT: Broad spreading tree with a short trunk and an open, rounded crown of a few large, often horizontally arranged branches; a tree of great beauty in its finest form.

RATE: Medium, 10 to 12' over a 5 to 8 year period.

TEXTURE: Medium in leaf; would probably be considered coarse in winter habit.

BARK: On old trunks, ridged and furrowed into a cork-like pattern, gray-brown in color; very beautiful and unusual bark pattern but does not develop until old age.

LEAF COLOR: Deep, often lustrous green in summer, changing to yellow or bronzy yellow in fall and persisting briefly.

FLOWERS: Dioecious, yellowish green, borne in 2 to 3 1/2" long, 1 1/2 to 3" wide panicles in late May to early June; not showy.

FRUIT: Subglobose, black, 1/2" diameter drupe, with strong odor when bruised; ripening in October and persisting into winter; borne only on female trees.

CULTURE: Transplants readily, has fibrous, shallow, wide-spreading root system; does well on many types of soils; withstands acid or alkaline conditions; drouth and polluted air; full sun; prune in winter; Dr. John Pair's Wichita KS tests provided data to support my long term observations that the tree is simply not as environmentally tough as given credit; authors, including me, have looked at the literature rather than the tree, over a 10-year period in KS tests the species averaged 4.7" per year, developed severe leaf scorch and often defoliated by August; also in nursery production trees produce a big trunk without much crown; interestingly Raulston reported 3 to 5' of growth per year on young plants.

DISEASES AND INSECTS: Unusually free of pests.

LANDSCAPE VALUE: Medium headed shade tree of unique interest for bark; excellent in parks and other large areas, possibly for residential landscapes with lots of 10,000 square feet or more; not for streets although has been used for that purpose; from my observations not as urban tolerant as the literature would have us believe.

CULTIVARS:

'Macho'—The first selection of *P. amurense* with moderately spreading growth habit, thick leathery dark green leaves, handsome corky bark, high resistance to insects and diseases, a male, Bill Wandell introduction.

PROPAGATION: Seeds germinate like beans without any treatment; I have directly sowed seed and also stratified seed and then planted; the differences in germination percentage were negligible although the percent was slightly higher with stratification.

NATIVE HABITAT: Northern China, Manchuria and Japan. Introduced 1856.

RELATED SPECIES:

Phellodendron lavallei, (fel-ō-den′dron la-val′ē-ī), Lavalle Corktree, tends to be more regular in outline than the above. The branches are more upright and the bark develops a corky characteristic but perhaps not as pronounced as *P. amurense*. The leaflets are duller green. I consider this a rather handsome tree and there are fine specimens in the Arnold Arboretum. Central Japan. Introduced 1862. Zone 5 to 7.

Phellodendron sachalinense, (fel-ō-den′dron sa-ka-len-en′sē), Sakhalin Corktree, tends to be more vase-shaped than the irregularly branched *P. amurense*. It also grows larger (50 to 60′ high). Although the literature states the bark is non-corky I do not find this to be true. There is a splendid specimen at the Arnold Arboretum. Minnesota Landscape Arboretum considers this species slightly hardier than *P. amurense* and has found it to be extremely fast growing. Korea, northern Japan and western China. Introduced 1877. Zone 3 to 7.

ADDITIONAL NOTES: The Arnold and Morton Arboreta have beautiful specimens of these species. Their effect is strongly oriental and the trees must be seen in the mature state to be fully appreciated. Some authorities relegated the two related species to variety status. In spite of what the books say the species treated here are difficult to separate. I collected samples of the various *Phellodendron* species at the Arnold, took them home, spread them out on the kitchen table, and armed with reference books, hand lenses and a degree of sanity attempted to separate them by leaf, bud and stem. If there were significant differences I did not locate them. *Phellodendron amurense* was once considered a good pollution tolerant tree but has not performed well as a city tree and almost languishes under hostile conditions. Given proper cultural conditions, it makes a fine tree.

Philadelphus coronarius — Sweet Mockorange
(fil-à-del′fus kôr-o-nā′ri-us)

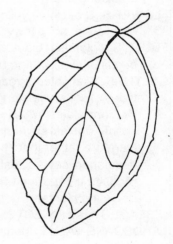

FAMILY: Saxifragaceae

LEAVES: Opposite, simple, ovate to ovate-oblong, 1 1/2 to 4″ long, 1/2 to 2″ wide, acuminate, broad cuneate or rounded at the base, remotely denticulate or dentate, dark green, glabrous except bearded in the axils of veins beneath and sometimes hairy on the veins; petiole—1/6 to 1/3″ long, hairy.

BUDS: Solitary, sessile, with 2 nearly valvate, mostly hairy scales, the terminal lacking.

STEM: Young branches glabrous or slightly pilose, dark reddish to chestnut-brown, exfoliating on old stems; pith—moderate, rounded, pale or white, continuous.

SIZE: 10 to 12′ by 10 to 12′.

HARDINESS: Zone 4 to 8.

HABIT: Large rounded shrub with stiff, straight, ascending branches that arch with age; often leggy, straggly.

RATE: Fast.

TEXTURE: Somewhat coarse in all seasons.

BARK: Exfoliating, orangish to reddish brown.

LEAF COLOR: Medium, may be non-descript green in summer, although is often dark green, no change in fall.

FLOWERS: Perfect, 4-petaled, white, 1 to 1 1/2″ across, very fragrant, May to early June, borne in 5 to 7-flowered racemes.

FRUIT: Four-valved dehiscent capsule, persisting.

CULTURE: Transplants readily; not particular as to soil; full sun or light shade; prefer moist, well drained soil supplied with organic matter and here make their best growth; should be pruned after flowering either by removing old wood or cutting to the ground; the root system on mockorange is more extensive and woody than the tops; I dug several large specimens out of our Illinois garden and simply could not believe the mass of roots.

DISEASES AND INSECTS: Canker, leaf spots, powdery mildews, rust, aphids, leaf miner and nematodes; none of these are serious.

LANDSCAPE VALUE: Old favorite for sweetly-scented flowers; does not have much to recommend it for the modern landscape; some of the floriferous cultivars are much better than the species.

CULTIVARS:

'Aureus'—Yellow foliage with typical fragrant white flowers, a real lemon in any garden, becomes yellow-green to green with heat of summer; widely used in England where it appears to be more suitable; Mr. Gary Koller, Arnold Arboretum, asked me to remove the real lemon comment, which was an attempt at subtle humor with "a peel".

'Nanus' ('Pumilus')—A rather handsome, compact (4'), haystack-shaped form with dark green foliage; it is rather sparse flowering; there may be several dwarf types in cultivation.

'Variegatus'—Leaves with an irregular border of creamy white, actually a weak grower but a rather dainty shrub when well grown, flowers fragrant, no foliage burn in Raleigh, NC.

PROPAGATION: In general, seed of all species can be directly sown; softwood cuttings taken in June and July and treated with 1000 ppm IBA-quick dip or talc root readily.

NATIVE HABITAT: Southeastern Europe and Asia Minor. Cultivated 1560.

Other *Philadelphus* types of some worth: Any treatment of *Philadelphus* species, hybrids and cultivars is superficial; for this I make minimal apology since the only redeeming character is fragrance and many cultivars do not offer this. New hybrids have been introduced from United States and Canadian programs and I have included most of these. A gardener's chances of locating, i.e., purchasing, more than 2 to 3 of those listed is quite dubious unless one locates a specialist *Philadelphus* grower who will be in business for about two weeks in May-June.

Philadelphus × *cymosus,* (fil-à-del′fus × sī-mō′sus), and the cultivars:
'Banniere'—Flowers semidouble, 1 1/2 to 2 1/2″ diameter, fragrant.
'Conquete'—Flowers single, 2″ diameter, very fragrant, one of the best.
'Norma'—Flowers single, 1 3/4″ diameter.
'Perle Blanche'—Flowering single, 1 1/2″ diameter, one of the most fragrant.
The plants in this group grow 6 to 8′ high; tend to be rather open and lanky; hardy in Zone 4 to 5; result of crosses between *P.* × *lemoinei* × *P. grandiflorus.*

P. × *lemoinei,* (fil-à-del′fus × le-moy′nē-ī), and the cultivars:
'Avalanche'—Flowers single, 1″ diameter, 4′ high with arching branches and one of the most fragrant.
'Belle Étoile'—Flowers single, 2 1/4″ diameter, 6′ high, fragrant, light maroon blotch at center.
'Boule d'Argent'—Flowers double, 2″ diameter, 5′ high, scarcely fragrant.
'Erectus'—Flowers single, 1″ diameter, 4′ high, good compact, upright habit, scarcely fragrant.
'Fleur de Neige'—Flowers single, 1 1/4″ diameter and very fragrant.
'Girandole'—Flowers double, 1 3/4″ diameter, 4′ high.
'Innocence'—Flowers single, 1 3/4″ diameter, 8′ high, one of the most fragrant forms, foliage sometimes with creamy white variegation.
'Mont Blanc'—Flowers single, 1 1/4″ diameter, 4′ high, one of the hardier forms.
'Sybille'—Flower white, purple stained, highly fragrant, almost squarish, arching shrub.
Plants grow 4 to 8′, are very fragrant and hardy in Zone 5. Result of crosses between *P. microphyllus* × *P. coronarius.*

P. × *virginalis,* (fil-à-del′fus × vĕr-jin-ā′lis), and the cultivars:
'Albatre'—Flowers double, 1 1/4″ diameter, 5′ high.
'Argentine'—Flowers very double, 2″ diameter, 4′ high.
'Bouquet Blanc'—Flowers single, 1″ diameter, 6′ high, moundlike habit and covered with flowers.

'Burford' ('Burfordensis')—Flowers single to semidouble, 2 1/4 to 2 1/2" diameter, not fragrant.

'Glacier'—Flowers double, 1 1/4" diameter, 5' high.

'Minnesota Snowflake'—Fragrant, white, double, 2" diameter flowers, 8' in height and clothed with branches. Supposedly withstanding temperatures as low as -30°F, G.D. Bush introduction.

'Virginal'—Flowers double, 2" diameter, 9' high, very fragrant.

Plants grow 5 to 9', are hardy in Zone 5. Result of crosses between *P. × lemoinei × P. nivalis* 'Plena'.

Several additional cultivars that cannot be categorized as to group include:

'Buckley's Quill'—Small erect branching shrub with compact clusters of fragrant white flowers, petals are narrow with pointed tips.

'Enchantment'—Large, semi-double, fragrant flowers, 6 to 7' high and well clothed with foliage to the ground.

'Frosty Morn'—Double, fragrant flowers on a 4 to 5' high shrub; introduced in 1953 by G.D. Bush of Minneapolis.

'Galahad'—A new selection with single white fragrant flowers on a compact 4 to 5' high rounded shrub.

'Marjorie'—Single, large, fragrant flowers, 9 to 10' high shrub; introduced by Morden Experiment Station in 1962.

'Miniature Snowflake'—Double, fragrant flowers on a compact, 3' high shrub, prolific flower production, dark green disease resistant foliage.

'Natchez'—In flower perhaps the handsomest of all mockoranges with 1 1/2" diameter slightly fragrant pure white flowers that cover the leaves in May and produce an avalanche, some tendency toward petaloid stamens but the four major petals dominate, large upright form easily 8 to 10' at maturity; have observed a great amount of *Cercospora* leaf spot in summer which disfigures foliage, good fertility and soil moisture reduce leaf spot incidence.

'Polar Star'—Semidouble, fragrant, white, 2 1/2" wide, May-June, again in autumn, 10 to 12' high, Zone 5 to 8, chance seedling from garden of late Herbert Fischer of Illinois.

'Snowdwarf'—A compact shrub, 1 1/2 to 2 1/2' high and 1 1/2' wide; flowers are pure white, 1 1/2 to 1 3/4" wide, with 20 petals, 6 sepals and no stamens, occur in clusters of 5; leaves are dark green, about 2" long, 1 1/4 to 1 3/4" long; should be hardy to -25°F; see *HortScience* 22: 163 (1987) for other details.

'Snowgoose'—A free flowering, winter hardy form with very fragrant, double (20 petals) pure white flowers; an upright shrub 4 to 5' high and 2 to 3 1/2' wide, foliage is dark green, 1 1/2 to 2 1/2" long, 3/4 to 1 1/2" wide, should be hardy to -25°F, a cross between 'Frosty Morn' and 'Bouquet Blanc' made in 1959; in Canada tests it was one of the most cold hardy cultivars, comparable to 'Galahad' and 'Siberregen' but more florally productive; *HortScience* 23: 785 (1988).

All *Philadelphus* types require about the same care—none. They are vigorous, easy to grow plants but are strictly of single season quality. In flower they are attractive to some but the rest of the year (about 50 weeks) are real eyesores. My garden space and labor are too valuable to waste on shrubs which only return a small interest. Consider these factors before extensively planting shrubs of this type.

Photinia serrulata — Chinese Photinia
(fō-tin′i-a̍ ser-ū-lā′ta̍)

FAMILY: Rosaceae

LEAVES: Alternate, simple, evergreen, lanceolate to oblong, 4 to 8" long, 1 1/2 to 3 1/2" wide, firm and leathery, acute, cuneate, finely serrate from base to apex, midrib prominent, lustrous dark green above, flat medium green below, glabrous; petiole about 1" long, clothed with whitish aging to brownish hairs.

BUDS: Flower—imbricate, 3/4 to 1" long, greenish red, conical with apex slightly crooked, 7 to 9 scaled, glabrous; laterals—small, obscure.

STEM: Stout, terete, glabrous, greenish brown, prominently dotted with brownish vertical lenticels; when bruised emits a prominent maraschino cherry odor; pith—solid, greenish white.

SIZE: 20 to 25' (30') high, about two-thirds that in spread, the largest of the commonly cultivated photinias; a 50 to 60' high specimen resides at the Bath Botanic Garden.

HARDINESS: Zone 7 to 9.

HABIT: Small tree or enormous multi-stemmed evergreen shrub that tends to engulf every structure or plant in close proximity.

RATE: Medium to fast.

TEXTURE: Coarse.

BARK: Blackish often exfoliating in large scales, relatively attractive.

LEAF COLOR: Emerging leaves green to bronze to reddish purple soon turning lustrous dark green; very handsome for the new leaves coincide with the flower; start to emerge in early to mid-March (Athens) depending on weather; usually a few reddish leaves present during winter.

FLOWERS: White, perfect, 5-petaled, each flower 1/3" across, borne in a 4 to 7" wide terminal corymbose panicle, malodorous like many of the hawthorns; odor quite offensive; contrast handsomely with the young foliage; early to mid-April; flowers last a good two weeks; open ahead of those of *P.* × *fraseri* and *P. glabra*.

FRUIT: Globose, 1/4" diameter red pome which matures in late summer and persists through spring of the following year, the large panicles of red are quite effective in the winter landscape; may turn black with time but this has not been the situation with plants I have observed.

CULTURE: Easily transplanted, well-drained soil; pH adaptable; full sun or partial shade; does not tolerate extremely wet soils; responds well to fertilizer; tends to exhibit nitrogen deficiency in landscape situations; does not form a great number of lateral breaks when pruned thus making it difficult to make a dense shrub.

DISEASES AND INSECTS: Mildew, leaf spots, fireblight, scales, and several other insects.

LANDSCAPE VALUE: Large hedge or privacy screen; could be used as a small tree; often used erroneously on the corners of small buildings; have seen it used in groupings around large campus buildings and it tends to soften some of the harsh architectural lines; can be used in groupings, screens; flowers are really foul smelling.

PROPAGATION: Seeds will germinate without cold treatment but 30 days of cold moist stratification unifies germination. Cutting information presented applies to *P.* × *fraseri* but is, no doubt, pertinent to *P. glabra* and *P. serrulata*. Many researchers have demonstrated the need for high IBA levels from 5000 to 10,000 ppm quick dip. Probably the best time to take cuttings is after the first flush of growth has firmed in late spring or early summer. However, cuttings can almost be rooted year-round. Use a well drained medium and mist. Cuttings root in 4 to 6 weeks.

NATIVE HABITAT: China. Introduced 1804.

RELATED SPECIES:

Photinia × ***fraseri,*** (fō-tin'i-à frā'zer-ī), Fraser Photinia, is the most popular photinia for southern gardens. In fact the words "red tip" mean only one thing: *P.* × *fraseri*. The name is derived from the red color of the new foliage. This plant is so overused that the term nauseous is not sufficiently applicable. Fraser Photinia grows 10 to 15' (20') high and about one-half that in spread. The outline is distinctly upright in youth and old age. Young plants when first set in the landscape are relatively open but fill in with time. Ideally plants should be pruned when young to encourage basal branching. This plant shows nitrogen stresses quite vividly, with off-color (yellowish) foliage. Flowers and fruits

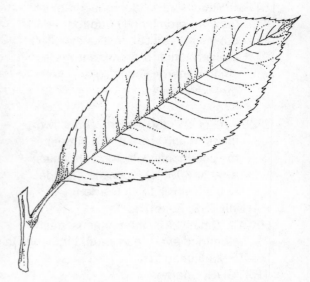

are intermediate between the parents. This plant is treated like privet and the flower buds are often removed in the pruning process. It is an undeniable fact that a hedge or screen fully clothed with the brilliant reddish foliage is an eye-catcher. The foliage does fade to deep green after 2 to 4 weeks; however, another flush of growth in summer or occasional spurious breaks will provide color. Basic problems and cultural requirements are the same as described under *P. serrulata.* This plant is a bread and butter item of many southern nurseries. *P.* × *fraseri* arose at the Fraser Nurseries, Birmingham, Alabama around 1940. All the seedlings agreed with the seed parent, *P. serrulata,* except one outstanding plant, which was propagated and put into commerce in 1955. The original selection was named 'Birmingham' and probably all plants grown in the south as *P.* × *fraseri* should be listed as *P.* × *fraseri* 'Birmingham' since it is a named cultivar and all plants are reproduced through vegetative means (cuttings). Undeniably tough plant except for leaf spot; I have observed it in almost impossible soil conditions and in heavy shade forming a respectable screen or hedge. The moist, humid weather in 1989 literally defoliated many plants in southern landscapes. A troublesome and often devastating leaf spot, *Entomosporium maculatum,* can wreak havoc on the species and complete defoliation may result. The disease is manifested by roundish lesions with purple halos that may coalesce and kill entire leaves. Spray schedules need to be vigorous to prevent the disease. Several relatively effective fungicides are available and it is best to check with the local extension agents. Several cultivars should be mentioned. 'Red Robin' is common in Europe but not in the United States. As I have seen it, the habit is more spreading than 'Birmingham' and the leaves are a rich ruby red but not as intense as 'Birmingham'. It was developed in New Zealand. 'Robusta' has coppery-red new leaves that become leathery dark green and resemble *P. serrulata,* also quite vigorous and grew 12' in 6 years, originated in Hazlewood Nursery, Sydney, Australia. 'Indian Princess' is slower growing, dense branching with orange-coppery new foliage, leaves are about one-half the size of 'Birmingham', a branch sport discovered at Monrovia Nursery Co. Zone 8 to 9.

Photinia glabra — Japanese Photinia
(fō-tin'i-à glā'brà)

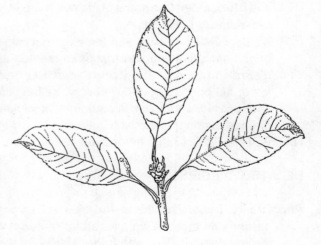

LEAVES: Alternate, simple, evergreen, narrowly oval to slightly obovate, 1 1/2 to 3 1/2″ long, one-third to half as wide, pointed, cuneate, regularly and shallowly serrate, bronzy red when emerging, finally glossy dark green, glabrous; petiole 1/4 to 1/2″ long.

Photinia glabra, Japanese Photinia, is the smallest version of the 3 evergreen photinias presented here, topping out between 10 and 12' high. In many respects it is quite similar to *P. serrulata* but the new growth is more red, the leaves smaller, finer toothed, glabrous, and the flowers and fruits smaller. The flowers also have the characteristic hawthorn odor and appear later and in smaller inflorescences. The petiole at maturity is glabrous compared to the pubescent petiole of *P. serrulata.*

'Rubens' has bright bronzy red leaves. Japan, China. Introduced 1914 by Wilson. Zone 8; definitely less cold hardy than previous two species, was killed to the ground or outright at -3°F.

ADDITIONAL NOTES: Photinias are ubiquitous throughout the south. When a customer asks a garden center employee for a good hedge plant these are recommended. Need I elaborate further. The flower odor is objectionable and the plant should not be located too close to entrances and walks. Over the past eight years I have learned the nuances of the species and hybrids. The following rankings are reasonably accurate. *Photinia serrulata* flowers before *P.* × *fraseri* before *P. glabra*. *P. serrulata* is more cold hardy (-5 to -10°F) than *P.* × *fraseri* (about -5°F) than *P. glabra* (0°F). *Photinia* × *fraseri* is more resistant to mildew than the other two species. *Photinia serrulata* is more resistant to *Entomosporium* than *P.* × *fraseri* and *P. glabra*. It is difficult to assess the actual degree of susceptibility of *P. glabra* since it is seldom grown in Zone 8 landscapes.

Photinia villosa — Oriental Photinia
(fō-tin′i-à vil-lō′sà)

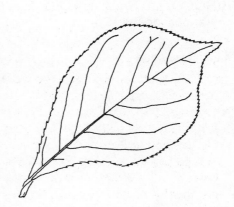

LEAVES: Alternate, simple, 1 1/2 to 3 1/2″ long, 3/4 to 1 1/2″ wide, obovate to oblong-obovate, acuminate, cuneate, finely and sharply serrate, each serration gland-tipped, glabrous and dark green above, villous beneath with 5 to 7 pairs of veins, firm at maturity; petioles 1/25 to 1/5″ long.

BUDS: Sessile, solitary, ovoid, acute, with about 4, somewhat keeled and mucronate scales; terminal lacking.

STEM: Moderate or rather slender, rounded, with large lenticels; pith rather small, continuous; leaf-scars 2-ranked, linear, crescent-shaped or somewhat 3-lobed, somewhat raised; 3 bundle traces.

SIZE: 10 to 15′ high, usually less in spread.

HARDINESS: Zone 4 to 7.

HABIT: A large shrub, but can be trained as a tree, often with an irregular, obovoid crown; usually taller than broad.

RATE: Medium.

TEXTURE: Medium throughout the year.

LEAF COLOR: Dark green above, villous beneath in summer changing to yellowish, reddish bronze and red in fall.

FLOWERS: White, 1/3″ across, May into June; borne in 1 to 2″ diameter corymbs terminating short side branches; inflorescence conspicuously warty.

FRUIT: Pome, bright red, 1/3″ long; effective in October and persist for a time if not consumed by the birds.

CULTURE: Best to move balled and burlapped; prefers well-drained acid soil; full sun or light shade; pruning is rarely required.

DISEASES AND INSECTS: Leaf spots, powdery mildews, fireblight; fireblight can be a very serious problem and for this reason the plant is often not grown.

LANDSCAPE VALUE: Makes a good specimen or shrub border plant; the fruits and fall color are attractive; extensive use limited by fireblight susceptibility.

PROPAGATION: Softwood, semi-hardwood, or hardwood cuttings will root without great difficulty; I have rooted the species from softwood cuttings in July using 1000 ppm IBA, peat:perlite, mist. Seed requires a 45 to 60 day cold treatment.

NATIVE HABITAT: Japan, Korea, China. Introduced about 1865.

RELATED SPECIES:

var. *laevis*, (lē′vis)—Leaves longer pointed, glabrous or only slightly downy, red fruits are 1/2″ long, most plants grown as *P. villosa* are var. *laevis*.

forma *maximowicziana*, (mak-sim-ō-wik-si-ā′nȧ)—Leaves almost sessile, rounded and abruptly acuminate, sometimes almost truncate at the apex, cuneate at base, veins deeply impressed, autumn color is described as yellow but as I observed it at the Arnold it was a good orange-red; the habit was that of a large, spreading shrub.

var. *sinica*, (sin′i-kȧ)—Downy young shoots, fruits egg-shaped, 1/2″ long, orange-scarlet, flowers borne in racemes, leaves color red in fall, 15 to 25′, represents species in central and western China.

Physocarpus opulifolius — Common Ninebark, also Eastern Ninebark
(fī-sō-kär′pus op-ū-li-fō′li-us)

FAMILY: Rosaceae

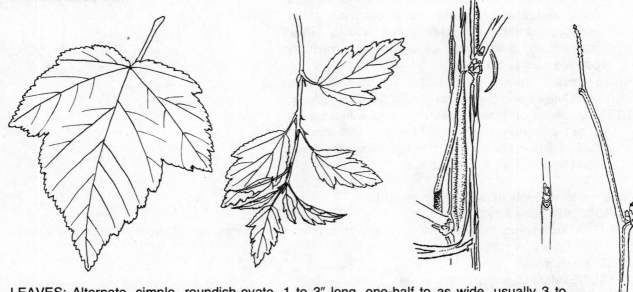

LEAVES: Alternate, simple, roundish-ovate, 1 to 3″ long, one-half to as wide, usually 3 to 5-lobed, sometimes slightly so or not at all, with crenate-dentate obtuse or acutish lobes, medium green, glabrous or nearly so beneath; petiole 1/4 to 3/4″ long.

BUDS: Imbricate, appressed, basically glabrous, usually 5-scaled, brown.

STEM: Young—shiny red-brown, glabrous; old—brown, exfoliating in papery strips; stems distinctly angled from base of leaf scars; pith—brownish.

SIZE: 5 to 10′ in height, spread 6 to 10′.

HARDINESS: Zone 2 to 7.

HABIT: Upright, spreading shrub with stiffly recurved branches, rounded and dense in foliage but quite ragged in winter.

RATE: Medium to fast.

TEXTURE: Medium in leaf, definitely coarse in winter.

BARK: Peeling in long papery sheets on older stems.

LEAF COLOR: Flat green (medium) in summer; fall color yellowish to bronze; usually not effective.

FLOWERS: White or pinkish, each flower about 1/4 to 1/3″ diameter, May-June, borne in many flowered, 1 to 2″ diameter corymbs, effective but not overwhelming, stamens purplish, numbering about 30.

FRUIT: Consist of 3 to 5 follicles, each 1/4″ long, inflated, glabrous, reddish, September-October, reasonably attractive; appears to be some variation in degree of red coloration.

CULTURE: Easily transplanted; adapted to difficult situations; full sun or partial shade; very tough individual resembling spirea in character; withstands acid and alkaline soils; dry situations; renew by cutting to ground in late winter.

LANDSCAPE VALUE: Quite coarse and therefore difficult to use in the small home landscape; massing, border, possibly a screen; limited in usefulness because of limited ornamental assets; bark on older stems (1/2″ diameter or larger) exfoliates into papery strips exposing a rich brown inner bark; unfortunately this character is masked by the foliage and dense tangle of stems.

CULTIVARS:

'Dart's Golden'—A more compact form than 'Luteus' with better yellow color; I have seen it in late June at Bernheim Arboretum and was quite impressed although the foliage color was yellow-green, it loses the yellow with time; possibly a good choice for spring and early summer foliage color but not superior to the golden foliaged forms of *Spiraea*.

var. *intermedius*—A handsome, low growing (4′), fine textured form with darker green and smaller leaves than the species; preferable for modern gardens because of refined and humble character; found in Minnesota, Colorado and Black Hills of South Dakota.

'Luteus'—Leaves initially yellow gradually changing to yellowish green and finally almost green, large shrub, easily growing 8 to 10′ tall and as wide.

var. *nanus*—Another dwarf from (2′) with smaller, less deeply lobed, dark green leaves.

PROPAGATION: Cuttings, easily propagated from softwood cuttings taken in summer; such cuttings rooted better in sand:peat than in sand, and better at 60°F than 70°F; November cuttings rooted 80% in 53 days without treatment. Seeds germinate readily without pretreatment.

NATIVE HABITAT: Quebec to Virginia, Tennessee and Michigan. Introduced 1687.

RELATED SPECIES:

Physocarpus monogynus, (fī-sō-kär′pus mon-og′i-nus), Mountain Ninebark, is an erect, much branched, compact, 2 to 3′ high and wide shrub of refined proportions. The small, 3/4 to 1 1/2″ long, roundish ovate, 3-lobed, irregularly and doubly toothed leaves remind of *Ribes alpinum*. The small, 1/4″ diameter, white or rose-tinted flowers occur in 3/4 to 1 1/3″ diameter few-flowered corymbs in May-June. Rather pretty small shrub for massing and low hedges. South Dakota and Wyoming to Texas and New Mexico. Introduced 1879. Zone 5.

ADDITIONAL NOTES: The Minnesota Landscape Arboreteum has a large collection of ninebarks and after looking over the entire group, I still came away with the opinion that about anything is better than a *Physocarpus*.

Picea — Spruce
Pinaceae

The spruces represent an interesting group of usually tall, symmetrical, conical trees. Numerous cultivars occur within selected species *(P. abies, P. glauca, P. pungens)* but are limitedly available in the trade. The genus includes nearly 40 species which are largely restricted to the cooler regions of the Northern Hemisphere. No less than 18 of these are confined to China but some of the newer Chinese species are difficult to separate. *Picea* is the ancient Latin name of the spruces, derived from pix = pitch. The wood is strong for its weight and is of primary importance in the manufacture of pulp and paper. The resinous bark exudations of *P. abies* furnish the so-called Burgundy pitch which is the basic compound for a number of varnishes and medicinal compounds; while the new leafy shoots are used in brewing spruce beer. Sounding boards for musical instruments are made from the wood of *P. abies*. Healing salves from gums and aromatic distillations of *P. glauca* and *P. mariana* are made, as well as ropes from the roots of *P. abies* and *P. glauca*.

MORPHOLOGICAL CHARACTERISTICS

Monoecious trees, pyramidal or conical; bark usually thin, scaly on old trees, sometimes furrowed at base; branches whorled; branchlets with prominent leaf-cushions (pulveni), separated by incised grooves and produced at the apex into a peg-like stalk bearing the leaf and left when the leaves fall; winter buds ovoid or conical; scales imbricated, with or without resin; leaves spirally, often pectinately arranged, on underside of branchlets, usually 4-angled, stomatiferous on all 4 sides or compressed and stomatiferous only on the upper or ventral side which appears by twisting of leaves to be the lower one; usually with 2 marginal resin-ducts; male flowers axillary; female flowers terminal; cones mostly hanging, ovoid to oblong-cylindrical, not shattering at maturity; scales suborbicular to rhombic-oblong, subtended by small bracts; seeds 2 to each scale, compressed; wing large, thin, obovate or oblong.

GROWTH CHARACTERISTICS

Most spruces are large trees of pyramidal to conical outline of a very formal nature. This tends to limit their usefulness as they dominate a small landscape because of their size and strong vertical lines. Retention of foliage and branches results in dense, attractive trees even after many years. *Picea glauca* 'Conica' is the most common dwarf type available in the trade. *Picea abies* alone contains over 150 cultivars, only a few of which possess merit for landscape use, or are sufficiently different from each other that anyone could notice the differences.

CULTURE

Spruces should be transplanted balled and burlapped and, because of the shallow, spreading root system, large specimens can be transplanted successfully. Spruces prefer a moderately moist, well drained soil although perform well in the clay soils of the midwest. They do not grow well under hot, dry, polluted conditions. Spruces are not adapted to culture in the southeast (Zone 8 to 10) although on occasion *Picea abies* will show prosperity. *P. omorika*, *P. orientalis* and *P. pungens* are more tolerant of dry conditions than other species. Usually little pruning is necessary but plants can be touched up in spring when the new growth is approximately one-half developed to create a denser plant. Selected species can be used for hedges as they tolerate heavy pruning.

DISEASES AND INSECTS

Canker *(Cytospora),* needle casts, rusts, wood decay, spruce gall aphid, cooley spruce gall aphid, other aphids, spruce budworm, spruce bud scale, spruce needle miner, pine needle scale, spruce epizeuxis, sawflies, white pine weevil, spruce spider mite and bagworm. The three most prevalent pests appear to be mites, aphids and bagworms.

PROPAGATION

Seeds of most *Picea* species germinate promptly without pretreatment, but cold stratification has been used for a few species. Cuttings have been used in isolated cases but percentages were usually low and this does not represent a practical method of propagation. Grafting is used on the cultivars of *P. abies* and especially the blue-foliaged forms of *P. pungens*. A side graft is used on seedlings of the species. Dirr and Heuser, 1987, present a detailed discussion of *Picea* propagation and should be consulted for specifics.

LANDSCAPE VALUE

Spruces are used extensively in large scale landscape plantings such as parks, golf courses, highways, and public buildings. The dense compact character of even older specimens provides attractive dependable evergreens which change little in effect over a long period of time. The symmetrical form results in plants with strong outlines and formal habit.

Textural variations are not great; however, some differences in branching habit can be used for different effect, i.e., the stiff branching of *P. pungens* contrasts with the pendulous branching of *P. abies*. Color contrasts are more distinctive and include light, dark, and yellow greens, and many shades of blue. Because of the conspicuous character of many of the so-called Blue Spruces, care and discretion should be used in locating these plants in the landscape. One of the stigmas of our landscapes has been the placement of these plants in prominent places especially in the front of the property, which detracts from all other plantings as well as the house.

Selected forms are effective as hedges, screens, windbreaks, specimens, and plantings near large buildings.

SELECTED SPRUCE SPECIES
(The best spruces for general landscape use)

Picea abies
Picea glauca
Picea omorika
Picea orientalis
Picea pungens

Picea abies — Norway Spruce
(pī'sē-á ā'bēz)

LEAVES: Persistent for several years, those on the upper side of the stem more or less overlapping and pointing forwards, those on the lower side spreading right and left and exposing the stem; rhombic in cross-section, 1/2 to 1″ long, stiff, straight or curved, ending in a blunt, horny point; light or dark green with 2 or 3 stomatic lines on each side, often shining green.
BUDS: Reddish or light brown, not resinous, scales often with spreading tips, about 1/4″ long, rosette shape.
STEM: Reddish brown or orangish brown, glabrous or with minute scattered hairs.
CONES: Pendulous, cylindrical, 4 to 6″ long, brown when mature; cone scales without undulations, persisting through winter.

SIZE: 40 to 60′ in height by 25 to 30′ spread; can grow to 100′ and more.
HARDINESS: Zone 2 to 7 (8), survives but is not well adapted to Zone 8 conditions.
HABIT: Pyramidal with pendulous branchlets; stiff when young, graceful at maturity.
RATE: Medium to fast especially in youth; may grow 75′ high after 50 years.
TEXTURE: Medium.
BARK: Usually thin on young trees; on old trees thick with small, thin gray flaking surface scales.
LEAF COLOR: Bright green in youth changing to lustrous dark green with 2 to 3 stomatic lines on each side.
FLOWERS: Monoecious, male flowers are axillary and infrequent whereas female flowers are terminal, spread on the crowns of the trees and reddish pink in color.
FRUIT: Cones are cylindrical, 4 to 6″ long, 1 1/2 to 2″ wide, pendulous, purple or green in youth, light brown at maturity.
CULTURE: The following applies to all spruces covered in this book unless other specifics are listed under a particular plant; transplant balled and burlapped in large sizes (3 to 4′ and greater); move readily because of shallow spreading root system; perform best in moderately moist, sandy, acid, well drained soils but can be planted in most average soils provided adequate moisture is available especially in the early years of establishment; prefer a cold climate; prune in early spring either by

removing a selected branch or, if a hedge is desired, by pruning the young growth; full sun or perhaps very light shade in south but plants become thin and ragged in heavy shade.

DISEASES AND INSECTS: Susceptible to red spider, spruce gall aphid, budworm and borers.

LANDSCAPE VALUE: Much overplanted, with old age may lose its form and its usefulness; commonly used as a windbreak, shelters or as a temporary specimen.

CULTIVARS: For a complete list see Den Ouden and Boom, Dallimore and Jackson, and Welch. The following are some that I have observed and which are also available in the trade. Iseli Nursery, Boring, OR, lists 36 forms of *P. abies*. For fun, I counted over 120 forms in Krüssmann's *Manual of Cultivated Conifers*.

'Argenteo-spica'—Really quite striking for the new shoots are creamy-white and finally turn to dark green; the first time I saw this was at the Morton Arboretum where it stood out from the other species and cultivars.

'Clanbrassiliana'—The earliest dwarf form of the Norway Spruce to be discovered (1836); it forms a low, dense, flat-topped mound usually wider than high, a 30-year-old plant may be less than 3' high; the original plant after 120 years was only 16 3/4' high; this is a rather handsome form.

'Maxwellii'—Originated from a witches broom, the true form makes a low, rounded cushion with thick, short branches, needles radially arranged, 1/2" long, somewhat roundish; another form selected from "loose" growth of the broom is stronger growing and much larger.

'Nidiformis'—Bird's Nest Spruce—Spreading, dense, broad plant of regular growth; usually a depression in center of plant that gives rise to the common name; quite common in commerce; after many years 3 to 6' high.

forma *pendula*—A rather heterogenous group including plants with pendulous branches to some degree or another; included here are 'Formanek', 'Inversa', 'Pendula', 'Pendula Major', 'Pendula Monstrosa' and 'Reflexa'; 'Inversa' is particularly interesting because the main and secondary branches are pendulous, if not trained it simply becomes a prostrate or trailing form.

'Procumbens'—Strong growing, flat-topped form with crowded, thin, stiff branchlets, 2 to 3' high.

'Pumila'—Dwarf, globular, flattened, compact, very broad, 3 to 4' high, lower branches spreading, upper ones nearly erect; branchlets dense, regularly set, directed slightly forward, stiff, flexible, light to reddish brown; several forms with various foliage colors, apparently quite a confused group.

'Repens'—A handsome, wide-spreading form which gradually builds up in the center, very uniform; there is a fine specimen at the Arnold Arboretum.

PROPAGATION: Seed does not require a stratification period and can be directly sown. Optimum period for rooting cuttings appears to be from November to February. Cuttings rooted better when taken in December. Cuttings root best when taken from the lower portion of old trees and should be made from the full length of the current year's growth. Cuttings generally rooted better if made with the basal cut at or slightly above the base of the current year's growth. Rooting was better in 1 sand:1 peat, than in sand. Hormonal treatments did not prove significantly beneficial for enhancing rooting.

NATIVE HABITAT: Northern and central Europe, growing in extended forests, in plains and in the mountains. Introduced in colonial times.

Picea glauca — White Spruce
(pī-sē-á glaw'ka)

LEAVES: Persistent for several years, crowded on the upper side of the stem, pale green or glaucous, 1/2 to 3/4" long, incurved, ending in an acute or roundish horny point; quadrangular in cross-section; 2 to 5 bands of stomata on each surface; fetid when bruised.

BUDS: Up to 1/4" long with rounded chestnut-brown scales, apex blunt, not resinous.

STEM: Slender, glabrous, often glaucous, becoming dark yellowish brown or pale brown in their second year.

CONES: Cylindric, blunt, 1 to 2 1/2" long and 1/2 to 3/4" in diameter, pale brown when ripe.

SIZE: 40 to 60′ in height by 10 to 20′ in spread; size descriptions for this species vary significantly with author; the largest trees I have seen were 40 to 50′ high.

HARDINESS: Zone 2 to 6.

HABIT: A broad, dense pyramid in youth, becoming a tall, fairly narrow, dense spire, compact and regular, with ascending branches.

RATE: Medium.

TEXTURE: Medium.

BARK: Thin, flaky or scaly, ashy brown; freshly exposed layer somewhat silvery.

LEAF COLOR: Glaucous green.

FLOWERS: Monoecious; staminate, pale red becoming yellow; pistillate purple.

FRUIT: Pendulous, cylindrical cones, 1 to 2 1/2″ long, 1/2 to 3/4″ wide, green when young and light brown when mature, scales thin, flexible, broad, rounded, almost entire at margins.

DISEASES AND INSECTS: Susceptible to trunk and root rot, spruce bagworm, European sawfly and red spiders.

CULTURE: Transplants readily; makes its best growth on moist loam or alluvial soils, and although found on many different sites, it is typical of stream banks, lake shores and adjacent slopes; one of the most tolerant spruces as it withstands wind, heat, cold, drought and crowding; best in full sun, but tolerant of some shade.

LANDSCAPE VALUE: Useful as a specimen, mass, hedge, windbreak; widely used in the plains states because of its adaptability; probably should be relegated to secondary garden status in the eastern states because of superior evergreen alternatives.

CULTIVARS:

var. *albertiana*—Slow growing, compact, narrow pyramidal tree; apparently there is considerable hybridization between *P. glauca* and *P. engelmannii* and this gives rise to numerous forms which have been classed as varieties by some authorities including *albertiana*.

'Conica'—Often called the Dwarf Alberta Spruce and Dwarf White Spruce. This natural dwarf (could be listed as var. *conica*) was found by J.G. Jack and Alfred Rehder at Lake Laggan, Alberta, Canada in 1904 as they awaited the train to bring them back to the Arnold Arboretum; the plants become broadly conical with time; the foliage (needles 1/4 to 1/2″ long) is light green, densely set, and the needles radiate around the stem; growth is very slow (about 2 to 4″ per year); interesting specimen or novelty plant; will grow about 10 to 12′ in 25 to 30 years. This is one of the most common dwarf conifers and is widely available in commerce; it is easily propagated from cuttings; mites can sometimes be a problem and I have seen it revert to the species on occasion; several bud sports have arisen and these have given rise to forms with smaller needles and slower growth.

'Densata'—This again could and often is listed correctly as var. *densata;* this is slow growing conical type reaching 20 to 40′ after 40 to 80 years; the few trees on the Illinois campus were much denser and more ornamental than the species; often called Black Hills Spruce.

PROPAGATION: Seed requires no pretreatment; cuttings collected in late July rooted 84 to 90% and better than cuttings taken earlier or later; treatment with IAA did not affect rooting; *P. g.* 'Conica' cuttings collected in December rooted better in sand:peat than sand, and the percentage was increased by 70 ppm IBA/24 hour soak; there are other reports which indicate this plant can be successfully rooted from cuttings.

NATIVE HABITAT: Labrador to Alaska, south to Montana, Minnesota, and New York. Introduced 1700.

RELATED SPECIES:

Picea brewerana, (pī′sē-à brew-er-ā′nà), Brewer Spruce, forms a stiff pyramidal tree in youth but with age the secondary branches become pendulous and the tertiary branchlets are perpendicularly pendulous and often 7 to 8′ long, hanging like curtains. It is truly one of the most striking spruces as it approaches maturity. It is limitedly represented in gardens. The 1/2 to 1″ long, 1/20 to 1/12″ wide needles point forward and radiate equally all around the stem. The needles are glossy dark green on one side and more or less gray-green on the other. The needles tend to be flattened or remotely 3-angled. The cylindrical-oval, 3″ long purple cones are composed of rounded, entire-margined scales. Found at about 7,000' altitude in the Siskiyou Mountains of California and Oregon. Introduced 1893. Zone 5.

Picea engelmannii, (pī'sē-à en-gel-man'ē-ī), Engelmann Spruce, is a large, narrow, almost spire-like, densely pyramidal tree with ascending branches. In the eastern states this species may grow 40 to 50' high in 40 to 60 years but in its native range can grow 100 to 120' tall. The needles are 4-sided, blue-green, about 1" long and emit a rank odor when crushed. The bark is thin and broken into large purplish brown to russet-red, thin, loosely attached scales. Maximum growth is made on deep, rich, loamy soils of high moisture content. Wyman considers this species one of the better spruces for ornamental planting. Several cultivars include 'Argentea' which has silvery gray needles and 'Glauca' with needles bluish to steel blue. British Columbia and Alberta to Oregon, Arizona and New Mexico. Introduced 1862. Zone 2 to 5.

Picea mariana, (pī'sē-à mār-ē-ā'na), Black Spruce, is a small to medium-sized tree which grows 30 to 40' tall and develops a limited spread. The habit is distinctly conical, spire-like. The needles are 4-sided, dull bluish green, more or less glaucous, 1/4 to 1/2" long. The cones are small, 3/4 to 1 1/2" long, ovoid, purplish and turn brown at maturity. The bark is broken into thin, flaky, grayish brown to reddish brown scales, 1/4 to 1/2" thick; freshly exposed inner scales somewhat olive-green. This is a cold climate tree and in the southern part of its range is commonly restricted to cold sphagnum bogs; in the far north it is found on dry slopes but makes its best growth on moist, well drained alluvial bottoms. The cultivar 'Doumetii" is a slow growing, densely pyramidal, bluish green form which can be propagated by cuttings. It is a beautiful cultivar that appears to do quite well in the heat of Zone 6 and 7. 'Nana' is commonly seen in gardens and makes a dense mound of dull gray-green needles, 1 1/2 to 2' high, slightly wider. 'Ericoides' is a rounded mound of small almost heath-like stems, needles average 3/8" long and are bluish gray. Labrador to Alaska, south to Wisconsin and Michigan and in the mountains of Virginia. Introduced 1700. Zone 2 to 5(6).

Picea rubens, (pī'sē-à rū'benz), Red Spruce, forms a broadly conical crown, 60 to 70' high under cultivation. Maximum development occurs in the southern Appalachians where humidity and rainfall are high. Under these conditions, a 162' high record tree was found. The 1/2 to 5/8" long, 4-sided, lustrous bright or dark green needles are acute and mucronulate. The green or purplish green cones mature to reddish brown and range from 1 1/4 to 2" long. This is a beautiful tree and is abundant in the high mountains of the Great Smokey Mountains National Park along Route 441. Not well suited to cultivation. Nova Scotia to the high peaks of North Carolina. Introduced before 1750. Zone 2 to 5.

Picea omorika — Serbian Spruce
(pī'sē-à ō-môr-ē'kà)

LEAVES: Overlapping and directed forwards on upper side of branchlets, 1/2 to 1" long, 1/16 to 1/12" wide, apex short pointed on young plants, rounded on older plants, compressed, flat, keeled on both sides, dark green, without stomata above; glaucous white with 4 to 6 distinct stomatic bands on either side of the midrib beneath.

SIZE: 50 to 60' by 20 to 25' spread after 50 to 60 years, can grow to 100'.
HARDINESS: Zone 4 to 7, is being grown at Minnesota Landscape Arboretum where it may winter burn in exposed sites.
HABIT: A tree with a remarkably slender trunk and short ascending or drooping branches forming a very narrow, pyramidal head; one of the most graceful and beautiful spruces.
RATE: Slow.

TEXTURE: Medium.

BARK: Thin, scaling off in platelets, coffee-brown in color.

LEAF COLOR: The upper surface is a glossy dark green in contrast to the lower with its two prominent white stomatic lines.

FLOWERS: Monoecious.

FRUIT: Cones are oblong-ovoid, 1 1/4 to 2″ long, blue-black when young, shining cinnamon brown when ripe, scales suborbicular, finely denticulate.

CULTURE: Prefers a deep rich soil that is both moist and well-drained; grows on limestone and acid peats, and will benefit from winter protection from strong winds; likes a dry atmosphere and semi-shade; supposedly tolerates city air; one of the most adaptable spruces.

DISEASES AND INSECTS: Subject to aphids, budworm and borers.

LANDSCAPE VALUE: Noted for its excellent foliage and narrow, pyramidal growth; considered excellent for the northeastern states; would make an excellent evergreen street tree; I have seen many fine specimens of the species, from the University of Maine campus (-30°F) to Louisville, KY where summer temperatures and humidity can be horrendous; the species is much more adaptable than given credit; as a specimen or in groups it is an excellent choice; this and *Picea orientalis* are my favorites among the spruces.

CULTIVARS:

'Expansa'—Interesting wide-spreading form with ascending branches and typical foliage, grows about 3′ high; may revert to the type and throw a normal leader.

'Nana'—A lovely conical to globose form of irregular outline eventually 8 to 10′ high; needles closely set, 3/8″ long, more or less radially arranged.

'Pendula'—A very beautiful, slender tree with drooping, slightly twisted branches.

PROPAGATION: Seed requires no pretreatment. Cuttings taken in winter from 4-year-old trees rooted moderately well; rooting was improved by treatment with 200 ppm IBA/24 hour soak.

ADDITIONAL NOTES: Perhaps the most handsome of the spruces. The habit is more graceful and refined than most. Should be used in preference to other spruces when it can be located.

NATIVE HABITAT: Southeastern Europe (Yugoslavia). Confined to a few stands in the limestone mountains on either side of the upper Drina. Introduced about 1880.

Picea orientalis — Oriental Spruce
(pī′sē-à ôr-i-en-tā′lis)

LEAVES: Very short, 1/4 to1/2″ long, 4-sided, lustrous dark green, blunt or rounded at the apex, quadrangular in cross section with 1 to 4 lines of stomata on each surface; shortest needles of the spruce species, arranged at and above the horizontal plane, upper appressed and hiding the stem.

SIZE: 50 to 60′ in height after about 60 years, can grow to 120′.

HARDINESS: Zone 4 to 7.

HABIT: A dense, compact narrow pyramid with horizontal branches that are often pendulous.

RATE: Slow.

TEXTURE: Medium.

BARK: Brown, exfoliating in thin scales.

LEAF COLOR: Lustrous dark green with 1 to 4 stomatic lines on each side, needles very short and tightly set.

FLOWERS: Monoecious, male carmine-red and resembling strawberries in youth.

FRUIT: Cones short stalked, nodding, ovoid-cylindrical, 2 to 4″ long by approximately 1″ wide, reddish purple when young turning brown when mature, scales entire at margin.

CULTURE: Will tolerate poor, gravelly soils; plant where winters are not excessively cold or dry; has done well in midwest as a young tree; protect from harsh winter winds.

LANDSCAPE VALUE: Because of its graceful and attractive habit it has value as a specimen spruce for small areas; much superior to Norway and White; may suffer browning of foliage in severe winters;

there are many fine specimens in Spring Grove, Cincinnati and Cave Hill, Louisville, Kentucky, also several magnificent 70′(?) high specimens at Biltmore Estate, Asheville, NC; once one sees this tree he or she wonders why Norway and White are ever planted.

CULTIVARS:

'Aurea'—Young shoots golden yellow in spring, changing to green, often with a general golden sheen all over the leaves.

'Gowdy'—More narrow, columnar form with small rich green leaves, slow growing, possibly 8 to 10′, I have seen a few plants labeled as 'Gowdy' which were wider than the typical description.

'Gracilis'—A slow growing, densely branched form developing into a small, conical tree, 15 to 20′ tall; needles radially set and bright grass green.

'Nigra Compacta'—Narrow dark green spire with glossy dark green needles.

'Pendula' (now called 'Weeping Dwarf')—A compact, slow-growing form with pendulous branchlets, the foliage is normal.

'Skylands'—Typical habit of the species but with golden needles that fade in the heat of the summer; may burn in hot climates.

PROPAGATION: Seed requires no pretreatment.

NATIVE HABITAT: Caucasus, Asia Minor. Introduced 1827.

Picea pungens — Colorado Spruce
(pī′sē-à pun′jenz)

LEAVES: Spreading more or less all around the stem, but more crowded above than below, stout, rigid, incurved and very prickly, 3/4 to 1 1/4″ long, varying in color on different trees, dull green, bluish or silvery-white, 4-sided with about 6 stomatic lines on each side, needles with acid taste when chewed.

BUDS: Broadly conical to nearly spherical, apex blunt, yellowish brown, not resinous; scales loosely appressed, apex often reflexed, the lowest ones keeled, long pointed.

STEM: Stout, without pubescence, glaucous at first becoming orange-brown with age.

CONES: Cylindrical but slightly narrowed at each end, 2 to 4″ long, pale shining brown when mature, scales wavy, oval, blunt and jaggedly toothed at apex.

SIZE: 30 to 60′ in height with a 10 to 20′ spread under average landscape conditions; 90 to 135′ in height by 20 to 30′ spread in the wild.

HARDINESS: Zone 2 to 7(8).

HABIT: A dense, regular narrow to broad pyramid with horizontal stiff branches to the ground; often becoming open, poor and dingy in age.

RATE: Slow-medium, 30 to 50′ after 35 to 50 years; very stiff and formal in outline.

TEXTURE: Medium to coarse.

LEAF COLOR: Usually gray-green to blue-green, young growth soft, silvery blue-gray.

FLOWERS: Monoecious, staminate orange, pistillate greenish or purple.

FRUIT: Cones oblong, cylindrical, short-stalked, 2 to 4″ long, 1 1/4″ wide, green when young turning light or yellow-brown when ripe, scales wavy and toothed at apex.

CULTURE: It prefers rich, moist soil in full sunlight although is more drought tolerant than other *Picea;* very adaptable.

DISEASES AND INSECTS: Subject to spruce gall aphid (causes tips of branches to die), spruce budworm and spider mite; *Cytospora* canker may infect lower branches.

LANDSCAPE VALUE: Overused; popular as a specimen but hard to combine well with other plants; acceptable in dry climates; can be used in groupings; one of the standard practices in past years has been the use of this plant or a blue-foliage type in the front yard where it immediately detracts from the rest of the landscape.

CULTIVARS:

'Argentea'—Foliage silvery white, a collective name for cultivars with silvery colored needles, probably not a valid term.

'Bakeri'—Deeper blue than foliage of 'Argentea' and possibly better than 'Moerheimii', after 32 years a specimen in the Arnold Arboretum was only 12′ tall and 6′ across.

'Fat Albert'—Dense upright pyramidal form with good blue needle color, have seen a block of these at Iseli Nursery and the uniformity was astounding, produced by cuttings.

f. *glauca* (var. *glauca*)—Foliage some variation of bluish green; in any population of seedlings variation in degree of blue or silver is evident; nurserymen often select these types and sell them at a higher price than the "normal" green types; it is from this forma or variety that the best cultivars have been selected and perpetuated by grafting; a nursery block of seed-grown trees is quite a sight for the foliage color often varies from green to silvery-blue.

'Glauca Globosa'—A compact (3′ high), rounded, flat-topped bush that at maturity is wider than high; the needles are bluish white and more or less radially disposed.

'Glauca Pendula' ('Glauca Procumbens', 'Glauca Prostrata')—I am a degree confused here for plants in this category more or less spread and sprawl over the ground becoming almost ground cover-like; the first listed has handsome silvery-blue needles, and makes a rather attractive, but somewhat gaudy, rock garden type plant; if lateral shoots of the species are propagated they tend to grow laterally or procumbently, so the production of these plants can be affected by selection of lateral growth from an otherwise normal tree; this type of growth response is termed topophysis.

'Hoopsii'—Dense, pyramidal form with spreading branches, foliage extremely glaucous (blue-white); perhaps the most glaucous form and the best grower, my number one choice.

'Hunnewelliana'—Dense pyramidal form of light blue foliage; thirty-two-year-old tree is 15′ tall and 8′ across.

'Iseli Foxtail'—Bushy blue twisted new growth, distinct tight upright habit, appears more heat tolerant and has prospered in Raleigh NC (Zone 8), Raulston reported 40″ vertical growth in 2 years while other cultivars grew 2 to 6″, also propagated from cuttings.

'Koster'—Plants I have observed never matched the quality of 'Thompsenii' and 'Hoopsii', plants were not uniform and dense, certainly this could have resulted from pruning and staking practices; selected as a group of blue seedling plants and so some variation is possible, at its best a regular conical form with silver-blue needles.

'Mission Blue'—Intense blue foliage color, compact, symmetrical grower with broad base.

'Moerheimii'—Compact, dense growing form with very blue foliage sometimes with longitudinal young shoots; retains blue color in winter; an irregular grower, ultimately 30′ or more.

'Montgomery'—A dwarf bush forming a broad cone; needles silver-blue and quite striking; given to the New York Botanical Garden by R.H. Montgomery of Coscob, CT; the original plant is still there.

'Thompsenii' ('Thompsen')—Symmetrical pyramidal tree of a whitish-silver-blue foliage color, more intense than the above varieties although somewhat similar to 'Hoopsii' with leaves at least twice as thick, one of the best.

PROPAGATION: Seed requires no pretreatment. Most of the cultivars are grafted onto seedling understocks. This is usually done in January and February in the greenhouse and the grafted plants are placed under lath or lined out in the spring.

NATIVE HABITAT: Southwestern United States; Rocky Mountains from Colorado to Utah to New Mexico and Wyoming. Introduced about 1862.

Pieris japonica — Japanese Pieris, also mistakenly called Andromeda
(pīēr′is ja-pon′i-k)à)

FAMILY: Ericaceae

LEAVES: Alternate, simple, evergreen, obovate-oblong to oblanceolate, 1 1/4 to 3 1/2″ long, 1/3 to 3/4″ wide, crenate-serrate, lustrous dark green above, lighter green beneath, glabrous, new growth is a bronze-green to reddish color.

FLOWERS: Buds form in summer prior to year of flowering and offer a valid identification characteristic.

SIZE: 9 to 12' in height by 6 to 8' in spread.
HARDINESS: Zone 5 to 8, does acceptably in
    Zone 4 with some protection.
HABIT: Upright evergreen shrub of neat habit
    with stiff, spreading branches and dense
    rosette-like foliage.
RATE: Slow, 4 to 6' in 5 to 8 years.
TEXTURE: Medium in all seasons.
LEAF COLOR: New growth a rich bronze, chang-
    ing to lustrous dark green at maturity; new
    foliage is almost the most aesthetic part of
    the plant and some of the new cultivars like
    'Mountain Fire' are spectacular.
FLOWER: Perfect, weakly fragrant, white, urn-
    shaped, 1/4" long, March-April, borne in 3
    to 6" long pendulous racemose panicles,
    effective for 2 to 3 weeks.
FRUIT: Dehiscent, 5-valved, 1/4" long capsule
    that persists into winter and is best removed
    after flowering.
CULTURE: Transplant balled and burlapped or
    as a container plant into moist, acid, well-
    drained soil which has been supplemented

with peat moss or organic matter; full sun or partial shade; not as fastidious for acid soil as other
ericaceous plants; prune after flowering; shelter from wind; well-drained soil is a must in the south
and plants are short-lived if grown in wet soils.
DISEASES AND INSECTS: Leaf spots, die back *(Phytophthora),* lace bug (very prevalent in eastern states
    where it has made the culture of *Pieris* very difficult, sucks juices from leaves and causes yellowing
    to browning of foliage), Florida wax scale, two-spotted mite, nematodes.
LANDSCAPE VALUE: Excellent large specimen broadleaf evergreen; works well in the shrub border, in
    mass, or blended with other broadleaf evergreens; does acceptably in south if sited in shade.
CULTIVARS: It is becoming increasingly difficult to keep up with the number of cultivars that are flooding
    the literature. How far they will travel in the nursery trade is questionable. The list has been expanded
    since the last edition.
    'Bert Chandler'—Young leaves at first salmon-pink, paling through cream and white and becoming
        normal green by summer; a seedling raised by the Australian nurseryman Bert Chandler around
        1936.
    'Bisbee Dwarf'—Leaves about 1/2 the size of the species, glossy dark green with a slight twist,
        reddish when young; compact, bushy plant.
    'Blush'—Rose-pink flowers that fade with maturity, open elegant habit, 5' by 5'.
    'Boltman's Pink'—Compact plant with bright red buds that open to blush pink flowers.
    'Christmas Cheer'—Flowers pink with the tips of the corolla a deeper pink creating a bi-color effect;
        good grower; imported from Japan; flowers early; a seedling of 'Daisen',
    'Coleman'—Pink flowered form with red flower buds that maintain this color through the winter.
    'Compacta'—Dense, compact form, leaves small, heavy flowering.
    'Crispa'—Wavy margined leaves, good white flowers.
    'Crystal'—Large thick glossy dark green leaves and beautiful white flowers; heat tolerant and
        Phytophthora resistant, Verkade introduction.
    'Daisen'—Flowers deep pink in bud paling as they open; leaves wider and smoother than those of
        'Christmas Cheer', color is best in some shade, from Japan.
    'Debutante'—Compact habit with dark green leaves, pure white flowers, dark green foliage.
    'Deep Pink'—Bright red buds and flower stalks brighten the plant through winter, open to good pink
        in spring.

'Dorothy Wycoff'—Compact form but strong growing, dark red flower buds opening to pale pink.

'Flamingo'—Deep rose-red non-fading flowers, foliage lustrous dark green.

'Geisha'—Gracefully slender leaves, pure white flowers.

'Grayswood'—Bronzy-green new shoots become dark green with maturity, white flowers in long arching racemes, freely borne, forms a dome shaped outline, 4 to 5' high.

'John's Select'—Compact, dark green leaves, red buds open to pure white flowers, grows about two-third's as tall as the species.

'Little Heath'—Slow growing, compact, leaves with yellowish green variegation, grows about 3' high, will revert to the green form which has been propagated and offered as 'Little Heath Green'.

'Mountain Fire'— New growth fire red, exceptional, flowers white, becoming common in commerce.

'Nana'—Low compact dwarf with small leaves.

'Pink Delight'—Pink buds, white flowers.

'Purity'—Unusually large pure white flowers, flowers heavily as a young plant, grows 3 to 4' high, foliage is light green, flowers and develops new shoots later in spring.

'Pygmaea' (f. *pygmaea*)—Leaves small, 1/2 to 1" long and very narrow, feathery in effect, grows about 3 to 4' high; white flowers.

'Red Bud'—Good vigorous form with showy red flower buds that open to light pink.

'Red Mill'—New leaves bright red turning mahogany then to lustrous dark green, leaves thick and leathery, maintains dense bushy habit in old age, supposedly quite insect and disease resistant, flowers white and last about 10 days longer than typical seed produced plants.

'Rosalinda'—Brownish red new shoots give way to glossy dark green leaves, flowers brown in bud due to colored calyx, pink in flower and holding the color, compact habit, about 4' by 4'.

'Scarlet O'Hara'—White flowered form with tall slender habit.

'Shojo'—Black-red flower buds open to red; said to be the darkest red flowers of any *Pieris,* from Japan.

'Spring Snow' (*P. japonica* × *P. floribunda*)—Flowers like those of *P. floribunda* with snow white corollas; leaves are like *P. japonica,* selected by Del Brown, Marysville, WA; introduced by Briggs Nursery.

'Temple Bells'—Slow-growing dwarf shrub with tiered branches, new foliage bronze-apricot maturing to lustrous dark green, large ivory-white flowers are borne in dense racemose-panicles, looks like a particularly fine form.

'Valentine's Day'—Early flowering form.

'Valley Fire'—Vivid colored new growth, large white flowers, vigorous grower.

'Valley Rose'—Deep green foliage and pastel-pink flowers, introduced by Bob Tichnor of Willamette Valley Experiment Station, Oregon State University, tall shrub of open habit, flowers described as silvery-rose passing to white.

'Valley Valentine'—From Dr. Robert Tichnor, Oregon State, considered best of his selections, rich maroon flower buds, long lasting deep rose-pink flowers abundantly borne on dense upright plants that grow 4' in 10 years; foliage is lustrous dark green.

'Variegata'—Leaves with white margins, will grow 10 to 12' with age, white flowers, actually rather pretty in a shady nook of the garden.

'White Cascade'—Long panicles of pure white flowers, effective for 5 weeks, very floriferous, seedling from Vermeulen Nursery in 1953, new leaves yellowish brown, glossy dark green later.

'White Pearl'—Distinct habit with erect branches and pure white flowers, dark green foliage.

'White Rim'—Compact habit, each leaf streaked light and dark green with uneven deep creamy white margins, young growth pinkish, flowers creamy white.

'White Water' ('Whitewater')—Floriferous white flowered form, spreading habit.

PROPAGATION: Seed, as discussed for *Calluna.* Cuttings root readily, see under *Leucothoe.* Seed was collected in November, 1975, and directly sown on peat and placed under mist; within 21 days excellent germination had occurred.

NATIVE HABITAT: Japan. cultivated 1870.

RELATED SPECIES:

Pieris floribunda — Mountain Pieris
(pīēr'is flō-ri-bun'da)

LEAVES: Alternate, simple, evergreen, elliptic-ovate to oblong-lanceolate, 1 to 3″ long, 1/2 to 1″ wide, acute or short acuminate, obtuse, crenate-serrulate, ciliate, glossy dark green above, paler beneath, with short black pubescence on each surface; petiole—1/4 to 3/8″long.

Pieris floribunda, Mountain Pieris, is a handsome evergreen shrub of neat, bushy habit, low and rounded, with rather stiff branches and dense, dark green, 1 to 3″ long leaves; will grow 2 to 6′ high with a similar or greater spread. Flowers are white, fragrant, borne in 2 to 4″ long, dense, upright racemose panicles; April for 2 to 4 weeks; very handsome small rounded shrub which has not been used enough in American gardens; not afflicted by the lacebug like the Japanese Pieris; also is tolerant of higher pH soils than most Ericaceae. Seed can be sown as soon as ripe, however, cuttings have proved somewhat difficult to root. 'Millstream' is a rather flat-topped, mounded, slow-growing form; it makes a splendid rock garden plant. Native from Virginia to Georgia. Introduced 1800. Zone 4 to 6.

An F_1 hybrid between the Japanese and Mountain Pieris has resulted in a clone called 'Brouwer's Beauty' which is dense and compact in habit; the leaves are dark green and shiny; the new foliage a distinct yellow-green. Panicles are horizontal but slightly arched. Flower buds are deep purplish red. Roots easier than *Pieris floribunda;* cuttings should be taken in the fall and placed in plastic tents and a peat:perlite medium. Previously, this clone was thought to be resistant to the lace bug but recent controlled tests have shown that the hybrid is susceptible when exposed to large numbers of lace bugs.

Pieris formosa, (pīēr'is fôr-mō'sa), Himalaya Pieris, although doubtfully adaptable in the eastern and southeastern United States will grow in the western U.S. and is one of the most colorful shrubs in the spring. Abundant literature is available from English references, particularly Bean, and should be consulted for specifics. In general leaves are larger (3 to 7″ long) and the ultimate size is 10′ and up. 'Wakehurst' has brilliant red new leaves in March and April fading to pink-crimson and then a chlorotic, almost albino condition before developing normal deep green. I have seen the plant in England particularly the fine old specimens at Wakehurst Place. It is difficult not to get excited about such a plant. 'Forest Flame' offers similar, perhaps not as brightly red colored foliage as the above, and is more compact and symmetrical in habit. Possibly a hybrid between *P. japonica* and *P. formosa* var. *forrestii.* Other cultivars with related parentage are known but are primarily of European garden interest. Hardiness possibly to Zone 8 but a cool even climate suits the plant best.

ADDITIONAL NOTES: The flower buds are formed the summer prior to flowering and are exposed all winter. They are quite attractive and do add ornamental appeal to the landscape.

Pinckneya pubens — Feverbark, Georgia Bark
(pink'nē-a̱ pū'benz)

FAMILY: Rubiaceae
LEAVES: Opposite, simple, elliptic to oblong-oval, 4 to 8″ long, 2 1/2 to 4 1/2″ wide, acute or short-acuminate, cuneate, entire, dark green and hairy above, pubescent below.
BUDS: Terminal—purple-brown, waxy, glabrous.
STEM: Gray-brown, pubescent.

SIZE: 10 to 20′ (30′) high.
HARDINESS: Zone (7) 8 to 9.
HABIT: Large shrub or small tree of rather open habit.
RATE: Slow to medium.

TEXTURE: Medium.

BARK: Gray-brown.

LEAF COLOR: Dark green in summer, no fall color.

FLOWERS: Perfect, yellowish-green, tubular, 1/2 to 1″ long, with 5 reflexed corolla lobes resulting in distinct trumpet-shaped flower; actual showy parts are the white, pink to rose sepals that become petal-like and remind of the bracts of poinsettia; full flower in June in Athens, beautiful for flower effect.

FRUIT: Dehiscent brown capsule, 3/4″ diameter, containing many small flattish seeds.

CULTURE: Transplant from a container, prefers moist, acid, well drained soil in partial shade.

DISEASES AND INSECTS: None serious.

LANDSCAPE VALUE: Unusual for flower effect, nice effect along edge of stream or pond, unfortunately not particularly hardy and -3°F killed the plant in my garden, but it did develop shoots from the roots.

PROPAGATION: Seeds require no pretreatment, I have grown many seedlings; cuttings at least from young plants root readily (June-July), 1000 ppm IBA, peat:perlite, mist.

NATIVE HABITAT: Low woods in South Carolina to Florida. Introduced 1786.

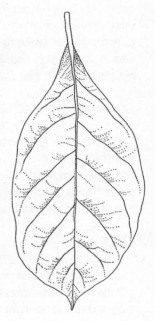

Pinus — Pine
Pinaceae

Of all the needle-type evergreens pines seem to show the greatest diversity of habit, distribution and ornamental characteristics. Approximately 90 species are distributed throughout the Northern Hemisphere from the Arctic Circle to Guatemala, the West Indies, North Africa and Malayan Archipelago. Most are large trees, however, several species are dwarfish or shrubby and over their native range may vary from dense, compact, slow growing types (3′) to large trees (75′, *Pinus mugo*). The pines are of primary importance in the production of timber, pulp, and paper manufacture. Turpentine, pine-wood oils, wood tars, and rosin are obtained from the wood of several species. The leaf oils of several species are used in the manufacture of medicines and the seeds of several others are suitable for food ("pine nuts"). Generally, pines are considered more tolerant of adverse soil and climatic conditions than species of *Picea* and *Abies*.

MORPHOLOGICAL CHARACTERISTICS

Evergreen, monoecious trees of various heights, tall, rarely shrubby; crowns of young to middle-aged trees pyramidal, older flat-topped or arched-umbelliformly branched; trunk of isolated trees usually large at base, rapidly tapering, that of forest-grown trees straight, lower branches shredding; bark usually thick, rough, furrowed or scaly; branches whorled; branchlets appearing as long shoots and as spurs; long shoots on seedling plants up to the third year with needle-like leaves, afterwards with dry-membranous (soon deciduous) scale-like leaves, in the axils of which arise the spurs; one year long shoots regularly grow from winter-buds producing a single internode, consisting of a leafless base, which often bears the male flowers, a longer upper part bearing foliage and ending in a terminal bud, surrounded by a whorl of smaller buds, one or more of which may be replaced by female flowers, or the shoot consisting of 2 internodes, each with a leafless base, a leaf-bearing portion, and a whorl of buds; some species produce occasional shoots that bear juvenile leaves until advanced in age; such often appear from adventive buds; terminal buds varying in different species regarding the shape and character of their scales, resinous or not; leaves of three kinds: leaves borne on seedling-plants, solitary, spirally arranged, linear lanceolate, entire or margin fringed, soon deciduous, except the basal portion; adult leaves, needle-like, borne in clusters of 2, 3 or 5, margin often minutely toothed, the section semi-circular in the 2-leaved species, triangular in the 3- to

5-leaved ones, persistent 2 or more years; sheaths of the leaf-bundles persistent, deciduous or partly so; cones variable in outline, symmetrical or oblique, remaining on the tree unopened for many years; scales thin, or thick and woody, the exposed part of each scale (apophysis) thickened, showing a terminal or dorsal protuberance or scar, called the umbo, which is often pointed with a prickly point, boss or stout hook; seeds 2 to each scale, nut-like or ovoid, appressed, the kernel surrounded by a shell, winged or not; cotyledons 4 to 15.

GROWTH CHARACTERISTICS

It is difficult to stereotype the growth habits of pines but the majority are pyramidal, more or less symmetrical trees in youth becoming more round-topped, open and picturesque with age. There is considerable interest in the dwarf types and many selections have been made among species. One of the most beautiful of all upright types is *Pinus strobus* 'Fastigiata' which carries its plume-like foliage on strongly ascending branches and maintains a full complement of branches into old age.

CULTURE

Pines, with the exception of small seedlings or liners, should be moved balled and burlapped. If large plants have been properly root pruned transplanting is accomplished with very little difficulty. Most pines will develop a tap root and therefore are difficult to transplant from the wild.

Pines are more tolerant of adverse soil, exposure, and city conditions than *Abies* and *Picea*. The two needle types are considered more tolerant than the three which are greater than the five. *Pinus sylvestris*, *P. taeda*, and *P. nigra* are adapted to many soil types while *P. mugo*, *P. pungens*, *P. banksiana* and *P. thunbergiana* are more satisfactory in sandy soils. *Pinus nigra*, *P. pungens*, *P. thunbergiana* and *P. virginiana* exhibit salt spray tolerance. Several species such as *P. jeffreyi*, *P. thunbergiana* and *P. wallichiana* are on the hardiness borderline in Zone 5.

Pines withstand pruning and can be maintained as hedges and screens. Removing one-half of the new candle-growth (usually in June) will result in the formation of lateral buds below the cut. Christmas tree growers use machete's or power equipment for pruning.

DISEASES AND INSECTS

Late damping-off and root rot, dieback, tip blight, stem blister rust, Comandra blister rust, canker, *Cenangium* twig blight, leaf cast, needle blight, needle rust, shrub pine needle rust, littleleaf, white-pine aphid, European pine shoot moth, Nantucket pine moth, sawflies, pine webworm, pine false webworm, pine needle scale, pine needle miner, pine spittlebugs, pine tortoise scale, red pine scale, pales weevil, pine root collar weevil, white pine shoot borer, white pine tube moth, white pine weevil, Zimmerman pine moth, bark beetles, pinewood nematode.

Physiological problems include:
White pine blight—browning of current season's needles especially in northeastern United States; primary cause is unknown.
Stunt—on *Pinus resinosa;* possibly from poor soil drainage.
Air pollutants—including sulfur dioxide and ozone, produce tip burn or speckling of leaves.
Salt—significant damage to trees located along highways which are heavily salted. Damage is usually evident only on side of tree facing the highway.

PROPAGATION

All species are grown from seed and the stratification requirements vary significantly (see specific requirements which are listed under each species). Recently there has been considerable interest in producing seed-grown dwarf types. Cones are collected from "witches' broom" type growths and the resultant progeny are usually dwarfish in habit.

Grafting is used on many of the cultivars. A side graft is usually used on seedlings of the species. Cuttings have also been rooted but the percentage was usually low.

LANDSCAPE USE

The tree species and cultivars of pine are used extensively in large scale landscape plantings such as parks, golf courses, estates, cemeteries, industrial grounds, shopping centers, and public buildings. More advantage is usually found in using a few or individual specimen plants, rather than mass planting, because of the interesting outlines and branching habits. Variations in color from blue to dark green and in texture from fine to coarse make possible the creation of many landscape effects.

Large dense specimens or groups should be used carefully, if at all, on small properties because of the massive and overpowering effects, unwanted shade in winter, and interference with air movement.

Selected forms can be used near the house or other small buildings, as hedges, screens, windbreaks, or specimens.

The continuing trend to large scale landscaping will increase the demand for high quality, landscape size pines in the future.

Pine List
According to Needle Number

FIVE NEEDLE TYPES
  PRIMARY

Pinus aristata	Bristlecone Pine
Pinus cembra	Swiss Stone Pine
Pinus flexilis	Limber Pine
Pinus koraiensis	Korean Pine
Pinus parviflora	Japanese White Pine
Pinus peuce	Balkan Pine
Pinus pumila	Japanese Stone Pine
Pinus strobus	Eastern White Pine
Pinus wallichiana	Himalyan Pine

  SECONDARY

Pinus balfouriana	Foxtail Pine

THREE NEEDLE TYPES
  PRIMARY

Pinus bungeana	Lacebark Pine

  SECONDARY

Pinus ponderosa	Ponderosa Pine
Pinus rigida	Pitch Pine
Pinus taeda	Loblolly Pine

TWO NEEDLE TYPES
  PRIMARY

Pinus densiflora	Japanese Red Pine
Pinus mugo	Swiss Mountain Pine
Pinus nigra or *P. nigra* var. *nigra*	Austrian Pine
Pinus resinosa	Red Pine
Pinus sylvestris	Scotch Pine

SECONDARY
Pinus banksiana	Jack Pine
Pinus echinata	Shortleaf Pine
Pinus pungens	Table Mountain Pine
Pinus thunbergiana	Japanese Black Pine
Pinus virginiana	Scrub Pine

Pinus aristata — Bristlecone Pine, also called Hickory Pine.
(pī'nus a̍-ris-tā'ta)

LEAVES: Borne 5 together, bluish green, persistent for 14 to 17 years, commonly dotted with white resinous exudations, 1 to 1 3/4″ long; leaf sheaths curling back into small rosettes, remaining 2 to 4 years at the base of the leaf.

SIZE: 8 to 20′ with an irregular spread; can grow to 40′ but this would take many years.
HARDINESS: Zone 4 to 7, should be protected from desiccating winds in cold climates as foliage will burn.
HABIT: Dwarf, shrubby and picturesque in youth and in old age, tremendous character in a young plant.
RATE: Slow, in fact extremely so, 16-year-old plant being only 4′ high.
TEXTURE: Medium.
LEAF COLOR: Dark green with white resinous exudations giving the leaf a bluish white cast.
FLOWERS: Monoecious.
FRUIT: Cones sessile, cylindrical-ovoid, 2 to 4″ long by 1 1/2″ broad, apex blunt, a bristle-like prickle at the edge of each pine scale.
CULTURE: Will succeed in poor, dry, rocky soils whether alkaline or acid; dislikes shade and will not tolerate smoke-polluted air.
DISEASES AND INSECTS: Refer to general culture sheet.
LANDSCAPE VALUE: Suitable for rock garden or use as an accent plant; could possibly be used as a foundation plant because of its picturesque growth habit; makes a nice bonsai or patio plant.
PROPAGATION: Seeds have no dormancy and will germinate immediately upon collection. I have raised many seedlings and the only requirement is that damping-off be controlled.
ADDITIONAL NOTES: Depending on what source you believe this species is one of the oldest living plants on earth. Estimates range from 2000 to 7000 years; however, several trees in the 4000 to 5000 year-old category have been adequately documented. One authority reported a 4900-year-old-tree in eastern Nevada. Trees may attain only an inch diameter in a century. Often referred to as a foxtail pine because of the length of needle retention and the bushy effect of the foliage. *Pinus balfouriana,* Foxtail Pine, is a related type but does not develop the resinous exudations.
NATIVE HABITAT: Southwestern United States from the mountains along the Nevada-California border east through the highlands of Nevada, Utah, Colorado, northern Arizona and northern New Mexico. Introduced 1861.

Pinus banksiana — Jack Pine
(pī'nus bank-sē-ā'na)

LEAVES: In pairs, persisting 2 to 4 years, olive green, stiff, curved or slightly twisted, 3/4 to 2″ long, margin with minute or rudimentary teeth, apex short-petioled, stomata on each surface.
BUDS: Dark brown, 1/8 to 1/4″ long, cylindrical, resinous with closely pressed scales.
STEM: Smooth, glabrous, pale yellowish green, reddish or brown the second year.

SIZE: 35 to 50′ in height, known to 70′; irregularly spreading but usually less than height.
HARDINESS: Zone 2 to 6 or 7.
HABIT: Pyramidal in youth; open, spreading, often shrubby and flat-topped at maturity.

RATE: Slow-medium.

TEXTURE: Medium; possibly coarse in winter as needles often color a sickly yellow-green.

BARK: Thin, reddish brown to gray on young stems, becoming dark brown and flaky; on old trunks furrowed into irregular thick plates.

LEAF COLOR: Young leaves light green to dull dark green; yellow-green in winter.

FLOWERS: Monoecious, staminate clustered, yellowish.

FRUIT: Pointing forward, slender, conical, curved at the tapered point, 1 to 2″ long, 3/4″ wide, yellowish brown on some trees, on some trees nearly all mature cones remain closed; on others most of them open; closed cones subjected to temperatures of 140°F will open.

CULTURE: Easily transplanted if root pruned; not good in limestone soils; but will survive in almost pure sand and extremely cold climates; full sun; dry, sandy and acid soils; grows in soils too poor for most plants.

LANDSCAPE VALUE: Not especially ornamental but adaptable for windbreaks, shelterbelts and mass plantings in sand; also valued for its extreme hardiness and suitability to the colder regions; I have seen considerable plantings in poor soil regions of southern Indiana.

CULTIVARS:

‘Uncle Fogy’—Weeping form, can be grafted to an upright standard and grown as a weeping tree or used as a ground cover; in 10 years, one plant had spread 15′ and was 2′ high.

PROPAGATION: Seeds have no dormancy, or only a slight one, and will germinate immediately upon collection after a light stratification.

ADDITIONAL NOTES: Species serves as a valuable pioneer tree on poor sandy soils, but, except on the very poorest, is eventually replaced by Red or White Pine. Parboiling the male flowers to remove excess resin supposedly makes them suitable for eating.

NATIVE HABITAT: Most northerly of North American species—grows near the Arctic Circle, south to northern New York and Minnesota. Introduced before 1783.

Pinus bungeana — Lacebark Pine
(pī′nus bun-jē-ā′na)

LEAVES: 3, remaining 3 to 4 years, stiff, apex sharp-pointed, 2 to 4″ long, 1/12″ wide, margins finely toothed, inside slightly rounded, made by the raised midrib, with stomatic lines on both sides, lustrous medium to dark green. Needles are very stiff and rigid as well as sharp to the touch.

STEM: Grayish green, shining, perfectly glabrous.

SIZE: 30 to 50′ with a 20 to 35′ spread, can grow to 75′.

HARDINESS: Zone 4 to 8, one plant on the Georgia campus is about 75 years old.

HABIT: Pyramidal to rounded, often with many trunks in youth; becoming open, picturesque, flat-topped and broad-spreading with age.

RATE: Slow, patience is a necessary virtue.

TEXTURE: Medium.

BARK: Exfoliating in patches like a planetree, young stems greenish with irregular whitish or brownish areas interspersed; one of the most handsome pines for bark character.

LEAF COLOR: Lustrous medium to dark green.

FLOWERS: Monoecious.

FRUIT: Cone, terminal or lateral, subsessile, ovoid, 2 to 3″ long, approximately 2″ across, light yellowish brown, scale-end broader than high, cross-keeled, with a reflexed, triangular spine.

CULTURE: Transplant balled and burlapped if root pruned; prefers well drained soils and sunny conditions; supposedly tolerates limestone.

DISEASES AND INSECTS: See culture sheet.

LANDSCAPE VALUE: A good specimen tree valued for its striking, showy bark; excellent on corners of large buildings, and places where bark can be viewed; may break up under heavy snow and ice loads.

ADDITIONAL NOTES: The National Arboretum, Washington, D.C., has many handsome specimens. Has a place in almost every garden; one of the most beautiful of introduced pines; first observed by Dr. Bunge near Peking in 1831, cultivated in a temple garden.
NATIVE HABITAT: China. Introduced 1846.

Pinus cembra — Swiss Stone Pine (Arolla Pine)
(pī′nus sem′brȧ)

LEAVES: 5, remaining 4 to 5 years, densely set, rather stiff, straight, 2 to 3″ (5″) long, scarcely 1/25″ wide, apex blunt-pointed, margins finely toothed, dark green outside, innersides with bluish white stomatic lines; leaf sheaths falling the first year, 3/4″ long.
STEM: Covered with dense, orange-colored pubescence the first year, becoming grayish brown to brownish black the second year.

SIZE: 30 to 40′ in height, occasionally 70′ with a spread of 15 to 25′.
HARDINESS: Zone 4 to 7.
HABIT: A narrow, densely columnar pyramid in youth, becoming open and flat-topped with spreading, drooping branches when mature; extremely upright in youth.
RATE: Slow, rarely reaches 25′ after 25 to 30 years.
TEXTURE: Medium.
LEAF COLOR: Lustrous dark green outside, innerside with bluish white stomatic lines.
FLOWERS: Monoecious, clustered and inconspicuous.
FRUIT: The cones are terminal, short-stalked, erect-ovoid, apex blunt, 2 to 3″ long by 1 1/2 to 2 1/4″ broad; greenish violet at first turning purplish brown when mature; cones never open but fall in the spring of the third year and seeds are released by birds or through decomposition of scales.
CULTURE: Requires a well-drained, loamy soil in full sun; transplants better than most other pines; soil must be well-drained and slightly acid; should be located in an open area with free air movement.
DISEASES AND INSECTS: See culture sheet.
LANDSCAPE VALUE: A picturesque and hardy tree; useful as a specimen or mass; very handsome pine but somewhat slow growing.
CULTIVARS:
    'Columnaris'—More narrow and columnar in habit than the species, at times seems to be the predominant form in cultivation.
PROPAGATION: Seed should be stratified in moist medium for 90 to 270 days at 33 to 41°F; there is some indication that direct sowing will result in a good germination.
ADDITIONAL NOTES: I was studying plants on a 6600′ high mountain outside of Lucerne, Switzerland when I came across this species. It formed a much more loose, open, pyramidal outline than what I am accustomed to seeing in cultivation. On this same mountain, were large, shrubby colonies of *Pinus mugo*.
NATIVE HABITAT: Mountains of central Europe and southern Asia. Introduced 1875.

RELATED SPECIES:

Pinus pumila, (pī′nus pū′mil-ȧ), Japanese Stone Pine or Dwarf Siberian Pine, a rather shrubby species, was at one time regarded as a geographical form of the European species, *P. cembra,* with which it has much in common. Needles 5, densely bundled, slightly curved and directed forward, 1 1/2 to 3″ (4″) long, apex blunt pointed, margin sparsely toothed or entire, green on outer surface, inner glaucous, and entire leaf appearing bluish green, sheaths falling after the first year. The cones are subterminal, clustered, short-stalked, spreading, ovoid, 1 1/2″ long, 1″ wide, purplish when young, finally dull reddish or yellowish brown and remaining unopened until shedding seeds. In general, it is a dwarf, more or less, dense, prostrate, 1 to 7.5′ high shrub of great beauty. There are several plants at the Arnold and all appear different. One particularly handsome specimen in the dwarf conifer collection is a dense, spreading procumbent evergreen with rich bluish green needles. Plants cone at a young age. Occurs in large groves on the tops of the highest mountain in Japan, widely distributed in the province Shinano, north through Hondo and Hokkaido, and in the valleys down to sea-level on Saghalin, on the seashore of Ochotosk, in continental Manchuria and northern Korea. Zone 5 and perhaps lower. Introduced 1807. The potential for the species is untapped. There are several named clones for which see Den Ouden and Boom and Welch.

Pinus densiflora — Japanese Red Pine
(pī′nus den-si-flō′ra)

LEAVES: 2, remaining 3 years, slender, twisted, soft, 3 to 5″ long, 1/25″ wide, apex acute, margins finely toothed, with inconspicuous stomatic lines on each side, lustrous bright to dark green, the needles appear as if tufted and are borne somewhat upright along the stems; sheath 1/4 to 3/8″ long, persistent, terminated by 1 or 2 slender threads.

BUDS: Cylindrical, resinous, reddish brown.

STEM: Initially glaucous green, glabrous or minutely downy, eventually orangish, glabrous.

SIZE: 40 to 60′ in height with a similar spread at maturity, can grow to 100′.

HARDINESS: Zone 3 to 7; some variation in hardiness but a strain introduced by the Forestry Experiment Station in Cloquet, MN has proven hardy.

HABIT: The trunks are frequently crooked or leaning, branches horizontally spreading and the crown is rather broad and flat; very irregular even in youth as it is an open, floppy grower.

RATE: Slow to medium.

TEXTURE: Medium.

BARK: Orangish to orangish red when young, peeling off in thin scales; in old age grayish at the base, fissured into oblong plates.

LEAF COLOR: Lustrous bright to dark green.

FLOWERS: Monoecious.

FRUIT: Cones sub-terminal, short-stalked, solitary or in clusters, conical-ovoid to oblong, somewhat oblique at the base, 1 1/2 to 2″ long by approximately 1″ broad, dull tawny yellow opening the second year and remaining 2 to 3 years on the tree.

CULTURE: Prefers a well-drained, slightly acid soil and sunny conditions.

DISEASES AND INSECTS: See culture sheet.

LANDSCAPE VALUE: Used as a specimen because of its interesting form and decorative orange-red bark; also favorite subject for bonsai; in my mind one of the handsomest pines; I had this species planted alongside *Pinus thunbergiana* in the Illinois test plots and after the 1976-77 winter (-20°F) the needles of the latter were completely brown (stem and buds not killed) while the former showed no injury.

CULTIVARS: Numerous forms have been selected in Japan. The following are a few that I have seen.

    'Globosa'—Rounded to hemispherical shrub, needles half as long as species, the trunk is semi-prostrate; slow growing (15′ in 50 years).

    'Heavy Bud' ('Large Bud')—Dwarf, broad-rounded top, like 'Umbraculifera' with larger red buds and lighter green needles.

    'Oculus-draconis'—Each leaf marked with two yellow lines (bands) and when viewed from above shows alternate yellow and green rings; can be rather attractive; especially in late summer and fall; I had a small plant in my Illinois garden and many people were fascinated by it; unfortunately it discolors to a muddied yellow-brown in winter.

'Pendula'—A rather effective weeping form with rich green needles; it can be used to drape over rock walls and raised planters; needs to be top-worked on a standard to form a true weeping character, needles about 4″ long.

'Tiny Temple' ('Temple')—Slow growing, about 4″ per year, 2 1/2″ long, very thin needles are dark green outside, gray-blue inside; habit wide pyramid.

'Umbraculifera'—Dwarf, umbrella-like head, to 9′ or more tall; branches densely borne, upright spreading, very beautiful especially when the orange bark color is developed; a 42-year-old plant at the Secrest Arboretum was 25′ high, unfortunately heavy snow broke many of the branches; goes by name of 'Tanyosho' in Japan, there is also a compact form of this cultivar.

PROPAGATION: Seeds require no stratification, I have grown many seedlings and with proper water and nutrition they grow quite rapidly.

NATIVE HABITAT: Japan, Korea, parts of China. Introduced 1854.

Pinus echinata — Shortleaf Pine
(pī′nus ek-i-nā′ta)

LEAVES: In fascicles of 2, but also in 3's on the same tree, occasionally the latter number predominates. 3 to 5″ long, dark bluish green, slender, finely toothed, flexible, persistent 2nd through 4th season, resin ducts medial, 1 to 4.

BUDS: Oblong-ovoid, 1/4″ long, apex acuminate, brown, slightly resinous or none, scales closely appressed.

STEM: First green and tinged with purple, glabrous, eventually reddish brown.

SIZE: 80 to 100′ in height; less under landscape conditions, perhaps 50 to 60′.

HARDINESS: Zone 6 to 9.

HABIT: Pyramidal in youth, developing a well formed trunk and a small, narrow pyramidal crown that opens with age, branches distinctly sinuous which permits easy separation from *P. taeda* which grows in a similar native range.

RATE: Fast.

TEXTURE: Medium-coarse.

BARK: Scaly, nearly black on young trees, with age reddish brown and broken into irregular flat plates, scaly on the surface, plates large, blocky and handsome.

LEAF COLOR: Dark bluish green.

FRUIT: Ovoid-oblong to conical, nearly sessile, 1 1/2 to 2 1/2″ long, 1 to 1 1/2″ wide, usually persistent for several years; umbo dorsal and armed with a small sharp, straight or curved, sometimes deciduous prickle.

CULTURE: Forms a deep taproot and therefore somewhat difficult to transplant, an 8-year-old tree may have a 14′ taproot; extremely adaptable and found on dry, upland soils; 8 to 10-year-old trees retain ability to sprout if stems are injured by fire or cutting.

DISEASES AND INSECTS: Nantucket pine-tip moth, southern pine beetle, littleleaf disease.

LANDSCAPE VALUE: Important timber species, probably inferior to Loblolly Pine for landscape use.

PROPAGATION: Seed requires no pretreatment.

NATIVE HABITAT: New York, south to Georgia, Texas, Oklahoma.

Pinus flexilis — Limber Pine
(pī′nus flek′-sil-is)

LEAVES: In fives, persisting 5 to 6 years, densely crowded on the ends of the branchlets, pointing forward, rigid, curved or slightly twisted, 2 1/2 to 3 1/2″ long, margins entire, apex sharp-pointed, 3 to 4 lines of stomata on each surface, dark green to a slight glaucous dark green.

BUDS: Ovoid, slender, sharply pointed, 3/8″ long.
STEM: Tough, flexible, glabrous or minutely tomentulous, actually can be tied in knots, shining green.

SIZE: 30 to 50′ in height by 15 to 35′ in spread.
HARDINESS: Zone 4 to 7.
HABIT: Dense, broad pyramid in youth; becoming a low, broad, flat-topped tree at maturity.
RATE: Slow.
TEXTURE: Medium.
BARK: In youth smooth, light gray or greenish gray, on old trunks grayish brown, separated by deep fissues into rectangular to nearly square, superficially scaled plates or blocks, looks similar to *P. strobus* bark.
LEAF COLOR: Dark bluish green, very attractive.
FLOWERS: Monoecious, staminate clustered, rose colored, female purple.
FRUIT: Cones subterminal, short-stalked, cylindric ovoid, 3 to 6″ long, 1 1/2″ wide, erect when young and pendulously-spreading when mature, light brown, quite resinous.
CULTURE: Transplants well balled and burlapped if root pruned; does best in moist, well-drained soil and prefers sun or partial shade; adapted for planting on rocky slopes; very adaptable species and one of the best for midwestern states.
DISEASES AND INSECTS: See culture sheet.
LANDSCAPE VALUE: A handsome specimen; this and *P. resinosa* were the only two pines that were not seriously wind-burned or injured in the Chicago region after the difficult winter of 1976–77; shows good adaptability and might be used more.
CULTIVARS:
   'Columnaris'—Upright, good for areas where lateral space to spread is limited.
   'Glauca'—Foliage bluish green, much more so than the species, quite attractive; probably a "catch-all" term for bluish green needled types.
   'Glauca Pendula'—I grew this in my Illinois garden where it scampered along the ground forming a wide-spreading rather irregular shrub of bluish green color; actually rather attractive.
   'Glenmore Dwarf'—Very slow-growing, forming a small, gray-blue, upright plant that becomes pyramidal with age; the main branches ascending or upswinging so that the growing tips are vertical or nearly so; needles are dense, about 1 1/2 to 1 3/4″ long, becoming shorter and tighter near the tips of the branches; averaged 5″ year, 6′ in 14 years at Longwood Gardens.
   'Nana'—Dwarf bushy form, extremely slow growing, needles about 1 1/4″ long.
   'Pendula'—A wide-spreading, weeping tree becoming quite large with time.
   'Vandewolf's Pyramid'—Upright form with good vigor, averaged 25″ per year and 17′ in 8 years, handsome blue-green foliage, needles twisted, Vermeulen introduction.
PROPAGATION: Seed should be stratified for 21 to 90 days at 35 to 41°F.

RELATED SPECIES: Categorized as one of the stone pines. A related species is *P. albicaulis,* (pī′nus al-bi-kaw′lis), White Bark Pine, which differs in its smaller ovoid cones, 2 1/2″ long, and the fact they remain closed at maturity; supposedly old specimens of *P. albicaulis* develop whitish bark. Weston Nurseries, Hopkinton, MA has offered the tree for a number of years.
NATIVE HABITAT: Rocky Mountains of western North America, Alberta to northern Mexico, east to Texas. Introduced 1861.

Pinus koraiensis — Korean Pine
(pī′nus kôr-ā-i-en′sis)

LEAVES: In 5's, persisting 3 years, 3 1/2 to 4 1/2″ long, lustrous dark green, with white stomatal lines on two inner surfaces giving an overall gray-green needle color, margins relatively coarse-toothed the entire length, apex bluntish; leaf sheaths 1/2″ long, soon falling.

STEM: Young shoots covered with a dense reddish brown pubescence which becomes dirty brown with age.

SIZE: 30 to 40′ under cultivation; may grow over 100′.

HARDINESS: Zone 4 to 7, surprisingly one of the hardiest pines but not well known.

HABIT: Loose, pyramidal outline; rather refreshing compared to many of the stiff-habit types; feathered to the ground with branches.

RATE: Slow.

TEXTURE: Medium.

BARK: Thin, gray or grayish brown, peeling off in irregular flakes, reddish brown beneath.

LEAF COLOR: Lovely bluish green; actually dark green on outside; inner surfaces grayish.

FRUIT: Cone subterminal, solitary or few-together, short-stalked, cylindric-conical, apex blunt, 3 1/2 to 6″ long, 2 to 2 1/4″ wide, lurid-brown when mature, resinous, opening when mature, falling with the stalk.

CULTURE: Tremendously adaptable and also extremely cold hardy.

DISEASES AND INSECTS: None serious.

LANDSCAPE VALUE: Fine specimen plant, groupings or screens.

PROPAGATION: Seeds will germinate without pretreatment although some cold may be valuable.

ADDITIONAL NOTES: I have real trouble separating this species from young *Pinus cembra* by needle characteristics. In general it is more openly branched and the needles are longer and are toothed to the apex. Cones are twice as long as those of *P. cembra.*

NATIVE HABITAT: Korea, mountainous areas on the main island of Japan. Introduced 1861.

Pinus mugo — Swiss Mountain Pine, Mugo Pine
(pī′nus mū′gō)

LEAVES: In pairs, persisting five or more years, rigid, curved, medium to dark green, 1 to 2″ (1 1/2 to 3″) long, margins finely toothed, apex short, blunt, horny point, stomatic lines on both surfaces, basal sheath up to about 3/5″ long.

BUDS: Oblong-ovoid, 1/4 to 1/2″ long with reddish brown scales encrusted with resin, scales closely appressed.

STEM: Young stems short, without down, green at first with prominent ridges, becoming brown to blackish brown.

SIZE: 15 to 20′ in height by 25 to 20′ spread; but can grow 30 to 80′ tall and as wide.

HARDINESS: Zone 2 to 7(8), have seen occasional plants in Zone 8 but they do not measure up to plants in the north.

HABIT: Very variable, prostrate or pyramidal; usually low, broad-spreading and bushy, at least the types available from nurseries.

RATE: Slow.

TEXTURE: Medium.

BARK: Brownish gray, scaly, split in irregular plates but not scaling off on old trunks; a good identification feature on 1/2″ to 2 to 3″ diameter stems are the regular bumpy protuberances which result when the leaves abscise.

LEAF COLOR: Medium green to dark green, often yellowish green in winter especially on the tips of the needles.

FLOWERS: Monoecious.

FRUIT: Cones, subterminal, sessile or short-stalked, erect, horizontal, or slightly pendulous, solitary or 2 to 3(4) together, ovoid or conical-ovoid, 1 to 2″ long by 1/2 to 1 1/2″ broad, apex surrounded by a darker ring, at maturity grayish black.

CULTURE: Moves well balled and burlapped if root pruned; many quality plants are being produced in containers, generally does not produce a tap root and is easy to transplant; prefers a deep, moist loam in sun or partial shade; can be pruned annually to thicken plant and keep dwarf habit; very calcareous soil tolerant.

DISEASES AND INSECTS: Subject to rusts, wood rots, borers, sawflies and especially scale (often very serious).

LANDSCAPE VALUE: The species is seldom used; valued chiefly for its dwarf cultivars which are useful in landscape plantings; especially for foundations, masses, groupings.

CULTIVARS: There are 15 to 20 named dwarfish clones but I defy anybody to separate them especially after they are butchered by the pruning shears. Most are seed-grown and it is fun to walk through a block of *Pinus mugo* where the variation in size is literally unbelievable. They range from the true dwarfs to rather large spreading shrubs. Many newer selections than those presented. A perusal of a good conifer producer will yield untold treasures.

'Compacta'—Very dense and globose, 40-year-old plant was 4' by 5'.

'Gnom'—Twenty-five-year-old plant was 15" high and 36" wide, forms a dense, globular, dark green mound.

'Mops'—Dwarf globose form as tall as wide, dark green 1 to 1 3/4" long needles, considered one of the better forms, grows about 3' high and 3' wide.

var. *mugo*—Low growing form of the species usually less than 8' tall and about twice that in width; variable due to seed source; found in eastern Alps and Balkans.

var. *pumilio*—Usually prostrate grower up to 10' wide, widely distributed in mountains of eastern and central Europe.

'Slavinii'—Forty-year-old plant is 3' by 5', dwarf, low, dense, needles crowded, dark green.

PROPAGATION: Seeds have no dormancy and will germinate immediately upon collection.

ADDITIONAL NOTES: Perhaps one of the most confusing pines for the homeowner because of tremendous variability in size. The cute, diminutive, prostrate plant that comes from the garden center and is placed in the foundation planting often becomes 10 to 15' tall although it was advertised as a 2 to 4' high, low-growing evergreen. One of the real problems with this and other plants is that they do not read the advertisements. This species includes a number of varieties or geographical forms which are difficult to classify, as the variations in habit are not always correlated with the character of the cones and appear to be due in many cases to soil, climate, and other growing conditions, or perhaps to hybridization with other species. Nomenclature is sometimes confused on this species as it is listed as *Pinus montana* var. *mugo* and other odd things. As I wandered atop a 6600' high mountain outside Lucerne, Switzerland, I came across numerous patches of Mugo Pine. The habit was dense, shrubby and wide-spreading. I saw no colonies more than 3 to 5' high. This could have been the geographical variety *pumilio*. I taught in Moline, Illinois and one of the local nurserymen showed me around an estate where a 35 to 45' high Mugo Pine was growing. It took me awhile to accept the fact that the plant was, in fact, *Pinus mugo*.

NATIVE HABITAT: Mountains of central and southern Europe from Spain to the Balkans. Introduced 1779.

Pinus nigra (Also listed as *P. nigra* var. *nigra, P. nigra* var. *austriaca*) — Austrian Pine
(pī′nus nī′grà)

LEAVES: In pairs, persisting about 4 (8) years, very dense on the branchlets, stiff, straight or curved, 3 to 5"(6") long, 1/16 to 1/12" wide, margins minutely toothed, apex a thickened horny point, sharp to the touch, 12 to 14 lines of stomata on each surface, dark green, sheath about 1/2" long.

BUDS: Ovoid to oblong or cylindrical, 1/2 to 1" long, abruptly contracted to a sharp point, scales light brown, resinous.

STEM: Young stems without down (pubescence), yellowish brown, ridged, the branchlets as they lose their leaves becoming roughened by the persistent leaf bases.

SIZE: 50 to 60' in height by 20 to 40' in spread but can grow to 100' or more.
HARDINESS: Zone 4 to 7, survives in Zone 8, although seldom seen.

HABIT: Densely pyramidal when young becoming a large, broad, flat-topped tree with a rough, short trunk and low, stout, spreading branches.

RATE: Medium, 35 to 50′ after 20 to 30 years; have seen 60 to 70′ trees under landscape conditions.

TEXTURE: Medium-coarse.

BARK: Dark brown furrows, usually with gray or gray-brown mottled ridges, quite attractive, one of the handsomest pines for bark.

LEAF COLOR: Lustrous dark green.

FLOWERS: Staminate clustered, yellow; pistillate yellow-green.

FRUIT: Solitary or in clusters, sub-sessile, ovoid, conical, 2 to 3″ long, 1 to 1 1/4″ wide before opening, tawny-yellow initially, becoming brown, scales about 1″ long, transversely keeled near the apex which often ends in a more or less persistent prickle.

CULTURE: A very hardy tree that withstands city conditions better than many other pines; very tolerant of soils, if moist; will stand some dryness and exposure; resists heat and drought; less fastidious in its soil requirements than most pines; will succeed in fairly heavy clay and alkaline soils; tolerates seaside conditions.

DISEASES AND INSECTS: In recent years this pine has exhibited severe dieback in midwestern states; some of the dieback as been attributed to *Diplodia* tip blight; however, whole trees have died in a single season so probably multiple factors are involved; recently a pine nematode has been reported; apparently the nematodes are transmitted by a beetle; they plug up the vascular system and an entire plant may die in a single season.

LANDSCAPE VALUE: An adaptable species with very stiff needles making a good specimen, screen or windbreak; can also be used for mass planting; develops its real character in old age when the branches become umbelliformly spreading and the bark colors develop fully.

CULTIVARS:

'Hornibrookiana'—Originated as a "witches' broom," needles 2 1/2″ long, very compact, dwarf, shrubby and rounded, 30-year-old plant is 2′ tall and 6′ across, found in Seneca Park, Rochester, New York by B.H. Slavin.

'Pyramidalis'—A narrow, pyramidal plant with closely ascending branches and 4 to 5″ long bluish-green needles.

PROPAGATION: Seeds have no dormancy and will germinate immediately upon collection.

ADDITIONAL NOTES: A somewhat confusing pine often listed as *Pinus nigra* var. *nigra* or *P. nigra* var. *austriaca*. It is another species somewhat like *P. mugo* and has many geographical varieties and subspecies. Den Ouden and Boom noted that it is a fine tree for garden planting and a forest tree with good economic properties. On the other side of the ledger, Dallimore and Jackson stated that under cultivation it is usually a rough, heavily branched tree, too sombre for ornamental planting and of little value as a timber tree as its wood is coarse and knotty. One wonders if these authorities are discussing the same plant. Variety *caramanica*, Crimean Pine, is not clearly distinguished from *P. nigra* but usually has larger cones up to 4″ long. It occurs in Asia Minor, the Caucasus, the Crimea, the Balkans and the southern Carpathians. Variety *maritima*, Corsican Pine, has a slender crown with horizontal branches. The needles are more slender and less rigid and may reach 6 to 7″ in length. Found in the southern part of the Italian peninsula, Sicily, Corsica and also Algeria. Excellent plant for afforesting sandy soils along coastal areas. Probably less hardy than the Austrian Pine, although it has grown quite fast at the Secrest Arboretum reaching 80 to 90′ in 67 years and withstood temperatures of -20 to -25°F. Variety *cebennensis* represents the western most race of *P. nigra*. It forms a small or medium-sized tree and is best distinguished by the orange stems and slender, 1/16″ diameter needles.

NATIVE HABITAT: It is a native of Europe, from Austria to central Italy, Greece and Yugoslavia. Introduced 1759.

Pinus parviflora — Japanese White Pine
(pī'nus par-vi-flō'ra)

LEAVES: 5, persisting 3 to 4 years, crowded, rather stiff, usually twisted, forming brush-like tufts at the ends of the branches, 1 1/4 to 2 1/2″ long, 1/25″ wide, apex usually blunt, margins finely toothed, without stomata outside, inner sides with 3 to 4 stomatic lines, leaf sheaths falling.
STEM: Greenish brown, finally light gray, short, minutely downy, older stems glabrous.

SIZE: 25 to 50′ in height with a similar or greater spread at maturity; 50 to 70′ in the wild.
HARDINESS: Zone 4 to 7, has survived -24°.
HABIT: Dense, conical pyramid when young developing wide-spreading branches, flat-topped head and picturesque character with age.
RATE: Slow.
TEXTURE: Medium.
BARK: On young trees smooth, gray, eventually becoming darker gray and platy, scaly on old trunks.
LEAF COLOR: Bluish green, sometimes grass green with 3 to 4 stomatic bands on inner sides of needles.
FLOWERS: Monoecious.
FRUIT: Cones nearly terminal, almost sessile, horizontally spreading, straight, ovoid to nearly cylindrical, 1 1/2 to 4″ long, spreading widely when ripe, remaining 6 to 7 years on the tree, scales few, broad wedge-shaped, thick, leathery-woody, brownish red, scale-end undulated, slightly incurved, umbo inconspicuous; often abundant even on the young trees.
CULTURE: Full sun, average moisture; good drainage essential; tolerant of most soils, even clay loam; salt tolerant.
DISEASES AND INSECTS: See culture sheet.
LANDSCAPE VALUE: A choice, extremely graceful small conifer whose low stature and fine-textured foliage make it a perfect tree for small places; good for the sea coast as it is salt tolerant; good accent or specimen conifer; artistic growth habit.
CULTIVARS:
  'Bergman'—Wide-spreading, rounded shrub with many leaders of uniform length, leaves bluish green, a 15-year-old plant was 16″ high and 36″ wide.
  'Brevifolia'—An ascending narrow tree with few branches; branchlets with short, very thick, stiff, blue-green 1″ long needles in tight bundles.
  'Glauca' (f. *glauca* is more accurate)—Perhaps the most common form in cultivation; it forms a wide-spreading tree with glaucous green foliage, can grow 45′ and greater; cones heavily in youth, at least trees I have seen show this characteristic.
PROPAGATION: Seed should be stratified for 90 days at 33 to 41°F in moist medium.
NATIVE HABITAT: Japan. Introduced 1861.

Pinus peuce — Balkan or Macedonian Pine
(pī'nus pū'cē)

LEAVES: 5, remaining 3 years, densely bundled, 3 to 4″ long, 1/36″ wide, apex pointed, straight, rather stiff, margin finely toothed, both inner sides with 3 to 5 lines, densely borne, pointing forward, dark green on upper side, grayish on inner surfaces.
STEM: Thickish, glossy, greenish, in the 2nd year grayish green or brownish gray, glaucous.

SIZE: 30 to 60′ in height with a relatively narrow spread; can grow to 100′ and specimens of this size grow in Bulgaria.
HARDINESS: Zone 4 to 7.
HABIT: Narrow pyramid, sometimes columnar in form, very handsome and reminding of *P. cembra* in youth.

RATE: Slow.

TEXTURE: Medium.

BARK: Gray-brown, thin, on old trees develops a scaly character.

LEAF COLOR: Dark green, overall appearance is blue-green.

FLOWERS: Monoecious.

FRUIT: Cones terminal, short-stalked, solitary or 3 to 4 together, spreading or deflexed, nearly cylindrical, 3 to 6″ long, light brown and resinous.

CULTURE: Full sun; moist soils with good drainage; move balled and burlapped if root pruned; quite adaptable.

LANDSCAPE VALUE: Specimen, handsome plant.

PROPAGATION: Seed may require no stratification or up to 60 days.

ADDITIONAL NOTES: Somewhat resembles *P. cembra* in outline; closely allied to *P. wallichiana,* but differs in its narrow habit, smaller branches, and shorter, stiffer needles which are less spreading; the green, glabrous shoots distinguish it from *P. cembra.*

NATIVE HABITAT: Balkans, confined to limited areas in Albania, Bulgaria, Greece and Yugoslavia. Introduced 1863.

Pinus ponderosa — Ponderosa Pine, Western Yellow Pine
(pī′nus pon-dēr-ō′så)

LEAVES: In three's, sometimes two's, remaining 3 years, densely crowded on the branchlets, rigid, curved, 5 to 10″ long, 1/20 to 1/12″ wide, margins minutely toothed, apex a sharp, horny point, stomatic lines on each surface, dark or yellowish green.

BUDS: Oblong, cylindrical, 4/5″ long, acute, resinous scales closely appressed, reddish brown.

STEM: Young stems stout, glabrous, orange-brown or greenish at first eventually becoming nearly black; with the odor of vanilla when bruised.

SIZE: Averages 60 to 100′ under cultivation, spread 25 to 30′; 150 to 230′ in height in the wild.

HARDINESS: Zone 3 to 6 or 7.

HABIT: Narrow, pyramidal when young; with time develops an irregularly cylindrical and narrow crown, with numerous short stout branches, the lower ones often drooping; very old trees have short, conical or flat-topped crowns and are devoid of branches for one-half or more of their height.

RATE: Medium, 75′ after 40 to 50 years.

TEXTURE: Medium to coarse.

BARK: Brown-black and furrowed on vigorous or young trees; yellowish brown to cinnamon-red and broken up into large, flat, superficially scaly plates separated by deep irregular fissures on slow-growing and old trunks.

LEAF COLOR: Dark or yellowish green.

FLOWERS: Monoecious, staminate clustered, yellow; pistillate red, in pairs.

FRUIT: Cones, terminal, solitary or 3 to 5 together, nearly sessile, spreading or slightly recurved, symmetrical, ovoid or oblong-ovoid, 3 to 6″ long, 1 1/2 to 2″ broad, light reddish brown, shining, after falling often leaving a few of the basal scales attached to the branchlet, umbo broad triangular, terminated by a stout usually recurved prickle.

CULTURE: Transplant balled and burlapped if root pruned; prefers a deep, moist, well-drained loam; sunny, open exposure; intolerant of shade; hurt by late frosts; resistant to drought; tolerates alkaline soils; has shown good salt tolerance in controlled studies.

LANDSCAPE VALUE: Valuable forest tree but not recommended for areas outside of which it is native, useful for mass planting and shelter belts.

PROPAGATION: Seeds have no dormancy and will germinate immediately upon collection.

ADDITIONAL NOTES: The most important pine in western North America. Furnishes more timber than any other American pine and is second only to douglas-fir in total annual production. Thrives under widely different conditions and in many kinds of soils with low elevations to a considerable altitude, on light and moist soils, on dry, arid land, on dried-up river-beds and lakes where there is a deep and rich soil, and on almost bare rocks. The most abundant growth takes place on light, deep, moist, well drained soils.

NATIVE HABITAT: Western North America. British Columbia to Mexico, east to South Dakota and Texas. Introduced 1827.

RELATED SPECIES:

Pinus cembroides, (pī′nus sem-broy′dēz), Pinyon or Mexican Nut Pine, is a rather bushy, small, 15 to 20′ high tree. I have seen it on the Kansas State and Colorado State campuses and was impressed by the good dark green needle color and attractive but rather stiff growth habit. The needles occur in 3's (sometimes 2's), are 1 to 2″ long, entire, the inner surfaces of the needles being pressed together. The cones are roundish, egg-shaped, 1 1/2 to 2″ long, 1 to 1 1/2″ wide with very few scales. The seeds are about 1/2″ long and edible. Southern Arizona to lower California and Mexico. Introduced 1830. Zone 5. Variety *edulis* has leaves chiefly in pairs instead of 3's and they are thicker; otherwise, it is similar to the above. Occurs in southern Wyoming to Arizona, Texas and northern Mexico. Introduced 1848. Zone 4. Variety *monophylla* has single needles (occasionally in pairs). It has a more westerly distribution than var. *edulis,* primarily in Utah, Arizona, Nevada and southern California and often forms pure strands of considerable extent. Introduced 1848. Zone 5. All the above are good choices for dry soil areas.

Pinus contorta, (pī′nus kon-tôr′tä), Lodgepole Pine, is widespread throughout western North America and from my limited observations more ornamentally attractive than *P. ponderosa.* It differs from *P. ponderosa* in that the needles are in fascicles of 2, 1 1/2″ long, yellowish green to dark green and twisted; the cones are about 1 1/2″ long, mostly remaining unopened and attached for many years. There are two distinct varieties: one termed *P. c.* var. *contorta,* Shore Pine (Zone 7), is a small tree, 25 to 30′ high characterized by a short contorted trunk and a dense, irregular crown of twisted branches, many of which extend nearly to the ground; the other *P. c.* var. *latifolia,* Lodgepole Pine (Zone 5), grows 70 to 80′ high and develops a long, clear, cylindrical trunk and short, narrow, open crown. The Shore Pine tends to establish in wet, boggy areas and is seldom found far from tidewater while the Lodgepole Pine performs best in moist, well drained, sandy or gravelly soils; although it grows on a variety of soils. Native habitat is western North America. Lodgepole is common in European gardens and makes an exceptionally handsome tree.

Pinus jeffreyi, (pī′nus jef′rē-ī), Jeffrey Pine, differs from the previous two species in the blue-green, 7 to 9″ long twisted needles (usually 3) and the 6 to 9″ long cones which open and fall at maturity. Similar to *P. ponderosa* in habit and other respects. Can endure great extremes of climate and is somewhat more frost hardy. The Morton Arboretum has several 40′ specimens which are rather attractive. Potentially can grow 90 to 100′ under favorable conditions. Native from southern Oregon to lower California. Introduced 1853. Zone 5.

Pinus resinosa — Red Pine
(pī′nus rez-in-ō′sa)

LEAVES: In two's, persisting 4 years, densely arranged on the branches, slender, snap when bent, 5 to 6″ long, margins finely and regularly toothed, apex sharp-pointed, stomata in ill-defined lines on each surface, medium to dark green; leaf sheaths 5/8 to 7/8″ long.

BUDS: Ovoid or narrow conical, about 1/2″ long, resinous, with some of the scales free at the tips.

STEM: Glabrous, stout, pale brown or yellowish green, roughened with the remains of the prominences on which each bundle was sealed.

SIZE: 50 to 80' in height with a variable spread; can grow to 125' and more; I have never seen a Red Pine larger than 50' in the midwest.

HARDINESS: Zone 2, can withstand seasonal variations of 40 to 60°F below zero to 90 to 105°F above; grows best in colder climates.

HABIT: When growing in the open the trunk is short and develops a heavily branched crown in youth; in old age the crown is somewhat symmetrically oval with the characteristic tufted foliage which separates it from the ragged, unkempt Jack Pines and the plumelike tops of the White Pine.

RATE: Medium, 50' after 25 to 30 years.

TEXTURE: Medium.

BARK: On young trees scaly, orange-red; eventually breaking up into large, flat, reddish brown, superficially scaly plates, irregularly diamond-shaped in outline.

LEAF COLOR: Medium to dark green.

FLOWERS: Monoecious, clustered; staminate red, pistillate reddish.

FRUITS: Cones subterminal, solitary or two together, sessile, horizontally spreading, symmetrical, ovoid-conical, narrowing rapidly to the apex, approximately 2″ long by 1 to 2″ broad and light brown.

CULTURE: Transplant balled and burlapped if root pruned; does well on exposed, dry, acid, sandy or gravelly soils; full sun; susceptible to sweeping winds; extremely cold tolerant (-40 to -60°F); susceptible to salt damage.

LANDSCAPE VALUE: A picturesque and desirable tree which survives under adversity; good on exposed and sterile soils; for groves and windbreaks; best in northern areas; unfortunately, with all the good press relative to environmental tolerances, it has not lived up to the clippings.

CULTIVARS:

'Globosa'—A compact, globe-shaped selection with short needles; I have seen many compact types derived from "witches' brooms".

PROPAGATION: Seeds have no dormancy and will germinate immediately upon sowing.

ADDITIONAL NOTES: Sometimes termed Norway Pine; it is said that early settlers mistook it for Norway Spruce, and also that it grew in abundance near the town of Norway, Maine. Very tolerant of sandy soils and ranks behind *P. banksiana* in its ability to invade cutover land.

NATIVE HABITAT: Newfoundland and Manitoba, south to the mountains of Pennsylvania, west to Michigan. Cultivated since 1756.

Pinus rigida — Pitch Pine
(pī'nus rij'i-dá)

LEAVES: In three's, lasting 2 to 3 years, spreading, rigid, slightly curved and twisted, 3 to 5″ long, margins finely toothed, ending in a horny point, dark green; leaf sheaths 1/3 to 1/2″ long.

BUDS: Cylindrical or conical, sharp-pointed, 1/4 to 3/4″ long, scales pressed together but often free at the tips, usually resinous.

STEM: Stout with many buds, green at first, becoming dull orange-brown in the second year, prominently ridged.

SIZE: Variable, 40 to 60' in height by 30 to 50' in spread although can grow to 100'; often dwarfed by its environment for on exposed sites it is very grotesque while in better situations a tall trunk and small open crown develop.

HARDINESS: Zone 4 to 7.

HABIT: Open, irregular pyramid in youth, becoming gnarled and more irregular with age.

RATE: Medium in youth becoming slower with age.

TEXTURE: Medium.

BARK: Initially dark and very scaly; eventually 1 to 2″ thick at the base of old trees and smoother with brownish yellow, flat plates separated by narrow irregular fissues.

LEAF COLOR: Yellowish green at first, becoming a dark green.

FLOWERS: Monoecious; staminate yellow, pistillate light green tinted rose.

FRUIT: Cones lateral, in whorls of 3 to 5, seldom solitary, 3 to 4″ long, stalked or nearly sessile, deflexed when young, spreading at right angles when mature, rather symmetrical, ovoid-conical, light brown and remaining 2 or more years on the tree.

CULTURE: Prefers a light, sandy, acid, moist, well-drained soil; however, is found along the coast on peat soils of Atlantic White-cedar *(Chamaecyparis thyoides)* swamps; open, sunny exposure; susceptible to sweeping winds; salt tolerant; able to survive on the driest, sandiest, most unproductive sites.

LANDSCAPE VALUE: Not highly ornamental but excellent for poor soils, wildernesses and solitary places.

CULTIVARS:

'Sherman Eddy' ('Little Giant')—A rather interesting compact 15′ high tree with pom-pom tufts of foliage; Weston Nurseries, Hopkinton introduced this clone and named it after the discoverer of the plant.

PROPAGATION: Seed requires no stratification.

ADDITIONAL NOTES: A tree of great diversity in form, habit, and development. One of the few conifers that produces sprouts from cut stumps or when injured by fire. Produces anywhere from 1 to 3 whorls of branches in a single season which is unusual for a pine. Also produces cones very early as 12-year-old trees often bear quantities of seeds. I have seen it all over Cape Cod in the sandiest of soils.

NATIVE HABITAT: Eastern North America in sandy uplands. New Brunswick to Georgia, west to Ontario and Kentucky. Introduced before 1759.

Pinus strobus — Eastern White Pine
(pī′nus strō′bus)

LEAVES: In five's, remaining 2 years, slender, bluish green, 2 to 4″(5″) long, margins finely toothed, white stomatic lines on the two inner surfaces, sheath about 1/2″ long, falling away.

BUDS: Ovoid, with a sharp point, 1/4″ long, resinous, some scales free at the tips.

STEM: Slender with tufts of short hairs below the insertion of the leaf bundles, usually without down elsewhere, greenish to light greenish brown, most of the pubescence falls away with time.

SIZE: 50 to 80′ in height by 20 to 40′ in spread; can grow to 150′ and more.

HARDINESS: Zone 3 to 8, grows reasonably well in Piedmont of Georgia but for inexplicable reasons trees die out; possibly related to heat and drought stress.

HABIT: In youth a symmetrical pyramid of soft, pleasant appearance; in middle-age and on old trees the crown is composed of several horizontal and ascending branches, gracefully plume-like in outline and very distinctive when compared to other conifers.

RATE: Fast, one of the fastest growing landscape pines; becoming 50 to 75′ tall in 25 to 40 years.

TEXTURE: Medium-fine.

BARK: Thin, smooth, grayish green when young, becoming darker with age; dark grayish brown on old trunks and deeply furrowed longitudinally into broad scaly, 1 to 2″ thick ridges.

LEAF COLOR: Light to bluish green; however, greatly variable; needles generally fall the second year in late summer-early fall and the interior of the tree harbors yellow-brown needles.

FLOWERS: Monoecious; staminate clustered, yellow; pistillate pink.

FRUIT: Cones subterminal, pendent, 6 to 8″ long by 1 1/2″ broad, stalked, cylindrical, often curved, apex pointed, resinous and light brown; mature in autumn of second year.

CULTURE: Easily transplanted because of wide-spreading and moderately deep root system with only a vestige of a taproot; makes its best growth on fertile, moist, well-drained soils, however, is found on such extremes as dry, rocky ridges and wet sphagnum bogs; light demanding but can tolerate some shade; humid atmosphere; quite susceptible to sweeping winds and branches are often lost in strong storms; is extremely intolerant of air pollutants (ozone, sulfur dioxide) and salts; may develop chlorosis in high pH soils.

DISEASES AND INSECTS: Two very serious pests include the White Pine blister rust, a bark disease, which eventually kills the tree; and the White Pine weevil which kills the terminal shoots thus seriously deforming the tree to the extent they become bushy and have been called "Cabbage Pines".

LANDSCAPE VALUE: A very handsome and ornamental specimen; valuable for parks, estates and large properties; also makes a beautiful sheared hedge; one of our most beautiful native pines; a well grown mature White Pine is without equal among the firs, spruces and other pines.

CULTIVARS: It is difficult to do even a half-baked job on the cultivars since there are so many and numerous others are waiting to be introduced. Mr. Al Fordham, former propagator, Arnold Arboretum, has conducted some fascinating research with "witches' brooms" of White Pine and the results of his work are many beautiful compact-growing types. Dr. Waxman, University of Connecticut, has a sizeable program in the same area and has introduced a number of *Pinus strobus* variants. Vermeulen Nursery, NJ, lists 21 different cultivars.

'Compacta'—A dense, rounded type, slow growing, appears to be a catch-all term for dwarfish clones.

'Contorta'—An open, irregular, pyramidal form with slightly twisted branchlets; 40-year-old plant is 18' high.

'Fastigiata'—Narrowly upright and columnar when young developing a wider character with age as the branches ascend at a 45° angle from the trunk; ultimately about three times as tall as wide; I have seen several large (70') specimens of this clone and they were beautifully formed and not at all harsh like many of the fastigiate plants, a beautiful cultivar.

var. *glauca*—Leaves are a light bluish green and of beautiful color; a specimen in the Arnold Arboretum is 60' high and 60' wide.

'Minima'—Dense, low-spreading type, wider than high, 1" per year, needles bluish green, 1" long.

'Nana'—A catchall term and I have seen several different types listed, usually compact, mounded or rounded.

'Pendula'—Very interesting weeping type with long branches which sweep the ground; must be trained in youth to develop a leader.

'Prostrata'—Another rounded, dwarf type; 20-year-old plant is 8' by 7'.

'Pumila'—Roundish plant with central shoot elongating.

PROPAGATION: Seed should be stratified for 60 days. Pines, in general, are difficult to root from cuttings; however, considerable work has been undertaken with White Pine. Cuttings can be rooted but the percentages were low averaging from 0 to 34% depending on the tree sampled. Several investigators have rooted fascicles with some success.

ADDITIONAL NOTES: Often produces cones at an early age, sometimes when not more than 10' high; very aggressive and quickly seeds in abandoned fields so much so it received the name "Old Field Pine". Largest of northeastern conifers and a very valuable timber species. Great variation in needle color, resistance to salts and air pollutants. Some trees are beautiful and keep their good bluish green color through the winter while others turn yellowish green. Selections could be made for superior traits and adaptability to various climatic and environmental conditions.

NATIVE HABITAT: Newfoundland to Manitoba, south to Georgia, Illinois and Iowa. Introduced about 1705.

Pinus sylvestris — Scotch Pine
(pī′nus sil-ves′tris)

LEAVES: In pairs, persisting about 3 years, variable in length, twisted, stiff, 1 to 3(4)" long, short pointed, margins minutely toothed, glaucous with many well-defined lines of stomata on the outer side, blue-green in color; leaf sheaths 1/4 to 3/8" long, persistent.

BUDS: Oblong-ovate, 1/4 to 1/2" long, pointed with lanceolate, fringed scales, the upper ones free at the tips, brown, resinous, reddish brown.

STEM: Green when young, dull grayish yellow or brown in the second year, marked with prominent bases of the scale leaves, glabrous.

SIZE: 30 to 60′ in height with a spread of 30 to 40′; can grow 80 to 90′ high.

HARDINESS: Zone 2 to 8, will grow in Zone 8 but is not well adapted.

HABIT: In youth an irregular pyramid with short, spreading branches, the lower soon dying, becoming in age very picturesque, open, wide-spreading and flat- or round-topped, almost umbrella-shaped.

RATE: Medium when young, slow with age.

TEXTURE: Medium.

BARK: On the upper portion of the stems orangish or orangish brown, thin, smooth, peeling off in papery flakes, thick towards the base, grayish or reddish brown, fissured into irregular, longitudinal scaly plates.

LEAF COLOR: Bluish green frequently changing to yellowish green in the winter; variable depending on seed source.

FLOWERS: Monoecious.

FRUIT: Cones mostly solitary to 2 to 3 together, long- or short-stalked, 1 1/2 to 3″ long, symmetrical or oblique, gray or dull brown, falling at maturity, umbo small, obtuse.

CULTURE: Transplants easily balled and burlapped if root pruned; will grow on a variety of soils as long as they are well-drained; poor, dry sites will support this tree; full sun; preferably acid soils.

LANDSCAPE VALUE: Valued for its picturesque character; useful as a distorted specimen or in masses and on waste lands; not suitable for underplanting or shelter belts; for displaying unique form and color among the pines it is outstanding; makes a good Christmas tree when plantation grown.

CULTIVARS:

'Argentea' (var. *argentea*)—Leaves are a pronounced glaucous or silvery hue; perhaps a catchall term for blue-needle types.

'Aurea'—Rather striking with yellowish green new growth that turns green in summer and then golden in winter, have seen in European gardens, not for the faint hearted.

'Beuvronensis'—Broad low dwarf bushy form that crops up in botanical gardens and commerce, needles bluish green, 3/4″ long, extremely slow growing about 1 to 2″ per year in youth, about 20″ in 25 years.

'Fastigiata'—Columnar, narrow in habit about the narrowest of any of the pines; often called Sentinel Pine, tends to break-up in heavy ice and snow, 25′ high and more if it lasts that long. Found in the wild in several European countries and correctly should be f. *fastigiata.*

'French Blue'—Listed by Monrovia as a select seedling strain with more uniform compact growth and brighter blue-green foliage that is retained through winter.

'Watereri'—A slow growing, densely pyramidal to flat-topped form with steel-blue needles, usually about 10′ but original plant is 25′ high and wide. Handsome selection and available in commerce.

PROPAGATION: Seeds have no dormancy and will germinate without stratification.

ADDITIONAL NOTES: One of the most popular pines for Christmas tree use; has largely superseded Balsam Fir and other pines as the number one tree. The great problem with Scotch Pine is the tremendous variability in needle length and color, hardiness, habit, and adaptability due to geographic races or strains. Five major groups of variants are recognized by Dallimore and Jackson and one starts to realize why some Scotch Pines have bluish needles, others yellowish green, etc., after reading their interesting discussion.

I checked many references and came away with the feeling that no authority has a distinct idea of the variation in *P. sylvestris.* Krüssmann offers the best lists of geographical varieties and cultivars. Supposedly over 150 varieties (not cultivars) have been described and Krüssmann lists over 40 cultivars. In Zone 8, Scotch Pine, at least the race (geographical variety) commonly planted is not heat tolerant. I have observed many trees that simply died for no explicable reason other than the drought(s) of the past ten years.

NATIVE HABITAT: One of the most widely distributed pines, ranging from Norway and Scotland to Spain, western Asia and northeastern Siberia; naturalized in some places in the New England states. Long cultivated.

Pinus taeda — Loblolly Pine
(pī′nus tē′då)

LEAVES: In fascicles of 3, occasionally 2, 6 to 10″ long, persistent until the second (3 to 4) autumn, slender, sometimes twisted, dark yellowish green, margins finely toothed, resin ducts usually 2, large, mostly medial, sheaths about 1″ long.

BUDS: Oblong-conical, apex long pointed, 1/4 to 1/2″ long, light reddish brown, not resinous, scales fringed, often reflexed.

STEM: Yellowish to reddish brown, glaucous, glabrous, strongly ridged.

SIZE: 60 to 90′ in height, usually smaller under landscape conditions, 40 to 50′.

HARDINESS: Zone 6 to 9; have seen it in central Illinois but it was barely surviving.

HABIT: Loosely pyramidal in youth losing its lower branches with age and forming a fairly open, oval-rounded crown at maturity.

RATE: Fast, one of the fastest growing southern pines.

TEXTURE: As pines go this is medium-coarse.

BARK: Variable, scaly and gray on young trees, later with rounded ridges and deep furrows.

LEAF COLOR: Dark green, becomes off-color in cold climates.

FRUIT: Cones, ovoid-cylindric to narrowly conical, sessile, 3 to 6″ long, umbo dorsal and armed with a stout, sharp spine, grouped 2 to 5 together.

CULTURE: Easy to transplant, may develop a short taproot but it ceases growth in favor of an extensive lateral root system; grows on a wide variety of soils, prefers those with deep surface layers having abundant moisture and poor drainage; prefers acid soils.

DISEASES AND INSECTS: None particularly serious in normal context of landscape; pine beetle can devastate plantings, fusiform rust, heart and butt rot.

LANDSCAPE VALUE: Not a graceful pine but very adaptable to extremes of soil and therefore valuable in south where the more graceful species do not thrive; good for fast screen in early years; one of the pioneer species along river bottoms; one particular abandoned bottomland agricultural field at the Georgia Botanical Garden was rapidly invaded by this species; is being used more frequently as a quick screen in southern landscapes, frequently container grown and is easily transplanted.

CULTIVARS:

'Nana'—Raulston describes several 30-year-old dwarf loblollies that originated from "witches' brooms", 8 to 15′ tall with dense rounded crowns; I have seen the plants and they are truly artistic and imbued with character.

PROPAGATION: Seeds germinate without pretreatment.

ADDITIONAL NOTES: One of the leading commercial timber species in the United States; on cutover areas in the south, the species has spread to a remarkable degree and is aggressive in forming pure stands in old fields; have seen it growing in the reddest of red clay where few other species proliferate.

NATIVE HABITAT: Southern New Jersey to Florida, eastern Texas and Oklahoma.

Pinus thunbergiana — Japanese Black Pine
(pī′nus thun-bēr′jē-ā′nå)

LEAVES: Two, persisting 3 to 5 years, densely crowded, twisted, more or less spreading, 2 1/2 to 4 1/2″ long, 1/12″ wide, apex stiff, fine pointed, rigid, margins finely toothed, with stomatic lines on each surface; very lustrous dark green; leaf sheaths 1/2″ long, ending in two long, thread-like segments, persistent.

BUDS: One of the few conifers in which the buds provide a good identification feature; the terminal buds characteristically ovoid-cylindrical, apex-pointed, 1/2 to 3/4″ long, not resinous, scales appressed, tips free, gray or silvery white (very prominent), fimbriated.

STEM: Light brown, glabrous, ridged with the scale leaves persisting during the first year; in the second and third year blackish gray.

SIZE: 20 to 80′ in height with a greatly variable spread, usually 20 to 40′ under cultivation.
HARDINESS: Zone 5 to 8(9), -10 to -15°F will burn the needles.
HABIT: In youth artistically uneven but more or less pyramidal, in old age with spreading often pendulous branches, however, young trees can be pruned into a full dense specimen.
RATE: Medium.
TEXTURE: Medium.
BARK: On old trees blackish gray, soon becoming fissured into elongated irregular plates.
LEAF COLOR: Dark green, very handsome.
FLOWERS: Monoecious.
FRUIT: Cones subterminal, solitary or clustered, short-stalked, spreading, symmetrical, ovoid to conical, 1 1/2 to 2 1/2″ long, 1 1/4 to 1 3/4″ wide; scale end flattened, shiny light brown; umbo depressed, small, obtuse or with a minute prickle.
CULTURE: Transplants easily balled and burlapped if root pruned; makes its best growth on moist, fertile, well drained soils; will grow on sandy soils and has been used for reclaiming sand dunes and other protective work near the shore; quite salt tolerant and has been used where foliar salts present a cultural problem; best in full sun; displays excellent heat and drought tolerance.
LANDSCAPE VALUE: Because of its tolerance of salt spray it is invaluable for seashore plantings and useful in stabilizing sand dunes; also a good accent or bonsai plant; in 1985 several 4 to 5′ plants were used as an irregular mass to screen a clay hillside at the University Botanical Garden, by fall of 1989 the plants had grown 10 to 12′ high and filled in without any pruning, their habit is somewhat irregular, the lustrous deep green needles and white candle-like buds are particularly handsome.
CULTIVARS:
'Compacta'—Dense irregular large shrub type.
'Globosa'—Large dense globe habit, dark green needles.
'Iseli' ('Aocha Matsu')—Gold variegated broad pyramidal form, 7′ by 3′.
'Majestic Beauty'—Habit like species with lustrous dark green needles, resistant to smog, cutting propagated, Monrovia introduction.
'Mini Mounds'—Good name for this 2 to 4′ high, 7 to 9′ wide, 23-year-old selection, closely spaced, 3 to 5″ (8″) long needles that are bunched to form mounds, Vermeulen.
'Mt. Hood Prostrate'—Dramatic low sweeping habit, dark green needles, 6 to 8′ high, 8 to 12′ wide, Iseli.
'Oculus-draconis'—Needles are banded with yellow like *P. densiflora* 'Oculus-draconis', very stiff appearance and wide spreading habit; for the collector.
'Pygmaea'—Compact form with rich green needles, 5′ to 4′, Iseli.
'Thunderhead'—Heavy bud set, i.e., white candle like buds above heavy, dense dark green needles, dwarf, broad habit, Angelica Nursery introduction.
PROPAGATION: Seeds have no dormancy and will germinate immediately upon planting.
ADDITIONAL NOTES: I conducted considerable salt tolerance research and in one comparative study between this species and *Pinus strobus* found that *P. thunbergiana* was tremendously salt tolerant. Apparently, it is able to exclude the sodium and chloride ions and thus resist injury. White Pine accumulated chloride at levels greater than 2 percent of needle dry weight and died. For a rather complete listing of salt tolerance plants see Dirr, *Journal of Arboriculture.* 2:209–216. 1976. See Townsend and Kwolek, *J. Arbor.* 13(9): 225–228 for a discussion of the salt-tolerance of 13 pine species.
NATIVE HABITAT: Japan. Introduced 1855.

Pinus virginiana — Virginia (Scrub) Pine, Jersey Pine, Spruce Pine, Poverty Pine
(pī′nus vĕr-jin′ē-ā′na)

LEAVES: In two's, remaining 3 to 4 years, twisted, spreading, stout, 1 1/2 to 3″ long, margins with minute, irregular teeth, apex sharp-pointed, yellow-green to dark green; sheath persistent, 3/16″ long.

BUDS: Ovoid with a short point, 1/3 to 1/2″ long, resinous with closely pressed scales.

STEM: Young-slender, reddish purple with a pale bloom; good way to separate it from *P. banksiana* and *P. sylvestris.*

SIZE: 15 to 40′ in height by 10 to 30′ spread.

HARDINESS: Zone 4 to 8.

HABIT: A broad, open pyramid, becoming flat-topped, the branches springing irregularly from the stem; finally low, straggling, scrubby, with long outstretched limbs.

RATE: Slow.

TEXTURE: Medium.

BARK: Thin and smooth, eventually scaly-plated, reddish brown, 1/4 to 1/2″ thick.

LEAF COLOR: Yellow-green to dark green; often sickly yellowish green in winter.

FLOWERS: Monoecious; staminate orange-brown, pistillate pale green.

FRUIT: Cones 2 to 4 together or solitary, short-stalked or sessile, spreading or deflexed, oblong-conical, symmetrical, 1 1/2 to 3″ long by 1 to 1 1/4″ broad, apex blunt, dark brown; maturing in the second autumn but often persistent after that; cones sharp due to prickly-like appendage.

CULTURE: Does well in poor, dry soils where other pines will not grow; best on clay loam or sandy loam; dislikes shallow, chalky soils; open, sunny exposure.

LANDSCAPE VALUE: Not very ornamental but valuable as a cover for dry and barren soils; serves as the basis for the Christmas tree industry in the southern states.

ADDITIONAL NOTES: Chief merit lies in its ability to reproduce and grow on heavy, clay land where few other plants will grow, both on virgin soil and impoverished farm land.

NATIVE HABITAT: Long Island, New York, southwestward to central Alabama, in the Appalachian, Ohio Valley, Piedmont, and part of the Coastal Plain regions. Introduced before 1739.

Pinus wallichiana — Himalayan Pine (Bhutan Pine); also called *P. griffithii.*
(pī′nus wăl-lik-ē-ā′na)

LEAVES: Five, persisting 3 to 4 years, on young shoots more or less erect, the older ones spreading or drooping, slender, flaccid, creating a feathery effect, 5 to 8″ long, apex sharp pointed, grayish green, margin minutely toothed, with glaucous-white stomatic lines inside, outside green, leaf sheaths about 3/4″ long, soon falling, needles often bent abruptly near base so greater part of needle is pendulous.

STEM: Stout, bluish green, glabrous, slightly ridged below each bundle of needles towards the apex.

SIZE: 30 to 50′ high under landscape conditions but can grow to 150′; spread is variable but the large specimens I have seen were 1/2 to 2/3's the height.

HARDINESS: Zone 5 to 7; shows considerable needle browning when temperatures drop below -15°F.

HABIT: Loosely and broadly pyramidal when young; graceful, of elegant habit and often feathered with branches to the ground in old age; tends to be more wide-spreading than many pines as it approaches maturity.

RATE: Slow-medium, in youth may grow 2 to 3′ per year.

TEXTURE: Medium.

LEAF COLOR: Gray-green.

FLOWERS: Monoecious.

FRUIT: Cones subterminal, solitary, on a 1 to 2″ long stalk, erect when young; pendulous the second year, cylindrical, 6 to 10″ long by approximately 2″ broad, light brown when ripe and very resinous.

CULTURE: Listed as somewhat difficult to transplant and should be moved as a young (2 to 3′ high) plant to a permanent location; soil requirements are similar to those for White Pine and a sandy, well drained, acid loam is best; full sun; not recommended for shallow, chalky soils; severe winter winds can result in needle browning; withstands atmospheric pollutants better than most conifers; in extremely exposed locations the top becomes thin and weak when the tree is 25 to 40′ high and, therefore, a sheltered position is desirable.

LANDSCAPE VALUE: Excellent and beautiful pine for large areas, very graceful in effect; a lovely specimen tree; apparently there are differences in hardiness among nursery-grown trees (related to origin of seed) for some trees will do well in the midwest and others succumb after a difficult winter; the Morton Arboretum has a lovely, well-formed specimen from which seed or scion wood should be collected for the midwestern states.

CULTIVARS: There is a yellow-banded clone which is listed as 'Oculus-draconis' by some authorities; however, Den Ouden and Boom categorize the clone as 'Zebrina' which they describe as having leaves barred, marked an inch below the apex with a cream-colored band, otherwise green and gold. I have seen this cultivar at the National Arboretum in the Gottelli Conifer Collection. Perhaps as striking and interesting a cultivar as one could hope to see among the pines. There are three 'Oculus-draconis' clones; one is *P. densiflora,* another is *P. thunbergiana,* and the above. All are interesting but difficult to blend into the average landscape. For the hobby gardener they offer a worthwhile challenge.

PROPAGATION: Seeds have no dormancy or a slight one and may require 15 days of stratification.

NATIVE HABITAT: Temperate Himalaya at 6,000 to 12,500′ elevation, extending westward to Afghanistan and eastward to Nepal. Introduced 1827.

RELATED SPECIES:

Pinus armandii, (pī′nus är-man′dē-ī), David's Pine, is closely allied to the above species and differs in its relatively broad, scarcely tapered, 4 to 8″ long, 2 1/2 to 3″ wide, thick-scaled cones. The needles occur in 5's, persistent for 2 to 3 years, 4 to 6″ long, glossy green on outside, glaucous on inner sides; pointed at apex and minutely toothed on the margin; the sheath soon falling away. It makes a broad pyramid in youth of graceful proportions. It is as handsome as *P. wallichiana* but supposedly less hardy. I am not sure this is the case and degree of hardiness would no doubt reflect the provenance of the seed. It is a beautiful tree that certainly deserves consideration for landscape use. The large cones are quite resinous and my initial introduction to the species came at the expense of resin-coated hands when I plucked a beautiful, unripened cone from a tree at the Arnold Arboretum. The cones are so large and heavy as to partially weigh down the branches. Western and central China, Burma, Formosa and Korea. Introduced 1895. Zone 5 to 7?

Pistacia chinensis — Chinese Pistache
(pis-tā′shi-à chī-nen′sis)

FAMILY: Anacardiaceae

LEAVES: Alternate, compound, even pinnate, about 10″ long, 10 to 12 leaflets, each leaflet 2 to 4″ long, 3/4″ wide, lanceolate, short-stalked, acuminate, oblique, entire, glabrous at maturity, lustrous dark green; petiole-puberulous.

BUDS: Terminal—1/4 to 3/8″ long, imbricate, brownish black, ovoid, composed of stout, mucronate keeled bud scales, glabrous to slightly pubescent; vegetative—1/8″ to 1/4″ long, similar to above in color, directly centered over leaf scar.

STEM: Stout, light brown, prominently covered with orangish lenticels, glabrous with prominent odor when bruised; leaf scars raised, shield shape; pith—white, solid, ample.

SIZE: 30 to 35′ high, spread 25 to 35′.
HARDINESS: Zone 6 to 9.

HABIT: Oval-rounded in outline; main branches may be upright-arching; have seen many specimens of the tree in the Athens-Atlanta areas and most were oval-rounded with upswept branches.

RATE: Medium, however, may grow 2 to 3′ per year under good cultural conditions.

TEXTURE: Medium.

BARK: Develops shallow furrows, the ridges becoming scaly, gray in color; as the scales flake off they expose a salmon to orange inner bark.

LEAF COLOR: Dark green in summer, often lustrous; hold rather late in fall, becomes brilliant orange and orange-red; for the southern states this is the closest thing to rivaling Sugar Maple for fall color; over the past eight years I have monitored the quality and progression of fall color, color will vary from yellow-green to vivid orange-red and the best forms need to be propagated, in the Athens area color develops about mid October and often extends into late November.

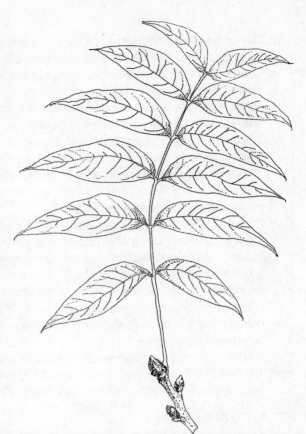

FLOWERS: Dioecious, small, greenish, male in dense, 2 to 3″ long panicles; female in 7 to 9″ long, loose panicles, not showy, April before leaves; flowers occur on previous year's wood.

FRUIT: A globose, obovoid, 1/4″ diameter drupe, typically maturing to robin's egg blue or red in the same fruit cluster; fruits are reasonably showy but certainly not the reason for using the tree, old fruit stalks persist on some trees and are less than aesthetic; fruits ripen in October and either fall or are taken by birds before late November.

CULTURE: Transplants well balled and burlapped or from containers; very adaptable species, tolerates a wide range of conditions but makes its best growth on moist, well-drained soils; very drought resistant; full sun; needs pruning in youth to form a good crown; in KS tests it averaged 1′1″ per year over a 10-year period and prospered in dry sandy soils.

DISEASES AND INSECTS: None serious.

LANDSCAPE VALUE: Too long neglected in the southern states for lawn, park, and street use; selections should be made for good habit and excellent fall color; its ability to withstand poor, droughty soils holds it in good stead as an urban tree; trees in Athens, Georgia are thriving; I am most impressed by its complete freedom from insects and diseases.

LANDSCAPE MAINTENANCE: As a young tree the habit is best described as gawky. Seedlings do not develop straight trunks and may produce multiple leaders. Some staking and pruning is necessary to produce a decent trunk. Once developed, the head seems to follow without a great deal of manicuring. My observations indicate that male trees are much neater and uniformly branched than the females. 'Keith Davey' has been described in a California publication as a selected male form that is neater and easier to shape.

PROPAGATION: One report stated that the pulp should be removed from the seeds, the seeds soaked in water for 16 hours then sown. From actual experience I have found the following to be reasonably foolproof. First and most important is the collection of sound seed. Only collect the bluish fruits for these have solid seed. I tried cut tests on a great number of reddish fruits and they were invariably hollow. Clean pulp from the seeds, place seeds in a moist medium at 41°F and observe for radicle emergence. In our work, 54 days proved optimum, for many seeds had germinated in the bag. These were then sown and the germination percentages were in the 80 to 90 percent range. Seed was sown directly and not a single one germinated. Cuttings: Morgan obtained 52% rooting of terminal cuttings with 1/3″ old wood attached, mid-May, 15000 ppm KIBA, mist, cuttings were collected from a mature,

45-year-old tree; with terminal new growth only, rooting was 20%; mid-June and August cuttings did not root as well. Grafting and budding have proven difficult.

ADDITIONAL NOTES: Have seen the species as far north as Urbana, Illinois where it was far from happy but did survive. It is really a tree for Zone 7 through 9. Is used in California to a considerable degree. Is used as an understock for the pistacio nut, *Pistacia vera,* of commerce. In China, the young shoots and leaves are eaten cooked as a vegetable. E.H. Wilson collected seeds of the species during his 1908 and 1910 expeditions to China. He noted that it turned a gorgeous crimson in the fall. Anyone interested in additional information should read Gary Koller's account in *Arnoldia* 38: 157–172 (1978). Also see McMillan Browse, *American Nurseryman* 167(1): 115–120 (1988) for excellent propagation and cultural discussion.

NATIVE HABITAT: Central and western China. Introduced about 1890.

Pittosporum tobira — Japanese or Tobira Pittosporum
(pit-o-spō′rum to-bī′rà)

FAMILY: Pittosporaceae

LEAVES: Alternate, simple, evergreen, obovate, 1 1/2 to 4″ long, 3/4 to 1 1/2″ wide, blunt or rounded at apex, tapering to a short petiole, glabrous, entire, leathery, lustrous dark green.

SIZE: 10 to 12′ high, spread 1 1/2 to 2 times height; picturesque spreading plants 20 to 25′ high have been reported.

HARDINESS: Zone 8, preferably lower portion, to Zone 10.

HABIT: Dense, compact, broad-spreading evergreen shrub of impenetrable proportions.

RATE: Slow.

TEXTURE: Medium.

LEAF COLOR: Lustrous dark green throughout seasons.

FLOWERS: Perfect, 5-petaled, fragrant (orange-blossom scent), creamy-white becoming yellow with age, 1/2″ diameter, borne in 2 to 3″ diameter clusters, April-May; somewhat inconspicuous but wonderfully fragrant.

FRUIT: Odd-looking, 3 valved, pear-shaped capsule, green changing to brown, September-October.

CULTURE: Easily transplanted from containers, adaptable, sandy soils to clays as long as well drained; acid or alkaline; used extensively in Florida; seems to thrive in sandy soils and hot, dry locations; full sun or heavy shade; withstands heavy pruning; tolerates salt spray.

DISEASES AND INSECTS: Tough, durable plant but can contract leaf spot disease and mealy bugs.

LANDSCAPE VALUE: Overused in warmer areas of south; mass plantings are popular, foundation use, in drifts under trees; hedges, screens, buffer or barrier planting; handsome plant for containers, patio tubs.

CULTIVARS:

'Variegata'—Leaf is edged with white, green areas take on a gray-green color, can be blended with green form for handsome effect, might not be as cold hardy as species; extremely popular and overused; grown as a house and conservatory plant in the north; flowers with same wonderful fragrance as species.

'Wheeler's Dwarf'—Compact form of the species growing 3 to 4′ high and wide; forms a compact mound of dark green foliage, all parts smaller than the species, not as cold hardy as species and generally not as adaptable, can be used as a houseplant. At 0 to 5°F, bark split devastated this cultivar; in Savannah, GA a large mass planting was killed outright at 10°F. This cultivar is a Zone 9 plant at best.

PROPAGATION: Use firm wooded cuttings, 1000 to 3000 ppm IBA-talc or solution, well drained medium, mist; have observed considerable "rot" under excessively moist propagation conditions.

NATIVE HABITAT: Japan, the Ryukyus, Formosa, Korea and China. Introduced 1804.

Platanus × *acerifolia* (Result of a cross between *P. orientalis* × *P. occidentalis,* sometimes listed as *P.* × *hybrida)* — London Planetree
(plat′ȧ-nus × a-ser-e-fō′le̅-ȧ)

FAMILY: Platanaceae

LEAVES: Alternate, simple, 6 to 7″ long, 8 to 10″ wide, 3 to 5 lobed, with triangular-ovate or broad triangular, not or sparingly toothed lobes, with acute or rounded sinuses extending 1/3 the length of the blade, truncate to cordate at base, glabrous or nearly so at maturity, medium to dark green; petiole 2 to 4″ long.

BUDS: Similar to *P. occidentalis.*

STEM: Similar to *P. occidentalis.*

BARK: Olive-green to creamy, exfoliating; actually the best asset of the tree.

FRUIT: Rounded, syncarp of achenes, 1″ across, 2 per stalk, rarely 1 or 3.

SIZE: 70 to 100′ in height with a spread of 65 to 80′ although can grow to 120′ or more.

HARDINESS: Zone 4 to 8 (9).

HABIT: Pyramidal in youth, developing with age a large, open, wide spreading outline with massive branches; does not spread as much as *P. occidentalis* but nonetheless is still not acceptable for street and small area use.

RATE: Medium, 35′ over a 20 year period, in Kansas tests grew 1′11″ per year over a 10-year period; under nursery production practices grows literally like a weed.

TEXTURE: Medium-coarse, but not particularly offensive; superb in winter when the bark is maximized.

BARK: Perhaps the handsomest of all large trees for winter character because of cream, olive, light brown bark; no two trees are exactly similar and as I write this large trees in Hyde Park, London; Berne, Switzerland; Mainau, Germany; and Cambridge, MA flash into view; all are spectacular, all remembered because of noble habit and unrivaled bark.

LEAF COLOR: Flat medium to dark green in summer, yellow-brown in fall.

FLOWERS: Monoecious, April, not showy, male and female similar in dense globose structures but on separate peduncles; develop with leaves.

FRUIT: Syncarp (multiple fruit) of elongated, obovoid achenes, ripening in October and persisting late into winter, usually borne 2 together although 3's and singles occur.

CULTURE: Easily transplanted; prefers deep, rich, moist, well-drained soils but will grow in about anything, withstands high pH conditions and pollutants; full sun or very light shade; prune in winter; withstands smoke and grime of cities and was so widely planted in London because of its adaptability that it acquired the name London Planetree.

DISEASES AND INSECTS: Cankerstain (very serious), *Botryosphaeria* canker, powdery mildew, American plum borer, and Sycamore lace bug; the London Planetree was once touted as a "Super" tree by many people and was soon overplanted; many diseases have caught up with it and its use should be tempered, the cankerstain fungus is especially troublesome and I have seen trees badly infested with lace bug; frost cracking is common in the midwest and anthracnose may occur on selected trees although the species generally shows good resistance.

LANDSCAPE VALUE: Acceptable for open areas in parks, golf courses, campuses; use as a street tree should be restricted for it grows too large; in some respects its use has approached monoculture status; the influx of disease problems should be closely monitored; considering that the tree is seed-grown it shows good uniformity but some segregation occurs and types resembling either parent result.

CULTIVARS: Considerable interest in better selections with uniform characteristics. Several new cultivars have been released since the last edition and *may be* superior to run-of-the-mill seedlings.

'Bloodgood'—Greater resistance to anthracnose than the species and after 10 years was the 10th rated tree in the Shade Tree Evaluation Tests at Wooster, Ohio; supposedly tolerates soil compaction, heat, drought, as well as severe pruning and is rapid growing; unfortunately the severe winters of 1976–77, 77–78 caused considerable injury and laboratory tests have indicated it is very susceptible to 0.5 to 1.0 ppm ozone, still a good selection and is being produced in greater numbers, 50′ by 40′ after 20 to 30 years, good dark green summer foliage, yellow-brown in fall.

'Columbia'—Original cross made by Dr. Santamour, U.S. National Arboretum in 1970 between *P. orientalis* (female) and *P. occidentalis* (male), pleasing pyramidal form in youth with dark green, mildew and anthracnose resistant foliage, compartmentalizes wounds well, grew 27′ in 12 years, 4″ diameter; 5 lobed leaves, length 80 to 90% of width; fruits in 2's and 3's; now being grown by American nurseries. See *HortScience* 19(6): 901–902 (1984) for more detailed information.

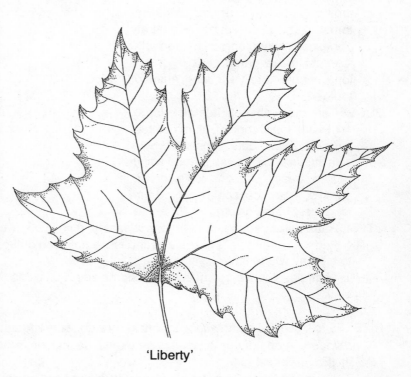

'Liberty'

'Liberty'—*P. orientalis* × *P. occidentalis* (bottomland tree), remotely 5-lobed leaves, fruits 1 to 2 with less than 1/3″ between fruits, resistant to anthracnose and powdery mildew, readily compartmentalizes against decay organisms; See *HortScience* 19(6):901–902 (1984) for details.

'Yarwood'—I don't know much about this form except it is supposedly mildew resistant, from California.

PROPAGATION: Seed requires a cold treatment for 45 to 60 days; there is some indication that seeds will germinate without pretreatment. Softwood and hardwood cuttings can be rooted and this appears to be standard practice in European countries; best to use 8000 ppm IBA, bottom heat, open bench with hardwoods. Myers and Still, *The Plant Propagator,* September 1979, p. 9–11, present interesting data relative to rooting June softwood cuttings; they collected the cuttings from a 45-year-old and a 20-year-old tree, dipped them in 50% alcohol solution, 8000, 16,000, 32,000 ppm IBA; best rooting occurred with the control and was 100% for the 20-year tree and 95% for the 45-year tree; IBA at the 2 lowest concentrations was also effective but not better than control; NAA proved valueless.

ADDITIONAL NOTES: The history of the plant is interesting and I suggest the reader consult Bean for a fine account. The first record of the tree was in 1663 when the hybrid was found growing in London. It is widely planted in Europe and especially England where in London it is the dominant street and park tree. My wife and I walked through Hyde Park on a cool September day and admired the great beauty of the bark and massive trunks. I think it is safe to say I have changed my opinion of the species over the years. When properly grown, it is a fine tree. The tree withstands heavy pruning and is often pollarded and pleached to form hedges and alleés. There is a magnificent alleé at the Jardin des Plantes, Paris, that every visitor to that city should see and experience.

Platanus occidentalis — American Planetree, also known as Sycamore, Buttonwood, and Buttonball-tree

(plat′a̦-nus ok-si-den-tā′lis)

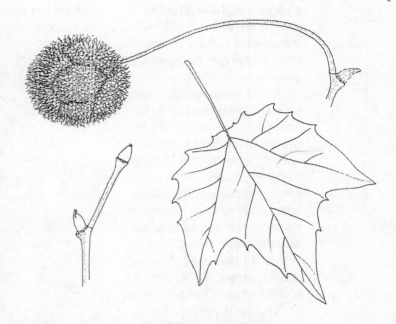

LEAVES: Alternate, simple, 4 to 9″ wide, often broader than long, 3- or sometimes 5-lobed with shallow sinuses and broad-triangular lobes, truncate or cordate, rarely cuneate, coarsely toothed or rarely entire, floccose-tomentulose when young, at maturity pubescent only along veins beneath, medium to dark green; petiole—3 to 5″ long, stipules 1 to 1 1/2″ long, entire or toothed.

BUDS: Terminal—absent, laterals—large, 1/4 to 3/8″ long, conical, blunt pointed, smooth, shiny dark reddish brown, with single visible scale formed within petiole base, second scale green, gummy, innermost scale covered with long rusty hairs; diverge at 45° angle.

STEM: Rather stout, round, smooth or pubescent, shiny yellow-orange-brown, generally zigzag.

BARK: Red to gray-grown and scaly near base, exfoliating on upper trunk exposing lighter colored (white to creamy white) inner layers.

FRUIT: Multiple, globose fruit of achenes, borne singly on a 3 to 6″ long peduncle, occasionally 2 fruits per stalk.

SIZE: 75 to 100′ in height with a similar or greater spread; can grow to 150′ and next to *Liriodendron tulipifera* is one of our tallest eastern native deciduous trees.

HARDINESS: Zone 4 to 9.

HABIT: Usually a tree with a large, massive trunk and a wide-spreading open crown of massive, crooked branches; a behemoth in the world of trees; a striking and impressive specimen especially in winter when the white mottled bark stands out against the cold gray sky; the best description of habit would be irregular.

RATE: Medium to fast, in KS tests averaged 1′11″ per year over a 10-year period.

TEXTURE: Coarse, but humanely so.

BARK: Mostly smooth, very light grayish brown, flaking off in large, irregular, thin pieces and exposing the grayish to cream-colored inner bark which gradually becomes whitish and produces the impressive mottled appearance.

LEAF COLOR: Flat medium to dark green in summer; fall color is tan to brown and unrewarding; leaves emerge late in spring.

FLOWERS: Similar to *P.* × *acerifolia*.

FRUIT: Also similar except the fruits are borne singly.

CULTURE: Similar to, but not as tolerant as *P.* × *acerifolia;* found native in bottomlands and along the banks of rivers and streams; attains its greatest size in deep, moist, rich soils.

DISEASES AND INSECTS: Anthracnose, leafspots, aphids, Sycamore plant bug, Sycamore tussock moth, scales, bagworms, borers, ad infinitum; anthracnose (*Gnomonia veneta*) is a serious problem as it affects developing leaves and stems; there is a dieback followed by a "witches' broom" type development beneath the dead area; excessive moisture is ideal for the spread of this disease.

LANDSCAPE VALUE: If native to an area do not remove the tree(s); however, do not plant it; have seen it used for street tree planting in Urbana, Illinois; the tree is simply too large and is constantly dropping leaves, twigs and fruits; if people only considered all the factors regarding each tree they plant perhaps much maintenance and trouble could be avoided, but...!; the city forester and I had several bouts over the removal of a plant that happened to be located in the tree lawn (parkway) bordering my property; I wanted to remove the tree and he did not approve; I did end up removing the lower branches; the tree was forever dropping part of its anatomy but was truly at its "best" when anthracnose kept it devoid of leaves until mid to late June; in a native situation especially along water courses it is an impressive sight in the landscape.

CULTIVARS:

'Howard'—Never knew one existed until the 1989 Georgia-South Carolina nursery meeting when a gentleman approached me about rooting a yellow-foliaged form; the new growth is a bright yellow that fades with the heat of summer; it is spectacular when the leaves first emerge.

PROPAGATION: Supposedly no pregermination treatment is necessary, although 60 days at 41°F has proven beneficial.

ADDITIONAL NOTES: The wood is heavy, hard, tough and coarse grained, and is used for furniture, boxes, crates and butcher's blocks. A beautiful tree in its finest form and as a child growing up in Cincinnati, Ohio, much pleasure was derived from climbing and hiding in the hollow trunks of the magnificent specimens that occurred along the stream along the back of our property.

NATIVE HABITAT: Ranges from Maine to Ontario and Minnesota, south to Florida and Texas. Introduced 1640.

RELATED SPECIES:

Platanus orientalis, (plat′a̶-nus ôr-i-en-tā′lis), Oriental Planetree, is one of the parents of *P.* × *acerifolia* and mentioned here because of its resistance to anthracnose which was apparently transmitted to the London Planetree. Similar to other species except the leaves are more deeply incised; the fruits are borne 3 to 6, rarely 2's; and the bark is a cream color. Not particularly hardy. Zone 7 to 9. Southeastern Europe and western Asia. I have seen a magnificent specimen at Kew Gardens and one can really appreciate the beauty of the tree in its mature state. It is not common in the United States.

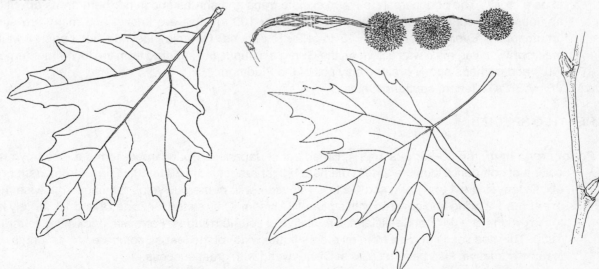

Podocarpus macrophyllus var. *maki* — Maki, Shrubby or Chinese Podocarpus
(pō-dō-kär′pus mak-rō-fil′us ma′kī)

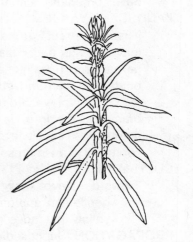

FAMILY: Podocarpaceae

LEAVES: Arranged spirally on stem, evergreen, needle like, 1/2 to 2 3/4″ long, 1/4 to 3/8″ wide, sharply acute, leathery, lustrous waxy dark green above with two wide glaucous stomatiferous bands beneath, glabrous; needles give a bottlebrush-like effect.

STEMS: Stout, green, grooved, glabrous.

SIZE: 20 to 35′ high, one-half this in spread; smaller in Piedmont.

HARDINESS: Zone 8 to 10, severely injured at -3°F on Georgia campus, many plants burned at 11°F at Sea Island, GA, most probably because of cambial damage (bark split).

HABIT: Upright oval to columnar evergreen shrub or tree; quite stiff and rigid.

RATE: Slow.

TEXTURE: Medium-fine.

LEAF: Lustrous dark green throughout the seasons.

FLOWERS: Dioecious, male catkin-like, cylindrical, yellow brown, 1 to 1 1/2″ long in clusters, female consists of a short stalk bearing a few scales of which only upper one are two are fertile; April-early May.

FRUIT: Naked seed, red to red-purple, 1/2″ long, have seen fruits with a pronounced bloom that gave them a bluish color, attached to a fleshy receptacle generally the same color as the seed; fruits are not poisonous and can be used to make preserves.

CULTURE: Transplants readily, prefers well-drained, fertile soils; like *Taxus* does not tolerate wet feet; full sun or moderate shade; tolerant of salt spray; displays excellent heat tolerance.

DISEASES AND INSECTS: Root rot in wet situations, scale has been reported.

LANDSCAPE VALUE: Makes a good hedge, screen, or small specimen tree where adapted; in upper reaches of Zone 8 is more shrubby and not particularly vigorous.

PROPAGATION: Seeds require 2 years to germinate. Hardwood cuttings root readily, handle like *Taxus;* also can be rooted in late summer and fall, 3000 to 8000 ppm IBA-talc, well drained medium, mist.

ADDITIONAL NOTES: *Podocarpus* belongs to the gymnosperms and bears a naked seed that is referred to as a "fruit". The podocarps are warm climate trees and shrubs and in northern areas are utilized as house and conservatory plants. Approximately 100 species are known and many are superb ornamentals. Even in Zone 8 (+10 to +20°F; Athens, Georgia) they do not perform well. *P. macrophyllus* var. *maki* was grown on the Georgia campus but suffered from the low winter temperatures and perhaps poorly drained clay soil of the Piedmont.

NATIVE HABITAT: Japan, southern China.

RELATED SPECIES:

Podocarpus nagi, (pō-dō-kär′pus nā′jī), Broadleaf or Japanese Podocarpus, forms a loose pyramidal outline of soft pendulous branches. Ultimate height ranges from 30 to 40′. The lustrous dark green, elliptic leaves are 1 to 3″ long and 1/2 to 1 1/4″ wide, with numerous veins running lengthwise. Fruits are about 1/2″ wide and covered with a plum-like bloom. Only suited for Zones 9 and 10, largely killed to the ground at +11°F at Sea Island, GA. Native of southern Japan, Formosa, and China. Introduced 1830. This species is distinct from all others in the width of the leaf as compared to its length. Bark is quite attractive. Has been utilized at Disneyworld with great success.

Polygonum aubertii — Silvervine Fleeceflower, Silver Lace Vine
(pō-lig'ō-num aw-ber'tē-ī)

FAMILY: Polygonaceae

LEAVES: Alternate, simple, 1 1/2 to 3 1/2″ long, ovate to oblong-ovate, hastate at base, usually undulate at margin, bright green; petioles 1 1/4 to 2″ long.

SIZE: 25 to 35′.

HARDINESS: Zone 4 to 7(8).

HABIT: Twining deciduous vine of rampant growth.

RATE: Fast, as much as 10 to 15′ in one growing season is not unreasonable.

TEXTURE: Medium in foliage; rather coarse in winter.

LEAF COLOR: Reddish, bronze-red when emerging and developing bright green when mature.

FLOWERS: Perfect, white or greenish white, sometimes slightly pinkish, fragrant, about 1/5″ diameter; borne in numerous, slender panicles along the upper part of the branches; July, August, and through September.

FRUIT: Three angled achene, not showy, not setting freely.

CULTURE: Easily transplanted; rapidly spreads by underground stems (rhizomes); the smallest segment of which will produce a new plant; full sun or shade; does well in dry soils; almost a weed because of its ebullient, vigorous habit.

DISEASES AND INSECTS: Japanese beetle can be a problem.

LANDSCAPE VALUE: A vigorous, rapid growing vine with good foliage; valued for its adaptability; makes a good, quick cover; this might be used where few other vines will grow.

PROPAGATION: Easily increased by stem cuttings or by division, seed requires no pretreatment.

ADDITIONAL NOTES: There were several *Polygonum* plantings on the University of Illinois campus which grew 1 to 2′ high and had pinkish flowers. They died back after a hard freeze and looked unsightly in the winter only to arise with reddish leaves in April. I noticed considerable variation in size, as some plants grew about a foot while others became almost vine-like and grew to 3′.

NATIVE HABITAT: Western China. Introduced 1899.

RELATED SPECIES: The nomenclature is confused within this group of plants and some of the names almost appear "homemade".

Polygonum baldschuanicum, (pō-lig'ō-num bald-shwa'ni-kum), Bokaravine Fleeceflower, is similar to *P. aubertii* in virtually every character and probably cannot be reliably separated. The inflorescences are glabrous and crowded toward the end of the shoots forming compound panicles. I have seen the plant in England on many occasions and believe that from a landscape standpoint it is similar to *P. aubertii*. Russia, Afghanistan, Pakistan. Introduced 1883. Zone 4 to 8.

Polygonum cuspidatum var. ***compactum,*** (pō-lig'ō-num kus-pi-dā'tum kom-pak'tum), Low Japanese Fleeceflower, grows to 2′ and has greenish white flowers and small reddish fruits. Wyman also reported a few roots which were planted in a vacant spot in the perennial border developed into an eight foot square in a short period of time. Often offered in the trade as *P. reynoutria.*

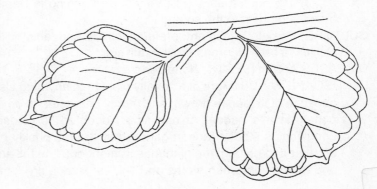

LEAVES: Alternate, simple, short-oval to orbicular-ovate, 3 to 6″ long, abruptly pointed, with an abrupt or truncate base; petiole about 1″ long.

Polygonum reynoutria, (pō-lig′ō-num rā-noo′trē-å), offers the biggest dilemma, for it is widely advertised in nursery catalogs but is limitedly discussed in botanical literature. Wyman and Bailey noted that *P. reynoutria* had pink flowers developing from deep red buds and grew only 4 to 6″ high.

Poncirus trifoliata — Hardy-orange
(pon-sī′rus trī-fō-li-ā′ta)

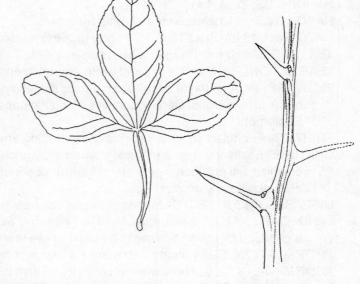

FAMILY: Rutaceae

LEAVES: Alternate, trifoliate, terminal leaflet obovate to elliptic, 1 to 2 1/2″ long, obtuse or emarginate, cuneate, crenulate, sub-coriaceous, the lateral ones similar, but smaller and usually elliptic-ovate, very oblique at base, lustrous dark green; petiole 1/3 to 1″ long, often winged.

BUDS: Glabrous, rather small, solitary, sessile, subglobose, with about 3 exposed scales; terminal lacking.

STEM: Glabrous, glossy green, triangular, dilated into the thorns at nodes, rather stout; pith large, white, homogeneous; leaf scars very small, elliptical, scarcely raised; bundle-trace 1, crescent-shaped; no stipule-scars; 1 to 4 stout spines, 1 to 2″ long; green stem color and very prominent broad-based spines are good winter identification characters.

SIZE: 8 to 20′ high, 2/3′s that in width.

HARDINESS: Zone 6 is more favorable; however, will grow in Zone 5 to Zone 9; have seen it killed to ground by -20°F.

HABIT: Small, oval shrub or tree with green spiny stems, usually low-branched and viciously spiny.

RATE: Slow to medium.

TEXTURE: Medium in leaf; medium to coarse in winter.

STEM COLOR: Young stems a distinct bright green with numerous spines, almost lethal to the touch.

LEAF COLOR: Lustrous dark green in summer changing to yellow or yellow-green in fall.

FLOWERS: Perfect, white, axillary, subsessile on previous year's branches, 1 1/2 to 2″ across, supposedly very fragrant, borne singly usually in late April to early May; in spite of what the literature states I cannot sense the sweet odor.

FRUIT: A modified berry (hesperidium), yellow, 1 1/2″ across, covered with soft down or glabrous, containing numerous seeds, very sour, ripening in September or October; ripens an unbelievable quantity of fruits in the south.

CULTURE: Easy to transplant, prefers well drained, acid soils; once established in the right situation it proves to be a vigorous grower; full sun.

DISEASES AND INSECTS: None serious.

LANDSCAPE VALUE: More of a novelty plant than anything else in the north, used in the south for hedging because of its dense growth and thorny character; even a dumb football player would not attempt to penetrate this hedge! At one time I doubted its landscape usefulness but have seen plants in Longwood's Mediterranean garden with yucca, prickly pear, sedum, and blue sheep's fescue that appeared to belong; the plant has tremendous late fall and winter character because of yellow fruits and interesting green stems and spines; spines are lethal and, doubtfully, should be used in high traffic areas. Recently visited Oklahoma State University campus and noticed the plant was used as a hedge. Hedges were so tightly pruned that one could walk on top.

CULTIVARS:
'Flying Dragon'—Interesting twisted stems, a novelty at best.

PROPAGATION: Seeds germinate like beans when stratified for 90 days at 41°F in a moist medium; one of my former students collected fruits from a tree in the Missouri Botanic Garden, St. Louis, and after stratification subsequent germination averaged 95 percent plus. I have also collected fruits in October from the Georgia Botanical Garden and sowed them directly, initial germination took 4 to 6 weeks and seeds were still coming up 3 months later; the cold period unifies and hastens germination more than anything else; also noted quite a number of albino seedlings, many more than occur in most seedling populations. Softwood cuttings taken in summer rooted after treatment with 50 ppm IBA/17 to 24 hour soak; cuttings taken in late October failed to root without treatment, but rooted 76 percent after treatment with 50 ppm NAA/24 hour soak.

ADDITIONAL NOTES: Introduced into commerce in U.S. by William Saunders of the USDA and P.J. Berckmans of Augusta, Georgia. It was listed by the Prince Nursery in 1823. Ripe fruits set aside for several weeks become juicy and develop a sprightly, slightly acid flavor. Serves as a substitute for lemon, pulp can be made into marmalade, and peel can be candied. After removing the numerous seeds there is not a whole lot of pulp left over.

NATIVE HABITAT: Northern China, Korea. Introduced about 1850. Seems incongruous that Prince Nursery listed it in 1823 but its introduction date corresponds to about 1850. Such is the nature of the literature.

Populus alba — White Poplar, Silver-leaved Poplar
(pop'ūlus âl'bà)

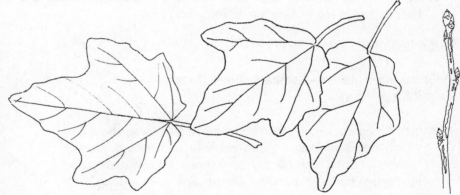

FAMILY: Salicaceae
LEAVES: Alternate, simple, on long shoots, palmately 3 to 5 lobed with triangular, coarsely toothed lobes, acute, subcordate or rounded at base, 2 to 5″ long, dark green above, white-tomentose beneath; on short branches, smaller, 1 to 2″ long, ovate to elliptic-oblong, sinuate-dentate, usually gray tomentose beneath; petioles—1/2 to 1 1/2″ long, tomentose.

BUDS: Imbricate, small, ovate to conical, light chestnut brown, appressed, shining or more or less covered especially toward base with cottony wool; laterals 1/5 to 1/4″ long, terminals larger.

STEM: Slender or sometimes stout, greenish gray, densely covered with thick whitish-cottony wool which can be readily rubbed off; pith—5 pointed, star-shaped.

BARK: On young trunks characteristically light greenish gray or whitish, often with dark blotches; base of older trunk deeply furrowed into firm dark ridges.

SIZE: 40 to 70′ in height with a similar spread; can grow to 90′ or greater.
HARDINESS: Zone 3 to 8(9).
HABIT: Usually a wide-spreading tree with an irregular, broad, round-topped crown; spreading abundantly by root suckers; tends to be weak-wooded and susceptible to breakage in storms.
TEXTURE: Medium-coarse in leaf; coarse in winter.
BARK: Greenish gray to whitish, marked with darker blotches, the bases of old trunks becoming fissured, with blackish ridges.

LEAF COLOR: Dark green above and silvery white beneath, the lower surface coated with a thick, matted tomentum; the leaves fall very early in the fall and usually show no coloration although yellowish and reddish have been listed by various authorities.

FLOWERS: Dioecious; male catkins 3″ long, females 2′ long.

FRUIT: Not important, see under *P. deltoides*.

CULTURE: Easy to grow, does well under any conditions but prefers moist, deep loam; pH adaptable; full sun; prune in summer or fall as it "bleeds" if pruned in winter and spring; air pollution tolerant; quite tolerant of salt spray.

DISEASES AND INSECTS: Poplars, in general, are affected by a whole host of diseases; they are poor ornamental trees and are continually dropping leaves, twigs and other debris; the following pests are the more common and include *Cytospora* canker, poplar canker, fusarium canker, hypoxylon canker, septoria canker, branch gall, leaf blister, leaf spots, leaf rusts, powdery mildew, dieback, aphids, bronze birch borer, poplar borer, red-humped caterpillar, poplar tent maker, scales and imported willow leaf beetle; if anyone plants poplars they deserve the disasters which automatically ensue.

LANDSCAPE VALUE: I hesitate to recommend this tree for anyone since it becomes a nuisance and liability after a time; wood is brittle, roots will clog drain tiles, sewers and water channels; avoid this pest.

CULTIVARS:

'Pyramidalis'—Columnar in habit, also called Bolleana Poplar; better than Lombardy Poplar but still of negligible quality; slightly broader than Lombardy.

'Richardii'—Upper surface of the leaves yellow, white beneath, slow growing, effective from a distance, have seen a time or two and always wanted to fertilize the tree.

PROPAGATION: Seed requires no pretreatment and germination will take place after dispersal. Cuttings root when treated with IBA but success may vary with timing; probably best in July-August.

NATIVE HABITAT: Central to southern Europe to western Siberia and central Asia. Long cultivated. Naturalized in North America. Introduced 1784.

RELATED SPECIES:

Populus nigra 'Italica'—Lombardy Black Poplar
(pop′ū-lus nī′gra)

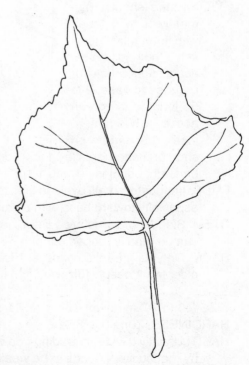

LEAVES: Alternate, simple, rhombic-ovate, 2 to 4″ long, about as wide, long-acuminate, broad cuneate to truncate, finely crenate-serrate, non-ciliate, dark green above, glabrous, light green beneath; petioles slender, 3/4 to 2 1/4″ long.

BUDS: Imbricate, small compared to other poplars, terminal 3/8″ long, laterals 1/3″ or less long, appressed, shiny, glutinous, reddish brown, glabrous.

STEM: Slender, round, lustrous brown.

GROWTH HABIT: Easily recognizable because of decidedly upright habit; often used for screen on old farm properties.

Populus nigra 'Italica', Lombardy Black Poplar, is an upright, fast growing, weedy cultivar that was introduced into this country in colonial times (1784); can grow to 70 to 90′ with a spread of 10 to 15′ in 20 to 30 years but seldom attains this size because of a canker disease which develops in the upper branches and trunk for which there is no cure. Substitutes might include *Populus alba* 'Pyramidalis', *Alnus glutinosa* 'Fastigiata', although none will grow as fast as Lombardy. Lombardy is a male clone and is propagated by cuttings. It apparently arose in the Lompardy district of Italy in the 1600's and was spread to other parts of Europe in the early 1700's. *Dothichiza populea* canker is a devastating disease which starts in the upper branches of the tree. It also infects Balsam, Black, and Eastern Cottonwoods. A form often listed as 'Thevestina' ('Theves') and sold as an improved Lombardy does resemble Lombardy in habit but tends to be more broad, has a whitish bark that becomes dark and slightly furrowed on old trunks, and is a female clone. A more correct name is 'Afghanica' for this form arose by mutation from a race of *P. nigra* native to central Asia. It is supposedly more resistant to the canker but I have seen no hard evidence to support this claim. Lombardy is hardy in Zones 3 to 9.

Populus deltoides — Eastern Cottonwood, also called Eastern Poplar.
(pop′ū-lus del-toy′dēz)

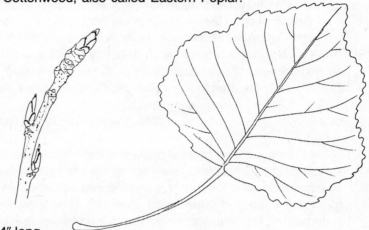

FAMILY: Salicaceae

LEAVES: Alternate, simple, deltoid-ovate or broad-ovate, 3 to 5″ long, about as wide, acuminate, subcordate to truncate and with 2 or 3 glands at base, coarsely crenate-dentate with curved teeth, entire at base and apex, densely ciliate, bright green below, glabrous; petioles flattened laterally, 2 1/2 to 4″ long.

BUDS: Imbricate, terminal—1/2 to 3/4″ long, 6 to 7 visible scales, conical, acute, shiny chestnut brown, resinous, balsam scented; laterals more or less flattened, appressed.

STEM: Stout, yellowish to greenish yellow to brown, round or marked especially on vigorous trees with more or less prominent wings running down from the two sides and bases of the leaf-scars; also quite ragged in appearance.

SIZE: 75 to 100′ in height spreading 50 to 75′.

HARDINESS: Zone 2 to 9.

HABIT: Pyramidal in youth but developing a broad vase-shaped habit in old age with the branching structure being somewhat open, irregular and ragged; often with massive, spreading branches.

RATE: Fast, 4 to 5′ a year in rich moist soil is not uncommon, in fact, in two years trees may attain heights of 30′ and diameters of nearly 5″.

TEXTURE: Medium-coarse in leaf, coarse in winter.

BARK: Ash-gray and divided into thick, flattened or rounded ridges separated by deep fissures on old trunks; young stems and trunks greenish yellow.

LEAF COLOR: Lustrous light to medium green in summer, abscising early in fall and usually only with a trace of yellow; in some regions good yellow.

FLOWERS: Applies to most *Populus;* dioecious, anemophilous, in pendulous catkins appearing before the leaves, individual flowers (both sexes) solitary, inserted on a disk and subtended by a bract; male flowers with either 6 to 12, or 12 to many stamens; female with a single pistil; up to 60 stamens on this species with attractive red anthers; usually opening in March-April before the leaves.

FRUIT: 3 to 4-valved dehiscent capsule, 1/4 to 1/3″ long, the seeds are tufted and represent the "cottony" mass which is seen under and around the trees at dispersal time; hence, the name Cottonwood.

CULTURE: Easily transplanted and grown, prefers moist situations along waterways but tolerates dry soils; very common on moist alluvial soils through the plains and prairie states; tolerates saline conditions and pollutants; very pH adaptable; a short-lived species and trees over 70 years old deteriorate rapidly.

LANDSCAPE VALUE: Little, except in the difficult plains states; a messy tree often dropping leaves, flowers, fruits, twigs and branches; will break up in storms as the wood is light, soft and weak; impressive in river bottoms and should remain there.

CULTIVARS: Many cottonless (male) forms and hybrids between *P. deltoides* and *P. nigra* have been selected and named. Pair evaluated six different forms over a 10-year period, his observations follow:
Species Male Clone—Averaged 3′4″ per year, subject to breakage.
'Lydick'—Averaged 4′ per year, female clone.
'NE-355'—Averaged 3′ per year.
'Noreaster'—Averaged 4′ per year, hybrid, with thicker bark and canker resistance.
'Robusta'—Averaged 4′1″ per year, vigorous, developed some canker.
'Siouxland'—Averaged 2′10″ per year, rust resistant, male form, introduced by South Dakota State University, apparently is susceptible to canker after 18 to 20 years; have observed in Spring Grove where 10-year-old trees averaged 30′ high and were quite pyramidal in outline, had dropped many interior leaves by late August and were not the most appealing specimens.
PROPAGATION: Seeds require no pretreatment; cuttings can also be used and apparently root with varying degrees of ease depending on the tree from which they were selected.
NATIVE HABITAT: Quebec to North Dakota, Kansas, Texas, Florida. Introduced 1750.

Other *Populus* of General Interest

There are about 30 species of poplars widely distributed in North America, Europe, North Africa and in Asia south to the Himalayas. There are numerous hybrids and named cultivars. In European countries they are commonly used for streets, parks, fence row, windbreak and canal plantings. They are important sources of pulpwood and other wood products. Their growth rates are phenomenal and the following figures are derived from information put out by the Minnesota Landscape Arboretum. Bolleana Poplar grew about 30′ in 9 years; 'Siouxland' 40′ in 9 years; Japanese Poplar 30′ in 9 years; *Populus nigra* 'Afghanica' ('Thevestina') 30′ in 9 years; *P. tremula* 'Erecta' 30′ high and 4′ wide in 10 years; *P. tremuloides* 25′ in 10 years; *P. trichocarpa* 20′ high and 7′ wide in 9 years.

Poplars can be divided into four groups:

1. White and gray poplars, aspens.
    Young trunks and main branches at first smooth, eventually pitted with numerous diamond shaped holes; leaves toothed or lobed; they can be further subdivided into:
    White or gray poplars—Leaves on long shoots woolly beneath, those of short shoots less woolly or almost glabrous, and of different shape; petioles, usually not flattened; included here are *P. alba, P. canescens,* (pop′ū-lus ka-nes′enz), and *P. tomentosa,* (pop′ū-lus tō-men-tō′s a).
    Aspens—Leaves glabrous or almost so beneath; uniform in size and with laterally flattened stalks which allow them to flutter in the slightest breeze; included are *P. grandidentata, P. tremula,* and *P. tremuloides.*
2. Leucoides
    The leaves are large and leathery, usually tomentose when young, and more or less the same size and shape; the bark is rough and scaly; *P. heterophylla,* (pop′ū-lus het-ēr-o-fil′ a), *P. lasiocarpa,* (pop′ū-lus lā-si-ō-kär′pa) and *P. wilsonii,* (pop′ū-lus wil-sō′nē-ī) belong here.
3. Balsam poplars
    The first to open in the spring, the buds and leaves very gummy, emit a pleasant balsam fragrance when expanding; usually whitish but not woolly beneath; petiole not compressed; *P. angustifolia,* (pop′ū-lus an-gus-ti-fō′li- a), *P. balsamifera,* (pop′u-lus bal-sam-if′ēr- a), *P. candicans,* (pop′ū-lus kan′di-kanz), *P. laurifolia,* (pop′ū-lus lâ-ri-fō′li- a), *P. maximowiczii,* (pop′ū-lus mak-sim-ō-wiks′ē-ī), *P. simonii,* (pop′ū-lus sī-mō′nē-ī), *P. trichocarpa,* (pop′ū-lus trī-kō-kär′pa), and others belong here.
4. Black poplars
    Leaves are green on both sides, petioles compressed, margins translucent and cartilaginous, trunks ridged and furrowed; *P. deltoides, P. nigra* and others belong here.

Populus × *canadensis* — Carolina Poplar
(pop′ū-lus × kan-a-den′sis)

Represents a large group of hybrids between *P. deltoides* and *P. nigra*. They are more vigorous than either parent and propagate easily from cuttings. 'Eugenei' is of a columnar habit with comparatively short spreading lateral branches; 'Florence Biondi', 'Gelrica', 'Marilandica', 'Noreaster' (only hybrid to show resistance in Dr. Pair's Wichita trials), 'Regenerata', 'Robusta' (small, vigorous, broad-oval), 'Serotina', 'Serotina Aurea' and 'Serotina de Selys' belong here. For a complete description see Bean.

Populus grandidentata — Bigtooth Aspen
(pop′ū-lus gran-di-den-tā′ta)

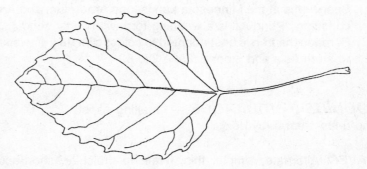

LEAVES: Alternate, simple, on long shoots, 3 to 4″ long, acuminate, truncate to broad-cuneate at base, coarsely sinuate dentate with callous mucronate teeth, dark green above, gray tomentose beneath at first, soon glabrescent and glaucescent, those of short branches elliptic, with sharper teeth; petiole glabrescent, 1 to 2 1/2″ long, slender, compressed toward the top.
BUDS: Imbricate, 1/8 to 1/4″ long, 6 to 7 visible scales, ovate to conical, pointed, generally divergent, dull, dusty-looking due to fine, close, pale pubescence especially at margin of scales.
STEM: Stout, round, reddish brown or somewhat yellowish brown, older stems greenish gray.

Populus grandidentata, Bigtooth Aspen, is normally a medium-sized tree reaching 50 to 70′, with a spread of 20 to 40′. Often pyramidal in youth with a central leader, developing an oval, open, irregular crown at maturity; very fast growing (65′/20 years); reaches best development on moist fertile soils but will grow on dry, sandy or gravelly soils; ornamental assets are few but it is valuable for pulp wood and other wood uses. Have seen good yellow fall color. Native from Nova Scotia to Ontario and Minnesota south to North Carolina, Tennessee, Illinois and Iowa. Introduced 1772. Zone 3 to 5(6).

Populus maximowiczii — Japanese Poplar
(pop′ū-lus mak-sim-ō-wiks′ē-ī)

Is a handsome, rather broad-spreading, large tree. The bark is smooth, light gray-green and attractive. It has proven to be one of the most promising and disease-free poplars in Minnesota's collection. The leaves open early in spring and persist late in fall. The leaves are slightly leathery, vivid green, whitish beneath and about 3 to 5″ long and wide. It has hybridized with other species and produced named selections including 'Androscoggin', 'Geneva', 'Oxford' and 'Rochester'. Northeast Asia, Japan. Introduction before 1890. Zone 3 to ?

Populus tremula 'Erecta' — Upright European Aspen
(pop′ū-lus trem′ū-la)

LEAVES: Alternate, simple, thin, suborbicular to ovate, 1 to 3″ long, rounded or acute at apex, truncate or subcordate at base, sinuately crenate-dentate, tomentose when emerging, quickly glabrous, dark

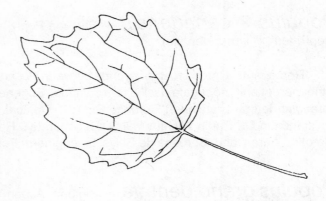

green above, glaucescent beneath, gray-
green; petioles flattened, glabrous, often as
long as the blade.

Populus tremula 'Erecta', Upright European
Aspen, is an excellent, narrowly fastigiate
tree which was found in the forests of
Sweden. It may prove to be a substitute for
the canker-infested Lombardy Poplar.
Based on evaluations of plants in the Illinois
trials, the leaves contract a severe leaf spot
and have been defoliated by early August.
Specimens at the Minnesota Landscape Arboretum and Arnold Arboretum appeared in outstanding
condition. 'Pendula' is a weeping form with stiffly pendulous branches and grayish purple catkins.
Perhaps the tree is best adapted to colder climates. The species is native to Europe, northern Africa,
western Asia and Siberia. Zone 2 to 5.

Populus tremuloides — Quaking Aspen
(pop′ū-lus trem-ū-loy′dēz)

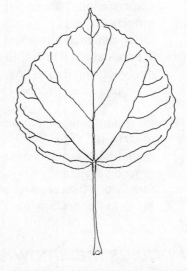

LEAVES: Alternate, simple, thin, ovate to orbicular, short-acuminate,
truncate to broad-cuneate at base, 1 1/2 to 3″ long and wide, finely
glandular-serrate, lustrous dark green above, glabrous and glaucescent beneath, leaves of suckers ovate, large, glabrous; petiole
slender, flattened, 1 to 2 1/2″ long.
BUDS: Terminal—imbricate, conical, sharp-pointed, sometimes very
slightly resinous, 6 to 7 scaled, reddish brown; laterals—incurved,
similar to terminal but smaller.
STEM: Slender, lustrous, reddish brown.
BARK: Smooth, greenish white to cream-colored; in old age furrowed,
dark brown or gray, roughened by numerous wartlike excrescences.

Populus tremuloides, Quaking Aspen, is the most widely distributed tree
of North America. It is fast growing, relatively short-lived and attains
heights of 40 to 50′ with a spread of 20 to 30′. Pyramidal and narrow
when young, usually with a long trunk and narrow, rounded crown
at maturity. Indifferent as to soil conditions and over its range can be found in moist, loamy sands to
shallow rocky soils and clay. The leaves flutter in the slightest breeze; hence, the name Quaking
Aspen. The fall color is a good yellow. Ornamentally not important because of disease and insect
problems but, nonetheless, an interesting tree. The wood is important for pulpwood and other uses.
Native from Labrador to Alaska, south to Pennsylvania, Missouri, northern Mexico and lower California. Introduced 1812. Zone 1 to 6(7); have seen a population in the Piedmont of Georgia.

Potentilla fruticosa — Bush Cinquefoil
(pō-ten-til′à froo-ti-kō′sà)

FAMILY: Rosaceae
LEAVES: Alternate, compound pinnate, 3 to 7 leaflets, usually 5, sessile, elliptic to linear-oblong, acute,
1/2 to 1″ long, with revolute margin, dark green, more or less silky.
STEM: Shiny brown, slender, wispy, exfoliating with age.

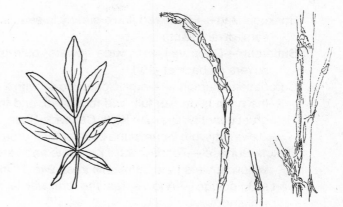

SIZE: 1 to 4′ in height and 2 to 4′ or larger in spread; dainty in size considerations.

HARDINESS: Zone 2 to 7, does not perform well in Zone 8.

HABIT: Very bushy shrub with upright slender stems forming a low, rounded to broad-rounded outline.

RATE: Slow.

TEXTURE: Fine in leaf, medium-fine in winter; refined, graceful appearance in foliage.

STEM COLOR: Interesting in winter if framed by a new snow; brown in color.

LEAF COLOR: Leafs out early in spring, silky gray-green when unfolding changing to bright to dark green in mature leaf; fall color is green to yellow-brown, not ornamental.

FLOWERS: Perfect, bright buttercup yellow, about 1″ across, June through until frost, borne singly or in few-flowered cymes, excellent color addition to any garden; numerous cultivars provide interesting color variation.

FRUIT: Achene, not showy, persistent.

CULTURE: Fibrous rooted, transplants well, of easy culture; withstands poor, dry soils and extreme cold; full sun for best flower although they seem to do well in partial shade; best in a fertile, moist, well-drained soil; most plants are container-grown; in the wild occasionally found in bogs but more common on wet or dry open ground especially that of calcareous origin; this is one of the reasons they perform so well in the midwestern states; remove one-third of the canes or renewal prune in late winter.

DISEASES AND INSECTS: Relatively free from insect and disease pests; there are several leave spots and mildews which affect the plant but they are rarely serious; spider mites can be troublesome.

LANDSCAPE VALUE: Shrub border, massing, edging plant, low hedge, perennial border, facer plant, can be integrated into the foundation planting and will add a degree of color unattainable with most plants, dainty clean foliage, good flower color and length of flowering period justify wider landscape consideration; can become ragged with time and proper pruning practices should be employed; I tried to grow 'Goldfinger' in my Georgia garden but the plant lacked vigor and never measured up to performance in Zone 4 to 6. High night temperatures may be the limiting factor.

CULTIVARS: I am hedging on my responsibility by including all the cultivars together but for ease of presentation have chosen this approach. Cultivars have been selected from several species, *P. arbuscula, P. davurica, P. fruticosa* and *P. parvifolia* as well as from hybrids between these. Since the 1983 edition, I have seen many new cultivars come onto the market, some good, others miserable. In addition, during sabbatical I carefully evaluated the entire collection at the Arnold Arboretum. Also, Bachtell and Hasselkus. *American Nurseryman* 153(3): 83–89 reported on their evaluations of *Potentilla* cultivars. Also used Bressingham Gardens catalog as a source for new introductions and consulted Krüssmann for more specifics. All of this information has been distilled and is presented here as a rather heterogeneous average that should serve as a reasonable guide to the selection of the best types.

'Abbotswood'—Dark bluish green foliage, spreading habit, large white flowers produced over a long period, considered one of the best whites, truly outstanding in flower, 3′ high.

'Abbotswood Silver'—Leaves with creamy white margins, the entire shrub rather handsome on close inspection, does not appear to be a vigorous grower and is not preferable to 'Abbotswood'; flowers are white, probably only good in cooler climates, 24 to 30″ by 24 to 30″.

'Bann Bannoch'—Strong bushy constitution, a continuum of primrose-yellow flowers, 30 to 36″ high.

'Beanii'—White flowers, shiny dark green leaves, medium height, irregular rounded form, severe dieback at -19°F.

'Beesii'—Buttercup yellow, 3/4″ diameter flowers, producing stamens only (should be fruitless), leaves rather silvery green, slow-growing to 2′ high.

'Boskoop Red'—Flame red flowers early in season becoming lighter later, bright green foliage on a semi-dwarf plant.

'Buttercup'—Deep yellow 1″ wide flowers, pale green leaves, low, mounded, fine-textured form, severe dieback at -19°F.

'Coronation Triumph'—A large clone, 3 to 4′, with a softer green foliage cast compared to 'Jackmanii'; the habit is dense, full, and mounded, and the bright yellow 1″ diameter flowers are borne in great quantity; Drs. Jim Klett, Colorado State University and Dale Hermann, North Dakota State University vote it one of the best for their area; in my Illinois garden it outperformed 'Jackmanii'.

'Dakota Sunrise'—Tends toward prostrate habit the first year, eventually dense and rounded, bright yellow flowers from June until frost, 2 to 3′, introduced in 1978.

'Dart's Golddigger'—A low spreading form with large golden flowers, raised in Darthuizer Nurseries, Holland.

'Daydawn'—Handsome form in a cool climate, peach pink, suffused with cream, flowers fade in heat to cream, tall mounded form with medium green leaves, 30″ high.

'Donard Gold'—Low spreading form, perhaps 20″ high but much wider, green foliage, large golden yellow flowers.

'Elizabeth' ('Arbuscula')—Flowers rich, soft yellow and up to 1 3/4″ diameter, flowering over a long period, leaves somewhat grayish green, bushy shrub to 3′, I have always liked this form, 'Sutters Gold' is same plant.

'Farreri' ('Gold Drop')—Flowers deep yellow, 3/4 to 1″ diameter, leaves very small, twenty-five year-old-plant—2′ tall and 3′ across, small bright green leaves, moderate flowering at Arnold.

'Farreri Prostrata'—Buttercup yellow, 1 1/4″ diameter flowers on a 1 1/2′ by 3′ shrub.

'Forrestii'—Medium yellow, large flowers, most abundant in late summer, gray-green leaves, coarse texture, low, mounded form, foliage may become bronzed and chlorotic in late summer.

'Friedrichsenii' ('Berlin Beauty')—Flowers creamy white to pale yellow, 1″ diameter, 58-year-old plant is 4 1/2′ high and 6′ across (hybrid origin), sparse flowered at Arnold, resembles 'Maanelys' but is more open.

'Gold Carpet'—Improved form of 'Arbuscula', mildew free with large deep yellow flowers.

'Gold Drop'—Often a common name for the yellow-flowered potentillas; in actuality a clone with 7/8″ diameter yellow flowers on a dwarf bushy framework.

'Goldfinger'—Compact, mounded, 3′ by 4′ shrub with large, bright yellow, 1 3/4″ diameter flowers that occur into fall, dark green foliage, it has proven to be a superior clone in the midwest.

'Goldstar' ('Gold Star')—This new form keeps cropping up in my European travels and I believe it will become popular in the future; deep yellow-gold, 2″ diameter flowers are borne in abundance particularly in cool climates, mildew resistant and trouble free, 3′ high, 2 to 2 1/2′ across, from West Germany.

'Goldteppich'—Somewhat similar to 'Dart's Golddigger' with smaller flowers and larger, deeper green leaves, golden yellow, 1 1/4 to 1 1/2″ diameter flowers are produced in great numbers.

'Grandiflora'—Flowers bright yellow, 1 3/8″ diameter, with large dark green leaves, ultimate height about 6′, abundant flowers, 3′ by 4′ at Arnold.

'Hollandia Gold'—Large, dark yellow flowers, medium green leaves, medium texture, low, mounded form, suffers chlorosis and leaf scorch under water stress.

'Hurstborne'—Bright yellow small flowers on a fine-textured, compact, globe form.

'Irving'—Golden yellow small flowers on a fine textured, dense, 3′ high shrub.

'Jackmanii' ('Jackman's Variety')—A larger form, 3 to 4′ high, good dark green foliage color, and a profusion of bright yellow, 1 1/4 to 1 1/2″ diameter flowers, has performed well in the midwest, stops flowering before 'Goldfinger' and 'Coronation Triumph' at least in the Urbana, Illinois area.

'Katherine Dykes'—A fine form with gracefully arching branches and seldom growing more than 2 to 3′ high, the medium green foliage is glaucous tinged and provides a framework for the lemon yellow, 1″ or slightly wider flowers that are freely produced, 4 1/2 by 3 1/2′ at Arnold, with age may become twiggy and unattractive.

'Klondike' ('Klondyke')—A dwarf, compact shrub about 2′ high is studded with 1 1/2″ diameter, deep yellow flowers, foliage is bright green above, bluish green below, not performing well at Arnold.

'Knaphill'—Small bright yellow flowers produced all season, medium green leaves, fine texture, dense low mounded form, rated highly by Bachtell and Hasselkus, showed good tolerance to water stress but suffered slight dieback at -19°F.

'Kobold'—Low, compact, fresh green leaves, masses of small yellow flowers from June into fall, 18″ or greater.

'Lady Daresbury'—Large bright yellow flowers, sparsely produced after initial strong showing, blue-green leaves, medium height and broad-spreading form, foliage chlorotic and bronzed under water stress.

'Logan'—Dark yellow flowers, pale green leaves, fine-textured, low, mounded form, may suffer from water stress.

'Longacre'—Similar to 'Elizabeth' but lower and more spreading, flowers large, bright sulfur-yellow, shiny dark green leaves, 3′ by 4′, heavy flowers at Arnold.

'Maanelys' ('Moonlight')—Soft yellow flowers about 1 1/4″ diameter fading as they age but remaining darker at the center, foliage soft gray-green and silky above, whitish underneath, flowers from May to July-August, considered a low, mounded grower although may reach 4 to 5′ by 8′; 4′ by 4′, 3/4″ diameter yellow flowers at Arnold.

'Manchu' (var. *mandshurica*)—White flowers, 1″ diameter, not prolific, a dense mounded shrub about 1 to 1 1/2′ high, grayish green foliage, a rather wispy, shabby shrub at the Arnold.

'McKay's White'—Creamy-white flowering sport that developed at McKay Nursery, WI.

'Mount Everest'—White flowers in spring and summer on an upright branching shrub.

'Northman'—Rich yellow flowers, sage-green leaves and small habit.

'Ochroleuca'—A seedling of 'Friedrichsenii' with bright green leaves and small cream-colored flowers, small erect shrub to 6′.

'Pink Pearl'—Large mid-pink flowers on a neat, mounded spreading shrub, 16 to 20″ high.

'Pretty Polly'—Small, salmon pink flowers on a compact shrub, 14 to 20″ high.

'Primrose Beauty'—A small (3′), free-flowering shrub with 1 3/8″ diameter primrose with deeper center flowers that pale with age, grayish green foliage, may grow 4 to 5′ high and 6′ wide, allied to 'Vilmoriniana' but is better and is considered one of the finest of all the garden hybrids, moderate flowering at Arnold.

'Princess'—Delicate pink flowers, white on the reverse, May into October but become smaller and may fade to white in the heat of summer, robust shrub 30″, Bressingham Gardens introduction, beautiful as I have seen it in England, doubtfully as nice in the heat of the United States.

'Pyrenaica'—Perhaps a misnomer but plants with this name are dwarfish, 6 to 18″ high, and have 1″ diameter, bright yellow flowers.

'Red Ace'—I would like to relate that this is a superior red-flowering form but unfortunately that is not the case. It was introduced through Bressingham Gardens, England, and described as having 1″ diameter, flaming vermillion petals, undercoated with yellow on an ultra-hardy, 2 1/2 to 2 1/2′ framework. In the U.S. it is a weak grower and the flowers in heat or drought bleach out to yellow or pale orange-red. It is also quite susceptible to mite damage and leaf scorch. I grew it in my Illinois garden and was woefully disappointed. Handsome in England where I have seen it in June; will fade there also in summer.

'Royal Flush'—A seedling from 'Red Ace' with rosy-pink, yellow-centered flowers on a compact 12 to 18″ high shrub, (twice as wide), leaves dark green, will lose its color and fade to soft pink or cream in hot weather.

'Sandra'—Ivory-white, 1 3/8″ diameter flowers on a 3′ high bushy shrub.

'Snowflake'—Flowers white, semidouble, 1″ diameter, not vigorous at Arnold.

'Stocker's Variety'—White flowers, sparsely produced, glossy dark green leaves, almost leathery in appearance, medium texture, dense, globe form.

'Sunset'—Pale yellow flowers tinged orange, retaining their unusual color but produced in small numbers, shiny medium green leaves, fine-texture, tall mounded form, foliage may be chlorotic under water stress, has been noted that color may fade to yellow in hot weather.

'Tangerine'—Medium yellow or flushed with orange-red (copper-red) under ideal conditions, in full sun, flowers are yellow, 1 1/4″ wide, gray-green leaves, 2′ by 4′, mounded, spreading shrub.

'Tilford Cream'—White flowers on a compact plant, 12 to 18″ high, leaves bright green.

'Vilmoriniana'—Flowers pale yellow to creamy white with a yellow center, up to 1 1/2″ diameter, silvery-green leaves, stiffly erect shrub, 4 to 5′ high, flowers borne sparsely over a long period.

'White Gold'—Medium yellow, large flowers, gray-green leaves, coarse-textured, low, mounded form, chlorosis and foliage bronzing may occur under water stress.

'William Purdom'—Canary-yellow flowers, with a deeper center, 1 1/8″ diameter, bright green leaves, fine-textured, large rounded, open, 4 to 6′ high.

'Woodbridge Gold'—Flowers buttercup-yellow, 1 1/4″ diameter, abundant over several months, leaves rich green and rather glossy, low growing to about 2′ by 3′.

PROPAGATION: Seeds require no pretreatment. Softwood cuttings rooted 100% under mist in peat:perlite when treated with 1000 ppm IBA; very easy to root from softwood cuttings but reduce the water as soon as they root.

ADDITIONAL NOTES: Wyman noted that one cultivar grown in the Arnold Arboretum in the same location for 60 years was 3′ tall and had never required pruning or spraying. I have seen the Arnold Arboretum's and the Minnesota Landscape Arboretum's extensive collections of *Potentilla fruticosa* and wondered how anyone could separate them without labels. Many look similar in flower color, habit, and foliage characteristics. The logical approach would be to select the best 5 to 10 and use this as a guide. From what I understand continued breeding and selection is occurring so, no doubt, more clones will inundate an already confused group of plants. The current edition includes 21 additional cultivars. Their extreme hardiness and summer flowering sequence make them valuable landscape plants.

NATIVE HABITAT: Northern Hemisphere.

Prinsepia sinensis — Cherry Prinsepia
(prin-sē′pi-à sī-nen′sis)

FAMILY: Rosaceae

LEAVES: Alternate on current season's growth, produced in clusters on the year old shoots, simple, ovate-lanceolate to lanceolate, 2 to 3″ long, about 1/2″ wide, long acuminate, entire or sparingly serrulate, finely ciliate, otherwise glabrous, bright green; slender petioled.

BUDS: Small, indistinctly scaly, concealed in brown hairs, buds may develop into spines.

STEM: Long and slender, round, spiny (1/4 to 2/5″ long), light gray-brown; pith chambered; on older stems the bark exfoliates to varying degrees.

SIZE: 6 to 10′ in height and as wide; specimen at Arnold is 10′ high and wide.

HARDINESS: Zone 3 to 7.

HABIT: Haystack to rounded, dense, spiny shrub well adapted for hedges and screens.

RATE: Medium.

TEXTURE: Medium in leaf, perhaps medium-coarse in winter.

BARK: On old stems brown and shredding off in long papery strips.

LEAF COLOR: Bright green in summer; fall color of little consequence, perhaps yellow-green; usually the first shrub to leaf out, have seen leaves in early to mid March at the Arnold Arboretum, also drops leaves early in fall.

FLOWERS: Perfect, small, light yellow, 5-petaled, almost creamy-yellow, borne in fascicles of 1 to 4 on previous year's wood in March-April, each flower about 3/5″ diameter, on a 1/2″ long pedicel, worthwhile but not overwhelming.

FRUIT: Red, cherry-like, 1/2″ long, subglobose or ovoid drupe which ripens in July, August and September and is effectively digested by birds; color is actually more orange than red, supposedly edible.

CULTURE: Easily transplanted, of undemanding culture, requiring only fertile, well-drained soil and open, sunny location; probably best to renewal prune when plants become overgrown; withstands pruning quite favorably.

DISEASES AND INSECTS: One of its principal merits is resistance to pests.

LANDSCAPE VALUE: Not a very common shrub but one certainly worth considering for hedges, screens or barriers; quite serviceable shrub and requires minimal maintenance; the endearing trait of being the first shrub to thrust its green leaves upon the spring landscape makes it worthwhile considering; no one characteristic is particularly outstanding but the sum of all the parts equals a good, serviceable shrub that could be utilized effectively on difficult sites.

PROPAGATION: Apparently seed germination is somewhat variable and the reports in the literature do not emphasize the best treatment; seeds will germinate when sown directly but a 2 to 3 month cold treatment definitely improves germination. Cuttings collected in June rooted 65 to 75% when treated with 3000 to 8000 ppm IBA; 100 percent rooting was obtained with August cuttings and 8000 ppm IBA, mist; apparently a higher hormone concentration is advisable.

Prinsepia uniflora appears more difficult to germinate and root; seeds will germinate if sown directly but cold treatments have produced variable results. Cuttings are difficult but can be rooted in July and August with high hormone and patience; during sabbatical I tried to root this species but was unable to induce a single root.

NATIVE HABITAT: Manchuria. Cultivated 1896.

RELATED SPECIES:

Prinsepia uniflora — Hedge Prinsepia
(prin-sē'pi-à ū-ni-flō'rà)

LEAVES: Alternate, simple, linear-oblong to narrow-oblong, 1 to 2″ long, 1/2 to 3/4″ wide, distinctly toothed, each serration terminated by a short bristle, lustrous dark green above, light green below, glabrous; petiole—1/4″ long.

BUDS: Small, indistinctly scaly, long, slender, scale-like appendages tend to mat together.

STEM: Slender, pale-gray to straw-brown, slight ridges, glabrous, small orangish bumps (lenticels); spines 1/2″ long, slender, sharp-pointed, borne singly above a node; pith—greenish white, finely chambered.

Prinsepia uniflora, Hedge Prinsepia, is a rather thorny, moderately dense aggregate of light gray branches growing 4 to 5′ high with a similar spread. The Minnesota Landscape Arboretum has both species growing side by side and the growth habit and foliage characteristic differences become immediately evident. The leaves are very dark green, 1 to 2″ long and not as densely borne as those of *P. sinensis.* The flowers are white, 3/5″ wide, 5-petaled, 1 to 3 together along with the leaves from nodes of the previous season's growth, on a 1/4″ long glabrous pedicel. The fruits are globose, about 1/2″ long, dark purplish red, bloomy, maturing in late summer. This species would also make a good hedge or barrier and on the basis of foliage color is superior to *P. sinensis.* Native to northwestern China. Introduced 1911. Zone 3 to 5(6). Rare in cultivation. The fruits are quite handsome and hang down from the branches in a rather pretty fashion. Interestingly, of two plants in the Arnold Arboretum, one fruited heavily, the other bore no fruits.

Prunus — Cherries, Peaches, Plums, Apricots, Almonds.
FAMILY: Rosaceae

The genus *Prunus* comprises over 400 species and numerous hybrids. The distinctions between species and cultivars are often difficult. Herein, I have presented an encapsulated treatment of the more popular ornamental types. The cherries provide a freshness to our gardens that is seldom achieved with any other plant. The delicate flowers pass quickly but in their finest hours are the equal of any ornamental tree. Unfortunately, *Prunus* as a group is beset with insect and disease problems and perhaps should not be looked upon as long term garden investments. Some, such as *Prunus subhirtella, P. sargentii* and selected *P. serrulata* types, can be expected to live for 30 to 50 years while *P. persica, P. cerasifera* 'Atropurpurea' and *P. glandulosa* may decline in 3 to 10 years.

ADDITIONAL NOTE: Two excellent books include Collingwood Ingram. 1948. *Ornamental Cherries.* Country Life, LTD, London, and Geoffrey Chadbund. 1972. *Flowering Cherries,* Collins, London. The first individual is considered the greatest force in ornamental cherry introduction and breeding. His 'Okame', correctly *P. × incamp* 'Okame' was introduced in 1947 and 40 some odd years later is receiving rave reviews from American gardeners. See discussion under *P. campanulata.* A trip through Ingram's book opens one's eyes to the beauty and diversity of flowering cherries.

Prunus americana — American Plum
(proo'nus a̓-mer-i-kā'na̓)

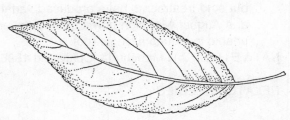

LEAVES: Alternate, simple, obovate to oblong-ovate, 2 to 4″ long, 1 1/4 to 1 3/4″ wide, acuminate, broad cuneate, sharply and doubly serrate, dark green and glabrous or slightly pubescent on midrib below; petiole—1/3 to 3/4″ long, pubescent, without glands.

Prunus americana, American Plum, is a common shrub, often forming large colonies along roadsides, in waste areas and other uncultivated habitats throughout its native range. I have seen the typical colonies which almost remind of sumacs the way they spread. Also, single stemmed, 15 to 25′ trees are evident. Flowers are pure white, about 1″ diameter, 2 to 5 together in sessile umbels, each flower on a slender 2/3 to 1″ long glabrous pedicel. Flowers open before the leaves in early to mid March in Athens and depending on temperature are effective for 5 to 7 up to 10 days. A pronounced difference in flowering times is evident as one colony will be spent while another is in full splendor. Flowers have that sickly sweet typical plum species odor. Fruits are generally yellow to red, rounded, +1″ diameter with yellow flesh that ripens in June-July. The fruits are utilized for jellies and jams. Obviously requires no special cultural requirements. Tends to thrive with neglect. Found from Massachusetts to Manitoba, south to Georgia, New Mexico and Utah. Cultivated 1768. Zone 3 to 8. *Prunus angustifolia,* Chickasaw Plum, is another suckering, colonizing shrub with comparable attributes. Branches are covered with thorn-like side branches. The leaves are 1 to 2″ long, one third as wide, oval-lanceolate, strongly trough shaped, acute, broad cuneate or rounded, lustrous dark green above. The white, 1/2″ diameter flowers occur 2 to 4 together before the leaves. Fruit is a 1/2″ diameter, rounded, lustrous red (yellow) drupe. Maryland and southern Delaware to Florida, west to Arkansas and Texas. Introduced around 1874. Zone 5 to 9.

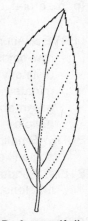

P. Angustifolia

Prunus avium — Mazzard or Sweet Cherry
(proo'nus ā'vi-um)

LEAVES: Alternate, simple, oblong-ovate, 2 to 6″ long, 1 1/2 to 2″ wide, acuminate, unequally serrate, dull dark green and often slightly rugose above, more or less pubescent beneath, of soft texture; petiole—1 to 1 3/4″ long with prominent often reddish glands near the blade.

Prunus avium, Mazzard or Sweet Cherry, is a large tree of conical shape growing to 70′ or more but usually under cultivation reaches 30 to 40′ with a similar spread. The emerging foliage is bronze, becoming deep green in summer and turns yellow to bronze in fall. Flowers are white, 1 to 1 1/2″ diameter,

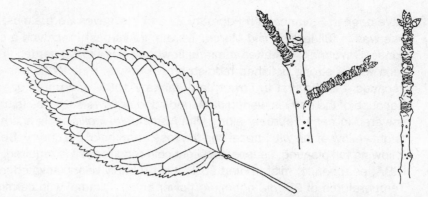

fragrant, mid to late April, in several flowered umbels. The fruit is a reddish black rounded drupe about 1″ in diameter. This is the species from which most of our popular sweet cherry clones are derived. 'Plena' has double white, 1 1/2″ diameter flowers with as many as 30 petals and is superior to the species for flower effect. The Arnold Arboretum had a tree that was spectacular when in flower. An enterprising nurseryman could sell this form. There are other clones of limited importance. Europe, western Asia. Cultivated since ancient times. Zone 3 to 8. Does reasonably well in Athens. One of the hardiest cherries and might be used where the Oriental types are not hardy.

Prunus besseyi — Western Sandcherry, Sand Cherry
(proo′nus bes′sē-ī)

LEAVES: Alternate, simple, oval, oval-lanceolate, sometimes obovate. 1 to 2 1/2″ long, shallowly serrate on upper two-thirds, glabrous, gray-green; petiole 1 1/2 to 4″ long.

Prunus besseyi, Western Sandcherry, is a suckering, spreading, 4 to 6′ high and wide shrub. The gray-green leaves are rather attractive and provide a different foliage color than most *Prunus* species. In late April-early May the shrub literally glows with pure white, 1/2″ diameter flowers that give way to sweet, purplish black, 3/4″ long fruits in July and August. I have only seen the plant in flower on one occasion and, indeed, it is attractive but cannot compete with the Oriental cherries. The species is found in the great plains and tolerates rather inhospitable, hot, dry conditions. It prefers a well-drained soil. Many cultivars have been selected for fruit quality. Manitoba to Wyoming, south to Kansas and Colorado. Introduced 1892. Zone 3 to 6.

Prunus campanulata — Bell-flowered or Taiwan Cherry
(proo′nus kam-pan-ū-lā′tȧ)

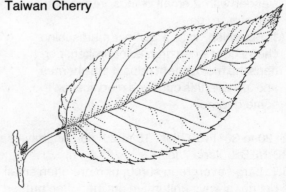

LEAVES: Alternate, simple, ovate, oval or slightly obovate, 2 1/2 to 4″ long, 1 to 1 3/4″ wide, slender-pointed, broadly wedge-shaped to slightly heart-shaped at the base, margins regularly set with fine forward-pointing or slightly incurved teeth, lustrous dark green, 6 to 8 vein pairs, glabrous; petiole—1/2 to 3/4″ long.

Prunus campanulata, Bell-flowered or Taiwan Cherry, is a small, graceful tree ranging from 20 to 30′ in height. The young leaves emerge rich green and become dark green at maturity and develop bronzy-red fall color. Before the leaves emerge, the deep rose, 3/4″ diameter flowers appear 2 to 6 together on 1/2 to 3/4″ long pedicels that arise from a 1 to 1 1/2″ long peduncle. The calyx tube is also deep rose and offers color after the petals have abscised. The red fruits are about 1/2″ long and about 3/8″ wide. In my mind, the flowers may be the most handsome of all ornamental cherries. I have seen flowers as early as late January in Athens, Georgia, but they usually open in February. I have been in Savannah on February 22 and the leaves were almost fully mature. In my garden the tree was in full leaf by mid March. Several years past I received a seedling from the late Mr. Jack Jones, Savannah, GA after admiring flowering trees in his garden. The tree is now 15′ high and as wide with 3 strong polished reddish brown trunks. It ranks as one of my all time favorites simply because it is the first to flower, late January 1989, and offers spectacular rose-carmine flowers. Because of the early flowering date, buds and/or flowers may be injured if they are too far open. Has flowered in early February along with *Hamamelis mollis.* This is a most effective combination, the bright yellow of the witchhazel and the rose-carmine of the cherry. Seeds will germinate in the spring following fall planting, I suspect a slight cold requirement is required. Early June cuttings, 5000 ppm KIBA, peat:perlite, mist, rooted 80%. It is probably best cultivated in the lower part of Zone 7 to 9. Temperatures of 0°F did not injure flower buds. 'Okame' with carmine-pink petals (March-April), a

rose-red calyx, and reddish flower stalks is hardier and very striking. Flowers are fully open by late February in Athens. It has performed well in the Middle Atlantic States and at the Georgia Botanical Garden. It is the result of a cross between *P. incisa* and *P. campanulata* raised by Collingwood Ingram. It definitely should be more widely planted for it also offers a good bronze to orange-red fall color.

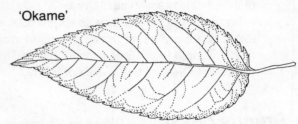

'Okame'

'Okame' received the prestigious Styer Award from the Pennsylvania Horticultural Society and is now common in commerce. Will mature between 20 and 30′ with a similar spread. *P. campanulata* is native to Formosa, southern China, Ryukyu Islands of Japan. Cultivated 1899. Zone (6)7 to 9.

Prunus caroliniana — Carolina Cherrylaurel
(proo′nus ka-ro-lin-i-ā′nȧ)

LEAVES: Alternate, simple, evergreen, oblong to oblong-lanceolate, 2 to 3″ (4″) long, 1″ wide, sharp apex, margin entire or with several spiny teeth toward apex, leaves on seedlings or young plants more toothed than those from mature plants, lustrous dark green; petiole— slender with 2 small glands, red in sun, green in shade.

STEM: Brownish, with a distinct maraschino cherry odor when bruised or broken, perhaps the most potent odor of the cherries and all have this odor or a modification to some degree.

SIZE: 20 to 30′ (40′) high, 15 to 25′ spread; have seen large trees 40′ high with a 30 to 40′ spread.
HARDINESS: Zone 7 to 10.
HABIT: Large evergreen shrub, or more often small tree of pyramidal-oval outline; usually dense and full but not always uniform in outline; often pruned into a hedge or screen.
RATE: Fast.
TEXTURE: Medium.
BARK: Dark gray to almost black.
LEAF COLOR: Lustrous dark green through the seasons, although will discolor in winter sun and wind; new growth rich yellow-green or bronze.

FLOWERS: Perfect, 5-petaled, white, sickenly fragrant, 1/4″ across, borne in 1 1/2 to 3″ long, 3/4 to 1″ wide racemes out of the leaf axils in March-April (usually late March to early April in Athens); flowers are not overwhelming but welcome by virtue of the early date.

FRUIT: Green maturing to lustrous dark black, 3/8 to 1/2″ diameter drupe, ripen in October, not particularly conspicuous as they are masked by the foliage; persist into winter and until flowering during the spring, abundant, birds deposit the seeds all over the landscape and consequently stray seedlings appear everywhere.

CULTURE: Easily transplanted, adaptable, prefers moist, well drained soils and here grows like a weed; pH adaptable; withstands heavy pruning; full sun to partial shade.

DISEASES AND INSECTS: Leaf spot, some damage from chewing insects, have not noticed any serious problems, subject to ice, snow, wind damage.

LANDSCAPE VALUE: Utilized widely for screens and hedges in the south; has been used to soften harsh vertical lines of large buildings; should not be planted too close to a residence, tends to overgrow its boundaries; used at Williamsburg by the early colonists; one of the few plants that can seed into a privet hedge and win; the weedy nature is something to be considered before making wholesale use of the plant; have seen it "everywhere" in the Coastal Plain of Georgia and South Carolina especially along fence rows and in waste areas, actually makes a pleasant small multiple-stemmed tree or large shrub.

CULTIVARS:

'Bright 'N Tight'—Compact tightly branched pyramidal form with smaller leaves than the species, leaves rarely have serrations, superior to the species for most situations; have seen 15 to 20 year old plants at Disneyworld about 20′ tall.

PROPAGATION: Seeds can be fall sown and will germinate the following spring; seeds with pulp removed, sown in November, germinated immediately; if a cold requirement exists it is indeed brief, probably 30 days would be sufficient. Softwood and greenwood cuttings will root and I suspect November-January or later hardwoods; cuttings collected on August 23 (Athens), 2000 ppm KIBA, 2 perlite:1 peat, mist, rooted only 50%.

ADDITIONAL NOTES: Distinct cherry odor is evident when stems are bruised; leaves carry a high concentration of hydrocyanic acid which makes the plant unpalatable and dangerous to livestock.

NATIVE HABITAT: Coastal Virginia to northern Florida and west to Louisiana.

RELATED SPECIES:

Prunus lusitanica, (proo′nus lū-si-tan′i-kȧ), Portuguese Cherrylaurel, is a large, bushy evergreen shrub or small tree 10 to 20′ high but occasionally larger. The ovate or oval, 2 1/2 to 5″ long, 1 1/4 to 2″ wide, glabrous, toothed, glossy dark green leaves are handsome throughout the year. The white, 1/3 to 1/2″ diameter fragrant flowers are produced in 6 to 10″ long, 1 to 1 1/4″ wide racemes in May-June from the ends of the previous season's growth 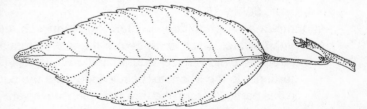 and from the axils of their leaves. The 1/3″ long, cone-shaped fruits are dark purple. This is a rather handsome plant and surprisingly has survived on the campus of Reinhart College, Walesca, Georgia where winter temperatures may range from 0 to -10°F. One reference reported that *P. lusitanica* was hardier than *P. laurocerasus.* There is a rather handsome variegated form but this is less hardy than the species. Spain, Portugal. Introduced 1648. Zone 7 to 9.

Prunus cerasifera — Cherry Plum or Myrobalan Plum
(proo′nus ser-as-if′ēr-à)

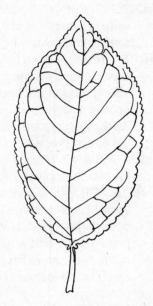

FAMILY: Rosaceae

LEAVES: Alternate, simple, ovate, elliptic or obovate, 1 1/2 to 2 1/2″ long, 1 to 1 1/4″ wide, apex pointed, broadly wedge-shaped or rounded, finely obtuse-serrate, glabrous above, green beneath, usually less than 6 vein pairs, pubescent on midrib and major veins beneath, petiole—about 1/2″ long; if glands are present they usually occur at base of the blade near the point of petiole attachment.

SIZE: 15 to 30′ by 15 to 25′.

HARDINESS: Zone (4)5 to 8.

HABIT: Small, shrubby tree, twiggy and rounded, with ascending, spreading branches.

RATE: Fast.

TEXTURE: Medium in all seasons.

LEAF COLOR: Light green in summer, no significant fall color.

FLOWERS: Perfect, white, 3/4 to 1″ across, sickeningly fragrant, sometime in April before the leaves, open around early to mid April (mid March in Athens); usually borne solitary.

FRUIT: Reddish, slightly bloomy edible drupe, approximately 1″ across, June, July or August.

CULTURE: This discussion applies to the *Prunus* species. Transplant bare root, balled and burlapped or container grown materials in spring; any average soil is acceptable but should be well drained; pH adaptable; full sun; prune after flowering although potential fruits will be cut off; keep trees vigorous as there are numerous serious insects and diseases associated with *Prunus;* they are not particularly pollution tolerant and in most cases are short-lived (approximately 20 years) although certain species are much more durable than others; if the gardener would think in decades instead of lifetimes the pleasurable experience of growing some of the *Prunus* would be just that.

DISEASES AND INSECTS: Almost hopeless to list them all but some of the worst include aphids, borers, scale, tent caterpillars, canker, leaf spots.

LANDSCAPE VALUE: The species has no value and is only known in cultivation, but the following cultivars are extensively (over-used) used for specimens, groupings, and in foundation plantings; there is something about a purple-leaved beast that excites people to spend money.

CULTIVARS:

'Alfred'—An unknown to me but described as white flowered, with 1 1/4″ wide fruit; upright spreading habit, 20′ by 15′.

'Atropurpurea'—Upright, dense branching form with reddish purple foliage and 3/4″ diameter, light pink flowers, which open before the leaves (usually); often called Pissard Plum ('Pissardii'); introduced into France around 1880 from Persia (now Iran) through the efforts of Mr. Pissard, gardener to the Shah; for best foliage color the purple-leaved forms should be sited in full sun; in this particular form the new unfolding leaves are ruby-red, later claret and finally dark reddish purple; the fruits are also purplish; it is shakily hardy in Zone 4 and a hard winter will produce some tip or branch dieback; found as a branch sport before 1880 and a number of selections have arisen from this selection either through hybridization or sports.

'Hessei'—Has narrow irregular reddish brown leaves with a yellowish margin and golden rim.

'Hollywood' (also called 'Trailblazer')—I have never been able to determine the exact nature of this selection and the literature is conflicting; flowers are light pink to white before the leaves, leaves dark green above, red purple below, distinct upright habit and may grow 30′ by 20′, red fruits 2 to 2 1/2″ wide, hybrid between *P. c.* 'Atropurpurea' and the 'Duarte' Japanese plum; have also seen the parentage listed as *P. cerasifera* 'Nigra' × 'Shiro' Japanese plum.

'Krauter Vesuvius'—Similar to 'Thundercloud' but more upright oval-rounded, light pink flowers before leaves, dark purple foliage, 20′ by 15′, supposedly quite heat tolerant.

'Mt. St. Helens'—A branch sport of 'Newport' with a straighter, stronger trunk, faster growing than 'Newport', leafs out earlier in spring, has longer and wider leaves than the parent, richer purple color that holds later in summer, flowers light pink, round headed tree, 20' by 20', a J. Frank Schmidt introduction.

'Newport'—Probably the hardiest of the purple-leaf types; a cross between *P. cerasifera* 'Atropurpurea' and the 'Omaha' Plum; introduced in 1923 by the University of Minnesota Horticultural Research Center; new growth light bronze-purple, finally changing to dark purple, pale pink to almost white flowers and dull purple 1" diameter fruits; a round-headed tree 15' (20') high; best in Zone 5 but can be grown in 4; appears to be the common form in the southern states, and has flowered before 'Atropurpurea' or *P.* × *cistena* even opened a single bud.

'Nigra'—Foliage very dark purple, color is retained through summer; flowers single, pink, 5/8" diameter; this may be the same as 'Vesuvius'; also 'Woodii' is similar.

'Purpusii'—Have seen several descriptions for the plant: the first called it a delicate scrambled mixture of plum-red and creamy white; the other bronze with yellow and pink variegation along the midrib and white flowers.

'Thundercloud'—Single pink flowers before the leaves, fragrant, retains its deep purple foliage through growing season; unfortunately not hardy at Madison, Wisconsin and I have observed injury at Urbana, IL, 20' by 20', introduced in 1987.

'Vesuvius'—Leaves dark green, well colored, large, similar to 'Nigra' but not as heavily flowered, perhaps hybridized by Luther Burbank.

PROPAGATION: *Prunus* seeds have an embryo dormancy and require a period of after-ripening to overcome it; generally 2 to 3 months at 40°F will suffice; seeds can also be cleaned and sown outdoors in fall with germination occurring the following spring. Cuttings show variable response depending on the species and cultivar; there is some indication that NAA may be more effective on *Prunus* than IBA but it is best to start with IBA and then experiment with NAA; in my own work, I have found the purple-leaf types easy to root with 1000 to 3000 ppm quick dip; this also applies to the evergreen *P. laurocerasus* and cultivars; *P.* 'Hally Jolivette' has proven easy; I know nurserymen who are producing 'Kwanzan', *P.* × *yedoensis* and others from softwood cuttings; from a practical standpoint it is better to establish many *Prunus* on their own roots to avoid possible graft incompatabilities; at Shadow Nursery, Winchester, TN, I have seen two-year-old rooted 'Kwanzan' cherries in the field that were 6 to 8' high; tremendous movement to own-root cherry and plum; slightly firmer cuttings seem to root in higher percentages than extremely soft May-June material, rooted cuttings will grow if lightly fertilized, overwintering does not appear to be a problem.

NATIVE HABITAT: Western Asia, Caucasia. Introduced before or about the 16th century.

RELATED SPECIES:

***Prunus* × *blireiana*,** (proo'nus blēr-ē-ā'nȧ), Blireiana Plum, is a hybrid between *P. cerasifera* 'Atropurpurea' and a double form of *P. mume*. It is a rounded, dense branching tree with reddish purple foliage that fades to green and double, light pink, 1" diameter flowers in March-April, before the leaves; fruits are purplish red and lost in the foliage so as not to be effective; 20' by 20'; Zone 5; put into commerce by Lemoine in 1906; 'Moseri' has deeper purple leaves and smaller flowers; strong growing.

***Prunus* × *cistena*,** (proo'nus × sis-tē'na), Purpleleaf Sand Cherry, is a cross between *P. pumila* and *P. cerasifera* 'Atropurpurea' and grows 7 to 10' tall usually with a slightly smaller spread. The foliage is intensely reddish purple and stays effective throughout summer. The flowers are single, pinkish, fragrant, borne after the leaves have developed in April-early May; fruits are blackish purple; Zone 2 to 8; introduced by Dr. N.E. Hansen of South Dakota State University in 1910; easily propagated from softwood cuttings; one of the hardiest purple leaf plants. 'Minnesota Red' has deeper red-

Prunus × *cistena*

dish purple leaf coloration that persists into fall. 'Big Cis' is a branch sport of *P.* × *cistena* that grows twice as fast producing a rounded dense 14′ by 12′ small tree, the reddish-purple leaves are larger, the trunk heavier. Flowers are pink like the parent. A J. Frank Schmidt introduction.

Prunus glandulosa — Dwarf Flowering Almond
(proo′nus glan-dū-lō′sa)

LEAVES: Alternate, simple, ovate-oblong or oblong to oblong-lanceolate, 1 to 3 1/2″ long, 3/4 to 1″ wide, acute, rarely acuminate, broad-cuneate at base, crenate-serrulate, medium green, glabrous beneath or slightly hairy on midrib;   petioles—1/4″ long; stipules linear with   gland-tipped teeth.

Prunus glandulosa, Dwarf Flowering Almond, is the bargain basement shrub of many discount stores. It grows 4 to 5′ tall and 3 to 4′ wide and is a spreading, weakly multi-stemmed, straggly shrub. The summer foliage is light green; flowers are pink or white, single or double; late April to early May, one or two together; fruits are dark pink-red, 1/2″ across and rarely produced; chief value is in the flower; basically a very poor plant, single season quality, appearing distraught and alone in summer, fall and winter; 'Alba' has pure white single flowers. 'Alba Plena' ('Alboplena') has double white flowers and 'Rosea Plena' ('Sinensis') double, 1 to 1/4″ diameter, pink; saw a single pink-white selection called 'Lawrence' in full flower in late March at Callaway Gardens, the double form nearby was still in tight bud; roots easily from cuttings. Central and northern China, Japan. Introduced 1835. Zone 4 to 8.

Prunus 'Hally Jolivette'
It is the result of a cross of *P. subhirtella* × *P.* × *yedoensis* backcrossed to *P. subhirtella* by Dr. Karl Sax of the Arnold Arboretum. It is a rounded, dense branching, shrubby tree growing 15′ and of relatively fine texture. The flowers are pink in bud, opening pinkish white, double, 1 1/4″ diameter and effective over a 10 to 20 day period in late April to early May as the flowers do not all open at once. I rooted a cutting and planted it in my Illinois garden. The plant grew 3′ or more a year and in the second year flowered. Still one of my favorite cherries and I have seen 20′ tall trees. Zone 5 to 7. 1940.

Prunus laurocerasus — Common Cherrylaurel, English Laurel
(proo′nus lâr-ō-sẽr-ā′sus)

LEAVES: Alternate, simple, evergreen, 2 to 6″ long, about 1/3 to 1/2 as wide, usually oblong or obovate-oblong, acuminate, cuneate to rounded at base, obscurely serrate to nearly entire, glabrous, lustrous medium to dark green above, two glands present on base of blade near point of attachment to petiole; petiole—1/2″ long.
BUDS: Solitary or collaterally multiple, sessile, subglobose or mostly ovoid with usually 6 exposed scales.

STEM: Slender or moderate, green, subterete or somewhat angled from the nodes, typical cherry odor when bruised; pith roundish or angled, pale or brown, continuous; leaf scars raised on a cushion flanked by the stipule vestiges or scars, half-round or half-elliptical, small; 3 bundle-traces, usually minute.

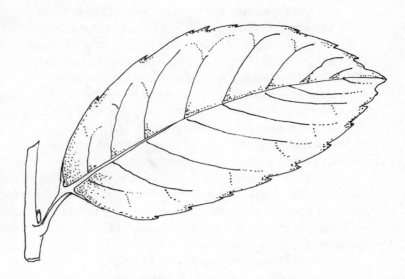

SIZE: Species can grow 10 to 18′ high and under ideal conditions might become 25 to 30′ wide but is smaller under cultivation and principally represented by the cultivars.

HARDINESS: Zone 6 to 8.

HABIT: Large, wide spreading evergreen shrub of solid, dense constitution, extremely bold element because of large lustrous dark green leaves.

RATE: Medium, 10′ in 5 to 6 years under good conditions.

TEXTURE: Medium in all seasons.

LEAF COLOR: Lustrous medium to dark green in summer; loses some of its sheen in cold climates.

FLOWERS: Perfect, white, each flower 1/4 to 1/3″ across, April-May, (early April, Athens) born in 2 to 5″ long, 3/4″ wide racemes from the leaf axils, sickeningly fragrant.

FRUIT: Conical-rounded drupe, purple to black, 1/3 to 1/2″ long, summer, often lost among the leaves.

CULTURE: Transplant balled and burlapped or from a container; lately I have seen most being sold in containers; although a great number of large plants are offered balled and burlapped from the West Coast; performs best in moist, well drained soil supplemented with organic matter; full sun or shade, salt spray tolerant; avoid excessive fertilization; withstands pruning very well.

DISEASES AND INSECTS: Not as susceptible to the problems which beset the tree *Prunus* but I have seen considerable foliage damage accomplished by insects, a shothole-type bacterium produces circular holes in the leaf that look like a shotgun was aimed at the plant; has become a significant problem in production nurseries where overhead watering is practiced, plants suffer from poorly drained soils and I have observed too many declining or dead plants because of this; several years past I was called to a large corporate site in Atlanta to assess the reason for many dying plants; 'Otto Luyken', a selection of the species was used in great numbers and bright brown plants were everywhere in evidence, plants were installed in January, I came in late May; I pulled one plant out of the ground and heard this slush, slosh, glush, glosh sound; obviously no drainage; moral: if the soil is not drained plant Baldcypress; root rot is also a problem that relates to inadequate drainage.

LANDSCAPE VALUE: Relatively handsome hedge plant; popular in the south; is not too successfully used north of Philadelphia; makes a good plant in the shade especially some of the cultivars, often used in groupings or masses; in fact, 'Otto Luyken' may be massed 50 to 100 in one location.

CULTIVARS: Numerous cultivars have been described from Europe. I have presented only those which are grown in this country or I have seen in my travels.

'Caucasica Nana'—Small compact shrub with full erect branching habit and thickly textured rich green leaves.

'Magnoliifolia' ('Latifolia', 'Macrophylla')—Large form with 10 to 12″ long, 3 to 4 1/2″ wide leaves; it may be trained into a tree; Dick Ammons, Florence, KY, mentioned that this was a shiny-leaved, hardy form; a massive 20 to 25′ high, 1 1/2 to 2 times as wide specimen has prospered at Kew Gardens, leaves remind of *Magnolia grandiflora* and are extremely lustrous, almost black-green; for textural effect this is a superb plant.

'Mt. Vernon'—Small, compact, 3' high and wide form with large species type leaves; I got so excited the first time I saw the plant at Carlson Nursery in Oregon; Mr. Carlson gave me 5 cuttings and all rooted, 5 years later in my garden the plants are 8 to 10" tall, grows very slowly and might be a good plant in a rock garden; Raulston suggests 3 to 5' high and 5 to 8' wide with age but J.C. and I will be pushing up Katsuratrees by that time.

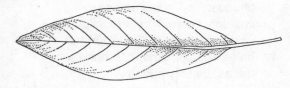

'Otto Luyken'—Quite a fine form of compact habit, leaves dark green, 4" long, about 1" wide; very free flowering; have seen it in heavy shade where it flowered profusely; grows 3 to 4' high and may spread 6 to 8'; introduced about 1968 by Hesse Nurseries, Weiner, Hanover, Germany, have seen 6' high by 10' wide plants in England, easily separated from 'Schipkaensis' and 'Zabeliana' because of the way the leaves are disposed at an upward, 60 to 45° angle to the stem. In the other two cultivars the leaves are more or less perpendicular to the stem or slightly drooping, usually the leaves of this form are not toothed toward the apex.

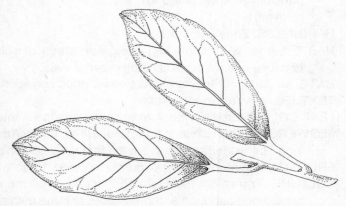

'Schipkaensis'—A dark green, narrow-leaved form found near the Shipka Pass in Bulgaria; it is probably the hardiest of the cherrylaurels and I have observed plants with good foliage after a winter of -6°F; the leaves are 2 to 4 1/2" long and 3/4 to 1 1/2" wide; it is more refined than the species and forms a rather wide-spreading plant at maturity probably seldom growing more than 4 to 5' (10') high; leaves may be entire or show only a few teeth toward the apex; Zone 5 to 8; at least 3 other 'Schipkaensis' forms are known and differ in growth habit, size and leaf characteristics.

'Variegata'—Leaves resembling those of the species and conspicuously mottled and variegated with creamy white, fairly robust and attractive, Zone 6 or 7, tends to revert; several white blotched and dotted forms are known, have seen them in Europe but not in the U.S.

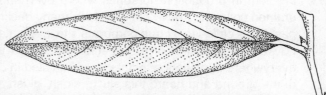

'Zabeliana'—Leaves dark green, narrow, entire, willow-like and, quite similar to 'Schipkaensis', very free flowering, may grow to 3' and spread 12'; plants 5' high and 25' wide are known; makes a good ground cover in dense shade; Zone 5 and does quite well in the south; put into commerce by Späth in 1898, along with 'Schipkaensis', the hardiest form, interestingly, laboratory hardiness tests indicated this was the most cold hardy cultivar.

PROPAGATION: Cuttings taken in late summer rooted 90 percent in sand:peat in 7 weeks without treatment; have rooted this successfully many times; seed requires a 2 to 3 month cold treatment, and radicles often emerge in the stratification medium; cuttings of the clone mentioned under additional notes were taken in early June and early July, 3000 and 5000 ppm IBA quick dip, respectively, peat:perlite, mist, with 100% rooting 4 weeks later.

ADDITIONAL NOTES: Collected seeds from 'Otto Luyken' in Oregon and grew 100 seedlings, saved the best four and planted them in my garden, only one proved superior with lustrous dark green foliage and tight rounded habit with leaves like 'Schipkaensis', interestingly none were similar to 'Otto Luyken'.

NATIVE HABITAT: Southeastern Europe and Asia Minor. Introduced 1576.

Prunus maackii — Amur Chokecherry
(proo'nus mak'ē-ī)

LEAVES: Alternate, simple, elliptic to oblong-ovate, 2 to 4″ long, acuminate, rounded, finely serrate, medium green, gland dotted below, and slightly hairy on veins; petiole—1/2″ long.

Prunus maackii, Amur Chokecherry, is an interesting, rounded, to almost mop-headed, dense branching tree that grows 35 to 45′ high. I have seen young trees that were pyramidal but with age the outline becomes more rounded. Although seldom credited with good flower characteristics, the white flowers occur in 2 to 3″ long racemes in great profusion around early to mid May. Numerous small, 1/4″ diameter red maturing to black fruits ripen in August. The bark is beautiful and I have seen all kinds of combinations and permutations. My first exposure to this tree occurred at the Royal Botanical Garden, Hamilton, Ontario, and on that tree the bark was a rich cinnamon brown and actually exfoliated in shaggy masses. Other trees I have seen showed minimal exfoliation. The color varies from brownish yellow to reddish brown to the cinnamon brown mentioned above. There are several magnificent trees near the old shrub collection at the Arnold and these will make believers out of any gardener. The tree requires a well drained soil and is best suited to cold climates. It can be rooted from June-July softwoods. Introduced 1878. Zone 2 to 6.

Prunus mandshurica — Manchurian Apricot (now *P. armeniaca* var. *mandshurica*)
(proo'nus man-shūr'i-kȧ)

LEAVES: Alternate, simple, broad-elliptic to ovate, 2 to 5″ long, acuminate, rounded or broad-cuneate, sharply and doubly serrate, with narrow elongated teeth, green beneath and glabrous except axillary tufts of hairs; petioles 1″ long, puberulous.

Prunus mandshurica, Manchurian Apricot, is a small (15 to 20′), spreading, round-headed tree that is most noteworthy for the single, pinkish, 1 1/4″ diameter flowers that occur in April or early May before the leaves. It is rather handsome in flower and where peach and other *Prunus* cannot be relied upon for flower this species might be considered. Manchuria, Korea. Cultivated 1900. Zone 3 or 4 and south.

Prunus maritima — Beach Plum
(proo'nus mȧ-rit'i-mȧ)

LEAVES: Alternate, simple, ovate or elliptic, 1 1/2 to 3″ long, 3/4 to 1 1/4″ wide, acute, cuneate, sharply serrate, dull green and glabrous above, paler and soft pubescent below; petiole—1/4″ long, pubescent, often glandular.

Prunus maritima, Beach Plum, is a rounded, dense suckering shrub growing to 6′ high and more. The flowers are white, single or double, 1/2″ across, May, 2 to 3 together; fruits dull purple, sometimes crimson, 1/2 to 1″ diameter, bloomy, ripening in August and relished for jams and jellies. This species abounds on Cape Cod, Massachusetts and is one of the Cape Codder's cherished plants. A good salt tolerant species which grows along the coast from Maine to Virginia. Introduced 1818. Zone 3 to 6. Variety *flava* is a yellow fruited form apparently found wild on the Cape.

Prunus mume — Japanese Apricot
(proo'nus mū'may)

LEAVES: Alternate, simple, broad-ovate to ovate, 2 to 4″ long, long acuminate, broad cuneate, finely and sharply serrate, rich green above, pubescent on veins below; petiole—1/2 to 3/4″ long, glandular.
STEM: Polished, shining green, glabrous.

Prunus mume, Japanese Apricot, is a favorite of Dr. J. C. Raulston's and his continuous exhortations have enthused me to the point that the plant must be included. Prior to J.C.'s proselytizing, I had only seen the plant once at the Missouri Botanic Garden in summer and all I remember was the polished green stems. However, in February of 1989, my graduate student and I discovered a double pink form in flower in the University's Botanical Garden. I have been converted. The habit is rounded with long, supple, green stems that produce 1 to 1 1/4″ diameter fragrant, pale rose flowers, singly or in pairs on naked stems in January-March. Chief attraction is the winter flowering character and the plant becomes obscure later. Have read several interesting thoughts on pruning the plant to obtain best flower. Cut back after flowering to produce long branches which will form next year's flower buds. From here, cut half the branches back every year so a guaranteed crop of flowers will be present while the other half (not cut back) will produce heavy bud set the following summer. Fruits are inedible, yellowish, globose, 1 to 1 1/4″ diameter drupes. A well drained reasonably fertile acid soil in full sun suits it best. Raulston mentioned that the Japanese have over 250 named cultivars in white, pink, rose, red, in single and double forms, on plants up to 20′ high. Habit may be normal, fastigiate, corkscrew or pendulous. Interestingly, almost impossible to locate in commerce in the United States but a few nurserymen are starting to grow the species. W.B. Clarke of California apparently selected a number of forms. Cultivars include 'Alba Plena' with double white flowers, 'Dawn' with large ruffled double pink flowers, 'Matsurabara Red' has double dark red flowers, 'Peggy Clarke' bears double deep rose flowers with extremely long stamens and red calyx, 'Rosemary Clarke' has double white flowers with red calyces, early to flower, 'W.B. Clarke' offers double pink flowers on a weeping plant. Easily rooted from softwood cuttings in summer. Seed requires a brief cold moist stratification. Japan, China. Introduced 1844. Zone 6 to 9, 10 in California.

Prunus nigra — Canada Plum
(proo'nus nī'gra)

LEAVES: Alternate, simple, elliptic to obovate, 2 to 4″ long, half as wide, acuminate, broad-cuneate to subcordate, coarsely and doubly obtuse-serrate, dark green and glabrous above, pubescent or nearly glabrous beneath, petiole—1/2 to 1″ long with two glands near point of attachment to blade.

Prunus nigra, Canada Plum, is a small 20 to 30′ high upright branched narrow headed tree. White, 1 1/4″ diameter flowers occur 3 to 4 together in the leaf axils on 1/2″ long reddish pedicels before the leaves in April-May. The fruit is a 1 to 1 1/4″ long, oval, yellowish red to red drupe. 'Princess Kay' is a double white flowered form that was found by Catherine Nyland in the wild in Itasca County, MN; the plant was introduced by the Minnesota Landscape Arboretum. It flowers heavily as a young plant and produces red fruit in August. The prominent lenticels, in combination with the black bark, add winter interest. Northeast and upper midwest into Canada. Introduced 1773. Zone 2 to 5(6)

Prunus padus — European Birdcherry
(proo'nus pā'dus)

LEAVES: Alternate, simple, obovate to elliptic, 2 1/2 to 5″ long, 1 1/2 to 2″ wide, apex abruptly taper pointed, base wedge-shaped, rounded or slightly cordate, teeth fine, very sharp, dull dark green above, grayish and hairless beneath or with axillary tufts; petiole 1/2 to 3/4″ long, glabrous, with 2 or more glands.

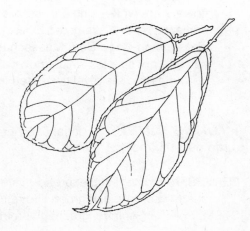

Prunus padus, European Birdcherry, is a medium sized (30 to 40′), rounded, low branched tree with ascending branches. The foliage is a dull dark green in summer and may become yellow to bronze in fall. The flowers are white, fragrant, 1/3 to 1/2″ across, mid April to early May; borne in drooping, loose, 3 to 6″ long racemes. The fruit is black, 1/4 to 1/3″ diameter drupe, July to August. This is one of the first trees to leaf out and the new, lustrous light green leaves are a welcome sight after a difficult winter. Black knot disease has been serious in Minnesota and would be a limiting factor in the use of the species. A pretty tree that flowers after the leaves have matured, somewhat diminishing the overall effectiveness. Several cultivars include:

'Albertii'—Pyramidal to rounded 30′ high tree, supposedly good for street tree use, Zone 3.

'Berg'—Tight globe headed form to 25′ high, new growth green quickly turning to crimson all summer, white flowers in 5 to 8″ long racemes, Zone 2.

'Colorata'—Offers bronze colored new leaves that turn dark green above, purplish below, stems are dark purple, flowers light pink.

var. *commutata*—Individual flowers 1/2″ in diameter and flowers 3 weeks before normal birdcherries.

'Plena'—Flowers large and double, remaining effective longer than any other form.

'Spaethii'—Racemes somewhat pendulous.

'Summer Glow'—Excellent red-purple leaf color through summer, strong semi-spreading growth habit has not exhibited suckering that is common to Schubert or Canada Red Chokecherry, well adapted to urban sites, 50′ by 35′, Zone 3 to 7, a Wandell introduction.

'Watereri'—Racemes 8″ long, quite effective in flower, have seen at Niagara Falls and was taken by the long and rather beautiful flowers.

NATIVE HABITAT: Europe, northern Asia, to Korea and Japan. Zone 3 to 6. Long cultivated.

Prunus pensylvanica — Pin or Wild Red Cherry
(proo′nus pen-sil-van′i-k à)

LEAVES: Alternate, simple, ovate, 3 to 4 1/2″ long, 3/4 to 1 1/4″ wide, long pointed, sharply serrate, teeth incurved and gland tipped, lustrous dark green, glabrous; petiole 1/2″ long, with 1 or 2 glands.
STEM: Slender, shining, glabrous, reddish, aromatic when bruised.

Prunus pensylvanica, Pin or Wild Red Cherry, is a small, slender, often shrubby tree with branches spreading at a broad angle forming a round-topped, oblong head. Size varies from 25 to 40′ in height by 18 to 25′ in spread. This is a very rapid grower and can quickly develop in abandoned areas. The leaves are a lustrous deep green in summer changing to yellow and red in fall. The flowers are white, 1/2″ across, May-June, borne in 2 to 5-flowered umbels or short racemes. Fruit is a light red, 1/4″ diameter, globose, sour drupe which ripens in July through August. Very adaptable species as it forms a pioneer association on cut-over or burned-over forest lands; intolerant of shade and soon yields to other species. A useful "nurse" type tree much in the mold of Gray Birch in this respect. 'Jumping Pond' is a form with drooping branches but it suffers from a leaf spot disease. 'Stockton' is a double-flowered, compact, round-headed form; the leaves turn red in fall. Native from Labrador west to British Columbia, south to North Carolina and Colorado. Introduced 1773. Zone 2 to 5(6).

Prunus persica — Common Peach
(proo′nus pĕr′si-kà)

LEAVES: Alternate, simple, elliptic-lanceolate or oblong-lanceolate, broadest about or slightly above the middle, 3 to 6″ long, 3/4 to 1 1/2″ wide, long-acuminate, broad cuneate, serrate or serrulate, glabrous, lustrous dark green; petioles 1/2″ long, glandular.

STEM: Offers a valid identification characteristic for the upper portion is often reddish while the lower part
is greenish, has a somewhat grainy appearance, glabrous.

Prunus persica, Peach, as most people know, yields luscious, succulent, tasty fruit in summer. Yet the
production of peaches is a highly specialized and technical art demanding considerable time,
investment and luck. Peaches are notoriously susceptible to insect and disease pests. The Common
Peach grows from 15 to 25′ tall and usually develops a spread equal to or greater than its height.
The habit is best described as one of ascending limbs and a low, broad, globular crown. The flowers
are pink, 1 to 1 1/2″ across, usually solitary, and develop in April (mid to late March, Athens) before
the leaves. Actually, a mature peach orchard in flower is a magnificent experience. Flowers are often
injured in cold winters or by late frosts. The fruit is a large, 3″ diameter, almost globular, yellow and/or
reddish, pubescent drupe which matures in June-July into August. Peaches present many problems
culturally and the homeowner should not be discouraged if they fail. The best approach is to avoid
peaches altogether. There are many single, semi-double or double flowered forms of the common
peach which are beautiful in flower but almost impossible to keep in good condition. The colors range
from white through pink to deep red to variegated. I watched a double pink peach flower spectacularly
for several years but consistent munching by the borers resulted in the death of the tree. The
temptation to buy these forms based on flower alone is overwhelming, but one's enthusiasm must
be tempered with the knowledge that the peach is prone to insects and disease. The peach is native
to China and has been cultivated since ancient times. Ideally provide well drained, acid, moist soil
and full sun. Zone 5 to 9. There are numerous cultivars of both the fruiting and double-flowered forms
and it is wise to check with the local nurseryman for the best types for your area. A few forms that I
have observed and/or are offered through the nursery industry include:

'Alba Plena'—Rather handsome double white form, flowers 2 to 2 1/2″ diameter and last 2 to 3 times
as long as single forms, occasional fruits are set, have heard it will come partially true to type
from seed; a fine form on the Georgia campus is 20′ by 20′, appears more resistant to insect
and disease problems.

'Early Double Pink', 'Early Double Red', 'Early Double White'—All offer the respective colors and
multiple petals early in the season.

'Helen Borchers'—Clear pink, 2 1/2″ wide flowers, late; have also seen this listed as semidouble with
rose flowers.

'Peppermint Stick'—I remember trying to sell this form 20 years past at a garden center in Columbus,
OH; flowers confused, being red and white striped, white or red often all on the same branch,
double.

'Royal Red Leaf' ('Foliis Rubris')—Reddish purple young leaves deepening to maroon, flowers deep
pink, fruit red-purple with a white flesh, edible; has been used as a rootstock to separate the
scion growth more easily, if all red obviously the graft or bud did not take.

'Weeping Double Pink', 'Weeping Double Red', 'Weeping Double White'—Have seen a few of these
types and generally they lack vigor or a strong constitution, perhaps in containers or as an
accent but with limited long term value.

Prunus sargentii — Sargent Cherry
(proo′nus sâr-jen′tē-i)

LEAVES: Alternate, simple, elliptic-
obovate to oblong-obovate, 3 to
5″ long, about one-half as wide,
long acuminate, rounded or
sometimes subcordate at base,
sharply serrate with acuminate
teeth, purplish or bronzy when

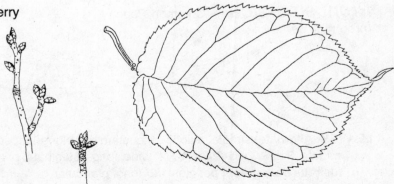

unfolding, dark green above, glabrous and glaucescent beneath; petiole 1/2 to 1″ long with 2 to 4 glands near the blade.
BUDS: Imbricate, conical-ovoid, reddish brown, sharply pointed, clustered at apex, often two buds at the nodes, one perhaps floral, the other vegetative.
STEM: Moderate, glabrous, reddish brown, marked with prominent lenticels, large gray-brown areas on stem.
BARK: Genuinely attractive, rich polished reddish to chestnut brown and marked with extended horizontal lenticels.

Prunus sargentii, Sargent Cherry, is one of the most useful cherries available. It grows 40 to 50′ in height with a spread approximately equal to height. Under cultivation 20 to 30′ high and wide would be more logical. The foliage is an excellent shiny dark green in summer and changes to bronze or red in the fall. The new leaves are reddish tinged as they emerge. The bark is rich, polished reddish to chestnut brown. The flowers are single pink, 1 1/4 to 1 1/2″ across; late April to early May; borne in 2 to 6 flowered sessile umbels on 1 to 1 1/4″ long pedicels. Fruit is a 1/3″ long, purple-black drupe which ripens in June and July. Both the species and 'Columnaris' (a narrow, columnar clone) have proved excellent in evaluations at the Shade Tree Evaluation Plots at Wooster, Ohio. I watched this most beautiful tree throughout the seasons at the Arnold Arboretum and decided it was the handsomest of the larger tree types for the northern states. The rich pink flowers open ahead of the leaves producing a frothy pink mass in the early spring landscape. Tremendous tree to work into a large border and perhaps underplant with bulbs and complimentary shrubs. Fall color as mentioned is superb for a cherry and often carries a mixture of yellow-bronze-red. Native to Japan. Introduced 1890. Zone 4 to 7. Perhaps the best of the larger cherries for general landscape use. 'Columnaris' forms an upright columnar to narrow vase-shape, although most trees I have seen were more vase-shaped than true columnar. Will probably grow 25 to 35′ by 10 to 15′. Flowers and foliage are similar to the species. 'Rancho' is narrower than 'Columnaris', 25′ by 5′ with large deeper pink flowers than the species, and was introduced by Ed Scanlon. Other selections with *P. sargentii* as one parent include:
'Accolade'—Semidouble, 12 to 15 petals, deep rose-pink in bud, opening blush pink, 1 1/2″ across, on 3/4 to 1″ long pedicels, dark green deeply serrated leaves, habit is open spreading, 20 to 25′, *P. sargentii* × *P. subhirtella.*
'Hillieri'—Single, blush pink, 1 1/4″ diameter flowers are borne on slender long hairy pedicels, leaves bronzy when emerging, later dark green, double toothed, hairy on veins below, developing good bronze-red fall color, broad-rounded tree, 25 to 30′ high and wide, probably *P. sargentii* × *P. × yedoensis.*
'Spire' ('Hillier Spire')—Soft pink flowers on a fastigiate tree, 27′ high, 10′ wide after 30 years, a sister seedling of 'Hillieri', yellow, orange, red fall color, originated around 1935.

Prunus serotina — Black Cherry
(proo′nus ser-ot′i-na)

LEAVES: Alternate, oblong-ovate to lance-oblong, 2 to 5″ long, 1 to 1 3/4″ wide, acuminate, cuneate, serrulate with small incurved callous teeth, lustrous medium to dark green above, light green beneath and often villous along the midrib; petioles—1/4 to 1″ long, glandular.

Prunus serotina, Black Cherry, is a common sight over much of the eastern United States. Distinctly pyramidal to conical in youth becoming oval-headed with pendulous branches, commonly growing

50 to 60′ tall but occasionally reaching 100′. The leaves are a lustrous dark green in summer and often a good yellow to red in fall. Flowers are white, 1/3″ across, May (April—Athens), borne in pendulous, 4 to 6″ long, 3/4″ diameter racemes. Fruits are red, changing to black, 1/3″ across, ripening in August and September and have a bitter-sweet and wine-like flavor and are often used for making wine and jelly. Valuable timber tree making its best growth on deep, moist, fertile soils but is also found growing on rather dry, gravelly, or sandy soils in the uplands. 'Spring Sparkle' has a dense growth habit with a decided weeping effect; abundance of white racemes in May-June, lustrous deep green leaves turn yellow to brilliant wine-red in October, 35-year-old tree was 26′ high and 22′ wide, a Wandell introduction. Can be a troublesome pest in the garden because of weedy, aggressive nature. Ontario to North Dakota, Texas and Florida. Introduced 1629. Zone 3 to 9.

Prunus serrula
(proo′nus ser′ū-là)

LEAVES: Alternate, simple, lanceolate, 2 to 4″ long, 1/2 to 1 1/4″ wide, long acuminate, rounded, finely and regularly serrated, lustrous dark green and glabrous above, pubescent along midrib or in vein axils below, 9 to 15 vein pairs; petiole—1/4 to 1/2″ long with 3 to 4 glands.

Prunus serrula is a small pyramidal to rounded tree growing 20 to 30′ high but seldom attains this size in the United States because of cankers, borers, etc. The main ornamental asset is the glistening surface of the red-brown, mahogany-like bark which ultimately peels. Flowers are white, 2/3″ diameter, produced in 2's and 3's, May, with the foliage. Fruit is a 1/2″ long red drupe. Very difficult to find commercially but worth seeking. Handsome in winter when the bark is maximally exposed. When properly grown it makes a tree of great beauty. Central China. Introduced 1908. Zone 5 to 6.

Prunus serrulata — Japanese Flowering Cherry, Oriental Cherry
(proo′nus ser-ū-lā′ta)

LEAVES: Alternate, simple, ovate to ovate-lanceolate, rarely obovate, 2 to 5″ long, 1 1/4 to 2 1/2″ wide, abruptly long acuminate, cuneate or rounded, serrate or often serrate with aristate teeth,

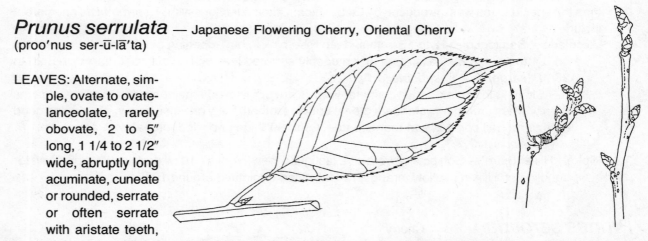

glabrous, reddish brown or bronze when unfolding, lustrous dark green; petiole—1/2 to 1″ long, usually with 2 to 4 glands, glabrous.

Prunus serrulata, Japanese Flowering Cherry or Oriental Cherry, is a large tree growing 50 to 75′; however, it is not a factor in the modern landscape for the numerous cultivars are much preferable. Most cultivars grow 20 to 25′ (35′) with a vase-shaped to rounded outline. The new foliage is often reddish tinged and eventually changes to lustrous dark green at maturity. Fall color is often a good bronze to subdued red. The flowers are greatly variable but range from single to doubles, white to pinks, and from 1/2 to 2 1/2″ diameter. They usually flower in April (mid April—Athens) to early May and are borne profusely along the stems, usually before or with the leaves. They are usually grafted on *P. avium,* Mazzard Cherry, at heights of 4 to 6′. The origin of many of the cultivars is lost to antiquity. I suggest the reader consult Wyman, Bean, Wilson and Ingram for a detailed discussion. Although the cultivars are not all true selections from *P. serrulata,* they are often treated that way for convenience.

'Amanogawa'—A form with the Lombardy Poplar type growth habit; flowers fragrant, pink, single to semi-double; sometimes developing the small black fruits; emerging leaves yellowish green, 20′ high, 4 to 5′ wide.

'Daikoku'—Double (+40 petals), deep pink, throat with light pink tinge, yellowish green new growth, open spreading habit, 30′, Zone 5.

'Fugenzo'—2 1/2″ diameter, rosy pink flowers fading to light pink, double with about 30 to 35 petals; leaves finely toothed, rich-coppery colored when young; habit spreading with a rounded crown.

'Hokusai'—Heavy semi-double (up to 12 petals), 2″ diameter, light pink to apricot, young leaves bronze, dark green and leathery at maturity, orange-red in fall; large rounded to spreading habit, 15 to 20′ by 30 to 35′.

'Kofugen'—Deep double pink, more stiffly upright and dense than 'Kwanzan', 25 to 30′ by 15 to 18′, in essence similar to 'Kwanzan' but more upright in habit, Zone 5.

'Kwanzan' ('Kanzan', 'Sekiyama', 'Hisakura')—The most popular and probably hardiest of all the double types; deep pink, double (30 petals), 2 1/2″ diameter flowers; very free flowering and utilized abundantly from Boston to Atlanta for every conceivable purpose; the new leaves are bronzy and may turn a good orange-bronze in fall; it is often grafted on *P. avium* about 4 to 6′ high and ends up looking like a manufactured tree; I have observed it on streets, along walks, etc., and it provides the uniformity (more or less) that every landscape architect dreams about; when grown on its own roots it makes a 30 to 40′ high and wide tree of great character and beauty; there is a splendid specimen on the Swarthmore campus; suffers from canker, virus and borers, often short lived.

'Mt. Fuji' ('Shirotae')—Pink in bud, open to white, fragrant, semi-double, 2″ wide, produced early; leaves pale green with a slight bronze tinge in youth; spreading habit, 15′ by 20′ or greater, Zone 5.

'Shirofugen'—Flowers pink in bud, white when open but aging to pink, 30 petals, leaves deep bronze when young; flat topped, wide-spreading crown, vigorous grower.

'Shogetsu' ('Shimidsu')—Double, 2″ diameter, blush pink flowers lighten to pure white, 30 petals, 3 to 6 flowers in long stalked corymbs, new leaves bronze-brown, serrations ending in long threadlike bristles, rounded habit, 18′.

'Tai Haku' (Great White Cherry)—Single white, 2 to 2 1/2″ diameter flowers, reddish bronze leaves when unfolding, up to 8″ long, turning yellow-orange in fall, coarsely branched, broad inverted cone shaped habit, 20 to 25′, slightly wider, Zone 5.

'Taoyama' ('Tao-yama', 'Taoyame')—Semidouble (up to 20 petals), soft shell pink, deep bronze emerging leaves, informal loose globe-like habit, 20′ high and wide-spreading, Zone 5.

'Ukon'—Semidouble to double, large, 1 3/4″ diameter greenish yellow flowers, new growth supposedly reddish brown but photographs indicate more greenish than brown.

No doubt the oriental cherries are among the most beautiful of all spring flowering trees. Unfortunately, 'Kwanzan' dominates the market when many other fine forms are available. In Japan, these cherries are called 'Sato Zakura', meaning "domestic cherries". Interestingly, I perused about 20 shade and ornamental tree nurseries and found only 'Amanogawa', Kwanzan', 'Mt. Fuji' and 'Shirofugen' listed. Growers are now rooting cuttings with variable success but firm wooded cuttings of 'Mt. Fuji' collected in late June, 1000 ppm KIBA, peat:perlite, mist rooted 22%. Japan, China, Korea. Zone 5 to 6 and south depending on the clone.

Prunus subhirtella — Higan Cherry
(proo′nus sub-hĕr-tel′lȧ)

LEAVES: Alternate, simple, ovate to oblong-ovate, 1 to 4″ long, about 1/2 as wide, acuminate, cuneate, sharply and often doubly serrate, lustrous dark green above, pubescent on veins beneath, with about 10 pairs of veins; petiole—1/4″ long, pubescent, glandular.

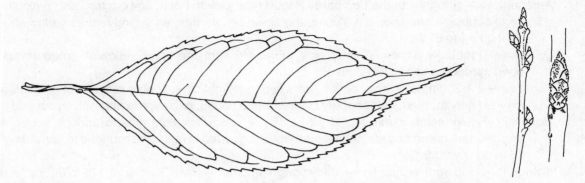

Prunus subhirtella, Higan Cherry, is seldom cultivated in the species form but is represented by the types var. *pendula,* var. *autumnalis,* and 'Yae-shidare-higan'. These types grow 20 to 40′ with a spread of 15 to 30′ or more. The var. *pendula,* Weeping Higan Cherry, is usually grafted about 6′ on the understock. The habit is gracefully weeping with single pink, 1/2″ diameter flowers in March-April (mid to late March, Athens) before the leaves, borne in 2 to 5-flowered umbels. The fruits are oval-rounded, 1/3″ diameter, red maturing to shining black. The var. *autumnalis* has semi-double (10 petals) pink flowers about 3/4″ in diameter which during a warm fall will open sporadically and then fully flower the following spring. Flowers are deep pink in bud, open to light pink and finally almost white. The habit on this tree is more like the species with forked trunk and erect twiggy branches with slender whiplike twigs. The cultivar 'Yae-shidare-higan' is a double-pink (20 to 25 petals) flowered type with pendulous branches and is quite floriferous with longer lasting flowers than var. *pendula.* The species is a very variable one giving rise to many different forms and flower colors. Variety *pendula* comes somewhat true from seed and selections such as 'Pendula Rosea' (pink flowers), 'Pendula Rubra' (deeper pink flowers), and 'Pendula Plena Rosea' (same as 'Yae-shidare-higan') have been selected. The double-pink weeping forms are attractive and the flowers last longer than those of var. *pendula.* 'Rosy Cloud' (same as 'Pink Cloud') has large, double, deep pink flowers, habit like 'Autumnalis', supposedly a cross between double weeping and 'Autumnalis', makes a good street or lawn tree. 'Whitcomb' is described as wide-spreading, horizontally branched with single pink flowers that fade to white, grows 20 to 25′ high, 30′ wide. Japan. Introduced 1894. Zone 4 to 8(9). Cherries are often described as short lived and many fit that tenet; however, the *P. subhirtella* types are among the most cold, heat, and stress tolerant of the group. Once establish, they are long lived, and offer the garden a sublimal quality unavailable from other ornamental trees. I can conjure visions of superb trees in the east, midwest, and south, especially 'Pendula' which even if it never flowered would be garden worthy. 'Pendula' might be likened to poor man's Weeping European Beech, with the artistically weeping gray-brown prominently horizontal-lenticelled branches. Growth rate is extremely fast and one does not have to wait until retirement to appreciate the ornamental virtues. The various cultivars can be rooted from firm wood cuttings in June and July.

Prunus tenella — Dwarf Russian Almond
(proo′nus te-nel′à)

LEAVES: Alternate, simple, obovate or oblong, 1 1/2 to 3 1/2″ long, 1/2 to 1″ wide, saw toothed, lustrous dark green above, pale beneath, glabrous; petiole 1/6″ long.

Prunus tenella, Dwarf Russian Almond, is a low, suckering shrub that may grow 2 to 5′ high. The principal value resides in the rosy-red, 1/2″ long, 1/2″ wide flowers that occur singly or up to 3 from each bud of the previous year's growth. 'Alba' has white flowers; 'Gessleriana' has intensely red, almost 1″ diameter flowers; and 'Fire Hill' which has been offered commercially in the U.S. has intense red flowers. These plants may be short-lived in American gardens. Southeastern Europe, western Asia to eastern Siberia. Introduced 1683. Zone 2 to 6.

Prunus tomentosa — Manchu Cherry, Nanking Cherry
(proo'nus tō-men-tō'så)

LEAVES: Alternate, simple, obovate to elliptic, 2 to 3″ long, 3/4 to 1 1/2″ wide, abruptly acuminate, unequally serrate, rugose, dull dark green and pubescent above, densely villous beneath; petiole 1/12 to 1/6″ long, glandular.

STEM: Covered with a soft villous pubescence.

Prunus tomentosa, Manchu or Nanking Cherry, is a broad spreading, densely twiggy shrub, becoming more open, irregular and picturesque with age. It grows 6 to 10′ high and spreads to 15′. The bark is shiny reddish brown and exfoliating. Leaves are dark green in summer and extremely tomentose on the lower surface. The flowers are pinkish in bud changing to white, fragrant, 3/4″ across; early to mid-April; one of the earliest flowering *Prunus* species. The fruits are scarlet, 1/3″ across, edible, ripening in June through July. Could be used in mass plantings or the shrub border for the early flowers and fruits are valuable. North and western China, Japan. Cultivated 1870. Zone 2 to 7? 'Leucocarpa' has white fruits. Seeds require about 2 months cold.

Prunus triloba var. *multiplex* — Double Flowering Plum, Flowering Almond
(proo'nus trī-lō'ba mul'ti-pleks)

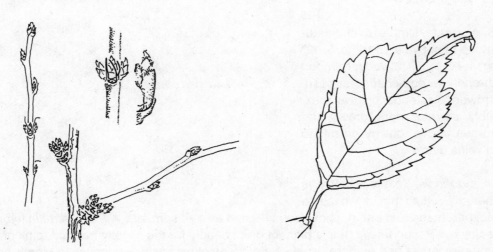

LEAVES: Alternate, simple, broad-elliptic to obovate, 1 to 2 1/2″ long, 3/4 to 1 1/4″ wide, acuminate or sometimes 3-lobed at apex, broad cuneate at base, coarsely and double serrate, medium green above, slightly pubescent beneath; petiole—1/2″ long, often with thread-like stipules.

Prunus triloba var. *multiplex,* Double Flowering Plum, is a large (12 to 15′), cumbersome, clumsy shrub with tree-like qualities. The foliage is medium green in summer and turns yellow to bronze in fall. The flowers are double, pinkish, about 1 to 1 1/2″ across, borne in April. They are often nipped by a late freeze and severely injured. I have never seen any fruit on the plants. This species has always been somewhat confusing. Rehder listed the double flowering type as *P. t.* var. *multiplex* and noted this was or is the original *P. triloba*. *P. t.* var. *simplex* is the single flowered type and bears 1/2″ diameter, downy, globose, red fruits. When right the flowers are rather impressive but it has nothing to recommend it beyond this. Variety *multiplex* was introduced from China in 1885. Zone 3 to 6(7).

Prunus virginiana — Common Chokecherry
(proo′nus vĕr-jin-ē-ā′na)

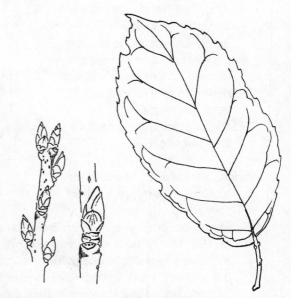

LEAVES: Alternate, simple, broad-elliptic to obovate, 1 1/2 to 5″ long, two-thirds as wide, abruptly acuminate, broad-cuneate to rounded at base, closely serrulate, dark green above, glaucescent or grayish green beneath, glabrous except axillary tufts of hair; petiole—1/2 to 3/4″ long, glandular.

Prunus virginiana, Common Chokeberry, can grow 20 to 30′ tall with a spread of 18 to 25′. It is a small suckering tree or large shrub with crooked branches and slender twigs forming an oval-rounded crown. Flowers are white, 1/3 to 2/5″ across; late April-May; in 3 to 6″ long, 1″ wide racemes. Fruit is red, finally dark purple, 1/3″ across. 'Schubert' ('Canada Red') is of pyramidal habit with dense foliage, green at first, and finally changing to reddish purple. Newfoundland, to Saskatchewan, North Dakota, Nebraska, south to North Carolina, Missouri and Kansas. Introduced 1724. Zone 2 to 6? The fruits have been used for making jams, jellies, pies, sauces and wine.

Prunus × yedoensis — Yoshino Cherry
(proo′nus yed-ō-en′sis)

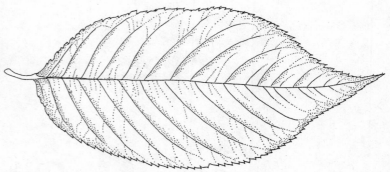

LEAVES: Alternate, simple, oval, broadly ovate to obovate, 2 1/2 to 4 1/2″ long, 1 1/2 to 2 1/2″ wide, rounded or broadly wedge-shaped at base, narrowed to a slender point at apex, doubly serrate, dark green and glabrous above, downy on midrib and veins below.

Prunus × yedoensis, Yoshino Cherry, is rather difficult to pin down as to exact parentage and origin. I have seen it listed as a *P. serrulata × P. subhirtella* hybrid but also *P. speciosa × P. subhirtella*. It is a plant of great beauty for the slightly fragrant, pink or white flowers occur in racemes of 4 or more usually before, sometimes with, the leaves in March-April. The habit is rounded, spreading and 40 to 50′ high. Fruits are globose, 1/2″ diameter, shining black drupes. 'Afterglow' is a handsome pink flowered form that originated as a seedling from 'Akebono', habit is upright spreading, 25′ by 25′, glossy bright green summer foliage followed by yellowish fall color. 'Akebono' has soft pink, supposedly double flowers and forms a rounded spreading 25′ high and 25′ wide tree, put into commerce by W.B. Clarke of California. 'Ivensii' is a distinct weeping form with white slightly fragrant flowers, the habit is almost broad umbrella shape with the ribs (branches) cascading to the ground to form a large mound. The first time I saw the plant in England I thought it was a form of *P. subhirtella*. Later at Kew Gardens another specimen jumped in my path, a virtual carbon copy of the first. Does not grow as large or wild as f. *perpendens*. A seedling of *P. × yedoensis* raised by Hilliers in 1925. 'Pink Shell' has shell pink petals that fade to a lighter shade. *Prunus ×* 'Snow Fountains' ('White Fountain' by Wayside) might be best included under *P. × yedoensis* although I do not know the exact parentage. The habit is semi weeping with snow white flowers on naked stems; will grow 6 to 12' high and wide at maturity, foliage is dark green and turns lovely gold and orange hues in fall, may produce a few black fruits. 'Shidare Yoshino' (f. *perpendens*) is the weeping form and often called Weeping Yoshino Cherry. A 10-year-old plant in the Georgia Botanical Garden was 15' tall and 20 to 25' wide with wildly arching branches; the plant is beautiful when covered with masses of white flowers in late March. 'Yoshino Pink Form' has flowers of a charming pink shade that open later than 'Pink Shell'. Seeds require a 2 month cold period and softwood cuttings are being rooted in abundance. The weeping form is usually staked and at a certain height allowed to weep. Zone 5 to 8. Found in Japan as a cultivated tree. Introduced 1902.

Pseudocydonia sinensis (*Cydonia sinensis*) — Chinese Quince
(soo-dō-sī-dō′ni-à̇ sī-nen′sis)

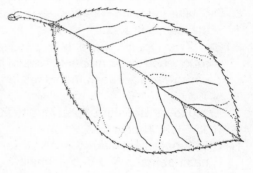

LEAVES: Alternate, simple, obovate, ovate or oval, 2 1/2 to 4 1/2″ long, 1 1/2 to 2 1/2″ wide, acute, cuneate, covered with pale brown hairs beneath at least when young, margin regularly and minutely serrate, teeth gland tipped, lustrous dark green above, glabrous, pale green below, with spreading hairs on principal veins, mid-vein impressed; petiole—1/2″ long, grooved, with distinct raised bristly glands.

BUDS: Small, 1/8″ long, imbricate, 3-scaled, glabrous.

STEM: Slender, lustrous brown, glabrous, epidermal skin peeling off, few lenticels.

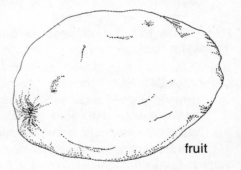

SIZE: 10 to 20′ (30 to 40′) high; one-half to two-third's that in spread.

HARDINESS: Zone 5 to 6 and into Zone 8; National, Tyler, and Morris Arboreta have notable specimens.

HABIT: Distinctly dense, upright-branching small tree or large shrub forming an oval to oval-rounded outline.

RATE: Slow-medium.

TEXTURE: Medium.

fruit

BARK: Quite beautiful, flaking off to produce a mosaic not unlike that of the plane-trees and Chinese Elm; trees I have observed also developed a fluted trunk; the bark alone is sufficient justification for using this plant; colors range from gray, green to brown; bark exfoliates on 2 to 3″ diameter trunks.

LEAF COLOR: Leafs out early and I have observed emerging leaves in late February on the Georgia campus, turns lustrous dark green, yellow to red in fall.

FLOWERS: Perfect, soft pink, 1 to 1 1/2″ across, solitary, borne on year-old shoots, April-May.

FRUIT: A large, 5 to 7″ long, egg-shaped, citron-yellow pome, October, highly aromatic, fruits developed the third year after planting in the Horticultural Garden.

CULTURE: Moist, acid, well-drained soil; site in full sun; microclimatize as much as possible especially in north.

DISEASES AND INSECTS: Fireblight is a major problem; trees were devastated by fireblight and had to be removed from campus.

LANDSCAPE VALUE: Excellent plant for bark effect; not extensively cultivated in the United States; excellent for winter effect.

PROPAGATION: Seed required a cold period of 2 to 3 months, seeds extracted from fruits which had been kept in a cooler during winter germinated immediately upon planting.

ADDITIONAL NOTES: Branches spineless which separate it from *Chaenomeles* species; not common in cultivation; bark is very attractive; a red fruited cultivar has been described; best specimen I have seen is at Tyler Arboretum, Lima, PA.
NATIVE HABITAT: China. Introduced about 1800.

Pseudolarix kaempferi (*P. amabilis*) — Golden-larch
(soo-dō-lār′iks kem′fẽr-ī)

FAMILY: Pinaceae
LEAVES: Scattered and spreading, often curved, 1 1/2 to 2 1/2″ long, 1/12 to 1/6″ wide, apex long pointed, soft, light green and rounded above, keeled beneath, margins thin with 2 conspicuous gray bands of stomata, singly and spirally on long shoots, in a radiating cluster on spur-like branches.
BUDS: Of long shoots ovoid, pointed, surrounded by long pointed brown scales with free tips which fall away soon after the leaves develop in spring; of short shoots similar in shape with persistent scales; axillary buds rounded with short-pointed deciduous scales.
STEM: Two types: long shoots thin, smooth, bloomy, brown in the second year, roughened by permanent bases of fallen leaves; short spurs longer than those of *Larix*, with a distinct constriction between the annual rings, with 15 to 30 umbelliformly sprreading leaves at the end.

SIZE: 30 to 50′ in height, spreading to 20 to 40′; can grow to 120′.
HARDINESS: Zone 4 to 7.
HABIT: Broad-pyramidal, deciduous conifer with wide-spreading horizontal branches and a rather open habit at maturity; I had a small (6′) specimen in my Illinois garden which was already quite open; Wyman noted that trees up to 30 to 40′ high may be almost as wide as tall; in some respects resemble a mature *Cedrus* in habit.
RATE: Slow, in fact a 100 year-old-tree was only 45′ tall.
TEXTURE: Medium.
BARK: On old trunks grayish to reddish brown and lightly ridged and furrowed with rather broad ridges.
LEAF COLOR: Soft, light green above, bluish green beneath in summer turning a clear golden yellow (orange-yellow) in autumn; fall color is brief but it is fantastic; peaked on October 16, 1978 at Arnold and was essentially gone by October 24.
FLOWERS: Monoecious, borne on separate branches of the same tree, opening in May or June; male flowers yellow in densely clustered catkins.
FRUIT: Cones solitary, ovoid, erect, 2 to 3″ long by 1 1/2 to 2″ wide, ripening in autumn of the first year; glaucous, bloomy, rich green to purplish during summer, ripening to golden brown, very beautiful but often borne in the upper reaches of the tree so as to be reduced in ornamental effectiveness; shattering soon after maturity.
CULTURE: Transplants readily balled and burlapped; requires a light, moist, acid, deep, well-drained soil; does not effectively tolerate high pH soils; prefers full sun although I have seen it in partially shaded situations; protect from wind; somewhat resistant to air pollutants.
DISEASES AND INSECTS: None serious.
LANDSCAPE VALUE: Truly a beautiful specimen in large areas; grows slowly enough that it can be integrated into the small landscape; the cones and fall color add seasonal interest; several magnificent trees along Bussey Brook in the Arnold Arboretum that are possibly the finest specimens in the country.
CULTIVARS:
  'Annesleyana'—Dwarf, bushy; short horizontal, pendent branches; leaves densely set.
PROPAGATION: Seeds are the usual method of reproduction; however, it is difficult to obtain fertile seeds. A specimen at the Missouri Botanic Garden has coned rather heavily but no viable seed has been produced. Den Ouden and Boom and Dallimore and Jackson noted that seeds were difficult to obtain

from China in a fresh state, but fertile seeds were frequently produced on trees grown in Italy. On a 1976 trip to the Holden Arboretum, Dick Munson, the former propagator, showed me numerous seedlings he had grown from seed collected off a grove of trees in Mentor, Ohio. He was kind enough to show me the parent trees and needless to say I was impressed. We discussed the problems of seed propagation and theorized that the trees are self-sterile and the fact that several seedling-grown trees were in close proximity contributed to cross pollination and viable seed production. Perhaps this is the reason the tree in the Missouri Botanic garden does not develop viable seed. Seeds may germinate without pretreatment, but 60 days at 41°F will result in more uniform germination; trees in the Arnold Arboretum produce abundant viable seeds.

NATIVE HABITAT: Eastern China at altitudes of 3000 to 4000′. Introduced 1854.

Pseudotsuga menziesii — Douglasfir (formerly listed as *P. douglasii* and *P. taxifolia*)
(soo-dō-soo′gȧ men-zē′zē-ī)

FAMILY: Pinaceae

LEAVES: Pectinate with a V-shaped arrangement between the 2 lateral sets, straight, 1 to 1 1/2″ long, thin, shining dark green above, with 2 white bands of stomata beneath, smelling of camphor when bruised.

BUDS: Ovoid-conical, imbricate, apex pointed, 1/4 to 1/3″ long, shining chestnut brown, mostly resinous at base.

STEM: Yellowish green initially, becoming gray to brown, minutely pubescent or almost glabrous.

CONES: Three to 4″ long, 1 1/2 to 2″ wide, light brown, bracts are prominent and extend beyond the scales, persistent into winter.

SIZE: Under landscape conditions will grow 40 to 80′ in height with a 12 to 20′ spread; can grow to 200′ and greater in its native habitat.

HARDINESS: Zone 4 to 6, depending on the seed source; there is a 25′ high tree on the Georgia campus (Zone 8) but it is not particularly vigorous.

HABIT: An open, spirey pyramid with straight stiff branches; the lower drooping, upper ascending; dense in youth becoming loose with age.

RATE: Medium, will grow 12 to 15′ over a 10 year period; this rate based on observations taken with trees growing on University of Illinois campus; one authority noted that the tree might grow 40 to 100′ high after 50 to 75 years and 1 to 2′ a year when young; he leaves a pretty safe estimating range!

TEXTURE: Medium.

BARK: On young stems smooth except for resin blisters; on old trunks often divided into thick reddish brown ridges separated by deep irregular fissures; becoming 6 to 24″ thick.

LEAF COLOR: Depends largely on the seed source; the Rocky Mountain, Colorado type is bluish green and hardy in Zone 4, this is the type which should be grown in the north; the other type is restricted to the Pacific slope where there is ample atmospheric moisture; this type has dark green foliage and is less hardy (Zone 6); this type is the largest growing and can grow to 300′ and more; types with yellow-green needles exist.

FLOWERS: Monoecious, on two year-old wood; staminate axillary, pendulous; pistillate terminal, with exerted, three-pointed bracts, handsome rose-red when young.

FRUIT: Cones pendulous, oval-ovoid, 4″ long by 1 1/2 to 2″ broad, three-pronged bracts, light brown.

CULTURE: Transplants well balled and burlapped; prefers neutral or slightly acid, well-drained, moist soils; fails on dry, poor soils; sunny, open, roomy conditions; injured by high winds; does best where there is an abundance of atmospheric moisture.

DISEASES AND INSECTS: Cankers (a number of species), leaf casts (similar to leaf spots), leaf and twig blight, needle blight, witches broom, aphids, Douglasfir bark beetle, scales, spruce budworm, pine butterfly, Zimmerman pine moth, tussock moth, gypsy moth, and strawberry root weevil.

LANDSCAPE VALUE: One of the noblest forest trees, very ornamental under cultivation; an excellent specimen, grouping or mass; not suited for underplanting or windbreaks; its use should be tempered in the dry windy areas of the midwest; makes a nice short needle Christmas tree.

CULTIVARS: Probably 30 to 40 cultivars with very few available except from specialty growers.

'Fastigiata'—Distinctly ascending, spire-like, branches crowded, branchlets erect, needles green with a hint of gray, densely radial, short; good looking clone; Dawes Arboretum, Newark, OH has several beautiful specimens.

'Fletcheri'—I suspect the most popular dwarf form with blue-green, 1/2 to 3/4" long needles and spreading flat-topped compact habit, 2 to 2 1/2' by 2 1/2 to 3', will grow 6' high and slightly wider at maturity.

var. *glauca*—More compact with slightly more ascending branches than the species; leaves bluish green; hardy to Zone 4.

'Pendula'—Branches and branchlets held close to the stem and hanging like curtains, not particularly attractive.

PROPAGATION: Several papers on rooting Douglasfir discuss various factors related to successful rooting and would make interesting reading for propagators. See *J. Amer. Soc. Hort. Sci.* 99:551–555; *The Plant Propagator* 24(2):9 (1978) and *PIPPS* 28:32(1978). Seeds will germinate without pretreatment although this may vary with seed source.

ADDITIONAL NOTES: There is considerable confusion related to the various types of Douglasfir and every individual seems to have a different story to tell. The following information is based on the current thinking of the foresters and coincides pretty well with what most knowledgeable plantsmen relate. *P. menziesii* includes two geographic varieties: (1) the Coast Douglasfir (var. *menziesii*) is fast growing, long-lived, and sometimes becomes over 300' tall and attains a diameter of 8 to 10'. The foliage is typically of a yellow-green color, although some trees show bluish green, and the cones are often 4" long and have straight, more or less appressed bracts; (2) the Rocky Mountain Douglasfir (var. *glauca*) is slower growing, shorter lived, and seldom exceeds 130' in height. The foliage is bluish green but others with yellowish green needles are found standing together. The cones are smaller, barely 3" in length, with much-exserted and strongly flexed bracts. Unfortunately in certain areas the two varieties overlap and here intermediate forms are found. Variety *glauca* is widely grown and used for Christmas trees and ornamental plantings in the northeastern United States.

At one time, the most important lumber producing tree in the United States. The wood has exceptional strength and is widely used for heavy structural timber; also used for plywood and pulp. One of the best short-needled Christmas trees because the needles do not easily fall off as is the case with *Abies* (fir) and *Picea* (spruce).

NATIVE HABITAT: Rocky Mountains and Pacific coast (British Columbia to Mexico). Introduced 1827.

Ptelea trifoliata — Hoptree, also called Wafer-ash, Stinking-ash or Water-ash
(tē'lē-à trī-fō-li-ā'tà)

FAMILY: Rutaceae

LEAVES: Alternate, trifoliate, leaflets ovate to elliptic-oblong, 2 1/2 to 5" long, narrowed at ends, sometimes acuminate, middle largest with a short petiolule, the lateral ones oblique at base, smaller, entire, or obscurely crenulate, sessile, lustrous dark green above and glabrous below; if

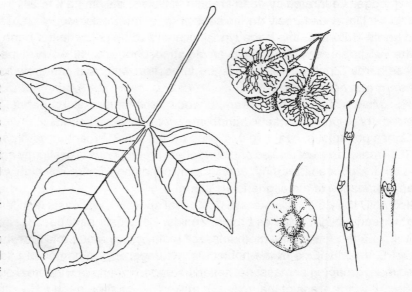

viewed with a hand lens while back-lighted distinct oil-glands are evident; pungent when bruised; petiole 2 to 4″ long.

BUDS: Closely superposed in pairs, very low-conical, sessile, hidden beneath petiole bases, breaking through the leaf scars, not distinctly scaly, silvery-silky; terminal lacking.

STEM: Glabrous, buff to reddish brown, moderate, warty and dotted, terete; pith rather large, roundish, continuous, white; leaf scars somewhat raised, rather long, horseshoe shaped when torn by buds; 3 bundle-traces.

SIZE: 15 to 20′ high and as wide; often 5 to 15′ high.

HARDINESS: Zone 3 to 9.

HABIT: Large shrub or small tree of a bushy, rounded nature; if tree-like usually low branched; has a tendency to sucker.

RATE: Slow to medium.

TEXTURE: Medium in leaf, medium-coarse in winter.

BARK: Dark gray, smooth, except for warty protuberances.

LEAF COLOR: Lustrous dark green in summer; yellow-green in fall; have observed good yellow on selected plants.

FLOWERS: Small, unisexual, greenish white, 1/3 to 1/2″ diameter, fragrant, borne in terminal 2 to 3″ diameter corymbs on short lateral branches, June, not particularly showy.

FRUIT: A compressed, broadly winged, suborbicular, 2-sided, 2/3 to 1″ diameter, indehiscent samara; brownish at maturity, rather conspicuous; effective August through September; the common name is derived from the shape and appearance of the parts; may persist into December and later.

CULTURE: Very adaptable species which performs maximally in well-drained soils; sun or shade; found in moist woodlands as an understory plant and for that reason makes a good choice for planting in heavy shade; I have seen plants in full sun and heavy shade and, in both situations, they made handsome specimens.

DISEASES AND INSECTS: Various leaf spots and a rust disease; none of which are serious.

LANDSCAPE VALUE: An interesting native plant covering much of the eastern United States; the cultivar 'Aurea' would be effective in the shrub border; this plant can grow on one after a while; I have developed a rather curious fondness for the species.

CULTIVARS:
> 'Aurea'—Quite a striking form with rich yellow young leaves fading to lime-green by August; not as obtrusive as many yellow-foliaged plants because the color subsides with time; can be rooted from softwood cuttings treated with 8000 ppm IBA-talc.

> 'Glauca'—Leaves blue-green and quite striking compared to the normal lustrous dark green leaves.

PROPAGATION: Seed requires a 3 to 4 month cold period; cuttings can be rooted with good success when collected in July and treated with 8000 ppm IBA-talc, mist; dug a plant from the wild for my garden and watched it grow like topsy in its new home. Moved it again and watched numerous shoots developing from remaining roots; this suggests root cuttings would work quite well.

ADDITIONAL NOTES: The fruits have been used as a substitute for hops; hence, the reason for the first common name. The bark has been utilized in medical preparations. The fruits and bark contain a bitter substance and the stems when bruised are rather pungent.

NATIVE HABITAT: Ontario and New York to Florida, west to Minnesota. Introduced 1724.

Pterocarya fraxinifolia — Caucasian Wingnut
(tēr-ō-kā′rē-a̅ frak-si-ni-fō′li-a̅)

FAMILY: Juglandaceae

LEAVES: Alternate, pinnately compound, 8 to 18″ long, leaflets 7 to 27, ovate-oblong to oblong-lanceolate, acuminate, rounded, sharply serrate, 3 to 5″ long, thin, glabrous except stellate hairs in the axils and along the midrib beneath, shiny, handsome dark green; rachis terete, glabrous.

BUDS: Red-brown, rather large, superposed, the upper distinctly stalked or elongating the first year, naked with folded leaves.

STEM: Red-brown, moderate or rather stout, rounded, glabrous; pith moderate, angular, chambered with rather close thin light brown plates; leaf scars elliptical or 3-lobed, large, rather low, 3 bundle-traces, crescent or horseshoe shaped, crenated, or fragmented.

SIZE: 30 to 50′ in height with a similar spread, can grow to 90′, 115′ high specimen is known.

HARDINESS: Zone 5 to 8 (9).

HABIT: Broad-spreading, rounded, often with several stems near the base; can be a beautiful tree with wide-spreading branches; has a tendency to sucker.

RATE: Medium, 12 to 15′ over a 10 year period.

TEXTURE: Medium in leaf and winter habit.

LEAF COLOR: Dark glossy green in summer, excellent summer foliage and apparently quite free of insects and diseases; fall color is yellow-green; plants in Zone 8 have produced no fall coloration

FLOWERS: Monoecious; male—5″ long greenish catkins; female to 20″ long, catkin-like, May-June.

FRUIT: Winged nut(let), reminds of a wing nut, wings 3/4″ diameter, roundish, oblique, horned at the top, green changing to brown, ripening in September-October; interesting as they hang on a slender, pendent 12 to 20″ long spike.

CULTURE: Transplant balled and burlapped into moist, well drained soil deep enough to accommodate the extensive root system; full sun; pH adaptable; will tolerate wind, drought and hard soil if the roots are well established; prune in summer; in the wild found in moist soil and there makes its best growth.

DISEASES AND INSECTS: None serious.

LANDSCAPE VALUE: Very handsome specimen plant which could be successfully used for large areas such as parks, schools, and golf courses; the largest specimen I have seen was very broad-spreading and made an excellent shade tree; much superior to ashes, honeylocusts and weak-wooded maples but little known; handsome foliage and interesting fruits that are not particularly messy; suspect suckering would limit landscape potential.

PROPAGATION: If seed is fresh some germination will take place upon sowing; as seed dries a period of cold (2 to 3 months) is probably necessary to insure uniform germination; I noticed that seeds from Arnold Arboretum trees were largely void while seeds from trees at the Georgia Botanical Garden were solid; this could be related to the length of the growing season and summer heat. Cuttings taken in summer and made from young shoots with a heel will sometimes root; probably best to collect cuttings in July and treat with high IBA concentration; the species shows a propensity to sucker which would indicate that root cuttings are a possibility.

ADDITIONAL NOTES: I first saw this at Vineland Station, Ontario, Canada, during a meeting of the American Society for Horticultural Science. No one could correctly identify the species until Dr. Lumis of the University of Guelph told us the identity. It was a massive, spreading specimen of great beauty. The root system is aggressive and the tree probably does not deserve consideration for residential or street use but in parks and large areas especially with abundant foot traffic, it might be utilized. I have observed the species or those treated under Related Species in European gardens, particularly in Germany where plants are quite common.

NATIVE HABITAT: Caucasus to northern Iran. Introduced 1782.

RELATED SPECIES: I have some doubts as to the correct identity of many of the specimens I have seen labeled as *P. fraxinifolia*. Many appear to be *P.* × *rehderana* or *P. stenoptera*.

Pterocarya stenoptera, (tēr-ō-kā′rē-à sten-op′tēr-à), Chinese Wingnut, has 11 to 21 (25) leaflets which are oblong or narrowly oval, finely and regularly toothed, 2 to 5″ long, and 1/3 to 2″ wide. The significant difference between this and *P. fraxinifolia* is the winged rachis with the wings sparsely toothed. Most Wingnuts I have seen show the winged character. China. Introduced about 1860. Zone 6 to 8.

Pterocarya × rehderana, (tēr-ō-kā′rē-à rā-dēr-ā′nà), Rehder Wingnut, is a hybrid between the above two species with *P. stenoptera* the maternal parent. Raised at the Arnold Arboretum from seeds received in 1879 from Lavallee's collection of Segrez. It is a rapid grower and tends to be prolific in its production of suckers. The rachis is winged but nowhere to the degree of *P. stenoptera* and not toothed. Apparently more vigorous and hardy than either parent. Zone (5) 6 to 8.

Pterocarya rhoifolia, (tēr-ō-kā′rē-à rō-i-fō′lē-a), Japanese Wingnut, carries 8 to 12″ long leaves with 11 to 21 leaflets, each 2 1/2 to 4″ long, 1 to 1 1/2″ wide, acuminate, rounded, finely and evenly toothed and dark green. The rachis is not winged. Differs from other species mentioned because buds have 2 to 3 large covering scales. Japan. Introduced 1888. Zone 5 to 8?

Pteroceltis tatarinowii — Tatar Wingceltis
(tēr-ō-sel′tis ta-tār-i-nō′ē-ī)

FAMILY: Ulmaceae

LEAVES: Alternate, simple, ovate to ovate-oblong, 2 to 4″ long, 3/4 to 2″ wide, acuminate, broad cuneate, three-nerved, irregularly and sharply serrate, upper medium to dark green, scabrous, lower with tufts of hairs on axils; petiole—1/4 to 1/3″ long.

Pteroceltis tatarinowii, Tatar Wingceltis, is a handsome 30 to 45′ high and wide tree with medium to dark green foliage. The species is closely allied to *Celtis* but differs in the winged, 1/2 to 3/4″ wide fruits. The gray-brown bark exfoliates in patches and is quite handsome. The only tree I have ever seen resides at the Morris Arboretum. For the plant collector this is a treasure to be unearthed. Northern and Central China. Introduced 1894. Zone 5 to 7?

Pterostyrax hispida — Fragrant Epaulettetree
(tēr-ō-stī′raks hiss′pi-dà)

FAMILY: Styracaceae

LEAVES: Alternate, simple, oblong to oblong-ovate, 3 to 7 1/2″ long, 1 1/2 to 4″ wide, acute or short-acuminate, rounded or cuneate at base, minutely denticulate, bright green and glabrous above, sparingly pubescent beneath at least on veins; petiole 1/2 to 1″ long.

BUDS: Terminal elongated, hairy, and naked, 1/2″ long, yellowish brown, sits at oblique angle to leaf scar; one or two smaller, ovoid, 2-scaled, brown, 1/4″ long buds subtending terminal.

STEM: Quickly shedding gray bark, rounded, rather slender with distinct fetid odor when bruised; pith off-white, continuous.

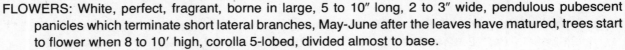

SIZE: 20 to 30′ tall with a similar or greater spread although can grow to 45′.

HARDINESS: Zone 4 to 8, has survived -22°F.

HABIT: A round-headed small tree which develops an open head, and slender spreading branches.

RATE: Medium, 12 to 14′ in about 8 years.

TEXTURE: Medium-coarse in leaf; medium-coarse in winter.

LEAF COLOR: Bright green above, silvery-green beneath in summer; yellow-green in fall and not effective; foliage is quite handsome and free of pest problems.

FLOWERS: White, perfect, fragrant, borne in large, 5 to 10″ long, 2 to 3″ wide, pendulous pubescent panicles which terminate short lateral branches, May-June after the leaves have matured, trees start to flower when 8 to 10′ high, corolla 5-lobed, divided almost to base.

FRUIT: A 1/2″ long, cylindric, 10-ribbed, densely bristly, dry drupe.

CULTURE: Transplant balled and burlapped in spring into moist, well-drained, preferably acid soil; full sun, have seen respectable plants in partial shade; in northern areas protect from strong winds and extremes of temperature; prune in winter; prefers hot, sunny conditions if good flowering is to occur.

DISEASES AND INSECTS: None serious.

LANDSCAPE VALUE: Quite difficult to locate in commerce, but it does have possibilities for the small residential landscape; the flowers are extremely handsome and develop when a limited number of plants are offering color; makes a rather handsome and unusual tree; it is much hardier than properly credited.

PROPAGATION: Seeds may germinate when directly sown but 3 months at 40°F is recommended to ensure more uniform germination. Softwood cuttings root easily and I have had 80 to 100 percent success with August cuttings treated with 3000 to 8000 ppm IBA-quick dip; the root systems were profuse and would serve as a model for any cutting one would every hope to root.

NATIVE HABITAT: Japan. Introduced 1875.

RELATED SPECIES:

Pterostyrax corymbosa, (tēr-ō-stī′raks kor-im-bō′sȧ), Little Epaulettetree, is distinguished from the above by the 1/2″ long, 3/8″ wide, 5-winged fruits that are covered by a close down. As I observed the two species there is not much ornamental difference. This species tends to be more shrub-like. This species also roots readily from softwood cuttings. Japan. Introduced 1850. Zone 5 to 8?

Punica granatum — Pomegranate
(pū′ni-kȧ grȧ-nā′tum)

FAMILY: Punicaceae

LEAVES: Alternate, opposite, or whorled depending on growth rate of shoot, oval-lanceolate, 1 to 3″ long, 1/3 to 1″ wide, entire, glabrous, lustrous dark green; petiole—short.

SIZE: 12 to 20′ high, spread equal to or less than height.

HARDINESS: Zone 8 to 10.

HABIT: Shrub or small tree of upright-oval to rounded outline; usually shrub-like in south.

RATE: Medium.

TEXTURE: Medium, perhaps almost fine.

LEAF COLOR: Lustrous dark green in summer, yellow-green fall color; leaves late to emerge in spring, also hold late in fall.

FLOWERS: Perfect, 5 to 7-petaled, petals crumpled; calyx with 5 to 7 lobes and a funnel-shaped base to which the numerous stamens are attached; effect is similar to a carnation; red in type, orange-red, pink, white, yellow or variegated in the cultivars; each flower an inch or more across, borne simgly or up to 5 at end of branches, May, June-July, usually starts to flower in late May-early June on the Georgia campus and may continue into fall, quite handsome; tubular portion of flower is fleshy.

FRUIT: A yellow, maturing to red (yellowish red), 2 to 3 1/2″ diameter berry with a thick leathery rind crowned by the persistent calyx; central pulpy mass formed by the fleshy outer seed coats; ripens in September-October.

CULTURE: Easily transplanted; tolerates extremes of soil from sand to clay providing they are well drained; pH adaptable; sun or partial shade (reduced flowering in shade); grows best in fertile, moist, well-drained soils; probably best to prune before flowering since it flowers on new growth.

DISEASES AND INSECTS: None serious.

LANDSCAPE VALUE: Truly a handsome shrub in flower; for some reason (cold hardiness) used sparingly in Piedmont area of Georgia; good plant for shrub border, grouping, or perhaps screening; should not be used for hedges; really brightens a landscape in June and later; makes a fine container or tub plant, would be great on a patio during the summer months; flowers prolifically on Georgia campus.

CULTIVARS: Several of the following may be found in commerce if one is tuned to treasure hunting.

 'Alba Plena'—Double creamy white or yellowish petals, waxy yellow calyx, new leaves bright green, 6 to 10′ high.

 'Albescens'—White flowers.

 'Chico'—Compact form with more refined branches, glossy leaves and double bright orange-red flowers over the summer.

 'Flavescens'—Yellow flowers, single.

 'Legrellei' ('Lagrelliae')—Double flowers with petals salmon-pink, variegated white (also described as red, striped yellowish white); apparently an unstable mutant from the double red, to which it reverts; has produced a branch sport with double white flowers; introduced before 1858 by Mme. Legrelle d'Hanis who obtained it from a friend, Mme. Parmentier, in Illinois.

 'Multiplex'—Double white flowers.

 var. *nana* ('Nana')—Red-orange, single flowers, smaller linear-lanceolate to linear leaves, smaller flowers and fruit, may only grow 18″ high but 3 to 4′ can be realized; apparently several (perhaps many) forms of this in cultivation; cultivated in 1723 in Kent, England; will come true when grown from seeds; makes a good glasshouse plant and will flower and fruit inside; has been described as hardier than the species; has flowered in October on Georgia campus and held leaves into mid November, some tip dieback after exposure to 0°F.

 'Pleniflora' ('Plena')—Double scarlet flowers.

 'Wonderful'—A good fruit producer, burnished red fruit, red-orange flowers, 8 to 12′ high, fountain-like habit.

PROPAGATION: Seeds germinate readily but progeny are extrremely variable; this would be a good species to work with as far as flower color improvements and compactness. Softwood cuttings root readily; I have had good success with cuttings taken in September.

ADDITIONAL NOTES: An "old" plant; grown for its fruits in southern Europe, northern Africa east to India from remote antiquity; needs sunny situation and a long warm growing season if fruits are to ripen; have seen it fruit heavily in Madison, Georgia; used abundantly at Williamsburg in the Governor's

Palace Garden; here it is planted with figs and espaliered pears; fruit was apparently a delicacy for the landed gentry.

NATIVE HABITAT: Lost to antiquity as far as origin; cultivated since time immemorial.

Pyracantha coccinea — Scarlet Firethorn
(pī-rȧ-kan'thȧ cok-sin'i-ȧ)

FAMILY: Rosaceae

LEAVES: Alternate, simple, evergreen, narrow-elliptic to lanceolate or oblanceolate, rarely ovate-oblong, 1 to 2 1/2″ long on long shoots, 1/2 to 1 1/2″ long on flowering ones, range from 1/4 to 3/4″ wide, acute, rarely obtusish, cuneate, closely crenulate-serrulate, lustrous dark green, slightly pubescent beneath at first; petiole 1/3″ long, downy.

STEM: Woolly at first, becoming glossy brown with spines 1/2 to 3/4″ long.

SIZE: 6 to 18′ in height with an equal spread; this shrub can get out of hand and considerable pruning is necessary to keep it in bounds.

HARDINESS: Zone 6 to 9, Zone 5 if a hardy cultivar is used, the hardiest types will probably be killed at around -20°F.

HABIT: Semi-evergreen to evergreen shrub with stiff, thorny branches and an open habit if left unpruned; can become wild and woolly unless pruned properly throughout its lifespan.

RATE: Medium to fast.

TEXTURE: Medium throughout the seasons.

LEAF COLOR: Lustrous dark green in summer becoming brownish in winter in unprotected areas; if sited well, will maintain considerable green foliage.

FLOWERS: Perfect, whitish, 1/3″ across, late April in Athens, late May-early June in Urbana, IL, borne in 1 to 2″ diameter, 2 to 3″ long compound corymbs on spurs along the stem of last year's growth; quite showy in flower as the inflorescences literally shroud the plants; malodorous, subdued odor but still like a hawthorn.

FRUIT: Berry-like rounded pome, 1/4″ diameter, orange-red, ripening in September and persisting into winter; often spectacular.

CULTURE: Move as a container plant in spring into well-drained soil; does quite well where soil is dry in summer; full sun for best fruiting although will do well in partial shade; pH 5.5 to 7.5; pruning can be accomplished anytime; very difficult to transplant and once established should be left in that area; makes a good plant for container production.

DISEASES AND INSECTS: Fireblight can be serious, scab affects the fruits turning them a dark sooty color, twig blight, leaf blight, root rot, aphid, lace bug, and scales.

LANDSCAPE VALUE: Often used as an informal hedge or barrier plant, good for espaliers on walls, trellises and the like; fruit is the outstanding attribute; hardiness is a problem and selected cultivars must be used; The Ohio State University campus has a large complement of *Pyracantha* that is spectacular in the fall.

CULTIVARS:

'Aurea'—Form with yellow fruits.

'Baker's Red'—Listed by Greenbriar Farms as their best red "berried" pyracantha for abundance of bright red fruit and cold hardiness.

'Chadwickii'—(Zone 5) Hardy form and a prolific fruiter, fruits are orange-red, 6′ high, spreading habit, one nursery noted it was hardier than 'Lalandei.'

'Kasan'—(Zone 5) Orange-red fruits, originated in Russia, one of the hardier forms, quite scab susceptible, spreading growth habit, 10′.

'Lalandei'—(Zone 5) Probably the most widely grown and one of the hardiest, with orange-red fruits, originated about 1874, vigorous to 10 or 15′, scab susceptible.

'Lalandei Monrovia'—Orange-red fruits and slightly less hardy than 'Lalandei', also saw a report that notes significantly less hardy, also quite scab susceptible.

'Red Column'—Upright growth habit and bright red fruits, listed as Zone 5 to 6 by Angelica Nursery.

'Royal'—Hardy, upright branched, orange fruited form.

'Runyanii'—Another orange-fruited form, highly scab and fireblight susceptible.

'Thornless'—Red fruiting, thornless form supposedly as hardy as 'Lalandei', highly susceptible to scab and fireblight.

'Wyattii'—Orange-red fruits prolifically produced, hardy to Zone 5, supposedly more cold hardy than 'Lalandei', 9 to 12' high, tolerant of poor soil, highly susceptible to scab and fireblight.

Other Cultivars Of Different Parentage. The above were primarily derived from *Pyracantha coccinea* but the following come from different parentage. Dr. Donald Egolf, U.S. National Arboretum and Dr. Elwin Orton, Rutgers University have hybridized a number of fine cultivars many of which are included here:

'Apache'—A semi-evergreen to evergreen compact shrub with 1/3″ diameter bright red fruits that ripen in September and persist until December and are not readily devoured by birds, resistant to pyracantha scab and fireblight, leaves are glossy dark green, grew 4 1/2 to 5' high and 6' wide after 14 years, a National Arboretum introduction; see *HortScience* 22:173–174 (1987), should be cold hardy in Zone 5/6.

'Cherri Berri' (*P. fortuneana*)—Large 3/8″ diameter cherry red fruits which persist into winter, large lustrous dark green leaves, 10' by 8', Zone 6 but I doubt this designation.

'Fiery Cascade'—An upright grower to 8' high and 9' wide, small glossy dark green leaves, abundant small red fruit, first orange in September, red in October and persisting, good disease resistance, hardy to -10°F, Dr. Orton, Rutgers, introduced this clone.

'Gnome'—(Obviously I had the parentage wrong in the last edition for a number of reasons but John Sabuco straightened out the problem. 'Gnome' is a seedling of *P. coccinea* 'Lalandei' × 'Aurea'? The patent tag read *P. angustifolia* 'Gnome' and in the disease update Oregon State listed it as *P. atalantioides.* Got it!) Medium sized shrub of compact, densely branched growth and somewhat spreading nature, 1/4 to 3/8″ diameter orange fruits, quite hardy and successful in Zone 5; highly susceptible to scab on leaves and fruits, 6' by 8'.

'Gold Rush'—Yellow fruited hybrid of *P. angustifolia* × *P. fortuneana* selected by Washington Park Arboretum, University of Washington and registered in 1976 after 20 years of testing; described as an intricately branched shrub to 10' high, persistent leaves and dense clusters of depressed-globular orange-yellow nearly 1/2″ diameter fruits that are so numerous the branches arch to the ground, resistant to scab and hardy to Zone 7.

'Golden Charmer'(*P. rogersiana* × *P. coccinea*)—Orange-yellow fruits, good lustrous dark green foliage, scab resistant, bred in Germany.

'Harlequin'—Pinkish white variegated new shoots settle down to a life of green and white in summer, turn pinkish in cold weather, 6' high and wide shrub; not as vigorous as the species, fruits are orange-red; as pyracanthas go this is at the bottom of the heap.

'Lowboy'—Vigorous-spreading, low-growing form, rich green foliage, orange fruit, extremely susceptible to scab, 2 to 3' high and wider at maturity.

'Mohave' (*P. koidzumii* × *P. coccinea* 'Wyattii')—Heavy flowers and huge masses of bright orange-red berries on a medium sized, densely branched, upright variety, grows 6 to 10' (9 to 12' high); based on tests in Illinois it is not hardy much below 0 to -5°F, quite resistant to scab and fireblight, lustrous dark green foliage, fruits exceptionally resistant to bird feeding, 8-year-old plant supposedly 13 1/2' by 16'.

'Navaho' (*P. angustifolia* × *P.* 'Watereri')—Low growing, 6' high and 7.5' wide, densely branched, mounded, rich orange-red fruits, resistant to scab and highly tolerant to fireblight.

'Orange Charmer' (*P. rogersiana* × *P. coccinea*)—Orange-red, 3/8″ diameter fruits that color in September, scab resistant, bred in Germany.

'Orange Glow' (*P. crenatoserrata* × *P. coccinea*)—A popular form in England which has proven quite hardy, quite free-flowering with masses of orange-red, 3/8″ diameter fruits which persist into winter, used frequently as an espalier on walls, 10' or more, scab resistant.

'Pauciflora'—Dense branching, low rounded form with small leaves and light crops of small orange fruits, 4' by 4'; this may be a rename.

'Pueblo'—A semievergreen to evergreen, dark green leaved, 6 to 7' high, 12' wide shrub (after 16 years) with 1/3 to 1/2" diameter, depressed globose orange-red persistent fruit, resistant to fireblight and scab; vigorous growing and heavy fruit producer, hardy to Zone 7, see *HortScience* 22:510–511 (1987).

'Red Elf'—Dwarf compact mounding habit; dark green foliage, bright red persistent fruits, low susceptibility to fireblight, Zone 7, Monrovia introduction.

'Ruby Mound'—Low mounding type with bright red fruits, Zone 7, Monrovia introduction.

'Rutgers'—A good, glossy dark green leaved form with abundant orange-red fruits and a spreading, sprawling growth habit, may reach 3' high and 9' wide, good disease resistance, roots easily from cuttings, shows good hardiness, much hardier that 'Mohave' and 'Navaho'; Introduced by Dr. Elwin Orton, Rutgers University.

'Shawnee'—An F2 seedling of *Pyracantha* 'San Jose,' which is a spontaneous hybrid of *P. koidzumii* and *P. fortuneana;* clear yellow to light orange fruit, semi-persistent foliage, resistance to fire blight and scab, original plant was 9' by 10'.

'Soleil d'Or'—Another European garden form with golden yellow fruits, 8 to 10' high.

'Teton' ('Orange Glow' × *P. rogersiana* 'Flava')—Quite unusual for its upright growth habit and yellow-orange fruits; growth habit and fruit color are somewhat affected by where it is grown; in south fruits are yellow-orange and habit is upright-spreading but nowhere as upright as shown and described in original cultivar release (see *HortScience* 13(4): 483–484); it is a strong grower and may become 16' high and 9' wide; resistant to scab and fireblight; reasonably hardy, in fact, may be the most cold-hardy pyracantha.

'Yukon Belle' *(P. angustifolia)*—Monrovia lists this form as the hardiest orange berried form, medium sized shrub with semi-evergreen tendencies, probably 6 to 10' high and wide, listed as Zone 4 but I doubt it.

PROPAGATION: Seed should be stratified for 90 days at 41°F. Softwood cuttings root readily under mist; treatment with 1000 to 3000 ppm IBA is recommended to hasten rooting.

ADDITIONAL NOTES: Pyracanthas make attractive fruiting shrubs but can become ratty with age. The disease ratings come from Ornamentals Northwest, December-January, 1977–78. A number of other cultivars were not included here because of their relative scarcity in commerce but are described in the publication.

NATIVE HABITAT: Italy to Caucasus. Introduced 1629.

Pyracantha koidzumii — Formosa Firethorn
(pī-rȧ-kan'thȧ koyd-zūm'ē-ī)

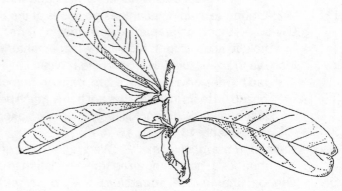

LEAVES: Alternate, simple, evergreen to semi-evergreen, oblanceolate, widest above the middle, 1 to 3" long, 1/2 to 3/4" wide, entire, or slightly serrate toward apex, apex often emarginate, lustrous dark green; easily separated from *P. coccinea* by the essentially entire leaf and emarginate apex; in clusters on old wood.

SIZE: 8 to 12' (20') high, 8 to 12' wide.
HARDINESS: Zone 8 to 10; this species is not reliably hardy in Zone 7; severely injured and in exposed locations killed to ground during 1981–82 winter in Athens when temperatures dropped to 0°F, same occurrence in 1983–84 at -3°F, some plants killed, others developed new shoots from base.

HABIT: Large multistemmed, stiff, upright-branched shrub that becomes unkempt with time unless properly pruned; like *P. coccinea* this is a rank grower and rather unruly.

RATE: Fast.

TEXTURE: Medium.

LEAF COLOR: May leaf out as early as late February in Athens, lustrous dark green; foliage may discolor
in colder areas of south.

FLOWERS: Perfect, 5-petaled, white, 1/4″ diameter, produced in small corymbose racemes in late
April-early May (Athens); an entire plant in flower is quite attractive, malodorous.

FRUIT: A globose, 1/4″ diameter, red pome that matures (colors) in September-October and persists
through the ensuing winter; the entire shrub is a great mass of red; many plants on the Georgia
campus are isolated specimens and they stand out like a sore thumb; birds apparently leave these
until they are desperately hungry.

CULTURE: Transplant from a container; *Pyracantha* is inherently impossible to move from the field;
prefers well drained soil and full sun; responds vigorously to good growing conditions; an
excellent choice for hot, dry areas; plants on the Georgia campus have survived numerous
droughts during the 1980's and fruited heavily; prune selectively; there is no one best time to
remove branches.

DISEASES AND INSECTS: Fireblight, lacebug, scab (affects fruit), mites in extremely dry situations, scale
and leaf rollers.

LANDSCAPE VALUE: Excellent for fruit effect and widely used for every conceivable landscape purpose;
single specimen, foundation plantings, hedges (a mistake), screens, masses, espaliers; requires a
great amount of maintenance to keep it looking nice; where space permits it is worth using; the most
widely used species in the southeast.

CULTIVARS:

'Low-Dense' ('Lowdense')—Mounded habit of growth to 6′, large orange-red fruits may be masked
by foliage, new growth light green, texture fine, severely injured or killed at 11°F during 1983–84
winter, true also for 'Red Elf' and 'Ruby Mound.'

'Santa Ana'—Dark red fruits, shiny large lustrous green foliage, 10′ by 10′, Zone 7.

'San Jose'—Wide spreading form, highly scab resistant.

'Santa Cruz'—Prostrate form with dark green leaves and red fruits, highly scab resistant; 2 1/2 to 3′
by 5 to 6′. Zone 7.

'Victory'—Vigorous form, upright arching growth habit, with dark red fruit, fruits among the last to
color but are retained for many months, Zone 7, 10′ or more, good scab resistance.

'Walderi Prostrata'—Prostrate growth habit, 4′, large red fruits.

'Watereri'—Parentage is suspect but probably *P. atalantioides* × *P. rogersiana;* vigorous, dense
shrub up to 8′ high and wide; dark red fruits on nearly thornless stems, leaves relatively small,
3/4 to 1 1/4″ long, 1/4 to 1/2″ wide, occasionally 2 1/2″ long.

PROPAGATION: Cuttings root readily especially from July to October when treated with 3000 ppm
IBA-quick dip.

ADDITIONAL NOTES: Many cultivars available; I have updated disease susceptibilities based on evaluations made in the Pacific Northwest.

NATIVE HABITAT: Formosa.

Pyrus calleryana 'Bradford' — Bradford Callery Pear
(pī′rus kal-er-ē-ā′na)

FAMILY: Rosaceae

This discussion is concerned with the cultivar Bradford and not the species.

LEAVES: Alternate, simple, broad-ovate to ovate, 1 1/2 to 3″ long, about as wide, rarely elliptic-ovate, short
acuminate, rounded, broad-cuneate, subcordate or truncate at base, crenate, usually quite glabrous,
leathery, lustrous dark green; petiole 1 to 1 1/2″ long.

BUDS: Large, terminal and laterals of approximately same size, ovoid, elongated, 1/2″ long, intensely woolly, dirty gray to gray-brown.

STEM: Stout, brownish sometimes exhibiting ridges running from base of leaf scar, generally white woolly pubescent, especially below terminal gradually changing to smooth, glossy brown at maturity, thornless.

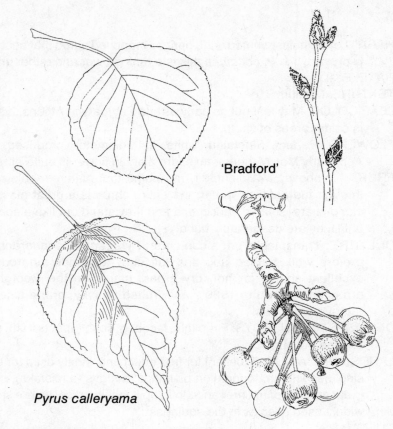

'Bradford'

Pyrus calleryama

SIZE: 30 to 50′ in height with a 20 to 35′ spread; 20 year old trees were 50′ high and 40′ wide.

HARDINESS: Zone 5 to 8(9).

HABIT: Moderately conical (pyramidal) in youth, and broadening with time.

RATE: Fast, 12 to 15′ over an 8 to 10 year period; a 12-year-old tree at the Secrest Arboretum was 24′ high, 22′ wide, and 7″ in diamater.

TEXTURE: Medium-fine in leaf, medium in winter.

BARK: Lustrous brown in youth, lightly ridged and furrowed and grayish brown at maturity.

LEAF COLOR: Outstanding glossy dark green in summer changing to glossy scarlet and purple shades in fall; very spectacular in fall color but variable; I have observed a great number of Bradford Pears in fall coloration and some were spectacular reddish purple, others yellow to red reminding of a persimmon orange; the leaves hold late and in northern areas color may not develop properly depending on the earliness of cold weather; in the south fall color is often an excellent glistening yellow to red and peaks in mid to late November.

FLOWERS: White, 3/8 to 3/4″ across, borne in 3″ diameter corymbs before or with the leaves, malodorous, in full flower in early to mid March in Athens, GA, and late April-early May in Urbana, Illinois, the tree looks like a white cloud in full flower; beautiful flowering tree.

FRUIT: Small rounded pome, 1/2″ or less across, russet-dotted, hidden by the foliage; not ornamentally effective; may be present in great quantities.

CULTURE: Easy to transplant balled and burlapped if moved in late winter or early spring; some nurserymen will not move them in leaf, very adaptable to many different soils; tolerates dryness, pollution, and should be sited in full sun; prune in winter or early spring.

DISEASES AND INSECTS: Resistant to fireblight which is so troublesome to the Common Pear, *Pyrus communis;* basically free of pests although I have seen tip dieback from fireblight in the south.

LANDSCAPE VALUE: In the second (1977) edition I commented that I hoped to see more Bradfords; little did I realize that this cultivar would literally inhabit almost every city and town to some degree or another; the tree is now approaching epidemic proportions and will no doubt be over-planted the way Green Ash, Silver Maple and Siberian Elm are/were; 'Bradford' is beautiful but not a panacea for urban planting; to some extent problems are now starting to appear that should give reason to temper enthusiasm for the cultivar; incompatability and severe splitting are occurring on older trees; Bradford tends to develop rather tight crotches and I have seen trees that were literally split in half; new cultivars have been introduced and several show promise; 'Bradford' is still popular but its limitations have been recognized by many knowledgeable plantsmen and nurserymen; unfortunately the buying public has not yet caught up; for short term use perhaps 10 to

15 years, 20 with luck, the tree is magnificent; the plant will literally fall apart because of the development of many branches around a common length of the trunk, plants manifest the problem by losing the distinct pyramidal shape and eventually becoming wide fan-shaped; plants have literally split in half before even reaching the fan shape; a move toward better pruning in the nursery has been advocated but economically and practically this has not worked out; genetically the tree is programmed to grow the way it does; if liabilities are understood then the plant is acceptable for use. 'Bradford' was the first selection of *P. calleryana* and was selected at the USDA Plant Introduction Station, Glenn Dale, MD from seedlings of Chinese seed, named in 1963, at that time the original tree was 44-years-old, 50′ high and 30′ wide; I suggest that the reader refer to Dirr, *American Nurseryman* 154(6), 1981. "What do we know about cultivars?"

PROPAGATION: Seeds of the species require cold (32 to 36°F) for 60 to 90 days. Seeds collected on January 17 from trees at the Atlanta Botanical Garden germinated 7 days after planting. Apparently the seeds had received sufficient natural cold moist stratification while still in the fruit. Much has been written about rooting cuttings and my graduate students and I have conducted considerable work. The best success I have seen was at Greenleaf Nursery, OK where the propagator Randy Davis took firm cuttings, treated them with 10,000 ppm IBA + 5000 ppm NAA quick dip, bark: sand, mist and achieved 70% rooting, with quality root systems.

OTHER CULTIVARS:

'Aristocrat'—Selection by William T. Straw, Carlisle Nursery, Independence, Kentucky; basically pyramidal to broad-pyramidal in outline, branches more horizontal and crotch angles wider, lustrous dark green leaves with a wavy edge and for that reason quite distinct from other *P. calleryana* selections; fall color is variable and ranges from yellow to red; trees I have seen were not as good as 'Bradford' although it is advertised as having better fall color; flowers are more sparsely borne but still quite attractive; tends to maintain a central leader and shows great vigor for 6-year-old trees may be 12′ high, 10′ wide with a 3″ trunk diameter; thornless; shows about the same cold and heat tolerance as 'Bradford'; is more fireblight susceptible than 'Bradford,' 36′ high and 16′ wide after 15 years, fireblight in the southeast during 1988 and 1989 has been devastating on this cultivar, many growers refuse to plant another 'Aristocrat'; in the north I have not noticed the problem to the degree it has occurred in the south.

'Autumn Blaze'—An introduction by Dr. Westwood, Oregon State, for consistent reddish purple fall color; it is also more cold hardy than 'Bradford'; supposedly with upright, pyramidal crown with lateral branches at about right angles to the central leader, trees I have seen have been more pyramidal-rounded, also will develop a few thorns, appears highly susceptible to fireblight, selected in 1969 at Oregon State, patented in 1980.

'Capital'—New introduction from the U.S. National Arboretum that is more upright than 'Whitehouse' and can be substituted for Lombardy Poplar; its leaves turn coppery in fall; see *HortScience* 16(6):799–800. 1981; early reports indicated it was a good selection; leaves are a lustrous dark green, show moderate to good fireblight resistance, grew 32′ high by 8′ wide after 15 years, possibly a good choice for narrow restricted growing areas, recent evaluations (1988 and 1989) reported tremendous fireblight susceptibility, in fact, so great that nurserymen are removing it from the fields in southern nurseries.

'Chanticleer' (same as 'Select, 'Cleveland Select' and 'Stone Hill')—A fine upright-pyramidal form that is much nar-

'Chanticleer'

rower than 'Bradford'; it flowers heavily and fall color may be a good reddish purple; the few times I have seen it in fall color it did not measure up to 'Bradford'; the leaves are longer and more ovate (see drawing) than 'Bradford' and thinner in texture; thornless; a fine tree and probably a better choice where lateral space to spread is limited; interestingly 'Chanticleer' hardens off earlier than 'Bradford' and may be less susceptible to early freezes, will grow 35' high, 16' wide in 15 years, has shown good fireblight resistance, a Scanlon introduction.

'Fauriei' *(P. fauriei)*—Often listed as a variety and by some authorities considered a species but because it is vegetatively propagated I will treat it as a cultivar; this is another tree that the literature said will be small (20') and round-headed; unfortunately the plant did not read the book and we know it will grow 30 to 40' and develop a pleasing pyramidal outline; the ovate leaves are lustrous dark green and thin; it tends to fall color (yellow or red) earlier than 'Bradford' and drop the leaves earlier; tends to develop a nice crown even in youth; its crotch angles are wider than 'Bradford' and it makes a less stiff, formal appearance in the landscape; supposedly it shows good urban soil tolerance; the buds on this form are distinctly different than the other *P. calleryana* types for they are reddish brown and show only a minor amount of gray pubescence; thornless; a fine tree in Spring Grove was devastated by storm damage; grew 32' by 25' in 15 years; in KS, averaged 1'4" per year over an 8-year-period.

'Paradise' (Dancer)—Young leaves silvery, changing to lustrous dark green, thick, elliptical and finely serrated, petiole permits fluttering in slightest breeze, develops a good main leader excellent branch angle and well-proportioned crown, white flowers 3 weeks later than 'Bradford', fruit size same as 'Bradford', about 3/8" across; 20' by 15'; Zone 5 to 7, a Wandell introduction.

'Princess'—I have only seen the tree on one occasion and it reminded of a 'Bradford', considered a rounded form of 'Bradford' but hardier, the original tree (25-years-old) was 28' high with an equal spread, a Scanlon introduction.

'Pzazz'—A smaller form than 'Bradford' with attractive bright green leaves and distinctive ruffled leaf margins, better branch structure than 'Bradford' or 'Redspire', 35' by 25', Zone 5 to 7, a Wandell introduction.

'Rancho'—Another Scanlon introduction with a columnar pyramidal form, fall color develops about 10 days earlier than 'Chanticleer', after 15 years averaged 32' high and 15' wide.

'Redspire'—A pyramidal form without the inherent stiffness of 'Bradford'; the ovate leaves are thick, shiny dark green and turn more yellow than red in fall; it colors ahead of 'Bradford'; and in my estimation makes a fine tree; thornless; slower growing and does not caliper as fast as 'Bradford'; unfortunately quite susceptible to fire blight; originated as a seedling of 'Bradford', ceases growth in early fall.

'Stonehill'—Apparently another name for 'Chanticleer', was informed by a Pennsylvania nurseryman that this is another rename.

'Trinity'—Tightly rounded head, profuse single white flowers, glossy light green leaves, orange-red fall color, negligible fruit, 30'.

'Whitehouse'—A U.S. National Arboretum introduction selected in 1969 from a population of 2500 seedlings resulting from an open pollination of 'Bradford' and other *P. calleryana* seedlings; it develops a columnar-pyramidal form with a strong central leader and fine, profuse, upward arching branches, a tree may be 14' high and only 3 1/2' wide, 35'

'Redspire'

by 14′ after 14 years; the leaves are glossy green, long pointed and narrower than 'Bradford'; fall color may range from red to reddish purple, colors earlier than other cultivars; in youth it is a faster grower than 'Bradford' because of the strong dominance of the central leader; thornless; see *HortScience* 12:591–592. 1977; flowers about 5 days later than 'Bradford'; leaf spot is terrible and disfigures leaves to the degree that trees are a liability; considerable hype has surrounded this tree and claims like "more urban tolerant and drought tolerant than 'Bradford' " have been made, unfortunately this form is less than desirable and several southern nurserymen who started to grow the plant in the early 1980's have quit.

Santamour and McArdle, *J. Arboriculture* 9(4):114–116 (1983) provide excellent background information on the species and cultivars. Also Haserodt and Sydnor, *J. Arboriculture* 4(6):160–163 (1983) profile the growth habits of 5 cultivars of *Pyrus calleryana*.

NATIVE HABITAT: *Pyrus calleryana* is native to Korea and China. Introduced 1908. 'Bradford' was raised from seed purchased in 1919 from Nanjing, China. The original reason for introducing *P. calleryana* was to breed fireblight resistance into the fruiting pears. This never materialized but the original effort resulted in several ornamental trees.

RELATED SPECIES:

Pyrus communis—Common Pear
(pī′rus kom-mū′nis)

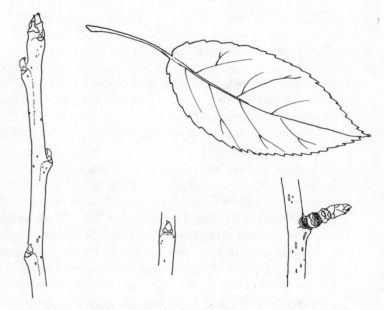

LEAVES: Alternate, simple, orbicular-ovate to elliptic, 3/4 to 3″ (4″) long, up to 2″ wide, acute or short acuminate, subcordate to broad-cuneate, crenate-serrulate, glabrous or villous when young, lustrous dark green; petiole 1 to 2″ long.

BUDS: Imbricate, conical, sharp pointed, smooth or slightly hairy, terminal about 1/3″ long, laterals—small, generally divergent and not flattened or at times on vigorous shoots both flattened and appressed.

STEM: Stout, glabrous or slightly downy, yellowish green or sometimes with tinge of brown; stubby-branched, slow-growing fruit spurs abundant.

BARK: Grayish brown, smooth on young branches, with age longitudinally fissured into flat-topped ridges which are further broken by transverse fissures into oblong scales.

FRUIT: A large fleshy pome, top-shaped to rounded, green to yellowish green.

Pyrus communis, Common Pear, is only mentioned here because it is sometimes trained as an espaliered plant. Tremendous fireblight susceptibility and not recommended for ornamental purposes although the white, 1 to 1 1/2″ diameter flowers are quite showy and malodorous. Very early flowering and I have seen it in full flower on February 22 at Savannah, GA, usually March 1–15 in Athens, GA. Tends to seed and can form thickets. Europe, western Asia. Long cultivated. Escaped and naturalized. Zone 4 to 8(9).

Pyrus kawakamii—Evergreen Pear

LEAVES: Alternate, simple, evergreen, ovate to obovate, 2 to 4″ long, finely and regularly serrate, lustrous dark green; petiole—1 1/4″ long.

Pyrus kawakamii, (pī′rus caw-a-cam′-ē-i), Evergreen Pear, is a small rounded evergreen tree that offers abundant white flowers in late winter or early spring. Tends toward a large shrub and the branches droop and sprawl. Used on the West Coast, particularly California. I have seen a few trees on the Georgia coast but they were decimated by fireblight. The branches may develop thorns. Fruit is globose, glabrous, about 1/2″ across and inedible. Native to China, Taiwan. Zone 8 to 10.

Pyrus pyrifolia—Chinese Sand Pear

LEAVES: Alternate, simple, ovate-oblong, 2 3/4 to 4″ long, about half as wide, acuminate, rounded or rarely subcordate, glabrous, margins conspicuously bristle-tipped, lustrous dark green above, petiole—1 1/4 to 1 3/4″ long.

Pyrus pyrifolia, (pī′rus pī-ri-fō′li-a̓), Chinese Sand Pear, is a rather large (40′), pyramidal-rounded tree that literally explodes into a white blanket in April. The tree reminds of a white cloud. The globular, 1 1/4″ long and wide fruits are brownish and spotted with white, quite hard and gritty. The lustrous dark green leaves turn excellent orange-red in fall. Wilson introduced it in 1909 when collecting for the Arnold and a magnificent specimen from his collection is located along the Chinese walk. Central and western China. Zone 5 to 8.

Pyrus salicifolia—Willowleaf Pear

LEAVES: Alternate, simple, narrow-lanceolate, 1 1/2 to 3 1/2″ long, 1/3 to 2/3″ wide, tapering at both ends, entire, covered with gray down when young, later upper surface shining green, lower pubescent; petiole–1/2″ or less long.
STEM: Covered with a grayish white pubescence which falls away with age.

Pyrus salicifolia, (pī′rus sal-is-i-fō′li-a̓), Willowleaf Pear, reaches 15 to 25′ and possesses graceful, silvery-gray, willow-like leaves. Unfortunately it is very susceptible to fireblight and is seldom seen in cultivation in the United States. I learned this tree in my plant materials course at Ohio State in 1962 and did not see it again until 1981 at Bodnant Garden, Wales. Habit is oval rounded with graceful arching branches. 'Pendula' with elegant drooping branches is probably more common in cultivation than the species. 'Silver Frost' is described as broadly weeping to pendulous, 12 to 15′ high, 10 to 12′ wide, with silver-gray foliage; I suspect it may be 'Pendula' with a fancy name. Flowers are pure white and closely packed in small rounded corymbs. Fruits are typical pear-shape and 1 to 1 1/4″ long and wide. Southeastern Europe, western Asia. Introduced 1780. Zone 4 to 7.

Pyrus ussuriensis—Ussurian Pear

LEAVES: Alternate, simple, orbicular-ovate to ovate, 2 to 4″ long, acuminate, rounded or slightly cordate, finely and regularly bristle-toothed, glabrous, lustrous dark green; petiole—1 to 2 1/4″ long.

Pyrus ussuriensis, (pī′rus ū-soor-ē-en′sis), Ussurian Pear, is the hardiest of all pears. The habit is dense, rounded, 40 to 50′; the leaves are a handsome, glossy dark green in summer changing to red and reddish purple in the fall. Flowers may be faintly pink in bud, finally white, 1 1/3″ across, April-May. The fruit is a 1 to 1 1/2″ diameter, greenish yellow, subglobose pome. It, along with *P. calleryana,* is the least susceptible to fireblight. For colder climates it would prove a valuable ornamental. Truly a handsome ornamental tree but has never been developed like *P. calleryana.* Northeastern Asia. Introduced 1855. Zone 3 to 6 or 7.

Quercus acutissima — Sawtooth Oak
(kwẽr′kus a-kū-tis′i-mȧ)

FAMILY: Fagaceae

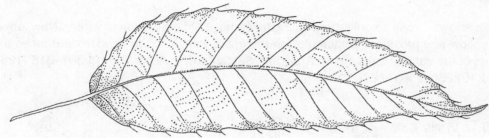

LEAVES: Alternate, simple, 3 1/2 to 7 1/2″ long, 1 to 2 1/4″ wide, obovate-oblong to oblong, acute, broad-cuneate or rounded at base, serrate with bristle-like teeth terminating the 12 to 16 parallel veins, lustrous dark green, glabrous above, glabrous beneath except axillary tufts of hairs, pubescent when unfolding; petioles 3/4 to 1″ long; leaf looks like a *Castanea* leaf in many respects and is often confused with same.

BUDS: Imbricate, pubescent, almost woolly, grayish brown, 1/4 to 1/3″ long; somewhat similar to *Q. velutina* in appearance, usually larger but not as angled.

SIZE: 35 to 45′ in height; I have seen trees taller than wide and others wider than tall; probably great variation in seed grown material although the trend is toward a broad, rounded outline.

HARDINESS: Zone 5 to 6 to 9.

HABIT: Dense, broad pyramidal in youth; varying in old age from oval-rounded to broad-rounded with low-slung, wide-spreading branches.

RATE: Initially medium, in 16 years grew 32′; in Wichita, KS tests averaged 2′3″ per year over a 7-year period.

TEXTURE: Pleasantly medium in foliage, medium to medium-coarse in winter.

BARK: Deeply ridged and furrowed, on old trunks appearing almost corky.

LEAF COLOR: Dark lustrous green in summer; often a good clear yellow to golden brown fall color, developing late, often in November; leaves open a brilliant yellow to golden yellow in spring, in late March-early April, Athens.

FLOWERS: Male, in 3 to 4″ long slender golden catkins in late March-early April with the emerging leaves.

FRUIT: Acorn, sessile, involucre with long, spreading and recurving scales, enclosing about 2/3's of the nut, about 1″ long, often heavy crops are borne, nut about 3/4″ long, lustrous rich brown, among the first acorns to ripen and fall.

CULTURE: Easily grown; I have seen it over a wide geographic area and it prefers acid, well-drained soils but appears quite adaptable; may develop chlorosis on high pH soils; thrives in the heat of the south.

DISEASES AND INSECTS: None serious.

LANDSCAPE VALUE: Nice, wide spreading, clean foliaged shade or lawn tree; could be used more than it is especially in south where it is fast growing; hardiness reports are somewhat conflicting and I estimate it will withstand -20°F once established; at a conference in Lincoln, Nebraska, where I lectured, a gentleman mentioned that the tree is growing in Blair, NE where winters can be extremely harsh; in spring the tree is covered with pendent, golden male catkins which are quite attractive; old leaves will persist throughout the winter; it also fruits heavily in the south showing an alternate year bearing tendency.

CULTIVARS: 'Gobbler' is the result of open-pollinated progeny that produce early and abundant acorns for wild turkey food.

PROPAGATION: Sow in fall, germination occurs in spring, root apparently emerges without cold treatment; shoot requires cold.

NATIVE HABITAT: Japan, Korea, China, Himalaya. Introduced 1862.

RELATED SPECIES:

Quercus variabilis, (kwĕr′kus vãr-i-ab′-i-lis), Oriental Oak, is a large (60 to 70′), fairly open tree with foliage similar to *Q. acutissima* except the upper surface is a dull dark green and the underside of the leaf is clothed with a distinct whitish tomentum and the teeth are shorter. The bark is very corky and deeply ridged and furrowed. Native to northern China, Korea, Japan. Introduced 1861. Zone 5 to 7.

ADDITIONAL NOTES: Shows strong juvenility and young trees may hold the leaves all winter. New leaves emerge a light yellow and provide a golden glow to the entire tree. Two worthwhile references that describe cultivars of the various oaks are McArdle and Santamour, *J. Arbor.* 11(10):307–315 (1985) and *J. Arbor.* 13(10):250–256 (1987).

Quercus alba — White Oak
(kwĕr′kus al′bà)

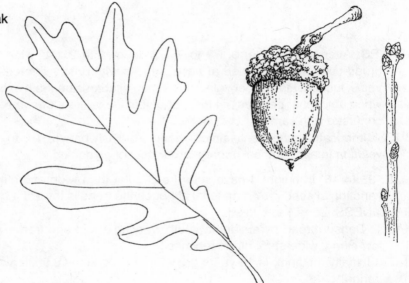

FAMILY: Fagaceae

LEAVES: Alternate, simple, obovate to oblong-obovate, 4 to 8 1/2″ long, about one-half as wide, narrowed at cuneate base, with 5 to 9 oblong and obtuse, entire lobes, dark green to almost dark blue-green above, pale or glaucous beneath; petiole 1/2 to 1″ long, yellowish green.

BUDS: Imbricate, broadly ovate, blunt, reddish brown to brown in color, 1/8 to 1/4″ long, sometimes slightly hairy especially at ends of bud scales.

STEM: Stout, brown to purple, angled, sometimes covered with a wavy grayish bloom.

SIZE: 50 to 80′ in spread; can grow well over 100′ in the wild; the Wye Oak in Maryland is 400-years-old, 95′ high, 165′ wide, 8′ in diameter.

HARDINESS: Zone 3 to 9.

HABIT: Pyramidal when young, upright-rounded to broad-rounded with wide-spreading branches at maturity; very imposing specimen when full grown, one of the most handsome oaks.

RATE: Slow to medium, 12 to 15′ over a 10 to 12 year period, very slow after first 20 to 30 years.

TEXTURE: Medium in leaf, medium to coarse in winter but with a strong, bold appearance.

BARK: On old trunks light ashy-gray, variable in appearance, often broken into small, vertically arranged blocks, scaly on the surface; later irregularly plated or deeply fissured, with narrow ridges; sometimes rather smooth and gray in spots; this is caused by a fungus.

LEAF COLOR: Grayish and pinkish when unfolding changing to dark green in summer, almost tends toward a blue-green; fall color varies from brown to a rich red to wine color and lasts for a long period of time; in fall of 1988 I saw the best fall color, a rich reddish purple on many White Oaks in the south.

FLOWERS: The following discussion concerns the flowers of the genus *Quercus* and is applicable to most species covered in this text. Monoecious, appearing on the old or new growth; staminate catkins pendent, clustered; individual flowers comprising a 4 to 7 lobed calyx which encloses 6 stamens, rarely 6 to 12; pistillate flowers solitary or in few to many-flowered spikes from the axils of the new leaves; individual flowers consisting of a 6 lobed calyx surrounding a 3 (rarely 4 to 5) celled ovary, the whole partly enclosed in an involucre.

FRUIT: Nut, solitary or paired, sessile or short stalked, 3/4 to 1″ long, ovoid-oblong, enclosed for 1/4 of its length in a light chestnut brown, bowl-like cup (involucre), involucre with raised "bumpy" scales rather than smooth overlapping scales like *Q. rubra,* nut colors a deep brown.

CULTURE: Transplant balled and burlapped as a small tree; found on many types of soil although performs maximally in deep, moist, well-drained soils; prefer acid soils, pH 5.5 to 6.5; full sun; prune in winter or early spring. There is a delicate balance in forest situations and when man encroaches and builds roads and houses in White Oak timber the trees often gradually decline and die. This is, in part, due to compaction, ruination of mycorrhizal associations and removal of the recycled organic matter from under the trees.

DISEASES AND INSECTS: The following is a list of problems reported occurring on oaks: anthracnose, basal canker, canker, leaf blister, leaf spots, powdery mildew, rust, twig blights, wilt, wood decay, shoe-string root rot, various galls, scales, yellow-necked caterpillar, pin oak sawfly, saddleback caterpillar, oak skeletonizer, asiatic oak weevil, two-lined chestnut borer, flatheaded borer, leaf miner, oak lace bug and oak mite; in spite of this inspiring list of pests, White Oak is a durable, long-lived tree.

LANDSCAPE VALUE: It is doubtful if this will ever become a popular ornamental tree unless it is native in a specific area; production is difficult, growth is slow, and transplanting can be a problem; a majestic and worthwhile tree for large areas; the state tree of Illinois; actually among the most handsome of oaks.

PROPAGATION: Seed requires no special treatment; direct sow after collection.

ADDITIONAL NOTES: The most important species of the White Oak group. The wood is used for furniture, flooring, interior finishing, boat building, wine and whiskey casks. The acorn is edible and is eaten by many kinds of birds and mammals. Best to boil in water to remove tannins.

NATIVE HABITAT: Maine to Florida, west to Minnesota and Texas. Introduced 1724.

RELATED SPECIES:

Quercus bicolor — Swamp White Oak
(kwẽr′kus bī′kul-ẽr)

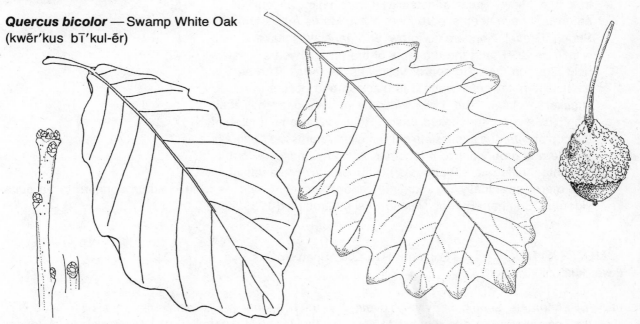

LEAVES: Alternate, simple, oblong-obovate to obovate, 3 to 7″ long, 1 1/4 to 4″ wide, acute or rounded cuneate, coarsely sinuate-dentate with 6 to 10 pairs of coarse obtuse teeth, or sometimes lobed halfway to the midrib, lustrous dark green above, whitish tomentose or grayish green and velvety beneath, midrib yellowish, leathery in texture; petiole 1/2 to 3/4″ long, yellowish.

BUDS: Imbricate, broadly ovate, light chestnut brown, 1/8″ long, coated with pale down above the middle; clustered buds often house needle- to strap-like appendages.

STEM: Stout to slender, yellowish brown to reddish brown, glabrous.

BARK: Flaky, grayish brown, divided by deep longitudinal fissures into rather long flat ridges; on old trunks rugged and handsome.

Quercus bicolor, Swamp White Oak, grows 50 to 60′ in height with an equal or greater spread; forms a broad, open, round-topped crown and a short, limby trunk; the acorn is about 1″ long, usually paired, covered about 1/3 by the involucre, shining light brown nut, borne on slender 1 to 4″ long peduncles; found in the wild in low lying and more or less swampy situations, often occurring in moist bottom lands and along the banks of streams; requires acid soil; I have observed very severe chlorosis on this species; there are mixed answers as to the ease of transplanting, several nurserymen said easy, others difficult; generally considered easier than *Q. alba.* Many beautiful specimens at Mt. Airy, Cincinnati, OH, fully 60 to 80′ high and 60 to 70′ wide. Excellent drought resistance is inherent in this species. Winter silhouette is more coarse than *Q. alba* because of the numerous short branches that develop from secondary branches. Normal fall color is yellow but have seen reasonable red-purple. Native Quebec to Georgia, west to Michigan and Arkansas. Introduced 1800. Zone 3 to 8.

Quercus cerris — Turkey Oak
(kwẽr′kus ser′ris)

LEAVES: Alternate, simple, oval or oblong, 2 1/2 to 5″ long, 1 to 3″ wide, coarsely dentate to pinnately lobed, teeth triangular and acute, lustrous dark green above, dull light green and pubescent below; petiole variable, 1/8 to 3/4″ long.

Quercus cerris, Turkey Oak, is a striking, round-headed, 40 to 60′ high and wide tree that shows great adaptability but is unknown outside of arboreta. I have seen superb trees at the Morris Arboretum and Spring Grove. Appears to grow well in clay soils and has withstood -25°F and the droughts of the past 10 years. Leaves hold late and die off green or yellow-brown in fall. The bark is especially noteworthy since it is blackish and occurs in raised checkered plates. The 1″ long acorns are enclosed half their length by a cup with reflexed scales. Reminds to some degree of the cup of *Quercus acutissima* only smaller. Acorns are generally sessile and grouped 1 to 4 together. A most handsome form is 'Argenteo-variegata' ('Variegata') with creamy-white blotches and margins; actually the marginal variegation often reaches to the midrib; appears to be quite vigorous. Southern Europe, western Asia. Introduced 1735. Zone 5 to 7 (?).

Quercus falcata — Southern Red Oak, Spanish Oak
(kwẽr′kus fal-kā′tȧ)

LEAVES: Alternate, simple, obovate to ovate, 5 to 9″ (12″) long, 4 to 5″ wide, either shallowly 3-lobed at the apex or more or less deeply 5 to 7-lobed, often falcate, the terminal lobe sometimes much longer than the laterals, apex acuminate or falcate, base rounded to broadly cuneate, lustrous dark green above, grayish green and tomentose below turning brownish with time; petiole—1 to 2″ long, often pubescent, yellowish.

BUDS: Imbricate, 1/4″ long, ovoid, acute, dusty reddish brown, pubescent especially toward apex.

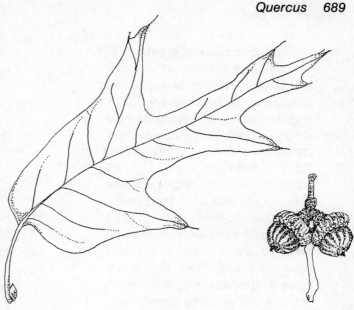

STEM: Reddish brown, angled, pubescent or nearly glabrous.

Quercus falcata, Southern Red Oak, is one of the most common upland southern oaks and is particularly characteristic of the drier, poorer soils of the Piedmont. There are a great number at the Georgia Botanical Garden and several large specimens on the Georgia campus. The species will grow 70 to 80′ and with time forms a rounded outline. The leaves hold late and fall color at best brown, perhaps with a tinge of red. The 1/2″ long, subglobose nut is borne either singly or paired. The cup is shallow and sits on the top of the nut. The nut is distinctly striate with alternating more or less parallel lines of light and dark brown to black. The variety *pagodifolia,* Cherrybark Oak, Swamp Spanish Oak, has leaves more uniformly lobed than the species, with the margins of the ribs at right angles to the midrib. The variety is found in a number of bottomland habitats but develops best on loamy ridges. The species is native from New Jersey to Florida, west to Missouri and Texas. Introduced before 1763. Zone (6)7 to 9. The variety runs from Virginia to Florida west to southern Illinois and Arkansas. Introduced 1904. Zone 7 to 9.

Quercus hemisphaerica — Laurel Oak
(kwĕr′kus hem-i-sfer′ik-à)

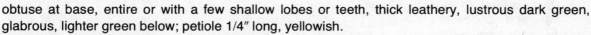

LEAVES: Alternate, simple, evergreen until February in Athens, lanceolate, elliptic to oblanceolate, obovate, or oblong-obovate, 1 1/4 to 4″ long, 1/2 to 1 1/4″ (2″) wide, acute or obtuse, usually with a bristle-tip, cuneate or obtuse at base, entire or with a few shallow lobes or teeth, thick leathery, lustrous dark green, glabrous, lighter green below; petiole 1/4″ long, yellowish.

BUDS: Imbricate, reddish brown, 1/16 to 1/8″ long, essentially glabrous, very small for oak buds, much more so than *Q. phellos* with which it can be confused.

STEM: Gray-brown, glabrous, dotted with small lenticels.

Quercus hemisphaerica, Laurel Oak, is reasonably common throughout coastal plain in the south. The habit is pyramidal-rounded with ultimate height ranging from 40 to 60′ and spread of 30 to 40′. Several trees on the Georgia campus are exceedingly handsome and are thriving in less than ideal locations. The lustrous dark green leaves persist into February and later depending on the severity of winter. Acorns are short stalked (virtually sessile), the nut subglobose to ovoid, about 1/2″ long, enclosed 1/4 to 1/3″ by the saucer-shaped cap.

It has found favor as a street tree in many cities of the south. It is not as long lived or sturdy as *Q. virginiana* but because of smaller size is a good choice for residential landscapes. There are no special soil requirements or pests. 'Darlington' is more compact and the leaves more persistent than the species. I have observed the above cultivar (debatable as to cultivar status, name derived from proximity of trees to Darlington, S.C.) as far north as Cincinnati, Ohio where it was distinctly deciduous. In the wild occupies well-drained, sandy soil with good water capacity. It occurs along the edges of rivers, swamps, and in flats. The rapid growth makes it a worthwhile choice for landscape use.

Great confusion abounds concerning the existence of this oak and *Q. laurifolia.* Many authorities considered *Q. laurifolia* the major species with *Q. hemisphaerica* simply lumped thereunder. Current status (see R.K. Godfrey, 1988. *Trees, shrubs and woody vines of northern Florida and adjacent Georgia and Alabama.* The University of Georgia Press, Athens, GA.) separates the two and possibly with good reason. *Q. laurifolia,* as I have observed it on the Georgia campus, loses all the leaves by December-January and is more open in out-

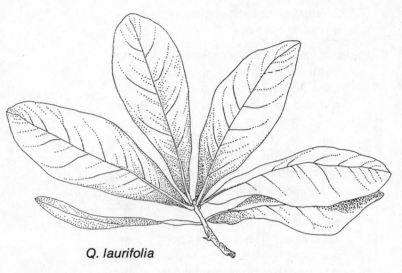

Q. laurifolia

line. Also, the leaves are larger and although many are similar to *Q. hemisphaerica,* others are almost diamond-shaped. Acorns are short stalked, much like *Q. hemisphaerica,* about 1/2″ long. Native to coastal plain and piedmont from southern New Jersey to Florida to east Texas and Southeast Arkansas. Zone 6 to 9.

Quercus imbricaria — Shingle Oak, also known as Laurel Oak
(kwĕr′kus im-bri-kā′ri-à)

LEAVES: Alternate, simple, oblong or lanceolate, 2 1/2 to 6″ long, 1 to 3″ wide, acute at apex with bristle-like tip, revolute margin, lustrous dark green and glabrous above, pale green or brownish and pubescent beneath; petiole 1/4 to 5/8″ long.

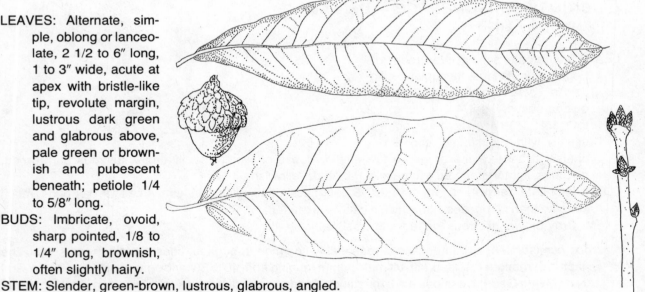

BUDS: Imbricate, ovoid, sharp pointed, 1/8 to 1/4″ long, brownish, often slightly hairy.
STEM: Slender, green-brown, lustrous, glabrous, angled.

SIZE: 50 or 60′ in height, developing a comparable or slightly greater spread, can grow 80 to 100′ in height.
HARDINESS: Zone 4 to 8.
HABIT: Pyramidal to upright-oval in youth assuming a broad-rounded outline in old age, often with drooping lower lateral branches.
RATE: Slow to medium, 1 to 1 1/2′ per year over a 10 to 20 year period.
TEXTURE: Medium in leaf, medium-coarse in winter.
BARK: Gray-brown, close, eventually with broad low ridges separated by shallow furrows.
LEAF COLOR: Reddish when first unfolding changing to a lustrous dark green in summer and assuming yellow-brown to russet-red colors in fall; old leaves often persisting through winter.

FRUIT: Nut, short-stalked subglobose, about 5/8″ long, the nut enclosed 1/3 to 1/2 in a thin bowl-shaped cup with appressed red-brown scales.

CULTURE: Transplants with less difficulty than many oaks; prefers moist, rich, deep, well-drained, acid soil although is tolerant of drier soils; somewhat tolerant of city conditions; full sun.

DISEASES AND INSECTS: See under White Oak.

LANDSCAPE VALUE: Does quite well in the midwest and has been used for lawn, street, park, golf course and other large areas; accepts pruning very well and can be used for hedges; the leaves persist into winter and aid in screening or breaking the wind, does not perform as well in Zone 8 as further north.

PROPAGATION: Seed, stratify in moist sand or peat for 30 to 60 days at 41°F or directly sow outside and germination will take place in spring.

ADDITIONAL NOTES: The wood of Shingle Oak was used to make shingles; hence, the common name.

NATIVE HABITAT: Pennsylvania to Georgia, west to Nebraska and Arkansas. Introduced 1724.

Quercus lyrata — Overcup Oak
(kwĕr′kus lī-rā′tȧ)

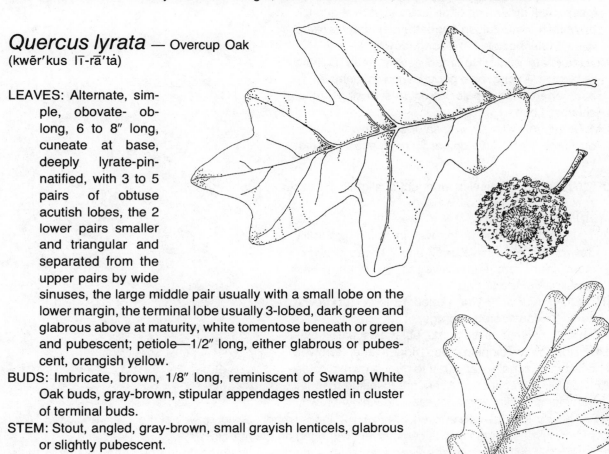

LEAVES: Alternate, simple, obovate- oblong, 6 to 8″ long, cuneate at base, deeply lyrate-pinnatified, with 3 to 5 pairs of obtuse acutish lobes, the 2 lower pairs smaller and triangular and separated from the upper pairs by wide sinuses, the large middle pair usually with a small lobe on the lower margin, the terminal lobe usually 3-lobed, dark green and glabrous above at maturity, white tomentose beneath or green and pubescent; petiole—1/2″ long, either glabrous or pubescent, orangish yellow.

BUDS: Imbricate, brown, 1/8″ long, reminiscent of Swamp White Oak buds, gray-brown, stipular appendages nestled in cluster of terminal buds.

STEM: Stout, angled, gray-brown, small grayish lenticels, glabrous or slightly pubescent.

Quercus lyrata, Overcup Oak, is a relatively obscure species but certainly worthy of consideration. The habit in youth is pyramidal-oval and oval-rounded to rounded at maturity. The branching is very uniform and a row of seedling-grown, 35′ high trees on the Georgia campus appear to be carbon copies of each other. The lower branches are upswept so minimal pruning is required compared to *Q. palustris.* These trees are growing in confined spaces on a slope and are thriving. The leaves are dark green and somewhat leathery. They turn a rich tannin-brown in fall and abscise earlier than those of other southern oaks. The common name is derived from the cup that almost completely encloses the nut. The nut is sub-globose to rounded, 3/4 to 1″ high, usually covered by the cup except for a small window at the base; other times the cup covers 3/4's of the nut. It is a bottomland species in the wild where it is found in sloughs and backwater areas. Apparently it will withstand considerable flooding. The ultimate size is 30 to 45′ high and wide. It might be worth considering for especially difficult sites. With selection and propagation this could become an important landscape tree. New Jersey to Florida, west to Missouri and Texas. Introduced 1786. Zone 5 to 9.

Quercus macrocarpa — Bur Oak, also called Mossycup Oak
(kwẽr′kus ma-krō-câr′pȧ)

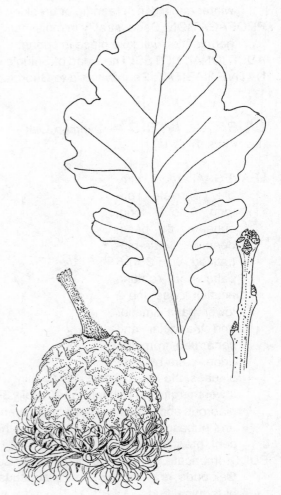

LEAVES: Alternate, simple, obovate to oblong-obovate, 4 to 10″ (12″) long, about 1/2 as wide, cuneate or rarely rounded at base, lower portion of leaf with 2 to 3 pairs of lobes, upper 5 to 7 pairs of ovate-obtuse lobes, dark green and often lustrous above, grayish or whitish tomentulose beneath, leaf shaped like a base fiddle; petiole 1 1/4″ long, downy.

BUDS: Imbricate, conical to broadly ovate, sharp pointed or blunt, 1/4″ long, pale pubescence covering entire bud, often with stipular structures arising out of clustered buds.

STEM: Stout, yellowish brown, smooth or downy, stems on some trees developing corky ridges after first year.

SIZE: 70 to 80′ in height with an equal or slightly greater spread, can grow to over 100′.

HARDINESS: Zone 2 to 8.

HABIT: Weakly pyramidal to oval in youth gradually developing a massive trunk and a broad crown of stout branches; impressive as an open grown specimen of the prairie.

RATE: Slow, over a 20-year-period 15 to 20′ of growth could be considered average.

TEXTURE: Coarse in all seasons, but majestically so.

BARK: Rough, developing deep ridged and furrowed character, usually dark gray to gray-brown in color.

LEAF COLOR: Often lustrous dark green in summer, fall color is dull yellow-green, yellow, to yellow-brown.

FRUIT: Nut, solitary, usually stalked, 3/4 to 1 1/2″ long, broadly ovoid, downy at the apex, enclosed 1/2 or more in a deep cup which is conspicuously fringed on the margin.

CULTURE: Difficult to transplant; very adaptable to various soils and is found on sandy plains to moist alluvial bottoms; on uplands, limestone soils are favored; succeeds well even in dry, clay soils; more tolerant of city conditions than most oaks; full sun.

DISEASES AND INSECTS: See under White Oak.

LANDSCAPE VALUE: Probably too large for the average home landscape; however, makes an excellent park or large area tree; very impressive and inspiring tree; there is one specimen in Urbana, Illinois over 90′ tall and estimated at 300 years of age.

PROPAGATION: No pretreatment is required although 30 to 60 days at 41°F in moist sand or peat is suggested.

ADDITIONAL NOTES: I have always been fascinated by variation within a species and when writing the identification features for many of the species in this book I literally cringe at the thought of presenting a stereotyped leaf, bud, stem, etc. I suggest the interested reader consult Dicke and Bagley, *Silvae Genetica* 29:171–196. 1980, for an interesting discussion of variation in Bur Oak. Professor Bagley told me that he has observed acorns on which the involucre is not fringed.

NATIVE HABITAT: Nova Scotia to Pennsylvania, west to Manitoba and Texas. Introduced 1811.

Quercus muehlenbergii — Chinkapin Oak, also called Yellow Chestnut Oak
(kwẽr'kus mū-len-berj'ē-ī)

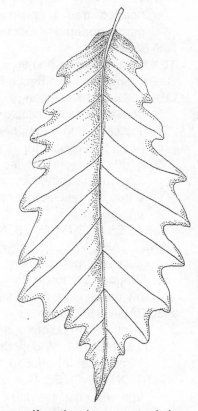

LEAVES: Alternate, simple, oblong to oblong-lanceolate, 4 to 6 1/2″ long, 1/3 to 1/2 as wide, acute or acuminate, usually rounded at base, coarsely toothed, with about 8 to 13 pairs of acute and mucronate often incurved teeth, lustrous dark yellow-green above, whitish tomentulose beneath; petiole—3/4 to 1 1/2″ long.

BUDS: Light brown or pale margined, ovoid or conical-ovoid, 1/6 to 1/4″ long.

STEM: Glabrous, brown, rounded, slender.

SIZE: 40 to 50′ under landscape conditions but can, and often does, grow 70 to 80′ tall in the wild, spread is usually greater than height at maturity.

HARDINESS: Zone 5 to 7.

HABIT: Weakly rounded in youth but of dapper outline; with maturity developing an open, rounded crown.

RATE: Medium in youth, slowing down with age.

TEXTURE: Medium in leaf; medium-coarse in winter.

BARK: Ashy-gray, more or less rough and flaky.

LEAF COLOR: Lustrous dark yellowish green in summer; fall color varies from yellow to orangish brown to brown.

FRUIT: Acorn, subsessile, globose-ovoid or ovoid, 3/4 to 1″ long, enclosed about 1/2 by the thin cup, scales small, depressed.

CULTURE: Like many oaks, somewhat difficult to transplant; in the wild is found on dry limestone outcrops and soils with an alkaline reaction; prefers rich bottomlands and there attains its greatest size.

DISEASES AND INSECTS: None particularly serious.

LANDSCAPE VALUE: Actually quite an attractive tree especially in old age; if native in an area it is worthwhile saving; I doubt if it will ever become a popular landscape tree; in Springfield, IL, I have seen 70 to 80′ mammoth specimens with large, bold scaly gray trunks and branches; trees are actually inspiring.

PROPAGATION: No seed pretreatment is necessary.

NATIVE HABITAT: Vermont to Virginia, west to Nebraska, Mexico and Texas. Introduced 1822.

Quercus myrsinifolia — Chinese Evergreen Oak
(kwẽr'kus mer-sin-i-fō' li-à)

LEAVES: Alternate, simple, evergreen, ovate to elliptic, 2 1/2 to 4″ long, 3/4 to 1 1/2″ wide, acuminate, rounded, bristle-tipped serrations, 10 to 16 vein pairs, the midrib scarcely impressed above, later nerves very slender, only slightly raised beneath, lustrous dark green above, glaucous green beneath; petiole—1/2 to 3/4″ long.

BUDS: Imbricate, slender-conical, gray-brown, pubescent at top, 1/4 to 3/8″ long.

STEM: Slender for an oak, shining brown, glabrous, prominently covered with small lenticels.

SIZE: 20 to 30′, spread slightly less or similar; have seen mature trees and most were round headed.

HARDINESS: Zone 7 to 9, the most cold hardy evergreen oak.

HABIT: Small, dapper, round headed tree that deserves much greater use for streets, parking islands, and containers.

RATE: Slow.

TEXTURE: Medium-fine throughout the seasons.

BARK: Smooth, gray, beech-like, actually smoother than a beech even in maturity.

LEAF COLOR: New foliage emerges purple-bronze, and changes to lustrous dark green with maturity; perhaps a slight discoloration in winter months.

FRUIT: Acorn, 2 to 4 together, 1/2 to 1″ long, oval-oblong, covered 1/3 to 1/2 by the glabrous cup which has 3 to 6 concentric rings.

CULTURE: Transplant balled and burlapped before buds break in winter or early spring, unbelievable soil tolerance: sandy, clay, acid, alkaline or dry, withstands tremendous summer heat, full sun although a tree on the Georgia campus is in 1/3 to 1/2 shade in a 15′ by 15′ restricted growing area and has prospered.

DISEASES AND INSECTS: None serious.

LANDSCAPE VALUE: Superb small street or lawn tree, used in Greenville, SC to soften large office buildings, plants are in raised planters, beautiful throughout the seasons; trees at the old USDA Bamboo Station in Savannah are 30 to 40′ high and have withstood the test of time; I planted two in my garden and with water and fertilizer the trees have averaged 18″ per year over the past 4 years.

PROPAGATION: Collect seed in fall and sow immediately or store and provide 1 to 2 months cold moist stratification before spring planting.

NATIVE HABITAT: Widely distributed in eastern Asia from Japan and Formosa through China and the Himalayas. Introduced 1807.

ADDITIONAL NOTES: Upon arrival in Georgia, I was introduced to several new evergreen oaks, although this one I had previously seen at the U.S. National Arboretum. Unfortunately, the nursery industry has confused the species and *Q. acuta, Q. glauca,* and *Q. myrsinifolia* are listed in various catalogs but in general describe the same oak, *Q. glauca.* The differences are adequately described under each species but for quick reference remember that the leaves of *Q. acuta* are entire, those of *Q. glauca* usually *coarsely* toothed one-third from the base to the apex. Also, *Q. myrsinifolia* is the most cold hardy, *Q. acuta* will grow only in Zone 9, if there, and *Q. glauca* was literally killed to the ground in Zone 8 at -3°F.

RELATED SPECIES:

Quercus acuta—Japanese Evergreen Oak
(kwēr′kus a-kū-tà)

LEAVES: Alternate, simple, evergreen, elliptic to ovate, 2 1/2 to 5 1/2″ long, 1 to 2 1/4″ wide, long acuminate, rounded to broad cuneate, entire, somewhat undulate, lustrous dark green above, yellowish green below, glabrous, 8 to 10 vein pairs; petiole—about 1″ long.

Quercus acuta, Japanese Evergreen Oak, is essentially non-existent in the southeast and the only place I have turned up a specimen was in the herbarium and it listed the location as a park in Albany, GA. For some unknown reason, this species is most often listed in nursery catalogs instead of *Q. glauca* and *Q. myrsinifolia,* which are the principal trees in commerce. In Europe, where I have seen the tree, it is always small and shrubby to 20′ high and wide, the leaves are handsome and the new growth emerges a purplish brown. Acorns are clustered like *Q. myrsinifolia* and the concentric ringed cup covers about 1/3 of the 3/4″ long nut. Japan. Introduced 1878. Zone 9.

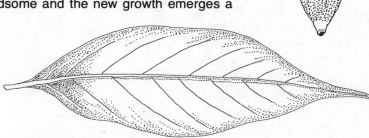

Quercus glauca—Blue Japanese Oak, Ring-cupped Oak
(kwĕr′kus glâ′kȧ)

LEAVES: Alternate, simple, evergreen, oblong, elliptic, to obovate-oblong, 2 1/2 to 5 1/2″ long, 1 to 2 1/2″ wide, strongly acuminate, slenderly tapered to rounded, strongly serrate in upper 1/2 to 2/3's, leathery, lustrous dark green above, gray-green beneath, pubescent, with 8 to 12 vein pairs, prominent beneath; petiole 1/2 to 1″ long, yellow.

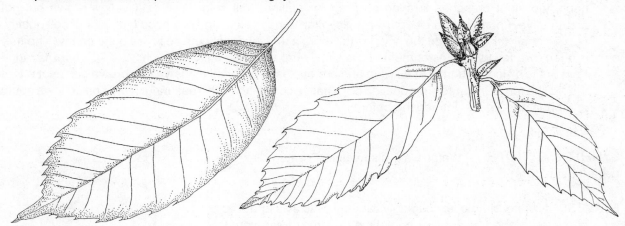

BUDS: Imbricate, abundantly clustered (5 to 7) at ends of stem, conical-angular, 5-sided, 1/4 to 1/2″ long, brown, glabrous, laterals diverge from stem at 45° angle.
STEM: Stout, slightly angular, dark olive-green, eventually becoming brown or purplish brown, glabrous, covered with small grayish lenticels; pith-solid, off-white.
FRUIT: Acorn, 1 to 3 in a cluster, 3/4″ long, enclosed 1/3″ in a downy cup with 6 to 7 raised concentric rings, ripens in one year.

Quercus glauca, Blue Japanese Oak, makes a handsome, almost shrubby appearance in the landscape. The habit is distinctly upright-oval with ultimate size approximately 20 to 30′ and spread about one-half this. The overall appearance is quite formal and the plant is best utilized in groupings. New foliage is either a rich green or bronze to purple green. Very handsome when the new foliage emerges which usually occurs in early April in the Piedmont. The emerging leaves may be injured by a late spring freeze. The leathery lustrous dark green leaves are handsome throughout the seasons. Tolerates heavy clay soils. Makes an excellent, large screen plant and requires a minimum of maintenance. The 1983–84 winter (-3°F in Athens) devastated the species and fine old specimens in Athens-Atlanta were killed. Was used at Atlanta Historical Society as a large screen and was effective and functional. Cold rendered these plants rubble. Japan and China. Introduced 1978. Zone 8 to 9.

Quercus marilandica — Blackjack Oak
(kwer'kus mar-i-lan'di-kȧ)

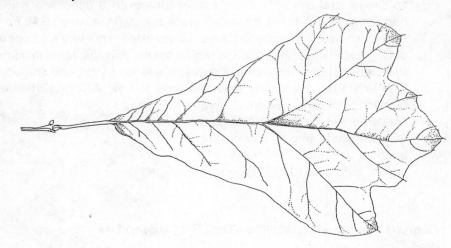

LEAVES: Alternate, simple,
broad obovate, 4 to 8″
long, often as broad at
the 3 to 5 lobed apex,
rounded at base, lobes
broad, entire or sparing-
ly toothed, lustrous dark
green and glabrous
above, brownish tomen-
tose beneath, finally al-
most glabrous and
yellowish green; peti-
oles 1/4 to 3/4″ long.

BUDS: Imbricate, ovoid,
coated with rusty brown hairs, 1/4 to 1/3″ long.

STEM: Stout, red-brown, pubescent initially, later brown to ash-gray.

Quercus marilandica, Blackjack Oak, is usually a scrubby tree with a Hounds-of-the-Baskervilles' gothic habit, the stout branches forming an irregular outline. Fall color is at best yellow-brown but not unattractive. Found in infertile, barren soils, often sandy veins, and is a good indicator of soil quality. I occasionally chance upon the species in Georgia and invariably the soils are quite sandy. The tree is often dwarfed by its environment and is somewhat shrublike but can reach 30 to 40′. Acorns range from 3/4 to 1″ long, about half as wide and are enclosed one-half in the yellow-brown cup. Not a tree that will be found in nursery production but if native certainly worth treasuring. New York to Iowa south to Florida and Texas. Introduced before 1739. Zone 6 to 9.

Quercus nigra — Water Oak, also called Possum Oak
(kwẽr'kus nī'grȧ)

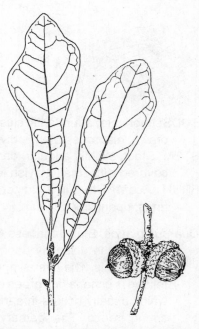

LEAVES: Alternate, simple, exceedingly variable as to size and shape,
obovate, 3-lobed at apex or sometimes entire, rarely pinnately
lobed above the middle, 1 1/2 to 4″ long, 1/2 to 2″ wide, dull bluish
green to lustrous dark green above, paler beneath, soon glabrous
except for axillary tufts of brown hairs; petiole 1/10 to 1/4″ long.

BUDS: Imbricate, ovoid, pointed, prominently angled, smooth, brown,
1/8 to 1/4″ long.

STEM: Slender, smooth, dull red to brown.

FRUIT: Acorn, usually solitary, 1/2″ long and wide, enclosed 1/3 in a
broad, shallow, short-stalked cup with appressed scales; nut with
alternating striated bands of brown and black.

Quercus nigra, Water Oak, is a conical to round-topped tree, 50 to 80′
high. It is popular in the south and has been effectively used on
the University of Georgia campus. Transplants readily and is quite
adaptable on moist to wet sites. Typically is it a bottomland species and is widespread and abundant along streams throughout the southeast from the Coastal Plain to the foothills of the mountains. Has been used effectively as a shade and street tree. The leaves persist quite late into fall and winter and I have observed a modicum of green foliage on trees in Spring Grove, Cincinnati, Ohio, as late as

December. The species is a weed tree in Zone 7 to 9 and can be found with Chinaberry in every abandoned location. The young juvenile seedling leaves are highly lobed and often evergreen. They *look nothing* like the species. This condition may persist for 3 to 6 years. The tree is also more weak-wooded than most oaks and limbs will break in wind, snow and ice. The inherent soil tolerance makes the species worth considering. A forester showed me a form of *Q. nigra* that looks just like *Carpinus betulus* 'Fastigiata'. Perhaps the species' best days are ahead. Mr. Rusty Allen, a former student, has had great success rooting a selected, compact dark green foliage form. His results are particularly encouraging. Water Oak extends from southern New Jersey, south to Florida, west to eastern Texas; and northward, in the Mississippi valley, to southeastern Missouri and eastern Oklahoma. Introduced 1723. Zone 6 to 9.

Quercus palustris — Pin Oak, also called Swamp Oak
(kwĕr′kus pa-lus′tris)

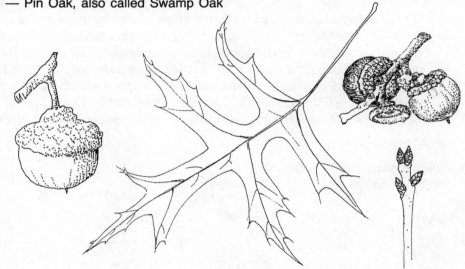

LEAVES: Alternate, simple, elliptic or elliptic-oblong, 3 to 6″ long, at times almost as wide, terminal lobe long acuminate, cuneate at base, sometimes truncate, 5 to 7 lobed, lustrous dark green above, lighter green beneath with axillary tufts of hair; key feature—major lobes "U"-shaped in comparison with "C"-shaped lobes of *Q. coccinea;* petiole up to 2″ long, slender.

BUDS: Imbricate, conical to ovate, sharp pointed, 1/8 to 1/4″ long, chestnut brown.

STEM: First year stems slender, greenish to brown; second and third year often greenish.

SIZE: 60 to 70′ in height with a spread of 25 to 40′, can attain a height of over 100′.

HARDINESS: Zone 4 to 8 (9).

HABIT: Strongly pyramidal, usually with a central leader; the lower branches pendulous, the middle horizontal, and the upper upright; in old age the tree assumes an oval-pyramidal form and loses many of the lower branches; very distinctive tree because of growth habit and widely planted as a lawn and street tree for this reason.

RATE: One of the faster growing oaks, 12 to 15′ over a 5 to 7-year-period; 'Sovereign' averaged 2′5″ per year over a 10-year period in Kansas tests.

TEXTURE: Medium in leaf, medium-coarse in winter.

BARK: Grayish brown, thinnish, smooth and with age develops narrow, relatively shallow ridges and furrows.

LEAF COLOR: Glossy dark green in summer changing to russet, bronze or red in fall; fall coloration is variable; great opportunity for selection if vegetative propagation techniques could be developed.

FRUIT: Nut, solitary or clustered, sessile to short-stalked, 1/2″ long and wide, nearly hemispherical, light brown, often striate, enclosed only at basal 1/4 to 1/3 in a thin, saucer-like cup.

CULTURE: Readily transplanted because of shallow, fibrous root system; will tolerate wet soils and is found in the wild on wet clay flats where water may stand for several weeks; actually prefers moist, rich, acid, well-drained soil; very intolerant of high pH soils and iron chlorosis can be a significant and disastrous problem with this species; somewhat tolerant of city conditions; tolerant of sulfur dioxide; full sun.

DISEASES AND INSECTS: Galls are often a problem; iron chlorosis can be serious but can be corrected; the use of capsules (ferric ammonium citrate) placed in the tree has proven very effective and has worked over a three-year-period.

LANDSCAPE VALUE: Probably the most widely used native oak for landscaping; a 1989 published survey by *American Nurseryman* magazine listed this as the most popular shade tree; possesses interesting habit and has been used for lawn, park, golf courses, commercial landscapes and streets; personally I feel there are many other superior oaks and tree species but this oak has outstanding customer appeal; correcting the chlorosis problem can be painful for the homeowner.

CULTIVARS:

'Crownright' ('Crown Right')—More upright habit, branches occur at a 30 to 60° angle to central leader and do not sweep ground; introduced by Princeton Nursery but not listed in spring, 1989 catalog.

'Sovereign'—The lower branches do not weep but are borne at a 90° to 45° angle to the main leader.

PROPAGATION: Seed, stratify at 32 to 41°F for 30 to 45 days; 'Sovereign' was originally grafted on Pin Oak seedlings; however, after several years a graft incompatability resulted; this was supposedly solved by grafting onto seedlings which had been produced from nuts collected from the original 'Sovereign' tree; from what I understand the incompatibility problem still occurs and this cultivar will probably be discontinued. Our early cutting propagation work indicated Pin Oak could be rooted, take cuttings when first growth flush hardens, 10000 ppm K-IBA, 2 perlite:1 peat, mist, with rooting 4 to 8 weeks later; see Drew and Dirr, *J. Environ. Hort.* 7:115-117 (1989).

NATIVE HABITAT: Massachusetts to Delaware, west to Wisconsin and Arkansas. Introduced before 1770.

RELATED SPECIES:

Quercus coccinea — Scarlet Oak
(kwẽr′kus cok-sin′ē-ȧ)

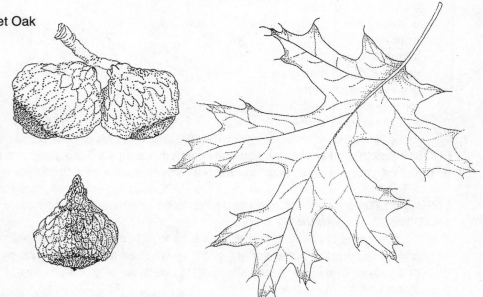

LEAVES: Alternate, simple, oblong or elliptic, 3 to 6″ long, 2 1/2 to 4 1/2″ wide, truncate or rarely broadly cuneate at base, with 7, rarely 9, bristle tipped lobes, lustrous dark green above, and glabrous beneath except tufts of hair sometimes occur in vein axils, major lobes "C" shaped; petiole 1 1/2 to 2 1/2″ long, glabrous, yellow.

BUDS: Imbricate, broadly ovate, blunt apex, 1/4 to 3/8″ long, dark reddish brown and glabrous below, pale woolly pubescent above middle, bud is shaped like a rugby ball.

STEM: Light brown to red-brown, glabrous, dotted with small gray lenticels, angled, older stems green with a luster.

Quercus coccinea, Scarlet Oak, grows 70 to 75′ in height by 40 to 50′ in width under landscape conditions but can reach 100′ in the wild, on the Georgia campus 70 to 80′ high and wide trees have withstood the test of time. Habit in youth is somewhat similar to Pin Oak but becomes more rounded and open at maturity; will grow 1 1/2 to 2′ per year over a 10 to 20 year period; foliage is an excellent glossy dark green in summer changing to scarlet in the fall, unfortunately some trees color russet red, if at all. Fruit is solitary or paired, short stalked, 1/2 to 1″ long, oval to hemispherical, reddish brown, rarely striate, often with concentric rings near the apex, 1/3 to 1/2 enclosed in a deep bowl-like cup; less tolerant of adverse conditions than Pin Oak and Red Oak and rarely available in the nursery trade;

Interestingly more nurseries are offering the species, although with difficulty in identification, it is difficult to determine if true Scarlet Oak is being sold; generally found on dry, sandy soils; usually does not develop chlorosis problems to the degree of Pin Oak; averaged 1'1" per year over 10 years in KS tests. Native range extends from Maine to Florida, west to Minnesota and Missouri. Zone 4 to 9. Introduced 1691.

Quercus shumardii — Shumard Oak
(kwẽr′kus shū-mar′dē-ī)

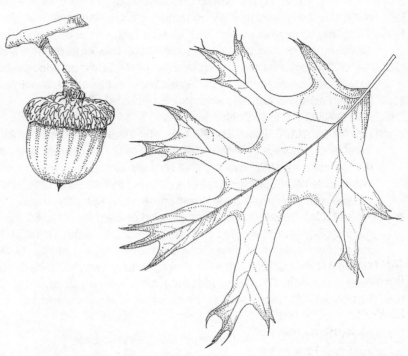

LEAVES: Alternate, simple, obovate to elliptic, 4 to 6" (8") long, 3 to 4" wide, usually with 7 lobes, occasionally 9, sinuses cut deeply to midrib, leathery, lustrous dark green above, glabrous except for axillary tufts of hairs below; petiole 1 1/2 to 2 1/4" long.

BUDS: Probably the only reliable aid to separate this species from *Q. palustris* and *Q. coccinea*; imbricate, angle-ovoid, 1/4" long, glabrous, gray or pale straw colored, never reddish brown.

Quercus shumardii, Shumard Oak, is a pyramidal tree becoming more spreading, much like Scarlet Oak, at maturity. Will grow 40 to 60' and wide at landscape maturity but can reach 100' or more in nature. Leaves may turn a good russet-red to red in fall. Acorns are ovate, 3/4 to 1" long, short-stalked and covered only at the base by a hemispherical shaped involucral cap. Considered a drought tolerant species and plantsmen in Oklahoma and Texas have extolled its virtues for use in those areas. Interestingly, in the wild, is found along streams, near swamps, or bodies of water in well drained soil. Grew 1'3.4" per year over a 10-year period in Kansas tests. Kansas to southern Michigan to North Carolina, Florida and Texas. Introduced 1907. Zone 5 to 9.

Quercus phellos — Willow Oak
(kwẽr′kus fel′ōs)

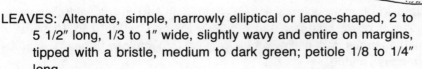

LEAVES: Alternate, simple, narrowly elliptical or lance-shaped, 2 to 5 1/2" long, 1/3 to 1" wide, slightly wavy and entire on margins, tipped with a bristle, medium to dark green; petiole 1/8 to 1/4" long.

BUDS: Imbricate, 1/8 to 1/4" long, ovoid, sharp-pointed, chestnut brown.

STEM: Slender, smooth, somewhat lustrous, reddish brown to dark brown.

BARK: Older, becoming gray and roughened by irregular furrows and thick, more or less scaly ridges.

SIZE: 40 to 60' high, 30 to 40' wide to a comparable spread, can grow 90 to 100' in ideal situations.

HARDINESS: 5 to 9, I still remember a handsome specimen on The Ohio State University Campus as well as older trees in Cincinnati that have been through -25°F.

HABIT: Pyramidal in youth, developing a dense oblong-oval to rounded crown at maturity.

RATE: Medium, 1 to 2' per year, may average 2' per year over a 10 to 20-year period, difficult tree to train to a central leader and requires considerable pruning in early years to make a respectable crown.

TEXTURE: Medium-fine through the seasons.

BARK: On old trunks, lightly ridged and furrowed, gray-brown.

LEAF COLOR: Light to bright green in spring changing to yellow, yellow-brown and russet-red in fall.

FRUIT: Acorn, solitary or paired, 1/2″ or less long and wide, subglobose, more or less stellate pubescent, enclosed at the base by a thin saucer-like cup, striated with alternating brown and blackish bands.

CULTURE: Transplants more readily than most *Quercus* species because of more fibrous root system, should still be moved in dormant season, preferably late winter, prefers moist and well drained soil but can adapt to virtually impossible habitats.

DISEASES AND INSECTS: None serious.

LANDSCAPE VALUE: From Zone 7 to 9, still the best oak for overall texture and form, finer textured than most and makes a splendid avenue, street or boulevard tree, also excellent for large area use, i.e., commercial establishments, golf courses and parks, many years past Milliken Corporation planted either side of I-85 in Spartanburg, SC and the effect is outstanding; I have mentioned the planting to people and they immediately remember driving by the trees.

PROPAGATION: Stratify seed in moist sand or peat for 30 to 60 days at 40°F or directly sow outside and germination will take place in the spring. Mr. John Drew, a former graduate student, conducted interesting work on rooting *Quercus* species from cuttings. *Q. phellos* was one of the easiest to root. He used firm cuttings after the first flush of growth hardened, 10,000 ppm KIBA-quick dip, 2 perlite:1 peat, mist, with 60 to 80% rooting in 10 weeks on *Q. phellos, Q robur,* and *Q. lyrata.*

NATIVE HABITAT: New York to Florida, west to Missouri and Texas. Introduced 1723.

Quercus prinus — Chestnut Oak, Basket Oak
(kwĕr′kus prī′nus)

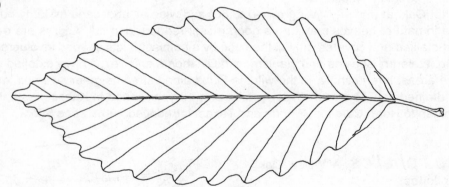

LEAVES: Alternate, simple, obovate to obovate-oblong, 4 to 6″ long, 1 1/2 to 3 1/2″ wide, acute or acuminate, cuneate or rounded at base, coarsely and regularly toothed, with 10 to 14 pairs of obtusish, often mucronate teeth, lustrous dark yellow-green, grayish tomentulose beneath; petioles 1/2 to 1″, yellow and color extends to midrib.

Quercus prinus (*Q. montana*), Chestnut Oak, is also called Rock Oak and Rock Chestnut Oak. This is a medium-sized tree reaching 60 to 70′ in height with a comparable, but irregular spread. The habit is rounded and relatively dense. The leaves are lustrous dark yellowish green in summer changing to orange-yellow to yellowish brown in fall. One tree (the only) in the fair city of Watkinsville, GA turns a reasonable reddish brown. Acorns are borne 1 to 2 on peduncles shorter than the petioles; ovoid, 1 to 1 1/4″ high, 3/4″ wide, enclosed 1/3 to 1/2 by the tuberculate cap. The nut is a rich dark brown. This is a tree of rocky places and is found on poor, dry, upland sites where it may form pure stands. Maximum growth is made in well-drained soils and other moist sites. It is often found in association with Scarlet and Black Oaks on the rocky slopes of mountains. This species can grow 12 to 15′ over a 7 to 10 year period. The acorns are sweet tasting and are relished by the gray squirrel, black bear, white-tailed deer and many other forms of wildlife. The bark is brown to nearly black and, on older trees, very deeply and coarsely furrowed. The bark is valuable, being richer in tannin content (11%) than that of any other oak species. Native from southern Maine and Ontario to South Carolina and Alabama. Cultivated 1688. Zone 4 to 8. A very lovely tree which does exceedingly well in dry, rocky soil. No seed pretreatment is necessary. *Quercus michauxii,* Swamp Chestnut Oak, is similar except it occurs in moister soils, grows larger and the involucral scales form a fringe round the rim. For ease of identification it might be better lumped with *Q. prinus.* Current thinking lumps *Q. prinus* under *Q. michauxii.*

Quercus robur — English Oak, Truffle Oak, Pedunculate Oak
(kwĕr′kus rō′bĕr)

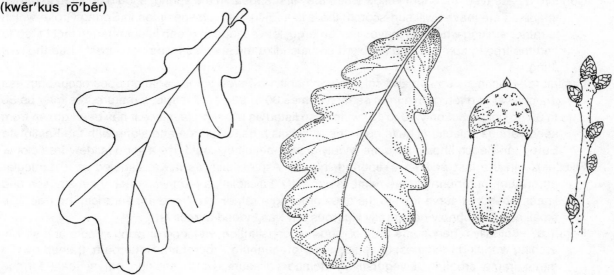

LEAVES: Alternate, simple, obovate to obovate-oblong, 2 to 5″ long, 3/4 to 2 1/2″ wide, auriculate to rounded base, 3 to 7 vein pairs of rounded lobes, glabrous, dark green above, pale bluish green beneath; key feature, ear-lobe-like leaf base (auriculate); petiole 1/6 to 1/3″ long.

BUDS: Imbricate, rounded, plump, angled, 1/4 to 3/8″ long, chestnut to reddish brown, scales fringed with hairs.

STEM: Glabrous, reddish brown, often purplish, angled, similar to White Oak.

SIZE: The species can reach 75 to 100′ or more in height with a comparable spread; in the United States averages 40 to 60′ under landscape conditions.

HARDINESS: Zone 4 to 8.

HABIT: Large, massive, broadly rounded, open-headed tree with a short trunk; too large for the average landscape; in youth pyramidal to rounded; have seen magnificent specimens in England.

RATE: Slow to medium, averaged 1′4″ per year over a 10-year period in KS tests.

TEXTURE: Medium in leaf, probably would be considered coarse in winter.

BARK: Deeply furrowed, grayish black.

LEAF COLOR: Dark green in summer; fall color is nil for the leaves either abscise green or persist and change to a nondescript brown.

FRUIT: Acorn, about 1″ long, narrow elongated-conical, enclosed 1/3 by the cup, one or several on a slender 2 to 5″ long peduncle, nut shiny brown.

CULTURE: Transplant balled and burlapped, prefers well-drained soil; pH tolerant; full sun.

DISEASES AND INSECTS: Mildew is often a serious problem on the species and 'Fastigiata'.

LANDSCAPE VALUE: The species is widely used in Europe; good tree for parks and other large areas; too many better native oaks to justify extreme excitement over this introduced species although 'Fastigiata' is a fine selection; does reasonably well in Zone 8 but cannot measure up to *Q. phellos, Q. lyrata,* and others; Dr. Dale Herman, North Dakota State University, mentioned that he had a good selection hardy to at least -35°F.

CULTIVARS:

'Atropurpurea'—Since the last edition (1983) this plant has jumped in my path many times in European gardens, the color is more brown-red than reddish purple and fades with time, leaves are slightly smaller than typical and the growth rate is slower, tree will probably mature between 20′ and 30′(40′); I am often confused by f. *purpurescens* which supposedly has young leaves and stems reddish and they become green (almost) with maturity.

'Attention'—Superior tight columnar growth form, does not broaden with age, dark green foliage exhibits mildew resistance, 60 to 80′ by 15′, Zone 5 to 8, a Wandell introduction, selection from 'Fastigiata'; John Barbour, Bold Spring Nursery, witnessed slight mildew susceptibility but this selection was much more resistant than typical 'Fastigiata' seedlings.

'Concordia'—Leaves are bright yellow when they first appear in the spring; should be sited in partial shade as the leaves will sun-scorch; there is a 25 to 30′ high specimen in Spring Grove which is rather striking when the leaves first emerge; leaves fade to green in summer, in fact I tried to find the tree in summer and it looked so much like the species I was not sure if I had the real thing.

'Fastigiata'—Distinctly upright and columnar in habit; however, some variation does occur because the cultivar is often grown from seed; it comes 80 to 90 percent true; a mature tree may be 50 to 60′ in height but only 10 to 15′ wide, also listed as f. *fastigiata;* since it has been grown from seed various selections have been made; this is a beautiful tree and along with the Fastigiate European Beech should be more widely grown; definitely could use a good mildew-free clone.

'Filicifolia'—In the last edition, I reported this as 'Asplenifolia' as it was labeled at a particular arboretum, unfortunately the name is correctly 'Filicifolia', a form with deeply cut sinuses and linear lobes that curve toward the apex creating a rather fern-frond appearance; the tree was small and is probably not greatly vigorous but was indeed attractive.

'Pendula'—Actually a handsome form of vigorous constitution with long growing shoots and widely arching weeping branches; have seen in Trompenburg Arboretum, Rotterdam, trained over a metal frame creating a vegetatively domed coliseum; worth seeking out at least for the specialist.

'Rose Hill'—Mildew free selection, leaf color different than typical with glossy pure green rather than dull blue-green that is typical for species; may not be as tight as typical 'Fastigiata'.

'Skymaster' ('Pyramich')—Narrow when young, becoming pyramidal, strong central leader and excellent lateral branch development, branches diverge at wide crotch angles, dark green leaves, 50′ by 25′, Schmidt Nursery introduction.

'Skyrocket'—A uniform, narrow, dark green foliaged form with yellow-brown fall color, will grow 45′ by 15′, a 1989 Schmidt introduction.

'Westminster Globe' ('Michround')—A broad spreading, round headed, symmetrical form with sturdy branch development, dark green leaves, 45′ by 45′, Schmidt Nursery introduction.

There are variegated and other cut-leaf forms but none are particularly outstanding. Most white variegated forms are rather weak growers and tend to produce reversion shoots. I visited a garden where the curator was proudly showing me a weeping White Oak. I took one look and saw the auriculate leaf base and quietly explained that he had a weeping English Oak. Sometimes it pays to learn these subtle identification characteristics.

PROPAGATION: Seed requires no pretreatment. Cultivars are grafted onto seedling understock.

NATIVE HABITAT: Europe, northern Africa, western Asia. Long cultivated.

RELATED SPECIES:

Quercus petraea—Durmast Oak
(kwẽr′kus pe-trē′à)

LEAVES: Alternate, simple, ovate to obovate, 3 to 5″ long, short and round lobed, truncate to broadly cuneate, dark green, almost blue-green above; petiole 3/8 to 1 1/4″ long, yellow.

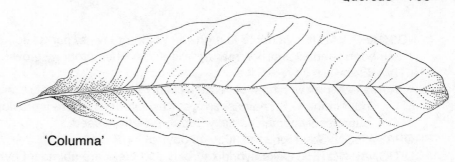

Quercus petraea, Durmast Oak, is similar to and hybridizes with the above. It differs in the comparatively long-stalked leaves, nearly stalkless acorns, and lack of an auriculate leaf base. The hybrid is listed as *Q.* × *rosaceae.* 'Columna', of fastigiate habit, like the Fastigiate English Oak, is often confused with it but differs by the characteristics enumerated. Also it is resistant to powdery mildew. Leaves are more sparse and it is not as handsome as *Q. robur* 'Fastigiata'. Europe, western Asia. Long cultivated. Zone 4 to 8.

'Columna'

Quercus rubra — Red Oak
(kwẽr′kus rū′bra)

LEAVES: Alternate, simple, oval or obovate, 4 1/2 to 8 1/2″ long, 4 to 6″ wide, 7 to 11-lobed, cuneate, sometimes rounded, lustrous dark green above, grayish or whitish or sometimes pale yellow-green beneath with axillary tufts of brownish hairs; petiole 1 to 2″ long, yellowish, glabrous.

BUDS: Imbricate, oval to ovate, 1/4 to 1/3″ long, chestnut to reddish brown, sharp-pointed, smooth or with rusty hairs at extreme apex; scale margin slightly hairy.

STEM: Stout, greenish to reddish brown, glabrous.

BARK: With distinct flat gray areas intermingled with ridged and furrowed areas.

SIZE: 60 to 75′ in height with a spread of 60 to 75′, although can grow to over 100′ in the wild.

HARDINESS: Zone 4 to 8.

HABIT: Rounded in youth, in old age often round-topped and symmetrical.

RATE: Another oak of fast growth, many individuals relegate the oaks to slow status; however, there are significant exceptions; Red Oak can grow 2′ per year over a 10 year period in moist, well-drained soil; however, in Wichita, KS tests averaged 11.5″ per year over a 9-year period.

TEXTURE: Medium in leaf and winter.

BARK: On old trunks brown to nearly black and broken up into wide, flat-topped gray ridges, separated by shallow fissures; on very old trees often deeply ridged and furrowed.

LEAF COLOR: Pinkish to reddish when unfolding, lustrous dark green in summer changing to russet-red to bright red in fall; sometimes disappointing and never passing much beyond yellow-brown.

FRUIT: Nut, solitary or paired, 3/4 to 1″ long, variable in shape, but usually subglobose, enclosed at the base in a flat, thick, saucer-like cup, acorns mature and fall early, nut is medium brown with grayish streaks.

CULTURE: Transplants readily because of negligible taproot; prefers sandy loam soils which are well-drained and on the acid side; withstands the polluted air of cities; full sun; good performer although not as widely planted as Pin Oak; will develop chlorosis in high pH soils.

DISEASES AND INSECTS: Basically free of problems, although the problems listed under White Oak are limitedly applicable to this species.

LANDSCAPE VALUE: Valuable fast growing oak for lawns, parks, golf courses and commercial areas; has been used as a street tree; excellent tree when properly grown.

CULTIVAR:

'Aurea'—A form with new leaves of a clear yellow; I have doubts about its success in intense summer heat in the U.S.; have seen it at Kew Gardens where it provides a golden glow during spring, supposedly comes partially true-to-type from seed.

PROPAGATION: Seed requires 30 to 45 days at 41°F.

ADDITIONAL NOTES: Oaks hybridize freely and there are abundant hybrids evident in landscapes and the wild. Red and Black Oak are associated in the wild and frequently hybrids occur.

NATIVE HABITAT: Nova Scotia to Pennsylvania, west to Minnesota and Iowa. Introduced 1800.

RELATED SPECIES:

Quercus velutina—Black Oak
(kwĕr′kus ve-lū′ti-nȧ)

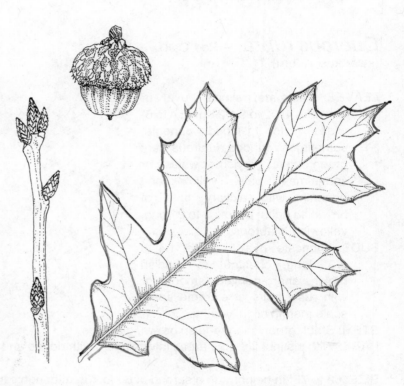

LEAVES: Alternate, simple, oblong-ovate to obovate, 4 to 10″ long, half to two-thirds as wide, cuneate to truncate, 7 to 9 lobes, lustrous dark green above, glabrous except in axils of veins; petiole 1 to 2 1/2″ long.

BUDS: Imbricate, ovate to conical, 1/4 to 1/2″ long, narrowed to a sharp point, generally 5-sided, strongly angled, covered with pale yellowish gray to dirty gray pubescence.

STEM: Stout, reddish brown or reddish, mottled with gray, tasting bitter if chewed and coloring saliva yellowish, downy when young, finally glabrous.

Quercus velutina, Black Oak, reaches 50 to 60′ in height and the spread is variable, for the crown is often quite irregular and can be narrow or wide-spreading, elongated or rounded; extensive tap root and for this reason is somewhat difficult to transplant; makes best growth on moist, rich, well-drained, acid soils but is often found on poor, dry, sandy, or heavy clay hillsides; not an important tree in commerce; fruit is solitary or paired, 1/2 to 3/4″ long, ovoid to hemispherical, often striate, light red-brown, 1/3 to 1/2 enclosed in a deep bowl-like cup; bark is nearly black on old trunks, deeply furrowed vertically, and with many horizontal breaks; inner bark bright orange or yellow; have found several 30 to 40′ high trees on the Georgia campus which have prospered under the stresses of the southeastern summers. Native from Maine to Florida, west to Minnesota and Texas. Introduced 1800. Zone 3 to 9.

Quercus stellata — Post Oak
(kwĕr′kus stel-lā′tȧ)

LEAVES: Alternate, simple, obovate, lyrately pinnatifid, 4 to 8″ long, 3 to 4″ wide, cuneate at base, rarely rounded, with 2 to 3 broad obtuse lobe pairs, the middle pair much larger and mostly with a lobe on the lower margin, separated from the lower lobes by wide, from the upper by narrow, sinuses, lustrous

dark green and rough above, with grayish to brownish, rarely white tomentum beneath, finally glabrescent; petiole—1/2 to 3/4″ long, pubescent; entire leaf has a cruciform appearance.
BUDS: Imbricate, subglobose to broadly ovoid, 1/8 to 1/4″ long, reddish brown, pubescent or glabrous.
STEM: Stout, dirty gray-brown, tomentose, dotted with numerous lenticels.

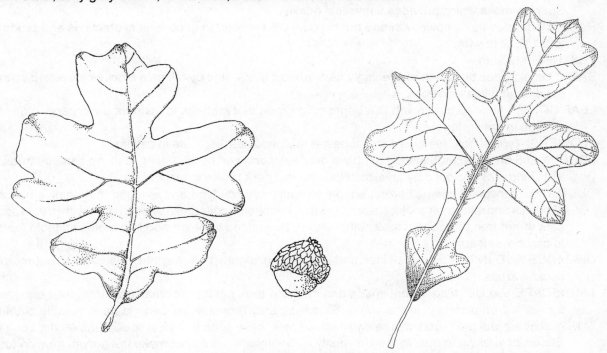

Quercus stellata, Post Oak, is seldom used in landscape situations but is frequently encountered in the wild throughout the southern states. Open grown trees have a dense round-topped crown with stout spreading branches. Average height is 40 to 50′. Fall color has, on occasion, been reasonable golden brown. Most often the color is so non-descript that no one notices. The sessile nuts appear singly or in pairs, are egg-shaped, 3/4 to 1″ long and are covered about 1/3 to 1/2 by the top-shaped cup, the scales of which are pointed, downy and appressed. It is typically found on dry, gravelly or sandy soils and rocky ridges. In the lower Mississippi Valley on silty loam soils it attains its greatest size. A distinct variety *mississippiensis* has been recognized. Variety *margaretta,* Sand Post Oak, is common in the Coastal Plain from Virginia to Texas and is a small scrubby tree. The lobes of the leaves are more rounded and less cruciform than those of the species. Native from southern Massachusetts to Florida, west to Iowa and Texas. Introduced 1819. Zone 5 to 9.

Quercus virginiana — Live Oak
(kwẽr′kus vẽr-jin-ē-ā′nȧ)

LEAVES: Alternate, simple, evergreen, elliptic-obovate, 1 1/4 to 3″ (5″) long, 3/8 to 1″ wide, entire or spiny, revolute, leathery, lustrous dark green above, glabrous, gray-green beneath, woolly pubescent, prominent yellowish brown midrib; petiole—1/4″ long, pubescent.
BUDS: Imbricate, slightly dome-shaped, reddish brown, glabrous or pubescent, 1/16″ long.
STEM: Slender, terete, gray, glabrous or pubescent toward tip.

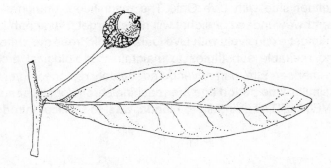

SIZE: Massive, ranging from 40 to 80′ high and 60 to 100′ wide.

HARDINESS: (7)8 to 10.

HABIT: Massive, picturesque, widespreading evergreen tree with magnificent horizontal and arching branches that form a broad-rounded canopy; a single tree constitutes a garden; often imbued with Spanish moss which provides a mystical quality.

RATE: Moderate; slows down with age but in youth will respond to good fertility practices and produce 2 to 2 1/2′ of growth.

TEXTURE: Medium.

BARK: On old trees becomes exceedingly dark, almost black, and develops a blocky characteristic in the mold of an alligator hide.

LEAF COLOR: New spring growth is a bright olive green that matures to lustrous dark green; old leaves all drop in the spring.

FLOWERS: Typical oak; females 1 to 5 together in axils of leaves; male in catkins.

FRUIT: 1 to 5 on a common stalk, but I have only seen one per 1/2 to 3″ long stalk on campus trees, 3/4 to 1″ long, 1/3 enclosed by an ellipsoidal cap, nut dark brown to black.

CULTURE: Transplant in small sizes; adapts to about any soil type and is found in its native haunts in sandhills and extremely moist soils; tolerant of compacted soils and has been used with great success as a street tree throughout the south; nursery trees need to be pruned to develop suitable leaders; tolerant of salt spray.

DISEASES AND INSECTS: A gall insect that is more unsightly than anything else and a root rot in the coastal areas.

LANDSCAPE VALUE: Magnificent shade and mansion tree, not for the small property; used extensively for street tree plantings in the south; Savannah and Thomasville, Georgia have notable plantings; makes a great park, golf course and campus tree; have seen beautiful specimens on the Louisiana State University campus; at the University of Georgia, trees do not make the growth they do further south; this is due in part to the colder temperatures.

PROPAGATION: Seeds are the preferred method although Texas A&M has experimented with cutting propagation; Morgan used 10000 ppm KIBA with great success on younger trees; see Dirr and Heuser, 1987 for details.

ADDITIONAL NOTES: State tree of Georgia, may live 200 to 300 years; considered a climax species in coastal Louisiana and along the east coast and outer banks of North Carolina; tolerant of saline conditions; the wood is exceedingly strong and one of the heaviest of native woods; was used for ribs and other hull parts of wooden ships; the acorns are eaten by many songbirds as well as quail, turkey, squirrel and deer. Several geographical varieties have been noted. Variety *fusiformis* is a small shrubby tree that occupies sandstone ridges in central Texas. Variety *maritima* integrades with the species and tends to be coastal from Virginia to Louisiana and Florida. Like many varieties, hairs are often being split in attempts to quantitatively separate them.

I was privileged to tour the city of Savannah with Mrs. Mary Helen Ray, Garden Club of Georgia and Mrs. Ruth Powers, Horticulturist. They showed me Live Oaks that dazzled my subconsciousness. I visited an old southern plantation, Wormsloe, where the drive leading to the house was lined on either side with Live Oak. The magnificent branches arched and crossed to produce a perfect archway. Indeed, a sight I will never forget. Savannah is a beautiful city but unfortunately is planted almost exclusively with Live Oak. The old trees are suffering and some have died. The city is looking for suitable substitutes to maintain the biological architecture but, alas, the Live Oak, like the American Elm, can never be adequately replaced. Interestingly, many of the trees were planted in a similar time period and are reaching chronological senescence.

NATIVE HABITAT: Virginia to Florida, west to Mexico. Introduced 1739.

Raphiolepis umbellata — Yeddo (Yedda) Raphiolepis, Indian Hawthorn
(raf-i-ō-le′pis um-bel-lā′tȧ)

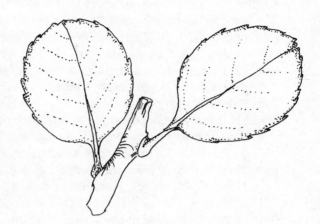

FAMILY: Rosaceae

LEAVES: Alternate, simple, evergreen, ovate to broad-ovate, 1 to 1 1/2″ (3″) long, 3/4 to 1 1/4″ (2″) wide, apex ranges from slightly acute to obtuse to emarginate, base rounded, leaves near end of stem entire, those lower on stem serrated to varying degrees, extremely leathery, glabrous, lustrous dark green above, dull beneath, in winter assuming a slight purplish tinge especially on margin; petiole— 1/4 to 1/2″ long, with small blackish stipules.

BUDS: Flower—terminal, imbricate, scales loose at tips, 1/4″ high, reddish purple, pubescent; laterals—small, almost imbedded in bark.

STEM: Stout, pubescent at tip, finally glabrous, brown, streaked vertically with gray epidermal layer; pith—solid, green.

SIZE: 4 to 6′ by 4 to 6′, some forms growing 10 to 15′ high.

HARDINESS: Zone 8 to 10, actually shaky in Zone 8; Mr. Will Corley, Georgia Experiment Station, evaluated 20 species and cultivars of *Raphiolepis* for hardiness and leaf spot resistance. In 1985, after -8°F, all were killed to the ground. At -3°F in 1983, the hardiest form was an unnamed, Plant Introduction (PI) accession from Japan. Interestingly, the PI showed near immunity to leaf spot while 'Majestic Beauty', 'Snow White' and 'Ovata' (var. *ovata*) showed good resistance; 'Enchantress', 'Fascination', and 'Pink Lady' the greatest susceptibility.

HABIT: Dense, mounded-rounded evergreen shrub; leaves clustered at ends of branches like *Pittosporum;* some forms loose, open, making small trees if trained.

TEXTURE: Medium, rather stiff in appearance.

LEAF COLOR: Glossy dark green in summer often assuming an off color during winter, somwhat of a subdued purple-green.

FLOWERS: Perfect, white, 3/4″ diameter, fragrant, borne in dense, upright, tomentose 2 to 3″ high and wide panicles or racemes; mid to late April, makes a respectable show but certainly not overpowering.

FRUIT: Subglobose, 3/8 to 1/2″ diameter, purple-black to bluish black, 1 to 2 seeded berry; ripen in early fall and persist attractively through winter.

CULTURE: Transplants readily from containers; prefers moist, well drained soils, pH 6 to 7; will tolerate drought; adaptable to containers and above ground planters; seems to tolerate restricted root space; good plant for coastal areas because of salt tolerance, injured at 0°F for many leaves were browned, probably best in Zone 8.

DISEASES AND INSECTS: Leaf spot in moist shady locations; have seen plants virtually defoliated.

LANDSCAPE VALUE: Have observed it in many landscape situations in the south; mass, unpruned hedge, containers, nice for textural effect; flowers and fruits are attractive; fruits tend to be lost in the dark green foliage especially when viewed at long distance.

CULTIVARS: Could be cultivars of *R. indica* or *R. umbellata.*

'Ballerina'—Vibrant rosy pink flowers with intermittent flowers in summer, foliage turns reddish color in winter, rounded habit 3 to 4′, *R. indica* form, killed at -3°F.

'Charisma'—Double, soft pink flowers, rich green foliage, tight mounded growth habit, a Monrovia introduction, killed at -3°F.

'Clara'—White flowers cover plant in spring, red new growth maturing to dark green, low evergreen shrub, 4′ high and 4′ wide, killed at -3°F.

'Coates Crimson'—Crimson-pink flowers, compact spreading, slow-growing, 2 to 4′ high and wide, killed at -3°F.

'Enchantress' ('Pinkie')—More compact than the species; rose-pink flowers in large panicles from late winter through early summer depending on geographic location, moderate to severe injury at -3°F.

'Fascination'—Compact, rounded form with large leaves and flowers; petals pink toward the edges, white in the center creating a star-like effect, moderate to severe injury at -3°F.

'Harbinger of Spring'—Deep pink flowers in loose panicles, 3″ long thick glossy green leaves, rounded habit, 5′ by 5′, moderate injury at -3°F.

'Indian Princess'—Broad bright pink flowers, fade to white, heavily tomentose new leaves become glabrous and bright green, compact broad mounded form, a Monrovia introduction.

'Jack Evans'—Vivid pink flowers in large panicles, strong upright habit, 4 to 5′ by 4′, killed at -3°F.

'Majestic Beauty'—Large form probably growing 8 to 10′ and larger, often trained into a small tree, leaves up to 4″ long, bronze turning deep green, flowers are pinkish and fragrant, has shown good resistance to leaf spot, killed at -3°F.

'Pink Cloud'—Pink flowers and compact growth habit, 3′ by 3 to 4′, may be the same as 'Springtime'?

'Pink Dancer'—Compact, mounding habit, 16″ by 36″, lustrous leaves with undulating margins, become bronze or maroon in cold weather, deep pink flowers.

'Pink Lady'—Deep pink flowers, vigorous form, 4 to 5′ by 4 to 6′, resistant to leaf spot, the same as 'Enchantress'?, slight to moderate injury at -3°F.

'Rosea'—Light pink flowers, loose more graceful habit, 3 to 5′ high and 5 to 6′ wide, new growth bronze; also a compact form with similar attributes ('Rosea Dwarf'); 'Rosea Dwarf' was killed at -3°F.

'Snow White'—Dwarf form with a spreading habit; pure white flowers from early spring into early summer; foliage lighter green than other cultivars, good resistance to leaf spot, moderate to severe injury at -3°F.

'Spring Rapture'—Rose-red flowers cover a compact, mounding shrub, a Monrovia introduction, slight to moderate injury at -3°F.

'Springtime'—More vigorous grower than the above cultivars; flowers pink, late winter to early spring; foliage—bronzy green, thick and leathery, moderate to severe injury at -3°F; same as 'Pink Lady'?

'White Enchantress'—Low-growing form with single white flowers, hardy to 0°F, moderate to severe injury at -3°F.

PROPAGATION: Seed collected in mid-February, pulp removed, direct down, germinated in high percentages. Cuttings: semi-hardwood to hardwood can be rooted, 2500 ppm IBA + 2500 ppm NAA, wound, has proved to be a very effective treatment. I have had miserable success rooting this genus and cuttings have been taken in fall and winter. An interesting Florida study mentioned that best rooting occurred from June to August with 10,000 to 20,000 ppm IBA quick dip, wound, perlite: vermiculite medium, 47% shade and mist. Rooting ranged from 90 to 100%.

NATIVE HABITAT: Japan, Korea. Introduced before 1864.

RELATED SPECIES: Based on my explorations around the south the *Raphiolepis* species are somewhat confused. Although *R. indica* is listed as the plant most in cultivation the technical description favors either the above or a hybrid *R. × delacourii*, (raf-i-ol′e-pis dē-là-koor′ē-ī), (*R. umbellata × R. indica*). It showed slight to moderate injury at -3°F. The hybrid was raised by Delacour, gardener at the Villa Allerton, Cannes, France. Numerous forms varying in leaf and flower color were raised. It displays moderate to good resistance to leaf spot.

Raphiolepis indica, (raf-i-ō-le′pis in′di-kà), Indian Hawthorn, is less hardy than *R. umbellata* and *R. × delacourii*. The 2 to 3″ long leaves are thinner and narrower, acute or acuminate, more sharply serrate and the flowers either white or pinkish. From a landscape standpoint this species is probably similar. I have not observed a single plant of the species on the Georgia campus. Southern China. Introduced 1806. Zone 9.

Rhamnus cathartica — Common Buckthorn
(ram′nus kȧ-thar′ti-kȧ)

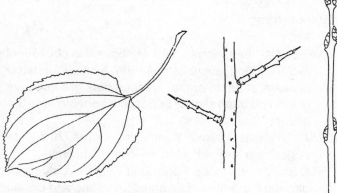

FAMILY: Rhamnaceae

LEAVES: Subopposite, simple, elliptic or ovate, 1 1/2 to 3″ long, half as wide, sometimes almost equal in width, acute or obtusish, rounded or subcordate at base, sometimes broad-cuneate, crenate-serrulate, dark glossy green above, light green and usually glabrous beneath, with 3 to 5 pairs of veins; petiole 1/4 to 1″ long.

BUDS: Imbricate, appressed, elongated, brownish black, glabrous, 1/4″ long.

STEM: Slender, somewhat grayish, glabrous, terminal bud a modified spine usually as long as or longer than the buds.

SIZE: 18 to 25′ in height with a comparable spread.

HARDINESS: Zone 2 to 7.

HABIT: Large shrub or low-branched tree with a rounded, bushy crown of crooked, stoutish stems.

RATE: Medium to fast.

TEXTURE: Medium in leaf, coarse in winter.

LEAF COLOR: Dark glossy green in summer, very clean foliage throughout the growing season, excellent if foliage is the only ornamental asset desired; fall color is a disappointing green to yellowish green, leaves hold quite late.

FLOWERS: Usually dioecious, small, yellowish green, 4-petaled, May, borne in 2 to 5 flowered umbels and forming a dense cluster at the base of the young shoot.

FRUIT: Berry-like drupe, 1/4″ diameter, black, not particularly effective, birds like them.

CULTURE: Easily transplanted, adapted to difficult conditions, withstands urban environments; a very tough, durable tree for areas where few other trees will survive; the fruits are eaten by the birds and the seeds deposited in hedge-rows, shrub borders and other out-of-the-way places; can actually become a weed.

DISEASES AND INSECTS: Leaf spots, rust, powdery mildew, aphids, scales; none are serious except the rust *(Puccinia coronata)* which can cause considerable damage to oats; eradication of buckthorn is the recommended control measure.

LANDSCAPE VALUE: Possibly as a background, screen or hedge under difficult growing conditions.

PROPAGATION: Seed, 60 to 90 days in moist peat at 41°F; cuttings are apparently somewhat difficult although 1000 ppm IBA or higher may suffice.

NATIVE HABITAT: Europe and western and northern Asia, naturalized in eastern United States.

RELATED SPECIES:

Rhamnus davurica, (ram′nus dȧ-vur′i-kȧ), Dahurian Buckthorn, is a 25 to 30′ high (usually smaller under cultivation), spreading shrub or small tree, with stout often spinescent stems; foliage lustrous dark green; fruit is black much like *R. cathartica;* extremely hardy and durable, well-adapted to difficult situations, limitedly available in commerce; differs only in longer and uniformly wedge-shaped leaves; have seen the plant literally consume waste areas; is a weed unless checked. Northern China, Manchuria, and Korea. Introduced 1817. Zone 2 to 6(7).

Rhamnus frangula — Glossy Buckthorn, also called
Alder Buckthorn
(ram'nus frang'-ū-lȧ)

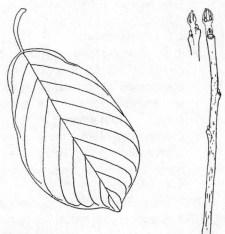

LEAVES: Alternate, simple, oval or obovate to obovate-oblong, 1 to 3″ (4″) long, about half as wide, acute, rounded or broad-cuneate at base, entire, lustrous dark green above, lighter green and often slightly pubescent beneath, with 8 or 9 pairs of veins; petiole 1/4 to 1/2″ long.

BUDS: Terminal—naked, pubescent, brownish, foliose, much larger than laterals; laterals—brownish, small.

STEM: Slender, pubescent on young stems, eventually becoming glabrous; prominently marked on young and old stems with gray, rectangular lenticels.

SIZE: 10 to 12′ possibly to 18′ in height and probably 8 to 12′ or greater in spread.

HARDINESS: Zone 2 to 7.

HABIT: Upright, spreading, large shrub or small, low-branched tree with long arching branches yielding an upright-oval outline; quite gangly and open.

RATE: Medium to fast.

TEXTURE: Medium in leaf, medium-coarse in winter.

LEAF COLOR: Dark glossy green in summer changing to greenish yellow or yellow in fall; the fall color is usually a poor greenish yellow.

FLOWERS: Perfect, creamy-green, parts in fives, 2 to 10 together in leaf axils of new growth, not showy, bees love them, May.

FRUIT: Berry-like drupe, 1/4″ across, in maturation passes from red to purple-black, effective from July through September.

CULTURE: Transplants well, adaptable, sun or partial shade, prefers well-drained soil; I noticed where students have made paths through the hedges *(Rhamnus frangula* 'Columnaris') a significant decrease in height is evident on either side of the path compared to nontrafficked areas.

DISEASES AND INSECTS: Until 1975 no serious problems had been reported. However, many of the hedge plants on the University of Illinois campus exhibited a dieback disorder typical of canker or wilt infestation. Don Schoeneweiss reported in the *Plant Disease Reporter* 58:937 that low temperature stresses predisposed Tallhedge to the fungus *Tubercularia ulmea.* He was consistently able to isolate the fungus from stem cankers that were girdling the shoots.

LANDSCAPE VALUE: Species is basically worthless for landscape considerations; falls into the weed character for the birds deposit the seeds everywhere and plants are found in unexpected places; cultivars offer some hope.

CULTIVARS:
'Asplenifolia'—Very fine texture, slow growing, but interesting, not common, will grow 10 to 12′ high and 6 to 10′ wide, leaves not cut but narrowed and with an irregular margin, offers an almost ferny texture to the landscape.

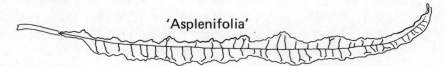

'Asplenifolia'

'Columnaris'—Narrow, upright deciduous shrub prized for hedges, has been overused in the midwest; referred to as Tallhedge Glossy Buckthorn, will come partially true to type from seed; is usually produced from cuttings.

PROPAGATION: Seed, 60 days in moist peat at 41°F; softwood cuttings collected in June or July will root well when treated with 8000 ppm IBA.

NATIVE HABITAT: Europe, western Asia, north Africa; naturalized in eastern and midwestern United States. Long cultivated.

RELATED SPECIES:

Rhamnus alaternus (ram′nus a-la-ter′nus), Italian Buckthorn, is a medium size evergreen shrub growing 10 to 12′ high. The oval to obovate dark glossy green leaves average 3/4 to 2″ long and 1/2 to 1″ wide. The species is seldom seen in cultivation but 'Argenteo-variegatus' is a pretty creamy-white margined form that grows 6 to 8′ high. I have seen it many times in Europe but never in the United States. Considered less cold hardy than the species. Mediterranean Region. Introduced about 1700. Zone 8 to 9?

Rhamnus caroliniana — Carolina Buckthorn, Indian Cherry
(ram′nus ka-rō-lin-i-ā′na)

LEAVES: Alternate, simple, elliptic-oblong or lance-oblong, 2 to 6″ long, acute or acuminate, rounded, serrulate or entire, lustrous dark green above, essentially glabrous, 8 to 10 vein pairs; petiole—1/2″ long, pubescent.

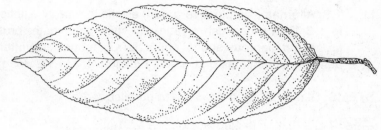

Rhamnus caroliniana, Carolina Buckthorn or Indian Cherry, is a handsome shrub or small tree with dark green, 8 to 10 vein-paired leaves. The real beauty resides in the 1/3″ diameter, globose, sweetish fruits that change from red to black as they mature. I have grown the plant for several years and am most impressed with the handsome foliage and interesting fruits. Fruits ripen in August (red) and remain on the plant until October or later by which time they have turned black. It is quite attractive in fruit and is often brought in for positive identification. It can supposedly grow 30 to 40′ high but in the Piedmont of Georgia I have seen plants in the 10 to 15′ range. New York to Florida, west to Nebraska and Texas. Introduced 1727. Zone 5 to 9.

Rhododendrons

The genus *Rhododendron* comprises over 900 species and infinite numbers of cultivars due to the ability of the species to freely hybridize. The improvements in rhododendrons (foliage, flower color and quality, hardiness and growth habit) have come about through hybridization. There is a need for cold hardy forms with good flower color. Many of the hardy types available are endowed with the lavender-purple-magenta colors offensive to many people. Rhododendrons are indigenous to many parts of the world but the strongest concentrations of hardy, colorful, useful types exist in China, Japan and the eastern United States. Greatest cultural success in the States is achieved in the Pacific Northwest and the eastern United States where soils and atmospheric conditions are close to optimum. The following list is not complete and was not intended to be. The types listed represent some of the hardier and more common forms. A good rhododendron display is without equal and a recent poll of gardeners (asking them their favorite shrub) indicated rhododendrons were *numero uno.* For additional information see Bower, Leach, Bean, Galle and join the American Rhododendron Society.

Differences in Rhododendrons and Azaleas

Actually, all azaleas are now included in the genus *Rhododendron.* There are no clear cut lines for distinguishing *all* azaleas from *all* rhododendrons but

1. True rhododendrons are usually evergreen but there are exceptions such as *R. mucronuclatum* and *R. dauricum*.
2. True rhododendrons have 10 or more stamens and leaves are often scaly or with small dots on their undersurface.
3. Azaleas are mostly deciduous.
4. Azalea flowers have mostly 5 stamens, leaves are never dotted with scales and are frequently pubescent.
5. Azalea flowers are largely funnel-form while rhododendron flowers tend to be bell-shaped.

Rhododendron carolinianum — Carolina Rhododendron
(rō-dō-den'dron ka-rō-lin-i-ā'num)

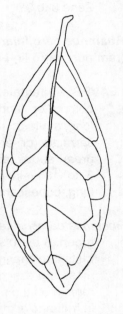

FAMILY: Ericaceae

LEAVES: Alternate, simple, evergreen, elliptic to narrow-elliptic, 2 to 3″ long, 1/2 to 1 3/4″ wide, acutish or abruptly short-acuminate, broad cuneate, dark green and glabrous above, entire, ferrugineous scaly often very densely so beneath, sometimes glaucescent; petiole 1/4 to 1/2″ long; leaves aromatic when bruised.

STEMS: Glabrous, often deep red to purplish red.

SIZE: 3 to 6′ in height with a similar or greater spread.

HARDINESS: Zone (4) 5 to 8.

HABIT: Small, rounded evergreen shrub of rather gentle proportions; not as coarse as Catawba hybrids, often loose and open.

RATE: Slow, 3 to 5′ over a 10 year period.

TEXTURE: Medium in all seasons.

LEAF COLOR: Dark green in summer, usually assuming a purplish tinge in cold climates.

FLOWERS: Perfect, varies from pure white to pale rose, rose and lilac-rose in color; borne in a terminal, 4 to 10-flowered, umbel-like, 3″ diameter raceme (truss), May, corolla 5-lobed, about 1 1/2″ wide.

FRUIT: Dehiscent 5-valved capsule, best to remove after flowers have faded.

CULTURE: Having tracked rhododendrons and azaleas from the midwest to east coast to the southeastern United States, I can unequivocally state that inadequate drainage is the most prominent factor limiting growth. If poor drainage does not directly kill plants, it predisposes them to insects and diseases such as root rot. They have fine silk-like roots, generally without root hairs, and are easy to transplant balled and burlapped or from a container; the root mass is usually profuse, which allows for successful planting; numerous plants are container-grown and the roots form a web (almost fabric-like) at the interface of the medium/container; if plants are left in the containers too long the root mass is so thick and matted it must be cut; ideally make vertical slits with a knife; this will insure contact with the soil when planted and, hopefully, root penetration into the native soil; I have observed azaleas and rhododendrons newly transplanted into a landscape that were wilted or dead; a simple tug on the plant and removal from the ground showed the plant was removed from the container and planted as a solid mass of roots; water uptake was severely limited as the planting hole became dry; I suspect more one gallon azaleas die this way than any other cause. Provide light shade in the north, even heavier shade in the south; have noticed tremendous lacebug infestations on plants exposed to full sun; the State Botanical Garden has a fine collection of ironclad *R. catawbiense* hybrids that were planted on a slope with the root balls above the soil and covered with pine bark; over the two years they have prospered but have received fertilizer and water as well as an occasional insect spray. Rhododendrons are extremely sensitive to salinity, high pH (chlorosis), and winter injury.

DISEASES AND INSECTS: *Botryosphaeria* canker, crown rot, dieback, dampening-off, azalea petal blight, azalea gall, leaf spots, leaf scorch, powdery mildew, rust, shoot blight, shoestring root rot, wilt, rhododendron aphid, azalea stem borer, azalea leaf tier, black vine and strawberry weevils, giant hornet, Japanese beetle, asiatic garden beetle, lace bugs, red-banded leafhopper, azalea leaf miner, rhododendron tip midge, mites, mealybugs, pitted ambrosia beetle, rhododendron borer, scales, thrips, rhododendron whitefly, nematodes, stem girdling caused by woodpeckers. Rhododendrons are troubled by many pests and their culture is often fraught with difficulty. Good cultural practices will reduce the incidence of disease and insect damage.

LANDSCAPE VALUE: Like all rhododendrons a nice plant for the shrub border, groupings, massing, foundations; should be sited in a slightly shaded area and out of strong winter sun and wind; survived -20°F in my Illinois garden and flowered nicely.

CULTIVARS:

var. *album*—White flowers.

var. *luten*—Mimosa yellow flowers.

PROPAGATION: See under *Calluna;* I have raised many seedlings with a minimum of effort. Like most rhododendrons this species exhibits great variation when grown from seed. Cuttings are somewhat difficult to root but when taken in August and treated with a hormone and fungicide will give a reasonable percentage.

NATIVE HABITAT: Blue Ridge Mountains of Carolinas and Tennessee. Cultivated 1815.

Rhododendron catawbiense — Catawba Rhododendron
(rō-dō-den′dron ka-taw-bi-en′sē)

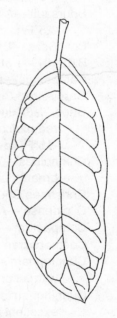

FAMILY: Ericaceae

LEAVES: Alternate, simple, evergreen, elliptic to oblong, 3 to 6″ long, 1 to 2″ wide, obtuse and mucronulate, rounded at base, entire, dark green above, light green below, glabrous, leathery texture; petiole 1/2 to 1 14″ long.

FLOWER BUDS: Large—1/2″ long, scaly, pointed, yellowish green

STEM: On new growth yellowish green changing to brown with age, glabrous.

SIZE: 6 to 10′ in height, rarely 15 to 20′, spread 5 to 8′ or more.

HARDINESS: Zone 4 to 8.

HABIT: Heavy evergreen shrub with large, dense foliage to the ground; often leggy in unfavorable locations; usually taller than wide although does assume a rounded outline.

RATE: Slow.

TEXTURE: Medium-coarse in all seasons.

LEAF COLOR: Dark green, very handsome; often in winter under exposed conditions will develop a yellow-green color.

FLOWERS: Lilac-purple, sometimes purplish rose, with green or yellow-brown markings on the inside of the corolla, 1 1/2″ long, 2 1/2″ broad; mid to late May in Urbana, IL (late April to late May in Athens, GA) depending on the cultivar, flowers borne in 5 to 6″ diameter umbel-like racemes (trusses).

FRUIT: Capsule, dehiscent, 5-valved.

CULTURE: See under *R. carolinianum.*

DISEASES AND INSECTS: See under *R. carolinianum.*

LANDSCAPE VALUE: Very handsome and aesthetic broadleaf evergreen; the flowers are beautiful but the foliage is equally valuable; beautiful when used in mass; hardy to about -20°F with proper cultivar selection.

CULTIVARS: Several are not *R. catawbiense* hybrids but are included here for convenience.

'A. Bedford'—Lavender-blue with dark blotch, -15°F.

'Album' (var. *album*)—A plant of great hardiness and vigor with buds flushed lilac, opening to pure white flowers with greenish yellow spotting, held in compact, rounded trusses; 6′ high, -25°F, excellent lustrous dark green foliage.

'Album Elegans'—White, -15°F.

'Alice'—Deep pink, -15°F.

'America'—Brilliant deep red, very floriferous, forming a broad bush, not as hardy as 'Nova Zembla', -15 to -20°F.

'Anah Kruschke' ('Purple Splendor' × *R. ponticum*)—Dense plant, glossy foliage, deep purple flowers form a tight truss, -15°F, performed well in Georgia Botanical Garden.

'Anna Baldsiefen'—Star shaped ruffled flowers are light rose with darker midribs and edges, upright growing, to 3'.

'Anna Rose Whitney'—(*R. griersonianum* × 'Countess of Derby'). This huge plant is impressive with its large full truss of deep rose-pink flowers with very light spotting on the upper lobes, -15°F.

'Antoon Van Welie'—Deep pink with a lighter blotch, -15°F.

'Autumn Gold'—Apricot Salmon.

'Baden Baden'—Red.

'Betty Wormald'—Pink with light center.

'Blue Diamond'—Lavender-blue.

'Blue Ensign'—Lavender-blue with a prominent dark blotch held in a rounded truss, the leaves are large and dark matte green, smaller than 'Blue Peter', 4 to 5' high, -15°F.

'Blue Jay'—Lavender-blue with brown blotch, -15°F.

'Blue Peter'—The flowers are a light lavender-blue with a striking purple flare, the leaves are dark green and glossy, 5 to 6' high, -15°F.

'Boursault'—A hardy plant that has lavender flowers in a rounded truss; good sturdy habit, 5' high, -25°F.

'Bow Bells'—Bright pink, -15°F.

'Butterfly'—Pale yellow, -15°F.

'Caractacus'—Red, -15°F.

'Cary Ann'—Coral-red, -15°F.

'Cheer'—('Cunningham's White' × red *R. catawbiense* hybrid). Shell pink flowers have conspicuous red blotches in conical trusses, the plant is rounded and compact with glossy leaves, 5' high, -15°F, flowers early in Georgia Botanical Garden, often flowers in fall.

'Chionoides'—White flowers have the yellow centers and make numerous dome shaped trusses. The broad, dense plant is easy to grow and has attractive, narrow foliage, 4' high, -20°F.

'Christmas Cheer'—Light pink, -20°F.

'Cilpinense'—Apple blossom pink, -20°F.

'Compactum'—This form stays less than 3' tall.

'Cosmopolitan'—Pink with a red blotch, -20°F.

'Cunningham's Blush'—Blush pink petals with light pink blotch, dark green leaves on this small shrub with a compact habit, -20°F.

'Cunningham's White'—Pink blushed buds open to white blooms blotched with greenish yellow, excellent foliage, low compact growth, -20°F.

'Cynthia'—(*R. catawbiense* × *R. griffithianum*). Showy conical trusses of rosy crimson flowers with blackish crimson markings, large and vigorous, 6' tall, -15°F, rather rank growing.

'Daphnoides'—Purple.

'Dora Amateis'—Floriferous white flowers, lightly spotted with green, slightly aromatic, vigorous, 3' high, twice as wide as tall, deep green dense foliage, -15°F.

'Dr. V. H. Rutgers'— Aniline red, a compact grower with good flowering capabilities, -20°F.

'Edward S. Rand'—Crimson-red with a bronze eye, -20°F.

'Elisabeth'—Red, -20°F.

'Elisabeth Hobbie'—Red, semi-dwarf, -20°F.

'English Roseum'—Light rose, vigorous yet compact, upright plant, large foliage, good growing habit, heat tolerant, -25°F.

'Evening Glow'—Light yellow, -15°F.

'Everestianum'—Rosy lilac, -20°F.

'Fastuosum Flore Pleno' ('Fastuosum Plenum')—Lavender-blue, semidouble, -20°F.

'Fred Hamilton'—Yellow with pink bands, -15°F.

'Furnivall's Daughter'—Pink with a sienna blotch, -20°F.

'Gomer Waterer'—Buds are slightly rose tinged, opening to white, dark green glossy leaves, broad and upright, 6' high, -15°F.

'Good News'—Crimson-red, -15°F.

'Grandiflorum'—Lilac, -20°F.

'Grierosplendour'—Plum, -15°F.

'Harvest Moon'—Pale yellow with red spots, -15°F.

'Ignatius Sargent'—Deep rose, -25°F.

'Janet Blair'—Delicate pink with brown blotch, -20°F.

'Jean Marie De Montague'—Bright scarlet blooms, dark green foliage, compact habit, -15°F.

'Jock'—Rosy pink, -15°F.

'Kluis Sensation'—Dark red, -15°F.

'Lady C. Mitford'—Peach pink, -15°F.

'Lavender Queen'—Lavender, -20°F.

'Lee's Dark Purple'—Buds very dark purple, opening to dark purple, surrounded by wavy foliage, grows into a broad compact bush, -20°F, common in the nursery trade.

'Lemon Ice'—Yellow, -20°F.

'Loder's White'—White, -15°F.

'Lord Roberts'—Red with a dark blotch, -20°F.

'Madame Carvalho'—White with green spots, -20°F.

'Madame Cochet'—Purple with a white center, -15°F.

'Madame Masson'—White with a yellow blotch, -20°F.

'Marchioness of Lansdowne'—Rose, -20°F.

'Mary Belle'—Light salmon buds open to peach, -20°F.

'Michael Waterer'—Dark red, -20°F.

'Mother of Pearl'—White, -15°F.

'Mrs. Betty Robertson'—Creamy yellow with red spots, -15°F.

'Mrs. C.S. Sargent'—Rich carmine-rose flowers, spotted yellow, a worthy selection for cold areas.

'Mrs. E.C. Stirling'—Silvery pink, -15°F.

'Mrs. Lady de Rothschild'—White, flushed pink, -15°F.

'Mrs. T.H. Lowinsky'—White with a reddish brown blotch, -20°F.

'Myrtifolium'—Medium pink, small, -20°F.

'Nova Zembla'—Red flowers, perhaps not as intense and with more lavender than 'America', quite cold tolerant and heat resistant, probably one of the best for the midwest and does well in the south, -25°F.

'Old Port'—Medium purple with a dark blotch, -20°F.

'Parson's Gloriosum'—Compact, conical trusses of lavender flowers, compact yet tall growth habit, dense, dark green foliage, -25°F.

'Pink Pearl'—Soft rose-pink, -15°F.

'Pink Petticoats'—China rose, -15°F.

'Pink Twins'—Light shrimp pink, -20°F.

'President Lincoln'—Lavender pink with a bronze blotch, -25°F.

'Prince Camille de Rohan'—Light pink, -20°F.

'Purple Lace'—Lacy purple with a light center, -15°F.

'Purple Splendour'—Dark purple with a black blotch.

'Purpureum Elegans'—Bishop's violet, dark green foliage, fine compact shape and the flowers open a clear pure color, -25°F.

'Rosamundi'—Light pink flowers in profusion, showy, small mounded shrub, -15°F.

'Roseum Elegans'—The old stand-by, lavender-pink flowers and reliability in flowering, withstanding temperature extremes without injury, more than one form under this name, -25°F, excellent heat tolerance.

'Roseum Pink'—Clear pale pink, similar to 'English Roseum'; strong grower making a broad well filled plant, -25°F.

'Roseum Superbum'—Rose lilac, -25°F.

'Roseum Two'—Pink, a strong grower with excellent bud set capabilities, bud sport in Wells Nursery.

'Sappho'—Mauve buds open to pure white flowers with a conspicuous blotch of violet overlaid with blackish purple, the plant habit is open and rather leggy, good background plant, 6 to 10' high, -10°F.

'Scarlet Wonder'—Scarlet-red, -20°F.

'Sham's Candy'—Bright pink with yellow-green blotch, -25°F.

'Shamrock'—Chartreuse blooms, extremely compact form, wider than high, -25°F.

'Spitfire'—Deep red with brown blotch, -20°F.

'The General'—Crimson with dark red blotch, -25°F.

'Trilby'—Deep crimson blooms with black blotches, small shrub with distinctive red stems, -20°F.

'Trude Webster'—Rich pink with dark spots, -15°F.

'Unique'—Reddish buds open to peach tinged yellow blooms, small, compact, mounded form, -15°F.

'Virginia Richards'—Large trusses open pale yellow with pink overtone, becoming deeper yellow with crimson blotch, small, compact shrub, -15°F.

'Vivacious'—Introduced by Vineland Experimental Station in Canada, hardy, compact and clearer red than 'Nova Zembla'.

'Vulcan'—Heavy trusses of brick red blooms, small, compact shrub with excellent mounded form, -20°F.

'Vulcan's Flame'—Bright red, -20°F.

'Wilgen's Ruby'—Red with brown blotch, -20°F.

PROPAGATION: Seed, as previously described; cuttings show great variation in rootability. I have had good success rooting various Catawba types by collecting cuttings in mid-August, wounding for about 1 to 1 1/2″, cutting leaf surface in half, treating with 1000 to 10,000 ppm IBA/50% alcohol for 5 seconds and placing the cuttings in peat:perlite under mist; rooting takes place in 2 to 4 months.

ADDITIONAL NOTES: One of the hardiest and best known of all the rhododendrons.

NATIVE HABITAT: Alleghenies, West Virginia, southwest to Georgia and Alabama. Introduced 1809.

Rhododendron mucronulatum — Korean Rhododendron
(rō-dō-den'dron mū-kron-ū-lā'tum)

FAMILY: Ericaceae

LEAVES: Alternate, simple, deciduous, elliptic to elliptic-lanceolate, 1 to 4″ long, 1/2 to 1 1/4″ wide, acute or obtusish, medium green, entire, very aromatic when crushed, thin textured; petiole 1/8 to 1/4″ long.

BUDS: Flower—rounded-ovoid, light brown, glabrous.

STEM: Slender, light straw-brown.

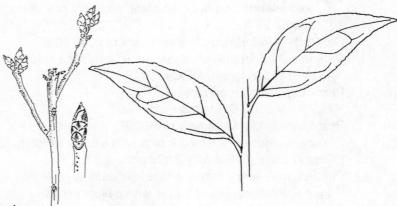

SIZE: 4 to 8' in height with a similar spread.

HARDINESS: Zone 4 to 7.

HABIT: Deciduous shrub of upright-oval to rounded outline with clean branching and foliage characteristics.

RATE: Slow, perhaps medium in youth.

TEXTURE: Medium-fine in foliage, medium in winter.

LEAF COLOR: Soft green in summer changing to shades of yellow and bronzy crimson in fall.

FLOWERS: Bright rosy purple, 1 1/2″ long and 1 1/2″ wide, mid to late March to early April, 3 to 6 together at the ends of the branches; flowers well before the leaves and often as the buds are opening a freeze will kill or injure them; siting is very important and a protected location where the south and southwestern sun will not hit them in February and March is recommended.

CULTURE: Trouble free plant, one of the hardiest.

DISEASES AND INSECTS: See under *R. carolinianum*.

LANDSCAPE VALUE: First of all the hardy rhododendrons and azaleas to flower in northeastern United States; very lovely in a shrub border; I had 5 scattered around the northeast corner of my home and they made nice foundation plants because of compactness and good foliage as well as lovely early flower.

CULTIVARS:

'Cama'—Large soft flowers that fade to white, unusual semi-evergreen leaves.

'Cornell Pink'—Phlox pink flowers, unadulterated by the magenta present in the flowers of the species; raised by Henry T. Skinner, Cornell University; named and put in commerce in 1952.

'Nana'—Clear purple flowers, dwarf to 2′, mahogany fall color.

'Pink Mucronulatum'—Lovely shades of pink, occurs in seed produced populations.

'Pink Peignoir'—Soft pink clone, opens early April, at least two week earlier than 'P.J.M.', opens and remains an unusually soft shade of pink that blends particularly well with the typical lavender color of the species, more subtle in the landscape than brighter pink clones such as 'Salem Hill Pink' and 'Cornell Pink', should be hardy to -25°F, 6′ in 20 years.

PROPAGATION: Seed, very easy; softwood cuttings collected in July rooted 50%. I have grown many seedlings of this species and also rooted many cuttings. One of the seedlings flowered in spring of 1975 and was a beautiful soft pink (apple-blossom like).

NATIVE HABITAT: Northern China, Manchuria, Korea and northern Japan. Introduced 1882.

Rhododendron schlippenbachii — Royal Azalea
(rō-dō-den′dron shlip-en-bȧk′ē-ī)

FAMILY: Ericaceae

LEAVES: Alternate, simple, usually 5 at ends of the branches, appear as if whorled, short-petioled, obovate or broad-obovate, 2 to 5 1/2″ long, 1 1/2 to 3″ wide, truncate or rounded to emarginate at apex, mucronate, cuneate, slightly undulate, sparingly pubescent when young, later glabrous except on veins beneath, dark green above, pale beneath.

SIZE: 6 to 8′ high and as wide at maturity, can grow larger but this seldom occurs in the U.S.

HARDINESS: Zone 4 to 7.

HABIT: Upright-rounded deciduous shrub.

RATE: Slow.

TEXTURE: Medium in all seasons.

LEAF COLOR: Dark green in summer, yellow, orange, crimson in fall.

FLOWERS: Pale to rose-pink, no trace of magenta, fragrant, early to mid-May; 3 to 6 together in a 2 1/4 to 3″ diameter inflorescence; one of the most delicate and beautiful of the azaleas for northern gardens; 10 stamens.

CULTURE: Seems to do better on high pH soils than other Ericaceae; pH 6.5 to 7 would be acceptable; may have a higher calcium requirement than other types.

LANDSCAPE VALUE: One of the finest azaleas, flowers open just as the leaves are expanding; no adequate way to do justice to the beauty of this plant by the written word.

PROPAGATION: Seed as previously described. Cuttings taken in late May and treated with a hormone (IBA) will give a fair percentage.

ADDITIONAL NOTES: This species comes fairly true from seed as it fails to hybridize freely with other species.

NATIVE HABITAT: Korea, Manchuria. Introduced 1893.

Other Rhododendrons and Azaleas

Rhododendron alabamense, (rō-dō-den'dron al-à-bam-en'sē), Alabama Azalea, is a deciduous shrub growing 5 to 6' (8') high. It tends toward compactness and may sucker. Colonies of 5 to 6 acres are known. The white, yellow-blotched (not always present), fragrant flowers appear with the new leaves. They occur 6 to 10 together in a terminal cluster. There are 10 stamens that are about twice as long as the 1″ long tubular funnel-shaped corolla. This is a beautiful plant in flower. Flowers from mid to late April. Possibly the most fragrant of the native azaleas. An 8 to 10' high and wide specimen at Biltmore House and Gardens is magnificent. Does not always appear true-to-type and should be purchased in flower. Found in dry open woodlands and rocky hill sites in north central Alabama and isolated areas in west central Georgia. Introduced 1922. Zone 7 to 8.

Rhododendron arborescens, (rō-dō-den'dron är-bō-res'enz), Sweet Azalea, is a deciduous, erect stemmed, loosely branched shrub growing from 8 to 20' in height with an equal spread; foliage is lustrous dark green in summer and may turn reddish in fall; flowers are white to light pink with a reddish style and pinkish to rose filaments, 1 1/2 to 2″ long, after the leaves in May, June-July, fragrant odor like heliotrope; best native white azalea what is hardy in the north; prefers light, consistently moist, acid soil; native from southern Pennsylvania to Georgia and Alabama; grows chiefly on the banks of mountain steams. Specialty growers offer pink, rose, smoky pink and yellow forms; also 'Hot Ginger' and 'Dynamite' selected for white flowers, pink stamens and intense fragrance; grew 6' by 5' in 18 years. Introduced before 1814. Zone 4 to 7.

Rhododendron atlanticum, (rō-dō-den'dron at-lan'ti-kum), Coast Azalea, makes a rather handsome 3 to 6' high and wide shrub of suckering habit. The leaves are a distinct bluish green and offer a handsome color contrast. The fragrant pinkish white (white to pink) flowers occur with or slightly before the leaves in April. Each flower is 1 to 1 1/2″ long and about 1 1/4 to 1 1/2″ wide with the stamens twice the length of the corolla. Corolla is covered with sticky glands and can be easily identified by this trait coupled with distinct foliage and later flowering. This is a beautiful azalea but like many of the natives it does not have the blatant flair of the hybrids. I have had good success rooting it from softwood cuttings. Found in the Coastal Plain from Delaware to South Carolina often in open pine woods. Used as a parent along with *R. periclymenoides* in the Choptank Hybrids. They are natural hybrids found wild in the vicinity of the Choptank River, Maryland, by Mr. and Mrs. Julian Hill. Several selections are apparently seedlings from the original wild selected plants. Cultivars include:

'Choptank Blend'—A scrumptious blend of cream, rose and yellow makes a charming flower, full and tall.

'Choptank C-1'—Mrs Julian Hill found this group of plants with delicate fragrant white flowers that perfume the garden, stoloniferous.

'Choptank Mellow'—Soft yellow flowers with lavender markings.

'Choptank River Belle'—Pink buds open to very fragrant white flowers flushed with pink, pink stamens, lovely blue-green foliage.

'Choptank Rose'—A fragrant rose and white flower with a golden blotch, plant is large and flowers are of good texture and fragrance.

'Choptank Yellow'—This offspring of 'C-1' is yellow with a slightly golden shading on the upper lobe, fragrant and hummingbirds flock to it.

'Choptank Yellow and Orange'—The yellow and orange colors mix and mingle in this huge ball truss, fragrant.

'Marydel'—Polly Hill's selected clone, deep pink buds, white flowers with a touch of pink, very fragrant.

'Nacoochee'—A selected Choptank seedling that has a fragrant white flower with a touch of pale pink.

'Pink Choptank'—A clear pink flower adorns this large plant which is an offspring of a selfed cross made years ago by the late George Beasley, Transplant Nursery, Lavonia, GA.

'Twiggy'—A descriptive name for a small, almost miniature plant that has white fragrant flowers, a Choptank seedling.

'Yellow Delight'—A choice seedling from an open pollinated *R. atlanticum,* large soft yellow with great fragrance and good growth habit.

Introduced about 1916. Zone 5 to 8 (9).

Rhododendron austrinum, (rō-dō-den'dron aw-strī'num), Florida Azalea, grows 8 to 10' high and forms a rather loose multistemmed shrub. The fragrant, clear yellow, cream, orange to almost pure red flowers occur 8 to 15 together, April-May. Flowers in my garden during mid April; colors are variable as mentioned. Each flower is 3/4" long and the tube somewhat cylindrical with 2" long stamens. Again this is a most beautiful native plant that makes a splendid addition to the shrub border. One of the easiest natives to grow, requires no pampering. Cultivars include:

'Adam's Orange'—Brightly colored deep orange selection.

'Austrinum Gold'—Early opening bright gold fragrant flowers, plant grows as wide as tall.

'Clyde's Yellow'—Huge clusters of beautiful large bright yellow flowers in the spring.

'Millie Mac'—The yellow center of each flower is bordered with a distinct white margin, found in Escambia County, AL by Mr. and Mrs. Floyd T. McConnell of Mobile, AL.

'Rushin's Austrinum'—Bright yellow flowers with clear yellow tubes herald spring with their aroma.

Northern and western Florida to southwest Georgia, southern Alabama and southeastern Mississippi. Introduced 1914. Zone 7 to 9.

Rhododendron bakeri, (rō-dō-den'dron bā'kēr-ī), Cumberland Azalea, is allied to *R. calendulaceum* but is more compact and tends to flower 2 or more weeks later, the 1 1/4 to 1 3/4" long, flowers are usually a good red but range from (yellow) orange to red. A compact, double red form is known. Have seen the species in flower on May 25 at Biltmore. Spectacular in flower. Does not tolerate excessive heat. Will grow 3 to 8' high, tends to be low growing with somewhat horizontal branches. Zone 5 to 7.

Rhododendron 'Boule de Neige' is listed as a Caucasian hybrid and is one of the finest white flowering types. The evergreen foliage is a dark, lustrous green and the habit is compact and of a rounded outline. Zone 5, possibly 4. Usually described as flower bud hardy to -15°F. As a graduate student at the University of Massachusetts, I was introduced to this taxon by Professor Thompson, who literally considered this the best of all rhododendrons for habit (5' by 8'), dark green foliage and large white flower trusses; he considered this the standard by which others should be judged; interestingly a 1988 article on rhododendrons by Peter Loewer, *Horticulture* essentially reiterated Professor Thompson's beliefs; for as many rhododendrons that are introduced each year, it is amazing how few really measure up.

Rhododendron calendulaceum, (rō-dō-den'dron ka-len-dū-lā'sē-um), Flame Azalea, is a deciduous, loosely branched shrub of upright habit, usually as wide as high (4 to 8' tall by a comparable spread to 10 to 15'). The summer foliage is medium green and the fall color subdued yellow to red; flowers average 2" diameter, May-June, in loose trusses; colors range from lemon to dark yellows, tawny, apricot, salmon, deep flesh color, pinkish, brilliant shades of orange and scarlet, non-fragrant. Most showy and one of the most notable American azaleas (a parent of the Ghent hybrid race); retains flowers for nearly two weeks, excellent in naturalistic setting or mass planting. Native to mountains of Pennsylvania south to Georgia. Zone 5 to 7, does not prosper in high heat. Cultivated 1800. Cultivars include:

Abbott azaleas [*R. calendulaceum* × *R. prinophyllum (R. roseum)*]—Super hardy hybrids created by Frank Abbott of Saxton's River, Vermont, withstood temperatures to -40°F.

'Carlsons Coral Flameboyant'—Large flowers in a bright shade of coral.

'Chattooga'—A natural hybrid of *R. calendulaceum* × *R. periclymenoides (nudiflorum),* the pink ruffled flowers with their yellow blotch gradually turn a soft yellow.

'Cherokee'—Soft apricot flowers with red stamens.

'Currahee'—Large shrub with orange flowers bordered with rosy pink; the buds are striped with red and yellow.

'Frank Lunsford'—Fuchia pink with white coloration, long stamens.

'Golden Sunset Flame'—A blend of orange, gold and yellow colors.

'Golden Yellow Flame'—A large companulate flower with crimped, pointed tips, the yellow background is accented with gold blotches.

'Lisa's Red Flame'—Tall, a big ruffled red flower with crimped edges.

'Scarlet Orange Flame'—Glows with its reddish orange blossoms.

'Smokey Mountaineer'—Compact form with excellent orange-red flowers; fall color is an excellent red.

'Soquee River'—Magnificent truss of orange, red and yellow at the same time, as wide as it is tall.

'Wahsega'—Darkest red form ever seen.

'Yellow Flame'—A large, clear bright yellow flower.

Rhododendron canadense, (rō-dō-den'dron kan-a-den'sē), Rhodora, is often a rather scrawny, erect-branched shrub that seldom grows more than 3 or 4' high. The leaves are a distinct gray-green and appear after the flowers. The principal beauty lies in the bright rosy purple, 1 to 1 1/2" wide flowers that occur aboutand appear after the flowers. The principal beauty lies in the bright rosy purple, 1 to 1 1/2" wide flowers that occur about 6 together at the end of the stem in April. A white form is known. The corolla is quite distinct from other members of the genus in having the 3 upper lobes almost united to the end and erect, the lower 2 narrow-oblong, divided to the base and spreading. There are 10 stamens. It is seldom seen in gardens but makes a lovely splash of color in April. In the wild it is often found in swamps and should be provided moist, acid soil in cultivation. Emerson said of this species "Beauty is its own excuse for being". Newfoundland and Labrador to central New York and Pennsylvania. Introduced before 1756. Zone 2 to ? Requires a cool climate.

Rhododendron canescens, (rō-dō-den'dron ka-nes'enz), Piedmont Azalea (also known as Florida Pinxter, Hoary Azalea), is a large shrub growing 10 to 15' high. The fragrant white to pink to almost rose flowers open in March-mid April. It is native in the Athens area where it inhabits open fields under power line cuts as well as stream banks under high shade. I have several on my property and find it an attractive species although many consider it an inferior landscape species. There is tremendous variation in corolla color and I have seen forms with white to deep rose-pink flowers. It is stoloniferous and a 10 acre colony has been described. It is the most abundant species in the southeast and the range extends from North Carolina, Tennessee to north Florida, Georgia, Alabama and Texas. Introduced around 1730. Zone 5 to 9. It hybridizes readily with other species.

Rhododendron dauricum, (rō-dō-den'dron dawr'i-kum), Dahurian Rhododendron, is a deciduous to semi-evergreen shrub that matures at about 5 to 6'. The small, 1/2 to 1 1/2" long, 1/4 to 5/8" wide, glossy dark green leaves are rather attractive and assume a purplish tinge in winter. The 1 to 1 1/2" diameter, bright rose-purple flowers appear singly from a cluster of buds at the end of last season's growth in February-March. Variety *sempervirens* is noted for holding the very dark green leaves through the winter. It flowers in March-April and like the above is not particularly showy but does provide a breath of color. It is one of the parents of the PJM rhododendron and has imparted its hardiness to that selection. Var. *album* has white flowers and was used by Edmund Mezitt in some of the newer compact cold hardy rhododendrons. Also 'Madison Snow' with creamy-white buds that open to pure white flowers and 'Snowy Morning Blues' with pure white flowers that open two weeks later than the species and both are available in commerce. The latter holds most of the shiny green leaves all winter. Altai Mountains of Korea, Manchuria and northern Japan. Cultivated 1780. Zone 4 to 5(6).

Rhododendron 'Exbury' and **'Knap Hill'** Hybrids are deciduous, upright growing types, 8 to 12' high and 2/3's to as wide, with medium green summer foliage and yellow, orange, red fall colors; flowers range from pink, creams, yellows, near whites or orange, rose and red, borne in 2 to 3" diameter, 18 to 30 flowered trusses in May.

These hybrids are the result of crosses involving several species including *R. calendulaceum, R. arborescens, R. occidentale, R. molle.* Zone 5 to 7 (8). The Exbury types do not display good heat tolerance but southern breeders are crossing them with native azaleas and producing heat tolerant lines. The Exbury Hybrids as well as the Knap Hill, Ilam, Windsor and Ghent types include a great number of selections. About the only way to find out if they will grow in a given region is to experiment with them. In general they are not suited for Zone 4 (considered flower bud hardy to -20°F, but depends on cultivar) and lower or Zone 8 and higher. Often imbued with mildew that renders them ugly.

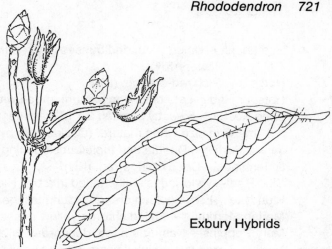

Exbury Hybrids

EXBURY (EX) AND KNAP HILL (KN) HYBRIDS

'Altair'—Large creamy white with yellow flare, very fragrant. (KN)

'Annabella'—Very fragrant deep golden yellow with dark bronze foliage. (KN)

'Anquistas'—Translucent light yellow outlined in pink, lightly fragrant.

'Avocet'—Fragrant white fringed with pink, large ruffled flowers. (KN)

'Banana Split'—Vanilla white surrounding a banana yellow blotch with a cherry throat.

'Basilisk'—Pink buds open cream, edged in pink, golden flare. (KN)

'Berryrose'—Fragrant, orange-red. (KN)

'Brazil'—Brilliant tangerine-red, strong grower, buds early, flowers frilled. (KN)

'Bullfinch'—Deep red. (KN)

'Buzzard'—Fragrant pale yellow, tinged with pink. Vigorous growing, wide upright, -24°F flower bud hardiness, resists mildew.

'Cannon's Double'—Double pink with light orange shading. (EX)

'Cecile'—Very large flowers in shades of salmon-pink and yellow, handsome form. (EX)?

'Clarice'—Pale pink fading to almost white, vigorous upright growth. (EX)

'Cockatoo'—Fragrant peach-apricot. (KN)

'Crimson'—Crimson-red, robust, upright-growing. (EX)

'Dawn's Chorus'—Pink buds open white with rays of dawn's pink. (EX)

'Desert Pink'—Pink. (KN)

'Exbury Evening Glow'—Frilled soft pink tinged with light yellow, golden throat.

'Fireball'—Bright shades of orange-red (scarlet); stronger growing plant than most red varieties; foliage is reddish bronze, then dark green when mature. (KN)

'Firefly'—Red. (EX)

'Fireglow'—Large orange-vermillion flowers, wine-red fall foliage. (KN)

'Flamingo'—Frilled fragrant deep pink with orange blotch, upright-growing. (KN)

'George Reynolds'—Enormous deep buttery yellow flowers with a deep golden throat. (KN)

'Gibraltar'—Spectacular flame-orange flower clusters with ruffled petals, by far the most heat tolerant and vigorous of the Knaphill group, does well as far south as Zone 8a, flowers later than Kurume azaleas. (KN), often listed as (EX).

'Gold Dust'—Bright deep yellow fragrant flower. (EX)

'Golden Dream'—Large open-faced flowers of soft clear yellow. (KN)

'Golden Eagle'—Bright orange with a yellowish orange flare. (KN)

'Golden Flare'—Vivid yellow with reddish orange blotch, to 2 1/2" diameter. (EX)

'Golden Oriole'—Brilliant yellow, deep orange blotch. (KN)

'Golden Sunset'—Vivid yellow, wide, upright habit. (KN)

'Harvest Moon'—Pale yellow with a deeper blotch. (KN)

'Homebush'—Unique rounded trusses of deep rose double flowers, vigorous upright shrub, superb in full flower. (KN)

'Hotspur'—Rich red-orange. (EX)

'Hotspur Red'—Late blooming nasturtium red with golden orange throat. (KN)

'Irene Koster'—Sweetly scented 2 1/2" diameter white blooms are flushed with strong pink coloring, medium size when mature. (Occidentale hybrid)

'Jackie Parton'—Double and triple buds opening to peach striped orange. (PN)

'J. Jennings'—Deep orange-red. (KN)

'King Red'—Vivid red, slightly ruffled in a ball-like truss. (EX)

'Klondyke'—Large golden orange, young foliage coppery red, wide upright, slow growing. (KN)

'Marion Merriman'—Frilled chrome-yellow trusses, orange blotch. (KN)

'Mary Poppins'—Nasturtium red, dark green foliage. (KN)

'Mavis'—Large dusty pink flowers in ball-shaped trusses. (KN)

'Orangeade'—Very full and frilly pure orange. (KN)

'Oxydol'—Large white flowers with soft yellow blotch, bronze foliage. (KN)

'Peppermint'—Deep peppermint pink with lighter shades of pink and white on the midribs of the petals, creating a soft striped bicolor effect. (KN)

'Royal Lodge'—Late-blooming vermillion red, wide-growing and upright.

'Salmon Pink'—Pink flowers, brilliant purple-red to yellow fall foliage, wide upright, vigorous. (EX)

'Satan'—Scarlet-red. (KN)

'Seville'—Orange-red flowers, notable for excellent fall color.

'Sham's Yellow'—Golden buds open to large frilled lemon-yellow flowers.

'Strawberry Ice'—Peach-pink with yellow shadings. (EX)

'Sun Chariot'—Buttercup yellow, darker blotch.

'Sunset Pink'—Large trusses of vivid red with yellow blotch.

'Sylphides'—Voluptuous pale pink and white with a touch of yellow in the throat, fragrant. (KN)

'Toucan'—Pale cream with yellow blotch, very fragrant, tall growing. (KN)

'Tunis'—Deep crimson with orange flare, fast-growing, upright.

'Tutti Frutti'—Rose with large red blotch. (EX)

'Violet Gordon'—Bright orange beauty with bronze tinted foliage. (KN)

'White Swan'—White with yellow blotch, very fragrant. (EX)

'White Throat'—Late-flowering frilled white, red fall foliage, slow-growing, wide spreading habit.

Rhododendron fastigiatum, (rō-dō-den′dron fas-tij-ē-ā′tum), Autumnpurple Rhododendron, is an excellent dwarf species for the rock garden with tiny leaves and small purple flowers.

Rhododendron flammeum (*R. speciosum*), (rō-dō-den′dron flam′ē-um), Oconee Azalea, grows 6′ high and wide and forms a rather attractive mounded shrub. The scarlet or bright red, funnel-shaped, 1 3/4″ long, non-fragrant flowers appear in April after *R. canescens.* The truss may contain up to 15 flowers. The stamens are about 2″ long. It has been confused with *R. calendulaceum* but differs in the slender corolla tube. The flower color ranges from yellow, pink, salmon to orange-red. 'Apricot Speciosum'— lovely soft shade of apricot with tangerine stamens is a perfect picture as the flowers cover the plant in late April; 'Harry's Speciosum'—a beautiful scarlet-red flower on a medium size plant, stoloniferous; 'Orange Speciosum'—a breathtaking sight with the huge round orange balls, full dense truss, hardy and a good grower; 'Pink Speciosum'—must be a cross with *R. canescens;* 'Red Speciosum'—a beautiful well clothed mounded planted with a brilliant red flower.

Rhododendron furbishi, (rō-dō-den′dron fẽr′bish-ī), is a very unusual native azalea, probably a hybrid between *R. bakeri* or a late *R. calendulaceum* type and *R. arborescens,* found in northern Georgia, mostly in orange and orange-red shades, a strong upright grower.

Rhododendron × gandavense, (rō-dō-den′dron × gan-dȧ-ven′sē), Ghent Azaleas, are deciduous, 6 to 10′ shrubby growers with flower colors ranging from pure white, pure yellow, to combinations of pink, orange and scarlet; flowers are single or double, the doubles with numerous overlapping petals, 1 1/2 to 2″ across. The hybrids were developed by crossing several species and some of the select clones are hardy to -20°F. Cultivars:

'Bouquet de Flore'—Orange-red flowers with yellow center, somewhat frilled, upright.

'Circus'—Yellow maturing to pink.

'Coccinea Speciosa'—Orange.

'Daviesi'—White to pale yellow, 2 1/4″ diameter flowers, tall growing, reasonable heat tolerance, fragrant.

'Fanny'—Violet-red, yellow center.

'Gloria Mundi'—Orange-yellow-red combination.

'Magic'—Yellow, maturing to orange.

'Nancy Water'—Large golden yellow.

'Narcissiflora'—Double yellow, hose-in-hose, fragrant, fine form, reasonable heat tolerance.

'Pallas'—Orange-red.

'Rainbow'—Yellow, maturing to orange-yellow.

Developed in Ghent, Belgium around 1820-1830 from *R. calendulaceum, R. molle, R. luteum, R. periclymenoides, R. viscosum,* and *R. flammeum.* In general the Ghent hybrids are best suited to cooler climates. 'Narcissiflora', as mentioned, is a fine form.

Rhododendron 'Gable Hybrids' are a mixed lot but offer a quality range of colors and they are considered the hardiest evergreen azaleas for Zone 5 conditions. They were developed by the late Joseph Gable, a rhododendron hybridizer at Stewartstown, Pennsylvania. These plants grow 2 to 4′ high and as wide. The foliage is a shiny dark green, about 1″ long, although there is considerable variation among clones. The flowers arrive in late April to early May and are about 2″ across. The following cultivars were synthesized from the literature and observations. Hybridizer is listed when known.

'Ben Morrison'—(Gable) Red and white striped.

'Big Joe'—Reddish violet.

'Boudoir'—(Gable) Watermelon pink, darker blotch, compact plant, 5′ by 4′, did well in my Illinois garden.

'Cadis'—Deep pink buds are a lovely contrast to large fragrant light pink flowers in flat trusses, large growing (rhododendron).

'Cameo'—Hose-in-hose pink.

'Carol'—Hose-in-hose violet-red flowers, low-spreading habit.

'Caroline'—(Gable) Large heavy textured pale orchid flowers, large leaves with wavy margins, does well in hot climates but appreciates partial shade, medium height (rhododendron).

'Cherokee'—Orange-red flowers, upright growing, medium height.

'Corsage'—Fragrant, light lavender, 2 1/2″ diameter, rounded dwarf plant, 4′ by 4′.

'David Gable'—(Gable) Red throated pink flowers in large dome-shaped trusses, floriferous, medium height (rhododendron).

'Forest Fire'—Hose-in-hose red.

'Herbert'—Possibly the hardiest of all Gable hybrids, vivid purple with darker blotch, hose-in-hose, 1 3/4″ long, dense rounded habit, 4′ by 4′, flower bud hardy to -20°F, has performed well in Zone 8, was the hardiest azalea in my Illinois garden.

'Karen'—Lavender pink, hose-in-hose, rounded habit, 4′ by 4′, excellent cold hardiness, similar to 'Herbert'.

'Keisrac Pink'—(Gable) Small leaves and flowers suggesting the pointed pink and white bloom of *Arbutus,* compact.

'Lorna'—(Gable) Masses of double pink flowers resembling rosebuds, compact low spreading habit.

'Louise Gable'—Double, deep salmon-pink, darker blotch, 2 1/2″ across, rounded dense habit, 3 to 4′ by 3 to 4′.

'Madame Greeley'—Single, large, white with green flecks in throat, 1″ wide, rounded compact habit, 3′ by 3′.

'Mary Dalton'—Orange-red.

'Mildred Mae'—(Gable) Large spotted lavender.

'Olive'—Orchid-purple flowers, hardy, compact and spreading.

'Purple Splendor'—(Gable) Purple, hose-in-hose.

'Robert Allison'—(Gable) Scented pink flowers with golden throats, large waxy green leaves on a rugged upright shrub, medium height.

'Rosebud'—(Gable) Silvery rose-pink, double, hose-in-hose, 1 to 2″ diameter, compact habit, 4′ by 4′, flowers resemble miniature roses, very popular cultivar.

'Rose Greeley'—Large hose-in-hose white flowers with chartreuse blotch, dense low growing and spreading plant, 3′ by 3′.

'Springtime'—(Gable) Clear pink, early blooming.

'Stewartstown'—(Gable) Vivid, brick-red, small single flowers, foliage dark green and wine-red in winter, rounded habit, 5′ by 4′; flowers later, although listed as very cold hardy it is distinctly less so than 'Herbert' and 'Karen', grew this in my Illinois garden and it was ruined above snow line; in Manchester, NH I was told this is an adaptable cultivar, possibly due to winter snow cover because low temperatures hover in the -25 to -30°F range.

Rhododendron impeditum, (rō-dō-den′dron im-ped-i′tum), Cloudland Rhododendron, forms a cushion of small dark green evergreen leaves upon which purple or bluish purple flowers are produced in April-May. It is an attractive, small rhododendron with good hardiness and for that reason should be considered in the colder regions of the country. 'Moerheim' is a *R. impedium* hybrid from Holland with small violet flowers and tiny leaves on a tight, compact dwarf. Western China. Cultivated 1918. Zone 5.

Rhododendron japonicum, (rō-dō-den′dron jȧ-pon′i-kum), Japanese Azalea, is a bushy shrub of rounded outline that grows 4 to 8′ high. The flowers are beautiful and range from yellow, orange-yellow, soft rose, salmon-red, orange-red to brick-red in color. Each flower is 2 1/2 to 3 1/2″ wide, and produced in trusses of 6 to 10 during May at the end of leafless stems. It is one of the parents of the Ghent hybrids and also figures in the Mollis hybrids *(R.* × *kosteranum).* The species has proven a fairly reliable flowerer at Minnesota (best in Zone 5). Japan, where it is found in open grassland, never in woods or dense thickets. Introduced 1861. *R. molle,* Chinese Azalea, is similar but differs in the conspicuous pubescence on the underside of the leaf and buds. It grows 2 to 5′ high and although hardy (Zone 5) is not as vigorous as *R. japonicum.* Flowers are yellow.

Rhododendron kaempferi, (rō-dō-den′dron kem′fĕr-ī), was formerly listed as *R. obtusum* var. *kaempferi* but is considered a species. The kaempferi hybrids can grow to 10′ high and 5 to 6′ wide after 5 to 10 years. The leaves are dark green, semi-evergreen to deciduous and turn reddish hues in fall and winter. The flowers range in color from salmon-red, orange-red, pink to rosy-scarlet and white; each flower 1 3/4 to 2 1/2″ long and wide, funnel-shaped, 1 to 4 per truss. This is a very variable species and apparently has interbred with *R. obtusum* producing large hybrid swarms which dot the mountainsides of Japan. Usually found in sunny positions on hillsides, by the sea, on active volcanoes and also in thickets, pinewoods and deciduous forests. The species is found wild on the main islands of Japan from sea-level to the lower hills below 2600′. Introduced 1892. Zone 5 to 8. Several cultivars of merit include:

'Alice'—Salmon-red.

'Annamarie'—Pure white, small flowers, bright yellow autumn foliage, widespreading, upright outline, 6′ high, -13°F bud hardiness.

'Atlanta'—Lovely large lavender-purple flowers, broad and spreading.

'Blue Danube'—Brilliant bluish violet, quite striking.

'Campfire'—Red, hose-in-hose.

'Carmen'—Red.

'Charlotte'—Dark orange-red.

'Christina'—Red, 2″ diameter, single, medium size shrub.

'Fedora'—Phlox-pink, with darker blotch, 2″ diameter, rounded habit, 6′ by 5 to 6′, reasonably common in commerce.

'Gretchen'—Reddish violet.

'Holland'—Single, large rich intense red, synonymous with 'Holland Red'.

'Johanna'—Red, 2″ diameter single flowers, medium size shrub.

'Juliana'—Deep pink.

'Kathleen'—Rosy red.

'Mary'—Violet-red.

'Mikado'—Dark red flowers, burgundy-red fall foliage, upright growth habit, synonymous with 'May King'.

'Norma'—Violet-red.

'Othello'—Red.

'Silver Sword'—Flowers vivid pink to red, approximately 2″ across, foliage deep green with creamy white margins, becoming more available.

Rhododendron keiskei, (rō-dō-den′dron kīsk′ē-ī), Keisk Rhododendron, grows 4 to 5′ high and is of scraggly habit; evergreen in foliage; lemon-yellow flowers, early to mid-May, 3 to 5 flowers per cluster; it is one of the few evergreen rhododendrons with pale yellow flowers; have observed it in flower in Urbana, IL, but it was less than inspirational. Japan. Zone 5.

Rhododendron kiusianum, (rō-dō-den′dron kī-oo′sē-ā-num), is a dwarf evergreen or semi-evergreen shrub, occasionally up to 3′, dense spreading habit. Leaves are dark green, small and oval shaped. Florets are funnel shaped, produced in clusters of 2 to 5. Colors range from red to purple, hardy to 0°F, flowers late May-June. Cultivars include:

'Album'—This dwarf plant has a small, delicate white flower.

'Benichidori'—A dwarf plant covered with small, bright reddish orange flowers.

'Benisuzume'—A reddish orange flower on a low, spreading plant.

'Hanekomachi'—Bright, pinkish red, Japanese selection.

'Harunoumi'—This small and dainty plant has soft pink flowers early in the season.

'Hinode'—Clearest red.

'Komo Kulshan'—Small flower with a pale pink center and a rose margin.

'Rose'—Rose flowers, small leaves and habit of the other Kiusianums but a slightly larger grower.

'Ukon'—This Japanese diminutive has delicate pink flowers.

Rhododendron × kosteranum — Mollis Hybrid Azaleas
(rō-dō-den′dron × kos-ter-ā′num)

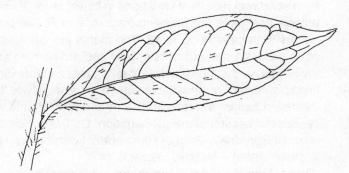

LEAVES: Alternate, simple, entire, 1 1/2 to 4″ long, obovate to oblong-ovate, apex bluntish, with a glandlike tip, base wedge-shaped, margin hairy on upper surface or becoming hairless, bristly-hairy on veins beneath.

BUDS: Large—1/4 to 1/2″, imbricate, tip of scales tinged brown.

Rhododendron × kosteranum, Mollis Hybrid Azaleas, are somewhat similar to the Exbury group in flower characteristics but usually smaller and not as hardy, although from observations in the midwest, I believe the hardiness is excellent; foliage is deciduous; resulted from crosses between *R. japonicum* × *R. molle*. Generally yellow to orange flower color. Cultivars worth considering include:

'Chevalier de Reali'—Maize yellow, fading to cream, fragrant.

'Christopher Wren'—Yellow.

'Consul Ceresole'—Rose-pink.

'Koster's Brilliant'—Orange-red.

'Lemon Twist'—A pleasing light yellow with uniquely twisted stems and branches, spreading growth.

'Queen Emma'—Large, light salmon-orange flowers, 10' high, vigorous, synonymous with 'Koningin Emma'.

'Snowdrift'—White.

Rhododendron × laetevirens, (rō-do-den'dron lē-ti-vī'renz), Wilson Rhododendron, is a small (2 to 4' by 2 to 6'), low growing, glossy leaved, evergreen shrub with pink to purplish flowers; makes a good, neat, small evergreen plant in the rock garden or for foundation planting. Actually one of the finest evergreen foliaged rhododendrons, unfortunately the flowers are third rate. Zone 4. Result of a cross between *R. carolinianum* × *R. ferrugineum*.

Rhododendron luteum, (rō-do-den'dron lū'tē-um), Pontic Azalea, is quite a handsome 8 to 10' (12') high shrub that produces fragrant, rich yellow, 1 1/2 to 2" diameter flowers on naked stems in May. It is truly beautiful in flower and I will always remember a particular striking specimen in the border along Meadow Road at the Arnold Arboretum. It is a vigorous species and has been used in hybridizing. Asia Minor, Caucasus, eastern Europe. Introduced 1792. Zone 5.

Rhododendron maximum, (rō-do-den'dron maks'i-mum), Rosebay Rhododendron, grows 4 to 15' in the north but can grow to 30'; habit is loose and open; leaves are large (4 to 8" long) and evergreen (dark green); flowers are rose, purplish pink to white, spotted with olive-green to orange, 1 to 2" across, June; requires moist, acid soil and shade protection. Occurs in abundance throughout the north Georgia mountains along streams. Requires cool, moist, well drained root run and is not ideally suited to "normal" landscape situations. Have observed many times in North Georga where it often forms pure thickets. The trunks are brown, lightly ridge and furrowed, somewhat twisted and quite beautiful in syncopated composition.

var. *album*—White flowers.

var. *purpureum*—Deep pink to purple flowers.

Native to Nova Scotia and Ontario to Georgia, Alabama and Ohio. Introduced 1736. Zone 3 to 7.

Rhododendron minus, (rō-do-den'dron mī'nus), Piedmont Rhododendron, has funnel shaped pink blooms in large trusses, growth habit dwarf and compact, 3 to 6' by 3 to 6', Zone 6 to 8.

Rhododendron 'Northern Lights' resulted from crosses between *R.* × *kosteranum* and *R. prinophyllum*. The original crosses were made in 1957 by the late Albert G. Johnson. Originally they were produced from seed with resultant variations in flower color. Flowers range from light to deep pink, lilac, yellow, orange and have the pleasing fragrance of *R. prinophyllum*. Each flower is about 1 1/2" long and occurs in trusses of up to 12. The plants are compact and grow 6 to 7' high and wide. The flower buds occur on naked stems in May and are nothing short of spectacular. I had one of the "culls" in my Illinois garden and it was fantastic. I realize fantastic is a relative term but when one lives in central Illinois and has an insatiable desire to grow flower bud hardy azaleas he has very few choices. 'Northern Lights' azaleas are hardy to -40°F. Plants are now quite common in commerce with the success of tissue culture propagation. Cultivars include:

'Apricot Surprise'—Bright yellow-apricot with orange shadings.

'Golden Lights'—Yellow, fragrant.

'Orchid Lights'—Semi-dwarf, bushy, lilac flowers.

'Rosy Lights'—Fragrant dark pink, rose-red shading.

'Spicy Lights'—Soft tangerine-orange, fragrant.

'White Lights'—Large, fragrant, floriferous white with yellow center.

Rhododendron oblongifolium, (rō-do-den'dron ob-long-i-fō'li-um), Texas Azalea, grows 6' high and has distinct obovate to oblanceolate, 1 1/2 to 4" long leaves. The slightly fragrant, funnel-shaped, pure white, 3/4 to 1" long flowers occur in 7 to 12 flowered trusses after the leaves. It is found in moist sandy woods or on the margins of sandy bogs and streams and even on limestone. Related to *R.*

viscosum and *R. serrulatum* and found in Arkansas, Oklahoma and Texas. Some taxonomists would argue that it is not a distinct species. Introduced 1917. Zone 7 (?).

Rhododendron obtusum, (rō-dō-den′dron ob-tūs′um), Hiryu Azalea, is a spreading, dense evergreen shrub with glossy green leaves up to 1 1/4″ long. The flowers are reddish violet, but bright red, scarlet and crimson forms occur. Each flower may be 3/4 to 1″ across, funnel-shaped, 1 to 3 per truss. Found wild in highly acid soil on three mountains in Kyushu, Japan. Introduced about 1844. Zone 6. There are a number of cultivars which have been derived from *R obtusum, R. kaempferi, R, kiusianum,* and *R. satense.* This group has the name Kurume Azaleas (see Kurume Hybrid list) and while often considered dwarf they will develop into dense, well-preserved, 4 to 6′ high plants. Many of the clones have been used for greenhouse forcing and are simply not hardy in the northern areas. The range of colors travels from white to pink, lavender, scarlet, salmon and all shades in between. As hybridization continues new and better cultivars will appear in the trade. The real crux is being able to separate the good flowering, hardy (at least to -10°F) types from the rest of the lot. Callaway Gardens has an excellent collection of Kurumes and their famous Azalea bowl is primarily planted with this group.

Rhododendron periclymenoides, (rō-dō-den′dron per-i-clī-men-oy′dēz), Pinxterbloom Azalea, is a low, much-branched, stoloniferous, deciduous shrub which averages 4 to 6′ in height but ranges from dwarfish (2′) to relatively large (10′) over the native habitat. The foliage is bright green in summer turning dull yellow in fall. The flowers vary in color from impure white or pale pink to deep violet and open in April or early May. Based on numerous visits to the azalea garden at Biltmore Estate, the flowers open with, or perhaps slightly later than *R. austrinum* and *R. canescens.* The flowers are fragrant, each about 1 1/2″ across, borne 6 to 12 together before the leaves. This species is adapted to dry, sandy, rocky soils. A useful plant for naturalizing, and along with *R. calendulaceum* and *R. viscosum* was used in the development of the Ghent hybrids. Native from Massachusetts to North Carolina and Ohio. Introduced 1730. Zone 3 to 8. Previously *R. nudiflorum.*

Rhododendron 'P.J.M.'
(rō-dō-den′dron 'P.J.M.')

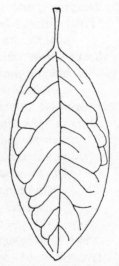

LEAVES: Small, 1 to 2 1/2″ long, usually elliptic, dark green above, changing to purple in winter, essentially hairless, rusty-scaly beneath, thick, leathery.
BUDS: Rounded and much smaller than those of *R. catawbiense.*

Rhododendron 'P.J.M.' Hybrids resulted from crosses between *R. carolinianum* and *R. dauricum* var. *sempervirens.* The P.J.M. Hybrids are a group of plants and, therefore, there may be differences in flower colors. The plant grows from 3 to 6′ in height and is of rounded outline; the foliage is evergreen, dark green in summer and turns plum purple in fall; the flowers are vivid, bright lavender pink and occur in mid to late April; the flowers occur heavily every year as the plant sets little or no seed. Zone 4 hardiness. Dr. Donald Wyman said the 'P.J.M.' Hybrids were the most promising rhododendrons that have originated in New England during the past 25 years. Originated in the Weston Nurseries, Hopkinton, Massachusetts, 1943. Many people do not like the "dirty, squalid lavender-pink flowers" but when the choice of rhododendrons is limited this is a bright element in the landscape. I grew 'P.J.M.' in my Illinois garden and it proved to be the hardiest broadleaf rhododendron. Minnesota Landscape Arboretum reported that it was the only flower bud hardy broadleaf rhododendron. It flowered in my garden along with daffodils and was a pleasant sight especially after a difficult midwestern winter.

MEZITT HYBRIDS
'Aglo'—Sister of 'Olga Mezitt', selected for its earlier flower and dark blotch, compact grower with light pink flowers.
'Balta' (*R. carolinianum* var. *album* × 'P.J.M.' Hybrid)—Small, glossy, partly convex evergreen leaves; compact and slow in growth; flowers a week after 'P.J.M.' hybrids, pale pink to almost white.

'Black Satin'—An F₃ hybrid of 'P.J.M.' hybrids, deep fall and winter foliage color, which is shiny coal-black, semi-upright in growth habit, flowers are a deep rose-pink.

'Counterpoint'—Sister of 'Marathon', deciduous upright spreading plant with semi-double bright pink flowers along the entire length of the stems.

'Desmit'—A sister seedling of 'Waltham', selected for one week earlier flowering time and appears less susceptible to the sunscalding leaf spot problem.

'Elite'—A most vigorous selection of 'P.J.M.', tall growing, blossoms are slightly pinker and open a few days later than 'Victor'.

'Henry's Red'—Very dark red, wide and upright with dark green foliage, have seen in Manchester, NH.

'Laurie' (*R. carolinianum* var. *album* × 'P.J.M.' hybrid)—Glossy green leaves turn red in fall and winter; compact and slow in growth; flowers pale pink to almost white with some branches exhibiting semidouble petaloid blooms just after 'P.J.M.'

'Low Red Frilled'—Medium red flowers with frilled edges, low growing, spreading and compact, dark green foliage.

'Marathon' (An F₂ hybrid of 'P.J.M.' × *R. mucronulatum* 'Cornell Pink')—Deciduous semi-upright habit, bright magenta flowers early, usually the day (April 19) of the Boston Marathon, which starts in sight of Weston Nursery, Hopkinton, MA.

'Mindaura' (*R. minus* var. *compacta* × *R. dauricum* var. *sempervirens*)—Evergreen foliage, green in summer, deep purple in fall and winter, foliage is thinner in texture than 'P.J.M.', wide spreading habit of growth, flowers a week after R. 'P.J.M.', discontinued and now used only for hybridizing.

'Molly Fordham'—Compact growing, white flowers, small glossy green foliage year-round, early May, named after Molly Fordham, wife of Alfred Fordham, the great propagator (now retired) at the Arnold Arboretum.

'Northern Rose' (*R.* 'Waltham' × *R. mucronulatum* 'Cornell Pink', crossed by Dr. Robert Ticknor)—Narrow evergreen foliage on a semi-upright plant, small bright pink flowers in abundance at or slightly after 'P.J.M.'; difficult to propagate but may become popular through tissue culture.

'Olga Mezitt' (*R. minus* var. *compacta* × *R. mucronulatum*)—Evergreen foliage turning light red in fall and winter, vigorous upright spreading plant, bright peach-pink flowers about the time of *R. carolinianum.*

'Regal'—A selection of 'P.J.M.', vigorous, wider spreading type of growth.

'Shrimp Pink Hybrids' (*R. carolinianum* var. *album* × *R. mucronulatum* 'Cornell Pink')—Green summer foliage turning light red in fall and retaining about 10% of the smaller leaves during the winter; upright spreading habit of growth, flowers in abundance a week after *R. mucronulatum.* The three selections are:
  'Caronella'—Strongest pink.
  'Llenroc'—Dusty pale pink to almost white.
  'Wally'—Soft pink.

'Victor'—A selection of 'P.J.M.', a compact slow-growing type, earliest to flower.

'Waltham' (*R. ferrugineum* × *R. carolinianum,* crossed by Dr. Robert Ticknor)—Deep green evergreen foliage on dense mound up to 3′ high. Flowers are pink *R. carolinianum* type, beautifully displayed about a week later. Leaves develop spotting when the plant is growing in full sun.

'Weston's Pink Diamond' (A petaloid 'P.J.M.' hybrid × *R. mucronulatum* 'Cornell Pink')—Semievergreen foliage and upright spreading habit of growth, flowers early, at time of *R. mucronulatum,* with frilled pink heavily double flowers.

'White Angel' (*R. carolinianum* var. *album* × *R. dauricum* var. *album*)—Semievergreen, upright plant; pale lavender buds opening white as they mature.

Rhododendron prinophyllum (formerly *R. roseum*), (rō-dō-den′dron prī-no-fil′um), Roseshell Azalea, is a deciduous, 2 to 8′, rarely to 15′ tall, much branched shrub with numerous spreading branches; spread is comparable to height; foliage is bright green in summer; green to bronze in fall; flowers are bright pink with clove-like scent, May, borne 5 to 9 per cluster before or with the leaves; superior to *R. periclymenoides* and *R. canescens;* extremely hardy, with marked tolerance to high pH. Native to New Hampshire and southern Quebec to Virginia, west to Illinois and Missouri. Introduced 1812. Zone 3 to 8.

Rhododendron prunifolium, (rō-dō-den'dron prūn'i-fō'li-um), Plumleaf Azalea, grows 8 to 10' (15') high and produces orange-red to red, funnel-shaped, 3/4 to 1" long flowers in July-August. The stamens are 2 to 2 1/2" long. The lateness of flower makes this a rather valuable addition to the garden. It is hardy to Boston but makes its best growth in the south and can be found in abundance at Callaway Gardens, Pine Mountain, GA. It is considered the most glabrous of all American azaleas and for that reason quite distinct. Found in sandy ravines along stream banks. Southwestern Georgia and eastern Alabama. Introduced 1918. Zone 5 to 9.
Cultivars include:
'Cherry Bomb'—Orange-red, July.
'Coral Glow'—Pink-orange, July.
'Lewis Shortt'—Scarlet red flower on a plant with plum leaf foliage; found and introduced by Mr. Shortt.
'Peach Glow'—Orange-pink, July.
'Pine Prunifolium'—Bright red flowers open in mid summer.

Rhododendron 'Purple Gem' is a rounded, dwarf, evergreen type with small leaves and light purple flowers in mid April. Hardy to -15°F; a cross between *R. fastigiatum* × *R. carolinianum.* 'Purple Imp' is similar to 'Purple Gem' but a truer blue; smaller and more alpine, low and dense.

Rhododendron racemosum 'Compactum' (rō-dō-den'dron ra-sem-ō'sum)—Compact form, 1 to 2' high, apple blossom pink, a rock garden gem.

Rhododendron 'Ramapo' is another compact form with glaucous foliage, bright violet-pink flowers in early April and −25°F hardiness.

Rhododendron serrulatum, (rō-dō-den'dron ser-ū-lāt'um), Sweet Azalea, is a medium to large-growing azalea, one of the latest blooming azaleas with flowers occurring after the foliage, from June through July. Flowers are 1 to 1 1/2" long, from pale pink to white and exceptionally fragrant. Does well in wooded swampy areas. Georgia to Florida and Louisiana. Introduced 1919. Zone 7 to 8.

Rhododendron smirnowii, (rō-dō-den'dron smēr-nōw'ē-ī), Smirnow Rhododendron, is an evergreen shrub growing 6 to 8' high and as broad in 15 years. The foliage is dark green above with thick woolly tomentum beneath. The flowers are rose or rosy-pink and the corolla is frilled; each flower is 1 1/2" long and 2" across; May; in 5 to 6" wide trusses. Very distinct and handsome rhododendron in flower. Has been used for breeding work because of good hardiness (Zone 4), flower and foliage. Will become increasingly evident in American gardens as its merits are extolled. Native to Caucasus, 5,000 to 8,000'. Introduced 1886.

Rhododendron vaseyi, (rō-dō-den'dron vā'zē-ī), Pinkshell Azalea, grows 5 to 10' in height; the habit is irregular upright; foliage is deciduous, medium green in summer changing to light red in fall, may develop excellent fall color and have observed deep red on plants in Arnold Arboretum; flowers are clear rose, bell-shaped with the two lower corolla lobes divided nearly at the base, before leaves, 1 1/2" diameter, early to mid-May, 5 to 8 flowers per inflorescence, 5 to 7 stamens, no fragrance; one of the hardy American types; var. *album* has white flowers; native to the blue Ridge Mountains of North Carolina. Zone 4 to 8. Makes a spectacular show when in flower; apparently does not hybridize.
Cultivars include:
'Pinkerbell'—Selected deep pink strain of the species.
'White Find'—A rare form, the white flowers have a greenish yellow blotch and are fragrant.

Rhododendrom viscosum, (rō-dō-den'dron vis-kō'sum), Swamp Azalea, grows 1 to 8' (average 5') by 3 to 8' and is of loose, open habit with numerous spreading, very hispid branches; flowers are white, rarely pink, clove-like scent, mid May to June, 4 to 9 flowers per inflorescence; have seen it growing along fresh water ponds on Cape Cod; leaves are lustrous green sometimes with a glaucous cast below; Maine to South Carolina, Georgia, Alabama, in swamps. Cultivated 1731. Zone 3 to 9.

'Lemon Drop'—A rare yellow form with spicy fragrant flowers in late June and July.

var. *montanum*—A low growing form only waist high; is responsible for many of the natural hybrids as it blooms with other species in June.

'Pink Rocket'—Red buds, slightly sweetly scented groups of small pink flowers in late June; wide, upright-growing; small ascending blue-green foliage with silvery undersides, turns bronze-red in fall, -29°F.

'Rosata'—Fragrant carmine-rose flowers, wide, upright.

Rhododendron weyricherii, (rō-dō-den'dron wâr-ich'ēr-ī) Weyrich Azalea, is a most unusual and beautiful deciduous azalea. Foliage is large, round and glossy with clusters of 2 to 3 leaves at end of the branches; funnel-shaped flowers usually brick-red with purple blotch adorning the plant before leaves appear in early spring. Native of Quelport Island, Korea.

Rhododendron 'Windbeam' is another very hardy (-25°F) evergreen type of low, semi-dwarf habit, with white flowers becoming suffused with pink. It is a cross between *carolinianum* and *racemosum,* will grow 4' by 4'. Leaves are roundish, small and aromatic. In Zone 8, foliage remains green in winter. In the last edition, I did not have much positive to say about performance in Zone 8 but over the past 7 years have altered my assessment. If given pine shade and a moist, well drained root run, it makes a handsome plant. It has not proven outstanding in Zone 8.

Rhododendron yakusimanum, (rō-dō-den'dron ya-koo-si-mā'num), is a dense, mounded, evergreen rhododendron growing about 3' tall and 3' wide. The foliage is dark green with a woolly indumentum beneath; the flowers are bright rose in bud opening to white in full flower (sort of an apple blossom effect), about 10 campanulate flowers in a truss; hardy from -5 to -15°F, used extensively in hybridizing and superior clones are available; one reference indicated a 20-year-old plant may be only 3' by 5'. Cultivars include:

'Mist Maiden'—(Leach) Rose colored buds open apple blossom pink and fade to white, a slightly faster growing form with beautiful indumentum.

'Yaku Duchess'—(Shammarello) Light red flowers in rounded truss, a low growing hybrid without indumentum.

'Yaku Princess'—(Shammarello) Low growing hybrid without indumentum, flower buds open light pink, turn to sparkling white.

'Yaku Queen'—(Shammarello) Another low growing hybrid without indumentum, vivid pink flower buds open to apple blossom pink, then fade to white.

Rhododendron yedoense var. ***poukhanense,*** (rō-dō-den'dron yed-ō-en'sē), Korean Azalea, grows 3 to 6' high and spreads that much or more; develops into a broad mat on exposed locations; foliage is dark green in summer; orange to red-purple in fall; flowers are rose to lilac-purple, 2" across, slightly fragrant, May, 2 to 3 flowers together. *R. yedoense* (Yodogawa Azalea) has double flowers of a similar color; native to Korea. Zone 4 to 5. Has performed well in Illinois and Georgia.

Azalea Cultivars and Hybrid Groups

In some respects, it is paralyzingly frightening to attempt to present the cultivars of azaleas. Numerous hybridizers using different progenitor species have produced hybrids that often bear their names. Mr. Fred Galle, in his great book *Azaleas* (1987), Timber Press, Portland, Oregon, presents the most comprehensive and up-to-date listing and description of azalea cultivars. I attempted to check the ones presented here (most derived from 1987-1989 nursery catalogs) against Mr. Galle's list. Surprisingly, many did not appear in his book, which indicates that this list will be outdated by the time the book is published. I used about 30 catalogs plus current literature to assemble the list which should reflect the more available cultivars. Anyone interested in azaleas, their history and development should consult Mr. Galle's book. It is the classic tome on the subject.

AICHELE HYBRIDS

'Laura'—Originally developed as a greenhouse forcing azalea, dense foliage and abundant, dark pink, 2″ diameter hose-in-hose flowers in early April, hardy in Zone 7 to 8.

'Posaman'—Medium sized shrub with 3″ diameter pink-white flowers.

BACK ACRE HYBRIDS

Plants are cold hardy to 0 to 5°F and are medium height, flowers open in late April in Georgia.

'Marian Lee'—Flower has white center with reddish pink border, 3″ diameter with the appearance of butterflies, medium size upright grower, habit similar to the Kurumes.

'Orange Flair'—Low-growing plant with very unusual flower, orange-pink with a white center and double.

'Target'—Upright grower with 3″ diameter scarlet-pink flowers.

BELTSVILLE (YERKES-PRYOR) HYBRIDS

'Eureka'—Flowers pink, hose-in-hose, medium, spreading.

'Guy Yerkes'—Hose-in-hose, salmon-pink, low growing, semievergreen.

'Polar Bear'—White, with slight yellow-green throat, hose-in-hose, wide upright, slow-growing, green leaves in summer become yellow in autumn; flower buds tested hardy to -13°F, common in the trade.

BROOKS HYBRIDS

Developed to endure hot, dry summers, hardy to 20°F.

'Flamingo Variegata'—Variegated red, hose-in-hose, late.

'My Valentine'—Rose, double, mid to late season.

'Pinkie'—Single, pink, hose-in-hose, late.

'Red Bird'—Large, red, ruffled, semi-double to hose-in-hose.

CARLA HYBRIDS

Developed at North Carolina State University, Raleigh, NC, Zone 7b-8a (USDA) (5 to 15°F). Flowering dates are based on observations in the Raleigh area. In July 1976 'Adelaide Pope', 'Carror', 'Elaine', 'Emily', 'Jane', 'Spalding', 'Pink Cloud', and 'Sunglow' were released. In 1982 'Autumn Sun', 'Cochran's Lavender', 'Pink Camellia' and 'Wolfpack Red' were released.

'Adelaide Pope'—Flowers deep rose-pink, single, medium-large, 1 to 5 per bud; plant medium-large, vigorous, compact; April 15-April 25.

'Autumn Sun'—Flowers bronze-red, hose-in-hose, 2 to 3 per bud; plant small to medium; upright-spreading, dense; April 15-25.

'Carror'—Flowers rose-pink, semi-double, medium sized, 1 to 4 per bud; plant medium sized, compact; April 25-May 1.

'Cochran's Lavender'—Flowers purplish pink, single, medium sized, 1 to 3 per bud; plant medium in size, spreading, dense; April 15-25.

'Elaine'—Flowers light pink, fully double, medium sized rose-bud type opening full wide in later development, 1 to 3 flowers per bud; plant medium sized; April 16-26.

'Emily'—Flowers deep rose-red, single, medium-small, 1 to 3 per bud, hose-in-hose; plant medium sized, compact; April 18-30.

'Fred D. Cochran'—Superior resistance to root rot.

'Greenthumb Peppermint'—Mid to late flowering, semidouble, hose-in-hose, 3″ diameter pinkish with white margins and a soft purplish pink inner pattern; typically plants develop sports of white and purplish pink, see *HortScience* 25: 236-237 (1990); not a Carla hybrid.

'Jan Cochran'—Compact shrub that resembles an English Boxwood in leaf; single rosy pink, 4/5 to 1″ long, 3/5 to 4/5″ wide, moderately resistant to *Phytophthora cinnamomi,* see *HortScience* 24: 717-718 (1989).

'Jane Spalding'—Flowers rose-pink, single, 1 to 3 per bud, medium sized; plant is medium sized; April 25-25.

'Pink Camellia'—Flowers light purplish pink, completely double, rosebud type, opening full in later development, 1 to 3 flowers per bud; plant medium sized; April 15-25.

'Pink Cloud'—Flowers light pink, predominantly single, large sized, 2 to 4 per bud; plants medium sized; April 15-25.

'Rachel'—Compact shrub with ascending-spreading branches, wine-red flowers, single to semi-double, up to 2″ diameter, 40 to 50% of the flowers are semidouble, moderately resistant to *Phytophthora cinnamomi,* see *HortScience* 24: 717-718 (1989).

'Sunglow'—Flowers deep rose-pink, single, medium large, 1 to 4 per bud; plant medium-large sized, vigorous; April 20-30.

'Wolfpack Red'—Flowers strong red, single, small, 1 to 4 flowers per bud; plant semi-dwarf, spreading; April 15-25.

GIRARD HYBRIDS

Excellent, large flowered, show-stopping evergreen azaleas for colder climates; flower bud hardiness ranges from -5 to -15°F; grew many of these in my Illinois garden, need more attention from northern gardeners; bred and introduced by Girard Nurseries, Geneva, OH.

'Girard Border Gem'—Beautiful deep rose-pink flowers that completely cover the dwarf azalea. When in bloom, the foliage and plant are completely hidden. Leaves are glossy dark green only 1/4 to 3/4″ long, turning a glossy scarlet during winter months. An early flowering beautiful dwarf azalea.

'Girard Chiara'—Clone originated in 1972. Received awards in three A.R.S. shows. Flowers are large, hose-in-hose, 2 1/2 to 3″ diameter. Color is clear rose, pleasingly ruffled and very floriferous. Foliage is glossy deep green type which holds very well. Plant takes on a dense broad growing habit; ideal for borders, foundation planting and rock gardens. Will withstand -15°F. Ideal for forcing.

'Girard Clare Marie'—Large ruffled single white flowers up to 3″ in diameter. Very vigorous upright grower, large light green foliage.

'Girard Crimson'—Large crimson flowers up to 2 1/2″ diameter, very large glossy green leaves, good winter color, on a good compact plant.

'Girard Dwarf Lavender'—Medium clear lavender florets. One of the most uniform and compact growing of all the evergreen azaleas. Excellent foliage, vigor and hardiness. Needs no or very little pruning. Excellent for small gardens and foundation plantings.

'Girard Fuchsia'—A beautiful shade of reddish purple, florets are beautifully waved and ruffled, of very heavy texture; foliage dark green and glossy, -15°F.

'Girard Hot Shot'—Fiery deep orange-red or scarlet flowers, 2 1/2 to 3″ diameter, heavily textured and completely covering the plants. Foliage 3/4 to 1″ long, medium green during summer changing to brilliant orange-red in fall. More upright habit than 'Girard Scarlet'.

'Girard Jeremiah'—Beautiful large hose-in-hose pink flowers with large dark green foliage turning red in winter. Excellent compact self-branching, prolific flowering. Extremely hardy and excellent for foundation plantings and gardens.

'Girard Kathy'—Good 2″ diameter single white flowers on a medium size shrub.

'Girard Leslie's Purple'—Large hose-in-hose purplish red flowers with dark spotting, 2 1/2 to 3″ diameter; foliage deep glossy green, semidwarf, low compact rounded habit, 3′ by 3′.

'Girard National Beauty'—Beautiful ruffled rose-pink florets, large dark green foliage and compact self-branching growth habit, matures to 24″ high, 3′ wide, hardy to -10°F.

'Girard Peter Alan'—Rich orchid florets with reddish shading to purplish black eye, strong upright habit; foliage is heavy rich green, hardy to -15°F.

'Girard Pink Dawn'—Large, hose-in-hose rose-pink, foliage is dark green in summer and assumes red tints in fall and winter; compact and vigorous, one of the hardiest.

'Girard Pink Delight'—Fragrant, vivid pink hose-in-hose with 20 to 24 florets forming a nice compact truss, tall growing.

'Girard Pleasant White'—Large 1 1/2 to 3″ diameter white flowers with a cream center, late flowering and vigorous, 2 to 2 1/2′ by 3′, dark green foliage, hardy.

'Girard Purple'—Purple flowers, superior color and habit compared to 'Herbert' or other lavenders, extremely vigorous and compact growing.

'Girard Renee Michelle'—Clear pink blossoms, 2 1/2 to 3″, foliage dark green, 1 1/2″ by 1/2″; plants are low, compact, a cross of 'Boudoir' and 'Gumpo Pink', beautiful flowers, flowered in my Illinois garden in a protected location, has withstood -10°F.

'Girard Roberta'—Double pink, ruffled petals, large to 3″ across.

'Girard Rose'—Rose, 2 1/2 to 3″ florets, slightly waved, foliage 1 1/2 to 2″ long by 3/4″ wide, deep green and glossy during the summer, taking on brilliant deep red tints in early fall, stems turn deep red in winter, vigorous, upright growth habit.

'Girard Salmon'—Large hose-in-hose salmon flowers, compact habit, more upright and taller than most Girard selections, vigorous.

'Girard Sandra Ann'—Reddish purple, 3″ diameter flowers, bright green foliage, broad rounded habit, 5′ by 6′.

'Girard Saybrook Glory'—Large pink flowers, 2 1/2 to 3″ ruffled florets, large dark green foliage, low compact plant.

'Girard's Scarlet'—Large flowers, strong red with deep orange-red glow, waxy textured, deep glossy green foliage, low compact plant, 1 1/2 to 2′ by 3′.

'Girard Unsurpassable'—Rose-pink flowers, compact with good dark green foliage, hardy.

'Girard Variegated Hotshot'—White and green variegated foliage and ruffled red florets similar to 'Hotshot', a vigorous low compact plant.

Deciduous types:

'Girard Crimson Tide'—Large double red flowers on a tight round head, vigorous grower and excellent flowerer.

'Girard Mount Saint Helens'—A blend of pink, salmon, with yellow and orange blotch exploding from all copper flower petals, very large trusses, 5″ by 6″, holding 12 to 15 large florets of very heavy texture; upright with good foliage that holds well until winter.

'Girard Red Pom Pom'—Fragrant, double red, forming a tight long-lasting truss, 4 1/2″ wide and 3 1/2″ long, compact, mildew resistant plant.

'Girard Salmon Delight'—Vivid rose flushed with yellow, florets 2 to 1/2″ diameter with 25 to 30 florets to each 5 to 5 1/2″ diameter truss; leaves medium green turning to yellow with orange tints, broad upright growth habit, appears mildew resistant.

'Girard Wedding Bouquet'—Unique apple blossom pink hose-in-hose frilled floret, 18 to 25 per truss, fragrant, medium growing, deciduous.

'Girard White Clouds'—Seedling white, vigorous, deciduous.

GLENN DALE HYBRIDS

Cold hardy for the Middle Atlantic States with flowers as large and as varied as those of the Southern Indica Azaleas! That was the aim of B.Y. Morrison, former head of the Plant Introduction Section at Glenn Dale, Maryland. To achieve that goal he selected and named over 400 Glenn Dale Hybrids from 70,000 seedlings. Some of the hardiest will withstand -10°F, however, they are often listed as flower bud hardy to 0°F. Flower from (April in Zone 8) May into June. Many have flecks or occasional stripes of a deeper complementary color that add considerable visual interest. Some will sport and produce branches with flowers that can be distinctively different in pattern and color.

'Alight'—Orange-pink.

'Aphrodite'—Rose-pink, single, 2″ diameter flower.

'Artic'— White.

'Aztec'—White.

'Baroque'—White flowers with striping of phlox-purple; broad and spreading, to 5' high; dark green leaves.

'Beacon'—Scarlet.

'Boldface'—White center with lavender margin.

'Buccaneer'—Orange-red.

'Carmel'—Spinel red with a blotch of Indian red dots, carries in garden effect as a burgundy red, very effective as accents to masses of light colors, tall and spreading.

'Cascade'—White, spotted rose-pink, hose-in-hose, 1 1/2" diameter, 4' by 4 to 6'.

'Colleen'—Pink.

'Copperman'—Orange-red, single flowers on medium-size, spreading, dense plants.

'Dayspring'—Pink.

'Delaware Valley White'—White, single, 2" diameter, one of the more common forms in commerce, mid-season.

'Delilah'—Begonia rose.

'Delos'—Rose-pink.

'Driven Snow'—Pure white flowers, 6' high.

'Eros'—Pink.

'Evensong'—Rose-pink.

'Everest'—White with pale chartreuse blotch, floriferous, 5' high.

'Fanfare'—Pink, hose-in-hose.

'Fashion'—Two inch diameter orange-red, hose-in-hose flower, medium sized shurb, 6' by 6', 0°F.

'Fawn'—White center, pink margin.

'F.C. Bradford'—Deep rose-pink with darker edges, blotch of purplish red dots, 5' high.

'Festive'—White striped with red.

'Glacier'—White petals with faint green tone to the throat, to 3" in diameter, vigorous grower to 6', erect to spreading habit, handsome lustrous foliage, one of the best Glenn Dale's, used frequently in the south.

'Gladiator'—Orange-red.

'Grace Freeman'—Pale pink.

'Greeting'—Ruffled coral-rose flowers, glossy dark green persistent leaves, erect and spreading, to 4' high.

'Guerdon'—Light lavender with a lavender-rose blotch, low spreading, to 2' high.

'H.H. Hume' (USDA, Beltsville hybrid)—White, with faint yellow throat, hose-in-hose, erect-spreading habit, 0 to +10°F.

'Illusions'—Lovely soft shades of pink, one of the hardiest, to 3' high.

'Jessica'—Rose-pink.

'Joya'—Rose-pink.

'Louise Dowdle'—Tyrian-pink.

'Manhattan'—Bold rose-pink flower, spreading to 4', wider than high, hardy.

'Martha Hitchcock'—White flowers with purple edge.

'Mary Margaret'—Orange-red.

'Masquerade'—White, striped with pink.

'Melanie'—Rose pink, hose-in-hose with rose blotch, upright and spreading, 5' high.

'Moonstone'—Profusion of cream-yellow blooms, compact mound, semi-dwarf.

'Morning Star'—Deep rose.

'Nectar'—Fragrant orange-pink.

'Niagara'—Exceptionally fine large frilled white flowers with a chartreuse blotch, dense growing, 3' high.

'Picotee'—White flowers with purple picotee edges, broad and spreading.

'Pinocchio'—White, striped red.

'Pixie'—White flowers with occasional stripes of bright pink, broad and spreading, 5' high.

'Polar Sea'—Frilled white flowers with chartreuse blotch, low and spreading, 3' high.

'Radiance'—Deep rose-pink.

'Refrain'—Rose-pink with white margin, hose-in-hose.

'Sagittarius'—Fine pink with salmon undertone, low spreading, 2′ high.

'Seafoam'—Frilled white flowers with chartreuse yellow throat, broad and low growing, 3′ high.

'Sea Shell'—Deep rose-pink.

'Silverlace'—White with a green blotch, a few purple stripes, broad and spreading, 5′ high.

'Snowclad'—White with ruffled margins and a chartreuse blotch, low and spreading, 3′ high.

'Sterling'—Deep rose-pink.

'Suwanee'—Rose-pink.

'Swashbuckler'—Red.

'Treasure'—White with very light pink edge, single flowers borne on spreading vigorous plants.

'Trophy'—Shell pink, very large, heavy informal double.

'Ursula'—Pink.

'Vespers'—Frilled white with chartreuse throat, broad and spreading, 5′ high.

'Vestal'—Large white flowers with chartreuse blotch, wide spreading habit, 4′ high.

'Violetta'—Light mallow-purple.

'Wildfire'—Red.

HINES HYBRIDS

Crosses of Belgian Indica with Southern Indica, vigorous, supposedly sun and salt tolerant.

'Cinnamon Sugar'—Single cinnamon-rose.

'Heather Lynn'—Double rose-purple which changes into white blushed lavender-pink with darker edges.

'Ida Marnion'—Double magenta.

'Jessie May'—Single to semi-double, purple with mottled throat and frilled petals.

'Jessie Shirar'—Undulate hose-in-hose, rose-red to pink.

'Lois Hines'—Frilled double, clear orange-desert rose with faint mottling.

'Stella Hines'—Ruffled single, Persian rose flowers.

'Stella Sue'—Ruffled, hose-in-hose, blush rose.

ILAM HYBRIDS

A strain of deciduous azaleas developed in New Zealand; rather large flowers completely cover plants in early spring, as hardy as the Exburys, Knaphills and Ghents; many of the plants produce fragrant flowers, have seen them in Wooster, Ohio where they were performing well, suspect -10 to -20°F flower bud hardiness.

'Copper Cloud'—Fragrant, deeply frilled orange, heavy flowering, medium habit.

'Martie'—Frilled dusky red.

'Peach Sunset'—Orange-pink suffused, early, brilliant color.

'Peachy Keen'—Fragrant, with subtle shades of peach-pink, compact semi-dwarf growth habit.

'Persian Melon'—Orange yellow, large trussed like 'Gibraltar', vigorous habit.

'Pink Williams'—Clear silvery pink, large slightly fragrant flowers, slow, compact-growing.

'Primrose'—Fragrant clear light yellow with golden flare, vigorous but lax grower.

'Red Letter'—Brilliant red, vigorous grower.

'Red Velvet'—Deep rich red, vigorous-growing, wide upright, red-purple fall foliage.

'Rufus'—Deep blood-red, foliage deep bronze.

INDICA TYPES

'Balsaminaeflorum' ('Rosaeflora')—Very low growing, large flowered, double, salmon pink.

'Flame Creeper'—Flowers are orange-red, becoming very popular as a ground cover.

'Macrantha'—Low, compact, double red, spreading growth habit, 3′ high.

'Macrantha Double'—Pretty double orange-pink flowers on compact plants.

'Macrantha Orange'—Bright orange-red blossoms produced late on medium size plants with bright green foliage.

'Macrantha Pink'—Bright pink blossoms produced late on medium size plants with bright green foliage.

'Macrantha Salmon'—Single, salmon-pink blossoms on medium size plants.

'Mrs. L.C. Fischer'—Red with darker blotch, single, hose-in-hose.

BELGIAN INDICA TYPES

These azaleas grow best when not exposed to direct sun. Small bushy plants are covered with bright green, lush foliage, an excellent background for spectacular masses of large blooms. Best in Zone 10, coastal California type climate; primarily greenhouse forcing types.

'Ambrosia'—Double, very dark red, prolific bloomer.

'Avenir'—Double, deep salmon-pink, large blooms.

'California Peach'—Large, double salmon-peach coloring, sport of 'California Sunset'.

'California Snow'—Double, pure white large blooms.

'California Sunset'—Double variegated white and deep pink, extremely showy.

'Chimes'—Semi-double, dark red flowers, same as 'Adventsclocke'.

'Charles Encke'—Variegated pink and white.

'Dr. Glazer'—Large, double, deep cardinal red.

'Eri'—Large, semi-double, mottled pink and white.

'Freckles'—Semi-double, hose-in-hose, delicate white, red mottling, profuse.

'Jezebel'—Semidouble, deep cardinal red, hose-in-hose.

'Kathryn Aileen'—Huge single red.

'Leuchtfeuer'—Single to semi-double, vibrant red.

'Marie-Louise'—Single, white sometimes splashed with pink, sport of 'Charles Encke'.

'Memoire John Hearrens'—Double, white edged with dark cerise.

'Mme. Alfred Sander'—Double, cherry red.

'Mme. Petrick'—Double red.

'Orange Chimes'—Semi-double, bright orange.

'Orange Sanders'—Double, orange sport of 'Fred Sanders'.

'Paul Schaeme'—Double light orange.

'Pink Ruffles'—Violet-red.

'Professor Wolters'—Single, variegated rose-red and white, ruffled edge.

'Red Ruffles'—Large, ruffled, double, hose-in-hose, deep red flowers; dark green, compact; semi-shade in extreme heat.

'Red Poppy'—Very large single to semi-double, bright deep red.

'Rose Glow'—Large, single, rose-red.

'Salmon Solomon'—Salmon flowers.

'Tickled Pink'—Single to hose-in-hose, rose-pink, edged in white.

'Triumph'—Double frilled red.

SOUTHERN INDICA TYPES

Best azaleas for high light areas, vigorous, upright growers, profuse spring flowers, hardy to 20°F.

'Albert-Elizabeth'—White with orange-red edges.

'Brilliant'—Single, watermelon red.

'Daphne Salmon'—Salmon flowers

'Duc de Rohan'—Single, salmon-pink.

'Elegans'—Light pink.

'Fielders White'—Large, single frosty white, 2 3/4″ diameter.

'Fisher Pink'—Pink flowers.

'Formosa'—Magenta with deep blotch, single, 3″ diameter flowers, large upright habit.

'G.G. Gerbing'—Pure white, single, 3″ diameter, sport of 'George L. Taber', more cold hardy than the typical Southern Indica.

'George L. Taber'—Very large, single, light orchid-pink, variegated, 3″ diameter, more cold hardy than most.

'Hexe de Saffelaere'—Red, hose-in-hose.

The 'Imperial' Family (Monrovia Nursery hybrid introductions)

Splendid varieties in exciting rich colors. Handsome, rich green foliage creates a lush, full plant, a pleasing mounded form. Generously covered with blooms in season and occasionally spotted with color throughout the year.

Imperial Countess— Single, hose-in-hose, deep salmon-pink, petal edges are crinkled, needs partial shade.

Imperial Duchess—Later than above, rose bud shaped flowers open to bright pink, then become soft pink; form is double, occasionally single, hose-in-hose, needs partial shade.

Imperial Princess—Lovely, long-lasting, large, single, rich pink flowers.

Imperial Queen—Double, pink flowers.

'Iveryana'—Single, white with orchid streaks, mid-season.

'Judge Solomon'—Pink, single, 3″ diameter flowers.

'Lady Formosa'—Large, single violet-red, weeping habit.

'Lawsal'—Salmon-pink,same as 'Daphne Salmon'.

'Little Girl'—Light pink, with silver tips to petals, double.

'Little John'—Large, single, burgundy red flowers, symmetrical form accented by eye-catching reddish purple foliage.

'Moss Point Red'—Large red flowers, broad spreading habit. Same as 'Triumphe de Lederberg'.

'New White'—White.

'Orange Pride'—Bright orange, single, listed also as 'Orange Pride of Dorking'.

'Phoenicia'—Single, lavender-purple.

'Pink Formosa'—A pink flowered sport of 'Formosa'.

'Pink Lace'—Petite, single, very compact, light rose-pink.

'Pink Ruffles'—Large, hose-in-hose, bright pink flowers borne on vigorous plants with large leaves.

'Plum Crazy'—Large, deep mauve single flowers have white and lilac-pink marbling with a blush of pale mauve overtone.

'President Clay'—Orange-red, single, 2 1/4 to 3″ diameter, same as 'President Claeys'.

'Pride of Dorking'—Single, brilliant carmine-red.

'Pride of Mobile'—Deep rose-pink, single 2 1/2″ diameter.

'Prince of Orange'—Heavy textured orange flowers.

'Red Formosa'—Deep violet-red flowers, large dark green foliage.

'Redwing'—Red, hose-in-hose, 3 to 4″ diameter flowers.

'Reverie'—Single, violet-pink, mid to late season.

'Rosa Belton'—Cream with bright lavender edges, large, single, profuse.

'Rosea'—Semi-double, rose-red flowers open from rose-like buds.

'Southern Charm'—Large, single, deep rose, a sport of 'Formosa'.

'Star Trek'—White, with very pale green throat, formal double.

'White April'—Large, single, pure white.

'White Grandeur'—Snow white, large, double flowers.

JANE ABBOT HYBRIDS (Weston Nurseries introductions)

'Jane Abbott Peach'—Large peach-pink fragrant flowers; vigorous, wide, upright-growing, -29°F.

'Jane Abbott Pink'—Cutting grown selections of *R. mollis* × *R. prinophyllum* hybrid. Large, fragrant flowers in shades of pink; wide, upright, robust, -29°F.

KURUME HYBRIDS

'Amoena Coccinea'—Small hose-in-hose, small and densely twiggy, red flowers, branches occasionally revert to purple flowers and should be removed; compact and low-growing; -8°F.

'Amoenum'—Flowers rich magenta, hose-in-hose, old cultivar, hardier than most.

'Appleblossom'—Light pink.

'Better Times'—Pink, hose-in-hose.

'Bridesmaid'—Salmon.

'Christmas Cheer'—Red, small hose-in-hose flowers produced on dwarf, medium-spreading plants.

'Coral Bells'—Coral pink, small, 1 1/2″ diameter hose-in-hose flowers produced on dwarf, low spreading plants, 3′ by 3 to 4′.

'Eileen'—Blush pink, semi-double to hose-in-hose.

'Eureka'—Pink.

'Flame'—Orange-red.

'Heather'—Attractive rose-lavender.

'Hershey's Red'—Early, large, 2″ diameter bright red, hardier than most, probably to -10°F, common in trade.

'Hexe Supreme'—Crimson, medium, hose-in-hose.

'Hino-Crimson'—Brilliant non-fading crimson flower, single, one of the hardiest, low growing compact with small deep glossy green leaves turning bronze in winter.

'Hinodegiri'—Vivid red, 1 1/2″ diameter flowers, dark green summer foliage turns wine-red in fall and winter, 3′ by 3 to 4′, flower buds test hardy to -8°F.

'Hinomayo'—Soft pink flowers in profusion, wide upright, slow-growing.

'Massasoit'—Single red flowers on dwarf, dense plants, Zone 7.

'Mauve Beauty'—Mauve hose-in-hose.

'Mildred Mae'—Pale lavender, large, single.

'Mother's Day'—Large red flowers, wide-growing.

'Peach Blossom'—Pale salmon-pink.

'Pink Pearl'—Pink, medium-sized hose-in-hose flowers on dwarf, upright plants.

'Red Bordeaux'—Red-orange.

'Salmon Beauty'—Salmon-pink, hose-in-hose.

'Sherwood Cerise'—Single, cerise.

'Sherwood Orchid'—Reddish violet with a darker blotch, single.

'Sherwood Pink'—Single, pink.

'Sherwood Red'—Orange-red, medium-size, single flowers on dwarf, low plants.

'Snow'—Pure white, hose-in-hose, vigorous grower, common.

'Sweetbriar'—Hose-in-hose pale pink flowers flushed red with a darker blotch, wide, upright.

'Tradition'—Clear light pink, double.

'Vesuvius'—Salmon-red.

'Ward's Ruby'—Brilliant ruby red, single.

LINWOOD HYBRIDS

'Linwood Blush'—Salmon-pink, semidouble.

'Linwood Lustre'—White, semidouble.

'Linwood Pink Giant'—Pink, hose-in-hose.

'Salmon Pincushion'—Luscious double, salmon pink.

'Slim Jim'—Double, pink, an upright grower.

PENNINGTON HYBRIDS

The late Ralph Pennington of Covington, Georgia produced these outstanding plants. A collection is housed at the University of Georgia Botanical Gardens.

'Beth Bullard'—Spreading plant with dark green foliage, 4″ diameter reddish pink flowers; an excellent low-growing azalea, 2 1/2′ tall with a spread of 4 to 5′.

'KJP'—Flowers light pink with dark pink stripes, 4″ diameter, foliage is like the Southern Indica, plants grow 5 to 6 high.

'Mrs. Anne G. Pennington'—A very late variable pink and white flower with blotches on a low growing plant; a late edition of 'KJP'.

'Mrs. R.W. Pennington'—A bright red flower on a low, bushy plant.

'Pennington Purple'—An early fragrant lavender flower on a well formed plant.

'Pennington Red'—A striking, early, all red flower on a medium shrub.

'Pennington White'—An early 2″ diameter frilled white flower that is the best of the early whites.

PERICAT HYBRIDS

The Pericat Hybrids are similar to Kurume Hybrids, with larger flowers.

'China Seas'—Pink.

'Dawn'—Phlox-pink.

'Distinction'—Salmon-pink, semi-double.

'Flanders Field'—Red.

'Fortune'—Red.

'Hampton Beauty'—Rose-pink.

'Hiawatha'—Hose-in-hose, red.

'Pericat Pink'—Pink.

'Pericat Salmon'—Salmon.

'Pericat White'—White.

'Pinocchio'—Rose.

'Sensation'—Violet-red.

'Splendor'—Phlox-pink.

'Sweetheart Supreme'—Blush pink, small semi-double buds resemble delicate rosebuds.

'Twenty Grand'—Violet-red, semi-double.

POLLY HILL'S NORTH TISBURY HYBRIDS

Since 1957, Mrs. Polly Hill, Martha's Vineyard, has been testing and selecting Japanese azaleas that she has grown from seed. Her objective has been to produce prostrate, hardy, evergreen forms that can be used as ground covers. Low growing azaleas with trailing branches that cascade over rocks or walls make suitable groundcovers. Most are hybrids of *R. nakaharai,* a prostrate evergreen species, that may reach 2 to 5″ in height in 10 years. As hybrids they are hardier than the species, benefitting from available snow cover. Flower in May-June.

'Alex'—A dwarf sport of 'Alexander', petite, prostrate and red.

'Alexander'—A low-growing spreading azalea eventually reaching 18″ high; flowers are salmon-red and bloom in late May and early June; excellent ground cover plant, cold hardy between 0 and -10°F.

'Andante'—A small to medium compact plant with salmon-pink flowers.

'Gabrielle Hill'—Light pink with a rosy crimson blotch, plant habit is airy, irregular and not too dense, original plant is 15″ tall and 5′ across.

'Hill's Single Red'—Salmon-red flowers on a compact, spreading plant.

'Hotline'—Large ruffled flowers, hot purple-red, 1 1/2′ by 4′ after 16 years.

'Jeff Hill'—Deep pink blossoms, plant is rounded, semi-dwarf and branching well, 17″ tall by 26″ wide in 13 years.

'Joseph Hill'—Bright red flowers, 12″ tall by 42″ wide in 13 years.

'Lady Locks'—Fragrant, lavender frilled flowers with large sepals.

'Late Love' ('Summertime')—Bright pink flowers, the latest blooming of the North Tisbury Hybrids.

'Libby'—A gorgeous fresh cool pink.

'Marilee'—Rose-red flowers, smoky purple-green leaves are retained well, 16″ tall by 50″ wide in 12 years.

'Michael Hill'—Late soft pink frilled flowers with dark throat, very dwarf and spreading, an excellent groundcover, 17″ tall by 45″ wide in 13 years.

'Mount Seven Star'—A vivid red with wavy lobes on a low, dense plant.

'Mrs. Hill's Flaming Mamie'—Red flowers.

'Pink Pancake'—Large bright pink wavy flowers on one of the fastest growing of all the North Tisbury Hybrids.

'Red Fountain'—Flowers are a strong red on branches that reach up at first, then arch down in a conspicuous fountain-like curve.

'Susannah Hill'—Deep red flowers with petaloid stamens, plant forms a vigorous low mound, 15″ tall by 52″ wide in 12 years.

'Trill'—Large ruffled medium red flowers, 14″ by 28″ in 12 years.

'Wintergreen'—Deep pink to light red flowers in late June, forms a circular mound 15″ by 39″ wide in 12 years.

'Yuka'—Another of Polly Hill's best 'Gumpo' seedlings, large flowers, most are pure white, some are striped with soft pink; others are nearly solid pink, low growing.

ROBIN HILL HYBRIDS

After some 50 years of hybridizing and selecting, Robert Gartrell succeeded in taking the flower characteristics of the Japanese Satsuki azaleas and producing a group of evergreens that are as lovely but more hardy and dependable. Their flowers are exceptionally large, open-faced and late blooming. Most are in soft, muted pastel tones. Their habits are low and prostrate. Considered hardy in the range of 0 to +10°F.

'Barbara M. Humphreys'—Pure white single flower covers bright green glossy leaves; one of the very best and is in much demand.

'Betty Ann Voss'—Lovely double light pink flowers on a plant that has a weeping habit and beautiful dark green foliage.

'Blue Tip'—Large lavender flower with a white center.

'Chanson'—Pink semi-double to double flowers.

'Christie'—Broad trumpet-shaped pink flowers, low mounding growth.

'Congo'—Vivid reddish purple flowers on a dwarf spreading plant.

'Conversation Piece'—Single, rich pink, 4″ diameter flowers with dots, blotches, sectors of pink, red and white, all at the same time, on a low to medium shrub, 25″ by 28″ in 10 years.

'Dorothy Hayden'—Single, open-faced white flowers with a distinct green throat, broader than tall, 15″ by 34″ in 10 years.

'Dorothy Rees'—This exquisite large single flower is pure white with a green throat and ruffled wavy margins.

'Early Beni'—Gorgeous coral-red hose-in-hose, semi-double with extra petals, 28″ by 36″ in 17 years.

'Eliza Scott'—Upright habit and pale pink-red single flowers.

'Eunice Updike'—Dwarf mounded, pale scarlet double flowers.

'Flame Dance'—A single large tubular red flower, habit has a weeping nature.

'Frosty'—The pink single flower with a distinct dark blotch has a frosty overtone.

'George Harding'—Vivid red flower with a white throat.

'Gillie'—Single, rose-salmon.

'Givenda'—Single, light pink.

'Glamora'—Large semi-double white flowers tinted lavender, 18″ by 36″ in 10 years.

'Glencora'—A medium red, double, 2 1/2″ diameter flower on a dwarf plant.

'Gresham'—A very large strong pink flower that has variable stripes and sectors on a compact, dwarf plant.

'Greta'—A low mound that is covered with dark pink single flowers with wavy margins.

'Gwenda'—Pale pink ruffled 3″ diameter flowers, mound shaped, semi-dwarf growth habit, 21″ by 36″ in 10 years.

'Hilda Niblett'—Absolutely perfect mounded growth habit and large pink and white flowers.

'Jeanne Weeks'—Fully double flowers of lavender-pink, opening flowers resemble rosebuds, compact mounded growth habit.

'La Belle Helene'—Strong pink flower that develops a white throat.

'Lady Louise'—Single to semi-double pink bloom with a darker blotch.

'Lady Robin'—Single white with variable stripes and sectors of bright pink, some will be white flushed pink or pink with white margins, with or without stripes or sectors, broad sprawling growth, 21″ by 36″ in 10 years.

'Laura Morland'—Soft warm pink semi-double flowers with occasional darker stripes, compact growth, 16″ by 23″ in 10 years.

'Maria Derby'—Bright red double flowers, dense compact growth.

'Mrs. Emil Hager'—Semi-double to double "hot" pink flower that is more vibrant than most Robin Hills, 12″ by 19″ in 10 years.

'Mrs. Villars'—A white frilled single flower with occasional pink splashing.

'Nancy of Robin Hill'—Light pink hose-in-hose flowers, broad growing, 16″ by 36″ in 10 years.

'Octavian' (Formerly 'Rosenkavalier')—A light creamy pink flower.

'Olga Niblett'—The two Nibletts are the last two Robin Hills Mr. Gartrell named; Olga is white with a yellowish cast and a yellow throat and is one of the best.

'Palmyra'—Delicate medium pink blooms, tall habit.

'Papineau'—White flower with a pale green throat stands out against the vigorous green foliage.

'Peg Hugger'—Soft pink double flowers on a compact plant.

'R-01-09'—This unnamed plant has a small white flower that opens with the Glenn Dales and Backacres.

'Redmond'—Flat faced large red single flower.

'Red Tip'—Single white flower with margin of strong rose-red.

'Robin Dale'—Wavy petaled white flower with a greenish throat, pink splashing throughout.

'Robin Hill Gillie'—Very ruffled flat faced scarlet flowers with dark blotch, dense foliage, 14″ by 36″ in 10 years.

'Roseanne'—Large ruffled white flowers with bright pink margins, broad and spreading.

'Sarah Holden'—Huge white single flower with ruffly margins.

'Scott Gartrell'—Orchid pink, hose-in-hose flower with a striking dark blotch.

'Sherbrook'—Large single, lavender flowers.

'Sir Robert'—Variable flower patterns that range from white to pink, flowers over a long period.

'Spink'—Delicate pink flower, the earliest of all the Robin Hill.

'Turks Cap'—A bright scarlet single flower on an upright plant.

'Verena'—Soft lavender single flower, rounded habit.

'Watchet'—A rich pink large flat single flower with ruffled margins, small leaves and mounded habit.

'Wee Willie'—Purplish pink single flowers with ruffled edges.

'Welmet'—Single lavender-pink flowers are large and flat-faced, as plants age they develop a white center.

'White Moon'—A lovely low mounded plant with huge flat wavy flowers that occasionally sport red specks or marks.

RUTHERFORDIANA HYBRIDS

Medium sized flowers, 2 to 4′ high shrubby plants with showy spring bloom, require mid-day shade, hardy to 20°F in protected location.

'Alaska'—Semi-double, pure white.

'Dorothy Gish'—Orange-salmon, semi-double, hose-in-hose.

'Gloria'—Variegated sport of 'Dorothy Gish'.

'Pink Ruffle'—Flowers pink-violet, semi-double, 2″ diameter.

'Red Ruffles'—Large, deep red ruffled flowers.

'Rose Queen'—Double, rose-pink.

'White Gish'—White sport of 'Dorothy Gish'.

SATSUKI HYBRIDS

Satsuki azaleas are lovely treasures from Japan, Satsuke meaning fifth month, the basic flowering period for most varieties. They are excellent evergreen spreading shrubs of dwarf size, featuring many flower forms and many color combinations on one plant. Large flowers appear in mid to late May to June in the Athens area.

'Amagasa'—Deep pink, 3 1/2″ diameter.

'Balsaminaeflorum'—Late double rose flowers with 40 petals or more and no pistil or stamens, low compact.

'Banka'—White flower with flecks of pink or a solid pink border on six rounded lobes.

'Beni-Kirishima'—Double orange-red flowers on a broad spreading plant.

'Bunkwa'—Flesh pink flowers, 2″ diameter, low grower.

'Chinzan' ('Chinsayii')—Warm pink flowers, outstanding shiny pointed little leaves, quite dwarf and compact.

'Coral Cascade'—Large, single coral-pink flower with white blotches, spreading, cascading branches.

'Daisetsu-zan'—Extremely large white flowers with yellow green centers adorn this dark green, heavy textured plant; collected by Dr. John Creech from the nursery of Mr. Yoshiyuki Shibahata in Japan.

'Eikan'—Extremely variable white ruffled, 4″ diameter flowers with all combinations of pink and rose, vigorous, spreading plant.

'Eiten'—Mallow purple.

'Flame Creeper'—Orange-red, low, dense.

'Fuku Ro Kuju'—Pristine white flowers with an occasional red fleck, shiny dark green leaves.

'Geisha'—White flowers often streaked with reddish purple, wide upright.

'Geisha Girl'—Deep rose and white.

'Getsutoku'—Large, single wavy petals are white with variegation of pink and salmon stripes or solid colors of shade mentioned.

GUMPOS

Gumpos are selections of *R. eriocarpum*. In the search through catalogs 'Gumpo Pink' and 'Gumpo White' were listed more times than all the Satsukis presented here.

'Gumpo Pink'—Most common Satsuki in south; soft pink ruffled petals on a compact plant.

'Gumpo Rose'—Darker rose flower, otherwise like above.

'Gumpo White'—Large single white frilled flowers with occasional purple flecks, dense habit, late flowering.

'Gunbi'—A sport of 'Gumpo' that is white with reddish flecks and stripes, large 3″ diameter flowers have ruffled lobes, compact habit.

'Gunrei'—Frilled showy white with pink flecks, low growing.

'Hakusen-No-Mai'—Semi-double white flower with green blotch, has the appearance of snowflakes.

'Haru-No-Hikari'—Huge salmon-white, variable, single.

'Heiwa'—White with shadings of pink and rose.

'Higasa'—Extremely large, 4 1/2″ diameter flat flower, deep rose-pink with paler pink on margins.

'Hitoya-No-Haru'—Large, rose-mauve variable single.

'Issho No Haru'—A variable flower of lavender and white with many forms and combinations.

'Juko'—Medium-large, single, wide pointed petals of light orchid-pink, speckled or striped with deeper pink; some solid blooms of pink or rose, or edged with white; small foliage, tight habit.

'Kayo-No-Homare'—Flower has a white center, bordered orange-red, with an occasional sport of white with pink stripes and deep pink solids; has slightly pointed petals; slow growing round habit.

'Keisetsu'—Strong red, 3″ diameter flowers with a light pink to white center, unusual variegated leaves.

'Kimi-Maru'—A light pink flower with deeper pink edges may have many variations, single with medium round petals; small leaves and a slightly open form.

'Kobai'—Large red flowers with occasional circles of white on six, round, overlapping lobes, descriptively called 'Red Plum'.

'Ko-Kinsai'—Lacy coral salmon single flower with split spider like petals, foliage is small and the plant has a low, bushy habit.

'Kokan'—Small growing plant with a 1 1/2″ long leaf that curls inward, making a tubed leaf.

'Mai-Hime'—Extremely variable flowers, rose pink to white, low grower.

'Matsu No Hikari'—White and orange-red with variable stripes and sectors on 3″ diameter ruffled flowers with overlapping petals.

'Mt. Baldy'—Single white flowers with a white throat and rose marking; unusual dense foliage with leaves curved inward for a tube-like effect.

'Myogi'—Flowers are light pink with dark pink stripes and flakes, 'Gumpo' type compact growth.

'Rukizon'—Small salmon-red flowers on a dense small plant with tiny 1/2" long leaves, also known as 'Kazan'.

'Shiko'—Large, wide, lavender-pink, variable, single.

'Shinkigen'—White flower with many variations of sectors and marks of pink and red with round overlapping petals.

'Shinnyo-No-Tsuki'—Large, white centers, rose border.

'Shira Fuji'—Unusual white markings on green foliage, white flowers, sometimes with purple.

'Tai Fuki'—White flower that may be one-half bright red.

'Tochi-No-Hikari'—Low growing plant with extremely deep red, 4 to 5" diameter flowers.

'Un-Getsu-No-Hikari'—Flower is salmon-pink edged with a spotted coral red throat and has small single pointed petal, slow growing.

'Wakaebisu'—Light salmon-pink flowers with deeper pink dots in the blotch, Zone 8.

WESTON HYBRIDS

Many azalea hybrids produced by the Nursery; flower times based on New England environment; 1990 catalog offers excellent, in depth descriptions, received too late for inclusion here.

'Bonfire'—Small orange-red.

'Golden Showers'—Lightly vanilla-scented, peach-yellow blooms; broad, upright growing; long, pointed, somewhat glossy green leaves, bronze in fall, -24°F.

'Independence'—Upright growing, small green leaves with bluish undersides; red buds, small fragrant dark pink flowers in ball-like heads; maturing silvery-pink in July.

'Iridescent'—Spicy-scented, silvery pink in mid-June, wide spreading, green foliage with a blue cast turns bronze-red in fall, -29°F.

'Lollipop'—Pink flowers with yellow flare, maturing silvery pink, with a sweet fragrance; green leaves have silvery undersides and change to long-lasting red-orange in September.

'Parade'—Sweet-scented dark pink flowers with orange eye, July, wide upright, -24°F.

'Popsicle'—Fragrant pink, -35°F.

'Ribbon Candy'—Wide upright-growing *R. viscosum* hybrid, spicy scented pink flowers with distinctive stripes in late June, medium green summer foliage turns burgundy red in autumn.

'Trumpeter'—Salmon-pink.

WINDSOR HYBRIDS

Originally from Windsor Great Park—Savill Gardens in England. Introduced into the US by Wells Nursery, Penrose, NC.

'Windsor Appleblossom'—An unusual multi-colored specimen that ranges from cream to deep pink, with a compact shape.

'Windsor Buttercup'—Brilliant clear yellow, heavy flowering, excellent shape.

'Windsor Daybreak'—A blend of dawn colors that is most fascinating, with a compact shape.

'Windsor Peach Glow'—A superb orange yellow, with an upright habit.

'Windsor Pink Souffle'—An extremely vigorous plant with soft pink flowers, trusses are large.

'Windsor Ruby'—A compact plant with large, deep red flowers.

'Windsor Sunbeam'—A darker yellow than 'Windsor Buttercup' with good shape and heavy flowering capabilities.

VUYKIANA HYBRIDS

Several plants were growing in Mt. Airy Arboretum, Cincinnati, OH before -25°F obliterated them, probably -5 to -10°F at best.

'Wilhelmina Vuyk'—Ivory-white, tall growing.

Miscellaneous Azaleas

COOLIDGE HYBRIDS

'American Beauty'—Double, holly berry red.

'Singing Fountain'—Single, rose-cerise.

GREENWOOD HYBRIDS
'Popcorn'—Sweet-scented white.
'Red Beauty'—Astonishingly large, bright red flowers up to 5″ across; long lasting semi-double to double flowers.

HARRIS HYBRIDS
'Pink Cascade'—An unusual salmon-pink azalea with long cascading limbs that make this an unusual hanging basket plant, also makes an excellent ground cover when planted on 3′ centers.

LOBLOLLY BAY HYBRIDS
'White Frills'—White with yellow-green blotch, hose-in-hose.

MAYO HYBRIDS
'Princess Augusta'—A large grower with light pink hose-in-hose, 2 1/2″ diameter flowers.

MISCELLANEOUS EVERGREEN HYBRIDS
'Barbara'—Single, rich pink, a selection of *R. tasaense.*
'Flat Out'—Vigorous late bloomer that blankets the ground with white, a ground hugging spreader, a perfect complement to the North Tisbury Azaleas.
'Kaempo'—Late blooming dwarf hot pink, particularly showy, *R. kaempferi* × *R.* 'Gumpo'.
'Pink Discovery'—Clear pink *R. poukhanense.*

NUCCIO HYBRIDS
'Garden Party'—Pink with peach flare.
'Nuccio's Happy Days'—Deep violet-purple double flower, heavy spring flowers.
'Nuccio's Pink Champagne'—Light pink, double, hose-in-hose.
'Nuccio's Wild Cherry'—Large single blooms, round petals of cherry red, rapid upright grower.

RUSTICA FLORA PLENO HYBRIDS
'Norma'—Late blooming double rose-red with a salmon glow and vivid stamens.

SLONECKER HYBRIDS
'Chetco'—Bright yellow flowers, orange blotch.

Rhododendron Hybrids

DEXTER HYBRIDS
Many of the rhododendrons that Charles O. Dexter of Sandwich, MA created from 1921 to 1943 were of a quality that had not previously been available. Noted for their fine, dense foliage, large stature and wonderful flowers and colors. Precise records of his crosses do not survive, but he appears to have used at least the following species: *R. decorum, R. discolor, R. griersonianum, R. haematodes,* and *R. fortunei.* The influence of *R. fortunei* is dominant in his plants, so much so that all widely distributed Dexter hybrids are referred to as Fortunei Hybrids. Hardy in the vicinity of -10°F and depending on cultivar has 5°F leeway from this number.
'Ben Moseley'—Slightly frilled bright pink flowers with dark blotch.
'Betty Arrington'—Large conical trusses of fragrant pink florets scented by ruby markings in the upper petals.
'Brown Eyes'—Paul Bosley, Sr., Mentor, OH, introduced this hardy pink with a brown blotch.
'Champaign'—Opulent creamy yellow, overlaid with pink, to 4′ high.
'Dexter's Purple'—Lovely lilac-purple blossoms of excellent substance.
'Gi-Gi'—Rose-red flowers covered with deep red spotting.
'Gloxineum'—Prolific flowering with enormous pastel pink flowers.

'Great Eastern'—Large light pink flowers, petals edged in light red, deeper red throat, floriferous, hardy.

'Janet Blair'—A lovely lavender-pink flower with a greenish throat, 6' high, -10°F.

'Kelley'—Light red flowers with attractive dark spotting on all petals, medium growth habit.

'Lady of Belfield'—Late blooming pink flowers with darker blotches adorn this tall pyramidal plant, magnificent foliage, 6' high.

'Mrs. W.R. Coe'—Intense pink.

'Parker's Pink'—Deep pink flowers shading darker at the margins and lighter near the center for a near bicolor effect.

'Pink Satin'—Deep, rich pink flowers with a satiny finish, large trusses on a compact plant.

'Powder Puff'—Candelabra effect as rosy buds elongate and open to soft lilac-pink, outstanding in the garden.

'Scintillation'—The best known of all Dexter rhododendrons and the most common in cultivation, luminous light pink flowers with an amber throat, good substance and heat resistance, lustrous dark green leaves on a compact plant, 6' high, excellent form and has performed magnificently in Zone 8.

'Skyglow'—Peach-edged pink.

'Todmorden'—Strikingly intense rose-pink and white flowers giving nearly a bicolor effect, tall growing.

'Tom Everett'—Frilled soft sensuous pink with pale yellow throat, extremely floriferous, low and spreading growth.

'Warwick'—Mauve-pink.

'Wheatley'—Frilled vivid pink flower with yellow blotch.

'Wissahickon'—Bright rose.

'Wyandanch Pink'—Shiny bright pink flowers, handsome rugose and convex leaves on an upright plant, 6' high, quite hardy.

LEACH HYBRIDS

Hybridized by Mr. David Leach, who is possibly the world's greatest authority on the subject. Mr. Leach is extremely discriminating and does not introduce a new cultivar unless it meets rigid standards of flower, foliage, habit and hardiness.

'Anna H. Hall'—A semidwarf, appleblossom pink and white.

'Bali'—Soft pink flowers with a creamy yellow throat, 6 1/2' by 9' in 30 years.

'Bravo'—Very hardy deep pink, described as "a huge, blowzy, Rubenesque sort of rhododendron with buxom trusses."

'Dolly Madison'—Early flowering white, strong, tall grower, very hardy.

'Hong Kong'—Pale yellow.

'July Jester'—Red, late bloomer.

'Lodestar'—Large white flowers with a prominent flare of green-gold flecks, dense foliage.

'Madrid'—Dark pink with maroon blotch, 5' by 6' in 10 years.

'Malta'—Small leaved form with small semidouble rose-like pink flowers.

'Nile'—Light yellow.

'Nuance'—A pastel blend of yellow, orange and pink.

'Small Wonder'—Compact, brilliant red.

'Sumatra'—Clear scarlet, dwarf, densely foliaged.

NEARING HYBRIDS

'Flamingo'—Rich coral.

'Mary Belle'—Ruffled flowers, mixed peach, coral and yellow.

'Mary Fleming'—Small-leaved variety, low and spreading to 3', flowers are pale yellow with blotches and streaks of salmon.

'Montchanin'—Graceful and willowy, adds diversity and interest, clusters of small white flowers near the ends of their slender branches make a welcome display.

'Wyanokie'—White.

SHAMMARELLO HYBRIDS

For more than 40 years A. M. "Tony" Shammarello hybridized and selected a group of large-leaved rhododendrons derived primarily from the standard ironclad cultivars. His goal was an extended season of flowers on compact bushy plants that are hardy around Lake Erie. He succeeded admirably. It is only a matter of time before they become more widely known and grown, not just as collectors items, but for their value as fine landscape plants.

'Belle Heller'—Enormous trusses of large glistening white flowers with throats flecked with gold, vigorous tall grower, tends toward loose open habit, has performed well in Zone 8.

'Besse Howells'—Ruffled burgundy red flowers accented by a dark red blotch, compact like 'Boule de Neige', very floriferous and hardy.

'Holden'—Rosy red flowers illuminated by a small dark red blotch, flowers fade to pink when fully open, one of the best for Zone 8, buds consistently every year; medium height with lustrous dark green foliage.

'Ice Cube'—Ivory white flowers accented with a lemon blotch, dark green foliage, medium height.

'Rocket'—Slightly ruffled, deep, radiant, coral-pink with a scarlet-red blotch, lustrous dark green foliage.

'Sham's Pink'—Light two-tone vivid pink flowers are darker at the edge with a light red blotch, low and spreading.

'Spring Parade'—Glowing scarlet-red flowers cover a compact plant, dark green leaves, very hardy.

MISCELLANEOUS RHODODENDRONS

'Bow Bells'—Deep pink buds open to light pink blooms, slow growing mounded small shrub, bronze-copper new growth.

'Jean Marie de Montague'—Showy bright red trusses, appearing on young plants; some shade prevents flowers from fading.

'Rosemarie'—A very fine blue-violet with larger flowers than 'Purple Gem' or 'Ramapo' but not quite as hardy, compact to 3'.

Rhodotypos scandens – Black Jetbead
(rō-dō-tī'pus skan'denz)

FAMILY: Rosaceae

LEAVES: Opposite, simple, ovate to ovate-oblong, 2 1/2 to 4" long, half as wide, acuminate, rounded at base, sharply and doubly serrate, bright green and glabrous above, lighter green and silky beneath when young; prominently parallel-veined (ribbed); petioled 1/8 to 1/4" long.

BUDS: Imbricate, brownish green, divergent, glabrous, slightly stalked, ovoid.

STEM: Young—green, glabrous, shiny, eventually turning brown; old—gray streaked, reddish brown, orangish lenticels.

SIZE: 3 to 6' in height by 4 to 9' in spread, in native haunts may grow to 15' but under cultivation I have never seen anything larger than 6'.

HARDINESS: Zone 4 to 8.

HABIT: Mounded, loosely branched shrub with ascending and somewhat arching branches, often of shabby appearance.

RATE: Medium to fast.

TEXTURE: Medium in leaf; coarse in winter.

LEAF COLOR: Various authors report dark green as the typical summer foliage color; however, I feel the color tends toward a bright green; fall color is green with a slight tinge of yellow; one of the first shrubs to leaf out in spring.

FLOWERS: Perfect, white, 1 to 2″ diameter, 4 petaled (unusual for Rosaceae), May to early June, borne singly at the end of short twigs, not outstanding but interesting upon close inspection.

FRUIT: Drupe, 1/3″ long, hard, 3 to 4 in a group, shining black, October and persistent into the following spring and summer; neither flowers nor fruits are showy but do offer a degree of interest in the garden.

CULTURE: Readily transplanted; very tolerant of differing soil conditions; tolerates full sun or shade; crowding and polluted conditions; pH adaptable; one of the better shrubs for adverse conditions and heavy shade.

DISEASES AND INSECTS: Trouble free.

LANDSCAPE VALUE: Tough, durable plant for rugged conditions; good in shady areas, shrub borders, massing on banks and under shade trees; there are too many superior ornamental shrubs to justify extensive use of this species.

PROPAGATION: Softwood cuttings taken in late spring root readily; actually easy to root any time the plant is in leaf. Seed apparently requires acid scarification and a cold period; the best treatments have not been established.

NATIVE HABITAT: Japan and central China. Introduced 1866.

Rhus aromatica — Fragrant Sumac
(roos a-rō-mat′ik-à)

FAMILY: Anacardiaceae

LEAVES: Alternate, trifoliate, leaflets subsessile, ovate, the terminal 1 1/2 to 3″ long, acute or acuminate, cuneate and often obovate; the lateral ones oblique and rounded at the base, about one half as large, all coarsely toothed, lower surface pubescent becoming glabrous, variable in leaf coloration but often a glossy medium to dark green; petiole—1 to 1 1/2″ long.

BUDS: Small, yellow, pubescent, covered by leaf scar.

STEM: Slender, pubescent, aromatically fragrant when bruised, leaf scars circular, distinctly raised.

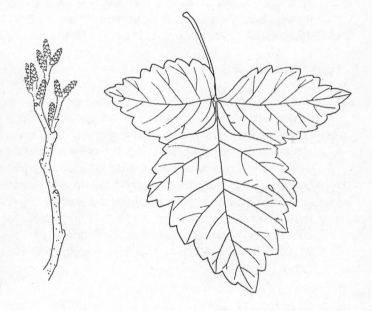

SIZE: 2 to 6′, possibly larger, with a spread of 6 to 10′, extremely variable in size over its native range; have seen 6′ high and wide mounded shrubs on occasion.

HARDINESS: Zone 3 to 9.

HABIT: Low, irregular spreading shrub with lower branches turning up at the tips; tend to sucker from the roots and produce a dense, tangled mass of stems and leaves.

RATE: Slow to medium.

TEXTURE: Medium in leaf, medium in winter habit.

LEAF COLOR: Medium green, almost blue-green effect, often glossy on the upper surface; fall color orange to red to reddish purple, coloring best on light soils.

FLOWERS: Polygamous or dioecious, yellowish, mid to late March-April, borne in approximately 1″ long catkins (male) or short panicles at ends of branches (female); male catkin persistent and exposed through late summer, fall and winter.

FRUIT: Red (female plants only), hairy drupe, 1/4″ diameter; August-September and may persist into winter but usually loses its good color.

CULTURE: Fibrous root system, easily transplanted; adaptable, withstands 1/2 to 3/4 shade or full sun; prefers acid soil.

DISEASES AND INSECTS: None serious although various wilts, leaf spots, rusts, aphids, mites, and scales have been noted.

LANDSCAPE VALUE: Excellent fast cover for banks, cuts and fills, massing, facing; could be used as ground cover especially the following cultivars; this plant has the ability to develop roots as the stems touch the soil and is therefore useful for stabilizing banks or slightly sloping areas.

CULTIVARS:

‘Green Globe’—Grows to 6′, forms a rounded, dense shrub.

‘Gro-low’—Low, wide-spreading habit, excellent glossy foliage, 2′ high, 6 to 8′ wide, good looking plant; a female with yellow flowers and hairy red fruits, fall color is a good orange-red, introduced by Synnesvedt Nursery, Glenview, Illinois; has become extremely popular in the midwest.

PROPAGATION: Seed, scarify for 60 minutes; and provide 1 to 3 months cold stratification or fall sow; softwood cuttings, July, 1000 ppm IBA gave 100% rooting in peat:perlite under mist; root cuttings will also work.

ADDITIONAL NOTES: In my mind this shrub is somewhat of a second class citizen but I have bumped into hundreds over the years and cannot remember any that were offensive. The bright yellowish flowers, especially on male plants, were always welcome after a difficult midwestern or eastern winter. The foliage has a certain sparkle and in fall, excellent reddish purple fall coloration may develop. I suspect when a planting becomes overgrown, it can be easily rejuvenated with a large mower, bush hog or other instrument of destruction.

NATIVE HABITAT: Vermont and Ontario to Minnesota, south to Florida and Louisiana. Introduced 1759.

RELATED SPECIES:

Rhus trilobata, (roos trī-lō-bā′ta) , Skunkbush Sumac, is quite similar to *R. aromatica* and appears to be its western ally. It is an upright or ascending shrub, 3 to 6′ high, with leaves and flowers smaller than *R. aromatica.* Flowers are more greenish and fruits slightly smaller than *R. aromatica.* The leaves are more unpleasantly scented. It makes a handsome and almost impenetrable mass which would lend itself to roadside and similar landscape sites. ‘Autumn Amber’ is low growing with prostrate branches, the plant tends to produce dense thickets, about 1 to 1 1/2′ high, the dark green leaves brilliant yellow and red in fall, greenish yellow flowers appear in early spring, sex is unknown but no fruits have been produced; originated from seeds collected near Littlefield, TX, found on limestone outcroppings and would be a good ground cover for high pH soils; hardy to Zone 4; see *HortScience* 21:1465–1466 (1986). Native from Illinois to Washington, California and Texas. Introduced 1877. Zone 4 to 6?

Rhus typhina — Staghorn Sumac
(roos tī-fē′na)

LEAVES: Alternate, compound pinnate, entire leaf 1 to 2′ long, 13 to 27 leaflets, often 19, each leaflet lance-oblong, 2 to 5″ long, 1 to 2″ wide, acuminate, serrate, bright green above, glaucous beneath, pubescent when young; petiole about 2″ long, hairy; in fact, entire rachis maintains some pubescence.

BUDS: Hairy, leaf scars not elevated and somewhat "C" shaped.

STEM: Stout, rounded, densely velvety hairy, concealing the lenticels, almost club-like; pith large, brownish, aromatic when broken.

SIZE: 15 to 25′ in a landscape situation; potential to 30 to 40′ in the wild; spread is usually equal to or greater than height.

HARDINESS: Zone 3 to 8.

HABIT: A large, loose, open, spreading shrub or a gaunt, scraggly tree with a flattish crown and rather picturesque branches resembling the horns on a male deer; hence, the name Staghorn.

RATE: Fast when development occurs from root suckers; slow to medium on old wood.

TEXTURE: Species—medium in summer, coarse in winter; cultivars ('Laciniata' and 'Dissecta') fine in foliage, coarse in winter.

STEM: Dense, velvety reddish brown pubescence persisting on 2 and 3-year-old branches; older stems gray and relatively smooth.

LEAF COLOR: Bright green in summer, yellow, orange and scarlet in fall; often spectacular; leafs out late in spring.

FLOWERS: Dioecious, greenish yellow, June to early July; female borne in dense hairy panicles, 4 to 8″ long; male in a bigger, looser, wider panicle.

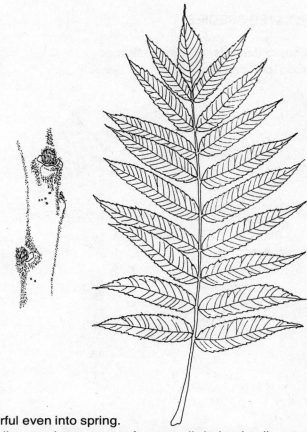

FRUIT: Crimson, late august through April, densely hairy drupe, closely packed in a pyramidal panicle; bright crimson in early fall, becoming darker red with cold weather and often still colorful even into spring.

CULTURE: Easily transplanted, adapted to many soil types; however, prefers a well-drained soil, not a plant for poorly drained areas; tolerates very dry, sterile soil; often seen along railroad tracks; suckers profusely and tends to form wide spreading colonies; tolerates city conditions; can be rejuvenated by cutting to ground in later winter.

DISEASES AND INSECTS: Same as described under *Rhus aromatica* except *Verticillium* is often prevalent in Staghorn Sumac.

LANDSCAPE VALUE: Massing, naturalizing, waste areas, perhaps banks, cuts and fills; actually hard to kill this plant due to its ability to sucker freely from roots; should not be used as a specimen, foundation or container plant; the cutleaf forms offer superb texture and even better yellow-orange-red fall coloration, quite coarse in winter and considerable thought should go into proper siting.

CULTIVARS:

'Dissecta'—Similar to 'Laciniata' but leaflets more deeply divided; discovered in the late 1800's by a Massachusetts nurseryman; foliage is quite beautiful and colors handsomely in fall; a female.

'Laciniata'—Leaflets deeply divided creating a fine-textured, ferny appearance; a female, much like 'Dissecta' which is perhaps more finely divided, had both in Illinois and had a difficult time differentiating especially from more than 10′ away.

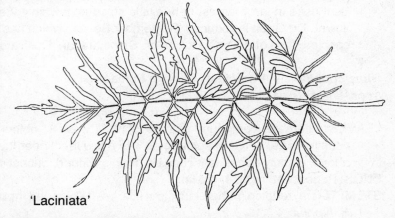

'Laciniata'

PROPAGATION: Seed—scarify for 50 to 80 minutes in sulfuric acid; cuttings, root pieces collected in December placed in moist sand:peat yielded plants in 2 months; the cultivars 'Dissecta' and 'Laciniata' are produced by root cuttings.

NATIVE HABITAT: Quebec to Ontario, south to Georgia, Indiana and Iowa. Cultivated 1629.

RELATED SPECIES:

Rhus chinensis — Chinese Sumac
(roos chī-nen′sis)

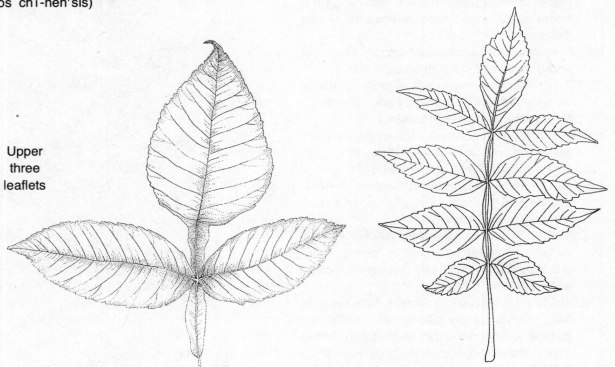

Upper
three
leaflets

LEAVES: Alternate, compound pinnate, 8 to 15″ long, 7 to 13 leaflets, subsessile, ovate to ovate-oblong,
2 to 5″ long, about half as wide, acute or short acuminate, coarsely crenate-serrate, lustrous bright
green above, brownish pubescent beneath, rachis and often the petiole conspicuously winged,
pubescent.
BUDS: Pubescent, almost woolly, gray-brown in color, leaf scars not elevated, "C" shaped.
STEM: Yellowish brown, glabrous to minutely pubescent, lenticels prominent.

Rhus chinensis, Chinese Sumac, is a loose, spreading, suckering shrub or flat-headed tree growing to 24′
in height. The foliage is bright green in summer and can change to orangish red tones in fall but this
color is seldom realized in the midwest; however, I have seen excellent yellow-red fall color on a plant
at the Arnold Arboretum. The flowers are yellowish white, August into September, borne in 6 to 10″
long and wide panicles. The fruit is a densely pubescent orange-red drupe which matures in October.
Best used in large areas, naturalistic settings, possibly the shrub border; valued mainly for its late
flower. Dr. Orton introduced 'September Beauty' which has immense panicles, and is superior to the
species. Also offers good fall color. China, Japan, Cultivated 1784. Zone 5 to 7(8).

Rhus copallina — Flameleaf (Shining) Sumac
(roos ko-pal-lī′nà)

LEAVES: Alternate, compound pinnate, 9 to 21 leaflets, oblong-ovate to lance-ovate, 1 3/4 to 4″ long,
usually acute, entire or sometimes with a few teeth near the apex, glabrous and lustrous dark green
above, usually pubescent beneath, rachis winged, pubescent.
BUDS: Pubescent, reddish brown.
STEM: Terete, reddish, puberulous, leaf scars—"U" shaped, not as coarse as *R. chinensis, R. glabra* and
R. typhina.

Rhus copallina, Flameleaf or Shining Sumac, is compact and dense in extreme youth becoming more and more open, irregular and picturesque as it ages, with crooked, ascending and spreading branches; broader at the top. Grows 20 to 30′ high with a similar spread. The foliage is lustrous dark green in summer changing to rich red, crimson, and scarlet in fall. Flowers (dioecious) are greenish yellow, July to August, borne in dense, 4 to 8″ long, 3 to 4″ wide panicles. The fruit is a pubescent, crimson drupe which ripens in September to October. One of the best sumacs; useful for dry, rocky places, banks, large areas, and naturalistic plantings. Probably the most ornamental of the sumacs but not commonly seen in gardens. Almost pestiferous in the south but certainly beautiful in the fall. A few disclaimers are needed to temper my exuberance. The species shows no penchant toward uniformity and usually forms large spreading colonies. For the small garden, it has no place. I have observed tremendous variation in fall color and believe the best form(s) should be vegetatively propagated. Use with discretion for the plant may turn on you tomorrow. Maine to Ontario in Minnesota south to Florida and Texas. Cultivated 1688. Zone 4 to 9.

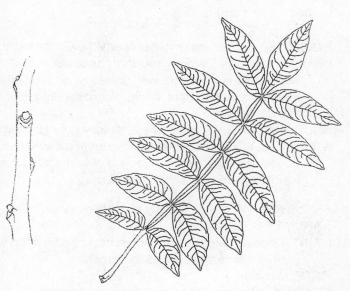

Rhus glabra — Smooth Sumac
(roos glā′brȧ)

LEAVES: Alternate, compound pinnate, 12 to 18″ long, 11 to 31 leaflets, lance-oblong, 2 to 5″ long, 1/2 to 3/4″ wide, acuminate, serrate, medium to deep green, glaucous beneath, rachis normally red.
BUDS: Pubescent, round, ovoid, with leaf scar almost completely encircling bud.
STEM: Stout (thick), glabrous, somewhat 3-sided, green to reddish and covered with a waxy bloom, leaf-scar horse-shoe shaped.

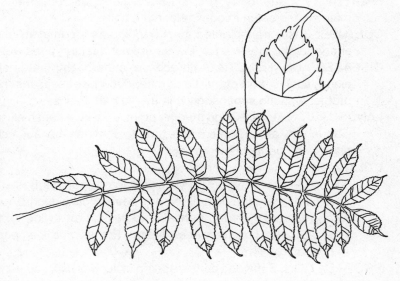

Rhus glabra, Smooth Sumac, grows 9 to 15′ high with a comparable spread. Usually grows in colonies as it suckers and develops in all directions from the mother plant. This is very evident in plantings which occur along railroad tracks and other waste areas. The foliage is medium green in summer changing to excellent orange-red-purple combinations in fall. Flowers are dioecious, greenish, June-July, borne in 6 to 10″ long panicles. Fruit is a scarlet, hairy drupe which persists late into winter. Good plant for mass plantings, highways, dry, poor soil areas. 'Laciniata' has leaflets which are deeply cut and lobed. It is female and will produce the bright scarlet fruits. It was discovered in the mid 1800's near Philadelphia. The essential difference between this species and *R. typhina* is the lack of pubescence on the young stems. This is the more common species, compared to *R. typhina,* in the Piedmont of Georgia. Maine to British Columbia, south to Florida and Arizona. Cultivated 1620. Zone 2 to 9.

Ribes alpinum — Alpine Currant
(rī'bēz al-pī'num)

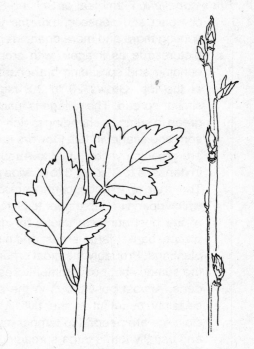

FAMILY: Saxifragaceae, more properly the Grossulariaceae(?).

LEAVES: Alternate, simple, roundish or ovate, 1 to 2″ long and wide, 3- rarely 5-lobed, with obtuse or acute dentate lobes, truncate or subcordate, bright green; petiole about 1/2″ long, glandular hairy.

BUDS: Stalked, large, imbricate, distinctly gray-tan in winter.

STEM: Light to chestnut brown, often lustrous, with conspicuous ridges running down from edges of leaf scars, unarmed, as stems mature, exfoliation may occur.

SIZE: 3 to 6′ (10′) high, usually as wide or wider.

HARDINESS: Zone 2 to 7.

HABIT: Densely twiggy, rounded shrub; erect in youth with stiffly upright stems and spreading branches.

RATE: Medium.

TEXTURE: Medium-fine in leaf; medium in winter.

STEM COLOR: Straw colored on young stems; old becoming deep brown and shredding.

LEAF COLOR: Deep bright green in summer, poor yellow in fall; one of the first shrubs to leaf out in spring.

FLOWERS: Dioecious, greenish yellow, April, staminate with 20 to 30 flowers in 1 to 2″ long racemes; female smaller, not showy, on racemes one half as long.

FRUIT: Juicy scarlet berry, 1/4 to 1/3″ diameter; June-July; attractive but seldom seen in cultivation as male clones seem to dominate; not edible.

CULTURE: Easily transplanted, best handled as a container plant; tolerant of any good soil; full sun or shade; prune anytime for flowers are not a factor; does well in calcareous soils.

DISEASES AND INSECTS: Anthracnose, cane blight, leaf spots, rust, currant aphid, imported currant worm, scales, and currant bud mite; during wet seasons leaf spot and anthracnose can be serious problems; male supposedly immune to rust diseases.

LANDSCAPE VALUE: Good hedge plant and is extensively used for that purpose, mass, good in semi-shady areas; male plants tend to dominate because of supposed rust resistance; occasionally plants with perfect flowers occur.

CULTIVARS:

'Aureum'—Dwarf type with yellowish leaves, colors best in full sun and supposedly maintains the color throughout summer; has been in cultivation since before 1881.

'Green Mound'—Dwarf, dense, 2 to 3′ high and wide form; male; shows good resistance to leaf diseases; have also seen 'Nana', 'Pumila' and 'Compacta' listed, essentially more compact than species.

PROPAGATION: Softwood cuttings taken in June or July rooted well when treated with 1000 ppm IBA and placed in sand under mist; seeds may be fall sown or provided 3 months cold stratification.

NATIVE HABITAT: Europe. Cultivated 1588.

RELATED SPECIES:

Ribes odoratum — Clove Currant
(rī'bēz ō-dôr-ā'tum)

LEAVES: Alternate, simple, ovate or orbicular-reniform, 1 to 3″ wide and as long, deeply 3 to 5 lobed, cuneate or truncate, with coarsely dentate lobes, glabrate or puberulous beneath, bluish green, thinnish; petiole 1/2 to 2″ long.

STEM: Pubescent, grayish brown.

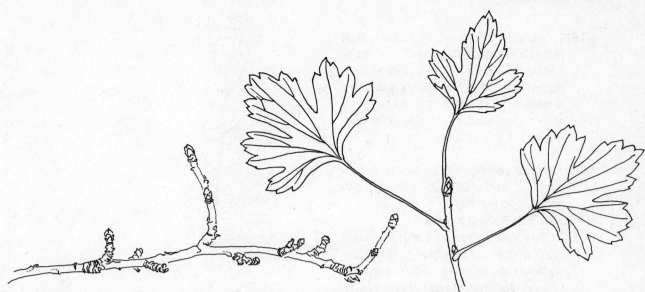

Ribes odoratum, Clove Currant, grows 6 to 8′ high and is an irregular shrub of ascending, arching stems, usually surrounded by a mass of young suckering growth, loose and open with age. It is not the neatest shrub and selection for dwarf attributes would be worthwhile. Foliage is bluish green in summer; briefly yellowish just before dropping in fall (could have reddish tones). Flowers (dioecious) are yellow, fragrant, odor of cloves; early to mid-April; borne in 5 to 10-flowered, usually nodding racemes. Fruit is a black berry, 1/3″ across, June or July. A yellow fruited forma, *xanthocarpum,* is known. Good shrub for the border or where early spring odor is desired. It is an alternate host for White Pine Blister Rust (*Cronartium ribicola*). South Dakota to western Texas, east to Minnesota and Arkansas. Zone 4 to 6(7).

Ribes sanguineum — Winter Currant
(rī′bēz san-gwin′e-um)

LEAVES: Alternate, simple, 3 to 5 lobed, 2 to 4″ wide, cordate, dark green above, whitish pubescent below; petiole—glandular pubescent.

Ribes sanguineum, Winter Currant, is a west coast species that is seldom seen in eastern gardens. The habit is upright-arching to rounded, maturing between 6 to 10′ (15′). The flowers of the better cultivars are exceptional. White, pink, rose-red flowers appear in pendulous 3″ long racemes along the length of the stems during April-May. Fruits are bloomy, bluish black, slightly glandular 1/3″ diameter berries. Plants prefer moist, well drained soil in full sun or partial shade and will tolerate a modicum of drought. As a shrub border plant, it is particularly attractive. 'King Edward VII' has red flowers and is quite compact, about 5 to 6′ high, while 'Brocklebankii' sports yellow leaves that fade with the heat of summer. Also leaves may scorch in hot sun. Flowers are pale pink. Numerous other forms are known but not widely available. British Columbia to northern California. Cultivated 1818. Zone 5 to 6(7).

Robinia pseudoacacia — Black Locust, also Common Locust, Yellow or White Locust
(rō-bin′ē-a̤ soo-dō-a̤-kā′sē-a̤)

FAMILY: Fabaceae
LEAVES: Alternate, pinnately compound, 6 to 14″ long, 7 to 19 leaflets, elliptic or ovate, 1 or 2″ long, entire, rounded or truncate and mucronate at apex, dark bluish green, glabrous beneath or slightly pubescent when young.
BUDS: Terminal—absent, laterals—minute, rusty-downy, 3 to 4 superposed, generally close together.

STEM: Slender, brittle, often zigzag, light reddish to greenish brown, smooth or nearly so, more or less angled with decurrent ridges from base and outer angles of leaf scars, generally spiny with paired stipular prickles at nodes, about 1/4 to 1/2" long.

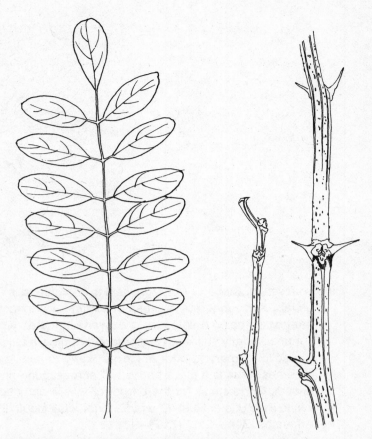

SIZE: Would average 30 to 50' in height with a spread of 20 to 35' although can grow 70 to 80' high.

HARDINESS: Zone 3 to 8(9).

HABIT: Often an upright tree with a straight trunk and a narrow oblong crown, becoming ragged and scraggly with age; will develop thickets as it freely seeds, and develops shoots from roots; some forms are spreading in habit with several trunks.

RATE: Fast, will average 2' or greater per year over a 10 year period.

BARK: Reddish brown to almost black, deeply furrowed into rounded, interlacing, fibrous, superficially scaly ridges.

LEAF COLOR: Dull, dark blue-green above, very strongly contrasting with the light and dark green of other trees; leaves show a slight yellow-green in fall and abscise early.

FLOWERS: Perfect, 1" across, white, extremely fragrant, borne in dense racemes, 4 to 8" long in May to early June, flowers at a young age, effective for 7 to 10 days.

FRUIT: Pod, flat, brown-black, 2 to 4" long, smooth, 4 to 10 seeded, maturing in October and persisting for a time.

CULTURE: Transplants very easily, extremely adaptable to varied soils and climates; will grow in about any soil except those that are permanently wet; reaches maximum development on moist, rich, loamy soils or those of limestone origin; tolerant of dry conditions and saline environments; will grow on sandy, sterile soils; has the ability to fix atmospheric nitrogen and in this way partially creates its own nitrogen supply; this is true for many legumes as well as alders, bayberry, sweetfern and others; prune in late summer or fall for locusts "bleed" in spring.

DISEASES AND INSECTS: Canker, dampening-off, leaf spots, powdery mildews, wood decay, witches' broom, locust borer, carpenterworm, locust leaf miner, locust twig borer, and scales; the most destructive pest is the locust borer which can riddle whole trees or whole plantations; the wood is extremely hard and durable yet this borer can destroy it like balsa wood; tree vigor is the important factor, for fast-growing trees exhibit the greatest resistance; leaf miner also turns the tree brown.

LANDSCAPE VALUE: An "alley cat" type tree which can survive under the toughest of conditions; good for stripped-mined areas, highway cuts and fills, sandy, poor soils, shelter plantations and afforestation purposes; not recommended for the home landscape, but definitely has a place in difficult areas; the flowers are exceedingly fragrant from which bees produce a delicious honey; several cultivars offer attractive foliage and flowers.

CULTIVARS: The Europeans have grown, appreciated and selected superior forms of this tree while Americans treated it as some pedestrian weed. In truth, it often makes, in the best forms, a handsome tree. Several of the cultivars have crossed my path. There are many others that I may never see but it will not be for a lack of trying. I understand that the U.S. Forest Service has developed borer resistant clones which as I write this will be hopefully increased through tissue culture.

'Aurea'—New leaves emerge yellow and the color persists for a time but eventually becomes lime-green, cultivated since 1864, found in Germany around 1859.

'Bessoniana'—Ovoid crown, well developed central leader, essentially unarmed stems, vigorous constitution and shy flowering characterize this form, in cultivation before 1871, have seen at Wisley Gardens.

'Decaisneana'—A vigorous tree with light rose flowers, first described in 1863, supposedly comes partially true to type from seed, considered more properly a hybrid and is listed under *R.* × *ambigua (R. pseudoacacia* × *R. viscosa),* branches slightly glutinous, stipular thorns small or absent.

'Frisia'—Leaves of a golden yellow color which hold (more or less) throughout the growing season, spines on young shoots red, discovered in an old nursery in 1935 at Zwollerkerspel, Holland; I noticed this form in abundance throughout Europe and it was a rather cheerful sight especially on some of the drab, dreary, rainy days; some older leaves become more yellow-green but overall it holds the yellow color as well as any colored foliage tree; displays excellent vigor.

'Purple Robe'—One of the prettiest forms with dark rose-pink flowers on a compact rounded tree that will probably never exceed 30 to 40', the new growth emerges bronzy red, have seen this form only once in Spring Grove, Cincinnati, OH; flower color is much deeper than *R. hispida* and *R. fertilis;* this form flowers about 10 to 14 days earlier than 'Idaho' and over a longer period.

'Pyramidalis'—A slender, medium sized (40 to 50'), columnar tree with closely erect spineless branches, sparse flowers, shoots essentially unarmed, Lombardy Poplar-like in habit.

'Semperflorens'—A large, vigorous tree which produces a major flower flush in June and a second in September or may flower continuously from midsummer on, put into commerce in 1874.

'Tortuosa'—A small tree with slightly twisted and contorted branches; the greatest concentration I have seen in the United States was at Cantigny Gardens, Wheaton, IL, the racemes are small and thinly set with flowers.

'Umbraculifera'—Forms a dense, umbrella-like canopy, 20' high and 20' wide, but bears few or no flowers; susceptible to borers and ice; essentially spineless; may be confused with 'Inermis' but is not the same thing; prominent in European landscapes.

'Unifoliola'—The leaves are reduced to a single large leaflet or subtended by 1 or 2 normalized leaflets. I am almost positive that this form was used as a street tree in Paris but on a bus at 35 miles an hour it is hard to be absolutely sure; the single leaflet may be as long as 4" and 1 1/2" wide; it can grow 40 to 60' high.

PROPAGATION: Seed dormancy is caused by an impermeable seed coat and seeds should be scarified in sulfuric acid, soaked in hot water or mechanically scarified. Root cuttings, 1/4 to 1" diameter, 3 to 8" long, gave 25% plants; the younger the tree and roots the better.

NATIVE HABITAT: Pennsylvania to Georgia, west to Iowa, Missouri, and Oklahoma. Introduced 1635.

RELATED SPECIES AND CULTIVARS:

Robinia fertilis
(rō-bin′ē-á̇ fĕr-til′is)

LEAVES: Alternate, compound pinnate, 9 to 15 leaflets, elliptic to oblong-ovate or oblong, 1 to 2" long, acute to obtusish, mucronate, dark blue-green above, slightly pubescent beneath.

Robinia fertilis, no common name, and *R. hispida,* (rō-bin′i-á̇ hiss′pi-dá̇), Bristly or Roseacacia Locust, are closely related species. *Robinia fertilis* sets fruits and seeds while *R. hispida* does not or only sparingly so. Most of my observations lead me to believe we are looking at *R. fertilis* and not the Bristly Locust. Both are small, spreading, suckering shrubs in the 6 to 10' category with prominent hispid petioles and branches; the foliage is a blue-green and the flowers rose colored or pale purple, scentless; borne in 2 to 4" long pendulous, hispid racemes; usually quite showy; their cultural requirements are similar to *R. pseudoacacia;* both are good plants for stabilizing sandy banks and sterile, dry, impoverished soils. *R. hispida* is native from Virginia and Kentucky to Georgia and

Alabama. 'Arnot' is a Soil Conservation Service selection that grows 3 to 8' high, forms dense thickets, has deep rose flowers, fixes nitrogen, and is good for stabilizing steep, sandy or gravelly slopes. 'Monument' is an old form of *R. fertilis* dating to the late 1940's when Wayside Gardens introduced it. The habit is small and compact with a narrow conical habit, flowers are rose colored, and the branches sparsely bristled, will grow 10 to 15' high, possibly a hybrid. 'Flowering Globe' is a supposed hybrid between *R. hispida* and *R. hispida* 'Macrophylla' with open, rather loose globe headed outline, dark pink 8 to 10" long racemes and larger leaves than the species, will grow 15 to 18' high and wide; no doubt grafted on *R. pseudoacacia* to produce a standard. 'Casque Rouge' is also listed as an improved *Robinia hispida* with purplish red flowers, pinkish new growth and stronger branches. *R. hispida* was introduced 1758. Zone 5 to 8, while *R. fertilis* ranges from North Carolina to Georgia. Cultivated 1900. Zone 5 to 8. Current thinking places *R. fertilis* as a variety of *R. hispida*.

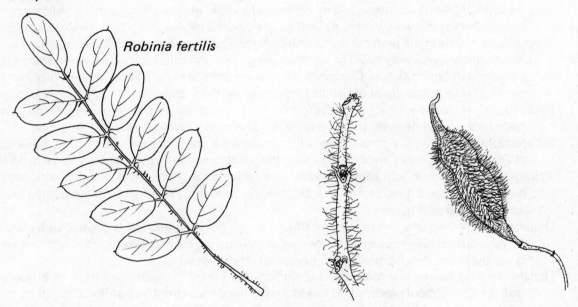

Robinia fertilis

Robinia 'Idaho', Idaho Locust, will grow 25 to 40' high with a spread of 15 to 30', tends to be more open than *R. pseudoacacia* in habit; flowers are rose-pink, fragrant, 1" long, borne in 6 to 8" long pendent racemes in May to early June; the parentage is presumably *R. pseudoacacia* and *R. hispida;* very popular in semiarid parts of the west that suffer extremes of heat and cold (Zone 3 and 4); supposedly meets the stringent requirements for street tree use; medium in growth rate; found a tree in Urbana, IL that fit the description and, in flower, was a rather pleasing experience.

ADDITIONAL NOTES: I am not a great fan of locust but there are situations where their use is warranted. I have observed miserable slopes along highways that were stabilized with *R. pseudoacacia* and it is doubtful that any other plant could have performed better. Variety *rosea* grows to 10' with pink to rose-pink flowers; var. *kelseyi* was introduced by and named for H.P. Kelsey in 1901 with rose flowers followed by reddish pods; *R. hartwigii* (*R. viscosa* var. *hartwigii*) grows to 12' although Krüssmann lists size at 25 to 30' high, and is shrublike with whitish to rosy-purple flowers; and *R. viscosa,* Clammy Locust, is a small tree (20 to 50') with pink flowers. See *Castanea* 49(4): 187–202 (1984) for a more absolute discussion of *Robinia* nomenclature.

Rosa — Rose

I considered dropping the rose section from this edition but decided to stay with the previous edition's treatment and add a select few new entries. The rose is a magnificent garden plant and will remain an essential element in gardens as long as there are gardens. Unfortunately, to keep them prosperous, a spray, fertilizer and pruning regime is essential. Over the years, I have observed our State Botanical

Garden attempt to properly care for a sizable collection of Hybrid Teas, Grandifloras and Floribundas. Some years the results were excellent; others abyssmal. Mildew, blackspot and canker cause the greatest concerns but thrips, Japanese beetles, deer (yes deer) and cold contribute mightily to decline. In recent years there has been an approach to market certain roses as "carefree" and with the Meidiland group the word *rose* is not used. Most interesting is the advertising campaign that describes them as "all new...all season, 'hybrid' flowering shrubs," with the word ROSE obvious by its absence.

Rosa multiflora — Japanese Rose, also referred to as Multiflora Rose
(rō′zȧ mul-ti-flō′rȧ)

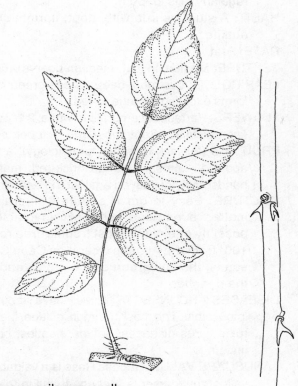

FAMILY: Rosaceae

LEAVES: Alternate, odd-pinnate, usually 9 leaflets, obovate to oblong, 1/2 to 1 1/4″ long, acute or obtuse, serrate, pubescent, lustrous bright green.

CANES: Usually with paired and occasionally scattered prickles; prickles short, recurved, more or less enlarged and flattened at base.

SIZE: 3 to 4 to 10′ in height and may spread 10 to 15′.

HARDINESS: Zone 5 to 8.

HABIT: A fountain with long, slender, recurving branches; eventually forming an impenetrable tangle of brush suitable only for burning.

RATE: Fast; too fast for most farmers who have this species in their fields.

TEXTURE: Medium in leaf; somewhat repulsive in winter (medium-coarse).

LEAF COLOR: Very lustrous bright green in summer; fall color, at best, is a sickly yellow.

FLOWERS: White, about 1″ across, fragrant; June; borne in many-flowered corymbs.

FRUIT: Red, 1/4″ globular to egg-shaped hip which is effective in August and into winter.

CULTURE: Same as described under *R. rugosa* although this species is more invasive; tolerates dry, heavy soils very well.

DISEASES AND INSECTS: None serious.

LANDSCAPE VALUE: None in the residential landscape; has received a lot of attention for conservation purposes; makes a good place for all the "critters" to hide, yet can be a real nuisance, for the birds deposit the seeds in fence rows and open areas, and soon one has a jungle; use this species with the knowledge that none of your gardening friends in the immediate vicinity will ever speak to you again.

CULTIVARS:

var. *cathayensis* has pale pink, 1/2 to 1″ diameter flowers which are borne in few- to many-flowered rather flat corymbs.

Variety *inermis* is a thornless type.

'Platyphylla'—Double form, flowers deep pink; according to Wyman, it is not a very vigorous grower.

PROPAGATION: Cuttings as described under *R. rugosa*. Seed should be stratified for 120 days.

NATIVE HABITAT: Japan, Korea. Escaped from cultivation in the United States. Introduced 1868.

Rosa rugosa — Rugosa Rose, also called Saltspray Rose, Beach Tomato
(rō'zà rū-gō'sà)

FAMILY: Rosaceae

LEAVES: Alternate, odd-pinnate, leaflets 5 to 9, elliptic to elliptic obovate, 1 to 2″ long, acute or obtusish, serrate, lustrous, rugose dark green and glabrous above, glaucescent, reticulate, and pubescent beneath, thick and firm; petioles tomentose and bristly.

CANES: Stout, densely bristly, prickly, downy.

SIZE: 4 to 6′ high by 4 to 6′ wide.

HARDINESS: Zone 2 to 7 (8); has been seen 100 miles from Artic Circle in Siberia where temperature regularly falls to -50°F.

HABIT: A sturdy shrub with stout, upright stems, filling the ground and forming a dense rounded outline.

RATE: Fast.

TEXTURE: Medium in leaf; medium-coarse when undressed.

LEAF COLOR: Lustrous, deep rugose green in summer then briefly yellowish to bronzish and in some forms excellent orange to red.

FLOWERS: Perfect, rose-purple to white, 2 1/2 to 3 1/2″ across, fragrant; June through August, often found sporadically in September and October; solitary or few in clusters.

FRUIT: Hip (for lack of better terminology), actually an urn-shaped structure which encloses achenes, about 1″ across, lustrous brick-red; maturing in August through fall. The flowers and fruit are handsomely displayed against the dark green foliage.

CULTURE: Easy to grow, prefers well-drained soil which has been supplemented with organic matter; sunny and open; pH adaptable, however, a slightly acid soil is best; salt tolerant; possibly one of the most trouble-free roses. I have seen the species growing in pure sand not 100′ from the Atlantic Ocean on Cape Cod, Mass. The plant really stands out against the white sands, the dull green beach grass, and silvery wormwood *(Artemesia).* In Japan, confined to the beaches.

DISEASES AND INSECTS: Roses have about as many problems as *Prunus* and a complete listing is impossible. The most common include: black-spot (a leaf disease), powdery mildew, various cankers, rusts, virus diseases, aphids, beetles, borers, leafhopper, scales, rose-slug, thrips, mites, ad infinitum.

LANDSCAPE VALUE: Rugosa Rose is a valuable plant for difficult sites: banks, cuts, fills, sandy soils, and saline environments. Very beautiful in foliage, flower and fruit. Has escaped from cultivation in the northeastern United States and is often apparent along the sandy shores of the ocean. It is also called Saltspray Rose because of its tolerance. Withstands pruning and is often used in hedges. Has been used in hybridization work because of its extreme vigor and ease of culture which would be worthwhile traits to impart to offspring. Have great affinity for this species and grew it for several years in my Georgia garden until the Japanese beetles reduced it to fodder.

CULTIVARS: Epping and Hasselkus, *American Nurseryman* 170(2):29–39 (1989) presented an excellent evaluation of *R. rugosa* and other shrub roses. Their particular focus was *R. rugosa,* hybrids and cultivars. Herein I present their observations. With over 50 cultivars in existence, they evaluated 30 of the most commonly available.

Recommended *Rosa rugosa* selections:

‘Albo-plena’ *(R. rugosa albo-plena)* is a selected mutation of *R. rugosa* ‘Alba’. ‘Albo-plena’ has double, pure white, fragrant flowers, dark green foliage and a dense, low habit. It grows up to 4′ tall. This cultivar does not produce hips, but it is highly resistant to blackspot and powdery mildew. ‘Albo-plena’ has yellow to orange fall color and is winter hardy at -15 to -20°F. It is a good white-flowered cultivar; its only drawback is its lack of hip production.

'Belle Poitevine' is an old (1894), hybrid cultivar. It has slightly fragrant, large, semidouble, light mauve-pink flowers with showy yellow stamens. The hips are not showy, and the foliage is dull, medium green. It has yellow to orange fall color and a dense compact habit, reaching 3 1/2 to 4' tall and wide. This cultivar is highly resistant to blackspot and powdery mildew and is hardy to -20°F. 'Belle Poitevine' is a tough cultivar with attractive flowers, foliage and form. Hips abscise shortly after they form.

'Blanc Double de Coubert' is very similar to 'Albo-plena', differing only in flower form and ultimate height. This hybrid has semidouble to double, pure white, fragrant flowers and showy yellow stamens. This shrub is a vigorous grower with glossy, dark green foliage, and yellow fall color. It grows 4 to 6' tall. It is highly resistant to blackspot and powdery mildew and is hardy to -20°F. 'Blanc Double de Coubert' also produces fairly heavy suckers and can get somewhat leggy. References don't indicate that it is sterile, but if hips do form, they abort before becoming showy.

R. × *calocarpa* is a hybrid *R. rugosa* with large, single, purplish crimson, fragrant flowers and showy stamens. This 4 to 5' tall cultivar has a dense, mounded habit and excellent burnt orange to red and maroon fall color. It produces attractive, orange-red hips that are somewhat oval and sparsely punctuated with tiny spines. The leaves are dull, medium green; they are more pointed, but less rugose, than those of the species. The twigs also have a finer texture than those of the species. *R.* × *calocarpa* is highly resistant to blackspot and powdery mildew and is hardy to -20°F. Plants were attacked by mites in the dry, hot summer of 1988.

'Frau Dagmar Hastrup' ('Frau Dagmar Hartopp') is a *R. rugosa* seedling that proved to be the best all-around performer of all cultivars evaluated. It is a prolific bloomer, with fragrant, light-pink, single flowers and showy yellow stamens. This cultivar produces very large red hips in great quantity that color as early as July. They appear along with the flowers and remain showy until November. 'Frau Dagmar Hastrup' has excellent yellow to orange fall color, rich dark green foliage, and a low, dense, mounded form growing 3 to 4' tall. It has the greatest resistance to blackspot and powdery mildew of any *R. rugosa* cultivar evaluated. It is very hardy with no winter injury at -21°F.

Acceptable cultivars:

'Delicata' is an old (1898), hybrid cultivar with large, semidouble, lilac-pink, slightly fragrant flowers and showy yellow stamens. The large orange-red hips are sparsely produced and sometimes occur with the flowers. The dark green foliage turns yellow in fall. 'Delicata' is a vigorous grower with a good, dense form (3 to 4' tall) and is winter hardy at -21°F. It is not as disease-resistant as 'Belle Poitevine', but it is useful when a darker pink flower is preferred. 'Delicata' was moderately infected with blackspot in late August and September 1987 but was disease-free during the drier 1988 growing season.

'Hansa' is a hybrid cultivar with semidouble, large, purplish red, very fragrant flowers. It produces many orange-red hips, often along with the flowers. This cultivar has dark green, glossy, blackspot-resistant foliage and yellow to orange fall color. The upright habit is often tall and leggy, and this shrub grows to an ultimate height of 5 to 6'. We did not observe any winter injury at -21°F and 'Hansa' is a good performer except for its leggy habit. This cultivar and 'Delicata' are rather similar, but 'Delicata' has lighter pink flowers and a better compact habit. 'Hansa' has a superior hip display and is more resistant to blackspot.

'Scabrosa' is a rather recent (1950) hybrid introduction. Its large, single, deep mauve-pink flowers have showy yellow stamens and usually appear in clusters of five. 'Scabrosa' produced attractive flowers and fruit, but not as freely as 'Frau Dagmar Hastrup'. The large, orange-red hips are abundant, and the bright green foliage is resistant to blackspot and powdery mildew. 'Scabrosa' has yellow to orange fall color and a dense, low, mounded form. It grows 3 to 4' tall. This cultivar is very hardy.

'Schneezwerg' ('Snowdwarf') is a floriferous hybrid with semidouble, small, white flowers and showy yellow stamens. Small, orange-red, showy hips often appear with the flowers. The dark green foliage has a finer texture than that of *R. rugosa* but is somewhat susceptible to blackspot.

'Schneezwerg' has a mounded, dense habit and ultimately grows 4 to 5' tall and wide. This cultivar is winter hardy to -20°F.

'Thérèse Bugnet' is a hybrid cultivar with large, double, medium pink, loosely clustered and very fragrant flowers. The red hips are rare, and the blue-green foliage is slightly susceptible to blackspot and turns yellow and orange in fall. The attractive, glossy red canes are somewhat susceptible to rose stem girdler attacks. The upright habit suckers to form dense thickets, and this shrub grows 5 to 6' tall. 'Thérèse Bugnet' is very attractive in the winter landscape due to its shiny red canes and is winter hardy to -20°F. Its biggest drawback is its susceptibility to rose stem girdler. This is not surprising since *R. acicularis*, one of its parents, can be extremely susceptible to this insect.

Further Evaluation Needed:

'Dart's Dash' has large, semidouble, mauve flowers and large, orange-red hips. The foliage is bright green and showed no sign of disease.

'Roseraie de l'Hay' is a cultivar of a sport of *R. rugosa* 'Rosea'. It has large, double, crimson-purple and very fragrant flowers. The sparse hips are not showy. No blackspot, powery mildew or other diseases on the light green foliage was evident. Krüssmann says this cultivar has a bushy form and reaches medium height. The cultivar is listed as hardy in Zone 2.

'Topaz Jewel' is a recent hybrid cultivar and one of the few yellow-flowered Rugosa Roses. It is a recurrent bloomer with semidouble, light yellow flowers and showy orange stamens. No hip production was noticed. The medium green foliage had no evidence of blackspot or other diseases. 'Topaz Jewel' is described as having a dense, bushy habit with arching canes. It grows up to 5' high and 7' wide.

Cultivars not recommended: Rather than describing attributes and liabilities, I chose to limply list those deemed unacceptable by Epping and Hasselkus. The reader may consult the original article for specifics.

'Agnes'	'Jens Munk'
'Alba'	'Martin Frobisher'
'Charles Albanel'	'Mrs. Anthony Waterer'
'David Thompson'	'Pink Grootendorst'
'Dr. Eckener'	'Rose a Parfume de l'Hay'
'F. J. Grootendorst'	'Sarah van Fleet'
'Flamingo'	'Sir Thomas Lipton'
'Grootendorst Supreme'	'White Grootendorst'
'Henry Hudson'	

PROPAGATION: The seeds (actually achenes) of most species exhibit dormancy which is principally due to seedcoat conditions rather than embryo dormancy. Cold stratification at 40°F for 90 to 120 days is recommended for *R. rugosa*. Cuttings can be effective with the species roses. Hardwood cuttings should be taken from November through early March, stored in sand or peat at 35° to 40°F and planted outside in spring, with only about 1" of the upper end of the cutting protruding. Softwood cuttings should be taken in July, August, and September with all but the top leaf removed. Rose cuttings respond to IBA and 1000 ppm IBA talc or quick dip is recommended.

ADDITIONAL NOTES: The species roses of which *R. rugosa* is a member, are not as prone to the diseases and insects as the hybrid types. They are more vigorous and less exacting as to culture. The fruits of *R. rugosa* are supposed to make the finest jelly.

NATIVE HABITAT: Northern China, Korea, Japan. Introduced 1845. Creech, *Amer. Nurseryman* 160(6): 77–79 (1984) says introduced around 1770.

Other Species Roses

Rosa banksiae — Lady Banks' Rose
(rō′zȧ bank′si-ȧ)

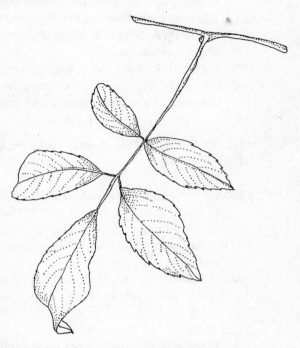

LEAVES: Alternate, compound pinnate, evergreen, elliptic-ovate to oblong-lanceolate, 3 to 5 leaflets, rarely 7, 1 to 2 1/2″ long, acute or obtusish, serrulate, glabrous except at base of midrib below, lustrous dark green; rachis pubescent.

Rosa banksiae, Lady Banks' Rose, is a common occurrence in southern gardens especially those with period (1850 to 1900) connotations. The species is a sprawling climber (15 to 20′) that requires restraint to be kept in bounds. The stems are nearly (in most cases completely) thornless. Used a great deal on fences, trellises and also espaliered against walls. The flowers are white or yellow, 1″ across, slightly fragrant, on smooth stalks in many flowered umbels from April into June. The double-flowered slightly fragrant yellow cultivar, 'Lutea', is the common represenative of this species in southern gardens and is also called "Lady Bank's Rose". 'Normalis' has single white flowers; 'Albo-plena' double white, fragrant; 'Lutescens' single yellow. The plant requires no special insect and disease control measures and actually appears to thrive with neglect. Tolerates a modicum of salt spray. Withstands full sun and partial shade. Roots readily from softwood cuttings. China. Zone 7 to 8.

Rosa blanda — Meadow Rose
(rō′zȧ blan′dȧ)

LEAVES: Alternate, compound pinnate, 5 to 7 leaflets, rarely 9, elliptic to obovate-oblong, 1 to 2 1/2″ long, acute, coarsely serrate, dull blue-green above, glabrous, paler and finely pubescent or glabrous below; stipules dilated.
CANES: Sparsely thorned or with scattered bristles to thornless with attractive red bark.
HABIT: Dense, mounded, strong growing, suckering, 4 to 5′ high.
FLOWERS: Single, light pink, fragrant, 2″ across, solitary or few together, May-June.
FRUIT: Subglobose to ellipsoidal, 1/2″ diameter, smooth bright red hips that color in late July and remain showy into winter.
ADDITIONAL NOTES: Epping and Hasselkus rated it one of the best roses for fruit display. Their only objection was late season blackspot susceptibility.
NATIVE HABITAT: Newfoundland to Pennsylvania, Missouri, North Dakota and Manitoba. Introduced 1773. Zone 2 to 6(7).

Rosa carolina — Carolina Rose, Pasture Rose
(rō′zȧ ka-rō-lī′na)

LEAVES: Alternate, pinnately compound, leaflets usually 5, rarely 7, elliptic to lance-elliptic, rarely oblanceolate, 1/2 to 1 1/4″ long, acute or obtuse, sharply serrate with ascending teeth, shiny rich green, glabrous beneath, pubescent on veins or nearly glabrous, stipules narrow; in autumn the leaves turn a dull red of varying shades.

CANES: Often covered with scattered and paired prickles and bristles when young, sometimes rather sparsely so later; prickles slender, usually not flattened except on vigorous branches, mostly straight.

HABIT: 3 to 6' high, freely suckering shrub composed of erect branches forming dense thickets.

FLOWERS: Pink, single, 2 to 2 1/2" across, solitary or 2 to 3 together, June into July. Variety *alba* has white flowers.

FRUIT: Red, 1/3" diameter, urn- or pear-shaped, persisting into winter and maintaining good color.

NATIVE HABITAT: Maine to Wisconsin, Kansas, Texas and Florida. Introduced 1826. Zone 4 to 9. Common in low wet grounds and borders of swamps and streams.

Rosa foetida — Austrian Brier Rose
(rō′zȧ fō-tē′dȧ)

LEAVES: Alternate, pinnately compound, 5, 7, or 9 leaflets, oval or obovate, 3/4 to 1 1/2" long, rounded or broad cuneate, edged with a few glandular teeth, brilliant parsley-green and glabrous or with scattered hairs above, glandular and more or less downy below.

CANES: Grayish, furnished with many slender, straight or slightly curved prickles abruptly widened at base and up to 3/8" long.

HABIT: Rather lax, with erect-arching canes, 6 to 7' high.

FLOWERS: Deep yellow, 2 to 3" across, usually solitary, May-June.

FRUIT: Rarely seen in culivation, listed as globose, red, 1/2" wide.

CULTIVARS:

'Bicolor' (Austrian Copper)—A magnificent rose with copper-red petals, yellow on the back side; often yellow or combination colored flowers occur on some branches; it is a tremendous experience to see it in full flower, perhaps no more handome rose.

'Persiana'—Double yellow flowers which are freely borne.

NATIVE HABITAT: Western Asia. Introduced before 1600. Zone 4 to 8. Has performed well in the State Botanical Garden.

Rosa × *harisonii* — Harrison's Yellow Rose
(rō′zȧ × hȧr-i-sō′nē-ī)

HABIT: Upright shrub growing 4 to 6' high.

FLOWERS: Yellow, double, about 2" diameter, borne over a two week period in early June; very dependable flowering shrub; has a somewhat unpleasant odor.

FRUIT: Nearly black, small, not ornamentally effective.

ADDITIONAL NOTES: The specific epithet is often spelled *harrisoni*. Zone 5.

Rosa hugonis — Father Hugo Rose
(rō′zȧ hū-gō′nis)

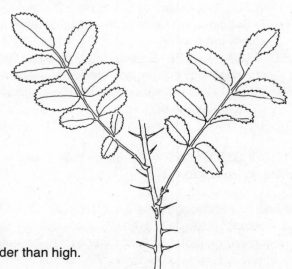

LEAVES: Alternate, pinnately compound, 5 to 13 leaflets, oval to obovate or elliptic, 1/4 to 1" long, obtuse, sometimes acutish, finely serrate, glabrous, or slightly villose on the veins when unfolding.

CANES: Often reddish, with scattered prickles, usually also bristly at least at base of non-flowering young growth; prickles stout, straight, flattened, often red.

HABIT: Medium sized (6 to 8') shrub with upright arching canes and a twiggy rounded habit; often broader than high.

FLOWERS: Single, canary yellow, 2 to 2 1/2″ diameter, solitary, May-June.

FRUIT: Scarlet turning blackish red, nearly globular, about 1/2″ across, ripening in August.

ADDITIONAL NOTES: One of the more common species roses; often found in older gardens. Good, free flowering, bright yellow shrub. Looks a little ragged when not in flower.

NATIVE HABITAT: Central China. Introduced 1899. Zone 5 to 8.

Rosa laevigata — Cherokee Rose
(rō′zȧ lē-vi-gā′-tȧ)

LEAVES: Alternate, pinnately compound, trifoliolate or with 5 leaflets, elliptic or ovate, 1 1/2 to 4″ long, half as wide, of thick, firm texture, toothed, lustrous dark green, glabrous.

CANES: Armed with hooked prickles, sometimes mixed with bristles on the branchlets.

HABIT: Spreading, arching, tangled, 8 to 10′ high shrub which will climb over and through trees; one plant on the Georgia campus was about 8 to 10′ high and 15 to 18′ wide and literally impenetrable.

FLOWERS: Pure white, fragrant, solitary, 3 to 4″ across, beautiful in flower, April-May.

FRUIT: Red, thickly set with bristles, pyriform, 1 1/2 to 1 3/4″ long, 3/4″ wide.

ADDITIONAL NOTES: The state flower of Georgia. It is a beautiful plant but with all the magnificent native plants in Georgia it seems strange that this would be chosen. Was cultivated about 1780 in Georgia. Not particularly cold hardy as -3°F in Athens killed the above described plant outright. A pink flowered form is available but is probably a hybrid.

NATIVE HABITAT: Southern China, Formosa, extending into Burma. Zone 7 to 9. Naturalized from Georgia to Florida to Texas.

Rosa moyesii — Moyes Rose
(rō′zȧ moy-es′ē-ī)

LEAVES: alternate, pinnately compound, 3 to 6″ long, 7 to 13 leaflets, ovate to roundish oval, 3/4 to 1 1/2″ long, singly or doubly toothed, glabrous except on midrib below which is downy and sometimes prickly, dark green above, pale or glaucous beneath; petiole glandular, sticky.

CANES: Erect, armed with stout, pale, scattered, broad-based prickles, abundant on non-flowering shoots, the lower part being furnished with fine needle-like prickles; flowering shoots less prickly.

HABIT: Medium-size to large, erect branched shrub of sturdy habit; grows 6 to 10′ high.

FLOWERS: Intense blood red, 2 to 2 1/2″ across, solitary or in pairs, June-July.

FRUIT: Red, 1 1/2″ long, crowned by the erect persistent sepals, glandular hairy.

ADDITIONAL NOTES: Popular species rose, and the parent of several hybrids.

   'Geranium'—is a compact, bushy form with lighter green foliage and clear geranium-red flowers; have seen frequently in English gardens, beautiful flower.

NATIVE HABITAT: Western China. Introduced 1894 and 1903. Zone 5 to 7, possibly 8.

Rosa omeiensis — Omei Rose
(rō′zȧ ō-mī-en′sis)

LEAVES: Alternate, pinnately compound, usually 5 to 9 leaflets, oblong or elliptic-oblong, 1/2 to 1 1/2″ long, acutish, cuneate, serrate, rich green, glabrous, puberulous on midrib beneath; petioles puberulous and prickly.

HABIT: Large spreading shrub with rich green, finely divided leaflets which give the plant a fern-like appearance. Can grow 10 to 15' high and as wide.

FLOWERS: White, single, 1 to 1 1/2" across, June, not overwhelmingly effective.

FRUIT: Pear-shaped, 1/3 to 2/3" long, glossy orange-red; borne on yellow stalks, maturing in July-August, falling soon after maturation.

ADDITIONAL NOTES: Fruits are especially beautiful as are the large; broad based, translucent, ruby-red prickles provide winter interest and make for interesting flower-arranging effects. Variety *chyrsocarpa* has yellow fruits. Variety *pteracantha* has much enlarged prickles often forming wide wings along the stem, reddish.

NATIVE HABITAT: Western China. Introduced 1901. Zone 4 to 7.

Rosa rubrifolia (*R. glauca*) — Redleaf Rose
(rō'zá rū-bri-fō'li-á)

LEAVES: Alternate, pinnately compound, 5 to 7 leaflets, ovate or elliptic, 1 to 1 1/2" long, toothed, glabrous, of a beautiful coppery or purplish hue.

CANES: Covered with a purplish bloom, armed with small decurved prickles; strong canes clad with bristles and needles.

HABIT: A 5 to 7' high, erect caned, eventually spreading shrub of good density.

FLOWERS: Clear pink, 1 1/2" wide, not effective especially against the reddish foliage backdrop.

FRUIT: Globose, red, 1/2" long, usually smooth.

ADDITIONAL NOTES: A fine addition to any shrub border because of interesting foliage color. It can be used in groups where it makes a great show. Interestingly, I have read descriptions of the flowers which state bright red but the plants I have seen were pink flowered. Abundant variation in flower color from seed grown specimens. I have grown a number of seedlings to flowering size and witnessed light pink to very deep pink flowers.

NATIVE HABITAT: Mountains of central and southern Europe. Introduced 1814. Zone 2 to 8.

Rosa setigera — Prairie Rose, also called Michigan Rose or Climbing Rose
(rō'zá se-tig'ēr-á)

LEAVES: Alternate, pinnately compound, leaflets 3, rarely 5, ovate to oblong-ovate, 1 1/4 to 3 1/2" long, short-acuminate, serrate, pubescent on veins beneath; lustrous dark green in summer; fall colors often a combination of bronze-purple, red, pink, orange and yellow.

CANES: With scattered or paired prickles; prickles strong, usually recurved, enlarged and flattened at base; stems, petioles and peduncles often glandular-pubescent; stems green or reddish, often dark purple with a bloom.

HABIT: A wide spreading shrub with arching and spreading canes which may extend 15' in a single season. May grow to 15' but usually shorter; when climbing over flat ground grows 3 to 4' in height.

FLOWERS: Deep pink fading to white, nearly scentless, single, about 2" across; borne in few-flowered corymbs in late June through early July.

FRUIT: Red, globular, 1/3" diameter, maturing in fall.

ADDITIONAL NOTES: One of the latest flowering species roses; quite hardy (Zone 4) and has been used in breeding work; might be a good plant for difficult areas along highways; definitely not for the small garden.

NATIVE HABITAT: Ontario to Nebraska, Texas and Florida. Introduced 1810.

Rosa spinosissima — Scotch Rose (by some authorities the correct name is *Rosa pimpinellifolia*)
(rō'zȧ spī̄-nō-sis'i-mȧ)

LEAVES: Alternate, pinnately compound, 5 to 11 leaflets, usually 7 to 9, orbicular to oblong-ovate, 1/2 to 1″ long, simply serrate, or doubly glandular-serrate, lustrous bright green, glabrous, sometimes glandular beneath; stipules entire, rarely glandular-dentate.

CANES: Densely covered with straight needle-like bristles and prickles.

HABIT: A dense, free-suckering shrub of mound-like, symmetrical habit, often forming thickets; may grow 3 to 4′ high.

FLOWERS: Pink, white, or yellow; solitary, single, but numerous on short branches along the stems, 1 to 2″ diameter; May-early June.

FRUIT: Black or dark brown, 1/2 to 3/4″ diameter; effective in September.

ADDITIONAL NOTES: One of the most widely distributed rose species; very variable and numerous cultivars are known; assets include low habit, profuse flowering, variation in flower color, size, doubleness; also of easy culture; is now used in commercial landscapes in the southeast as a ground cover and mass planting.

NATIVE HABITAT: Europe, western Asia, naturalized in northeastern United States. Cultivated before 1600. Zone 4 to 8.

Rosa virginiana — Virginia Rose
(rō'zȧ vĕr-jin-ē-ā'na)

LEAVES: Alternate, pinnately compound, 7 to 9 leaflets, elliptic to obovate, 1 to 2 1/2″ long, usually acute at ends, serrate with ascending teeth; upper stipules dilated.

CANES: Reddish, with mainly paired prickles, sometimes variously prickly; prickles thick based, flattened, straight or often hooked.

HABIT: A low to medium-sized shrub which often forms a dense mass of erect stems. Will grow 4 to 6′ in height.

FLOWERS: Pink, single, solitary or 2 to 3 together, 2 to 2 1/2″ across; June.

FRUIT: Red, about 1/2″ diameter, ripening late and persistent through winter.

ADDITIONAL NOTES: One of the more handsome native roses. The summer foliage is excellent glossy dark green and changes first to purple then orange-red, crimson and yellow in autumn. The fruits are a bright glistening red and persist into winter. The canes are reddish with many paired prickles and are attractive in winter. Can be used as an effective barrier or low hedge, and when it has overstepped boundaries it can be cut to the ground and will develop quickly to excellent form; excellent in sandy soils, particularly by the sea.

NATIVE HABITAT: Newfoundland to Virginia, Alabama and Missouri. Introduced before 1807. Zone 3 to 7(8).

Rosa wichuraiana — Memorial Rose, Sunshine Rose
(rō'zȧ wi-shur-ē-ā-nȧ)

LEAVES: Alternate, pinnately compound, 7 to 9 leaflets, suborbicular to broad-ovate or obovate, 1/2 to 1″ long, usually obtuse, coarsely serrate, lustrous dark green above and beneath, glabrous, stipules dentate.

CANES: With scattered prickles; prickles sparse, strong, and recurved.

HABIT: A procumbent shrub, of semi-evergreen nature, with long green canes trailing over the ground and rooting; will climb if supported. Probably stays in the 8 to 16′ category from a height aspect.

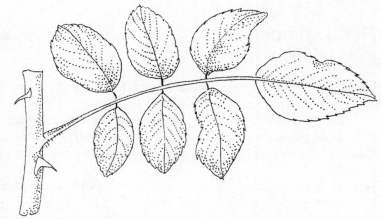

FLOWERS: Pure white with rich yellow stamens in the center, fragrant, single, about 2″ across, borne in few-to many-flowered pyramidal corymbs in June and July.

FRUIT: Red, about 1/2″ long, egg-shaped; maturing in September-October.

ADDITIONAL NOTES: This species makes an excellent ground cover. I have seen it used on highway slopes where it does an excellent job of holding the soil as well as adding a touch of beauty. Has been used in breeding work and is a parent of many of the modern climbers. Good plant because of its ease of culture and freedom from insects and diseases.

NATIVE HABITAT: Japan, Korea, Taiwan, Eastern China. Found on beaches and low hills along the coast in southern parts of Japan. Introduced in 1891 into North America by the Arnold Arboretum. Zone 5 to 8.

NEW LOWER MAINTENANCE ROSES

The name rose conjures maintenance and Conard-Pyle, West Grove, PA, the introducer of the new Meidiland series wanted to avoid the connotation. The jury is still out on their absolute carefree nature but to date the reports have been favorable. They are definitely black spot and mildew resistant. However, early spring and midsummer fungicide applications are recommended.

Bonica ('Meidomonac')—The first in the series with medium pink buds that open to pastel pink, fully double (50 petals), 3″ wide flowers; considered everblooming with cycle highest in spring and late summer-fall, produce bright orange-red hips (remained green in Madison, WI); upright, arching habit, 5′ by 4 1/2 to 5′; small glossy dark green leaves do not develop fall color, hardy to Zone 4 to 5; in Wisconsin tests -12°F caused tip die back of at least 12″; -21°F killed plants to the ground but they did resprout to 3′ and flower by mid June.

Carefree Beauty ('Beubi')—Becoming more common in gardens. It is not a Meidiland selection. In Wisconsin tests, it produced semi-double, fragrant, medium pink flowers from June to frost. The hips remained green; foliage is thickish, glossy medium green and does not develop fall color; resistant to black spot and powdery mildew; habit is somewhat open, 3 to 4′ high and wide. Hardiness response was akin to 'Bonica'; the cultivar has been included in the evaluation plots at the University Botanical Gardens and, after a healthy start, the deer decimated the plant.

Ferdy ('Keitoli')—Produces profuse coral-pink, 1 to 1 1/2″ diameter double flowers over a 4 week period in spring; flowers so heavily that the glossy medium green foliage is almost obscured, in fall the leaves turn shades of red; grows 3 1/2 to 5′ by 3 to 4′ with a graceful cascading effect; Zone 4.

Pink Meidiland ('Meipoque')—Represents a more upright form, 3 to 4′ by 1 1/2 to 2 1/2′, that can be used as a buffer, mass or unpruned hedge; the single, 2 to 2 1/2″ diameter pink with white center flowers open from spring to frost and are followed by reddish fruits that provide winter interest; foliage is slightly glossy medium green and densely borne; Zone 4 to 5.

Scarlet Meidiland ('Meikrotal')—Double, 1 to 1 1/2″ diameter, scarlet flowers occur in profusion for 4 weeks in early summer and sporadically until frost; grows 3 to 4′ by 5 to 6′ and makes an excellent cover, abundant glossy rich green foliage adds to the plant's aesthetic qualities; Zone 4 to 5.

White Meidiland ('Meicoublan')—Was prospering in the State Botanical Garden tests until the deer reduced it to rubble; a low growing almost groundcover type with dense lustrous, leathery dark green leaves and up to 4″ wide, double pure white flowers from June into fall; will grow 1 1/2 to 2′ high by 4 to 5′ wide, makes a good mass or ground cover; Zone 5.

A FINAL ROSE NOTE

For years Agricultural Canada has introduced cold hardy, disease free roses for Canada and the northern United States. As long as I can remember Felicitas Svejda had her name attached to many (perhaps all?) the new introductions. The introductions were tested at several locations in Canada and the northern United States over a number of years to assess floriferousness, hardiness and disease resistance.

'Champlain'—Combines winter hardiness with the flowering habit and attractive flowers of Floribunda Roses; grows 3′ high with 2 to 2 3/4″ diameter, 30 petaled, dark red, fragrant flowers; leaves are abundant, lustrous and dark yellow-green.

'Charles Albanel'—Derived from 3 cycles of open pollination of *R. rugosa* 'Souvenir de Philemon Cochet', grows 3′ by 3 1/2′, flowers are 3 to 4″ diameter, 20 petaled, fragrant, medium red; the leaves are rugose dark green and abundant; stems are prickly and bristly; high blackspot and mildew resistance, long flowering period, fragrance and vigor are principal attributes; interestingly, Epping and Hasselkus found this selection unacceptable.

'John Davis'—A trailing growth habit to 6 to 8′ long, medium pink, perfume fragrance, 3 to 4″ diameter, 40 petaled flowers occur in clusters of approximately 17, unopened bud is bright red and unfurls to pink; leaves are leathery, glossy dark green, resistant to black spot.

'J.P. Connell'—A vigorous shrub, 3 to 5′ high and 2 1/2 to 3 1/2′ wide; flowers are yellow, 30 to 70 petaled, 3 to 4″ diameter, fragrant; foliage is dark green; this is the first yellow flowered form introduced from the Plant Research Centre of Agricultural Canada; it is susceptible to black spot; interestingly 24 parental types were used in breeding this selection, this represents a long term commitment to a breeding program; see *HortScience* 23:783–784 (1988) for additional information about this and 'John Davis'.'

'Rugosa Ottawa'—Introduced in 1984 as a source of insect and disease resistance for breeding roses; offers resistance to the 2-spotted spider mite, strawberry aphid, blackspot and mildew; flowers are purple, habit is rounded-mounded, 5′ by 5′; cold hardy and flowers repeatedly but sparingly; see *HortScience* 19:896–897 (1984).

'William Baffin'—A cold hardy, disease resistant, strong climber; grows 9 to 10′ high; 2 1/2 to 3″ diameter, 20 petaled, deep pink flowers open in spring with a second flush in late summer; leaves are glossy dark green, see *HortScience* 18:962 (1983), probably Zone 4.

Rosmarinus officinalis — Rosemary
(rōs-mȧ-rī′nus o-fis-i-nā′lis)

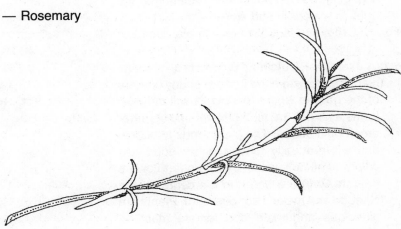

FAMILY: Lamiaceae

LEAVES: Opposite, simple, evergreen, 3/4 to 2″ long, 1/16 to 1/8″ wide, linear, sessile, narrow, entire, revolute margin, lustrous dark green above, white-tomentose beneath (gray-green effect), thick, aromatically fragrant when bruised.

Rosmarinus officinalis, Rosemary, forms a 2 to 4′ high (to 6 to 7′ in favorable climates) and wide, irregular evergreen shrub. The needle-like foliage is gray-green and contrasts nicely with other dark green foliage shrubs. The leaves when bruised emit a potent, unmistakable aromatic odor. The light blue, 1/2″ long flowers are borne in the leaf axils from fall to spring. Flower effect is often reduced because flowers blend with foliage. Easily cultured. Withstands drought and about any soil except those that are permanently wet. Full sun. Displays excellent salt tolerance. Withstands pruning and can be fashioned into a low hedge. has numerous uses in the garden but often kind of wild and woolly in appearance. This is not particularly bad because so many southern landscape plants look like they were dressed in tuxedos. 'Prostratus' is more trailing and irregular than the species and less hardy (Zone 8). I have become increasingly fond of this species over the years and offer the following cultivars for consideration.

'Beneden Blue'—Offers vivid blue, almost gentian-blue flowers, narrow leaves and semi-erect habit.
'Blue Spire'—Light green narrow leaves and clear blue flowers on an erect compact shrub.
'Huntington Carpet'—Blue flowers, dark green leaves that are silvery beneath on a compact semi-prostrate, dwarf mounding shrub that grows less than 1' tall; introduced by Huntington Botanical Garden, San Marino, CA.
'Lockwood de Forest'—Akin to 'Prostratus' in habit but has lighter green foliage and bluer flowers.
'Majorca Pink'—Lilac-pink flowers, relatively broad leaves on an erect shrub.
'Miss Jessopp's Upright'—Erect, robust form with broad, deep sea green leaves, considered one of the hardiest.
'Severn Sea'—Fine blue flowers on a free flowering, arching-spreading shrub.
'Tuscan Blue'—Clear blue flowers, light green rather broad leaves on an erect shrub.
I have grown the plant in my Georgia garden and no winter injury has been observed at 15°F. However, in Massachusetts the plant winter-killed at -5 to -10°F. Excellent garden plant because of foliage color and fragrance. Use the better blue flowered forms. Have seen it used in containers and other places where it can cascade. The aromatic leaves are employed in cooking, sachets, etc. Easily rooted from cuttings about any time of year with a rooting hormone; the rooting medium should not be excessively moist. Southern Europe, Asia Minor. Cultivated for centuries. Zone 6 to 8(9).

Ruscus aculeatus — Butcher's Broom
(rus'kus ä-kū-lē-ā'tus)

FAMILY: Liliaceae
LEAVES: Actually not really leaves but modified stems called cladodes, evergreen, ovate, 3/4 to 1 1/2" long, 1/4 to 3/4" wide, dark green, slightly glossy on both sides, tapering at the apex to a slender stiff spine.
STEMS: Grooved, dark olive-green, glabrous.

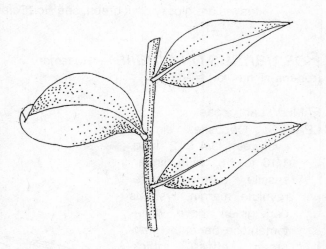

Ruscus aculeatus, Butcher's Broom, is an unusual plant that can be used in deep shady corners of the garden where few plants will thrive. It forms a neat, 1 1/2 to 3' high mound of rather erect, rigid stems. The plant tends to sucker and will gradually form a rather good-size colony. The dull white, 1/4" diameter flowers (March-April) are borne in the center of the cladode and make a curious sight. Plants are dioecious and male and female must be present if fruit set is to occur. The oblong fruits (berry) are bright red, about 1/2" long and borne in the center of the cladode. They ripen in September-October and persist into the following spring. Fruits are genuinely handsome and appear as small red cherries studding the branches. This species, although not spectacular, does quite well in Zone 8. One particular plant on campus was literally smothered by shade but nonetheless maintained a rather dense and healthy constitution. The plant is quite prickly. It is frequently dried, dyed red, and sold for Christmas decorations. Apparently bisexual forms are in commerce. Europe, northern Africa and the Near East. Cultivated before 1750. Zone 8 to 9.

Salix alba — White Willow
(sā′liks al′bà)

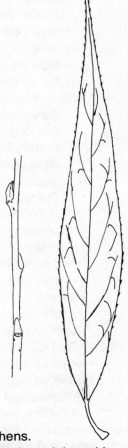

FAMILY: Salicaceae

LEAVES: Alternate, simple, lanceolate, 1 1/2 to 4″ long, 1/4 to 5/8″ wide, acuminate, cuneate, serrulate, bright green above, glaucous and silky beneath; petiole 1/4 to 1/2″ long, with small glands; stipules—lanceolate.

BUDS: Terminal—absent, laterals about 1/4″ long, oblong, rounded at apex, smooth, more or less silky-downy, flattened and appressed against stem, a single bud scale visible, rounded on back, flattened toward the twig, yellow to yellowish brown.

STEM: Rather slender, light yellow-green, smooth and shining or dull with more or less dense covering of fine silky hairs, bitter to taste.

SIZE: 75 to 100′ in height with a spread of 50 to 100′.

HARDINESS: Zone 2 to 8 or 9.

HABIT: Large, low branching tree with long branches and flexible stems forming a broad, open, round-topped crown.

RATE: Extremely fast, 3 to 4′/year over a 20-year-period.

TEXTURE: Fine in leaf, medium in winter.

BARK: Yellowish brown to brown, somewhat corky, ridged and furrowed; there is a beautiful specimen at Smith College Botanic Garden, Northampton, Massachusetts, with a distinctly corky-textured bark, the correct identity of the Smith tree may be *S.* × *chrysocoma*.

LEAF COLOR: Bright green above, glaucous green beneath (silvery) in summer; may turn excellent golden yellow in fall, often variable; willows are one of the first plants to leaf out in spring and the last to drop their leaves in the fall; have seen new leaves by late February and old leaves into early January in Athens.

FLOWERS: Dioecious, entomophilous and also anemophilous; male and female borne in upright catkins; the males are quite showy and represent the "Pussy" willow character which is familiar to everyone; most are insect pollinated.

FRUIT: Two-valved capsule containing a number of cottony or silky hairy seeds.

CULTURE: Easily transplanted because of fibrous, spreading, suckering root system; prefer moist soils and are frequently found along streams, ponds, rivers and other moist areas; full sun; pH adaptable but do not like shallow, chalky soils; prune in summer or fall.

DISEASES AND INSECTS: Willows like poplars are afflicted by numerous problems such as bacterial twig blight, crown gall, leaf blight, black canker, cytospora canker, many other cankers, gray scab, leaf spots, powdery mildew, rust, tar spot, aphids, imported willow leaf beetle, pine cone gall, basket willow gall, willow lace bug, willow flea weevil, mottled willow borer, willow shoot sawfly, willow scurfy scale and other selected insects.

LANDSCAPE VALUE: One of the best upright willows for landscape use; good for moist, wet places where little else will grow; wood is actually tougher than *Populus* but still very susceptible to ice and wind storms; tends to be a dirty street tree as do all willows because leaves, twigs, branches and the like are constantly dropping throughout the season.

CULTIVARS:

f. *argentea* ('Sericea')—Leaves with an intense silvery hue; I saw many willows in The Netherlands and Germany that had the silvery leaf color; apparently this form occurs occasionally in the wild where it is usually of dwarf habit, both surfaces are covered with silvery pubescence, saw 40 to 60′ high trees in Germany.

'Britzensis' ('Chermesina')—First year stems reddish, must be cut back heavily for good stem color only occurs on young stems, male; the literature is really confusing and contradictory with one reference noting that 'Britzensis' is a distinct cultivar, another saying 'Chermesina' and

'Britzensis' are the same; 'Britzensis' as I have seen it has more orange-red stems and then only on the new growth of the season, it must be pruned or pollarded to encourage the extension shoots that color so vibrantly during winter; grown by the German nurseryman Späth at Britz, near Berlin.

'Caerulea'—Only mentioned because it is used for making cricket bats; the leaves are green above, bluish gray below, a female, will grow 80 to 100', pyramidal and erect branching compared to the species.

'Tristis'—Called the Golden Weeping Willow and certainly one of the hardiest and most beautiful of the weeping types; sometimes listed as *S. vitellina* var. *pendula* and *S. alba* 'Niobe' in the trade; this form is also listed as *S.* × *chrysocoma* or *S.* 'Chrysocoma'; a hybrid between *S. alba* and *S. babylonica;* this is essentially the standard weeping willow and has largely supplanted the other weeping types in gardens; will grow 50 to 70'(80') and produce a broad canopy of graceful golden weeping branches. 'Tristis' is an enigmatic species with confusing botanical background. The typical tree as I have seen it throughout the U.S. is immense with large stout ascending (45 to 60° angle) branches with secondary branches steeply pendulous and often sweeping the ground, the whole tree rather dignified and majestic; for point of reference the flowers are male or female on the same or separate branches, or female flowers occupying the terminal part of the catkin, or with bisexual (perfect) flowers; the botanical uncertainties swept aside, it is a handsome tree but can suffer severe breakage and is likely to drop limbs at the drop of a hat.

'Vitellina' (var. *vitellina*)—Bright yellow stems, almost egg-yoke yellow, must be cut back like 'Britzensis', apparently several clones with the characteristics enumerated belong here.

'Vitellina Tristis'—Semi-pendulous form of the above, in commerce before 1815.

PROPAGATION: Seeds have no dormancy and germinate within 12 to 24 hours after falling on moist or wet sand; there is no dormancy known in any species; all willows are easily propagated by soft or hardwood cuttings at anytime of the year; just collect the cuttings and stick them; the stems have preformed root initials.

A "willow rooting substance" that is quite effective in promoting rooting of difficult-to-root plants especially when used in combination with IBA has been described; the young willow stems are cut into small pieces, steeped in water; the cuttings to be rooted are then placed in the extract and allowed to absorb for a period of time; IBA may also be applied in conjunction with the willow extract.

NATIVE HABITAT: Central to southern europe to western Siberia and central Asia. Naturalized in North America. Long Cultivated.

RELATED SPECIES: The willows are not extensively treated in this text. There are about 250 species generally confined to the northern hemisphere and about 75 species grow in North America. They hybridize freely and it is often difficult to distinguish hybrids from species. Bean and Krüssmann offer excellent treatments of *Salix* and should be consulted. Santamour and McArdle, *J. Arbor.* 14(7): 180-184 (1988) attempt to delineate the various weeping types. I considered following their lead but am not convinced that anyone has a solid grasp on *Salix* nomenclature. Their paper is worth reading. The following are used in landscaping to one degree or another but are not enthusiastically recommended by this author.

Salix babylonica — Babylon Weeping Willow
(sā'liks bab-i-lon'i-ka)

LEAVES: Alternate, simple, lanceolate to linear-lanceolate, 3 to 6" long, 1/2 to 3/4" wide, acuminate, cuneate, serrulate, light green above, grayish green beneath, with distinct venation, glabrous; petiole 1/5" long, stipules rarely developed, ovate-lanceolate.

STEM: Long, pendulous, glabrous except at nodes, brown, on upper surface reddish brown and *never* yellow as in *S. alba* 'Tristis'.

Salix babylonica, Babylon Weeping Willow, grows 30 to 40′ with a comparable spread; a very graceful, refined tree with a short, stout trunk and a broad, rounded crown of weeping branches which sweep the ground; true *S. babylonica* is an enigma and appears almost to be a plant of the past. In European countries and the U.S., it is almost nowhere to be found. In fact, trees that I have seen labeled as *S. babylonica* were usually something else. The normal form is a female. 'Crispa' ('Annularis') is a cultivar with spirally curled leaves. I have read several historical renderings concerning this tree and am almost convinced it does not exist in gardens except in the minds of those who wish to associate it with the hanging gardens of Babylon and the tree described therein was *Populus euphratica.* Apparently, three different clones, maybe more, exist under this name. The bottom line translates to another weeping willow other than *S. babylonica.* Santamour and McArdle, *J. Arboriculture* 14(7): 180-184 (1988) propose the cultivar name 'Babylon' for the tree described above. Introduced 1730. China. Zone (5)6 to 8.

Salix × blanda, (sā′liks × blan′da), perhaps more correctly listed as 'Blanda', Wisconsin Weeping Willow, is a hybrid between *S. babylonica* and *S. fragilis* with increased hardiness (Zone 4). It is not truly weeping although the branches are somewhat pendulous. The leaves are glossy dark green, rather thick and bluntly toothed. There is some indication this may be a hybrid between *S. babylonica* and *S. pentandra.* This is a female clone. First described around 1867. To my knowledge not available in commerce in the U.S.

Salix caprea — Goat Willow
(sā′liks kap′rē-a)

LEAVES: Alternate, simple, broad-elliptic to oblong, 2 to 4″ long, 1 to 2 1/4″ wide, acute, rarely rounded at base, irregularly and slightly toothed or nearly entire, pubescent at first, finally glabrate, rugulose and dark green above, gray-pubescent beneath and reticulate; petiole 1/3 to 2/3″ long; stipules oblique-reniform, serrate.

BUDS: Stout at maturity, 1/4 to 1/2″ long, colored and clothed as the twigs, purplish brown.

STEM: Stout, yellowish brown to dark brown, pubescent to glabrescent.

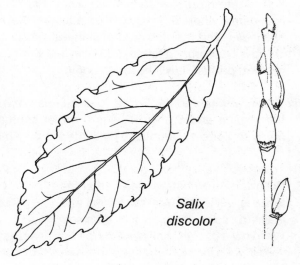

*Salix
discolor*

Salix caprea, Goat Willow, is an erect small tree growing 15 to 25′ with a 12 to 15′ spread; the only asset is the large (1 to 2″ long) male catkins which appear in March and early April and are affectionately referred to as Pussy Willows because of their silky softness. This species is often confused with *S. discolor,* the true Pussy Willow, which is native to wet areas over much of the eastern United States, but that species has deep brown branches and very glaucous (almost bluish white) lower leaf surface. *Salix discolor* is quite susceptible to canker and is considered inferior for landscape use although neither species is a plant of the first order. 'Pendula' ('Kilmarnock') is a handsome weeping form (female) that can be used as a ground cover or raised on a

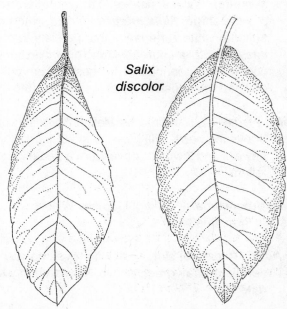

*Salix
discolor*

standard to produce a small weeping tree. This clone was discovered on the banks of the River Ayr before 1853 and was put into commerce by Thomas Lang of Kilmarnock, Ayrshire. There are two clones under the the above name; one female, the other male. The female is the most common form in cultivation in the U.S. *S. caprea* is adapted from Zone 4 to 8. Roy Lancaster named the female form 'Weeping Sally'. The cultivars are often grafted on a standard to produce a rather pretty small weeping tree. When not grafted or staked, the plant forms a large-trailing mound and serves almost a ground cover function.

Salix elaeagnos — Rosemary or Hoary Willow
(sā′liks el-ē-ag′nos)

LEAVES: Alternate, simple, linear to narrow lanceolate, 1/8 to 7/8″ wide, tapered at both ends, appearing narrower because of the revolute margins, finely serrate, rather lustrous dark green and glabrous above, covered with a white wool below; petiole—1/4″ long.

Salix elaeagnos, Rosemary or Hoary Willow, is a dense, medium sized shrub with long, linear, "Rosemary-like" leaves. The leaves are initially grayish and finally dark green above and whitish beneath. The stems are a distinct reddish brown. This is a handsome willow because of the pretty leaves and is recommended for wet areas where few other shrubs can be successfully grown. Mountains of central and southern Europe, Asia Minor. Zone 4 to 7. I first learned the plant as *S. rosmarinifolia* which is a fine name when one takes into account the similarity of the leaves to Rosemary, *Rosmarinus officinalis.* This is a fine garden plant with wispy gray-green foliage and a delicate texture. Ideally the shrub is best pruned to the ground in late winter to promote the long shoot growth. If not occasionally renewal pruned, it will become leggy.

Salix × elegantissima, (sā′liks × el-e-gan-tis′i-mȧ), Thurlow Weeping Willow, is a hybrid between *S. babylonica* and *S. fragilis.* It is a rather confusing entity and may represent several clones. it is hardy to Zone 4. Doubtfully cultivated in the United States.

Salix exigua, (sā′liks ex′i-gwa), Coyote Willow, of the western states offer intense silvery gray narrow leaves that maintain color through the summer. Will grow 10′ high. **Salix hastata** (sā′liks has-tā′tȧ) 'Wehrhahnii' presents silver gray male catkins that turn yellow when the stamens open, the leaves are fresh green, the habit bushy and spreading, 6′ by 12′. **Salix helvetica** (sā′liks hel-vet′i-kȧ) also offers silver-gray leaves and golden catkins on a 2′ high and 3′ wide shrub. **Salix integra** (sā′liks in-teg′rȧ) 'Albomaculata' produces salmon-pink new shoots aging to white variegation that persists through summer. Will grow 10′ high but is best cut back in late winter to encourage strong growth in spring and summer. All the willows listed above will require cool growing conditions for best foliage color/performance. I suspect in Zone 7 to 8 most would develop the consistency of a soggy potato chip.

Salix 'Flame'—Discovered by Melvin Bergeson of Fertile, MN. The habit is oval with a compact dense branching habit. Will grow 15 to 20′ high. Bark is orange-red in winter. The tips of the branches curl upward and inward. Leaves turn a beautiful golden yellow in fall, long after those of other trees have fallen.

Salix gracilistyla — Rosegold Pussy Willow
(sā′liks gras-il-is′til-ȧ)

LEAVES: Alternate, simple, oblong, oval, narrow ovate, 2 to 4″ long, 1/2 to 1 1/4″ wide, acute at ends, serrulate, gray-green above, grayish and pubescent below; petiole—1/4″ long, stipules—semicordate.

Salix gracilistyla, Rosegold Pussy Willow, is allied with *S. discolor* and *S. caprea* by virtue of being grown for its showy, 1 1/4″ long, male, pinkish or reddish tinged catkins produced in March-April. The catkins are quite attractive and there is much variation in the degree of pinkish or reddish suffusion of the gray catkins. It is lower growing (6 to 10′) than *S. caprea* and for this reason may be better suited to the small landscape. The leaves are grayish or bluish gray and offer a foliage contrast not available from many species. 'Variegata' is a rather pretty white margined form that will revert to the species. Raulston mentioned that the variegation only appears on strong shoots exposed to full sun; catkins are twice as long as the normal pussy willow grown in the nursery trade. Japan, Korea. Cultivated 1900. Zone 5 to 8.

Salix lanata — Woolly Willow
(sā′liks lȧ-nā′tȧ)

LEAVES: Alternate, simple, oval, roundish or obovate, 1 to 2 1/2″ long, 3/4 to 1 1/2″ wide, abruptly pointed, cuneate, although sometimes rounded or heart-shaped, entire or essentially so, silvery gray pubescence on both surfaces; petiole—1/8 to 1/4″ long, stipules 1/3″ long, ovate, entire, prominently veined.

Salix lanata, Woolly Willow, has *never* been seen by the author in a U.S. garden, but appears like privet in European gardens. It is a small, 2 to 4′ high and slightly wider shrub that offers wonderful gray foliage. Among the traditional green foliaged evergreens and deciduous shrubs it genuinely piques interest. The 1 to 2″ long, 1/2″ thick male catkins are bright golden and occur at the end of the previous season's growth. No doubt, it requires a cool climate and the heat and humidity of the midwest and southeast would prove disastrous. Another gray foliage type is 'Stuartii' which is probably a form of *S. lanata*. In my travels I have seen several handsome willows in Mr. Adrian Bloom's great garden at Bressingham that would be of interest to the intrepid willow-o-phile. *Salix cinerea* 'Tricolor' has young leaves that are mottled pink, white and creamy yellow. Plants should be cut back in winter to encourage new growth. Apparently variegation is lost during summer and another pruning to induce new shoots is warranted. Will grow 6 to 10′ high if not pruned. Northern Europe and Northern Asia. Cultivated 1789. Zone 3 to 5.

Salix matsudana — Hankow Willow
(sā′liks mat-sū-dā′nȧ)

LEAVES: Alternate, simple, linear-lan-ceolate, 2 to 4″ long, 1/3 to 3/5″ wide, long acuminate, rounded or rarely cuneate, sharply glandular serrate, bright green above, glaucous and glabrous below; petiole—1/4″ long.
STEM: Yellowish in youth, later olive-green to greenish brown, glabrous.

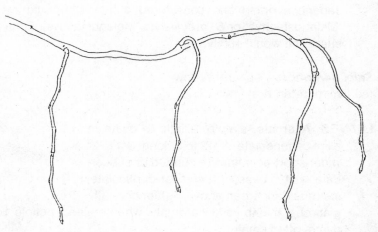

Salix matsudana, Hankow Willow, develops an oval-rounded head of fine textured branches. The emerging leaves are bright green, turn darker green and yellow-green in fall. The species is seldom encountered in the United States. It is closely allied with *S. babylonica* and differences are based on 2 nectaries in the female flower of *S. matsudana* compared to a single of *S. babylonica*. It is more drought tolerant than most willows and for that reason might be worth considering. The species matures between 40 and 50′. Several cultivars include:
'Golden Curls' is a hybrid between *S. alba* 'Tristis' and *S. matsudana* 'Tortuosa' that tends toward a shrubby nature although I have seen small trees. The golden stems have a slight tortuosity and semi-pendulous nature while the leaves are somewhat curled. This is a possibility for cut branches; Raulston predicted it might grow 40′ high and this is certainly possible considering

the parentage. Have seen 30′ by 15′ size categorization. Probably correctly listed as *S.* × *erythroflexuosa.* Apparently discovered in Argentina around 1971 and brought into the trade by Beardsley Nursery, Perry, OH. Zone 5 to 8.

'Navajo' (Globe Navajo Willow)—A large 20′ high round-topped tree that is tough and hardy. Apparently, this form is used in the southwestern United States. Same as 'Umbraculifera'?

'Pendula'—The branches are pendulous, the young branches green and the flowers female; a male pendulous form is also known.

'Scarlet Curls'—Probably has *S. matsudana* 'Tortuosa' as one parent and perhaps *S. alba* 'Britzensis' as the other. The stems are red (scarlet) in winter and the older branches golden brown. The leaves are curled somewhat like those of 'Golden Curls'. Will grow 30′ by 15 to 20′. Zone 5 to 8.

'Snake'—A great plant name, sure to inspire confidence in the buying public; not well known but supposedly an improved form of *S. m.* 'Tortuosa' with perhaps greater branch contortions and canker resistance.

'Tortuosa' (Dragon's Claw Willow)—At one time I looked upon this contorted stemmed tree with a habit similar to the species as a third class citizen but in recent years have come to appreciate the interesting architecture it brings to the winter landscape. The gray-brown branches are distinctly gnarled and contorted and make a great conversation piece. The tree may grow 50′ high but 20 to 30′ appears more typical. In a sense, the tree might be pruned heavily in youth like the Europeans pollard the bright red and yellow stemmed willows. The more vigorous shoots tend to have the greatest degree of contortions. Possibly this might be of use as a plant for the cut branch (florist) market. The fast growth is a distinct advantage over plants like *Corylus avellana* 'Contorta'. Unfortunately, in Zone 8 the tree is short lived. A female clone.

'Umbraculifera'—A bushy almost broad-rounded form without a central leader that will grow 25 to 35′ high; after 6 years in the Arnold Arboretum a plant was 20′ high and 30′ wide.

Salix melanostachys, (sā′liks mel-an-ō-stak′ē-ōs), Black Pussy Willow, is a 6 to 10′ shrub, the stems of which in winter assume a rich purple-black color. In spring the male catkins open a deep purple-black with brick red anthers and finally show yellow. It is an attractive and rather curious shrub. It is of Japanese origin and considered a hybrid. Should perhaps more correctly be listed as *Salix* 'Melanostachys' or *S. gracilistyla* 'Melanostachys'. Zone (4) 5 to 7. Have not seen it in Zone 8 but suspect it would survive.

Salix pentandra — Laurel Willow
(sā′liks pen-tan′drȧ)

LEAVES: Alternate, simple, elliptic to ovate to elliptic-lanceolate, 1 1/2 to 5″ long, 3/4 to 2″ wide, short-acuminate, rounded or subcordate at base, glandular-denticulate, lustrous dark green above, lighter beneath, glabrous, midrib yellow aromatic when bruised; petiole 1/4 to 1/2″ long, glandular; stipules oblong-ovate, often small.

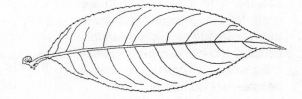

STEM: Lustrous, greenish brown, glabrous.

Salix pentandra, Laurel Willow, has the most handsome foliage of all the willows. The leaves are a lustrous, polished, shimmering dark green in summer; grows to 60′ but usually much less (30 to 35′) with a compact oval form. The few I have seen in central Illinois were so infested with leaf disease that by August there were no leaves on the tree. Where leaf diseases do not present a problem it could be an interesting specimen. Native to Europe. Often listed as hardy in Zone 2 and probably best in 2 to 5. Long cultivated.

Salix 'Prairie Cascade'—Originated at the Morden Research Station in Canada. Apparently a hybrid between *S. pentandra* and *S.* 'Blanda' with hardiness and glossy green foliage of *S. pentandra* and weeping habit and stem color of the weeping willow. Will grow 35 to 45′ high and wide. Zone 3 to 5(6).

Salix purpurea — Purpleosier Willow
(sā′liks pĕr-pū′rē-á)

LEAVES: Alternate or occasionally opposite, simple, oblanceolate, rarely oblong-obovate, 2 to 4″ long, 1/8 to 1/3″ wide, acute or acuminate, cuneate, serrulate toward the apex, lustrous dark blue-green above, pale or glaucous beneath, glabrous or slightly pubescent at first, turning black upon drying; petiole 1/6 to 1/3″ long; stipules small or wanting.
BUDS: Small, appressed, purplish, glabrous.
STEM: Slender tough branches, purplish at first, finally light gray or olive-gray, glabrous.

Salix purpurea, Purpleosier Willow, is a rounded, dense, finely branched shrub, 8 to 10′ (18′) high. Can look horrendous unless properly maintained. When specimens become overgrown it is best to cut them to the ground. The long shoots are supple and with the fine-textured leaves can be rather attractive. Good plant for wet areas especially to stabilize banks along streams or ponds. The stems are used in basket making. 'Nana' is a compact form usually less than 5′ high and wide with blue-green leaves; often called 'Artic Blue Leaf' Willow. 'Pendula' is a more or less wide-spreading weeping form that is often grafted on a standard; makes a rather attractive plant when used in this manner. 'Streamco' is a Soil Conservation Service, USDA introduction for stabilizing banks along waterways. Grows 12 to 15′ by 10 to 12′ and suckers and layers producing dense mats that resist erosion. Native to Europe, northern Africa to central Asia and Japan. Long cultivated. Zone 3 to 6(7).

Salix sachalinensis 'Sekka'
(sā′liks sa-ká-len-en′sis sē′kā)

LEAVES: Alternate, simple, lanceolate, 4 to 6″ long, 3/4″ wide, acuminate, cuneate, serrate, lustrous dark green above, glabrous; petiole—1/2 to 1″ long.
BUDS: Purplish red.
STEM: Reddish purple when exposed to the sun, lustrous, glabrous.

Salix sachalinensis 'Sekka', Japanese Fantail Willow, is a large broad-rounded shrub or small tree with uniquely twisted branches that are sometimes flat. The species is native to Japan. Introduced 1905. Zone 4 to 7. It grows 10 to 15′ high and forms a wide spreading shrub. It is a male clone. The branches are sometimes used for flower arranging.
ADDITIONAL NOTES: The use of any willow should be tempered with the knowledge that serious problems do exist. Many are short-lived and require much maintenance to keep them presentable. All are fast growing and somewhat weak wooded. The weeping willows do add a light, graceful touch around ponds and streams. Extract of willow bark is one of the precursors of aspirin.

Sambucus canadensis — American Elder
(sam-bū′kus kan-á-den′sis)

FAMILY: Caprifoliaceae
LEAVES: Opposite, compound pinnate, usually 7 leaflets, each 2 to 6″ long, 1/2 to 2 1/2″ wide, short stalked, elliptic to lanceolate. acuminate, sharply serrate, bright green, slightly puberulous on the veins beneath or nearly glabrous; lowest pair of leaflets frequently 2 or 3-lobed.
BUDS: Solitary or multiple, terminal mostly lacking, brown, few-scaled, small, 1/8″ long.
STEM: Stout, pale yellowish gray, heavily lenticellate, glabrous; pith—white; leaf scars broadly crescent-shaped or 3- or 4-sided, large, more or less transversely connected.

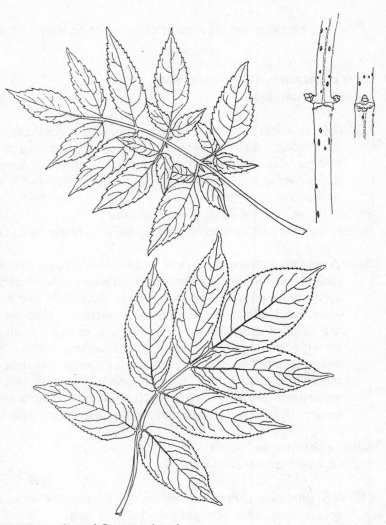

SIZE: 5 to 12', quite variable in size, varies significantly with habitat.

HARDINESS: Zone 3 to 9.

HABIT: Stoloniferous, multistemmed shrub, often broad and rounded with branches spreading and arching.

RATE: Fast.

TEXTURE: Medium in foliage (usually quite dense); very coarse in winter.

LEAF COLOR: Bright green in summer, leafs out early in spring; fall color is generally an insignificant yellow-green.

FLOWERS: Perfect, white, actually more yellow-white due to stamens, June-July, borne in 5-rayed, slightly convex, 6 to 10″ wide, flat-topped cymes; usually quite profuse and covering the entire plant; in the Orlando, FL area I saw the plant in flower in March and November and wondered whether it was some mysterious species; it checked out to *S. canadensis* and apparently flowers out of synchronization with the usual June-July sequence so common in Zone 4 to 7(8), have seen it listed as *S. simpsonii* in a Florida reference book but the plant looks like nothing more than a southern extension of *S. canadensis*.

FRUIT: Purple-black, August-September, berry-like, about 1/4″ in diameter.

CULTURE: Transplants well, does best in moist soils although will tolerate dry soils; thrives under acid or alkaline conditions; suckers profusely and requires constant attention if it is to be kept in presentable, decent condition.

DISEASES AND INSECTS: Borers, cankers, leaf spots, powdery mildew.

LANDSCAPE VALUE: Fruit is good for jellies, wine and attracting birds; difficult to utilize in home landscape situations because of its unkempt habit; potential near wet areas, naturalizing effect, roadside plantings.

CULTIVARS:

'Acutiloba'—Leaflets very deeply divided, rather handsome plant, appears to be a weak grower, is nice for foliage effect.

'Adams'—Numerous fruits in large clusters, excellent for jams, pies and wine, selected by William M. Adams of Union Springs, NY.

'Aurea'—Cherry red fruit, broad golden yellow leaves, grows vigorously and looks good throughout the growing season.

'Maxima'—Flower clusters 10 to 18″ in diameter, leaves 12 to 18″ long, rose-purple flower stalks, vigorous, may have 11 leaflets instead of the normal 7.

'Rubra'—A red fruited form, introduced before 1932 by A.P. Wezel, Smith College.

PROPAGATION: Seed, 60 days at 68°F plus 90 to 150 days at 41°F in moist sand. Cuttings, softwood root well; hardwood taken in late winter also root well.

NATIVE HABITAT: Nova Scotia and Manitoba to Florida and Texas. Introduced 1761. Found in damp, rich soil.

RELATED SPECIES:

Sambucus caerulea — Blueberry Elder
(sam-bū′kus ser-ū′lē-à)

LEAVES: Opposite, compound pinnate, 6 to 10″ long,
5 to 7(9) leaflets, 2 to 6″ long, 1/2 to 2″ wide,
coarsely serrate, bright green, glabrous.

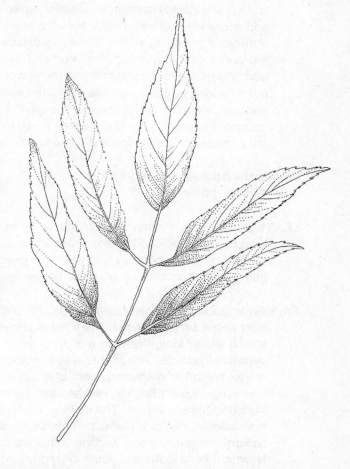

Sambucus caerulea, (*S. glauca*), Blueberry Elder, is
a large shrub or small tree often growing 15 to 30′
high and larger. Several years past, while jogging
on some back roads near Portland, OR, I noticed
the plant in abundance. This was August and the
dusty-coated, blue-black berries were dripping
from the plants. Fruits make good jam, jelly, pie
and wine. The yellowish white flowers occur in
convex, 5-rayed, 4 to 6″ wide cymes. Have not
seen on east coast but for an elder collector could
be worthwhile. British Columbia, east to Montana
and Utah. Cultivated 1850. Zone 5.

Sambucus nigra — Common or European Elder
(sam-bū′kus nī′grà)

LEAVES: Opposite, compound pinnate, 4 to 12″ long,
leaflets 3 to 7, usually 5, short-stalked, elliptic to
elliptic-ovate, 1 1/2 to 5″ long, 3/4 to 2″ wide,
acute, sharply serrate, dark green above, lighter and sparingly hairy on the veins beneath; of
disagreeable odor when bruised.

Sambucus nigra, European Elder, is a large multistemmed shrub or tree ranging from 10 to 20′ (30′) high.
The foliage is dark green in summer and of a disagreeable odor when bruised. Flowers are yellowish
white, of a heavy odor, and borne in 5 to 8″ diameter, 5-rayed, flat-topped cymes in June. The fruit is
lustrous black, 1/4″ diameter, September. There are numerous cultivars associated with this species
including white variegated, yellow-leaf,
purple-leaf, cutleaf, yellow fruited and
others. The Strybing Arboretum, San Francisco had several cultivars that were quite
handsome. I have observed the species all
over the British Isles and continental
Europe growing along roadsides, in ditches
and in open fields. Apparently it deserves
the same weed status as *S. canadensis.* A
few of the cultivars are worth mentioning.
'Aurea' offers bright yellow new foliage that
fades with time and heat. 'Laciniata' (f.
laciniata) presents finely dissected green
leaflets not unlike those of *Acer palmatum*
var. *dissectum* 'Filigree Lace'. A wonderfully fine textured shrub that attracts considerable attention from members of our
European garden tours. In 'Marginata' the

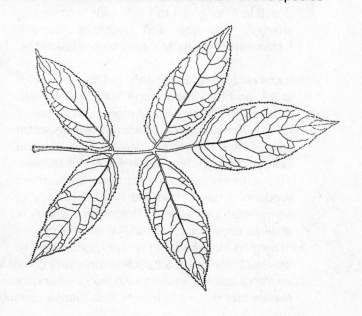

leaflets are initially margined yellowish white, fading to creamy white. This is a most handsome form and probably requires heavy root moisture and partial shade in the eastern-southeastern U.S. 'Aureomarginiata' is akin to the above except the leaflets are bordered with a yellow-golden border. 'Purpurea' probably should be listed as f. *purpurea* since several purple leaf forms are known. The new shoots are bronze-purple and the flower petals are pinkish. The color does not hold well in heat but for spring effect is worthwhile. All the above except 'Laciniata' are best cut back in late winter to encourage strong, highly colored shoots. For shrub borders, they offer a different touch. I have seen abundant aphids on the Black Elder, much more so than on *S. canadensis.* Spider mites and aphids are particularly troublesome in hot weather. Europe, northern Africa, western Asia. Zone 5 to 6(7).

Sambucus pubens — Scarlet Elder
(sam-bū′kus pū′benz)

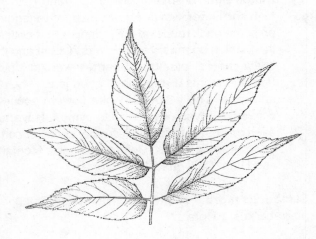

LEAVES: Opposite, compound pinnate, 5 to 7 leaflets, ovate-oblong to oblong-lanceolate, 2 to 4″ long, stalked, serrate, lustrous dark green, pubescent or sometimes glabrous below.

Sambucus pubens, Scarlet Elder, grows 12 to 25′ high with a similar spread. The flowers are yellowish white, May, borne in a 5″ long ovoid to pyramidal panicle. The fruit is a red or scarlet drupe, 1/5 to 1/4″ diameter, ripening in late June into July, quite effective. White and yellow-fruited forms are known. The cultivar 'Dissecta' has deeply divided leaflets. The buds are solitary, 4-scaled, brown and the stems are light brown with a brown pith. Found in rocky woods from Newfoundland to Alaska, south to Georgia and Colorado. Handsome plant in fruit and certainly worth leaving if native. Introduced 1812. Zone 4 to 6. It is closely allied to *S. racemosa.*

Sambucus racemosa — European Red Elder
(sam-bū′kus ra-se-mō′sà)

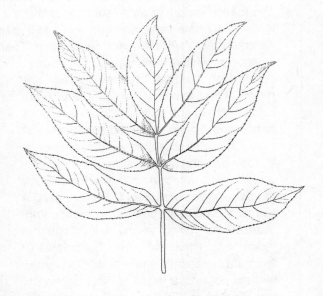

LEAVES: Opposite, compound pinnate, 6 to 9″ long, 5 to 7 leaflets, ovate or elliptic to ovate-lanceolate, 2 to 4″ long, 3/4 to 1 3/4″ wide, acuminate, sharply, coarsely and regularly serrate, lustrous dark green, glabrous on both surfaces.

Sambucus racemosa, European Red Elder, grows 8 to 12′ and has flowers and fruits similar to *S. pubens,* the fruits usually more tightly packed on the infructescence. 'Redman' is a selection with finely dissected leaves. 'Sutherland Golden' has golden yellow finely cut leaflets. This appears to be a good plant for northern gardens. I have observed it at University of Minnesota Landscape Arboretum where it showed good vigor. 'Tenuifolia' forms a mound of arching branches with finely divided, fern-like leaves. This, too, is a beautiful form but I do not know its adaptability to hot, dry conditions. It is not a strong grower. 'Plumosa Aurea' is a handsome form with finely cut leaflets and bright yellow new leaves that mature to green. This form is common in Europe and is frequently cut to the ground in late winter to encourage vigorous shoots. Interestingly, I saw the plant in June at Sissinghurst and it literally jumped out and grabbed me. On a September visit, I had trouble locating the same plant; the yellow coloration had completely dissipated. 'Plumosa' is described with large leaflets up to 5″ long by 1 1/4″ wide and the serrations reaching half way to the midvein. This is a green leaf form. A recent introduction is 'Golden Locks' from Canada, a dwarf form with golden foliage. Native to Europe, western Asia. Cultivated 1596. Zone 3 to 6 or 7.

Santolina chamaecyparissus — Lavender Cotton
(san-tō-lī′nȧ kam-e-sip-âr-is′us)

FAMILY: Asteraceae
LEAVES: Alternate, pinnate, evergreen, 1/2 to 1 1/2″ long, 1/8″ or less wide, with short-oblong-obtuse, 1/24 to 1/12″ long segments, whitish tomentose; strong aromatic odor when bruised; easily identified by virtue of subshrub nature and silvery gray-green foliage.

SIZE: 1 to 2′ high, spread 2 to 4′.
HARDINESS: Zone 6 to 9.
HABIT: Evergreen subshrub forming a broad mound; almost cushion-like when properly grown.
RATE: Slow.
TEXTURE: Fine.
LEAF COLOR: Silvery gray-green through the seasons, a bit off color in winter.
FLOWERS: Perfect, button-shaped, 1/2 to 3/4″ diameter, yellow heads cover the plant like lollipops; usually in June-August; borne on 4 to 6″ long stalks above the foliage; quite showy but should be removed after they fade; no ray florets present.
FRUIT: Achene, not important.
CULTURE: Transplants readily; adaptable but prefers relatively dry, low fertility soils; will grow in pure sand; in excessively fertile soils becomes rank and open; full sun; prune after flowering or just about anytime during growing season to shape the plant; displays some salt tolerance.
LANDSCAPE VALUE: Quite a tough plant; have observed it used in a multiplicity of sites from pure sand on Cape Cod to heavy clay in Illinois; excellent in mass or for low hedge or border; works well in rock walls or rock gardens; have grown this along with *S. virens* in Urbana, Illinois and the Green Santolina did not prove as cold hardy; both are beautiful and elicit a positive response from the public.
CULTIVARS:
var. *nana*—Forms a low (1 to 1 1/2′), dense, more compact mound than the species.
PROPAGATION: Seeds germinate readily; cuttings can be rooted about anytime; very important to keep medium on the dry side; too much moisture spells failure.
NATIVE HABITAT: Southern Europe. Cultivated 1596.

RELATED SPECIES:

Santolina virens, (san-tō-lī′nȧ vī′renz), Green Santolina, is essentially a "dead ringer" for the above species except for the deep green, glabrous foliage and slightly more compact growth habit. Leaves are a degree longer (to 2″). The bright yellow, 3/4″ diameter flowers borne on 6 to 10″ long stalks are highlighted against the rich green foliage during July. Can be used in the same fashion as *S. chamaecyparissus.* Southern Europe. Cultivated 1727. Zone 7 to 8(9); not as hardy as *S. chamaecyparissus,* requires same cultural manipulations. I have grown this a number of years and generally cut it back after flowering when it tends to open up and become floppy. 'Primrose Gem' is listed with pale primrose-yellow flowers.

Sapindus drummondii — Western Soapberry
(sap'in-dus drum-mon'dē-ī)

FAMILY: Sapindaceae

LEAVES: Alternate, compound and even pinnate, 10 to 15" long, 8 to 18 leaflets, each short stalked, obliquely lanceolate, 1 1/2 to 3 1/2" long, 1/2 to 1" wide, acuminate, entire, lustrous medium green, glabrous above, pubescent beneath, each leaflet slightly curved or sickle-shaped not unlike pecan; rachis has no margin (wing).

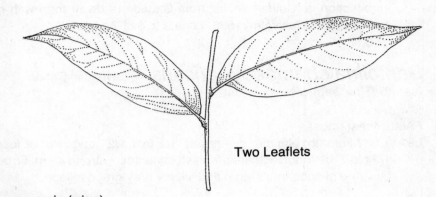

Two Leaflets

SIZE: 25 to 30' high with a similar spread, have seen 40 to 50' specimens.

HARDINESS: Zone 5 but best in Zone 6 to 9.

HABIT: Single-stemmed or low-branched tree with a broad-oval to rounded crown similar to *Koelreuteria paniculata;* makes a rather graceful small shade tree.

RATE: Medium.

TEXTURE: Medium.

BARK: Shallowly furrowed, develops platy or scaly condition, as these fall they create a patchwork of gray-brown, orange-brown to reddish brown.

LEAF COLOR: Glossy medium green in summer, deep yellow-gold in fall; excellent fall color.

FLOWERS: Yellowish white, about 1/5" across, borne in loose, 6 to 10" long, pubescent, terminal, pyramidal panicles in May to June; apparently there is an initial growth flush and with increasing day length the terminal portion turns reproductive.

FRUIT: Subglobose, 1/2" diameter, translucent yellow-orange drupe that ripens in October; remains on tree through winter and into spring but the flesh may turn black; the seeds are black, rounded, 1/4 to 1/3" wide, with one (sometimes 2 to 3) in each fruit; a single 30' high, 40' wide tree resides in Athens that sets prodigious quantities of fruit every year; *Sapindus drummondii* is supposedly unisexual and for argument's sake I know this one tree is female; the question then arises as to the source of pollen for effective fruit set unless fruiting is parthenocarpic; Rehder mentions that the genus, not this particular species, is polygamous, so it is possible that the Athens tree is polygamo-dioecious with sufficient pollen supplied by the polygamous flowers.

CULTURE: Easily transplanted, adaptable to varied soils and is native to infertile, dry soils throughout portions of the southwest; extremely tolerant of urban sites and should be utilized more widely; wood is close-grained and strong, making the tree very wind resistant; seedlings may be objectionable.

DISEASES AND INSECTS: None serious, appears trouble-free as leaves are as clean in October as when first emerging in spring.

LANDSCAPE VALUE: Excellent choice for dry soil areas in south and southwest; should be considered for use in urban situations; recommended as a shade and ornamental tree in dry areas of country; have reservations about recommending it for patio or street use because of the fruit litter; remember picking fruits off the ground in December at Missouri Botanical Garden; much better tree than *Melia azedarach.*

PROPAGATION: The seeds have been described as doubly dormant and two hours scarification in sulfuric acid followed by 90 days at 40°F is recommended. I collected seed, removed the fleshy fruit wall by soaking, followed by extraction in a blender; the seeds were then placed in moist peat in poly bags at 41°F. After 54 days radicles had emerged in cold stratification. At this time the seeds were planted and about 95 out of 100 germinated. Seeds that received no cold treatment were also sown but only

2 to 3 seedlings emerged. Another test was conducted and it became evident that 30 days was sufficient time to induce some radicles to emerge. Based on the work I estimate 45 to 60 days cold to be sufficient. No scarification is necessary. Cuttings have also been rooted when collected in May-June, treated with 16,000 ppm IBA talc preparation; takes 5 to 6 weeks for rooting. In Kansas work, early June cuttings rooted equally well with a 10,000 to 30,000 ppm treatment.

ADDITIONAL NOTES: Generic name is derived from the nature of the fruits. When crushed in water they develop a lather. The West Indian natives used the saponin-rich fruits of *S. saponaria* as a soap substitute.

NATIVE HABITAT: Southern Missouri, Kansas, New Mexico, and Arizona to Louisiana, Texas and northern Mexico. Cultivated 1900.

Sapium sebiferum — Chinese Tallow Tree, Popcorn Tree
(sā′pi-um se-bif′er-um)

FAMILY: Euphorbiaceae

LEAVES: Alternate, simple, broadly rhombic-ovate or suborbicular, 1 1/2 to 3″ long and broad, abruptly acuminate, entire, glabrous, broad-cuneate, medium green; petiole—1 to 2″ long, slender, with 2 glands on petiole at junction of blade.

BUDS: Small, appressed, brownish.

STEM: Wispy, green, finally brown, glabrous, glaucous, dotted with small brownish lenticels.

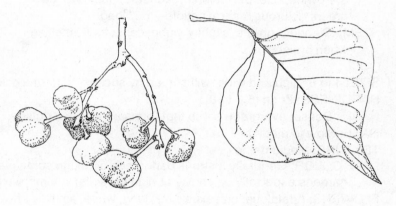

Sapium sebiferum, Chinese Tallow Tree, is seldom seen in the Piedmont area of Georgia but becomes almost pestiferous in the Coastal Plain from South Carolina to Florida and Louisiana. The medium green leaves are shaped much like a poplar and the first impulse is to relate this tree to that genus. The leaves emerge later in spring than most deciduous trees. The leaves turn reddish purple in the fall. Fall color in the Athens area has been disappointing for seldom do all the leaves color at the same time; leaves toward the interior color first with a progression toward the periphery; often yellow, orange-red and purple-red are intermingled on the same tree; some trees show limited coloration. Leaves fall by late October on the Georgia campus and are in full coloration in late December in Orlando, Florida. The gray bark is ridged and furrowed with the ridges becoming flattened. The yellow green 2 to 4″ long catkin-like flowers (male at apex, 1 to 5 females at base) are followed by brown, 1/2″ wide, 3-valved capsules which open to expose the white, oval, waxy seeds (October). The tree is known as "Popcorn Tree" because of the appearance of the seeds. The seeds are not messy but do persist into winter and eventually result in numerous seedlings where conditions permit. Chinese Tallow Tree is adaptable to moist, dry, acid, and alkaline soils but must be located in full sun. It is a *rapid* grower easily making 2 to 3′ and more a year especially in youth. The general shape is pyramidal-rounded and the canopy thin and airy. Grass can be grown up to the trunk. The ultimate height approximates 30 to 40′ (60′). Makes a good, but not long lived tree for fall color in the southern states. The milky sap is poisonous. The waxy coat on the seeds is extracted by the Chinese for use in soaps and candles; hence, the name tallow. It has also been suggested as a source of oil and one estimate I read said it could supply 5% of the U.S. oil needs. In our work, it became immediately evident that Chinese Tallow Tree was easy to propagate. I collected seeds with the white, waxy seed coat intact and directly sowed them. Within 4 weeks, most seeds had germinated. The seedlings exhibit tremendous vigor. I would speculate that because of the very rapid growth the species might have possibilities as a biomass source. The tree was injured at 0°F and -3°F during the 1981-82 and 83-84 winters, respectively. Plants tend to harden late and early fall freezes may result in injury. A

California reference listed 10 to 15°F as the breakpoint. Considerable deadwood was evident after the spring growth flush occurred. Will grow in Zone 7 but best in 8 to 10. China. Cultivated 1850. *Sapium japonicum* is similar except the female flowers occur singly on 1/2″ long pedicels, rather than in the cymose clusters like those of *S. sebiferum*. I have only seen the plant once and the fall color was a handsome reddish purple. Maybe a better tree than *S. sebiferum* for fall coloration but is proabably less cold hardy. China, Japan, Korea. Zone 9(?).

Sarcococca hookerana — Himalayan Sarcococca, Sweetbox
(sar-ko-kōk'a̠ hook-er-ā'na̠)

FAMILY: Buxaceae

LEAVES: Alternate, simple, evergreen, coriaceous, lance-oblong to narrow-lanceolate, 2 to 3 1/2″ long, 1/2 to 3/4″ wide, slender-pointed, cuneate, lustrous dark green, glabrous, entire; petiole—1/3″ long.

STEM: Slender, green, slightly pubescent, foul smelling when bruised.

SIZE: 4 to 6′ high and wide, will spread by suckers to form a colony.

HARDINESS: Zone (5)6 to 8.

HABIT: Dense, evergreen shrub that forms a mounded outline.

RATE: Slow to medium.

TEXTURE: Medium-fine.

LEAF COLOR: Generally lustrous dark green although some plants have lighter green foliage; in English gardens especially on chalky or high pH soils, in a more exposed location, foliage is lighter green.

FLOWERS: Apetalous, unisexual, 1/2″ long, white, actually off-white, fragrant, in the leaf axils, the female flowers below the male flowers, may open in fall but usually in March-April, essentially unnoticed as they occur under the foliage, only the sweet fragrance advertises their arrival.

FRUIT: Have only seen on a few plantings and suspect the species may be self sterile; globose, 1/4 to 1/3″ wide, shiny black drupe that persists into winter, not showy and literally visible only then the leaves are parted.

CULTURE: Transplant from containers into loose, acid, high organic matter, moist, well drained soils; will tolerate higher pH soils but does not appear as prosperous, partial shade to shade, will become off color in full sun; appears to tolerate polluted atmospheric conditions.

DISEASES AND INSECTS: None serious.

LANDSCAPE VALUE: Nowhere common but at its best a worthy evergreen ground cover that offers handsome foliage, and fragrant flowers; stoloniferous nature is not aggressive and can be kept in bounds; Longwood Gardens used it along a path above the rock garden with *Cornus florida* planted on either side, makes an excellent combination.

CULTIVARS: Variety *digyna* is more compact than *S. hookerana*, perhaps 3′ high and wide, at least plants I have seen, with greenish shoots and narrow-elliptic to oblong-lanceolate lustrous green leaves about 1 3/4 to 3 (4 1/2″) long, 1/2 to 1″ wide. The key difference is the presence of two styles (i.e. *digyna*) compared to 3 for the species; flowers are fragrant, plant is more hardy than *S. hookerana* but less hardy than var. *humilis*, it is easily rooted from cuttings as described below. Variety *humilis* is often treated as a separate species but current thinking provides varietal status. This is the best of the *Sarcococca* species for northern gardens because of cold hardiness; at -3°F this species was unfazed while *S. hookerana*, var. *digyna* and *S. confusa* were virtually defoliated in the piedmont of Georgia; var. *humilis* grows 18 to 24″ high, is stoloniferous, smaller in all its parts than *S. hookerana*, and is black fruited; native to western China. Introduced 1907. Zone 5 to 8.

PROPAGATION: Seeds will germinate without pretreatment. Cuttings of all species root readily. Have collected cuttings of variety *humilis* in November and February, 3000 ppm IBA-quick dip, peat:perlite, mist with 100% success. The root systems were profuse. Suspect cuttings can be rooted year round if stems are firm.

NATIVE HABITAT: Western Himalayas and Afghanistan. Cultivated 1884.

RELATED SPECIES:

Sarcococca confusa
(sar-ko-kōk'á con-fū'sá)

LEAVES: Alternate, simple, evergreen, 1 1/4 to 2″ long, 1/2 to 3/4″ wide, elliptic, elliptic-lanceolate to obovate, long acute to acuminate, obtuse to cuneate, lustrous green above, light green below; petiole—1/4″ long.

Sarcococca confusa forms a 3 to 5′ high and wide densely branched evergreen shrub. The flowers are sweetly scented and based on olfactory comparisons, are more fragrant than *S. hookerana*. They occur in late February-early March in Zone 8. The female flowers have either 2 or 3 stigmas. Fruits are glossy black. Where well grown this is a handsome plant but is considerably less cold hardy than var. *humilis* and should only be grown in Zone (7)8.

Sarcococca ruscifolia — Fragrant Sarcococca
(sar-ko-kōk'á rus-ki-fō'lē-á)

LEAVES: Alternate, simple, evergreen, ovate, 1 to 2 1/2″ long, half as wide, acuminate, rounded, perhaps cuneate, 3-nerved at base, glabrous, lustrous dark green above, lighter beneath; petiole—1/8 to 1/4″ long.

Sarcococca ruscifolia, Fragrant Sarcococca, is a 3′ high and wide shrub with handsome foliage and milk-white, fragrant flowers in the axils of the terminal leaves. There are consistently 3 stigmas. Fruits are rounded, red, 1/4″ diameter. A handsome plant but not sufficiently cold hardy for inclusion in gardens below Zone (7)8. Central and Western China. Variety *chinensis* has longer narrower leaves and is the common form in cultivation.

Sassafras albidum — Common Sassafras
(sas'á-fras al'bi-dum)

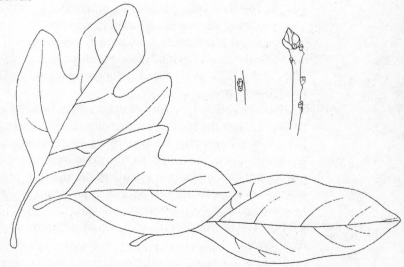

FAMILY: Lauraceae

LEAVES: Alternate, simple, ovate to elliptic, 3 to 7″ long, 2 to 4″ wide, acutish or obtuse, cuneate at base, bright green above, glabrous and glaucous beneath, entire, mitten-shaped or three lobed; mittens occur in left and right hand models; petiole 1/2 to 1 1/2″ long.

BUDS: Terminal, solitary, ovoid, sessile, about 4 to 6 exposed scales, green-tinged with red toward tip, 1/3″ long; lateral buds small, divergent, green; terminal is the flower bud.

STEM: Bright yellowish green, often reddish where exposed to light, glabrous and glaucous; spicy-aromatic to both smell and taste; sympodial branching.

SIZE: 30 to 60′ in height with a spread of 25 to 40′, can grow larger.

HARDINESS: Zone 4 to 9.

HABIT: Pyramidal, irregular tree or shrub in youth, with many short, stout, contorted branches which spread to form a flat topped, irregular, round-oblong head at maturity; often sprouting from roots and forming extensive thickets.

RATE: Medium to fast, 10 to 12′ over a 5 to 8 year period.

TEXTURE: Medium in all seasons, very intriguing winter silhouette results from the sympodial branching habit.

BARK: Dark reddish brown, deeply ridged and furrowed, forming flat corky ridges that are easily cut across with a knife; bark almost a mahogany-brown, handsome when mature.

LEAF COLOR: Bright to medium green in summer changing to shades of yellow to deep orange to scarlet and purple in fall; one of our most outstanding native trees for fall color; a sassafras thicket in October is unrivaled.

FLOWERS: Usually dioecious, yellow, weakly fragrant, developing before the leaves in April (late March, Athens), borne in terminal racemes, 1 to 2″ long, apetalous, calyx about 3/8″ long and wide, with 6 narrowly oblong lobes, 9 stamens in male; 6 and aborted in the female; flowers are actually quite handsome and can be readily distinguished in the early spring landscape.

FRUIT: Drupe, 1/2″ long, dark blue, ripening in September but quickly falling or devoured by birds; the fruit stalk (pedicel) is scarlet and very attractive at close range; many people think the pedicel is the fruit.

CULTURE: Move balled and burlapped in early spring into moist, loamy, acid, well drained soil; have observed chlorosis in high pH soils; full sun or light shade; in the wild often found in acid, rocky soil; has a strong tendency to invade abandoned fields and form dense thickets; as a pioneer tree it is somewhat intolerant and gives way to other species after a time; prune in winter; it is difficult to establish (transplant) from the wild because of the deep tap root and the few spreading, lateral roots; could possibly be container grown and thus many of the transplanting problems would be alleviated; if a single trunked tree is desired be sure to remove the suckers (shoots) that develop.

DISEASES AND INSECTS: Cankers, leaf spots, mildew, wilt, root rot, Japanese beetle, promethea moth, sassafras weevil and scales have been reported. Sassafras has appeared remarkably free of problems except for occasional iron chlorosis.

LANDSCAPE VALUE: Excellent for naturalized plantings, roadsides, and home landscaping; with a little extra cultural effort one will be rewarded many fold.

CULTIVARS:

   var. *molle*—The young branches and under surface of the leaf are downy, called Silky Sassafras; in my mind somewhat difficult to separate from the species; occurs throughout the range of the species but is more prevalent in the south.

PROPAGATION: Seeds exhibit strong embryo dormancy which can be overcome with moist stratification at 41°F for 120 days. Root cuttings collected in December and placed in 2:1:1; peat:loam:sand produced plants.

ADDITIONAL NOTES: The bark of the roots is used to make sassafras tea and the "oil of sassafras" is extracted from the roots. Some concern that the extract from *Sassafras* is carcinogenic, but then what isn't, since living can be construed as dangerous to one's health. Interestingly, many medicinal attributes were attributed to the species. In Rockville, IN, an October festival offers numerous concoctions of sassafras including candy, tea, bread, et al. Certainly a great native plant and on numerous back roads throughout the eastern United States there is no more inspiring sight than a sassafras thicket in full flaming fall color.

NATIVE HABITAT: Along with var. *molle* distributed from Maine to Ontario and Michigan, south to Florida and Texas.

Sciadopitys verticillata — Umbrella-pine or Japanese Umbrella-pine
(sī-à-dop′it-is vẽr-ti-si-lā′tà)

FAMILY: Pinaceae

LEAVES: Of 2 kinds, some small and scale-like scattered on the shoot, but crowded at its end and bearing in their axils a whorl of 20 to 30 linear flat leaves, each 2 to 5″ long, 1/8″ wide, furrowed on each side, more deeply beneath with a glaucous-green groove, dark glossy green, thick, almost prehistoric in appearance; the way the needles radiate around the stem creates an "umbrella" effect.

STEM: At first green, later brown, glabrous, stout, flexible, striated, with prominent protuberances on stem.

BARK: Thin, nearly smooth, orangish to reddish brown, exfoliating in long strips, quite handsome but essentially hidden by the foliage.

SIZE: 20 to 30′ by 15 to 20′; can grow 60 to 90′ high.

HARDINESS: Zone 4 to 8, not as prosperous in Zone 8 as further north.

HABIT: Variable, from spirelike to broadly pyramidal tree in youth, with a straight stem and horizontal branches spreading in whorls, stiff and twiggy, the young branchlets with the leaves crowded at the ends; with age the branches become more pendulous and spreading and the whole habit loose; have also observed multiple-stemmed versions.

RATE: Slow, extremely slow, perhaps 6″ a year.

TEXTURE: Medium-coarse, one of the most interesting conifers for textural effect.

BARK: Rich orangish to reddish brown and exfoliating in long shreds or strips; handsome but generally unnoticed since hidden by foliage.

LEAF COLOR: Dark green and glossy above throughout the year, persisting about 3 years.

FLOWERS: Monoecious; female solitary, terminal and subtended by a small bract, male flowers in 1″ long racemes.

FRUIT: Cones oblong-ovate, upright, 2 to 4″ long, 1 to 2″ wide, scales with broad reflexed margins; cones are green at first, ripening to brown the second year, each scale bears 5 to 9 narrowly winged seeds.

CULTURE: Transplant balled and burlapped, prefers rich, moist, acid soils and sunny, open locations; late afternoon shade is advantageous in hot areas; protection from wind is desirable.

DISEASES AND INSECTS: None serious.

LANDSCAPE VALUE: F.B. Robinson called it "a queer tree of odd texture; can be used as an accent or specimen."; L.H. Bailey termed it "one of the most handsome and distinctive of conifers"; for foliage effect as well as texture this conifer ranks among the best; could be integrated into a foundation planting, rock garden or border; the plant will grow in Zone 8 but prefers light pine shade; its unusual texture makes it a valuable addition to the list of needled conifers.

CULTIVARS: Several forms are described in the literature but are not common in commerce, even from specialty producers.

    'Pendula'—Listed as a remarkable tree with pendulous branches; have not seen it but would like to secure a plant.

PROPAGATION: Either warm stratification for 100 days in moist sand at 63 to 70°F or cold for 90 days in moist, acid peat at 32 to 50°F have been recommended for inducing prompt germination. A combination of the two may be more effective. Seedlings kind of sit there for a while and look at you before deciding to "grow up". Cuttings taken in January rooted 92% in sand:peat in 20 weeks after treatment with 100 ppm NAA for 24 hours. Cuttings from 7-year-old trees collected in January and treated with 20 ppm IBA rooted 70% in 8 months. In 32 weeks there was 43% rooting of untreated cuttings taken in August. See Waxman, *PIPPS.* 28:546–550 (1978) for a detailed report on cutting propagation. In brief, Dr. Waxman noticed tremendous tree-to-tree rooting variability. The best rooting occurred when the cuttings were immersed in water and allowed to soak. There appeared to be a correlation between the amount of resin and rootability. Low resin correlated with high rooting. Hormones did not prove that critical. February-March and July-August were the best times.

NATIVE HABITAT: Restricted in a wild state to the Valley of the Kiso-gawa in central Hondo, and to Koya-san and its immediate neighborhood in east central Hondo; the best trees being found in steep, rocky, sheltered situations. Introduced 1861.

Securinega suffruticosa
(se-cūr-in-ē′gȧ su-frū-ti-kō′sȧ)

FAMILY: Euphorbiaceae
LEAVES: Alternate, simple, elliptic or ovate to lance-ovate, 3/4 to 2″ long, 1/3 to 1″ wide, acute or obtuse, cuneate, entire, bright yellowish green, glabrous, petiole—1/8″ long.

Securinega suffruticosa is a virtual unknown in American gardening and probably will remain buried in anonymity. I first saw the plant at the Missouri Botanic Garden, St. Louis, and was taken by the fresh green foliage and upright arching branches and rather dense constitution. For use as a foliage mass, it has possibilities. The plant can be pruned in late winter to entice long shoot extensions. The greenish white flowers (July-August) and greenish capsules are not showy. Any well-drained soil and full sun suit it best. Northeast Asia to central China. Introduced 1783. Zone 5 to 7(8).

Sequoia sempervirens — Redwood
(sē-kwoi′ȧ sem-pēr-vī′renz)

FAMILY: Taxodiaceae
LEAVES: Evergreen needles spirally arranged on the terminal leader, about 1/4″ long, slightly appressed to spreading, 2 ranked on the lateral shoots, 1/4 to 7/8″ long, 1/20 to 1/8″ wide, with an abrupt point, lustrous dark green, almost bluish green above with two broad whitish stomatal bands below.

SIZE: Difficult to ascertain under landscape conditions on east coast, perhaps 40 to 60′; in west 300′; 378′ is the tallest tree on record.
HARDINESS: Zone 7 to 9.
HABIT: Imposing conifer, densely branched and gracefully pyramidal in youth, with time losing the lower branches and devoid of branches 50 to 100′ from the ground with a still relatively narrow pyramidal crown.
RATE: Slow to medium in east, fast in west.
TEXTURE: Medium.
BARK: Exquisite on old trees being a rich red-brown and fibrous on the surface, with deep furrows and irregular ridges; I saw mature redwoods in Muir Woods, north of San Francisco, and walking in the shadows of these behemoths provided pause for reflection on man's coming and going; a living legacy that has held court over 30 generations of mankind and has never passed a negative verdict; yet man has attempted, albeit sometimes unintentionally, to destroy what is beyond his realm of reasoning or appreciation.
LEAF COLOR: Dark green through the seasons, some forms show a distinct bluish green cast.
FLOWERS: Male flowers axillary and terminal with numerous spirally arranged stamens; female terminal with 15 to 20 peltate scales.
FRUIT: A 3/4 to 1″ long, somewhat egg-shaped brownish cone that ripens the first year; seeds reddish brown.
CULTURE: Generally container grown in west coast nurseries and should be transplanted as such; prefers moist, acid, deep, well drained soils in areas of high atmospheric moisture; will never perform in eastern states like it does in native habitat or British Isles.
DISEASES AND INSECTS: None serious.
LANDSCAPE VALUE: Only for specimen use as a noble conifer where room to ascend and spread is ample, a few of the compact cultivars are more suitable for smaller gardens.
CULTIVARS:
‘Adpressa’—Has 1/4 to 3/8″ long loosely appressed needles, the young shoots are tipped creamy white, often listed as a dwarf conifer but will produce vertical shoots and unless removed will become treelike, may also be listed under names like ‘Albospica’ and ‘Albospicata’, may grow 4′ by 4′ in ten years; however, a 73′ high tree has been described which indicates somebody

forgot to prune; Raulston mentioned that this cultivar survived the -9°F winter while the species was killed; introduced before 1867 in France.

'Aptos Blue'—Foliage is dark bluish green, secondary branches distinctly horizontal with tertiary branchlets pendulous.

'Cantab' ('Prostrata', 'Pendula Nana')—Arose as a branch sport at the Cambridge Botanic Garden, semi-prostrate habit, distinct blue-green or gray-green 1/2" long needles, about one-half as wide, unstable and will send up vertical shoots with needles akin to 'Cantab'.

'Santa Cruz'—Strong pyramidal-cone shaped tree, soft textured, pale green needles, distinct horizontal secondary branches.

'Soquel'—Pyramidal habit, fine-textured dark green foliage, bluish on underside, holds good color in winter.

PROPAGATION: Seeds require no pretreatment. Cuttings of 'Santa Cruz' rooted 70% with 16,000 ppm IBA, 47% on 'Soquel' with 6000 ppm IBA + 6000 ppm NAA. Cuttings must be staked and pruned to develop a leader.

NATIVE HABITAT: Confined to the fog belt along the Pacific Ocean from southern Oregon to California around San Francisco. Introduced 1843.

RELATED SPECIES:

Sequoiadendron giganteum, (sē-kwoi'a-den'dron jī-gan'tē-um), Big Tree, Sierra Redwood, Wellingtonia, is another west coast giant growing 250 to 300' in the wild but much less, perhaps 60', under cultivation in the east. In England, numerous + 100' high trees are common. The habit is dense and pyramidal-oval in youth, losing its lower branches with a narrow-pyramidal crown of foliage in the upper reaches at maturity. The bluish green needles vary in length from 1/8 to 1/2" and are usually awl shaped and triangular in cross section, tapering from the base to a fine point. Needles point forward toward the apex and completely cover the stem and spiral in 3 longitudinal rows. Needles persist 3 to 4 years. Cones are 1 1/2" to 3" long, 1 1/4 to 2" wide, reddish brown at maturity, upright the first year, pendulous the second, the flattened seeds shining pale to yellowish brown. The bark is spongy in texture and rich reddish brown. This species succeeds better in the eastern United States and Longwood Gardens has a number of 30 to 40' high trees. The species withstands drier conditions than *Sequoia sempervirens.* Tyler Arboretum, Lima, PA has a 100' tall specimen. Several cultivars are known but the most common is 'Pendulum' with an erratic leading stem that zigs, zags, arches, bends, dips and dives to form a piece of living sculpture. The secondary branches hang mop (mane)-like. The whole plant leaves much to the imagination. California in the Sierra Nevada Mountains at elevations of 4500 to 8000'. Introduced 1853. Zone 6 to 8.

Serissa foetida — Yellow-rim
(ser-ē'sa fet'i-da)

FAMILY: Rubiaceae

LEAVES: Opposite, simple, evergreen, ovate to elliptic, 1/2 to 3/4" wide, acute, rounded, entire, glabrous, deep green above, lighter below, with clusters of leaves in axils, virtually sessile.

STEM: Fine, gray, glabrous, malodorous when bruised.

Serissa foetida, Yellow-rim, is a small, rounded, 3 to 4' high, fine-textured evergreen shrub with dark green leaves and 4 to 6 lobed, 1/3" diameter white flowers in May-June. The plant has been growing on the Georgia campus for numerous years without an identity. It has survived −3°F and droughts too numerous to recount, all in the shadow and root competition of a 30 to 40' high *Quercus virginiana.* In Japan it is used as a hedging plant. Dr. Raulston has succeeded with the plants at Raleigh and is collecting various cultivars for evaluation. Adaptable and will withstand about any site conditions except permanently wet. Southeastern Asia. Introduced 1878. Zone (6)7 to 9.

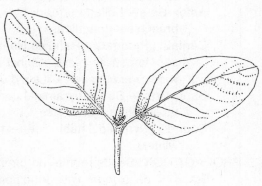

Shepherdia canadensis — Russet Buffaloberry
(she-pēr′di-a̍ kan-a-den′sis)

FAMILY: Elaeagnaceae

LEAVES: Opposite, simple, 1/2 to 2″ long, 1/4 to 1″ wide, elliptic to ovate, obtuse, dark green and sparingly scurfy above, silvery stellate pubescent below, often much of the pubescence is brown (brownish scales); petioles—1/8 to 1/6″ long, stellate pubescent.

BUDS: Rather small, solitary or multiple, stalked, oblong, with 2 or 4 valvate scales.

STEM: Red-brown, scurfy, scaly, not spiny, nearly terete, rather slender; leaf scars half-round, minute, slightly raised; 1 bundle-trace; pith—small, round, continuous.

SIZE: 6 to 8′ high and as wide, varies from 3 to 9′ high.

HARDINESS: Zone 2 to 6.

HABIT: Small, loosely-branched shrub of rounded outline.

RATE: Slow to medium.

TEXTURE: Medium in all seasons.

LEAF COLOR: Silver-green to gray-green in summer; upper surface green, lower silvery mixed with brown scales, like most members of the Elaeagnaceae does not color well in the fall.

FLOWERS: Dioecious, small, yellowish, 1/6″ across; in short axillary spikes or the pistillate often solitary, April to early May, not showy.

FRUIT: Drupe-like achene, yellowish red, insipid, ovoid, 1/6 to 1/4″ long; effective in June and July.

CULTURE: Easily grown and tolerates the poorest of soils; does well in dry or alkaline situations; prefers sunny open position; has the ability to fix atmospheric nitrogen.

DISEASES AND INSECTS: Several leaf spots, powdery mildew, and a rust have been reported but are not serious.

LANDSCAPE VALUE: Actually of no value where the soil is good and better shrubs can be grown; has possibilities along highways and other rough areas where poor soils, lousy maintenance, and salt are the rule, good plant for dry, high pH soils.

CULTIVARS: 'Xanthocarpa'—Yellow-fruited type.

PROPAGATION: Seeds of both species has an embryo dormancy and should be stratified for 60 to 90 days at 41°F; the seed coats are hard and an acid scarification for 20 to 30 minutes proves beneficial. July cuttings of the yellow-fruited form treated with 8000 ppm IBA-talc rooted 100%.

NATIVE HABITAT: Newfoundland to Alaska, south to Maine, Ohio, northern Mexico and Oregon. Introduced 1759.

RELATED SPECIES:

Shepherdia argentea — Silver Buffaloberry
(she-pēr′di-a̍ är-jen′tē-a̍)

LEAVES: Opposite, simple, elliptic, 1 to 2″ long, 1/8 to 5/8″ wide, obtuse, entire, covered with silver or silver-brown scales, densely pubescent; petiole 1/4 to 1/2″ long.

BUDS: Loosely scaly, 2-4-6 scaled, elongated, silvery to silvery brown, 1/4″ long, densely pubescent.

STEM: Young—terete, silver tomentose; old—brown, bark flaking and appearing like an onion skin; pith brown, excavated; spines 1 to 2″ long, terminating leafy branches.

Shepherdia argentea, Silver Buffaloberry, is a thorny shrub, sometimes nearly tree-like, growing 6 to 10′ high, although it may reach 18′. The foliage is silvery on both surfaces and much more gray in appearance than *S. canadensis.* The flowers and fruits (red or orange) are similar to the above species with only minor exceptions. The fruits of both species have been used for jellies. Native to Minnesota and Manitoba to Sasketchewan, Kansas and Nevada. Introduced 1818. Zone 2 to 6.

ADDITIONAL NOTES: I have seen both species, but only in arboreta or on campuses and was not intrigued by either. They are extremely cold- and drought-tolerant as well as alkaline soil adaptable and should be used in areas where these conditions prevail. For fruit set both male and female plants are required.

Sinojackia xylocarpa — Jacktree
(sī-nō-ja′kē-ȧ zī-lō-car′pȧ)

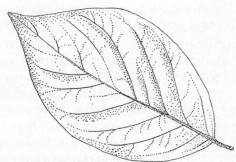

FAMILY: Hamamelidaceae

LEAVES: Alternate, simple, elliptic to elliptic-obovate, 1 1/4 to 3″ long, short acuminate, rounded, denticulate, dark green and glabrous above; petiole—1/4″ long.

Sinojackia rehderiana

Sinojackia xylocarpa, Jacktree, offers potential as a large shrub or small tree, probably 15 to 20′ high at maturity. I have seen the plant at North Carolina State Arboretum in October and at that time the foliage was still dark green. The white, 1″ wide flowers occur in 3 to 5 flowered cymes at the ends of lateral shoots in April-May. The woody drupe is 3/4″ long and 1/2″ across with a broad conical obtuse apex. Appears to thrive in full sun and well drained soil. A plant of the future? Eastern China. Introduced 1934. Zone (6)7 to 8.

Skimmia japonica — Japanese Skimmia
(skim′i-ȧ ja-pon′i-kȧ)

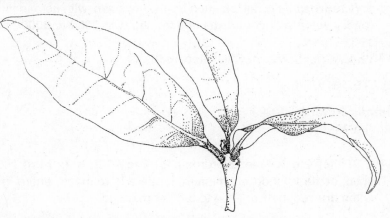

FAMILY: Rutaceae

LEAVES: Alternate, simple, evergreen, crowded at end of branches and appearing whorled, elliptic-oblong to oblong-obovate, 2 1/2 to 5″ long, 3/4 to 2″ wide, bright green upon emerging, finally dark green above, yellowish green beneath, entire, glabrous, dotted with pellucid glands; aromatic when bruised; petiole—short, 1/4″ long, glabrous, reddish purple.

BUDS: Imbricate, covered with red scales, glabrous, 1/16 to 1/8″ long.

STEM: Stout, green with an overcast of reddish purple, glabrous, spicy-fragrant when bruised; pith— ample, excavated, green.

SIZE: 3 to 4′ with a similar spread; have seen plants 6′ and larger.

HARDINESS: Zone (6) 7 to 8 (9).

HABIT: Dense, rounded to haystack-shaped (dome-shaped), evergreen shrub of rather gentle garden proportions.

RATE: Slow.

TEXTURE: Medium.

LEAF COLOR: Arguably dark green, although often stands out as a light green when compared to other broadleaf evergreens.

FLOWERS: Dioecious, glossy red-maroon in bud, creamy-white when open, weakly fragrant, each flower 1/3″ across and borne in 2 to 3″ long, 1 to 2″ wide upright panicles; March-April (early April in Athens); flowers on male plants larger and more fragrant; selections have been made for this trait; peduncle and pedicels are glabrous and glossy reddish purple; almost more showy than flowers.

FRUIT: Only on female plant, bright red, 1/3″ wide, globose drupe that ripens in October and persists into the following spring; fruit is borne at end of shoots in panicles described above and is very effective; about one male to 6 females is necessary for good fruit set.

CULTURE: Transplant from containers; prefers moist, acid, high organic matter soils although will supposedly thrive in chalky (limestone) soils; partial shade or full shade is beneficial especially in winter when foliage is apt to discolor; in northern areas provide some winter protection.

DISEASES AND INSECTS: Mites can disfigure foliage.

LANDSCAPE VALUE: Beautiful evergreen shrub of dainty proportions for use in foundations, planter boxes, mixed broadleaf evergreen plantings.

CULTIVARS: Several are known but to my knowledge none are common in the United States.

　'Bronze Knight'—A male clone with flowers similar to 'Rubella', the leaves, however, more lustrous dark green and sharply pointed.

　'Formanii'—Vigorous form with broad-obovate leaves and large clusters of brilliant red fruits; more properly *S. japonica* × *S. reevesiana* hybrid, flowers white; 2 to 3′ by 2 to 3′; flowers usually female although bisexual flowers occur.

　'Nymans'—Free fruiting form with oblanceolate leaves and comparatively large red fruits; may be the best fruiting form but a male is required to insure fruit set.

　'Rubella'—A male clone with large, 3″ long, 2 1/2″ wide at base panicles of red buds through winter, peduncle and pedicels deep shiny bronze-red, opening to 4-petaled white with yellow anthers in spring, very fragrant; leaves dark green, 3 to 4″ long, petiole dark red; also listed as *S. reevsiana* clone.

　'Ruby Dome'—Considered an improvement on 'Rubella' because it produces abundant pollen.

PROPAGATION: Seeds when cleaned and sown germinate readily without treatment. Have collected fruits of *S. reevesiana* in fall, cleaned from pulp, sown, with germination in 3 to 4 weeks. Cuttings root quite readily when collected in fall and treated with 3000 to 8000 ppm IBA-talc; rooting should approach 100 percent.

NATIVE HABITAT: Japan. Cultivated 1838.

RELATED SPECIES:

Skimmia laureola — Skimmia
(skim′i-a̦ lâ-rē-ō′la)

LEAVES: Alternate, simple, evergreen, 2 1/2 to 4 1/2″ long, 1 to 1 1/2″ wide, oblong-obovate or oblong-elliptic, acute to short acuminate, cuneate to rounded, entire, glabrous, rich green above, aromatic when bruised; petiole—1/4 to 3/8″ long, green.

Skimmia laureola, Skimmia, forms a compact, low growing handsome foliaged shrub about 2 to 3′ high and wide. The sweet scented, creamy green flowers occur in lax, pyramidal, 4″ long, 3″ wide panicles in spring, although I saw plants in full flower in January in England. The fruit is purplish black but has not been seen on cultivated plants. Apparently all(?) forms in cultivation are male. 'Kew Green' is a handsome form with large panicles of greenish flowers, larger than normal and quite unusual, no trace of reddish pigment in flowers; leaves are large dark green and densely set. Probably only adapted to Pacific Northwest and have never seen the species in the eastern corridor. Some speculation that *S. laureola* as described by Bean from plants in Kew Gardens are, in fact, hybrids. Himalayas. Cultivated 1868. Zone 7(?) to 9.

Skimmia reevesiana — Reeves Skimmia
(skim′i-a̍ rēv′si-ā′na̍)

LEAVES: Alternate, simple, evergreen, lanceolate or oblong lanceolate, 1 to 4″ long, 3/4 to 1″ wide, acuminate, cuneate, entire,
dark green above, light green beneath.

Skimmia reevesiana, Reeves Skimmia, is a low growing 1 1/2 to 2′
high and 2 to 3′ wide evergreen shrub. It tends to be more loose
and open than *S. japonica.* The flowers are white, fragrant,
bisexual, 1/2″ diameter, parts in 5's, and produced in 2 to 3″
terminal panicles. The oval to pear-shaped, 1/3″ long rich
crimson fruits persist into winter, Because of the bisexual
nature of the flowers a lone plant will set fruit. It requires a rich,
moist, acid soil. China. Introduced 1849. Zone 7 and considered more cold hardy than *S. japonica.* There is a
variegated form with white-margined leaves.

Sophora japonica — Japanese Pagodatree, often called Scholar-tree
(so-fō′ra̍ ja-pon′i-ka̍)

FAMILY: Fabaceae
LEAVES: Alternate, pinnately compound, 6 to 10″ long, 7 to 17
leaflets, ovate to lance-ovate, 1
to 2″ long, half as wide, acute,
broad cuneate to rounded at
base, entire, medium, almost
bright, green and lustrous
above, glaucous beneath and
closely appressed-pubescent.
BUDS: Blackish, woolly, sessile, indistinctly scaly, concealed by the
leaf scar, end bud lacking; base of petiole swollen and enclosing bud.
STEM: Slender, essentially glabrous, green on 1 through 4 and 5-year-old wood, grayish lenticels, nodes
prominently protruding; pith solid, greenish.

SIZE: 50 to 75′ in height with a comparable spread although great variation occurs.
HARDINESS: Zone 4 to 8.
HABIT: Usually upright-spreading with a broadly rounded crown at maturity; casts a relatively light shade;
many seedling trees have been planted on the Georgia campus and are rather open the first 2 to 3
years but form a decent canopy in the 4th and 5th years.
RATE: Medium to fast, 10 to 12′ in a 5 to 6 year period; has been faster than this in Zone 8, probably 3′
per year the first 5 years.
TEXTURE: Medium-fine in leaf; medium in winter.
BARK: On old trunks somewhat Black Locust-like except pale grayish brown in color.
LEAF COLOR: Bright to medium lustrous green in summer; green color holds late and little fall color
develops; I have trouble with the shade of green, looks more bright green than anything.

FLOWERS: Perfect, creamy-white, mildly fragrant; borne in 6 to 12″ long and wide terminal panicles (have measured them 12″ high and 14″ wide) in July through mid-August; each flower 1/2″ long, calyx 1/8″ long, green, bell-shaped, very showy in flower.

FRUIT: Pod, bright green changing to yellow and finally yellow brown, 3 to 8″ long, 3 to 6 (10) seeded; October, and may remain all winter; after the pods abscise the inflorescence remains.

CULTURE: Transplant balled and burlapped as a young specimen; prefers loamy, well-drained soil; actually somewhat tender to cold when young but once over 1 1/2″ caliper diameter seems to be fine; once established withstands heat and drought well; also tolerant of polluted conditions; prune in fall; tends to be a "floppy" grower and is somewhat difficult to train into a central leader with a nice head; have watched with great satisfaction the inclusion of the species, primarily seedlings, throughout the Georgia campus and the resultant outstanding performance without supplemental water; the literature is full of comments about the lateness to flower, i.e., needs to grow 10 years or more; 3 to 5 year old trees have produced *heavy* crops of flowers and fruits; perhaps most impressive has been the growth rate in the southeast, probably 3′ per year during the first 5 years after transplanting; more urban tolerant than given credit; a number of plantspeople are taking a closer look at its attributes.

DISEASES AND INSECTS: Canker, damping-off of seedlings, twig blight, powdery mildew and leaf hoppers; the potato leaf hopper can kill young stems and this in turn results in a witches' broom.

LANDSCAPE VALUE: Good tree for city conditions, lawns, poor soil areas, parks, golf courses; excellent flower and good foliage are principal assets; could be considered messy for petals, fruits, leaves, rachises and pods drop differentially; flowers create a creamy carpet under the tree for a time in July-August.

CULTIVARS:

'Columnaris' ('Fastigiata')—Upright growth habit, have never observed but young trees often show an upright outline.

'Pendula'—Weeping form, seldom flowers, quite interesting when used as an accent or formal specimen; comes relatively true-to-type from seed; I have collected seed from a plant at Bernheim Arboretum and a surprising number of the seedlings exhibited various degrees of pendulousness; my only regret is I gave them to my friends and did not save one for my garden; often grafted on a standard, will grow 15 to 25′ high.

'Princeton Upright'—All the good qualities of 'Regent' with a compact upright branching system, 40 to 50′.

'Regent'—Selection by Princeton Nurseries for fast growth rate, often twice the rate of seedling trees, straight growth habit, large oval-rounded crown, glossy deep green leaves, and earliness to flower (6 to 8 years old); in Zone 8 this occurs after 1 to 3 years in the nursery; good plant and it flowers heavily in the Athens area.

'Variegata'—White speckled leaves; saw for the first time in Berlin Botanic Garden, for the dedicated collector.

PROPAGATION: Seeds supposedly require a weak scarification in acid to break down the impermeable seed coat, easy to grow from seed; I have grown numerous seedlings by sowing them as soon as they are removed from the pod; cultivars are budded.

ADDITIONAL NOTES: Last of the large ornamental trees to flower in the north; used around Buddhist temples; yellow dye can be extracted from the flowers by baking them until brown and then boiling them in water. A very distinctive and aesthetically handsome tree in flower; should be used more extensively. Bean mentioned that the tree does not flower until 30 to 40 years of age. American references have stated 10 to 14 years. I have a sneaking suspicion that high summer heat, perhaps warm nights, foster early flowering. All authors, including this one, tend to pass along time honored information without determining, first hand, the actual response in question.

NATIVE HABITAT: China, Korea. Introduced 1747.

Sorbaria sorbifolia — Ural Falsespirea
(sôr-bā′ri-ȧ sôr-bi-fō′li-ȧ)

FAMILY: Rosaceae

LEAVES: Alternate, pinnately compound, 8 to 12″ long, 13 to 25 leaflets, 2 to 4″ long, 1/2 to 1″ wide, lanceolate to ovate-lanceolate, long acuminate, double and sharply serrate, usually glabrous or nearly so beneath, green on both surfaces; resembles mountainash foliage.

STEM: Young—usually green or pink, often somewhat downy, gray-brown when old and glabrous; pith—large, brown, continuous.

SIZE: 5 to 10′ in height with a similar spread.

HARDINESS: Zone 2 to 7(8).

HABIT: Erect, rather coarse multistemmed shrub, with foliage similar to European Mountainash; spreads rapidly by suckers, forming colonies.

RATE: Fast.

TEXTURE: Many people say the texture is coarse but I feel if the shrub is properly pruned and maintained the texture is at worst medium in summer; tends toward coarseness in winter.

LEAF COLOR: Has a reddish tinge when unfolding gradually changing to deep green in summer; fall color is not effective; leafs out early and I have seen emerging leaves as early as late March in central Illinois.

FLOWERS: Perfect, white, 1/3″ across; late June into July; borne in large, terminal, fleecy, 4 to 10″ long panicles; very effective and, in fact, outstanding in flower, flowers turn brown upon senescing; flowers occur on new wood of the season.

FRUIT: Dehiscent follicles.

CULTURE: Transplants readily, very fibrous rooted, suckers and spreads profusely; prefers moist, well drained, organic soil; tends to become dwarfed in dry soils; full sun or light shade; pH adaptable; prune in early spring before growth starts as the flowers are produced on current season's growth; cut off old flowers; relatively easy plant to grow, however, it is not widely known.

DISEASES AND INSECTS: None serious.

LANDSCAPE VALUE: Excellent plant for the shrub border, for massing, grouping, might make a good bank cover as it freely suckers and spreads; is one of the first shrubs to leaf out in spring; needs considerable room to spread and is not suitable for small planting areas.

PROPAGATION: Easy to root from softwood, greenwood or hardwood cuttings, preferably in sand under mist; division is a good method; seeds can be sown as soon as ripe and will germinate.

NATIVE HABITAT: Northern Asia from Ural to Japan. Cultivated 1759.

RELATED SPECIES:

Sorbaria aitchisonii, (sôr-bā′ri-ȧ atch′i-sō′nē-ī),

Single leaflet

Kashmir Falsespirea, is a rather graceful, 6 to 9′ (12′) high shrub with 11 to 23 sharply toothed and tapered, 2 to 4″ long, 1/4 to 5/8″ wide, single serrate leaflets, in a 9 to 15″ long leaf. The young glabrous stems are usually a rich red. The white flowers occur in large, conical, 1 to 1 1/2′ long and 8 to 14″ wide panicles in (June) July and August. Handsome in full flower with the large billowy white panicles. Flowers age to brown and there always seems to be a transition between white and brown, never continuous white changing to brown. Possibly best to remove the old flower panicles. This is a handsome shrub which could be planted more than it is, especially in large masses along highways or in open spaces. Afghanistan, Western Pakistan, Kashmir. Introduced 1895. Zone (5)6 to 7.

Sorbaria arborea, (sôr-bā′ri-ȧ ar-bō′rē-ȧ),
Tree Falsepirea, is a large spreading shrub to 15′ with 13 to 17 slender-pointed leaflets. The white flowers are produced in large 12 to 15″ long and wide panicles similar to the previous species. Leaflets and stems are more pubescent than the previous species. Central and western China. Introduced 1908 by Wilson. Zone 5 to 7, hardier than the above.

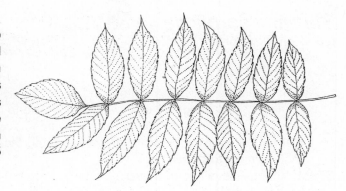

Sorbus alnifolia — Korean Mountainash
(sôr′bus al-ni-fō′li-ȧ)

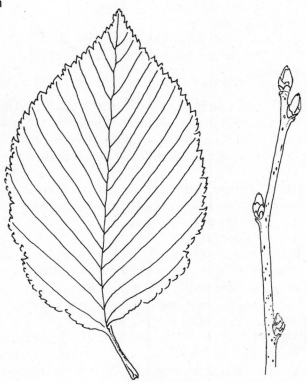

FAMILY: Rosaceae

LEAVES: Alternate, simple, 2 to 4″ long, 3/4 to 1 1/2″ wide, ovate to elliptic-ovate, short-acuminate, rounded at base, unequally serrate, glabrous above, glabrous or slightly pubescent beneath, on vigorous shoots sometimes pubescent, with 6 to 10 pairs of veins, leaf shape resembles *Fagus* to a degree, lustrous dark green; petiole 1/2 to 3/4″ long.

BUDS: Oblong, terminal bud scarcely larger than the lateral, solitary, sessile, with several dark margined scales, the inner of which are more or less pubescent with long hairs often matted in gum.

STEM: Moderate, lustrous reddish brown, prominent small gray lenticels; on older stems lenticels become distinctly diamond-shaped.

SIZE: 40 to 50′ in height by 20 to 30′ (50′) in spread although can grow to 60′.

HARDINESS: Zone 3 to 7, growing successfully at Minnesota Landscape Arboretum.

HABIT: Pyramidal when young developing a weakly pyramidal-oval to almost rounded outline at maturity; have also seen broad rounded trees.

RATE: Medium to fast, 10 to 12′ over a 5 to 7 year period.

TEXTURE: Medium in all seasons.

BARK: Gray on old trunks, almost beech-like; the first time I witnessed Korean Mountainash was at the Arnold Arboretum and was instantly taken by the beautiful foliage, flowers, bark and habit; one of my favorite all around trees; unfortunately, not very well known.

LEAF COLOR: New leaves a rich bright fresh spring green; lustrous dark green in summer changing to yellow, orange, and golden brown in fall; the leaves are simple and do not look anything like what we normally consider a mountainash leaf; look like beech or hornbeam leaves.

FLOWERS: Perfect, white, 1/2″ diameter, borne in 6 to 10 flowered, flat-topped, 2 to 3″ diameter corymbs in May, beautiful in flower but shows an alternate sequence, heavy one year, lighter the next.

FRUIT: Roundish or obovoid pome, pinkish red to orangish red to scarlet, bloomy, speckled with dark lenticels, 3/8 to 5/8″ long, September-October and persisting, spectacular, at its best perhaps the handsomest of all mountainash for fruit effect.

CULTURE: Transplant balled and burlapped into any well drained soil; very pH adaptable; does not withstand polluted conditions; prune in winter or early spring; Donald Wyman noted that it was one of the most successful of the flowering trees introduced by the Arnold Arboretum from Japan and required little cultural attention.

DISEASES AND INSECTS: Discussed under *Sorbus aucuparia,* the least susceptible to borer injury; Hasselkus, Wisconsin, reported fireblight susceptibility.

LANDSCAPE VALUE: Specimen tree for lawns; not for streets or downtown city areas; the best of the mountainash; difficult to believe it is even related to the genus *Sorbus,* botanically placed in the section Micromeles.

CULTIVARS:
    'Redbird'—Listed as having rosy red fruits that persist into winter and serve as a food source for birds.

PROPAGATION: Seeds require 3 months or more of cold stratification at 41°F in moist medium.

ADDITIONAL NOTES: Like most mountainash there is always the threat of fireblight and borer damage. Probably best not to utilize the tree in high stress environments (urban settings) where it would be predisposed to insect or disease infestations. I monitored the trees in the Arnold's collection during sabbatical and seldom a day would pass when I did not give them a caring inspection. The fruits can be spectacular and, during a heavy flowering year, it is the equal of any fruiting tree. The Arnold also has an upright form that is somewhat broad-columnar. To my knowledge it does not have a cultivar name although the name 'Skyline' appears in some literature.

NATIVE HABITAT: Central China to Korea and Japan. Introduced 1892.

Sorbus aucuparia — European Mountainash, Rowan
(sôr′bus aw-kū-pā′ri-à)

LEAVES: Alternate, pinnately compound, 5 to 9″ long, 9 to 15 (19) leaflets, 3/4 to 2 1/2″ long, oblong to oblong-lanceolate, acute or obtusish, serrate, usually entire in lower third, dull dark green above, glaucescent beneath and pubescent, at least when young.

BUDS: Terminal—large, woolly, 1/2″ long, lateral often reduced with several scales, the inner of which are more or less pubescent, reddish brown.

STEM: Young branches pubescent, becoming glabrous, grayish brown and shiny when older.

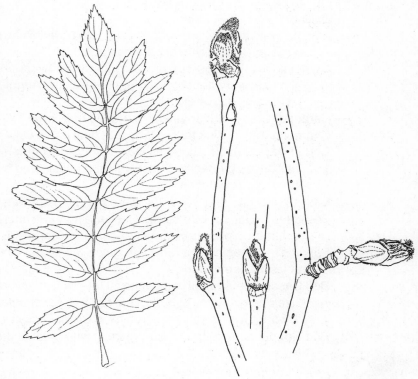

SIZE: 20 to 40′ (60′) in height with a spread of 2/3's to equal the height.

HARDINESS: Zone 3 to 6 or 7; excessive summer heat induces problems.

HABIT: Erect and oval in youth forming an ovate or spherical, gracefully open head at maturity.

RATE: Medium, 25 to 30′ over a 20 year period.

TEXTURE: Medium-fine in leaf, medium or medium-coarse in winter.

BARK: Light grayish brown in color, usually smooth, both often somewhat slightly roughened on old trunks.

LEAF COLOR: Flat, dull dark green in summer; fall color ranges from green to yellow to reddish, often a fine reddish purple.

FLOWERS: White, 1/3″ across, malodorous, borne in 3 to 5″ diameter flat-topped corymbs in May; effective, but not outstanding; not as showy as *S. alnifolia*.

FRUIT: Small, berry-like pome, 1/4 to 3/8″ diameter, orange-red; late August into September, very handsome, frequented by birds and seldom persisting for any time.

CULTURE: Transplant balled and burlapped into well drained loam; prefers acid soils and is often short-lived on chalky soils; have seen far too many problems on the species especially where stress is common, does not fare well in compacted soils, polluted atmospheres and the like; high summer temperatures appear to limit growth, I have not seen a single mountain ash in Zone 8 and generally those in Zone 7 are short lived; stress apparently predisposes the species to canker and borer.

DISEASES AND INSECTS: Fireblight can be devastating, crown gall, canker, leaf rusts, scab, aphids, pear leaf blister mite, Japanese leafhopper, roundheaded borer, mountainash sawfly, and scales; borers are serious in weakened and poorly growing trees; the best line of defense is a vigorous, healthy, actively growing tree.

LANDSCAPE VALUE: Excellent for fruit effect but its use should be tempered by the knowledge that it is susceptible to many pests; use in northern climates.

CULTIVARS: There are numerous cultivars, some of which were branch sports and others which came about through hybridization. The following represent a small complement of the different types. In this edition I added cultivars that were listed in 1988 and 1989 nursery catalogs.

'Apricot Queen'—Apricot colored fruit.

'Asplenifolia'—Leaflets doubly serrate and supposedly deeply divided; however, the one tree I saw was just a degree more saw-toothed than the species.

'Beissneri'—A graceful variety with pinnately lobed leaflets; leaf petioles and branchlets bright red, stems and trunk a rich copper-brown color.

'Black Hawk'—A strong columnar form with thick dark green leaves and large orange fruits, appears to be resistant to sun-scald, 30′ by 20′.

'Brilliant Pink'—Pink fruit.

'Brilliant Yellow'—Golden yellow fruit in 3 to 5″ wide infructescences, 30′ by 20′, oval outline, offered by Lake County Nursery Exchange.

'Cardinal Royal'—Vigorous grower with symmetrical upright narrow-oval habit, leaves dark green above, silvery beneath, brilliant red fruits in August-September, introduced by Michigan State University, 35′ by 20′.

'Carpet of Gold'—Sulfur-yellow to orange fruit, hybrid with *S. cashmiriana*.

'Charming Pink'—Pink fruit, 30′ by 20′, oval habit, Lake County Nursery offering.

'Coral Fire'—Notable attributes include thick dark green leaves, bright red fall color, coral-red fruits, introduced by Pacific Coast Nursery, considered a *S. hupehensis* selection and listed here for ease of presentation.

'Edulis'—Fruit larger (1/3 to 3/8″ diameter) than species and used for preserves in Europe.

'Fastigiata'—Upright with strongly ascending branches, dark green leaves, good large sealing wax red fruits; slow-growing, rather coarsely branched.

'Pendula'— Weeping in a rather irregular, unkempt manner and fruiting quite heavily, 15 to 20′ high at landscape maturity.

'Red Cascade'—A small compact oval tree with small orange-red fruits and yellow-orange fall color, size approximates 6′ by 8′, listed as a *S. tianshanica* form in Schmidt Nursery 1988-89 catalog, 'Dwarfcrown' is cultivar name, Red Cascade is the trademark name.

'Red Copper Glow'—Bright scarlet fruits with coral and copper overtones, 30′ by 20′, Lake County Nursery offering.

'Scarlet King'—Scarlet fruit.

'Wilson'—Dense columnar form, red fruit, 30′.

'Xanthocarpa'—Yellow fruits, more properly amber-yellow.

PROPAGATION: Seeds require 60 to 120 days of cold, moist stratification at 38°F. Cultivars are budded or grafted onto seedling understocks.

NATIVE HABITAT: Europe to western Asia and Siberia, and naturalized in North America.

RELATED SPECIES:

Sorbus americana — American Mountainash
(sôr′bus   à-mer-i-kā′nà)

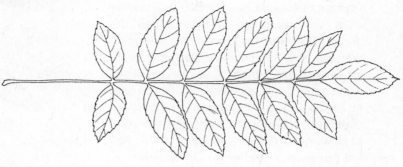

LEAVES: Alternate, compound pinnate, 6 to 12″ long, 11 to 17
leaflets, 1 1/2 to 4″ long, 1/2 to
3/4″ wide, lance-oblong to
lanceolate, acuminate, sharply serrate, dark green and
glabrous above, paler be-
neath, pubescent or glabrous,
generally serrated almost to
the base, where on *S. aucuparia* the serrations start about 1/3 from the base.

Sorbus americana, American Mountainash, is a northern species that grows from 10 to 30′ high and is
usually a small tree or shrub with a short trunk of spreading slender branches that form a narrow,
open, round-topped crown. Hardy to Zone 2 (-35 to -50°F), it frequents borders of cold swamps and
bogs, or grows in a stunted form on relatively dry soils; grows slowly and is short-lived; flowers are
white; fruit is a brilliant orange-red; ranges from Newfoundland to Manitoba, south to Michigan, and
North Carolina along the Appalachian Mountains. Have observed on the top of the highest mountain
(Brasstown Bald) in Georgia; attractive in the right situations. Cultivated 1811.

Sorbus aria — Whitebeam Mountainash
(sôr′bus   är′ē-à)

LEAVES: Alternate, simple, 2 to 4″ long, one-half to two-thirds as wide, elliptic to broad-elliptic or ovate,
obtuse or acute, cuneate or rounded, double serrate except at base, lustrous dark green above,
covered with whitish tomentum below, 8 to 13 parallel vein pairs; petiole—1/2 to 1″ long.

Sorbus aria, Whitebeam Mountainash, is a tree which develops a broad-pyramidal or ovoid head. This
species grows 35 to 45′ tall and has simple, leathery, lustrous dark green leaves (upper surface)
while the lower surface is white-tomentose in summer. Fall color varies from pale green to golden
brown to reddish. Flowers are white, about 1/3″ across, borne in 2 to 3″ terminal corymbs in May.
Fruit is 1/2″ diameter, orange-red or scarlet, ovoid or rounded berry-like pome that ripens in September through October. The leaves are quite different from what we associate with a "normal"
mountainash leaf. Native to Europe, long cultivated. Zone 5. There are several cultivars of note:
'Aurea'—a type with yellow foliage; var. *majestica*—fruits are as much as 5/8″ in diameter and the
leaves reach 7″ in length; others are noted.

Sorbus cashmiriana — Kashmir Mountainash
(sôr′bus kash-mēr-ē-ā′nà)

LEAVES: Alternate, compound pinnate, 3 1/2 to 7″ long, 13 to 19 leaflets, 1 to 2″ long, 3/8 to 5/8″ wide,
lanceolate to oblong, acute, sharply serrate to base, rich green above and glabrous, gray-green
below.

Sorbus cashmiriana, Kashmir Mountainash, develops a conical crown and grows 20 to 40′ high with an
equal spread. The flowers are pinkish white, 3/4″ diameter, and borne in mid to late May. In fall the
leaves may change to a good red. The white fruits are about 3/8″ diameter and are often tinged pink;
the fruit stalks are pink to red in color. This species has been used in hybridizing with *S. aucuparia*
by European nurserymen. Some of the cultivars include 'Carpet of Gold', yellow fruits; 'Kirsten Pink',

dark pink fruits; and 'Maidenblush', pale pink fruits. Native to Himalayas; introduced 1949 into the Arnold Arboretum. Zone 4. Wyman considers this species well worthy of a trial wherever mountainashes are grown. The exact taxonomic status is questionable; the trees I have seen are more loose and open than *S. aucuparia* types with smaller, fine-textured leaflets and bear large loose 5 to 7″ wide corymbs that are eventually laden with the handsome white to pinkish fruit. Other species of some interest but limited landscape acceptability include *S. commixta* (sôr′bus com-miks′ta),

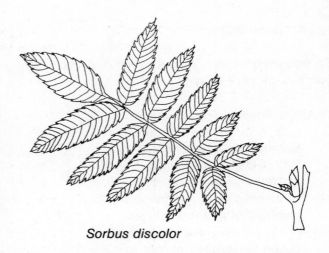

Sorbus discolor

Japanese Mountainash, with white flowers in 4 to 6″ wide inflorescences and globose, 3/8″ wide, lustrous bright red fruits, 20 to 30′, Zone 5; *S. decora* (sôr′bus de-ko′ra), Showy Mountainash, with white flowers and red fruit. Bailey Nursery considers it the hardiest of the mountainash grown in the United States, 20 to 25′, Zone 2 to 5; and *S. discolor,* (sôr′bus dis′kul-er), Snowberry Mountainash, with white flowers, 2 to 4(6″) wide bright scarlet fruit clusters, 20 to 30′, Zone 2. I have seen these species and was quite impressed by their fruit displays and fall color especially in the case of *S. commixta.*

ADDITIONAL NOTES: *Sorbus* presents a real challenge to the taxonomist and horticulturist. There are numerous hybrids and cultivars and even intergeneric hybrids with *Aronia* (× *Sorbaronia),* *Cotoneaster* (× *Sorbocotoneaster)* and *Pyrus* (× *Sorbopyrus).* The treatment I have presented is not extensive and I recommend the reader consult Bean and Wyman for additional information. I have observed so many European Mountainashes decimated by fireblight and borers in the midwest that it became somewhat discouraging to recommend the tree to the gardener. The Arnold Arboretum had a significant collection and I delighted in the magnificent fruit displays that ranged in color from white, pink, yellow, orange to red and the excellent fall color on species like *S. commixta* and *S. esserteauiana.* In Europe, and especially England, they are planted in abundance. The cool, moist climate is more to their liking. In the U.S., extreme heat and drought predispose them to many problems.

Unfortunately, since moving south, *Sorbus* has been removed from my gardening vocabulary simply because the plants do not prosper (survive) in Zones 7 to 9. In fruit, there are few trees that equal the mountainash especially some of the white, pink and coral-pink colored forms. In January 1989, I heard Dr. Hugh McAllister present a lecture on *Sorbus* at the Pershore Nursery Conference, Pershore, England. He provided an excellent overview of the garden attributes and discussed the confusion in identification. There are 120 or so species and since *Sorbus* reproduces apomictically (without normal fertilization), numerous microspecies are known which further confound taxonomy. In brief, the best advice to gardeners is to enjoy the mountainash for their lovely fruit and fall color.

Two other *Sorbus* that appear in northern latitudes and are often listed by nurseries include *S.* × *hybrida* and *S. thuringiaca.* Both are medium size, pyramidal oval trees about 25 to 35′ high and two thirds as wide. *S.* × *hybrida* is a tetraploid apomictic species and reproduces true to type from seed. The leaves are deeply lobed and essentially simple, but often cut to the midvein, the overall effect somewhat oak-like. Generally, they are lobed toward their end, lobes increasing in depth toward the base. Size ranges from 3 to 3 1/2″ long, 2 to 2 1/2″ wide, dull dark green above, white pubescent below, with a 1/2 to 1″ long petiole. White flowers occur in 2 to 5″ wide corymbs and are followed by globose 1/2 to 5/8″ wide deep red fruits. *S. thuringiaca* is often called the Oakleaf Mountainash and may be a hybrid between *S. aucuparia* and *S. aria.* The habit is upright with numerous ascending branches forming with time a dense, rhombic crown, eventually 20 to 40′ high. White flowers occur in 3 to 5″ wide corymbs, followed by 3/8″ wide, globose or ellipsoidal bright red fruits. The leaves are leathery dark green above covered with dull whitish tomentum below. Leaves average 3 to 6″ long and have the lobing pattern of *S.* × *hybrida.* Leaves are 2 to 2 1/2 times as long as wide. 'Fastigiata' is similar to the species but differs in more fastigiate form perhaps twice as tall as wide at maturity. Both species (hybrid) were originated in or native to Europe. Zone (3)4 to 5.

Spiraea albiflora — Japanese White Spirea
(spī-rē′a̱ al-bi-flō′ra̱)

LEAVES: Alternate, simple, lanceolate, 2 1/2″ long, one third to half as wide, acuminate, cuneate, coarsely or sometimes double serrate, with callous-tipped teeth, rich bright green above, glabrous and bluish green beneath; short petioled.

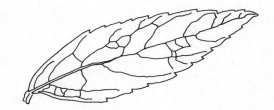

Spiraea albiflora, Japanese White Spirea, could be equated with a white flowered 'Anthony Waterer'.
The habit is low (2 to 3′), rounded, dense and the white corymbs which appear in late June and July (late May-early June, Athens) are effectively foiled against the handsome foliage. Makes an excellent facer plant, mass, or filler in the shrub border. Flowers on new wood so can be effectively rejuvenated in early spring. Cultivated in Japan. Introduced before 1868. Zone 4 to 8. Sometimes listed as *S. japonica* var. *alba* or 'Alba'. Roots very readily from cuttings and is infinitely superior to the large, cumbersome, unkempt, straggly spireas. Have seen tremendous chlorosis in some areas of the midwest. Requires acid soil for best growth. It is probably more correctly listed as a cultivar ('Albiflora') of *S. japonica* but in this edition I have chosen to stay with the species treatment. Has performed well in Zone 8 and the overall foliage color is brighter green than *S.* × *bumalda* types. The pure white flowers are particularly handsome framed by the rich green leaves. 'Leucantha' is a seedling of *S. albiflora* with larger leaves and inflorescences.

Spiraea × *billiardii* — Billiard Spirea
(spī-rē′a̱ × bil-yard′ē-ī)

Billiard Spirea resulted from crosses between *S. douglasii* and *S. salicifolia*. It is an upright (6′) shrub that shows a propensity to sucker. The chief beauty resides in rose-colored flowers which occur in narrow, dense-pyramidal, 4 to 8″ long panicles in June to August. The flowers fade to a rather ugly brown and should be removed. It is susceptible to iron chlorosis and should only be planted in acid soil. Other than the pretty flowers, there is little to recommend it. Originated before 1854. Zone 3 to 6. 'Triumphans' has purplish rose flowers in dense, conical panicles and is considered among the finest of late flowered spireas. 'Macrothyrsa' with bright pink flowers in 6 to 8″ long panicles is included here. These hybrids and west coast species do not appear as well adapted to the heat and humidity of the southeast.

Spiraea bullata — Crispleaf Spirea
(spī-rē′a̱ bū-lā′ta̱)

Crispleaf Spirea makes a rather intriguing, low (12 to 15″), groundcover type plant. The foliage is thickish and bullate, dark almost bluish green above, grayish green beneath. Leaves average 1/2 to 1 1/4″ long, up to 3/4″ wide and are coarsely toothed. Flowers are deep rosy-pink, borne in small, dense corymbs which form a terminal 1 1/2 to 3″ diameter corymb; June-July. Valuable as a dwarf shrub, especially in a rock garden setting. Japan. Cultivated 1880. Zone 4 to 8. Considered a selection from *S. japonica*. Often aphid infested and less than desirable in hot climates, best in colder areas.

Spiraea × *bumalda* — Bumald Spirea (Result of a cross between *S. albiflora* and *S. japonica*)
(spī-rē′á bū-mǎl′dá)

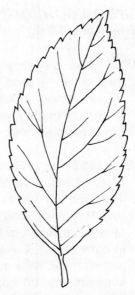

FAMILY: Rosaceae

LEAVES: Alternate, simple, 1 to 3″ long, ovate-lanceolate, apex pointed, base narrowed, teeth mostly double, sharp, pinkish-red-purple when young, finally dark green, almost bluish green.

STEM: Brown, slightly angled in cross section, somewhat lined or ridged, glabrous.

SIZE: 2 to 3′ high and 3 to 5′ wide.

HARDINESS: Zone 3 to 8.

HABIT: A broad, flat-topped, low shrub, densely twiggy with erect branches, often mounded in habit, clean, relatively refined shrub.

RATE: Fast.

TEXTURE: Medium-fine in all seasons.

LEAF COLOR: Pinkish to reddish when unfolding changing to dark bluish green at maturity; leaves tend to show cream to yellow variegation patterns; often turning bronzy red to purplish in fall; seldom spectacular; very early leafing as is true for many spireas, showing leaf color by early March in Athens.

FLOWERS: White to deep pink, June into August, borne in 4 to 6″ diameter flat-topped corymbs; flowers on new growth; flowers mid to late May into early June in Athens, often sporadically thereafter.

FRUIT: Dry, brown follicle, not ornamental, maintained on large infructescence through winter.

CULTURE: Easy to transplant; tolerant of many soils except those which are extremely wet; prefers full sun and open areas; pruning must be based on type of wood upon which flowers are produced; *S. × bumalda* should be pruned in early spring before growth starts if pruning is required, after flowers fade, remove them, and a second flush of growth is stimulated that will also produce additional flowers.

DISEASES AND INSECTS: Subject to many of the problems that afflict other members of the Rosaceae; fireblight, bacterial hairy root, leaf spot, powdery mildews, root rot, spirea aphid, oblique-banded leaf roller, scales, caterpillars and root-knot nematode; based on my experience it is difficult to kill a spirea.

LANDSCAPE VALUE: Good filler or facer plant, can be used as a low massing plant, possibly as a bank cover for it suckers from the roots; like most spireas has been overused.

CULTIVARS: *Spiraea* × *bumalda* is almost an enigma, and most European authorities place its cultivars (such as 'Anthony Waterer' and 'Froebelii') under *S. japonica*. In the hybrid form, *S. × bumalda* is considered a cross between *S. japonica* and *S. albiflora*. Since most American nursery catalogs and popular refernce books call the plant *S. × bumalda,* I will maintain similar consistency.

    S. × bumalda was described in 1891. England's Kew Gardens received it in 1885 from Karl Froebel of Zurich. (The original *S. × bumalda* was a dwarf plant, and a high proportion of the leaves were either marked with yellow or were totally yellow.) The emerging leaves of *S. × bumalda* are brownish red and essentially hairless and mature to a bluish green.

    The flowers are carmine-pink. Many authors have noted the instability of this clone, remarking that all the plants propagated throughout the world from this one plant are not the same due to the numerous branch sports.

'Anthony Waterer'—Originated from the original *S. × bumalda* described above. This cultivar also produces branch sports. The best form reaches 3 to 4′ high and 4 to 5′ wide at maturity. 'Anthony Waterer' has 4 to 6″ diameter, essentially flat-topped, carmine-pink inflorescences. The new leaves are brownish red changing to bluish green. They may turn wine-red to russet-red in fall. The leaves emerge in Georgia in early to mid-March. Flowers appear in late May and in June, and the reddish purple fall color is apparent by early November. The richly polished brown stems add a degree of winter interest. Based on many observations, I am convinced there are numerous (yes, numerous) forms floating around in the nursery trade. At the Georgia Botanical Garden, a so-called 'Anthony Waterer' planting develops puny, 2" diameter inflorescences and the strangest yellow-green leaf patterns imaginable. Some shoots are completely yellow, others are yellow and green, and some are even completely green. Another form listed as 'Anthony Waterer' does not develop branch sports and has long-lasting deep cerise-red flowers. Flower color is another variable trait, with certain plants displaying flowers of a deep carmine-pink. In the heat of the south, the plants' pigmentation is not as vibrant as that of plants farther north.

'Coccinea'—Is a bud mutation of 'Anthony Waterer' that has deep carmine-red flowers, decidedly more colorful than 'Anthony Waterer'; I first saw it at Bressingham Gardens in England and, although some literature says it differs very little in color, the plant I witnessed was much deeper red; maybe smaller than 'Anthony Waterer; perhaps 2 to 3' high; has developed branch sports.

'Crispa'—Is not well-known, and my first introduction to the plant occurred at the Morton Arboretum in Lisle, IL. In most respects, 'Crispa' is similar to 'Anthony Waterer'. However, its leaves are slightly twisted and deeply incised, giving the plant a slightly finer-textured appearance than 'Anthony Waterer'. I grew 'Crispa' in my Illinois garden and gave a plant to my sister in Cincinnati but never brought it into my Georgia garden. The plant in Cincinnati is 3 1/2' high and 4 to 5' wide. It has shown the yellow-green variegation pattern typical of most 'Anthony Waterer' clones. I suspect 'Crispa' originated as a branch sport of *S. × bumalda* or 'Anthony Waterer' but cannot locate corroborating evidence in the literature. At Wakehurst Place, England, I observed a plant labeled *S. japonica* 'Walluff' that looked exactly like 'Crispa'. This plant is listed in the literature as *S. × bumalda* 'Wallufii' and 'Walluf'. 'Walluf' is described as having a compact growth habit, young leaves reddish without variegation, flowers bright pink-red but lighter than 'Anthony Waterer'. There is no mention of the finely cut leaves on 'Walluf' and I suspect the plant at Wakehurst was labeled incorrectly. 'Crispa' develops chlorosis in high pH soils.

'Dart's Red'—A branch sport of 'Anthony Waterer' with deep carmine-red flowers paling somewhat as they fade; introduced by Darthuizer Nursery, Holland.

'Dolchica'—Was sent to me by Michael Epp who had read an article that I published on the summer flowering spireas [see *Amer. Nurseryman* 163(2):53–61 (1986)]. The plant, in most respects, has the same fine cutleaf character of 'Crispa' with deep purple-red (bronzy-purple) new growth and fine pink flowers; appears to be more stable, i.e., no variegated shoots and will mature between 1 1/2 and 2 1/2' high, 2 to 4' wide; the plant in my garden has performed admirably, but contracts aphids more so than other cultivars.

'Froebelii'—Has the same characteristics as 'Anthony Waterer', but its habit is slightly taller, 3 to 3 1/2' high, its leaves are slightly larger, its flowers are brighter (at least in the true form), and its inflorescences are smaller. New growth is brownish red and never develops variegated shoots. My observations of U.S. plants indicate that there is not a great deal of difference between the two, although the origin of 'Froebelii' is different from that of 'Anthony Waterer.' 'Froebelii' was distributed before 1894 by Froebel. Donald Wyman, author of *Shrubs and Vines for American Gardens,* noted that growth after flowering is vigorous enough to cover the dead flower heads. Dr. Harold Pellett, University of Minnesota Landscape Arboretum, believes that 'Froebelii' is probably the hardiest. He also believes that it is the best adapted to heat and drought. Wilson Nurseries Inc., Hampshire, IL, discovered a compact form of 'Froebelii' that is smaller and neater in habit. The selection has been called 'Dwarf Froebel' by this author, but more properly 'Gumball.' I am growing this form in my Georgia garden, and the plant is now 3' high and 4' wide; plants in the Botanic Garden are 3 1/2' high and wide; the plant definitely grows larger than originally advertised. The flowers are light pink, but this could be due to the heat. Most 'Froebelii' types do not have deep flower color compared to 'Anthony Waterer'.

'Goldflame'—Is one of the most popular forms and appears to be on fire when the leaves emerge in spring. Russet-orange to bronze-red leaves change to soft yellow, yellow-green and, finally, green. In Georgia, the summer leaf color is green; in England, it is yellowish. The spring leaf colors are often repeated in fall, making a rather handsome display. Leaves hold late, often into December in Athens. Will grow 2 to 3'(4') high and slightly wider at maturity. Its flowers are smaller than those of 'Anthony Waterer' and 'Froebelii' and are a rather sickly pink. In England,

I have observed the pink flowers in combination with the yellow-green leaves, and eyes and tummy became jaundiced and nauseous, respectively. The bright spot in the makeup of 'Goldflame' is its high heat tolerance. Leaf burn has not occurred on plants I have grown or observed in the southeast. Like other selections, 'Goldflame' displays the propensity to produce variegated green-and-gold shoots and leaves. It also produces green shoots, which must be removed. This phenomenon seems to occur more frequently on European than on American plants. Perhaps climate affects the stability of this clone. 'Goldflame' flowers about a week later than 'Dwarf Froebel' ('Gumball') in my garden.

'Limemound'—Is a new introduction from Monrovia Nursery Co., Azusa, CA, that arose as a branch sport of 'Goldflame'. In spring, dense, slender branches display lemon-yellow leaves with a russet tinge. The leaf color becomes lime-green when the leaves mature, and autumn foliage is orange-red on reddish stems. The branches form a uniform dwarf mounded outline. Supposedly, 'Limemound' is one zone more cold-hardy than 'Goldflame', which is hardy to Zone 4. Looks like a winner and will probably mature around 2' by 3'.

'Norman'—Is another mystery selection, but both Wyman and Brian Mulligan (formerly of the University of Washington Arboretum) describe it as a small, 10 to 12" high, compact plant with rosy pink flowers and raspberry-purple to red fall color that lasts for a month. It may be a form of *S. japonica*. Mrs. Wister has a plant in her Swarthmore, PA garden and indeed it fits the description to a "T". The fall foliage is particularly attractive. Leaves are much smaller than the typical *S.* × *bumalda* and *S. japonica*.

'Superba'—Is not well-known but is listed in the literature. The only plant I observed was at the Arnold Arboretum in Jamaica Plain, MA. In general, it resembles 'Anthony Waterer', the only difference being that 'Superba' bears flowers of a lighter pink. Technically, it is a hybrid between *S. albiflora* and *S. corymbosa,* although I have seen it listed as a *S.* × *bumalda* type.

I have a great interest in the dwarf spireas and have grown 'Anthony Waterer', 'Crispa', 'Dolchica', 'Goldflame', 'Gumball', 'Nyewoods', *S. j.* var. *alpina, S. j.* var. *a.* 'Little Princess, and *S. j.* 'Atrosanguinea'. They offered color (June-July) when other shrubs were in the green summer doldrums. Interestingly, 'Goldflame' became almost normal green in August while I observed the plant on Cape Cod in August and it was distinctly yellow-green. The summer heat has a great influence on whether yellow shrubs stay yellow, purple-purple and so forth. The compact spireas are excellent for modern landscapes where space is at a premium.

Spiraea cantoniensis 'Lanceata' — Double Reeves Spirea
(spī-rē'à kan-tō-ni-en'sis)

LEAVES: Alternate, simple, rhombic-oblong to rhombic-lanceolate, 1 to 2 1/2" long, 1/2 to 3/4" wide, cuneate, incised serrate, glabrous, bluish green above, pale bluish green beneath; petiole—1/3" long.

Spiraea cantoniensis 'Lanceata', Double Reeves Spirea, is more prominent in the south than the species. The habit is mounded-rounded with graceful, wispy, arching branches. Height ranges from 4 to 6' and the spread is similar. The leaves are bluish green and hold late in the fall without coloring. May be almost evergreen in deep south and part of California. The showy white, 1/2" diameter, many petaled flowers appear in abundance during early April (Georgia) in upright terminal corymbs. The flowers open before those of *S.* × *vanhouttei*. Often leaves and flowers emerge so early (March) that the tender flower buds are killed by a hard freeze. The flowers often overlap those of Vanhoutte. Pruning should be accomplished after flowering. This species displays excellent heat tolerance and its only requirements are full sun and well drained soil, although plants in half-shade are presentable. Have collected cuttings in July, treated them with 3000 ppm IBA quick dip, peat:perlite, mist and rooting was 100 percent. Grows extremely fast and would be a good filler in a shrub border. Should not be used for hedges. The species is one of the parents of the ubiquitious *S.* × *vanhouttei* and is seldom cultivated. China, Japan. Introduced 1824. Zone 6 to 9.

Spiraea × cinerea 'Grefsheim'
(spī-rē′à sin-e-rē′à)

Spiraea × cinerea 'Grefsheim' is about as handsome an early flowering spirea as one could ever hope to
find. The small, white flowers clothe the leafless branches in April presenting the entire shrub as a
white cloud. Flowers occur about 10 days ahead of *S. arguta*. In my opinion it is superior to *S. ×
arguta* and *S. thunbergii*. It forms a rather dense shrub with arching stems, 4 to 5′ high and wide.
The hybrid originated before 1884 and the cultivar is of Norwegian origin. Zone 4 to 7(8). Leaves are
narrow-elliptic or lanceolate, narrowed at both ends, almost entire, or with a few teeth at the apex;
about 1″ long, 1/3″ wide, soft sea green, appressed silky hairs beneath. Result of a cross between
S. cana and *S. hypericifolia*.

Spiraea japonica — Japanese Spirea
(spī-rē′à ja-pon′i-kà)

var. *alpina*

LEAVES: Alternate, simple, ovate to ovate-
oblong, 1 to 3″ long, acute, glaucescent
beneath and usually pubescent on the
veins; petioles about 1/8″ long.

Spiraea japonica, Japanese Spirea, is almost excessively variable and defies any
reasonable description. It is most often considered a 4 to 5′ high shrub with rounded,
flattened or angled, glabrous or hairy
branches. The leaves range from 1 to 3″
long with distinct, sharp serrations.

Normal flower color is rosy pink, with inflorescences in some of the garden forms
measuring as large as 12″ in diameter.
Ohwi, in his *Flora of Japan,* noted that the
species is common and variable where it is found in the mountains of Hokkaido, Honshu, Shikoku,
and Kyushu. It is also found in Korea, and in China north to the Himalayas. This wide geographic
range no doubt offers wonderful opportunities for the selection of different forms.

Spiraea japonica var. *alpina* (sometimes listed as *S. j.* 'Alpina' or 'Nana') is a rather handsome
variety that has hybridized with *S. × bumalda* cultivars to produce several interesting new selections.
In the common form, the shrub makes a dainty, fine-textured, low-growing mass with pink flowers in
late May (in Athens), June or July. It leafs out and flowers later than the *S. × bumalda* types, usually
5 to 10 days later.

The small, five-veined, light blue-green leaves cover the plant thickly and provide a fine foil for the
pink flowers. The leaves measure a half-inch or less but range to 1″ in some types.

The plant ranges from 15 to 30″ high to as much as 6′ in diameter. Over the years, I have allowed
it to cascade over walls and used it as a low facer and as a ground cover.

The origin of the plant is not clear. It was described in 1879 from a plant found wild on Mt. Hakone
in the central island of Japan. It had procumbent or erect stems and grew a "hand-breadth" high. The
general consensus is that the form of *S. j.* var. *alpina* in cultivation is of garden origin. The form in
cultivation does not come true from seed, with seedlings being more lax and possessing larger
leaves. Bean has treated var. *alpina* as a cultivar and listed it as 'Nana' ('Alpina').

One objection to *S. j.* var. *alpina* is posed by its retention of old seed heads, which give the plant
a rather shabby appearance. In late summer, the plant can look pretty ragged.

'Atrosanguinea' is a beautiful, deep rose-red form with 4 to 5″ diameter inflorescences. I grew this plant in Illinois and found the flower color slightly deeper than the "best" 'Anthony Waterer'. The growth habit is more stiff and upright than that of 'Anthony Waterer'. Pellett also mentioned this spirea as one of the best for deep rose-red flower color. Will grow 3 to 4′ high and wide.

'Coccinea' is often listed, but I am not exactly sure how different it is from *S. j.* 'Atrosanguinea'. It is a compact bushy plant growing about 2′ tall and wide, and it has rich crimson flowers. It is described as being similar to 'Froebelii' by W.J. Bean in *Trees and Shrubs Hardy in the British Isles.*

'Fortunei' was the first representative of *S. japonica* in Western gardens. it was sent from China to England by Robert Fortune in 1849. It was the commonest from in cultivation but has largely lost favor. I have not observed it in American gardens. The deep pink flowers occur in large inflorescences. *S. japonica* 'Fortunei' is one of the largest garden forms, often growing to about 5′.

'Glabrata' is described as a vigorous form with rosy pink flowers in 12″ diameter (or larger) corymbs. The broad-ovate leaves can reach 4 to 5″ long and 2 1/2 to 3″ wide. The plant's origin is unknown.

'Goldmound' is a hybrid between *S. j.* var. *alpina* and *S.* × *bumalda* 'Goldflame'. It was introduced by W.H. Perron Co. Ltd., Laval, Quebec, Canada. 'Goldmound' is a low-mounded form reminiscent of *S. japonica,* with pink flowers in May and June and golden leaves throughout the growing season. The golden leaf color fades in summer to a yellow-green. One report noted that 'Goldmound' burns badly in the heat of the south. From 1987 to 1989 this plant has been growing in the *Spiraea* test garden at the Botanical Garden and performing magnificently. The bright yellow coloration fades to yellow-green but even in August is still decidedly yellow and not green like 'Goldflame'. Best of all, no foliage burn has been observed and 1987 and 1988 were two of the driest and hottest years on record in the southeast. Might prove a great color addition to shrub and perennial borders, or any spot in full sun where some brightness is welcome, will mature around 2 1/2 to 3 1/2′ by 3 to 4′.

'Golden Princess' is a new introduction from Bressingham Gardens, England, and is protected by United Kingdom Plant Breeders Rights. The new leaves are bronze-yellow and then change to yellow. I do not know how the plant fares in America but suspect some reduction in yellow coloration occurs. The flowers are pink. The habit of 'Golden Princess' is gently mounded with an ultimate height of about 30″. The leaves appear to be slightly smaller than those of 'Goldflame'; I have seen the plant many times in England and it appears to offer the same fine qualities as 'Goldmound'. Apparently a seedling of 'Goldflame'.

'Little Princess'—From Holland is one of several closely related forms. This selection has larger leaves and deeper pink flower color than *S. j.* var. *alpina*. After repeated observations it became evident that 'Little Princess' grew faster, larger, and had larger leaves, to 1″ long, than var. *alpina*. Ultimate size will approach 30″ or greater.

'Macrophylla' has leaves as large as those of 'Glabrata' that display a distinctly inflated (bullate) condition. The leaves supposedly color well in autumn, but the flowers are small.

'Nyewoods'—Is considered to be the same as *S. j.* var. *alpina,* and, according to an article in *Dendroflora,* 1977, it is a synonym for *S. j.* var. *alpina.* I have observed 'Nyewoods' at several gardens in Ohio, and the proprietors insisted that 'Nyewoods' was different. The 'Nyewoods' I saw offered blue-green foliage, pink flowers and a compact habit. From a landscape viewpoint, the differences are probably not worth fighting over. The Holden Arboretum, Mentor, OH; Millcreek Valley Park, Youngstown, OH; and Wakehurst Place, England, display the plant as a distinct entity. If anything, 'Nyewoods' approximates 'Little Princess' more so than var. *alpina*.

A final note on *S. j.* var. *alpina* concerns the iron chlorosis that the plants often develop. In the midwest, I have observed some wonderfully golden forms, and they were not meant to be that way. I have not noticed problems in the south on *S. japonica* or on 'Little Princess'. Of course, soil pH in the Athens area is 4.5 to 6.0.

'Ovalifolia', is sometimes listed as *S. j.* var. *ovalifolia,* offers white flowers in 3 to 5″ diameter corymbs.

'Ruberrima' has dark rose flowers in downy corymbs; the plant grows to 3′ and develops a mounded outline.

'Shirobana' is an interesting selection that offers deep rose, pink and white flowers on the same plant. Individual inflorescences often have mixed colors. I first saw the plant at the University of British Columbia Botanical Garden, Vancouver, BC, Canada, in August 1985. The plant grows 2 to 3′ (4′) high and forms a handsome mound. I have grown the plant for several years and am most impressed by the recurrent flowering that continues through the summer sporadically even if the old inflorescences are not removed. The leaves are a lustrous deep green and probably the handsomest of any *S. japonica* form. The multiple colored flowers may not hold true depending on origin of propagation wood. The flowers are striking at their best.

NOTE: Additional cultivars with *S.* × *bumalda, S. japonica* et al. parentage were introduced by W.H. Perron and Co., Laval, Quebec, Canada. Their descriptions were published in *HortScience* 3(3): 455 (1988), and are presented here for reader awareness.

'Flaming Globe' (*S. japonica* 'Nana' and *S.* × *bumalda*)—Selected because of its rich, coppery-pink young foliage, which turns bright yellow in summer and bright red in autumn; fast-growing, dense shrub that forms a 12″ globe in 3 years; flowers are rarely produced.

'Flaming Mound' (*S.* × *bumalda* 'Goldflame' with *S. japonica* 'Nana')—Selected because of flaming red foliage, red flower buds turning yellow, and small, dark pink flowers; has 3″ by 3/4″ leaves and forms a 24″ high and 24″ diameter mound.

'Flowering Mound'—Selected because of young, reddish leaves, which turn yellow, and abundant, dark pink flower clusters during June, July, and August; foliage turns pink-orange after frost; softwood cuttings grow into saleable plants in 17 months; forms a compact, bushy mound 28″ high by 36″ across in 7 years.

'Glowing Globe' (*S.* × *bumalda* 'Goldflame' with *S. japonica* 'Nana')—Selected because of reddish pink foliage, which turns salmon in the sun; becomes green-yellow in shade; forms a strong, bushy, globose plant 12″ in diameter in 3 years.

'Glowing Mound' (*S.* × *bumalda* with *S. japonica* 'Nana')—Selected because of yellow leaves with a pinkish glow; change to a coppery-pink after the first frost; flowers sparingly, with small, pink flowers; forms a mound, 30″ high by 36″ across after 3 years; leaves are 2 1/2″ by 1/2 to 3/4″.

'Golden Carpet' (*S.* × *bumalda* 'Goldflame' with *S. japonica* 'Nana')—Selected because of creeping habit and golden leaves, which are 3/5″ long by 1/3″ broad; forms a carpet 3″ thick by 8″ in diameter in 3 years; in contact with soil, branches root easily.

'Golden Globe' (*S.* × *bumalda* 'Goldflame' with *S. japonica* 'Nana)—Chosen for salmon-pink new growth, which changes to golden yellow; color holds until fall, when it turns pink; in sunny, dry locations it forms a dense, globose shrub 10″ high by 10″ across.

'Green Globe' (*S.* × *bumalda* and *S. japonica* 'Nana')—Selected because of vigorous, compact habit and small, bright green leaves (1″ by 1/2″), which turn to brilliant purple-red in early fall; produces small, light pink flowers from June to September; forms a dense globe 7 to 8″ tall by 10″ in diameter in 4 years.

'Lightened Mound' (*S. japonica* 'Nana')—Selected because of creamy-lemon leaves, which turn to lime in summer; does best in partial shade, as it sunburns in hot summers; flowers rarely; forms dense mounds 18″ tall by 20″ in diameter in 2 years.

'Sparkling Carpet' (*S.* × *bumalda* 'Goldflame' and *S.* × *bumalda*)—Selected because of dense, prostrate habit and reddish pink leaves which turn yellow; the branches are stronger and denser than those of 'Golden Carpet' and the leaves are smaller (3/4″ long by 1/3″ broad); the plant forms a multicolored carpet 4″ thick by 11″ across in 3 years; flowers are rare or nonexistent.

Spiraea nipponica 'Snowmound' — Snowmound Nippon Spirea
(spī-rē′à nip-pon′i-kà)

LEAVES: Alternate, simple, narrowly oblong-obovate, 1 to 1 1/2″ long, 3/8 to 1/2″ wide, toothed at the rounded apex, rarely entire, cuneate, dark blue-green; petiole 1/6 to 1/8″ long.

Spiraea nipponica 'Snowmound', Snowmound Nippon Spirea, has performed admirably and appears to be a superior replacement for *S.* × *vanhouttei*. The plant grows 3 to 5′ high and as wide, with small dark blue-green leaves and white flowers appearing in late May into June. It maintains a neater, denser outline than Vanhoutte. There have been reports of isolated branches dying out but I have not observed this. Have had reasonably good success with 'Snowmound' on the Georgia campus. 'Rotundifolia' is considered the typical state of the species with broadly obovate or oval, sometimes nearly round, 1/2 to 1″ long, sometimes entire, but usually with a few broad teeth at the rounded apex. In variety *tosaensis,* which I believe is confused with 'Snowmound', the leaves are linear-oblong, tapered at the base, entire or with 2 or 3 teeth at the apex, 3/8 to 1″ long, 1/8 to 1/4″ wide. It is not a profuse flowerer. 'Halward's Silver' is more compact than the species and densely branched, will grow 30 to 36″ in 3 to 5 years, covered with abundant white flowers, introduced by Royal Botanic Garden, Hamilton, Ontario. Native to the island of Shikoku, Japan. Zone 3 to 8.

Spiraea prunifolia — Bridalwreath Spirea
(spī-rē′à prū-ni-fō′li-à)

LEAVES: Alternate, simple, elliptic to elliptic-oblong, 1 to 2″ long, 1/2 to 3/4″ wide, acute at ends, denticulate, lustrous dark green and glabrous above, finely pubescent beneath; petiole about 1/8″ long.
STEM: Zig-zag, slender, shiny borwn, glabrous.

Spiraea prunifolia, Bridalwreath Spirea, is an old favorite (I do not know why) growing 4 to 9′ tall and 6 to 8′ wide. It is an open, coarse, straggly shrub, often leggy, upright and limitedly spreading with foliage on the upper 50% of the plant. The foliage is shiny dark green in summer and may turn yellow-orange to purplish bronze in fall but is never overwhelming. The flowers are white, double, 1/3″ diameter, 3 to 6 together and virtually cover the leafless stems in mid to late April; in Athens it starts to show color in February and is usually in full flower by early March. I really see no use for this plant in modern gardens; it belongs to the "Over the hill gang". The single flowered form is listed as var. or forma *simpliciflora* and is rarely cultivated; 'Plena' is the form described here. Korea, China, Formosa. Cultivated 1864. Zone 4 to 8.

Spiraea thunbergii — Thunberg Spirea
(spī-rē′à thun-bēr′jē-ī)

LEAVES: Alternate, simple, linear-lanceolate, 1 to 1 1/2″ long, 1/8 to 1/4″ wide, acuminate, sharply serrate,glabrous, pale green.
STEM: Extremely slender and fine, slightly angled, zig-zag, light brown, downy to glabrous, primarily the latter on cultivated plants.

Spiraea thunbergii, Thunberg Spirea, grows 3 to 5′ tall and 3 to 5′ wide. It is a bushy, slender-branched, tiny leaved shrub, rather loosely spreading and arching and very twiggy. Foliage is yellowish green in summer and turns yellowish, tinged with orange and bronze in fall and holds late (not very effective). Flowers are white, 1/3″ across, March-April (early to mid March, Athens) before the leaves; usually the first spirea to flower; borne in 3 to 5 flowered sessile umbels. Definitely requires pruning to keep the plant in good condition

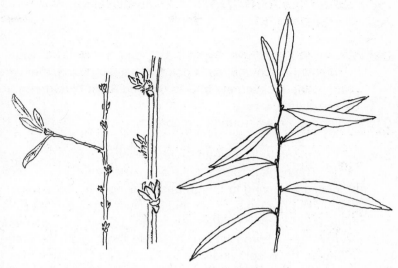

as it becomes straggly and open. My fondness for the species has increased since coming to Georgia. The wispy fine textured foliage of light green contrasts with the darker greens of most shrubs. Have seen mass plantings and was impressed by the effect. Another species, *S.* × *arguta,* (spī-rē′á är-gū′tá), Garland Spirea, is similar to the above but larger growing and, in fact, is a cross between *S.* × *multiflora* × *S. thunbergii.* I cannot see a great deal of difference in the two. The leaves of *S. thunbergii* appear to be serrated throughout their length while in *S.* × *arguta* the serrations are lacking or occur only above the middle. The oblanceolate leaves are 3/4 to 1 1/2″ long, 1/4 to 1/2″ wide, light green and glabrous above. *S.* × *arguta* flowers later than *S. thunbergii.* It was raised sometime before 1884. The cultivar 'Compacta' grows to 4′ tall. All flower on old wood and pruning should be accomplished after flowering. This is also true for *S. prunifolia* and *S.* × *vanhouttei.* Native to Japan, China. Introduced 1830. Zone 4 to 8.

S. × *arguta*

Spiraea trilobata — Threelobe Spirea
(spī-rē′á trī-lō-bā′tá)

LEAVES: Alternate, simple, roundish, 1/2 to 1″ long (1 to 1 1/2″ rarely), about as wide, coarsely toothed, sometimes obscurely 3 or 5-lobed, base rounded or sometimes slightly heartshape, glaucous green.
STEM: Zig-zag, round.

Spiraea trilobata, Threelobe Spirea, is a relatively small (4 to 5′) shrub of dense compact habit with slender spreading branches. The small, usually rounded to 3-lobed leaves are bluish green. The pure white flowers occur in 3/4 to 1 1/2″ diameter umbels and appear in great profusion during May. In many respects the flowers remind of *S.* × *vanhouttei.* 'Swan Lake' is considered more floriferous than the species and a degree more compact. Based on photographs I've seen it might be an excellent alternative to Vanhoutte and the larger growing spireas. It will probably mature between 3 and 4′. 'Fairy Queen' is a compact 3′ high and wide shrub with dark green lobed leaves and frothy masses of white flowers in May-June. Northern China to Siberia and Turkestan. Introduced 1801. Zone 3 to 7. One of the parents of Vanhoutte. Apparently withstands considerable shade and still flowers well.

Spiraea × *vanhouttei* — Vanhoutte Spirea
(spī-rē′a̲ van-hoot′ē-ī)

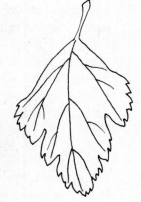

LEAVES: Alternate, simple, 3/4 to 1 3/4″ long, 1/2 to 1 1/4″ wide, rhombic-ovate
or somewhat obovate, apex pointed, base tapering, teeth irregular, coarse,
often incised, obscurely to 3 to 5-lobed, dark blue-green above, glaucous
below, glabrous.

STEM: Slender, brown, rounded, glabrous.

Spiraea × *vanhouttei,* Vanhoutte Spirea, grows 6 to 8′ (10′) high and spreads 10
to 12′. The habit is fountain-like or vase-shaped, round-topped with arching
branches recurving to the ground, making a tall broad mound. Foliage is a
dull bluish green in summer and fall color is nonexistent or perhaps with an
overcast of purple. Flowers are white, 1/3″ across; April-May (early to mid
April, Athens); borne in many flowered 1 to 2″ diameter umbels. Very showy
in flower. I was spraying weed killer and had a bit left over and decided to
apply the rest to the Vanhoutte Spireas which were left by the previous owner. To my surprise the
herbicide did not affect the plant in the slightest. I think this says something about its toughness. This
is undeniably the most popular of all the spireas and is a hybrid between *S. trilobata* × *S. cantoniensis.* The arching, fountain-like habit coupled with the profusion of white flowers has contributed to its
popularity with the masses. Zone 3 to 8(9). Raised by Billiard in about 1862.

PROPAGATION: All spireas root readily from softwood cuttings taken in June or July; IBA treatment
usually improves rooting but is not necessary in most cases; I have had great success with all the *S.
× bumalda* and *S. japonica* forms. Seed requires no special treatment and will germinate readily
when directly sown although, if dried, a one-month cold stratification is beneficial.

OTHER *SPIRAEA* SPECIES

Spiraea decumbens, (spī-rē′a̲ dē-kum′benz), literally jumped into my life during a June visit to Germany. The habit is compact spreading, probably no taller than 8″ high with prostrate branches. It
was covered with frothy masses of white flowers. Might be an ideal ground cover species for full
sun and certainly could be used in rock gardens. The flowers are only 1/4″ diameter but occur in 2″
wide flat-topped corymbs. The green leaves are obovate or oval, tapered at both ends, and rather
coarsely toothed toward the apex, glabrous with a 1/8″ long petiole. Found on limestone soil in the
wild. Southeastern Europe. Cultivated 1830. Zone 5 to 8.

Spiraea betulifolia var. ***aemiliana,*** (spī-rē′a̲ bet-ū-li-fō′li-a̲ a̲-mil′ē-ā′na̲), Birchleaf Spirea, is a compact mounded rather dense shrub probably 2 to 2 1/2′ at maturity. The white flowers occur in flattish
corymbs after the leaves have matured. The principal ornamental characteristic is the long persistent gold, yellow and bronze fall color. I have obtained a plant and look forward to evaluating its
performance. True var. *aemiliana* is generally smaller (8 to 12″ high) than the species, however,
the plant I have seen in cultivation listed as the variety favors the above description.

Spiraea fritschiana (spī-rē′a̲ frit-shē-ā′na̲) is virtually unknown in the United States but offers dark
green foliage and 1 to 3″ diameter flat-topped white flowers in May-June on a 2 to 3′ high compact
mounded shrub. I have grown this in Illinois and Georgia with success and know that it grows in
Fargo, ND which attests to hardiness. Worth a try in difficult climates. Leaves are elliptic or
elliptic-ovate to elliptic-oblong, 1 to 3 1/2″ long, acute to acuminate, cuneate, simple serrate, with
a 1/4″ long petiole. This species is closely related to *S. betulifolia.* Central China to Korea.
Introduced 1919. Zone (3)4 to 8.

Staphylea trifolia — American Bladdernut
(staf-i-lē′á trī-fō′li-á)

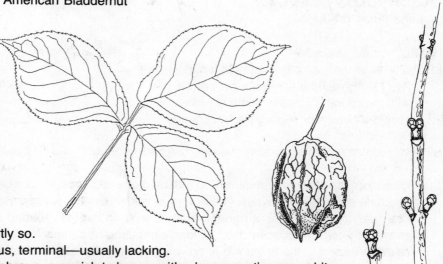

FAMILY: Staphyleaceae

LEAVES: Opposite, compound pinnate, 3 leaflets, ovate to broadly ovate, 2 to 4″ long, acuminate, sharply and unequally serrate, dark green above, pubescent beneath, sometimes glabrate at maturity, the middle leaflet long stalked, the laterals shortly so.

BUDS: Solitary, ovoid, glabrous, terminal—usually lacking.

STEM: Moderate, rounded, glabrous, greenish to brown; pith—large, continuous, white.

SIZE: 10 to 15′ in height, usually taller than wide at maturity.

HARDINESS: Zone 3 to 8.

HABIT: Upright, heavily branched, suckering shrub with smooth striped bark forming a solid aggregate of brush; sometimes wide spreading; actually a rather attractive shrub.

RATE: Medium to fast.

TEXTURE: Medium in leaf; medium-coarse in winter.

BARK: Light, greenish gray with linear white fissures, branchlets at first pale green with white lenticels, downy, later brownish purple, finally ashen gray, glabrous.

LEAF COLOR: Bright green when emerging eventually turning dark green in summer; developing pale dull yellow in fall.

FLOWERS: Perfect, greenish white, bell-shaped, borne in nodding, 1 1/2 to 2″ long panicles, abundant, April-May.

FRUIT: A 3-lobed, 1 to 1 1/2″ long, inflated capsule, pale green changing to light brown, effective in September; usually containing several hard, yellowish brown, 3/16″ diameter rounded seeds.

CULTURE: Prefers moist, well-drained soils; performs better under cultivation than in native haunts; in the wild is often loose and open, but under cultivation takes on a more dense, vigorous nature; have found it in heavy shade just above the flood plain in the Georgia Botanical Garden.

DISEASES AND INSECTS: None serious.

LANDSCAPE VALUE: Not a great deal; could be used in naturalizing; best reserved for parks and other low maintenance areas; rather nice for foliage effect.

PROPAGATION: Seed apparently possesses a double dormancy; do not allow the seed to dry out before stratification; 3 months warm followed by 3 months at 40°F is recommended. Softwood and hardwood cuttings root easily.

NATIVE HABITAT: Quebec to Ontario and Minnesota, south to Georgia and Missouri. Cultivated 1640.

RELATED SPECIES:

Staphylea colchica, (staf-i-lē′á kōl′chi-ká), Colchis Bladdernut, is somewhat similar to the above but the leaflets are usually in 5′s and the orange-blossom fragrant flowers are borne later, usually in May or June. It, too, is a suckering, upright shrub growing 6 to 10′ high. The flowers occur in erect panicles, the largest up to 5″ long and wide. The seeds are 1/3″ long and pale brown. It is quite handsome in flower. 'Coulombieri' may be a hybrid between *S. colchica* and *S. pinnata*. The leaves are composed of 3 to 5 dark green leaflets. Flowers and fruits are intermediate between the parents. I saw *S. colchica* in flower at Rockingham Castle, England, in mid-May. It was easily 10′ high and 15 to 18′ wide and made a fine display.

ADDITIONAL NOTES: The most curious aspect of bladdernuts is the inflated, balloon-like fruit.

Stachyurus praecox
(sta-che-ū′rus prē′koks)

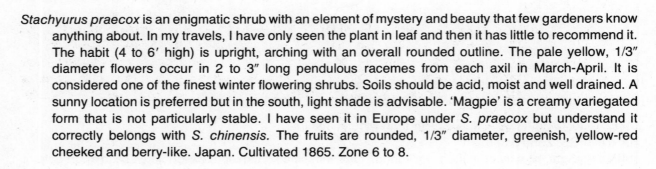

FAMILY: Stachyuraceae
LEAVES: Alternate, simple, ovate-lanceolate,
3 to 7″ long, acuminate, rounded, serrate
with spreading teeth, lustrous dark
green, glabrous or slightly pubescent on
veins below.
STEM: Reddish brown to chestnut-brown, lustrous, glabrous.

Stachyurus praecox is an enigmatic shrub with an element of mystery and beauty that few gardeners know
anything about. In my travels, I have only seen the plant in leaf and then it has little to recommend it.
The habit (4 to 6′ high) is upright, arching with an overall rounded outline. The pale yellow, 1/3″
diameter flowers occur in 2 to 3″ long pendulous racemes from each axil in March-April. It is
considered one of the finest winter flowering shrubs. Soils should be acid, moist and well drained. A
sunny location is preferred but in the south, light shade is advisable. 'Magpie' is a creamy variegated
form that is not particularly stable. I have seen it in Europe under *S. praecox* but understand it
correctly belongs with *S. chinensis*. The fruits are rounded, 1/3″ diameter, greenish, yellow-red
cheeked and berry-like. Japan. Cultivated 1865. Zone 6 to 8.

Stephanandra incisa—Cutleaf Stephanandra
(stef-a-nan′dra in-sīz′a)

FAMILY: Rosaceae

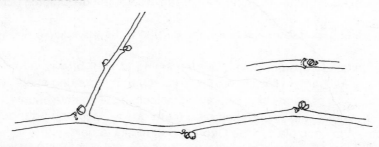

LEAVES: Alternate, 2-ranked, simple, ovate, long-acuminate, cordate to truncate, 1 to 2″ long, or on shoots
to 3″ long, less in width, incisely lobed and serrate, the lower incisions halfway to the midrib, bright
green above, pubescent on the veins beneath; petioles 1/8 to 1/2″ long; stipules linear, toothed, 1/4″
long.
BUDS: Small, superposed, ovoid, with about 4 scales.
STEM: Terete, or somewhat 5-lined from the nodes, slender, zig-zag, warm brown, glabrous.

SIZE: 4 to 7′ high with an equal or greater spread.
HARDINESS: Zone 3 to 7(8).
HABIT: Graceful shrub with dense, fine to medium-textured foliage and wide spreading, arching slender
branches; tends to form a haystack-like mound; suckers freely from the base.
RATE: Fast.
TEXTURE: Medium to fine in leaf; medium in winter.
STEM COLOR: Warm brown.
LEAF COLOR: Tinged reddish bronze when unfolding, later bright green; red-purple or red-orange in fall,
not particularly effective.
FLOWERS: Yellowish white, small; May-June; borne in loose terminal panicles, 1 to 2 1/2″ long; not
particularly showy, in fact, I did not know the two small plants in my garden were flowering, although

I walked past them every day, until I was doing some hand weeding and inadvertently gazed upon the flowers.

FRUIT: Follicle, not showy.

CULTURE: Easy to transplant, best moved as a container plant; prefers moist, acid, well-drained soil that has been supplemented with peat moss or leaf mold, although tolerant of most soils; full sun or light shade; in exposed, windswept areas the very delicate young branches may be killed, at least near the tips, in winter; simply prune back to live tissue before new growth starts; tends to root wherever the stems touch the soil; will develop chlorosis in high pH soils.

DISEASES AND INSECTS: None serious.

LANDSCAPE VALUE: The species could be used for hedges, massing, screens, or in the shrub border while the low growing cultivar 'Crispa' makes an excellent facer, bank cover, or ground cover plant.

CULTIVARS:

'Crispa'—Handsome form which grows 1 1/2 to 3' tall and forms a low, thick tangle of stems; it makes an excellent mass or ground cover planting, more common than the species in cultivation.

PROPAGATION: Roots readily from cuttings taken at any time of the year. I have used softwood (June and July collected) cuttings and had 100% success; seeds appear to require a warm/cold period or perhaps light scarification followed by about 3 months cold; 3 months warm followed by 3 months cold produced 89% germination.

NATIVE HABITAT: Japan, Korea. Cultivated 1872.

RELATED SPECIES:

Stephanandra tanakae, (stef-à-nan'drà tà-nà'kē), Tanaka Stephanandra, is larger (6'), more vigorous growing than *S. incisa* with larger, 3 to 5″ long, 3 to 5-lobed and incisely toothed leaves. It is rather attractive but not preferable to *S. incisa.* Japan. Introduced 1893. Zone 5 to 7.

Stewartia ovata — Mountain Stewartia
(stū-är'ti-a ō-vā'ta)

FAMILY: Theaceae

LEAVES: Alternate, simple, ovate or elliptic to ovate-oblong, 2 to 5″ long, about half as wide, acuminate, usually rounded at the base, serrulate almost to base, dark green above, sparingly pubescent and grayish green beneath, thickish with a rubbery texture; petiole 1/8 to 3/5″ long, winged.

BUDS: Solitary or superposed, sessile, compressed-fusiform, with 2 or 3 exposed scales, brown.

STEM: Moderate, subterete, in youth tinged with red above, green or creamy below, distinctly zig-zag; pith—rounded, somewhat spongy.

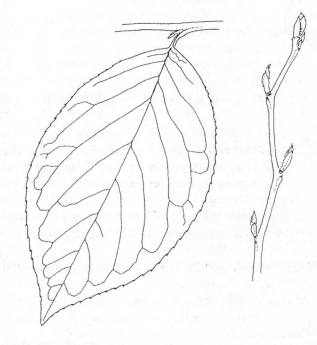

SIZE: 10 to 15' high and wide.

HARDINESS: Zone 5 to 9.

HABIT: Large shrub or small tree with spreading branches and a bushy habit.

RATE: Slow.

TEXTURE: Medium in leaf and winter.

BARK: Not particularly handsome compared to the other species, brown.

LEAF COLOR: Dark green in summer; beautiful orange to scarlet in fall, although this species is not as colorful as *S. pseudocamellia.*

FLOWERS: Perfect, white, 5, often 6, concave, obovate petals, each crimped and crenulated, filaments whitish to purple; each flower 2 1/2 to 3″ wide, up to 4″ on some plants, July to August; June-July in Athens.

FRUIT: Woody, sharply 5-angled, 1/2 to 1″ long, dehiscent capsule, each chamber containing up to 4 seeds.

CULTURE: Applies to *Stewartia* in general, somewhat difficult to transplant and should be moved as a small (4 to 5′ or less) container or balled and burlapped plant in early spring; the soil should be moist, acid (pH 4.5 to 6.5), abundantly supplemented with leaf mold or peat moss; they do best where there is sun most of the day, but shade during the hottest periods; they seldom require pruning; *S. ovata* is found as an understory shrub along stream banks and occurs in the wild about 20 miles north of Athens, GA; I checked specimens in the Botany Department's herbarium and discovered that plants have been found in rocky, moist soils on the walls of a canyon.

DISEASES AND INSECTS: Basically free of problems.

LANDSCAPE VALUE: *Stewartia,* in general, make specimen plants and should not be hidden in some obscure corner of the landscape; the flowers, fall color and bark are among the best; I have seen plants used in shrub borders or on the edges of woodlands; some shade, at least in hot climates, is probably a necessity; observations in Zone 8 indicate *S. monadelpha, S. ovata* and *S. malacodendron* are the best; over the years, several *S. pseudocamellia* have been planted in the Botanical Garden and none have lived; summer drought and high night temperatures may contribute to decline; the beautiful exfoliating cream, tan, rich brown bark of *S. koreana* or *S. pseudocamellia* is unparalleled among *Stewartia* species.

CULTIVARS:

var. *grandiflora*—Has larger flowers than the species, up to 4″ diameter, and purple stamens; it is beautiful in flower, and may have up to 8 petals. I do not believe everyone is in agreement as to whether this is a true variety for people I have talked with say purple stamens occur in wild populations of the true species; it is best to use var. *grandiflora* as a name to distinguish purple-stamened types.

PROPAGATION: Seeds require a warm/cold treatment and 3 to 5 months warm followed by 3 months cold is probably best; personally I have not had much success with seed although a nurseryman friend, Mr. Don Shadow, Winchester, TN had tremendous success planting seeds in the fall with germination taking place the second spring following planting; the backyard gardener would do well to put the seeds in a clay flower pot, sink it in the ground, and practice the same patience as Mr. Shadow. Cuttings are, to say the least, a challenge; most species can be rooted from softwood cuttings at 70 to 90 percent using high IBA levels (1 to 2%), peat:perlite, mist; it is quite critical that the cuttings are not moved after rooting but allowed to go through a dormancy period; when new growth is initiated, they should be transplanted; this genus has driven me to the brink of propagation insanity; too many times cuttings have been successfully rooted only to lose them during the overwintering period; I have followed every precaution and have one *S. monadelpha* that has been successfully overwintered, probably out of 1000 rooted cuttings. Also seeds can be manipulated by warm/cold treatments to germinate but the resulting seedlings are reluctant to grow; many times I have had bags of seeds with root radicles evident yet have no plants to show; as far as I am concerned nurserymen deserve any price they charge.

NATIVE HABITAT: North Carolina to Tennessee and Florida. Cultivated 1800.

RELATED SPECIES:

Stewartia koreana — Korean Stewartia
(stū-är′ti-a̍ kôr-ē-ā′na̍)

LEAVES: Alternate, simple, elliptic to broad-elliptic, 1 1/4 to 4″ long, 3/4 to 3″ wide, abruptly acuminate, broad-cuneate or rounded, remotely serrate, dark green and glabrous above, slightly pubescent below.

Stewartia koreana, Korean Stewartia, is a small (20 to 30′), dense, somewhat pyramidal tree that maintains an upright character into old age. The dark green leaves may turn excellent red to reddish purple in fall although I have seen trees with little color and others that were spectacular. The white, 3″ diameter, 5 to 6 petaled, yellow-stamened flowers occur on 3/4″ long, glabrous pedicels in June-July. The flowers tend to be flattened rather than cup-shape and appear over a long time period. The best feature is the rich flaky bark that, in spite of what the books say (reddish brown) ranges from soft grays and browns to orangish brown with often all colors intermingled on the same tree. In my mind this species is fairly similar to *S. pseudocamellia* and the differences are, at best, slight. E.H. Wilson introduced this species from Korea in 1917. Zone 5 to 7.

Stewartia malacodendron — Silky Stewartia
(stū-är′ti-á mal-ak-ō-den′dron)

LEAVES: Alternate, simple, elliptic to elliptic-oblong, 2 to 4″ long, acute or short acuminate, cuneate, serrulate and ciliate, dark green and glabrous above, light green and pubescent beneath; petiole 1/4″ long, pubescent.

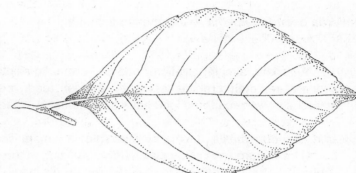

Stewart malacodendron, Silky Stewartia, is a southeastern United States native found principally in the Coastal Plain. Herbarium sheets I checked noted that it is found on the side of streams but also in drier areas. The habit is that of a large shrub or small tree growing 10 to 15′ (18′) high. There is a splendid specimen at Biltmore Estate, Asheville, NC; have seen the plant in Savannah, GA performing well. The 2 1/2 to 3 1/2″ diameter, white petaled, purple-filamented, blue-anthered flowers appear singly from the leaf axils in July and August (June, Asheville, NC). The fruit is a woody, egg-shaped, 1/2″ diameter, 5-valved capsule and the lustrous brown seeds are wingless. The bark is gray-brown, not effective compared to *S. koreana, S. pseudocamellia, S. monadelpha* and *S. sinensis.* Differs from *S. ovata* in leaf shape and the united styles. Virginia and Arkansas to Florida and Louisiana. Cultivated 1752. Zone (6)7 to 9.

Stewartia monadelpha — Tall Stewartia
(stū-är′ti-á mon-á-del′fá)

LEAVES: Alternate, simple, elliptic to oblong-elliptic, 1 1/2 to 3″ long, 5/8 to 1 1/4″ wide, acute, rounded or broad cuneate, finely serrate, dark green above, grayish green and pubescent below; petiole 1/2″ long.

Stewartia monadelpha, Tall Stewartia, was little more than an afterthought in the last edition, but after observing it in the southeast, I believe gardeners should be growing this instead of *S. pseudocamellia.* I have an 8 to 10′ tall plant that has provided tremendous satisfaction over the last 8 years. The habit is pyramidal, rounded and almost shrubby although older trees at Callaway Gardens are more open and horizontally branched and about 20 to 25′ high after 30-plus years. The dark green leaves have developed outstanding deep reddish, almost maroon fall color on 3 or 4 occasions in my garden. The leaves hold into December and may be killed at 20 to 25°F. The bark is given short shrift in most references but in youth is rich brown and scaly. The scales are small and exfoliation is not as manifest as on *S. pseudocamellia.* However, with age, the older trunks become rich, almost cinnamon-brown and smooth. I can focus in on this species more easily by bark than many of the other species. Interestingly, the species displays *excellent* heat tolerance and should be considered for southern gardens. The flowers are the smallest of the species treated here, being 1 to 1 1/2″ wide, white with yellowish stamens. Flowers tend to remain cupped and do not open as wide as *S. koreana, S. pseudocamellia.* Flowers open over 4 weeks starting in early June in my garden. Fruit is a small, 5-valved, 1/2″ long woody beaked capsule covered with appressed pubescence. Best in partial shade but will take full sun. Japan. Cultivated 1903. Zone 6 to 8.

Stewartia pseudocamellia — Japanese Stewartia
(stū-är′ti-à soo-dō-ka-mēl′e-à)

LEAVES: Alternate, simple, elliptic or obovate-elliptic to elliptic-lanceolate, 2 to 3 1/2″ long, acuminate, cuneate, remotely crenate, serrulate, thickish, dark green and glabrous above, light green and glabrous or with scattered long hairs below; petiole 1/8 to 3/8″ long.

Stewartia pseudocamellia, Japanese Stewartia, is a magnificent small to medium-sized pyramidal-oval tree. The mature landscape size is 20 to 40′ but, in the wild, it will grow 60′ high. The dark green leaves may turn yellow, red to dark reddish purple in fall. The 2 to 2 1/2″ diameter white flowers with white filaments and orange anthers occur in July. Fruit is a broad-ovoid, 1″ long, hairy, 5-valved capsule. This is possibly the best tree for the garden and is commercially available. Several fine specimens at the Dawes Arboretum have withstood -22°F. The plant pretty much speaks for itself with maturity. The bark is outstanding and develops a rather sinuous, musclely character with the wonderful exfoliating bark fragments painting a lovely portrait. As I write this I reflect on beautiful specimens at the Arnold Arboretum, Hershey Gardens, Swarthmore...each an individual. As mentioned under *S. ovata,* I have reservations about its performance in Zone 8. The bark is much like that of *S. koreana* and provides excellent winter color. Japan. Introduced 1874. Zone (4)5 to 7.

Stewartia sinensis — Chinese Stewartia
(stū-är′ti-à sī-nen′sis)

LEAVES: Alternate, simple, elliptic-obovate to oblong-elliptic, 1 1/2 to 4″ long, 5/8 to 1 3/4″ wide, acuminate, cuneate or rarely rounded, remotely serrate or crenate-serrate, medium green and glabrous above, bright green below; petiole 1/8 to 1/4″ long, hairy.

Stewartia sinensis, Chinese Stewartia, is a small (15 to 25′) tree or large shrub with a rich, smooth, light tan-white bark. The medium green leaves may turn reddish in fall but the few trees I have observed were a subdued reddish and certainly not the rich crimson as described in some references. This is a delightful small landscape plant that should be more widely used. The white, fragrant, cup-shaped, 1 1/2 to 2″ diameter flowers are smaller than those of the other species treated here, with the exception of *S. monadelpha.* The ovoid, 5-angled and 5-beaked, 3/4″ wide capsule is about the largest of the genus. Considerable travel was necessary before I was able to straighten the confusion between this and *S. monadelpha.* The bark in the finest form is choice and a plant at Wakehurst Place, England, is my type specimen for comparing all others. Bean terms the bark "as smooth as alabaster and the color of weathered sandstone" and, indeed, I have stroked the trunk and branches feeling I had touched polished marble. On young plants, the bark exfoliates in relatively long sheets. Hardy to Boston and should be pursued by discriminating gardeners. *S. sinensis* is native to central China. Introduced 1901. Zone 5 to 7.

ADDITIONAL NOTES: All are wonderful garden plants and are worth seeking. I believe a moist, well-drained, high organic matter, acid soil is important. They have no serious pests and once established, offer many years of season-long beauty. Stewartias can easily be categorized among the crème de la crème of woody flowering shrubs/trees. Unfortunately, their availability in commerce is limited and in one 1988 nursery catalog a 4 to 5′ high *S. pseudocamellia* was costed at $135.00. Even at that price it is a bargain, for the years of enjoyment provided, it is an inexpensive price to pay. Gossler Farms Nursery, 1200 Weaver Road, Springfield, OR 97478-9663 offers the finest assortment and most reasonable price available.

Another species that the collector might want to track includes *S. serrata* . . . with dull green, incurved, serrated, 1 1/2 to 3″ long leaves and 2 to 2 1/2″ wide, creamy white, yellow-anthered stamens. I have not seen this species in flower but note that Gossler Farms offers it. As a final note, I recommend Spongberg's article on *Stewartia* in the *Journal of the Arnold Arboretum* 55: 182–214 (1978) for the true afficiendo.

Stranvaesia davidiana — Chinese Stranvaesia
(stran-vē′zi-á dā-vid-i-ā′ná)

FAMILY: Rosaceae
LEAVES: Alternate, simple, semi-evergreen to evergreen, elliptic-ovate, 2 to 5″ long, 3/8 to 1″ (1 3/4″ wide), acute, rounded, entire, lustrous dark green above, pale beneath, glabrous or pubescent on veins; petiole—1/4 to 1/2″ long, grooved above, pubescent, 2 persistent stipules.
BUDS: 2 to 3 scaled, appressed, red, 1/4″ long, remind of willow buds; set directly above the leaf scar.
STEM: Stout, pubescent, red-purple, showing 3-decurrent ridges that run from base and sides of leaf scar; 2nd year stems brown; pith—green, solid.

Stranvaesia davidiana, Chinese Stranvaesia, is a large shrub or small tree that may grow 30 to 35′ in height. In the U.S. it tends to be rather shrub-like and is doubtfully preferable to many evergreen shrubs. The leaves are not particularly dense which results in an open, less than ideal specimen. The leaves turn red before falling and occur on the inside of the plant, presenting a rather handsome two-toned effect. The 1/4″ diameter white flowers occur in lax, hairy, 3″ diameter corymbs in summer. The globose, 1/4 to 3/8″ wide, bright red fruits are attractive. The fruits make a good show and persist for a long period. It prefers a moist, slightly acid, organic, well drained soil. Seeds apparently require a 2 month cold period and softwood cuttings taken in June-July can be rooted. 'Fructu Luteo' is a yellow fruited form. 'Prostrata' is a vigorous prostrate form that can be used as a ground cover. I have seen it at the Arnold Arboretum. 'Palette' has reddish pink shoots that develop light green, pink and cream leaves; it flowers and bears red fruits; grows 4 to 6′ high, a branch sport discovered in Holland. Western China. Introduced 1917. Zone (5)6. Not cultivated to any degree in the U.S. May be susceptible to fireblight. Bean describes 'Redstart' as a relatively new clone that may have great promise in the United States. It is the result of a cross between *Stranvaesia davidiana* 'Fructu Luteo' and *Photinia* × *fraseri* 'Robusta'; 'Redstart' offers red new shoots, free flowering (white) in May-June and pendent clusters of red, yellow tinged fruits. Correctly it is listed as × *Stranvinia* 'Redstart'. Should mature 8 to 10′ (15′). Raulston describes it as easy to root from stem cuttings.

Styrax japonicus — Japanese Snowbell
(stī′raks ja-pon′i-kus)

FAMILY: Styracaceae
LEAVES: Alternate, simple, broad-elliptic to elliptic-oblong, 1 to 3 1/2″ long, 1/2 to 1 1/2″ wide, acute to acuminate, cuneate, remotely denticulate to almost entire, glabrous except axillary tufts beneath, medium to dark green above, glabrous, with axillary tufts below; petiole 1/3″ long.
BUDS: Small, sessile, naked, scurfy, superposed, 1/6 to 1/4″ long.
STEM: Rounded, zig-zag, rough-scurfy; pith small, rounded, continuous, green; leaf scars—2 ranked, at first torn, narrow, and shrivelled, finally broadly crescent-shaped.

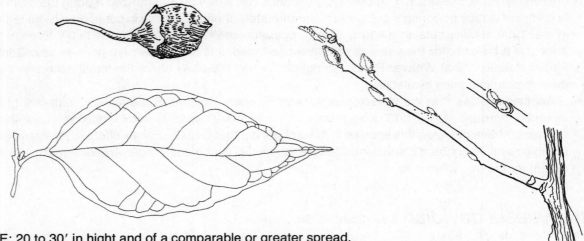

SIZE: 20 to 30′ in hight and of a comparable or greater spread.

HARDINESS: Zone 5 to 8, injured at -20°F, very few flowers opened, wood was not killed.

HABIT: A lovely, small, low-branched tree which develops a rounded to broad-rounded crown and a distinct horizontal appearance because of the wide-spreading branches; a very dainty tree which will grace any landscape.

RATE: Medium, 9 to 10′ over a 7 to 10 year period; I have grown this at Illinois and with proper water and fertilizer it can easily grow 2 to 3′ per year in youth.

TEXTURE: Medium-fine in leaf; medium in winter.

BARK: Quite handsome gray-brown of smooth consistency but showing irregular, orangish brown, and interlacing fissures; excellent addition to winter landscape.

LEAF COLOR: Medium to dark green in summer, unusually pest free; changing to yellowish or reddish in the fall; foliage is borne on the upper part of the branches and does not significantly detract from the flowers which are pendulous; I have not seen good fall color on this species; leaves hold late and are often killed by an early freeze.

FLOWERS: Perfect, 3/4″ wide, white, yellow-stamened, slightly fragrant, bell-shaped, corolla 5-lobed being united near base, each flower borne on a 1 to 1 1/2″ long pendulous stalk, occurring on short lateral shoots, each with 3 to 6 flowers, May-June and of great beauty. I have always considered this a most beautiful and delicate flowering tree yet is not well known outside of arboreta and botanical gardens.

FRUIT: Dry drupe, ovoid, about 1/2″ long, grayish in color and somewhat attractive; effective in August and falling by November; containing a single shiny brown hard seed.

CULTURE: Transplant balled and burlapped in early spring into a moist, acid, well-drained soil which has been abundantly supplemented with peat moss or organic matter; full sun or partial shade; prune in winter; site carefully in cold climates; probably best in partial shade in Zone 7 and 8.

DISEASES AND INSECTS: Amazingly trouble-free; Dr. Darrel Apps mentioned a borer that had devastated plants in the Philadelphia area.

LANDSCAPE VALUE: A handsome small tree for any situation; excellent near the patio, in the lawn, or in the shrub border; it is another of the unknown trees that is worthy of extensive landscape use; Bean called it a tree of singular grace and beauty; can be planted on hillsides or slopes where the flowers are seen firsthand by passersby; the leaves are perched like butterflies on the upper part of the stem so the pendulous flowers are not masked.

CULTIVARS: Several rather handsome and unusual cultivars have found their way into the U.S. and should be available to the gardening public in a few years.

'Pendula'—A small (8 to 12′) weeping tree with foliage and flowers similar to the species; I have seen one of the early introductions and am quite impressed by the general refined nature and gracefulness; I believe 'Carilon' is a rename of 'Pendula'.

'Pink Chimes'—Offers pink flowers on an upright shrub.

'Rosea'—A clear pink-flowered form that occurred as a bud sport, the parent plant was only 4′ high and the growth habit somewhat upright, perhaps same as 'Pink Chimes'.

'Sohuksan'—Introduced in 1985 by Dr. J.C. Raulston and U.S. National Arboretum collecting team from Korea; have seen the plant and leaves are larger, more leathery and darker green than typical. Flowers are also larger.

I have also heard of double-flowered, variegated and dwarf forms.

PROPAGATION: Seeds exhibit a double dormancy and warm stratification for 5 months followed by cold for 3 months is recommended; I have germinated seeds of *S. obassia* but they proved to be doubly dormant and after several transfers from warm to cold to warm to cold to warm finally secured a modicum of seedlings. Try cuttings first for they prove as easy as forsythia. Seeds could be fall sown and germination will take place the second spring; if collected fresh and sown immediately they may come up the next spring. Softwood cuttings, treated with IBA will root readily under mist; *S. obassia* rooted well when collected in mid-July. *S. americanus, S. japonicus* and *S. obassia* are extremely easy to root from softwood cuttings; about 1000 to 3000 ppm IBA-quick dip, peat:perlite, mist proved optimum; cuttings are readily transplanted and will continue to grow.

NATIVE HABITAT: China, Japan. Introduced 1862.

RELATED SPECIES:

Styrax americanus — American Snowbell
(stī′raks ȧ-mer-i-kā′nus)

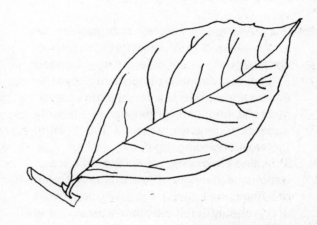

LEAVES: Alternate, simple, narrow oval to obovate, 1 1/2 to 3 1/2″ long, 1/2 to 1 1/4″ wide, acute or acuminate, cuneate, entire or serrulate, bright green, sparingly stellate-pubescent below; petiole 1/8″ long.

BUDS: Superposed, larger bud set at an oblique angle to stem, 1/16 to 1/8″ long, quite similar to *S. japonicus* in overall morphology.

STEM: Slender, light brown, glabrous or slightly scurfy, zig-zag, developing stringy condition; pith—green, solid.

Styrax americanus, American Snowbell, is a small, slender-stemmed, rather wispy, 6 to 8′ (10′) high rounded shrub. The bright green leaves do not develop any significant fall color. The beautiful white, bell-shaped flowers with highly reflexed lobes hang from the leaf axils in June or July. Each flower is 1/2 to 3/4″ long, 3/4 to 1 1/4″ wide, produced 1 to 4 at the ends of short branches on 1/4 to 1/2″ long pedicels. The petals are quite narrow, usually about 1/4″ wide. The 1/3″ long, obovoid, grayish pubescent drupe develops in August-September. I consider this a beautiful shrub and if given a cool, moist, acid root run will reward the gardener many-fold. It is found in the wild in lowlands bordering streams. I have found it along a stream in Bishop, GA just south of Athens. In this situation it looks rather forlorn but when freed from competition it makes a fine garden shrub. Variety *pulverulenta* (separate species according to some) has more pubescent leaves. Virginia to Florida, west to Missouri, Arkansas and Louisiana. Introduced 1756. Zone 5 to 9, although some tip dieback may occur in severe winters. Extremely easy to root from softwood cuttings in June-July. Seeds sown in fall will germinate the following spring.

Styrax grandifolius — Bigleaf Snowbell
(stī′raks gran-di-fō′li-us)

LEAVES: Alternate, simple, elliptic to obovate, 2 1/2 to 7″ long, short acuminate, cuneate, denticulate or almost entire, dark green above, grayish tomentose below; petiole 1/4 to 1/2″ long.

Styrax grandifolius, Bigleaf Snowbell, is found along the banks of streams from Virginia to Georgia. I have discovered it mixed with *Kalmia* in the Piedmont of Georgia. The habit is shrub-like and it occurs as an understory plant. Size ranges from 8 to 12′ (15′) in height. The leaves remind of *S. obassia* and range from 2 1/2 to 7″ long. The beautiful white, fragrant, 3/4 to 1″ wide flowers occur in 7 to 12-flowered, 4 to 8″ long nodding racemes in May-June. This would be a good choice for southern gardens but is not commonly available from nurseries. Not as "tough" as *S. obassia* and for that reason tends to labor in obscurity. Have attempted to root May cuttings from a local native population but with no success. Introduced 1765. Zone 7 to 9.

Styrax obassia — Fragrant Snowbell
(stī′raks ō-bās′ē-à)

LEAVES: Alternate, simple, suborbicular to broad-ovate, 3 to 8″ long, from 2/3's to as wide, abruptly acuminate, usually rounded at the base, remotely denticulate above the middle and sometimes tricuspidate at apex, glabrous and dark green above, densely pubescent beneath; petiole 1/3 to 1″ long, the base enclosing the bud.
BUDS: Scales enveloping rather than imbricate, tomentose, dirty gray-brown, usually 2 buds at a node, the larger 1/4 to 5/16″ long, ovoid and probably floral; the other smaller, 1/8 to 3/16″ long, appressed to the larger bud.
STEM: Stout, glabrous, lustrous reddish brown, exfoliating to expose greenish brown inner bark; pith—solid, green; second year smooth, lustrous brown; third year becoming gray-brown and developing prominent fissures.
BARK: Relatively smooth, gray to gray-brown, marked with shallow, vertical fissures; similar to bark of *S. japonicus,* very handsome.

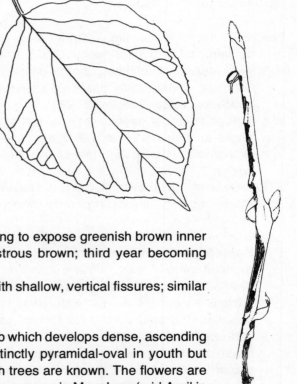

Styrax obassia, Fragrant Snowbell,is a small tree or shrub which develops dense, ascending branches and can grow 20 to 30′. Plants are distinctly pyramidal-oval in youth but become more open and rounded with age. 50′ high trees are known. The flowers are white, fragrant, borne in 4 to 8″ (10″) long, drooping racemes in May-June (mid April in Athens). The leaves are dark green and quite large and detract slightly from the quality and intensity of the flowers. The leaves do not develop a good fall color. The fruit is a 3/4″ long, ovoid, dry, pubescent drupe. Native to Japan. Introduced 1879. Zone 5 to 8. This species is not considered as hardy as *S. japonicus* although I have observed them in the same collections where temperatures dropped as low as -25°F and both survived. I have noticed that it flowers ahead of *S. japonicus* opening its flowers in late May-early June at the Arnold while *S. japonicus* was in full flower around mid-June. Over the observational years, I have come to the conclusion that *S. obassia* is more cold hardy than *S. japonicus.* More stem damage is evident on *S. japonicus* than on *S. obassia* after a difficult winter. For the past 8 years, *S. obassia* has been a regular fixture in my garden and is one of my wife's and my favorite conversation pieces. Unfortunately, it leafs out early, about early April in Athens, and is injured 1 out of 3 years, the leaves being rendered potato-chippy and the flowers useless. New growth follows from latent buds and full foliage is realized by June. Also, in fall an early freeze can render the leaves crispy gray-brown before their time. Architecturally, the smooth gray branches with numerous twists, turns and sinuations are handsome for winter effect. The flowers are also interesting as they appear to peek out from under the large leaves on slightly curve-shaped racemes that open from the base to the apex over a 2 to 3 week period. Ideally provide ample moisture and high organic matter soil in partial shade, although full sun is acceptable. The less stress the better for maximizing appearance through the summer months. Creech, *Amer. Nurseryman* 163(5):48–49 (1986), reported that *S. obassia* occurs widely in Northern Honshu and extends into Hokkaido, across the Sea of Japan into Korea and Manchuria. This indicates that *S. obassia* should be more cold hardy than *S. japonicus.*

ADDITIONAL NOTES: I have observed the four species listed above and believe that *S. japonicus* is the most aesthetic; experiences with *S. americanus* and *S. japonicus* in my Georgia garden have been less than satisfactory. I had sited them in full sun and obviously partial shade and a cool, moist root run would have served better. At the Arnold Arboretum, *S. americanus* and *S. japonicus* make superb specimens. For additional information see Dirr. *American Nurseryman* 147(2):7, 8, 87–90. 1978. "The exquisite snowbells."

Sycopsis sinensis
(sī-cop'sis sī-nen'sis)

FAMILY: Hamamelidaceae
LEAVES: Alternate, simple, evergreen, elliptic-ovate to elliptic-lanceolate, 2 to 4″ long, 1/3 to 1/2 as wide, acuminate, broad cuneate, entire or remotely toothed above the middle, leathery, lustrous dark green and glabrous above, pale green and glabrous or with scattered pubescence below; petiole 1/3″ long.

Sycopsis sinensis, is a pretty, glossy-leaved evergreen shrub that grows 10 to 15′ high and wide under cultivation. I have seen it used at Disney World, Orlando, FL in mass plantings and informal hedges. Apparently it is amenable to pruning and would make an excellent screen in warmer climates. The small yellowish flowers have red anthers and are surrounded by dark reddish brown tomentose bracts. Flowers open in February-March. Fruit is a 1/3″ long, two-valved, dehiscent pubescent capsule. Any well drained soil is acceptable and I have observed plants in full sun in Zone 9. For southern gardens this plant might be worth a longer look. Hardiness is somewhat suspect but plants in Savannah, Ga have withstood 10°F with minimal injury. An interesting intergeneric hybrid, × *Sycoparrotia semidecidua,* between *Sycopsis sinensis* and *Parrotia persica,* is known. It is a rather loose, arching, semi-evergreen (has been evergreen in my garden), 10 to 15′ (20′) high shrub with 1 to 5″ long, 2″ wide lustrous dark green leaves that although described as intermediate, tend toward the *Parrotia* parent. Flowers are particularly attractive and occur in February-March along the length of the stems. The color effect is reddish brown from a distance. Have seen

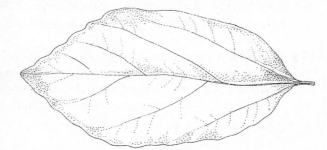
× *Sycoparrotia semidecidua*

plants in Europe but only in Zone 8 and 9 in the United States. Certainly not a plant for every garden but does have botanical and horticultural interest. Partial shade and well drained soil appear ideal. Developed from seed around 1950 in the nursery of P. Schonholzer, Basel, Switzerland. Zone (7)8 to 9. *Sycopsis sinensis* is native to central and western China. Introduced 1907. Zone (7)8 to 9.

Symphoricarpos albus — Common Snowberry
(sim-fō-ri-kär′pos al′bus)

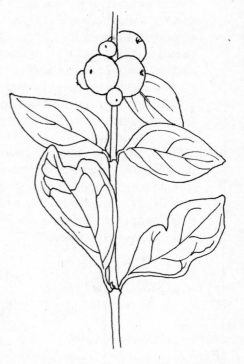

FAMILY: Caprifoliaceae

LEAVES: Opposite, simple, oval to elliptic-oblong, 3/4 to 2″ long, obtuse, roundish, on shoots often sinuately lobed, dark almost blue-green above, pubescent beneath; petiole 1/8 to 1/4″ long.

STEM: Slender, rounded, pubescent; pith—brownish, escavated.

SIZE: 3 to 6′ by 3 to 6′.

HARDINESS: Zone 3 to 7.

HABIT: Bushy, rounded to broad rounded shrub with numerous ascending shoots, densely fine and twiggy; tends to sucker and colonize.

RATE: Fast.

TEXTURE: Medium in leaf; however, in winter extremely sorrowful; needs a brush.

LEAF COLOR: Bluish green in summer; no effective fall color.

FLOWERS: Perfect, pinkish, 1/4″ long, June, borne in terminal spikes on current season's growth, basically inconspicuous.

FRUIT: Berry-like drupe, white, 1/2″ diameter, September through November; most ornamental asset of this shrub; fruit can persist into winter but is often discolored by a fungus.

CULTURE: Transplants easily, very tolerant of any soil; native on limestone and clay; full sun to medium shade; suckers profusely and tends to spread extensively; prune in early spring so current season's growth can produce flowers.

DISEASES AND INSECTS: Anthracnose (two genera affect the host; one causes a discoloration of the fruit, the other a spotting of the leaves), berry rot (fruits turn yellowish or brown and are affected by a soft, watery rot), leaf spots, powdery mildews, rusts, stem gall, aphids, snowberry clearwing, scale and glacial whitefly.

LANDSCAPE VALUE: Not a very valuable plant but fruit can be interesting; useful in shaded situations and for holding banks, cuts, fills; the hybrids and cultivars have greater landscape appeal.

CULTIVARS:

var. *laevigatus*—Taller (6′), leaves larger (3″ long) and broader, fruit larger and more abundant, vigorous grower; have seen *S. albus* var. *laevigatus* listed as *S. rivularis;* I do not know the validity of the name change.

PROPAGATION: Immersion in sulfuric acid for 40 to 60 minutes followed by warm and then cold stratification will assist in breaking seed dormancy; cuttings are extremely easy to root, softwood taken in June, July, August, rooted readily; the entire group roots easily from softwood cuttings.

NATIVE HABITAT: Nova Scotia to Alberta, south to Minnesota and Virginia. Introduced 1879.

RELATED SPECIES:

Symphoricarpos × *chenaultii,* (sim-fō-ri-kär′pos × she-nō′e-ī), Chenault Coralberry, is a cross between S. microphyllus × S. orbiculatus. The plant is a low-spreading, arching shrub growing about 3 to 6′ high. Flowers are pink; fruit is pink or white and tinged pink; the cultivar 'Hancock' is a beautiful low growing type with small leaves and good ground cover possibilities, a 12-year-old plant may be 2′ tall and 12′ wide; have not seen mildew on this form, raised about 1940 at Hancock Nurseries, Cookville, Ontario, Canada. Chenault Coralberry fruits differ from those of Indiancurrant Coralberry in that the side away from the sun is white. Zone 4 to 7. The fruit is more rose-red than pinkish as mentioned above but variation exists. The leaves are quite small, dark blue-green, ovate, 1″ long and pubescent below.

Symphoricarpos × ***doorenbosii,*** (sim-fō-ri-kär′pos doo-ren-bo′sē-ī), are hybrids among *S. albus* var. *laevigatus, S. orbiculatus,* and *S.* × *chenaultii.* Plants were raised by G.A. Doorenbos before 1940 and the first was named in 1940. 'Mother of Pearl' is vigorous, semipendulous, 5 to 6′ high shrub with broad elliptic or obovate leaves and dense clusters of 1/2″ wide white-pink cheeked fruits; 'Magic Berry' is a compact, spreading shrub with abundant rose-pink (rose-lilac) fruits; I saw this clone in Amsterdam and was impressed by the fruit display; 'Erect' is a vigorous, compact, upright form with rose-lilac fruits; 'White Hedge' grows 5′ high, stiff and upright, and bears large white fruits primarily in terminal clusters above the foliage. Their fruit effect justifies consideration for shady areas of the garden but availability is limited in the United States. All should be hardy to -30°F and will probably prove adaptable to Zone 7.

Symphoricarpos orbiculatus — Indiancurrant Coralberry or Buckbrush
(sim-fō-ri-kär′pos or-bi-kū-lā′tus)

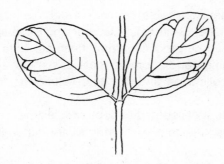 

LEAVES: Opposite, simple, elliptic or ovate, 1/2 to 1 1/4″ long, 1/4 to 3/4″ wide, obtuse or acutish, rounded at base, dull dark green above, glaucescent and pubescent beneath; petiole 1/12″ long.

Symphoricarpos orbiculatus, Indiancurrant Coralberry or Buckbrush, grows 2 to 5′ high by 4 to 8′ wide and develops into a spreading arching shrub. The foliage is a dull green (possibly blue-green) in summer and hangs on late in fall. I observed this species loaded with mildew growing next to *S.* × *chenaultii* which had none. The flowers are yellowish white, flushed rose, borne in June or July, in dense and short axillary clusters and terminal spikes. The fruit is a purplish red, 1/6 to 1/4″ diameter berry-like drupe, maturing in October and persisting late into winter; 'Leucocarpus' has white or whitish fruit. 'Variegatus' is a weak growing, irregularly yellow-margined form, the leaves becoming creamy white margined in full sun; I have grown this for a number of years and am pleased with the performance; definitely more vigorous than given credit; also listed as 'Foliis Variegatus'. New Jersey to Georgia, Kansas and Texas, west to South Dakota. 1727. Zone 2 to 7(8).

ADDITIONAL NOTES: The *Symphoricarpos* have limited ornamental value but fruit and shade tolerance are definite assets. Should be used sparingly; however, the cultivar 'Hancock' deserves further use as well as the *S.* × *doorenbosii* hybrids.

Symplocos paniculata — Sapphireberry or Asiatic Sweetleaf
(sim-plō′kos pan-ik-ū-lā′ta)

FAMILY: Symplocaceae

LEAVES: Alternate, simple, elliptic or obovate to oblong-obovate, 1 1/2 to 3 1/2″ long, 3/4 to 1 3/4″ wide, acute or acuminate, broad-cuneate, finely serrate, dark green and glabrous above, conspicuously veined beneath and usually pubescent, rarely glabrous; petiole 1/8 to 1/3″ long, hairy.

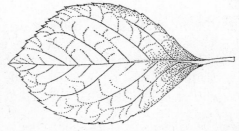

BUDS: Small, gray-brown, imbricate.

STEM: Grayish, slender, glabrous or pubescent.

BARK: On older plants develops gray flat ridges and darker fissures, becomes slightly stringy; reminds of the bark of *Lonicera maackii*.

SIZE: 10 to 20' high with a similar spread.

HARDINESS: Zone 4 to 8, has withstood -20 to -25°F and flowered normally.

HABIT: Large shrub or small, low-branched tree becoming wide-spreading at maturity; a particularly handsome specimen at the Arnold is 20' high and 30' wide.

RATE: Slow.

TEXTURE: Medium.

BARK: Gray, ridged and furrowed, resembling that of *Lonicera maackii*.

LEAF COLOR: Dark green in summer; no appreciable fall color.

FLOWERS: Perfect or unisexual, 5 petaled, 30 stamens, about 1/2" diameter, creamy white, fragrant, flowers are borne in 2 to 3" long panicles in late May-early June on growth of previous season; the flower effect is much superior to honeysuckles.

FRUIT: Ellipsoidal, 1/3" long, one-seeded drupe that color-wise can be categorized as ultramarine, sapphire, bright turquoise-blue and lapis-lazuli blue, September-October and often stripped by the birds; the color is unique among fruiting shrubs; fruit production may fluctuate from plant to plant because of the nature of the flowers, some being perfect, others male or female; several shrubs should be planted to insure adequate cross pollination and the best solution is to vegetatively propagate.

CULTURE: Easily transplanted from a container or as a balled and burlapped specimen; light or heavy, well-drained soil is acceptable; pH 5 to 7; full sun; best to prune during winter although some flower buds will be lost.

DISEASES AND INSECTS: None serious, have never seen a scratch on this shrub.

LANDSCAPE VALUE: Probably best used in the back of the shrub border, as an unpruned screen or as a small specimen tree; this is an excellent plant for attracting birds; specimens are long-lived and require essentially no maintenance; plant several seedlings or different clones to insure cross-pollination; have a lone plant in my Georgia garden that flowers well but sets little fruit; suspect another seedling is necessary for cross pollination.

PROPAGATION: Softwood cuttings root readily and I have had 100 percent success with July cuttings, 1000 ppm IBA-quick dip, peat:perlite, mist; cuttings should root in 6 to 8 weeks and should be hardened off in a cooler or cold frame, and transplanted when new growth occurs; over the years have successfully rooted this plant numerous times, yet have been unable to overwinter the cuttings. Seeds appear to be double dormant and require 3 to 4 months warm, followed by 3 months cold. In Mt. Airy, Cincinnati, OH, numerous stray seedlings are evident around several large shrubs.

NATIVE HABITAT: Himalayas to China and Japan. Introduced 1875.

ADDITIONAL NOTES: Certainly one of the handsomest of fruiting shrubs and should be used in every park, bird sanctuary and the like. A plant in full fruit is truly spectacular. See Dirr, *American Nurseryman* 150(12):42, 44, 46, 48. 1979. "Sapphireberry has true blue fruit."

RELATED SPECIES:

Symplocos tinctoria — Horse-sugar
(sim-plō'kos tink-tō'ri-à)

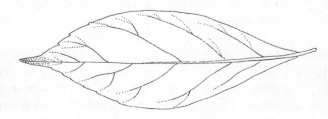

LEAVES: Alternate, simple, elliptic to oblong-lanceolate, 3 to 6" long, half as wide, acute or acuminate, cuneate, entire or obscurely serrate, thickish, lustrous dark green above, paler and pubescent below.

Symplocos tinctoria, Horse-sugar, is a semi-evergreen shrub or small tree that occurs in woods, swamps and bottomlands from Delaware to Florida and Louisiana. The lustrous dark green leaves are rather attractive and to one degree or another persist into spring. There are several colonies in the Georgia

Botanical Garden that show a distinct suckering tendency. The 1/3″ diameter yellowish, fragrant flowers occur in dense axillary clusters on the previous season's growth during April-May. The fruits, which I have not seen on the Georgia plants, are orange or brown, 1/4″ long, ellipsoidal drupes. Rather interesting native plant, probably best in a naturalized landscape. See Weaver. *Arnoldia* 44:34–35 (1984) for a good overview. Cultivated 1780. Zone 7 to 9.

Syringa meyeri — Meyer Lilac, in the trade often referred to as *S. palibiniana* or possibly *S. velutina*.
(si-ring′gȧ mī′ẽr-ī)

FAMILY: Oleaceae

LEAVES: Opposite, simple, 3/4 to 1 3/4″ long, not quite as wide, elliptic-ovate to sometimes elliptic-obovate, acute or obtusish, entire, glabrous above, scarcely paler beneath and pubescent on the veins near base, with 2 to 3 pairs of veins from base nearly to apex, dark green, somewhat lustrous with a reddish purple rim around margin of young leaves; petiole about 1/3″ long.

SIZE: 4 to 8′ high and 1 1/2 times that in spread.

HARDINESS: Zone 3 to 7, although I have seen it growing at Callaway Gardens (Zone 8).

HABIT: Small, dense, neat, broad-rounded, mounded shrub; excellent clean branch structure, one of the best lilacs for uniform, pristine outline in summer and winter.

RATE: Slow.

TEXTURE: Medium-fine in leaf; medium in winter.

LEAF COLOR: New leaves rimmed with a purplish margin, finally turning dark green; fall color is nonexistent.

FLOWERS: Violet-purple (I see pink in them but most of the botanical descriptions do not); each 1/2″ long, 1/4″ wide, flowers are densely packed in 4″ long and 2 1/2″ wide panicles, May, effective for 10 to 14 days, fragrant but not the soft fragrance associated with Common Lilac; literally cover the entire plant and are spectacular; one of the best for flower effect if not adulterated by the vagaries of weather.

FRUIT: Capsule, warty, 1/2 to 3/4″ long.

CULTURE: Does well in the midwest and east, does not contract mildew like other species, requires little or no maintenance; possibly one of the easiest lilacs to grow, also suited to culture in the south.

LANDSCAPE VALUE: Very handsome lilac, will start to flower when about one foot high; extremely floriferous; best used in shrub border with an evergreen background, flowers before leaves are fully developed; the flower buds emerge very early and can be injured by a late freeze.

CULTIVARS:

'Palibin'—The compact form of the species that is prevalent in the trade; will grow 4 to 5′ high, 5 to 7′ wide; reddish purple buds open whitish pink, since there was significant confusion as to what constituted true *S. meyeri*, Dr. Peter Green, *Curtis's Botanical Magazine*, 183. Part III. New Series 116–120, provided a degree of order by providing the above name.

PROPAGATION: Lilacs in general are not easy to root from cuttings and timing is critical; ideally softwood cuttings should be collected before end leaves mature, treat with 1000 to 5000 ppm IBA talc or quick dip, well drained medium and mist; my successes with various *Syringa* species is minimal; Dirr and Heuser, 1987 offer a detailed discussion of the vagaries of lilac propagation. Seeds of most species should be provided 1 to 3 months cold, moist stratification.

ADDTIONAL NOTES: A good discussion of cultivated *Syringa* along with notes on introduction and identification was presented by Griffin and Maunder. *The Plantsman* 7(2): 90–113. (1985).

NATIVE HABITAT: Northern China. Introduced 1908 and known only in cultivation.

RELATED SPECIES:

Syringa microphylla — Littleleaf Lilac
(si-ring'gȧ mī-krō-fil'ȧ)

LEAVES: Opposite, simple, orbicular-
ovate to elliptic-ovate, 1/2 to 2"
long, 1/3 to 1 1/4" wide, obtuse
or abruptly acuminate, broad-
cuneate to rounded at base,
slightly pilose and medium
green above, grayish green and
pubescent beneath, at maturity
only on the veins, ciliolate, or
nearly glabrous; petiole 1/6 to
1/3" long; quite distinct from the
previous and following species
by virtue of leaf color and pubescence but often confused with those species.

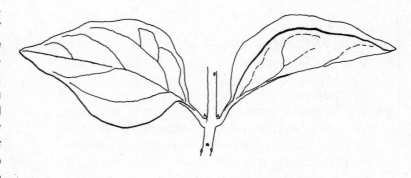

Syringa microphylla, Littleleaf Lilac, is a very handsome, broad spreading, dense shrub usually about 1 1/2
to 2 times as broad as tall, 6' by 9 to 12'; the medium green leaves are about one half the size of
those of *S. vulgaris;* flowers are rosy-lilac, fragrant, borne in 2 to 4" long, 1 1/2 to 2" wide panicles in
May into early June and often flowering sporadically again in September. Makes a nice plant for the
shrub border, in groupings, possibly a free-standing hedge; 'Superba' has single deep pink (pink-red)
flowers, grows twice as broad as tall and is quite floriferous; another versatile, adaptable, heat
tolerant, mildew resistant species that is worthy of consideration. Native to northern and western
China. Introduced 1910. Zone 4 to 7(8).

Syringa patula — Manchurian Lilac (previously *S. velutina*)
(si-ring'gȧ pat'ū-lȧ)

LEAVES: Opposite, simple, elliptic to ovate-
oblong, larger than those of *S. meyeri* or *S.
microphylla,* 2 to 5" long, 1/2 to 2" wide,
acuminate, broad-cuneate or rounded at
base, entire, dull dark green and slightly
pubescent to glabrous above, densely
pubescent beneath or pilose only on midrib
or veins; petiole 1/4 to 1/2" long.

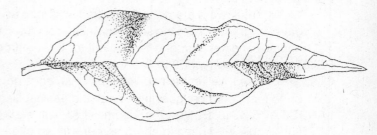

STEM: Purplish young shoots, slightly downy or glabrous at maturity.

Syringa patula, Manchurian Lilac, is frequently confused with the above two species. *S. patula* is a more
upright, vigorous shrub (9') than *S. meyeri* and *S. microphylla.* Panicles often in pairs from the
terminal pair of buds of the previous season's shoots, each 4 to 6" long and rather thinly set with
lilac-purple flowers of pleasing fragrance in May-June. 'Miss Kim' is listed as growing 3' high and 3'
wide with 3" long panicles of purple buds which open to fragrant icy blue flowers. I have seen this
clone growing in the Holden Arboretum and, at that time, it was 6' high and 4 to 5' wide. I saw the
parent plant at the Horticultural Farm at the University of New Hampshire and it was about 8 to 10'
high and oval-rounded. It may develop a reasonably good fall color. Northern China, Korea. Cultivated 1902. Zone 3 to 8. The so called *S. palibiniana* as used in the nursery trade does not really
exist. One is buying either *S. meyeri* or *S. patula* or, perhaps, *S. microphylla.* Have seen the species
at Callaway Gardens.

Syringa reticulata — Japanese Tree Lilac, formerly *S. amurensis* var. *japonica*
(si-ring′gȧ re-tik-ū-lā′ta)

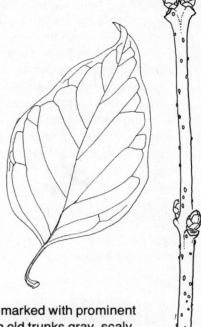

LEAVES: Opposite, simple, entire, broad-ovate to ovate, 2 to 5 1/2″ long, about half as wide, acuminate, rounded or subcordate, dark green above, grayish green and reticulate beneath and glabrous or slightly pubescent; petiole 1/2 to 1″ long.

BUDS: Sessile, subglobose, with 4 pairs of scales, end bud frequently absent, brownish.

STEM: Stout, shiny brown, heavily lenticelled resembling cherry bark, glabrous.

SIZE: 20 to 30′ in height; 15 to 25′ in spread.

HARDINESS: Zone 3 to 7, have not observed a plant in Zone 8.

HABIT: Large shrub or small tree with stiff, spreading branches developing a somewhat oval to rounded crown; with time branches and leaves become somewhat arching, the entire tree much more graceful.

RATE: Medium, 9 to 12′ over a 6 to 8 year period.

TEXTURE: Medium in all seasons.

BARK: Cherry-like, reddish brown to brownish on young and old stems, marked with prominent horizontal lenticels, good feature to separate it from other lilacs; on old trunks gray, scaly.

LEAF COLOR: Dark green in summer; like most lilacs no good fall color.

FLOWERS: Perfect, creamy white, fragrant, early to mid-June, effective for 2 weeks, borne in large terminal 6 to 12″ long and 6 to 10″ wide panicles, extremely showy in flower, odor somewhat akin to that of privet, petals turn brown with age and appear rather untidy toward the end of their tenure; a long pole pruner does wonders for the tree's appearance.

FRUIT: Warty, glabrous, scimitar-shaped, dehiscent, 3/4″ long capsule, blunt at apex.

CULTURE: This discussion applies to the lilac species in general; transplant balled and burlapped or from a container, actually lilacs are easy to move; soil should be loose, well drained and slightly acid although lilacs are pH adaptable; full sun for best flowering; pruning should be accomplished after flowering or if a plant is overgrown (applies to multi-stemmed clones) cut it to the ground for complete rejuvenation; should be good air movement; prefer cool summers.

DISEASES AND INSECTS: Bacterial blight, *Phytophthora* blight, leaf blights, leaf spots, powdery mildew (bad on Common Lilac, Persian Lilac), wilt, other minor pathological problems, ring spot virus, witches' broom, frost injury (in late spring the young leaves may be injured by near freezing temperatures), graft blight (occurs on lilacs grafted on privet), leaf roll necrosis (caused by various air pollutants), lilac borer, leopard moth borer, caterpillars, giant hornet, lilac leaf miner, scales and several other insects of negligible importance; it should be evident that lilacs require a certain degree of maintenance; I have seen the borer and scale insects decimate large shrubs and entire plantings.

LANDSCAPE VALUE: Possibly the most trouble-free lilac; excellent specimen tree, street tree, good in groups or near large buildings; one of my favorite lilacs; I think there is a need for selection of superior flowering and foliage types within the species; have seen the species performing magnificently on the Nebraska campus at Lincoln as well as in Burlington, Vermont; I consider it the toughest of the lilacs but the flower fragrance is somewhat privet-like which turns many people off; is resistant to mildew, scale and borer, which is an unbridled recommendation.

CULTIVARS:

'Chantilly Lace'—Margins on young leaves pale yellow, maturing to creamy yellow, margin width varying from 1/5 to 4/5″, central portion of leaf blotched dark green with light green halo, leaves may burn in hot sunny locations. Introduced by Herrmann Nursery, Limehouse, Ontario.

'Ivory Silk'—A 1973 selection by Sheridan Nursery, Ontario, Canada, that flowers at a young age and is a rather sturdy and compact, rounded dense form, deep green leaves, heavy flowering, 20 to 25′.

var. *mandschurica*—Tends toward a shrubby nature, 6 to 8′ (12′) high, leaves and flowers smaller than those of the species.

'Regent'—An exceptionally vigorous upright form, Princeton Nursery introduction.

'Summer Snow'—Offers compact rounded crown, profuse large panicles of fragrant creamy white flowers, handsome glossy cherry-like bark, good small street or lawn tree, 20′ high, 15′ wide, a Schichtel Nursery introduction.

PROPAGATION: Seed dormancy is variable but cold stratification for 30 to 90 days at 34°F to 41°F is recommended; I have attempted to grow this lilac from seed; however, all attempts met with failure; the seed, in all cases, was purchased from an unknown source and perhaps this was the problem. Cuttings which I collected in June rooted 90 percent when treated with 10,000 ppm (1%) IBA/50 percent alcohol and placed in sand under mist. Root formation was extremely profuse. Work in Canada indicated that early July, 8 to 10″ long cuttings rooted 87% after treatment with 8000 ppm IBA.

NATIVE HABITAT: Japan. Introduced 1876.

RELATED SPECIES:

Syringa pekinensis — Pekin Lilac
(si-ring′gȧ pē-kin-en′sis)

LEAVES: Opposite, simple, ovate to ovate-lanceolate, 2 to 4″ long, 1 to 2″ wide, acuminate, cuneate, dark green above, grayish green beneath and scarcely veined, quite glabrous; petiole 1/2 to 1″ long.

Syringa pekinensis, Pekin Lilac, is somewhat similar to the above but smaller (15 to 20′) with a more informal (multistemmed) habit and finer texture throughout. With only an exception or two, plants I've observed were multistemmed, upright arching, loose and open. Have seen good tree forms at Minnesota and Arnold Arboreta. The leaves and stems are smaller and finer. The flowers are yellowish white (creamy) and appear before *S. reticulata* in 3 to 6″ long panicles. I have seen plantings in various arboreta where the two plant types were flowering at about the same time. The habit tends to be bushy, spreading and rounded. The bark is often quite handsome and adds significantly to the plant's landscape assets. Bark may be similar to *S. reticulata* or on some trees exfoliate in rich brown flakes or sheets. There is a clone named 'Pendula' with drooping branches. 'Summer Charm' is a tree form with fine textured foliage and impressive creamy white flowers that was introduced by Bill Wandell. Northern China. Introduced 1881. Zone 3 to 7.

ADDITIONAL NOTES: Both plant types deserve further use. The Pekin Lilac is interesting but from what I can gather little known and grown, although the potential for superior selections could change its relative obscurity.

Syringa villosa — Late Lilac
(si-ring′gȧ vil-lō′sȧ)

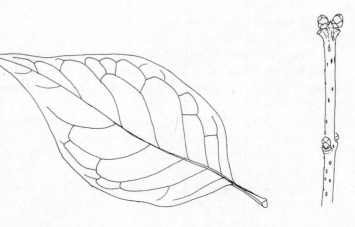

LEAVES: Opposite, simple, broad-elliptic to oblong, 2 to 7″ long, 1 to 2 1/2″ wide, entire, acute at ends, dull dark green above, glaucescent beneath and usually pubescent near the midrib, rarely glabrous, veins impressed creating a pleated appearance; petiole 1/4 to 1 1/4″ long.

SIZE: 6 to 10′ high and 4 to 10′ wide.

HARDINESS: Zone 2 to 7.

HABIT: Bushy shrub of dense rounded habit with erect or ascending, stout, stiff branches.

RATE: Slow to medium.

TEXTURE: Medium in leaf and winter.

LEAF COLOR: Medium to dull dark green in summer.

FLOWERS: Rosy lilac to white, not as fragrant as *S. vulgaris,* with a curious odor similar to privet; mid to late May possibly into early June; borne in dense pyramidal 3 to 7″ long panicles, forms a true terminal bud and 3 panicles often occur at the end of the shoot, flowers are borne on the current season's growth rather than last season's wood like *S. vulgaris.*

FRUIT: Capsule, 1/2″ long.

CULTURE: See under *S. reticulata.*

DISEASES AND INSECTS: See under *S. reticulata.*

LANDSCAPE VALUE: Nice lilac for the shrub border; performed well in midwest, seldom used in contemporary gardens.

NATIVE HABITAT: China. Cultivated 1802.

CULTIVARS: The Preston Lilacs *(S. × prestoniae)* are the result of crosses between *S. villosa* and *S. reflexa.* They are extremely hardy (Zone 2) and possess many of the morphological features of *S. villosa.* Developed by Isabella Preston of Ottawa in 1920's and later. Many new cultivars continue to be developed; however, somewhere along the line there needs to be a stopping point for the glut becomes mind-boggling. Krüssmann listed 43 cultivars.

'Audrey'—Light magenta-pink outside, almost white within, in 9″ long dense conical panicles.

'Coral'—Single, light pink flowers, considered best pink.

'Desdemona'—Single, purplish flowers.

'Donald Wyman'—Deepest pink to almost reddish flowers with buds and flowers the same color, 6″ by 4″ panicles.

'Isabella'—Single pinkish lilac flowers in large (1′ long, 8″ wide) pyramidal panicles.

'Jessica'—Single violet flowers, 7″ long, 5″ wide panicles.

'Patience'—Single lilac flowers.

'Redwine'—Single magenta flowers, considered darkest red form.

PROPAGATION: See *S. meyeri.*

RELATED SPECIES:

Syringa josikaea — Hungarian Lilac

(si-ring′gà jos-ik′ē-à)

LEAVES: Opposite, simple, broad-elliptic to elliptic oblong, 2 to 5″ long, acute to acuminate, broad cuneate to rounded, ciliolate, entire, lustrous dark green above, glaucescent (whitish) below, sparingly hairy on veins or glabrous; petiole about 1/3″ long.

Syringa josikaea, Hungarian Lilac, is a 8 to 10′ high, 8 to 12′ wide, spreading, arching multi-stemmed shrub that offers slightly fragrant lilac-violet flowers in 4 to 7″ (8″) long narrow panicles from late May into June. The leaves, habit and flowers remind of *S. villosa* but the color is usually deeper at least on plants I have seen. The loose panicles are handsome for late season effect. Has been used as a parent in the development of many late flowering hybrids. Hungary. Introduced about 1830. Zone 5 to 7.

Syringa reflexa — Nodding Lilac

(si-ring′gà rē-flek′sà)

LEAVES: Opposite, simple, oval-oblong to oblong-lanceolate, 3 to 6″ (8″) long, half as wide, acuminate, cuneate, entire, dark green and glabrous above, villous on veins beneath and paler; petiole 1/2″ long.

Syringa reflexa, Nodding Lilac, is a large 10 to 12′ high and wide, stout-stemmed shrub with handsome foliage and 4 to 10″ long, 1 1/2 to 4″ wide cylindrical or narrowly pyramidal panicles of purplish pink flowers that age pink with a white interior. Flowers are packed in a series of whorls along the length of the terminal, leafy, arching to pendulous panicle. I cannot pick up any fragrance of consequence. A parent of *S.* × *prestoniae* and other late flowering hybrids. For the lilac collector a worthwhile addition; for the gardener with space for one lilac, forget it. Central China. Introduced 1901. Zone 5 to 7.

Syringa sweginzowii — Chengtu Lilac
(si-ring′ga̍ sweg-in-zō′ē-ī)

LEAVES: Opposite, simple, entire, oblong or ovate, 2 to 4″ long, 1 to 2″ wide, abruptly acuminate, broad-cuneate to rounded, thinnish, dark green and glabrous above, light green below and pilose pubescent on veins; petiole 1/4 to 1/2″ long.

Syringa sweginzowii, Chengtu Lilac, is another of the late flowering species that offers 6 to 8″ long panicles of rosy lilac, fading to flesh pink. The panicles occur at the end of the shoot with a few lateral ones developing further down the stem. The inflorescence is extremely loose and the flowers tend to hang and do not always present themselves in the most aesthetic manner. The habit is elegantly upright with landscape size approximately 10 to 12′ by 10 to 12′. With *S. reflexa,* it resulted in the hybrid grex, *S.* × *swegiflexa.* Northwestern China. Introduced 1914. Zone 5 to 6.

ADDITIONAL NOTES: Despite the lack of overwhelming fragrance this group of lilacs deserves landscape consideration because of lateness and quantity of flowers. All are quickly recognizable by the impressed veins, rather loose inflorescences, late flowers, and inflorescences that appear on the new growth of the season. All can be separated from each other by floral characteristics which, for example, come down to anthers not protruding from the corolla in *S. sweginzowii,* while those of *S. villosa* do.

Syringa vulgaris — Common Lilac
(si-ring′ga̍ vul-gā′ris)

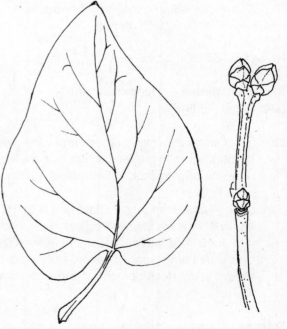

LEAVES: Opposite, simple, ovate or broad-ovate, 2 to 5″ long, 3/4′s to as wide, acuminate, truncate or subcordate to broad-cuneate, entire, dark green almost bluish green, glabrous; petiole—3/4 to 1 1/4″ long.

STEM: Stout, angled, lustrous brown, glabrous.

SIZE: 8 to 15′ in height (to 20′) with a spread of 6 to 12′ (15′).

HARDINESS: Zone 3 to 7(8).

HABIT: Upright leggy shrub of irregular outline but usually devoid of lower branches after a time and forming a cloud-like head of foliage.

RATE: Medium.

TEXTURE: Medium to coarse in leaf depending on age and size of plant; coarse in winter.

FLOWERS: Lilac, extremely fragrant, early to mid-May (early April, Athens); borne in 4 to 8″ long panicles, usually in pairs from the terminal buds.

FRUIT: Smooth, 5/8″ long, beaked dehiscent capsule.

CULTURE: Best soil is one close to neutral and supplemented with peat or leaf mold; old flowers should be cut off as soon as flowers fade.

DISEASES AND INSECTS: See *S. reticulata.*

LANDSCAPE VALUE: Flowers of only value, probably best reserved for the shrub border or in groupings; considerable nostalgia attached to this shrub, often associated with Grandmother or Mom; my Mom would always pick large bouquets for the house and the fragrance literally permeated every room, I have tried to convince myself to plant one but in Zone 8 the plant is not prosperous, lacks vigor and does not flower reliably from year to year.

CULTIVARS:

There are over 400, possibly 800 to 900 different clones (a recent publication said 2,000 clones) and it is hopeless to attempt to list them. Donald Wyman has a valuable list in his *Shrubs and Vines for American Gardens* based on observations of the lilac collection at the Arnold Arboretum. Also Krüssmann, *Manual of Cultivated Broadleaved Trees and Shrubs III* and Bean present extensive lists of cultivars. A recent (1988) book on lilacs by Father Fiala is another worthy reference. An interesting historical perspective is provided by Torer, *Horticulture* 61(5): 25 (1983). The following list of the more popular types was gleaned from Rogers, *American Horticulturist* 57(2):13–17. 1978. This list resulted from a survey conducted by Mr. Frank Niedz in 1970 to determine the most popular types. Also, John H. Alexander, III, and the Arnold Arboretum permitted me to use a list of lilacs, "Fifty of the best lilacs for the gardens of New England", that appeared in *Arnoldia* 49(2) 2-7 (1989).

COLOR	DOUBLE	SINGLE
White	'Ellen Willmott'	'Vestale'
	'Edith Cavell'	'Ian Van Tol'
	'Mme. Lemoine'	'Mont Blanc'
Violet	'Violetta'	'De Miribel'
	'Maréchal Lannes'	'Cavour'
Blue	'Ami Schott'	'President Lincoln'
	'Olivier De Serres'	'Firmament'
	'Prés. Grévy'	'Decaisne'
Lilac	'Victor Lemoine'	'Christophe Columb'
	'Henri Martin'	'Jacques Callott'
	'Léon Gambetta'	
	'Alphonse Lavallée'	
Pink	'Mme. Antoine Buchner'	'Lucie Baltet'
	'Katherine Havemeyer'	'Macrostachya'
	'Montaigne'	
	'Belle De Nancy'	
Magenta	'Paul Thirion'	'Capitaine Baltet'
	'Charles Joly'	'Mme F. Morel'
	'Prés. Poincairé'	'Congo'
Purple	'Adelaide Dunbar'	'Ludwig Spaeth'
	'Paul Hariot'	'Mrs. W.E. Marshall'
		'Night'
		'Monge'

John Alexander's List

Cultivar	Flower Type
VIOLET BLOSSOMS	
Henri Robert	Double
Louvois 0	Single
Mieczta	Single
"BLUE" BLOSSOMS	
Dr. Chadwick 0	Single
Laurentian + 0	Single
Maurice Barres	Single
Madame Charles Souchet	Single
President Lincoln +	Single
PURPLE BLOSSOMS	
Adelaide Dunbar +	Double
Paul Hariot	Double
President Roosevelt +	Single
Sarah Sands	Single
Sensation	Single
Zulu	Single
MAGENTA BLOSSOMS	
Charles Joly +	Double
Glory	Single
Mme. F. Morel	Single
Paul Thirion	Double
Ruhm von Horstenstein +	Single
"YELLOW" BLOSSOMS	
Primrose	Single
"PINK" BLOSSOMS	
Catinat + 0	Single
Charm	Single
Churchill 0	Single
General Sherman +	Single
Katherine Havemeyer +	Double
Lucie Baltet	Single
Mme. Antoine Buchner	Double
Scotia 0	Single
Vauban + 0	Double
Virginite	Double
WHITE BLOSSOMS	
Jan Van Tol	Single
Jeanne d'Arc	Double
Joan Dunbar	Double
Krasavitsa Moskvy	Double
Marie Legraye	Single
Maude Notcutt	Single
Miss Ellen Willmott	Double
Mme. Lemoine	Double
Saint Margaret	Double
Sister Justena 0	Single

LILAC BLOSSOMS

Alphonse Lavallée	Double
Assessippi + 0	Single
Excel + 0	Single
Hippolyte Maringer	Double
Hugo Koster	Single
Hyazinthenflieder	Single
Michel Buchner	Double
Nokomis 0	Single

+ indicates a high degree of fragrance
0 indicates an early-blooming hybrid

TEN FAVORITE UNCOMMON LILACS (from Alexander's Article)

The "best fifty" list includes only cultivars of *Syringa vulgaris* and the early-flowering *S.* × *hyacinthiflora* because they have the general appearance of the traditional or common lilac. Hybrids and selections of the species listed below have leaves, flowers and fragrance that are different, and offer adventurous gardeners the opportunity to break with tradition.

Syringa laciniata
S. meyeri
S. meyeri 'Palibin'
S. microphylla 'Superba'
S. patula 'Miss Kim'
S. pekinensis
S. × *prestoniae* 'Agnes Smith'
S. × *prestoniae* 'Miss Canada'
S. pubescens
S. reticulata

HEAT TOLERANT, LOW CHILL CULTIVARS

The Descanso hybrids were developed in Southern California for good flower production in mild winter environments. The following forms would be worth testing in Zone 8 and 9 of the southeast.

'Blue Boy'—Blue flowers.
'Chiffon'—Lavender flowers.
'Lavender Lady'—Lavender-purple, single, fragrant flowers, open growth habit, result of cross between *S. vulgaris* × *S. laciniata;* heat tolerance imparted by the latter parent.
'Mrs. Forrest K. Smith'—Light lavender flowers.
'Sylvan Beauty'—Rose-lavender flowers.

FATHER FIALA'S LILACS

The following cultivars were selected for color, size, form, fragrance, habit of growth and disease resistance. They are being produced through tissue culture by Knight Hollow Nursery, Madison, WI. Please see Fiala's *Lilacs: The Genus Syringa,* Timber Press, 1988 for additional details.

White

'Avalanche'—Large white florets, fine lingering fragrance, rounded to upright habit, about 9' high, *S. vulgaris* type.

Bicolor

'Albert F. Holden'—Deep violet flowers with a silvery blush on the reverse of the petals, good fragrance, large loose-open, somewhat reflexed panicles, dark green foliage, moderately rounded to 7', *S. vulgaris* type.

Blue

'Blanche Sweet'—Ethyl blue buds open to whitish blue petals tinged with pink, fine fragrance, good foliage, upright to 10′, a *S.* × *hyacinthiflora* selection.

'Wedgewood Blue'—Lilac-pink buds open to the blue background of English Wedgewood pottery, excellent fragrance, large somewhat wisteria-like panicles, lower growing to 6′, *S. vulgaris* type.

'Little Boy Blue' ('Wonder Blue')—Sky-blue flowers of good fragrance on a compact rounded 4 to 5′ high shrub, *S. vulgaris* type.

Magenta and Purple

'Arch McKean'—Bright reddish purple, individual flowers, 4/5 to 1 1/5″ wide, in large upright panicles, heavy flowering, moderate fragrance, dark green leaves, practically non-suckering, 8′ high, *S. vulgaris* type.

'Yankee Doodle'—Deepest and darkest purle, 1 to 1 1/5″ diameter individual flowers in 8″ long panicles, profuse flowering, upright habit to 8′, *S. vulgaris* type.

S. juliana 'George Eastman'—Rich wine-red buds open to deep cerise-pink flowers, color is the same on inside and outside of the petals, a compact 5′ high plant with horizontal spreading branches.

PROPAGATION: If only a plant or two are needed simply divide and replant sucker(s); for commercial considerations see *S. meyeri;* tissue culture has been successful with this species.

NATIVE HABITAT: Southern Europe. Cultivated 1563.

RELATED SPECIES:

Syringa × **chinensis** — Chinese Lilac
(si-ring′gȧ × chī-nen′sis)

LEAVES: Opposite, sim-
ple, ovate-lanceo-
late, 1 1/2 to 3″
long, to 1 1/4″ wide,
acuminate, cuneate
or rounded, entire,
medium to dark
green, glabrous; petiole 1/3 to 1/2″ long.
BUDS: Smaller and more refined than those of *S. vulgaris.*

Syringa × *chinensis,* Chinese or Rouen Lilac, also listed as *S. rothomagensis,* is a hybrid between *S.* × *persica* and *S. vulgaris.* The shrub is graceful, broad spreading, round-topped, with arching branches, more delicate and more profuse in flower than *S. vulgaris.* Grows 8 to 15′ tall and as wide. Flowers are purple-lilac, fragrant, mid-May, borne in large and loose 4 to 6″ long panicles from the upper nodes producing an elongated, arching compound panicle that results in a shroud of color; have seen excellent plantings in midwest; not as coarse as *S. vulgaris* in habit; one of the more handsome hybrid lilacs and often spoken of as the first hybrid lilac, originated as a chance seedling at Rouen, France, 1777. Midway in leaf size and habit between Persian and Common Lilac. Can become ratty looking like *S. vulgaris* and proper pruning techniques are a must. The cultivar 'Alba' has light pink almost white flowers, and 'Saugeana' has lilac-red flowers and is more colorful than the species. The latter is also available in commerce. Zone 3 to 7. Variable mildew susceptibility.

Syringa × **hyacinthiflora,** (si-ring′gȧ × hī-ȧ-sin-thi-flō′rȧ), is the grex name for *S. oblata* and *S. vul-garis* hybrids. They were first raised by Lemoine in 1876 but have since been produced by Clarke of San Jose, California, Dr. Frank Skinner of Dropmore, Manitoba and Elizabeth Preston at the Dominion Experiment Station, Ottawa. They are extremely hardy and flower before the *S. vulgaris* types. The leaves may turn reddish purple in fall. In general they grow to be large shrubs approaching 10 to 12′ high and wide. Many cultivars; suitable for Zone 3 to possibly 7; better in cold climates; considered quite resistant to leaf curl necrosis.

Syringa laciniata — Cutleaf Lilac
(si-ring′gȧ lȧ-sin-ē-ā′tȧ)

LEAVES: Opposite, simple, all or partly 3 to 9 lobed, very interesting and different leaf texture for a lilac; first leaves always lobed, later often not.

Syringa laciniata, Cutleaf Lilac, is a somewhat confused entity and at one time was listed as a variety of *S.* × *persica*. The habit is low, dense, rounded-mounded and 6 to 8′ high. The small, pale lilac fragrant flowers are often borne in 3″ long loose panicles all along the stems in May. The lacy, fine-textured foliage is an unusual asset and quite striking when one considers the usual foliage complement of most *Syringa.* Hardy to at least Zone 4 as I have seen a thriving specimen in the Wisconsin Landscape Arboretum. It is one of the best lilacs for Zone 8 conditions and is frequently encountered in Athens and Atlanta, GA where it flowers in late March-early April. Displays excellent heat tolerance and will provide reliable flower in partial shade. Considered native to Turkestan and China.

Syringa oblata — Early Lilac
(si-ring′gȧ ob-lā′tȧ)

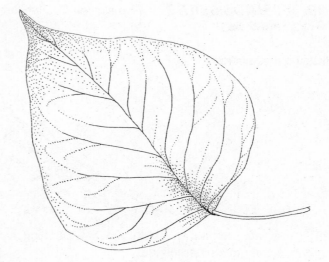

LEAVES: Opposite, simple, orbicular-ovate to reniform, often broader than long, 2 to 4″ broad, abruptly acuminate, cordate to subcordate, entire, glabrous, dark green, almost bluish green; petiole—3/4 to 1″ long.

Syringa oblata, Early Lilac, is a large (10 to 12′) shrub or small tree related to *Syringa vulgaris.* The young leaves are often bronzish and change to dark green in summer followed by muted reddish to reddish purple tones in fall. The pale to purple-lilac flowers occur in rather broad 2 to 5″ long panicles from the upper-most nodes of the previous year's wood in April-May, usually opening 7 to 10 days ahead of *S. vulgaris.* This is a rather coarse lilac but is valuable for breeding work as well as the rather handsome fall color. Northern China. Introduced 1856. Zone 3 to 6. Variety *dilatata* is more common and tends to be more shrubby with longer leaves and a longer, more slender corolla tube than the species. I had the variety in my Illinois garden and have seen it at the Arnold and University of Maine where the bronzy red to purple fall color was quite beautiful. Raulston mentioned that var. *dilatata* had proven reliable in Raleigh, NC with early and profuse flowering every year. Korea. Introduced 1917. Zone 3 to 6.

Syringa × persica — Persian Lilac
(si-ring′gȧ pẽr′si-kȧ)

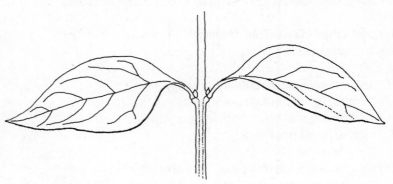

LEAVES: Opposite, simple, lanceolate or ovate-lanceolate, (rarely
3-lobed), 1 to 2 1/2″ long, 1/3 to
1/2″ wide, acuminate, cuneate,
entire, dark green above,
glabrous, often infested with mildew to a degree that the leaves
assume a whitish cast; petiole
1/3″ long.

Syringa × persica, Persian Lilac, is a graceful shrub with upright, arching branches reaching 4 to 8′ in
height and spreading 5 to 10′. The foliage is dark green; flowers are pale lilac, fragrant, mid-May (has
opened from early to late April, Athens), borne profusely in 2 to 3″ long and wide panicles from the
upper nodes of the previous season's growth. A nice small lilac with a mass of flower when properly
grown, good plant for the shrub border. Cultivated since time immemorial. Introduced 1614. Zone 3
to 7. According to Wyman this may not be a true species and, in fact, may be a hybrid between *S.
afghanica × S. laciniata* since it is almost completely sterile and probably has not been found wild
in any country. 'Alba' is a white-flowered form.

ADDITIONAL NOTES: Four of the nicest lilac collections I have seen are located at the Arnold Arboretum;
Royal Botanic Garden, Hamilton, Ontario, Canada; Swarthmore College; and the Minnesota
Landscape Arboretum.

Tamarix ramosissima — Five-stamen Tamarix or Tamarisk, formerly listed as *T. pentandra*.
(tam′ȧ-riks ram-ō-sis′i-mȧ)

FAMILY: Tamaricaceae

LEAVES: Alternate, simple, lanceolate to ovate, 1/8″ long, acute, glaucous, small, usually scale-like, bright
green, similar to juniper foliage.
BUDS: Small, sessile, rounded, compressed against twig, solitary or quickly becoming concentrically
multiple, with about 3 exposed scales.
STEM: Slender, elongated, rounded; pith small, rounded, continuous.

SIZE: 10 to 15′ high, usually less in spread, have observed 20 to 25′ high specimens along North Carolina
and Georgia coasts.
HARDINESS: Zone 2 to 8; the hardiest species of *Tamarix*.
HABIT: Usually a wild growing, very loose, open shrub; can be attractive with its fine-textured foliage, but
definitely needs to be hidden when defoliated.
RATE: Fast.
TEXTURE: Fine in foliage; needs to be disguised in winter (coarse).

LEAF COLOR: Light green, scale-like; creating a feathery appearance.

FLOWERS: Perfect, rosy-pink, 5-petaled, borne in dense or slender 1 to 3″ long racemes which form large terminal panicles, June-July; quite attractive, the entire flowering shoot may approximate 3′ in length; normally in full flower by early to mid April in Athens.

FRUIT: Capsule, inconsequential.

CULTURE: Root systems are usually very sparse and, for this reason, care should be exercised in planting; container-grown plants are the best bet; prefer acid, well-drained, low fertility soil; full sun; not really particular as to soil and can grow in sand; ideal for seashore plantings as they are fantastically salt tolerant; prune back this species in early spring since it flowers on new growth; I have seen heavy flowering on new growth; I have seen heavy flowering on plants that were pruned to the ground the previous winter; however, from the early flowering date in the south, it is obvious that flowers arose from previous years buds; apparently the plant can go both ways which is somewhat unusual; have observed 25′ high plants growing in pure sand less than 100 yards from the Atlantic Ocean on Georgia's St. Simons Island; indeed saline and dry soil tolerant.

DISEASES AND INSECTS: Cankers, powdery mildew, root rot, wood rot, and scales.

LANDSCAPE VALUE: Interesting for foliage effect as well as flowers but its uses are limited; perhaps best reserved for saline environments where it does amazingly well; have seen it used at Cantigny Gardens, Wheaton, IL where it had been treated like a herbaceous perennial to stimulate vegetative growth; for textural quality it is beautiful when handled this way; the flowers may last 4 to 6 weeks but show their age toward the end of the cycle.

CULTIVARS:

'Cheyenne Red'—Deeper pink flowers than the species.

'Pink Cascade' has slightly richer pink flowers than 'Rosea' and is quite vigorous.

'Rosea' has rosy-pink flowers, each 1/8″ across, arranged in slender, variable length (1 to 5″ long) racemes; flowers occur late and may develop as late as July-August in the north, considered one of the hardiest cultivars; ideally cut back in late winter and a 6 to 10′ tall plant will bear profuse flowers in mid to late summer.

var. *rubra*—Deeper pink flowers than the species, a branch sport of 'Rosea'; 'Summerglow' may be the same plant.

PROPAGATION: Fresh seeds usually germinate within 24 hours after imbibing water; no pretreatment is necessary; softwood cuttings, placed in peat:perlite under mist root easily; the rooting may be sparse and the roots coarse and somewhat difficult to handle; hardwood cuttings can also be rooted.

NATIVE HABITAT: Southeastern Europe to central Asia where it usually occurs on saline soils. Cultivated 1883.

RELATED SPECIES:

Tamarix parviflora, (tam′a-riks pär-vi-flō′rȧ), Small-flowered Tamarix, grows 12 to 15′ high, flowers on previous year's growth and should be pruned immediately after flowering. The 4-petaled flowers are light pink and usually develop in late May through early June. Supposedly very similar to *T. odessana* except it is larger in size and flowers earlier. Native to southeastern Europe. Cultivated 1853. Zone 4 to 8.

ADDITIONAL NOTES: This genus does not require high fertility soils, and I have noticed decline in container-grown specimens under high nutritional status. The plants also become more open and leggy than normal when grown under high fertility. This is a genus which has a distinct place when salt presents a cultural problem. The entire genus is rather taxonomically similar and from a landscape viewpoint there is little to differentiate the species, unless one considers the type of wood upon which the flowers are borne. In August, several students and I were hiking through Hidden Lake Gardens, Tipton, MI and came upon a 25′ high and 25′ wide flowering specimen of *T. ramosissima,* or so I spouted until my graduate student read the label . . . *T. africanus,* . . . as I said, not the easiest plants to separate . . . ahem!

Taxodium ascendens — Pondcypress (Deciduous), also called Pond Baldcypress.
(taks-ō′di-um ȧ-sen′denz)

FAMILY: Taxodiaceae

IDENTIFICATION CHARACTERISTICS: Similar to *T. distichum* except bark is light brown and deeply furrowed; deciduous branchlets erect; leaves appressed or incurved, awl-shaped, 3/8″ long, bright green, rich brown in autumn.

SIZE: 70 to 80′ in height, probably 15 to 20′ wide.

HARDINESS: Zone (4)5 to 9.

HABIT: Narrowly conical or columnar with spreading branches and erect branchlets; a deciduous conifer.

RATE: Slow to medium (18′ in 20 years); sufficient evidence to indicate that with ample moisture and fertility 2′ of growth per year in the early years is possible.

TEXTURE: Fine in foliage; medium in winter.

LEAF COLOR: Bright green changing to rich brown (orangish brown) in autumn; late leafing, as late as late May-early June in the midwest.

FLOWERS: Monoecious; male flowers ovoid, forming terminal and drooping panicles; female flowers scattered near the ends of branches of the previous year, sub-globose; male flowers appear as slender pendulous catkins (4 to 5″ branched spikose panicle), often more prevalent in the upper reaches of the tree, March–April.

FRUIT: Cones short-stalked, globose or ovoid, 1/2 to 1 1/4″ across, purplish and resinous when young, ripening the first year and turning brown.

CULTURE: Nurseryman mentioned that the tap root makes this and *T. distichum* difficult to transplant; however, suspect root pruning at an early age would alleviate the problem; have seen far too many successfully transplanted specimens; adaptable, prefers moist acid soils; performs well on upland soils; full sun and open areas, extremely wind firm.

DISEASES AND INSECTS: None serious.

LANDSCAPE VALUE: Specimen for parks, large areas, wet and dry places; I used to look at this species as totally secondary to *T. distichum* but have questioned my conventional wisdom in recent years; have seen groves, groupings, isolated specimens and leave with strong positive impressions; tree is decidedly columnar compared to *T. distichum* with scaffold (secondary branches originating at right angles to central leader); also have not noticed the gall on this species which is so common on *T. distichum.*

CULTIVARS:

'Nutans'—Branches short, horizontal, some ascending parallel with the trunk; branchlets crowded, closely set, more or less pendulous.

'Prairie Sentinel'—An Earl Cully, Jacksonville, IL introduction; very tall in relation to width, 60′ tall and 10′ wide with very soft, fine-textured foliage; does well on upland soil and on very moist sites; Mr. Cully mentioned that the selection was not particularly cold hardy.

PROPAGATION: *Taxodium* seeds exhibit an apparent internal dormancy which can be overcome by 90 days of cold stratification; softwood cuttings have been rooted but success is variable and, doubtfully, commercially viable; hardwood cuttings have been used in England; grafting is the most reliable method for reproducing the cultivars, with bench grafting using 2 to 3-year old seedlings, whip-and-tongue graft, and allow to heal at 55 to 60°F; see *The Plant Propagator* 9(1):11 (1962) and *PIPPS* 17:376 (1967).

ADDITIONAL NOTES: This species is now listed as a variety by several authors under the name *nutans.* I have treated it as a species; however, this may not be the case although everyone does not agree on the classification. The "knees" supposedly do not form to the degree they do on *T. distichum.*

NATIVE HABITAT: Virginia to Florida and Alabama, on more upland areas, i.e., around ponds rather than in them, although the species occur in mixed company. Cultivated 1789.

Taxodium distichum — Common Baldcypress (Deciduous)
(taks-ō′di-um dis′ti-kum)

LEAVES: Spirally arranged on the branchlets, 2-ranked on the deciduous shoots (branchlets), linear-lanceolate, apicu-late, 1/3 to 3/4″ long, 1/16 to 1/12″ wide, bright yellow-green in spring, soft sage green in summer, rich brown in autumn.

BUDS: Alternate, near tip of stem rounded, with overlapping, sharp-pointed scales; smaller lateral buds also present, and from them leafy, budless branches (branchlets) arise which fall in autumn.

STEM: Of two kinds: later branchlets green, deciduous; young branchlets green, becoming brown the first winter.

SIZE: 50 to 70′ high by 20 to 30′ wide, can grow to 100′ and more.

HARDINESS: Zone 4, Baldcypress has been planted far north of its natural range. There are specimens in Minnesota, southern Canada and a few 75-year-old trees in Syracuse, New York; some of these trees have withstood temperatures of -20 to -30°F, to Zone 9.

HABIT: A lofty, deciduous conifer of slender, pyramidal habit, almost columnar in youth, with a stout, straight trunk buttressed at the base and short, horizontal branches, ascending at the ends, the lateral branchlets pendulous; sometimes becoming irregular, flat-topped and picturesque in old age.

RATE: Medium, 50 to 70′ high in 30 to 50 years; amazing growth rate in Wichita, KS tests where it averaged 2′7.4″ per year over a 9 year period.

TEXTURE: Medium-fine in leaf, medium in winter.

BARK: Rather attractive reddish brown, fibrous bark; the trunk becoming strongly buttressed especially in wet areas; I have observed specimens in the Coastal Plain of Georgia growing in wet areas that were magnificent; there is something hauntingly beautiful about a "grove" of Baldcypress; it should be mentioned that the "cypress knees" occur only near water; I have not seen them on trees planted under normal conditions in cultivation; it has been shown that the "knees" are not necessary for gaseous exchange.

LEAF COLOR: Bright yellow-green in spring; it darkens in summer to a soft sage green; in autumn it becomes a russet, soft brown to a mellow orangish brown.

FLOWERS: Monoecious, staminate in drooping, 4 to 5″ long panicles; March-April; pistillate cones are subglobose, comprising several spirally arranged peltate scales, each bearing 2 erect, basal ovules.

FRUIT: Cones globular or obovoid, short stalked, approximately 1″ across, green to purple and resinous when young; brown at maturity, mature in one year.

CULTURE: Transplants readily balled and burlapped as a small root pruned nursery-grown plant; see comment under *T. ascendens;* makes it best growth on deep, fine, sandy loams with plenty of moisture in the surface layers and moderately good drainage; in the wild it is seldom found on such places and occurs primarily in permanent swamps where it forms pure stands; very adaptable tree to wet, dry and well drained soil conditions; requires a sunny location; soils should be acid for chlorosis will occur on high pH soils; several trees on the Illinois campus were almost golden yellow and when treated with a trunk injection of ferric ammonium citrate they greened up within a month; exceptionally wind firm and even winds of hurricane force rarely overturn them.

DISEASES AND INSECTS: Twig blight, wood decay, cypress moth, spider mites, and a gall forming mite.

LANDSCAPE VALUE: A stately tree, a decided accent of texture and form; in parks or large estates it makes a distinctive specimen; good for wet areas; possibly a worthwhile highway plant or state tree; have seen used in groupings and groves around lakes and the effect is spectacular; interestingly the knees form in the shallow water at lake's edge and seldom on the other side.

CULTIVARS:

'Monarch of Illinois'—Truly a handsome specimen; wide spreading, the parent tree has a limb spread of 65′ and a height of 85′; this type of growth habit is unusual for this species.

'Pendens'—Pyramidal form; branches nearly horizontal, nodding at the tips, branchlets drooping.

'Shawnee Brave'—Form with narrow pyramidal habit; parent tree is 75' tall and 18' across; has street tree and single specimen possibilities, have seen 20' high trees in Spring Grove that were beautiful.

PROPAGATION: As previously discussed under *T. ascendens.* I have rooted cuttings with 30 to 40% success using very soft growth, 1000 ppm IBA, peat:perlite, mist.

ADDITIONAL NOTES: Several years past, I journeyed to Germany and visited gardens and parks with the denominator being *Taxodium distichum* in common use. Many trees were easily 50 to 60' high and a match for plants in the wild. The Germans are great at reproducing habitat gardens and *T. distichum* was used with other plants of wet soil or geographical affinity. In fact, as I write this, the wonderful Planten und Blumen in Hamburg comes to mind with a tremendous number of *T. distichum* reflecting a southeastern habitat.

Interestingly, the plant is usually columnar to pyramidal without great variation but I have seen trees with broad-spreading canopies. Many years past I walked the Kansas State University campus with Dr. Steve Still and could not reconcile the broad spreading habit. Also, this is often the common habit in swamps along I-95 through coastal Georgia, the plants often draped with Spanish moss. Amazing plants in San Antonio, TX along the River Walk, some 100' high.

NATIVE HABITAT: Delaware to Florida, west to southern Illinois, Missouri, Arkansas and Louisiana. Introduced 1640.

Taxus — Yew
Taxaceae

Taxus includes the highest quality needle type evergreens in landscape use. The quality characteristics include slow to medium growth rate, resistance to insects and diseases, excellent year-round color, wide variations in form, compact growth habit, winter hardiness, and ease of propagation. *T. canadensis, T. floridana,* and *T. brevifolia* are native to this country; however, the important ornamental cultivars are found in the species *T. cuspidata* and *T. × media* with a few excellent types in the species *T. baccata.* Many of the *T. baccata* types are tender and may be damaged or discolor during winter in the midwest. In addition to the factors mentioned above, the colorful red seed is an effective ornamental feature on some cultivars. Literature has it that Robin Hood made his bows from the yew tree.

Unfortunately the nomenclature of *Taxus* is as confused as any genus. This has come about because of the lack of distinguishing features between cultivars, and the indiscriminate naming of cultivars by numerous plantsmen. This problem is particularly serious in the *T. cuspidata* and *T. × media* types; whereas the naming of *T. baccata* types, which have been under cultivation for hundreds of years, is less confused. A collection of *Taxus* was begun at the Ohio Agricultural Research and Development Center in Wooster in 1942. This collection, containing over 100 cultivars, is the largest in the world and is intended to serve as a base for selecting outstanding forms which, after positive identification, are being disseminated throughout the world.

MORPHOLOGICAL CHARACTERISTICS

Evergreen trees and shrubs with reddish to brown bark and spreading and ascending branches. Branchlets are green. Leaves are glossy or dull dark green above, lighter green below, flat and needle-like, abruptly pointed or tapering and acute. *T. baccata* types usually have sickle-shaped leaves. Leaves are arranged radially or in a flat plane. Winter buds are small and scaly. With rare exceptions, plants are dioecious with the *male flowers globose* and the *female flowers appearing as small stalked conical buds.* The seeds are brown and nut-like, covered by an attractive fleshy red aril, ripening the first year; cotyledons 2. If one is interested in securing "fruiting" plants, the morphological differences italicized above are worth remembering.

GROWTH CHARACTERISTICS

Wide variation in habit, size, growth rate, and textural effects occurs. Practically all cultivars are compact and retain a dense character with age, without extensive pruning. In addition to overall form, line and textural effects vary because of differences in branching habit and degree of compactness. Foliage color is essentially dark green with some variations to lighter greens and a few cultivars with yellow foliage. *Taxus* retain high quality characteristics indefinitely and, under good conditions, will continue to increase in value with age.

CULTURE

Taxus are most effectively moved balled and burlapped and can be planted in spring or fall with good success. Some growers are producing container yews and this represents an alternate choice to balled and burlapped specimens. However, most yews are field grown, then dug and placed in containers for ease of handling during the marketing process. Yews require a fertile soil, sufficient moisture, and *excellent* drainage. Anything less than *excellent* drainage results in growth reductions or death of yews. Yews do equally well in sun or shade but should be kept out of sweeping winds. Often, in winter, the needles will brown or yellow because of desiccation. All, except some of the *T. baccata* cultivars, are reliably hardy in the midwest. Very few yews are used in Minnesota and areas with similar low temperatures. Conversely, yews are seldon used in the southern states for they do not tolerate the extreme heat. Several garden designers have reported success in the Atlanta area but for large scale corporate landscapes, the plant should not be used. One species, *Taxus floridana,* Florida Yew, occurs in a narrow area along the Apalachicola River in northwestern Florida. It becomes almost tree-like and may grow 20 to 24′ high. There is a fine specimen at the Biltmore Estate, Ashville, NC.

Many of the cultivars are naturally compact and symmetrical and relatively little corrective pruning is necessary. *Taxus* can be pruned severely and it is possible to maintain plants at determined sizes and shapes by frequent pruning or shearing. This is particularly advantageous in the culture of formal *Taxus* hedges or screens where early spring pruning followed by removal of "feather growth" in the summer will maintain the desired form. Although it is common practice to shear *Taxus* into tight, formally shaped plants, more interesting and attractive plants will result from pruning rather than shearing to retain the natural habit and appearance of the cultivar. The tight pruning results in the formation of green meatballs, cubes, rectangles, and other odd shapes. Overgrown plants have been pruned 12 to 24″ from ground and developed new shoots and filled in quite well.

DISEASES AND INSECTS

Needle blight, twig blight, root rot, other fungus diseases, twig browning, black vine weevil, strawberry root weevil, taxus mealybug, grape mealybug, scales, ants, termites, and nematodes.

PROPAGATION

Although *T. cuspidata* var. *capitata* is usually propagated from seed, all other cultivars are propagated by cuttings taken in the late summer through winter and rooted in cold frames and greenhouses. Specific recommendations are listed under *T. canadensis.*

LANDSCAPE VALUE

Probably the only negative comment one can apply to yews is that they are overused. Their ubiquitous landscape uses make them a favorite choice of designers. They appear, almost to the point of monotony, in hedges, foundations, groupings, broad masses and as facer plants.

The moderate growth rate, uniform habit, high quality appearance, and maintenance free aspect result in *Taxus* being classed as the best shrubby needle-type evergreen for landscape use. However, it should be emphasized that *T. baccata, T. cuspidata* and *T. × media* can grown 40 to 50′ in height. Proper pruning does wonders to keep the plants in bounds.

Taxus baccata — English Yew (Common Yew)
(taks'us ba-kā'tȧ)

LEAVES: Spirally arranged, spreading all around in erect shoots but appearing more or less 2-ranked on horizontal shoots or on plants grown in shade, linear, 1/2 to 1 1/4″ long, 1/16 to 1/4″ wide, convex and shining dark, almost black-green on the upper surface, with recurved margins and a prominent midrib, paler and yellowish green beneath with ill-defined lines of stomata, gradually tapering at the apex to a horny point.

STEM: Branchlets surrounded at the base by brownish scales.

SIZE: 30 to 60′ high by 15 to 25′ spread; usually smaller; tremendous number of clones all varying in size and shape; large plants up to 85′ high and 8 1/4′ in girth have been recorded.

HARDINESS: Zone (5)6 to 7.

HABIT: Tree or shrub-like, wide-spreading and densely branched; broad-rounded, or shrubby; indescribably beautiful in the best forms with a dense, dark, somber pyramidal outline and often a massive, fluted, rich reddish brown trunk; I have seen nothing in the States to match the splendid old trees in England, often church yards house the most magnificent specimens; the many cultivars offer a multitude of shapes from wide-spreading to distinctly columnar.

RATE: Slow.

TEXTURE: Medium.

BARK: Reddish brown, furrowed, thin, scaly, flaky; often fluted on old trunks.

LEAF COLOR: Dark green and lustrous above.

FLOWERS: Usually dioecious, male strobili stalked, globose, arising from the axils of the leaves on the undersides of the branchlets of the previous year, each consisting of 6 to 14 stamens with short filaments; female strobili solitary, green, from the leaf axils, usually opening in March-April.

FRUIT: Seeds solitary, bi- seldom tri- or quadrangular, slightly compressed, 1/4″ long, 1/5″ broad, olive-brown; aril roundish, red.

CULTURE: Does well on calcareous soils as well as acid soils; prefers a moist, well-drained, sandy loam; see under culture in the introductory remarks.

DISEASES AND INSECTS: *Taxus* mealybug, black vine weevil, *Taxus* scale, yew-gall midge.

LANDSCAPE VALUE: Useful in gardens and parks, in shade, for undergrowth, hedges, screens and foundation plantings; used extensively for topiary work in England; not outstandingly hardy in Zone 5 and inferior to *T* × *media* and *T. cuspidata* types for that reason.

CULTIVARS: Den Ouden and Boom list over 100 cultivars of this species. Apparently cultivated in England for over 1000 years and numerous selections have been made. The following might be considered among the best.

'Adpressa'—Wide spreading, dense habit, dark green needles only 1/4 to 1/2″ long, 1/10″ wide, abruptly pointed at apex, will make a large shrub or small tree, plants as large as 30′ high are known, female; several 'Adpressa' variations are known including 'Aurea', 'Erecta', 'Pyramidalis' and 'Variegata'.

'Adpressa Fowle' (Midget Boxleaf English Yew)—Handsome, compact form rather stiffly branched but clothed with short, heavy textured, lustrous black green needles, grows slowly, introduced by Weston Nurseries, Hopkinton, Mass; original plant 7 1/2′ high and 16′ wide.

'Aurea' (f. *aurea*)—Apparently several different yellow-foliaged types are included here; the few I have seen are golden in the new growth which eventually fades to green.

'Cheshuntensis'—Narrow columnar with small blue-green needles, faster and hardier than the Irish Yew, female, listed in 1988 Weston Nurseries catalog, not in 1989.

'Dovastoniana'—Tree form (may be shrub-like), usually short-trunked, widely spreading branches, pendulous branchlets, blackish green needles, male form, apparently becomes immense with age for the original plant measured in 1929 was 56′ wide and 12′ in trunk circumference, a male but on occasion a branch produces seeds.

'Fastigiata'—This is one of the most fascinating of all yews and certainly one of the most common especially in European countries; it is fastigiate with all branches rigidly upright, needles blackish green above, streaked with dull green and a narrow shining midrib beneath; generally 15 to 30' high, 4 to 8' wide; have seen it used at Filoli Gardens, California where it is a fine biological accent to the formal architecture of the house; it is a female but male flowers may occur on isolated branches; several cultivars have been raised from seed of this form, 'Fastigiata' occurred sometime around 1780.

'Fastigiata Aurea'—Similar in habit but with golden foliage on the young shoots of the season; several selections have been made.

'Fructu-luteo'—Arils are orange-red, otherwise similar to the species, first noted about 1817.

'Nana'—Dwarf form not exceeding 3', pyramidal, needles smaller and darker green than species.

'Pygmaea'—Dwarf form to 15" high, wide, dense habit, needles less than 1/2" long, radially arranged.

'Repandens'—Dwarf, wide-spreading form with the tips of the branches pendulous, sickle-shaped needles shining dark green above, dull green below, probably the hardiest form of English Yew (Zone 5); widely used in the United States with some of the finest plants located at Longwood Gardens; may grow 2 to 4'(6') high and 12 to 15' across; I have seen plants considerably larger than this; excellent landscape plant, known before 1887, female.

'Standishii'—Somewhat similar to Irish Yew but slower growing and smaller in size; needles yellow, crowded, considered the best golden yew for small gardens.

'Summergold'—Foliage predominantly golden in summer, even in sun, semi-prostrate habit, raised from seed in Holland.

'Washingtonii'—Open, loose form, branchlets yellowish green, leaves tinted a rich gold, finally yellow-green, female, wide-spreading form, 5 to 6' high.

PROPAGATION: Most clonal selections of yews are propagated by cuttings, which root easily. Seedling propagation is little used, owing to the variation appearing in the progeny, the complicated seed dormancy conditions, and the slow growth of the seedlings. Side or side-veneer grafting is practiced for those few cultivars which are especially difficult to start by cuttings.

ADDITIONAL NOTES: Yews are among the most toxic of plants. They appear to be poisonous all seasons of the year. The toxic principal is taxine. Foliage, bark or seeds, whether dry or green, are toxic to people and to all classes of livestock. The fleshy red arils are not poisonous as the toxic principal is contained in the hard part of the seed. This is not digested and is passed so no harm is done. I had a veterinarian in one of my off-campus courses and while discussing yews he mentioned he had seen cows who had died from eating yew foliage and the amount removed from their stomach was very small in relation to their total body weight.

NATIVE HABITAT: Europe, northern Africa, western Asia. Cultivated since ancient times.

Taxus canadensis — Canadian Yew
(taks'us kan-à-den'sis)

LEAVES: Densely set, in 2 ranks, 1/2 to 3/4" long, 1/16 to 1/12" wide, apex abruptly short pointed, with a slightly raised midrib above and below, glossy dark green above, paler green beneath, assuming a reddish tint in winter, short stalked.

SIZE: 3 to 6' by 6 to 8' broad, often twice as wide as high at maturity.
HARDINESS: Zone 2 to 6.
HABIT: Often prostrate, loose, straggling; leaders prostrate and rooting in the ground; very straggly shrub compared to other yew types.
RATE: Slow.
TEXTURE: Medium.
LEAF COLOR: Glossy dark green assuming a reddish tint in winter, almost reddish brown not unlike the worst Andorra juniper color.
FLOWERS: See *T. baccata*.

FRUIT: Seeds broader than high, aril light red.

CULTURE: Moist, sandy loam; transplant balled and burlapped; will not tolerate heat and drought; requires winter shade.

DISEASES AND INSECTS: None serious.

LANDSCAPE VALUE: Suitable as a ground cover but only for underplanting in cool, shaded situations; the hardiest of the yews; probably the least desirable of the yews for landscape purposes.

CULTIVARS:

'Stricta' ('Pyramidalis')—Branches stiffly upright yet the plant is wider than high at maturity.

PROPAGATION: Yew seeds are slow to germinate, natural germination not taking place until the second year. Seeds have a strong but variable dormancy that can be broken by warm plus cold stratification. One recommendation is to hold the seeds for 90 to 120 days at 60°F followed by 60 to 120 days at 36 to 41°F. Another recommendation specifies prechilling the seed for 270 days at 36° to 41°F. Most yews root readily from cuttings and the recommended practice is to procure wood from October through January. The cuttings are treated with a hormone dip or powder (IBA, 5000 to 10,000 ppm talc or quick dip) and placed in sand or sand:peat. Misting is used although I have placed flats of yew cuttings under the bench, watering them only when other plants need water and had excellent success. Rooting time is rather long and 2 to 3 months would probably represent an average time span from sticking to rooting.

NATIVE HABITAT: Newfoundland to Virginia, Iowa and Manitoba. Introduced 1800. I have found it growing out of sandstone cliffs in deep shade in Turkey Run State Park, Marshall, Indiana. In the midwest, this is probably its southernmost location.

Taxus cuspidata—Japanese Yew
(taks′us kus-pi-dā′tà)

LEAVES: Short-stalked, mostly not distinctly 2-ranked, upright and irregularly V-shaped, straight or slightly curved, slightly leathery, apex rather abruptly sharp-pointed, 1/2 to 1″ long, 1/12 to 1/8″ wide, dull to dark lustrous green above, paler beneath with 2 yellowish green bands.

BUDS: Ovoid-oblong, chestnut brown, composed of overlapping, concave, ovate scales more or less keeled on the back.

SEEDS: Ovoid, about 1/3″ long, aril—red; hard seed.

SIZE: 10 to 40′ with an equal or greater spread; usually smaller depending on cultivar—see cultivar list for specifics; in native haunts it may grow 40 to 50′ high.

HARDINESS: Zone 4 to 7.

HABIT: Crown erect or flattened, broad or narrow, of irregular habit and spreading or upright-spreading branches; can be grown as a tree or multistemmed shrub.

RATE: Slow.

TEXTURE: Medium.

BARK: On old tree-like specimens is a handsome reddish brown, exfoliating in scales or longer strips.

LEAF COLOR: Dark lustrous green above, yellowish green beneath.

FLOWERS: Dioecious, see *T. baccata* for description.

FRUIT: Seeds ovoid, about 1/3″ long by 1/6″ broad, compressed, aril red.

CULTURE: Transplants well balled and burlapped; the roots of the yews are rather thick but abundant and a large mass of roots is normally present around the base of young plants which allows for successful transplanting; prefers a moist, sandy loam although adaptable, must be well-drained; shade or sun; superior to other conifers in shade; sun and wind may cause needles to turn yellowish brown; furthermore, it endures the dust and smoke of city atmospheres surprisingly well and withstands any amount of pruning.

DISEASES AND INSECTS: None serious.

LANDSCAPE VALUE: Excellent for many purposes; foundation plantings, hedges, screens, bonsai, masses, groupings, bank covers.

CULTIVARS:

'Aurescens'—Low, compact, slow-growing form, 1 by 3', leaves of the current year's growth deep yellow, after first season changing gradually to green, male.

'Capitata'—Usually a pyramidal form, can be maintained in a tightly pruned form, however, will grow 40 to 50', a common form in cultivation and certainly a functional landscape plant.

'Cross Spreading'—A form selected by Cross Nurseries, Lakeville, MN that is highly resistant to winter burn; grows 3 to 4' high and 8 to 10' wide.

'Densa'—Low shrub form, two times as broad as tall with extremely dark green leaves; 40-year-old specimen is 4 by 8'; fruiting clone, one of the best dwarf forms.

'Expansa'—According to Wyman a name applied to many *Taxus cuspidata* seedlings with a vase-shaped habit; this form has an open center, loose foliage and branches at a 45 to 60° angle from the base; about 1 1/2 to 2 times as broad as high; male and female clones available.

'Intermedia'—Dwarf, round, compact, slow-growing form, leaves densely set, resembles 'Nana' with the same heavy plump dark green leaves; starts growth earlier in the season and grows faster.

'Jeffrey's Pyramidal'—Heavy fruiting, pyramidal form.

'Nana'—Slow-growing form with spreading branches, needles radially arranged; twice as wide as high; forty-year-old plant—10 to 20' high; excellent fruiting form; in Minnesota has shown some resistance to winter burn.

'Pyramidalis'—Pyramidal form with dark green leaves; introduced by Hill's, Dundee, IL.

'Thayerae'—Slow-growing, wide-spreading form (8' high, twice as wide) with branches at a 30° angle with ground and forming a flat-topped head, centers are full; some consider this a *T* × *media* type; raised in Massachusetts around 1916–1917.

'Winston Peters'—Lower, broader, faster growing than 'Densiformis' with lighter shiny green needles; supposedly with excellent root system and quite easy to transplant.

PROPAGATION: Cuttings of most clones will root readily. *Taxus cuspidata* var. *capitata* is often grown from seed as it comes fairly true-to-type. Cuttings from *capitata* should be collected from vertical terminal growth as laterally-spreading cuttings will develop into spreading types.

ADDITIONAL NOTES: The new growth on *Taxus* is a lovely soft yellow-green which develops in May and is effective for about one month. The emphasis on well-drained soil cannot be stressed enough. *Taxus* do not tolerate "wet feet" for any period of time. Even if they do not die the growth is often reduced. About the best advice is to plant high if the soil is hopelessly wet and use raised beds. Pruning can be accomplished about any time but early in the growing season is often recommended. Hard, close pruning is not recommended as this results in the formation of a shell of foliage and a very formal appearance. The best way is to hand prune removing the longest growth every other year and thus creating an "unpruned" effect.

NATIVE HABITAT: Japan, Korea, Manchuria. Introduced 1853.

Taxus × *media* — Anglojap Yew (*T. cuspidata* × *T. baccata*)
(taks'us × mē'di-à)

Similar to *T. cuspidata* in many respects, however, differing in olive color of the branchlets which do not change to brown the second year, the blunt bud scales and the distinct two-ranked leaves.

SIZE: Variable, 2 to 3' high to 20' high; every cultivar is different.

HARDINESS: Zone 4 to 7.

HABIT: Broad-pyramidal, medium-sized tree to large shrub, of spreading habit often with a central leader. Actually, it is very difficult to ascertain the exact habit and size of the Anglojap types since they are hybrids and the growth characters they exhibit are variable. I have seen the excellent *Taxus* collection at Wooster, Ohio, and it is here that growth differences are very evident. The plants have not been pruned and have developed naturally. It is extremely difficult to identify *Taxus* by needle characteristics and when they have been pruned into little squares, balls and hedges in the landscape, there is no hope. Often nurserymen sell *Taxus* "spreaders" which could be about anything.

RATE: Slow.

TEXTURE: Medium.

LEAF COLOR: Similar to *T. cuspidata;* dark green, often lustrous above, lighter green beneath.

FLOWERS: Dioecious, see under *T. baccata.*

FRUIT: Fleshy, red aril covers hard brown seed.

CULTURE: Transplants well balled and burlapped; prefers a moist, sandy, acid to neutral loam; must be well-drained; shade or sun.

DISEASES AND INSECTS: See culture sheet.

LANDSCAPE VALUE: Depending on the cultivar, may be used for hedges, screens, foundations, and mass plantings.

CULTIVARS:

'Amherst'—Male clone, slow-growing, dense, compact form; 12-year-old specimen is 6' by 9'.

'Andersonii'—Spreading type to 4 to 5' high, deep green foliage, excellent winter color, considered Zone 4 hardy.

'Angelica'—A slow, low growing form with good dark green needles, considered extremely hardy.

'Anthony Wayne'—Wild columnar form with light green new shoots, relatively fast growing, female, landscape effect is similar to 'Hatfield' but growth is faster.

'Berryhillii'—A female clone, dense growing spreading type, 20-year-old plant is 5' by 9', resembles *T. cuspidata* 'Nana'.

'Brownii'—Male clone with a densely rounded habit, foliage dark green, 9' by 12' after 15 to 20 years; easily pruned and can be maintained at any height, common form in midwest; have seen it listed as female but have not observed fruit set.

'Chadwickii'—Low growing compact spreader with handsome lustrous dark green foliage that holds up well in winter, 2 to 4' by 4 to 6', named after Dr. L.C. Chadwick, one of my mentors at The Ohio State University.

'Densiformis'—Dense, shrub-like form, twice as wide as high, needles bright green, first year branchlets greenish brown in winter, 3 to 4' high, 4 to 6' wide.

'Everlow'—A dark green needled, low-growing spreader, resistant to wind desiccation, may be a good substitute for *T. baccata* 'Repandens' in colder climates, 1 1/2' by 4 to 5'.

'Flemer'—Good dark green needles, color holds well in winter, similar to 'Sebian' but with full center, more dense and compact, female form, 6' by 10' in 20 years.

'Flushing'—Slender, stately form with thickish, lustrous dark green needles and red seeds.

'Green Wave'—Dark green foliage and low mounded spreading habit with distinctive, graceful, arching branches, considered a good substitute for *T. baccata* 'Repandens', offered by Angelica Nursery.

'Halloran'—Broad, compact form, branches erect, sprays erect, leaves densely set, dark green, 6' by 6' in 20 years.

'Hatfieldii'—Dense, broad pyramidal form, leaves dark green; 20-year-old plant is 12' by 10'; a very excellent clone; predominantly male.

'Hicksii'—Male and female clones, columnar in habit, needles lustrous dark green above, lighter green beneath; similar to the Irish Yew but more hardy; 20' high after 15 to 20 years; raised at former Parsons Nursery, Flushing, NY; selected and introduced by Henry Hicks; fairly narrow in youth becoming fatter with age.

'Kelseyi'—Erect, dense, compact form taller than broad, free fruiting female form; very dark green needles; 20-year-old plant is 12' by 9'.

'L. C. Bobbink'—Fine textured, glossy dark green needles, color holds well in winter, globe to mound shaped, 6' high, 6 to 8' wide, female.

'Meadowbrook'—Columnar growth habit and fine needle texture, 4' by 18" in 10 years, found on an estate on Long Island, NY.

'Moon'—Upright-rounded habit, branches and shoots ascending, densely arranged.

'Old Westbury'—Handsome form with deep green needle color, narrow upright column, branches tight and compact.

'Sebian'—Straight dark green needles, intermediate compact spreading form with flat top, good winter hardiness (Zone 4), 6' by 12' in 20 years, male.

'Sentinalis'—Very narrow form, female; 10-year-old plant is 8' by 2'.

'Stoveken'—Male, excellent columnar form; 20-year old specimen is 12' by 6'.

'Tauntonii'—Spreading form about 3 to 4' high; most interesting because it is about the only *T.* × *media* type to show resistance to winter burn; on the other side of the ledger, it is the only *T.* × *media* type performing well in the heat of Zone 8.

'Vermeulen'—Female, slow-growing, rounded type; 20-year-old plant is 8' by 9'.

'Viridis'—Slow growing narrow columnar form, foliage lighter green than typical, new growth bright yellow-green, needles twisted.

'Wardii'—Wide-spreading, flat topped, dense form, foliage dark green; 20-year-old plant is 6' by 19', female.

PROPAGATION: Propagate vegetatively (cuttings) to maintain trueness-to-type.

ADDITIONAL NOTES: A hybrid species first raised by T.D. Hatfield of the Hunnewell Pinetum, Wellesley, Massachusetts about 1900. Since that time numerous selections have been made and often it is difficult to tell if one is looking at a *T. cuspidata, T. baccata* or *T.* × *media* type. Unfortunately nurserymen have confounded the issue by indiscriminately naming clones which they thought were better and introducing them. When one sees a whole nursery block of a certain yew next to another block, specific differences are noticeable such as foliage color, needle density, and habit; but once they have been massacred in the landscape by the hedge shears (worst landscape tool ever invented), there is no effective way to distinguish between and among different clones.

"A Study of the Genus *Taxus*" is available from the OARDC, Wooster, Ohio, as Research Bulletin 1086. The publication contains a wealth of information on the *Taxus* collection at Wooster, early history of yews, the development of the Hatfield yews, morphology, sex and fruiting characteristics, propagation, culture and an extensive treatment of *Taxus* species, clones, and cultivars. Written by Drs. R.A. Keen and L.C. Chadwick and should prove invaluable for anyone interested in this most important group of landscape evergreens. Anyone interested in hardiness evaluations should consult *Nursery Notes* Vol. II (4). July-August 1978. The Ohio State University. Drs. Chadwick and Smith performed a genuine service by evaluating the extensive *Taxus* collection after the devastating winters of 1976–77, 77–78.

Ternstroemia gymnanthera (usually sold as *Cleyera japonica*) — Japanese Ternstroemia,

(tĕrn-strō'mi-à jim-nan'thĕr-à)

FAMILY: Theaceae

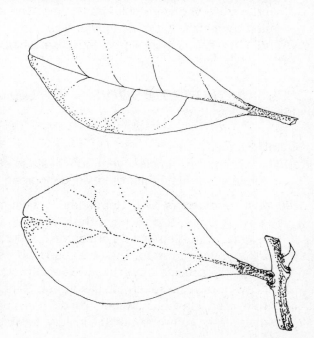

LEAVES: Alternate, simple, evergreen, leathery, narrow-oblong to ovate-oblong, 2 1/2 to 4" long, 1/2 to 1 1/2" wide, bluntly pointed at the apex, narrowly wedge-shaped at the base, entire, glabrous, lustrous deep green above, paler beneath; petioles—about 3/4" long, stout, red or reddish purple in color; leaves appear whorled at end of stem.

SIZE: 8 to 10' high, 5 to 6' wide; may grow 15 to 20' high; can be maintained at a 4 to 6' height indefinitely with proper pruning.

HARDINESS: Zones 7 to 9 and into 10; severely injured at -3°F; many old 10 to 15' high plants on the Georgia campus were killed to the ground.

HABIT: Distinctly upright-oval to oval-rounded, densely branched evergreen shrub; may be grown as a small tree but most plants I have seen were shrub-like.

RATE: Slow.

TEXTURE: Medium.

LEAF COLOR: Emerging leaves bronze to red, changing to lustrous dark (midnight) green at maturity, assuming a rich reddish bronze color in winter; leaves tend to be clustered at the end of the branch resulting in a whorled or tufted appearance; considerable variation in new leaf color since plants are seed grown.

FLOWERS: Perfect, white to yellowish white, 1/2″ across, borne 1 to 3 together from the leaf axils on the previous year's wood, or on short spurs, pedicels about 1/2″ long, petals fleshy, May-June.

FRUIT: Egg-shaped, 1/2″ diameter, 1″ long, green to red berry that ripens in September.

CULTURE: Container-grown and easily transplanted; prefers moist, well-drained soils; appears to do best in shade or partial shade on east or north side of structures; responds well to pruning; essentially intolerant of wet, poorly drained soils.

DISEASES AND INSECTS: None serious.

LANDSCAPE VALUE: Good accent plant, can be used for screens and hedges; foliage is attractive; definitely best used in shady situations; a group of these plants sited in full sun on the Georgia campus is yellow-green, purple-green and green in the winter; the plant is grown from seed and variation results.

CULTIVARS:

'Variegata' ('Tricolor')—A very beautiful but perhaps excessively gaudy cultivar, the dark green leaves are marbled gray and possess a creamy-white to yellowish margin that turns to rose-pink with the advent of cold weather; not as vigorous as the species.

PROPAGATION: Cuttings collected late in summer or fall can be rooted; seed collected in fall and planted germinates readily the following spring, seeds are the primary method of propagation; have seen whole nursery blocks in Mobile, AL and the variation was maddening.

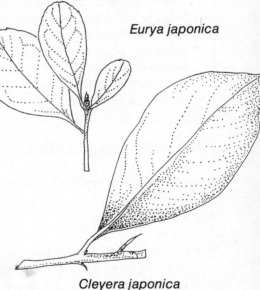

Eurya japonica

ADDITIONAL NOTES: Totally confused in the nursery trade. What is called *Cleyera japonica* is actually *Ternstroemia gymnanthera.* The differences between the two species reside in various minute floral characters. True *Cleyera* has a smaller leaf and is less cold hardy. Another closely related genus is *Eurya. Eurya* differs by virtue of unisexual flowers and toothed leaves. The few plants I have observed were quite handsome. There are dwarf and compact forms of *Eurya japonica.*

NATIVE HABITAT: Japan, Korea, Formosa, China, India, Borneo.

Cleyera japonica

Teucrium chamaedrys — Wall Germander
(tū′kri-um kam-ē′dris)

FAMILY: Lamiaceae

LEAVES: Opposite, simple, evergreen, ovate to oblong-ovate, 1/4 to 1″ long, 1/2 as wide, acute, broad-cuneate, serrate or almost lobed, dark green and pubescent on both surfaces.

Teucrium chamaedrys, Wall Germander, is best classified as an evergreen subshrub of mounded habit growing about 12 to 15″ high. The dark green leaves are present throughout the year. The rose-purple flowers (June-September) are borne in whorls of 4 from the axils of the uppermost leaves and form a 2 to 5″ long raceme. They are reasonably showy but are not the principal reason for growing the plant. The species is best used as edging material or a low hedge. It also fits nicely into a rock garden. I have grown the species in Illinois and Georgia with mixed success. In Urbana, Illinois the extreme cold killed it to the snowline but it did come back. In Georgia it performed more satisfactorily. Easily rooted from softwood cuttings in June provided there is not excessive moisture. Variety *prostratum* supposedly grows only 8″ high or less, spreads 2 to 3′, and flowers heavily. Central and southern Europe, northern Africa, western Asia. Cultivated 1750. Zone 5 to 8(9).

Thuja — Arborvitae
Cupressaceae

The genus *Thuja* constitutes a major group of small to medium size evergreens used extensively in landscape plantings, especially in the midwest and east. Many cultivars of different form, size, and with varied foliage color are available. Five species in cultivation are native in North America and Eastern Asia. *T. orientalis* is the least hardy of the species and is used extensively on the west coast and in the south. Some cultivars of *T. occidentalis* are of good quality; however, many types have a tendency to discolor in the winter, with center foliage browning in the fall. *T. plicata* and *T. standishii* have the best foliage characteristics of the species. *T. koraiensis* is not common in cultivation, but had proven hardy in the lower midwest. *T. occidentalis* and *T. plicata* are important timber trees, the wood being used extensively for shingles, shakes, siding and poles. Arborvitaes are not considered to be of the highest quality because of winter discoloration, loss of foliage and a thin and "ratty" appearance with age. Because of this, many types tend to decrease rather than increase in value, especially in congested planting sites. *Thuja occidentalis* cultivars 'Emerald' ('Smaragd'), 'Nigra', and 'Techny' are very valuable for they maintain good dark green foliage color in all seasons.

MORPHOLOGICAL CHARACTERISTICS

Evergreen small trees and shrubs with thin scaly bark and spreading or erect branches. Juvenile leaves are needle-like and the mature foliage scale-like and imbricate in four rows with glands sometimes on the back. The lateral leaves nearly cover the facial ones with branchlets flattened in one plane. Flowers are monoecious with male types yellow and female types rounded and forming a rounded cone. Cones solitary, ovoid or oblong; scales 8 to 12, with a thickened apical ridge or process, the 2 or 3 middle pairs fertile; seeds 2 to 3 beneath each scale, thick, wing broad or thick, or seeds wingless; cotyledons 2.

GROWTH CHARACTERISTICS

Arborvitaes are usually dense, pyramidal trees but vary from narrow- to broad-pyramidal. Numerous cultivars have been selected from *T. occidentalis* and *T. orientalis* and a selected few are available in the trade. Cultivars range from dwarf, round, globe, to narrow-upright types with foliage colors of yellow, bluish and various shades of green.

CULTURE

Arborvitaes should be planted in fertile, moist, well drained soils, although in the wild the species may be found on wet and dry soils; however, maximum growth is not realized on these sites. They are easily transplanted balled and burlapped or as container grown plants about any time of year. Arborvitaes perform best in full sun, although light shade is acceptable. In heavy shade plants become loose, open and lose their dense constitution. The characteristic winter browning of *T. occidentalis* and cultivars results in an unsightly plant. *T. orientalis* also suffers from low temperature stresses and probably should be avoided in Zone 5 gardens although it is frequently sold in the local mass market outlets. Pruning can be accomplished prior to growth in the spring. Usually extensive pruning is not necessary and if heavy pruning is practiced the result is similar to that achieved with tightly pruned yews.

DISEASES AND INSECTS

Leaf blight, juniper blight, tip blight, arborvitae aphid, cedar tree canker, arborvitae leaf miner, mealybug, scales, bagworms, and other pests.
Physiological Diseases:
Leaf browning and shedding—inner leaves may drop in the fall.
Winter browning—caused by rapid temperature changes, desiccation of needles caused by sun and wind.
In general, arborvitaes exhibit few serious insect and disease problems.

PROPAGATION

Seeds do not usually require a stratification period although selected seed lots have exhibited dormancy. Stratification in a moist medium at 34 to 41°F for 40 to 60 days will stimulate prompt germination. Cuttings are taken in late summer through early winter. See specific recommendations under the species descriptions. Cultivars are also rooted from cuttings.

LANDSCAPE USE

Arborvitaes have received wide acceptance in landscaping and are commonly used in foundations and as screens, windbreaks, accent plants, or hedges. They make excellent tall hedges and screens and, to a degree, have become stereotypes in these roles. The yellow-foliaged forms should be used with discretion for they detract from surrounding plantings. Arborvitaes will always be popular landscape plants but some of the new cultivars should be used in preference to the seedling-grown material.

Thuja occidentalis — Eastern Arborvitae, American Arborvitae, White Cedar
(thew′ya̱ ok-si-den-ta̅′lis)

LEAVES: Scale-like, about 1/12″ long, abruptly pointed, those on the main axis conspicuously glandular; on the branchlets sometimes inconspicuously so, shiny bright green above, pale green below, emitting a tansy-like odor when bruised.
BRANCHLETS: Alternate, compressed, flat; sprays horizontal, laterally compressed; 3 to 4 times divided.
CONES: Oblong, 1/3 to 1/2″ long, yellowish and erect when young, brown and pendent when mature at the end of the first summer, scales 8 to 10, usually 4 fertile, with a minute mucro at apex; differs from *T. orientalis* which has a distinct spine-like hook on the back of each cone scale near the apex.

SIZE: 40 to 60′ high, usually less, by 10 to 15′ spread; realistically under cultivation 20 to 30′ is more accurate.
HARDINESS: Zone 2 to 8, but not vigorous under Zone 8 conditions.
HABIT: A dense, often broad-pyramidal tree with short ascending branches to the ground which end in flat, spreading, horizontal sprays; usually there is one trunk but multiple trunks do occur; this is a good feature for separating this species from *T. orientalis* which develops many leaders and takes on a more dense bushy appearance with the sprays borne in strong vertical planes.
RATE: Slow to medium.
TEXTURE: Medium-fine.
BARK: Reddish to grayish brown, 1/4 to 1/3″ thick, fibrous, forming a more or less close network of connecting ridges and shallow furrows, grayish on the surface.
LEAF COLOR: Flat dark green in summer changing to yellow-brown-green in winter.
FLOWERS: Monoecious, terminal, solitary.
FRUIT: Cones oblong, 1/3 to 1/2″ long, light brown; scales 8 to 10, usually 4 fertile, with a minute mucro at apex; seeds 1/8″ long, compressed; wing round the seed, narrow, emarginate.

CULTURE: Readily transplanted from containers or balled and burlapped if root pruned; should be grown in areas with considerable atmospheric moisture as well as soil moisture; requires a deep, well-drained soil; thrives in marshy loam; full sun; tolerant of pruning; susceptible to strong wind, snow or ice damage; very tolerant of limestone soils; in spite of the absolute admonitions about this species and the cultivars, it will, once established, take considerable heat and drought.

DISEASES AND INSECTS: Subject to bagworm, heart rot and red spider mites; see culture sheet.

LANDSCAPE VALUE: Useful as a specimen or accent, good for hedges, shelter-belts and commonly used as a foundation plant; at times over-used in landscape plantings; 'Emerald', 'Nigra' and 'Techny' are excellent for cold climates' several Februaries past, Dr. Harold Pellett, University of Minnesota, and I were walking around the Minnesota Landscape Arboretum; near the visitor's center, surrounded by snow, were several Techny arborvitaes that were still a good dark green color even with the reflected light from the snow, wind and cold; interestingly on the ride from the Minnesota airport I was thinking how ugly the yellow-brown arborvitaes looked in many of the home landscapes; moral: plant the superior cultivars.

CULTIVARS:

Many, and I become confused trying to separate the various forms. I suspect there are 80 to 100 cultivars, some of worth, about 90% deserving of trash heap status. I used the literature, nursery catalogs and my eyes in assembling this list. Many of the smaller forms are collector's items or suitable for small scale landscapes or rock garden situations. Occasionally, I read the literature and see mention of shade tolerance. I don't believe it for a minute and neither does the plant for with time arborvitaes become thin, open, and generally ratty.

'Aurea'—Broad conical shrub with golden yellow leaves, 2 1/2 to 3' by 2 1/2 to 3'.

'Boothii'—Dwarf, globular, dense, foliage bright green, broader than tall, flat-topped at maturity, 6 to 10' high, named in 1874.

'Canadian Green'—Good globose-rounded form with better bright green foliage color than the old standard 'Woodwardii', listed as 3' high, Zone 3.

'Douglasii Aurea'—Pyramidal, slender, 30 to 45' tall, branchlets spreading; sprays yellow, grading to yellowish green at base; leaves golden yellow, bronzed in winter, developed by D. Hill Nursery Co., Dundee, IL before 1923.

'Elegantissima'—Narrow pyramidal form with dark green foliage that is tipped yellow which turns bronze during winter, 10 to 15' high, 4 to 5' wide.

'Ellwangeriana'—Juvenile form, conical, sometimes broad-pyramidal, 6 to 9' tall, leaves on developed branches and branchlets—scale-like, other leaves linear, spreading, acicular; a golden needled, slow growing form is known ('Ellwangeriana Aurea').

'Emerald' ('Smaragd')—Out of Denmark, saw 8 to 10 years past at Iseli Nursery, Boring OR and realized it had potential; many nurserymen are now growing it; narrow compact pyramidal form, 10 to 15' by 3 to 4', bright lustrous emerald green foliage in more or less vertical sprays, does not discolor in winter like many forms; also displays excellent heat tolerance, cold hardy to at least -40°F; introduced in 1950. Could this be a hybrid with *T. orientalis*?

'Ericoides'—Juvenile form, dwarf, compact, rounded, 3' tall and wide, leaves linear, spreading in pairs, flat, apex sharp pointed, yellowish green in summer, brownish in winter.

'Filiformis'—Weeping habit to the dense branches that hold loose tufts of long threadlike drooping branchlets, new growth bright green.

'Globosa'—Dwarf, globular, 4.5 to 6' high and wide; leaves green, slightly grayish green in winter.

'Hetz Midget'—A dense, globe-shaped form that doubtfully will ever grow more than 3 to 4' high; it has a fine rich green foliage and is quite an attractive selection, originated about 1928 as a chance seedling at Fairview Nurseries.

'Holmstrup'—Compact, slow growing, pyramidal form with bright green, tight, bunchy vertically arranged foliage, 5' by 2', eventually to 10' high, good for low hedges; have seen abundant cones on relatively young plants.

'Little Gem'—Dwarf, globose, dense form, broader than tall, 3' high and 4.5 to 6' in diameter, leaves dark green, slightly brown in winter.

'Little Giant'—Slow growing, globe-shaped small form with rich green foliage.

'Lutea'—Pyramidal, narrow, 30 to 36' high, sprays and leaves golden yellow, light yellowish green on underside of branchlets, old name was 'George Peabody', developed before 1873 in Geneva, NY.

'Nigra'—Pyramidal form with good dark green foliage persisting through the winter, 20 to 30' high, 4 to 5' wide.

'Pendula'—An attractive small pyramidal form with rather open ascending-arching branches and pendulous branchlets, a first class plant for accent use, ±15' high.

'Pyramidalis'—Narrow pyramidal, formal in outline with bright green soft textured foliage, susceptible to winter burn; a catch-all term?

'Rheingold'—A slow-growing ovoid or conical shrub 4 to 5' high by 3 to 4' wide; the foliage primarily adult and rich deep gold; it is quite similar to 'Ellwangeriana Aurea' except smaller in stature. No doubt propagated from the juvenile shoots of that form, turns copper to brownish yellow in winter.

'Rosenthalii'——Pyramidal, compact, slow-growing, 9 to 15' high, leaves shining dark green; good hedge form; one reference said no more than 6 to 9' in 50 years.

'Sherwood Forest'—According to Raulston, a variegated form, vigorous and fast growing.

'Spiralis'—Narrow pyramidal, slender, 30 to 45' high, branches short; branchlets spirally arranged, sprays somewhat fernleaf-shaped, leaves dark green.

'Sudwelli'—Irregular outline with green, gold-tipped foliage, quite similar to 'Lutea'.

'Techny' ('Mission')—Broad based pyramidal form to 10 to 15', excellent dark green foliage year-round, good hedge plant, slow growing; probably the best form for northern gardens, extremely popular.

'Umbraculifera'—Dwarf, globose, depressed, compact form, 2 to 2 1/2' high, 4 to 5' wide, glaucous, bloomy, probably most glaucous form.

'Wareana'—Pyramidal, low, dense, leaves bright green, without a brown tinge; 35-year-old plant is 8' tall; good for northern areas.

'Wintergreen'—Columnar pyramidal form holding good green winter color, coarser than other selections, 20 to 30' high, 5 to 10' wide.

'Woodwardii'—Globular form, wider than high, foliage dark green, turning brown in winter, 72-year-old plant—8' by 18'; a popular form; not preferable to some of the smaller globose or rounded types.

PROPAGATION: Cuttings made from current year's wood, taken with a heel, rooted well when taken each month in November through March. Cuttings taken in and after January rooted a little more quickly.

NATIVE HABITAT: Eastern North America (Nova Scotia to Manitoba, south to North Carolina, Tennessee and Illinois). Introduced about 1536.

RELATED SPECIES: For the purpose of further education, I offer several additional species which may appear occasionally in arboreta and botanic gardens. They are inferior to the better forms of the three primary species. *Thuja koraiensis,* Korean Arborvitae, is usually a broad, rather irregular, 2 to 5' high spreading shrub of no great beauty. I have seen it in the midwest during the winter where it pales by comparison with 'Techny', 'Nigra' and others. The foliage is bright green above with distinct whitish markings. The shoots are quite flattened and the branches procumbent-ascending. Wilson mentioned seeing the species in Korea from sprawling shrubs to slender, graceful, narrowly pyramidal trees reaching a maximum height of 25 to 30'. Korea. Introduced 1910. Zone 5 to 7(8).

Also worth mentioning is *Thuja standishii,* Japanese Arborvitae, with a broadly conical crown, slender trunk and shaggy deep red bark. The branch sprays arch, ultimate divisions are 1/16" wide, sprays are bright green on upper side and glaucous with whitish spots beneath. Cones are oblong, about 10 scaled and 3/8" long. Probably 20 to 30' under cultivation, larger in the mountains of Honshu and Shikoku to 100'. Introduced 1860. Zone 5 to 6(7). The broad head may be the greatest difference from the other species.

Thuja orientalis — Oriental Arborvitae (This plant has had its name changed to *Biota orientalis* and *Platycladus orientalis,* the latter being more correct. I am staying with the old name because it keeps similar plants together.)
(thew′yȧ ôr-i-en-tā′lis)

LEAVES: Smaller than those of other species, distinctly grooved on the back, those on main axis about 1/12″ long, triangular, ending in a blunt point, not pressed close to the shoot, those on the finer spray about 1/16″ long, closely pressed, green on both surfaces, bearing minute stomata, giving off a slightly resinous odor when bruised. Branchlets arranged in a vertical plane.

CONES: Ovoid, fleshy, glaucous green before ripening, 3/4″ long, 6 to 8 scales, each with horn-like process or hook.

SIZE: 18 to 25′ high by 10 to 15′ in width; however, can grow 30 to 40′ high but this is seldom realized under cultivation.

HARDINESS: Zone (5)6 to 9.

HABIT: A large shrub or small tree of dense, compact, conical or columnar habit when young with the branchlets held vertically, becoming in age loose and open and not so markedly vertical; composed of many slender branches which tend to bend and break in ice and snow.

RATE: Slow to medium.

TEXTURE: Medium-fine.

LEAF COLOR: Bright yellow-green to grass-green in youth changing to a darker green when older, often discolors in northern climates becoming yellow-green-brown.

FLOWERS: Monoecious, terminal, solitary.

FRUIT: Cones roundish egg-shaped, 3/4″ long, fleshy, bluish before ripening; scales usually 6, ovate, each with a horn-like projection, the uppermost sterile; seeds 2 to each scale, ovoid, about 1/8″ across, wingless; the wingless seeds distinguish it from the other *Thuja* species.

CULTURE: Transplant balled and burlapped or from a container; tolerant of most soils except those that are extremely wet; needs less moisture than *T. occidentalis;* best if the winter atmosphere is dry, protect from sweeping winds; pH adaptable; does quite well in southeast and southwest; in Key West, FL, yes, Key West, I saw the species on several occasions, robust, full-bodied and as obvious as a sore thumb; obviously it requires no significant chilling to satisfy any bud rest; also the plants were growing in/on coral/sand/sea shells and appeared to flourish; I have seen the plant all over Savannah, GA, particularly in cemeteries.

DISEASES AND INSECTS: Bagworm and red spider mites, see list on general culture sheet.

LANDSCAPE VALUE: Useful for hedges and specimens but not of value in the north central states although commonly sold; used extensively in the south and southwest where it is more adaptable; several worthwhile cultivars that are a cut above the species.

CULTIVARS:

'Aurea Nana' (Berckman's Golden Arborvitae)—Dwarf, dense, globular to ovoid form to 5′ tall, foliage golden yellow and finally light yellow-green, slightly brownish in winter.

'Baker'—Bright green foliage, densely set needles and broad conical shape; does well in hot dry places; grows 5 to 8′ high in 8 to 10 years.

'Beverlyensis'—Upright cone shaped to globe outline with time, soft golden yellow foliage turning bronzy gold in winter, may grow 10′ high and wide with age.

'Blue Cone'—Upright pyramidal form with compact sprays of flattened branchlets of green foliage with a bluish cast; my eyes see more green than blue.

'Bonita'—Dwarf form, broadly conical, new growth yellow-green, later light green at tops, darker green below, 3′ high.

'Compacta'—Pyramidal, dense, formal, slow-growing form, foliage glaucous green, tips plum colored in winter.

'Conspicua'—A medium-size to large shrub of dense, compact, conical habit with the sprays strongly vertical; foliage golden yellow and holding longer than most yellow selections; probably the true "Berckman's Golden Biota".

'Elegantissima'—Narrow pyramidal, foliage in flat sprays, emerges bright golden yellow, maturing to yellow-green, brown in winter.

'Filiformis Aurea'—Similar to 'Filiformis Erecta' but having more yellow-green foliage in summer.

'Filiformis Erecta'—When young, plants have upright cord-like branching habit, eventually forming upright oval-shaped shrub with light green foliage, more brownish in winter.

'Fruitlandii'—Upright-conical shape, rich deep green foliage.

'Golden Ball'—Dwarf loosely rounded habit, soft golden foliage in summer, vivid orange-brown tints in winter.

'Golden Globe'—Semidwarf, golden globe, supposedly none burning, 3' by 3'.

'Green Cone'—Upright oval, bright green foliage produces abundant cones.

'Juniperoides'—Dense feathery blue-gray in summer changing to purplish plum in winter; rounded bushy habit.

'Meldensis'—Tight globose to broad columnar, feathery light green foliage, dwarf growing, juvenile form.

'Minima Glauca'—Narrow pyramidal form, becoming 3 to 4' high and nearly as wide at maturity, blue-green foliage on flat sprays on vertical branches.

'Pyramidalis'—Over the years I have been confused by a large tree form with potential to grow 30 to 40' and rather loose, open, stringy foliage compared to the typical form; at Griffin, GA, Mr. Will Corley has grown several seedlings of this form for 15 to 20 years, they appear to be related to anything but the species; open, loose, gangly with bright green foliage, the cones are typical.

'Sieboldii'—Bright green foliage on a dense mounded plant that rarely exceeds 6' in height.

'Sudworthii'—Tight pyramidal, golden yellow that bronzes in winter, 7 to 10' by 3', probably larger at maturity.

'Sunkist'—Dwarf globose form, dense flattened foliage with bright golden tips, 2' by 2'.

'Westmont'—Compact, globe-shaped, slow growing type with rich dark green foliage tipped with yellow from spring to fall.

PROPAGATION: Seed germination is relatively easy but stratification of seeds for 60 days at about 40°F may be helpful. Cuttings of this species are more difficult to root than those of *T. occidentalis*.

ADDITIONAL NOTES: Always look ragged in midwest, especially during the winter; best reserved for southern and western states. The scientific name is listed by some authorities as *Biota orientalis* or *Platycladus orientalis*.

NATIVE HABITAT: Korea, Manchuria and northern China. Introduced before 1737.

Thuja plicata — Giant (Western) Arborvitae
(thew'yá plī-kā'tá)

LEAVES: On leading shoots, parallel to the axis, ovate, long-pointed, each with an inconspicuous resin gland on the back, up to 1/4" long, the points free; those on the ultimate divisions smaller, about 1/8" or less long, ovate, short and bluntly pointed, closely overlapping and often without glands, glossy dark green above, usually faintly streaked with white beneath but on some branches remaining green; emitting a tansy-like odor when bruised.

STEM: Branches horizontal, often pendent at the ends; branchlets in the same plane, much divided, the small lateral shoots falling after 2 or 3 years; often fern-like or stringy in appearance.

SIZE: 50 to 70' high and 15 to 25' wide; can grow in areas of the northwest to 180 to 200' high.

HARDINESS: Zone 5 to 7.

HABIT: A narrow, pyramidal tree with a buttressed base and often with several leaders; usually maintaining the lower branches; have seen old 80 to 100' high trees that were anything but narrow; still maintained branches and foliage to the ground.

RATE: Slow to medium.

TEXTURE: Medium.

BARK: Cinnamon-red on young stems; gray-brown to red-brown on old trunks, 1/2 to 1″ thick, fibrous, and forming a closely interlacing network.

LEAF COLOR: A good dark green in summer and winter.

FLOWERS: Monoecious, small, inconspicuous; staminate-yellowish, pistillate-pinkish.

FRUIT: Cones erect, cylindric-ovoid, 1/2″ long, green in summer, brown in winter; scales 8 to 10, elliptic-oblong with usually the middle pair fertile; seeds winged, the wing notched apically.

CULTURE: Transplants readily balled and burlapped; prefers moist, well drained, fertile soils and in the wild is found on moist flats, slopes, the banks of rivers and swamps, and is even found in bogs; occasionally found on dry soils but growth is usually stunted; moist atmosphere; full sun or partial shade; pH adaptable; have seen the species in the Vancouver, BC area and it grew everywhere from the steep slopes to the deep fertile valleys; truly an imposing evergreen if given optimum cultural conditions, handsome plants exist in the midwest and east coast and the species may be more adaptable than given credit; Raulston reported 2 to 4′ of growth per year at Raleigh, NC.

DISEASES AND INSECTS: Bagworm and heart rot.

LANDSCAPE VALUE: Useful as a specimen or for hedges in formal and semi-formal plantings, groupings, screens; a beautiful conifer when properly grown.

CULTIVARS:

Many more selections in Europe, especially England. The few that I have seen or are currently grown in the United States include:

'Atrovirens'—Possibly the best of the large, pyramidal arborvitae types, excellent shining dark green foliage, an excellent hedge form.

'Canadian Gold'—Broad pyramidal, brilliant gold foliage.

'Cuprea'—Dwarf broad pyramidal form, green with yellow new growth, 3′ high.

'Fastigiata' ('Hogan')—A good columnar clone with a straight slender outline and dense foliage.

'Pygmaea'—Dwarf bush, blue-green foliage, irregular branching, 2 to 2 1/2′ high, 1 to 1 1/2′ wide.

'Semperaurea'—Compact, rounded outline with golden foliage holding color in winter, will grow to 10′.

'Stoneham Gold'—Broad conical form, semidwarf, interior foliage dark green, bright yellow new growth, 6′ by 2′.

'Stribling'—Dense thick column that grows 10 to 12′ high, 2 to 3′ wide.

'Zebrina'—Kind of like an old friend, it tends to crop up in unexpected places, broad pyramidal outline with yellowish striped sprays (actually variable variegation pattern), have seen 30′ tall plants in England, plants 60 to 70 ′ are known; the effect from a distance is a rather pleasing yellow-green.

PROPAGATION: Dormant seed lots have been encountered occasionally on which stratification in a moist medium at 34 to 41°F for 30 to 60 days stimulated prompt germination (variation among seed lots). Cuttings rooted well when taken in January. Best to collect currings after cold weather has set in. Raulston mentioned 95% rooting on December-January cuttings with 8000 ppm IBA talc and mist.

ADDITIONAL NOTES: Extremely handsome conifer; probably better than *T. occidentalis* from an ornamental standpoint. Principal timber tree used for shingle manufacture in the United States and Canada. Is used for poles, posts, piling, boxwood, house-building, garden buildings, summerhouses and green houses because of its durability. The Indians used the split trunks for totem poles and hollowed-out trunks for canoes. They used the inner bark for fiber which was woven into mats, baskets and hats. The roots are so tough that they were used for fish hooks.

NATIVE HABITAT: Alaska to northern California and Montana. Introduced 1853.

Thujopsis dolobrata — Hiba Arborvitae, False Arborvitae
(thewyop′sis dol′ō-brā-tȧ)

FAMILY: Cupressaceae

LEAVES: Shining dark green above, flat ones glandless on the back, oblong-spathulate, with a green keel and a hollowed silvery white stripe of stomata on each side; the side leaves larger, hatchet-shaped, ovate or linear-oblong, bluntly keeled, the more appressed part on the underside of branchlets with a broad white stripe.

BRANCHLETS: Arranged in opposite rows, the ultimate divisions much flattened, about 1/4″ wide, sprays spreading in one plane.

SIZE: 30 to 50′ high, 10 to 20′ wide.

HARDINESS: Zone 5 to 7.

HABIT: Dense pyramidal evergreen of great beauty; the most magnificent specimen I have seen is located at the Isle of Mainau in Germany; in all appearances, at least from a distance, it resembles a fine *Thuja plicata*.

RATE: Slow.

TEXTURE: Medium.

LEAF COLOR: Lustrous dark green on the upper surface and prominently marked with whitish streaks on the lower surface.

FRUITS: Subglobose, 1/2 to 3/4″ long cones with 6 to 8, thick, woody scales, each ending in a horn-shaped boss, seeds winged.

CULTURE: Readily transplanted from a container; prefers moist, acid, organic soil and protection from sweeping winds; full sun but will tolerate considerable shade; found in moist forests in Japan; prefers high atmospheric moisture; the further south the plant is grown, ideally the more shade should be provided.

DISEASES AND INSECTS: None serious.

LANDSCAPE VALUE: To my knowledge the species is seldom found in the U.S.; it is a beautiful plant but, from a practical standpoint, probably not worth the commercial effort when there are so many other conifers that offer similar landscape effects; a good plant for the collector.

CULTIVARS:

‘Nana’ (‘Laetevirens’)—Dwarf form of rounded-mounded outline to 3′ high, good dark green foliage, as I have seen and propagated it; several references say lighter green foliage than the species; perhaps there are several dwarf forms.

‘Variegata’—The sprays marked with creamy white blotches, interesting plant but supposedly reverts rather readily to the green form.

PROPAGATION: Seeds are described as difficult. I have collected cuttings of ‘Nana’ in November, 3000 ppm IBA-quick dip, peat:perlite, mist and in 10 weeks had 100 percent rooting; the variegated form is also easy to root; apparently even large forest trees are easily propagated by cuttings.

NATIVE HABITAT: Central Japan. Introduced 1861 to America.

Thymus serpyllum — Mother-of-Thyme
(thī′mus sēr-pī′lum)

FAMILY: Lamiaceae

LEAVES: Opposite, simple, ovate or elliptic to oblong, 1/4 to 1/2″ long, about one half as wide, obtuse, broad-cuneate, glabrous beneath or pubescent and ciliate, short petioled; dotted with oil glands.

SIZE: 1 to 3″ high.

HARDINESS: Zone 4 to 8.

HABIT: Prostrate, weak subshrub or nearly herbaceous perennial; spreading, trailing, with rooting stems which ascend at the ends.

RATE: Slow.

TEXTURE: Fine in leaf; hardly noticeable in winter.

LEAF COLOR: Medium green although the numerous cultivars offer grayish, bluish, yellowish green, whitish margined, and yellowish colored foliage.

FLOWERS: On the species rosy-purple, 1/4″ long; June through September; borne in dense terminal heads. The flowers are beautiful and one can walk by Thyme without ever noticing it underfoot but the bright flowers make it come alive. The bees appreciate the flowers and from same manufacture a delicious honey.

CULTURE: Easily moved as clumps or from containers in spring; prefers dry, calcareous, well drained soil in a summy location; if over-fertilized or the soil is too rich the stems become tall and weak and the plant loses its dainty character; plant 6 to 12″ apart and they will fill in adequately in one growing season; makes an excellent cover for gentle slopes, a filler among rocks, dry walks, ledges or a crevice plant for walls, terraces, sidewalk cracks and the like.

DISEASES AND INSECTS: Apparently there are very few problems associated with the species although root rot and the ground mealybug have been noted.

LANDSCAPE VALUE: My first thorough introduction to this plant came as a graduate student when I took care of the Amherst, Massachusetts, Garden Club's 18th Century Garden. It was always a delight to watch the barren, sterile small stems yield the soft green and gray foliage in May after a long Massachusetts winter. As discussed under culture this species and the many cultivars are well adapted for rocky, dry slopes, as an edging plant, ground cover or among stepping stones; will endure a modicum of mowing and occasional tramping.

CULTIVARS: I have had great difficulty locating specific names for many of the different flowering and foliage clones which exist.

'Albus'—Possesses white flowers.

'Citriodorus' (Lemon Thyme)—Lemon odor, will grow into a spreading small shrub about 1′ high.

'Coccineus'—Has bright red flowers.

'Lanuginosus'—A type with gray-pubescent leaves and the appropriate name, Woolly Mother-of-Thyme.

'Roseus'—A pink flowering clone.

Other clones with lavender flowers, white leaf margins, and yellow coloring in the leaves are known.

PROPAGATION: Very easy to root from cuttings or simply divide the plant.

RELATED SPECIES: Other species include *Thymus lanicaulis,* (thī′mus lan-i-kaw′lis), Woolly-stem Thyme, and *Thymus vulgaris,* (thī′mus vul-gā′ris), Common Thyme, which has been used for seasoning since earliest times. Both species are ornamentally inferior to *T. serpyllum* but are worth the effort for the collector and the true plantsman.

NATIVE HABITAT: Europe, western Asia, northern Africa. Cultivated for centuries.

Tilia americana — American Linden or Basswood
(til′i-à à-mer-i-kā′nà)

FAMILY: Tiliaceae

LEAVES: Alternate, simple, broad-ovate, 4 to 8″ long, almost as wide, abruptly acuminate, cordate to truncate at base, coarsely serrate with long-pointed teeth, dark green and glabrous above, light green beneath, with tufts of hair in the axils of the lateral veins, wanting at base; petiole 1 to 3″ long, glabrous.

BUDS: Terminal-absent, laterals—1/4 to 1/3″ long, somewhat flattened, often lopsided, divergent, brown, reddish brown or greenish, smooth or slightly downy at apex, bud shaped like a teardrop, about 2-scaled.

STEM: Moderate, smooth gray-brown, shining brown or greenish red, covered with a bloom, generally zigzag, glabrous.

SIZE: 60 to 80′ in height with a spread of 1/2 to 2/3's the height, but can grow to 100′ or more.

HARDINESS: Zone 2 to 8(9).

HABIT: Tall, stately tree with numerous, slender, low hung spreading branches; pyramidal in youth; at maturity the lower drooping down then up, forming a deep, ovate, oblong, or somewhat rounded crown.

RATE: Medium, 20 to 30′ over a 20 year period although some authorities indicate the tree may grow 2 to 3′ over a 10 to 20 year period; soil conditions largely govern the growth rate; in Minnesota tests both the species and 'Pyramidalis' ('Fastigiata') were 25′ high after 8 years from 1 1/4 to 1 3/4″ diameter whips.

TEXTURE: Coarse in all seasons, in this edition I bent a degree, perhaps medium-coarse.

BARK: Gray to brown, broken into many long, narrow, flat-topped, scaly ridges, very tough and fibrous.

LEAF COLOR: Dark green above, paler green beneath, sometimes changing to pale yellow in the fall; usually the leaves fall off green or yellow-green; leaves on some trees tend to develop a brownish cast in mid-September and actually become unsightly; this seems even more pronounced if the summer was extremely dry.

FLOWERS: Perfect, pale yellow, 1/2″ wide, fragrant, borne in 5 to 10 flowered, 2 to 3″ wide, pendulous cymes in mid to late June; bees supposedly make the finest honey from these flowers; bracts spathulate, 3 to 4″ long.

FRUIT: Not clearly defined, but termed a nutlike structure, 1/3 to 1/2″ long, grayish tomentose, of no ornamental value, thick-shelled, without ribs.

CULTURE: Transplants readily; prefers deep, moist, fertile soils and here reaches maximum size but will grow on drier, heavier soils and is often found in the wild on the slopes of hills, even in rocky places; pH adaptable; full sun or partial shade; not particularly air pollutant tolerant.

DISEASES AND INSECTS: Anthracnose occasionally occurs on the European lindens, leaf blight, canker, leaf spots, powdery mildew, *Verticillium* wilt, linden aphid, Japanese beetle, elm calligrapha, European linden bark borer, linden borer, walnut lace bug, caterpillars, basswood leaf miner, elm sawfly, scales and linden mite can be and often are serious problems; the foliage feeding insects can damage the trees as they strip them of almost all foliage.

LANDSCAPE VALUE: Limited because of size; too many superior European species which are more tolerant and ornamental; a good and handsome native tree which should be left in the woods; definitely not for the small property; perhaps parks, golf courses and other large areas.

CULTIVARS:

'Dakota'—A round-headed form introduced by Ben Gilbertson, Kindred, South Dakota.

'Douglas'—Luxuriant deep green foliage, upright specimen tree growth with little staking or pruning, develops into broad pyramid, a Klehm introduction.

'Fastigiata'—A distinct pyramidal form which could be used in restricted growing areas; not a bad looking tree; spreads out a bit with age, selected in Rochester Parks about 1927.

'Legend'—Distinctly pyramidal with a central leader and excellent branching structure; thick dark green leaves are resistant to late season discoloration which often renders those of the species unsightly, winter stem and bud color is red, 55-year-old parent tree is 55′ high and 36′ wide, a Wandell introduction.

'Lincoln'—Slender-upright compact form with lighter green foliage, 27′ by 14′ after 24 years, a Klehm introduction.

'Redmond'—Originally listed as a *T.* × *euchlora* form but more properly included here; densely pyramidal with large leaves that are intermediate between *T. americana* and *T.* × *euchlora;* introduced by the Plumfield Nurseries of Fremont, Nebraska in 1927; makes a handsome street or lawn tree; I have thoroughly examined this cultivar and find it to differ from *T.* × *euchlora* in stem color (gray-brown-maroon on top, underside often greenish brown) and buds (glossy, ovoid, 3/8″ long, reddish). The leaves approximate those of *T. americana* rather than *T.* × *euchlora* in size and color; in Kansas tests, this was slow to establish and averaged only 9.6″ per year over a 10-year period.

'Rosehill'—An improved selection, fast growing and developing an open crown.

PROPAGATION: *Tilia* seed shows a delayed germination because of an impermeable seed coat, a dormany embryo, and a tough pericarp. Seed treatments that consistently result in good germination have not been developed. Recommendations include removing the pericarp, etching the seed coat in concentrated sulfuric acid for 10 to 15 minutes, and then stratifying in a moist medium for 3 months at 34° to 38°F. Seeds will germinate the following spring if picked before fruit wall and bract turn gray to brown. Cuttings have been rooted using mid-May to late June softwoods (Kansas), wound, 20000 to 30000 ppm IBA quick-dip, perlite:peat, and mist. See *The Plant Propagator* 24(2): 15 (1978) for details. Typically the cultivars are summer budded on seedling understock.

NATIVE HABITAT: Canada to Virginia and Alabama, west to North Dakota, Kansas and Texas. Introduced 1752.

RELATED SPECIES:

Tilia heterophylla — Beetree Linden, White Basswood (Now merged with *T. americana*)
(til′i-à het-ēr-ō-fil′à)

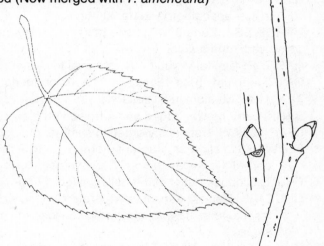

LEAVES: Alternate, simple, ovate, 3 to 6″ long, about as wide, gradually acuminate, obliquely truncate or rarely subcordate at base, finely serrate, with aristate teeth, lustrous dark green and glabrous above, beneath with close thick white tomentum or often brownish on the upper leaves, and with small tufts of reddish brown hairs; petiole 1 to 1 1/2″ long, glabrous.

BUDS: Terminal-absent, laterals 1/4 to 1/2″ long, prominently pointed, reddish maroon, glabrous.

STEM: Glabrous, relatively stout, reddish maroon.

Tilia heterophylla, Beetree Linden, also called White Basswood, is similar to the preceding but is typically a southern species. Morphologically, very similar except for undersurface of leaf, which is densely whitish; flowers smaller (1/4″ long) and 10 to 25 per inflorescence. I have reason to suspect that many trees labeled *T. americana* are, in fact, *T. heterophylla* and possibly were bought from southern nurseries. At Illinois, I taught this and *T. americana* with students forever bringing me samples to identify. Many specimens were not clear-cut and apparently some forms of *T. heterophylla* are almost hairless below. Indeed, the tree is handsome but in my own mind probably does not deserve species rank. Mr. Bill Wandell introduced a handsome upright form, 'Continental Appeal', with a distinct oval form and a tremendous heavy crown, the large lustrous leaves being distinctly silvery on the underside, an excellent plant where lateral space to spread is limited, quite urban tolerant and transplants readily. Current thinking includes this species with *T. americana* which means 'Continental Appeal' would be a cultivar of *T. americana*. Native from West Virginia to northern Florida, Alabama and Indiana. Cultivated 1755. Zone 5 to 9.

ADDITIONAL NOTES: The wood of these trees is used for many purposes including furniture, boxes, cooperage, wooden ware, veneer and food containers. The tough inner bark is sometimes used for making rope. Since the last edition several valuable papers concerning *Tilia* have been published. Some of the information is utilized herein but for in depth information, see Santamour and McArdle, *J. Arboriculture* 11:157–164 (1985); Muir, *The Plantsman* 5:206–242 (1985); and Muir, *The Plantsman* 10:104–127 (1988).

Tilia cordata — Littleleaf Linden
(til′i-à kôr-dā′tà)

LEAVES: Alternate, simple, suborbicular, 1 1/2 to 3″ long, almost as wide and sometimes broader than long, abruptly acuminate, cordate, sharply and rather finely serrate, dark green and glabrous and

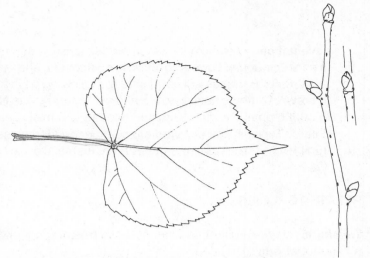

somewhat lustrous above, glaucous or glabrescent and glabrous beneath except axillary tufts of brown hairs; petiole 3/4 to 1 1/4″ long, slender, glabrous.

BUDS: Similar to *T. americana*—small, brown, about 1/4″ long.

STEM: Slender, lustrous brown, color continuous from current season's growth inward; may be greenish brown.

SIZE: 60 to 70′ in height and 1/2 to 2/3's that in spread; can grow 80 to 90′ high.

HARDINESS: Zone 3 to 7; have observed a few newly planted trees in Athens and Atlanta, some have lived, others died.

HABIT: Pyramidal in youth; upright-oval to pyramidal-rounded and densely branched in old age.

RATE: Medium, 10 to 15′ over a 5 to 10 year period.

TEXTURE: Medium in all seasons.

BARK: Gray-brown, ridged and furrowed on older trunks.

LEAF COLOR: Dark shiny green in summer changing to yellow in fall; often, at best, only yellow-green.

FLOWERS: Yellowish, fragrant, borne in 5- to 7-flowered, pendulous, 2 to 3″ wide cymes in late June or early July; flowers before *T. tomentosa;* floral bract 1 1/2 to 3 1/2″ long, 3/8 to 3/4″ wide.

FRUIT: Globose nutlet, thin-shelled, slightly or not ridged, covered with a gray pubescence.

CULTURE: Readily transplanted; prefers moist, well drained, fertile soil; full sun; pH adaptable; found on limestone in the wild; quite pollution tolerant; one of the best street and city trees and widely used for same.

DISEASES AND INSECTS: See under *T. americana;* aphids and Japanese beetles are often a problem.

LANDSCAPE VALUE: Excellent shade tree for lawn, large areas, streets, planters, malls and about any place a real quality tree is desired; can be pruned (and quite effectively) into hedges; the Europeans tend to use the tree much more as a hedge than do the Americans.

CULTIVARS:

'Bicentennial'—Tight pyramidal-conical form with acute branch angles, small typical dark green leaves; Ohio Shade Tree Tests mentioned an upright oval habit.

'Bohlje' ('Erecta')—Form of narrow, upright habit that supposedly is well suited to street tree use in urban areas; leaves small, orbicular, coloring yellow and holding late in fall.

'Chancellor'—Fastigiate in youth becoming pyramidal with age, fast growing, has good crotch development.

'Corinthian'—Compact pyramid, formal shape created by uniform spacing of limbs around straight central leader, dense branching, lustrous dark green leaves, leaves smaller, thicker and more lustrous than species, 45′ by 15′, Lake County introduction.

'DeGroot'—Sturdy, upright tree with compact head, glossy dark green foliage, slower growing than most lindens, 40′ by 25′.

'Fairview'—Strong, straight rapid growth, thick leathery dark green leaves are slightly larger than the species, well proportioned crown; matures as a linear about one grade larger than most *Tilia* of the same age.

'Glenleven'—Fast growing selection with a straight trunk; more open than typical *T. cordata,* leaf 1 1/2 to 2 times size of 'Greenspire'; introduced by Sheridan Nurseries, Ontario, Canada, 50′ by 35′; possibly a *T. × flavescens* selection.

'Green Globe'—A bushy round-headed form that is top grafted at 6 to 7′ on *Tilia* understock; foliage is dark green, 15′ by 15′.

'Greenspire'—Maintains a single leader with a nice branching habit, widely used as a street tree, result of a cross between cultivar 'Euclid' and a selection from the Boston Parks, does well under difficult conditions; good dark green foliage; handsome tree; probably commands 80 to 90% of the market; grew only 9.5″ per year over a 10-year period in Kansas tests; 40′ by 30′, have seen some of the early trees at Princeton Nursery which have maintained excellent form.

'Handsworth'—Young stems are a light yellow-green; quite striking especially on young trees.

'June Bride'—According to the introducers, Manbeck Nurseries, Inc., New Knoxville, Ohio, this clone is distinguished from other clones by the "unique combination of substantially pyramidal habit of growth, maintaining an excellent straight central leader, the branches are evenly spaced around the leader; the small-sized leaves are more glossy than those of the species, and flowers more abundant with 3 to 4 times as many"; have seen in Spring Grove in flower, it is a handsome tree.

'Morden'—Dense pyramidal crown; quite hardy; introduced by Morden Research Station in 1968, slowest growing in Minnesota tests over an 8 year period.

'Olympic'—Symmetrical form with better branching, glossy dark green leaves, 40′ by 30′.

'Pendula Nana'— Dwarf compact habit with pendent branches, strictly for the collector, Girard Nursery introduction.

'Prestige'—Excellent form, shape and limb structure, slightly broader than 'Greenspire' but with controlled shape, fast growing, easily headed in nursery production, shiny bright green leaves, 60′ by 40′.

'Rancho'—An upright-oval clone with small, glossy green leaves, good crotch development, and a medium-fine branch texture, has proven to be a good selection, flowers heavily with very fragrant small yellow flowers.

'Salem'—Upsweeping branches form rounded head, brilliant deep green foliage, 35′ high.

'Shamrock'—Supposedly stouter but more open crown than 'Greenspire'; strong pyramidal outline, typical foliage, 40′ by 30′.

'Swedish Upright'—Narrow, upright in outline, old trees become pyramidal.

'Turesi'—Strong growing pyramidal form.

PROPAGATION: See under *T. americana;* cultivars are budded on seedling understocks.

ADDITIONAL NOTES: Pellett et al., *J. Environ. Hort.* 6(2):48–52 (1988) presented valuable growth data on *T. americana, T. cordata, T. × europaea* and *T. platyphyllos* species and cultivars after 8 years. The information is difficult to compare because the liners were slightly different sizes at the time of planting. Perhaps the most striking aspect is the similarity in growth among the many *Tilia cordata* cultivars.

NATIVE HABITAT: *T. cordata* is native to Europe and has been planted as a shade tree since ancient times.

RELATED SPECIES:

Tilia × euchlora — Crimean Linden
(til′i-å × ū-klō′rà)

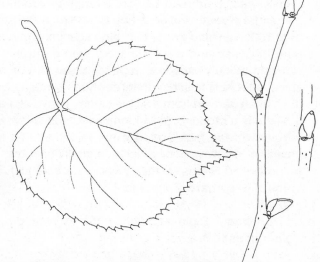

LEAVES: Alternate, simple, roundish ovate, 2 to 4″ long and as wide, abruptly short-acuminate, obliquely cordate, finely and sharply serrate with mucronate teeth, lustrous dark green and glabrous above, pale green and glabrous beneath, except axillary tufts of brown hairs; petiole 1 to 2″ long, glabrous.

BUDS: Glabrous, 1/4″ long or greater, yellowish red to reddish above, green beneath.

STEM: Glabrous, slender, greenish yellow on bottom, light reddish brown on top, almost rose-brown.

Tilia × euchlora, Crimean Linden, is the result of a cross between *T. cordata × T. dasystyla.* This tree grows to 40 to 60′ and half that in spread. Graceful in habit with the lower branches skirting the ground.

Not as stiff as *T. cordata*. The leaves are a lustrous dark green. Other features are similar to *T. cordata*. Flowers produced 3 to 7 in 2 to 4″ long cymes in July. The floral bract is linear-oblong, or narrowly lance-shaped, 2 to 3″ long, 1/4 to 5/8″ wide, glabrous, short stalked. A bud may form at the point of insertion of peduncle into bract, and also in the first division of the inflorescence. The ovoid fruits are tapered to a point, covered with pale brown wool, and 1/4″ long, slightly 5-ribbed. This is a rather handsome tree and in my opinion superior to *T. cordata*. Unfortunately, many trees are grafted and the basal suckers and sprouts become unslightly and a maintenance problem. The foliage is truly beautiful but like most lindens dies off green or yellow-green and never offers outstanding fall color. Still (Ohio State) has successfully rooted this species from cuttings which could alleviate the suckering problem on grafted trees. Interestingly, in England this species is free of the troublesome aphid infestations that wreak havoc on *T. cordata*. The sooty mold that develops after the aphids finish feeding colors the branches almost black. Recent English literature mentions a bleeding canker that has killed large trees. It is tolerant of air pollution and hot, dry conditions. Zone 3 to 7. Originated about 1860 but its parentage is not clear cut. 'Laurelhurst' is vigorous with straight, strong trunk; even, compact, broadly pyramidal crown; glossy dark green leaves.

Tilia × europaea — Common or European Linden, also listed as *T. vulgaris*.
(til′i-à × ū-rō′pēà)

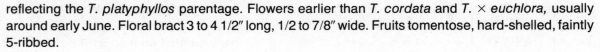

LEAVES: Alternate, simple, broad-ovate, 2 to 4″ long, about as wide, short-acuminate, obliquely cordate or nearly truncate, sharply serrate, dark green and glabrous above, bright green beneath and glabrous except axillary tufts of hair; petioles 1 to 2″ long, glabrous.

Stems and buds glabrous, usually intensely red-maroon, buds and stems smaller, more refined than those of *T. heterophylla*. Occasionally stems are slightly pubescent, reflecting the *T. platyphyllos* parentage. Flowers earlier than *T. cordata* and *T. × euchlora*, usually around early June. Floral bract 3 to 4 1/2″ long, 1/2 to 7/8″ wide. Fruits tomentose, hard-shelled, faintly 5-ribbed.

Tilia × europaea, European Linden, is another hybrid with *T. cordata* and *T. platyphyllos* the parents; pyramidal in youth and develops a more rounded habit in old age than the previous species. Will grow over 100′ with time and a 150′ high specimen grows at Duncombe Park, Yorkshire. Tends to sucker from the base and also forms burls on the trunk. Probably not preferable to *T. cordata* and her cultivars. Widely used in Europe for allees, street, parks, formal areas. Susceptible to aphid and red spider attacks with subsequent sooty mold infestation. Produced by stooling and most trees in Europe have been derived from a single clone. In my estimation, it is inferior to *T. cordata* and *T. × euchlora*. 'Pallida' is a broadly conical form with reddish brown branchlets and leaves whose undersurface is yellowish green, highly rated in the Ohio Shade Tree Evaluation tests. 'Wratislaviensis' produces new growth of a yellow color which eventually becomes green; there is a plant at the Arnold Arboretum. In the United States, certainly not preferable to *T. americana, T. × euchora* and certainly the best forms of *T. cordata*. Zone 3 to 7.

Tilia platyphyllos — Bigleaf Linden
(til′i-à plat-i-fil′us)

LEAVES: Alternate, simple, roundish ovate, 2 to 5″ long, about as wide, abruptly acuminate, obliquely cordate, sharply and regularly serrate, dark green and short pubescent or glabrous above, light green and pubescent beneath, especially on the veins, rarely nearly glabrous; petiole 1/2 to 2″ long, pubescent.

BUDS: Terminal-absent, laterals — 1/4″ long, reddish green-brown.

STEM: Reddish green-brown, pilose on young stems, rarely glabrous.

FLOWERS: Borne about the same time as *T. × europaea;* generally the earliest flowering linden and soon followed by tomentose, 5-ribbed, hard-shelled, pyriform, 1/3 to 1/2″ long fruits.

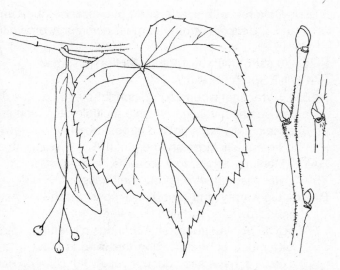

Tilia platyphyllos, Bigleaf Linden, grows 60 to 80′ high and larger; not extensively planted in the United States although the few large specimens I have seen were extremely beautiful in foliage (dark green) and outline (similar to *T. cordata*). It has the largest leaves of the European species but in no way compares in size to our American species. Yellowish white flowers occur in 3, sometimes 6-flowered, pendent, 3/4″ long cymes and are about the first to open. Floral bracts are 2 to 5″ long, 1/2 to 1 1/4″ wide. Very variable and numerous types have arisen. Cultivars include:

'Aurea'—Young twigs and branches yellow, must be viewed close-up to be appreciated.

'Fastigiata'—Upright-oval in habit, branches strongly ascending.

'Laciniata'—Irregularly lobed leaves and considerably smaller tree than the species, not particularly handsome; several cut-leaf forms exist.

'Rubra'—Young stems red in winter.

'Tortuosa'—The branches are curiously curled and twisted, not a particularly handsome tree, Minnesota Landscape Arboretum has grown this for a number of years.

This species is supposedly easy to identify by the pubescent stems and leaves but this is not always true. The degree of pubescence varies tremendously from densely pubescent to almost glabrous. The ribbed nutlets may be the best feature when separating it from *T. cordata, T. × euchlora* and *T. × europaea.* At the gardens of Fountainbleu, numerous *T. platyphyllos* form extended alleés. Most of the trees I examined were densely pubescent. Planted in Europe for centuries. In Germany, the species is quite common. In my perusal of American nursery catalogs, I did not find a single listing of this or the cultivars. Santamour and McArdle, *J. Arboriculture* 11:157–164 (1985) listed 25 valid cultivars.

Tilia tomentosa — Silver Linden
(til′i-à tō-men-tō′sà)

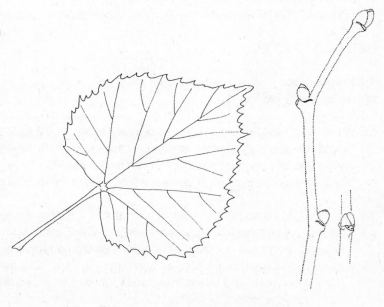

LEAVES: Alternate, simple, suborbicular, 2 to 5″ long, about as wide, abruptly acuminate, cordate to nearly truncate at base, sharply and sometimes doubly serrate or even slightly lobulate, dark green and slightly pubescent above at first, white tomentose beneath; petiole 1 to 1 1/2″ long, tomentose.

BUDS: Often partially covered with soft, short pubescence, green-red-brown in color, about 1/4″ long.

STEM: Covered with a soft, short pubescence; the dense, short pubescent stems separate this species and *T. petiolaris* from the other commonly grown lindens.

SIZE: 50 to 70′ high by 1/2 to 2/3's that in spread.

HARDINESS: Zone 4 to 7.

HABIT: Pyramidal when young, upright-oval to pyramidal-oval in old age; one of my favorite shade trees; can be effectively grown as a multiple-stemmed specimen for in this way the light gray, smooth bark is maximally enjoyed; the largest tree I have seen is located in the Arnold Arboretum and grows next to an equally large and beautiful *T. cordata;* both are about 60′ in height with upright oval habits.

RATE: Medium, similar to *T. cordata.*

TEXTURE: Medium throughout the seasons.

BARK: Light gray and smooth, almost beech-like on trunks up to 8 to 10″ and eventually becoming gray-brown, ridged and furrowed.

LEAF COLOR: Lustrous, shimmering, glistening, gleaming dark green on the upper surface, silvery tomentose beneath; when the wind is blowing a nice effect is created as both leaf surfaces are exposed; have seen decent yellow fall color on occasion.

FLOWERS: Yellowish white, fragrant, supposedly narcotic to bees; late June to early July; borne in 7 to 10-flowered pendulous cymes, generally the last *Tilia* to flower, bract 1 1/2 to 2 1/2″ long.

FRUIT: Egg-shaped with a short point, 1/3 to 3/8″ long, whitish pubescent, minutely warted, faintly 5-angled.

CULTURE: See under *T. cordata.*

DISEASES AND INSECTS: See under *T. cordata.*

LANDSCAPE VALUE: Good street tree as it tolerates heat and drouth better than other lindens; I highly recommend this for residential plantings as it is a very beautiful ornamental shade tree.

CULTIVARS:

'Brabant'—Broad conical crown with a strong central leader, leaves dark green with yellow fall color, excellent street tree.

'Erecta' ('Fastigiata')—An upright clone, as I have seen it not too different from the species especially with age.

'Green Mountain'—An improved rapid growing form, develops a handsome, dense-headed tree that is heat and drought tolerant, dark green leaves with silvery undersides, Princeton introduction.

'Satin Shadow'—Gilted green leaves, with silver underside, 50′ by 40′; Lake County introduction.

'Sterling'—Impressive, sculptured broad pyramidal crown with lustrous dark green leaves, silvery on the underside, young leaves silvery, 30-year-old tree 45′ by 24′, handsome grayish bark and uniform winter silhouette, resistant to Japanese beetle and Gypsy moth, a Wandell introduction.

PROPAGATION: See under *T. americana.*

NATIVE HABITAT: Southeastern Europe, western Asia. Introduced 1767.

RELATED SPECIES:

Tilia mongolica—Mongolian Linden
(til′i-å mon-gōl′i-kå)

LEAVES: Alternate, simple, ovate to broadly ovate, 1 1/2 to 3″ long and as wide, acuminate, truncate or cordate, coarsely serrate, serrations triangular, with slender points, often 3 to 5 lobed especially on vigorous shoots, lustrous dark green and glabrous above, paler and glabrous below except for tufts of pubescence in axils of veins; petiole 1″ long, glabrous, reddish.

Tilia mongolica, Mongolian Linden, is a small (30′), graceful, round-headed tree. The leaves are small and deeply cut (almost lobed), which makes the leaf unlike any linden leaf. The glabrous stems supposedly turn a good red in winter although most stems I have examined were reddish brown. Leaves turn good yellow in autumn. Also is resistant to aphids. This tree received rave reviews early in its career but nurserymen and others have found it hard to grow, tends to flop, must be trained, grafted on *T. cordata.* In addition it is subject to storm damage, ice and snow. I have changed my assessment of this species and recommend growers and homeowners temper their enthusiasm. Perhaps the most notable aspect is that the leaf does not look like a Linden. A leaf spot has also been reported. Native to China, Mongolia. Introduced 1880. Zone 3 to 5(6).

Tilia petiolaris—Pendent Silver Linden
(til'i-à pet-i-ō-lā'ris)

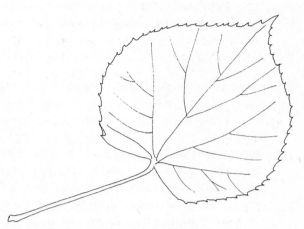

Tilia petiolaris, Pendent Silver Linden, is closely allied to *T. tomentosa,* but differs chiefly in the pendulous, graceful branches. It makes a beautiful specimen tree and perhaps the finest in the country are located at Swarthmore College and the University of Illinois. Interestingly this species exhibited the best fall color of all the lindens in the Arnold's extensive collection. It was a uniform golden yellow and extremely effective. I highly recommend the tree for the individual who wants something different and better than the standard *Tilia cordata* syndrome. The petioles are longer than those of *T. tomentosa* but this is not a black and white trait for separating the species. I believe *T. petiolaris* is nothing more than a selection of *T. tomentosa* and should correctly be listed as a cultivar. Santamour and McArdle listed this as 'Pendula'. Supposedly the bees find the flowers narcotic or poisonous and can be found in large numbers on the ground under such trees. I did not notice strange "bee-behavior" around the Illinois tree. It is interesting to note that although this tree is listed as a species, it is usually grafted. I would be interested in knowing what percentage of seed-grown trees exhibit the weeping tendency. 'Orbicularis' has somewhat more pendulous branches and a more conical crown; the petioles are shorter and undersides gray; may be a hybrid between *T. petiolaris* and *T.* × *euchlora.* Dr. Donald Wyman considered it the most beautiful of the lindens. Native to southeastern Europe and Western Asia. Introduced 1840. Zone 5 to 7.

Trachelospermum jasminoides — Confederate or Star Jasmine
(trā-ke-lō-spēr'mum jaz-min-oy'dēz)

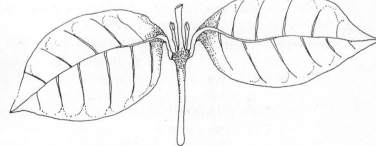

FAMILY: Apocynaceae
LEAVES: Opposite, simple, evergreen, ovate-rounded, 1 1/2 to 3 1/2" long, 1/2 to 1" wide, abruptly acute, cuneate to rounded, entire, glabrous, leathery, lustrous dark green above, pale green beneath, with veins darker green creating a prominent mosaic; petiole—1/4" long, pubescent.
BUDS: Imbricate, 1/32 to 1/16" long, brown.
STEM: Slender, rounded, dark brown, pubescent, exuding a milky sap when cut.

Trachelospermum jasminoides, Confederate or Star Jasmine, is a twining evergreen vine or ground cover (10 to 12') with lustrous dark green leaves and fragrant, one-inch diameter, 5-petaled white flowers that occur in slender stalked cymes. The flowers open from May to June and sporadically thereafter and provide a delightful fragrance. The plant requires support and will make an effective cover on any type of latticework. Pruning is a necessary prerequisite every year if the plant is to be kept in bounds. Has been used on the Georgia campus in a courtyard area where the fragrant flowers hold court. Can also be used as a ground cover in shaded situations. Prefers partial or full shade and moist, well-drained soils but is adaptable to a wide range of conditions. Have observed a very pretty form on which the leaves are bordered and blotched with white ('Variegatum'), the interior of the leaf is gray-green, exterior creamy. In winter creamy areas turn pinkish red to carmine. Can be used for a multiplicity of purposes. Easily rooted from softwood cuttings in June or July and could probably be rooted about anytime of year. Often grown as a glasshouse plant in the north. Japan, China. Zone 8 to 9. Actually tender in the vicinity of Athens, Georgia and should be sited carefully. Leaves were killed at -3°F but stems and buds survived.

RELATED SPECIES

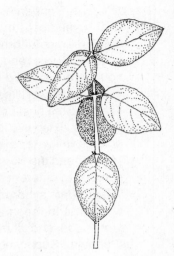

Trachelospermum asiaticum, (trā-ke-lō-spēr'mum ā-shi-at'ī-kum) Japanese Star Jasmine, is a degree hardier but to my knowledge is not as common in the southern landscape. The leaves are smaller (3/4 to 2″ long, 3/8 to 3/4″ wide) and the main veins are almost white. It is apparently not as precocious as *T. jasminoides* and the flowers are yellowish white and fragrant. Have seen it used effectively as a ground cover on the Louisiana State University campus. The calyx lobes are erect; in *T. jasminoides* they are larger and reflexed. Can be used in similar landscape situations. In 'Nortex' ('Nana'), the leaves are more lance-shaped. A creamy-white variegated form is known which recently has been utilized on the Georgia campus in a shady corner for ground cover purposes. The actual leaf color is similar to *T. jasminoides* 'Variegatum'. Japan, Korea. Cultivated 1880. Zone 7 to 9.

Tripterygium regelii — Regels Threewingnut
(trip-te-rēg'i-um rē'jil-ē-ī)

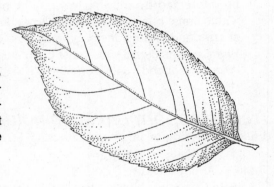

FAMILY: Celastraceae
LEAVES: Alternate, simple, oval or ovate, 2 1/2 to 6″ long, 1 1/2 to 4″ wide, acuminate at apex, broadly wedge-shaped to rounded at the base, rounded, blunt, incurved teeth, dark green and glabrous above except with minute down on the midrib when young; petiole 1/4 to 3/4″ long.
STEM: Angular, warty, brown.

Tripterygium regelii, Regels Threewingnut, is a rather rank-climbing or rambling deciduous shrub-vine (scandent shrub). The yellowish white 1/3″ diameter flowers are produced in large terminal panicles and these in turn are supplemented by flowers in the axils of the terminal leaves, the entire inflorescence up to 8 or 9″ long and 2 to 3″ wide, July-August. It is an attractive plant in flower and appears to be adaptable to varied soils. The 3-angled, greenish white, winged fruits are 5/8″ long and 1/4″ wide. There was a fine plant at the Arnold Arboretum that served as my first and only field specimen. Obviously, it is not common in commerce. Manchuria, Korea, Japan. Introduced 1904. Zone 4 to 7.

Trochodendron aralioides — Wheel-tree
(trō-kō-den'dron ȧ-rā-li-oy'dēz)

FAMILY: Trochodendraceae
LEAVES: Alternate, clustered, simple, evergreen, rhombic-obovate to elliptic-lanceolate, 3 to 6″ long, obtusely acuminate, cuneate, crenate-serrate at terminal end, leathery, lustrous dark green above, paler beneath; petioles 1 to 3″ long.

BUDS: Terminal about 1/4 to 1/3″ long, imbricate, pointed, reminding of a *Rhododendron catawbiense* flower bud.

STEM: Green year-round, glabrous, aromatic when bruised.

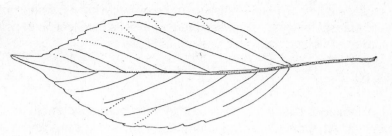

Trochodendron aralioides, Wheel-tree, is a virtual unknown in American gardens but occasionally appears (like Brigadoon) in collections. The habit is distinctly shrublike, probably no larger than 10 to 20′ high and half as wide. In the wild it supposedly reaches 60′ or greater. The branching is somewhat horizontal and almost sympodial like a sassafras. The most aesthetic aspect is the handsome foliage which although listed as dark green is a more vibrant rich green that appears to stand out from other evergreens. Flowers are a bright green and occur in 2 to 3″ long racemes in April-May. The fruit is a 3/4″ diameter follicle. The few plants I have seen in cultivation were in shady protected locations free from winter sun and desiccating winds. I suspect moist, well drained, acid soil suits it best. Probably only use is a novelty or collector's item in a semi-shady area of the garden. Found in mountain forests in Japan and Korea. Introduced 1894. Zone 6 to 8.

Tsuga—Hemlock
Pinaceae

If I were forced to select one conifer for my garden it would certainly be *Tsuga canadensis*. The species has multitudinous uses and the infinite variation in seed-grown material has resulted in the selection of many excellent cultivars. The number of *Tsuga* species used in landscaping is small but they are considered among the most graceful and beautiful of large evergreen conifers. Fourteen species have been reported, four occurring in the United States and the others in the Himalayas, China, Taiwan, and Japan. *Tsuga heterophylla* is the most important timber-producing species. Hemlock bark contains between 7 and 12 percent tannin, and in the United States that of *T. canadensis* was one of the principal commercial sources for many years.

MORPHOLOGICAL CHARACTERISTICS

Evergreen trees of graceful pyramidal habit with slender horizontal to drooping branches. The bark is cinnamon-red color and furrowed. Buds are rounded and not resinous. Needles, borne on petioles, spirally arranged, more or less 2 ranked, flattened and grooved above, with 2 white stomatic bands below. Needle margin is toothed or entire and the apex is rounded, notched, or blunt pointed. Male flowers are catkins and axillary on previous year's shoots. The greenish female flowers are terminal on previous year's lateral shoots with imbricated scales. Cones are pendulous and often produced in abundance.

According to Jenkins in *Arnoldia* 6:11–12 (1946) the name *Tsuga* is derived from a Japanese word, composed of the elements 'tree' and 'mother', meaning Tree-mother. Concerning the common name Hemlock, Sudworth states that the New York Indians use the descriptive name Oh-neh-tah, pronounced Hoe-o-na-dia or Hoe-na-dia, while the Indian name for the North Country (now Canada) was also Hoe-nadia, which means a land of the Hemlock.

GROWTH CHARACTERISTICS

Generally, the *Tsuga* species are stately, graceful, pyramidal trees and maintain their good characteristics in old age. The cultivars range from low ground cover types ('Coles Prostrate') to gracefully weeping ('Sargentii' or 'Pendula') to distinctly upright ('Fastigiata'). There are various globose types and the foliage colors may be whitish to yellow especially on the new growth. The Arnold Arboretum, Jamaica Plain, Massachusetts, has assembled an excellent collection of hemlock variants. It is well worth the trip just to observe and study this one group of plants.

CULTURE

Hemlocks should be moved balled and burlapped in either spring or fall. They can be planted on many soil types; however, good drainage, cool, acid soils, and adequate moisture are necessary. They will not thrive under hot, extremely dry conditions. Sweeping winds may be detrimental. They will withstand full shade; however, partial shade is preferable and best growth is attained in full sunlight. They will not withstand air pollution and are susceptible to salt damage. Pruning can be accomplished in spring or summer. Hemlocks withstand heavy pruning and for this reason are often used for hedges.

DISEASES AND INSECTS

Leaf blight, cankers, blister rust, needle rust, sapwood rot, hemlock borer, hemlock looper, spruce leaf miner, hemlock fiorinia scale, grape scale, hemlock scale, spider mites and other pests. In recent years a woolly adelgid (*Adelges tsugae*) has wreaked havoc on the species in some New England and Middle Atlantic States; over time infestations lead to decline and death.
Physiological diseases:
Sunscorch, drought injury—Hemlocks are more sensitive to drought than most other narrow leaf evergreens especially when sited in southern exposures and rocky slopes.

PROPAGATION

Seed dormancy is variable in hemlock, with some seed lots requiring pregermination treatment and other germinating satisfactorily without treatment. Cold stratification of mature seeds shortens incubation time and may substantially increase germinative energy, and is therefore recommended. General recommendation for *T. canadensis, T. caroliniana, T. heterophylla,* and *T. mertensiana* is 60 to 120 days at 41°F in moist sand. Some success has resulted from the use of cuttings but timing is critical and the rooting percentages are low. Most of the cultivars are grafted onto species understocks. For a detailed discussion of *Tsuga* propagation see Dirr and Heuser, 1987.

LANDSCAPE USE

Tsuga canadensis is used extensively for specimen, hedge, screen and grouping purposes. Often it is used in foundation plantings but care must be exercised in keep it in bounds over the years. This is quite simple for it can be maintained at a height of 3 to 5′ by judicious pruning. *Tsuga caroliniana* is less common in landscapes but, by some authorities, is considered a better plant because of greater pollution tolerance. The habit of Carolina Hemlock is a bit more stiff than Eastern Hemlock. *Tsuga canadensis* makes one of the best evergreen hedges especially if pruned correctly. If individual shoots are removed every year (rather than shearing the entire plant) a more aesthetically pleasing effect is achieved.
Bean separated the two cultivars 'Pendula' and 'Sargentii', but according to Jenkins the nurseryman's stock has all been derived from the 4 original plants found near the summit of Fishkill Mountain (near Beacon City, on the Hudson River) by General Joseph Howland about 1870. The finder grew one in his own garden at Matteawan, N.Y., gave the second to Henry Winthrop Sargent (after whom the plant was named), of Fishkill; the third to H.H. Hunnewell, of Wellesley, Mass., and the fourth to Prof. C.S. Sargent of the Arnold Arboretum. The second and third are dead but the first and fourth have made fine specimens. Most of the plants in cultivation have been grown from grafts; however, there are also seedlings, so some variation can be expected. The fascinating story of the Weeping Hemlock is told by Del Tredici, *Arnoldia* 40:202–223. 1980.

Tsuga canadensis — Canadian (Eastern) Hemlock
(tsoo′gȧ ka-nȧ-den′sis)

LEAVES: Almost regularly 2-ranked, linear, obtuse or acutish, 1/4 to 2/3″ long, 1/12 to 1/8″ wide, obscurely grooved, lustrous dark green above, with 2 whitish bands beneath, toothed, with a short petiole.

BUDS: Minute, ovoid, with hairy scales, light brown.

STEM: Young stems slender, grayish brown, hairy.

CONES: Small, ovoid, 1/2 to 1″ long on slender pendulous stalks, light to medium brown.

SIZE: 40 to 70′ in height by 25 to 35′ in spread; known to 100′ or more.

HARDINESS: Zone 3 to 7 (8); actually languishes in heat of Zone 8 although occasional good specimens occur.

HABIT: Softly and gracefully pyramidal in youth with tapering trunk becoming pendulously pyramidal with age; one of the most beautiful conifers.

RATE: Medium, 25 to 50′ in 15 to 30 years.

TEXTURE: Fine.

BARK: Flaky and scaly on young trees, brown, soon with wide, flat ridges; on old trees heavily and deeply furrowed; freshly cut surfaces showing purplish streaks.

LEAF COLOR: New spring growth light yellow-green changing to a glossy dark green, underside of needles with two glaucous bands.

FLOWERS: Monoecious; staminate light yellow, pistillate pale green.

FRUIT: Cones slender, stalked, ovoid, apex nearly blunt, 1/2 to 1″ long by approximately 1/4 to 1/2″ broad, brown at maturity; hang like small ornaments from the branches.

CULTURE: Transplants well balled and burlapped if root pruned; amenable to pruning; an excellent subject for moist, well-drained, acid soils, rocky bluffs or sandy soils; English literature lists this species as more lime tolerant than any other *Tsuga;* in Urbana IL there were many handsome specimens growing in calcareous soils; unlike most conifers tolerates shade well; can grow in full sun as long as it has good drainage and organic matter in the soil and there is no strong, drying wind to contend with; heavy soil from which water is unable to drain is not suitable; does not tolerate wind or drought; plant in sheltered locations, avoid windswept sites and polluted conditions.

DISEASES AND INSECTS: Leaf blight, cankers, blister rust, needle rust, sapwood rot, hemlock borer, hemlock looper, spruce leaf miner, hemlock fiorinia scale, grape scale, hemlock scale, spider mites, bagworm, fir flat headed borer, spruce budworm, gypsy moth, hemlock sawfly, and woolly adelgid. Two physiological problems include sunscorch which occurs when temperatures reach 95°F and above. The ends of the branches may be killed back for several inches. Another problem is drought injury for hemlocks are more sensitive to prolonged periods of dryness than most other narrowleaf evergreens. Plants may die during extended dry periods. For all the problems mentioned, hemlocks under landscape conditions prove to be reliable, handsome ornamentals if given proper cultural care.

LANDSCAPE VALUE: Makes an extremely graceful evergreen hedge of value in almost any situation except city conditions; excellent for screening, groupings, accent plant and foundation planting; the most commonly planted of the hemlocks, popular over a wide area; one of our best evergreens.

CULTIVARS: At one time I considered including a long list of cultivars but decided against such a move when the long list looked end "list". There are prostrate, globose, mounded, weeping, fastigiate and variegated forms. I refer the reader to Welch and Den Ouden and Boom.

Since the last edition, more cultivars have been introduced and several new or revised books, including Del Tridici, Swartley,and Krüssmann offer greater coverage than this book. In the summer of 1988, I had an opportunity to verify the collections in Mt. Airy Arboretum, Cincinnati, OH and the conifer collection, especially *Tsuga canadensis* cultivars were neigh impossible to accurately verify. So many clones are virtually the same and when the differences are based on growth habit, i.e., compact, more compact, most compact, one is easily confused. Even 'Jeddeloh' in three or four areas did not look exactly similar. Iseli Nursery, Boring OR listed 27 cultivars of *T. canadensis* while John Vermeulen and Son Nursery, Neshanic Station, NJ listed 38. Even a small specialty producer like

Washington Evergreen Nursery, Leicester, NC lists 24 and perhaps one of the premier growers of hemlock in New England, Weston Nurseries, Hopkinton, describe only four, but their 'Westonigra' strain which I have seen in the fields of Hopkinton, with extremely good dark green needle color in winter, may be the best around. The moral is that more is not necessarily better, only more.

'Sargentii' (var. *sargentii*)—A magnificent, broadly spreading, weeping form that is among the most handsome of all conifers; I have seen it used by water where it produced the effect of a green waterfall; as a single specimen or grouping it can be most effective; by no means a small plant although can be kept that way with judicious pruning; will grow 10 to 15' high, twice as wide. The late Professor C.E. Lewis of Michigan State likened it to a ghost, gracefully sweeping across the landscape; really an eye-catching plant and one that is frequently available in commerce. See *Arnoldia* 40:202–223. 1980.

PROPAGATION: Seed dormancy is variable so to insure good germination it is advisable to stratify the seeds for 2 to 4 months at about 40°F. Layering has also been used successfully. Cuttings have been successfully rooted but timing is important. Hormonal treatment is necessary. Percentages ranged from 60 to 90% depending on sampling time and hormonal strength.

NATIVE HABITAT: Nova Scotia to Minnesota, south along the mountains to Alabama and Georgia.

RELATED SPECIES:

Tsuga diversifolia — Northern Japanese Hemlock
(tsoo'gȧ dī-ver-si-fō'li-ȧ)

LEAVES: Densely arranged, generally shorter and more densely borne than *T. canadensis,* 1/4 to 5/8" long, 1/10" wide, distinctly notched at the apex, margins entire, glossy dark green and furrowed above, with two clearly defined chalk white bands of stomata below.

Tsuga diversifolia, Northern Japanese Hemlock, is a graceful, pyramidal tree that makes an excellent specimen in the landscape. Plant is broad pyramidal and gracefully branched. The branches are reddish brown, pubescent, while those of *T. sieboldii,* (tsoo'gȧ sē-bōl'dē-ī), are glabrous, grayish to yellowish brown. The egg-shaped cones are 1/2 to 3/4" long. The finest plants I have seen were at Millcreek Valley Park, Youngstown, Ohio and based on their beauty and performance would have no trouble recommending the tree for general landscape use. Average landscape height would approximate 35 to 60'. Neither tree is common in commerce and with so many excellent forms of *T. canadensis* it is difficult to compete. Japan. Introduced 1861. Zone 5 to 6.

Tsuga heterophylla — Western Hemlock
(tsoo'gȧ het-er-ō-fil'ȧ)

LEAVES: More or less in 2 ranks (rows), although set all around the stems, 1/4 to 3/4" long, 1/20 to 1/16" wide, rounded at apex, entire, shining dark green and grooved above, broad white bands below.

Tsuga heterophylla, Western Hemlock, is a handsome tall tree with a narrow pyramidal crown, slightly semipendulous branchlets and fine textured dark green needles with two whitish bands below. I have seen the tree in Vancouver, BC and all over Europe and it makes an imposing specimen. The 3/4 to 1" long cones are sessile but hang from the branch tops. Best growth occurs in a moisture laden atmosphere and at cooler summer temperatures than are found in the eastern United States. The stems are yellow-brown, change to dark red-brown and remain pubescent for 5 to 6 years. Southern Alaska to Idaho and California. Introduced 1851. Zone 6 to ?

Tsuga mertensiana — Mountain Hemlock
(tsoo′gȧ mḗr-ten′si-ā-nȧ)

LEAVES: Radially spreading, 1/3 to 3/4″ long, 1/16″ wide, obtuse apex, convex above and often keeled, almost round in cross section, entire, stomatal lines on both surfaces resulting in a blue-green to gray-green color.

Tsuga mertensiana, Mountain Hemlock, is possibly the least adaptable of the hemlocks treated herein. In the wild, a tree 50 to 90′ high, but much less under cultivation. Prefers cool, moist root run and cooler air temperatures. Have seen plants in the Netherlands that appeared native they were so robust. Foliage color is distinctly different than other species and 'Argentea', 'Blue Star' and 'Glauca' are more silvery or blue needled forms. 'Blue Star', as I witnessed, was as handsome as the blue forms of *Picea pungens* var. *glauca.* Unfortunately not a tree for the eastern United States. Southern Alaska to northern Montana, Idaho and California. Introduced 1854. Zone 5 to ?

Tsuga caroliniana — Carolina Hemlock
(tsoo′gȧ ka-rō-lin-ē-ā′nȧ)

LEAVES: Radiating around the stem, linear, 1/4 to 3/4″ long, about 1/12″ wide, apex blunt or slightly notched, glossy green above, with 2 distinct white bands beneath, margins entire.
BUDS: Ovoid to roundish, apex blunt, pubescent.
STEM: Light reddish brown when young, finely pubescent or nearly glabrous.

SIZE: 45 to 60′ in height by 20 to 25′ spread.
HARDINESS: Zone 4 to 7.
HABIT: Airy, spiry-topped tree with a tapering trunk and short, stout, often pendulous branches forming a handsome, evenly pyramidal head; often more compact and of darker green color than *T. canadensis.*
RATE: Slow to medium, not as fast as *T. canadensis.*
TEXTURE: Medium.
BARK: Reddish brown, deeply fissured, scaly.
LEAF COLOR: Glossy green above, with two silvery bands below.
FLOWERS: Monoecious, inconspicuous.
FRUIT: Cones short-stalked to sessile, oblong-cylindrical, 1 to 1 1/2″ long, 1″ wide, scales radiating out from center.
CULTURE: Transplants well balled and burlapped if root pruned; needs moist, well-drained soils; partially shaded, sheltered exposure and will not tolerate droughty conditions.
LANDSCAPE VALUE: Performs better than *T. canadensis* under city conditions, and probably as good a landscape plant but not as well known; tends to be more stiff and rigid although I have seen plants that rival the best *T. canadensis;* qualities may be overstated for it has never found its way into the mainstream.
CULTIVARS:
  'Arnold Pyramid'—Pyramidal, dense, with a rounded top, 25 to 35′ high.
  'Compacta'—Dwarf, low growing and very dense, wider than high.
PROPAGATION: Same as for *T. canadensis.*
ADDITIONAL NOTES: Easily separable from *T. canadensis* by the way the foliage radiates around the stem forming a bottlebrush-like effect, the larger cones and entire needles.
NATIVE HABITAT: Southeastern United States (southwestern Virginia to northern Georgia in the Blue Ridge Mountains). Introduced 1881.

Ulmus americana — American Elm, also known as White, Gray, Water, or Swamp Elm
(ul′mus ȧ-mēr-i-kā′nȧ)

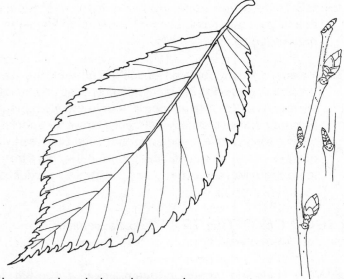

FAMILY: Ulmaceae

LEAVES: Alternate, simple, ovate-oblong, 3 to 6″ long, 1 to 3″ wide, acuminate, unequal at base, doubly serrate, lustrous dark green, glabrous and rough or smooth above, pubescent or nearly glabrous beneath; lateral veins crowded, straight, running out to teeth; petioles about 1/4″ long.

BUDS: Terminal—absent; laterals—imbricate, ovate-conical, pointed, 1/4″ long, slightly flattened and more or less appressed against the stem, light reddish brown, smooth and shining or slightly pale-downy; flower buds stouter, obovate, appearing as if stalked, scales generally with darker and more or less hairy-edge margins.

STEM: Slender, round, red-brown, pubescent at first, becoming glabrous (sometimes maintaining pubescence); leaf scars with 3 distinct bundle traces that result in a "cat-face" configuration.

SIZE: 60 to 80′ with a spread of 1/2 to 2/3's the height, may grow larger.

HARDINESS: Zone 2 to 9.

HABIT: Three distinct habits are recognized and include the vase-shaped form in which the trunk divides into several erect limbs strongly arched above and terminating in numerous slender often pendulous branchlets, the whole tree a picture of great beauty and symmetry; a form with more widely spreading, less arching branches, often called the "oak-form"; and a narrow form with branchlets clothing the entire trunk.

RATE: Medium to fast, 10 to 12′ in 5 years; this rate of growth is common for many elms.

BARK: Dark gray with broad, deep, intersecting ridges, or often scaly; outer bark in cross section shows layers of a whitish-buff color alternating with thicker dark layers.

LEAF COLOR: Lustrous dark green in summer, yellow in fall; great variation in intensity of fall coloration.

FLOWERS: Perfect, greenish red, in fascicles of 3 or 4, March, interesting but not showy.

FRUIT: Rounded, notched, disc-shaped samara, 1/2″ long, maturing in May through June, not ornamental, greenish, but may have reddish tinge, fringed with hairs.

CULTURE: Easily transplanted because of shallow, fibrous, wide spreading, gross feeding root system; prefers rich, moist soils but grows well under a variety of conditions; in the wild the tree is a common inhabitant of wet flats where standing water may accumulate in the spring and fall; prune in fall; pH tolerant; shows good soil salt tolerance.

DISEASES AND INSECTS: The elms are, unfortunately, subject to many pests and I have often wondered why they have been treated as royalty when they are so fallible. Many of the pests are devastating and control measures are simply not effective or available. The following list should provide an idea of the protential problems which may beset "your" elm. Wetwood (*Erwinia mimipressuralis*) is a bacterial disease which appears as a wilt, branch dieback, and internal and external fluxing of elms. A pipe is often placed in the tree to relieve the tremendous gas pressure that builds up; no control known. Cankers (at least 8 species cause cankers and dieback of stems and branches), Dutch elm disease (devastating and uncontrollable), bleeding canker, leaf curl, leaf spots (there are so many fungi that cause leaf spots that only an expert can distinguish one from another), powdery mildews, *Cephalosporium* wilt, *Verticillium* wilt, woody decay, phloem necrosis (apparently caused by a mycoplasm), mosaic, scorch, woolly apple aphid, elm leaf curl aphid, Japanese beetle, smaller

European elm bark beetle, elm borer, spring canker worms, fall cankerworms, elm cockscomb gall, dogwood twig borer, elm leaf miner, gypsy moth, leopard moth borer, white marked tussock moth, elm calligrapha, mites and scales (many species infest elms).

LANDSCAPE VALUE: At one time extensively used as a street and large lawn tree. The streets of the New England towns and cities were arched with this tree but the Dutch elm disease has killed many of the trees. People somehow have the notion that all the American elms were destroyed. This is by no means true and many cities have extensive maintenance programs. Having gone to school in Massachusetts I can appreciate the legacy of these elms and the pride that people take in them. The elms, unfortunately, have not stopped dying and since the 1983 edition I have observed many old, venerable specimens succumb to Dutch elm disease. I can remember a fine planting of 'Ascendens' on the Amherst College campus which as a graduate student at the University of Massachusetts from 1969–1972 I photographed frequently. They are now gone. Urbana, IL was called the city of the elms and the Illinois campus was extensively planted. There may be no American elms left on campus for most of the remaining ones had died during my seven years on campus. In some respects it seems only a matter of time before Dutch elm disease wins. There are fine, established plantings on many campuses that are being maintained by systematic spray programs. Eventually because of age and/or disease these will pass and the search for a suitable substitute will continue. In my opinion, there is no substitute (presently) for the American elm. See *Arnoldia* 42(2), 1982, for a good discussion of the American Elm.

CULTIVARS:

'Ascendens'—Upright form, 4 to 5 times as tall as wide, branches high up on trunk.

'Augustine'—Fast growing, columnar form, branched to ground, 3 times as high as broad.

'Delaware #2'—Highly resistant to Dutch elm disease, vigorous with a broad spreading crown, 70 to 80' high, introduced by Nursery Crops Research Laboratory, Delaware, OH; Princeton is the only nursery I have seen offering this and the cultivar 'Washington'.

'Lake City'—Upright form, wide at top and narrow at base, however, not the typical vase-shaped form.

'Liberty'—Described as Dutch elm disease resistant by Elm Research Institute, Harrisville, NH 03450, however, the plants are seed produced and young trees may show resistance; I am hopeful but skeptical since the disease seems to catch up, several different clones in the series.

'Littleford'—Columnar, 3 times as high as wide.

'Moline'—Good, rugged, moderately vase-shaped form, one of the last of the American elms to succumb to Dutch elm disease on the Illinois campus.

var. *pendula*—Pendulous branches, but vase-shaped habit.

'Princeton'—Large leathery foliage, vigorous, and supposedly resistant to elm leaf beetle (foliage feeder).

'Washington'—Selected for crown resistance to Dutch elm disease, good glossy foliage, 70 to 80' high, selected by Dr. Horace V. Webster, former plant pathologist, National Park Service, Washington, DC.

PROPAGATION: Seeds of some lots show dormancy and should be stratified at 41°F for 60 to 90 days in moist medium although some seeds do not require any treatment. In the long run it is probably safer to stratify. Cuttings can be rooted; those taken in early June rooted 94% with IBA treatment. Stong juvenility effect is evident with *U. americana* cuttings collected from stump sprouts (6 to 7 1/2' or 1' from ground) and a mature tree which rooted 64, 83, and 38%, respectively.

NATIVE HABITAT: Newfoundland to Florida, west to the foot of the Rockies. Introduced 1752.

RELATED SPECIES:

Ulmus rubra — Slippery Elm
(ul'mus rū'brȧ)

LEAVES: Alternate, simple, obovate to oblong, 4 to 8″ long, about half as wide, long acuminate, very unequal at base, doubly serrate, dark green and very rough above (scabrous), densely pubescent beneath; petioles 1/4 to 1/3″ long.

BUDS: Terminal-absent, laterals about 1/4″ long, dark brown, nearly black at tips of scales, long rusty hairs at tip of bud; flower buds more or less spherical.

STEM: Rather stout, light grayish brown, pubescent, roughened by numerous raised lenticels, strongly and characteristically mucilaginous if chewed.

FRUIT: Orbicular or obovate, 1/3 to 3/4″ long samara, slightly notched at apex, center covered with red-brown hairs, glabrous elsewhere.

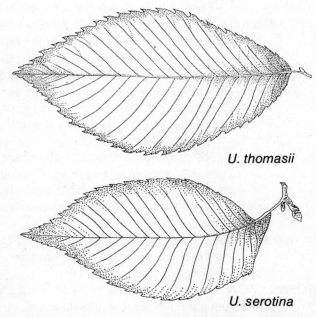

Ulmus rubra, Slippery Elm, is a close cousin of the American Elm and often goes under the names Red, Gras, or Moose Elm. The tree grows 40 to 60′ high with a somewhat vase-shaped habit but the branchlets are more ascending (upright) than those of American Elm. The ornamental value is limited and this species actually becomes a weed as it tends to infest unkempt shrub borders, hedges, fence rows and other idle ground; prefers moist, rich, bottomland soils but also grows on dry, limestone soils. The name "Slippery" developed because of the mucilaginous inner bark which was chewed by the pioneer to quench thirst. It is susceptible to Dutch elm disease. Native from Quebec to Florida, west to the Dakotas and Texas covering much of the same range as *Ulmus americana.* Cultivated 1830. Zone 3 to 9.

Two other native elm species worth mentioning include *Ulmus thomasii,* (ul'mus tom-as'ē-ī) Rock or Cork Elm, and *U. serotina,* (ul'mus ser-ot'i-nà), September or Red Elm. The former has an oblong crown and the trunk usually remains unbranched; it is found on dry gravelly uplands and rocky slopes but attains its best development in rich bottomland soils; the wood is heavy, hard and tough; the finest of all woods; hence the name Rock Elm. The wood was used in the construction of automobile bodies and refrigerators. It is now used for furniture, agricultural implements, hockey sticks, ax handles and other items which require a wood which will withstand strains and shocks. Native from Quebec to Tennessee, west to Nebraska. Introduced 1875. Zone 2 to 7. The latter elm, *U. serotina,* is a southern species ranging from Kentucky to Alabama, north to Georgia and southern Illinois. Cultivated 1903. Zone 5 to 8. Both are susceptible to Dutch elm disease.

U. thomasii

U. serotina

ADDITIONAL NOTES: The extensive use of one tree such as the American Elm is an example of foolhardy landscaping. The tree is tremendously ornamental and was overplanted. The diseases caught up with the tree and the results were disastrous. Unfortunately, people do not seem to learn by their mistakes and now Honeylocust, Bradford Pear, Green Ash, and Planetree are being used in wholesale fashion for cities, residences and about everywhere. I strongly urge a diversified tree planting program encompassing many different species and cultivars.

Other Elms

Ulmus alata — Winged Elm
(ul′mus a̍-lā′ta̍)

LEAVES: Alternate, simple, ovate-oblong to oblong-lanceolate, 1 1/4 to 2 1/2″ long, half as wide, acute or acuminate, unequal, doubly serrate, leathery, dark green and glabrous above, with axillary tufts below; petiole 1/10″ long.

BUDS: Almost like miniature versions of *U. americana*—imbricate, reddish brown.

STEM: Gray to brown, glabrous, slender with two opposite corky wings but not always present; pronounced on young vigorous shoots.

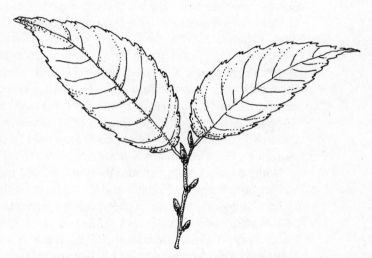

Ulmus alata, Winged Elm, is a medium-sized, 30 to 40′ high tree with spreading branches that form a round-topped, oblong head. It is common in the south and especially noticeable for the 2 broad opposite corky wings that develop on the branches. The dark green, 1 to 2 1/2″ long leaves may turn dull yellow in fall but are often infected with powdery mildew and remind of a Common Lilac in its best mildew condition. The mildew susceptibility is a variable trait for some trees approach whiteness while others are not affected. The greenish red flowers open in mid to late February (Athens) and are followed by oval 1/3″ long villous samaras with 2 inward curving beaks at apex. Virginia to Florida, west to Illinois and Texas. Introduced 1820. Zone 6 to 9.

Ulmus carpinifolia — Smoothleaf Elm
(ul′mus kär-pī-ni-fō′li-a̍)

LEAVES: Alternate, simple, elliptic to ovate or obovate, 1 1/2 to 4″ long, 1 to 2″ wide, acuminate, very oblique at base, doubly serrate with about 12 pairs of veins, lustrous dark green and smooth above, glabrous when young; petioles 1/4 to 1/2″ long, usually pubescent.

BUDS: Imbricate, terminal-absent, laterals— 1/8″ long, deep brown to black, ovoid, bud scales covered with soft silky pubescence, edges of scales often finely ciliate.

STEM: Brown, slightly pubescent, older branches turning ashy-gray.

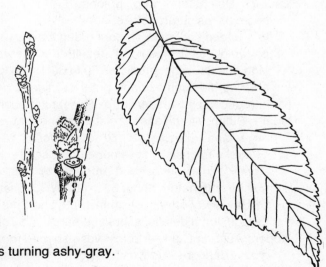

Ulmus carpinifolia, Smoothleaf Elm, is native to Europe, North Africa and western Europe. The tree will grow 70 to 90′ with a straight trunk and slender ascending branches forming a weakly pyramidal tree; personally I find the tree attractive but again it is an elm and subject to all the pests although considered intermediate in resistance to Dutch elm disease; the foliage is a lustrous dark green in summer. The following cultivars are largely hybrids from various breeding programs and include mixed parentage:

'Bea Schwarz'—Broad upright crown, 2 to 4″ long deep green leaves, 9 to 12 vein pairs, selected around 1935, resistant to Dutch elm disease, *U.* × *hollandica* type.

'Christine Buisman'—Broadly erect form with central leader, 2 to 3 1/4″ long leaves, base very oblique, developed by Boskoop Experimental Station around 1945, 60′ by 45′, Zone 4, resistant to Dutch elm disease, a *U.* × *hollandica* type.

'Dampieri'—Narrow conical form, leaves crisped, clustered on short shoots, broad-ovate, 2 to 2 1/2″ long, rough and deep green above, originated in Belgium around 1863, somewhat resistant to Dutch elm disease; 'Dampieri Aurea' ('Wredei') has yellow leaves and is slower growing; have seen both in English gardens, *U.* × *hollandica* type, Rehder lists it as a *U. carpinifolia* selection.

'Groeneveld'—Like 'Commelin' but with tighter upright habit, dense crown, regular branching, 40 to 50′ high, averaged 2′1″ per year over a 10-year period in Kansas tests, resistant to wind and Dutch elm disease, from Boskoop Experiment Station, Holland, *U.* × *hollandica* type.

'Homestead'—Dutch elm disease and phloem necrosis resistant, symmetrical somewhat pyramidal crown to oval-arching, dense dark green foliage may turn straw yellow in fall, rapid growth rate, 12-year-old tree was 36′ high and 25′ wide, considered Zone 5 to 7, although will probably grow in Zone 8, result of complex parentage involving *U. pumila, U.* × *hollandica* and *U. carpinifolia;* see *HortScience* 19:897–898 (1984) for all details; introduced by Nursery Crops Research Laboratory in 1984, have seen 25′ high plants in Cincinnati, has a pleasing form and good foliage, unfortunately, susceptible to elm leaf beetle, true for 'Pioneer' and 'Urban'.

'Jacan'—An *U. davidiana* var. *japonica* form with excellent hardiness (-30 to -40°F), vase-shaped outline with strong branches, tolerant to Dutch elm disease, 1977 introduction from Morden, Manitoba, Canada; see *Can. J. Plant Sci.* 59:267–268 (1979).

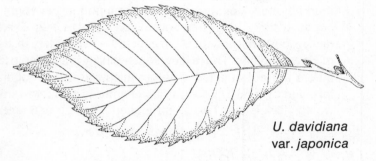

U. davidiana var. *japonica*

'Pioneer'—Dutch elm and phloem necrosis resistant, globe shaped to rounded crown, large dark green leaves with empire yellow fall color, dense canopy, grows as rapidly as 'Homestead', result of *U. glabra* × *U. carpinifolia* cross, 11-year-old tree is 27′ high and 28′ wide, predicted 50 to 60′ by 50 to 60′, Zone 5 to 7(8); has survived in Minneapolis area as did 'Homestead', but was injured; see *HortScience* 19:900 (1984) for more details, introduced by Nursery Crops Research Laboratory; Delaware, OH in 1984.

'Regal'—Dutch elm disease resistant clone that resulted from a cross between 'Commelin' (*U.* × *hollandica* 'Vegeta' × *U. carpinifolia* #1) with N 215 (*U. pumila* × *U. carpinifolia* 'Hoersholmiensis'); develops strong central leader and rather open growth habit without the dignity or majesty of good American or Chinese Elms; will probably maintain a pyramidal-oval outline and mature about 50 to 60′ by 30′; mature leaves are a dusty spinach green; introduced by University of Wisconsin in 1983; see Smalley and Lester, *HortScience* 18:960–961 (1983) for additional details, should be hardy into Zone 4.

'Sapporo Autumn Gold'—Upright vase-shaped form resembling a densely branched American Elm; glossy dark green leaves turn golden in fall, 50 to 60′, averaged 2′ per year over a 7-year-period in Kansas tests.

'Sarniensis'—Narrowly upright conical in habit; 1 3/4 to 2 1/2″ long, glossy dark green leaves, rather good looking form, susceptible to Dutch elm, still relatively common in areas of Middle Atlantic and New England States, 60 to 70′.

'Umbraculifera'—Usually grafted high on species, forms a single-trunked tree with a densely globose head; leaves smaller than the species, 1 to 2 1/2″ long, 20 to 30′, *U. carpinifolia* type.

'Urban'—Result of crossing among *Ulmus × hollandica* var. *vegeta × Ulmus carpinifolia × Ulmus pumila*, resistant to Dutch elm disease. Developed by ARS Shade Tree Laboratory, Delaware, Ohio. Grows fast on various soil types, has dark green foliage, and is tolerant of drought, pollution, soil compaction and restricted root space. Should make a good tree for heavily urbanized areas. Based on my observations,

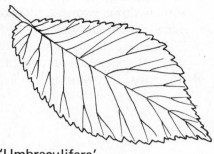

'Umbraculifera'

it is not a very handsome tree and is completely lacking in the grace, beauty and dignity of American Elm. I would plant something else before opting for this form. Tends toward stiff oblong-rounded head, 50′ by 35′, has not received the nursery acceptance of 'Homestead' and 'Pioneer', grew 2′6″ per year over a 7-year-period in Kansas tests.

'Variegata'—Rather handsome form with white streaked and flecked leaves, 30′.

ADDITIONAL NOTES: In Europe, particularly the Netherlands, elms are common throughout the cities and countryside. In Amsterdam, the canals are lined with elms that I suspect are of hybrid origin. Many were produced by Dutch breeding programs. In addition to those listed above 'Dodoens', 'Lobel' and 'Plantyn' are at best moderately resistant to the aggressive strain of Dutch elm disease while 'Commelin' has no resistance. Interestingly, in Dr. Pair's Kansas field tests, 'Commelin' averaged 2′7″ per year over a 10-year period.

Ulmus glabra — Scotch Elm
(ul′mus glā′brȧ)

LEAVES: Alternate, simple, oblong-ovate to elliptic or obovate, 3 to 7″ long, 1 1/2 to 4″ wide, abruptly acuminate, very unequal at base, sharply and double serrate, dark green and scabrous above, pubescent beneath, rarely nearly glabrous, 14 to 20 vein pairs; petioles—1/8 to 1/4″ long.

BUDS: Imbricate, terminal-absent, laterals—1/4″ long, vegetative buds dark chestnut brown to brown-black with hispid bud scales.

STEM: Dark gray-brown with bristle-like pubescence, distinctly hairy.

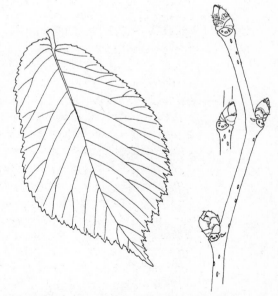

Ulmus glabra, Scotch Elm, is a large, massive, rather open tree growing from 80 to 100′ with a spread of 50 to 70′. The foliage is dark green in summer and green to yellow, to brown in fall. I would not recommend the species but the cultivars 'Camperdownii' and 'Pendula' are worthwhile. The former is a round-headed, pendulous-branched type that is usually grafted about 6 to 7′ high on the understock while the latter, although often confused with 'Camperdownii', is a flat-topped tree with horizontal branches and pendulous branchlets. The original of 'Camperdownii' is interesting for it apparently originated as a seedling and was discovered creeping along the ground at Camperdown House, near Dundee, Scotland in the first half of the 19th century. I have seen plants of 'Horizontalis' (Tabletop Elm) that were 33′ across and no more than 15′ high. *Hortus III* lists 'Camperdownii' under *U. × vegeta* (*U. carpinifolia × U. glabra*).

I am staying with the old nomenclature. I have seen tremendous crops of fruit on 'Horizontalis' but not on 'Camperdownii'. Most of the plants labeled as 'Camperdownii' are 'Horizontalis' at least as I have observed them in the U.S. I saw the most magnificent planting of 'Horizontalis' near the Cathedral of Notre Dame, Paris. When used properly it makes a rather handsome and eye-catching plant. 'Exoniensis', an upright form with leaves folded along the midrib and clustered, grew 1' per year over a 10-year-period in Kansas tests. Native to northern and central Europe, western Asia. Zone 4 to 6.

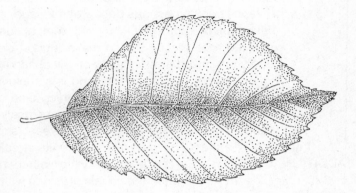

Ulmus × *hollandica* — Dutch Elm
(ul′mus × hol-lan′di-kȧ)

Is a group of trees which resulted from crossing *U. carpinifolia* × *U. glabra* with the progeny supposedly intermediate between the two parents. Selections have been made from the group. Quite confused taxonomically and generally of little landscape interest in the U.S. I have tried to make sense of the taxonomy of this grex but it is too complex to be presented in a condensed version. Bean simply lists the old hybrid or pure clones as 'Belgica' (Belgium or Holland), 'Dampieri' (also a golden form); 'Hollandica' (Dutch); 'Smithii' ('Downton'), 'Vegeta' ('Huntingdon'); all, unfortunately, are susceptible to Dutch elm disease and many splendid specimens have been lost.

Ulmus parvifolia — Chinese Elm, Lacebark Elm
(ul′mus pär-vi-fō′li-ȧ)

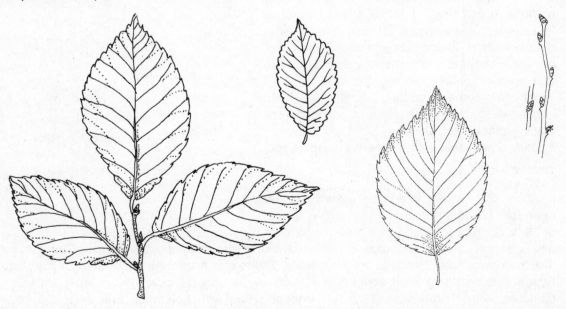

LEAVES: Alternate, simple, elliptic to ovate or obovate, 3/4 to 2 1/2″ long, 1/3 to 1 1/3″ wide, acute or obtusish, unequally rounded at base, simply or nearly simply serrate, lustrous dark green and smooth above, pubescent beneath when young, subcoriaceous at maturity, 10 to 12 vein pairs; petioles 1/4 to 1/2″ long.

BUDS: Small, 1/10 to 1/8″ long, brown, smallest buds of any elm, slightly pubescent.

STEM: Gray-brown, glabrous to slightly pubescent, slender, very fine in texture.

FLOWERS: Easy to recognize because of late flower and fruit dates—August-September.

BARK: Mottled (rather than rigid and furrowed like other elms), exfoliating in irregular patches, exposing lighter bark beneath, trunks sometimes fluted.

SIZE: 40 to 50′ high and wide; have seen 70′ high trees that were about 40′ wide.

HARDINESS: Zone 4 to 9.

HABIT: Rather graceful round-headed tree often with pendulous branchlets; some forms are upright-spreading, almost American elm like; others broader than tall.

RATE: Medium to fast depending on moisture and fertility levels; grew 1′6″ per year over a 10 year period in Kansas tests.

TEXTURE: Medium-fine throughout the seasons.

BARK: Magnificent and often a beautiful mottled combination of gray, green, orange and brown; variable and selections could be made for superior traits.

LEAF COLOR: Lustrous dark green changing to yellowish and reddish purple in fall; fall color is usually not outstanding but appears to be better on southern grown trees than those I have observed in the north; leaves hold late and I have photographed trees in late November in fall color in Athens, Georgia.

FLOWERS: Inconspicuous, appearing in axillary clusters during August-September, essentially masked by the foliage.

FRUIT: Samara, elliptic-ovate, 1/3″ long, glabrous, notched at apex, seed in middle, ripens in September-October.

CULTURE: Easily transplanted, adaptable to extremes of pH and soil; best growth is achieved in moist, well drained, fertile soils; shows excellent poor soil tolerance and should be considered for urban areas.

DISEASES AND INSECTS: Shows considerable resistance to Dutch elm disease and also the elm leaf and Japanese beetle; in comparing Siberian Elm, Japanese Zelkova, and this species for elm leaf resistance I have found *U. parvifolia* the best followed by *Zelkova serrata* and *U. pumila* which did not even place; have noticed glyphosate (Roundup) damage on young trees for lateral shoots develop spine-like condition.

LANDSCAPE VALUE: Excellent, tough, durable tree for about any situation; do not confuse it with the inferior *U. pumila,* Siberian Elm, which by the nursery trade is often offered as "Chinese" Elm; several authors have suggested the name Lacebark Elm to delineate it from *U. pumila* and provide a suitable description of its most beautiful morphological trait; some of the great gardens of the world consider this a superior tree and now we need to alert the nursery industry; Disney World, Orlando, FL., has used the tree extensively throughout the grounds; in my opinion, it has received a bad rap for supposed susceptibility to ice, snow and storm damage; I have *never* seen extensive damage and in February, 1979 a devastating ice storm hit Athens and caused extensive damage to pines, Water Oak, Siberian Elm, Silver Maple, and other trees; *U. parvifolia* was not damaged and the Georgia campus contains some of the largest, oldest and finest specimens in the country; since the last edition the Chinese elm has risen from its biological grave and at least 5 new cultivars have been introduced; nurserymen, landscape architects and gardeners are taking a much closer look at the tree's attributes rather than treating it as another ELM; the gene pool is large and the variation in habit, leaf quality and hardiness almost unbelievable; some of this genetic variation is being exploited and I predict the species will provide some of our most beautiful shade trees in the years ahead; in fact I will crawl out on a limb and predict a bright future in the 21st century.

CULTIVARS:

'Across Central Park' (misnamed in original publication, correctly 'A. Ross Central Park')—The parent tree was planted in New York's Central Park over 100 years ago. The tree is 59′ tall with a trunk that measures a little over 4 1/2′ in diameter at breast height. The branching habit is spreading, with strong angular branches that fan out from where the crown originates. The tree has strong wood; rarely do its stems or branches break in a storm. The bark of young trees is dark gray and smooth. The parent tree's bark is light gray to light brown fissured into irregular plates. The mature 1 to 1 3/5″ long, elliptical, round-serrated leaves are thick and leathery. They are a lustrous spinach green, turning mimosa yellow in fall. Hardy to Zone 5 and can be used as far north as the New York City area without suffering winter damage. Karnosky reported branch and twig dieback at -20°F; young trees were killed outright at -25°F. Softwood cuttings, 3 to 5″ long, root with high frequency in one month. Treat them with 3000 ppm IBA talc and place them in an equal mix of peat and perlite under mist. The plant grows 2 to 4′ high in two growing seasons or between 1 1/2 to 2′ per year under typical nursery conditions. Young trees head early in the nursery bed but require pruning to develop crowns at suitable heights. See *HortScience* 23:925–926 (1988).

'Brea'—Described as having an upright habit and larger leaves than 'Drake', 'True Green' and 'Sempervirens'. Apparently, Keeline-Wilcox Nurseries, Inc. in Brea, CA, originally listed 'Brea' in its 1982 winter catalog. According to Green [*Arnoldia* 24:41–80 (1964)] this selection is the same as 'Drake'. Also, Monrovia Nursery Co., Azusa, CA, described what seemed to be 'Brea' in its 1952–53 catalog but called the cultivar 'Drake'. Are 'Brea' and 'Drake', in fact, the same plant? I have not seen 'Brea' in commerce or at arboreta.

'Burgundy'—Selected from the University of Georgia campus as were 'Emerald Isle' and 'Emerald Vase' by Dirr and Richards for outstanding foliage and habit. This form has large, thick dark green leaves that turn deep burgundy fall coloration. The habit is distinctly broad rounded with uniform branch development and extremely fast growth. The parent tree is approximately 8-years-old and grows in a barren parking lot island. Tree is now 18′ high and 20′ wide. The bark has started to develop the exfoliating character and is a rich orangish brown. The characteristic flaking and mixed mottle are also apparent. Cuttings root readily and in 1989, percentages averaged over 90 using 5000 ppm KIBA, 2 perlite: 1 peat medium, and mist. Many nurserymen visit our campus and this tree has piqued their aesthetic senses. Possibly a tree of the future.

'Drake'—Used in the lower south and California and, according to one source, is probably not hardy below Zone 7. Whitcomb and Hickman reported that 'Drake' was severely injured during the 1983–84 winter in Stillwater OK, when temperatures fell to -8°F on December 23 and -31°F on January 14. Although 'Drake' is listed as hardy in Zone 6, I find this extremely dubious. 'Drake' offers rich dark green foliage on spreading branches that grow more upright than those of regular evergreen cultivars ('Sempervirens') but still approach a weeping tendency. Young trees in containers develop long arching branches. The tree is more or less evergreen in California and stays evergreen through most winters except when it loses its leaves during unusual cold snaps. This cultivar develops an attractive round-headed form of medium size for lawn and street tree use. Bark exfoliates early and is quite handsome.

'Dynasty'—The result of a controlled cross between two trees of seedling origin at the US National Arboretum. The parent trees were grown from seed from the 1929 introduction PI 92487 from the Forest Experiment Station, Keijo, Japan. 'Dynasty' is distinctly vase-shaped. After 16 years, it grew to 30′ high and 30′ wide with a 12″ trunk diameter at 39″ from the ground. Summer leaves and fruits are typical of the species. Fall color has been red in cooler climates, a notable trait since typical fall color is seldom effective. The bark is dark gray on young stems and starts to exfoliate when stem diameters approach 2″ or greater. Unfortunately, some say that the bark's patchiness does not approach a degree of color contrast that could be considered ornamental. One nurseryman told me that the cultivar's bark does not compare with the bark of 'Emerald

Isle' and 'Emerald Vase'. 'Dynasty' is cold hardy in Zone 5 and perhaps lower, but it has not been thoroughly tested under Zone 4 conditions. The cultivar is easily propagated from softwood cuttings using an 8000 ppm IBA talc formulation, coarse medium, and mist. These factors are important since authors have reported great variation in rooting different clones. See *HortScience* 19:898–899 (1984).

'Emerald Isle'—A broad-spreading elm with a rounded crown resulting in a pleasing globe-shaped outline. It measures 30' high and 54' wide. At 3' from the soil line, the mature tree has a 30″ diameter trunk and an 88″ circumference. The bark exfoliates 2' from the ground in a puzzle-like pattern exposing light gray and gray-green to orangish brown colors. The bark is flecked with orangy brown, corky lenticels. The trunk's base develops a rough, blocky, gray-black bark. The leathery, lustrous dark green (almost black) foliage is densely borne at the ends of the fine branches, creating a dense canopy. The leaves are more leathery and a darker green than the typical phenotype. Fall coloration is bronze-brown and not really effective. 'Emerald Isle' has shown no symptoms of leaf scorch during the 1986–88 summers, which have been the driest on record in the southeast. The tree is also highly resistant to Dutch elm disease and elm leaf beetle. The leaves are alternate and simple, measuring 1 to 2″ long and 1/2 to 7/8″ wide. They are ovate to slightly obovate and lustrous dark green, almost black-green on the top and gray-green on the bottom. They are oblique and have simple rounded serrations. They are glabrous on both sides and exhibit 10 to 16 vein pairs. The petioles are 1/8 to 1/4″ long, light green and often pubescent. The cultivar's chestnut brown buds are ovoid, imbricate, slightly pubescent, 1/8″ long and slightly divergent. In the first year, the stems are fine textured, terete, brown, and pubescent. By the second year, the stems turn gray-brown and glabrous with small orangy brown lenticels. The pith is small, solid and brown.

'Emerald Vase'—An upright-spreading tree with an outline similar to that of American elm. It measures 70' high and 59' wide. At 4' from the soil line the mature tree has a 35″ diameter trunk and a 110″ circumference. The bark exfoliates in a puzzle-like pattern exposing light gray, slate gray, gray-green and orangy brown colors; it is flecked with burnt orange corkish lenticels. The exfoliation begins at the base of the trunk and continues upward to include upper branches 1 to 2″ in diameter. Surface roots also exfoliate. Unlike the typically rounded trunk of the species, the trunk is irregularly fluted. The lustrous rich green foliage is densely borne at the ends of the fine branches, creating a dense canopy. Leaf color and texture are typical of the species. Fall color is subdued yellow. Despite the record drought conditions, no leaf scorch of dieback symptoms occurred. In addition, the parent tree is thriving in an 18 by 18' area surrounded by concrete. 'Emerald Vase' is also highly resistant to Dutch elm disease and elm leaf beetle. The leaves are alternate and simple, 3/4 to 2″ long and 3/8 to 3/4″ wide. They are ovate to slightly obovate, lustrous bright green on the top and gray-green on the bottom. They can be acute or obtuse, and they are oblique, with simple serrations that are slightly more pointed than those on 'Emerald Isle'. The leaves are glabrous on both sides and show 11 to 16 vein pairs. The petioles are 1/8 to 1/4″ long, light green and pubescent. The chestnut brown buds are ovoid, imbricate, slightly pubescent, 1/8″ long and slightly divergent. During the first year, the stems are fine textured, terete, brown and pubescent. In the second year they turn glabrous and gray brown, with small orangy lenticels. The pith is small, solid and brown.

'King's Choice'—The only patented form I am aware of (PP# 5554, granted Sept. 10, 1985). A gentleman walked into my office and introduced himself as Ben King. He said that he knew I liked Chinese Elm, and he wanted me to evaluate his new selection. After considerable discussion, he escorted me to his station wagon and handed me 18 strong 4 to 6' high liners, which are now being tested at a local Athens nursery. King selected the tree from 1,000 Chinese Elms seedlings that were planted at King's Men Tree Farm, Hampstead, MD, in April 1978. The tree had grown at twice the rate of the other seedlings and was saved for evaluation. It grew 22' high and 16' wide in seven years and developed an oval-rounded outline. The patent describes the branching pattern as "a single bole, which divides into laterals at angles greater than 90° above the horizon, which then droops to a canopy silhouette much like [that of] American elm." A photograph that accompanies the patent description does not clearly show this trait. The leaves of this selection are up to 2 1/2" long, leathery, semiglossy and dark green and turn a dull yellow in autumn. After 8 years, the bark had not developed an exfoliating character but had regular vertical fissures. The bark's color is described as grayed orange, which means little until one looks at the Royal Horticultural Society Colour Chart. From the information given in the patent description, this tree may not develop the typical bark of a Chinese Elm until it is much older. Softwood cutting root 90% compared with 60 to 80% for the other Chinese Elms King tested. The hardiness is unknown, but a Zone 6 designation—possibly even 5—is probable. Laboratory hardiness testing indicates tolerance to at least -22°F.

'Milliken'—May be the finest selection of all; the parent tree resides in a grassy field in Spartanburg, SC and reminds of the outline of a White Oak from a distance; parent tree probably 50' by 40' with dark green foliage; bark is superlative with brown, orange, tan mosaic on 2" diameter branches and the mature trunk; has withstood ice, hurricane force winds, and the ravages of time; extremely uniform outer tracery of fine branches lends a well tailored profile.

'Prairie Shade'—Selected from 800 seedlings planted in 1973. Researchers initially selected 13; only two of these exhibited good form and were easy to propagate from cuttings. Seven-year-old trees propagated from cuttings measure 30' tall and 20' wide, with 8" diameter trunks 6" above the soil line. The habit is upright-spreading. 'Prairie Shade' has leathery, dark green leaves that are smaller then typical for the species. The irregular bark character develops slowly, with only moderate flaking when branches are 2 to 3" in diameter. The cultivar is resistant to anthracnose (*Gnomonia ulmea*) and elm leaf beetle. It survived the 1983–84 winter in Stillwater, OK, and no ice or wind damage has occurred. The tree has performed well in Lubbock, TX; Guymon, OK; and Dodge City and Manhattan, KS. See *HortScience* 21:162–163 (1986). Recent reports from Oklahoma indicate significant susceptability to anthracnose.

'Sempervirens'—Sometimes listed as a variety, but taxonomic references do not consider this valid. Generally the epithet refers to the semi-evergreen to evergreen nature of the foliage. The cultivar is described as a medium-sized, round-headed shade tree with graceful, broad-arching branches that assume a weeping tendency at the ends. The leaves are dark green. Older trees shed their bark in patches, somewhat like sycamores. This tree, or a reasonable facsimile, is widely grown in California and Florida but is listed as hardy in Zone 6. Hickman and Whitcomb reported severe injury at -8°F and -31°F during the 1983–84 winter in Stillwater, OK. Realistically, this tree is hardy in Zone 8 and possibly in Zone 7. Apparently 'Sempervirens' is extremely variable in form, which suggests it is seed-grown. The cultivar appears to have characteristics similar to those of 'Pendens' (forma *pendula*), which Rehder described in 1945 as having long, loosely pendulous branches.

'True Green'—More evergreen then 'Sempervirens' or 'Drake' and also less hardy, although listed for Zone 7. At -4°F, the tree was severely injured in Stillwater, OK. 'True Green' develops a graceful, round-headed outline and has small, glossy, deep green leaves. Unfortunately, the bark characteristics of 'True Green' are unknown. I have observed older Chinese Elms in California and Florida with semievergreen tendencies that developed respectable exfoliating bark. However, there was no way to determine whether the trees were any of the above.

PROPAGATION: If seed is collected fresh (green to greenish brown stage) it germinates in good quantities; however, if left to dry it requires about 2 months cold. I have experimented with the seed and found the above to be the best prescription for success. Cutting procedures vary with investigator; ideally take cuttings in May-June, 5000 to 10000 ppm K-IBA, peat:perlite, mist. See Dirr and Richards, "In search of the perfect Chinese Elm," *American Nurseryman* 169(3):37–49 (1989) for additional propagation information.

ADDITIONAL NOTES: A fine tree whose use is limited only by the confusion the nursery industry has perpetuated. Superior selections can be made for a number of good features. I consider it a tree of the future. See Dirr, *American Nurseryman* 155(4):75–79 for an in-depth analysis of this and *U. pumila.* Dr. Pair, Kansas State, reported it is a good tree for Kansas. See Dirr and Richards, *Amer. Nurseryman* 169(3):37–49 (1989) for a detailed discussion. I remarked in the 1983 edition that *Ulmus parvifolia* had a great feature. It is obvious from the new cultivars that others believed similarly. Dr. John Pair, Kansas State University, Wichita Field Station, has evaluated the tree for many years and has several good clones.

NATIVE HABITAT: Northern and central China, Korea, Japan. Introduced 1794.

RELATED SPECIES:

Ulmus crassifolia, (ul′mus kras-i-fō′li-à), Cedar Elm, like the above, also flowers and fruits in the fall. It makes a large, 50 to 70′ high, 40 to 60′ wide tree of oval-rounded outline. The 1 to 2″ long, 1/2 to 1 1/4″ wide leaves are lustrous dark green, stiff and rough (scabrous) to the touch. The tree may have possibilities for use from Zone 7 to 9 for it withstands drouth and heavy, infertile soils. It is susceptible to Dutch elm disease, and elm leaf

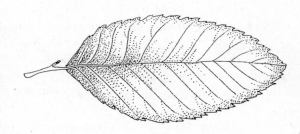

beetles may cause damage. It is probably not preferable to *U. parvifolia* but does offer a useful alternative. It is confused with *Ulmus alata,* Winged Elm, but does not have the pronounced corkiness on the young branches and flowers in fall. Corky wings are often opporite each other along the stem. I saw numerous specimens in San Antonio, TX. Used as a street and shade tree throughout southwest. Mississippi to Arkansas and Texas. Introduced 1876.

Ulmus procera — English Elm
(ul′mus prō-sē′rà)

LEAVES: Alternate, simple, ovate or broad-elliptic, 2 to 3 1/2″ long, two-thirds as wide, short acuminate, oblique, doubly serrate, dark green and scabrous or smooth above, soft pubescent beneath and with axillary tufts of white pubescence, 12 vein pairs; petiole 1/4″ long, pubescent.

Ulmus procera, English Elm, has always been a mystery to me for what I was taught as English Elm never jibed with the published description. The answer to the problem is that plants do not read books and teachers should. I encountered a good guide to the elms commonly grown in England at the Chelsea Flower Show. It is entitled "Field recognition of British elms" by J. Jobling and A.F. Mitchell, Forestry Commission Booklet 42, available from HMSO, 49 High Holborn, London WCIV 6HB. It is worth the 85 pence for the serious student. The book describes the English Elm as broadest near the top, dense, either open umbrella in form or billowing hemispheres; the bark finely fissured into small rectangles, tissues seldom dominantly vertical, dark brown. There are creamy-white marked and yellow leaf cultivars but they, like the species, have suffered the ravages of Dutch elm disease and I noticed in the *Hillier Colour Dictionary of Trees and Shrubs* that only one elm is presented with the comment that "the planting of elms has virtually ceased." England, one of the early introductions to America but difficult to locate. Interestingly the tree is apparently wholly sterile and it is reproduced from suckers. The validity of this species has been questioned and it has been theorized it may be a hybrid between *U. carpinifolia* and *U. glabra* which should place it in the *U.* × *hollandica* group (?). Zone 4 to ?

Ulmus pumila — Siberian Elm
(ul′mus pū′mi-là)

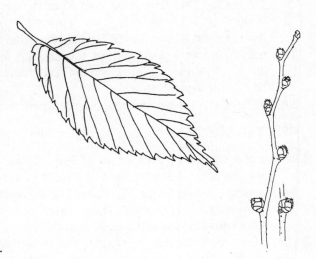

LEAVES: Alternate, simple, elliptic to elliptic-lanceolate, 3/4 to 3″ long, 1/3 to 1″ wide, acute or acuminate, usually nearly equal at base, nearly simply serrate, with the teeth entire or with only one minute tooth, dark green and smooth above, glabrous beneath or slightly pubescent when young, firm at maturity; petioles 1/12 to 1/6″ long.

BUDS: Large, globose flower buds, 1/4″ long, blackish brown, with ciliate hairs along the edge of bud scales.

STEM: Slender, brittle, very light gray or gray-green, usually glabrous, can be slightly hairy, roughened by lenticellar projections.

FRUIT: Circular or rather obovate samara, 1/2″ across, seed almost centered, deeply notched at the top.

Ulmus pumila, Siberian Elm, is a 50 to 70′ high tree with a spread 3/4's to equal the height. The habit is rather open, with several large ascending branches with flexible, breakable, pendulous branchlets. The growth is fast and the wood brittle; the tree grows under any kind of conditions; the foliage is dark green and loved by insects; a poor ornamental tree that does not deserve to be planted anywhere! Resistant to Dutch elm disease and phloem recrosis; one of, if not, the world's worst trees; I have seen whole streets and cemeteries planted with this species; the initial growth is fast but the ensuing branch breakage, messiness, and lack of ornamental assets appalling. Several cultivars have been introduced which would seem to have preference over the species. They include:

'Chinkota'—A cold hardy form introduced by South Dakota State University.

'Coolshade'—Resistant to breakage in ice storms compared to species (*U. pumila* × *U. rubra*).

'Dropmore'—Fast growing form with small neat foliage, hardy in Dropmore, Manitoba, Canada; original selection made by Dr. Frank Skinner.

'Hamburg Hybrid'—Stronger wooded than species, fast growing, 4 to 6′ per year (*U. americana* × *U. pumila*).

'Improved Coolshade'—Fast growing, uniform habit, hardy, drought resistant and resistant to breakage from wind and ice (*U. pumila* × *U. rubra*).

'Mr. Buzz'—Selection by Westerveldt Tree Co, Selma, AL for dense crown, dark green foliage, and vigorous growth, have seen photographs and looks too good to be true.

'Pendula'—Pendulous branches.

The principal attribute is for breeding Dutch elm disease resistance into hybrids like 'Regal', 'Urban' and others. I grew up with the species in the midwest and fretted constantly about the potential for brain damage engineered by cascading branches. Upon arrival in Athens, I thought the blight was removed but, alas, the tree appeared with the same vengeance. Interestingly, in 10 years, several large campus and city specimens have transpired. I have noticed tremendous elm leaf beetle damage; more than I remember from the midwest. Some of the resistance is evident for a tree next to the University's agronomy greenhouses remains green into fall while others assume a skeletonized gray-brown. I may cut it (the good one) down before a breeder tunes in.

Native to eastern Siberia, northern China, Manchuria, Korea and, unfortunately, was not left there. Cultivated 1860. Zone 4 to 9.

Vaccinium corymbosum — Highbush Blueberry
(vak-sin'i-um kôr-im-bō'sum)

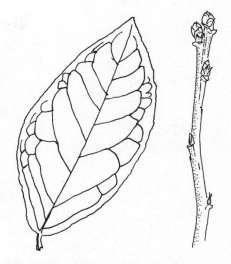

FAMILY: Ericaceae

LEAVES: Alternate, simple, ovate to elliptic-lanceolate, 1 to 3 1/2″ long, half as wide, acutish, cuneate, entire, dark green above, paler beneath, pubescent on midrib and veins; short petioled.

STEM: Slender, yellow-green to reddish in winter, granular; pith—solid, green; overall effect is quite handsome in winter.

SIZE: 6 to 12′ in height with a spread of 8 to 12′.

HARDINESS: Zone 3 to 7 (8).

HABIT: Upright, multi-stemmed shrub with spreading branches forming a rounded, dense, compact outline, especially under cultivation.

RATE: Slow.

TEXTURE: Medium in all seasons.

LEAF COLOR: Dark green, almost dark blue-green in summer changing to yellow, bronze, orange or red combinations in fall; very excellent fall coloring shrub.

FLOWERS: White, possibly tinged pink or pinkish, urn-shaped, 1/3″ long, May, just before leaves completely unfold; borne in axillary racemes in great quantities.

FRUIT: Berry, blue-black, bloomy, rounded, 1/4 to 1/2″ across depending on the cultivar, edible but require a complement of sugar; July through August.

CULTURE: Transplant balled and burlapped or from a container into moist, acid, organic, well-drained soils (pH 4.5 to 5.5); native to somewhat swampy soils but does extremely well under acid, sandy conditions; chlorosis is a significant problem and pH of the soils should be the first concern of anyone desiring to culture blueberries; actually they are very easy to grow if given the above conditions; mulch to reduce injury around roots and preserve moisture; prune after fruiting; full sun or partial shade.

DISEASES AND INSECTS: Actually the cultivated blueberries are subject to a number of insects and diseases; if the shrub is being grown for ornamental rather than commercial purposes no extensive control program is necessary and there are usually sufficient fruits for a few pies, jams, and the birds.

LANDSCAPE VALUE: Could blend well into the shrub border or small garden plot; two or three plants will provide many quarts of berries; it is wise to check with the local extension service or the state university to determine the best cultivars for a given area.

CULTIVARS:

Numerous selections and hybrids have been named and are preferable to the wild types. When selecting cultivars for your garden, write or call your county extension service to find out which are best for your area. Note that the cultivars also vary in shape, vigor and productivity as well as size, color, and taste of the fruit. Although single cultivars can be planted, more than one cultivar should be planted for best pollination.

'Berkeley'—Midseason, vigorous, spreading, and productive. Light-blue fruits of good quality are largest of all berries. Berries store well and generally ripen one week after 'Blueray'.

'Bluecrop'—Midseason. Hardier and more drought resistant than most. Upright bushes are unusually productive to the point of overbearing. Medium to large, light-blue fruit of good quality. Fruit flesh is firm, resistant to cracking, and flavor is good. Plants are vigorous, spreading and consistently productive. The ripening time is similar to 'Blueray'. 'Blueray' and 'Bluecrop' appear to be a good combination for cross-pollination.

'Blueray'—Midseason. Very hardy, upright, exceptionally vigorous bush produces large, light-blue, highly flavored tart fruit. It ripens 1 to 2 weeks after 'Bluetta', depending on vigor. 'Blueray' grows to heights of 4 to 5′, and its diameter is similar. Summer leaf color is a glossy, dark green, giving

'Bluetta'—Medium vigor, productive bush which ripens in June.

way to bright red in fall. Its very red stems stand out in the winter. It is a very neat, compact grower.

'Burlington'—Late. Vigorous, upright, moderately productive shrub. Small to medium, light-blue fruit of fair dessert quality.

'Collins'—Ripens with 'Bluetta'. Fruit is light blue, sweet, and has an excellent flavor.

'Coville'—Late. Very vigorous, spreading bush with large, light-blue berries of good quality when fully ripe.

'Dixi'—Late. Vigorous, spreading bush that is not very hardy. Large, medium-blue berries are of excellent quality but subject to cracking.

'Earliblue'—Early. Vigorous, upright bush with large, good quality, sweet berries.

'Elliot'—More upright, reaching 6′ high and spreading as much as 4 to 5′ in diameter. Leaf color during summer is bluish green, turning to orange-red in fall.

'Herbert'—Late. Vigorous, upright bush. Medium-blue berries are among the largest and best quality. Fruit is resistant to cracking and does not shatter. Ripening time is late June.

'Jersey'—Late. An old favorite and perhaps the most widely grown. Vigorous, upright, very productive bush. Large, light-blue berries are acidic when picked early but sweet when fully ripe. 'Jersey' and 'Rubel' are the only cultivars to survive bad winter and late-spring frosts at Geneva, NY.

'Northland'—Can be used from the Canadian provinces through most of the southern states. It has bright green, oval leaves that turn orange in the fall. Its height exceeds 4′, and it spreads to a 5′ diameter.

'November Glo'—Developed by the late Dr. Arthur Elliott in Michigan, it was named for retaining the fiery red foliage throughout November and December. Plants reach heights of 4 or 5′ and can be used as accent plants and hedges. The foliage has good color on its graceful, lance-shaped leaves.

'Pemberton'—Late. Unusually vigorous, erect bush that bears a year or two earlier than most. Productive, but medium-blue berries are difficult to pick and subject to cracking in wet weather.

'Weymouth'—Early. Erect bush of below average vigor with medium-size, dark-blue berries of poor dessert quality that fall off the plant.

Southern Highbush Varieties

These plants flower and ripen their berries before rabbiteye (*V. ashei)* blueberries.

'Avonblue'—Very early season, ripens one week after 'Sharpblue'. It is very prone to overbearing and pruning is necessary to balance the fruit load. Young plants must be defruited to obtain good growth. 'Avonblue' blooms a week after 'Sharpblue'. 400 chilling hours (45°F or below) required to satisfy bud rest and allow flowers to open and develop normally.

'Flordablue'—Very early season, it is difficult to propagate and grow. It ripens one week after 'Avonblue'. 300 chilling hours required.

'Sharpblue'—Very early season. Self-fertile, therefore, it may be planted in solid blocks. It does not grow as fast as rabbiteyes and the fruit must be stripped when the plants are young to obtain good growth. It is also necessary to prune off excess flowers on older plants. It must be grown on well-drained soil to prevent root rot. 'Sharpblue' is subject to early blooming and bird damage. The fruits have a wet scar when picked, but can be shipped with careful management. Grows as far south as Homestead FL. It is slow growing, maturing at a height of 4 to 5′. It has the typical glossy green leaves that change to orange-red in fall. With its compact growth, large leaves and neat growing habit, it makes an altogether satisfactory landscape plant. 300 chillding hours required.

PROPAGATION: Seed, some species germinate immediately, others germinate over a long period of time. Seeds of *V. corymbosum* do not require pretreatment. Cuttings, especially softwood, collected in June root readily under mist in peat:perlite when treated with 1000 ppm IBA; I have had good success this way; a rooting hormone may not be necessary but is always a good safeguard.

NATIVE HABITAT: Maine to Minnesota, south to Florida and Louisiana. Introduced 1765.

RELATED SPECIES:

Vaccinium angustifolium — Lowbush Blueberry
(vak-sin′i-um an-gus-ti-fō′li-um)

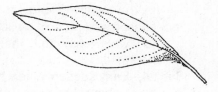

LEAVES: Alternate, simple, lanceolate, 1/3 to 3/4″ long, acute at
    ends, serrulate with bristle-pointed teeth, lustrous dark green
    above essentially glabrous on both surfaces; var. *laevifolium*
    has larger leaves about 3/4 to 1 1/2″ long and represents more
    southerly distributed members.

Vaccinium angustifolium, Lowbush Blueberry, is a low, straggly, open growing shrub reaching 6″ to 2′ in
    height and spreading 2′. The foliage is lustrous dark to blue-green in summer changing to bronze,
    scarlet and crimson in fall. The flowers are white, tinged red, 1/4″ long, April-May. The fruit is a bluish
    black, bloomy, very sweet berry, 1/4 to 1/2″ across. Does extremely well in dry, acid, poor soils and
    is the main fruit crop in the state of Maine (6 to 9 million dollar enterprise). Newfoundland to
    Sasketchewan, south to the mountains of New Hampshire and New York. Introduced 1772. Zone 2
    to 5(6).

Vaccinium arboreum — Farkleberry
(vak-sin′i-um är-bō′rē-um)

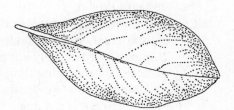

LEAVES: Alternate, simple, obovate to oblong, evergreen to
    deciduous depending on location, 1/2 to 2″ long, about half
    as wide, acute or obtuse, entire or obscurely denticulate,
    leathery, lustrous dark green and glabrous above, slightly
    pubescent beneath or downy.

Vaccinium arboreum, Farkleberry, is abundant in the Georgia Botanical Garden as an understory plant in
    rather dry woods. It ranges from a spreading shrub to a 15 to 20′ small tree. The 1/2 to 2″ long, leathery
    dark green leaves turn rich red to crimson in fall. The 1/4″ long white flowers are followed by 1/4″
    diameter, black, inedible, persistent fruits. The bark exfoliates and is composed of grays, rich browns,
    oranges and reddish brown. Virginia to North Carolina to Florida, southern Illinois and Texas.
    Introduced 1765. Zone 7 to 9.

Vaccinium ashei, (vak-sin′i-um ash′ē-ī), Rab-
    biteye Blueberry, is best described as the
    southern equivalent of *V. corymbosum* in
    modern taxonomy. In general, Rabbiteye is
    similar to Highbush but is better adapted to
    culture in the southern states. Many selec-
    tions have been made for superior fruiting
    characteristics. The foliage of some selec-
    tions is a glaucous blue-green and genuine-

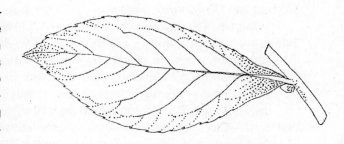

ly attractive. The plants color well in the fall and are enthusiastically recommended by this author for
    the home landscape. Because the rabbiteye blueberry requires cross-pollination for maximum fruit
    set, plant 3 or more cultivars with a minimum of 2 cultivars. Chill hours refer to the number of hours
    at 45°F or below necessary to satisfy bud rest and allow flowers to open and develop normally.
    Cultivars include:
'Baldwin'—Late season, vigorous and upright with fruit of medium size. The ripening season may
        extend into August and September and is an excellent choice for you-pick operations where
        late season fruit is desired. It is not recommended for mechanical, fresh market harvest. (450
        to 500 chill hours).

'Beckyblue'—Early season, a University of Florida release for the fresh fruit trade. It blooms early. (300 chill hours).

'Bluebelle'—Mid-season, plants are moderately vigorous with upright growth. Berries are large, round, light blue, and have excellent flavor. Fruit ripening beginning in mid-season and extends over a relatively long period. Under favorable conditions the berries size well throughout the season and production is high, thus being an excellent pick-your-own variety. Berries tend to tear when harvested. Therefore, this variety is not recommended for shipping. (450 to 500 chill hours).

'Bonita'—Early season, a new fresh fruit shipping variety from Florida. The shrubs are vigorous and ripen about three days after 'Climax.' It blooms early so it is best planted by 'Woodard' or 'Beckyblue'. (About 300 chill hours).

'Brightwell'—Early season, introduced by the University of Georgia Coastal Plain Experiment Station in 1982. Plants are vigorous and upright. The berries are medium in size, have small, dry stem scars and good flavor. 'Brightwell' ripens over a relatively short period beginning after 'Climax' and about the same season as 'Woodard.' It is suitable for mechanical harvest. (350 to 400 chill hours).

'Briteblue'—Mid-season, moderately vigorous and grows upright and open. Berries are light blue, large, and very firm with good flavor when fully ripe. The season of ripening is generally before 'Tifblue.' Berries are easily hand picked because they grow in clusters. Mature berries have a long retention on the plant and are an excellent choice for pick-your-own operations. (400 to 650 chill hours).

'Climax'—Early season, plants grow upright and open. Berries are medium in size and medium dark blue in color, have a small scar and good flavor. Fruit ripening begins 3 to 5 days before 'Woodard'. It has concentrated ripening with few shriveled or overripe fruit. This cultivar is excellent for mechanical harvesting. (450 to 550 chill hours).

'Delite'—Late season, moderately vigorous, producing an upright plant. Berries are light blue, sometimes being a reddish blue when ripe. They are large and firm, and have excellent flavor, not sharply acid before fully ripe. Its season is slightly later than 'Tifblue'. (500 chill hours).

'Powderblue'—Mid-to-late season, height averaging 6 to 10', spreads to 5 or 6' in diameter and does not sucker at the base. The leathery oval leaves are bluish, coloring from bright yellow to orange in fall. The stem color after leaf drop is green to yellow. It is similar enough to 'Tifblue' in appearance, quality, season and mechanical harvesting charcteristics that the two can be harvested together and used as pollinators for each other.

'Premier'—Early season, a release from North Carolina State University. The bushes are vigorous and productive, but the canes may be too limber to support the fruit load. It is similar in growth habit to 'Powderblue' except that its lanceolate leaves are a deeper green that turn to orange-red in the fall. The stem color varies from red to burgundy. (About 550 chill hours).

'Tifblue'—Mid-to-late season, plants make vigorous, upright growth. This has been the best commercial variety from the standpoint of appearance, productivity, and shipping qualities. However, most years the fruit ripens too late to receive high fresh market prices. The large, light blue berries are very firm and are highly flavored. Berries of this variety, like 'Woodard,' are very tart until fully ripe. Berries remain on the plant several days after fully ripe. (550 to 650 chill hours).

'Woodard'—Early season, plants are the shortest and most spreading of the rabbiteye varieties. The plant sprouts over an area of 3 to 4' in 6 to 10 years. Plants do not grow as tall as 'Tifblue', so they may be hand picked more easily. Berries are light blue and are large early in the season. The quality of the berries is excellent when they are fully ripe but are very tart until ripe. 'Woodard' ripens 7 to 10 days before 'Tifblue'. It is a poor choice for fresh market sales, because it is too soft. (350 to 400 chill hours).

Other *Vaccinium* (blueberry) hybrids and cultivars

'Northsky'—About 10 to 18" tall. It is dense, with glossy, dark green summer foliage that turns dark red in the fall. 'Northblue' is similar but taller, growing to 25". It produces more fruit than

'Northsky'. 'Northcountry' is similar to 'Northblue'. The University of Minnesota states that they can survive -40°F. These cultivars may grow slightly taller in warmer areas.

'Ornablue'—According to a West Virginia University publication, it is a hybrid between *V. corymbosum* and *V. pallidium* collected from the wild in Alabama. During its 12th season in the field, it was about 3′ tall and 5 1/2′ in diameter, making it suitable for specimen planting. 'Ornablue' manifests all the attributes of the blueberry family in a pronounced manner. This plant was declared unfit for competition with commercial fruit varieties. However, someone fell in love with its beauty, and it was saved from being grubbed out.

'Top Hat'—A release from Michigan State University developed at the South Haven Experimental Station. This plant was named for its neat, very dense growth, which is reminiscent of that of *Viburnum opulus* 'Nanum'. 'Top Hat' is a result of crosses between *V. corymbosum* and *V. angustifolium.* It has small leaves and matures at about 16″. This plant has the same plus factors of all blueberry plants, namely glossy leaves, white bell-shaped flowers, delicious berries and fiery fall color. Besides being used in landscapes where a low plant is desired, it can also serve as a container plant for the patio and as an excellent bonsai subject.

Several good extension publications exist and those desirous of additional information should write the Horticulture Department, Coastal Plain Experiment Station, University of Georgia, Tifton, GA. Zone 8 to 9, possibly parts of 7.

Vaccinium crassifolium, (vak-sin′i-um kras-i-fō′li-um), Creeping Blueberry, is scarcely a household name in American gardening circles but might deserve consideration for ground cover use; the lustrous dark green, finely serrate, 1/3 to 3/4″ long, 1/8 to 3/8″ wide oval leaves are spaced about 1/4″ apart along the stem. The reddish petiole is only about 1/16″ long. The rosy-red, 1/4″ diameter flowers occur in short lateral and terminal racemes in May. The evergreen nature makes it a good candidate for groundcover use in the southeastern United States. If provided a sandy, well drained situation it might prove adaptable. Will probably grow 6″ high and has the potential to spread many times its height. 'Wells Delight' offers lustrous elliptic dark green leaves and outstanding disease tolerance; 'Bloodstone' is a *V. crassifolium* subsp. *sempervirens* form with reddish new growth that matures to lustrous dark green, will grow 6 to 8″ high and makes a rather pretty groundcover. In winter, the maturing foliage assumes an attractive reddish cast and the stems become distinctive dark red. Susceptible to *Phytophthora* and stem anthracnose. My observations indicate that these cultivars require a well drained soil. See *HortScience* 20:1138–1140 (1985) for specifics on both cultivars. North Carolina to Georgia. Introduced 1787. Zone 7 to 8.

ADDITIONAL NOTES: There are about 130 species of *Vaccinium* and it is quite difficult to separate many of the types without a road map. Many make great garden shrubs because of fruit and fall color. In general they prefer an acid soil and if provided this reward one for many years. I remember a retired professor in Urbana, Illinois who was determined to grow *V. corymbosum* at all costs in the calcareous, high pH soil of the area. He went so far as to use HCl (hydrochloric acid) to acidify the soil in his garden and still had chlorotic plants. The best way to handle the problem under conditions like his is the use of raised beds and a medium like pine-bark, peat moss or some other acid organic. On a magnificent October day I scouted a Maine bog with Professor Bill Mitchell of the University of Maine and saw *V. corymbosum* in fluorescent fall color growing in what appeared to be the wettest and most acid of soils.

Vaccinium macrocarpon — American Cranberry
(vak-sin′i-um mak-rō-kär′pon)

FAMILY: Ericaceae
LEAVES: Alternate, simple, evergreen, 1/4 to 3/4″ long, 1/8 to 1/3″ wide, elliptic-oblong, flat or slightly revolute, slightly whitened beneath,

lustrous dark green in summer assuming reddish purplish hues in fall and winter; short petioled.

BUDS: Small or minute, solitary, sessile, with 2 apparently valvate scales or the larger with some half-dozen scales.

STEM: Slender, very obscurely 3- or 5-sided or distinctly angled; pith small, nearly round, continuous; leaf-scars small or minute, half-rounded or crescent-shaped, somewhat elevated; 1 bundle-trace.

SIZE: 2 to 6″ in height, spread is indefinite.

HARDINESS: Zone 2 to 6.

HABIT: Low, dense, small-leaved evergreen ground cover.

RATE: Slow to medium; I have grown plants in containers with excellent success.

TEXTURE: Beautifully fine in all seasons.

LEAF COLOR: Glossy medium to dark green in summer; new growth is often bronzy; during cold weather the foliage takes on reddish bronze to reddish purple hues.

FLOWERS: Perfect, pinkish, corolla deeply 4-cleft with revolute linear-oblong lobes; borne solitary, axillary, nodding, jointed with pedicel; May-June; not showy but interesting from a morphological viewpoint.

FRUIT: Berry, red, 1/2 to 3/4″ across; ripening in September or October.

CULTURE: Transplant as a container grown plant into a moist, high organic matter soil; in the wild is found growing in moist sphagnum bogs; full sun, possibly light shade; most important to keep the roots cool and moist.

DISEASES AND INSECTS: Several associated with commercial production but nothing of consequence for the homeowner to worry about.

LANDSCAPE VALUE: A novelty evergreen ground cover which is quite handsome. I have had good success with container-grown plants which were transplanted into a 1/2 soil:1/2 sphagnum peat mixture.

PROPAGATION: Seeds require 3 months cold stratification for best germination. Cuttings are extremely easy to root. Softwood cuttings treated with 1000 ppm IBA, placed in peat:perlite under mist rooted 80 percent in 6 weeks.

ADDITIONAL NOTES: The American Cranberry is the source of the cranberries which we relish during the holidays and for that matter the rest of the year. Massachusetts is the leading state in cranberry production and a trip to Cape Cod at harvesting time (or for that matter any time) is well worth the effort. Very interesting crop as far as cultural and nutritional practices are concerned and anyone interested should consult a text on modern fruit production.

NATIVE HABITAT: Newfoundland to Sasketchewan, south to North Carolina, Michigan and Minnesota. Introduced 1760.

RELATED SPECIES:

Vaccinium vitis-idaea — Cowberry
(vak-sin′i-um vī′tis ī-dē′a)

LEAVES: Alternate, simple, oval to obovate, 3/8 to 1″ long, half as wide, often notched at apex, leathery, lustrous dark green, lower surface sprinkled with black dots; short stalked.

Vaccinium vitis-idaea, Cowberry, may grow to 10″. The evergreen foliage is lustrous dark green above and paler dotted beneath; turns metallic mahogany in winter. The flowers are white or pinkish, campanulate, 4-lobed, 1/4″ long; May through June; borne in short sub-terminal nodding racemes. The fruit is a dark red, 3/8″ diameter berry with an acid, bitter taste; ripens in August. Culturally it performs best on moist, peaty soil and in full sun. The variety *minus,* Mountain Cranberry, is lower growing (4″ rarely 8″) and hardier (Zone 2) than the species. The variety ranges from Labrador to Massachusetts to Alaska and British Columbia (Cultivated 1825) while the species is native to Europe and northern Asia. Cultivated 1789. Zone 5. I have seen the variety *minus* in Maine and have come to cherish and appreciate it for the refined, dainty habit and the excellent evergreen foliage.

Viburnum — Viburnum
Caprifoliaceae

A garden without a vibrunum is akin to life without music and art. I have a special fondness for this great group of plants that numbers about 120 species and contains numerous cultivars. They range in size from 2 to 3′ to 30′, in odor from the sweetest perfume to the stenchiest stink, in flower from white to pink (rose), and in fruit color from yellow, orange, red, pink, blue and black. Dr. Donald Egolf, U.S. National Arboretum, has introduced some superior types most of which are presented here. For many years viburnums were slighted in the mid south region but I now see *Viburnum plicatum, V. p.* var. *tomentosum, V. macrocephalum, V.* × *burkwoodii* and many of Dr. Egolf's excellent selections becoming almost commonplace. For additional information see Wyman, Krüssmann, Bean, and Dirr, *American Nurseryman* 150(9), 1979, and Plants and Garden Handbook 37(1):32–35, 1981.

Viburnum acerifolium — Mapleleaf Viburnum
(vī-bēr′num ā-sēr-i-fō′li-um)

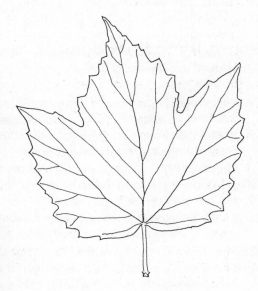

LEAVES: Opposite, simple, suborbicular to ovate, 3-lobed, sometimes slightly so, 2 to 4″(5″) long, about as wide, rounded to cordate at base, the lobes acute to acuminate, coarsely dentate, slightly pubescent above and dark green, more densely so and with black dots beneath; petiole 1/2 to 1″ long, pubescent.
BUDS AND STEM: Remind of *V. dentatum,* glabrous, gray-brown.

Viburnum acerifolium, Mapleleaf Viburnum, is a low, sparsely branched shrub growing 4 to 6′ tall and 3 to 4′ wide. The foliage is bright to dark green in summer changing to reddish purple in fall. The flowers are yellowish white, early June (early May, Athens), borne in 1 to 3″ diameter long-stalked flat-topped cymes. The fruit is a black, 1/3″ long drupe which ripens in September and often persists into winter. An extremely shade tolerant species reserved for naturalizing. The habit could best be described as suckering for it develops rather large, loose, open colonies in the wild. Is adapted to shade and rather dry soils as it occurs in the understory of the forest in southern locales. It is an excellent plant for use in heavily shaded situations and I find the range of fall colors (creamy-pink, rose, red to grape-juice purple) intriguing. Roots well from June-July cuttings. New Brunswick to Minnesota, south to North Carolina and Georgia. Introduced 1736. Zone 3 to 8.

Viburnum alnifolium — Hobblebush (Now *V. lantanoides* but I consider the name repulsive)
(vī-bēr′num al-ni-fō′li-um)
(vī-bēr′num lan-tā-noy′dēz)

LEAVES: Opposite, simple, broad-ovate to suborbicular, 4 to 8″ long, nearly as wide, short acuminate, cordate, irregularly denticulate, stellate-pubescent above at first, late glabrous and dark green, more densely pubescent beneath, chiefly on the veins; petioles 1 to 2 1/2″ long, scurfy.

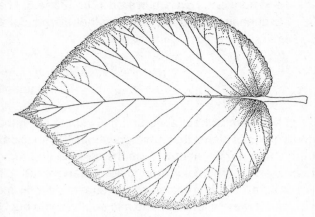

Viburnum alnifolium, Hobblebush, is a straggling
shrub with pendulous outer branches; often
develops a procumbent habit and roots
develop where the branches touch the ground;
reaches 9 to 12′ in height. The summer foliage
is medium to dark green and develops reddish
to deep claret in fall although I saw plants in
Maine in rather deep shade that were beautiful
rose-gold, green-gold to pinkish purple. The
flowers are borne in flat-topped, 3 to 5″
diameter cymes-the outer flowers of which are
sterile, white, about 1″ diameter and produced
in mid-May. The fruit is a red, finally purple-
black drupe about 1/3″ long which matures in
September. This species is maximally adapted to shady, moist areas. Native to New Brunswick and
Michigan to North Carolina in the mountains. Introduced 1820. Zone 3 to 5(6). This is a shrub that
one has to adapt to for it lacks the symmetry of many viburnums. Probably best adapted to a
naturalized situation.

Viburnum × burkwoodii — Burkwood Viburnum
(vī-bēr′num × bērk-wood′ē-ī)

LEAVES: Opposite, simple, oblong to ovate, 1 1/2 to 4″ long, 3/4 to
1 3/4″ wide, acute or obtuse, rounded or heart shape, indistinctly
toothed, lustrous dark green above, a bit rough to the touch, much
lighter beneath and tomentose, veins—often rusty brown in color;
petiole 1/4 to 1/2″ long, scurfy-pubescent.
BUDS: Vegetative-foliose, naked, tomentose.
STEM: Light tan in color, tomentose.
FLOWERS: Clustered (cymose), 1/2″ across, grayish pubescent.

SIZE: 8 to 10′ with spread about 2/3′s height.
HARDINESS: Zone 4 to 8; has been injured at Minnesota Landscape
Arboretum but is about the hardiest of the semi-snowball fragrant
types.
HABIT: Upright, multistemmed, often tangled mass of stems yielding a
somewhat straggly appearance; never as dense as *V × juddii* and
V. carlesii as the young growth extensions are elongated and seldom branched.
RATE: Slow to medium.
TEXTURE: Medium in foliage, yields a medium-coarse appearance in winter, primarily because of its
irregular growth habit.
LEAF COLOR: Lustrous dark green above; light gray-brown beneath; holds green color late, tends toward
a semi-evergreen character especially in southern states (Zone 8); fall color may be a sporadic
wine-red.
FLOWERS: Pink in bud to white in flower, spicy, aromatic, almost *Daphne odora* fragrance, April, effective
for 7 to 10 days, hemispherical cyme approximately 2 to 3″ across, each flower 1/2″ wide, with 5
spreading, rounded lobes; often opens in late March in Athens.
FRUIT: Red changing to black, July-August, drupe, usually sparsely produced and of insignificant ornamental importance; have seen respectable fruit when other plants of a similar nature were in close
proximity thus facilitating good cross pollination.
CULTURE: Most viburnums require a slightly moist, well-drained soil, are pH adaptable but prefer a slightly
acid situation; probably should be moved balled and burlapped or as a container specimen, small

plants can be handled bare root; avoid sulfur sprays as many viburnums are defoliated by them; a very serviceable group of plants of easy culture provided the soil is well-drained; nematodes in the south can be problematic.

DISEASES AND INSECTS: Bacterial leaf spot, crown gall, shoot blight, leaf spots, powdery mildew, rusts, downy leaf spot, spot anthracnose, spray burn (caused by sulfur sprays), viburnum aphid, asiatic garden beetle, citrus flatid planthopper, tarnished plant bug, thrips, potato flea beetle, dogwood twig borer, and seven scale species; although the list is impressive the viburnums are relatively free of major problems.

LANDSCAPE VALUE: Excellent choice for the shrub border, works well with broadleaf evergreens, fragrance permeates the entire garden; thrives even in a polluted environment. The more I travel the more convinced I am that this is an excellent garden plant; it is often considered a second class citizen among fragrant viburnums but its heat and cold tolerance are notable assets; it is definitely one of the best viburnums in the midwest and south; some pruning is necessary to keep it looking good.

CULTIVARS:

'Anne Russell'—Resulted from a back bross between *V. carlesii* with *V.* × *burkwoodii* made in 1951 at L.R. Russell Ltd., England. The habit is compact and will grow 6′ high and 8′ wide; the pink-budded, fragrant, 3″ wide flowers open several weeks before 'Fulbrook'.

'Chenaultii'—An extremely confused entity and in many respects resembles *V.* × *burkwoodii* except the leaves are smaller. I have seen specimens labeled as *Viburnum* × *chenaultii* but always thought they were *V.* × *burkwoodii*. Rehder does not list this species in his *Manual of Cultivated Trees and Shrubs* and *Hillier's Manual of Trees and Shrubs* lists the plant as a cultivar and not a species. Several specimens I have seen were actually larger in size than the normal *V.* × *burkwoodii* but a bit more compact in the density of branching and leaves. The flowers are borne in great profusion and literally cover the shrub in late April or early May just slightly later than *V.* × *burkwoodii*. I have seen plants at Callaway Gardens, GA, that were still pink in bud while *V.* × *burkwoodii* was full and open white.

'Fulbrook'—Parentage supposedly as in 'Anne Russell' with comparatively large, sweet-scented, pink-budded flowers that open white, each flower 5/8″ wide, the cyme 3″ across; 8′ high and 10′ wide, leaves like *V. carlesii* with more luster, strongly serrated, 3 to 4″ long, 2 to 3″ wide.

'Mohawk'—Resulted from a backcross of *V.* × *burkwoodii* × *V. carlesii* made in 1953. The cultivar was selected for the dark red flower buds which open to white petals with red-blotched reverse; abundant inflorescences; strong, spicy clove fragrance; compact growth habit; and foliage resistant to bacterial leaf spot and powdery mildew. The brilliant red flower buds appear several weeks before the flowers begin to open, and extend the effective ornamental period of the plant to several weeks rather than a few days 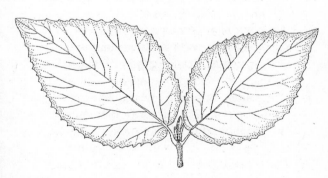 as with *V. carlesii* types. The strong, spicy clove fragrance is very pleasant and a noteworthy attribute of 'Mohawk'. The glossy, dark green leaves, which turn a brilliant orange-red in autumn are highly resistant to bacterial leaf spot and powdery mildew. Leaves favor *V. carlesii* in shape and color. The original plant is a compact shrub, 7′ in height with spreading branches to 7 1/2′. 'Mohawk' has been hardy as far north as Ithaca, New York. In colder regions the plant may survive, but the naked flower buds may be frost damaged. I have seen the plant in flower in late April at the Strybing Arboretum, San Francisco. Has performed well in Zone 8 and is slightly later flowering than *V.* × *burkwoodii*. Plants have reached 7 to 8′ tall in 4 years after planting as 3′ high shrubs. It is every degree as handsome as the above description especially the glistening dark red buds; an Egolf introduction.

'Park Farm Hybrid'—Similar to *V.* × *burkwoodii* but differing in its larger, 3 to 5″ diameter pinker budded inflorescences and the wide-spreading habit; it may grow 4′ high and 7′ wide, some literature noted it as tall as typical *V.* × *burkwoodii.*

PROPAGATION: In general seeds of viburnums are not the easiest to germinate; they show a double dormancy and require warm/cold periods of different duration; 3 to 5 months warm followed by 3 months cold is sufficient for many; it is best to place the cleaned seeds in warm stratification and watch for radicle emergence; when this occurs the seeds should be transferred to the cold. I have rooted cuttings from June-July collected wood with 100% efficiency; cuttings were dipped in 1000 ppm IBA/50% alcohol solution; in general cuttings of most viburnums are easy to root. See Dirr and Heuser (1987) for a good discussion.

ADDITIONAL NOTES: The species was developed in England by Albert Burkwood and Geoffrey Skipwith in 1914 and introduced in 1924. It is a cross between *V. carlesii* and *V. utile,* the latter having proved to be of little worth as a garden shrub but a fine parent in breeding programs.

RELATED SPECIES:

Viburnum utile — Service Viburnum
(vī-bēr′num ū′ti-lē)

LEAVES: Opposite, simple, ovate to oblong, 1 to 3″ long, 1/4 to 1 1/4″ wide, obtuse, rarely acutish, broad-cuneate or rounded, entire, leathery, lustrous dark green and glabrous above, prominently veined (5 to 6 pairs) and white beneath with a dense covering of stellate hairs; petiole 1/6 to 1/3″ long.

Viburnum utile, Service Viburnum, is a small (6′) evergreen shrub of rather straggly habit. The leaves have a rather wavy and at times almost inrolled appearance. The white flowers occur in April-May in 5-rayed, 2 to 3″ diameter, rounded cymes. The fruit is a 1/4″ long, bluish black drupe. This species has been most important in breeding work and has given our gardens the above species and cultivars, *V.* × *pragense,* 'Chesapeake', 'Conoy', and 'Eskimo'. The species is seldom seen in gardens and is not the handsomest of plants owing to the open habit, small leaves and rather non-descript flowers. However, it carries genes for heat tolerance and old plants at Callaway Gardens and in Aiken, SC attest to this. Also, the fine glossy foliage character appears often in the off-spring. Central China. Introduced 1901. Zone 6 to 8.

'Chesapeake'—Compact, mounded, twice as wide as high, leathery lustrous dark green leaves, foliage long persistent; pink buds open to white fragrant flowers, 2 to 3 1/2″ diameter cymes, dull red to black fruit; 6′ high and 10′ wide in 16 years, result of a cross between 'Cayuga' × *V. utile* made in 1962, introduced by U.S. National Arboretum, an Egolf selection; see *HortScience* 16:350. 1981; I had great hopes for this when it was first planted in our Horticulture Garden in 1982 but it has not measured up to expectations. The plant is about 8 by 10′, large, billowy and with medium density. Foliage tends toward a semi-evergreen nature with leaves at end of stems persistent. Leaves are undulating (wavy)

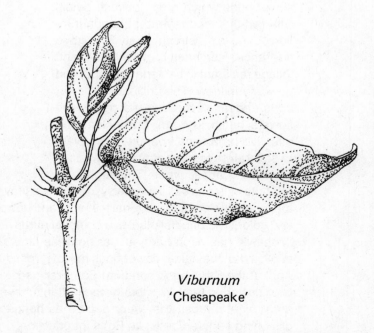

Viburnum
'Chesapeake'

with a slight twist to the long axis. Flowers are small, actually about 2″ diameter and fragrant. They peak in mid April in Athens but have opened in early April and as I pen this are still effective on April 25, 1989. 'Chesapeake' has not been as hardy as 'Eskimo', a sister seedling, and I suspect -10 to -15°F is the break point. Actually, I have received mixed reports on hardiness and the plant supposedly survived -25°F in Cincinnati but in Winchester, TN was killed to the ground at -20°F.

'Conoy'—A spreading dense branched evergreen shrub with glossy dark green, 1 1/2 to 2 1/2″ long leaves that assume a dark maroon tinge in winter; the undersides of the leaves are pale blue-green and covered with stellate pubescence; the flowers occur in April with dark red buds opening to creamy white, flowers are slightly fragrant and occur in 2 to 2 1/2″ diameter cymes, 70 to 75 florets per inflorescence; the 1/3″ long glossy ovoid drupes ripen in August changing from red to black at maturity and persist 5 to 8 weeks, 5′ by 8′ in 17 years; has been resistant to bacterial leaf spot; has withstood -9°F without injury; in southern climates foliage does not color in winter; result of a backcross between *V. utile* × *V.* × *burkwoodii* 'Park Farm Hybrid', see *Hortscience* 23:419–421 (1988) for additional information; a Don Egolf/National Arboretum introduction.

'Eskimo'—Dense compact form, 4 to 5′ high and 5′ wide in 12 years, semi-evergreen at ends of stems, coriaceous, lustrous dark green leaves, pale cream buds have a touch of pink on edges, open to pure white, globose, snowball, 3 to 4″ diameter inflorescences composed of 80 to 175 tubular flowers, fruits dull red to black, resistant to bacterial leaf spot, a U.S. National Arboretum introduction, see *Hort-Science* 16:691. 1981; parentage is 'Cayuga' × *V. utile;* I believe this selection will win out over time for it is hardier, offers bigger, more abundant flowers on young plants and stays relatively compact. The leaves are flat without the waviness of 'Chesapeake'. Plants grown in containers appear prosperous and are show-stoppers in flower. Interestingly, the flowers are not in the least fragrant.

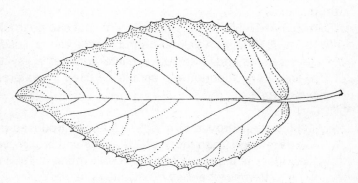

Viburnum carlesii — Koreanspice Viburnum
(vī-bēr′num kär-lē′sē-ī)

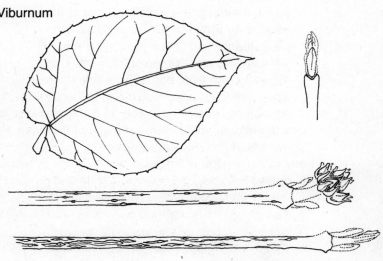

LEAVES: Opposite, simple, broad-ovate to elliptic, 1 to 4″ long, 3/4 to 2 1/2″ wide, acute, usually rounded to subcordate at base, irregularly toothed, dull dark green and stellate pubescent above, densely so and paler beneath; petiole—1/4 to 1/2″ long.

BUDS: Vegetative-foliose, naked, hairy; flower buds large—1/4 to 1/2″ wide.

STEM: Light brown to gray, stellate pubescence on young stem; old stems are gray and exhibit a characteristic fissuring.

SIZE: 4 to 5′ possibly to 8′ in height, by 4 to 8′ in width, have seen plants 10′ high and wide.

HARDINESS: Zone 4 to 7 (8).

HABIT: Rounded, dense shrub with stiff, upright spreading branches.

RATE: Slow.

TEXTURE: Medium in summer and winter, clean in appearance.

LEAF COLOR: Dull dark green, very pubescent on the upper surface; reddish to wine-red in fall color, not consistent in coloration and usually disappointing.

FLOWERS: Perfect, pink to redddish in bud, opening white, each individual flower 1/2″ across; late April to early May; in dense hemispherical cymes, 2 to 3″ across, often termed semi-snowball type flowers; flowers are at their best when leaves are 1/2 to 2/3′s mature size; fragrance almost like *Daphne odora,* truly outstanding.

FRUIT: Drupe, 1/3″ long, egg-shaped, flattened, red changing to black (not effective), August to September.

CULTURE: Transplant balled and burlapped or as a small bare root plant; best in well-drained, slightly acid soil with even moisture; full sun to partial shade; prune after flowering; plants used to be grafted on *V. lantana* and I have seen the scion consumed by the understock; be careful to buy own-root plants.

DISEASES AND INSECTS: Bacterial leaf spot can be troublesome.

LANDSCAPE VALUE: A valuable shrub for fragrance; I used it in a foundation planting along a walk at my Illinois home and for ten days in late April-early May it was a joy; some of the newer cultivars and *V. × juddii* are superior and should be used in preference; not as adaptable as *V. × juddii* or *V. × burkwoodii.*

CULTIVARS:

'Carlotta'—Improved form of *V. carlesii;* introduced by W.B. Clarke Co., San Jose, CA; the leaves are larger than those of *V. carlesii* and broad-ovate in outline.

'Cayuga'—Is the result of a backcross made in 1953 of *V. carlesii × V. × carlcephalum* (*V. carlesii × V. macrocephalum*). 'Cauyga' is distinct in producing abundant inflorescences with pink buds that open to white flowers in late April; compact growth habit; and medium textured foliage, with tolerance to bacterial leaf spot and powdery mildew. The leaves, which are less susceptible to bacterial leaf spot and powdery mildew than those of *V. carlesii,* are a darker green, smaller and not as coarse as those of *V. × carlcephalum,* their greater numbers present a mass effect and a more ornamental plant. The 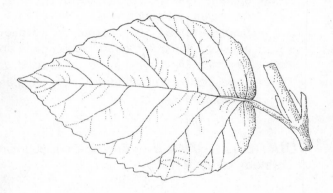 flowers open from one side of the inflorescence in such a way that nearly all inflorescences have pink buds accenting the white, waxy flowers. Although 'Cayuga' is described as a compact spreading, deciduous shrub to 5′ high, plants in the Georgia Botanical Garden are distinctly upright oval and somewhat leggy at the base. Plants have been hardy as far north as Ithaca, New York; an Egolf introduction.

'Compactum'—One of the best dwarf clones available but is rarely found in modern landscapes; it grows 2 1/2 to 3 1/2′ high and wide and produces exceptionally dark green leaves and flowers about the same size as the species; shows greater resistance to leaf spot; introduced by Hoogendoorn Nurseries, Inc., Newport, R.I. in 1953.

Other cultivars include 'Aurora', 'Charis' and 'Diana' which are the result of 25 years selection by Leslie Slinger, Slieve Donard Nursery, Newcastle, Northern Ireland. 'Aurora' has intense red buds, pink when open and turning white with a strong fragrance at maturity. 'Charis' is similar but very vigorous. 'Diana' is similar to 'Charis' but the flowers are strongly scented.

PROPAGATION: Generally considered difficult but June-July cuttings treated with 8000 ppm IBA-talc rooted 80 percent and all were successfully transplanted after going through a dormancy cycle; this appears to be one of those plants that dislikes root disturbance after rooting.

NATIVE HABITAT: Korea. Introduced 1812.

RELATED SPECIES:

Viburnum bitchiuense — Bitchiu Viburnum
(vī-bēr′num bitch-i-ū-en′sē)

LEAVES: Opposite, simple, ovate, 1 to 3″ long, 1/2 to 3/4″ wide, obtuse, cordate, dentate especially toward apex, dark green above, pubescent on both surfaces, 6 to 7 vein pairs.

Viburnum bitchiuense, Bitchiu Viburnum, is somewhat similar to *V. carlesii* but with smaller leaves, more slender stems, looser habit and smaller pinkish white flowers (1 1/2 to 2″ across) in looser clusters. Bitchiu is considered inferior to *V. carlesii* but selected forms may rival Koreanspice. Height varies from 8 to 10′. The dark bluish green foliage may turn dull reddish purple in fall but is usually not effective. The red, changing to black, fruit is produced sparsely. Bitchiu has imparted some of its good characteristics to *V.* × *juddii.* Japan, Korea. Cultivated 1909. Zone 5 to 7.

Viburnum × _carlcephalum,_ (vī-bēr′num kärl-sef′a̕-lum), Carlcephalum or Fragrant Viburnum, grows 6 to 10′ high with an equal spread. Habit is somewhat open and loose. Foliage is dark green with a slight luster in summer changing to reddish purple in fall. The flowers are pink in bud, finally white, fragrant, late April to early May, borne in 5″ diameter hemispherical 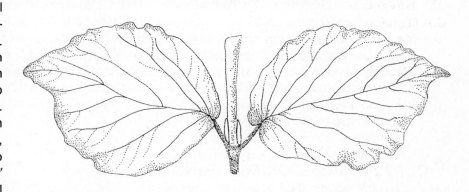 cymes. One of the best descriptions I read termed the inflorescences lumpy. Fruit is a drupe which changes from red to black; however, it is seldom effective. Reasonable plant for the garden. Result of a cross between *V. carlesii* × *V. macrocephalum* var. *keteleeri.* Originated in England in 1932 at the Burkwood and Skipwith Nursery and introduced into the U.S. about 1957. It is relatively easy to root from softwood cuttings. It is the latest of the semi-snowball types to flower. Hardiness is somewhat suspect and a Zone (5)6 to 8 rating is safest. Usually somewhat coarse and in no way as fine a garden shrub as *V.* × *juddii,* 'Eskimo' or 'Mohawk'. Have seen on occasion in south and was pleased with floral performance.

Viburnum × _juddii_ — Judd Viburnum
(vī-bēr′num × jud′ē-ī)

Viburnum × *juddii,* Judd Viburnum, is the result of a cross between *V. carlesii* and *V. bitchiuense* with the best features of both parents. I feel it is superior to *V. carlesii* and may eventually replace it in northern and southern areas. The habit is full and rounded with mature height approaching 6 to 8′. It is more resistant to bacterial leaf spot and roots much more readily from softwood cuttings. The inflorescence ranges from 2 1/2 to 3 1/4″ wide and when open is highly fragrant. I have heard people say that the fragrance of *V.* × *juddii* is not as pronounced as that of *V. carlesii* but am hard-pressed to distinguish between the two. This hybrid was raised at the Arnold Arboretum by William H. Judd, propagator, in 1920; flowered for the first time in 1929 with it was 6′ high and named in 1935. Nurserymen are selling this hybrid in greater numbers and someday it may replace *V. carlesii* as the dominant semi-snowball viburnum. Zone 4 to 8. Over the past 5 years has proven an adaptable and floriferous shrub in the State Botanical Garden. It is located by a walk that leads from the parking area and many people stop to sample its delicious perfume.

Viburnum macrocephalum — Chinese Snowball Viburnum
(vī-bēr′num mak-rō-sef′à-lum)

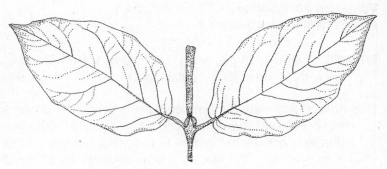

LEAVES: Opposite, simple, deciduous or semi-evergreen, ovate or elliptic to ovate-oblong, 2 to 4″ long, 1 1/4 to 2 1/2″ wide, acute or obtusish, rounded at base, denticulate or entire, dark green and nearly glabrous above, stellate-pubescent beneath; petiole—1/2 to 3/4″ long.

Viburnum macrocephalum, Chinese Snowball Viburnum, is a dense, rounded shrub growing 6 to 10′ high. The flowers are white, non-fragrant, each indivual floret 1 1/4″ across, May to early June, (mid-April in Athens), borne in 3 to 8″ diameter hemispherical cymes. Extremely showy in flower but requires a protected location and well-drained soil. I have seen it flowering in Columbus, Ohio, in a protected area. The foliage is semi-evergreen in the south. In the southern states the plant may grow 12 to 15′ (20′) high and form a massive rounded shrub. It tends to flower in the fall during warm weather in the south. In full flower it is a spectacular shrub and certainly worthy of consideration in larger gardens. It is relatively easy to root from June-July cuttings using 3000 to 5000 ppm IBA-quick dip but resents disturbance after rooting and should be left in place until the second year. Does not fruit as the flowers are sterile. The var. (forma) *keteleeri* is the wild form and has sterile marginal flowers and fertile inner flowers. China. Introduced 1844. Zone 6 to 9.

Viburnum cassinoides — Witherod Viburnum
(vī-bēr′num kas-i-noy′dēz)

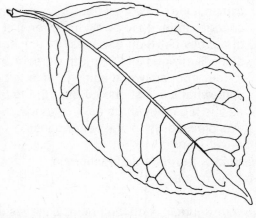

LEAVES: Opposite, simple, elliptic or ovate to oblong, 1 1/2 to 3 1/2″ long, 3/4 to 2 1/4″ wide, acute or bluntly acuminate, rounded or wedge shaped, obscurely dentate or denticulate, dull dark green above, nearly glabrous, somewhat scurfy beneath; petiole 1/4 to 3/4″ long, scurfy.
BUDS: Valvate, flowers with a bulbous base terminating the shoots, similar to *V. lentago;* vegetative-long, narrow, without the fattened base.
STEM: Gray to brown, scurfy in youth, finally glabrous.

Viburnum cassinoides, Witherod Viburnum, grows 5 to 6′ tall with a similar spread but can reach 10′ or greater in height. It is a handsome dense shrub, compact and rounded, with spreading, finally slightly arching branches. The dull dark green foliage changes to orange-red, dull crimson, and purple in fall. The emerging leaves are often bronze or purple-tinted. The flowers are creamy white, June to early July, borne in 2 to 5″ diameter flat-topped cymes. The fruit is the most beautiful attribute as it changes from green to pink, then from red to blue before becoming black in September. Often all colors are present in the same infructescence (fruiting cluster). A very lovely but little used shrub which has a place in naturalizing, massing, and the shrub border. I have seen it used effectively in a mass planting at the Holden Arboretum, Mentor, Ohio. In Maine, I saw it growing along the roadside and while trekking the highest mountain in Georgia discovered it in full fruit all along the route. A few plants I have observed were in the 12 to 15′ range although most books do not allow the species to grow over 12′. This is a fine viburnum and in fruit is spectacular. Newfoundland to Manitoba and Minnesota south to Georgia. Introduced 1761. Zone 3 to 8. A closely related species, *V. nudum,* Smooth Witherod, is equally beautiful and perhaps more so because the leaves are more lustrous. The leaves and stems may also be less pubescent but this appears to be somewhat variable. I grew this species in my Illinois garden where it survived -20°F. The red to reddish purple fall color is also attractive. 'Winterthur' is an improved form selected at Winterthur Gardens, Delaware. Dr. Darrell Apps, Chadds Ford, PA had several outstanding *V. nudum* seedlings in his garden that

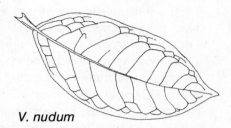

V. nudum

developed outstanding fall color. With selection this could become a well received garden plant. Long Island to Florida, west to Kentucky and Louisiana. Introduced 1752. Zone 5 to 9. Current thinking merges *V. nudum* under *V. cassinoides.* For purposes of discussion, I have kept them separate.

Viburnum davidii — David Viburnum
(vī-bēr′num dā-vid′ ē-ī)

LEAVES: Opposite, simple, evergreen, narrowly oval or slightly obovate, 2 to 6″ long, 1 to 2 1/2″ wide, acuminate, cuneate, conspicuously 3-veined, toothed toward apex, leathery, dark green, almost dark bluish green above, pale beneath, glabrous except for axillary tufts of hair below; petiole 1/4 to 1″ long.

Viburnum davidii, David Viburnum, forms a low, compact, 3 to 5′ high mound of thick, dark blue-green evergreen foliage. It is a beautiful viburnum and if it never flowered or fruited it would still be a plant of the first order. I have seen it in abundance throughout Europe but seldom in the U.S. In Athens, GA and Aiken, SC where I observed plantings, it is still subject to the vagaries of weather and the flowers and leaves may be injured. It appears to require a more moderate, even climate than can be offered in most parts of the U.S. Ideally it is suited to the Pacific Northwest. The pink-budded, finally dull white flowers occur in dense, 2 to 3″ wide cymes in April-May. The 1/4″ long, oval fruits are a beautiful shade of blue. Unfortunately the plant is either functionally dioecious or requires cross pollination from another clone for fruit is not set unless the proper conditions are met. In England, clones have been designated "male" and "female". The plant in fruit is spectacular and the first impulse is to locate a source for one's own garden. I have seen the plant used in combination with other broadleaf evergreens and it was effective. The Isle of Mainau in Germany has several large specimens. 'Jermyn's Globe' is now considered a hybrid of *V. davidii* × *V. calvum* and the original plant is low, compact and rounded. Western China. Introduced 1904. Zone 8 to 9.

Viburnum dentatum — Arrowwood Viburnum
(vī-bēr′num den-tā′tum)

LEAVES: Opposite, simple, suborbicular to ovate, 2 to 4 1/2″ long, 1 to 4″ wide, short acuminate, rounded or subcordate, coarsely dentate, glabrous, lustrous dark green above, glabrous beneath or bearded in the axils of the veins, with 6 to 10 pairs of veins; petiole 1/2 to 1″ long.
BUDS: Imbricate, usually appressed, green to brown, small, lower bud scale forming a "V"-shaped notch, glabrous, almost glossy.
STEM: Glabrous at maturity, gray, leaf scars with ciliate hairs around the margins.

SIZE: 6 to 8′ to 15′ in height in favorable locations, spread 6 to 15′.

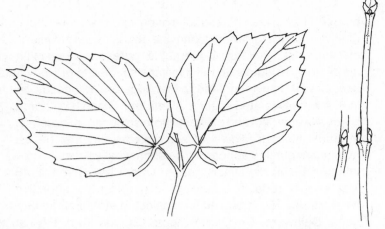

HARDINESS: Zone 2 to 8.

HABIT: Multistemmed, dense, rounded shrub with spreading, finally arching branches.

RATE: Medium.

TEXTURE: Medium in leaf and winter habit; some specimens are so delicately branched as to appear medium-fine in winter.

LEAF COLOR: Lustrous dark green in summer, sometimes without the sheen, fall color ranges from yellow to glossy red to reddish purple; selections for superior clones both in habit and foliage could be made for there is great variability within this species; I have seen poor fall colored specimens growing next to brilliant glossy red forms; the differences were not attributable to soils or climate but genetics.

FLOWERS: White, actually yellow stamens create a creamy color rather than pure white, no fragrance, May to early June, effective 10 to 14 days, borne in 2 to 4″ diameter, flat-topped, 7-rayed cymes on 1 1/2 to 2 1/2″ high raised peduncles.

FRUIT: Drupe, oval-rounded, 1/4″ long, blue or bluish black, late September through October; birds like the fruits and seeds are found germinating in many out-of-the-way places; some plants have particularly striking blue fruits, actual seed (stone) has a narrow deep groove on one side.

CULTURE: Fibrous rooted, transplants well, adapted to varied soils (possibly most durable viburnum for midwest), prefers well-drained conditions; sun or partial shade; suckers freely from the base and may have to be restricted from getting out of bounds.

DISEASES AND INSECTS: None serious, have not noticed any problems.

LANDSCAPE VALUE: Valued for durability and utility, the ornamental characters are secondary to other viburnums, good in hedges, groupings, masses, filler in shrub border; University of Illinois has effectively employed this shrub for screening parking lots; its utilitarian and adaptable nature is readily evident for I have observed it growing in the sands of Cape Cod, not too far removed from the salt spray, but never forming the first or second line of defense; in Nebraska it withstands the high pH, heavy soils and the vagaries of that climate; without a doubt it is one of the most functional viburnums.

PROPAGATION: Seed, 180 to 510 days at fluctuating temperatures of 68 to 86°F, followed by 15 to 60 days at 41 to 50°F. Softwood cuttings are easy to root, 1000 to 8000 ppm IBA have given good results.

NATIVE HABITAT: New Brunswick to Minnesota, south to Georgia, Introduced 1736.

RELATED SPECIES:

Viburnum molle — Kentucky Viburnum
(vī-bēr′num mol′lē)

LEAVES: Opposite, simple, suborbicular to broad-ovate, 2 to 5″ long, 1 3/4 to 3 3/4″ wide, short acuminate, deeply cordate, coarsely dentate with 20 to 30 teeth per margin, lustrous dark green and glabrous above, paler and slightly pubescent below; petiole 1/2 to 2″ long.

Viburnum molle, Kentucky Viburnum, is a loose, open, multi-stemmed shrub reaching 10 to 12′ in height. The bark exfoliates in thin flakes exposing a brownish inner bark. The leaves are dark green in summer. The flowers are whitish, borne in long-stalked, 2 to 3″ diameter cymes in May-June. The fruit is a bluish black, 1/2″ long dupe which is effective in August through September. Much like *V. dentatum* except for the bark, the long petioled leaves and often a pair of stipules on the petiole.

ADDITIONAL NOTES: Indians used the strong shoots which developed from the roots for the shafts of their arrows; hence, the name Arrowwood. There are a great number of closely related species that do not differ significantly at least from a landscape standpoint although there are those who will disagree with this contention. If the readers can envision this group as a north-south, east-west continuum showing slight differences in pubescence, habit and size but possessing similar creamy-

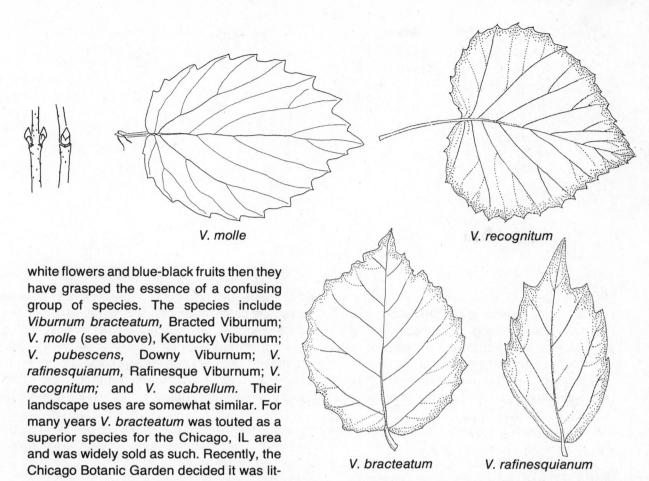

V. molle

V. recognitum

V. bracteatum

V. rafinesquianum

white flowers and blue-black fruits then they have grasped the essence of a confusing group of species. The species include *Viburnum bracteatum*, Bracted Viburnum; *V. molle* (see above), Kentucky Viburnum; *V. pubescens*, Downy Viburnum; *V. rafinesquianum*, Rafinesque Viburnum; *V. recognitum;* and *V. scabrellum*. Their landscape uses are somewhat similar. For many years *V. bracteatum* was touted as a superior species for the Chicago, IL area and was widely sold as such. Recently, the Chicago Botanic Garden decided it was little more than a superior form of *V. dentatum*. I have seen the plant and its merits are worthwhile perpetuating vegetatively.

Viburnum dilatatum — Linden Viburnum
(vī-bẽr′num dī-là-fā′tum)

LEAVES: Opposite, simple, suborbicular to broad-ovate to obovate, 2 to 5″ long, to about half as wide, abruptly short acuminate, rounded or subcordate at base, coarsely toothed, dark green above, often lustrous, hairy on both sides, with 5 to 8 pairs of veins; petiole 1/4 to 3/4″ long.

BUDS: Inbricate, slightly pubescent, 4 to 6 bud scales, blunt, brownish, often with a tinge of red in the scales.

STEM: Young branches hispid, brown, lenticels—orange (prominent).

SIZE: 8 to 10′ in height, 2/3's to equal that in spread, actually have observed a few plants wider than tall.

HARDINESS: Zone (4)5 to 7, possibly in Zone 8 where some shade is helpful but does not appear well adapted, have seen in Zone 9 but the plants were languishing.

HABIT: Often upright, somewhat leggy and open; also dense and compact in other forms; selection is the key within this species; the newer cultivars are superior to run-of-the-mill seedlings.

RATE: Slow-medium.

TEXTURE: Medium in leaf, medium to coarse in winter.

LEAF COLOR: Dark green, often lustrous, changing to an inconsistent russet-red in fall, may range from bronze to burgundy, leaves hold late.

FLOWERS: White, 1/4″ diameter, May to early June, effective 7 to 10 days, borne in pubescent (pilose), flat-topped, 3 to 5″ diameter, mostly 5-rayed cymes; often profusely produced and literally smothering the plant in a veil of creamy white.

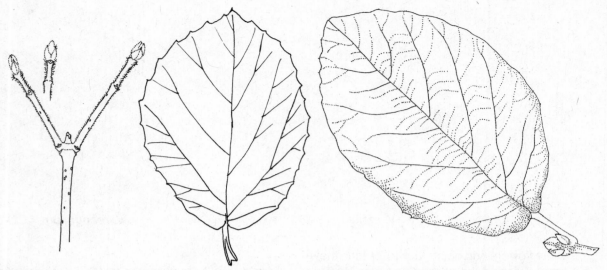

FRUIT: Drupe, 1/3″ long, ovoid, bright red, cherry red or scarlet (excellent color), September to October and often persisting into December when fruits may take on the appearance of withered red raisins; I have seen fruiting cymes heavy enough to bend the branches; plant several clones for best fruiting; superior selections are available that hold their fruit color through winter; Don Shadow, Winchester, TN has a fine, somewhat upright selection that maintains the glossy rich red fruit color through winter while one of the outstanding U.S. National selections, 'Erie', loses its rich red fruit color; I have compared these two forms as they grew side-by-side in the nursery in late January and the differences were quite striking.

CULTURE: Easily transplanted; best in moist, slightly acid, even-moistured soils but will do well in higher pH situations; full sun or partial shade; seems to prefer cooler climates but can be grown in Zone 8 if sited properly; ideally in Zone 8 provide moist soil and partial shade.

DISEASES AND INSECTS: None serious.

LANDSCAPE VALUE: Specimen, shrub border, all purpose shrub, ornamentally valuable in three seasons; outstanding for fruits, however, little used compared to the normal garden variety (forsythia, deutzia) shrubs; some of the new selections are outstanding and should be used in preference to seed-grown materials.

CULTIVARS:

'Catskill'—Is a dwarf *V. dilatatum* seedling selection made in 1958 from plants raised from seed obtained from Japan. 'Catskill' was selected for the compact growth habit; smaller and rounder leaves; and good autumn coloration. The compact, wide spreading growth habit has been constant. The smaller, dull, dark green leaves, which are more nearly rounded than on most *V. d.* plants, assume good yellow, orange, and red fall coloration. The creamy-white inflorescences are produced in May on new growth. The dark red fruit

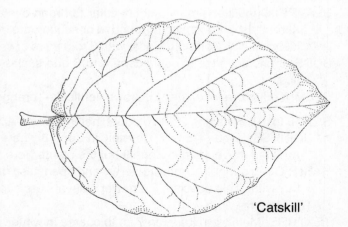

'Catskill'

clusters, which are dispersed over the plant, ripen in mid-August and provide a display until mid-winter. The original plant, at 13 years old, was 5′ high and 8′ wide. This selection did not do well in the Illinois field tests; however, it has performed well in Tennessee, see *Baileya* 14:109–112 (1966).

'Erie'—Rounded-mounded shrub, 6′ high and 10′ wide in 14 years, dark green leaves assume good yellow, orange and red fall color, white flowers in 4 to 6″ wide flat-topped cymes, prolific red fruits which after frost become coral and persist as coral to pink; highly resistant to diseases and insects. See *HortScience* 10:430–431 (1957).

'Iroquois'—Resulted from a cross of two *V. d.* selections made in 1953. The cultivar was selected for large, thick textured, dark green leaves; abundant inflorescences of creamy-white flowers; large, glossy, dark scarlet fruits; and dense, globose growth habit. The heavy textured foliage is ornamental in all seasons, glossy green in summer, and orange-red to maroon in autumn. In mid-May the inflorescences transform the plant into a mound of creamy-white. The glossy red fruits are larger than those on *V. d.* plants. The flat, wide-spreading fruit clusters contrast well with the dark green leaves. The fruit, which ripens in late August, persists after the leaves have fallen, and often the dried fruits are in abundance in mid-winter if not eaten by birds earlier. The original specimen is 9' high and 12 1/2' wide. Excellent form based on my observations; have seen fruit so heavy it weighs the branches down; see *Baileya* 14:109–112 (1966).

'Mt. Airy'—Possibly a great treasure for the future; while surveying the *Viburnum* collection at Mt. Airy Arboretum, Cincinnati, OH, I discovered a stray, misnamed seedling with lustrous leathery dark green foliage and abundant large bright red fruits; interestingly about 30' away were plants of 'Erie' that were not close in fruit size and abundance; obviously ample opportunities existed for cross pollination so if good fruit were to occur, it should have; the new clone was 6 to 7' high and wide with pleasing upright rounded outline; cuttings have been rooted and I look forward to this plant's competitive chances in the years to come; appears to be nothing more than a bird planted seedling, has all the characteristics of true *V. dilatatum*.

'Oneida'—Resulted from a cross of *V. dilatatum* × *V. lobophyllum* made in 1953. This deciduous shrub was selected for the abundance of flowers in May and sporadic flowers throughout the summer; the glossy, dark red fruit that persists until late winter; and the thin textured foliage that turns pale yellow and orange-red in autumn; and upright growth habit with wide spreading branches. Because of the two or three sporadic flowering periods, abundant fruit is produced that ripens in August and persists on the plant until mid-winter. The original plant has grown to a height of 10' and a width of 9 1/2'. It has not proven as impressive as 'Erie' and 'Iroquois' but is still a good choice. My more recent field notes are more positive including comments about a 10' high plant with excellent red fruit on September 27 at Brooklyn Botanic Garden and a Swarthmore plant with fruit as good as any typical *V. dilatatum*. Also the leaves and stems are more glabrous than typical *V. dilatatum* due to *V. lobophyllum* parent.

'Xanthocarpum'—Form with yellow to almost amber-yellow fruits which are not produced in great abundance and do not make the show of the better red-fruited types; as I have seen the fruits, scarcely yellow in the classical sense, more yellow-orange.

PROPAGATION: Seeds require about 5 months warm/3 months cold but even then germination is not guaranteed; softwood cuttings, 8000 ppm IBA, peat:perlite, mist equals high rooting; I have rooted this species without difficulty; on July 24 collected cuttings of 'Erie' and 'Mt. Airy' in Cincinnati, OH, 10000 ppm K-IBA, 2 perlite:1 peat with 100 and 80% rooting, respectively, and 100% overwinter survival.

NATIVE HABITAT: Eastern Asia. Introduced before 1845.

RELATED SPECIES:

Viburnum wrightii — Wright Viburnum
(vī-bĕr′num rīt′ē-ī)

LEAVES: Opposite, simple, ovate or broad-ovate, 3 to 5″ long, 1 to 2 1/2″ wide, abruptly acuminate, rounded or broad-cuneate at base, coarsely dentate, dark green and glabrous above, essentially glabrous beneath, except tufts of hairs in axils of veins, 6 to 10 vein pairs; petiole 1/4 to 3/4″ long.
STEM: Essentially glabrous which permits easy separation from *V. dilatatum*.

Viburnum wrightii, Wright Viburnum, is similar to the above but differs in its larger leaves and the relative absence of pubescence on the stem and inflorescence. I have only seen true *V. wrightii* a couple of times and it was distinctly different from *V. dilatatum*. The habit is upright-rounded, 6 to 10' high. The round-ovoid red fruits average about 1/3″ in length and are quite showy. The dark metallic green leaves may turn a good red in fall; variety *hessei* ('Hessei') is a compact form with attractive foliage and sealing-wax red fruits. Apparently many plants were grown from seed collected by C.S. Sargent, Arnold Arboretum, by Hesse Nurseries, Germany. 'Hessei' has occasionally been listed as superior, but one person's 'Hessei' may not be the same as another's. Japan and Korea. Introduced 1909. The species is native to Japan. Introduced 1892. Zone 5 to 7.

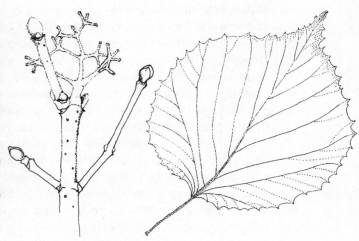

Viburnum farreri — Fragrant Viburnum
(vī-bĕr′num fãr′er-ī)

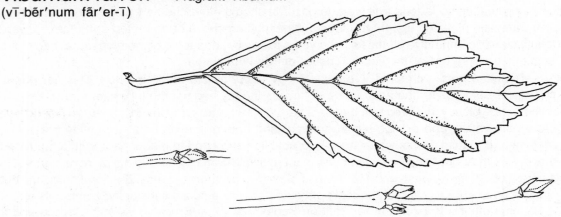

LEAVES: Opposite, simple, obovate or oval, 1 1/2 to 4″ long, 1 to 2 3/4″ wide, acute, broad-cuneate or cuneate, serrate with triangular teeth, sparingly pubescent above and pubescent on veins beneath, finally glabrous or nearly so, with 5 to 6 pairs of veins and the veinlets impressed above and below, dark green; petiole 1/3 to 3/4″ long, purplish.

Viburnum farreri (V. fragrans), Fragrant Viburnum, grows 8 to 12′ tall with a similar spread and is often rather loose, unkempt and unruly. The foliage emerges bronzy-green and matures to dark green in summer changing to reddish purple in fall. The fragrant flowers are pinkish red in bud opening to white tinged with pink, early to mid-April before the leaves, borne in a 1 to 2″ long panicle; one of the earliest viburnums to flower. Fruit colors red, finally black and is effective in July to August but I have never seen a good display. 'Candidissimum' ('Album') has pure white flowers and the leaves do not show the reddish pigment of the species and are much lighter green. 'Nanum' is a dwarf type growing 2 to 3′ tall and 4 to 6′ across with pinkish buds and flowers that fade to pinkish white. The flowers often open in the fall on a rather sporadic basis and push forth full force in spring at the first sign of warm weather. Unfortunately, late frosts wreak havoc on the species and it is seldom that the flowers are not browned to one degree or another. I grew the species in my Illinois garden and enjoyed the foliage more than the flowers which suffered from the vagaries of the midwestern winters. I have had good success rooting the species and 'Candidissimum' from softwood cuttings. *Viburnum × bodnantense* 'Dawn' is a hybrid of *V. f. × V. grandiflorum.* It is pink flowered

'Dawn'

and suffers the same fate as *V. farreri* from the vagaries of weather. It was raised at Bodnant Gardens, Wales about 1935. 'Dawn' receives an unbelievable amount of press for the rather undistinguished but fragrant flowers. Even in England, where it flowers in January, the shrub is valued only for winter wake-up and fragrance value. I have a small plant that flowered in February, 1989 and is worthwhile for cuts for a winter bouquet. Plants in England were 8 to 10′ high so it is by no means "dainty." 'Deben' and 'Charles Lamont' are of the same parentage, the former with shell pink buds opening white with a pink blush; the latter considered better than 'Dawn' with more abundant bright pink flowers. Northern China. Introduced 1910. Zone (4)5 to 8.

Viburnum japonicum — Japanese Viburnum
(vī-bẽr′num ja-pon′i-kum)

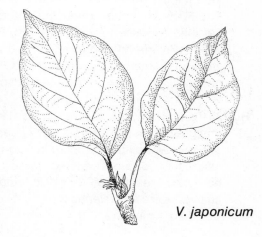

LEAVES: Opposite, simple, evergreen, leathery, ovate to roundish, 3 to 6″ long, half to as wide, abruptly pointed or short acuminate, rounded or tapering, entire or remotely toothed toward apex or wavy, glabrous, dark glossy green above, paler beneath with numerous small black dots; petiole 1/2 to 1 1/4″ long.

V. japonicum

Viburnum japonicum, Japanese Viburnum, is a sturdy evergreen shrub that matures between 10 to 15′ in height. It is extremely dense in habit and would make a fine screen. The lustrous dark green foliage is attractive throughout the seasons. The fragrant, white, 3/8″ wide flowers are produced in 3 to 4 1/2″ diameter, rounded, short-stalked, 7-rayed cymes. The fruit is a 1/3″ long, oval-rounded, red drupe. A small plant in my Zone 8 garden did not fare well and succumbed to cold. At Griffin, GA a 10′ high specimen was killed out-

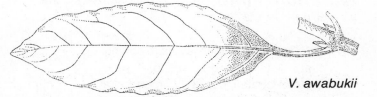

V. awabukii

right at -5 to -10°F during the 1983–84 winter. The viburnum is considered hardy to 0 to -10°F, so the abnormal weather wreaked havoc. Raulston has promoted *Viburnum awabuki* which is a large lustrous dark green leaf form of great beauty. He mentions observing "large pendulous masses (6 to 10″ diameter) of bright red fruits hanging in the 15′ tall plant like ornaments on a Christmas tree." I have a gift plant from Dr. Raulston that over the past two winters (lowest about 10°F) showed no injury. It could be a winner if cold hardy. Several Georgia Nurserymen, most notably Mr. John Barbour, have started to grow the plant. Young field-grown plants are indeed impressive. Unfortunately, the nomenclature of this form is somewhat confusing, being a Japanese continuum of the widely distributed *V. odoratissimum. Hortus III* reduces it to variety *awabuki.* I checked the leaves on the plant in my garden and, indeed, the veins to not run out of the leaf which is characteristic for *V. japonicum.* Perhaps the var. *awabuki* should be more properly classified under *V. odoratissimum.* This is a hand-

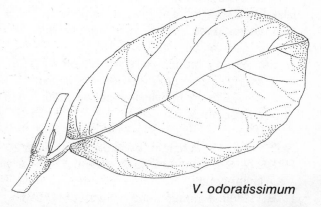

V. odoratissimum

some viburnum and probably best suited to the lower parts of Zone 8 and into 9. It is often confused with *V. odoratissimum* but the young wood is not so warted, the secondary veins run to the margin, and the inflorescence is rounded, cymose rather than paniculate. Japan. Introduced 1879.

RELATED CULTIVARS: An arbitrary system since the following two clones have *V. japonicum* as a common parent and are most logically included here.

'Chippewa' is a hybrid between *V. japonicum* × *V. dilatatum* with semi-evergreen leaves and a dense branched, multistemmed nature; parent plant was 8′ high and 10′ wide after 10 years; leaves are leathery glossy dark green, 2 to 4 1/2″ long, 1 1/2 to 3″ wide, and turn dark maroon to bright red in autumn; the white flowers occur in 4 to 7 1/2″ wide, 5 to 7 rayed cymes containing 200 to 300 flowers per inflorescence; oblong dark red, 3/8″ long, 1/3″ wide fruits ripen in August and persist into winter, no winter damage has occurred at -10°F but foliage is deciduous; have seen young plants and still do not have a good fix on relative landscape worth. Have not been overly impressed.

'Huron' (*V. lobophyllum* × *V. japonicum*) is a semi-evergreen, dense branched, multiple stemmed shrub that grew 7 1/4′ by 9 1/4′ after 17 years; leaves are leathery dull dark green turning rich purple in late autumn; white flowers occur in 4 to 6′ wide, 6 to 7 rayed cymes containing 250 to 400 florets per inflorescence; ovoid dark red, 1/4 to 1/3″ long, 1/3″ wide fruits ripen in August and persist into winter; hardy to at least −10°F at which temperature it will be deciduous; for additional information on both cultivars see *HortScience* 22:174–176 (1987). Based on the article, 'Huron' has a narrow, more ovate leaf than 'Chippewa'.

Viburnum lantana — Wayfaringtree Viburnum
(vī-bẽr′num lan-tā′na)

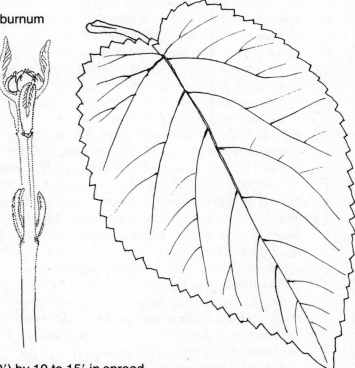

LEAVES: Opposite, simple, ovate to oblong-ovate, 2 to 5″ long, 1 1/2 to 4″ wide, acute or obtuse, cordate to rounded at base, rather closely denticulate, dark green and sparingly stellate-pubescent and wrinkled above, stellate-tomentose beneath; petiole 1/2 to 1 1/2″ in long; very uniform serrations and a strong reticulate venation pattern are good identification features.

BUDS: Naked, foliose, grayish tomentose; flower buds similar to *V. carlesii* but larger and coarser.

STEM: Young branches light gray-brown, scurfy pubescent, older branches gray, usually heavily lenticelled, stout, coarse, thick.

SIZE: 10 to 15′ in height (possibly as large as 20′) by 10 to 15′ in spread.

HARDINESS: Zone (3)4 to 8, does not appear vigorous in Zone 8, in fact not well suited in the mid and lower south.

HABIT: Multistemmed shrub with stout spreading branches, usually rounded in outline.

RATE: Medium.

TEXTURE: Medium in leaf, often quite ragged in winter habit, appearing coarse.

LEAF COLOR: Dull dark green (almost a bluish green), leaves quite pubescent below and somewhat leathery in texture; fall color tends toward purplish red; however, very inconsistent in midwest and east, often poor.

FLOWERS: White, no fragrance, actually creamy due to numerous yellow stamens, early to mid-May, 10 to 14 days, borne in 3 to 5″ diameter flat-topped cymes; flowers profusely in midwest and one of the better viburnums for that area.

FRUIT: Drupe, 1/3″ long, yellow changing to red and finally black, often all colors present in same infructescence, August to late September, outstanding attribute of this plant; I have noticed that fruit set is best when several different clones are in close proximity.

CULTURE: Fibrous rooted, readily transplanted; withstands calcareous and dry soils better than other viburnums; sun or 1/2 shade; prefers well-drained, loamy situation.

DISEASES AND INSECTS: None serious.

LANDSCAPE VALUE: Used for hedges, screens, massing, shrub border; foliage persists until November in parts of midwest; winter coarseness should be considered before this species is used extensively.

CULTIVARS:

'Aureum'—The young shoots rather handsome golden yellow, later becoming green; have seen on occasion, not too offensive.

'Mohican'—A seedling selected in 1956 from a population frown from *V. lantana* seed received from Poland. The plant, as a deciduous shrub, was selected for compact growth habit; thick dark green leaves; fruit that turns orange-red and maintains an effective display for 4 or more weeks; and resistance to bacterial leaf spot. The creamy-white flowers and expanding pale green leaves appear together for a week in early May. The orange-red fruit begins to ripen in early July and remains effective for 4 or more weeks, whereas fruits on other *V. l.* plants pass rapidly from red to black. The original specimen in 15 years had grown 8 1/2′ high and 9′ wide. An Egolf introduction and has become extremely propular in the nursery trade.

'Rugosum'—Leathery leaf form with larger, darker green leaves which are more handsome than those of the species; tends to become open and rather ragged with age.

PROPAGATION: Cuttings, softwood, root easily. This species is often grown from seed.

NATIVE HABITAT: Europe, western Asia, occasionally escaped from cultivation in eastern United States. Long cultivated.

Viburnum lentago — Nannyberry Viburnum, Sheepberry
(vī-bēr′num len-tā′gō)

LEAVES: Opposite, simple, ovate to elliptic-obovate, 2 to 4″ long, half as wide, acuminate, broad cuneate to rounded at base, finely toothed, lustrous dark green and glabrous above, glabrous or scurfy on the veins beneath; petiole—1/2 to 1″ long, mostly winged with wavy margin.

BUDS: Vegetative-valvate in nature, long pointed, slightly curved, lead-gray in color; flower buds—fat at base and tapering to a long point, both about 1″ long.

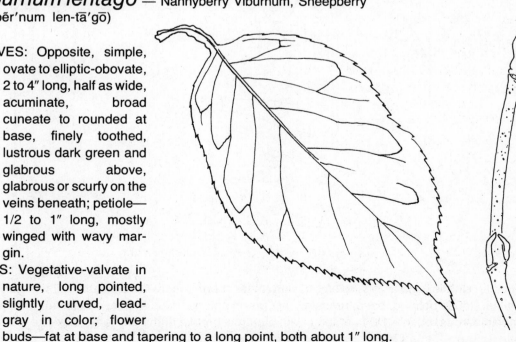

STEM: Slightly pubescent to essentially glabrous, brownish in color.

SIZE: 15 to 18' possibly to 30' in height, spread quite variable, often 6 to 10' and more.
HARDINESS: Zone 2 to 8, seldon grown in Zone 8.
HABIT: Shrub or small tree with slender finally arching branches, somewhat open at maturity, often suckering.
RATE: Medium.
TEXTURE: Medium in leaf, medium-coarse in winter.
LEAF COLOR: Soft yellow-green when unfolding, gradually changing to glossy dark green; fall color develops purplish red but is not guaranteed, often poor green and falls off as such.
FLOWERS: White, appearing creamy due to yellow stamens, early to mid May, 7 to 10 days, borne in 3 to 4 1/2" diameter, flat-topped cymes; flower is good but color is typical of many viburnums.
FRUIT: Drupe, oval, 1/2" long, bluish black, bloomy, September to October and often December; common name is derived from smell of the fruits; the color actually starts out green and in the coarse of maturation may show tinges of yellow, rose and pink before finally becoming bluish black; actually most handsome in the early stages of coloring.
CULTURE: Fibrous rooted, transplants readily, often suckers profusely forming a thicket; adaptable to a wide range of conditions; sun or shade; native species of great durability; moist or dry soils.
DISEASES AND INSECTS: Often covered with mildew especially when grown in shaded area; usually no serious problems are encountered.
LANDSCAPE VALUE: Ideal shrub for naturalizing, works well in shrub borders, as a background or screen plant and limitedly for specimen use; good winter food for the birds.
CULTIVARS: 'Pink Beauty' has pink fruits maturing to violet; I have never seen the cultivar but Krüssmann mentions that it is quite attractive.
PROPAGATION: Seed, 150 to 270 days at 68 to 86°F fluctuating temperatures followed by 60 to 120 days at 41°F. Cuttings, softwood; from personal experience this species roots easily from softwood cuttings.
NATIVE HABITAT: Hudson Bay to Manitoba, south to Georgia and Mississippi. Introduced 1761.

Viburnum opulus — European Cranberrybush Viburnum
(vī-bēr'num op'ū-lus)

LEAVES: Opposite, simple, similar to *V. trilobum,* with rather shorter, more-toothed lobes, 2 to 4" long, as wide or wider, lobes pointed, base truncate, dark green and glabrous above, pubescent beneath or sometimes glabrous; petiole 1/2 to 1" long, with a narrow groove and a few large disk-like glands of a concave nature.

BUDS: Plump, 2 scaled, green-red-brown, glabrous, shiny, scales connate (fused at edges).
STEM: Light gray-brown, glabrous, smooth, ribbed, rather stout.

SIZE: 8 to 12' possibly 15' in height, spread 10 to 15'.
HARDINESS: Zone 3 to 8.
HABIT: Upright, spreading, multistemmed shrub, often with arching branches to the ground creating a rounded habit.
RATE: Medium.
TEXTURE: Medium in foliage; medium to coarse in winter, can look "ratty" in winter.
LEAF COLOR: Good glossy dark green in summer, changing to yellow-red and reddish purple in fall; not a consistent fall coloring shrub, often leaves show no change, simply falling off green.
FLOWERS: White, outer ring of 3/4" diameter flowers sterile and showy, inner flowers fertile and inconspicuous, anthers yellow, creating a pin-wheel effect, May, borne in 2 to 3" diameter, flat-topped cymes, flowers are handsome and interesting because of unique combination of sterile and fertile flowers in same inflorescence.
FRUIT: Berry-like drupe, bright red, ripening in September-October and persisting into winter, each fruit is about 1/4" diameter and globose in shape; the fruits often shrivel through the winter months and take on the appearance of dried red raisins.
CULTURE: Transplant balled and burlapped, one of the easiest viburnums to grow; adaptable to extremes of soil and in its native haunts is particularly rampant in wet or boggy situations; pH adaptable; large canes should be thinned out; fruits best in full sun but will stand partial shade.
DISEASES AND INSECTS: Often infested with aphids (plant lice) but this is more common on the cultivar 'Roseum'; can be controlled with malathion or similar compounds; borer has been a problem in the midwest.
LANDSCAPE VALUE: Shrub border, screen, large areas, massing, excellent for its showy flower and fruit display; the following cultivars are excellent landscape plants.
CULTIVARS:
'Aureum'—New growth a reasonably good yellow but soon fading to rather sickly yellow-green, the color is either lost or the foliage may burn in hot climates, slower growing than the species, rather limited landscape appeal, flowers and fruits like the species, to 12' high, needs some shade.
'Compactum'—Excellent plant where space is limited, 1/2 the size of the species in height and extremely dense in habit, excellent in flower and fruit, fruit makes a brilliant show; excellent in masses, probably should be considered over the species in the smaller, more restricted planting areas of the modern landscape; have been told that stem borers can be a problem, very fine plant when properly grown.
'Nanum'—Dwarf form, much branched and dense, 18 to 24" in height and 1 1/2 times that in spread; I have seen specimens between 4 and 5' high; supposedly never flowers or fruits but, again, I have seen several isolated flowering and fruiting specimens, makes a good filler or facer plant; can be used for low hedges; will not withstand wet, poorly drained conditions, and in wet weather contracts significant leaf spot; leaves range from 3/4 to 1 1/2" in width.

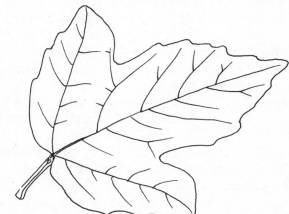

'Notcutt'—More vigorous than the species with larger flowers, fruits and excellent maroon-red fall color.
'Roseum'—The European Snowball or Guilder-rose, a form with sterile flowers which is extremely showy in flower; the 2 1/2 to 3" diameter inflorescences literally cover the shrub in mid-May (mid

to late April, Athens); an old favorite more apt to be located around older residences; aphids infest this form quite heavily and often distort the young leaves and stems; the flowers are an apple green in the early stages and change to white, they remain effective for a long period; a 20-year-old specimen in Fargo, N.D. showed no dieback although temperatures dropped as low as -30°F; there is a reported pink-flowered form but this I have not observed; sometimes the aging inflorescence assumes a slight pink tinge, also listed as 'Sterile', known since the 16th century, grows 10 to 12′ high, vigorous form.

'Xanthocarpum'—Form with yellowish gold fruits, quite attractive, and often persistent; a nice color compliment to the red-fruited type; have seen in England on several occasions, worth considering, will grow 8 to 10′ high; 'Fructo-luteo' with lemon-yellow fruits is listed.

PROPAGATION: Seed, 60 to 90 days at fluctuating temperatures of 68 to 86°F followed by 30 to 60 days at 41°F. Cuttings are easy to root. I have had 100% success with softwood and greenwood cuttings.

NATIVE HABITAT: Europe, northern Africa and northern Asia.

Viburnum plicatum var. *tomentosum* — Doublefile Viburnum
(vī-bēr′num plī-kā′tum var. tō-men-tō′sum)

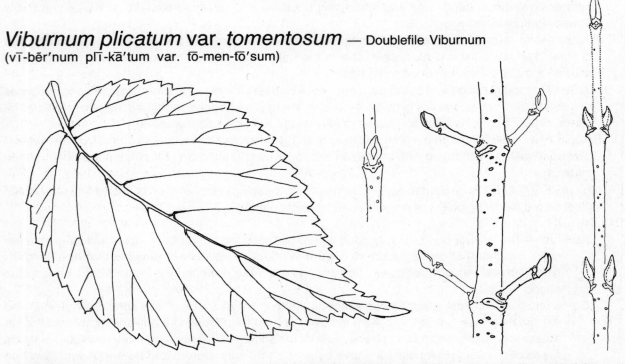

LEAVES: Opposite, simple, broad-ovate to oblong-ovate, sometimes elliptic-obovate, 2 to 4″(5″) long, 1 to 2 1/2″ wide, acute or abruptly acuminate, rounded to broad-cuneate to cordate, dentate-serrate, dark green and nearly glabrous above, stellate-pubescent beneath, with 8 to 12 pairs of nearly straight veins; petiole—1/2 to 1″ long.

BUDS: Vegetative buds-naked, foliose, pubescent; flower buds—valvate, angular, tan-brown, hairy, appressed to stem or divergent.

STEM: Young branches stellate tomentose; older branches dark gray or brownish, orangish lenticels, many small branches (2 at node) forming a fishbone effect.

SIZE: 8 to 10′ in height, usually slightly wider than tall at maturity (9 to 12′), one old plant at Bicton outside Bristol, England, was 10′ tall and 20′ wide; have seen this plant run the gamut in terms of size.

HARDINESS: Zone 5 to 8.

HABIT: Horizontal, tiered branching, creating a stratified effect, appearing rounded to broad-rounded at maturity.

RATE: Medium.

TEXTURE: Medium in foliage, medium in winter, can prove quite handsome in winter because of clean grayish brown branches and horizontal habit.

LEAF COLOR: Leaves emerge early, often by the first or second week of March in Athens, GA; dark green with maturity, veins are impressed creating a ridge-furrow effect; fall color is consistent reddish purple, leaves are borne opposite along the stems and tend to hang down creating a "dog-eared" effect.

FLOWERS: White, no fragrance, outer flowers sterile, 4 to 5 lobes, 3/4 to 1 1/2" wide, pure snow white; inner flowers fertile, not showy, May (mid-April, Athens), borne in 2 to 4" (up to 6") diameter flat-topped cymes which are borne on 2" long peduncles above the foliage creating a milky way effect along the horizontal branches; a choice specimen of Doublefile Viburnum is without equal.

FRUIT: Drupe, egg-shaped, 1/3" long, bright red changing to black, July and August, usually devoured by birds before completely ripened; one of the earliest viburnums to display excellent fruit color.

CULTURE: Fibrous rooted, transplants well, demands moist, well-drained soil; from my own observations this plant will not tolerate heavy, clayey, poorly drained soils; I have grown well-branched, 3 to 4' high specimens in two growing seasons from cuttings without special care; at a recent lecture received several comments about stem dieback which does occasionally occur; old overgrown or ratty specimens on campus are cut back to 12" from the ground and rejuvenate quite nicely; in Zone 8 the plant is spectacular in April and May but heat and drought of the summer often induce marginal leaf necrosis; some shade and supplemental water are recommended in the south.

DISEASES AND INSECTS: None serious, although I have observed stem dieback in wet areas; I am not sure if the problem was of a pathological or physiological nature.

LANDSCAPE VALUE: Possibly the most elegant of flowering shrubs; easily the biggest resides at Swarthmore College, fully 15 to 18' high and 20' or more wide; A choice specimen when placed near red brick buildings where the snow-white flowers are accentuated; massing, screen, shrub border; blends well into a border as the horizontal lines break up the monotony of upright growing shrubs; could be integrated into foundation plantings especially corner plantings where it would help to soften vertical lines and make the house appear longer; I witnessed tremendous winter kill during the difficult winters of 1976–77, 77–78 throughout the midwest (-20 to -25°F); large, well established, 8 to 10' high plants in the President's Garden on the Illinois campus were killed; I am estimating the break point for injury in the -15°F or lower range.

CULTIVARS: The species, *V. plicatum,* Japanese Snowball Viburnum, by all botanical standards, should not be considered as such since it possesses sterile, 2 to 3" diameter white flowers and, hence, cannot reproduce itself since fruits are not formed and therefore does not fit the definition of a species. Similar in all respects to Doublefile except for carnation-like snowball flowers and upright growth hahbit to 15' high. The flowers are borne in 2-ranks along the arching branches and make a spectacular show in May for 2 to 2 1/2 weeks. This has proven to be an excellent plant for Zone 8 conditions provided there is ample root moisture. Several plants on the Georgia campus are 15' high and wide and are spectacular when they flower. Generally, flowers 2 to 3 weeks later than *V. p.* var. *tomentosum.*

'Chyverton'—Low wide spreading habit, flowers all sterile as in typical *V. plicatum,* a mature plant grew 4' high and 20' wide in 24 years; at Stourhead, England, there is also a relatively low growing, wide spreading form with abundant flowers; this form might be welcome in American gardens since the principal form in cultivation is upright, large and coarse.

'Grandiflorum'—A fine form with abundant, slightly larger flower heads than *V. plicatum;* the plants I have seen showed an accentuated horizontal branching pattern; this form is worth seeking out.

'Roseace'—Selected and introduced around 1953 by Carl Kern of Wyoming Nursery, Cincinnati, Ohio for its medium-pink flower and bronze tinged foliage; plants I have seen appeared less vigorous than the species; there is some indication that the pink color results from aging and soil conditions. I believe this is the same as 'Kern's Pink' and 'Pink Sensation', as I saw 'Kern's Pink' the color was on off-pink with some inflorescences pink, others white and still others mixed.

'Rotundifolium'—A form with round leaves which are 1 to 2" long and 1 to 1 1/2" wide; it is more refined than *V. plicatum.*

V. p. var. *tomentosum* types:

'Cascade'—A seedling of 'Rowallane' with wide spreading branches, ultimately taller than 'Mariesii'; inflorescences umbrella-shaped, 2 1/2 to 4″ across, with large sterile outer flowers, red fruits are produced in abundance, good burgundy fall color.

'Lanarth'—Larger flowered from than typical doublefile with strong horizontal branching habit, ray flowers up to 2″ diameter and larger, is probably confused with 'Mariesii'; as I have observed it a very beautiful selection, 12 to 14′ by 12 to 14′.

'Mariesii'—Ray flowers large, up to 1 3/4″ diameter, raised on a 2 1/2″ high peduncle that brings the flowers above the foliage; habit is distinctly horizontal and a plant in full flower is a magnificent sight; the leaves may turn reddish purple in fall, this form is available in commerce; introduced in the late 1870's, I have read accounts that state 'Mariesii' is the best fruiting form and also that fruit is sparsely set; I have not resolved this discrepancy in my own mind; like many viburnums lack of fruit set may be due to absence of cross pollinator; leaves perhaps lighter green in summer than other types; many plants offered as 'Mariesii' are, in fact, something else; lower growing than 'Lanarth'.

'Nanum Semperflorens' ('Watanabei')—A compact form introduced from Wada's nursery in Japan; habit dense, flowers smaller than the type but making a good display; may grow 5 to 6′ high, flowers on and off through summer, sparse fruit set.

'Newport' ('Nanum Newport')—I know very little about this form but have seen it a number of places in the midwest; the habit is extremely dense, mounded, with smaller dark green leaves than the species that turn burgundy in fall; flowers are produced sparingly; probably 5 to 6′ by 5 to 6′.

'Pink Beauty'—Handsome form with pink petals; the only specimen I have observed had leaves and flowers slightly smaller than doublefile but the deep pink petal color was outstanding; somewhat upright in habit, generally smaller in all its parts, flower color develops as petals age.

'Roseum'—The sterile flowers open white and gradually fade to an excellent deep pink, smaller leaf, less vigorous than the type; in several respects 'Pink Beauty' and 'Roseum' are similar and may be one and the same; from Brooklyn Botanic Garden.

'Rowallane'—Less vigorous than 'Lanarth' and 'Mariesii' with smaller, broadly ovate, short acuminate leaves; flowers not as wide but the ray-florets are still large and form a uniform circle around the sparse, fertile inner flowers; supposedly fruits heavier than 'Mariesii'; selected before 1942 in Rowallane Park, Northern Ireland.

'Shasta'—A tremendous new (1979) introduction from the U.S. National Arboretum and Don Egolf's breeding program; it is a broad, horizontally branched shrub being 6′ high and about 10 to 12′ wide at maturity; the abundant, 4 to 6″ wide inflorescences have sterile, marginal, pure white florets about 1 1/4 to 2″ wide and 5 to 15, 1/2 to 1 1/2″ wide, inner florets dispersed among the fertile flowers; the flowers are followed in July by bright red maturing to black fruits; this is an excellent plant and should become extremely popular as it becomes better advertised, see *HortScience* 14(1):78–79, 1979, for additional information; for the past 5 years I have nurtured a supposed specimen of 'Shasta' into a 7′ by 8′ specimen only to decide it was just the species or a cheap imitation; my garden heart was broken especially when I saw the real McCoy with wide-spreading horizontally accentuated branches and immense inflorescences that literally smothered the leaves; in the south what is being passed as 'Shasta' is anything but.

'Shoshoni'—A seedling of 'Shasta' with all the attributes of that form on a smaller scale; in 17 years the parent plant was 5′ high and 8′ wide; the dark green leaves are 2 1/2 to 6″ long, 1 1/4 to 2 1/2″ wide, and turn dull purplish red in fall; the flowers occur in 3 to 5″ wide flat topped cymes in April-May; the 5 to 7 outer sterile showy florets average 3/4 to 1 1/4″ long and 1 to 1 3/4″ wide with 50 to 130 greenish white perfect flowers in the center; the ovoid 1/3″ long, 1/5″ wide drupe ripens red and matures to black; will be hardy to at least -5°F; a Don Egolf/National Arboretum introduction, see *HortScience* 21:1077–1078 (1986) for additional information.

'St. Keverne'—Large form like var. *tomentosum,* 10 to 12′ high and wide, inflorescences umbrella-shaped, seldom produces fruit; better than typical species.

'Summer Stars' ('Fujisanensis')—Also may be the same as 'Nanum Semperflorens' and 'Watanabei'; the University of British Columbia Botanical Garden has gone overboard renaming plants to suit marketing needs; I am thoroughly confused and have a hunch that all names may lead to the same plant; Tsk! Tsk! to such a fine institution; definitely more compact (4 to 6' at maturity) than the type with a continuum of flowers from April into November in the south; have seen photographs and must admit it is a handsome plant deserving of garden consideration; supposedly sets good quantities of bright red fruits but has not done so with regularity in the south.

'Triumph'—More compact form, 3 to 4' high and 3 to 4' wide, white typical flowers, few fruits, Lake County introduction; could there be a rename?

PROPAGATION: Cuttings—I have taken cuttings throughout the growing season and achieved 100% success with 1000 ppm IBA, peat: perlite, mist; one of the easiest viburnums to root.

NATIVE HABITAT: China, Japan. Introduced 1865; the sterile form in 1844 by Robert Fortune.

Viburnum prunifolium — Blackhaw Viburnum
(vī-bēr'num prū-ni-fō'li-um)

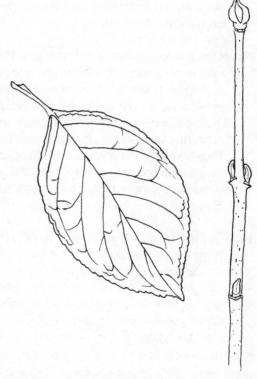

LEAVES: Opposite, simple, broad-elliptic to ovate, 1 1/2 to 3 1/2" long, 1 to 2" wide, acute or obtuse, rounded at base or broad-cuneate, serrulate, lustrous dark green above, pale below, glabrous or nearly so; petiole not narrowly winged, 1/3 to 3/4" long, reddish.

BUDS: Vegetative and flower buds short pointed, valvate, lead colored, about 1/2" long, flower buds with a bulbous base.

STEM: Glabrous, usually short and stiff in nature, gray-brown, side branches present a hawthorn-like appearance.

SIZE: 12 to 15' in height by 8 to 12' in width, can grow 20 to 30' high.

HARDINESS: Zone 3 to 9.

HABIT: Round headed tree or multistemmed shrub, stiffly branched, similar to *Crataegus* in growth habit; Robinson described this species as a "puritan with a rigidity of character similar to some of the hawthorns"; have seen 20 to 25' high plants in tree form that were quite handsome.

RATE: Slow to medium.

TEXTURE: Medium in leaf; handsomely coarse in winter.

LEAF COLOR: Dark green, handsome, clean foliage in summer changing to purplish to reddish purple in the fall; various authorities have described the fall color as shining red, dull deep red to bronze; variable from plant to plant.

FLOWERS: White, actually creamy due to numerous yellow stamens, May, borne in 2 to 4" diameter, flat-topped cymes; not overwhelming but certainly attractive.

FRUIT: Drupe, oval, up to 1/2" long, pinkish, rose and at maturity bluish black, bloomy, September through fall, fruit is palatable and has been used for preserves since colonial days.

CULTURE: Transplants well, adaptable to many soil types; sun or shade; does well in dry soils.

DISEASES AND INSECTS: None serious.

LANDSCAPE VALUE: Interesting as a small specimen tree, massing, shrub border, groupings; habit is somewhat similar to hawthorns.

NATIVE HABITAT: Connecticut to Florida, west to Michigan and Texas. Introduced 1727.

RELATED SPECIES:

Viburnum rufidulum—Rusty Blackhaw Viburnum
(vī-bēr′num rū-fid′ū-lum)

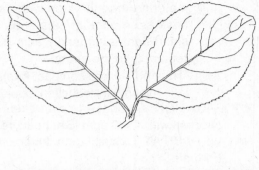

LEAVES: Opposite, simple, oval, ovate to obovate, 2 to 4″
    long, 1 to 1 1/2″ wide, sometimes almost as wide as
    long, obtuse, broad cuneate to almost rounded,
    leathery, serrulate, lustrous dark green above, pubes-
    cent below initially, finally glabrous; petiole 1/4 to 1/2″
    long, more or less winged, with rusty pubescence.
BUDS: Much like *Viburnum prunifolium* in shape and size
    but covered with short, dense rusty brown hairs that set this species apart from the closely allied *V.
    prunifolium* and *V. lentago*.

Viburnum rufidulum, Southern or Rusty Blackhaw, has handsome lustrous dark green leathery foliage,
    more pubescent plant parts, and is slightly less hardy (Zone 5 to 9) than the above species; worthwhile
    specimen where it can be grown. I have developed a real fondness for this species and found it wild
    in the Athens, GA environs. The buds are covered with a deep rich rusty brown pubescence which
    distinguishes it from any viburnum in this book. The habit can be shrubby or tree-like and larger
    branches develop a blocky, *Cornus florida*-like bark. The leaves may turn a rich burgundy in fall.
    Excellent plant and should be used more widely. Will grow 10 to 20′ high under typical landscape
    conditions but may reach 30 to 40′ in the wild. Occurs as an understory plant in the Piedmont of
    Georgia and tends toward an open habit in such locations. In full sun, it becomes more dense.

Viburnum × rhytidophylloides — Lantanaphyllum Viburnum
A hybrid of *V. lantana × V. rhytidophyllum*.
(vī-bēr′num ×   rī-tī-dō-fil-oy′dēz)

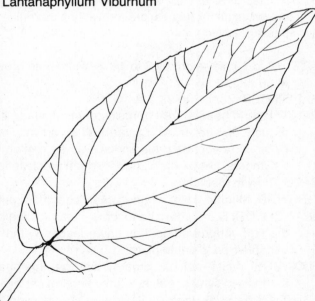

Similar to *V. rhytidophyllum* except leaves
broader and less rugose, not as elongated and
a degree less dark green and leathery. Another
good trait is the flower bud which is tightly
clustered like a cauliflower where *V.
rhytidophyllum* is larger and looser. Usually
deciduous.

SIZE: 8 to 10′, possibly 15′ in height, spread
    would probably equal height at maturity;
    robust shrub often exceeding the first
    mentioned size range.
HARDINESS: Zone 4 to 8 depending on cul-
    tivar.
HABIT: Upright, spreading shrub with slightly
    arching branches; eventually somewhat rounded in outline; large, robust and coarse.
RATE: Medium.
TEXTURE: Medium to coarse in summer and winter.
LEAF COLOR: Dark leathery green above, light gray to gray-brown and extremely tomentose beneath,
    the foliage has a bold coarseness which is quite attractive, leaves hold late often into November.
FLOWERS: White (creamy), borne in 3 to 4″ diameter flat-topped cymes; flowers in early to mid-April in
    Athens; mid-May, Urbana, IL.

FRUIT: Drupe, reddish changing to black, late August through September into fall, can be excellent depending on cultivar and the presence of a pollinator; actually much like *V. lantana* in color transformations.

CULTURE: Transplants well, adaptable; sun or partial shade; best sited in a protected location; much hardier than *V. rhytidophyllulm;* has performed well in the heat of Zone 8; can be located in full sun with good success.

LANDSCAPE VALUE: Possibly should replace *V. lantana* because of excellent foliage; could be utilized for screen, foundation plant, blended with other broad-leaf evergreens; I had never seen a good fruiting specimen prior to 1977; since that time I have observed some magnificent specimens with a fruit character not unlike that of *V. lantana,* i.e., yellow-red-black; I have noticed that if *V. lantana, V. rhytidophyllum* and other clones of *V. × rhytidophylloides* are close, fruit set is significantly better; many viburnums must be cross pollinated for good fruit set to occur; planting several plants of the same clone is not the answer.

CULTIVARS:

'Alleghany'—A selection from an F$_2$ *V. rhytidophyllum × V. lantana* 'Mohican' seedling population in 1958. Plants have very dark green, coriaceous leaves; abundant inflorescences; resistance to bacterial leaf spot; hardiness; and vigorous, dense, globose growth habit. The foliage, which tends to be deciduous to semi-persistent, is intermediate between the patental species. It is smaller than *V. r.,* and is more leathery than *V. l.* The rugose, coriaceous leaves are resistant to leaf spot and are highly ornamental. The abundant, yellowish white inflorescences in May are effectively displayed above the dark green foliage. For several weeks in September and October the fruit becomes brilliant red as ripening advances to black at maturity. In 13 years the original plant has attained a height of 10 1/2′ and a spread of 11′. This has proven to be an outstanding selection and is being successfully grown as far north as the University of Minnesota Landscape Arboretum although is not perfectly cold hardy. Has been a stalwart in Zone 8 but little known or grown. It is so superior to normal *V. lantana* that I do not understand the reasons for planting that species; a Don Egolf/U.S. National Arboretum introduction.

'Holland'—Only presented here for historical purposes; it was apparently one of the first named hybrids between the two species; raised about 1925.

'Willowwood'—A form with excellent lustrous rugose foliage and arching habit. Has performed admirably in the midwest. Has at times come through the winter with foliage in good condition. I have seen this cultivar flowering in October on the Purdue University campus at West Lafayette, Indiana. Result of a cross made by Henry Tubbs of Willowwood Farm, Gladstone, New Jersey.

PROPAGATION: Cuttings, softwood and greenwood, 1000 ppm IBA solution, rooted 100%; the cultivars are extremely easy to root from cuttings.

Viburnum rhytidophyllum — Leatherleaf Viburnum
(vī-bēr′num rī-tī-dō-fil′um)

LEAVES: Opposite, simple, evergreen, ovate-oblong to ovate-lanceolate, 3 to 7″ long, 1 to 2 1/2″ wide, acute or obtuse, rounded or subcordate at base, entire or obscurely denticulate, lustrous dark green, glabrous and strongly wrinkled above, prominently reticulate beneath and gray or yellowish tomentose; petiole—1/2 to 1 1/4″ long.

BUDS: Vegetative—large, rusty colored, tomentose, foliose; flower buds borne in semi-rounded cymes, 1 1/2 to 2″ across, evident throughout winter and rather open compared to *V. × rhytidophylloides.*

STEM: Gray to brown in color with stellate pubescence on young stems, older stems glabrous.

SIZE: 10 to 15′ in height with a similar spread.

HARDINESS: Zone 5 to 8, although in severe winters will be killed to the ground; usually develops new shoots the following spring as the roots are not injured; -10 to -15°F is about the break point.

HABIT: Upright, strongly multistemmed shrub, often somewhat open with age, usually upright-rounded in outline.

RATE: Medium.

TEXTURE: Coarse throughout the year.

LEAF COLOR: Dark lustrous leathery green above, gray to brownish tomentose beneath, essentially evergreen in the north and with proper siting (in a micro-climate) will maintain most of its foliage; evergreen in the south.

FLOWERS: Yellowish white, mid May (mid April, Athens), borne in 4 to 8″ diameter, 7 to 11 rayed, flat-topped cymes; the color is not outstanding but the quantity and size of the flowers are ornamental assets; the naked flower buds are formed in July-August-September of the year prior to flowering and are interesting because of large cymes on which they are borne; flowers are slightly fragrant.

FRUIT: Drupe, oval, 1/3″ long, red changing to black, September, October through December; prior to 1973 I had never observed good fruiting on this species; in 1973 I found three specimens on the north side of a house in Urbana, Illinois, literally weighted down with beautiful red fruits; often viburnums are self-sterile and do not fruit heavily unless different clones are present; perhaps what I stumbled upon are three clones of Leatherleaf.

CULTURE: Transplants well, well-drained soil aids hardiness; shelter from wind and winter sun, tolerates heavy shade (3/4's); −10°F will injure leaves; best where it is offered some protection; prune to ground to rejuvenate.

DISEASES AND INSECTS: None serious.

LANDSCAPE VALUE: Excellent specimen where it can be grown without coddling; blends well with other broadleaf evergreens; possibly massing or as a background plant; everything is relative in life and even my great emotional ties to viburnums have influenced me unfairly in appraising the merits of this shrub; in the north it was welcome for the reasons enumerated; in the south the competition is so ferocious from other broadleaf shrubs that it is second class; I refuse to part with a 10′ high plant in my garden that my wife, Bonnie, loathes.

CULTIVARS:

var. *roseum*—Has pink flower buds that open yellowish white; have seen this form in England and indeed the buds are an attractive pink.

'Variegatum'—I had high hopes for this creamy white irregularly variegated shrub but after seeing it in England a few times, came away disappointed; the plant reverts and it is often difficult to locate the variegated leaves; for the collector who has time to prune away the green shoots.

PROPAGATION: Cuttings, I have taken firm cuttings throughout the growing season and achieved 100% success; use 1000 to 3000 ppm IBA to improve rooting.

NATIVE HABITAT: Central and western China. Introduced 1900.

RELATED SPECIES:

Viburnum × pragense, (vī-bēr′num prag-en′sē), Prague Viburnum, is the result of a cross between *V. rhytidophyllum* and *V. utile.* It is an attractive evergreen shrub with lustrous, dark green, elliptic, 2 to 4″ long leaves. The flowers are pink in bud, opening creamy-white, slightly fragrant and produced in terminal 3 to 6″ wide, essentially flat-topped

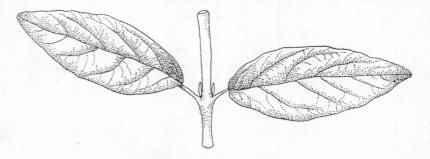

cymes in mid April in Athens. This hybrid was raised in Prague in the 1950's and is extremely hardy. There was a plant in the woody plant test plots at the Univeristy of Illinois which help up well under the rigors of midwestern winters. It survived -6°F in the Arnold Arboretum without foliage discoloration. I observed severe leaf burn (no stem or bud damage) at Spring Grove after exposure to -17°F. It will grow 10' or more and is suited to culture in Zone 5 to 8. It definitely looks like a good plant for the future. It is easily propagated from softwood cuttings. The species has received considerable attention in the mid to lower south and is now grown by several major nurseries. The habit is upright oval to oval-rounded. The growth extensions are so vigorous that they must be pruned to achieve reasonable density. Extremely fast growing and makes a good screen, grouping or accent plant. Has much more ornamental charm than *V. rhytidophyllum* and based on my observations is hardier than either parent. In fact, in the Arnold Arboretum's viburnum collection, *V.* × *pragense* was 8 to 10' high, *V. rhytidophyllum*—a die-back shrub and *V. utile*-did not exist.

Viburnum sargentii — Sargent Viburnum
(vī-bĕr′num sär-gen′tē-ī)

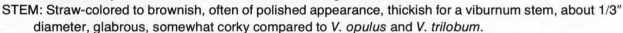

LEAVES: Opposite, simple, similar to *V. opulus* but of thicker texture and often larger, 2 to 5″ long, the upper ones usually with much elongated entire middle lobe and short spreading lateral lobes, sometimes oblong-lanceolate and without lobes, medium to dark green and glabrous above, lighter beneath and slightly pubescent below; petiole 3/4 to 1 3/4″ long with large disk-like glands, pinkish or reddish in color.

BUDS: Oblong or flask-shaped, mostly appressed, scurfy, scales closely valvate or connate as a closed sac, green to red in color.

STEM: Straw-colored to brownish, often of polished appearance, thickish for a viburnum stem, about 1/3″ diameter, glabrous, somewhat corky compared to *V. opulus* and *V. trilobum.*

SIZE: 12 to 15' high and 12 to 15' in width.

HARDINESS: Zone 3 to 7.

HABIT: Multistemmed upright-rounded to rounded shrub of relatively coarse texture; somewhat similar to *V. opulus* but not as handsome.

RATE: Medium, I noticed a specimen at Purdue's Horticultural Park which exhibited extreme vigor.

TEXTURE: Would have to be rated coarse in all seasons.

LEAF COLOR: New spring growth often bronze-purple; medium to dark green in summer; often assuming yellowish to reddish tones in fall.

FLOWERS: White, borne in flat-topped 3 to 4″ diameter cymes on 1 to 2″ long stalks; sterile outer flowers about 1″ or slightly greater in diameter; the anthers are purple and differ from the yellow anthers of *V. opulus,* May.

FRUIT: Scarlet, 1/2″ long, globose, berry-like drupe; effective in August through October.

CULTURE: Similar to other viburnums especially *V. opulus;* definitely not heat tolerant and is best suited to colder climates.

DISEASES AND INSECTS: None particularly serious.

LANDSCAPE VALUE: More vigorous than *V. opulus* and more resistant to aphids; interesting species but a degree too coarse in comparison to other viburnums with similar ornamental characters; the fruits are excellent and of a bright, translucent red, lasting well into winter.

CULTIVARS:

'Flavum'—A type with yellow anthers and golden yellow translucent fruits; Wyman has an interesting anecdote concerning a trial he conducted growing seedlings from the yellow-fruited form, he noted that many seedlings showed yellowish leaf petioles and others reddish; the seedlings with yellowish petioles fall colored yellowish green; those with reddish petioles fall colored red. Obviously the fruit will also follow the same trends exhibited in petiole color.

'Onondaga'—A U.S. National introduction distinguished by the velvety, fine-textured, dark maroon young foliage that maintains a maroon tinge when mature; flowers in 2 to 5″ diameter flat topped cymes, buds red, opening creamy white with a trace of pink, with 10 to 17 outer, 1 1/4 to 1 3/4″ wide, sterile florets; the red fruits are sparsely produced; forms a globose shrub 6′ high and wide, introduced 1966, probably will grow larger than original size description.

'Susquehanna'—A U.S. National introduction best described as a select *V. sargentii* with a heavy-branched, corky trunk; coriaceous, dark green foliage; abundant flowers and fruits; and upright growth habit; appeared as a seedling in population of 209 raised from seed obtained from Province Matsu, Hondo, Japan; it is a large shrub (12 to 15′ high) approximating the species in size; I have seen it in fruit and the effect is striking; probably too large for the average landscape but good for parks, campuses and large areas.

PROPAGATION: Easily propagated by cuttings. Seed probably possesses a double dormancy similar to *V. opulus* and a warm stratification of 60 to 90 days followed by cold for 30 to 60 days should suffice.

NATIVE HABITAT: Northeastern Asia. Introduced 1892.

Viburnum setigerum — Tea Viburnum
(vī-bēr′num se-tij′ēr-um)

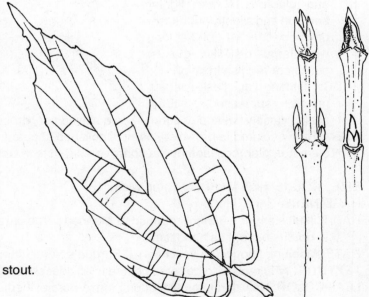

LEAVES: Opposite, simple, ovate-oblong, 3 to 6″ long, 1 1/4 to 2 1/2″ wide, acuminate, rounded at base, remotely denticulate, flat, soft blue-green to dark green above, glabrous except silky hairs on the veins beneath with 6 to 9 pairs of veins; petiole 1/2 to 1″ long, glabrous or hairy like midrib.

BUDS: Imbricate, terminal—green with red; lateral—green with red tip, large and glabrous, very prominent, usually with 3 to 5 visible scales.

STEM: Glabrous, smooth, gray and usually stout.

SIZE: 8 to 12′ tall, 2/3's that in width.

HARDINESS: Zone 5 to 7, have seen plants in Zone 9.

HABIT: Upright, multistemmed, often leggy at the base, but if used properly the leggy character is minimized.

RATE: Slow, possibly medium.

TEXTURE: Medium-coarse in foliage; coarse in winter.

LEAF COLOR: Flat, soft blue-green foliage in summer; fall color is inconsistent but can develop reddish purple.

FLOWERS: White, mid to late May, borne in 1 to 2″ diameter, 5-rayed, flat-topped cymes; limitedly ornamental.

FRUIT: Drupe, egg-shaped, 1/3″ long, bright red, September-October into late fall, very effective, possibly the most handsome fruiter among the viburnums.

CULTURE: Similar to other viburnums.

DISEASES AND INSECTS: None serious.

LANDSCAPE VALUE: Shrub border situations because of leggy habit, fruit is outstanding; derives its name from the fact that the leaves were used for making tea.

CULTIVARS:

'Aurantiacum'—Orange-fruited form, handsome in fruit but like the species often leggy.

PROPAGATION: I have rooted this species from leafy cuttings collected as late as September.

ADDITIONAL NOTES: I have seen branches so heavily laden with fruit that they literally arched and almost touched the ground. Unfortunately, this is not a very popular viburnum but when used correctly it can hold its own against any, especially in fall.

NATIVE HABITAT: Central and western China. Introduced 1901.

Viburnum sieboldii — Siebold Viburnum
(vī-bẽr′num sē-bōl′ dē-ī)

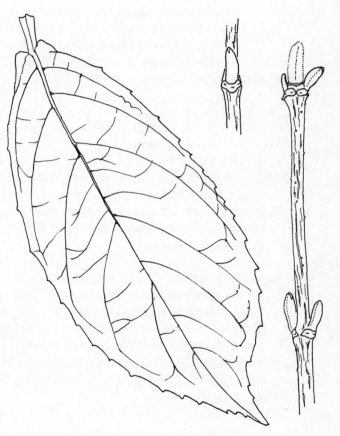

LEAVES: Opposite, simple, elliptic or obovate to oblong, 2 to 5″(6″) long, 1 1/2 to 3″ wide, acute, broad-cuneate, coarsely crenate-serrate, lustrous dark green and glabrous above, stellate pubescent chiefly on the veins beneath, with 7 to 10 pairs of prominent veins; petiole 1/4 to 3/4″ long; leaves when crushed emitting a fetid odor.

BUDS: Flower large, valvate, angled, 4-sided, gray-green-brown, slightly pubescent.

STEM: Slightly pubescent, stout, leaf scars connecting around the stem, usually grayish in color.

SIZE: 15 to 20′ in height, spread 10 to 15′, can reach 30′ in height.

HARDINESS: Zone 4 to 7(8); has been grown successfully at Minnesota Landscape Arboretum.

HABIT: Large shrub or small tree of open habit with stiff, stout, rigid branches.

RATE: Medium, possibly fast under ideal growing conditions.

TEXTURE: A rugged, handsome coarseness in summer and winter.

LEAF COLOR: Lustrous dark green, extremely clean looking foliage, very fetid if crushed, fall color is usually nonexistent (green); however, various authors indicated red-purple a possibility and I saw one specimen at the University of Maine with an ashy-purple color; tends to hold leaves late often into November.

FLOWERS: Creamy-white, late May, borne in 3 to 6″ diameter flat-topped long stalked cymose-paniculate clusters; excellent effect because flowers are borne in great abundance literally masking the bright green foliage.

FRUIT: Drupe, oval, 1/3 to 1/2″ long, rose-red to red changing to black, effective for two weeks in August through early October, birds seem to devour the fruits; however, the inflorescences are handsome rose-red and remain effective for two to four weeks after the fruits are gone; the fruit must be seen to be fully appreciated and the result is usually love at first sight.

CULTURE: Transplants well, adaptable, prefers moist, well-drained soils; tolerates partially shady situations; definitely needs sufficient moisture as leaf scorch will develop under dry soil conditions; pH
adaptable.

DISEASES AND INSECTS: None serious.

LANDSCAPE VALUE: Specimen, against large buildings, blank walls, groupings; open habit, excellent
foliage, flowers and fruits make it worthy of consideration for many landscape situations.

CULTIVARS:

'Seneca'—Resulted from a self-pollination of *V. s.* The plant was selected for the abundant, large,
pendulant inflorescences of firm red fruit on red pedicels which persist on the plant up to 3
months before turning black and falling. The massive, creamy-white panicles are produced in
May to early June as the young foliage unfolds. The panicles are supported on stout, spreading
branches that are picturesque at all seasons. The pendulant, multiple-colored clusters of
orange-red ripening to blood-red fruits are spectacularly displayed above the coriaceous, green
foliage. Birds normally eat the fruit of *V. s.* before it has matured, leaving only the red pedicels
which provide an ornamental display. However, the fruit of 'Seneca' is very firm and is not
devoured by birds even when the fruit becomes fully ripe. Although 'Seneca' is tree-like and has
attained a height of 14′ and a width of 13 1/2′, the plant can be trained with several branches
from the base and kept as a large spreading shrub. This cultivar will undoubtedly equal in size
plants of the species and be as much as 30′ with a gnarled trunk.

PROPAGATION: Cuttings, softwood-root easily.

NATIVE HABITAT: Japan. Cultivated 1880.

Viburnum suspensum — Sandankwa Viburnum
(vī-bēr′num su-spen′sum)

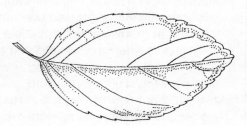

LEAVES: Opposite, simple, evergreen, ovate to oval, 2 to 5″
long, 1 1/2 to 3″ wide, pointed, rounded or broadly wedge-
shaped, toothed in the upper two-thirds or scarcely at all,
leathery lustrous green, glabrous, 4 to 5 vein pairs;
petiole 1/4 to 1/2″ long.

Viburnum suspensum, Sandankwa Viburnum, is a 6 to 12′ high
evergreen shrub that is used in the Coastal Plain and frequently seen in Florida gardens. The white,
faintly tinged pink, fragrant flowers occur in a 2 1/2 to 4″ long and wide corymbose panicle. The
globose fruits are red. I have seen it used for hedges in Florida. It appears to prefer a hot dry climate
and also seems well suited to sandy soils. I see the species everywhere in Florida all the way to Key
West where it is used for screens, specimens and the ubiquitous hedge. Interestingly, sizeable plants
were killed to the ground or outright on the Georgia coast at 11°F. Ryukyus. Introduced 1850. Zone
9 to 10.

Viburnum tinus — Laurustinus
(vī-bēr′num tī′nus)

LEAVES: Opposite, simple, evergreen, narrowly ovate to oblong, 1 1/2 to 4″ long, 3/4 to 1 1/2″ wide, entire,
lustrous dark green above, paler beneath, axillary tufts below; petiole 1/3 to 3/4″ long, usually
pubescent.

Viburnum tinus, Laurustinus, is a fine upright-rounded evergreen species that reaches 6 to 12′ in height
and usually less in spread. The lustrous dark green leaves are handsome throughout the year. The
pink-budded, 2 to 4″ diameter flowers open to white and often flower in January-February in the south.
The flowers are followed by ovoid, metallic blue fruits that mature to black. It is an excellent plant for

screening, hedging and withstands considerable shade as well as salt spray. It is hardy to 0°F once established and appears to be insect and disease free. 'Eve Price' is a compact form with smaller leaves than the species and attractive buds and pink-tinged flowers. 'Variegata' is a handsome clone with conspicuous creamy-yellow variegations. 'Compactum' will grow one half to three quarter's the size of the species and has slightly smaller leaves than the species. 'Spring Bouquet' may be the same as 'Compactum' and offers dark red flower buds that open to white on a 5 to 6' high and wide compact plant. 'Robustum' is larger in habit (15') and leaf (4"). This is a variable species in degree of pubescence, leaf size, etc. It is not common in the south but does make a handsome evergreen shrub. It can be used for screening, hedging, and massing. I noticed the plant was frequently used in England. Southern Europe, primarily in the Mediterranean region, northern Africa. Cultivated since 16th century in England. Zone (8)9 to 10. Since the last edition, I have observed numerous plants, especially in English gardens. It is a serviceable evergreen shrub for Mediterranean climates or where winter temperatures seldom drop below + 10°F. Over my 10 years in Athens, GA, I have watched a 7' high specimen disappear to its root tips. The University grounds department tried several plants of 'Spring Bouquet' in a protected area only to have them succumb to the vagaries of a southern winter. I do not believe the plant hardens off eary enough in fall to avoid the early fall freezes.

Viburnum trilobum — American Cranberrybush Viburnum
(vī-bēr'num trī-lō'bum)

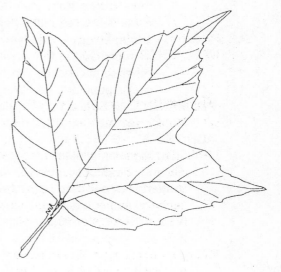

LEAVES: Opposite, simple, 3-lobed, broad-ovate, 2 to 5" long, lobes acuminate, rounded or truncate at base, coarsely dentate, sometimes the middle lobe elongated and entire, dark green and usually lustrous above, pilose on the veins beneath, or nearly glabrous; petiole 1/2 to 1" long with shallow groove and small dome-shaped, usually stalked glands.

BUDS: Similar to *V. opulus,* sometimes sticky, green-reddish and smooth, with 2 connate outer scales.

STEM: Gray-brown, glabrous, with a waxy appearance.

SIZE: 8 to 12' in height, spread 8 to 12'.

HARDINESS: Zone 2 to 7, can grown in 8 but not well adapted to the heat.

HABIT: Similar to *Viburnum opulus,* round-topped and fairly dense.

RATE: Medium.

TEXTURE: Medium in foliage; medium to coarse in winter.

LEAF COLOR: Lustrous medium to dark green changing to yellow through red-purple in fall; new growth has a reddish tinge.

FLOWERS: White, similar to *V. opulus,* mid to late May, 3 to 4 1/2" diameter, flat-topped cymes; extremely handsome, possibly better than *V. opulus* but the plant is not as available through nurseries.

FRUIT: Drupe, nearly globose, 1/3" long, bright red, early September through fall into February, holds better than *V. opulus,* edible, used for preserves and jellies.

CULTURE: Native species, transplants well; prefers good, well-drained, moist soil; sun or partial shade; should be more adaptable than *V. opulus* due to wide native range; however, limitedly planted.

DISEASES AND INSECTS: A stem blight can kill plant in warm humid states.

LANDSCAPE VALUE: Excellent plant for screening and informal hedging; like *V. opulus* it becomes too large for the small landscape; I have seen it used to define boundaries between houses in subdivisions and it really affords a good privacy screen and at the same time offers excellent flower, fruit and foliage; if subjected to excessive water stress it declines rapidly and makes a rather poor specimen.

CULTIVARS:

'Compactum'—Excellent compact, dwarf form with good flowering and fruiting habit; the stems are much more slender and uniformly upright-spreading than its counterpart, *V. opulus* 'Compactum'; grows about one-half the size of the species (6′); fall color is not particularly good and is usually yellow at best. The entire taxonomy of this group is rather confusing and I am not sure I can "unconfuse" it. In my Illinois garden, 'Compactum' grew with passion and flowered and fruited without any significant fall color. Along comes . . . I think . . . several new forms, the one called 'Alfredo' which is similar to 'Compactum' but with a denser, broader habit, good summer foliage and excellent red fall color. Flower and fruit set are sparse. Unfortunately, I have read literature that said fruit set was good. Another form is 'Bailey Compact' (Bailey Nursery, St. Paul, MN) with compact habit and deep red fall foliage. No mention is made of flower and fruit characteristics.

Also, there is some confusion about true 'Compactum' which is alternately listed as virtually sterile and heavy flowering and fruiting. I have a suspicion that lack of fruit set on 'Compactum' may be the result of the lack of a suitable cross pollinator.

'Andrews', 'Hahs', 'Wentworth'—Have been selected for larger fruits; the story goes deeper than that for in early 1900's a Mr. Hahs and Mr. Andrews (there may have been others) selected the above three plants from over 3000 seedlings, cuttings and divisions in 1922; apparently the initial collections took place near the White Mountains of New Hampshire; they are early, mid, and late ripening, respectively, and were selected for edibility; I have bserved 'Wentworth' and it is beautiful as the fruit passes from a yellow-red to bright red but, in my mind, is no better than other plants I have seen in various locations, may have best red fall color; 'Hahs' has large fruits and is popular in the Chicago region; 'Hahs' matures at a smaller size than the species.

PROPAGATION: Seeds require the normal warm/cold routine but cuttings are easy to root; softwood cuttings in late July, 1000 ppm IBA-quick dip, peat:perlite, mist, rooted 100 percent in 6 weeks.

ADDITIONAL NOTES: I have refrained from giving recipes primarily because I like Snicker's bars better than ornamental plant concoctions. I relent here and present what sounds like a recipe for a fine jam. Simmer cleaned fruit for 10 minutes in 1/3 its weight of water; put through a sieve, use a little more water to remove pulp from seeds; add sugar to equal weight of cleaned fruit; boil to 222°F; pour into jars and immediately seal; yields beautiful ruby jam with distinctive flavor.

NATIVE HABITAT: New Brunswick to British Columbia, south to New York, Michigan, South Dakota and Oregon. Introduced 1812.

Vinca minor — Common Periwinkle
(ving′kȧ mī′nôr)

FAMILY: Apocynaceae

LEAVES: Opposite, simple, evergreen, elliptic, oblong or ellip-tic-ovate, 1/2 to 1 1/2″ long, 1/2 to 3/4″ wide, acutish or obtuse, rounded or cuneate, entire, lustrous dark green above, lighter green beneath; petiole short—1/2 to 1 1/4″ long, exuding a milky juice when broken.

STEM: Shining green, glabrous.

SIZE: 3 to 6″ high ground hugging plant.

HARDINESS: Zone 3 to 8(9), can be grown further north when protected by snow.

HABIT: Low growing, prostrate, mat forming evergreen ground cover, spreading indefinitely.

RATE: Medium to fast; in a loose, organic, well drained soil will fill in very fast.

TEXTURE: Medium-fine in all seasons.

LEAF COLOR: New growth emerges early, often March in Athens and is a handsome yellow green maturing to lustrous green in summer, often losing some of the sheen in winter.

FLOWERS: Perfect, lilac-blue, 1″ diameter, March-April, borne solitary on 1/2 to 1 1/4″ long pedicels; very attractive in flower and sporadically flowering over a long period.

FRUIT: Follicle, not ornamental, seldom set on cultivated plants.

CULTURE: Transplant from pots or as a bare root plant into moist, well drained soil abundantly supplemented with organic matter; supposedly does equally well in full sun or shade, but I have seen considerable leaf discoloration (yellowing and browning) in winter under full sun conditions; can tolerate poor soils but will not develop and fill in as fast.

DISEASES AND INSECTS: Blight, canker and dieback, leaf spots, and root rot; the canker and dieback (*Phomopsis livella*) disease have been significant problems; the shoots become dark brown, wilt, and die back to the surface of the soil.

LANDSCAPE VALUE: Excellent ground cover in spite of problems; the dainty blue flowers are handsome as is the lustrous foliage; plant on 1′ centers; makes its best growth in shade and here can form large carpets under the leafy canopy; the new growth emerges a rich spring green and the flowers appear at the same time; flowers over a long period; never really spectacular unless viewed close up, too often large seas of the plant are used in dense shade; I have seen mixed plantings with daffodils and other bulbs that bring the carpet to life in spring; I suspect that *Colchicum* species would do nicely and perhaps even *Lycoris radiata* in more southerly locations.

CULTIVARS:

‘Alba’—White flowering form representing a nice change from the lilac-blue of the species; ‘Alba Plena’ with double white flowers is known.

‘Alba Variegata’—White flowers and leaves edged with light yellow, old cultivar.

‘Argenteo-variegata’—Blue flowers and leaves margined with white; leaves shorter and broader than typical species.

‘Atropurpurea’—Deep plum-purple flowers, rather handsome form, flowers are large and have good substance, first recorded in 1826.

‘Aureo-variegata’—Blue flowers and leaves with yellow blotches and stripes.

‘Azurea Flore Pleno’—Sky-blue double flowers.

‘Bowles White’—Flowers flushed pink in bud, white when open, large.

‘Gertrude Jekyll’—A form with glistening white flowers, quite attractive, flowers freely borne; flowers and foliage smaller than typical.

‘Green Carpet’ (‘Grüner Teppich’)—Apparently a non-flowering form of *V. minor* with luxuriant rich green leaves that are larger than the type.

‘La Grave’—Large, up to 1 1/2″ diameter, lavender-blue (deep mauve) flowers; this is also the same, according to the literature, as ‘Bowles Variety’ which is listed as having larger azure-blue flowers, vigorous growth habit but more clumpy rather than spreading like the species; I received ‘La Grave’ from Dr. Raulston and indeed it is superior in size and color, the petals having more substance than the typical species type; the ‘Bowles Variety’ I have seen in commerce is not the same as ‘La Grave’ but the plant does not always match up with the name; true ‘La Grave’ is a more handsome plant and is worth pursuing; collected by E.A. Bowles in the 1920’s in the churchyard of La Grave in the Dauphine.

‘Multiplex’—Plum-purple double flowers.

‘Onland Blue’—Form with large light violet-blue flowers, narrower in the petals than ‘La Grave’, see *The Garden* 109:426–429 (1984) for a Wisley Garden “Trial of *Vinca* cultivars”.

‘Ralph Shugert’—Uniform creamy white to white margins on dark green leaves; more regular marginal variegation and darker green, smaller leaves than ‘Argenteo-variegata’, introduced by David Mackenzie, Spring Lake, MI.

‘Rosea’—Flowers violet-pink, smaller leaves.

‘Rosea Plena’—Flowers violet-pink, double.

‘Shademaster’—A dense evergreen ground cover with purple flowers, a Princeton Nursery introduction.

PROPAGATION: Fresh seeds of ‘Gertrude Jekyll’ were give a 24 hour soak in Gibberillic acid (GA) at 0 or 1000 ppm and/or stratified for 0, 30, 60, 90 days; 1000 ppm GA, plus 90 days cold stratification resulted in 70% germination in 30 days; neither GA nor cold alone induced germination. Division, also extremely easy from cuttings.

NATIVE HABITAT: Europe and western Asia, cultivated since ancient times; escaped from cultivation.

RELATED SPECIES:

Vinca major — Large Periwinkle
(ving′kȧ mā′jôr)

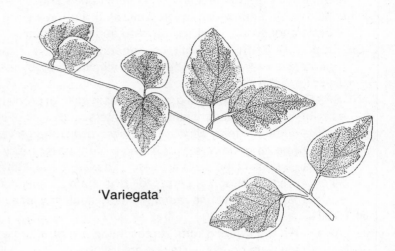

'Variegata'

LEAVES: Opposite, simple, evergreen, ovate, 1 to 3″ long, half to two-thirds as wide, acute or obtusish, often nearly cordate, entire but often with ciliate hairs, lustrous dark green and glabrous above, lighter beneath; petiole 1/3 to 1/2″ long.

Vinca major, Large Periwinkle, is essentially a large carbon copy of the above. The plant averages between 12 to 18″ high. It flowers well in full sun and the flowers often occur sporadically over the growing season. *Vinca major* prefers moist, well-drained soils and shade. Makes a good ground cover in dense shade. 'Variegata' ('Elegantissima') has leaves that are blotched and margined irregularly with creamy-white markings. 'Variegata' is as hardy and vigorous as the species and the flowers are similar. Have seen 'Variegata' used at a residence in Columbus, Ohio with some success. Near the foundation it overwintered in good condition but was obliterated 3 to 4′ from the foundation. Should be cut back in spring. Used for window boxes, containers and urns; cascades gracefully over their edges. In the 1983 edition, I commented that this species was more drought resistant than *V. minor.* After observing both species during the two hottest and driest back-to-back summers on record in the south, I give the adaptability nod to *V. minor.* *V. major* showed pronounced wilting. Have also seen a a narrow petaled, deep purple form in England termed 'Oxyloba'. 'Aureomaculata' has a central blotch of yellow green. 'Jason Hill' has deeper violet-blue flowers.

Vitex negundo — Chastetree
(vī′teks nē-gun′dō)

FAMILY: Verbenaceae

LEAVES: Opposite, compound palmate, leaflets usually 5, sometimes 3 to 7, 1 1/4 to 4″ long, stalked, elliptic-ovate to lanceolate, entire or serrate, grayish green, tomentulose beneath; petiole 3/4 to 2″ long.

BUDS: Superposed, sessile or the upper commonly developing the first season, subglobose, the 1 or 2 pairs of leaf-rudiments or scales concealed in pubescence.

STEM: Compressed at nodes, quadrangular with obtuse or flattened angles, rather slender; pith relatively large, more or less angled, white, continuous and homogeneous; leaf-scars U-shaped, rather small, low; the surface usually torn and the solitary bundle-trace indistinct.

SIZE: Difficult to predict in the north since the plants are often frozen to the ground; the height in one growing season might be 3 to 5′ but if no damage is done, over the years the plant may grow 10 to 15′.

HARDINESS: Zone 6, often listed as 5 but shakily so, does well in southern states.

HABIT: Not a bad looking plant in leaf; develops a loosely branched, airy, open outline.

RATE: Fast.

TEXTURE: Medium-fine in leaf; medium-coarse in winter; tends to leaf out late.

LEAF COLOR: Grayish green cast in summer; nothing to speak of in the way of fall color.

FLOWERS: Small, lilac or lavender, in loose clusters forming slender spikes collected into terminal 5 to 8″ long panicles; effective in July-August (June in Athens).

FRUIT: A small drupe of no consequence.

CULTURE: Transplant as a container plant into loose, moist, well-drained soil; full sun; prefer hot weather; well-drained situation definitely aids in reducing winter injury; if pruning is necessary, cut the plant to within 6 to 12″ of the ground in spring or back to live wood on old plants.

DISEASES AND INSECTS: Several leaf spots and a root rot have been reported but are not serious.

LANDSCAPE VALUE: Possibly a plant for the shrub border; should almost be treated as a herbaceous perennial in the north; interesting foliage texture and late season flowers.

CULTIVARS:

'Heterophylla'—The leaflets are gray-green and finely divided creating a graceful, airy texture especially when treated as a herbaceous perennial and grown primarily for its foliage; based on my evaluations at the Arnold, this form appears hardier than *V. agnus-castus* var. *latifolia*.

PROPAGATION: Softwood cuttings root like weeds but must not be left in the mist too long after rooting; this applies to *V. a.* var. *latifolia;* seeds can be directly sown.

NATIVE HABITAT: Actually rather wide-ranging from southeast Africa, Madagascar, eastern and southeastern Asia, Philippines. Introduced 1697.

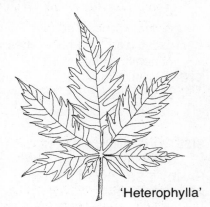

'Heterophylla'

RELATED SPECIES:

Vitex agnus-castus — Chastetree
(vī′teks ag′nus-kās′tus)

LEAVES: Opposite, compound palmate, digitate (finger-like) in appearance, 5 to 7 radiating leaflets, each lanceolate, 2 to 4″(5″) long, 1/2 to 1″ wide, tapering at the apex and base, entire or toothed toward apex, dark gray-green above, grayish beneath with a fine pubescence, leaves aromatic when bruised; petiolule 1/4″ long or less.

Vitex agnus-castus, Chastetree, is not as hardy as the above species. The flowers are more prominent, lilac or pale violet, fragrant, and occur from June-July through September. Flowers occur in 3 to 6″ long racemes from the ends and leaf axils of the current season's growth resulting in 12 to 18″ long and slightly less in spread panicles. This species grows 8 to 10′ high. The cultivars include 'Alba' with white flowers, 'Rosea' with pink flowers, and 'Silver Spire' with white flowers and good vigor. A variety *latifolia* is supposedly more vigorous and hardier than the species. I remember learning the variety in my plant material courses at Ohio State, for it was always necessary to hunt through the old Horticultural garden to see if there were a few live branches. In the south, it makes a fine small tree 15 to 20′ high and is spectacular in flower. The bark on old plants is grayish and develops a blocky characteristic. There are many fine specimens on the Georgia campus. Native to southern Europe and western Asia. Introduced 1570. Zone (6)7 to 8(9).

ADDITIONAL NOTES: The *Vitex* species makes good summer flowering garden plants but do not seem to be widely available. See Dirr, *American Nurseryman* 150(3):11, 75–78, 1979 for additional information. Good plant for hot climates and might even be grown as a small tree. Will flower recurrently during late summer as long as new growth develops. Not a bad idea to remove spent flowers since this may result in a late season flush of growth.

Weigela florida — Old Fashioned Weigela
(wī-gē′là flôr′i-dà)

FAMILY: Caprifoliaceae

LEAVES: Opposite, simple, elliptic to ovate-oblong, or obovate, 2 to 4 1/2″ long, 3/4 to 1 1/2″ wide, acuminate, rounded to cuneate at base, serrate, medium green and glabrous above except on mid-rib, pubescent or tomentose on veins beneath; petiole short.

STEM: With 2 rows of hairs running from node to node, gray-brown, scurfy, with large circular lenticels; pith—moderate, pale brown, continuous.

SIZE: 6 to 9′ high by 9 to 12′ wide; smaller in exposed and harsh situations.

HARDINESS: Zone 4 to 8 (9).

HABIT: Spreading, dense rounded shrub with coarse branches that eventually arch to the ground.

TEXTURE: Medium in summer, at times almost offensive in winter.

LEAF COLOR: Nondescript medium green, no fall color of consequence.

FLOWERS: Perfect, funnelform-campanulate, 1 to 1 1/4″ long, abruptly narrowed below the middle, rosy-pink outside, paler within, with rounded spreading lobes, May-June (mid to late April, Athens), singly or several in axillary cymes on short twigs from last year's branches, also flowering sporadically on current season's growth, have seen flowers as late as mid October.

FRUIT: Two-valved, glabrous capsule of no ornamental value; seeds unwinged.

CULTURE: Transplant bare root or from a container; extremely adaptable but prefers a well-drained soil and full sun; often considerable dieback occurs and considerable pruning (after flowering) is necessary to keep it in shape; quite pollution tolerant.

DISEASES AND INSECTS: None serious.

LANDSCAPE VALUE: Best used in the shrub border, for grouping or massing; have seen it used frequently as a foundation planting in older sections of cities; really appears forlorn in the winter landscape; looks like it needs a place to hide.

CULTIVARS: One truly needs a score card to keep track of the many cultivars that have resulted from hybridization among the various species. A glance at the list is sufficient reason to throw the hands in the air and give up. Krüssmann mentions that there are 170 known hybrids that resulted from the work of van Houtte, Billard, Lemoine and Rathke. New cultivars are coming primarily from Holland and Canada. Svejda from Agriculture Canada has introduced several cold hardy, compact, free flowering forms since the 1983 edition of the *Manual.* The cultivars listed here are not necessarily progeny of *W. florida.*

'Abel Carriere'—Large rose-carmine flowers flecked gold in the throat, free flowering, buds carmine-purple, 1876, Lemoine.

'Avalanche'—Vigorous, free flowering white form, the flowers with pink tinge, 1909, Lemoine.

'Boskoop Glory'—Large, trumpet shaped, salmon-pink flowers, about 7 to 8′ at maturity.

'Bristol Ruby'—Ruby-red flowers, erect growth habit, free flowering, a hybrid between *W. florida* and 'Eva Rathke,' 7′ high, good hardiness, 1954.

'Bristol Snowflake'—White, with some pink, more vigorous than 'Candida', 1955.

'Candida'—Pure white in bud stage and older flowers, foliage light green, 1879.

'Centennial'—Robust shrub to 9′ with erythrite red flowers to tips of branches, cold hardy form introduced in 1967, hybrid between 'Dropmore Pink' and 'Profusion'.

'Conquerant'—Very large deep pink flowers almost 2″ long, spreading habit, 1904, Lemoine.

'Dame Blanche'—Almost pure white but with a pink tinge, large flowers, 1902, Lemoine.

'Dart's Colordream'—Cream and rose-red, while others are mixed, will be in the medium size category, probably 4 to 6′ high.

'Dropmore Pink'—Hardy pink strain developed by Dr. Skinner using a Manchurian strain for hardiness, 1951.

'Eva Rathke'—A slow growing cultivar of compact habit with bright crimson-red flowers with yellow anthers, opening over a long period, 1892, Rathke.

'Eva Supreme'—Vigorous grower with bright red flowers; hybrid of 'Eva Rathke' and 'Newport Red', supposedly only 5′ high, limited repeat flower, quite cold hardy, 1958, Holland.

'Evita'—Resembles 'Eva Rathke' in flower color (red), but is dense and spreading in habit, 2 to 3′ high, flowers profuse in May-June, with recurrent bloom later.

'Floreal'—Clear rose-pink outside, deep carmine-pink throat, large flowered, floriferous, buds 1901, Lemoine.

'Foliis Purpureis'—Pink flowers with purplish green foliage, dwarf, for a 20-year-old plant is purple-red, densely rounded and 4′ tall, a *W. florida* form; buds carmine-red, same as 'Java Red'.

'Gracieux'—Erect, free flowering, salmon-rose with sulfur-yellow throat, large flowered, floriferous, 1904, Lemoine.

'Java Red'—Somewhat confused in my mind, may be the same as 'Foliis Purpureis'.

'Lawrence'—Exceptional hardiness, floriferous, pale blue flowers with white keels?, original plant 20′ by 10′, discovered in Brantford, Ontario, 1970; I have difficulty reconciling the reported flower color with the typical range.

'Looymansii Aurea'—Is a form that jumps in my path in many European gardens; the leaves are bright golden yellow with a narrow red marginal rim, foliage will fade with heat and probably scorch in the heat of the U.S. summers, flowers are pink and habit is more restrained than *W. florida* but still 4 to 6′ high at maturity.

'Lucifer'—A compact form, 3 to 5′ high with dark green foliage and large, 1 3/4″ long deep red flowers.

'Minuet'—Very dwarf compact form with dark ruby red flowers profusely borne over the purple tinged dark green foliage, flowers slightly fragrant, 30″ high, has shown excellent cold hardiness, flowers are ruby-red on outside of corolla, lobes lilac-purple, throat yellow, 1 1/2″ long, 1 1/4″ wide; released by Agricultural Canada, parentage 'Foliis Purpureis' × 'Dropmore Pink'; see *Canadian J. Plant. Sci.* 62:249–250 (1982).

'Mont Blanc'— Vigorous form with large white, fragrant flowers; often considered the best white, 1898, Lemoine.

'Newport Red'—Similar to 'Eva Rathke', flowers not as bright and more purple-red, vigorous grower, winter stems green, the same as 'Vanicek' and, in fact, introduced by V.A. Vanicek, Newport, RI, 5 to 6′ high, good hardiness.

'Pink Delight'—Deep pink flowers that do not fade as blatantly as many forms, more compact habit, greater cold hardiness, from Mission Gardens, IL.

'Pink Princess'—A pink (actually lavender-pink) flowered hardy selection from Iowa, 5 to 6′ high, spreading, loose, open.

'Polka'—Develops into a 3 to 4′ high, 4 to 5′ wide shrub, foliage is dark green, leaves 2 1/2 to 3″ long, 1 1/2 to 2″ wide, flowers are pink on outside of the corolla with a yellow inner throat and average 1 3/4″ long, 1 1/4 to 1 1/2″ wide, suffered 7% winter injury in Ottawa and flowered for 10 to 11 weeks in 16 weeks from June to September, counted 12 progenitor taxa in this clone's makeup, Wow!; see *HortScience* 23:787–788 (1988) for additional details.

'Red Prince'—Good red flower that does not fade, recurrent flowering in late summer, upright growing when young, 5 to 6′, hardier than 'Newport Red' ('Vanicek'), introduced by Iowa State University.

'Rubigold'—Have seen this at Bressingham Gardens in England and find the yellow or yellow-green splashed foliage/red flowers a degree indigestible but for those who want bright foliage and flowers it might be worth a shot; might cook in heat of south or at least fade quickly, a branch sport of 'Bristol Ruby'.

'Rumba'—A vigorous, compact spreading shrub, 3' by 3 1/2' wide, yellow-green leaves with purple edges, 3" long by 1 1/2" wide, flowers dark red with a yellow throat, 1 3/4" long and 1 to 1 1/4" wide, winter hardy and flowers for 8 weeks from June to September; see *HortScience* 20:149 (1985); result of cross between 'Foliis Purpureis' and 'Dropmore Scarlet'.

'Samba'—A compact, vigorous, well formed shrub that grows about 3' high and wide, leaves are dark green with purple tips and edges, 2 1/2 to 3" long, 1 to 1 1/2" wide, flowers are red with a yellow throat, 1 3/4" long, 1" wide, displays excellent winter hardiness, a hybrid between 'Rumba' and 'Eva Rathke', see *HortScience* 21:166 (1986) for details.

'Seduction'—Magenta-rose, buds dark red, heavy flowering.

'Styriaca'—Small carmine-rose flowers freely borne on arching branches, smaller shrub, foliage light green.

'Tango'—Compact shrub, 2' high by 2 1/2' wide, leaves 2 1/2 to 5" long, 3/4 to 2" wide, purple on the upper surface, dark green below, purple is predominant and maintained throughout the growing season, flowers are red on the outside, yellowish in the throat, 1 1/4 to 1 1/2" long, 3/4 to 1" wide, has shown a maximum of 4% winter injury in Ottawa, Canada, and flowered for 3 to 4 weeks in June (Canada); see *HortScience* 23:787–788 (1988) for more details; interestingly, this clone resulted from four progenitor taxa.

'Vanicek'—Same as 'Newport Red'.

'Variegata'—Flowers deep rose, leaves edged pale yellow to creamy white, compact grower, about 4 to 6' high although have seen 10' tall plants.

'Variegata Nana'—Most dwarf of the weigelas—3' tall—same foliage as above, again have seen larger specimens than the norm.

var. *venusta*—Leaves smaller, flowers rosy pink, very hardy, free flowering, Zone (3) 4.

PROPAGATION: Seeds can be directly sown; softwood cuttings in June, July, August root readily; one of the easiest plants to root.

NATIVE HABITAT: Japan. Introduced 1860.

RELATED SPECIES:

Weigela middendorffiana, (wī-gē'là mid-en-dôr-fi-ā'nà), Middendorf Weigela, is a small (3 to 5' high) shrub of note for the 1 to 1 1/2" long sulfur-yellow flowers, dotted orange on the lower lobes. I have seen it at the Arnold Arboretum and, although interesting, cannot compete with the better hybrids. Manchuria, northern China, Japan. Introduced 1850. Zone 4(5) to 7?

Wisteria floribunda — Japanese Wisteria
(wis-tē'ri-à flôr-i-bun'dà)

FAMILY: Fabaceae

LEAVES: Alternate, pinnately compound, 10 to 15" long, (11) 13 to 19 leaflets, ovate-elliptic to ovate-oblong, 1 1/2 to 3" long, acuminate, rounded at base, rarely broad cuneate, entire, bright green above, appressed pubescent when young, soon nearly glabrous; petiole flattened at base.

BUDS: Narrowly oblong and acute at the tip with 3 outer scales, one scale usually surrounding the entire bud, reddish brown, pubescent, appressed.

STEM: Twines clockwise, somewhat angled, light tan or brown changing to gray-brown, 2 spine-like projections at the top sides of the leaf scar.

SIZE: 30' or more, essentially limited by structure on which it is allowed to grow; have seen plants 40 to 50' high in trees.

HARDINESS: Zone 4 to 9.

HABIT: Stout vine, climbing by twining stems which turn clockwise developing twisted woody trunk several inches in diameter and requiring considerable support.

RATE: Fast, as is true with most vines; will grow 10′ or more, especially in south, in a single season once established.

TEXTURE: Medium in leaf, somewhat coarse in winter.

BARK: On old trunks a grayish color, smooth and sometimes irregularly fluted; almost reminiscent of the bark of *Carpinus caroliniana*.

LEAF COLOR: Bright green, usually late to leaf out, no fall color of any consequence, a tad of yellow; new growth often bronze or purplish.

FLOWERS: Perfect, violet or violet-blue, on old wood on short leafy shoots, each flower 1/2 to 3/4″ long, slightly fragrant, April-May (early to mid April, Athens), borne in slender 8 to 20″ long racemes, the flowers opening from the base to the apex; very lovely as the flowers open before or just as leaves

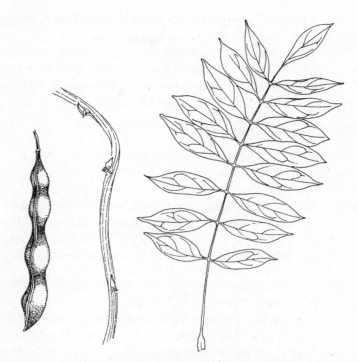

emerge; not too many vines rival it for flower effect; flowers occasionally on new growth of the season.

FRUIT: Pod, brown, 4 to 6″, October, persisting into winter, velvety.

CULTURE: Supposedly hard to transplant and slow to establish; however, I have grown many in containers and have had no difficulty establishing them; plant in deep, moist, well-drained loam; pH adaptable although supposedly does better at a higher pH; in order to insure successful culture it is wise to use nitrogen sparingly for this promotes excess vegetative growth, use superphosphate, root prune, cut back vigorous growth leaving only 3 to 4 buds, plant in full sun and use named cultivars rather than seedling grown material; if left to its own devices, the plant can consume fences, trellises, arbors and people; indeed it is one of the most beautiful of all flowering vines and deserves first consideration where it can be maintained; although all types of horticultural voodoo and folk art are recommended to keep it flowering, in the south it is unstoppable, for two weeks in April in Athens the plant appears as common as Japanese Honeysuckle.

DISEASES AND INSECTS: Crown gall, leaf spots, stem canker, powdery mildew, root rot, tobacco mosaic virus, sweet potato leaf beetle, Japanese mealybug, citrus flata planthopper, fall webworm, black vine weevil and scale.

LANDSCAPE VALUE: Excellent flowering vine, nice over patios, on large structures, or trained into a tree form; needs ample support and metal pipe is recommended for it will actually crush wood supports with time; not the easiest plant to keep flowering and cultural practices must be fairly precise.

CULTIVARS:

'Alba'—Racemes 11″ long, moderate fragrance, dense, white, 13 leaflets.

'Issai'—Racemes 12″ long, moderate fragrance, violet to bluish violet, 17 leaflets, have seen 'Issai' described as having 24 to 30″ long racemes.

'Ivory Tower'—White flowers, abundantly produced, heady fragrance.

'Kyushaku'—Racemes 26″ long, fragrance fair, reddish violet to violet.

'Lawrence'—Flowers pale blue with white keels, selected because of exceptional hardiness and floriferousness.

'Longissima Alba'—Racemes 15″ long, good fragrance, 13 leaflets, white.

'Macrobotrys'—Racemes 18 to 36″ (48″) long, fragrance excellent, reddish violet to violet.

'Murasaki Noda'—Racemes 10″ long, fragrance fair, 15 leaflets, reddish violet to violet.

'Rosea'—Pale rose, tipped purple, excellent fragrance, in long racemes to about 18″.

'Royal Purple'—Violet-purple, 12 to 14″ long, slightly fragrant, 15 leaflets.

'Texas Purple'—Violet-purple, precocious, a Monrovia offering.

'Violacea Plena'—Double flowers, violet-blue; flowers rosetted, slightly fragrant, 13 leaflets, racemes 10 to 12″ long.

PROPAGATION: Seeds germinate readily without treatment; I have collected seed in fall and direct sowed them with good results; if seed is quite dry and hard, a 24 hour soak in warm water is recommended, June to July cuttings rooted without treatment. Cultivars are also grafted.

NATIVE HABITAT: Japan. Introduced 1830.

RELATED SPECIES:

Wisteria frutescens — American Wisteria
(wis-tē′ri-à froo-tes′enz)

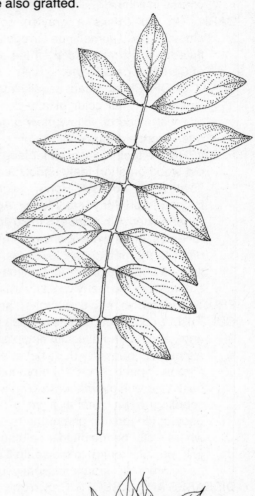

LEAVES: Alternate, compound pinnate, 7 to 12″ long, 9 to 15 leaflets of uniform size, elliptic-ovate to oblong or oblong-lanceolate, 1 1/2 to 2 1/2″ long, to 1 1/4″ wide, glabrous and bright green above, slightly pubescent below.

Wisteria frutescens, American Wisteria, is a vigorous climbing vine that may reach 30′ or more. The fragrant, 3/4″ long, pale lilac-purple flowers have a yellow spot and are compressed into 4 to 6″ long dense villous racemes in June-August on the current season's growth. The pods are compressed, 2 to 4″ long, and glabrous with the seeds more rounded than those of *W. floribunda* and *W. sinensis.* Tends to be less vigorous in cultivation than the Asiatic species. 'Nivea' is a white flowered form. Virginia to Florida and Texas. Introduced 1724. Zone 5 to 9.

Wisteria sinensis — Chinese Wisteria
(wis-tē′ri-à sī-nen′sis)

LEAVES: Alternate, pinnately compound, 10 to 12″ long, 7 to 13 leaflets, usually 11, ovate-oblong to ovate-lanceolate, 2 to 4″ long, 1/2 to 1 1/2″ wide, abruptly acuminate, usually broad-cuneate at base, ciliate, densely appressed-pubescent at first, deep green and glabrous above, somewhat hairy beneath, especially on the midrib.

Wisteria sinensis, Chinese Wisteria, is similar to *W. floribunda* except the flower is blue-violet, about 1″ long, not as fragrant, May, borne in dense, 6 to 12″ long racemes, all flowers of one raceme opening at about the same time; fruit is a pod, 4 to 6″ long, densely velutinous with 1 to 3 seeds; var. *alba* has white flowers; 'Jako' is a selected form of *alba* with extremely fragrant flowers; 'Black Dragon' has double dark purple flowers; and 'Plena' has double, rosette-shaped, lilac flowers. China. 1916. Zone 5 to 8. Twines counter-clockwise. The exact identity of this species has brought much hand wringing to the author especially when confronted with a shoot and no flower. It would seem that leaflet numbers should be a good criterion for separation from *W. floribunda.* I have seen true *W. sinensis* in the Netherlands and England and, indeed, the flowers open more or less at the same time along the axis of the raceme compared to the differential opening of *W. floribunda* from base to apex. The clockwise *(W. floribunda)* and counter-clockwise *(W. sinensis)* turnings also leave room for interpretations. Most plants I see in cultivation and escaped into the wild are *W. floribunda,* not *W. sinensis. W. sinensis,* according to Bean is more vigorous than *W. floribunda.* Perhaps this is true in England but is not the case in this country.

Wisteria venusta — Silky Wisteria
(wis-tē'ri-a̍ ve-nus'ta̍)

LEAVES: Alternate, compound pinnate, 8 to 14″ long, 9 to 13 leaflets, usually 11, elliptic to ovate, 1 1/2 to 3 1/2″ long, 1/2 to 1 1/2″ wide, short acuminate, rounded, pubescent on both surfaces, bright green above.

Wisteria venusta, Silky Wisteria, offers 1″ long, white, slightly fragrant flowers that are borne in 4 to 6″ long, 3 to 4″ wide racemes; all flowers opening about the same time. The 6 to 8″ long pod is compressed and densely velutinous; var. *violacea* is the wild form with violet flowers. Japan, where it (white) was only known in cultivation; before 1900. Zone 5 to 8.

ADDITIONAL NOTES: The wisterias are lovely vines but do require considerable care. In the south (Zone 7 and higher) they are pernicious pests and *W. floribunda* can be found strangling everything in its grasp. Admittedly, it is quite pretty draped over and around trees especially during April. Must be used with a certain amount of discretion and a commitment to proper culture and pruning. Good articles on *Wisteria* selection and culture appeared in *Horticulture* 63(4):38–40 (1985), and in *The Plantsman* 6(2):109–122 (1984).

Xanthoceras sorbifolium — Yellowhorn
(zan-thōs-ēr'as sôr-bi-fō'li-um)

FAMILY: Sapindaceae
LEAVES: Alternate, compound pinnate, 5 to 9″ long, 9 to 17 leaflets, narrow elliptic to lanceolate, 1 1/2 to 2 1/2″ long, deeply and sharply serrate, dark green above, lighter beneath.

Xanthoceras sorbifolium, Yellowhorn, is a striking tree but virtually unknown in commerce and gardens. It tends to be upright in habit and the branching pattern is rather stiff and coarse. Size ranges from 18 to 24′. The beautiful, slender-stalked, 3/4 to 1″ diameter flowers occur in 6 to 10″ long racemes in May. Each flower is composed of 5, rather thin white petals with a blotch at the base that changes from yellow to red. It is a striking tree in flower and one which any gardener would be proud to display. Adaptable to any good loamy soil even those of calcareous origin (high pH). Supposedly has the reputation for being difficult to transplant. Should be sited in full sun. The fruit is a 3-valved, thick-walled, 2″ long capsule; each cell contains several globose, dark brown pea-sized seeds. At a conference in Nebraska, I talked with a gentleman who said the tree was growing well in Blair, Nebraska where winter lows reach -25 to -30°F. Seed apparently requires no pretreatment although 2 to 3 months at 40°F may unify and hasten germination. Root cuttings offer a feasible means of vegetative propagation. The lustrous green leaves remain late in fall. I have only seen the tree in flower around mid May at the Wister Garden, Swarthmore, PA and Winterthur Gardens, DE. It is striking at this time and certainly the rival of any flowering tree. In many respects, the foliage characteristics and growth habit remind of *Koelreuteria paniculata.* Northern China. Introduced 1866. Zone (3)4 to 6 (7).

Xanthorhiza simplicissima — Yellowroot
(zan-thō-rī′zȧ sim-pli-cis′i-mȧ)

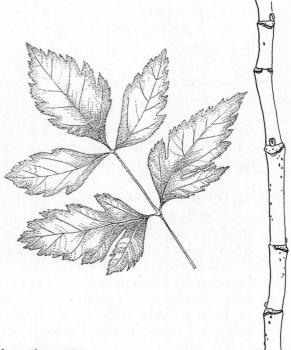

FAMILY: Ranunculaceae

LEAVES: Alternate, compound pinnate, or appearing bipinnate, leaflets usually 3 to 5, 1 1/2 to 2 3/4″ long, the basal pair 2 to 3 lobed, ovate to ovate-oblong, incisely toothed, sometimes serrate, lustrous bright green.

BUDS: Lateral buds solitary, sessile, ovoid-oblong, compressed and flattened against stem, with about 3 scales; terminal buds much larger, fusiform, terete, with about 5 scales, red-brown.

STEM: Outer bark yellowish brown, inner bark yellow, branchlets pale greenish gray; pith large, round, continuous; leaf-scars low, slightly curved, more than half encircling twig; about 11 bundle-traces.

ROOT: Long, slender, deep yellow; hence, the name Yellowroot.

SIZE: 2 to 3′ in height and spreading freely as it suckers from the roots.

HARDINESS: Zone 3 to 9, in laboratory tests survived -55°F.

HABIT: A flat-topped groundcover with erect stems and celery-like leaves, filling the ground as a thicket; magnificent plant for difficult as well as normal sites especially where shade is a problem.

RATE: Medium.

TEXTURE: Medium in all seasons.

STEM AND ROOT COLOR: The inner bark and roots are yellow.

LEAF COLOR: Lustrous bright green in summer; very handsome foliage, fall color may develop golden yellow and orange; holds late, have seen foliage in early December in Boston.

FLOWERS: Brownish purple, 1/6 to 1/4″ across, star-shaped, usually occurring before the leaves in March-April, borne in 2 to 4″ long racemes, forming a racemose panicle, not showy but interesting.

FRUIT: Follicle, not effective.

CULTURE: Transplant in spring or fall; best to divide old plants and space these 18 to 24″ apart; prefers moist, well-drained soils and here makes its best growth; will do well in heavy soils; does well under average conditions but is less invasive in dry soils; full sun or partial shade; thrives along streams and moist banks; avoid high pH soils for it will develop chlorosis.

DISEASES AND INSECTS: None serious.

LANDSCAPE VALUE: A very desirable ground cover for moist areas; little known and grown; makes a very solid mat; the more I see it the more I believe it has been slighted by American gardeners; had several clumps in my Illinois garden where it did quite well; did notice chlorosis in a high pH pocket of soil; have seen tremendous plantings at Arnold Arboretum, Smith College and Heritage Plantation that would be sufficient to entice anyone to find a place for it in their landscape; abundant in southeast along water courses in the dense shade of large trees; appears to savor a cool, moist root run; sometimes develops a slight purple fall color.

PROPAGATION: Most effective method is by division of the parent plant; root cuttings will also work and June shoot cuttings treated with 8000 ppm IBA rooted in high percentages.

ADDITIONAL NOTES: From the juice (sap) the Indians extracted a yellow dye.

NATIVE HABITAT: New York to Kentucky and Florida. Introduced 1776.

Yucca

There is a certain reluctance on my part to include these sword-like members of the Agavaceae but their use in landscaping, especially in the southeast, southwest and west, is an undeniable and often horrible fact. When I see them in a landscape a feeling of old Mexico or the desert southwest arises. Several are native to the southeast and they are treated here. Too many Yuccas are sufficient reason to cause one to YUK!

Yucca filamentosa — Adam's-needle Yucca
(yuk'à fil-à-men-tō'sà)

LEAVES: Sword-like and ready for battle, 1 to 2 1/2′ long, 1 1/2 to 4″ wide, abruptly narrowed at the apex where the margins are usually infolded (cusped); from the margins curly thread-like filaments, 2 to 3″ long break away and are especially numerous toward the base.

Yucca filamentosa, Adam's-needle Yucca, is a low evergreen shrub with stiffly erect and spreading leaves, the stem of which does not rise above ground level. The real attraction occurs during May-June (Athens), July-August (Urbana) when the 3 to 6′ high, erect, conical panicles are covered with 2 to 3″ diameter yellowish white pendulous flowers. It is best used in mass and is not particular as to soil as long as it is not excessively wet. This is a very hardy species and can be grown as far north as Minnesota with some protection. It has long been confused with *Y. smalliana* but that species has thinner, flatter, narrower leaves, 7/8 to 1 3/4″ wide, long-tapered at apex. The central axis of the panicle is pubescent and the flowers are smaller (2″ long). 'Ivory Tower' forms a mounded rosette of sword-like leaves 3 to 4′ high, tall panicles of ivory-white flowers occur in summer, from Monrovia. Also listed by Monrovia is 'Starburst' with narrow long green leaves striped with creamy-yellow, tinged with pink in cooler weather; flowers like the species.

Another closely related species is *Y. flaccida,* Weakleaf Yucca, but the leaves of this species are 1 to 1 3/4′ long and 1 to 1 1/2″ wide and bent downwards, above the middle, long-pointed, with straight marginal thread-like fibers. The flowers are similar to *Y. f.* but occur in a downy, shorter panicle. 'Golden Sword' has a green margin and yellow center while in 'Bright Edge' the color patterns are reversed. As near as I can determine they are *Y. flaccida* selections. *Y. filamentosa* occurs from South Carolina to Mississippi and Florida. Cultivated 1675. Zone 3 to 9. *Y. flaccida* tends to be more inland from North Carolina to Alabama. Introduced 1816. Zone 4 to 9. *Y. smalliana* occurs from North Carolina, west to Louisiana and Tennessee. Zone 5 to 9.

Yucca glauca — Small Soapweed
(yuk'à glâ'kà)

Yugga glauca, Small Soapweed, is an evergreen shrub with a low, often prostrate stem that carries a hemispherical head of leaves 3 to 4′ in diameter. The glaucous green leaves are narrow linear, 1 to 2 1/2′ long and 1/2 to 3/4″ wide. They taper to a fine point with whitish margins beset with a few threads, the dull greenish white, 2 1/2 to 3″ long, pendulous flowers occur on an erect, 3 to 4 1/2′ high, rarely branched raceme. Flowers occur in July-August. Variety *striata* is a vigorous form with a more branched inflorescence; in 'Rosea' the flowers are tinted pink on the outside. South Dakota to New Mexico. Introduced about 1656. Zone 4 to 8. This is a rather attrractive species especially for its foliage.

Yucca gloriosa — Spanish-dagger, Moundlily Yucca
(yuk′ȧ glō-ri-ō′sȧ)

Yucca gloriosa, Spanish-dagger, is often encountered in the southeast where it forms an evergreen shrub
6 to 8′ high. I have seen it branched but it often produces a single, thick fleshy stem that is crowned
with stiff, straight 1 1/2 to 2′ long, 2 to 3″ wide, glaucous green, spine-tipped leaves. The leaves are
usually entire. The pendulous, creamy-white, often tinged red or purple, 4″ diameter flowers occur
on an erect, narrowly conical, 3 to 8′ high, 1′ wide panicle from July to September. *Y. recurvifolia,*
Curveleaf Yucca, is similar except the upper leaves are recurved rather than straight as in *Y. gloriosa.*
It is found along the coast of Georgia and Mississippi. Introduced 1794. Zone 6 to 9. *Y. gloriosa* occurs
from South Carloina to northeast Florida often on sand-dunes. Introduced 1550. Zone 6 to 9. There
are variegated forms of both but I have not seen them in cultivation in the southeast.

Propagation of the various species are best effected by dividing the fleshy roots (stems) and placing
them horizontally in a suitable medium; shoots and roots regenerate from these pieces. Pollination
of most species is effected by the pronuba moth. The moths emerge from the pupae before the
flowering of the species with which they are associated. The female gathers pollen and rolls it into a
ball; she then lays her eggs in the ovary of another flower and places the pollen-ball in the stigmatic
chamber of the ovary. The grubs feed on the ovules but leave enough to supply adequate seeds. The
yucca is entirely dependent on the moth and vice-versa. The seeds are black, compressed and
remind of little wafers. They usually occur in great numbers.

Yucca identification is scarcely straight lined and I have a difficult time separating the various species.
Dr. Wilbur Duncan, Professor Emeritus, Department of Botany, University of Georgia supplied the following
key to southeastern yucca species that might prove helpful to yuccaphiles.

Key to Southeastern Yucca Species

1. Leaves rigid, margin minutely but sharpely serrate; mature fruits fleshy . . . . 1. *Y. aloifolia*

1. Leaves pliable, leathery, margin entire and often frayed into filamentous threads;
 mature fruits dry 2

2. Leaf margin set with a thin, very narrow light brown strip (eroding with age), usually
 lacking curved or curled fibers; fruits not splitting open when mature 3

3. Leaves erect to spreading, often drooping at ends with age; fruits mostly pendent,
 seeds glossy . . . . .2. *Y. gloriosa*

3. Leaves mostly recurved, only the upper younger ones erect to spreading; fruits
 erect, seeds dull . . . . .3. *Y. recurvifolia*

2. Leaf margin green to whitish, not extremely thin, usually with filamentous curved or
 curly fibers; fruits splitting open when mature. 4

4. Inflorescence a raceme, rarely a panicle, reaching just below to a little above
 tip of upper leaves . . . . .4. *Y. arkansas*
 (*Y. glauca* var. *mollis*)

4. Inflorescence a panicle, rarely a raceme, held prominently above tip of upper leaves 5

5. Leaves stiffly pliable, minutely scabrous on both surfaces,
 the tips cusped . . . . .5. *Y. filamentosa*
 (*Y. concava*)

5. Leaves quite pliable, sometimes rough but not scabrous,
 the tip long-tapering and not cusped 6

6. Leaves 1/2 to 2 1/2″ wide; styles oblong, whitish . . . . 6. *Y. flaccida*
 (*Y. smalliana*)

6. Leaves 3/8 to 1 1/4″ (1 1/2″) wide; styles swollen, greenish . . . . 7. *Y. louisiansis*

Zanthoxylum americanum — Prickly-ash, Toothache Tree
(zan-thō-zī′lum à-mēr-i-kā′num)

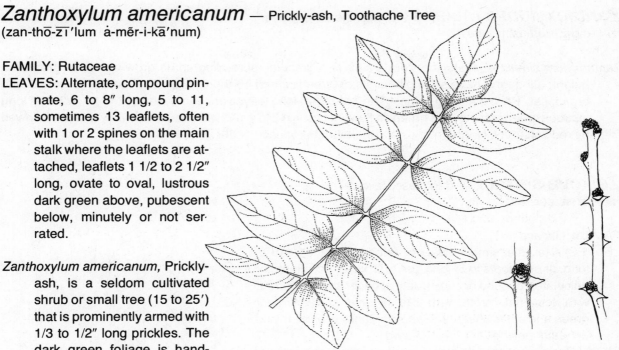

FAMILY: Rutaceae

LEAVES: Alternate, compound pinnate, 6 to 8″ long, 5 to 11, sometimes 13 leaflets, often with 1 or 2 spines on the main stalk where the leaflets are attached, leaflets 1 1/2 to 2 1/2″ long, ovate to oval, lustrous dark green above, pubescent below, minutely or not serrated.

Zanthoxylum americanum, Prickly-ash, is a seldom cultivated shrub or small tree (15 to 25′) that is prominently armed with 1/3 to 1/2″ long prickles. The dark green foliage is handsome and not susceptible to insect or disease problems. The yellowish green flowers occur in axillary clusters before the leaves on the previous season's wood. This is a dioecious species. The 2-valved, 1/5″ long black capsule matures in July-August and contains small lustrous black seeds. This species might be used in poor soil areas or where a barrier plant is needed. Supposedly the stems and fruits were chewed by the Indians to alleviate toothache for the acrid juice has a numbing effect. From a landscape standpoint this is the least desirable of the species treated here. Quebec to Nebraska and Virginia. Introduced about 1740. Zone 3 to 7.

Zanthoxylum piperitum — Japanese Prickly-ash
(zan-thō-zī′lum pī-pēr′i-tum)

Zanthoxylum piperitum, Japanese Prickly-ash, is perhaps the most ornamental member of the genus. It forms a compact, dense shrub or small tree about 8 to 15′ high and is clothed with handsome lustrous dark green leaves. Each 3 to 6″ long leaf contains 11 to 23 sessile leaflets that average 3/4 to 1 1/2″ long. The greenish yellow flowers occur in small 1 to 2″ long corymbs in June. The fruits are reddish. The black seeds are ground and used as a pepper in Japan. The stems are armed with 1/2″ long flat spines that occur in pairs at each node. This is a rather handsome plant, the leaves of which may turn yellow in the fall. Northern China, Korea, Japan. Cultivated 1877. Zone 5 to 7.

Zanthoxylum schinifolium — Peppertree
(zan-thō-zī′lum skī-ni-fō′li-um)

Zanthoxylum schinifolium, Peppertree, is a graceful medium-sized shrub growing 10′ or more. The 3 to 7″ long leaves are composed of 11 to 21, 3/4 to 1 1/2″ long deep green leaflets. The green-petaled flowers occur in 2 to 4″ diameter flattish corymbs in July-August and are followed by greenish or brownish (red) fruits. The 1/2″ long spine is solitary at the node thus differentiating this species from *Z. piperitum*. Japan, Korea, eastern China. Cultivated 1877. Zone 5 to 7.

Zanthoxylum simulans — Flatspine Prickly-ash
(zan-thō-zī'lum sim'ū-lanz)

Zanthoxylum simulans, Flatspine Prickly-ash, is a graceful, spreading shrub growing 10' or greater in
height, although I have seen plants almost tree-like and 15 to 20' high. The stems are armed with
broad, flat, 1/4 to 3/4" long spines. The 3 to 5" (9") long leaves are composed of 7 to 11, 1/2 to 2" long
lustrous green leaflets. The greenish flowers occur in 2 to 2 1/2" wide panicles in July and are followed
by reddish fruits. Northern and central China. Introduced 1869. Zone 5 to 7.

Zelkova serrata — Japanese Zelkova
(zel-kō'và ser-rā'tà)

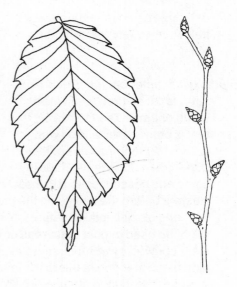

FAMILY: Ulmaceae
LEAVES: Alternate, simple, ovate to oblong-ovate, 1 1/4 to 2"
   long, or on shoots to 5" long, 3/4 to 2" wide, acuminate or
   apiculate, rounded or subcordate at base, sharply serrate
   with acuminate teeth, with 8 to 14 pairs of veins, dark
   green and somewhat rough above, glabrous or nearly so
   beneath; petioles 1/12 to 1/4" long.
BUDS: Ovoid, acutish, with many imbricate, shiny dark brown,
   broad scales; diverge at 45° angle from stem.
STEM: Pubescent when young, glabrous at maturity, brown.
BARK: Beautiful, smooth-gray initially, finally resembling that
   of Chinese Elm but usually not as exfoliating.

SIZE: 50 to 80' in height with an equal spread.
HARDINESS: Zone 5 to 8.
HABIT: In youth, a low branched, vase-shaped tree; in old age maintaining a similar form with many
   ascending branches.
RATE: Medium, possibly fast in youth, 10 to 12' over a 4 to 6 year period, have seen 3 to 4' of growth on
   young trees.
TEXTURE: Medium-fine in leaf; medium in winter.
BARK: In youth cherry-like, reddish brown, heavily lenticelled; in old age often exfoliating with a character
   not unlike that of Chinese Elm, *U. parvifolia*.
LEAF COLOR:Dark green in summer; yellow-orange-brown in fall, possibly deep red to reddish purple; in
   Athens fall color is maximized from early to mid November.
FLOWERS: Monoecious, male clustered in axils of lower leaves, female in axils of upper leaves, not showy,
   flowers in April with the leaves; in Athens have charted full flower as early as February 24 with some
   years the second week of March.
FRUIT: A small drupe, about 1/6" across, ripening in fall.
CULTURE: Transplants readily balled and burlapped; prefers moist, deep soil; pH adaptable; once
   established very wind and drought tolerant; young trees are susceptible to frost; prune in fall; displays
   reasonable pollution tolerance; in Kansas tests 'Village Green' averaged 11.6" per year over a 9 year
   period.
DISEASES AND INSECTS: Susceptible to some of the problems which beset the elms; however, resistant
   to Dutch elm disease; the trees I have observed were much cleaner than the elms; shows good
   resistance to elm leaf beetle and Japanese beetle; English reference mentioned that it was proving
   susceptible to Dutch elm disease.
LANDSCAPE VALUE: Very handsome tree because of good foliage, interesting growth habit and handsome bark; well suited to lawns, residential streets, parks, large areas; considered as a replacement
   for the American Elm but this has not, and will never, come about; there are beautiful specimens at

the Arnold, Spring Grove, Cave Hill, Bristol, R.I. area; does quite well in the south and should be used more for streets and urban areas than it is.

CULTIVARS:

'Autumn Glow'—Well proportioned head, good leaf texture, deep purple fall color.

'Green Vase'—Vase shaped with upright arching branches, very vigorous, producing a taller more graceful tree than 'Village Green', good dark green foliage, orange-brown to bronze-red fall color, 60 to 70' by 40 to 50', grows twice as fast as 'Village Green' as a young tree and 2-year old trees are 2 to 3 times higher; received the prestigious Styer Award in 1988 from the Pennsylvania Horticultural Society.

'Halka'—Have seen 'Green Vase', 'Village Green' and this form in the same nursery with 'Green Vase' and 'Halka' the fastest growing and the most graceful; this form may emulate the American elm as closely as any form because of the long, gracefully arching branches; medium to dark green summer foliage, yellowish fall color, 50' by 30'.

'Parkview'—A selection with a good vase-shape; size similar to species; Dr. Hasselkus reported that it winterkilled in Madison, Wisconsin.

'Spring Grove'—A handsome vase-shaped form with arching branches that appear slightly stiffer than 'Green Vase' and 'Halka'; the parent tree in Spring Gove, Cincinnati, OH puts other mature zelkovas to shame because of handsome dark green foliage, wine-red fall color, excellent branch structure and bark; parent tree is probably 80' with a 50 to 60' spread; has been produced in limited quantities and young trees outplanted in Spring Grove show excellent form.

'Variegata'—Weak growing, small-leaved (3/4 to 1 1/2" long) form with a narrow white rim around the margin of the leaf; might be a good bonsai subject.

'Village Green'—Selected by Princeton Nurseries, the tree grows more rapidly than ordinary seedlings and develops a smooth, straight trunk; the dark green foliage turns a rusty red in fall; much hardier than trees of Japanese origin and is highly resistant to Dutch elm disease and to leaf eating and bark beetles; I studied this selection closely during sabbatical and it is superior to the normal *Z. serrata;* it is vigorous and I recorded as much as 3' of new growth in 1978; interestingly the fall color was a reasonably good wine-red while every other *Z. serrata* in the Arnold and Boston environs was a golden brown; in laboratory hardiness tests (Dr. Harold Pellett, University of Minnesota), we found that it was not as cold hardy as some seedling material in the Arnold's collections; probably could be grown in Chicago area without too much trouble; was killed at Madison, Wisconsin; listed in 1988 Princeton Nursery catalog as one zone hardier than 'Green Vase'.

PROPAGATION: Seeds germinate without pretreatment but percentage is better when stratified at 41°F for 60 days (this was my own personal experience). I have rooted cuttings taken from seedlings with 100% success when treated with 1000 ppm IBA. Cuttings from older trees root 50 to 60% (70%). Cultivars are budded on seedling understock.

RELATED SPECIES:

Zelkova carpinifolia — Elm Zelkova
(zel-kō′vȧ kär-pī-ni-fō′li-ȧ)

LEAVES: Alternate, simple, ovate or oval, 1 1/2 to 3" long, 3/4 to 1 3/4" wide, acute, rounded or subcordate, coarsely crenate-serrate, dark green with scattered hairs above, paler and more downy below, 6 to 8 vein pairs; petiole about 1/8" long.

Zelkova carpinifolia, Elm Zelkova, forms an ovoid or oblong head or rather upright branches, 50 to 75' high, with a short beech-like trunk. It is a beautiful tree with dark green leaves that have 6 to 8 vein pairs. The bark is smooth and gray like a beech but flakes with age. There is a magnificent specimen in Kew Gardens, London. Introduced 1760. Zone 6 to ?

Zelkova schneideriana, (zel-kō'vȧ shnī-dĕr-ē-ā'nȧ), Schneider Zelkova, is a virtually unknown entity in the United States but may prove worthy of consideration. A tree in the Morris Arboretum developed excellent wine-red fall color. At first, I thought the tree was *Z. serrata* 'Village Green', but the label said otherwise. The habit is akin to *Z. serrata.* The dark green 1 3/4 to 4″ long, 3/4 to 2″ wide leaves have 7 to 14 indented vein pairs. Leaves are quite scabrous on their upper surface, much like sandpaper. Eastern China. Introduced 1920. Zone 6 to 8.

Zelkova sinica — Chinese Zelkova
(zel-kō'vȧ sin'i-kȧ)

LEAVES: Alternate, simple, elliptic to oblong, 1 to 2 1/2″ long, 2/3 to 1 1/8″ wide, acuminate or apiculate, rounded or broad cuneate, sharply serrate with acute or apiculate teeth, dull dark green and scabrous above, grayish green and pubescent below, 7 to 10 vein pairs; petiole short, pubescent.

Zelkova sinica, Chinese Zelkova, is smaller (probably 20 to 40′ high under cultivation) than the other species and sometimes multi-trunked. The dark green leaves have 7 to 10 vein pairs. The bark is probably the handsomest of the genus and on old trunks assumes a rich mottle of gray, orange, and rich brown. One key difference I noted between this and *Z. serrata* is that the winter buds are more plump and rounded while those of *Z. serrata* are ovoid and pointed. There is a specimen at the Morton Arboretum that indicates the species may be hardier than the Zone 6 rating it was originally given. Central and eastern China. Introduced 1908.

Zenobia pulverulenta — Dusty Zenobia
(zen-ō'bi-ȧ pul-vĕr-ū-len'tȧ)

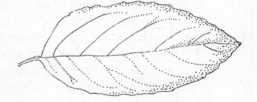

FAMILY: Ericaceae
LEAVES: Alternate, simple, semi-evergreen to deciduous, oval to oblong, 1 to 3″ long, obtuse or acutish, usually rounded at base; entire to serrulate-crenate, glabrous and covered more or less with a glaucous bloom on both surfaces appearing bluish green to gray green.
STEM: Glabrous, glaucous, bloomy, often arching.

Zenobia pulverulenta, Dusty Zenobia, is a 2 to 3′ high (6′) gracefully arching shrub. The glaucous green leaves are particularly attractive and in fall may turn yellowish with a tinge of red. The 3/8″ broad, white, anise-scented flowers occur on slender, nodding, 3/4″ long stalks in axillary clusters during May-June. It is difficult to root from cuttings but will come readily from seed. Requires acid, moist, well-drained soil for best growth. Often available from native plant nurseries. Some nurseries offer selected dusty blue foliage forms and appear to have no trouble rooting them. North Carolina to Florida. Zone 5 to 9. Introduced 1801.

Ziziphus jujuba — Chinese Date (The generic name is also spelled *Zizyphus*)
(ziz'i-fus jö-jö'bȧ)

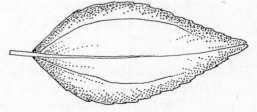

FAMILY: Rhamnaceae
LEAVES: Alternate, simple, oval, ovate to ovate-lanceolate, 1 to 2 1/2″ long, acutish or obtusish, oblique, 3-nerved at base, crenate-serrulate, lustrous dark green, glabrous, firm; petiole 1/8 to 1/4″ long.

STEM: Glabrous, flexuose, with paired spines at the nodes, the larger straighter ones to 1 1/4", the shorter—decurved.

Ziziphus jujuba, Chinese Date, is a rather unique large shrub or small tree with handsome lustrous green foliage, rounded outline, and 15 to 20' (25') ultimate size. Leaves may turn good yellow in fall. The small, 1/4" diameter yellowish flowers occur 2 to 3 together from the leaf axils of the current season's growth. The edible fruits, which I have been fooled by on previous occasions, are plum-like to egg-shaped in outline, 1/2 to 1" long and generally listed as dark red to black when ripe. A former student's, Mr. Mark Callahan, greatest joy was trying to ruin my Monday by attacking me with some unusual plant from the vicinity of Hazelhurst, GA. The fruits he brought were more brownish than red or black. The species will grow in any well drained soil and based on observations at Tennessee Valley Nursery, Winchester, TN is hardy to -15°F. Obviously this is a plant for the collector and will never find its way into the gardening mainstream. However, at least four individuals wanted to know why it was left out of the book. Well, I couldn't take the pressure and relented. Happy Chinese Dating. Seeds are the usual means of propagation and apparently require 3 months warm/3 months cold for best germination. Cultivars are grafted to seedling understocks. 'Lang' is precocious and bears 1 1/2 to 2" long fruits while 'Li' has 2" long fruits. Southeastern Europe to southern and eastern Asia. Introduced about 1640. Zone 6 to 9.

BIBLIOGRAPHY

Adams, William D. 1976. *Trees for Southern Landscapes.* Pacesetter Press, Houston, TX. 85 p.

Adams, William D. 1979. *Shrubs and Vines for Southern Landscapes.* Pacesetter Press. Houston, TX. 70 p.

Agricultural Research Service. U.S.D.A. 1970. *Crabapples of Documented Authentic Origin.* Washington, D.C. 107 p.

Agricultural Research Service. U.S.D.A. 1973. *International Checklist of Cultivated Ilex.* Supt. of Doc., U.S. Gov. Printing Office. Washington, D.C. 84 p.

Allan, Mea. 1974. *Plants That Changed Our Gardens.* David and Charles. North Pomfret, VT.

Allen, Gertrude E. 1968. *Everyday Trees.* Houghton Mifflin. Boston. 47 p.

American Horticultural Society. 1976. *Environmentally Tolerant Trees, Shrubs and Ground Covers.* AHS. Mt. Vernon, VA. 27 p.

Angelo, Ray. 1978. *Concord Area Shrubs.* Concord Field Station Museum of Comparative Zoology Harvard University. Cambridge, Massachusetts. 128 p.

Apgar, Austin C. 1892. *Trees of the Northern United States.* American Book Co., N.Y. 224 p.

Apgar, Austin C. 1910. *Ornamental Shrubs of the United States.* American Book Co., N.Y. 352 p.

Arno, Stephen F. and Ramona P. Hammerly. 1977. *Northwest Trees.* Mountaineers, Seattle. 161 p.

Arnold, Henry F. 1980. *Trees in Urban Design.* Van Nostrand Reinhold, N.Y. 168 p.

Arthurs, Kathryn. 1979. *Sunset Lawns and Ground Covers.* Lane Publ. Co. Menlo Park, Calif. 96 p.

Atkinson, Robert E. 1970. *The Complete Book of Groundcovers: Lawns You Don't Have to Mow.* McKay, N.Y. 210 p.

Baerg, Harry J. 1973. *How to Know the Western Trees.* W. C. Brown Co. Dubuque, Iowa. 179 p.

Bailey, Liberty Hyde. 1914. *The Standard Cyclopedia of Horticulture.* Vols. I, II, III. Macmillan Co. N.Y. 3639 p.

Bailey, Liberty Hyde. 1923. *The Cultivated Evergreens.* Macmillan Co. N.Y. 434 p.

Bailey, Liberty Hyde. 1933. *How Plants Get Their Names.* Macmillan Co. N.Y. 209 p.

Bailey, Liberty Hyde. 1934. *Gardener's Handbook.* Macmillan Co. N.Y. 292 p.

Bailey, Liberty Hyde. 1948. *The Cultivated Conifers in North America.* Macmillan Co. N.Y. 404 p.

Bailey, Liberty Hyde. 1949. *Manual of Cultivated Plants.* Macmillan Co. N.Y. 1116 p.

Bailey Hortorium. 1976. *Hortus III.* Macmillan Co. New York. 1290 p.

Barber, Peter N. and C. E. Lucas Phillips. 1975. *The Trees Around Us.* Follett. Chicago. 191 p.

Barnes, Burton V. 1981. *Michigan Trees: A Guide to the Trees of Michigan and the Great Lakes Region.* Univ. Michigan Press. Ann Arbor. 383 p.

Bärtels, Andreas. 1986. *Gardening With Dwarf Trees and Shrubs.* Timber Press. Portland, Oregon. 294 p.

Bawden, H. E. and J. E. G. Good. 1980. *Dwarf Shrubs: A Gardener's Guide.* Alpine Garden Society. Woking, Surrey, England. 121 p.

Bean, W. J. Variable dates. *Trees and Shrubs Hardy in the British Isles,* 8th Ed. Vols. I, II, III, IV and Supplement. John Murray Ltd. London.

Beckett, Kenneth A. 1975. *The Love of Trees.* Octopus Books. London. 96 p.

Beckett, Kenneth A. 1981. *The Complete Book of Evergreens.* Ward Lock Ltd. London. 160 p.

Benson, Lyman. 1959. *Plant Classification.* D. C. Heath and Co., Lexington, MA. 688 p.

Berg, Johann and Lothar Heft. 1969. *Rhododendron and Evergreen Deciduous Trees.* E. Ulmer. Stuttgart, 284 p.

Berns, E. R. 1967. *Native Trees of Newfoundland and Labrador.* St. John's, Newfoundland. 74 p.

Berry, James Berthold. 1966. *Western Forest Trees.* Dover. N.Y. 238 p.

Blackburn, Benjamin. 1952. *Trees and Shrubs in Eastern North America.* Oxford University Press. N.Y. 358 p.

Blakeslee, Albert Francis, and Chester Deacon Jarvis. 1972. *Northeastern Trees in Winter.* Dover Publications. Inc. N.Y. 264 p.

Blanchard, Robert O. and Terry A. Tattar. 1981.*Field and Laboratory Guide to Tree Pathology.* Academic Press, Inc. New York. 285 p.

Bloom, Adrian. 1986. *Conifers and Heathers for a Year-Round Garden.* Aura Books and Floraprint Ltd. London. 78 p.

Bloom, Adrian, *Conifers for Your Garden.* American Garden Guild. 145 p.

Bloom, Alan. 1976. *Plantsman's Progress.* T. Dalton. Lavenham, England. 142 p.

Boddy, Frederick A. 1974. *Ground Cover and Other Ways to Weed Free Gardens.* David and Charles. North Pomfret, VT. 184 p.

Bonar, Ann. 1973. *Shrubs for All Seasons.* Hamlyn, London. 64 p.

Boom, Dr. B. K. and H. Kleijn. 1966. *The Glory of the Tree.* George G. Harrap and Co. Ltd. London. 128 p.

Bonnie, Fred. 1976. *Flowering Trees, Shrubs, and Vines: A Guide for Home Gardens.* Oxmoor House. Birmingham, AL. 96 p.

Bowers, Clement Gray. 1960. *Rhododendrons and Azaleas.* Macmillan Co. N.Y. 525 p.

Brickell, C. D. and Brian Mathew. 1976. *Daphne: the Genus in the Wild and in Cultivation.* The Alpine Garden Soc. Lye End Link, St. John's, Woking. GU21 1 SW, Surrey. 194 p.

Britton, Nathaniel Lord and Addison Brown. 1912. *Illustrated Flora of the Northern United States, Canada and the British Possessions,* Vols. I, II, III. Charles Scribner's Sons. N.Y.

Brooklyn Botanic Gardens' Plants and Gardens Handbooks covering a multitude of subjects. Book list available from Brooklyn Botanic Garden, 1000 Washington Avenue, Brooklyn, N.Y. 11225.

Brown, Clair Alan. 1966. *Mississippi Trees.* Mississippi Forestry Commission, Jackson. 938 p.

Brown, George E. 1972. *The Pruning of Trees, Shrubs & Conifers.* Faber and Faber. London. 351 p.

Brown, H. P. 1075. *Trees of New York State.* Dover Publications, Inc. New York. 433 p.

Brown, H. P. 1938. *Trees of Northeastern United States.* Christopher Publishing House. Boston, Mass. 488 p.

Brown, Russell G. and Melvin L. Brown. 1972. *Woody Plants of Maryland.* Univ. Maryland, College Park. 347 p.

Buckley, A. R. 1980. *Trees and Shrubs of the Dominion Arboretum.* Agriculture Canada, Research Branch. 237 p.

Burns, George Plumer and Charles Herbert Otis. 1979. *The Handbook of Vermont Trees.* Tuttle. Portland, VT. 244 p.

Bush, Charles S. 1972. *Flowers, Shrubs and Trees for Florida Homes.* Florida Dept. Agr. and Consumer Services. Tallahassee, FL. 176 p.

Butcher, D. 1964. *Knowing Your Trees.* American Forestry Assoc. Washington, D.C. 349 p.

Campbell, Christopher S., Fay Hyland and Mary L. F. Campbell. 1977. *Winter Keys to Woody Plants of Maine.* University of Maine Press, Orono. 52 p.

Carpenter, Philip L., Theodore D. Walker, and Frederick O. Lanphear. 1975. *Plants in the Landscape.* W. H. Freeman. San Francisco. 481 p.

Carter, Cedric J. 1964. *Illinois Trees: Their Diseases.* III. Nat. Hist. Survey. Urbana, Ill. 96 p.

Carter, Cedric J. 1970. *Illinois Trees: Selection, Planting and Care.* III. Nat. Hist. Survey. Urbana, Ill. 123 p.

Chadbund, Geoffrey. 1972. *Flowering Cherries.* Collins. London. 160 p.

Clapham, A. R., T. G. Tutin, and E. F. Warburg. 1962. *Flora of the British Isles.* University Press. Cambridge. 1269 p.

Clark, Ross C. 1962. *A Distributional Study of the Woody Plants of Alabama.* Univ. North Carolina Press. Chapel Hill, NC. 269 p.

Clark, Ross, C. 1972. *The Woody Plants of Alabama.* Missouri Bot. Gar. Press. St. Louis. 242 p.

Clouston, Brian (ed.) 1977. *Landscape Design and Plants.* Heinemann, London. 456 p.

Clovis, Jesse F. 1977. *The Woody Plants of the Core Arboretum.* West Virginia University, Morgantown. 83 p.

Coats, Alice M. 1964. *Garden Shrubs and Their Histories.* E. P. Dutton & Co., Inc., N.Y. 416 p.

Collingwood, George Harris. 1978. *Knowing Your Trees.* Amer. Forestry Assoc. Washington, D.C. 392 p.

Compton, James. 1987. *Success with Unusual Plants.* William Collins, Sons and Company Ltd. London. 192 p.

Cope, Edward A. 1986. *Native and Cultivated Conifers of Northeastern North America.* Cornell University Press. Ithaca, New York. 231 p.

Core, Earl L. and Nelle P. Ammons. 1958. *Woody Plants in Winter.* Boxwood Press, California. 218 p.

Courtright, Gordon. 1979. *Trees and Shrubs for Western Gardens.* Timber Press. Forest Grove, OR. 329 p.

Cox, Peter A. 1973. *Dwarf Rhododendrons.* Macmillan. N.Y. 296 p.

Cox, Peter S. and Kenneth N. E. Cox. 1988. *The Encyclopedia of Rhododendron Hybrids.* Timber Press, Portland, OR. 384 p.

Crittenden, Mabel and Jack Popovich. 1977. *Trees of the West.* Celestial Arts, Millbrae, CA. 212 p.

Crockett, James Underwood. 1972. *Evergreens.* Time-Life Series. Time-Life Books. N.Y. 160 p.

Crockett, James Underwood. 1972. *Flowering Shrubs.* Time-Life Series. 160 p.

Crockett, James Underwood. 1972. *Lawns and Ground Covers.* Time-Life Series. 160 p.

Crockett, James Underwood. 1972. *Trees.* Time-Life Series. 160 p. (Numerous other books in Time-Life Series.)

Curtis, Carlton C. and S. C. Bausor. 1943. *The Complete Guide to North American Trees.* Collier Books. New York, N.Y. 342 p.

Curtis, Ralph W., John F. Cornman, and Robert G. Mower. 1962. *Vegetative Keys to Common Ornamental Woody Plants.* New York State College of Agriculture. Cornell University, Ithaca, N.Y. 83 p.

Dallimore, W. and Bruce A. Jackson. 1967. *A Handbook of Coniferae and and Ginkgoaceae.* St. Martin's Press, N.Y. 700 p.

Dallimore, W. 1978. *Holly, Yew and Box.* John Lane Co, The Bodley Head. New York & London. 284 p.

Dame, Lorin L. and Henry Brooks. 1972. *Trees of New England.* Dover Publications, Inc. N.Y. 196 p.

Daniels, Roland. 1975. *Street Trees.* Penn State Univ. State College, PA. 47 p.

Davis, Brian. 1987. *The Gardener's Illustrated Encyclopedia of Trees and Shrub.* Viking. Penguin Books Ltd. England. 256 p.

Davis, Donald E. and Norman D. Davis. 1975. *Guide and Key to Alabama Trees.* Kendall Hunt. Dubuque, Iowa. 136 p.

Dayton, William A. and Harlan P. Kelsey. 1942. *Standardized Plant Names.* J. Horace McFarland Co., Harrisburg, PA. 675 p.

Deam, Charles C. 1921. *Shrubs of Indiana.* State of Indiana Publication No. 44. Indiana. 350 p.

Dean, Blanche E. 1968. *Trees and Shrubs in the Heart of Dixie.* Southern University Press. Birmingham, AL. 246 p.

Dean, F. W. and L. C. Chadwick. *Ohio Trees.* Ohio State University. Columbus, Ohio. 127 p.

Degraaf, Richard M. and Gretchin M. Witman. 1979. *Trees, Shrubs, and Vines for Attracting Birds: A Manual for the Northeast.* Univ. Mass. Press. Amherst. 194 p.

denBoer, Arie F. 1959. *Ornamental Crabapples.* American Association of Nurserymen. 226 p.

Dirr, Michael. 1984. *All About Evergreens.* Ortho Books. San Francisco, California. 96 p.

Dirr, Michael A. 1983. *Manual of Woody Landscape Plants.* 3rd Edition. Stipes. Champaign, IL. 826 p.

Dirr, Michael A. 1978. *Photographic Manual of Woody Landscape Plants.* Stipes. Champaign, IL. 376 p.

Dirr, Michael A. and Charles W. Heuser, Jr. 1987. *The Reference Manual of Woody Plant Propagation.* Varsity Press, Inc. Athens, GA.

Duble, Richard and James C. Kell. 1977. *Southern Lawns and Groundcovers.* Pacesetter Press. Houston, TX. 91 p.

Duncan, Wilbur H. 1975. *Woody Vines of the Southeastern United States.* Univ. Georgia Press. Athens. 75 p.

Duncan, Wilbur H. and Marion B. Duncan. 1987. *The Smithsonian Guide to Seaside Plants of the Gulf and the Atlantic Coasts.* Smithsonian Institution Press, Washington, D.C. 409 p.

Duncan, Wilbur H. and Marion B. Duncan. 1988. *Trees of the Southeastern United States.* University of Georgia Press, Athens, GA. 322 p.

Easterly, Nathan William. 1976. *Woody Plants of the Oak Openings.* Dept. of Biological Sciences, Bowling Green State University. Bowling Green, Ohio. 143 p.

Ebinger, J. E. and H. F. Thut. 1970. *Woody Plants of East Central Illinois.* Kendall Hunt. Dubuque, Iowa. 135 p.

Edlin, Herbert L. 1970. *Know Your Conifers.* Forestry Commission Booklet 15. HMSO. London. 64 p.

Edlin, Herbert L. 1976. *Trees and Man.* Columbia Univ. Press. N.Y. 269 p.

Edlin, Herbert L. 1978. *The Illustrated Encyclopedia of Trees: Timbers and Forests of the World.* Harmony Books. N.Y. 256 p.

Edlin, Herbert L. 1978. *The Tree Key: A Guide to Identification in Garden, Field, and Forest.* Scribner, N.Y. 280 p.

Egolf, Donald R. and Anne O. Andrick. 1978. *The Lagerstroemia Handbook Checklist.* Amer. Assoc. Bot. Gardens and Arbor. 72 p.

Elias, Thomas S. 1981. *Illustrated Guide to Street Trees.* The New York Botanical Garden. Bronx, New York. 107 p.

Elias, Thomas S. 1980. *The Complete Trees of North America: Field Guide and Natural History.* Van Nostrand Reinhold. N.Y. 948 p.

Elwes, Henry John and Augustine Henry. 1906–1913. *The Trees of Great Britain and Ireland.* VII volumes with index plus VII accompanying volumes of photographs. Magnificent Work. Privately printed.

English, L. L. 1970. *Illinois Trees and Shrubs: Their Insect Enemies.* Ill. Nat. Hist. Survey. Urbana, Ill. 91 p.

Evelyn, John. 1979. *Silva: et. al.* Strobart and Son. London. 235 p.

Everett, Thomas H. 1980. *The New York Botanical Garden Illustrated Encyclopedia of Horticulture.* Garland STP. Press. N.Y.

Farrer, Reginald. 1938. *The English Rock-Garden.* Vol. 1 & 2. C. & E. C. Jack, Ltd. Edinburgh. 524 p. and 504 p.

Feathers, David L. and Milton H. Brown. 1978. *The Camellia (History, Culture, Genetics and a Look Into Its Future Development.)* R. L. Bryan Co., Columbia, South Carolina. 476 p.

Ferguson, Barbara (Ed.). 1982. *All About Trees.* Ortho Books. San Francisco, California. 112 p.

Fernald, Merritt Lyndon. 1950. *Gray's Manual of Botany.* 8th ed. American Book Co. 1632 p.

Fiala, John L. 1988. *Lilacs.* Timber Press, Portland, Or. 372 p.

Finch, Irene. 1969. *Autumn Trees.* Longmans, London. 79 p.

Fish, Margery. 1970. *Ground Cover Plants.* David and Charles. North Pomfret, VT. 144 p.

Foley, Daniel J. 1969. *The Flowering World of "Chinese" Wilson.* Macmillan. N.Y. 334 p.

Foley, Daniel J. 1972. *Ground Covers for Easier Gardening.* Dover Publ. Inc., N.Y. 224 p.

Foley, Daniel J. 1974. *Gardening by the Sea.* Chilton Book Co., Radnor, Penn. 295 p.

Forest Service, U.S.D.A. 1974. *Seeds of Woody Plants in the United States,* Agriculture Handbook No. 450. Supt. of Doc. U.S. Gov. Printing Office. Washington, D.C. 883 p.

Forsberg, Junius L. 1979. *Diseases of Ornamental Plants.* Univ. Ill. Press. Urbana-Champaign. 222 p.

Frederick, William H., Jr. 1975. *100 Great Garden Plants.* Knopf. N.Y. 207 p.

Galle, Fred C. 1985. *Azaleas.* Timber Press. Portland, Oregon. 486 p.

Garden and Landscape Staff, Southern Living Magazine. 1980. *Trees and Shrubs, Gound Covers, Vines.* Oxmoor House. Birmingham, Ala. 260 p.

Gault, S. Millar. 1976. *The Color Dictionary of Shrubs.* Crown Publishing, Inc. New York. 208 p.

Gilmour, J. S. L. 1980. *International Code of Nomenclature of Cultivated Plants.* International Assoc. for Plant Taxonomy. Utrecht. Netherlands. 32 p.

Godfrey, Robert K. 1988. *Trees, Shrubs, and Woody Vines of Northern Florida and Adjacent Georgia and Alabama.* Univ. of Georgia Press. Athens and London. 734 p.

Gorer, Richard. 1971. *Multi-season Trees and Shrubs.* Faber and Faber. London. 192 p.

Gorer, Richard. 1976. *Trees and Shrubs: A Complete Guide.* David and Charles. North Pomfret, VT. 264 p.

Graetz, Karl E. 1973. *Seacoast Plants of the Carolinas for Conservation and Beautification.* U.S.D.A. Soil Conservation Service. Raleigh, North Carolina. 206 p.

Graves, Arthur Harmount. 1956. *Illustrated Guide to Trees and Shrubs.* Harper and Row. N.Y. 271 p.

Green, Charlotte Hilton. 1939. *Trees of the South.* The University of North Carolina Press, Chapel Hill, NC. 551 p.

Greene, Wilhelmina F. and Hugo L. Blomquist. 1953. *Flowers of the South.* The University of North Carolina Press. Chapel Hill, NC. 208 p.

Grimm, William Carey. 1962. *The Book of Trees.* Stackpole Co. Harrisburg, PA. 493 p.

Grimm, William Carey. 1966. *Recognizing Native Shrubs.* Stackpole Company. Harrisburg, PA. 319 p.

Grimm, William Carey. 1969. *Recognizing Flowering Wild Plants.* Stackpole Co. Harrisburg, PA. 319 p.

Grimm, William Carey. 1970. *Home Guide to Trees, Shrubs and Wildflowers.* Stackpole Books. Harrisburg, PA. 320 p.

Grounds, Roger. 1974. *Shrubs and Decorative Evergreens.* Ward Lock. London. 127 p.

Grounds, Roger. 1974. *Trees for Smaller Gardens.* Dent, London. 269 p.

Halfacre, R. Gordon and Anne R. Shawcroft. 1989. *Landscape Plants of the Southeast.* Sparks Press, Raleigh, N.C. 426 p.

Hansell, Dorothy E., ed. 1970. *Handbook on Hollies.* The American Horticultural Magazine. Mt. Vernon, VA. 333 p.

Hardwicke, Denis, A. R. Toogood, and A. J. Huxley. 1973. *Evergreen Garden Trees and Shrubs.* Macmillan, N.Y. 216 p.

Harlow, William M. 1942. *Trees of the Eastern United States and Canada.* Whittlesey House, N.Y. 512 p.

Harlow, William M. 1946. *Fruit Key and Twig Key.* Dover Publications, Inc. N.Y. 56 p.

Harlow, William M. and Ellwood S. Harrar. 1969. *Textbook of Dendrology,* 5th Ed. McGraw-Hill Book Co. 512 p.

Harrar, Ellwood S. and J. George Harrar. 1962. *Guide to Southern Trees,* 2nd Ed. Dover Publications, Inc., N.Y. 709 p.

Harris, Cyril Charles, ed. 1979. *An Illustrated Guide to Flowering Trees and Shrubs.* Orbis, London. 444 p.

Harris, Richard W. 1983. *Arboriculture: Care of Trees, Shrub, and Vines in the Landscape.* Prentice-Hall, Inc. Englewood Cliffs, N.J. 688 p.

Harrison, Charles E. 1975. *Ornamental Conifers.* Hafner Press, N.Y. 224 p.

Harrison, Richmond E. 1974. *Handbook of Trees and Shrubs.* Reed Wellington. 409 p.

Harrison, Richard E. and Charles R. Harrison. 1972. *Trees and Shrubs.* Reed Wellington. 199 p.

Hartmann, Hudson J. and Dale E. Kester. 1975. *Plant Propagation: Principles and Practices.* 3rd Ed. Prentice-Hall, Inc., Englewood Cliffs, N.J. 662 p.

Haworth-Booth, Michael. 1959. *The Hydrangeas.* Constable Publishers, London. 185 p.

Hay, Roy and D. M. Synge. 1975. *The Color Dictionary of Flowers and Plants for Home and Garden.* Crown. N.Y. 584 p.

Helmer, Jane Coleman and John L. Threlkeld. 1979. *Pictorial Library of Landscape Plants.* Merchants Publ. Co. Kalamazoo, MI. 335 p.

Helwig, Larry. 1975. *Native Shrubs of South Dakota.* 97 p.

Heptig, George H. 1971. *Diseases of Forest and Shade Trees of the United States.* Agricultural Handbook No. 386. U.S.D.A. Forest Service. Supt. of Doc. U.S. Gov. Printing Office. Wash. D.C. 658 p.

Hicks, Ray R. and Scott Swearingen. 1978. *Woody Plants of the Western Gulf Region.* Kendall/Hunt. Dubuque, Iowa. 339 p.

Hightshoe, Gary L. 1978. *Native Trees for Urban and Rural America: A Planting Design Manual for Environmental Designers.* Iowa State, Ames. 370 p.

Hillier and Sons. 1977. *Hilliers' Manual of Trees and Shrubs.* David and Charles, Inc. North Pomfret, VT. 575 p.

Hillier and Sons. 1981. *The Hillier Colour Dictionary of Trees and Shrubs.* David and Charles, Inc., North Pomfret, VT. 323 p.

Hoag, Donald, G. 1965. *Trees and Shrub for the Northern Plains.* N. Dakota Institute for Regional Studies. Fargo. 376 p.

Hora, Bayard. 1981. *The Oxford Encyclopedia of Trees of the World.* Oxford Univ. Press. Oxford. 288 p.

Hosie, R. C. 1973. *Native Trees of Canada.* Queens Printer. Ottawa. 380 p.

Hudak, Joseph. 1980. *Trees for Every Purpose.* McGraw-Hill, New York. 229 p.

Hume, H. Harold. 1954. *Gardening in the Lower South.* The Macmillan Co. New York. 377 p.

Huxley, Anthony (ed.). 1973. *Deciduous Garden Trees and Shrubs.* Macmillan Publishing Co., Inc. New York. 216 p.

Huxley, Anthony (ed.). 1973. *Evergreen Garden Trees and Shrubs.* Macmillan Publishing Co., Inc. New York. 181 p.

Hyams, Edwards. 1965. *Ornamental Shrubs for Temperate Zone Gardens.* A.S. Barnes and Co. N.Y. 315 p.

Hyland, Fay. 1977. *The Woody Plants of Sphagnous Bogs of Northern New England and Adjacent Canada.* Univ. Maine Press, Orono. 110 p.

Ingram, Collingwood. 1948. *Ornamental Cherries.* Country Life Ltd. London. 259 p.

Janick, Jules. 1986. *Horticultural Science.* 4th Edition. W. H. Freeman and Co. New York. 746 p.

Jaynes, Richard A. 1975. *The Laurel Book.* Hafner Press. N.Y. 180 p.

Jaynes, Richard A. 1988. *Kalmia The Laurel Book II.* Timber Press. Portland, Oregon. 220 p.

Jefferson, Roland M. and Alan E. Fusonie. 1977. *The Japanese Flowering Cherry Trees of Washington D.C.; A Living Symbol of Friendship.* U.S.D.A. Washington, D.C. 66 p.

Jefferson-Brown, M. J. 1957. *The Winter Garden.* Faber and Faber. London. 156 p.

Jennings, Neal A. 1978. *Broadleaf Trees for Nebraska.* Coop. Ext. Service, Univ. Nebraska. Lincoln. 58 p.

Jobling, J. and A. F. Mitchell. 1974. *Field Recognition of British Elms.* Forestry Commission Booklet 42. HMSO. London. 24 p.

Johns, Leslie. 1973. *Garden Trees.* David and Charles. North Pomfret, VT. 172 p.

Johnson, Hugh and Paul Miles. 1981. *The Pocket Guide to Garden Plants.* Simon and Shuster. N.Y. 192 p.

Johnson, Hugh. 1973. *The International Book of Trees.* Simon and Shuster, Inc. N.Y. 286 p.

Johnson, Hugh. 1979. *The Principles of Gardening.* Simon and Shuster, New York. 272 p.

Johnson, Warren T. and Howard H. Lyon. 1976. Insects That Feed on Trees and Shrubs. Comstock Publishing Assoc., Division of Cornell University Press. Ithaca, N.Y. 463 p.

Johnstone, G. H. 1955. *Asiatic Magnolias in Cultivation.* The Royal Horticultural Society. London. 160 p.

Jones, Almut G. and David T. Bell. 1976. *Guide to Common Woody Plants of Robert Allerton Park.* Stipes Publishing Company. Champaign, Illinois. 36 p.

Jones, George Neville. 1971. *Flora of Illinois.* University of Notre Dame, Notre Dame, Indiana. 401 p.

Jones, Ronald K. and Robert C. Lamb. *Diseases of Woody Ornamental Plants and Their Control in Nurseries.* Cooperative Extension Service, University of Georgia. Athens, Georgia. 130 p.

Jones, Samuel B. and Arlene E. Luchsinger. 1986. *Plant Systematics.* McGraw-Hill Book Co. 512 p.

Jones, Samuel B. and Leonard E. Foote. 1989. *Native Shrubs and Woody Vines of the Southeast.* Timber Press, Portland, OR. 199 p.

Keeler, Harriet L. 1916. *Our Northern Shrubs.* Charles Scribner's Sons. N.Y. 519 p.

Keith, Rebecca McIntosh, and F.A. Giles. 1980. *Dwarf Shrubs for the Midwest.* University of Illinois at Urbana-Champaign, College of Agriculture Special Publication 60. 163 p.

Kelly, George W. 1979. *Shrubs for the Rocky Mountains: A Manual of the U.S. and Care of Shrubs in the Rocky Mountain Area.* Rocky Mountain Horticultural Publ. Co. Cortez, Colo. 171 p.

Kelly, George W. 1970. *A Guide to the Woody Plants of Colorado.* Purett Publ. Co. Boulder. 180 p.

Kelsey, Harlan P. and William A. Dayton. 1942. *Standardized Plant Names,* 2nd Ed. J. Horace McFarland Co. Harrisburg, PA. 675 p.

Kent, Adolphus H. 1900. *Veitch's Manual of the Coniferae.* James Veitch and Sons, Ltd. Chelsea, England. 562 p.

Knobel, Edward. 1972. *Identify Trees and Shrubs by Their Leaves.* Dover Publications, Inc. N.Y. 47 p.

Koller, Gary L. and Michael A. Dirr. 1979. *Street Trees for Home and Minicipal Landscapes. Arnoldia* 39:73–237.

Krüssmann, Gerd. 1982. *Pocket Guide to Choosing Woody Ornamentals.* Timber Press, Portland OR. 140 p.

Krüssmann, Gerd. 1985. *Manual of Cultivated Broad-Leaved Trees and Shrub.* Vol. I-III. Timber Press. Portland, Oregon.

Krüssmann, Gerd. 1985. *Manual of Cultivated Conifers.* Timber Press. Portland, Oregon. 361 p.

Kumlier, Loraine L. 1946. *The Friendly Evergreens.* Rinehart. N.Y. 237 p.

Labadie, Emile L. 1978. *Native Plants for Use in the California Landscape.* Sierra City Press. Sierra City, California. 244 p.

Lamb, Samuel H. 1975. *Woody Plants of the Southwest.* Sunstone Press. Sante Fe. 122 p.

Lancaster, Roy. 1974. *Trees for Your Garden.* Charles Scribner's Sons., New York. 145 p.

Lanzara, Paolo. 1978. *Simon and Shuster's Guide to Trees.* Simon and Shuster. N.Y. 327 p.

Lawrence, George H. M. 1951. *Taxonomy of Vascular Plants.* Macmillan Co. N.Y. 823 p.

Leach, David G. 1961. *Rhododendrons of the World.* Charles Scribner's Sons. N.Y. 544 p.

Lee, Frederic P. 1965. *The Azalea Book.* D. Van Nostrand Company, Inc. Princeton, N.J. 435 p.

Lemmon, Robert S. 1952. *The Best Loved Trees of America.* The American Garden Guild. Garden City, N.Y. 254 p.

Lentz, A. N. *Common Forest Trees of New Jersey.* Ext. Bull. 396. Coop. Ext. Service Rutgers Univ. New Brunswick, N.J.

Li, Hui-lin. 1963. *The Origin and Cultivation of Shade and Ornamental Trees.* Univ. of Penn. Press. Philadelphia, PA. 282 p.

Li, Hui-lin. 1972. *Trees of Pennsylvania, The Atlantic States and the Lake States.* Univ. of Pennsylvania Press. Philadelphia, PA. 276 p.

Little, Elbert L. 1968. *Southwestern Trees—A Guide to the Native Species of New Mexico and Arizona.* U.S.D.A. Forest Service. Washington, D.C. 109 p.

Little, Elbert L. 1977. *Atlas of United States Trees.* U.S.D.A. Superintendent Documents. Washington, D.C.

Little, Elbert L. 1980. *The Audubon Society Field Guide to North American Trees, Eastern Region.* Knopf, N.Y. 714 p.

Little, Elbert L. 1980. *The Audubon Society Field Guide to North American Trees, Western Region. Knopf, N.Y. 639 p.*

Logan, Harry Britton. 1974. *A Traveler's Guide to North American Gardens.* Charles Scribner's Sons. New York. 253 p.

Loudon, John C. 1836. *Arboretum et Fruticetum Britannicum.* VII volumes plus index. A. Spottiswoode. London.

Lyons, C. P. 1952. *Trees, Shrubs and Flowers to Know in British Columbia.* J. M. Dent & Sons Ltd. Canada, 194 p.

Lyons, Chester Peter. 1956. *Trees, Shrubs, and Flowers to Know in Washington.* Dent. Toronto. 211 p.

Macdonald, Bruce. 1986. *Practical Woody Plant Propagation for Nursery Growers.* Timber Press. Portland, Oregon. 669 p.

Maki, Mary M., P. Bischoff, E. H. Emerson, L. T. Grady, B. L. Hoadley, H. W. Lanphear and M. A. Livingston. 1975. *Trees in Amherst.* Garden Club of Amherst. Amherst, Massachusetts. 1160.

Makins, F. K. 1948. *The Identification of Trees and Shrubs.* E. P. Dutton and Co., N.Y. 350 p.

Maino, Evelyn and Frances Howard. 1955. *Ornamental Trees.* Univ. Calif. Press. Berkeley. 219 p.

Marshall, Humphry. 1967. *Arbustum Americanum: The American Grove.* Hafner Publishing Co. N.Y. and London. 278 p.

Mayer, A. M. and A. Poljakoff-Mayber. 1982. *The Germination of Seeds.* Pergamon Press. New York. 211 p.

McClintock, Elizabeth and Andrew T. Leiser. 1979. *An Annotated Checklist of Woody Ornamental Plants of California, Oregon and Washington.* Univ. Calif. Berkeley. 134 p.

McMillan, Browse, P. D. A. 1979. *Hardy Woody Plants from Seeds.* Grower Books, London. 163 p.

Menninger, Edwin A. 1970. *Flowering Vines of the World: An Encyclopedia of Climbing Plants.* Hearthside Press, N.Y. 410 p.

Miller, Howard A. and H. E. Jacques. 1978. *How to Know the Trees.* Wm. C. Brown. Dubuque, Iowa. 263 p.

Miller, Howard A. and Samuel H. Lamb. 1985. *Oaks of North America.* Naturegraph Publishers, Inc. Happy Camp, California. 327 p.

Mitchell, A. F. 1972. *Conifers in the British Isles.* Forestry Commission Handbook 33. HMSO London. 322 p.

Mitchell, A. F. 1974. *A Field Guide of the Trees of Britain and Northern Europe.* Collins. London. 415 p.

Mitchell, A.F. 1985. *The Complete Guide to Trees of Britain and Northern Europe.* Dragon's World Ltd. Surrey, Great Britain. 208 p.

Mohlenbrock, Robert H. 1972. *Forest Trees of Illinois.* State of Ill. Dept. of Conservation. Div. of Forestry. 178 p.

Montgomery, F. H. 1970. *Trees of Canada and the Northern United States.* Ryerson, Toronto. 144 p.

Moore, Dwight M. 1972. *Trees of Arkansas.* Arkansas Forestry Commission, Little Rock. 142 p.

Mulligan, Brian O. 1977. *Woody Plants in the University of Washington Arboretum, Washington Park.* Univ. Washington. 183 p.

Neelands, R. W. 1968. *Important Trees of Eastern Forests.* U.S.D.A.-Forest Service Southern Region. Atlanta, Georgia. 111 p.

Nelson, W. R., Jr. 1975. *Landscaping Your Home.* Circ. 111. U. of I. Coop. Ext. Service. Champaign, IL. 246 p.

Newcomb, Lawrence. 1977. *Newcomb's Wildflower Guide.* Little, Brown. Boston. 490 p.

Nicholson, Barbara E. and Arthur R. Clapham. 1975. *The Oxford Book of Trees.* Oxford University Press, London. 216 p.

Notcutt, R. C. 1926. *A Handbook of Flowering Trees and Shrubs for Gardeners.* Martin Hopkinson and Co. Ltd. Covent Garden. 245 p.

Notcutts Nurseries Ltd. 1981. *Notcutts Book of Plants.* The Thelford Press Ltd., London and Thelford. 328 p.

Novak, F. A. 1965. *The Pictorial Encyclopedia of Plants and Flowers.* Crown Publishers, Inc. New York. 589 p.

Odenwald, Neil G. and James R. Turner. 1980. *Plants for the South: A Guide for Landscaping Design.* Baton Rouge, LA. 565 p.

Odenwald, Neil G. and James R. Turner. 1987. *Identification, Selection and Use of Southern Plants for Landscape Design.* Claitor's Publishing Division. Baton Rouge, Louisiana. 660 p.

Ohwi, Jisaburo. 1965. *Flora of Japan.* Smithsonian Institution. Washington, D.C. 1067 p.

Osborne, Richard. 1975. *Garden Trees.* Lane Publ. Co., Menlo Park, CA. 96 p.

Otis, Charles Herbert. 1954. *Michigan Trees.* Univ. of Michigan Press. Ann Arbor. 333 p.

Ouden, P. Den and B. K. Boom. 1965. *Manual of Cultivated Conifers.* M. Nijhoff. The Hague. Netherlands. 526 p.

Outdoor World. 1973. *Trees of America.* Outdoor World. Waukesha, Wisconsin. 192 p.

Partyka, R. E. 1980. *Woody Ornamentals: Plants and Problems.* Chemlawn Corp., Columbus, OH. 427 p.

Peattie, Donald Culross. 1950. *A Natural History of Trees.* Houghton Mifflin Co., Boston. 606 p.

Peattie, Donald Culross. 1953. *A Natural History of Western Trees.* Houghton Mifflin Co., Boston. 751 p.

Peterson, Russell. 1980. *The Pine Tree Book.* The Brandywine Press. New York. 144 p.

Petrides, George A. 1972. *A Field Guide to Trees and Shrubs, 2nd Ed.* Houghton Mifflin Co. Boston, Mass. 428 p.

Philips, Roger. 1978. *Trees in Britain, Europe, and North America.* Ward Lock. London, 224 p.

Philips, R. and M. Rix. 1989. *Shrubs.* Random House, N.Y. 288 p.

Pirone, Pascal P. 1978. *Diseases and Pests of Ornamental Plants,* 5th Ed. Wiley, N.Y. 566 p.

Pirone, P. P., J. R. Hartman, M. A. Sall, and T. P. Pirone. 1988. *Tree Maintenance.* Oxford University Press. New York. 514 p.

Platt, Rutherford. 1952. *A Pocket Guide to Trees.* Pocket Books, New York. 256 p.

Plumridge, Jack. 1976. *How to Propagate Plants.* Lothian Publishing Company Pty Ltd. Tattersalls Lane, Melbourne. 214 p.

Pokorny, J. 1974. *A Color Guide to Familiar Flowering Shrubs.* Octopus Books, London. 191 p.

Pokorny, Jaromír. 1973. *A Color Guide to Familiar Trees—Leaves, Bark and Fruit.* Octopus Books. London. 184 p.

Poor, Janet Meakin (ed.). 1984. *Plants That Merit Attention Vol. I—Trees.* Timber Press. Portland, Oregon. 400 p.

Powell, Thomas and Betty. 1975. *The Avant Gardener.* Houghton Mifflin Co. Boston, Mass. 263 p.

Preston, Richard J. 1940. *Rocky Mountain Trees.* Iowa State College Press. Ames, Iowa. 285 p.

Preston, Richard J. 1976. *North American Trees.* 3rd Ed. Iowa State University Press. Ames. 399 p.

Preston, Richard J. and Valerie G. Wright. 1976. *Identification of Southeastern Trees in Winter.* North Carolina Agr. Ext. Serv., Raleigh. 113 p.

Prime, Cecil T. and Richard John Deacock. 1970. *Trees and Shrubs: Their Identification in Summer or Winter.* Heffer, Cambridge. 131 p.

Radford, Albert E., Harry E. Ahles and C. Ritchie Bell. 1978. *Manual of the Vascular Flora of the Carolinas.* The University of North Carolina Press, Chapel Hill. 1183 p.

Randall, C. E. and H. Clepper. 1976. *Famous and Historic Trees.* Amer. For. Assoc. Washington, D.C. 90 p.

Reader's Digest Editorial Staff. 1978. *Reader's Digest Encyclopedia of Garden Plants and Flowers.* Reader's Digest Assoc. Ltd. London. 800 p.

Rehder, Alfred, 1940. *Manual of Cultivated Trees and Shrubs,* 2nd Ed. Macmillan Co. N.Y. 996 p.

Reisch, Kenneth W., Philip C. Kozel, and Gayle A. Weinstein. 1975. *Woody Ornamentals for the Midwest.* Kendall/Hunt, Dubuque, Iowa. 293 p.

Robinette, Gary. 1967. *The Design Characteristics of Plant Materials.* American Printing and Publishing, Inc. Madison, Wisc. 244 p.

Robinson, Florence B. 1941. *Tabular Keys for the Identification of Woody Plants.* Garrard Press. Champaign, Ill. 156 p.

Robinson, Florence B. 1960. *Useful Trees and Shrubs.* Garrard Publishing Co. Champaign, Ill.

Rogers, Matilda. 1966. *Trees of the West Identified at a Glance.* The Ward Ritchie Press. 126 p.

Rogers, Walter E. 1935. *Tree Flowers of Forest, Park, and Street.* Dover Publications, Inc. New York. 499 p.

Rosendahl, Carl Otto. 1963. *Trees and Shrubs of the Upper Midwest.* Univ. Minn. Press, Minneapolis. 411 p.

Sabuco, John J. 1987. *The Best of the Hardiest.* 2nd-Edition. Good Earth Publishing Ltd. Flossmoor, Illinois. 368 p.

Salley, Homer and Harold Greer. 1986. *Rhododendron Hybrids.* Timber Press, Portland, OR 484 p.

Santamour, F. S., Jr., H. D. Gerhold, and S. Little. 1976. *Better Trees for Metropolitan Landscapes.* U.S.D.A. Forest Service General Technical Report NE-22. 256 p.

Sargent, Charles Sprague. 1947. *The Silva of North America.* 14 Vols. Peter Smith, N.Y.

Sargent, Charles Sprague. 1965. *Manual of the Trees of North America,* Vols. I and II. Dover Publications, Inc. N.Y. 934 p.

Schaffner, John H. 1950. *Field Manual of Trees.* Long's College Book Co. Columbus, Ohio. 160 p.

Schuler, Stanley. 1973. *The Gardener's Basic Book of Trees and Shrubs.* Simon and Schuster. N.Y. 319 p.

Seabrook, Peter. 1975. *Shrubs for Your Garden.* Scribner, N.Y. 144 p.

Settergren, Carl and R. E. McDermott. 1969. *Trees of Missouri.* Agr. Exp. Sta. Univ. of Missouri. Columbia, MO. 123 p.

Shosteck, Robert. 1974. *Flowers and Plants.* New York Times Book Co. N.Y. 329 p.

Smith, Alice Upham. 1969. *Trees in a Winter Landscape.* Holt, Rinehart and Winston of Canada, Ltd. 107 p.

Snyder, Leon C. 1978. *Gardening in the Upper Midwest.* Univ. of Minnesota Press. Minneapolis, Minnesota. 292 p.

Snyder, Leon C. 1980. *Trees and Shrubs for Northern Gardens.* University of Minnesota Press, Minneapolis. 411 p.

Stafleu, F. A., C. E. B. Bonner, and R. McVaugh. 1969. *International Code of Botanical Nomenclature.* Oosthoek, Utrecht. 426 p.

Steele, Frederic L. and Albion R. Hodgdon. 1975. *Trees and Shrubs of Northern New England.* Society for the Protection of New Hampshire Forests. Concord, New Hampshire. 127 p.

Stephens, H. A. 1967. *Trees, Shrubs and Woody Vines in Kansas.* Univ. Press of Kansas. Lawrence, Kansas. 250 p.

Stephens, H. A. 1973. *Woody Plants of the North Central Plains.* Univ. Press of Kansas, Lawrence. 530 p.

Stresau, Frederic B. 1986. *Florida, My Eden.* Florida Classics Library. Port Salerno, Florida. 299 p.

Stupka, Arthur. 1964. *Trees, Shrubs, and Woody Vines of Great Smokey Mountains National Park,* Univ. Tennessee Press. Knoxville, 186 p.

Sudworth, George B. 1967. *Forest Trees of the Pacific Slope.* Dover Publications, Inc., N.Y. 455 p.

Sunset Editorial Staff. 1971. *Rhododendrons and Azaleas.* Lane Books, Menlo Park, California. 80 p.

Sunset Editorial Staff. 1984. *New Western Garden Book.* Lane Publishing Co. Menlo Park, California. 512 p.

Swain, Roger B. 1989. *The Practical Gardener: A Guide to Breaking New Ground.* Little, Brown and Company. Boston, Massachusetts. 268 p.

Symonds, George W. D. 1958. *The Tree Identification Book.* William Morrow and Co. Inc. N.Y. 272 p.

Symonds, George W. D. 1963. *The Shrub Identification Book.* M. Barrows and Co. N.Y. 379 p.

Tattar, Terry A. 1978. *Diseases of Shade Trees.* Academic Press. N.Y. 361 p.

Taylor, Norman. 1961. *Taylor's Encyclopedia of Gardening.* Houghton Mifflin Co. Boston, Mass.

Taylor, Norman. 1965. *The Guide to Garden Shrubs and Trees.* Houghton Mifflin Company. Boston. 450 p.

Taylor, Norman. 1988. *Taylor's Guide to Trees.* Houghton Mifflin Co. Boston. 479 p.

Taylor, Sally L. 1979. *Garden Guide to Woody Plants.* Connecticut College. New London, Connecticut. 100 p.

Tehon, Leo R. 1942. *Field Book of Native Illinois Shrubs.* Nat. Hist. Survey Div. Urbana, Ill. 300 p.

Thomas, Graham Stuart. 1977. *Plants for Ground-Cover.* J.M. Dent and Sons Ltd. 282 p.

Del Tredici, Peter. 1983. *A Giant Among the Dwarfs—The Mystery of Sargent's Weeping Hemlock.* Theophrastus. Little Compton, Rhode Island. 108 p.

Trelease, William. 1931. *Winter Botany,* 3rd Ed. Dover Publications, Inc. N.Y. 396 p.

Treseder, Neil G. 1978. *Magnolias.* Faber and Faber, London. 243 p.

Treshow, Michael, Stanley L. Welsh, and Glen Moore. 1970. *Guide to the Woody Plants of the Mountain States.* B.Y.U. Press, Provo, Utah. 178 p.

Valavanis, William N. 1976. *The Japanese Five-Needle Pine.* Symmes Systems. Atlanta, Georgia. 68 p.

van Gelderen, D. M. and J. R. P. van Hoey Smith. 1986. *Conifers.* Timber Press, Inc. Portland, Oregon. 385 p.

Van Melle, P. J. 1943. *Shrubs and Trees for the Small Place.* Charles Scribner's Sons. New York. 298 p.

Verey, Rosemary. 1981. *The Scented Garden.* Van Nostrand Reinhold Co. New York 167 p.

Vertrees, J. D. 1987. *Japanese Maples.* Timber Press, Forest Grove, Oregon. 189 p.

Viereck, Leslie A. and Elbert L. Little. 1972. *Alaska Trees and Shrubs.* Agricultural Handbook No. 410, U.S.D.A. Forest Service. Supt. of Doc. U.S. Gov. Printing Office. Wash. D.C. 265 p.

Vines, Robert A. 1960. *Trees, Shrubs, and Woody Vines of the Southwest.* Univ. Texas Press. Austin. 1104 p.

Voigt, T. B., Betty R. Hamilton and F. A. Gills. 1983. *Groundcovers for the Midwest.* Univ. of Illinois Printing Division. Champaign, Illinois. 184 p.

Wait, D. Dwight. 1977. *Ornamental Plants, Their Care, Use, Propagation, and Identification.* Kendall/Hunt. Dubuque, Iowa. 426 p.

Walheim, Lance (Ed.). 1977. *The World of Trees.* Ortho Books. San Francisco, California. 112 p.

Walker, Egbert H. 1976. *Flora of Okinawa and the Southern Ryukyu Islands.* Smithsonian Institution Press. Washington D.C. 1159 p.

Walker, Mary C. and F. A. Giles. 1985. *Flowering Trees for the Midwest.* University of Illinois. Champaign, Illinois. 102 p.

Wandell, Willet N. 1989. *Handbook of Landscape Tree Cultivars.* East Prairie Publishing Co. Gladstone, Illinois. 318 p.

Watkins, John V. 1969. *Florida Landscape Plants: Native and Exotic.* Univ. Florida Press. Gainesville. 368 p.

Watkins, John V. and Herbert S. Wolfe. 1968. *Your Florida Garden.* Univ. of Florida Press. Gainesville. 382 p.

Watkins, John V. and Thomas John Sheehan. 1975. *Florida Landscape Plants: Native and Exotic.* Univ. Florida Press. Gainesville. 520 p.

Weaver, Richard E. 1972. *A Guide to City Trees in The Boston Area.* The Arnold Arboretum. Jamaica Plain, Massachusetts. 97 p.

Weiner, Michael A. 1975. *Plant a Tree: A Working Guide to Regreening America.* Macmillan, N.Y. 276 p.

Welch, H. J. 1966. *Dwarf Conifers.* Charles T. Branford Co. Mass. 334 p.

Welch, H. J. 1979. *Manual of Dwarf Conifers.* Theophrastus. Little Compton, RI. 493 p.

Welles, J. C. 1985. A Dictionary of the Flowering Plants and Ferns, Student Edition. Cambridge University Press. England. 1245 p.

Wharton, Mary E. and Roger W. Barbour. 1973. *Trees and Shrubs of Kentucky.* Univ. Press of Kentucky, Lexington. 582 p.

Whitcomb, Carl E. 1984. *Plant Production in Containers.* Lacebark Publications. Stillwater, Oklahoma. 638 p.

Whitcomb, Carl E. 1985. *Know It and Grow It.* Lacebark Publications. Stillwater, Oklahoma. 740 p.

Whitehead, Stanley B. 1956. *The Book of Flowering Trees and Shrubs.* Frederick Warne and Co. Ltd. N.Y. 246 p.

Wigginton, Brooks E. 1963. *Trees and Shrubs for the Southeast.* University of Georgia Press, Athens. 280 p.

Wilder, Louise Beebe. 1974. *The Fragrant Garden.* Dover Publications, Inc. New York. 407 p.

Wilson, Ernest Henry. 1920. *The Romance of Our Trees.* Doubleday. Garden City, NJ. 278 p.

Wilson, Ernest Henry. 1925. *America's Greatest Garden: The Arnold Arboretum.* The Stratford Co. Boston. 123 p.

Wilson, Ernest Henry. 1926. *Aristocrats of the Garden.* The Stratford Co. Boston. 312 p.

Wilson, Ernest Henry. 1927. *Plant Hunting.* Vols. I and II. The Stratford Co. Boston.

Wilson, Ernest Henry. 1928. *More Aristocrats of the Garden.* The Stratford Co. Boston. 288 p.

Wilson, Ernest Henry. 1929. *China Mother of Gardens.* The Stratford Co. Boston. 408 p.

Wilson, Ernest Henry. 1930. *Aristocrats of the Trees.* The Stratford Co. Boston. 279 p.

Wilson, Ernest Henry. 1931. *If I Were to Make a Garden.* The Stratford Company. Boston. 295 p.

Wyman, Donald. 1954. *The Arnold Arboretum Garden Book.* D. Van Nostrand Co., Inc. 354 p.

Wyman, Donald. 1956. *Gound Cover Plants.* Macmillan Co., N.Y. 175 p.

Wyman, Donald. 1965. *Trees for American Gardens.* Macmillan Co. N.Y. 502 p.

Wyman, Donald. 1969. *Shrubs and Vines for American Gardens.* Macmillan Co. N.Y. 613 p.

Wyman, Donald. 1971. *Wyman's Gardening Encyclopedia.* Macmillan Co. N.Y. 1221 p.

Wyman, Donald. 1975. *Dwarf Shrubs.* Macmillan Co. N.Y. 137 p.

GLOSSARY OF TAXONOMIC TERMS COMMONLY EMPLOYED
IN THE IDENTIFICATION OF WOODY PLANTS

a-: prefix indicating not or without.

abortive: defective, barren, not developed.

abruptly pinnate: without a terminal leaflet.

abscission: the separating of a leaf from a self healing, clean-cut scar.

acaulescent: stemless or apparently so. Ex: *Taraxacum, Dodecatheon, Primula.*

accessory buds: those found beside or above the true bud at a node.

accessory fruit: one whose conspicuous tissues have not been derived from those comprising the pistil of the fl. Ex: in strawberry *(Fragaria)* the fleshy part of the fr. is of receptacular and not of pistillate origin. An accessory fr. may or may not also be an aggregate fr. (it is so in the strawberry and not so in the banana).

accessory parts of a flower: the petals and sepals.

achene: a dry indehiscent one-seeded fruit. Ex: fr. of members of the Compositae.

acicular: needle-shaped. Ex: lvs. of *Pinus,* spines of some cacti.

acorn: the fruit of oaks, a thick walled nut with a woody cup-like base.

actinomorphic: of regular symmetry, applied to perianth whorls, as opposed to zygomorphic.

aculeate: prickly.

acuminate: having an apex whose sides are gradually concave and tapering to a point.

acute: having an apex whose sides are straight and taper to a point.

adherent: a condition existing when two dissimilar organs touch each other (sometimes seemingly fused) but not grown together.

adnate: fused with unlike parts, as in the fusion of a filament to a petal.

adventitious: arising from an unusual or irregular position.

aerial rootlets: those produced above ground, especially as in climbing organs of a vine.

aestivation: the arrangement of floral parts (especially sepals and petals) in the bud.

aggregate flower: a flower heaped or crowded into a dense cluster.

aggregate fruit: one formed by the coherence or the connation of pistils that were distinct in the flower (as in *Rubus*) when the pistils of separate flowers (as in mulberry) make up the fr. it is designated as a multiple fruit.

akene: a small dry indehiscent fruit with one seed free inside the thin pericarp.

alternate: an arrangement of leaves or other parts not opposite or whorled; parts situated one at a node, as leaves on a stem: like parts succeeding each other singly with a common structure.

ament: see catkin.

amplexicaul: encircling the stem.

anastomosing: netted, applied to the veins of a lf.; the marginal reticulations closed.

androecium: stamens of a fl. as a unit.

anemophilous: describes flowers that are pollinated by wind.

angiospermous: having seeds borne within a pericarp.

angular: of pith; not rounded in cross section.

annual: maturing and living one season only.

annular: shaped like a ring.

anterior: on the front side, away from the axis, toward the subtending bract.

anther: pollen-bearing part of a stamen, borne at the top of a filament, or sessile.

anthesis (an-thee-sis): that period of fl. development when pollen is shed from the anther; also used to designate the act of flowering or the time of fl. expansion.

apetalous: without petals. Ex: fls. of grasses.

apex: the tip or terminal end.

apical: describes the apex or tip.

apiculate: ending abruptly in a short pointed tip.

apocarpous: having separate carpels; frequently applied to a gynoecium of several pistils.

apophysis: that part of the cone scale that is exposed when the cone is closed.

appressed: pressed close to the stem, not spreading.

arboreal, arboreous: treelike or pertaining to trees.

arching: curving gracefully.

arcuate venation: pinnate, with the secondary veins curving and running parallel to the margin.

areole: small pit or raised spot, often bearing a tuft of hairs, glochids, or spines.

aril: a fleshy appendage of the seed.

aristate: bearing a stiff bristle-like awn or arista, or tapered to a very slender stiff tip. Ex: awns of many grasses, apices of many calyx-teeth.

armed: provided with a sharp defense such as thorns, spines, prickles or barbs.

aromatic: fragrantly scented, at least if broken or crushed.

articulate: having nodes or joints where separation may naturally occur.

ascending: curving indirectly or obliquely upward. Ex: branches of *Taxus canadensis.*

assurgent: rising at an angle, not straight upwards.

attenuate: showing a long gradual slender taper; usually applied to apices, but equally appropriate for bases of leaves, petals, etc.

auriculate: bearing ear-like appendages, as the projections of some leaf and petal bases.

awl-shaped: tapering to a slender stiff point.

awn: a bristle-like appendage.

axil: belonging to the axis. See placentation.

axillary: in the axil.

axis: the main stem or central support of a plant.

baccate: pulpy, fleshy.

barbed: bristles, awns, etc. provided with terminal or lateral spine-like hooks that are bent sharply backward. Ex: pappus on fruits of beggar's ticks.

bark: a dead outer protective tissue of woody plants, derived from the cortex. Varies greatly in appearance and texture; often including all tissue from the vascular cambium outward.

basal: pertaining to the extremity of an organ by which it is attached to its support; said of lvs. when at base of plant only. See rosette.

basifixed: attached basally as ovules or anthers.

beak: a long prominent point. Ex: on lettuce *(Lactuca)* or dandelion *(Taraxacum)* frs.

beaked: ending in a point, especially on fruits.

bearded: having long hairs.

berry: a fleshy indehiscent pulpy multi-seeded fr. resulting from a single pistil. Ex: tomato.

bi-: prefix indicating twice or doubly.

biennial: of two season's duration, normally flowering, fruiting and dying the second growing season from time of seed germination.

bifid: two-cleft, as in apices of some petals and leaves. Ex: petals of some *Lychnis* or leaves of *Bauhinia.*

bifurcate: forked, as some Y-shaped hairs.

bilabiate: two-lipped, often applied to a corolla or calyx: each lip may or may not be lobed or toothed. Ex: corolla of snapdragon *(Antirrhinum)* and most members of the mint family *(Labiatae).*

bipinnate: twice pinnate.

bisexual: stamens and pistil present in the one fl.

biternate: twice ternate; a structure basically ternate, but whose primary divisions are again each ternate. Ex: lvs. of some columbines *(Aquilegia)* and meadow-rues *(Thalictrum).*

bladder-like: inflated, empty with thin walls.

blade: the expanded part of lf. or petal; lamina.

bloom: a waxy coating found on stems, leaves, flowers and fruits, usually of a grayish cast and easily removed.

bole: stem of a tree.

boss: a raised usually pointed projection.

bract: a much-reduced lf., often scale-like and usually associated with a fl. or infl.

branch: one of the coarser divisions of a trunk or main branch.

branchlet: smaller, a division of the branch.

bristle: a stiff hair.

broad-elliptic: wider than elliptic.

broad-ovate: wider than ovate.

bronzing: turning a metallic bronze or coppery color, especially of foliage after a winter.

bud: a structure of embryonic tissues, which will become a leaf, a flower, or both, or a new shoot. Especially the stage in which a growing point spends the winter or a dry season. May be naked or enclosed in scales.

bud scale: a modified leaf or stipule (there may be one, a few, or many) protective of the embryonic tissue of the bud.

bud scale scar: the mark left by the sloughing off of the bud scale.

bulb: a modified underground stem comprised of shortened central axis surrounded by fleshy scale-like lvs.

bulbil: small bulbs arising around parent bulb.

bulblet: small bulbs arising in leaf axils.

bullate: with the surface appearing as if blistered between the veins. Ex: Savoy cabbage.

bundle scar: seen in the leaf scar, the broken ends of the woody vascular strands that connected the leaf and the stem.

bur: any rough or prickly seed envelope.

burl: a knot or woody growth of very irregular grain.

bush: a low several stemmed shrub with no single trunk.

caducous: falling off early or prematurely.

calcarate: having a spur.

calcicole: a plant growing best on limey soils.

callus: a hard protuberance, or the new tissues formed in response to a wound.

calyx: the outer set of perianth segments or floral envelope of a flower, usually green in color and smaller than the inner set.

campanulate: bell-shaped.

cane: a long woody pliable stem rising from the ground.

canescent: having a gray hoary pubescence.

capillary: hair-like; very slender.

capitate: headlike, in a dense rounded cluster.

capsule: a dry dehiscent fruit produced from a compound pistil. Ex: fruit of a tobacco, *Catalpa*, *Dianthus*.

carinate: keeled; with longitudinal ridge or line.

carpel: one of the foliar units of gynoecium. See pistil.

carpophore: elongated axis bearing a gynoecium and projecting between the carpels.

caryopsis: the fruit of members of the grass family; not basically distinct from an achene.

castaneous: dark brown.

catkin: a spike-like infl. comprised of scaly bracts subtending unisexual fls., often somewhat flexuous and pendulous but not necessarily so. Ex: infl. of willows *(Salix)* and poplars *(Populus)*.

caudate: bearing a tail-like appendage. Ex: spadices of some aroids.

caulescent: having an evident leaf-bearing stem above ground.

cauliflorous: flowering from the trunk or main branches directly or on short specialized spurs.

cauline: of or belonging to the stem.

ceriferous: waxy.

cernuous: drooping or nodding.

cespitose: growing in tufts or dense clumps.

chalaza: basal part of ovule, where it is attached to the funiculus.

chaff: dry, thin, membranous bract, particularly those subtending the fls. of the *Compositae*.

chaffy: covered with small thin dry scales or bracts.

chambered: of pith, divided into empty horizontal chambers by cross partitions.

channeled: grooved lengthwise.

chartaceous: of papery or tissue-like texture.

ciliate: marginally fringed with hairs, often minutely so and then termed "ciliolate."

cinereous: ash colored.

circinate: rolled coil-wise from top downward. Ex: unopened fern fronds.

circumscissile: opening or dehiscing by a line around the fr. or anther, the top (valve) coming off as a lid. Ex: fr. of *Portulaca* or *Plantago.*

cladophyll: a flattened, foliaceous stem having the form and function of a leaf, but arising in the axis of minute bract-like often caducous true leaf. Ex: the so-called leaves of *Ruscus* and *Asparagus.*

clasping: a stalkless leaf, with the base partly surrounding the stem.

clavate: club-shaped, as a baseball bat.

claw: the constricted petiole-like base of petals and sepals of some flowers. Ex: petals of flowers of mustard family, of *Cleome.*

cleft: divided to or about the middle into divisions.

cleistogamous: describes a small, closed self-fertilized flower, usually near the ground.

climbing plant: one which raises its foliage by supporting itself on surrounding objects, by twining stem or tendrils, grasping rootlets, or scrambling.

clone: a group of plants derived vegetatively from one parent plant, identical to each other and to the parent.

close bark: not broken up or scaly.

clustered: of leaves, crowded so as not to be clearly opposite or alternate, also said of whorled condition.

coalescent: two or more parts united.

coarse (texture): consisting of large or rough parts.

coherent: two or more similar parts or organs touching one another in very close proximity by the tissues not fused. Ex: the two ovaries of asclepiadaceous flowers. (By some the term treated as if synonymous with connate.)

collateral buds: accessory buds to either side of the true lateral bud at a node.

columella: the carpophores in umbellifer fruits.

column: the structure formed by union of filaments in a tube (as in mallows) or of the filaments and style of orchids.

commisure: the edge or face of two adjoining structures.

comose: tufted with hairs. Ex: milkweed seeds.

compact: arranged in a small amount of space, dense habit.

complete flower: one which has corolla, calyx, stamens and one or more pistils.

composite: compound.

compound leaf: a leaf of two or more leaflets, in some cases (Citrus) the lateral leaflets may have been lost and only the terminal lft. remain. *Ternately compound* when the lfts. are in 3's; *palmately compound* when three or more lfts. arise from a common point to be palmate (if only three are present they may be sessile); *pinnately compound* when arranged along a common rachis or if only three are present at least the terminal lft. is petioled; *odd-pinnate* if a terminal lft. is present and the total number of lfts., for the lf. is an odd-number; *even-pinnate* if no terminal lft. is present and the total is an even number.

compound pistil: a pistil comprised of two or more carpels. The number of cells or locules within the ovary may or may not indicate the number of carpels. An ovary having more than one complete cell or locule is always compound, but many one-celled ovaries are compound also. A pistil having a one-celled ovary, but more than one placenta or more than one style or more than one stigma, or any combination of these duplicities, may be presumed to be compound insofar as taxonomic considerations are concerned.

compressed: flattened from the sides.

concave: curved like the inner surface of a sphere.

conduplicate: folded together lengthwise.

cone: a coniferous fruit, having a number of woody, leathery, or fleshy scales, each bearing one or more seeds, and attached to a central axis.

conelet: a young, immature first season cone, in the pines.

conical: cone shaped, as the young form of many spruces.

coniferous: cone bearing.

confluent: blending together, not easily distinguishable as separate.

connate: like parts fused together into one, fused into a tube. Ex: filaments of a mallow androecium, or anthers of a Composite flower.

connective: the tissues between the two anthers of a stamen, often much elaborated when the anther cells are separated. Ex: *Salvia.*

connivent: a synonym of coherent.

constricted: squeezed or compressed as if by shrinking or tightening.

continuous pith: solid and without interruption.

convex: curved like the outer surface of a sphere.

convulate: rolled up lengthwise; in flower buds when overlapping of one edge of a perianth segment by the next while the other margin is overlapped by its preceding member.

coppice: growth arising from sprouts at the stump, bushy.

cordate: heart-shaped, with a sinus and rounded lobes; properly a term applied only to bases of leaves and bracts, but frequently employed to designate a structure of ovate outline and heart-shaped base.

coriaceous: of leathery texture. Ex: *Buxus* lf.

corky ridges: elongated warts or strips of soft springy wood.

corm: a solid bulb-like underground stem not differentiated into scales, often depressed-globose in form, bearing scale-like buds on surface, usually tunicated. Ex: *Gladiolus, Crocus.*

cormel: small corm arising from base of parent corm.

corolla: the usually petaloid, inner whorl or floral envelopes; when the parts are separate and distinct they are petals and the corolla is said to be *polypetalous;* when connate in whole or in part the distal parts are teeth, lobes, divisions, or segments and the corolla is said to be gamopetalous.

corona: a crown; an appendage or extrusion that stands between the corolla and stamens; an outgrowth of perianth tissue in the ''cup'' of *Narcissus,* or of the androecium in the milkweeds.

corymb: a more or less flat-topped indeterminate infl. whose outer fls. open first. Ex: *Viburnum,* some verbenas.

costate: having longitudinal ribs or veins.

cotyledon: the primary leaves of the embryo, present in the seed.

creeping: running along at or near the ground level and rooting occasionally.

cremocarp: a dry dehiscent 2 seeded fruit of the *Umbelliferae,* each half a mericarp.

crenate: rounded teeth on mgn. Ex: lvs. of some *Coleus.*

crenate-serrate: having a mixture of blunt and sharp teeth.

crenulate: having very small rounded teeth.

crested: with an elevated and irregular or toothed ridge; found on some seeds or some floral parts.

crisp-hairy: with kinky hair or tomentum.

crown: the upper mass or head of a tree, also a central point near the ground level of a perennial herb from which new shoots arise each year.

cruciform: cross shaped.

cucullate: hooded.

culm: stem of grasses and sedges.

cultigen: a plant arising through domestication and cultivation.

cultivar: a cultivated variety.

cultivated: maintained by man.

cuneate: wedge-shaped with essentially straight sides, the structure attached at the narrow end.

cuspidate: with an apex somewhat abruptly and concavely constricted into an elongated sharp-pointed tip.

cuticle: an outer film of dead epidermal cells, often waxy.

cyathium: the infl. characteristic of *Euphorbia,* the fls. condensed and congested within a bracteate envelope, emerging at anthesis.

cymbiform: boat-shaped.

cyme: a more or less flat-topped determinate infl. whose outer fls. open last. Ex: elderberry *(Sambucus).*

cymose: of or arranged on cymes.

cymule: a diminutive cyme. Ex: *Armeria.*

deciduous: falling off, as lvs. of a tree.

decompound: more than one compound.

decumbent: reclining on ground with tip ascending.

decurrent: extending down the stem.

decussate: with alternating pairs at right angles to each other, as pairs of opposite lvs. on a stem.

deflexed: synonym of reflexed.

defoliation: casting off or falling off of leaves.

dehiscent: splitting open, the sides or segments of the splitting organ usually termed valves; *loculicidally* dehiscent when the split opens into a cavity or locule, *septicidally* dehiscent when at point of union of septum or partition to the side wall, *circumscissilely* when the top valve comes off as a lid. *Poricidally* when by means of pores whose valves are often flap-like. The term is commonly applied to anthers or seed pods.

deliquescent: the primary axis or stem much branched. Ex: branching of an elm tree.

deltoid: triangular.

dense: crowded together, thick, compact.

dentate: having marginal teeth whose apices are perpendicular to the margin and do not point forward.

denticulate: slightly or minutely dentate.

denuded: naked through loss of covering.

depressed: flattened, as if compressed somewhat.

determinate: said of an inflorescence when the terminal flower opens first and the prolongation of the axis is thereby arrested.

di-: prefix indicating two.

diandrous: having an androecium of two stamens.

diaphragmed pith: having horizontally elongated cells with thickened walls spaced throughout the pith like the rungs of a ladder.

dichlamydeous: having both a corolla and a calyx.

dichotomous: forked in pairs.

diclinous: with unisexual flowers.

dicot: angiospermous plant having two cotyledons.

didynamous: in two pairs of different length.

diffuse: loosely or widely spreading, an open form.

digitate: palmate.

dimorphic: having two forms.

dioecious: having unisexual fls., each sex confined to a separate plant, said of species.

disarticulate: to fall away leaving a clear cut scar.

discoid: having only disk fls. as an infl. of a member of the Compositae family.

disk: (1) a glandular elevation about the base of a superior ovary; (2) the flattened receptacle of the infl.; (3) a flattened extremity as a stigma or as on the tendrils of some climbing vines.

disk flower: the tubular fl. in the center of the usual Composite infl. Ex: daisy, aster.

disposed: arranged.

dissected: divided in narrow, slender segments.

distal: toward the apex, away from the base.

distichous: two-ranked, with lvs., lfts. or fls. on opposite sides of a stem in the same plant.

distinct: separate, not united with parts of like kind. Compare with "free".

diurnal: blossoms opening only during the day.

divaricate: spreading very wide apart.

divergent: spreading broadly.

divided: separated to the base into divisions.

dormant: in a restive or non vegetative state, especially a winter condition.

dorsal: the black or outer surface.

dorsiventral: referring to a front-to-back plane.

dotted: describes the underside of a leaf having a pattern of spots or hair glands visible.

double flower: one with more than the usual number of petals, colored sepals or bracts.

double serrate: serrations bearing minute teeth on margins.

doubly compound: bi-pinnate.

diadelphous: in two sets, applied to stamens. In many legumes the androecium is comprised of 10 stamens: 9 in one set, 1 in the other.

doubly crenate, dentate, or serrate: having small teeth of the given kind within the larger ones.

downy: pubescent with fine soft hairs.

drooping: hanging from the base, suggesting wilting.

drupaceous: drupe-like.

drupe: a fleshy indehiscent fr. whose seed is enclosed in a stony endocarp. Ex: date, cherry.

drupelet: a small drupe. Ex: raspberry.

duct: generally, a water conducting tube, also a canal through the wood carrying resin, latex or oil.

dwarf: an atypically small plant.

dwarf shoots: spur shoots.

ebracteate: without bracts.

echinate: with stout bluntish prickles.

eglandular: without glands.

ellipsoid: three dimensional shape of ellipse, football shaped.

elliptic-oblong: a shape between the two forms.

elliptical: having the outline of an ellipse, broadest at middle and narrower at each end.

elongate: lengthened.

emarginate: with a shallow notch at the apex.

emergences: appendages other than hairs.

endemic: confined to a small geographic area.

endocarp: the inner layer of the pericarp.

ensiform: sword-shaped.

entire: having a margin without teeth or crenations.

entomophilous: describes flowers that are pollinated by insects.

ephemeral: persisting for one day only, of short duration. Ex: fls. of *Neomarica, Tradescantia.*

epidermis: the outer superficial layer of cells.

epigynous: borne on the ovary; said of the fl. when the ovary is inferior, or of stamens when apparently borne on the gynoecium.

epitrophic: more nourished and developed on the upper side.

equitant: overlapping in two ranks. Ex: lvs. of *Iris.*

erect: upright habit of growth.

erose: having a margin appearing eroded or gnawed; of a jaggedness not sufficiently regular to be toothed. Ex: leaf apices of the fish-tail palm *(Caryota).*

espalier: any plant trained lattice fashion in one plane.

established: growing and reproducing without cultivation.

estipulate: without stipules.

evanescent: describes veins grown very faint near the margin.

even-pinnate: results in a lack of the terminal leaflet, since each one is paired.

evergreen: having green foliage throughout the year.

excavated: describes pith which is hollow between the nodes.

excurrent: extending beyond the margin or tip. Ex: awns of some grasses.

exfoliate: to peel off in shreds or thin layers, as bark from a tree.

exotic: foreign, not naturalized.

exserted: projecting beyond, as stamens beyond a corolla.

exstipulate: without stipules.

extrorse: facing outward from the center; in the case of anthers, dehiscing outward; a character most accurately determined by a cross-section of the anther.

falcate: sickle-shaped.

falls: outer whorl of perianth segments of an iridaceous fl., often broader than the inner and, in some *Iris,* drooping or flexuous.

farinaceous: with a powdery or mealy coating.

fasciated: abnormally much flattened, and seemingly several units fused together.

fascicle: a close cluster. Ex: lvs. of white pine.

fastigiate: branches erect and close together.

felty: having compressed matted fibers.

fenestrate: perforated with opening or with translucent areas. Ex: lvs. of *Monstera deliciosa.*

ferrugineous: rust colored.

fertile: capable of producing fruit and seed.

fibrous: having long narrow shreds or flakes.

filament: that portion of a stamen comprising the stalk.

filamentous: thread-like.

filiform: long and very slender; thread-like.

fimbriate: fringed.

fine texture: consisting of small rather delicate parts.

firm bark: close, not broken into loose or shaggy parts.

fissured bark: torn lengthwise, with vertical furrows.

fistulose: hollow and cylindrical.

fistulous: describes a hollow stem with excavated pith.

flabellate: fan-like.

flaccid: limp.

flaking: shreddy, with shorter fragments.

flat: a low horizontal habit of growth.

fleshy: applied to a fruit somewhat pulpy or juicy at maturity, as opposed to a dry hard or papery fruit.

flexous: waxy.

floccose: having surface with tufts of soft woolly hair, often rubbing off easily.

floret: technically a minute flower; applied to the flowers of grasses and Composites.

flower: an axis bearing one or more pistils or one or more stamens or both: when only the former, it is a *perfect flower* (I.E. bisexual or hermaphroditic). The androecium represents a series or whorls, derived from a spiral condition adjoining the pistil. When this perfect flower is surrounded by a perianth represented by two floral envelopes (the inner envelope comprising the corolla, the outer the calyx), it is a *complete flower.*

flower scar: marks remaining after the abscission of the flower parts.

fluted: having rounded lengthwise ridges.

foliaceous: leaf-like in color and form.

foliage: leaves.

-foliate: -leaved.

-foliolate: -leafleted.

follicle: a dry dehiscent fruit opening only along one suture and the product of a single carpel (simple ovary). Ex: peony, columbine, milkweed.

form: a subdivision of a species which occurs occasionally in the wild, seldom breeds true, and does not develop a natural population or distribution.

foveola: a pit.

fragmented: not continuous, especially of vascular bundle scars.

free: separate in that it is not joined to other organs; as petals free from calyx or calyx free from capsule. Contrast with "distinct".

free-central: see placentation.

fringed: ciliate with glands or scales rather than hairs.

frond: a leaf, once applied only to leaves of ferns but now to leaves of palms also.

fruit: technically a ripened ovary with its adnate parts, the seed-containing unit characteristic of all Angiosperms. The term is also employed loosely for all similar structures as the "fruit" of a Cycad which in reality is a naked seed or the "fruit" of the Blue Cohosh (an Angiosperm) which also is a naked seed: all are functionally fruiting structures.

fruticose: shrubby, in sense of stems being woody.

fugacious: falling or withering very early.

fulvous: tawny, a dull grayish yellow color.

funiculus: the stalk by which an ovule is attached to the ovary wall.

funnelform: the tube gradually widening. Ex: corolla of morning-glory.

furcate: forked.

furrowed: having longitudinal channels or grooves.

fuscous: grayish brown.

fusiform: spindle-shaped; tapering to each end from a smaller mid-section.

galea: a helmet. Ex: *Aconitum.*

gamopetalous: the petals united, at least at base, to form a corolla of one piece; the corolla coming off from the fl. as a single unit.

geniculate: bent like a knee.

genus: a group of species possessing fundamental traits in common but differing in other lesser characteristics.

gibbous: swollen on one side, usually basally. Ex: snapdragon corolla.

glabrate: becoming glabrous with maturity, but as seen under a lens is noted to be not quite so prior to maturity.

glabrous: not hairy. Note: a glabrous surface need not be smooth, for it may be bullate or rugose.

gland: a general term applied to oil-secreting organs, or sometimes an obtuse projection or a ring at base of a structure.

glandular: bearing glands.

glandular-pubescent: glands and hairs intermixed.

glandular-punctate: see punctate.

glaucescent: slightly glaucous.

glaucous: covered with a waxy bloom or whitish material that rubs off readily. Ex: the bloom on many sorts of grape.

globose: having a round or spherical shape.

globular: circular.

glochid: a minute barbed spine or bristle. Ex: the components of the tawny hair-like tufts on many species of *Opuntia.*

glomerate: in dense or compact clusters, usually applied to flowers.

glossy: shining, reflecting more light than if lustrous.

glume: a stiff chaff-like bract, usually applied to the two empty bracts at base of grass spikelets.

glutinous: sticky.

granular: minutely roughened.

grooved: marked with long narrow furrows or channels.

ground cover: a plant that grows near the ground densely, and spreads.

gum: a fluid sticky resin.

gymnospermous: plant bearing naked seeds without an ovary.

gynoecium: collectively the female element of a fl.; a collective term employed for the several pistils of a single fl. when referred to as a unit; when only one pistil is present the two terms are synonymous.

gynophore: a stalk bearing a pistil above point of stamen attachment. Ex: *Cleome.*

habit: the general aspect or mode of growth of a plant.

habitat: the type surrounding in which a plant grows.

hair: superficial outgrowth, trichome.

hairy: pubescent with longer hairs.

hardened: conditioned by various factors to withstand environmental stresses; contrast with succulent growth which is very vulnerable.

hardy: capable of enduring winter stresses.

hastate: having the shape of an arrow-head and the basal lobes pointed outwards at or nearly at right angles to the mid-rib.

head: a short dense infl. of variable form, as in *Compositae* (daisy) family, *Eryngium,* or many clovers.

helicoid: spiraling like a snail shell.

herb: a plant dying to the ground at the end of the season; one whose aerial stems are soft and succulent without appreciable parenchymatous xylem tissue; a plant not woody in texture.

herbaceous: having no persistent woody stem above ground.

herbage: vegetative parts of an herb.

hermaphrodite: bisexual.

hesperidium: a fleshy berry-like fr. with hard rind and definite longitudinal partitions. Ex: orange.

heterogamous: bearing two kinds of flowers.

heterogeneous: not uniform in kind of flowers.

hidden bud: bud covered by the petiole base and therefore inconspicuous.

hilum: the scar on a seed marking its point of attachment.

hip: fruit of the rose.

hippocrepiform: horseshoe-shaped.

hirsute: with rough coarse hairs, usually rather long.

hirtellous: minutely hirsute.

hispid: with stiff or bristly hairs.

hispidulous: minutely hispid.

hoary: with a close white or whitish pubescence.

hirsute: pubescent with coarse or stiff hairs.

hollow: describes pith with a central cavity.

homogamous: bearing only one kind of flower.

homogeneous: all of one kind and texture, continuous pith.

hooked: bent like a hook, having a hook.

horizontal: with broad faces parallel to the ground.

humifuse: spreading over the ground.

husk: outer covering of the seed or fruit.

hyaline: translucent when viewed in transmitted light.

hybrid: plant resulting from a cross between two or more other plants which are more or less alike.

hydrophyte: an aquatic plant.

hypanthium: the cup-like "receptacle" derived from the fusion of perianth parts and on which are seemingly borne the stamens, corolla, and calyx. Ex: fuchsia, plum.

hypocrateriform: see salverform.

hypogynous: borne on the torus or receptacle, beneath or at base of ovary; said of stamens, petals or calyx when the ovary is superior or above their point of attachment.

hypotrophic: more nourished and developed on the under side.

imbricated: overlapping, as shingles on a roof.

imperfect flower: one which lacks either stamens or pistils.

impressed: bent inward, furrowed as if by pressure.

incised: cut by sharp and irregular incisions more or less deeply, but intermediate between toothed and lobed.

included: not protruding as stamens not projecting beyond a corolla; opposed to exserted.

incomplete flower: one which lacks any one or more of these parts: calyx, corolla, stamens, and pistils.

incumbent: having cotyledons which within the seed lie face to face with the back of one lying against the hypocotyl; anthers are incumbent when turned inwards.

incurved: bent into an inward curve.

indehiscent: not opening regularly, as a capsule or anther.

indeterminate: said of those kinds of infl. whose terminal fls. open last, hence the growth or elongation of the main axis is not arrested by the opening of first flowers.

indigen: plant native and original to a region.

indumentum: with a generally heavy covering of hair: a general term without precise connotation.

indurate: hardened.

indusium: the epithelial excrescence that, when present, covers or contains the sporangia of a fern when the latter are in sori.

inferior: beneath, below; said of an ovary when situated below the apparent point of attachment of stamens and perianth; a fl. having such an ovary is said to be epigynous.

inflated: bladder like, loose and membraneous about the seed.

inflorescence: the method of flower-bearing; the disposition of flowers on the axis (or axes).

infundibular: funnel-shaped.

inner bark: cortical tissues inside the protective outer layers but outside the wood.

internode: the part of an axis between two nodes.

interrupted: not continuous, smaller parts or lack of parts between normal ones.

introduced: brought intentionally from another region for purposes of cultivation.

introrse: turned or faced inward, toward the central axis; said of stamens whose anthers dehisce on the side facing inward.

involucel: a secondary involucre.

involucral: of the involucre.

involucrate: having an involucre.

involucre: one or more whorls or series of small lvs. or bracts that are close underneath a fl. or infl.; the individual bracts termed phyllaries by some. Ex: subtending the heads of most members of the *Compositae.*

involute: a longitudinal curving or rolling upwards as opposed to revolute.

irregular flower: a flower that can be cut longitudinally into two equal halves at only one place; one having some parts different from other parts in the same series; a flower that is not symmetrical when in face view; a zygomorphic flower.

isodiametric: as broad as tall.

jointed: having nodes or points of real or apparent articulation.

jugum: a pair, as of leaflets.

junctures: winter nodes.

juvenile: an early phase of plant growth, usually characterized by non-flowering, vigorous increase in size, and often thorniness.

keel: of a papilionaceous corolla, the two front petals united along lower margin into a boat-shaped structure enveloping the pistil and stamens.

key: a small indehiscent fruit with a wing.

knees: pointed or domelike outgrowths from baldcypress roots, rising above the water.

labellum: a modified petal; the enlarged spreading or pouch-like lip of the orchid flower.

labiate: lipped, as in the corolla of most mints; as a proper noun, a member of the *Labiatae* family.

lacerate: irregularly torn or cleft.

laciniate: slashed into narrow pointed incisions.

lactiferous: milky.

lacuna: a cavity, hole or gap.

lageniform: gourd-shaped.

lamellae: thin flat plates or laterally flattened ridges.

lamellate: made up of thin plates.

lamina: a blade.

lanate: woolly; with long intertwined curly hairs.

lanceolate: much longer than wide, broadest below the middle and tapering to the apex.

lanuginose: cottony or woolly; downy, the hairs somewhat shorter than in lanate.

lanulose: very short woolly.

lateral: borne at or on the side, as flowers, buds or branches.

lateral bud: a bud borne in the axil of a previous season's leaf.

latex: milky sap.

lax: loose; the opposite of congested.

leader: the primary or terminal shoot, trunk of a tree.

leaf: the whole organ of photosynthesis, characterized by an axillary bud most of the year.

leaflet: a foliar element of a compound leaf.

leaf ratio: the fraction obtained by dividing length by width.

leaf scar: the mark remaining after the leaf falls off a twig.

legume: a dry fruit dehiscing along both sutures and the product of a single carpel (simple ovary). Ex: pea, most beans.

lemma: the outer or lowermost bract of the two immediately inclosing a grass flower.

lenticel: a small corky spot on young bark made of loosely packed cells, providing gaseous exchange between the inner tissues and the atmosphere.

lenticular: lens-shaped, the sides usually convex.

lepidote: covered with minute scurfy scales.

liana: a tropical woody vine.

lignified: woody, hardened.

ligulate: strap-shaped; a leaf blade with the sides essentially parallel and abruptly terminated.

ligule: (1) a strap-shaped organ; (2) (in grasses) a minute projection from the top of the leaf sheath; (3) the strap-shaped corolla in the ray flowers of Composites.

limb: the expanded, and usually terminal, part of a petal (as in *Dianthus*), or of a gamopetalous corolla as distinguished from the often constricted tube.

linear: long and very narrow, as in blades of grass.

lineate: lined; bearing thin parallel lines.

lined: lightly ridged or ribbed.

lingulate: tongue-shaped.

lip: one of the parts of an unequally divided corolla or calyx; these parts are usually two, the upper lip and the lower lip, although one lip is sometimes wanting; the seemingly lower lip of orchid fls. (the labellum) has this position because of a twisting of the pedicel or receptacle.

lobe: a projecting part or segment of an organ as in a lobed ovary or stigma; usually a division of a lf., calyx, or petals cut to about the middle (i.e. midway between margin and midrib).

locule: a cell or compartment of an ovary, anther or fruit.

loculicidal: see dehiscent.

lodicule: minute, gland-like structure at base of grass ovary.

loment: a legume constricted between the seeds (as in peanut) or which separates into one-seeded articulations (as in *Desmodium* or *Lespedeza*).

loose: not compact, irregularly formed.

lorate: strap-shaped.

lunate: crescent-shaped, as a quarter moon.

lustrous: having a slight metallic gloss, less reflective than glossy.

lyrate: having a pinnately compound leaf with the terminal lft. much larger than the lateral lfts. and the latter becoming progressively smaller basally.

macrospore: the larger of two spores (as in *Selaginella*) which on germination produces the female gametophyte; synonymous with megaspore.

marcescent: withering, but the remains persisting.

margin: the edge of a leaf.

marginal: pertaining to the margin.

matted: growing densely, forming a low close ground cover or compact tufts.

mature: a later phase of growth characterized by flowering, fruiting, and a reduced rate of size increase.

mealy: having a mottled, granular appearance.

membranaceous: of parchment-like texture.

meristem: nascent tissue, capable of developing into specialized tissues.

-merous: referring to the number of parts; as fls. 3-merous, in which the parts of each kind (as petals, sepals, stamens, etc.) are 3 each or in multiples of 3.

metamorphosed: changed from one state to a different one.

microspore: the smaller of two kinds of spores (as in *Selaginella*) which on germination produces the male gametophyte; sometimes applied to a pollen grain.

microsporangium: the microspore-containing case; an anther sac.

midrib: the primary-rib or mid-vein of a leaf or lft.

milky sap: whitish in color, often thicker than water.

monadelphous: said of stamens when united by their filaments. Ex: hollyhock.

moniliform: constricted laterally and appearing bead-like.

monocarpic: fruiting once and then dying. Ex: some palms and most bamboos.

monocot: angiospermous plant having only one cotyledon.

monoecious: a species with unisexual fls., having both sexes on the same plant. Ex: corn.

monogymous: having a gynoecium of one pistil.

monopodial: continuing growth from a terminal bud each year.

mossy: describes a matted growth habit, with small overlapping foliage.

mound: plant having a massive form, full to the ground.

mucilaginous: slimy.

mucro: a short, sharp, abrupt tip.

mucronate: abruptly terminated by a mucro.

mucronulate: minutely mucronate.

multiple buds: a terminal or lateral bud crowded by many accessory buds.

multiple fruit: one formed from several fls. into a single structure having a common axis, as in pineapple or mulberry.

mummy: a dried shrivelled fruit.

muricate: rough, due to presence of many minute spiculate excrescences on the epidermis.

muriform: with markings, pits, or reticulations arranged like bricks of a wall; as on some seed coats and achenes.

mutation: a sudden change in genetic material resulting in an altered individual. Generally disadvantageous to survival.

naked bud: one without scales.

naked flower: one having no floral envelopes (perianth).

nascent: in the act of being formed.

native: inherent and original to an area.

naturalized: thoroughly established, but originally from a foreign area.

navicular: coat-shaped, as glumes of most grasses.

nectary: a nectar-secreting gland; may be a protuberance, a scale, or a pit.

needle: the slender leaf of many conifers.

nerve: a slender rib or vein, especially unbranched.

netted venation: the veins reticulated and resembling a fish net; the interstices close.

neutral flower: a sterile fl. consisting of perianth without any essential organs.

nocturnal: opening at night and closing during the day.

nodding: drooping, bending over.

node: a joint on a stem, represented by point of origin of a leaf or bud; sometimes represented by a swollen or constricted ring, or by a distinct leaf scar.

nodulose: having small, swollen knobs; knot-like.

notched: with v-shaped indentations.

nut: a dry, indehiscent, 1-celled, 1-seeded fruit having a hard and bony mesocarp; the outermost endocarp may be fibrous or slightly fleshy.

nutlet: diminutive nut; applied to one of the four nucules of the fruit of the mint family.

ob-: prefix indicating the inverse.

obcordate: the apex being cordate.

oblanceolate: inversely lanceolate.

oblate: flattened at the poles.

oblique: lop-sided, as one side of a leaf base larger, wider or more rounded than the other.

oblong: longer than broad; rectangular; the sides nearly parallel.

oblong-lanceolate: a shape in between the two forms.

oblong-obovate: a shape in between the two forms.

obovate: inversely ovate, broadest above the middle.

obovoid: three dimensional shape of obovate, pear shaped.

obsolete: rudimentary.

obtuse: rounded, approaching the semi-circular.

ochrea: a nodal sheath formed by fusion of the two stipules. Ex: *Rumex, Polygonum.*

odd-pinnate: see compound.

odoriferous: aromatic but questionably pleasant.

oligo-: a prefix meaning few, as oligospermous—few-ovuled.

opposite: two at a node, as leaves.

operculate: provided with a cap or lid (the operculum).

orbiculate: circular or disk-shaped. Ex: leaf of common nasturtium.

orthotropous: said of an ovule or seed when straight and erect, the hilum at the base and micropyle at the apex.

osier: a long lithe stem.

oval: twice as long as broad, widest at the middle, both ends rounded.

ovary: the ovule-bearing part of a pistil; one borne above the point of attachment of perianth and stamens is a *superior ovary:* when below attachment of these floral envelopes it is an *inferior* or *hypogenous ovary:* when intermediate or surrounded by an hypanthium it is a *half-inferior* or *perigynous ovary.*

ovate: egg-shaped in outline, broadest below the middle, like an oval.

ovate-oblong: a combination of the two forms.

ovoid: said of a solid that is three-dimensionally egg-shaped.

ovulate: bearing ovules.

ovule: the egg-containing unit of an ovary, which after fertilization becomes the seed.

paired: occurring in twos.

palate: the projecting part of the lower lip of a bilabiate corolla that closes the throat of the corolla or nearly does so. Ex: toad-flax, snapdragon.

palea (Palet): the inner of the two bracts immediately subtending a grass flower; the lower one is the lemma.

palmate: digitate, radiating, fan-like from a common point, as leaflets of a palmately compound lf. or veins or palmately-veined lf.

palamatifid: cut palmately about half-way down.

pandurate: fiddle-shaped.

panicle: an indeterminate infl. whose primary axis bears branches of pedicelled fls. (at least basally so); a branching raceme.

paniculate: bearing panicles.

papilionaceous: having a pea-like corolla that is comprised of standard, wings and keel.

papillate: bearing minute, pimple-like protuberances (Papillae).

pappillose: with small nipple-like projections.

pappus: the modified calyx of Composites, borne on the ovary (usually persisting on the achene) and represented by hairs, bristles, awns, scales, or others.

parallel: especially of veins, running side by side from base to tip.

parallel venation: the veins extending in more or less parallel fashion from base to apex.

parenchyma: unspecialized living cells, present in the pith.

parietal: borne on the side walls of an ovary (or capsule), or on invaginations of the wall that form incomplete partitions or septae within the ovary.

parted: cleft or cut not quite to the base.

pectinate: comb-like or pinnatifid with very close narrow divisions or parts; also used to describe spine conditions in cacti when small lateral spines radiate as comb-teeth from areole.

pedate: a palmately divided or compound lf. whose two lateral lobes are again cleft or divided.

pedicel: the stalk of a flower or fruit when in a cluster or when solitary.

peduncle: the stalk of a fl. cluster or a single fl. when that fl. is solitary, or the remaining member of a reduced infl. (as in *Euphorbia* where a constriction designates the "break" between peduncle and pedicel).

pellucid: clear or translucent, said of minute glandular dots that can nearly be seen thru when viewed in transmitted light.

peltate: having the petiole attached inside the margin, such a lf. is typically shield-shaped.

pendulous: more or less hanging or declined.

penniveined: pinnately arranged.

percurrent: the main trunk continuing through to the top.

perennial: of three or more seasons duration.

perfect flower: having both functional stamens and pistils.

perfoliate: the leaf-blade surrounding the stem. Ex: *Uvularia perfoliatus.*

perianth: the two floral envelopes of a fl.; a collective term embracing both corolla and calyx as a unit; often used when it is not possible to distinguish one series from the other (as in most monocots) and the parts then called tepals.

pericarp: a term used by some to designate a fruit; technically, the ovary wall.

periderm: a protective layer of corky cells.

perigynous: borne around the ovary but not fused to it, as when calyx, corolla and stamens are borne on the edge of a cup-shaped hypanthium. Ex: coral-bells, fuchsia, evening-primrose.

persistent: adhering to position instead of falling, whether dead or live.

personate: concealed; a corolla whose tube is closed by a palate, as in snapdragon.

perulate: scale-bearing, as a scaly bud.

petal: one unit of the inner floral envelope or corolla of a polypetalous fl., usually colored and more or less showy.

petaloid: a structure not a petal (for example a sepal) that is of the color and shape of a petal; resembling a petal.

petiole; leaf-stalk.

petiolule: leaflet-stalk.

phylloclad: a branch, more or less flattened, functioning as a leaf. Ex: Christmas cactus.

phyllodium: a flattened, expanded petiole without blade and functioning as a lf. Ex: some spp. *Acacia.*

phyllotaxy: arrangement of lvs. or of floral parts on their axis.

picturesque: striking in an unusual way.

pilose: shaggy with soft hairs.

pinked: notched.

pinna: the lft. of a compound lf.; of ferns, the primary division attached to the main rachis; feather-like.

pinnate: compounded with the lfts. or segments along each side of a common axis or rachis; feather-like.

pinnatifid: pinnately cleft or parted.

pinnatisect: pinnately cut to midrib or almost to it.

pinnule: the lft. of a pinna; a secondary lft. of a pinnately decompound lf.

pistil: the unit of the gynoecium comprised of ovary, style and stigma: it may consist of 1 or more carpels; the former with a single placenta is a *simple pistil,* the latter with 2 or more carpels is a *compound pistil.* See carpel or ovary.

pistillate: having no functional stamens (staminodia may be present) in the flower.

pith: the central part of a twig, usually lighter or darker than the wood.

pitted: marked with small depressions.

placenta: that place in the ovary where ovules are attached. A location, not a structure.

placentation: the arrangement of ovules within the ovary. Several types are recognized, among them are: *parietal placentation* (see parietal), *axile placentation,* the ovules borne in the center of the ovary on the axis formed by the union and fusion of the septae (partitions) and usually in vertical rows; in 2-celled ovaries they are borne in the center and on the cross partition or on a proliferation of it often filling the loculi; *free central placentation,* the ovules borne on a central column with no septae present; *basal placentation,* the ovules few or reduced to one and borne at the base of the ovary, the solitary ovule often filling the cavity; *lamellate placentation,* the ovules completely sunken in spongy ovarian and receptacular tissues with only the discoid stigmas exserted.

plicate: folded, as in a folding fan, or approaching this condition.

plugged pith: having cross partitions at the nodes.

plumose: feather-like, plumy.

pod: a dry dehiscent fruit; a general term.

pollen: microspores contained within an anther; sometimes agglutinated into a mass.

pollinium: an agglutinated, coherent mass of pollen. Ex: milkweeds, orchids.

polycarpic: flowering and fruiting many times. See monocarpic.

polygamo-dioecious: having male and female fls. on separate plants, but these plants having perfect flowers as well.

polygamous: bearing unisexual and bisexual flowers on the same plant.

polypetalous: with a corolla of separate petals. See corolla.

polysepalous: having a calyx of separated sepals.

pome: a type of fleshy fruit represented by the apple, pear and related genera, resulting from a compound ovary.

poricidal: see dehiscence.

porrect: said of cactus spines when the laterals are at right angles to the central one of an areole.

posterior: at or toward the back; opposite the front; nearest the axis; away from the subtending bract.

preformed: already having definite structure, such as leaves within a bud.

prehensile: clasping or coiling in response to touch.

prickle: an excrescence of bark that is small, weak, and spine-like.

prominent: projecting outward, conspicuous.

primocane: the first year's shoot or cane of a biennial woody stem. Ex: *Rubus.*

procumbent: lying flat on the ground but the stem not rooting at nodes or tip.

prostrate: lying flat on the ground; a general term.

protandrous: with anthers maturing before the stigma.

protogynous: having stigma receptive to pollen before pollen is released from anthers of same fl.

proximal: toward the base, away from the apex.

pruinose: having a coarse, granular, dust-like, waxy bloom.

pseudo-terminal bud: seemingly the terminal bud of a twig, but actually the upper-most lateral bud with its subtending lf. scar on one side and the scar of the terminal bud often visible on opposite side.

puberulent: minutely pubescent as viewed with a lens.

pubescent: covered with short soft hairs; a general term.

pulvinate: cushion-shaped.

pulvinus: a minute gland or a swollen base of the petiole or petiolule responding to vibrations. Ex: sensitive-plant *(Mimosa).*

punctate: with translucent or covered dots, depressions, or pits.

pungent: terminated by a sharp stiff point; sharp and acid to taste or smell.

pustular: blistery, usually minutely so.

pyramidal: broadest at base, tapering apically; pyramid-shaped.

pyrene: the pit or "seed" of a drupelet.

pyriform: pear-shaped.

pyxidium: pyxis: a capsule dehiscing circumscissilely.

quadrangular: four angled, of pith or a twig.

raceme: a simple indeterminate inflorescence with pedicelled flowers.

racemose: having flowers in racemes.

rachilla: a diminutive or secondary axis; a branch of a rachis; the minute axis bearing the individual florets in grass and sedge spikelets; the secondary axes of decompound fern fronds.

rachis: axis bearing leaflets or the primary axis of an infl.; the axis bearing pinnae of a fern frond.

radial: arranged around and spreading from a common center.

radiate: (1) said of a Composite infl. when bearing ray fls.; (2) star-shaped or spreading from a common center.

radical: of or pertaining to the root.

radicle: the embryonic root of a seed.

ramified: branched.

ramiform: branching.

ranked: foliage is arranged in longitudinal planes around the stem.

raphides: needle-like crystals in plant tissues.

ray: (1) the ligulate or lorate corolla of some composite flower; (2) the fl. of a Composite having a ligulate or strap-shaped corolla; (3) the axes of an umbel or umbel-like inflorescence.

receptacle: a torus; the distal end of a flower-bearing axis, usually more or less enlarged, flattened, or cup-like on which some or all of the flower parts are borne. Ex: *Compositae, Onagraceae.*

reclining: having an axis that is falling back or bent down from the vertical.

recurved: bent or curved backward, usually roundly or obtusely so. See reflexed.

reduced: smaller or simpler than normal.

reduplicate: said of buds whose components have their edges rolled outward in aestivation.

reflexed: bent abruptly backward or downward.

regular flowers: (1) a flower that can be cut longitudinally into two equal halves along an indefinite number of radii; (2) one having the parts of any one series all alike and uniformly disposed about the axis, as petals all alike, sepals all alike, etc.; a symmetrical or actinomorphic fl.

remote: widely spaced.

reniform: kidney-shaped.

repandate: having a weakly sinuate margin, one slightly uneven.

repent: creeping along the ground and rooting at the nodes.

replum: the partition separating the two loculi or cells or cruciferous fruits.

resin duct: a lengthwise or transverse canal carrying resins.

resinous: secreting a viscid exudate.

reticulate: like a net, the interstices closed.

retrorse: turned back or downwards, usually applied to armament or vesture.

retuse: notched slightly at a usually obtuse apex.

revolute: rolled toward the back, as a margin tightly or laxly rolled along the lower side.

rhizome: an underground stem distinguishable from a root by presence of nodes, buds or scale-like lvs.

rhombic: with four nearly equal sides, but unequal angles, diamond shaped.

rhombic-ovate: somewhere between egg and diamond shaped.

rhomboidal: of the shape of a rhomboid.

rib: conspicuous vein of a lf.; a prominent ridge.

root: the descending axis of the plant, without nodes and internodes, usually underground.

rootlet: a subdivision of a root, also an aerial root.

rosette: a crown of lvs. radiating from a st. and at or close to the surface of the ground.

rostellum: a small beak: a projection from the distal edge of the stigma in many monandrial orchids.

rostrate: beaked.

rosulate: in rosettes, or rosette-like in form.

rotate: wheel-shaped, a corolla whose limb flares out at right angles to the fl. axis and with no conspicuous tube produced; a flat circular or disc-like limb.

rotund: orbicular and inclining to be oblong.

rudiment: the beginning of an undeveloped member.

rufous: reddish brown.

rugose: wrinkled, usually covered with wrinkles.

ruminate: mottled in appearance, in a surface or tissue due to dark and light zones or irregular outline.

runcinate: pinnatifidly incised, the incision sharp and pointing backward. Ex: some *Taraxacum* leaves.

runner: a slender trailing shoot that usually roots at the tip and some nodes.

saccate: bag-shaped, pouchy.

sagittate: shaped like an arrow-head with the basal lobes pointing directly downward (backward) or inward.

salverform: said of a corolla with a slender tube and an abruptly expanded flat limb extending at right angles to the tube. Ex: *Phlox, Galium,* most primulas.

samara: a dry indehiscent fruit bearing a wing (the wing may be limb-like or envelop the seed and be wafer-like). Ex: maple, ash, *Ptelea.*

sarmentose: producing long flexuous runners.

scabrous: rough or gritty to the touch; rough-pubescent.

scalariform: said of pits or pith partitions when arranged like ladder rungs.

scale: a small and usually dry bract or vestigial leaf or a structure resembling such.

scandent: climbing, usually without tendrils.

scape: a leafless peduncle arising from the basal rosette of a few or no basal leaves; sometimes a few scale-like lvs. or bracts may be borne on it; a scape may be one or many-flowered.

scapose: bearing its fls. on a scape.

scar: the mark left from a former attachment.

scarious: thin, dry, membranous and usually translucent margins or parts that are not green in color.

scattered: not in any patterned arrangement, especially of vascular bundle scars.

schizocarp: a dry dehiscent fr. that splits into two halves. Ex: maple.

scorpioid-cyme: a determinate infl. (often seemingly indeterminate) that is coiled with the fls. 2-ranked and borne alternately at the right and the left. Ex: forget-me-not, heliotrope.

scrambler: plant that climbs without twining or grasping in some way.

scurfy: describes a surface covered with bran-like particles.

scutate: like a small shield.

secund: one-sided, in that the fls. are seemingly borne in a one-sided infl.

seed: a fertilized ripened ovule that contains an embryo.

segment: a portion of a leaf or perianth that is divided but not compound.

semi-cordate: partly heartshaped.

semi-evergreen: green for only a part of the winter, or only part of the foliage fully evergreen.

sepal: one of the units comprising the calyx; a usually green foliaceous element subtending the corolla.

septate: divided by partitions.

septicidal: see dehiscence.

septum: a partition.

sericeous: see silky.

serotinous: produced late in the season, late to open; having cones that remain closed long after the seeds are ripe.

serrate: saw-toothed, the teeth pointing forward.

serrulate: minutely serrate.

sessile: without a stalk.

seta: a bristle.

setaceous: bristle-like.

setose: covered with bristles.

shaggy: covered with or resembling long rough woolly hair.

sheath: any elongated, more or less tubular structure enveloping an organ or part.

shrub: a woody plant that is never tree-like in habit and produces branches or shoots from or near the base.

silicle: the short fr. of some crucifers, which is usually not more than 1 1/2 times as long as wide.

silique: the elongated fr. of some crucifers, usually 3 times as long as wide or longer.

silky: covered with soft appressed fine straight hairs; sericeous.

simple: said of a lf. when not compound, of an infl. when unbranched.

sinuate: with a strongly wavy margin.

sinus: the space between two lobes, segments, or divisions; as of lvs. or perianth parts.

smooth: not roughened, not warty.

solitary: occurring alone, not paired or clustered.

sori: see sorus.

sorus: cluster of sporangia (of ferns), appearing usually as a dot on the dorsal surface of a frond.

spadix: a fleshy usually club-shaped axis on which are borne fls. and which is generally enveloped by a spathe; the infl. of most *Araceae;* sometimes employed for the branched infl. of palms.

spathe: the bract or modified leaf surrounding or subtending a flowering infl. (usually a spadix); it may be herbaceous, colored, and "flower-like" as in the calla-lily or the anthurium, or hard, dry and woody in many palms. By some the term is restricted to members of the *Araceae.*

spathe valves: one or more herbaceous or scarious bracts that subtend an inflorescence or a flower.

spatulate: spoon-shaped.

species: a natural group of plants composed of similar individuals which can produce similar offspring; usually including several minor variations.

spicate: with spikes.

spicula: a cymule or small cyme.

spike: (1) a usually unbranched, elongated, simple, indeterminate infl. whose fls. are sessile; the fls. may be congested or remote; (2) a seemingly simple infl. whose "fls." may actually be composite heads (Liatris).

spikelet: (1) a secondary spike; (2) one part of a compound infl. which of itself is spicate; (3) the floral unit, or ultimate cluster, of a grass infl. comprised of fls. and their subtending bracts.

spine: an excrescence of st., strong and sharp-pointed. Ex: spines of hawthorns.

spinescent: more or less spiny.

spinose: beset with spines.

spirally arranged: the actual pattern of alternate leaves.

spongy: porous, as parenchyma cells of the pith.

sporangium: a spore-containing case, as in ferns.

spore: a minute reproductive body comprised of a single gametophytic cell.

sporocarp: a body containing sporangia or spores.

sporophyll: a spore-bearing leaf.

spray: a branchlet with foliage.

spreading: growing outward or horizontally.

spur: a tubular or sac-like projection from a fl. and usually from a sepal or petal.

squamate: with small scab-like projection from a fl. and usually from a sepal or petal.

squamose: covered with small scales, more coarsely so than when lepidote.

squarrose: with branches spreading and recurved at the ends.

stalk: a supporting structure of a leaf, flower or fruit.

stalked bud: a bud whose outer scales are attached above the base of the bud axis.

stamen: the unit of the androecium and typically comprised of anther and filament, sometimes reduced to only an anther; the pollen-bearing organ of a seed plant.

staminate: describes an imperfect flower with only functional stamens, male.

staminate flower: see flower.

staminode (staminodium): a sterile stamen reduced to a non-functional filament-like stalk, a gland, or sometimes expanded and petal-like; borne in the same or adjacent whorl as the functional stamens.

standard: (1) of a papilionaceous fl., the upper usually expanded, more or less erect petal; (2) the erect petals of an iris fl. as opposed to the broader and often drooping falls.

stellate: star-like; stellate hairs having radiating branches or are separate hairs aggregated in star-like clusters; hairs once or twice forked often are treated as stellate.

stellate-pubescent: with hairs in small starlike tufts.

stem: the primary axis of a plant having foliage and flowers opposed to the root axis.

sterigma: the raised base from which some small evergreen leaves finally fall (spruces).

sterile: barren, not able to produce seed.

stigma: the usually distal end of the pistil that receives the pollen, of varied shapes and surfaces.

stipe: (1) a naked stalk; (2) the petiole of a fern frond.

stipel: a stipule of a lft.

stipellate: having stipels at the base of the leaflets.

stipular, stipulate: having stipules at the base of the leaves.

stipule: a basal appendage of a petiole, usually one at each side, often ear-like and sometimes caducous. (falls off early) Sometimes spine like Caragana

stipule scar: a pair of marks left after the stipules fall off, to either side of the leaf scar.

stolon: a horizontal stem that roots at its tip and there gives rise to a new plant.

stoloniferous: bearing slender stems just on or under the ground which roots at the tips.

stoma: a minute pore in the epidermis, especially in the lower surface on the leaf.

stomatiferous: bearing stomata.

stone: the hard usually one-seeded endocarp of a drupe.

stratified: arranged in horizontal layers.

striate: with fine longitudinal lines, channels or ridges.

strict: rigidly erect.

strigose: with sharp, stiff, straight and appressed hairs.

strobilus: a cone.

style: the more or less elongated part of a pistil between the stigma and the ovary.

stylopodium: a disk-like enlargement at the base of a style.

subcontinuous pith: with occasional but not regular gaps.

submerged bud: a bud hidden by the petiole or embedded in the callus of the leaf scar.

subopposite: pairs of leaves close but not exactly at the same level on the stem.

subpetiolar: under the base of the petiole.

subtend: to stand immediately beneath.

subulate: awl-shaped.

succulent: thickened, juicy, fleshy tissues that are more or less soft in texture.

sucker: a shoot arising from the roots or from beneath the surface of the ground; also the adhering discs of a vine.

suffrutescent: a plant whose stems are woody basally but herbaceous above, dying back to the woody portion at the close of each growing season. Ex: *Alyssum saxatile,* rock rose, *Pachysandra.*

sulcate: deeply grooved lengthwise.

superficial: on the surface, not connected to inner tissues.

superior ovary: see ovary.

superposed bud: accessory bud above the true lateral bud.

supine: lying flat, face upwards.

suture: a line of dehiscence or groove marking a face of union.

syconium: the fruit of a fig.

symmetrical: actinomorphic or regular (flower) to the extent that the parts of the several series (calyx, corolla, stamens) are each of the same number.

symmetrical flower: one having the same number of parts in each envelope (calyx and corolla).

sympetalous: the petals united at least at the base; synonym for gamopetalous.

sympodial: continuing growth by the development of an axillary bud and not the terminal bud, season after season.

sympodial inflorescence: a determinate infl. that simulates an indeterminate infl., as if a scorpioid cyme were straight rather than circinate.

syncarp: a fleshy aggregate fruit.

syncarpous: having a gynoecium with all the carpels united.

syngenesious: stamens connate by their anthers in a cylinder about the style. Ex: *Compositae* family.

tailed: said of anthers having caudal appendages.

tapering: gradually decreasing towards an end.

taxonomy: the area of botany dealing with the classifying and naming of plants.

tendril: a modified stem or leaf, usually filiform, branched or simple, that twines about an object providing support.

tepal: a segment of perianth not differentiated into calyx or corolla. Ex: tulip, magnolia.

terete: cylindrical, or at least circular in cross section.

terminal: at the tip or distal end.

ternate: in threes.

testa: the outer coat of a seed.

tetradynamous: with an androecium of 6 stamens, four longer than the other two, as in Cruciferae.

texture: the effect of the surface structure.

thallus: a foliaceous organ, not differentiated into the stem and foliage and not bearing true roots.

thicket: a dense growth of shrubs, a copse.

thorn: a modified twig which has tiny leaf scars and buds; can be single or branched.

throat: the opening into the lower end of a gamopetalous corolla, the point where the limb joins the tube.

thyrse: compact panicle-like infl. whose distal end is indeterminate and the lateral branches determinate. Ex: lilac *(Syringa vulgaris).*

tomentose: densely woolly, the hairs soft and matted.

tomentulose: diminutive of tomentose; delicately tomentose.

tomentum: the dense matted hairs.

toothed: the margin broken up into small rather regular segments.

torsion: twisting.

torose: cylindrical with constrictions at intervals, slightly moniliform.

torulose: twisted or knobby; irregularly swollen at close intervals.

torus: see receptacle.

trailing: prostrate and not rooting.

translucent: transmitting light but diffuse enough to distort images.

transverse ridge: one which runs across the stem from one leaf scar to its pair on opposite twigs.

tree: a woody plant with one main stem at least 12 to 15 feet tall, and having a distinct head in most cases.

triangular-ovate: a flattened angular egg shape.

trichoma: a bristle.

trifid: three-cleft.

trifoliate: three-leaved. Ex: *Trillium.*

trifoliolate: with a leaf of three lfts.

tripinnate: with compounded pinnules.

triternate: a biternate lf. again divided in 3's. Ex: many spp. *Thalictrum.*

triquetrous: three-angled.

truncate: as if cut off at right angles to the primary axis; a term applicable to bases or apices.

tuber: a short, thickened organ, usually—but not necessarily—an underground stem.

tubercle: a miniature tuber, tuber-like body or projection.

tubular: having petals, sepals, or both united into a tube.

tuft: a clump of hairs growing close together.

tumid: swollen.

tunic: a coat about an organ, often fibrous or papery. Ex: about the crocus corm or tulip bulb.

tunicated: with concentric layers, often of fleshy scales. Ex: onion bulb.

turion: a young shoot or sucker. Ex: asparagus stalk.

turbinate: inversely conical, top-shaped.

turgid: swollen to firmness.

twig: the shoot of a woody plant representing the growth of the current season.

twiggy: having many divergent twigs.

twig scar: mark left by the sloughing of a length of dead twig tissue.

twining: the stem winding about a support.

umbel: an indeterminate infl., usually but not necessarily flat-topped with the pedicels and peduncles (termed rays) arising from a common point, resembling the stays of an umbrella.

umbellate: having umbels.

umbellet: a secondary umbel.

umbo: a conical projection arising from the surface.

unarmed: without a sharp defense such as spines or bristles.

uncinate: hooked at the tip.

undulate: wavy, as a leaf margin.

unguiculate: narrowed into a petiole-like base; clawed.

unijugate: a compound lf. reduced to a single pair of leaflets.

unilateral: one-sided.

unilocular: one-celled or with a single cavity.

unisexual flowers: of one sex only. See flower.

urceolate: urn-shaped; constricted at the throat.

utricle: a small dry thin-walled, usually dehiscent, 1-seeded fruit; an achene whose pericarp is loose and readily removed. Ex: *Amaranthus.*

vaginate: sheathed.

valvate: (1) dehiscing by valves; (2) meeting by the edges without overlapping, as lvs. or petals in the bud.

valve: a separable part of a dehiscent fruit or stamen; the unit into which a capsule splits or divides in dehiscing.

variegated: striped, margined or mottled with a color other than green, where green is normal.

variety: subdivision of a species having a distinct though often inconspicuous difference, and breeding true to that difference. More generally also refers to clones.

vascular bundle: a discrete group of conducting vessels.

vascular bundle scar: a minute spot within the leaf scar where the vessels were positioned.

vasiform: an elongated funnel-shaped object.

vein: a vascular rib of the leaf.

velutinous: clothed with a velvety indumentum comprised of erect straight dense moderately firm hairs.

venation: arrangement of veins.

ventral: relating to the anterior or inner face or part of an organ, the opposite of dorsal.

ventricose: a one-sided swelling or inflation, more pronounced than gibbous.

venulose: with very fine veins.

vernal: related to spring.

vernation: the arrangement of leaves within a bud.

verrucose: having a wart-like surface.

versatile: moving freely because of attachment near the middle, as an anther attached crosswise medianly to the filament.

vertical: having broad faces perpendicular to the earth.

verticil: a whorl.

verticillate inflorescence: one with the flowers in whorls about the axis, the whorls remote from one another (as in many salvias) or congested into head-like structures (catnip). Such whorls are false-whorls since they are actually sessile cymes arranged opposite one another in the axils of opposite bracts or leaves.

verticillate: arranged in whorls.

vesicle: a small bladdery sac or cavity filled with air or fluid.

vestige: the remains of an exhausted or dead member.

vesture: any substance on or arising from the surface rendering it other than glabrous.

vexillum: the petal of a papilionaceous corolla known also as the standard; the upper broad petal.

villous: having long, soft, shaggy hairs that are not matted.

vine: a slender-stemmed climbing or trailing plant.

virgate: wand-like; long straight and slender.

viscid: sticky or with appreciable viscosity.

vittatae: the oil tubes of *Umbelliferae,* especially of their fruits.

voluble: twining.

warty: marked with rounded tubercles, rougher than granules.

watery sap: thin and clear.

wavy: alternating concave and convex curves.

weeping: dropping conspicuously, pendent.

whorl: arrangement of three or more structures arising from a single node.

whorled: in a whorl, as leaves.

wilt: to become limp and lose turgor through a deficit of water.

wing: (1) the lateral petal of a papilionaceous flower; (2) a dry, thin, membranous appendage.

wither: to dry up and shrivel.

wood: a dead, hard xylem tissue.

woolly: having long, soft, more or less matted hairs; like wool.

x: indicates a hybrid.

zig-zag: bent back and forth at the nodes.

zone: an area restricted by a range of annual average minimum temperatures, used in describing hardiness.

zygomorphic: irregular, not symmetrical.

SCIENTIFIC NAME INDEX

992

COMMON NAME INDEX